Oxford Dictionary of
National Biography

Volume 45

Oxford Dictionary of National Biography

IN ASSOCIATION WITH
The British Academy

From the earliest times to the year 2000

Edited by
H. C. G. Matthew
and
Brian Harrison

Volume 45
Pote–Randles

OXFORD
UNIVERSITY PRESS

OXFORD

UNIVERSITY PRESS

Great Clarendon Street, Oxford OX2 6DP

Oxford University Press is a department of the University of Oxford.
It furthers the University's objective of excellence in research, scholarship,
and education by publishing worldwide in

Oxford New York

Auckland Bangkok Buenos Aires Cape Town
Chennai Dar es Salaam Delhi Hong Kong Istanbul Karachi
Kolkata Kuala Lumpur Madrid Melbourne Mexico City Mumbai Nairobi
São Paulo Shanghai Taipei Tokyo Toronto

Oxford is a registered trade mark of Oxford University Press
in the UK and in certain other countries

Published in the United States
by Oxford University Press Inc., New York

British Library Cataloguing in Publication Data
Data available

Library of Congress Cataloging in Publication Data
Data available: for details see volume 1, p. iv

ISBN 0-19-861395-4 (this volume)
ISBN 0-19-861411-X (set of sixty volumes)

Text captured by Alliance Phototypesetters, Pondicherry
Illustrations reproduced and archived by
Alliance Graphics Ltd, UK
Typeset in OUP Swift by Interactive Sciences Limited, Gloucester
Printed in Great Britain on acid-free paper by
Butler and Tanner Ltd,
Frome, Somerset

LIST OF ABBREVIATIONS

1 General abbreviations

AB	bachelor of arts
ABC	Australian Broadcasting Corporation
ABC TV	ABC Television
act.	active
A$	Australian dollar
AD	*anno domini*
AFC	Air Force Cross
AIDS	acquired immune deficiency syndrome
AK	Alaska
AL	Alabama
A level	advanced level [examination]
ALS	associate of the Linnean Society
AM	master of arts
AMICE	associate member of the Institution of Civil Engineers
ANZAC	Australian and New Zealand Army Corps
appx *pl.* appxs	appendix(es)
AR	Arkansas
ARA	associate of the Royal Academy
ARCA	associate of the Royal College of Art
ARCM	associate of the Royal College of Music
ARCO	associate of the Royal College of Organists
ARIBA	associate of the Royal Institute of British Architects
ARP	air-raid precautions
ARRC	associate of the Royal Red Cross
ARSA	associate of the Royal Scottish Academy
art.	article / item
ASC	Army Service Corps
Asch	Austrian Schilling
ASDIC	Antisubmarine Detection Investigation Committee
ATS	Auxiliary Territorial Service
ATV	Associated Television
Aug	August
AZ	Arizona
b.	born
BA	bachelor of arts
BA (Admin.)	bachelor of arts (administration)
BAFTA	British Academy of Film and Television Arts
BAO	bachelor of arts in obstetrics
bap.	baptized
BBC	British Broadcasting Corporation / Company
BC	before Christ
BCE	before the common (*or* Christian) era
BCE	bachelor of civil engineering
BCG	bacillus of Calmette and Guérin [inoculation against tuberculosis]
BCh	bachelor of surgery
BChir	bachelor of surgery
BCL	bachelor of civil law

BCnL	bachelor of canon law
BCom	bachelor of commerce
BD	bachelor of divinity
BEd	bachelor of education
BEng	bachelor of engineering
bk *pl.* bks	book(s)
BL	bachelor of law / letters / literature
BLitt	bachelor of letters
BM	bachelor of medicine
BMus	bachelor of music
BP	before present
BP	British Petroleum
Bros.	Brothers
BS	(1) bachelor of science; (2) bachelor of surgery; (3) British standard
BSc	bachelor of science
BSc (Econ.)	bachelor of science (economics)
BSc (Eng.)	bachelor of science (engineering)
bt	baronet
BTh	bachelor of theology
bur.	buried
C.	command [identifier for published parliamentary papers]
c.	*circa*
c.	*capitulum pl. capitula*: chapter(s)
CA	California
Cantab.	Cantabrigiensis
cap.	*capitulum pl. capitula*: chapter(s)
CB	companion of the Bath
CBE	commander of the Order of the British Empire
CBS	Columbia Broadcasting System
cc	cubic centimetres
C$	Canadian dollar
CD	compact disc
Cd	command [identifier for published parliamentary papers]
CE	Common (*or* Christian) Era
cent.	century
cf.	compare
CH	Companion of Honour
chap.	chapter
ChB	bachelor of surgery
CI	Imperial Order of the Crown of India
CIA	Central Intelligence Agency
CID	Criminal Investigation Department
CIE	companion of the Order of the Indian Empire
Cie	Compagnie
CLit	companion of literature
CM	master of surgery
cm	centimetre(s)

Cmd	command [identifier for published parliamentary papers]
CMG	companion of the Order of St Michael and St George
Cmnd	command [identifier for published parliamentary papers]
CO	Colorado
Co.	company
co.	county
col. *pl.* cols.	column(s)
Corp.	corporation
CSE	certificate of secondary education
CSI	companion of the Order of the Star of India
CT	Connecticut
CVO	commander of the Royal Victorian Order
cwt	hundredweight
$	(American) dollar
d.	(1) penny (pence); (2) died
DBE	dame commander of the Order of the British Empire
DCH	diploma in child health
DCh	doctor of surgery
DCL	doctor of civil law
DCnL	doctor of canon law
DCVO	dame commander of the Royal Victorian Order
DD	doctor of divinity
DE	Delaware
Dec	December
dem.	demolished
DEng	doctor of engineering
des.	destroyed
DFC	Distinguished Flying Cross
DipEd	diploma in education
DipPsych	diploma in psychiatry
diss.	dissertation
DL	deputy lieutenant
DLitt	doctor of letters
DLittCelt	doctor of Celtic letters
DM	(1) Deutschmark; (2) doctor of medicine; (3) doctor of musical arts
DMus	doctor of music
DNA	dioxyribonucleic acid
doc.	document
DOL	doctor of oriental learning
DPH	diploma in public health
DPhil	doctor of philosophy
DPM	diploma in psychological medicine
DSC	Distinguished Service Cross
DSc	doctor of science
DSc (Econ.)	doctor of science (economics)
DSc (Eng.)	doctor of science (engineering)
DSM	Distinguished Service Medal
DSO	companion of the Distinguished Service Order
DSocSc	doctor of social science
DTech	doctor of technology
DTh	doctor of theology
DTM	diploma in tropical medicine
DTMH	diploma in tropical medicine and hygiene
DU	doctor of the university
DUniv	doctor of the university
dwt	pennyweight
EC	European Community
ed. *pl.* eds.	edited / edited by / editor(s)
Edin.	Edinburgh

edn	edition
EEC	European Economic Community
EFTA	European Free Trade Association
EICS	East India Company Service
EMI	Electrical and Musical Industries (Ltd)
Eng.	English
enl.	enlarged
ENSA	Entertainments National Service Association
ep. *pl.* epp.	*epistola(e)*
ESP	extra-sensory perception
esp.	especially
esq.	esquire
est.	estimate / estimated
EU	European Union
ex	sold by (*lit.* out of)
excl.	excludes / excluding
exh.	exhibited
exh. cat.	exhibition catalogue
f. *pl.* ff.	following [pages]
FA	Football Association
FACP	fellow of the American College of Physicians
facs.	facsimile
FANY	First Aid Nursing Yeomanry
FBA	fellow of the British Academy
FBI	Federation of British Industries
FCS	fellow of the Chemical Society
Feb	February
FEng	fellow of the Fellowship of Engineering
FFCM	fellow of the Faculty of Community Medicine
FGS	fellow of the Geological Society
fig.	figure
FIMechE	fellow of the Institution of Mechanical Engineers
FL	Florida
fl.	*floruit*
FLS	fellow of the Linnean Society
FM	frequency modulation
fol. *pl.* fols.	folio(s)
Fr	French francs
Fr.	French
FRAeS	fellow of the Royal Aeronautical Society
FRAI	fellow of the Royal Anthropological Institute
FRAM	fellow of the Royal Academy of Music
FRAS	(1) fellow of the Royal Asiatic Society; (2) fellow of the Royal Astronomical Society
FRCM	fellow of the Royal College of Music
FRCO	fellow of the Royal College of Organists
FRCOG	fellow of the Royal College of Obstetricians and Gynaecologists
FRCP(C)	fellow of the Royal College of Physicians of Canada
FRCP (Edin.)	fellow of the Royal College of Physicians of Edinburgh
FRCP (Lond.)	fellow of the Royal College of Physicians of London
FRCPath	fellow of the Royal College of Pathologists
FRCPsych	fellow of the Royal College of Psychiatrists
FRCS	fellow of the Royal College of Surgeons
FRGS	fellow of the Royal Geographical Society
FRIBA	fellow of the Royal Institute of British Architects
FRICS	fellow of the Royal Institute of Chartered Surveyors
FRS	fellow of the Royal Society
FRSA	fellow of the Royal Society of Arts

FRSCM	fellow of the Royal School of Church Music	ISO	companion of the Imperial Service Order
FRSE	fellow of the Royal Society of Edinburgh	It.	Italian
FRSL	fellow of the Royal Society of Literature	ITA	Independent Television Authority
FSA	fellow of the Society of Antiquaries	ITV	Independent Television
ft	foot *pl.* feet	Jan	January
FTCL	fellow of Trinity College of Music, London	JP	justice of the peace
ft-lb per min.	foot-pounds per minute [unit of horsepower]	jun.	junior
FZS	fellow of the Zoological Society	KB	knight of the Order of the Bath
GA	Georgia	KBE	knight commander of the Order of the British Empire
GBE	knight or dame grand cross of the Order of the British Empire	KC	king's counsel
GCB	knight grand cross of the Order of the Bath	kcal	kilocalorie
GCE	general certificate of education	KCB	knight commander of the Order of the Bath
GCH	knight grand cross of the Royal Guelphic Order	KCH	knight commander of the Royal Guelphic Order
GCHQ	government communications headquarters	KCIE	knight commander of the Order of the Indian Empire
GCIE	knight grand commander of the Order of the Indian Empire	KCMG	knight commander of the Order of St Michael and St George
GCMG	knight or dame grand cross of the Order of St Michael and St George	KCSI	knight commander of the Order of the Star of India
GCSE	general certificate of secondary education	KCVO	knight commander of the Royal Victorian Order
GCSI	knight grand commander of the Order of the Star of India	keV	kilo-electron-volt
GCStJ	bailiff or dame grand cross of the order of St John of Jerusalem	KG	knight of the Order of the Garter
GCVO	knight or dame grand cross of the Royal Victorian Order	KGB	[Soviet committee of state security]
		KH	knight of the Royal Guelphic Order
GEC	General Electric Company	KLM	Koninklijke Luchtvaart Maatschappij (Royal Dutch Air Lines)
Ger.	German		
GI	government (*or* general) issue	km	kilometre(s)
GMT	Greenwich mean time	KP	knight of the Order of St Patrick
GP	general practitioner	KS	Kansas
GPU	[Soviet special police unit]	KT	knight of the Order of the Thistle
GSO	general staff officer	kt	knight
Heb.	Hebrew	KY	Kentucky
HEICS	Honourable East India Company Service	£	pound(s) sterling
HI	Hawaii	£E	Egyptian pound
HIV	human immunodeficiency virus	L	lira *pl.* lire
HK$	Hong Kong dollar	l. *pl.* ll.	line(s)
HM	his / her majesty('s)	LA	Lousiana
HMAS	his / her majesty's Australian ship	LAA	light anti-aircraft
HMNZS	his / her majesty's New Zealand ship	LAH	licentiate of the Apothecaries' Hall, Dublin
HMS	his / her majesty's ship	Lat.	Latin
HMSO	His / Her Majesty's Stationery Office	lb	pound(s), unit of weight
HMV	His Master's Voice	LDS	licence in dental surgery
Hon.	Honourable	*lit.*	literally
hp	horsepower	LittB	bachelor of letters
hr	hour(s)	LittD	doctor of letters
HRH	his / her royal highness	LKQCPI	licentiate of the King and Queen's College of Physicians, Ireland
HTV	Harlech Television		
IA	Iowa	LLA	lady literate in arts
ibid.	*ibidem*: in the same place	LLB	bachelor of laws
ICI	Imperial Chemical Industries (Ltd)	LLD	doctor of laws
ID	Idaho	LLM	master of laws
IL	Illinois	LM	licentiate in midwifery
illus.	illustration	LP	long-playing record
illustr.	illustrated	LRAM	licentiate of the Royal Academy of Music
IN	Indiana	LRCP	licentiate of the Royal College of Physicians
in.	inch(es)	LRCPS (Glasgow)	licentiate of the Royal College of Physicians and Surgeons of Glasgow
Inc.	Incorporated		
incl.	includes / including	LRCS	licentiate of the Royal College of Surgeons
IOU	I owe you	LSA	licentiate of the Society of Apothecaries
IQ	intelligence quotient	LSD	lysergic acid diethylamide
Ir£	Irish pound	LVO	lieutenant of the Royal Victorian Order
IRA	Irish Republican Army	M. *pl.* MM.	Monsieur *pl.* Messieurs
		m	metre(s)

m. *pl.* mm.	membrane(s)
MA	(1) Massachusetts; (2) master of arts
MAI	master of engineering
MB	bachelor of medicine
MBA	master of business administration
MBE	member of the Order of the British Empire
MC	Military Cross
MCC	Marylebone Cricket Club
MCh	master of surgery
MChir	master of surgery
MCom	master of commerce
MD	(1) doctor of medicine; (2) Maryland
MDMA	methylenedioxymethamphetamine
ME	Maine
MEd	master of education
MEng	master of engineering
MEP	member of the European parliament
MG	Morris Garages
MGM	Metro-Goldwyn-Mayer
Mgr	Monsignor
MI	(1) Michigan; (2) military intelligence
MI1c	[secret intelligence department]
MI5	[military intelligence department]
MI6	[secret intelligence department]
MI9	[secret escape service]
MICE	member of the Institution of Civil Engineers
MIEE	member of the Institution of Electrical Engineers
min.	minute(s)
Mk	mark
ML	(1) licentiate of medicine; (2) master of laws
MLitt	master of letters
Mlle	Mademoiselle
mm	millimetre(s)
Mme	Madame
MN	Minnesota
MO	Missouri
MOH	medical officer of health
MP	member of parliament
m.p.h.	miles per hour
MPhil	master of philosophy
MRCP	member of the Royal College of Physicians
MRCS	member of the Royal College of Surgeons
MRCVS	member of the Royal College of Veterinary Surgeons
MRIA	member of the Royal Irish Academy
MS	(1) master of science; (2) Mississippi
MS *pl.* MSS	manuscript(s)
MSc	master of science
MSc (Econ.)	master of science (economics)
MT	Montana
MusB	bachelor of music
MusBac	bachelor of music
MusD	doctor of music
MV	motor vessel
MVO	member of the Royal Victorian Order
n. *pl.* nn.	note(s)
NAAFI	Navy, Army, and Air Force Institutes
NASA	National Aeronautics and Space Administration
NATO	North Atlantic Treaty Organization
NBC	National Broadcasting Corporation
NC	North Carolina
NCO	non-commissioned officer
ND	North Dakota
n.d.	no date
NE	Nebraska
nem. con.	*nemine contradicente*: unanimously
new ser.	new series
NH	New Hampshire
NHS	National Health Service
NJ	New Jersey
NKVD	[Soviet people's commissariat for internal affairs]
NM	New Mexico
nm	nanometre(s)
no. *pl.* nos.	number(s)
Nov	November
n.p.	no place [of publication]
NS	new style
NV	Nevada
NY	New York
NZBS	New Zealand Broadcasting Service
OBE	officer of the Order of the British Empire
obit.	obituary
Oct	October
OCTU	officer cadets training unit
OECD	Organization for Economic Co-operation and Development
OEEC	Organization for European Economic Co-operation
OFM	order of Friars Minor [Franciscans]
OFMCap	Ordine Frati Minori Cappucini: member of the Capuchin order
OH	Ohio
OK	Oklahoma
O level	ordinary level [examination]
OM	Order of Merit
OP	order of Preachers [Dominicans]
op. *pl.* opp.	opus *pl.* opera
OPEC	Organization of Petroleum Exporting Countries
OR	Oregon
orig.	original
OS	old style
OSB	Order of St Benedict
OTC	Officers' Training Corps
OWS	Old Watercolour Society
Oxon.	Oxoniensis
p. *pl.* pp.	page(s)
PA	Pennsylvania
p.a.	per annum
para.	paragraph
PAYE	pay as you earn
pbk *pl.* pbks	paperback(s)
per.	[during the] period
PhD	doctor of philosophy
pl.	(1) plate(s); (2) plural
priv. coll.	private collection
pt *pl.* pts	part(s)
pubd	published
PVC	polyvinyl chloride
q. *pl.* qq.	(1) question(s); (2) quire(s)
QC	queen's counsel
R	rand
R.	Rex / Regina
r	recto
r.	reigned / ruled
RA	Royal Academy / Royal Academician

RAC	Royal Automobile Club
RAF	Royal Air Force
RAFVR	Royal Air Force Volunteer Reserve
RAM	[member of the] Royal Academy of Music
RAMC	Royal Army Medical Corps
RCA	Royal College of Art
RCNC	Royal Corps of Naval Constructors
RCOG	Royal College of Obstetricians and Gynaecologists
RDI	royal designer for industry
RE	Royal Engineers
repr. *pl.* reprs.	reprint(s) / reprinted
repro.	reproduced
rev.	revised / revised by / reviser / revision
Revd	Reverend
RHA	Royal Hibernian Academy
RI	(1) Rhode Island; (2) Royal Institute of Painters in Water-Colours
RIBA	Royal Institute of British Architects
RIN	Royal Indian Navy
RM	Reichsmark
RMS	Royal Mail steamer
RN	Royal Navy
RNA	ribonucleic acid
RNAS	Royal Naval Air Service
RNR	Royal Naval Reserve
RNVR	Royal Naval Volunteer Reserve
RO	Record Office
r.p.m.	revolutions per minute
RRS	royal research ship
Rs	rupees
RSA	(1) Royal Scottish Academician; (2) Royal Society of Arts
RSPCA	Royal Society for the Prevention of Cruelty to Animals
Rt Hon.	Right Honourable
Rt Revd	Right Reverend
RUC	Royal Ulster Constabulary
Russ.	Russian
RWS	Royal Watercolour Society
S4C	Sianel Pedwar Cymru
s.	shilling(s)
s.a.	*sub anno*: under the year
SABC	South African Broadcasting Corporation
SAS	Special Air Service
SC	South Carolina
ScD	doctor of science
S$	Singapore dollar
SD	South Dakota
sec.	second(s)
sel.	selected
sen.	senior
Sept	September
ser.	series
SHAPE	supreme headquarters allied powers, Europe
SIDRO	Société Internationale d'Énergie Hydro-Électrique
sig. *pl.* sigs.	signature(s)
sing.	singular
SIS	Secret Intelligence Service
SJ	Society of Jesus

Skr	Swedish krona
Span.	Spanish
SPCK	Society for Promoting Christian Knowledge
SS	(1) Santissimi; (2) Schutzstaffel; (3) steam ship
STB	bachelor of theology
STD	doctor of theology
STM	master of theology
STP	doctor of theology
supp.	supposedly
suppl. *pl.* suppls.	supplement(s)
s.v.	*sub verbo* / *sub voce*: under the word / heading
SY	steam yacht
TA	Territorial Army
TASS	[Soviet news agency]
TB	tuberculosis (*lit.* tubercle bacillus)
TD	(1) *teachtaí dála* (member of the Dáil); (2) territorial decoration
TN	Tennessee
TNT	trinitrotoluene
trans.	translated / translated by / translation / translator
TT	tourist trophy
TUC	Trades Union Congress
TX	Texas
U-boat	*Unterseeboot*: submarine
Ufa	Universum-Film AG
UMIST	University of Manchester Institute of Science and Technology
UN	United Nations
UNESCO	United Nations Educational, Scientific, and Cultural Organization
UNICEF	United Nations International Children's Emergency Fund
unpubd	unpublished
USS	United States ship
UT	Utah
v	verso
v.	versus
VA	Virginia
VAD	Voluntary Aid Detachment
VC	Victoria Cross
VE-day	victory in Europe day
Ven.	Venerable
VJ-day	victory over Japan day
vol. *pl.* vols.	volume(s)
VT	Vermont
WA	Washington [state]
WAAC	Women's Auxiliary Army Corps
WAAF	Women's Auxiliary Air Force
WEA	Workers' Educational Association
WHO	World Health Organization
WI	Wisconsin
WRAF	Women's Royal Air Force
WRNS	Women's Royal Naval Service
WV	West Virginia
WVS	Women's Voluntary Service
WY	Wyoming
¥	yen
YMCA	Young Men's Christian Association
YWCA	Young Women's Christian Association

2 Institution abbreviations

All Souls Oxf.	All Souls College, Oxford
AM Oxf.	Ashmolean Museum, Oxford
Balliol Oxf.	Balliol College, Oxford
BBC WAC	BBC Written Archives Centre, Reading
Beds. & Luton ARS	Bedfordshire and Luton Archives and Record Service, Bedford
Berks. RO	Berkshire Record Office, Reading
BFI	British Film Institute, London
BFI NFTVA	British Film Institute, London, National Film and Television Archive
BGS	British Geological Survey, Keyworth, Nottingham
Birm. CA	Birmingham Central Library, Birmingham City Archives
Birm. CL	Birmingham Central Library
BL	British Library, London
BL NSA	British Library, London, National Sound Archive
BL OIOC	British Library, London, Oriental and India Office Collections
BLPES	London School of Economics and Political Science, British Library of Political and Economic Science
BM	British Museum, London
Bodl. Oxf.	Bodleian Library, Oxford
Bodl. RH	Bodleian Library of Commonwealth and African Studies at Rhodes House, Oxford
Borth. Inst.	Borthwick Institute of Historical Research, University of York
Boston PL	Boston Public Library, Massachusetts
Bristol RO	Bristol Record Office
Bucks. RLSS	Buckinghamshire Records and Local Studies Service, Aylesbury
CAC Cam.	Churchill College, Cambridge, Churchill Archives Centre
Cambs. AS	Cambridgeshire Archive Service
CCC Cam.	Corpus Christi College, Cambridge
CCC Oxf.	Corpus Christi College, Oxford
Ches. & Chester ALSS	Cheshire and Chester Archives and Local Studies Service
Christ Church Oxf.	Christ Church, Oxford
Christies	Christies, London
City Westm. AC	City of Westminster Archives Centre, London
CKS	Centre for Kentish Studies, Maidstone
CLRO	Corporation of London Records Office
Coll. Arms	College of Arms, London
Col. U.	Columbia University, New York
Cornwall RO	Cornwall Record Office, Truro
Courtauld Inst.	Courtauld Institute of Art, London
CUL	Cambridge University Library
Cumbria AS	Cumbria Archive Service
Derbys. RO	Derbyshire Record Office, Matlock
Devon RO	Devon Record Office, Exeter
Dorset RO	Dorset Record Office, Dorchester
Duke U.	Duke University, Durham, North Carolina
Duke U., Perkins L.	Duke University, Durham, North Carolina, William R. Perkins Library
Durham Cath. CL	Durham Cathedral, chapter library
Durham RO	Durham Record Office
DWL	Dr Williams's Library, London
Essex RO	Essex Record Office
E. Sussex RO	East Sussex Record Office, Lewes
Eton	Eton College, Berkshire
FM Cam.	Fitzwilliam Museum, Cambridge
Folger	Folger Shakespeare Library, Washington, DC
Garr. Club	Garrick Club, London
Girton Cam.	Girton College, Cambridge
GL	Guildhall Library, London
Glos. RO	Gloucestershire Record Office, Gloucester
Gon. & Caius Cam.	Gonville and Caius College, Cambridge
Gov. Art Coll.	Government Art Collection
GS Lond.	Geological Society of London
Hants. RO	Hampshire Record Office, Winchester
Harris Man. Oxf.	Harris Manchester College, Oxford
Harvard TC	Harvard Theatre Collection, Harvard University, Cambridge, Massachusetts, Nathan Marsh Pusey Library
Harvard U.	Harvard University, Cambridge, Massachusetts
Harvard U., Houghton L.	Harvard University, Cambridge, Massachusetts, Houghton Library
Herefs. RO	Herefordshire Record Office, Hereford
Herts. ALS	Hertfordshire Archives and Local Studies, Hertford
Hist. Soc. Penn.	Historical Society of Pennsylvania, Philadelphia
HLRO	House of Lords Record Office, London
Hult. Arch.	Hulton Archive, London and New York
Hunt. L.	Huntington Library, San Marino, California
ICL	Imperial College, London
Inst. CE	Institution of Civil Engineers, London
Inst. EE	Institution of Electrical Engineers, London
IWM	Imperial War Museum, London
IWM FVA	Imperial War Museum, London, Film and Video Archive
IWM SA	Imperial War Museum, London, Sound Archive
JRL	John Rylands University Library of Manchester
King's AC Cam.	King's College Archives Centre, Cambridge
King's Cam.	King's College, Cambridge
King's Lond.	King's College, London
King's Lond., Liddell Hart C.	King's College, London, Liddell Hart Centre for Military Archives
Lancs. RO	Lancashire Record Office, Preston
L. Cong.	Library of Congress, Washington, DC
Leics. RO	Leicestershire, Leicester, and Rutland Record Office, Leicester
Lincs. Arch.	Lincolnshire Archives, Lincoln
Linn. Soc.	Linnean Society of London
LMA	London Metropolitan Archives
LPL	Lambeth Palace, London
Lpool RO	Liverpool Record Office and Local Studies Service
LUL	London University Library
Magd. Cam.	Magdalene College, Cambridge
Magd. Oxf.	Magdalen College, Oxford
Man. City Gall.	Manchester City Galleries
Man. CL	Manchester Central Library
Mass. Hist. Soc.	Massachusetts Historical Society, Boston
Merton Oxf.	Merton College, Oxford
MHS Oxf.	Museum of the History of Science, Oxford
Mitchell L., Glas.	Mitchell Library, Glasgow
Mitchell L., NSW	State Library of New South Wales, Sydney, Mitchell Library
Morgan L.	Pierpont Morgan Library, New York
NA Canada	National Archives of Canada, Ottawa
NA Ire.	National Archives of Ireland, Dublin
NAM	National Army Museum, London
NA Scot.	National Archives of Scotland, Edinburgh
News Int. RO	News International Record Office, London
NG Ire.	National Gallery of Ireland, Dublin

NG Scot.	National Gallery of Scotland, Edinburgh
NHM	Natural History Museum, London
NL Aus.	National Library of Australia, Canberra
NL Ire.	National Library of Ireland, Dublin
NL NZ	National Library of New Zealand, Wellington
NL NZ, Turnbull L.	National Library of New Zealand, Wellington, Alexander Turnbull Library
NL Scot.	National Library of Scotland, Edinburgh
NL Wales	National Library of Wales, Aberystwyth
NMG Wales	National Museum and Gallery of Wales, Cardiff
NMM	National Maritime Museum, London
Norfolk RO	Norfolk Record Office, Norwich
Northants. RO	Northamptonshire Record Office, Northampton
Northumbd RO	Northumberland Record Office
Notts. Arch.	Nottinghamshire Archives, Nottingham
NPG	National Portrait Gallery, London
NRA	National Archives, London, Historical Manuscripts Commission, National Register of Archives
Nuffield Oxf.	Nuffield College, Oxford
N. Yorks. CRO	North Yorkshire County Record Office, Northallerton
NYPL	New York Public Library
Oxf. UA	Oxford University Archives
Oxf. U. Mus. NH	Oxford University Museum of Natural History
Oxon. RO	Oxfordshire Record Office, Oxford
Pembroke Cam.	Pembroke College, Cambridge
PRO	National Archives, London, Public Record Office
PRO NIre.	Public Record Office for Northern Ireland, Belfast
Pusey Oxf.	Pusey House, Oxford
RA	Royal Academy of Arts, London
Ransom HRC	Harry Ransom Humanities Research Center, University of Texas, Austin
RAS	Royal Astronomical Society, London
RBG Kew	Royal Botanic Gardens, Kew, London
RCP Lond.	Royal College of Physicians of London
RCS Eng.	Royal College of Surgeons of England, London
RGS	Royal Geographical Society, London
RIBA	Royal Institute of British Architects, London
RIBA BAL	Royal Institute of British Architects, London, British Architectural Library
Royal Arch.	Royal Archives, Windsor Castle, Berkshire [by gracious permission of her majesty the queen]
Royal Irish Acad.	Royal Irish Academy, Dublin
Royal Scot. Acad.	Royal Scottish Academy, Edinburgh
RS	Royal Society, London
RSA	Royal Society of Arts, London
RS Friends, Lond.	Religious Society of Friends, London
St Ant. Oxf.	St Antony's College, Oxford
St John Cam.	St John's College, Cambridge
S. Antiquaries, Lond.	Society of Antiquaries of London
Sci. Mus.	Science Museum, London
Scot. NPG	Scottish National Portrait Gallery, Edinburgh
Scott Polar RI	University of Cambridge, Scott Polar Research Institute
Sheff. Arch.	Sheffield Archives
Shrops. RRC	Shropshire Records and Research Centre, Shrewsbury
SOAS	School of Oriental and African Studies, London
Som. ARS	Somerset Archive and Record Service, Taunton
Staffs. RO	Staffordshire Record Office, Stafford

Suffolk RO	Suffolk Record Office
Surrey HC	Surrey History Centre, Woking
TCD	Trinity College, Dublin
Trinity Cam.	Trinity College, Cambridge
U. Aberdeen	University of Aberdeen
U. Birm.	University of Birmingham
U. Birm. L.	University of Birmingham Library
U. Cal.	University of California
U. Cam.	University of Cambridge
UCL	University College, London
U. Durham	University of Durham
U. Durham L.	University of Durham Library
U. Edin.	University of Edinburgh
U. Edin., New Coll.	University of Edinburgh, New College
U. Edin., New Coll. L.	University of Edinburgh, New College Library
U. Edin. L.	University of Edinburgh Library
U. Glas.	University of Glasgow
U. Glas. L.	University of Glasgow Library
U. Hull	University of Hull
U. Hull, Brynmor Jones L.	University of Hull, Brynmor Jones Library
U. Leeds	University of Leeds
U. Leeds, Brotherton L.	University of Leeds, Brotherton Library
U. Lond.	University of London
U. Lpool	University of Liverpool
U. Lpool L.	University of Liverpool Library
U. Mich.	University of Michigan, Ann Arbor
U. Mich., Clements L.	University of Michigan, Ann Arbor, William L. Clements Library
U. Newcastle	University of Newcastle upon Tyne
U. Newcastle, Robinson L.	University of Newcastle upon Tyne, Robinson Library
U. Nott.	University of Nottingham
U. Nott. L.	University of Nottingham Library
U. Oxf.	University of Oxford
U. Reading	University of Reading
U. Reading L.	University of Reading Library
U. St Andr.	University of St Andrews
U. St Andr. L.	University of St Andrews Library
U. Southampton	University of Southampton
U. Southampton L.	University of Southampton Library
U. Sussex	University of Sussex, Brighton
U. Texas	University of Texas, Austin
U. Wales	University of Wales
U. Warwick Mod. RC	University of Warwick, Coventry, Modern Records Centre
V&A	Victoria and Albert Museum, London
V&A NAL	Victoria and Albert Museum, London, National Art Library
Warks. CRO	Warwickshire County Record Office, Warwick
Wellcome L.	Wellcome Library for the History and Understanding of Medicine, London
Westm. DA	Westminster Diocesan Archives, London
Wilts. & Swindon RO	Wiltshire and Swindon Record Office, Trowbridge
Worcs. RO	Worcestershire Record Office, Worcester
W. Sussex RO	West Sussex Record Office, Chichester
W. Yorks. AS	West Yorkshire Archive Service
Yale U.	Yale University, New Haven, Connecticut
Yale U., Beinecke L.	Yale University, New Haven, Connecticut, Beinecke Rare Book and Manuscript Library
Yale U. CBA	Yale University, New Haven, Connecticut, Yale Center for British Art

3 Bibliographic abbreviations

Adams, *Drama* W. D. Adams, *A dictionary of the drama*, 1: *A–G* (1904); 2: *H–Z* (1956) [vol. 2 microfilm only]

AFM J O'Donovan, ed. and trans., *Annala rioghachta Eireann / Annals of the kingdom of Ireland by the four masters*, 7 vols. (1848–51); 2nd edn (1856); 3rd edn (1990)

Allibone, *Dict.* S. A. Allibone, *A critical dictionary of English literature and British and American authors*, 3 vols. (1859–71); suppl. by J. F. Kirk, 2 vols. (1891)

ANB J. A. Garraty and M. C. Carnes, eds., *American national biography*, 24 vols. (1999)

Anderson, *Scot. nat.* W. Anderson, *The Scottish nation, or, The surnames, families, literature, honours, and biographical history of the people of Scotland*, 3 vols. (1859–63)

Ann. mon. H. R. Luard, ed., *Annales monastici*, 5 vols., Rolls Series, 36 (1864–9)

Ann. Ulster S. Mac Airt and G. Mac Niocaill, eds., *Annals of Ulster (to AD 1131)* (1983)

APC *Acts of the privy council of England*, new ser., 46 vols. (1890–1964)

APS *The acts of the parliaments of Scotland*, 12 vols. in 13 (1814–75)

Arber, *Regs. Stationers* F. Arber, ed., *A transcript of the registers of the Company of Stationers of London, 1554–1640 AD*, 5 vols. (1875–94)

ArchR *Architectural Review*

ASC D. Whitelock, D. C. Douglas, and S. I. Tucker, ed. and trans., *The Anglo-Saxon Chronicle: a revised translation* (1961)

AS chart. P. H. Sawyer, *Anglo-Saxon charters: an annotated list and bibliography*, Royal Historical Society Guides and Handbooks (1968)

AusDB D. Pike and others, eds., *Australian dictionary of biography*, 16 vols. (1966–2002)

Baker, *Serjeants* J. H. Baker, *The order of serjeants at law*, SeldS, suppl. ser., 5 (1984)

Bale, *Cat.* J. Bale, *Scriptorum illustrium Maioris Brytannie, quam nunc Angliam et Scotiam vocant: catalogus*, 2 vols. in 1 (Basel, 1557–9); facs. edn (1971)

Bale, *Index* J. Bale, *Index Britanniae scriptorum*, ed. R. L. Poole and M. Bateson (1902); facs. edn (1990)

BBCS *Bulletin of the Board of Celtic Studies*

BDMBR J. O. Baylen and N. J. Gossman, eds., *Biographical dictionary of modern British radicals*, 3 vols. in 4 (1979–88)

Bede, *Hist. eccl.* *Bede's Ecclesiastical history of the English people*, ed. and trans. B. Colgrave and R. A. B. Mynors, OMT (1969); repr. (1991)

Bénézit, *Dict.* E. Bénézit, *Dictionnaire critique et documentaire des peintres, sculpteurs, dessinateurs et graveurs*, 3 vols. (Paris, 1911–23); new edn, 8 vols. (1948–66), repr. (1966); 3rd edn, rev. and enl., 10 vols. (1976); 4th edn, 14 vols. (1999)

BIHR *Bulletin of the Institute of Historical Research*

Birch, *Seals* W. de Birch, *Catalogue of seals in the department of manuscripts in the British Museum*, 6 vols. (1887–1900)

Bishop Burnet's History *Bishop Burnet's History of his own time*, ed. M. J. Routh, 2nd edn, 6 vols. (1833)

Blackwood *Blackwood's [Edinburgh] Magazine*, 328 vols. (1817–1980)

Blain, Clements & Grundy, *Feminist comp.* V. Blain, P. Clements, and I. Grundy, eds., *The feminist companion to literature in English* (1990)

BL cat. *The British Library general catalogue of printed books* [in 360 vols. with suppls., also CD-ROM and online]

BMJ *British Medical Journal*

Boase & Courtney, *Bibl. Corn.* G. C. Boase and W. P. Courtney, *Bibliotheca Cornubiensis: a catalogue of the writings … of Cornishmen*, 3 vols. (1874–82)

Boase, *Mod. Eng. biog.* F. Boase, *Modern English biography: containing many thousand concise memoirs of persons who have died since the year 1850*, 6 vols. (privately printed, Truro, 1892–1921); repr. (1965)

Boswell, *Life* *Boswell's Life of Johnson: together with Journal of a tour to the Hebrides and Johnson's Diary of a journey into north Wales*, ed. G. B. Hill, enl. edn, rev. L. F. Powell, 6 vols. (1934–50); 2nd edn (1964); repr. (1971)

Brown & Stratton, *Brit. mus.* J. D. Brown and S. S. Stratton, *British musical biography* (1897)

Bryan, *Painters* M. Bryan, *A biographical and critical dictionary of painters and engravers*, 2 vols. (1816); new edn, ed. G. Stanley (1849); new edn, ed. R. E. Graves and W. Armstrong, 2 vols. (1886–9); [4th edn], ed. G. C. Williamson, 5 vols. (1903–5) [various reprs.]

Burke, *Gen. GB* J. Burke, *A genealogical and heraldic history of the commoners of Great Britain and Ireland*, 4 vols. (1833–8); new edn as *A genealogical and heraldic dictionary of the landed gentry of Great Britain and Ireland*, 3 vols. [1843–9] [many later edns]

Burke, *Gen. Ire.* J. B. Burke, *A genealogical and heraldic history of the landed gentry of Ireland* (1899); 2nd edn (1904); 3rd edn (1912); 4th edn (1958); 5th edn as *Burke's Irish family records* (1976)

Burke, *Peerage* J. Burke, *A general [later edns A genealogical] and heraldic dictionary of the peerage and baronetage of the United Kingdom* [later edns *the British empire*] (1829–)

Burney, *Hist. mus.* C. Burney, *A general history of music, from the earliest ages to the present period*, 4 vols. (1776–89)

Burtchaell & Sadleir, *Alum. Dubl.* G. D. Burtchaell and T. U. Sadleir, *Alumni Dublinenses: a register of the students, graduates, and provosts of Trinity College* (1924); [2nd edn], with suppl., in 2 pts (1935)

Calamy rev. A. G. Matthews, *Calamy revised* (1934); repr. (1988)

CCI *Calendar of confirmations and inventories granted and given up in the several commissariots of Scotland* (1876–)

CCIR *Calendar of the close rolls preserved in the Public Record Office*, 47 vols. (1892–1963)

CDS J. Bain, ed., *Calendar of documents relating to Scotland*, 4 vols., PRO (1881–8); suppl. vol. 5, ed. G. G. Simpson and J. D. Galbraith [1986]

CEPR letters W. H. Bliss, C. Johnson, and J. Twemlow, eds., *Calendar of entries in the papal registers relating to Great Britain and Ireland: papal letters* (1893–)

CGPLA *Calendars of the grants of probate and letters of administration* [in 4 ser.: *England & Wales, Northern Ireland, Ireland,* and *Éire*]

Chambers, *Scots.* R. Chambers, ed., *A biographical dictionary of eminent Scotsmen*, 4 vols. (1832–5)

Chancery records chancery records pubd by the PRO

Chancery records (RC) chancery records pubd by the Record Commissions

CIPM	*Calendar of inquisitions post mortem*, [20 vols.], PRO (1904–); also *Henry VII*, 3 vols. (1898–1955)
Clarendon, *Hist. rebellion*	E. Hyde, earl of Clarendon, *The history of the rebellion and civil wars in England*, 6 vols. (1888); repr. (1958) and (1992)
Cobbett, *Parl. hist.*	W. Cobbett and J. Wright, eds., *Cobbett's Parliamentary history of England*, 36 vols. (1806–1820)
Colvin, *Archs.*	H. Colvin, *A biographical dictionary of British architects, 1600–1840*, 3rd edn (1995)
Cooper, *Ath. Cantab.*	C. H. Cooper and T. Cooper, *Athenae Cantabrigienses*, 3 vols. (1858–1913); repr. (1967)
CPR	*Calendar of the patent rolls preserved in the Public Record Office* (1891–)
Crockford	*Crockford's Clerical Directory*
CS	Camden Society
CSP	*Calendar of state papers* [in 11 ser.: domestic, Scotland, Scottish series, Ireland, colonial, Commonwealth, foreign, Spain [at Simancas], Rome, Milan, and Venice]
CYS	Canterbury and York Society
DAB	*Dictionary of American biography*, 21 vols. (1928–36), repr. in 11 vols. (1964); 10 suppls. (1944–96)
DBB	D. J. Jeremy, ed., *Dictionary of business biography*, 5 vols. (1984–6)
DCB	G. W. Brown and others, *Dictionary of Canadian biography*, [14 vols.] (1966–)
Debrett's Peerage	*Debrett's Peerage* (1803–) [sometimes *Debrett's Illustrated peerage*]
Desmond, *Botanists*	R. Desmond, *Dictionary of British and Irish botanists and horticulturists* (1977); rev. edn (1994)
Dir. Brit. archs.	A. Felstead, J. Franklin, and L. Pinfield, eds., *Directory of British architects, 1834–1900* (1993); 2nd edn, ed. A. Brodie and others, 2 vols. (2001)
DLB	J. M. Bellamy and J. Saville, eds., *Dictionary of labour biography*, [10 vols.] (1972–)
DLitB	Dictionary of Literary Biography
DNB	*Dictionary of national biography*, 63 vols. (1885–1900), suppl., 3 vols. (1901); repr. in 22 vols. (1908–9); 10 further suppls. (1912–96); *Missing persons* (1993)
DNZB	W. H. Oliver and C. Orange, eds., *The dictionary of New Zealand biography*, 5 vols. (1990–2000)
DSAB	W. J. de Kock and others, eds., *Dictionary of South African biography*, 5 vols. (1968–87)
DSB	C. C. Gillispie and F. L. Holmes, eds., *Dictionary of scientific biography*, 16 vols. (1970–80); repr. in 8 vols. (1981); 2 vol. suppl. (1990)
DSBB	A. Slaven and S. Checkland, eds., *Dictionary of Scottish business biography, 1860–1960*, 2 vols. (1986–90)
DSCHT	N. M. de S. Cameron and others, eds., *Dictionary of Scottish church history and theology* (1993)
Dugdale, *Monasticon*	W. Dugdale, *Monasticon Anglicanum*, 3 vols. (1655–72); 2nd edn, 3 vols. (1661–82); new edn, ed. J. Caley, J. Ellis, and B. Bandinel, 6 vols. in 8 pts (1817–30); repr. (1846) and (1970)
DWB	J. E. Lloyd and others, eds., *Dictionary of Welsh biography down to 1940* (1959) [Eng. trans. of *Y bywgraffiadur Cymreig hyd 1940*, 2nd edn (1954)]
EdinR	*Edinburgh Review, or, Critical Journal*
EETS	Early English Text Society
Emden, *Cam.*	A. B. Emden, *A biographical register of the University of Cambridge to 1500* (1963)
Emden, *Oxf.*	A. B. Emden, *A biographical register of the University of Oxford to AD 1500*, 3 vols. (1957–9); also *A biographical register of the University of Oxford, AD 1501 to 1540* (1974)
EngHR	*English Historical Review*
Engraved Brit. ports.	F. M. O'Donoghue and H. M. Hake, *Catalogue of engraved British portraits preserved in the department of prints and drawings in the British Museum*, 6 vols. (1908–25)
ER	The English Reports, 178 vols. (1900–32)
ESTC	*English short title catalogue, 1475–1800* [CD-ROM and online]
Evelyn, *Diary*	*The diary of John Evelyn*, ed. E. S. De Beer, 6 vols. (1955); repr. (2000)
Farington, *Diary*	*The diary of Joseph Farington*, ed. K. Garlick and others, 17 vols. (1978–98)
Fasti Angl. (Hardy)	J. Le Neve, *Fasti ecclesiae Anglicanae*, ed. T. D. Hardy, 3 vols. (1854)
Fasti Angl., 1066–1300	[J. Le Neve], *Fasti ecclesiae Anglicanae, 1066–1300*, ed. D. E. Greenway and J. S. Barrow, [8 vols.] (1968–)
Fasti Angl., 1300–1541	[J. Le Neve], *Fasti ecclesiae Anglicanae, 1300–1541*, 12 vols. (1962–7)
Fasti Angl., 1541–1857	[J. Le Neve], *Fasti ecclesiae Anglicanae, 1541–1857*, ed. J. M. Horn, D. M. Smith, and D. S. Bailey, [9 vols.] (1969–)
Fasti Scot.	H. Scott, *Fasti ecclesiae Scoticanae*, 3 vols. in 6 (1871); new edn, [11 vols.] (1915–)
FO List	*Foreign Office List*
Fortescue, *Brit. army*	J. W. Fortescue, *A history of the British army*, 13 vols. (1899–1930)
Foss, *Judges*	E. Foss, *The judges of England*, 9 vols. (1848–64); repr. (1966)
Foster, *Alum. Oxon.*	J. Foster, ed., *Alumni Oxonienses: the members of the University of Oxford, 1715–1886*, 4 vols. (1887–8); later edn (1891); also *Alumni Oxonienses … 1500–1714*, 4 vols. (1891–2); 8 vol. repr. (1968) and (2000)
Fuller, *Worthies*	T. Fuller, *The history of the worthies of England*, 4 pts (1662); new edn, 2 vols., ed. J. Nichols (1811); new edn, 3 vols., ed. P. A. Nuttall (1840); repr. (1965)
GEC, *Baronetage*	G. E. Cokayne, *Complete baronetage*, 6 vols. (1900–09); repr. (1983) [microprint]
GEC, *Peerage*	G. E. C. [G. E. Cokayne], *The complete peerage of England, Scotland, Ireland, Great Britain, and the United Kingdom*, 8 vols. (1887–98); new edn, ed. V. Gibbs and others, 14 vols. in 15 (1910–98); microprint repr. (1982) and (1987)
Genest, *Eng. stage*	J. Genest, *Some account of the English stage from the Restoration in 1660 to 1830*, 10 vols. (1832); repr. [New York, 1965]
Gillow, *Lit. biog. hist.*	J. Gillow, *A literary and biographical history or bibliographical dictionary of the English Catholics, from the breach with Rome, in 1534, to the present time*, 5 vols. [1885–1902]; repr. (1961); repr. with preface by C. Gillow (1999)
Gir. Camb. opera	*Giraldi Cambrensis opera*, ed. J. S. Brewer, J. F. Dimock, and G. F. Warner, 8 vols., Rolls Series, 21 (1861–91)
GJ	*Geographical Journal*

Gladstone, *Diaries*   *The Gladstone diaries: with cabinet minutes and prime-ministerial correspondence*, ed. M. R. D. Foot and H. C. G. Matthew, 14 vols. (1968–94)

GM   *Gentleman's Magazine*

Graves, *Artists*   A. Graves, ed., *A dictionary of artists who have exhibited works in the principal London exhibitions of oil paintings from 1760 to 1880* (1884); new edn (1895); 3rd edn (1901); facs. edn (1969); repr. [1970], (1973), and (1984)

Graves, *Brit. Inst.*   A. Graves, *The British Institution, 1806–1867: a complete dictionary of contributors and their work from the foundation of the institution* (1875); facs. edn (1908); repr. (1969)

Graves, *RA exhibitors*   A. Graves, *The Royal Academy of Arts: a complete dictionary of contributors and their work from its foundation in 1769 to 1904*, 8 vols. (1905–6); repr. in 4 vols. (1970) and (1972)

Graves, *Soc. Artists*   A. Graves, *The Society of Artists of Great Britain, 1760–1791, the Free Society of Artists, 1761–1783: a complete dictionary* (1907); facs. edn (1969)

Greaves & Zaller, *BDBR*   R. L. Greaves and R. Zaller, eds., *Biographical dictionary of British radicals in the seventeenth century*, 3 vols. (1982–4)

Grove, *Dict. mus.*   G. Grove, ed., *A dictionary of music and musicians*, 5 vols. (1878–90); 2nd edn, ed. J. A. Fuller Maitland (1904–10); 3rd edn, ed. H. C. Colles (1927); 4th edn with suppl. (1940); 5th edn, ed. E. Blom, 9 vols. (1954); suppl. (1961) [see also *New Grove*]

Hall, *Dramatic ports.*   L. A. Hall, *Catalogue of dramatic portraits in the theatre collection of the Harvard College library*, 4 vols. (1930–34)

Hansard   *Hansard's parliamentary debates*, ser. 1–5 (1803–)

Highfill, Burnim & Langhans, *BDA*   P. H. Highfill, K. A. Burnim, and E. A. Langhans, *A biographical dictionary of actors, actresses, musicians, dancers, managers, and other stage personnel in London, 1660–1800*, 16 vols. (1973–93)

Hist. U. Oxf.   T. H. Aston, ed., *The history of the University of Oxford*, 8 vols. (1984–2000) [1: *The early Oxford schools*, ed. J. I. Catto (1984); 2: *Late medieval Oxford*, ed. J. I. Catto and R. Evans (1992); 3: *The collegiate university*, ed. J. McConica (1986); 4: *Seventeenth-century Oxford*, ed. N. Tyacke (1997); 5: *The eighteenth century*, ed. L. S. Sutherland and L. G. Mitchell (1986); 6–7: *Nineteenth-century Oxford*, ed. M. G. Brock and M. C. Curthoys (1997–2000); 8: *The twentieth century*, ed. B. Harrison (2000)]

HJ   *Historical Journal*

HMC   Historical Manuscripts Commission

Holdsworth, *Eng. law*   W. S. Holdsworth, *A history of English law*, ed. A. L. Goodhart and H. L. Hanbury, 17 vols. (1903–72)

HoP, *Commons*   *The history of parliament: the House of Commons* [*1386–1421*, ed. J. S. Roskell, L. Clark, and C. Rawcliffe, 4 vols. (1992); *1509–1558*, ed. S. T. Bindoff, 3 vols. (1982); *1558–1603*, ed. P. W. Hasler, 3 vols. (1981); *1660–1690*, ed. B. D. Henning, 3 vols. (1983); *1690–1715*, ed. D. W. Hayton, E. Cruickshanks, and S. Handley, 5 vols. (2002); *1715–1754*, ed. R. Sedgwick, 2 vols. (1970); *1754–1790*, ed. L. Namier and J. Brooke, 3 vols. (1964), repr. (1985); *1790–1820*, ed. R. G. Thorne, 5 vols. (1986); in draft (used with permission): *1422–1504, 1604–1629, 1640–1660*, and *1820–1832*]

IGI   *International Genealogical Index*, Church of Jesus Christ of the Latterday Saints

ILN   *Illustrated London News*

IMC   Irish Manuscripts Commission

Irving, *Scots.*   J. Irving, ed., *The book of Scotsmen eminent for achievements in arms and arts, church and state, law, legislation and literature, commerce, science, travel and philanthropy* (1881)

JCS   *Journal of the Chemical Society*

JHC   *Journals of the House of Commons*

JHL   *Journals of the House of Lords*

John of Worcester, *Chron.*   *The chronicle of John of Worcester*, ed. R. R. Darlington and P. McGurk, trans. J. Bray and P. McGurk, 3 vols., OMT (1995–) [vol. 1 forthcoming]

Keeler, *Long Parliament*   M. F. Keeler, *The Long Parliament, 1640–1641: a biographical study of its members* (1954)

Kelly, *Handbk*   *The upper ten thousand: an alphabetical list of all members of noble families*, 3 vols. (1875–7); continued as *Kelly's handbook of the upper ten thousand for 1878* [1879], 2 vols. (1878–9); continued as *Kelly's handbook to the titled, landed and official classes*, 94 vols. (1880–1973)

LondG   *London Gazette*

LP Henry VIII   J. S. Brewer, J. Gairdner, and R. H. Brodie, eds., *Letters and papers, foreign and domestic, of the reign of Henry VIII*, 23 vols. in 38 (1862–1932); repr. (1965)

Mallalieu, *Watercolour artists*   H. L. Mallalieu, *The dictionary of British watercolour artists up to 1820*, 3 vols. (1976–90); vol. 1, 2nd edn (1986)

Memoirs FRS   *Biographical Memoirs of Fellows of the Royal Society*

MGH   Monumenta Germaniae Historica

MT   *Musical Times*

Munk, *Roll*   W. Munk, *The roll of the Royal College of Physicians of London*, 2 vols. (1861); 2nd edn, 3 vols. (1878)

N&Q   *Notes and Queries*

New Grove   S. Sadie, ed., *The new Grove dictionary of music and musicians*, 20 vols. (1980); 2nd edn, 29 vols. (2001) [also online edn; see also Grove, *Dict. mus.*]

Nichols, *Illustrations*   J. Nichols and J. B. Nichols, *Illustrations of the literary history of the eighteenth century*, 8 vols. (1817–58)

Nichols, *Lit. anecdotes*   J. Nichols, *Literary anecdotes of the eighteenth century*, 9 vols. (1812–16); facs. edn (1966)

Obits. FRS   *Obituary Notices of Fellows of the Royal Society*

O'Byrne, *Naval biog. dict.*   W. R. O'Byrne, *A naval biographical dictionary* (1849); repr. (1990); [2nd edn], 2 vols. (1861)

OHS   Oxford Historical Society

Old Westminsters   *The record of Old Westminsters*, 1–2, ed. G. F. R. Barker and A. H. Stenning (1928); suppl. 1, ed. J. B. Whitmore and G. R. Y. Radcliffe [1938]; 3, ed. J. B. Whitmore, G. R. Y. Radcliffe, and D. C. Simpson (1963); suppl. 2, ed. F. E. Pagan (1978); 4, ed. F. E. Pagan and H. E. Pagan (1992)

OMT   Oxford Medieval Texts

Ordericus Vitalis, *Eccl. hist.*   *The ecclesiastical history of Orderic Vitalis*, ed. and trans. M. Chibnall, 6 vols., OMT (1969–80); repr. (1990)

Paris, *Chron.*   *Matthaei Parisiensis, monachi sancti Albani, chronica majora*, ed. H. R. Luard, Rolls Series, 7 vols. (1872–83)

Parl. papers   *Parliamentary papers* (1801–)

PBA   *Proceedings of the British Academy*

Pepys, *Diary* — *The diary of Samuel Pepys*, ed. R. Latham and W. Matthews, 11 vols. (1970–83); repr. (1995) and (2000)

Pevsner — N. Pevsner and others, Buildings of England series

PICE — *Proceedings of the Institution of Civil Engineers*

Pipe rolls — *The great roll of the pipe for . . .*, PRSoc. (1884–)

PRO — Public Record Office

PRS — *Proceedings of the Royal Society of London*

PRSoc. — Pipe Roll Society

PTRS — *Philosophical Transactions of the Royal Society*

QR — *Quarterly Review*

RC — Record Commissions

Redgrave, *Artists* — S. Redgrave, *A dictionary of artists of the English school* (1874); rev. edn (1878); repr. (1970)

Reg. Oxf. — C. W. Boase and A. Clark, eds., *Register of the University of Oxford*, 5 vols., OHS, 1, 10–12, 14 (1885–9)

Reg. PCS — J. H. Burton and others, eds., *The register of the privy council of Scotland*, 1st ser., 14 vols. (1877–98); 2nd ser., 8 vols. (1899–1908); 3rd ser., [16 vols.] (1908–70)

Reg. RAN — H. W. C. Davis and others, eds., *Regesta regum Anglo-Normannorum, 1066–1154*, 4 vols. (1913–69)

RIBA Journal — *Journal of the Royal Institute of British Architects* [later *RIBA Journal*]

RotP — J. Strachey, ed., *Rotuli parliamentorum ut et petitiones, et placita in parliamento*, 6 vols. (1767–77)

RotS — D. Macpherson, J. Caley, and W. Illingworth, eds., *Rotuli Scotiae in Turri Londinensi et in domo capitulari Westmonasteriensi asservati*, 2 vols., RC, 14 (1814–19)

RS — Record(s) Society

Rymer, *Foedera* — T. Rymer and R. Sanderson, eds., *Foedera, conventiones, literae et cuiuscunque generis acta publica inter reges Angliae et alios quosvis imperatores, reges, pontifices, principes, vel communitates*, 20 vols. (1704–35); 2nd edn, 20 vols. (1726–35); 3rd edn, 10 vols. (1739–45), facs. edn (1967); new edn, ed. A. Clarke, J. Caley, and F. Holbrooke, 4 vols., RC, 50 (1816–30)

Sainty, *Judges* — J. Sainty, ed., *The judges of England, 1272–1990*, SeldS, suppl. ser., 10 (1993)

Sainty, *King's counsel* — J. Sainty, ed., *A list of English law officers and king's counsel*, SeldS, suppl. ser., 7 (1987)

SCH — Studies in Church History

Scots peerage — J. B. Paul, ed. *The Scots peerage, founded on Wood's edition of Sir Robert Douglas's Peerage of Scotland, containing an historical and genealogical account of the nobility of that kingdom*, 9 vols. (1904–14)

SeldS — Selden Society

SHR — *Scottish Historical Review*

State trials — T. B. Howell and T. J. Howell, eds., *Cobbett's Complete collection of state trials*, 34 vols. (1809–28)

STC, 1475–1640 — A. W. Pollard, G. R. Redgrave, and others, eds., *A short-title catalogue of . . . English books . . . 1475–1640* (1926); 2nd edn, ed. W. A. Jackson, F. S. Ferguson, and K. F. Pantzer, 3 vols. (1976–91) [see also Wing, *STC*]

STS — Scottish Text Society

SurtS — Surtees Society

Symeon of Durham, *Opera* — *Symeonis monachi opera omnia*, ed. T. Arnold, 2 vols., Rolls Series, 75 (1882–5); repr. (1965)

Tanner, *Bibl. Brit.-Hib.* — T. Tanner, *Bibliotheca Britannico-Hibernica*, ed. D. Wilkins (1748); repr. (1963)

Thieme & Becker, *Allgemeines Lexikon* — U. Thieme, F. Becker, and H. Vollmer, eds., *Allgemeines Lexikon der bildenden Künstler von der Antike bis zur Gegenwart*, 37 vols. (Leipzig, 1907–50); repr. (1961–5), (1983), and (1992)

Thurloe, *State papers* — *A collection of the state papers of John Thurloe*, ed. T. Birch, 7 vols. (1742)

TLS — *Times Literary Supplement*

Tout, *Admin. hist.* — T. F. Tout, *Chapters in the administrative history of mediaeval England: the wardrobe, the chamber, and the small seals*, 6 vols. (1920–33); repr. (1967)

TRHS — *Transactions of the Royal Historical Society*

VCH — H. A. Doubleday and others, eds., *The Victoria history of the counties of England*, [88 vols.] (1900–)

Venn, *Alum. Cant.* — J. Venn and J. A. Venn, *Alumni Cantabrigienses: a biographical list of all known students, graduates, and holders of office at the University of Cambridge, from the earliest times to 1900*, 10 vols. (1922–54); repr. in 2 vols. (1974–8)

Vertue, *Note books* — [G. Vertue], *Note books*, ed. K. Esdaile, earl of Ilchester, and H. M. Hake, 6 vols., Walpole Society, 18, 20, 22, 24, 26, 30 (1930–55)

VF — *Vanity Fair*

Walford, *County families* — E. Walford, *The county families of the United Kingdom, or, Royal manual of the titled and untitled aristocracy of Great Britain and Ireland* (1860)

Walker rev. — A. G. Matthews, *Walker revised: being a revision of John Walker's Sufferings of the clergy during the grand rebellion, 1642–60* (1948); repr. (1988)

Walpole, *Corr.* — *The Yale edition of Horace Walpole's correspondence*, ed. W. S. Lewis, 48 vols. (1937–83)

Ward, *Men of the reign* — T. H. Ward, ed., *Men of the reign: a biographical dictionary of eminent persons of British and colonial birth who have died during the reign of Queen Victoria* (1885); repr. (Graz, 1968)

Waterhouse, *18c painters* — E. Waterhouse, *The dictionary of 18th century painters in oils and crayons* (1981); repr. as *British 18th century painters in oils and crayons* (1991), vol. 2 of *Dictionary of British art*

Watt, *Bibl. Brit.* — R. Watt, *Bibliotheca Britannica, or, A general index to British and foreign literature*, 4 vols. (1824) [many reprs.]

Wellesley index — W. E. Houghton, ed., *The Wellesley index to Victorian periodicals, 1824–1900*, 5 vols. (1966–89); new edn (1999) [CD-ROM]

Wing, *STC* — D. Wing, ed., *Short-title catalogue of . . . English books . . . 1641–1700*, 3 vols. (1945–51); 2nd edn (1972–88); rev. and enl. edn, ed. J. J. Morrison, C. W. Nelson, and M. Seccombe, 4 vols. (1994–8) [see also *STC, 1475–1640*]

Wisden — *John Wisden's Cricketer's Almanack*

Wood, *Ath. Oxon.* — A. Wood, *Athenae Oxonienses . . . to which are added the Fasti*, 2 vols. (1691–2); 2nd edn (1721); new edn, 4 vols., ed. P. Bliss (1813–20); repr. (1967) and (1969)

Wood, *Vic. painters* — C. Wood, *Dictionary of Victorian painters* (1971); 2nd edn (1978); 3rd edn as *Victorian painters*, 2 vols. (1995), vol. 4 of *Dictionary of British art*

WW — *Who's who* (1849–)

WWBMP — M. Stenton and S. Lees, eds., *Who's who of British members of parliament*, 4 vols. (1976–81)

WWW — *Who was who* (1929–)

Pote, Joseph (1704–1787), bookseller and printer, was born in the parish of St Clement Danes, London, the son of Joseph Pote (*d.* 1716), staymaker, and his wife, Elizabeth (*née* Booden or Bowden), and was baptized in that parish in March 1704. Joseph was apprenticed to Daniel Brown, bookseller, on 4 August 1718 and almost as soon as he was out of his apprenticeship on 7 December 1725, he opened his own bookshop 'at the Golden Door, over against Suffolk House, Charing Cross' (Plomer, 201).

In 1729 Pote moved to premises at Isaac Newton's Head, 'the corner of Suffolk Street near Charing Cross' (Plomer, 201). At about the same time, however, he became involved with the bookselling business previously owned by Thomas Bartlet at Eton. Bartlet had died in 1727 and it appears that Pote then helped Bartlet's widow to run the business. At some point Pote married Bartlet's daughter, Ann (*d.* 1771), and their son Joseph was baptized on 1 February 1730 at St Martin's-in-the-Fields in London. It is not clear when Pote moved permanently to Eton.

Pote published several schoolbooks and classical texts throughout his career but there were also scholarly works aimed at a wider public than the boys at Eton College. Remarkably soon after his arrival in Eton he published *Catalogus almunorum … de Etona* (1730) and later, a revised edition of William Cave's *Historia literaria* (1735), and there were a few popular works—*The Foreigner's Guide to London* (1728) and the *History and Antiquities of Windsor Castle* (1749). A new venture began in 1745 when he started a twice-weekly newspaper, the *Eton Journal, or, Early Intelligencer*, with the chief purpose of providing information about the Jacobite rising. The title was changed in 1746 to the *Windsor and Eton Journal* and after the battle of Culloden the paper became a weekly.

Publications apart, Pote's main business was bookselling to the scholars at Eton and he soon became well known to members of the college. They used to chant:

Jos[eph] Pote of Eton, a man of great renown,
Buys a book for sixpence, and sells it for a crown.
(Lyte, 309)

He also dealt in stationery (particularly to supply the needs of the college), wallpaper, and patent medicines; and, never one to miss a business opportunity, he ran a small boarding-house for boys.

Pote had four sons (Joseph, Thomas, John, and Edward Ephraim) and four daughters (Ann, Catherine, Elizabeth, and Mary). His wife died in 1771 and he married Martha Belk in 1778. His son Joseph became a fellow of King's College, Cambridge, while Thomas (who was freed as a member of the Stationers' Company by his father in 1754) helped in the business. In 1769 Pote assigned most of the business to Thomas to devote more time to publishing. Pote died at Eton on 11 March 1787, leaving the business to Thomas, but because of their 'unnatural behaviour' to their mother and family, Joseph and Ann were cut off with 5*s.* each (will, fol. 194*v*). JOHN R. TURNER

Sources R. A. Austen-Leigh, 'Joseph Pote of Eton and Bartlet's *Farriery*', *The Library*, 4th ser., 17 (1936–7), 131–54 · H. R. Plomer and others, *A dictionary of the printers and booksellers who were at work in England, Scotland, and Ireland from 1726 to 1775* (1932); repr. (1968) · *Monthly Review*, 11 (1754), 235 · *GM*, 1st ser., 57 (1787), 365 · K. G. Burton, *The early newspaper press in Berkshire* (1954) · Nichols, *Lit. anecdotes* · H. C. M. Lyte, *A history of Eton College, 1440–1875* (1877) · R. Birley, *The history of Eton College Library* (1970) · will, PRO, PROB 11/1153, sig. 230

Potenger, John (1647–1733), legal official and writer, was born on 21 July 1647 in Winchester, the son of John Potenger DD (*d.* 1659), headmaster of Winchester College from 1 August 1642 to 1652, and Anne Withers. He was admitted to Winchester College in 1658, matriculated at Corpus Christi College, Oxford, on 26 May 1664, where he obtained a Hampshire scholarship, and graduated BA on 1 February 1668. He was admitted to the Inner Temple and called to the bar on 28 November 1675.

By the favour of Sir John Ernley, then chancellor of the exchequer, Potenger purchased at the price of £1700 the comptrollership of the pipe, and was sworn in in Hilary term 1676. Subsequently he obtained the post of master in chancery, but sold it again for £700. In 1685 he was appointed secretary to the chancellor of the exchequer. In the reign of James II he was removed from the commission of the peace for Middlesex for refusing to support the king's religious policy, but was restored again by William III. He married Philadelphia (*c.*1654–1692), second daughter of Sir John Ernley, on 2 July 1678. Their only daughter Philadelphia (1678–1757) married Richard Bingham (1666–1735) of Melcombe Bingham, Dorset, in 1695.

Potenger was the author of *A Pastoral Reflection on Death* (1691) and of many unpublished poems and translations from Latin authors (Bodl. Oxf., MS Eng. poet. d. 161). His *Life of Agricola* was published in 1698, while translations from poetry appeared anonymously, from Statius, *Silvae*, 5.4 in Nahum Tate's miscellany (N. Tate, *Poems by Several Hands*, 1685), and Horace, *Odes*, ii.14 in the Dryden–Tonson second miscellany (*Sylvae*, 1685). The latter was included by John Nichols in his *Select Collection of Miscellaneous Poems* along with two letters from Dr South praising his compositions; both translations appear in *The Oxford Book of Classical Verse in Translation* (ed. A. Poole and J. Maule, 1995). His memoirs were edited with the title *The Private Memoirs of John Potenger, Esq.* (1841) by his descendant Charles William Bingham, vicar of Sydling St Nicholas, Dorset, and contain interesting information on the state of education at Winchester and Oxford during the seventeenth century. As early as 1893 the book was rare (Fowler, 234, n. 1), but extracts concerning the University of Oxford are reproduced by Quiller-Couch and Feingold. Potenger died on 18 December 1733 and was buried with his wife in Blunsden church, Highworth, Wiltshire.

C. H. FIRTH, *rev.* ANNA CHAHOUD

Sources Foster, *Alum. Oxon.* · L. M. Quiller-Couch, ed., *Reminiscences of Oxford by Oxford men, 1559–1850*, OHS, 22 (1892), 53–6 · M. Feingold, 'The humanities', *Hist. U. Oxf. 4: 17th-cent. Oxf.*, 211–358, esp. 225, 284, 342 · M. Feingold, 'The mathematical sciences and new philosophies', *Hist. U. Oxf. 4: 17th-cent. Oxf.*, 359–448 · T. Fowler, *The history of Corpus Christi College*, OHS (1893), 234–5; repr. in T. Fowler, *Corpus Christi* (1898), 148–50 · J. L. Chester and J. Foster, eds., *London marriage licences, 1521–1869* (1887), 1079 ff. · F. A. Inderwick and R. A. Roberts, eds., *A calendar of the Inner Temple records*, 3 (1901), 105, 298, 325 · D. Lemmings, *Gentlemen and barristers: the inns of court and the English bar, 1680–1730* (1990), 59 · S. Gillespie, 'A

checklist of Restoration English translations and adaptations of classical Greek and Latin poetry, 1660–1700', *Translation and Literature*, 1 (1992), 52–67 • M. L. Clarke, *Classical education in Britain, 1500–1900* (1959), 61, 97–8 • A. Chalmers, ed., *The general biographical dictionary*, new edn, 32 vols. (1812–17)
Archives Bodl. Oxf., letters, poems, and translations

Pott, Alfred (1822–1908), Church of England clergyman and college head, was born on 30 September 1822 at Norwood, Surrey, the second son of Charles Pott of Norwood and Anna, daughter of C. S. Cox, master in chancery. From 1838 he was educated at Eton College under Edward Craven Hawtrey, and he matriculated at Balliol College, Oxford, on 15 December 1840. Having been elected to a demyship at Magdalen College in 1843, he graduated BA in 1844 with a second class in *literae humaniores*, and in the following year he won the Johnson theological scholarship. He was treasurer in 1844 and president and librarian in 1845 of the Oxford Union. He proceeded MA in 1847, and BD in 1854. Ordained deacon in December 1845 and priest in the following year, in 1847 he became curate of Cuddesdon, and in 1852 vicar on the nomination of Bishop Samuel Wilberforce. In 1853 he was elected a fellow of Magdalen College.

In 1851 Wilberforce had given Pott the task of building a theological college opposite the bishop's palace in Cuddesdon, near Oxford. As first principal he stressed the task of 'forming character and moulding habits' (Chadwick, 32), which subsequently influenced theological education far beyond Cuddesdon. Because of his own modesty, his work as rural dean, and his lengthy periods of illness, he was somewhat overshadowed by his far more uncompromising vice-principal, Henry Parry Liddon. As principal he lectured on the New Testament and he also published a number of sermons and addresses he had given to the people of the village; his *Confirmation Lectures* (1852) reached a fifth edition in 1886. On 5 July 1855 he married Emily Harriet (*d.* 1903), daughter of Joseph Gibbs, vicar of Clifton Hampden, Oxfordshire. Their only daughter was Gladys Sydney *Pott (1867–1961), anti-suffragist and civil servant.

Pott resigned as principal owing to ill health shortly after Charles Pourtales Golightly had called attention to ritualist and Romanizing practices of the Cuddesdon system. Pott's judicious defence against these charges, together with his high standing in the diocese and his appointment of Edward King (1829–1910) as chaplain 'to change the tone' of the college, did much to allay the fears among the clergy, and to secure the future of residential graduate theological education.

In 1858 Pott accepted the living of East Hendred, Berkshire, though he once again took on the running of Cuddesdon College following his successor's death in 1862 until Edward King's appointment in 1863. He became vicar and rural dean of nearby Abingdon in 1867, remaining so until 1875. Bishop Wilberforce appointed Pott one of his examining chaplains (a position he retained on Wilberforce's translation to Winchester in 1869). He was made an honorary canon of Christ Church in 1868, and in 1869 Wilberforce preferred him to the archdeaconry of

Berkshire. Wilberforce had hoped to have Pott elevated to the episcopate, but after his sudden death in 1873, Pott lost his chief mentor. He subsequently held the benefices of Clifton Hampden (1875–82) and of Sonning, Berkshire (1882–99). He resigned the archdeaconry in 1903, but retained his honorary canonry. In convocation, though only an occasional speaker, Pott was a recognized authority on ecclesiastical law; and as archdeacon he showed wisdom, justice, and judgement. Although a high-churchman, he was never a party man and enjoyed the friendship of those of widely divergent opinions. After the publication of R. G. Wilberforce's *Life of the Right Revd Samuel Wilberforce* in 1882 Pott destroyed all his own private papers and diaries for undisclosed reasons, and wrote a brief autobiographical sketch (now lost) for the use of the family.

Pott died at his home, Woodside, Windlesham, Surrey, on 28 February 1908, and was buried at Clifton Hampden churchyard. G. S. WOODS, *rev.* MARK D. CHAPMAN

Sources O. Chadwick, *The founding of Cuddesdon* (1954) • R. G. Wilberforce, *Life of the right reverend Samuel Wilberforce … with selections from his diaries and correspondence*, 3 (1882) • H. P. Liddon, *The life of Edward Bouverie Pusey*, ed. J. O. Johnston and others, 4 vols. (1893–7) • Ripon College, Cuddesdon, Cuddesdon College archives • *Correspondence relating to Cuddesdon Theological College in answer to the charges of the Revd C. P. Golightly and the report of the commissioners thereon* (1858) • S. C. Gayford, *Cuddesdon College, 1854–1929: a record and a memorial* (1930) • H. E. C. Stapylton, *The Eton school lists, from 1791 to 1850*, 2nd edn (1864) • Foster, *Alum. Oxon.* • Bodl. Oxf., MSS Wilberforce • *The Guardian* (4 March 1908), 365 • *CGPLA Eng. & Wales* (1908) • A. Atherstone, 'Charles Golightly (1807–1885): church parties and university politics in Victorian Oxford', DPhil diss., U. Oxf., 2000, ch. 6
Archives Bodl. Oxf., Wilberforce MSS • Pusey Oxf., Liddon MSS • Ripon College, Cuddesdon, archives
Likenesses photograph, Clifton Hampden church, Oxfordshire • two photographs, Cuddesdon College, Oxfordshire
Wealth at death £51,815 17s. 9d.: resworn probate, 19 March 1908, *CGPLA Eng. & Wales*

Pott, Gladys Sydney (1867–1961), anti-suffragist and civil servant, was the only daughter of the Venerable Alfred *Pott (1822–1908), archdeacon of Berkshire, and his wife, Emily Harriet, *née* Gibbs (*d.* 1903). She had a private education and never married. One acquaintance, Helen Moyes, described her as 'very able, good speaker, quite impressive, in fact a bit formidable … not particularly feminine' (Harrison, 131). But though she resembled an archetypal late-Victorian feminist, Gladys Pott emerged on the opposite side as a staunch and articulate campaigner against the enfranchisement of women. After becoming secretary of the north Berkshire branch of the Women's National Anti-Suffrage League in 1908 Gladys Pott came to the attention of the leading anti-suffragists lords Cromer and Curzon who admired her industriousness, organizing abilities, and imaginative tactics. Following the amalgamation of the male and female anti-suffrage organizations in 1910 she served on the executive committee and became secretary in 1913–14. Gladys Pott liked to take the battle into the enemy camp by asking questions at Women's Social and Political Union meetings; as a result she was invited to speak for the antis but protested 'I did not know how'. However, she quickly took to debating with leading suffragists including Cicely Hamilton and Millicent Fawcett. In her frequent letters to *The Times* Gladys Pott attacked Millicent Fawcett for acquiescing in suffragette violence; she warned that the suffragists would not rest content with a limited vote for women but would end by demanding complete adult suffrage; and she took pains to refute claims that working women would gain higher wages once they were enfranchised.

However, the key tactical expedient with which Gladys Pott was associated was the canvass of female municipal electors. At a time when the majority of MPs had been converted to women's suffrage its opponents felt it necessary to shore up their crumbling position by demonstrating that most ordinary women continued to lack interest in winning the vote. Gladys Pott's north Berkshire branch claimed that 1085 women electors opposed enfranchisement, while only 75 were in favour and 63 neutral in a total of 1291. She repeated the exercise in 1912 with a canvass of four London boroughs with similar results. Although Pott's methods, including the reply-paid postcard, were criticized by opponents, she succeeded in restoring some credibility to the anti-suffragists' case and maintaining doubt in the minds of wavering MPs. In spite of this the antis were fighting a rearguard action and by 1912–13 the league had begun to suffer serious internal divisions and resignations. With Curzon's support Gladys Pott attempted to reorganize the league at this stage; in particular she tried to win more press publicity and to co-ordinate the efforts of the MPs by forming a parliamentary committee similar to that organized by the suffragists.

However, the outbreak of war led Gladys Pott to abandon anti-suffragism in favour of war work. With her friend Dame Muriel Talbot she helped to organize the Women's Land Army, and from 1916 to 1919 she worked as a woman inspector under the women's branch of the Board of Agriculture and Fisheries. By the end of the war her combination of organizational experience and conventional political views made her an attractive and reassuring figure for politicians now anxious to place women on official boards and committees. Consequently a whole new career opened up, and, as with her Edwardian campaigns, it involved fighting a losing cause. Gladys Pott became secretary and chairman of the Society for Oversea Settlement of British Women from 1920 to 1937. Originally an independent organization, the society was invited to accept a grant of public money and thus became absorbed into a department of state. As a result Gladys Pott worked as chief woman officer of the oversea settlement department of the Dominions Office helping to promote emigration to the empire. Her work took her to India and South Africa in 1921 and to Australia and New Zealand in 1923. In 1926 she formed part of the British government delegation to the eighth session of the International Labour Conference at Geneva when she acted as woman adviser to the delegates; in that year her work was recognized by her appointment as OBE. On her retirement in 1937 Gladys Pott was made a CBE. She died at her home, Little Place, Clifton Hampden, Oxfordshire, aged ninety-four, on 13 November 1961.   MARTIN PUGH

Sources *The Times* (14 Nov 1961) · *The Times* (17 Nov 1961) · *Anti-Suffrage Review* (1908–14) · B. Harrison, *Separate spheres: the opposition to women's suffrage in Britain* (1978) · *Jus Suffragii* (Aug–Sept 1926) · d. cert. · *WWW*

Wealth at death £26,205 5s.: probate, 6 Feb 1962, *CGPLA Eng. & Wales*

Pott, Joseph Holden (1758–1847), Church of England clergyman, was born on 27 October 1758 in Smithfield, London, the third son of Percivall *Pott (1714–1788), an eminent surgeon, and his wife, Sarah, daughter of Robert Crittenden. He was educated at Eton College from 1767, becoming a scholar in 1776. About that year he entered St John's College, Cambridge, where he secured Sir William Browne's medal, graduated with first-class classical honours in 1780, and proceeded MA in 1783. By 1786 he had published *Poems* (1779), *Elegies, with Selmane, a Tragedy* (1782), *Essay on Landscape Painting* (1782), and *The Tour of Valentine* (1786). He was ordained deacon by the bishop of Peterborough in 1781 and priest by the bishop of Lincoln in 1782. He was appointed rector of Beesby in the Marsh, Lincolnshire, in 1783, and of Bratoft in 1784, and chaplain to Lord Chancellor Thurlow in 1784. Bishop Thurlow of Lincoln collated him to the prebendal stall of Welton Brinkhall in Lincoln Cathedral in 1785. He resigned Bratoft for St Olave Jewry and St Martin Pomeroy, Ironmonger Lane, in London in 1787. In 1789 Bishop Porteus of London appointed him archdeacon of St Albans, and he resigned Beesby in 1790. In 1797 Porteus appointed him rector of Little Burstead in Essex, and he resigned his City parishes. In 1806 he accepted the vicarage of Northall in Middlesex, and resigned Little Burstead. In 1812 Bishop Randolph appointed him vicar of St Martin-in-the-Fields. In 1813 he exchanged the archdeaconry of St Albans for that of London, and in 1814 resigned his prebendal stall at Lincoln. In 1822 Bishop Howley appointed him a prebendary of St Paul's, and he resigned the vicarage of Northall; in 1824 he accepted the vicarage of Kensington, and resigned St Martin-in-the-Fields. In 1826 Archbishop Manners-Sutton appointed him a prebendary and chancellor of Exeter Cathedral. He resigned as vicar of Kensington and archdeacon of London in 1842.

Pott was regarded as an exceptionally efficient administrator and a good preacher. He was a member of the Hackney Phalanx, and was associated with many of their reforming projects. As archdeacon of St Albans he was much concerned with education and the role of the clergy. Contemporaries regarded him as an exemplary archdeacon. As a governor of the Society for Promoting Christian Knowledge he was associated with Joshua Watson, William Van Mildert, and Christopher Wordsworth in establishing district committees of clergy and laity in each diocese to broaden the membership of the society, and to increase its income and influence. He was subsequently treasurer of the society and attempted to organize parliamentary support for missionary work in India, but was opposed by Bishop Randolph of London. He was one of the initiators of the Incorporated Church Building Society, launched in 1818 to assist in providing grants for building churches in newly developing urban areas, and he was appointed a member of the commission established by Lord Liverpool's government to administer the £1 million grant to build new churches and to establish new parishes. Pott was a key member of the commission, serving on its most important committees. His relations with Bishop Blomfield from 1828 were frosty. He was regarded as the last survivor of the Hackney Phalanx. He was an active residentiary at Exeter, where he was involved in the dispute between Bishop Phillpotts and the dean and chapter over the interpretation of the Book of Common Prayer ornaments rubric during the Exeter 'Surplice riots' in 1842.

Pott had a reputation as a theologian, publishing *Remarks on Two Particulars in a Refutation of Calvinism* in 1811, in response to Sir George Pretyman-Tomline's *Refutation of Calvinism*, and *The Testimony of St Paul Concerning Justification* in 1846, in addition to at least seven collections of sermons. He died, unmarried, aged eighty-eight, in his house in Woburn Place, Holborn, on 16 February 1847, and was buried in St Mary Aldermary, with his parents. He left estate valued at £20,000. W. M. JACOB

Sources DNB · Venn, *Alum. Cant.*, 2/5 · *GM*, 2nd ser., 28 (1847) · Allibone, *Dict.* · C. Dewey, *The passing of Barchester* (1991) · W. K. L. Clarke, *A history of the SPCK* (1959) · E. A. Varley, *The last of the prince bishops: William Van Mildert and the high church movement of the early nineteenth century* (1992) · A. Burns, *The diocesan revival in the Church of England, c.1800–1870* (1999) · G. C. B. Davies, *Henry Phillpotts, bishop of Exeter* (1954) · M. H. Port, *Six hundred new churches: a study of the church building commission, 1818–1856, and its church building activities* (1961) · R. A. Austen-Leigh, ed., *The Eton College register, 1753–1790* (1921), 429

Likenesses J. Porter, mezzotint, pubd 1843 (after W. Owen), BM, NPG · W. Owen, oils

Wealth at death approx. £20,000: *GM*

Pott, Percivall (1714–1788), surgeon, only son of Percivall Pott (1681–1717), a notary and scrivener of London, was born on 6 January 1714 in Threadneedle Street, City of London, now the site of the Bank of England. The house was probably destroyed when the east and west wings of the bank were built between 1766 and 1788. Members of the Pott family, originally from Cheshire, settled in London in the late seventeenth century as grocers and vintners. In 1712 Pott's father had married Elizabeth (*d.* 1745), daughter of William Symonds, a vintner, and widow of Benjamin, son of Sir John Houblon, the first governor of the Bank of England. Benjamin Houblon, an army officer, died in Lisbon in 1708, leaving his widow and a daughter, also named Elizabeth. The early death of Pott's father in 1717 left his mother a widow for the second time and, it is believed, her young family in straitened financial circumstances.

Education and early career Fortunately, Elizabeth Pott and her two children were assisted by a distant relative, Dr Wilcox, bishop of Rochester, and, at the age of seven, Percivall was sent to a private school at Darenth in Kent. Sir James *Earle, Pott's son-in-law and former apprentice, stated in a short biography preceding the 1790 edition of

Percivall Pott (1714–1788), by Sir Joshua Reynolds, 1784

Pott's collected works that Pott formed an early taste for classical knowledge and was recommended to enter the church where his prospects of preferment were considerable. This he declined for a compelling interest in surgery and, aged fifteen years in 1729, he was bound apprentice to Edward Nourse for a premium of 200 guineas. Nourse was then assistant surgeon to St Bartholomew's Hospital and, unlike most of his colleagues, gave lectures on anatomy and surgery, delivering them at London House in Aldersgate Street where it was Pott's duty to prepare dissections for demonstration. These early anatomical studies combined with wide reading, daily exposure to clinical problems, and practical surgery, allied to an excellent memory, soon gained Pott professional respect. Earle reports that during his later apprenticeship, Pott being 'confident in the fair prospect of industry, hired a house of considerable rent in Fenchurch Street, and took with him his mother and her daughter by her first husband' (Earle, x). When Pott presented himself to the court of examiners of the Barber–Surgeons' Company in 1736, it was recorded,

> not having waited on all the Governors and Examiners to desire the favour of their presence at his examination, and it appearing to the Court that Mr. Pott had been sent for out of town to attend Sir Robert Goodesall's lady, where he was detained so long as not to be able to return within the time limited … It was resolved that the Court would proceed to the examination of the said Mr. Pott notwithstanding his default in attending the Examiners: But this is not to be taken as a precedent … to any other person. (Dobson, 55)

This confirmed an established reputation, for he received not only his freedom of the company but, on the same day,

7 September 1736, passed the difficult grand diploma. At this time he was still in Fenchurch Street, but when he took the livery of the company in 1739 he had moved to Bow Lane. With growing expertise and practice he applied for a post as assistant surgeon at St Bartholomew's Hospital and, after an initial failure, was successful in 1745. That same year was important for the breakup of the Barber–Surgeons' Company and the formation of the Company of Surgeons, later the Royal College of Surgeons. In 1753 Pott and William Hunter were elected the first lecturers in anatomy to the new company; Pott became a member of the court of examiners in 1763, and master of the company in 1765.

At St Bartholomew's Hospital Pott saw many patients and acquired the profound clinical experience so evident in his later written work. After moving to Watling Street he began informal classes for private pupils in anatomy and surgery. Initially lecturing with hesitation and reserve, according to Earle, he later developed confidence, eloquence, and a manner which 'gave importance to every subject, and impressed his audience with the idea, that the art which he taught was worthy of their highest ambition' (Earle, xxiii). Appointment to full surgeon at St Bartholomew's in 1749 enabled him to challenge long established and painful therapeutic measures, in particular to restrict the use of hot iron cauteries, of caustic applications, and of dangerous mechanical equipment employed to reduce major joint dislocations.

An accident inspires authorship On a cold January day in 1756 Pott sustained an injury which proved a turning point in his career and a stimulus to the original contributions associated with his name. In the words of Earle:

> As he was riding in Kent-street, Southwark, he was thrown from his horse, and suffered a compound fracture of the leg, the bone being forced through the integuments. Conscious of the dangers attendant on fractures of this nature, and thoroughly aware how much they may be increased by rough treatment, or improper position, he would not suffer himself to be moved until he had made the necessary dispositions. He sent to Westminster, then the nearest place, for two chairmen, to bring their poles; and patiently lay on the cold pavement, … In this situation he purchased a door, to which he made them nail their poles. When all was ready he caused himself to be laid on it, and was carried through Southwark, over London-bridge, to Watling-street, near St Paul's [over a mile], … At a consultation of surgeons, the case was thought to be so desperate as to require immediate amputation. Mr Pott, convinced that no one could be a proper judge in his own case, submitted to their opinion; and the instruments were actually got ready, when Mr. Nourse, who had been prevented from coming sooner, fortunately entered the room. After examining the limb, he conceived there was a possibility of preserving it; an attempt to save it was acquiesced in, and succeeded.   (Earle, xiv–xv)

Commenting on compound long bone fracture in *Fractures and Dislocations* (1768) Pott stated that it 'either unites or heals as it were by the first intention, which is the case of some lucky few (as was my own) or it is attended with high inflammation'. This statement and Earle's words suggest that the fracture sustained was not, as often alleged, a Pott's fracture, or fracture-dislocation of the ankle as meticulously analysed in his writings—a Pott's fracture is not a fracture of the leg, meaning the shin in eighteenth century parlance. It is of interest that three well-known surgeons, Ambroise Paré, Richard Wiseman, and Pott avoided amputation after compound tibial fractures at a time when dismemberment was commonly advised.

Necessarily confined to bed and home for three months or so Pott started to write an essay on hernias, published in late 1756 as *A Treatise on Ruptures*. Prior to this, his only communication was a short paper in the *Philosophical Transactions of the Royal Society*, in 1741, entitled 'An account of tumours which rendered the bones soft'. The book's immediate success generated a series of monographs during the succeeding twenty-eight years which analysed ophthalmic, neurological, genito-urinary, orthopaedic, and traumatological subjects. Fortuitously, the enforced rest of his fracture revealed a talent for writing which otherwise might not have flourished.

Surgical renown In 1764 Pott's second paper, 'An account of a hernia of the urinary bladder, including a stone', was published by the Royal Society, which elected him a fellow. Succeeding Nourse as senior surgeon at St Bartholomew's Hospital in 1765 enabled Pott to give his course of surgical lectures publicly to large audiences; these became celebrated and, coupled with his writings, disseminated his views and methods widely.

With a growing private practice Pott moved house to Lincoln's Inn Fields in 1769 and finally to Princes Street, Hanover Square, in 1777. Among important patients he saw David Garrick, Samuel Johnson, and Thomas Gainsborough. He confirmed, with William Cruikshank, that Johnson had a solid tumour (sarcocoele) of the testis and not a simple hydrocele and, with John Hunter, that Gainsborough had inoperable cancer involving the neck. Earle stated that Pott's evenings were often occupied answering letters of consultation on cases in Europe, Russia, Turkey, and India. In 1786 the Royal College of Surgeons of Edinburgh made him an honorary fellow, the first such fellowship to be awarded, and in 1787 the Royal College of Surgeons in Ireland made him an honorary member. At the age of seventy-three he resigned from St Bartholomew's Hospital, having walked its wards for fifty-eight years. He was made a hospital governor and continued in private practice until his death. John Hunter and Henry Park were both pupils of Pott.

In 1746 Pott married Sarah, daughter of Robert Cruttenden, and they produced five sons, including Joseph Holden *Pott, archdeacon of London, and four daughters. According to Earle:

> The labours of the greatest part of his life were without relaxation; an increasing family requiring his utmost exertion: of late years he had a villa at Neasden; and in the autumn usually passed a month at Bath, or at the sea-side. (Earle, xliv)

And: 'The person of Mr Pott was elegant, though lower than middle size: his countenance animated and expressive; his manners and deportment were graceful' (Earle, xliii). His kindness of heart was proverbial, and he is said to have had at one time three needy surgeons living in his house. His high character and blameless life helped to raise the surgeon's social standing in this country.

Surgical concepts and philosophy Pott was an experienced and proficient lecturer and doubtless his lecture notes were the source of later publications. This is borne out in copies of Pott's lectures which survive in the manuscript hand of students, deposited in the Royal College of Surgeons of England, St Bartholomew's Hospital, and the Royal Society of Medicine; similarities between these notes and his publications are often close. One student recorded Pott's humane approach to patients thus:

> in performing an operation, always remember you have a diseased body, endowed with the greatest degree of sensibility and feeling; give therefore the least possible pain imaginable, be not too quick to strive to show your dexterity, by doing which you may cut parts which ought not to be cut, but be calm and moderate, and let this be a general rule with you. If it is well done, it is soon done.   ('Surgical lectures')

Pott's conception of surgery demanded continuous improvement, towards which he contributed by objective analysis of hard gained experience. He challenged colleagues who accepted, automatically, earlier authors with most of whom Pott was familiar, due to his command of Latin and French. In the preface to *A Treatise on Fistula in ano* (1765) Pott wrote:

> The honour of our art and the moral character of its professors suffer, whenever we pay blind deference to anyone, as prevents us from using our own judgement, and from declaring freely the results of our enquiries or experiments. Truth, as Lord Bacon has said, is not the child of authority but of time. And were we to allow ourselves to suppose (let the subject be what it may) that nothing more, or new, could be taught, it is pretty clear that nothing more, or new, would be learnt.

And he added in the preface to *Chirurgical Observations* (1775): '[It is by] careful attention to the cases of individuals, and from an observation of diseases ... that true and extensive judgement can be acquired'.

In the preface to *A Treatise on Ruptures* (1756) Pott remarked:

> The ancient surgery was coarse, and loaded with a farrago of external applications, some of which were horribly, and yet unnecessarily painful, and others altogether useless; whilst the operative part of the art was encumbered with a multitude of awkward unmanageable instruments, and pieces of machinery. The practitioners of the present time have brought the practice into a much narrower compass ... by a sedulous application to anatomy, by the frequent examination of dead morbid bodies, by making such experiments on the living, as they had just reason to think would prove beneficial ... and not persisting in tormenting their fellow-creatures merely for gain.

Pott's style of writing frequently won him praise. However, in the preface to *Hydrocele, or, Watry Rupture* (1767) Pott claimed:

> The character of an elegant writer I make no pretension to: that of a skilful surgeon ... I should be extremely glad to deserve. ... When ... information is intended to be conveyed to many people of different capacities, it may be necessary to set the same object in several different lights; and to repeat the same thoughts many times in different words: to those who have not been much conversant with the thing treated of, a studied brevity would become a perplexing obscurity;

however satisfied such readers might be with the stile of the writer, they would not be sufficiently acquainted with the subject; they might be pleased but they would not be informed.

In further advice to the profession given in his preface to *Observations on … Fistula lachrymalis* (1758) Pott emphasized:

> The operative part of surgery is far from being the whole of it: and I cannot help thinking, that by attending a little more to what is called common or practical surgery [that is, venesection, catheterization, and so on], our art might still be considerably improved, practitioners rendered expert, and mankind much benefitted. … It is a false idea which the bystanders at an operation generally have of chirurgic 'dexterity'; to which word they annex no other idea than that of quickness. This had produced a most absurd custom of measuring the motion of a surgeon's hand, as jockeys do that of the feet of a horse, viz. by a stop watch.

Ever sensitive to the sufferings of patients and anxious to diminish the pain of operative procedures, Pott criticized the management of *fistula in ano* in his preface to *A Treatise on Fistula in ano* (1765), writing:

> The term Cutting for a Fistula, conveys to a patient a terrible idea; this terror is not a little increased by his incapacity to see the part diseased. The majority of writers have greatly increased, rather than lessened, this dread: and as the operation is (under their direction) sometimes performed, it is, indeed, a very severe one: … A more serious reflection … would lead us to a more rational method of treating it, and to a more easy and expeditious cure.

Pott's publications Pott spurned publication of a systematic surgical textbook in favour of single subject studies which, he maintained, promoted greater attention to detail. Further, these relatively short books appeared at prices appealing to students: 1s. 6d. has been quoted. Each monograph debated a burning topic of the day and their popularity is evident from the numerous editions, translations into German, French, Dutch, and Italian, and several issues of collected works, lastly in 1819.

If Pott's *Treatise on Ruptures* (1756) first drew attention to his ability as a surgical author, it lacked the detailed references of later works and the individual clinical case observations of several others. None the less, Pott's vigorous challenge to old ideas and methods, his concern for patients mishandled by ignorant practitioners, and his overall lucidity set a pattern repeated in later monographs. Pott's advocacy of early operation for strangulated inguinal hernia must have saved numerous lives yet, after reduction of the hernia, he did not repair the defect. If indicated, gangrenous bowel was sutured to the wound margin, a dressing was applied, and the patient was kept horizontal until the wound healed. Rarely the scarring repaired the hernia naturally; most patients needed a steel truss permanently. Unhappily, repair sutures left at depth, prior to antiseptic techniques, usually festered, with uncertain results.

Pott's *Account of a Particular Kind of Rupture Frequently Attendant upon New-Born Children* (1757) is a short work on congenital hernias; it contains no references and was criticized harshly by William Hunter, who claimed that Pott failed to acknowledge Hunter's prior description at student lectures given in 1756. He wrote: 'It was what any of my pupils might have written … it bore strong marks of second-hand observations, and of time-serving hurry in the composition' (Hunter, 70). Hunter later apologized for any unintended offence, accepting Pott's probity in the matter. In the event, both deferred to an earlier suggestion of Samuel Sharp and the work of Albrecht von Haller who coined the term hernia congenita in *Opuscula pathologica* (1755).

Pott's next publication was *Observations on that Disorder of the Corner of the Eye, Commonly called Fistula lachrymalis* (1758). This was followed by *Observations on the Nature and Consequences of Wounds and Contusions of the Head and Fractures of the Skull Concussion of the Brain, etc* (1760). This has a preface but no case observations or plates, unlike a revised publication on the same subject published eight years later. The 1760 works is of interest for a long preface debating Pott's wider surgical tenets and views on head injury. He wrote:

> The symptoms brought on by the pressure of a piece broken off from the inner table of the skull, are scarcely distinguishable from those produced by blood or lymph pressing on the brain, each of which is certainly a very different cause of mischief. These combinations of causes and symptoms, and the uncertainty … make this a very disagreeable part of surgery: but merely lamenting, will never mend it; and as the inconvenience which we feel is great, our attempts to get information ought to be in proportion.

Practical remarks on the hydrocele or watry rupture, and some other diseases of the testicle, its coats and vessels, etc (1762) is a long treatise that defines swellings of the scrotum and their treatment. Well referenced, it is amplified by thirty-six detailed case observations, increased to fifty-one in later editions. Here, as in other treatises, Pott provides excellent anatomico-pathological descriptions based on accurate clinical records enhanced by careful post-mortem studies. He limited the false or spurious rupture either to fluid swellings around the testis or to solid testicular swellings known as sarcoceles. To discharge hydrocele fluid Pott favoured a trocar and cannula, in preference to uncertain lancet puncture. For radical cure he introduced a seton of fine lint to excite local inflammation and obliterative scarring of the hydrocele cavity; in 1771 he wrote *An account of the method of obtaining a perfect or radical cure of the hydrocele … by means of a seton*, which illustrated improved instrumentation for inserting silk threads. When diagnosed early, sarcocele due to a scirrhus (tuberculosis) or cancer was treated by orchidectomy to avoid a miserable demise; he deplored local applications of caustic and uncertain ulcerative mortification. Pott's manuscript of the second edition (1766) was deposited in the Royal College of Surgeons.

Pott's *Remarks on the Disease Commonly called Fistula in ano* (1765) referred particularly to contemporaneous French authors but without case observations. In the preface, he said:

> I have, on this occasion, carefully perused almost every writer of character on the subject; and think, that I may venture to say, that they are all either defective, or erroneous: they either pass the disease over slightly … or subject it to a method of cure, which is operose, painful, tedious, and unnecessarily productive of future evil.

Pott said that many surgeons believed, erroneously, that every perineal sinus was fistulous and hence operated precipitately. If surgery was necessary he opposed the blind use of probe scissors inside the anal canal and recommended a curved probe pointed knife; later he devised a more sophisticated probe blade with movable guard. Benjamin Bell considered Pott's monograph the first to treat the subject with precision.

Observations on the Nature and Consequences of those Injuries to which the Head is Liable from External Violence (1768) is one of Pott's longest and most important treatises, incorporating his preliminary study of 1760 but enlarged with forty-three case observations, references, and illustrations. Acknowledging the work of Henry-François Le Dran, Pott emphasized that brain injury and not skull damage dictated outcomes. Recommending early skull decompression, he was criticized for operating prophylactically by contemporaries such as William Dease in *Observations on Wounds of the Head* (1776). Comparison of his twenty-five observations with Pott's forty-three shows that most of Dease's patients had been assaulted while Pott's had been victims of a wider range of injuries including animal kicks and falls from horses, vehicles, scaffolding, and ladders, and two boys struck accidentally with cricket bats. Pott's cases were probably more severe; most deaths were subjected to post-mortem examination. Curiously 44 per cent of Dease's and 42 per cent of Pott's patients recovered, yet Dease trephined 80 per cent and Pott only 63 per cent, although several of Pott's patients had repeated procedures. Of those trephined, only 30 per cent of Dease's compared to 63 per cent of Pott's patients recovered; of those trephined early (within 24 hours), four of five of Dease's patients and two of six of Pott's died. Perhaps Pott's technique of trephining was more accurate and less inclined to infection. Others reporting detailed histories, including John Hunter, did not achieve Pott's success with the trephine. Pott noted that undisplaced closed fractures often formed epidural collections which suppurated to form a swelling, described as 'a puffy, circumscribed, indolent tumour of the scalp, and a spontaneous separation of the pericranium from the skull under such tumour' (P. Pott, *Observations on the Nature and Consequences of those Injuries to which the Head is Liable from External Violence*, 1768, 53). 'Pott's puffy tumour' was considered a bad sign requiring early surgery.

In *Some Few General Remarks on Fractures and Dislocations* (1768) Pott wrote: 'it is by no means my intention to write a regular treatise on fractures … I only mean to throw out a few hints' (8). However, this monograph of 126 pages is considered by many to be his most important contribution, for two reasons. First, he argued that long bone fractures subjected to powerful extension developed deforming muscle tension and were better managed without extension by relaxing the limb in flexion. As an example he drew attention to fractures of the humerus which healed routinely with the elbow flexed in a sling. His drawing shows that femoral and tibial fractures were positioned on their side with the knee and foot flexed before final splinting. This method introduced a need to splint joints both above and below tibial fractures, a fundamental concept which persisted. His scheme, popular in Britain and France, proved less so in America. At the end of the twentieth century conservative fracture management combined extension and the physiological doctrine of Pott: thus for the lower limb plaster was applied and traction apparatus was designed to permit partial knee flexion, although the foot was held in neutral.

Second, Pott drew attention to a particular fracture of the lower fibula combined with disruption of the inner ankle ligaments and dislocation of the tibia from the joint. Rarely, the lower tibia protruded through skin and gangrene was possible; if recovery followed conventional treatment, flat foot deformity, a permanent iron support, and disabling lameness were probable. Pott believed that a side posture on pillows with the knee flexed promoted reduction of the dislocation and a corrected stable result. This is Pott's fracture, a term used daily in every accident department in Britain to encompass almost all fractures at ankle level; very few recall the specificity of Pott's original description.

Chirurgical observations relative to the cataract, the polypus of the nose, the cancer of the scrotum, the different kinds of ruptures, and the mortifications of the toes and feet appeared in 1775. For cataract Pott counselled long established lens couching or depression instead of a recently introduced lens extraction procedure. Suffering himself from nasal polypi he counselled care in assessing their suitability for extraction; he employed a polypus forceps. Pott's pioneering account of scrotal cancer brought attention to an occupational disease caused by chimney soot. Cure was possible if early excision of the ulcerated scrotal sore was performed before testicular involvement. On ruptures he described twenty-four further case observations. For gangrene of the toes and feet he recommended opium by mouth twice daily which alleviated pain and often produced a local healing reaction. This regime persisted, in Britain at least, for more than a century.

Remarks on that kind of palsy of the lower limbs which is frequently found to accompany a curvature of the spine (1779) was followed in 1782 by his *Farther remarks on the useless state of the lower limbs in consequence of a curvature of the spine: being a supplement to a former treatise on that subject.* These two tracts generated the eponymous description, Pott's disease of the spine, *le mal vertébral de Pott* of the French, despite a similar description given by J.-P. David in his *Dissertation sur les effets du mouvement et du repos dans les maladies chirurgicales* in 1779; this work was overlooked until much later. Pott associated changes in the spine with a strumous or scrophulous disposition, combined with local abcesses in the loin, groin, and thigh, and his treatment included the formation of issues, made by caustic, to discharge adjacent to the vertebral angulation; this involved rest in bed which doubtless contributed to healing; at the same time he discouraged the use of splints and apparatus. The

1782 publication, illustrated with plates of spinal pathology, included healed vertebrae from a patient, after Pott's issue therapy, who died from other reasons. St Bartholomew's Hospital museum displays carious spinal specimens either prepared by Pott or taken from patients under his care. Pott described the spastic nature of the palsy and lamented many victims of the disease in infancy and childhood, observing: 'a malady which, when an infant becomes its victim, renders all the care and tears, all the tenderness and anxiety of the fondest parent absolutely unavailing' (*Farther remarks on the useless state of the lower limbs*, 3). He claimed that issues encouraged cure and, in children, perhaps paravertebral abcesses were drained; on recovery they were mobilized in his 'go-cart', a form of baby-walker which kept the child upright. Once criticized for a neglect of splintage, his direct drainage technique was revised later, under antibiotic cover, as a method of choice in the twentieth century.

Pott's remarks on amputation were a response to doubts raised throughout Europe by Johann Ulrich Bilguer's book (1764) on the inutility of amputation. Pott accepted the terrible nature of amputation through sound flesh but concluded that it was 'in certain circumstances, absolutely and indispensably necessary' (*Remarks on … Palsy of the Lower Limbs*, 16). Careful selection and early operation were emphasized. Unlike John Hunter he experienced poor results after ligature of lower limb aneurysms and recommended amputation. For scrophulous (tuberculous) joints, amputation was generally accepted, for Henry Park's pioneering joint excisions were not reported until 1783, curiously enough in a letter specifically addressed to Pott, entitled 'An account of a new method of treating diseases of the joints of the knee and elbow'.

Conclusion In severe weather on 11 December 1788 Pott visited a patient 20 miles from London and came back with a cold. On developing a fever he curtailed further visits but matters worsened and he died at his house in Hanover Square on 22 December, probably of pneumonia; his burial took place on 7 January 1789 at St Mary Aldermary, where a commemorative tablet was erected. He was survived by his wife. Remarkably, no full-length biography of Pott has been published. T. J. Horder commented in 1894: 'Our knowledge of Pott's life is by no means extensive. It does not seem to have been of that kind which invites the pen of the biographer' (Horder, 165). If Pott's personal life is sketchy, his surgical activities are documented in detail and remain a basis for further studies.

Pott introduced a wholesome scepticism into surgical practice, placing emphasis on personal observations described with clarity and accuracy, illuminated by a mastery of macroscopic anatomy and diligent post-mortem dissection. Unlike many contemporaries he recorded success and failure alike, believing more was gleaned from an unfavourable than a favourable case. Over fifty years of practice Pott's workload was prodigious, his opinion eagerly sought, and his teaching at the bedside and at lectures widely acclaimed. He devised and simplified many instruments. Without antiseptic wound care his operative results were often remarkable. Before statistical methods evolved he judged the probability of events by attentive comparison of similar cases. He promoted ethical standards, stating that surgeons had a duty to inform relatives fully of their motives and conduct.

Critics suggest that Pott's surgery had no scientific basis, comparing him unfavourably to immediate British successors, including John Hunter, Benjamin Bell, John Abernethy, and Astley Cooper. However, their improvements and Pott's were of the same mould; indeed they were students of Pott's and built on his foundations. If they all achieved renown, for different reasons, Pott at least equalled them clinically and excelled them in his mastery of previous authors, and in the quality of his written work. Over two centuries later Pott's fracture and Pott's disease persist in everyday surgical language. His publications achieved a refreshing impact on contemporary practice and remain a rich source central to our understanding of eighteenth-century surgical progress.

JOHN KIRKUP

Sources J. Earle, ed., 'A short account of the life of the author', in P. Pott, *The chirurgical works*, 3 vols. (1790), 1.i–xlv · *DNB* · J. Dobson, 'Percivall Pott', *Annals of the Royal College of Surgeons of England*, 50 (1972), 54–65 [incl. complete list of works and trans.] · G. M. Lloyd, 'The life and works of Percivall Pott', *St Bartholomew's Hospital Reports*, 66 (1933), 291–336 · T. J. Horder, 'Life and works of Percivall Pott', *St Bartholomew's Hospital Reports*, 30 (1894), 163–87 · A. R. Jones, 'Percivall Pott', *Journal of Bone Joint Surgery*, 31B (1949), 465–70 · E. S. Flamm, 'Percivall Pott: an 18th century neurosurgeon', *Journal of Neurosurgery*, 76 (1992), 319–26 · J. M. Potter, 'Percivall Pott on head injuries, 1760', *St Bartholomew's Hospital Journal*, 64 (1960), 331–3 · N. Capener, 'Percivall Pott: the forerunner', *St Bartholomew's Hospital Journal*, 78 (1974), 38–40 · M. M. Ravitch, 'Invective in surgery', *Bulletin of the New York Academy of Medicine*, 50 (1974), 797–816 · 'Surgical lectures of Percivall Pott', RCS Eng., MS, n.d., 42.d.32 · W. Hunter, *Medical commentaries, part 1* (1762) · W. Dease, *Observations on wounds of the head, with a particular enquiry into the parts principally affected* (1776) · *The case books of John Hunter*, ed. E. Allen, J. L. Turk, and R. Murley (1993), vols. 1 and 5 · W. Wadd, *Nugae chirurgicae, or, A biographical miscellany* (1824), 252 · N. Moore, *The history of St Bartholomew's Hospital*, 2 vols. (1918) · B. Bell, *A system of surgery*, 3rd edn, 5 vols. (1787), 2.336 · J. -P. David, *Dissertation sur les effets du mouvement et du repos dans les maladies chirurgicales* (1779) · J. U. Bilguer, *A dissertation on the inutility of the amputation of limbs* (1764) · H. Park, *An account of a new method of treating diseases of the joints of the knee and elbow* (1783)
Archives MHS Oxf., lecture notes · RCP Lond., lecture notes · RCS Eng., lecture notes and treatise · Wellcome L., lecture notes
Likenesses G. Romney, oils, *c.*1782–1786, RCS Eng. · J. Reynolds, oils, 1784, St Bartholomew's Hospital, London [*see illus.*] · stipple, 1790 (after J. Heath), Wellcome L. · P. Hollins, marble bust, 1836, RCS Eng. · N. Dance, oils, RCS Eng.

Potter, Barnaby (*bap.* 1577, *d.* 1642), bishop of Carlisle, son of Thomas Potter, mercer and alderman of Kendal, Westmorland, was baptized on 11 August 1577. After schooling at Kendal with Mr Maxwell, 'a Puritane' (Lloyd, 153), on 3 May 1594 he matriculated at Oxford from the Queen's College. He graduated BA on 24 April 1599, proceeded MA on 30 June 1602, and was elected fellow on 1 March 1604.

For some years Potter lived at Bowden, in Totnes, Devon, in the house of Sir Edward Giles, MP for the town. There he became a preacher 'much followed by the precise party' (Wood, *Ath. Oxon.*, iii.22). Early in 1610 he declined

the principalship of St Edmund Hall, Oxford. Potter proceeded BD on 5 July 1610, but continued to live mostly in Devon. In 1613 he published a funeral sermon, *The Baronets Buriall*, with a dedication to Sir Edward and Lady Mary Giles, in which he commented that 'the more learned are the more loath to leave any thing in print to the view of the world'. This may explain his failure to publish systematic series of sermons on scripture attributed to him by Lloyd (Lloyd, 156).

The year 1615 was critical in Potter's life. On 29 May he was presented by James I to the rectory of Diptford, Devon. He proceeded DD on 27 June. On 21 August he married at Dean Prior, Devon, Elizabeth (*d.* 1673), daughter of Walter Northcote of Crediton, a clothier, and widow of Edward Yard of Churston Ferrers. Sir Edward Giles, connected by marriage with the Yards, had moved to Dean Prior, and on 4 October 1615 he presented Potter to the vicarage there. The Potters had one son, who died in 1623, and six daughters, almost all baptized at Dean Prior between 1616 and 1625, of whom Grace and Amye were celebrated by Robert Herrick, Potter's successor, in his poem 'Hesperides'.

On 14 October 1616 Potter was elected provost by the fellows of Queen's, who rejected Archbishop Abbot's recommendation of Dr Pilkington. Over ten years he saw through repairs and material improvements, but kept his family in Devon. He became chaplain to King James and continued in that position initially under Charles I, becoming known as the 'Penetential Preacher' (Lloyd, 154).

Thomas Crosfield of Queen's College remarked in early June 1626 on Potter's influence at court (Queen's College, MS 390, fol. 18*v*). It may have been in expectation of preferment as well as for personal reasons that he resigned the headship of Queen's on 17 June 1626, having secured the succession of his nephew, Christopher *Potter, chaplain to Lord Keeper Coventry. He was appointed chief almoner to Charles I on 4 July 1628. The king seems to have held Potter, despite his consistent Calvinism, in some regard, although Laud claimed credit at his trial for his appointment as bishop of Carlisle. At Potter's consecration on 15 March 1629, Christopher Potter preached.

The new bishop was financially embarrassed and borrowed £100 from his college. He was reputed the 'Puritanical Bishop', and it was said that 'the noise of an Organ would blow him out the Church' despite a personal love of music (Lloyd, 153). His visitation articles of 1629 were published. Enjoying good relations even with Catholic recusants, he was reputed 'indulgent to tender consciences' among protestants (ibid., 154–5). Reporting on his diocese in January 1636 he blamed churchwardens and justices of the peace for failure to achieve due attendance at services, and dropped a broad hint that he wanted a better diocese. Charles I's marginal comments suggest dissatisfaction with Potter's performance. When his diocese was stricken by plague that year the bishop was in Devon and the king had to insist in August that he return to the north.

Potter was one of the bishops who recommended acceptance of Strafford's attainder to the king in 1641. He died in January 1642 at Covent Garden lodgings and was buried on 6 January in the churchyard of St Paul's, Covent Garden. He was to be held up as an exemplary prelate by Bishop Joseph Hall in 1644. A. J. HEGARTY

Sources W. Jones, *Dr. Barnaby Potter, bishop of Carlisle: a short biography* (privately printed, Exeter, 1888) [two copies at Queen's College, Oxford] • Wood, *Ath. Oxon.*, new edn, 3.21–3 • D. Lloyd, *Memoires of the lives … of those … personages that suffered … for the protestant religion* (1668), 153–7 • *Reg. Oxf.*, 1.212, 290; 2/2.202; 2/3.214 • *The diary of Thomas Crosfield*, ed. F. S. Boas (1935) • J. R. Magrath, *The Queen's College*, 1 (1921), 242–4 • R. H. Hodgkin, *Six centuries of an Oxford college: a history of the Queen's College, 1340–1940* (1949), 87 • N. W. S. Cranfield, 'Chaplains in ordinary at the early Stuart court: the purple road', *Patronage and recruitment in the Tudor and early Stuart church*, ed. C. Cross (1996), 120–47 • B. Potter, *The baronets buriall, or, A funerall sermon preached at the solemnitie of that honourable Baronet Sr Edward Seymours buriall* (1613) • [B. Potter], *Articles to be enquired of, in the diocesan visitation of … Barnabie … lord bishop of Carlisle* (1629) • C. Worthy, *Devonshire parishes, or, The antiquities, heraldry and family history of twenty-eight parishes in the archdeaconry of Totnes*, 2 vols. (1887–9), 2.68–70 • J. Hall, *The shaking of the olive tree* (1660), 341 • Queen's College, Oxford, MS 390

Likenesses oils, Queen's College, Oxford

Potter, (Martha) Beatrice. *See* Webb, (Martha) Beatrice (1858–1943).

Potter [*married name* Heelis], **(Helen) Beatrix** (1866–1943), artist, children's writer, and sheep breeder, was born on 28 July 1866 at 2 Bolton Gardens, South Kensington, London, the elder child and only daughter of Rupert William Potter (1832–1914), a lawyer specializing as equity draftsman and conveyancer until he inherited a large fortune in 1883. A close friend of John Everett Millais and a gifted amateur photographer, Rupert Potter had in 1863 married Helen Leech (1839–1932), the youngest surviving daughter of the late John Leech, a prosperous cotton merchant from Stalybridge, near Manchester.

Beatrix, known by her second name to distinguish her from her mother, had a lonely childhood, looked after by nurses and taught by governesses. She was delicate and often ill, but she found great comfort in drawing and painting, encouraged by her parents, both amateur artists. When she was nearly six a brother, Walter Bertram, was born, although as soon as he was old enough he was sent away to school. Every summer the family took a large house in Perthshire and at weekends they visited Beatrix's grandfather, Edmund *Potter, at his home, Camfield House, Hatfield. Both children soon became fascinated with the natural world, observing and recording the habits of animals and birds and, from an early age, they cared for a variety of pets. From 1881 to 1897 Beatrix kept an encrypted journal which, decoded in 1958 by Leslie Linder, provided valuable details of Potter's formative years, during which she was constantly drawing and painting.

In 1882 the family spent their first holiday in the Lake District, a part of England with which Potter would become identified. Her interests now included fossil-hunting, photography, and in particular the study of fungi. By 1893 she was painting and recording fungi in detail, encouraged by Charles McIntosh of Dunkeld, and in 1897, with the assistance of Sir Henry Roscoe (1833–

(Helen) Beatrix Potter (1866–1943), by Delmar Banner, 1938

1915), who was married to her aunt, Lucy Potter, she submitted a paper to the Linnean Society of London. 'On the germination of the spores of *Agaricineae*' by Miss Helen B. Potter was read on 1 April 1897, not by Potter herself, as women could not attend. Nor was the paper published—though on 24 April 1997, one hundred years later, recognition was finally given to Potter's research by the Linnean Society with a lecture by Professor Roy Watling of the Royal Botanic Garden, Edinburgh, entitled 'Beatrix Potter as mycologist'.

Whenever she was away from London, Potter sent illustrated letters to the children of her last governess, Annie Moore, and it is the story from one of these, written on 4 September 1893 to Noel Moore, that became her first published book. Rejected by a number of publishers, *The Tale of Peter Rabbit* was issued privately by Potter herself on 16 December 1901, in an edition of 250 copies, all the illustrations but the frontispiece in black and white. A small reprint followed in February 1902, and then a privately issued edition of *The Tailor of Gloucester*, before Frederick Warne & Co. persuaded Potter to redo the illustrations for *The Tale of Peter Rabbit* in colour for the publication in a trade edition on 2 October 1902. It was the first of twenty-two uniformly produced 'little books' by her, published by Warne, nineteen of them by 1913. With many of them featuring her own pets—Peter Rabbit, Benjamin Bunny, Mrs Tiggy-Winkle, and Samuel Whiskers—Potter's books have become classics of children's literature, with their sharp prose, their strong story lines, and their exquisite, freshly painted, and beautifully observed pictures.

In 1905 39-year-old Potter became engaged to her editor, Norman Warne, who died only four weeks later of leukaemia. She fled to Near Sawrey in the Lake District, to a working farm, Hill Top, that she had recently purchased with her royalties. It was the start of a new interest in her life, farming. Though still living with her now ageing parents in London, Potter spent as much time as possible at Hill Top, working on new books for Warne, adding to her farm stock, and acquiring land. On 15 October 1913, aged forty-seven, she married a local solicitor, William Heelis (1871–1945), son of the late John Heelis, rector of Kirkby Thore, and settled in Castle Cottage, Near Sawrey, keeping Hill Top as a place in which to draw and to store her treasures.

Over the next thirty years, Beatrix Heelis built up her Lake District property, improving the stock on her farms and becoming a prize-winning breeder of Herdwick sheep, president-elect of the Herdwick Sheepbreeders' Association, and a notable judge at local agricultural shows. She also bought up extensive tracts of land to save it from development by builders, often working in close association with the National Trust. She alerted them to properties and estates coming on the market and, through the sale of drawings (mainly to the USA), raised the money to buy pieces of land for them. In 1930 she purchased the 5000 acre Monk Coniston estate, on condition that the trust bought half of it from her as soon as they were able to raise the money. She then managed the entire estate herself for the next six years.

Beatrix Heelis died on 22 December 1943 at Castle Cottage of a heart attack following severe bronchitis. She was cremated in Blackpool nine days later, and her ashes were scattered on her land by her shepherd, Tom Storey. In her will she left everything to her husband, William Heelis, and on his death her fifteen farms, numerous cottages, and over 4000 acres of land to the National Trust. Hill Top was to be preserved as it stood and the sheep stock on her fell farms to be of the pure Herdwick breed. The copyright in all her published work was bequeathed to Norman Warne's nephew, Frederick Warne Stephens, and was ceded to Frederick Warne & Co. in 1970. Over sixty years after her death, Beatrix Potter's original artwork is held in national collections, the largest in the Victoria and Albert Museum in London and the Free Library of Philadelphia. Her books are available in thirteen languages and the characters from them feature on an extensive range of merchandise. The Beatrix Potter Society, formed in 1980, has a worldwide membership.   JUDY TAYLOR

Sources J. Taylor, *Beatrix Potter: artist, storyteller and countrywoman* (1986); new edn (1996) • M. Lane, *The tale of Beatrix Potter*, 1946, rev. edn (1985) • L. Linder, *A history of the writings of Beatrix Potter*, 1971, rev. edn (1987) • *The journal of Beatrix Potter*, ed. L. Linder, 1966; rev. edn (1989) • A. S. Hobbs, *Beatrix Potter's art* (1989) • J. Taylor, J. I. Whalley, A. S. Hobbs, and E. M. Battrick, *Beatrix Potter, 1866–1943* (1987) • *The letters of Beatrix Potter*, ed. J. Taylor (1989) • J. C. Morse, ed., *Beatrix Potter's Americans: selected letters* (1982) • *Letters to children from Beatrix Potter*, ed. J. Taylor (1992) • E. Jay, M. Noble, and A. S. Hobbs, *A Victorian naturalist* (1992) • 'So I shall tell you a story …': *encounters with Beatrix Potter*, ed. J. Taylor (1993) • A. S. Hobbs and J. I. Whalley, eds., *Beatrix Potter: the V&A collection* (1985) • d. cert. • *Westmorland Gazette* (Jan 1944)
Archives Beatrix Potter Gallery, Hill Top, Hawkshead, drawings, literary MSS, and papers • BL • Free Library of Philadelphia, corresp., drawings, literary MSS, and papers • National Trust Historic Buildings, Grasmere, Ambleside, Cumbria, corresp. and literary papers • Penguin Books, London, Frederick Warne archive • priv. coll. • Tate collection • V&A NAL, corresp. and papers • V&A NAL, letters | Cumbria AS, Carlisle, letters to the Moscrop family • NL Scot., letters to Charles Macintosh • V&A Book Trust, Linder collection • V&A NAL, Linder bequest
Likenesses R. Potter, photographs, 1870–1913, Frederick Warne archive, Penguin Books, London • D. Banner, oils, 1938, NPG [*see illus.*] • D. Banner, oils, National Book League, London • D. Banner, watercolour, NPG • photographs, Beatrix Potter Society, London • photographs, V&A • portraits, priv. coll.
Wealth at death £211,636 4*s*. 10*d*.: probate, 2 March 1944, *CGPLA Eng. & Wales*

Potter, Charles (1634–1663). *See under* Potter, Christopher (1590/91–1646).

Potter, Christopher (1590/91–1646), college head and dean of Worcester, nephew of Barnaby *Potter (*bap.* 1577, *d.* 1642), was born at Kendal, Westmorland. After schooling at nearby Appleby he entered Queen's College, Oxford, in early 1606, obtained a 'poor boy's' scholarship on 29 October 1609, and graduated BA on 30 April 1610. Ordained deacon in May 1613, he became a college chaplain on 5 July and proceeded MA on 8 July. He was elected a fellow on 22 March 1615 and ordained priest the following June.

Potter was much influenced by the thoroughly Calvinist provost of Queen's College, Henry Airay. In 1618 he published Airay's *Lectures upon the Whole Epistle of St. Paul to the Philippians*, with a dedication to Archbishop George Abbot evincing a characteristic dislike of polemic. Foreshadowing his own later defence of clerical property, Potter published in 1621 the late provost's *Just and necessary apology touching his suit in law for the rectory of Charlton on Otmore in Oxfordshire*. Potter meanwhile became a zealous and popular lecturer at Abingdon in Berkshire. In December 1616 he was nominated by Matthew Sutcliffe to his college at Chelsea for controversies against Catholics and sectaries.

Potter obtained his BD degree and a university preaching licence on 9 March 1621. In 1623, with permission from Queen's, he travelled to France and the Low Countries, visiting Antwerp and probably Paris. He became familiar with the Dutch Remonstrant position and with controversies in the Catholic church. The experience possibly initiated his rejection of extreme predestinarianism and adoption of eirenic approaches to religious differences.

On 17 June 1626 Barnaby Potter resigned as provost of Queen's, having canvassed for Christopher to succeed him. As a chaplain to Lord Keeper Coventry and a potential channel of ecclesiastical patronage, the nephew was duly elected. Within a few months, aided by Coventry, the earl of Carlisle, and Sir George Goring, and exploiting his knowledge of French to write to the queen, he obtained from Charles I through Henrietta Maria the advowsons of three rectories and three vicarages in Hampshire for the college; he himself became rector of Stratfield Saye. Three of Coventry's sons were later entrusted to Queen's, and Potter became by his influence chaplain to Charles I. The provost regularly received intelligence from Coventry and other friends at court in the years ahead. Potter's *The

Christopher Potter (1590/91–1646), attrib. Gilbert Jackson, 1634

History of the Quarrels of Pope Paul V. with the State of Venice (1626), a translation of Paolo Sarpi, was dedicated gratefully to Coventry.

On 17 February 1627 Potter obtained his DD degree, but received from John Prideaux, regius professor of divinity, slights on doctrinal grounds which he later often recalled as unjust and unchristian. At an unknown date between his election as provost and July 1628 he married Elizabeth (d. 1692), daughter of Charles Sunnybanke, canon of Windsor. The couple had three sons, Charles [see below], Christopher, and Edward, and one daughter, Anne.

Queen's became a magnet for young men of promise, as Provost Potter improved academic discipline, promoted study of Hebrew, Arabic, and Greek, and insisted on regular preaching by turns in the chapel. He also proved a judicious administrator: his memorandum book shows concern to collect debts and maximize income from property.

In 1631 Potter succeeded his brother as rector of Binfield, Berkshire, but significantly exchanged it after a few weeks for a prebend of Chichester Cathedral with the approval of Bishop Richard Montagu, a bugbear of committed protestants. Anthony Wood's assertion that Potter was a creature of Bishop William Laud, and thus regarded as an Arminian (Wood, *Ath. Oxon.*, 3.180), muddies a complex relationship and Potter's religious position. Thomas Crosfield believed Laud had prevented Potter obtaining a prebend at Ely in 1626, while Potter preferred Coventry as

university chancellor in 1630. When Laud obtained that office there was friction when in 1631 Queen's elected a new principal of St Edmund Hall with what Laud saw as indecent haste to pre-empt his interference. However, while Potter made some objections to Laud's university statutes of 1634 and 1636, in 1635 he wrote him a shrewd letter praising his projected metropolitical visitation of Oxford and simultaneously seeking to shield Queen's behind the archbishop of York's peculiar visitatorial jurisdiction.

Despite ongoing frictions, 1631 probably saw the turning point in the relationship. Potter had felt himself under siege for abandoning the shibboleth of Calvinist orthodoxy since at least December 1628. He published his sermon at the episcopal consecration of his uncle in March 1629, widely regarded as Arminian, to reassure the fathers of Queen's men, but in July he felt obliged to write a vindication (later printed in J. Plaifere, *Appello evangelium*, 1650) to an old friend and Queen's man Mr Vicars, who suspected he had turned Arminian for mercenary motives. Potter denied he was an Arminian; though he also stated, 'I love *Calvin* very well, and, I must tell you I cannot hate *Arminius*' (*Appello evangelium*, 413). In June 1630 he privately recommended to the college non-polemical debate of the eternal decree of reprobation and of free will. Reported outside, this provoked bitter attacks by Oxford Calvinists, especially at the Act that summer. On 25 August he produced a manuscript apologia rejecting the absolute decree of reprobation as 'repugnant to … Scripture, … contrary to the … mercy of … God, … contrary to the constant judgm[en]t of antiquity, of many reformed Churches, and of plaine reason' (MS Rawl. C. 167, 227r). In the same month he criticized the proceedings of the Synod of Dort (Queen's College, MS 390, 51v). He shared the enthusiasm for Grotius of Lord Falkland's Great Tew circle, in which Coventry's sons were involved, and encouraged Thomas Crosfield and Francis Coventry during 1631 to translate that author's *True Religion Explained*, which was published anonymously the next year. In 1631 he himself published anonymously a new edition of the *Stratagemata Satanae* of Jacobus Acontius, a humanistic and heterodox Italian protestant who held that there were very few essential articles of faith, and that those were to be found only in scripture, and who advocated general tolerance. Much of Oxford would have known Potter was behind this.

Events came to a head in summer 1631 when Giles Thorne traduced Potter as a Pelagian in a Latin university sermon. When Thorne and others were tried before Charles I at Woodstock on 22 August, Potter insisted he had directed Queen's men to Augustine and other anti-Pelagian writers of antiquity. His case was accepted and the hearing seems to have produced greater trust between him and Laud, who approvingly entered into his account of his chancellorship the improvements to Queen's chapel between 1630 and 1636. In September 1632 Laud entrusted his godson, William Chillingworth, to Potter for resolution of doubts preparatory to reception back into the Church of England. In 1633 he was prepared to help Potter obtain a Windsor canonry, even against his protégé, Peter Heylyn, although the expected vacancy did not occur. Potter published in that year *Want of Charity* in answer to *Charity Mistaken* by the Jesuit Edward Knott (Matthew Wilson). Undertaken 'in obedience to your Ma[jes-]ties particular commandement', it was dedicated to the king, and expressed too ecumenical and inclusive an attitude to non-Jesuitical Catholics for many protestants. For a second edition in 1634 Potter sought and used Laud's criticisms, a point not lost on William Prynne at the archbishop's trial. A response to Knott's reply was left to Chillingworth in his *Religion of Protestants*, which Laud had Potter examine in 1637. While, however, Potter subscribed to a form of 'rational theology' akin to that of Chillingworth, they by no means agreed on everything.

Meanwhile, Potter pursued, and received abuse for, his individualist theological stance. In September 1632 he was named in satirical verses, 'The academicall army of epidemicall Arminians', scattered around the university, while in November he contrasted favourably in college the doctrinal latitude allowed by the Church of England with the narrowness of the Irish and French protestant churches. A 1636 Oxford squib claimed that at Queen's, 'Dr. Potter is converted and they preach much of the salvation of the Heathens' (U. Nott. L., MS C1. c, 84b). Gerard Langbaine, in dedicating his *A Review of the Councell of Trent* (1638) to the provost, indicated that this translation of Gallican Guillaume Ranchin was at Potter's suggestion. It needed a preface disclaiming Catholic doctrinal content.

Potter concurred with Laud on academic discipline, exhorting his college in August 1634 to obey the chancellor's new statutes and promoting conformity to dress codes. His suggestion of the usefulness of portable statutes for students possibly inspired the broadsheet printed *Synopsis* of 1635, and Potter certainly had Crosfield prepare for publication in early 1638 on Laud's behalf a volume entitled *Statuta selecta* for student use. Moreover, in 1634 he encouraged bowing at the name of Jesus, praised the beautifying of churches, and guided discussion on defence of church property which led to outspoken attacks on the sacrilegious behaviour of Henry VIII and Elizabeth I.

With Laud's backing Potter was presented by the king to the deanery of Worcester on 31 December 1635. In 1637 he was chosen a JP for Oxford. Having declined Laud's offer of the vice-chancellorship in 1638 on the grounds of ill health, Potter finally accepted in 1640 only to face a troubled tenure answerable to a critical parliament. However, he refined procedure in public examinations for the BA degree, finished improvements to the Convocation House, and vindicated university control over Oxford markets against a hostile city. On 30 April 1641 Potter presented the university's petition in support of episcopacy and cathedral establishments to the king at Whitehall and received a supportive response. Finally the beleaguered Laud timed his own resignation as chancellor for the end of Potter's mandate so as to save him from the tender mercies of his certain successor, the earl of Pembroke.

Potter proved a firm royalist. He was one of seven heads who subscribed to the 1642 protestation only with reservations. In July 1642 he personally lent £400 to the king and ensured his college provided £800 by making up a deficiency himself. It appears from a repayment made to his son in 1662 that he lent at least another £1000 on security. Potter's arrest was ordered by parliament on 12 July 1642. That year he resigned the college rectory of Bletchingdon, Oxfordshire, which he had held since 1632, and became rector of his father-in-law's old parish of Great Haseley.

According to Hearne, Potter later preached at Uxbridge before the treaty commissioners. In April 1645 he was one of those commissioned by the governor of Oxford to take an oath of loyalty from academics. His Worcestershire property was sequestered by parliament for delinquency. He was nominated dean of Durham by the king in January 1646, but he died at Queen's College on 3 March of that year prior to installation, and was buried in the college chapel.

David Lloyd described Potter as 'a strict Puritan ... when preacher at *Abingdon*, in his doctrine, and always one in his life' (Lloyd, 544). By his will of 21 February 1646 Potter declared that he died

abhorring all secte, sideinge and tyranny in Religion and holding Communion with all holy Christians through the world that love the same Lord Jesus in sincerity, ... Agreeing with all such in things that are necessary ... (which I take to bee but fewe and cleerely revealed in the New Testam[en]t). (Oxford University Archives, arch. wills OP, 84)

After small benefactions to his college, the poor, and relatives, the residue of goods and lands went to his wife, three sons, and daughter. His widow soon married his successor as provost, Gerard Langbaine.

Charles Potter (1634–1663), courtier, eldest son of Christopher Potter and his wife, Elizabeth Sunnybanke, was born at Queen's College and admitted there in summer 1646, shortly after his father's death. Chosen student of Christ Church in 1647, he graduated BA on 27 June 1649, and proceeded MA on 15 July 1650. His 'Theses quadragesimales', defending in exercises Pythagorean positions, much commended at the time but according to Wood really the work of his tutor, Thomas Severne of Christ Church, was published at Oxford in 1651 and dedicated to his stepfather, Gerard Langbaine.

Potter travelled abroad, joining the exiled court of Charles II and the household of James Crofts, later duke of Monmouth. Correspondence received by Joseph Williamson in France suggests that his stepfather and others were very worried about his living extravagantly there and mortgaging property to support his lifestyle during 1657 and 1658. He became a Roman Catholic, and at the Restoration was made usher to the queen mother, Henrietta Maria. In early 1662 he was repaid money lent by his father to Charles I and awarded another sum for faithful service, amounting to £2000. He died at lodgings in Duke Street, the Strand, London, in December 1663, and was buried in St Paul's, Covent Garden, near his great-uncle, Barnaby Potter.   A. J. HEGARTY

Sources *DNB* · Queen's College, Oxford, MS 390 [diary of Thomas Crosfield] · *The diary of Thomas Crosfield*, ed. F. S. Boas (1935), esp. introduction and notes · *The life and times of Anthony Wood*, ed. A. Clark, 1, OHS, 19 (1891), 74–5, 77, 125–6 · A. Wood, *The history and antiquities of the University of Oxford*, ed. J. Gutch, 2 (1796), 325, 382, 425, 440, 457 · *The works of the most reverend father in God, William Laud*, 5, ed. J. Bliss (1853), 4, 34–6, 50, 62, 84, 132–5, 143, 165, 184–5, 284–5, 287, 291–2, 295–8 · D. Lloyd, *Memoires of the lives … of those … personages that suffered … for the protestant religion* (1668), 544 · A. Milton, *Catholic and Reformed: the Roman and protestant churches in English protestant thought, 1600–1640* (1995), 92, 155–7, 166, 249–50, 263, 329, 342–3, 435, 446–7 · PRO, SP 16/178, 122r; 16/247, 43r–44v; 16/257, 201r–v; 16/291, 94r–95v; 16/317, 215r–216v; 16/237, 77r–78v; 16/367, 260v; 16/387, 12r; 16/390, 135r; 16/436, 117r–v; 16/470, 177r; 16/499, 166r–167v; 18/179, 73r–v; 18/180, 178r · Wood, *Ath. Oxon.*, new edn, 3.179–82, 648–9 · *Reg. Oxf.*, 1.269; 2/2.290; 2/3.294 · PBA, memorandum book of Provost Christopher Potter, Queen's College Archives · N. W. S. Cranfield, 'Chaplains in ordinary at the early Stuart court: the purple road', *Patronage and recruitment in the Tudor and early Stuart church*, ed. C. Cross (1996), 120–47 · Bodl. Oxf., MS Rawl. C. 167 · U. Nott., MS Cl. c · chancellor's court wills, Potter, Oxf. UA
Likenesses attrib. G. Jackson, oils, 1634, Queen's College, Oxford [*see illus.*]
Wealth at death £40 to poor of several places; family and personal bequests approx. £30; books valued at £10 to Queen's College; 'goods, chattells, money, plate, bookes and household stuff whatsoever, together with the reversion of certeine coppie holds, messuages and lands, parcell of the Mannor of Borraston in the Countie of Worcester', and property at Devizes, Wiltshire, to wife and children: chancellor's court will, Oxf. UA; M. A. E. Green, *Calendar of the proceedings of the committee for compounding*, 1.553; 4.2498

Potter, Christopher (*c.*1751–1817), ceramic manufacturer and contractor, was probably the son of George Potter of Bethnal Green, London. He was the owner in 1777 of the estate of New Barns, near Ely, Cambridgeshire, devoted to the culture of woad. At first his property was cultivated by itinerant woadmen, but afterwards by his own agricultural labourers—in his view, an innovation. He also manufactured orchel dyes at Bethnal Green. During the American War of Independence he was one of the principal victualling contractors for the British army. In 1780 he unsuccessfully contested the parliamentary representation of Cambridge. In 1781 he was returned for Colchester, but on petition was unseated for corrupt practices. In 1784 he was again returned, but was again unseated, on the grounds of having been declared bankrupt, and of possessing no property qualification. On a new writ being issued he was candidate for a third time, but was defeated. His candidature seems to have led to the passing of the act disqualifying government contractors.

Potter settled in Paris, where in 1789 he established potteries, including the Manufacture du prince de Galles, in the rue de Crussol; he may also have been involved in potteries at Forges-les-Eaux and Montereau. He assumed or received credit for the invention of printing on porcelain and glass, though this had been practised at Worcester and Liverpool as early as 1756–7. Backed by the Academy of Sciences and by Jean Sylvain Bailly, the mayor of Paris, in 1791 he petitioned the national assembly for a seven years' patent, promising to give a quarter of the profits to the poor, and to teach his process to French apprentices. No action was taken on his petition, but he enjoyed for years a virtual monopoly. In 1792 Potter reopened the Chantilly potteries, closed through the emigration of the Condé family at the beginning of the French Revolution. Here he employed 500 men and reputedly produced 9000 dozen plates a month, for which he is said to have earned £6000 a year (*Annual Biography and Obituary*, 1818, vol. 2, p. 352). In 1793, when the English in France were arrested as hostages in response to the British support for the royalist uprising at Toulon, he was imprisoned at Beauvais and Chantilly. In 1796 he was the bearer to Lord Malmesbury at Paris of an offer from Jean-Nicolas-Paul-François de Barras to conclude peace for a bribe of 500,000 livres.

At the industrial exhibition of 1798 on the Champ de Mars, the first held in Paris, Potter was awarded one of twelve chief prizes for white pottery—the composition, shape, and varnish being highly commended. In 1802 he was one of twenty-five gold medallists who dined with Bonaparte. Very few specimens of his ware survive, but at the Musée National de la Céramique, Sèvres, there is a cup, ornamented with designs of flowers and butterflies, which bears his initials, surmounted by prince of Wales's feathers.

In 1811 Potter advocated the culture of woad in France, citing his Cambridgeshire experience, and between 1794 and 1812 he took out five patents for agricultural and manufacturing processes, some of them in association with his son, Thomas Mille Potter. (No details of a marriage have been established.) By all accounts Potter appears to have been an agreeable man. Lord North described him in 1778 as 'a gentleman of business and of very fair character in the City … a good friend to Government upon all occasions' (HoP, *Commons, 1754–90*, 3.309). William Cole, the Cambridge antiquary, noted in 1780 that he was a man 'eloquent to a great degree, of a most captivating conversation and behaviour' (ibid.). He died, apparently in London, on 18 November 1817. His obituary described him as a person 'whose opportunities and abilities should have fixed him at the summit of wealth', but who was 'too eccentric and speculative to hoard a fortune' (*GM*).

J. G. ALGER, *rev.* SUSAN E. GORDON

Sources *GM*, 1st ser., 87/2 (1817), 569 · T. Cromwell, *History and description of the ancient town and borough of Colchester*, 2 vols. (1825) · HoP, *Commons, 1754–90* · J. G. Alger, *Napoleon's British visitors and captives, 1801–1815* (1904) · C. S. Manning, 'The farm or grange of New Barns in the manor of Ely, pt 2: Christopher Potter (*c.*1751–1817)', *Cambridgeshire Local History Society Bulletin*, 44 (1989), 9–19 · C. S. Manning, 'The farm or grange of New Barns in the manor of Ely, pt 3: Christopher Potter (*c.*1751–1817) and others', *Cambridgeshire Local History Society Review*, new ser., 1 (1992), 11–26 · R. de Plinval de Guillebon, *Faïence et porcelaine de Paris, XVIIIe–XIXe siècles* (Paris, 1995) · R. G. Hagger, *The concise encyclopedia of continental pottery and porcelain* (1960) · J. Fleming and H. Honour, eds., *The Penguin dictionary of decorative arts*, new edn (1989) · C. S. Manning, 'The farm or grange of New Barns in the manor of Ely and Richard Tattersall (1724–1795)', *Cambridgeshire Local History Society Bulletin*, 43 (1988), 20–28 · G. de Luc, *Porcelaine tendre de Chantilly au XVIIIe siècle* (Paris, 1996) · L. Jewitt, *The ceramic art of Great Britain* (1883) · W. Burton, *Porcelain: its nature, art and manufacture* (1906) · VCH Essex, vol. 9 · *Annual Biography and Obituary*, 2 (1818), 352
Archives Cambs. AS, land tax registers, ref. 297/04 · CUL, church commissioners' deeds, nos. 94104–94107
Wealth at death a man 'whose opportunities and abilities should have fixed him at the summit of wealth … [but] He was too

eccentric and speculative to hoard a fortune; and in that respect may be likened to "the man who heapeth up riches and cannot tell who shall gather them." ': *GM*

Potter, (Philip) Cipriani Hambley (1792–1871), composer and pianist, was born in London on 3 October 1792, the fifth child (and third son) of the seven children of the flautist, violinist, and teacher Richard Huddleston Potter (1755–1821), and his wife, Charlotte, *née* Baumgarten (1757–1837); his paternal grandfather was the flute maker Richard Potter (1726–1806). The name Cipriani, by which he was generally known, came from his godmother, said to have been a sister of the artist Giovanni Baptista Cipriani (1727–1785); he was familiarly known as Chip or Little Chip because of his small stature. He was one of the leading composers and pianists of the 1820s and 1830s.

At the age of seven Potter began to study music under his father. He later had lessons from Thomas Attwood and William Crotch, and studied for a five-year period from 1805 with Joseph Wölfl (1773–1812), his most influential teacher; he may also have had lessons with John Wall Callcott. On attaining his majority in 1813 he became an associate of the recently founded Philharmonic Society, and he was elected to full membership on 29 May 1815. His overture in E minor, a society commission, was performed at the concert of 11 March 1816; seven weeks later, on 29 April 1816, he made his début as a pianist in a performance of his own sextet for piano, flute, and strings, op. 11, another society commission.

At the end of 1817 Potter left England to study composition abroad. His first destination was Vienna, where he met Beethoven, who commented favourably on him in a letter of 5 March 1818 to Ferdinand Ries. At Beethoven's suggestion he studied counterpoint with Aloys Förster. After about eight months in Vienna and other Austrian and German cities he moved on to Italy, returning to London in the spring of 1819. He married Emily Caroline Thomson (1802–1867) on 4 October 1822; they had eight children.

In 1820 Potter resumed his involvement with the Philharmonic Society. He played a Mozart concerto on 20 March 1820, and appeared frequently as a soloist at the society's concerts until around 1836, giving the English premières of many Mozart piano concertos and of the first, third, and fourth concertos of Beethoven. Many of his major orchestral works were performed at Philharmonic Concerts, and he also frequently appeared as a conductor.

As a composer, Potter's most active period was between his return to Britain and 1837, when he virtually gave up composition. In 1855, when Wagner conducted his symphony in G minor at a Philharmonic Society concert, Potter struck him merely as a 'rather old-fashioned but very amiable composer' with an almost pathetic desire to please (Wagner, 521). His published works, consisting largely of piano music, give a misleading impression of his output. His most significant compositions are his nine extant symphonies, all unpublished in their original form in his lifetime. These show many effective touches of orchestration and a good deal of counterpoint and imitation. His other works include three overtures on Shakespearian themes; a cantata, *Medora e Corrado*, to a libretto by his friend Gabriele Rossetti (1783–1854); some chamber music; and a substantial amount of piano music in a variety of genres. The manuscripts of his unpublished music are mostly in the British Library and the Royal Academy of Music.

Potter was also active as an arranger and editor and as an occasional writer on music. In 1831 he arranged and provided additional accompaniments for a staged production of Handel's *Acis and Galatea* at the Queen's Theatre. As his own creativity as a composer waned, he turned his attention to editing the works of others. His collected edition of Mozart's piano music, which began to appear in 1836, was his most significant achievement in this area; he also prepared editions of keyboard music by Beethoven, Handel, and J. S. Bach. In 1836 and 1837 he contributed articles on Beethoven and the orchestra to early issues of the *Musical World*.

Potter is also remembered as an influential teacher and for his long association with the Royal Academy of Music, which he served for thirty-six years from its foundation in 1823. Initially appointed principal piano teacher to the male students, he became director of orchestral practice on the dismissal of Nicholas Charles Bochsa in 1827, and succeeded Crotch as principal on his resignation in 1832. He remained principal until 1859. Among his many pupils were William Sterndale Bennett (1816–1875) and G. A. McFarren (1813–1887), each in his turn later to be principal of the academy. He resigned in 1859, at the age of sixty-six. A man of kindness, ready wit, charm, and modesty, he was respected and loved by colleagues and pupils alike.

Potter spent the remaining years of his life in quiet retirement. On 10 July 1871, less than three months before his death, he participated in the first performance in England of Brahms's Requiem, at the home of Kate Loder (Lady Thomson), when he and his hostess played the orchestral part in an arrangement for piano duet. Potter was elected a member of the Royal Society of Musicians in 1817. He was a member of the Society of British Musicians from its foundation in 1834 and of the Bach Society from its foundation in 1849; from 1854 to his death he was the musical director of the Madrigal Society. He died on 26 September 1871 at his home, 3 Craven Hill, Hyde Park, London, and was buried at Kensal Green cemetery, on 2 October.   PHILIP OLLESON

Sources P. H. Peter, 'The life and work of Cipriani Potter, 1792–1871', PhD diss., Northwestern University, 1972 · G. A. Macfarren, 'Cipriani Potter: his life and work', *Proceedings of the Musical Association*, 10 (1883–4), 41–56 · F. Corder, *A history of the Royal Academy of Music from 1822 to 1922* (1922) · A. W. Thayer, *Thayer's life of Beethoven*, rev. E. Forbes, 2 vols. (1964), 210, 682–4 · R. Wagner, *My life*, trans. A. Gray (1983), 521–2 · R. Wagner, *On conducting*, trans. E. Dannreuther (1887), 24–5 · M. B. Foster, *History of the Philharmonic Society of London: 1813–1912* (1912) · R. Elkin, *Royal Philharmonic: the annals of the Royal Philharmonic Society* (1946) · C. Ehrlich, *First philharmonic: a history of the Royal Philharmonic Society* (1995) · W. H. Holmes, *Notes upon notes* (1885) · W. Macfarren, 'The past principals of the Royal Academy of Music', *Royal Academy of Music Club Magazine*, 1 (1900),

5–7 · [J. S. Sainsbury], ed., *A dictionary of musicians*, 2 vols. (1824) · *New Grove*

Archives Royal Academy of Music, London | BL, Royal Philharmonic Society papers, corresp. with the Philharmonic Society, loan 48

Likenesses Bendixen, lithograph, 1838, repro. in Corder, *A history of the Royal Academy of Music*; coloured copy, Royal Academy of Music, London · J. T. Hart, bust, 1856, Royal Academy of Music, London · tinted photograph, *c*.1859, Northwestern University; repro. in Peter, 'The life and work of Cipriani Potter' · portrait (in old age), repro. in *Royal Academy of Music Club Magazine* (1905)

Wealth at death under £20,000: probate, 12 Oct 1871, *CGPLA Eng. & Wales*

Potter, Dennis Christopher George (1935–1994), journalist and playwright, was born on 17 May 1935 at Joyford Hill, off Berry Hill, Forest of Dean, Gloucestershire, the eldest child and only son of Walter Edward Potter (1906–1975), coalminer, and his wife, Margaret Constance, *née* Wale (*b*. 1910). Brought up a protestant he attended the local Salem chapel, and went to Christchurch junior school where he passed the eleven-plus entrance examination to Bell's Grammar School at Coleford. He then went, in 1949, to St Clement Danes in London, while the family lived for a time with his maternal grandfather in Hammersmith. Potter was a shy, quiet boy and later in life he made repeated references to the summer of 1945, when he suffered sexual abuse. The culprit was his homosexual and drunken Uncle Ernie, his mother's brother Ernest Wale, with whom he had to share a bed while living temporarily with his grandfather on an earlier occasion.

In 1953, conscripted into the army for national service, Potter entered the intelligence corps and achieved A-level standard in Russian. He served out his time at the War Office. In 1956 he won a scholarship to New College, Oxford, where he read philosophy, politics, and economics, and in 1958 edited *Isis*. A tall, lean young man with red hair, he was described by his economics tutor as a 'cross between Jimmy Porter and Keir Hardie' (Carpenter, 96). He always retained his Gloucestershire burr. On 10 January 1959 he married Margaret Amy Morgan (1933–1994) at Christchurch parish church.

Having left Oxford with a BA (second-class honours), he became a BBC trainee in radio and then television journalism, during which he collaborated on a short film for *Panorama* about the closure of coalpits in the Forest of Dean. Television journalism was not his forte, however, and he resigned, but he was commissioned to dramatize excerpts from contemporary novels for the series *Bookstand*. Working for the left-wing *Daily Herald* from August 1961 he became a television critic for that paper and for its successor, *The Sun*. But he was soon back in television, writing sketches for the satirical show *That Was The Week That Was*.

In 1962 Potter was struck down with the uncommon hereditary disease psoriatic arthropathy, a crippling and debilitating condition of unknown cause, marked by eruption and flaking of the skin and paralysis of the joints. Believing that his future lay in politics he had been selected to stand as Labour candidate for Hertfordshire

Dennis Christopher George Potter (1935–1994), by Trevor Leighton, 1989

East in the 1964 general election. It was a safe Conservative seat, however, and was comfortably held by the sitting member. Potter, excited by the possibilities of television drama, decided to give up both politics and journalism and become a playwright. His imagination had been fired partly by the 1963 Granada TV version of Tolstoy's *War and Peace*, based on Erwin Piscator's celebrated stage production. Potter had called it 'surely the most exciting evening that TV has ever given us' (*Daily Herald*, 27 March 1963).

Potter's earliest plays were commissioned for the BBC 'Wednesday Play' and 'Play for Today' series. They included *Stand Up, Nigel Barton* and *Vote, Vote, Vote for Nigel Barton*, tragicomedies about a young Labour candidate's campaign for office, and attracted favourable notice, but his next offerings were upstaged by seminal television works from other sources: Kenneth Loach's *Cathy Come Home* and John Hopkins's *Talking to a Stranger*, which were the most discussed television dramas of the decade after their transmission in 1966. Nevertheless, in that year Potter won the Writers' Guild writer of the year award.

While other talented writers and directors deserted television for more lucrative contracts elsewhere, Potter remained loyal to television and was to become the medium's most prolific, innovative, and controversial playwright. 'Television', he said, 'is the only medium that counts for me. It's the only one that all people watch in all sorts of situations. Television is the biggest platform and you should fight and kick and bite your way on to it' (Gilbert, 26).

By this time Potter and his wife had a son and two daughters and were living in Norfolk, but they returned to their roots in 1967, when Potter bought Morecambe Lodge at Ross-on-Wye, where he and Margaret lived for the rest of their lives. His illness worsened; psoriasis is aggravated by emotional stress. The arthritic element had contorted his hands into clenched fists and he could hold a cup or glass only between the knuckles of both hands. In and out of hospital he needed a stick to walk with, was sometimes unable to eat because his jaws seized up, and was constantly plagued by his flaking and itchy skin. He wrote in 1968 that until the previous few days 'the most burning issue in my mind had undoubtedly been whether to turn over in bed or not' (*The Sun*, 30 Sept 1968). But he kept working between bouts of pain, nausea, and diarrhoea, clutching a pen in his clawed fist and writing in surprisingly neat longhand. 'I can't use a typewriter', he said, 'because my trailing fingers would hit more than one key at once' (Carpenter, 224).

The script of *Son of Man* (1969), mostly written in hospital, was delivered with drops of blood and cortisone grease splashed on it. An agnostic interpretation of events leading to Christ's death, it represented Jesus as full of self-doubt. Despite inevitable reaction against the play from predictable quarters (Mary Whitehouse of the National Viewers' and Listeners' Association urged prosecution of the author for blasphemy), it won the European Broadcasting Union's play of the year award and a Writers' Guild award, and was subsequently adapted for the stage. The peak of Potter's career was aided by a succession of new drugs that dramatically eased his physical symptoms, but one of them was found to be a cause of cancer in the experimental control group.

Where Adam Stood, based on Edmund Gosse's autobiography, *Father and Son*, was an imaginative treatment of its key themes. It was among Potter's finest works and one of three plays by him planned for transmission in 1976; another was *Brimstone and Treacle*, written earlier but postponed because of nervousness about its controversial nature. Rescheduled for showing on 6 April, it was again withdrawn, and although promptly adapted for the stage and produced at the Crucible Theatre, Sheffield, its television première was delayed for eleven years. Described by the author as a black comedy it concerns a couple with a crippled and brain-damaged daughter who are visited by a devil in ingratiatingly human form, who rapes the girl, increasing her awareness and making her speak. If this effect had been produced by an angel, Potter said later, reaction to it would have been sanctimonious. He had presented an extreme illustration of the paradox that good can come out of evil. Nevertheless, when the play was finally transmitted in 1987, it resulted predictably in uproar.

Meanwhile, the BBC had produced Potter's serials *Pennies from Heaven* and *The Singing Detective*, and the play *Blue Remembered Hills*. The first of these (1978) was a groundbreaking original with actors miming to recordings (sometimes by singers of the opposite sex) of popular songs of the 1930s, contrastingly palliative as the story became increasingly cheerless. The tale concerned a commercial traveller in sheet music during the depression—a frustrated dreamer who ends up on the scaffold. The script lacked discipline, and this death of a salesman was

pathetic rather than tragic. *Blue Remembered Hills* (1979) successfully used adult actors to play children. Both *Pennies from Heaven* and *Blue Remembered Hills* won BAFTA awards for their author.

The Singing Detective (1986), in which Potter again employed the device of miming to popular songs, was his most accessible work. The chief character is a playwright suffering from psoriasis and going through a journey of self-discovery. Potter consistently denied writing autobiographically but he grafted imaginative ideas onto the flesh of his own experience and few authors have laid their souls so bare. He dramatized Martin Cruz Smith's novel *Gorky Park* for the cinema and wrote a screenplay, *Dreamchild*, in which he revisited the relationship between Lewis Carroll and Alice Liddell with considerably more skill and sensitivity than in his early play *Alice*. Some considered *The Singing Detective* his masterpiece but his best work was that dealing with real people other than himself (Jesus, Edmund Gosse, Lewis Carroll, among others) because these scripts demanded restraint and a tight rein on his self-indulgence and more outrageous flights of fancy.

Potter did not become a playwright because of his illness but clearly he would have been a different playwright if it had not been for his physical and mental ordeals. Psoriasis and the sexual abuse of children occur repeatedly in his plays, which also convey a strong sense of place, the Forest of Dean forming a backcloth almost as powerful as Hardy's Wessex. 'I knew Cannop Ponds by the pit where Dad worked, I knew that was where Jesus walked on the water; I knew where the Valley of the Shadow of Death was, that lane where the overhanging trees were' (Potter, 8). In 1987 he was made an honorary fellow of New College, Oxford.

Controversy was par for the course with Potter's works. After *The Singing Detective* Mary Whitehouse urged the government to include broadcasting in the Obscene Publications Act, and the four-part serial *Blackeyes* brought Potter the most vitriolic criticism of his career, earning him the tabloid press nickname Dirty Den, after a character in a current soap opera. Judged a failure by most critics, the serial seemed guilty of the crime that Potter claimed to be condemning: the objectification of women. Sexual fantasy was a powerful element in both his life and his work, and its repeated and explicit portrayal on television offended many, but the critic Maurice Wiggin had perceptively identified Potter, early in his career, as 'a moralist … with a religious basis to his work' (*Sunday Times*, 3 Nov 1966).

Nevertheless, Potter was a man of irascible and misanthropic temperament, capable of almost Swiftian ferocity and exploitation of others for his own ends. He displayed a hair-raising compulsion to bite the hands that fed him. Though professionally rewarding (he was paid £14,000 per episode for *The Singing Detective* in 1984) his relationship with the BBC was never easy, and the direction in which the corporation was moving became intellectually abhorrent to him. In his James MacTaggart memorial lecture at the Edinburgh International Television Festival in August

1993 he described the then BBC chairman, Marmaduke Hussey, and its director-general, John Birt, as 'a pair of croak-voiced Daleks'. His spleen, however, was mainly reserved for the Rupert Murdoch media empire.

In February 1994 Potter, whose wife had been given three years to live after a mastectomy in 1993, was also handed a death sentence. Told that he had cancer of the pancreas and liver, his life expectation was a mere three months. Having unwisely sunk a great deal of his own money into the making of an unsuccessful film, *Midnight Movie*, he agreed, for a fee of about £20,000, to be interviewed by Melvyn Bragg for Channel 4. Frail but dignified, entirely without self-pity but with a characteristic dash of self-promotion, he broadcast his final testament between defiant chain-smoking and swigs of liquid morphine, and left his admirers anxiously willing him time to complete his last works. In fact they were virtually finished already. The interview, recorded on 15 March, was shown on 5 April. Potter died at his home on 7 June, aged fifty-nine, only nine days after his wife. Both were cremated, and their ashes buried in Ross-on-Wye churchyard.

Potter went on mesmerizing television audiences from beyond the grave, in more ways than one. The four-part serials *Karaoke* and *Cold Lazarus* were produced jointly by the BBC and Channel 4 in accordance with his wishes. Both concern a writer, Daniel Feeld, whose dying words in the first serial are 'No biography!' In the second, his severed head, preserved by cryogenic science for nearly 400 years, produces sounds and images from its reactivated brain. In a world run by Murdoch-type media moguls, news-hungry investigators seek the worst possible interpretations of the signals emitted.

Potter's reputation, like John Osborne's, will outlast his plays, which were never destined to swell the ranks of great dramatic literature; but the impact of his work at the time cannot be overestimated, and at the end of the twentieth century, when British television had sunk to abysmally low standards, Potter's challenging originality was sorely missed. BRIAN BAILEY

Sources W. S. Gilbert, *Fight & kick & bite: the life and work of Dennis Potter*, pbk edn (1996) · H. Carpenter, *Dennis Potter* (1998) · D. Potter, *Seeing the blossom* (1994) · b. cert. · m. cert. · d. cert.
Archives BFI, corresp. with Joseph Losey · Ransom HRC, screenplay of John Fowles's *The French lieutenant's woman* and related corresp. |FILM BBC and Channel 4 recordings of plays, interviews, etc. |SOUND BBC recordings of radio broadcasts
Likenesses photographs, 1958–78, Hult. Arch. · T. Leighton, photograph, 1989, NPG [*see illus.*] · photograph, repro. in Gilbert, *Fight & kick & bite*
Wealth at death £541,204: probate, 11 Oct 1994, *CGPLA Eng. & Wales*

Potter, Edmund (1802–1883), calico printer and politician, was born on 25 January 1802 at Ardwick, Manchester, the second of six children of James Potter, merchant, and his wife, Mary, and was baptized at Cross Street Unitarian Chapel on 28 April 1802. On 3 October 1829 he married Jessy Crompton (1800–1891) of Lune Villa; they had four sons (Edmund Crompton, Rupert, Walter, and William Henry) and three daughters (Clara, Mary, and Lucy). Beatrix Potter was their granddaughter.

Little is known of Potter's early life; he claimed to have had 'a sound education and a severe apprenticeship'. In 1825 he went into partnership with his cousin Charles as a calico printer at Dinting Vale, Glossop. The business failed in 1831 and the partnership was dissolved, but Potter continued under administration, discharged his final debts in 1836, and resumed trading on his own account. In the 1840s Potter was at the forefront of the shift from block to cylinder printing, and over the ensuing thirty years, although he increasingly left the business in the hands of his managers, Dinting Vale grew to be reputedly the largest calico printing works in the world. Its cloths were well regarded for their designs and innovative use of new dyes.

Potter was a spokesman of the practical calico printers and took considerable interest in design education. He helped establish the Manchester School of Design (later School of Art), serving as president from 1855 to 1858, and wrote several pamphlets on calico printing and design education, including *Calico Printing as Art and Manufacture* (1852) and *A Lecture on the Positions of Schools of Art* (1855). In 1856 he was elected a fellow of the Royal Society as the representative of scientific calico printing, and he also gave evidence to various parliamentary inquiries, including the select committees on design (1840) and schools of art (1864). He was the driving force behind the 1857 Manchester Art Treasures Exhibition, recalling later that he 'gave two years' hard labour' to it.

Deputation and committee work, rather than platform advocacy, were Potter's métier. Hence, although he was remembered as one of the founders of the Anti-Corn Law League, and an indefatigable worker for it and for the Liberal interest in south Lancashire, this activity took place largely behind the scenes. His pivotal role as a broker between the league party and the Palmerstonians brought him to prominence briefly in 1859–60 when he engineered, first through the Manchester Reform Association, and then the Lancashire (later National) Reform Union, an alliance between these factions and moderate working-class radicals—an early local expression of the Gladstonian Liberal alignment. During this period he was also an active campaigner on the cotton supply question, and served as president of the Manchester chamber of commerce (1859–62).

From 1861 to 1874 Potter was Liberal MP for Carlisle, predominantly as a representative of commerce. In this regard he retained an unshakeable commitment to *laissez-faire* and faith in 'enlightened self-interest, competition and individual energy', except in respect of sanitary reform and education. He was one of the parliamentary mouthpieces of the National Federation of Associated Employers of Labour (founded in 1873), and, as illustrated by several pamphlets written in the 1850s and 1860s, remained an outspoken critic of trade unions, co-operation, and limited liability legislation.

Between 1842 and 1861 Potter resided at Dinting Vale, but after his election to parliament he lived increasingly in London, his house a meeting-place for radical Liberals. In 1873, in steadily deteriorating health, he relinquished oversight of the Dinting Vale works to his son Edmund (1830–1883), a noted art collector. The following year he retired from parliament to Camfield Place, Hatfield, Hertfordshire, an estate he had purchased in 1866. He died there on 26 October 1883, and was buried on 31 October at Gee Cross, Hyde, Cheshire. He was survived by his wife.

M. HEWITT

Sources J. G. Hurst, *Edmund Potter … and Dinting Vale* (1948) · G. R. Searle, *Entrepreneurial politics in mid-Victorian Britain* (1993) · *Annual Reports* [Manchester Chamber of Commerce] (1856–61) · Q. Bell, *The schools of design* (1963) · *Manchester Examiner and Times* (29 Oct 1883)
Archives Derbys. RO, Edmund Potter & Co. MSS · Lpool RO, George Melly MSS · Man. CL, George Wilson MSS · V&A, department of textiles and dress, Edmund Potter & Co. pattern book · W. Sussex RO, Cobden MSS
Likenesses L. Potter, photograph, 1859, repro. in Hurst, *Edmund Potter* · portrait, 1862, repro. in Hurst, *Edmund Potter* · portrait, repro. in Hurst, *Edmund Potter*
Wealth at death £441,970 19s. 9d.: probate, 17 Jan 1884, *CGPLA Eng. & Wales*

Potter, Francis (1594–1678), Church of England clergyman, instrument maker, and experimentalist, was the second son of the Revd Richard Potter (d. 1628), prebendary of Worcester, and his wife, who belonged to the Horsey family of Clifton, Dorset. He was born at Mere vicarage, Wiltshire, on 29 May (Trinity Sunday) 1594, and educated at the King's School, Worcester. In 1609, he went up as a commoner to Trinity College, Oxford, where his elder brother, Hannibal *Potter (1592–1664), was a scholar; Francis graduated BA in 1613 and MA in 1616. In 1625 he proceeded BD. He succeeded his father as rector of Kilmington, which was then in Somerset, though there is some confusion regarding the exact date. Archives in Trinity College, Oxford, give Richard Potter's death as 1628 ('Blakiston's register', ref. 73), though a list of rectors in Kilmington church, compiled in the early twentieth century, with no sources cited, gives Francis Potter's induction date into the parish as 4 November 1626. Wood (2.612), however, gives the date as 1637, which is almost certainly incorrect. But it is known that Potter did not make his home at Kilmington for some time after becoming rector. He continued to reside in Trinity College, and to pay his annual 40 shillings 'caution money' until 1631.

Potter escaped sequestration during the civil war and interregnum. He had been sickly, especially when younger, but his health improved with age, though he subsequently became blind. He did not marry. His friend John Aubrey provides in *Brief Lives* the most detailed and intimate portrait of Potter, whom he greatly admired. Aubrey describes him as 'like a monk', and as 'pretty long visagd, and pale cleare skin, gray eie'. In old age, Potter preferred to be looked after by his servants who 'were kind to him' rather than by his kinsfolk who 'did begrudge what he spent'.

Potter was a practical mechanician and inventor, and admired Dr John Wilkins. He made quadrants, and invented a beam compass which could divide an inch into a thousand parts. The compass was later given to Aubrey. He experimented with blood transfusion in the 1640s, and

Aubrey sent him a surgical lancet for this work. Potter hoped to use transfusion to cure diseases, and later communicated his results to the Royal Society via John Aubrey. He was proposed for fellowship of the Royal Society on 18 March 1663, and admitted on 11 November of that year. He probably made the fine dial (probably seen in Loggan's view in *Oxonia illustrata*) on the north side of the original quadrangle of Trinity College, Oxford. He also drew and painted; the copy of the founder's portrait in Trinity College hall is his work, and Aubrey said that he devised an instrument for drawing in perspective, which was afterwards reinvented by Wren. He was fond of chess, which he played with a contemporary at Trinity, Colonel Bishop, who was accounted by Aubrey 'the best in England'. Potter also cultivated and experimented with bees; he and Aubrey examined them under the microscope.

Potter was interested in computing the number of the beast, connecting 25, the 'appropinque' square root of 666, with various institutions in the Roman Catholic church. His ideas were elaborated in a manuscript which was read in 1637 by Joseph Mede, and commended as a wonderful discovery, the 'happiest that ever yet came into the world', and as calculated to 'make some of your German speculatives half wild' (Mede to S. Hartlib, 29 Jan 1638, Mede, 1077). It was published as *An Interpretation of the Number 666*, by Leonard Lichfield of Oxford in 1642, with a symbolical frontispiece, an opinion by Mede prefixed, and a preface date from Kilmington. Wood (2.612) wrote that it was translated into French, Dutch, and Latin, printed in a small octavo at Amsterdam in 1677, and attributed to Thomas Gilbert (1613–1694) of St Edmund Hall, Oxford. Potter's work on the number of the beast was read in November 1666 by Pepys, who considered it to be 'mighty ingenious'. It continued to be influential and was reprinted in Worcester as late as 1808.

Potter lived through fast-moving political and intellectual times, and his interests in science, medicine, and biblical eschatology spanned some of the deepest concerns of the age. He died in April 1678, and was buried in the same month in the chancel of Kilmington church.

ALLAN CHAPMAN

Sources F. Potter, *An interpretation of the number 666* (1642) · Wood, *Ath. Oxon.* · *Aubrey's Brief lives*, 2nd edn, ed. O. L. Dick (1950) · J. Aubrey, *The natural history of Wiltshire*, ed. J. Britton (1847) · R. C. Hoare, *The history of modern Wiltshire*, 1 (1822) · J. Mede, *The works of … J. Mede … being discourses on divers texts of scripture* (1664) · M. Poole, *Synopsis criticorum aliorumque s. scripturae interpretum*, 4/2 (1676) · M. Hunter, *The Royal Society and its fellows, 1660–1700: the morphology of an early scientific institution* (1982) · D. Loggan, *Oxonia illustrata* (1675) · M. Hunter, *John Aubrey and the realm of learning* (1975) · C. Webster, *The great instauration: science, medicine and reform, 1626–1660* (1975) · Trinity College, Oxford
Archives Bodl. Oxf., Ashmole 243 · Bodl. Oxf., letters to John Aubrey

Potter, George (1832–1893), trade unionist and journalist, was born in Kenilworth, Warwickshire, the son of Edmund William Potter, a carpenter, and his wife, Anne. As one of seven children, he had to leave the local endowed school after only a few years to find paid work, before following his father into the woodworking trade through an apprenticeship with a joiner in Coventry. He left for London in 1853, found well-paid employment, and in 1857 married the daughter of a Warwick shoemaker. He settled in Pimlico, and soon became a leading member of the small Progressive Society of Carpenters and Joiners which met at the Rose and Crown in Tottenham Court Road. While serving as this society's chairman, Potter helped to initiate a movement for the nine-hour day among the London building trades, and became its chief spokesman during the widely publicized lock-out which followed in the winter of 1859–60, ending in an honourable compromise. The combination of an intellectual appearance and restrained oratory with militant views and effective actions made Potter an instant celebrity and allowed him to launch a national trade union newspaper, *The Bee-Hive*, which from 1861 to 1878 provided him with an unusually prominent platform.

At first *The Bee-Hive* served as the organ of the London Trades Council, but in the mid-1860s Potter's principle of supporting local strikes brought him into increasing conflict with the more strategic approach of the leaders of the new amalgamated craft societies, who emphasized instead national discipline and a more responsible public image. This difference of opinion raised the question of Potter's claim to leadership as he was no longer an elected union official and, following a particularly serious disagreement over the conduct of a Staffordshire ironworkers' strike in 1865, the London Trades Council announced that *The Bee-Hive* no longer represented its views. Potter responded by setting up the London Working Men's Association in 1866, mainly to give *The Bee-Hive* the appearance of representing a significant organization though it did receive some support from among the smaller craft societies. Paradoxically this widening of ambition from largely industrial matters to wider political questions began to blur the distinction between the rival groups of leaders. For example, it was Potter who initiated the unification of franchise campaigners into the Reform League, even though it soon became dominated by the London Trades Council leaders. Similarly, it was Potter who effectively secured the appointment of a commissioner friendly to the unions on the 1867 royal commission on trade unions, even though his own appearances before it were soon overshadowed by the more carefully planned presentations of the secretaries of the amalgamated societies.

Later historians looking for an alternative to the new style of responsible leadership in the middle of the nineteenth century were therefore misguided in elevating Potter to that position. First he did not represent any permanently organized body of workers, and second his policies were not in general very unusual: the conflicts were ones of personal ambition within a movement going in a broadly agreed direction. Indeed, realizing that his own bid for leadership had failed, Potter soon moved towards an accommodation with the mainstream, through co-operation with the radical manufacturer Samuel Morley and participation in the campaigns of the Reform League and the middle-class Reform Union. This paved the way for an explicit reconciliation during and after the general election of 1868 when Potter supported Gladstonian Liberalism, allowed the London Working Men's Association to lapse, and re-established *The Bee-Hive* as the organ of the Labour Representation League and the parliamentary committee of the TUC: the one substantial shift in position being the abandonment of support for local strikes in favour of the strategy of the leaders of the amalgamated societies.

This turned *The Bee-Hive* into an important national forum, drawing established labour leaders and middle-class sympathizers into debates characterized by a high level of intellectual argument, with an unprecedented influence on the educated working men of the day. Potter himself took his place within the official leadership of the movement, as president of the TUC in 1871 and chairman of its parliamentary committee for the following year, and as one of the group of Labour candidates in the 1874 general election, in which he was unsuccessful. However he was elected to the Westminster school board on his second attempt in 1873, having declared himself a Congregationalist, and held his seat until 1882 promoting nonconformist educational policies. After *The Bee-Hive* (by then named the *Industrial Review*) was forced to close in 1878 he devoted himself to commercial publishing and ceased to play a prominent role in national labour politics, such appearances as he did make, for example as a candidate for Preston in the 1886 election, being as an official Gladstonian Liberal.

Potter played an important role as a newspaper proprietor and editor in the trade union cause, and thus left an invaluable legacy for later historians. He was a thin, pale, intense-looking man, able to speak and write forcefully but without any great intellectual originality. After the death of his wife in 1886, he moved to live with his married daughter in Clapham, where he died at home, at 21 Marney Road, Lavender Hill, on 3 June 1893.

ALASTAIR J. REID

Sources S. Coltham, 'Potter, George', *DLB*, vol. 6 · S. Coltham, 'George Potter, the Junta, and the Bee-hive', *International Review of Social History*, 9 (1964), 391–432 · S. Coltham, 'George Potter, the Junta, and the Bee-hive', *International Review of Social History*, 10 (1965), 23–65 · *CGPLA Eng. & Wales* (1893) · d. cert. · *The Times* (5 June 1893)
Archives Bishopsgate Institute, London, letters to George Howell
Wealth at death £520 14s.: probate, 22 June 1893, *CGPLA Eng. & Wales*

Potter, George (1887–1960), Church of England clergyman and religious superior, was born at 6 Park Terrace, Cavendish Road, Clapham, London, on 13 April 1887, the youngest of five children of George Potter, railway clerk, and his wife, Eliza Jeannette Fairey (1842?–1924). He was brought up by his mother after the early death of his father, and was educated at St Mary's School, Balham, until the age of fourteen. He then worked as a clerk with various firms in the City of London before becoming secretary to Canon Bates, vicar of St Mary's, Balham, who helped to foster his vocation to the priesthood. He studied at the House of the Sacred Mission, Kelham, for eighteen months from 1909, but had to leave because of ill health. However, he studied for a further two years as a day student at King's College, London, becoming an associate in 1912. In the same year he was ordained deacon, and in 1914 priest, serving as assistant curate of All Saints', Wimbledon. He served as an army chaplain in France and Egypt in 1915, but apart from this his entire ministry was in poor parts of south London in the diocese of Southwark. In 1917 he became assistant curate of St Bartholomew's, Camberwell, and in 1923 vicar of St Chrysostom's, Peckham. Potter resigned the incumbency in 1938 because of overwork and ill health, but remained honorary curate of St Chrysostom's until his death on 15 February 1960. He was made an honorary canon of Southwark Cathedral in 1954.

Potter renovated St Chrysostom's Church and established a vicarage, which he shared with his mother (until her death in 1924) and his two sisters. He was an outstanding slum priest, but is chiefly remembered for his work with homeless boys and boys in care. Beginning informally, this work led to the establishment of a hostel in south London and a holiday home at Southwick, Sussex, where his sisters took charge. Potter was noted for combining kindness with discipline, and many of those who came into his care later made good and kept contact long afterwards. He and his lay helpers evolved into a small religious community, the Brotherhood of the Holy Cross. This received official recognition from Bishop Parsons of Southwark in June 1933, with Potter as superior. The brotherhood followed a simple rule of life based on the principles of St Francis of Assisi, to whom Potter always had a great devotion. Close relations were established with other Anglican Franciscan communities, but the Brotherhood of the Holy Cross remained apart when the Society of St Francis was formed in 1937.

George Potter combined firm Anglo-Catholic convictions with a strong belief in personal commitment and evangelism. He was a keen supporter of the Scouts and, particularly in later years, much in demand for parish missions and prison visiting. All who knew him well testify to his great sense of humour, his love for animals, and his deep sense of devotion combined with an easy informality. Much of his personality comes across in his autobiography, *Father Potter of Peckham* (1955), while the sequel, *More Father Potter of Peckham* (1958), says much about life in the parish and the brotherhood. He had a gift for making a point by story-telling, usually drawing from his own experience. The towel used by Christ to wash the disciples' feet was a particularly meaningful symbol to Potter, who regarded it almost as a banner of Christian service.

From 1938 Potter devoted himself to the work of the brotherhood and the hostel. This work continued during the Second World War despite the hostel sustaining damage during the blitz. Potter died where he had lived at Nunhead, London, on 15 February 1960. As a religious, he never married. His sisters died at Southwick in 1944. The Brotherhood of the Holy Cross did not long survive; three of the surviving members joined the Society of St Francis in 1963.   BARRIE WILLIAMS

Sources G. Potter, *Father Potter of Peckham* (1955) · G. Potter, *More Father Potter of Peckham* (1958) · private information (2004) · B. Williams, *The Franciscan revival in the Anglican communion* (1982) · P. Dunstan, *This poor sort: a history of the European province of the Society of St Francis* (1997) · b. cert.
Archives Bodl. Oxf., Brotherhood of the Holy Cross archives
Likenesses photograph, repro. in Potter, *Father Potter* · photograph, repro. in Potter, *More Father Potter*, jacket · photographs, priv. coll.
Wealth at death probably nominal

Potter, Gillie [*real name* Hugh William Peel] (1887–1975), comedian and broadcaster, was born at 27 Weston Street, St Paul, Bedford, on 14 September 1887, the eldest son of the Revd Brignal Peel, a Wesleyan minister, and his wife, Elizabeth Stimson. He was educated at Bedford modern school and, briefly, Worcester College, Oxford, before embarking on the stage career that first made his name.

He first appeared in E. M. Royle's *The White Man* at the Lyric Theatre, London, thereafter in touring theatre, musical comedy, concert parties, and pantomime, and in 1915 was George Robey's understudy at the Alhambra. He served as a lieutenant in the Royal Fleet Auxiliary from February 1917. Returning to music-hall after the war he developed his highly individual comedic style and stage persona, described by critic James Agate as 'that sham Harrovian who bears upon his blazer the broad arrows of a blameful life' (Mosley, 116). In straw boater, wide grey flannel trousers (he claimed to have invented 'Oxford bags' at the London Coliseum in 1920), and 'Old Borstolian' blazer (blue, with white convict arrow on the breast pocket), and generally carrying notebook and rolled umbrella, he lectured his audience in deadpan tones on unlikely and esoteric themes peppered with literary, historical, and linguistic allusion. Though a classical education was needed fully to appreciate his act, it was widely popular: in 1930 he appeared in the royal variety performance, and the following year made his radio début.

At a time when the BBC was seeking new variety styles beyond the broad humour typical of inter-war music-hall, Potter's literate and allusive humour, with its echoes of *Punch* and 'Beachcomber', was hailed as the radio comedy of the future. He was soon one of the most popular radio entertainers in Britain, one of the pioneer generation that included Leonard Henry, Mabel Constanduros, A. J. Alan, and Ronald Frankau. His celebrated opening catchphrase, 'Good evening England. This is Gillie Potter speaking to you in English', signalled his principal themes of the English language and character. His act included at various times the adventures of 'my brother who was educated at Borstal', burlesques of 'society snippets', and parodies of *Who's Who* entries. However, his fame rests chiefly on his chronicles of the mythical English village of Hogsnorton—the name a typically arcane reference to the proverbial Oxfordshire village where 'pigs play on the organ' (*Brewer*, 523)—its noble but impoverished ancestral family, the Marshmallows of Hogsnorton Towers, and their disorderly world of inverted logic and improbable situations. Potter's combination of mock erudition, absurdity, and nostalgia struck a chord with inter-war audiences and made him a household name. When the BBC evacuated much of its staff to Wood Norton Hall, near Evesham, on the eve of the Second World War, its new base was known, inevitably, as Hogsnorton.

Beyond the comedy routines the English language, history, and people were an abiding passion in Potter's life. He was an authority on heraldry, genealogy, and church history, a knight templar, a member of the Middle Temple and the Society of Genealogists, a vice-president of the Royal Society of St George and the Society of King Charles the Martyr, as well as for many years parish clerk of the church of St Botolph, Aldgate, London. His letters to *The Times* from the 1930s to 1960s attest both to his eclectic scholarship (topics on which he offered his expertise ranged from the iconography of St Cuthbert to the heraldic derivations of the bunting celebrating the centenary of Waterloo Station) and his distaste for modern trends. He deplored the 'alien' pollution of the English comedic tradition by European and particularly American influences. Though he continued to broadcast throughout the Second World War, he felt increasingly out of sympathy with 'this era of Priestley and "Penguins"' (*The Times*, 10 Aug 1940). After the war, writing from what he termed 'unoccupied England', his targets included the adoption of the word 'university' by new scientific higher education institutions and the plans for the new Coventry Cathedral (a 'cross between a super-cinema and an abattoir'; *The Times*, 27 Nov 1951). His anger at what he considered the BBC's declining moral standards made him an unlikely spokesman for the Popular Television Association, which campaigned in the early 1950s for a commercial alternative to the BBC. He once considered standing for parliament as an independent on the platform of 'England for the English', with special reference to the theatre.

Potter's style of comedy, and the attitudes that coloured it, were increasingly hard to accommodate in the post-war years. His love of language and eye for the absurd led to his being called the English Thurber, but his comedy lacked Thurber's humanism and seemed increasingly dated, particularly on stage. He retired from live performance, it was said, after a chastening experience at the London Palladium performing to an audience of young girls impatient for the headline act Danny Kaye (*The Guardian*). He was increasingly at odds with the BBC, partly because of his outspoken criticism of its output, partly because he resisted undertaking any broadcasting other than series, partly—mostly, he believed—because of his political views. He completed his last radio series, *Mr Gillie Potter*, in 1952, and the following year made his last broadcasts as a comedian, *Coronation at Hogsnorton* for radio and *A Little of What you Fancy* for television.

Potter was married to Beatrice Fanny Scott; they had two children, a son (J. H. B. Peel, a *Daily Telegraph* writer on country matters) and a daughter. In the early 1960s he retired to Bournemouth, occasionally appearing on talks programmes but refusing to speak to the press. His last broadcast appearance was in the panel game *Sounds Familiar* in 1970. He died on 4 March 1975, aged eighty-seven, at Douglas House, 84 Southbourne Road, Bournemouth.

SIÂN NICHOLAS

Sources *The Times* (5 March 1975) · *Daily Telegraph* (5 March 1975) · *The Guardian* (5 March 1975) · G. Potter, correspondence and news reports, *The Times* (1934–66) · files, BBC WAC · S. A. Mosley, ed., *Who's Who in Broadcasting* (1933) · C. Brown, *The spice of variety* (1949) · matriculation record, 15 Oct 1907, Oxf. UA · undergraduate register, Oxf. UA · *Oxford University Gazette* (1907–8) · E. S. Craig and W. M. Gibson, eds., *Oxford University roll of service*, 3rd edn (1920) · S. Hibberd, *This … is London* (1950) · *BBC Year Book, 1931* (1931) · *Brewer's dictionary of phrase and fable*, 15th edn (1995) · P. Scannell and D. Cardiff, *A social history of British broadcasting*, [1] (1991) · B. Took, *Laughter in the air: an informal history of British radio comedy* (1976) · A. Briggs, *The history of broadcasting in the United Kingdom*, 2–4 (1965–79) · *CGPLA Eng. & Wales* (1975) · b. cert. · d. cert.

Archives BBC WAC | SOUND BL NSA, performance recordings

Likenesses photograph, repro. in *BBC Year Book* (1931) · photograph, repro. in *The Times*

Wealth at death £11,274: probate, 22 July 1975, *CGPLA Eng. & Wales*

Potter, Hannibal (1592–1664), college head, was born at Mere vicarage, Wiltshire, the eldest son of Richard Potter (*c*.1557–1637), prebendary of Worcester. In 1607 he was sent to Trinity College, Oxford, where his father had held a fellowship from 1579 to 1585. Two years later he was elected to a scholarship, while his younger brother Francis *Potter (1594–1678) entered as a commoner. Potter was elected to a fellowship in 1613; the simple monasticism of the life suited him well. He and Francis shared a room until the latter succeeded to their father's living in 1637. A man of great piety Hannibal Potter took his BD in 1621 and his DD in 1630, and was unfailingly conscientious in his religious duties. He was appointed rector of Over Worton in Oxfordshire in 1624 and of Wootton, Northamptonshire, in the following year; in 1635 he preached at Gray's Inn.

When the president of Trinity, Ralph Kettell, died in 1642, Potter had been senior fellow for twelve years and was thus an obvious candidate to succeed. Contemporary gossip had it that the fellows' vote had been in favour of the more dynamic William Chillingworth, but Potter was the choice of the visitor, Walter Curll, whom he had previously served as chaplain. As a fellow, Potter came before parliamentary questioners several times, and showed skill in picking his path carefully. To be head of house in the civil war was far from easy, and the ever-timorous Potter approached the daily difficulties of the role with a mixture of heroic endurance and nervous cat-and-mouse resistance. It was a surprisingly effective combination. By nature reluctant to get involved in controversy, sometimes his will to resist needed bolstering by men such as Richard Baylie of St John's—for example, when he spoke against the visitors' contempt for learning and was ordered to submit a copy of his speech to Westminster. As pro-vice-chancellor during the imprisonment of Dr Fell he often found himself in the limelight. In October 1647 he urged convocation to show Christian patience and inoffensive behaviour. When ordered into custody in January 1648, he could not be found. A week later he appeared before the commissioners in London and was found guilty of high contempt, a verdict of which he was in turn contemptuous. On 13 April 1648 he reduced a violent ejection from his lodgings to a mere formality by the expedient of fleeing in advance, and the puritan Robert Harris was imposed on the college in his place.

Potter endured twelve painful years as an exile from Oxford. He automatically lost the presidential living of Garsington. One Captain Coleford obtained for him the curacy of Broomfield, Somerset, but he was soon removed, either for using the liturgy or for 'insufficiency' (Neal, 315). At times he despaired. He was in debt, unable to study, and felt futile and worthless. But at the same time his strong faith and devotion to duty never wavered; and he found time and energy to follow with increasing concern his brother's growing reputation as an eccentric scientist, and to rebuke him for neglecting his vocation and the souls of his flock.

On 3 August 1660 Potter was reinstated to the presidency of Trinity College, the appointment again sealed by an old friend—on this occasion Robert Skinner, bishop of Oxford, who had been a contemporary of Potter's as scholar and fellow. It was quietly done, and the last years of his life were tranquil. Trinity's finances were consolidated, the work ably assisted by Ralph Bathurst, fellow and patently the president-in-waiting. Potter died on 1 September 1664 and was buried in the college chapel. A dirge composed by Samuel Dugard gives the impression of a man much loved in the frailty of his old age. His will was simple, leaving everything to his brother-in-law Thomas Taylor of Worcester. Francis was not mentioned.

CLARE HOPKINS

Sources A. Wood, *The history and antiquities of the University of Oxford*, ed. J. Gutch, 2 (1796), pt 2 • H. E. D. Blakiston, *Trinity College* (1898) • J. Walker, *An attempt towards recovering an account of the numbers and sufferings of the clergy of the Church of England*, 2 pts in 1 (1714) • H. Potter, letters to John Aubrey, Bodl. Oxf., MSS Aubrey 13/162–163 • S. Dugard, 'Epicedes on the Rev. Dr Potter', Bodl. Oxf., MS Rawl. poet. 152.40 • A. Wood, *The history and antiquities of the colleges and halls in the University of Oxford*, ed. J. Gutch (1786) • *John Aubrey: 'Brief lives'*, ed. J. Buchanan-Brown (2000) • will, Bodl. Oxf., O.U. Arch. wills OP [microfilm] • I. Roy and D. Reinhart, 'Oxford and the civil wars', *Hist. U. Oxf.* 4: *17th-cent. Oxf.*, 687–732 • Kettell's register, Trinity College archive, Oxford • D. Neal, *The history of the puritans or protestant nonconformists*, 2nd edn, 2 vols. (1754)

Potter, John (1673/4–1747), archbishop of Canterbury, was born in what was subsequently called Black Rock House, in Market Place, Wakefield, Yorkshire, the son of Thomas Potter, a linen draper of that town. There he was educated at the Queen Elizabeth Grammar School. The non-juror Thomas Hearne claimed that Potter's father was a 'rank Presbyterian and a continual frequenter of their meetings' (*Remarks*, 2.5); it has also been claimed that Potter was brought up a dissenter and was perhaps even destined for the presbyterian ministry. Despite his nonconformist background, in 1688 Potter entered University College, Oxford, as a servitor, aged fourteen, and on 18 May he matriculated. He must therefore have subscribed to the Thirty-Nine Articles, and while at Oxford he wrote to his

father telling him of his decision to conform to the Church of England. As the letter is not dated it is unclear when this took place but it was possibly about mid-1690. Similarly it is unclear whether his conversion to Anglicanism was recent or whether he had made the decision earlier but had concealed the fact from his family. It is probable that through the influence of the Anglican clergyman Edward Clarke, who had been his tutor at school, he had secretly decided to conform before he left Wakefield in 1688; his decision to do so, however, caused a serious rift with his father, which may have left him in financial difficulties. He had matriculated without paying the standard fee, since he was considered a 'pauper', and following his announcement to his father financial support from his family may have been withdrawn, thus forcing him to become the tutor of Gilbert Jackson of Forest Hill.

Potter went on to gain his BA on 23 January 1692 and his MA in 1694. On 2 May of that year he was elected Yorkshire fellow of Lincoln College, a position which he held until 23 June 1706. While at Oxford he was a pupil of two other natives of Wakefield, Thomas Bateman (*d.* 1690) and Joseph Bingham. It was perhaps due to Bingham that Potter, who had become skilled in Greek from an early age, developed his interest in classical history and patristics. These studies led him to write his *Variantes lections at Notoe and Plutarchi librum de audiendis poetis*, which he published in 1694 on the advice of Arthur Charlett, master of University College, Oxford. Charlett also paid for the publication costs and gave copies as new year gifts to his students and friends. During his lifetime Potter also published a number of other classical works, including his *Archaeologia Graeca* in 1697 and 1698, and his *Klementos Alexandros ta Euriskomena* in 1715.

In 1697 Potter was made rector of Greens Norton, Northamptonshire, where he remained until 1700; at the same time he gained the vicarage of Coleby, Lincolnshire, which he held until 1709. In 1698 he was made deacon, and a year later he was ordained priest by John Hough, bishop of Coventry, to whom he was chaplain. On 8 July 1704 he gained his BD and moved to Lambeth to be chaplain to the archbishop of Canterbury, Thomas Tenison. His career advanced quickly under Tenison's patronage, and two years later he gained his DD, on 18 April 1706, and became chaplain-in-ordinary to Queen Anne. Also in 1706 he resigned his fellowship at Lincoln College and was made rector of Mongeham, Kent; on 17 February the following year he was moved to the rectory of Monks Risborough, Buckinghamshire.

Potter was a high-churchman. He had an elevated role of the clerical estate, upheld the independent rights of the church, and was committed to the authority of the ancient fathers and the example of the primitive church. These views were expressed most notably in 1707, when he published *The Discourse on Church Government*, a work which, according to Stephen Taylor, prompted Potter's dissenting father to start writing a refutation, although he never completed the work. Despite his high-church outlook in religious matters Potter was a committed whig in political affairs. It is probably for this reason that Thomas Hearne called him a 'famous Low Church Man' (*Remarks*, 2.79) and frequently criticized him. During the reigns of George I and George II whig ministers were keen to promote a close relationship between the political administration and the Church of England, and Potter's political affiliation ensured that he enjoyed the patronage of a number of leading whigs, of whom his principal clerical supporter, Tenison, was one. He also enjoyed the influential patronage of John Churchill, duke of Marlborough. In January 1707 Robert Harley, speaker of the House of Commons, to whom Potter had dedicated the first volume of his *Archaeologia Graeca*, offered him the regius chair of Greek, a position which he refused as he was by that time more interested in divinity than in classics. Due to the influence of the duke of Marlborough he was made regius professor of divinity, on 8 January 1708, and a few weeks later, on 29 January, he was installed as canon of Christ Church. At the same time he was appointed rector of Newington, Oxfordshire, a position which he held until his elevation to the primacy in 1737.

While at Christ Church, Potter married a Miss Venner, with whom, according to Hearne, he had ten children, of whom six or seven survived (*Remarks*, 9.238). However, only four outlived their father, two daughters and two sons. Potter's first son, John (d. 1770), entered the church and was advanced considerably by his father, attaining the archdeaconry of Oxford in 1741. However, John lost his father's goodwill and patronage when he married a domestic servant from Lambeth, a marriage which Potter considered unsuitable. Potter bestowed similar patronage on his son-in-law Jeremiah Milles, who later became vicar of Merstham in Surrey as well as of West Tarring in Sussex, and dean of Exeter. Potter's second son, Thomas *Potter (1718?–1759), became a barrister of the Inner Temple, registrar of the province of Canterbury, recorder of Bath, and a member of parliament for St Germans, Aylesbury, and also Okehampton.

It was again through the influence of the duke of Marlborough that Potter was made bishop of Oxford; installed on 9 May 1715, he moved to Cuddesdon. On 1 August 1715 he was asked to preach before the House of Lords on the first anniversary of George I's accession to the throne. His whig principles, which expressed themselves on this occasion in his firm commitment to the Hanoverian succession and the new administration, ensured that he became a regular preacher at court and at Westminster. He was later to preach at the coronation of George II and Queen Caroline on 11 October 1727. A chance for further advancement came in September 1719, when the dean of Christ Church, George Smalridge, died and many people, including William Wake and Francis Atterbury and those within the ministry, urged Potter to take over the position, despite his already being bishop. However, Potter appeared reluctant, due to ill health and poor eyesight, which had plagued him throughout his life, and the king disposed of the position to Hugh Boulter. Similarly in 1727 he was offered the bishopric of Bath and Wells and again

he declined. According to Hearne, Potter was already hoping for the archbishopric of Canterbury, but Hearne's assessment may be unreliable.

During his time at Oxford, Potter became embroiled in the Bangorian controversy. Despite his prominence and his learning he had tended to remain aloof from public controversies in religious matters, particularly those between the high and low church, preferring to concern himself with his pastoral duties. But, following the publication of Benjamin Hoadly's infamous sermon on the nature of the kingdom of Christ, delivered on 31 March 1717, and the protracted dispute that ensued, Potter became involved. At his triennial visitation to the clergy of his diocese in 1719 he delivered a charge in which he indirectly condemned Hoadly's arguments and denounced Arianism, which he believed was threatening the Church of England. He was reluctant to be drawn further into the controversy but agreed to publish his charge when urged to do so by his clergy. However, when Hoadly printed a condemnation of Potter's views the bishop of Oxford was moved to write a defence of his charge, which he published in the same year.

In 1734 the bishopric of Winchester became vacant and, according to Lord Hervey, Potter hoped to be given that position, primarily because of the great cathedral library there. His hopes were not to be fulfilled, since the government decided to appoint Benjamin Hoadly, in return for his service to the whigs. In 1737 the archbishop of Canterbury, William Wake, died and the ministry had to find a successor; there were a number of candidates. Lord Hervey recommended Potter for the position, telling Walpole that 'Potter is a great man of undoubted learning' who was committed to the Hanoverian succession; he went on to say: 'his Character will support you in sending him to Lambeth, and his capacity is not so good, nor his temper so bad as to make you apprehend any great danger in his being there' (Barnard, 89). L. W. Barnard believes that 'Potter may have appeared as a mild, cautious, scholarly, almost a non-political choice' (ibid.) and that Hervey believed that he would be a compliant archbishop. He was also a great favourite of Queen Caroline, which may have been influential. He was installed as archbishop on 28 February 1737 at St Mary-Le-Bow and returned to Lambeth House.

As archbishop Potter opposed church reform. In March 1738 he resisted calls for the reform of the liturgy along the lines of the 1689 proposals, and throughout the 1740s he was opposed to pressure for convocation to initiate reform. He did not always receive a sympathetic or flattering assessment from contemporaries. Thomas Hearne was a regular critic, calling him 'an ambitious, conceited, proud man' (*Remarks*, 2.107) who had been elevated within the church in order to promote the interests of the whigs but who was 'far from being a truly great man upon any account' (ibid., 9.367). The Arian William Whiston wrote in his memoirs that when asked by Queen Caroline about Potter's suitability for the newly vacated archbishopric he had praised him, claiming that he was a man 'of great *Piety*, *Learning*, and *Moderation*; and an excellent pastor of a parish' and so had recommended him for the position (Whiston). Whiston went on to say that the new position had made Potter 'high and pontifical' and he criticized him for not taking action against the rise of Athanasianism (ibid., 300–01). While bishop Potter had attempted to remain aloof from the politics of London, despite his prominent position within the church and his political support for the whig ministry, for which he was rewarded. Instead he preferred where possible to remain in his diocese and attend to ecclesiastical matters there. As he wrote to William Wake, then archbishop, on 20 October 1723, he did not spend as much time at court and parliament as many of his brethren, since 'for several years past I have found I could be altogether as serviceable both to the church and state whilst I remained here in the Country as in town' (Barnard, 62). His nineteenth-century biographer Robert Anderson claimed that Potter 'took care not to involve himself too much in secular matters, but devoted his chief attention to the affairs of the church' (Anderson, ix). This lack of involvement in secular matters continued during his years as primate and led to criticism from his peers, particularly during the period of danger from French invasion in 1743 and during the Jacobite rising of 1745—when contemporaries such as the bishop of London, Edmund Gibson, condemned his lack of involvement and leadership. However, as both bishop and archbishop Potter appears to have fulfilled his spiritual duties diligently, while being committed to raising the pastoral quality of the clergy.

Towards the end of his career Potter became isolated at court, much to his frustration. It may have been for this reason that he was involved in the Leicester House opposition to the ministry in 1747. Both Thomas Gooch, bishop of Ely, and Thomas Herring, archbishop of York, mentioned this involvement in their private correspondence. Gooch claimed that the withdrawal of Frederick, prince of Wales, from the election for the chancellorship at the University of Cambridge in 1747 was a personal defeat for Potter. It may have been Potter's involvement in this political struggle that prompted the duke of Richmond, on Potter's death later that year, to write to the duke of Newcastle, saying that the archbishop had 'died in good time, because he was growing an old Rogue' (BL, Add. MS 32713, fols. 277–8).

Potter died suddenly, of an apoplectic fit, at Lambeth House on 10 October 1747, his wife having predeceased him. He was buried in the chancel of Croydon parish church; a simple white plaque, inscribed with his name and life dates, was placed over his grave but it was destroyed, probably in a fire of 1870. He left a sizeable fortune on his death, of between £70,000 and £90,000. He bequeathed £100 to his old school at Wakefield and left the majority of the rest to his second son, Thomas, thus disinheriting his elder son, John. His will later became the subject of a legal trial when one of his chaplains, John Chapman, attempted to use his position as executor to promote himself by using the archbishop's options, although he failed when Potter's family won their legal case against him.   REBECCA LOUISE WARNER

Sources L. W. Barnard, *John Potter: an eighteenth-century archbishop* (1989) • S. Taylor, 'Archbishop Potter and the dissenters', *Yale University Library Gazette*, 67 (1993), 118–26 • R. Anderson, *The memoir of the life and writings of John Potter, D.D., lord archbishop of Canterbury* (1824) • M. H. Peacock, *The history of the free grammar school of Queen Elizabeth at Wakefield* (1892) • Foster, *Alum. Oxon.* • J. L. Sisson, *Historic sketch of the parish church, Wakefield* (1824) • *Remarks and collections of Thomas Hearne*, ed. C. E. Doble and others, 11 vols., OHS, 2, 7, 13, 34, 42–3, 48, 50, 65, 67, 72 (1885–1921), vols. 1–2, 9 • W. Whiston, *Memoirs of the life and writings of Mr William Whiston: containing memoirs of several of his friends also*, 2nd edn, 2 vols. (1753) • Wood, *Ath. Oxon.*, 2nd edn, vol. 2 • Nichols, *Illustrations*, vol. 3

Archives BL, abstract of his register and corresp., Add. MSS 6108, 5143 • LPL, household and personal vouchers, sermons • LPL, papers | BL, Birch MSS • BL, Cole MSS • BL, corresp. with duke of Newcastle, Add. MS 32691–32710, *passim* • Bodl. Oxf., Add. MSS • Bodl. Oxf., Ballard MSS • Bodl. Oxf., North MSS • Bodl. Oxf., MSS Rawl. • Bodl. Oxf., St Amard MSS

Likenesses G. Vertue, line engraving, 1727 (after M. Dahl), BM, NPG • T. Gibson?, oils, *c.*1737–1747, LPL • T. Hudson, oils, 1742–4, Examination Schools, Oxford • T. Hudson, oils, 1744–6, LPL • T. Hudson, portrait, 1744–6, Christ Church Oxf. • T. Hudson, oils, *c.*1746, Bodl. Oxf. • G. Vertue, line engraving (after T. Gibson), BM, LPL, NPG

Wealth at death under £90,000: Barnard, *John Potter*

Potter, John (b. 1734?, d. after 1813?), writer and composer, born in London, was probably the son of the John Potter from Kent who was vicar of Cloford, Somerset, and author of works on mathematics and theology. He was probably also related to the family of John *Potter (1673/4–1747), archbishop of Canterbury. Potter is said to have received a good classical education; he 'studied mathematics and physic principally with his father, and afterwards made some progress in the science of music' (Baker, Reed, and Jones, 1.578). Baker claims that he published some poems at the age of twenty in 1754. About two years later he settled in the west country, and at Exeter in 1756 established a weekly paper, the *Devonshire Inspector*. When he returned to London he read the music lecture at Gresham College in the Easter and Trinity terms of 1761. He was not appointed to a professorship but the substance of the lectures was published in Potter's *Observations on the present state of music and musicians ...; to which is added a scheme for erecting and supporting a musical academy in this kingdom* (1762). His advocacy of the professional training of musicians, one of the earliest proposals of its kind, attracted favourable comment from the *Critical Review*.

Potter wrote the music for the pantomime *The Rites of Hecate* (Drury Lane, December 1763) and probably contributed music to *Hymen*, written to celebrate the marriage of Princess Augusta to the prince of Brunswick (Drury Lane, January 1764). He was also responsible for the text of *The Choice of Apollo*, a serenata, with music by William Yates (Haymarket, March 1765). At this period he became acquainted with David Garrick and this connection with the theatre led to his writing a number of dramatic prologues and epilogues. Through Garrick's patronage, Potter was introduced to Jonathan Tyers, the proprietor of Vauxhall Gardens. For the entertainments there Potter wrote 'several hundreds of songs, ballads, cantatas, &c' (Baker, Reed, and Jones, 1.578). Collections of these Vauxhall songs were published annually between 1765 and

1774 (with the possible exception of 1770). Potter's connection with Vauxhall lasted until some conflict with Tyers's successors led to his resignation in 1777.

Potter also quarrelled rather more publicly. In November 1766, as theatrical critic of the *Public Ledger*, he attacked Garrick's managerial style in an anonymous piece entitled 'The Rosciad, or, A Theatrical Register'. Garrick found out and an angry correspondence ensued, in which Potter threatened to publish a statement on the subject and claimed that Garrick had slandered him to his employer Tyers as 'a *Bad & Dangerous* Man'. Garrick denied all allegations and reminded his former protégé: 'I had a Regard for you and always Shew'd it when in my power. You best know if You have return'd it in a proper manner' (*Letters*, 2.550). Potter did not allow matters to rest and outlined his side of the case in *The Hobby Horse* (1766), cast in Hudibrastic verse. Another victim of Potter's published satire was J. A. Fisher, who, after a quarrel over the music to the latter's oratorio *Providence* (1777), duly appeared as the main target in *Music in Mourning, or, Fiddlestick in the Suds* (1780).

Potter's theatrical criticisms for 1771–2 were collected and published under the title *The Theatrical Review, or, A New Companion to the Playhouse* (2 vols., 1772). These pieces, ostensibly written by 'a Society of Gentlemen Independent of Managerial influence' (but actually by Potter himself), constitute a valuable, because almost complete, record of the performances at Drury Lane and Covent Garden that season. Other works which Potter published at this period include *The Words of the Wise* (1768); a modernized and expurgated version (1768) of Edmund Gayton's venerable *Festivous Notes on Don Quixote*; and the first examples of his comic novels, *The History and Adventure of Arthur O'Bradley* (1769) and *The Curate of Coventry* (1771).

Potter went to Europe about 1780, possibly for financial reasons, at about the time that his membership of the Royal Society of Musicians (of which he had been a member since 1771) lapsed through non-payment of his annual fees. Baker asserts that while away Potter was retained as a government spy. On his return to Britain three more novels were published: *The Virtuous Villagers* (1784), *The Favourites of Felicity* (1785), and *Frederic, or, The Libertine* (1790). Potter's life at this time is uncertain but at this stage he seems to have made a radical career change by studying medicine and to have graduated MD at Edinburgh. (A short thesis, apparently his, entitled *Dissertatio medica inauguralis, quaedam de sedentariae vitae malis, amplectens*, Edinburgh, 1784, is listed in the *Eighteenth-Century Short-Title Catalogue*.) He was admitted subsequently as a licentiate of the Royal College of Physicians, London, on 30 September 1785, when he was described as a native of Oxfordshire. He is said to have practised at Enniscorthy, Ireland. Potter left about the time of the 1798 uprising and returned to London, where he is perhaps to be identified with the John Potter of 47 Albemarle Street, author of *Thoughts Respecting the Origin of Treasonable Conspiracies, &c* (1803). A final novel, published as by John Potter MD, was *Olivia, or, The Nymph of the Valley* (1813).

Potter's biographer in the *Dictionary of National Biography*

confessed that aspects of his life were 'contradictory and confusing'. He remains something of a puzzle, especially after 1780, and the possibility that he has been muddled with at least one other John Potter who published in the late eighteenth and early nineteenth centuries cannot be dismissed. Modern bibliographies and library catalogues tend to list him under two or three different headings: as musician, physician (or surgeon), and by his Albemarle Street address. According to Reuss, Potter was author of *A Journal of a Tour through Parts of Germany, Holland, and France* and *A Treatise on Pulmonary Inflammation* (both undated). Potter was evidently an industrious updater of several standard reference works, including Thomas Salmon's *The Modern Gazetteer* (9th edn, 1773) and Ogilby's and Morgan's important seventeenth-century survey of roads which he published as *The Traveller's Pocket-Book* (17th edn, 1775; with several further editions, up to at least 1780). Some of Potter's songs, mostly pastoral in character, appeared in *The Spinnet, or, Musical Miscellany* (1750), occasionally in the *Universal* and *London* magazines, the *Gentleman's Magazine* (between 1767 and 1770), and in *Polyhymnia, or, The Complete Song Book* (1769). He died probably some time after 1813. JOHN RUSSELL STEPHENS

Sources D. E. Baker, *Biographia dramatica, or, A companion to the playhouse*, rev. I. Reed, new edn, rev. S. Jones, 3 vols. in 4 (1812) • [D. Rivers], *Literary memoirs of living authors of Great Britain*, 2 (1798) • J. D. Reuss, *Alphabetical register of all the authors actually living in Great-Britain, Ireland, and in the United Provinces of North-America*, 2 vols. (1804) • H. Mendel and A. Reissmann, eds., *Musikalisches Conversations-Lexikon: eine Encyklopädie der gesammten musikalischen Wissenschaften*, 12 vols. (Berlin, 1870–83), vol. 8 • *The letters of David Garrick*, ed. D. M. Little and G. M. Kahrl, 3 vols. (1963) • *The private correspondence of David Garrick*, ed. J. Boaden, 2 vols. (1831–2) • L. Baillie and R. Balchin, eds., *The catalogue of printed music in the British Library to 1980*, 62 vols. (1981–7), vol. 45 • Highfill, Burnim & Langhans, *BDA* • J. C. Kassler, 'Potter, John', *New Grove* • G. W. Stone, ed., *The London stage, 1660–1800*, pt 4: *1747–1776* (1962) • *European Magazine and London Review*, 7 (1785), 38, 283 • DNB

Archives V&A, Forster collection, corresp. with David Garrick

Potter, John Phillips (1818–1847), anatomist, the only son of the Revd John Phillips Potter (1793–1861), was born on 28 April 1818 at Southrop, Gloucestershire, while his father was acting as curate there. He was educated partly by Dr Morris at Brentford, and partly at the Kensington proprietary school of the Revd J. T. Evans. He entered University College, London, as a student in 1831, and in his first year he attained a high position in the class of experimental and natural philosophy. He was awarded the gold medal in chemistry for the year 1834/5, and in the following year he was a private pupil of Richard Quain (1800–1887), professor of anatomy. He obtained the highest honours in the session of 1836/7, spent three years in the wards of the hospital, and became house surgeon to Robert Liston. In 1841 he took the degree of bachelor of medicine with the highest honours at the University of London and became MRCS. Potter was appointed junior demonstrator of anatomy for 1843/4 and became FRCS in August 1845. On 3 May 1847 he was appointed assistant surgeon to University College Hospital. Unfortunately Potter received a wound while dissecting for Liston the body of the dwarf Harvey Leach, and he died of pyaemia on 17 May 1847. He was buried at Kensal Green cemetery on 22 May 1847.　　　　　　　　　　　D'A. POWER, *rev.* KAYE BAGSHAW

Sources *The Lancet* (22 May 1847), 576–7 · V. G. Plarr, *Plarr's Lives of the fellows of the Royal College of Surgeons of England*, rev. D'A. Power, 2 vols. (1930) · private information (1896) · *GM*, 2nd ser., 28 (1847), 100
Archives UCL, lecture notes
Likenesses T. Campbell, bust, 1847, UCL · T. H. Maguire, lithograph (after T. Campbell), NPG

Potter, Joseph (*c*.1756–1842), architect, began his career as a joiner in Lichfield. He was employed by James Wyatt as clerk of works in the restoration of Lichfield Cathedral (1787–93) and later at Hereford Cathedral (1790–93) and St Michael's Church, Coventry (1794); and in 1794 he succeeded Wyatt as cathedral architect at Lichfield, a position he held for the rest of his life. In this capacity he was responsible for the repair of the spires, the choir and transepts, and other structural work, but he made few major alterations to the fabric. Through Wyatt's influence he carried out work in the Gothic style at Plas Newydd, the Anglesey seat of the first marquess of Anglesey, in 1793–9 and again in 1805–9 and 1823–6; he was subsequently employed by Lord Anglesey to design the new baths and assembly rooms in Caernarfon (*c*.1822–1828).

From 1797 until his death Potter was county surveyor of Staffordshire, and he also served for many years as engineer to the Grand Trunk Canal Company. His official commissions include the lunatic asylum (1818; dem.) and house of correction (1832–3) at Stafford and two graceful cast-iron bridges over the River Trent, at Alrewas (1823–4) and Armitage (1829–30). He also ran a successful private practice in Staffordshire and Warwickshire, designing several schools, parsonages, and country houses in the Tudor–Gothic style, of which he was an able if not a very original practitioner. But his main claim to fame comes from his involvement in the design of St Mary's College for training Roman Catholic priests at New Oscott, near Birmingham (1835–8).

Apparently a Catholic himself, Potter was employed by the Catholic priest John Kirk, missioner at Lichfield, to design or extend Catholic churches at Tamworth (1829–30), Newport, Shropshire (1832), and Lichfield itself (1835) in the wake of Catholic emancipation. Through Kirk he was introduced to Thomas Walsh, vicar apostolic of the midland district from 1826, and it was Walsh who conceived the idea of Oscott as a focal point of the Catholic revival. Potter's buildings at New Oscott were competently designed in the 'collegiate Gothic' style favoured for such establishments throughout the nineteenth century; in 1839, however, he was superseded by that most passionate of Gothic revivalists A. W. N. Pugin, and it was Pugin who was responsible for the chancel and decoration of the chapel, as well as the gate lodges.

Potter was essentially a provincial builder–architect in the eighteenth-century mould. He spent his whole working life in Lichfield; he became a city councillor in 1835 and died there in St John's Street on 18 August 1842. He had three sons: Robert (*c*.1795–1854), who established an architectural practice in Sheffield; Joseph (*c*.1797–1875), who took over his father's practice in Lichfield; and James (1801–1857), a civil engineer. His pupils included the Lichfield architect Thomas Johnson (1794–1865).

GEOFFREY TYACK

Sources Colvin, *Archs.* · R. B. Lockett, 'Joseph Potter: cathedral architect at Lichfield', *Transactions of the South Staffordshire Archaeological and Historical Society*, 21 (1979–80), 34–44 · G. Jackson-Stops, 'Plas Newydd', *Country Life*, 159 (1976), 1686–9 · G. Jackson-Stops, 'Plas Newydd', *Country Life*, 160 (1976), 18–21 · J. F. Champ, *Oscott* (1987) · R. O'Donnell, 'Pugin at Oscott', *Oscott College, 1838–1988: a volume of commemorative essays*, ed. J. F. Champ (1988), 45–66 · *VCH Staffordshire*, vols. 5, 14 · d. cert.
Archives RIBA · Sheff. Arch.

Potter, Lewis (1807–1881), shipping agent and banker, was born on 27 May 1807 at Falkirk, the son of James Potter, a timber merchant and brick manufacturer, and his wife, Janet, *née* Wilson. He was apprenticed to David Chapman, a shipping agent in Glasgow, who had a small fleet of coastal sailing smacks trading down the west coast to Liverpool. Potter became a partner in the firm in 1832, when its name was changed to Chapman and Potter. Five years later the firm extended its agencies to include Dublin and the Isle of Man, and in 1839 Potter became sole partner. He married Margaret Muirhead and had at least three sons and one daughter.

During the early 1840s in Glasgow there was intense speculation in Australian investments. To take advantage of the 'mania', Potter set up a new merchant and shipowning business in 1848 in partnership with Andrew Wilson—Potter, Wilson & Co. Wilson left within less than two years, and Potter took his eldest son, Andrew, into the partnership. Later they were joined by another son, John A. Potter. Together they soon became one of the largest Antipodean shippers in the west of Scotland, acting as agents for most of the leading Glasgow merchants and shipowners in the trade, including James Nicol Fleming, and Buchanan, Wilson & Co. Through their agent, Glen Walker, they speculated heavily in Australian land and became wealthy men. Potter was reputed to have an annual income of over £17,000 or £18,000 and the partners sometimes to earn commissions of over £100,000.

Between 1857 and 1859 Potter purchased Udston and adjoining properties for £40,000 to form a large estate near Hamilton in Lanarkshire. Coal was soon found on the estate, raising its value to £120,000. Although his bankers were the National Bank of Scotland and the British Linen Bank, he was invited to join the board of the City of Glasgow Bank in 1859 after payments had been suspended the year before. The object of this invitation was to bring together the bank's Australian interests with those of Potter to form the Australian Land and Investment Company. When the company in turn merged with James Morton's New Zealand interests in 1866 in the wake of the Overend Gurney crisis to form the New Zealand and Australian Land Company, Potter became a director with a shareholding of over £60,000. The new firm continued to speculate heavily in land, borrowing enormous sums from the City of Glasgow Bank, which raised funds by extending its branch network throughout the west of Scotland. Little of the borrowing by either the Potters or the New Zealand and Australian Land Company was secured by the bank. Several of the more able directors, sensing that the bank was committing the cardinal sin of lending long and borrowing short, resigned in the late 1860s and early 1870s. Potter and his friends, who knew little of sound banking, were left in control. Potter on his own admission began to withdraw from business in the early 1870s, handing over to his son Alexander.

The economy spiralled downwards in the 1878 recession, and the City of Glasgow Bank collapsed on 1 October with debts of over £5 million, sending shock waves throughout the banking world. Since the bank was unlimited, each shareholder faced eventual calls of £2750 for every £100 of stock. Many families were ruined, and throughout 1879 lists of shareholders who had to meet further calls or no longer had any resources appeared regularly in the Glasgow press. Only 254 of the 1819 shareholders remained solvent when the affairs of the bank were finally wound up, though the depositors were paid in full. 'The collapse of the bank was a traumatic experience for Glasgow: nearly 2000 families suffered severe loss; many were ruined' (Checkland, 471). The catastrophe had similar repercussions in both New Zealand and Australia.

Potter, personally, and his businesses were heavily indebted to the bank. In the processes of winding up the bank's affairs he was declared bankrupt and his property sold. Udston House was purchased by Robert McAlpine. Along with his fellow directors he was tried for fraud early in 1879 in a blaze of publicity, when it emerged that the accounts had been deliberately falsified, probably since 1866. Although he denied knowledge of the bank's reckless advances for foreign speculations, Potter was found guilty. As it was believed that he was more culpable than his fellow directors, he was sentenced to eighteen months' imprisonment. He was released, apparently in good health, from Perth prison in July 1880, but died a broken man a year later, on 17 June 1881, at 15 Warrender Park Road, Edinburgh. Unlike other contemporary fraudsters—Jabez Balfour or Whittaker Wright—there were many, including the lawyer and investment manager David Murray, who believed Potter, an old man, had been harshly treated for crimes that were more a reflection on the management than on the directors of the bank.

The collapse of the City of Glasgow Bank arguably precipitated the worst British financial crisis of the nineteenth century, and all the Scottish banks suffered a very substantial fall in their paid-up capital. It also led to a major inquest into Scottish banking and necessitated the introduction of new banking legislation.

MICHAEL S. MOSS

Sources *Report of the trial of the directors of the City of Glasgow Bank* (1879) · *List of shareholders and biographies of the directors of the City of Glasgow Bank* (1878) · *Edinburgh Courant* (18 June 1881), 4, col. 6 · R. E. Tyson, 'Scottish investment in American railways: the case of the City of Glasgow Bank, 1856–1881', *Studies in Scottish business history*, ed. P. L. Payne (1967) · R. E. Tyson, 'The City of Glasgow Bank and the crisis of 1857', *Enterprise and management: essays in honour of Peter L. Payne*, ed. D. H. Aldcroft and A. Slaven (1995) · bankruptcy (sequestration) proceedings, 1879, NA Scot. · press cuttings of the trial of directors, U. Glas. L., special collections department, David Murray collection · S. G. Checkland, *Scottish banking: a history, 1695–1973* (1975) · parish register, Falkirk, 10 June 1807 · d. cert.
Archives U. Glas. L., special collections department, David Murray collection, reports of trial of the directors of the City of Glasgow Bank and press cutting books
Likenesses pen-and-ink sketch, repro. in Checkland, *Scottish banking*, 472

Potter [*née* Attenborough], **Marian Anderson** [Mary] **(1900–1981)**, painter, was born on 9 April 1900 at Rockford, Barnmead Road, Beckenham, Kent, the second of the four children of (John) Arthur Attenborough (1873–1940), solicitor, and his wife, Kathleen Mary, *née* Doble (1872–1957). She was educated at St Christopher's, Beckenham, and at Beckenham School of Art. She won a scholarship to the Royal College of Art but out of preference went to the Slade School of Fine Art instead. When she arrived there in October 1918, she was taught by Professor Henry Tonks, who believed that students should learn to paint exactly what they saw; Mary would argue furiously with him but thought him a wonderful teacher and in turn became a star pupil. She won a near record number of prizes. At the Slade she was extremely popular and was remembered as a great party-goer. Her 'turn' was to sing songs and accompany herself on the ukulele. She became known as Att (short for Attenborough), a name which remained with her until her fifties. After leaving the Slade she shared a studio in nearby Fitzroy Street and became an early member of the Seven and Five Society. She exhibited with it on at least three occasions but resigned early on, never liking to align herself with any kind of movement. She also exhibited at the New English Art Club. Very few of these early paintings can be traced, but according to the critic P. G. Konody her work was 'competent and accomplished'.

At a boat race party given by A. P. Herbert, Mary Attenborough met the critic and radio producer Stephen Meredith *Potter (1900–1969), whom she married on 7 July 1927. They rented from the Herberts a tiny house overlooking the Thames in Chiswick Mall. Mary painted the world around her—a vase of flowers on a window sill with the river in the background, or an ornament on a bookcase. She and her husband later moved into a bigger house—Thames Bank, a few doors along Chiswick Mall. Two sons were born: Andrew in 1928 and Julian in 1931. Bringing up a family made inroads into her painting. None the less on a normal day she would paint at least throughout the morning. Records of over 100 Chiswick oils exist: undoubtedly she painted many more. Her first solo exhibition was at the Bloomsbury Gallery, London, in 1932, followed by a second in 1939 at Arthur Tooth & Sons. With the onset of war Mary and her husband, who was working for the BBC, moved to Manchester. Opportunities to paint were limited but she sold *The Golden Kipper* to the Tate Gallery at this time, and two pictures to the Manchester City Art Gallery. In 1941 the Potters moved to a farmhouse deep in the Essex countryside, where Mary had more freedom to work. She received commissions for a number of portraits, mostly of local friends. Her talent for portrait painting had been recognized by Henry Tonks, who had set up commissions for her when she left the Slade. She liked to paint her closest friends, of whom the actress Joyce Grenfell was one whose portrait she painted extremely successfully, capturing her humour as well as her depth of character. While she undertook portrait commissions for financial reasons, she continued with her other work. At the end of the war the Potters moved to a flat in Harley Street, London. The Essex paintings, together with the first of many views of Regent's Park and of Harley Street, were shown at Arthur Tooth & Sons in 1946. Over half were sold, including a series of paintings of the windswept seafront at Brighton in winter. She was slow to build up enough paintings for a further show because of family distractions. Her next exhibition was at the Leicester Galleries, in Leicester Square, London.

In 1951 Mary Potter and her husband moved to the Red House in Aldeburgh, Suffolk. Stephen Potter already knew Benjamin Britten through his work at the BBC, and it was not long before the Potters took part fully in Aldeburgh life, serving on the council of the music festival. Sessions of the Aldeburgh Music Club were held either at the Red House or at Crag House, Britten's home on the seafront. Every summer Britten, Peter Pears, and the Potters formed the nucleus of countless tennis parties on the grass court at the Red House. From this time until his last illness Britten became Mary's very close friend. Other friends made at this time included Sir Laurens van der Post, who was living at Aldeburgh, a tennis opponent as well as a collector of her work. Many years later he attended all her exhibitions at the New Art Centre in Sloane Street, London. With more time to paint, Mary Potter began a regime of long hours of work every day which was to become ever more unrelenting over the next thirty years. In 1954 her husband asked for a divorce, which became effective in 1955. As the Red House was too large and too expensive for one person, it was decided that she and Britten should swap houses, and in 1957 she moved to Crag House. Her work was shown regularly at the Leicester Galleries, and her pictures were sold to many leading collectors and museums.

In 1963 Bryan Robertson, director of the Whitechapel Art Gallery, London, proposed that Mary Potter should have an exhibition there and persuaded her that she was capable of developing in new directions, on a larger scale. A retrospective exhibition of her work opened at the gallery in October 1964 and was a brilliant success. The accompanying catalogue had a foreword by Sir Kenneth Clark and the exhibition toured to Sheffield, King's Lynn, and Chichester. At this time Mary Potter moved into a studio house commissioned by Benjamin Britten and designed by Peter Colleymore in the garden of the Red House, her old home. As her reputation grew steadily she continued to be involved in the Aldeburgh festival. She held exhibitions, and painted many portraits of musicians such as Janet Baker and Britten. Seeking to change her exhibiting arrangements, and on the recommendation of Sir Kenneth Clark, another great friend, she approached the New Art Centre in Sloane Street, London, where both the directors of the gallery responded enthusiastically to her work. From 1967 until 1980 an exhibition of her work was mounted every two years at the gallery, and for each exhibition she produced about fifteen new paintings.

Using beeswax mixed with paint Mary Potter achieved a chalky luminous quality in her paintings, and from the 1950s her range of colours was pale and subtle. She always put strict instructions on the back of each painting not to varnish or glaze the work, abhorring the use of shiny varnish or gloss, both widely used by many artists to give their work a false depth. Her later paintings became more diffuse and abstracted; their misty colours were never bright and very seldom pure. She painted in an evocative shorthand, the lines and half-shapes suggesting the whole. Certain images continued to appear in her work, such as a leaf-shape, a fraction of tree trunk, or the misted disc of a sun. Her paintings at this time expressed joy, beauty, and freedom, and some of her best and most original work was produced in these last years.

Honours and wider recognition came during this period: in 1979 Mary Potter was made an OBE, and in 1980 the Tate Gallery held an exhibition of her work, in two of its rooms, which included many of the paintings it owned, together with loans from other museums. In May the following year the Arts Council of Great Britain organized a full-scale retrospective of her work at the Serpentine Gallery in London. With its magical light filtered through the leaves of the trees of Kensington Gardens, the space was a perfect setting for her paintings. The show received outstanding critical acclaim and was attended by 25,000 people before it went on tour. Critically ill with the lung cancer which caused her death four months later, she went to London for the hanging and the private view. Mary Potter died on 14 September 1981 at her home, the Red Studio, Golf Lane, Aldeburgh, and was cremated on the 16th at Ipswich crematorium.

MADELEINE BESSBOROUGH

Sources private information (2004) [family, friends] · J. Potter, *Mary Potter: a life of painting* (1998) · New Art Centre Sculpture Park and Gallery Archive, Salisbury · *CGPLA Eng. & Wales* (1982) · b. cert. **Archives** Tate collection, corresp. with Lord Clark **Wealth at death** £63,626: probate, 26 March 1982, *CGPLA Eng. & Wales*

Potter, Mary Cecilia (1847–1913), Roman Catholic nun, was born at Jamaica Row, Bermondsey, London, at midnight on the night of 21 November 1847; her birthday is normally celebrated on the 22nd. She was the fifth child of William Norwood Potter, a pawnbroker, and Mary Anne Potter, *née* Martin (1816–1900). She was baptized a Catholic at the church of the Most Holy Trinity, Bermondsey, on 12 December 1847. Her father abandoned the family home soon after her birth, emigrating to Australia about 1849–50. She was educated at Cupola House, a small Catholic boarding-school in Southwark, London, before moving with her mother and brother Thomas (1842–1917) to Southsea, Portsmouth. She became engaged to Godfrey King in 1867, but the engagement did not last.

With the support and assistance of Bishop Thomas Grant (1816–1870), Mary Potter entered the Sisters of Mercy Convent in Brighton in 1868, remaining there until 23 June 1870, when she returned to her brother's home. Her departure from the Mercy community was not voluntary: as her brother wrote to her, her superior believed she had 'neither the health nor the temperament for religious life' (T. Potter to M. C. Potter, 12 Oct 1902, Little Company of Mary archives, box 1, ser. 0002). After her departure, it was recorded in the Brighton community's log book that 'she was exceedingly good and holy, but quite unable for the duties, besides which, her mind was weak and she was nervous and imaginative, and this most probably would have increased in her' (Archives of the Sisters of Mercy).

After regaining her health, Potter ran a small school in Southsea. She began to follow the spiritual teaching of St Louis-Marie Grignon de Montfort (*d.* 1716). Subject to a variety of mystical experiences from 1872 to 1874, during which time she felt herself to be filled with the love of God and drawn into ever closer union with him, she became convinced that she was called to establish a new order of Catholic Sisters, dedicated to praying and caring for the dying. In 1872 she sought spiritual guidance from Monsignor John Vertue (1826–1900), chaplain to the garrison in Portsmouth, but he was dismissive of both her spiritual experiences and her convictions. Gaining a reputation as a somewhat unstable visionary, she also failed to find support from either Bishop James Danell of the Southwark diocese, or the cardinal archbishop of Westminster, H. E. Manning, but was unshaken by opposition. She was befriended by Father Edward Selley in 1876, the year in which she published her *Path of Mary*. Selley, a Marist Father of St Anne's, Spitalfields, London, supported her endeavours and together they gathered a group of like-minded women who were interested in her vision of a new religious congregation. In January 1877 she approached the bishop of Nottingham, Edward Bagshawe, who gave her permission to begin work within his vast and under-staffed diocese. Taking possession of a disused stocking factory in the village of Hyson Green, Nottingham, she quickly set about gathering recruits. On 2 July 1877 she and three companions received the habit of the Little Company of Mary and began work in the diocese, teaching and nursing. Bagshawe's interference in the workings of the new order proved difficult and Potter turned to Rome for help.

In 1882, the year in which she published *The Spiritual Exercises of Mary*, Potter went to the Vatican to seek approbation of her rule. Pope Leo XIII encouraged her venture and invited her to remain in Rome and to open a hospital for the English community there. She and the sisters stayed, and began caring for sick members of the English and Italian community either in their own homes or in rented premises. According to contemporary accounts, they gave their services 'to rich and poor alike. No fees were charged' (Dougherty, 215). A hospital was finally established in via San Stefano Rotondo in 1908; it became the first Italian school for professional nurses.

Before final approbation of the Congregation in 1893,

Mother Mary Potter sent Little Company of Mary sisters throughout the world. Communities were established in Australia (1885), Ireland (1888), the United States (1893), and Malta (1894). A mission was established in South Africa in 1904. Of the sixteen or more devotional books which she published in her lifetime, the *Path of Mary* (1876), *The Spiritual Exercises of Mary* (1882), and *Mary's Call* (1880) were the most frequently republished, and probably the most influential. Mary Potter died of cancer, heart disease, and general debility in Rome on 9 April 1913. First buried in San Lorenzo cemetery, Verano, her body was transferred in 1917 to the crypt of the Mother House of her community, San Stefano Rotondo, in Rome; in December 1997 it was reinterred in the Roman Catholic cathedral of St Barnabas, Nottingham. The cause for her canonization was begun in 1942; she was declared venerable by Pope John Paul II on 8 February 1988. ELIZABETH WEST

Sources personal letters and papers, Little Company of Mary, London, boxes 1–46B, 001-0334.002 · annals of the Brighton community, 1868–70, Archives of the Sisters of Mercy, Bermondsey, London · P. Dougherty, *Mother Mary Potter: foundress of the Little Company of Mary* (1961) · E. Healy, *The life of Mother Mary Potter: foundress of the congregation of the Little Company of Mary* (1935)

Archives Little Company of Mary, London, archives · Sacra Congregazione di Propaganda Fide, Rome · Ryde, Little Company of Mary archives, Australian Province | Nottingham Roman Catholic diocese, Wilson House, Nottingham, diocesan archives

Likenesses window, St Anne's Church, Underwood Road, London

Potter, Richard (1778–1842). *See under* Potter, Thomas Bayley (1817–1898).

Potter, Richard (1799–1886), university professor, was born in Manchester on 2 January 1799, the son of Richard Potter, from Westmorland, a corn merchant and afterwards a brewer in Manchester. He attended Manchester grammar school from 1811 to 1815, and later worked in a Manchester warehouse, but his business ventures were not particularly successful. However, in his leisure time he studied optics and chemistry, becoming a student of John Dalton. In the early 1830s he wrote several scientific papers, three of which he presented at the first meeting of the British Association in 1831. The interest generated by these contributions encouraged him to apply to Queens' College, Cambridge, which admitted him in 1834 and granted him a scholarship. In 1838 he graduated BA as sixth wrangler, and in January 1839 he was elected a foundation fellow of his college and obtained the medical scholarship, with the intention of studying medicine. He proceeded MA in 1841, being then a licentiate of the Royal College of Physicians, but did not practise medicine. Instead, in October of that year, he was appointed to the chair of natural philosophy and astronomy at University College, London. On 11 April 1843, at St Pancras Church, London, he married Mary Ann (*d.* 1871), daughter of Major Pilkington of Urney, King's county, Ireland. They had no children.

In the same year the college senate granted him leave to study mathematics in order to cope with the increasingly mathematized branches of physics. Having accepted a position at King's College, Toronto, he emigrated to Canada but returned to University College in 1844 due to an improved financial arrangement. He retained his professorship until 1865, but he was generally viewed as an incompetent teacher who could not control his students. Much of his research was on optics, but his work was often criticized by contemporaries who adopted the mathematically demanding wave theory of light and did not share his enthusiasm for the corpuscular theory. He published four books and over sixty papers, but made no significant contributions to science. Following his retirement in 1865 he moved to Cambridge where he died at his house, 10 Trumpington Road, on 6 June 1886.

GEOFFREY CANTOR

Sources *Manchester Guardian* (18 June 1886) · Venn, *Alum. Cant.* · H. H. Bellot, *University College, London, 1826–1926* (1929) · senate minutes, UCL · G. Cantor, *Optics after Newton* (1983) · *CGPLA Eng. & Wales* (1886)
Likenesses photograph, *c*.1856, UCL
Wealth at death £4410 14*s*. 7*d*.—effects in England: probate, 4 Sept 1886, *CGPLA Eng. & Wales*

Potter, Robert (1721–1804), translator and Church of England clergyman, was born in 1721 in Podimore, Somerset, the third son of John Potter (*fl.* 1676–1723), prebendary of Wells. His mother was descended from the Liversedge and Newborough families of Somerset. According to Potter's own account he was educated by his father, and at Sherborne, before proceeding to Emmanuel College, Cambridge, in July 1737. However, Venn lists Scarning School, Norfolk (where he later worked as a schoolmaster). Potter took his degree in 1740, and graduated BA in 1742. He was ordained by Bishop Wynne of Bath and Wells, and served briefly as 'Chaplain to a colony of colliers at Ashwick on Mendip' (NL Wales, MS 12502). In 1742 his friend Richard Hurd was made fellow of Emmanuel College, and offered his curacy of Reymerston, Norfolk, to Potter. Hurd also used his influence to secure for him the vicarage of Melton Parva, one of the poorest college livings, giving a combined annual income of less than £50.

Potter married Elizabeth Colman (*d.* 1786), daughter of a neighbouring clergyman, and the couple had nine children, several of whom survived into adulthood. Much of their life was spent in attempts to curry favour with the rich and powerful to secure a better living to support the ever-growing family. They were only partially successful, obtaining a succession of poverty-stricken livings and falling deeper into debt. It was not until 1788, two years after Elizabeth's death, that Robert secured financial independence.

In 1754 Potter was presented to the rectory of Crostwight, and in June 1761 became the master of the Scarning Free School, increasing his income to £90. Potter's appointment caused a riot by the local populace who favoured another candidate, but in time he achieved considerable local respect. The following year he was also appointed curate of this parish, but had to resign Reymerston. He likewise held two livings in Somerset, but claimed they cost him more than they brought in.

Potter gained a literary reputation among the Norfolk gentry and their patronage to publish his poetry, including *Retirement: an Epistle* (1748), *A Farewell Hymne to the Country* (1749 and 1750), *Holkham* (1758), *Kymber* (1759), and his *Collected Poems* (1773). He also ventured into religious controversy with his sermon *On the Pretended Inspiration of the Methodists* (1758), which attracted sufficient attention to elicit rejoinders by John Wesley and Cornelius Cayley. These he answered in *An Appendix* to his sermon, but such controversy was not to his taste. He likewise dabbled in politics and took an active part in the unsuccessful election campaign of Sir Armine Wodehouse during 1768. He wrote *A Letter to John Buxton*, one of the many anonymous pamphlets published in Norwich at that time, and various election squibs, which attracted acrimonious responses. However in later years he made no mention of such publications, and tried to play down his political activities. In 1775 Potter became involved in a campaign to establish a workhouse in Launditch hundred, and published a graphic account of the plight of the rural poor, which, according to the *Norwich Mercury*, caused an inquiry to be made into the existing Suffolk and Norfolk houses of industry.

Potter however achieved fame through his blank-verse translations of the Greek tragedians. His edition of Aeschylus was published to great acclaim in 1777 and brought him to the notice of London literary society. Elizabeth Montagu befriended the poor curate, and encouraged and financed him to produce a commentary on the plays which was presented to subscribers, and then included within a second edition in 1779. He then embarked upon Euripides, but this project was interrupted in 1779 to assist Hans Stanley with a translation of Pindar's *Odes*, in the hopes that in return Stanley might secure him a more prosperous living. Their collaboration was a success, and the task was completed, but Potter's hopes were dashed by Stanley's suicide in a fit of depression.

The delayed translation of Euripides, published in two volumes during 1781 and 1782, had to compete with Michael Wodhull's version. Potter's edition was not as well reviewed as his Aeschylus, although it is considered superior to that of Wodhull. As a result the work was not a financial success, and despite promises, no preferments were forthcoming from his literary friends. He decided to abandon Greek tragedy, and rather translate one of the Pindaric odes with an accompanying essay on contemporary lyric poetry. Under Mrs Montagu's influence this work was transformed into one of the chorus of pamphlets attacking Johnson's *Lives of the Poets* published during 1783, although it was the most thoughtful and well argued of these. (Potter's mixed views of Johnson's work were later elaborated in his *The Art of Criticism*, 1789.) In 1785 he translated two odes from the book of Isaiah, but it was not long before encouragement was forthcoming for him to complete a new translation of Sophocles. This was published early in 1788 and was moderately well received.

Shortly afterwards Potter received the offer from Lord Thurlow of a prebend's stall at Norwich, with a stipend twice his existing income. He retired from his offices of schoolmaster and curate, and his other livings, and graduated as MA. In June 1789 Bishop Bagot also presented him with the extremely valuable vicarage of Lowestoft, where he moved in 1790. His old age was spent in comfort and prosperity. He published two further commemoration sermons, in 1793 and 1802, the first of which attacked Thomas Paine's *Rights of Man*, and died quietly at the vicarage on 9 August 1804.

According to the antiquary Craven Ord, Potter was 'rather an entertaining and well behaved gentleman with some singularities of thinking' (BL, Add. MS 14823, fol. 137); his correspondence shows him to have been witty, kind, and thoughtful. Yet his considerable abilities were for many years unrecognized by his contemporaries and his wish to ingratiate himself with the rich and famous sometimes excited their contempt. There are several surviving anecdotes of his having been snubbed or otherwise humiliated by, among others, Dr Johnson and Lord Thurlow. He was however well loved by his parishioners at Lowestoft who subscribed for a mural monument to his memory, placed in the churchyard.　　　DAVID STOKER

Sources D. Stoker, 'Greek tragedy with a happy ending: the publication of Robert Potter's editions of Æschylus, Euripides and Sophocles', *Studies in Bibliography*, 46 (1993), 282–302 • D. Stoker, 'Robert Potter's attack on Dr Johnson', *British Journal for Eighteenth-Century Studies*, 16 (1993), 179–83 • H. G. Wright, 'Robert Potter as a critic of Dr Johnson', *Review of English Studies*, 12 (1936), 305–21 • L. Bettany, ed., *Edward Jerningham and his friends: a series of eighteenth century letters* (1919), 325–74 • Nichols, *Lit. anecdotes*, 2.306 • Venn, *Alum. Cant.*, 1/3.385 • M. F. L. Prichard, 'The misappropriation of Scarning School', *N&Q*, 195 (1950), 115–17 • G. A. Carthew, *The hundred of Launditch and deanery of Brisley, in the county of Norfolk*, 3 (1879), 362 • M. L. Clarke, *Greek studies in England, 1700–1830* (1945), 147 • [J. Chambers], *A general history of the county of Norfolk*, 2 vols. (1829), 107, 834 • BL, Add. MS 14823, fol. 137 • NL Wales, MS 12502 • C. B. Jewson, *The Jacobin city: a portrait of Norwich in its reaction to the French Revolution, 1788–1802* (1975), 40

Archives NL Wales, notes on his biography | BL, letters to Charles Poyntz, Althorp MS E28 • Hunt. L., corresp. with Elizabeth Montagu • NL Wales, corresp. with Robert Conway Potter • NL Wales, notes and corresp. regarding collaboration with Hans Stanley

Likenesses G. Romney, portrait, 1779 • D. Turner, etching (after A. Payne), BM, NPG

Potter, Stephen Meredith (1900–1969), writer and radio producer, was born on 1 February 1900 at 36 Old Park Avenue, Battersea, London, the only son of Frank Collard Potter (1856/7–1939), chartered accountant, and his wife, Elizabeth Mary Jubilee (Lilla) Reynolds (d. 1950), who named Potter after George Meredith, whom she was reading while pregnant. He was educated at Clapham high school, Rillo Road preparatory school, and Westminster School, where he did not excel but where, he proudly relates, he 'won the pancake' (Potter) in the annual Shrove Tuesday contest the Greaze, where boys fight to catch a pancake. He left just in time to be trained and gazetted as a second lieutenant in the Coldstream Guards before demobilization returned him to civilian life in 1919. After a few uneasy months in his father's office learning bookkeeping he followed his sister Muriel to Oxford, where he took

a second in English language and literature in 1922 at Merton College. In what he called 'Shakespeare's missing years' he taught at a private boys' school and for a time he acted as secretary to the playwright Henry Arthur Jones, until in 1926 he was appointed a lecturer in English at Birkbeck College, London.

On 7 July 1927 Potter married Marian Anderson Attenborough (1900–1981), the painter, professionally known as Mary *Potter and by Potter himself as Att; they had two sons. Potter's first book, *The Young Man* (1929), was the inevitable autobiographical novel and caused little stir. In 1930 he published a good short study of D. H. Lawrence, then turned his attention to Coleridge, editing the Nonesuch Press *Coleridge* (1933) and Sara Coleridge's letters to Thomas Poole in *Minnow among Tritons* (1934). In 1941 he wrote a play, *Married to a Genius*, based on the Coleridge marriage. His main work on the subject, and his most important critical book, *Coleridge and S.T.C.* (1935), was an acute discussion of the duality in the poet's nature. In 1937 he published *The Muse in Chains: a Study in Education*, a humorous attack on the way English was taught in universities. G. M. Young wrote of it: 'if I were suddenly commissioned by some Golden Dustman to organize a new University, I think I should send for Mr. Potter and offer him the Chair of English literature forthwith' (*Daylight and Champaign*, 1937, 130).

All seemed set for a distinguished career as teacher and critic, but marriage and children made financial demands which these pursuits could not resolve, and in 1938 Potter joined the British Broadcasting Corporation (BBC) as a writer–producer in the features department (later he became editor of features and poetry). His broadcasting career was long and increasingly successful. Literary features and war documentaries occupied him initially; then in 1943 appeared the first of twenty-nine 'How' programmes, written with Joyce Grenfell. They dealt satirically with everyday subjects, such as 'How to Talk to Children', 'How to Woo', 'How to Give a Party'; and in 1946 'How to Listen to Radio' was the first broadcast heard in the newly created Third Programme (later Radio 3).

Potter's light touch did a great deal to move radio features on from a rather static form of presentation to an impressionism with natural dialogue and minimal use of sound-effects which was lively, immediate, imaginative, and vivid. Particularly successful were his series of *Professional Portraits*, and *New Judgments*, as well as the broadcast of Nevill Coghill's version of *The Canterbury Tales*. As a radio producer Stephen Potter was clear and unfussy, inspiring confidence and enthusiasm.

In 1945 Potter did a stint as theatre critic for the *New Statesman and Nation*, and in 1946 a year as book critic on the *News Chronicle*. He was also an occasional and useful member of the BBC *Critics* panel. When he had enjoyed the subject under discussion he said so, in refreshing contrast to the superior and grudging assessments of some of his colleagues.

A ten-day power-cut at the beginning of 1947 cancelled all broadcasting and gave Potter the opportunity to dash off, on odd scraps of paper, the book which gave a new word to the language and a new concept to the whole world of sport. This was *The Theory and Practice of Gamesmanship, or, The Art of Winning Games without Actually Cheating*, published in November 1947. In it he described how the idea crystallized when he and his friend C. E. M. Joad managed to defeat at tennis two younger and more agile opponents, by subtle and entirely legal ploys which put them off their game. Potter left the BBC after the success of the book, and apart from a short term as editor of *The Leader* magazine, which folded in 1950, he now faced the prospect of being a full-time writer. From *Gamesmanship* the idea was extended to many other aspects of life. *Some Notes on Lifemanship* (1950) was followed by *One-Upmanship* (1952) and *Supermanship* (1958). By this time the concept and the suffix '-manship' had travelled the world (Potter himself toured America in 1950), and the foreign policy of the American secretary of state John Foster Dulles was universally known as 'brinkmanship'. Fowler's *Modern English Usage* notes that Potter invented 'the conceit of making facetious formations by treating -manship as the suffix'. For Potter the joke was played out, but for the rest of his life he found it difficult to speak or write naturally, so accustomed had he grown to the jocose gambits and ploys of his own invention.

Potter's first marriage was dissolved in 1955 and on 20 May of that year he married Heather Jenner, director of a marriage bureau, whom he had met while editor of *The Leader*. They had one son who died aged sixteen. A book on his lecture tour of America appeared in 1956 and then *Steps to Immaturity* (1959), an attractive evocation of his Edwardian boyhood and Georgian schooldays. His choice of title showed a disarming self-awareness, for in many ways he never grew up, and always seemed an immensely likeable overgrown boy. He was such an obsessive games player (squash, tennis, golf, croquet, and always snooker at the Savile Club) that his friends wondered how he managed to do any work at all. Later, and minor, publications included an anthology, *Sense of Humour* (1954), and *The Complete Golf Gamesmanship* (1968).

Potter was tall and rangy, with rough fair hair which stood on end in spite of absent-minded attempts to dampen and flatten it. In a memorial broadcast Roy Plomley said: 'There was something very special about his trousers. Some men have the kind of hips which keep a waistband neatly in place: Stephen hadn't.' He smoked in a perilous manner, disregarding ashtrays. On 2 December 1969 Potter died at 11 Fellows Road, Hampstead, London, of pneumonia, after suffering bad health for the last few years of his life.

JOYCE GRENFELL, rev. CLARE L. TAYLOR

Sources S. Potter, *Steps to immaturity* (1959) · A. Jenkins, *Stephen Potter: inventor of gamesmanship* (1980) · *The Times* (3 Dec 1969) · b. cert. · m. cert. · d. cert. · personal knowledge (1981) · private information (1981)
Archives Ransom HRC, corresp. and literary papers | University of Bristol, corresp. and statements relating to the trial of *Lady Chatterley's lover*

Likenesses photograph, *c.*1947, Hult. Arch. · D. Low, pencil caricatures, NPG · photographs, repro. in Jenkins, *Stephen Potter*
Wealth at death £4767: administration with will, 28 Sept 1972, CGPLA Eng. & Wales

Potter, Thomas (1718?–1759), wit and politician, was born at Cuddesdon, Oxfordshire, probably in 1718, the second son of John *Potter (1673/4–1747), bishop of Oxford and later archbishop of Canterbury, and his wife, the granddaughter of Thomas Venner. His older brother was disinherited after making an unsuitable marriage, and Thomas inherited all his father's wealth, estimated to have been between £70,000 and £100,000. He matriculated from Christ Church, Oxford, on 18 November 1731, aged thirteen, graduated BA in 1735 and MA in 1738, was admitted to the Middle Temple on 27 February 1735, and was called to the bar on 8 November 1740. Later he held the recordership of Bath. On 17 February 1740 Potter married unwillingly, at his father's behest, Anne (*bap.* 1716, *d.* 1744), the daughter of Thomas Manningham, rector of Slinfold, Sussex, and his wife, Mary. He wrote 'I am … unhappy, miserable beyond remedy. In short I am married—and married to a woman I despise and detest.' It was said that he treated her with calculated brutality, though he claimed on her death on 4 January 1744 that he had been 'deprived of what was most dear to [me] in the world'. They had one son, Thomas (*d.* 1801), who was educated at Emmanuel College, Cambridge, and became a judge. On 14 July 1747 Potter married Anne, the daughter of Francis Lowe of Brightwell, Oxfordshire, who brought with her a fortune of £50,000; they had two daughters.

Potter used his inheritance, and his post of principal register to the province of Canterbury, to embark upon a career in politics. He was initially an adherent of the prince of Wales, and after the prince's death of the Grenville faction. Between 1747 and 1754 he sat for the borough of St Germans in Cornwall, through the patronage of the Eliot family, and from 1748 until the prince's death in 1751 was secretary to the prince of Wales. Potter made an immediate impact in parliament in his first session by attacking the conduct of the duke of Newcastle, who was accused of having exercised undue influence in the 1747 election at Seaford in Sussex. Lady Hervey commented on the incident:

> Mr Potter the lawyer is a second Pitt for fluency of words. He spoke well and bitterly, but with so perfect an assurance, so unconcerned, so much master of himself, though the first sessions of his being in parliament and first time of opening his mouth there, that it disgusted more than it pleased. (*Letters of Mary Lepel*, 110–11)

The speech was widely published and elicited an anonymous response from Horace Walpole in the form of *A Letter to a Certain Distinguished Patriot, and most Applauded Orator* (1748).

Potter's second noteworthy contribution in parliament was over the proposed bill for removing the assizes from Aylesbury to Buckingham, a result of the contest between Lord Chief Justice Edward Willes and the Grenville faction. In 1751 Potter himself proposed an additional duty of 2*s.* on spirits, and in the session 1753–4 he introduced a

Census Bill which, though it passed the Commons, was thrown out by the Lords. The scheme was not successfully revived until 1801. In 1757 he criticized the ill-fated expedition against the port of Rochefort, which led to a pamphlet war with Henry Seymour Conway. From 1754 to 1757 Potter sat for the borough of Aylesbury, and he soon allied himself with Pitt the elder. He was on Pitt's list of candidates for high office, but was initially barred by the king. In 1756, however, he was re-elected at Aylesbury and appointed paymaster-general of the land forces. The following year he was appointed joint vice-treasurer of Ireland, a post he held until his death.

It is, however, chiefly for his behaviour outside parliament for which Potter is particularly remembered. Though in poor health, he was thought extremely good-looking and witty. According to John Nichols, he is believed to be the handsome candidate depicted in Hogarth's election series. In the early 1750s he was one of George Bubb Dodington's constant guests at La Trappe and was 'among the more vicious of Bubb's intimates' (Fuller, 114). He was also a member of the bizarre fraternity established by Sir Francis Dashwood known as the Medmenham Monks, or Hellfire Club. This set was a secret society which met in the ruins of St Mary's Abbey, Medmenham, and held obscene and blasphemous orgies parodying the Roman Catholic mass. Other members included the earl of Sandwich, Lord Orford, and John Wilkes.

Potter was one of the most enthusiastic members of this club, and was frequently held responsible for the moral and financial ruin of his close associate Wilkes. Potter, described as Wilkes's 'evil genius' (Thomas, 4), has been seen as the instigator of Wilkes's early excesses, for 'richer, looser, and more a man of the world, he initiated him [Wilkes] into a circle which scandalized even the eighteenth century ... It is clear ... that it was he and not Wilkes who was the leader' (Postgate, 23). Even Potter's best friends remonstrated with him at his behaviour, but his response to such pleadings was typical: 'It is injudicious to tell a Sinner that he must imitate a Saint. The impossibility makes him too desperate even to begin the attempt' (Fuller, 116). Potter was not responsible for writing the scurrilous *Essay on Woman*, for which Wilkes was prosecuted for obscenity in 1763. The *Essay* had been written by Wilkes in 1754 and met with Potter's approval; he wrote to Wilkes on 27 October that year: 'I have read your parody, for the ninety-ninth time, and have laughed as heavily as I did at the first' (Thomas, 4).

As well as introducing Wilkes to the Hellfire Club and the Grenville faction, Potter was involved with the triangular deal that established him in parliament. In July 1757 a vacant seat at Bath was occupied by Pitt, leaving Pitt's seat at Okehampton free for Potter, which opened Aylesbury to Wilkes. The arrangement cost Wilkes some £7000, and to pay for it Potter introduced him to the Jewish financiers, who later contributed to his financial ruin.

Potter died 'of a long Decay' at Ridgmont, near Woburn, on 17 June 1759, 'unrepentant to the end' (Fuller, 168). According to his wishes, his body was dissected, and his lungs and liver were found to be much decayed. He was buried on 25 June in the churchyard at Ridgmont 'at the west end of the belfry, in a place where no one was used to be buried'. He was borne by six labourers, representing three counties, and his body was interred in three coffins, one of which was lead. His estate passed to his daughter Mariana and her husband, Malcolm Macqueen (*d.* 1829), a physician. R. D. E. EAGLES

Sources L. B. Namier, 'Potter, Thomas', HoP, *Commons, 1715–54* · L. B. Namier, 'Potter, Thomas', HoP, *Commons, 1754–90* · R. Fuller, *Hellfire Francis* (1739) · R. Postgate, *That devil Wilkes* (1930) · P. D. G. Thomas, *John Wilkes: a friend to liberty* (1996) · G. Rudé, *Wilkes and liberty* (1962) · *Letters of Mary Lepel [sic], Lady Hervey*, ed. J. W. Crooker (1821) · H. Walpole, *Memoirs of the reign of King George the Third*, ed. G. F. R. Barker, 4 vols. (1894) · H. A. C. Sturgess, ed., *Register of admissions to the Honourable Society of the Middle Temple, from the fifteenth century to the year 1944*, 3 vols. (1949) · Nichols, *Lit. anecdotes* · J. Nichols, *Biographical anecdotes of William Hogarth, and a catalogue of his works chronologically arranged with occasional remarks*, 3rd edn (1785) · Foster, *Alum. Oxon.* · IGI

Archives BL, Add. MSS 30865–30896 | BL, letters to John Wilkes, Add. MSS 30867, 30876 · PRO, letters to the first earl of Chatham, 30/8

Likenesses W. Hogarth, group portrait, oils, 1754?

Potter, Sir Thomas (1774–1845). *See under* Potter, Thomas Bayley (1817–1898).

Potter, Thomas Bayley (1817–1898), politician, was born on 29 November 1817 at Manchester, the younger son of **Sir Thomas Potter** (1774–1845), merchant and first mayor of Manchester, and his second wife, Esther, the daughter of Thomas Bayley of Booth Hall, Blackley, near Manchester. The Potters originated from Tadcaster, Yorkshire, where Thomas Potter senior had managed his father's farm until 1802, when, endowed with capital of some £7000 from his father, he moved to Manchester to set up a textile warehouse with his brothers William (who soon left the partnership) and **Richard Potter** [*nicknamed* Radical Dick] (1778–1842). Under Thomas's direction, this firm became by repute Manchester's largest mercantile business by the early 1840s, dominating the home trade and gradually moving into the foreign trade.

Both Thomas and Richard also played a leading part in the town's civic affairs, at the centre of the radical dissenting nucleus which contested the power of Manchester's entrenched tory-Anglican élite. They took a prominent part in the campaigns for religious equality, free trade, and municipal and parliamentary reform in Manchester, while also helping to found both the *Manchester Guardian* and what became the *Manchester Examiner and Times*. Richard, who married Mary Seddon on 25 September 1815 and was the grandfather of Beatrice Webb, in particular devoted himself to politics, and having become involved in the attempt to reform the constituency of Wigan in 1830, he was elected as its MP in 1832. In the house he proved a stalwart supporter of civil and religious liberty, free trade, the cotton industry, and national education but resigned on account of ill health in March 1839, before dying at Penzance from a brain tumour on 13 July 1842. Sir Thomas Potter, with Richard Cobden and others, played a leading part in the bitter struggle for the incorporation of

Thomas Bayley Potter (1817–1898), by Elliott & Fry

Manchester and in 1838 became the first mayor elected under the Municipal Corporations Act of 1835; he was knighted by Queen Victoria in 1840. Despite the growing moderation of his political views, he played a key role in the anti-corn law movement in Manchester, and generously contributed to Anti-Corn Law League funds before his death at Buile Hill, Salford, where he lived, on 20 March 1845. He was buried at Ardwick cemetery, Manchester. His elder son, Sir John Potter (1815–1858), took over many of his civic and business interests, served as mayor in 1848–51, and was knighted on the occasion of Queen Victoria's visit to Manchester in 1851. Sir John Potter's readiness to engage in the outward display of office exposed him to charges of snobbery from some of his former radical allies; his growing separation from the 'Manchester school' was accentuated by the Crimean War and culminated in his famously defeating John Bright in the Manchester election of 1857. Ironically, however, Sir John's younger brother Thomas Bayley 'Principles' Potter, although at this time a firm supporter of Sir John against 'league tyranny', was later to become Cobden's closest political heir and 'the personification of the Manchester School' (*Economic Journal*, 8, 1898, 590).

Thomas Bayley Potter was first educated at Mr John's school, George Street, Manchester, before joining several more Mancunian Unitarians at Dr Lant Carpenter's school at Bristol (1827–31). He went on to attend Rugby School (1831–2) and University College, London (1833). He was soon actively engaged in Manchester's radical politics, especially the universal suffrage movement, while also serving his apprenticeship in the family firm. He became its principal partner on the death of his brother in 1858, but he seems increasingly to have depended upon Francis Taylor (1818–1872) for its day-to-day management. Shortly after the latter's death, and in the light of unfavourable business conditions, Potter gave up his part in the firm in favour of his political interests. From the late 1850s Potter had been anxious to heal the breach between himself and the Manchester school, and his vigorous support of the Northern cause in the American Civil War, as president of the Union and Emancipation Society, revived his friendship with Cobden and Bright as well as bringing him to national prominence. He also supported European 'friends of liberty' and visited Garibaldi at Caprera (which he had helped to purchase) in 1864. Residual rivalries in Manchester politics deterred him from standing for Salford in 1865, but later that year he succeeded Cobden as MP for Rochdale, a seat he would hold until 1895. Potter, friendly with J. S. Mill, was now a keen 'out of doors' advocate of an extensive parliamentary reform bill. Within parliament, while neither orator nor debater, Potter proved a popular and attentive MP, and his girth marked him out (like one of his late twentieth-century Liberal successors at Rochdale, Cyril Smith) as the Commons' 'greatest' figure. He was active among the radical advocates of religious equality and land law reform, firmly backed Gladstone's leadership of the party, and in 1886, despite earlier reservations, supported home rule.

Potter's real political influence, however, lay outside the house and above all through the organization of the Cobden Club, formed in honour of its hero in 1866. Potter, 'its author and its soul' (Bright to Potter, 3 April 1874, Potter letters), envisaged the club as an equivalent political organization to the National Association for the Promotion of Social Science. It proved an important focus for Liberal MPs and their political allies, a forcing-house on important policy issues such as land and fiscal reform, on which it published an influential series of weighty tomes. It also funded a notable set of university prizes, designed to stimulate the study of political economy. But above all the club became the bastion for the defence of free trade in Britain, and for its advocacy in Europe, the British empire, and America. Under Potter's energetic guidance, it did much to repel the challenge of fair trade in the late 1870s and 1880s, with its popular propagandist activities aimed especially at the newly enlarged rural electorate in the 1885 general election. Potter's own concern for the state of British agriculture was a constant thread in his political career. The club's most obvious public profile came through its regular political dinners, which provided the opportunity for morale-boosting speeches and for the cultivation of international links. But such 'mere annual orgie[s]' (Mallet to Morier, 16 Jan 1866[7], Morier

MSS, Oxford, Balliol College) also provided the opportunity for poking fun at Potter, the florid-faced gourmand hoping to win the world to free trade through its stomach. Potter also proved an indefatigable (if often illegible) correspondent, and kept up a wide array of contacts and occasionally exerted some influence on government policy. He travelled extensively in Europe, especially in France and Italy, and in 1879 visited the United States, although his and the Cobden Club's advocacy of free trade proved largely counter-productive in the face of a growing Anglophobic economic nationalism.

Potter remained the linchpin of the Cobden Club until his death, but the club's later years were marked by growing intellectual and policy rifts, especially between the individualistic free-traders such as Sir Louis Mallet and Potter's more pragmatic and radical associates. The club's dinners were less frequent by the late 1880s, but on issues such as the sugar bounties it still achieved considerable public prominence. Potter himself, while often derided, held the club together in a way a less single-minded and more subtle politician might not have done. Suitably in 1890 the club honoured him with a commemorative address presented by Gladstone, who had been a keen supporter of the club's work.

In February 1846 Potter had married Mary (b. c.1820), the daughter of Samuel Ashton, cotton master, of Pole Bank, Gee Cross, Hyde, Cheshire, and the brother of Thomas Ashton, memories of whose murder at the time of a strike in 1831, the family resentfully felt, had been deliberately revived in Mrs Gaskell's *Mary Barton* (1847). The lives of their children proved largely unremarkable, although one of the four sons journeyed to the north pole. Believing that 'Manchester was no place for a man out of business' (Potter to Carnarvon, 15 Jan 1877, PRO 30/6/21), Potter moved to London. He sold the family home at Buile Hill, Pendleton (an impressive Greek revival villa built for his father by Sir Charles Barry in 1828, and later home of the Salford School of Mining), having already disposed of his Scottish hunting-lodge at Pitnacree, where between 1862 and 1874 he had entertained Cobden, Bright, and other political friends. Following Mary's death at Cannes in 1885, Potter married on 10 March 1887 Helena, the daughter of John Hick, of Bodmin, Cornwall. They later combined living in London with a rural retreat, The Hurst, Midhurst (close to Cobden's old Sussex home), where Potter died on 6 November 1898, following a paralytic stroke the previous June. He was buried at Heyshott parish church on 10 November, his wish to rest near Cobden at West Lavington having been refused by its vicar. His second wife survived him.　　　A. C. HOWE

Sources W. Sussex RO, Cobden papers · Man. CL, Potter letters · A. C. Howe, *Free trade and liberal England, 1846–1946* (1997) · M. J. Turner, *Reform and respectability: the making of middle-class liberalism in early nineteenth-century Manchester*, Chetham Society, 3rd ser., 40 (1995) · BL, Gladstone MSS, Add. MS 44282 · *Manchester Guardian* (8 Nov 1898) · *Rochdale Observer* (9 Nov 1898) · *Rochdale Observer* (12 Nov 1898) · A. K. Potter, 'The Potter family', 1983, Man. CL · 'Portrait, autograph & record of Mr Thomas Bayley Potter', *Monthly Record of*

Eminent Men (1890) · G. Meinertzhagen, *From ploughshare to parliament* (1908) · Richard Potter papers, BLPES, Coll. misc. 0146 · *Manchester City News* (4 Feb 1865) · *City Lantern* (24 May 1878) · J. V. Crangle, 'Potter, Thomas Bayley', *BDMBR*, vol. 2 · m. certs. · T. Baker, *Memorials of a dissenting chapel* (1884) · *Manchester Examiner and Times* (22 March 1845) · *Manchester Examiner and Times* (29 March 1845)

Archives BL, corresp., Add. MS 43678 · Man. CL, letters, MS 923.2 Br13 | BL, corresp. with W. E. Gladstone, Add. MS 44282 · Bodl. Oxf., corresp. with Lord Kimberley · L. Cong., D. A. Wells MSS · McMaster University, Hamilton, Ontario, letters to Lord Amberley and Lady Amberley · Mitchell L., NSW, Parkes MSS, corresp. · PRO, Carnarvon MSS, corresp. · W. Sussex RO, corresp. with Richard Cobden

Likenesses M. Noble, marble bust, 1860, Rochdale town hall · W. Sickert, painting, c.1880 · Elliott & Fry, carte-de-visite, NPG [*see illus.*] · Spy [L. Ward], cartoon (*The Manchester school*), NPG; repro. in *VF* (2 June 1877) · oils, Dunford House, West Sussex · photograph, repro. in *Manchester Faces and Places* (Dec 1898), facing p. 50

Wealth at death £66,550 10s. 3d.: probate, 16 Jan 1899, CGPLA Eng. & Wales

Potter, Thomas Joseph (1828–1873), poet and novelist, born on 9 June 1828 at Scarborough, Yorkshire, was the son of George Potter and his wife, Amelia Hunt. His parents intended him to take orders in the Church of England, but, on 24 February 1847, he was received into the Roman Catholic church at Stockeld Park, Beverley, East Riding of Yorkshire, and joined Stonyhurst College. On 24 October 1854 he entered All Hallows' College, Dublin, and was ordained a priest on 28 June 1857. He was appointed professor of *belles-lettres* and sacred eloquence, and later director of All Hallows' College.

While on the staff of All Hallows', Potter began to contribute religious verses to *The Lamp* and other Catholic periodicals, and in 1860, his first novel, *The Two Victories*, appeared. It was followed a year later by *The Rector's Daughter, or, Love and Duty*, a didactic romance, and *Legends, Lyrics, and Hymns*, a collection of short stories and hymns, was published in 1862. The publication of two of Potter's collections of religious poetry, *Light and Shade* and *The Panegyrick of St Patrick*, followed in 1864. Potter's first real literary success, however, came with *Percy Grange, or, The Dream of Life*, published in 1865 with subsequent posthumous editions in 1876 and 1884. This success was followed by *Sir Humphrey's Trial, or, The Lesson of Life* (1870), a collection of poems and short stories based upon biblical and Irish legends which ran to four editions by 1884.

In 1868 Potter wrote a guidebook drawing upon his professional experience at All Hallows', *Sacred Eloquence, or, The Theory of Preaching*, which became a standard text for trainee priests and was reissued three times by 1870. He provided a companion volume in *The Spoken Word, or, The Art of Extempore Preaching* (1872). He died at All Hallows' on 31 August 1873. *Rupert Aubrey of Aubrey Chase*, a historical novel set in 1681, was published posthumously in Dublin in 1874, with a second edition in 1876. After his death, some of his poems were set to music and sung as hymns: in New York, in 1971, Virgil T. Ford published a musical score together with Potter's poetry, called *Jesus, Lord and Master*.　　　D. J. O'DONOGHUE, rev. KATHERINE MULLIN

Sources Gillow, *Lit. biog. hist.* · Allibone, *Dict.* · Boase, *Mod. Eng. biog.* · D. J. O'Donoghue, *The poets of Ireland: a biographical dictionary*

with bibliographical particulars, 1 vol. in 3 pts (1892–3) • V. T. Ford, *Jesus, lord and master* (1971)

Likenesses portrait, repro. in T. J. Potter, *Sir Humphrey's trial* (1870)

Wealth at death under £800: probate, 21 Oct 1873, *CGPLA Ire.*

Potter, Thomas Rossell (1799–1873), antiquary and journalist, son of John Potter (*c.*1773–1827), a farmer, of West Hallam, Derbyshire, and his wife, Mary Rossell (*c.*1772–1840), was born at West Hallam on 7 January 1799. He was educated at the grammar schools at Risley and Wirksworth. When he was fifteen his parents moved to Wymeswold in Leicestershire, where Potter lived for the rest of his life. He married, on 14 January 1836, Frances Sarah (1807–1896), daughter of Leonard Fosbrooke of Shardlow Hall, Derbyshire, and Ravenstone Hall, Leicestershire. They had five sons and four daughters; two of their children died in infancy.

Potter's intention of taking holy orders was frustrated by his father's death in 1827. Instead, he started a school at Wymeswold, which proved successful, and, with the exception of a few years devoted entirely to literary work, he spent the remainder of his days as a schoolmaster and a newspaper editor. From his schooldays he had developed literary tastes and was much interested in antiquities and geology. In 1842, owing to an outbreak of fever, he temporarily moved his school from Wymeswold to a house in Charnwood Forest. While living here he collected notes on the history, antiquities, natural history, and geology of that district for his book *The History and Antiquities of Charnwood Forest* (1842). This, his largest work, shows considerable depth of research. Encouraged by its reception, Potter planned a new edition of John Nichols's *History and Antiquities of Leicestershire* (1790), revised and brought up to date, but his effort proved abortive; only *The Physical Geography and Geology of Leicestershire* (1866), written by D. T. Ansted as part of the project, was ever published.

Potter was fond of field sports and regularly rode with the Quorn hunt. He contributed papers and poems to the *Sporting Magazine* from 1827 until 1840, under the pseudonym of Old Grey. Afterwards he wrote for the *Sporting Review*. One of the best of his sporting pieces was a poem entitled 'The Meltonians' (1835). Potter was also editor of the *Leicester Advertiser* from 1849, of the *Ilkeston Pioneer* from 1856, and of the *Leicester Guardian* from 1858. In 1865 he was editor of the *Loughborough Monitor*, which, on amalgamation with another paper, became the *Loughborough Monitor and News*. Some lyrical ballads by Potter, in which local legends were incorporated, were collected in a volume of *Poems* after his death by his son Charles Neville Potter in 1881. His other works included *Walks Round Loughborough* (1840), *The Genius of Nottinghamshire* (1849), and *Rambles Round Loughborough*, reprinted from the *Loughborough News* (1868).

Potter died on 19 April 1873, at The Hermitage, Wymeswold, and was buried in Wymeswold on 23 April.

W. G. D. FLETCHER, *rev.* JANETTE C. SHEPHERD

Sources L. Jewitt, 'Thomas Rossell Potter: a memory', *The Reliquary*, 14 (1873), 17–20 • S. P. Potter, *A history of Wymeswold* (1915),
112–15 • parish register, Wymeswold, 1813–1909, Leics. RO [baptism, burial] • *The Antiquary* (10 May 1873) • *Leicestershire Advertiser* (26 April 1873) • Burke, *Gen. GB* • W. G. D. Fletcher, *Leicestershire pedigrees and royal descents* (1887), 156 • IGI

Likenesses photograph, *c.*1870, repro. in Potter, *History of Wymeswold*, 114

Potter, Vincent (*c.*1614–1661?), parliamentarian army officer and regicide, was born, apparently in Warwickshire, of unknown parents. Potter was an original member of the Massachusetts Bay Company, and in mid-May 1635 he sailed out of London on the *Elizabeth and Ann*, bound for New England. In midsummer this vessel arrived at Boston, Massachusetts, where Potter settled and was employed as a soldier at the nearby Castle Island Fort for £10 per year. He probably fought in the Pequot War, and though his wife is unknown he had a brother-in-law named Thomas Fowle residing in Boston before the civil war. In June 1639 Potter prepared to return to England, placing his apprentices with other settlers.

Potter set sail for England from Massachusetts Bay in the *Fellowship* on 10 October 1639. A fellow passenger later recalled his quibbling over a shipboard sermon (Lindholdt, xix). From a devotional text reportedly carried by him throughout the civil wars, Potter was apparently a strict puritan. The ship landed in Devon on 24 November after a passage marred by cold weather: 'our deck in a morning ore-spread with hoaries frost, and dangling Isickles hung upon the Ropes' (Lindholdt, 25). Potter continued to trade with New England until the outbreak of civil war when he joined the parliamentarian army. Robert Greville, second Baron Brooke, commissioned Potter a captain of horse on 30 January 1643 at Warwick. After Brooke's death at Lichfield, Potter continued to serve under the parliamentarian Warwickshire county committee in Colonel William Purefoy's regiment of horse. The assessments of the villages of Snitterfield and Hatton were among those assigned to maintain his troop, which on one occasion ventured into Oxfordshire to support Sir William Waller's army at Abingdon. On 5 December 1644 Potter was among the 200 horse that burned the house of Lionel Cranfield, earl of Middlesex, at Milcote, Warwickshire, allegedly to prevent the royalists from garrisoning it.

Potter gave up his troop on 25 July 1645 and succeeded his brother Captain John Potter as parliamentary commissioner to the army on 14 July. These commissioners were accountable to the committee for the army chaired by Robert Scawen MP. They were intermediaries between parliament and the New Model Army and, if required, were empowered to stop soldiers' pay. Potter was extremely diligent in his duties and joined his new colleague, Thomas Herbert, at Basingstoke on 10 October 1645. He purchased horses for Sir Thomas Fairfax and arranged supplies for Oliver Cromwell's leaguer before Basing House. Potter was a strict disciplinarian and repeatedly condemned the practice of free quarter, pointing out that if it continued, the New Model Army would fall 'Parallel to the Enimy, who in nothing more then free Quarter has forfeited the affeccons of the Countrys' (PRO,

SP 28/129/10). On 5 November he wrote to Edward Massey requiring him to discipline his plundering troops who had looted some 'poore men but well affected to our Armies' (PRO, SP 28/129/10). Potter's efficient administration of supplies and his realization that the people would favour the side that most refrained from plunder and free quarter helped ensure the speedy success of the New Model Army's western campaign.

Potter subsequently became the foremost administrator in settling army pay arrears, formulating 'Potter's lists' of former soldiers. He continued as army commissioner during the second civil war, and after the battle of St Fagans on 8 May 1648 he was appointed a county commissioner for Pembrokeshire. Potter attended the high court of justice that tried Charles I on seventeen occasions and signed the king's death warrant [see also Regicides]. On 6 March 1649 he also signed the death warrants of the royalist peers Arthur Capel, first Baron Capel of Hadham, James Hamilton, first duke of Hamilton, Henry Rich, first earl of Holland, and George Goring, first earl of Norwich. Having been promoted to a colonelcy by June 1649, he co-ordinated the receipt of provisions for Cromwell's Irish campaign. On 17 August he was appointed with Herbert to state the accounts of officers of the Train during service in Ireland, under the same conditions as they had in England.

In June 1650, after his return to England, Potter arranged Cromwell's travel northwards to organize the forthcoming campaign against the Scots. He was dispatched on 27 August to join Cromwell in Scotland, empowered to superintend the issuing and receipt of provisions to each of the regimental accounts. On 5 March 1651, on Cromwell's personal recommendation, Colonel Potter was appointed commissioner for improving lands in Scotland brought under the power of the English forces there; and on 29 April 1652 Potter and Herbert were commissioned to Irish affairs once more.

In 1660 a Robert Howcott claimed his reward for assisting in the arrests of Potter and his fellow regicide John Downes. Potter was tried as a regicide on 16 October 1660. At his trial Potter declared, 'I will deny nothing; I confess the fact, but did not contrive it' (State trials, 5.1214–15). Owing to intense pain from kidney stones Potter complained he could not speak: 'I am not in a condition to declare what I know, and would speak; I am mighty full of pain … I beseech you let me go to ease myself' (State trials, 5.1214–15) but the court refused him permission to urinate. Found guilty, he was sentenced to death and imprisoned in the Tower of London. He escaped the horror of being hanged, drawn, and quartered as he died there, probably in 1661, before his sentence could be carried out.   ANDREW J. HOPPER

Sources Greaves & Zaller, BDBR · DNB · account book of Vincent Potter, PRO, Commonwealth exchequer papers, SP 28/129/10 · P. J. Lindholdt, ed., John Josselyn, colonial traveller: a critical edition of two voyages to New England (1988) · C. E. Banks, ed., The planters of the Commonwealth, 1620–1640 (1984) · W. L. Sachse, 'The migration of New Englanders to England, 1640–1660', American Historical Review, 53 (1947–8), 251–78 · CSP dom., 1650–52; 1660–61 · The writings and speeches of Oliver Cromwell, ed. W. C. Abbott and C. D. Crane, 1 (1937) ·

C. H. Firth and R. S. Rait, eds., Acts and ordinances of the interregnum, 1642–1660, 3 vols. (1911), vol. 2 · Note-book kept by Thomas Lechford, esq., lawyer, in Boston, Massachusetts Bay, from June 27, 1638, to July 29, 1641, ed. [E. E. Hale jun.] (1885); repr. (1988) · J. Camden Hotten, ed., The original lists of persons of quality; emigrants; religious exiles; political rebels … and others who went from Great Britain to the American plantations, 1600–1700 (1986) · State trials, 5.1214–15
Archives PRO, state papers, account book, SP 28/129/10 | Warks. CRO, Denbigh MSS, CR2017/C9/16, 17, 18, 40

Potter, William (fl. 1650–1651), advocate of paper currency in England, whose origins are unknown, was one of several writers on trade and money during the Commonwealth. He contributed to the widespread debate on banking and finance in the Tudor and Stuart period. Given his interest in monetary matters, it is possible that this may be the same William Potter who, prior to 1656, had been appointed registrar of debentures for the sale of the late Charles I's lands, and who was in that year appointed to assist a commission for discovering fraud regarding the debentures. However, there is no evidence to show that these two William Potters are one and the same. Nothing else is known of his life.

Potter explained his scheme at greatest length, but least clarity, in his pamphlet The Key of Wealth, or, A New Way for Improving of Trade, published in London in September 1650. He believed that the nation's wealth could be increased by reviving trade, which was languishing. The key to this, he argued, was to improve the speed of trade and, crucially, to increase the number of transactions by providing a greater supply of money or credit. The heart of his plan was that groups of merchants should undertake to issue bills of a fixed value—say £10—payable to the bearer, so that they could circulate freely. He thus anticipated by over forty years certain essential characteristics of the first notes issued by the Bank of England on its foundation in 1694.

Much of Potter's reasoning was naïve; none the less, he addressed ideas which became central to later economic theory, for example in his discussions of the mechanisms of supply and demand, or the use of trade to stimulate employment. He also implicitly recognized the risk of inflation, and argued that increasing the money supply, circulation, and the number of transactions would lead to a rise in the number of goods for sale, thus preventing price rises. This foreshadowed the quantity theory of money as expressed by Fisher in 1920, which attempted to explain the relation between the supply of money, the velocity of circulation, and the level of prices.

Potter's scheme did not necessarily require banks, but he acknowledged that if his plan for issuing bills spread beyond London to the main towns of England, this would effectively result in the creation of banks. Here he once again anticipated future events, for in the late eighteenth and early nineteenth centuries small private banks did open up across England, many started by merchants. But he had reservations—also prophetic—about such a system, warning that bankers were 'lyable to hazard … whereby thousands are in danger of ruin at once' (The Key of Wealth, bk 4, p. 71).

As *The Key of Wealth* was intended not only for parliament but for the general public, Potter elaborated his ideas with much repetition, parable, and biblical justification. He presented his economic arguments much more succinctly in two further pamphlets. Published in London in October 1650, *The trades-man's jewel, or, A safe, easie, speedy and effectual means for the incredible advancement of trade, and multiplication of riches* was a condensed version of *The Key of Wealth*. In *Humble Proposalls to the Honorable Councell for Trade*, published the following year, he was somewhat more positive about the advantages of banks throughout the country, but again emphasized that these were not essential for the issue of the bills, which were the central feature of his plan.

Potter wrote at a time of much concern over improving the finances of the Commonwealth. In *The Key of Wealth* he referred to the ideas of Henry Robinson, who published several tracts on this theme, while Potter's own work inspired Samuel Hartlib's *Essay upon Master W. Potter's design: concerning a bank of lands to be erected throughout this Commonwealth* (reprinted in Hartlib's *Discoverie for Division or Setting out of Land*, London, 1653). Potter himself did not promote the notion of a land bank, only mentioning in passing in *The Key of Wealth* the possibility of backing bills by the value of land.   VIRGINIA HEWITT

Sources W. Potter, *The key of wealth, or, A new way for improving of trade* (1650) · W. Potter, *The trades-man's jewel, or, A safe, easie, speedy and effectual means for the incredible advancement of trade, and multiplication of riches* (1650) · W. Potter, *Humble proposalls to the honorable the councell for trade: and all merchants and others who desire to improve their estates* (1651) · R. D. Richards, *The early history of banking in England* (1929); repr. (1958), chap. 4 · J. K. Horsefield, *British monetary experiments, 1650–1710* (1960), 94–5 · S. Hartlib, 'An essay upon Master W. Potter's designe: concerning a bank of lands to be erected throughout this Common-wealth', *A discoverie for division or setting out of land, as to the best form* (1653), 27–33 · *CSP dom.*, 1656–7 · M. Ashley, *Financial and commercial policy under the Cromwellian protectorate*, 2nd edn (1962) · *DNB*

Pottinger, Eldred (1811–1843), army officer in the East India Company and diplomatist, was born in Ireland on 12 August 1811, the eldest son of Thomas Pottinger of Mount Pottinger, co. Down, and his first wife, Charlotte (d. 1813), only daughter of James Hamilton Moore. He was educated at Addiscombe College from 1826 to 1827, and entered the Bombay artillery in 1827.

After some regimental service Pottinger was appointed to the political department and became assistant to his uncle Colonel Henry *Pottinger, then resident at Cutch. In 1837 the latter granted his request to travel in Afghanistan. Disguised as a horse dealer, with a few companions he travelled via Peshawar to Kabul and Herat. Soon after his arrival at Herat in September 1837 the city was besieged by a Persian army, which was accompanied by Russian officers. Pottinger then made himself known to Yar Mahammad Khan, the wazir and commander of the forces under Shah Kamran, ruler of Herat, and offered his services for the city's defence. These were accepted, and, largely through Pottinger's energy, a stubborn resistance was organized. At the same time a British-Indian naval demonstration was made in the Persian Gulf, and the siege was ended by the Persians in September 1838. Pottinger's services were highly appreciated, and Lord Auckland, the governor-general, thanked him as one 'who, under circumstances of peculiar danger and difficulty, has by his fortitude, ability, and judgment honourably sustained the reputation and interests of his country' (Pottinger, 62). Though only a subaltern, Pottinger received a brevet majority and was created CB; he was appointed political agent at Herat, but left the city in 1839, being replaced by Major D'Arcy Todd.

In 1841 Pottinger was sent back to Afghanistan as political officer in Kohistan, a district north of Kabul. On 2 November the uprising against the British protégé Shah Shuja and the British broke out at Kabul. The same day insurgents attacked Pottinger's residence at Laghman, and he fled to Charikar, the neighbouring town, which was occupied by the 4th Gurkhas, part of Shah Shuja's force and commanded by Christopher Codrington. There they were besieged. Codrington was killed on 6 November and succeeded by John Colpoys Haughton; Pottinger was wounded in the leg. On the 14th the Gurkhas evacuated the town, and despite great difficulties Pottinger and Haughton, both severely wounded, escaped to Kabul, arriving on the 15th. There, on 23 December 1841, the British envoy Sir William Macnaghten was murdered by Akbar Khan, and Pottinger succeeded to Macnaghten's dangerous post. Supplies were short and demoralization was widespread; the British-Indian garrison, under General Elphinstone, was helplessly inactive, and against his better judgement and advice Pottinger negotiated the British-Indian withdrawal from Kabul. On 6 January 1842 the retreat began towards Jalalabad, but Akbar detained Pottinger as one of three hostages. He thus escaped the massacre in which the retreating army was destroyed. He was kept prisoner at Kabul until Major-General Pollock's army arrived there on 17 September 1842, and returned with it to India in October. His services received scant recognition from the new governor-general, Lord Ellenborough, who was hostile to those involved in the Afghanistan disaster. However, the court of inquiry exonerated Pottinger and praised his character and conduct.

With no worthwhile employment in sight Pottinger visited his uncle Sir Henry Pottinger at Hong Kong. There he died, after a brief illness, on 15 November 1843. He was buried at Hong Kong. Sir Henry Lawrence wrote of him:

> India, fertile in heroes, has shown since the days of Clive, *no man of greater and earlier promise* than Eldred Pottinger. Yet, hero as he was, you might have sat for weeks beside him at table and not have discovered that he had seen a shot fired. (Macrory, 270)

WILLIAM BROADFOOT, *rev.* JAMES LUNT

Sources J. Houghton, *Char-ee-kar* (1841) · G. Pottinger, *The Afghan connection* (1983) · J. A. Norris, *The First Afghan War, 1838–1842* (1967) · P. Macrory, *Signal catastrophe: the story of a disastrous retreat from Kabul, 1842* (1966) · Lady Sale, *A journal of the disasters in Affghanistan* (1843) · J. C. Pollock, *Way to glory: the life of Havelock of Lucknow* (1957) · J. W. Kaye, *History of the war in Afghanistan*, 2 vols. (1851) · H. Havelock, *Narrative of the war in Affghanistan in 1838–39*, 2 vols.

(1840) · W. Hough, *A narrative of the march and operations of the army of the Indus* (1841) · H. M. Vibart, *Addiscombe: its heroes and men of note* (1894)
Archives PRO NIre., letters to his family · SOAS, notes and papers relating to the tribes of Burma
Likenesses oils, c.1840 (after G. Beechey), NAM · V. Eyre, print, chromolithograph, c.1842, NAM; repro. in V. Eyre, *Prison sketches: comprising portraits of the Cabul prisoners and other subjects* (1843) · G. D. Beechey, oils, NPG

Pottinger, Sir Henry, first baronet (1789–1856), army officer in the East India Company and colonial governor, was born at Mount Pottinger, co. Down, Ireland, on 3 October 1789, the fifth son of Eldred Curwen Pottinger, a descendant of the Pottingers of Berkshire, and his wife, Anne, daughter of Robert Gordon of Florida Manor, co. Down. He was educated at Belfast Academy, which he left when twelve years old, and went to sea. In 1803 he travelled to India to join the marine service there, but friends persuaded Lord Castlereagh in 1804 to substitute a cadetship in the East India Company's army. Meanwhile he studied in Bombay, and acquired a knowledge of Indian languages. He worked well, became an assistant teacher, and on 18 September 1806 was made an ensign, and promoted lieutenant on 16 July 1809.

In 1808 Pottinger was sent on a mission to Sind under Nicholas Hankey Smith, the British political agent at Bushehr. In 1809, when Sir John Malcolm's mission to Persia was postponed, Pottinger and a friend, Captain Charles Christie, offered to explore the area between India and Persia in order to acquire information lacking to the government, which accepted the offer. The travellers, disguised as Indians, and accompanied by a local horse dealer and two servants, left Bombay on 2 January 1810, journeying by sea to Sind, and from there by land to Kalat. They were immediately recognized as Europeans, and even as having belonged to the embassy at Sind, but safely reached Nushki, near the boundary between Afghanistan and Baluchistan; here Christie diverged northwards to Herat, and proceeded thence by Yazd to Esfahan, while Pottinger, keeping in a westerly direction, travelled through Kerman to Shiraz, and joined Christie at Esfahan. Christie was directed to remain there, and was killed in a Russian attack on the Persians in 1812. Pottinger, returning via Baghdad and Basrah, reached Bombay in February 1811. He reported the results of his journey, published as *Travels in Beloochistan and Sinde* (1816). Pottinger married, in 1820, Susanna Maria (1800–1886), daughter of Captain Richard Cooke of Dublin, whose family was a branch of the Cookes of Cookesborough, co. Westmeath. They had a daughter and three sons; the eldest son died in infancy.

Pottinger was next appointed to the staff of Sir Evan Nepean, governor of Bombay, by whom he was sent as assistant to Mountstuart Elphinstone, the British resident at Poona. On 15 October 1821 he was made captain. He served during the Anglo-Maratha War, and at its close became collector of Ahmednagar. He was promoted major on 1 May 1825, and in the same year was made resident in Cutch. He was promoted lieutenant-colonel on 17 March

Sir Henry Pottinger, first baronet (1789–1856), by Sir Francis Grant, 1845

1829, and brevet colonel on 23 January 1834. While resident in Cutch he conducted a mission to Sind in 1831, successfully negotiating a commercial treaty. He conducted further missions in 1833–4 and 1836–7, being appointed political agent there in 1836, negotiating the treaty of 1839 which achieved domination of Sind. Out of sympathy with what he saw as Auckland's excessively coercive approach, Pottinger left India in 1840, ill health being given as the reason for his return. He was created a baronet on 27 April 1840.

Pottinger accepted Lord Palmerston's offer of the post of envoy and plenipotentiary in China and superintendent of British trade, thus superseding Captain Charles Elliot. The First Anglo-Chinese War had begun in January 1840. After Elliot, the British representative, had seized the forts by Canton (Guangzhou), a preliminary treaty had been drawn up in January 1841, but it was disavowed by both governments. Palmerston directed Pottinger to replace this treaty by one which would open China to British trade, but before he reached China hostilities had recommenced. Major-General Sir Hugh Gough arrived in March 1841 to command the expeditionary force from India. Gough took the four forts defending Canton in May 1841, and while he was preparing to attack the town itself, Pottinger reached Macau (Macao) (9 August). He deemed it essential to the success of his mission to make a further display of force, and he co-operated with Gough and Admiral Sir William Parker (1781–1866) in the capture of Amoy (Xiamen), Chushan, Chintu (Chengdu), and Ningpo (Ningbo). On 13 June 1842 Pottinger, with Parker, entered the Yangtze (Yangzi) River with the object of taking Nanking (Nanjing). After many successes by the way, an assault on that city was imminent in July, when Pottinger announced that the Chinese were ready to treat for peace on a satisfactory basis. The Chinese diplomatists had already found that Pottinger could not be trifled with: an intercepted letter from the chief Chinese negotiator to his government stated that 'to all his representations the barbarian, Pottinger, only knit his brows and said "No"'. Eventually peace was signed on 29 August 1842 on board HMS *Cornwallis* before Nanking. By this treaty of Nanking, China agreed to pay an indemnity of $21 million, Hong Kong was ceded to England, and the five 'treaty ports'— Canton, Amoy, Foochow (Fuzhou), Ningpo, and Shanghai—were opened to British traders, and were to receive British consuls. In recognition of his successful conduct of negotiations Pottinger was made GCB (2 December 1842), and on 5 April 1843 was appointed the first British governor of Hong Kong.

Pottinger returned to Britain in the spring of 1844, and was much honoured: he was sworn of the privy council (23 May 1844), was presented with the freedom of many cities, and in June 1845 the House of Commons voted him £1500 a year for life. On 28 September 1846 he succeeded Sir Peregrine Maitland as governor of the Cape Colony. He stayed there less than six months, and apparently without reputation or distinction in the view of G. M. Theal, according to whom Pottinger left the colony 'without the esteem of a single colonist' (Lehmann, 279). On 4 August 1847 he returned once more to India as governor of Madras and attained the rank of lieutenant-general in 1851. He held the post until 1854, when he returned to Britain in broken health. His government of Madras had not been a success. He was resistant to change and had become dilatory in the discharge of public business, failing to recognize the need for essential improvements. He was better fitted to deal with a crisis than with ordinary administration. He died at Malta on 18 March 1856, and was buried at Valletta. His two surviving sons successively succeeded to the baronetcy.

WILLIAM BROADFOOT, *rev.* JAMES LUNT

Sources Burke, *Peerage* (1907) • *Hart's Army List* • M. E. Yapp, *Strategies of British India: Britain, Iran and Afghanistan, 1798–1850* (1980) • J. A. Norris, *The First Afghan War, 1838–1842* (1967) • H. Pottinger, *Travels in Beloochistan and Sindi* (1816) • A. Burnes, *Travels into Bokhara*, 3 vols. (1834) • A. Burnes, *Cabool: residence, 1836–8* (1842) • Fortescue, *Brit. army*, vol. 12 • A. J. Smithers, *The Kaffir wars* (1973) • G. M. Theal, *History of South Africa*, 11 vols. (1915–20); facs. edn (Cape Town, 1964) • J. H. Lehmann, *Remember you are an Englishman: a biography of Sir Harry Smith* (1977)
Archives PRO, corresp. and papers, FO 705 | BL, corresp. with Lord Aberdeen, Add. MS 43198 • BL, letters to Sir John Hobhouse, Add. MS 36478 • BL OIOC, letters to Mountstuart Elphinstone, MSS Eur. F 87–9 • BL OIOC, corresp. with Sir John Hobhouse, MS Eur. F 213 • NL Scot., corresp. with Sir Thomas Cochrane • NMM, letters to Sir William Parker • PRO, corresp. with Lord Ellenborough, PRO 30/12 • U. Durham L., corresp. with third Earl Grey • U. Southampton L., letters to Lord Palmerston
Likenesses F. Grant, oils, 1845, Gov. Art Coll. [*see illus.*] • H. Griffiths, stipple, pubd 1846 (after a lithograph by S. Laurence, 1842), NG Ire. • J. Brown, line engraving, NG Ire. • L. Dickinson, lithograph (after S. Laurence), BM, NPG • portrait (after F. Grant), Oriental Club, London • portrait (after F. Grant), possibly government house, Hong Kong • portrait (after F. Grant), priv. coll.

Pottinger, Israel (*fl.* 1759–1761), playwright, of whose early life nothing is known, was first an apprentice to a bookseller named Worral. He then set up for himself in Paternoster Row, London, and planned a variety of periodicals. One of them, the *Busy Body*, was published three times a week for 2d. at the Dunciad, Paternoster Row. Oliver Goldsmith contributed to it in 1759. Not meeting with much success, Pottinger then opened a circulating library near Great Turnstile, Holborn, and at Islington performed for a time George Alexander Stevens's popular *Lecture on Heads*. He subsequently suffered from a mental disorder, but supported himself in his lucid intervals through his writing. In 1761 he published an unacted comedy called *The Methodist*, which he described as 'a continuation or completion of the plan of [Samuel] Foote's *Minor*'. It was a scurrilous attack on George Whitefield. A third edition appeared within the year. In the same year a farce by Pottinger, entitled *The Humorous Quarrel, or, The Battle of the Greybeards*, was performed at Southwark fair, and subsequently published. *The Duenna*, a comic opera in three acts, a parody on R. B. Sheridan's play, published in 1776 and 'acted by his majesty's servants', is supposed to have been by Pottinger. A new edition appeared within the year. He was probably also the author of *The Critic* (1780), a political burlesque of Sheridan's play of the same name.

G. LE G. NORGATE, *rev.* MICHAEL BEVAN

Sources D. E. Baker, *Biographia dramatica, or, A companion to the playhouse*, rev. I. Reed, new edn, rev. S. Jones, 1 (1812), 580; 2 (1812), 178; 3 (1812), 40 • J. Forster, *The life and times of Oliver Goldsmith*, 5th edn, 2 vols. (1871)

Potts, Edward (1839–1909), architect, was born at Bolton Street, Bury, Lancashire, on 2 March 1839, the younger son of Edward Potts, a draper, and his wife, Mary, *née* Diggle. He was educated locally, then moved to Oldham and was taken into partnership by the well-known local architect George Woodhouse. On 31 July 1861 he married Sarah (1838–1898), the daughter of William Ackroyd; they had at least three sons and seven daughters.

As Oldham became the world's leading mill town during the 1860s, Potts found ample scope for his talents. He secured custom not merely by subscribing from 1871 to more shares than any other architect in the new 'Oldham limiteds' but also by actively promoting the flotation of such companies. Thus he became a pioneer of the contractors' company, which was formed by a group of tradesmen with a direct interest in the construction, equipment, and supply of a new cotton mill. Thereafter he was the architect for fourteen new mills during the borough's greatest mill-building boom (1871–5).

Potts's innovations began with his design of the Prince of Wales mill in 1875, 'one of the most complete and well-arranged mills in Oldham' (*Textile Manufacturer*, 11, 15 May 1878, 151), employing unusually narrow longitudinal ceiling vaults in place of the deep arch patented in 1871 by his older rival A. H. Stott. These vaults transferred all the thrust from a lateral to a vertical direction and at the same time reduced the amount of shadow in the spinning room. After the end of the Oldham boom Potts extended his interests to the nearby towns of Ashton (from 1875), Dukinfield (from 1877), Stalybridge (from 1881), and Shaw (from 1882).

In 1880 Potts established the new firm of Potts, Pickup, and Dixon in partnership with George Pickup and Frederick William Dixon, who, like Potts, were Methodists. In 1882 the partnership built the textile mill at Chadderton, equipped with 91,000 spindles, as a 'showcase mill'. In the same year Potts opened an office in Manchester in order to extend the range of his clientele. From 1883 he pioneered the use of ferroconcrete in mill flooring and wholly abandoned the use of the brick arch. The new technique of fireproof and waterproof construction proved to be stronger, safer, and cheaper than the older method. Such advantages led to its speedy general adoption, especially after Potts failed to secure the grant of a patent in 1884. In consequence the window area was enlarged and the proportion of glass to wall expanded to a maximum, improving the lighting of the spinning rooms. In 1884 Potts applied the new technique in the construction of the Palm mill, which was built in the record time of ten months and became Oldham's pioneer ring-spinning firm, equipped with 80,000 Rabbeth spindles.

From 1884 Potts extended his interests to Middleton, Rochdale, Heywood, and Stockport, and also to the continent. In Rouen he built in 1884 the first mill on the Oldham model, while in Lille he established in the 1890s the firm of Potts, Son, and Hodgson. His growing reputation secured him a large number of contracts. In Oldham he designed many public buildings, including the infirmary (1870) and the town hall extension (1879–80), with an impressive façade, as well as banks, board schools, and chapels. He also served as the architect for the Manchester corn exchange (1891) and for Blackpool town hall (1895–1900). He became a fellow of the Royal Institute of British Architects (RIBA) in 1888 and took his eldest son, William Edward Potts (1862–1932), into partnership, establishing in 1899 with Arthur W. Hennings the new firm of Potts, Son, and Hennings. W. E. Potts became an associate of the RIBA in 1890 and was an active Methodist, holding from 1885 onwards almost all the offices open to a layman (*Methodist Who's Who*, 1915, 241).

During the Edwardian boom of 1904–7 Potts undertook his final contracts in the Oldham district for John Bunting, the leading mill magnate of Lancashire. The Bell mill (1904), with 130,176 spindles, was the largest mill so far built and was the 162nd mill designed by Potts. The Iris mill (1907) was built in the record time of four months and became the first ring mill in the Bunting group. In 1907–8 Potts designed for Bunting the Times mill no. 2 at Middleton which, with 160,000 spindles, fulfilled Bunting's wish to become the proprietor of the world's largest mill. Potts opened an office in Bolton in 1896 and built mills there as well as in Leigh, the industry's final area of expansion. During a career of forty-nine years he built some 200 mills, for both private employers and limited companies, for both fine and coarse spinning, and for firms abroad as well as at home: he extended the range of his foreign clients from France to Germany, Russia, China, and Mexico. He ranks with P. S. Stott as the greatest mill architect of Victorian Lancashire.

Potts moved from Oldham to Bowdon in 1877 and then to Eccles in 1891. Wherever he resided he played an active part in public life. He may have been 'deaf with one ear but sharp with the other' (Oldham census returns, 1871). He remained nevertheless 'a man with a broad and sympathetic heart' (*Eccles and Patricroft Journal*, 16 April 1909), especially receptive to the claims of the weak and the poor. The causes of better education, better health, and better living attracted his support. In Oldham he served as a director of the Lyceum (1862–70). In Bowdon he inspired the building of a Methodist chapel. For forty years he served as a Sunday school teacher, and he also held every office his church could give him. In Eccles he was a Liberal member of the borough council (1902–5), the first chairman of its library committee (1904), and a JP (1906). From Andrew Carnegie he secured in 1906 a grant of £7500 to finance the construction of a public library. He then designed free of charge a handsome building in Renaissance style (adjoined by a grand public hall which was never built), which he opened on 19 October 1907. Potts expressed the hope that the building would become 'the Eccles University' in harmony with Carlyle's dictum of 1841 that the true university was a collection of books. He presented five large etchings in order to provide the nucleus of an art gallery. As a keen supporter of the cause of temperance, he inaugurated in Eccles popular Saturday-night concerts in order to provide cheap and wholesome entertainment during the winter months. Himself the father of a large family, he sought to reduce the local incidence of infant mortality: in December 1906 he offered a sovereign to the mother of every infant attaining the age of one year. He honoured the pledge and died at his home, Quorndon, Brackley Road, Monton, near Eccles, on 15 April 1909. He was buried in Chadderton cemetery, Oldham, on 17 April.　　　　D. A. FARNIE

Sources D. Gurr and J. Hunt, eds., *The cotton mills of Oldham*, 3rd edn (1998) · *Eccles and Patricroft Journal* (16 April 1909), 10d · *Eccles and Patricroft Journal* (23 April 1909), 9f · *Manchester Guardian* (16 April 1909), 9f · *Manchester Courier* (16 April 1909), 8c · *Oldham Chronicle* (17 April 1909) · *Oldham Standard* (17 April 1909), 13c · *Methodist Times* (29 April 1909), 15 · *Methodist Recorder* (6 May 1909), 27 · *Methodist Recorder* (28 April 1932), 19 · *Textile Manufacturer*, 11 (May 1878), 151 · *Textile Manufacturer*, 11 (Aug 1885), 397 · W. B. Tracy and W. T. Pike, *Manchester & Salford at the close of the 19th century: contemporary biographies* (1899), 218 · W. E. Potts, 'Notes on the construction of modern industrial buildings', *Journal of the Textile Institute*, 5 (1914), 363–74 · census returns for Oldham, 1871 · *Methodist Who's Who* · b. cert. · m. cert. · d. cert.
Likenesses portrait, repro. in Tracy and Pike, *Manchester & Salford*, 218 · portrait, repro. in *Eccles and Patricroft Journal* (25 Oct 1907), 10

Wealth at death £24,930 12s. 3d.: probate, 8 June 1909, *CGPLA Eng. & Wales*

Potts, Laurence Holker (1789–1850), surgeon and inventor of a process for sinking foundations, the son of Cuthbert Potts, surgeon, and Ethelinda Margaret Thorpe, daughter of John *Thorpe (1715/16–1792), was born in Pall Mall, London, on 18 April 1789. He was educated at Westminster School and at a school in Northamptonshire before being apprenticed in 1805 to Mr Birch, surgeon, of Warwick. In 1810 he became a house pupil of Sir Benjamin Brodie at St George's Hospital, London; William Frederick Chambers and Charles Locock were house pupils at the same time. Potts was admitted to the Royal College of Surgeons in 1812, and he graduated MD at King's College, Aberdeen, in 1825.

In 1812 Potts was appointed surgeon to the Royal Devon and Cornwall Miners' militia, then quartered in Ireland. The regiment returned to Truro in 1814 and was subsequently disbanded, and Potts started in practice in the town. He had always taken a great interest in scientific pursuits, and in 1818 he took an active part in founding the Royal Institution of Cornwall. He gave several courses of lectures there and made a habit of gratuitously analysing minerals for the miners.

In 1820 Potts married Anne Wright, of Lambessow, Cornwall; they had four daughters and two sons who survived him. In 1828 he became superintendent and physician of the Cornwall County Lunatic Asylum at Bodmin. He resigned in 1837, and moved in the following year to Vanbrugh Castle, Blackheath, near London, where he established an institution for the treatment of spinal diseases. Here he established a workshop for the manufacture of various appliances and apparatus, of which he devised many new forms. He had at the same time a London town house, 9 Buckingham Street, Strand, to which a workshop was attached. His increasing interest in his inventions diverted his attention from his patients, and Vanbrugh Castle was eventually given up.

Potts's minor inventions included his patent no. 9642 of 1843 for a suspended railway, velocipede, and manual paddle boat. But the invention for which his name is generally remembered is a method of sinking foundations under water, for which he obtained a patent in 1843 (no. 9975). This involved the sinking of hollow piles of iron, open at the lower end and closed at the top by a cap. A partial vacuum being then formed within the tube by means of a pump, the coastal or river-bed materials such as shingle and sand were caused to flow up through the pile by the pressure of the atmosphere, the rush of water from below breaking up the soil and undermining the lower edges of the pile. The pile descended by its own gravity, assisted by atmospheric pressure on its closed end, and, when filled, its contents were discharged by a pump. As the tube descended the cap was removed and a fresh length attached. The tubes could be of large size, forming an alternative to cofferdams in constructing foundations. Potts claimed to have first considered the idea while in Cornwall, and may have developed it from observing the sinking of wrought iron tubes for mine shafts through sand off the coast of Cornwall, a practice which was introduced about 1801.

Potts's invention was well received, and at first it promised to be a great success. Potts gave evidence on 10 June 1844 before the commission on harbours of refuge, and James Walker, president of the Institution of Civil Engineers and a member of the commission, was impressed by the ingenuity of the idea, though he remained uncertain about its practical application. The matter was taken up by Trinity House, to which Walker was consultant, and on 16 July 1845 an experimental tube 2 feet 6 inches in diameter was driven into the Goodwin Sands, to a depth of 22 feet, in two or three hours. A cluster of such piles was used to form the foundation of a beacon, which was completed on 26 August 1847. Several small beacons were erected on sands lying near the mouth of the River Thames in 1845–6. Sir John Burgoyne also took an interest in the invention, and a trial cylinder 4 feet in diameter was sunk at the Goodwin Sands as a possible foundation for a fortification.

Although Potts may originally have had maritime applications in mind, others saw alternative uses for his idea. In 1845 Potts became acquainted with Charles Fox of the firm of Fox and Henderson. The firm invested heavily in developing the device and attempted to use it wherever there was an opportunity. Undoubtedly the hope was that it would provide a cheaper alternative to the expensive temporary construction of cofferdams generally used for bridge foundations. The first large work upon which it was employed was the viaduct carrying the Chester and Holyhead Railway across Malltraeth Bay in the Isle of Anglesey. Nineteen tubes, 1 foot in diameter and 16 feet long, were successfully sunk in the sand during the summer of 1847. Potts's method was also employed successfully for sinking the piers for a railway bridge over the River Ouse at Huntingdon. Ground conditions were evidently favourable in both locations, but the system failed at the bridge over the River Nene at Peterborough: here there were boulders in the clay forming the river bed. The foundations for the south-western railway bridge over the Thames between Datchet and Windsor were laid by the same process, but on 12 August 1849, when the line was ready to be opened, one of the tubes suddenly sank, causing a fracture in the girder resting upon it. G. W. Hemans tried the operation with cylinders 10 feet in diameter in 1850, during the construction of a bridge over the River Shannon at Athlone, on the Midland Great Western Railway of Ireland, but it proved very expensive because of the cost of pumping out the air. Trouble was again caused by boulders, which the trial borings had failed to indicate. These later examples all involved cylinders of much larger diameter.

Potts read a paper on his method before the Society of Arts on 10 May 1848, for which he received the Isis gold medal. He devoted the last years of his life and a considerable fortune almost exclusively to the perfecting of his invention. Unhappily it was not a financial success, and experience soon proved that its application was very limited. It had, however, one very important result, as it incidentally gave rise to the system of sinking foundations by compressed air, an invention of great importance. It was intended to employ Potts's method to sink the piers of Rochester Bridge (commenced about 1849), but it was found that the river bed was encumbered with the remains of a very ancient bridge, and that the cylinders could not be forced through the obstructions. It then occurred to John D'Urban Hughes (1807–1874), Fox and Henderson's engineer in charge of the work, to reverse the process, and to pump air into the cylinders to force the water out, so that the men could work at the bottom of the cylinders, as in a diving bell. As the material was excavated from the space covered by the cylinders they sank by their own weight. An 'air-lock' provided the means of access to and from the cylinders. Although Hughes first developed the idea independently, compressed air had already been used to sink mine shafts in France by J. Triger (1801–1867) in 1838, and Hughes became aware of this through Andrew Ure's *Dictionary* and was able to make use of this information in applying the invention to bridge foundations. Hughes went on to become an acknowledged expert in the application of compressed air to foundations.

Through his links with Fox, Potts was able to send his sons John Thorpe and Benjamin Langford Forster (1839–1910) to Fox and Henderson for training as engineers. B. L. F. Potts worked closely with E. A. Cowper of this firm for many years. Potts died at 9 Buckingham Street, Strand, London, on 23 March 1850.

R. B. PROSSER, *rev.* MIKE CHRIMES

Sources H. Clark, *Mining manual and almanack* (1851), 198 · G. R. Burnell, *Supplement to the theory, practice, and architecture of bridges* (1850), 98–107 · W. J. M'Alpine, 'The supporting power of piles', *PICE*, 27 (1867–8), 275–319, esp. 298–303 · R. Glossop, 'The invention and early use of compressed air to exclude water from shafts and tunnels', *Geotechnique*, 26 (1976), 253–80 · J. Hughes, 'On the pneumatic method adopted in constructing the foundations of the new bridge across the Medway at Rochester', *PICE*, 10 (1850–51), 353–69 · *Civil Engineer and Architect's Journal*, 13 (1850), 144 · *New Scientist* (19 Feb 1970), 366 · W. Humber, *A complete treatise in cast and wrought iron bridge construction*, 3rd edn (1870), 180–247 · 'Lighthouse on the Goodwin sands', *Mechanics Magazine*, 43 (1845), 96 · 'Pneumatic pile driving', *Civil Engineer and Architect's Journal*, 10 (1847), 388–9 · A. Findley, 'On lighthouses and beacons', *Transactions of the Society of Arts*, 56 (1847), 269–71 · *Civil Engineer and Architect's Journal*, 13 (1850), 392 · 'Failure of a cast iron girder bridge', *Mechanics Magazine*, 51 (1849), 166 · d. cert.
Archives Inst. CE, J. G. James collection

Potts, Robert (1802x4–1885), mathematician, was born at Lambeth, the son of Robert Potts, and grandson of the head of a textile firm specializing in Irish linen. He entered Trinity College, Cambridge, on 27 June 1827 as a sizar, and graduated BA as twenty-sixth wrangler in 1832, proceeding MA in 1835. Potts was married soon after taking his degree; his wife's name was Jeannetta. They lived near Parker's Piece, Cambridge, and he became a successful private tutor in the university. A strenuous advocate of attempts to open up the university to groups previously excluded, he actively supported most of the university reforms that were carried out in his time. He acquired a wide reputation as the editor of Euclid's *Elements*, which

he brought out in a large edition in 1845, followed in 1847 by an appendix. His school edition appeared in 1846, and was republished a number of times in the following years. The book had an immense circulation in the British colonies and in America, and the William and Mary College of Virginia conferred the honorary degree of LLD upon Potts 'in appreciation of the excellence of his mathematical works'. The merits of his edition of Euclid consisted in the clear arrangement and division of the component parts of the propositions, and in the admirable collection of notes. He also published *Elementary Arithmetic* (1876) and *Elementary Algebra* (1879), both with brief historical notes. His non-mathematical publications can be divided into two categories: those concerning the University of Cambridge and those on theology. Of the former, *Liber Cantabrigiensis* appeared in two parts between 1855 and 1863, followed in 1866 by *A brief account of the scholarships and exhibitions open to competition in the University of Cambridge*. In the latter category he edited the 1543 edition of William Turner's *Huntyng and Fyndyng out of the Romish Fox* (1851), *King Edward VI on the Supremacy … with his Discourse on the Reformation of Abuses* (1874), and other theological works, including an edition of William Paley's *View of the Evidences of Christianity* and the *Horae Paulinae*, which he published together in 1850 with some specimens of Cambridge exam papers.

Potts had long campaigned for university recognition of residence hostels. In 1884 he received a royal charter to open a hostel, to be called St Paul's Hostel, to house students who were 'natives of India', but did not live to implement his plan. He died at his home, Park Terrace, Parker's Piece, Cambridge, on 4 August 1885 in his eighty-second year. He was survived by his wife.

CHARLES PLATTS, *rev.* ADRIAN RICE

Sources private information (1896) · Venn, *Alum. Cant.* · *The Times* (7 Aug 1885), 1b · Boase, *Mod. Eng. biog.* · Ward, *Men of the reign* · *CGPLA Eng. & Wales* (1885)
Archives CUL, letters to Hugh Godfrey
Wealth at death £8561 16s. 9d.: resworn administration with will, Sept 1886, *CGPLA Eng. & Wales* (1885)

Potts, Thomas (*fl.* 1610–1614). *See under* Pendle witches (*act.* 1612).

Potts, Thomas (1778–1842), compiler of reference works, was the son of Edward Potts (1721–1819) of Glanton, near Alnwick, Northumberland. Thomas Potts was a solicitor, and at one time was connected with Skinners' Hall. In 1803 he lived in Camden Town, and he later lived at Chiswick and other places, and had chambers in Serjeants' Inn.

Potts published *A compendious law dictionary … intended for the use of country gentlemen, the merchant, and the professional man* in 1803; it was reissued in 1814 and in 1815 a new edition was enlarged by Thomas Hartwell Horne. His next work, *The British Farmers' Cyclopaedia, or, Complete Agricultural Dictionary* (1806), with forty-two engravings, was judged to be an advance on preceding works and ran to two editions. His *Gazetteer of England and Wales … with Maps* followed in 1810.

Potts died at Upper Clapton, London, on 8 November 1842 and was described then as 'of Haydon Square, Minories' (*GM*, 1842, 672).

G. LE G. NORGATE, *rev.* ELIZABETH BAIGENT

Sources *GM*, 2nd ser., 18 (1842), 672 · Allibone, *Dict.* · J. Donaldson, *Agricultural biography* (1854) · *GM*, 1st ser., 89/1 (1819), 279

Pouch, Captain. *See* Reynolds, John (*d.* 1607).

Poulett, John, first Baron Poulett (1586–1649), local politician and royalist army officer, was the eldest son and heir of Sir Anthony Poulett (or Paulet; 1561/2–1600) of Hinton St George, Somerset, governor of Jersey from 1588 until his death, and his wife, Catherine (*d.* 1602), daughter of Henry *Norris, first Baron Norris of Rycote. Poulett's paternal grandfather was Sir Amias *Paulet, the gaoler of Mary, queen of Scots, and Elizabethan privy councillor. While in wardship following his father's death on 22 July 1600 John matriculated at University College, Oxford, in 1601, aged fifteen, and travelled abroad in 1603. Already established in Somerset county society with a colonelcy of militia cavalry in 1608, he was admitted specially at the Middle Temple in January 1611. By 1613 he was a justice of the peace, and in 1616 sheriff of Somerset. He was a deputy lieutenant at least from 1624. His social position was reinforced by his financially advantageous marriage, about 1614, to Elizabeth (1593?–1663?), daughter of Christopher Ken or Kenn, of Kenn Court, Somerset, with whom he had five daughters and three sons.

Poulett sat for Somerset in the last six weeks of the 1610 session of parliament and appears not to have spoken in debate. He was returned, again for the county, to the parliament of 1614. It was a brutal election, in which he was returned instead of Sir Robert Phelips, whom he had promised not to oppose. Phelips was forced to sit for Saltash. The election ruptured the slight friendship that had existed between Poulett and Phelips, and began a rivalry which dominated Somerset for two decades. Poulett's parliamentary service in 1614 was no more than being named to the committee for the oath *ex officio* and speaking once on the last day, while Phelips's parliamentary career began in earnest. In 1621 Phelips sat for Bath and Poulett sat for Lyme Regis. While Phelips achieved prominence in 1621 Poulett figured not at all in debate. He did not again attend a parliament until he took his seat in the Lords in 1628, and was there no more voluble than he had been in the lower house.

Both Poulett and Phelips aspired to political power in Somerset, the former by assiduous and often obsequious cultivation of contacts at court, the latter by bold and exaggerated defence of the 'country's' interests. Phelips's appeal was broader and more populist; Poulett's more narrowly focused on the county's numerous and prosperous gentry. There was little ideological distinction between them. Poulett was not involved in the sedition of Edmond Peacham, vicar of Hinton St George, among whose papers was found a sermon he had written foretelling the king's death as a divine judgment. Peacham had been presented to the living by Poulett's grandfather Sir

Amias a quarter-century earlier, and Poulett's examinations by the privy council in 1614–15 were merely an exercise of its routine prudence. Poulett was no more a 'popular man' in 1640 than the rest of the aristocracy who realized the regime could not stop the Scots without a parliament. In their rivalry for local power Poulett and Phelips divided the county's magnates along lines of kinship and affinity and of office. Poulett, as the principal deputy lieutenant to a non-resident lord lieutenant, controlled the lieutenancy; Phelips regularly carried a majority of the magistrates with him. But they made no appeals to higher loyalty or to sectarian principles. By the same token both were substantially indifferent to the larger issues which were in train towards revolution.

Poulett's advancement was sudden and considerable. Charles I visited him at Hinton in 1625, and at the king's request Poulett entertained the exiled Huguenot military commander Benjamin de Rohan, seigneur de Soubise, at Hinton from October 1625 to September 1626. Soubise, agitating for a major expedition to relieve La Rochelle, was an embarrassment to the king, and his rustication removed him from court. One of Poulett's opponents remarked that the king had 'committed Monsieur de Soubize to Mr Poulettes custodie, because hee knewe him to bee a good gaoler' (PRO, SP 16/40/58). So he was, for Poulett kept Whitehall informed of his guest's restlessness, and when Soubise finally bolted, Poulett despaired. However, largely for his painful service, Poulett was created first Baron Poulett on 23 June 1627.

Peerage gave Poulett extraordinary standing in a county with only one other resident peer, one who took no active part in county politics or administration. But it did not save his hunting when the disafforestation of Neroche Forest ended his office as warden there, and his uncharacteristic complicity in popular opposition to the project very nearly brought his disgrace at court in 1631. His command, from May to September 1635, of the king's ship *Constant Reformation* in the earl of Lindsay's ship money fleet in the channel was gratifying. But the round of personally expensive on-board entertainment and short sallies to force Dutch merchantmen to strike their colours ended with his illness, the accolade of knighthood for himself and his eldest son, John [*see below*], in 1635 being slight consolation. Poulett's choleric temperament repeatedly caused him to overreact to Phelips's challenges. Even with the court's favour, in virtually every confrontation with Phelips—over the payment of the muster master, pressing of Phelips's adherents as soldiers, sacking a friend of Poulett as a militia officer, deputy lieutenants' warrants, churchales, disafforestation—Poulett lost, both in the county and at the council table.

In the first civil war Poulett achieved something of an apotheosis. With the militia ordinance of 1642 he withdrew from the Lords, signed the York manifesto in June, and joined the marquess of Hertford at Wells in executing the commission of array. As the roundheads slowly reduced Somerset, Poulett fortified Hinton St George in September and put up a stiff fight before retreating with two cannons to Sherborne. In March 1643 parliament impeached him for treason while he was in Wales and the marches with Hertford. The earl of Essex captured Poulett in October in Shropshire. After escaping he served under Sir Ralph Hopton, recruiting a sizeable force around Oxford which invaded Dorset, besieging Lyme Regis with Prince Maurice. After Essex raised the siege in June 1644 Poulett retreated to Exeter and was commissioner there until the city's fall in April 1646, when he was taken prisoner. Thanks to the good offices of Sir Thomas Fairfax, Poulett was treated leniently by parliament, being ordered to pay a £2742 fine, £1500 compensation for destroying Lady Drake's house in Dorset, and an annuity of £200 to Lyme Regis. He was allowed to retire to Hinton, where he died on 20 March 1649. He was buried in Hinton, and his memorial is the chapel dedicated to his memory in the parish church.

All three of Poulett's sons—John, Francis, and Amias—were solid royalists. His youngest daughter, Elizabeth, married the eldest son of John Ashburnham, who having married Poulett's relict in 1649 was both father-in-law and stepfather of Elizabeth.

John Poulett, second Baron Poulett (c.1615–1665), royalist army officer, matriculated at Oxford from Exeter College in 1632, without apparently graduating; in March 1643 he was awarded an honorary MD degree at Oxford. He was knighted with his father in 1635 and took no active part in Somerset affairs until he was returned for the county in the Long Parliament. But he had travelled on the continent, and in February 1640 was with Lord Conway's army in the north. He figured only slightly in the Commons, and withdrew with his father to do battle in Somerset in the summer of 1642, being impeached in September. Appointed to the council of Munster, he commanded a regiment against the Catholic confederate insurgents which was sent to Bristol after the 1643 armistice. He and his younger brother Amias served valiantly in the battles of 1644 in Somerset. John was in the Winchester Castle garrison that surrendered to Cromwell in October 1645. He joined his father at Exeter, and with its fall in April 1646 was barely allowed composition under the articles of capitulation. But it was his marriage to Sir Thomas Fairfax's sister-in-law, Catherine (1612/13–1648×53), daughter of Sir Horace *Vere and widow of Oliver St John, which had taken place in March 1641 (by marriage licence dated 6 March 1641) that moved Fairfax's several interventions to save the Poulett fortunes. John and Catherine had two sons and three daughters. She was alive in March 1648 but had died by 30 January 1653 when he married Anne (b. 1635, d. in or before 1711), the second daughter and coheir of Sir Thomas Browne.

Having succeeded to the barony in 1649 Poulett remained a stalwart, though circumspect royalist: he was imprisoned in 1655 in Major-General Disbrowe's sweep of Somerset royalists, and again in 1658 though under more lenient conditions. A deputy lieutenant after the Restoration, he died on 15 September 1665 at his house at Court de Wick in the parish of Yatton, Somerset, and was buried on 24 October at Hinton St George. John Poulett, his eldest

son with Catherine, succeeded as third baron, and was the father of John *Poulett, first Earl Poulett.

The Pouletts were very wealthy. In 1638 the estate was worth £2100 per annum clear. The second baron's properties in Somerset, Dorset, Berkshire, and Essex were settled on him during his father's life, and were valued at £1500 per annum. Besides the great house at Hinton St George and the commodious house of Court de Wick (or Courtaweek), the house and lands in Chiswick, Middlesex, served for the London season. The first baron made generous provision for his daughters and two younger sons. He made his son and heir both executor and residual legatee of all other chattels, real and personal, demonstrating a deep affection and trust forged in the comradeship of arms.   THOMAS G. BARNES

Sources Som. ARS, Poulett MSS, DD/PT · Som. ARS, Sanford MSS, DD/SF · quarter sessions order books, Som. ARS · quarter sessions rolls, Som. ARS · state papers, James I, PRO, SP 14 · state papers, Charles I, PRO, SP 16 · privy council register, PRO, PC 2 · inquisition post mortem of Anthony Powlett, PRO, C 142, 42 Eliz 260, 143 · will, PRO, PROB 11/207, sig. 45, fols. 335v–337r · Foster, *Alum. Oxon.* · GEC, *Peerage* · S. R. Gardiner, ed., *Parliamentary debates in 1610*, CS, 81 (1862) · E. R. Foster, ed., *Proceedings in parliament, 1610*, 2 (1966) · M. Jansson, ed., *Proceedings in parliament, 1614* (House of Commons) (1988) · W. Notestein, F. H. Relf, and H. Simpson, eds., *Commons debates, 1621*, 7 vols. (1935) · M. F. Keeler, M. J. Cole, and W. B. Bidwell, eds., *Lords proceedings, 1628* (1983) · F. H. Relf, ed., *Notes of the debates in the House of Lords … AD 1621, 1625, 1628*, CS, 3rd ser., 42 (1929) · T. G. Barnes, *Somerset, 1625–1640: a county's government during the personal rule* (1961) · D. Underdown, *Somerset in the civil war and interregnum* (1973) · S. W. Bates-Harbin, *Members of parliament for the county of Somerset* (1939) · Keeler, *Long Parliament* · L. Stone, *The crisis of the aristocracy, 1558–1641* (1965) · J. Collinson, *The history and antiquities of the county of Somerset*, 3 vols. (1791), vols. 2–3 · M. Kishlansky, *Parliamentary selection: social and political choice in early modern England* (1986), 85–101

Archives Som. ARS, MSS, DD/PT | Bristol RO, letters to Thomas Smyth

Likenesses E. Harding, stipple, BM, NPG; repro. in J. Adolphus, *The British cabinet*, 1 (1799) · attrib. Myttens, group portrait (with his family), Hinton House, Somerset · attrib. Van Dyck, oils · engraving

Wealth at death personalty: over £3000; realty: at least £5000, though already settled: will, PRO, PROB 11/207, sig. 45, fols. 335v–337r; M. F. Keeler, *The Long Parliament, 1640–1641: a biographical study of its members* (Philadelphia, 1954), p. 313; Som. ARS, Poulett MSS, DD/PT

Poulett, John, second Baron Poulett (c.1615–1665). *See under* Poulett, John, first Baron Poulett (1586–1649).

Poulett, John, fourth Baron and first Earl Poulett (c.1668–1743), politician, was the only son of John, third Baron Poulett (d. 1679), and his second wife, Susan, the daughter of Philip Herbert [*see under* Herbert, Philip, first earl of Montgomery and fourth earl of Pembroke (1584–1650)]. He succeeded to the barony in 1680, but only took his seat in the Lords on 24 November 1696, when under threat of committal for non-attendance. He was a tory, and a friend and supporter of Robert Harley (afterwards earl of Oxford). By licence dated 23 April 1702 he married Bridget, the only daughter and coheir of Peregrine Bertie of Waldershare, Kent, with whom he had four sons and four daughters.

On the accession of Queen Anne Poulett was appointed

lord lieutenant of Devon, and on 10 December 1702 was sworn of the privy council. He was described by Macky in 1705 as 'certainly one of the hopefullest Gentlemen in England; is very learned, virtuous, and a Man of Honour; much esteemed in the Country', although 'a mean Figure in his Person' and 'not handsome' (GEC, *Peerage*, 10.620). On 2 April 1706 he was elected FRS, and on 10 April he was appointed one of the commissioners to negotiate the treaty of union with Scotland. He was created Viscount Hinton St George and Earl Poulett on 24 December. From 8 August 1710 to 30 May 1711 he was first lord of the Treasury in Harley's administration, and from June 1711 to August 1714 he served as lord steward of the household. On 25 October 1712 he was elected, and on 4 August 1713 he was installed, KG.

Poulett seldom spoke in parliament, although he worked hard and enthusiastically as a manager between the houses, whipping up good attendances on special occasions. On 11 January 1711 he raised the issue of the reverse at Almanza, which formed the subject of the second debate on the progress of the war in Spain, and on 27 May of the following year he defended the duke of Ormond while accusing Marlborough of squandering the lives of his officers for personal gain. Marlborough challenged him to a duel, which caused him some agitation. His wife communicated the circumstance to Lord Dartmouth, who prevented the meeting by placing Poulett temporarily under arrest. He lost his places on the accession of George I, during whose reign he hardly spoke in parliament except to oppose the Septennial Bill on 14 April 1716 and the bill of pains and penalties against Atterbury on 15 May 1723. However, while Oxford was in the Tower following his impeachment, Poulett was instrumental in persuading certain peers to vote for his friend's acquittal.

During the reign of George II, Poulett lived the life of a country gentleman, but was rallied to the court party by the gift of a lord of the bedchamber's place to his eldest son, John, who entered the Lords as baron of Hinton St George on 17 January 1734. On 10 December 1742 Poulett spoke in support of the proposal to take Hanoverian troops into British pay. He died on 28 May 1743 and was buried on 3 June at Hinton St George, Somerset.

J. M. RIGG, *rev.* M. E. CLAYTON

Sources C. Jones, ed., *Party and management in parliament, 1660–1784* (1984) · G. S. Holmes, *British politics in the age of Anne* (1967) · C. Jones and D. L. Jones, eds., *Peers, politics and power: the House of Lords, 1603–1911* (1986) · I. Cassidy, 'Poulett, Hon. John (c.1641–79)', HoP, *Commons, 1660–90*, 3.268 · R. O. Bucholz, *The Augustan court: Queen Anne and the decline of court culture* (1993) · GEC, *Peerage*, new edn

Archives BL, corresp. with second Lord Oxford, Add. MS 70393
Likenesses P. Angelis, group portrait, oils, c.1713 (*Queen Anne and the Knights of the Garter, 1713*), NPG · J. M. Rysbrack, bust on monument, 1745, St George's Church, Hinton St George, Somerset · J. B. Closterman, oils (as a youth), Yale U. CBA

Poullain, Valérand (*c.*1509–1557), Reformed minister and theologian, was born in Lille, one of five children of Jacques Poullain, a Burgundian who had become a citizen of the town. He matriculated at the University of Louvain in March 1531, and by 1540 he had become a priest. In that year Charles V recommended Poullain to the bishop of Namur for a benefice. However, he was converted to the Reformation and by 1543 had taken refuge in Strasbourg. He became a firm supporter, regular correspondent, and friend of Calvin. Poullain played an important role encouraging Reformed ideas in the Netherlands, circulating two hundred copies of Calvin's *Petit traité* in 1544. When the Reformed communities of Valenciennes and Tournai appealed for a minister, Pierre Brully was dispatched, and Poullain took over responsibility for the French church in Strasbourg. However this was only a temporary role, and after Brully's arrest Poullain was rejected by the congregation, which elected Jean Garnier as their minister. In January 1545 Poullain left Strasbourg and was employed by Calvin on a mission to the archbishop of Cologne and to settle a dispute at Wesel. By 1546 he was in the service of Jacques de Bourgogne, seigneur de Falais, but Poullain became embroiled in a scandal over his promise to marry Isabelle de Haméricourt, a member of Bourgogne's entourage. Isabelle's youth and their different social status led to the case being referred to the marriage tribunal in Basel. However, by July 1547 Poullain had left Basel, possibly for Zürich. Poullain returned to Strasbourg, and in January 1548 he married a relation of Anne t Serclaes, the wife of Bishop John Hooper; their son was baptized at Frankfurt in 1554.

In the wake of the Interim of Augsburg, Charles V's attempt of 1548 to impose a religious settlement upon the Holy Roman empire, Poullain sought exile in England. Hopes of being offered a chair at Oxford were not realized, so he remained in London where he continued writing, and was also tutor to the earl of Derby's son. In 1551 the duke of Somerset established a community of Walloon protestant weavers at Glastonbury to help the local economy by introducing continental textile techniques. Poullain was appointed superintendent and minister of the community, and in December 1551 received a letter of denization. A liturgy and ecclesiastical discipline for the community were drawn up in Latin by Poullain and published in London in 1551, while two revised editions of his *Liturgia sacra* were later published in Frankfurt for the use of the community there. The work was based upon the liturgy used by the French church in Strasbourg, and also included a codification of customs similar to those which had been used there since Calvin's time. With the accession of Mary Tudor the Glastonbury community was evicted (September 1553) and Poullain returned to London, where he took part in the Westminster disputation, later publishing a translation of John Philpot's account of the meeting.

Accompanied by twenty-four families from Glastonbury, Poullain went into exile, and after travelling via Antwerp and Wesel to Cologne, in the spring of 1554 arrived at Frankfurt. The council gave them permission to settle and meet for worship in the town. However the influx of refugees to Frankfurt served to alter the character of the French congregation as well as to provoke hostility from local craftsmen, which was encouraged by the town's

Lutheran ministers. Calvin was concerned about the disputes within the French congregation, attacking Poullain's opponents as being petty and legalistic in arguing that Poullain had assumed the ministry without a proper election. As the situation deteriorated Calvin intervened directly in September 1556. A commission examined the charges against Poullain and broadly found in his favour, but there was some criticism of the minister which prompted Poullain to resign. Although the majority of the commission urged him to remain, Calvin stayed silent, and the resignation was accepted. Poullain was replaced by François Pérussel in January 1557. This caused a rift in the former's friendship with Calvin which remained unresolved at the time of Poullain's death.

Poullain remained in Frankfurt, where he entered into the heated dispute over sacramental doctrine between the Lutherans, championed by Joachim Westphal, and the Swiss reformers. His *Antidotus versus Joachim Westphal* justified the position of the stranger church, and was published in 1557 when this controversy was at its peak. Westphal quickly responded in his *Apologia adversus veneratum antidotum Valerandi Pollani*, but Poullain died in the early autumn of 1557. ANDREW SPICER

Sources P. Denis, *Les églises d'étrangers en pays rhénans, 1538–1564* (Paris, 1984) · K. Bauer, *Valérand Poullain* (1927) · A. Pettegree, *Foreign protestant communities in sixteenth-century London* (1986) · A. Pettegree, 'The London exile community and the second sacramentarian controversy', in A. Pettegree, *Marian protestantism: six studies* (1996), 55–85 · C. Rahlenbeck, 'Valérand Poullain', *Biographie nationale*, 18 (Brussels, 1904) · E. Haag and E. Haag, *La France protestante*, 10 vols. (Paris, 1846–59) · F. de Schickler, *Les églises du réfuge en Angleterre*, 3 vols. (Paris, 1892) · M.-P. Willems-Closset, 'Le protestantisme à Lille jusqu'à la veille de la révolution aux Pays-Bas, 1521–1565', *Revue du Nord*, 52 (1970), 199–216 · R. S. DuPlessis, *Lille and the Dutch revolt: urban stability in an era of revolution, 1500–1582* (1991) · H. J. Cowell, 'The French–Walloon church at Glastonbury, 1550–1553', *Proceedings of the Huguenot Society*, 13 (1923–9), 483–515 · V. Poullain, *Liturgia sacra*, ed. A. C. Honders (1970) · *Matricule de l'Université de Louvain*, 4, ed. A. Schillings (1961)

Poulson, George (1783–1858), topographer, produced his first publication, the copiously illustrated *Beverlac, or, The antiquities and history of the town of Beverley … and the collegiate establishment of St. John's*, in 1829, with the assistance of Charles Frost (1781/2–1862). This was followed by his principal work, *The history and antiquities of the seigniory of Holderness, in the East Riding of the county of York, including the abbies of Meaux and Swine, with the priories of Nunkeeling and Burstall* (1840–41). This was based on original records and the unpublished manuscripts of the Revd William Dade (1740–1790) in the library of Burton Constable, and it contains valuable, if not always accurately transcribed, material which is now lost. Poulson also edited Henry William Ball's *Social History and Antiquities of Barton-upon-Humber* (1856). He died at Barton upon Humber on 12 January 1858. THOMPSON COOPER, *rev.* WILLIAM JOSEPH SHEILS

Sources GM, 3rd ser., 4 (1858), 449 · C. R. J. Currie and C. P. Lewis, eds., *English county histories: a guide* (1994), 440–46
Archives Bodl. Oxf., corresp. relating to *Beverlac*

Poulson, John Garlick Llewellyn (1910–1993), architect and criminal, was born on 14 April 1910 at Hill Top, Knottingley, near Pontefract, Yorkshire, the elder of the two sons of Charles Ernest Austrick Poulson, an earthenware manufacturer and lay Methodist preacher, and his wife, Sarah Garlick. He was bullied by his father, and in his turn became an arrogant and insecure bully himself. He retained the stern Methodism of his upbringing, but did not absorb its lessons of moral probity. He was educated at Woodhouse Grove Methodist public school at Apperley Bridge, near Bradford, and at the Leeds School of Art, where he failed to complete the course. In 1927 he was articled to a firm of architects, Garside and Pennington (subsequently Hustler and Taylor), in Pontefract. Despite doubts about his son's talent as an architect, his father's funding enabled Poulson to open a small architectural office in Pontefract in 1932; by 1939 it had become moderately successful in the manner of small town practices. On 30 September 1939 he married Cynthia Irene Sykes (*b.* 1914/15), a teacher; they had two daughters. Excused military service on medical grounds, he used the war years to expand his practice and develop his technique of cultivating the support of people who could award work to his growing practice. With no formal training, Poulson was registered as an architect under the Architects Registration Act (1939), as previous practice was then acceptable in lieu of an architectural education. In 1942 he became a licentiate member of the Royal Institute of British Architects (RIBA).

By the late 1950s Poulson's practice, still based in Pontefract, was one of the largest in the United Kingdom, and he was recognized as a successful businessman and architect. He was responsible for the design of hospitals, shopping centres, housing, and many other buildings in Britain and abroad, including the Arndale Centre, Leeds, the redevelopment of Cannon Street Station in London, the Aviemore tourist centre in Scotland, and the Victoria Hospital at Gozo, Malta. Few are considered to have any lasting architectural merit, yet in some ways Poulson was a visionary entrepreneur in the development of his postwar practice. He was one of the first architects to see the advantages to his clients in combining in a single organization all construction professionals: architects, engineers, surveyors, and planners. This he did so effectively that his practice at its peak was the largest in the country, with 750 staff and offices in London, Middlesbrough, Newcastle, Edinburgh, Beirut, and Lagos. By the 1980s the multidisciplinary professional design practice was accepted as the best and perhaps the only way to operate a successful large international professional design consultancy. In the 1960s Poulson's company, Open System Building, offered his clients a package deal combining design with construction. (At that time involvement in commercial construction by architects was expressly forbidden by the RIBA code of conduct; by the end of the century, such involvement was not only permitted, but encouraged.)

Yet Poulson's was a flawed character. From the outset of his professional life he believed that everyone had their price, and he had the knack of knowing what it would be and how it could benefit his practice. He began before the war by bribing local councillors and businessmen (who often had small personal incomes but large public budgets). During the war he moved on to more profitable liaisons with government officials; and in the post-war construction boom Poulson's standard practice was to bribe those individuals (from peers and MPs to civil servants and local officials) who were able to grant or influence lucrative contracts. But he overreached himself, and in 1972 he filed for bankruptcy. The bankruptcy hearings exposed his practices, and in 1973 he was put on trial for corruption. It was the biggest corruption trial in the twentieth century, and ended with Poulson's conviction and eventual sentencing to seven years' imprisonment. But the ramifications were widespread: among those brought down with Poulson were civil servants (including George Pottinger, sentenced to five years), local government officials (most notably T. Dan *Smith of Newcastle, sentenced to six years), and three MPs: the Labour member Albert Roberts was severely criticized in parliament for his involvement with Poulson, the Conservative John Cordle resigned in disgrace, and Reginald Maudling, the home secretary, who had chaired two of Poulson's companies, resigned in July 1972. In total, some twenty-one people were convicted on corruption charges in connection with the case. Summing up Poulson's character, the prosecuting barrister said: 'John Poulson was an ambitious, ruthless and friendless man whose object in life was to get as much money and work as he could by bribery and corruption' (*The Independent*, 4 Feb 1993), while the judge, in passing sentence, remarked that such corruption undermined the entire system of government. Poulson served a little over three years in prison before being released on parole in May 1977. In 1981 he published a self-justificatory book, *The Price*, which was withdrawn in the face of threatened libel proceedings. He died in the General Infirmary, Pontefract, on 31 January 1993, survived by his wife and daughters.

Little political capital was made of the Poulson case, perhaps because he distributed his bribes without regard to political ideology. But he made a lasting impression on the face of British towns, particularly in the north, where old civic centres were destroyed in the name of urban improvement but often in fact to line the pockets of Poulson and his associates.   OWEN LUDER

Sources *The Times* (4 Feb 1993) · *The Independent* (4 Feb 1993) · M. Tomkinson and M. Gillard, *Nothing to declare: the political corruption of John Poulson* (1980) · R. Fitzwalter and D. Taylor, *Web of corruption: the story of John Poulson and T. Dan Smith* (1981) · E. Milne, *No shining armour: the story of one man's fight against corruption in public life* (1976) · M. Parris, *Great parliamentary scandals* (1995) · personal knowledge (2004) · private information (2004) · b. cert. · m. cert. · d. cert.
Likenesses photograph, 1972, Hult. Arch. · photograph, *c.*1973, repro. in *The Times* · photograph, *c.*1973, repro. in *The Independent*
Wealth at death £7008: probate, 20 Sept 1993, CGPLA Eng. & Wales

Poulter, John (1715?–1754), thief, was probably born in Newmarket, Suffolk. His early life is obscure, and nothing

is known of his parents, his siblings, or his education. He seems to have been married, but his wife's name is uncertain: at his trial in 1746 it was said of his co-defendant, Elizabeth Bradbury, that she 'goes for his Wife', but that 'several Women have come and claimed him for their Husband besides her' (*Old Bailey Sessions Papers*, Dec 1746); just before his execution in 1754 he asked to see his wife, who was living at Bath, but her name was not recorded. Between 1728 and 1739 he may have worked in the stables of the duke of Somerset, Lord James Cavendish, and Colonel John Lumley, the brother of the earl of Scarbrough. He may have then been a sailor on ships out of Bristol to Africa and America.

By 1746 Poulter was keeper of the Gatehouse prison in London, and in that year he was sentenced to transportation for fourteen years at the Old Bailey for receiving stolen property. He presumably sailed on the *St George* in January 1747, although if he arrived in the North American colonies he did not stay long. In 1749 he was allegedly back in England being measured for a waistcoat when a gun, which was concealed in his coat, went off. No one was injured, but the tailor, who was 'very much surprized' (*Discoveries*, 3), went to report the incident, and Poulter, well aware that returning early from transportation was a capital offence, fled to Ireland. There he may have worked in alehouses, but went back to England, probably in November 1751, when the authorities discovered that he was also involved in smuggling. Avoiding London, where he might have been recognized by one of the city's many thieftakers, he joined a gang with a relatively fluid membership, the nucleus of which came from sailors (along with their wives and partners) who fought in the 'Royal Family' squadron of privateers disbanded at the end of the War of the Austrian Succession in 1748. Although the gang operated mainly in the south and west of England, its members, including Poulter, travelled as far north as Newcastle upon Tyne, and on one occasion a horse stolen from near Marlborough was taken to Rotherham to be sold. The gang's itinerary was largely determined by the location of fairs and horse-races at which members undertook fairly elaborate confidence tricks. These journeys also enabled them to engage in opportunist thefts of items, such as luggage left unattended outside The Crown inn at Blandford and a silver tankard from The George inn at Corsham, and they occasionally robbed other travellers. The gang sought refuge in, and disposed of much of its booty at, inns across the south and west of England.

Poulter was eventually arrested and condemned to death in August 1753 at the Somerset assizes held in Wells for the robbery of Dr Hancock and his daughter on Claverton Down near Bath in February 1753. 'A lusty well-set Man, about five Feet ten Inches high … and a Scar on each cheek' (*Bath Journal*, 26 March 1753), Poulter pleaded guilty, probably because he had been led to expect a pardon in exchange for information about the gang. Indeed, although condemned to death, he was granted a respite by the trial judge, Baron Smythe, who, along with various Bath dignitaries including Richard 'Beau' Nash, supported the granting of a pardon. The respite was later extended until 1 March 1754 while he was examined and the value of his information tested. This confession was presumably the basis for *The Discoveries of John Poulter*, which was reprinted at least seventeen times between 1753 and 1779 and ensured Poulter's notoriety survived his death. Its revelations about the mobility and organization of criminal gangs, the network of receivers, the ease with which offenders could evade arrest, and the apparent futility of the sentence of transportation shocked readers, moving one to lament, 'what an extensive Scene of Combinations in Villainy, have we before our Eyes?' (*Letter to a Member of Parliament*). It also contains a cant dictionary which has proved an invaluable source for lexicographers. Eventually the government decided there was not sufficient justification for a pardon, and, although Poulter made accusations against almost fifty people, no one seems to have been convicted on his evidence. Shortly after hearing that he was to hang, Poulter escaped from the prison at Ilchester. He headed for Wales, presumably with the intention of going to Ireland, but got hopelessly lost. Tired and hungry he stumbled into The Ring-of-Bells inn at Wookey, Somerset, where he was recognized and arrested. On his return to prison, the gaoler, who ran the risk of a fine whenever a prisoner escaped, and the local people petitioned for the date of the execution to be brought forward. The government agreed and Poulter was hanged in Ilchester on 25 February 1754, probably at Gallows Five Acres on the west side of the Yeovil Road. It was reported that at the place of execution he declared the truth of the declarations published in *The Discoveries of John Poulter*.   PHILIP RAWLINGS

Sources *The discoveries of John Poulter*, 9th edn (1754) · *Devon, (to wit) the voluntary information, examination, and confession of John Poulter* (1753) · *A further information, examination, and confession of John Poulter* (1753) · P. Rawlings, *Drunks, whores and idle apprentices: criminal biographies of the eighteenth century* (1992), 139–77 · *A letter to a member of parliament, upon the subject of the present reigning enormities of murders and robberies* (1754)

Archives PRO, petition for mercy, SP 36/123, pt 2, fols. 11–12, 43–4

Poulton, Sir Edward Bagnall (1856–1943), zoologist, was born at Reading on 27 January 1856, the second child and only son of William Ford Poulton, architect, and his wife, Georgina Selina Bagnall. From a young age he showed a keen interest in natural history, and especially in entomology. However, such interests were not encouraged at Oakley House, Reading, and school was 'a long dreary interval in a happy life' (Carpenter, 665). In addition, his father wished him to become an architect, and only reluctantly allowed him to study science. In 1873 Poulton won a scholarship at Jesus College, Oxford, where he was placed in the first class in natural science in 1876 and where he was president of the union in 1879.

In 1876 Poulton became a demonstrator in comparative anatomy under George Rolleston, whose brilliant lectures had greatly inspired him. However, the inadequacy of his salary led to him to accept the Burdett-Coutts scholarship in geology in 1878—as a result of which he worked for a time under Joseph Prestwich. Thus it came about that his first published researches, in 1880, were on Tertiary remains in a Yorkshire cave. However, geology was not a passion, and he returned to zoology later in 1880 with an appointment as lecturer at Jesus and Keble colleges. The following year he married Emily (*d.* 1939), eldest daughter of George *Palmer, biscuit manufacturer and Liberal member of parliament for Reading; they had two sons and three daughters. Poulton quickly attracted attention at Oxford by morphological studies on the tongues of marsupials and by discovering in the embryos of the duck-billed platypus (*Ornithorhynchus*) the rudiments of teeth. His last work on vertebrate zoology, in 1894, was a paper on the bill and hairs of *Ornithorhynchus*, with a discussion of the homologies and origin of mammalian hair.

Poulton's first entomological paper appeared in 1884— on his favourite subject, the colours, markings, and protective attitudes of caterpillars. His interest in this was stimulated by finding that some observations he had made as a boy were in accord with the studies of August Weismann. Throughout his life he emphasized the need for observation of the living insect, especially its behaviour. He wrote a series of papers on insects that alter their coloration to camouflage themselves. Essays by A. R. Wallace turned his attention to the importance of protective colouring in all its forms, concealing, warning, and mimetic, and this is the subject of which he became the foremost exponent.

As a student Poulton had been warned off Darwinism by John Obadiah Westwood, leading entomologist and first Hope professor of zoology at Oxford, because it was too speculative. But under the inspiration of Wallace and Weismann, Poulton made the study of evolution more rigorous by using both careful fieldwork and experiments to analyse adaptation. These methods advanced a newer ecological approach to the study of evolution. Poulton argued for the importance of natural selection as the main mechanism of evolution and, like Weismann, attacked the neo-Lamarckian theory that acquired characteristics could be inherited. He publicized Weismann's work, helping to arrange the publication of *Essays upon Heredity and Kindred Biological Subjects* (1889), translated from Weismann's original text. In 1890 Poulton produced *The Colours of Animals*, which concisely and simply explained the many forms of coloration in terms of natural selection; these forms he ingeniously summarized in a comparative table introducing terms which became the standard nomenclature.

The Royal Society elected Poulton a fellow in 1889, and in 1893 he was appointed Hope professor of zoology at Oxford. Over the next forty years he corresponded with many naturalists who, stimulated by his enthusiasm, sent to Oxford the large collections which greatly aided him in the study of warning colours and mimicry, especially in tropical Africa.

While Poulton always emphasized the need for observation and experiment in the field, he often found it possible to make important deductions from museum specimens. His explanation of the extraordinary differences, found in African *Precis* butterflies, between the forms occurring in wet or dry seasons was a good example of his careful work. He showed that the form appearing in the dry season, the period of greatest danger to the individual insect, while better concealed than the wet season form, could be seen to be derived from it if the minute details of pattern were carefully traced. Such seasonal forms had hitherto been classed as distinct species, until Guy Anstruther Knox Marshall, in 1898, bred one from the other. Poulton's self-revealing comment on this was:

> Under the shock of Mr. Marshall's discovery … the systematist may well feel doubts about the foundations upon which his science has been erected. In these distracting circumstances a firm belief in natural selection will be found to exercise a wonderfully calming and steadying influence. (Cited in Carpenter, 668)

Poulton also became deeply interested in the study of the wide variations of African mimetic butterflies collected in localities where the species mimicked were much less common than the mimickers. He put forward the suggestion that natural selection was here in abeyance. Mimicry is not maintained in the absence of the models because there is no greater selective pressure upon one variant than upon another. It was a bionomic discovery that gave Poulton great pleasure. As a Darwinian he was greatly interested in sexual selection, and under his influence much knowledge was gained of the courtship of insects and of the special structures used for that purpose.

After 1900 two new theories, the mutation theory of Hugo de Vries and Mendelian theory, appeared to challenge the Darwinian idea of origin of species by selection of small variations. Poulton disagreed vehemently with the way the proponents of these new theories disparaged traditional lines of research in natural history. He argued that Mendelism merely extended ideas advanced by Weismann, and hence was not an abrupt departure from Darwinism. His critique of the limitations of the new science was published as an introduction to his collection of papers, *Essays on Evolution, 1889–1907* (1908). Starting in 1913 Poulton began a debate with Reginald C. Punnett, who used Mendelian theory to explain mimicry. Poulton emphasized the compatibility between Darwinism and Mendelism. His work on mimicry influenced Ronald Aylmer Fisher, a founder of theoretical population genetics. Fisher developed the ecological genetics of mimicry in collaboration with Edmund B. Ford, who had been Poulton's student in the 1920s.

Wide recognition came to Poulton as a leader. He was a vice-president of the Royal Society for 1909–10 and its Darwin medallist in 1914. He presided over the Linnean Society of London from 1912 to 1916 and was awarded the Linnean medal in 1922. He was three times president of the Entomological Society of London, which elected him honorary life president in 1933 when the title 'Royal' was conferred upon it. The second International Congress of Entomology met under his guidance in 1912, as did the Association of Economic (later Applied) Biologists in 1922–3. He was for many years a member of the British Association, and he presided over it in 1937, having been

president of the zoology section in 1931. He was a commander of the Swedish order of the Pole Star, and an honorary member of many foreign learned societies. The universities of Reading, Durham, Dublin, and Princeton conferred honorary degrees upon him; he was knighted in 1935. He died at his home, Wykeham House, 56 Banbury Road, Oxford, on 20 November 1943. The only child to survive him was his second daughter. The elder son, Edward Palmer Poulton, a distinguished physician, was on the staff of Guy's Hospital. The younger son, Ronald William *Poulton, who took the name Poulton-Palmer, was a famous rugby football blue and international; he was killed in action in the First World War.

G. D. H. CARPENTER, *rev.*

Sources G. D. H. Carpenter, *Obits. FRS*, 4 (1942–4), 655–80 · W. C. Kimler, 'Poulton, Edward Bagnall', *DSB*, suppl., 18.721–7 · E. B. Poulton, *John Viriamu Jones and other Oxford memories* (1911) · personal knowledge (1959) · *CGPLA Eng. & Wales* (1944)
Archives Linn. Soc., corresp. and notes · Oxf. U. Mus. NH, Hope Library, corresp., diaries, and notes · RBG Kew, corresp. · Royal Entomological Society of London, corresp. and papers as editor of Royal Entomological Society journals | Oxf. U. Mus. NH, corresp. with W. A. S. Lambourn · Oxf. U. Mus. NH, letters to Robert McLachlan · Royal Entomological Society of London, corresp. with Herbert Druce · Royal Entomological Society of London, entomological and genealogical letters to C. J. Wainwright · UCL, letters to Sir Francis Galton · University of Bristol Library, letters to Conwy Lloyd Morgan
Likenesses F. A. de Biden Footner, portrait, priv. coll. · W. Rothenstein, drawing, Jesus College, Oxford · photograph, repro. in S. A. Neave, *The history of the Entomological Society of London, 1833–1933* (1933), frontispiece
Wealth at death £16,258 10s. 4d.: probate, 17 Aug 1944, *CGPLA Eng. & Wales*

Poulton [*later* Poulton-Palmer], **Ronald William** (1889–1915), rugby player, was born at Wykeham House, Oxford, on 12 September 1889, the second son and fourth of the five children of Edward Bagnall *Poulton (1856–1943), Hope professor of zoology in the University of Oxford, and his wife, Emily, *née* Palmer (*d.* 1939). He was educated at Oxford preparatory school and Rugby School before in 1908 entering Balliol College, Oxford, from where he graduated in 1911 with a second-class honours degree in engineering.

In one of English rugby's most successful periods, Poulton was perhaps its most gifted and charismatic player. He won three blues (1909–11) for Oxford University and played seventeen times (1909–14) for England; he captained the team in four matches in 1914. His club rugby was played for Harlequins (1908–13) and Liverpool (1913–14). Poulton's unorthodox style of three-quarter play was known to confuse team-mates as well as opponents: one team-mate recalled, 'Hanged if I ever knew where he was going' (Sewell, *Rugger*, 78). This unpredictability, which made it difficult to fit him into a team pattern, cost Poulton a blue in 1908, his first year at Oxford. His devastating attacking abilities were shown in subsequent years. The game against Cambridge in 1909 is remembered as 'Poulton's match' (Frost, 44) for his five tries, a record for the fixture. He scored a total of eight tries in three matches against Cambridge. England were quicker to accommodate unpredictable brilliance. He was capped in 1909, only a few weeks after his exclusion by Oxford. In 1913 and 1914 he was the outstanding individual in the first team to win all four five nations' internationals in consecutive seasons. He scored eight tries and one dropped goal, a total of 28 points, for England.

Tall by the standards of his time (5 feet 11 inches) and fair-haired, Poulton was described as having 'a curiously even, yet high-stepping motion; his head thrown back, the ball held in front at full arm's length' (Poulton, 169). His effectiveness rested on deception rather than pure speed. The Welsh journalist W. J. T. Collins called him 'a man apart' with 'a quality of unexpectedness which played havoc with the defence' (Collins, 167). One opponent asked 'How can one stop him when his head goes one way, his arms another and his legs keep straight on?' (Poulton, 211).

His close friend William Temple, later archbishop of Canterbury, described Poulton as having a 'wonderful buoyancy and freedom from self-consciousness' (Poulton, 8) and 'a genius for evoking affection' (ibid., 5). At the same time Poulton was serious-minded, with a strong interest in the Boys' Club movement. His politics were Liberal and his bequests included one to the Workers' Educational Association. In 1912 he argued publicly that rugby union's rules on professionalism effectively excluded working-class players, writing that 'rugby is too good a game to be confined to any particular class' (Poulton, 214).

On leaving Oxford, Poulton went to work for the family firm, the biscuit manufacturers Huntley and Palmer, and spent several months training as an engineer with Mather and Platt in Manchester. His change of name in 1914 to Poulton-Palmer followed the death, in October 1913, of his uncle George William Palmer, a member of the biscuit manufacturing firm and Liberal MP for Reading, who left him an annual income of £4000. A territorial member of the Royal Berkshire regiment from June 1912, Poulton-Palmer was called up as a lieutenant on the outbreak of war in August 1914 and sent to the front in Flanders on 30 March 1915. He was killed by sniper fire in Ploegsteert Wood, near Armentières, in the early hours of 5 May 1915 and buried the following day in the Berkshire cemetery there. He never married. Among the most memorable figures in the 'lost generation' destroyed in the First World War, he was commemorated in a biography by his father, published in 1919.   HUW RICHARDS

Sources E. B. Poulton, *The life of Ronald Poulton by his father* (1919) · E. H. D. Sewell, *Rugby football international roll of honour* (1919) · E. H. D. Sewell, *Rugger: the man's game*, rev. O. L. Owen, 3rd edn (1950) · D. Frost, *The Bowring story of the varsity match* (1988) · W. J. T. Collins, *Rugby recollections* (1948) · M. G. Brock, epilogue, *Hist. U. Oxf.* 7: *19th-cent. Oxf.* pt 2
Likenesses photographs, repro. in Poulton, *Life*
Wealth at death £22,310 0s. 7d.: probate, 22 June 1915, *CGPLA Eng. & Wales*

Pouncey, Philip Michael Rivers (1910–1990), art connoisseur, was born in Oxford on 15 February 1910, the second of the three sons (there were no daughters) of the Revd George Ernest Pouncey, a bank manager who had decided to take holy orders, and his second wife, Madeline Mary, daughter of Albin Roberts, cloth-maker. He was educated at Marlborough College and at Queens' College, Cambridge, where he obtained a third class in part one (1930) and a second (division two) in part two (1931) of the English tripos. He then worked as a volunteer in the Fitzwilliam Museum, Cambridge, until 1934, when he was appointed assistant keeper in the National Gallery, London. He began by working on the catalogue of fourteenth-century Italian paintings, but as successive volumes of the catalogue (all published after he left the gallery) show, his interests extended over the entire Italian school.

In the latter part of the Second World War Pouncey was seconded to the Government Code and Cypher School at Bletchley Park, but for the first two years he was in charge of that part of the National Gallery collection moved for safety to the National Library of Wales at Aberystwyth. The drawings from the British Museum print room and the Royal Library at Windsor were also there under the care of A. E. Popham, then deputy keeper of the print room, who took the opportunity of starting work on the catalogues of the Italian drawings in both collections. As problems arose Popham discussed them with two eminent art historians, Johannes Wilde and Frederick Antal, then also in Aberystwyth. Pouncey naturally took part in these discussions and realized that drawings, surviving as they have in far larger numbers than paintings and posing more difficult problems of attribution, offered greater scope for his particular gift for connoisseurship.

After the war he accordingly transferred to the British Museum and continued, now on an official basis, to collaborate with Popham on the catalogue of Italian drawings. The first volume, of fourteenth- and fifteenth-century drawings of all schools, appeared in 1950. Two later volumes, both in collaboration with J. A. Gere, were *Raphael and his Circle* (1962) and *Artists Working in Rome, c.1550–c.1640* (1983). In 1954 he became deputy keeper, but succession to the keepership was blocked and he would have had to retire at sixty. The prospect of freedom from official routine and of again working with paintings led him in 1966 to join Sothebys as a director, but he kept in close touch with his old department and continued to work there regularly on the third volume of the catalogue.

While still at Marlborough, Pouncey had studied the classic history of Italian Renaissance painting (1864–71) by Sir Joseph Crowe and G. B. Cavalcaselle. This pioneer work was the first to survey the field in a spirit of rigorous scientific enquiry, taking into account all available evidence, both documentary and stylistic. Pouncey's approach was similarly untheoretical and matter-of-fact. He saw the subject in terms of the complex interaction of a host of individual artistic personalities whose identification was the primary duty of the historian. His approach was that of connoisseurship; he held that no critical generalization about an artist can be valid until his *œuvre* is correctly defined.

In the drawing-cabinets of Europe and the USA perplexed students see with relief inscriptions in his familiar neat handwriting. (It is estimated that in the Louvre alone he restored some 500 Italian drawings to their proper authors.) These annotations and his carefully indexed notes constitute the principal record of his life's work. Apart from the three British Museum catalogues, his publications were limited to short articles dealing with specific points, usually of attribution, and an occasional review (including a *tour de force*, of the 1964 Italian edition of Bernard Berenson's *The Drawings of the Florentine Painters*). His one monograph, on the drawings of Lorenzo Lotto (1965), is an essay of only fifteen pages, but in them the essential facts are stated with concise clarity. His reluctance to publish was more than offset by the number and importance of his discoveries and by the encouraging generosity with which he always shared them with fellow students. A French friend described 'son allure juvénile et son air latin'. In spite of his solidly English descent, there was something *méridional* about his dark hair and pale lively features, his rapid speech, and flashing brown eyes—an effect in no way diminished by his invariable London uniform of dark suit, bowler hat, and high stiff collar.

In 1937 Pouncey married Myril, daughter of Colonel Albert Gros, a staff officer in the French army. She shared all his interests, and was felicitously described in an obituary notice as 'wife and colleague'. They had twin daughters, one of whom married Dr Marco Chiarini, director of the Galleria Palatina (Palazzo Pitti) in Florence. In 1975 Pouncey was elected a fellow of the British Academy and in 1987 he was appointed CBE. His seventy-fifth birthday was celebrated at the Fitzwilliam Museum (where he was honorary keeper of Italian drawings from 1975) by a loan exhibition of his reattributions; and after his death at his house, 5 Lower Addison Gardens, Kensington, London, on 12 November 1990, he received the unique distinction of being similarly honoured by the Louvre (1992), the Uffizi (1992), and the British Museum (1994). He left an estate valued at £6,493,705.   J. A. GERE, *rev.*

Sources J. A. Gere, 'Philip Pouncey, 1910–1990', *PBA*, 76 (1990), 530–44 · *The Independent* (16 Nov 1990) · *The Times* (20 Nov 1990) · *Art Newspaper* (Dec 1990) · *WWW, 1981–90* · *CGPLA Eng. & Wales* (1991)
Likenesses photograph, repro. in Gere, 'Philip Pouncey', 536
Wealth at death £6,493,705: probate, 29 July 1991, *CGPLA Eng. & Wales*

Pouncy, Benjamin Thomas (*d.* 1799), draughtsman and engraver, may have studied engraving with his father, Edward Pouncy. He was certainly a pupil of William Woollett, and is said (in the *Gentleman's Magazine* of 1799) to have been his brother-in-law; his wife's name was Ann. Pouncy's place and date of birth are unknown but the evidence of his work and a portrait of him by Henry Edridge in the British Museum indicate a birth date of about 1750. He was one of a group of London-based artists with Kentish associations which included Woollett, Thomas Hearne, William Alexander, and Edridge.

Pouncy has been described as 'a feeble draughtsman' (Grant, 163), but his topographical watercolours are of a high quality. Among a number of Kentish views shown by him at the Society of Artists and Royal Academy exhibitions between 1772 and 1789 was *The Gate of Dandelion, Near Margate* (exh. RA, 1788), a subject also drawn by Alexander, Edridge, and the young Turner. Pouncy's picture is most probably the watercolour exhibited as *A Haycart Approaching a Castle Gateway* in London in 1978 at Agnew's annual exhibition of watercolours and drawings. A group of watercolours by him is in the collection of the Kent Archaeological Society, and there are good examples in the Fitzwilliam Museum, Cambridge, the Whitworth Art Gallery, Manchester, and the Victoria and Albert Museum. A large *View of Margate Harbour* in the British Museum shows him to have been a highly accomplished master of the gentle pencil, pen, and watercolour wash technique so popular with topographical artists towards the end of the eighteenth century.

As a printmaker Pouncy produced large reproductive plates imitative of the style of Woollett, plates to illustrate a number of antiquarian and travel books, and some etchings and engravings after his own designs. The large plates are of classical, landscape, and seascape themes after such artists as Richard Wilson, Solomon Delane, and Robert Cleveley. His technique of overlaying line engraving on an etched design is identical to Woollett's, and several plates, such as an *Apollo and the Seasons* (1777), after Wilson and John Hamilton Mortimer (held in the British Museum), are collaborative enterprises, Pouncy having engraved the landscape and Woollett the figures. In the 1770s Pouncy formed a link with Lambeth and provided architectural and archaeological illustrations for the historian Andrew Coltee Ducarel, the librarian at Lambeth Palace. One of his earliest Lambeth works is his illustration of the *Monument of John Tradescant* in St Mary's churchyard, dated 1773, for John Nichols's *Bibliotheca Topographica Britannica* (1782–8). After this date he worked regularly for Ducarel, although he did not live in Lambeth until 1780 and it is not clear whether he was ever employed as a member of staff at Lambeth Palace Library.

Pouncy's steady hand and keen eye for detail were also well employed in the production of facsimile illustrations—some of his copies of medieval manuscripts for Thomas Astle's *The Origin and Progress of Writing* (1784) being of exceptional quality. Towards the end of his life he engraved some of the finest plates to Sir George Staunton's *An Authentic Account of an Embassy from the King of Great Britain to the Emperor of China* (1797), after drawings by William Alexander. The engraver and watercolourist Joseph Powell (*fl.* 1796–1833) gave his address 'At Mr Pouncey's, Pratt Street, Lambeth' in 1797, and may therefore have been a pupil of the artist. Pouncy died at this address on 22 August 1799 and was buried in the churchyard of St Mary's, Lambeth. Witnesses to his will were Joseph Powell and Elizabeth Woollett.   SUSAN SLOMAN

Sources *GM*, 1st ser., 69 (1799), 726 · L. A. Fagan, *A catalogue raisonné of the engraved works of William Woollett* (1885) · Mallalieu, *Watercolour artists* · PRO, PROB 11/1333, fols. 100–01 · M. Hardie, *Water-colour painting in Britain*, ed. D. Snelgrove, J. Mayne, and B. Taylor, 1: *The eighteenth century* (1966) · I. O. Williams, *Early English watercolours and some cognate drawings by artists born not later than 1785* (1952) · S. Legouix, *Image of China: William Alexander* (1980) · Graves, *Soc. Artists* · Graves, *RA exhibitors* · M. H. Grant, *A dictionary of British etchers* (1952) · Nichols, *Lit. anecdotes* · private information

(2004) [Robin Myers] • private information (2004) [R. J. Palmer, LPL]

Archives BM • FM Cam. • V&A

Likenesses H. Edridge, pencil and ink wash drawing, BM

Pound, Sir (Alfred) Dudley Pickman Rogers (1877–1943), naval officer, was born on 29 August 1877 at Park View, Wroxall, Isle of Wight, the eldest child of Alfred John Pound, barrister, and his wife, Elizabeth Pickman, daughter of Richard Saltonstall Rogers of Boston, Massachusetts. Pound received most of his early education at Fonthill School in East Grinstead. In his youth he enjoyed riding and fishing, and had enough family connections to receive an offer from an uncle to find a place for him in the firm of Pierpont Morgan. But close proximity to the sea and the lure of a more glamorous career proved a stronger call. In January 1891 Pound entered the Royal Naval College, Dartmouth, as a cadet, embarking on a lifelong career as a naval officer.

Early career Varied service, ranging from China to the channel, from the training squadron under sail to specialization as a torpedo officer and service at the Admiralty, led to promotion to commander at the age of thirty-two in June 1909. Along the way Pound made useful friendships as he expanded his range of experience. His next notable appointment was as instructor at the new Naval Staff College in 1913, where he first encountered a most important factor in his advancement: fate. By accepting an offer from William Fisher to become his commander in the battleship *St Vincent*, Pound found himself at sea under a useful patron when the First World War broke out. Promoted captain in December 1914, he served at the Admiralty in the first half of 1915 as second naval assistant to the first sea lord, the pugnacious 'Jackie' Fisher. Pound thus saw at first hand the titanic struggle between his masters, as Fisher squared off with the first lord, Winston Churchill, in a battle that saw both men ousted from office. Pound surely drew some conclusions about how not to handle ministers, in particular Churchill, which years later he would find useful.

Later that year Pound returned to sea as flag captain of the Grand Fleet, in the battleship *Colossus*. In that vessel he fought in the battle of Jutland on 31 May 1916, being commended for his service that day. Then in 1917 fate again brought Pound back to the fast track with an appointment that marked him out for future high command. He was selected to launch what became in due course the plans division of the Admiralty, charged with foreseeing and thinking out operations and problems that the navy might have to face. This was the first such division dedicated to this important task, a major step in the modernization of the navy, and it was a feather in Pound's cap to secure the billet. He soon moved on, at the end of 1917, to be director of operations (home), where he ended what was for him personally a very good war.

Pound's subsequent peacetime career followed the pattern laid down for those being considered for the very top positions in the navy, a mixture of staff, shore, and sea appointments. In 1920 he took command of the battle

Sir (Alfred) Dudley Pickman Rogers Pound (1877–1943), by unknown photographer

cruiser *Repulse*. In 1922 he returned to the Admiralty as director of the plans division. In 1925 he was named chief of staff to Lord Keyes, who was now the commander-in-chief, Mediterranean Fleet; in that appointment Pound was promoted to flag rank in March 1926. He then spent two more years in the Admiralty as assistant chief of naval staff from 1927 to 1929. He returned to sea in May 1929 to command the battle-cruiser squadron of the Atlantic Fleet. Detached service as a naval representative to the ill-fated general conference on disarmament in 1932 helped bring Pound back to the Admiralty in August of that year as second sea lord. He was appointed KCB in 1933.

This mix of appointments in a dozen years gave Pound both the sea time he needed to round out his qualifications for high command and staff appointments that brought him in touch with all the great naval and international issues of the time: the naval limitation negotiations, naval aviation, imperial defence, the future of capital ships, to name a few. He succeeded well enough all around to be nominated in September 1935 for one of the two most coveted commands in the service, as commander-in-chief, Mediterranean Fleet.

The Dudley Pound who accepted this attractive appointment was by now a seasoned 58-year-old full admiral, a character and personality developed through forty-five years of service. The most marked feature of that character was Pound's total dedication to the navy. In 1908 he had married Bessie Caroline Grace (*d.* 1943), daughter of John Livesay Whitehead, a physician from Ventnor, Isle of Wight. Their married life was apparently happy but little is known of it; references to his wife note how much she helped him and the service but little else. They had a daughter and two sons, the older of whom followed his father into the Royal Navy, while the younger took a commission in the Royal Marines. Pound continued to enjoy fishing and now also shooting, but as he rose in rank and responsibility took less and less time off to indulge these interests. The picture seems clear: for this man, the navy was his life. In that service he was seen as sharp but not brilliant, an indefatigable worker, a good listener, a driver rather than a delegator, and above all utterly loyal to his superiors. He had an immense capacity for work and revelled in carrying out in hands-on fashion even the myriad duties of higher appointments. Personally, colleagues found him serious, reserved, not hard to work with but difficult to befriend. Subordinates respected rather than idolized him, many remembering the care he took to look after their interests, enquire after their families, and nurture their careers. Pound seems to have had limited social graces and narrow intellectual horizons. His sense of fun, such as it was, emerged in his other passion: driving automobiles at breakneck speed, especially with a passenger aboard to be suitably unnerved. The image that emerges is of a thorough but narrow professional, entering the service too young and throwing himself into it too completely to develop a fully rounded character.

It would be quite wrong to see Pound as personally ambitious. For all his faults, he consistently put the service before himself. That was made clear when he offered to delay his appointment to the Mediterranean command in order not to disrupt the fleet; the change of command coincided with the onset of the international crisis provoked by Italy's attack on Ethiopia. Pound acted as chief of staff to Fisher until finally assuming command in March 1936, a situation which must have had awkward moments with two full admirals on the scene but had no apparent repercussions. Pound gave further evidence that personal ambition did not consume him when in 1938 he calmly received the news that he was not seen as a probable first sea lord. Given a choice, he opted to take the offer of a one-year extension in command in the Mediterranean, followed by retirement, rather than a transfer to one of the home port commands for a final three years. As commander-in-chief, Mediterranean, Pound enjoyed perhaps his happiest years in the navy, relentlessly training his fleet for war by leading from the bridge as much as possible. When the fleet was handed over to the command of Andrew Browne Cunningham, he noted that it was 'in great fettle and obviously in a high state of efficiency' (Cunningham, 207). It was left to Cunningham to take this fleet to war while fate, in one last twist, brought Pound to the summit of his service after all.

First sea lord A succession of untimely deaths and disabilities left Pound the only possible choice for an appointment the navy had not intended him to assume. Concerns about his physical fitness, his perceived inability to see different sides to a question, and his tendency to take too much into his own hands all had to be set aside when he emerged as the only senior admiral with the range and depth of experience to become the professional head of the service. Pound took office as first sea lord and chief of the naval staff in June 1939, being promoted to admiral of the fleet the next month. Within two months events forced him to lead the navy into the Second World War. The rest of his life was taken up by the demanding job which made him a figure of historical significance, directing the senior service in a global total war which stretched it beyond its strength almost from the start.

Pound was *ex officio* a major figure in the central direction of the war as a member of the chiefs of staff committee. It is also fair to say that the strain upon him was greater than that on his army and air force counterparts, for two reasons. First, the war at sea knew no boundaries and only from the centre could it be co-ordinated, the Admiralty acting as an operational headquarters and intervening directly in battle by issuing orders to fleets at sea. Second, geography pushed the Royal Navy to the forefront of both the defence of the home islands and any attempt to carry the war to the enemy. In these circumstances anyone holding Pound's appointment would have become a controversial figure in history. For most of his tenure the allies seemed to be losing the war. As professional head of the navy he had to take or be involved in decisions which many feel aggravated rather than reversed that trend; this plus his own personality and deportment made Pound a uniquely controversial first sea lord. Three themes dominated his direction of the navy in total war: his role in British grand strategy, his role in the conduct of fleet operations, and his working relationship with Churchill.

As a maker of grand strategy it cannot be said that Pound ever developed a broad outlook or mastered the challenge of seeing problems from other than a naval perspective. On the other hand, he understood that the maritime war must be related to a co-ordinated grand strategy. Colleagues from other services noted, sometimes in exasperation, how stolidly Pound argued any naval brief and how completely prepared he was to weigh in with the naval perspective on any broader issue. Yet his own subordinates sometimes became frustrated at the first sea lord's insistence on reaching a consensus among the chiefs of staff, even at times by making compromises the naval staff considered uncomfortable. But not even his fiercest critics ever denied that he saw from the start the foundation of the maritime dimension of grand strategy: in Pound's own words, 'if we lose the Battle of the Atlantic we lose the war' (Barnett, 460). The struggle to secure the lifeline by which alone the United Kingdom could be maintained, and any great counter-offensive prepared, never strayed from the centre of his efforts to contribute to the central direction of the war.

The degree to which Pound contributed to a war-winning grand strategy remains a complicated question. The major complication was the relative weakness of the Royal Navy, indeed of British empire forces in general, after the defeat of France in June 1940. Forced now to cope with an expanded surface and submarine threat in the Atlantic, the imminent threat of invasion of the homeland, a new war in the Mediterranean, and possible trouble in the Far East, Pound became markedly cautious. He had to be persuaded to drop a call to abandon the eastern Mediterranean, which secured the Suez Canal and the vital oil supplies of the Middle East, before any direct threat even materialized. Despite his emphasis on the battle of the Atlantic, Pound for too long did not do all he might have done to master that struggle. Not until November 1942 did he appoint a really first-rate commander—Admiral Sir Max Horton—to take charge of the pivotal convoy struggle. Above all he allowed the all-important struggle to secure more effective support from the Royal Air Force to drag on so long as to threaten the whole war effort.

Burdens of leadership Nevertheless Pound won the confidence, respect, and even friendship of his chiefs of staff colleagues, and was generous enough to make way as chairman of the committee when it became clear the chief of the Imperial General Staff, Alan Brooke, would be more effective. Yet that in itself also indicated that Pound could not translate his understanding of the need to work together into anything more helpful than an ever more defensive emphasis on naval problems. Nor did Pound prove very successful in helping to direct global coalition warfare when the entry of the United States into the war led to the formation of the combined chiefs of staff. He did not really win the confidence of his American opposite number, Admiral Ernest J. King—admittedly a difficult task for any British naval officer—and the combined efforts of the two navies to secure a determined commitment to the Atlantic convoy battle as a priority in grand strategy suffered as a result. Not until early 1943 did the battle at last receive the definitive priority, and the air support, that it required. But the most frequent criticism of Pound as grand strategist is that he was too much the navy man, while his most dangerous failure was to take too long to secure full national commitment to the navy's most vital campaign. As a result, only one conclusion seems fair: as a grand strategist, Pound was barely adequate.

One important mitigating factor was the fact that Pound had the heaviest burden to carry among the chiefs of staff. The tension between fleet commanders at sea wanting to run their own show and a first sea lord at home feeling the responsibility on his shoulders and wanting to play a direct role in operations was nothing new. It was almost assumed wisdom in the Royal Navy that seniority conferred greater insight as well as authority, and only the Admiralty could see the 'full picture'. The fact that Pound and the Admiralty often enjoyed the advantage of more reliable information, provided especially by signals intelligence, only reinforced this assumption. On occasion it was not unjustified, as for example during the hunt for the German battleship *Bismarck*. But there seems little doubt that Pound was predisposed, by personality as well as naval tradition, to take too much into his own hands. One critic went as far as to argue that he 'ran the Navy as if he were the executive officer of a ship' (Barnett, 732).

Pound's style in running the Admiralty displayed his strengths and weaknesses. He commanded the respect of his subordinates and helped train his wartime staff to a high level of efficiency; if anything he became too comfortable with them, and was reluctant to suffer changes in his entourage. Nor did he ever shirk from taking personal responsibility for Admiralty decisions great or small, regardless of what advice he received. But it must be said that his inability to delegate was a serious mistake, given the sheer scope and strain of his responsibilities. He blocked the appointment of a deputy chief of the naval staff until July 1942, too long for his stamina to hold up against the strain of the job. His principal fleet commanders respected the frankness with which he discussed matters with them and enjoyed generally satisfactory personal relations with him, but came for the most part to resent what they regarded as his undue and unwise interference in fleet operations.

As a fighting admiral Pound reflected the conventional wisdom of the navy and adjusted to the lessons of war with reasonable promptness. He entered the war still focused on the dominance of the capital ship and the big gun, paying not enough attention to air weapons and the submarine. But his confidence in the ability of surface vessels to defend themselves against aircraft did not survive the Norway campaign of spring 1940. By 1941 the first sea lord was at least rating the need for stronger anti-submarine forces as of equal importance to maintaining the battlefleet. And only one direct intervention by Pound in an ongoing operation at sea can really be argued to have led to avoidable disaster. The decision to scatter convoy PQ17 in July 1942 on the basis of negative intelligence—the fear that the battleship *Tirpitz* might be at sea on its trail in the absence of confirmation by signals intelligence that it was not—did indeed show Pound at his worst. He never really grasped the limitations of signals intelligence nor how best to apply it, made up his mind too rigidly and readily in the face of conflicting advice, and overruled the commander on the spot without adequate justification. But other heavy defeats suffered by the Royal Navy were not directly attributable to intervention by the first sea lord. The sinking of the *Hood* hit all as a shock, the decision to send force Z to Singapore was taken over Pound's fierce opposition, and the heavy losses suffered by the Mediterranean Fleet in 1941 did not result from Admiralty intervention. The broadly critical reception of Pound as operations supervisor stemmed more from the general pattern of his behaviour than any specific cases, from the manner of his day-to-day handling of fleet operations and orders from the top which taken in sum unsettled the fleet. Perhaps the single most important cause of this perception was the problem that amounted to Pound's most important challenge and heavily affected all his other tasks: his working relationship with Churchill.

Handling Churchill Pound had to answer to the most self-confident and interventionist political master any first sea lord has ever worked for. Churchill worked hard to maintain control of the broad direction of grand strategy in his own hands, and constantly involved himself in fleet operations even to the point of issuing orders and instructions personally to fleet commanders. The struggle to help harness the positive energy of this human dynamo yet prevent him from making impulsive decisions that might lead to disaster, or meddling in operations to the point where the fleet had no idea to whom it answered nor confidence in its direction, may have been Pound's greatest contribution to victory. Yet it is in his pattern of 'handling' Churchill that many at the time and since found the cause of Pound's most serious errors.

In general Pound's approach to handling Churchill was never to oppose any idea or suggestion directly unless there was absolutely no other choice. Unwise proposals would be sent to an irritated and overworked staff to be examined thoroughly, while the first sea lord carried on a slow lobby of suggestion to lead his master to safer ground. Pound tried to strike a balance, to let Churchill vent his frustration on matters not vital, to shield subordinates as much as possible without provoking an open dispute with the prime minister, and to keep control of the maritime war yet retain the confidence of his mercurial boss. This led to subordinates such as Cunningham and James Somerville being shaken in their faith in Pound when they were badgered by unfair telegrams from the top, and there were whispers that sometimes Pound let his personal feelings get in the way when he allowed someone to be damaged by prime ministerial wrath. But Pound never allowed Churchill to remove someone in whom he had confidence, and usually prevented him from changing strategy when he disagreed.

On some crucial matters Pound did fall short. Force Z went east despite his determined opposition to sending out a force too important to lose but too weak to hold off the Japanese. And the effort to secure consistent and sufficient priority for the Atlantic struggle dragged on in part because he was reluctant to push matters to the point of an open breach. This has to be seen as a judgement call. Pound saw the weapon of a threat to resign as an act of desperation, dangerously close to the abandonment of duty, and indeed it was not to be bandied about lightly amid total war. He also realized that whatever his faults no one else could lead the war with the same fire and resolve as Churchill. Yet critics on both sides have not been fair to Pound on this issue. It was the very manner of Pound's handling of Churchill that provoked the controversy, some inevitably seeing it as, on balance, too compliant. Only on the Atlantic issue does this seem right. When Pound finally did make the ultimate threat, very quietly, in October 1942, results soon followed. But he received little credit for this from a navy already convinced he had allowed Churchill to bully it for too long. To balance this, Pound deserves credit for restraining Churchill as much as he did while retaining his confidence as well as he did.

Working with Churchill no doubt aggravated the final controversy surrounding Pound, his fitness for the demanding job fate thrust upon him. This arose because of his increasingly obvious fatigue as the war went on, and behaviour that suggested his powers were fading. He suffered from osteoarthritis, a painful condition which must have sapped his energy. Though medically certified fit to assume his appointment in 1939, he rarely took time off for real relaxation. Pound's tendency to put his head down and appear to be asleep in meetings became more pronounced from 1941. His defenders argue that this was in fact a way of concentrating, and insist that whenever any issue bearing on the navy came up, the first sea lord became fully alert and intervened in the discussion. Yet at best this would confirm the argument that Pound's participation in the central direction of the war was too narrow; at worst it spread the belief that he could not bear the strain.

Last months The death of his wife in July 1943 hit Pound very hard. But the condition that finally killed him was malignant glioma, a slowly developing brain tumour. Pound suffered a stroke in early September and was forced to tell Churchill on 8 September that he was no longer fit to serve. It is not possible to be definitive about whether this was the case. Supporters who argue that Pound remained fit until near the end are offset by critics who insist he was unfit long before. Whatever evidence he himself might have left went up in smoke when his personal papers were destroyed by burning, shortly after the war, by his fellow admirals Cunningham and Geoffrey Blake—possibly to conform with another naval tradition.

Death came for Pound in the Royal Masonic Hospital, Ravenscourt Park, London, on 21 October 1943, Trafalgar day—surely a last and most appropriate intervention by fate for this most devoted servant of the Royal Navy—and he was buried at sea on 27 October. He refused the late offer of a peerage, further testimony to lack of personal ambition, and died with the tide of war having truly turned. But as it was his lot to guide the navy during the difficult years of overstretch, so it has remained his fate to be a controversial figure among historians. The burning of his papers ruled out a definitive biography and made it more difficult to weigh Pound's role in the controversies of his career. Yet the mass of documentation surrounding any first sea lord has produced a long debate on Pound's life and career. The forgiving reception accorded by the post-war generation, which stressed his part in laying the foundations for victory, has now become a more critical discourse—should it have taken so long to win and at such cost, were serious errors made, and if so why? Assessments have ranged from calling Pound one of the weakest professional heads of the navy ever to lead the service in war to the claim that he did a more than adequate job when it fell to him. The most balanced view seems to be that for better or worse he was a product of the service to which he gave his life. The navy certainly could have benefited from stronger leadership at the top, but Pound was not a failure. He helped both to build a navy able to contribute to victory and to make sure no irreversible blunder was ever made. Pound's wartime successes and failures were those of the navy he led; he and it were inseparable.

BRIAN P. FARRELL

Sources R. Brodhurst, 'Admiral Sir Dudley Pound (1939–1943)', *The first sea lords: from Fisher to Mountbatten*, ed. M. H. Murfett (1995), 185–99 • P. Kemp, 'Admiral of the Fleet Sir Dudley Pound', *Men of war: great naval leaders of World War II*, ed. S. Howarth (1992) • C. Barnett, *Engage the enemy more closely: the Royal Navy in the Second World War* (1991) • S. Roskill, *Churchill and the admirals* (1977) • S. W. Roskill, *The war at sea, 1939–1945*, 3 vols. in 4 (1954–61) • A. J. Marder, *From the Dardanelles to Oran: studies of the Royal Navy in war and peace, 1915–1940* (1974) • A. J. Marder, M. Jacobsen, and J. Horsfield, *Old friends, new enemies: the Royal Navy and the imperial Japanese navy*, 2 vols. (1981–90), vol. 1 • M. Stephen, *The fighting admirals: British admirals of the Second World War* (1991) • P. Beesly, *Very special intelligence: the story of the admiralty's operational intelligence centre, 1939–1945* (1977) • A. Cunningham [first Viscount Cunningham], *A sailor's odyssey: the autobiography of admiral of the fleet, Viscount Cunningham of Hyndhope* (1951) • W. Jackson and Lord Bramall, *The chiefs: the story of the United Kingdom chiefs of staff* (1992) • B. P. Farrell, *The basis and making of British grand strategy, 1940–1943: was there a plan?* (1998) • *CGPLA Eng. & Wales* (1944) • *WWW*, 1941–50

Archives CAC Cam., corresp. and papers, incl. material collected for a biography • IWM, diary of service on HMS *St Vincent* | BL, corresp. with Viscount Cunningham, Add. MSS 52560–52561 • BL, corresp. with Sir Roger Keyes • CAC Cam., corresp. with A. V. Alexander • CAC Cam., corresp. with Sir James Somerville • NMM, corresp. with Sir Geoffrey Blake • NMM, corresp. with Lord Chatfield • PRO, Admiralty MSS, incl. series ADM 1, ADM 116, ADM 199, ADM 205 | FILM BFI NFTVA, actuality footage; documentary footage; news footage • IWM FVA, actuality footage • IWM FVA, news footage | SOUND IWM SA, oral history interview

Likenesses W. Stoneman, photograph, 1920, NPG • E. Kennington, pastel drawing, 1940, IWM • W. Stoneman, photograph, c.1940, NPG • O. Birley, oils, c.1945–1948, Royal Naval College, Greenwich, Greenwich Collection • D. Ewart, oils, United Service Club, London • photographs, IWM [*see illus.*]

Wealth at death £3810 8s. 4d.: administration with will, 8 April 1944, *CGPLA Eng. & Wales*

Pound, Ezra Loomis (1885–1972), poet, was born on 30 October 1885 in the family home at Hailey, Idaho, USA, the

Ezra Loomis Pound (1885–1972), by Alvin Langdon Coburn, 1913

only child of Homer Loomis Pound (1858–1942), assayer, and his wife, Isabella (1860–1948), daughter of Harding Weston and Mary Parker. Pound's paternal grandfather, Thaddeus C. Pound (1832–1914), was a merchant in the lumber and railroad industries of the American midwest, a member of the Wisconsin state legislature, and republican congressman for north-west Wisconsin from 1878 to 1884. On his mother's side Pound claimed descent from an early British settler family, the Wadsworths, who migrated to America in the 1630s, and in his disguised autobiographical fragment *Indiscretions* (1923) proposed 'that one could write the whole social history of the United States from one's family annals'.

Education and early career Homer Pound was appointed an assayer at the Philadelphia mint in 1889 and moved his family to Wyncote, a suburb of Philadelphia, where Pound attended dame-schools before moving on to Wyncote public school (1895–7), and Cheltenham Military Academy (1897–1901). In 1898 Pound's abiding interest in European culture was nourished by a cherished great-aunt, Frances Weston, who took him and his mother on a tour of Europe. His early academic record was undistinguished, apart from a facility for Latin, but he began undergraduate studies at the University of Pennsylvania (1901–3) a few weeks before his sixteenth birthday, then transferred to Hamilton College at Clinton in New York state, graduating BPhil in 1905. He returned to the University of Pennsylvania to pursue an MA course in Romance languages, graduating in 1906, and then registered as a PhD student. A combative student in conflict with the pedagogical orthodoxies of the time, his academic record did not allow him to proceed and he left the university after one year. He did, however, begin a lifelong friendship with the poet William Carlos Williams while at Pennsylvania, and with the poet H. D. (Hilda Doolittle), to whom he was briefly engaged. Though nurturing an early ambition to be a writer, he began an academic career as a teacher of Romance languages at Wabash College, Crawfordsville, Indiana, in autumn 1907 but lost this post through an alleged incident of moral misconduct in February 1908.

Pound left the United States in April 1908, and spent the summer of that year in Venice, where he joined his friend the pianist Katherine Ruth Heyman and her company, and acted as her unofficial manager. His first book of poems, *A lume spento* ('With tapers quenched'), was published there in 1908 at his own expense, its title commemorating his friend the painter William Brooke Smith of Philadelphia, who died of consumption at twenty-five. Later that year he moved to London to be near the poet W. B. Yeats, whom he regarded as the best poet then writing in English, and because London seemed to offer an ideal literary culture in which it would be possible to establish himself. His friendship with Yeats flourished, and he is usually credited with helping Yeats move from the late romantic poetry of the Celtic Twilight into the early modernist idioms and forms of his middle and later years. London became Pound's place of permanent residence for the next twelve years, though he made frequent journeys into France, Italy, and Germany, and spent eight months from June 1910 to February 1911 back in the United States. Pound's brief experience as a university teacher was his only full-time paid occupation, and from 1908 to his death he earned his living by his prolific writing and editing, supported for many years by a small monthly income from his father, whose own financial resources were very modest, and by his wife's annual allowance from her parents.

Modernism and early poetry Pound's London years are part of the extraordinary story of the emergence of modernist literature both in his own work and through his involvement with many of the writers, artists, and musicians responsible for the innovative and experimental arts of the early twentieth century—most notably T. S. Eliot, James Joyce, Wyndham Lewis, Ford Madox Ford, T. E. Hulme, and the French sculptor Henri Gaudier-Brzeska. It took some years before Pound's own poetry developed a distinctly modernist character, however. His earliest collections were obsessed with the idioms and culture of European poetry from the twelfth to the nineteenth centuries, and his practice was to compose in the 'personae' or voices of the poets of the past in order to develop his own unique voice. He often used an archaic vocabulary and an inverted syntax stylistically anchored in an antiquated poetic diction. If this way of working was partly a matter of temperament, it was also a product of his education and training in Romance languages and literature. His poetic models were Homer's epics and the Latin poets Catullus, Ovid, and Propertius, the French poet Villon, the Italians Dante and Guido Cavalcanti, and the troubadour poets of twelfth-century Provence, particularly Arnaut

Daniel. Wyndham Lewis observed that Pound was interesting not so much for his forward thinking about the arts but for how far he went back in time to find the true measures of artistic excellence, for Pound believed nothing new could be created without a knowledge of the 'tradition'. These convictions were shared by T. S. Eliot, notably in Eliot's classic essay 'Tradition and the individual talent' (1919). Pound's own reading of the tradition was given in a series of evening lectures at the London Polytechnic in 1909, published as *The Spirit of Romance* (1910). The audience for these lectures included Olivia Shakespear, a novelist and close friend of Yeats, and her daughter Dorothy Shakespear (1886–1973), an artist, whom Pound married on 20 April 1914.

From 1910 Pound's interest in avant-garde theories and practices across the arts merged with his convictions about the tradition, and he became a prominent propagandist for the new in contemporary writing, painting, sculpture, and music. For Pound the great writers of the tradition were the innovative writers of their time, and it was by their standards of originality that he thought writing in his own time should be measured. It is at this point that the celebration of the tradition and Pound's invocation to his own contemporaries to 'make it new' takes its force. His visits to Europe introduced him to the revolutionary developments in the visual arts of post-impressionism, cubism, and abstract art, and in London the geometric forms of Wyndham Lewis's painting and the sculpture of Gaudier-Brzeska and Jacob Epstein. His propaganda for the new was carried out in articles in a variety of magazines, such as both issues of Wyndham Lewis's journal *Blast* in 1914 and 1915, for which he also wrote poems. The typographical style and iconoclastic idiom of *Blast* owes something to the manifestos of the Italian futurists, whose meetings in London in 1910 and 1912 under the leadership of F. T. Marinetti were attended by Pound and Lewis. Though Lewis disputed the originality of futurist 'machine age' art, Pound was deeply impressed by the polemical energy of the futurist movement. He invented the term 'vorticism' to describe the British manifestation of European futurism [*see* Vorticists (*act.* 1914–1919)].

At the same time Pound was editing anthologies of contemporary writing such as *Des imagistes* (1914), a practice maintained for many years. The imagist poems of Pound and his young contemporaries H. D., Richard Aldington, and others were short, intense lyrics, devoid of interpretative content and the rhetorical excess Pound identified as bad practice in much contemporary poetry. By 1914 Pound had met his compatriot T. S. Eliot in London, and published *Catholic Anthology* in 1915 with the express intention of getting 'some fifteen pages or so of Eliot into print' when publishers and editors in London were baffled by Eliot's poems. In 1917, at Pound's prompting, Eliot published a short commentary on Pound's work, *Ezra Pound: his Metric and Poetry*, and in 1922 Pound edited the manuscript of Eliot's *The Waste Land*, for which Eliot honoured him with the dedication 'il miglior fabbro' ('the better maker'). Pound's editorial intervention in the manuscript of *The Waste Land* was potent, suggesting wholesale cuts in various sections, and innumerable changes in words and phrases throughout, most of which Eliot accepted, so Pound contributed significantly to the shape and language of the poem as we know it. In later years Eliot edited and introduced Pound's *Literary Essays* (1954), and their relationship survived until Eliot's death in 1965. Pound also espoused the cause of James Joyce. Through his agency as corresponding editor of the American magazine the *Little Review*, and as literary editor of *The Egoist* in London, he arranged for episodes of Joyce's *Ulysses* to be published in these two journals at a time when Joyce could not easily place his work. Later Pound helped raise money for the first publication of *Ulysses* in book form in Paris in 1922.

Of Pound's collections of shorter poems *Riposte* (1912) is regarded as a break-through volume in which Pound moved from the courtly diction of his earliest work towards a more contemporary language as the proper vehicle for poetry, in sympathy with imagist theory. It includes his version of the eighth-century Anglo-Saxon poem 'The Seafarer', which, like his translations from the Latin, Italian, French, and Chinese, has upset scholars who complain of his blunders in translating particular words or because he is ignorant about the cultural context of the original. Pound did not seek to versify a literal translation of originals, and in 'The Seafarer' gives a modern English version which recreates the sound of the words and the rhythmic pattern of the original through what is called a 'phonic simulacrum'. Pound's practice in his translations inspired poets throughout the twentieth century, and was central to his creative enterprise. His translation *Sonnets and Ballate of Guido Cavalcanti* was published in 1912, and *Cathay*, translations of Chinese poetry based on the notes of the American Sinologist Ernest Fenellosa, in 1915. In 1919 he published 'Homage to Sextus Propertius', a version of the Latin poet done initially for the benefit of an aspiring young American poet who had no Latin. Trounced by Latinists for its errors, as a 'homage' to Propertius like the eighteenth-century British practice of the verse 'imitation', its larger purpose is to imitate Propertius in taking an anti-militaristic attitude during the early years of the First World War. In *Lustra* (1916) imagist poems and brief versions from the Chinese accompany his familiar use of poetic strategies and personae from Italian courtly love poetry and the troubadour tradition in poems such as 'Near Perigord' and 'Provincia deserta', now in a language closer to contemporary speech. *Lustra* also marks the onset of his repudiation of London as a cultural capital, a rejection formally articulated in *Hugh Selwyn Mauberley* of 1920. This complex suite of poems organized in two contrasting sections is a critical anatomy of late Victorian and Edwardian culture and a critique of the difficulties of the artist in meeting the demands of the age. Composed in tight rhyming quatrains with passages of free verse, it contains a moving lament for the dead soldiers of the First World War. His significant prose studies of this period include his *Memoir of Gaudier-Brzeska* (1916), and *'Noh', or, Accomplishment* (1916), a study of the classical

theatre of Japan developed from manuscripts of Fenellosa.

The *Cantos* and later life Pound left London at the end of 1920 and settled in Paris for the next four years. His major work thereafter was on the *Cantos*. Versions of some early cantos were published in 1917, 1919, and 1921, with the first complete sequence, *A Draft of XVI Cantos*, privately published by William Bird's Three Mountains Press in Paris in 1925. From 1933 commercial editions of each sequence of *Cantos* were published in Britain by Faber and Faber. Other projects intervened. With editorial help from a young American composer, George Antheil, Pound wrote an opera, *Le testament de Villon* (1921). Friends who knew him to have no formal musical training were incredulous, though he had served as music critic, among other roles, for the *New Age* during his London years, and it was at a concert in this capacity that he first encountered the American violinist Olga Rudge (1895–1996). By 1923 Pound and Rudge had started their lifelong relationship; they had a daughter, Mary, in 1925. In 1926 Dorothy Pound had a son, Omar, with an unnamed father. Pound and Dorothy left Paris at the end of 1924 and settled in Rapallo in Italy, while Olga Rudge moved to Venice. Pound returned to Italy for practical and intellectual reasons: the cost of living was low, he wanted to continue archival research on Cavalcanti, and he was increasingly drawn to Mussolini and fascist politics, as well as to the social credit theory of economics developed by C. H. Douglas, whom Pound had first met in 1919. While composition of the *Cantos* continued, with three further sequences published between 1930 and 1940, Pound published a succession of prose works on literary, economic, political, and cultural topics. These included *How to Read* (1931), *ABC of Reading* (1934), *ABC of Economics* (1933), *Social Credit* (1935), *Jefferson and/or Mussolini* (1935), *Make it New* (1934), and *Guide to Kulchur* (1938). His literary and cultural prose works show Pound to be an inveterate if unorthodox teacher: *ABC of Reading* is an abrasive guide to what he considered the literature of ancient and modern Europe worth reading, and *Guide to Kulchur* proposes a 'new paideuma', a field of new learning based principally on the writings of Confucius and the modern German ethnologist and cultural theorist Leo Frobenius.

Pound visited the United States in 1939 and while there was awarded an honorary doctorate by Hamilton College in recognition of his literary accomplishments, but his attempt to promote social credit economics and to prevent American involvement in a future European war alienated his friends. In 1941 Pound was allowed by Mussolini to broadcast talks on Rome Radio aimed at discouraging American involvement in the Second World War, and in 1943 he was indicted for treason by the American government for broadcasting what was considered to be axis propaganda. In 1945 he was arrested by Italian partisans and taken to the American detention training centre at Pisa, prior to his captive return to the USA to face trial for treason. In Pisa, under extraordinarily punitive conditions—he was imprisoned in an open-air wire cage, without protection from the weather, for six weeks—he composed *The Pisan Cantos* (1948), widely admired as the best sequence of cantos and awarded the Bollingen prize for poetry in 1949. At his trial he was found unfit to plead on grounds of insanity and thenceforward was confined in St Elizabeth's Hospital, Washington, DC, until 1958. In that year his indictment for treason was dismissed, an event aided by support for his cause by many of America's eminent poets and writers. Dorothy Pound moved to Washington to be near her husband throughout his incarceration, and from that time forward had legal control of his estate. During his years in St Elizabeth's, Pound was allowed to continue writing, received visits from an extensive network of family, friends, poets, and scholars, and maintained a copious correspondence. He completed two further sections of the cantos, *Section: Rock-Drill* (1955) and *Thrones: de los cantares* (1959), and published a translation of the odes of Confucius under the title *The Classic Anthology Defined by Confucius* (1954) and a version of Sophocles' play *Women of Trachis* (1956). A collection of his miscellaneous writings was published as *Pavannes and Divagations* (1958), and the first collection of *The Letters of Ezra Pound*, edited by D. D. Paige, appeared in 1950. On his release from St Elizabeth's, Pound returned to Italy to live with his daughter, and from spring 1962 with Olga Rudge in Sant'Ambrogio above Rapallo, and in Venice. In ill health for much of the last decade of his life, he became obsessed by a profound sense of failure, and lapsed into silence. The final, incomplete, sequence of cantos appeared in 1969: *Drafts and Fragments of Cantos CX–CXVIII*. He died at the hospital of SS Giovanni e Paolo in Venice on 1 November 1972, and was buried on 3 November in the municipal cemetery of San Michele, Venice.

Reputation Pound early cultivated the bohemian image of the poet in his dress and public demeanour. He generally wore brightly coloured clothes, went open-shirted, or wore floppy hand-painted ties or cravats, unconventional hats such as a sombrero, and from the mid-twenties used a malacca cane. A tallish figure with eyes variously described as green, blue, aquamarine, and sapphirine, and a reddish beard which matured to grey then white in his later years, with large hands and long, well-shaped fingers, he was a dramatic social presence. His bohemianism, allied to his aggressive self-advertising manner, due in some measure to his midwestern American origins, sees him as a flamboyant rooster in the cockpit of London literary life, where he was admired by his modernist contemporaries and loathed by the cultural establishment, who eventually silenced him through neglect. Entrepreneurial self-promotion went hand in hand with a selfless effort to promote the best work across the spectrum of the arts, a disinterested labour devoid of competitive animus. His prose writings at this time were invigorated by a desire for public good.

From the early 1930s, however, Pound's commitment to social credit economics and Italian fascist politics became obsessive. Given some fascist pamphlets by F. T. Marinetti in Rome in 1932, he was excited by the achievements of Mussolini's regime in public administration and reform, and thereafter would talk of little but the centrality of economics and politics in human affairs, to the despair of his friends. These obsessions were accompanied by an increasingly vocal and vituperative antisemitism. On his visit to America in 1939 he spent time in New York with the writer E. E. Cummings, who reported Pound as 'gargling anti-semitism from morning till morning', though the Jewish American poet Louis Zukofsky wrote that he 'never felt the least trace of anti-semitism in his presence'. In origin Pound's antisemitism was of the kind common to non-Jewish racial cultures, but its expression became violently intensified in his reading of monetary policies and banking practices in American and European history. Usury is first cited in the 'Hell cantos', numbers 14–16, a Dantescan vision of a modern inferno, and elaborated in the 'Usura cantos', numbers 45 and 51, though in all these cantos the connection between Jewish practices and usury is implied rather than explicit. At the end of his life Pound recanted his antisemitism, describing it as a foolish 'suburban prejudice', an inadequate apology in the face of the evidence. These obsessions in the thirties and forties led many to think Pound had gone mad. (Diagnoses of his mental health by psychiatrists at the Pisa detention centre found no evidence, however, of psychosis, neurosis, or psychopathy, but rather of superior intelligence, friendliness, and co-operation, though he was thought lacking in 'personality resilience'. This was later confirmed by psychiatrists who examined him prior to his trial and thereafter at St Elizabeth's.)

Although crucially damaged by his commitment to Mussolini's fascist politics, and his antisemitism, Pound's reputation rests on the *Cantos*. At its core is an idealistic ambition: to adduce from history and the present the best examples of good practice in all aspects of life and to denounce bad practice. This project is applied to government and economics, to all the arts, and across civilizations remote from each other in time and place. Its religious temper is polytheistic and mystical, its ethical project anti-militaristic. It is what Pound called a 'periplum', a circumnavigation or 'sailing after knowledge' to discover and record the centre of values across human history. It contains a multitude of voices, for Pound worked by citing history through quotations from public and private documents, books, records, proclamations, letters, diaries, and other written artefacts from a vast array of sources. It opens with a recall of Odysseus as the type of heroic wanderer, but its primary heroes are what Pound called 'factive' personalities, an idiosyncratic choice of figures from history whose energies have charged their times with vital and beneficent qualities, such as the Chinese sage Confucius, the Renaissance Italian condottiere Sigismundo Malatesta, the poets Ovid, Dante, and Cavalcanti, the second American president, John Adams, and the Italian dictator Mussolini. It is at its most personal in the *Pisan Cantos* sequence, and in some of the last and incomplete cantos. While the thickly meshed web of historical evidence through which each sequence is composed often proves difficult for the uninitiated reader, there are compensatory qualities in Pound's command of a simple language of lyric intensity which speaks unerringly of the pleasures and pains of the human condition.

LIONEL KELLY

Sources J. J. Wilhelm, *The American roots of Ezra Pound* (1985) · J. J. Wilhelm, *Ezra Pound: the tragic years, 1925–1972* (1994) · H. Carpenter, *A serious character: the life of Ezra Pound* (1998) · m. cert.
Archives Indiana University, Bloomington, Lilly Library, corresp., papers, and diaries · L. Cong., Washington, DC, manuscript division, MSS · National Records Center, Washington, DC, MSS · St Elizabeth's Hospital, Washington, DC, MSS · University of Pennsylvania, Philadelphia, papers · University of Toledo, MSS | BL, letters to Patricia Hutchins, Add. MS 57725 · BL, corresp. with Graham Seton Hutchison, Add. MS 74270 · BL, letters to D. Marsden, RP3387 · University of Kent, Canterbury, letters to H. Johnson · W. Sussex RO, letters to W. S. Blunt
Likenesses photographs, c.1910–1967, Hult. Arch. · A. L. Coburn, collotype, 1913, NPG [*see illus.*] · H. Gaudier-Brzeska, marble head, 1914, Kettle's Yard, Cambridge · photographs, 1914, National Museum of Photography, Film and Television, Bradford, Royal Photographic Society collection · W. Lewis, oils, 1938–9, Tate collection · W. Roberts, group portrait, oils, 1961–2 (*The Vorticists at the Restaurant de la Tour Eiffel, spring 1915*), Tate collection; *see illus. in* Vorticists (*act.* 1914–1919) · A. L. Coburn, photograph, repro. in E. Pound, *Lustra* (1916), frontispiece

Pound, James (1669–1724), astronomer, was baptized on 2 March 1669 at Bishop's Canning, Wiltshire, the son of James Pound and his wife, Mary. He matriculated at St Mary Hall, Oxford, on 16 March 1687, graduated BA from Hart Hall on 27 February 1694 and MA from Gloucester Hall in the same year, and obtained a medical diploma and MB on 21 October 1697. He practised medicine only briefly, but, perhaps in consequence, enjoyed the courtesy title of Dr Pound; he took holy orders and entered the service of the East India Company as chaplain to the merchants of Fort George, Madras. From India he was sent to Chushan Dao, an island south of Shanghai, where he arrived in 1700.

During his voyages Pound made what simple astronomical observations he could and noted the changing magnetic variation. He corresponded with John Flamsteed, the astronomer royal, who hoped that Pound would be able to provide observations of the southern stars, and for this purpose oversaw the construction of a fine 3 foot quadrant in the workshops of Thomas Tuttle. It was shipped to Pound in 1700, but its arrival was delayed by the vagaries of weather, and it reached him, sadly corroded, only in 1704.

In 1702 Pound joined a group of merchants who built a fort and settlement on Pulo Condore, one of a group of islands now known as Con Son, off the Mekong delta. He possessed an 18 inch quadrant and a clock, and was able to send observations to Flamsteed as well as specimens of plants and animals to Dr Charlett of Oxford University. But on 3 March 1705 the native troops attacked the settlement, setting fire to the buildings. Pound was one of eleven Europeans who escaped, having lost all their possessions, and fled the island in the sloop *Rose*, making for Malacca and eventually Batavia. He reached England in July 1706. The year after his return Pound was presented to the rectory of Wanstead, Essex. When Flamsteed died in 1720 he vacated it, and Lord Chancellor Parker presented him to Flamsteed's former living of Burstow, Surrey. He married on 14 February 1710 Sarah (*d.* 1715), the widow of Edward Farmer. Their firstborn son died at birth; a daughter, Sarah, died unmarried at Greenwich on 19 October 1747.

Pound had been elected fellow of the Royal Society on 20 December 1699, so that his admission was delayed until 30 July 1713, by which time he possessed a 15 foot telescope and had sufficient reputation as an astronomer to be invited on to the board of visitors for the Royal Greenwich Observatory. Edmond Halley presented Pound's observations of the total solar eclipse of 3 May 1715 to the Royal Society, the first of three reports from Pound to be published in *Philosophical Transactions* that year; the others dealt with the occultation of a star by Jupiter and an eclipse of the moon on 30 October. In 1716 and 1717 he made various planetary observations. In 1717 the Royal Society lent Pound the 123 foot focal length lens which Huygens had made; he mounted this in Wanstead Park as the objective of an aerial telescope (one with no tube), supporting it on the maypole lately removed from the Strand, in Westminster, and procured for the purpose by Isaac Newton. Such ungainly apparatus was inconvenient to use, but Pound managed to master it to the extent that his observations of the five known satellites of Saturn enabled Halley to correct his own calculations. Newton employed Pound's micrometrical measurements of Jupiter's disc, of Saturn's disc and ring, and of the elongations of their satellites, in the third edition of his *Principia* (1726), and obtained from him data for correcting the places of the comet of 1680. Pound recorded two payments of 50 guineas from Newton in 1719 and 1720 for these or other services. The French astronomer Laplace also employed Pound's observations of Jupiter's satellites in determining the planet's mass, and Pound himself compiled in 1719 a set of tables for the first satellite, introducing an equation for the transmission of light.

Pound's second marriage, in October 1722, was to Elizabeth (1673–1740), the daughter of Matthew Wymondesold; she possessed her own estate of £10,000, while her brother, Matthew Wymondesold, was a successful speculator in South Sea stock and the proprietor of the Wanstead estate. There were no children of this marriage. Pound was responsible for encouraging a love of astronomy in his nephew James *Bradley (*bap.* 1692, *d.* 1762). He had paid for Bradley's education, and nursed him through smallpox; many of their observations were made together at Wanstead, among them those of the opposition of Mars in 1719 and of the transit of Mercury on 29 October 1723. Their measurement of gamma Virginis in 1718, the first made of the components of a double star, was part of their search for solar parallax; Pound may have aided in planning the observations of gamma Draconis which led Bradley to his discovery of the aberration of light. He was a frequent visitor of Samuel Molyneux (1689–1728), promoter of reflecting telescopes, at Kew. He was commissioned by the Royal Society in July 1723 to test John Hadley's reflecting telescope, and reported favourably on its performance. Pound died at Wanstead on 16 November 1724. His widow resided with Bradley at Oxford from 1732 to 1737; she died on 10 September 1740 and was buried at Wanstead. ANITA MCCONNELL

Sources Bodl. Oxf., MS 16428 (Bradley 24) · J. H. von Mädler, *Geschichte der Himmelskunde*, 2 vols (Brunswick, 1873); repr. (Walluf bei Wiesbaden, 1973), vol. 1, pp. 408–10, 428–9; vol. 2, p. 444 · *Miscellaneous works and correspondence of the Rev. James Bradley*, ed. [S. P. Rigaud] (1832); repr. (1972) · Foster, *Alum. Oxon.* · F. Baily, *An account of the Revd John Flamsteed, the first astronomer-royal* (1835); repr. (1966), 218, 261, 308, 334–6
Archives Bodl. Oxf.

Pound, William (*bap.* 1807, *d.* 1881), headmaster and religious writer, was the son of Matthew Pound, gentleman. A William Pound, son of Matthew Pound and his wife, Sarah, was baptized at Great Stanmore, Middlesex, on 18 March 1807. After attending Grantham School, Pound entered St John's College, Cambridge, in 1829, holding the Newcome exhibition (1829–36) and the Baker exhibition (1832–4), and being admitted Robinson scholar in 1832. He graduated BA as sixth wrangler in 1833, ill health contributing to his failure to achieve the anticipated highest mathematical honours. He was Naden divinity student from 1833 to 1836, when he proceeded MA. Pound was fellow (and sometime librarian) of the college from then until 1839, vacating before his marriage in January 1840 to Charlotte Augusta, fourth daughter of Richard Furley, a wharfinger from Gainsborough. The couple had two sons, Robert William (*b.* 1843) and Alfred John (*b.* 1847), and one daughter, Amelia Dorothena (*b.* 1845). Pound was ordained deacon in 1835, becoming a priest in 1836. In 1839 Archbishop Musgrave appointed him headmaster of Old Malton grammar school, Yorkshire, then in a decayed condition and suffering from local competition. Pound moved the school to Norton, let the old schoolroom, and effectively conducted a private school, although he admitted without payment Malton boys wishing to study classics only. This policy generated local opposition. While at Malton, Pound served as official to the archdeacon of the East Riding, Robert Isaac Wilberforce.

In the 1850s Pound was a prominent campaigner for the revival of diocesan synods. He helped organize the well-attended synodal consultative meetings held at Derby, London, Gloucester, and Warrington in 1851–2, and wrote much of the literature circulated by the provisional committee, of which he was secretary. Pound also edited and largely wrote the *Synodicon* (1854–6), in which contemporary issues were considered with reference to synodical action. A high-churchman but not a ritualist, Pound saw the diocesan synod—'A whole diocese standing before its king'—as the heart of an ideal Anglo-Saxon church polity, which had subsequently been debilitated by a combination of papal usurpation and state interference (of which convocation was a manifestation):

> By synodical action within the diocese, in mixed assemblies of clergy and laity, the old Saxon independent action of the Church will be attained, and supply to the state a bulwark of truth to fall back on, when the combined tide of expediency

and centralisation shall have recoiled upon the state with irrepressible violence. (Pound, *Papal Aggression … Repelled by the Revival of Diocesan Synods*, 1852, 8)

It was only among his clergy that a bishop exercised his proper authority. Pound developed a scheme for diocesan synods elaborately organized to energize the existing diocesan structure, and with lay participation. He believed such synods would counteract the growth of church party, restore church discipline, and support education. In other writings on this last subject Pound upheld the moral and religious content of education, which he considered to be under threat from government proposals in the late 1860s. Diocesan synods figured here as a means of ensuring the moral content in education and preventing damaging centralization.

In 1866 Pound transferred his teaching activities to Appuldurcombe House on the Isle of Wight, so saving the ancestral home of the Worsleys from demolition. He remained principal of the school until in 1876 he handed over to his elder son, hoping to devote his remaining years to scriptural researches. A 'complication of maladies' frustrated these plans, but Pound had already produced his most ambitious publication, *The Gospels in Unity* (1870). This sought to demonstrate the infallibility and inspiration of the evangelists' narratives through an elaborate explanation of apparent inconsistencies in chronology as the result of similar incidents occurring at different times in Christ's life. The *Literary Churchman* dismissed it as 'a last desperate effort to construct a perfect harmony of the Gospels'. Pound was an active campaigner for the Conservatives on the island, organizing a Conservative association at Ventnor. In 1871 he assumed the duties of lecturer at St Catherine's, Ventnor, in which post he remained until his death at Appuldurcombe on 23 October 1881. He was buried at Godshill. ARTHUR BURNS

Sources *The Guardian* (26 Oct 1881), 1519 · Crockford (1881) · Venn, *Alum. Cant.* · Boase, *Mod. Eng. biog.* · D. J. Lloyd, H. Fox, and A. Kirby, *History of Malton grammar school* (1965) · *British Magazine*, 17 (1840), 232 · D. J. Salmon, ed., *Malton in the early nineteenth century* (1981), 72 · *Isle of Wight Journal and Newport Times* (29 Oct 1881), 5 · IGI
Archives Pusey Oxf., Denison MSS, letters to George Anthony Denison, DEN 2 P33
Wealth at death £11,072 11s. 3d.: resworn probate, April 1883, *CGPLA Eng. & Wales* (1882)

Pounde [*alias* Duke, Harrington, Gallop, Wallop], **Thomas** (1539–1615), Jesuit lay brother, was born on 29 May 1539 in Belmont, Hampshire. His father, William Pounde, was a wealthy landowner and his mother, Anne, was the sister of Thomas Wriothesley, earl of Southampton. As a student of Winchester College, Pounde allegedly composed an ode to welcome Elizabeth I. If so he greeted her during her visit to the city of Winchester shortly after her accession: she did not visit the college until 1570.

From Winchester, Pounde entered Lincoln's Inn on 16 February 1560. Heir to extensive estates upon the death of his father about 1564, Pounde squandered much in an attempt to gain influence at court. For the same reason he conformed to the established church. During twelfth night celebrations in 1570 Pounde directed plays, games, and masques at court, some of which, according to Simpson, he wrote. An attempt to repeat an intricate dance step at the queen's request resulted in an embarrassing fall. All laughed as Elizabeth ordered him to stand with 'Rise, Sir Ox'. In a voice loud enough for bystanders to hear Pounde muttered 'Sic transit gloria mundi' and quickly abandoned the court for Belmont.

With the same zeal with which he formerly pursued worldly honours Pounde now threw himself into prayer, mortification, almsgiving, and works of charity. Impressed by accounts of Jesuit missionary activity, Pounde decided to apply for the society. In approximately 1574 he travelled to London to tidy up affairs before his departure for the continent. The evening before his crossing an official from Edwin Sandys, bishop of London, summoned him for questioning regarding his religious convictions. His cousin Henry Wriothesley, earl of Southampton, secured his release from prison after six months on condition that he would neither leave the country nor interfere with religious matters, and that he would confine himself to Belmont. Violation of the second condition resulted in a summons from Robert Horne, bishop of Winchester; after two months spent incarcerated in Winchester, Pounde was sent to Marshalsea prison, London, on the bishop's warrant on 11 March 1576. In 1578 his friend Thomas Stephens, a Jesuit since 1575, interceded with Everard Mercurian, Jesuit general, on Pounde's behalf. Mercurian granted the request for admission to the society on 1 December 1578 but urged Pounde to 'keep your secret to yourself until better times shine forth' (Foley, 3.585–6). Robert Persons visited Pounde in prison some time in late June 1580 and may have received his vows as a Jesuit. At Pounde's recommendation Persons and Edmund Campion prepared statements for public release in the event of their capture. Pounde distributed copies entrusted to him among his friends and was thus responsible for the wide circulation of Campion's 'Brag'.

Encouraged by Campion's example Pounde petitioned the privy council in September 1580 for a public disputation on religious matters and challenged the protestant preachers Henry Tripp and Robert Crowley, who harangued Catholic prisoners in Marshalsea. His 'Six reasons' was intended to demonstrate that religious controversies could not be settled by scripture alone: scripture bore witness to the truth but the judge was the church. Pounde was consequently transferred from Marshalsea to the dungeons of Bishop's Stortford Castle, Hertfordshire. For the next two decades he was transferred from prison to prison: Marshalsea, Counter, Gatehouse, White Lion, the Tower of London, and Wisbech and Framlingham castles (with the exception of a period from approximately May 1585 until September 1586 when he was released on bail and restricted to his mother's residence, first in Hampshire and then in Newington). Initially, either through bribery or trust, Pounde was often allowed to leave prison during the day, but having been labelled a dangerous man because of his challenge, henceforth he was periodically tortured or kept in solitary confinement.

Pardoned and released from Framlingham Castle at the accession of James I in March 1603, Pounde was again in trouble in late 1604 because of a memorial in which he detailed cruel sentences and punishments against Roman Catholics by justices in Lancaster. It is not known whether the petition ever reached the king's hands, but Pounde was summoned before Star Chamber in November 1604 and charged with calumny for his criticism. Having been found guilty he was pilloried and condemned to life imprisonment unless he conformed to the established church; the intercession of Catholic ambassadors prevented harsher punishment.

In early 1609 Pounde explained how he had suffered imprisonment for his faith 'half these sixty-eight years' (Foley, 3.614) and recited his tour of English prisons. Now he requested release from James I. By 3 June he had returned to Belmont. What remained of his fortune and estate after years of recusant fines he made over to two nephews, whom he educated as Catholics although their parents were not, and prepared to cross to a Jesuit house on the continent. He cancelled his trip because of orders from his Jesuit superior (either Richard Holtby or Robert Jones). He remained at Belmont with his nephews until his death there on 5 March 1615.

THOMAS M. McCOOG

Sources T. M. McCoog, *English and Welsh Jesuits, 1555–1650*, 2 vols., Catholic RS, 74–5 (1994–5) · T. M. McCoog, ed., *Monumenta Angliae*, 1–2 (1992) · H. Foley, ed., *Records of the English province of the Society of Jesus*, 7 vols. in 8 (1875–83) · *The Elizabethan Jesuits: Historia missionis Anglicanae Societatis Jesu (1660) of Henry More*, ed. and trans. F. Edwards (1981) · *Report on manuscripts in various collections*, 8 vols., HMC, 55 (1901–14), vol. 3 · R. Simpson, 'Biographical sketch of Thomas Poundes', *The Rambler*, new ser., 7 (1857), 24–38, 94–106 · W. P. Baildon, ed., *The records of the Honorable Society of Lincoln's Inn: admissions*, 1 (1896) · T. F. Kirby, *Annals of Winchester College, from its foundation in the year 1382 to the present time* (1892) · PRO, SP 14/21/48 · Archives of the British Province of the Society of Jesus, London, MSS Anglia III, 95 · Archivum Romanum Societatis Iesu, Rome, Fl. Belg. 2

Archives Archivum Romanum Societatis Iesu, Rome | Bodl. Oxf. · PRO, state papers

Wealth at death seemingly gave all to nephews before death

Poundmaker (1842–1886). *See under* Big Bear (*c*.1825–1888).

Pounds, John (1766–1839), cobbler and ragged-school teacher, was born in St Mary Street, Portsmouth, on 17 June 1766, the son of a naval dockyard sawyer. With little education, Pounds was apprenticed at the age of twelve to a shipwright. The turning point in his life came in 1781 when he was permanently injured by a fall into a dry dock. Left permanently disabled, Pounds resorted to the more sedentary occupation of shoe-mending. From 1803 he lived and worked in a small weatherboarded shop in St Mary Street, one of the poorest parts of Portsmouth, which became famous as one of the first ragged schools. It was estimated that between 1818 and 1839 Pounds provided free schooling for approximately 500 street children.

Pounds's philanthropy was recounted in a long obituary and afterwards inspired anecdotal memoirs and eulogies in Britain and America. In particular, the Scottish philanthropist Thomas Guthrie acknowledged the inspiration of

Pounds in his *Pleas for Ragged Schools* in 1847, 1849, and 1860. Charles Dickens's portrayal of the schoolmaster in *The Old Curiosity Shop* may have been based upon Pounds.

Pounds began his charitable work for outcast children of Portsmouth in 1818, teaching his disabled nephew and a friend to read. While continuing to trade as a cobbler, he possibly taught as many as forty pupils at a time, accepting only the poorest and most ragged. Pounds used an interrogative approach to teach simple Bible study, morality, reading, writing, arithmetic, and nature study. He taught cookery to the girls and shoe-mending to the boys, and fed and cared for them when they were ill. Pounds's own poverty was illustrated by his use of discarded books, scraps of newspapers, and handbills as teaching aids, although he later accepted books from the local Unitarian High Street Chapel. A Unitarian himself, Pounds encouraged children to attend services and Sunday school at the chapel.

An idealistic oil painting by the journeyman shoemaker H. S. Sheaf, widely distributed in a lithograph engraved by W. S. Charpentier, depicted Pounds with black hair and strong unlined features, surrounded by industrious children. However, Hawkes's memoir probably gives a more accurate picture of Pounds as self-neglected, lame, thin, dirty, and grey haired, with a heavily lined face and a harsh, strident voice. He never married.

Pounds died suddenly on 1 January 1839 at the Portsmouth home of his friend Edward Carter. He was buried in the High Street Chapel graveyard, on 5 January. His fame drew hundreds to his funeral. An inscribed plaque in the chapel and monument on his grave were paid for by subscriptions from Britain and abroad. Portsmouth subsequently established a number of ragged schools in his name.

Pounds was not the founder of ragged schools but was one of a number of working-class pioneers in the early history of the movement. He cared for the bodies, minds, and souls of his pupils, and some aspects of his work can be seen in the later development of the Ragged School Union.   JANET SHEPHERD

Sources *Christian Reformer, or, Unitarian Magazine and Review*, 6 (1839), 191–3 · *GM*, 2nd ser., 11 (1839), 213–14 · H. Hawkes, *Recollections of John Pounds: memoir* (1839) · T. Guthrie, *Seedtime and harvest of ragged schools, or, Third plea with new editions of first and second pleas* (1860) · *Memorable Unitarians* (1906) · P. Harwood, *The poor shoemender* (1839) · W. H. Saunders, *Annals of Portsmouth* (1880) · D. H. Webster, 'The ragged school movement and the education of the poor in the nineteenth century', PhD diss., University of Leicester, 1973 · C. J. Montague, *Sixty years in waifdom* (1904) · R. E. Jayne, *The story of John Pounds* (1925) · *Autobiography of Thomas Guthrie*, ed. D. K. Guthrie and C. J. Guthrie, 2 vols. (1874–5) · M. Carpenter, *Reformatory schools for the children of the perishing and dangerous classes* (1851) · E. A. G. Clark, 'The early ragged schools and the foundation of the Ragged School Union', *Journal of Educational Administration and History*, 1/2 (1969), 9–21

Archives City Museum and Records Office, Portsmouth, architect's plan of John Pounds's shop in St Mary Street, Portsmouth · City Museum and Records Office, Portsmouth, watercolours of interior of John Pounds's shop

Likenesses H. Anelay, group portrait, woodcut (with children), NPG · W. S. Charpentier, engraving (after an oil painting by H. S. Sheaf), repro. in A. Tropp, *The school teachers* (1957) · D. H. Webster,

photograph, repro. in Webster, 'The ragged school movement and the education of the poor' · statuette, repro. in Jayne, *The story of John Pounds*

Wealth at death none: Hawkes, *Recollections*; DNB

Povey, Charles (*bap.* 1651?, *d.* 1743), writer and entrepreneur, may have been the Charles Povey, son of John and Elizabeth Povey, baptized at St Andrew's, Holborn, on 27 July 1651. Povey himself was ambiguous about his ancestry, claiming only that his birth was neither noble nor ignoble. His brother, Josiah (*d.* 1727), was a clergyman at Telscombe, Sussex. Povey was married—his wife's name was Anne—but had no children. His first published works were political tracts directed against James II. For these writings he was gaoled in the 1680s but he continued to write about Jacobitism in *A Challenge to All Jacobites* (1689) and *A Challenge in Vindication of the Revolution* (1690).

More is known about Povey from the late 1690s when he turned to economic subjects. He published *Proposals for Raising one Thousand Pounds* (1699) and entered Britain's thriving coal trade as a wholesaler in 1700. Povey was harassed by coal-dealers in Wapping, where he was living. He had designed a hoist, which supplanted lightermen, for the job of unloading ships at his wharf at Execution Dock, enabling Povey to sell coal priced below the going rate. After being convicted for selling false measure in May 1700, Povey maintained the charges had arisen only because he would neither pay bribes to officials nor price like his competitors. He defended his discount pricing in *A discovery of indirect practices in the coal-trade, or, A detection of the pernicious maxims and unfair dealings of a certain combination of men, who affirm, it is a cheat to be just, and just to cheat* (1700); but he traded coal no more. In 1701 he published *The Unhappiness of England as to its Trade by Sea and Land*, a work lamenting the impact of monopolistic practices on shipowners and their crews. Povey increasingly came to believe that government regulation was needed to avoid unfair practices in the British coal trade. His next two publications were on religious topics: *Meditations of a Divine Soul* (1703) and *Holy Thoughts on a God-Made Man* (1704). The latter of these also illustrates Povey's lifelong interest in astronomy, a topic to which he would return in *The Opinions of Ancient Philosophers about the Substance and Nature of the Sun* and *An Enquiry into the Nature … of the Heavenly Bodies*.

By 1705 Povey was at Hatton Garden, near Holborn, in a rented building he called the Traders' Exchange House. There Povey matched lenders with debtors, connected those wishing to sell properties with those wishing to buy them, and generally operated as a middleman. In conjunction with that business Povey edited a single-sheet newspaper, the *General Remark on Trade* (containing mostly advertisements), the first number of which appeared on 23 October 1705. It continued under that title through to issue number 213 of 7 July 1707 and as *General Remark on Trade: with an Extract of Foreign News and Observations on Publick Affairs*, and similar titles with expanded contents, until at least 22 December 1708. Advertisements became secondary to tables of currency exchange, stock valuations, commodity prices, export and import figures, lists of ships 'Arriv'd at, and Departed from several Ports of England', foreign news from papers such as the *Paris Gazette*, lists of 'Christenings and Burials', columns of miscellany, brief descriptions of various English towns, counties, and of the universities at Oxford and Cambridge, and running essays on topics such as the trade of England and Scotland. All of that was pitched with Povey's characteristic twist of charitable concern:

> Favour our Undertaking … because out of the Profits arising by the sale of it, 20 Poor Boys, most Orphans … are Cloathed, kept to School, allowed 2s. 6d. a Week each, and at Two Years End, Five Pounds a piece given, to put them out Apprentices to Trades, and Twenty others taken in their Room.

These same boys comprised Povey's delivery team. Povey relied, as well, on the labour of others for some of the paper's content, which he admitted was reprinted from 'the Old Athenian Mercuries'.

Povey's scheming mind would not be contained and he became caught up in the excitement over insurance companies. In May 1706 Povey floated his own life-insurance scheme, proposing that it would 'bring *The Traders Exchange-House* into far greater Credit and Business than ever' and also make the *General Remark on Trade* 'sell all over England, more than any other'. It would also fulfil a philanthropic role by 'increasing the Store of the Rich, bettering the Circumstances of Persons in a middle Station, and maintaining many who are reduced to want, by Losses, Oppression, or Wrong'. From the quarterly premiums collected from 4000 subscribers, Povey proposed to pay claims on a quarterly basis and also to use profits to construct 'a Structure in or some where about *London*, containing 100 Rooms of £1,000 Value; and the said Structure is to bear the Name of the TRADERS EXCHANGE-HOUSE-COLLEGE', that would house 100 of the most needy policy-holders and their families.

In 1708 Povey began a new project that would insure 'Moveables, Goods, Merchandizes and Wares from Loss by Fire'. The Exchange House Fire Office long outlived Povey's involvement. Povey organized a group of 'Exchange House Men' who, 'able Bodied' and chosen 'out of different Parishes, in the Cities and Suburbs of London and Westminster', would 'be ready at Hand, to give immediate Assistance, where-ever a FIRE shall break forth, in Removing and Securing the Moveable Goods, Merchandizes and Wares, of all … Subscribers'. Subscribers' homes were identified by 'a Mark representing the SUN, nailed up against their Houses'. In 1709 Povey gave up part ownership of the Exchange House Fire Office, or the Sun Fire House as it was popularly known, to raise capital for yet another enterprise.

On 4 October 1709 Povey started his Half-penny Carriage of Letters, a business that infringed upon the monopoly of the royal post. Povey's service delivered letters and parcels between depots in London, Southwark, and Westminster, where patrons identified Povey's mail carriers by their ringing bells. Accused in late 1709 by the Post Office authorities of infringing on their monopoly, a number of letters were exchanged in the *London Gazette* between Povey and his accusers. Povey's halfpenny post continued

to operate for a number of months during this clamour, but eventually was stopped.

On 21 August 1710 Povey had printed the first number of *The Visions of Sir Heister Ryley, with Other Entertainments*. Described by Povey himself as an imitator of Richard Steele's *The Tatler*, *The Visions* was published thrice weekly in two quarto leaves and continued for eighty numbers until 21 February 1711. In the preface to the first number Povey explained that he thought 'it adviseable to steer a middle Course, between the Rocks of Padantick Elocution, and the Shallows of a mean Utterance; so as to adapt his Compositions to the Genius of every Capacity'. His design was 'to instill into the Mind of the Reader sound Principles of Morality, under the Vail of a pleasing Vision, an apposite Allegory, or a lively Emblem'.

In 1714 Povey published, anonymously, his *An Inquiry into the Miscarriages of the Four Last Years Reign* (1714), in which he summarized his long-standing literary goal to supplant vice for virtue:

> I have writ Five large *Quarto* and *Octavo* volumes, with many other treatises to recommend Vertue, Loyalty, Wit, Honour, Truth, and Moderation, and to extinguish Vice, Rebellion, Bribery, Pride and Ambition; and yet I see Men of Figure and Fortune still more degenerate in their Morals.

That work was followed by others, such as *A Memorial of the Proceedings of the Late Ministry* (1714), *The English Parliament Represented in a Vision* (1715), *The Subject's Representation* (1717), *English Inquisition* (1718), and *Britain's scheme to make a new coin of gold and silver to give in exchange for paper money and South Sea stock* (1720), directed against the ruling whigs.

Povey continued to contrive and market devices of various sorts well into his old age. In 1723 he designed a 'fire-annihilator', essentially a water bomb, for extinguishing fires. Almost twenty years later he invented a self-playing organ, a device that was announced in the *Daily Advertiser* on 23 November 1742. He also had begun to look back at his earlier years, publishing a number of books that made reference to his past deeds and tribulations, such as *The Secret History of the Sun Fire Office* (1733), *England's Memorial to Obtain Right and Property* (1737), and *The Torments after Death, upon Atheism and Charity* (1740), a book that commented on his various charitable projects.

Povey's last major publication was *The Virgin in Eden* (1741), a book written against Samuel Richardson's popular epistolary novel *Pamela*. Povey considered Richardson's to be far from a moral tale, writing in his preface: '*Good God! what can Youths and Virgins learn from* Pamela's *Letters, more than Lessons to tempt their Chastity; those Epistles are only Scenes of Immodesty, painted in Images of Virtue; Disguises in Masquerade, as I shall prove.*' Povey's book concluded with a catalogue listing forty of his works. Another short section, headed 'Universal Charity imitates the Saviour of the World', is informative of the mind behind his writings. Povey declared his ruling belief that:

> no Man can be a Christian in Life and Doctrine, that judges or censures any Speech or Language in Points of Religion, or Principles of Faith. Neither can we be perfect, unless we are invested with a Spirit of Mercy and Pity to all living Creatures in Distress and Pain.

It is in that spirit that:

> the Author most humbly petitions the Publick in Christ's Name, to make one Act of Charity universal in this Island. That as often as any Housekeeper, or other Person, boils any Butcher's Meat, and makes no Use of the Liquor in their own Families, that they would be so good to engage their Servants not to waste or fling the same away as usual, but give it to poor Families.

Povey died on 4 May 1743 in Little Alie Street, Goodman's Fields, London. His will, dated 13 January 1742, was published, by his request, in the *London Daily Post*, where it appeared on the front page on 1 and 8 July 1743. Povey left his self-playing organ to the parish of St Mary, Newington, and money for the parish charity school, for the poor of Whitechapel, and for his executors, Elizabeth Smith, his niece, and Margaret Stringer, a widow. For 100 poor tradesmen's and ministers' widows, Povey left money and a copy each of *The Virgin in Eden* and *Torments after Death*. Povey was buried beside his wife on 8 May at St Mary's, Newington.

MARK G. SPENCER

Sources P. G. M. Dickson, *The Sun Insurance Office, 1710–1960* (1960), 17–31 · F. B. Relton, *An account of the fire insurance companies … also of Charles Povey* (1893), 261–84, 447–543 · R. Turner, 'English coal industry in the seventeenth and eighteenth centuries', *American Historical Review*, 27 (1921), 1–23 · W. Lewins, *Her majesty's mails: an historical and descriptive account of the British post-office* (1864), 82–4 · T. Keymer and P. Sabor, eds., *The Pamela controversy: criticisms and adaptations of Samuel Richardson's 'Pamela', 1740–1750*, 6 vols. (2001), vol. 2, pp. xvii–xix · M. M. Goldsmith, 'Public virtue and private vices: Bernard Mandeville and English political ideologies in the early eighteenth century', *Eighteenth-Century Studies*, 91 (1976), 477–510 · F. Staff, *The penny post, 1680–1918* (1992), 53–4 · *The new Cambridge bibliography of English literature*, [2nd edn], 2, ed. G. Watson (1971), 1272, 1321 · *National Union Catalog pre-1956 imprints*, vol. 468, pp. 280–81 · *IGI* · will, PRO, PROB 11/726, sig. 172

Povey, Thomas (*b*. 1613/14, *d*. in or before 1705), colonial entrepreneur and administrator, was the son of Justinian Povey (*d*. *c*.1652), auditor of the queen's revenue and auditor of the exchequer, and his second wife, Anne Keterick (*d*. 1657). One of a family of at least nine children, he seems originally to have been destined for the law and entered Gray's Inn in 1633. Believing the civil war to be unjustifiable, he had at first taken up a non-partisan stance, expounding his views in a pamphlet, *The Moderator, Expecting Sudden Peace or Certaine Ruine* (1643), which elicited three hostile responses, the last entitled *Neutrality is Malignancy, by J.M.* (1648). Povey was elected an MP for Liskeard in March 1647, only to be secluded at Pride's Purge in December 1648. As the English revolution progressed, moderation became ever more suspect; Povey was thought to be disloyal to the council of state and in 1650 a warrant was issued for his arrest. Trade now seemed a safer and more profitable pursuit than politics, particularly since Povey possessed, so he avowed, a fortune hardly sufficient to support him. There was a family connection with the colonies; his father had been appointed a commissioner of the Caribbee Islands in 1637.

In 1654 Povey helped to fit out the 'western design' fleet, working closely with the London merchant-capitalist Martin Noell, principal banker to the government and, as

Thomas Povey (*b*. 1613/14, *d*. in or before 1705), by John Michael Wright, 1658

Povey noted, a man in 'extraordinary favor' with Cromwell (Andrews, 50). Two of Povey's brothers accompanied the fleet, and although this expedition was, in many respects, an ill-organized fiasco, the débâcle did not hurt the Poveys. Richard and William Povey acquired minor offices in Jamaica and Barbados respectively and Thomas himself soon became a recognized expert on matters colonial. He was to remain at the centre of colonial affairs for the next decade.

A whole series of papers concerning the proper governance and commercial exploitation of England's colonies flowed from Povey's pen. It was probably he who first proposed a council of trade, to which he was duly appointed in 1655, and he became the chairman, secretary, and most active member of the council for America (1657). Throughout the vicissitudes of protectorate, restored Commonwealth, and restored monarchy, Povey kept his nerve, built up his contacts and tailored his 'overtures' and 'propositions' to suit the situation. He maintained an extensive correspondence with governors and other colonial officials and acted as a minor patronage broker, although he modestly disclaimed to be anything but a 'Journeyman', with 'little power' but 'greater industrie' (Bliss, 261).

Povey continued to invest in colonial trading schemes with Noell and others, some profitable, some not (the Nova Scotia Company was probably among the latter). His fortune grew; he had found that the marriage market could offer as much as the colonial in the disordered days of the late 1650s and in 1657 he married Mary, daughter of John Adderly, widow of John Agard of King's Bromley, Staffordshire, 'a handsome old woman that brought him money' (Pepys, 4.297). An elegant house next door to the residence of the earl of Northampton was built for the Poveys on Arch Row, the most fashionable part of Lincoln's Inn Fields. A daughter, Frances, married Giles Bland, executed in 1677 for his role in the Virginia rebellion.

In February 1659 Povey was elected to Richard Cromwell's parliament as an MP for Bossiney. A year later he was among the MPs secluded in 1648 who took their seats in the reassembled Long Parliament. To the moderate-minded Povey, the Restoration was both pleasing and profitable. In 1661 he was granted the receiver-generalship for the rents and revenues in Africa and America, the office 'being framed by him and he much versed in plantation affairs' (*CSP dom.*, 1661–2, 94; 1663–4, 408). His colonial expertise was also recognized by an appointment to the council of trade (1660) and the secretaryship of the committee for foreign plantations (1661). In 1660 he became treasurer of the duke of York's household, and in 1662 treasurer of Tangier and surveyor-general of its victualling department. In 1662 also he was made a master of requests extraordinary, with the promise of the next ordinary vacancy.

Such prodigious pluralism took its toll, however. Povey was clearly overextended and in 1665 he resigned the treasurership of Tangier to Pepys: they were to share the profits equally. In 1666 he lost his place as the duke of York's treasurer, being replaced by Sir Allan Apsley. According to Pepys (a not entirely disinterested observer), Povey had neglected all his business and committed it to unfit hands (Pepys, 7.191–2) and it is clear that his accounts were in substantial disarray. Not surprisingly, Pepys found Povey 'mightily discontented … about his disappointments at Court' in this period (Pepys, 7.228). His career never recovered. As recorder of Thetford, he botched the management of the Thetford election in 1669; Sir Joseph Williamson, client of the powerful Arlington, had to look elsewhere for assistance. Understandably, an application in 1673 to discuss the transference of Williamson's council clerkship to Povey upon the former's elevation to a secretaryship of state was unsuccessful; there was a petulant tone to Povey's letter as he bewailed the fact that the good will and power of his friends had not as yet recommended him to some advantageous station (Christie, 2.5–6). It was becoming clear in this period that he could gain patronage and office only for his talented nephew, William Blathwayt, and not for himself. On James II's accession (1685) he lost his mastership of requests, although he remained a member of the queen dowager's council.

There was much more to Povey than his offices, however. Pepys found him 'most excellent in anything but business' (Pepys, 6.215). He was a gentleman of fashion and a 'nice contriver of all elegancies' (Evelyn, 4.84). The house in Lincoln's Inn Fields was a marvel: its cabinet work, wine cellar, stables, and pictures, especially the *trompe-l'œil* perspectives, all gained universal admiration.

Povey was a generous, if garrulous, host, always ready to retail the latest court gossip and to offer advice on social niceties. He was a connoisseur and collector (he donated thirty-eight rare volumes to the College of Arms) and an original member of the Royal Society, serving on its council in 1663, 1679, and 1691. Fascinated by things mechanical, in 1669 he applied with John Prichard for a patent for an engine for raising water and he perfectly conforms to the definition of the 'virtuoso': intensely curious, interested, as were Evelyn and Pepys, in the 'rare' and the 'wonderful', a man of taste and discrimination and possessed of the funds to indulge them. In 1701 the financier Sir Stephen Fox congratulated Povey on his memory and his letter writing: 'No man in England of 87 years' could compare (Glos. RO, MS D1799/C9). His last appearance in the Royal Society's membership lists is 1702. Administration of his estate was granted to his nephew, William Blathwayt, in July 1705. BARBARA C. MURISON

Sources C. M. Andrews, *British committees, commissions, and councils of trade and plantations, 1622–1675* (Baltimore, MD, 1908) · R. M. Bliss, *Revolution and empire: English politics and the American colonies in the seventeenth century* (1990) · Pepys, *Diary* · BL, Egerton MS 2395 · *CSP dom.*, 1661–4 · M. Hunter, *The Royal Society and its fellows, 1660–1700: the morphology of an early scientific institution*, 2nd edn (1994) · G. A. Jacobsen, *William Blathwayt: a late seventeenth-century English administrator* (1932) · Glos. RO, Blathwayt MS D1799 · *CSP col.* · Evelyn, *Diary* · HoP, *Commons, 1660–90* · W. D. Christie, ed., *Letters addressed from London to Sir Joseph Williamson*, 2, CS, new ser., 9 (1874) · D. Underdown, *Pride's Purge: politics in the puritan revolution* (1971) · PRO, PROB 6/81, fol. 149 · M. Coate, *Cornwall in the great civil war and interregnum, 1642–1660* (1933) · *DNB* · Venn, *Alum. Cant.*
Archives BL, corresp. relating to the West Indies, Add. MS 11411 · BL, papers, Sloane MSS · BL, papers relating to the colonies, Egerton MS 2395 · JRL, papers relating to revenues of duke of York | Coll. Arms, heraldic and genealogical collections, B1–B38 · Glos. RO, Blathwayt MS D1799
Likenesses J. M. Wright, oils, 1658, Dyrham Park, Gloucestershire [*see illus.*] · portrait (after J. M. Wright), Dyrham Park, Gloucestershire
Wealth at death reasonable; half profits from treasurership of Tangier, £400 p.a. pension after resigning as treasurer to duke of York; but was extravagant and perhaps financially strained; sold country house 1671, and 500 books and ninety-three pictures in 1693 (for £500): *Dyrham guide*, 39 · experienced 'comparative narrowness', 1701: Fox, Glos. RO, Blathwayt MS D1799/C9

Powderham [*alias* Exeter, Poydras, Tanner], **John** (*d.* 1318), impostor, was the son of an Exeter tanner who attained notoriety by treasonably claiming to be the rightful king of England in 1318. Records are meagre: on 20 July William Montagu, the king's steward, was ordered to take him (under the name of John Exeter) from Northampton gaol for trial. All further information comes from chronicle sources, which show a reasonable correspondence of detail.

Powderham, who took his name from a hamlet about 5½ miles south of Exeter, first made his claim in Oxford in June 1318. Variously described as *literatus* or *scriptor*, perhaps attracted from Exeter to make his living as a scribe on the fringes of Oxford's university community, he went to the King's Hall there, which had recently been granted to the Carmelites, and ordered them to leave his house, claiming to be the true heir of Edward I. His claim was confused, being reported both as a claim to be Edward II's brother, and as a claim to be the real Edward II, changed in the cradle following injury through the negligence of his nurse. He was first imprisoned in the Bocardo in Oxford, then in Northampton. The king treated him with derision, but the queen and the magnates took him seriously in the tense political situation of 1317–18. A trial was held before Montagu; Powderham's parents were brought from Exeter and swore he was their son; he then allegedly confessed to association with the devil, who he said had persuaded him to make the claim; and he was executed by hanging about 24 July. Franciscan and Dominican writers used the episode as an excuse to preach on the vanity of dreams and on false prophets, but in general chroniclers were sceptical about witchcraft, and the canon of Bridlington considered him weak in the head.

The Lanercost chronicler raised the question of whether Powderham was manipulated by others. His advent certainly came at a delicate political time. England hovered on the edge of civil war in 1317 and early 1318, with relations between Edward and Thomas of Lancaster at their lowest ebb. However, mediation intensified in June and July 1318, largely due to the need to face the Scots, who had retaken Berwick in April. By 23 June the first set of talks had failed, but on 11 and again on 18 July the archbishop of Canterbury expected success. It is exactly in these months that the impostor appeared. Agreement was finally reached on 29 July, just after his execution. If he was, as most chronicle reports seem to suggest, a foolish, half-educated man, who had convinced himself that the devil came to him in dreams, he might easily be manipulated, but if so, by whom? The king's favourites did not particularly want a peace settlement with Lancaster if it included a confirmation of the ordinances, but it is not easy to see how an attack on the king's position would help them, unless they hoped to attribute the attack to Lancaster. It is conceivable that Lancaster or some of his supporters might encourage an attack on the king if they thought it would weaken him, and bring reconciliation on Lancaster's terms. There is in fact no evidence that either side had any connection with Powderham, nor of what effect his appearance had on negotiations. The impostor was an embarrassment to Edward, but it is unlikely that anyone saw the deposition of Edward as a practical possibility at this time, and, whatever Edward's faults, it is highly doubtful that any manipulator would seriously think that a man whose background appears to have been an upbringing in an Exeter craft family, and who believed he was in contact with the devil, would be more suitable. Edward's initial reaction, to see him as a court jester, might well have been the right one in normal times.

WENDY R. CHILDS

Sources W. Childs, '"Welcome my brother": Edward II, John of Powderham and the chronicles, 1318', *Church and chronicle in the middle ages: essays presented to John Taylor*, ed. I. Wood and G. A. Loud (1991), 149–63 · *CPR, 1317–21*, 273 · W. R. Childs and J. Taylor, eds., *The Anonimalle Chronicle, 1307 to 1334: from Brotherton collection MS 29*, Yorkshire Archaeological Society, 147 (1991) · PRO, E 37/4 m.3

Powel [Powell], **David** (1549×52–1598), Church of England clergyman and historian, was the son of Hywel ap Dafydd ap Gruffudd of Denbighshire (his father's family possessed a pedigree stretching back to beyond 1073) and of Katherine, the daughter of Gruffudd ab Ievan ap Dafydd. At the age of sixteen, some time between 1566 and 1568, David Powel went to study at Oxford University although his initial college membership is not known. He migrated to Jesus College upon its foundation in 1571 and is thought to be its first graduate, receiving the degree of BA on 3 March 1573 and that of MA on 6 July 1576. In the meantime Powel married Elizabeth, the daughter of Cynwrig of Marchwiail before 1570. The couple had at least three sons—Daniel, the eldest and a layperson, and two clerics, Samuel (1570–1600) and Gabriel (1576–1611). Powel's scholarly talents were considerable enough to attract the support of the church. Even before his graduation he was named vicar of Ruabon in Denbighshire in 1570, and the rectory of Llanfyllin in Montgomeryshire followed in 1571. In 1579 he exchanged Llanfyllin for the vicarage of Meifod, and he also held two prebends in St Asaph Cathedral. Such support allowed Powel to pursue further studies in theology so that in 1583 he earned the degree of BTh from Oxford on 19 February and proceeded DTh on 11 April. Between about 1584 and 1586 Powel was at Ludlow, serving as private chaplain to Sir Henry Sidney, president of the council of Wales.

Although Powel did not enjoy a long life, he contributed significantly to the development and preservation of Welsh culture and helped to plant the seeds of protestantism in Wales. As both a staunch Welsh patriot and a committed protestant Powel engaged in many activities and projects to forward those interests. In particular, he supported efforts to translate the entire Bible into Welsh, a project that was finally completed in 1587. Its translator William Morgan gratefully acknowledged Powel's assistance. During 1588 he was mentioned as one of three preachers working in the diocese of St Asaph and for years he kept the privy council informed about illegal and possibly treasonous books, libels, and prophecies that circulated among Welsh Roman Catholics.

Powel was also a respected scholar and early on became associated with the group of geographers that included John Dee and Richard Hakluyt. He may be the 'D. P.' who wrote the elementary tract *Brief Rules of Geography for the Understanding of Maps and Charts* (1573). When John Dee left England in September 1573, Powel inherited the project of preparing for publication a manuscript in the possession of Sir Henry Sidney. It was the English translation by the antiquary Humphrey Llwyd of some medieval Welsh chronicles. With the help of William Cecil, Lord Burghley, who provided him with access to important documents, Powel went further and greatly expanded Llwyd's work in both depth of detail and in chronological coverage. In doing so he was careful to make his additions typographically distinct. The result was Powel's *magnum opus*, The *Historie of Cambria, now called Wales* (1584), the first printed history of Wales. It remained a major and popular source for medieval Welsh history until the early nineteenth century. In it Powel showed his ardent support of the Tudor dynasty. *The Historie of Cambria* also popularized the legend of the discovery of America by the Welsh prince Madoc about 1170. Powel, along with Dee, personally supported the authenticity of the Madoc story which served to justify English encroachments on Spanish America as Hakluyt showed in his *Discourse on Western Planting* (1584). It also for centuries spawned countless tales of encounters with Welsh Indians on the American frontier.

The next year, 1585, saw Powel publish an omnibus volume containing editions of Ponticus Virunnius's *Historia Britannica*; Gerald of Wales's *Itinerarium Cambriae* and *Descriptio Cambriae* (omitting its negative comments about the Welsh); and the letter entitled *De Britannica historia recte intelligenda*. This volume he dedicated to Sir Henry Sidney, who now employed him as his personal chaplain. According to his son Daniel and the Welsh lexicographer Dr John Davies, Powel also worked on a Welsh dictionary throughout his life which was never published. He died early in 1598 at Ruabon and was buried there.

RONALD H. FRITZE

Sources DNB · DWB · D. Powell [D. Powel], 'Epistle dedicatorie' and 'To the reader', in *The historie of Cambria, now called Wales*, ed. D. Powell, trans. H. Lhoyd [H. Llwyd] (1584) · Wood, *Ath. Oxon.*, new edn · M. McKisack, *Medieval history in the Tudor age* (1971) · G. A. Williams, *Madoc: the making of a myth* (1979) · G. Williams, 'Religion and Welsh literature in the age of the Reformation', *The Welsh and their religion* (1991), 138–72 · Foster, *Alum. Oxon.*

Powell. *See also* Powel, Powle.

Powell, Sir (George) Allan (1876–1948), public servant, was born on 1 February 1876 at Mile End, London, the son of Richard Powell, labourer, later school caretaker, and his wife, Mary Anne Clouter. He was educated at Bancroft's School and King's College, London, and was called to the bar at Gray's Inn in 1907. On 24 May 1904 Powell married Jeannie Jack (*b.* 1878/9), daughter of John Marshall, a Stepney physician and surgeon; they had one son.

Powell worked for the Metropolitan Asylums Board from 1894, reaching the post of assistant clerk to the board by 1914. Throughout the First World War he was resident officer-in-charge of the government war refugees camp at Earls Court, where he had charge of a shifting refugee community of 4000 allied soldiers and civilians. For this work he was made a CBE in 1920, and was also awarded the order of Leopold of Belgium, the white eagle of Serbia, and the médaille de la Reconnaissance Française. He published a book on his experiences, *Four Years in a Refugee Camp*, in 1924.

During the inter-war years Powell made his name as a distinguished public servant. He was clerk to the Metropolitan Asylums Board from 1922 until its transfer to the London county council (LCC) in 1930, and published its history, *The Metropolitan Asylums Board and its Work, 1867–1930*, in 1930. Between 1930 and 1932 he organized a new department of public assistance for the LCC. Meanwhile, he was a member of the royal commission on food prices from 1924 to 1925, a member of the night baking committee in 1925, and in 1929, after four years as vice-chairman of the National Food Council and chairman of its executive committee (during which time he was knighted, in 1927), came to public prominence as its chairman (1929–32).

From 1932 to 1939 Powell served full-time on the import duties advisory committee, acting as an unofficial liaison between the chairman of the committee, Lord May, the economic adviser Sir Sydney Chapman, and the consumer. He was appointed president of the state medicine and industrial hygiene section of the Public Health Congress in 1933, and chairman of the Institute of Public Administration conference in 1934, and sat on the committee on key industries duties in 1935. Elected to the council of the royal borough of Kensington in 1932, he was twice mayor, in 1937–8 and 1938–9.

In March 1939 Neville Chamberlain appointed Powell to the chairmanship of the board of governors of the BBC, where he succeeded R. C. Norman on 18 April 1939. Despite his successful administrative career Powell was not considered an obvious choice for the post: he memorably acknowledged on accepting the appointment that 'I know nothing of radio. Frankly, I don't know how many valves my set has got' (Briggs, *Governing the BBC*, 67). The question of his qualifications to arrange the variety programmes was raised in parliament, and the press did not fail to compare his new job with his previous responsibilities at the Metropolitan Asylums Board. The outbreak of war placed additional and unanticipated burdens on the post of chairman, notably from 1939 to 1941 when the number of governors was reduced from seven to two and the BBC's very independence came under government challenge.

Powell's role as the wartime BBC chairman remains ambiguous. He maintained a genial and uncontroversial public profile during the war, but his accommodating attitude to the government was a persistent source of concern within the corporation, notably his assurance to the minister of information Lord Macmillan in September 1939 that he accepted the direction of the government in all matters pertaining to the war effort, and his good relations with Churchill (one of the principal advocates of a 'controlled' BBC). Although he worked actively behind the scenes to reappoint a far stronger and more influential full board of governors in April 1941, mistrust persisted as he oversaw the extension of closer ties between the BBC, Ministry of Information, and the intelligence services, assuming powers increasingly greater than those of the BBC director-general himself. In particular his 'feud' with Director-General Frederick Ogilvie and his role in the latter's resignation in January 1942 (in order to facilitate reorganization of the corporation) fuelled internal concerns despite Ogilvie's recognized shortcomings in the post. Nevertheless, the BBC's fears of government control were not ultimately realized and, probably in part owing to Powell's willingness to compromise—though also to the decision by the minister of information Brendan Bracken not to press home his advantage—the BBC emerged from the war having played an essential part in maintaining public morale, and with its public reputation and status not simply secure but immeasurably enhanced.

Describing himself as simply an 'ordinary listener' (Briggs, *Governing the BBC*, 154), Powell impressed contemporaries with his energy and his courtly charm. A large, genial man, Powell was said to be a born chairman of committees, with the ability to bring out the best in others. He believed strongly in the future of broadcasting, and predicted as early as 1943 that television would be in every home after the war. He was reappointed to the chairmanship in 1944 and was made a GBE in the same year. He also maintained his wider interests in the field of public administration. As well as serving as chairman of the radio and cinema section of the British Association conference in 1943, he was a member of the committee on industrial alcohol in 1943, and in 1944 and 1946 again chaired the Institute of Public Administration conferences. Other positions held during his career included chairman of Briggs Motor Bodies Ltd, vice-president of the Royal Sanitary Institute (1939), and honorary fellow of the American Public Health Association.

Having overseen the opening day of post-war BBC television on 7 June 1946 (during which he—like many other experienced public speakers new to the cameras—momentarily 'dried' on air), Powell retired from the BBC and in effect from public life on 31 December 1946. He died at his home, Mead Cottage, Ridgeway, Gerrards Cross, Buckinghamshire, on 24 January 1948. He was survived by his wife and their son Donald. Among many others at his memorial service, at St Mary Abbots, Kensington, were the director-general of the BBC, Sir William Haley, many officials and members of staff of the BBC, officials of the LCC, and the mayor and mayoress of Kensington.

SIÂN NICHOLAS

Sources *The Times* (14 March 1939) · *The Times* (26 Jan 1948) · A. Briggs, *The history of broadcasting in the United Kingdom*, 4 vols. (1961–79), vols. 3–4 · A. Briggs, *Governing the BBC* (1979) · A. Briggs, *The BBC: the first fifty years* (1985) · *The Listener* (29 Jan 1948) · CGPLA Eng. & Wales (1948) · WWW · d. cert. · m. cert.
Archives BBC WAC, corresp., memoranda, working papers
Likenesses photograph, repro. in *The Times* (14 March 1939), 12e
Wealth at death £17,560 18s. 5d.: probate, 20 March 1948, CGPLA Eng. & Wales

Powell, Anthony Dymoke (1905–2000), writer, was born on 21 December 1905 at 44 Ashley Gardens, Westminster, London, the only child of Lieutenant-Colonel Philip Lionel William Powell (1882–1959) CBE DSO, of the Welch regiment, and Maud Mary (1867–1954), second daughter of Edmund Lionel Wells-Dymoke, whose family owned land in Lincolnshire. A passionate genealogist, who said his hobby underlined 'the vast extent of human oddness' (Powell, *Infants of the Spring*, 2), Powell claimed descent from the medieval Welsh chieftain Rhys ap Gruffydd (1132–1197), ruler of south Wales. By Elizabethan times, when the family had begun to call itself Powell (pronounced 'Poel'), their estate had shrunk to a few hundred acres on the marches. It disappeared entirely in the eighteenth century, after which the Powells left the principality for good. But Powell considered himself Welsh and was angry when people disputed this.

Although privileged in many respects, Powell experienced just enough of the 'moderate unhappiness in childhood' (Powell, *Under Review*, 304) he thought a writer needed to get him going. His father was largely to blame for this. Like the narrator's father in *A Dance to the Music of Time*, Colonel Powell was a difficult man, highly strung, caustic, often morose. His wife, fifteen years older, dedicated herself to his welfare, a task made no easier by the number of times the family had to move in the course of his career. Powell was not exactly neglected as a child, but, brought up never to draw attention to himself, he was often rather bored and lonely.

Powell had a gentleman's education, beginning in 1916 at the New Beacon preparatory school in Kent, which he loathed, continuing at Eton College, which he enjoyed, and concluding at Balliol College, Oxford, in which he was disappointed. At Eton, where he overlapped with Eric Blair (pseudonym George Orwell), Cyril Connolly, Henry Yorke (pseudonym Henry Green), and Harold Acton, his happiest hours were spent in the studio, a meeting place for boys of all ages 'whose adventures took place in the world of the imagination' (Powell, *New English Review*, 11 Sept 1945, 468). It was here that Powell began to grasp what an exciting period this was for the arts. At Oxford he was handicapped by being neither rich nor homosexual, and despite attending some amusing parties was often sunk in gloom. Later he concluded that 'to the egotism of adolescence … there is nothing to be offered short of growing up and a life of one's own' (Powell, 'Youth in the twenties', *TLS*, 9 Nov 1951, 703).

Powell left Oxford with a third in history and in 1926 joined Duckworth, the publishers, where one of his jobs was to read unsolicited manuscripts. He said he learned more about writing from this chore than from reading the classics. Another influence was Hemingway, who, as Powell said, 'cleared the ground of extraneous matter in the Twenties' (Powell, *Miscellaneous Verdicts*, 225). But first Powell had to grow up, a process that accelerated once he graduated from débutante dances to bohemian routs, with their quota of what were once referred to as 'Arts, Barts, Smarts, Tarts and Upstarts'. He captured the seedier side of this milieu in his first novel, *Afternoon Men* (1931), described as 'the party novel to end all party novels' ('From a chase to a view', *TLS*, 16 Feb 1951). Two other novels quickly followed, *Venusberg* (1932) and *From a View to a Death* (1933); all three were distinguished by their deadpan humour and underlying melancholy. But by now the party was over for young writers like Powell whose commitment was to literature, not politics. His marriage on 1 December 1934 to Lady Violet Georgiana Pakenham (1912–2002), third daughter of the fifth earl of Longford, was the one bright spot in an otherwise depressing pre-war period when he struggled to make himself heard above the clamour for a popular front.

Much to his regret Powell never saw action in the Second World War, his military career duplicating that of Jenkins in the *Music of Time*: eighteen months as an infantry subaltern in Ulster, followed by four years in the intelligence corps as military liaison officer to various allied governments in exile. This, he maintained, was the hardest work he had ever done in his life. He was demobilized in the rank of major and awarded the orders of the White Lion (Czechoslovakia), Leopold II (Belgium), and Oaken Crown and Croix de Guerre (Luxembourg).

Fiction was out of the question for Powell in wartime, but he did manage to assemble some notes for his first post-war book: *John Aubrey and his Friends* (1948), a biography of the seventeenth-century antiquary and biographer whose intense curiosity about his fellow men he shared. He then began to write *A Question of Upbringing* (1951), the first instalment of *A Dance to the Music of Time*, the twelve-volume novel on which his reputation rests. This covers more than fifty years in the life of Nicholas Jenkins, who is, like Powell himself, an urbane, yet sharply observant novelist married to the daughter of a peer. But the novel is less about Jenkins than about the world he belongs to, in which the more raffish elements of the establishment commingle with the upper echelons of bohemia, the usual catalysts being their wives, mistresses, and lovers. Observing how these incoherent bodies interact, and the bizarre unions that result, Jenkins discerns a pattern dictated by the rhythm of life—hence the theme of the novel, which is that its characters, like the Seasons in Poussin's painting, are engaged in a ritual dance to the music of time.

His contemporary Evelyn Waugh likened Powell's huge cast to 'a continuous frieze in high relief, deep cut and detailed' (E. Waugh, *Essays, Articles and Reviews*, 1983, 548). One figure in particular stands out: that of Widmerpool, the obtuse, inelegant, yet indefatigable striver, living by the will, dedicated to 'getting on'; his quietus in the final chapter bears out another of the novel's themes, that 'in the end most things in life—perhaps all things—turn out to be appropriate' (Powell, *Casanova's Chinese Restaurant*, 1960, 2). What was not appropriate, in Powell's view, was the way in which people would try and 'pin his characters down', particularly Widmerpool, whose supposed identity was the subject of endless debate. Paradoxically, he gave his own opinion on this contentious subject to a character of his who does appear to have been drawn from life, X. Trapnel, a projection of the Fitzrovian writer Julian Maclaren-Ross. 'Human beings aren't subtle enough to play their part', says Trapnel. 'That's where the art comes in' (Powell, *Books do Furnish a Room*, 1971, 215).

For Powell, literary art was like alchemy, a mysterious indefinable process by which the commonplace was transmuted. But art alone was not enough. Writing a novel, so he said on several occasions, was 'appallingly hard work' and there were times when, like Kipling (a favourite of his), he would get up from his chair feeling he would never be able to write another line. But of course there he would be next morning, in front of the typewriter. It was all a question of guts.

Powell was a conscientious and prolific literary journalist. From 1947 until 1952 he supervised fiction on the *Times Literary Supplement*, leaving to become literary editor of *Punch* under Malcolm Muggeridge, who had recommended the *Music of Time* to Powell's publisher, Heinemann. Powell was created CBE in 1956 and in 1958 his novel *At Lady Molly's* won the James Tait Black memorial prize. Also in 1958 he left *Punch* and for the next thirty years reviewed a book every other week in the *Daily Telegraph*. He also wrote a good deal about art, in which he took as much pleasure as in writing. From 1962 until 1976 he was a trustee of the National Portrait Gallery, which contains a drawing of him by Hubert Freeth. Powell was also drawn by Augustus John, Nina Hamnett, and Adrian Daintrey, and painted by his brother-in-law Henry Lamb.

In 1974 Powell was made an honorary fellow of Balliol College, Oxford, and awarded a DLitt at the University of Wales and several other universities. *Temporary Kings*, the penultimate volume of the *Music of Time*, won the W. H. Smith award. Powell was made a Companion of Honour in 1988. Two large collections of his essays and reviews, *Miscellaneous Verdicts* and *Under Review*, were published in 1990 and 1991.

Powell thrived on gossip, and in a long life he accumulated an impressive haul. Some of this found its way into his *Memoirs* and *Journals*, which should be read by anyone interested in the cultural history of twentieth-century Britain. The *Journals*, begun in 1982 when he was seventy-seven, are also notable for their spleen, which up until then had been largely absent from his writing. The last work of his to appear was *A Writer's Notebook*, published posthumously but dating from about 1930, containing ideas, aphorisms, and quotations which had taken his fancy.

Of medium height, with bushy eyebrows, a long upper lip, and plenty of white hair which he would smooth back with both hands when being interviewed, Powell was once described as looking like a cross between a duke, a don, and an actor. His Edwardian upbringing left its mark on him: he was courteous, but not pliable, and by no means everyone felt at ease with him. But to those who were on his wavelength he was the best of company: amusing, generous, loyal, and as eager to hear a good story as to tell one, at which he excelled. He was a good judge of wine, liked making curries, and was particularly fond of cats (he had a theory that people who preferred dogs craved power). In 1952, having lived in London since their marriage, he and Lady Violet, together with their two sons, moved to The Chantry, a grey stone Regency house in its own grounds near Frome in Somerset. Powell died at The Chantry on 28 March 2000 and following his cremation his ashes were scattered on the lake there. Lady Violet died on 12 January 2002.   MICHAEL BARBER

Sources A. Powell, *Infants of the spring* (1976) · A. Powell, *Miscellaneous verdicts* (1990) · A. Powell, *Under review* (1991) · A. Powell, *Journals, 1982–86* (1995); *1987–89* (1996); *1990–92* (1997) · A. Powell, *A writer's notebook* (2000) · Burke, *Gen. GB* · *Paris Review* (spring/summer 1978) · *Summary* (autumn 1970) · G. Lilley, ed., *Anthony Powell: a bibliography* (1993) · *The Times* (30 March 2000) · *Daily Telegraph* (29 March 2000) · *The Guardian* (30 March 2000) · private information

(2004) • personal knowledge (2004) • A. Powell, *Faces in my time* (1980)

Archives Lincs. Arch., corresp. and papers relating to Wells Dymoke families | U. Leeds, Brotherton L., letters to the *London Magazine* • UCL, corresp. with George Orwell • University of Bristol, corresp. and statements relating to trial of *Lady Chatterley's lover* | SOUND BL

Likenesses N. Hamnett, drawing, 1927 • A. Daintrey, drawing, 1931 • L. Morley, bromide print, 1963, NPG • M. Boxer, caricature • H. A. Freeth, pencil, NPG • A. John, drawing • H. Lamb, oils • O. Lancaster, caricature • N. Mee, oils • J. S. Monagan, photograph • W. Pye, bust • photographs, NPG

Wealth at death £1,617,713: probate, 10 Oct 2000, *CGPLA Eng. & Wales*

Powell, Baden (1796–1860), physicist and theologian, was born at Stamford Hill, Hackney, Middlesex, on 22 August 1796, the eldest son of Baden Powell (1767–1841), wine merchant and, in 1831, high sheriff of Kent, and his first cousin Hester Powell (1776–1848). The Powell family circle included leading representatives of the Hackney Phalanx, the group of conservative high-churchmen of considerable influence on church politics in the early nineteenth century. Thomas Sikes, Joshua Watson, and Henry Handely Norris were Powell's relatives. Powell entered Oriel College, Oxford, in the spring of 1814, and started residence in January 1815. William Van Mildert, bishop of Llandaff and a family friend, recommended him to the provost, Edward Copleston, and to Richard Whately, at the time firm allies of the conservative Phalanx. Powell became Whately's pupil and lifelong friend. Having graduated in 1817 with first-class honours in mathematics he proceeded MA and was ordained in 1821. He had started his clerical career in December 1820 as curate of Midhurst, Sussex, then in 1821 took the vicarage of Plumstead, Kent, a living to which he was presented by his family. There he conducted experiments on radiant heat and wrote his early contributions to conservative journals financed by the Hackney Phalanx. He married, on 17 July 1821, Eliza Rivaz, but the poor health of his wife forced him to leave Plumstead in 1824, and take residence in Clapton, London.

Powell's early experimental work concentrated on radiant heat and the wave theory of light. In papers published in the *Philosophical Transactions of the Royal Society* and elsewhere he argued that radiant heat could be intercepted by a glass screen, whereas the light emitted by hot bodies, being capable of passing through the screen, increased the heating effect of the source. His work on heat attracted little attention and almost no support, whereas his experiments on the dispersion of light carried on in the early 1830s as exemplification of Cauchy's wave theory of light met with qualified approval. However, he was unable to keep pace with the increasing mathematical sophistication of contemporary physics; his papers submitted to the Royal Society in the late 1830s contained serious mathematical flaws. 'Several times under similar circumstances I have felt determined … never again to meddle with science,' he wrote to Lubbock in February 1839, acknowledging his 'want of command of analysis' (Royal Society, Lubbock MSS, fols. 301, 294). Nevertheless,

he published 137 scientific papers between 1822 and 1860 in numerous journals, eleven with the Royal Astronomical Society (RAS).

A fellow of the Royal Society since 1824 (vice-president in 1853), upon being elected Savilian professor of geometry at Oxford in 1827 Powell resigned his living. He was an active member of metropolitan scientific bodies such as the Geological and Astronomical societies and was a leading participant in the 1850 royal commission for the reform of British universities. He contributed widely to the British Association for the Advancement of Science with surveys of current research on heat, or on issues fashionable in the mid-century such as the fall of meteorites. He served the association as a local secretary at Oxford in 1832, and was a council member in 1837, vice-president, and president of section A in 1847. From the early 1840s Powell increasingly chose for himself the gentlemanly role of commentator on philosophical, scientific, and theological issues, and on the way they impinged upon the social and political condition of England.

Powell's fame rested on his role as commentator on theological issues. He was a fierce critic of the Tractarian movement, and to the dismay of high-church relatives such as Edward Churton he gained the controversial reputation of being an early proponent of what was to become known as broad church theology. Yet his early sermons, his anonymous contributions to the *British Critic* and the *Christian Remembrancer* of the 1820s, and the essay *Rational Religion Examined* (1826) fully reflected the conservative stand of the Hackney Phalanx as interpreted by the Oriel school. On the one hand Powell affirmed that scriptural prophecies and miracles attested to the truth of the gospels; he therefore argued that it was impious to submit their content to the test of fallible human reason, as atheists and Unitarians were doing. On the other hand, natural theology was at best a pious exercise; at worst, a concession to unbelievers. While accepting that true rational Christians had no other consistent choice but to submit to the literal wording of the scriptures, following Dugald Stewart, Powell maintained that necessary truths were attained only by deduction from mathematical definitions. Thus he held that knowledge of the natural world was inevitably contingent, since man's definitions of phenomena were bound to be limited; hence, no result of scientific endeavour could be construed as contradicting the scriptural narrative.

These theological debates were further complicated by social pressures which spilled over into the pulpit. The Catholic Emancipation Bill of 1829 broke the alliance between Oriel College—by and large favourable to the measure—and the Hackney Phalanx. Powell became convinced that his family circle did not understand the need to adapt to the climate of change pervading the country. In a sermon preached in 1833, *Revelation and Science*, he forcefully expressed the view that the social and theological leadership of the Anglican church could not be defended by repressive measures, but only through a well considered reform of Christian apologetics centred on the authority of scientific progress. This view reflected his engagement in the early 1830s in the reform movement at Oxford University, where he pleaded for scientific subjects to be given higher curricular consideration. Powell was public examiner in 1828 and 1831, effectively the only representative of mathematics, and, beside Charles Daubeny and Richard Walker, of physical science in the university. Quiet in manner, an excellent and popular lecturer, he was outspoken in his views. Once all hopes for reforming the curriculum were crushed, Powell took advantage of the 1832 British Association meeting at Oxford to appeal to the intelligentsia of the country. This infuriated conservative dons. Moreover his opposition to the mounting wave of the Tractarian movement also contributed to his increased isolation at Oxford. Powell's personal ties to Richard Whately were reinforced by marriage. His first wife having died on 13 March 1836, on 27 September 1837 he married Charlotte Pope, the younger sister of Whately's wife, Elizabeth; they had one son, Thomas Baden Henry (b. 1841), later judge of the chief court, Lahore, and three daughters.

Powell articulated his philosophy of science and of Christian apologetics which had evolved from an epistemology based on deduction from axiomatic like premises and his initial opposition to the argument from design, to a natural theology founded on induction, therefore accessible to all rational beings including the intellectual industrial élites and also the leaders of the emerging working-class movement. He argued that the progress of discovery bespoke of a God operating through natural laws and that developments in the physical, the natural, and the social sciences all showed the ultimate beneficial results of an arrangement that men had the duty to understand. Therefore, to Powell a belief in miracles increasingly became the symptom of primitive ignorance—to him embedded in the Old Testament—of the natural causes at the bases of ordinary or extraordinary phenomena.

During the late 1830s and the 1840s, frequent visits to London and Dublin made up for his loss of influence in Oxford. Family tragedy, remarriages, and his intellectual life prolonged his stay in the capital, to where he finally moved in 1854, while retaining his chair. His second wife had died on 14 October 1844 leaving him four infants. From at least 1829 Powell had been a visitor to John Lee's Hartwell House, had there befriended the family of Captain William Henry Smyth RN (1788–1865), and was a regular attender and council member with Lee and Smyth at the RAS, of which Powell was vice-president from 1856 to 1857, and its dining club. On 10 March 1846, at the age of fifty, Powell married Henrietta Grace (1824–1914), whom he had watched grow up as the accomplished sixth of nine children (including the astronomer Charles Piazzi Smyth) of Captain Smyth and his wife, Annarella (1799–1873). Of seven sons and three daughters born of this marriage, two and one respectively died in infancy. Among the survivors were Sir George Smyth Baden-*Powell and Robert Stephenson Smyth Baden-*Powell (1857–1941), first Baron Baden-Powell of Gilwell (Henrietta adopted the name Baden-Powell about ten years after her husband's death);

Robert became founder of the Boy Scouts. Powell preached regularly at Trinity Church, Paddington, and on several occasions at Kensington Palace, at Prince Albert's invitation.

In the political and social climate of the late 1840s and the 1850s Powell felt reassured that Britain was not going to fall victim to the revolutions and extreme working-class movements proliferating in continental Europe. Together with new friends like William Benjamin Carpenter, Robert Chambers, Francis Newman, William Rathbone Greg, or the *Westminster Review* group, he felt that the intellectual conservatism of his former high-church allies represented a serious obstacle to the reforming strategy aimed at making timely concessions to avoid political upheavals. He was convinced that innovations in science, such as the evolution theory propounded by Chambers in his 1845 *Vestiges of the Natural History of Creation*, or in Charles Darwin's *Origin of Species* (1859), had to be embraced by the élites because they constituted further evidence that nature, as well as society, was governed by iron laws and not by capricious will. He could neither understand nor tolerate Adam Sedgwick's and William Whewell's charge of atheism against Chambers and evolutionism. In the *Order of Nature* (1859) Powell spoke of a society where religion expressed itself following the levels of intellectual and moral development of its members. It was therefore acceptable that the masses should believe in miracles and in paternal providence, whereas the well-educated rulers wisely believed in the religion of a natural order created by a benevolent rational being.

A series of essays published in the 1850s, and especially the *Essay on the spirit of inductive philosophy, the unity of worlds and the philosophy of creation*, made Powell a well-known figure at London intellectual soirées and at court; he mixed with literary lions such as Charles Dickens, George Eliot, and George Henry Lewes, Baron von Bunsen and Thomas Henry Buckle, and famous scientists such as Charles Babbage, John Frederick Herschel, Charles Lyell, and Roderick Impey Murchison. Powell's outspoken denial of miracles, and his enthusiastic comments on Darwin's theory in 'On the study of the evidences of Christianity' which he contributed to the famous 1860 issue of *Essays and Reviews*, marked the breaking up of relations with Whately, and made Edward Bouverie Pusey doubt that Powell was still a Christian. His death prevented his involvement in the prosecution brought against several contributors to *Essays and Reviews*, as well as his intention to take part, a week later, in the Oxford meeting of the British Association for the Advancement of Science, where he would most certainly have defended Darwin's theories against Bishop Wilberforce's strictures. On 9 March 1860 he presided at his last dinner as president of the RAS Club. He died of bronchitis followed by heart failure on 11 June at his home, 6 Stanhope Street, Hyde Park Gardens, London, three weeks after the birth of his youngest son. He was buried at Kensal Green, London. Contemporaries described him as a kind-hearted person, 'happy as a child' when discussing his favourite theological or scientific ideas, though younger naturalists such as Joseph Dalton

Hooker and later generations unfairly looked upon him as a typical example of a cleric meddling with scientific theories which he was ill-equipped to judge.

PIETRO CORSI

Sources B. Powell, journal, 1816–60, priv. coll. · *PRS*, 11 (1860–62), xxvi–xxix · *Notices of the life of … Baden Powell* [1886] · E. Powell, *Pedigree of the family of Powell* (1891) · P. Corsi, *Science and religion: Baden Powell and the Anglican debate, 1800–1860* (1988) · I. Ellis, *Seven against Christ: a study of 'Essays and reviews'* (1980) · *DSB* · *Monthly Notices of the Royal Astronomical Society*, 21 (1860–61), 103–5 · J. Morrell and A. Thackray, *Gentlemen of science: early years of the British Association for the Advancement of Science* (1981) · *Hist. U. Oxf. 6: 19th-cent. Oxf.* · m. cert. · d. cert.

Archives MHS Oxf., corresp. · priv. coll. | CUL, letters to Sir George Stokes · RS, Lubbock · U. St Andr. L., corresp. with James David Forbes · UCL, letters to Society for the Diffusion of Useful Knowledge

Wealth at death under £3000: probate, 8 Aug 1860, *CGPLA Eng. & Wales*

Powell, Cecil Frank (1903–1969), physicist, was born in Tonbridge, Kent, on 5 December 1903, the elder child and only son of Frank Powell, gunsmith, of 99 High Street, Tonbridge, and his wife, Elizabeth Caroline Bisacre. His father, from a family long established as gunsmiths in Tonbridge, had been bankrupted by a lawsuit arising from a shooting accident, so family circumstances were severely straitened in Powell's childhood. Nevertheless, encouraged by his grandfather George Bisacre, a schoolmaster, who gave him second-hand (and rather ancient) scientific texts, and inspired by the engineering talents of two paternal uncles, one of whom had constructed the first successful motor car in the Tonbridge district, he contrived to have a garden-shed chemical laboratory while a schoolboy.

At eleven Powell won a scholarship to Sir A. Judd's Commercial School, Tonbridge, whence state and college open scholarships took him to Sidney Sussex College, Cambridge, where he obtained first-class honours in parts one (1924) and two (1925) of the natural sciences tripos, and was placed second in his year for physics. He followed this with research in Rutherford's Cavendish Laboratory, under the direction of C. T. R. Wilson. In 1928 he moved, as research assistant to Professor A. M. Tyndall, to the newly opened H. H. Wills Physics Laboratory of the University of Bristol. There he spent the rest of his career, becoming lecturer (1931), reader (1946), Melville Wills professor of physics (1948–63), Henry Overton Wills professor of physics and director of the H. H. Wills Physics Laboratory (1964–9), and a pro-vice-chancellor of the university (1964–7). He was elected to the Royal Society in 1949 and received the Nobel prize for physics in 1950. He was elected president of the Association of Scientific Workers in 1954 and of the World Federation of Scientific Workers in 1957. He married, in 1932, Isobel Therese (1907–1995), daughter of Johann Artner, an Austrian business executive with I. G. Farbenindustrie. They had two daughters. Isobel was to become an important member of his research team.

Powell's earliest research work, with C. T. R. Wilson, which aimed at improving the performance of cloud

Cecil Frank Powell (1903–1969), by Elliott & Fry, 1950

chambers, had an engineering spin-off in application to the discharge of steam through nozzles. With Tyndall, during Powell's first four years in Bristol, the nature of gaseous ions was greatly clarified. His research interests then diverged in two very different directions—seismology and nuclear physics. In 1935 he went as seismologist on the joint Colonial Office and Royal Society expedition to Montserrat, West Indies. Another such expedition to Dominica was being planned in 1939, but was frustrated by the war, and at that point Powell's career as a seismologist ended.

Concurrently, Powell undertook the construction of a Cockcroft generator to produce a 700 keV proton beam, and the associated cloud chamber, evidence of his considerable skill and enjoyment in working with his hands. His high-voltage set came into service in 1939 but was dismantled in 1940 because space was needed for other war-related work. However, it was in use for long enough to launch him into what was to be his principal line of research. Before the cloud chamber was ready he recorded his proton beam in the emulsion of a photographic plate, tangentially exposed. Then he used the same technique to determine the energy spectrum of a neutron source by registering the tracks of 'knock-on' protons in the emulsion, and at the same time he participated in experiments registering events produced by the cosmic rays in photographic plates stored on high mountains.

It was generally thought at the time that the registration of fast particle tracks in emulsion was only suitable for qualitative demonstrations and could give no results of worthwhile precision, but Powell persisted in following his belief that, with better microscopes, better used, with improved processing techniques, and with the development of new thicker and more silver-rich emulsions, the accuracy and sensitivity of the method could be greatly improved. He was correct, and was rewarded with an important harvest of new phenomena observed in the cosmic rays in the years following the war. The method had an intrinsic advantage over all others for the observation of particle transformations occurring after very short time intervals (because of the high magnification under which the tracks were seen). The resolution of the meson paradox in 1947, revealing that there was a strongly interacting π-meson which transformed spontaneously into a weakly interacting and relatively long-lived μ-meson. won him his Nobel prize. These observations were made in balloon-borne stacks of photographic emulsion, a method which was to reveal a new world of transient 'fundamental' particles during the next decade.

Powell built up a team of more than twenty researchers from all over the world, and collaborated with many others. An integral part of his group were the dozen or so female 'scanners', headed by his wife and known in the department as 'Cecil's beauty chorus'. He treated all his team as equals and was punctilious in acknowledging co-workers. From his position thus established as a leader in European collaborative research Powell then played a leading role in the establishment of the Conseil Européen de Recherches Nucléaires (CERN) at Geneva as fundamental particle research entered the era of giant accelerator machines too expensive for any one nation in Europe to develop. He was chairman of the scientific policy committee of CERN from 1961 to 1963. To the end of his life he continued to play an active part both in the science and in the forward planning of research on fundamental particles.

Powell's politics had been on the left, but in a speech in 1955 on the hydrogen bomb and the future of mankind, later published as a pamphlet by the London Co-operative Society, he said:

> We are in a situation of great difficulty and danger in which it is very important to create a serious and informed body of opinion, all over the world ... [which] must, if it is to be effective, embrace people with conflicting opinions on almost all other issues but who can be united on this.

This represented his political position from then onwards. He was importantly involved in the discussions leading up to the Russell–Einstein declaration of 9 July 1955, of which he was one of the eleven original signatories, and in the setting up of the Pugwash series of conferences on science and world affairs, commencing on 7 July 1957. He was elected chairman in 1967 but had in fact been the working chairman from the beginning, as deputy to Bertrand Russell who, prevented by age from attendance, usually guided the conferences from a distance. All such duties Powell performed with great charm, tact, and literary style.

Of medium height, and cheerfully serious disposition, Powell's hobbies included landscape drawing and making furniture, preferably from a difficult wood like yew. He had a well-developed sense of humour and was a skilled raconteur: at parties he enjoyed being asked to recite 'The Barge' or to tell some story about his inventive Uncle Horace. As chairman of an awkward confrontation he knew how to lower the temperature with a well-timed joke. He was one of Bristol University's leading statesmen at the time of student unrest in 1968, helping to allay suspicions of professors and students alike. He had a love for good English, and particularly liked to find an apposite quotation from the essays of Bacon. One of his greatest joys was an unplanned audience reaction when he gave a lecture on the cosmic rays at Oxford. After he had entered the Sheldonian Theatre with the vice-chancellor and bedells in robed procession, his innocent opening words, 'Coming from outer space', brought the house down.

The Royal Society awarded Powell the Hughes medal in 1949 (the year of his election as a fellow) and the royal medal in 1961; he gave the Bakerian lecture in 1957, and a tercentenary lecture in 1960. The Physical Society of London awarded him the Charles Vernon Boys prize in 1947, and (as the Institute of Physics and the Physical Society) the Guthrie medal and prize in 1969. He was elected a foreign member of the Academy of Sciences of the USSR in 1958 and received its Lomonosov gold medal in 1967, and was elected a foreign member of the Yugoslav Academy of Sciences and Arts in 1966. He was an honorary member of the Royal Irish Academy (1959) and an ordinary member of the Leopoldina Academy, Halle (1964), and received honorary doctorates from the universities of Dublin (1950), Bordeaux (1952), Warsaw (1959), Berlin (1960), Padua (1965), and Moscow (1966). He was also an honorary fellow of Sidney Sussex College, Cambridge (1966), and of the Institute of Physics and the Physical Society (1962). He was chairman of the nuclear physics board of the British Science Research Council from 1965 to 1968. In addition to many scientific papers and published lectures, Powell published, in 1947, with G. P. S. Occhialini, *Nuclear Physics in Photographs*, and, in 1959, with P. H. Fowler and D. H. Perkins, *The Study of Elementary Particles by the Photographic Method*.

On 9 August 1969, eight days after he retired from the Bristol chair, Powell died of a heart attack on an Italian mountainside, at Alpe Giumello, Commune di Casargo, Lago di Como. A commemorative plaque donated by the Clifton and Hotwells Improvement Society marks his place of residence from 1946 to 1954 at 1 Downside Road, Clifton, Bristol. CHARLES FRANK, *rev.*

Sources F. C. Frank, D. H. Perkins, and A. M. Tyndall, *Memoirs FRS*, 17 (1971), 541–63 · *Selected papers of Cecil Frank Powell, Nobel laureate, FRS*, ed. E. H. S. Burhop, W. O. Lock, and M. G. K. Menon (1972) · W. O. Lock, 'Origins and early days of the Bristol school of cosmic ray physics', *European Journal of Physics*, 11 (1990), 193–202 · *The Times* (11 Aug 1969) · *The Times* (16 Aug 1969) · *Scientific World*, 13 (1969) · *Science Today* (Dec 1969) · personal knowledge (1981) · m. cert.

Archives University of Bristol, corresp., papers, and notebooks | CAC Cam., corresp. with Sir James Chadwick

Likenesses Elliott & Fry, photograph, 1950, NPG [*see illus.*] · D. H. Fountain, plaque, University of Bristol, H. H. Wills Physics Laboratory · B. Hailstone, oils, Judd School, Tonbridge, Kent · C. Hewer,

sculpture, priv. coll. • M. Levy, drawing, priv. coll. • photograph, repro. in Frank, Perkins, and Tyndall, *Memoirs FRS*, facing p. 541
Wealth at death £18,934: probate, 13 Nov 1969, *CGPLA Eng. & Wales*

Powell, Colin Trevor [Cozy] (1947–1998), rock musician, was born on 29 December 1947 at Cirencester, Gloucestershire. Adopted, he never discovered the identity of his natural parents. He was married but divorced.

Cozy Powell was one of rock's most celebrated drummers. His powerful style was a feature of many of the biggest rock groups of the 1970s and 1980s, including Rainbow, Whitesnake, and Black Sabbath. He also epitomized the flamboyant rock star. Lean and muscular, his dark hair worn long, Powell loved to drive fast cars and motor cycles and was photographed in racing leathers and astride a powerful 'superbike' on the cover of Rainbow's 1980 album *Down to Earth*, the most successful recording of his thirty-year career. He had raced formula 3 cars before joining Rainbow in 1975.

As a teenager Powell played in a variety of groups, including Big Bertha and the Sorcerors, before he was recruited by leading British guitarist Jeff Beck, who had been Eric Clapton's replacement in the Yardbirds. Powell appeared on two albums by the Jeff Beck Group, *Rough and Ready* (1971) and *Jeff Beck Group* (1972). Both albums sold well in America but less so in Britain, and when Beck split the group Powell formed his own heavy rock band, Bedlam, with singer Frank Aiello, guitarist Dave Ball, and bassist Dennis Ball. Bedlam released one album, simply titled *Bedlam*, on the Chrysalis label in 1973.

Powell was also in demand as a session musician, and played uncredited on numerous pop records of the early 1970s. Noted producer Mickie Most hired him to work on singles by Donovan and Hot Chocolate, and encouraged Powell to make a solo recording. His first solo single, 'Dance with the Devil', was a number three hit in the UK in December 1973—a rare distinction indeed for a drummer. Powell formed a new ensemble, Cozy Powell's Hammer, to capitalize on his success with a British tour. Two more top twenty hits followed in 1974 ('The Man in Black', which reached number eighteen, and 'Na na na', a second top ten hit) before Powell accepted an invitation from former Deep Purple guitarist Ritchie Blackmore to join his new group, Rainbow.

With Rainbow, Cozy Powell's star rose to its highest point. The first album he recorded with the band, *Rainbow Rising*, peaked at number eleven in the UK chart and is widely acknowledged as a classic example of 1970s rock. Powell's contribution to the track entitled 'Stargazer' helped to establish the song as Rainbow's defining moment and confirmed Powell as one of the leading rock musicians of his generation, a worthy successor to Led Zeppelin's formidable drummer, John Bonham.

Powell recorded three more albums with Rainbow: *On Stage* (1977), *Long Live Rock 'n' Roll* (1978), and *Down to Earth* (1979). The latter produced two hit singles in 'Since You Been Gone', which reached number six in September 1979, and 'All Night Long', which peaked at number five in

February 1980 and featured a typically powerful performance from Powell, whose solo single 'Theme One' became his final British chart entry in November 1979. In August 1980 Rainbow topped the bill at the inaugural Monsters of Rock festival at Castle Donington racetrack in Leicestershire, drawing an audience of 50,000.

Despite the group's success, Powell quit Rainbow near the end of 1980 and joined the Michael Schenker Group, led by the acclaimed guitarist whose reputation had been established in German hard rock act Scorpions and with British band UFO. This liaison lasted for two years and two 1981 albums: *MSG* and *One Night at Budokan*. Then Powell was tempted to work with another former Deep Purple star, singer David Coverdale, in Whitesnake. In a turbulent time for the group Powell appeared on the album *Slide it in* (1984), which laid the foundation for Whitesnake's huge success in North America in the late 1990s. He also starred on a solo album by The Who's vocalist, Roger Daltrey, entitled *Under a Raging Moon* and dedicated to the memory of Daltrey's late bandmate Keith Moon, whose aggressive style of drumming had a profound influence on Powell. His sometime collaborator Neil Murray wrote that Powell was 'the most powerful drummer I have played with … [he] always tried to get "his" sound captured on record, which used a lot of room acoustic to achieve a huge sound'. Live, he 'liked to put on a very visual show … and … became famous for his drum solos, which incorporated explosions, strobes and flame jets, which many other drummers copied'. Powell's musical tastes were eclectic, and his shows 'usually included him playing along to pieces of music such as Tchaikovsky's 1812 Overture' (Siegler).

Powell was a member of Whitesnake when the band took top billing at Castle Donington in 1983 and at the Rock in Rio festival in 1985, but at the close of 1985 he joined Keith Emerson and Greg Lake in reactivating virtuoso progressive rock trio ELP. In 1989 Powell was lured by another legendary rock band, Black Sabbath, which he left two years later having suffered an injury in a riding accident. He appears on three Black Sabbath albums: *Headless Cross* (1989), *Tyr* (1990), and *Forbidden* (1995).

In the 1990s Cozy Powell recorded and toured with former Queen guitarist Brian May (he is featured on May's 1993 album *Back to the Light* and 1998's *Another World*) and with former Fleetwood Mac guitarist Peter Green's Splinter Group. Powell, noted for his likeable personality, secured Green's return to the stage following a drug-related breakdown in the late 1960s.

Powell recorded four solo albums: *Over the Top* (1979), *Tilt* (1981), *Octopus* (1983), and *The Drums are Back* (1992). He also played on former Led Zeppelin vocalist Robert Plant's *Pictures at Eleven* (1982), Gary Moore's *After the War* (1989), and Judas Priest guitarist Glenn Tipton's *Baptism of Fire* (1998).

Shortly before his death Powell sustained several broken ribs when his new Harley Davidson motor cycle collided with a tractor on a narrow country lane. Unfortunately, the accident did not dampen his enthusiasm for high-speed driving. On the night he died—5 April 1998—Powell was reported to have been travelling at close to 100 m.p.h. on the M4 near Bristol when his Saab vehicle veered from the road. It was also reported that he had been using a mobile phone, the safety of which devices in motor vehicles was a matter of public debate at the time. He died from his injuries at Frenchay Hospital, and his body was cremated in Wiltshire on 18 April 1998; a memorial concert was held in Buxton on 1 May 1999.

PAUL ELLIOTT

Sources P. Gambaccini, T. Rice, and J. Rice, *British hit singles*, 14th edn (2001) · D. Oliver and A. Jasper, *The international encyclopedia of hard rock and heavy metal*, rev. edn (1991) · *The Times* (9 April 1998) · *Daily Telegraph* (9 April 1998) · J. Siegler, www.cozypowell.com [official Cozy Powell home page; incl. N. Murray, 'A tribute to Cozy Powell'] · *The Independent* (8 April 1998) · www.deus.net/~bjb/CozyPowell · d. cert.

Powell, David. *See* Powel, David (1549x52–1598).

Powell, (Elizabeth) Dilys (1901–1995), film critic, was born on 20 July 1901 at Lloyd's Bank, Bridgnorth, Shropshire, the daughter of Thomas Powell, bank manager, and his wife, Mary Jane, *née* Lloyd. She was educated at Bournemouth high school and at Somerville College, Oxford (1921–4), where she read modern languages and wrote for the magazine *Isis*. After graduating with first-class honours she was employed as secretary and literary assistant to Lady Ottoline Morrell before joining the literary department of the *Sunday Times* in 1928. While at Oxford she had met Humfrey Gilbert Garth *Payne (1902–1936), archaeologist, son of Edward John Payne, barrister. They married on 2 January 1926. From 1931 to 1936 Powell divided her time between Oxford and Greece when Payne was appointed director of the British School of Archaeology in Athens. They had no children. The marriage ended with Payne's sudden death from blood poisoning in 1936. Powell returned to Greece many times thereafter and was inspired to write several books with personal, Grecian themes, including *Remember Greece* (1941) and *An Affair of the Heart* (1957). On 12 June 1943 she married Leonard Frederick Russell (1906–1974), associate editor and chief literary editor of the *Sunday Times*. They had no children.

Powell was appointed film critic for the *Sunday Times* in 1939, and held the post until 1976. Although she claimed to have little knowledge of cinema, she built on the enthusiasm she had developed for the medium as a child and at Oxford. In her reviews she aimed to entertain and amuse readers but also to be serious and truthful, providing balanced accounts that were also characterized by wit and irony. Her appreciation of experimentation with the visual properties of cinema was marked throughout her career. In her early reviews she admired *Citizen Kane* (1941), and the films of Luis Buñuel and Jean Renoir. She also enjoyed the films of Buster Keaton, whom she preferred to Charlie Chaplin.

Powell contributed to BBC radio broadcasts and to *Sight and Sound*, activities which consolidated her position as Britain's leading film critic, rivalled only by C. A. Lejeune, film critic for *The Observer*. While she admired British directors including Carol Reed and the films of Michael Powell and Emeric Pressburger, she was concerned about the

(Elizabeth) Dilys Powell (1901–1995), by Fred Daniels, 1947

tendency for many British films to be unimaginative adaptations of literary classics. To this end she argued that British cinema should develop its own visual style, particularly that of documentary realism, while at the same time including fantastical elements such as in Ealing's *Dead of Night* (1945) and *Hue and Cry* (1946). Powell praised the 'free cinema' movement of social realist documentaries at the end of the 1950s and *Room at the Top* (1958), a film she correctly predicted would herald a 'renaissance' in British cinema.

Powell's ability to forecast trends and spot talent was accurate and astute. An admirer of American detective thrillers, she was an early observer of the cinematic potential of Raymond Chandler's novels, which became source texts for the *film noir* genre. In her review of *Niagara* (1952), Powell praised Marilyn Monroe's performance in one of her earliest roles. She also noted the talent of Steven Spielberg in a review of *Duel* (1971), one of his first films as a director, and was quick to appreciate the early work of key independent American directors, including Robert Altman, Francis Ford Coppola, and Terence Malick. As well as welcoming films distinctive for their experimentation, she wrote enthusiastically about westerns, musicals, and horror films. Her highly positive review of *Psycho* (1960) differed from that of several other critics, who deplored Hitchcock's apparent switch from adventure thrillers to horror. Some films which were huge box-office successes, including *Gone with the Wind* (1939) and *The Sound of Music* (1965), were not Powell's personal favourites but she always measured her views against what she perceived might be compensatory factors. Her famous description in the *Sunday Times* in February 1972 of

Ken Russell as 'an appalling talent' (Cook, 149) expressed her ambivalence about his use of shocking but striking images. In a few rare exceptions she did not conceal her dislike of a film, the most notorious cases being her reviews of Michael Powell's *Peeping Tom* (1959) and Sam Peckinpah's *Straw Dogs* (1971), whose violence led her to conclude, in the *Sunday Times* in January 1972, 'For the first time in my life I felt concern for the future of the cinema' (ibid., 391).

In 1976 Powell ceased writing weekly reviews for the *Sunday Times* and became film reviewer for *Punch* until that magazine's demise in 1992. Nevertheless she continued to review films broadcast on television for the *Sunday Times* until 1989. She was on the board of governors of the British Film Institute (1948–52) and became a fellow of the British Film Institute in 1986. She was president of the Classical Association (1966–7) and was awarded an honorary fellowship by Somerville College, Oxford, in 1991. She was made CBE in 1974. Highly respected for her modesty and unfailing commitment to her profession, she impressed generations of filmgoers. Her contribution to the informed appreciation of cinema was immense. Above all, her aim was to encourage people to see a film, even when she had reservations about its merits, and in so doing she was a key influence on the establishment of film culture in Britain. In later years she suffered a series of strokes; she died on 3 June 1995 at St Charles Hospital, Kensington, London.   SARAH STREET

Sources C. Cook, ed., *The Dilys Powell reader* (1991) · microfiche on Dilys Powell including all key obituaries and background press articles, BFI · G. Perry, ed., *The golden screen: fifty years of films* (1989) · *The Times* (5 June 1995) · *The Independent* (5 June 1995) · *The Independent* (15 June 1995) · b. cert. · m. certs. · d. cert.
Archives BFI, papers relating to first London Film Festival, also files on actors and directors · University of Bristol, corresp. and statements relating to trial of *Lady Chatterley's lover* | BFI, corresp. with Joseph Losey | SOUND BL NSA
Likenesses P. de Jong, caricature, watercolour, c.1932, repro. in R. Hood, *Faces of archaeology in Greece* (1998) · F. W. Daniels, bromide print, 1947, NPG [see illus.] · photograph, 1947, Hult. Arch. · photograph, repro. in R. Hood, *Faces of archaeology in Greece* (1998) · photograph, repro. in *The Times* · photograph, repro. in *The Independent* (5 June 1995)
Wealth at death £805,410: probate, 11 Aug 1995, *CGPLA Eng. & Wales*

Powell, Edward (c.1478–1540), Roman Catholic priest and martyr, was born in Wales and was educated at Oxford University, where he graduated MA, became a fellow of Oriel College by 1495, and proceeded DTh on 26 June 1506. In 1501 he had been granted leave to study in Paris, where he began his theological course. He also held several administrative posts at Oriel, including those of collector of rents (1494–5), junior treasurer (1499–1500), chaplain (1499–1501), and dean (1500–01), and was made commissary to the chancellor of the university on 8 June 1508. He was ordained priest in 1499. Powell was involved in two university scandals, although neither proved damaging to his career: in 1510 he was implicated in an embezzlement scheme involving the university proctors and the keepers of the university chests, while in 1522 he was the object of a writ of *praemunire* obtained in a secular court by a

scholar called Roger Cruge, leading Archbishop Warham to defend his jurisdiction as chancellor over all civil cases in the university.

After resigning as college chaplain Powell became rector of Bleadon, Somerset, in 1503, and in that same year was made a canon of Lincoln, where he held several prebendaries in the years that followed. In June 1507 he was made a canon of Salisbury, where he also held several prebendaries as well as being provost of St Edmund's College, Salisbury, from 1509 to 1534. His other livings included the vicarage of Powerstock, Dorset, 1522–6, the vicarage of Melksham, Wiltshire, 1526–34, and the rectorship of Radipole, Dorset, from 1526 to an unknown date. To allow for all his simultaneous livings Powell was granted a papal dispensation in November 1514 to hold three incompatible benefices.

After Henry VIII's accession in 1509 Powell became a frequent preacher at court, but his real fame began in the 1520s as an early leader in the English fight against Lutheranism. In 1521 he was commissioned to write a treatise against Luther, and in 1522 he sent Cardinal Wolsey the first instalment of his manuscript entitled *De immunitate ecclesiae*. This work won high praise, being offered to Henry VIII by the university as the best work of its kind to be written there, and it was expanded and published in 1523 as *Propugnaculum summi sacerdotii evangelici … adversus Martinum Lutherum*, a three-part dialogue between Powell and Luther defending the holiness of the pope and the seven sacraments. The book also included a lengthy list of past heresies adopted by Luther, an anti-Lutheran epigram by the Cambridge scholar William Dynham, and a preface by the prominent humanist Sir Thomas Elyot.

Powell's reputation for theological conservatism, while helpful in the 1520s, made him extremely controversial in the 1530s. He became one of Katherine of Aragon's theological counsellors during the king's divorce proceedings, and in 1533 he was one of the few English theologians who gave an unfavourable opinion of the king's divorce case. In that same year, when Hugh Latimer preached fiery protestant sermons at Bristol, Powell, William Hubberdyne, and Nicholas Wilson were hired by local conservatives to preach against him. In one of his sermons Powell allegedly condemned civil rulers who 'corrupteth and infecteth the people with open sinning and ill example of living, as he that doeth put away his first wife and taketh another without assent or dispensation of the Church'. In another sermon, he argued that by virtue of the sacrament of holy orders, 'princes are subject to priests and prelates' (PRO, SP 6/3, fol. 57r). In 1534 he preached again in Bristol, in defence of pilgrimages.

Powell refused to take the oath of succession, and was thus deprived of all his benefices and committed to the Tower of London on 10 June 1534. He was attainted of treason on 3 November 1534. He was shortly thereafter moved to Dorchester gaol, where he lived in appalling conditions, set in stocks and without a bed to lie on. He was moved back to the Tower in 1535, probably as a result of his plaintive letter to Sir Thomas Arundell dated 12 April. In the Tower his conditions improved, but his gilt chalice and richly finished pax were stolen from him, allegedly by an agent of Thomas Cromwell. Powell passed the remainder of his life there, resolutely refusing to acknowledge the royal supremacy or the validity of the king's remarriage. He was executed for treason at Smithfield on 30 July 1540 as part of the king's symbolic, simultaneous execution of three protestants for heresy and three papalists for treason. Powell was brought from the Tower to Smithfield tied together with the protestant Robert Barnes, leading to the anonymous publication, soon after their deaths, of a satirical pamphlet, *The Metynge of Doctor Barons and Doctor Powell at Paradise Gate* (1540). Powell was beatified by the Roman Catholic church in 1886.   ETHAN H. SHAGAN

Sources E. Powell, *Propugnaculum summi sacerdotii evangelici … adversus Martinum Lutherum* (1523) · J. E. Paul, *Catherine of Aragon and her friends* (1966) · W. T. Mitchell, ed., *Epistolae academicae, 1508–1596*, OHS, new ser., 26 (1980) · PRO, SP 6/3, fol. 57r · *LP Henry VIII* · R. Rex, 'The English campaign against Luther in the 1520s', *TRHS*, 5th ser., 39 (1989), 85–106 · Emden, *Oxf.*, vol. 3 · Foster, *Alum. Oxon.* · *The metynge of Doctor Barons and Doctor Powell at paradise gate and of theyr communicacion bothe drawen to Smithfylde from the Towar* (1540)

Powell, Edward [*called* Anderson of the Fens] (*bap.* **1608**, *d.* in or after **1642**), protester, was baptized on 8 May 1608 in the parish of Holy Trinity, Ely, Cambridgeshire, the illegitimate son of Mary Powell (*d.* 1645?), who later, in 1613, married John Anderson. As Anderson of the Fens he was prominent in protest against the drainage and enclosure of the fens around the Isle of Ely.

Powell spent his life in Ely, where he married Margery Marshall on 19 May 1633 and raised a family. A labourer, he was described in 1637 as a poor man when he received relief from an Ely charity. Like others in the city he had cattle which he was able to common on the surrounding fens but, again like others, he was threatened by the implementation of a major drainage and enclosure scheme in the Great Level, of which the Cambridgeshire fens formed part, led by Francis Russell, first earl of Bedford. A legal ruling in spring 1638 that Bedford had failed to perfect the drainage scheme seems to have encouraged the commoners to renew their destruction of the works and provides the background to Powell's involvement. At the beginning of June 1638 a crowd of over 200, drawn from Ely and surrounding villages and taking the name Anderson's Camp, destroyed drainage ditches on Whelpmore Fen. They did so under the guise of a game of football, a violent form of sport that often supplied a pretext for organized protest, and following rumours that Anderson was to bring the football and a hundred men.

Powell was arrested by the authorities at Ely in a preemptive move and was not present at the attack but his subsequent examination revealed why the event was popularly nicknamed Anderson's Camp. Earlier, in Lent that year, Powell had paid the town crier to summon the town's inhabitants to go to petition the king, then at Newmarket, that the losing of their fens would be the losing of their livelihoods. The next day in Ely market place Powell, cudgel in hand and at the head of a crowd of some sixty men similarly armed, defied the call of a local JP to disperse, claiming that the king had personally instructed

him to report any who hindered his petition. Among his fellow commoners, it was reported, Powell claimed to have had 'ordinary access and speech' with the king and that Charles I, on learning of the fenland commoners' plight, had wept on his shoulder (PRO, SP 16/409/50). Powell had managed to forestall further legal action then by going to London and entering a recognizance for his good behaviour. Examined following his later arrest in June, he refused to give up his claim to common in the fens unless he could be shown the king's signet to the grant to the undertakers of the drainage work. The declaration of loyalty to the king he then made carried with it a hint of social levelling: 'I will obey God and the King, but no man els, for we are all but subjects' (PRO, SP 16/409/50). Powell certainly showed a defiant attitude in his dealings with the authorities at Ely; as he told the JPs, they were but the bishop's justices and not the king's, a reference to the bishop of Ely's right to appoint justices in the isle. Powell spent three weeks in gaol before being bailed, a local clergyman acting as surety for him, to appear in court at Ely in late July 1638. Perhaps because of the threat posed by popular actions to the drainage scheme over which the king had assumed control, Powell was tried on the direct advice of the attorney-general and the solicitor-general. He was fined the heavy sum of £200 and sentenced to imprisonment.

Partly because of a fear that he might be the subject of a rescue attempt, Powell was transferred to the Newgate prison in London, from where he twice sent letters to his local minister asking him to read an appeal to his fellow inhabitants to raise a collection to secure his release or to provide him, his aged mother, wife, and children with a weekly pension. He was finally released in June 1639 and returned to Ely, where he last appears as putting his mark to a petition in 1642 from some of the inhabitants of Ely against the dean and chapter of the cathedral. Powell has been described by the historian of opposition to the drainage as 'evidently an educated, literate man who was reasonably articulate and had some familiarity with the law' (Lindley, 103). Although it is now known that Powell was unable to sign his name, his brief career demonstrated that he knew what it took to become a charismatic leader. As he asked of his interrogators at examination, 'may not a man be inspired? Then, why not I to do the poore good about their Commons?' (PRO, SP 16/409/50).

JOHN WALTER

Sources K. Lindley, *Fenland riots and the English revolution* (1982) · R. Holmes, *Cromwell's Ely* (1975) · parish registers, Holy Trinity, Ely, Cambs. AS, Cambridge, P67/1/2 [baptism, marriage] · transcript records, Parson's Charity, Ely, Cambs. AS, Cambridge · PRO, SP 16/392/45, 16/409/50 · CUL, Ely records, E 10/3 and 4 · PRO, PC 2/50, p. 341

Powell, (John) Enoch (1912–1998), politician, was born on 16 June 1912 in Flaxley Lane, Stetchford, Birmingham, the only child of Albert Enoch Powell (1872–1956), schoolmaster, and his wife, Ellen Mary (1886–1953), daughter of Henry Breese, a policeman, of Liverpool, and his wife, Eliza. The Powells were of Welsh descent, though by the time of John Enoch's birth had lived in the Black Country

(John) Enoch Powell (1912–1998), by Jane Bown, 1968

for four generations, working first as miners and then in the iron trade. He grew up in a household where learning and self-improvement were prized. His father was an elementary school headmaster, and his mother gave up her own teaching career on her marriage. As soon as her son could grasp the letters of the alphabet, she put them up on cards around her kitchen and taught them to him. By six he was a precocious reader, and would lecture his parents on the subjects of his previous week's reading each Sunday evening. Thanks largely to his mother's coaching he won a scholarship to King Edward's School in Birmingham in 1925; and after a term there she taught him Greek (in which she herself was self-taught) so he could transfer to the classical side of the school. He also became an accomplished clarinettist, and contemplated a career in music. However, by the time he left school in 1930, on a scholarship to Trinity College, Cambridge, he had collected almost all the school prizes for classics, and had begun his own translation of Herodotus. That achievement and a love of Thucydides made him decide on a career as a scholar. Since there was already a well-known classicist named J. U. Powell—and J. E. Powell feared confusion with him—the boy known as Jack to his parents now began to style himself J. Enoch Powell, in confident anticipation of his own fame in his chosen field.

Academic and military career Powell maintained this academic excellence at Cambridge, whence he graduated with first-class honours in the classical tripos in 1933. At

university as at school he was a loner, obsessed with scholarship. From the start of his undergraduate career he was submitting articles analysing fragments of Greek texts to learned journals. In his spare time he also undertook papyrological research. He had very little social life. Under the influence of A. E. Housman he developed his skills as a textual critic, an arid branch of study but one that gave the logician in Powell great satisfaction. He became the first freshman ever to win Trinity's Craven scholarship, which he soon followed with the college's Greek prose prize. He won many such trophies at Cambridge, notably the Porson prize and the Sir William Browne medal.

Powell for a time considered a career in the diplomatic service, his linguistic skills already extending beyond the classics and into French, German, and Italian. However, he accepted his father's advice that the fellowship Trinity offered him after a year of postgraduate study, and at the remarkably early age of twenty-two, was too good to turn down. None the less, he found Cambridge suffocating. He spent much of his three and a half years as a fellow of Trinity studying ancient manuscripts in Italian libraries, mainly in the course of work on Thucydides. His translation of that author was published in 1942, and his other main work of research, his *Lexicon to Herodotus*, appeared in 1938. His translation of Herodotus into the English of the Authorized Version of the Bible—not an affectation, but a means of accentuating its antiquity—did not appear until 1949.

As an emotional outlet, Powell started to write poetry, lyrics that appear heavily, if not extremely, influenced by Housman. There is not just a metrical similarity, but also a thematic one, Powell (like the author of *A Shropshire Lad*) being obsessed with early death and echoing a repressed sexuality. Two volumes were published before the war, *First Poems* in 1937 and *Casting off* in 1939. His poetry was influenced by his belief that the First World War had been interrupted, not ended, and that battle would be rejoined soon. His other main cultural obsession was with German thought and literature, though he developed a distaste for Germany after the rise of Hitler. Attracted to atheism as a schoolboy reading *The Golden Bough*, he was confirmed in that mindset by a thorough reading of Nietzsche in his twenties.

Powell determined to beat Nietzsche's record of securing a professorship by the age of twenty-four. However, universities to which he applied rejected him as soon as they discovered his age. Eventually one took the bait: and in the winter of 1938, still aged twenty-five, Powell was on the flying boat to Australia, to become professor of Greek in the University of Sydney. On arrival he stunned the vice-chancellor by informing him that war would soon break out in Europe, and that when it did he would be heading home to enlist in the army. The next eighteen months were a time of torture for Powell, as he witnessed from afar the abasement of his country before Hitler, yet felt powerless to do anything to expiate the shame. On 4 September 1939 he kept his promise, and started for England. With no military experience he had trouble enlisting, eventually doing so as a private soldier in the Royal

Warwickshire regiment, but only after passing himself off as an Australian. Selected for officer training within weeks, he was commissioned second lieutenant in May 1940, and began a long and unsuccessful struggle to be posted to the front line. Recognizing this officer's superior intellectual abilities—he had by now added various other languages, from Russian to medieval Welsh, to his armoury—the army had no intention of allowing Powell to do anything other than staff jobs. Though he found these frustrating, he nevertheless played an important part in the war.

In October 1941 Powell was posted to Cairo, where he was soon promoted major. For the next two years he helped mastermind the attack on Rommel's supply lines that contributed so much to his defeat and the German evacuation of north Africa. The hardest time for Powell was seeing brother officers go to their deaths at El Alamein, while he remained in comparative safety. He was promoted lieutenant-colonel in August 1942 and given command of an intelligence group, MI (Plans). In this capacity he attended the conference between Franklin D. Roosevelt and Winston Churchill at Casablanca in the spring of 1943, an event that would have a profound intellectual effect upon him. He confronted the American political mind for the first time, and it made him profoundly anti-American. He believed from that moment that America's main war aim, and in the peace that followed its main foreign policy aim, was to extinguish British imperial and strategic power.

With the war effectively over in north Africa, Powell determined to be posted to India, for a chance of fighting the Japanese. Although he secured the posting, he was no more successful at seeing action. He arrived in Delhi in August 1943, having been appointed a military MBE for his work in north Africa, and soon set about helping to plan the war in the Far East. Despite having pressed his case with General Orde Wingate, he was kept at staff work to the end of the war and beyond. However, he found India deeply rewarding. He loved the country, its cultures and peoples. He learned Urdu and immersed himself in the native literature, and it was in India that he acquired the love of architecture that became a main antiquarian interest in later life. By 1945, promoted brigadier, he was one of a small commission charged with settling the shape of the Indian army after the war, the report on which he wrote single-handedly. With early independence that hard labour, too, bore less fruit than it might have done. The commander-in-chief in India, Sir Claude Auchinleck, offered Powell the commandant's post at what was intended to be the Indian equivalent of Sandhurst. Powell turned this down, and returned to England in February 1946. Even at this late stage he still had an unshakeable belief that India would remain British indefinitely. He had formed the ambition to be viceroy, and thought that the best way to accomplish this was from the House of Commons.

Into politics Despite having voted for Attlee in the 1945 election—not for ideological reasons, but to punish those responsible for Munich—Powell was a visceral tory, and it was to the Conservative Party that he went on his arrival in London. As a brigadier and former fellow of Trinity he cut an impressive figure. He was immediately appointed to the party's parliamentary secretariat, later merged into the research department. He shared an office with Iain Macleod and Reginald Maudling, and together they set about shaping the party's policies for its renaissance in the 1950s.

Powell's viceregal ambitions crumbled in February 1947, when Attlee announced that Indian independence was imminent. Powell was shocked by the change of policy, so much so that he spent the whole of the night after it was announced walking the streets of London, trying to take it in. He came to terms with it by becoming fiercely anti-imperialist, believing that once India had gone the whole empire should follow it. This logical absolutism explained his later indifference to the Suez crisis, his contempt for the Commonwealth, and his urging that Britain should scrap any remaining pretence that she was a world power.

Although he could no longer achieve his main ambition, Powell had unintentionally stumbled upon a new, more passionate love, that of parliament itself. Being a member of parliament would now be an acceptable end in itself. That same winter he fought a hopeless by-election for the Yorkshire mining seat of Normanton, and then set out to find a seat he could win at the next general election. It was not easy. Despite his political, academic, and military qualifications, his manner was off-putting. A spare man of medium height, he had his hair cut *en brosse* which, with his intently staring eyes and stern demeanour when not among intimates, made him rather terrifying. He spoke in an exact way, with a slight but metallic west midlands accent. He had little small talk, and at that stage no point of contact with women. When he finally secured the nomination for a seat—Wolverhampton South-West, in December 1948—the agent advised the selection committee not to be put off by his 'short hair on end and his bulging eyes' (Heffer, 126).

For the next year Powell nursed the constituency carefully, cutting down and finally resigning from his work at the research department. He was returned at the general election of 1950 after a campaign run like a military operation. He became an active opponent of the government, and with Macleod and other new members formed the One Nation group of MPs. In June 1950 he rebelled against his party by refusing to support the Schuman plan, adoption of which would have made Britain one of the founder members of the European Coal and Steel Community, forerunner of the European Union. This act of independence set back his career, but was indicative of Powell's anti-careerist view of politics. Through One Nation he articulated a radical, free-market Conservatism for which there was then little sympathy in the party. He and Macleod both specialized in the health and social services, but it was Macleod who, to Powell's chagrin, was invited to become minister of health in the spring of 1952, barely six months after the Conservative Party had regained power. Later that year Powell refused a job at the Home Office with responsibility for Welsh affairs, saying that he was interested only in an economic ministry. He had to wait three years for another offer, while his contemporaries clambered up the greasy pole.

Powell's emotional life had been somewhat unconventional. A religious experience in 1949 caused him to abandon his militant atheism. His poetry revealed turbulent inner forces that he otherwise kept repressed. A double volume of it was published in 1951: *Dancer's End*, a collection of verse written during the war, and *The Wedding Gift*, written in a period of 'epic struggle' with his emotions in the summer of 1950 (Powell, ix). The 'struggle' had been to persuade the first woman with whom he had fallen in love—at the age of thirty-eight—to marry him. He failed. He had earlier had two intense friendships with men, one a pupil at Cambridge and the other a brother officer in India, but there is no evidence that they had a physical side. He married, on 2 January 1952, Margaret Pamela Wilson (*b.* 1926), a former colleague from Conservative central office, who provided him with the settled and happy family life essential to his political career. They had two daughters.

In the Commons, Powell demonstrated a wide range of expertise in his speeches and interventions, whether on his pet social services interests, or on defence, or on the constitutional questions that were becoming of deep interest to him. He believed his speech in March 1953 on the Royal Titles Bill was the finest of his life. He argued in it that the substitution of the idea of the queen's 'realms' for 'realm' was 'literally meaningless' (*Hansard 5C*, 512.242). It was an early example of his opposition to the idea of a Commonwealth as a sticking plaster for the wound left by the amputation of empire, and helps explain why he was not one of those tories distressed by the failure of the Suez operation in 1956.

Into government In 1954 One Nation published a pamphlet entitled *Change is our Ally*, mostly written by Powell and his friend and colleague Angus Maude. It argued for a fast retreat from the planned economy in order to maximize efficiency. However unclubbable and intellectually isolated Powell was, his sheer ability could not be ignored indefinitely. On 21 December 1955 Anthony Eden appointed him parliamentary secretary to Duncan Sandys at the Ministry of Housing. He soon mastered the detail of the Housing Subsidies Bill then before parliament. He took charge of measures on slum clearance and, finally, oversaw the Rent Bill. This was a measure close to Powell's radical heart, deregulating leaseholds and decontrolling many rents after years of wartime and post-war state control. Such was the assurance and technical mastery Powell displayed that, after barely a year, he was promoted on 14 January 1957 to the most important departmental post outside the cabinet, that of financial secretary to the Treasury.

There, Powell could take on the Keynesian forces whose essentially socialist doctrine still underpinned the Conservative government. With sterling depressed after the débâcle of Suez in late 1956 and the country living beyond its means, tough measures were needed to steady the economy. Together with the economic secretary, Nigel Birch, Powell impressed upon the chancellor, Peter Thorneycroft, that inflation was the government's doing. The three men agreed in the summer of 1957, largely under Powell's guiding influence, that inflation was a monetary phenomenon; and that only by strict control of the money supply could it be eliminated and sound money restored. Two basic tools were used to enforce this discipline. First, the bank rate was increased in September 1957 from 5 to 7 per cent. Second, Thorneycroft told his cabinet colleagues in the summer of 1957 that they would have to pare back government spending in 1958–9 to the levels of the previous year. Fearing political damage, they were reluctant to agree, and the prime minister, Harold Macmillan, was at best ambivalent. This studied freedom from conviction by the then prime minister, whom Powell regarded as an actor–manager rather than as a politician, would be at the root of Powell's later intense—and reciprocated—dislike of him.

Powell had long been attracted by the economic ideas of the Manchester Liberals of the nineteenth century, tying in as they did with his belief in the individual over the corporate state. It was also, for him, a matter of logic that inflation was caused by having too much money in circulation, and therefore by governments. He reinforced these views with later readings of Hayek and Adam Smith, but he came to them largely by his own reasoning. As financial secretary, he had to deal directly with the spending bids of ministers. The matter came to a head in a series of cabinet meetings at the turn of 1957–8, when Thorneycroft—armed with intellectual arguments by Powell—refused to back down from demanding that a further £50 million of spending cuts had to be found. On 6 January 1958, when Macmillan refused to back the chancellor, Thorneycroft and his two colleagues resigned. Powell's doubts about Macmillan, although he served him again, matured into contempt.

In this first period on the back benches after holding office, Powell suffered increasing frustration, though he continued to make a name for himself as both a thinker and a politician. He used his time to return to some literary work put aside earlier. Since the late 1940s he had been working on a history of the House of Lords, and he took up that task again wholeheartedly, though it was not published until 1968, and then only covered the period to 1540. He also wrote a shorter book entitled *Great Parliamentary Occasions* (1960), reflecting his love of the institution. More substantially, in 1959–60 he wrote an important tract of liberal economics, *Saving in a Free Society* (1960); and, after a relative parliamentary silence in 1958 (once he had signalled his opposition to the legislation introducing life peerages), he began once more to make weighty contributions from the back benches in 1959. The most significant of these was his speech in July 1959 on the Hola Camp massacre in Kenya, in which he attacked British policy in the colony. In it, he argued that the government could not:

> have African standards in Africa, Asian standards in Asia and perhaps British standards here at home ... we must be

consistent with ourselves everywhere … we cannot, we dare not, in Africa of all places, fall below our own highest standards in the acceptance of responsibility. (*Hansard 5C*, 610.237)

The Hola Camp speech won Powell many new admirers on all sides of the house, and distanced him further from the old imperialist tory party. He had repudiated the Suez Group of tory MPs, even before Suez, having detected as early as 1954 an unwillingness and incapacity on Britain's part to defend what remained of its empire. It was the logical end of his idea that, once India had gone, there was no point in preserving the rest of the empire, of which India had been the focal point. During the Suez crisis itself in 1956 he took no part, recognizing the futility of the convulsions through which most of his colleagues were going. He had felt, and recovered from, such pains in 1947, when India went. His attack on the treatment of the Kenyans in Hola is difficult to reconcile with later accusations that he was a man motivated by theories of racial superiority. Powell believed that, where British rule still pertained, so too should a principle of *civis Romanus sum*, with the same standards of justice that applied in Britain applying in her colonies too, irrespective of the race of those governed.

When Thorneycroft was brought back into the cabinet on 27 July 1960 as minister for aviation, Powell felt that he could in honour return to serve Macmillan. His three years as minister of health were intellectually satisfying for him, as he set about at reforming the National Health Service and making it more responsive to its patients. He suspected that the service was run more for the benefit of its staff than of its clients, and his subsequent experiences confirmed him in this—and compelled him to try to improve matters. He won the funding for a ten-year hospital building programme, which he announced in 1962. He established a programme to close and demolish the Victorian lunatic asylums, which he found offensively dehumanizing. He instituted regular meetings with chairmen of regional health authorities, and often toured hospitals to meet health service staff. In July 1962 he was promoted, in the same post, to the cabinet: although Macmillan found him uncongenial, he could not ignore Powell's prodigious talent in a party that was short of it.

In a parliamentary career of thirty-seven years Powell had just fifteen months in the cabinet. Once he found his feet he proved a powerful force for radicalism, outarguing more experienced and less ideological colleagues for a programme based on liberal economics and the dismantling of the socialist state. Even he, though, had to make compromises. Under collective responsibility he supported an incomes policy in which he did not believe—for he felt, as a monetarist, that it had no effect on inflation. It caused him great intellectual, as well as political, difficulty when nurses threatened industrial action in the spring of 1963 over pay limits. As the party prepared for the election due by the autumn of 1964, Powell's was a rare voice arguing for a return, effectively, to the liberal economics of the period before 1914. Such calls were met with incomprehension from colleagues,

and derision from economists for whom Keynesianism was the only possible orthodoxy.

In the leadership campaign in the Conservative Party caused by the resignation of Macmillan in October 1963, Powell and Macleod, who had fallen out in previous years, made common cause to try to have R. A. Butler made the next leader. Butler was an odd choice, given the scale of their divergence on policy. However, Powell felt a personal loyalty to him that dated back to his time in the research department in the late 1940s. He regarded him as having the most intellectual and moral integrity of any of the available candidates. Butler had also, like Powell, seen through Macmillan early on. When Butler failed to press his case, Powell, like Macleod, refused to serve under Lord Home. Powell harboured no animosity towards Home, but felt that having opposed his candidacy so strongly it would be hypocritical to serve under him: 'I'd have to go home and turn all the mirrors round' was how he justified his position (Heffer, 331).

Opposition Powell used his new-found freedom to argue in public for policies and remedies he had hitherto advocated in private. As well as pleading for his party to be released from the pointless strait-jacket of incomes policies, he advocated other courses that became the basis of Thatcherism over a decade later—denationalization and deregulation chief among them. Although this won him new followers on the intellectual right, his former colleagues regarded his interventions as unhelpful, with Quintin Hogg likening his ideological fervour to that of Chairman Mao. Noting, for almost the last time, the dangers his individualism might pose to his party, Powell remained anonymous when he wrote three articles under the byline 'A Conservative' for *The Times* in April 1964. All attacked the lack of ideas, decisiveness, and principle in his party, and made a strong impact. Powell was widely supposed to have been the author of at least one of the articles: but he denied having any hand in them, and the truth was revealed only after his death.

When the Conservatives went into opposition in October 1964, Powell returned to the front bench as transport spokesman. He spent an unhappy nine months in that post, estranged from the issues on which he felt so passionately. When Douglas-Home resigned from the leadership in July 1965, Powell joined Edward Heath and Reginald Maudling in the party's first elective leadership contest. He came a distant third with just fifteen votes, but observed 'I left my visiting card' (Heffer, 385)—by which he meant that he had laid down a marker for the future on behalf not only of himself, but also of his liberal-nationalist values. It was at this time that the term 'Powellism' first came into vogue to describe his doctrine: the coinage itself a tribute to Powell's intellectual influence. The doctrine was consolidated by the publication in July 1965 of the first of several collections of his speeches, *A Nation Not Afraid*, subtitled *The Thinking of Enoch Powell*.

Heath offered Powell the pick of shadow portfolios. To general surprise, Powell—who might have been thought, given the burden of many of his speeches, to covet the post of shadow chancellor—asked to be defence spokesman. This was not only because he was interested in the disposition of the armed forces, but also because he wished to alert his party to the changed role of Britain in the world through the prism of the country's defences. In addition to the economic heresies he believed his party was committing, he felt equally strongly that it had not yet recognized the realities of Britain's post-imperial condition. This policy brought him into immediate conflict with Heath. A speech at the party's annual conference in October 1965, in which Powell advocated British withdrawal from east of Suez, caused shock waves in America. Heath, who had initially praised the speech, felt forced, under diplomatic pressure, to repudiate his colleague within days. Powell believed passionately in a European-based defence strategy; and in the election campaign of 1966 he attacked the notion that the Wilson government might be preparing to send British troops to Vietnam to assist the Americans. Although Powell did this at the urging of Conservative central office, Heath felt embarrassed by this, too, and sought to distance the party from what Powell appeared to have been saying.

After Heath had lost the election in 1966, he was urged by some colleagues to sack Powell from the front bench; Heath summoned his defence spokesman and asked him to follow the party line more closely in his pronouncements. He also asked him not to comment on matters within the portfolios of others. It was not merely that there were disagreements over defence. Keen still to repudiate socialist control, Powell had stepped up his advocacy of denationalization, and had been seeking to expose the futility both of incomes policies and of general economic planning in a free society. The Conservative Party, being in a quandary about the alternatives, was reluctant to depart from the consensual orthodoxy on any of these questions. Whatever assurances Powell may or may not have given Heath at his meeting, he continued to advocate the principles in which he firmly believed, on defence or on anything else. He felt that collective responsibility could not, under the British constitution, exist for an opposition in the same way as for a government; and that it was the job of experienced politicians like himself to try to develop policy irrespective of their nominal shadow responsibilities. In saying this he was merely following the precedent of how Churchill had conducted opposition in Powell's time in the parliamentary secretariat and the research department. Fatally, Powell chose to ignore the fact that Heath, being far less self-confident as a politician than Churchill and with no comparable record of achievement, was less happy to give colleagues a free rein.

The Birmingham speech Since the mid-1950s, Powell had, when in government, argued on departmental committees that mass immigration was having a damaging effect on certain parts of the country where immigrants tended to settle. His own experience in Wolverhampton confirmed him in this view. Powell's detractors later falsely claimed that he had, in fact, encouraged such immigration to staff the National Health Service during his time as minister of health. The truth was that ever since he had, as a party official, advised the then home affairs spokesman, Sir David Maxwell-Fyfe, to oppose the British Nationality Bill of 1948, Powell had worried about the capacity of British communities to absorb and integrate large concentrations of immigrants without causing social unrest. He had believed this in 1948 not because of racism on his part, but because of the impossibility, as he saw it, of offering British citizenship to the hundreds of millions of people living in the old empire. He felt, too, that there was a lack of logic in giving such a privilege to those who, because their countries were becoming independent, no longer had any allegiance to the crown. Later, when he came to sit for Wolverhampton South-West, he also had the empirical evidence of the strains and difficulties he witnessed among his own constituents. He argued, too, that his objections would be the same even if substantial numbers of Europeans arrived in one community *en masse*.

In the spring of 1968, at a time when his relations with Heath and many of his colleagues were strained in any case, Powell expressed dissatisfaction with his party's relatively conciliatory position on the Race Relations Bill which was then going through parliament. He felt that the Conservative leaders, few of whom sat as he did for constituencies with large immigrant populations, simply did not understand the unhappiness of many people at what was being done to their communities without their having been consulted. Heath and Hogg, the home affairs spokesman, thought that they had dealt successfully with Powell's reservations, since Powell gave them no indication at a meeting of the shadow cabinet where the question was discussed that he had any unresolved difficulties on the matter. However, on 20 April 1968 Powell made a speech at the Midland Hotel, Birmingham, about immigration. This speech thereafter defined his place in British political culture. He told the story of a little old lady, the last white woman in her street, who was taunted by immigrants and had excrement pushed through her letterbox. Sensing the chorus of execration that was about to break over him, he said that he had no right to remain silent when things such as this were happening to his electors. He predicted that, unless something was done to stop mass immigration, there would be a breakdown in public order. 'Like the Roman,' he told his audience, quoting Virgil, 'I seem to see the River Tiber foaming with much blood' (Powell, *Freedom and Reality*, 1969, 213–19).

Heath, angry at being caught unawares by the speech, decided that it was racist in tone, and sacked Powell the next day. The political class sided with Heath, but there was widespread public support for Powell. A month after his speech Gallup found that 74 per cent of people agreed with Powell, 15 per cent disagreed, and 11 per cent did not know (Gallup, 1026). He received over 100,000 letters in the weeks after his speech, only a small proportion of which disagreed with him. Heath, by contrast, had the obloquy of his party's grass roots heaped upon him. Trade unionists, to the embarrassment of the Labour leadership, marched to the Commons from the London docks and the Smithfield meat market in support of Powell. Although the furore was hard on Powell and particularly upon his wife and two daughters, he came to terms with his sudden celebrity, and sought to take advantage of the freedom his new position on the back benches allowed him.

> I felt like a man walking down a street who is hit on the head by a tile falling from a roof ... I saw it immediately that I would never hold office again; and I determined to make the best use I could of my circumstances. (*The Independent*, 9 Feb 1998)

Much criticism was directed at Powell for his use of the 'little old lady'. Despite the best efforts of the press, she was never traced; nor was her daughter-in-law, who lived in Northumberland, and who had written the letter highlighting the old lady's concerns. The letter itself was not found in Powell's papers after his death, though he meticulously kept all other significant documents. To opponents of Powell's, some details in the letter seemed incredible. There was also suspicion that it was a hoax, and that Powell had failed to check its, and her, bona fides. In future speeches on the question he was careful to give chapter and verse when citing examples of tension provided to him by correspondents.

After the Birmingham speech Powell stepped up his programme of political speeches around the country, though for years he was pursued by demonstrators who attempted to disrupt his meetings. Despite the forces ranged against him in the liberal establishment and the media, he succeeded in establishing himself as a formidable political force, thanks largely to his powers of communication. He became adept at the television and radio interview, and carefully timed his speeches to command press attention. As his Birmingham speech showed, he was an early master of the sound bite. His message was enhanced by the drama of his public performances—an intensely charismatic style based on his hypnotic combination of staring eyes and a metallic tone of voice. His language was memorable, his convictions clear, his naked patriotism a direct appeal to the masses. His friend and political opponent Tony Benn later observed that 'people listen to him fascinated by his intellect and clarity and he mesmerises Labour MPs like rabbits caught in a headlamp' (Benn, 55).

At the Conservative Party conference at Blackpool in 1968 the evidence of support for Powell within his party disconcerted the leadership. Although heckled by a few, Powell was rapturously received when he dismissed the caution and lack of radicalism of his former colleagues with the Nietzschean observation: 'Whatever the true interest of our country calls for is always possible' (Heffer, 483). Powell was no longer bound by any sort of collective responsibility, and did not in future allow his thought or his words to be trammelled by any considerations of party orthodoxy, or of loyalty to its leadership. This meant that, in expounding matters of policy, he could steal an initiative, and appear to have trumped the less radical impulses of his colleagues. A coherent framework of ideology was,

by the late 1960s, fully in place, rooted in economic liberalism and social nationalism. It was not a menu from which it was possible to dine à la carte. One who admired him greatly, Margaret Thatcher, recalled that 'the very fact Enoch advanced all his positions as part of a coherent whole made it more difficult to express agreement with one or two of them' (Thatcher, 147). None the less, by the time Mrs Thatcher left office, almost the only parts of the Powell doctrine she had not come to embrace were his anti-Americanism and his opposition to the death penalty.

After 1968 Powell fought to acquit himself of the charge of racism, with the support of unlikely friends such as Michael Foot, a prominent left-wing Labour MP. However, it was a badge that was uncritically attached to him by his opponents, for the rest of his life. Powell was infuriated when anyone referred to his speeches on 'race', for he claimed that he had never offered any opinions on the subject. 'It so happens that I never talk about race', he said during the 1970 election campaign. 'I do not know what race is' (*The Guardian*, 6 June 1970). His speeches, he said, were about immigration. He had no time for genetic or scientific theories of race, but relied on analysing the demographic and cultural effects of mass immigration on an area with a distinctly different culture. He was most concerned not about absolute numbers of immigrants, but at the pace of growth in an immigrant population overwhelmingly comprising people of child-bearing age. Powell was strongly influenced by what he perceived to be the racial tensions in America caused by the creation of ghettos, and was concerned that such a phenomenon should not be allowed to happen in Britain. Over the next few years he returned in his speeches frequently to immigration, his task made easier by less than honest presentation of the immigration figures by the government. The Commonwealth Immigrants Act of 1971, passed by the next Conservative government in a belated attempt to limit immigration, was in part the result of Powell's raising of public consciousness on the question. However, even as late as 1985 he urged a policy of voluntary repatriation, to prevent areas of Britain having Asian or African-descended populations that were a third of the total. Otherwise, he warned, 'it will be a Britain unimaginably wracked by dissension and violent disorder, not recognizable as the same nation as it has been, or perhaps a nation at all' (*The Times*, 21 Sept 1985). Powell was speaking in the wake of riots at Handsworth in Birmingham, a predominantly immigrant-populated suburb. These riots were but the latest in a string of inner-city disturbances in the early 1980s that many thought justified another component in Powell's objections to mass immigration: its effect on public order.

Eventually Powell's reliance on statistics and facts in his speeches, and his avoidance of anything smacking of prejudice or of what was conventionally understood to be racism, forced his opponents to take him seriously in a way they would not have done had he been a simple bigot. He highlighted practical problems of housing, education, and crime caused by the concentration of immigrants in geographically small areas like his own constituency. These were issues to which politicians had no choice but to respond. The Labour cabinet minister Anthony Crosland, for one, recognized the deep feelings of his party's own working-class supporters, with whom Powell was striking a chord. Angered by the self-righteousness with which these sentiments were labelled 'fascist', he wrote in 1973 that 'to condemn such feeling as racialist is libellous and impertinent. They [sic] reflect a genuine sense of insecurity, and anxiety for a traditional way of life' (The Observer, 21 Jan 1973). However, the emotion with which Powell invested his pronouncements on immigration undeniably whipped up unhealthy sentiment among some of the less discerning of his audience. He could not be held responsible for the actions of those who took his words, contrary to their intention, to legitimize hostility towards immigrants. None the less, many blamed him for the racist feeling that grew in Britain in the late 1960s and beyond. Powell himself believed that the growth of such feeling was the consequence of failing to act on the problem he had identified at Birmingham. He also believed firmly that he did not, as a parliamentarian, have the right to remain silent. He shared with Walter Bagehot a belief that parliament should mirror national opinion, and debate national concerns. In a speech on 7 September 1968 he warned that 'people rightly look to see their wishes and views voiced and discussed in parliament and if, over a long period, they feel this is not happening a dangerous estrangement can set in between electorate, Parliament and Government' (Sunday Times, 8 Sept 1968).

It was not just on immigration that Powell felt that parliament was ignoring the concerns of the people: he felt it was true on foreign policy, the Commonwealth, free trade, taxation, and crime too. As a result, and in his new-found populist clothes, he was keen to attack the political orthodoxy on an even broader basis than before. The unifying theme was his regard for the freedoms, integrity, constitution, and customs of the British nation, and his mounting sense that the public shared that regard. His attack on immigration was the first salvo on this nationalist front, and he continued to stress the integrity and identity of the nation in speeches on that and other topics. He said at Wolverhampton on 9 June 1969 that 'we have an identity of our own, as we have a territory of our own ... the instinct to preserve that identity, as to defend that territory, is one of the deepest and strongest implanted in mankind' (The Times, 10 June 1969).

On the fringe of the Conservative Party conference in 1968 Powell delivered his 'Morecambe budget'. In it he argued that with drastic cuts in public spending, and the reduction of the role of the state, the standard rate of income tax could be halved (from 8s. 3d. to 4s. 3d. in the pound). That autumn he put himself at the head of a cross-party movement to prevent the House of Lords from being reformed as a result of a deal done by the two front benches in the House of Commons. So successfully was the government impeded during the committee stage of the Parliament (No. 2) Bill early in 1969 that the prime

minister, Harold Wilson, was forced to abandon the measure.

In March 1969 Powell opened a new front, on the possibility that Britain might join the European Economic Community. This drew great criticism from his own side, for opposition to entry had hitherto been confined largely to the Labour Party. As supporters of Heath pointed out, Powell had sat quietly in the cabinet in 1962–3 when Macmillan had, unsuccessfully, tried to take Britain in. Powell argued that he was consistent: he had voted against the Schuman plan in 1950 and had supported entry hitherto only because he had been convinced that the Common Market was simply a means to secure free trade. Now it was clear to him that the sovereignty of parliament was in question, as was Britain's very survival as a nation. This nationalist analysis powerfully attracted millions of grass-roots Conservatives and others, and as much as anything else made Powell the implacable enemy of Heath, a fervent pro-European.

When Wilson went to the country in June 1970, Powell was at odds with his party's leadership on almost all the main questions. His second collection of speeches, Freedom and Reality (1969), was selling well and had been reprinted, indicating the following he could command by his dissent. Under his economic influence, however, his party was preparing to fight on a manifesto—hammered out at a meeting at the Selsdon Park Hotel early in 1970—that deferred to the free market more than had any manifesto since the war. Powell's election address in Wolverhampton mentioned the Conservative Party only once: his was a personal manifesto that went well beyond what Labour caricatured as 'Selsdon man'.

The Heath government Heath's victory, predicted by almost no one, was a shattering blow to Powell. He felt his chance of leading his party—a notion that had come to seem more feasible to him as he examined his postbag and witnessed the great displays of admiration that met him as he tirelessly toured the country—was at an end. Until early in 1971 he licked his wounds and made relatively few public pronouncements. He was waiting for Heath to make mistakes, and only then would he attack. Such opportunities soon came. Since 1968 Powell had been an increasingly frequent visitor to Northern Ireland, and in keeping with his general British nationalist viewpoint sided strongly with the Ulster Unionists in their desire to maintain British rule. From early in 1971 he opposed, with increasing vehemence, Heath's approach to Ulster, the greatest breach with his party coming over the imposition of direct rule in 1972. By then, though, other matters had caused Powell and his party to undergo a divorce in all but name.

The Common Market was the main cause. The Conservatives had promised at the 1970 election to negotiate about entry, that entry to be accomplished only with the full-hearted consent of the British parliament and people. When Powell saw Heath sign an accession treaty before parliament had even debated the issue, when the second reading of the bill to put the treaty into law passed by just eight votes on second reading, and when it became clear that the British people would have no further say in the matter, he declared open war on his party's line. He voted against the government on every one of the 104 divisions in the course of the European Communities Bill. When finally he lost this battle, he decided he could no longer sit in a parliament that was not sovereign. In the summer of 1972 he prepared to resign.

As he was about to do so, Powell changed his mind. He felt compelled to stay in parliament to articulate the fears of his supporters about a new wave of mass immigration, caused by the expulsion of Asians from Uganda by the dictator Idi Amin. Powell argued, and in law was correct, that Britain had no legal obligation to accept these refugees: but the government dismissed his objections and admitted the Ugandan Asians for humanitarian reasons. The issue was the subject of a noisy debate at the party conference in October 1972, at which Powell spoke. Unusually, a vote was taken, in which a two-to-one victory for the leadership barely disguised the support Powell commanded at the grass roots.

In the following month the issue that brought down the Heath government, not least because it gave Powell his most formidable line of assault against it, blew up. Heath had told the country in 1970 that he would not countenance an incomes policy. Having expanded the money supply at the astonishing rate of 30 per cent a year, Heath came to the House of Commons in November 1972 to announce the introduction of prices and incomes controls, in an attempt to counter the rampant inflation that had resulted. The government would not, however, admit to having caused the problem, which went back to the unlearned lessons of 1957–8. Powell could see at once not just a flagrant breach of promise, but an utterly futile and politically damaging measure in the making. In an electric moment he asked Heath, on the floor of the Commons, whether he knew 'that it is fatal for any Government or party or person to seek to govern in direct opposition to the principles on which they were entrusted with the right to govern'. He asked, further, whether Heath had 'taken leave of his senses' (*Hansard 5C*, 845.631–2). The personal breach between the two men, hitherto kept largely private, was out in the open.

From then until the government lost the general election of February 1974, Powell's position of open dissent became a matter of keen public and media interest. Substantial grass-roots dissatisfaction with Heath led to various 'Powell for prime minister' campaigns, which Powell ignored. However, he maintained his high-profile attacks on various elements of government policy in speeches inside and outside the Commons, which led colleagues loyal to Heath to demand that he have the whip withdrawn from him. However, Heath and his chief whip, Francis Pym, did not wish to make Powell more of a martyr than he already was. A speech by him at Stockport in June 1973 seemed the final straw, for he signalled clearly in it that his party no longer merited the loyalty of its supporters. He rode out the wave of anger that this provoked, though some in his constituency by this time felt that he was trying their patience. At his constituency party's annual general meeting in December 1973 he successfully faced down criticism, and gained the support of his activists for his campaign, though some remained implacably hostile. He argued that he was fighting on the platform on which he and his party had been elected in 1970, a platform that Heath had largely abandoned. He disappointed his association officers by refusing to tell them what he would do if Heath called an early election. It had become apparent to them that Powell would have difficulty standing as a Conservative in such an election, but he maintained that he saw no prospect of one being called. This was disingenuous, for he well knew that in the following eighteen months he would have to make up his mind.

The matter was forced far more quickly than anyone had expected. An essential part of Heath's new strategy was to impress upon trade unions that they had to accept pay restraint. With grim inevitability this provoked a confrontation with the miners that came to a head in December 1973 – January 1974. A shortage of coal caused Heath to announce a three-day working week for industry, and power cuts for domestic consumers. Powell believed that, having adopted this confrontational stance, Heath would now follow it through to maintain his political authority. However, when Heath called an election on what was represented as the issue of 'who governs?', Powell was outraged. Though it had long been hard to see how he could ever have stood again as a Conservative, given his extensive disagreements with the leadership, his hand was now forced. As soon as he heard that the election had been called, he sent a letter to his association in Wolverhampton saying that he would not be a candidate. His supporters there felt a keen sense of betrayal, as did adherents of Powellism across the country, who felt that that was no time for him to be ditching the Conservative Party—not least for his own sake.

For the first fortnight of the three-week campaign Powell said nothing in public, except to deliver a theological sermon at a church service. However, in the five days before the poll he made two speeches, at Birmingham and at Saltaire in Yorkshire, to anti-EEC rallies. At both he implied heavily that people should vote Labour, as Labour was committed to a referendum on continued membership of the EEC, which Britain had joined thirteen months earlier. At the second meeting, when Powell compared Heath unfavourably with Wilson, a heckler cried out: 'Judas!' Powell shouted back: 'Judas was paid! Judas was paid! I am making a sacrifice!' (Heffer, 709).

Heath stayed in office for four days after the election, trying to form a minority government. Powell took great pleasure in his failure to do so, but had also to confront the fact that he had apparently ended his own political life too, and was despised by many Conservatives. There could be no possibility of any reconciliation while Heath remained leader, or while the party remained committed to Europe and to failed methods of economic management. Several Conservative associations approached Powell and asked him to be their candidate, but he declined all such offers. He was also approached by representatives of the Unionist coalition in Northern Ireland. They suggested he might be a Unionist candidate in the election the minority Labour government was expected to call within months. Powell agreed, and when a vacancy arose for a candidate in the Down South seat he was adopted to fill it. At the election of 10 October 1974, after seven months in the wilderness, he was back in the Commons.

Northern Ireland As an Ulster Unionist MP, Powell had to devote much of his time to a cause in which he firmly believed—the maintenance of British rule in Ulster—but this inevitably took him away from mainstream political issues. A posthumous victory for Powellism in the removal of Heath from the Conservative leadership seemed to bring him no comfort, even though Heath's successor, Margaret Thatcher, set about establishing policies drawn straight from Powellite economic doctrine. Speaking of their ideological sympathies, she said that 'economically we both hold the same views … I originally got them from Enoch, but also of course Keith Joseph took them up, and we developed them' (*Odd Man Out*). Joseph, too, had learned them from Powell, who had directed him towards the Institute of Economic Affairs during the 1960s. Joseph's influence on Mrs Thatcher was profound, and through him, therefore, Powell's was more profound still. Nevertheless, for some years Powell was hostile to Mrs Thatcher, partly because he felt that women were unsuited to the House of Commons and to high politics, but also because he doubted the strength of the ideological conversion of those who had sat happily in the Heath cabinet. Inevitably, many also felt that his feelings stemmed from pique at having missed a golden opportunity for himself.

Powell regained some of his clout during the 1974–9 parliament by persuading his Unionist colleagues to support the Labour government after it lost the slim majority it had won at the October 1974 election. Although this support was given in return for favours to Ulster, and undeniably advanced the Unionists' interests, it deepened the sense of betrayal that Conservatives felt towards Powell. His greatest achievement was to secure increased parliamentary representation for Northern Ireland at Westminster. In the end, though, even he could no longer bring himself to support the Callaghan government. The Unionists were instrumental in its losing the vote of confidence on 28 March 1979.

Powell was returned for Down South a second time at the election of May 1979, but regarded Mrs Thatcher's victory as 'grim' (Heffer, 820). Her clear majority meant that an influential role for the Unionists in general, or for Powell in particular, was over. Powell maintained a big national following, and was still greatly in demand as a speaker, as a journalist, and as a television and radio performer. As he approached his seventies there were signs of his mellowing, the public face of unbending, logical sternness now and then complemented by revelations of the poetical side of his character. He also took up new political interests, not least his sponsorship of a private member's bill in the 1984–5 session of parliament to ban embryo experimentation. The bill failed, but only after a long battle in which every trick of parliamentary procedure was used to try to keep it alive.

In time Powell reached an accommodation with the Conservative government, giving warm support not just to its monetarist economic policies but also to Mrs Thatcher's determination to retake the Falkland Islands after the Argentinian invasion of April 1982. He had regular meetings with Mrs Thatcher, who valued his counsel highly. As a result of this relationship he was again able to advance Ulster's cause with Downing Street. However, his public denunciation of the 1985 Anglo-Irish agreement as an act of treachery put relations back into the freezer, where they remained for some years until finally thawed. In response to that agreement Powell reluctantly joined all his Unionist colleagues in resigning his parliamentary seat and fighting a by-election in January 1986. He had won in 1983, but his majority had narrowed thanks to a growing nationalist vote and to his being opposed by a Democratic Unionist. In the by-election Powell had no Unionist opponent, and won. However, at the general election of 1987 Powell's thirty-seven-year parliamentary career ended when he lost the seat to his Social Democratic and Labour Party opponent. Although he had known victory was uncertain, he was devastated by the result. He was offered a life peerage, which was regarded as his right as a former cabinet minister, but declined it. He argued that, as he had opposed the bill that established life peerages in 1958, it would be hypocritical for him to take one.

Instead, Powell resumed a life of scholarship. He had long wanted to write a study of the Greek New Testament, and began with a controversial book, *The Evolution of the Gospel* (1994), on the gospel according to St Matthew, which among other things called into question whether there had literally been a crucifixion of Christ. He published his *Collected Poems* in 1990, the availability of some of which after half a century out of print made him 'glad in a vaguely melancholy sort of way' (*Collected Poems*, vii). He continued to speak at public meetings regularly into his eighties, and assumed a unique place as a public figure—though one who, to the end, provoked fierce emotions.

In 1994 Powell was diagnosed as suffering from Parkinson's disease. He fought the affliction with his customary resolution, despite mounting incapacity. For the last few years of his life he managed occasional pieces of journalism, co-operated in a television documentary about his life in 1995, and began but did not complete work on a study of the gospel according to St John. He died on 8 February 1998 in the King Edward VII Hospital for Officers in London. Dressed in his brigadier's uniform, he was buried in his regiment's plot in Warwick cemetery on 18 February 1998. He was survived by his wife and two daughters.

Powell's legacy Powell claimed that 'all political lives, unless they are cut off in midstream at a happy juncture, end in failure, because that is the nature of politics and of human affairs' (Powell, *Joseph Chamberlain*, 1977, 151). Not only did Powell not become prime minister, or even leader of his party: he served in the cabinet for only fifteen months, and it was usually by his own will that he did not hold higher offices. He made no concessions to those who might otherwise have tentatively explored his way of politics. Also, when he entered into conflict with Heath and his supporters after 1968, much of that conflict, while rooted in ideology, took on a personal tone that indicated a strong animus on Powell's part against some of his rivals. He himself revealed that, on the morning after the general election of February 1974, he went to his bathroom 'and sang the Te Deum' on reading that Heath had failed to secure a majority—something he in part attributed to his own role in that campaign. He added: 'I didn't mean it vindictively', though towards the end of his life he admitted 'I had had my revenge on the man who had destroyed the self-government of the United Kingdom' (Heffer, 710–11).

Powell was also prevented from maximizing his influence during his political prime because of what many felt to be the contradictory nature of his philosophy: the contrast of his liberal economics with his high tory social policy, notably on immigration. At the height of his popularity, induced as it was by his views on immigration, he often spoke over the heads of some of the audiences who came to hear him by treating them to detailed discourses on, for example, the theory of floating exchange rates. He also allied himself with causes that allowed his opponents to stigmatize him as reactionary and anti-populist. He was, for example, opposed to legislation to prevent discrimination against women, though he took this view for precisely the same reasons for which he opposed laws against race discrimination. He found them an affront to individual liberty, and believed that the market, if allowed to work, would eliminate discrimination through a meritocratic pursuit of profit. Such rarefied arguments were seldom appreciated by the general public, though on greater reflection their logic became more apparent.

However, as a populist figure Powell had few rivals in his generation, and his long-term political influence was considerable. Much of the programme of what came to be called Thatcherism was propagated by Powell during the twenty years before Mrs Thatcher came to power. In British political terms he was the father of monetarism and privatization. His example spurred on a group on the Thatcherite right of the Conservative Party who exposed and attacked the moral and logical contradictions of the policy of John Major, particularly towards Europe. The shift to the right by the party under William Hague brought it more into line with Powell's doctrine than ever before, highlighting the Powellite mixture of liberal economics and social conservatism. Nor was Powell's influence confined just to what had once been his own party. In the months before his death he saw a Labour chancellor of the exchequer pursuing precisely the monetary policy he, Thorneycroft, and Birch had advocated, and so been forced to resign. His warnings of the constitutional dangers of British membership of the European Union came to be recognized as having some validity in the late 1980s and 1990s, after the Single European Act and the treaty of Maastricht. In an age when the presentation of policy often took on greater importance than the policy itself, Powell exemplified the ability of the well-organized, coherent politician to survive attack by the media, and ultimately to capture them and put them to work for his own cause.

On the issue with which Powell's name is inevitably most associated—that of the risks of conflagration provoked by mass immigration—his worst predictions have not come true, though he argued to the end of his life that the early part of the twenty-first century would see him vindicated. None the less, like Joseph Chamberlain and scarcely anyone else in the twentieth century, he established with the public a reputation as a political figure that is usually accorded only to prime ministers. His main motivations—patriotism, and a profound understanding of how the people of England valued their liberties and wished to be left alone by the state—touched an undeniably popular chord. His was above all a career that demonstrated how a superfluity of principle and a loathing of pragmatism preclude success in politics by any conventional measure. It also showed how intellectual originality and the radicalism it strives to beget were for much of the twentieth century regarded with suspicion, and even fear, in British political life. 'I may have failed', he told a television interviewer in 1989. 'That does not mean I was wrong' (*The Independent*, 9 Feb 1998).   SIMON HEFFER

Sources S. Heffer, *Like the Roman: the life of Enoch Powell* (1998) · J. E. Powell, *Collected poems* (1990) · T. Benn, *Against the tide: diaries, 1973–1976* (1989) · M. Thatcher, *The path to power* (1995) · G. H. Gallup, ed., *The Gallup international public opinion polls: Great Britain, 1937–75*, 2 (1976) · M. Cockerell, *Odd man out*, 11 Nov 1995, BBC 2 · *The Observer* (21 Jan 1973) · *The Independent* (9 Feb 1998) · *The Times* (10 June 1969) · *The Times* (21 Sept 1985) · *The Times* (9 Feb 1998) · *The Guardian* (6 June 1970) · *The Guardian* (9 Feb 1998) · *Daily Telegraph* (9 Feb 1998) · *WWW* · personal knowledge (2004) · private information (2004) [Margaret Powell, widow] · d. cert.

Archives CAC Cam., papers · priv. coll., papers · PRO NIre., Down South constituency corresp., speeches, and papers · Staffs. RO, Wolverhampton constituency papers · U. St Andr. L., speeches | BLPES, interview with Anthony Seldon · King's Lond., Liddell Hart C., corresp. with Sir B. H. Liddell Hart · NL Wales, letters to Professor S. J. Stephens as co-editor of 'Ilyfa Blegynryd' | FILM BBC, London · Independent Television News | SOUND BBC, London

Likenesses H. A. Freeth, etching, 1937, NPG · H. A. Freeth, chalk drawing, 1940, priv. coll. · H. A. Freeth, etching, 1951, priv. coll. · photographs, 1956–86, Hult. Arch. · H. A. Freeth, oils, 1959, priv. coll. · H. A. Freeth, oils, 1966, priv. coll. · J. Bown, photograph, 1968, priv. coll. [*see illus.*] · G. Scarfe, ink and collage on paper, 1971, NPG · F. Topolski, oils, 1976, priv. coll. · A. Newman, bromide print, 1978, NPG · C. Cutner, photograph, 1979, priv. coll. · N. Sinclair, bromide print, 1992, NPG · M. Cummings, pen-and-ink drawing, NPG · P. Friers, pen-and-ink drawing, NPG · D. Waugh, colour print, NPG · photograph, repro. in *The Times* (9 Feb 1998) · photograph, repro. in *The Independent* · photograph, repro. in *The Guardian* (9 Feb 1998) · photograph, repro. in *Daily Telegraph*

Wealth at death £246,603: probate, 23 March 1998, *CGPLA Eng. & Wales*

Powell, Foster (*bap.* 1734, *d.* 1793), pedestrian, was baptized at Horseforth, near Leeds, West Riding of Yorkshire, on 12 December 1734, the son of William Powell (*b.* 1706?). Details of his education are unknown. In 1762 he travelled to London where he worked as a clerk to an attorney in the

Foster Powell (*bap.* 1734, *d.* 1793), by Sylvester Harding, pubd 1788

Temple before moving to live with his uncle at New Inn. Later that decade he began his career as a pedestrian, walking 50 miles along the London to Bath road in 7 hours. In November 1773 he made the first of four timed walks from London to York and back, completing the journey in 5 days and 18 hours; five years later he is recorded as having run 2 miles in 10 minutes. The high point of Powell's career came in the late 1780s. In 1786 he walked 100 miles on the Bath road in 23 hours, 15 minutes; in 1787 he covered the 122 miles between London Bridge and Canterbury (and back) in 24 hours; in 1788 he improved his time for 100 miles to 21 hours 35 minutes, and completed his second London to York expedition, the same journey being undertaken once more in 1790. His best performance for this latter walk was made on his final attempt in 1792 when he walked from Shoreditch church to York Minster in a time of 5 days, 15 hours, and 15 minutes. On longer walks Powell, described as 'tall and thin, very strong downward [and] well-calculated for walking', fortified himself with five hours sleep a night, 'light food', and brandy (Wilson, 3.275).

Powell does not appear to have profited greatly from his walks, despite considerable popular interest in his athleticism. His final journey to York brought him £10, said to be the largest sum he ever received. Other wagers, such as that for a second walk to Canterbury in 1792, were lost

when on the return to London he took the wrong road at Blackheath. On this occasion donations from sympathetic friends exceeded the original bet. However, such gifts proved insufficient to keep him from poverty, 'his constant companion in his travels … to the hour of death'. He died at New Inn on 15 April 1793 at the age of fifty-nine. His funeral procession on 22 April 1793 'was characteristically a *walking* one from New-inn, through Fleet-Street, and up Ludgate Hill' to his place of burial at St Faith's Church in St Paul's Churchyard (*GM*).   PHILIP CARTER

Sources H. Wilson, *Wonderful characters*, 3 vols. (1821) · *GM*, 1st ser., 63 (1793) · *Particulars of the late Mr Foster Powell's journey on foot from London to York and back again* (1793) · *DNB*
Archives PRO, deeds and papers, some relating to Foster Powell, C 107/174
Likenesses etching, pubd 1771, NPG · S. Harding, etching, pubd 1786, BM · S. Harding, engraving, pubd 1788, priv. coll. [*see illus.*] · R. Cooper, engraving (after an unknown portrait), repro. in Wilson, *Wonderful characters*, vol 1. p. 272 · etching, NPG
Wealth at death died in poverty; 'rather indigent circumstances': Wilson, *Wonderful characters*

Powell, Frederick York (1850–1904), historian, born on 14 January 1850 at 43 Woburn Place, Bloomsbury, was the eldest child and only son of Frederick Powell and Mary (*d.* 1910), daughter of Dr James York (*d.* 1882), a physician who was also a Spanish scholar. His father, a commissariat merchant, who had an office in Mincing Lane, came of a south Wales family. Much of Powell's early life was spent at Sandgate, Kent, where he learned to love the sea and formed lifelong friendships with some fishermen. In the autumn of 1859 he went to the Manor House preparatory school at Hastings. In 1864 he entered Dr Jex Blake's house at Rugby, but though he gained a name for esoteric learning he never rose above the lower fifth and left, chiefly for reasons of health, in July 1866. The next two years were fruitfully spent in travel and self-education. There was a visit to Biarritz, and a tour in Sweden which gave Powell, who had read Sir George Webbe Dasent's translation of *Burnt Njal* at Rugby, occasion to learn and practise a Scandinavian language. At eighteen he began to work on Old French, German, and Icelandic with Henry Tull Rhoades at Bonchurch. He was already a strong socialist and agnostic, and had formed most of the tastes and prejudices which accompanied him through life—an interest in old armour, a special attraction for the art of William Blake, a passion for northern and medieval literature, and an aversion to philosophy, except for Kant and Schopenhauer.

Powell went to Oxford in 1868, and after a year spent with the non-collegiate students migrated to Christ Church. He gained a first class in law and modern history in the Trinity term of 1872. After graduating, he spent two years (1872–4) at his father's house in Lancaster Gate in London. He entered the Middle Temple on 8 November 1870, and was called to the bar on 6 June 1874.

Powell's first academic appointment was to teach one of the few subjects in which he had no enthusiastic interest. In 1874 he was appointed to a lecturership in law at Christ Church, and save for a year's interlude as history lecturer at Trinity College, where his teaching method was felt to

Frederick York Powell (1850–1904), by Sir William Rothenstein, 1896

be 'too irregular and haphazard' by some of the students (Elton, 1.27), his official teaching in Oxford was, until 1894, confined to the uncongenial subjects of law and political economy. He had, however, attracted the attention of Mandell Creighton, who invited him to contribute a volume on early English history to Longman's Epochs of English History, of which Creighton was editor. The book, *Early England to the Norman Conquest*, published in 1876, delighted Creighton, who praised its clarity of style. These were to be the years of Powell's best work. In 1869 he had met Gudbrandur Vigfússon, who had come to Oxford in 1866 to edit the *Icelandic–English Dictionary* for the Oxford press. In 1877 Powell engaged with Vigfússon upon the prolegomena to an edition of *Sturlunga saga*, 'taking down across the table', said Vigfússon, 'my thoughts and theories, so that though the substance and drift of the arguments are mine, the English with the exception of bits and phrases here and there is Mr. Powell's throughout.' An *Icelandic Prose Reader*, the notes to which were mainly the work of Powell, followed in 1879, and two years later the *Corpus poeticum boreale*, an edition of the whole of *Ancient Northern Poetry*, with translations and a full commentary. The translations were provided by Powell and exhibited his command of a style reminiscent of Dasent's early work.

The first volume contains the old mythological and heroic poetry: the poems of the *Poetic Edda* and similar texts. The second volume is a collection of the poems composed, chiefly by Icelanders, in honour of successive kings of Norway and other important figures. Powell here brought to bear his knowledge of Scandinavian history. These poems were used as authorities by the early historians of Norway (such as Snorri Sturluson); the introductions to the different sections, in the second volume of the *Corpus*, containing biographical information about the poets, formed the only original work in English on this portion of Scandinavian history at that time. It is hardly possible to describe the extraordinary variety of contents in the editorial part of the two volumes—essays on mythology and points of literary history. They show an unsurpassed breadth of imagination, even if they are too unreliable to form any foundation for subsequent scholarship.

The *Corpus poeticum boreale* at once made Powell's name as a northern scholar and was intended to be the prelude to an even more ambitious work. In August 1884 he spent a fortnight with Vigfússon in Copenhagen examining Icelandic manuscripts, with the aim of producing an edition and translation of the classics of northern prose, a proposal for which had been submitted to the Clarendon Press. The work advanced steadily and most of the *Origines Islandicæ* was already in proof when Vigfússon died in 1889. So long as Vigfússon was alive Powell was kept steadily working at his Scandinavian task, but with the loss of his friend and associate his study was no longer directed and he gave himself up to miscellaneous reading; 'he missed the double harness in which he had pulled so long' (Elton, 1.106). The result was that the work was never concluded and was only published in 1905 after Powell's death. The Clarendon Press would only allow a list of corrigenda rather than the substantial revision which Craigie felt it needed; consequently it is unusable for serious scholarly purposes. Powell's procrastination was typical of the later period of his life—projects were initiated but never brought to conclusion. The text of the prose sagas is substantially the work of Vigfússon, 'the ordering, the English, and many of the literary criticisms, portraits, and parallels are Powell's' (Elton, 1.101). Powell seems to have deferred to the Icelander's fine, technical scholarship; but he did not check Vigfússon's wilder speculations nor was he able to provide much philological method. The translation remains readable, if error prone, only occasionally lapsing into archaism; but the notes are 'littered with York Powell's inspired but deluded guesses' (Sutcliffe, 81).

Meanwhile, in 1884, through the influence of Dean H. G. Liddell, Powell had been made a student of Christ Church. His official duties as law lecturer were to teach for the law school, to look after Indian Civil Service candidates, and to lecture on political economy for the pass school. His real and congenial avocations extended far beyond this narrow circuit. Besides his work on Scandinavian literature, he taught Old English, Old French, and even for a time Old German, for the Association for Education of Women in Oxford, took a leading share in founding the *English Historical Review* (1885), and published a history of *England from the Earliest Times to the Death of Henry VII* (1885), designed for 'the middle forms of schools'. A series of little books, *English History from Contemporary Writers*, was begun under his editorship in 1885.

Powell built for himself a contemporary reputation as one of the most profound scholars in medieval history and literature in England. When J. A. Froude died in 1894, and S. R. Gardiner, the prime minister's first choice, declined the chair, the regius professorship of modern history was conferred on Powell on the recommendation of Lord Rosebery (December 1894). Powell's scout identified the prime minister's letter as a tradesman's bill and put it aside for a while until enquiries from Downing Street brought it to light. The post was accepted with misgivings. Powell had no gift either for public lecturing or for organization. His inaugural lecture was only thirty minutes long and virtually inaudible. He was shy of an audience which he did not know, and although both in his inaugural lecture and upon subsequent occasions he pleaded for the scientific treatment of history, for the training of public archivists, and for the divorce of history and ethics, his practice differed from his theory; in his journalism he frequently relied on opinion and moral feeling rather than historical fact.

As professor of history, Powell was a disappointment. He made no special contribution to the advance of historical knowledge or method and failed to make any general impression upon the undergraduates as a teacher. Indeed, from the age of forty until the end of his life he published only two works: a translation of the *Færeyinga saga* (1896), dedicated jointly to H. G. Liddell, dean of Christ Church, and Henry Stone, an old fisherman at Sandgate; and a rendering of some quatrains from 'Umar Khayyam (1901). Powell was, however, the most generous as well as the most unambitious of men. His time was his friends' time, and the hours which might have been spent upon his own work were squandered on helping and advising others. Oliver Elton translated the first nine books of Saxo Grammaticus at his suggestion, and the bulk of the introduction was Powell's work. Again, as delegate of the Clarendon Press, an office which he held from 1885 until his death, Powell was able to render some service to the advancement of learning, though his procrastination and failure to answer letters hindered some projects; his interference with Q's editing of the *Oxford Book of English Verse* caused the other delegates considerable irritation.

As professor Powell regularly lectured in his rooms at Christ Church on the sources of English history, and on every Thursday evening was at home to undergraduates. In his pleasant rooms in the Meadow Buildings of Christ Church, with their stacks of books and Japanese prints, he would discourse freely on any subject which came up, from boxing and fencing to the latest Portuguese novel. His knowledge of foreign, especially of Romance, literature was singularly wide. A founder of the Rabelais Club, he had a rich fund of Rabelais stories which he recounted at its monthly dinners. He brought Verlaine to lecture in Oxford in 1891, and as a curator of the Taylor Institution (from 1887) procured an invitation to Stéphane Mallarmé to give a lecture there on 28 February 1894. Powell found

Mallarmé most congenial and translated his lecture into English in a single evening. The Belgian poet Verhaeren and the French sculptor Rodin were likewise at different times Powell's guests at Christ Church. He had also studied Old Irish, and was one of the presidents of the Irish Texts Society. On 7 April 1902 he lectured in Dublin to the Irish Literary Society on Irish influence in English literature, and in December of the same year went to Liverpool to speak for the endowment of Celtic studies in the university. Meanwhile, he learned Persian, had dabbled in Maori and Romani, and had assembled a valuable collection of Japanese prints. Robert Bridges described Powell's rooms as 'a veritable knick-knackatory of Japanese carvings, old Psalters, Parisian advertisements, etc. etc.' (Sutcliffe, 82). He wrote numerous reviews for the daily and weekly press, principally for the *Academy*, and after 1890 for the *Manchester Guardian*.

The radical side of Powell's versatile nature is illustrated by the preface which he wrote to *A Penny Garland of Songs of Labour*, published in 1893 and written by his Oxford friend William Hines, chimney sweeper, herbalist, and radical agitator, and by the active share which he took in the foundation of Ruskin College, an institution devised to bring working men to Oxford. Powell presided over the inaugural meeting at the town hall on 22 February 1899, and acted from the first as a member of the council of the college. In religion Powell described himself as a 'decent heathen Aryan', in politics as 'a socialist and a jingo'. He was an advocate of home rule, and of the Second South African War, and the first president of the Oxford Tariff Reform League. He was made an honorary LLD of Glasgow in 1901.

In 1874 Powell married Florence Batten, *née* Silke (d. 1888), a widow with two young daughters. Mrs Powell did not live in Oxford; for many years Powell spent the middle of the week during term time in Oxford and the weekend with his family in London. In January 1881 he moved from 6 Stamford Grove West, Upper Clapton, to Bedford Park, an aesthetic urban development in the Queen Anne style, popular with painters, actors, poets, and journalists. Here he resided until 1902; his only child, a daughter, Mariella, was born there in 1884. Four years later Powell's wife died. In the summer of 1894 he visited Ambleteuse on the coast of Normandy for the first time, and for the next ten years spent much of his summers there. In December 1902 Powell gave up his London house and settled in north Oxford with his daughter. The next year came warnings of heart trouble. He died on 8 May 1904 at his home, Staverton Grange, Banbury Road, Oxford. He was buried at Wolvercote cemetery, Oxford, without religious rites by his own desire; the delegates of the Clarendon Press processed from Walton Street to pay their respects. His large library was sold by Blackwells bookshop, which issued three special sale catalogues.

In appearance Powell resembled a sea captain. He was broad, burly, and bearded, brusque in manner, with dark hair and eyes, and a deep rich laugh, 'a big, untidy, generous man' (Starkie, 22). In the sphere of learning he is chiefly remembered for his services to northern literature, for his support of Vigfússon, and for the general stimulus which he gave to the study of medieval literature in Great Britain, rather than for outstanding or lasting scholarship.

H. A. L. FISHER, rev. CAROLYNE LARRINGTON

Sources O. Elton, *Frederick York Powell*, 2 vols. (1906) · P. Sutcliffe, *The Oxford University Press: an informal history* (1978) · E. Starkie, 'Verlaine and Mallarmé at Oxford', *Harlequin*, 1 (1949), 22–3, 37 · J. A. B. Townsend, 'The Viking Society: a centenary history', *Saga-book of Viking Society*, 234 (1992), 180–212 · B. Benedikz, 'Gudbrandr Vigfússon: a biographical sketch', *Ur dölum til dala: Gudbrandur Vigfússon centenary essays*, ed. R. McTurk and A. Wawn (1989), 11–34 · *The Times* (10 May 1904) · *Manchester Guardian* (10 May 1904) · *Oxford Magazine* (18 May 1904) · A. L. P. Norrington, *Blackwell's 1879–1979: the history of a family firm* (1983) · *CGPLA Eng. & Wales* (1904)
Archives CUL, letters to Lord Acton · U. Oxf., faculty of English language and literature, list by him of Icelandic bibles in British Museum and British and Foreign Bible Society
Likenesses J. B. Yeats?, oils, 1892, Oriel College, Oxford · W. Rothenstein, lithograph, 1896, BM, NPG [*see illus.*] · Spy [L. Ward], caricature, chromolithograph, NPG; repro. in *VF* (21 March 1895) · J. Williamson, portrait, priv. coll. · J. B. Yeats, portrait, priv. coll. · photographs, repro. in Elton, *Frederick York Powell*
Wealth at death £2210 0s. 5d.: probate, 21 July 1904, *CGPLA Eng. & Wales*

Powell, Gabriel (*bap.* 1576, *d.* 1611), Church of England clergyman and polemicist, was born at Ruabon, Denbighshire, and baptized on 13 January 1576, the son of David Powell (1549x52–1598) [*see* Powel, David], vicar of Meifod, and his wife, Elizabeth, daughter of Cynwrig ap Robert ap Hywel. He entered Jesus College, Oxford, in Lent term 1592, and graduated BA on 13 February 1596. He then spent some time in foreign universities, and probably, from 1601, at his sinecure rectory of Llansanffraid-ym-Mechain, Montgomeryshire, which he held until 1607, and which his father had also held. On 2 March 1605 he supplicated for a BD degree from St Mary Hall, Oxford, but it is not known whether he obtained it.

That year Powell became domestic chaplain to Richard Vaughan, bishop of London, and in 1606 rector of Chellesworth, Suffolk, a crown living. He was collated on 14 October 1609 to the prebend of Portpool in St Paul's, by Bishop Thomas Ravis of London, and on 15 October 1610 he was admitted vicar of Northolt, Middlesex, by Bishop George Abbot of London.

Powell was highly regarded by most contemporaries for his learned and virulently anti-papal polemics. He opposed any toleration of 'Romanism' as an idolatrous and even heathenish religion. His *Consideration of the Papists* (1604) predicted dire consequences for England should Prince Henry marry a Catholic. The following year he labelled the Roman church the 'synagogue of Antichrist' and declared himself 'as certain that the pope is Antichrist as that Jesus Christ is the son of God and redeemer of the world' (*Disputationum … de Antichristo et eius ecclesia*, dedicatory epistle). This treatise won the admiration of Matthew Sutcliffe and Thomas Holland, and was sent to Venice when that city appeared on the verge of converting to protestantism. Forty years later Archbishop Laud would denounce Powell's 'peremptoriness', quoting with distaste his equation of the pope with Antichrist as an example of 'foul language in controversies' which he doubted 'did ever yet convert an understanding papist' (*Works*, ed. W. Scott and J. Bliss, 1847–60, 4.309). Certainly Powell never minced words; to his own generation, however, he was simply enunciating orthodoxy.

Theologically a staunch Calvinist, Powell defended particular election, reprobation, and assurance of salvation. Taken together, the zeal of his antipopery, Laud's denunciation, and his authorship of a popular treatise of practical piety, *The Resolved Christian* (1600), written to 'recall the worldling' from a 'voluptuous, foolish, prodigal, passionate' life (*Resolved Christian*, 7) and in its seventh edition by 1617, may explain why some nineteenth-century historians (following Benjamin Brook, *Lives of the Puritans*, 1813) mistook him for a puritan. In fact, Powell directed his polemical ire against protestant nonconformists as well as Catholics, and has been more aptly placed 'at the centre of the ecclesiastical establishment', a 'government apologist' for the state church and its ceremonies (Milton, 56, 111). In *De adiaphora* (1607), one of three treatises directed against the puritan William Bradshaw, he condemned the 'seeds of discord' sown by 'factious and giddie brains' who scrupled at the surplice, sign of the cross, and kneeling at communion (*De adiaphora*, 13.60). These are things indifferent, resisted only by 'factious frequenters of private conventicles' (*A Rejoynder unto the Mild Defence … of the Silenced Ministers*, 1607, 100). In the interests of unity and order Powell defended the 'absolute power and authority' given by God to the church to establish ceremonies and rites (*De adiaphora*, 9). Underlying much of his anti-Catholic writing was his message to nonconformists that ceremonies and liturgy did not make the Church of England less than thoroughly protestant; he was himself a living emblem of the English church's tradition of denouncing popish superstition while maintaining liturgical order. The theme he hammered home in his exchanges with Bradshaw was that nonconformists undermined the battle against the true enemy, the Roman Antichrist, by creating dissension in the protestant camp and paving the way to separatism.

Powell always made it clear, however, that popery was the greater threat. He stressed both the common theological ground between puritans and conformists and their common devotion to the king. Puritans were merely 'factious brethren', while papists were 'bloody traitors' faithful only 'unto the pope and the devil' (*Consideration of the Deprived and Silenced Ministers*, 1606, 10–11). Powell died in 1611. The exact date is unknown, but his successor was admitted to the Northolt living on 18 December.

MARGO TODD

Sources Wood, *Ath. Oxon.*, new edn, 2.24–6 · Wood, *Ath. Oxon.: Fasti* (1815), 269, 303 · Foster, *Alum. Oxon.* · J. Foster, ed., *Index ecclesiasticus, or, Alphabetical lists of all ecclesiastical dignitaries in England and Wales since the Reformation* (1890) · A. Milton, *Catholic and Reformed: the Roman and protestant churches in English protestant thought, 1600–1640* (1995) · N. Tyacke, 'Religious controversy', *Hist. U. Oxf.* 4: *17th-cent. Oxf.*, 569–620, esp. 575–6

Powell, Geoffry Charles Hamilton (1920–1999). *See under* Chamberlin, Peter Hugh Girard (1919–1978).

Powell, George (1668?–1714), actor and playwright, was apparently the son of Martin Powell (*d. c.*1698), an actor in the King's Company. His date of birth is uncertain, but he is identified most plausibly as the George Powell who was born on 17 January 1668 and baptized in St Giles-in-the-Fields five days later, ten months after a Martin Powell had married Elizabeth Heath at St Clement Danes. About the time that he began his acting career George Powell married Mary (*d.* in or after 1723), who became a reliable actress for Christopher Rich's company, beginning in the 1695–6 season. Her first known part was as Gammer Grime in Aphra Behn's *The Luckey Chance* in April 1686, and she may have left the stage or played small parts for the next nine years. Almost nothing is known about her.

Actor Powell began acting in the 1686–7 season and may have appeared in a few plays before his first recorded performance as Don Cinthio in Behn's *Emperor of the Moon* (March 1687). Hannah Lee, a Bartholomew fair booth manager, claimed that he began acting there for her mother. He acted a large number of parts for the United Company and began to be given numerous prologues to speak, a sure sign of popularity and stardom. Tall, handsome, and with a fine voice and body, Powell was well suited for the stage and for heroic parts. In his early years he played such parts as Friendly in *The Widow Ranter*, Cassander in *The Rival Queens*, and the title roles in *Valentinian* and *Edward III*.

When his friend William Mountfort was murdered by a rival for Anne Bracegirdle's attention in 1692 Powell was given many of his parts. He was then often cast opposite Susanna Mountfort in an attempt to make them the new leading couple (Holland, 152). Among the roles Powell took over were Granger in Dryden's *Marriage à-la-mode*, the rake Bellmour in William Congreve's *The Old Batchelor*, and male leads such as Clerimont in Thomas D'Urfey's *Love for Money*.

When he chose to stay with Christopher Rich at the time of the secession of Thomas Betterton and the majority of the most experienced players in the United Company in 1695, Powell was given many of Betterton's parts. Rich and his partner Sir Thomas Skipwith rewarded his loyalty with additional money as well as the parts and put him in charge of rehearsals. Among Powell's skills was 'taking off' Betterton. Soon after the division of the companies he acted Heartwell in Congreve's *The Old Batchelor*, mimicking Betterton throughout; the intention, which succeeded, was to draw an audience away from the newly formed company at Lincoln's Inn Fields. Cibber, who acted Fondlewife as Thomas Doggett, wrote that Powell 'was allow'd to have burlesqu'd [Betterton] very well'. Powell also acted Falstaff as Betterton. In a prologue in 1698, allegedly in retaliation for a 'scurrilous' prologue spoken against him at 'Betterton's Booth', he mocked the ageing Betterton's taking the parts of heroic lovers:

As when a nauseous Vizor in the Pit,
Grossly abuses, without Sense or Wit,

All justifie her merited disgrace,
If they unvail the grievance of the place,
And shew the drab in her own ugly face.
If in Return of a dam'd dull Abuse,
We pluck the Vizor off from t' other house:
And let you see their natural Grimmaces
Affecting Youth with pale Autumnal Faces.
Wou'd it not any Ladies Anger move
To see a Child of sixty-five make Love (Grunting like B).
(*Fatal Discovery*, late February 1698; Danchin, 3.481)

In this, his mid-career, Powell was playing Montezuma in *The Indian Queen*, Aboan in *Oroonoko*, Worthy in *The Relapse*, Cornavo in *The Fatal Discovery*, Jaffeir in *Venice Preserv'd*, and the title roles in *Caligula*, *Macbeth*, and *Achilles*. His parts tended to be those of the second man, not the lead, perhaps because of his rather unruly personality. Typical parts were Cassio in *Othello* and Lothario in *The Fair Penitent*. He was a virtuoso actor, however, and the newspapers often mentioned his appearances in new, successful plays. Steele once wrote tellingly of one of his benefits:

this Day the haughty *George Powell* hopes all the Good-natured Part of the Town, will favour him whome they Applauded in *Alexander*, *Timon*, *Lear* and *Orestes*, with their Company this Night, when he hazards all his Heroic Glory for their Approbation in the humbler Condition of honest *Jack Falstaff*.   (R. Steele, *The Spectator*, 7 April 1712)

Both Addison and Steele wrote about Powell's frequent appearances as Alexander in various plays, and once included him in a fantasy performance in which he was to ride a 'Dromedary, which nevertheless Mr. *Powell*' was to call 'Bucephalus' to fight the comedian William Pinkethman as King Porus mounted on an elephant (*The Spectator*, 5 April 1711). In spite of his irregular life, he continued to add roles until the end of his career. Among these were Portius in *Cato* and Cassius in *The Albion Queens*.

Drinker and brawler The irrepressible Powell seems to have alternated theatrical triumphs with scrapes with the law. In spite of his immense talent and considerable ambition and competitiveness, he drank heavily and by 1696 occasionally even appeared drunk on stage. In that year he played himself in *The Female Wits*, was cast as the actor the women fought over, but was depicted as drinking in the early morning and unashamed of regarding 'neither Times nor Seasons in Drinking' (act 1, scene xiii). Powell spent a great deal of his time at the bar of the Rose tavern. Thomas Davies wrote that he:

often toasted to intoxication, his mistress, with bumpers of Nantz-brandy; he came sometimes so warm, with that noble spirit, to the theatre, that he courted the ladies, so furiously on stage, that, in the opinion of Sir John Vanbrugh, they were almost in danger of being conquered on the spot. (Davies, 3.416)

Vanbrugh described Powell as having begun drinking at six in the morning and 'wadling' on stage; he made a joke of the warmth of Powell's lovemaking when under the influence of alcohol:

I confess I once gave *Amanda* [played by Jane Rogers] for gone, and am since (with all due Respect to Mrs. *Rogers*) very

sorry she scap't; for I am confident a certain Lady ... who highly blames the Play, for the barrenness of the conclusion, wou'd then have allowed it, a very natural Close.
(J. Vanbrugh, preface to *The Relapse*)

It is impossible to give a complete list of Powell's legal difficulties. As one of the king's servants, as all actors at the patent theatres were, he was subject to arrest and punishment by the lord chamberlain and the House of Lords alone, and that fact probably saved him from gaol on several occasions. For example, two people were ordered to be apprehended on 23 April 1690 for arresting Powell without the lord chamberlain's permission. Some of his problems stemmed from debt. In the early 1690s the journalist Abel Roper took him to court for £10, and Daniel and Elizabeth Tofield carried on a three-year campaign to recover £10 that he owed them for a purchase, and another man claimed £30. About 1703 he was in a dispute with Christopher Rich over his pay and was not allowed to leave the company until he had paid his debts to it. Cibber said he was 'so hunted, by the sheriffs officers, for debt, that he usually walked the streets with his sword in his hand (sheathed)', and sometimes they would yell to him as he menaced them, 'We do not want you *now*, Master Powell' (Davies, 3.453).

Powell was a witness to the murder of William Mountfort, and he himself had a propensity for violence. He was arrested on 1 May 1698 for assaulting one of William Davenant's sons, probably Ralph, the treasurer of the company, or, less likely, Thomas, the nominal manager, 'with the intention, as [it] seem'd, to kill him', and then drawing his sword on Lieutenant-Colonel Stanhope, who tried to intervene (Milhous and Hume, 1.329–30). For this offence, he was confined briefly in the Gatehouse, and the bond was set at a rather high £200 for himself and £100 each for two friends who would swear for his good behaviour. Ralph was murdered by would-be robbers on 18 May 1698, and that may have ended the case. Powell was one of the actors ordered suspended for assaulting Aaron Hill on 2 June 1710. Hill had been made manager of William Collier's company, and the actors reacted with violence to Hill's style. Hill's complaint read, 'Powell had shortened his sword to stab me in the Back & had cut a Gentlemans hand through who prevented the thrust' (Highfill, Burnim & Langhans, *BDA*, 12.113). The lord chamberlain noted in his order to discharge Powell from 'her Majesty's Company' that he had been 'formerly guilty of the like offenses' (ibid.). For both of these assaults Powell was suspended from acting for several months. Once when Drury Lane employed him before the suspension had expired the lord chamberlain shut the theatre down. In 1698 his actions contributed to Lord Monmouth moving in the House of Lords that actors should not be allowed to wear swords.

Like many actors of his generation, Powell was occasionally in legal trouble for trying to change companies without permission or for giving a performance or two at a small theatre. He was confined to the Porter's Lodge, a place often used to gaol minor offenders against the crown, privy council, or parliament, for leaving Lincoln's Inn Fields in June 1704, and was arrested in November 1705 for refusing to act at the Queen's Theatre. The annotation with this apprehension suggests his unusually violent temper; it charges him with attempting to incite a riot in the company, and ten days later, on 24 November, the companies were ordered not to employ him because he 'behav'd himself with great insolence'. Cibber described him as one of the company with 'contempt of all discipline' when Wilks became manager. Wilks 'was reduced to the necessity of challenging and fighting several amongst the ring-leaders', including Powell, who refused to fight (Davies, 3.452). He was, however, indisputably an excellent, desirable actor. Congreve and Vanbrugh were complained against for trying to hire Powell in December 1705, and in 1707 Drury Lane was silenced once again for letting him perform before his suspension was up.

Playwright—and plagiarist? Powell wrote *The Treacherous Brothers* (1689), *Alphonso, King of Naples* (1690), *A Very Good Wife* (1693), *Bonduca* (1695), and *The Imposture Defeated* (1697). Both *The Treacherous Brothers* and *Alphonso* are violent tragedies with big doses of the time's popular rant and pathos. *The Treacherous Brothers* includes romantic love, a poisoning, and a scene of Menaphon impaled on spikes. *Alphonso* features rival lovers killing each other and then an emotional scene for the heroine, who stabs herself and speaks her last lines 'bleeding, her hair hanging loose'. Powell used music well in his plays, and in 1696 he and John Verbruggen rewrote Nahum Tate's *Brutus of Alba* into an opera. The piece shows their canny business and theatrical sense, for they used popular elements from Tate's and other plays, got Daniel Purcell to write some of the songs, and used four sets from Dryden's *Albion and Albanius*, two from Shadwell's *Psyche*, one from Settle's *Fairy Queen*, and pieces of sets from other lavish productions. The stunning machinery came from *Albion* and *The Fairy Queen* (Holland, 45).

A Very Good Wife, a play Powell whipped up to take advantage of the demand for new satiric comedies in the 1692–3 season, is composed of chunks of Richard Brome's *The City Wit* and *The Court Beggar* and James Shirley's *Hide Park*. Brome's Crasy becomes Courtwit, 'A Gentleman, who by his Generous Temper, has wasted his Fortunes, and put to his shifts', a premier part for Powell (Holland, 159). Mary Pix accused him of plagiarizing most of *Imposture Defeated* from her *The Deceiver Deceived* while it was still in manuscript. Pix had offered her play to Drury Lane when Powell had the power to reject it, and his *Imposture Defeated* was produced in September 1697. Her play was performed at Lincoln's Inn Fields in late November. In his preface 'To the reader' Powell writes that the play was 'only a slight piece of Scribble, purely designed for the Introduction of a little Musick, being no more than a short weeks work'. He avers he never read her play, although he did as she requested and asked the company to consider it before 'she very mannerly carry'd the Play to the other House'. In the part of Bondi, by whatever means conceived, he created another virtuoso role for himself. He insisted that both he and Pix got the plot from an unnamed novel, and Laura Rosenthal has pointed out that no playwright in that time feared any legal action for plagiarism (Rosenthal, 181–2). The prologue at Lincoln's Inn Fields begins:

Our Authoress, like true Women, shew'd her Play
To some, who, like true Wits, stole't half away,

and this may be the 'abuse' that Powell was answering in the prologue that mocked Betterton. Pix, known for her unattractive face and figure, may be the 'nauseous Vizor' who 'merited disgrace'. Unlike Pix's play, Powell's play emphasizes farcical debauchery and drunkenness rather than her intrigue comedy plot about arranged marriages. It also depends upon music for much of its entertainment and includes *Endimion … a Masque* (act v, scene i).

Powell's career was marked by irascible, erratic behaviour, and, after the actors' secession, he changed theatres often. In the winter of 1701 he moved from Drury Lane to Lincoln's Inn Fields, returned to Drury Lane in June 1704, then in April 1705 went to the Queen's Theatre, and, after a suspension, back to Rich's Drury Lane in February 1707, where he spent the rest of his career except for brief appearances such as those at Pinkethman's Greenwich Theatre. Powell died on 14 December 1714 and was buried four days later at St Clement Danes. His funeral was paid for by the Drury Lane Theatre and the expenses included 5 quarts of white port, 5 quarts of red, and 4 quarts of sack. Obituaries ranked him in talent with Betterton and Charles Hart; Joseph Addison declared him 'excellently form'd for a Tragedian, and, when he pleases, deserves the Admiration of the best Judges' (J. Addison, *The Spectator*, 16 April 1711), and Thomas Davies summed him up as 'an actor of genius' (Davies, 3.453). His wife acted at least until the year of Powell's death and survived him by a number of years.

PAULA R. BACKSCHEIDER

Sources W. Van Lennep and others, eds., *The London stage, 1660–1800*, 5 pts in 11 vols. (1960–68) • P. Danchin, ed., *The prologues and epilogues of the Restoration, 1660–1700*, 7 vols. (1981–8), vol. 6 • P. Holland, *The ornament of action: text and performance in Restoration comedy* (1979) • D. F. Bond, ed., *The Tatler*, 3 vols. (1987) • R. Steele and J. Addison, *The Spectator*, ed. D. Bond, 5 vols. (1965) • L. Rosenthal, *Playwrights and plagiarists in early modern England: gender, authorship, literary property* (1996) • T. Davies, *Dramatic miscellanies*, 3 (1784), vol. 3 • J. Milhous and R. D. Hume, eds., *A register of English theatrical documents, 1660–1737*, 2 vols. (1991) • C. Cibber, *An apology for the life of Colley Cibber*, new edn, ed. B. R. S. Fone (1968) • Highfill, Burnim & Langhans, *BDA*, vol. 12

Powell, Sir George Smyth Baden- (1847–1898), politician and author, born at Oxford on 24 December 1847, was the third son of Professor Baden *Powell (1796–1860) and his third wife, Henrietta Grace (1824–1914), daughter of Admiral William Henry *Smyth. Major-General Robert Stephenson Smyth Baden-*Powell, founder of the Boy Scouts, was his younger brother. The Powells were a large family whose wealth was earned by Sir George's great-grandfather David Powell (1725–1810), a London merchant who left £300,000 and fathered fourteen children. George was admitted to St Paul's School on 17 September 1858,

Sir George Smyth Baden-Powell (1847–1898), by unknown photographer, 1889

and to Marlborough College in April 1864. Owing to a burst blood vessel suffered through strenuous sporting activity, he was obliged to leave school at midsummer 1866. He travelled abroad for three years, visiting India, Australasia, South Africa, and Spain, Portugal, Norway, and Germany. In 1872, at the age of twenty-five, he published his observations on Australia and New Zealand under the title *New Homes for the Old Country*, notable for its information on natural history. On 18 October 1871 he matriculated from Balliol College, Oxford, graduating BA in 1875 and MA in 1878. In 1876 he obtained the chancellor's prize for an English essay on the subject of *The Political and Social Results of the Absorption of Small Races by Large*. In the same year he entered the Inner Temple as a student; but in 1877 he became private secretary to Sir George Fergusson Bowen, governor of Victoria. A convinced free-trader, in 1879 he published *Protection and bad times with special reference to the political economy of English colonisation*, in which he attacked the notion that while free trade was good for a manufacturing country like England, it was unsuited to newer communities. In 1880 Baden-Powell was appointed as commissioner to inquire into the effect of the sugar bounties on West India trade, visiting the West Indies in 1880–81. One outcome was his book *State*

Aid and State Interference (1882), a strong protest against protection, which made use of his observations on the West Indies. In November 1882 he was appointed joint commissioner (with Colonel Sir William Crossman) to inquire into the administration, revenue, and expenditure of the West India colonies. The commission's report, completed by Easter 1884, was published in five blue books, and for his services Baden-Powell was created a KCMG in 1888. In January 1885 he went to South Africa to assist Sir Charles Warren in the pacification of Bechuanaland, afterwards making a tour of investigation of Basutoland and Zululand.

At the general election of November 1885 Baden-Powell was elected as a Conservative for the Kirkdale division of Liverpool, a heavily nonconformist seat created in the redistribution of 1885. He successfully held the seat at the three subsequent general elections, until his death three years after that of 1895. As a parliamentarian he was a popular local member, overcoming initial discomfort among constituents towards a 'carpetbagger' who had no previous connections with Liverpool. His position as a strong proponent of free trade was well regarded locally, as were his imperial links and what obituary tributes described as his 'staunch support of the Protestant Church'.

In 1886 Baden-Powell travelled to Canada to assist in the establishment of a line of steamers between Vancouver and Yokohama. He worked vigorously for this scheme, which was subsidized by the government and reduced the length of a journey to Japan from forty-two to twenty-two days. In 1887 he was appointed (with Sir George Bowen) special commissioner to arrange the details of the new Maltese constitution; all the recommendations of the commissioners were adopted and they received the thanks of the government.

During his visit to the Pacific coast of Canada in 1886 Baden-Powell had become interested in Britain and Canada's dispute with the American government over the Bering Sea fisheries, and had visited Washington on his way back to England to call attention to the question. In June 1891, when the controversy became acute, Lord Salisbury appointed him and a representative of the Canadian government to proceed to the Bering Sea to investigate the subject. The British claims were founded on their reports, and in December 1892 Baden-Powell was appointed British member of the joint commission in Washington; in the spring of 1893 he was chosen to advise those preparing the British case before arbitrators in Paris. For these services he received the thanks of parliament; and in 1892 he was made honorary LLD of Toronto University.

On 8 April 1893 Baden-Powell married, at Cheltenham, Frances Annie (d. Oct 1913), the only child of Charles Wilson of Glendowan, Cheltenham; they had a son and a daughter. Wilson had been a wealthy Australian pastoralist prior to returning to England, and was the brother of Sir Samuel Wilson, one of the richest men in Australia. An enthusiastic yachtsman, in 1896 Baden-Powell took a party of astronomers to Novaya Zemlya on his steam yacht, the *Ontario*, to observe the total eclipse of the sun on 9 August. He was also a prolific writer—apart from the books already noted, he was the author of over forty articles in the leading journals of the day, such as the *Quarterly*, *Westminster*, *Fortnightly*, and *National* reviews, dealing chiefly with imperial topics. In 'Postal universities', published in *Temple Bar* in November 1872, he advocated a correspondence university for colonists in remote parts of the empire. He also edited *The Truth about Home Rule* (1888), a collection of essays attacking Irish nationalism, and was a frequent writer for *The Times* and other journals. Baden-Powell died of a kidney malignancy, at the age of only fifty-one, at his residence, 114 Eaton Square, London, on 20 November 1898, and was buried in Kensal Green cemetery. W. D. RUBINSTEIN

Sources *Liverpool Mercury* (21 Nov 1898) · *Liverpool Mercury* (22 Nov 1898) · *Liverpool Mercury* (25 Nov 1898) · *Liverpool Courier* (23 Nov 1898) · *Liverpool Courier* (24 Nov 1898) · *Wellesley index* · *ILN* (26 Nov 1898) · Boase, *Mod. Eng. biog.* · *DNB* · d. cert.
Archives HLRO, papers
Likenesses photograph, 1889, priv. coll. [*see illus.*] · photograph, repro. in *The Porcupine* (26 Nov 1898) · woodcut, repro. in *The Porcupine* (7 Oct 1893)
Wealth at death £4636 2s. 3d.: resworn probate, April 1900, *CGPLA Eng. & Wales* (1899)

Powell, Griffith (1560/61–1620), college head, was the third of four sons of John ap Hywel of Prysg Melyn, Llansawel, Carmarthenshire, and his wife, Annes, daughter of Gruffydd ap Henry. He matriculated at Jesus College, Oxford, on 24 November 1581, graduated BA on 28 February 1584, and proceeded MA on 21 June 1589, BCL on 12 July 1593, and DCL on 23 July 1599. From the time he entered Jesus College, of which he became a fellow in 1589 or 1590, his life was spent at Oxford. Under Francis Bevans (1586–1602) and John Williams (1602–13) he played a large part in the running of the college. He was 'an energetic and capable tutor' and a 'noted philosopher', writing two important works on Aristotle, *Analysis analyticorum posteriorum* and *De sophisticis elenchis*, published respectively in 1594 and 1598. He also showed himself 'very diligent, industrious and careful' for the good estate of the college. Powell succeeded Williams as principal in 1613. His careful management of legacies and endowments made it possible to establish more resident fellowships and scholarships, and Jesus College became popular particularly with students from south Wales in Powell's time. His appeal to the Welsh clergy and gentry raised £764 5s. 6d., which was used to build the hall, buttery, and kitchens, and the outer quadrangle of the college, with the chapel, was completed within a year of Powell's death. He died, unmarried, at Oxford on 28 June 1620, and was buried in St Michael's Church, Oxford. By a nuncupative will made on the day of his death, and proved on 15 June 1621, he left his estate of £648 17s. 2d. to the college; it was used to buy land in Flintshire to maintain a fellowship at the college.

BARRIE WILLIAMS

Sources E. G. Hardy, *Jesus College* (1899) · Foster, *Alum. Oxon.* · *Heraldic visitations of Wales and part of the marches … by Lewys Dwnn*, ed. S. R. Meyrick, 2 (1846) · *DWB* · J. T. Jones, *Geiriadur bywgraffyddol o enwogion Cymru*, 2 vols. (1867–70) · Wood, *Ath. Oxon.*, new edn, vol. 2

Archives Jesus College, Oxford, 'The Estate of Jesus College in Oxon', ES 1/1
Wealth at death £648 17s. 2d.: Wood, *Ath. Oxon.* 3rd edn (1815), 2

Powell, Hugh (1798–1883), maker of optical instruments, was born on 21 November 1798 in St Marylebone, Middlesex, the son of Thomas and Elizabeth Powell. Nothing is known of his education or apprenticeship. On 3 June 1824 he married Elizabeth Lealand; they had three children, Elizabeth Jane (*b.* 1827), Thomas (*b.* 1834), and Hugh Peter (*b.* 1838). During the 1830s, Powell was making microscopes for certain retailers in London, and traded as mathematical, optical, and philosophical instrument maker, offering microscopes and achromatic object glasses from 24 Clarendon Street, Somers Town. By 1840 he was signing his microscopes Hugh Powell, and he began in 1840 to date his instruments, a practice that was continued by him, and then his son, into the twentieth century. With the exception of one known telescope and one crystal goniometer, the sole product of the firm was microscopes. In 1841 he took into partnership his brother-in-law, Peter H. Lealand, and in December 1841 the names of Powell and Lealand were linked in the account of a new design of mounting for a microscope. Subsequent instruments were signed 'Powell & Lealand'.

The first innovation under the name of Hugh Powell was the design of a fine adjustment acting on the stage of a microscope, for which he received, in 1834, a silver medal of the Society of Arts. In this design a wedge was advanced under the stage by a micrometer screw, but this was not a satisfactory method because the illumination of the specimen was thereby altered. Powell was producing microscopes that were derived from the late eighteenth-century form of instrument, where the body tube was not held rigidly. The new design of achromatic objective produced to the specification of Joseph Jackson Lister (1786–1869), which was published in 1830, meant that the resolving power of the instrument became much greater, and in consequence it could become a truly scientific instrument, provided the stand were redesigned. A prototype Powell microscope in the Museum of the History of Science at Oxford showed clearly the transition from the old to the new form of stand, which Powell exploited from 1841. He was awarded the silver medal of the Society of Arts in 1841 'for his mode of mounting the body of a microscope'.

The Microscopical Society of London (from 1866 the Royal Microscopical Society), which was founded in September 1839, ordered the best microscopes then obtainable from the three leading makers, Powell, Ross, and Smith. Powell delivered his microscope in December 1841; the massive stand, with six achromatic objectives, including one of 1/16 inch, cost the society £94 10s., and became part of the society's collection at Oxford.

In November 1843 there was published in the *London Physiological Journal* a description of 'Powell and Lealand's new microscope'. This was a radically new design, which became the basis of the firm's instruments for over sixty years. There is a true tripod support carrying the body on trunnions, which gave the necessary stability and ease of manipulation when the user was seated. The Powell tripod was adopted by other makers from the later nineteenth century well into the twentieth. In the 1860s the model became 'the large compound microscope', popularly known as the 'P & L No. 1 stand'. Four models were sold: the No. 1, which had all possible refinements to the highest possible standard of craftsmanship; the No. 2, which was less fully equipped, and therefore less costly; the No. 3, which was a smaller version; and the No. 4, a portable model similar to the No. 3. Two simpler stands were the No. 5, which was mainly for the use of students and did not have a fine adjustment, and the No. 6, a cheaper student's microscope.

Powell was the pioneer of very high powers in objectives. The first high-powered achromatic objective by a British manufacturer was Powell's of 1/16 inch as early as 1840. With his eldest son, Thomas, he made one of 1/25 inch in 1860, and four years later one of 1/50 inch. The first of the latter design was made for Lionel Smith Beale, and is dated 15 October 1864. This high resolution objective had a numerical aperture of 0.97, very close to the theoretical limit of 1.0 for a non-immersion lens, and cost £31 10s. In 1869 the firm was also the first to produce in Britain a water immersion objective of 1/16 inch with a numerical aperture of 1.22. Medals for these objectives were awarded at international exhibitions in London (1862) and Moscow (1872). The high opinion of the firm's products was expressed in 1878 by the Belgian professor Henri van Heurck:

> Messrs Powell & Lealand occupy quite a unique position in the microscopic world. Their workshops are very small, the number of instruments which they produce are few, but every piece of apparatus, marked with their name, is an artistic production, perfect in all its details. Moreover, both instruments and objectives of these makers are in the greatest request, and are used in England by all serious microscopists. (van Heurck, 163)

Powell died at his home, 170 Euston Road, Somers Town, London, on 14 November 1883. His son Thomas took over the business, which effectively faded out of existence by 1914. The workshop was from 1832 to 1846 at 24 Clarendon Street, and from 1846 to 1901 at 170 Euston Road, which was named 4 Seymour Place, Euston Square, before 1857.

G. L'E. TURNER

Sources G. L'E. Turner, 'Powell & Lealand: trade mark of perfection', *Proceedings of the Royal Microscopical Society*, 1 (1966), 173–83 · G. L'E. Turner, *The great age of the microscope: the collection of the Royal Microscopical Society through 150 years* (1989) · *The Times* (28 Nov 1883), 6 · *English Mechanic and World of Science* (30 Nov 1883) · H. Powell, 'Fine adjustment for the stage of a microscope', *Transactions of the Society of Arts*, 50 (1836), 108–10 · 'Description of Messrs. Powell and Lealand's newly-constructed achromatic microscope', *The Microscopic Journal and Structural Record for 1841*, 1 (1842), 177–81 · 'Description of Powell and Lealand's new microscope', *London Physiological Journal* (Nov 1843), 63 · H. van Heurck, *Le microscope*, 3rd edn (1878), 163 · parish register (baptism), 20 Jan 1799, St Marylebone, London · parish register (marriage), 3 June 1824, St Pancras, London · d. cert.
Archives MHS Oxf., collection of the Royal Microscopical Society, twenty-four microscopes with accessories, equipment from the firm, Powell's silver medal, 1841

Likenesses portrait, repro. in *Journal of the Royal Microscopical Society* (April 1899), frontispiece, 209

Wealth at death £1435 10s. 10d.: probate, 21 Feb 1884, *CGPLA Eng. & Wales*

Powell, Humphrey (*d.* in or after 1566), printer, of whose parentage nothing is known, was working near Holborn conduit, Middlesex, in 1547–9, from where he published *An Holesome Antidotus* and *Certayne Litel Treatises* (both 1548), and *Oecolampadius's Sermon* and *Barclay's Eclogues* (both undated). Soon afterwards Powell moved to Dublin, as printer to the king. In July 1550 a warrant was issued giving him £20 towards setting up, and he established the first printing press in Ireland, residing first in the great tower by the crane (probably Crane Lane). The only book to emerge from this press, in 1551, was a verbal reprint of the English common prayer of 1549. Powell's work probably consisted mainly of broadsides, for nothing is known before a broadside of 1561 against Shane O'Neill and another in 1564 against the O'Connors. In 1566, giving his address as St Nicholas Street, Powell issued an eight-leaf tract, *A Brefe Declaration of Certein Articles of Religion*, namely the eleven articles of 1559.

It is not known if Powell was related to William and Thomas Powell, printers in London, but he was certainly a business associate of William and in 1553 they were joint defendants in an action brought in the court of common pleas concerning a printing house. Powell was also named as an original member of the Stationers' Company in its charter of 1556. He died, presumably in Dublin, in or after 1566.   A. F. POLLARD, *rev.* ANITA McCONNELL

Sources H. R. Plomer, 'An inventory of Wynkyn de Worde's house, "The Sun in Fleet St" in 1553', *The Library*, 3rd ser., 6 (1915), 228–34 · E. G. Duff, *A century of the book trade* (1905), 124 · *STC, 1475–1640*, 3.136 · J. Ames, T. F. Dibdin, and W. Herbert, eds., *Typographical antiquities, or, The history of printing in England, Scotland and Ireland*, 4 vols. (1810–19), vol. 4, pp. 543–5 · C. H. Timperley, *Encyclopaedia of literary and typographical anecdote*, 2nd edn (1842); repr. (1977), 314, 325 · W. C. Hazlitt, *Hand-book to the popular, poetical and dramatic literature of Great Britain* (1867), 156, 588

Powell [Renaud], **Jane** (*c.*1761–1831), actress, was born about 1761. Conflicting stories in contemporary biographies describe her birth in Cranbrook, Kent, and her early life as a series of amorous adventures. Whatever the truth of these she made her first appearance at the Haymarket as Alicia in Nicholas Rowe's *Jane Shore*, on 29 August 1788. The following day's *Public Advertiser* identified her as Mrs Farmer, while the *Morning Chronicle* gave her name as Miss Palmer. From the Haymarket she went to Drury Lane in the autumn of 1788. Appearing there as Mrs Farmer, she played Anne Bullen to the Queen Katharine of Sarah Siddons, Virgilia in *Coriolanus*, and Leonora in Edward Young's *The Revenge*.

During the summer of 1789 she performed in Liverpool, where she married William Powell (1762–1812), a prompter there and at Drury Lane; the two returned to London, where Jane Powell retained her engagement with the Drury Lane company until 1811. As the primary support for Sarah Siddons, her forte lay in heavy and intense tragedy. Among many others, her roles included Andromache in *The Distrest Mother*, Mrs Haller in *The Stranger*, and

Almeria in *The Mourning Bride*. When Siddons refused to play Edmunda in Ireland's Shakespearian counterfeit *Vortigern*, Powell took the part (2 April 1796). That season she performed Hamlet for her benefit to Dorothy Jordan's Ophelia, and garnered some praise. In addition, she created Matilda in *The Curfew* and the title role in *Adelgitha*. In the *Dramatic Mirror*, Thomas Gilliland described her as 'majestically beautiful', with 'a full mellow-toned voice'. He further complimented her brilliant conversation and engaging manner, and mentioned that she had a country house at Norwood. A critic for the *Thespian Dictionary* (1805) and other commentators noted her usefulness to the theatre and her tall and elegant figure.

Some time before 1808, Jane Powell separated amicably from her husband. Following his death in 1812, she married John James Renaud (*d.* 1834), a provincial actor, on 31 January 1813 at St George's, Bloomsbury. They were soon separated, but she continued to perform using his name after 1814.

After travelling for two years in the provinces, Jane Renaud settled in 1818 in Edinburgh, where she had previously acted in the summer of 1802. The parts for which she was chiefly cast were the same intense roles she had made her own in the capital: Meg Merrilies in *Guy Mannering*, Lady Macbeth, Gertrude in *Hamlet*, and Belvidera in *Venice Preserv'd*. The parts she created in Edinburgh included Helen Macgregor in *Rob Roy*, the Queen in *The Heart of Midlothian*, Elspat in *The Antiquary*, Lady Douglas in *Mary Stuart*, and Janet in *The Twa Drovers*. She was credited with providing splendid support to Edmund Kean and other great London tragedians who made starring visits to the Scottish capital.

Jane Renaud displayed in her old age a rare dignity of bearing, correct elocution, and a telling voice, although she became increasingly incapacitated. She appeared for the last time on 30 September 1829, when she acted Gertrude to Kean's Hamlet. The *Gentleman's Magazine* reported that her Edinburgh manager continued to pay her 2 guineas a week until her death, which occurred in London, on 31 December 1831, when she was 'aged about 70'.   K. A. CROUCH

Sources Highfill, Burnim & Langhans, *BDA* · C. B. Hogan, ed., *The London stage, 1660–1800*, pt 5: *1776–1800* (1968) · Genest, *Eng. stage* · T. Gilliland, *The dramatic mirror, containing the history of the stage from the earliest period, to the present time*, 2 vols. (1808) · J. Roach, *Roach's authentic memoirs of the green room* (1796) · [J. Haslewood], *The secret history of the green rooms: containing authentic and entertaining memoirs of the actors and actresses in the three theatres royal*, 2 vols. (1790) · *GM*, 1st ser., 102/1 (1832) · *Monthly Mirror*, 3 (May 1797), 311 · B. Crosby, *Crosby's pocket companion to the playhouses* (1796) · *Morning Chronicle* (30 Aug 1788) · *Public Advertiser* (30 Aug 1788) · *European Magazine and London Review*, 14 (1788), 218 · *The thespian dictionary, or, Dramatic biography of the present age*, 2nd edn (1805)

Likenesses J. Alais, engraving (as Euphrasia in *The Grecian daughter*), repro. in Roach, *Authentic memoirs*, 2nd edn (1807) · T. Cheesman, engraving (as Matilda in *The curfew*; after Sharpe), repro. in Gilliland, *Dramatic mirror* · S. De Wilde, oils (as Boadicea), Garr. Club · S. De Wilde, oils (as Douglas), Garr. Club · S. De Wilde, oils (as Mary Queen of Scots), Garr. Club · S. De Wilde, watercolour (as Adelgitha in *Adelgitha*), Garr. Club · W. Leney, engraving (as Mary Queen of Scots; after S. De Wilde), repro. in J. Bell, *Bell's British theatre* (1791–7), plate · G. Murray, engraving (after Cruikshank), repro. in *Roach's authentic memoirs* (1799) • W. Ridley, engraving, repro. in J. Parson, *Minor theatre* (1804), plate • Thornwaite, engraving (after oils by S. De Wilde), repro. in J. Bell, *Bell's British theatre* (1791–7), plate

Powell, Sir John (1632/3–1696), judge, was the son of John Powell of Pentre Meurig, Llanwrda, Carmarthenshire. As a boy Powell was taught by Jeremy Taylor at a school at Newton Hall, whence he entered Gray's Inn on 12 November 1650, and also probably matriculated at Jesus College, Oxford, on 7 December 1650. He graduated BA on 29 March 1653, and MA in 1654 from King's College, Cambridge. He was called to the bar on 13 November 1657, becoming an ancient in 1676.

Nothing is known of Powell's legal practice, but in James II's reign he was marked out for rapid promotion. In April 1686 he was made a serjeant-at-law, appointed a judge of common pleas on the 24th, and knighted the next day. In the following Trinity term, in company with the other judges, he was asked his opinion of the dispensing power in the case of *Godden* v. *Hales*. At first he reserved judgment, but then he concurred with the majority opinion. On 13 April 1687 he was transferred to king's bench. In that capacity he was among the judges who sentenced the earl of Devonshire to a fine of £30,000 for his assault on Colepeper, and presided over the trial of the seven bishops for seditious libel. On the latter occasion he showed himself hostile to the notion of a suspending power in ecclesiastical matters as set out in the declaration of indulgence because 'if this be once allowed of, there will need no parliament; all the legislature will be in the King' (*State trials*, 11.427). As regards the bishops, 'if the King hath no such power (as clearly he hath not in my judgement), the natural consequence will be, that this petition is no diminution of the King's regal power, and so not seditious or libellous' (Keeton, 443). Several altercations with other judges followed from this, and as one of the Verneys' correspondents wrote, 'Powell spoke so much that some asked if he were Advocate for the Bishops' (Verney, 1.458). Not surprisingly, Powell received his quietus on 2 July 1688, soon after the trial ended.

The revolution revived Powell's fortunes and on 18 March 1689 he was appointed a judge of common pleas. He faced some difficult moments when called before the House of Lords on 6 May 1689 to explain his decision to fine Devonshire, which was voted a violation of the privilege of the peerage, against Magna Carta, and the fundamental laws of the nation. However, he begged the house's pardon, claiming that 'he was misguided by some books, which he looked on as authorities' (*State trials*, 11.1369). On 14 June 1689 he was called before the Commons to explain why he had been turned out of office by James II, to which he supposed 'it was about my opinion of the dispensing power', and 'upon giving my judgement about several *quo warrantos* where the borough chose members of parliament by prescription' (Cobbett, *Parl. hist.*, 5.311).

Powell died at Exeter of the stone, on 7 September 1696, aged sixty-three, and was buried on the 26th at Broadway, near Laugharne, Carmarthenshire, where his epitaph

made mention of the offer of the great seal should he have changed his course. He left his estate to his son, Thomas (d. 1720), created a baronet in 1698, 'the better enabling him to discharge the estate of Llaugharne purchased by him of Sir William Russell' (will).   STUART HANDLEY

Sources Sainty, *Judges* • Baker, *Serjeants* • *The whole works of the Right Rev. Jeremy Taylor*, ed. R. Heber, 1 (1822), xxvi, cccxv–vi • J. Foster, *The register of admissions to Gray's Inn, 1521–1889, together with the register of marriages in Gray's Inn chapel, 1695–1754* (privately printed, London, 1889), 255 • R. J. Fletcher, ed., *The pension book of Gray's Inn*, 1 (1901), 421 • G. W. Keeton, *Lord Chancellor Jeffreys and the Stuart cause* (1965), 356, 439, 443 • F. P. Verney and M. M. Verney, *Memoirs of the Verney family during the seventeenth century*, 2nd edn, 4 vols. in 2 (1907), vol. 2, p. 458 • *State trials*, 11.1198, 1369; 12.426–7 • Cobbett, *Parl. hist.*, 5.311–12 • N. Luttrell, *A brief historical relation of state affairs from September 1678 to April 1714*, 1 (1857), 382, 444, 447–9, 530; 4 (1857), 108 • will, PRO, PROB 11/430, sig. 38 • Foster, *Alum. Oxon.* • Foss, *Judges*, 7.337–40 • *N&Q*, 7 (1853), 262

Likenesses oils (after original, *c*.1690–1695), NPG

Powell, Sir John (1645–1713), judge and politician, was born on 26 May 1645 in Gloucester, the eldest son of John Powell (d. 1666) of Dewsall, Herefordshire, and also Gloucester, and his wife, Bridget (d. in or after 1666). Powell's father was mayor of Gloucester in 1663 after the corporation had been purged. Powell was possibly the man admitted to Brasenose College, Oxford, on 21 May 1664, and he definitely entered the Inner Temple in 1664 and was called to the bar in 1671. He had succeeded his father in 1666. He was elected a common councilman of Gloucester in 1672, under the new charter, and was town clerk from 1674 to 1685. Powell was elected to the 1685 parliament by the freemen of Gloucester in defiance of the duke of Beaufort. Beaufort had him removed from the town clerkship in September 1685, but Powell took legal action and regained his place in 1687. Beaufort believed that Powell supported James II's religious policies and he was probably the John Powell who agreed to all three of James II's 'three questions', and who was nominated as a commissioner of inquiry into recusant fines in Herefordshire and Shropshire in December 1687. He was also recommended as a court candidate for the abortive parliament of 1688.

Powell was created a serjeant-at-law in May 1689. He ceased to be Gloucester's town clerk on his appointment as a baron of the exchequer on 31 October 1691, and he was knighted on 4 November 1691. Originally he had been intended as a judge of common pleas, but the master of the rolls, Sir John Trevor, had objected. Powell was transferred to common pleas on 26 October 1695 and following the accession of Queen Anne he was promoted to queen's bench. As a judge he thus took part in the *Ashby* v. *White* case over the franchise at Aylesbury, the Tutchin case over the publication of *The Observator*, and the prosecution of the Sacheverell rioters. Swift described him to Stella in July 1711 as 'an old fellow with grey hairs, who was the merriest old gentleman I ever saw, spoke pleasing things and chuckled till he cried again' (*DNB*). In 1712 he memorably quashed the prosecution for witchcraft of one Jane Wenham who was alleged to be able to fly with the comment 'you may—there is no law against flying' (ibid.). On 2

June 1713 Powell was discharged from his duties, presumably on account of his age and ill health because he died a few days later on 14 June at his house in Gloucester after returning from Bath.

Powell's will revealed that most of his estate had been settled on the marriage earlier in 1713 of John Snell MP with his 'niece' Anna Maria, the daughter of Robert Huntindon, bishop of Raphoe. Powell was buried in Gloucester Cathedral and a monument was erected by Snell to his memory.   STUART HANDLEY

Sources HoP, *Commons, 1660–90*, 1.242, 3.268–9 · J. Stratford, *Gloucestershire biographical notes* (1887), 76–88 · Sainty, *Judges*, 36, 79, 127 · Baker, *Serjeants*, 450, 531 · will, PRO, PROB 11/535, sig. 168 · will, PRO, PROB 11/322, sig. 168 · Foster, *Alum. Oxon.* · Foss, *Judges*, 7.399–401 · A. Boyer, *The political state of Great Britain*, 5 (1713), 399 · J. E. Martin, ed., *Masters of the bench of the Hon. Society of the Inner Temple, 1450–1883, and masters of the Temple, 1540–1883* (1883), 53 · N. Luttrell, *A brief historical relation of state affairs from September 1678 to April 1714*, 5 (1857), 358, 380, 492, 519; 6 (1857), 603 · M. Goldie, 'James II and the dissenters' revenge: the commission of enquiry of 1688', *Historical Research*, 66 (1993), 53–88, esp. 85 · G. Duckett, ed., *Penal laws and Test Act*, 1 (1882), 265, 450 · *DNB*

Likenesses W. Sherwin, mezzotint, 1711, repro. in *N&Q*, 4th ser., 1/1 (1868), 128, 196 · T. Green, marble statue on monument, Gloucester Cathedral · W. Sherwin, line engraving, BM, NPG

Powell, John (*fl.* **1769–1785**), portrait painter, of whose parents nothing is known, entered the Royal Academy Schools in November 1769. He was a pupil and assistant of Sir Joshua Reynolds, and painted reduced-size copies of Reynolds's portraits which he occasionally exhibited at the Royal Academy. The portrait of the duke of Cumberland in the National Portrait Gallery, after Reynolds, was once stated to be the work of Powell, although the reason for this assertion is now obscure.

Powell copied Reynolds's family group of the duke and duchess of Marlborough with their children, now at Blenheim Palace, Oxfordshire. The original, while in Powell's charge, was seized by his creditors, and narrowly escaped being cut up to pay his debts. According to Northcote, Reynolds, on seeing Powell's copy, perceived some important errors in his own composition which he subsequently corrected.

A portrait in the National Gallery of Ireland, of the fifth earl of Harrington, is attributed to Powell.

L. H. CUST, *rev.* PAUL A. COX

Sources Graves, *RA exhibitors* · C. R. Leslie and T. Taylor, *Life and times of Sir Joshua Reynolds*, 2 (1865), 213–14 · G. Scharf, *Catalogue raisonné, or, A list of the pictures in Blenheim Palace* (1860) · S. C. Hutchison, 'The Royal Academy Schools, 1768–1830', *Walpole Society*, 38 (1960–62), 123–91, esp. 134 · *Illustrated summary catalogue of paintings*, National Gallery of Ireland (1981)

Powell, John Hardman (1827–1895). *See under* Hardman family (*per. c.*1820–1935).

Powell, John Joseph (*bap.* **1753**, *d.* **1801**), legal writer, was baptized on 9 April 1753 at St Martin-in-the-Fields, Westminster, the only son of James Powell of Queen Street, Westminster, and his wife, Ann. Admitted to the Middle Temple on 25 April 1775 he became a pupil of the conveyancer Charles Fearne, and was called to the bar on 5 May 1780. While in practice as a conveyancer Powell became

one of the most prolific writers of legal treatises at a time when, following the publication of Sir William Blackstone's *Commentaries*, a number of writers were attempting to portray the common law as a science based on reason and principle. Powell wrote several works on aspects of property law, including *A Treatise upon the Law of Mortgages* (1785), *An Essay on the Learning Respecting the Creation and Execution of Powers* (1787), and *An Essay upon the Learning of Devises* (1788). In addition he brought out new editions of Edward Wood's *A Complete Body of Conveyancing* (1790–93) and Fearne's *An Essay on the Learning of Contingent Remainders* (1795).

Powell's most important work was his *Essay upon the Law of Contracts and Agreements* (1790), which was the first comprehensive treatise on its subject. Beginning with the premise that 'all reasoning must be founded on first principles' (*Essay upon the Law of Contracts*, iii), Powell defined his notion of contract, laying particular stress on the importance of agreement, and then structured his book in such a way as to analyse the component parts of his definition. Although Powell used civilian sources for his work, and was influenced by the work of the French jurist R. J. Pothier, he limited his citations in general to English case law. He took the view that the fundamental principles of English law should be regarded with a 'sacred veneration' (ibid., vii), and held that the good administration of private law was essential for the preservation of the constitution. At the same time he felt free to criticize the decisions in cited cases where he felt the judges had erred in their principles. For instance, he attacked Lord Mansfield's decision in *Corbett* v. *Poelnitz* (1785), in which it was held that a *feme covert* who lived separately from her husband and had her separate maintenance could be sued on a contract made by her. Powell strongly criticized the judgment, dismissing Mansfield's notion that modern times required new developments, and concluded that it 'would be endless to pursue this idea through all its legal ABSURDITIES' (*Essay upon the Law of Contracts*, 98). The case was overruled in 1800.

Although Powell believed that legal rules could be modelled and adapted by the process of construction, he was very hostile to the blending of legal and equitable rights, which he associated especially with Mansfield. Commenting on Mansfield's decision in *Corbett*, he wrote, 'when a court of equity furnishes ample relief, there seems no *reason* why a court of law should *extend* its power, by overthrowing both the *soundest principles* and *clearest precedents*, merely because the parties have mistaken the remedy' (*Essay upon the Law of Contracts*, 108). Powell's work on contract was popular on both sides of the Atlantic, and reached a sixth edition in America in 1825. However, despite its early importance the work was too rooted in eighteenth-century property law, and devoted too little attention to modern commercial transactions, to have an enduring success, and it was superseded in the early nineteenth century by the work of others, notably Joseph Chitty the younger and Charles Greenstreet Addison.

Powell died on 21 June 1801 at his home in Guildford

Place, St Pancras, London, and was survived by his wife, Mary. She was a beneficiary of his will, but no more is known about her.   MICHAEL LOBBAN

Sources P. S. Atiyah, *The rise and fall of freedom of contract* (1979) · A. W. B. Simpson, 'The rise and fall of the legal treatise: legal principles and forms of legal literature', *University of Chicago Law Review*, 48 (1981), 632–79 · M. Lobban, 'The English legal treatise and English law in the eighteenth century', *Iuris Scripta Historica*, 13 (1997), 69–88 · D. Lieberman, *The province of legislation determined: legal theory in eighteenth-century Britain* (1989) · *GM*, 1st ser., 71 (1801), 674 · H. A. C. Sturgess, ed., *Register of admissions to the Honourable Society of the Middle Temple, from the fifteenth century to the year 1944*, 1 (1949) · J. Hutchinson, ed., *A catalogue of notable Middle Templars: with brief biographical notices* (1902), 197 · PRO, PROB 11/1360 · *IGI* · *Browne's General Law List* (1797) · P. Barfoot and J. Wilkes, eds., *The universal British directory of trade, commerce, and manufacture* (1791), 1.364

Powell, Joseph (1780–1834), watercolour painter and printmaker, may possibly have been a son of the Joseph Powell and Mary March who married at St Marylebone in September 1776, and it is likely that he had family connections with Herefordshire and Worcestershire. He often painted there, and his sketchbook in the Victoria and Albert Museum is signed 'J. Powell, Salop, Bridgnorth'. Despite having been Powell's pupil, Samuel Redgrave misnamed him John in his *Dictionary of Artists* and confused him with an enamel painter, J. Powell. The incorrect forename was repeated in the *Dictionary of National Biography*. When Powell first exhibited at the Royal Academy in 1796 and 1797, he was living in the Lambeth house of Benjamin Thomas Pouncy (d. 1799), the engraver and topographer, whose pupil he probably was. He was also connected with the watercolour painter Michael 'Angelo' Rooker, publishing an engraving after Rooker's drawing of Netley Abbey in 1800. He also etched after such old masters as Domenichino, Salvator Rosa, and Gaspar Poussin, and about 1810 made a series of soft-ground etchings of Egyptian scenes. There is, however, no other intimation that he ever travelled abroad. It is likely that some of his oil paintings and watercolours have been credited to more prestigious names, but his known watercolours are often both impressive and poetic. He was a very accomplished sketcher. By 1800 Powell had moved to Old Cavendish Street, and after living in John Street and Great Poland Street in 1819 he settled at 14 Allsop's Buildings, between Baker Street and Regent's Park. This remained his London address. Family tradition had it that a quarrel with William Turner of Oxford led to Powell's being blackballed at the Society of Painters in Water Colours. There is no record of this in the Old Watercolour Society's archives, but he aspired to membership of the Associated Artists (1808–11) and was the first president of the New Society of Painters in Water Colours set up in 1831 to combat what he and his fellows regarded as the selfish monopoly of the older body. He exhibited with them until 1834, and appears to have died towards the end of that year. His wife's first name was Harriet, and their eight children were baptized at St Marylebone. They were Charlotte Harriet (*bap.* 1820), Richard Foulkefs [*sic*] (1822), Joseph Rubens (1823–1896), Emma Roslin (1825), Clara (1827), Louisa Caroline (1828), Agnes (1830), and Adelaide (1832). Joseph

Rubens Powell studied at the Royal Academy Schools from 1844, exhibited precociously from 1835 to 1871, and worked for the most part in oil. He died at Canterbury on 26 January 1896, leaving his effects to his spinster daughters and son John Christopher Powell, a machine manufacturer. The British Museum and Victoria and Albert Museum, London, Brighton Art Gallery, and Manchester City Galleries hold examples of Joseph Powell's work.

       HUON MALLALIEU

Sources J. Mayne, *Burlington Magazine*, 90 (1948), 267–8 · Redgrave, *Artists*, 2nd edn · *IGI*

Powell, Lawrence Fitzroy (1881–1975), literary scholar and librarian, was born at 235 Cowley Road, Oxford, on 9 August 1881. He was the youngest of the seven children of Harry Powell (1830–1886), a trumpeter, who was wounded in the charge of the light brigade of 1854 and who published his *Recollections* in 1876, and his wife, Anne Budd, of Oxford. Powell was named after two of Harry Powell's regimental officers. He was educated at a board school in London.

Powell began work in the library of Brasenose College, Oxford, in 1893, and in 1895 became a boy helper at the Bodleian Library, under E. W. B. Nicholson. In 1901 he joined the team of William Craigie on the *New English Dictionary*. On 31 July 1909 he married Ethelwyn Rebecca (1873/4–1941), writer, daughter of James Slatter Steane, wine merchant, of Oxford. They had one son. In 1914 Powell was declared unfit for active service, but joined the Admiralty in 1916. After the war he returned to the *New English Dictionary*. In 1921, supported by Joseph Wright and Charles Firth, he was appointed librarian of the Taylor Institution, Oxford, from which he retired in 1949. Thereafter he supervised many graduate research students, and was recognized by honorary fellowships at St Catherine's and Pembroke colleges in 1966, and an Oxford DLitt in 1969. It was one of his few boasts that he had never taken an academic examination in his life.

Powell's lexicographical work under Craigie laid the foundations of his scholarship, enforcing an interest in Samuel Johnson. In 1923 R. W. Chapman invited him to revise the edition by G. Birkbeck Hill of James Boswell. The four volumes were published in 1934, and acknowledged with the award of a DLitt by Durham University in 1935. Thereafter, as for Johnson, the title was inseparable from his name. The emergence of more Boswellian material from Malahide Castle and Fettercairn House led to a full edition of Boswell's *Tour to the Hebrides*. A motoring tour of Scotland with James Marshall Osborn in 1935 was followed by annual excursions with Esmond de Beer to Raasay, where Powell prepared articles and papers in tranquil surroundings and pursued the intricacies of highland genealogy. This edition was published in 1950 as volume 5 of his *Boswell*, together with a separate index volume to the whole.

Powell's scholarship ranged over work on the sections M–N, Q–R, Si–St, and U–V, for the *Oxford English Dictionary*; an edition of the translation by Nicholas Love of Bonaventure's *Meditationes vitae Christi* of *c.*1410; studies of the

Adventurer of John Hawkesworth; the bibliography of Samuel Johnson, Thomas Percy, Thomas Pennant, and Robert Southwell; contributions to the *Cambridge Bibliography of English Literature*, vol. 2 (1940), and the Yale edition of Johnson (1963); and a collaboration with John Munro on the London Shakespeare (1958). His published works are listed in *Johnson, Boswell and their Circle* (1965), a Festschrift celebrating his eighty-fourth birthday. Equally important contributions are recorded in the acknowledgements of Johnsonian and Boswellian scholars, who benefited from his advice.

The career of L. F. (as he was generally known) displayed native tenacity. An orphan boy with few material advantages, he was largely self-taught, undeterred by difficulties, ever alert for information, and he kept his memory in full activity. A formidable indexer, he rightly considered his memory superior to card indexes, and drew together disparate source material, references, and recondite information, with effortless skill. For his pupils he resembled Johnson without the danger: cheerfulness was always evident. He was eminently clubbable, loved a *bon mot* or anecdote, and despised gossip. He defied the doctors of 1914 with energetic pedestrianism, and in his eighties would sometimes trick unwary visitors by suggesting a stroll. He was a shrewd and learned editor, a patient mentor, and a courteous friend; his *Boswell* is a lasting memorial.

In 1969 Powell became seriously ill and in February 1970 was moved to the Tracy Nursing Home in Banbury, from where he continued to collect material for a further edition of *The Life of Johnson*. He died there, aged ninety-three, on 17 July 1975.   J. D. FLEEMAN, *rev.*

Sources M. M. Lascelles, ed., *Johnson, Boswell and their circle: essays presented to Lawrence Fitzroy Powell in honour of his eighty-fourth birthday* (1965) • M. C. Hyde, ed., *Our friend L. F.: recollections of Lawrence Fitzroy Powell* (privately printed, 1976) • J. S. G. Simmons, 'Lawrence Fitzroy Powell, 1881–1975: a tribute', *New Rambler* (1976) • personal knowledge (1993) • m. cert. • WWW

Archives Bodl. Oxf., letters to R. W. Chapman; letters to K. M. Chapman

Likenesses photograph, repro. in Simmons, 'Lawrence Fitzroy Powell'

Wealth at death £20,540: probate, 21 Oct 1975, *CGPLA Eng. & Wales*

Powell, Martin (*d.* in or before **1725**), puppet-showman, came to notice early in the eighteenth century. He had established a theatre in Bath by 1709, which apparently attracted a fashionable audience and was alluded to in the pages of *The Tatler*. In 1710 he gave a season in London, and in 1711 he opened Punch's Theatre in the Little Piazza at Covent Garden, probably at no. 20 in the south-east corner. Here the sexton at St Paul's Church was assumed by Steele to have written a letter to *The Spectator* complaining that the congregation at the church took the warning of his bell morning and evening as notice that Powell was about to perform. This was clearly a joke, but it hints at the popularity of the show with a middle-class and aristocratic public.

Powell performed in London only for three seasons of six months each, but during this time he produced twenty plays. Some of these were based on legendary tales from ballads and chapbooks, such as *The History of Sir Richard Whittington* or *King Bladud, the Founder of the Bath*, which were the staple fare of puppet shows everywhere. These traditional stories were, however, alternated with more sophisticated satires of contemporary society, such as *Poor Robin's Dream, or, The Vices of the Age Exposed*, based on a ballad of the day, in which the gallants, the whores, and the quacks were miraculously reformed, and poets had guineas in their pockets. And then there was a series of operatic burlesques such as *The False Triumph, or, The Siege of Troy*, in which Signor Punchanella appeared in the role of Jupiter, descended from the clouds in a chariot drawn by eagles, and sang an aria in Punch's squeaky voice to Paris; or a dig at a recent production of *Hydaspes*, in which Nicolini had fought a lion on the stage, with a scene in which Punch danced a minuet with a live pig. Powell was, indeed, a master of satire, and Lord Chesterfield recalled how:

> there was a great number of fanatics, who said they had, and very possibly actually thought they had, the gift of prophecy … The then ministry … were however wise enough not to disturb these madmen, and only ordered one Powell, who was the master of a famous puppet-show, to make Punch turn prophet, which he did so well, that it soon put an end to the prophets and their prophecies. (*Miscellaneous Works*, 2.528)

A contemporary complained that 'Mr. Powell, by subscriptions and full house, has gathered such wealth as is ten times sufficient to buy all the poets in England, and that he seldom goes out without his chair' (*Les soupirs de la Grande Bretagne*), but his fourth Covent Garden season closed early, and almost nothing is known of his later career. He had died by 1725, and his son succeeded him, but only at the fairgrounds.

In 1714 Thomas Burnet and George Duckett published *A Second Tale of a Tub, or, The History of Robert Powel the Puppet-Show-Man*. This was really a political satire aimed at Robert Harley, but it incorporated a few apparently true references to the real Powell. By the time it appeared Powell was no longer performing in London, but he may be said to have founded a tradition of puppet satire which was continued during the eighteenth century by Charlotte Charke, the daughter of Colley Cibber; by Henry Fielding, using the *nom de théâtre* of Madame de la Nash; and by Samuel Foote and Charles Dibdin. He also helped to develop the character of Punch, which had been introduced to England in 1662, and which reached its climax in the Punch and Judy show of the next century.

GEORGE SPEAIGHT

Sources G. Speaight, *The history of the English puppet theatre*, 2nd edn (1990), 92–103, 285–7 • G. Speaight, 'Powell from the Bath', *Studies in English theatre history* (1952), 38–51 • G. Speaight, 'A reconstruction of Powel's stage', *Puppetry*, 1944–45, ed. P. McPharlin, 33–4 • *The Tatler* (12 April 1709); (14 May 1709); (24 May 1709); (19 July 1709); (2 Aug 1709); (4 Aug 1709); (4 Oct 1709); (31 Dec 1709); (7 March 1709/10) • *The Spectator* (16 March 1711); (23 March 1711); (5 April 1711); (9 April 1711); (2 June 1711); (17 Jan 1712); (29 April 1712); (7 May 1712); (13 May 1712) • [T. Burnet and G. Duckett], *A second tale of a tub, or, The history of Robert Powel the puppet-show-man* (1714) • *The letters of*

Thomas Burnet to George Duckett, 1712–1722, ed. D. N. Smith (1914) • *Les soupirs de la Grande Bretagne, or, The groans of Great Britain* (1713) • *Miscellaneous works of the … earl of Chesterfield*, ed. M. Maty, 2 (1777), 528, 555
Likenesses portrait, repro. in Burnet and Duckett, *Second tale of a tub*, frontispiece

Powell, Michael Latham (1905–1990), film director, was born on 30 September 1905 at Howletts, Bekesbourne, near Canterbury, Kent, the second son and younger child of Thomas William Powell, farmer, and his wife, Mabel, daughter of Frederick Corbett, of Worcester. He was educated at King's School, Canterbury, where he was a king's scholar, and at Dulwich College. Powell started work with the National Provincial Bank in 1922, but entered the film business in 1925, when he joined Rex Ingram, a Hollywood director who was working at the Victorine Studios in Nice, and Harry Lachman, a Chicago-born painter who secured employment for Powell with British International Pictures. The contact with Ingram was made through Powell's father, who owned a hotel in Nice. In 1927 Powell married Gloria Mary Rouger, an American dancer; they were married in France and stayed together for only three weeks. In 1931 Powell formed Film Engineering with Jerry Jackson, an American lawyer, to produce 'quota quickies', British films given a market by the Cinematograph Act of 1927. In just five years he worked on approximately twenty-three films, gaining valuable experience and making useful contacts in the film world.

After a successful contract with Gaumont-British, one of Britain's major film production companies, Powell directed a personal project shot on the island of Foula in the Shetlands, *The Edge of the World* (1937), produced by the American Joe Rock. The film received good reviews and a cup for the best direction of a foreign film at the 1938 Venice film festival. This led to a contract with Alexander Korda, who facilitated Powell's first collaboration with the screenwriter Emeric *Pressburger on *The Spy in Black* (1939), about a German plan to sabotage the British fleet anchored off the Orkney Islands in the First World War, the first of twenty-one films they made together; they formed their production company, the Archers, in 1943. But before their partnership was more permanently forged Powell co-directed a propaganda film, one of the first to be completed after the beginning of the Second World War, *The Lion has Wings* (1939). The film was much admired by Winston Churchill for its patriotism. Powell then co-directed Korda's spectacular adventure film *The Thief of Bagdad* (1940). This gave him the opportunity to explore the potential of Technicolor, the preferred technique in many of his subsequent films, and also the use of the pre-recorded soundtrack. It also encouraged his fascination with modernist, self-reflexive devices which he developed in later films. On 1 July 1943 Powell married Frances May Reidy (1909/10–1983), daughter of Jerome Reidy, a medical practitioner. They had two sons.

During the Second World War Powell and Pressburger produced some of their finest work, including *Forty Ninth Parallel* (1941), *One of our Aircraft is Missing* (1941), and *The Life*

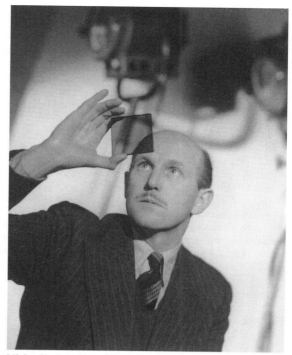

Michael Latham Powell (1905–1990), by Fred Daniels, 1940s

and Death of Colonel Blimp (1943), a film which was criticized by Churchill and the Ministry of Information for its satirical portrayal of the military. The films were imaginative, creative, cinematic, and rather unconventional. Whereas most British films were made in realistic style, Powell and Pressburger used fantastical situations, dream sequences, bold colour, and disjointed narratives. Powell's break with the realist tradition (of which *The Lion has Wings* was part) left both audiences and critics puzzled. The Archers also broke new ground with *A Canterbury Tale* (1944), a lyrical meditation for the post-war world which suffered from studio cuts to render it more conventional. Although Powell's films were considered to stray beyond what was expected from British films, the Rank Organization nevertheless gave the Archers a firm production base and considerable freedom in the development of their projects. Powell excelled at location shooting and had a particularly poetic response to landscape. When location shooting was not possible or appropriate, Powell devised ingenious experiments in the studio to create fantasy environments. Pressburger's screenplays gave him ample opportunities to develop these skills, and he always preferred narratives based on fantasy and the imagination rather than on fact.

At the end of the war Powell directed *I Know Where I'm Going!* (1945), a film which employed location shooting on the western isles of Scotland and impressive studio effects to create a dramatic storm sequence. This was followed by his favourite film, the spectacular *A Matter of Life and Death* (1946), starring David Niven as a British pilot on the verge of death who has to argue his case in 'heaven' in order to be allowed to live. It was an aesthetic experiment involving imaginative sets and innovative film techniques to represent the pilot's hallucinations. For this film Powell used the German art director Alfred Junge, with whom he had first collaborated on *Contraband* (1940). Junge and Powell worked towards creating a distinctive and imaginative setting for both 'heaven' and earth, alternating between black and white and colour to stress the difference. Another collaborator with whom Powell worked on many successful occasions was the cinematographer Jack Cardiff, who did his best work for the Archers. *A Matter of Life and Death* was Cardiff's first film for Powell and Pressburger, and used his experience of working with Technicolor for several years to stunning effect.

In a spirit of resourceful creativity *Black Narcissus* (1946), based on Rumer Godden's novel, reproduced the Himalayas in a Pinewood studio. Seeking to avoid an awkward mix of two styles, Powell turned down the opportunity to go to India for location shots, in favour of a studio experiment. Powell, Junge, and Cardiff again rose to the challenge, creating stunning sets and evoking an atmosphere of alluring sensuality. The film was the subject of intense controversy in the USA, where the Legion of Decency, a Catholic organization, lobbied to have it banned because of its allegedly sacrilegious portrayal of a religious order. A cut version was released there to placate this powerful pressure group. Their next film, *The Red Shoes* (1948), was an extravagant gamble. Rank allowed the Archers to produce a high-budget film about ballet at a time when the British film industry was enjoying a brief period of protection against US film imports. Its excess stretched the limits of the relationship with Rank and ended the Archers' partnership with the studio until *The Battle of the River Plate* in 1956. *The Red Shoes* is significant for its experimentation with the idea of the 'composed' film, whereby the film is conceived and shot on the basis of an existing musical score. Powell had used elements of this method in earlier films, but employed the technique to an unprecedented extent with *The Red Shoes*. The film was also ambitious in its use of British and European locations, and dealt with the tempestuous world of ballet, in which dedication and personal sacrifice are demanded for art. The film was extremely successful in the USA, appearing as the highest-earning British film in top box-office lists for many years. Powell repeated the strategy of the composed film several times, particularly in *The Tales of Hoffman* (1953), an experimental adaptation of Jacques Offenbach's opera. He was also involved in the development of a technical special effects device known as the 'independent frame', which aimed to reduce costs by creating a multiplicity of effects in the studio.

From 1948 to 1955 Powell worked with Alexander Korda again on *The Small Back Room* (1949) and *The Tales of Hoffman*. In 1950 two costume films, *Gone to Earth* and *The Elusive Pimpernel*, suffered from Korda's involvement with the American independent producers Sam Goldwyn and David O. Selznick. Selznick insisted on two versions of *Gone to Earth*, resulting in an American version which related more closely than the British to the source novel by Mary Webb. *The Elusive Pimpernel* was not released in the USA until 1955 in a black and white version that was shorter than the British version released in 1950, and retitled *The Fighting Pimpernel*. Powell's last film with Pressburger was a wartime drama, *Ill Met by Moonlight* (1956), produced by Rank. Powell felt constrained with a narrative based on fact and was dissatisfied with the results. The Archers' partnership ended in 1956 after disagreements during the filming of *Ill Met by Moonlight*. Over the previous few years there had been a mutual distancing, and several unsuccessful attempts to raise finance for film projects.

In 1959 Powell directed the controversial *Peeping Tom*, later widely regarded as a classic but at the time considered to be sadistic cheap horror. It was based on a story by Leo Marks about a young cameraman who photographs victims as he kills them with the point of his tripod. The film was controversial because it encouraged sympathy for the murderer. Powell also indulged his fascination for self-reflexivity with the inclusion of home-movie footage of himself as a child with his father. Its immediate reception was so bad that Powell could get no further funding for his work and had to go to Australia in 1966 to make two films: *They're a Weird Mob* (1966) and *The Age of Consent* (1969), the last feature film he was to direct. Despite its initial poor reception, *Peeping Tom* has subsequently been praised by critics as an important advance in the horror genre and a meditation on voyeurism in cinema. In the 1970s Powell's talent was fully recognized by film-makers and critics, especially Martin Scorsese, Brian de Palma, and David Thompson, who encouraged him to move to the USA in 1980 to teach at Dartmouth College, New Hampshire. Powell's passion for experiment, risk taking, and creative use of colour influenced many film directors in both Britain and the United States. In 1981 Powell became director-in-residence at Francis Ford Coppola's Zoetrope Hollywood studio, where he also worked on his boastful and vengeful autobiographies *A Life in Movies* (1986) and *Million-Dollar Movie* (1992).

Powell was remarkable for his liveliness, enthusiasm, and passion for both cinema and Rudyard Kipling. He was a fierce champion of cinema as an art form and resented producers who placed restrictions, creative and budgetary, on his films. Above all, he insisted that a good film was the product of many talents, remarking in his autobiography that 'one of my missions in life is to convince my fellow film directors that collaboration is an art, and that the movies is the greatest of collaborative arts' (Powell, *Million-Dollar Movie*, 421). He particularly admired the films of Akira Kurosawa, Luchino Visconti, John Huston, David Lean, Carol Reed, Francis Ford Coppola, and Martin Scorsese. Despite his reputation as an imaginative director who acknowledged the importance of collaboration, however, Powell was difficult to work with, and antagonized many actors with his lack of respect and his self-centredness. The partnership with Pressburger was remarkable for its longevity, even though it was not entirely free from friction. When the work of Powell and Pressburger was being re-evaluated from the 1970s Pressburger often felt that Powell, the consummate self-publicist, dominated billings and events for retrospectives. Yet when interviewed about the partnership Powell always expressed a huge debt to the quality of the screenplays, upon which he worked closely with Pressburger to ensure their most striking realization. In acknowledging the importance of their collaboration Powell remarked that 'I am the teller of the tale, and not the creator of the story' (Macdonald, 155), insisting that above all he was a craftsman in film art. Powell likened their relationship to a marriage which on the whole was characterized by mutual dependence and respect. Powell's physical appearance was distinctive: he had clear blue eyes, ruddy cheeks, and a moustache, and was bald from an early age. He loved the outdoors and always shot on location when possible.

In recognition of his work Powell received a number of awards, including fellowship of the Royal Geographic Society, honorary doctorates from the universities of East Anglia (1978) and Kent (1984) and the Royal College of Art (1987), and the British Film Institute's special award in 1978 and a fellowship in 1983. He married for a third time on 19 May 1984; his wife was the film editor Thelma Colbert Schoonmaker (b. 1939/40), daughter of Bertram Schoonmaker, a clerical worker in the Standard Oil Company. He also lived for many years with the actress Pamela Mary *Brown. Powell died from cancer on 19 February 1990 at his home at 1 Lee Cottages, Avening, Gloucestershire. His third wife survived him.   SARAH STREET

Sources I. Christie, *Arrows of desire* (1985) · M. Powell, *A life in movies: an autobiography* (1986) · M. Powell, *Million-dollar movie: the second volume of his life in movies* (1992) · K. Macdonald, *Emeric Pressburger* (1994) · I. Christie, *A matter of life and death* (2000) · private information (2004) · b. cert. · m. certs. [Frances May Reidy, Thelma Colbert Schoonmaker] · d. cert.
Likenesses F. Daniels, photograph, 1940–49, BFI NFTVA [*see illus.*]
Wealth at death £26,261: probate, 28 Nov 1990, CGPLA Eng. & Wales

Powell, Dame Muriel Betty (1914–1978), nurse, was born on 30 October 1914 at Ruspidge, East Dean, Gloucestershire, the third child of Wallace George Powell (1878–1969), a stonemason, and his wife, Annie Elizabeth Harriet Florence Jones, *née* Stewart (1889–1959). She was one of seven children, the second of four daughters. At her first school she was remembered as a quiet, sensitive child who found pleasure in music and in literature. At East Dean grammar school in Cinderford she was determined to become a missionary and, in preparation for the Universities Mission to Central Africa, she started Swahili lessons; her decision to become a nurse instead astonished her family. She embarked on her career by training as a probationer nurse at St George's Hospital, London (1934?–1937). In 1947 she was to return, aged thirty-two, as its matron. She was qualified as a staff nurse then ward sister by 1939. Her pacifism prevented her joining the forces, but while a nurse tutor at Ipswich she worked on the land in the evenings and at weekends. In 1942 she took a diploma in nursing at London University. From a post at Manchester Royal Infirmary, where she was principal tutor, she returned in 1947 to St George's, where she remained

Dame Muriel Betty Powell (1914–1978), by Godfrey Argent, 1970

for twenty-three years, for the last three as chief nursing officer. She was appointed CBE in 1962 and DBE in 1968.

Powell was a slight, good-looking, charismatic woman, who deeply believed in the value and dignity of each person. As Dame Muriel she became the most famous nurse in Britain since the First World War. To the general public she was the matron who enabled patients to remain, unawakened, in bed in hospital until seven o'clock in the morning. This simple concession for the sick in hospital, from her manual on nursing, caught the public imagination through the popular press. She became well known throughout the 1960s and 1970s to national radio audiences for her wise and sensible responses to enquiries from broadcasters and journalists about the various news items concerning sickness and the National Health Service. Her successor said 'she really made an impact on the public and not just on the nursing profession' by changing the general practice of nursing (Joan Clague, *Nursing Times*, 2039). A deeply committed Christian, she also regularly spoke in religious broadcasts; her contributions were always infused with dedication to caring and to her beliefs, yet she had a lightness of touch that enabled her to impart these to listeners with gentle humour. Her name and opinions became bywords to the public. During this time she wrote, with her co-author, the Revd Paul Gliddon, a former chaplain at St George's, *Called to Serve*, 'a book for all who care for the sick and who must face the problem of suffering'.

Recognized by her professional colleagues as *primus*

inter pares, Powell became the president of the Association of Hospital Matrons from 1958 to 1963, and deputy president of the Royal College of Nursing, which latter office may be considered as recognition by the 'other ranks' organization. In 1963 and 1964 she also served on the Nurses and Midwives Whitley Council that determined the salaries and conditions of employment. For eleven years, from 1958 to 1969, she served on the Central Health Services Advisory Council as chairman of the standing nursing advisory committee of the Ministry of Health. She was also on the council of the King's Fund, the University of London's advisers panel on nursing. With a high national profile it was natural that she should move onto the international stage as a member of the World Health Assembly's expert advisory committee on nursing. She was also a director of the International Council of Nurses, and she travelled the world both officially and by invitation.

Nationally Powell was a member of the committee chaired by Sir Harry Platt that produced *A Reform of Nursing Education*, and of the committee under the chairmanship of Sir Brian Salmon on senior nursing staff structure. With her background in teaching she maintained that education was the key to better nursing. She introduced into St George's a shortened programme for university graduates, sponsored by the Ministry of Health. This enabled her hospital to form a partnership with the University of Surrey, combining an honours degree in biology with a nursing training.

By 1970 plans were advanced for the transfer of St George's from Hyde Park Corner to the suburb of Tooting. At fifty-five Powell could have sought retirement, but she elected to apply for the post of chief nursing officer for Scotland. She was appointed and moved north. Life as a senior civil servant was vastly different from her previous experience. She missed the contact with patients—she had always carried out unaccompanied ward rounds—but with her small team of nursing officers in Edinburgh she set about new tasks. Music continued to be her recreation.

Sadly, there is little doubt that, from the time of her acceptance of this last appointment, she was already experiencing the first symptoms of Alzheimer's disease in small ways that were detectable to her closest nursing colleagues. The decision seems to have been made in the Scottish Office that she should be supported until her retirement date, despite increasingly obvious signs of her waning powers.

When, in 1976, she finally retired to the family home in her beloved Gloucestershire, it became increasingly obvious that she needed both help and support in her daily living. These were gallantly provided by a former colleague, John Greene, who had succeeded her as president of the Association of Nurse Administrators (the former Association of Hospital Matrons). He was then the chief nursing officer of the nearby Coney Hill Hospital, where, lovingly cared for and cherished, she died on 8 December 1978. She was buried at Cinderford. The service of thanksgiving for her life, held at St Paul's, Knightsbridge, London, on 2 February 1979, attracted a huge congregation of citizens from all walks of life, as well as her numerous professional colleagues. PEGGY D. NUTTALL

Sources 'Dame Muriel Powell', *Nursing Times* (14 Dec 1978), 2039 · personal knowledge (2004) · private information (2004) [family] · WWW · b. cert. · d. cert. · *CGPLA Eng. & Wales* (1979)
Likenesses G. Argent, photograph, 1970, NPG [*see illus.*] · photograph, repro. in 'Dame Muriel Powell', *Nursing Times*
Wealth at death £66,159: probate, 19 April 1979, *CGPLA Eng. & Wales*

Powell, Nathaniel. *See* Powle, Nathaniel (*d.* 1622).

Powell, Olave St Clair Baden- [*née* Olave St Clair Soames], **Lady Baden-Powell** (1889–1977), leader of the world Girl Guide movement, was born on 22 February 1889 at Stubbing Court, near Chesterfield, Derbyshire, the third child and younger daughter of Harold Soames (1855–1918), and his wife, Katherine Mary Hill (1851–1932). Her father, an educated and artistic man, had been able to sell his family business, the Brampton Brewery Company, in his early thirties, and thereafter was able to live comfortably off his investments. Her mother, a conventional, fashion-conscious woman, was her husband's opposite, and increasingly they lived separate lives. As her parents moved almost every year from one large rented property to the next, until settling at Grey Rigg, Lilliput, near Bournemouth, and as she received almost no formal education except through a German governess, Friede Dentzelmann, she had a lonely and emotionally confusing childhood. Not conventionally beautiful, and less favoured than her sister in her mother's affections, trust in her father was shattered by his affair with her first female role model, Jean Graham, who had been acting as her informal tutor. Spending much of her childhood in the country, she grew up an athletic and sporting young woman, naïve in worldly matters and inexperienced emotionally, with little sense of personal direction. She was much influenced by Sybil Mounsey-Heysham, a Soames family friend, a woman of eccentric dress and masculine habits, reputed to be the third best duck shot in England. Throughout her life, Olave was attracted by vigorous, athletic, unaffected, independently minded women, with whom she would quarrel on occasion. In 1911 she was briefly engaged to her cousin Noel Soames.

In January 1912, while accompanying her father on a cruise on the SS *Arcadian*, she met Lieutenant-General Sir Robert Baden-*Powell (1857–1941), hero of the defence of Mafeking during the Second South African War and founder of the Boy Scout movement. Although he was thirty-two years her senior, they were immediately attracted to one another and had become secretly engaged by the end of the voyage. Despite Baden-Powell's briefly doubting the wisdom of his actions, a public engagement was announced, and the couple were married on 31 October 1912 at St Peter's Church, Parkstone, Dorset, to the disapproval of their surviving parents. Each brought complementary qualities to what became a happy, companionate marriage. For her husband, Olave brought a vigorous,

Olave St Clair Baden-Powell, Lady Baden-Powell (1889–1977),
by Karl Pollak, *c.*1948

unaffected, and youthful independence of spirit combined with an unquestioning belief in his individual genius and heroic status. For her, Baden-Powell was an ideal older man whom she could both support and defer to, and who gave a focus and purpose to her life for the first time. They had three children, Peter, Heather, and Betty.

Upon her marriage Olave gave herself totally and unquestioningly to the work of her husband and the two movements he had founded, the Boy Scouts and the Girl Guides. She did voluntary work at the scout recreation hut at Étaples in France during the early part of the First World War. At the same time she built up her own position within the Girl Guides: moves that created tensions with her sister-in-law Agnes Baden-Powell, its first president. In early 1916 she assumed a leading role, first as county commissioner for Sussex (which she systematically reorganized along scout lines), then as chief commissioner for the United Kingdom from the end of that year, and finally as chief guide of the British empire from 1918. She also at times chaired the executive committee of the Girl Guides' Association in the absence of her husband. As a result she increasingly dominated the work of the association nationally in the period of its most rapid expansion, principally through her selection of women to take up the position of county commissioners across the country. Internationally she was also influential as head of the overseas department from January 1920. As with the earlier expansion of the Boy Scout movement between 1908 and 1910, the dramatic growth of the guide movement after 1916

created considerable personal tensions within the headquarters among the small and intimate band of strong-minded leading women at what one historian has called 'the Court of Queen Olave' (Jeal, 478). In disputes over policy, Olave was able to refer to the authority of her husband; on matters of personnel, he usually deferred to her intuitions.

From the late 1920s Olave Baden-Powell became less closely involved with the running of the UK association and spent more time supporting the international work of her husband, a role confirmed by her election as world chief guide in 1930, paralleling Baden-Powell's own position as chief scout of the world. She travelled extensively, initiated the guide and scout cruises, and ministered to the needs of her now elderly husband. In addition she had responsibility for an extended family, following the suicide of her sister Auriol early in 1919. Having settled at Pax Hill, Bentley, Hampshire, in January 1919, Olave ran a relaxed, rural household, supported by a loyal staff, ministering to her husband, five or six children, and a continuous stream of scout and guide guests. On the one hand, it was a happy unfussy, slightly eccentric community; on the other, Olave made some of the mistakes of her own mother, in clearly preferring her younger daughter, and showing a deep disappointment that her son could not live up to the heroic qualities of his father. Her dislike of sophistication and fashion, and the wholesomeness of the domestic environment, created difficulties in late adolescence for two of her children, and she was never reconciled to her son, Peter, whose funeral in 1962 she did not attend. On moving to Kenya in October 1938, the Baden-Powells settled at Paxtu, Nyeri, where Olave nursed and supported her husband until his death in January 1941.

As a widow of fifty-two, Olave had to rebuild her life. At first she was completely distraught, unable to attend his funeral. After initially engaging in voluntary work with the East Africa Women's League, she returned to the UK in September 1942, determined to devote the remainder of her life to sustaining her husband's work and reputation. This she did continuously and energetically until forced into semi-retirement by diabetes in 1970. In many ways this was her greatest achievement. As world chief guide, she had no defined authority in any national association or within the world organization. Nevertheless, her presence was always sought as an increasingly matriarchal figure for both movements, a role she fulfilled with charm, vigour, and charisma. Equally at ease with a small group of children or at a large adult international gathering, she was able to communicate the ideals of scouting and guiding and the unique vision (as she saw it) of her late husband in ways that remained in the minds of those present throughout their lives. Aided by a phenomenal memory for individuals, she maintained a vast ungrammatical and idiosyncratically typed correspondence from the grace-and-favour apartments she had accepted in Hampton Court Palace in December 1942. It is estimated that she travelled 488,000 miles between 1930 and 1977.

In personal terms Olave Baden-Powell had an almost completely untrained intelligence, which she combined with powerful intuitions, and an uncomplicated direct-ness and eloquence, which had little patience with com-plexity or ambiguity. She had little time for discussions about details, policies, or bureaucratic structures. A lover of animals (but not cats), who delighted in the outdoor life and country dancing, and had a talent (if little used in later life) for the violin, she was not a reading woman. A con-ventional Anglican, although impatient—like her hus-band—of denominational detail, she nevertheless used mediums to communicate with the spirit of her husband after his death. In political terms, she shared some of the prejudices of her age and class as she grew older. But from the moment of their meeting in 1912, her values were those of her husband as expressed through scouting and guiding. Not surprisingly some of the changes introduced to update the scout movement in the 1960s were distress-ing to her, especially alterations in the wording of the scout laws and promise. As a result, she donated a consid-erable portion of her husband's archive and personal effects to the Boy Scouts of America, whom she thought more appreciative of his memory, and, possibly as a recog-nition of the fact that they had largely paid for her travel as world chief guide. In August 1973 she moved into a nursing home at Birtley House, near Guildford, Surrey, where she died on 25 June 1977. After her funeral at Bent-ley church on 1 July, her ashes were interred in her hus-band's grave at Nyeri, Kenya, in August. She had been cre-ated GBE in 1932 and received many other national hon-ours around the world. There is a joint memorial tablet in Westminster Abbey.

Although she always presented herself as simply the vehicle of her husband's vision, Olave Baden-Powell made her own distinctive contribution in two main ways. First, as a young woman of little formal education, she demon-strated to a whole generation of women (many of whom were unmarried) after 1918 that they could be construct-ive and effective as workers with girls and young women without having to subscribe to all the conventional con-straints of Edwardian gentility in forms of dress and behaviour. Whatever the ambiguities of guiding's mes-sage for women (and it had many variants around the world), it remained a movement for girls and young women led by women of all social ranks and opinions. Although not uncontested, Olave Baden-Powell signifi-cantly aided that development as an enthusiast and role model. Second, in her later life, as an international ambas-sador on behalf of the ideals of her late husband after 1942, she supported and sustained the reputations of both movements as instruments of international harmony and reconciliation, so that despite the enormous cultural and political differences between national associations, almost all their members could affirm that what they had in common was more important than what distinguished them one from another.　　　　　ALLEN WARREN

Sources O. Baden-Powell and M. Drewery, *Window on my heart* (1973) · E. K. Wade, *Olave Baden-Powell* (1971) · T. Jeal, *Baden-Powell* (1989) · R. Kerr, *The story of the Girl Guides* (1932) · A. Warren, '"Mothers for the Empire"? The Girl Guides Association in Britain, 1909–1939', *Making imperial mentalities: socialisation and British imperi-alism*, ed. J. Mangan (1990), 96–110 · *CGPLA Eng. & Wales* (1977) · *DNB* · private information (2004)
Archives Girl Guide Association, letters and papers · priv. coll., papers, scrapbooks, and diaries | London, archives of Girl Guide Association | FILM BFI NFTVA, advertising film footage · BFI NFTVA, news footage | SOUND BL NSA, news recordings
Likenesses L. Sprink, portrait, 1912 · D. Jagger, portrait, 1930 · K. Pollak, photograph, *c*.1948, NPG [*see illus.*] · Mrs Wheatley, por-trait
Wealth at death £7346: probate, 21 Oct 1977, *CGPLA Eng. & Wales*

Powell, Richard (1766–1834), physician, was born at the end of 1766 and baptized on 11 May 1767, the son of Joseph Powell, gentleman, of Thame, Oxfordshire, and his wife, Francis, formerly Smith. He was educated at Thame gram-mar school and proceeded in 1781 to Winchester College. He matriculated at Pembroke College, Oxford, on 19 Janu-ary 1785, and in the same year he migrated to Merton Col-lege, where he graduated BA on 23 October 1788, MA on 31 October 1791, BM on 12 July 1792, and DM on 20 January 1795. He went on to study medicine at St Bartholomew's Hospital, London, having spent some time at the Edin-burgh Royal Infirmary; at Barts he was one of the founders of the Medical and Philosophical Society, afterwards named the Abernethian Society, which existed until about 1986.

Powell was elected a fellow of the Royal College of Phys-icians on 30 September 1796, and in 1799 he delivered the Goulstonian lectures. They were published in 1800, under the title of *Observations on the Bile and its Diseases, and on the Oeconomy of the Liver*, and show careful observation and sound judgement. The method of clinical examination of the liver which he proposed was excellent; and he was the first English medical writer who demonstrated that gall-stones may remain fixed in the neck of the gall bladder, or even obliterate its cavity, without well-marked symptoms or serious injury to the patient. Powell lectured at St Bar-tholomew's from 1796 and on the resignation of Dr Rich-ard Budd he was, on 14 August 1801, elected physician to the hospital, an office which he retained until 1824. He was a censor at the Royal College of Physicians in 1798, 1807, 1820, and 1823; was Lumleian lecturer from 1811 to 1822; and delivered the Harveian oration in 1808. In the same year he was appointed secretary to the commission for regulating madhouses.

Powell had considerable chemical knowledge and pub-lished *Heads of Lectures on Chemistry* in 1796. He was one of the revisers of the *Pharmacopoeia Londinensis* in 1809, and he published a translation from Latin to English of that edition. On 13 April 1810 he read, at the Royal College of Physicians, *Observations upon the Comparative Prevalence of Insanity at Different Periods*, afterwards published in the sixth volume of *Medical Transactions of the Royal College of Physicians of London*. In the same volume he published *Observations on the Internal Use of Nitrate of Silver*, in which he recommended its use in chorea and in epilepsy, an opin-ion which he modified in a subsequent paper on further cases of the same diseases, read on 17 April 1815. On 20 December 1813 he had read *Observations upon some Cases of*

Paralytic Affection (*Medical Transactions*, vol. 5), in which simple facial palsy was described for the first time. Sir Charles Bell, in the course of his researches on the nervous system, afterwards redescribed and explained this affliction, but the credit of its first clinical description belongs to Powell, who also initiated a method of treatment by warm applications which was often efficacious. On 2 December 1814 Powell read 'Some cases illustrative of the pathology of the brain', a description of thirteen cases of interest, including that of one patient with tuberculous meningitis and of another with a pituitary tumour.

A fellow of the Society of Antiquaries, Powell gave some attention to the study of the history of St Bartholomew's Hospital; and on 27 November 1817 a communication by him was read to the society describing the most ancient charter preserved in the hospital (a grant from Rahere in 1137), and its seal. The whole text of this charter was printed in the nineteenth volume of *Archaeologia*. Powell lived in London in Bedford Place for some years, and, after he retired from practice in 1824, in York Terrace, Regent's Park, where he died on 18 August 1834.

NORMAN MOORE, rev. KAYE BAGSHAW

Sources Munk, *Roll* · Foster, *Alum. Oxon.* · V. C. Medvei and J. L. Thornton, eds., *The royal hospital of Saint Bartholomew, 1123–1973* (1974) · 'Richard Powell (1767–1834)', *Journal of the American Medical Association*, 208/2 (1969), 353–4 · F. G. Lee, *History and antiquities of the church of the blessed Virgin Mary of Thame* (1883), col. 623 · *GM*, 2nd ser., 2 (1834), 554 · T. F. Kirby, *Winchester scholars: a list of the wardens, fellows, and scholars of … Winchester College* (1888), 273

Likenesses J. Lonsdale, oils, 1821, St Bartholomew's Hospital, London · J. Jenkins, stipple, pubd 1839 (after J. Lonsdale), BM, NPG · engraving, RCP Lond.; repro. in Medvei and Thornton, eds., *Royal Hospital of Saint Bartholomew*

Powell, Sir Richard Douglas, first baronet (1842–1925), physician, born at Walthamstow on 25 September 1842, was the second but only surviving son of Captain Scott Powell of the 23rd Royal Welch Fusiliers, and his wife, Eliza, daughter of Richard Meeke. Much of his boyhood was spent at Toft, near Cambridge, and there he laid the foundations of the interest in natural history and sport (fishing and shooting) which were the chief relaxations of his later life. Educated privately at Streatham he gave up his wish to follow his father's profession, entered University College, London, and continued his course at University College Hospital, becoming physician's assistant to Sir William Jenner, to whom he owed much in his early professional career. He graduated MB in 1865 and qualified for the gold medal at the MD (1866) examinations.

Powell was appointed in 1867 to take temporary charge of out-patients, and in 1869 he applied unsuccessfully for a vacancy as assistant physician at University College Hospital. Two years later (1871) he was elected assistant physician and lecturer on materia medica to Charing Cross Hospital. He resigned both posts in 1878 on being appointed assistant physician to the Middlesex Hospital, becoming physician in 1880 and consulting physician in 1900. Thus for nearly thirty years he taught medical students, being a stimulus to the thoughtful rather than a source of dogmatic answers for those interested only in satisfying examiners. As resident clinical assistant, assistant physician (1868), physician (1875), and consulting physician (1889) he was attached to the Brompton Hospital for Consumption and Diseases of the Chest, and was much in demand as a consultant in thoracic disease. For thirty-eight years he was connected with the court, being appointed in 1887 physician-extraordinary in the place of Wilson Fox, and in 1899 physician-in-ordinary to Queen Victoria, whom he attended in her last illness (1901); he continued to serve in the latter capacity Edward VII and George V.

A hard worker, Powell's published writings extended over a period of fifty-six years and included articles on diseases of the chest contributed to Russell Reynolds's *System of Medicine* (1879), and to the two later editions (1898–9 and 1909). His chief work was *On the Principal Varieties of Pulmonary Tuberculosis with Practical Comments* (1872) which went through six editions up to 1921. His Lumleian lectures, delivered in 1898 at the Royal College of Physicians of London, appeared as *The Principles which Govern Treatment in Diseases and Disorders of the Heart* (1899).

In the medical life of London, Powell was continuously at work from the time when he was a junior at the Pathological Society, of which he was secretary (1877–9). Later he was successively president of the Medical Society of London (1891), the Clinical Society of London (1899–1901), and the Royal Medical and Chirurgical Society (1904–6), and he was active in the arrangements for amalgamating seventeen metropolitan medical societies into the Royal Society of Medicine (1907). Powell also lent his help to the formation, initiated by Sir William Osler, of the Association of Physicians of Great Britain and Ireland, and was its first president (1907). At the Royal College of Physicians of London he became a member (1867) and a fellow (1873), held several offices, was president (1905–10), and delivered the Harveian oration in 1914. He was deputy chairman (1899–1925) of the Clerical, Medical, and General Life Assurance Society, and in 1896 was president of the Life Assurance Medical Officers' Association. He was closely connected with the Conservative and Unionist Association of the University of London for more than thirty years, and was its president 1909–19. He was created a baronet in 1897 and KCVO in 1901, and received several honorary degrees from English, Scottish, and Irish universities.

Powell was a striking personality. Tall, slight, with an ascetic, clean-shaven, pale face, charming in manner and voice, reticent, correct, cautious, dignified, and kindly, he was widely recognized as an impressive leader. He married twice: first, on 30 October 1873, Juliet (d. 1909), second daughter of Sir John *Bennett, sheriff of London and Middlesex, with whom he had three sons and two daughters; second, on 16 October 1917, Edith Mary Burke (d. 1935), younger daughter of Henry Wood, of 10 Cleveland Square, Hyde Park, London, where they afterwards lived. He died there after a short illness on 15 December 1925, contributions from his pen to the medical press appearing three days before and two weeks after his death. He was succeeded as second baronet by his eldest son, Douglas

(1874–1932), brevet lieutenant-colonel, Royal Welch Fusiliers. The second son was killed in the Second South African War, the third in the First World War.

H. D. ROLLESTON, rev. ANITA McCONNELL

Sources *The Times* (16 Dec 1925), 19a · *The Times* (19 Dec 1925), 15c · *The Times* (23 Dec 1925), 7a · Munk, *Roll*, 4.218–19 · *The Lancet* (26 Dec 1925), 1361–2 · *BMJ* (19 Dec 1925), 1201–2 · personal knowledge (1937) · m. cert. [Juliet Bennett] · m. cert. [Edith Mary Burke] · d. cert.
Archives BL, corresp. with Sir Sydney Cockerell, Add. MS 52743 · Bodl. Oxf., letters to S. A. Acland
Likenesses O. Edis, photograph, c.1905, NPG · W. Stoneman, photograph, 1917, NPG · Spy [L. Ward], caricature, chromolithograph, NPG; repro. in *VF* (28 April 1904) · S. Watson, oils (replica), RCP Lond.
Wealth at death £43,679 2s. 3d.: probate, 29 Jan 1926, CGPLA Eng. & Wales

Powell, Robert (*fl.* 1609–1642), lawyer and legal writer, styled himself, in 1634, an attorney of Wells (Somerset) who had been practising for twenty-five years and who was also a member of New Inn, one of the inns of chancery in London. But apart from what can be learned from his published works little is known about his education or life.

Powell published three short books, a feat that was unusual, but not unique, among members of his branch of the legal profession at the time. Composed in the early to mid-1630s they combine the perspective of a country lawyer, sometimes aiming at a 'vulgar' audience, with a more metropolitan interest in pre-conquest British history and conceptions of the state. Inspired by the work of Sir Thomas Skene, Powell frequently quoted Bracton, parliamentary statutes, and the popular classical authors Cicero and Seneca, as well as more recent historians including Camden and Bacon. He did not often refer to court records or law reports, but his first book, *The Life of Alfred* (1634), combined a narrative based on Asser's contemporary works with an appreciation of Anglo-Saxon laws as translated by the Elizabethan William Lambarde. Dedicated to Walter Curll, the bishop of Winchester, the work stresses the depredations of war while depicting Alfred as an enlightened monarch who founded University College, Oxford, and who eventually reduced the confused 'kingdom to the subordinate rule of orderly government' (Powell, *Alfred*, 70) by instituting national laws and dividing the country into its most ancient units of local government: shires, hundreds, and tithings. In a final section, moreover, Powell attempted to draw detailed parallels between the reign of Charles I and that of Alfred, asking in his conclusion 'where there are such glorious Soveraignes, would it not well become their people to be gracious subjects' (ibid., 153).

The next of Powell's works to be published, *Depopulation Arraigned, Convicted and Condemned by the Lawes of God and Man* (1636), which was dedicated to Attorney-General Sir John Bankes, was an unsolicited apology for the Caroline policy of issuing commissions to investigate enclosures and rural depopulation. Less interesting as a factual account of the contemporary problem than for its approach to political economy, the book pointed to historical examples from the ancient Greeks onwards of attempts by states to protect agriculture. In Powell's view, when people lost their homes and means of making a living it ultimately caused them to become 'aliens and strangers to their nationall government, and the kingdome by that means is in a manner dispeopled and desolated' (Powell, *Depopulation*, 7). He also argued that no claim based on the sanctity of private property rights could stand in the way of using measures such as the royal commissions to find a solution to the problem.

Powell's third book, *A Treatise of the Antiquity, Authority, Uses and Jurisdiction of the Ancient Courts of Leet*, was composed at roughly the same time as the *Life of Alfred*, but various delays prevented it from being published until 1642. Although similar in many respects to previous treatises on leet jurisdiction Powell's historical introduction developed the importance of Alfred as a founder of legal institutions and traced the history of the leet from his time down to the present. The publication also reflects a shift in Powell's political opinions since it includes a lengthy 'Explanation of The old Oath of Legeance', which develops at some length the theory that the subject's duty of obedience was directly related to the sovereign's obligation to protect civil and religious liberties. Castigating the illegality of ship money Powell provided a number of historical examples of clashes between monarch and people over such issues, but his conclusion expressed the hope that King Charles's decision to call parliament would lead to a period of reform and reconciliation.

CHRISTOPHER W. BROOKS

Sources DNB · R. Powell, *The life of Alfred or Alured: the first institutior of surordinate government in this kingdome, and refounder of the University of Oxford. Together with a parallell of our soveraigne lord, K Charles untill this year, 1634* (1634) · R. P. [R. Powell], *Depopulation arraigned, convicted and condemned by the lawes of God and man: a treatise necessary in these times by R. P. of Wells, one of the Societie of New Inne* (1636) · R. Powell, *A treatise of the antiquity, authority, uses and jurisdiction of the ancient courts of leet, or view of franck-pledge, and of subordination of government derived from the institution of Moses, the first legislator: and the first imitation of him in this island of Great Britaine by King Alfred and continued ever since. Together with additions and alterations of the moderne lawes and statutes inquirable at those courts, untill this present yeare, 1642. With a large explication of the old oath of allegiance and the kings royall office of protection annexed* (1642)

Powell, Robert Stephenson Smyth Baden-, first Baron **Baden-Powell** (1857–1941), army officer and founder of the Boy Scouts and Girl Guides, was born at 6 Stanhope Street, Paddington, London, on 22 February 1857, the sixth son of the Revd Baden *Powell (1796–1860), Savilian professor of geometry at Oxford, and his third wife, Henrietta Grace (1824–1914), eldest daughter of Admiral William Henry *Smyth (1788–1865), who claimed descent (almost certainly incorrectly) from John Smyth of Virginia (1580–1631), and who also incorrectly claimed she was a great-niece of Nelson. Sir George Smyth Baden-*Powell was his brother. His father, a liberal theologian, died in 1860. Robert was brought up within a large, closely-knit family, dominated by his mother, who governed her children's

Robert Stephenson Smyth Baden-Powell, first Baron Baden-Powell (1857–1941), by Sir Hubert von Herkomer, 1903

lives well beyond childhood. Manipulative, and obsessively concerned with social status and family advancement, she moved to London and attempted on limited means—her total income was between £700 and £800 p.a.—to promote the careers of her sons. She wrote, 'I am determined not to make any new friends unless very choice people indeed' (Jeal, 24). In 1869 she changed the family name from Powell to Baden-Powell, partly to set her own children apart from their half-siblings and cousins. She also quartered the Powell arms with those of the duke of Baden, to which she was not entitled: surprisingly, the College of Arms agreed to this. Henrietta was not close to Robert (known as Stephe, pronounced Steevie), and he grew up craving parental affection and esteem. He was to show considerable theatrical talents, combined with a deep emotional reserve.

Education   Baden-Powell was educated at home until 1864, at dame-school in Kensington Square, London, and in 1867 briefly at a small private school in Cheshire, before going in 1868 to his father's old preparatory school, Rose Hill, in Tunbridge Wells. In 1870 he was sent to Charterhouse School as a gownboy, on the nomination of the duke of Marlborough, so receiving a free education on the Charterhouse Foundation. He showed little interest in his studies, but was a successful goalkeeper in the school football eleven. He was a keen cadet, and shot for the school at Wimbledon. The school, which moved from London to Godalming, Surrey, in 1872, allowed him to explore local woods, giving him a taste for outdoor adventure, an enthusiasm encouraged by the headmaster, William Haig

Brown (1823–1907). At the same time he showed talent for acting and mimicry, as well as sketching and drawing ambidextrously. Baden-Powell acquired a number of nicknames and was seen as 'a bit of a card'. He made almost no close friends among his peers, but remained a loyal Old Carthusian and was later president of the Old Carthusian Club.

Early army career   Baden-Powell's mother planned he should attend Oxford University, then enter the army as a university candidate. In 1876 he failed the entrance examinations to Balliol College and Christ Church, Oxford, a fact which he later omitted from his autobiography. However, he succeeded in the army examinations, passing second into the cavalry and fifth into the infantry. Excused Sandhurst, because war with Russia seemed imminent and more officers were wanted, he was gazetted lieutenant in the 13th hussars, then stationed in Lucknow, on 11 September 1876. He left England on 30 October. Baden-Powell did not enjoy his first two years: he failed to make friends, was bullied, and found the regiment's élitism overbearing. He went home on sick leave in December 1878. Failing to change regiment, he attended a musketry course at Hythe, Kent, before returning to India in the spring of 1880. Stationed at Kandahar in Afghanistan, in the aftermath of the Second Anglo-Afghan War, he was mainly involved in mapping and reconnaissance work, laying the foundations of his later military reputation. Upon moving to Quetta in the summer of 1881 he met another young officer of the regiment, Kenneth McLaren (d. 1924), whom he nicknamed 'the Boy' for his youthful looks. Sharing enthusiasm for polo and pigsticking, on which Baden-Powell later wrote an authoritative handbook, *Pig Sticking and Hog Hunting* (1889), they lived together and were almost inseparable. The friendship was one of the most important relationships in Baden-Powell's life. He served as an adjutant from 1882 to 1886, and was promoted captain in May 1883. Keen to be noticed, and to supplement his income, he published *Reconnaissance and Scouting* (1883) and regularly sent sketches to the *Daily Graphic*. In November 1884 Baden-Powell's regiment was ordered to Natal in readiness to support Sir Charles Warren's Bechuanaland expedition. He published *Cavalry Instruction* in 1885, which was well received, and returned to England in November.

Baden-Powell had yet to make his mark, and his next nine years were frustrating. His poor academic training led to his failing to secure admission to staff college in November 1886—he blamed an attack of fever—and, lacking a military patron, he was forced in November 1887 to accept the position of aide-de-camp (later he was promoted military secretary) to his uncle, Sir Henry Smyth (1825–1906), the commander-in-chief of Cape Colony. He joined an expedition against the Zulu, and came to admire their discipline, physical beauty, and prowess. He found his official duties irksome, but enjoyed colonial informality. Lacking an alternative, he followed his uncle to Malta in October 1890, with the rank of brevet major. He undertook a number of gentlemanly espionage trips in the eastern Mediterranean between 1890 and 1893, embellished accounts of which appeared in *My Adventures as a Spy* (1915). Promoted major in 1892, he was stationed in Ireland from late 1893.

Baden-Powell's fortunes changed in November 1895, when he was picked by the commander-in-chief, Lord Wolseley, to raise and command the native levy for Sir Francis Scott's expedition against King Prempeh of Asante, inland from the Gold Coast. Heavily dependent on Chief Andoh of Elmina, Baden-Powell's thousand-strong pioneer force participated in the successful invasion of Asante. Scott secured the submission of Prempeh who, to Baden-Powell's regret, chose not to fight. His later account, *The Downfall of Prempeh* (1896), was dedicated to Chief Andoh. It was on this campaign that he began wearing his distinctive wide-brimmed pointed hat: balding, he preferred to be photographed hatted. Still eager to earn more money, he was the *Daily Chronicle*'s correspondent on the expedition, and he sold his sketches to *The Graphic*. Promoted brevet lieutenant-colonel, he was appointed in April 1896 chief staff officer to Sir Frederick Carrington (1833–1913), who had been charged with the suppression of the Ndebele (Matabele) uprising in Southern Rhodesia. He reached Bulawayo in June and was responsible for the administration of logistics. He undertook reconnaissance in the Matopos and was nicknamed by Ndebele 'Impeesa' ('hyena'): in his later accounts he changed it to 'the wolf that never sleeps'. He was in battle, and met Rhodes, whom he greatly admired. Commanding a column of the 7th hussars and others in the Somabula Forest, 100 miles north-west of Bulawayo, he ordered in September 1896 the court martial of, and confirmed the death sentence on, the captured rebel chief Unwini, whom he believed largely responsible for the continuation of the uprising in the area. Unwini was shot. Baden-Powell's action may have shortened the uprising but was of doubtful legality since martial law had not been proclaimed, and it might have destroyed his career. He was exonerated by a court of inquiry but criticized by the British radical press, especially Henry Labouchere's *Truth*. His military reputation enhanced, Baden-Powell returned to England in January 1897 and quickly wrote *The Matabele Campaign* (1897).

In February 1897, on his promotion to lieutenant-colonel, Baden-Powell took command of the 5th dragoon guards. On arrival in India he reduced regimental drill and ceremonial, gave attention to reconnaissance and training (ideas later incorporated into his *Aids to Scouting*, 1899), and was unusual in taking a close personal interest in the welfare of his men. He built them a soda water factory and a temperance club, warned them against venereal disease, and tried unsuccessfully to dissuade them from visiting the local brothel. He also continued his amateur dramatics and practical jokes.

The siege of Mafeking In July 1899, as the situation worsened in South Africa, Baden-Powell was selected for special duties. With the title commander-in-chief, north-west frontier forces, he raised 500 irregulars, with the aim of tying down Boer troops, and maintaining the loyalty of the local natives. On arrival Baden-Powell, extremely vulnerable to Boer attack, decided to occupy the border town of Mafeking, with its 1500 white and 5500 black inhabitants. Because the town was not easily defended, Baden-Powell had to improvise defence works, at the same time maintaining civil and native morale and continuing to harry the Boers besieging the town. It is estimated that during October and November 1899 some 6000 to 8000 Boer troops were in the vicinity, deployments which significantly reduced their military strength in other areas. The siege lasted 219 days, and Baden-Powell's reports, with their cheeky and jaunty style, increasingly attracted public interest at home.

As the siege lengthened Baden-Powell's priorities had to be the sustaining of morale as food supplies diminished, while remaining prepared for a Boer attack. This he achieved largely through force of personality, using fully his theatrical, reconnaissance, and organizational abilities. He ordered the attack (26 December) on the Boer outpost, the Game Tree Fort. The operation was bungled, causing unnecessary casualties: the worst blunder of the siege. In early January his difficulties increased on his being told by his military superiors to hold out until May 21, six to eight weeks longer than he had been led to expect. News of Mafeking's final relief reached London on the evening of 18 May, and provoked an outburst of popular patriotism throughout the country, and in many other parts of the English-speaking world. Baden-Powell acquired a heroic status. Later historians have disagreed about the significance of the Mafeking crowds, but the celebrations clearly crossed existing class, religious, and political divides. The *Manchester Guardian* concluded:

> And the story is all the more moving because the defence is an achievement not so much of professional soldiers as, to a great extent, of men and women before the war we should not have been able to distinguish from the average Englishmen in the colonies. (*Manchester Guardian*, 19 May 1900, 9b)

Baden-Powell's role in the defence of Mafeking gave him a unique status for the rest of his life.

Baden-Powell was promoted major-general in August 1900 and ordered by the new commander-in-chief, Lord Roberts, to form a police force to aid pacification once the war was concluded. In setting up the South African constabulary—for which he designed an idiosyncratic uniform with American stetsons and special badges—Baden-Powell, with his views on training and welfare, faced much obstruction from the military and civilian authorities, still engaged in fighting the war. In June 1901 he had to take home leave from exhaustion, and by his return in January 1902 the force was fully established.

Inspector-general of cavalry In late 1902 Baden-Powell was appointed inspector-general of cavalry (from May 1904 redesignated inspector of cavalry), his first War Office posting. He did not enjoy it, disliking a desk-bound routine, and having little talent for military politics. His popular status created jealousies, and senior cavalry officers resisted his attacks on their expenses. His principal concern was with the quality of cavalry training, and as part of his efforts at improvement he founded in 1904 the cavalry training school at Netheravon on Salisbury Plain,

Wiltshire, and in 1906 was one of the founders of the *Cavalry Journal* (see Warren, *EngHR*, 1986, 384, n. 1). In the contemporary debates about the future role of the cavalry Baden-Powell expressed his belief that it would have to adopt a more individualistic and reconnaissance role, using the rifle as its main weapon, rather than retain its traditional emphasis on mass formations, *esprit de corps*, and the use of the lance. His *Cavalry Training* (1904), reflecting these views, prompted fierce resistance from the conservatives, led by Lieutenant-General Sir John French (1852–1925) and Major-General Douglas Haig (1861–1928). In subsequent editions the offending sections were removed. Baden-Powell later acknowledged that he had not anticipated the effects of mechanization on the role of the cavalry.

Scouting for Boys Baden-Powell's popular status also made him an attractive figure to voluntary organizations seeking his endorsement. In particular he became aware that his military manual *Aids to Scouting* (1899) was being used by church organizations, such as the Boys' Brigade and the Young Men's Christian Association (YMCA), and also that the popular press could be useful in promoting his own reputation and ideas. He became a vice-president of the Boys' Brigade in May 1903, and conducted a major inspection at Glasgow in April 1904. Gradually he became convinced that his training methods, with their focus on individual responsibility, fitness, and reconnaissance, could be used in a non-military environment. He also absorbed domestic concerns about physical deterioration, moral degeneracy, juvenile crime, blind-alley employments, 'wasters' and 'slackers'. R. B. Haldane (1856–1928), secretary of state for war, persuaded him that character training should be at the centre of any scheme of boy instruction. Although pressed by Roberts and the National Service League to back the campaign for compulsory military training, Baden-Powell had already identified the scout's training as the best way to train future citizens. Meetings with the Legion of Frontiersmen and the American naturalist Ernest Thompson Seton (1860–1946)—founder of the American boys' organization the Woodcraft Indians—gave him more ideas and encouraged him to place his training ideas in an outdoor context, something consistent with his upbringing and professional experience. A growing contact with the newspaper magnate Sir C. Arthur Pearson (1866–1921) led him to write a training manual for boys in the summer of 1907, and to hold an experimental camp on Brownsea Island in Poole harbour, Dorset, in July. Twenty-two boys from public schools and the local Boys' Brigade were divided into four patrols with animal and bird names, and did swimming, fieldcraft exercises, scouting games, and survival training, led by Baden-Powell, wearing long shorts and an old trilby, assisted by 'Boy' McLaren: six of the Brownsea boys later died on the western front. *Scouting for Boys* was published in fortnightly parts in January 1908. Within each of its chapters (or camp fire yarns, as they were called) Baden-Powell brought together all his training ideals, placing them in an attractive camping and frontier-based environment. Linked to this were recommendations on how the individual scout might improve himself in the company of other scouts, so as to become a happier individual and better citizen. Underpinning this approach was a personal pledge to keep the scout promise (that 'on his honour' he would be loyal to God and the king, that he would help other people at all times, and keep a series of simply expressed scout laws). Separate sections were included for church and youth leaders on how to use these ideas in their own programmes. The book was an eclectic potpourri of advice, stories, and games in the style of the popular boys' journalism of the day, and was an immediate success. Through its many editions and translations it has remained continuously in print, and is estimated to have sold more copies worldwide than almost any other text, excluding the Bible.

The growth of scouting and guiding Scout troops sprang up quickly around the country, some independently and others attached to existing organizations such as the Boys' Brigade and the YMCA. Early examples included those in Glasgow, Birkenhead, and Croydon. Possibly to his surprise, Baden-Powell found himself impelled to form his own organization, the Boy Scouts, during 1908. From then on his life was inextricably connected with the movement he had founded. He designed a scout uniform that was practical, attractive, and redolent of frontier adventure: soon it was recognized everywhere, and it was used virtually unchanged until the 1960s. Having been promoted lieutenant-general in June 1907 he was commander of the Northumbrian division of the new Territorial Force from 1908 to 1910. As scout troops were set up around the country he found the small office in London, paid for by Pearson, increasingly inadequate. Rivalries and misunderstandings proliferated, of which the most troublesome was with Sir Francis Vane, bt (1861–1934). Centred on London, and involving clashes of personality as well as principled arguments about militarism and the hierarchical nature of the early headquarters structure, this dispute threatened the existence of the fledgeling organization in the late autumn of 1909. A small breakaway association, the British Boy Scouts, was established with Vane as its president. Impatient with bureaucratic structures, Baden-Powell found himself forced into forming a national committee to support the growing number of local associations. The team was brought together after the first national rally of scouts at the Crystal Palace, London, in September 1909. Sea Scouts were introduced in 1910 with Baden-Powell's brother Warington (1847–1921) writing their training manual. In March 1910 Baden-Powell retired from the army to devote himself fully to the scouts. He secured royal patronage, George V reviewed scouts in Windsor Great Park in July 1911, and a royal charter was granted in January 1912. It is estimated that there were some 100,000 scouts by 1910.

Such was the public interest generated that girls also wanted to become scouts. At first Baden-Powell seems to have anticipated a co-educational movement, but facing criticism that a scout's training would encourage tomboyish attitudes, he agreed to produce a separate training manual for girls, in association with his sister Agnes. Even so, many elements of *Scouting for Boys* were included in *How Girls can Help Build up the Empire: a Handbook for Girl Guides* (1912).

The Girl Guides Association was formally incorporated in September 1915, and both movements spread widely, at first largely in the English-speaking world, but also in Europe, and later in Africa and Asia. Within the United Kingdom Girl Guides Baden-Powell's wife, Olave (1889–1977) [*see* Powell, Olave St Clair Baden-, Lady Baden-Powell], whom he had married in 1912, became increasingly dominant; with his backing she replaced and excluded Agnes Baden-Powell and became chief commissioner in 1916.

Baden-Powell always insisted that individual character training was at the centre of his scouting method, rejecting accusations of militarism and resisting overtures from Roberts and others. Nevertheless among the early scouting volunteers his ideas were capable of more than one interpretation, and Baden-Powell steered a slightly uneven course on the militarism question between 1908 and 1910. Many of his adult enthusiasts came from among existing church workers with boys. As a result his character-training scheme had to acquire a more explicit religious and moral underpinning than was contained in *Scouting for Boys*, yet without losing its non-denominational character. Before and during the First World War Baden-Powell resisted attempts to incorporate the scouts into a national cadet scheme. Rather he argued that a war requiring mobilization of the nation's resources created opportunities for trained civilian war-service by boys and girls. Of the many examples the scouts' national coast-watching scheme was the best known. Under pressure to form a section for younger boys, Baden-Powell in 1916 started the Wolf Cubs, based partly on his friend and admirer Rudyard Kipling's *Jungle Books*: Kipling became an honorary scout commissioner. Baden-Powell later provided for young men over eighteen, which he did less convincingly around the theme of chivalric dedication and service in his *Rovering to Success* (1922). A lasting advantage of the scout movement has been its benefactors' generosity, locally and nationally. For example, the 6th Richmond, founded in 1916, still uses the building donated by Lady Archer. In 1918 the movement received a major benefaction, Gilwell Park, Essex, bought for it by a Scottish rubber magnate, W. F. de Bois MacLaren. There Baden-Powell established the movement's national and international training centre for scouters. He preferred it to the London Imperial Headquarters and was often there. By 1918 scouts and guides were established features of national life in Britain and the empire, and, with variations, throughout the world.

The inter-war years From 1918 to 1939 the scout and guide movement grew worldwide, though banned in totalitarian states. In Britain the movement's rivals, the older uniformed organizations and the newer left-wing organizations including the Woodcraft Folk and the Young Communist League—the latter in 1927 sent Baden-Powell a coffin—did not approach them in popularity. With their global appeal and unifying philosophy scouts and guides were well placed to express the prevalent internationalism, in ways which included great international camps (jamborees), of which the first was held at Olympia, London, in August 1920, and at which Baden-Powell was proclaimed chief scout of the world. Scouting and guiding were seen as a junior League of Nations, and Baden-Powell and his wife travelled much, encouraging and supporting both movements, and being accorded a reception similar to that of a head of state. Nor were these activities simply symbolic. As the founder, Baden-Powell tried to resolve differences and disputes in very different cultural, political, and religious circumstances, particularly in India and South Africa, where he was only partially successful. By 1939 the total world membership of the scout and guide movement was about 5 million.

Marriage and family life Before his return to England in 1902 Baden-Powell's life had been almost exclusively military and familial, the latter dominated by his mother. His closest personal relations had been with McLaren, and he had had no intimate female liaisons. Increasingly put under pressure to marry by his mother, he was attracted by the idea of family life and having his own children, and he made several proposals of marriage. He was apparently not attracted to women of his own age, preferring older widows or much younger women. It has been alleged that he was a repressed homosexual. In January 1912, on a world tour, he met on SS *Arcadian* Olave St Clair Soames. Thirty-two years his junior, she also had had a complicated family and emotional upbringing. They were immediately attracted to each other. For her, he represented a heroic figure, cast in a mould of idealism; for him, she reflected energetic, enthusiastic, unconventional, physical femininity. They were married at St Peter's Church, Parkstone, Dorset, on 31 October 1912. Nervous prior to his engagement, Baden-Powell found early married life difficult, its physical side giving him intense headaches and disturbing dreams, which only ceased on their sleeping apart. But after the birth of their three children (a boy, followed by two girls), it was a happy, supportive, companionate partnership, in which each was dedicated, almost exclusively, to scouting and guiding. Baden-Powell wanted to have the ideal scouting and guiding family, but his status and hopes were apparently an oppressive burden for his son, (Arthur Robert) Peter Baden-Powell (1913–1962), despite the great efforts made by his now elderly father to adjust his excessive ambitions for his son. All his children married in his lifetime, and his younger daughter, Betty, later took over her parents' role as head of the movement's first family.

Old age Baden-Powell was increasingly honoured at home and internationally. Having been knighted in 1909, he became a baronet in December 1922, GCVO in 1923, and, recommended by Ramsay MacDonald, first Baron Baden-Powell of Gilwell in September 1929, an honour announced at the international jamboree held at Arrowe Park, Birkenhead, to celebrate the 'coming of age' of scouting. Later he was appointed to the Order of Merit (1937), and awarded the Carnegie Wateler peace prize (1937). Previously, he had been master of the Mercers' Company (1913). He received many honorary degrees—including an Oxford DCL (1923) and a Cambridge LLD (1931)—and foreign decorations. Throughout the inter-war period Baden-Powell continued to write extensively on scouting, as well as commenting on contemporary affairs in a light, journalistic style. At first he admired the apparent dynamism of Mussolini's Italy and Hitler's Germany, but later he revised his opinion. Nevertheless he continued to be naively optimistic about the value of continuing the contacts between youth organizations across Europe. Like many of his generation he was more fearful of Bolshevism than fascism, and he supported the Munich agreement. His opinions on national and international politics attracted leftist criticism then and later. Not a systematic thinker, Baden-Powell failed to see that equality of opportunity could not be achieved by voluntary action alone. In fact, he had little time for politics of any kind. In matters of religion he was formally an Anglican, but was extremely intolerant of denominational differences, founding his simple faith on the worship of nature and doing good to others.

In October 1938 Baden-Powell and his wife retired to their bungalow Paxtu, at Nyeri in Kenya. There he lived quietly, reading and corresponding; typically, his last memorandum was in protest against a proposed compulsory state youth training service in late 1940. He gradually weakened, and he died peacefully at Paxtu on 8 January 1941. He was buried in St Peter's churchyard, Nyeri, the next day, as was his widow in 1977. Among many memorial plaques, both lives are commemorated in Westminster Abbey. He was succeeded as baron by his son, Peter, who defied his own mother's wish that he should not take his father's title 'since there was only one Lord Baden-Powell' (Jeal, 575).

Personality Baden-Powell was slim and spare in physique, and of medium height. Although he enjoyed the uniforms and insignia of success his personal tastes were simple, tending to the austere. He slept on an open verandah for most of his married life. His principal recreations were fishing and sketching. He could be stubborn and eccentric, and not everyone enjoyed his taste for practical jokes and amateur dramatics, but almost all his later scouting associates were inspired by his vision, versatility, and energy which, in many cases, transformed their lives; he remained for them, simply, 'the Chief'.

Assessment Baden-Powell's remarkable career has been more argued over since his death than during his lifetime. In 1900 he was a popular patriotic hero, seen as exemplifying all that was best in the British character. In 1941 he died, lauded as a figure of global significance, having founded the two largest youth organizations in the world. Since 1941 both reputations have been attacked. Some historians (Gardner, Willan, and Pakenham) have alleged that at Mafeking his theatrical style was merely self-promotion, covering military incompetence and indecision, as well as hiding racial assumptions, which led him

to starve Africans, and expose them to greater danger than white inhabitants. The most detailed and balanced examination of the evidence (Jeal) refuted these charges, while recognizing that Baden-Powell failed in his later accounts to acknowledge sufficiently the African, especially BaRolong, military contribution. Baden-Powell's successful defence of Mafeking was not strategically significant after its first two months: it proved, however, to be a heroic episode of considerable domestic importance in one of the first wars in which civilian reaction to military events was a critical factor in the overall conduct of war. Commentators have also focused on Baden-Powell's intentions in writing *Scouting for Boys*. For some, the book reflected all the anxieties of the Edwardian governing classes—physical deterioration, the threat of class-based politics, fears of military and imperial weakness—and the need to establish new forms of social control (Springhall, Rosenthal). For others, it was an innovative book, providing an imaginative, recreative training programme in the outdoors, based on non-denominational religious and moral principles (Warren, Wilkinson, Jeal). In these interpretations, the book's broader social purpose lay in the better training of future citizens and happier, more fulfilled individuals. This was to be achieved through personal self-improvement and team participation, linked to a readily understood moral and spiritual code, based on an inclusive brotherhood. Both interpretations can find supporting evidence in Baden-Powell's writings between 1900 and 1910.

Taking the longer view, the Boy Scout and Girl Guide movements remained very much the creation of their founder, even though both he and they showed a considerable capacity to adapt and change. Each was dedicated to the individual development of character through a training scheme which was based on the small group (the patrol), and each focused on ideas of voluntary social or civic service as a means of individual fulfilment and social improvement. Both sought the development of the whole person, physically, mentally, and spiritually, and were committed to ideals of a common humanity, believing that this informal training in personal development could be best achieved through camping and outdoor activities. As such, both organizations were seen as a progressive force by almost all commentators in their founder's lifetime. Only in his final years, in the United Kingdom at least, did it become clear that scouting and guiding had to be part of the range of voluntary and statutory provision for the development of future citizens.

ALLEN WARREN

Sources T. Jeal, *Baden-Powell* (1989) · *DNB* · W. Hillcourt and Olave, Lady Baden-Powell, *Baden-Powell: two lives of a hero* (1964) · E. E. Reynolds, *Baden-Powell: a biography of Lord Baden-Powell of Gilwell, OM, GCMG, GCVO, KCB* (1942) · R. S. S. Baden-Powell, *Scouting for boys: a handbook for instruction in good citizenship* (1908) · H. Collis, F. Hurll, and R. Hazlewood, *B.-P.'s scouts: an official history of the Boy Scouts Association* (1961) · R. Kerr, *The story of the Girl Guides* (1932) · J. Springhall, *Youth, empire, and society: British youth movements, 1883–1940* (1977) · B. Gardner, *Mafeking, a Victorian legend* (1966) · T. Pakenham, *The Boer War* (1979) · B. Willan, 'The siege of Mafeking', *The South African War: the Anglo-Boer War, 1899–1902*, ed. P. Warwick and S. B. Spies

(1980), 139–60 · A. Warren, 'Sir Robert Baden-Powell, the Scout movement and citizen training in Great Britain, 1900–1920', *EngHR*, 101 (1986), 376–98 · A. Warren, 'Citizens of the empire: Baden-Powell, the Scouts, Guides and an imperial ideal', *Imperialism and popular culture*, ed. J. M. Mackenzie (1986), 232–57 · A. Warren, '"Mothers for the Empire"? The Girl Guides Association in Britain, 1909–1939', *Making imperial mentalities: socialisation and British imperialism*, ed. J. Mangan (1990), 96–110 · A. Warren, 'Popular manliness: Baden-Powell, scouting and the development of manly character', *Manliness and morality: middle class masculinity in Britain and America, 1880–1940*, ed. J. A. Mangan and J. Walvin (1987), 199–220 · A. Warren, 'Baden-Powell: two lives of a hero or two heroic lives?', *Exemplary lives*, ed. G. Cubitt and A. Warren (2000) · M. Dedman, 'Baden-Powell, militarism and the "invisible contributors" to the Boy Scout scheme', *Twentieth Century British History*, 4/3 (1993), 201–23 · M. Rosenthal, *The character factory: Baden-Powell and the origins of the Boy Scout movement* (1986) · R. H. MacDonald, *Sons of the empire: the frontier and the Boy Scout movement, 1890–1918* (1993) · P. Wilkinson, 'A study of English uniformed youth movements, 1883–1935', MA diss., U. Wales, 1968 · Burke, *Peerage* (1999) · *Hart's Army List* (1891) · *Army List* (1920) · T. M. Proctor, '(Uni)forming youth: Girl Guides and Boy Scouts in Britain, 1908–39', *History Workshop Journal*, 45 (1998), 103–34 · *CGPLA Eng. & Wales* (1941)

Archives Mercers' Hall, London, corresp. and papers · NAM, staff diaries and papers · Scout Association, London, corresp. and papers relating to scouting | BL, papers relating to siege of Mafeking, Add. MS 50255 · BL, corresp. with Macmillans, Add. MS 55252 · Bodl. Oxf., corresp. with H. A. Gwynne · Bodl. Oxf., letters to Lord Hanworth · Bodl. RH, letters to Sir Edward Garraway · CUL, corresp. with Lord Hardinge · NAM, letters to Earl Roberts · NL Scot., daily orders issued at Mafeking · NRA Scotland, priv. coll., letters to Sir J. S. Ewart · W. Sussex RO, letters to F. I. Maxse | FILM Scout Association, Baden-Powell House, Queen's Gate, London | SOUND Scout Association, Baden-Powell House, Queen's Gate, London

Likenesses G. F. Watts, oils, exh. RA 1902, Charterhouse School, London · H. von Herkomer, oils, 1903, NPG [*see illus.*] · S. Slocombe, chalk drawing, 1916, NPG · A. Drury, bronze bust, 1918?, Baden-Powell House · W. Stoneman, photograph, 1927, NPG · D. Jagger, oils, 1929, Baden-Powell House, London · D. Jagger, oils, 1930, Mercers' Company, London · A. G. Atkinson, bronze relief, c.1931, Mercers' Company, London · S. Elwes, oils, 1931, Girl Guides Association headquarters, London · bronze bust, c.1931, Girl Guides Association headquarters, London · A. John, drawing, 1936, collection of the 13th/18th royal hussars · stained-glass window, after 1941, St James-the-Less, Sussex Gardens, London · D. Potter, statue, 1961, Baden-Powell House, London · Ape Junior, caricature, Hentschel-colourtype, NPG; repro. in *VF* (19 April 1911) · Drawl, caricature, chromolithograph, NPG; repro. in *VF* (5 July 1900) · W. Stoneman, photographs, NPG · group portrait, photograph, NPG

Wealth at death £7613 8s. 2d.: probate, 11 Nov 1941, *CGPLA Eng. & Wales*

Powell, Roger (1896–1990), bookbinder, was born in London on 17 May 1896, the elder of the two sons of Oswald Byrom Powell (*b*. 1867) and his wife, Winifred Cobb. Between 1907 and 1915 he was educated at Bedales School, of which his father was a co-founder. After leaving school he served in the First World War, first in the Royal Hampshire regiment, later in the Royal Flying Corps in Egypt, where he became 'a very competent signals officer' (Pickwoad, 3). On leaving the army he did not immediately take up bookbinding, but ran a poultry farm with his brother between 1921 and 1930. On 8 September 1924 he married Rita Glanville Harvey (*d*. 1988). They had a son, David, and twin daughters, Ann and Jill.

Powell began training as a binder in 1930 at the Central School of Arts and Crafts, London, where he was taught by Peter McLeish, George Frewin, William Matthews, and Douglas Cockerell. When Powell's own first bindery, in Welwyn Garden City, ran into financial difficulties in 1935, Cockerell invited him to join the firm of Cockerell & Son in Letchworth. Powell became a full partner only a year later. During the 1930s he also taught part-time at the Central School, and in 1943 he took over Sandy Cockerell's position at the Royal College of Art, where he remained until his retirement in 1956. He was noted for teaching less by demonstration than by discussion and anecdote. Peter Waters remembers that:

> A typical Powell day at the RCA was heralded by the sound of his cane in the corridor leading to the bindery, accompanied by a mixture of whistling and humming in perfect harmony from his part in the latest production of a Gilbert and Sullivan operetta … He … would remove his coat, then sit down to finish *The Times* crossword. I might be binding a book across the room and he would look up and say, 'I don't think that's a very good idea do you?' and then, after completing the crossword, expound at length on what I was doing. (Donnelly and Waters, *New Bookbinder*, 82)

Other colleagues remember that he would frequently bring in a shoulder-bag of his own honey for sale to staff and students, while others have commented on his distinctive appearance. A photograph taken on his ninetieth birthday shows him with a long, strong-boned face and marvellously alive and humorous eyes, and with the exceptionally bushy eyebrows which he himself jokingly attributed to the fumes from the egg glair used in gold-tooling (ibid., 84).

After dissolving his partnership with Cockerell in 1947 Powell moved to The Slade, Froxfield, in Hampshire. It was here that he did much of the work for which he is now remembered. In 1953 he was commissioned to rebind the Book of Kells for Trinity College, Dublin. His successful completion of this exceptionally demanding job led to further work on early manuscripts for the Royal Irish Academy, the University of Aberdeen, and Lichfield Cathedral, among others. It also earned him an honorary master of arts degree from Trinity College. In 1956 Powell entered into a business partnership with Peter Waters, which lasted until 1971. They were known both for their conservation and for their design work. As well as receiving commissions to bind a Cranach Press *Hamlet*, an Ashendene Press *Golden Asse*, and a Kelmscott *Chaucer*, among many others, both Waters and Powell played an important role in the rescue and conservation of the books damaged in the Florence flood of 1966.

For Powell the conservation and design aspects of the craft were complementary; as Nicholas Pickwood observes, Powell's design sense was 'very much fashioned by his knowledge of technique and function, inclining towards a formality of design which matches the formality required by an efficient working structure' (Pickwoad, 4). Thus, Powell's resignation of his honorary fellowship of Designer Bookbinders in February 1979 was indicative of a wider dispute about the purpose of binding. While many binders have, since the 1950s or 1960s, increasingly been drawn to treat the book as an art object, Powell was always highly resistant to 'anything which is likely to prejudice [the book's] durability or ease of handling' (Pickwoad, 11). It is perhaps for this reason that—despite his designs for the *Divina commedia*, for Blake's *Jerusalem*, and for *Troilus and Cressida* during the 1970s—he concentrated increasingly on conservation in the last two decades of his working life. In what has at times been an acrimonious dispute among binders, it says much for Powell's achievement that even his opponents concede his importance to the craft, and to the collector and binder Bernard Middleton he is simply 'one of the most important and influential bookbinders of the last hundred years and, arguably, of any period' (Middleton, 87). Powell was made an OBE in 1976. He died at his home in Froxfield on 16 October 1990.   JANE GRIFFITHS

Sources A. Donnelly and P. Waters, 'Roger Powell, 1896–1990: reminiscences of his family and working life', *Roger Powell, the compleat binder: liber amicorum*, ed. J. L. Sharpe (1996) • B. Middleton, 'Roger Powell: an appreciation', *New Bookbinder*, 11 (1991), 87–90 • N. Pickwoad, 'Powell multiscient', *New Bookbinder*, 2 (1982), 3–16 • R. H. Lewis, *Fine bookbinding in the twentieth century* (1984) • D. A. Harrop, 'Craft binders at work III: Roger Powell', *Book Collector*, 22 (1973), 479–86 • C. Clarkson, 'Annotated bibliography of works by and about Roger Powell', *Roger Powell, the compleat binder: liber amicorum*, ed. J. L. Sharpe (1996), 57–67 • G. Pedlurbridge, 'The compleat binder: the arts and crafts legacy of Roger Powell', *Roger Powell, the compleat binder: liber amicorum*, ed. J. L. Sharpe (1996), 34–56 • A. G. Cains, 'Roger Powell's innovation in book conservation: the early Irish manuscripts repaired and bound, 1953–81', *Roger Powell, the compleat binder: liber amicorum*, ed. J. L. Sharpe (1996) • N. Barker, *The Independent* (19 Oct 1990) • A. Donnelly and P. Waters, 'Roger Powell, 1896–1990: reminiscences of his family and working life', *New Bookbinder*, 11 (1991), 81–7 • H. M. Nixon, *Roger Powell and Peter Waters* (The Slade, Froxfield, 1965)

Likenesses photographs, repro. in Middleton, 'Roger Powell' • photographs, repro. in Donnelly and Waters, 'Roger Powell' (1996)

Wealth at death house at Froxfield worth several hundred thousand pounds; apparently poor business skills and frequent cash flow problems: Donnelly and Waters, 'Roger Powell'

Powell, Thomas (*d. c.*1635), lawyer and writer, of Welsh parentage, came from the same family as Sir Edward Powell, who became master of requests in 1622. Thomas Powell was described as 'Londino-Cambrensis' on a number of his works and, when he entered Gray's Inn in London on 30 January 1593, his home was given as Diserth, Radnorshire. Nothing is known of his early life and education.

Powell published his first work, a long poem, *Loves Leprosie*, in 1598, dedicating the work to Sir Robert Sidney. The poem tells the story of the death of Achilles, treacherously slain by Paris, after he had arranged to meet Polyxena in the temple of Apollo. Achilles' death was in revenge for his killing of Hector, who, in turn, had prevented the marriage of Achilles and Polyxena. A second long poem, *The Passionate Poet, with a Description of the Thracian Ismarus* (1601), was dedicated to Lady Frances, countess of Kildare (who is later mentioned in *Vertues Due*, and so may have been one of Powell's early patrons). It is another work inspired by classical settings and consists mainly of a series of descriptions of the variety of trees—including vine, olive, myrtle, oak, bay—found near Athens.

Powell's verse has not fared well at the hands of the few critics who have read his work, and he is generally considered to be incompetent and obscure as a writer (though this may be because he tried to imitate the harsh rhythms and style fashionable among young writers in London in the 1590s). He wrote little more separately published poetry—though his later published works are interspersed with a number of poems—probably because his legal career started to take off. His first prose work was *A Welch Bayte to Spare Provender, or, A Looking Back at the Times* (1603), dedicated to Henry Wriothesley, earl of Southampton, a warning of the dangers to the state from both Catholics and dissenters; Powell praised Elizabeth's moderate religious policy, warned of the impending dangers of the succession, and looked forward to James's plans to unite the people of England and Scotland. The book, containing poems to Lady Elizabeth Brydges, Sir Thomas Knevet, and Sir Edward Dyer, was called in and the publisher, Valentine Simms, was ordered to pay a fine of 13*s*. 6*d*. for printing it without a licence. The entry in the Stationers' register also refers to a collection of ballads printed by Simms, which probably indicates that Powell had infringed others' rights to the material rather than incurred any official objection to the work. In the same year Powell published *Vertues Due, or, A True Modell of the Life of the Right Honourable Katherine Howard*—dedicated to her widower, Charles Howard, earl of Nottingham, the lord high admiral. This lament for Katherine Howard's death was written in sestets and emphasized her chastity, comparing her to Diana and Astrea. A Latin dedicatory poem by 'T. P.', prefaced to John Ford's *Fames Memoriall, or, The Earle of Devonshire Deceased* (1606) may also be by Powell.

Powell was appointed solicitor-general in the Welsh marches on 13 November 1613, a position he held until 5 August 1622. He appears to have been searching assiduously through the legal records in the chancery, the Tower of London, and the exchequer in this period—research which was to form the basis of his most important works. In 1622 he published *Direction for the Search of Records Remaining in the Chancerie, Tower, Exchequer, &*, prefaced with dedicatory poems to James, Prince Charles, William Noy, reader at Lincoln's Inn, Sir James Ley, lord chief justice, Sir Edward Powell, master of his majesty's requests, James, Viscount Doncaster, and Sir Thomas Coventry. In the address to the reader Powell refers to his twenty years' work in these archives in order to help lawyers prepare for court cases.

In 1623 Powell published *The Attourneys Academy, or, The Manner of Proceding upon any Suite*, 'The first printed treatise on common-law proceedure' (Baker, 96). This work was again dedicated to the king and others such as Sir James Ley and Francis, Lord Verulam, Viscount St Albans, and was reprinted three times in the next seven years. It listed and described all the procedures to be followed in English courts, giving details of the requisite fees and locations, in order to benefit all the king's subjects. There was an extensive table appended for ease of use. He also published *Wheresoever you See mee, Trust unto your Selfe, or, The Mysterie* of *Lending and Borrowing*, a survey of all the types of creditor and debtor, dedicated to 'the two famous universities, the seminaries of so many desperate debtors, Ram Ally and Milford Lane'. This may have been satirical in intent, but it provides a wealth of information about credit practices in the early 1600s.

On 14 September 1623 Powell petitioned James to request the co-operation of judges and court officers to give him all the necessary information on court fees and other details so that his manuscript, 'Direction for the search of records', a work that Powell claimed would be more useful than the Domesday Book, could be completed. James granted the request and *The Reporterie of Records at Westminster* (1631), an extensive catalogue of the records in the chancery, the Tower, and the exchequer, was the result (though it is clear that not all the work is by Powell).

In 1627 Powell published *The Attornies Almanacke*, a list of courts designed to help those who have to move 'any person, cause, or Record, from an inferior Court to any of the higher Courts at Westminster'. In the same year he is mentioned in a letter from the mayor of Monmouth to the privy council dated 7 September, indicating that he had not paid his share of the loan money assessed on the town. *Tom of All Trades, or, The Plain Pathway to Preferment* was published in 1631, a dialogue between the author's fictional persona and a gentleman from Northampton dealing with the way to bring up children, provide for their education, and prepare them for a trade or profession. It contains significant information on English education, schools, and the expectations of the minor gentry in Caroline England, and was reprinted in 1635 as *The Art of Thriving, or, The Plaine Way to Preferment* (together with *The Mysterie of Lending and Borrowing*). Powell died probably about 1635, leaving 'The Breath of an Unfeed Lawyer, or, Beggers Round' in manuscript (Cambridge University Library).   ANDREW HADFIELD

Sources CSP dom., 1580–1625 · STC, 1475–1640 · *The reports of Sir John Spelman*, ed. J. H. Baker, 2, SeldS, 94 (1978), vol. 2 · Arber, *Regs. Stationers*, vols. 2–3 · W. C. Hazlitt, *Hand-book to the popular, poetical and dramatic literature of Great Britain* (1867) · E. Brydges, *The British bibliographer*, 4 vols. (1810–14) · J. P. Collier, ed., *A bibliographical and critical account of the rarest books in the English language*, 2 vols. (1865) · T. Warton, *The history of English poetry*, rev. edn, ed. R. Price, 4 vols. (1824) · J. Ritson, *Bibliographia poetica* (1802) · N&Q, 10 (1854), 366–7 · DNB

Powell, Thomas (1776–*c*.1863), composer and instrumentalist, was born in London. He studied composition and the cello, and in 1799 was elected a professional member of the Royal Society of Musicians. In 1811 he married, and settled for a time in Dublin as a teacher of music, his pupils including the duke of Leinster and a son of Lord Leitrim. He then spent some time in Edinburgh and Glasgow before eventually returning to London in 1826. It is reported that he performed his own cello concerto at the Haymarket Theatre and, on one occasion, stood in at the last minute for the celebrated Robert Lindley there.

Powell's compositions are numerous, and include arrangements of popular and classical airs for piano, violin, and harp, as well as for the cello. Other, more substantial, works include an overture for full orchestra, an *Introduction and Fugue for the Organ as Performed at the Cathedrals of Christchurch and St Patrick at Dublin* (1825), *Three Grand Sonatas for Pianoforte, with Obbligato Accompaniment for Violoncello*, op. 15 (*c*.1825), duets and trios for combinations of violins and cellos, and fifteen violin concertos. Powell was apparently a very proficient artist on several instruments and also possessed a bass voice with a wide range. His style of cello playing was likened at the time to that of the prominent B. H. Romberg. He died in Edinburgh in or about 1863.   DAVID J. GOLBY

Sources [J. S. Sainsbury], ed., *A dictionary of musicians*, 2 vols. (1824) · Brown & Stratton, *Brit. mus.* · [Clarke], *The Georgian era: memoirs of the most eminent persons*, 4 (1834), 546 · J. D. Champlin, ed., *Cyclopedia of music and musicians*, 3 vols. (1888–90) · DNB

Powell, Thomas (1779–1863), coal owner, was born in Monmouthshire (at Monmouth or Chepstow) on 6 January 1779, the son of John Powell. No records of his early life and education have been found. His substantial achievement was to lay the foundations of the Powell Duffryn Company, the most widely known name in the Welsh coal industry.

Powell began his commercial career around 1810 as a timber merchant. He became interested in Monmouthshire's newly developing bituminous (house) coal industry, which at the time was mostly operated through single, small-scale enterprises. Powell's ambitions were wider. In 1837, along with Thomas Protheroe and Joseph Latch, he made a determined effort to control Monmouthshire coal prices by forming the Newport Coal Company, through which the main proprietors were to sell their coal. Before 1840 he had already become the greatest single figure in the bituminous coal trade, and by 1841 he owned four collieries—Gelli-gaer, Gelli-groes, Bryn, and, in partnership with Protheroe, Buttery Hatch—which employed 431 men and boys.

Powell was also exceptionally quick to recognize the potential of the new trade in steam coal from Cardiff, and perceptive in not following its legendary pioneer, Lucy Thomas, into the Merthyr valley in the 1830s. Instead he moved to the virtually unworked Aberdâr (Cynon) valley and rapidly opened a succession of collieries to serve this new market: Old Dyffryn (Tir Ffounder) was sunk first (1840–42), then came Upper Dyffryn (1844–6), Middle Dyffryn (1850), Lower Dyffryn and Cwm Pennar (1850–54), Abergwawr (1855), and Cwmdare (1852–4). Thomas Powell was unique at this stage of the development of the coal industry of south Wales. By the time he was sixty and heavily handicapped by deafness he had built up a similar supremacy in the business of steam coal to the one he had achieved in the bituminous coal trade. At a time when even the most enterprising were unlikely to be involved in more than two collieries, he ruled over a multi-pit undertaking.

Powell's other activities—in banking, docks, and railways (he was on the original board of the Taff Vale Railway)—were influenced by and undertaken to support his coal enterprises. By 1862 he owned sixteen pits and exported 700,000 tons of coal a year. After his death his property passed to his three sons (his will was stolen but dramatically recovered by a policeman disguised as a woman), who avoided their obligations by selling, for £365,000, all the steam-coal collieries in the Aberdâr valley, together with the New Tredegar colliery in the Rhymni valley, to a group headed by Sir George Elliot; and on 28 July 1864 the Powell Duffryn Steam Coal Company was formed.

Thomas Powell lived a long life of frugality and industry: the day before his death at the age of eighty-three he had been at work in his Newport office. He left a personal estate of about £250,000. Even the most celebratory books on the coal pioneers, however, hint at something more dubious than an industrious approach. It is not surprising, therefore, to find the colliery owner John Nixon complaining that Powell had simply reneged on paying him an agreed commission for marketing Powell's coal in France. Nixon recorded Powell's blunt response: 'I had a law suit with Lord Bute, and I beat him … I never in my life made an agreement that I could not get out of' (Vincent, 152). This was not entirely accurate: in 1841 Powell had been obliged to pay substantial damages to Sir Charles Morgan of Tredegar for moving coal under his land without a wayleave. More creditably, after an explosion killing twenty-eight people at Dyffryn in 1845, Powell rejected a public subscription to care for the five widows, instead giving them an allowance of 9s. a week with housing and coal.

Powell was one of the first six aldermen of Newport under the 1835 act. He was a member of the Church of England, and was married three times (although his family life is obscure). He is known to have had three sons and at least two daughters. The eldest son was, with his family, murdered in Abyssinia in 1869; the youngest disappeared without trace while in a hot-air balloon over the English Channel in 1881; and the middle son later died following a blow from a horse. Thomas Powell died at home at The Gaer, in the parish of St Woolos, Newport, on 24 March 1863, survived by his third wife, Anne Powell.

JOHN WILLIAMS

Sources J. H. Morris and L. J. Williams, *The south Wales coal industry, 1841–1875* (1958) · *Cardiff Times* (27 March 1863) · W. W. Price, 'History of Powell Duffryn in Aberdare valley', *P. D. Review* (1942–3) · *Glamorgan, Monmouth and Brecon Gazette, and Merthyr Guardian* (1840–59) · *Monmouthshire Merlin* (1840–59) [various dates in 1840s and 1850s] · 'Royal commission on children's employment in mines and manufactories: first report', *Parl. papers* (1842), vol. 17, no. 382 · Cardiff City Library, Bute MSS, vol. 3 · J. E. Vincent, *John Nixon: pioneer of the steam coal trade in south Wales* (1900) · *Powell Duffryn Steam Coal Company Ltd, 1864–1914* (1914) · C. Wilkins, *The south Wales coal trade and its allied industries* (1888)
Wealth at death under £250,000: resworn probate, July 1864, CGPLA Eng. & Wales (1863)

Powell, Vavasor (1617–1670), Independent minister, was born at Cnwclas (Knucklas) in the parish of Heyope, near Knighton in Radnorshire, the son of Richard Powell (d. before 1630?), a freeholder. Penelope Powell, Vavasor's mother, was the daughter of William Vavasor of Newtown, Montgomeryshire: her grandfather had been sheriff of the county in 1564, and was the first of his name to settle in Wales, having moved from Yorkshire. Others of Vavasor Powell's ancestral family had been sheriffs, stewards, and educated clergy, although his later detractors persisted in alleging he came from the common people. He was probably educated at Christ's College, Brecon, and may possibly have attended Jesus College, Oxford, although there is no written record of his having done so. He was never ordained in any of the orders of the Church of England, but probably worked as a schoolmaster in Clun, no more than 10 miles from Cnwclas, under the auspices of his great-uncle, Erasmus Powell, puritan vicar of Clun until 1637. During his time in Clun he was converted, making a conscious acceptance of God's grace after an acute sense of his own sinfulness. He had been greatly influenced by the works of Richard Sibbes and by the preaching of Walter Cradock, who had established a congregation at nearby Llanfair Waterdine. Powell had begun preaching by 1640 and in that year was arrested with fifty or sixty hearers for causing a disturbance through preaching.

The civil war On 2 February 1642 Powell married Joan Quarrell, widow of a Presteigne merchant and Hereford freeman, Paul Quarrell. In 1642 he appeared at Presteigne great sessions charged with nonconformity, but was found not guilty. He must have left shortly afterwards for London, and was there by August 1642, ahead of the refugees from the Llanfaches congregation of Monmouthshire, the first Independent church in Wales. Once there, he signed articles accusing his persecutors in Radnor of anti-parliamentarian activities. He preached in the parish of St Anne and St Agnes, Aldersgate, and in Crooked Lane, in the City, before moving to Dartford, in Kent, where he was vicar between mid-1643 and January 1646. As his sympathies were with Independent varieties of protestantism, this could only have been a temporary haven. If he had not already met Morgan Llwyd, the Welsh Independent minister and writer, he probably did so in 1644, as the latter sailed that year from Kent as part of the parliamentarian force relieving Pembrokeshire.

In 1646 Powell left Dartford to join the New Model Army forces besieging Oxford, having resigned from his living, but on 11 September he received a certificate of approval from the Westminster assembly as to his fitness for the ministry in Wales and his ability to preach in Welsh. Already, however, Thomas Edwards in *Gangraena* had noted 'many erroneous things' in his theology and reported Powell's harsh way with his opponents (Edwards, 3.97). That Powell could at this point accept presbyterian authority, and that the assembly felt able to endorse him despite the attacks on him in *Gangraena*, indicate that he was willing to present himself as orthodox. In June 1648 he, Ambrose Mostyn, and Llwyd were awarded maintenance from the tithes of six Montgomeryshire parishes to preach in the north Wales counties, shortly after he had signed a declaration by Montgomeryshire gentry, freeholders, and ministers to adhere to parliament and suppress the revolt which had broken out in May. He attached himself to the army of Thomas Mytton, and was injured at the siege of Beaumaris in October 1648. In the heat of the action he heard a voice telling him that he was chosen to preach the gospel; he later attributed his survival to divine intervention on account of his calling.

The propagation of the gospel Powell was in London in the winter of 1649–50 and preached before the lord mayor on 2 December 1649; his sermon called upon the city fathers to inaugurate the godly commonwealth. About this time he was invited by some parishioners to the living of Clyro, Radnor, but he declined it on learning that the incumbent had received his appointment from the committee for plundered ministers in London. On 22 February 1650 Powell was named twenty-third in the list of approvers under the Act for the Propagation of the Gospel in Wales, and six days later preached before the House of Commons. He remained a wholehearted enthusiast for the Commonwealth, and with Walter Cradock went to the north of England with a troop of horse to defend the new state against the forces of Charles Stuart. The Welsh propagation experiment allowed Powell's Independency to develop unchallenged, and like that of other leading figures in that dispensation, his outlook was deeply millenarian. In the petitioning against the propagators, which began as a complaint to parliament in 1652 and then fanned out to become a campaign in print against them, the name of Vavasor Powell was prominent. He was the target specifically of Alexander Griffith, a displaced Anglican clergyman, who alleged that Powell disregarded the common law, had made a huge fortune from trading in church lands and tithes, taught heresy, employed unseemly and obscene language in the pulpit, and (after December 1653) spoke disloyally of the protector. The last point in this litany of offences hit harder than most of the others, and was given force by Powell's undoubted and scarcely concealed distaste for the protectorate of Oliver Cromwell, which encouraged his enemies in mid-Wales to resort more frequently to the printing press.

The other charges levelled at Powell were informed by Griffith's bitter personal animosity. There was no question of Powell's immediacy as a preacher, at least part of which owed much to his capacity to employ to good effect the popular idiom, both in Welsh and English. Colonel John Jones, a commissioner of parliament in Dublin, hoped in vain that Powell would undertake a preaching mission to Ireland, and that he would grow weary of theological disputations. The title 'metropolitan of the itinerants' (*Strena Vavasoriensis*, 1654, title-page) bestowed upon him by his enemies, was not undeserved. He was said to preach often in two or three places a day in his counties of Brecon, Radnor, and Montgomery. As for his giving short shrift to the ways of the law, he was associated during this period with controversial figures such as Colonel Philip Jones, the dominant force in south Wales politics (although they had little in common in their religious outlook), and certainly had a regard for military-backed solutions to local difficulties of authority, even when the problem was to extract rent from his own tenant. After 1660 he

admitted buying confiscated property, but his own gloss that his purchases were modest is borne out by evidence that they were confined to parcels of crown land in Old Radnor, which he bought in 1651 for £252, and which yielded him £70 a year. From a perspective of several centuries later, his attitude to tithes was ambivalent. He refused the living of Penstrowed, Montgomeryshire, in 1647 on the grounds that he was unable to accept a maintenance by tithes, but was an enthusiast for the propagation commission, which deployed confiscated tithes to fund an itinerant ministry. Powell never directly received tithes, nor a settled salary, but received an annually fluctuating award for his labours from a fund of pooled tithe income. The attitude of William Erbery, who, after accepting an award from the commissioners, in 1652 came to deplore the use of all tithes for religious purposes, seems more consistent.

Opposition to the protectorate Powell looked forward with eager anticipation to what might be achieved by the nominated assembly of 1653, viewing it as a progressive development after the shortcomings of the Commonwealth government, and worked with Thomas Harrison and others to compile a slate of millenarian sympathizers to serve for Wales at Westminster. All Powell's choices were successful, and he was thus an important influence on the radical element in this parliament. His fury at the termination of the assembly by its moderate elements, and at the dawn of the protectorate of Oliver Cromwell, was immediate. Three days after Cromwell had been installed as lord protector Powell and other millenarian preachers, including Daniel Feake, met at Blackfriars in London to denounce the new regime. Powell deployed the book of Daniel to vilify Cromwell as the 'vile person' (*CSP dom.*, 1653–4, 305) mentioned in that portion of scripture and urged his hearers to ask God whether he would 'have Oliver Cromwell or Jesus Christ to reign over us?' (ibid., 306). He was arrested on 21 December, and was released on the twenty-fourth. He made his way back to Wales on 10 January 1654 and began a programme of preaching in mid-Wales which entrenched his opposition to the new government. His enemies sent ample evidence of his hostility and customary vehemence of language, but noted also the element of respect he commanded among the magistrates of mid-Wales. By March 1654 he had devised a petition against the government, and he and ten sympathizers were summoned before Montgomery great sessions for this activity against the protectorate. There was no prospect of his joining any alliance with royalists, however, for all his dislike of the new regime. In the spring of 1655 he was again in arms against insurgent royalists, accompanied by men of Wrexham: he was wounded in a skirmish.

After the scheme of the superintendent major-generals had been established, as a direct result of royalist unrest, Powell's movements were monitored by James Berry, major-general for the Welsh counties. Berry's judgement on the preacher's attitude to the government must have been coloured by Powell's readiness, despite everything, to fight for it, and it led him to underestimate his capacity still to make trouble. Information that Powell was busy in three mid-Wales counties fomenting an armed rising was implausible, but he could still wield the pen to damaging effect. Berry interviewed Powell at Worcester late in November 1655, and was assured that a petition in the making from Wales was simply a matter of conscience. Powell preached four sermons in the city that day, and Berry continued to take a relaxed attitude to Powell even after the petition, *A Word for God*, was published. It turned out to be a bitter denunciation of the protectorate, in which the theme of betrayal of the godly was dominant. It undoubtedly had more impact in London than in Wales, but its text and the furore it provoked exposed Berry's insouciance. Powell was its principal draughtsman and chief promoter, and the petition drove a wedge between former clerical colleagues of Powell's, such as Cradock and Llwyd, who could accommodate themselves to a tithe-supported ministry, and Powell himself. *A Word for God* also stimulated a print debate, in which Henry Vane the younger and William Sedgwick were notable contributors, on the legitimacy and authority of the government.

Independent and open-communion Baptist In the last years of the interregnum Powell lived at Goetre, in the parish of Kerry, Montgomeryshire, and continued to travel Wales and England to preach and dispute. His first encounter with a Quaker, Richard Hubberthorne, came on 14 November 1653 at Chirk, and it began a series of well-documented disputations with Friends, especially between 1656 and 1658. Powell emphasized the need for repentance for sin on these occasions, and thus on matters of doctrine remained resolutely orthodox, unlike Llwyd, who evinced sympathy for the spiritual insights of the Quakers. Llwyd was also more willing than Powell to think the best of the lord protector, and relations between the two men cooled a little, even if they never chilled, in the late 1650s. Powell's targets in the pulpit were not only the Quakers: in Oxford in July 1657 he preached against the universities, as had William Erbery in the same place nearly ten years previously. On this occasion, Powell denounced Henry Hickman, fellow of Magdalen College, for admitting that the Church of Rome was a true church. Later, Anthony Wood's account attributed to Powell the view that only Independents and Roman Catholics 'had religion' (Wood, *Ath. Oxon.*, 3.918)—probably a garbling of the 1657 incident.

Powell may have held fast to Calvinist orthodoxy longer than did either Erbery or Llwyd, but his own ecclesiology, at least, developed in new directions from the Independency he had promoted during the propagation and earlier. By this time he had on the question of church membership moved towards Baptist principles. Unlike John Miles, who restricted access to the ordinance of communion to those who had been baptized as adults by total immersion, Powell taught that adult baptism was a rite that every believer should undergo, but that it was neither necessary for salvation nor a condition of admission to the Lord's supper. This placed him in an intermediate position between the Independents, who held with infant baptism, and the Strict Baptists of Miles. Nevertheless, he

was still considered enough of an Independent to be invited in 1658 to the assembly to devise a declaration of faith. His response, on 26 August, was a guarded willingness to convey the invitation to churches where he had influence, but he warned against the dangers of the churches becoming too close to the government: 'If you go upon political and worldly accounts or by a humane spirit, to work, you may expect God to blast the work' (Peck, 2.13.25–6). His suspicion that this letter would be intercepted because it travelled near Cromwell's court suggests that his distrust of the protector's establishment was more that of a 'country' critic than of one, like William Erbery, with a principled distaste for state power.

The Restoration, imprisonment, and death the restoration of Charles II was a personal disaster for Powell, who may have been arrested as early as February 1660, and was certainly detained by 23 April that year. The new government feared his influence and rounded up a number of his followers at Bala. After a period of imprisonment at Shrewsbury, Powell resumed his preaching in June 1660, and when rearrested refused to take the oaths of supremacy and allegiance at Shrewsbury assizes. Despite the clearest signals that he was *persona non grata* to the restored monarchy he published a repudiation of the authority of bishops and Book of Common Prayer. He was moved to the Fleet prison and wrote there *The Bird in the Cage Chirping*, an apologia for the propagation era. It vindicated his former colleagues and honestly analysed the difficulties they had encountered in making the experiment work. It also explained the Restoration in terms of a squandering by the godly of divine mercies: 'We have been stomachful, sick and surfeited with the sweet and fat things of God's house … we trampled and trod under foot the good pastures' (*The Bird in the Cage Chirping*, 1662, 8–9). On 30 September 1662 he was moved to Southsea Castle by yacht, and remained there for five years, unrepentant and still inclined to a millenarian analysis of events. He believed himself to be incarcerated 'for foretelling calamities in 1666' (*CSP dom.*, 1665–6, 191). The downfall of Edward Hyde, earl of Clarendon, seems to have provided a reason for freeing long-term prisoners of conscience like Powell, and in November 1667 the preacher at last walked free.

Even this long period in prison had failed to daunt Powell, and in March 1668 he was reported to have preached to a congregation of Fifth Monarchists at Blue Anchor Alley, Old Lane, London. In September, returning from a sojourn in Bath, where he was taking the waters for health reasons, Powell preached to gatherings at Newport, Monmouthshire, and Merthyr Tudful. At the instigation of the incumbent of Merthyr, Powell was arrested there, and on 17 October was examined by deputy lieutenants meeting at Cowbridge, in the Vale of Glamorgan. Before these former cavaliers Powell defended himself against charges of unlawful preaching with some verve, and was re-examined on 8 November 1668 and 13 January 1669. Powell managed to impose on these examinations something of the character of a religious disputation. He resisted taking the oaths of supremacy and allegiance on the grounds that he had taken them before and that they had been tendered to him by an officer without lawful authority. He also took exception to the practice of laying a hand on the Bible to swear an oath. The examinations, or 'conventions' (*Life*, 182–8) as Powell called them, had one inevitable outcome, and he returned to prison at Cardiff. A writ of *habeas corpus* procured by a friend of his provided the authority necessary to move Powell from Glamorgan to London, where it was evidently thought he stood a better chance of a permanent acquittal. It was not to be, however, and Powell was committed to the Fleet on 24 May 1669. He continued to correspond with friends, and may have exercised the liberty of daily parole to frequent old haunts, and even to preach a little. By December 1668 he had married again after the death of his first wife. His second wife was Katherine Gerard (*bap.* 1638), fifth daughter of Gilbert Gerard, parliamentarian governor of Chester, who was twenty-one years younger than Powell. There were no children from either of his marriages. His last sermons were preached in London on 25 September 1670, by which time he was seriously ill. He died in London on 27 October, of a disease of the alimentary canal involving haemorrhaging and thrush. He was buried at Bunhill Fields, where a marble gravestone once recorded the fact, quoting Revelation 6: 10:

> Christ him released, and now he's joyned among
> The martyred Souls, with whom he cries, How long?
> (*Proceedings … Bunhill Fields Burial-Ground*, 83)

Although a Welsh speaker, Powell only published in English, and his fifteen works consisted of polemical pieces, sermons before civil authorities, and orthodox evangelical tracts. Some unpublished English verse thought, if not known, to be by him, certainly follows his style in elevating the 'saints' in combative terms, and setting them in the political context of the period. He preferred to invest his energies in preaching and disputation rather than authorship, holding that he 'would not neglect for the printing of a thousand books, the preaching of one sermon' (V. Powell, *Christ and Moses Excellency*, 1650, sig. A2). Some at least of this preference derived from his temperament, described by friends and foes alike as fiery and impetuous. He may have helped Walter Cradock prepare a Welsh version of the New Testament in 1647, although there is no direct evidence that he did, and he had in preparation a concordance to the Bible, which others completed after his death. His closeness to civil authority before December 1653 may have contributed to his adherence in general to theological orthodoxy while others of the Welsh 'saints' moved towards antinomian positions: he was a regular preacher at assizes and civic occasions. But his strong belief in the value of the godly magistrate and soldier was balanced by an unshakeable conviction that the purpose of godly secular authority was to protect and nurture the people of God, a minority in the nation. When from December 1653 it seemed to him that secular power was no longer being deployed in the interests of the godly, he withdrew his consent to the government, and moved into permanent opposition, which could only

intensify after 1660. An anonymous contemporary described Powell as:

> a man indefatigably industrious, unweariedly laborious in his studies, and in his ministerial performances: for a long time of great strength of body, and equal vigour of mind, both of which, while out of prison, he restlessly employed in the service of God. (*A Winding-Sheet for Mr. Baxter's Dead*, 1685, 10)

He was said to have been short in physical stature. His personal seal was 'a skeleton or figure of death, holding in the right hand a dart, in the left an hourglass; sitting upon the tree of life' (Peck, 2.13.26). STEPHEN K. ROBERTS

Sources *The life and death of Mr Vavasor Powell* (1671) • A. Griffith, *Strena Vavasoriensis* (1654) • *Vavasoris examen et purgamen* (1654) • R. T. Jones, *Vavasor Powell* (1971) [in Welsh] • Thurloe, *State papers*, vols. 2–4 • Wood, *Ath. Oxon.*, new edn, vol. 3 • *Proceedings in reference to preservation of Bunhill Fields burial ground* (1867) • CSP dom., 1653–4 • F. Peck, ed., *Desiderata curiosa*, 2 (1735), bk 13, pp. 25–6 • T. M. Rees, *Welsh painters, engravers, sculptors (1527–1911)* (1912) • T. Richards, *A history of the puritan movement in Wales* (1920) • T. Richards, *Religious developments in Wales, 1654–1662* (1923) • *Calendar of the correspondence of Richard Baxter*, ed. N. H. Keeble and G. F. Nuttall, 1 (1991), 90–91; 2 (1991), 253 • T. Edwards, *Gangraena, or, A catalogue and discovery of many of the errours, heresies, blasphemies and pernicious practices of the sectaries of this time*, 3 vols. in 1 (1646) • DWB • G. Ormerod, *The history of the county palatine and city of Chester*, 2nd edn, ed. T. Helsby, 2 (1882), 132
Wealth at death small bequests: will, 3 Aug 1671, Jones, *Vavasor Powell*, 189

Powell, William (1735/6–1769), actor and theatre manager, was born in 1735 or 1736 in Hereford, the son of William Powell (1704–1784), who died at Charlotte Street, Rathborne Place, London, on 31 July 1784. It is uncertain whether or not his mother was the Theodosia Brand (*d.* 1784) referred to in Powell senior's will, dated 16 April 1784, as 'now Theodosia Powell my lawful wife' (Highfill, Burnim & Langhans, *BDA*). The actor was educated at Hereford grammar school and at Christ's Hospital, London. He was then employed in a City counting-house by Sir Robert Ladbrooke, who was president of Christ's Hospital. He worked for Sir Robert for ten years and was 'so clever in business that his master would have taken him in partner' (*Letters of Horace Walpole*, 5.379). The young Powell, however, was a keen participant in amateur theatricals and gained both the friends and the experience, through the spouting clubs he attended, to make his sudden and meteoric change of career in 1763 a possibility. In 1759, while still working for Ladbrooke, he had married Elizabeth Branson (or Branston); by 1761 he had two daughters, Elizabeth Mary and Anne, as well as his wife to support from his secure City employment. Two years later he turned his back on the counting-house and ventured on a career as a professional actor.

Charles Holland, a friend from the spouting clubs who had become established at Drury Lane Theatre, introduced Powell to David Garrick, who at that time was looking for a young player to tutor in some of his leading roles. Garrick himself wanted to make a tour of the continent and needed someone to fill in for him while he was gone. He was impressed by Powell and coached him during the summer of 1763 before leaving for Paris. Powell's début as the eponymous hero in Colman's adaptation of Beaumont and Fletcher's *Philaster* was a sensation. As William Hopkins, the Drury Lane prompter, observed in his diary: 'A greater reception was never shown to anybody.' It is clear that from the outset Powell's appeal was as an emotive and dynamic actor:

For young Philaster *feels* his Part,
And follows Nature more than art.
(*Public Advertiser*, 11 March 1766)

He performed Philaster thirteen times during October and November, including a royal command performance on 20 October. During his first season he took on sixteen further roles, notably that of Othello, the role he chose for his first benefit at Drury Lane, on 31 March 1764. In spite of criticisms of wildness, of overstraining, and of feelings and tears choking his articulation, his power to draw and hold audiences was immense. Theatre receipts relating to his appearances were consistently high (first-night receipts for ten of his major roles ranged from £231 19*s*. to £268 11*s*.), and during the course of the season Powell's salary was raised from £3 to £8 per week. At his benefit there was, according to William Hopkins, 'one of the greatest overflows that ever was known'. Among the roles he performed during this first season, those which were especially praised for their 'great feeling', 'tenderness', 'pathos', and 'strong emotions' included Posthumus in *Cymbeline*, Lusignan in Aaron Hill's *Zara*, the King in 2 *Henry IV*, Castalio in Thomas Otway's *The Orphan*, and Shore in Nicholas Rowe's *Jane Shore*. However, it was as Jaffier in Otway's *Venice Preserv'd* that he seems to have caught the audience's imagination most consistently:

his Distraction on hearing his Friend was to die—his Prayer for Belvidera—his Execution at the tolling of the Bell—his last parting from his Wife, I think were the most masterly strokes of Acting I ever beheld; and indeed the Audience seemed full as sensible of it; for profound Silence and Attention filled the House, while the big Drops rolled down from almost every Eye. (*Public Advertiser*, 31 Jan 1764)

This was one of the roles that was to stay in Powell's repertory throughout his brief career. He performed it eight times during his first season at Drury Lane and sixteen times during ensuing seasons, often 'by Particular Desire'. It was the role he chose, when he became involved in the management of Covent Garden, for his first acting appearance there in 1767. It also featured regularly in his summer seasons at Bristol, and in 1769 was the last role he ever performed on the stage.

Between the close of his first season and the opening of his second season at Drury Lane, Powell acted at the Jacob's Wells Theatre in the Hotwells district of Bristol. It was the beginning of an important five-year relationship with the city. For his benefit there on 13 August 1764 he played King Lear, a role he was to add to his London repertory five months later. Lear's curse near the end of act I and his reconciliation with Cordelia towards the end of the play were highlights of his portrayal, and featured prominently in accounts of the time. It was in the mad scenes, however, that he clearly excelled:

With such Variety! such Strength! such Taste!
That in quick Whirlwinds more and more increas'd;
Till Reason like a shatter'd Vessel tost,
Amid the Mind's mad Hurricanes was lost.
(*Felix Farley's Bristol Journal*, 15 Aug 1767)

Many of the roles Powell performed during his second season at Drury Lane (1764–5) seem to have been chosen to exploit, or build upon, his ability to delineate extreme states of mind or feeling: Lothario in Rowe's *The Fair Penitent*, Orestes in Ambrose Philips's *The Distrest Mother*, Herod in Elijah Ferton's *Marianne*, Leontes in *The Winter's Tale*, and, on 2 January 1765, King Lear. In contrast, towards the end of January Powell appeared in a new comedy, Elizabeth Griffith's *The Platonic Wife*, playing Lord Frankland, which was his first original role. On the opening night the play 'was not well received' (Victor, 3.60), but after some revision it ran for five further performances.

After a second summer at the Jacob's Wells Theatre, Powell returned to Drury Lane for a third season (1765–6), his first alongside, and under the gaze of, David Garrick. His roles in the early months of the season, after Garrick's return, were Castalio, Jaffier, Lusignan, and Lear. He did not add any roles to his repertory until 11 November (Moneses in Rowe's *Tamerlane*) and 26 November (Alcanor in James Miller's *Mahomet*). On 23 January 1766 Garrick retrieved the part of Lusignan from Powell for a royal command performance, where the presence of Jean Jacques Rousseau in Garrick's box 'fronting his Majesty' caused a stir (*GM*, 1st ser., 36, 1766). However, Powell was playing the role again at Drury Lane by 19 April. In Colman and Garrick's *The Clandestine Marriage*, which had a continuous run at Drury Lane from 20 February to 13 March, Powell was the original Lovewell. On 20 March he played the title role in *King John*, and on 22 March Antony in Dryden's *All for Love*.

In Bristol, Powell became involved, together with Matthew Clarke and John Arthur, in the management of the newly built Theatre Royal, which opened on 30 May 1766. After a quarrelsome summer Arthur was replaced by Powell's friend Charles Holland. Over the next two years the new management established this theatre as an important and fashionable centre in Bristol. Powell's interest in management extended to London in 1767, when, at the end of his last season at Drury Lane, he bought a quarter share in the patent and property of Covent Garden. This second venture as a theatre manager—in partnership with George Colman, Thomas Harris, and John Rutherford—proved even more acrimonious, fuelled by Harris's desire to advance his mistress's career, and eventually led to litigation by Harris and Rutherford against Colman (whom Powell supported). The case was settled in Colman's favour in 1770, a year after Powell had died. As Kathleen Barker has observed, Powell's 'educational and business background needs to be borne in mind and weighed against the rather derisive remarks made by Garrick and some of his biographers about Powell's lack of culture and qualifications for theatre management' (Barker, 73).

Powell was the leading actor at Covent Garden under the new management. He delivered an inaugural prologue at the opening on 14 September 1767, played Jaffier on 16 September, and then over the next four months appeared in twenty-two different roles, including Honeywood in the première of Oliver Goldsmith's *The Good-Natured Man*. From 1768 onwards he was often ill, and during the summer at Bristol he was unable to perform at all for two weeks. During his second season at Covent Garden (1768–9) he added eight new roles to his repertory, among them two originals—Cyrus in John Hoole's play of the same name and Courtney in Charlotte Lennox's *The Sister*. But in Bristol the following summer he acted only twice at the Theatre Royal, his last appearance being in *Venice Preserv'd*. On 3 July 1769, after a month's illness, he died in lodgings in King Street, Bristol, from pneumonia, at the age of thirty-three or thirty-four. On 6 July his hearse was carried in procession, preceded by a choir, from College Green to his burial-place, Bristol Cathedral, where the dean conducted the funeral service. 'The spectators were too numerous to observe silence and decorum' and were impatient 'to take a final look at him, to whom they had been indebted for so many hours of elegant entertainment' (*Sarah Farley's Bristol Journal*, 8 July 1769).

Powell left no will. His widow, Elizabeth, erected a monument to her husband in 1771, in the north aisle of Bristol Cathedral, on which is inscribed an epitaph composed by 'a faithful friend', George Colman.

LESLIE DU S. READ

Sources Highfill, Burnim & Langhans, *BDA* · K. Barker, 'William Powell, a forgotten star', *Essays on the eighteenth-century English stage*, ed. K. Richards and P. Thomson (1972), 73–83 · G. W. Stone, ed., *The London stage, 1660–1800*, pt 4: 1747–1776 (1962) · *Public Advertiser* (31 Jan 1764) [review] · *Public Advertiser* (11 March 1766) [review] · *Felix Farley's Bristol Journal* (15 Aug 1767) [review] · *Sarah Farley's Bristol Journal* (8 July 1769) · review, *GM*, 1st ser., 36 (1766) · *The letters of Horace Walpole, fourth earl of Orford*, ed. P. Toynbee, 16 vols. (1903–5); suppl., 3 vols. (1918–25) · B. Victor, *The history of the theatres of London and Dublin*, 3 vols. (1761–71)
Archives Folger, William Hopkins's diary
Likenesses J. H. Mortimer, group portrait, 1768 (with family), Garr. Club · J. H. Mortimer, painting, 1768? (as King John), Garr. Club · caricature, 1768 (as Red King of Hearts), BM · J. Dixon, mezzotint, pubd 1769 (after T. Lawrenson), BM, NPG · engraving, 1769 (as Lovewell) · J. H. Mortimer, group portrait, Garr. Club · S. Okey junior, engraving (after R. Pyle), Garr. Club · R. Pyle, oils, Garr. Club · B. Wilson, group portrait (with family), Garr. Club · J. Zoffany, painting (as Posthumus), priv. coll.; repro. in *The Georgian playhouse* (1975) [Hayward Gallery] · miniatures, Garr. Club · prints, BM, NPG

Powell, William Samuel (1717–1775), college head, was born at Colchester on 27 September 1717, the elder son of the Revd Francis Powell and his wife, Susan, the daughter of Samuel Reynolds (*d.* 1694), MP for Colchester, and widow of George Jolland. He was educated at Colchester grammar school, under the Revd Palmer Smythies, and admitted pensioner at St John's College, Cambridge, on 7 July 1734. In November 1735 he was elected a foundation scholar, and he held exhibitions from his college in November 1735, 1736, and 1738. He graduated BA (1739), MA (1742), BD (1749), and DD (1757). He was admitted as a fellow of St John's on 25 March 1740.

In 1741 Powell became private tutor to Charles Townshend (second son of Viscount Townshend), who later became chancellor of the exchequer. At the end of that year he was ordained deacon and priest, and was presented to the rectory of Colkirk in Norfolk on 13 January 1742 by Lord Townshend. In 1742 he returned to college life, and was assistant tutor for two years, becoming principal tutor in 1744; in 1745 he acted as senior taxor of the university. His closest Cambridge friends were Thomas Balguy and Richard Hurd; he tutored at St John's the poet William Mason, who later became an important figure in the Hurd circle. On 3 November 1760 he became a senior fellow of the college; he resigned his fellowship in 1763, having left Cambridge for a house in London in 1761, when he inherited the property of a cousin. This inheritance later provoked comment when Powell himself died, leaving some £30,000 in his will. The inheritance came through his mother's eldest brother's marriage to Frances, daughter of Charles Pelham of Brocklesby, Lincolnshire, a member of the duke of Newcastle's family. On the death of their son, Charles Reynolds of Peldon Hall, Essex, that estate, along with other Essex property in Little Bentley and Wix, came to Powell.

On 25 January 1765, backed by the influence of the duke of Newcastle, Powell was unanimously elected master of St John's College, where, following his inheritance, he lived for the rest of his life in some style. Powell had been admitted a fellow of the Royal Society on 15 March 1764; in November 1765 he succeeded to the vice-chancellorship of Cambridge. In December 1766 he was appointed to the archdeaconry of Colchester by the crown. In 1768 he somewhat controversially claimed for himself the rich college rectory of Freshwater on the Isle of Wight (worth £500 a year), which was in the master's option, resigning the benefice of Colkirk in the process. Freshwater was naturally a living coveted by the fellows, and Powell's tactless action was defended by a later biographer, Thomas Hughes, as necessary in guaranteeing that his successor as master could afford to entertain on a scale commensurate with his standing. The consequent ill feeling in the college was mitigated by Powell's personal gift of some £500 to rebuild the first court and to lay out the college grounds under the care of Capability Brown. A strict disciplinarian and a careful steward of the college's revenues, he secured the first place in the university for St John's College. In his first year as master he established college examinations, for which he drew up the papers, and which he always made sure to attend in person. This encouraged applications to a college which was thus seen to be committed to improving academic standards, and it was jealousy of the position thereby achieved that led Powell vigorously to oppose John Jebb's proposal for annual examinations for all students of the university in general subjects. Powell published anonymously in 1774 *An Observation on the Design of Establishing Annual Examinations at Cambridge*, to which Mrs Jebb replied in *A Letter to the Author*. Powell, a firmly committed Johnian, helped out several of his students financially, enabling them to complete their studies. He also bestowed college prizes at his own expense. All students, whatever their year might be, had to pass an examination in one of the gospels or the Acts of the Apostles.

He attended chapel throughout the year, at six o'clock in the morning. He was a man of rigid and unbending manners.

In addition to the engagement with the Jebbs, Powell provoked two serious controversies at Cambridge, the first of which inadvertently initiated the major controversy concerning undergraduate and clerical subscription to the Thirty-Nine Articles which led to the Feathers tavern petition in 1772. This was effected through a sermon preached before the university on Commencement Sunday in 1757, and which was published that year as *A Defence of the Subscriptions Required in the Church of England*; it was reprinted in 1758, 1759, and 1772. He argued that the articles were studiedly general and indeterminate, providing a means of reading the scriptures which conformed to 'the general voice of learned men through the nation'. Powell argued that latitude in the expression of the articles allowed for those improvements in theology which required latitude in their turn. Orthodox critics disliked Powell's latitudinarian position on the matter, while Francis Blackburne, an ultra-latitudinarian and Powell's chief critic, denounced his arguments as being casuistical in the extreme, acting as the denial of religious and moral freedom. In *Remarks* on the sermon which he published in 1758 Blackburne questioned the wisdom of Powell's choice of theme for a commencement sermon, since it revived a controversy which did little credit to the Church of England.

The second controversy was of an altogether more personal, indeed collegiate character (it became increasingly difficult to separate the two interests during Powell's years as a fellow and then as master). The Lucasian professorship of mathematics had become vacant in 1760, and among the candidates were Edward Waring of Magdalene College and William Ludlam of St John's College. Waring distributed a portion of his *Miscellanea analytica* in support of his candidature, which Powell anonymously attacked in order to serve the interests of Ludlam, a fellow Johnian, in *Observations on the First Chapter of a Book called 'Miscellanea analytica'* (1760). Waring replied to the piece, to which Powell retorted, again anonymously, in his *Defence of the Observations*, which Waring answered in a *Letter*. Waring had much the better of the debate.

Powell had a stroke of apoplexy in 1770, and died in his chair from paralysis on 19 January 1775. He was buried in the college chapel on 25 January, the anniversary of his election as master, and a flat blue stone, with an epitaph by Balguy, was placed over his vault. He was unmarried and left his property to his niece, Miss Jolland, who had lived with him. An annuity of £150 was left to his sister, Susanna Powell, a matron of the Chelsea Hospital, from whom he was early distanced: they were too alike in character to get on. He also left £1000 to Dr Balguy, and a sum to be equally divided between six fellows and four members of the college who had been his contemporaries. These collegiate legacies were the subject of some disapproving comment at the time. Jeremiah Markland, the classical scholar, a notably charitable fellow of Peterhouse, thought that an unmarried divine leaving such a

sum in his will looked decidedly 'unscriptural' (*GM*, 1785). Powell's books were left to four of the college's fellows.

Besides the works mentioned above Powell wrote two others. *The Heads of a Course of Lectures on Experimental Philosophy*, published anonymously in 1746 and 1753, demonstrated a particular interest in optics, and was the result of the still comparatively rare practice of providing intercollegiate lectures at Cambridge. A posthumous work, *Discourses on Various Subjects*, (1776), was edited by Dr Balguy, who provided an outline of Powell's life and work by way of an introduction. Powell's controversial commencement sermon was included in the collection. They were reprinted, together with the discourses of the Revd James Fawcett, by Thomas Hughes in 1832, who also provided a somewhat defensive account of Powell's career by way of introduction.

                                                        B. W. YOUNG

Sources Nichols, *Lit. anecdotes* · *GM*, 1st ser., 45 (1775), 47 · *GM*, 1st ser., 55 (1785), 290, 339 · T. Baker, *History of the college of St John the Evangelist, Cambridge*, ed. J. E. B. Mayor, 2 vols. (1869) · C. Wordsworth, *Social life at the English universities in the eighteenth century* (1874) · C. Wordsworth, *Scholae academicae: some account of the studies at the English universities in the eighteenth century* (1877) · B. W. Young, *Religion and Enlightenment in eighteenth-century England: theological debate from Locke to Burke* (1998) · *The works, theological and miscellaneous of … Francis Blackburne*, ed. F. Blackburne, 7 vols. (1804–5) · J. Gascoigne, *Cambridge in the age of the Enlightenment* (1989) · *The early letters of Bishop Richard Hurd, 1739–1762*, ed. S. Brewer (1995)
Archives St John Cam. | BL, letters to second earl of Hardwicke and Charles Yorke, Add. MSS 35607, 35637, 35640, 35657, 35680, *passim* · BL, corresp. with duke of Newcastle and others, Add. MSS 32557, 32957–33072, *passim*
Wealth at death £30,000: T. Hughes, *Life* (1832) · £30,000–£40,000: Nichols, *Lit. anecdotes*; *GM*

Power, Sir Arthur John (1889–1960), naval officer, was born in London on 12 April 1889, the son of Edward John Power, corn merchant, and his wife, Harriet Maud Windeler. He entered the *Britannia* in 1904 and won the king's gold medal for the best cadet of the year. In his sub-lieutenant's courses he gained first-class certificates in each subject and in 1910 he was promoted lieutenant. In 1913 he was appointed to the *Excellent* to specialize in gunnery. His service in the war included appointments as gunnery officer of the battleship *Magnificent*, the cruiser *Royal Arthur*, the monitor *Raglan* in which he took part in the Dardanelles operations, and the battle cruiser *Princess Royal* in the Grand Fleet.

Power was promoted commander in 1922 and served for two years in the Admiralty as assistant to the director of naval ordnance. He was selected for a staff college course in 1924 and, after passing, joined the battle cruiser *Hood* as executive officer. From 1927 to 1929 he was on the instructional staff of the Royal Naval College, Greenwich, and after promotion to captain in 1929 became naval member of the ordnance committee. He commanded the cruiser *Dorsetshire* from 1931 to 1933 as flag captain and chief staff officer to E. A. Astley-Rushton, rear-admiral commanding 2nd cruiser squadron, and to his successor Percy Noble. He was appointed to the Imperial Defence College as naval member of the directing staff in 1933, and from 1935 to 1937 commanded the naval gunnery school *Excellent*. He was in charge of the naval party which drew the gun carriage at the funeral of George V in January 1936 and was appointed CVO.

In January 1938 Power was appointed to command the new aircraft-carrier *Ark Royal* and was still holding this appointment at the outbreak of the Second World War. The target for many attacks by the German air force which claimed her sinking many times, she was torpedoed off Gibraltar in November 1941. Meanwhile Power was called to the Admiralty in May 1940 as assistant chief of naval staff (home) and was promoted rear-admiral one month later.

In August 1942 Power returned to sea to fly his flag in the *Cleopatra* as flag officer commanding 15th cruiser squadron, but early in 1943 was appointed flag officer, Malta, as acting vice-admiral, a post of particular importance at that time since it was in Malta that the planning and organization of the invasions of Sicily and Italy were being prepared. Power's keen brain and his gifts of quick decision making and high organizing ability did much to ensure the rapid success of both invasions with remarkably few casualties. After the surrender of Italy he went to sea again in command of the naval force occupying Taranto and was appointed head of the allied military mission for administration to the Italian government. His promotion to vice-admiral was dated 4 August 1943, and for a brief period he acted as second in command of the Mediterranean Fleet.

In January 1944 Power arrived in Ceylon as second in command of the Eastern Fleet. Many of the bombardments and naval air strikes carried out against the Japanese positions in the East Indies were under his active leadership. On the formation of the British Pacific Fleet in November 1944 Power became commander-in-chief, East Indies, initiating many of the naval strikes and assaults which brought the Japanese to defeat in Borneo and Malaya. Flying his flag in the *Cleopatra* he entered Singapore on 3 September 1945, the first ship of the Royal Navy to do so since 1942.

Power returned to England in 1946 and for the next two years was a lord commissioner of the Admiralty and second sea lord, an appointment in which he was in charge of the complicated run-down of the personnel of the navy to its peacetime strength. He was promoted admiral in 1946 and in 1948 took command of the Mediterranean Fleet. In 1950–52 he was commander-in-chief at Portsmouth and while holding this post was promoted admiral of the fleet (1952). He was also in that year allied commander-in-chief, channel and southern North sea. The previous year he had been made first and principal naval aide-de-camp to the king.

Power was twice married: in 1918 to Amy Isabel (*d.* 1945), daughter of Colonel D. A. Bingham, with whom he had three sons; second, in 1947, to Margaret Joyce, a second officer in the WRNS, daughter of A. H. St C. Watson, of Hendon. Power died at the Haslar Royal Naval Hospital, Hampshire, on 28 January 1960.

According to his *Times* obituarist Power was recognized as one of the leading naval officers of his generation.

'Good looks, a strong character, and a complete mastery of every branch of his profession in which he had served, combined to make him a man of mark' (*The Times*, 29 Jan 1960). For his war services he was appointed CB (1941), KCB (1944), and GBE (1946). He was promoted GCB in 1950 and held a number of foreign decorations.

PETER KEMP, *rev.*

Sources *The Times* (29 Jan 1960) · *WWW* · personal knowledge (1971) · S. W. Roskill, *The war at sea, 1939–1945*, 3 vols. in 4 (1954–61) · *CGPLA Eng. & Wales* (1960)
Archives BL, corresp., diaries, notebooks, and papers, Add. MSS 56093–56098 | FILM BFI NFTVA, 'Singapore surrender', British News, 31 Sept 1945 · BFI NFTVA, news footage · IWM FVA, actuality footage
Likenesses O. Birley, oils, *c.*1945–1948, Royal Naval Staff College, Greenwich · W. Stoneman, photograph, 1947, NPG · K. Hutton, photograph, 1949 (with Louis Mount-Batten), Hult. Arch.
Wealth at death £18,681 3*s.* 10*d.*: probate, 24 May 1960, *CGPLA Eng. & Wales*

Power, Beryl Millicent Le Poer (1891–1974), civil servant, was born on 17 September 1891 at Dunham Massey, Cheshire, the youngest of the three daughters of Philip Ernest Le Poer Power (*b.* 1860), a stockbroker, and his wife, Mabel Grindlay Clegg (1866–1903). Her eldest sister was Eileen *Power, and her second sister was Rhoda *Power (1890–1957). She was educated at Bournemouth Church High School, Bournemouth high school, and Oxford High School for Girls. The sisters were cared for and supported by their maternal grandparents and several aunts after their father's conviction for fraud in 1891 and their mother's death in 1903. In 1910 Beryl Power entered Girton College, Cambridge, where she obtained an upper second in the second part of the history tripos in 1913.

When Miss Power left university she became an organizer and speaker for the National Union of Women's Suffrage Societies, the non-militant wing of the women's suffrage movement, and described the work as 'valuable as a training in propaganda and public speaking, often under difficult conditions' (letter to Dr Donald S. Howard, 14 Nov 1945, Power MSS). Most active suffrage campaigning stopped at the outbreak of the First World War, and in 1915 she was appointed to the office of trade boards at the Board of Trade as an inspector, third class, primarily dealing with the enforcement of the controversial Trade Boards Acts of 1909 and 1918. By 1920 she had become a deputy chief inspector in the Ministry of Labour (created in 1916 and into which parts of the Board of Trade had been incorporated) and in the same year was offered the Rose Sidgwick memorial fellowship by the United States Association of Collegiate Alumnae. She planned to study minimum wage legislation in the United States, but the Ministry of Labour would not release her.

However, in 1925 Miss Power was awarded the Laura Spelman Rockefeller memorial fellowship. One of its main purposes was to enable the holders to travel extensively throughout the United States, so she arranged a wide programme of research mainly into the labour conditions of women and children. Although she was not required to write up her research she produced two reports at the request of her principals at the Ministry of

Labour. The reports were praised for their quality, and R. H. Tawney, at the time a colleague of her sister Eileen at the London School of Economics, proposed that she submit them as a PhD thesis. However, she was advised that the material was too confidential for publication. She was herself against publication, noting that the report was largely narrative and that, as some of its conclusions were not favourable to some US state officials, she did not want to abuse their hospitality by appearing to criticize them.

In 1929 Miss Power was the only woman appointed to the royal commission on Indian labour, chaired by J. H. Whitley, visiting India and Burma. Her correspondence offers perceptive insights into contemporary British attitudes towards India against the background of the independence movement. At the end of the commission she was asked by the Anglo-Persian Oil Company to study its welfare arrangements in the Persian oilfields and refineries. She also studied the indigenous industries in Persia and in Palestine, where she visited Jewish and Arab enterprises and toured some of the Jewish agricultural collectives. She recorded her travels in a series of letters and photographs.

Between 1931 and 1945 Power seems to have acted as a civil service trouble-shooter, serving in different departments of the Ministry of Labour for short periods. In 1932 she made a short visit to the Soviet Union to study welfare and education arrangements. She wrote a vivid account of her visit, commending the humanitarian measures adopted by the communist government while expressing reservations when it was obvious that she was being fed propaganda. She was impressed by the enthusiasm of many of the people she met, although she was equally aware that many workers were exhausted despite the improvements in their conditions, and she described the result of the visit as sobering.

By 1938 Power was an assistant secretary—only the second woman to achieve that position at the Ministry of Labour—in charge of the central register. The register was an extensive compilation, drawn up in conjunction with university appointment boards, of the names of all those whose technical, scientific, or professional qualifications might make them useful to the state in time of war; by the time that war was declared in 1939 it comprised about 80,000 cards. One of Miss Power's colleagues at that time recalled that she was 'a very forceful person' and another described her as 'solid rather than tall, dark hair, spectacles, good bust, she walked very upright. She was a little too forceful in saying what she thought without thinking too much of the effect on others' (Hennessy, 95).

In 1940 Power was appointed director of selection at the short-lived Children's Overseas Reception Board, set up to organize the evacuation of British children to the Commonwealth, but its work was curtailed after HMS *City of Benares* was torpedoed on 17 September 1940 with the loss of more than seventy children. She then joined the Ministry of Food to oversee the implementation of schemes for providing refreshments for people in air raid shelters. After the successful organization of the feeding schemes she was assigned to the Ministry of Supply, where she took over the housing and welfare branch, organizing hostel accommodation and other amenities for war workers.

In 1945 the Foreign Office requested Power's secondment to the staff of the United Nations Relief and Rehabilitation Administration (UNRRA), China, and she was appointed as an adviser on administrative and welfare policies for the Chinese national relief and rehabilitation administration under the auspices of the Chinese ministry of social affairs. She combined her observational and investigative skills with considerable diplomacy, and was instrumental in reconciling differences between various agencies and departments of the Chinese government. At the end of her period of secondment, in 1947, the Chinese government asked that she be allowed to continue her work, and she remained there on secondment to the International Labour Organization until 1949. Her work was praised by the Chinese minister of social welfare, C. K. Ku, and by Eleanor Hinder, the US attaché for UNRRA affairs. She also worked in Thailand for the United Nations Economic Commission for Asia and the Far East.

Beryl Power retired in 1951 and became involved in charitable causes, primarily housing for the elderly and education. She endowed a number of trusts and charities from her savings, especially those concerned with research into racial intolerance. She retained a deep affection for Girton College, where she endowed a feast for distinguished historians.

Power published articles connected with her work, including one, 'Indian labour conditions', in the *Journal of the Royal Society of Arts* (June 1932), which was awarded the silver medal of the RSA. Most of her writing took the form of official or semi-official reports but despite her self-deprecatory comments on her work the reports show her ability to combine careful and open-minded assessments of situations and people with a lively narrative. She stressed the importance of 'patient and persistent personal investigation', maintaining that it was 'the duty of every woman, as of every man, not to rest content until she has made herself a part of an informed public opinion' (lecture at the annual meeting of the Bengal Presidency Council of Women, Calcutta, February 1930, Power MSS).

Beryl Power died at her home, 42A Clarendon Road, Kensington, London, on 4 November 1974, of self-administered alcohol and barbiturate poisoning. At her request there was no memorial service; the notice of her death, which she had written herself, appeared in *The Times* only after she had been cremated at a private ceremony.

                          ELAINE HARRISON

Sources Girton Cam., Power MSS · K. T. Butler and H. I. McMorran, eds., *Girton College register, 1869–1946* (1948) · M. Berg, *A woman in history: Eileen Power, 1889–1940* (1996) · *The Times* (15 Nov 1974) · WWW · *The Vote* · records of the Children's Overseas Reception Board, PRO · *The story of U.N.R.R.A.* (1948) · P. Hennessy, *Whitehall* (1989) · b. cert. · d. cert. · *CGPLA Eng. & Wales* (1974) · *The Times* (11 Nov 1974)

Archives Girton Cam., MSS | priv. coll., corresp. with Eileen Power

Likenesses photographs, Girton Cam.

Wealth at death £43,926: probate, 28 Nov 1974, *CGPLA Eng. & Wales*

Power, Cyril Edward Mary (1872–1951), architect and linocut artist, was born on 17 December 1872 at 14 Redcliffe Street, Chelsea, London, the son of Edward William Power, architect and grandson of Edward Power, architect, of Bristol, and his wife, Amelia Poole Berry. Educated in Kensington and encouraged to draw from a young age, he followed the family tradition by joining his father's architectural practice. His early abilities were recognized in 1900 with the award of the Soane medallion by the Royal Institute of British Architects (RIBA) for his design of an art school. In 1902 he was elected an associate member of the RIBA and for the next twenty years he pursued a career in architecture. On 27 August 1904 he married Dorothy Mary Margaret (*b.* 1882/3), daughter of George Frederic Roper Nunn, agent, of Bury St Edmunds, Suffolk, with whom he had three sons and one daughter. From 1905, among other public works, he worked on designing and building the General Post Office King Edward VII Building in King Edward Street, central London, with Sir Richard Allington in the Ministry of Works. During this period Power was a part-time lecturer in architectural history and design in the school of architecture at University College, London, under Professor Simpson, and also at Goldsmiths' College. Academically minded, he published *English Mediaeval Architecture* (1912), a two-volume history largely illustrated with his pen-and-ink sketches.

In 1916 Power was commissioned into the Royal Flying Corps, where he supervised the repair workshops at Lympne aerodrome, near Folkestone. On demobilization he moved with his family to Bury St Edmunds, where he resumed his architectural practice, in 1920 designing the library extensions at Bradwell Manor, near Mistley, Essex, for his patron Lord Iveagh. In 1922 when nearly fifty, Power suddenly abandoned architecture, his wife, and four children (the youngest of whom was born in December 1921) and returned to London, with the idea of becoming an artist. He took with him a 24-year-old art student, **Sybil Andrews** (1898–1992), whom he had met the year before. Born in Bury St Edmunds on 19 April 1898, she was the daughter of Charles Andrews (1861–1922), ironmonger, and Beatrice Martha Trigg (1868–1929). Andrews did war work as an oxy-acetylene welder on aeroplanes in Bristol and began her art education in 1918 with John Hassall's correspondence course. Power helped the young Andrews with compositional drawing and design; they held a joint exhibition of their watercolours and pastels inspired by local subjects at the Crescent House, Angel Hill, in Bury St Edmunds in December 1921.

In 1922 Power and Andrews enrolled at Heatherley School of Fine Art, where Iain Macnab was co-principal. Here they declared their artistic beliefs in a joint unpublished paper 'Aims of the art of to-day'; inspired by the rhetoric of the Italian futurists, they called for an art of the modern age that was expressed through dynamism and movement. In October 1925 Macnab appointed Power to teach the principles of perspective for artists and to provide courses on architectural history at his newly opened Grosvenor School of Modern Art at 33 Warwick Square, Pimlico, London; Andrews was appointed as the school secretary. When Claude Flight joined the staff in the following year, Power and Andrews were among the most gifted students in his popular linocut classes. They participated in Flight's 'First Exhibition of British Lino-Cuts' at the Redfern Gallery, London, in 1929; thereafter they regularly exhibited their dynamic linocuts of modern speed and movement in group shows during the 1930s. Power and Andrews achieved wider critical recognition with their joint exhibition of monotypes and linocuts at the Redfern in 1933; under the pseudonym Andrew-Power, they also collaborated on several lithographic posters for sports venues commissioned by the London Passenger Transport Board.

Andrews established her studio at 2 Brook Green, Hammersmith, London, which she shared with Power from 1928 until their partnership came to an end in July 1938. At Brook Green they closely collaborated on the themes, colours, and designs of their linocuts; in 1934, a critic for the *Morning Post* observed, 'They are co-workers in the same studio, each inspiring the other in the conception of ideas and their pictorial realisation' (12 July 1934, 15). By virtue of his wider experience and maturity Power was perhaps the more creative force of the partnership in the development of ideas while Andrews was technically superior in the cutting and registering of the printing blocks. A romantic about the medieval past, Power was equally at home in expressing the modernity of his own age. He took to heart the dynamism of the metropolitan rush; among his most striking images were those inspired by the London underground, where his architectural training informed the bold, architectonic forms and sweeping rhythms. By contrast Andrews's themes, drawn mainly from her native Suffolk, expressed the agricultural cycle and the rhythms of seasonal change. Musically gifted and intensely interested in all things medieval, Power learned to play the viola da gamba and the recorder; he also spent many hours transcribing early music manuscripts in the British Museum Library. The Brook Green studio became a meeting place for the Recorder Society and for those interested in early music, including the Dolmetsch family.

When their artistic partnership broke up in 1938, Andrews moved to Norley Wood near Lymington in the New Forest to a cottage that Power had renovated for her. Power, then aged almost sixty-six, returned to his family at New Malden, Surrey, for the final thirteen years of his life. Although he lectured to local art societies and continued to paint in oils and watercolours until his death, he ceased to make linocuts. A highly cultivated dilettante without the income, Power perhaps dissipated his energies over too wide a field. On 20 May 1951 Power died at his home, 24 Howard Road, New Malden, aged seventy-eight. His obituary in the *Surrey Comet* (26 May 1951) was entitled 'Artist, architect and musician. Death of Mr C. E. Power'.

In 1943 Andrews married Walter Morgan, a shipyard worker whom she had met in the shipyards near Southampton while doing war work; in 1947 they emigrated to

Canada, settling in Campbell River, a remote logging township on Vancouver Island, British Columbia. After initial years of hardship she built a studio and eventually resumed her career as a linocut artist. In 1980 a solo exhibition of her prints was held at the Michael Parkin Gallery, London. A major travelling retrospective organized in 1982–3 by the Glenbow Museum, Calgary, brought her national recognition in Canada. Her notes and thoughts on art gained from her private teaching at Campbell River since 1960 were published in London as *Artist's Kitchen* (*c*.1986). Andrews died at Campbell River on 21 December 1992. A few months before her death she donated a large collection of her linocuts to the British Museum; the Glenbow Museum holds a complete representation of her work in all media.   STEPHEN COPPEL

Sources S. Coppel, *Linocuts of the machine age: Claude Flight and the Grosvenor School* (1995) · S. Coppel, 'Claude Flight and the linocut', in F. Carey and A. Griffiths, *Avant-garde British printmaking, 1914–1960* (1990), 73–89 [exhibition catalogue, BM, 1990] · C. E. Power, *English mediaeval architecture*, 2 vols. (1912) · C. E. Power and S. Andrews, 'Aims of the art of to-day', typescript, 29 pp., priv. coll. · S. Andrews, *Artist's kitchen* [n.d., *c*.1986] · P. White, *Sybil Andrews: colour linocuts / linogravures en couleur* (1982) [exhibition catalogue, Glenbow Museum, Calgary, and elsewhere] · G. Samuel and R. Gault, *The linocuts of Cyril Edward Power, 1872–1951* (1989) [incl. chronology by artist's youngest son, Edmund Berry Power; exhibition catalogue, Redfern Gallery, London, 1989] · C. Reeve, *Something to splash about: Sybil Andrews in Suffolk* (1991) [exhibition catalogue, St Edmundsbury Museums, Bury St Edmunds, 1991] · 'Mr Richard Eurich's fine painting', *Morning Post* (12 July 1934), 15 · *Surrey Comet* (26 May 1951) · M. Parkin and D. Hooker, *Sybil Andrews: paintings and graphic work* (1980) [exhibition catalogue, Michael Parkin Fine Art, London, 22 Oct – 15 Nov 1980] · b. cert. · m. cert. · d. cert. · *CGPLA Eng. & Wales* (1952)

Archives Glenbow Museum and Archives, Calgary, work notebooks, papers, blocks, prints [Sybil Andrews]

Likenesses photograph, 1918 (Sybil Andrews), repro. in Reeve, *Something to splash about*, inside front cover · H. Glicenstein, drypoint etching, *c*.1923 (Sybil Andrews), BM · E. R. Roper Power, photograph, 1936, priv. coll. · C. E. Power, self-portrait, linocut, Redfern Gallery, London; repro. in Coppel, *Linocuts of the machine age*

Wealth at death £369 7s. 6d.: probate, 12 July 1952, *CGPLA Eng. & Wales*

Power, Sir D'Arcy (1855–1941), surgeon and historian, was born at 3 Grosvenor Terrace, Pimlico, London, on 11 November 1855, the eldest of six sons and five daughters of Henry Power, then assistant surgeon at the Westminster Ophthalmic Hospital, and his wife and first cousin, Anne, daughter of Thomas Simpson, a banker and shipowner of Whitby, Yorkshire. Power was educated at Merchant Taylors' School and entered New College, Oxford, in 1874 as a commoner. As biology was not taught at New College he transferred to Exeter College, in 1877, with an open exhibition; he obtained his BA with first-class honours in natural science (physiology) in 1878. That year he entered St Bartholomew's Hospital medical school, and he qualified BM in 1882. Power married in 1883, Eleanor (*d.* 1923), younger daughter of George Haynes Fosbroke, a medical practitioner of Bidford, Warwickshire. They had two sons, the younger of whom died of wounds received in action at the second battle of Ypres

in 1915, and one daughter, who died aged two of whooping cough. The elder son became an air vice-marshal in the Royal Air Force Medical Service.

Power spent the whole of his surgical professional life at St Bartholomew's. He was house surgeon to W. S. Savory, and ophthalmic house surgeon to his father. He served as curator of the museum, as demonstrator in operative surgery, and as demonstrator in surgical pathology. He was appointed assistant surgeon in 1898, surgeon in charge of the throat and nose department from 1902 to 1904, and full surgeon in 1904. He resigned this last appointment in 1920, when he was elected consultant surgeon and a governor to the hospital. In 1934 he was appointed the hospital archivist and began a systematic survey of the hospital's medieval muniments. At the Royal College of Surgeons, Power obtained his FRCS in 1883, served as examiner, was a member of Council from 1912 to 1928, and was vice-president in 1921 and 1922. He gave the Bradshaw lecture for 1919, the Vicary lecture for 1920, and was the Hunterian orator in 1925. He was appointed honorary librarian in 1929 and a trustee of the Hunterian Museum in 1930. Power joined the Volunteer Medical Staff Corps in 1888 and was commissioned major on formation of the Royal Army Medical Corps's Territorial Force in 1908. During the First World War he was lieutenant-colonel and surgeon to the officers hospital at Fishmongers' Hall from 1914 to 1916, and then at the 1st London General Hospital until 1920. He published *Wounds in War* in 1915 and was appointed KBE in the peace gazette of June 1919.

Power took a leading part in many professional and learned societies. At various times he was president of the section of the history of medicine and of the section of comparative medicine at the Royal Society of Medicine (1926–8), president of the Bibliographical Society (1926–8) and of the Harveian Society, chairman of the Royal Medical Benevolent Fund, and the holder of various offices in the Pathological Society. He was a corresponding member or honorary fellow of many learned societies both at home and overseas. A keen freemason, he served as consultant surgeon to the Freemasons' Hospital (later the Royal Masonic Hospital). He was elected fellow of the Society of Antiquaries in 1897. Power visited the USA in 1924 and 1930, lecturing on the foundations of medical history, and he went to Australia in 1935.

As a surgeon Power was a rapid and skilful operator, and an early pioneer of abdominal and paediatric surgery in this country. He was at his best in emergency operations. Power wrote extensively on surgery, including a number of textbooks, but his real mark was as a scholar and historian of medicine. He contributed a historical article to almost every number of the *British Journal of Surgery* from its beginning in 1913; some 200 'lives' to the *Dictionary of National Biography*; numerous historical articles (many unsigned) to the *British Medical Journal*; and he edited the *Lives of the Fellows of the Royal College of Surgeons of England*, published in 1930. He also wrote the entries for the subsequent (1930–51) volume of the *Lives*, between 1930 and 1940, almost up to his death; it was published in 1953. Among his historical publications are *William Harvey*

(1897), one of the best short studies of this subject, *Portraits of Dr William Harvey* (1913), *Foundations of Medical History* (1931), *A Short History of Surgery* (1933), and *Mirror for Surgeons*, an anthology (1939). Power edited and in 1910 published the manuscripts of the English works of the fourteenth-century surgeon, John of Arderne; he also translated his Latin treatises (published in 1922).

Power was a modest unselfish man. Having been poor in his early life, he remained simple and approachable. He was widely loved and trusted for his integrity and friendliness. Power was of middle height, small featured, wore a moustache, and had keen blue eyes. During the second half of his life, he lived in a small house in Chandos Street, Cavendish Square, next door to the Medical Society of London. His home contained his large collection of books, including a remarkable collection of editions of the *Regimen of Salerno*. He developed heart failure soon after his eighty-fifth birthday; his house had been damaged in air raids in the autumn of 1940, and he moved to his son's home, 53 Murray Road, Northwood, Middlesex, where he died on 18 May 1941. He was cremated and his ashes were buried in his wife's grave at Bidford, Warwickshire. The following month his library was sold at Sothebys.

HAROLD ELLIS

Sources D'A. Power and W. R. Le Fanu, *Lives of the fellows of the Royal College of Surgeons of England, 1930–1951* (1953) · *The Times* (19 May 1941) · *British Journal of Surgery*, 29 (1941), 1 · *BMJ* (31 May 1941), 836–7 · D'A. Power, *Selected writings, 1877–1930* (1931); repr. (New York, 1970) · *WWW* · *DNB*
Archives Duke U., Perkins L. · RCS Eng. · Wellcome L.
Likenesses W. Stoneman, photograph, 1917, NPG · photograph, 1930, repr. in Power, *Selected writings* (1970) · M. Thompson, oils, 1934, RCS Eng. · M. Ayoub, group portrait, oils (*Council of the Royal College of Surgeons of England of 1926–27*), RCS Eng.
Wealth at death £20,722 3s. 1d.: probate, 21 Aug 1941, CGPLA Eng. & Wales

Power, Edward Joseph [Ted] (1899–1993), radio engineer and art collector, was born on 11 September 1899 at Maryborough, Queen's county, Ireland, one of the four children of Patrick Power, an army sergeant in the Leinster regiment, and his wife, Jane, formerly Heart. The family moved to England in 1907, when the regiment was transferred, but his parents later separated, and in 1910 his mother took the children to Manchester. Power was educated probably at Xaverian College, Manchester, leaving in 1916 to take a short course at Wilmslow Radio School before joining the navy as a wireless operator. After the war he joined the merchant navy, leaving in 1922 to set himself up as a manufacturer of crystal sets and transformers. On 22 November 1924 he married Irene (Rene) Cordelia Bevan (1899/1900–1978), wig maker and hairdresser. They had four children. He worked as chief engineer for McMichael Radio from 1926, before setting up a business in Slough repairing wirelesses and making radio receivers.

In 1928 Power joined his friend Frank Murphy, a former Post Office engineer, in setting up Murphy Radio Ltd in Welwyn Garden City, as partner and chief engineer. The first Murphy sets were produced in 1930, and Murphy and

Power then approached the furniture maker Gordon Russell in their search for a good modern designer for their radio cabinets. The cabinets designed by R. D. Russell, Gordon Russell's brother, for Murphy radios, became classics of industrial design. When Frank Murphy resigned in 1937 Power became chairman.

During the Second World War Murphy Radio played an important part in the development of radar, manufacturing high-power valves and experimenting with valve technology. After the war the company resumed its expansion into television production, which had begun in 1937; in 1949, when it was floated on the stock market, Power became a wealthy man. He remained chairman until 1962, when he allowed the Rank Organization to buy control of the company.

Power began to collect modern art in 1951, and by the mid-1950s had acquired a large collection of paintings, mainly by as yet unknown contemporary French artists. He particularly admired Jean Dubuffet, eighty of whose works he bought between 1956 and 1960. He sought out the newest art he could find on frequent trips to Paris, mainly in the company of Peter Cochrane, a director of Tooth's Gallery. He amassed large collections of works by individual artists in order to try to understand their ideas, and he bought experimentally to see whether he liked a work, and if he did not he sold it. As Lawrence Alloway, deputy director of the Institute of Contemporary Arts, wrote in 1956: 'this collector works … in the spirit in which his artists paint—impulsively, experimentally, to see what will happen' (Arts Council exhibition catalogue, *New Trends in Painting: some Pictures from a Private Collection*, 1956, 5).

In the late 1950s Power turned his attention to American art, buying works by de Kooning and Rothko, and he was one of the first British collectors to buy paintings by Jackson Pollock, Ellsworth Kelly, and Barnett Newman. He also became a close friend of the Danish artist Asger Jorn, twenty-nine of whose paintings he bought between 1956 and 1960. In the 1960s he bought works by R. B. Kitaj, Howard Hodgkin, Claes Oldenburg, and Roy Lichtenstein, and he owned a number of early paintings by Andy Warhol, including *Soup Can*, which he bought in 1964. Although he continued to buy—and sell—until the end of his life, after 1968 he no longer tried to collect the best of contemporary work, but he kept in touch with the latest trends. Power believed in the vital importance of contemporary art and donated many paintings to the Tate Gallery, where he was a trustee from 1968 to 1975. Although he was one of the most important British collectors of modern art in the 1950s and 1960s he shunned publicity and few knew the scale of his collection.

Power died on 16 September 1993 at Oakwood House Hospital, Old Watton Road, Colney, Norfolk. Two sons and a married daughter survived him. His estate was valued at over £26 million.

ANNE PIMLOTT BAKER

Sources J. Mundy, ed., *Brancusi to Beuys: works from the Ted Power collection* (1996) · R. Allwood and K. Laurie, *R. D. Russell, Marian Pepler* (1983), 6–7 [exhibition catalogue, Geffrye Museum, London, 9 Sept – 23 October 1983] · G. Russell, *Designer's trade* (1968), 145–52 ·

N. Pevsner, 'Broadcasting comes of age: the radio cabinet, 1919–1940', *ArchR*, 87 (1940), 189–90 · *The Independent* (18 Sept 1993) · *The Independent* (25 Oct 1993) · b. cert. · m. cert. · d. cert. · *CGPLA Eng. & Wales* (1995)

Likenesses H. Hodgkin, oils, 1969–73, Tate collection · photograph, *c.*1979, repro. in Mundy, ed., *Brancusi to Beuys* · P. Blake, oils, 1987–9, repro. in Mundy, ed., *Brancusi to Beuys* · photograph, repro. in *The Independent* (18 Sept 1993)

Wealth at death £26,357,872: probate, 9 Jan 1995, *CGPLA Eng. & Wales*

Power [*married name* Postan], **Eileen Edna Le Poer** (1889–1940), economic historian, was born at home at Parkdale, Dunham Massey, Altrincham, Cheshire, on 9 January 1889, the eldest of three daughters of Philip Ernest Le Poer Power (*b.* 1860), stockbroker, and his wife, Mabel Grindlay Clegg (1866–1903). She was the granddaughter of the Revd Philip Bennett Power (1822–1899), originally from Waterford, Ireland, who made his name as a prolific writer of evangelical tracts. Philip Power was imprisoned for fraud in 1891, and Mabel Power, faced with scandal and financial ruin, moved with her daughters to Bournemouth. There they lived with and were financially supported by her father, Benson Clegg. Eileen Power and her sisters started school in Bournemouth, but on Mabel Power's death in 1903, Benson Clegg moved with one of his spinster daughters and his granddaughters to Oxford. There Eileen and her sisters Rhoda Dolores Le Poer *Power and Beryl Millicent *Power attended the Oxford High School for Girls, founded by the Girls' Public Day School Company.

Eileen Power went to Girton College, Cambridge, from 1907 to 1910, on a Clothworkers' scholarship, and took a first in both parts of the historical tripos. She was awarded the Gilchrist research fellowship, and studied at the University of Paris and the École des Chartes from 1910 to 1911. On her return to Britain she was awarded the Shaw research studentship at the London School of Economics (LSE) (1911–13), where she studied medieval women. She became director of studies in history at Girton in 1913, and remained there until 1921, but during that time also held the Pfeiffer research fellowship, (1915–18). She wrote her book *Medieval English Nunneries* (1922) and the early versions of several major essays on medieval women during the time she was in Cambridge. She was awarded the Albert Kahn travelling fellowship in 1920–21, and reported on her world travels during that year, which included China, in her *Report to the Trustees of the Albert Kahn Travelling Fellowship, September 1920 – September 1921* (1921). In 1921 she was appointed lecturer in economic history at the London School of Economics, and remained there until her death: she became reader in 1924 and professor in 1931. She was made a corresponding member of the Medieval Academy of America in 1936, and was Ford lecturer in English history at Oxford in 1938–9. She was awarded an honorary LLD at Manchester in 1933, and another at Mount Holyoke College in 1937.

While Eileen Power was a student at Cambridge she was a close friend of Margaret Garrett (later Spring-Rice), niece of Millicent Garrett Fawcett, and of Karin Costelloe (later Stephen), niece of Alys Russell. These friendships took her

Eileen Edna Le Poer Power (1889–1940), by unknown photographer

into suffrage politics, and onto the edges of the Bloomsbury circle. She campaigned for the National Union of Women's Suffrage Societies, and joined the women's peace movement. Her interests in women's medieval history and in internationalism were formed in this context, and in her personal response to the First World War. Her experience in the Kahn travelling fellowship, especially in India and China, also developed a new interest in comparative and world history. From this time she also argued for the role of history in spreading internationalist political ideals, and undertook the series of editions for children the Broadway Travellers (1926–38), the Broadway Medieval Library (1928–31), and the Broadway Diaries, Memoirs and Letters (1929–31). With her sister Rhoda she wrote children's history books, of which the most famous was *Boys and Girls of History* (1926). She was part of literary London, wrote widely in the press, and was a popular lecturer. During the 1920s she also started the memorable BBC schools history broadcasts which she made with Rhoda. The international aspects of medieval history, medieval trade, comparative economic history, and world history, as well as women's and social history, which Eileen Power made her own, were always made immensely attractive and immediately accessible to broad audiences by her extensive use of literary references and personal portraits. Her broadcasts continued until 1936, when she came into conflict with her producers over the political and pedagogical directions of the programmes.

When Eileen Power moved to the LSE the predominantly literary, cultural, and social framework of her history was challenged under the influence of the social sciences then being fostered there. She became part of a remarkable group of scholars developing the social sciences in new directions. She reshaped the economic history courses and seminars in partnership with R. H. Tawney, and later with Sir Michael Moïssey *Postan, whom she later married. Academic collaboration and friendship with Harold Laski, Bronislaw Malinowski, and Charles Webster developed in the pre-departmental days at the LSE, and in the social gatherings in both Tawney's and Power's houses in Mecklenburgh Square. Power also worked closely with several of these in working groups and other initiatives to foster close connections between economic and social history and the social sciences. From the early 1930s she ran the famous medieval economic history seminar together with Postan.

Eileen Power made a number of significant contributions to her discipline. She developed economic history within the framework of medieval history. She avoided the contemporary traditions of legal and constitutional history, and initially followed an inclination towards literary history and the history of religious life. Her early work had a clear political framework in her commitment to the women's peace campaigns of the inter-war years. Her book *Medieval English Nunneries*, major essays on medieval women's history, especially the well-known chapter 'The position of women' in C. G. Crump's and E. F. Jacob's *The Legacy of the Middle Ages* (1926), and other essays brought together long after her death in *Medieval Women* (ed. M. M. Postan, 1975), were conceived and written in this framework. Her most successful and famous work of social history, *Medieval People* (1924), which went into ten editions, was the culmination of the first phase of her approach to social history. Its genesis lay in her feminist and pacifist political commitment, and in the methodology she developed of history as literature. The book was a social history deploying literary devices, but even more significantly it was a social history written to spread a message of internationalism.

At the LSE, Power worked in partnership with R. H. Tawney to develop an extended course structure for economic history, as well as graduate seminars, social science discussion groups, and collaborative research projects. Economic history was enormously popular during the time she taught, and indeed it came for a time to be identified with the LSE. Her personality contributed to this success. Tawney commented that it was not just 'her brilliance as a lecturer, it was personal contact which best revealed her magic. She possessed to an extraordinary degree the gift of not merely drawing out different personalities, but of fusing them into an organic group' (*DNB*). The keynote of Power's teaching at the LSE remained internationalism and comparative history, especially that between the East and the West. In another collaboration with M. M. Postan from the later 1920s she also moved economic history forward into discussion with the social sciences, especially sociology and anthropology. She developed her comparative method through analogies between current underdeveloped economies, especially China and India, and medieval societies, and she also drew on the comparative regional studies developed by historians from the German historical school, especially the Austrian Alfons Dopsch. Her project should be seen as parallel to the work in France of Marc Bloch and Lucien Febvre, founders of the *Annales* school of history, and Bloch and Power recognized the similarity of their goals.

Throughout this period Power concentrated on the study of long-distance trade and merchants. The inspiration on which she drew for this work, and for the place she saw for it in explanations for the transition out of feudal economic limitations to capitalist development, was Henri Pirenne. Pirenne attributed to the medieval merchant–entrepreneur the origins of the dynamism which would eventually lead to economic growth. For Power this position provided further connections between economic history and her internationalist political views. She associated trade and merchants with international connection and peace. Her research and publications over this period reflected this search for the origins of merchant capitalism before industrialization: *English Trade in the Fifteenth Century* (ed. E. E. Power and M. M. Postan, 1933), *The Wool Trade in English Medieval History* (published posthumously in 1941), and the first volume of *The Cambridge Economic History of Europe* (ed. E. E. Power and J. H. Clapham, 1941). *The Cambridge Economic History of Europe* was the first great collaborative project in comparative economic history; it was also a great international enterprise which succeeded despite the Second World War.

Eileen Power's idea of social history from the time she arrived at the LSE thus developed away from simply revealing the lives of ordinary people towards offering a historical analysis of social structures. Thus she turned to the analysis of the underlying trends of medieval agrarian society and to comparative commercial and industrial development, linking it to the new discipline of economic history. She also took a professional attitude to the development of her discipline. She took a major role in the founding in 1926 of the Economic History Society; she helped to establish its journal, the *Economic History Review*; and she edited the first wartime number herself. She worked in archives, and raised research funding from the Rockefeller Foundation to start major new archive collections, including a registry and depository of London business archives. She developed research projects, set up her research seminar to pursue these, and left behind a group of research students who in the following two decades published work on medieval trade and commercial history. Other students and colleagues whom she had influenced wrote the big books of social history and women's history which were not overtaken until the 1970s and 1980s—Alice Clark, Dorothy George, Ivy Pinchbeck, Dorothy Marshall, and H. S. Bennett among them.

During a second trip to China in 1929 Eileen Power became engaged to Reginald *Johnston, the tutor to the last emperor of China. He returned to Britain in 1930, but the engagement was finally ended in 1932. She then turned to a closer involvement with her former student and research assistant, by now a lecturer at the LSE, Sir Michael Moïssey Postan (1897/8–1980), who was nine years her junior. They married on 11 December 1937, and a few months later Michael Postan became professor of economic history at Cambridge. They built a house in Cambridge, but kept on the house in Mecklenburgh Square, as Eileen Power continued to teach at the LSE.

While Power continued to support the League of Nations, and attended an assembly in Geneva in 1939, she was also a critic of fascism and was part of a prominent anti-appeasement circle in the later 1930s. She turned to lecturing and writing against appeasement, including her famous lecture to the Cambridge History Club 'The eve of the dark ages: a tract for the times', later reprinted in a posthumous edition of *Medieval People*. At the outbreak of war she returned to Cambridge when part of LSE was evacuated there. She died on 8 August 1940, on the way to the Middlesex Hospital, London, after a sudden heart attack, and was cremated at Golders Green, Middlesex, on 12 August.   MAXINE L. BERG

Sources M. Berg, *A woman in history: Eileen Power, 1889–1940* (1996) · J. H. Clapham, 'Eileen Power, 1889–1940', *Economica*, new ser., 7 (1940), 355–9 · R. H. Tawney, 'Eileen Power', address delivered at Golders Green crematorium, 12 Aug 1940 · *DNB* · C. K. Webster, 'Eileen Power (1889–1940)', *Economic Journal*, 36 (1926), 317–20 · K. T. Butler and H. I. McMorran, eds., *Girton College register, 1869–1946* (1948) · b. cert. · m. cert. · d. cert.

Archives BLPES, personal file · CUL, papers, incl. indexes relating to historical work, notes, and transcripts · Girton Cam., MSS · NRA, priv. coll., MSS · Nuffield Oxf., Economic History Society MSS | BBC WAC, Eileen Power and Rhoda Power MSS · BL, corresp. with Sir Sydney Cockerell, Add. MS 52743 · BLPES, R. H. Tawney MSS

Likenesses photograph, 1933, BBC · photograph, BLPES [*see illus.*]

Wealth at death £1194 8s. 6d.: probate, 6 Jan 1941, *CGPLA Eng. & Wales*

Power, Henry (*c.*1626–1668), natural philosopher and physician, was born in Annesley, Nottinghamshire, the eldest son of John Power (*d.* 1638) of Halifax, cloth merchant and landlord, and his wife, Jane (*née* Jennings). After attending school in Halifax, Power matriculated at Christ's College, Cambridge, on 15 December 1641 when his age was given as fifteen. He graduated BA in 1644 and MA in 1648. At Cambridge the physician and author Thomas Browne, a friend of his father, advised him to pursue medicine, and Power complied, declaring his intention to 'review the whole body of Philosophy, especially Naturall' (*Works*, 256–7), as he did so. Browne recommended that his protégé read works by Harvey, but also by Paracelsians such as Croll and Hartmann. As a result, even as Power pursued his medical studies he became fascinated by the intricate wonders revealed by practical anatomy, chemical philosophy, and botany. Such interests were being fostered by a number of Cambridge virtuosi, especially the physician Francis Glisson, who had become the focus of a medical and natural philosophical circle in which Power now participated to the full. He came

increasingly to feel that the key to appreciating Creation was to be sought in a synthesis of Cartesian and Paracelsian approaches. This was hardly Browne's view; but Power did inherit something of Browne's rich prose style, and his eagerness to draw elaborate imaginative analogies across the natural order.

Power graduated MD in 1655, and settled in Halifax. He married, at a date unknown, Margaret, daughter of Anthony Foxcroft. His interests in natural philosophy and natural history were furthered by friendship with another gentleman impressed by the Cartesian philosophy, Richard Towneley of Towneley Hall, near Burnley. The Towneleys were a Catholic family that had pursued such interests since before the civil war. Now they and Power co-operated in natural philosophy, procuring expensive equipment from London to facilitate their investigations. By 1661, Power said, they had '4 as rare telescopes (as England affordes)' (Webster, 158). In the 1650s they conducted experiments on the atmosphere, inspired by Jean Pecquet's *Experimenta nova anatomica* (Paris, 1651), a primarily medical work that also included an account of Pascal's Puy de Dôme trial. Their investigations may have led to the issuing of a report in the autumn of 1661 entitled *Mercurial Experiments Made at Towneley Hall in the Years 1660, and 1661*; no copies survive, but the report later became part of Power's *Experimental Philosophy*.

The nascent Royal Society in London was in need of men such as Power and Towneley. John Tillotson informed the society of their activities; Croune, the society's register, was forthwith ordered to open a correspondence with Power. The latter responded by forwarding some of his by now extensive experimental researches, which were read at the society. The experiments on air were of especial interest, since they arrived at a moment of international controversy over Robert Boyle's researches on the subject. The society immediately recruited Power as a helper in its experimental and natural historical work, and he was elected a fellow on 1 July 1663 (having been proposed as early as May 1661).

Power visited the society in June 1663, and demonstrated his microscopical observations before the virtuosi. During his London stay he arranged for publication of these and other observations by the society's new 'printers' (strictly speaking, booksellers), John Martyn and James Allestry. The result was Power's only surviving publication, the book on which his reputation is founded: *Experimental Philosophy* (1664 [1663]). This work incorporated material dating back over the previous decade. Its three books dealt respectively with microscopy, the air, and magnetism. Its reputation, then and since, has chiefly rested on the first of these, which was the first book in English about microscopy, and included a number of pioneering descriptions of microscopic observations.

However, Power's descriptions were soon eclipsed by the splendidly illustrated pages of Robert Hooke's *Micrographia*, which meant that the source of *Experimental Philosophy*'s initial fame was also the cause of its later obscurity. Readers inevitably tended to assume that both books were aiming at the same ends, and that Hooke's was 'an aggrandized version of the *Experimental Philosophy*' (Webster, 161). Yet Power's elaborate descriptions were really more akin to the literary conceits of Browne than the visual world of Hooke (Samuel Butler used Power's style as a vehicle for satirizing the experimental enterprise in general). Power's descriptions were perhaps intended as aids to a kind of rhapsodic reflection while readers peered through microscopes, rather than as substitutes for such observing. When Samuel Pepys read Power, for example, he did so with a new microscope to hand, as he and his wife struggled together to master 'the manner of seeing anything' through it (*Diary*, ed. R. Latham and W. Mathews, 1970–83, 5.241); this experience does not seem to have been the case when he read Hooke. Moreover, in Power's eyes the sections on the air and magnetism were also important. Each illustrated a central element of his peculiar Cartesian/Helmontian philosophy: infinite divisibility, the elasticity of air (and the absurdity of a vacuum), and the use of electricity and magnetism to refute a geostatic cosmology such as that of Jacques Grandami.

The publication of his research marked the peak of Power's involvement with the London experimental community. In 1664 he transferred his medical practice to Wakefield, and contacts with both the Towneleys and the Royal Society diminished. In relative seclusion, Power synthesized his earlier work on anatomy and chemical physiology into a general treatise, which he entitled *Historia physico-anatomica*. Dedicated to Lord Delamere, it was never published, and was preserved only in manuscript. Its explanations were couched in terms of the kind of circulating system beloved of mid-seventeenth-century thinkers. Power envisaged 'Animal Spirits' that were subtle enough to bridge the divide between the corporeal and the incorporeal. These spirits were a central unifying theme of the *Experimental Philosophy*. Simultaneously both physical and chemical, Power believed that they had been the first products of Creation. They permeated the universe, circulated within the bodies of all living creatures, and were 'the main (though invisible) Agent in all Natures three Kingdoms Mineral, Vegetal, and Animal' (Power, 61).

Power died in December 1668, and was buried on 23 December at the church of All Saints, Wakefield. His work shows both the variety of opinions among the first generation of experimental philosophers and the vitality of natural philosophy beyond London and the Royal Society. Power's philosophy was a creative appropriation of both Paracelsian and Cartesian principles, inspired by what may always have been his prime interest, medicine.

ADRIAN JOHNS

Sources H. Power, *Experimental philosophy in three books, containing new experiments microscopical, mercurial, magnetical …* (1664); repr. with corrections (1966) • *The works of Sir Thomas Browne*, new edn, ed. G. Keynes, 4 (1964), 254–70 • T. Birch, *The history of the Royal Society of London*, 4 vols. (1756–7), vol. 1 • T. Cowles, 'Dr. Henry Power, disciple of Sir Thomas Browne', *Isis*, 20 (1933–4), 344–66 • C. Webster, 'Henry Power's experimental philosophy', *Ambix*, 14 (1967), 150–78 • J. T. Hughes, 'Henry Power (1626–1668) of New Hall, Elland and experiments on barometric pressure', *Transactions of the Halifax Antiquarian Society*, new ser., 10 (2002), 14–26
Archives BL, Sloane MSS, corresp. and papers • RS, papers

Power, Jane [Jennie] **Wyse** [*née* Jane O'Toole] (**1858–1941**), Irish nationalist and feminist, was born in May 1858 in Main Street, Baltinglass, co. Wicklow, the youngest of the seven children, three daughters and four sons, of Edward O'Toole, provision dealer, and his wife, Mary Norton. She grew up in Dublin, where her father set up shop in 1860 in the St Stephen's Green area, and probably attended a local convent school. She was well educated, articulate, and in appearance tall and dark-haired. Her first political involvement was in the Ladies' Land League (1881–2), of which she became a central executive member. While the male leaders were imprisoned from October 1881 to May 1882 the Ladies' Land League, headed by Anna Parnell, sister of Charles Stewart Parnell, ran the land campaign. Anna became estranged from her brother, owing to different interpretations of land league policy, but O'Toole remained devoted to both. On 5 July 1883 she married John Wyse Power (*c*.1859–1926), journalist and member of the Irish Republican Brotherhood. They had four children, three daughters and a son, none of whom left any children.

In 1893 Jennie Wyse Power and her husband became active members of the Gaelic League. In 1899 she set up a business, the Irish Farm Produce Company, with restaurant attached, at 21 Henry Street, Dublin. The family lived above the business, which became a nationalist meeting-place. A feminist and suffragist, Wyse Power was a member of the Irishwomen's Suffrage and Local Government Association, founded in 1876, and later of the Irish Women's Franchise League, founded in 1908. When eligibility for women as poor-law guardians was achieved in 1896, she was elected as a guardian in Dublin South and served from 1903 to 1911. In 1900 she was a founding member of Inghinidhe na hEireann (Daughters of Ireland), founded to facilitate women's active participation in the male-dominated nationalist movement. Its first president was Maud Gonne. In 1905 she became a founder and executive member of the National Council, from 1908 called Sinn Féin ('we ourselves'), who were committed to Irish self-reliance and self-government. She took a middle position in debate among feminist-nationalist women as to which took priority. She believed that the demand to include women's suffrage should not be pushed before the Home Rule Bill was passed, in case it held up the bill's passage, but once passed she was ready to campaign for its inclusion.

Wyse Power became a member, and later president, of Cumann na mBan (League of Women), established in 1914 as an auxiliary to the Irish Volunteers. She was among the Cumann members who shared the belief that the First World War was an opportunity for Irish nationalism. The 1916 proclamation was signed at her house, and she and her family actively supported the 1916 rising. After that date she became an executive member of the new Sinn Féin, now an umbrella group for nationalists committed to separation from England. When it won the 1918 election and set up its own parliament (Dáil Éireann) and government, she acted as treasurer of the party and as a judge in the Sinn Féin courts. She was elected to Dublin corporation in 1920.

One of a minority in Cumann na mBan who accepted the Anglo-Irish treaty of 1921 as a stage towards complete independence and a united Ireland, she resigned and joined the pro-treaty Cumann na nGaedheal Party and became a member of the Seanad (senate) of the Irish Free State. Disillusioned with her party when the boundary commission of 1924 failed to make any change in the partition of Ireland, she resigned in 1925 to become an independent. When Eamonn De Valera's party, Fianna Fáil, came into government in 1932 she liked its policies of economic self-sufficiency and of dismantling aspects of the treaty. She joined it in 1936, and became a Fianna Fáil senator. She remained a consistent supporter of women's rights, opposing policies of both Cumann na nGaedheal and Fianna Fáil governments which restricted women's full citizenship and employment opportunities. When Fianna Fáil abolished the Seanad in 1936 her public political life ended.

John Wyse Power had died in 1926, and in 1929 Jennie sold her business and lived with her daughter Nancy at 15 Earlsfort Terrace, Dublin. She died in Dublin on 5 January 1941 and was buried in Glasnevin cemetery beside her husband and her daughter Maura. MARY CULLEN

Sources M. O'Neill, *From Parnell to De Valera: a biography of Jennie Wyse Power, 1858–1941* (1991) · Seanad (Irish senate) debates, 1922–36
Likenesses photograph, *c.*1882, priv. coll. · S. C. Harrison, portrait, 1926, priv. coll.
Wealth at death £5308 5s. 4d.: probate, 14 Feb 1941, CGPLA *Éire*

Power, Sir John Cecil, first baronet (1870–1950), company director and public benefactor, was born at Eldon, co. Down, on 21 December 1870, the younger son of William Taylor Power and his wife, Cecilia, daughter of Colonel John Burgoyne. At ten Power went to London where, with his brother, he was later to enter the firm of Power, Power & Co., export merchants with considerable business in the East.

As a young man Power was delicate and had to spend three years in Italy, a sojourn which implanted in him a love of other countries and of travel which he was later to indulge whenever possible. In 1902 he married Mabel Katherine Louisa, daughter of John Hartley Perks JP of London and Wolverhampton; they had two sons and three daughters. After his marriage he bought a villa in the south of France to which he would go as often as business and, subsequently, parliamentary duties allowed. He paid a series of visits to the United States and went to Canada, India, and South Africa, afterwards lecturing and writing on his experiences. He served for many years as a member of the executive of the Travel and Industrial Development Association.

Real estate soon tempted Power away from the family business; he had an unerring flair for property, together with considerable financial talent. His name is associated particularly with Kingsway, a London thoroughfare which opened up what had hitherto been slum property between Holborn and Aldwych. A number of its imposing buildings, such as Adastral House, were of Power's provenance.

Power's success in real estate made him a wealthy man and enabled him to become a generous benefactor. His first great gift was in 1920, an anonymous benefaction prompted by the historian A. F. Pollard of £20,000 towards the founding of an institute of historical research in London. Next, in 1923, came a gift of £10,000 to the British (later Royal) Institute of International Affairs, for the erection of a lecture hall at the rear of the mansion (given by Colonel and Mrs R. W. Leonard) in St James's Square, London, which became known as Chatham House. Power was honorary treasurer of the institute from 1921 to 1943 and during his long association made many other gifts to the organization which included, in 1938, the leasehold premises of his own house in Chesham Place. This house he had hitherto made available to the British Council (before it moved to larger premises) of which he was honorary treasurer from 1934 to 1950. On the outbreak of war in 1939 the house in Belgrave Square, in which he was then living, was lent to the government for use as offices.

Power was for many years associated with the League of Nations Union, serving on the executive committee from 1929 to 1936 and, at various times, on its appeals, finance, and parliamentary committees. In addition he was a member of the committee of the Royal Humane Society and, from 1934 to 1949, a director of the Royal Insurance Company.

Politics early claimed Power's attention and in 1924, the year in which he became a baronet, he was elected Conservative member for Wimbledon, a seat which he held until 1945 when, his health beginning to fail, he withdrew to his country home in Hampshire.

Power's friends came from all walks of life; he enjoyed good company and was a generous host. The personal tastes of this tenacious and indomitable Irishman were simple; apart from golf and cricket, he had few hobbies save music. He had fallen under the spell of the opera as a young man and would talk nostalgically of the days when he had frequented the gallery of La Scala. Opera remained his abiding delight, and he was regularly to be seen at Covent Garden in the London season. He never fully recovered from the shock of his wife's death in 1945. He continued, however, to make occasional visits to Villa Fressinet at Grasse, where he died on 5 June 1950. He was succeeded, as second baronet, by his elder son, Ivan McLannahan Cecil (1903–1954). I. S. MACADAM, *rev.*

Sources *The Times* (9 June 1950) · personal knowledge (1959) · private information (1959) · *WWW* · CGPLA *Eng. & Wales* (1950)
Archives NL Wales, corresp. with Thomas Jones
Likenesses O. Birley, oils, 1934, Royal Institute of International Affairs, Chatham House, London · S. Charoux, bronze bust, 1944, Royal Institute of International Affairs, Chatham House, London

Wealth at death £306,329 0s. 8d.: probate, 11 Sept 1950, *CGPLA Eng. & Wales*

Power, Joseph (1798–1868), librarian, was the fifth son of John Power MD, of Market Bosworth, Leicestershire, where he was born on 5 October 1798. He entered Clare College, Cambridge, as a pensioner in 1817, and in 1821 he graduated as tenth wrangler. In 1823 he was elected a fellow of his college. On 13 June 1824 he was ordained deacon at Norwich. But as there was no teaching post available at Clare, in 1829 he removed to Trinity Hall, a society then dominated by the study of civil law. There he taught mathematics, and acted as one of two tutors, until he was able to return to a vacancy in his first college in 1844.

In 1845, on the resignation of John Lodge, the university librarian, on account of ill health, Power was put forward to succeed him. In an unusually hard-fought election, in which his ultimate opponent was J. J. Smith of Gonville and Caius College, a prominent figure in local antiquarian circles and well known for his industry as well as for his outspokenness, wits spoke of a choice between work without power and power without work. Power was elected, and remained in office until he resigned in 1864. Lodge had transformed the library, overseeing the erection of the new Cockerell building and a great increase in the numbers of books acquired. Power, more relaxed, left a reputation that suffered further at the tongues and pens of his successors J. E. B. Mayor and Henry Bradshaw. Nevertheless, under his eye (albeit at a time when the library was run more by the university than by the librarian) the staff was increased; arrangements were made, with the advice of Antonio Panizzi, for the more efficient gathering of copyright deposit books under the Copyright Act of 1842; reforms in the library's management pre-empted the recommendations of the Cambridge University commissioners' report of 1852; the first volume of a printed catalogue of manuscripts appeared in 1856; an extension was erected, to the designs of George Gilbert Scott; and, not least importantly, Henry Bradshaw was appointed to care for the manuscripts and early printed books.

Corpulent and sociable, Power preferred Cambridge society to travel. His published work consisted mainly of various mathematical papers contributed to the Cambridge Philosophical Society. In 1856 he was presented to the Clare College living of Litlington, Cambridgeshire, which he held until 1866, when the college presented him to the richer living (of which it had bought the advowson in 1836) of Birdbrook, Essex. He remained rector until his death there, after prolonged illness, on 7 June 1868. He never married, and was buried at Birdbrook.

DAVID McKITTERICK

Sources *Reminiscences of the Rev. Joseph Power*, ed. J. M. Chapman (privately printed, 1868) • D. McKitterick, *Cambridge University Library, a history: the eighteenth and nineteenth centuries* (1986) • Venn, *Alum. Cant.* • Crockford (1868), 532 • Boase, *Mod. Eng. biog.*
Archives CUL, letters to Sir George Stokes
Likenesses photograph, repro. in Chapman, ed., *Reminiscences of the Rev. Joseph Power*
Wealth at death under £9000: probate, 8 Aug 1868, *CGPLA Eng. & Wales*

Power, Lionel (*c.*1375×80–1445), composer, is of unknown origins, and his early training and professional experience are also unrecorded. By September 1418 he was a lay singing man and master of the choristers of the household chapel of Thomas, duke of Clarence. He may have been recruited to this chapel at its inception in 1411–13; his service until its disbandment on 29 September 1421, following the duke's death, included a spell in northern France (October 1419 to spring 1421). His employment immediately after 1421 remains unidentified; in all probability he moved to other aristocratic service at a comparable level, quite probably in the household chapel of John, duke of Bedford. In 1438 he became the first master of the newly inaugurated lady chapel choir at Canterbury Cathedral (eight boys, with a few appropriately skilled monks), and in this semi-retirement post he stayed until his death. The fact that Canterbury sources style him esquire and gentleman indicates that he remained a layman.

Power's output exhibits mastery of many of the styles cultivated over a lengthy period of about fifty years. He became, with John Dunstaple, a leading contributor to the emergence and development of a body of English compositional practice which from *c.*1420 to *c.*1450, in terms of both style and content, was received in continental Europe not only with admiration, but also with emulation by contemporaries; English manuscripts were extensively copied.

Between thirty-five and forty surviving works are attributable to Power, of which some twenty-two occur in the English Old Hall manuscript (BL, Add. MS 57950, *c.*1418, additions *c.*1421–5). As well as Marian votive antiphons written in a relatively direct and simple descant style incorporating the plainsong they include movements from the ordinary of the mass composed to exploit the ample resources offered by Clarence's chapel: isorhythmic pieces based on mathematically complex dispositions of the *cantus firmus*; richly scored items for four or even five voices; and pieces modelled in style on the contemporary French secular chanson, some involving the elaborate syncopations and intricate proportional notations of the *ars subtilior*.

Few of Power's early works were known outside England; by contrast, virtually all of his later pieces survive only in continental sources (especially north Italian). Such transmission may have been facilitated by lengthy sojourns between 1419 and 1438 with aristocratic employers in the conquered regions of France; however it was plainly triggered by Power's role in the contemporary application of a sweetly consonant harmonic style to a novel homogeneity and grandeur of musical conception, which together constituted the much admired *contenance angloise*. Already by *c.*1419 he was composing paired movements of the ordinary of the mass, and within another few years he and his contemporaries had developed the unified mass cycle, of which Power's mass *Alma redemptoris mater* is possibly the earliest surviving example. This was the first multi-movement polyphonic form in music history; by lifting composition from the realm of the miniaturist to that of the formulator of broad plans and grand designs, it provided the foundation on which European emulators, particularly Guillaume Dufay and Johannes Ockeghem, were to develop the continental Renaissance style later in the fifteenth century.

From the last years of Power's career came four or five late Marian votive antiphons appropriate to performance in Canterbury Cathedral lady chapel, and also a vernacular treatise prescribing a course of instruction for teaching singing boys the skills of improvising at sight a counterpoint to plainsong. Power died at Canterbury on 5 June 1445 in one of the cathedral's guest lodgings, and was buried the following day in the lay cemetery within the precinct.

ROGER BOWERS

Sources M. Bent, 'Power, Leonel', *New Grove* · R. Bowers, 'Some observations on the life and career of Lionel Power', *Proceedings of the Royal Musical Association*, 102 (1975–6), 103–27 · *Complete works: Leonel Power*, ed. C. Hamm, Corpus Consuetudinum Monasticarum, 50 (1969), xi–xviii · C. Hamm, 'The motets of Leonel Power', *Studies in music history: essays for Oliver Strunk*, ed. H. S. Powers (1968), 127–36 · J. Caldwell, *From the beginnings to c.1715* (1991), vol. 1 of *The Oxford history of English music*, 120–26, 130–34 · S. B. Meech, 'Three musical treatises in English', *Speculum*, 10 (1935), 235–69 · A. Hughes and M. Bent, 'The Old Hall manuscript: a re-appraisal and an inventory', *Musica Disciplina*, 21 (1967), 97–147 · W. G. Searle, ed., *Christ Church, Canterbury*, 1: *The chronicle of John Stone, monk of Christ Church*, Cambridge Antiquarian RS, 34 (1902) · R. Bowers, *English church polyphony: singers and sources from the 14th to the 17th century* (1999), 10–11

Archives BL, Add. MS 57950

Power, Sir Manley (1773–1826), army officer, was born at Hill Court, near Ross, Herefordshire, the son of Thomas Bolton Power (1735–1801), captain in the 20th regiment, of Hill Court, and his wife, Ann Corney, daughter of Captain Corney. His great-grandparents were John Power (d. 1712) and Mercy Manley, daughter of Thomas Manley, of Erbistock, Denbighshire. Manley's first commission as ensign in the 20th foot was dated 27 August 1783, when apparently he was between nine and ten years old. He was promoted lieutenant in 1789 and captain of an independent company in 1793. After his transfer to the 20th foot on 16 January 1794, he was promoted major in 1799 and lieutenant-colonel in 1801.

Power saw much active service. After two years (1795–7) in Halifax, Nova Scotia, he served with the unsuccessful expedition to the Netherlands in 1799 and went to Minorca in 1800. In 1801 his regiment joined the force in Egypt commanded by Sir Ralph Abercromby. He was present at the siege and French surrender (31 August 1801) at Alexandria. On 25 October 1802 he was placed on half pay but from 1803 to 1805 he acted as assistant adjutant-general at the Horse Guards, London. On 6 June 1805 he was made lieutenant-colonel of the 32nd foot, and became colonel in the army in 1810. He took part in the Peninsular War, serving with the duke of Wellington's army in Spain. He was ordered to return for assignment in England, but owing to his experience in commanding Portuguese troops, he was re-assigned to a Portuguese brigade under Lieutenant-General William Carr Beresford. He commanded such a brigade at Salamanca and later at Vittoria, Nivelle, and Orthes. In June 1813 he was promoted major-general. He was awarded a cross and clasp and was made knight-commander of the Portuguese order of the Tower and Sword and made KCB (2 January 1815). Later he served on the staff in Canada and was lieutenant-governor of Malta.

On 5 June 1802 Power married Sarah, daughter of J. Coulson, and they had three daughters and a son, Manley (1803–1857), who became a lieutenant-colonel commanding the 85th regiment. In 1818 he married, second, Anne, daughter of Kingsmill Evans, colonel in the Grenadier Guards, of Lydiart House, Monmouthshire, and they had two sons. Their eldest son, Kingsmill Manley Power (1819–1881), was captain in the 9th and 16th lancers and served with distinction in the Gwalior and Sutlej campaigns. He was promoted lieutenant-general in May 1825. Power died at Bern, Switzerland, on 7 July 1826.

WILLIAM BROADFOOT, *rev.* GORDON L. TEFFETELLER

Sources Fortescue, *Brit. army*, vols. 4–10 · *Supplementary despatches (correspondence) and memoranda of Field Marshal Arthur, duke of Wellington*, ed. A. R. Wellesley, second duke of Wellington, 15 vols. (1858–72), vols. 1–11 · Army lists · *GM*, 1st ser., 96/2 (1826), 182–3 · J. Philippart, ed., *The royal military calendar*, 3rd edn, 3 (1820), 312

Archives Herefs. RO, corresp. and papers | BL, corresp. with Earl Bathurst, loan 57 · NL Scot., corresp. with Sir G. Brown

Power, Marguerite Agnes (1815?–1867), writer, was a daughter of Colonel Robert Power (b. c.1792), and his wife, Agnes Brooke, and niece of Marguerite *Gardiner, countess of Blessington (1789–1849). Little is known about her childhood, which was probably spent in Ireland. Her mother was the daughter of Thomas Brooke, first member of council at St Helena. Her father had an army career, and afterwards became agent for the Blessington estates in co. Tyrone. He was later given a posting in Canada by Lord Durham. In 1839 Marguerite Power and her sister Ellen moved to London to live permanently with Lady Blessington at Gore House. As a result of her aunt's extensive literary connections, Marguerite Power became a friend of many of the most influential people of the day, including Walter Savage Landor, Charles Dickens, William Thackeray, Prince Louis Napoleon, and Benjamin Disraeli. During the 1840s she was a regular contributor to the annuals, particularly *The Keepsake* and Heath's *Book of Beauty*. After the breakup at Gore House in April 1849, Marguerite Power and her sister accompanied their aunt to Paris. Marguerite Power wrote a memoir of Lady Blessington, prefixed to Lady Blessington's novel *Country Quarters* (1850) and reprinted in the *Journal of the Conversations of Lord Byron with the Countess of Blessington* (1893).

After Lady Blessington's death in June 1849, Marguerite Power remained in Paris, supporting herself as a journalist and novelist. From 1851 to 1857 she edited *The Keepsake*, to which Dickens contributed 'To be Read at Dusk' in 1852. The annual's folding came as a great financial blow and, despite an extensive literary output, she struggled financially for the rest of her life. She continued to write for periodicals and annuals, including four stories and a poem for *Household Words*, and miscellaneous pieces for *Once a Week*, the *Forget-me-Not*, the *Irish Metropolitan Magazine*, and *All the Year Round*. In 1853, at Thackeray's recommendation, she was given the job as Paris correspondent for the *Illustrated London News*. According to Charles Mackay, this was something of a sympathy posting, but he noted that she distinguished herself well in the position, becoming the first journalist to announce the engagement of Louis Napoleon (Mackay, 2.296).

Marguerite Power published her first novel, *Evelyn Forester*, in 1856; it was favourably compared to the works of Lady Blessington. This was followed by *The Foresters* (1858), the pseudonymous *Letters of a Betrothed* (1858, signed Honoria), *Nelly Carew* (1859), and *Sweethearts and Wives* (1861).

In 1857 Dickens, Thackeray, and John Forster raised a subscription of £200 for her from among the old friends of Lady Blessington (*Letters of Charles Dickens*, 8.497). Later, Dickens helped secure a publisher for her final book. In 1860 she published a poem, 'Virginia's Hand', dedicated to John Forster. It was evidently written under the influence of Mrs Browning's *Aurora Leigh*. Landor highly praised her poetical efforts, especially a poem written by her in Heath's *Book of Beauty*. Her last publication was an account of a winter's residence in Egypt, entitled *Arabian Days and Nights, or, Rays from the East* (1863). It is dedicated to Janet and Henry Ross, with whom she stayed at Alexandria. A fall from a horse caused a severe spinal injury from which she never fully recovered. She died at Bushey Heath, Bushey, Hertfordshire, on 1 July 1867 after a long battle with cancer.

In its obituary notice, the *Gentleman's Magazine* faults Marguerite Power's writing for a lack of 'literary individuality or merit' (*GM*, 266). However, by the accounts of her contemporaries and friends, she was respected as a writer and editor. Camilla Toulmin Crosland defends her against the charge that she was responsible for the folding of *The Keepsake* (C. T. Crosland, 121), and Dickens published her contributions in his periodicals. It was no doubt her extended financial hardships that gave her a 'pensive and taciturn' quality noticed by her friends (N. Crosland, 181). She lacked 'hopeful eagerness' and 'buoyancy of youth', and was 'calm, earnest, and dignified, even in her girlhood' (C. T. Crosland, 100). She was praised by all her friends especially for her intelligence, sense of humour, warmth, tact, and unfailing generosity.

ELIZABETH LEE, *rev.* SAMANTHA WEBB

Sources Mrs N. Crosland [C. Toulmin], *Landmarks of a literary life, 1820–1892* (1893), 97–122 · N. Crosland, *Rambles round my life: an autobiography*, 2nd edn (1898), 180–82 · C. Mackay, *Forty years' recollections of life, literature, and public affairs, from 1830 to 1870*, 2 (1877), 296–7 · R. R. Madden, *The literary life and correspondence of the countess of Blessington*, 3 vols. (1855) · M. Sadleir, *The strange life of Lady Blessington* (1947) [American edn of *Blessington–D'Orsay: a masquerade*] · *The letters of Charles Dickens*, ed. M. House, G. Storey, and others, 12 vols. (1965–2002) · D. J. O'Donoghue, *The poets of Ireland: a biographical and bibliographical dictionary* (1912), 388 · *GM*, 4th ser., 4 (1867), 266 · A. Lohrli, ed., *Household Words: a weekly journal conducted by Charles Dickens* (1973), 402 · S. C. Hall, *A book of memories of great men and women of the age*, 2nd edn (1877), 405 · d. cert.
Likenesses W. H. Egleton, stipple, pubd 1842 (after W. Drummond), BM · D. Maclise, drawings, 1844–5 · Count D'Orsay, portraits · W. H. Egleton, stipple (after W. Drummond), BM, NPG; repro. in *Heath's book of beauty* · E. Landseer, drawing · portrait, repro. in Countess of Blessington [M. A. Power], ed., *Heath's book of beauty* (1842), 135 · portrait, repro. in M. A. Power, ed., *The Keepsake*, 1 (1849)

Power, Rhoda Dolores Le Poer (1890–1957), broadcaster and children's writer, was born on 29 May 1890 at Parkdale, Dunham Massey, Altrincham, Cheshire, the second of the three daughters of Philip Ernest Le Poer Power (*b.* 1860), stockbroker, of Altrincham, Cheshire, and his wife, Mabel Grindlay Clegg (1866–1903). She was the sister of the historian Eileen *Power (1889–1940) and of Beryl *Power (1891–1974). The family came originally from Waterford, Ireland, but there is no evidence that it was connected to the Le Poer family of Waterford. In 1891 her father was sent to prison for five years for forgery, and was declared bankrupt, and was imprisoned again in 1905 for another five years. Rhoda did not see her father again after 1891. The family moved to London, and then Bournemouth, and in 1899 went to Switzerland, where her mother was treated for tuberculosis. After their mother's death, Rhoda and her sisters moved to Oxford with their maternal grandfather, and were educated at Oxford High School For Girls. She studied languages and political economy at St Andrews University from 1911 to 1913, and won a distinction in economic history. After leaving university, she taught for a year in the United States, and in 1916 went to Russia as governess to the daughter of a businessman in Rostov-on-Don. In *Under Cossack and Bolshevik* (1919) she described her experiences there during the Russian Revolution, when Rostov, a Cossack town, was attacked by Bolshevik forces. After the war she worked as a freelance journalist, lived in Palestine for a time, and wrote travel guides.

In the mid-1920s Rhoda and Eileen Power started a series of history books for children. The first of these, *Boys and Girls in History* (1926), was an attempt to illustrate life in England through the lives of children, based on contemporary accounts. Other books written together included *Twenty Centuries of Travel* (1926) and *Cities and their Stories* (1927). In the 1930s she continued to write children's histories on her own, including *Great People of the Past* (1932) and *The Kingsway Histories for Juniors* (1937).

Rhoda Power's career with the BBC began in 1927, at the time of the BBC inquiry into the value of broadcast lessons for schools, when she was asked by Mary Somerville to give six talks, 'Boys and girls of other days'. She worked on a freelance basis until July 1937, when she was appointed as a part-time assistant and scriptwriter in the school broadcasting department. Her contribution to developing school history broadcasting was the idea of the illustrated history lesson, augmenting the talk with sound effects, music of the period, and dialogue, and introducing the dramatic interlude. While Eileen checked the programmes for historical accuracy, Rhoda did a great deal of research herself, especially for the interludes: as she pointed out, it was a struggle to keep up to date as her 'special subject' was 4000 BC to the present day. She preferred to do the reading first, and then get her ideas for the broadcasts, and her sources included contemporary accounts wherever possible. She wanted to make history come to life, determined that it should no longer be regarded as the 'dry bones of the past', and she wanted to show children that history was the story of human life, and not just facts and events. She shared with Eileen a belief in the importance of teaching world history, and her World History series, started in 1932, was one of her most successful. She became a passionate advocate of school broadcasting, travelling round the country talking at teacher training colleges, visiting schools, talking to teachers and children. She regarded school broadcasting as a co-operative venture, working with teachers, making suggestions for how to use her lessons, wanting to relate her programmes to the work done in the classroom, to complement the work of the teacher, and not to replace it.

Rhoda Power became a full-time member of the school broadcasting department with the outbreak of war in 1939, and moved to Bristol with the department in 1940. As well as writing scripts for the British History and World History series, she developed *How Things Began* and *If You were Chinese*: this latter was prepared in close consultation with the Chinese community in England. She also published *Ten Minute Tales* (1943) and *The American Twins of the Revolution* (1943) in the twins series started by Lucy Fitch Perkins. By the end of the war she was exhausted—she estimated that she had written 340 scripts between 1939 and 1946—and she was also frustrated at the lack of time to browse and try out new ideas, feeling her technique had become stereotyped. After a year off from 1946 to 1947, travelling in South and North America, she arranged to have three months' unpaid leave every year.

Highly regarded by historians and educationists such as H. A. L. Fisher and R. H. Tawney for her contribution to the teaching of history, Rhoda Power was appointed MBE in 1950. Although she suffered from chronic deafness, which got worse after an unsuccessful operation in America in 1947, she continued to write scripts and develop new series, while publishing books based on her broadcasts, including *We Were There* (1955), stories told by imaginary eye-witnesses. She also contributed to children's television programmes.

Rhoda Power died very suddenly on 9 March 1957 at 72 Westbourne Park Road, Paddington, London. She was unmarried. She left her collection of books to the BBC's school broadcasting department, which created a Rhoda Power Library at Portland Place.

ANNE PIMLOTT BAKER

Sources M. Berg, *A woman in history: Eileen Power, 1889–1940* (1996) · files, BBC WAC · R. Palmer, *School broadcasting in Britain* (1947), 83–97 · K. Fawdry, *Everything but Alf Garnett: a personal view of BBC school broadcasting* (1974) · A. Briggs, *The history of broadcasting in the United Kingdom*, rev. edn, 2 (1995) · R. Power, 'Broadcasting history lessons', 25 Feb 1933, BBC WAC [unpubd lecture] · *The Times* (11 March 1957) · *The Times* (13 March 1957) · b. cert. · d. cert.
Archives BBC WAC
Likenesses photograph, repro. in Palmer, *School broadcasting* · photograph, repro. in Berg, *A woman in history*
Wealth at death £36,513 0s. 11d.: probate, 28 May 1957, CGPLA Eng. & Wales

Power, Richard, first earl of Tyrone (1629/30–1690), nobleman, was the eldest son of John Power, fifth Baron le Power and Coroghmore (d. 1665), of Curraghmore, co. Waterford, and his wife, Ruth (d. 1641), daughter of John

Pypho of St Mary's Abbey, Dublin, and his wife, Kinbrough Valentine; he was said to be twelve in a document dated 17 June 1642. About the time of his birth his father became a lunatic and in December 1641, shortly after the outbreak of the Irish rising, his pregnant mother died of shock when a party of rebels burst into Curraghmore. The dominant influence on Richard's upbringing was therefore his grandmother Kinbrough Pypho. During the turbulent years of the rising and Commonwealth, it was the lunacy of Lord Power that saved the Curraghmore estate from confiscation: he was placed under the protection of the lords justices in 1642, and was exempted from transplantation by order of the lord protector in 1654.

The allegiance of the Powers, as Catholic landowners, would naturally have been to the Irish Catholic confederation. Richard, however, was too young to take part in the rising and after the victory of the parliamentary army he 'demeaned himself inoffensively to the English, [and hath] slain (with the assistance of his father's tenants) divers tories [rebels] and brought others prisoners to the English garrisons where they have been executed' (*In the House of Lords*, no. 16). He appears to have taken his religious loyalties as lightly as his political ones, for in 1654 he contracted a very favourable marriage with Dorothy, eldest daughter of Arthur *Annesley, the future earl of Anglesey, an alliance which placed him firmly among the new Anglo-Irish protestant establishment. There were four children of this marriage: Arthur (died in Waterford), Dorothy (died in London), John, and James.

The Restoration brought prosperity to Curraghmore. In 1661 Power was appointed governor of the city and county of Waterford and elected MP for the county. He succeeded his father as Baron le Power in 1665. A letter at Curraghmore from Lord Anglesey to his daughter, dated 1 May 1666, shows how Anglicized the family had become:

> I am glad to find by your husband that you have chosen an English nurse for the child you go with. He writes me word that he is upon making his house English. … I wish you had a good chaplain and then I doubt not God would bless all the rest. (cited in Girouard, 257–8)

Power's sister Catherine married in 1658 John FitzGerald of Dromana, proprietor of the vast estate of Decies in the western half of the county. They had one child, a daughter Catherine. Upon the deaths of her mother in 1660 and her father in 1664, guardianship of the little heiress passed to her uncle Richard. In May 1673 Richard made a bold stroke to unite the Curraghmore and Dromana estates by marrying his ward and niece to his eldest surviving son, John. Catherine was about twelve and her cousin a mere seven, but Archbishop Sheldon allowed a marriage ceremony to be performed before him in Lambeth Chapel. In October Power was created earl of Tyrone and Viscount Decies (the title formerly borne by the FitzGeralds and now given by courtesy to the child-bridegroom).

In May 1675 Catherine appeared again before Sheldon and repudiated the contract. She was then kept under house arrest by Lord Anglesey, but on Easter eve 1677 she escaped from his house and was married the same day to

Edward Villiers, eldest son of the third Viscount Grandison. Chancery proceedings followed, and Tyrone was forced to give up the title-deeds of the Dromana estate, and his family to vacate the Decies title. The case formed an important precedent in cases regarding the validity of child marriages.

Tyrone's skill in walking the religious tightrope turned against him in 1679 when he was accused of involvement in the Popish Plot. He was indicted at Waterford in August 1679 and again in March 1680, and taken to England, where his impeachment was decided on by the House of Commons and he was imprisoned in the gatehouse at Westminster. He remained there until the beginning of 1684 when he was released on bail. Public reaction against the plot, and the king's death, saved him from further trouble on that score.

Tyrone's protestantism did not survive the accession of James II. He became colonel of a regiment of foot, was made a privy councillor in May 1686, and was lieutenant of the county and city of Waterford. He sat as a peer in the Irish parliament of May 1689, at which most of the protestant landowners were attainted. With his regiment he took part in the battle of the Boyne and the siege of Waterford in July 1690. On the approach of King William's army Tyrone's son and heir John Power fled to the royal camp at Carrick-on-Suir, where he obtained from the king a letter confirming that he was and had always been a protestant, and had been 'extremely oppressed' by his father on account of his religion. The king's support undoubtedly saved Curraghmore once again from confiscation.

Upon the surrender of Waterford the Jacobite force there joined the defenders of Cork, where they soon found themselves under siege from John Churchill, later duke of Marlborough. The defence of Cork, brave as it was, proved to be a rash mistake, and in order to prevent an all-out Williamite assault Tyrone and Lord Rycault negotiated terms of surrender. They were harsh: the entire garrison of about 4000 men became prisoners of war on 28 September and were shipped off to England. Prison conditions for the ordinary soldiers were grim and many members of Tyrone's regiment died of malnutrition and disease. The senior officers were lodged in the Tower of London, where Tyrone died on 14 October 1690. He was buried on 3 November at Farnborough in the Annesley vault.

Tyrone was succeeded by his elder son John, second earl (hero of the celebrated 'Beresford ghost story'), who died unmarried in 1693. Tyrone's younger son, James, now succeeded as third earl, but died without a male heir in 1704. The earldom of Tyrone then became extinct, while the barony of le Power passed to a different branch. Curraghmore was inherited by James's daughter Catherine, who in 1717 married Sir Marcus Beresford; their descendants, the marquesses of Waterford, still occupy Curraghmore. By his energy and resourcefulness—and opportunism—Tyrone restored the ailing fortunes of his family and preserved them through turbulent times. To this end he was apparently prepared to sacrifice religion, principles, and the happiness of his children. However, in the final phase of his public life—his role in the defence of Cork and the negotiations for its surrender—he displayed courage and nobility.

JULIAN C. WALTON

Sources DNB · Edmond, first Count De la Poer, chapter on Richard Power in MS history of the Power family, Beaminster, Dorset, collection of Anthony, fourth Count De la Poer · In the House of Lords: barony of Le Power and Coroghmore in the peerage of Ireland, copies of documents, extracts and translations lodged by the petitioner, John William Rivallon De la Poer, in support of his case [n.d., 1920?] · GEC, Peerage · Burke, Gen. Ire. (1976) · N. K. De la Poer, 'The Powers of Curraghmore, co. Waterford: their origins and their history', Irish Genealogist, 10/4 (2001), 388–95 · Anne, Lady Tyrone, letter, 5 June 1708, TCD, MS 1218, no. 11 · M. Girouard, 'Curraghmore, co. Waterford, Eire', Country Life (7–21 Feb 1963) · 'Power papers, the property of Count De la Poer', Analecta Hibernica, 25 (1967), 59–75 · will of Kinbrough Pypho, 1665; letters written to subject; letter of William III, 23 July 1690, MSS of the marquess of Waterford, Curraghmore · The information of Hubert Bourk gent, touching the popish plot in Ireland carried on by the conspiracies of the earl of Tyrone (1680) · The information of John Macnamara gent, touching the popish plot in Ireland (1680) · The several informations of John Mac-namara, Maurice Fitzgerrald and James Nash relating to the horrid popish plot in Ireland (1680) · T. Sampson, A narrative of the late popish plot in Ireland (1680) · D. Ó Murchadh, 'The siege of Cork, 1690', Journal of the Cork Historical and Archaeological Society, 254 (Jan–Dec 1990) · M. Bacon, A new abridgment of the law (1740), vol. 3, pp. 119–20 · W. R. Young, Fighters of Derry (1932), 310

Power, Richard (1724–1794), judge and politician, was the second of three sons of John Power (d. 1743), a landowner of Barretstown, co. Tipperary, and his wife, Elizabeth, daughter of the Revd John Congreve. A member of the Church of Ireland, he was educated at Trinity College, Dublin, entered the Middle Temple in 1752, and was called to the Irish bar in 1757. He became usher of the court of chancery in 1763, and a king's counsel in 1768, receiving the degree of doctor of laws honoris causa from Trinity in 1769. He was MP for Monaghan Borough (1767–8) and for Tuam, co. Galway (1768–72), purchasing his seat on both occasions. Noted in Baratariana as a prominent supporter of the Townshend administration (1767–72), and a close associate of Sir George Macartney, chief secretary (1769–72), he was lampooned for his verbose and theatrical speeches. On one occasion in the House of Commons he made a vigorous attack on William Blackstone, and damaged a copy of Blackstone's Commentaries by thumping it against the benches while displaying 'the vociferation of a Bedlamite and gesture and attitude nicely copied from the state kettle-drummer' (Baratariana, 152). In another debate he showed more statesmanlike qualities by making a speech of great clarity, in favour of the administration, to explain an important alteration to a controversial money bill of 1769; the bill, however, was rejected by the Commons because it was not drawn up in that chamber, leading Townshend to prorogue parliament until February 1771. The pamphlet A Comparative State of the Two Rejected Money Bills in 1692 and 1769 (1770) has been attributed to Power.

During his parliamentary career Power made little secret of his desire to be a judge, and he was rewarded for his loyalty to the Townshend administration by being appointed second baron of the court of the exchequer in

1772, while retaining his chancery position. Some observers regarded his behaviour on the bench as excessively austere, but his defenders claimed that this was simply a result of his insistence on legal precision and regularity. When Lord Carlisle and William Eden came to office in December 1780 they immediately decided to assert their authority, and in May 1781 recommended Power's dismissal on the grounds of his continued absence from duty, but he managed to hold onto his offices.

From 1771 to 1794 Power lived successively in Stephen's Street and Kildare Street, Dublin; he was well known as a connoisseur of the fine arts in Dublin. It was thought that he would probably receive a peerage in 1791 but this came to nothing. A contemporary described him as 'a morose, fat fellow, affecting to be genteel: he was very learned, very rich, and very ostentatious' (Gilbert, 3.290). Much of his fortune came from the lucrative office of usher of the court of chancery, a position mainly remunerated by interest which accrued on lodgements in the court. In a case between the duke of Chandos and his tenants, Power was entrusted with a large sum of money lodged by the tenants under a court order. After several years the tenants won and were declared entitled to the fund. Power returned the principal but, in right of his office, withheld the interest, which amounted to almost £3000. The tenants presented a petition against this to the lord chancellor, John Fitzgibbon, who ordered Power to appear before him on 5 February 1794 to explain his actions. Power remonstrated strongly against this summons, claiming that as a judge he should not be subject to such an indignity, but the chancellor insisted on seeing him. An arrogant man, Power had often clashed with the equally arrogant Fitzgibbon, and the prospect of appearing before him threw him into a panic. According to one account Power then decided to murder Fitzgibbon (Daunt, 2.146), and drove to his house at Ely Place with a pair of loaded pistols in his pockets. Not finding Fitzgibbon at home Power then resolved on suicide; friends believed that two recent bouts of illness had also influenced his resolve to die.

On Sunday 2 February 1794 he spent the morning arranging his papers and made his will. Accompanied by his groom he rode to Dublin's South Wall, one of his favourite rides, where he dismounted and instructed his servant to walk the horse to Ringsend to await his return. Power waited until he was alone, then filled his pockets with pebbles, walked into the sea, and was drowned. It was said that he carried an umbrella to protect himself from the rain as he walked off the pier. His body was discovered next day on the strand, near the Pigeonhouse. Although it was widely known in Dublin that he had committed suicide, the coroner's jury recorded a verdict of accidental death. His fortune was estimated at £60,000: he left £10,000 of this to Lord Macartney, his patron in the Townshend administration, and, as he had no children, the remainder went to his nephews. His elder brother, Ambrose Power of Barretstown, had been killed by the Whiteboys in 1775; his younger brother, John Power of Tullamaine, co. Tipperary, was aide-de-camp to Lord Clive at the battle of Plassey.   JAMES QUINN

Sources F. E. Ball, *The judges in Ireland, 1221–1921*, 2 (1926) · J. T. Gilbert, *A history of the city of Dublin*, 3 (1861), 290 · *GM*, 1st ser., 64 (1794), 186–7 · [H. Grattan and others], *Baratariana: a select collection of fugitive political pieces*, ed. [Rev. Simpson], 2nd edn (1773) · *Public Register, or, Freeman's Journal* (8 Feb 1794) · *Annual Register* (1794) · W. J. O'Neill Daunt, *Personal recollections of the late Daniel O'Connell MP*, 2 (1848), 145–6 · J. Kelly, *Henry Flood: patriots and politics in eighteenth-century Ireland* (1998) · Burke, *Peerage* (1912), 1552 · E. Keane, P. Beryl Phair, and T. U. Sadleir, eds., *King's Inns admission papers, 1607–1867*, IMC (1982) · D. Large, 'The Irish House of Commons in 1769', *Irish Historical Studies*, 11 (1958–9), 18–45 · Burtchaell & Sadleir, *Alum. Dubl.*
Wealth at death approx. £60,000: *Annual Register*

Power, (William Grattan) Tyrone (1797–1841), actor, was born near Kilmacthomas, co. Waterford, Ireland, on 2 November 1797. His father was a member of a well-to-do Waterford family, and died in America before Tyrone was a year old. His mother, Marie, the daughter of a Colonel Maxwell, who fell in the American War of Independence, settled, on her husband's death, in Cardiff, where she had a distant relative named Bird, a printer and bookseller. On the voyage from Dublin she and her son were wrecked off the Welsh coast, and narrowly escaped drowning. Power may have served an apprenticeship to Bird's business in Cardiff. Bird was printer to the local theatre, and seems to have introduced Power to the company of strolling players which, to the great grief of his mother, he joined in his fourteenth year. He was handsome and well made, and creditably filled the role of a 'walking gentleman'.

In 1815 Power visited Newport, Isle of Wight, where he made his début as Alonzo in Sheridan's *Pizarro*, and where he also became engaged to Anne Gilbert (1798–1876), the third daughter of John Gilbert of that town. He married her in 1817 when he was nineteen and she was a year younger. After appearing in various minor characters he undertook in 1818 at Margate the part of a comic Irishman, Looney Mactwoler, in Colman's *The Review*. His first attempt in the role, in which he was destined to make a great reputation, was a complete failure. Want of success as an actor led him at the end of the year, when his wife succeeded to a small fortune, to quit the stage. He sailed for the Cape of Good Hope in 1820 and spent twelve months ineffectively in South Africa, but returned to England and the stage in 1821. He made his first appearance at the English Opera House, London, in 1822, as Charles Austencourt in *Man and Wife*. In the same year he performed at the Olympic, of which he also became stage-manager for a while. He continued to obtain small engagements in the London theatres, and in 1824 made a second and somewhat successful attempt in Irish farce as Larry Hoolagan, a drunken scheming servant, in *The Irish Valet*. In 1826, while filling small roles at Covent Garden, his opportunity came. Charles Connor, the leading Irish comedian on the London stage, died suddenly of apoplexy in St James's Park on 7 October 1826. At the time he was fulfilling an engagement at Covent Garden. Power was allotted Connor's parts as Serjeant Milligan in *Returned Killed* and O'Shaughnessy in *The One Hundred Pound Note*. His success was immediate. Henceforth he confined himself to the delineation of Irish characters, such as Sir Lucius O'Trigger in Sheridan's *The Rivals*, Dr O'Toole in *The Irish*

(William Grattan) **Tyrone Power** (1797–1841), by John Simpson, in or before 1833

Tutor, and Dennis Brulgruddery in Colman's *John Bull*, in which he is said by contemporary critics to have been superior to Connor, and at least the equal of John Henry Johnstone. He appeared at the Haymarket, Adelphi, and Covent Garden theatres, fulfilling long engagements at £100 and £120 a week, and he paid annual visits to the Theatre Royal, Dublin, where he was always received with boundless enthusiasm. Between 1833 and 1835 he made a tour of the principal American towns and cities, and repeated the visit in 1837 and 1838.

On his return to London after his first tour of America, Power published *Impressions of America* (2 vols., 1836). He had previously published three romances—*The Lost Heir* (1830), *The Gipsy of Abruzzo* (1831), and *The King's Secret* (1831). He also wrote the Irish drama *St Patrick's Eve, or, The Orders of the Day* (1832); a comedy entitled *Married Lovers*; and the Irish farces *Born to Good Luck, or, The Irishman's Fortune, How to Pay the Rent, Paddy Carey, the Boy of Clogheen* (1833), and *O'Flannigan and the Fairies* (1836), all of which he produced himself.

Power's last appearance on the London stage was at the Haymarket on the evening of Saturday 1 August 1840, when he filled the roles of Captain O'Cutter in Colman's *The Jealous Wife*, Sir Patrick O'Plenipo ADC in Kenney's *The Irish Ambassador*, and Tim More (a travelling tailor) in *The Irish Lion*. He then paid a fourth visit to America, in order to look after some property he had purchased in Texas and £3000 he had invested in the United States Bank, which had stopped payment. His performance at the Park Theatre, New York, on 9 March 1841, as Gerald Pepper and Morgan Rattler, was to be his last appearance on stage. On 11 March 1841 he left New York on the return voyage in the

President, the largest steamer then afloat. There were 123 persons on board. The steamer was accompanied by the packet ship *Orpheus*, also bound for Liverpool. On the night of 12 March a storm rose and raged during the whole of Saturday the 13th. Before the break of dawn on Sunday the 14th the *President* disappeared, and no vestige of her was afterwards recovered. Power was forty-three years old at the date of the disaster. He left a widow and four sons and three daughters. His eldest son, Sir William Tyrone Power KCB, became for some time agent-general for New Zealand and was the author of various books of travel. His second son, Maurice, went on the stage, and died suddenly in 1849.

Tyrone Power was about 5 feet 8 inches in height; his form was light and agile, with a very animated and expressive face, light complexion, blue eyes, and brown hair. He was best in representations of blundering, good-natured, and eccentric Irish characters; but his exuberant, rollicking humour and his inexhaustible good spirits he infused into every comedy and farce, however indifferent, in which he acted.

MICHAEL MACDONAGH, *rev.* NILANJANA BANERJI

Sources T. A. Brown, *History of the American stage* (1870) • B. N. Webster, ed., *The acting national drama*, 2 (1838) • *Era Almanack and Annual* (1877) • P. Hartnoll, ed., *The concise Oxford companion to the theatre* (1972) • P. Hartnoll, ed., *The Oxford companion to the theatre* (1951); 2nd edn (1957); 3rd edn (1967) • *The biography of the British stage, being correct narratives of the lives of all the principal actors and actresses* (1824) • J. W. C., 'Tyrone Power: a biography [pts 1–3]', *Dublin University Magazine*, 40 (1852), 257–73, 577–81, 715–34 • T. Marshall, *Lives of the most celebrated actors and actresses* [1846–7] • Walford, *County families*

Likenesses J. Simpson, portrait, in or before 1833, priv. coll. [*see illus.*] • C. Turner, mezzotint, pubd 1833 (after J. Simpson), BM • Count D'Orsay, lithograph, pubd 1839, NG Ire. • Count D'Orsay, lithograph, BM, NPG • A. Edouart, silhouette, NPG • portrait, repro. in *Oxberry's Dramatic Biography* • portrait, repro. in Cumberland, *Minor theatre* (1829) • portrait, repro. in Webster, ed., *Acting national drama* • portrait, repro. in *Actors by Daylight* (14 April 1838), plate • prints, BM, NPG

Power, (Frederick) Tyrone Edmond (1869–1931), actor, was born in London on 2 May 1869, the son of Harold Power and his wife, Ethel Levenu, mildly successful entertainers, who in 1877 crossed the Atlantic to seek their fortune with American audiences. He formed the third generation of a theatrical dynasty which originated in the early nineteenth century with his grandfather the first Tyrone Power (1797–1841), and continued into the late twentieth century with his son Tyrone (1914–1958), the popular film star, and his actress granddaughters, Romina and Taryn, and grandson Tyrone jun. (*b*. 1958).

His parents did not wish Power to endure the hardships of life on the stage, so after a nominal education at Dover College until 1883 he was packed off to an orange ranch in Florida in order to learn the business of fruit-farming. He soon ran away and attached himself to the stock company of a theatre at St Augustine, with which he made his acting début as Gibson in Charles Hawtrey's *The Private Secretary* on 29 November 1886. With similar enterprise and aplomb he then proceeded to fashion a rewarding professional career for himself, gaining valuable early experience with two of the leading companies of the day. He had three seasons in 1888–91 with the formidable Czech actress Fanny Janauschek, one of the last great tragediennes in the 'grand style', for whom he opened as Dominie Sampson in *Guy Mannering* (an adaptation of Sir Walter Scott's novel) at Montreal; he subsequently toured throughout Canada and the United States in tragedies, comedies, and melodramas. He then contrived to obtain a letter of recommendation from Ellen Terry. This he presented to Augustin Daly, the celebrated playwright–director–impresario, whose company he joined in May 1891 to play Sir Oliver Surface in *The School for Scandal* and with which he remained associated until November 1898, while fulfilling occasional engagements elsewhere. Under Daly he took a full part in the manager's characteristically mixed repertory of contemporary plays and classics, accompanying him on American and European tours and playing a wide range of major and supporting roles. These included Posket in Sir Arthur Wing Pinero's *The Magistrate* and Brooke Twombley in *The Cabinet Minister* by the same author, Much the Miller in Tennyson's *The Foresters*, Frederick in *As You Like It*, Holofernes in *Love's Labour's Lost*, Antonio in *Much Ado about Nothing*, Christopher Sly in *The Taming of the Shrew*, Caliban in *The Tempest*, and the Host of the Garter Inn in *The Merry Wives of Windsor*. In 1894 he gave his first performance with the company in London, where in June he also took the bold step of hiring the Princess's Theatre to mount and assume the lead in his own play, *The Texan*; the venture was not a success. He then appeared in several productions with Herbert Beerbohm Tree, both on tour and at Her Majesty's, and acted in a command performance before Queen Victoria at Balmoral.

After returning to America, Power became a member of Minnie Maddern Fiske's company, appearing in Hermann Sudermann's *Magda*, *Frou-Frou* by Henri Meilhac and Ludovic Halévy, and other plays, before securing a particular triumph at the Fifth Avenue Theatre in September 1899 with his characterization of Lord Steyne in *Becky Sharp*, an adaptation by Langdon Mitchell from Thackeray's *Vanity Fair*. In 1900–02 he undertook an extensive tour of Australia and New Zealand, co-starring with his first wife, Edith Crane (whom he had married in 1898) in an astutely chosen repertory programme, which included *inter alia* dramatizations of Thomas Hardy's *Tess of the D'Urbervilles* and George Du Maurier's *Trilby*, H. J. Byron's comedy *Our Boys*, *The Taming of the Shrew*, and a current sensation, *The Only Way*, F. C. Wills and F. Langbridge's version of *A Tale of Two Cities*. This was followed by an engagement in June/July 1902 at the Lyceum Theatre in London as Bassanio in *The Merchant of Venice*, opposite Sir Henry Irving as Shylock and Ellen Terry as Portia. Back in New York, Power rejoined Mrs Fiske as Judas Iscariot in her production of William Winter's *Mary of Magdala* at the Manhattan Theatre in November, and played the title-role in a tour of Stephen Phillips's verse drama *Ulysses*, which opened at the Garden Theatre in September 1903. Power then acted as leading man to a succession of starring actresses: to

Julia Marlowe in Maria Lovell's *Ingomar the Barbarian* and Paul Kester's *When Knighthood was in Flower* in 1904, to Mrs Leslie Carter in David Belasco's *Adrea* in 1904–5, and to Henrietta Crosman in *The Christian Pilgrim*, a morality play based on *The Pilgrim's Progress*, in 1907. Other conspicuous successes in the ensuing years included his Robert Smith, the Drainman, in C. R. Kennedy's *The Servant in the House* in 1908, Brutus in William Faversham's production of *Julius Caesar* in 1912–13, and Abu Hasan in the American première of Oscar Asche's *Chu-Chin-Chow* (music by Frederick Norton) in 1917.

After the First World War, with the advent of greater realism in performance, Power's romantic, somewhat rhetorical style of acting seemed increasingly outdated, and his stage work became more intermittent, although he repeated his Brutus in revivals of *Julius Caesar* in 1918 and 1927, and in 1922 could still command such important roles as Sir Anthony Absolute in *The Rivals*, and Claudius in *Hamlet*. Turning to the cinema, he moved to Hollywood, where he appeared in numerous silent films, notably D. W. Griffith's *Dream Street* (1921), Henry King's *Fury* (1923), Raoul Walsh's *The Wanderer* (1925), and J. S. Blackton's *Bride of the Storm* (1926). He was beginning to adapt to sound, as in Walsh's *The Big Trail* (1930), when he died in Hollywood of a heart attack on 30 December 1931. By then his personal life had become increasingly turbulent, plagued by alcoholism and financial troubles. After the untimely death in January 1912 of Edith Crane, to whom he was happily married for almost fourteen years, he had contracted other, shorter-lived marriages, first to the actress Patia (Helen Emma) Reaume, with whom he had a son but from whom he was divorced in 1920, then, following a long, adulterous affair, to Bertha Knight, whom he married in 1921. Blessed with a tall, imposing physique, handsome features, a strong, resonant voice, and a natural dignity of bearing, Power was without doubt an accomplished actor in his prime. Though ultimately denied the accolade of greatness, he none the less made a distinctive contribution to the character of the American theatre while significantly enriching his own family traditions.

DONALD ROY

Sources W. Winter, *Tyrone Power* (New York, 1913) • *DAB*, vol. 15 • W. Hood, 'Power, Tyrone', *ANB* • S. D'Amico, ed., *Enciclopedia dello spettacolo*, 8 (Rome, 1961) • *Who was who in the theatre, 1912–1976*, 3 (1978) • D. Hines and H. P. Hanaford, *Who's who in music and drama* (1914) • G. Bordman, ed., *The Oxford companion to American theatre*, 2nd edn (1992) • D. B. Wilmeth and T. L. Miller, eds., *Cambridge guide to American theatre* (1993) • B. Sobel, ed., *The theatre handbook and digest of plays* (1940) • L. Reed and H. Spiers, *Who's who in filmland* (1931) • *New York Times* (31 Dec 1931) • *New York Herald Tribune* (31 Dec 1931) • *Dover College Register* [centenary edition]

Likenesses O. Sarony, four photographs, *c.*1888–1912, repro. in Winter, *Tyrone Power* • two photographs, 1902–3, repro. in Winter, *Tyrone Power* • White, photograph, repro. in Winter, *Tyrone Power*

Power, William (1873–1951), writer and journalist, was born at 16 Arlington Street, Glasgow, on 30 August 1873, the eldest of the five children of William Power (1839/40–1886/7), shipmaster, and his wife, Ada, *née* Denham

(1839/40–1904). Both parents came from Brechin, Forfarshire. He attended Woodside School in the west end of Glasgow, but had to leave at the age of fourteen as a result of his father's death at Gibraltar from west African fever. In 1887 he obtained a position with the Royal Bank of Scotland in Glasgow, where he was employed for twenty years. On 20 August 1906, he married Giulia Dick (1871/2–1922), a schoolteacher, and the following year, encouraged by the success of essays he had contributed to the *Glasgow Herald*, he joined the paper as a full-time member of its editorial staff and remained there as essay and leader writer for nearly another twenty years. His first wife died in 1922, and in 1924 Power married Williamina Mills (*d.* 1946); there were no children of either marriage. In 1926 Power resigned from the *Glasgow Herald* to become editor of the *Scots Observer*, a new weekly supported by the Scottish churches. The paper was not successful and he left the editorship in 1929 to work for Associated Newspapers.

William Power was much more than a journalist. Although forced by circumstances to be largely self-educated, he had a wide knowledge of his country's history and literature, and of literature generally, together with a keen critical understanding, qualities developed through his mother's love of the songs and sayings of her native Forfarshire. He was a considerable essayist and critic himself, and a supporter of the new writing of the inter-war Scottish cultural revival—he was in touch with all the major figures of the 'Scottish renaissance'. His autobiography is significant for its contemporaneous perspectives on the events of that period, both within and outside of Scotland. His first published work, in 1893, was an extended blank verse poem, *Clutha*, about the river-spirit of the Clyde. Among his many subsequent writings about Scotland, his principal publications include *The World Unvisited* (1922), *Robert Burns and other Essays and Sketches* (1926), *My Scotland* (1934), *Scotland and the Scots* (1934), *Literature and Oatmeal* (1935), *Should Auld Acquaintance … : an Autobiography* (1937), and *The Culture of the Scots: its Past and Future* (1943). He stood unsuccessfully as Scottish nationalist candidate in the parliamentary by-election in Argyll in 1940, and was associated with the movement for a parliament in Edinburgh as chairman and then president of Scottish Convention.

Power was no narrow nationalist, however. Like Hugh MacDiarmid and Neil Gunn he saw nationalism and internationalism as being essentially complementary. He was a founder member of Scottish PEN and its president (1935–8), and was latterly a president of the Glasgow Esperanto Society. Other interests are seen in his presidency of the Scottish Ramblers' Federation (1934) and his membership of the Glasgow Art Club and Edinburgh Arts Club.

Power lived principally in Glasgow and later at Corra Linn, Stirling. He died in hospital in Alloa, Clackmannanshire, on 13 June 1951; his funeral service was held at Glasgow Cathedral on 16 June, and he was buried in Old Eastwood cemetery, Glasgow. Obituaries commented on his intellectual curiosity, his kindness towards young writers, his humour, his love for his country, and on his being 'a good European and a world citizen'. His own words from his autobiography make a fitting epitaph: 'To help in the restoration of national culture was my central aim'.

MARGERY PALMER MCCULLOCH

Sources W. Power, *Should auld acquaintance: an autobiography* (1937) · *Scottish biographies* (1938) · b. cert. · m. cert. [Giulia Dick] · d. cert. · *Glasgow Herald* (14 June 1951) · *Daily Record and Mail* (14 June 1951) · *Glasgow Herald* (10 Sept 1926) · *Glasgow Herald* (5 Dec 1938) · H. MacDiarmid, *Lucky poet* (1943)
Archives NL Scot., corresp. and literary papers · NL Scot., MS essay | NL Scot., letters to various correspondents, incl. Gunn, Gibbon, Ray Mitchell, Douglas Young · NL Scot., letters to William Soutar
Likenesses A. Paterson, photograph, 1937, repro. in Power, *Should auld acquaintance*, frontispiece · photograph, repro. in *Glasgow Herald* (14 June 1951)
Wealth at death £8280 12s. 11d.: confirmation, 12 Nov 1951, *CCI*

Power, Sir William Henry (1842–1916), epidemiologist and civil servant, was born at 1 Tillotson Place, London, on 15 December 1842, the eldest son of William Henry Power (1811–1877), surgeon, and his wife, Charlotte Smart. He was educated at University College School, London, and was one of the fifth generation in his family to take up a medical career. After serving an apprenticeship with his father he undertook further study at St Bartholomew's Hospital, and in 1864 he qualified MRCS and LSA. In 1871, after various hospital appointments, he became an inspector in the medical department of the Local Government Board. He made his subsequent career within the department, becoming assistant medical officer in 1887 and medical officer in 1900. He retired in 1908, retaining an active interest in public health and epidemiology. On 8 June 1876 he married Charlotte Jane (1849/50–1882), daughter of Benjamin Charles Godwin, a solicitor. They had two daughters.

Power's distinctive abilities as an epidemiologist were demonstrated during his time as a medical inspector between 1871 and 1887. A keen ornithologist and the possessor of an extremely logical mind (there was a strong mathematical streak in the family), Power used his knowledge of natural history and his analytical abilities to elucidate the epidemiological puzzles presented to him. Four investigations from this period stand out for their original contributions to epidemiological knowledge. First, in 1876, his inquiry into a diphtheria outbreak at Brailes, Warwickshire, demonstrated not only that the disease was passed on mainly by personal contact, but also that the village day school had played a central part in the spread of the infection. As a result of this discovery, 'school influence' was widely recognized as a critical factor in the spread of children's diseases. Second, between 1881 and 1886 Power was involved in investigating the causes and incidence of smallpox in London. He demonstrated an association between local incidence and isolation hospitals, which led to the latter being moved out of London. Third, and in these years also, he detected and described the transmission of streptococcal infections from cows to humans through milk from infected animals, at a time when bovine tuberculosis infection was still disputed, and the transmission route of Malta fever was as yet unknown. Finally, between 1887 and 1892 Power originated and co-ordinated an extensive investigation into lead poisoning through public water supplies derived from moorland sources, which had caused widespread plumbism in several Yorkshire cities. Also in 1887 he used his knowledge of natural history to resolve the longstanding problem of eels in the East London Water Company's water pipes.

Power's translation to 'headquarters' work in 1887 ended his active career as an epidemiologist. From then on he concentrated his energies on educating and assisting the department's junior staff, and in consolidating the wider work of the department. He fostered among the staff a policy of inquiring so thoroughly into subjects that its investigations became standard works, and as back-up to the royal commission on sewage disposal he supported a scientific research programme that revolutionized the understanding and practice of sewage disposal. He was instrumental in guiding the Local Government Board to the creation of the sub-department of food inspection in 1905, and he took an active part in the royal commission on tuberculosis. Yet Power's profile during his years at the centre of public health administration was decidedly low: contemporaries were unanimous in the opinion that the extent of his influence on international public health was immense, but that it would never be fully known or appreciated. Power loathed publicity of any kind; he would accept no acknowledgement of his work or assistance; he would not appear at any occasion where he would be prominent before an audience; and he would not allow himself to be photographed.

Despite Power's intensely private attitude he received due recognition from his peers. He was elected a fellow of the Royal Society in 1895, created CB in 1902, and knighted on his retirement in 1908. He was a formidable figure—6 feet 5 inches tall, with a fine physique; in his youth he had a distinguished sporting record. His favourite recreation was duck shooting from a small yacht off the east coast, and in retirement and illness his principal occupation was the study of birds through a pair of powerful field-glasses. He died at his home, Holly Lodge, East Molesey, Surrey, on 28 July 1916, and was buried on 1 August at Brookwood cemetery, Woking.   ANNE HARDY

Sources *BMJ* (5 Aug 1916), 203–8, 223 · S. M. C., *PRS*, 90B (1917–19), i–viii · *The Lancet* (5 Aug 1916), 244–6 · b. cert. · m. cert.
Archives Wellcome L., lecture notes and papers
Wealth at death £10,199 11s. 5d.: probate, 12 Oct 1916, *CGPLA Eng. & Wales*

Powerscourt. For this title name *see* Wingfield, Richard, Viscount Powerscourt (d. 1634).

Powhatan (c.1545–1618), leader of the Powhatan Indians, was born to unknown parents probably in the 1540s near the fall line of the James River in modern Virginia. Also known as Wahunsonacawh and Wahunsonacock, he was the principal headman of the Algonquian peoples neighbouring the English colony of Jamestown.

Familiar in popular culture as the father of *Pocahontas (c.1596–1617), Powhatan was the paramount chief of Tsenacommacah, an extensive Chesapeake Bay domain conforming to the present-day boundaries of Tidewater Virginia and containing about 20,000 American Indians, collectively known as Powhatans. Inheriting six original tribes, Powhatan extended his authority by alliance and conquest over two dozen others, probably motivated by European attempts at settlement in the region after 1570.

By the founding of Jamestown in 1607 Powhatan ruled the strongest chiefdom along the Atlantic coast as both hereditary leader and head priest, while his sons and siblings served as regional governors, collecting a vast tribute in foodstuffs, furs, and freshwater pearls. At his capital at Werowocomoco, along the York River, Powhatan presided over a regal court, attired in a huge robe of raccoon skins.

Powhatan sustained the Jamestown colonists for over two years, expecting to use their ships and firearms against his American Indian foes. The ceremony in which Pocahontas 'saved' Captain John Smith from a feigned 'execution' formally invested Smith as a Powhatan chieftain and officially made all colonists subordinate tribespeople. Peace prevailed until August 1609, when Captain Smith could not control hundreds of new, hungry, and aggressive Englishmen, who invaded Powhatan's villages, abused his people, and stole precious food supplies.

The resulting First Anglo-Powhatan War (August 1609–April 1614) pitted the American Indians' superior numbers against the Englishmen's superior technology. Powhatan nearly annihilated the Jamestown garrison with a five-month siege (the infamous 'Starving Time'), forced the brief abandonment of that settlement, and threatened England's fragile foothold in North America. Finally weakened by a war of attrition and the destruction or desertion of key allies, Powhatan reluctantly agreed to a mutually face-saving peace in 1614, marked by the marriage of an Anglicized Pocahontas to colonist John Rolfe.

An aged, dispirited Powhatan abdicated in 1617 soon after the death of Pocahontas in London, and he was ultimately succeeded by his more militant kinsman *Opechancanough. In April 1618 Rolfe reported that his father-in-law had died in a secluded retirement at an unknown location.

Powhatan is significant because he was the first American Indian leader to explore the full range of options—from voluntary accommodation to retaliatory aggression to coerced acquiescence—in coping with the unprecedented challenges of English colonization. Knowing the difference between 'Peace and Warre better then any', he asked the colonists: 'What will it availe you to take … by force [what] you may quickly have by love, or to destroy them that provide you food. What can you get by warre …?' (*Complete Works of Captain John Smith*, 2.196). Although such rhetoric was embellished in Smith's writings, Powhatan's policies were truly eloquent expressions of wisdom, forbearance, pragmatism—and ultimate futility. In the light of the fate of later Native Americans over several centuries, Powhatan's political losses and personal sacrifices seem all the more poignant.

J. FREDERICK FAUSZ

Sources *The complete works of Captain John Smith (1580–1631)*, ed. P. L. Barbour, 3 vols. (1986) · P. L. Barbour, ed., *The Jamestown voyages under the first charter, 1606–1609*, 2 vols., Hakluyt Society, 2nd ser., 136–7 (1969) · R. Hamor, *A true discourse of the present state of Virginia* (1615); repr. with an introduction by A. L. Rowse (1957) · W. Strachey, *The historie of travell into Virginia Britania*, ed. L. B. Wright and V. Freund, Hakluyt Society, 2nd ser., 103 (1953) · S. Purchas, *Hakluytus posthumus, or, Purchas his pilgrimes*, 20 bks in 4 vols. (1625); repr. 20 vols., Hakluyt Society, extra ser., 14–33 (1905–7) · S. M. Kingsbury, ed., *Records of the Virginia Company*, 4 vols. (1906–35) · J. F. Fausz, 'Powhatan', *ANB* · P. L. Barbour, *Pocahontas and her world* (1969) · H. C. Rountree, *The Powhatan Indians of Virginia* (1989) · J. F. Fausz, 'An "abundance of blood shed on both sides": England's first Indian war, 1609–1614', *Virginia Magazine of History and Biography*, 98 (1990), 3–56
Likenesses engravings, repro. in J. Smith, *The generall historie of Virginia, New-England, and the Summer Isles* (1624), following pp. 20, 40

Powicke, Sir (Frederick) Maurice (1879–1963), historian, was born at Alnwick, Northumberland, on 16 June 1879, the eldest child of Frederick James Powicke (1854–1935), a Congregational minister and historian of seventeenth-century puritanism, and his wife, Martha, youngest daughter of William Collyer of Brigstock, Northamptonshire. He was named Maurice after F. D. Maurice. In 1886 the family moved to Hatherlow, near Stockport, and Powicke was educated at Stockport grammar school until, in 1896, he went to the University of Manchester. There he came under the influence of T. F. Tout, who turned him into a historian. It was in these years also that Powicke first experienced the pleasure of working in a scholar's library among the books of E. A. Freeman, whose library formed one of the earliest departmental libraries in an English university.

In 1899 Powicke went to Balliol College, Oxford, Tout's old college. He became a Brackenbury scholar of the college and read classics with only moderate success, obtaining a second class in *literae humaniores* in 1902. He then returned to history and achieved a first class in that subject in 1903. Meanwhile he had become a Langton research fellow at Manchester University, a fellowship which he held from 1902 to 1905. This allowed him to do his first serious piece of historical research on Furness Abbey for the Victoria county history of Lancashire.

With the exception of Tout, who supported him throughout, Powicke at this time was undervalued by those who made academic appointments. From 1905 to 1906 he was assistant lecturer at the University of Liverpool, but he failed to get his position renewed, and Tout brought him back to Manchester as assistant lecturer from 1906 to 1908. His election to a prize fellowship at Merton College, Oxford, in 1908 was the turning point in his career and Powicke never ceased to feel a warm attachment to the college which had rescued him from obscurity. A series of important articles in the *English Historical Review* from 1906 to 1909 laid the foundations of his academic reputation and from this date his troubles in getting employment were over. From 1909 to 1919 he was professor of modern history at Queen's University, Belfast; from 1919 to 1928 professor of medieval history at Manchester; and from 1928 until his retirement in 1947 regius

Sir (Frederick) Maurice Powicke (1879–1963), by Walter Stoneman, 1945

professor of modern history at Oxford. After his retirement he received *Studies in Medieval History Presented to Frederick Maurice Powicke*, edited by R. W. Hunt, W. A. Pantin, and R. W. Southern (1948), which contains a full bibliography of his publications to that date. He was given a room in Balliol where he continued to work until shortly before his death. He left his books to Balliol College.

In his inaugural lecture at Oxford, Powicke described his ideal of a degree in history as combining the 'two kinds of experience which historical study can provide, namely the lessons suggested by the historical treatment of political science and of general historical developments, and the discipline implied in the careful intensive study of a special historical subject' ('Historical study in Oxford', reprinted in F. M. Powicke, *Modern Historians and the Study of History*, 1955, 173), but his persistent failure to get the undergraduate course divided into two parts on the Manchester model clouded his Oxford years. His individual genius as a teacher ensured that he made a greater contribution to the study of history at the university than any professor since Stubbs, and that Oxford replaced Manchester as the leading centre for medieval studies. Illuminating and suggesting rather than explaining, and encouraging graduate students to follow their own way while remaining the most important single influence in their work, he produced a generation of distinguished medievalists often very different in style from himself.

In his writing Powicke showed himself the first influential British historian to be aware of the range of continental scholarship. He seems to have reacted against the record-based English administrative history of Tout, and of his own successor in the regius chair, V. H. Galbraith, whom he had taught at Manchester. His interest he declared to be 'the interplay of experience and ideas in the formation of medieval political societies' (F. M. Powicke, *Ways of Medieval Life and Thought*, 1949, 5), and his method can be described as a narrative of events, explained in terms of the personalities and values of the people who shaped them. His first book, *The Loss of Normandy* (1913), attributed Philip Augustus's ability to seize Normandy from King John in 1204—an event which he saw as crucial to the formation of both the French state and the English nation—to the chivalry, art, and intellect of France.

In Powicke's next book, *Stephen Langton*—his Ford lectures at Oxford in 1926–7, begun as a study of Langton's part in the struggle for Magna Carta—he found himself seeking to bring his subject:

> into relation with the common man in England and with the intellectual life of Europe, [and] to break down the barriers which prevent us from considering as a whole, in the light of the influences that played upon them, the men and affairs of politics and religion.   (*Langton*, 161)

Langton's 'clear, sensible, penetrating, but not original mind' (ibid., 160) was seen as being sharpened in the schools of Paris, in disputations about the extent of papal power, the duty of the church to aid kings in a just and urgent cause, and the restraints which natural law and judicial custom placed on monarchy. In 1936 he produced in collaboration with A. B. Emden another work of lasting importance: a new edition of *The Universities of Europe in the Middle Ages* (1895) by Hastings Rashdall, in which he described the 'intense intellectual life of the schools' as 'a process of incessant wisdom and folly' throwing up 'ideas and ways of thought and speech' still profoundly influencing the modern world (*Universities of Europe*, 1.xxxvii). By these books and his catalogue *The Medieval Books of Merton College* (1931) he opened up for British historians the whole subject of scholastic history, but he left it to others to acquire the expertise to pursue it in depth.

In the 1930s some of Powicke's energy was taken up in promoting co-operative historical scholarship through the Royal Historical Society, whose president he became in 1933 on a reforming programme in that rarest of events for such a body, a contested election. The society's series of guides and handbooks, notably *The Handbook of British Chronology* (1939), which he himself edited, are the result of his initiative. Of importance for church history was his project for a new edition of the *Concilia* (1737) of David Wilkins, which he announced in his Raleigh lecture of 1931 and which began to appear in 1964, the year after his death. He was also continuing to produce the type of essays written for a wider public at which he excelled: an early example was *Christian Life in the Middle Ages* (1926), the book which he thought had caused Stanley Baldwin to offer him the regius chair. His interest in evoking the personalities and purposes of individuals—Pope Boniface

VIII, for instance, or Gerald of Wales—is evident in this book, as also in his edition of Walter Daniel's life of Abbot Ailred of Rievaulx (1922 and 1950), which glows with his liking for the man and love of the place. In his article 'The murder of Henry Clement [in 1235] and the pirates of Lundy island', published in *History* (vol. 25, 1941), he confessed:

> sometimes, as I work at a series of patent and close rolls, I have a queer sensation; the dead entries begin to be alive. It is rather like the experience of sitting down in one's chair and finding that one has sat on the cat. These are real people.
> (*Ways of Medieval Life*, 67)

The rewards and dangers of this imaginative sympathy with figures of the past, even to talk of them as friends, and of the intuitive recreation of their ideas and motivation are exemplified in the two massive books which appeared at the end of Powicke's career and on which his reputation largely rests: *King Henry III and the Lord Edward* (1947), and *The Thirteenth Century* in the Oxford History of England (1953). The first is an episodic, 'Proustian' narrative of the century from Henry's accession to the early years of Edward's reign, hauntingly written, and most successful in its evocation of the culture of the western European governing class as manifested in the politics of the kingdom of England. The principal explanation of political change given here is generational change among the aristocracy. But Powicke's aspiration to make the book 'a study in social history, not in the sense in which the term is generally used, but in the sense of social life, relations, and forces in political action' (*King Henry III*, v), ran up against the difficulty of finding an unprejudiced vocabulary for insights into the attitudes of a remote age. He could have no impression of the motivation of the mass of the population, and there seems to be a touch of nostalgia for a lost England in the values he attributed, in the gloom of the Second World War, to medieval aristocrats. He was convinced that the thirteenth century was a harmonious and 'happier time' when 'England coped with herself' ('England and Europe in the thirteenth century', *Ways of Medieval Life*, 117) despite the extremism of Simon de Montfort and his 'commissars', and he was too impressed by the concept of the 'community of the realm' which he found in the records. Many have found inexplicable his belief, evinced in both his last books, in Edward's generosity and respect for right, even in his dealings with the Welsh and Scots. In 1965 K. B. McFarlane demolished Powicke's 'feeble attempt to extenuate' Edward's treatment of earldoms for his own and his family's material advantage, and showed how little community there was even in the group around the king ('Had Edward I a "policy" towards the earls?', *History*, 50, 1965, 149–50).

The Thirteenth Century, which carries the narrative down to Edward I's death in 1307, has some of the previous book's weaknesses. The extensive work of economic historians on what was a largely peasant society still makes little impact. Indeed, Powicke argued in the *Economic History Review* (vol. 14, 1946) that the emphasis of economic history 'on the particular interests of persons and groups tends to incoherence'; the strength of English parliamentary government, 'the most stable form of government in the world' so far, lay 'in its capacity to deal with our economic life as part of the community' ('The economic motive in politics', *Modern Historians and the Study of History*, 247). *The Thirteenth Century* is different from *King Henry III and the Lord Edward*, however, in weaving into the narrative discussions of the work being done in legal and administrative history, with which he was fully conversant. The result is a difficult book, but one that comes nearest to the ambition Powicke had expressed in his presidential address to the Royal Historical Society in 1936 to write the history of the English state as 'more than a complex of institutions': rather as 'the relations between men with a capacity to be influenced in their normal daily life by abstractions' and able 'to discuss, plead and act together in councils, law courts, armies and business' ('Reflections on the medieval state', *TRHS*, 4th ser., 19, 1936, 5). Despite the criticism, the two late books have together established the enduring image of thirteenth-century England, and also support a claim that Powicke added a new dimension to medieval historiography by his combination of wide scholarship with imaginative insight into the springs of action.

In personal appearance Powicke was noticeably small and deceptively fragile; his voice was soft and fluty; he read well, especially such favourite authors as Dickens, and he had a relish for the ridiculous which went with a somewhat macabre and elfish sense of humour. He liked walking and was deeply attached to the Lake District, where for many years he and his family spent most of the summer at their cottage in Eskdale. On 8 September 1909 he married Susan Irvine Martin Lindsay (*d.* 1965), daughter of the Revd Thomas M. Lindsay, principal of the United Free College of Glasgow, and the sister of his friend A. D. Lindsay. For many years the Powickes' house at 97 Holywell, Oxford, was a place of resort for large numbers of pupils and visiting historians. They had one son, who to Powicke's lasting grief was killed in a road accident in 1936. Of his two daughters one, Janet, married the historian Richard Pares.

Powicke was elected a fellow of the British Academy in 1927 and knighted in 1946. He was an honorary fellow of his three Oxford colleges, Merton (1932), Balliol (1939), and Oriel (1947), an honorary doctor of many universities, and a corresponding member of foreign academies in France, Germany, and America. He died in the Radcliffe Infirmary, Oxford, on 19 May 1963, after a brief illness.

R. W. SOUTHERN, *rev.* ALAN HARDING

Sources R. W. Southern, 'Sir Maurice Powicke', *PBA*, 50 (1964), 275–304 • personal knowledge (1981) • private information (1981) • M. T. Clanchy, 'Inventing thirteenth-century England: Stubbs, Tout, Powicke – now what?', *Thirteenth Century England* [ed. P. R. Coss and S. D. Lloyd], 5 (1995)
Archives JRL, papers | JRL, letters to the *Manchester Guardian* • PRO NIre., letters to J. C. Beckett • U. Glas., letters to E. L. G. Stones • U. Reading L., letters to Sir Frank Stenton and Lady Stenton
Likenesses R. Schwabe, drawing, 1944, Oriel College, Oxford • W. Stoneman, photograph, 1945, NPG [*see illus.*] • Ramsey & Muspratt, photograph, *c.*1947, NPG • W. Stoye, drawing, 1947, priv.

coll. • J. Oppenheimer, drawing, 1955, U. Oxf., history faculty library • J. Oppenheimer, drawing, 1955, Balliol Oxf.
Wealth at death £9716 7s. 0d.: probate, 18 Oct 1963, *CGPLA Eng. & Wales*

Powis. For this title name *see* Herbert, Percy, second Baron Powis (1598–1667); Herbert, William, styled first marquess of Powis and Jacobite first duke of Powis (*c.*1626–1696); Herbert, William, second marquess of Powis and Jacobite second duke of Powis (1657x61–1745); Clive, Edward, first earl of Powis (1754–1839); Herbert, Edward, second earl of Powis (1785–1848).

Powis, William Henry (1808–1836), wood-engraver, was born in London. He learned his craft from George Wilmot Bonner and soon became established as 'one of the best wood-engravers of his time' (Chatto and Jackson, 544). Linton, who worked alongside him for a year, observed that 'most noticeable in Powis's work is ... that everything has been cut at once. In this he differed notably from [John Orrin] Smith, who depended on after-toning' (Linton, 194). With Bonner, Powis produced some facsimile engravings after Hans Holbein's work for Francis Douce's *The Dance of Death*, printed at the Chiswick Press in 1833; contemporaries deemed his contributions to be of 'remarkable excellence' (Linton, 193).

After leaving Bonner, Powis undertook work for John Jackson, who, according to Linton, often signed Powis's engravings. He produced many engravings of animals for Jackson, including several in James Northcote's *Fables* (1833), such as *Elephant* and *Wolf*, and in Edward Turner Bennett's *The Gardens and Menageries of the Zoological Society Delineated* (1830–31), for instance, *Palm Squirrel* and *Barn Owl*. Powis was probably best known for his topographical views, many of them biblical scenes. A number adorned Richard Westall and John Martin's *Illustrations of the Bible* (1833). Linton thought such landscapes 'perhaps the best ... for their size up to that time engraved in wood' (Linton, 194). Certainly the publishers regarded Powis's work as excellent, paying him, according to Chatto and Jackson, 15 guineas instead of the more usual fee of 12, for his engraving of *The Deluge*, after Martin. Later, Powis engraved William Harvey's illustration to accompany the poem 'Vesuvius: Across the Bay' in Charles Latrobe's *The Solace of Song* (1837). His contemporaries thought him less gifted in his figure subjects, and Linton considered them 'weakly drawn' (Linton, 194).

Throughout his working life Powis was established in London. The London trade directories record him working from 94 St John Street Road (1832–4) and later from 59 St John Street Road (1836). Although many early sources, including Samuel Redgrave, suggest that Powis's early death at the age of twenty-eight in 1836 was caused by overwork, Linton claimed that he had always been unhealthy and probably died of consumption. There are proof impressions of the engraver's work in the British Museum and the Victoria and Albert Museum, London; these are characteristically signed either 'W. H. POWIS, Sc' or 'W. POWIS, Sc.' SUSANNA AVERY-QUASH

Sources *DNB* • W. J. Linton, *The masters of wood-engraving* (1889), 192–4 • W. Chatto, J. Jackson, and H. G. Bohn, *A treatise on wood-*

engraving, 2nd edn (1861), 544, 546 • R. K. Engen, *Dictionary of Victorian wood engravers* (1985) • G. K. Nagler, ed., *Neues allgemeines Künstler-Lexikon*, 22 vols. (Munich, 1835–52) • Redgrave, *Artists* • Bryan, *Painters* (1903–5) • Bénézit, *Dict.* • Thieme & Becker, *Allgemeines Lexikon*

Powle, George (*fl.* 1764–1771), etcher and miniature painter, was a pupil of Thomas Worlidge (1700–1766). Powle imitated his tutor's delicate and highly finished Rembrandtesque style of etching. Worlidge's series of plates from antique gems, issued in 1768, was to a large extent the work of Powle. Although he worked in London, Powle was resident initially in Hereford and later Worcester. He designed views of both cities that were engraved by James Ross in 1778. While in Worcester, Powle was commissioned in 1771 to etch portraits of both John Berkeley of Spetchley, described as the only 'true' likeness that he produced (Anderton catalogues, 5, no. 1165), and the judge Sir Robert Berkeley. It was John Berkeley, in his letters to James Granger, who spoke highly of Powle's character and skill. Among Powle's drawings are portraits of Lady Pakington, Sir Edwin Sandys, and Sir John Perrot, which were engraved by Valentine Green. Powle's plates (most of which are in the British Museum) are not numerous but include portraits of Thomas Popplewelt and Thomas Belasyse, Lord Fauconberg; *Mademoiselle d'Hamilton, the Comtesse de Grammont*, after Lely, and *Old Parr*, after Rubens; two candlelight subjects, after Schalken; and a plate in Dr Hunter's *Anatomy of the Gravid Uterus*. Two anonymous plates in T. R. Nash's *History of Worcestershire* (1781) are also ascribed to him. His only known mezzotint (British Museum) is a portrait of Mrs Elizabeth Worlidge, his tutor's third wife. Powle exhibited portrait miniatures with the Society of Artists in 1769 and 1770, and with the Free Society in 1764, 1766, and 1768.

F. M. O'DONOGHUE, rev. JULIA NURSE

Sources Bénézit, *Dict.* • Thieme & Becker, *Allgemeines Lexikon* • Graves, *Artists* • *Engraved Brit. ports.*, 1.176 • D. Foskett, *A dictionary of British miniature painters*, 1 (1972), 455–6 • J. C. Smith, *British mezzotinto portraits*, 3 (1880), 1006 • Anderton catalogues, vol. 5, nos. 1163–6; vol. 6, no. 1245 [exhibition catalogues, Society of Artists, BM, print room] • A. Whitman, *Valentine Green* (1902), nos. 57–9 • *Letters between Rev. James Granger … and many of the most eminent literary men of his time*, ed. J. P. Malcom (1805)

Powle, Henry (*bap.* 1630, *d.* 1692), politician, was baptized on 18 October 1630 at Shottesbrooke, Berkshire, the second son of Henry Powle (*d.* 1646), landowner, of Shottesbrooke and his wife, Katherine (*d.* 1659), daughter of Matthew Herbert of Monmouth. Sir Richard Powle MP was his elder brother. Powle matriculated at Christ Church, Oxford, on 16 December 1646 and was admitted to Lincoln's Inn on 11 May 1647, being called to the bar on 31 May 1654.

Opposition politician In 1657 Powle succeeded his uncle, William Powle, at Quenington, Gloucestershire, and that same year he purchased the manor of Williamstrip from his brother Richard. In 1659 he married the Hon. Elizabeth Newport (1627–1672), daughter of Richard *Newport, first Baron Newport. They had one daughter, Katherine, who married Henry Ireton, son of the regicide. Powle's two

Gloucestershire manors gave him an interest in the parliamentary borough of Cirencester for which he was returned in the Convention of 1660. His only speech of note occurred on 9 July when he opposed the established religion according to the Thirty-Nine Articles, an early indicator of his sympathy for a broader church. Powle was elected FRS, probably in 1663 (he was expelled in 1685). He was not returned in the 1661 election. In 1667 he had the reputation of a gambler and a rake, and in 1670 he was removed from the Gloucestershire bench, probably because of his reluctance to enforce the Conventicle Acts, although he was reinstated the following year.

Powle was returned to parliament again at a by-election for Cirencester on 3 January 1671. He made at least one speech during the session, on 22 March 1671, over the fining of juries, and acted as a teller and chair of several select committees. Powle really began to make his mark as an opposition speaker during the 1673 session, peppering his speeches with a detailed knowledge of parliamentary precedents. As Bishop Burnet put it, 'Powle was very learned in precedents, and parliament journals, which goes a great way in their debates' (*Bishop Burnet's History*, 2.84). In 1673 Powle particularly opposed the king's declaration of indulgence, favouring a temporary parliamentary indulgence for protestant dissenters, and arguing on 10 February 'that the king could not dispense, much less suspend, the laws in being' (*Diary of Sir Edward Dering*, 115). On a related matter, Powle was a keen supporter of the bill preventing the growth of popery (the Test Act), even suggesting on 21 March 1673 that supply legislation be delayed so that this bill could be completed.

Parliament was summoned to meet again on 20 October 1673, and on the eve of the session Sir William Temple thought Powle a leader of a moderate group of MPs whose aims were to safeguard religion and end the war with the Netherlands. Powle thwarted the court's plan for an immediate prorogation on the 20th and proceeded to move for an address that the duke of York's marriage with Mary of Modena might not be consummated. Parliament was prorogued later that day for a week, and when the new session began on the 27th Powle was again at the forefront of the opposition. On 30 October he opined that 'when money is given, or any good thing done, still popery spoils all' (Grey, 2.195–6). He continued to stress the danger from popery and the grievance of the standing army before parliament was again prorogued on 4 November 1673.

When parliament reconvened in January 1674, Powle was again at the head of the attack on the court, and especially the conduct of the dukes of Buckingham and Lauderdale. On 13 January he spoke of 'a pernicious design to alter the government … these councillors having brought us to the brink of destruction' (Grey, 2.239–40), and moved for an address that Lauderdale be removed from the king's presence for ever. On the 14th he supported moves to have Buckingham stripped of all the offices he held during royal pleasure. He was less forward in promoting the case against the earl of Arlington, arguing that what was done should be 'just and regular' (ibid., 2.323–4). He described the war against the Dutch as hanging 'over our heads like a comet' (ibid., 2.334–5). He supported a general test bill to distinguish between protestants and papists and a habeas corpus bill, but described the Lords' bill for regulating the trial of peers as likely to set them up as kings should it pass.

The parliamentary session which began in April 1675 saw Powle return to the attack on ministers, especially Lauderdale. Despite claiming 'an unwillingness to accuse great men' (Grey, 3.41–2), on 26 April, he nevertheless supported the impeachment of Lord Treasurer Danby. Other targets for Powle included the danger from France, pensioners, and Lauderdale again (who remained in power). Powle was critical of the king's advisers, believing that there was a design to rule without parliament, and that there were those whose 'boundless ambition makes them hate parliaments' (ibid., 3.132).

Powle continued his opposition in the next session. On 20 October 1675 he supported a bill for the royal children to be educated as protestants. On the 21st he made the point about royal finances: 'it seems prodigy to him, that having no war, and such a revenue, there should be such debts' (Grey, 3.318). On the need for a supply for a ship-building programme, he thought money should not be voted for all the ships requested because then there would be no need to summon parliament, and 'the prospect of the coming of a parliament keeps things in order' (ibid., 3.331).

In 1677 the earl of Shaftesbury thought Powle 'doubly worthy', but Powle did not endorse Shaftesbury's contention that the fifteen-month prorogation of parliament to February 1677 constituted a dissolution. He was not, however, willing to support the grant of a supply until grievances had been redressed. He was perturbed by the misuse of previous grants of supply, complaining on 21 February that money was 'not laid out for the purpose it was given' (Grey, 4.126–7), and on 26 March argued for the need to formulate a system of alliances which would secure 'the reduction of the French power to an equality with their neighbours' (ibid., 4.310–11).

When parliament sat again in January 1678, Powle's speech on the 29th encapsulated the case for a restrictive grant of supply: 'whilst we give small sums, there will be still recourse to parliaments for more, but giving of great sums will make parliaments useless' (Grey, 5.23–5). He then argued for redress of grievances before money was granted for the king's foreign policy. On 4 February he defended the right of the Commons to advise the king on foreign policy, and in March consistently pressed for more information on the king's foreign policy and for a war with France. Following a short adjournment in May 1678 he continued to resist a grant of supply without redress of grievances, arguing on 1 June, 'I think it can never be suitable to our trust to give money and leave men's minds unquiet as to the growth of popery' (ibid., 6.48–51). On 8 June he summed up the frustration of the Commons with Charles II's foreign policy: 'we desired a war, and we have a peace. We desired to lessen the power of the French king, and we make peace to greaten him' (ibid., 6.76–7).

In the last session of the Cavalier Parliament Powle was one of a number of MPs associated with Lord Arlington and Prince Rupert who were encouraged to attack Lord Treasurer Danby, probably in Powle's case because of his ambition to secure a place on the Treasury commission. Initially he was sceptical of the Popish Plot, noting on 6 November 1678 his belief that 'this plot has come in by the connivance of the government' (Grey, 6.154). However, he was soon supporting a whole raft of opposition policies for safeguarding the state and the protestant religion, including the Test Act depriving Catholics of their parliamentary seats, and raising the militia as an alternative to a standing army, which he hoped to see disbanded. He defended the former courtier and now MP Ralph Montagu on 19 December, perhaps partly to protect his own contacts with the French ambassador, Paul Barillon, which had been begun via Montagu and which subsequently led to him receiving £500 from Barillon for his opposition to the court. He then helped to promote Danby's impeachment.

Expedients not exclusion On 11 February 1679 Powle was re-elected to parliament for Cirencester, and three days later he was defeated at East Grinstead where he stood on that part of the Sackville interest espoused by the dowager countess of Dorset. Following Charles II's initial refusal to accept Edward Seymour as speaker, Powle was actually nominated, though not chosen, as an alternative on 8 March. On 19 March he wanted the journals inspected and a report on the events of the previous session laid before the house for the benefit of new MPs. On 1 April he opposed an investigation into the army, wishing to see the troops disbanded quietly, and the punishment of those that counselled raising them. On 7 April he was seated on petition at East Grinstead, but did not choose between his two seats before the end of the parliament. In the middle of the session, on 21 April 1679, Powle was one of a group of former members of the opposition who were admitted to the privy council. The duke of York was encouraged by this move regarding Powle 'as a man of honour' (Dartmouth MSS, 1.31). The new privy councillors, however, were now placed in the position of being royal spokesmen in the Commons, but without the full support of the king. Powle thus faced a difficult time being heard in the house, particularly when arguing for a supply to be granted to the king. In the debate on excluding the Roman Catholic duke of York from the throne on 11 May 1679, he argued for limitations to be placed on a royal successor, not for exclusion, which he voted against.

Powle's first wife having died on 28 July 1672, following the end of the parliamentary session he married, by a licence of 28 June 1679, Frances (d. 1687), daughter of Lionel *Cranfield, first earl of Middlesex, and the widow of Richard Sackville, fifth earl of Dorset. They had no children. The king dissolved parliament in July 1679, and on 19 August Powle was re-elected for Cirencester. Despite being married to a Sackville, he came bottom of the poll at East Grinstead. In December 1679 Barillon thought him 'a man fit to fill one of the first posts in England; he is very eloquent and able' (Dalrymple, 1.338). Charles II's refusal to allow the new parliament to meet led to Powle's resignation from the privy council on 31 January 1680. When parliament eventually met in October 1680 he was again an unsuccessful candidate for the speakership. He was probably a moderate exclusionist, being appointed to draw up the second Exclusion Bill, but not speaking for it. He was a manager of the impeachment of Lord Stafford in December 1680, summing up on the 4th 'in a vehement oration' on the 'Jesuitical doctrine of holding it not only lawful but meritorious to murder an heretic king' (Evelyn, 3.229–30). He also supported the Comprehension Bill and the impeachment of Lord Chief Justice Scroggs, but he appeared to be losing his influence to the more ardent exclusionists.

Elected for both Cirencester and East Grinstead in February 1681, in the week-long Oxford parliament Powle spoke on 24 March 1681 in favour of 'expedients' over exclusion. After the accession of James II, Powle stood at Cirencester in March 1685, and was easily defeated. He retained his seat on the Gloucestershire bench, but was absent from the county when the 'three questions' were asked concerning the repeal of the Test Act and penal laws. In September 1688, however, the earl of Sunderland recommended Powle as a court candidate for New Windsor.

Powle had been in contact with The Hague before the invasion of William of Orange in November 1688. Together with Sir Robert Howard he travelled to the prince's camp at Windsor on 16 December 1688, and after a long audience carried a letter back from the prince to the common council of London, which disapproved of James II's return to the capital and ensured that the authorities took precautions to secure the city for William. Powle took the chair of the meeting summoned by William of all the members of Charles II's parliaments on 26 December 1688 in order to find a method of calling a 'free parliament'. Powle clearly impressed in this role, the Dutch ambassador, Van Citters, describing him as a 'man of excellent understanding and probity' (Schwoerer, 136).

Speaker of the house Powle was elected to the Convention Parliament for New Windsor on 11 January 1689, and was chosen speaker on the 22nd. There was an attempt to have him removed from the speakership by overturning his election for New Windsor, but it was confirmed by the house without a division on 2 May. Powle was appointed on 14 February 1689 to the privy council, was named master of the rolls on 13 March, and reappointed on 14 June. He had been made a bencher of Lincoln's Inn on 13 May of the same year. As well as presiding over the succession debates, Powle presented the Bill of Rights to William and Mary on 16 December 1689.

In the 1690 election Powle was returned for Cirencester, but despite support among some whig backbenchers he was not re-elected to the chair. On 26 April he supported the Abjuration Bill because it was aimed only at those people employed in the government, and 'they who are to act ought to be zealous in it' (Grey, 2.85–6). Unseated on petition on 25 November 1690, Powle died on 21 November 1692, after a few days' illness, and was buried at Quenington. His great collection of precedents, parliamentary journals, and manuscripts on English history was split up, eventually part of it finding its way into the Lansdowne collection, and part to the Bodleian Library.

STUART HANDLEY

Sources HoP, Commons, 1660–90 · G. W. Marshall, ed., The Genealogist, 7 (1883), 11, 13 · A. Grey, ed., Debates of the House of Commons, from the year 1667 to the year 1694, 10 vols. (1763) · Foster, Alum. Oxon. · Sainty, Judges · M. Hunter, The Royal Society and its fellows, 1660–1700: the morphology of an early scientific institution (1982), 164–5 · W. R. Williams, The parliamentary history of the county of Gloucester (1898), 162 · A. L. Browne, 'The forbears of Sir Henry Powle', Journal of the British Archaeological Association, new ser., 39 (1933), 362–81 · The manuscripts of the earl of Dartmouth, 3 vols., HMC, 20 (1887–96), vol. 1, pp. 30–31 · R. Beddard, ed., A kingdom without a king: the journal of the provisional government in the revolution of 1688 (1988), 51–6 · Bishop Burnet's History · M. J. Knights, Politics and opinion in crisis, 1678–81 (1994) · L. G. Schwoerer, The declaration of rights, 1689 (1981), 32, 136–41, 173 · The parliamentary diary of Sir Edward Dering, 1670–1673, ed. B. D. Henning (1940), 115 · J. Dalrymple, Memoirs of Great Britain and Ireland, new edn, 3 vols. (1790), vol. 1, pp. 338, 381 · The life of the the Lord Keeper North by Roger North, ed. M. Chan (1995), 110 · Evelyn, Diary, 3.227–30 · K. H. D. Haley, The first earl of Shaftesbury (1968), 319, 336–7, 398, 418, 457, 565 · J. R. Jones, The first whigs (1961) · C. J. Phillips, History of the Sackville family, 2 vols. [1930], 424–5

Archives BL, historical collections and papers, Lansdowne MSS 315–318 · Folger, legal and historical papers · Yale U., Beinecke L., commonplace book

Likenesses G. Vertue, line engraving, 1737 (after G. Kneller), BM, NPG

Powle [Powell], **Nathaniel** (d. 1622), colonist in America, was apparently the son of Thomas Powle of Holton St Mary, Suffolk. The parish register does not record his baptism but does include between 1593 and 1609 the baptisms of Thomas and five other children of Thomas Powle, and between 1627 and 1635 names four Nathaniels in the family. Details about his early life are unknown. He arrived in Virginia in 1607, being described as a gentleman.

In Virginia, Powle was busily employed. In February 1608 he attended Christopher Newport when the latter met Powhatan, leader of the neighbouring American Indians. Later in the year (July–September) he accompanied Captain John Smith on his second exploration of Chesapeake Bay, and at the very end of the year he went with Smith to the Pamunkey Indians on the occasion when Smith outfaced Powhatan's military chief, Opechancanough. During this expedition he was sent to the Mangoaco in search of Sir Walter Ralegh's lost colony, but could only report that they were all dead. When Smith came to compose his account of these events, he made use of Powle's records.

As we know from his own report, Powle took part in 1616 in a punitive campaign against the Chickahomini Indians. On 20 October 1617 he was appointed sergeant-major-general in Virginia, and, commenting on his death, Smith later described him as 'a valiant Souldier' (Barbour, 2.295).

When Argall, the acting governor, left for England in early April 1619, he appointed Powle as his temporary replacement. Sir George Yeardley, the new governor, arrived within a fortnight and at once added Powle to his council, an appointment that the company confirmed when they issued instructions on 24 July 1621 to Sir Francis Wyatt, Yeardley's successor.

About this time Powle married Joyce Tracy (d. 1622), the daughter of another councillor, William Tracy, who had come to the colony with her parents in January 1621. In March 1622, when the Powhatan Indians launched their attack on the colony, Nathaniel and Joyce were living at Powle-brooke, his 600 acre estate at Bikers Point in Charles City county. Along with ten others at the settlement, both Powle and his pregnant wife were killed on 22 March. The attack ultimately saw the destruction of about one-sixth of the colony's population.

When the news reached England, Powle's brothers and sisters petitioned the company for his estate. Referring to him as 'a man of extraordinary merritt' and to his siblings' poverty, the company's court instructed the council in Jamestown to take special care in the matter (Kingsbury, 2.107), but clearly nothing was done at that time, for on 21 July 1626 Nathaniel's brother Thomas for himself and his 'poor distressed' brothers and sisters asked the privy council for an order to the governor and council for the recovery of their brother's estate (CSP col., 1.81). It was then said to be in the hands of Mr Blany, who had married the widow of a William Powell, who was no kin to them. Ultimately they were successful: the Virginia land books record that on 12 February 1639 William Barker, mariner, and his associates bought from John Taylor, citizen and girdler of London, the estate in Virginia which Taylor had earlier bought from 'Thomas Powell, yeoman', of 'Howlton' in Suffolk (Nugent, 70, 100).   DAVID R. RANSOME

Sources S. M. Kingsbury, *Records of the Virginia Company of London* (1906–35) · *The complete works of Captain John Smith (1580–1631)*, ed. P. L. Barbour, 3 vols. (1986) · *CSP col.*, vol. 1 · N. M. Nugent, *Cavaliers and pioneers*, 1 (1963) · parish registers, Holton St Mary, Suffolk

Powle, Sir Stephen (c.1553–1630), administrator, was born at Cranbrook, Essex, the youngest son of the chancery clerk Thomas Powle (1514–1601) of St Anne's, Aldersgate, London, and Jane Tate (1521–1577) of Wraxham, Norfolk. About 1564 Stephen went to Broadgates Hall, Oxford, where he was admitted BA (March 1569) and MA (December 1572). In November 1574 he entered the Middle Temple, lodging for some time with the young Walter Ralegh. Despite success in his legal studies, Powle left London in 1579 for Geneva, where he attended Beza's lectures, thus demonstrating his Calvinist leanings. He then spent six months at Basel University before enrolling as a student at Strasbourg in early 1581. After study at Strasbourg, and excursions to Speyer and Heidelberg, he went to Paris in late 1581, and was back in England by March 1582.

Powle now entered the service of the lord treasurer, Burghley, but by April 1583 he had gone north to Scotland, where he spent six months studying under Andrew Melville at New College, St Andrews. In early 1585 he returned to Heidelberg as Burghley's agent at the court of Duke Casimir, where he passed his time at the university until

in March 1586 Casimir entrusted him with letters for England. As his next assignment, in March 1587 Powle was dispatched by secretary Walsingham as an agent to Venice, from where he sent regular newsletters, reporting on papal plots against Elizabeth. Within a year, however, he was recalled from Venice and once more languished in London, living with his father in Maiden Lane. Eager for employment, in early 1589 he sought Burghley's permission to return to Switzerland, while Walsingham suggested service with the duke of Brandenburg; a rumour that he was to be sent as ambassador to Scotland came to nothing.

At last Powle decided to remain in England. In March 1590 he married Elizabeth Hobart (1556–1590) of Wraxham, Norfolk, but she died on Christmas eve the same year, following childbirth. In late 1593 he married an Essex widow, Margaret Smyth (née Turner), and settled with her at Smyth Hall, Blackmore, Essex, where he lived the life of a country gentleman and served as a JP. He became a friend of the Essex poet Nicholas Breton, who dedicated *The Court and Country* (1618) to him. Following concerns about his elderly father's neglect of his chancery duties, in April 1596 Stephen was appointed deputy clerk of the crown in chancery, and in 1601 Thomas surrendered his six clerkships to his son. On 8 July 1604 Stephen Powle was knighted by James I at Theobalds. In March 1609 he enrolled as an 'adventurer' in the Virginia Company and subsequently served on its London council; he also invested in an expedition to Guiana.

Powle divided his time between Blackmore and his houses in Chancery Lane and at Mile End, Middlesex, until April 1621, when his wife, Margaret, died and Smyth Hall passed to her heirs. In May 1623 he married Ann (d. 1631), widow of Sir Richard Wigmore, and they settled in her house in King Street, Westminster, where Powle passed his declining years. He died intestate, and was buried at St Margaret's, Westminster, on 26 May 1630. Powle's papers, including several commonplace books and travel journals, are preserved in the Tanner manuscripts in the Bodleian Library, Oxford.   P. R. N. CARTER

Sources V. F. Stern, *Sir Stephen Powle of court and country* (1992) · PRO, SP 12/222/77, 92; SP 12/223/1 · BL, Lansdowne MSS 75, 100 · W. J. Jones, *The Elizabethan court of chancery* (1967) · D. B. Quinn, 'Notes by a pious colonial investor, 1608–1610', *William and Mary Quarterly*, 16 (1959), 551–5
Archives BL, Lansdowne MSS · Bodl. Oxf., Tanner MSS 168, 169, 246, 309 · Exeter College, Oxford, Exon MS 88 · PRO, Italian letters, SP 101/81

Powles, John Diston (1787/8–1867), company promoter and speculator, was particularly active in South America. His earliest speculations were connected with the movements of Spanish American emancipation at the close of the Napoleonic wars. In 1817 he sold arms and the corvette *Emerald* to the Venezuelan patriots. His operations became more extensive in the early 1820s, when the emergent Spanish American republics began to borrow large sums on the London market, and when many mining companies were promoted on the mistaken assumption that access to British capital and technology would transform the production and profitability of the gold and silver mines concerned.

Powles was the moving spirit in a number of these ventures, and besides government loans and mining in Gran Colombia (later New Granada, Venezuela, and Ecuador) his interests included the settlement of a Scottish agricultural colony at Topo, near Caracas (a predictable failure, whose sufferings he did little to alleviate), tobacco speculations in New Granada (later Colombia) and Venezuela, and the educational projects for a time pursued under Bolívar's patronage in Caracas by the educationist Joseph Lancaster. Before the 1826 crash of Spanish American speculations, the first debt defaults, and the severe falls in the value of mining shares, Powles orchestrated a promotional campaign and the publication of reviews and newspapers in London and in the republics concerned; the publisher John Murray was heavily involved with him, and he employed as pamphleteer the young Benjamin Disraeli, whose first published work, *An Inquiry into the Plans, Progress and Policy of American Mining Companies*, he commissioned. There is a description of Powles's Spanish American dealings and boostings in Disraeli's novel *Vivian Grey*.

Despite numerous reverses, Powles carried on in business for the next half century. The chief sufferers in 1826, and in many of his subsequent failures, were the shareholders. Powles himself and his immediate associates, both in government loans and in mining ventures, made money through commissions, subcontracting to management companies under their own control and other forms of insider dealing; his mines in New Granada continued to operate through the successive bankruptcies of the companies that nominally owned them and their consistent failure to pay any dividends. He also engaged in occasional short-term high-interest lending to governments of the region, while at the same time representing the holders of their defaulted bonds. His company trading in New Granadan tobacco did not survive the crisis of 1857–8. In the aftermath of this debacle, he visited Colombia and attempted without success various speculations in the disturbed circumstances that followed the local civil war of 1859–61. In 1863, by then chairman of the Committee of Spanish American Bondholders, he published a short work on the republic's prospects, *New Granada: its Internal Resources*.

A foray in 1855 by Powles into London politics as an 'administrative reformer' produced from one aggrieved shareholder a pamphlet containing a sharp attack on his character and business methods; it lists, besides Colombian mining and river transport enterprises, mines in Mexico and Brazil, and interests in Pacific whaling and Australian copper. The author of the pamphlet, a Mr Richardson, noted that Powles was 'a great speechifier, &c. at religious meetings' and a subscriber to the Society for the Propagation of the Gospel in Foreign Parts.

In the closing years of his career Powles was prominent in the service of various bondholders' committees engaged in the conversions and reschedulings that accompanied the gradual reappearance in these years of Spanish American governments as borrowers on the London market. Many of his business operations would now be considered fraudulent, but they were not illegal by the looser standards of his time. He shared, and did not create, the illusions about Spanish American prospects in the early years of the region's independence, and never entirely shed them. It was not in his interest to do so.

Powles was married, but nothing is known about his wife or children. He died on 14 September 1867 at Borehamwood, Elstree, at the age of seventy-nine.

MALCOLM DEAS

Sources F. G. Dawson, *The first Latin American debt crisis* (1990) · M. Deas, *Vida y opiniones de Mr William Wills*, 2 vols. (Bogota, 1996) · H. English, *General guide to the companies working foreign mines* (1825) · H. English, *A complete view of the joint stock companies formed during the years 1824 and 1825* (1827) · B. Disraeli, *Vivian Grey* (1826) · B. Disraeli, *An inquiry into the plans, progress, and policy of American mining companies* (1825) · C. Richardson, *Mr John Diston Powles, or, The antecedents, as a promoter and director of foreign mining companies, of an administrative reformer* (1855) · H. Rheinhamer Key, *Topo: historia de la colonia escocesa en las cercanias de Caracas, 1825–1827* (Caracas, 1986) · R. K. Porter, *Caracas diary, 1825–1842* (1966) · E. Vaughan, *Joseph Lancaster en Caracas, 1824–1827*, 2 vols. (1989) · D. Morier Evans, *The history of the commercial crisis, 1857–1858, and the stock exchange panic of 1859* (1859) · d. cert.
Likenesses W. Ward, engraving (after J. Jackson), BM

Powlett, Charles. See Paulet, Charles, second duke of Bolton (c.1661–1722).

Powlett [Paulet]**, Charles, third duke of Bolton** (1685–1754), politician, was born on 3 September 1685 at Chawton, Hampshire, the eldest son of Charles *Paulet or Powlett, second duke of Bolton (c.1661–1722), and his second wife, Frances Ramsden (d. 1696). Styled marquess of Winchester from 1699, he was educated at The Palace, Enfield. In 1700 its master, Robert Uvedale, wrote that Winchester 'declines all business, and refuses to be governed, absenting himself from school, and by no persuasion will be prevayl'd upon to follow his studies, but takes what liberty hee thinks fitt upon all occasions' (*Leeds MSS*, 151). According to Narcissus Luttrell, Winchester subsequently travelled on the continent with Anthony Ashley Cooper, third earl of Shaftesbury, returning to England in August 1704. Luttrell expected him to serve as a volunteer in Portugal, but on 27 April 1705 Winchester was appointed colonel of a regiment of horse by Marlborough, suggesting that he was then in the Low Countries. On 7 December that year he was elected member of parliament for Lymington, Hampshire; he moved to sit for one of the Hampshire county seats in 1708.

On 21 July 1713 Winchester married a much sought-after heiress, Anne (d. 1751), only daughter of John *Vaughan, third earl of Carbery. 'Exstreemly good, and very handsome, and very modist and vertuously brought up' (*Complete Letters of Lady Mary Wortley Montagu*, 1.236n.), the new marchioness had little in common with her pleasure-loving husband and his 'provoking' (*Portland MSS*, 5.328) conduct: 'he made her an early confession of his aversion' (*Complete Letters of Lady Mary Wortley Montagu*, 1.236–7) and the couple separated within a few weeks of their wedding. There were no children.

In 1714 Winchester was appointed a lord of the bedchamber to George Augustus, prince of Wales, and in 1715 became member of parliament for Carmarthenshire, inheriting the Carbery interest there. That year he also became lord lieutenant of Carmarthenshire and Glamorgan, governor of Milford Haven, and vice-admiral of south Wales. At the breach between George I and the prince in 1717, Winchester leant towards the king, and was rewarded with the colonelcy of the regiment of Royal Horse Guards (8 March) and a summons to the House of Lords (12 April). This was intended as a writ of acceleration by which he would have taken a seat in his father's barony of St John of Basing, but a drafting error resulted in his being summoned in a new barony, Pawlet of Basing, instead. He resigned his place in the prince's household in December.

On 21 January 1722 Winchester succeeded his father as duke of Bolton, and was also appointed to his father's places as lord lieutenant of Hampshire and Dorset and warden of the New Forest. He was also elected KG, on 10 October. Bolton inherited substantial landholdings and political influence in Hampshire. He wrote to Charles Spencer, third earl of Sunderland, assuring him of his loyalty and his help in building a coalition: 'I find not only the Whig Gentlemen butt even some of the Tory Interest very zealous and ready to serve me' (Bolton to Sunderland, 25 Feb 1722, BL, Add. MS 61496, fol. 130). After Sunderland's death he moved towards the Walpole–Townshend administration, becoming a privy councillor and constable of the Tower of London in 1725 and governor of the Isle of Wight (in place of the Tower appointment) in 1726.

Bolton was probably representative of many major landowners in that politics was not a passion but an expression of his rank. He controlled only a small number of seats, but his territorial dominance in Hampshire made him useful, although not essential, to ministers. More heartfelt were his enthusiasms for the hunt—'such long chases and hard riding was never known nor spoke of' (John Leheux, 1725, *Various Collections*, 8.393)—horse-racing, and the pursuit of women. During 1728 he became entranced by Lavinia *Fenton (1710–1760), an actress whose portrayal of Polly Peachum in *The Beggar's Opera* had taken the town by storm. Bolton was depicted by William Hogarth watching Fenton's performance in his painting of the Newgate scene in the play. On 19 June it was announced that Fenton had retired from the stage. Bolton lived quietly but openly with Fenton at a succession of town houses and at Westcombe Park, near Greenwich; the couple had three sons, all of whom were known by the surname Powlett, the form preferred by Bolton for himself and his brothers.

Bolton's relationship with Walpole was always born of his desire to hold offices and enjoy their incomes, but his overconfidence in his political position as a duke and patron led him to vote against the excise in 1733. Walpole retaliated by dismissing him from all his positions. His loss was unregretted, at least by John, Baron Hervey, who wrote that Bolton, 'as vain as if he had some merit, and as necessitous as if he had no estate'—although he had lost large sums in the South Sea Bubble—'was troublesome at Court, hated in the country, and scandalous in his regiment' (Hervey, 176), alluding to his allegedly unparalleled trafficking in officerships as colonel of the Royal Horse Guards. Bolton was one of the founders of the Beefsteak Club of opposition whigs, which first met on 15 January 1734, but he never took to opposition. He conceivably maintained contact with the ministry through his brother Lord Harry Powlett, a lord of the Admiralty from 1733. He was certainly corresponding with the duke of Newcastle by 1739 and in 1740 his return to the fold was rewarded with the minor office of captain of the gentleman pensioners, a place in the cabinet, and a pension of £1200 a year. At the fall of Walpole in 1742 he again became lord lieutenant of Hampshire, warden of the New Forest, and governor of the Isle of Wight, with a pension increase to £2000 a year. In November 1745 he was promoted lieutenant-general and raised a regiment in Hampshire in response to the Jacobite rising. Although Newcastle had helped bring Bolton back into government in 1740, Bolton preferred to follow John Carteret, second Earl Granville, in cabinet. This may have been because Granville was closer to the king than were Newcastle and his brother Henry Pelham, and Bolton wanted to emphasize his loyalty to the monarch over party. None the less, in February 1746 Bolton lost his place in the cabinet, as well as the governorship of the Isle of Wight. He never held cabinet office again.

On 25 March 1751 Bolton, whose feet and legs had been weak for some time, wrote to Newcastle that 'I have bien told that a Warmer Climate and a Clearer Air such as the South of France, wou'd give me better health than I have had for some year's' (BL, Add. MS 32724, fol. 212). He left for France accompanied by Lavinia Fenton and the critic and clergyman Joseph Warton. The latter was expected to marry Bolton and his mistress as soon as news came of the death of the duchess of Bolton. Warton found it impossible to study as he had intended and left before the duchess died on 20 September 1751. Bolton married Lavinia Fenton at Aix-en-Provence on 20 October; the news broke in London earlier than Bolton had wished, as it revealed his disregard for his first wife's memory, but was welcomed by Granville and Newcastle.

Bolton's quest for patronage in his later years was conducted on behalf of his sons: Charles, who first entered the army and then the church; Percy, a naval officer; and Horatio Armand, in the army. Bolton died at Tunbridge Wells on 26 August 1754 and was buried on 14 September at Basing, Hampshire. He was succeeded in all his titles, except the Pawlet of Basing barony, which became extinct, by his brother Harry. His widow died on 24 January 1760 at Westcombe Park.   MATTHEW KILBURN

Sources BL, Newcastle MSS, Add. MSS 32692, 32693, 32711, 32722, 32723, 32724, 32725, 32728, 32733 · P. Watson, 'Powlett, Charles', HoP, *Commons, 1715–54* · GEC, *Peerage* · John, Lord Hervey, *Some materials towards memoirs of the reign of King George II*, ed. R. Sedgwick, 3 vols. (1931) · BL, Blenheim MSS, Add. MSS 61293, 61496,

61589, 61603 · *The complete letters of Lady Mary Wortley Montagu*, ed. R. Halsband, 3 vols. (1965–7) · J. B. Owen, *The rise of the Pelhams* (1957) · J. W. Wilkes, *A whig in power: the political career of Henry Pelham* (1964) · N. Luttrell, *A brief historical relation of state affairs from September 1678 to April 1714*, 5 (1857), 460 · C. E. Pearce, *Polly Peachum* (1913) · *The manuscripts of his grace the duke of Portland*, 10 vols., HMC, 29 (1891–1931), vol. 5, pp. 325, 328, 547 · *Report on manuscripts in various collections*, 8 vols., HMC, 55 (1901–14), vol. 8, pp. 393–4 · *Biographical memoirs of the late Rev Joseph Warton*, ed. J. Wooll (1806) · J. H. Plumb, *Sir Robert Walpole*, 2 vols. (1956–60) · *Manuscripts of the earl of Egmont: diary of Viscount Percival, afterwards first earl of Egmont*, 3 vols., HMC, 63 (1920–23), vols. 2–3 · *DNB*

Archives Hants. RO, appointments | BL, Newcastle MSS, corresp. with duke of Newcastle, Add. MSS 32692–32733 · BL, Blenheim MSS, Add. MSS 61293, 61496, 61589, 61603 **Likenesses** W. Hogarth, group portrait, oils, 1728–9 (*The Newgate scene from The beggar's opera*), priv. coll.; versions, Birmingham Museums and Art Gallery, National Gallery of Art, Washington, Yale U. CBA

Powlett [Paulet], **Harry**, sixth duke of Bolton (1720–1794), naval officer, was born on 6 November 1720, the second son of Harry Paulet, fourth duke of Bolton (1691–1759), and Catherine Parry (*d.* before March 1758), daughter of Charles Parry of Oakfield, Berkshire. He was brother of Charles Paulet, fifth duke of Bolton (*c.*1718–1765), and nephew of Charles Paulet, third duke. He was educated at Winchester College (1728–9), and in August 1733 was enrolled as a scholar in the Royal Naval Academy in Portsmouth Dockyard. On 4 March 1740 he was promoted fourth lieutenant on the *Shrewsbury*, and on 15 July 1740 captain of the *Port Mahon* (20 guns), attached to Rear-Admiral Nicholas Haddock's fleet off Cadiz. In late July 1741 he moved to the *Oxford* (50 guns), which he commanded in the action off Toulon on 11 February 1744. In the subsequent courts martial Powlett's evidence was strongly against Richard Lestock.

In March 1745 Powlett was appointed to the guardship *Sandwich* (90 guns), at Spithead, and a few months later to the *Ruby* (50 guns). Accompanied by the *Defiance* and *Salisbury* he was sent from Plymouth on 11 April 1746 to reinforce Admiral William Martin off Brest. Having failed to find the admiral, Powlett cruised off the port, captured the French frigate *Embuscade* (40 guns), and gained news of French forces, which he dispatched to England by his French prize; he finally found Martin on 22 May. In November 1746 he was appointed to the *Exeter* (60 guns) in which he went out to the East Indies to serve under admirals Thomas Griffin and Edward Boscawen. On his return to England in April 1750 he brought charges of misconduct against Griffin for failing to engage eight French ships at Cuddalore at a time—June 1748—when Griffin was commander-in-chief on that station. Although Powlett was Griffin's chief accuser, there had been general disagreement among Griffin's captains at his decisions. Griffin, who was found guilty of negligence, and temporarily suspended from his rank, regarded Powlett's action as 'the inveterate malice of a capricious turbulent young man' (Rodger, 249). He retaliated by bringing Powlett to a court martial for cowardice and other serious charges. In spite of Powlett's attempts to avoid it by going on half pay, the court martial assembled on 1 September 1752. But

after five years Griffin could produce no witnesses to support his accusations, the charge failed for want of evidence, and Powlett was acquitted. The incident produced a volley of pamphlets on both sides, and ultimately resulted in a duel on Blackheath in 1756.

Powlett's meteoric progress to command was the result of family influence. His father's loyal support of Sir Robert Walpole had been rewarded with a seat at the Admiralty in 1733, a year which marked the beginning of Harry Powlett's naval education and career. He was promoted post captain only four months after being made lieutenant, while his father was at the Admiralty. Family influence, which enabled him as a junior officer to take an active part in the courts martial of two of his superiors without fear of blighting the duke of Portland's promotions during the late 1750s.

Powlett was appointed to the guardship *Somerset* at Chatham in January 1753; and on 28 August 1754, by his father's succession to the dukedom, he became, by courtesy, Lord Harry Powlett. On 4 February 1755 he was appointed to the *Barfleur* (80 guns), which formed part of Sir Edward Hawke's fleet in July, which was cruising to prevent a junction between the Brest and Toulon French fleets and de la Motte's squadron returning from America. On 22 August Powlett was ordered to chase a sail that was seen to the south-east; during the night he lost sight of the fleet, and for the next two days he cruised independently. On 25 August he went to Hawke's rendezvous, to await his return. But the carpenter reported the stern-post of the *Barfleur* loose and dangerous. Powlett ordered an examination and, acting on the report of the first lieutenant and the master, returned to Spithead for repairs. Here, on 20–22 October, he was court martialled for separating from the fleet and returning to port unjustifiably. On the former charge he was admonished, but on the latter he was acquitted. The carpenter was dismissed as incompetent, but public opinion blamed Powlett as the real author of the carpenter's report. Henceforth he was nicknamed Captain (later Admiral) Stern-post; it is also thought that he was the subject behind Captain Whiffle in Smollett's *Roderick Random* (1748).

Between 26 November 1751 and 1754 Powlett had been MP for Christchurch, Hampshire, in the government interest, and from 17 January 1755 to 27 March 1761 he represented the family seat of Lymington. In June 1755, just before the stern-post incident, he solicited the duke of Newcastle's help towards promotion to flag rank, urging his and his family's attachment to government. At the end of 1755, and again in March 1756, his father pressed Newcastle for him to succeed to one of the two vacancies at the Admiralty and in March 1756 Powlett again urged Newcastle to forward his promotion. Despite the stern-post incident, political influence proved decisive: on 4 June 1756 he was promoted rear-admiral and on 14 February 1758 vice-admiral of the white. However, political influence could not eradicate the professional impact of his recent court martial and despite the outbreak of war he remained without employment. Boscawen is reported to have wished Powlett to accompany him to the Mediterranean in 1756 as second in command, but it is said George II, who was supposed to have agreed with the popular judgement on Powlett, refused to sanction the appointment.

The political influence of Powlett's family sustained him after his active service career ended. Powlett, MP for Winchester between 1761 and 1765, generally remained a government supporter, though his interventions in Commons debates, chiefly on naval subjects, were undistinguished, sometimes confused, marked by bathos, and too often greeted with derision by fellow members. Powlett was in favour of the peace proposals of 1763; but the support he and his elder brother gave to John Wilkes between 1763 and 1764, his opposition to the naval estimates, and his quarrel in the House of Commons with George Grenville in 1765 may reflect residual resentment at a lack of employment. Powlett supposedly persuaded his brother to join Lord Temple and William Pitt in their opposition to Grenville. But his brother's death on 5 July 1765, and his own accession to the title as sixth duke of Bolton, brought a reputed change of heart. He declared he was now free of all political connection and his attachment was solely to the crown. In this vein he supported successive ministries and became vice-admiral of Hampshire and Dorset in 1767, admiral of the blue on 18 October 1770, and vice-admiral of the white on 31 March 1775.

From 1778 Bolton was in opposition to the government's conduct in the American War of Independence. With Lord Bristol he organized and signed the memorial to the king of twelve admirals, protesting at the court martial of Admiral Augustus Keppel in December 1778. In March 1779 the death of Bolton's eldest daughter, Mary, the wife of Viscount Hinchingbrooke, heir to the fourth earl of Sandwich since 1772, dissolved a connection already weakened by the events of the preceding year. Bolton's involvement in active politics waned from 1780 onwards, and by 1784 he retained a political interest only in Totnes through his friend Colonel Jennings (later Jennings Clerke). From 1782 to 1791 Bolton was governor of the Isle of Wight, an office he had previously held between 1766 and 1770, and from 1782 until his death he was lord lieutenant of Hampshire, an office previously held by his uncle, father, and brother.

Bolton was twice married, first on 7 May 1752 to Mary Nunn of Eltham, Kent, who died on 31 May 1764; they had one daughter, Mary (1753–1779). His second marriage, on 8 April 1765, was to Katherine Lowther (1736?–1809), youngest sister of the first earl of Lonsdale. They had two daughters. Bolton died on 25 December 1794 at Hackwood House, his Hampshire seat, and was buried at St Mary's Church, Basing, on 2 January 1795.

His reputation as a naval officer was irrevocably tarnished by the stern-post incident. Horace Walpole thought him 'a silly, brutal, proud man, yet whose valour was … problematical' (GEC, *Peerage*, 2.215, n. b). Nor did he shine in the political sphere. The laudatory but disingenuous inscription on his monument in St Mary's Church, Basing, refers to his 'excellent understanding and firm

persevering disinterested attachement to the liberty of his country'.

At his death the dukedom became extinct but all other honours devolved on his distant cousin and male heir, George Powlett of Amport, Hampshire. The illegitimate daughter of his brother, the fifth duke, became heir to Bolton Castle and other estates, her husband, Thomas Orde, taking the name of Powlett after Orde, by royal licence on 7 January 1795. Bolton's widow died on 21 March 1809, and was buried at Basing on 29 March, aged seventy-three.

P. K. CRIMMIN

Sources D. Syrett and R. L. DiNardo, *The commissioned sea officers of the Royal Navy, 1660–1815*, rev. edn, Occasional Publications of the Navy RS, 1 (1994) · GEC, *Peerage* · P. Watson, 'Powlett, Harry', HoP, *Commons, 1715–54* · L. B. Namier, 'Powlett, Harry (1720–94)', HoP, *Commons, 1754–90* · J. E. Doyle, *The official baronage of England*, 1 (1886), 204–5 · H. W. Richmond, *The navy in the war of 1739–48*, 3 vols. (1920) · D. Lyon, *The sailing navy list: all the ships of the Royal Navy, built, purchased and captured, 1688–1860* (1993) · *The Hawke papers: a selection, 1743–1771*, ed. R. F. Mackay, Navy RS, 129 (1990) · *VCH Berkshire*, vol. 3 · *VCH Hampshire and the Isle of Wight*, vol. 4 · N. A. M. Rodger, *The wooden world: an anatomy of the Georgian navy* (1986) · BL, Newcastle MSS, Add. MS 32855, fol. 340; Add. MSS 32864, fols. 30, 101
Archives BL, Egerton MSS, Add. MSS 3438, fol. 243 · BL, Newcastle MSS, Add. MSS 32855, 32864
Likenesses F. Cotes, portrait, Metropolitan Museum of Art, New York · Flaxman, marble bust on monument, St Mary's Church, Basing, Hampshire · portrait, repro. in 'Tête-à-tête', *Town and Country Magazine*, 10 (1781), 289
Wealth at death see will, PRO, PROB 11/1254, fol. 32

Powlett, Lavinia. *See* Fenton, Lavinia (1710–1760).

Powlett, Thomas Orde-, first Baron Bolton (1746–1807), politician, the elder son of John Orde (d. 1784), a landowner, of East Orde and Morpeth, Northumberland, and his second wife, Anne Marr (d. 1788) of Morpeth, was born on 30 August 1746 at Morpeth, where he was baptized Thomas Orde on 2 October. He was descended from a prominent Northumbrian family—his great-uncle William represented Berwick upon Tweed between 1713 and 1715—and he had a half-brother, William, from his father's first marriage, to Mary Ward, and a younger brother, John *Orde, who became first baronet. He was educated at Eton College from 1755 until he went up in 1765 to King's College, Cambridge, where he was made a fellow in 1768 and graduated BA in 1770 and MA in 1773. A competent artist, he became known for his etched caricatures of local celebrities in Cambridge; these were published by his drawing-master, James Bretherton. Having been admitted to Lincoln's Inn in 1769, he was called to the bar in 1775. In the intervening years he travelled in France, Switzerland, and Italy (1772–3) and Flanders, the Netherlands, and Germany (1774). On 7 April 1778 he married Jean Mary Browne Powlett (d. 1814), the natural daughter of Charles Powlett, fifth duke of Bolton, and Mary Browne Banks, on whom the greater part of the Bolton estates was entailed.

The holder of a succession of offices in the duchy of Lancaster from 1772, which he owed to the patronage of Lord Hyde, later earl of Clarendon, who was a personal friend, Orde also owed his entry to parliament to the influence of

Thomas Orde-Powlett, first Baron Bolton (1746–1807), by John Jones, pubd 1786 (after George Romney, 1777)

powerful patrons. He was elected to represent the borough of Aylesbury in 1780 on the nomination of the earl of Chesterfield, to whom he had been recommended by John Robinson. Robinson allocated a substantial sum of secret service money to defray the cost of his election to this 'venal and expensive borough' (Namier, 232). Though a reluctant parliamentary performer, Orde was a loyal and not inactive supporter of Lord North's ministry in its final years. He seconded the address on 27 November 1781 defending the government's American policy, but his major contribution was made in the secret committee established on 2 May 1781 to investigate the causes of the war in the Carnatic. Although this was chaired by Henry Dundas and included Charles Jenkinson among its membership, Orde 'took over the detailed work of the committee' (ibid., 233). It was a task for which he was eminently suited, as Nathaniel Wraxall noted when he observed of the fifth report of the committee, which was attributed to Orde, that it was 'one of the most able, well-digested, and important documents ever laid upon the table of the House of Commons' (*Historical and Posthumous Memoirs*, 2.108). Publicly complimented for his efforts by Dundas, Orde was made under-secretary to Lord Shelburne at the Home Office on the creation of the short-lived Rockingham ministry, and on the formation of a new ministry under Shelburne in July 1782 he was promoted to the position of secretary to the Treasury. Orde and Shelburne established a close attachment arising out of their period in office together, so much so that, when William Pitt came to form a new ministry on the dismissal of the Fox–

North coalition in December 1783, Orde declined Pitt's request that he should resume his place at the Treasury. A number of other offers and requests for help at this time merely underlines the point that he was identified in the corridors of power as a man of ability. In spite of his expectation that he would soon be without a seat in the House of Commons should a general election be called— he could not sustain an expensive election contest at Aylesbury out of his own resources without government backing—he declined every invitation until the newly appointed lord lieutenant of Ireland, the duke of Rutland, approached him through Shelburne with the request that he should become his chief secretary. This assured him of the support he required, and he was returned for the Treasury borough of Harwich in the general election of 1784.

Orde accompanied Rutland to Ireland in February 1784. On the face of it, they were an unlikely combination. Rutland was better known for his prodigal lifestyle than for his political skill, but his style, convivial disposition, and lack of interest in the daily grind of administration well complemented Orde's strengths. As Irish chief secretary Orde was particularly attentive to the detail of business, and though he demonstrated a perturbing readiness to indulge in self-pity when things got difficult it never eclipsed his strong commitment to duty. Where hard work and application were sufficient, he ensured that the work of government was conducted efficiently. His judgement of men and measures was less secure; he was prone to lose perspective when the matter at issue was complex and contested, and his lack of social grace ensured that he was never very good at the task of man management, which was an essential part of the work of an Irish chief secretary. These limitations became apparent only with time. In the short term Orde worked well with the conservative men of business that Rutland's predecessor, Lord Northington, had introduced into the Irish executive.

The greatest challenge the new administration faced in 1784 was to deflect the demand for a reform of the representative system that was promoted by a loose coalition of patriot parliamentarians and middle-class radicals. In common with his colleagues on the Irish administration, Orde believed that any liberalization of the representative system must exacerbate the task of maintaining English control in Ireland, so when the rejection by the Irish parliament in the late spring of popular measures for the reform of parliament and for protecting duties prompted a prolonged bout of public disorder, he was easily convinced that its purpose was 'to weaken the government and to sever the bonds of union between the two countries' (Bolton MS 16355, fols. 1–4). Indeed, Orde was so persuaded by evidence gleaned from intercepted correspondence and spy reports that there was a conspiracy afoot involving 'connections and confederacies' (ibid., fols. 10– 12) of Roman Catholics, Presbyterians, and the French crown that, when Pitt contemplated responding with a plan of reform that would provide for the increased admission of protestants to the political process, he categorically condemned the suggestion as inappropriate and counter-productive. 'The measure could not succeed here without the most extreme hazard, not the administration merely, but the British government in the kingdom', he pronounced at the outset of an exhaustive 27-page rebuttal (Chatham MS 30/8/329, fols. 145–59). Orde's disposition to indulge in self-pity under pressure was first manifested at this point. Distressed by the death of his father and harassed by his inability to get to the root of the disorder that continued to disturb the streets of Dublin, he confided to Henry Dundas that 'never was a man placed in a situation which he more cordially detested, or where he makes a more complete sacrifice of his feelings, his habits and comforts' (Melville MS 54, fol. 25). However, he vowed 'to endure all rather than to risk my character … or … the success of the King's government' (ibid.), and before the year was out he had the satisfaction of witnessing the return of order to the city streets and the virtual disintegration of the parliamentary reform movement.

Because, as chief secretary, he was the key link in the chain that bound the British and Irish executives, Orde enjoyed little respite from the pressures of high office. Arising out of his conviction that the Anglo-Irish relationship had been left dangerously undefined as a result of the concession of legislative independence in 1782, William Pitt's determination to bind Britain and Ireland in a commercial union demanded the total engagement of the Irish chief secretary in its elaboration and presentation. It was Orde who provided the prime minister with 'a short state of the case' upon the commercial points around which Pitt devised his initial outline of a settlement. Subsequently he unsuccessfully advised the prime minister against including a provision for an annual financial payment from the Irish to the British exchequer. As Orde forecast, this proved the sticking point with the Irish parliament when on 7 February 1785 he presented the scheme in the form of ten propositions 'in a most correct and masterly manner' (Rutland MSS, 3.175). Determined that it should not fail at the first hurdle, Orde agreed to the inclusion of an additional proposition to ease Irish anxieties, but the perception in Britain that this put an Irish financial contribution at risk was a serious complication. It little impressed ministers that the modified propositions were warmly endorsed by the Irish parliament. Pitt insisted that a formula was devised that secured a contribution from Ireland. Orde was so deflated by this and by criticism of the amended propositions that he contemplated resignation. There was no question of his resignation being sought or accepted, but the resulting tortuous efforts to devise an acceptable strategy to ensure a secure financial contribution from Ireland, which necessitated his departure for London in March, in an 'unpleasant hurry' (Bolton MS 16352, fol. 9), proved difficult and distressing.

Obliged to represent the English case in Ireland and the Irish case in England, Orde felt he was engaged, he explained to Pitt, 'in a perpetual scene of warfare both on the one side and on the other' (Bolton MS 16358, fols. 93–6). Matters became even more difficult following Pitt's decision to respond to pressure at home by recasting and expanding the propositions to take account of wider imperial and domestic vested interests. Orde attended to the myriad issues that arose out of this with scrupulous care, but he continued to find this task and that of endeavouring to keep political interests in Ireland on side extremely trying: 'My brain is almost unsettled by the endless conversations and explanations which I am obliged to endure' (ibid., fols. 119–20), he conceded to George Rose on 3 June. Despite this, and occasional bouts of debilitating illness that necessitated recourse to an amanuensis, a broadly acceptable bill for a commercial settlement was finally drafted in the late summer, and Orde was ready to present it to the Irish parliament on 12 August. The task that faced him that day would have tested even the most expert of parliamentarians, and Orde failed to rise to the occasion. According to 'Memory' Woodfall, who was present to record the debate, the chief secretary was 'so far unintelligible that, had I not known the business practically before, I could not have conceived its true tendency' (Journal and Correspondence of … Auckland, 1.79). Irish dislike of the proposal rather than Orde's poor performance ensured that the measure did not advance beyond first reading stage. None the less, the chief secretary's limitations in the Commons and inattention to man management reinforced the perception that he was not possessed of the qualities necessary in an Irish chief secretary. Arising out of this, Pitt suggested to the duke of Rutland late in 1785 that he might wish to replace Orde, but the lord lieutenant's stout defence of his beleaguered chief secretary ensured his survival, and Pitt signalled his support by nominating him to the British privy council shortly afterwards.

Encouraged by their experiences in 1785, the Irish administration 'attempted nothing out of the common course' (Rutland MSS, 3.264) during the 1786 parliamentary session. The commercial arrangement was quietly shelved, and Orde overcame his increasing susceptibility to illness to oversee the ratification of a measure that provided for the introduction of a government-controlled police force for Dublin city. He had become convinced of the necessity for such a body by the disorder that gripped the city in 1784, and his identification and implementation of this pioneering experiment in policing, in the teeth of strong opposition, emphasized his skills and capabilities as an administrator. He demonstrated this further by developing a suggestion made to him by the earl of Shelburne that he should reform Irish education. Persuaded by his own observations, as well as by reports of the serious failings of existing institutions, that an enhanced educational system would serve both to dispel 'the mists of ignorance' (Giffard, 29) and to attach Catholics to the state, he presented the Irish parliament on 12 April 1787 with a plan for a five-tier educational system encompassing parish, provincial, diocesan, and collegiate schools and two universities. Orde conceded that it was not possible 'to accomplish the whole system at once' (Bolton MS 16360, fol. 1). Considerable efforts were made to overcome the opposition of vested interests during the summer of 1787 and to secure funding, but Orde's own capacity to engage with the subject was restricted by illness. His departure from Ireland was assured even before the death of the duke of Rutland in October brought down the curtain on the Rutland administration and on Orde's eventful and significant chief secretaryship.

Orde left Ireland with a pension of £1200. Ill health and his own political limitations ensured he never again held major office; while he continued to act as MP for Harwich in the government interest until 1796, he rarely contributed to debates. He was appointed governor of the Isle of Wight in succession to his father-in-law in 1791, and the Bolton estates passed to him in right of his wife on the death of the sixth duke of Bolton on 24 December 1794. On 7 January 1795 he took the additional name of Powlett, and on 20 October 1797 he was created Baron Bolton of Bolton Castle, Yorkshire. His last appointment was to the lord lieutenancy of Hampshire in 1800. He died on 30 July 1807 at his home, Hackwood Park, near Basingstoke, some seven years before his wife (who died on 14 December 1814) and was buried on 8 August 1807 at Old Basing, Hampshire. He was succeeded by William Powlett Orde (1782–1850), the elder of his two sons.   JAMES KELLY

Sources NL Ire., Bolton MSS, 16350–16360, 15800–15978 · *The manuscripts of his grace the duke of Rutland*, 4 vols., HMC, 24 (1888–1905), vol. 3 · L. B. Namier, 'Orde, Thomas', HoP, *Commons, 1754–90* · R. G. Thorne, 'Orde (afterwards Orde Powlett), Thomas', HoP, *Commons, 1790–1820* · PRO, Chatham MSS, 30/8/329 · NL Ire., Melville MSS, MS 54 · J. Kelly, *Prelude to Union: Anglo-Irish politics in the 1780s* (1992) · J. Kelly, 'The context and course of Thomas Orde's plan of education of 1787', *Irish Journal of Education*, 20 (1986), 3–27 · J. Kelly, 'Parliamentary reform in Irish politics, 1760–90', *The United Irishmen: republicanism, radicalism and rebellion*, ed. D. Dickson and others (1993), 74–87 · S. Palmer, *Police and protest in England and Ireland, 1780–1850* (1988) · *The historical and the posthumous memoirs of Sir Nathaniel William Wraxall, 1772–1784*, ed. H. B. Wheatley, 5 vols. (1884) · *The journal and correspondence of William, Lord Auckland*, ed. [G. Hogge], 4 vols. (1861–2) · *Correspondence between the Right Honourable William Pitt and Charles, duke of Rutland, … 1781–1787*, ed. Lord Mahon (1890) · GEC, *Peerage* · *DNB* · J. Giffard, *Mr Orde's plan of an impressed system of education in Ireland* (1787) · J. Ingamells, ed., *A dictionary of British and Irish travellers in Italy, 1701–1800* (1997) · Venn, *Alum. Cant.*
Archives Bodl. Oxf., scheme for a 'system of education in Ireland' · Hants. RO, corresp. and papers · HLRO, papers relating to Ireland · Isle of Wight County RO, Newport, corresp. relating to government and defence of Isle of Wight · N. Yorks. CRO, corresp. and papers · NL Ire., corresp. and papers · Yale U., journal of Italian tour [copy] | Belvoir Castle, Rutland, Rutland papers · BL, corresp. with first earl of Liverpool, Add. MSS 38218–38224, 38308–38310, 38407, 38447–38448, 38471, *passim* · Bowood, Calne, Wiltshire, Shelburne papers · Hunt. L., letters to Lord Pery · NL Ire., letters to second earl of Glandore · NRA, priv. coll., letters to Lord Lansdowne · PRO, letters to William Pitt, PRO 30/8 · PRO, Chatham papers
Likenesses P. Batoni, oils, 1773, priv. coll. · J. Jones, mezzotint, pubd 1786 (after G. Romney, 1777), BM, NPG [*see illus.*] · Bretherton, etching · G. Romney, oils · oils (after Romney), King's Cam.

Pownall, Sir Henry Royds (1887–1961), army officer, was born in London on 19 November 1887, the second son of Charles Assheton Whately Pownall of St John's Park, Blackheath, London, and his wife, Dora Bourne Royds. C. A. W. Pownall was consulting engineer to the railway

Sir Henry Royds Pownall (1887–1961), by Walter Stoneman, 1941

bureau of Japan, and between the ages of three and eight Henry lived in Japan. He was educated at Rugby School, entered the Royal Military Academy, Woolwich, in 1904, and was commissioned into the Royal Field Artillery in 1906. From 1914 to 1919 he served continuously in France and Belgium, acting as brigade major, Royal Artillery, 17th division, in 1917–18. He was mentioned in dispatches, and was awarded the MC and DSO (1918). On 10 December 1918 Pownall married Lucy Louttit (d. 1950), daughter of William Henderson of Aberdeen and the widow of Captain John Gray, 36th Sikhs, Indian army, killed at Kut al-Amara in 1916; they had one son.

Pownall was brigade major, school of artillery (1924–5) and on the directing staff (general staff officer, grade 2) of the Staff College, Camberley (1926–9): an excellent horseman, he gained the prestigious appointment of whip to the Staff College drag. In 1931 he won a bar to his DSO in action on the north-west frontier of India. From 1933 to 1936 he served on the secretariat of the committee of imperial defence (CID) under Sir Maurice Hankey, who would have been prepared to recommend Pownall as his successor had he not preferred to return to service with troops. From mid-1936 he was commandant of the school of artillery, Larkhill, Salisbury Plain, with the rank of brigadier.

In the 1930s Pownall consistently argued—against the policy of 'limited liability' advocated by Captain Basil Liddell Hart and others and favoured by Chamberlain, most other politicians, and many officers—that a continental commitment of the army was probably unavoidable; and he played an important part in eventually getting it accepted as government policy. He wrote in his diary in May 1934 on Chamberlain, 'his ideas on strategy would disgrace a board school' (Bond, *British Military Policy*, 200). In January 1938 he wrote of the 'most dangerous heresy … of "limited liability" in a war … It will be 100%—and even then we may well lose it' (ibid., 218). He also bitterly criticized Liddell Hart, and impugned his motives. He disliked his criticism of orthodox officers, and believed that his proposed strategy was wrong and that his role of *éminence grise*, outside adviser to Leslie Hore Belisha (secretary of state for war, 1937–40), was improper and irresponsible, and that his influence increased the general staff's difficulties in preparing for a continental commitment. Pownall also disliked Liddell Hart's 'confused writing and his usual false deductions from History' (*Chief of Staff*, 151). Later, during the war, Pownall and other senior officers opposed his proposed appointment as adviser to David Margesson when secretary of state for war (1940–42).

Pownall's three years at the CID had established his reputation as an exceptionally able staff officer. In the five years before the war he was promoted five times, and his appointment as director of military operations and intelligence at the War Office in January 1938 was a jump of over a hundred places in seniority. Long convinced that war with Germany was inevitable—in 1933 he had guessed that war might come in 1940—he strove first to secure a definite continental commitment for the army. In January 1938 he wrote in his diary, '*My* view is that support of France is home defence—if France crumbles we fall' (Bond, *British Military Policy*, 286). Nevertheless he distrusted French politicians and the French army. In the few months remaining (April–August 1939), he worked all-out to prepare the British expeditionary force (BEF) to go to France.

At the War Office Pownall enjoyed excellent relations with Lord Gort VC (chief of the Imperial General Staff, 1937–9) whom he much admired, and Gort selected him as his chief of staff (CGS) when appointed to command the BEF on the outbreak of war; although this entailed—as in 1914—that the two men who knew most about military organization and planning were suddenly removed from the War Office. Pownall, Gort, and other officers detested Hore-Belisha, believing him conceited, ignorant, self-seeking, and untrustworthy. Pownall in May 1939 in his diary contrasted Gort and Hore-Belisha: 'a great gentleman and an obscure, shallow-brained, charlatan, political Jewboy' (*Chief of Staff*, 203). He wrote that Hore-Belisha intended 'to bitch up the higher organization of the Army in order to make the position of CIGS impossible' (ibid., 206).

After the 1939 'pill box affair'—during which Gort and other senior officers expressed resentment at what they considered unjustified criticism and interference by Hore-Belisha on the BEF's construction of concrete 'pill box' defences in France—Pownall played a considerable part behind the scenes in securing Chamberlain's dismissal of Hore-Belisha (4 January 1940). He wrote in his diary, 'it's no good being Old School Tie with H-B, you have to fight him with his own weapons' (*Chief of Staff*, 264). During the 1940 retreat to Dunkirk, Pownall set an admirable example of calmness and foresight, working closely with Gort in the final phase to extricate the BEF from encirclement. He was mentioned in dispatches and appointed KBE (1940).

Unlike Gort, Pownall retained Churchill's confidence, and he was given a succession of important commands in potential trouble-spots. After a few months as the first inspector-general of the Local Defence Volunteers (later the Home Guard) he was commander-in-chief of British forces in Northern Ireland (1940–41) when German invasion was still a real possibility. When the threat had waned he returned to the War Office in May 1941 as vice-chief of the Imperial General Staff. In November 1941 the replacement of Sir John Dill by Sir Alan Brooke as chief of the Imperial General Staff led to a reshuffle of senior officers at the War Office and Pownall was appointed commander-in-chief, Far East. However, Japan entered the war against Britain and the United States before he could effectively take up his command, and in January 1942 he became chief of staff to Wavell in the short-lived south-west Pacific command. He was promoted lieutenant-general in 1942 and in April took over the Ceylon command, a post he held for exactly a year. Once again the enemy robbed him of the opportunity to demonstrate his capacity as a commander, and when the Japanese advance had clearly been arrested he was appointed commander-in-chief, Persia–Iraq, succeeding Sir Henry Maitland Wilson, but he wanted to escape from what he regarded as a backwater into the Mediterranean theatre.

In the summer of 1943 Mountbatten had been appointed to the new south-east Asia command, and Brooke—with Churchill's approval—selected Pownall as a highly experienced staff officer, 'a wise old head', to supply a steadying influence as chief of staff: Pownall saw his role as, in his favourite phrase, 'to keep, Mountbatten on the rails' (*Chief of Staff*, xiv). This proved an excellent choice so far as personal relations with Mountbatten and the creation of the large and complex SEAC inter-allied staff headquarters were concerned; but in strategic terms Pownall's term of office was largely characterized by frustrating changes of plan due to the theatre's low priority in the allies' grand strategy. In November 1944 Pownall's health broke down, and he retired from the army early in 1945, receiving a KCB (1945). From 1942 to 1952 he was colonel commandant, Royal Artillery.

Pownall was a first-class staff officer, orthodox, not an original thinker, and between the wars lukewarm on mechanization. He was aptly described by his friend and successor as deputy secretary to the CID, Lord Ismay, as 'one of the best brains of my vintage in the Army, courageous, competent and cool as cucumber' (Ismay, 124). Lieutenant-General Sir Wilfrid Lindsell, who served with 'Henry', as he was universally known, as quartermaster-general of the BEF in 1939–40, wrote of him:

> He certainly possessed all the qualities for success in any branch of Staff work or in Command. He had the essential basis of sturdy commonsense, a well-balanced knowledge of his profession, no fear of taking responsibility and plenty of initiative and energy … of a serious turn of mind and always

imperturbable in a crisis … Quick and precise in manner, he was an energetic worker, bringing to the solution of all his problems a clear well-ordered mind. To all who served under him he was a quiet, courteous and sympathetic chief. He had a remarkable memory and was a masterly writer of minutes and reports.   (*Royal Artillery Regimental News*, Aug 1961, 297–8)

Wavell also found him an ideal senior staff officer.

Pownall was appointed chief commissioner of the St John Ambulance Brigade in 1947, and became vice-chancellor of the order of St John in 1950 and chancellor in 1951. He was chairman of Friary Meux Ltd and a member of the committee of Lloyds Bank. For six years he assisted Churchill as military consultant on the *History of the Second World War*. His chief relaxations were skiing, fly-fishing, and golf. He was an accomplished linguist and a delightful conversationalist with a dry sense of humour. Pownall died in London on 9 June 1961.

BRIAN BOND, rev.

Sources *The Times* (10 June 1961) · *Royal artillery regimental news* (Aug 1961) · *Chief of staff: the diaries of Lieutenant-General Sir Henry Pownall*, ed. B. Bond, 2 vols. (1972–4) · private information (1981) · B. Bond, *British military policy between the two world wars* (1980) · *WWW* · Burke, *Peerage* (1959) · B. Bond, *Liddell Hart: a study of his military thought* (1977) · R. J. Minney, *The private papers of Hore-Belisha* (1960) · M. Howard, *The continental commitment* (1974) · D. French, *The British way in warfare, 1688–2000* (1990) · H. Strachan, *The politics of the British army* (1997) · [H. L. Ismay], *The memoirs of General the Lord Ismay* (1960) · *CGPLA Eng. & Wales* (1961)

Archives King's Lond., Liddell Hart C., diaries | FILM BFI NFTVA, news footage · IWM FVA, actuality footage · IWM FVA, news footage

Likenesses W. Stoneman, photograph, 1941, NPG [*see illus.*] · J. W. Pownall-Gray, miniature, tempera, 1950, priv. coll. · S. Elwes, portrait, priv. coll.

Wealth at death £46,425 10s.: probate, 10 Aug 1961, *CGPLA Eng. & Wales*

Pownall, Robert (1520–1571), Church of England clergyman and translator, was born in Dorset, not Somerset as formerly believed—a detail furnished by his signature on the list of English exiles at Aarau. Little is known of his life and career before the reign of Mary. He fled abroad as a student, but soon achieved a certain prominence through his activities in several exile centres. On reaching the continent he settled first in Calais: in 1557 he penned to his former fellow citizens *An Admonition to the Town of Calais* (*STC*, *1475–1640* 19078) threatening them with plagues such as had afflicted Israel in the time of Jezebel:

> When as I call to remembrance how many wayes God hath sought to induce thee to repentance, … and on the other side thine indurate rebellion in following in the footsteps of thy mother England, I cannot but with tears lament thyne emynent destruction.   (sig. A1r)

But Calais, at this time still under English rule, was hardly a safe haven, and by 1556 Pownall had moved on to Wesel, a small German Rhineland town which had already earned a reputation as a hospitable place of safety for religious exiles. Now a considerable colony of English gathered in the city, and the young Pownall soon found himself raised to a leadership role. The first ministers of the church were Miles Coverdale and William Barlow, both former bishops, but this notwithstanding the Wesel church adopted a church order modelled not on the Edwardian prayer book but on John à Lasco's *Forma ac ratio*, the church order of the Edwardian London stranger churches. Barlow as minister was assisted by two 'adiutors' or under-ministers, seven elders, and two deacons; Pownall was named among the elders.

Alongside his duties in the management of the congregation, Pownall's most signal service during his time in Wesel came in the form of his writings and translations. During these years a concerted effort was made to make Wesel, alongside Emden, one of the two centres of production for vernacular protestant propaganda aimed at those left behind in England. Its strategic location on Europe's principal artery of trade in one respect made it well suited for this task, although, like Emden, there was no previous tradition of printing within the city. Unlike Emden, the exile community did not number among its members veterans of the London printing trade, and were therefore forced to rely on local men with little previous experience of English-language work. These Wesel editions tend to be of a more rudimentary appearance than the accomplished Emden work; nevertheless, the exiles managed to bring some twenty editions to the market during the course of little over two years. To this Pownall contributed four significant works: the *Admonition to Calais* and three translations from the French. Of these, the most substantial was an edition (1555) of Wolfgang Musculus's famous work, *The Temporiser*, first translated into French from the original Latin by Valérand Poullain, minister of the French church in Frankfurt and a fellow refugee from England. This was a work entirely typical of this phase of the exile, an admonition to those true Christians who had remained behind in England to abandon their temporizing or 'Nicodemism' and join the exodus abroad. In an introductory epistle Pownall attempted to fathom what had brought about such a transformation in England, 'where worthy Magistrates, nobility and rulers turned into faint hearted persons … and thy infinite number of gospellers and faithful Christians, into dissembling hypocrites and hollow-hearted persons' (sig. A4). In his perplexity Pownall spoke for many of the exiles, but he had little to propose but admonition to rejoin the right path: 'Wo worth those oxen, that farme, that wife, or any other worldly pleasure, that shall stay us from coming to that celestial supper' (sig. A7).

Pownall also translated from the French two further works in the same vein: *A most Pithy and Excellent Epistle to Animate All Trew Christians unto the Cross of Christ* (1556) and the *Little Dialogue of the Consolator* of Pierre du Val, minister of the French church in Emden. Where Pownall learned his French is unknown, possibly even in his short stay in Calais (in the *Admonition* he refers to Calais as 'thow towne of myne education'), but there was also a sizeable French exile congregation in Wesel. The fact that Pownall chose for translation works of du Val and Poullain, ministers of the French churches in Emden and Frankfurt respectively, is an indication of the close communication between the various exile groups.

Wesel proved ultimately an unhappy refuge for the English and French exile congregations. The Lutheran town council soon appeared to regret the privileges they had extended and, as relations deteriorated, members of the congregation began to look for a new place of refuge. In the summer of 1557 the bulk of the congregation migrated in a body to Aarau, in the Swiss confederation. Here Pownall was appointed one of the ministers of the church under Thomas Lever, whom he had earlier accompanied on a visit to the English community in Geneva. He had by this time married and had three children, one of whom died in Aarau. On 5 October 1557 Pownall and seven of his companions wrote to Heinrich Bullinger, thanking him for the dedication of a volume of his writings to the dispersed English congregations. On 16 January 1559, after the death of Mary, he again joined his companions in a letter to the English church of Geneva accepting their proposition that all English exiles should adopt a uniform attitude on disputed ceremonies.

After the accession of Elizabeth, Pownall returned to England, and was ordained priest by Edmund Grindal, bishop of London, on 1 May 1560. Perhaps surprisingly in view of his distinguished service in exile, Pownall's name never features among those discussed for high office in the new church, notwithstanding his willing conformity. On 31 January 1563 he subscribed the newly prepared Thirty-Nine Articles, and from 1562 until his death he was rector of Harbledown in the Kentish hundred of Westgate. In 1570 he was one of the six preachers of the cathedral church of Canterbury. He died in the following year, having asked in his will for burial in the cathedral, next to the vehemently protestant antiquary John Bale, another of the six preachers, who had died in 1563. Pownall's widow was given a life pension by the cathedral authorities. ANDREW PETTEGREE

Sources C. H. Garrett, *The Marian exiles: a study in the origins of Elizabethan puritanism* (1938) · R. A. Leaver, *'Goostly Psalmes and Spirituall Songes': English and Dutch metrical psalms from Coverdale to Utenhove, 1535–1566* (1991), 197, 200 · E. J. Baskerville, *A chronological bibliography of propaganda and polemic published in English between 1553 and 1558* (1979) · *STC, 1475–1640*, nos. 10432, 7376.5, 18312, 19078 · P. Collinson, 'The protestant cathedral, 1541–1660', *A history of Canterbury Cathedral, 598–1982*, ed. P. Collinson and others (1995), 154–203

Pownall, Thomas (1722–1805), colonial governor and politician, was born on 4 September 1722 in St Mary Magdalen's parish, Lincoln, eldest son of William Pownall (1692–1735), an army officer, and his second wife, Sarah (*d.* 1762), daughter of John Burniston, deputy governor of Bombay. From Pownall's paternal grandfather, Thomas Pownall (1650–1706), who overcame imprisonment for Jacobitism to serve in the armies of William III and Anne, his family inherited modest lands at Saltfleetsby and Dally in Lincolnshire; however, poor management and the untimely death of Pownall's father led to a decline in fortunes. Despite his family's penury—or perhaps because of it—Pownall grew up with a boundless ambition that was made the more conspicuous by his average stature and rotund girth.

Thomas Pownall (1722–1805), by Richard Earlom, pubd 1777 (after Francis Cotes)

After attending Lincoln grammar school, he entered Trinity College, Cambridge, in 1740 as a pensioner, and graduated BA in 1743.

Introduction to America Following a brief, frustrating attempt at restoring the family estate in Lincolnshire, Pownall sought out wider horizons in London, obtaining a clerkship at the Board of Trade, where his younger brother John Pownall (1724–1796) was secretary. Pownall quickly gained the confidence of the board's president, George Montagu Dunk, second earl of Halifax, and in 1753 became private secretary to Halifax's brother-in-law, Sir Danvers Osborne, the newly appointed governor of New York. Coming on the brink of the Seven Years' War (1756–63)—Britain's final, decisive struggle with France for control of North America—Pownall arrived at a propitious moment, but Osborne's suicide, days after their New York landfall on 6 October 1753, created even greater opportunities. Pownall used his freedom from official duties to the full, visiting the principal cities on the American seaboard, attending the Albany congress of 1754, and forming lasting friendships with influential colonists, including Benjamin Franklin and Lewis Evans. During the autumn of 1755 he also became embroiled in the quarrel between Sir William Johnson, British superintendent for Indian affairs, and William Shirley, governor of Massachusetts and commander of the British forces in North America, over the management of Indian affairs. Although Shirley had extended him a warm welcome in 1754, Pownall sided with his rival, using his connections at the Board of Trade to question Shirley's military judgement and hasten the governor's dismissal as British commander in February 1756.

Partly as a result of his own expanding connections in America, and partly through the continued support of his brother at the Board of Trade, Pownall was named lieutenant-governor of New Jersey in May 1755. In February 1756 he returned to England where, after declining the governorship of Pennsylvania, he was made 'secretary extraordinary' to the new British commander in America, John Campbell, earl of Loudoun. Although Loudoun's high-handed policies occasioned hostility in the colonies and criticism at home, Pownall used the position to enhance his own reputation, making another trip to London in August 1756, gaining the confidence of the new prime minister, William Pitt, and establishing himself as an expert in colonial affairs. With Loudoun's blessing, he also pursued his campaign to discredit Shirley, who had been recalled to England in September 1756. Pownall's repeated attacks, which included giving testimony in the House of Commons, contributed to an unsavoury reputation for 'artful and insinuating' behaviour (Schutz, *Thomas Pownall*, 71); however, such accusations were not enough to prevent his being named to succeed Shirley as Massachusetts governor in February 1757. As it happened, Pownall's appointment as governor came close on the heels of his paternal grandmother's death in January 1757, an event that made him sole proprietor of his late grandfather's modest holdings in Lincolnshire. He thus returned to America not only as a man who seemed destined for great things as an 'imperial politician' but as one who could claim—if only just—the coveted status of 'landed gentleman'.

Governor of Massachusetts Pownall's three years as Massachusetts governor (1757–9) were dominated by the strains of war. Like most colonial governors Pownall enjoyed broad powers in theory but few other resources beyond what the Massachusetts legislature was willing to give him. As a result he had to steer a careful course between satisfying the demands of his superiors at home and avoiding policies that might unnecessarily jeopardize his relations with the colony's leaders. Towards that end Pownall worked assiduously to soften the burdens of Britain's war with France, limiting the navy's impressment of local seamen, reducing military penalties for Massachusetts soldiers, and securing British subsidies to help pay the costs of the colony's own campaigns. Shortly after his appointment he also successfully defused a confrontation with Lord Loudoun caused by the British commander's threat to occupy Massachusetts if the provincial legislature refused to provide housing for the army's recruiting parties. In exchange Pownall was able to secure the assembly's support for large annual supplies and levies of troops. During the summer of 1759 he also organized and led a provincial expedition to the Penobscot River in Maine, despite the colony's refusal to appropriate the necessary funds. In each instance he demonstrated a keen awareness of the precariousness of his own position, along with a willingness to accommodate colonial fears over any policy that could be construed as an abuse of power or a stretch of the governor's prerogative.

Despite a reputation for personal vanity Pownall was aided in his executive duties by a tendency towards informality in conducting public business. Less helpfully, he gained a name as a womanizer and giver of lavish parties—'that fribble', in the words of one hostile New Englander (Sawtelle, 235). True to his liberal Anglican principles, however, Pownall also distinguished himself with his assiduous cultivation of the province's established Congregational clergy. Although he attempted to stand apart from the factionalism of Massachusetts politics, Pownall was inevitably drawn into the struggle between the province's 'court' and 'popular' parties. At first he sought the good will of the former group, many of whom had supported Governor Shirley, and even gave his consent for the court leader Thomas Hutchinson to be appointed lieutenant-governor. None the less, lingering resentment over Shirley's dismissal, along with the need to secure legislative support for the war with France, gradually forced him into an alliance with the court's opponents, especially the merchant Thomas Hancock, with whom the governor formed a close friendship. His willingness to co-operate with the popular party was not greeted with universal approval at the Board of Trade; nor was Pownall himself entirely comfortable with having to choose sides in a struggle that threatened to weaken the already fragile basis of British authority in America. Years later John Adams described him as 'the most constitutional and national Governor' ever to represent the crown in Massachusetts (*Works of John Adams*, 10.243), but Pownall's experience also showed him the inadequacy of Britain's colonial administration and the pressing need for reform.

Political and literary career in England Following the conquest of Quebec, Pownall began seeking a new position and, in November 1759, was appointed governor of South Carolina. However, convinced that his best prospects for advancement lay at home, he chose to return to England and resign the South Carolina governorship in favour of a lucrative post as commissary for the British forces in Germany, to which he was appointed on 29 June 1760. The wealth Pownall derived from his two years with the army was sufficient to draw charges of mismanagement from John Wilkes's *North Briton*, no. 40 (5 March 1763), but a Treasury inquiry cleared him of all wrong doing. On 25 August 1765 Pownall consolidated his personal fortune by marrying Harriet, *née* Churchill (1726–1777), widow of the wealthy diplomat Sir Everard Fawkener and mother of four children. Not only did his marriage to Lady Fawkener—as she continued to be known—enable him to lease a house in London's fashionable Albemarle Street, where Horace Walpole, Thomas Almon, and Benjamin Franklin were regular guests, but it also gained him an introduction to many of the leading families of England. Probably with the assistance of his friend Hugh Boscawen, second Viscount Falmouth, a shrewd electioneer, Pownall entered parliament as the member for Tregony, Cornwall, where he won a by-election on 4 February 1767. He was defeated during the general election of 1774 but, through the efforts of Lord North—who may have engineered his defeat at Tregony in order to gain his support for the government's colonial policies—he won another by-election later that same year at Minehead in Somerset, which he represented until his retirement in 1780.

Despite his improved finances and election to parliament, Pownall never realized the expectations fostered by his term as Massachusetts governor. Indeed, as he found himself thwarted in his quest for preferment in England, he came to regret his decision to leave the colonial service where, he believed, greater opportunities existed for ambitious men of modest means. None the less, he remained an acknowledged expert on Britain's colonial affairs in general, especially the American colonies that declared independence in 1776. Pownall's most influential statement in this respect was his *Administration of the Colonies*, first published in 1764 and subsequently enlarged in five revised editions (1765, 1766, 1768, 1774, and 1777). As in his later speeches to parliament, Pownall consciously sought in this work to identify himself as a supporter of American liberty. Although he feared that Britain was losing control of its colonies, he wrote that the Americans were entitled to the same rights of representative government as their fellow subjects in England, Scotland, and Wales. At the same time, Pownall insisted that the military protection that the colonists received from Britain created equally extensive obligations to help pay for some of the cost. He was also convinced of the need for a strong, central legislature capable of making common policies that would be binding for every member of the British empire, including the fractious provinces in North America. Pownall eventually decided that the only solution lay in creating an imperial parliament with representatives from both Britain and the colonies (Pownall, *Administration of the Colonies*, 4th edn, 1768, 174). Although he was not the only British commentator to embrace the idea of an imperial parliament, most Americans found it anathema, so much so that John Dickinson singled out his centralized plan of legislative reform for particular criticism in his influential *Letters from a Farmer in Pennsylvania* (1768).

Throughout this period Pownall searched for possible solutions to the crisis in America. In the House of Commons, where his first speech was on the dangers of forcing New York to quarter British troops, he established a reputation as a staunch pro-American. He also remained in close contact with many colonists, including New Englanders on both sides of the looming divide, as well as Franklin, who was a colonial agent in London. In addition, although the allegation has never been proved, Pownall may have had a part in writing the Junius letters, which attacked successive ministries during the later 1760s and early 1770s, and in publishing the incriminating correspondence that contributed to Thomas Hutchinson's departure as governor of Massachusetts in 1774. As the situation in the colonies deteriorated, Pownall supported some of Lord North's policies, including the Boston Port Act (1774)—though not the rest of the 'Intolerable Acts'—

and the conciliatory plan of early 1775. He also aspired to lead a mission to negotiate a reunion with the rebellious colonies, an honour that instead went to Frederick Howard, fifth earl of Carlisle. In December 1777 Pownall finally broke with Lord North and demanded a liberal treaty recognizing American independence.

Somewhat surprisingly, in view of his literary reputation, Pownall was a notoriously difficult author to read. While he was still governor of Massachusetts, one Boston satirist claimed that his convoluted style seemed calculated to produce a 'most excruciating head-ach' (Schutz, *Thomas Pownall*, 177); twenty years later John Adams went so far as to 'translate' one of his pamphlets on the American War of Independence (*A Translation of the Memorial to the Sovereigns of Europe*, 1781). If Pownall's prose was not always easy to understand, however, he produced a great deal of it, on topics ranging far beyond the crisis in America. In 1773 he published a pamphlet on the East India Company, in which he called for the crown to be given administrative responsibility for Bengal and the other Mughal provinces under British rule. Starting in the early 1770s he sought ways to reduce the high price of grain in England, co-authoring with Edmund Burke a new regulatory law (1773) and embracing the cause of free trade during the mid-1790s. He was likewise an early, if somewhat critical, admirer of Adam Smith's *Wealth of Nations* (1776). Following his own acceptance of American independence, Pownall turned his attention to the conflict's implications for Europe and the Americas, predicting, among other developments, the emergence of independence movements in Latin America and the formation of a new Atlantic community based on commerce and treaties among equal, sovereign states (Schutz, 'Thomas Pownall's proposed Atlantic federation', 264–8). At various points Pownall also wrote on geography and antiquarianism, with works on North American topography, Atlantic Ocean currents, and Roman antiquities. In addition he was an amateur artist, and Paul Sandby acknowledged his drawings as the basis for several engravings in a folio of views of North America and the West Indies, which appeared in 1761 (*DNB*).

Later years Pownall's first wife, Lady Fawkener, died in 1777 and was buried at Lincoln Cathedral, complete with a sarcophagus for which Pownall wrote a lavish inscription. On 2 August 1784 he married Hannah, *née* Kennett (*d.* 1807), widow of Richard Astell, a prosperous landowner with property in Huntingdonshire and Bedfordshire, and two manors, Everton Mosbury and Everton Biggin. The Pownalls made Everton House in Bedfordshire their country home. They also travelled widely, living in France between 1785 and 1787. Pownall continued to maintain a large circle of friends and acquaintances, including Franklin and Francisco de Miranda, the Latin American revolutionary. His final years were marked by gout and rheumatism, which led him to spend progressively longer stays at Bath. It was during one such visit that he died, on 25 February 1805. Following his own wishes he was buried at St Michael's Church, Walcot, Bath. Neither of Pownall's marriages produced children. He left a life interest on his estate to his widow; upon her death two years later, it passed to his brother John's elder son, Sir George Pownall.   ELIGA H. GOULD

Sources J. A. Schutz, *Thomas Pownall, British defender of American liberty* (1951) · J. A. Schutz, 'Pownall, Thomas', *ANB* · L. W. Labaree, 'Pownall, Thomas', *DAB* · *DNB* · W. O. Sawtelle, 'Thomas Pownall', *Proceedings of the Massachusetts Historical Society*, 63 (1929–30), 233–84 · J. A. Schutz, 'Thomas Pownall's proposed Atlantic federation', *Hispanic American Historical Review*, 26 (1946), 263–8 · D. Baugh and A. G. Olson, *The administration of the colonies* (1993) · G. H. Guttridge, 'Thomas Pownall's *The administration of the colonies*: the six editions', *William and Mary Quarterly*, 26 (1969), 31–46 · S. M. Pargellis, *Lord Loudoun in North America* (1933) · C. A. W. Pownall, *Thomas Pownall, MP, FRS, governor of Massachusetts Bay, author of the 'Letters of Junius'* (1908) · *The works of John Adams, second president of the United States*, ed. C. F. Adams, 10 vols. (1850–56), vol. 10, p. 243

Archives Boston PL, papers · Mass. Hist. Soc., papers · Massachusetts Commonwealth Archives, Boston, papers | BL, letters to Samuel Cooper, Kings MS 203 · BL, letters to Lord Hardwicke, Add. MSS 35614–35625, *passim* · Hunt. L., letters to James Abercrombie · Hunt. L., letters to John Campbell, earl of Loudoun · Lincs. Arch., letters to J. C. Brooke, papers · PRO, letters to first earl of Chatham and William Pitt, PRO 30/8

Likenesses R. Earlom, mezzotint, pubd 1777 (after F. Cotes), Smithsonian Institute, Washington, DC, National Portrait Gallery [*see illus.*] · Cotes, oils, priv. coll. · H. C. Pratt, engraving (after his portrait) · H. C. Pratt, portrait, Pownalborough, Maine · portrait, Mass. Hist. Soc.

Wealth at death reportedly land at North Lynn, Norfolk, and leasehold in Albemarle Street; heir was second wife, and after her death elder son of his brother: Pownall, *Thomas Pownall*

Pownoll, Philemon (*b.* in or before **1734**, *d.* **1780**), naval officer, was the son of Israel Pownoll (*d.* 1779), master shipwright of Plymouth yard (1762–5) and Chatham (1775–9). The family's precise origins remain obscure. However, it is known that his father owned property in Shadwell and Clerkenwell which, together with his name, suggests that Philemon was descended from the Independent seamen and merchants who populated the Shadwell and Wapping area in the mid-seventeenth century and had strong links with New England. This connection may account for the statement by Edward Locker, the late-eighteenth-century naval antiquary, that Pownoll (or Pownell) was 'a Gentleman of American extraction' (NMM, CLU/8). He entered the navy about 1748 on the *Mars* (64 guns) and his passing certificate of 7 April 1755 gives his age as 'upwards of twenty'. He was promoted lieutenant on 7 October 1755 and appointed second lieutenant of the *Weymouth* (60 guns) and then the *Royal George* (100 guns). In 1758, in the opening stages of the Seven Years' War, he was transferred to the *Namur* (74 guns), flagship of Admiral Edward Boscawen, who became his patron and promoted him quickly from fourth to first lieutenant. Then on 6 August 1759 he was promoted commander of the sloop *Favourite*.

In July 1761 the *Favourite* was part of a squadron off Cadiz under the command of Captain Charles Proby, when it captured the French ships *Achille* (64 guns) and the frigate *Bouffonne*. In the following May the *Favourite* was dispatched by Admiral Sir Charles Saunders with several other cruisers to guard Cape St Vincent. On 15 May 1762

the *Favourite*, in company with the frigate *Active* commanded by Captain Herbert Sawyer, captured a Spanish register ship, the *Hermione*, off Cape St Mary. The vessel had sailed from the Peruvian coast before the outbreak of war and was found to be carrying an extremely valuable cargo, including bags of dollars, gold coin, ingots of gold and silver, cocoa, and blocks of tin. When the vessel was condemned as a prize, her contents, hull, and fittings were sold for a total of £519,705 10*s*. 0*d*. Pownoll's share alone came to £64,872, one of the largest individual sums obtained in the period. Both Pownoll and Sawyer became very rich men overnight, and subsequently married two sisters, daughters of a Lisbon merchant. Pownoll also invested his prize money by purchasing the estate at Sharpham, at Ashprington, Devon, where he built a large house, still extant.

At the end of 1775, following the outbreak of the American War of Independence, Pownoll was appointed to the frigate *Blonde* (32 guns)—an unusual act for monied officers for which he was praised by the earl of Sandwich in the House of Lords. In the *Blonde*, on the recommendation of Boscawen's brother, Lord Falmouth, he agreed to take on board the young midshipman Edward Pellew, who had been turned out of his previous ship. During a storm in February 1776 the frigate was nearly swept from her moorings at Chatham and was saved only by prompt action from Pownoll, who was on board at the time. In April the *Blonde*, together with the frigate *Juno*, was sent to St Helen's to collect a convoy of twenty transports carrying troops of General Burgoyne's army bound for America. In 1776 Pownoll was appointed to command the frigate *Apollo* (32 guns). On 31 January 1779 she engaged the French frigate *Oiseau* in a very close range action off the coast of Brittany during which both the French commander and Pownoll were wounded—Pownoll being shot in the chest by a musket ball which remained there for the remainder of his life.

On 15 June 1780 the *Apollo* chased and engaged the French privateer *Stanislaus* off Ostend. Pownoll was killed by a cannon ball during the action, which was brought to a successful conclusion by his first lieutenant, Edward Pellew. A highly respected officer known for his consideration to his men and his skills as a trainer, Pownoll was widely mourned. Following the action Pellew wrote to the earl of Sandwich, first lord of the Admiralty:

> The loss of Captain Pownoll will be severely felt. The ship's company have lost a father. I have lost much more, a father and a friend united; and that friend my only one on earth. Never, my lord, was grief more poignant than that we all feel for an adored commander. Mine is inexpressible. (Osler, 52)

Admiral John Jervis judged him 'the best officer, & most excellent, kind hearted man in the Profession', and claimed that he had 'lost the best Partizan, if not the best officer under every line of description in the Service' (BL, Add. MS 29914, fols. 140, 143). In 1804 Jervis (now the earl of St Vincent) promoted Pownoll's grandson, John Bastard, in honour of his grandfather's contribution to the navy. That reputation also influenced Edward Pellew and John Borlase Warren—Warren also served under Pownoll in the *Apollo*—who themselves became frigate captains of great merit and commanders of frigate squadrons during the French Revolutionary Wars.   TOM WAREHAM

Sources C. N. Parkinson, *Edward Pellew, Viscount Exmouth, admiral of the red* (1934) · E. Osler, *The life of Admiral Viscount Exmouth* (1835) · J. S. Corbett, *England in the Seven Years' War: a study in combined strategy*, 2 vols. (1907) · C. G. Pitcairn Jones, 'List of commissioned sea officers of the Royal Navy, 1660–1815', NMM, NMM 359 (42) (083.81) GRE, vol. 9 · W. L. Clowes, *The Royal Navy: a history from the earliest times to the present*, 7 vols. (1897–1903) · NMM, The papers of John, earl Sandwich, NMM SAN · M. Duffy and others, eds., *The new maritime history of Devon*, 1 (1992) · R. Beatson, *Naval and military memoirs of Great Britain*, 2nd edn, 3 (1804), vol. 3, p. 417 · R. Perkins and K. J. Douglas-Morris, *Gunfire in Barbary* (1982) · J. Marshall, *Royal naval biography*, 4 vols. (1823–35) [with 4 suppls.] · G. W. Allen, *A naval history of the American revolution*, 2 vols. (1913)
Likenesses J. Spilsbury, etching, 1781, NMM · E. Hunt, engraving, pubd 1865 (after J. Reynolds), NMM · J. Reynolds, portrait; Christies, 16 March 1984, lot 93

Powys. For this title name *see* Vernon, Henry, styled sixth Baron Powys (1548–1606).

Powys [*née* Girle], **Caroline** (1738–1817), diarist, was born on 27 December 1738, the only child of John Girle (*d.* 1761), surgeon, of Beenham, Berkshire, and his wife, Barbara (1715–1801), daughter of John Slaney of Yardley and Ludsley, Worcestershire. Her father built a house in Lincoln's Inn Fields, London, and they moved there in 1754. After his death she moved to Caversham, Oxfordshire, with her mother, but following her marriage in 1762 to Philip Lybbe Powys (1734–1809), the eldest of the three sons of Philip Powys (1704–1779) and his wife, Isabella Lybbe (1713–1761), of Hardwick House, Whitchurch, Oxfordshire, she became mistress of Hardwick House, which had been in the Lybbe family since 1526. Isabella Lybbe, as the only child, had inherited the house from her father, Richard Lybbe.

Caroline Powys had two sons, Philip Lybbe (1765–1838), who was commissioned into the Grenadier Guards, and Thomas (1767–1817), a clergyman, and one daughter, Caroline (*b.* 1775), who married the Revd Edward Cooper, later rector of Hamstall Ridware, Staffordshire. Another daughter died in infancy. After her sons left home she and her husband let Hardwick House, and in 1784 moved to Fawley rectory, Buckinghamshire, 13 miles away, to live with her brother-in-law, the Revd Thomas Powys, a bachelor.

It was Caroline Powys's father who taught her to keep a diary, starting in 1756. While still living in Lincoln's Inn Fields in 1761 she saw Earl Ferrers being taken from the Tower of London to Tyburn to be hanged for murder, and saw the hearse return; also in 1761 she describes the coronation procession of George III. After her marriage the diary records social life in the country, with visits to neighbouring country houses, often newly built, with gardens laid out by Capability Brown, such as Caversham Park; assemblies and balls during the Henley winter season, with lists of those attending; visits to Bath and London, with plays and concerts, including performances by Mme Catalani in Bath and Mrs Sheridan in London; travels, always in England, including a visit to Ramsgate in 1801,

Caroline Powys (1738–1817), by W. Spornberg, 1807

where she could hear Nelson bombarding French ships off Boulogne; local events, as when she watched Cliveden burn down in 1795; details of alterations to the gardens at Hardwick, with lists of fruit trees planted; recipes, including one for lavender drops, a cure for the palsy; and menus, including that for a dinner given in 1798 by her brother-in-law in Canterbury for Prince William of Gloucester. After a ball in the Upper Assembly Rooms in Bath in January 1791 her list of all the members of the nobility there fills more than a page, 'besides baronets and their wives innumerable'.

Caroline Powys's diary has been dismissed as of little interest, but although she rarely comments on political events, it is none the less a fascinating record of upperclass life in the second half of the eighteenth century. She wrote over 150,000 words, but had no pretensions to literary style: 'if the rusticity of a dull pen, like a piece of rough Marble, may be polished by exercise, then … may I, in time, perhaps have the honorary title of an expert journalist' (U. Powys, *Reading Mercury*, 7 Nov 1959). The diary ends in December 1808, when the rheumatism in her right hand stopped her from writing any more. The death of her husband on 12 April 1809 was followed six months later by that of her brother-in-law, who had been dean of Canterbury since 1797 (always referred to as 'the Dean'). She moved to Henley-on-Thames, and her son Thomas was given the living of Fawley in 1810. On 17 August 1817 Thomas died, leaving a widow and eleven children, including six-year-old triplets, and Caroline returned to Fawley rectory to help her daughter-in-law. She died there three months later, and was buried in her husband's grave at Whitchurch on 7 November 1817. A volume of passages from the diary was first published in 1899.

ANNE PIMLOTT BAKER

Sources C. Powys, *Passages from the diaries of Mrs Philip Lybbe Powys of Hardwick House, Oxfordshire, 1756 to 1808*, ed. E. J. Climenson (1899) · U. Powys, 'The eighteenth century re-created', *Reading Mercury* (22 Aug–7 Nov 1959) · A. Ponsonby, *English diaries: a review of English diaries from the sixteenth to the twentieth century with an introduction to diary writing*, 2nd edn (1923), 252–3 · W. Matthews, *British diaries: an annotated bibliography of British diaries written between 1442 and 1942* (1950), 89 · Burke, *Gen. GB* (1894) · IGI

Archives BL, corresp., journals, and travel notebooks, Add. MSS 42610–42673 · Hardwick House, Oxfordshire, Powys–Lybbe MSS
Likenesses W. Spornberg, miniature, engraving, 1807, repro. in Climenson, ed., *Passages* [see illus.]
Wealth at death inherited property at Beenham, Berkshire, house in Lincoln's Inn Fields from father; inherited one third of an estate at Lulsley, Worcestershire, from mother (1801); she inherited money from both her parents

Powys, Horatio (1805–1877), bishop of Sodor and Man, born on 28 November 1805, was the third son of Thomas Powys, second Baron Lilford (1775–1825), and Henrietta Maria, eldest daughter of Robert Vernon Atherton of Atherton Hall, Lancashire. He was educated at Harrow School and at St John's College, Cambridge, matriculating in 1824 and graduating MA in 1826; he was created DD in 1854. His father presented him to the family living of Warrington, Lancashire, in 1831, and he was for some time rural dean of Cheshire. Strongly impressed with the necessity for improved education, he succeeded in establishing a training college at Chester and an institution for the education of the daughters of the clergy at Warrington. On 5 July 1854 he was nominated to the bishopric of Sodor and Man. A plan for its amalgamation with the diocese of Carlisle had been dropped in 1836, but the future of the see remained insecure. Powys successfully maintained its independence and involved himself in much litigation. He supported the revival of a convocation for the north of England. He printed two charges, *A Pastoral Letter to the Congregation at Warrington* (1848), and two sermons.

Powys married, on 21 February 1833, Percy Gore, eldest daughter of William Currie of East Horsley Park, Surrey; they had three sons—Horace (*d.* 1857); Percy William, rector of Thorpe-Achurch, Northamptonshire; Henry Lyttleton, lieutenant-colonel of the Oxfordshire light infantry—and five daughters. Powys died at Bewsey House, Bournemouth, on 31 May 1877, and was buried at Warrington on 5 June.   G. C. BOASE, rev. H. C. G. MATTHEW

Sources Venn, *Alum. Cant.* · *The Guardian* (6 June 1877), 772 · *Manx Sun* (2 June 1877) · *Manx Sun* (9 June 1877) · *Men of the time* (1875), 820 · D. A. Jennings, *The revival of the Convocation of York, 1837–1861*, Borthwick Papers, 47 (1975)
Wealth at death under £9000: resworn double probate, Nov 1877, *CGPLA Eng. & Wales*

Powys, John Cowper (1872–1963), novelist and writer, was born on 8 October 1872 at the vicarage, Shirley, Derbyshire, the eldest of eleven children of the Revd Charles Francis Powys (1843–1923) and his wife, Mary Cowper (1849–1914), daughter of William Cowper Johnson, rector of Yaxham, Norfolk, through whom Powys inherited the blood of the poets John Donne and William Cowper. Through both parents he came from several generations of country parsons. The Powys family, connected in England with the barony of Lilford, was of ancient Welsh origin. In 1879 John's father took a curacy at Dorchester, Dorset, in order to be near his mother in Weymouth; in 1885 he became vicar of Montacute, Somerset. Thus the west country was the major conditioning environment of John and his brothers Theodore Francis *Powys (1875–1953)

John Cowper Powys (1872–1963), by unknown photographer

and Llewelyn *Powys (1884–1939), all aware in their writings of the impact of landscape on personality. John was educated at Westbury House preparatory school, Sherborne, and Sherborne School (1883–91). He read history at Corpus Christi College, Cambridge, from 1891 to 1894, 'years of an unbalanced and chaotic idealism' (Powys, *Autobiography*), and was awarded a second-class degree. While walking in Cambridgeshire, Powys experienced 'a beyond sensation', which was 'to do with some secret underlying world of rich magic and strange romance. In fact I actually regarded it as a prophetic idea of the sort of stories that I myself might come to write'. In 1896 he married Margaret Alice Lyon (1874–1947), sister of a Cambridge friend, T. H. Lyon; they had one son, Littleton Alfred (1902–1954), who entered the Anglican and afterwards the Roman Catholic priesthood.

From lecturing in girls' schools near Brighton, Powys moved to Oxford University extension lecturing from 1898 and to the American Society for the Extension of University Teaching from 1905. From 1909 to 1934 he spent the large part of each year in the USA, normally returning each summer to his family. As an enthralling, theatrical lecturer, Powys could draw American audiences of 2000 people. Recognition in the USA of his fame and critical intelligence is indicated by his being called, for example, as expert defence witness at court cases on the publication of Theodore Dreiser's *The 'Genius'* (1915) and James Joyce's *Ulysses* (1922), and his being filmed with Bertrand Russell in *Debate: is Modern Marriage a Failure?* (1929).

Powys began his literary career with a small collection

of lyric poems, *Odes and other Poems* (1896), and continued to publish small volumes (in 1899, 1916, 1917, and 1922). His first novel was *Wood and Stone* (1915), followed by *Rodmoor* (1916). These coincided with his first works of non-fiction: three books of literary criticism including *Visions and Revisions* (1915) and *Suspended Judgments* (1916), and one of self-analysis, *Confessions of Two Brothers* (with Llewelyn Powys) (1916). Thereafter he published steadily throughout his lifetime, growing in power.

In America in 1921, a meeting with Phyllis Playter (1894–1982), one of several powerful, intellectual American women friends, led to a lifelong companionship in which she served as Powys's secretary, influential literary critic, and muse. Critical opinion, supported by evidence in his diaries, is that Phyllis Playter's advice helped to raise the quality of Powys's novels, starting with the first of the 'great' ones, *Wolf Solent* (1929), written from 1925 to 1928. This novel may in part reflect the contrasting natures of Margaret Alice Lyon and Phyllis Playter in its principal women characters. Retiring from 4 Patchin Place, New York, his base of seven years, in 1930 Powys moved with Phyllis Playter to Phudd Bottom, upper New York state, where, with 'the life-blood of his home', he wrote the massive works for which he is generally most admired, *A Glastonbury Romance* (1932), *Autobiography* (1934), and *Weymouth Sands* (1934). Phyllis Playter accompanied Powys on his return to Britain in 1934, moving with him to Wales for his final years.

Powys did not win the Nobel prize with *A Glastonbury Romance*, as he anticipated. Instead he was financially crippled by an out-of-court payment of the novel's royalties and more to a Glastonbury dignitary who thought himself portrayed in the novel. *Weymouth Sands* was published in England not under the title of place, but of its main protagonist, *Jobber Skald*. A year in Dorchester produced *Maiden Castle* (1937). When Powys retreated to north Wales, he identified himself with the Welsh in *Obstinate Cymric* (1947), and wrote the Wales-based novels *Owen Glendower* (1940) and *Porius* (1951), his 'masterpiece' set in one week in AD 499. His latest fiction was also removed from contemporary life, including *Atlantis* (1954), *Homer and the Aether* (1959), and a space fantasy, *All or Nothing* (1973).

In tandem with his fourteen full-scale novels and other fiction, Powys produced fourteen 'philosophical' works to guide the 'common man' through the stresses of modern urban life, such as *The Art of Happiness* (1923), *The Meaning of Culture* (1929), *In Defence of Sensuality* (1930), *A Philosophy of Solitude* (1933), *The Art of Growing Old* (1944), and *In Spite Of* (1953). Literary criticism continued, including *The Pleasures of Literature* (1938), *Dostoievsky* (1947), and *Rabelais* (1948). The latter two subjects give some clue to the mixed ingredients of Powys's outstanding works—some six novels and his astonishing *Autobiography*. *Autobiography* is a self-portrait without reticence, without excuse, virtually without women (Frances Gregg, with whom he had a passionate friendship from 1912 to her death in 1945, appears fleetingly when dressed in boy's costume), and with more than his 'touch of caricature'. Here, at sixty, he declared his ambition in fiction to break down fossilized attitudes,

putting his readers at pleasant unease by writing a 'mystic-humorous, Pantagruelian, Shandean, Quixotic Romance'. It is a fact that Powys's novels can be and are read for their dynamic representation of the landscapes he knew well ('Glastonbury herself' he declared the 'hero' of that 'story'), for occasional animation of the inanimate, and for their series of spectacular scenes mingling the trivial, the unexpected, the comic, and the sublime, crowded with increasingly large arrays of intriguing and eccentric characters in tortuous relationships. This is their strength but also only their surface: he had a great gift for investing even the inanimate with complex personality. In his lifetime Powys received appreciative reviews, such as Conrad Aiken's praise of *Wolf Solent* as 'leisurely, copious, humorous', and the *Times Literary Supplement* critic's contrast of it with *Ulysses* as arousing 'disgust' but leaving us 'with a realisation of the beauty not the ugliness of the world' (1929). Yet, as Angus Wilson put it in 1963, Powys's enthusiastic critics failed him in their expression of 'amazement rather than comprehension'.

John Cowper Powys was strikingly handsome in appearance as in personality. The painting by Raymond Jonson (1917) and numerous photographs for dust-jackets, including the National Portrait Gallery's choice, may better represent the novelist than the portrait by his sister Gertrude (1944; NMG Wales), the drawing by Augustus John, and the bust by Jonah Jones of the 1950s.

Official recognition was slight and late: Powys received the plaque of the Hamburg Free Academy of Arts in 1958 and was made DLitt by the University of Wales in 1962. He received a stream of visitors, eminent writers and ordinary readers, to his houses in Corwen (1935–54), and Blaenau Ffestiniog. He died on 17 June 1963 at the Memorial Hospital, Blaenau Ffestiniog. His ashes were scattered on the sea off Chesil Beach, Abbotsbury, Dorset.

Since Powys's death he has been progressively perceived as ahead of or out of his time: that is, as an interwar novelist with Proust, Woolf, and Joyce; as an antinovelist in a line from Homer, Rabelais, Spenser, and Sterne; as an ultra-Wordsworthian, 'green' novelist who is pervasively aware of the vital interaction of nature and man, inanimate and animate worlds, as a magic realist, and, finally, as a poet-novelist who not only presents individual man's fictive imagination as his liberation but is a teasing creator who gives his reader the novel as a fictive game. He is seen as the 'terrifyingly formidable genius' he claimed to be.

BELINDA HUMFREY

Sources J. C. Powys, *Autobiography* (1968) · B. Humfrey, ed., *Recollections of the Powys brothers* (1980) · R. P. Graves, *The brothers Powys* (1983) · K. Hopkins, *The Powys brothers* (1967) · *Powys Review*, 1–32 (1977–) · L. Marlow, *Welsh ambassadors: Powys lives and letters* (1936) · J. C. Powys, *Letters to Louis Wilkinson, 1935–56* (1958) · J. C. Powys, *Letters to his brother Llewelyn, 1902–39*, 2 vols. (1975) · J. C. Powys, *Letters to Frances Gregg*, 2 vols. (1994–6) · *Powys to Sea-Eagle: the letters ... to his sister Philippa* (1996) · J. C. Powys, *The diary 1930* (1987) · J. C. Powys, *The diary 1931* (1990) · J. C. Powys, *Petrushka and the dancer: the diaries of John Cowper Powys 1929–1939* (1995) · *The Dorset year: the diary of John Cowper Powys, June 1934 – July 1935*, ed. M.. Krissdóttir and R. Peers (1998) · B. Humfrey, ed., *John Cowper Powys's Wolf Solent, critical studies* (1990) · B. Humfrey, ed., *Essays on John Cowper Powys* (1972) ·

S. Rands, *John Cowper Powys, the Lyons and W. E. Lutyens* (2000) • D. Langridge, *John Cowper Powys: a record of achievement* (1966)
Archives CAC Cam., corresp. and papers • Colgate University Library, Hamilton, New York, literary papers • Hunt. L., literary papers • NL Wales, corresp. and papers • NL Wales, diaries • NL Wales, papers • Oxf. UA, lecturer's reports • priv. coll., MSS • Ransom HRC, letters to his mother and his sisters, Gertrude and Philippa, MS essays • Syracuse University, corresp. and literary MSS • U. Leeds, Brotherton L., letters • U. Mich., Harlan Hatcher Graduate Library, letters • University of Calgary Library, Alberta, Canada, family corresp. • University of Connecticut Library, Storrs, Connecticut, family papers | BL, letters to Vera Wainwright, Add. MS 54330 • Bodl. Oxf., letters to G. Wilson Knight • Col. U., Rare Book and Manuscript Library, letters to Cyril Clemens and literary MSS • CUL, letters to Ichiro Hara • NL Wales, letters to Marjorie L. Gay • NL Wales, corresp. with Gwyn Jones • NL Wales, letters to Susanne Lane • NL Wales, letters to I. C. Peate • NL Wales, letters to Phyllis Playter • NL Wales, letters to Laurence Pollinger • NL Wales, letters to Evan Roberts • NL Wales, letters to Lloyd Emerson Siberell • NL Wales, letters to Marjorie Tilden • NL Wales, letters to Margaret Thorpe • U. Leeds, Brotherton L., letters to Jessie Cormack
Likenesses R. Jonson, oils, 1917, repro. in Humfrey, ed., *Essays*, frontispiece • photograph, c.1920, NPG; repro. in Humfrey, ed., *Essays*, p. 2 • G. Powys, oils, 1944, NMG Wales • A. John, drawing, 1955 • J. Jones, bronze bust, 1957, NMG Wales • photographs, priv. coll. [*see illus.*]
Wealth at death £6089 18s.: probate, 18 Nov 1963, CGPLA Eng. & Wales

Powys, Sir Littleton (1647–1732), judge, was the eldest son of Thomas Powys (1618/19–1672) of Henley, Shropshire, serjeant-at-law, and his second wife, Mary (d. in or before 1668), daughter of Sir Adam Littleton, first baronet, of Stoke St Milborough, Shropshire. He matriculated at St Edmund Hall, Oxford, on 25 November 1663, aged fifteen, was admitted to Lincoln's Inn on 12 May 1664, and was called to the bar on 16 May 1671. On 3 December 1674 in the Temple Church he married Agnes Carter (c.1656–1720) of St Dunstan-in-the-West, the sister of John Carter, grocer, of London.

Little is known about Powys before the revolution of 1688, in which he took an active part, reading the prince of Orange's declaration at Shrewsbury. His reward was an appointment on 22 July 1689 as second justice of Chester. He was created a serjeant-at-law in April 1692, and knighted later that year on 4 December. On 28 October 1695 he was appointed a baron of the exchequer and, despite rumours in September 1697 that he would be transferred to common pleas, he remained there until raised to king's bench on 26 January 1701. He was reappointed following Queen Anne's accession, and took part in most of the controversies before king's bench during the reign, most notably the Aylesbury case. He was reappointed on 20 November 1714 following the accession of George I, Lord Cowper advising that he should be kept on and his half-brother Sir Thomas *Powys discarded: 'Sir Littleton, the elder brother, is a man of less abilities and consequence, but blameless' (Holmes and Speck, 64), whereas Thomas was more culpable in the actions of the previous tory ministry. Others were also unimpressed by Littleton's abilities, notably Dudley Ryder, who confided to his diary a distaste for Powys's methods. Powys was elected a fellow of the Royal Society in 1724. He surrendered his office on 26 October 1726, although he continued to draw his salary.

He made his will, in his eighty-fifth year, in April 1731, when in pretty good health, 'gout excepted' (PRO, PROB 11/651/116). He died between 13 and 16 March 1732 at Bitterley and was buried in Bitterley church, near to his country home at Henley Hall, Shropshire. He died childless, having invested most of his personal estate in the Bank of England and South Sea companies, at one point owning £15,000 worth of bank stock.   STUART HANDLEY

Sources Sainty, *Judges*, 36, 127 • Baker, *Serjeants*, 451, 532 • J. L. Chester and J. Foster, eds., *London marriage licences, 1521–1869* (1887), 1086 • Foster, *Alum. Oxon.* • *The register of the Temple Church of London*, Harleian Society, new ser., 1 (1979), 67 • W. P. Baildon, ed., *The records of the Honorable Society of Lincoln's Inn: admissions*, 1 (1896), 292 • W. P. Baildon, ed., *The records of the Honorable Society of Lincoln's Inn: the black books*, 3 (1899), 72 • PRO, PROB 11/651, sig. 116 • W. R. Williams, *The history of the great sessions in Wales, 1542–1830* (privately printed, Brecon, 1899), 62 • D. Lemmings, *Gentlemen and barristers: the inns of court and the English bar, 1680–1730* (1990), 147, 158, 188 • N. Luttrell, *A brief historical relation of state affairs from September 1678 to April 1714*, 4 (1857), 283; 5 (1857), 358, 380, 519 • G. Holmes and W. Speck, eds., *The divided society: parties and politics in England, 1694–1716* (1967), 64 • Foss, *Judges*, 8.52–5
Archives Shrops. RRC, letters to Henry Mitton • Shrops. RRC, bishop of Shipton MSS

Powys, Llewelyn (1884–1939), writer, was born on 13 August 1884 at Rothesay House, South Walks, Dorchester, the fifth son and eighth child among the eleven children of Revd Charles Francis Powys (1843–1923), vicar of Montacute, Somerset, and his wife, Mary Cowper Johnson (1849–1914). His mother was the daughter of the Revd William Cowper Johnson of Yaxham, Norfolk, who was related to the poet William *Cowper (1731–1800). Llewelyn Powys's elder brothers were the novelists John Cowper *Powys (1872–1963), and Theodore Francis *Powys (1875–1953). Llewelyn Powys was educated first at Sherborne preparatory school (1895–9) and then at Sherborne School, Dorset (1899–1903), before he went on to Corpus Christi College, Cambridge (1903–6). At none of these places did he show an aptitude for scholarship. He was a slow starter, and his personality, indulged by his older sisters and brothers, responded mainly to nature, companionship, and passing pleasures. This was shown in the cultivation, at Cambridge, of important early friendships, such as that with Louis Wilkinson, and with his founding of an epicurean society, the Club of the Honest Cods, in 1904. But it also resulted in his 'ploughing' the Cambridge tripos and having to re-sit the finals for a pass BA degree in November 1906.

On leaving Cambridge, Powys drifted rather forlornly into schoolmastering, first at Broadstairs and then at Bromsgrove (1907), before becoming a private tutor to a family at Calne, Wiltshire (1908) (which he described in *Confessions of Two Brothers*). Partly to release him from the drudgery of an uncongenial profession, his brother John arranged for him to visit America on a lecturing programme in December 1908. Here he spoke on the English poets and on some contemporary writers in Philadelphia and in New York state for four months, but was ill-equipped to cope with the task. He returned disheartened to school teaching at Sherborne preparatory school

(1909), where his brother Littleton had become headmaster.

On 3 November 1909 the direction of Llewelyn Powys's life suddenly changed when he suffered a serious haemorrhage due to contracting pulmonary tuberculosis. In December he was sent to Clavadel sanatorium, Davos Platz, Switzerland, where he remained for sixteen months. In addition to combating his illness, he had the leisure to read extensively and to cultivate the writing skills which he needed to fulfil his ambition to be a writer. His admired brother John encouraged him in this pursuit, and Powys began to keep a diary which became a remarkable testament to his life's struggle at this time, and a quarry for some of his later writing.

On returning to England, Llewelyn Powys spent a summer and autumn of recuperation at the family home at Montacute and with his brother Theodore at East Chaldon, Dorset (a period about which he wrote revealingly in *Skin for Skin*). A return to Switzerland in early 1912 brought on a further haemorrhage when Powys unwisely walked over a mountain pass between Arosa and Davos, but he recovered sufficiently to return to England in March. Here, in convalescence in the summer and winter of 1912–13, he began writing in earnest 'for the papers'—mostly stories and vignettes in the style of Guy de Maupassant, the first of which to be published was 'Death' in the *New Age* in April 1913.

In 1914, after his mother's death and to help his recovery from consumption, Powys travelled to join his brother William on his farm in the East Africa Protectorate. However, with the outbreak of the First World War and his brother volunteering to fight, he was left to manage a stock ranch, and so remained in Africa for the duration of the war. In 1916 he published *Confessions of Two Brothers*, which was written with John and in which Llewelyn's section consisted of short autobiographical fragments.

After the war Powys returned to England for a year and then sailed for America, where he spent another five years, mostly in New York but also in California. He gained a considerable reputation between 1921 and 1924 on the east coast, through his journalism and book reviews for periodicals such as *The Dial*, *The Freeman*, and *The Mentor*, as well as for notable New York newspapers such as the *New York Evening Post* where he wrote vividly about his experiences in Africa. *Ebony and Ivory*, his first book, containing some of the early stories of 1912–13, came out in America in 1923, with *Black Laughter*, which made his name there, following in 1924.

On 30 September 1924 Llewelyn Powys married Alyse Gregory (1884–1967), the managing editor of *The Dial*, and returned with her to England and to a coastguard cottage on a Dorset headland called the White Nothe near Weymouth. There were no children. Powys published the autobiographical *Skin for Skin* in 1925 and *The Verdict of Bridlegoose*, about his experiences in America, in 1926. In 1927 Powys and Gregory briefly returned to New York, where Powys was appointed visiting critic of the *New York Herald Tribune* (books section) for a four-month period, at a time when his reputation in America was at its height. He

also began an affair with the poet Gamel Woolsey, which resulted in a miscarried pregnancy. Powys's letters to Woolsey were published as *So Wild a Thing* in 1973; her letters to him were published in 1983.

After returning briefly to England, Powys and Gregory travelled through Europe to Palestine. In consequence of this visit Powys, who for most of his life was an anti-Christian rationalist, wrote three books of religious observation, including *The Cradle of God* (1929), a survey of the Old Testament, and *The Pathetic Fallacy* (1930), a 'study of Christianity'. The culmination of this period was *Impassioned Clay* (1931), a philosophical meditation on the origin and purpose of the human condition, which Powys always regarded as one of his most important works. While Powys was brought up in the Christian faith he spent much of his life rejecting its tenets. He was a convinced agnostic and humanist who nevertheless believed in a cosmic 'mystery'.

In 1931 Powys and Gregory travelled in the West Indies, but for much of the 1930s Powys was ill with recurring bouts of blood-spitting and digestive disorders. In 1931 he and his wife moved to Chydyok, a cottage on the Lulworth estate between East Chaldon and the sea, next door to Powys's sisters, Gertrude, a painter, and Philippa, a poet. In December 1936 they travelled to Clavadel, Switzerland, for a last bid to save his health. In these years Powys was a prolific writer of essays and articles for local and national papers, on country themes, literary by-ways, and rationalist thought. Some of these were collected in books such as *Dorset Essays* (1935), *Somerset Essays* (1937), and *Rats in the Sacristy* (1937). In Switzerland he continued with this intensive output of work, composing lovingly recalled reminiscences of his Somerset childhood, in the collection *A Baker's Dozen* (1939), and re-imagining his early life in a quasi-autobiographical novel, *Love and Death* (1939), which drew on his affair with Woolsey.

On 2 December 1939 Llewelyn Powys died in Clavadel of a burst duodenal ulcer, and was cremated in Davos. After the Second World War his ashes were brought back to Dorset and buried on the cliffs above the sea near Chydyok. In 1949 a stone was erected over the ashes, carved by the sculptor Elizabeth Muntz, with wording from Isaiah, 'The Living. The Living. He Shall Praise Thee'. 　　P. J. Foss

Sources M. Elwin, *The life of Llewelyn Powys* (1946) · R. P. Graves, *The brothers Powys* (1982) · *The letters of Llewelyn Powys*, ed. L. Wilkinson (1943) · L. Marlow, *Welsh ambassadors: Powys lives and letters* (1936) · *The letters of John Cowper Powys to his brother Llewelyn*, ed. M. Elwin, 2 vols. (1975–82) · P. J. Foss, *A study of Llewelyn Powys, his literary achievement and personal philosophy* (1991) · K. Hopkins, *The Powys brothers* (1967) · B. Humfrey, *Recollections of the Powys brothers* (1980) · A. Gregory, *The cry of a gull* (1973) · J. C. Powys, *Autobiography* (1934) · J. C. Powys and L. Powys, *Confessions of two brothers* (1916) · L. Powys, *Skin for skin* (1925) · L. Powys, *The verdict of Bridlegoose* (1926)

Archives Colgate University, Hamilton, New York · Dorset County Museum, Dorchester, Powys Society archive, Bissell collection · Ransom HRC | CUL, MSS · priv. coll., magazine publications · Yale U., Alyse Gregory papers

Likenesses J. J. Hunt, photograph, 1908, priv. coll. · G. M. Powys, pencil drawing, 1911, priv. coll. · T. B. Zadig, wood-engraving, 1924, repro. in S. Sherman, *Critical woodcuts* (1926); priv. coll. · G. M. Powys, oils, *c*.1926, priv. coll. · D. Ulmann, photograph, 1928,

repro. in Elwin, *Life of Llewelyn Powys* • photograph, 1934, repro. in Elwin, *Life of Llewelyn Powys*; priv. coll. • E. L. Kirchner, oils, 1938, repro. in Foss, *Study of Llewelyn Powys*; priv. coll.
Wealth at death £3623 1s. 6d.: probate, 27 March 1940, *CGPLA Eng. & Wales*

Powys, Theodore Francis (1875–1953), novelist and short-story writer, was born on 20 December 1875 at the vicarage, Shirley, Derbyshire, the third child and third son of the eleven children—who included John Cowper *Powys (1872–1963) and Llewelyn *Powys (1884–1939)—of the Revd Charles Francis Powys (1843–1923), son of the Revd Littleton Charles Powys, rector of Stalbridge, Dorset. Theodore Powys's mother was Mary Cowper Johnson (1849–1914), daughter of the Revd William Cowper Johnson, rector of Yaxham, Norfolk. The 'Cowper' derives from the family of poet William Cowper; there was a distant Welsh strain in both sides of the marriage.

Charles Francis Powys became curate of St Peter's Church, Dorchester, Dorset, in 1879, and vicar of Montacute, Somerset, in 1885. Theodore Powys was educated at Hardye's School, Dorchester, and at Sherborne preparatory school, in Dorset, and then at Eaton House School, Aldeburgh, Suffolk, where he met Louis Wilkinson, a son of the master, who became a lifelong friend of the Powyses. After training Powys farmed near Sweffling, Suffolk, from 1895. In 1901 he retired to Studland on the Dorset coast to read and write, and moved inland to Chaldon Herring on the Dorset downs in 1904. On 19 April 1905 he married Violet Rosalie Dodds (b. 1886/7), the eighteen-year-old daughter of a local solicitor. They had two sons and later adopted a daughter.

There are Nietzschean undertones in Powys's early biblical commentaries, of which only *An Interpretation of Genesis* (1907) reached publication. Early in the century he turned to fiction, but none of it was published before 1923, although *The Soliloquy of a Hermit* (1918) carried an advertisement that a novel, *Mr Tasker's Gods* (1925), was forthcoming. Between 1923 and 1932 only one year did not see the issue of at least one title. Many of Powys's stories have never been published.

Powys is best known for the novel *Mr Weston's Good Wine* (1927), but *Mark Only* (1924) and *Unclay* (1931) are also outstanding among his longer fictions. The most praised collection of his countless short stories is *Fables* (1929). The setting of most of the tales is an elemental Dorset, and the characters are elemental cartoons that interact against that background to convey allegories of the search for everlasting truths. Elaborate allusions drawn from Powys's wide reading play on deliberately down-to-earth village commonplaces in seemingly artless and often cryptic sentences. Much of the dialogue is in dialect. Powys had an eye for the bizarre and was a sardonic humorist. Although he read the freethinking literature of his time, he was never a rationalist and questioned all newfangledness. His personal values never strayed far from the evangelicalism of the rectory, and he was a persistent churchgoer.

Powys was of medium height, and darkish in his farming years, when he had a moustache. Later he was stocky, clean-shaven, and white-haired, his characteristic expression being that of one always ready to be amused. His talk, like his prose, was pithy and quirky. Powys had a stroke in 1937 and in 1940 moved to Mappowder, north Dorset. In 1953 his health worsened, and he died at his home, The Lodge, Mappowder, on 27 November of that year. He was buried in Mappowder churchyard, and was survived by his wife.   BERNARD JONES

Sources R. P. Graves, *The brothers Powys* (1983) • K. Hopkins, *The Powys brothers* (1967) • J. C. Powys, *Autobiography* (1934) • L. Marlow, *Welsh ambassadors: Powys lives and letters* (1936) • L. Marlow, *Seven friends* (1953) • P. Riley, *A bibliography of T. F. Powys* (1967) • M. Elwin, *The life of Llewelyn Powys* (1946) • J. Stinton, *Chaldon Herring* (1988) • *CGPLA Eng. & Wales* (1954)
Archives Dorset County Museum, Dorchester, corresp. and literary papers | BL, letters to Vera Wainwright, Add. MS 54330 • LUL, letters to Charles Lahr and literary MSS • NL Wales, letters to John Cowper Powys • U. Aberdeen L., letters to J. B. Chapman
Likenesses P. Evans, pen-and-ink drawing, c.1929, NPG • G. M. Powys, oils and pen-and-ink portrait, c.1929, NPG? • A. John, oils, c.1932, Tate Collection • H. Coster, photographs, 1934, NPG • E. Muntz, stone bust, 1934, Bristol City Museum and Art Gallery • E. Muntz, marble bust, 1949, Bristol City Museum and Art Gallery
Wealth at death £6294 12s. 5d.: probate, 29 Jan 1954, *CGPLA Eng. & Wales*

Powys, Sir Thomas (1649–1719), judge and politician, was born at Lilford, Northamptonshire, the second son of Thomas Powys, serjeant-at-law, of Henley, Shropshire, and Anne, daughter of Sir Adam Littleton, chief justice of north Wales, and younger half-brother of Sir Littleton *Powys. He was educated at Shrewsbury School, matriculated at Queen's College, Oxford, on 20 May 1664, and was admitted to Lincoln's Inn on 19 February 1666. He was called to the bar on 24 April 1673, elected a bencher of his inn on 27 April 1686, and served as treasurer during 1687, the year in which he was appointed attorney-general to James II. He had been appointed solicitor-general and knighted on 23 April 1686. He was created serjeant-at-law in 1702 and held the office of queen's serjeant from 1702 to 1713. In 1710 he wrote to Robert Harley expressing his desire to be appointed attorney-general if Sir Simon Harcourt should be appointed lord chancellor. In recommending himself to his patron, Powys told Harley that the office was a 'place [he] could make easy, by wholly applying [himself] to the execution of [the] office' (Powys to Harley, 16 Oct 1710, *Portland MSS*, 4.614–15). Powys never became a law officer under Queen Anne but on 8 June 1713 he was appointed a judge of the queen's bench, an office he held only until George I's accession, being removed on 14 October 1714 on Lord Chancellor Cowper's advice. However, a series of letters of appeal to the lord chancellor led to his appointment as king's serjeant on 28 October 1714 (Powys to Cowper, 21, 23, and 25 Oct 1714, Panshanger MSS, D/EP F149/12–16). The reason for his removal from the bench seems to have been that he had held the office of attorney-general to James II until the abdication and during that period had been 'zealously instrumental in most of the steps which ruined that prince and brought … great dangers on the kingdom'. From 1717 he held the office of prime serjeant. He became a freeman of Ludlow in 1677 and of Portsmouth in 1700. He was appointed recorder of Ludlow in 1707.

During the reign of James II Powys was active in promoting the king's policies, a role which may justify Burnet's writing of him as 'a compliant young aspiring lawyer' (*Bishop Burnet's History*, 3.97). He appeared for the crown in *Godden* v. *Hales*, a test case in which the king sought to establish the legality of the dispensing power. In this instance Sir Edward Hales, a Roman Catholic officer, was prosecuted for holding office contrary to law but invoked in his defence the king's dispensing power. As an officer of his inn, Powys encouraged his fellow benchers in sponsoring the call of Roman Catholics to the bar. As attorney-general he prosecuted in June 1688 for seditious libel the seven bishops who, on the ground that it was an exercise of the disputed dispensing power, had opposed the reading in churches of the declaration of indulgence extending religious toleration to dissenters. The unpopularity of the proceedings and the acquittal of the defendants were no reflection upon Powys, for he was said to have 'acted his part in this trial as fairly as his post could admit of' (ibid., 3.234). Powys's practice at the bar mirrored the loyalty he had displayed towards James II. During the reign of William III he built up his practice by defending state prisoners, among them Sir John Fenwick, the author of the Jacobite plot of 1696, and his practice developed such that in the last years of Queen Anne's reign Powys's fees were said to amount to nearly £4000 a year. That sum was augmented by investment in the financial markets when he held no legal office.

Powys stood for parliament for the first time in January 1701 and was returned at the top of the poll as member for Ludlow after a three-cornered contest with two tories, one of whom had questioned his loyalty to the government. He was nominated for Truro at the general election of 1702 as his fate in his native Shropshire seemed uncertain (BL, Add. MS 28055, fols. 3–4). He was, however, returned at both Truro and Ludlow but chose to serve for the latter. Powys's prominence and his legal ability were reflected in his activities in parliament so that many of his numerous committee appointments were to committees of address and to drafting committees. Powys supported the ministry after its reorganization in 1704, was listed as a placeman in 1705, and was re-elected in that year for Ludlow. His attitude to the speakership vote on 25 October 1705 was neutral such that he would vote neither for the court candidate nor for the tory, withdrawing from the house before the question was put. On the resignation of Harley and his supporters in February 1708, Powys reverted to opposition and spoke on 9 March against the bishop of Carlisle's Cathedrals Bill, which was widely regarded as a party cause. Powys's restoration to the rank of king's serjeant in 1714 marked the end of his parliamentary career as he returned to his practice at the bar and did not stand again.

Historians have disagreed sharply about Powys. Macaulay, in a passage in which his whig sympathies are all too apparent, describes him as 'an obscure barrister, who had no qualification for high employment except servility' (Macaulay, 2.736), a judgement not qualified by Burnet's comment on his lack of ill nature (*Bishop Burnet's History*, 3.97). A modern historian on the other hand speaks of him as '[a barrister] in the very highest flight' (Holmes, *Augustan England*, 125). Less contrasting are the estimates of Powys's abilities supplied by two of his near-contemporaries. Arthur Onslow as a young man heard Powys when in December 1711 he appeared as counsel with Serjeant Pratt for the duke of Hamilton in the House of Lords. Powys and Pratt were instructed by Hamilton to advance the legal argument which preceded the debate on whether the English title of duke of Brandon conferred on him by the queen in September 1711 entitled him to sit in the House of Lords: the vote went against the duke but Onslow recorded that Powys's speech 'was deemed a great performance. He exerted all his strength and left very little for Pratt to say although one of the most able advocates of that time' (*Bishop Burnet's History*, 6.86n.). Peter Wentworth was less impressed, saying that 'they both [Powys and Pratt] seem'd as if they lay under difficulty, that they had no lawyers to answer, but was to suppose what objections were to be made' (Cartwright, 226–7). That observation may perhaps have been more a comment upon the constraints under which counsel were labouring than an estimate of their oratorical powers.

Powys married twice: on 4 June 1685 he married Sarah, daughter of Ambrose Holbech of Mollington, Warwickshire, who died in March 1694; on 2 October 1698 he married Elizabeth, daughter of Sir Philip *Meadows, of Chattisham, Suffolk. He had three sons and three daughters with his first wife and two sons with his second. He died on 3 or 4 April 1719 and was buried at Lilford. His tomb, which bears an effigy in robes and an inscription by Matthew Prior, was moved to St John Baptist Church, Thorpe Achurch, also in Northamptonshire, in 1778.

ROGER TURNER

Sources W. P. Baildon, ed., *The records of the Honorable Society of Lincoln's Inn: the black books*, 3 (1899), 88, 156, 158 · W. P. Baildon, ed., *The records of the Honorable Society of Lincoln's Inn: admissions*, 1 (1896), 297 · Baker, *Serjeants*, 532 · D. Lemmings, *Gentlemen and barristers: the inns of court and the English bar, 1680–1730* (1990) · *The manuscripts of his grace the duke of Portland*, 10 vols., HMC, 29 (1891–1931), vol. 4, pp. 614–15 · *Bishop Burnet's History*, 3.97, 234; 6.86n. · E. Foss, *Biographia juridica: a biographical dictionary of the judges of England … 1066–1870* (1870), 533–4 · Burke, *Peerage* (1916) · Herts. ALS, Panshanger MSS, D/EP F149/12–16 · BL, Add. MS 28055, fols. 3–4 · T. B. Macaulay, *The history of England from the accession of James II*, new edn, ed. C. H. Firth, 6 vols. (1913–15), vol. 2, p. 736 · Sir Thomas Powys, HoP, *Commons* [draft] · G. Holmes, *Politics, religion and society in England, 1679–1742* (1986), 89–92 · G. Holmes, *Augustan England* (1982), 125, 127, 129, 187 · *The Wentworth papers, 1705–1739*, ed. J. J. Cartwright (1883), 226–7 · IGI
Archives Herts. ALS, Panshanger MSS · Shrops. RRC, letters to Henry Mitton · Shrops. RRC, bishop of Shipton MSS
Likenesses R. Hartshorne, statue, 1720, St John Baptist Church, Thorpe Achurch, Northamptonshire

Powys, Thomas Littleton, fourth Baron Lilford (1833–1896), ornithologist, was born on 18 March 1833 at 14 Great Stanhope Street, Mayfair, Westminster, the eldest son of Thomas Atherton Powys, third Baron Lilford (1801–

1861), and his wife, Mary Elizabeth (1806–1891), daughter of Henry Richard Fox, third Baron Holland, and Elizabeth Vassall, his wife. He was educated at Dr Bickmore's school, Berkswell, Warwickshire, from 1843 to 1848, and at Harrow School until midsummer 1850, when he went to reside with a tutor at Lausanne, Switzerland. He then matriculated at Christ Church, Oxford, on 12 June 1851, but left the university without taking a degree.

At an early age Powys manifested a love for animals; at Harrow he kept a small menagerie, and also began contributing to *The Zoologist*. He kept a larger menagerie at Oxford, and all his spare time, during vacations and subsequently through life, as far as his health would permit, was devoted to travel for the purpose of studying animals, especially birds. In 1853 he visited the Isles of Scilly, Wales, and Ireland, and becoming acquainted with Edward Clough Newcome, the best falconer of his day, shortly afterwards took up falconry himself. His aviaries at Lilford Park in Northamptonshire were the envy of field ornithologists, and especially noted for the collection of birds of prey.

In 1854, on the embodiment of the militia, Powys joined that of his county and served at Dublin and Devonport, giving up his commission at the end of 1855. From 1856 to 1858, accompanied by the Hon. Hercules Rowley, he made an extended yachting cruise in the Mediterranean. He returned to England in the following year, and married, on 14 June 1859, Emma Elizabeth (d. 1884), youngest daughter of Robert William Brandling, of Low Gosforth, Northumberland. He succeeded his father as fourth Baron Lilford on 15 March 1861.

Between 1864 and 1882 Lilford paid frequent visits to Spain and the Mediterranean, rediscovering the rare gull *Larus audouini*. Together with his friend Leonard Howard Loyd *Irby, he was a pioneer in Spanish ornithology. The death in 1882 of his eldest son, Thomas Atherton, and in 1884 of his wife, greatly distressed him, and his lifelong malady, gout, subsequently rendered him a permanent invalid. His affliction was somewhat relieved by the devoted attention of his second wife, Clementina Georgiana (1839–1929), daughter of Ker Baillie Hamilton CB, whom Lilford married on 21 July 1885.

Lilford had been elected a fellow of the Zoological Society in 1852, and of the Linnean Society in March 1862. He was one of the founders of the British Ornithologists' Union in 1858, and its president from March 1867. He was also a liberal supporter and first president of the Northamptonshire Natural History Society, founded in 1876, and a prominent member of the 'Old Hawking Club'.

Lilford's zeal for his favourite science never flagged. In addition to some two dozen papers on ornithological subjects, contributed to the *Ibis* (of which he was a generous supporter), the *Proceedings of the Zoological Society*, and other scientific journals, he was author of: *Coloured Figures of the Birds of the British Islands*, in seven volumes (1885–97)—which was completed by Osbert Salvin and included a biography by the zoologist Alfred Newton— and *Notes on the Birds of Northamptonshire and Neighbourhood* (1895). He

died at Lilford Hall on 17 June 1896, and was buried three days later at Achurch, near Lilford. He was succeeded by his son, the Hon. John Powys.

B. B. WOODWARD, rev. YOLANDA FOOTE

Sources C. M. P. Drewitt, *Lord Lilford Thomas Littleton, (fourth Baron FZS, president of the British Ornithologists' Union)* (1900) • Lord Lilford [T. Powys], 'Coloured figures of the birds of the British Isles (1885–97)', *The Ibis*, 7th ser., 2 (1896), 593 • *Proceedings of the Linnean Society of London* (1896–7), 59 • Burke, *Peerage* (1931) • Boase, *Mod. Eng. biog.* • W. H. Mullens and H. K. Swann, *A bibliography of British ornithology from the earliest times to the end of 1912* (1917)
Archives McGill University, Montreal, papers on birds of Spain • NHM, diaries, notebooks, and papers | Hunt. L., letters to Grenville family • NHM, letters to Albert Gunther and R. W. T. Gunther • NHM, letters to Osbert Salvin [copies] • Northants. RO, letters to G. V. Charlton
Likenesses portrait, repro. in Drewitt, *Lord Lilford Thomas Littleton* • portrait, repro. in Lord Lilford, 'Coloured figures of the birds of the British Isles'
Wealth at death £53,278 6s. 10d.: probate, 7 Nov 1896, CGPLA Eng. & Wales

Poy. *See* Fearon, Percy Hutton (1874–1948).

Poyer, John (d. 1649), merchant and army officer, was a Welshman from near Narberth in Pembrokeshire. About 1640 he was both a wealthy merchant regularly trading with Bristol and an industrial entrepreneur who claimed to employ 'more poor … in making cloth than any other man in those parts' (Leach, 44). Having become mayor of Pembroke in 1641–2, he effectively continued in office for another six years, usurping the position of his successor. Aided by what some of his local enemies described as 'a loose rabble of the meaner sort', he also took possession of Pembroke Castle (*A Declaration of Divers Gentlemen …*, April 1648, BL, E436/7, 2).

In 1642 Poyer was prominent in staying ships and arresting Catholics bound to and from Ireland. He was once detained for staying two ships bound for Galway, but was quickly released on 27 June by order of the House of Commons. Under Poyer's rule Pembroke survived several royalist sieges and blockades during the first civil war. In 1643 he lost one of his own ships in a vain attempt to acquaint the lord admiral the earl of Warwick with Pembroke's plight. However, he did at least frustrate the threat of the earl of Carbery's soldiers to roll him into Milford Haven in a barrel of nails, and in March 1644 he succeeded in capturing Carew Castle. This apparent triumph was later to occasion charges from his local enemies that he had illegally appropriated to himself some revenues of its demesne. Carew Castle was to be retaken by the royalists in May 1645 as part of a spectacular campaign by Sir Charles Gerrard which was again to put Pembroke at risk. Poyer was later to maintain that he had impoverished himself by personally financing the defence of Pembroke Castle though his critics averred that this had been done out of the sale of confiscated ships and goods and other exactions. Be this as it may, Poyer's petition for reimbursement was sympathetically received in February 1647 by the House of Lords and recommended—apparently unavailingly—to the attentions of the lower house. For all his grievances, Poyer played no part in the insurgency in south Wales in the summer of 1647 and it was not until the following year that the resentment which he shared with Major-General Rowland Laugharne, exacerbated by the projected disbandment of the parliamentary forces in south Wales, boiled over into active revolt.

In February 1648 Sir Thomas Fairfax's suspicions about Poyer's intentions impelled him to send down Colonel Fleming to replace him as governor of Pembroke Castle. Poyer's refusal to co-operate unless paid what he claimed to be due to him and his soldiers produced an ultimatum at the beginning of March that he hand over the castle within twelve hours on pain of being declared a traitor. Poyer's response was decisive; sallying forth from the castle he routed Fleming's force, some of whom he captured along with artillery pieces brought to subdue the castle. Having raised more men at a muster on 9 April, Poyer now moved to Carmarthen to join forces temporarily with Colonel Rice Powell. Their combined force was estimated at between 3000 and 4000 men, many of them, if Poyer's opponents are to be believed, reluctant and ill-armed conscripts. Poyer's and Powell's increasingly pro-royalist stance is evidenced by their appeal to the prince of Wales (*Powells and Poyers Letter to the Prince of Wales*, April 1648, BL, E436/14). But while this produced a favourable response from the prince, it seems to have cut little ice with the Welsh royalist élite who despised Poyer in particular as a plundering social upstart. As a letter of early April puts it, 'not many Gentlemen of note or Men of Estates … come in to Poyer or … give him any visible Countenance' (Rushworth, 7.1051). To such gentlemen the aims of these roundhead renegades amounted to no more than 'the advancement of their owne wretched & mechanick ambitions' (*The Declaration … of Col. John Poyer*, May 1648, BL, E441/6, 3), a view not notably different from that of a parliamentary news sheet of mid-January which describes Poyer as standing 'neither for the king, parliament or army, but his own interest and free booting' (*Heads of Chiefe Passages in Parliament*, no. 2, 12–19 Jan 1648, BL, E423/11, 12). In pursuit of these ends he regularly dispatched his so-called 'bullies' to plunder the cattle and property 'of any Gentlemen he bore a spleen to' (*A Declaration of Divers Gentlemen …*, BL, E436/7, 3).

As for his religion, Poyer was described as 'a stiffe maintainer of the Booke of Common Prayer', which he and Powell declared to be 'the sole comfort of the People here' in south Wales (*Heads of Chiefe Passages in Parliament*, no. 2, 12–19 Jan 1648, BL, E423/11, 11; *The Declaration of Col. Poyer and Col. Powel*, April 1648, BL, E435/9, 4–5, 6). A hostile account tells a more cynical story, albeit one which confirms Poyer's anti-puritan credentials. After challenging a gentleman as to whether he was an Independent or a Presbyterian, he heard the latter reply, 'Neither, for he was a Protestant'. 'Why, so am I, quoth Poyer, therefore let us be Merry. So in they went, and drunk so hard that neither was able to stir in Four and twenty Hours after' (Rushworth, 7.1033).

At the beginning of May, with Cromwell already *en route* to quell the various insurgents in south Wales, Poyer reportedly boasted that he would be 'the first that shall

charge against Ironsides (viz. Cromwell), saying that if he had a back of steel and a breast of iron, he durst and will encounter with him' (*The Declaration … of Col. John Poyer*, May 1648, BL, E441/6, 6). He was soon to be joined in Pembroke Castle by Laugharne, whose force had been smashed at St Fagans by Colonel Horton on 8 May. They were an ill-assorted couple. Poyer was described by his critics as at best a protean character: 'a man of two Dispositions every Day … in the Morning Sober and Penitent, but in the Afternoon, Drunk and full of Plots' (Rushworth, 7.1033). Laugharne, on the other hand, had a distinguished record as a parliamentary major-general, even if he was also subject to fits of something approaching paranoia in face of real or imagined slights. Rumour soon had it that, in the course of one dispute, he had run Poyer through with his sword. Nevertheless, while Powell capitulated at Tenby on 7 June, Pembroke held out for more than a month longer, Poyer striving to encourage the garrison through the vain hope of relief from Sir Marmaduke Langdale's northern royalists. On 14 June Cromwell assured Speaker Lenthall that the garrison would be starved out within a fortnight. Deserters predicted that Poyer's throat would soon be cut and the danger of mutiny appeared to be confirmed by the cry heard from within the walls: 'Shall we be ruined for two or three men's pleasure? Better it were we should throw them over the walls' (Carlyle, 1.269–70). On 10 July Cromwell sent his final summons to surrender and Poyer yielded on the following day.

Poyer, Laugharne, and Powell were placed at parliament's mercy and on 13 August the prince of Wales requested Fairfax to intervene to the end that 'such moderation may be used towards them as becomes souldgers to one another'. But the lord general replied that he was powerless to act since they had 'betrayed the trust … reposed in them to the ingaging the Kingdom againe in War & Blood' (BL, Add. MS 19399, fols. 58, 60; Rushworth, 7.1233). After many delays a court martial condemned them to death on 10 April 1649, but it was ruled that only one should die, and that lots should be drawn to decide who this should be. This was done on 21 April when the fatal lot fell to Poyer who, following the rejection of his wife Elizabeth's appeal for his life, 'was shot to death in *Covent-Garden* and died very penitently' on 25 April (Whitelock, 384*b*). In June 1661 his impoverished widow petitioned Charles II, claiming that her late husband had lost £8000 in the royal service. On 25 August 1663 she was granted £100 and soon after a further £3000 to be paid in ten annual instalments.

ROBERT ASHTON

Sources A. L. Leach, *The history of the civil war (1642–1649) in Pembrokeshire and on its borders* (1937) • *A declaration of divers gentlemen of Wales concerning Collonell [sic] Poyer*, April 1648, BL, E 436/7 • *The declaration of Col. Poyer and Col. Powel [sic]*, April 1648, BL, E 435/9 • *The declaration and resolution of Col. John Poyer*, May 1648, BL, E 441/6 • J. Rushworth, *Historical collections*, new edn, 7 (1721), 7 • *JHC*, 5 (1646–8) • *JHL*, 10 (1647–8) • *Heads of chiefe passages in parliament*, no. 2, 12–19 Jan 1648, BL, E423/11 • *Heads of chiefe passages in parliament*, no. 7, 16–23 Feb 1648, BL, E428/16 • BL, Add. MS 19399, fols. 58, 60 • Bodl. Oxf., MSS Tanner 57–58 • *A declaration from the Isle of Wight concerning the kings majesty and the proceedings of Col. Poyer*, April 1648, BL,

E435/26 • J. R. Phillips, *Memoirs of the civil war in Wales and the marches, 1642–1649*, 2 vols. (1874) • [B. Whitelocke], *Memorials of the English affairs* (1682) • *Oliver Cromwell's letters and speeches*, ed. T. Carlyle, 1 (1857), 269–70 • *Colonell Powells and Col. Poyers letter to the prince of Wales*, April 1648, BL, E436/14 • *A bloody slaughter at Pembrooke [sic] Castle in Wales*, March 1648, BL, E433/5 • CSP dom., 1660–65
Archives Bodl. Oxf., MSS Tanner 57–58
Wealth at death left widow impoverished

Poynder, John (1779/80–1849), lawyer and evangelical activist, was the eldest son of a City of London tradesman and his evangelical wife. He was educated briefly at the Newington Butts school of Joseph Forsyth, where he imbibed a lasting love of literature. As a young man he hoped to become an Anglican clergyman but he was persuaded by family pressures to become a solicitor instead, and for nearly forty years he served as clerk and solicitor to the royal hospitals of Bridewell and Bethlem. On 15 September 1807 he married Elizabeth Brown of Clapham, Surrey, the daughter of low-church parents.

Poynder was one of the earliest members of the Church Missionary Society in the days when it met in London in the Revd William Goode's rectory at St Ann Blackfriars. Poynder first came to public attention in 1803 with the publication of *A Serious Address to the Public on the Present Times*, an attack on the proposed admission of Roman Catholics to political office and on the East India Company's toleration of idolatry in India. These remained abiding concerns throughout his life, so much so that on his death the Revd William Jay of Bath, a friend for over fifty years, observed fondly that 'Never was there a more determined enemy to Popery, and its half-sister, Puseyism' (*Autobiography of … William Jay*, 447). Jay was a whig and a dissenter whereas Poynder was a tory and a devout churchman, but nevertheless it was one of Jay's sermons which prompted Poynder to take up the cudgels against the East India Company's policy of religious toleration in India. A sermon by Claudius Buchanan, the most fiery of the company's 'pious chaplains', also spurred him on. Poynder wrote numerous articles attacking the company's refusal to prohibit the rite of suttee (widow immolation), its collection of pilgrim taxes from Hindu shrines, and its requirement that civilian and military employees occasionally put on a show of respect at certain Hindu temples. In 1813, when the company's charter was due for renewal, Poynder set out his arguments in a series of letters to *The Times* under the name Laicus (published separately as *Christianity in India* in 1813). Over the next thirty-five years he pressed the court of directors with petitions and appeals on the subject of idolatry, and he was highly influential in the court's decision of 1827 to outlaw suttee and its dispatch of 1833 ordering the abandonment of pilgrim taxes. After these victories Poynder continued to agitate against the company's lingering connections with the Jagannath temple at Puri in Orissa. He also served on the committees of the Lord's Day Observance Society, the Reformation Society, and the Protestant Association.

Poynder was for three years under-sheriff of London and Middlesex, a post which often took him to Newgate prison and provided him with a vast store of anecdotes on London's social and moral climate. These interests were reflected in his three-volume *Literary Extracts from English and other Works* (1844, 1847), a miscellany of quotations, sermons, and aphorisms which had appealed to him in the course of his life. His other publications included works of religious controversy. His wife, Elizabeth, died, aged sixty, on 22 September 1845, after which Poynder rarely left his house. He loved her dearly and in an autobiographical fragment written after her death paid moving tribute to her companionship and affection during their thirty-eight years of marriage. After many years of suffering from bronchitis and other ailments, Poynder died at his home, Montpelier House, South Lambeth, Surrey, on 10 March 1849. He was survived by several children, including two sons who became clerics: Frederick, chaplain of Bridewell Hospital from 1849 to 1858 and second master of Charterhouse School from 1858 to 1872; and Leopold (1818–1896), chaplain in India from 1847 to 1866.

The extent of Poynder's eclectic literary tastes was revealed in January 1850 when Sothebys took three days to sell his remarkable library. The collection included first editions of Shakespeare and many volumes with autograph letters and memoranda, including an edition of the *Phaenomena et diosemeia* of Aratus Solensis, autographed and annotated by Milton.

W. P. COURTNEY, rev. KATHERINE PRIOR

Sources J. Poynder, 'A fragment of autobiography', *Christian Observer* (1847), 400–10 • *Christian Observer* (1849), 354–6 • *The autobiography of the Rev. William Jay*, ed. G. Redford and J. A. James, 2nd edn (1855) • GM, 1st ser., 77 (1807), 887 • GM, 2nd ser., 24 (1845), 544 • GM, 2nd ser., 31 (1849), 547 • Foster, *Alum. Oxon., 1715–1886* [Frederick Poynder] • Venn, *Alum. Cant.* [Leopold Poynder] • D. M. Lewis, ed., *The Blackwell dictionary of evangelical biography, 1730–1860*, 2 vols. (1995)
Archives BL OIOC, 'Parliamentary papers on heathen sacrifices in India', owned and heavily annotated by Poynder, MSS Eur. E. 150 • GL, office day-books as clerk and solicitor to Bridewell and Bethlem Royal hospitals, and personal papers mostly relating to his private law practice
Wealth at death library sold after death: DNB

Poynder, John Poynder Dickson-, Baron Islington (1866–1936), politician and colonial administrator, was born at Ryde, Isle of Wight, on 31 October 1866, the only son of the four children of Rear-Admiral John Bourmaster Dickson (1815–1876), and his first wife, Sarah Matilda (who died in childbirth with John), third daughter of Thomas Poynder of Hilmarton Manor, Calne, Wiltshire. On his father's side John Dickson came of a family which had distinguished itself in the fighting services, the most notable member being his great-uncle Major-General Sir Alexander Dickson. He succeeded to his uncle's baronetcy in 1884. His mother's family had made its mark in commerce and had attained considerable wealth in the East India trade. From his uncle, Thomas Poynder, of Hilmarton, Wiltshire, whom he succeeded in 1887, he inherited a large fortune, and in 1888 he assumed by royal licence the additional surname Poynder. He was educated at Harrow School and then entered Christ Church, Oxford, in 1885, but did not take a degree. He settled down at Hartham Park, near Chippenham, Wiltshire, where the Poynder lands were extensive. It was said to be characteristic of

John Poynder Dickson-Poynder, Baron Islington (1866–1936), by unknown photographer

him that when he came of age he remitted a year's rent to all his tenant farmers. On 30 September 1892 he was elected as the Conservative member for the Chippenham division. He retained this seat until his resignation in 1910. On 30 September 1896 he married Ann Beauclerk (d. 1958), third daughter of Robert Henry Duncan Dundas, of Glenesk, Midlothian, and granddaughter of Robert Cornelis Napier, first Baron Napier of Magdala. They had one daughter.

After leaving Oxford, Dickson-Poynder had been commissioned in the 3rd Royal Scots regiment and afterwards joined the Wiltshire yeomanry, serving from 1900 to 1901 as aide-de-camp to P. S. Methuen, third Lord Methuen, in the Second South African War. For his services during the campaign, which involved a good deal of dispatch riding in enemy country, he was appointed DSO. He was elected for the third time at Chippenham while at the front in 1900.

Having chosen politics, rather than the military or business, as a career, Dickson-Poynder had selected to enter parliament as a Conservative in an area where his family influence was strong. But he 'had rather a cross-bench mind which prevented him from fitting comfortably into either the Conservative or the Liberal Party' (The Times, 8 Dec 1936, 11). In 1905 he crossed the floor of the house on the tariff reform issue and joined the Liberal Party. But he

showed his independence again by opposing the land taxation clauses of the Liberal 1907 budget. He was a moderate (Conservative) member of the London county council from 1898 to 1904, representing St George's, Hanover Square. There he showed a deep concern for social issues. He was chairman of the housing committee and was also a member of the committee on the feeding of schoolchildren. The report of that committee formed the basis for parliamentary legislation in 1906. He was also a member in 1903–4 of the royal commission on London traffic.

Having not achieved government office in the House of Commons, Dickson-Poynder in 1910 accepted the offer of appointment as governor-general of New Zealand, and, on 27 April 1910, was created Baron Islington of Islington. In 1911 he was sworn of the privy council and appointed KCMG. But in 1912 he resigned his governorship in order to become chairman of the royal commission on the public services in India. He was appointed GCMG in 1913 and in 1914–15 was under-secretary of state for the colonies. From 1915 to 1918 he was under-secretary of state for India.

In 1915 Islington was promoting himself as a possible new viceroy for India, with the support of the secretary of state, Austen Chamberlain. But the prime minister, Asquith, wrote to Venetia Stanley: 'What folly! They wd never do' (Letters to Venetia Stanley, 406). This perhaps reflected agitation over what was described as Islington's tendency to be 'changeable in some things—he could be a vigorous champion to-day and a vehement opponent tomorrow' (The Times, 12 Dec 1936, 19) as well as concerns about his wife. Asquith was not the only one to have this opinion. Hearing the news that the Islingtons were being considered, the Australian governor-general, Munro-Ferguson, commented that: 'It is hard to imagine anything worse' (Letters to Venetia Stanley, 407).

In 1920 Islington became chairman of the National Savings Committee, touring the country on its behalf until his resignation in 1926, when he was appointed GBE. He had acquired a position of some authority in the House of Lords. He obtained the house's approval in June 1922, against the opposition of the ex-prime minister, Lord Balfour, for a motion against acceptance of the British mandate for Palestine 'until such modifications had been effected as would comply with British pledges to the Arabs'. As The Times noted, Islington was notable for his 'devotion to the cause of Palestine Arabs' (The Times, 12 Dec 1936, 19).

Islington also served for twenty-one years (1891–1912) as chairman of the board of management of the Royal Northern Hospital in Islington. He died at his home, 18 Hyde Park Gardens, London, on 6 December 1936, and was buried at Hilmarton church, Calne, Wiltshire, on 10 December.   ALTRINCHAM, rev. MARC BRODIE

Sources The Times (8 Dec 1936) · The Times (11 Dec 1936) · personal knowledge (1949) · Burke, Peerage · H. H. Asquith: letters to Venetia Stanley, ed. M. Brock and E. Brock (1982) · J. Turner, British politics and the Great War: coalition and conflict, 1915–1918 (1992) · J. Foster, Oxford men, 1880–1892: with a record of their schools, honours, and degrees (1893) · CGPLA Eng. & Wales (1937)

Archives NRA, papers | BL OIOC, corresp. with Sir Harcourt Butler, MSS Eur. F 116 · BL OIOC, letters to Sir Louis Kershaw, MSS Eur. D. 1056 · Bodl. Oxf., corresp. with Lewis Harcourt · CUL, corresp. with Lord Hardinge · U. Birm. L., corresp. with Austen Chamberlain
Likenesses J. Russell & Sons, photograph, c.1915, NPG · W. Stoneman, photograph, 1932, NPG · photograph, repro. in *The Times* (8 Dec 1936) · photograph, NPG [*see illus.*]
Wealth at death £136,661: probate limited to settled land, 8 April 1937, CGPLA Eng. & Wales · £87,880 1s. 7d.: probate save and except settled land, 17 Feb 1937, CGPLA Eng. & Wales

Poynings, Sir Adrian (1512?–1571), soldier, was born in Ghent, Flanders, the youngest of seven illegitimate children, three of them boys, of Sir Edward *Poynings (1459–1521), military commander, courtier and diplomat to Henry VII and Henry VIII. Thomas *Poynings, first Baron Poynings, was his brother. Adrian's sister Jane married Thomas, eighth Baron Clinton; their only son was Edward Clinton (d. 1585), the future lord admiral. Adrian attended Gray's Inn in 1533. He began his military career as an officer in the retinue of his eldest brother, Thomas, who was marshal of Calais. He also served with him during the Boulogne campaign, which led to the appointment of Thomas as governor of the town. His brother Edward became captain of the guard at Boulogne, but was killed in action in January 1546 and was replaced by the younger Thomas Wyatt. Adrian became Wyatt's lieutenant in February 1546. The earl of Surrey noted his bravery during the defence of the lower town, and in June 1546 he became captain of the citadel and was pardoned from all responsibility for the debts of his brothers. He was appointed captain of the town a year later. In 1548 his nephew Lord Clinton became governor, and he served at Boulogne until it was handed back to the French in 1550, when he became lieutenant of Calais Castle.

Poynings married Mary, daughter of Sir Owen West of Wherwell, Hampshire. In 1552 his services to the crown were recognized by an annual grant of 200 marks, but following the suppression of Thomas Wyatt's rebellion he appeared on the pardon roll of October 1554 and was required to pay a fine of £22. He served in the St Quentin campaign of 1557. A strong protestant, he sat in the Commons for Tregony in 1559, perhaps through Bedford's or Clinton's patronage. Elizabeth knighted him on her accession, and on 1 December 1560 granted him the office of keeper and captain of the town, island, and new castle of Portsmouth. In July 1562 the government ordered a force of 1960 troops and 17 vessels to assemble at Portsmouth in preparation for the occupation of Le Havre in Normandy. Poynings was appointed high marshal and granted his own company. On inspecting the troops he complained to Cecil that '500 or 600 have been ill chosen' (*CSP for.*, 1562, no. 698). Until the arrival of the designated commander, Ambrose Dudley, earl of Warwick, Poynings held overall command; and as Dudley lacked experience, he was directed by the privy council to be instructed by his marshal.

The force sailed on 26 September 1562, but strong winds delayed them and they did not disembark at Le Havre until 4 October. Poynings took possession of the town and

castle from the Huguenot commander, who demanded support for the forces besieged in Rouen. On 6 October he reported to the queen that he had secured the town and was dispatching help to Rouen, which contravened his instructions. A number of small English vessels transported the Huguenot garrison, English mercenaries in Huguenot service, and a company of Poynings's men under Thomas Leighton up the Seine, where they were all killed or captured when Rouen was stormed. The queen was angered that Poynings had not sent more troops, while blaming him for disobeying her instructions.

The fortifications of Le Havre were much weaker than expected, and Poynings and the military engineer, Richard Lee, recommended a substantial work programme. Cost and appalling weather prevented its being fully implemented, and pioneers sent to assist were diverted to assist the Huguenots besieging Caen. Warwick arrived in late October 1562, and Poynings complained that he was 'loath to punish, glad to give, loath to deny anything' (*CSP for.*, 3 Nov 1562). In late November Poynings was replaced by Sir Hugh Paulet, but remained as knight marshal and a member of the military council. On 25 March 1563, as the siege around Le Havre tightened, he was ordered to London to brief the privy council on the situation. Despite a heroic defence, Warwick was ordered to surrender on 27 July; no blame attached to Poynings. In 1564 he was granted denization in recognition of his services. He held his post as governor of Portsmouth until his death, at either Portsmouth or Lulworth, on 15 February 1571. He was also appointed vice-admiral for Hampshire. His widow, Mary, was granted her husband's lands in Dorset and elsewhere, and the wardship of their three daughters.

M. A. STEVENS

Sources CSP for., 1562–3 · CPR, 1560–63 · LP Henry VIII, vol. 21/2 · CSP dom., 1547–80 · 'Poynings, Sir Edward', DNB · 'Poynings, Thomas, Baron Poynings', DNB · Burke, *Peerage* · E. Tenison, *Elizabethan England* (1933) · T. Glasgow, 'The navy in the French wars of Mary and Elizabeth I [pt 2]', *Mariner's Mirror*, 54 (1968), 281–96 · W. T. MacCaffrey, *The shaping of the Elizabethan regime: Elizabethan politics, 1558–1572* (1968), 130–31 · HoP, *Commons*, 1558–1603, 3.241–2
Wealth at death manor of Ludworth (Lulworth), Dorset; ten other manors in Dorset and the county of Southampton: CSP dom., 1564

Poynings, Sir Edward (1459–1521), administrator, soldier, and diplomat, was born in the autumn of 1459, probably at his father's house in Southwark.

Origins and early service to Henry VII Poynings was the only son of Robert *Poynings (c.1419–1461) [*see under* Poynings, Michael] and his wife, Elizabeth Paston (1429?–1487/8), who married in 1458. His father, who had been carver and sword-bearer to Jack Cade, was killed at the second battle of St Albans in February 1461, after which his estates in Kent and Sussex were seized by his cousin Eleanor, countess of Northumberland, who retained many of them until her death in 1484. Poynings was brought up by his mother, who in 1466 married Sir George Brown of Betchworth, Surrey. She later appointed him her executor. In October 1483 he was prominent in the rising against Richard III in Kent, probably being drawn in by his stepfather. He was attainted in the parliament of January 1484, but escaped abroad, and joined Henry Tudor in Brittany. He led the English party in Vannes in October 1484 when Henry fled into France.

Poynings's later reputation as an outstanding administrator and experienced military commander grew out of his trusted position in Henry Tudor's court in exile. He landed with Henry at Milford Haven in August 1485, where he was knighted. Thereafter he combined membership of the king's council with household office. His attainder was reversed by parliament in November. He also recovered his father's estates, and in 1488 secured a life interest in six manors of Sir Guy Brian's inheritance. These twelve manors, mainly in Kent and Sussex, were worth £427 a year, but in September the king also rewarded him, as knight of the body, with a lavish grant of seven manors in the midlands forfeited by Humphrey Stafford, and in 1491 Poynings was created knight of the Garter. He was commissioned to inspect the ordnance at Calais, Guînes, and Hammes in August 1488, and in 1492 he had command of 12 ships and 1500 troops sent to the Netherlands to aid Maximilian against a French-instigated revolt. After clearing the sea of pirates preying on English commerce from the rebel base at Sluys, Poynings laid siege to Sluys in August, while the duke of Saxony blockaded it by land. After hard fighting the two castles defending the town were surrendered to Poynings, who then negotiated the rebels' submission to Maximilian. Poynings then joined Henry VII before Boulogne, but in November the treaty of Étaples ended the French War. Poynings was appointed deputy lieutenant of Calais, the scene of Yorkist plotting, and in July 1493, he was sent with William Warham on embassy to Flanders in a vain attempt to expose Perkin Warbeck, who was harboured there by Marguerite of Burgundy, and to procure his expulsion from the Netherlands. Archduke Philip would only promise not to support Warbeck but disclaimed any power to intervene in Marguerite's affairs.

Appointment to Ireland and early problems In Ireland, however, the situation was even more problematic, with continued Yorkist plotting and the recrudescence of an old feud between the lordship's leading families, the Butlers and Geraldines. Warbeck had already made one descent on this traditional Yorkist stronghold in a bid to improve on Lambert Simnel's unsuccessful invasion of England in 1487, and since then successive attempts to strengthen royal control over the English lordship of Ireland and to restore order had all failed. Thus by the summer of 1494 Henry felt that sterner measures were needed. It was to be for his service in Ireland that Poynings was chiefly remembered and where his skills as a soldier–administrator were most effectively deployed. In September he was appointed deputy to the king's son, Henry, the nominal lieutenant of Ireland. At the request of the prelates, magnates, and other notables of Ireland—so Henry informed Charles VIII of France—he was to lead an expedition to impose order among the wild Irish, establishing there the same justice and good rule as in England. Yet his retinue of

427 men was very small for this purpose, even when reinforced by 226 soldiers already in Ireland. In reality Poynings had instructions to reduce the lordship to royal control and to destroy the king's enemies and rebels there. He was also accompanied by a handful of skilled administrators to reform the Dublin administration. Indeed, with the appointment of three experienced lawyers, headed by Henry Deane, bishop of Bangor, as chancellor and chief justices, and of Sir Hugh Conway as treasurer, the Irish council was dominated by English outsiders.

Poynings landed at Howth on 13 October 1494 and almost immediately summoned a parliament to meet at Drogheda on 1 December. Initially affairs ran smoothly. Leading lords, English and Gaelic, came in to the deputy and chiefs surrendered pledges for peace, but in November the deputy led a hosting into Ulster, where Ó hAnluain and Mág Aonghusa remained aloof and Ó Domhnaill was intriguing with James IV of Scotland. Accompanied by the earl of Kildare, Gerald Fitzgerald (d. 1513), and Sir James Ormond, Poynings invaded the country of Ó hAnluain, who eventually submitted, as did Mág Aonghusa shortly afterwards. Yet the deputy then learned of communications between Kildare and the chiefs immediately before their submission and, in view of Kildare's previous record, suspected treachery. This breach with Kildare ended any real hopes that Poynings's more ambitious military objectives might be realized.

Poynings' law Later generations remembered Poynings best for an act (10 Henry VII c. 9) of the parliament he convened, known as Poynings' law. This provided that in future no parliament could be held in Ireland without the king's prior consent signified under the great seal of England, and that only bills similarly approved by the council in England could be considered. Its obscure wording may simply reproduce verbatim the king's instructions to Poynings about this before he left for Ireland, and the elaborate operational procedure for Poynings' law was worked out only later. Yet its purpose was to prevent parliament's unauthorized use by governors like Kildare to further private interests, in particular to prevent Warbeck from using parliament, as Simnel had, to legitimize a *coup d'état*. Subsequently the local community came to see Poynings' law as a bulwark against arbitrary rule by English governors, and still later as a restraint on parliament's legislative freedom, but no one anticipated that Poynings' law would survive, with modifications, until 1782. Another statute (10 Henry VII c. 39), sometimes also called Poynings' law, likewise had a long history, though its original purpose is unclear. It ordained that all statutes for the common weal of late made in England should apply in Ireland. Possibly a particular application to Ireland was intended of recent English legislation curbing magnate retaining (also regulated by other statutes of Poynings's parliament), but the act was later used to justify a more general application of English statutes passed before 1494. Otherwise, the forty-nine acts of Poynings's parliament had a shorter lifespan, although much of the legislation was politically important and of official origin. One act enjoined obedience to the king's commands under his

English seals, and repealed a statute of the Yorkist parliament of 1460 to the contrary. The chief judges and financial officers were to hold office during pleasure, not for life. It was made treason to incite the Irish to levy war against the governor. Custody of the chief royal castles was restricted to those born in England. Finally, many statutes re-enacted, with slight modifications, previous legislation for fostering the use of English law, customs, and weapons and proscribing Gaelic practices, notably by confirming the Statutes of Kilkenny of 1366. Overall, the legislation strengthened the king's control over the lordship and the Dublin administration.

Military success and administrative reform   By spring 1495, however, Poynings was increasingly preoccupied with the worsening military situation, and Bishop Deane as chancellor presided over the later sessions of parliament, which was dissolved in April. Kildare was eventually arrested in late February, and shipped to England. Within days his brother, Sir James Fitzgerald, had seized Carlow Castle and Poynings and Ormond besieged it throughout the spring, eventually retaking it in July. The terms of Kildare's attainder for treason highlighted the growing danger from Warbeck: he was accused of plotting the deputy's murder, holding communications with the king's enemies, and conspiring with the king of Scots and the earl of Desmond for an army of Scots to invade Ireland and overthrow the deputy and the king's true subjects. During the spring Desmond and Lord Barry were organizing a rising in Munster on Warbeck's behalf, and Gaelic chiefs throughout the west and north were also restive; but without reinforcements, Poynings could do no more than defend the pale. In late June, Desmond besieged Waterford, just as Warbeck sailed from Flanders. Warbeck's eventual arrival with a fleet on 23 July intensified the city's blockade and the king, responding to renewed appeals from Poynings, promised reinforcements. Yet in the crisis the deputy was forced to call out levies from the pale and Gaelic troops from Leinster as he marched south to confront the rebels. He broke the siege on 3 August, dispersing the blockading forces with his artillery and capturing three of Warbeck's ships. Warbeck retreated westwards and then retired to Scotland, while Poynings conducted mopping-up operations until his recall in December. In military terms Poynings's main achievement in Ireland was undoubtedly the crushing of the Yorkists. Yet an unsuspected legacy of his deputyship was probably the concept of 'the English pale', meaning the closely delineated and defended area of 'the four obedient shires' around Dublin. The first reference to the Calais pale dates from 1494, during Poynings's deputyship there; and following his transfer to Ireland, a statute of Poynings's parliament for 'diches to be made aboute the Inglishe pale' marks the first recorded reference to a pale in Ireland.

Concurrently with the military crisis Poynings's administration was attempting to meet the king's demands for financial and administrative reform. The foundations for this had been laid in parliament, with an act of resumption, and the grant of a double subsidy based on a revised

extent which yielded Ir£1500 per annum over five years. Yet, since the king spent £12,000 on Irish affairs between August 1494 and December 1495, chiefly on the army, efforts to raise more money in Ireland were intensified, notably in April 1495 when the offices of under-treasurer and treasurer-at-war were revived for two associates of Poynings, William Hatteclyffe and John Pympe. As peace was restored during the autumn, military expenditure was curtailed, the value of crown lands recovered, and reform of the customs also swelled revenue from that source. Thus for the year 1495–6 the Irish revenues yielded Ir£3056, or about double its usual value. Yet even this substantial increase was not sufficient, and those captains and officials remaining after Poynings's departure were now needed for the defence of the English north against Warbeck and James IV.

Administrative and diplomatic service, 1496–1516   Leaving from Ireland in December 1495 Poynings returned to his native Kent, where he had earlier been appointed lieutenant of Dover Castle, close by Warbeck's attempted landing at Deal in early July 1495. He had been on the Kent peace commission since Henry's accession, was promoted constable of Dover in September 1504, and became deputy warden of the Cinque Ports in 1505; but, in the king's last decade, he also attended the council more regularly. In 1500 he was present at Henry VII's interview with Archduke Philip at Calais, and in October 1501 was among those who conducted Katherine of Aragon to London. In 1508 he likewise conducted the Flemish ambassadors who came to conclude the projected marriage of Henry's daughter Mary to Prince Charles of Castile. Some time before the king's death, he became comptroller of the household and was one of the trusty councillors recommended by Henry in his will to his son.

Poynings attended Henry VIII's coronation as comptroller of the household. He was also promoted lord warden of the Cinque Ports, but soon emerged as a leading diplomat. He witnessed the renewal of the treaty with Scotland on 29 August 1509. In June 1511 he had command of the ships and 1500 soldiers dispatched to the Low Countries to assist Maximilian in suppressing revolt in Guelderland. His expedition embarked at Sandwich on 18 July, and enjoyed some success, reducing several towns and castles. Poynings returned to England in the autumn. He sat in the parliament of 1512–14, probably as knight of the shire for Kent, and led the Commons delegation which announced its choice of speaker to the chancellor in the Lords. From May to November 1512 he was travelling in the Netherlands as one of four commissioners negotiating a league against France. He returned there early in 1513, with Sir Richard Wingfield, to conclude negotiations for Maximilian's inclusion on 5 April in the Holy League. With a retinue of 500 men he was present at the capture of Thérouanne on 22 August, and on 24 September of Tournai, of which he was appointed lieutenant with a garrison of 5000 men. For most of 1514 he was engaged in diplomatic work in the Netherlands. He resided chiefly in Tournai, where he uncovered a plot to betray the city to the French.

His duties there precluded his attendance at the third session of parliament, where he secured an act (5 Henry VIII c. 18) annulling all suits prejudicial to his landed possessions determined in his absence.

In February 1515 Poynings finally returned to England, having been replaced as governor of Tournai by Lord Mountjoy. He requested leave to go on a pilgrimage to Rome, but on 7 May he was appointed ambassador, with Dr William Knight, to renew the league of 1505 with Prince Charles. They arrived in Bruges on 23 May, but returned to England after four months' unsuccessful negotiation. Almost immediately, however, the French victory at Marignano once more cemented the league of her enemies, and Poynings, recommissioned ambassador to Charles (now king of Spain) on 21 February 1516, succeeded in concluding a treaty with him on 19 April. Charles also granted him a pension of 1000 livres.

Last years, death, and legacy This was the last of Poynings's important negotiations. Thereafter he spent most of his time in the Cinque Ports or at his manor of Westenhanger, Kent, where he rebuilt the castle. In 1517 he became chancellor of the Order of the Garter, and in June he was at Calais deciding disputes between English and French merchants and dealing with violations of the treaty. In 1518 he was treating for the surrender of Tournai. Poynings was promoted treasurer of the household in 1519, and Henry considered raising him to the peerage, but he never became Lord Poynings, although he was occasionally so styled. As warden he supplied ships to transport Henry VIII to Calais in 1520 and attended him at the Field of Cloth of Gold. He was also present at Henry's meeting with Charles V at Gravelines. He died at Westenhanger on 22 October 1521.

Poynings had married, before 1485, Isabella (Elizabeth), daughter of Sir John *Scott [see under Scott family], comptroller of the household, and sister of Sir William Scott, warden of the Cinque Ports; she died on 15 August 1528, and was buried in Brabourne church, where she is commemorated by a brass. They had one child, John, who predeceased Poynings childless, but Poynings left seven illegitimate children—three sons, including Sir Adrian *Poynings, and four daughters. He provided for them in his will of 27 July 1521, leaving Westenhanger to his eldest son, Thomas, to whom the king also regranted some lands; but most of Poynings's estates reverted to Henry Percy, fifth earl of Northumberland. Thomas *Poynings was in 1545 created Lord Poynings and appointed lieutenant of Boulogne. His two brothers also served as captains there. Of Poynings's daughters, Jane married Thomas, eighth Lord Clinton (d. 1517), and Poynings paid £135 for the wardship of his grandson, Edward, ninth Lord Clinton.   STEVEN G. ELLIS

Sources A. Conway and E. Curtis, *Henry VII's relations with Scotland and Ireland, 1485–1498* (1932) · I. Arthurson, *The Perkin Warbeck conspiracy, 1491–1499* (1994) · S. G. Ellis, *Reform and revival: English government in Ireland, 1470–1534*, Royal Historical Society Studies in History, 47 (1986) · C. G. Cruikshank, *The English occupation of Tournai, 1513–1519* (1971) · HoP, *Commons, 1509–58* · CPR · LP Henry VIII · S. G. Ellis, 'Henry VII and Ireland, 1491–1496', *England and Ireland in the later middle ages: essays in honour of Jocelyn Otway-Ruthven*, ed. J. Lydon (1981), 237–54 · J. Gairdner, ed., *Letters and papers illustrative of the reigns of Richard III and Henry VII*, 2 vols., Rolls Series, 24 (1861–3) · J. M. W. Bean, *The estates of the Percy family, 1416–1537* (1958) · E. Hasted, *The history and topographical survey of the county of Kent*, 2nd edn, 12 vols. (1797–1801); facs. edn (1972) · R. Jeffs, 'The Poynings–Percy dispute: an example of the interplay of open strife and legal action in the fifteenth century', *BIHR*, 34 (1961), 148–64 · *DNB*

Archives BL, Royal MS 18 C.xiv

Poynings [Ponyngs], **Michael**, **first Lord Poynings** (c.1318–1369), soldier, of Poynings and Slaugham, Sussex, was the eldest son of Sir Thomas Poynings and his wife, Agnes, daughter and coheir of Richard Rokesley of Preston and Ruxley, Kent. Michael Poynings served in Flanders from 1338 to 1340. Thomas Poynings having died at the siege of Honnecourt in the Vermandois on 10 October 1339, the king gave Michael his marriage and livery of his lands, although he was still under age, in consideration of his father's good service. Poynings was summoned to campaign in Scotland in December 1341, and to attend council meetings in February 1342, July 1352, July 1353, and June 1358. He went on the expedition to Brittany of 1342, and on the Crécy–Calais campaign of 1346–7, where he served with forty-five men, including his uncle Michael Poynings. From August 1347 to September 1351 he had the keeping of the property of Margery, widow of Nicholas Beche, forfeited by her husband, Sir John Dalton, following their unlicensed marriage. The Daltons had abducted Margery from a manor house near Reading in March 1347, in the process slaying Michael, the uncle of Lord Poynings; a number of the latter's men were charged with the killing until he personally vouched for them.

From November 1348 Poynings was summoned to parliament as Lord Poynings. By the end of that year he had married Joan, née Ruxley (d. 1369), the childless widow of John Moleyns; she brought with her properties in Wiltshire and Buckinghamshire. Their eldest son, Thomas [see below], was born at Slaugham in the following year. A frequent commissioner in Sussex, Kent, and the Cinque Ports from 1351, in that and the following year Poynings was a guardian of the Sussex coast. He campaigned in France in 1355 and 1356, fighting at Poitiers, and with his brothers Richard and Luke among his company, took part in Edward III's invasion of France of 1359–60. He was a signatory to the treaty with Castile in June 1362. In the last seven years of his life Poynings made preparations for the future: in November 1362 his plans to found a chantry at Mottenden, Kent, laid as far back as 1347, at last came to fruition. In February 1366 he paid £1000 to Queen Philippa for the wardship of William, son and heir of Lord Bardolf, in order to marry him to his daughter Agnes. Poynings died on 7 March 1369 and was buried in Poynings church, having left 200 marks in his will to finance its rebuilding. He had acquired considerable property in Norfolk, Sussex, and Kent.

Michael Poynings's nineteen-year-old son **Thomas Poynings**, **second Lord Poynings** (1349–1375), who was heir to his father's properties in Kent and Sussex, became a royal ward; he was coheir with his twelve-year-old brother, Richard [see below], to the property held by Kentish gavelkind tenure. Their mother Joan died on 16 May 1369, when her estates in Wiltshire and Buckinghamshire reverted to the Moleyns family. Thomas Poynings succeeded to his father's title, as second Lord Poynings, but died in June 1375 at the age of twenty-six, possibly in consequence of being immured for two years in a Castilian prison after he was captured in the sea battle of La Rochelle in 1372. There were no children of his marriage to Blanche, daughter of John (II) Mowbray, Lord Mowbray. Thomas was succeeded by his brother **Richard Poynings**, third Baron Poynings (*c*.1355–1387), who went to Spain with John of Gaunt, duke of Lancaster, in 1386 (making a will at Plymouth, as the army prepared to sail, in which he made careful provision both for the payment of his debts and the future of his younger children), and died there on 25 May 1387. His wife was Isabel, daughter and heir of Robert Grey (Robert Fitzpayn), a younger son of Richard, Lord Grey of Codnor.

Richard's son and heir **Robert Poynings**, fourth Baron Poynings (1382–1446), was summoned to parliament in 1404, and is several times recorded as attending council meetings under Henry IV. He served regularly in France, taking custody of the duke of Bourbon in 1420, and fighting at Cravant in 1420, and at the recovery of Crotoy and the battle of Verneuil in 1424. He married twice. With his first wife, whose name is unknown, he had two sons, Richard, who was killed in France in 1429, and **Robert Poynings** (*c*.1419–1461). The second Robert's life was dominated by his struggle to acquire the Kentish manors of Tirlingham, Newington, Eastwell, and Westwood, which his father had settled on Eleanor (1428–1484), daughter of Robert's elder brother, Richard, and wife of Henry Percy, third earl of Northumberland and, by right of his wife, fifth Baron Poynings. Robert claimed these manors as heir by gavelkind. He also claimed Great Perching in Sussex. In the summer of 1450 he was one of a handful of gentry to join the Cade rebellion, apparently acting as Cade's carver and sword-bearer. He may have been motivated by another feud, this time with his stepbrother, William Crowmer (whose mother had been the fourth Lord Poynings's second wife), over the fourth Lord Poynings's moveables (Crowmer was a particular target of the rebels). Robert did not take out a pardon until 1457, in the meantime suffering outlawry and imprisonment, but this did not prevent him from sitting as MP for Sussex from October 1450 to May 1451. In 1458 he married Elizabeth (1429?–1487/8), daughter of Judge William Paston, with whom he had a son, Edward *Poynings, the future lord deputy of Ireland. Robert was killed fighting for the Yorkists at the battle of St Albans on 17 February 1461.

PETER FLEMING

Sources GEC, *Peerage*, new edn, 10.660–64 · *Chancery records* · *CIPM*, 8, no. 231; 12, nos. 404–5 · J. H. Round, 'The lords Poynings and St. John', *Sussex Archaeological Collections*, 62 (1921), 12–19 · R. Jeffs, 'The Poynings–Percy dispute: an example of the interplay of open strife and legal action in the fifteenth century', *BIHR*, 34 (1961), 148–64 · N. Saul, *Scenes from provincial life: knightly families in Sussex, 1280–1400* (1986) · J. M. W. Bean, *The decline of English feudalism, 1215–1540* (1968), 143 · S. Walker, *The Lancastrian affinity, 1361–1399* (1990) · P. E. Russell, *The English intervention in Spain and Portugal in the time of Edward III and Richard II* (1955)

Archives PRO, Paston letters

Poynings, Richard, third Baron Poynings (*c*.1355–1387). *See under* Poynings, Michael, first Lord Poynings (*c*.1318–1369).

Poynings, Robert, fourth Baron Poynings (1382–1446). *See under* Poynings, Michael, first Lord Poynings (*c*.1318–1369).

Poynings, Robert (*c*.1419–1461). *See under* Poynings, Michael, first Lord Poynings (*c*.1318–1369).

Poynings, Thomas, second Lord Poynings (1349–1375). *See under* Poynings, Michael, first Lord Poynings (*c*.1318–1369).

Poynings, Thomas, first Baron Poynings (1512?–1545), soldier and courtier, was one of the three illegitimate sons of Sir Edward *Poynings (d. 1521) of Westenhanger, Kent. Sir Adrian *Poynings was his brother. His mother could have been Rose Whetehill of Calais, who was left an annuity of 40 marks in Sir Edward's will of 1521. The two may have met during Sir Edward's time in Calais in the late 1480s and early 1490s. Thomas was probably born in 1512, as Sir Edward provided in his will that the revenues of the manor of Westenhanger should be enjoyed by his servant Edward Thwaytes for twelve years until Thomas came of age. This also corresponds to Thomas's first appearance at court.

Poynings served at the coronation of Anne Boleyn in June 1533 and was made a knight of the Bath during the coronation celebrations. His listing as a sewer-extraordinary in a document dated by the editors of *Letters and Papers, Foreign and Domestic, of the Reign of … Henry VIII* to 1516 is a mistake: the document has subsequently been redated to 1535. Poynings continued his father's close links with Kent and its gentry families. He was on the sheriff roll for the county in 1533 and chosen in the following year. During the northern rising of 1536 he contributed 150 men for the royal army, serving alongside other leading Kentish members of the royal affinity. His links with Sir Thomas Wyatt were especially close; while Wyatt was abroad as ambassador at the imperial court during 1537–9, Poynings acted as his agent, petitioning Cromwell for the payment of Wyatt's annuity. Indeed, there is evidence that he may have served with Wyatt abroad, receiving a diet as an ambassador between 19 March 1537 and 2 June 1539. He continued to have close contacts with the court throughout the late 1530s, being present at both the christening of the future Edward VI and the funeral of Jane Seymour in 1537, and jousting in a tournament in May 1540. Some time before 1539 he married Katherine, daughter and coheir of John, second Lord Marney, and widow of George Ratcliffe.

In 1540 it appears that the king decided to establish Poynings as a power in the west country, possibly based around the Marney lands in Dorset and Somerset which had descended to his wife. In August of that year he exchanged Westenhanger for a grant of monastic land in Dorset. He also acquired lands in Wiltshire, Cornwall, and Somerset. Within weeks, however, it was decided that he could best serve the king abroad: in October he was dispatched to Calais as marshall. Presumably, he had demonstrated both the military prowess, probably during the suppression of the Pilgrimage of Grace, and diplomatic skills, perhaps while serving with Wyatt, that the position at Calais demanded. In December 1540 he took temporary charge of the important castle at Guînes on the death of William, Lord Sandys. He remained at Guînes until 1544, frequently taking part in border skirmishes with the French. During the invasion of France in 1544 he led a contingent from Dorset. It was during this campaign that his martial reputation was firmly established: he was involved in heavy fighting around Montreuil in July, and was responsible for the tactics of the assault on Boulogne which captured that town on 13 September.

On 30 January 1545 Poynings was raised to the peerage as Baron Poynings, in preparation for his appointment as lieutenant of Boulogne 'as the most experienced in wars with the Frenchmen upon the frontiers and as speaking their language' (LP Henry VIII, 20/1, no. 121). He continued to serve in the front line while lieutenant: in July his horse was shot from under him during one attack. That year he was nominated for the Garter by the dukes of Norfolk and Suffolk and the earls of Arundel, Hertford, Essex, and Surrey. But he was not elected, and his career was cut short when he contracted dysentery and died, still at Boulogne, on 17 August 1545. His only child, a son christened in March 1539, probably died in infancy.

DAVID GRUMMITT

Sources LP Henry VIII • W. G. Davis, 'Whetehill of Calais [pt 1]', New England Historical and Genealogical Register, 102 (1948), 241–53 • W. G. Davis, 'Whetehill of Calais [pt 2]', New England Historical and Genealogical Register, 103 (1949), 5–19 • H. Miller, Henry VIII and the English nobility (1986) • J. Guy, Tudor England (1988) • E. Hasted, The history and topographical survey of the county of Kent, 2nd edn, 8 (1799) • GEC, Peerage • DNB • state papers, domestic series, Henry VIII, PRO, SP 1 • will, PRO, PROB 11/20, fols. 157–8 [Sir Edward Poynings] • chancery, inquistions, PRO, 142, post mortem, ser. II, 84, nos. 10, 35–6
Archives PRO, letters to Henry VIII, SP 1/217–225

Poynter, Agnes, Lady Poynter (1843–1906). See under Macdonald sisters (act. 1837–1925).

Poynter, Ambrose (1796–1886), architect, was born on 16 May 1796 in London, the second son of Ambrose Lyon Poynter and Thomasine Anne Peck. The family was of Huguenot origin, his father's great-great-grandfather Thomas Pointier of St Quentin in France having settled in England in 1685. Poynter's architectural education was thorough: pupillage between 1814 and 1818 in the office of John Nash, then foreign travel in 1819–21, in Italy, Sicily, and the Ionian Islands. In 1821 he attended out of courtesy the funeral in Rome of Keats, whom he did not know. A few years after returning to Britain, Poynter set up in practice at 1 Poet's Corner, Westminster. In 1830–32 he lived in Paris, where his associates included Richard Parkes Bonington, Baron Denon, the engraver Boucher-Desnoyers, and others. From about 1846 his London house and office were at 12 Park Street (later 1 Queen Anne's Gate). He married, in 1832 at the British embassy chapel in Paris, Emma, daughter of the Revd E. Forster and Lavinia, the only child

of the sculptor Thomas Banks. With her he had one son, Sir Edward John *Poynter, president of the Royal Academy, and three daughters, of whom Clara, wife of Robert Courtenay Bell, attained distinction as a translator. Emma died in 1848, and in 1850 Poynter married Louisa Noble (d. 1874), the daughter of General Robert Bell, with whom he had a daughter.

Poynter was closely involved in the development of the architectural profession. One of the founder members of the Institute of British Architects in 1834, he was an early member of its council, and in 1840, 1841, and 1844 served as its secretary. He read markedly diverse papers at its meetings, and in 1842 his anonymous essay 'On the general introduction of iron in buildings' won the institute's silver medal; despite this interest, however, Poynter's numerous buildings demonstrate no particular precocity or adventurousness in the use of iron. He also contributed papers to the proceedings of the Archaeological Institute, of which he was an original member. He was frequently employed on arbitration cases, notably in 1844–55 as one of three official referees appointed under the Metropolitan Building Act. Deteriorating eyesight from 1858 compelled him to retire by 1860; several commissions then in hand were completed by William Burges.

Poynter was chiefly an architect of churches and country houses. His best-known London work is the Tudor Gothic-style hospital and chapel of St Katharine in Regent's Park (1827); other London churches, Christ Church, Westminster (1841), and the French protestant church in Bloomsbury Street (1845), have been demolished. Elsewhere the greatest concentrations of his work are in Cambridge and Flintshire in north-east Wales. In Cambridge he is said to have built early in his career an observatory for his friend the mathematical 'coach' William Hopkins (1793–1866). Between 1837 and 1843 he built three Cambridge churches, St Paul's, Christ Church, and St Andrew the Great, and in 1835 he competed unsuccessfully for the building of the Fitzwilliam Museum. In Flintshire he built churches, schools, and houses, many of them, including Mostyn Hall (1846–7), for the first Lord Mostyn. Of other country houses his work at Pynes House, Devon (1849, for Sir Stafford Northcote), is significant; restorations or additions to Warwick Castle (1830–31) and Crewe Hall were destroyed by fire during Poynter's lifetime. His other restoration schemes include Waltham Abbey, Essex (1851–c.1855), and the Maison Dieu, Dover (begun 1858). In his later career he was architect to the National Provincial Bank of England, for which he designed several premises. Poynter's buildings are competent but rarely inspired essays in the conventional Renaissance and (especially) English medieval idioms of the day, in which he was content to follow rather than lead; his Cambridge churches fell foul of the fashion for more accurate imitation of medieval forms, however, for which he was ridiculed by The Ecclesiologist (2, 1843, 137).

Poynter's architectural draughtsmanship was exceptionally fine, and he was also an accomplished watercolourist, having studied under Thomas Shotter Boys. His papers include extensive notes and fine drawings of English medieval architecture, made in the later 1820s, apparently with a view to publication. However, his most widely read writings were articles on literature, science, and art in Charles Knight's mass-market *Pictorial History of England* (1837–44); he also provided illustrations for the work, and for Knight's edition of Shakespeare (1838–41). He was an original member of the Arundel Society and the Graphic Society, and an amateur of heraldry.

Poynter was also involved with the government schools of design. In 1845–8 he served as a somewhat undistinguished inspector of the provincial schools, then run as satellites of the main school in Somerset House, London. His chief shortcoming was the failure effectively to modernize their curricula to accommodate the claims of commercial design. For this and for his contradictory official reports he was accused in 1849 of slackness and duplicity in the *Journal of Design*, a mouthpiece of the reformer Henry Cole (2, 1849, 142–5). Although Poynter served on successive reforming committees in 1848–51, it was Cole who effectively reorganized the schools thereafter. Poynter died at his home, 3 Marine Place, Dover, on 20 November 1886, and is presumed to have been buried at Kensal Green, London, where he had bought a plot.

L. H. CUST, *rev.* SIMON BRADLEY

Sources T. H. Lewis, 'The late Ambrose Poynter', *Journal of Proceedings of the Royal Institute of British Architects*, new ser., 3 (1886–7), 113–15, 137 • Pevsner • Colvin, *Archs.* • Q. Bell, *The schools of design* (1963) • *The Builder*, 51 (1886), 787 • *Dir. Brit. archs.* • RIBA BAL, drawings collection [especially C3, H3/S3] • Graves, *RA exhibitors* • S. MacDonald, *The history and philosophy of art education* (1970) • private information (2004) • A. Brooks, 'The stained glass designs of Sir Edward Poynter', *Victorian Society Annual* (1996), 27–36 • *CGPLA Eng. & Wales* (1887)

Archives Col. U., Avery Architectural and Fine Arts Library • RIBA, drawings collection • RIBA BAL, architectural notebooks, papers, and sketches • Yale U. CBA | Bodl. Oxf., letters to Robert Finch

Wealth at death £10,299: probate, 15 Jan 1887, *CGPLA Eng. & Wales*

Poynter, Sir Edward John, first baronet (1836–1919), painter and arts administrator, was born on 20 March 1836 in Paris, the second child and only son of Ambrose *Poynter (1796–1886), an architect, and his first wife, Emma Forster (1800–1848). He came from an artistic family and many commentators subsequently emphasized the inherited nature of his ability. His father's interests extended beyond architecture to include watercolour painting and illustration. His mother was the granddaughter of the neo-classical sculptor Thomas Banks (1735–1805), and both she and her mother were talented amateur artists.

Education and training in Paris Poynter's childhood was marked by poor health and interrupted study at Westminster School (1847–9), Brighton College (1849–50), and Ipswich grammar school (1851–2). In 1852 he began his artistic training under the watercolourist Thomas Shotter Boys, a friend of his father; he also attended Leigh's academy. During the following year, he spent the winter in Rome where he met the painter Frederic Leighton.

Sir Edward John Poynter, first baronet (1836–1919), by Ralph W. Robinson, pubd 1891

Inspired by the example of Leighton's large-scale academic painting, Poynter returned to London to continue his training at Leigh's and at the studio of W. C. T. Dobson. In 1855 he entered the Royal Academy Schools but a visit to the Paris Universal Exhibition in the same year convinced him of the superiority of contemporary French painting. He returned to Paris in 1856, becoming a pupil in the atelier of Charles Gleyre (1806–1874) and enrolling in the École des Beaux-Arts. Poynter's three-year period in Paris with fellow students James McNeill Whistler, George Du Maurier, Thomas Lamont, and Thomas Armstrong was later celebrated in Du Maurier's best-selling novel *Trilby* (1894). During this period Poynter received his first commissions for decorative work in the form of painted furniture and stained glass. He continued to design stained glass after his return to England in 1860, principally for James Powell & Sons of Whitefriars glassworks. His friend the architect William Burges also employed him on several decorative projects, of which the most important were the stained glass designs for the Maison Dieu, Dover (1860–1861), and the painted ceiling of Waltham Abbey, Essex (1860). Poynter also joined the ranks of the black and white illustrators of the 1860s, contributing drawings to several magazines, such as *Once a Week* and *London Society*, and executing twelve plates for the Dalziel brothers' prestigious *Bible Gallery* (eventually published in 1880).

Early career and marriage In 1861 Poynter exhibited his first work at the Royal Academy, and during the following years he made his name with pictures of Egyptian and classical subjects. A typical example is *Faithful unto Death* (1865; Walker Art Gallery, Liverpool), illustrating a dramatic scene set in ancient Pompeii. He also produced paintings in watercolour, chiefly portraits and landscapes, which were regularly exhibited at the Dudley Gallery in London. In 1867 Poynter completed the large and elaborate biblical painting *Israel in Egypt* (Guildhall Art Gallery, London), which enjoyed enormous popular success and established his reputation. He followed this with *The Catapult* (1868; Laing Art Gallery, Newcastle upon Tyne), another impressive depiction of ancient history. Both works demonstrate characteristic features of Poynter's art, such as his technical proficiency, careful attention to archaeological detail, and commitment to the academic ideal of the nude. These works ensured his election in 1869 as ARA.

Poynter's career as a decorative artist also flourished. Indeed, he emerges as a significant figure in the 'mosaic revival' of the 1860s. The majority of his decorative works were commissioned by the South Kensington Museum, London. These included designs for the mosaics of *Phidias* and *Apelles* (1864) in the south court (for the series known as the Kensington Valhalla), the innovative tile decoration and metal grill for the grill room (or Dutch kitchen) (1866–c.1874), and his proposed mosaic scheme for the apse of the lecture theatre (1867–71). In preparation for this latter work—an ambitious multifigured hemicycle—Poynter travelled to Italy in 1868 to study Venetian mosaics. Unfortunately, the only part of the scheme eventually to be completed was the ornamental soffit (1877). Two further decorative projects from this period were Poynter's design for part of the frieze of the Royal Albert Hall (1869) and the cartoon for the *St George* mosaic in the houses of parliament (1869).

The same decade witnessed Poynter's marriage, on 9 August 1866, to Agnes [see Poynter, Agnes, *under* Macdonald sisters], daughter of the Revd G. B. Macdonald. Remembered as 'a lady of great beauty and musical talent' (*DNB*, 440), Agnes's charm was to prove a considerable social asset for her husband, whose tall and distinguished appearance was offset by a deeply reserved and forbidding manner. Agnes Poynter achieved a certain status in her own right as one of the Macdonald sisters, a title which alluded to the sisters' later fame as wives or mothers of eminent Victorians. Agnes's sisters included Louisa Baldwin (mother of Stanley Baldwin), Alice Kipling (mother of Rudyard Kipling), and Georgiana Burne-Jones (wife of Edward Burne-Jones). Edward and Agnes Poynter's eldest child, Ambrose, was born in 1867; he was followed by a second son, Hugh, in 1882.

As an art educator In 1871 Poynter was appointed the first Slade professor at University College, London. During his five-year tenure he was responsible for introducing the principles of French art education into the English system. His Slade lectures upheld the continued relevance of the academic tradition, while also addressing practical issues, such as the importance of life drawing. These lectures were well received and later published under the title *Ten Lectures on Art* (1879). Poynter's promotion of his friend the French artist Alphonse Legros (1837–1911) as his successor at the Slade ensured the continuation of his teaching philosophy. Poynter retired from the Slade professorship in 1875, following his appointment to the influential position of director and principal of the National Art Training School at South Kensington. In his new role administering the government art system, he again took on an agenda of reform. This included a greater emphasis on fine art training within the schools and was also reflected in his appointment of new teachers such as the French sculptor Jules Dalou (1838–1902) as head of the modelling class. While at South Kensington, Poynter was responsible for the publication of a series of drawing books and several art history text books.

Major works Many of the ideas which Poynter expounded in his role as an educator were evident in his major works of the 1870s. These included the fresco in St Stephen's Church, south Dulwich (1872–3), depicting the trial and martyrdom of the saint. Recognized as a rare example of the *buon fresco* technique in Britain, this work's heroic figures and expressive gestures embody the principles of history painting, the most prestigious of the genres. Poynter's most important commission of the decade was the execution of four large oil paintings to decorate the billiards room at the earl of Wharncliffe's seat, Wortley Hall, near Sheffield. Between 1872 and 1879 Poynter exhibited these paintings—*Perseus and Andromeda* (1872), *The Fight between More of More Hall and the Dragon of Wantley* (1873), *Atalanta's Race* (1876), and *Nausicaa and her Maidens Playing at Ball* (1879)—at the Royal Academy. The last of these pictures reflects the influence of the aesthetic movement in its frieze-like composition and flowing draperies. Nevertheless, Poynter's strong emphasis on narrative and dramatic action distinguished his classical paintings from those of his contemporaries, such as Leighton and Moore. Many considered these paintings to be Poynter's greatest success as an exponent of 'high art'; certainly they contributed to his election as RA in 1876. During the early 1880s Poynter completed the Wharncliffe commission by designing an elaborate ornamental scheme for the billiards room interior.

Poynter's next important work was *A Visit to Aesculapius* (1880; Tate collection), a large classical painting celebrating the female nude which was acquired by the Chantrey bequest. Between 1878 and 1884 he collaborated with Frederic Leighton on a proposal to decorate the dome of St Paul's Cathedral in mosaic. Both artists designed large cartoons illustrating an apocalyptic theme, but when viewed *in situ* these efforts were judged unsuitable and the scheme was abandoned. This project was followed by Poynter's most ambitious painting, *The Visit of the Queen of Sheba to King Solomon* (1890; Art Gallery of New South Wales, Sydney). A vast canvas, which included over fifty figures, this painting is reminiscent of his earlier reconstructions of antiquity, although far more grandiose in terms of technical skill and the wealth of archaeological detail. After taking over six years to complete, the work sold for £3000—the highest payment Poynter ever received for one of his paintings. While working on the canvas, Poynter's interest in the ancient world was reinforced by his acceptance in 1889 of the position of honorary secretary to the Society for the Preservation of the Monuments of Ancient Egypt.

The majority of Poynter's later works tended to be small-scale classical paintings such as *On the Terrace* (1889; Walker Art Gallery, Liverpool), and *When the World was Young* (1891; priv. coll.), which were frequently likened to the anecdotal, Graeco-Roman pictures of Lawrence Alma-Tadema. This predilection for classical genre was matched by an increased interest in portraiture (including some highly original portrait medallions in bronze) and landscape painting. Poynter became a regular exhibitor at the Grosvenor and New galleries and at the Society of Painters in Water Colours, sending examples in a range of media, including designs and studies. These latter works enhanced his reputation as a fine and versatile draughtsman. His interest in decorative design also continued. In 1892–3 he collaborated with Alma-Tadema on a scheme of neo-Pompeian decoration for a series of rooms in the Athenaeum; the following year he created some reverses for the proposed new coinage.

As director of the National Gallery and president of the Royal Academy The 1890s saw Poynter become more actively involved in public office. In 1894 he was the last practising artist to be appointed director of the National Gallery, London. In spite of legislative changes which had curtailed the director's discretionary powers, Poynter still made a valuable contribution to the collection. His most notable acquisitions included Pisanello's *The Vision of St Eustace*, Antonello's *St Jerome in his Study*, Mantegna's *Agony in the Garden*, Titian's *Portrait of a Man*, and Rembrandt's portraits of Jacob Trip and his wife. Moreover, his unusual breadth of taste resulted in the gallery purchasing works by Lorenzo Monaco, Dürer (ascribed), Zurbaran, Jan Steen, Goya, and Alfred Stevens. Before his retirement in 1904, Poynter edited the first complete illustrated catalogue of the collection (1899) and was responsible for the display and opening of the Tate Gallery in 1897.

In recognition of his experience and talents as an artist, educator, and administrator, Poynter was elected president of the Royal Academy in December 1896, following the death of Millais; in the same year he was knighted, becoming a baronet in 1902. During his presidency the academy was increasingly challenged by more progressive elements in the arts community. This is reflected, for example, by the appointment in 1904 of a select committee to inquire into the academy's administration of the Chantrey Fund. Poynter remained in office for twenty-two years, until ill health and failing eyesight led to his reluctant resignation in 1918. In the same year, his fine collection of old master drawings was sold at Sothebys on 24–5 April 1918. Poynter died on 26 July 1919 at his house and studio, at 70 Addison Road, Kensington, and was buried in St Paul's Cathedral, London, on 30 July. His studio sale was held at Christies on 19 January 1920.

Conclusion Poynter was unfortunate in outliving most of his generation, for he became a target of the modernists in their rejection of Victorian art. His reputation as a teacher and academic draughtsman, however, did survive into the twentieth century: William Gaunt described him as 'one of the best draughtsmen of his age' (Gaunt, 16). It was not until the revival of interest in Victorian art during the 1970s that Poynter's role as a leading figure of the English classical revival was again recognized. Recent scholarship has continued to focus on aspects of Poynter's classicism, such as his assimilation of contemporary developments in archaeology or his advocacy of the nude. This emphasis on Poynter as a 'Victorian Olympian' has tended to obscure his equally important activities as a decorative artist and public official. It should not be forgotten that during his lengthy career—which extended over sixty years—Poynter achieved distinction not only as a painter in oil and watercolour, but also as an academic draughtsman, a decorative designer in stained glass, mosaic, fresco, and ceramic tiles, a modeller of medals and coinage, an etcher, a graphic illustrator, a portrait painter, and a theatre designer. He also added the roles of educator, administrator, and museum official to his many achievements. He deserves recognition as one of the great Victorian polymaths. Poynter's works are held in most major British collections, including the Tate collection, the Victoria and Albert Museum, the Walker Art Gallery in Liverpool, Manchester City Galleries, and the British Library. He is also represented in many Commonwealth art collections.

ALISON INGLIS

Sources C. Monkhouse, 'The life and work of Sir Edward J. Poynter: president of the Royal Academy', *Easter Annual* (1897), 1–32 • F. H. Jackson, 'The work of Sir E. J. Poynter viewed mainly from the decorative side', *ArchR*, 2 (1897), 3–13, 50–63, 118–30, 155–66, 224–31 • A. W. Baldwin, *The Macdonald sisters* (1960) • *DNB* • M. Bell, *Drawings of Sir E. J. Poynter Bart, P.R.A.* (1905) • [M. H. Spielmann], 'The studies of Sir Edward J. Poynter', *Magazine of Art*, 21 (1897), 1–7, 289–94 • L. Lusk, 'Sir E. J. Poynter as a water-colourist', *Art Journal*, new ser., 23 (1903), 187–92 • P. Connor, '"Wedding archaeology to art": Poynter's *Israel in Egypt*', *Influences in Victorian art and architecture*, ed. S. Macready and F. H. Thompson (1985), 112–20 • A. Inglis, 'Sir Edward Poynter and the earl of Wharncliffe's billiard room', *Apollo*, 126 (1987), 249–55 • J. Kestner, 'Poynter and Leighton as aestheticians: the ten lectures and addresses', *Journal of Pre-Raphaelite and Aesthetic Studies*, 2/1 (1989), 108–20 • A. Smith, *The Victorian nude: sexuality, morality and art* (1996) • W. Gaunt, 'A set of drawings by Sir Edward Poynter', *The Connoisseur*, 153 (1963), 16–20 • R. P. Asleson, 'Classic into modern: the inspiration of antiquity in English painting, 1864–1918', PhD diss., 2 vols., Yale U., 1993 • H. Smith, *Decorative painting in the domestic interior in England and Wales, c.1850–1890* (1984) • M. Liversidge and C. Edwards, eds., *Imagining Rome: British artists and Rome in the nineteenth century* (1996) • *The Times* (28 July 1919) • *The Times* (31 July 1919) • *Morning Post* (28 July 1919) • C. Arscott, 'Poynter and the arty', *After the Pre-Raphaelites: art and aestheticism in Victorian England*, ed. E. Prettejohn (1999), 135–51 • B. Boucher, 'Lawrence Alma-Tadema, Edward Poynter and the redecoration of the Athenaeum Club', *Apollo*, 150 (Oct 1999) • A. S. Inglis, 'The decorative works of Sir Edward Poynter and their critical reception', PhD diss., 3 vols., University of Melbourne, 2000 • A. Smith, ed., *Exposed: the Victorian nude* (2001) • A. Inglis, 'Archaeology and empire: Edward Poynter's Visit of the queen of Sheba to King Solomon', *Melbourne Art Journal*, 5 (2001), 25–40 • J. Flanders, *A circle of sisters: Alice Kipling, Georgiana Burne-Jones, Agnes Poynter and Louisa Baldwin* (2001)

Archives Hunt. L., letters · National Gallery, London, MSS, papers, corresp. · RA, MSS, papers, corresp. · Tate collection, MSS, papers, corresp. · V&A, MSS, papers, corresp. | BL, letters to Sir A. H. Layard, Add. MSS 38994–39100, *passim* · Bodl. Oxf., corresp. with Sir William Harcourt and Lewis Harcourt · Castle Howard, North Yorkshire, letters to ninth earl of Carlisle · JRL, letters to M. H. Spielmann · PRO, MSS of Department of Science and Art and Board of Education · PRO, MSS of Office of Works · PRO, Royal Mint records · Sheff. Arch., letters to Lord Wharncliffe · U. Birm. L., letters to M. H. Spielmann · U. Glas., Whistler MSS · V&A NAL, Cole MSS · V&A NAL, letters relating to the Royal Academy winter exhibition of works by Anthony Van Dyck · V&A NAL, letters to Sir I. Spielmann · Worcs. RO, Baldwin MSS

Likenesses A. Legros, etching, *c.*1877, BM, NPG; repro. in *The portfolio*, 8 (1877), 12 · Lock & Whitfield, woodburytype, 1880, NPG; repro. in T. Cooper, *Men of mark: a gallery of contemporary portraits* (1880) · J. P. Mayall, photograph, 1882, NPG; repro. in F. G. Stephens, *Artists at home* (1884) · E. J. Poynter, self-portrait, oils, 1882, Aberdeen Art Gallery, Aberdeen · E. J. Poynter, self-portrait, oils, exh. RA 1888, Uffizi, Florence · R. W. Robinson, photograph, pubd 1891, NPG; repro. in *Members and associates of the Royal Academy of Arts, 1891* [*see illus.*] · Spy [L. Ward], chromolithograph caricature, 1897, NPG; repro. in *VF* (4 March 1897), 153 · H. Herkomer, group portrait, oils, 1908 (*The council of the Royal Academy*), Tate collection · P. Burne-Jones, oils, 1909, NPG · A. S. Cope, oils, 1911, RA · S. Lucas, oils, 1911, RA · H. J. Brooks, group portrait, oils (*Private view of the Old Masters Exhibition, Royal Academy, 1888*), NPG · Elliott & Fry, cabinet, NPG · J. Russell & Sons, photograph, NPG · W. Stoneman, photograph, NPG · J. Watkins, photograph, NPG

Wealth at death £20,608 13s. 2d.: probate, 5 Sept 1919, *CGPLA Eng. & Wales*

Poynter, Frederick Noël Lawrence (1908–1979), librarian and medical historian (known as Noël to family and friends), was born in London on 24 December 1908, the seventh of nine children of Herbert William Poynter and his wife, Margaret, *née* Gurry (1875/6–1924), originally from Cork. His father, employed in the London docks, was the son of a draper in Wareham and had served in the merchant navy before his marriage. His mother, a firm believer in self-improvement, was the driving force of the family. Poynter later reacted strongly against his early Roman Catholic upbringing. He was educated at West Ham secondary school and, from 1927 to 1929, studied history at King's College, London. After a spell of preparatory school teaching he joined the Wellcome Historical Medical Library as a junior assistant in November 1930 and participated in the final phase of Sir Henry Wellcome's omnivorous collecting, sometimes representing the library in the salerooms. The library was closed to readers and housed in congested conditions in a former wireless factory near Willesden Junction, in north-west London. Poynter's enthusiasm and efficiency quickly gained him the esteem of the librarian, the scholarly and reclusive S. A. J. Moorat; he resumed work for his degree and in 1936 took the London University diploma in librarianship. On completing his BA in 1938 he was promoted to sublibrarian, and in the following year he married (Kate L.) Ruth Marder (*d.* 1966), a sculptor. They had no children.

The outbreak of war brought the Viennese historian Max Neuburger to the Wellcome staff; he proved a significant influence on Poynter's development into a historian. In 1941 space was allocated to the library in the Wellcome building in London, in the Euston Road, and Poynter had started to organize the transfer of books before being conscripted into the RAF educational branch. While absent he completed his professional qualifications by becoming a fellow of the Library Association, in 1942. On his release early in 1946 he found that Moorat was about to take early retirement (though he continued to serve the library until 1973 as honorary keeper of western manuscripts) and was to be succeeded by W. J. Bishop from the Royal Society of Medicine. Poynter was promoted to deputy librarian and developed a successful partnership with Bishop. After the library's formal opening, in December 1949, they worked hard to develop its services and to attract readers, as well as raising its profile through the medical section of the Library Association. Both took a leading part in organizing the first International Congress on Medical Librarianship, in 1953, and Poynter edited the proceedings, which were published the following year. They were also active in research in medical history and bibliography. However, the Wellcome pharmaceutical company had suffered a financial crisis in 1948 and throughout the 1950s the library was hampered by shortage of funding and space. Makeshift fittings installed in 1945 remained for many years. There was also friction between the library and its parent body, the Wellcome Historical Medical Museum, and its director, Dr E. Ashworth Underwood. Bishop resigned in frustration at the end of 1953, to make a career as a writer, and Poynter succeeded as librarian.

One of Poynter's first acts was to found in 1954 *Current Work in the History of Medicine*, a quarterly bibliography of recent publications, and in the same year he published a catalogue of the library's incunabula. He was steadily consolidating his position as a medical historian, specializing particularly in the sixteenth and seventeenth centuries. In 1956 he was awarded a PhD from Westfield College, London, for a bibliography of Gervase Markham; it was published in book form in 1963. Other publications included: *Selected Writings of William Clowes* (1948); *A Seventeenth-Century Doctor and his Patients* (with Bishop, 1951), based on the casebooks of John Symcotts; a translation of William Harvey's *Lectures on the Whole of Anatomy* (with C. D. O'Malley and K. F. Russell, 1961); and *The Journal of James Yonge, Plymouth Surgeon* (1963). Nicholas Culpeper was another long-standing interest. For younger readers Poynter produced *A Short History of Medicine* (with K. D. Keele, 1961).

In 1958 Poynter was involved in the foundation of the faculty of the history of medicine and pharmacy of the Society of Apothecaries; he served as secretary, edited the proceedings of the faculty's annual conferences, and became chairman in 1970. The faculty's success led to the foundation of the British Society for the History of Medicine in 1965. In 1961, on Bishop's death, Poynter succeeded him as editor of *Medical History*, the first British journal devoted exclusively to the subject.

Prospects for the library improved in 1961 when it and the museum were taken over by the Wellcome Trust, the research charity set up under Sir Henry Wellcome's will. The library became independent of the museum, Poynter was designated chief librarian, and in 1962 the library was elegantly refurbished, so that it at last had a worthy setting. The same year saw the publication of the first volume of the library's *Catalogue of Printed Books* up to 1640, under Poynter's editorship. In 1964 Poynter succeeded Underwood as director of the museum and was able to initiate a programme of revitalization and expansion, weeding out irrelevant material and planning new displays. In 1968 the academic status of the museum and library was underlined by the adoption of the title Wellcome Institute of the History of Medicine. The institute's pivotal position in its field was very much Poynter's achievement. He was capable of great charm and had a gift for stimulating productive discussion and research. He was elected to numerous national and international societies, serving as president of both the International Academy of the History of Medicine (1970–73) and of the British Society for the History of Medicine (1971–3), and was much in demand as a lecturer. He was awarded the honorary degrees of DLitt from the University of California in 1967 and MD from the University of Kiel in 1968.

Poynter reached the climax of his career in September 1972 when he presided over the 23rd International Congress of the History of Medicine. However, his final months before retirement were clouded with disappointment when negotiations were initiated to transfer the Wellcome Museum (though not the library) to the Science Museum. With hindsight it can be seen that his work had highlighted the scale of support needed to maintain the standards he had set, which at that time would have strained the resources of the Wellcome Trust. Poynter retired to France in September 1973, restoring a house in the Dordogne valley. His wife Ruth had died in 1966, but he found happiness in his second marriage, in 1968, to Dodie Barry, *née* McClellan. He died at Brive, Corrèze, after a short illness, on 12 March 1979. He did not live to complete his various research projects, including studies of Culpeper and of medicine in Tudor England, nor to see the successful reopening of the Wellcome Museum in its new home in 1981. His name is perpetuated by the Poynter memorial lecture of the British Society for the History of Medicine, and by the Poynter Room, the Wellcome Library's special collections reading room.

JOHN SYMONS

Sources personal knowledge (2004) · private information (2004) · Wellcome Library records, Wellcome L. · *Medical History*, 23 (1979), 352–4 · *Journal of the History of Medicine and Allied Sciences*, 34 (1979), 463–5 · *Archives Internationales d'Histoire des Sciences*, 32 (1982), 99–100 · *Clio Medica*, 14 (1979), 1–3; 5–6 · *Bulletin of the History of Medicine*, 53 (1979), 140 · L. G. Stevenson, 'Retirement of F. N. L. Poynter', *Bulletin of the History of Medicine*, 47 (1973), 205–6 · W. F. Bynum, *Gesnerus*, 37 (1980), 145–6
Archives Wellcome L., administrative MSS, corresp., etc |SOUND Wellcome L.
Likenesses R. Poynter, bust, priv. coll. · photographs, Wellcome L.

Poynter, John (1600–1684), clergyman and ejected minister, was apparently born in London of an armigerous family. According to Edmund Calamy, 'his mother devoted him to the ministry from the womb' (*Nonconformist's Memorial*, 1.216), for 'she promised to bring him up to be a preacher of God's Word, if he proved fit for it and inclined to it' (Calamy, *Continuation*, 1.102). When she died in 1608 Poynter was taken by his brother-in-law, William Hancock, a mercer of Coventry, to that city to enter the grammar school there. Poynter matriculated at Brasenose College, Oxford, on 28 March 1617 and graduated BA on 2 July 1618. Instead of pursuing an MA degree, he left Oxford to board with the venerable nonconformist John Dod, at Canons Ashby, Northamptonshire. When less than a year later Timothy Dod, John's son, left his father's house to study with William Ames at Leiden, Poynter accompanied him and remained about a year until illness forced him to return to England.

Poynter was ordained deacon in London and priest in Lichfield in December 1625, and shortly after became lecturer at St Mildred, Bread Street, London, where he preached twice on Sundays. At the time of William Laud's first episcopal visitation in 1628 Poynter was ordered to produce his preaching licence, if indeed he had one, and to clarify whether he was curate or lecturer to St Mildred's, at which point owing to the opposition of the incumbent he appears to have quitted the lectureship. He returned to Hanwell, Oxfordshire (from which living John Dod had been suspended in 1604), from which he was called in 1630 to a lectureship at Wootton Wawen, Warwickshire, where he remained two years. Again forced out, he went to Hornton, near Hanwell, where the presence of fevers led him to move with his wife and three children to Warwick, where he is recorded as having preached.

On advice from his father (who was apparently a member of the London Mercers' Company), Poynter then competed with eight other candidates for the vacant lectureship at Huntingdon, recently endowed by Richard Fishborne, and was elected on 12 August 1634. Four years later, on 8 May 1638, Poynter appeared before the Mercers' court to announce that he had been suspended from preaching by the archbishop's visitor, and, while the Mercers attempted to obtain his restoration, Poynter resigned from the lectureship on 1 November 1639. However, on 10 February 1641 Oliver Cromwell and William Spurstow appeared from the House of Commons committee for religion to request that Poynter be continued in his lectureship, to which the company readily agreed, and, barring the interruption occasioned by the civil war, Poynter remained there until 1645.

Although Poynter apparently did not take the covenant and took no part in the ecclesiastical controversies of those years, he had no hesitation in finally accepting a cure and on 4 April 1646 became vicar of the sequestered living of Bures, Suffolk, where he remained until recurrent fevers led him to surrender the living in 1653. The following year he was appointed assistant to the Hertfordshire commission and on 13 October presented to the rectory of Houghton Conquest, Bedfordshire, by Cromwell. In 1655 Cromwell presented him to a vacant canonry at Christ Church, Oxford, on condition that he 'promise that he would take as much pains in his ministry, as he had done at Huntingdon, which promise he fulfilled' (Calamy,

Continuation, 1.103–4), preaching regularly at Christ Church, St Thomas's, and Great St Mary's as well as in surrounding parishes.

In 1660 Poynter resigned the canonry and is reported never to have preached again. Although Calamy claimed that he was very studious, he apparently published nothing. He lived on in his house in New Inn Hall Lane, Oxford, until his death on 2 January 1684. In his will of 21 September 1683 he left property in Oxfordshire and Warwickshire to his three sons, Theophilus, John the younger, and Timothy, and made gifts to his married daughter Johanna Farrall; Poynter's wife, whose name is unknown, had evidently predeceased him and is not mentioned. A pious puritan to the end, Poynter:

> beseech[ed] my said sons upon my knees by all endearing mercies of God and merits of Jesus Christ to fear and obey God and keep his sabbaths and get to hear his word preached and sacraments administered constantly and read the sacred Scriptures and pray in their families morning and evening … and labour to be rooted and built up in Jesus Christ and to live in charity. (PRO, PROB 11/375/33)

His last thought, however, was for 'poor Timothy, my loving and afflicted son', whom he asked Theophilus and John to counsel and help. P. S. SEAVER

Sources E. Calamy, *A continuation of the account of the ministers … who were ejected and silenced after the Restoration in 1660*, 2 vols. (1727) • *The nonconformist's memorial … originally written by … Edmund Calamy*, ed. S. Palmer, [3rd edn], 3 vols. (1802–3) • *Calamy rev.* • acts of court, Mercers' Hall, London, 1631–7, 1637–41, 1641–5 • Foster, *Alum. Oxon.* • Wood, *Ath. Oxon.: Fasti*, new edn • will, PRO, PROB 11/375/33

Wealth at death lands in Oxfordshire and Warwickshire plus small bequests: will, PRO, PROB 11/375/33

Poynter, William (1762–1827), Roman Catholic bishop and vicar apostolic of the London district, was born at Petersfield, Hampshire, on 20 May 1762, the son of John Poynter, a coachmaker and his wife, Mary, *née* Todd; he was baptized a Catholic on 24 May. Educated initially at Petersfield grammar school, he entered the English College at Douai on 3 August 1775. He was ordained a priest in 1786 and took the degree of DD, becoming prefect of studies at the college. In 1793 he and the other seminarians were moved by the French revolutionary authorities to the castle of Dourlens, and then held prisoner in the Irish College at Douai. These adventures were afterwards recounted by Poynter in the *Catholic Magazine and Review* (1831). On 25 February 1795 the seminarians were sent to England, where they landed on 2 March.

Upon his return to England, Poynter was nominated by Bishop Douglass to be vice-president of Old Hall Green College, near Ware in Hertfordshire. When Dr Gregory Stapleton was made vicar apostolic of the midland district, Poynter became president of Old Hall Green College (March 1801) and afterwards served as Stapleton's vicar-general. On 3 March 1803 he was appointed coadjutor to Dr John Douglass, vicar apostolic of the London district, by a papal brief; he was consecrated bishop of Halia *in partibus* at Old Hall Green College on 29 May. When Douglass died, on 8 May 1812, Poynter also succeeded to the vicariate *per coadjutoriam*.

Poynter's fluency in French, knowledge of Italian, training in theology and canon law, and love of scholastic disputation well prepared him for the theological and political debates then plaguing the English Catholic community. A 'man of polished manners, and proverbial coolness and moderation' (Ward, *Eve of Catholic Emancipation*, 1.28), his refined style and subtle distinctions contrasted sharply with the rancorous activities and quick judgements of the vicar apostolic of the midland district, Bishop John Milner. The two clashed repeatedly when Poynter counselled Douglass to take a moderate and canonically precise approach to the London-exiled French clergy who criticized the papacy's 1801 concordat with Napoleon.

Poynter consistently tried to mediate between the leading Catholic laymen, who were willing to grant some political securities to the government in exchange for Catholic emancipation, and Milner and the Irish bishops, who would accept no compromises. His struggle to interpret the political and theological issues of the day in an orthodox yet open manner may be seen in his published controversy with the Irish radical priest Charles O'Conor (*A Theological Examination of the Doctrine of Columbanus*, 1811) and the large collection of unpublished letters and comments on parliamentary petitions held in the archives of the archbishop of Westminster. When Milner accused him of schismatic tendencies and publicly attacked the other vicars apostolic, Poynter composed his 'Apologetical epistle' to Cardinal Litta, prefect of the propaganda, dated 15 March 1815. The document was not intended to be made public, but was translated and printed, without his knowledge, by Charles Butler, who published it in 1820 as part of his *Historical Memoirs of the English Catholics* (vol. 4, appx, n. 1). In addition to his annual publications in the *Laity's Directory* (1813–28) and numerous pastoral addresses, from 1813 Poynter worked actively with the leading laity in the Catholic Bible Society to publish a popular stereotyped edition of the New Testament, for which he wrote a preface in 1815. Although Milner vigorously objected, this work was never condemned in Rome.

In 1823 the Holy See appointed Dr James Yorke Bramston as Poynter's coadjutor, *cum jure successionis*. Along with other English and Scottish Catholic prelates, Poynter issued the famous *Declaration of the Catholic Bishops, the Vicars Apostolic, and their Coadjutors in Great Britain* (1826). He died in Castle Street, Holborn, London, on 26 November 1827, and was buried first (on 11 December 1827) in the church of St Mary Moorfields, London, where a monument was erected to his memory, and then at Old Hall Green, near Ware (1903). His funeral sermon, which was preached by the Revd Lewis Havard, was printed. In addition to Poynter's occasional contributions to Catholic magazines, he was also responsible for putting together *The Catholic Soldier's and Sailor's Prayer Book* (repr. 1858). J. P. CHINNICI

Sources B. N. Ward, *The eve of Catholic emancipation*, 3 vols. (1911–12) • B. Ward, *The dawn of the Catholic revival in England, 1781–1803*, 2 vols. (1909) • G. Anstruther, *The seminary priests*, 4 (1977) • C. Butler, *Historical memoirs of the English, Irish, and Scottish Catholics since the*

Reformation, 3rd edn, 4 (1822), 379, 469–523 · Gillow, *Lit. biog. hist.* · J. Connell, *The Roman Catholic Church in England, 1780–1850* (1984) · J. Hodgson and W. Poynter, 'Narrative of the seizure of Douay College', *Catholic Magazine and Review*, 1 (1831), 1–8, 397, 457 · *GM*, 1st ser., 97/2 (1827), 571

Archives Ushaw College, Durham, corresp. relating to Ushaw College · Venerable English College, Rome, archives · Westm. DA, corresp. and papers · Westm. DA, corresp. and papers relating to St Edmund's College | Archivio Vaticano, Vatican City, archives of Propaganda Fide · Old Hall Green College archives, Ware, Hertfordshire · Ushaw College, Durham, letters to E. Winstanley · Westm. DA, corresp. with Bishop Douglass

Likenesses H. Meyer, stipple, pubd 1818 (after J. Ramsay), BM · R. Fenner, engraving (after an unknown portrait), repro. in *Catholic Miscellany*, 4 (1825), frontispiece · J. Ramsay, oils, Old Hall Green College, Ware; repro. in Ward, *The eve of Catholic emancipation*, vol. 2, frontispiece · stipple, NPG

Wealth at death £450: will, 1827, Anstruther, *Seminary priests*

Poynting, John Henry (1852–1914), physicist, the youngest son of Thomas Elford Poynting, Unitarian minister at Monton, near Manchester, and his wife, Elizabeth Long, of Bath, was born at Slack Lane, Monton, on 9 September 1852. He received his early education at the school kept by his father, and then went in 1867 to Owens College, Manchester. He took the BSc degree of London University in 1872. In the same year he gained an entrance scholarship at Trinity College, Cambridge, and entered in October. In 1876 he graduated third wrangler in the mathematical tripos and returned to Owens College as demonstrator in the physical laboratory under Balfour Stewart.

Elected a fellow of Trinity College in 1878, under James Clerk Maxwell in the Cavendish Laboratory, Poynting began experiments on the mean density of the earth, which occupied much of his time for the next ten years. In the next two years he also published work on the use of balances, the sonometer, the saccharimeter, and on the change of state from solid to liquid. Those articles advanced the understanding of both the physics and mathematics of those areas. He remained at Cambridge until 1880, when he was elected to the chair of physics in the new Mason College, later the University of Birmingham, a post he held until his death. There he developed his interests in improving scientific instruments, and later supervised the construction of new physical laboratories.

Poynting married on 9 June 1880, Maria Adney (b. 1857/8), daughter of John Cropper, a Unitarian minister, of Stand, near Manchester. They had one son and two daughters. In 1887 Poynting received the ScD of Cambridge, continued to act as an examiner for that university, and won their Adams prize in 1893 and the Hopkins prize in 1903. In 1888 he was elected a fellow of the Royal Society. He was president of section A of the British Association in 1899, of the Physical Society in 1905, and in 1907 was a founder of the National Physical Laboratory. In 1905 he received a royal medal from the Royal Society 'for his researches in physical science, especially in connexion with the constant of gravitation and the theories of electrodynamics and radiation'. He was a vice-president of the Royal Society in 1910–11.

Poynting's most important contributions to physics were two papers communicated to the Royal Society: 'On the transfer of energy in the electromagnetic field' (*PTRS*, 1884) and 'On the connexion between electric currents and the electric and magnetic induction in the surrounding field' (*PTRS*, 1885). These papers revolutionized ideas about the motion of energy in the electric field. For example, it was previously supposed that when a charged Leyden jar was discharged by connecting the inside and outside by a wire, the energy travelled along the wire. Poynting's explanation was that the energy spread out from the glass between the coatings of the jar and then converged sideways into the wire, where it was converted into heat. He showed that there was a general law for the transfer of energy, according to which it moves at any point perpendicularly to the planes containing the direction of the electric and magnetic forces, and the amount crossing unit area per second is equal to the product of these forces multiplied by the sine of the angle between them and divided by 4π. The line which represents in direction and magnitude the flow of energy at any point is now known as the Poynting vector and is of fundamental importance in electromagnetic questions.

Poynting did work which was important at the time on the pressure of radiation. This helped to confirm earlier work by Maxwell, but was later more usually explained in terms of the quantum theory of radiation. Poynting established the existence of the tangential force produced when light is reflected from a surface at which there is some absorption, and the existence of a torque when light passes through a prism. He succeeded in demonstrating the recoil from light of a surface giving out radiation. These experiments, in which he was associated with William Henry Barlow, are a good example of Poynting's practical skill. He had exceptional mechanical ability and an excellent knowledge of the capabilities of instruments.

Throughout his life Poynting was engaged on researches connected with gravitation. As well as his early experimental work on determining the density of the earth, he investigated whether the gravitational attraction between two crystals depended on the orientation of their axes, and whether the attraction was affected by temperature. He also made important contributions to the theory of the change of state in matter (*Philosophical Magazine*, 1881) and to osmotic pressure (*Philosophical Magazine*, 1896). He took great interest in the philosophical basis of physics and chose this as the subject of his presidential address to section A of the British Association in 1899. There he argued for physicists to move away from a mechanical cause–effect view of scientific laws, and that the aim should be to reduce the number of laws. He used as examples the notions of corpuscle and wave as applied to light.

Poynting's *Collected Scientific Papers* was published by Cambridge University Press in 1920. In addition he wrote *On the Mean Density of the Earth* (Adams prize essay, 1893), *The Pressure of Light* (1910), *The Earth* (1913), and, in conjunction with J. J. Thomson, a series of textbooks on physics. Poynting was very successful as a teacher, and his sound judgement and conspicuous fairness and courtesy were of great service to the University of Birmingham. He became dean of the science faculty when Mason College was made the University of Birmingham, and held the office for twelve years.

Poynting suffered from diabetes for twenty years. To improve matters he lived for some time at a small farm in Alvechurch in Worcestershire where he pursued his interests in farming and natural history. He was for some time chairman of the Birmingham Horticultural Society. He died of diabetes at his home, 10 Ampton Road, Edgbaston, Birmingham, on 30 March 1914. He was survived by his wife.   J. J. THOMSON, *rev.* GRAHAM I. BIRLEY

Sources O. J. Lodge, *Nature*, 93 (1914), 138 · J. L. [J. Larmor], 'John Henry Poynting', *London, Edinburgh, and Dublin Philosophical Magazine*, 6th ser., 27 (1914), 914–16 · J. J. T. [J. J. Thomson], *PRS*, 92A (1916), i-ix, esp. ii · *DSB* · *Report of the British Association for the Advancement of Science* (1899) · *Report of the British Association for the Advancement of Science* (1913) · J. H. Poynting, 'Presidential address to section A, mathematical and physical science', *Report of the British Association for the Advancement of Science* (1899), Transactions, 615–24 · E. Hecht and A. Zajac, *Optics* (1974) · F. K. Richtmyer, E. H. Kennard, and T. Lauritsen, *Introduction to modern physics* (1955) · Lord Rayleigh [J. W. Strutt], *Theory of sound*, 1 and 2 (1896) · J. H. Poynting, 'On the graduation of the sonometer', *London, Edinburgh, and Dublin Philosophical Magazine*, 5th ser., 9 (1880), 59–64 · J. H. Poynting, 'On the change of state: solid–liquid', *London, Edinburgh, and Dublin Philosophical Magazine*, 5th ser., 12 (1881), 32–48 · b. cert. · m. cert. · d. cert.

Archives U. Birm. L., family and personal papers | Trinity Cam., corresp. with Sir Joseph John Thomson · UCL, corresp. with Sir Oliver Lodge

Likenesses portrait, repro. in J. J. T., *PRS*

Wealth at death £1206 14s. 11d.: probate, 24 July 1914, *CGPLA Eng. & Wales*

Poynton, **Sir Arthur Hilton** (1905–1996), civil servant, was born on 20 April 1905 at 3 Fyfield Road, Oxford, the younger son in the family of two sons and three daughters of Arthur Blackburne Poynton (1867–1944), fellow of University College, Oxford, and his wife, Mary, daughter of J. Y. Sargent, fellow of Magdalen and Hertford colleges. His father was a distinguished classicist, curator of the Bodleian Library (1912–37), and master of University College (1935–7). Poynton's elder brother, John Blackburne Poynton (1900–1995), was also a gifted classical scholar, but chose to be a schoolmaster at Winchester College in preference to an Oxford career.

Poynton was educated at Marlborough College and Brasenose College, Oxford, where he obtained a first in classical moderations (1925) and a second in *literae humaniores* (1927). He joined the civil service in 1927, spent two years at the Department of Scientific and Industrial Research, and moved to the Colonial Office in 1929, his professional home for most of the next three and half decades. He was seconded to Sierra Leone in 1933–4 and to the Dominions Office for a short period in 1935. Between 1941 and 1943 he was on loan as a private secretary, first to Lord Beaverbrook, the minister of supply, and then to Oliver Lyttelton, the minister of production. On his return to the Colonial Office in 1943, he became an assistant secretary and head of its defence department. He was promoted assistant under-secretary of state in 1946. As deputy

under-secretary of state between 1948 and 1959 he had overall responsibility for the economic division of the Colonial Office. In 1959 he became permanent under-secretary of state, a post that he held until his retirement in August 1966. He was appointed CMG in 1946, KCMG in 1949, and GCMG in 1964. On 12 July 1946 he married Elisabeth Joan (*b.* 1915/16), daughter of the Revd Edmund Williams, Congregational minister, of Exmouth; they had three children, John (*b.* 1947), Christopher (*b.* 1949), and Elisabeth (*b.* 1954).

Poynton was the last head of an independent Colonial Office, the latter merging with the Commonwealth Relations Office to form the Commonwealth Office in 1966, before this department in turn merged with the Foreign Office in 1968 to create the Foreign and Commonwealth Office. At the beginning of his career colonial administration from London was concerned with good government, law and order, and sound finance. During and after the war the promotion of colonial development and welfare became another priority. By the end of his career—and especially during the 'wind of change' era of the early 1960s, when no fewer than eighteen territories (all but eight of them African) became independent—the work of the Colonial Office had become highly political. Poynton presided over this transition and indeed participated in it. He spent hours behind the scenes at Marlborough House conferences working on the details of independence constitutions. But it was not a climate that he particularly enjoyed: an old-fashioned and rather patrician administrator, he belonged to a different world.

Over the whole of his career Poynton left a mark in three areas. First, he was a dogged opponent of the notion that colonial powers should be internationally accountable. At San Francisco in 1945 he played a significant role in drafting those chapters of the United Nations (UN) charter that dealt with non-self-governing territories. His defence department at the Colonial Office had been assigned responsibility for post-war reconstruction in this area of policy, and the British intention at the time was to keep UN supervision at arm's length. As the international critics of colonialism gathered strength at the UN in the 1950s and 1960s, Britain found itself under attack. Poynton, however, stood firm. He observed in 1962 that what he objected to was not 'international scrutiny of affairs in our Colonies in all circumstances but international scrutiny prompted solely by the fact that the territories are Colonial' (Hyam and Louis, 2.347). His stand was not welcome to some on his own side. Sir Hugh Foot, the United Kingdom representative at the UN, complained that 'Poynton in particular seems obsessed by the need to resist any attempt by the people at the UN to interest themselves in British colonial affairs'. According to Foot, Poynton saw no need to work closely on such matters with the Americans or Commonwealth countries, and he regarded the new countries of Africa and Asia as 'irritating busybodies' (ibid., 2.339).

Poynton's second legacy concerned the future of the Colonial Office itself. As the number of territories for which it was responsible shrank, he was determined that the Colonial Office should not be reduced to what he described in 1963 as a 'rocks and islands Department' (Hyam and Louis, 1.338). He fought the Colonial Office corner, insisting at the time of the 1966 merger that his officials would have much to offer through their specialist expertise and advisory services.

Finally, at the end of his career Poynton devoted considerable time to the future of those very small colonial territories for which independence was ruled out because they were either too small or too poor and very often both. He would not countenance any abdication of Britain's responsibilities. In 1959 the Treasury and the Commonwealth Relations Office wanted for financial reasons to transfer the Pacific colonies to Australia and New Zealand. Poynton responded:'I don't mind "giving up" a territory in favour of another Commonwealth administration if that provides a more efficient administration & is what the people want. I *do* object to being asked to "give up" territories just because they are thought to be a nuisance to the Treasury or others!' (Hyam and Louis, 2.721).

Upon retirement Poynton served between 1968 and 1977 as the director of the overseas branch of St John Ambulance. He was also a governor of the London School of Hygiene and Tropical Medicine from 1965 to 1977. Always somewhat donnish in manner, he was able to pursue his lifelong interest in classical literature. Between 1967 and 1976 he was treasurer of the Society for the Promotion of Roman Studies. He died of bronchopneumonia and heart failure at Mayday Hospital, Croydon, on 24 February 1996. He was survived by his wife and their three children.

S. R. ASHTON

Sources R. Hyam and W. R. Louis, *The conservative government and the end of empire, 1957–1964*, 2 pts (2000) · S. R. Ashton and D. Killingray, eds., *The West Indies* (1999), ser. B/6 of British documents on the end of empire · D. Goldsworthy, *The conservative government and the end of empire, 1951–1957*, 3 pts (1994) · J. M. Brown and W. R. Louis, *The Oxford history of the British empire, 4: The twentieth century* (1999) · C. Jeffries, *The colonial office* (1965) · C. Jeffries, *Whitehall and the colonial service: an administrative memoir, 1939–1965* (1972) · *The Times* (8 March 1996) · *Daily Telegraph* (6 March 1996) · *WWW* · Burke, *Peerage* · b. cert. · m. cert. · d. cert.
Archives BLPES, interview · Bodl. RH, interview | PRO, Colonial Office records
Likenesses photograph, repro. in *Daily Telegraph* · photograph, repro. in *The Times*
Wealth at death £190,618: probate, 30 April 1996, *CGPLA Eng. & Wales*

Poyntz, Sir Anthony (*c.*1480–1532/3), naval commander, was the eldest son of Sir Robert *Poyntz (*b.* late 1440s, *d.* 1520) and Margaret, the illegitimate daughter of Anthony *Woodville, second Earl Rivers. He was descended from a cadet branch of the family based at Iron Acton in Gloucestershire since the early fourteenth century. Poyntz served Henry VIII as a naval officer and played a minor part in Wolsey's ceremonial diplomacy between 1518 and 1521. In 1513 he commissioned and led a small flotilla of ships from Bristol as part of the fleet in Edward Howard's ill-fortuned expedition against Brittany. He was

knighted the same year. Nine years later, as captain of the *Santa Maria*, he joined the force led by Howard's brother, the earl of Surrey, on another raid against the Breton coast and participated in the small but bloody battle of Morlaix. In 1523 he was given the *ad hoc* title of vice-admiral, and between April and September was entrusted with the task of intercepting the duke of Albany should he attempt to bring French support to Scotland. That Albany succeeded in transporting 5000 soldiers via the Irish Channel was largely the responsibility of the admiral, Sir William Fitzwilliam, who denuded the western seas by leading a fruitless raid against Tréport.

Poyntz's diplomatic duties were purely ceremonial. He took part in the festivities arranged to celebrate the peace of London in November 1518, although he was not included in the embassy subsequently dispatched to France. He was also among Henry's entourage at his meetings with François I at the Field of Cloth of Gold and the emperor Charles V at Gravelines, both held in July 1520. The few records remaining that detail Poyntz's administrative and judicial activities are no doubt a poor reflection of the responsibilities that as a leading member of the gentry he almost certainly undertook. In May 1521 he sat on the jury at Bristol that indicted the duke of Buckingham. He was appointed sheriff of Gloucestershire in 1527 and in 1530 was part of the commission appointed to inquire into Wolsey's possessions. He married twice: first, before 1510, Elizabeth, daughter of Sir William Huddesfield of Shillingford, Devon, with whom he had a son and heir, Nicholas; and second, by April 1527, Joan, widow of Sir Richard Guildford. He died between September 1532 and February 1533.

LUKE MACMAHON

Sources LP Henry VIII · J. Maclean, *Historical and genealogical memoir of the family of Poyntz* (1886) · J. G. Nichols, ed., *The chronicles of Calais* (1846) · *Hall's chronicle*, ed. H. Ellis (1809) · D. Starkey, ed., *Henry VIII: a European court in England* (1991) · G. Walker, 'The "expulsion of the minions" of 1519 reconsidered', *HJ*, 32 (1989), 1–16 · D. M. Loades, *The Tudor navy* (1992)

Poyntz, Charles (1734/5–1809), Church of England clergyman, was baptized in July 1735, the second son of Stephen *Poyntz (*bap.* 1685, *d.* 1750) and his wife, Anna Maria Mordaunt (*d.* 1771). (Margaret) Georgiana *Spencer (1737–1814) was his sister. The godson of Princess Amelia, as a child Poyntz moved in royal circles; his father was governor to the duke of Cumberland, his mother had been maid of honour to Queen Caroline. With his elder brother, William, he was sent abroad, on Cumberland's bidding, to complete his education after the death of their father. Poyntz matriculated at Christ Church, Oxford, on 13 December 1752, aged seventeen; he graduated BA in 1756, and proceeded MA in 1759 and DD in 1769. Though from a whig family, while at university he entered the circle of high-churchmen such as Samuel Glasse, George Horne, and William Jones, who were slightly older than himself. Their influence left an enduring impress on his churchmanship. Poyntz took holy orders and his friend George Horne wrote for him 'A Letter to a Young Gentleman Just

Admitted into Holy Orders', dated 9 October 1759. As a charming and personable young man, the scion of a well-connected family, Poyntz might have expected to go far in his chosen career. As his mother put it in the early 1760s: 'If there was a Bishop of Hereford, and the Town could choose him, Charles would be the man, for he is adored here' (Maclean, 214). But Charles Poyntz was not chosen. His maturity coincided with the demise of Pelhamite power and he was left with patrons unable to help him.

Poyntz lived as a country parson all his adult life. He was named rector of North Creake, Norfolk, in 1760 and remained in post until his death, nearly half a century later. He was conscientious in his duties, for instance trying to hold monthly communion services for the people of North Creake, preaching occasionally in Norwich Cathedral, taking private pupils (such as Lord Duncannon in 1779), planting trees and walks on his glebe lands, and corresponding with friends. Though he was the brother of the first Countess Spencer, Poyntz was never able to obtain much in the patronage stakes beyond prebendal stalls at Llandaff (1769) and at Durham (1784). He preached in Oxford at the invitation of the vice-chancellor (George Horne) in 1780, and there was talk of his name going forward for the deanery of Worcester, which fell vacant while his political allies of the Fox–North coalition held office in 1783, but nothing came of it; had the whigs taken power in 1788–9, during the regency crisis, and had the second Earl Spencer gone to Dublin as lord lieutenant, Poyntz would have been favourite as chaplain. That scheme, too, was a non-starter. A lucrative additional promotion, to alleviate his troubled financial affairs, was his constant hope, but he obtained nothing further except occasional duties as one of the deputy clerks of the closet. He had taken on many of his mother's debts while chronically unable (like other members of his family) to handle money himself. Poyntz was a spendthrift, albeit a charitable one, and he invariably helped friends in financial need, such as George Berkeley, vice-dean of Canterbury. Periodically he took refuge abroad from his creditors. He passed the years 1800–07 on the continent, mainly in Göttingen, and died, unmarried, at the London house of his sister, the dowager Lady Spencer, on 10 May 1809. Despite the creation of a family trust his debts by that date were immense and Poyntz was begging his sister for ready money. On his death his executors were confronted with innumerable demands on his estate. He had once written, 'I am not that sad man the world suspects me to be' (Spencer MSS, E. 16), but though his friends knew other sides to him he could not dispel that overriding impression.

NIGEL ASTON

Sources Foster, *Alum. Oxon.* · H. L. Thompson, *The Poyntz family* (1879) · J. Maclean, *Historical and genealogical memoir of the family of Poyntz* (1886) · Walpole, *Corr.*, 2.208 · correspondence of Revd Charles Poyntz, BL, Spencer MSS · *The later correspondence of George III*, ed. A. Aspinall, 5 vols. (1962–70), vol. 4, p. 186
Archives BL, corresp. and papers | BL, Spencer MSS, accounts and papers at North Creake, E. 35 · BL, Spencer MSS, letters and papers of Georgiana, first Countess Spencer, F. 5, F. 175
Likenesses group portrait, drawing (with his siblings), priv. coll.

Wealth at death died in debt; estate bequeathed to sister: will, 8 July 1809, BL, Spencer MSS, E. 36; Maclean, *Historical and genealogical memoir*, 214

Poyntz, Sir Francis (*c*.1487–1528). *See under* Poyntz, Sir Robert (*b*. late 1440s, *d*. 1520).

Poyntz, John (*c*.1485–1544). *See under* Poyntz, Sir Robert (*b*. late 1440s, *d*. 1520).

Poyntz, John (*fl.* 1639–1665). *See under* Poyntz, John (1629/30–1712).

Poyntz, John (1629/30–1712), naval officer, travelled 'in the greatest part of the Caribee Islands and most parts of the Continent of America, and almost all his majesty's foreign plantations' (Poyntz, *Prospect*, sig. A2*v*) and was especially involved in proposals to settle the island of Tobago. Several men named John Poyntz were active in the Caribbean in the later seventeenth century, but this John Poyntz was probably the third son of Sydenham Poyntz's youngest brother, Newdigate (*bap*. 1608, *d*. 1643), a royalist killed at Gainsborough, and his first wife, Sarah, daughter of Francis Foxley, of Harringworth, Northamptonshire (*d*. 1636). If so, he was baptized at nearby Benefield on 3 January 1630 and married Alice (*d*. 1712), *née* Brown, of Dartford, Kent, probably died at Dartford, and was buried there on 12 August 1712. His wife has been buried three weeks earlier. Maclean, in his exhaustive history of the various branches of the Poyntz family (1886), makes no mention of any connection with Tobago, but the relevant calendars of colonial state papers were published only later (1898–1912).

In 1666 four English ships commanded by a Captain John Poyntz captured a Dutch settlement on Tobago. They left behind a small garrison, which was forced to surrender to a French party from Grenada, who then abandoned the island. In a much later memorial to the council of trade and plantations (17 November 1699) Poyntz claimed that he had made eleven voyages to Tobago (many from Barbados) up to 1680, on one of which (1678–9) the local 'emperor' (of Trinidad) had named his only son after him. On 20 September 1681 Poyntz, on behalf of a group of London merchants, signed a treaty with the agent in England of the duke of Courland, to whom Charles II had granted Tobago, for 120,000 acres on the island, on which liberty of conscience would be given to all save Catholics.

In 1683 Poyntz published *The Present Prospect of the Famous and Fertile Island of Tobago* (2nd edn, 1695), a very well informed survey of the climate, flora, fauna, and timber of the island, which included a recommendation for barracuda, with a helpful warning to beware of its teeth, and prospects for growing cocoa, sugar-cane, and tobacco. On 26 February he petitioned the king about the colours and standards he should use there. Poyntz later alleged that his grant had aroused the hostility of the duke of York, so that an order of the commissioners of the admiralty (15 December) stopped his ship, the *Fountain*, from sailing to Tobago from Gravesend; but it might have been held up pending negotiations for the treaty of Aix-la-Chapelle (1684). Several hundred settlers from Barbados had already moved to Tobago before the king blocked Poyntz's project; they were returned to Barbados. On 2 February 1686 Poyntz granted 1000 acres on Tobago to the antiquary John Aubrey as a reward for services he had done for Poyntz with the earls of Pembroke and Abingdon; among Aubrey's papers is a note that under William III Abingdon was to buy Poyntz's claim to Tobago.

The crown questioned the duke of Courland's claim to Tobago, given the many changes of possession and occupation it had seen. In answer to a further petition from Poyntz, the privy council declared (1686) that the king's grant of Tobago to the duke of Courland was void; a memorial from the Courland envoy in London (12 April 1687) also rejected the contract made with Poyntz. In his 1699 petition (2 May), which attempted to revive the scheme, Poyntz said he had considerably developed the planting and settling of Tobago, despite heavy losses during the recent war with France. Among the benefits he claimed would arise from his activities would be added security to the neighbouring English plantations in wartime, an increase in crown revenue and in the endowment of the recently constructed naval hospital at Greenwich. His settlement would also employ the poor and provide refuge for dispossessed French Huguenots.

Poyntz aimed to gain possession of the whole island and grant it to a charitable foundation for converting the Indians to Christianity and, in England, suppressing vice and debauchery, augmenting the salaries of indigent clergy and endowing a hospital in London for the blind poor. But the privy council declared that a free-port in Tobago would be prejudicial to the English colonies, especially Barbados, a line taken by the council of trade and plantations as early as 1686. In 1702 Poyntz made his final petition, but his claim to Tobago was conclusively rejected. In 1692–3 a Captain John Poyntz filed three patents: no. 320 of 1693 for the invention of engines to remove bars, sandbanks, mud, and other obstructions that stop up ports and harbours; no. 297 of 1692 for taking up ships sunk at sea; and no. 327 of 1693 for raising water to perform mill-work.

Another **John Poyntz** (*fl.* 1639–1665), also a naval officer, was recommended by Admiral Robert Blake, in the reorganization of the fleet early in 1653, for naval employment as a clerk of the cheque, on the basis of his fourteen years' service at sea—presumably all or mostly in the merchant service. Having been clerk of the cheque in the *Happy Entrance* (April 1653) and lieutenant of the *Dover* on William Penn's expedition to the West Indies (1654), he was lieutenant of the *Portland* in the West Indies (April 1655) and became captain of the fly-boat *Mary* (or *Mayfly*). He wrote to the council of state (15 November 1656) about settling planters from Nevis, St Kitts, and New England on Jamaica, and, on his return from the West Indies in March 1657, Poyntz certified (5 March) that, in the *Mayfly*, he had settled 1500 planters, including the governor of Nevis, around Port Morant, Jamaica. This activity suggests he may have been a kinsman of Sydenham Poyntz, who was governor of the Leeward Islands (1650–51) and, though he

effectively disappears from history at that date, was possibly a resident of Antigua in the 1650s and was mentioned as governor of Antigua as late as 1661–3. While captain of the *Providence* (April 1657), serving off Dunkirk and in the channel, he twice (15 February and 22 June 1658) wrote to the commissioners of the admiralty. From December 1658 to 1660 he was captain of the *Wakefield*.

After the Restoration William Coventry damned Poyntz as 'an enemy and plunderer' (Coventry MS 98, fol. 69) and he was dropped from the service. In the Second Anglo-Dutch War Poyntz was hired by the navy as captain of the merchant ship *Maryland* and wrote to Pepys (14 November 1664) asking for £18 expenses he had incurred in pressing 140 men into the *Maryland*. But Coventry described him as 'naught' (Coventry MS 99, fol. 92) and another captain was commanding the *Maryland* in 1665. He may have been the John Poyntz who wrote to Pepys from Dartmouth (8 February 1668), in a very assured style, undertaking to build a lighthouse and a castle on the Goodwin Sands, at his own expense, in return for ownership of the island and a levy on each ship to help maintain the light. There is a draft of a letter on this to the navy commissioners, in Pepys' shorthand, but no more seems to have been heard of the proposal.

BASIL MORGAN

Sources *CSP col.*, vols. 11–12, 17, 21 • J. Maclean, *Historical and genealogical memoir of the family of Poyntz* (1886) • *CSP dom.*, 1652–3; 1656–7; 1664–5; 1667–8 • G. Carmichael, *History of the West Indian Islands of Trinidad and Tobago* (1961) • *Aubrey's Brief lives*, ed. O. L. Dick (1962) • C. Hollis, *A brief history of Trinidad under the Spanish crown* (1941) • *DNB* • J. Poyntz, *The present prospect of the famous and fertile island of Tobago*, 2nd edn (1695)

Poyntz, Sir Nicholas (*b.* in or before **1510**, *d.* **1556**). *See under* Poyntz, Sir Robert (*b.* late 1440s, *d.* 1520).

Poyntz, Sir Robert (*b.* late **1440s**, *d.* **1520**), courtier and landowner, was the son of John Poyntz (*d.* 1465/6), landowner, of Iron Acton, Gloucestershire, and his wife, Alice Cocks, who came from a Bristol merchant family. While a minor his wardship and marriage were granted to Thomas Herbert of Little Troy in Herefordshire in reward for service to the Yorkist cause. A grant of wardship in 1467 indicates that Poyntz was born in the late 1440s. His prominence stemmed more from his marriage in 1479 to Margaret, an illegitimate daughter of Anthony *Woodville, second Earl Rivers (*c.*1440–1483), and Gwenllian. The couple had five sons, including Sir Anthony *Poyntz (*c.*1480–1532/3), John Poyntz [*see below*], and Sir Francis Poyntz [*see below*], and four daughters. His dependence on Rivers, Edward IV's brother-in-law, led to his advancement to local office in Hampshire, where Rivers held the lordship of the Isle of Wight, first as constable of Carisbroke Castle and then in 1482 as sheriff of the county.

Following Edward's unexpected death and the usurpation of Richard III in spring 1483, Poyntz was replaced as sheriff on the instructions of the new king. Whatever the nature of his involvement in Henry Stafford, second duke of Buckingham's rebellion, by which men hitherto adherents of the Yorkist regime expressed their disillusionment with Richard, he found it expedient to seek sanctuary at Beaulieu Abbey in Hampshire, and it was as 'of Beaulieu' that in 1484 he sued out a pardon. Poyntz seems not long after to have gone into exile, where he joined the group of English dissidents centring on Henry Tudor, second earl of Richmond, in Brittany. He was a member of Richmond's expeditionary force landing at Milford Haven in summer 1485, and for his valour at the battle of Bosworth he was knighted on the field by the new king. As a proven supporter of Henry VII, and particularly after the marriage in January 1486 of the king to *Elizabeth of York (1466–1503), one of his kinswomen, Poyntz belonged to the small circle of trusted men upon whom the Tudor dynasty relied in its formative years. Restored to the bulk of his offices, he took his place as a knight of the body at court while also assuming the role played by his forebears in Gloucestershire. In 1486 he entertained Henry and Elizabeth at Iron Acton while they were travelling to Bristol.

On the marriage of Arthur, prince of Wales, to Katherine of Aragon in 1504, Poyntz and his eldest son, Anthony Poyntz, obtained appointments in their household. Poyntz was successively vice-chamberlain and chancellor of the household to Katherine, remaining in her service until his death on 5 November 1520 when he was aged seventy or more. His last major appearance as a member of her entourage was early in 1520 at the Field of Cloth of Gold, where he received a gift of plate from François I. At least one other of his sons, John Poyntz, entered Katherine's service, being one of her sewers by 1520. A third son, Francis Poyntz, seems to have benefited from the enlightened educational system promoted by Katherine and to have had sufficient command of Latin to undertake, on his elder brother's suggestion, a translation of a text, then wrongly attributed to the Greek philosopher Cebes, on how a man should conduct his life. He could speak Spanish and French. Of Sir Robert Poyntz's own intellectual achievements there is only one clue, his employment in 1520 of the astronomer and maker of scientific instruments Nicholas Kratzner to provide a design for a sundial at Iron Acton. Poyntz's eldest son, Sir Anthony Poyntz, succeeded him. In turn, he was succeeded by his own heir, Sir Nicholas Poyntz [see below].

John Poyntz (c.1485–1544), courtier and landowner, was Sir Robert Poyntz's second son. He was returned to the parliament of 1529 as a representative of the Wiltshire borough of Marlborough, which belonged to Katherine as queen consort. He cut a figure in the parliament early in 1533 when he expressed reservations about the important bill in restraint of appeals to Rome. His alignment with other Aragonese supporters evidently did not harm his advancement to the Gloucestershire bench or his marriage prospects, which led to his acquisition of an estate in Surrey. His first marriage, by 1528, to Elizabeth (d. in or before 1544), daughter of Sir Matthew Browne of Betchworth in Surrey, linked him distantly with Sir Henry

*Guildford (1489–1532), comptroller of the royal household. The couple had four sons, including Matthew Poyntz (b. after 1528, d. 1605), and three daughters. On 1 May 1544 he made his marriage settlement with Margaret (d. in or after 1558), daughter of Nicholas Saunders of Charlwood, Surrey. They had no children. Poyntz's modern fame rests not on his political activity but on a surviving drawing of him by Hans Holbein the younger and an epistolary satire addressed to him by Sir Thomas Wyatt the elder, in which the poet extols the virtues of country living away from 'the press of courts'. He fought in the military campaign of 1544, which culminated in the capture of Boulogne. He died on 19 November 1544, either during the final stages of his service abroad or shortly after his return. His eldest son, Henry Poyntz, then aged sixteen, was unable to inherit because he was mentally handicapped, leading to Matthew Poyntz's recognition as heir. Another of his sons was the Roman Catholic theologian Robert *Poyntz (b. c.1535, d. in or after 1568).

Sir Francis Poyntz (c.1487–1528), diplomat, was Sir Robert Poyntz's third son. He followed his father to court, where by 1516 he was an esquire of the body to Henry VIII, rising in 1521 to be a carver. In 1526 the king granted him the manor of Holborn, Middlesex, during the minority of Edward Stanley, third earl of Derby, and some lands formerly in the possession of Edward Stafford, third duke of Buckingham. Like his oldest brother, Sir Anthony Poyntz, he was also employed in diplomacy. In 1527 the king sent him to Charles V with instructions to negotiate peace between France and the empire. As a mark of the trust shown in him, Henry knighted him. He had an audience with the emperor on 2 July, and although authorized to threaten war if Charles was unresponsive, he failed to persuade him of the reasonableness of his mission. Travelling back from Madrid he met François in Paris. He died of the plague in London on 26 January 1528, leaving as widow Joan, who was the sister of his brother John Poyntz's wife, Elizabeth: his marriage clearly had formed one of a series linking his family to the Guildfords. There were no children.

Sir Nicholas Poyntz (b. in or before 1510, d. 1556), courtier and landowner, was the eldest son of Sir Anthony Poyntz, naval commander, and his first wife, Elizabeth (d. in or before 1527), daughter of Sir William Huddesfield of Shillingford, Devon. On 24 June 1527 he married Joan (d. in or after 1556), daughter of Thomas Berkeley, de jure fifth Baron Berkeley. The couple had five or six sons, including Sir Nicholas Poyntz (c.1528–1585), and three daughters. The Berkeley family was staunchly Catholic and the connection strengthened Poyntz's local connections in Gloucestershire, but disputes arising out of which properties had been settled on his wife soured his dealings with her kin as well as with his neighbours. These disputes prompted an official investigation by the privy council in October 1541, together with a report on him by the king's council in the marches of Wales. Pending their outcome he was committed to the Fleet prison, but early in 1542 he was released on condition that he resided within 40 miles of London, only to be re-committed several months later. He was finally released following his wife's appearance to plead on his behalf. Although instructed to make amends over two of the properties concerned, he failed to do so, and the matter went to litigation during Edward VI's reign.

Nicholas Poyntz's career was an almost seamless continuation of his father's. In 1532 he accompanied Henry to Calais for the meeting with François. He was often at court, where by 1539 he had become a groom of the bedchamber. During the 1530s and 1540s he was present for the principal state occasions. He often saw active service on land and at sea. In 1534 he served in Ireland together with other Gloucestershire men, and in 1536 he was a member of the county contingent directed to help suppress the Pilgrimage of Grace. Notwithstanding his initial selection to join the military force sent to the Low Countries in 1543, he was appointed to the naval patrol protecting the Bristol Channel. During 1544 Poyntz saw both military and naval action against the Scots, and his prowess at Calais earned for him the praise of John Russell, Baron Russell. In 1549 he led forces against the western rebellion. His last appearance as a soldier seems to have been in 1554, when he helped to defend the Tower of London against Sir Thomas Wyatt the younger's supporters.

Poyntz seems to have been brought up in the reformist zeal shared by so many of his closest relatives, an aunt in 1522 engaging William Tyndale as tutor to her children. He was prominent among the group of evangelical sympathizers living in the Severn area. Poyntz endowed lectures at his parish church. He displayed his contempt for traditional religious observances by incorporating in several of his properties, including Ozleworth, Gloucestershire, stones from smashed crosses from churches. In August 1535 the king and Anne Boleyn visited him at Iron Acton as part of a progress intended to promote religious change. To accommodate them he erected a new wing which reflected the current Renaissance or 'antique' fashion at Whitehall Palace. It was sumptuously equipped with Italian maiolica and Venetian glass. He may have received his knighthood at the culmination of this visit. Poyntz was drawn by Holbein wearing a gold chain denoting his knighthood. His extravagant lifestyle far outstripped his income. He acquired property at the dissolution of the monasteries for £1000, but by 1546 he was forced to surrender part of his property to the crown in settlement of arrears. Poyntz nearly succumbed to his creditors. In October 1541 he was sent to the Fleet prison over a property dispute, and on his deathbed he owed his creditors £700. Poyntz was twice elected to parliament. While knight of the shire for Gloucestershire from 1547 he was imprisoned in the Tower during the winter of 1551–2 as a close adherent of Edward Seymour, duke of Somerset, and in December 1555, while MP for Cricklade, he voted with the opposition to defeat a major government bill penalizing religious exiles. Even so, during the succession crisis in 1553 he did not rally to the protestant Lady Jane Grey against the Catholic Mary Tudor. Poyntz was suspected of complicity in the Dudley conspiracy early in

1556, but his death on 27 or 28 November may have prevented any allegation against him from being investigated. He left some eight surviving children.

ALASDAIR HAWKYARD

Sources LP Henry VIII · GEC, Peerage · R. Horrox, Richard III: a study in service (1989) · HoP, Commons, 1386–1421 · HoP, Commons, 1509–58, 3.147–50 · J. Maclean and W. C. Heane, eds., The visitation of the county of Gloucester taken in the year 1623, Harleian Society, 21 (1885) · J. Gairdner, History of the life and reign of Richard the Third, rev. edn (1898) · C. Rawcliffe, The Staffords: earls of Stafford and dukes of Buckingham (1978) · D. R. Starkey, ed., Henry VIII: a European court in England (1991) · PRO, PROB 11/19, fols. 223r–227v · PRO, PROB 11/30, fols. 149r–151v · PRO, PROB 11/39, fols. 170r–172r · PRO, C142/35/8, 9; C142/70/27; C142/50/98; C142/107/51 · PRO, E315/239/24 · D. M. Loades, Two Tudor conspiracies (1965)
Archives Bristol, Gloucestershire, draft notes and artefacts from Iron Acton archaeological excavation
Likenesses H. Holbein, drawing (John Poyntz), repro. in S. Foister and others, Holbein and the court of Henry VIII, 87–8 [exhibition catalogue, Queen's Gallery, Buckingham Palace, 1978–9] · H. Holbein, drawing (Nicholas Poyntz), repro. in S. Foister and others, Holbein and the court of Henry VIII, 88–9 [exhibition catalogue, Queen's Gallery, Buckingham Palace, 1978–9]

Poyntz, Robert (b. c.1535, d. in or after 1568), Roman Catholic theologian, son of John *Poyntz (c.1485–1544) [see under Poyntz, Sir Robert] and his first wife, Elizabeth Browne (d. in or before 1544), was born at Alderley, Gloucestershire. He was educated at Winchester College and was admitted to New College, Oxford, as a perpetual fellow on 21 August 1554, graduating BA on 5 June 1556 and MA on 27 May 1560. A devout Roman Catholic, he left the country soon afterwards and settled at Louvain. There in 1566 he published his Testimonies for the real presence of Christ's body and blood in the blessed sacrament of the altar, a work that formed part of a concerted Catholic response to the sermon at Paul's Cross in 1559 in which John Jewel challenged his Catholic adversaries to produce evidence of the antiquity of the doctrine of transubstantiation. Poyntz's work consisted of relevant passages translated from the Latin fathers. In April 1568 Poyntz was preparing to go on pilgrimage to Jerusalem in the company of the Oxford doctor Richard Smith, the uncle of Richard Smith, later bishop of Chalcedon. In his will of 14 April 1568 Smith named Poyntz as his 'particular friend'. The date of Poyntz's death is unknown.   G. MARTIN MURPHY

Sources J. Maclean, Historical and genealogical memoir of the family of Poyntz (1886) · Foster, Alum. Oxon. · A. F. Allison and D. M. Rogers, eds., The contemporary printed literature of the English Counter-Reformation between 1558 and 1640, 2 (1994), 129, no. 649 · A. C. Southern, Elizabethan recusant prose, 1559–1582 (1950) · P. Milward, Religious controversies of the Elizabethan age (1977) · Munk, Roll, 1.67–8 · Bodl. Oxf., MS Rawl. D. 130, fol. 63 · will, PRO, PROB 11/52, sig. 11 [Richard Smith]

Poyntz, Sir Robert (bap. 1588, d. 1665), royalist writer, was born at Iron Acton, Gloucestershire, and baptized there on 26 October 1588, the first son and heir of Sir John Poyntz (c.1560–1633), later MP for Gloucestershire, and his second wife, Elizabeth Sydenham (d. 1595). On 14 June 1604 he married Frances Gibbons (d. 1638), and he matriculated at Brasenose College, Oxford, on 15 March 1605. In February 1626 he received the Order of the Bath at Charles I's coronation, and he was returned for Gloucestershire to the 1626 parliament. The following year he refused to pay the forced loan or to serve as a commissioner and was imprisoned, first in the Fleet in London, and then in Northamptonshire. He was released in time to sit once again for Gloucestershire in the parliament of 1628–9. He was not an active member, although he did draw the Commons' attention to one of Roger Manwaring's sermons in favour of the forced loan, and was appointed to a committee to draw up charges against him.

During the 1630s Poyntz became involved in a protracted chancery suit over his wife's inheritance and in May 1637 he was briefly imprisoned in the Fleet after insulting one of the judges, Sir Richard Hutton. Later that year he was appointed sheriff for Gloucestershire, but warned that opposition to ship money was such that if he had to 'committ all the refusers, and distraine all their chattell … there will not be found either prisons or pinfoldes enow in the country to receive them' (PRO, SP 16/386/88). Poyntz did not sit in either the Short or Long parliaments: in 1642 he became a royalist and was summoned before the Commons for refusing to act as a parliamentarian deputy lieutenant. He was at Bristol for part of the civil war, and in the spring of 1649 he compounded for £723 under the Bristol articles. His first wife had been buried on 12 March 1638, and by 1645 Poyntz had married his second wife, Cicely Smith (d. 1678).

In 1661, Poyntz published *A vindication of monarchy and the government long established in the church and kingdome of England*. This tract warned of 'the danger that cometh by the abuse of Parliaments' (p. 35) and argued that 'the best limited power … is regulated by the soundest, most perfect and equal lawes between the Prince and the people' (p. 143). He regarded 'unity in religion' as 'the chiefest pillar that upholdeth the joynt obedience of the subjects to their soveraign, and to the lawes' (p. 8). He insisted that 'no pretences whatsoever can be just ground of a Civil War or Rebellion' (p. 153), and argued that 'by innovations … the peace of the Church and Common-wealth [is] indangered, if not destroyed' (p. 4). Poyntz was buried at Iron Acton on 10 November 1665.   DAVID L. SMITH

Sources DNB · State Papers domestic, Charles I, PRO, SP 16 · M. A. E. Green, ed., *Calendar of the proceedings of the committee for advance of money, 1642–1656*, 3, PRO (1888), 1384 · M. A. E. Green, ed., *Calendar of the proceedings of the committee for compounding … 1643–1660*, 3, PRO (1891), 1942 · 'Poyntz, Sir Robert', HoP, *Commons, 1604–29* [draft] · R. Poyntz, *A vindication of monarchy and the government long established in the church and kingdome of England* (1661) · *JHC*, 1 (1547–1628) · *APC*, 1627–8 · R. C. Johnson and others, eds., *Proceedings in parliament, 1628*, 6 vols. (1977–83) · 'Extracts from parish registers, no. V: Iron Acton', *Gloucestershire Notes and Queries*, 3 (1887), 51–5 · J. Maclean, *Historical and genealogical memoir of the family of Poyntz* (1886) · J. J. Clarke, 'Poyntz, Sir John', HoP, *Commons, 1558–1603*
Wealth at death assessed at the rate of one sixth, at £723, in 1649, which suggests that his annual income was three times that figure, that is, roughly £2169: Green, ed., *Calendar of the proceedings of the committee for compounding*, 3 (1889), 1942

Poyntz, Stephen (*bap.* 1685, *d.* 1750), diplomatist and courtier, was born in Cornhill, London, and baptized in November 1685, the second son of William Poyntz, an upholsterer, and his second wife, Jane, the daughter of Stephen Monteage, a merchant of London and Buckingham. He was educated at Eton College and at King's College, Cambridge (1703–6). He served as a diplomat only between 1724 and 1730, yet his correspondence shows both judgement and ability and he enjoyed connections and respect without ever having great employments. Poyntz entered diplomacy through his early connection with Lord Townshend, first as tutor to Townshend's sons, from 1709, and then as his patron's private secretary. In 1712 he wrote, anonymously, a very long, informed, and closely reasoned book, *The Barrier-Treaty Vindicated*, strongly advocating strategic defence against France, popery, and the Pretender. In July 1716 he was made commissary to James, first Earl Stanhope, then secretary of state, while remaining in correspondence with Horace Walpole and Townshend. After the fall of John Carteret in April 1724, Townshend had the direction of British foreign policy, and employed Poyntz to avert Russian attempts to control Sweden. In July of that year the post of envoy-extraordinary and plenipotentiary to Sweden was given to Poyntz, who complained: 'The variety of cares which this disagreeable employment brings upon me putts me almost beside myself' (Weston MSS, 1).

During his exile in Stockholm Poyntz endured the usual deprivations of the expatriate, badgering his correspondents for news and books. The diplomat Thomas Robinson arranged a shipment of wine for him, professing a high value for his acquaintance. From November 1725 he spent eighteen months defending the reputation of Admiral Sir John Norris against a calumny by the new Russian envoy in Sweden, Count Golowitz, 'a most noted Jacobite' (BL, Add. MS 28156, fol. 143). The charge related to 1719, when the navy of Peter the Great of Russia was terrorizing the Swedish coast near Stockholm, and Norris's squadron lay at Copenhagen. There was Swedish discontent that the British navy had failed to prevent the raids, and Golowitz fostered this with the story that the tsar had bribed Norris with money and jewels to stay in port. Poyntz was ordered by George I to clear Norris's honour, conduct, and reputation. He appears to have had considerable success in managing the affair, which even came before the Swedish senate in February 1726, a battle in the war between Britain and Russia to win hearts and minds in Sweden. Immersing himself in Swedish concerns, and spending British government money freely to secure support, Poyntz gained the approval of both Townshend and George I. Poyntz's mission was over in June 1727 and he was already awaiting recall when he heard of the death of George I. In July 1727 he arranged to set out for London, in a frigate provided by a grateful Norris, who had finally arrived in Sweden. Poyntz declared himself 'at present able to form no guess what my lott is to be' (BL, Add. MS 28156, fol. 227), and in the event he was retained at Stockholm until the end of September.

In June 1728 Poyntz was sent as one of the plenipotentiaries to the Congress of Soissons, which lasted until July 1729, though the more significant discussions were taking place with Cardinal Fleury in Paris. He never presented formal credentials to the French court. None the less, along with his fellow commissioner William Stanhope, he claimed to be out of pocket by several thousand pounds on the 'Vast Expence we have been at in order to make the same Appearance here as the Ministers of other Powers' (Newcastle MSS, BL, Add. MS 32757, fol. 516). Poyntz showed himself to be adept in the detailed etiquette and protocol of the conference. He was also successful in promoting the two chief British interests of the negotiations after the formal business at Soissons was over. One was to get the French to demolish the fortifications of Dunkirk, as promised in the 1717 treaty of the triple alliance, and the other, following the November 1729 treaty of Seville, was to support Spain against Austria in Italy, if necessary by attacking Austria there. A delighted duke of Newcastle congratulated Poyntz on securing 'so expeditiously and seasonably' a French order to demolish the Dunkirk fortifications, a tactical triumph in Westminster politics. 'You cannot imagine', Newcastle told him, 'what a Victory it has given us over our Enemies, and how their Batteries, which were with some Skill and Success, raised against us, have now turned upon themselves' (Newcastle MSS, BL, Add. MS 32766, fol. 50). Stanhope, now first Earl Harrington, was persuaded by regard for Poyntz to rejoin him in Soissons in February, and together they canvassed an attack upon the Austrian forces in Sicily, with the approval of George II. On 9 June 1730 Harrington left for England, replaced by Walpole, with whom Poyntz braved the browbeatings of Germain-Louis de Chauvelin, the anti-British foreign minister.

After his return to England in August 1730, Poyntz was not employed again in formal diplomacy. At midsummer 1731, when the household of the ten-year-old duke of Cumberland was established, Poyntz was made its governor and steward, beginning a long and close connection. As late as May 1745, on the sensitive issue of reinforcements for the army of the duke in Flanders, the draft instructions were sent for approval to the king and also to Poyntz. His governorship put him on friendly terms with Queen Caroline, and in February 1733 he married a maid of honour to the queen, Anna Maria Mordaunt (d. 1771), the daughter of Brigadier-General Lewis Mordaunt. She was a beauty, who inspired Samuel Croxall's poem 'The Fair Circassian', dedicated to her in extravagant terms. Poyntz's rooms in St James's gave the couple the benefit of society and preserved their intimacy with the crown. Two sons, including Charles *Poyntz were born in the first two years of marriage, both of whom had royal godparents, which meant that noble ladies and gentlemen had to be found to act as proxies at the actual ceremony. After the second birth, Poyntz jokingly wrote: 'I have threatened Mrs. P. to have no more children if there must be all this stately fuss about making them Christians' (Stephen Poyntz to Thomas Townshend, 8 July 1735, James Marshall and Marie Louise Osborn Collection, Beinecke Library, Yale University). In 1734, when the king was not in full agreement with his ministers over the current war, Poyntz was employed to carry private messages between George II and Caroline and the Austrian envoy Count Kinsky. In 1735 he was sworn of the privy council and

given the lucrative post of receiver-general and cashier of excise. Poyntz was a frequent visitor to Bath on account of his own bad health and his wife's recurrent bouts of the stone. He was keen to retire from the city: 'A very good house and Garden, with gravell wood and water and a small Estate of £200 or £300 a year about, if within 30 miles of London, would I think make the remainder of my days happy, as well as help to prolong them' (Stephen Poyntz to Thomas Townshend, 4 Feb 1736, James Marshall and Marie Louise Osborn Collection, Beinecke Library, Yale University). He was baulked in his attempt to purchase Tetcham, by competition from the duke and duchess of Cleveland, but soon after purchased his estate at Midgham, near Newbury. A daughter, Margaret, was born in 1737 [see Spencer, (Margaret) Georgiana, Countess Spencer (1737–1814)]. In November 1740 Mrs Poyntz was delivered of their fifth child, a third son, and Poyntz, then in his mid-fifties, commented: 'my own age and infirmity admonish me to look on this as almost a posthumous child' (ibid., Stephen Poyntz to Thomas Townshend, 23 Nov 1740).

Walpole, reporting his death, ten years later, said that Poyntz was:

> ruined in his circumstances by a devout brother, whom he trusted, and by a simple wife, who had a devotion of marrying dozens of her poor cousins at his expense … Mr. Poyntz was called a very great man, but few knew anything of his talents, for he was timorous to childishness. The duke has done greatly for his family and secured his places for his children, and sends his two sons abroad, allowing them £800 a year. (Walpole, 20.208)

A more positive panegyric was pronounced by a friend who had great obligations to Poyntz: 'he was endowed with every Quality, and adorn'd with every Virtue, that could render the Patriot esteemed, the Parent respected, the Friend beloved, and the whole Man, in every Station of Life, truly amiable' (Epistle to Poyntz, 5). Poyntz certainly remained to the end of his life an ardent patriot. In 1747 he celebrated the news, sent to him by an agent of the duke of Newcastle, of Vice-Admiral George Anson's victory off Cape Finisterre: 'I have spread the News this morning, and have sett the Bells ringing Six Miles round me' (Newcastle MSS, BL, Add. MS 32711, fol. 69). In 1748 he sent reports of disaffection in the Scottish lowlands and other political information to Lord Hardwicke, despite what he referred to in November as 'my late affliction' (BL, Add. MS 35590, fols. 56, 194). He died at his home, Midgham, on 17 December 1750.

PHILIP WOODFINE

Sources J. Maclean, *Historical and genealogical memoir of the family of Poyntz* (1886) • BL, Newcastle MSS, Add. MSS 32686–32769 • letters to Sir John Norris, BL, Add. MS 28156, fols. 143, 227 • Yale U., Lewis Walpole Library, Weston papers • John, Lord Hervey, *Some materials towards memoirs of the reign of King George II*, ed. R. Sedgwick, 3 vols. (1931) • *An epistle to the late Right Honourable Stephen Poyntz, Esq: occasion'd by the compleat victory obtain'd by the duke over the rebels, written in the year 1746, and now first published* (1751) • Burney, *Hist. mus.*, vol. 4 • D. B. Horn, ed., *British diplomatic representatives, 1689–1789*, CS, 3rd ser., 46 (1932) • schedule of his estate, 1751, BL, Add. MS 25086 • BL, Add. MS 35590, fols. 56, 194 • Walpole, *Corr.*

Archives BL, corresp. and papers | BL, corresp. with duke of Newcastle etc., Add. MSS 32686–32769 • BL, letters to Sir John Norris, Add. MS 28156 • BL, letters to Sir Thomas Robinson, Add. MS

23780 · BL, corresp. with Lord Townshend, Add. MSS 48981–48982 · Yale U., Lewis Walpole Library, letters to Edward Weston · Yale U., Beinecke L., Osborn MSS, letters to Thomas Townshend **Likenesses** J. Faber junior, mezzotint, 1732 (after J. Fayram), BM, NPG · attrib. J. B. van Loo?, oils, 1732, Althorp House, Northamptonshire · J. Faber, mezzotint (after portrait by J. B. Van Loo (attrib.), 1732), BM, NPG **Wealth at death** properties and loan transactions: schedule of estate, BL, Add. MS 25086

Poyntz [Poynts], **Sydenham** [Sednham] (*bap.* **1607**), parliamentarian army officer, was baptized on 3 November 1607, the fourth son of John Poynts of Reigate, Surrey, and his wife, Anne Skinner. His own spelling of his name was Sednham Poynts. Although he was of an established family little wealth remained and Poyntz was apprenticed to a London tradesman. This became the subject of chancery proceedings in light of a report that he had died at Rotterdam in July 1625. The proceedings suggest that Poyntz arrived in the Netherlands to escape either ill-treatment or prosecution for theft. Whatever the truth of his apprenticeship experience Poyntz was to record his military service on the continent between 1625 and 1636 in his fitfully accurate 'Relation'. The report that he had died might have stemmed from a period of captivity which Poyntz, in his 'Relation', said occurred between 1626 and 1632.

During his military service Poyntz rose through the ranks and, according to his *Vindication* of 1646, was eventually knighted on the battlefield. In his 'Relation' Poyntz claimed to have served first in English regiments in the Netherlands, entering Lord Vaux's regiment as a private soldier under a Captain Reysby, and soon after that the earl of Essex's regiment under Captain William Baillie. He went on to join the army of Count Mansfeld in Germany and Hungary, and it was following the break up of the army that, he later claimed, he became a prisoner of the Turks. Poyntz was present at the battle of Breitenfeld in 1631 alongside the forces of John George of Saxony, but some time afterwards he changed sides and entered the service of the imperial army, appearing as one of Wallenstein's captains at Lutzen in 1632. Such was the ferocity of that clash with the Swedes that Poyntz recorded that he had only three officers left out of twelve. Poyntz accompanied Wallenstein during his 1633 campaign in Silesia and was also present at Nordlingen in 1634. Although he left Germany after the peace of Prague in 1636 it is probable that at some point thereafter Poyntz returned to the continental wars.

While fighting on the continent Poyntz recorded his first two marriages. The first, to a rich German merchant's daughter about 1633, ended with her death in childbirth. In 1635 Poyntz married another German, whose name John Aubrey rendered as 'Anne Eleanora de Court Stephanus de Cary in Würtemberg …' (Aubrey, 4.212–13). Poyntz, though not naming her, recalled she was 'rich in Land and mony, but of a higher birth and spirit, and therefore would live at a higher rate than our meanes would well afford …' (Goodrick, 14.125). However, she and their child were killed by French troops returning from Italy through the estates which Poyntz had bought, probably in the vicinity of Schorndorf. It is possible that he married his third wife, Elizabeth, during his time on the continent for she was to describe herself in a letter to Speaker Lenthall in 1647 as a 'stranger in your kingdom' (Cary, 1.300–01).

In 1636, after the death of his second wife, Poyntz went back to England and wrote his 'Relation' in the house of the recusant Sir Lewis Tresham, brother of the gunpowder plotter Francis Tresham. The 'Relation' indeed makes much of Poyntz's conversion to Roman Catholicism after his escape from captivity: 'that holy Church … wherein by Gods grace I mean to dy' (Goodrick, 54). Ten years later in his *Vindication* Poyntz was to deny charges that he was a papist, declaring that 'my constant Profession … from my first years, according to the Instructions of this my native Countrey have been in the Reformed Protestant Religion, and accordingly [I] have for many years been an elder of the Dutch church as is very well known' (ibid., 145). But Poyntz's stay in England seems to have been brief: the 'Relation' ends with Poyntz, unable to find employment as a soldier in England, bidding 'a Longum Vale to my Country' (ibid., 130), and he almost certainly returned to his old career on the continent.

It is unclear when Poyntz returned to England again. The fact that he was voted £200 by the Commons on 22 May 1645 for arrears suggests, however, that he had returned at the latest by some point in 1644. On 27 May 1645 the Commons ordered Poyntz to have command of regiments of horse and foot in the northern association. This was followed by his appointment as commander-in-chief of that army with the title of colonel-general. On 19 August 1645 Poyntz was nominated governor of York. However, despite their being more regularly paid than they had ever been under Lord Fairfax it was only under Poyntz's command that the troops mutinied.

Following Naseby Poyntz was ordered to follow the king, and he eventually forced an engagement with the royalists at Rowton Heath, Chester. In his letter of 25 September to Lenthall Poyntz explained how they had discovered the enemy within 3 miles of Chester. As he advanced towards them Poyntz encountered a part of the enemy force which he routed. The main engagement resulted in the destruction of the royalist force: the earl of Lichfield was killed and those captured included Sir Thomas Glenham, Sir Thomas Dacre, and Sir Philip Musgrave. In gratitude the Commons voted Poyntz £500—a payment which Lenthall confirmed by letter of 30 September 1645.

The day before Poyntz had outlined to the committee for war at York the general military situation, including his worries about the discontent among his Nottinghamshire regiment, the king's expectation of 5000 'rebels' from Ireland, and rumours of the approach of a royalist force from Newark. However, on the advice of Colonel Hutchinson Poyntz proceeded to Shelford House. Finding his summons returned in a scornful manner by the governor, Colonel Phillip Stanhope, and meeting stiff early resistance, Poyntz declared that no quarter would be given. Amid general slaughter Shelford was taken. The next day Wiverton House in Nottinghamshire, fearing similar treatment, yielded upon terms. Writing to Lenthall on 9 November 1645 Poyntz related that the strength of the garrison had meant that he gave them fair quarter. Having stressed his concern that no foot had arrived from the eastern garrisons Poyntz also expressed his dissatisfaction that he was more than £400 out of purse. Poyntz moved on to lay siege to Newark. On 5 May 1646, while still undertaking that enterprise, Poyntz reported to Lenthall that the king had taken refuge with the Scots.

In February 1646 Poyntz published a *Vindication* to counter charges of ambition, debauchery, oppression of the country, and, in particular, about his religion. Denounced by some as a papist, Poyntz was accused by others of being neither religious himself, nor respecting it in others. Such claims were linked to the efforts of the 'presbyterian' leaders in the Commons to include Poyntz's troops in their plans to dismantle or crush the New Model Army. In March 1647 the Commons declared that Poyntz's horse regiment was to be one of the four retained in England. The Commons had also voted Poyntz £300 p.a. However, the 'presbyterian' leaders had made the mistake of judging the troops by their commander.

In communication with the New Model, and aware of the increasing rift between the parliament and their southern comrades, the northern troops took the initiative. Although crucially aided by men from outside their ranks, such as Major Henry Lilburne, younger brother of the Leveller John, it is clear that the northern troops were also led by their own militants. A leading figure in the rebellion against Poyntz was Captain John Hodgson of Lionel Copley's regiment, the surgeon (and later Quaker) who was a close confidant of Colonel John Lambert. Lambert had originally been a leading officer in the northern army; he was now taking a leading role in the political action of the New Model. Poyntz informed Lenthall on 17 June that 'a surgeon of colonel Copley's regiment marched with the aforesaid colonel's own troop through Leeds to a rendezvous … the chirurgeon drew some papers out, and read to the soldiers, and told them, that the army in the south desired they should join with them …' (Cary, 1.233–5). At a second rendezvous the next day agitators were chosen.

The northern troops later justified their action by recounting how Poyntz had acted in concert with the Yorkshire presbyterian MP Philip Stapleton. They particularly focused on his removal of Lieutenant-Colonel Charles Fairfax, the kinsman of Sir Thomas Fairfax, and John Lambert, as governor of Clifford's Tower garrison in York who had been replaced with an ally, the lord mayor of York, Thomas Dickenson. Their action was also prompted by Poyntz's abuse of the New Model and of Fairfax, his recruiting of a reformado company (that is, a company of unemployed former soldiers) and his harsh treatment of soldiers whose political allegiance he suspected.

At the end of June 1647 Poyntz complained, to both Lenthall and Fairfax, that agitators from the New Model had stirred up his own troops: 'the soldiers are misinformed and deluded by such as are come out of the South, And some of our inferior officers in these parts' (Bodl. Oxf., MS Tanner 58, fol. 272). He informed Fairfax that he had orders from parliament to apprehend them. On 28 June Poyntz told his officers of Lilburne and Hodgson's attempt to 'putt this Army into confusion and distraction, pretending they were sent with authoritie from Sir Thomas Fairfax …' (Firth, 1891, 143). However, Poyntz' complaint to Fairfax did not receive a sympathetic response. What particularly infuriated Poyntz, as he related it to Lionel Copley, was that the militants in his forces were preparing to present their grievances to Fairfax who had failed to denounce their actions, probably in the knowledge of Poyntz's willingness to turn on the New Model.

On 8 July 1647 Poyntz was seized at his York headquarters, and his wife, Elizabeth, was left to complain to Fairfax of how her husband had been 'carried away in his slippers …' (Cary, 1.300–01). Poyntz was taken to Fairfax at Reading and charged with having 'endeavoured to reimbroyle this Kingdom in a 2d warr … to justify the 11 accused Members and kept correspondency with them …' (Firth, 1891, 168–9). Having been released by Fairfax, Poyntz submitted his resignation in a letter to Lenthall. John Lambert was appointed, in his place, as commander of the northern association.

Poyntz arrived in London and with Edward Massey and Sir William Waller played a prominent role in the attempted counter-revolution. On 2 August entering the Guildhall yard Poyntz and the reformadoes under his control attacked a crowd of Independent-minded citizens who had come to present a petition for peace to the common council. Although one pamphlet claimed that Poyntz had acted in self defence against what was a 'rude rabble of Anabaptists' others claimed that Poyntz and his troops 'in a cruel manner with their Swords hacked and hewed' the crowd (*The Army Anatomized*, 24; Rushworth, 7.741).

Unable to resist the New Model and abandoned by their City allies, Poyntz and Massey, before fleeing, expressed their bitterness in their 'declaration' of 9 August 1647. In a last plea from Amsterdam in May 1648 Poyntz claimed 'it would almost make a man desperate to see how I am slighted in place of the great rewards which the honourable houses were pleased to promise me' (Cary, 1.418). He played no role in the second civil war. Following his flight to the Netherlands, Poyntz was recorded as accompanying Lord Willoughby to the West Indies in 1650. There he became governor of the Leeward Islands, establishing himself at St Kitts. With the arrival of Sir George Ayscue's fleet and Willoughby's consequent surrender of Barbados, Poyntz, facing military defeat, supposedly fled to Virginia. However, the generous articles granted by Ayscue gave Poyntz the option of returning to Antigua with any others who had estates there. It is not clear whether he took advantage of these articles and though Poyntz is mentioned as governor of Antigua between 1661 and 1663 there is little evidence to support the conjecture that he filled this role. Indeed Poyntz effectively disappears from the historical record after his flight in the face of Ayscue.

D. N. FARR

Sources H. Cary, ed., *Memorials of the great civil war in England from 1646 to 1652*, 2 vols. (1842) • *The Clarke papers*, ed. C. H. Firth, 1, CS, new ser., 49 (1891) · *The Clarke Papers*, ed. C. H. Firth, 2, CS, new ser., 54 (1894) · Bodl. Oxf., MS Tanner 58, fol. 272 · A. T. S. Goodrick, ed., *The relation of Sydnam Poyntz, 1624–1636*, CS, 3rd ser., 14 (1908) · J. Maclean, *Historical and genealogical memoir of the family of Poyntz* (1886) · R. Ashton, *Counter-revolution: the second civil war and its origins, 1646–8* (1994) · I. Gentles, *The New Model Army in England, Ireland, and Scotland, 1645–1653* (1992) · *The vindication of Colonel-General Poyntz* (1646) · *The declaration of Generall Massey and Colonell Generall Poyntz* (1647) [Thomason tract E 401(12)] · *The army anatomized* (1647) · L. Hutchinson, *Memoirs of the life of Colonel Hutchinson*, ed. J. Sutherland (1973) · G. Parker, *The Thirty Years' War* (1994) · J. Rushworth, *Historical collections*, 2nd edn, 4/2 (1701), 741 · *The manuscripts of his grace the duke of Portland*, 10 vols., HMC, 29 (1891–1931), vol. 1 · *A letter from Colonell Generall Poyntz* (1645) · *Severall letters from Colonell Generall Poyntz* (1645) · *DNB* · J. Aubrey, *The natural history and antiquities of the county of Surrey*, 4 (1718) · D. N. Farr, 'John Hodgson: soldier, surgeon, agitator and Quaker?', *Journal of the Friends' Historical Society*, 58 (1997–9), 220–34

Archives Bibliothèque Nationale, Paris, MS 'Relation' · U. Nott. L., letters | Bodl. Oxf., Tanner MSS, corresp.

Likenesses line engraving, BM, NPG; repro. in J. Vicars, *England's worthies* (1647) · pen-and-ink drawing, NPG · plate, repro. in J. Ricraft, *A survey of England's champions* (1647); copy, line engraving, BM, NPG · two oil paintings, Althorp, Northamptonshire

Praed [*née* Murray-Prior], **Rosa Caroline** [*known as* Mrs Campbell Praed] (**1851–1935**), novelist, was born on 27 March 1851 on her father's cattle property, Bromelton, near Brisbane, New South Wales, Australia, the third of eleven children of Thomas Lodge Murray-Prior (1819–1892), pastoralist and MP, and his first wife, Matilda (1828–1868), daughter of Thomas Harpur and his wife, Rosa Adams. Educated mostly by her mother and by governesses, Rosa Murray-Prior lived on a succession of pastoral and farm properties and in Brisbane, where her father became postmaster-general and a member of the legislative council of the newly declared state of Queensland. Experience of both pioneering bush conditions and Brisbane's élite social and political circles was stored for later use in fiction. In 1872 she married Arthur Campbell Bulkley Praed (1846–1901), known as Campbell Praed, a younger son of an English brewing and banking family, and went with him to live on his cattle run, Monte Christo, on Curtis Island off the Queensland coast. Lonely and unhappy there, Praed was delighted when in 1875 Campbell Praed decided to sell up and return to England.

Encouraged by her mother to write, Praed as a teenager had produced a number of romance novelettes for the family's handwritten, monthly 'Maroon Magazine'. On arrival in England she resumed writing and submitted Australian sketches to various publishers. Encouragement from George Meredith and Frank Chapman led to the publication of her first novel, *An Australian Heroine*, in 1880. Over the next thirty-five years Praed published almost fifty books, including four in collaboration with the Irish politician and author Justin McCarthy. Their attempt to produce a novel, 'The Right Honourable' (1886), which combined the insights of male and female, led to a close friendship terminated by McCarthy's death in 1912. Praed edited his letters to her as *Our Book of Memories* (1912).

Praed had a lifelong interest in the supernatural. She was involved with the Theosophical Society in London in the early 1880s and hosted meetings of the society in her house. Occult themes appear in her novels of this period such as *The Brother of the Shadow* (1887) and *The Soul of Countess Adrian* (1892), and continue throughout her later books. In 1899 she left her husband to live with another writer, Anne (Nancy) Harward (1864–1927). Praed believed Nancy to be the reincarnation of a Roman slave girl whom Praed herself, in an earlier life, had oppressed. The Roman past revealed by Nancy in a series of séances was fictionalized as *Nyria* (1904) and recounted in more documentary form as *Soul of Nyria* (1931). Although not as committed to astrology as Nancy, Praed was convinced of the reality and importance of the spiritual plane. An unpublished book consists of the teachings of nature spirits with whom Praed communicated.

Praed's literary reputation peaked about 1890 on the basis of her Australian stories such as *Policy and Passion* (1881), which describes the tensions between a self-made Australian politician and his Anglophile daughter, *The Head Station* (1885), and *Outlaw and Lawmaker* (1893). She also achieved a reputation for sensational psychological studies of victimized or tragic women, as in *Nadine* (1882), *Moloch* (1883), *The Bond of Wedlock* (1887; dramatized in London as *Ariane*), and *Christina Chard* (1893). *Affinities* (1885), with its protagonist based on Oscar Wilde, reflects the prominent social and artistic circles in which she moved at this time. After revisiting Australia in the mid-1890s she published an autobiographical account of her Australian days in *My Australian Girlhood* (1902), in which she bids farewell to the pioneer era, her own youth, and the Australian Aborigines, then believed to be dying out. Praed thought the lasting value of her work was in its investigations of the supernatural. Fitfully reprinted since the 1980s, she is now valued for her energetic Anglo-Australian literary sensibility, as a critic of female oppression, and as a complex example of late Victorian sexual ambiguity.

An unenthusiastic mother, Praed bore four children before separating from her husband in 1899. Three sons predeceased her, one dying in a car crash in California, one in a hunting accident in South Africa, and one, racked by terminal cancer, shooting himself. Her daughter was placed in a mental asylum. All died childless. Praed herself died on 10 April 1935 at her home, 12 Lower Erith Road, Torquay, Devon, and was buried with Nancy in Kensal Green cemetery, London. CHRIS TIFFIN

Sources C. Roderick, *In mortal bondage* (1948) · Mrs Campbell Praed [R. C. Praed], *My Australian girlhood* (1902) · Mrs Campbell Praed [R. C. Praed], *Our book of memories* (1912) · Mrs Campbell Praed [R. C. Praed], 'My literary beginnings', *Brisbane Grammar School Magazine*, 2 (1900), 15–22 · J. McCarthy, 'Mrs Campbell Praed', *English Illustrated Magazine*, 30 (1904), 686–8 · C. Tiffin, *Rosa Praed (Mrs Campbell Praed): a bibliography* (1989) · W. T. Stead, 'An outstanding find: Mrs Campbell Praed', *Review of Reviews for Australasia*, 25 (1904), 157 · P. Clarke, *Rosa! Rosa! A life of Rosa Praed, novelist and spiritualist* (1999) · *The Argus* [Melbourne] (16 April 1935) · *New York Times* (14 April 1935) · *Sydney Morning Herald* (16 April 1935) · *The Times* (15 April 1935) · d. cert. · will · bap. cert.

Archives State Library of Queensland, South Brisbane, John Oxley Library · State Library of Queensland, South Brisbane, corresp. and papers | Mitchell L., NSW, Murray-Prior MSS · NL Aus., Murray-Prior family MSS

Praed, William Mackworth (1747–1833), banker and politician, was born on 24 June 1747 and baptized the following month at the London Foundling Hospital. He was the eldest of six children of Humphrey Mackworth Praed (1718?–1803), MP and banker, and Mary, daughter of William Forester of Dothil Park in Shropshire, and widow of Sir Brian Broughton Delves, baronet, of Broughton in Staffordshire.

Educated at Eton College and at Magdalen College, Oxford, in 1774 Praed was elected MP for St Ives, the family seat. However, after allegations of bribery the result was declared void and he was unseated. On 19 June 1778 he married Elizabeth Tyringham (1749–1811), daughter of a banker, Barnaby Backwell of Tyringham in Buckinghamshire, at St George's, Hanover Square. Elizabeth had just inherited the family estate at Tyringham after the death of her brother, and this became the family home. William and Elizabeth were to have twenty children, only seven of whom reached their majority. In 1792 the old manor house was pulled down and a new one built by Sir John Soane.

In July 1779 Praed became a junior partner of his father's bank, the Cornish Bank at Truro. In 1802 shortly before his father's death he became the senior partner, and soon afterwards opened a second branch at Falmouth, known as the Cornish Naval Bank. In 1780 he was again elected MP for St Ives, and remained so until 1806. He usually supported the Pitt ministry, but was best known for guiding enabling legislation for the Grand Junction Canal through the House of Commons. This important canal linked London and the midlands, and Praed was noted for his obsession with its success. For his work in parliament he was awarded a piece of plate by the canal shareholders, and, in 1813, in honour of his work as the company chairman, his portrait was commissioned for the boardroom. In 1801 he also became one of the company treasurers. In 1808 he was a leading proponent of the Grand Union Canal which linked the Grand Junction Canal and the Leicestershire and Northamptonshire Union Canal. After 1823 he no longer attended meetings of the Grand Junction Canal Company, but his sons and London banking partners retained a close interest on his behalf. Praed Street in Paddington, where the canal terminated, is another memorial of his enthusiasm.

In 1801 William Praed formed a banking partnership with Philip Box, Kendon Digby, and Benjamin Babbage, and opened a bank at 189 Fleet Street, London, the building being designed by Sir John Soane. There were several changes of partner, but Praed was always the senior partner, and he brought other members of the family into the firm. Many of the bank's customers came from the west country or Buckinghamshire, and the bank provided treasurers, lent money, and invested in shares for the Grand Junction Canal. After 1850 the bank traded as Praed & Co., and it was taken over by Lloyds in 1891.

In 1803 his father died and Praed inherited the family estate at Trevethow, but he disposed of it soon afterwards to Sir Christopher Hawkins, and gave up representing St Ives. Instead he stood for election in the closed borough of Banbury in Oxfordshire. In 1806 he won this seat, ousting Dudley North, but in 1807 there was a double return, and Praed was ousted by North in the fresh election ordered in 1808. He was never an MP thereafter. He concentrated on his other activities, but during the 1820s he may have withdrawn from active management, as his sons took on more responsibility. Near the end of his life he may have retired to Trevethow, which had been acquired once more, for he died there on 9 October 1833, and was buried at the local parish church in Lelant. His eldest son, James Backwell Praed, inherited the estate at Tyringham, while his father's banking interests, while another son, William Tyringham Praed, was also involved in the London banking firm, and became treasurer to the Grand Junction Canal Company.   K. R. FAIRCLOUGH

Sources R. G. Thorne, 'Praed, William', HoP, *Commons, 1790–1820*, 4.880–81 [see also various articles in other HoP *Commons* vols.] · F. G. Hilton Price, *A handbook of London bankers* (1876) · minute books of Praed & Co. (Truro), 1774–1830, Lloyds Bank archives, 53/58 · partners ledger of Praed & Co. (London), 1802–89, Lloyds Bank archives, A 19b/1 · Praed's alphabet of Praed & Co. (London), 1806–36, Lloyds Bank archives, A 19b/9 · records of Grand Junction Canal Company, PRO, RAIL 845 · records of Grand Union Canal Company, PRO, RAIL 831 · baptism registers of London Foundling Hospital, PRO, RG 4/4396 · will of William Praed, PRO, PROB 11/1825, sig. 778 · L. S. Presnall, *Country banking in the industrial revolution* (1956) · A. H. Faulkner, *The Grand Junction canal* (1972) · Boase, *Mod. Eng. biog.* · D. Hudson, *A poet in parliament: the life of Winthrop Mackworth Praed, 1802–1839* (1939)
Likenesses C. Turner, mezzotint, pubd 1816 (after painting by W. Owen), BL, department of prints and drawings
Wealth at death see will, PRO, PROB 11/1825, sig. 778

Praed, Winthrop Mackworth (1802–1839), poet and politician, was born on 26 June 1802 at 35 John Street, Bedford Row, London, the fourth of the five children of William Mackworth Praed (1756–1835), serjeant-at-law and long-time chairman of the Audit Office, and his wife, Elizabeth (1767–1810), daughter of Benjamin Winthrop, merchant and governor of the Bank of England. Praed was the product of an old family with roots in Rutland and Cornwall. His father was wealthy enough to afford a fashionable address in London as well as Bitton House, an 18 acre estate in Teignmouth, Devon. Praed was a remarkably precocious but delicate child. In 1810 he started at Langley Broom School, near Colnbrook, where he quickly distinguished himself. He went to Eton College in March 1814, and remained there until July 1821. Praed was a legendary Etonian, who left as indelible a mark on his schoolmates there as George Canning had done a generation earlier. In 1820 he founded a manuscript journal, the 'Apis Matina', and accounted for at least half of the contributions to its six numbers. Later the same year, he started *The Etonian*, a more ambitious journal which Charles Knight agreed to

Winthrop Mackworth Praed (1802–1839), by Daniel Maclise, c.1830–35

publish, and once again he dominated its pages, contributing some thirty-five articles and a dozen poems. Knight later described Praed the Etonian as:

> natural and unaffected in his ordinary talk; neither shy nor presuming; proud, without a tinge of vanity; somewhat reserved, but ever courteous; giving few indications of the susceptibility of the poet, but ample evidence of the laughing satirist; a pale and slight youth, who had looked upon the aspects of society with the keen perception of a clever manhood.   (Knight, 1.282–3)

Praed followed up his Eton career with an equally brilliant one at Cambridge. Breaking with family tradition, he chose Trinity College over St John's, and there he read classics alongside Macaulay. He won four medals for Greek odes and epigrams and two more for English parody, as well as a declamation prize. He narrowly missed winning the university scholarship, and in 1825 was bracketed third in the classical tripos. An active member of the Cambridge Union Society, Praed was widely praised for his witty and offhand manner in debate. While he lacked the physical stamina to match Macaulay's soaring eloquence, he could argue his case tenaciously when provoked into doing so, and he often took the radical side on political issues. Praed's good looks undoubtedly contributed to his popularity at Cambridge. 'In person he was of spare habit', according to his sister Susan:

> complexion pale, features strongly marked, symmetrical, but thin and somewhat sharply cut. His forehead was clear and well built; finished above by an uncommon beauty: his eyes large, and very expressive; face almost pointed, from

the unusual prolongation of the lower outline. (Hudson, 66)

His singular features, his self-confidence, and the ease with which he seemed to master any subject that interested him all combined to make him a legend. He 'was to the University what Byron was to the world', Bulwer Lytton recalled. '[T]here was a fascination in the very name of this young man which eclipsed the repute of his contemporaries' (ibid., 67–9).

After leaving Cambridge in March 1825, Praed served as tutor to Lord Ernest Bruce, second son of the marquess of Ailesbury, and eventually accompanied his charge to Eton. During this interval Praed contributed several political squibs to the whig *Morning Chronicle*. He also began a long relationship with the *New Monthly Magazine*, where many of his poems first appeared, and composed verse for Alaric Watts's *Literary Souvenir*, the most popular of the illustrated annuals. Praed also made time to read for a Trinity fellowship, to which he was elected in 1827. After leaving Eton late in 1827, Praed went to London, where he began work as a pupil of John Bayley, a Middle Temple barrister. He had little patience with the drudgery of legal work, but persevered in his studies and was called to the bar in May 1829. Praed decided to go the Norfolk circuit, and, like most new barristers, started off with few briefs and considerable time on his hands.

Praed's flirtation with political radicalism had ended by the time he left Cambridge. He was an enthusiastic supporter of Catholic emancipation, but by the late 1820s had become convinced that wholesale parliamentary reform could only lead to social chaos. An admirer of Canning, Praed lauded him in verse after he suddenly died shortly after reaching the premiership in 1827. Praed essentially remained a Canningite for the rest of his short life by subsequently professing his devotion to Sir Robert Peel. Like his two heroes, he was committed to practical improvements while deploring what he considered the dangerous constitutional tinkering of the whigs and their radical associates. The tories were aware of Praed's debating skills, and, thinking that he would provide a counterweight on the Commons floor to the likes of his old schoolfriend Macaulay, in December 1830 they offered him the use of the pocket borough of St Germans for two years in exchange for £1000. He accepted the offer, and thus became one of very few promising young men who took a seat opposite the new Grey ministry. Praed lost little time in making himself useful to the tory cause. In a series of verse satires published in *The Alfred* and *The Albion* he established his anti-reform credentials:

> We're sick of this distressing state
> Of order and repose;
> We have not had enough of late
> Of blunder, or of blows;
> We can't endure to pass our life
> In such a humdrum way;
> We want a little pleasant strife—
> The Whigs are in to-day!
> …
> It's time for us to see the things
> Which other folk have seen;
> It's time we should cashier our kings,

And build our guillotine;
We'll abrogate Police and Peers,
And vote the Church away;
We'll hang the parish overseer—
The Whigs are in to-day!
('The New Order of Things', 1830, stanzas 1 and 4, reprinted in
Praed, *Political and Occasional Poems*, 123–4)

On 14 February 1831 Praed delivered a celebrated maiden speech on the cotton duties, supporting his argument against the government's plans for altering them with an impressive array of statistics. But his chief preoccupation at this time was the Reform Bill. Resentful that his borough had been slated for extinction under schedule A, he fought vigorously against the main provisions of the bill, and tried but failed to narrow their scope through amendment. After the disfranchisement of St Germans, Praed stood for the borough of St Ives, but lost to the incumbent, James Halse, in a bitter contest. While he was out of parliament he remained deeply involved in partisan politics, frequently contributing anti-whig satires to the *Morning Post* and serving as the *Post's* chief leader writer from early 1833 until late 1834. By this time his political celebrity had greatly enhanced the value of his legal practice; his barrister's income trebled the year after he entered the Commons, and it continued to grow thereafter. Praed returned to the Commons as MP for Great Yarmouth in 1834, and served as secretary to the Board of Control in Peel's short-lived ministry of 1834–5. After retiring from this constituency in 1837, he was subsequently returned for Aylesbury, conveniently taking over the seat previously held by his cousin James. Already plagued by symptoms of consumption, Praed refused to slow down the hectic pace of his life; he still possessed sufficient energy to attack the Melbourne government's Canada policy and to champion the National Society's working-class education schemes.

What little spare time Praed allowed himself he devoted to raising a family. On 7 July 1835 he married Helen Bogle, a wealthy young beauty whose sugar merchant father, George, had retired to Effingham, Surrey. Two daughters were born to them over the next next three years, Helen Adeline and Elizabeth Lilian. In order to accommodate his growing family, Praed purchased a spacious house in south-west London, 64 Chester Square. His health was already rapidly deteriorating when they moved in, but he insisted on carrying on his legal and political duties as best he could, and was still attending Commons debates only a few weeks before his death. He died on 15 July 1839 at his Chester Square residence.

Praed is best remembered for what he might have become had he not died young; indeed, he came to be seen as a tragic archetype—the young man of promise cut down before his prime. He carried his schoolboy reputation with him into parliament, and managed to preserve it there through occasional flashes of brilliance. Had he lived, he might well have risen to a commanding position within Peel's Conservative ministry in the early 1840s. As it happened, at the time of his death he was best known for his poetry. Although he often dismissed himself as a mere versifier, Praed sketched the manners and mores of the polite society he knew so well with a graceful nonchalance. While his poetry is now virtually unknown, it was popular enough in the Victorian era to merit the publication of several collections on both sides of the Atlantic. American collections appeared in 1844, 1850, and 1859. Praed's close friend Derwent Coleridge was responsible for the first British edition in 1864, and his nephew Sir George Young edited *Political and Occasional Poems* in 1888. It is altogether appropriate that Praed, a boy wonder whom fate would not permit to grow old, left behind him some of the most vivid paeans to the golden youth of the early nineteenth-century leisured classes:

I wish that I could run away
From House, and court, and levee,
Where bearded men appear to-day,
Just Eton boys, grown heavy;
That I could bask in childhood's sun,
And dance o'er childhood's roses;
And find huge wealth in one pound one,
Vast wit in broken noses;
And play Sir Giles at Datchet Lane,
And call the milk-maids Houris;—
That I could be a boy again,
A happy boy, at Drury's!
('School and schoolfellows', 1829, ll.77–89)

PHILIP HARLING

Sources D. Hudson, *A poet in parliament: the life of Winthrop Mackworth Praed, 1802–1839* (1939) · *Selected poems of Winthrop Mackworth Praed*, ed. K. Allott (1953) · D. Coleridge, ed., *Poems of Winthrop Mackworth Praed, with a memoir*, 2 vols. (New York, 1865) · *Political and occasional poems of Winthrop Mackworth Praed*, ed. G. Young (1888) · G. Saintsbury, *The collected essays and papers of George Saintsbury, 1875–1920*, 4 vols. (1923), 2.31–52 · C. Knight, *Passages of a working life during half a century*, 3 vols. (1864–5), vol. 1, pp. 281–94 · E. R. Bulwer-Lytton, first Earl Lytton, *The life, letters and literary remains of Edward Bulwer, Lord Lytton*, 1 (1883), 233–5
Archives Eton College, corresp., literary MSS, and papers | BL, letters to Sir Robert Peel and others · CKS, corresp. with J. C. Herries · CKS, letters to Lord Mahon · Wilts. & Swindon RO, letters to Lord Ernest Bruce
Likenesses G. Hamilton, caricature, c.1819, priv. coll. · D. Maclise, watercolour drawing, c.1830–1835, NPG [*see illus.*] · M. Gauci, lithograph, 1832, Eton College · W. Hamilton, miniature, 1834, priv. coll. · D. Maclise, pencil drawing, c.1835, priv. coll. · W. Drummond, lithograph, pubd 1837 (after H. Mayer), NPG · H. N. O'Neil, group portrait, oils, 1869 (*The billiard room of the Garrick Club*), Garr. Club · R. Smith, medallion on tomb, Kensal Green cemetery, London

Praeger, Robert Lloyd (1865–1953), naturalist and author, was born on 25 August 1865 at The Crescent, Holywood, co. Down, the second of the six children of Willem Emil Praeger (d. 1884), linen merchant, and his wife, Maria, daughter of Robert Patterson. Praeger's father was of Dutch extraction and had emigrated to Belfast in 1860 to set up a linen exporting business, in partnership with his brother in The Hague. His maternal family, the Pattersons, were prosperous Belfast dissenters with many interests in the fields of antiquities, art, local history, and natural history. In 1866 the Praegers moved to Croft House in Holywood, a large house on the southern shore of Belfast Lough owned by Robert's maternal uncle Robert Lloyd Patterson (1836–1906), himself an avid naturalist. Here

Robert, or Robin, enjoyed extra-curricular tuition in natural history so that by the age of six, he later claimed, he could identify the quartz, feldspar, and mica in a specimen of granite from the Mourne Mountains (Praeger, *The Way*, 8). Early membership of the Belfast Naturalists' field club brought him into contact with other amateur naturalists from his area and provided opportunities for wider exploration in the north-east of Ireland.

Following his early education at a private primary school in Holywood run by the local Unitarian minister, Praeger attended the Royal Belfast Academical Institution (1876–1882) before proceeding to Queen's College, Belfast, where he graduated BA (1885) and BEng. (1886). His first employment was as an engineer working on the enlargements to Belfast harbour between 1886 and 1888; this gave him an opportunity to study fossil shells in the estuarine clays and stimulated a lifelong interest in Quaternary history. At this period he also conducted botanical research on the ferns of Ulster with William H. Phillips and the flowers of the Mourne Mountains with Samuel Alexander Stewart.

In 1888 Praeger passed up the opportunity of a permanent contract in engineering and began to cast around for an alternative which would allow him to devote his main energies to natural history. He eventually secured a position in 1893 as a librarian at the National Library in Dublin, where he worked until 1923. This was the beginning of a prolific period of fieldwork, publishing, and organizing of scientific societies. The establishment of a monthly journal, *The Irish Naturalist*, by Praeger and George Herbert Carpenter in 1892 provided the natural history movement with an outlet for regular publication of sightings, finds, and distributional papers. In 1895 Praeger launched the Irish Field Club Union, uniting all the field clubs in Ireland, in order to co-ordinate fieldwork and to report on progress in the different branches of natural history. Praeger's energies, as well as his indifference to bad weather and physical discomfort, were now famous in field club circles: a friend celebrated his calf muscles to contemporaries as 'one of the seven wonders of Dublin' (Aleyn Reade to Praeger, 1 May 1941, Praeger Collection, 10:77); on a trip to Fermanagh in 1904, when three-and-a-half out of five days rained, he decided 'not to mind it; so I put in an average of twelve hours' field work each day, and every evening returned, dripping but happy' ('Among the Fermanagh Hills', *The Irish Naturalist*, 13, 1904, 232).

While Praeger continued with research into estuarine clays and glacial deposits, botany and Irish plant distribution became his major interest. His *Irish Topographical Botany* appeared in 1901 following a marathon programme of summer fieldwork lasting five years. He subsequently concentrated on the floral communities of Irish islands and organized a multidisciplinary survey of Lambay Island, co. Dublin, in 1907. The results of this survey included ninety additions to the Irish flora and fauna, including seventeen new British species and five which were new to science. These findings prompted the Royal Irish Academy, where Praeger was already an influential member, to sponsor a larger survey of Clare Island in Clew

Bay, co. Mayo. When it finally appeared under Praeger's editorship the Clare Island survey (1911–15) listed 3219 plant species and 5269 animal species of which 11 and 109, respectively, were new to science. Despite these findings the survey failed in its stated aim to demonstrate endemism on Clare Island.

On a holiday visit to Germany in 1901 Praeger met Hedwig (Hedi), daughter of the artist Christian Carl Magnussen. They were married the following year and set up home at Lisnamae, Zion Road, in Rathgar, a prosperous Dublin suburb. The Praegers had no children, but theirs was a companionate marriage, with Hedwig accompanying her husband on many of his travels; accordingly he dedicated his 1937 masterpiece, *The Way that I Went*, to her, his 'dear companion in many wanderings'.

The move to Rathgar also marked the beginning of Praeger's work as a gardener and a specialist in succulents. The garden at his new home provided him with the opportunity of growing many native and exotic species, and here he took a special interest in houseleeks (*Sempervivum*) and stonecrops (*Sedum*). His cultivated collection of stonecrops eventually numbered 1500 specimens and formed the basis of his taxonomic study of the genus *Sedum*, published by the Royal Horticultural Society of London in 1921. This sedentary pursuit was suited to a period of war and upheaval in both Ireland and Europe with the restrictions placed on fieldwork.

In 1923, following the creation of the Irish Free State, Praeger retired from his position as head librarian at the National Library and was free to pursue botanical fieldwork full time. During the 1920s Praeger and his wife made several visits to the Alps, the Canary Islands, Madeira, and the Balkans for a second taxonomic study, *An Account of the Sempervivum Group* (1932). This taxonomic work earned him an international reputation as a botanist.

Having published several sketches of his foreign travels in periodical and then in book form (*Beyond Soundings*, 1930), Praeger discovered a facility for impressionistic prose. He committed this talent to a topographical survey of Ireland, *The Way that I Went* (1937), based largely on personal experience; this is the book by which Praeger is known to a general readership. His findings on Irish plant distribution and habitat types culminated in *The Botanist in Ireland* (1934); he also published a further volume of reminiscences, *A Populous Solitude* (1941), a biographical dictionary, *Some Irish Naturalists* (1949), and a *Natural History of Ireland* (1950).

During Praeger's retirement he and his wife lived at 19 Fitzwilliam Square, Dublin, where they had moved in 1922. The central location suited the Praegers, who were never car owners, as it afforded quick access to the museums, libraries, and other institutions with which Praeger had connections. In later life Praeger enjoyed many honours for his contributions to natural history, but the one which gratified him most was his election as president of the Royal Irish Academy in 1931. Twice president of the Dublin field club, he received the gold medal of the Royal Horticultural Society of Ireland in 1940 and became its president in 1949–50. He continued to enjoy vigorous physical health into the 1930s, working in a voluntary capacity as a gardener at the zoological gardens and continuing his fieldwork on Irish plant distribution. In his final years increasing deafness contributed to a brusqueness of manner while arthritis of the knee joints eventually reduced his mobility.

Following his wife's death in 1952 Praeger settled his affairs in Dublin and returned to the north-east of Ireland, where he spent his last months at his sister Rosamond's house, Rock Cottage, Craigavad, co. Down. He died at the Musgrave and Clark Clinic, Belfast, on 5 May 1953.

SEÁN LYSAGHT

Sources T. Collins, *Floreat Hibernia: a bio-bibliography of Robert Lloyd Praeger, 1865–1953* (1985) · S. Lysaght, *Robert Lloyd Praeger: the life of a naturalist* (1998) · R. L. Praeger, *Beyond soundings* (1930) · R. L. Praeger, *The way that I went* (1937) · R. L. Praeger, *A populous solitude* (1941) · J. W. Foster, ed., *Nature in Ireland: a scientific and cultural history* (1997) · C. Mollan, W. Davis, and B. Finucane, eds., *Some people and places in Irish science and technology* (1985) · *CGPLA Eng. & Wales* (1953) · *Belfast News-Letter* (26 Aug 1865)
Archives National Botanic Gardens, Glasnevin, Dublin, corresp. and field notes · National Botanic Gardens, Glasnevin, Dublin, herbarium · RBG Kew, archives, corresp. · Royal Irish Acad., collection | Royal Irish Acad., Robert A. Phillips MSS · Ulster Museum, Belfast, Robert Welch collection
Likenesses R. Welch, photographs, 1889–1910, Ulster Museum, Belfast; repro. in Collins, *Floreat Hibernia* · Irish school, bronze bust (after S. R. Praeger), NG Ire. · S. R. Praeger, bronze bust, Royal Irish Acad.; repro. in Collins, *Floreat Hibernia* · photographs, Royal Irish Acad.; repro. in Collins, *Floreat Hibernia*
Wealth at death £690 11s. 10d. in England: Northern Irish probate sealed in London, 25 Nov 1953, *CGPLA Eng. & Wales* · £1060 10s. 0d.: probate, 28 Oct 1953, *CGPLA NIre.*

Prain, Sir David (1857–1944), botanist, was born on 11 July 1857 at Fettercairn, Kincardineshire, the elder child of David Prain, a native of Inchture near Dundee, and his wife, Mary, daughter of George Thomson, farmer and miller, of the Vale of Alford, Aberdeenshire. For at least two hundred years Prain's ancestry on both sides had been country people. His father, who had a saddlery business, was also clerk to the parish council and to the school board in Fettercairn. Prain was educated until the age of fifteen at the Fettercairn parish school, then for one year at the Aberdeen grammar school in order to be accepted as a clerk in the Royal Bank of Scotland. However, in 1873 he went to the University of Aberdeen where he obtained an MA (1878), with honours in natural science, botany being his strongest subject. A bursary had made it possible for him to enter the university and in vacations he added to his means by teaching. He had intended to become a schoolmaster but after two years of teaching at Chatham House School, Ramsgate, he returned to the university to study medicine. He qualified MB and CM at Aberdeen in 1883 with the highest honours; he also qualified LRCS (Edinburgh) the same year.

Prain was persuaded by his mentor at Aberdeen, Professor J. W. H. Traill, to seek admission to the Indian Medical Service in the expectation of opportunities to transfer to botanical research. Accepted in October 1884, he left the following spring for India where for the next two and a

Sir David Prain (1857–1944), by Walter Stoneman, 1917

half years he served in military hospitals except for a few months in 1885 when he temporarily filled the post of curator of the herbarium at the Royal Botanic Garden, Calcutta. In January 1887 he was recalled to the same position in the garden under Sir George King, the then superintendent. Since he showed an active interest in economic botany, the government of Bengal requested Prain to submit a report on Indian hemp. This was followed by other official investigations on wheat, mustards, pulses, and indigo. In 1887 he married Margaret Caird (*d.* 1942), daughter of the Revd William Thomson, of Belhevie, Aberdeen. They had a son, Theodore, who was killed in the First World War.

When King retired in 1898 Prain succeeded him as director of the botanic garden (as the post had by then been renamed) and of the botanical survey of India. Prain had already replaced King as professor of botany at the medical college of Calcutta in 1895. In his role as government quinologist, he reorganized the management of the cinchona factory in Sikkim, making it once more commercially viable. As botanist on Sir Francis Younghusband's Sikkim–Tibet boundary commission in 1903, Prain had the opportunity to collect plants on the Tibetan plateau. His travels through the Indian subcontinent, Burma, Ceylon, and the Andaman and Nicobar islands extended his knowledge of the Indian flora which he reviewed in articles in *Annals of the Royal Botanic Garden, Calcutta* and *Journal of the Asiatic Society of Bengal. Bengal Plants* (1903), published at his own expense, described nearly 3000 species. In 1905 he was elected FRS and retired from Indian service with the rank of lieutenant-colonel. In June 1906 he was appointed CIE.

In December 1905 Prain succeeded Sir William Thiselton-Dyer as director of the Royal Botanic Gardens at Kew. The staff there were still suffering from Thiselton-Dyer's autocratic administration and someone with Prain's tolerance and diplomacy was needed to restore harmony. His willingness to delegate responsibility was especially appreciated; he was happy to leave decisions regarding the layout of the gardens to the curator and his assistant director, Arthur Hill. During Prain's term of office a medicinal garden was formed in the grounds of Cambridge Cottage, a large tank for aquatic plants was installed, and the Japanese gateway, made for the Japan–British exhibition in 1910, was acquired. Also in 1910 Cambridge Cottage was converted into a museum of British forestry and timbers. Much of Prain's time at Kew was devoted to editorial duties: he revived the *Kew Bulletin* which had been languishing for several years; he abandoned the practice of the *Index Kewensis* in making taxonomic judgements regarding synonymy; he edited *Curtis's Botanical Magazine* and Hooker's *Icones plantarum*; he collaborated with I. H. Burkill in *An Account of the Genus Dioscorea in the East* (1936); and he contributed to the *Flora Capensis* and *Flora of Tropical Africa*.

Prain, who retired in 1922, served as the first chairman of the advisory council of the Imperial Institute on plant and animal products from 1926. During all his time at Kew and to the end of his life he was especially interested in the John Innes Horticultural Institution, being chairman of its council from 1909. He did not much less for the Imperial College of Tropical Agriculture, Trinidad. He was president (1916–19) of the Linnean Society, from which he received the Linnean medal (1935); vice-president from 1919 of the Royal Horticultural Society which awarded him the Victoria medal of honour (1912) and a Veitch memorial medal (1933); treasurer of the Royal Society (1919–29); a trustee of the British Museum (1924–36); president of the Imperial Botanical Conference in 1924; and a member of the council of the British Association (1907–14), its vice-president (1931), and president of the botany section in 1909. His many honours included appointment as CMG in January 1912 and knighthood in June of the same year; he was a knight of the royal Swedish order of the Pole Star (1908) and a commander of the Belgian order of Leopold II (1919). The honorary degree of LLD was conferred upon him by the universities of Aberdeen (1900) and St Andrews (1911); he received the Albert medal of the Royal Society of Arts (1925), and was an honorary member of many foreign learned societies.

Prain's modest demeanour, his courtesy, and many kindly acts won him the support of his staff at Kew, where he brought stability, and consolidated the achievements of his predecessors. He died at his home, Well Farm, Godstone Road, Whyteleafe, Surrey, on 16 March 1944 and was buried at Putney Vale cemetery five days later.

RAY DESMOND

Sources I. H. Burkill, *Obits. FRS*, 4 (1942–4), 747–70 · I. H. Burkill, *Proceedings of the Linnean Society of London*, 156th session (1943–4),

223–9 · *Yearbook of the American Philosophical Society* (1944), 379–83 · W. W. Smith, *Year Book of the Royal Society of Edinburgh* (1943–4), 22–4 · *Chronica Botanica*, 10 (1946), 374–6 · R. Desmond, *Kew: the history of the Royal Botanic Gardens* (1995) · F. A. Stafleu and R. S. Cowan, *Taxonomic literature: a selective guide*, 2nd edn, 4, Regnum Vegetabile, 110 (1983), 376–9 · *The Times* (22 March 1944)

Archives RBG Kew, archives, corresp. and papers · Royal Botanic Gardens, Calcutta | RBG Kew, archives, letters to A. T. Gage · U. Glas., Archives and Business Reward Centre, letters to F. O. Bower

Likenesses W. Stoneman, photograph, 1917, NPG [*see illus.*] · F. A. de Biden Footner, crayon drawing, 1929, RBG Kew; repro. in Burkill, *Obits. FRS*, 746 · black and white photograph, RS · portrait, repro. in E. Nelmes and W. Cuthbertson, *Curtis's Botanical Magazine dedications, 1827–1927* (1931), 290

Wealth at death £5667 15s. 8d.: administration, 17 Aug 1944, CGPLA Eng. & Wales

Prance, Miles (*fl.* 1678–1688), perjurer, was born in Eastwood in the Isle of Ely. His father was Simon Prance, gentleman, a Roman Catholic convert of royalist sympathies. In his youth Miles Prance was apprenticed to a gold- and silversmith and in the early 1670s he was a servant-in-ordinary to Queen Catherine of Braganza. By the late 1670s he was living in Prince's Street, Covent Garden, with a wife and family.

As a Catholic himself, and having referred to Jesuits as 'honest fellows' (Boys, 10), news of the death of the magistrate Sir Edmund Berry Godfrey in October 1678 made Prance an object of suspicion. Many people believed that the murder was part of a plot by the papists. Prance was arrested on 21 December 1678 after inquiries at his home, where his lodger, John Wren (who owed Prance money), maliciously revealed that his landlord had been absent at the time of the murder. Prance's problems were further compounded when the opportunistic fabricator of Romanist conspiracies William Bedloe accused him of being one of the men he had seen about the body of Godfrey as it lay in Somerset House. After a short examination, in which Prance denied being a party to any murder, he was committed to Newgate and there harshly treated. He subsequently confessed his involvement in the crime, only to recant this confession. While still in Newgate he claimed that the clergymen William Boys, Gilbert Burnet, and William Lloyd had visited him, and on 12 January 1679 Prance once more confessed, later claiming that 'It was purely the fear of Death, and the misery of my condition, that wrought upon me to foreswear myself, without any thought of reward' (L'Estrange, 3.128).

In his new confession Prance maintained that the design against Godfrey came to his notice through two Irish priests: Girald, or Fitz-girald, and Kelly. Also brought into the business were Henry Berry, porter to the queen at Somerset House, Robert Green, an Irishman employed in the Queen's Chapel, and Lawrence Hill. Prance said that the group had followed Godfrey as he went about his business in the week of his death. Finally, while Prance kept watch, Godfrey had been strangled on the evening of Saturday 12 October in a yard at Somerset House. The body was then hidden in the palace until it could be placed in a manner so that whenever it should be found it might be supposed that Godfrey had committed suicide and so discredit him and any evidence against Catholics. Prance claimed that this had been done on the following Wednesday, when they had laid the corpse in a ditch near Primrose Hill and put Godfrey's own sword through his body.

Prance now became responsible for the arrest and deaths of Berry, Green, and Hill. He gave evidence against them at their trial on 5 February 1679 and also shared with Bedloe the reward given for the discovery of the murderers. Thereafter Prance informed on a number of Catholics under the influence of Bedloe and Titus Oates, the principal instigator of the Popish Plot. On 13 June 1679 he gave evidence against two Jesuits, Harcourt and Fenwick, in support of Bedloe and Stephen Dugdale, the Popish Plot witness, and on 10 January 1680 he obtained a pension of £50 from the crown. In September 1679 he helped Sir William Waller to election victory at Westminster and later assisted Oates in trying to discredit Sir Roger L'Estrange. Prance published a number of pamphlets defending his evidence against the accusations of Elizabeth Cellier and purporting to explain its contradictions, but with the ebbing of the Popish Plot he faded from view.

Retribution followed in the next reign. On 15 June 1686 Prance was found guilty of perjury and sentenced to be fined £100, pilloried, and whipped. He stood in the pillory at Westminster on 21 June 1686, but the last part of his sentence was not carried out because the 'Queen dowager hath beg'd of the king the remission of the last punishment … [as she was persuaded that Prance had] … return'd to the church of Rome' (Clark, 3.189), having previously converted to the Church of England. In December 1688 Prance tried to escape abroad, but was arrested in the company of some other Catholics in a ship off Gravesend. Interrogated by the House of Lords, he was subsequently released and seems to have fled to the continent, where he died in obscurity.

As Prance 'had not the brand upon him of an infamous Course of Life, to blast his Evidence as his Fellow-witnesses had', he was more readily believed by the authorities (L'Estrange, 3.126). While his story of the Godfrey murder was startling in its detail and provided an easy solution to the mystery, it also caused the deaths of the innocent Berry, Green, and Hill. It is highly unlikely that his claims were genuine. Prance's evidence had been gained under extreme pressure. While he knew something of the particulars of Godfrey's death, he appears to have gained much circumstantial evidence by being a member of the club at the White House, close to Primrose Hill, where the body of the magistrate was discovered and where the inquest had been held. Moreover his version of Godfrey's death, particularly the timing of the disposal of the body, contains a number of improbabilities. Despite his perjury Prance's apparently unconditional return to the Catholic church has led some historians to claim he was a Catholic agent throughout the events in which he was entangled. It is far more likely that Prance was merely yet another unfortunate caught up in circumstances not of his own making and used by those more powerful than

himself. In this respect his return to the Catholic church, sanctioned by Queen Catherine herself, was an act of forgiveness rather than anything sinister.

ALAN MARSHALL

Sources R. L'Estrange, *A brief history of the times* (1688) • M. Prance, *A true narrative and discovery of several very remarkable passages relating to the horrid Popish Plot as they fell within the knowledge of Mr Miles Prance* (1679) • M. Prance, *The additional narrative of M. Prance … who was the discoverer of the murther of Sir E. Godfrey* (1679) • M. Prance, *Mr Prance's answer to Mrs Cellier's libel* (1680) • M. Prance, *The anti-protestant, or, Miles against Prance, being a solemn protestation of M. Prance concerning the murder of Sir E. Godfrey* (1682) • J. Warner, *The history of English persecution of Catholics and the presbyterian plot*, ed. T. A. Birrell, trans. J. Bligh, 2 vols., Catholic RS, 47–8 (1953) • *A succinct narrative of the murder of Sir E. G. Octob. 12 1678, with the various … circumstances … relating to the said murder … collected out of the depositions given upon oath by Miles Prance and Captain W. Bedloe* (1683) • *The life and times of Anthony Wood*, ed. A. Clark, 5 vols., OHS, 19, 21, 26, 30, 40 (1891–1900) • W. Boys, *The narrative of M. W. Boys, citizen of London, faithfully relating what came to his knowledge concerning the late horrid Popish Plot* (1680) • *Eleventh report*, HMC (1887) • *Twelfth report*, HMC (1890) • W. Smith, *Contrivances of the fanatical conspirators in carrying on their treasons under the umbrage of the Popish Plot laid open* (1685) • J. Kenyon, *The Popish Plot* (1972)
Likenesses R. White, line engraving, BM, NPG • engraving, repro. in Prance, *A true narrative*

Prasad, Rajendra (1884–1963), president of India, was born at Zeradei, a village in the Saran district of Bihar, on 3 December 1884, the youngest son of Mahadev Sahai, who owned a small *zamindari* (landed estate) and practised Indian medicine. Prasad learned Persian at home and then joined first the district school at Chapra and then a private school at Patna. In 1897 he married Rajbansi Devi; they had two sons.

Gaining a scholarship, in 1902 Prasad moved to Presidency College in Calcutta, graduated in 1906, and went on to take an MA degree in English literature. After teaching for a year at a college in Muzaffarpur he returned to Calcutta to take a degree in law and set up a legal practice in 1911. He also taught at the law college.

Living in Calcutta, Prasad was influenced by the agitation from 1905 over the partition of Bengal; and in 1911 he joined the Indian National Congress. But his interests were mainly in his home province. In 1913 he presided over the Bihar students' conference in Monghyr and the next year was active in flood relief operations. In 1916 he shifted his legal practice to Patna, where a high court had been set up. The next year he came into contact with Mahatma Gandhi, who had interested himself in the agitation of the workers in the indigo plantations at Champaran; this marked a turning point in Prasad's life. In 1920 he joined Gandhi's non-co-operation movement and gave up his legal practice. As the movement required the boycott of educational institutions managed or subsidized by the government, Prasad established a National College at Patna and was its first principal. He also started *Desh* ('Nation'), a Hindi newspaper.

In 1924 Prasad served as chairman of the Patna municipal committee; but his primary concerns in the twenties were the promotion of *khaddar* (handspun cotton) and the propagation of Hindi to replace English as the all-India language. In 1928 he visited Britain to assist an old client whose case came up before the privy council, and thereafter travelled in Europe. At an anti-war conference in Graz, Austria, he was beaten up by right-wing elements.

In 1930 the Congress again engaged in a civil disobedience campaign led by Gandhi; Prasad was arrested in July and served a sentence of six months in Hazaribagh gaol. He was in the same prison again from January to July 1932, and from January 1933 to 15 January 1934. On the day of his release there was a massive earthquake in Bihar, followed by floods. Prasad's organization of relief operations brought him to national attention. He was elected president of the Congress for the annual session at Bombay in October.

For the next few years Prasad was at the centre of policy making in the Congress. He was regarded as an unquestioning follower of Gandhi, a leader of the right-wing group in Congress and the man acceptable to all sides in compromise settlements. In April 1939 he was re-elected president of the Congress in the crisis caused by the resignation of Subhas Chandra Bose following differences with Gandhi, and served in that capacity until March 1940.

In August 1942 Prasad, being a member of the Congress working committee which was outlawed by the government at the start of the Quit India campaign, was arrested and detained in Bankipore gaol until June 1945. From his early youth a sufferer from asthma, his poor health did not permit his joining the other members of the working committee in detention in Ahmednagar Fort, and the conditions under which he was detained were less stringent. In gaol he wrote in Hindi a book on the possible consequences of a partition of the country, later translated and published in English as *India Divided* (1946), and completed his autobiography, which he had begun in the early forties.

After his release Prasad was a Congress participant in the negotiations with the British government. In September 1946, when the Congress decided to join the interim government, he took charge of the food and agriculture portfolio. He was also, on 11 December 1946, elected president of the newly formed constituent assembly. But he left the government in December 1947 again to become president of the Congress, when the party was riven by a dispute between the organizational and governmental wings.

On 26 January 1950, when India became a republic, Prasad was elected president of the republic, and was re-elected in 1952 and 1957. But on each occasion he was elected by a majority in the Congress Party against the wishes of the prime minister, Jawaharlal Nehru. Prasad was a conservative Hindu conformist out of tune with the secular socialist views of Nehru. In consequence, relations between the president and the government were not happy. Prasad did not reconcile himself to the opinion of legal experts that he was bound to accept ministerial advice in all cases. He was particularly opposed to changes in Hindu personal law granting women the rights of divorce and inheritance; and in 1951 Nehru prevailed only by threatening resignation.

Prasad was tall, well-built, muscular, and of a dark complexion. He at no time enjoyed good health and in 1961 was seriously ill. After retirement in 1962 he returned to Patna and died there at the Sadaqat *ashram* on 23 February 1963.   S. GOPAL

Sources R. Prasad, *Rajendra Prasad: autobiography* (Bombay, 1957) · K. K. Datta, *Rajendra Prasad* (1970) · V. Choudhary, *Dr Rajendra Prasad: correspondence and select documents*, 21 vols. (1984–95)
Archives National Archives of India, New Delhi | FILM BFI NFTVA, news footage
Likenesses A. Bose, portrait, Rasthrapati Bhavan, New Delhi · H. S. Trivedi, portrait, Parliament House, New Delhi

Prasutagus (*d. AD 59/60*). *See under* Roman Britain, British leaders in (*act. 55 BC–AD 84*).

Pratt [*married name* Pearless], **Anne** (1806–1893), botanist, born on 5 December 1806 in Strood, Kent, the second of three daughters of Robert Pratt (1777–1819), a wholesale grocer of that town, and his wife, Sarah Bundock (1780–1845), of Huguenot descent. Her childhood and youth were passed at Chatham and she was educated by a Mrs Roffey at the Eastgate House School, Rochester. Her delicate health—'a stiff knee'—rendered her unfit for active pursuits and she devoted herself to literary study. A Scottish friend, Dr Dods, undertook to teach her botany and she soon became an ardent student. Aided by her elder sister, who collected plants for her, she formed an extensive herbarium and supplemented her collection by

Anne Pratt (1806–1893), by unknown photographer

making sketches of the specimens. The drawings afterwards formed illustrations for her books.

Anne Pratt left Chatham in 1846 and went to live with friends at Brixton and other places, but subsequently settled at Dover in 1849. There she wrote her principal work, *The Flowering Plants and Ferns of Great Britain*. Other changes of residence followed. On 4 December 1866 she married John Pearless of East Grinstead, Sussex. They lived at East Grinstead for two and a half years, after which they settled for some years at Redhill, Surrey. Anne died on 27 July 1893 at Rylett Road, Shepherd's Bush, London.

Anne Pratt's works were written in popular style but were said to be accurate. They were also instrumental in spreading a knowledge and love of botany, and were at one time acknowledged by a grant from the civil list. Her first, *The Field, the Garden, and the Woodland*, was published in 1838 and reached a third edition in less than ten years. Perhaps her most popular, especially among children, *Wild Flowers* (2 vols., 1852), was also issued in sheets for hanging up in schoolrooms. *The Flowering Plants and Ferns of Great Britain*, published in five volumes from 1855, was widely regarded as the best popular botanical work of her time.　　　　　　　B. B. WOODWARD, *rev.* GILES HUDSON

Sources *Journal of Horticulture, Cottage Gardener and Home Farmer*, 27 (1893), 102 · *Journal of Botany, British and Foreign*, 32 (1894), 205–7 · Desmond, *Botanists*, rev. edn

Likenesses photograph, Linn. Soc. [*see illus.*] · portrait, Carnegie Mellon University, Pittsburgh, Hunt Botanical Library

Charles Pratt, first Earl Camden (1714–1794), by Nathaniel Dance, 1767–9

Pratt, Charles, first Earl Camden (1714–1794), lawyer and politician, was born in Kensington, London, and baptized there on 21 March 1714, the third son of Sir John *Pratt (1657–1725), MP and later lord chief justice of king's bench, and his second wife, Elizabeth (*d.* 1728), daughter of the Revd Hugh Wilson, vicar of Trefeglwys and a canon of Bangor Cathedral. He was educated at Eton College (1725–31) and King's College, Cambridge (BA, 1736; MA, 1740), and developed an early interest in the constitution as a safeguard of liberty which was to characterize his life. Always destined for the law, in accordance with his father's wishes, he was entered at the Inner Temple in 1728 and was called to the bar in 1738. He so failed to prosper at king's bench and on the western circuit that he despaired of his profession and thought of the church, until in the mid-1740s his career was given a much-needed boost by a friendly senior counsel, Robert Henley, later as Lord Northington his predecessor as lord chancellor. Once established in his profession Pratt made an advantageous marriage on 4 October 1749 to Elizabeth (*d.* 1779), daughter of Nicholas Jeffreys and eventually heir of Brecon Priory, an estate that commanded a leading political interest in Brecknockshire: they had a son, the politician John Jeffreys *Pratt, and four daughters.

Champion of liberty By the 1750s Pratt was involved in cases of political import before the House of Commons and at Westminster Hall, notably the prosecution in 1752 of Alexander Murray for libel, when he first argued, successfully for the defence, that the jury rather than the judge should assess the intent of a libel and not merely the fact of publication, a legal contention he helped to bring

to a triumphant conclusion forty years later. Appointed a king's counsel in 1755, Pratt was drawn into politics by William Pitt, a friend at Eton who often consulted him on legal and constitutional issues. Pitt's connection with the opposition Leicester House court of the young prince of Wales led in 1756 to Pratt's appointment as attorney-general to the prince, in preference to a judgeship offered him by the duke of Newcastle, the prime minister. In July 1757 Pitt, when forming his famous wartime coalition with Newcastle, insisted on the appointment of Pratt as attorney-general over the head of the solicitor-general, Charles Yorke, son of Newcastle's ally Lord Hardwicke, the former lord chancellor, who earlier had hindered the career of Yorke's perceived rival.

The two men perforce had to work together in the routine legal business of government, and the Pratt–Yorke judgment of 24 December 1757 was a landmark in imperial history. The crown's law officers distinguished between territories acquired by conquest, where the property as well as the dominion was vested in the crown, and those acquired by private treaty, where the crown enjoyed only sovereignty: this opinion, which related to the East India Company, was subsequently applied elsewhere in the British empire.

Pratt was brought into the House of Commons as MP for the burgage borough of Downton, but was rarely called upon to defend the successful war ministry in parliamentary debate. He sponsored the Habeas Corpus Amendment Bill of 1758, designed to extend that measure to cover civil and political as well as criminal cases. It was favoured by Pitt but rejected by the House of Lords. In the same year Pratt as attorney-general successfully prosecuted both Florence Hensey, an Irishman who was a French spy, and the libeller John Shebbeare when, though not defence counsel, he still maintained that the decision be taken by the jury. In 1760 Pratt led the famous prosecution of Lord Ferrers, a peer convicted and hanged for murdering a servant, to the astonishment of European high society. But Pratt's chief activity in these years was the development of a flourishing practice in the court of chancery which gave him financial security, and about this time he bought the estate of Camden Place in Kent.

The time of quiet prosperity and growing reputation ended in 1761. Pratt's political predicament when his mentor, Pitt, left the ministry in October proved to be brief, for the death on 15 December of the lord chief justice of common pleas opened a vacancy to which he could retreat from the political scene. Resigning his parliamentary seat, accepting the concomitant honours of a knighthood on 28 December, and being sworn of the privy council, Pratt took the judicial post in January 1762. The court of common pleas, by contrast with that of king's bench, seldom dealt with cases of political import, and Pratt may well have thought his brief political career to be over. But when John Wilkes was arrested on 30 April 1763 under a general warrant for an alleged seditious libel in the forty-fifth number of the *North Briton*, it was to the obviously sympathetic judge at common pleas that application was made for his release. Judge Pratt freed Wilkes, declaring him immune as an MP from arrest on such a charge. The popularity Pratt thereby acquired with the London mob went to his head, encouraging him during the summer of 1763 to incite juries into awarding excessive damages, quite disproportionate to any inconvenience suffered, to printers mistakenly arrested in the same case. On 6 December, Pratt followed up this behaviour by condemning the use of general warrants for the search of houses and other buildings, Wilkes being awarded £1000 in damages by the jury. The contemporary press celebrated this victory for liberty. 'By this important decision, every Englishman has the satisfaction of seeing that his home is his castle' (*St James's Chronicle*, 8 Dec 1763). Two years later he confirmed and strengthened this ruling by his judgment in the landmark *Entinck* v. *Carrington* case. This arose not, as is often stated, out of the *North Briton* affair, but from a ministerial attempt in 1762 to prosecute the weekly periodical *Monitor*. On 27 November 1765 he condemned as 'contrary to law' the use of a general warrant to search for and seize papers in charges of seditious libel. Of greater significance even than the verdict was the reason for his decision. He refuted 'the argument for state necessity' by declaring that 'the common law does not understand that kind of reasoning', thereby confirming the common law as the best defence against arbitrary government (Holdsworth, *Eng. law*, 670).

By then Pratt had re-entered parliament, being created Baron Camden on 17 July 1765. His peerage was one of the measures by which the incoming ministry of Lord Rockingham vainly sought to win the support of William Pitt. Camden declined to speak in the first Lords debate on the American Stamp Act crisis, but attended the Commons debate of 14 January 1766 to ascertain Pitt's line. The subsequent speeches of the two men on 3 February were so similar that contemporaries thought they had been prepared together. In his maiden Lords speech that day Camden argued that taxation was founded on consent, and therefore depended on representation. He was one of the minority of five peers who then voted against the ministerial resolution asserting what was the generally accepted right of parliament to tax all British territories. But Camden logically supported the administration in the Lords debate of 11 March over repeal of the Stamp Act, when he claimed that the colonial resistance had been aroused by hardship caused by that taxation, an unconvincing contention in the light even of contemporary knowledge.

Lord chancellor It was from Camden that George III in May 1766 ascertained that Pitt was willing to form a ministry, but Camden was absent on the midland circuit when the change of administration took place in July. It was generally assumed that Pitt, now to become earl of Chatham, would make Camden his lord chancellor, and he accepted the office when he returned to London, stipulating an additional allowance of £1500 and the reversion of a lucrative exchequer tellership for his elder son John Jeffreys Pratt, to whom the office reverted in May 1780. Camden became lord chancellor on 30 July 1766. It was a post that, as well as sitting on the woolsack as *de facto* speaker of the House of Lords, involved several discrete legal functions. He presided over the court of chancery, and although his speciality was common law, his judgments in the equity cases that now came before him have been deemed sound, if not innovative. As head of the law lords Camden also presided over appeals and other legal cases referred to the House of Lords. In 1767 he secured unanimous approval for the opinion of Lord Mansfield that the City of London should not fine dissenters for refusing to serve as corporate officials when they were disqualified by the Corporation Act, a reinforcement of religious liberty. Camden's political impartiality was demonstrated when in 1768 a complaint of John Wilkes about serving two prison sentences as consecutive and not concurrent was dismissed. In 1769 he overrode both public opinion and evidential probability when finding for the mother in his judgment on the notorious Douglas legitimacy case. Camden continued to play a leading role in such cases even after leaving the woolsack. Of long-term significance was his decisive 1774 opinion that authors had no perpetual literary copyright, since that would handicap the advance of knowledge, and he played a part in rejecting a Copyright Bill of the same year.

As a politician the new lord chancellor was soon exposed to criticism that questioned his role as a champion of liberty against state power. A parliamentary ban on the export of corn expired on 26 August 1766, and the combination of a poor harvest and the resumption of exports provoked widespread disorder through fears of high prices and of possible starvation. The Chatham ministry, acting through the privy council and with the support of Lord Chancellor Camden, decided upon a royal proclamation of 26 September prohibiting corn exports until after parliament met on 11 November. But this action breached the 1689 Bill of Rights provision that forbade the crown to suspend laws, and the matter was promptly raised in both houses of parliament. Camden found Chatham and himself accused of tyrannical behaviour. The plea of necessity, so contrary to Camden's own famous legal opinion of the previous year, did not allay parliamentary resentment, especially when Camden unwisely claimed that it had been only 'a forty days tyranny', and the ministry had to pacify criticism by the humiliation of an act of indemnity.

Camden's reputation as a champion of liberty was soon further weakened over the American problem. Although the Chatham group had opposed the 1766 Declaratory Act they now accepted it as the law, and sundry acts of colonial defiance hardened Chatham's attitude to America. Camden as usual followed his lead, his Lords speeches of 1767 urging a firm but prudent stance. On the key issue of colonial taxation the lord chancellor was a member of the cabinet that endorsed Charles Townshend's 1767 scheme of taxation by port duties, as meeting the supposed American distinction of internal and external taxes. Edmund Burke later recalled that 'Lord Camden … contended that these were external' and so acceptable to the colonies (*Correspondence*, 1.280n.). Yet when in 1768 the American challenge to all parliamentary taxation showed that claim to have been a delusion, Camden promptly adopted the view that colonial taxation was 'inexpedient'. A letter of 4 October 1768 to the acting prime minister the duke of Grafton reeked of indecision:

> I do not know what to advise … I submit to the declaratory law, and have thought it my duty, upon that ground, as a minister, to exert my constitutional power to carry out the duty act into execution. But as a member of the legislature I cannot bring myself to advise violent measures.

The American crisis coincided with the final end of the Chatham ministry, and Camden promptly transferred his allegiance. 'You are my Pole Star, Lord Chatham being eclipsed. I had rather see your Grace at the head of government than any other man in the kingdom' (*Autobiography … of Grafton*, 215–17). Since Chatham gave ill health as the reason for his resignation in October 1768, Camden and others of his followers could continue in office under the Grafton ministry without embarrassment. The reshuffled cabinet was finely balanced on America between advocates of coercion and conciliation. Camden was foremost among the latter, opposing hardline proposals of the American secretary, Hillsborough, and playing an important role in devising the tax concessions decided upon by the cabinet on 1 May 1769. He was deemed personally responsible for the public promise that no future taxes would be levied on the colonies, and he voted in the cabinet minority that vainly sought to include the tea duty with the other Townshend duties to be repealed. Those concessions sufficed to allay the colonial discontent in 1770, but the tea tax remained a hostage to fortune.

By that time America had long been eclipsed as a political issue by the second Wilkes case of the Middlesex election. The return of John Wilkes for Middlesex on 28 March 1768 was a shock to the ministry. Camden, absent in Bath, commented to Grafton that 'the event is disagreeable, and unforeseen'. He was as aghast as his colleagues that 'a convict and an outlaw' could be elected. Although Camden stated that expulsion might be according to precedent he feared the consequences if Wilkes should then be re-elected, and advised that the best tactic would be to ignore him (*Autobiography … of Grafton*, 199–200). When the ministry decided on expulsion Camden, whether through timidity, love of popularity, or knowledge of Chatham's opinion, parted company with Grafton on the issue, writing on 9 January 1769: 'Your Grace and I have unfortunately differed … I had rather pardon Wilkes than punish him. This is a political opinion independent of the case' (ibid., 201). Camden thereafter distanced himself from his colleagues on the matter, seemingly being absent from cabinet and silent in parliament.

In opposition In July 1769 Camden's political allegiance reverted to Chatham, whose return then to health was marked by denunciation of ministerial policies on Wilkes and America. Only royal pressure kept Camden in office until the end of 1769, with the lord chancellor generally being considered as in open opposition. When the new parliamentary session began on 9 January 1770 Chatham moved in the Lords an opposition amendment to the address. The lord chancellor thereupon left the woolsack to break his self-imposed silence:

> I have often drooped and hung down my head in Council, and disapproved by my looks those steps which I knew my avowed opposition could not prevent … I now proclaim to the world, that I entirely coincide in the opinion expressed by my noble friend … respecting this unconstitutional and illegal vote of the House of Commons. (Cobbett, *Parl. Hist.*, 16.644)

Camden, on the advice of his friends, did not resign, but George III was scandalized that a lord chancellor should oppose the king's government, and insisted upon his dismissal, on 17 January 1770.

Camden may well have expected a prompt return to that office if, as expected, the combined opposition parties of Chatham, Rockingham, and Grenville brought down the king's ministry: but although Grafton resigned, Lord North successfully took over, and Camden began twelve years of opposition to his administration. Since after early 1770 Chatham seldom attended parliament for some years, and Camden's relationship with his deputy, Lord Shelburne, was on the cool side, Camden often found himself playing a lone hand. Much of the parliamentary session of 1770–71 was taken up by a dispute over the law of libel, highlighted by a personal controversy between Camden and an old legal adversary, Lord Chief Justice Mansfield of king's bench. The issue was again whether a jury should decide whether an alleged libel was criminal or innocent or, as Mansfield maintained, merely the fact of publication: but a much-anticipated Lords confrontation between the two lawyers never took place. During the next two sessions Camden adopted a low political profile, although in 1772 he did oppose the provision of the Royal Family Marriage Act extending it to all descendants of George II, pointing out the future impracticability of the clause.

The American crisis of 1774 brought Camden back into the forefront of politics. When the Lords debated the Boston Port Bill on 28 March he criticized as mischievous the tea duty that had led to the defiance of the Boston Tea Party. Although this view was consistent with his cabinet opinion of 1769 he was continually reminded afterwards that he had been lord chancellor when the tax was first introduced. In reply he maintained that he had personally never consented to any American taxation, resorting in 1776 to the quibble that he had been absent from the relevant cabinet meeting of 1767. The Chathamite group at first supported the coercive legislation of 1774, and on 11 May Camden sided with the ministry over the Massachusetts Government Bill. 'I am too much of an Englishman not to pray for the success of this country let her cause be good or bad' (Lord Camden's speech in the House of Lords, BL, Add. MS 35912, fols. 221–2). But Chathamite fears that the Massachusetts Justice Bill would provoke colonial resistance led Camden into opposing that measure on 18 May. Thereafter the Chathamite group opposed ministerial policy on America, and Camden played a full part in parliamentary debates. His major speech on America, timed at ninety minutes, was on 16 February 1775 against the New England Trade and Fishery Bill, designed to coerce the northern colonies by crippling their economy. The speech was widely thought to have been concocted with Benjamin Franklin for American consumption. The former Massachusetts governor Thomas Hutchinson scornfully commented: 'I never heard a greater flow of words, but my knowledge of facts in this controversy caused his misrepresentations and glosses to appear in a very strong light.' Camden admitted that both parliament and public opinion were behind government policy, which he condemned as being not a trade bill but 'a bill of war; it draws the sword, and in its necessary consequences plunges the empire into civil and unnatural war'. He quoted John Locke's opinion that resistance to tyranny was justified, and declared the military conquest of America, a free people in a vast country, to be impossible:

My lords, it is evident that England must one day lose the dominion of America. It is impossible that this petty island can continue in dependence that mighty continent … To protract the time of separation to a distant day is all that can be hoped. (Simmons and Thomas, 5.540–52)

Later in the session Camden, responding to a petition from a minority of British settlers, on 17 May 1775 moved the repeal of the Quebec Act as incompatible with the religion and constitution of Britain: it is not known whether he had opposed its passage in 1774, for no reports of relevant Lords debates survive. Camden now gave vent to deep prejudices, claiming the secret purpose was to create a popish army in Canada to subdue the protestant British

colonies, an accusation so absurd as to be deemed unworthy of a reply. The motion was defeated by eighty-eight votes to twenty-eight after proxies had been called for.

The outbreak of the American War of Independence reduced the Chathamite group to despair, and Camden withdrew from parliament for a while. 'America is lost and the war afoot' he wrote on 24 January 1776 to Grafton, whose personal friendship he had retained since their political split in 1770 and who had now quit government for opposition (*Autobiography … of Grafton*, 279). The Chathamite line during the war was to advocate conciliation, deploring equally the idea of American independence and the attempt to prevent it. Camden spoke often and at length in parliament on these themes, although less so from 1778 after the death of Chatham and French intervention in the conflict. He remained in the forefront of the political battle, and his speech on 27 November 1781 was rated excellent even by political opponents. But, nearing seventy, Camden did not claim his old post of lord chancellor when Lord North's fall in March 1782 was followed by a coalition ministry of the two former opposition factions led by Rockingham and Shelburne. He became lord president of the council, a cabinet post of high rank and little work. In Lords debates Camden supported both the programme of economical reform, designed to reduce government corruption of parliament, and the legislative independence of Ireland. But the ministry was an uneasy alliance, and Prime Minister Rockingham's death on 1 July merely precipitated its collapse. Camden continued in office, as Shelburne's new administration essentially had a Chathamite base; but after Commons defeats in February 1783 over the American peace terms Camden advised Shelburne to resign, emphasizing the point by doing so himself. Camden went into active opposition to the ensuing Fox–North coalition ministry and, denouncing the measure as a patronage job, played a leading role in the Lords debate of 9 December 1783 on Fox's India Bill that resulted in its defeat and the dismissal of the ministry. Camden then waived his claim to office to facilitate the ministerial arrangements of the younger William Pitt, son of his old political mentor. But a year later he accepted once more the post of lord president, which he retained until his death nearly a decade later, being raised to Earl Camden on 13 May 1786, with an additional peerage of Viscount Bayham so that his son could enjoy that courtesy title. Camden favoured Pitt's Parliamentary Reform Bill of 1785, and defended in Lords debates his Irish trade proposals of the same year. Then, as his parliamentary career was beginning to fade away, Camden was suddenly propelled to the forefront of the political scene by the prevarication of Lord Chancellor Thurlow in the Regency crisis, when George III in November 1788 suffered the illness then thought to be insanity and subsequently diagnosed as porphyria. As lord president he conducted the privy council examination of the king's doctors. It was then Camden who, because of Thurlow's behaviour, had to put forward in the House of Lords the ministerial contention that parliament should appoint the regent, as against the opposition's claim for the immediate right of the prince of Wales, their ally, so to act. Camden's resolution to that effect was carried in the Lords by ninety-nine votes to sixty-six on 23 December 1788; and on 22 January 1789 he carried by ninety-four to sixty-eight another that the prince should be appointed regent only under restrictions, so as to avoid inconvenience if the king should recover. George III did so the next month, obviating the need for that arrangement.

Thereafter Camden took little part in parliamentary debate, with the notable exception of his support for Fox's Libel Act of 1792, that established as law one of his own long-cherished opinions: that the jury, not the judges, should decide whether or not a publication was a libel. In the Lords debate of 16 May 1792 on the second reading Camden argued that the issue was intention, and a jury should decide that, as it did in murder cases. Moving from legal to political argument, he then said that the people of England, represented by a jury, must take care of the liberty of the press, not judges, who were possibly susceptible to government influence. Camden's speech was deemed instrumental in securing a Lords majority of fifty-seven to thirty-two, despite the unanimous opinion of the judges to the contrary. Camden maintained a regular attendance at cabinet, which was sometimes held at his own house to allow for the ill health that led him to move from Camden Place in Kent to his town house in Hill Street, Berkeley Square, London, where he died on 18 April 1794. He was buried at Seal, Kent, near the Pratt family home of The Wildernesse.

Significance Legal historians have acclaimed Lord Camden as a great lord chancellor, Lord Campbell perhaps because he allowed his whig and even radical prejudices to sway his judicial opinions. Sir William Holdsworth, in his magisterial *History of English Law*, rated Camden as 'a great constitutional lawyer, a great legal historian, and a great common lawyer—a worthy successor, by virtue both of his learning and his principles, of such predecessors as Coke and Hale and Holt' (Holdsworth, *Eng. law*, 10.672). But a cynical view more recently propounded is that Camden's legal opinions were delivered to accord with Chatham's political views. Certainly in parliament he faithfully followed Chatham's views on Wilkes and America, and a town in Maine, USA, was named after him in 1791. His loyalty to Chatham, too, was tempered by a propensity, evinced in 1761 and 1768, to cling to office after Chatham had resigned. Altogether he served fifteen years in cabinet, under five different premiers.

In appearance Camden was a small, well-made man, with a pleasant face. He eschewed the vices of lechery and gambling characteristic of his time, but had a reputation for physical laziness and gluttony. His modes of relaxation were music, the theatre, romantic fiction, conversation, and food: that he was an epicure is shown by his scathing criticism of French cuisine, after a visit to France in 1783, for the use of sauces to disguise the poor quality of the meat. Camden, a younger son of a second marriage, died a man of wealth, derived from his legal career and his wife's inheritance, which included the area of London later known as Camden Town.   PETER D. G. THOMAS

Sources H. S. Eeles, *Lord Chancellor Camden and his family* (1934) · J. Campbell, *Lives of the lord chancellors*, 8 vols. (1845–69), vol. 5 · Holdsworth, *Eng. law*, vol. 10 · R. C. Simmons and P. D. G. Thomas, eds., *Proceedings and debates of the British parliaments respecting North America, 1754–1783*, 6 vols. (1982–7) · *Autobiography and political correspondence of Augustus Henry, third duke of Grafton*, ed. W. R. Anson (1898) · *The correspondence of Edmund Burke*, 1, ed. T. W. Copeland (1958) · P. D. G. Thomas, *John Wilkes: a friend to liberty* (1996) · P. D. G. Thomas, *British politics and the Stamp Act crisis: the first phase of the American revolution, 1763–1767* (1975) · P. D. G. Thomas, *The Townshend duties crisis, 1767–1773* (1987) · P. D. G. Thomas, *Tea party to independence: the third phase of the American Revolution, 1773–1776* (1991) · P. Brown, *The Chathamites* (1967) · H. V. Bowen, 'A question of sovereignty: the Bengal land revenue issue, 1765–67', *Journal of Imperial and Commonwealth History*, 16 (1987–8), 155–76 · J. Oldham, *The Mansfield manuscripts and the growth of English law in the eighteenth century*, 2 vols. (1992) · GEC, *Peerage*, new edn, 2.500

Archives CKS, corresp. and papers | BL, letters to first and second earls of Hardwicke, Add. MSS 35594–35682, *passim* · BL, corresp. with duke of Newcastle and first earl of Chichester, Add. MSS 32940, 32991, 33089, *passim* · NRA, priv. coll., letters to Lord Lansdowne · PRO, letters to Lord Chatham and Lady Chatham and to William Pitt, PRO 30/8 · PRO NIre., letters to Lord Castlereagh, D3030 · Sheff. Arch., letters to marquess of Rockingham · Suffolk RO, Bury St Edmunds, letters to duke of Grafton · U. Nott. L., letters to second duke of Newcastle

Likenesses B. Wilson, oils, 1759, Harvard U., law school · T. Hudson, oils, 1764, Exeter Guildhall · J. Reynolds, oils, 1764, Guildhall Art Gallery, London · J. G. Haid, mezzotint, pubd 1766 (after J. Reynolds), BM, NPG · N. Dance, oils, 1767–9, NPG [*see illus.*] · R. Stewart, mezzotint, pubd 1779 (after unknown artist), BM, NPG · J. Ogborne, stipple, pubd 1794 (after G. Dance), BM, NPG · W. Behnes, bust, 1846, Eton · J. S. Copley, drawing, Metropolitan Museum of Art, New York · N. Dance, chalk drawing, BM · J. Faber junior, mezzotint (after A. Ramsay), BM, NPG · J. Faber junior, mezzotint (after unknown artist), NPG · T. Gainsborough, portrait; formerly in the possession of Lord Northbourne, in 1896 · mezzotint (after unknown artist), NPG · oils (after J. Reynolds), NPG · Wedgwood medallions, Wedgwood Museum, Stoke-on-Trent

Wealth at death Brecon Priory and estates in London to wife (seemingly entailed); £11,000 to one daughter, £500 to others; Camden Place, Kent, to son

Pratt, Sir Charles (1768–1838), army officer, was reportedly of an Irish family which may have been distantly connected with the earls of Camden. After becoming an ensign on 14 April 1794 he was promoted lieutenant, 5th foot (later Northumberland Fusiliers) on 3 September 1795, captain on 28 February 1798, major on 25 August 1804, lieutenant-colonel on 25 March 1808, colonel on 4 June 1814, major-general on 27 May 1825, and lieutenant-general and colonel of the 95th foot (later the Derbyshire regiment) on 23 December 1834.

Pratt commanded the 1st battalion of the 5th foot which embarked at Cork in May 1812, and landed at Lisbon to join the army under Wellington in the Peninsula. He took a prominent part in a long series of brilliant engagements. Both battalions of the 5th shared in the honours and triumphs of Salamanca on 22 July 1812; and he and his men further distinguished themselves at Vitoria on 21 June

1813. In 1814 he was present in command of the 1st battalion at the battles of Nivelle and Orthez, and at the crowning victory of the war, the battle of Toulouse. Pratt was made a CB. He remained with his regiment, serving in the army of occupation in France until 1818. In 1819 the 5th embarked for St Vincent. Pratt returned home in May 1825. In 1830 he was made KCB but declined command of the troops in Jamaica. He died (childless) of an apoplectic fit at Brighton on 25 October 1838.

B. H. SOULSBY, rev. DAVID GATES

Sources *Army List* · *GM*, 2nd ser., 11 (1839), 210 · *The Times* (29 Oct 1838) · R. Cannon, ed., *Historical record of the fifth regiment of foot, or Northumberland fusiliers* (1838) · D. Gates, *The Spanish ulcer: a history of the Peninsular War* (1986) · R. Muir, *Britain and the defeat of Napoleon, 1807–1815* (1996)
Archives NRA, priv. coll., corresp. and papers

Pratt, Hodgson (1824–1907), peace campaigner and co-operative movement activist, born at Bath on 10 January 1824, was the eldest of five sons of Samuel Peace Pratt and his wife, Susanna Martha Hodgson (d. 1875). After education at East India College, Haileybury, where he won a prize for an English essay in his first term, he matriculated at London University in 1844. In 1847 he joined the East India Company's service at Calcutta. In 1848 he became assistant magistrate and collector at Murshidabad, and the following year he married Sarah Caroline Wetherall, daughter of an Irish squire. In 1851 he was superintendent of the land revenue survey of Monghyr, in 1853 he was joint magistrate and deputy collector there, and in 1854 he became under-secretary to the government of Bengal and inspector of public instruction there.

Following Sir Charles Wood's establishment of national education for India, Pratt became inspector of public instruction for the lower provinces. He was concerned to stimulate the educational and social development of the province of Bengal, and urged on the Bengalis closer relations with British life and thought. In 1851 he helped to found the Vernacular Literature Society, which published Bengali translations of standard English literature, including Macaulay's *Life of Clive*, *Robinson Crusoe*, Lamb's *Tales from Shakespeare*, and selections from the *Percy Anecdotes*. Pratt acted as the society's secretary until 1856. He also started a school of industrial art in Calcutta. In 1857 Pratt was at home on leave and at the close of that year he contributed to *The Economist* articles and letters dealing with Indian questions, social, political, educational, and religious, which were published collectively in a pamphlet. He founded, with Mary Carpenter, the National Indian Association, supporting nationalist demands for self-government, and remained closely involved with it until 1905. The spread of the Indian mutiny recalled Pratt hurriedly to India, which he left finally in 1861; he resigned from the Indian Civil Service in 1863.

On settling in Britain, Pratt immediately threw himself into the industrial co-operative movement, in association with Edward Vansittart Neale and George Jacob Holyoake. He was a member of the first central board of the modern co-operative movement and, with Thomas Hughes, was a

Hodgson Pratt (1824–1907), by Felix Moscheles, 1891

guarantor of the London Co-operative Agency, established to supply wholesale to southern co-operative societies. In 1874 he helped to establish a London branch of the Co-operative Wholesale Society and throughout the 1870s and 1880s he worked to found new stores and societies in metropolitan and suburban London. Pratt was elected chairman of the council of the Guild of Co-operators (1878), established to disseminate co-operative knowledge, and later succeeded Benjamin Jones as its secretary. Pratt originated the idea of the International Co-partnership Alliance, supported the Labour Co-partnership Association, founded the Co-operative Permanent Building Society in 1884, and advocated the formation of a co-operative college to provide craft, technical, and academic education.

In 1864 Pratt met Henry Solly and became a member of the council of the Working Men's Club and Institute Union (founded by Solly in June 1862). In its interest he travelled up and down the country, encouraging struggling branches and forming new ones. He was president from 1885 to 1902. With Solly he also started trade classes for workmen in St Martin's Lane, London, in 1874. In 1867 he was a vice-president with Auberon Herbert, W. E. Forster, George Joachim Goschen, and others of the Paris excursion committee, through whose efforts over 3000 British workmen visited the Paris Exhibition of that year.

At the same time Pratt, who had a perfect command of French, was an ardent champion of international arbitration. On the outbreak of the Franco-Prussian War of 1870 he pleaded for a peaceful settlement of the dispute. Two years later he joined in an appeal to M. Thiers, the French premier, for the release of Elisée Reclus, the geographer, who had supported the commune and been taken prisoner. In 1880 he joined William Phillips and others in founding the International Arbitration and Peace Association, and became first chairman of the executive committee. Four years later (1 July 1884) he founded, and for some time edited, the association's *Journal* (later entitled *Concord*). On behalf of the association he visited nearly all the countries of Europe and helped in the formation of many kindred continental societies—in Belgium, Italy, Germany, Austria, and Hungary. He took part in many international peace congresses at Paris and elsewhere from 1889 onwards. For the association Pratt produced translations of works by Elie Ducommun and Descamps, published respectively as *The Programme of the Peace Movement* (1896) and (summarized in English) *The Organisation of International Arbitration* (1897).

Notwithstanding his disinterested and retiring disposition, Pratt's persuasive advocacy of international arbitration and industrial co-operation was appreciated by governments and peoples at home and abroad and he was recommended for the Nobel peace prize in December 1906. He was a fellow of the Royal Geographical Society, vice-president of the National Association for the Promotion of State Colonisation (1886) the Sunday Society, and the Workmen's Peace Association, and an executive member of the Travelling Tax Abolition Committee.

In 1892 Pratt married his second wife, Monica, daughter of the Revd James Mangan DD LLD. He spent the last years of his life at Le Pecq, Seine et Oise, France, and died at his home, 12 avenue du Pavillon, Sully-Le-Pecq, on 26 February 1907. His wife and their daughter survived him. He was buried in Highgate cemetery. The Hodgson Pratt memorial fund was established in 1910, awarding annual scholarships to the co-operative college and prizes for essays on peace; an annual Hodgson Pratt memorial lecture was also founded.   W. B. OWEN, *rev.* MATTHEW LEE

Sources Concord [International Arbitration and Peace Association] (March 1907) • *The Times* (5 March 1907) • *The Times* (14 Nov 1907) • H. Solly, *'These eighty years', or, The story of an unfinished life*, 2 vols. (1893) • B. T. Hall, *Our fifty years* (1912) • J. Saville, 'Pratt, Hodgson', *DLB*, vol. 1 • J. J. Dent, *Hodgson Pratt* (1932) • H. L. Malchow, *Agitators and promoters in the age of Gladstone and Disraeli: a biographical dictionary* (1983) • CGPLA Eng. & Wales (1907)
Archives Bishopsgate Institute, London, letters to George Howell • Co-operative Union, Holyoake House, Manchester, papers relating to the Hodgson Pratt Memorial Fund
Likenesses F. Moscheles, oils, 1891, NPG [*see illus.*] • F. Moscheles, oils, 1912, Club and Institute Union, Clerkenwell Road, London
Wealth at death £27,718 10s. 6d.: resworn probate, 25 April 1907, CGPLA Eng. & Wales

Pratt, Sir John (1657–1725), judge, was born in Oxford, the son of Richard Pratt (1629–1692) and his first wife, Elizabeth Skaye (d. before 1662). The family had been adversely affected by adherence to the royalist cause in the civil wars, Pratt's grandfather John Pratt (d. 1673) being forced to sell Carswell Priory in Devon. Pratt was educated at Oxford at Magdalen Hall (1673) and Wadham College (1674); he graduated BA in 1676, became a fellow of Wadham in 1678, and proceeded MA in 1679. While at Oxford he became associated with the whig cause, being

reproved in a local coffee house for proposing a toast 'to the confusion of all popish princes' (*Life and Times of Anthony Wood*, 2.497–8) and when challenged specifically citing the duke of York. He entered the Inner Temple in 1675 and was called to the bar in 1682. Henceforth he pursued a legal career, first in London, until he reputedly fell foul of Lord Chief Justice Jeffreys, and then in Exeter. On 17 November 1683 he married Elizabeth (d. 1705), daughter and coheir of Henry Gregory, rector of Middleton Stoney, Oxfordshire. They had five sons and four daughters. He later married Elizabeth (d. 1728), daughter of Hugh Wilson, vicar of Trefeglwys, Monmouthshire, and canon of Bangor. They had four sons and four daughters.

Following the revolution of 1688 Pratt made steady progress in his profession, and was chosen by the attorney-general, Sir Thomas Trevor, as one of the crown's counsel before the House of Lords during the trial for high treason of the Jacobite conspirator Sir John Fenwick. The leading whig lawyer, Lord Keeper Sir John Somers, approached Sir George Treby, chief justice of common pleas: 'I know your Lordship has a favour for him, and therefore I hope you will send for him and advise him what he is to say, and how he is to manage himself in that place' (*Fitzherbert MSS*, 44). Pratt duly appeared before the Lords in December, although he may have found the experience somewhat daunting as in 1702 Bishop Nicolson recollected him 'swooning' during the trial. Thenceforth Pratt appeared intermittently as counsel before the Lords, most notably in June 1698 against the passage of the bill settling the trade to the East Indies, until 1704 when his appearances began to increase markedly. His legal talent was recognized on 1 October 1700 when he was made a serjeant-at-law. Pratt made his first significant land purchase, the estate at Wildernesse (formerly Stidulfe's Place), Kent, which was sold pursuant to a private act passed in 1704. By 1705 his reputation was such that he was grouped among the 'great counsel' (*Portland MSS*, 4.176). On 3 December 1708 he appeared before the Commons as counsel for the petitioners in the case of the right of the eldest sons of Scottish representative peers to sit in the Commons. With an enhanced profile among the Scots in the following January he was counsel before the Lords over the objection made to the duke of Dover's (Queensberry) voting in the elections for Scottish representative peers. On 17 January 1710 the House of Lords approved Pratt's appointment as counsel for the outspoken tory cleric Dr Henry Sacheverell, who was being impeached by the Commons, but one week later Pratt withdrew from the case owing to Sacheverell's determination to milk the situation for the political advantage of the tories. Pratt's withdrawal may have hindered his chances of securing a seat at Marlborough in the general election held in the following autumn.

In December 1711 Pratt was again embroiled as counsel in a matter of great significance for the Scots: the eligibility of the duke of Hamilton to sit in the Lords by virtue of his patent as duke of Brandon. Although Bishop Burnet described him as 'one of the most able advocates of that time', Pratt was content to play second fiddle to Sir

Thomas Powys in arguing Hamilton's case. On 28 December 1711 Pratt was elected to parliament in a by-election for Midhurst, a seat he owed to the whiggish duke of Somerset. Pratt's career in the Commons was low key, although in January 1712 he exerted himself in defence of the duke of Marlborough who was under attack for corruption. Indeed, in April it was rumoured that should Marlborough be prosecuted through the courts then Pratt would be one of his counsel. Pratt contributed to the whig cause outside the Commons in February 1713 when he joined an array of distinguished whig lawyers in the defence of the journalist George Ridpath for articles which appeared in the *Flying Post*. Pratt added to his landed estates in 1714, as a result of a private act authorizing the sale of Bayham Priory on the Sussex–Kent border.

The Hanoverian succession saw a resurgence in Pratt's fortunes. His knighthood (11 October 1714) was the precursor of his appointment as a justice of king's bench (20 November). In April–May 1718 he served for twenty-five days as a commissioner of the great seal in the hiatus following Lord Cowper's resignation, and following Parker's assumption of the chancellorship he succeeded him as lord chief justice (19 May 1718). He became a privy councillor on 9 October 1718. Pratt's first significant case concerned the claim by George I to control the education and marriage of members of the royal family. Pratt found that as the crown had an undoubted right in respect of marriage it 'is a natural and necessary consequence' that it also had the care of their education (*State trials*, 15.1216). In 1721 Pratt stepped into the breach following the resignation of John Aislabie as chancellor of the exchequer following the South Sea Bubble crisis, and held the office for longer than the usual period of a few days. In November 1722 he presided over the trial for treason of Christopher Layer, acquiring a certain reputation for harshness in keeping the prisoner in chains. Indeed, upon sentencing Layer he thought the accused's crimes even more heinous because of his legal training, which ought to have brought him to a proper understanding of 'the excellency of our happy constitution and government' (ibid., 16.320). Pratt also presided over the cause between Richard Bentley and Cambridge University, which saw him resist pressure from the whig ministry to protect one of Bentley's whig antagonists, John Colbatch. Pratt died on 24 February 1725 at his house in Ormond Street, London, death depriving him of the chancellorship which Parker was soon to relinquish. His heir was John, the fourth son from his first marriage. Charles *Pratt, his son from his second marriage, became lord chancellor and was created Lord Camden. Jane, his daughter from his second marriage, married Nicholas *Hardinge, while Anna Maria, the third daughter of this marriage, married Thomas Barrett Lennard, sixteenth Lord Dacre.   STUART HANDLEY

Sources HoP, *Commons* [draft] · H. S. Eeles, *Lord Chancellor Camden and his family* (1934) · John, Lord Campbell, *The lives of the chief justices of England*, [2nd edn], 2 (1858), 181–4 · *The manuscripts of the House of Lords*, new ser., 12 vols. (1900–77), vols. 2–10 · Baker, *Serjeants*, 532 · Sainty, *Judges*, 12, 36 · *State trials*, 15.1216–17; 16.97–8, 290–320 · G. S. Holmes, *The trial of Doctor Sacheverell* (1973), 105–7 · S. M. Cooper, 'The Premonstratensian abbey of Bayham', *Sussex Archaeological Collections*, 9 (1857), 145–81, esp. 181 · E. Hasted, *The history and topographical survey of the county of Kent*, 4 vols. (1778–99) · D. Lemmings, *Gentlemen and barristers: the inns of court and the English bar, 1680–1730* (1990), 196 · *The life and times of Anthony Wood*, ed. A. Clark, 2, OHS, 21 (1892), 431, 497–8, 508–9 · DNB
Likenesses M. Dahl, portrait, repro. in Eeles, *Lord Chancellor Camden* · T. Murray, portrait, NPG · oils (after M. Dahl?, c.1718), NPG

Pratt, John (1772–1855), organist, the son of Jonas Pratt, a music-seller and teacher, was born at Cambridge. In 1780 he was admitted as chorister of King's College, Cambridge, and studied under John Randall, whom he succeeded as organist to the college in 1799. In the same year he was appointed organist to Cambridge University, and in 1813 he held the same post at St Peter's College, Cambridge. Pratt composed sacred music, including a morning and evening service, which he chose not to publish. He made compilations for the use of choirs in college chapels, and published in 1810 *A Selection of Ancient and Modern Psalm Tunes*, which became widely known and generally used, principally in the form in which it was republished, about 1820, under the title *Psalmodia Cantabrigiensis*. His other works included *A collection of anthems in score selected from the works of Handel, Haydn, Mozart, Clari, Leo, and Carissimi*, published about 1825, and *Four double chants, the responses to the commandments as performed at King's College, Cambridge*. Pratt retired many years before he died, at Belmont Place, Cambridge, on 9 March 1855, in his eighty-fourth year.

L. M. MIDDLETON, *rev.* NILANJANA BANERJI

Sources Brown & Stratton, *Brit. mus.* · Grove, *Dict. mus.* · J. D. Brown, *Biographical dictionary of musicians: with a bibliography of English writings on music* (1886) · D. Baptie, *A handbook of musical biography* (1883) · *Cambridge Independent Press* (10 March 1855) · [J. S. Sainsbury], ed., *A dictionary of musicians*, 2 vols. (1824)

Pratt, John Burnett (1799–1869), Scottish Episcopal clergyman and antiquary, born at Cairnbanno, New Deer, Aberdeenshire, was the son of a working tradesman. After graduating MA at Aberdeen University he took orders in the Scottish Episcopal church, and obtained a living at Stuartfield in 1821. In 1825 he was elected to St James's Church, Cruden, Aberdeenshire, where he remained until his death. He was also examining chaplain to the bishop of Aberdeen and domestic chaplain to the earl of Erroll. Aberdeen University conferred on him the honorary degree of LLD in 1865. Pratt edited *The Communion Office for the Use of the Church of Scotland* (1866), and, in addition to a volume of sermons, published *The Old Paths, where is the Good Way* (3rd edn, 1840), *Buchan* (1858), which embodied the results of many years of antiquarian and topographical research in the district, and *The Druids* (1861); his *Letters on the Scandinavian Churches, their Doctrine, Worship, and Polity* (1865) reflected an unusual interest. Pratt died at the parsonage, Cruden, on 20 March 1869.

E. I. CARLYLE, *rev.* H. C. G. MATTHEW

Sources A. Pratt, 'Memoir of the author', in J. B. Pratt, *Buchan*, ed. A. Pratt, 3rd edn (1870) · *Aberdeen Free Press* (23 March 1869) · *Fraserburgh Advertiser* (26 March 1869)
Wealth at death £352 15s. 0d.: inventory, 23 July 1869, NA Scot., SC 1/36/65/91

Pratt, John Henry (*bap.* **1809**, *d.* **1871**), Church of England clergyman and mathematician, was baptized on 30 June 1809 at St Mary Woolnoth, London, one of two sons of Josiah *Pratt (1768–1844), Church of England clergyman, and his wife, Elizabeth, formerly Jowett. He was educated at Oakham School, Rutland, and entered Gonville and Caius College, Cambridge, in 1829, graduating BA in 1833 as third wrangler. He was elected to a fellowship, and proceeded MA in 1836. After taking orders he was appointed through the influence of Daniel Wilson, bishop of Calcutta, a chaplain of the East India Company in 1838. He became Wilson's domestic chaplain and in 1850 archdeacon of Calcutta.

While at Cambridge Pratt had been concerned with the figure of the earth as an oblate spheroid; his *Mathematical Principles of Mechanical Philosophy* was published in 1836 (and expanded in 1860 as *A Treatise on Attractions, Laplace's Functions, and the Figure of the Earth*). Taking account of the Newtonian force of attraction, and local gravitation anomalies caused by irregularities in the crust, he had produced values for the equatorial and polar diameters of the earth which were close to those accepted today. In 1847 George Everest, head of the great Indian survey, published results of a measurement of a meridian arc in which he noted a discrepancy of 5.236 seconds of arc between the value given by astronomical methods and that derived from the triangulation surveys. Everest believed the discrepancy to arise from errors of measurement, but Pratt decided to investigate the matter, and in 1854 sent a long letter to the Royal Society outlining his ideas and the method he had followed to resolve the discrepancy. He began by considering that the plumb-bobs of the astronomical and geodetic instruments were deflected from the vertical by the gravitational attraction of the mass of the nearby Himalaya mountains, but that this would disturb the vertical astronomical observations more than the horizontal readings for the triangulation. He then calculated the mass of the Himalayas, assuming a density similar to that estimated in a similar investigation in 1772 on Mount Schiehallion in Scotland, and arrived at a figure of 15.885 seconds of arc—a far larger discrepancy than the Indian survey had recorded. Even when he reduced his estimates for the density and mass of the Himalayas, Pratt could not reconcile his answers with Everest's figure, and he could only suppose that the Indian arc was in some way unusual.

The problem was then taken up by George Biddell Airy, astronomer royal, who considered the relative densities of an earth whose thin crust overlay a denser fluid interior. He concluded that any mountainous mass would sink through such a crust, unless it was underlain by a balancing light mass, 'like a raft floating on water' (Greene, 241), and so proposed the 'roots of mountains' hypothesis, also known as 'Airy isostasy'. In 1859 Pratt published in the *Philosophical Transactions* his own further thoughts on this subject, now known as the hypothesis of uniform depth of compensation, or 'Pratt isostasy'. He assumed a crust between 800 and 1000 miles thick, undergoing secular cooling, and overlaying a substratum of the same material

which was less dense because it was hotter. He considered that the crust would be most depressed in the coolest regions, and that the uplands represented the warmer material. Pratt had no way of testing this hypothesis, but eventually he decided that the discrepancy was not caused by the Himalayas but by the plumb-bobs of the apparatus being deflected at coastal stations by anomalously high density under the adjacent oceans. There the matter rested for some years, being revived only after Pratt's death and broadly confirmed by advances in geophysical techniques.

Pratt was a conscientious pastor, 'one of the ablest theologians and most devoted divines ... that England ever sent to India ... a quiet earnest worker, solitary in his habits ... a wise counsellor ... and an ardent, though undemonstrative contraversialist' according to his *Times* obituarist. He was elected FRS in 1866. He never married, and died of cholera on 28 December 1871, while on a visitation to Ghazipur, where he was buried the following day. Although his paper of 1855 has been used to justify his reputation as 'the father of isostasy', this concept is not mentioned until 1859, following the hypothesis of Airy, who himself took no further interest in the subject.

ANITA MCCONNELL

Sources M. T. Greene, *Geology in the nineteenth century* (1982) • *The Times* (1–29 Jan 1872) • I. Todhunter, *A history of the mathematical theories of attraction and the figure of the earth* (1873); repr. (1962) • J. H. Manheim, 'Pratt, John Henry', *DSB* • J. H. Pratt, 'On the deflection of the plumbline in India ... and its modification by the compensating effect of a deficiency of matter below the mountain mass', *PTRS*, 149 (1859), 745–78 • S. G. Brush, 'Nineteenth-century debates about the inside of the earth', *Annals of Science*, 36 (1979), 225–54 • parish register (baptism), London, St Mary Woolnoth, 30 June 1809 • burial register, Ghazipur, BL OIOC, IOR N/1/138, fol. 154
Archives CUL, letters to Sir George Stokes
Wealth at death under £10,000 in England: resworn probate, May 1874, *CGPLA Eng. & Wales* (1872)

Pratt, John Jeffreys, **first Marquess Camden** (**1759–1840**), politician, was born on 11 February 1759 at 34 Lincoln's Inn Fields, London, and baptized on 13 March, the eldest child and only son of Charles *Pratt, first Earl Camden (1714–1794), politician and judge, of Camden Place, Chislehurst, Kent, and Elizabeth (*d.* 1779), daughter and heir of Nicholas Jeffreys of Brecon Priory, Brecknockshire.

Early career, to 1794 The Hon. John Pratt, as he was known after his father became Baron Camden in 1765, was educated by the Revd Thomas Powys, later dean of Canterbury, at Fawley, Buckinghamshire, and may also have attended Eton College about 1773. He entered Trinity College, Cambridge, on 11 November 1776 and graduated MA three years later. Among his university friends was William Pitt the younger, the second son of his father's closest political associate. In March 1779 Pratt became an ensign in the West Kent militia, and was promoted lieutenant in the following May, but he resigned his commission in June 1782. On 21 May 1780 he succeeded to one of the tellerships of the exchequer, a lucrative sinecure, the reversion to which had been secured for him fourteen years earlier by Camden on the latter's resignation as chief justice of common pleas.

John Jeffreys Pratt, first Marquess Camden (1759–1840), by Sir Francis Legatt Chantrey, 1835

Pratt, who supported the aims of the association movement at the Kent county meeting on 22 April 1780 and joined Brooks's Club in May, was returned to parliament as MP for Bath, where his father had a substantial interest, at the general election later that year. A young man about town, he initially took little interest in politics and failed to live up to expectations in the Commons. However, on 12 June 1781 he spoke against the war with the American colonies, and on 6 May 1782 for economies in the management of the exchequer, despite his own vested interest. Having voted regularly with the opposition to Lord North's administration, in July 1782 he was appointed a lord of the Admiralty in Lord Shelburne's ministry, in which his father served as lord president. He voted with his colleagues in favour of the peace preliminaries on 17 February 1783 and left office with them on the accession of the Fox–North coalition. He voted for Pitt's parliamentary reform motion on 7 May and against Fox's India Bill on 27 November 1783. Like Camden he resumed his former office on the appointment of Pitt as prime minister in December 1783.

On 31 December 1785, at Lord Lucan's house in Charles Street, Berkeley Square, Westminster, he married Frances (1766–1829), daughter and heir of William Molesworth of Wembury, Devon, and Anne Elizabeth Smith. Owing his position mostly to his connection with Pitt, Viscount Bayham (as he was styled from 1786) remained a solid and popular, if undistinguished and almost entirely silent, junior minister. He left the Admiralty to be a lord of the

Treasury in August 1789, and was sworn of the privy council on 21 June 1793 on being named a member of the Board of Trade. He succeeded his father as second Earl Camden on 18 April 1794 and inherited estates in Kent, including Wildernesse, near Sevenoaks, where he had lived since his marriage. No longer MP for Bath, he followed his father as recorder of the borough (until 1835) and for many years exercised the electoral patronage over one of its seats. He relinquished his position in the government but continued to give it his support and, having been introduced to the House of Lords on 13 May, he seconded the address of thanks there on 30 December 1794.

Lord lieutenant of Ireland, 1795–1798 Camden, whom Pitt had previously approached with a view to taking on the role, was appointed lord lieutenant of Ireland on 11 March 1795. His tenure in Dublin was more significant for the events that immediately preceded and followed it than for the uninspired application during it of the twin policies of concession and repression, which as usual characterized British attitudes towards its nearest colony. Yet the period also witnessed developments of vital importance for the future of the sister kingdom. Aged just thirty-six and lacking appropriate experience for so demanding a position as viceroy, Camden nevertheless impressed the ascendancy with his character, being described by Lord Charlemont as 'a plain, unaffected, good humoured man, of pleasing conversation and conciliatory address' (*Charlemont MSS*, 2.264). He displayed considerable assiduity in fulfilling his functions, as well as a good deal of personal bravery, not least during the riot that greeted his arrival in Ireland on 31 March, when he was admitted to the privy council there. But, taking over at a difficult time, his talents were insufficient for the task confronting him and he was ill served both by the largely distracted ministry in London and by the government, or 'Castle', interest in Dublin.

During his short administration Camden's predecessor, Earl Fitzwilliam, who was drawn from the whig contingent of Pitt's wartime coalition, had raised hopeless expectations among opposition politicians and leading representatives of the majority Catholic population. As instructed by George III and Pitt, Camden reversed Fitzwilliam's ill-advised changes, reassuring the protestant élite by reinstating the so-called Irish cabinet of senior office-holders, upon whom he was thereafter largely dependent. As expected, and believing that the times made any such steps impracticable, he also crushed the attempt to enable Catholics to sit in parliament and to hold high office, Henry Grattan's motion being defeated in the Irish Commons by 155 votes to 84 on 5 May 1795. In line with the long-term policy of securing the loyalty of the Catholic priesthood, as well as in compensation for the defeat of Catholic emancipation, he oversaw the opening of St Patrick's College, Maynooth, later that year and laid the foundation stone of its new building on 20 April 1796.

Yet rural violence continued, with the sectarian struggle reaching a new peak on 21 September 1795, when the battle of the Diamond, near Loughgall, in co. Armagh, between Catholic Defenders and protestant Peep o'Day Boys led to the formation of the Orange Order. The arming of the secret society of United Irishmen, which except in the north was mainly Catholic in composition, made it necessary to pass the Insurrection Act (24 March 1796) and the Habeas Corpus Suspension Act (26 October), the main legislative measures in an extensive programme of repression. In addition, despite his own reservations, Camden introduced late in that year a new system for raising county yeomanry corps; largely protestant in character, these were intended for civilian peacekeeping duties as well as national defence. The abortive attempt to land French forces, accompanied by the revolutionary Theobald Wolfe Tone, at Bantry Bay in December 1796 was the most significant invasion scare during Camden's time in Ireland. The delicate European situation and the fear of domestic unrest in Britain strengthened the hand of those demanding firm action, and in March 1797 he ordered the forcible disarming of the peasantry in Ulster. However, the general election passed off peacefully that summer and on 9 January 1798 he opened what proved to be the last Irish parliament until the early twentieth century.

The Irish rising of 1798 Alarmed at the extent of the outrages that swept Ireland at the start of 1798, Camden was hesitant to act on the basis of conflicting intelligence reports and before damning legal proof of treasonable activity could be ascertained. However, bowing to pressure from Dublin Castle he closed down the United Irishmen's newspaper, *The Press*, ordered the arrest of the leaders of its Leinster directory in Dublin on 12 March, and issued a proclamation declaring martial law on the 30th. Critical of the conduct of the Irish gentry and magistracy—by turns timid and vindictive—his sentiments coincided with the view of the commander of British forces in Ireland, Sir Ralph Abercromby: that firm but disciplined measures of pacification were preferable to acts of exemplary harshness. But he could not long protect Abercromby from the furore that greeted his condemnation of the Irish army's lack of discipline, and he ultimately had little control over the excesses subsequently meted out in the name of the king's government.

In short Camden came across as irresolute in a crisis; in a remark that was typical of the criticisms voiced against him the southern magnate Lord Shannon wrote to his son on 11 April that 'Things look as bad as possible, and his Excellency very undecided, where vigour and decision are so necessary' (*Shannon's Letters*, 81). Although the arrest on 19 May of Lord Edward Fitzgerald (whose family blamed Camden for his death shortly afterwards) crippled the attempted full-scale uprising, a limited one began in earnest on the night of 23–4 May. There followed one of the most unsavoury episodes in Irish history, in which sporadic fighting and bloodthirsty outrages on both sides marked an unpredictable contest between disorganized rebels and an almost equally disorderly force of loyalists and semi-professional soldiers. Bewildered and despondent, Camden applied urgently for reinforcements from England, and more than once offered to resign so as to enable General Cornwallis to become joint viceroy and commander-in-chief. On Camden's repeating his offer the king agreed to the recall of the 'too much agitated' lord

lieutenant (*Later Correspondence of George III*, 3.1755). Cornwallis's strong military grip and steady assertion of undivided political authority rapidly restored order after his succeeding Camden on 20 June 1798.

Among Irish commentators there was some sympathy for Camden, who regretted that he had departed before his conduct could be vindicated by the ending of the uprising. As Sir Jonah Barrington recollected:

> Earl Camden was of a high mind, and of unblemished reputation: his principles were good, but his talent was not eminent;—he always intended right, but was repeatedly led to do wrong; he wished to govern with moderation, but he was driven by his council into most violent proceedings. (Barrington, 2.244–5)

By contrast Anglo-Irish loyalist opinion was especially hostile in its judgement. The author of a popular pamphlet, *Considerations of the Situation to which Ireland is Reduced*, blamed him for tergiversation, observing that:

> though some men thought a system of *coercion* more likely to succeed than a system of *concession*;—and some again gave a preference to the latter; yet, that there was one mode of proceeding which by all honest men of every party was equally condemned, and that was a system which, by *weakly* attempting a mixture of both, became neither *coercion* nor *concession*. (p. 28)

In essence, however, Camden's role was that of a largely powerless agent faced with tumultuous political challenges, and his influence probably did little either to provoke or to contain the uprising. Indeed it could be argued that his most important legacy as lord lieutenant was in bringing to the fore—first as private secretary and then as acting replacement chief secretary to the ailing Thomas Pelham—his sister's brilliant young stepson, Viscount Castlereagh. Anxious not to appear a scapegoat for the Irish rising Camden, on his return to England, secured a seat in the cabinet (without portfolio) and the promise of a Garter (which he was awarded on 14 August 1799), while also letting it be known that he had refused a marquessate. Subject to vociferous criticisms in the British parliament he defended his record in the Lords on 19 March 1799, when he argued that he was not responsible for the murderous atrocities, many of which occurred after the end of his mandate.

Cabinet minister, 1798–1812 Camden was a firm supporter of the plan for legislative union between Britain and Ireland that Pitt had originated at the time of the uprising and praised it in parliament on 8 May 1800. Cautiously in favour of Catholic emancipation, he resigned from office with Pitt in the following February on George III's refusal to countenance such a policy, and privately blamed the outgoing prime minister for having failed to prepare the ground with the king well in advance of the union settlement. Following his chief's line of not opposing Henry Addington's administration outright he stated, in the Lords on 13 May 1802, that he approved the principle but not the details of the peace preliminaries. He returned to office with Pitt in May 1804 and was made secretary of state for war and the colonies, an office in which he was little more than a cipher, as the premier handled the most important matters. He moved the second reading of the

Additional Forces Bill on 24 June 1804 and, among other departmental interventions, commented on the state of the national defences on 15 February and 8 March 1805. On 10 May of that year he remarked that the times were not apposite for granting Catholic relief.

Camden succeeded his uncle Thomas Pratt to the family estate of Bayham Abbey, on the Kent and Sussex border, in 1805, and this became his principal residence. Always declining to return to Ireland, he served from July 1805 to February 1806 in the largely decorative office of lord president of the council. Known as Lord Chuckle (Gray, 96), he was not reckoned among the chiefs of the remaining Pittites but opposed the Grenville ministry, defending the Additional Forces Act on 20 May 1806. In March 1807 he resumed the lord presidency under the duke of Portland, and he continued occasionally to speak for the government in the House of Lords. He was named lord lieutenant and custos rotulorum of Kent in June 1808. An indefatigable intriguer, he was invariably privy to the negotiations that attended the rise and fall of statesmen and administrations, and among his papers can be found many of the memoranda and letters in which he provided self-justificatory accounts of his conduct on these occasions.

The most disgraceful affair in which Camden was implicated was the proposed reshuffle that culminated in the duel of 1809 between Castlereagh and his ambitious rival, George Canning. With less excuse than his cabinet colleagues, given what had hitherto been his close connection with Castlereagh, he connived at the ministerial deceit practised upon his nephew, who was soon to be ousted. When the brouhaha became generally known it was to Camden that Canning addressed his public explanation in the form of *A Letter*, published in *The Times* on 28 November 1809 and then in pamphlet form. The affair exposed Camden as a liability, and Canning, ever an opponent, in that year described him, along with Lord Westmorland, as 'useless lumber' in the ministry (*Diary and Correspondence*, 2.180). However, Camden retained his post under Spencer Perceval from that time until April 1812, and was a minister without portfolio in Lord Liverpool's cabinet from then until the close of the year. He retired from high office with the consolation of a promotion in the peerage, being made Marquess Camden on 7 September 1812.

Later life, 1812–1840 Camden expressed himself cautiously in favour of granting Catholic emancipation on 1 July 1812. From that time onwards he spoke rarely in parliament but backed Liverpool's tory government, applauding the Habeas Corpus Suspension Bill on 19 June 1817 and the Irish Insurrection Bill on 9 February 1822. Reiterating his former views on the Catholic question he again supported it on 17 May 1825 and, having advocated concessions at the Kent county meeting on 24 October 1828, he spoke and voted for it in the house on 10 April 1829. He divided against the Grey ministry's parliamentary reform bills on 7 October 1831 and 13 April 1832, and thereafter continued to act with the duke of Wellington's Conservative opposition in parliament. On 14 August 1833 he was appointed

one of the original members of the judicial committee of the privy council. Having received a doctorate of laws from Cambridge in 1832 he became chancellor of the university on 12 December 1834, and many of his later parliamentary interventions were on the subject of higher education.

Camden's tellership had long been the object of radical condemnation, particularly because of its inflated wartime profits, which rose ten-fold from about £2500 in 1782 to about £24,000 in 1808. However, he had voluntarily contributed £7000 a year in taxes between 1798 and 1802 and had remitted a third of the revenues from 1812 until the end of the war in 1815. On 11 February 1817 Castlereagh told the Commons that his uncle had decided to renounce all the revenue paid to him except for a salary of £2500 a year, and this arrangement was given statutory form in Marquess Camden's Tellership Act of 1819 (59 Geo. III c. 43). He was thanked by parliament on 21 May 1819 for this 'large sacrifice of public fortune to the service of his country' (*JHC*) and received numerous public accolades for his munificent gesture. Because of the extraordinary size of his contribution, which amounted to just under £245,000 in 1834, he was exempted (by clause 30) from the abolition of the office under the Exchequer Receipt Act of 1834 (4 and 5 Wm. IV c. 15), and his income from the now defunct office finally lapsed only on his death.

Camden, who was elected FSA in 1802, held numerous minor and charitable offices. In 1805 he was chosen an elder brother of Trinity House, of which he was master three times (1809–16, 1828–9, and 1831–7). He was appointed a governor of Charterhouse in 1811, a director of Greenwich Hospital in 1815, and a trustee of the British Museum in 1826. As well as seeing service in various troops of the Kent yeomanry during the French revolutionary and Napoleonic wars he was colonel of the West Kent militia from 1827 to 1832. Remembered for his financial beneficence, Camden died at Wildernesse on 8 October 1840 and was buried in nearby Seal church on 17 October. In addition to a surviving daughter (two others predeceased him) he left an only son, George Charles Pratt (1799–1866), who inherited the marquessate and estates in Kent and elsewhere, as well as the bulk of personal wealth sworn under £40,000, but failed to fulfil his father's ambitions for him in national politics. S. M. FARRELL

Sources CKS, Camden MS U840 [with memoranda, etc. at O102–127 and O2566] · BL, Add. MSS 33101–33112; 33119, fols. 161–76; 33441 · R. Willis, 'William Pitt's resignation in 1801: note and document', *BIHR*, 44 (1971), 239–57 · *The later correspondence of George III*, ed. A. Aspinall, 5 vols. (1962–70) · *The correspondence of George, prince of Wales, 1770–1812*, ed. A. Aspinall, 8 vols. (1963–71) · *Memoirs and correspondence of Viscount Castlereagh, second marquess of Londonderry*, ed. C. Vane, marquess of Londonderry, 12 vols. (1848–53) · Lord Dunfermline [J. Abercromby], *Lieutenant-General Sir Ralph Abercromby KB, 1793–1801: a memoir* (1861) · *The diary and correspondence of Charles Abbot, Lord Colchester*, ed. Charles, Lord Colchester, 3 vols. (1861) · *The manuscripts of J. B. Fortescue*, 10 vols., HMC, 30 (1892–1927), vols. 3–10 · *The manuscripts and correspondence of James, first earl of Charlemont*, 2, HMC, 28 (1894), 264 · *Lord Shannon's letters to his son*, ed. E. Hewitt (1982), 81 · J. Barrington, *Historic memoirs of Ireland; comprising secret records of the national convention, the rebellion, and the* *union*, 2 vols. (1833) · *Considerations of the situation to which Ireland is reduced by the government of Lord Camden*, 5th edn (1798) · G. Canning, *A letter to the Earl Camden; containing a full, correct, and authentic narrative of the transactions connected to the late duel* (1809) · *JHC*, 74 (1818–19), 470 · Cobbett, *Parl. hist.*, vols. 30–36 · W. Cobbett, *Parliamentary debates*, 41 vols. (1804–20), vols. 1–41; new ser., 25 vols. (1820–30), vols. 1–25; 3rd ser., 356 vols. (1831–91), vols. 1–55 · T. Packenham, *The year of liberty: the great Irish rebellion of 1798*, rev. edn (1997) · R. B. McDowell, *Ireland in the age of imperialism and revolution, 1760–1801* (1979) · A. P. W. Malcomson, *John Foster: the politics of the Anglo-Irish ascendancy* (1978) · N. J. Curtin, *The United Irishmen: popular politics in Ulster and Dublin, 1791–1798* (1994) · P. M. Geoghegan, *The Irish Act of Union: a study in high politics, 1798–1801* (1999) · J. Ehrman, *The younger Pitt*, 3 vols. (1969–96) · A. D. Harvey, *Britain in the early nineteenth century* (1978) · D. Gray, *Spencer Perceval: the evangelical prime minister, 1762–1812* (1963) · H. S. Eeles, *Lord Chancellor Camden and his family* (1934), 190–265 · *GM*, 2nd ser., 13 (1840), 651–2 · *The Times* (12 Oct 1840) · *DNB* · *GEC, Peerage*

Archives CKS, corresp. and papers [copies at TCD and PRO NIre. T2627/4] · TCD, 'secret ministerial' letter-books | BL, letters to Lord Bathurst, loan 57 · BL, corresp. with earl of Chichester, etc., Add. MSS 33101–33119, *passim*; 33441 · BL, Gordon MSS, Add. MSS 49500–49505, *passim* · BL, corresp. with Lord Grenville, Add. MSS 58935, 59253–59254, 59254A · BL, corresp. with earl of Liverpool, Add. MSS 38243–38291, *passim*; 38311, 38473, 38578 · BL, corresp. with Sir Robert Peel, Add. MSS 40221–40406, *passim* · BL, letters to Lord Spencer · BL, corresp. with Lord Wellesley, Add. MSS 13470–13471, 13714, 37286–37313, *passim* · Bodl. Oxf., letters to Richard Heber · CKS, letters to William Pitt · CKS, corresp. with Lord Romney · Cumbria AS, Carlisle, letters to earl of Lonsdale · Harrowby Manuscript Trust, Sandon Hall, Staffordshire, letters to Lord Harrowby · Hunt. L., letters to Grenville family · NA Scot., corresp. with Henry Dundas · PRO, letters to William Pitt, PRO 30/8/119, 325, 326, 366, 373 · PRO, Home Office MSS, HO 100/53–81, *passim* · PRO NIre., corresp. with Lord Castlereagh, D3030 · PRO NIre., letters to marquess of Downshire, D607, D671 · PRO NIre., corresp. with John Foster, D207/55 · Royal Arch., letters to George III · Southampton Archives Office, letters to J. G. Smyth · TCD, corresp. with duke of Portland · U. Southampton L., letters to first duke of Wellington

Likenesses N. Dance, oils, 1767, Bayham Abbey, Sussex · T. Gainsborough, oils, *c*.1786, Bayham Abbey, Sussex; repro. in Eeles, *Lord Chancellor Camden*, 132 · J. Reynolds, oils, 1786, Bayham Abbey, Sussex · O. Humphrey, miniature, *c*.1800, Old Gwernyfed · T. Lawrence, oils, 1802, NG Ire.; version, Trinity Cam. · J. Hoppner, oils, 1806, Bayham Abbey, Sussex · W. Ward, mezzotint, pubd 1807 (after Hoppner), BM, NPG · G. Cruickshank? and J. Marshall, three caricatures, 1820, BM · F. L. Chantrey, pencil drawing, 1830, NPG · T. Dighton, etching, 1834, Trinity Cam. · F. L. Chantrey, drawings, 1834–5 · F. L. Chantrey, marble bust, 1835, NPG [*see illus.*] · J. R. Wildman, oils, 1839, Bayham Abbey, Sussex · F. L. Chantrey, bust, AM Oxf. · G. Hayter, group portrait, oils (*Trial of Queen Caroline*, 1820), NPG · K. A. Hickel, group portrait, oils (*The House of Commons, 1793*), NPG

Wealth at death under £40,000 personal wealth: IR 26/1544/787; probate record, CKS, Camden MSS U840, T240; statement of property at death (1840) MSS U840, T304

Pratt, John Tidd (1797–1870), barrister and civil servant, was born in London on 13 December 1797, the second son of John Pratt, surgeon, of Kensington. He was admitted a student at the Inner Temple in 1819 and called to the bar in 1824. He married on 20 May 1821 Anne, daughter of Major Thomas Campbell.

In 1828 Tidd Pratt was appointed as consulting barrister to the national debt commissioners and an act of that year

John Tidd Pratt (1797–1870), by Maull & Polyblank, 1855

gave him the duty of certifying the rules of savings banks, which hitherto had simply been submitted to quarter sessions. The following year legislation added to his duties that of certifying the rules of friendly societies, along with the task of receiving their returns of sickness and mortality quinquennially. In subsequent years the certification of the rules of loan societies (1835), building societies (1836), and societies for the pursuit of literature, science, and the fine arts were also added to Tidd Pratt's responsibilities. Because of this widening of his duties, from 1846 he was remunerated by salary instead of through fees, and provision was made for the employment of clerks and the running of a permanent office. This enabled copies of registered rules, returns, and the like to be held centrally instead of being deposited only with local justices of the peace. By this time arrangements had to be made for the keeping of about 30,000 sets of rules and amendments. The scope of his duties continued to increase, the most important later addition being the registration of industrial and provident (or co-operative) societies from 1852.

The enormous expansion of Tidd Pratt's official functions reflected growing national needs, but the way in which these were met—essentially the shape and form of a new government department—was largely due to the personality, vigour, and influence of the man himself. He wrote extensively on the need for good management of thrift organizations. An act of 1855 required the registrar of friendly societies to submit an annual report to parliament, and this set of reports served to provide not only a mass of official statistics but also a good deal of advice on the prudent conduct of friendly and other societies. The need for the collection, analysis, and understanding of the statistical basis for reliable sickness and life insurance among working people was often little understood among friendly society members. Tidd Pratt did much to encourage improvement and the greater reliability of clubs as insurers. He campaigned against such social habits as the payment of liquid rent for the hire of club rooms at public houses—in other words a club's agreeing to buy a quantity of beer in return for the use of a private room.

The conduct of burial societies, some of them very large, was a particular cause of concern to him, for, while they carried on their activities registered as friendly societies, they were often controlled by an 'irresponsible board over which the secretary usually reigns supreme'. Tidd Pratt believed that such organizations were designed for the benefit of the managers and collectors, not for the members, and that special legislation was needed to control them. The affiliated orders, the Oddfellows, Foresters, and the like, which grew rapidly from the middle of the nineteenth century, felt that they had no friend in Tidd Pratt. Legislation did not in his time permit the registration of affiliated orders as such but treated each local lodge or court as the object of registration. This led to problems which he did little to try to ease and certainly he did not seek to have the law amended.

After Tidd Pratt's forty-one years of public service, his death in 1870 inevitably raised the question of the future shape and form of an office which had been so closely associated with one man's personality and attitudes. A royal commission was appointed which reported in 1874. Describing Tidd Pratt as 'minister of self-help to the whole of the industrious classes' (Royal Commission on Friendly Societies, *Fourth Report*, C 961, Appendix 1.22), it pointed out that by the middle years of the nineteenth century whether a man joined a savings bank, a friendly society, or a trade union, shopped at a co-operative store or bought his house through a building society, Tidd Pratt's certificate would follow him. The legislation based on the report built on and extended the work he had accomplished and formed the basis for the state's relationship with self-help organizations well into the twentieth century.

Tidd Pratt was the author of numerous legal manuals, and published on the law relating to savings banks (1828), friendly societies (1829), the poor (1833), and highways (1835). Active in London's cultural life, he was one of the founders of the Reform Club, a trustee of the Soane Museum, and a fellow of the Royal Society of Literature and of the Society of Antiquaries. The Institute of Actuaries made him an honorary fellow. He died at his home, 29 Abingdon Street, Westminster, on 9 January 1870. His wife died on 25 November 1875. Their eldest son, William Tidd Pratt (1823–1867), a barrister, published on the law of friendly societies, building societies, and income tax. Another son, Charles Pallmer Tidd Pratt (1829–1886), vicar of Bracknell, gave evidence to the 1874 commission. A daughter, Maria, married the theologian M. F. Sadler.

PETER GOSDEN

Sources *ILN* (22 Jan 1870), 107 · *ILN* (5 Feb 1870), 152 · Ward, *Men of the reign*, 732 · *Law Times* (12 Feb 1870), 305 · *Solicitors' Journal*, 14 (1869–70), 223 · *Annual reports* (registrar of friendly Societies, 1856–69) · E. W. Brabrook, *Provident societies and industrial welfare* (1898), 9–18 · P. H. J. H. Gosden, *Friendly societies in England, 1815–1875* (1961), 190–93 · P. H. J. H. Gosden, *Self-help* (1973), 70–73 · J. F. Wilkinson, *Mutual thrift* (1891), 102–6 · E. J. Cleary, *The building society movement* (1965), 31–33

Archives PRO, Registry of Friendly Societies MSS · W. Sussex RO, letters to duke of Richmond

Likenesses Maull & Polyblank, photograph, 1855, NPG [*see illus.*] · C. Baugniet, lithograph, BM, NPG · black and white pen sketch, repro. in *ILN* (5 Feb 1870), 152

Wealth at death under £50,000: probate, 1 Feb 1870, *CGPLA Eng. & Wales*

Pratt, Joseph Bishop (1854–1910), engraver, was born on 1 January 1854 at 4 College Terrace, Camden New Town, London, the son of Anthony Pratt, a mezzotint engraver, and his wife, Ann, *née* Bishop. From 1868 he was apprenticed for five years to the noted mezzotint engraver John Lucas, of whom he made a portrait drawing (priv. coll.). Pratt's first published plate was *Maternal Felicity*, after Samuel Carter, issued in December 1873, proofs of which cost 4 guineas. It was exhibited at the Royal Academy in 1874, when his address was given as 24 Kentish Town Road, London. On 26 August 1878 Pratt married Caroline Almader James, with whom he had six children. His eldest son, Stanley Claude Pratt (1882–1914), trained under his father, and also became an engraver.

Pratt was a prolific and successful engraver who declared more than a hundred plates to the Print Sellers' Association. He worked in mezzotint, line, and mixed-method engraving. He was also significant for his work in colour, and also for engaging with new technology through his hand photogravures. His prints were signed in roughly equal proportion either 'Joseph B. Pratt' or 'Bishop Pratt'. He was known particularly for his engravings of animal and landscape pictures by Peter Graham, Sir Edwin Landseer, Frank Paton, Briton Rivière, and Rosa Bonheur, all issued by the leading print publishers of the day. From the mid-1890s he devoted himself increasingly to mezzotint, and executed a series of successful prints in this medium after the portraits of Reynolds, Gainsborough, Romney, Lawrence, Raeburn, and Hoppner, artists who were then enjoying renewed critical interest. Pratt generally chose unengraved subjects, and in his employment of mezzotint sought to evoke the prints of that period. Such plates often sold for the relatively high price of 10 guineas for an artist's proof.

Throughout his career Pratt's skill was widely admired, and exhibitions of his work were held by Agnews at Manchester and Liverpool in 1902, and by Vicars in Bond Street in 1904. A large collection of his prints is held by the British Museum. From 1878 until the mid-1890s he lived in Dartmouth Park Avenue, first at Lonsdale House and from 1891 at Northover. From 1897 his address was Carlton House, Harpenden, Hertfordshire, but in 1907 he moved to High Firs, Brenchley, Kent. He died on 23 December 1910 at 25 Dorset Square, London, following an operation, leaving an estate valued at almost £22,000. He was survived by his widow.

ROBERT UPSTONE

Sources DNB · *The Times* (24 Dec 1910), 11 · R. K. Engen, *Dictionary of Victorian engravers, print publishers and their works* (1979) · Print Sellers' Association lists · *CGPLA Eng. & Wales* (1911)

Wealth at death £21,893 6s. 10d.: resworn probate, 14 March 1911, *CGPLA Eng. & Wales*

Pratt, Josiah (1768–1844), Church of England clergyman, second son of Josiah Pratt, a Birmingham manufacturer, was born at Birmingham on 21 December 1768. His parents were pious evangelicals. With his two younger brothers, Isaac and Henry, Josiah was educated at Barr House School, 6 miles from Birmingham. When he was twelve years old his father took him into his business, but his religious impressions deepened, and at the age of seventeen he obtained his father's permission to enter holy orders. After some private tuition, he matriculated on 28 June 1789 from St Edmund Hall, Oxford, at that time the only stronghold of evangelicalism at the university. His college tutor was Isaac Crouch, a leading evangelical, with whom he formed a lifelong friendship. He graduated BA and was ordained deacon in 1792, and became assistant curate to William Jesse, rector of Dowles, near Bewdley on the borders of Shropshire and Worcestershire. He remained at Dowles until 1795, when, on receiving priest's orders, he became assistant minister under Richard Cecil, the evangelical minister of St John's Chapel, Bedford Row, London.

On 7 September 1797 Pratt married Elizabeth, eldest daughter of John Jowett of Newington, and settled in London, at 22 Doughty Street. There he received pupils, among them being Daniel Wilson, afterwards bishop of Calcutta, with whom he maintained a close friendship. In 1799, at a meeting of the Eclectic Society, which met in the vestry of St John's Chapel, he argued that a periodical publication would signally serve the interests of religion. A pilot edition, the first number of the *Christian Observer*, appeared in January 1802 under his editorship. In about six weeks he resigned the editorship to Zachary Macaulay.

Pratt had also taken part in those meetings of the Eclectic (18 March and 12 April 1799) at which the Church Missionary Society was formulated. On 8 December 1802 he was elected secretary of the missionary society in succession to Thomas Scott. He filled the office, which became the chief occupation of his life, for more than twenty-one years, and displayed a rare tact and business capacity in the performance of his duties. From 1813 to 1815 he travelled through England, successfully pleading the cause of the society. He also took a leading part in the establishment in London of the seminary at Islington for the training of missionaries, which was projected in 1822 and opened by him in 1825. At last, on 23 April 1824, he resigned his arduous post to Edward Bickersteth, the assistant secretary. Bickersteth was also an evangelical, and Pratt believed that the society should be kept in evangelical hands. Pratt devised, and for some time conducted, the *Missionary Register*, of which the first number appeared in January 1813.

Pratt likewise helped to form the British and Foreign

Josiah Pratt (1768–1844), by Samuel William Reynolds senior, pubd 1826 (after Henry Wyatt)

Bible Society in 1804; he was one of the original committee, and was its first Church of England secretary, but he soon retired in favour of John Owen (1766–1822). In 1811 he was elected a life-governor, and in 1812 he helped to frame the rules for the organization of auxiliary and branch societies, and of Bible associations.

In 1804 Pratt ceased to be assistant to Richard Cecil, and became a lecturer at St Mary Woolnoth, in Lombard Street. Here John Newton, another evangelical leader, whose health was failing, was rector. Next year he became Newton's regular assistant curate. In 1804 he also undertook two other lectureships: the evening lecture at Spitalfields church, and the Lady Campden lecture at St Lawrence Jewry. In 1810 he was made by Hastings Wheler, the proprietor, incumbent of the chapel of Sir George Wheler, or 'Wheler Chapel', in Spital Square, which had been shut up for some time. For sixteen years he enjoyed this humble preferment. He established in connection with it the Spitalfields Benevolent Society, and among his hearers were Samuel Hoare of Hampstead, friend of the Wordsworths, and Thomas Fowell Buxton. At Pratt's suggestion Buxton left the Society of Friends, and was baptized into the Church of England.

Pratt's interest in church affairs abroad was always keen. He worked actively in promoting an ecclesiastical establishment in India, stimulating Dr Claudius Buchanan to renew his efforts and urging the Church Missionary Society to give practical aid when Dr Thomas Fanshaw Middleton was appointed bishop of Calcutta. At a time when there was considerable controversy over the powers of bishops in relation to the Colonial Missionary Society, Pratt defended episcopacy even though, unlike some of his fellow evangelicals, he did not believe that it was absolutely necessary. In 1820 Pratt corresponded with two American bishops (Dr Griswold and Dr White), and warmly welcomed Dr Philander Chase, bishop of Ohio, on his visit to England; and it was largely through his efforts that an American missionary society was established. He similarly took the warmest interest in the mission of his brother-in-law, William Jowett (1787–1855), to Malta and the Levant, and may be regarded as founder, in conjunction with Dr Buchanan, of the Malta mission.

In 1826, when Pratt was fifty-eight, he at last became a beneficed clergyman. The parishioners of St Stephen's, Coleman Street, who had the privilege of electing their own vicar, had chosen him as early as 1823. But legal difficulties had arisen, and were not overcome for three years. Pratt retained his lectureship at St Mary Woolnoth until 1831. He established various Christian and benevolent institutions in St Stephen's parish, showed his opposition to the Oxford Movement, and took part in the formation of the Church Pastoral Aid Society. To the last Pratt remained a prominent leader of the evangelicals. Alexander Knox described a meeting with him at Hannah More's, and called him 'a serious, well-bred, well-informed gentleman, an intimate friend of Mrs. More's and Mr. Wilberforce's'. By the word 'serious' Knox disclaims meaning 'disconsolate or gloomy' (*Remains of Alexander Knox*, 4.68).

In spite of his many and varied occupations, Pratt found time for literary work. In 1797 he issued A Prospectus, with Specimens, of a New Polyglot Bible for the Use of English Students, a scheme for popularizing the labours of Brian Walton. The *British Critic* attacked him for presuming to trespass on that scholar's province. Pratt published his *Vindication*; but the scheme fell through. He edited the works of Bishop Hall (10 vols., 1808), of Bishop Hopkins (4 vols., 1809), Cecil's *Remains* (1810), and Cecil's *Works* (4 vols., 1811). He also published A Collection of Psalms and Hymns, 750 in number, for the use of his parishioners in public worship, of which no fewer than 52,000 copies were sold.

Pratt died in London on 10 October 1844, and was buried in 'the vicars' vault' in the church of St Stephen, Coleman Street. He had two sons; Josiah was his successor at St Stephen's, and John Henry *Pratt became a chaplain to the East India Company.   J. H. OVERTON, *rev.* IAN MACHIN

Sources J. Pratt and J. H. Pratt, *Memoir of the Rev. Josiah Pratt, B.D.* (1849) · H. Cnattingius, *Bishops and societies: a study of Anglican colonial and missionary expansion, 1698–1850* (1952) · J. H. Overton, *The English church in the nineteenth century, 1800–1833* (1894) · C. Hole, *The early history of the Church Missionary Society for Africa and the East to the end of AD 1814* (1896) · E. Stock, *The history of the Church Missionary Society: its environment, its men and its work*, 1–3 (1899) · W. Canton, *A history of the British and Foreign Bible Society*, 5 vols. (1904–10) · R. G. Cowherd, *The politics of English dissent* (1959) · *The Times* (1 Jan 1872), 5 · Venn, *Alum. Cant.* · *Remains of Alexander Knox*, ed. [J. J. Hornby], 4 vols. (1834–7), vol. 4

Archives U. Birm. L., corresp.

Likenesses S. W. Reynolds senior, mezzotint, pubd 1826 (after H. Wyatt), BM, NPG [*see illus.*] · H. Turner, lithograph (after E. U. Eddis), BM

Pratt, Sir Roger (*bap.* 1620, *d.* 1685), architect, was baptized on 2 November 1620, at Marsworth, Buckinghamshire, the son of the lawyer Gregory Pratt (*d.* 1640) and his wife, Theodosia West (*née* Tyrell). He was the nephew of Francis, the holder of the family seat at Ryston, near Downham, Norfolk. He was educated at Magdalen College, Oxford, where he matriculated on 12 May 1637, and entered the Inner Temple in 1639. His father died in 1640, leaving him an estate which produced a small income which enabled him to travel from 1643 until 1649 in France, Italy (where he met John Evelyn, the diarist), Flanders, and the Netherlands, avoiding the civil war and to 'give myself some convenient education' (Gunther, 3). Although he matriculated in the faculty of law at Padua in 1645 and upon his return to Britain kept chambers at the Inner Temple until 1672, his travels laid the foundation not for a legal but for an architectural career, for which he was rewarded by a knighthood in 1668.

Although Roger Pratt has been characterized as a gentleman architect, which suggests to the modern reader an element of the dilettante, his approach, in the early days of the development of the architectural profession, was analytical, practical, and systematic. His essays on architecture and building, drawing on both continental and English experience and unpublished in his own day, were written principally in 1660 and 1665, possibly with the intention of publication as a treatise. They show him taking pains to master all aspects of the design process and building practice, as well as advertising his own experience. He advises prospective builders first to

> resolve with yourself what house will be answerable to your purse and estate … then if you be not able to handsomely contrive it yourself, get some ingenious gentleman who has seen much of that kind abroad and been somewhat versed in the best authors of Architecture: viz. Palladio, Scamozzi, Serlio etc. to do it for you, and to give you a design of it in paper.   (Gunther, 60)

Pratt's particular interest lay in planning and the organization of circulation. In his five known houses, built over a period of only fifteen years, he sought to effect a balance between large and small rooms, grand staircases and discreet backstairs, public display and private function, within an arrangement both symmetrical and hierarchical. Coleshill, Berkshire (*c.*1658–62; dem. 1952), astonishing in its assurance and repose as the first known work of the architect, represents the supreme example of the double-pile house, two ranges deep, a form which had been popular in England throughout the seventeenth century, which Pratt particularly recommended as convenient and economical since 'it seems of all others to be the most useful … for that we have there much room in a little compass … and there may be a great spare of walling' (Gunther, 24). But Coleshill was never an exemplar, and in a house of this size economy was a relative concept: this was a pre-eminent and inimitable work of art. Pratt did not invent features at Coleshill but brought together elements which were already part of the currency of European domestic architecture: the rooftop platform and cupola, dormered attics, half-sunk basement, astylar elevation, and symmetrically placed apartments. The house was the more remarkable for the beauty of its façade, the grandeur of its two-storey staircase hall and the provision of central corridors on all floors which enabled rapid and effective progress, separating suites of apartments from each other and avoiding the use of private rooms as through-rooms.

Coleshill's answer to the problem of preventing accidental contact between family, visitors, and servants, a matter of some concern to architects of the later seventeenth century, was atypical: Pratt did not repeat his uncompromising corridors. His three principal later houses presented different planning solutions. Kingston Lacy, Dorset (1663–5; altered 1835–41), and Horseheath Hall, Cambridgeshire (1663–5; dem. 1792), had tripartite plans with a central two-storey hall, large stair compartments to each end, and self-contained apartments at the angles. At Horseheath the circulation was severely restricted by the inclusion of a chapel in one corner. Clarendon House, Piccadilly, London (1664–7; dem. 1683), built for Edward Hyde, was Pratt's greatest commission and his most influential and copyable design. This larger house represented a summation of the planning developments of the previous fifty years. Here Pratt combined aspects of his own earlier plans, a central double-pile with grand staircases at each end, and pavilions at each corner disposed in a manner premonitory of the grander houses of the later seventeenth century: Belton House, Lincolnshire, is the most notable of the Clarendon derivatives. John Evelyn, who referred to Pratt as 'my old acquaintance at Rome' (*Diary of John Evelyn*, 360), expressed qualified approval, finding 'my L:Chancellors new Palace' (ibid., 488), when almost complete, 'a goodly pile to see … but had many defects as to the Architecture' (ibid., 503). Evelyn does not specify the problems, but one of them may have been the increase in size without a commensurate increase in scale. Clarendon, with a single-storey hall, was internally less inventive and spatially complex than the earlier houses in which Pratt had fitted single-storey rooms around a two-storey hall, and in adding the pavilions he risked monotony by increasing the frontage from nine to fifteen equally spaced bays. Clarendon was a handsome and important house, but its façade bore no comparison with the rhythms of Coleshill, and its plan offered few surprises. In the opinion of Roger North, it was 'without one large or good room, as one would expect in so great a fabrick' (Colvin and Newman, 77).

While engaged in private practice, Pratt was involved in an official capacity in advising the commissioners for the repair of St Paul's Cathedral, shortly before the great fire of 1666. After the fire he was (with Sir Christopher Wren and Hugh May) one of the three commissioners appointed by the king to supervise the rebuilding of the City, in which capacity he urged the formation of wider streets. In 1668 he married Ann (1643–1706), daughter and coheir of Sir Edmund Monins bt, of Waldershare in Kent, and the

following year began for himself the rebuilding of Ryston Hall, Norfolk, on the estate which he had inherited from his cousin Edward, who had died in 1664. This, his last recorded house (1669–72; remodelled 1787–8), built to a double-pile plan, was distinguished by a whimsical, segmentally pedimented centrepiece of French derivation, crowned by a small turret.

Pratt's later years were spent in leading the life of a country gentleman. He died at Ryston on 20 February 1685 and was buried in the parish church. His three sons, Roger, Monins, and Theodore, all predeceased him and the estate passed to Edward Pratt, a descendant of Sir Roger's great-grandfather. His widow then married Sigismund Trafford of Lincolnshire, who erected a monument at Ryston to her memory upon her death in 1706.

Pratt's portrait by Sir Peter Lely is preserved at Ryston along with his manuscript notebooks, not only on architecture, which were published by R. T. Gunther in 1928, but also on his later enthusiasms, farming and estate management. Although he did not leave a school of architecture behind him, Sir Roger Pratt has a significant place in English architectural history as the author of the notebooks which, together with those of Roger North, provide us with the most informed commentary on the domestic architecture of the period; as the designer of the short-lived but influential Clarendon House, a building of great typological significance in the development of the English country house; and as the architect of one unique masterpiece, Coleshill.   JOHN BOLD

Sources Colvin, *Archs.* · R. T. Gunther, ed., *The architecture of Sir Roger Pratt* (1928) · N. Silcox-Crowe, 'Sir Roger Pratt, 1620–1685', *The architectural outsiders*, ed. R. Brown (1985), 1–20 · J. Newman, 'Pratt, Sir Roger', *The dictionary of art*, ed. J. Turner (1996) · F. Blomefield and C. Parkin, *An essay towards a topographical history of the county of Norfolk*, [2nd edn], 11 vols. (1805–10), vol. 7 · O. Hill and J. Cornforth, *English country houses: Caroline, 1625–1685* (1966) · F.-E. Keller, 'Christian Eltester's drawings of Roger Pratt's Clarendon House and Robert Hooke's Montagu House', *Burlington Magazine*, 128 (1986), 732–7 · *The diary of John Evelyn*, ed. E. S. De Beer (1959) · J. Bold, 'Privacy and the plan', *English architecture public and private*, ed. J. Bold and E. Chaney (1993), 116–17 · private information (1998) · *Of building: Roger North's writings on architecture*, ed. H. Colvin and J. Newman (1981), 77
Archives NRA, priv. coll., accounts and memoranda · Ryston Hall, Norfolk, notebooks
Likenesses P. Lely, oils, Ryston Hall, Norfolk

Pratt, Samuel (1658–1723), dean of Rochester, was born in London on 2 June 1658 and baptized on 10 June at St Gabriel Fenchurch, the third and youngest child of Daniel Pratt, painter, and his second wife, Jane. There were also, it appears, five children from his father's previous marriage. After attending Merchant Taylors' School from 1666 to 1677 Pratt probably studied at Cambridge. He married young: Samuel, the eldest child of Pratt and his wife, Anne, was born on 29 June 1680. They had six more children.

Pratt was ordained deacon and priest (London) on 4 March 1683 and was inducted as rector of Kenardington, Kent, six days later. He resigned on becoming vicar of All Hallows, Tottenham, Middlesex, where he was instituted on 18 November 1693. He was listed as chaplain to two regiments of dragoons: in 1685 Colonel John Berkeley's and in 1687 the princess's. The Treasury paid for printing his contribution to the recoinage debate, *The Regulating Silver Coin* (1696): Pratt supported William Lowndes's case for devaluation, which John Locke mistakenly persuaded the government to resist. On 25 February 1697 he was chosen minister of the Savoy, and by royal mandate, dated 20 April, was created DD at Cambridge from St Catharine's College.

Pratt was one of Princess Anne's chaplains and tutor to her son, William Henry, duke of Gloucester. At Tunbridge Wells in summer 1697 Pratt 'studied Fortification very hard, and made a pentagon, with out-works, in a wood near the Wells, for the Duke's improvement and entertainment' (Lewis, 96–7). At Anne's request he was named canon of Windsor on 27 November 1697, and on 28 July 1698 he was made almoner to the duke of Gloucester. When his elder brother John, a lawyer, died in 1699 Pratt inherited his estate at Stratford Langhorne, Essex.

Between 1697 and 1704 Pratt published five sermons. In 1706 Queen Anne presented him to the deanery of Rochester, where he was installed on 9 August, and made him clerk of the closet. Francis Atterbury, who became his bishop, appears to have disliked him: he recommended young Samuel Pratt to Jonathan Trelawny as being 'no ways like his father' (2 Nov 1717, in Atterbury, 3.339). He was vicar of Goudhurst, Kent, from 15 August 1709 until his resignation in 1713 and of Twickenham, Middlesex, from 21 January 1713 until his death.

After many years' work Pratt's two-volume *Grammatica Latina in usum principis juventis Britannicae* (which reprints the popular Latin grammar known as William Lily's, with extensive notes and conjectures) was published in 1722 and a compendium of it the following year. A rival, Solomon Lowe, attacked him in *A Proposal for Perfecting a Latin Grammar* (1722). Pratt died on 14 November 1723 and was buried ten days later in St George's Chapel, Windsor, where a memorial to him was erected. His will, dated 4 October 1723, gave £50 to Christ's Hospital, London, as well as making bequests to his wife and family.

HUGH DE QUEHEN

Sources Mrs E. P. Hart, ed., *Merchant Taylors' School register, 1561–1934*, 2 (1936), vol. 2 · R. Newcourt, *Repertorium ecclesiasticum parochiale Londinense*, 2 vols. (1708–10), vol. 1 · E. Hasted, *The history and topographical survey of the county of Kent*, 4 vols. (1778–99), vol. 3 · J. Lewis, *Memoirs of Prince William Henry, duke of Gloucester* (1789) · *CSP dom.*, 1697, 114, 343; 1700–02, 497–8 · W. A. Shaw, ed., *Calendar of treasury books*, 10, PRO (1935), 1693–6, 1415–17 · *The epistolary correspondence, visitation charges, speeches, and miscellanies of Francis Atterbury*, ed. J. Nichols, 5 vols. (1783–90), vol. 3 · *Fasti Angl., 1541–1857*, [Canterbury] · *Fasti Angl.* (Hardy), vol. 3 · C. Dalton, ed., *English army lists and commission registers, 1661–1714*, 2 (1894) · diocese of London, ordination registers, 1675–1809, GL, MS 9535/3 · diocese of Canterbury, induction book, 1662–1792, Canterbury Diocesan Archives, MS F/B/2 · parish register, St Gabriel Fenchurch, 10 June 1658, GL [baptism] · N. Luttrell, *A brief historical relation of state affairs from September 1678 to April 1714*, 4 (1857) · J. Swift, *Journal to Stella*, ed. H. Williams, 2 vols. (1948) · M.-H. Li, *The great recoinage of 1696 to 1699* (1963) · E. Carpenter, *Thomas Tenison, archbishop of Canterbury* (1948) · E. H. Fellowes and E. R. Poyser, eds., *Register of St George's Chapel* (1957)

Archives St George's Chapel, Windsor, thanksgiving sermons, M.25

Pratt, Samuel Jackson [*pseud.* Courtney Melmoth] (1749–1814), writer and actor, was born at St Ives, Huntingdonshire, on 25 December 1749. He was the son of a brewer in that town who twice served as high sheriff of his county, and apparently died in 1773. His mother was a niece of Sir Thomas Drury. He was educated in part at Felsted School in Essex, is said to have been for some time under the private tuition of Hawkesworth, and was ordained in the English church. His poem entitled 'Partridges, an Elegy', often included in popular collections of poetry, was printed in the *Annual Register* for 1771 (p. 241) as by the 'Rev. Mr. Pratt of Peterborough' and he is described as 'an esteemed and popular preacher' (Britton and Brayley, 485).

About 1772 Pratt eloped with a 'pretty boarding school miss, whose Christian name was Charlotte (*b.* 1749, *d.* 1805 or 1823) and whose family name perhaps was Melmoth, the pseudonym Pratt was to adopt for his stage ventures and under which she also acted' (Highfill, Burnim & Langhans, *BDA*, 10.181). His parents disapproved of the alliance, and the family property was much impaired by constant dissensions and litigation. Pratt soon abandoned his clerical profession, and in 1773 appeared, under the name of Courtney Melmoth, on the boards of the theatre in Smock Alley, Dublin, taking the part of Marc Antony in *All for Love*. He 'cut a tall and genteel figure but lacked conviction in his acting' and his success was not great (ibid.). At the end of the season he took a company to Drogheda, but after three months' lack of success the theatre was closed. In 1774 and 1775 he assumed at Covent Garden Theatre the parts of Philaster and Hamlet, again without success, and he also appeared as a reciter. Courtney and Charlotte Melmoth often appeared as a duo: in November 1774 as Leontes and Hermione of *The Winter's Tale*, and in March 1776 as Jaffeir and Belvidera in *Venice Preserv'd*, at the Theatre Royal, Edinburgh. They performed also in Bath (1778–9), again in Edinburgh (1779), and probably again in Dublin, 'where Mrs. Melmoth was engaged regularly from 1780–81 and 1788–9' (ibid., 10.182). Courtney Melmoth's failure as an actor was perhaps due, says Taylor, to his walk, 'a kind of airy swing that rendered his acting at times rather ludicrous' (Taylor, 1.45–6; Highfill, Burnim & Langhans, *BDA*, 10.182). Subsequently he and Mrs Melmoth travelled about the country telling fortunes, and they resorted to various other expedients to gain a livelihood. Some time after 1781, the couple, 'who no doubt had never been married by ceremony, separated', she emigrating to the United States in 1793, and he travelling to the continent 'to glean ideas for future literary efforts' (Highfill, Burnim & Langhans, *BDA*, 10.182). They retained, however, feelings of 'cordial and confidential amity' (L'Estrange, 1.33–5).

From 1774, when he published verses deploring the death of Goldsmith, Pratt depended largely on his pen for support. At first he generally wrote under his stage name.

Samuel Jackson Pratt (1749–1814), by Sir Thomas Lawrence, *c*.1805

About 1776 he was at Bath, in partnership with a book-seller called Clinch, in the old established library, subsequently known as Godwin's library, at the north-west corner of Milsom Street. On Clinch's death Pratt's name remained as a nominal partner in the business under the style of Pratt and Marshall, but after a few years he left Bath for London.

Pratt's voluminous works, well catalogued in the *New Cambridge Bibliography of English Literature*, assume many forms. Some works are tributes, such as *The Tears of Genius, on the Death of Dr Goldsmith* (1774); 'Garrick's Looking-Glass' (1776); *An Apology for the Life and Writings of Hume* (1777); and *The Shadowe of Shakespeare* (1780?). His plays include *Joseph Andrews* (1778), a two-act farce; *The Fair Circassians* (1781); and *The School for Vanity* (1783). One novel, entitled *Emma Corbett, or, The Miseries of Civil War*, appeared anonymously in 1780, was translated into French in 1783, and ran into many editions. Among his efforts at landscape poetry are *Landscapes in Verse, Taken in Spring* (1785), *Gleanings through Wales, Holland, and Westphalia* (1795–9); and *Gleanings in England* (1801).

One remarkable division of Pratt's diverse publications is that reflecting his humanitarian interests. Although Pratt was personally insupportable to many of his acquaintances, in print his persona could be gentle and caring. This streak in an already multi-faceted personality probably originated with *Liberal Opinions on Animals, Man, and Providence*, otherwise known as *Liberal Opinions, or, The History of Benignus* (6 vols., 1775–7), which traced the adventures of Benignus, considered by many to be an autobiographical character. *Sympathy, a Poem* (1788) was many times corrected and enlarged, and was marked by 'feeling,

energy, and beauty' (Polwhele, 1.132). Also included in this group are: *The Triumph of Benevolence* (1786); *Humanity, or, The Rights of Nature* (1788); *Bread, or, The Poor* (1801); and *The Lower World* (1810).

Pratt's contemporaries varied in their esteem for the man and his works. When his plays were produced at Drury Lane, he became intimately acquainted with Potter, the translator of Aeschylus, George Colman the elder, James Beattie, and John Wolcot. His popular poem, 'Sympathy', was first handed to Thomas Cadell, the publisher, by Gibbon. Pratt travelled at home and abroad; in 1802 he was at Birmingham, making detailed enquiry into its manufactures and the lives of its artisans. Pratt possessed considerable talents, but his necessities left him little time for reflection or revision. Some severe lines on his poetry and prose were in the original manuscript of Byron's *English Bards and Scotch Reviewers*, but they were omitted from publication.

One twentieth-century commentator states that 'to know [Pratt], it seems, was most often to despise him, a fact to which Byron's letters … attest' and reveals that the actress Sarah Siddons and the poet Anna Seward loathed him, accusing him of abandoning a wife and child in Dublin in 1773 (London, 357). Byron made sarcastic allusions to Pratt's posthumous patronage of the poet Joseph Blacket in a letter to Mr Dallas of 21 August 1811 (*Works*, 2.53–4). Charles Lamb condemned Pratt's *Gleanings* as 'a wretched assortment of vapid feelings' and wrote sarcastically of the credibility of Pratt's benevolent involvement in the Humane Society in a letter to Southey of 28 November 1798 (*Letters of Charles and Mary Lamb*, 1.151). To readers with less privileged information than Byron or Lamb, however, Pratt 'maintained a public reputation of a genial, kindly, and even sentimental presence' (London, 357). Robert Taylor thought well of him, opining that, 'if Pratt had been born to a fortune, a great part of it would have been devoted to benevolence', but even so, inevitably, Pratt 'injured his relationships by displays of rancour and viciousness, especially in his correspondence' which was too often earmarked by impetuous begging-letters (Highfill, Burnim & Langhans, *BDA*, 10.184). The public and the private Pratts, it would seem, were two different Pratts altogether.

After a long, diverse, and prolific career in the arts, Pratt became ill after a fall from his horse in Birmingham in 1814. After a long decline, he died there at an address on Colmore Row, on 4 October 1814.

There is much more room for speculation about the death date of Charlotte Melmoth, as Highfill traces her career until her death in 1823, and states that the *Dictionary of National Biography* is simply incorrect in setting her death in 1805. This earlier date had been chosen because a letter from Pratt to Mr Mitford refers to the death of Mrs Pratt, whom Pratt had not seen for some twenty years, as occurring in 1805. Moreover, Pratt's will of 1806 uses the phrase 'my late wife, Mrs. Pratt'. One could surmise that there were two Mrs Pratts, or that Pratt used the phrase to keep her out of his estate, but no definite conclusions can be drawn.   GRANT P. CERNY

Sources Highfill, Burnim & Langhans, *BDA* · A. London, 'Samuel Jackson Pratt', *British novelists, 1660–1800*, ed. M. C. Battestin, DLitB, 39/2 (1985), 356–63 · will, PRO, PROB 11/1566, sig. 150 · A. G. L'Estrange, ed., *The friendships of Mary Russell Mitford: as recorded in letters from her literary correspondents*, 2 vols. (1882), 1.33–5 · *GM*, 1st ser., 43 (1773), 54 · *GM*, 1st ser., 84/2 (1814), 398–9 · *N&Q*, 6th ser., 6 (1882), 212 · J. Taylor, *Records of my life*, 1 (1832), 38–47 · *The letters of Charles and Mary Lamb*, ed. E. W. Marrs, 3 vols. (1975–8), vol. 1, p. 151 · J. Britton, E. W. Brayley, and others, *The beauties of England and Wales; or, Delineations topographical, historical, and descriptive, of each county*, [18 vols.] (1801–16), vol. 7, p. 485 · R. Polwhele, *Traditions and recollections; domestic, clerical and literary*, 1 (1826), 132 · *The works of Lord Byron*, ed. T. Moore and J. Wright, 2 (1832), 53–4; 7 (1832), 244n · R. E. M. Peach, 'Bath booksellers', *Bath Herald* (15 Dec 1894) · *DNB*
Archives Bodl. Oxf., corresp. | BL, letters to Royal Literary Fund, loan 96 · Bodl. Oxf., letters to John Nichols · JRL, letters to Sir John Caldwell
Likenesses C. Turner, mezzotint, pubd 1802 (after J. Masquerier), BM, NPG · T. Lawrence, portrait, *c.*1805; Sothebys, 8 March 1989, lot 59 [*see illus.*] · C. Watson, stipple, pubd 1805 (after T. Lawrence), BM, NPG · W. Ridley, stipple (after T. Beach), BM, NPG; repro. in *Monthly Mirror* (1803)

Pratt, Sir Thomas Simson (1797–1879), army officer, was the son of Captain James Pratt and Anne, daughter of William Simson, and was educated at the University of St Andrews. He was gazetted an ensign in the 26th regiment on 2 February 1814, and served in the Southern Netherlands in the same year as a volunteer with the 56th regiment. He was present at the attack on Merxem on 2 February and the subsequent bombardment of Antwerp. He purchased his captaincy on 17 September 1825. Pratt married, in 1827, Frances Agnes, second daughter of John S. Cooper; they had two sons and one daughter. He was with the 26th regiment in the China expedition, and as brevet major commanded the land forces at the assault and capture of the forts of Chuenpe (Chuanbi) on 7 January 1841, and again at the capture of the Bogue (Humen) forts on 26 February. In the attacks on Canton (Guangzhou), from 24 May to 1 June, he was in command of his regiment, and was present also at the demonstration before Nanking (Nanjing), and at the signing of the treaty of peace on board HMS *Cornwallis*. On 28 August 1841 he was gazetted lieutenant-colonel, and on 14 October 1841 was made a CB. From 5 September 1843 to 23 October 1855 he was deputy adjutant-general at Madras.

In October 1858 Pratt was promoted major-general, and in 1859 appointed to command the troops in Australia and New Zealand. He reached Melbourne in January 1860. When, in early July, he learned of the serious reverses suffered by British troops in the Waitara district of Taranaki, New Zealand, he himself went, with reinforcements, to direct operations. His operations were cautious. Avoiding his predecessor's mistake of fighting in the open, he reduced the Maori *pa* with minimum casualties by using earthworks to provide cover. This was slow, unspectacular, and successful. The New Zealand command was separated from that of Australia, and a new commander arrived early in 1861; by then the Taranaki revolt had been suppressed. Pratt returned to Australia in April, and continued to command there until 1863, when he returned to England and was appointed to the colonelcy of the 37th regiment. For services in New Zealand, he was made KCB

on 16 July 1861. In the first ceremony of its kind in Australia, he was publicly invested on 15 April 1862 by Sir Henry Barkly, governor of Victoria, who in 1860 had married Pratt's daughter, Anne Maria. He was promoted general on 26 May 1873, and in October 1877 retired from active service. Pratt died at his residence, 13 Cavendish Place, Bath, on 2 February 1879.

G. C. BOASE, *rev.* JAMES FALKNER

Sources *Army List* · *The Times* (6 Feb 1879) · *Hart's Army List* · S. H. F. Johnston, *The history of the Cameronians*, 1 (1957) · *AusDB* · Boase, *Mod. Eng. biog.*
Archives CUL, corresp. and papers, journal
Wealth at death under £20,000: probate, 24 Feb 1879, *CGPLA Eng. & Wales*

Pratten, Robert Sidney (1824–1868), flautist, was born on 23 January 1824 in Bristol, the second son of a professor of music who was for many years flautist at the Bristol theatre. His mother's maiden name was Sidney. He was considered a prodigy on the flute, and on 25 March 1835, at Clifton, made an early début, playing Charles Nicholson's arrangement of 'O dolce concento'. When only twelve he performed at concerts in Bath and Bristol. After engagements as first flute at the Dublin Theatre Royal and with other musical societies in the city, he arrived in London in 1846. The duke of Cambridge and Lady Tonkin were interested in his talent, and he was sent to Germany to study composition. Pratten's popular piece for flute and piano accompaniment *L'espérance* was published in Leipzig in 1847. Upon his return to London in 1848, he soon rose to the front rank of his art. He played first flute at the Royal Italian Opera, the English Opera, the Sacred Harmonic Society, the Philharmonic Society, and other concerts and musical festivals, including the Musical Society of London and Alfred Mellon's concerts. Contemporaries praised his powerful tone and brilliant execution. He also wrote instruction books for his instrument, among them special studies for Siccama's diatonic flute (1848) and for his own perfected flute (1856), as well as a *Concertstück* (1852) and many arrangements of operatic airs for flute in combination with other instruments.

On 24 September 1854 Pratten married Catharina Josepha Pelzer, a guitarist born at Mülheim on the Rhine. She made her reputation as a child artist in Germany, and in her ninth year appeared at the King's Theatre, London, eventually settling in the capital as a teacher of the guitar, for which she composed a number of pieces and wrote instruction manuals. She died on 10 October 1895.

Pratten died after a long illness on 10 February 1868 at 21 Paragon, Ramsgate. His younger brother Frederick was an eminent double bass player engaged in London's principal orchestras, who died in London on 3 March 1873.

L. M. MIDDLETON, *rev.* DAVID J. GOLBY

Sources *Musical World* (22 Feb 1868), 125 · *Musical World* (15 Feb 1868), 108 · J. D. Brown, *Biographical dictionary of musicians: with a bibliography of English writings on music* (1886), 483 · *CGPLA Eng. & Wales* (1868) · Grove, *Dict. mus.*
Likenesses H. Watkins, carte-de-visite, NPG · photograph, BM
Wealth at death under £600: probate, 13 March 1868, *CGPLA Eng. & Wales*

Preece, Isaac Arthur (1907–1964), biochemist and brewing scientist, was born on 19 March 1907 at 90 Worcester Street, Birmingham, to Isaac Arthur Preece, a master bassinette maker, and his wife, Isabel Wright. He was educated at Birmingham Central secondary school and at the University of Birmingham, from which he graduated BSc in 1927, MSc in 1928, and PhD in 1931. He was an assistant lecturer in the department of biochemistry at the University of Birmingham from 1928 until 1931, when he was appointed to a lectureship in the chemistry department at Heriot-Watt College, Edinburgh, with special responsibility for teaching brewing, biochemistry, and botany. In 1945 Preece was made head of an independent department of brewing, and in 1950 awarded a new chair of brewing and applied biochemistry at Heriot-Watt, founded with the financial support of the Brewers' Association of Scotland. He was elected fellow of the Royal Society of Edinburgh in 1949 and was awarded an honorary DSc from the University of Birmingham in 1950.

Under Professor Ling in the department of biochemistry at Birmingham, Preece received a wide-ranging training, which encompassed botany, biochemistry, and brewing. He maintained this breadth of perspective in his wider professional activities and in his approach to teaching and research, which spanned brewing, biology, and chemistry. Between 1946 and 1947 he was chairman of the Scottish section of the Institute of Brewing, and president of the same section from 1953 to 1955. He regularly gave lectures to the European Brewery Convention as well as to Irish, American, and Canadian malting and brewing societies, yet continued to give refresher lectures to the Scottish section of the Institute of Brewing almost annually.

In 1949 Preece became editor of the *Journal of the Institute of Brewing*, which he maintained at a professionally scientific standing until his death. The Institute of Brewing recognized his contributions with the award, in 1964, of the Horace Brown medal, the highest honour it could bestow. In addition Preece was a council member of the Royal Institute of Chemistry from 1949 to 1950, and chairman of the Edinburgh and south-east Scotland section of the institute from 1950 to 1952; this he immediately followed with a spell as president of the Scottish branch of the Institute of Biology from 1953 to 1955. Preece was particularly involved in the educational committee of this body and was instrumental in establishing the national certificates in biology. In 1963 he was elected vice-president of the Institute of Biology. This versatility was acknowledged in his being elected to fellowships of both the Royal Institute of Chemistry and the Institute of Biology.

Preece established a thriving school and research centre for brewing and biochemistry at Heriot-Watt College, which acquired an international reputation, attracting postgraduate students from as far afield as Poland, Rhodesia, and Pakistan. He tried to instil a more scientific understanding of brewing into this very traditional industry by requiring his students to undertake a basic training in the principles of biology and chemistry; his textbook, *The Biochemistry of Brewing* (1954), became recognized as a

classic work. Preece published some forty original papers in biochemical, brewing, and chemical journals, either individually or with research students, and, in 1957, a monograph entitled *Cereal Carbohydrates*. His research centred on questions relating to malting—specifically the role of large structural molecules, and enzymes involved in processes of germination in the barley grain—and made fundamental contributions to several difficult fields. He began by studying amylases and non-starchy polysaccharides, but his most significant research was on the hemicellulases, for which he was made an honorary DSc. These enzymes help to break down the cell wall components of the endosperm during germination, which makes the starch molecules available for metabolism, which in turn produces the malt. His later work was on phytin metabolism, phosphatases, and the enzymes which break down proteins in barley grains, and bore on the enduring nitrogen question in brewing. Preece tried to bring his wider perspective to bear on the large problems which he addressed and was firmly committed to the ideals of scientific method, yet recognized the imperatives of the industrial context and was suspicious of simplistic solutions. He sought steadily, if slowly, to replace empiricism with experimentally validated procedures.

Preece was married, with two sons, and enjoyed a variety of sporting and musical pastimes. He played rugby as a young man, tennis and cricket in later life. He was a skilled musician, playing the viola and, for a time, singing in the choir of St Mary's Cathedral, Edinburgh. Close colleagues wrote warmly of his sociability and good humour and were shocked by his sudden death from a heart attack, on 12 August 1964, while holidaying in Switzerland.

KEITH VERNON

Sources *Journal of the Institute of Brewing*, 70 (1964), 381–2 · A. M. MacLeod, *Year Book of the Royal Society of Edinburgh* (1963–4), 33–4 · H. B. Nisbet, *Chemistry and Industry* (10 Oct 1964), 1727 · *Nature*, 204 (1964), 1035 · I. A. Preece, 'An original inquirer to the manner born', *Journal of the Institute of Brewing*, 70 (1964), 477–84 · b. cert.
Likenesses photograph, repro. in *Chemistry and Industry*
Wealth at death £10,081 11s. 7d.: probate, 22 Dec 1964, *CGPLA Eng. & Wales*

Preece, Sir William Henry (1834–1913), electrical engineer and administrator, was born on 15 February 1834 at Bryn Helen near Caernarfon, Wales, the eldest son of Richard Matthias Preece (1797–1854), stockbroker and politician, and his wife, Jane (1799–1870), daughter of John Hughes of Caernarfon. In 1845 the family moved to London, where William entered King's College School and, in 1850, King's College. His father had intended to secure William a commission in the army, but financial reverses made this impossible, and Preece left King's College in 1852. The Preeces had by then become friendly with Latimer Clark, who was to marry William's sister Margaret in 1854. Clark was an assistant to his brother Edwin, chief engineer of the Electric Telegraph Company, and together they secured Preece a job on their engineering staff in 1853.

Preece later liked to say he had learned about electricity 'at the feet of Faraday', but his contact with Michael

Sir William Henry Preece (1834–1913), by unknown
photographer, 1900s

Faraday was limited to a stint in 1853 helping with some
telegraphic experiments, and he in fact acquired his
knowledge of electricity on the job. After three years in
London, Preece was appointed superintendent of the Electric Telegraph Company's south-western district at Southampton, in 1856. He also supervised the telegraphs of the
London and South Western Railway and, from 1858 to
1862, the cables of the Channel Island Telegraph Company.

While at Southampton, Preece met (Ann) Agnes Mary
Pocock (1843–1874), the daughter of a local solicitor. They
married on 28 January 1864, and had four sons and three
daughters before her death in childbirth in 1874. Grief-
stricken, Preece left Southampton and soon settled with
his children at Gothic Lodge, Wimbledon Common,
Surrey. He had by then begun his long service with the
Post Office telegraph system, having been named engineer for the southern district when the government bought
out the private telegraph companies in 1870. He became
electrician to the Post Office system in 1877 and spent the
next two decades directing the expansion and improvement of the British telegraph network. He was promoted
to engineer-in-chief in 1892, and on retirement in 1899
was made a KCB. He continued as a government consultant until 1904, and was also active, along with his sons Llewellyn and Arthur, in the engineering firm of Preece and
Cardew.

Preece introduced several valuable technical advances,
particularly in railway signalling, but his most important

work was as an administrator, writer, and public speaker.
He published a widely used handbook on telegraphy
(1876, with James Sivewright), two books on the telephone
(1889, 1893), and over a hundred papers and lectures. He
was president of the Society of Telegraph Engineers in
1880, and again (after it had become the Institution of
Electrical Engineers) in 1893, and was elected a fellow of
the Royal Society in 1881.

Of average height, stocky, and with a round face usually
adorned with small wire-rimmed spectacles, Preece was a
lively and impressive lecturer, and excelled at making
complex subjects seem simple and understandable.
Although he took great interest in new technologies, he
was often complacent about the superiority of existing
methods, particularly those used by the Post Office. Thus,
although he had been the first in Britain to demonstrate a
working telephone, he told a parliamentary inquiry in
1879 that he foresaw little demand for the device in Britain, saying the telegraph and a 'superabundance of messengers, errand boys and things of that kind' already met
the need. Like other Post Office officials, Preece resisted
anything that might undercut the existing telegraph system, an attitude that did much to delay the spread of the
telephone in Britain.

In 1887 Preece began a long and bitter feud with the
physicist and electrical engineer, Oliver Heaviside. Heaviside had found theoretically that the clarity of telegraph
and telephone signals could be greatly improved by loading transmission lines with extra inductance. Reasoning
from inadequate experiments, Preece had already declared inductance to be prejudicial to clear signalling; he
not only dismissed Heaviside's theory as empty mathematics, but took steps to block its publication. Enraged,
Heaviside thereafter missed no opportunity to denounce
Preece's mendacity and scientific ignorance. American
telephone engineers later made inductive loading a great
practical success, but Preece always refused to give Heaviside any credit for the innovation.

Preece had pioneered an early method of wireless telegraphy, using induced currents, and in 1896 he gave an
enthusiastic reception to Guglielmo Marconi's new system using Hertzian waves. Although his public praise and
provision of Post Office experimental facilities did much
to establish Marconi as the early leader in wireless telegraphy, Preece did not secure government control of
Marconi's patents, a failure that later drew criticism.

Preece spent his last years at Penrhos, Waenfawr, his
summer home near Caernarfon. He was awarded an honorary DSc degree by the University of Wales in 1911. After a
long period of failing health, he died at Penrhos on 6
November 1913 and was buried on the 11th in Llanbeblig
churchyard, Caernarfon.   BRUCE J. HUNT

Sources E. C. Baker, *Sir William Preece, F.R.S., Victorian engineer
extraordinary* (1976) • D. G. Tucker, 'Sir William Preece (1834–1913)',
Transactions [Newcomen Society], 53 (1981–2), 119–36 • *The Times* (7
Nov 1913), 9c • *The Electrician* (14 Nov 1913), 253–5 • *Nature*, 92 (1913–
14), 322–4 • H. G. J. Aitken, *Syntony and spark: the origins of radio*
(1976) • P. J. Nahin, *Oliver Heaviside: sage in solitude* (1988) • D. G.
Tucker, 'The first cross-channel telephone cable: the London–Paris
links of 1891', *Transactions* [Newcomen Society], 47 (1974–6), 117–

32 • B. J. Hunt, *The Maxwellians* (1991) • J. Kieve, *The electric telegraph: a social and economic history* (1973) • m. cert. • d. cert. • *CGPLA Eng. & Wales* (1913)

Archives Gwynedd Archives, Caernarfon, papers • Inst. EE, archives, corresp. and papers • Royal Mail Heritage, London, papers | CUL, corresp. with Lord Kelvin • ICL, letters to S. P. Thompson • UCL, corresp. with Sir Oliver Lodge

Likenesses B. Bright, oils, 1899, Sci. Mus. • photograph, 1900–10, Sci. Mus. [*see illus.*] • photograph, repro. in *The Sketch* (6 July 1904) • photographs, repro. in 'Lost Dialogues from the "New Republic" of Plato': no. 1 — Mr W. H. Preece on the Duties of Corporations', *Lightning* (1 Dec 1892), 348, 349

Wealth at death £32,320 2s. 2d.: probate, 18 Dec 1913, *CGPLA Eng. & Wales* • £22,074—net personalty: 23 Dec 1913, *The Times*

Prelleur, Peter (*bap.* 1705?, *d.* 1741), musician and composer, was probably the Pierre Preleur baptized at the French protestant church, Threadneedle Street, London, on 16 December 1705, the son of Jacque Preleur, a weaver, and his wife, Françoisse, of 'over against Crispin Street, Stepney parish' (Colyear-Ferguson, 206). Prelleur's life ran almost entirely within the Spitalfields area of east London, reflecting his origins in the Huguenot refugee community from which he came. His parents are likely to have left France after 1685, following the revocation of the edict of Nantes and the subsequent proscription of protestants.

Prelleur's career suggests that he enjoyed a prosperous background and a good education; it is likely that he was apprenticed to his father, or possibly attended one of the local dissenting schools. He then became a writing-master in Spitalfields, but also played the harpsichord at the Angel and Crown tavern, Whitechapel. His first known musical success arrived in 1728 with his election as organist at St Alban's Church in Wood Street; this may have been the occasion of his first organ voluntaries—which appear in several sources, some named, but often in fragments.

Prelleur is chiefly remembered for the publication of *The Modern Musick-Master, or, The Universal Musician* in 1730, which was commissioned by the publishers John Cluer and William Dicey. This beautifully produced book is almost entirely unoriginal: it amalgamates earlier tutors (without acknowledgement) with recent tunes, which were updated with successive reprints. It successfully captured the interest of the amateur music-lover eager for self-improvement. *The Modern Musick-Master* included a brief history of music, a short musical dictionary, and instructions on singing, and on playing the violin, flute, recorder, oboe, and harpsichord—with occasional extra sections for the bassoon and cello. Much of its appeal lay in its suitability for amateurs: none of the tunes is difficult or needs more than one performer. In 1732 Prelleur and B. Smith wrote a set of undistinguished hymns entitled *The Harmonious Companion* which may have been intended for local children attending the charity schools in east London, who sang in local church choirs and annually for their benefactors.

Prelleur must have been working at Goodman's Fields Theatre, then under the management of Thomas Odell, for some time before his benefit concert on 13 May 1731,

which was shared with the box-keeper John Giles. He retained his involvement with the theatre after it was rebuilt in 1732 by Henry Giffard. His first ascribed theatrical composition was *A Masque of Musick*, first performed there on 7 May 1733. The following year Prelleur shared a benefit concert with the actor James Excell at the Swan tavern music society in Whitechapel (22 March 1734), and on 24 January 1735 Excell took the leading role in the pantomime *Jupiter and Io* at Goodman's Fields Theatre, written by Prelleur and the theatre's leading violinist John Christian Eversman. Prelleur regularly attended the Swan tavern music society, which was frequented by dissenting tradesmen.

On 9 February 1736 one of Prelleur's medley overtures was performed in Dublin, and that year several were advertised for sale in London. The most important development in Prelleur's career that year was his election as organist to Christ Church in Spitalfields, a cause of some local controversy as Prelleur, a French protestant, was not a member of the Church of England. Prelleur, a member of the Society of Schoolmasters, was probably involved with teaching the charity children of Spitalfields, some of whom later sang at his funeral.

Goodman's Fields Theatre had closed following the Licensing Act of 1737, but a new management opened Goodman's Fields Wells (or 'New Wells') nearby in 1739, and claimed to produce only music and dancing. For this, Prelleur wrote his only complete surviving ascribed theatrical work: *Baucis and Philemon*, which includes an overture and several songs, with arrangements for flutes or recorders. Prelleur also wrote music for *Harlequin Hermit, or, The Arabian Courtezan* for the New Wells in 1739, from which a few songs survive. He also became a founder member of the Royal Society of Musicians, which assisted needy musical performers. After this, his last known music was written for *Harlequin Student, or, The Fall of Pantomime*, first performed at the reopened Goodman's Fields Theatre on 3 March 1741.

Much of Peter Prelleur's musical life remains obscure; at some time he wrote a set of seven concerti grossi of fairly high quality, which are now in the Fitzwilliam Library in Cambridge, and the overtures, dances, and concertos in BL, Add. MS 31453, can be ascribed to Prelleur through the stylistic and compositional resemblances to his concerti grossi and organ voluntaries and the trumpet concerto at the Sächsische Landesbibliothek, Dresden. He died, presumably in London, on 25 June 1741, and was buried at Christ Church, Spitalfields, on 27 June 1741.

WILLIAM SUMMERS

Sources R. Platt, 'Prelleur, Peter [Pierre]', *New Grove*, 2nd edn • Highfill, Burnim & Langhans, *BDA* • J. Hawkins, *A general history of the science and practice of music*, new edn, 3 vols. (1853); repr. in 2 vols. (1963) • T. C. Colyear-Ferguson, ed., *The registers of the French church, Threadneedle Street, London*, 3, Publications of the Huguenot Society of London, 16 (1906), 268 • Burney, *Hist. mus.* • A. H. Scouten, ed., *The London stage, 1660–1800*, pt 3: *1729–1747* (1961)

Prence, Thomas (*c.*1600–1673), colonial governor, was born about 1600, the son of Thomas Prence (*d. c.*1630), carriage maker, of Lechdale, Gloucestershire, who emigrated to Leiden as a puritan while his son was still young. The younger Thomas Prence emigrated to New Plymouth in 1621 aboard the *Fortune* and resided in the colony towns of Plymouth, Duxbury, and Eastham. While the New World offered immigrants unusual opportunities for improving their lot, few rose as high from undistinguished origins as did Prence. Within six years of his arrival he was chosen as one of eight 'undertakers' responsible for discharging the colony's debt in exchange for exclusive rights to American Indian trade. He later joined William Bradford and others in a lucrative partnership in a trading post on Maine's Kennebec River. In 1632 he joined the colony's government through election as an assistant, and he served as either assistant or governor of the colony every year thereafter until his death.

Undoubtedly Prence's marriages to daughters of leading settlers propelled his own rise to prominence. S. E. Morison declared that Prence showed a 'genius for marrying' well (Morison, 172). On 5 August 1624 he married Patience Brewster (*d.* 1634), daughter of William *Brewster, Plymouth's ruling elder and the most learned man in the colony. Thomas and Patience had four children, Rebecca, Thomas, Hannah, and Mercy. Patience died in 1634, and on 1 April 1635 he married Mary Collier (*d.* in or before 1644), daughter of wealthy settler William Collier. Their children were Jane and Mary. There has been some confusion about his remaining marriages and children, but in 1904 Ella Florence Elliot determined that Prence had married not three but four times and that his last two wives were Apphia Quick, the divorced wife of Samuel Freeman, and Mary Howes (*d.* 1695), the widow of Thomas Howes. Which mother bore the three children of these last two marriages—Judith, Elizabeth, and Sarah—remains unclear.

No record exists of any formal education for Prence, a deficit he felt keenly. Cotton Mather declared that 'the want and worth of *Acquired Parts* was a thing so sensible unto [Prence], that *Plymouth* perhaps never had a greater *Maecenas* of *Learning* in it' (Mather, 2.2.209). Like his first father-in-law, he amassed a sizeable library, valued at over £214 at probate. In addition, he left funds to be used for grammar schools to teach 'humane learning, and good literature' (ibid., n.).

As governor, an office he filled in 1634, 1638, and from 1657 to 1672, Prence tightened laws restricting Quaker worship and backed legislation mandating town financial support of Congregational ministers. These actions may account for the characterization of him as 'a terror to evil doers' by a contemporary (Morison, 172). He showed similar severity in dealing with a threatened Indian uprising in 1671. He ordered confiscation of all Indian arms and imposed a fine of £100 on the Wampanoag sachem Philip (Metacom), a humiliation and hardship that, some historians believe, contributed significantly to the sachem's instigation of King Philip's War four years later. In addition to his service as governor and assistant, he was a commissioner for the United Colonies of New England in 1645, 1650, 1653–8, 1661–3, and 1670–72. He died in New Plymouth on 29 March 1673, and was buried there on 8 April, leaving an estate of £422, in addition to over 300 acres of land throughout Plymouth Colony.

JENNY HALE PULSIPHER

Sources R. C. Anderson, ed., *The great migration begins: immigrants to New England, 1620–1633*, 3 vols. (Boston, MA, 1995) · S. E. Morison, *The story of the 'old colony' of New Plymouth* (1956) · C. Mather, *Magnalia Christi Americana*, ed. E. W. Miller and K. B. Murdock, new edn (1977) · G. D. Langdon, *Pilgrim colony: a history of New Plymouth, 1620–1691* (1966) · J. Savage, *A genealogical dictionary of the first settlers of New England*, 4 vols. (1860–62) · Mass. Hist. Soc., Winslow MSS · Mass. Hist. Soc., John Davis MSS
Archives Mass. Hist. Soc., John Davis MSS · Mass. Hist. Soc., Winslow MSS
Wealth at death £422 10s. 7d.; plus over 300 acres: Plymouth Colony probate records 3:1:60–70, cited Anderson, *Great migration begins*, 3.1521

Prendergast, Sir Harry North Dalrymple (1834–1913), army officer, second son of Thomas *Prendergast (1807/8–1886) of the Madras civil service, and his wife, Lucy Caroline Dalrymple, was born in India on 15 October 1834. On their mother's death in 1839, Harry and his brother Hew were sent to Brighton to live with their grandfather, Major-General Sir Jeffrey Prendergast, Madras army. Educated at Cheam School and at Brighton College, Harry followed Hew to Addiscombe College and Chatham. He obtained a commission in the Madras engineers in 1854.

Prendergast took part in the Anglo-Persian War (1857), and in the Indian mutiny served with the Malwa and Central Indian field forces. During the battle of Mandasor (21 November 1857) he saved the life of Lieutenant Dew, and was severely wounded. For this and for heroism at Bhima and Betwa he received the Victoria Cross. Aide-de-camp to Sir Hugh Henry Rose, Prendergast saw constant action until, perilously wounded a second time, he was invalided home in April 1858. Thereafter, his left arm was virtually useless, not that that stopped him volunteering (unsuccessfully) for the Austrian army in 1859 to fight the Italians or for the Anglo-Chinese War of 1860: 'I can play cricket so I can fight', he protested. In 1867 he was, however, appointed field engineer to the Abyssinian expedition, saw action at Magdala, and, mentioned by the commander-in-chief as having rendered singularly valuable assistance, was promoted brevet lieutenant-colonel. Prendergast had married at Bangalore on 11 October 1864 Emilie Rachel Simpson. They had five children; their daughter Ella married Sir Harry Aubrey de Vere Maclean.

In 1878 Prendergast led the Indian sappers sent to Malta and Cyprus at the time of the Congress of Berlin. Then followed a series of posts and commands: military secretary, Madras (1878–80), the Western Districts (1880–81), the Ceded Districts (1881–2), quartermaster-general, Madras (1882–3), the British Burma division (1883–4), and the Hyderabad subsidiary force (1884–5). Emphasis on musketry, mapmaking, and manoeuvres showed Prendergast a modern major-general and explain his eyebrow-raising selection in October 1885 to lead the Burma field force; no Madras officer had been entrusted with field command since 1857. Equally unusual were his instructions from the viceroy, Lord Dufferin, to take the capital and dethrone

This self-effacing soldier died of pneumonia, at his residence, 2 Heron Court, Richmond, Surrey, on 24 July 1913 and was buried four days later at Richmond cemetery.

ALFRED COCHRANE, *rev.* MARTIN D. W. JONES

Sources H. M. Vibart, *The life of General Sir Harry N. D. Prendergast* (*the happy warrior*) (1914) · A. T. Q. Stewart, *The pagoda war: Lord Dufferin and the fall of the kingdom of Ava* (1972) · *Field operations in Upper Burma* (Rangoon, 1886) · M. D. W. Jones, 'The war of lost footsteps', *Bulletin of the Military Historical Society*, vol. 40/no. 157 (1989), 36–40 · *The Times* (26 July 1913) · *CGPLA Eng. & Wales* (1913)

Archives NAM · Royal Engineers, Brompton barracks, Chatham, Kent | BL OIOC, Lewin Bowring portfolios · BL OIOC, Grant Duff collection · BL OIOC, corresp. with Sir E. B. Sladen, MS Eur. E 290 · BL OIOC, Sir George White MSS · Bodl. Oxf., corresp. with Lord Kimberley

Likenesses Desanges, oils, 1858–9, Royal Engineers, London · photograph, *c.*1860, NAM [accession no. 6272] [*see illus.*] · photograph, *c.*1865, NAM · Ball, photograph, *c.*1886, repro. in T. E. Tooney, *Heroes of the Victoria cross* (1895) · Byrne and Co., photograph, *c.*1902, repro. in Vibart, *Life of General Sir Harry Prendergast*

Wealth at death £5010 2*s.* 4*d.*: administration with will, 22 Oct 1913, *CGPLA Eng. & Wales*

Sir Harry North Dalrymple Prendergast (1834–1913), by unknown photographer, *c.*1860

King Thibaw 'rather by the display than the use of force'. Prendergast had to overcome modern blockhouses guarding the Irrawaddy and reach Mandalay before the Burmese could block the river. Fierce fighting at Minhla (17 November) showed that, outmatched in everything but courage, Burma intended to fight. But the Third Anglo-Burmese War, the most audacious example of forward policy in India, was launched so rapidly that Prendergast seized every vantage point first. Unconditional surrender was offered on 27 November, Mandalay occupied on the 29th and the royal family deported that night.

Prendergast was showered with congratulations and created KCB, but annexation (1 January 1886) provoked extensive insurgence. With a 9000-man force, Prendergast was suddenly expected to conquer a kingdom the size of France, with no cavalry, no mules, and no reinforcements. War correspondents gleefully attacked military inadequacies and ruined several reputations, Prendergast's included. Although promoted lieutenant-general (1886) and general (1887), he remained unemployed from April 1886. Through the kindnesses of friends, he filled in as acting resident in Travancore, Mysore, Baroda, and Baluchistan. Relegated to the supernumerary list, however, he quit India in 1892, aged only fifty-seven.

While Prendergast supported campaigns for imperial conscription and cadet corps in schools, bitterness proved preferable to boredom. Many saw his GCB (1902) as the army making amends; 1908 saw him appointed colonel commandant, Royal Engineers. But he would never be commander-in-chief in India, as some had once hoped.

Prendergast, John Patrick (1808–1893), historian and barrister, was born on 7 March 1808 at 37 Dawson Street, Dublin. His parents were Francis Prendergast (1768–1846), registrar of the court of chancery, Ireland, and Esther (1773/4–1846), eldest daughter of John Patrick of 27 Palace Row, Dublin. He had two younger brothers, Francis and William, who were also lawyers, and three sisters about whom little is known except that on their parents' death they moved to Plymouth, where they lived for a time in reduced circumstances. He had also a half-brother, Jeffrey (*d.* 1879), from his father's first marriage to Maria Reynolds, a sister of Thomas *Reynolds the informer (of 1798). The Prendergasts traced their roots to Maurice de Prendergast, a companion of Richard de Clare, known as Strongbow, under Robert Fitzstephen; but the more immediate origins of the family's rise may be attributed to Thomas Prendergast, John Patrick's grandfather, who conformed to the established church in the eighteenth century and who had subsequently prospered in the legal profession.

Prendergast was educated in Reading, England, under Dr Valpy (his mother had an antipathy towards Irish education) from about 1817 to 1821; he passed on to Trinity College, Dublin, graduated in 1825, and was called to the Irish bar in 1830. He spent many enjoyable years on the Leinster circuit, learning to overcome a natural shyness and becoming an effective public speaker. In later life he would regale his guests with amusing and sometimes scurrilous tales of the barristers and judges he had known. In 1836 he succeeded his father and grandfather in the agency of Lord Clifden's estates, which he administered for many years. The knowledge and experience gained in this practical work made him a firm advocate of tenant rights and a sympathizer with the schemes of the early land reformers in Ireland. He was particularly incensed by the notorious Derryveagh and Glenveagh evictions in co. Donegal in 1861, and he travelled there to hear the story at first hand.

In 1840 Prendergast was commissioned to undertake

some genealogical researches in the county of Tipperary and this led to a study of the settlement of Ireland at the restoration of Charles II, and also of the Cromwellian settlement. His researches culminated in the publication of *The History of the Cromwellian Settlement of Ireland* in 1863 (2nd edn, 1875; reprint edn, 1996). This work was based on extensive original research in London and Dublin, and while its tone was undoubtedly polemical, it was a pioneering venture into the law of Irish real property, and remains a valuable contribution to the history of the Irish land question.

In 1864 Prendergast was appointed by Lord Romilly, a historical manuscripts commissioner, to select official papers relating to Ireland for transcription from the voluminous Carte manuscripts in the Bodleian Library, Oxford. Fearing allegations of partiality, Romilly—to Prendergast's chagrin—brought in as co-editor the Revd Dr Russell, president of the Catholic seminary St Patrick's College, Maynooth, co. Kildare. The relationship between Prendergast and Russell was never cordial: the former, convivial and outgoing, was repelled by what he regarded as the latter's primness; none the less, their collaboration proved a success. For five summers in the 1860s Prendergast travelled with his wife, Caroline, to the Bodleian Library where he selected the documents and she transcribed them. At the same time Dr Russell made his selection, and the report of the commissioners was published in 1871. Russell and Prendergast continued to calendar these state papers until 1877, when Russell died. Prendergast worked on at the task, though without realistic prospect of publication, until 1880. Meanwhile he had brought out for private circulation *The Tory War in Ulster* (2 pts); and in 1881 he wrote some account of the life of his close friend Charles Halliday, the antiquary and book collector, which served as an introduction to the latter's *Scandinavian Kingdom of Dublin*. In 1887 Prendergast published *Ireland from the Restoration to the Revolution*.

Although Prendergast's chief historical work was concerned with the seventeenth century he was also an authority on Irish genealogy and archaeology, and contributed numerous papers to the journal of the Kilkenny Archaeological Society. In addition he published a series of anonymous articles in the Dublin press (1884–90) concerning the old houses of Dublin.

In politics Prendergast was a Liberal but with a strong tinge of O'Connellite nationalism. He contributed to *The Nation* newspaper and in 1872–4 wrote a series of devastating reviews of the work on Irish history by J. A. Froude. So successful was he at combating Froude's anti-Irish and anti-Catholic slurs that a ballad ('to the air of the White Cockade') was published in his honour. Entitled 'Froude's Lies Refuted', it concluded:

> So here's to John P. Prendergast
> Who strikes for Ireland hard and fast
> Come friend as with trumpet blast
> Hurrah for John P. Prendergast.

His attack on Froude and his earlier work on the Cromwellian settlement had gained Prendergast, like his friend W. E. H. Lecky, whom he had assisted in his researches, the reputation of being a strong nationalist. But like Lecky he was never a home ruler, and from 1878 on he was a violent opponent of Parnell's general policy. An Irish parliament, he argued, would be fatal for both England and Ireland; he was a passionate defender of the Irish viceroyalty; and, curiously, he advocated the formation of a regiment of Irish guards, clad in 'rebel green', as a way of binding the two countries together. His letters (collected in six manuscript volumes) written to his friend Philip Henry Bagenal, in the last twenty years of his life, reflect his increasing and ultimately crushing disillusion with Irish and English politics.

Prendergast was a brilliant talker, full of anecdote and reminiscence. His racy—and unpublished—autobiography gives a very full account of his experiences of the Irish bar. The flavour may be gained from such remarks of Prendergast as that 'I look upon every woman and first think what kind of bedfellow she would make. I then in imagination strip her naked', and by his reference to the Irish jurist Chief Justice Whiteside as 'Chief Justice Backside ... for he was a bare-arsed foundling picked up by an old watchman from the gutters of St James Street'. However, his account of his life has also considerable historical interest, as he was an eyewitness to the Young Ireland rising of 1848 and he has much to say about the influx of Catholic barristers into the profession after Catholic emancipation in 1829.

Prendergast married on 1 September 1838 Caroline (*d.* 1875), second daughter of George Ensor of Ardress, Loughgall, co. Armagh. His bride was of Presbyterian stock and they had known one another from youth. Prendergast held off asking for her hand as 'I got a kind of fear of not making a wife happy': when he did get round to asking her to marry him she reproached him with 'Why didn't you marry me sooner?' She died on 5 February 1875. They had one son, Francis (1841–1897), who after completing an engineering degree at Trinity College, Dublin, emigrated to the United States, where he pursued a very successful career as a railroad engineer. He married Mary M. Childs in 1873 and they had seven children.

After his wife's death Prendergast lived contentedly at 127 Strand Road, Sandymount, Dublin, where he enjoyed a wide circle of friends. Standish O'Grady arranged a meeting in the mid-1870s between Prendergast and Philip Henry Bagenal, who shared Prendergast's interests in tenant rights and Irish history, and there ensued a rich friendship which, despite the disparity in age—Bagenal was many years his junior—endured until Prendergast's death. It was at Bagenal's urging that Prendergast got his papers in order, and he compiled his autobiography 'for the purpose of enabling you [Bagenal] when I was gone to write a notice of me'. Following a fall down the steps of the King's Inn Library in 1892, Prendergast died at his home on 6 February 1893, and was buried beside his wife in Mount Jerome cemetery, Dublin; his son was also later buried there. Bagenal wrote his obituary for *The Times* (8 February 1894), acted as his literary executor, and sought to have Prendergast's 'life and times' published. In 1926

Bagenal learned from Blackwoods, the Edinburgh publishing house, that they would not 'with regret' be undertaking this project, and shortly afterwards Prendergast's papers and books were, in accordance with his instructions, given in to the King's Inn Library, where they remain a century later.   THOMAS BARTLETT

Sources DNB · King's Inn, Dublin, Prendergast MSS · *The Nations* (14 Dec 1872) · *The Nations* (21 Dec 1872) · *The Nations* (9 May 1874) · *The Nations* (16 May 1874)
Archives King's Inns, Dublin, MSS, typescript autobiography, letters, and pamphlets | TCD, letters to W. E. H. Lecky

Prendergast [Pendergrass], Sir Thomas, first baronet

(c.1660–1709), army officer and Jacobite conspirator, was the third son of Thomas Prendergast (1614?–1725) and his wife, Eleanor (d. in or before 1705), daughter of David Condon. He was possibly born at Croane, co. Tipperary, and had three brothers and at least three sisters. The Prendergasts, a prosperous Catholic family, had been based at Newcastle, co. Tipperary, but lost their property in the Cromwellian confiscations. Prendergast's father's elder brother Jeffery was transplanted to Connaught, and later emigrated to France with his Jacobite officer sons after the treaty of Limerick. Prendergast's father himself may have been the Thomas Prendergast who in 1665 occupied a one-hearth dwelling near the ruined family seat at Newcastle; the situation would have many Irish parallels. Jonathan Swift (who retrospectively hated Prendergast as a supposed false witness even before his anticlerical son offended him) described the elder Thomas Prendergast as a cottager narrowly saved from the gallows at Clonmel assizes for stealing cows by his protestant landlord Moore, and accused Prendergast himself of having worked as a shoeblack and footman.

During the Irish war of 1689–91 Prendergast became a captain in the Jacobite cavalry. Many officers saw the war as furnishing a career, not a cause; military honour rather than Jacobitism or Catholicism provided their basic morality. A Captain Thomas Pendergrass was among 100 Jacobite officers who entered William's service after the final surrender of Limerick. By June 1693 it was intended to send them to fight for the Venetians in Greece, which would have practically amounted to perpetual banishment. At some point during the war, Prendergast was in France. A prisoner frantically seeking pardon in 1696 claimed that a 'Pendergrass' was involved in the plots to kidnap William in late 1693, but attributed to him another man's actions. In England Prendergast joined the Jacobite debauchee George Porter as a highwayman. They operated from a Jacobite safe house in Hampshire run by William O'Brian (whose wife became their mistress about 1695). Prendergast felt himself under the greatest obligation to Porter.

In February 1696 Prendergast was called to London from Hampshire by Porter, who brought him into the assassination plot devised by Sir George Barclay. Prendergast was chosen for the party of eight men under Barclay who would attack William III's coach, and received a musketoon with which to fire repeatedly into it.

Late on 14 February 1696, the eve of the attempt, Prendergast secretly went to Whitehall, where he broke the news of the plot to William's confidential adviser Hans Willem Bentinck, earl of Portland. He told him that William must be prevented from hunting next day, but that the same honour and conscience which made him, a Catholic Jacobite, give the warning prevented him from testifying against, or even naming, his fellow conspirators, particularly one of them (Porter). Portland had earlier disregarded a similar general warning, but believed Prendergast and, with difficulty, persuaded William to cancel his hunting. After learning from their spies at Kensington that no alarm had been raised, the plotters prepared to try again a week later. A double agent, Francis Delarue, confirmed Prendergast's story, and when Prendergast went to Kensington Palace late on 21 February to give another warning, he was brought to the king. William told him that unless he revealed more details of the plot, he himself would not be safe should the assassins change their method and timing. With a promise that he should not be a witness unless he chose, Prendergast was persuaded to name the conspirators.

The next day, Prendergast was among them as they prepared to depart to ambush William at Turnham Green. When their Kensington agent brought them word that William's hunting was again cancelled, amid rumours of a plot, they agreed to disperse. Prendergast warned Portland of this, and retreated to Surrey with Porter and Porter's servant Thomas Keyes. As a cover, £1000 was offered for his capture in the government's proclamation. The three men were captured (without collusion) on 27 February at Leatherhead. Porter immediately offered to turn king's evidence, and on 28 February implicated his comrades, including Prendergast. The latter, now that his friend was safe (though both remained some weeks in Newgate), agreed to be a witness. However, a latecomer to the plot, he testified only at the first trial, that of Robert Charnock, Edward King, and Keyes on 11 March, and at that of the conspirators' quartermaster Charles Cranburne. He received a pardon on 28 April 1696. After William O'Brian carried off to France Cardell Goodman, a witness against Sir John Fenwick, Prendergast persuaded Mrs O'Brian in early 1697 to follow as a spy.

William, with immense experience of informers, apparently believed that Prendergast's motives and scruples had been genuine, and distinguished him from the other witnesses. On 5 May 1696 he granted him £3000 and ordered the Irish government to find for him a forfeited Jacobite estate worth £500 a year. On 23 April 1697 Prendergast was finally granted one at Gort, co. Galway, where he supplanted not only the forfeited Jacobite owner, Roger O'Shaughnessy, but the Williamite Colonel Gustavus Hamilton (later Viscount Boyne), temporarily given it for services in the Irish war. As post-war depression had reduced the yearly value of the Gort estate by almost £200, Prendergast, after petitioning, was additionally granted on 18 July 1698 other forfeited properties in several counties, theoretically worth £334 a year.

Prendergast married at Dublin, by licence of 10 August

1697, Penelope (d. 1746), only daughter of the Dublin lawyer Henry Cadogan, of Liscarton, co. Meath, and sister of William *Cadogan, later Earl Cadogan. He at some time converted to protestantism, and others of his close-knit family, whose fortunes he was restoring, apparently followed. He lived largely in Dublin.

On 23 September 1697, the Irish House of Commons passed a resolution of thanks to Prendergast. On 15 July 1699 he was created a baronet. The Act of Resumption of 1700 exempted his estates. In the Irish parliament of 1703 he became MP for Monaghan. He repurchased family properties, and began buying forfeited estates in various counties from the Hollow Sword Blade Company with loans it granted.

By 1706 Prendergast was lieutenant-colonel of the earl of Orrery's new infantry regiment, where he was joined by relatives. He could be a harsh disciplinarian. On 24 February 1707 he became colonel of his regiment. It was ordered to Flanders in April 1708, and was subsequently quartered at Oudenarde. On 1 January 1709 Prendergast was promoted brigadier-general. He fought bravely in the battle of Malplaquet on 11 September 1709 NS, and was mortally wounded while leading his regiment against the French troops entrenched in the wood of Blaregnies; he was presumably buried near Malplaquet. A tradition, whose details vary, claimed that he had a strong premonition of his death, linked to the plot of 1696. He left one son, Thomas [see below]; his three daughters were later all married: Juliana (d. 1758) to Chaworth Brabazon, sixth earl of Meath (a love match); Elizabeth first to Sir John Dickson Hamon, bt (d. 1728) and second to Charles Smyth, MP for Limerick, with whom she had four children; and Anne to Samuel Hobson, of Muckridge. Among the provisions of his will was a £14 annuity to his elderly father.

Swift in 1720 described Penelope, Lady Prendergast, as 'the greatest Widow Blacacre [obsessive litigant] now in Christendom' (Correspondence, 2.341). She had little choice if she was to protect her son, as Earl Cadogan plundered his nephew's estate. It owed large sums to the Hollow Sword Blade Company. Roger O'Shaughnessy's rights in the Gort estate had been limited, and the family made repeated, though ultimately unsuccessful, legal attempts to reclaim it. Lady Prendergast died in Dublin between June and October 1746. Her will indicates fear that her son would embezzle her main bequest, to her faithful serving-maid, unless he thought it inconsiderable.

Prendergast's son, **Sir Thomas Prendergast**, second baronet (bap. 1702, d. 1760), politician, was baptized at St Peter's and St Kevin's Church, Dublin, on 20 May 1702 and became a child ensign in his father's regiment. He was admitted a fellow-commoner at Clare College, Cambridge, on 21 May 1719, and entered the Inner Temple in 1721. He lobbied Charles Lennox, second duke of Richmond, who had married his cousin Lady Sarah Cadogan, for a seat in the British parliament, and was returned to the Commons in March 1733 as MP for Chichester. In his first week, he voted against the government over the Excise Bill because Sir Robert Walpole would not make him Irish postmaster-general. Walpole covertly ensured

his defeat in the 1734 general election. George II called him 'an Irish blockhead' (Sedgwick). Meanwhile, Prendergast was defeated in October 1733 in a by-election for the Irish Commons at Clonmel by Guy Moore, grandson of his grandfather's benefactor. The Commons reversed this on petition, and he sat for Clonmel until his death; this was one of several such setbacks to the Moore family's government-backed campaign to make it their pocket borough. Swift, however, blamed the 'parson-hunters', Prendergast's fellow anti-clericals. His Commons antics in 1736 provoked Swift in the poems 'Noisy Tom' and 'The Legion Club' to assail vituperatively both father and son:

the spawn of him who shamed our isle,
the traitor, assassin, informer vile.
(*Complete Poems*, 550)

On 11 January 1739, Prendergast married Anne (d. 1770), daughter and heir of Sir Griffith Williams, sixth baronet, of Marle, Caernarvonshire (where he stood unsuccessfully in the 1747 election). In 1754 he at last became Irish postmaster-general. He was lieutenant-governor of co. Galway. He died childless at his home in Merrion Street, Dublin, on 23 September 1760, while his patent as Viscount Clonmell was being prepared. His nephew and heir, John Prendergast Smyth (1741–1817), the son of his sister Elizabeth, was created first Viscount Gort in 1816.

PAUL HOPKINS

Sources DNB · State trials, vols. 12–13 · Burke, *Peerage* (1999) · GEC, *Peerage* · R. R. Sedgwick, 'Prendergast, Sir Thomas', HoP, *Commons, 1715–54* · W. A. Shaw, ed., *Calendar of treasury books*, 10–14, PRO (1933–5) · CSP dom., 1696–1702 · *The complete poems of Jonathan Swift*, ed. P. Rogers (1983) · *Prendergast Chronicles* [Prendergast Association] (1981–6) [periodical] · U. Nott. L., Portland MSS, PwA · W. P. Burke, *History of Clonmel* (1907) · C. Dalton, ed., *English army lists and commission registers, 1661–1714*, 6 vols. (1892–1904) · J. G. Simms, *The Williamite confiscation in Ireland, 1690–1703* (1956) · MSS of John Ellis, BL, Add. MS 28881 · will, PRO, PROB 11/521, fols. 125–6 · will, PRO, PROB 11/752, fols. 389–90 [Penelope Prendergast, wife] · Hardwicke papers, BL, Add. MSS 35584, 35591, 36047, 36051 · N. Luttrell, *A brief historical relation of state affairs from September 1678 to April 1714*, 6 vols. (1857) · *Journals of the House of Commons of the Kingdom of Ireland*, 8–11 (1753–61) · Earl of March [C. H. G. Lennox], *A duke and his friends: the life and letters of the second duke of Richmond*, 2 vols. (1911) · T. Laffan, *Tipperary's families: being the hearth money records for 1665–6–7* (1911) · R. Simmington, ed., *The civil survey: county Tipperary*, 2 vols. (1931–4) · H. Manners Sutton, ed., *The Lexington papers, or, Some account of the courts of London and Vienna* (1851) · *The correspondence of Jonathan Swift*, ed. H. Williams, 5 vols. (1963–5) · Marlborough MSS, BL, Add. MSS 61320, 61336 · T. P. Power, *Land, politics and society in eighteenth century Tipperary* (1993) · *Faulkner's Dublin Journal*, 3483 (23 Sept 1760)
Wealth at death estates in Galway (£300–£500 p.a.), Tipperary, and other Irish counties; but some titles insecure, and heavy borrowings from the Hollow Sword Blade Company: BL, Add. MS 36047, fols. 28v–30

Prendergast, Sir Thomas, second baronet (bap. **1702**, d. **1760**). See under Prendergast, Sir Thomas, first baronet (c.1660–1709).

Prendergast, Thomas (1807/8–1886), East India Company servant and writer on language learning, was the son of Sir Jeffrey Prendergast (1769–1856) and his wife, Elizabeth, daughter of Hew Dalrymple of Nunraw, East Lothian; they married in 1804. His father was born at Clonmel, was in the service of the East India Company, and became colonel of the 39th native infantry in 1825. He served in the Anglo-Mysore War, was knighted in 1838, was promoted to be a general in 1854, and died in 1856.

Thomas was nominated a writer in the East India Company's service on 23 June 1826, and became assistant to the collector of Tanjore, Madras presidency, in 1828. He was acting head assistant to the collector of Nellore on 16 January 1829, and head assistant on 9 February 1830. In 1830 he became acting sub-collector and joint magistrate of Nellore, in 1833 acting assistant judge at Guntur, and on 8 August 1834 assistant judge of Tinnevelly (or Tinnevelly), where he remained until 1838. His wife, Lucy Caroline, *née* Dalrymple, died in 1839, and their two sons, Hew and Harry, were sent to live with their grandfather Sir Jeffrey. He was afterwards for many years collector and magistrate at Rajahmundry until his retirement on the annuity fund in 1859. On his arrival in England he settled at Cheltenham, and about 1861 became totally blind. Despite this misfortune, he devoted himself to literary work, and invented what he called the mastery system of learning languages. This system is based upon the process pursued by children in learning to speak. They are impelled by instinct to imitate and repeat the chance sentences which they hear spoken around them, and afterwards to interchange and transpose the words so as to form new combinations. By frequently repeating conversational sentences Prendergast had himself acquired the Madras vernacular, Tamil, and Telugu. The system was to some extent a development of the Ollendorffian, but Prendergast elaborated its details on original lines. His success was considerable, and the various manuals in which he practically expounded his views went through numerous editions.

Prendergast's key works are *The Mastery of Languages, or, The Art of Speaking Foreign Tongues Idiomatically* (1864; 3rd edn, 1872) and *Handbook to the Mastery Series* (1868; 5th edn, 1882). The Mastery Series itself covered French (1868; 12th edn, 1879); Spanish (1869; 4th edn, 1875); German (1868; 8th edn, 1874); Hebrew (1871; 3rd edn, 1879); and Latin (1872; 5th edn, 1884).

Prendergast died at Meldon Lodge, The Park, Cheltenham, on 14 November 1886, and was buried in the town's new cemetery on 18 November. His son, Sir Harry North Dalrymple *Prendergast (1834–1913), GCB VC, was commander in Burma from 1883 to 1886.

G. C. BOASE, rev. JOHN D. HAIGH

Sources E. Dodwell and J. S. Miles, *Madras civil servants* (1839), 226 · *The Times* (19 Nov 1886), 6 · *The Academy* (20 Nov 1886), 345 · *Cheltenham Chronicle* (20 Nov 1886), 2 · d. cert. · CGPLA Eng. & Wales (1887)
Wealth at death £4152 13s. 7d.: probate, 21 Jan 1887, CGPLA Eng. & Wales

Prentice, Archibald (1792–1857), journalist and free-trader, was born on 17 November 1792 at Covington Mains, a farm in the Upper ward of Lanarkshire, Scotland. He was one of seven children born to the yeoman farmer Archibald Prentice and his second wife, Helen, daughter of John Stoddart of Carnwath. Prentice's religious upbringing was Presbyterian, with paternal ancestral roots stretching back to the Commonwealth period.

There is no contemporary description of his appearance, but an autographed illustration of him in the frontispiece to his *Tour of the United States* (1849) shows an earnest-looking man, bespectacled, with a broad forehead.

Prentice served as apprentice to a baker (1804–5) and a woollen draper (1805–8) and, despite his rudimentary education, in 1808 he received a position in the Glasgow textile firm of Thomas Grahame. Rising steadily in the business, he oversaw its move to Manchester, where he became a partner in 1815. As he settled into life in Manchester he married Jane, daughter of James Thompson of Oatridge, near Linlithgow, Scotland, on 3 June 1819. Meanwhile, participation in the Manchester Literary and Philosophical Society put him in contact with Edward Taylor, the first editor of the *Manchester Guardian*, and Absalom Watkin, both of whom were later associated with advanced reforms in Manchester. This contact with Taylor, who invited him to write for his paper, introduced Prentice to journalism and the importance of newspapers as shapers of public opinion. Prentice's editorials for the paper advanced the reforms of Jeremy Bentham, and especially the movement for free trade.

Impatient with Taylor's cautious approach to reform, in 1824 Prentice established a rival journal, the *Manchester Gazette*, later renamed the *Manchester Times*. Against the background of the Peterloo massacre of 1819, Prentice joined a growing number of editors of provincial weeklies who were attempting to mould popular thinking about economic distress and the need for parliamentary reform. Prentice, in particular, tried to merge the interests of both manufacturers and workers. In arguing against governmental waste, for example, he said that such inefficiencies simultaneously reduced the value of workers' wages and stifled the entrepreneurial efforts of the manufacturers. Similarly, he attacked the 1815 corn law because it raised the price of bread for the poor while inhibiting employment and industrial expansion.

Prentice's ardent devotion to reform efforts, however, proved to be his undoing as a commercially successful newspaperman. Although his newspapers turned a profit in their early years, his single-minded use of them for reformist causes, to the exclusion of lighter and more attractive features, drove down circulation, and his propagandizing alienated many. This partly explains the *Manchester Gazette*'s failure in 1828 and the subsequent inability of the *Manchester Times* to compete with John Bright's more moderate *Manchester Examiner*.

Although Prentice supported a variety of reforms, he made his reputation as a founder of the Anti-Corn Law League. In 1838 the free-trade campaign began in earnest in Manchester when Prentice joined six others to form the Anti-Corn Law Association (later League). Notwithstanding his identification with its work, questions have arisen about his true prominence in the organization (McCord, 34, 35). Certainly he was its leading publicist and later wrote the *History of the Anti-Corn Law League*. However, he did not serve in any leadership capacity and was at odds with other members, especially Richard Cobden. In 1841, for example, when the tories assumed office, Cobden had to restrain Prentice from pressing greater demands on Robert Peel for tariff reform. Similarly, as league moderates strove to focus on repeal, Prentice and other extremists were accused of diverting the public's attention to other reform issues.

Nevertheless, Prentice's contribution to the anti-corn law effort was well recognized by contemporaries. Cobden's view of him as an earnest, hard-working, and principled man did not, however, go far enough for Prentice's long-time friend, John Childs. Annoyed that Bright and others had set up the rival *Manchester Examiner* in 1846 against Prentice's *Times*, Childs pointed out that Prentice had devoted his life to the league and wondered what Cobden and Bright would have done without him.

As a reformer Prentice derived his inspiration from several sources. His dissenting background led him to favour religious toleration and to support Catholic emancipation and an end to the Test and Corporation Acts. He encouraged temperance, even total abstinence, and was later treasurer of the Manchester Temperance League. He was also an early supporter of parliamentary reform and eventually joined Joseph Sturge's complete suffrage movement in 1841. However, as a hard-headed follower of Bentham's educational reform ideas he advocated a literacy test for voting. He sponsored mechanics' institutes for Manchester's workers as well as elementary education, although as a Presbyterian he opposed any curricula lacking religious instruction.

Also consistent with Prentice's middle-class radicalism was his desire to reach out to the working class. This gesture was not reciprocated by the unenfranchised, who distrusted Prentice's intentions, believing that he was more committed to the manufacturers than to the operatives. In 1830, when Prentice helped form a shopkeeper-dominated political union favouring piecemeal parliamentary reform, the workers established their own union calling for universal suffrage, annual parliaments, and vote by ballot. Also, despite Prentice's pledge that corn law repeal would benefit both masters and men, Chartists viewed him with suspicion.

It has been suggested that Prentice's estrangement from the workers was due, in part, to his inability to speak to them in a language they understood. Although he claimed to speak for the workers, he had the habit of addressing them in a condescending, even scolding, tone. William Cobbett described him and his friends as priggish, while Bentham had to admit that he was well intentioned but 'juggical' (Read, 60). Prentice's criticism of aspects of the new poor law and his sensitivity to the plight of the workers did not change the perception of him as cold and antiseptic.

Unable to compete for readers with the *Manchester Examiner*, Prentice left *The Times* in 1847. A brief tour of the United States in 1847 followed, which was later recounted in his *A Tour of the United States*, published in 1849. Upon his return from America, his impecunious state forced him to seek employment at the Manchester gas office, where he received an annual salary of £150. This income provided

him the security to continue his writing, which took the form of *Historical Sketches and Personal Recollections of Manchester from 1792 to 1832*, published in 1851, and his *History of the Anti-Corn Law League*, which appeared in 1853. Although modern and more objective accounts have eclipsed Prentice's work, no other contemporary work has provided such a detailed record of the league's activities.

In Prentice's later years he and his wife were supported by an annuity of £100 provided by friends and admirers. He died in Manchester on 22 December 1857 of what has been described as brain congestion (*DNB*) and was buried at Rusholme Road cemetery, Manchester.

PAUL R. ZIEGLER

Sources A. Prentice, *History of the Anti-Corn Law League*, 2 vols. (1853); repr. with introduction by W. H. Chaloner (1968) • A. Prentice, *Historical sketches and personal recollections of Manchester intended to illustrate the progress of public opinion from 1792 to 1832*, 3rd edn (1970) [incl. introduction by D. Read] • N. McCord, *The Anti-Corn Law League, 1838–1846* (1958) • D. Read, *Peterloo: the 'massacre' and its background* (1958) • R. Dunlop, 'Archibald Prentice: a page in the history of journalism', *Macmillan's Magazine*, 60 (1889), 435–43 • A. Prentice, *A tour of the United States with two lectures on emigration*, 6th edn (1849) • *DNB* • L. Brown, *The board of trade and the free-trade movement, 1830–42* (1958) • D. Ayerst, *Guardian: biography of a newspaper* (1971) • N. C. Edsall, *Richard Cobden: independent radical* (1986)
Archives Man. CL, Manchester Archives and Local Studies, Anti-Corn Law League, letter-book • W. Sussex RO, corresp. with Richard Cobden • W. Yorks. AS, Wakefield, Todmorden Anti-Corn Law Association, resolutions, roll books, and rules • W. Yorks. AS, Calderdale, Anti-Corn Law League, Halifax, minutes and MSS
Likenesses portrait, repro. in Prentice, *Tour of the United States*, frontispiece
Wealth at death under £600: will, 23 April 1858, *CGPLA Eng. & Wales*

Prentice, Joan (*d.* 1589). *See under* Essex witches (*act.* 1566–1589).

Prentis, Edward (*bap.* 1797, *d.* 1854), painter, was baptized on 19 August 1797 at Earl Street Presbyterian Church, Maidstone, Kent, the son of Walter Prentis and Anne Sweatman. He was the brother of Stephen *Prentis (1800–1862), poet. He first exhibited two pictures at the Royal Academy in 1823, *Girl with Matches* and *Boy with Oranges*. He exhibited at the Society (later Royal Society) of British Artists from 1826 until 1850, having been made a member of the society in 1827, and he remained a steady supporter of the society throughout his life. According to the society's catalogues he lived in Kensington, London, first at 5 Hornton Street (1826–33) and later at 9 Hornton Street (1833–45); the Royal Academy catalogue for 1823 gives his address as 2 Tavistock Row, Covent Garden, London. He painted genre scenes of domestic life, often with allegorical meaning, and his works were accompanied in the exhibition catalogues with quotations from literature. Among the pictures he exhibited at the Society of British Artists were *The Nervous Miser* (1826), *The Wife* and *The Daughter* (1836), engraved as a pair by J. C. Bromley in 1837, and *The Folly of Extravagance* (1850). His painting *The Sick Bed* is in the Glasgow Art Gallery. Prentis also executed for the trustees of the British Museum a series of highly finished drawings of the ivory objects found at Nimrud, Turkish Mosul. These were engraved on wood by J. Thompson and published in A. H. Layard's *Monuments of Nineveh* (1849). Prentis died in December 1854, leaving property to his wife, Sarah, with whom he had eleven children.

JOHN SUNDERLAND

Sources Graves, *Artists* · Graves, *RA exhibitors* · Wood, *Vic. painters*, 3rd edn · *IGI* · private information (2004) [J. D. Pickles] · will, PRO, PROB 11/2205, fols. 145v–146v

Prentis, Stephen (1800–1862), poet, son of Walter Prentis and Anne Sweatman, was born at Rochester, Kent, on 21 July 1800 and baptized there on 16 September 1800. He was educated at Greenwich and then admitted as a pensioner on 12 March 1819 (he matriculated at Easter 1820) to Christ's College, Cambridge, where he became a scholar in 1821 and graduated BA in 1824 and MA in 1830. He was living at Maidstone, Kent, in 1829, and for many years resided at Dinan in Brittany. He was the author of numerous short poems of considerable merit, which he printed for private circulation among his friends.

Prentis's works, some of which were published in London but most privately in Dinan, are extremely scarce; they include *An Apology for Lord Byron, with Miscellaneous Poems* (1836), *Tintern, Stonehenge: 'Oh! think of me at times!'* (1843), *The Wreck of the 'Roscommon'* (1844), *A Tribute to May* (1849), *Le grand bey* (1849), *Winter Flowers* (1849), *The Flight of the Swallow* (1851), *The Revel of the Missel-Thrush* (1851), and *The Prince and the Prayer-Book: an Episode in the Life of Napoleon III* (1858). In 1850 he edited a quarterly publication, the *Dinan Magazine*; but it did not survive. He died at Dinan on 12 June 1862. THOMPSON COOPER, *rev.* REBECCA MILLS

Sources *IGI* · Venn, *Alum. Cant.*, 2/5.185 · J. Peile, *Biographical register of Christ's College, 1505–1905, and of the earlier foundation, God's House, 1448–1505*, ed. [J. A. Venn], 2 (1913), 393 · T. Cooper, *A new biographical dictionary: containing concise notices of eminent persons of all ages and countries* (1873), 967 · H. R. Luard, ed., *Graduati Cantabrigienses*, 7th edn (1884), 420 · J. Romilly, ed., *Graduati Cantabrigienses* (1846), 254 · Allibone, *Dict.* · private information (1896)

Pre-Raphaelite women artists (*act.* 1848–1870s) is the name given by late twentieth-century scholars to a group of female contemporaries of the Pre-Raphaelite Brotherhood (PRB), founded in 1848. A major exhibition of Pre-Raphaelite art at the Tate Gallery, London, in 1984 included the work of only one woman, Elizabeth *Siddal, although several of the male artists represented were linked only marginally with Pre-Raphaelitism. It was to redress this misleading imbalance—and to correct the commonly held view that the women associated with members of the PRB were exclusively models and mistresses—that the Manchester exhibition 'Pre-Raphaelite Women Artists' (1998) was organized by Jan Marsh and Pamela Gerrish Nunn. In this the work of twenty women artists more or less connected with the PRB and with Pre-Raphaelite style was examined. Few examples survive from the artwork of several of the women linked with early Pre-Raphaelitism (1848–*c*.1857) (Anna Mary *Howitt and Eliza Florance Bridell-*Fox) and with its second phase (1857–1870s) (Rebecca Solomon and Emma Sandys), making the degree of stylistic connection, in some cases, difficult to establish.

Pre-Raphaelitism: the first phase, 1848–*c*.1857 The group of women associated with the initial phase of Pre-Raphaelitism shared both background and interests. The painter Eliza Fox and the artist and women's activist Barbara Leigh Smith *Bodichon were both from prominent Unitarian families, and the painter Anna Mary Howitt, together with her parents—the writer William *Howitt and his wife, the writer and translator Mary *Howitt—converted to Unitarianism in the mid-1840s. The feminist commitment of these young women (a group which also included the writer Bessie Rayner Parkes [see Belloc, Elizabeth Rayner]), and their belief in literature and art as instruments of moral and spiritual reform, stem from a shared interest in radical Unitarianism. This incorporated a set of cultural and political beliefs formulated by Eliza's father, William Johnson *Fox, and his circle from the 1830s and widely disseminated in the 1840s, through personal contact and journalism, by William and Mary Howitt. The regeneration of art proposed by the Pre-Raphaelites appealed strongly to Eliza Fox, Barbara Leigh Smith, and Anna Mary Howitt.

The art education of these three women and of other women artists connected with the Pre-Raphaelite movement often coincided. Eliza Fox and Anna Mary Howitt both attended classes run between 1844 and 1847 by F. S. Cary at Henry Sass's drawing school, where Walter Deverell, Dante Gabriel *Rossetti, and Henry Wallis were also pupils. (As the Fox and Rossetti households were both in Charlotte Street, Bedford Square, in the early 1840s it is possible they met.) By 1849 and until 1859 Eliza Fox ran practice sessions (and subsequently lessons) in drawing from the nude in her father's library. These were attended by Barbara Leigh Smith (whose family was acquainted with the Howitts from 1845), Anna Mary Howitt, and another woman artist from a prominent Unitarian family, Anne Laura *Herford (1831–1870). In 1849 Smith and Joanna Boyce [see Wells, Joanna Mary], the sister of the Pre-Raphaelite artist George Boyce, attended ladies' classes run by Cary at the newly founded Ladies' College in Bedford Square, and in the early 1850s Joanna Boyce and Anna Blunden (1829–1915) both received instruction at James Mathews Leigh's painting school in Newman Street. In May 1850 Howitt and Jane E. Benham, an ironmonger's daughter who married the artist William Milton Hay in October 1851, becoming **Jane E. Hay** [known as Jane Benham Hay] (*b.* 1829), went to Munich to study art and were given work space in the studio of Wilhelm von Kaulbach. Benham remained until December 1850, Howitt until May 1852. Eliza Fox's plan to accompany them was not realized, but Smith visited in September 1850. Echoing, perhaps, the formation of the Pre-Raphaelite Brotherhood two years earlier, in September 1850 Howitt, Smith, and Benham planned a 'beautiful sisterhood in Art' in which a core of women artists would be provided for by an outer band of women workers in a female co-operative community—all united by high moral purpose (Howitt-

Watts, 1.92). This scheme was undoubtedly influenced by Tennyson's *The Princess*—whose heroine Ida presides over a college for women—a work favourably reviewed by William Howitt in 1848 and with which Howitt, Smith, and Parkes were much preoccupied in the same year. The plan was apparently not put into practice.

In 1849 or early 1850 Howitt became engaged to marry Edward La Trobe Bateman, a decorative designer and illuminator who was an intimate associate of the PRB, whose members he may have introduced to the Howitt family. D. G. Rossetti, Holman *Hunt, and Thomas *Woolner were all visitors at 28 Avenue Road, Regent's Park, the Howitt family's home between 1848 and 1852, and J. E. Millais visited them at the Hermitage, Highgate, where they moved in 1852. Siddal, then emerging as an artist in her own right, was introduced to the Howitt circle at this time. In 1854 Howitt and Smith were two of only four women (the others being Louisa Anne *Beresford, marchioness of Waterford, and Eleanor Vere *Boyle) invited to join the Folio Club, a sketching club formed by members of the PRB. While Howitt and Smith were certainly acquainted with members of the PRB (Rossetti in particular—their best documented meeting was during a visit to Hastings in 1854 when Howitt and Smith sketched Siddal), it is difficult to establish definite personal connections between members of the PRB and the other women artists associated with the Pre-Raphaelite movement—with the obvious exception of Elizabeth Siddal. Nevertheless, all the women artists mentioned above may be linked through style or theme (or both) with early Pre-Raphaelitism.

The first two volumes of Ruskin's *Modern Painters* (1843–6), with their insistence on minute observation of nature, not only influenced the Pre-Raphaelites but were extremely encouraging to women artists, who were, for the most part, deprived of a classical art education and access to proper study from the life. The 'Academy of Nature' referred to in a letter from Howitt to Smith (Hirsch, 43) was open to everyone. In landscapes, portraits, and accessorial natural detail, Ruskin's influence, and by extension that of the Pre-Raphaelites, is apparent in the work of many of these artists [see also Women artists in Ruskin's circle].

Howitt and Jane Benham Hay both attached importance to meticulous observation in art. Thus the latter's first exhibited work at the Royal Academy, *Studies from Nature* (1848), was described in the *Art Union* as 'a very skilful copy of objects scarcely deserving the pains that have been bestowed upon them' (*Art Union*, 10, 1848, 167). In Munich the two spent much time drawing from nature. Several critics (for example, those writing in the *Illustrated London News*, *The Athenaeum*, and *The Critic*) commented on Pre-Raphaelite influence in Howitt's first exhibited work, *Margaret Returning from the Fountain* (exh. Portland Gallery, National Institution of Fine Arts, London, 1854).

Barbara Leigh Smith, primarily a watercolour painter, received instruction in oil painting from Howitt in 1854. While staying with Howitt at Scalands Farm (Smith's home in Hastings, Sussex) in May that year, Smith herself

commented on the Pre-Raphaelite nature of her work. *Quarry by the Sea*, her contribution to the Folio Club in July, on the theme of desolation, was much admired by the Rossetti brothers, and her coastal scene exhibited at Crystal Palace in 1856 was described by W. M. Rossetti as 'full of real Pre-Raphaelitism, that is to say, full of character and naturalism in the detail as well as in the multiplicity of it' (W. M. Rossetti, 1856, 245). This phase was short-lived, however.

The most conscientious female followers of Ruskin's truth to nature precept were Rosa *Brett and Anna *Blunden [see under Women artists in Ruskin's circle]. As early as 1852, John Brett noted in his diary that his sister had 'lately made a few first-rate sketches on Preraffaelite [sic] principles' (MS, priv. coll.). Her first Royal Academy exhibit, *The Hayloft* (exh. 1858), was praised by Woolner and by Frederick Stephens, who referred to 'minute picking out of every detail' and 'punctilious finish' (*The Spectator*, 5 June 1858, 604). Brett's surviving work—primarily landscapes and still lifes—suggests that, like her brother, she adhered closely to Ruskinian principles until her death in 1882.

Sincerity to nature extended also to portraiture. It was primarily as a portrait painter that Eliza Fox exhibited between 1846 and 1858. In 1858 she drew Elizabeth Barrett Browning—one of the Pre-Raphaelite 'immortals'—in Rome. Joanna Boyce, described by D. G. Rossetti as 'a wonderfully gifted woman' (*Reflections of a Friendship*, 169), admired Ruskin's *Modern Painters* and early Pre-Raphaelite work. Her paintings, and particularly her portraits of the 1850s, have been related to Pre-Raphaelitism because of their vivid colouring and minute delineation. Her first exhibit at the Royal Academy was a head entitled *Elgiva* (1855; priv. coll.). A simple, unornamented, and yet careful study, it received praise from Ford Madox Brown and Ruskin. Other portraits by her, such as *Portrait of Sidney Wells* (1859; Tate collection) and *Head of Mrs Eaton* (1861; Yale U. CBA), are executed in a similar style, which may be compared with that of Elizabeth Siddal in her self-portrait (1853/4; priv. coll.). David Masson, in the *British Quarterly Review*, described another particularity of Pre-Raphaelite art as a tendency to 'archaism' which commonly took the form of a 'relish for mediaevalism' (Masson, 206, 208), expressed initially in Christian themes and subsequently in literary subjects. Shakespeare, Tennyson, Keats, Browning, and Scott's *Minstrelsy of the Scottish Border* provided frequent sources. Elizabeth Siddal used all these. Howitt also favoured literary themes, from Goethe's *Faust*, Shelley's *Sensitive Plant*, and Tennyson's *Boadicea*. Boyce's interest in medieval or archaic subjects is apparent from such titles as *Rowena Offering the Wassail Bowl to Vortigern* (1856; destroyed). Her most successful work was *The Florentine Procession* (known as 'The burning of the vanities'; exh. French Gallery, 1867; Homerton College, Cambridge), probably based on a scene from George Eliot's *Romola*. Jane Benham Hay illustrated Longfellow, among other writers, in the early 1850s. Several artists also wrote themselves, *The Germ*—to which Howitt was invited to contribute—providing the most obvious example of the literary nature of the group. Bodichon, Howitt, and Boyce all published on art, social issues, or both, and Siddall wrote fifteen more or less completed poems.

Recent feminist scholarship has focused on depictions of women by women artists associated with the early Pre-Raphaelite movement and has either related these to, or contrasted them with, the predominantly idealizing representations by male artists of the group. Most of these women artists certainly wanted greater freedom and more opportunities for women; the Unitarian background of the original group was an important factor here, helping to explain the 'sisterhood in Art' project. Boyce was unwilling to give up her independence when, in 1857, she married the portrait painter Henry Tanworth *Wells. Hay's visit to Munich with Howitt and her espousal of the cause of Italian independence (which Fox and Herford also supported) suggest a background of free thought. In 1854 Bodichon had formed the Langham Place Group (with which Howitt and Fox were also connected) to campaign for women's rights, and in the early 1850s she and the Howitt circle were preoccupied with prostitution.

Moral issues and specifically the theme of 'fallen' women appear in the work of several artists associated with the early Pre-Raphaelite movement. Examples by women included Howitt's *Margaret Returning from the Fountain*, which was shown in 1854 at the Portland Gallery with a quotation from Goethe's *Faust*: 'Margaret, having heard the harsh judgment of her companions at the city fountain returns home tortured by self-accusation'; Howitt's *The Castaway* (exh. RA, 1855), showing a desolate woman with mud and a discarded rose symbolic of her degradation; and Siddal's *Pippa Passing the Loose Women* (1854; AM Oxf.), from Browning, which has been described as offering 'a female perspective' on the subject (Marsh and Nunn, 115). Women artists also depicted women as outcasts or outsiders in other contexts in works such as Howitt's *The Lady—vide Shelley's Sensitive Plant* (exh. Portland Gallery, National Institution of Fine Arts, London, 1855) and *Boadicea* (modelled by Bodichon; exh. Crystal Palace, 1856), and Boyce's *The Outcast, or, No Joy the Blowing Season Gives* (Tennyson) (exh. RA, 1858).

From 1857—when D. G. Rossetti initiated what has been called the second phase of Pre-Raphaelitism with his Oxford Union Society project—the women artists connected with Pre-Raphaelitism's first phase became gradually dissociated from the group. Bodichon spent long periods abroad after her marriage in 1857, and around the same time Hay moved to Italy for at least ten years. Howitt last exhibited in 1858. From the same year, 1858, Fox spent long periods in Italy. Boyce died in 1861, Siddal in 1862. By this time, however, aspects of early Pre-Raphaelite art were being widely imitated in the broader art world, not least among women artists: thus in 1861 a reviewer of the Society of Female Artists exhibition alluded to the 'frantic Pre-Raphaelite attempts' which had proliferated during the preceding years (*English Woman's Journal*, 7, 1861, 56–7).

Pre-Raphaelitism: the second phase, c.1857–1870s The second phase of the Pre-Raphaelite movement saw a shift to a more aesthetic and decorative emphasis (influenced by classicism and sixteenth-century Venetian painting) most commonly associated with the work of D. G. Rossetti, Edward Burne-Jones, and William *Morris, and with Morris's firm, established in 1861. This development extended beyond the immediate Pre-Raphaelite circle. The women artists whose work may be most closely linked with this style, however, were all to a greater or lesser extent personally connected with D. G. Rossetti in the 1860s and 1870s. The photographer Julia Margaret *Cameron would have had the opportunity to meet members of the PRB at the Prinsep's salon at Little Holland House (her sister was married to Thoby Prinsep). Her work of the 1860s and 1870s echoes early Pre-Raphaelite interest in literary subjects, as well as Pre-Raphaelite compositional arrangements. Her association with Pre-Raphaelitism is suggested most effectively by her own words: she strove for 'High Art' in her photography, she wrote, 'by combining the real and Ideal and sacrificing nothing of Truth by all possible devotion to Poetry and beauty' (Ford, 140).

Rebecca Solomon (1832–1886) was born on 26 September 1832 in Bishopsgate Street, London, the second among the three children of Michael Solomon (b. 1779) and his wife, Catherine Levy (d. 1886). Her father was a businessman and prominent member of the Jewish community in the City of London. Her two brothers, Abraham *Solomon and Simeon *Solomon were also artists. She trained at the Spitalfields School of Design and worked as an assistant and copyist to her brother Abraham until his death in 1862. She also made copies for other artists, including Millais. Between 1850 and 1874 she exhibited widely in London and the provinces, initially in oil and then, for financial reasons, diverting to watercolour and illustrative work from 1863. Through her younger brother, Simeon, with whom she lived after Abraham's death, she came into contact with the circle of D. G. Rossetti. She was an exponent primarily of literary and historical genre, and Pre-Raphaelite influence may be seen in some of her work of the 1860s and 1870s, specifically in paintings she exhibited at the Dudley Gallery, such as *Primavera* (exh. 1865; priv. coll., Japan) and *The Wounded Dove* (exh. 1866; University College of Wales, Aberystwyth). She died in London on 20 November 1886 after having been hit by a cab in the Euston Road.

Emma Sandys (1843–1877) was born in Norwich, the daughter of Anthony Sands (bap. 1804, d. 1883), a local artist who was formerly a dyer, and his wife, Mary Ann Brown (d. 1883), and the younger sister of (Anthony) Frederick *Sandys. In 1853 the family added a 'y' to their surname, implying (wrongly) a connection to an ancient Cumbrian family. Taught by her father, Emma was advised by Frederick, an associate of Pre-Raphaelite circles from 1857. She specialized in portraits and female heads in oil, often in medieval or period costume against decorative backgrounds; examples are *Elaine* (c.1862–5; Lanhydrock, Cornwall, National Trust collection), *Lady in Yellow Dress* (c.1870; Norwich Castle Museum), and *Viola* (c.1870; Walker Art

Gallery, Liverpool). Sandys worked from about 1862 and exhibited in London and Norwich between 1867 and 1874. She died in Norwich, where she had continued to live throughout her career, in November 1877.

Lucy Madox Brown [see Rossetti, (Emma) Lucy Madox Brown] (1843–1894), who married W. M. Rossetti in 1874, her half-sister Catherine, and Marie Spartali [see Stillman, Marie], were all trained in art by Ford Madox Brown in the 1860s and thus came into contact with D. G. Rossetti and his associates. Shakespearian subjects, aesthetic themes, richness of colouring, and decorative treatment of background connect Lucy Madox Brown's work with Pre-Raphaelitism. The most prolific of the three, Spartali depicted single female figures from literature and history, and as symbols (often with symbolic attributes) against rich decorative backgrounds. Her most ambitious and highly acclaimed paintings were multi-figure compositions with themes drawn from the *Morte d'Arthur* and Italian literature, often in D. G. Rossetti's translations. Her two Arthurian themes exhibited at the Royal Academy in 1873 led Henry James to describe her as 'a spontaneous, sincere, naïve Pre-Raphaelite' (James, 93). **Catherine Emily Madox Brown** [*married name* Hueffer] (1850–1927) was born on 11 November 1850 and baptized on 18 April 1852, the first child of Ford Madox *Brown (1821–1893) and Emma Matilda Hill (*b.* 1829) (later his second wife), and the second of Brown's three surviving children. As an infant and during her girlhood she modelled for her father, and after leaving Queen's College, a girls' school in Harley Street, she trained under her father, for whom she continued to work as a model and studio assistant. Between 1869 and the mid-1870s she exhibited portraits and subject pictures, chiefly in watercolour, at the Royal Academy and the Dudley Gallery, and also in Manchester and Liverpool. After her marriage in 1872 to the musicologist Francis (Franz) *Hueffer (*d.* 1889), and the birth of their three children, her exhibition appearances became rare. Her best-known work, an outdoor portrait, *Ford Madox Brown at the Easel* (1872; priv. coll.), strongly recalls her father's own work. After resuming her career in the 1890s she exhibited for the last time in 1901. She died in 1927.

Marie Terpsithea Zambaco [*née* Cassavetti] (1843–1914) was born in London, the daughter of Demetrius Cassavetti (*d.* 1858) and his wife, Euphrosyne, *née* Ionides. Like Spartali she was a member of the wealthy Greek community in London; her uncle was the noted art collector and patron Alexander Ionides. She inherited a fortune from her businessman father and in 1861 married Demetrius Zambaco, a physician in Paris, with whom she had two children. They separated in 1866, when Marie returned with her son and daughter to London. Having modelled for the Pre-Raphaelites, she began to paint, and probably received instruction from Edward Burne-*Jones, with whom she was romantically involved from 1868 to 1870. Later she trained as a sculptor under Alphonse Legros, exhibiting in London from 1886 and in Paris from 1888. The expressive style of her cast medals has been compared with that of the Pre-Raphaelite sculptors Woolner and Alexander Munro, and her association of female

portraits with symbolic flower imagery (as in her medal of 1886 depicting Marie Spartali; BM) was a frequent Pre-Raphaelite practice. About 1906 she moved to Greece and thence back to Paris, where she died in 1914.

Numerous artists in various media, many women among them, were influenced by Pre-Raphaelitism in the late nineteenth and early twentieth centuries. The most successful female exponents of Pre-Raphaelite style emerged after D. G. Rossetti's death. They were not members of a group, artistic or feminist, nor were they in general linked closely (in a personal sense) with key Pre-Raphaelite figures. All, however, were strongly influenced by the style of particular Pre-Raphaelite painters. The style of Evelyn De *Morgan, for example, recalls Burne-Jones, while the moral seriousness of her themes evokes G. F. Watts. It is also worth noting that all were professionally trained at art schools and may thus be said to have benefited from the campaigns of their forebears.

Marianne Stokes [*née* Preindelsberger] (1855–1927) was born at Graz, Austria. She studied at the city's art academy and won a prize that enabled her to continue her studies in Munich, then in 1880 she moved to Paris, where she attended the Trélat and Colarossi academies. The influence of Pascal Dagnan-Bouveret's 'square brush' technique was evident in works she exhibited at the Paris Salon, where she made her début in 1884, and at the Royal Academy from 1885. While painting *en plein air* in Brittany she met the British painter Adrian Stokes (1854–1935), whom she married in 1884. From 1886 to 1900 they lived at St Ives, Cornwall, and she continued to exhibit at the Royal Academy, the New Gallery, and the Institute of Painters in Oil, as well as in Liverpool. A devout Catholic, she turned to religious themes, finding inspiration in early Italian art on a visit to Italy in 1887, with paintings such as *Angels Entertaining the Holy Child* (1893; Pyms Gallery, London). *St Elizabeth of Hungary Spinning Wool for the Poor* (exh. New Gallery, 1895; priv. coll.) is related to Pre-Raphaelitism not only because of its theme (the saint was depicted by James Collinson, Millais, Rossetti, and Charles Collins) but also stylistically on account of the shallow space and flattened figure reminiscent of Rossetti's *Girlhood of Mary Virgin*. From the late 1890s Stokes favoured romantic medieval themes such as *The Page* (exh. New Gallery, 1896; priv. coll.), from Heinrich Heine, *Aucassin and Nicolette* (exh. New Gallery and Liverpool Academy, 1898; Carnegie Institute, Museum of Art, Pittsburgh), from Thomas Malory, and *Tristram's Death* (1902), from Tennyson. These were executed in a tempera technique which achieved Pre-Raphaelite brilliance of colour and with minute Pre-Raphaelite attention to detail. Her subject matter and naivety of style led Alice Meynell to describe her as 'a Primitive in art and heart' (Meynell, 242). With her husband Marianne Stokes went to the Netherlands in 1899 and in 1905 made the first of five visits to Hungary, which resulted in a jointly illustrated book, *Hungary* (1909), and an exhibition in Budapest in 1910. Marianne Stokes died in London in 1927.

Kate Elizabeth *Bunce (1856–1927) was influenced by

Rossetti and Burne-Jones in her choice of medieval subjects and themes from Rossetti's poems, for example, *How May I, When Shall He Ask?* (exh. RA, 1887), from the ballad *An Old Song Ended*. The highly decorated style of the second phase of Pre-Raphaelitism may be seen in works such as *Melody (Musica)* (c.1895; Birmingham Museum and Art Gallery). Bunce was a founder member in 1901 of the Society of Painters in Tempera in Birmingham, an interest she shared with Marianne Stokes and Christiana *Herringham.

Most widely known and perhaps most representative among women artists of the late Pre-Raphaelite style favoured by John Byam Shaw and Alfred Waterhouse is Eleanor Fortescue *Brickdale. An enthusiastic admirer of Millais, she focused mainly on romantic, but also sacred, themes from literature.

Early Pre-Raphaelite ideals appealed to a group of relatively liberated Unitarian women—several of whom were personally acquainted with the PRB—and to others whose backgrounds remain unexplored. Aspects of Pre-Raphaelitism (medievalism, poetical reference, vivid colour, naturalistic detail), and especially the works of Rossetti and Burne-Jones, appealed to female as well as male artists throughout the nineteenth century and into the twentieth. Considerable impetus was given to the style by the impact of Burne-Jones's pictures at the Grosvenor Gallery in 1877 (in reinforcing the classical dimension he linked Pre-Raphaelitism with academic practice) and by the arts and crafts movement. The latter stimulated the Birmingham and Glasgow schools, of which women were an important constituent [see Glasgow Girls]. Women artists may be said to have played a significant role in the late nineteenth-century reversion, within the Pre-Raphaelite tradition, to original moral and artistic earnestness.

CHARLOTTE YELDHAM

Sources *Pre-Raphaelite women artists* (1997) [exhibition catalogue, Man. City Gall., 22 Nov 1997–22 Feb 1998] • *The Pre-Raphaelites* (1984) [exhibition catalogue, Tate Gallery, London, 1984] • J. Marsh and P. G. Nunn, *Women artists and the Pre-Raphaelite movement* (1989) • D. Cherry, *Painting women: Victorian women artists* (1993) • D. Gaze, ed., *Dictionary of women artists*, 2 vols. (1997) • J. Marsh, *Pre-Raphaelite women: images of femininity in Pre-Raphaelite art* (1987) • J. Marsh, *Pre-Raphaelite sisterhood* (1985) • J. Marsh, *The legend of Elizabeth Siddal* (1989) • P. Hirsch, *Barbara Leigh Smith Bodichon, 1827–1891: feminist, artist and rebel* (1998) • *Sublime and instructive: letters from John Ruskin to Louisa, marchioness of Waterford, Anna Blunden and Ellen Heaton*, ed. V. Surtees (1972) • B. R. Belloc, *In a walled garden* (1895) • *An exhibition of paintings by Joanna Mary Boyce (Mrs H. T. Wells), 1831–1861* (1936) [exhibition catalogue, Tate Gallery, London, 1935] • W. M. Rossetti, *Some reminiscences* (1906) • C. R. Woodring, *Victorian samplers: William and Mary Howitt* (1952) • Mrs Howitt-Watts [A. M. Howitt], *An art student in Munich*, 2nd edn, 2 vols. (1880) • A. Lee, *Laurels and rosemary: the life of William and Mary Howitt* (1955) • *Mary Howitt: an autobiography*, ed. M. Howitt, 2 vols. (1889) • W. M. Rossetti, *Preraphaelite diaries and letters* (1900) • W. M. Hardinge, 'A reminiscence of Mrs. William Michael Rossetti', *Magazine of Art*, 18 (1895), 341–6 • H. James, *The painter's eye: notes and essays on the pictorial arts* (1956) • A. Meynell, 'Mrs. Adrian Stokes', *Magazine of Art*, 25 (1901), 241–7 • *Evelyn de Morgan drawings* (1970) [exhibition catalogue, Hartnoll and Eyre Gallery, London, 1970] • Mrs A. M. W. Stirling, *William de Morgan and his wife* (1922) • D. Masson, 'Pre-Raphaelitism in painting and literature', *British Quarterly Review*, 16 (1852), 197–220 • R. Garnett, *The life of W. J. Fox, public teacher and social reformer, 1786–*

1864 (1910) • B. R. Parkes, *Poems*, 2nd edn (1855) • IGI • G. L. Taylor, *Centenary exhibition of works by Eleanor Fortescue-Brickdale, 1872–1945* (1972) [exhibition catalogue, AM Oxf., 1 Dec 1972–7 Jan 1973] • *Reflections of a friendship: John Ruskin's letters to Pauline Trevelyan, 1848–1866*, ed. V. Surtees (1979), 169 • C. Ford, *The Cameron collection: an album of photographs by Julia Margaret Cameron presented to Sir John Herschel* (1975)
Archives Girton Cam., corresp. and papers • Women's Library, London, letters | Bodl. Oxf., corresp. with Sir Henry Taylor • CKS, letter • Girton Cam., corresp. with Bessie Rayner Parkes and others • NRA, priv. coll., corresp. with Sir Norman Moore and Amy (Leigh Smith) Moore • RS, corresp. with J. F. W. Hershel

Prescott, E. Livingston. *See* Jay, Edith Katherine Spicer (1847–1901).

Prescott, Henry (1649–1719), ecclesiastical administrator and diarist, was born on 9 June 1649 at Rough Park, near Upholland, Lancashire, the fifth son and seventh child of Thomas Prescott (b. 1604), gentleman, and his wife, Margaret Hey (b. 1604). The devoutly royalist Prescott family suffered under the Commonwealth, having been loyal supporters of James Stanley, seventh earl of Derby (executed 1651), but after 1660 the eighth earl was a generous patron of those who had sided with his father. Henry was accordingly educated from about 1661 to 1666 at Winwick grammar school, which had close Stanley connections, and in 1677, using the earl's influence, he obtained a place in the diocesan registry at Chester. From that year, encouraged by the deputy registrar, William Wilson, he studied law at Trinity College, Dublin (graduating in 1682). When Wilson died in 1686 Prescott succeeded him as deputy registrar and held that post for the rest of his life, his attempts to become registrar being thwarted because his family connections were comparatively inferior.

In Dublin in 1682 Prescott had married Lydia Peake, widow of John Williamson. She and their newborn son died at Wigan on 18 May 1685; for the rest of his life he mournfully commemorated the birthdays and deathdays of his beloved Lydia. On 11 August 1687 he married Susanna, daughter of Sir John Puleston of Hafod-y-Wern in Denbighshire. Between 1688 and 1707 she bore fourteen children, of whom six died young. Theirs was a marriage of deep love and mutual esteem, reflected not only in the number of their progeny but also in a frequent correspondence during his long absences, their shared participation in the social life of Cheshire from their residences at Abbey Green in Chester and Ayrfield, Upholland, and the many affectionate references to her in his diaries.

Prescott was an assiduous and effective administrator, personally overseeing the great variety of detailed work undertaken by the diocesan registry, making frequent visitations around the archdeaconry of Chester and occasionally into the largely autonomous archdeaconry of Richmond, and ensuring that the legal processes of the church were speedily performed. His efficiency and hard work were instrumental in ensuring that during the first two decades of the eighteenth century the diocese of Chester was better administered than at any time since its creation in 1541. In February 1712 he became, in plurality, registrar of the diocese of St Asaph, an appointment obtained with the help of influential Chester friends and connections by marriage in north-east Wales and one which helped to compensate for his failure to become registrar of Chester.

Prescott read voraciously, showing a taste for the classical authors, sermons and meditations, and religious history, but historical biography and English history in general were also a special enthusiasm. He was, although strictly in an amateur sense, an early antiquary, collecting coins and archaeological artefacts and on his travels often visiting, as a tourist, places of historical significance. Underpinning Prescott's work was his extremely active social life. He shone brightly as a conversationalist, dinner guest, country-house visitor, and, above all, as a drinking companion. His capacity for alcohol was awesome even by the standards of the age, and it fuelled his insatiable appetite for gossip and news. Every day when in Chester he drank and dined with leading figures in church, city, and county life and all important people who passed through the city *en route* for and from Dublin took wine with him. He was at the centre of a complex network of social, political, and ecclesiastical connections and was thus a much more influential figure in local, regional, and even national affairs than his comparatively modest official position might imply.

From at least 1689 Prescott kept a copious diary, detailing the people he met, where and how much he drank, the administrative business he transacted, who was passing through Chester, and which national and international news had arrived that day. The diaries, a source of major historical importance, are continuous from 1704 onwards. They recount great and stirring events such as the rising of 1715, when the city was seized by hysterical panic as the Jacobites advanced south through Lancashire. In 1716, though, they reveal Prescott's Damascene conversion from vehement loathing of the rebels to outright support for the exiled Stuarts. The diaries thus expose a complex figure of abundant energies and talents: an instinctive high-church Anglican tory; a loyal supporter of Queen Anne who initially welcomed the Hanoverian accession yet later abhorred it; a dedicated servant of the establishment who, judging people above all else for their personal qualities and companionship, was a devoted friend of the crypto-Catholic Bishop Cartwright. Prescott was modest and sober (at least, in his judgement), his keen eye for landscape and improvement being accompanied by a particular distaste for lavish display and ostentation. He was a good and kindly man, ahead of his times in his detestation of cruelty to beast and human alike, a loving father and husband, and a loyal friend. He died at Wrexham, survived by his second wife, and was buried at Upholland on 9 June 1719.

ALAN G. CROSBY

Sources *The diary of Henry Prescott, LLB, deputy registrar of Chester diocese*, ed. J. Addy and others, 1, Lancashire and Cheshire RS, 127 (1987), vii–xxviii · *The diary of Henry Prescott, LLB, deputy registrar of Chester diocese*, ed. J. Addy and others, 3, Lancashire and Cheshire RS, 133 (1997), ix–xiii, 1105 · *The parish registers of Upholland*, Lancashire Parish Register Society, 23 (1905) · *The parish registers of Ormskirk*, Lancashire Parish Register Society, 98 (1960)

Archives Ches. & Chester ALSS, corresp., diaries, and papers · priv. coll., diaries and other personal papers | Ches. & Chester ALSS, Chester diocesan records · Flintshire RO, Hawarden, St Asaph diocesan records

Likenesses portrait, repro. in Addy, *The diary of Henry Prescott*, 127; priv. coll.

Prescott, Sir Henry (1783–1874), naval officer, son of Admiral Isaac Prescott (1737–1830), who commanded the *Queen* as flag-captain to Sir Robert Harland in the action off Ushant on 27 July 1778, and his wife, daughter of the Revd Richard Walter, editor of *Anson's Voyage Round the World*, was born at Kew, Surrey, on 4 May 1783. He entered the navy in February 1796 on board the *Formidable*, with Captain George Cranfield Berkeley. In 1798 he was moved to the *Queen Charlotte*, and in 1799 to the *Penelope*, with Captain Henry Blackwood; he was present at the capture of the *Guillaume Tell* on 30 March 1800. In 1801, in the *Foudroyant*, he was present at the operations on the coast of Egypt, and on 17 February 1802 Lord Keith appointed him acting lieutenant of the brig *Vincejo*. In April 1803 Prescott was appointed to the *Unicorn*, in the North Sea, and in December 1804 to the *Aeolus*, one of the squadron under Sir Richard John Strachan which, on 4 November 1805, captured the four French ships of the line that had escaped from Trafalgar. In 1806 he was moved to the *Ajax*, and then transferred to the *Ocean*, flagship of Lord Collingwood in the Mediterranean. On 4 February 1808 he was promoted to be commander of the brig *Weasel*, and for the next three years served on the west coast of Italy. On 25 July 1810, at Amantea, in company with the frigate *Thames*, and the *Pilot*, he commanded the boats of the squadron in the capture or destruction of thirty-two store-ships and seven gunboats. For his gallantry then Prescott was promoted captain, dated to the day of the action. From August 1811 to June 1813 he commanded the *Fylla* (20 guns), on the Jersey station; and from 1813 to 1815 the *Eridanus*, in the Bay of Biscay. In 1815 he married Mary Anne Charlotte, eldest illegitimate daughter of his commander-in-chief, Vice-Admiral Philip d'Auvergne, prince de Bouillon, and they had several children. On 4 June 1815 he was nominated a CB. From 1821 to 1825, in command of the frigate *Aurora*, he was senior officer at Rio de Janeiro, or on the west coast of South America, under Sir Thomas Hardy. In 1822 he was chiefly responsible for the successful resistance of the British merchants to the imposition of a forced loan of $200,000 by the Peruvian congress. In October 1822 he was voted a testimonial of the value of $1500 by the British merchants at Lima, for his protection of British interests. From 1834 to 1841 he was governor of Newfoundland; a period of political quarrels and sectarian animosities which he was unable to allay.

On 24 April 1847 Prescott was promoted rear-admiral, and in June was appointed a lord of the Admiralty, an office he resigned in December to become admiral-superintendent of the Portsmouth Dockyard, where he remained until 1852. Prescott was appointed to the board at a time when the whigs were unable to find a suitable whig flag-officer prepared to contest a seat in parliament on Sir Charles Adam's retirement. His move to Portsmouth was inevitable. However, when Lord Auckland replaced him with Alexander Milne, then only a captain, he began the process of breaking the link between a seat on the board and active political support for the government in the House of Commons.

Prescott was promoted vice-admiral on 15 April 1854, was nominated a KCB on 4 February 1856, became admiral on 2 May 1860, and on 9 June following was retired with a pension. On 2 June 1869 he was made a GCB. He died in London, at his residence, 7 Leinster Gardens, Hyde Park, on 18 November 1874.

Prescott was an able officer, well suited to the administrative demands of colonial government and dockyard management. He lacked the political or personal influence for an active command afloat, but his services were highly valued. His belated GCB was for his work of the 1840s.   J. K. LAUGHTON, rev. ANDREW LAMBERT

Sources PRO, Russell MSS · G. S. Graham and R. A. Humphreys, eds., *The navy and South America, 1807–1823*, Navy RS, 104 (1962) · G. R. Balleine, *The tragedy of Philip d'Auvergne* (1973) · A. D. Lambert, *The last sailing battlefleet: maintaining naval mastery, 1815–1850* (1991) · *CGPLA Eng. & Wales* (1874)
Likenesses portrait, repro. in D. W. Prowse, *A history of Newfoundland from the English, colonial and foreign records* (1895)
Wealth at death under £50,000: resworn double probate, Feb 1875, *CGPLA Eng. & Wales* (1874)

Prescott, Oliver (1731–1804), physician and revolutionary army officer in America, was born on 27 April 1731 in Groton, Massachusetts, the son of Benjamin Prescott and his wife, Abigail Oliver. He attended Harvard College, graduated in 1750, and studied medicine for a time with Ebenezer Robie of Sudbury. He settled in Groton, where he successfully practised medicine for the rest of his life. In 1753 he received a master's degree from Harvard. He married Lydia Baldwin on 19 February 1756; they had seven children. Evincing an interest in matters military and political, he served in the Massachusetts militia during the Seven Years' War, and held the offices of town clerk and selectman in Groton for many years. As tensions grew between Britain and America, Prescott emerged as a leader of colonial protests. During the Stamp Act crisis in 1765 he was chairman of Groton's committee appointed to oppose British taxation, and nine years later served as clerk of the town's committee of correspondence in opposition to the 'Intolerable Acts'.

At the outbreak of the American War of Independence in 1775, Prescott was appointed brigadier-general of Middlesex county militia by the Massachusetts revolutionary government. He was put in charge of some military supplies evacuated from Concord before the British arrived there on 19 April 1775, and he tended American casualties in the battles of Lexington and Concord, and at Bunker Hill on 17 June 1775. In the same year he was appointed justice of the peace and of the quorum by the Massachusetts government. He was elected to the board of war on 30 October but declined to serve, choosing instead to remain with his troops at the siege of Boston. When the

American army marched to New York in 1776, Prescott remained in Massachusetts, serving as a leader of the state's militia. In 1778 he was appointed a major-general of Massachusetts militia and retained the position until the end of the war. Meanwhile, he held numerous civilian offices. In 1777 he was elected to the Massachusetts executive council and served for three years. In that office he also acted as a member of the Harvard College board of overseers. He was appointed a probate judge in Middlesex county in 1779, and remained in the office until his death.

In 1780 Prescott helped incorporate the American Academy of Arts and Sciences, and a year later he was an original founder of the Massachusetts Medical Society. Later he was made an honorary member of the New Hampshire Medical Society. In addition, he was president for many years of the Middlesex Medical Society and of the Western Society of Middlesex Husbandmen. Interested in education, he was one of the first trustees of Groton Academy and the first president of the school's board. His medical practice continued during these years. It covered an extensive territory and required Prescott to make long and exhausting trips on horseback. In 1791 he was awarded by Harvard College an honorary doctorate in medicine for his many contributions to medical practice in New England. He served for a final time in the military in 1786, acting as a recruiter of militiamen to quell disturbances in Middlesex county that were associated with Shays's rebellion in western Massachusetts. During his last years he was corpulent and became deafer with age, but he remained active in his medical practice and other pursuits. He was a tall, kind, gentlemanly man, who was appreciated by his fellow citizens for both his medical knowledge and his pleasing manners. He died at Groton on 17 November 1804 of pectoral dropsy; his wife survived him.   PAUL DAVID NELSON

Sources E. H. Christianson, 'Prescott, Oliver', *ANB* · C. K. Shipton, *Sibley's Harvard graduates: biographical sketches of those who attended Harvard College*, 12 (1962), 569–73 · J. Thatcher, *American medical biography*, vol. 1 (1828) · P. Cash, *Medical men at the siege of Boston, April, 1775–April, 1776* (1973) · S. A. Green, *A history of medicine in Massachusetts* (1881) · P. Cash and others, eds., *Medicine in colonial Massachusetts, 1620–1820* (1980) · *Columbian Centinel* (21 Nov 1804) · E. E. Curtis, 'Prescott, Oliver', *DAB*

Prescott, Oliveria Louisa (1842–1917), composer and writer, was born on 3 September 1842 at 13 Oxford Square, Paddington, Middlesex, the daughter of Frederick Joseph Prescott of the War Office and his wife, Elizabeth Oliveria, *née* Russell. Little is known about her early life before she entered the Royal Academy of Music in 1871 as a composition student. She remained at the academy for at least eight years, studying with George Macfarren among others. Several of her works were performed at academy concerts, including a symphony and a Magnificat for solo voices, chorus, orchestra, and organ. Her first published work appeared in 1873 and other music published while she was still a student included two anthems, a piano duet version of an orchestral concert finale, partsongs, and songs. In 1879 Prescott became a teacher of harmony at the Church of England High School for Girls, Upper Baker Street, London, a post which she retained until 1893. She also worked as Macfarren's amanuensis and as a contributor to *Musical World*. A collection of her articles from this weekly paper was published as *Form or Design in Music* (1880). She regarded form in music as a progressive and fluid concept and made an interesting distinction between form as heard and as seen written down.

In the early 1880s Prescott concentrated on writing vocal music, including *Lord Ullin's Daughter* (1884), a dramatic choral ballad with orchestral accompaniment. In the later 1880s and 1890s she focused on instrumental music, most of which was never published and has not survived. Her chamber music, including three string quartets, was frequently heard at the concerts given by the Musical Artists' Society, and for several years she was the only woman to serve on the council of this organization. Her orchestral music included an overture, *In Woodland— by Beech, and Yew, and Tangled Brake*, performed at the Bristol Popular Concerts in 1890.

Prescott frequently gave lectures to various organizations and was appointed lecturer in harmony and counterpoint to the correspondence course of Newnham College, Cambridge. She was determinedly professional in her approach to her career, joining the Society of Professional Musicians and becoming one of the few women to belong to the Society of British Composers. Her second book, *About Music and What it is Made of: a Book for Amateurs* (1904), includes discussion of women's contribution to musical life. One of her last published works was a musical comedy in three acts, *Carrigraphuga: the Castle of Fairies* (1914).

Prescott herself modestly described her musical career in an article she published in 1890:

> My own little life of music is a very quiet one; chiefly comprised within the walls of my study, from whence I look out as from a watch tower upon the struggles, the sorrows, hopes, and joys of my fellows, having those of my own which they perhaps have little knowledge of.   ('Brothers and sisters', *Musical World*, 70/4, 1890, 66)

Her many contributions to the professional musical world led the way towards women's increasing involvement in all aspects of British musical life. She died of bronchitis on 11 January 1917 at her brother's house, Brantyngeshay, Hambledon, Surrey.   SOPHIE FULLER

Sources *Musical News* (24 Feb 1917) • A. De Ternant, 'Short sketches of contemporary women composers: Oliveria Prescott', *Englishwoman's Review*, 18 (1887), 53–60, esp. 59–60 • *Society of British Composers: Year Book* (1912) • Brown & Stratton, *Brit. mus.* • b. cert. • d. cert.

Wealth at death £4807 8s. 9d.: probate, 16 March 1917, *CGPLA Eng. & Wales*

Prescott, Robert (1726/7–1815), army officer and governor-in-chief of British North America, was born in Lancashire. His father is often given as Richard Prescott, a cavalry officer, but on what grounds is not clear. He is also sometimes described as the brother of Colonel William Prescott (1725–1795) but as this Prescott was from an American family it is unlikely. Robert joined the British army as ensign in the 15th foot on 22 June 1745 and was promoted lieutenant three years later and captain on 22 January

1755. During the Seven Years' War he participated in an expedition in 1757 against Rochefort, France, and the next year in the seizure of Louisbourg, Cape Breton Island (Île Royale). In May 1759 he became aide-de-camp to Major-General Jeffrey Amherst, colonel of his regiment, whom he accompanied in 1760 on the advance to Montreal. On 22 March 1761 Prescott was gazetted major in the 95th foot, which was ordered to Martinique in 1762. That July he exchanged into the 27th and on 10 November he was promoted lieutenant-colonel in the 72nd. After the war ended he spent the following decade unattached to a regiment and probably in Britain.

On the outbreak of the American War of Independence Prescott was appointed lieutenant-colonel of the 28th foot on 8 September 1775 and took part in engagements in New York: on Long Island, in Westchester county, and at Fort Washington. Promoted brevet colonel in August 1777, he joined the expedition against Philadelphia, fighting at the battle of Brandywine the following month, and remained with the army of occupation until it retreated in 1778. That November he led the 1st brigade in an assault on the French island of St Lucia and from August 1779 to spring 1780 he commanded British troops in the Leeward Islands. He became colonel of the 94th foot on 13 October 1780 and major-general in November 1782. With the coming of peace in 1783 and disbandment of his regiment, he returned to Britain and was placed on half pay. On 6 July 1789 he was gazetted colonel of the 28th foot.

When war with revolutionary France broke out Prescott was promoted lieutenant-general in October 1793 and given command in Barbados. Joining the expeditionary force against the French West Indies in 1794, led by Lieutenant-General Sir Charles Grey and Vice-Admiral Sir John Jervis, Prescott participated in the capture of Martinique and was made the island's governor. Opinionated and irascible, he clashed with Grey over the scale of arrests and deportation of inhabitants deemed security risks, asserting his independent authority in outraged, insubordinate language. Despite this dispute Grey appointed him that September governor of Guadeloupe, captured the previous April. Soon engaged in fighting resurgent French republicans, a disheartened, sickly Prescott sought to return home. This sparked further acrimonious correspondence with Grey, until the British withdrawal from Guadeloupe in December and the departure of both men for London, where they continued their rancorous exchanges.

On 21 January 1796 Prescott was appointed lieutenant-governor of Lower Canada and, by a revised commission of 15 December, both governor-in-chief and commander of British forces in North America. Promoted general in January 1798, he was deeply concerned about Quebec's security against external invasion and internal subversion by disaffected French Canadians. Co-operating with Chief Justice William Osgoode and other members of the Anglophone élite, he responded to rioting by summary arrests and the exemplary execution of David McLane, an American spy. Controversy with his councillors over a scheme to resolve the chaos in land granting led to

Prescott's recall in April 1799, though he remained governor-in-chief until 1807 without returning to Canada. Resolute in action and forthright in opinion, Prescott had capabilities that were vitiated by a cantankerous temperament.

George Thomas Landmann of the Royal Engineers, who met Prescott in Quebec, recalled 'a little man, not exceeding five feet four or five inches high, very slender and certainly not much under eighty years of age; he was nevertheless active, a good officer, but exceedingly peppery' (Landmann, 1.240). Married to Susanna (d. 18 April 1817), with at least one daughter (who married a Captain Baldwin) and a son, he died in his eighty-ninth year on 21 December 1815 at Rose Green, near Battle, Sussex, and was buried at Winchelsea.   PETER BURROUGHS

Sources *Army List* (1754–1816) · NA Canada, Robert Prescott collection, MG23-GII17 · *GM*, 1st ser., 31 (1761), 238 · *GM*, 1st ser., 53 (1783), 271 · *GM*, 1st ser., 67 (1797), 979 · *GM*, 1st ser., 86/1 (1816), 88 · military officers' widows' pensions, 1815–56, PRO, WO 23/105 · G. Landmann, *Adventures and recollections of Colonel Landmann*, 1 (1852), 240–48 · original corresp., governor to secretary of state, Lower Canada, 1795–9, PRO, CO 42/105–113 · entry books, secretary of state to governor, Lower Canada, 1794–8, PRO, CO 43/17–18 · P. D. Nelson, *Sir Charles Grey, first Earl Grey: royal soldier, family patriarch* (1996) · F. M. Greenwood, *Legacies of fear: law and politics in Quebec in the era of the French Revolution* (1993) · letters to first Earl Grey, U. Durham, Grey MSS, Prescott file · NA Canada, Thomas Carleton collection, MG23-D3 · H. J. Morgan, *Sketches of celebrated Canadians, and persons connected with Canada* (1862), 129–30

Archives Montreal Historical Society, letter-books · NA Canada, corresp. and papers | Bodl. Oxf., letters to John Charles Brooke · PRO, Colonial Office records, CO 42/105–113; CO 43/17–18 · U. Durham L., letters to first Earl Grey · U. Mich., Clements L., corresp. with Sir John Vaughan

Likenesses J. Bogle, miniature, 1776, NPG

Pressburger, Emeric [Imre Josef] (1902–1988), author and screenwriter, was born Imre Josef Pressburger at 3 St Peter's Street, Miskolc, Hungary, on 5 December 1902, the only son (he had one elder half-sister from his father's previous marriage) of Kálmán Pressburger, estate manager, and his second wife, Kätherina Wichs. The family were Jewish. Pressburger attended a boarding-school in Temesvár, where he was a good student, excelling at maths, literature, and music. He then studied mathematics and engineering at the universities of Prague and Stuttgart before his father's death forced him to abandon his studies.

Pressburger moved to Berlin in 1926 to work as a journalist and writer of short stories and film scripts. UFA, the major European film studio, employed him as a contract writer, and his first screen credit was for *Abschied* (1930), co-written with the novelist Erich Kästner and directed by Robert Siodmak. The film was a drama-documentary shot in 'real time', representing one and a quarter hours in the lives of people living in a Berlin boarding-house. Although not a great success, it ensured Pressburger's continued employment by UFA in their script department at a time when film jobs were scarce. Pressburger was not listed on the credits for a screen adaptation of Kästner's *Emil and the Detectives* (1931), which was signed by Billy Wilder. A key

experience at UFA was working on musical comedy adaptations of operettas, thereby beginning a fascination with the links between music and film which continued all his life. When UFA did not renew Pressburger's contract for 1933, and in a context of escalating antisemitism in Germany (where he changed his forename to Emmerich), he decided to settle in France, beginning again in another country as an émigré writer. Although Pressburger managed to obtain film work, life was difficult; he was threatened with deportation and faced imprisonment for debt. Intermittent film employment prevented this, and one script, *Monsieur Sans-Gêne* (1934), directed by Karl Anton, was a major success in France. It was remade in Hollywood by Jesse L. Lasky and released as *One Rainy Afternoon* (1936).

Pressburger entered Britain in 1935, on a stateless passport. One of his screenplays, *La vie parisienne* (1935), an adaptation of an operetta by Jacques Offenbach, had been filmed in English and French versions, and Pressburger had travelled to Britain to work on the English version with Arthur Wimperis, an associate of Alexander Korda, of London Film Productions, one of the largest British film companies. Pressburger was eventually to work for his fellow Hungarian. He decided to settle in Britain, and changed his name in 1938 to Emeric. On 24 June that year he married Agnes (b. 1917/18), daughter of Andol Donath, a general merchant. The marriage was dissolved in 1941.

Pressburger's first British assignment for Korda was *The Challenge* (1938), a film about a race to reach the summit of the Matterhorn. In 1938 he met Michael *Powell, his director and collaborator for the next eighteen years. Their first joint project was *The Spy in Black* (1939), a First World War espionage thriller based on a novel by Storer Clouston. Filmed at Denham Studios, it starred Conrad Veidt and Valerie Hobson. Powell was hired to direct the film as a replacement for Brian Desmond Hurst, and Korda invited Pressburger to work on the script. After this successful collaboration their next joint venture was *Contraband* (1940), another vehicle for the popular stars Veidt and Hobson. From then onwards Pressburger's most successful work was with Powell. In 1943 they formed a production company, the Archers, which became known for its distinctive film trademark of a red, white, and blue archery target with eight arrows, a ninth one thrusting into it. Their partnership was egalitarian; both men shared the financial rewards and creative responsibility for all the films, the credits stating that they were 'written, produced and directed' by Michael Powell and Emeric Pressburger.

Pressburger's screenplays provided excellent scope for Powell's distinctive visual style, which employed colour in an imaginative way and used fantasy and spectacle, complex and challenging narrative structures, and flamboyant visual and camera devices. Several films were produced under the aegis of the Ministry of Information, a connection which prevented Pressburger from being deported as a foreigner. The most notable films produced by Powell and Pressburger during The Second World War were *Forty Ninth Parallel* (1941), *One of our Aircraft is Missing* (1941), *The Silver Fleet* (1943), *The Life and Death of Colonel*

Blimp (1943), based on the cartoon character created by David Low, *A Canterbury Tale* (1944), and *I Know Where I'm Going!* (1945). In many respects Pressburger was patriotic, an Anglophile who celebrated the freedom he had found in his adopted country. His ability to see Britain from the point of view of a fascinated outsider suited the films' quizzical perspective on British society and history.

A recurrent theme in Pressburger's writing was a journey by a leading character into unknown territory. Now regarded as a classic in a mystical tradition, *A Canterbury Tale* was misunderstood at the time of release, a misunderstanding that helped initiate the Archers Company reputation as film-makers who were ahead of their time, and whose work was characterized by wit, fantasy, ambition, and originality. The film celebrated British heritage and freedom, two themes that were extremely important to Pressburger. *I Know Where I'm Going!* shared a similar fascination with self-discovery and mysticism, charting the journey of a young woman from Manchester to Scotland, where she discovers that the path in life she believed she was destined to follow has been mistaken. The screenplay for *The Life and Death of Colonel Blimp*, Pressburger's favourite Archers film, proved to be controversial. Its portrayal of the British officer class as anachronistic led to accusations that the film was pro-German. The film's release was delayed in the United States, where it was cut and advertised inappropriately. During the war Pressburger's involvement with the Screenwriters' Association and the Association of Cine Technicians became more active. He mixed with other left-wing émigrés and in 1942 was involved with the Free German League of Culture, a group which organized a rally, the Pageant of Four Freedoms, at the New Theatre, Oxford.

Pressburger (who was naturalized in 1946) married again on 29 March 1947. His second wife was Gwynneth May (Wendy) Zillah (*b.* 1911/12), former wife of Abraham Jacob Greenbaum, and daughter of Edward Regnald Orme, army officer. They had two daughters, one of whom died as a baby in 1948. The marriage was dissolved at Reno, Nevada, in 1953, and in Britain in 1971.

In 1946 *A Matter of Life and Death* became the film chosen for Britain's first charity royal film performance. Although it was originally conceived as a wartime propaganda film, its production was delayed because Technicolor was not available. Starring David Niven as an RAF pilot on the borderline between life and death, the film is an imaginative meditation on love, grief, and war. Pressburger's ability to deal with broad, challenging themes was further demonstrated when he explored a clash of communities and values in *Black Narcissus* (1946), about a group of nuns in the Himalayas living in an atmosphere of hysteria and repressed sexuality. Perhaps the most daring experiment was *The Red Shoes* (1948, based on a Hans Christian Andersen story), set in the tempestuous and exacting world of a ballet company. This film in particular showed how Powell's sense of colour could be assisted by Pressburger's ambitious screenplay. Pressburger first started working on the screenplay for *The Red Shoes* in 1939 but the project was disrupted by the war. In 1946 the Archers bought the rights from Korda for the project and began a productive collaboration with art director Alfred Junge and Robert Helpmann, a dancer at Sadler's Wells. Most of Pressburger's subsequent screenplays were also not based on original material. *The Red Shoes* was followed by adaptations of challenging material for *The Tales of Hoffman* (1953, adapted from a Jacques Offenbach opera at the suggestion of Sir Thomas Beecham) and *Oh Rosalinda!* (1955, based on Johann Strauss's operetta *Die Fledermaus*). These films separated the Archers from the conventional canon of British film production, often to their cost, for puzzled critics were inclined to dismiss their work as pretentious, extravagant, and confusing. In 1952 Pressburger directed for the only time, but the film, *Twice upon a Time*, was generally regarded as a disastrous project. On the other hand, *The Battle of the River Plate* (1956), directed by Powell, was chosen for the royal film performance in 1956. After their last Archer collaboration, *Ill Met by Moonlight* (1956), a wartime drama, Powell and Pressburger parted. Their work was beginning to lose its experimental edge and the two agreed to separate as their interests began to diverge.

Pressburger then wrote and produced *Miracle in Soho* (1957) and published his first novel, *Killing a Mouse on Sunday* (1961), a story about a terrorist set in the Spanish Civil War, on which Fred Zinnemann based his film *Behold a Pale Horse* (1964). The novel's controversial subject matter led to Pressburger being banned from entering Franco's Spain. Pressburger's critical success with *Killing a Mouse on Sunday* was not repeated with his second novel, *The Glass Pearls* (1966), a more personal book about Nazi Germany. He continued writing, but could not find a publisher for a subsequent novel, 'The Unholy Passion'. Many of his projects in the 1960s were never completed. Pressburger accompanied David Lean to India to conduct research for a screenplay about the life of Gandhi, but Lean rejected the script he eventually produced. He worked again with Powell in 1966 on *They're a Weird Mob* (1966), shot in Australia, and again in 1972, when they collaborated on a film for the Children's Film Foundation, *The Boy who Turned Yellow*, and on a novel of *The Red Shoes* (1978). None of these projects revived their former ingenuity. Pressburger more or less retired after this, but enjoyed the critical appreciation of his work encouraged by Martin Scorsese and Francis Ford Coppola. Key events in the reappraisal of the Archers' work were a retrospective of their work at the National Film Theatre in 1971, and the showing of a restored print of *The Life and Death of Colonel Blimp* at the National Film Theatre in 1978. A documentary on Powell and Pressburger was shown on BBC2 television in 1981.

Powell was always keen to stress that his skill as a director was stretched to the best advantage when Pressburger had written the screenplay. Their general method was for Pressburger to write the story and devise the structure, and then he would collaborate with Powell on scripting the dialogue. Pressburger was involved in all stages of a production, a process that engendered creativity out of conflict. As Pressburger commented, 'Our films were born out of disagreement' (Macdonald, xvii). Powell described

Pressburger's talent for storytelling as that of 'a screen-writer with the heart and mind of a novelist. He was a born dramatist and writer, and he didn't learn as much from me as I did from him' (ibid., 155). Nevertheless, Pressburger often felt that Powell put himself at the centre of events organized to reappraise their work. However, their earlier collaborations were marked by a mutual sense of trust and a shared desire to explore the boundaries of word and image. Pressburger commented on how they inspired each other's work: 'He knows what I am going to say even before I say it—maybe even before I have thought it—and that is very rare' (ibid., 156). Pressburger was a diffident and private person, who at times, particularly later on in his life, could be hypersensitive and prone to bouts of melancholia. This was in contrast to Powell, who was more of a self-publicist. A keen gastronome, Pressburger loved French food, enjoyed music, and possessed a great sense of humour. In appearance he was short, wore glasses, and had a sagacious, bird-like facial expression. He was a keen supporter of Arsenal football team, a passion he developed soon after arriving in Britain.

Pressburger received the British Film Institute special award (with Powell) in 1978 and fellowships from the British Academy of Film and Television Arts in 1981 and the British Film Institute in 1983. He won an Oscar in 1942 for best original story, for *Forty Ninth Parallel*. He died of bronchial pneumonia on 5 February 1988 in the Foxearth Lodge Nursing Home, Little Green, Saxtead, Woodbridge, Suffolk.   SARAH STREET

Sources I. Christie, *Arrows of desire* (1985) · M. Powell, *A life in movies* (1986) · M. Powell, *Million-dollar movie* (1992) · K. Macdonald, *Emeric Pressburger* (1994) · I. Christie, *A matter of life and death* (2000) · private information (2004) · m. certs. · d. cert. · *CGPLA Eng. & Wales* (1988)
Archives BFI, papers
Wealth at death £164,578: probate, 1988, *CGPLA Eng. & Wales*

Prest, Godfrey (*fl.* **1395–1399**). *See under* Broker, Nicholas (d. 1426).

Prest, Thomas Peckett (1809/10–1859), writer and playwright, was probably the Thomas Prest who was born on 13 May 1810, the son of William Prest and his wife, Ann. His family background remains obscure, but he appears in London in the early 1830s, writing and performing songs for the saloons and singing clubs, and working as a general literary hack for minor publishers of the unstamped press. He edited and largely wrote ephemeral penny periodicals, including *The Weekly Penny Comic Magazine, or, Repertory of Wit and Humour* (1832), *The London Singer's Magazine and Reciter's Album*, volume 1 (1834?), *The Magazine of Curiosity and Wonder* (1835–6), and *Tales of the Drama* (1836–7). He also wrote melodramas for the Pavilion Theatre.

Prest's quest for new material drew him to the work of Dickens, and in 1836 Edward Lloyd, then a minor publisher of ephemera, issued Prest's *The Sketch Book*, by 'Boz' in penny numbers. In April 1837, a year after Dickens (Boz) had begun *Pickwick Papers* (1836–7) in monthly shilling parts, Prest began writing a penny weekly serial, *The Posthumourous Notes of the Pickwick Club, or, The Penny Pickwick*,

by 'Bos' (1837–8). Prest's version freely adapted and expanded Dickens's work for a working-class readership. Aided by spirited woodcuts by the popular cartoonist C. J. Grant, 'this disgraceful fabrication', as G. A. Sala noted, 'had an immense sale' (Sala, 74). At over 850 pages it was considerably longer, and at the time probably sold more copies, than Dickens's original. Prest followed this success with other adaptations, including *Oliver Twiss* (1838), *Nickelas Nicklebery* (1838), *Pickwick in America!* (1839), *A Legend of the Tower of London* (1840) by 'J. H. Hainsforth' after the novel by W. H. Ainsworth, and a plagiarism of Henry Cockton's *Valentine Vox*, *The Adventures of Valentine Vaux* by Timothy Portwine (1840).

These penny serials established Edward Lloyd as a popular publisher, and alerted him and his rivals to the potential of cheap fiction written specifically for the rapidly expanding mass urban readership of the time. Lloyd commissioned Prest to write more sensational novels, paying 10s. a number, money which is said to have financed Prest's drinking at his favourite tavern, the White Swan, Salisbury Court, Fleet Street. Prest has been commonly credited with being the author of *Sweeney Todd, the Demon Barber of Fleet Street*, but recent scholarship has revealed that the tale was actually the work of James Malcolm Rymer. Prest's most popular single work, the gypsy romance *Ela the Outcast* (1839–40), was followed by over sixty 'bloods' written for Lloyd in the 1840s. These showed a remarkable versatility in adapting literary genres—historical fiction after Scott in *The Hebrew Maiden* (1840), naval in *Gallant Tom* (1840), Gothic in *The Death Grasp* (1841), and domestic in *Emily Fitzormond* (1841), while a novel like *The Death Ship, or, The Pirate's Bride and the Maniac of the Deep* (1846) combines them all. Possibly as a result of ill health his fiction output decreased in the 1850s, and his last major novel was *Grace Walton, or, The Wanderers of the Heath* (1857). He continued to write melodramas, notably *The Miser of Shoreditch* (the Standard Theatre, 1854) and *Lucy Wentworth* (prize-winning play, the City of London Theatre, 1857).

Although not possessing a major creative talent Prest wrote vigorous, stylized prose that popularized penny fiction at the moment when an increasingly literate working-class public were tiring of political and educational reading and looking for entertainment. With his knowledge of popular taste and in particular melodrama he adapted middle-class writing for a popular audience, facilitating a significant stage in the development of literature for the masses. He died of phlebitis at his home, 9 George Street, Thornhill Bridge, Islington, London, aged forty-nine, on 5 June 1859.

LOUIS JAMES and HELEN R. SMITH

Sources H. R. Smith, *New light on Sweeney Todd, Thomas Peckett Prest, James Malcolm Rymer and Elizabeth Caroline Grey* (2002) · Boase, *Mod. Eng. biog.* · G. A. Sala, *Charles Dickens* (1870) · T. Frost, *Forty years recollections literary and political* (1880) · F. Jay, *Peeps into the past* (1945) [extracts from the *London Journal*] · W. O. G. Lofts, 'James Malcolm Rymer and Thomas Pecket Prest: two writers of Gothic "bloods"', *Reckless Ralph's Dime Novel Roundup* (Feb 1973), 18–23 · J. Medcraft, *Bibliography of penny bloods of Edward Lloyd* (1945) · E. S. Turner, *Boys will be boys* (1948) · L. James, *Fiction for the working man, 1830–1850*

(1963); rev edn (1974) · E. James and H. R. Smith, *Penny dreadfuls and boys' adventures* (1998) · d. cert. · PRO, Family Records Centre **Archives** BL, Barry Ono collection · Dickens House, London, Lesley Staples collection **Likenesses** J. W. Gear, lithograph, repro. in *The Pickwick songster*, pt 1, no. 2

Prest, William (1830–1885), football administrator and wine merchant, was born in York, probably on 1 April 1830, one of five sons of John Prest, a successful merchant in the city, and his wife, Arabella. He attended private schools in York from c.1840 to 1848. His father bought William's older brother John Beevor Prest into a partnership with a Sheffield wine merchant as Prest and Porter in 1850, and William Prest succeeded Porter in 1855. The business, which flourished, was continued by William after his brother's death, in partnership with E. C. Viner from London.

Prest was a keen cricketer—a good batsman and a speedy fielder—and attended in 1854 the meeting at which Bramall Lane was established as a venue for cricket. He played in the inaugural match the following year, but failed to score on that occasion. He also played for Yorkshire County Cricket Club. A talented athlete, he managed during an annual Sheffield sports day to carry off eleven prizes, one of which bore the inscription 'Toujours Prest'.

During his lifetime Prest was best-known for his interest in the local rifle volunteers. In 1859 he helped to establish the Hallamshire volunteer rifle corps, joining as an ensign and second in command to his friend Nathaniel Creswick (1831–1917). Before long he was promoted to the rank of major, and it was as Major Prest that he was generally known. In 1884, shortly before his death, he was promoted lieutenant-colonel.

Prest came to be more widely remembered, however, for his part in the founding of Sheffield Football Club, later recognized as the first association football club of the modern era. According to Creswick's recollections, it was while he and Prest were taking a summer walk that the idea of a football club was discussed as a winter sport to complement cricket. They wrote to Cambridge University and those public schools known to play versions of football, asking for copies of their rules. These were used in drawing up their own code, which was confirmed at the inaugural meeting of Sheffield Football Club in October 1857 (the most widely accepted date of the club's formation). Creswick was duly elected honorary treasurer and secretary and Prest was also elected to a committee dominated by fellow businessmen and men from the professions. Opponents in the early years were thin on the ground before the formation of Hallam Football Club two years later; Prest played in one of the early matches between the two clubs in 1861.

In later years Prest's interest in football gave way to his business, the rifle volunteers, and politics. He was a member of the executive and finance committee of the Sheffield conservative and constitutional association, but according to an obituarist 'he was never accused of being an offensive politician' since his views 'were always put temperately and with much good humour'. Perhaps for this reason he made 'but a slight stir on the public affairs of the borough'.

An Anglican—his brother Edward Prest (1824–1882) was archdeacon of Durham—Prest never married. He died in Market Place, Sheffield, on 10 February 1885 at the age of fifty-four, his four brothers having predeceased him. Thanks to the range of his interests he was said to have had a wide circle of friends and, although a disciplinarian with the rifle volunteers, he was liked for his good humour and kindness. Perhaps his relaxed, tory, gentlemanly approach quickly became incompatible with the serious, often rigid puritanism of those who came to dominate Sheffield football in the late Victorian period; his business activities would not have endeared him to temperance militants in the local football world such as Charles Clegg. It would be an exaggeration to say that without Prest the history of the world's biggest sport would have been markedly different, but in his typical Victorian, voluntarist way Prest earned his place in the history of the game.

NICHOLAS FISHWICK and ROLAND FISHWICK

Sources *Sheffield obituary notices*, 1885, Sheffield Central Library, vol. 1 · P. M. Young, *Football in Sheffield* (1962) · K. Farnsworth, *Before and after Bramall Lane* (1988) · R. S. Holmes, *The history of Yorkshire county cricket* (1904) · F. Walters, *History of Sheffield football club, 1857–1957* (1957)

Prestage, Edgar (1869–1951), historian and Portuguese scholar, was born in Manchester on 20 July 1869, the only surviving child of John Edward Prestage (1828/9–1915), solicitor, and his wife, Elizabeth Rose (1843/4–1917), both of High Wycombe, Buckinghamshire. Towards the end of his life he attributed the awakening of an interest in Portugal to the reading of stories of adventure, particularly Vasco da Gama's voyage to India. While still at school at Radley College, he began to study Portuguese, using a shilling grammar. He was converted to Roman Catholicism with his mother in 1886, and in 1891 he first visited Portugal, where the kindness of his reception, at a time when Lord Salisbury's ultimatum had caused a wave of anti-British feeling, gave him a permanent bond with the Portuguese. Religion, he said, proved a closer tie than nationality. His lecture 'Portugal: a pioneer of Christianity' (1933) was perhaps the fruit of this early approach.

From Balliol College, Oxford, Prestage graduated with a second class in modern history in 1891, and from 1896 to 1907 practised as a solicitor in his father's firm, Allen, Prestage, and Whitfield, at Manchester. His first published work (1893) was a translation from the French of the celebrated *Letters of a Portuguese Nun* ('Marianne Alcoforado'), now generally considered the work of a professional writer rather than the lovesick nun of Beja to whom Prestage himself, in common with tradition from the seventeenth century, had originally attributed the work. Prestage became convinced that the book was a literary fabrication and refused to allow further editions of his translation after the third. He also translated for the Hakluyt Society the fifteenth-century chronicler of the discoveries, Azurara, in collaboration with C. R. Beazley (2 vols., 1896–9). Between 1891 and 1906 he often visited Lisbon, mainly for historical research, and made friends with a number of prominent Portuguese scholars and writers, including most of those forming part of the celebrated coterie *Os Vencidos da Vida* ('the Vanquished in Life'). He had already, in the 1890s, been elected to the Portuguese Royal Academy of Sciences. He was introduced in Lisbon to the salon of Dona Maria Amália Vaz de Carvalho, herself a distinguished writer and widow of the Brazilian (Parnassian) poet Gonçalves Crespo. In 1907 Prestage married their only daughter, Maria Cristina. His mother, who had a strong influence over him, opposed his intention of settling in Portugal, but his wife, who is said not to have been accepted in English society owing to her non-European blood, was unhappy in Southport, Lancashire, and they soon returned to Lisbon. There they occupied the flat over Dona Maria Amália's in the Travessa Santa Catarina until, in the wake of his wife's suicide in 1918, Prestage returned to England.

During the period of his permanent residence in Lisbon, between 1907 and 1919, Prestage saw little of the English colony, identifying himself with his adopted country. He worked continuously at his researches in the Portuguese state and private libraries. A traditionalist by temperament, he was much attached to the monarchy, and never reconciled himself to the first Portuguese republic. He later supported the dictator Salazar, while remaining friendly with the exiled king Manuel II, whose three volumes on early Portuguese printed books he helped to revise. Prestage published many articles in Portuguese historical reviews, completed his long biography, in Portuguese, of the great seventeenth-century writer Don Francisco Manuel de Melo (1914), and published some of the Lisbon parish registers. From 1917 to 1918 he was press officer at the British legation in Lisbon.

In 1923 Prestage was appointed as the first Camões professor of Portuguese at King's College, London. There was almost no undergraduate teaching in the nascent department of Portuguese for many years, and the chief work of the professorship consisted in giving public lectures at which the Portuguese or Brazilian ambassadors presided, and in conducting the research to publish books and pamphlets. In 1924 Prestage married Victoria, daughter of Charles Davison Cobb, who was half-Spanish and had family connections with Oporto. They settled down at her Queen Anne house in London, 16 Holland Street, Kensington, visiting Lisbon frequently in the spring of each year.

At this time Prestage's main publications were connected with the period of the Portuguese restoration of 1640. He printed much of the relevant diplomatic correspondence, including (in collaboration) that of João F. Barreto, *Relação da Embaixada a França em 1641* (1918), and F. de Sousa Coutinho, *Correspondência diplomática* (1920, 1926, vol. 3 unpublished). His account of the *Diplomatic Relations of Portugal with France, England and Holland from 1640 to 1668* was published at Watford in 1925 and in Coimbra in 1928. It is a valuable survey of the whole subject, skilfully reduced to readable proportions, but limiting itself mainly to the narrative of events. In 1929 he published an account of Afonso de Albuquerque, which was followed

by a general survey of the Portuguese discoveries, *The Portuguese Pioneers* (1933), which was translated into various languages. He delivered the Norman MacColl lectures at Cambridge in 1933, and his short although rather incomplete account of the Anglo-Portuguese alliance was presented as a lecture to the Royal Historical Society and included in the society's *Transactions* for 1934.

After this Prestage wrote no major work, for in his later years he was more concerned with his lifelong commitment to Catholicism than with his further research, although he contributed chapters to several publications, and compiled a bibliography on Portugal and the War of the Spanish Succession. He remained professor until 1936. He was elected FBA in 1940, was a grand officer of the order of Santiago, a corresponding member of the Lisbon Academy of Sciences, the Portuguese Academy of History, and the Lisbon Geographical Society. He died at his London home, 16 Holland Street, Kensington, on 10 March 1951.

Prestage was a devoted and meticulous scholar, who, like many of those who pioneered the study of foreign countries in Britain in the late nineteenth and early twentieth centuries, displayed remarkable sympathy and identification with an adopted people and language. With Aubrey Fitzgerald Bell, he was the chief early pioneer of Portuguese and Lusophone studies, but the dryness of his writing style, and the limited range of the subjects to which he applied himself, meant that his impact on making things Portuguese known in Britain was limited.

H. V. LIVERMORE, *rev.* C. A. R. HILLS

Sources E. Prestage, in H. V. Livermore and W. J. Entwistle, *Portugal and Brazil* (1953) [autobiographical memoir] · personal knowledge (1971) · private information (2004) · Prestage MSS, King's Lond. · *CGPLA Eng. & Wales* (1951) · J. F. Laidlar, 'Edgar Prestage: Manchester's Portuguese pioneer', *British Historical Society of Portugal: 23rd Annual Report and Review, 1996* (1997), 55–75
Archives Harvard U., Houghton L., commonplace book · JRL, corresp. · King's Lond., corresp. · King's Lond., corresp. and papers relating to the history of Portugal | U. Edin. L., corresp. with Charles Sarolea
Likenesses W. Stoneman, photograph, 1943, NPG
Wealth at death £26,087 9s. 2d.: probate, 23 May 1951, *CGPLA Eng. & Wales*

Preston. For this title name *see* Graham, Richard, first Viscount Preston (1648–1695).

Preston, Sir Amyas (*d.* 1609), naval commander, was a member of the Preston family of Cricket, Somerset. No reference to his birth or education has been found and the earliest reference to him is his marriage on 4 June 1581 to Julian Burye (*d.* 1614?), widow, of the city of London, at St Dunstan and All Saints, Stepney. In 1588 he took part in the operations against the Spanish Armada, commanding the flotilla of ships' boats sent by Lord Howard to attack the great galleass the *San Lorenzo*, stranded outside Calais. He is said to have been severely wounded in this fight, although he and his men made sure that the galleass could not take part in the battle again and recompensed themselves by taking anything moveable from the ship. On 23 June 1589, in accordance with regulations intended to prevent the export of iron guns, Preston entered into a bond of £60 to cover the arming of his ship the *Julyan Goodspeed* with 2 sakers and 6 minions. These regulations were primarily aimed at merchant ships and their captains, some of whom had been accused of arming their ships and then selling the guns once they were in a foreign port. Preston's appearance in a list of captains who had not redeemed their bonds suggests that he may have armed a ship for foreign trade, or perhaps for privateering, on his own account.

In 1595 he led a voyage to the Spanish main together with Sir George Somers. Not even the author of *The Victorious Voyage of Captaine Amias Preston … and Captaine George Sommer to the West Indies* could make this expedition into anything more than a not very successful raiding party. Damage was done to some of the Spanish settlements and the town of Santiago de León, now known as Caracas, was burnt, but very little plunder was taken back to England after six months at sea.

In 1596 Preston sailed as captain of the *Ark* under Lord Howard in the Cadiz expedition, and was among the sixty-four men knighted by Howard and the earl of Essex in Cadiz. He is said to have taken part the following year in the attack on the Azores known as the Islands voyage, but the sources differ as to whether he commanded a ship. He seems however to have been associated with court factions surrounding the earl of Essex and the Howard family. About the time of Essex's rebellion, with Ralegh's cousin Sir Ferdinando Gorges, he became involved in a quarrel with Sir Walter Ralegh and allegedly challenged Ralegh to a duel, although no fight seems to have taken place. In 1601 he was vice-admiral under Sir Richard Leveson of the fleet which was commissioned to guard the channel, commanding the *Adventure* and later the *Dreadnought*. In the autumn he commanded the *Garland* as part of the fleet which was detached to defend Kinsale in Ireland against the attempted Spanish invasion, again acting as vice-admiral under Leveson. In the spring of 1602 he succeeded Leveson as admiral in the Irish fleet, commanding the *Swiftsure*.

Preston was appointed storekeeper to the ordnance on 17 May 1603, but the office quarter books do not show him as being active or paid as a member of the board until the March 1604 quarter. He served until his death, the last payment of his allowances being for the September quarter of 1609. In May 1609 he was one of those who petitioned for the incorporation of the second Virginia Company, and he was appointed a member of the new management council. Between 12 and 15 July, however, 'being sick but of perfect mynde and memory', he made his oral will in the presence of one Holliland and Roger Knight, leaving all his property to his wife, but asking her to give his black rapier and dagger to his brother Edward Preston, his gilt rapier and dagger to his godson Amyas Preston and 'his gylt faulcheon or semiterie with a greene velvet Scaberd' to the son of his elder brother. Probate was granted to his wife on 15 September 1609.   SARAH BARTER BAILEY

Sources DNB · R. Hakluyt, *The principal navigations, voyages, traffiques and discoveries of the English nation*, 10, Hakluyt Society, extra ser., 10 (1904); repr. (1969), 213–26 · J. K. Laughton, ed., *State papers relating to the defeat of the Spanish Armada, anno 1588*, 2 vols., Navy RS, 1–2 (1894) · quarter books of the board of ordnance, for the years 1603–1612, PRO, WO 54, 4, 5, 6 · will, PRO, PROB 11/114, sig. 85 · *The naval tracts of Sir William Monson*, ed. M. Oppenheim, 1–2, Navy RS, 22–3 (1902) · A. Brown, ed., *The genesis of the United States*, 2 vols. (1890) · J. L. Chester and G. J. Armytage, eds., *Allegations for marriage licences issued by the bishop of London*, 1, Harleian Society, 25 (1887) · T. Colyer-Ferguson, ed., *The marriage registers of St Dunstan's, Stepney* (1898) · F. T. Colby, ed., *The visitation of the county of Somerset in the year 1623*, Harleian Society, 11 (1876) · T. Lediard, *The naval history of England*, 2 vols. (1735) · W. A. Shaw, *The knights of England*, 2 (1906); repr. (1971) · E. Edwards, *The life of Sir Walter Ralegh … together with his letters*, 2 vols. (1868) · *The letters of John Chamberlain*, ed. N. E. McClure, 2 vols. (1939) · Burtchaell & Sadlier, *Alum. Dubl.* · PRO, E101/64/23

Preston, Charles (1660–1711), botanist, was born in Lasswade, Edinburghshire, on 12 July 1660, the second son in a family of at least four sons and two daughters of Sir Robert Preston and his second wife, Margaret Bothwell. George *Preston (1664/5–1749), who succeeded him as professor of botany at Edinburgh, was his younger brother. In 1663 Robert Preston, younger son of Sir John Preston of Valleyfield, obtained a charter for the lands of Preston, establishing an estate called Gorton on the banks of the North Esk in Edinburghshire. Presumably Charles Preston spent his childhood there, but nothing is known of his early life; his father was knighted in 1672.

Preston studied at the University of Edinburgh in the early 1680s and his interest in botany is mentioned in the journal of John Erskine of Carnock. Preston studied medicine at various universities in the Netherlands, France, and Flanders, and was granted the degree of MD from the University of Rheims on 14 July 1696. On his way back from the continent he stayed for a time in London, where he met Hans Sloane, with whom he established a lengthy correspondence. He also corresponded with the apothecary and botanist James Petiver. With both men he exchanged plants and seeds as well as books and information. Three of his letters were conveyed to the Royal Society and published in the *Philosophical Transactions* at this period.

On his return to Edinburgh in the summer of 1697 Preston attempted to establish a medical practice, but was cited by the Edinburgh College of Physicians for practising medicine without its licence. The college fined him £5 sterling for illicit practice but the fine was apparently never paid. Preston despaired of succeeding in a medical practice in Edinburgh and wrote to Sloane in 1702 requesting his assistance in obtaining a post at a military hospital, but this did not transpire; Preston was eventually elected a fellow of the Edinburgh College of Physicians in 1704.

Preston's main interest was not in medicine but in botany. About 1700 he established a botanical garden on the family estate at Gorton. He was already known to his contemporaries for his botanical knowledge. In 1700 Leonard Plukenet in his *Opera omnia botanica* referred to a specimen obtained from and identified by Preston, whom he called a most learned explorer and erudite Scot. In his *Methodus plantarum* (1703) John Ray called Preston 'eruditissimus vir et curiosissimus stirpium observator' ('a most learned man, and a most diligent observer of plants'; *Methodus plantarum*, 89) and referred to his opinions several times in the text. Preston was influenced by the French botanist Joseph Pitton de Tournefort, with whom he may have studied in Paris.

On the retirement of James Sutherland in 1706 as professor of botany in the University of Edinburgh, Preston was appointed his successor, which included charge of the town Physic Garden and the university's botanical garden. Like Sutherland, Preston lectured in the summers to medical and surgical students. Preston seems to have spent less effort in developing the Physic Garden than had Sutherland, but like his predecessor he was diligent in promoting the interests of his students. His letters to Sloane and Petiver frequently mention a young man (often the bearer of the missive) seeking employment or training in London.

Preston never married, and probably lived near the Physic Garden, which was next to Trinity Hospital. He died suddenly in December 1711, at the age of fifty-one. He left his small estate, totalling about £100 Scots, to his brother George.

ANITA GUERRINI

Sources J. M. Cowan, 'The history of the Royal Botanic Garden, Edinburgh: the Prestons', *Notes from the Royal Botanic Garden Edinburgh*, 19/92 (1935), 63–134 • A. Bower, *The history of the University of Edinburgh*, 3 vols. (1817–30) • A. Grant, *The story of the University of Edinburgh during its first three hundred years*, 2 (1884)

Archives Royal Botanic Garden, Edinburgh, corresp. | BL, corresp., Sloane MSS 4036–4042, 4060, 4063–4065, 4067

Wealth at death approx. £100 Scots: will, NA Scot., inventory, CC 8/8/85, p. 142r

Preston, (Sydney) Denis (1916–1979), jazz critic and record producer, was born Sidney Denis Prechner on 16 November 1916 at 13 Paget Road, Stoke Newington, London, the only son and second child of Louis (Lou) Prechner, businessman, and his wife, Sarah (Cissie), *née* Hobsbaum, teacher. His parents were English, his father of Alsatian descent. He grew up in Vienna and Brighton, but his father left when the children were small, and he and his sister were brought up by their mother. By the early 1930s they had moved to Sydenham, south London; he attended school there and left early, intending to become a professional musician. He studied the viola under Hubert Menzies and did some professional playing, but had no regular occupation and drifted into the theatre, becoming assistant stage manager at the Festival Theatre, Cambridge. On 6 September 1939 he married Ruth Queenie Pearl (b. 1915/16), daughter of Adolf Pearl, commercial traveller; she was a violinist from New Zealand and leader of the Boyd Neel Orchestra strings. Shortly thereafter he changed his surname and the spelling of his first name, by deed poll.

Preston was a passionate jazz fan who had his first encounter with 'live' American music when he saw Louis Armstrong in London in 1932. He soon got to know the coterie of serious young jazz enthusiasts; Max Jones, especially, became a close friend and associate, and when Jones and Albert McCarthy started the publication *Jazz Music*, Preston contributed pungent articles about black music and literature. After listening to the country blues

on rare imported records, he wrote powerfully about the connection between vernacular African-American music and enslavement, and developed a reputation for being a stern and insightful critic.

Preston began broadcasting in wartime, compiling and presenting musical programmes for the BBC, notably the weekly *Radio Rhythm Club* on which he played records and discussed trends in jazz. When Fats Waller died in 1943 he hosted a tribute programme in the company of Waller's colleague, the African-American songwriter and British resident Spencer Williams, and later introduced talks with other leading jazz authorities. His radio programmes were distinguished by their historical and sociological content. He also continued to write prolifically, for *Musical Express* and *Melody Maker*, and by 1945 had become aware of several Caribbean musicians who had settled in London. When he sponsored a ragtime concert that year, he featured the Guyanese reed musician Freddy Grant; he also found work for the Trinidadian guitarist Lauderic Caton. Through them he met and on 16 September 1946, following a divorce, married Helen Nontando (Nonie) Jabavu (b. 1918/19), a journalist; she was the daughter of Davidson Jabavu, professor of languages, and the granddaughter of South African nationalist John Tengo Jabavu, who had founded that country's first African newspaper.

In 1948 Preston travelled to New York to establish London Records for the British Decca Record Company. In Harlem he heard authentic Trinidadian calypso, an experience that sparked a new enthusiasm. On his return he made his début in the recording business, producing a series of calypsos by Lord Kitchener (Aldwyn Roberts) and Lord Beginner (Egbert Moore), both of whom had arrived on the *Empire Windrush* that summer. He continued to record black British musicians for almost two decades. He was responsible for guiding the repertory of the calypsonians and in 1950 he supervised what was probably the first commercial recording to feature the steel drum. He formed close working relationships with Guyanese pianist Mike McKenzie and Trinidadian bass player and arranger Rupert Nurse, employing them for his sessions, recorded the Jamaican folklorist Louise Bennett, and pioneered in other musical fields; he produced the Yoruba guitarist Ambrose Campbell and his West African Rhythm Brothers and, in 1952, a series of collaborations between Freddy Grant's calypsonians and the jazz trumpeter Humphrey Lyttelton. On 20 April 1954, his second marriage having ended in divorce, he married Laurel Patricia (Pat) Clarke (b. 1927), a state registered nurse from Jamaica; she was the daughter of Lincoln Clarke, landowner. They had two children, Richard (b. 1956) and Tracey (b. 1959).

Preston was primarily a businessman, but with little money to be made from speculative record production many of his endeavours were fired by enthusiasm and the urge to educate the listening public. When, in 1956, he persuaded the Nixa label to issue a series of recordings by leading British modern jazz musicians, he knew these could only sell modestly, yet as an inspired merger of mainstream and modern jazz styles they remained cameos of excellence.

It was when he turned his attention to the burgeoning market for skiffle, the amateur 'folk' music that presaged rock and roll, that Preston's fortunes changed. Lonnie Donegan's *Cumberland Gap* paved the way and other hit records followed. In 1958 he opened Lansdowne Recording Studios, becoming the first totally independent jazz record producer in Europe to operate from his own premises. With the controversial Joe Meek as his main engineer, he recorded a wide range of material as well as jazz and blues, but 'trad', the commercial form of traditional jazz exemplified by the Somerset clarinettist Acker Bilk, remained his mainstay. Outstanding among his productions in the 1960s were experimental albums by the innovative Jamaican saxophonist Joe Harriott; these included *Indo-Jazz Fusions*, the result of collaborations with the violinist John Mayer. Other imaginative projects included recordings of a solo album by the Ghanaian percussionist Guy Warren, of poetry and jazz, of the pianist Stan Tracey with a brass ensemble, and of American composer Bill Russo with the London Jazz Orchestra.

A neat, bespectacled man who wore a moustache and patronized a good tailor, Preston was a hard-nosed entrepreneur who did not suffer fools gladly. Despite this, he was generous to musicians he liked. He found 'unnecessary' recording sessions for those fallen on hard times and gave financial assistance to Harriott and the clarinettist Archie Semple. His success enabled him to indulge in driving a Mercedes but he continued to provide exposure for artists in whom his interest was aesthetic. A lifelong enthusiast for literature by and about African-Americans, he was more than an armchair theorist when it came to matters of racial integrity. He succeeded in having the book *Little Black Sambo* removed from school libraries, and in 1958 helped found the Stars' Campaign for Inter-Racial Friendship, formed in response to the Notting Hill racial disturbances of that year. This was essentially a jazz lovers' initiative, its main protagonists including Preston and his first cousin Eric Hobsbawm, the historian, the musicians Johnny Dankworth and Cleo Laine, and the Trinidadian journalist Claudia Jones. He died of cancer at 84 Ashdown, Eaton Road, Hove, on 21 October 1979, and was survived by his wife, Pat, and their two children.

VAL WILMER

Sources P. Leslie, 'The man behind the trad boom', *Scene*, 17 (26 Jan 1963), 6–9 • J. Asman, 'Radio jazz', *Challenge* (1 June 1946), 6 • E. Cook, *Jazz Journal* (Dec 1979), 3 • J. Cowley, 'London is the place for me', *Black music in Britain*, ed. P. Oliver (1990), 65–72 *passim* • J. Godbolt, *A history of jazz in Britain, 1919–50* (1984) • personal knowledge (2004) • private information (2004) • b. cert. • m. certs. • d. cert.
Likenesses photograph, 1940–44, repro. in Godbolt, *A history of jazz in Britain* • photographs, *c*.1946, priv. coll.
Wealth at death £303,170: probate, 9 Jan 1980, *CGPLA Eng. & Wales*

Preston, George (1659?–1748), army officer, was the second son of George Preston (*d.* 1679) of Valleyfield, who was descended from the Prestons of Craigmillar and was created a baronet of Nova Scotia on 31 March 1637. His mother was Marion Sempill, only child of Hugh Sempill, fifth Lord Sempill. He was captain in the service of the states general in 1688, and accompanied William, prince of Orange, in his expedition to England. Subsequently he served in the foreign wars of King William and Queen Anne, and at the battle of Ramillies he was severely wounded. In 1706 he was made colonel of the Cameronian or 26th regiment, and he retained that office until 1720. At the outbreak of the rebellion in 1715 he was sent from London to take command of the castle of Edinburgh, and was finally appointed deputy governor of the castle, 'with a salary of ten shillings per day'. He served for some years as commander-in-chief of the forces in Scotland. Despite his great age, Preston remained in his post at Edinburgh Castle as late as 1747. After the battle of Prestonpans in 1745 the victorious Jacobites laid siege to the castle. According to some accounts, the governor, General Joshua Guest, encouraged the siege as a way of delaying the rebels' advance into England. Other accounts claim that Guest was deterred from surrender only by his deputy's firmness. Indeed, Preston's robust conduct during the siege did much to ensure that the castle held out. By now in his eighties, he inspected the guards every two hours in a wheelchair propelled by a party of soldiers. More questionably, he responded to the blockade the highlanders threw around the castle by bombarding Edinburgh town with his guns. The damage, panic, and casualties that this caused did not deter Preston from repeating the ploy, until Charles Edward Stuart agreed to allow supplies to pass. Preston parried the rebels' threat to damage his Valleyfield estate in Fife by promising to have Wemyss Castle, the ancestral home of Lord Elcho, one of Charles's generals, razed by naval bombardment.

Preston died at Valleyfield on 7 July 1748. He left no children. He had paid off the encumbrances on the estate of Valleyfield, and thus acquired the right of the entail of the property, which he duly executed in favour of the heirs, male and female, of his brother Sir William and his nephew Sir George.

T. F. HENDERSON, *rev.* TIMOTHY HARRISON PLACE

Sources *Scots Magazine*, 10 (1748), 355 • F. J. McLynn, *Charles Edward Stuart: a tragedy in many acts* (1988) • J. Home, *The history of the rebellion in the year 1745* (1802) • *Army List* (1743) • *Army List* (1744) • *Army List* (1747) • N. B. Leslie, *The succession of colonels of the British army from 1660 to the present day* (1974) • GEC, *Baronetage*

Preston, George (1664/5–1749), apothecary and botanist, was the sixth child and fourth son of Sir Robert Preston and his second wife, Margaret Bothwell. Charles *Preston (1660–1711), professor of botany in the University of Edinburgh, was his older brother. The place of his birth is not recorded, although the Preston family lived at this time at Gorton, near Lasswade, on the banks of the North Esk in Edinburghshire. Presumably George Preston spent his childhood there, but nothing is known of his early life.

On 14 May 1684 he was apprenticed to Alexander Hay, king's apothecary in Edinburgh. At the end of his apprenticeship, on 15 June 1691, he was appointed surgeon of a regiment known as Cunningham's dragoons, later the 7th hussars. About 1698 he married Marion, daughter of John Wauchope, macer, and by her right Preston was appointed burgess of Edinburgh and guild brother apothecary. His name was entered in the burgess roll of Edinburgh on 4 May 1698. Their daughter, Isabella, married John Lauder, surgeon, but died young; a son, George, became a surgeon.

Preston practised as an apothecary in Edinburgh for many years; his shop was in Smith's New Land in Edinburgh, next to Blackfriar's Wynd, according to a 1701 advertisement in the *Edinburgh Gazette*. On 16 February 1703 he was appointed surgeon-major to her majesty's forces in Scotland, a position he held until his death.

Like his brother Charles, Preston was an enthusiastic botanist. When Charles died in December 1711, Preston applied for his position as professor of botany in the University of Edinburgh and intendant of the town Physic Garden and of the university's botanical garden; on 4 January 1712 the town council voted to appoint Preston, at a yearly salary of £10 sterling, out of which he paid £40 Scots for rental of the Physic Garden. He supplemented this salary by teaching and by selling plants and drugs. He taught materia medica to medical and surgical students at the garden during the summer months from 5 a.m. to 7 a.m. He apparently also retained his practice as an apothecary.

In 1712 Preston issued his only publication, a catalogue of the garden's holdings, *Catalogus omnium plantarum quas in seminario medicinae dicato*. The first edition is very rare, and a second edition appeared in 1716. This is one of the earliest lists of plants grown in Scotland. In the university library in Edinburgh are manuscript lectures on botany which may be Preston's. He corresponded with many botanists and was an active collector of plants but does not appear to have been an innovator in his field.

Although Preston introduced few new plants to the Physic Garden (particularly in comparison with his brother's predecessor James Sutherland), he physically improved it, adding a greenhouse. The garden continued to be the personal responsibility of the intendant, with the Edinburgh town council providing little financial support. The duties in this garden caused Preston to neglect the university's garden, which was transferred to others in 1724. Preston resigned his positions as professor and intendant in 1738 and retired to the family estate at Gorton, where he died on 16 February 1749, aged eighty-four. His estate, totalling over £700 sterling in value, was left to his grandson George Lander, who was executor of Preston's will.   ANITA GUERRINI

Sources J. M. Cowan, 'The history of the Royal Botanic Garden, Edinburgh: the Prestons', *Notes from the Royal Botanic Garden Edinburgh*, 19/92 (1935), 63–134 · A. Bower, *The history of the University of Edinburgh*, 3 vols. (1817–30), vol. 1, pp. 119–22, 362–84; vol. 2, pp. 40–42 · A. Grant, *The story of the University of Edinburgh during its first three hundred years*, 2 (1884), 380
Archives BL, corresp., Sloane MSS 4039, 4065, 4067 · U. Edin. L., 'Introduction to materia medica' lecture, c.1736
Wealth at death over £700; incl. £675 18s. money and £56 6s. 6d. in goods: will: NA Scot., inventory, CC 8/8/112, pp. A–G

Preston, George Dawson (1896–1972), physicist, was born on 8 August 1896 at Bardowie, Orwell Park, Rathgar, Dublin, the eldest of the three children of Professor Thomas *Preston (1860–1900), physicist, and his wife, Katherine Mary *Preston, née McEwen (1868–1951), eldest daughter of Thomas McEwen, headmaster, of Baldernock, Stirlingshire, and his first wife, Eliza Gray Mann; at the time of George's birth his mother was lecturer in Italian and she later became lady principal of Alexandra College, Dublin.

Preston's father died in 1900 leaving the family in reduced circumstances until 1910, when they inherited family property in co. Armagh. He attended school in Dublin and at thirteen won a scholarship to Oundle School, chosen on advice from his father's successor as HM inspector of schools, Sir Robert Blair, that it was the best school for science in the UK. In 1915 Preston won a scholarship to Gonville and Caius College, Cambridge, but, against the advice of his headmaster, Dr Sanderson, chose to enlist instead. Soon after, in a near-fatal hand-grenade incident, Preston lost his right patella, resulting in a permanent 'gammy' leg and a 75 per cent pension from his military service; he was also infected with tuberculosis. Preston was posted to the Ministry of Pensions, but at the armistice—by then a lieutenant and assistant adjutant of 49 squadron, Royal Flying Corps—decided to 'desert', as he described it, and went to Jamaica for a year to recuperate.

Preston finally took up his place at Gonville and Caius in 1920. In Cambridge he met Margaret Chrystal (1898–1994), also a physicist, and daughter of Captain Alexander Chrystal; they were married in 1924 after a four-year engagement. Preston was awarded a double first in the natural sciences tripos and became Sir Ernest Rutherford's graduate student working in the new field of X-ray crystallography.

In 1922 Preston moved to the department of metallurgy at the National Physical Laboratory (NPL), where until 1943 he pursued topics within the emerging mainstream of X-ray crystallography as well as in a branch of related research, electron microscopy. His interests ranged from the study of molecular structures by X-ray methods to thermal vibrations in the crystal lattice and oxidization in metals. One result of his early career, the Gunier–Preston layer, a clustering of solute atoms during precipitation hardening, was named after him.

In 1938 Preston was promoted to senior scientific officer at the NPL and from this time, although still active in other research, he led British work on electron microscopy. His pioneer apparatus had a magnification of only about × 600 diameters, roughly the limit of optical microscopy. Funding for this was withdrawn in the year prior to the outbreak of the Second World War: the decision, ultimately made by the Home Office on a cost-cutting initiative, meant that American research soon outstripped the British effort, producing the Metro-Vic electron microscope which magnified × 15,000 diameters. Preston was elected by fellow scientists to the Whitley Council in 1940 to represent them in negotiations with the relevant government bodies. He felt that the decision to cut funds for electron microscopy had been a political one, on the grounds that there was no practical application for such a device, but its true worth soon became apparent. By 1941 two Metro-Vic microscopes had been sent from the United States on separate ships; the first became a U-boat casualty, but the second machine was used under Preston's supervision.

The initial focus of research was on war-related issues, and the apparatus was used to study viral and bacterial specimens in conjunction with agricultural research at Rothamsted, especially in response to crop diseases and the overall food shortage. Other research was in metallurgy and mineralogy, notably of coal. At the time of Dunkirk some Bren gun breech-blocks were exploding and crews were reluctant to fire them. The NPL metallurgy team soon found the cause and Preston, as a veteran, was able to convince the military that the new block was safe.

In 1942, despite his role in halting research four years earlier, home secretary Sir J. Anderson planned to visit Preston's laboratory and to become the first non-scientist in Europe to witness the capabilities of electron microscopy. On 26 December, just prior to the visit, Preston preempted him by smuggling his own young son Tom past NPL security to secretly claim this first. Anderson was subsequently informed by Preston that he had not actually been the first non-scientist in Europe to see beyond the limits of light.

In 1943 Preston was appointed by St Andrews University to the Harris chair of natural philosophy at Queen's College, Dundee. He had proceeded ScD of Cambridge University in that year. In Scotland he continued work in electron microscopy, X-ray crystallography, and diffraction grids, becoming a fellow of the Royal Society of Edinburgh and fellow of the Institute of Physics in 1944. As chairman of the 1947 Electron Microscope Society meeting, Preston remarked that 'as three dimensional images can be made with electrons, it ought also to be possible to do so with light'. Later Dennis Gabor, inventor of holography, attributed his idea of 'incoherent light in contrast to coherent electrons' to Preston's words.

Although his appointment was for life Preston retired when he was about seventy. His main intellectual activity and hobby was the study of quaternions while for exercise he gardened at his mansion, Craigellie, Alyth, in Perthshire. He shunned the limelight, declining potential honours, finding it convenient to say that the ceremonies would be too tiring on his old war wound. He died at Meigle Cottage Hospital, Perth, on 22 June 1972, survived by his widow and four children, Margaret, Thomas, Mary, and George.   TALAL DEBS and THOMAS PRESTON

Sources WWW · The Times (29 June 1972), 18h · The Times (13 July 1972), 18g · Reports on the metallurgy department for the years 1936 to 1943, National Physical Laboratory, Teddington (1937–44) · J. Venn and others, eds., Biographical history of Gonville and Caius College, 5: Admissions from 1911 to 1932 (1948), 172 · 'Gunier-Preston zones', Chambers materials science and technology dictionary, ed. P. M. B. Walker (1997) · personal knowledge (2004)
Archives priv. coll.
Likenesses photograph, University of Dundee, department of electronic engineering and physics

Wealth at death £58,918.68: confirmation, 27 Sept 1972, CCI

Preston, Sir Gilbert of (b. in or before **1209**, d. **1274**), justice, came of a family which took its name from the village of Preston Deanery in Northamptonshire, and which was part of a holding of two knights' fees belonging to the honour of Huntingdon, which the Prestons had held since at least the mid-twelfth century. A holding of two knights' fees at Little Billing and Hulcote in the same county, which formed part of the honour of Chokes, had been held by the family since the time of the Domesday Book. Gilbert of Preston was the son of the **Walter of Preston** (d. 1230), who obtained a fee farm grant of the Northamptonshire royal demesne manor of Gretton in 1204, and was sheriff of Northamptonshire between 1206 and 1208; Walter rebelled against King John but procured the restoration of his lands in 1217, and was subsequently involved in other local administrative activities on behalf of the crown until his death, which had occurred by October 1230.

Gilbert of Preston began his career in the king's service by acting as one of the collectors of an aid in Northamptonshire in 1235/6, and in 1240 he received his first appointment as a royal justice. Between 1240 and 1254 he was employed almost continuously as one of the puisne justices on successive eyre circuits led by William of York, Roger of Thirkleby, and Henry of Bath, and in the common bench at Westminster; he also received a number of miscellaneous judicial and administrative commissions. In most years he received some payment from the king, but was not put on a regular salary (of £40 a year) until 1253. This was at a time when arrangements started being made for the regular payment of most royal justices.

In the autumn of 1254 Preston became the senior justice of an eyre circuit for the first time, though he also continued, when not on eyre, to act as a puisne justice of the Westminster bench. It was not until Michaelmas term 1260 that he sat for the first time as senior justice of that court. Shortly before this (in February 1260) his salary had been raised to 100 marks a year. Between Michaelmas term 1261 and Michaelmas term 1267 Preston sat continuously as senior justice of the common bench, except when sessions of the court were suspended because of political disturbances, but between the beginning of 1268 and the end of 1272 he once again left Westminster to lead an eyre circuit. He returned to Westminster only when eyres were suspended on the death of Henry III. His final period as chief justice of the common bench was during 1273, the last year of his life.

Preston's wife, Alice, was the daughter of Christine, the daughter and heir of Wischard Ledet, lord of the barony of Chipping Warden, and her first husband, Henry of Braybrooke (d. 1234). They were married by 1239. There is no evidence that they had any children: there was a donor to the priory of St Andrew, Northampton, called Sybil, daughter of Gilbert of Preston, but she was probably the daughter of an earlier namesake belonging to the same family. The justice's heir was Laurence of Preston, the son of his (predeceased) younger brother, William. Gilbert of

Preston also had a second brother, Michael, whose lands, forfeited for adherence to the Montfortians, were granted to him in 1265; Michael was subsequently admitted into the king's peace at the request of Roger Leyburn (in 1266). Gilbert of Preston probably died early in January 1274. He had made provision some years before his death for the welfare of his soul through a grant of land in Lincolnshire to the prior of Sempringham in return for the provision of a canon of the order to celebrate at Sempringham for the donor, his ancestors, and heirs, and also by a grant of property at Gretton in Northamptonshire to support a chantry in the parish church there.   PAUL BRAND

Sources *Chancery records* · unpublished records, PRO · W. Farrer, *Honors and knights' fees … from the eleventh to the fourteenth century*, 1 (1923), 95–9 · *CIPM*, 2, no. 69

Preston, Jennet (*d.* 1612). *See under* Pendle witches (*act.* 1612).

Preston, John (*d.* 1434), justice, was the younger son of John (perhaps Sir John) Preston of Preston Patrick and Preston Richard, Westmorland. His father lived until some time between 1392 and 1395, and is often hard to distinguish from his namesake and son. Although the younger John became his father's heir when his elder brother, Richard, died in 1390, giving him northern prospects and interests which he did not neglect, this did not prevent his pursuing a career as a lawyer in the south of England; his first commission, to investigate the seizure of nets in the Thames, came in February 1391. He soon acquired powerful patrons and employers. In 1393 he became steward of the Sussex estates of John of Gaunt, duke of Lancaster, and by 1397, and probably earlier, he was steward of the archbishop of Canterbury's Kentish manors of Otford and South Malling. Preston also acted for the crown, on 19 July 1394 receiving £2 6s. 8d. for securing the conviction of a multiple killer, and such additional rewards as the wardship and marriage of the heir of Henry Michelgrove, a landowner in Kent and Sussex. Preston himself acquired estates in the latter county, at Ringmer, South Malling, and Framfield. He retained links with Westmorland and Yorkshire, in November 1398 securing a powerful commission to act against adversaries there who were allegedly conspiring against his life. But his interests in the south remained paramount. He was appointed to the Sussex bench in 1397, and his Lancastrian ties were doubtless responsible for his being elected to represent Sussex in the parliament of 1399 which saw Henry Bolingbroke become king as Henry IV.

Preston's connections with Sussex were inevitably weakened in 1404, when he lost his position as steward of the duchy of Lancaster's estates in that county, presumably for reasons connected with his being arrested and taken to London for questioning shortly after his dismissal. Instead he became increasingly involved in the government of London, where he had been appointed the city's recorder by 9 July 1406. In 1407 or 1408 he was admitted to the livery of the Mercers' Company, and he also acquired London property, in the parish of St Botolph, Aldersgate. Preston remained recorder until August or

September 1415, and was regularly appointed to Newgate gaol deliveries until January 1425. On 11 January 1414, immediately after Sir John Oldcastle's rising, he was one of the commissioners appointed to act against Lollardy in the city. By this time he was a serjeant-at-law, having been ordered to take up that position on 3 February 1412. Three years later, on 16 June 1415, he was appointed a justice of the common pleas (reappointed on 1 October 1422); he was subsequently summoned among the justices to every parliament for which records survive until July 1427.

Following his appointment to the common bench, Preston was appointed to a large number of commissions in many counties, in a large number of which he also became a JP. As a justice of assize and gaol delivery he acted in the west midlands as well as in the northern counties. But although in May 1425 he acquired the manor of Farnborough and other estates in Kent, during the 1420s his interests became perceptibly more concentrated in the north, just as his activities as a justice of assize and gaol delivery, and as a commissioner, were increasingly confined to the northern counties. In 1424, for instance, he was appointed to investigate claims to Yorkshire lands forfeited in 1415 by Henry, Lord Scrope of Masham. In 1421 he was granted the custody of the Westmorland and Yorkshire estates of Sir John Lumley, during the minority of the heir, a trust he was later charged with abusing. On 28 January 1428 Preston was licensed to retire, in response to his own petition, which complained of age and infirmity. However, he lived until 29 September 1434; he probably died in Westmorland. It was almost certainly in the intervening period that he planned a chantry in the chapel of St George in Preston Richard, to be served by two priests and maintained from Preston's London property. However, nothing came of this plan. With an unknown wife Preston had three sons, Richard, who was probably the eldest, since he inherited his father's lands in Sussex and Westmorland, Robert, and John.

HENRY SUMMERSON

Sources HoP, *Commons, 1386–1421*, 4.137–9 · *Chancery records* · W. Farrer, *Records relating to the barony of Kendale*, ed. J. F. Curwen, 2, Cumberland and Westmorland Antiquarian and Archaeological Society, record ser., 5 (1924) · R. R. Sharpe, ed., *Calendar of letter-books preserved in the archives of the corporation of the City of London*, [12 vols.] (1899–1912), vols. I, K · *Lists of various common-law records* (1970) · F. Devon, ed. and trans., *Issues of the exchequer: being payments made out of his majesty's revenue, from King Henry III to King Henry VI inclusive*, RC (1837) · N. L. Ramsay, 'The English legal profession, c.1340–1450', PhD diss., U. Cam., 1985, xviii · Sainty, *Judges*

Preston, John, of Penicuik, Lord Fentonbarns (*d.* 1616), judge, was the son of John Preston (*fl.* 1533–1585), burgess and dean of guild of Edinburgh, and his wife, Marion Nicoll. He matriculated at St Leonard's College, St Andrews, in 1564, and graduated BA in 1566 and MA in 1568. Admitted advocate in 1575, his first judicial appointment was in 1580 to the commissary court of Edinburgh, which had jurisdiction in testamentary and consistorial causes. He was elected a senator of the college of justice on 8 March 1596 on James VI's nomination, and took his seat in the court of session on 12 March. He took his judicial title of Lord Fentonbarns from a property in East Lothian he had acquired in 1579, and continued to use it after his purchase of the barony of Penicuik, Midlothian, in 1604. Exceptionally he continued as one of the four commissaries until 1599. Appointed to the privy council in 1596, he became one of its most active members, serving on numerous commissions and committees.

In 1598 Sir George Home of Wedderburn, the comptroller, had severe problems in financing the royal households. On 31 October he entered into a contract with Preston by which the latter agreed to take on Home's offices of collector-general of the thirds of benefices and treasurer of the new augmentation. Any surplus from the revenue, which derived from ecclesiastical benefices and temporalities, was to be applied towards furnishing the households. Preston may have owed his formal appointment a month later to the friendship of John Erskine, eighteenth earl of Mar. In February 1599 James was reportedly angered by the refusal of the treasurer, the comptroller, and the collector, all of them Mar's friends, to give surety for the price of diamonds purchased from George Heriot, goldsmith. In July 1600 he was again said to be angry with the treasurer and collector 'for that they give him not money enough' (*CSP Scot.*, 1597–1603, 673). Nevertheless, Preston was nominated on 2 October 1601 as one of eight commissioners to assist the new treasurer, Sir George Home of Spot.

Preston also had a supporting role in James's ecclesiastical policy, beginning with his appointment in March 1596 as one of the king's two commissioners to the general assembly. In December 1596 James empowered him to make overtures to the ministers of Edinburgh following the riot there, and on 6 January 1597 he was appointed to advise the magistrates on the trial of those involved. Over the next ten years he represented the king at various synods and provincial assemblies. In January 1606 he was an assessor at the trial of the ministers accused of convoking an illegal general assembly at Aberdeen, dissenting from two rulings by the justice-depute. At the convention of estates in December 1606 he made 'a large discourse of the paines and travells which his majestie had tane in the effaires of the kirk', ending 'with exhortatioun to give his Hienesse satisfactioun' (Calderwood, 6.605). He was appointed to the new courts of high commission in 1610.

On 23 December 1607 the lords of session elected Preston to be vice-president in Lord President Balmerino's absence. He was an assessor at Balmerino's trial for treason in March 1609, and following his conviction the lords of session elected Preston as best qualified to succeed him, on 6 June 1609. By then Preston's financial offices were of diminished importance, owing partly to the restoration of temporalities to the bishops in 1606 and partly to substantial grants of former church lands and revenues. Preston himself had pensions amounting to £1087 10s. Scots and 24 'bolls' of meal from various abbacies for his own and his eldest son's lifetimes. On 15 November 1610 George Home, earl of Dunbar, was appointed to the combined offices of treasurer, comptroller, collector, and treasurer of the new augmentation. Though requiring Preston to demit his offices, thereby ceasing to rank as an officer of state, James preserved his status by stipulating that he was to continue as a member of the privy council and its president in the lord chancellor's absence. Preston was also one of the seven assessors nominated to assist the treasurer-depute in Dunbar's absence. After Dunbar's death he was one of eight commissioners, known as the New Octavians, appointed in April 1611 to manage the royal finances. Later that year, when told that the king expected to have some surplus revenue from Scotland, Preston commented: 'I wald thai[r] wer money, but it must not go to England' (Laing, 1.282). The treasury commission terminated in December 1613, but Preston retained his presidencies of the court of session and privy council until his death on 14 June 1616.

Preston had three wives, each the widow of an advocate. He married first, in 1583, Elizabeth Fawside, widow of Clement Little, who died in the same year after giving birth to his eldest son, John. About 1588 he married Lilias Gilbert, widow of Alexander Mauchan, who was the mother of his other children, Michael, George, James, and Catherine. She had died by 1609, when he married Margaret Collace, widow of Sir John Shairp of Houston, who survived him, dying on 25 September 1617. Margaret owned the estate of Muirtown, near Forres, Moray, which passed to the son of her first marriage to Walter Reid, commendator of Kinloss. Though Penicuik had been destined for Preston's second son, Michael, he had agreed with his elder brother in 1612 to exchange it for Fentonbarns. It thus passed to Sir John Preston of Airdrie, who sold it in 1647. He had acquired the estate of Airdrie in Fife by marrying Elizabeth Turnbull, the heiress, and was created a baronet in 1628. Sir Michael Preston of Fentonbarns married Marion, daughter of John Hay of Kennet, in 1616. Catherine, who married Robert Nairn, advocate, was the mother of Robert Nairn of Strathord, first Lord Nairne (*d.* 1683).   ATHOL MURRAY

Sources M. D. Young, ed., *The parliaments of Scotland: burgh and shire commissioners*, 2 (1993), 569–71 · *Reg. PCS*, 1st ser., vols. 3–10 · *CSP Scot., 1595–1603* · J. M. Thomson and others, eds., *Registrum magni sigilli regum Scotorum / The register of the great seal of Scotland*, 11 vols. (1882–1914), vols. 4–9 · G. Brunton and D. Haig, *An historical account of the senators of the college of justice, from its institution in MDXXXII* (1832), 234–6 · F. J. Grant, ed., *The Faculty of Advocates in Scotland, 1532–1943*, Scottish RS, 145 (1944), 145, 173, 189 · *Original letters relating to the ecclesiastical affairs of Scotland: chiefly written by … King James the Sixth*, ed. D. Laing, 2 vols., Bannatyne Club, 92 (1851) · D. Calderwood, *The history of the Kirk of Scotland*, ed. T. Thomson and D. Laing, 8 vols., Wodrow Society, 7 (1842–9) · C. P. Finlayson, *Clement Litill and his library* (1983) · books of sederunt, NA Scot., CS 1/4/1–2 · register of deeds, 1st ser., NA Scot., RD 1 · J. Stuart, ed., *Records of the monastery of Kinloss*, Society of Antiquaries of Scotland, 9 (1872) · J. Grant, *Cassell's old and new Edinburgh*, 3 vols. [1880–83]
Wealth at death pensions of over £1087 10s. Scots

Preston, John (1587–1628), Church of England clergyman, was born at Upper Heyford, Northamptonshire, in October 1587 and baptized at the parish church of Bugbrook on 27 October, the son of Thomas Preston, a farmer, and his wife, Alice, daughter of Lawrence Marsh of Northampton. His father died before Preston was thirteen, but his mother's rich uncle, Cresswell, who was childless, took a

The true Picture of Iohn Preston, Dʳ in Diuinity, and ſometimes Preacher of Lincolnes-Inn.

John Preston (1587–1628), by unknown engraver

liking to him, and sent him to the free school in Northampton.

Early years at Cambridge After further tuition in Bedfordshire, Preston on 5 July 1604 matriculated as a sizar from King's College, Cambridge. There he also studied music with particular devotion to the lute. Unhappy in this, he moved in 1606 to Queens' College, where he studied natural philosophy and graduated BA early in 1608. A business venture, for which he had sold land inherited from Cresswell, came to nothing, and so he returned to Aristotelian philosophy. What became a characteristic strictness of life emerged early: his tutor reprimanded him for excessive studying to the neglect of his body. However, he was rewarded in 1609 with a fellowship of the college.

In 1610 Preston was made a lay prebendary of Lincoln Cathedral, an office he held until his death. However, at this time he had no intention of seeking ecclesiastical preferment and, according to Thomas Ball, writing later as one of his devoted disciples, Preston 'thought it below him to be a minister, & held the study of Divinity to be a kind of honest silliness' (Ball, 7). Instead, he turned to the study of medicine and astrology. He proceeded MA in 1611. However, about 1611 or 1612 'as he was in the Caelestial

contemplations', he was rudely awakened by the 'hotter sort of Protestant' (ibid., 16). When John Cotton preached a plain, evangelical university sermon in Great St Mary's, it met with widespread disapproval from an audience seeking more ostentatious rhetoric, and Cotton returned dejected to his fellow's accommodation in Emmanuel College. Suddenly, however, Preston 'knocks at his door, and coming in, acquaints him with his spiritual condition, and how it had pleased God to speak effectually unto his heart by that Sermon' (J. Norton, *Abel being Dead yet Speaketh*, 1658, 14). Not only did Preston and Cotton become lifelong friends, but Preston's view of the Christian ministry and the study of divinity was transformed, and soon he was immersing himself in the works of the schoolmen, delighted to find there so frequently quoted his old friend Aristotle. He was ordained deacon in the diocese of Peterborough on 19 June, and priest on 20 June 1614.

Court contacts and the question of conformity Soon afterwards Preston began to attract notice outside Cambridge. Samuel Harsnett, master of Pembroke College and vice-chancellor of the university, prevailed upon him to engage in a public philosophical disputation at Cambridge before King James in March 1615. Preston excelled and gained the king's favour, debating the question as to 'whether Dogs could make syllogismes' (Ball, 23). However, when Preston was offered a place at court he declined. This indifference to the allurements of the court offended many, and a few suspected that 'some inclination to puritanisme' lay behind his reserve (ibid., 29), but at this point no tangible evidence seems to have been given in support of the charge, other than his opposition to one of his pupils appearing in a stage play as a woman.

Five years later, however, Preston nearly lost his place at Queens' owing to accusations of being 'a Non-Conformist' and 'an enemy to formes of Prayer' (Ball, 45, 53). On 23 January 1620 he clashed with Robert Newcome, commissary of the archdeacon of Ely, and with Lancelot Andrewes, recently departed bishop of Ely, over his failure to use the Book of Common Prayer at a lecture in St Botolph's Church, Cambridge, and his preaching a sermon when explicitly forbidden to do so by Newcome. Yet Preston reaffirmed his full allegiance to the prayer book at St Botolph's, in what was made to be seen as an enforced recantation sermon, and he signed a written apology to Newcome. He thereby evaded the moves by Andrewes to have him expelled from the university. As if to play to both galleries, Preston in this sermon endorsed set forms of prayer and extempore prayer as each being useful in its own place. Preaching before James I at Hinchingbrooke that year, as is clear from the more reliable 1644 edition of the sermon *Plenitudo fontis*, he delivered what was largely anti-Arminian polemic, but towards the end he obliged with a defence of liturgical prayer, and an exhortation to obey the commands of the church. Both aspects of the sermon pleased the king.

John Hacket, later bishop of Coventry and Lichfield, claimed Preston was 'not well affected to the Church' and was 'zealous for a new Discipline, and given to Change'; he wanted the marquess of Buckingham to help him 'strenuously lop off from this half-reformed Church, the superfluous Branches of Romish Superstition, that much disfigured it' (Hacket, *Scrinia reserata*, 1693, 1.203). However, writing in the 1650s, Hacket cited no sources for this narrative, and its accuracy is impossible to assess. Preston was indeed close to Buckingham, and the effect of this and other contacts is evident from the fact that the St Botolph's incident did nothing to hinder his rapid promotion: Sir Fulke Greville, among others, became his patron, strategic contacts at court continued, and his reputation as a theologian grew.

Later in 1620 Preston proceeded BD, and he soon became dean and catechist at Queens'. The longest item in Preston's manuscript legacy—a system of theology as taught to his Cambridge pupils—dates from about this time (Emmanuel College, Cambridge, MS 181). It has been suggested that Preston's anti-papal activities extended to writing, if only in a joint-authorship capacity, one of the most outspoken tracts against the Spanish match, possibly that known as 'Mr Alured's' letter against the Spanish match, numerous copies of which survive. On 9 May 1621 James Ussher, then vice-chancellor of Trinity College, Dublin, chose Preston as professor of theological controversies there but, having deliberated until 20 July, Preston declined. But he did not refuse another offer that same year to enter the court, and was made chaplain-in-ordinary to Prince Charles, thanks to his sermon before the king and his relationship with Buckingham.

Preacher, pastor, and absentee academic On 21 May 1622 Preston was elected to succeed John Donne as preacher to the Honourable Society of Lincoln's Inn, where he officiated regularly for the rest of his life. He exerted a considerable influence through this prestigious congregation, and even the newly rebuilt chapel was soon bursting at the seams. On 3 October, following a legal but hurried and secret election behind locked gates, Preston was also admitted master of Emmanuel College, Cambridge. His court connections gave Emmanuel the prestige it needed to offset its growing notoriety as a subversive 'puritan' institution. Yet Preston later fell out of favour with the fellows who had elected him, because he was so absorbed with court affairs that he had little time to bring in the reforms to the college statutes that the fellows were expecting. His predecessor, Laurence Chaderton, may have continued to discharge many of the master's functions.

Meanwhile, Preston had caught the eye of Arthur, Lord Chichester, who in 1623 requested the king for the company of Preston on his proposed mission to Cologne to negotiate an end to war in the Palatinate. Chichester, Sir Edward Conway, and Buckingham then obtained for Preston, through a personal mandate of the king dated 15 July, a degree of DD, conferred on 17 July. It was thought improper for a master of a university college to be seen abroad without one.

About this time Preston turned down an offer of the deanery of Westminster, seeing it as no use for the cause of 'the godly'. His desire to place a higher priority on preaching than on financial gain was very evident in 1624 when the lectureship at Holy Trinity Church, Cambridge, became vacant. By now suspicious of the use Preston would make of such a position, the king and bishops not only promised Paul Micklethwaite, fellow of Sidney Sussex, a reward if he would campaign for it, but also tried to deflect Preston with an offer of any bishopric or other preferment he desired. This ploy failed, not because of any stated unease on Preston's part with the episcopal office itself—indeed, he maintained close and enduring friendships with numerous bishops—but rather because he believed that God's cause was better served in other spheres. His heart was set on preaching, and he was finally confirmed lecturer at Trinity by Nicholas Felton, bishop of Ely, amid much controversy and opposition from the vice-chancellor.

Preston's ministry there and elsewhere had a significant impact, including influencing ordinary people. Many attributed their spiritual awakening to his preaching, among them Thomas Shepard of New England fame. Furthermore, although Preston was never given a cure of souls, he was much sought after as a spiritual counsellor concerning the inward motions of the human heart. His most demanding service in this area was probably the infamous case of Joan Drake, who in the early 1620s was understood to be in the grip of Satan and suicidal until she was apparently delivered through the prolonged counselling of Preston, John Dod, Thomas Hooker, and James Ussher. Preston also had close and long-lasting friendships with those renowned for a more defiant stance towards their mother church. He may or may not have shared the nonconformist tenets of Cotton or Arthur Hildersam, but he was sufficiently behind them to negotiate their liberty to preach again after they had been silenced in the 1610s and 1620s.

Last years By the mid-1620s Preston had reached the peak of his career. It seems fair to say that theological concerns overrode his more natural inclinations to prolong this period of political favour. In April 1625 Joseph Mede could still describe Preston as 'a man in speciall favour with the king' (BL, Harley MS 389, fol. 428), and for a while Buckingham continued to seek his preferment. That year he nominated Preston for the newly vacant position of lord keeper, although Sir Thomas Coventry, formerly of Emmanuel College, finally received the post. However, Buckingham was quietly undergoing a change of allegiance in an anti-Calvinist direction. At the York House conference in February 1626 Preston played a leading if, to his supporters, disappointing role, but Richard Montague, accused of popery and Arminianism, escaped the clutches of his would-be oppressors, and Buckingham's new agenda became clear to Preston. He committed to writing his new assessment of the duke and court politics in general but the letter fell into the hands of Sir Henry Spiller, who alerted the duke. A wedge was driven between him and Preston, and the latter's influence at court began to wane, so much so that he even considered escaping to Basel. But Preston remained in England and, although direct evidence is lacking, it is probable that he went on to become a key leader behind the formation in

1626 of the feoffees for impropriations, who aimed to gather endowments for the establishment of preaching ministries.

Soon after this Preston's health began to fail. On 27 May 1628 Richard Sibbes, fellow feoffee and preacher at Gray's Inn, wrote to Ussher, now archbishop of Armagh, informing him that Preston was 'inclining to a consumption' (probably tuberculosis) and that his state was 'thought doubtful to the physicians' (J. Ussher, *Works*, 1864, 16.522). Preston spent his last months travelling to see friends, hoping that the country air would do him good. He finally returned to his home county of Northamptonshire and to his friend Sir Richard Knightley at Fawsley, enabling him to renew his fellowship with Dod, who prayed with him on his deathbed. He was also visited by Chaderton and Lord Saye and Sele. At five o'clock in the morning on 20 July, Preston died at Knightley's home in Fawsley—a bachelor, and just short of his forty-first birthday. He was buried on 28 July in Fawsley parish church, intentionally without elaborate ceremony. Dod preached the funeral sermon, 'and a world of Godly people came together' (Ball, 175). Preston's will, made on 30 July 1618 and proved on 30 July 1628, was indicative both of that world and of his primary concerns. Beneficiaries included Chichester, Saye and Sele (his executor), Dod, Sibbes, Cotton, Hooker, and other 'godly preachers', with £50 going to Queens' College. A codicil left £200 to Emmanuel College to support two poor scholars.

Legacy and reputation Undoubtedly Preston's greatest legacy was the subsequent flood of published editions of his sermons, through which he continued to have a great influence on 'the godly' in England and New England. His works, all published posthumously, comprise mainly sermonic as opposed to systematic material, and were critical in establishing a new spiritual genre of protestant devotional publications, through Dutch-language editions among others. When Lord Saye and Sele visited him on his deathbed, Preston chose four men as his editors, Sibbes and John Davenport for his Lincoln's Inn sermons, and Thomas Goodwin and Ball for all his other sermons. Collections of the former first appeared as *The New Covenant* (1629); a treatise on prayer, *The Saints Daily Exercise* (1629); *The Breast-Plate of Faith and Love* (1630); and *The Saints Qualification* (1633). The other authorized collections of sermons were *The Golden Scepter* (1638); a series on indwelling sin, *The Doctrine of the Saints Infirmities* (1636); an incomplete treatise on the divine attributes, *Life Eternall* (1631); and an important collection of court sermons, *Sermons Preached before his Majestie* (1630). To the dismay of the authorized editors, twice as many titles in Preston's name were to come from unauthorized editors, who included Preston's great admirer William Prynne. The unauthorized editions are not inherently or generally unreliable, however, although *The Fulnesse of Christ for Us* (1639, 1640) was purged to make it appear that Preston had not preached against Arminianism before the king; the 1644 edition, *Plenitudo fontis*, corrects this. Other more important unauthorized publications include: a treatise on the sovereignty of grace, *Irresistibilitate gratiae convertentis* (1639; English translation, 1654); *Remaines* (1634); a thorough treatment of the mortification of sin, *Sins Overthrow* (1633); and a collection of assorted sermons, *Riches of Mercy* (1658), the last of Preston's works to be published in the seventeenth century. This brought the total number of editions of his material to over 100.

In terms of theology he has often been misrepresented, but his printed legacy reveals that the mature Preston embraced the system of English hypothetical universalism. This was a modified and moderate form of Calvinism, which he had learned from Ussher and Bishop John Davenant in reaction to rigorous Elizabethan particularism (which he seems to have once held) and which arose from the perceived need for a Reformed and Lutheran consensus in the light of a rising Arminianism. He held that in one sense Christ died for all without exception, and that God desires to save all hearers in the preaching of the gospel. He was a self-conscious and influential covenant theologian, and promoted a greater emphasis on human responsibility in the covenant relationship. His evangelical impulse led him to attack the formalism he saw in the state church, and dominant themes in his preaching were preparation for salvation, the quest for full assurance of faith, and the need for thorough self-examination prior to partaking of the Lord's supper.

Preston's relationship to the established church remains more elusive. He has been described as 'one of the more enigmatic figures in the history of religion, and of politics' (Bendall, Brooke, and Collinson, 215); in the historiography of dissent, by 1702 Preston was being heralded as 'one of the greatest Men in his Age' (C. Mather, *Marginalia Christi Americana*, 1702, 3.16); there was 'scarcely an eminent Puritan divine of fifty years after Preston's death who does not refer to him as one of the greatest authorities' (Hill, 244). He later became enshrined as a 'sufferer for nonconformity' (D. Neal, *History of the Puritans*, 1822, 2.128). Yet this was without evidence: Thomas Fuller gave no grounds for styling Preston as the 'Patriarch of the Presbyterian Party' (T. Fuller, *The Church-History of Britain*, 1655, pt 11, 131). Preston nowhere seems to have spoken against episcopacy, and neither does there appear to be any surviving evidence of his attitude to vestments or the signing of the cross in baptism.

On the other hand, Preston shows himself to have been definitely the 'hotter sort of Protestant'. The zeal of his youth continued into his later preaching and Heylyn singled him out as a renowned sabbatarian. His plain-style preaching was on occasions militantly anti-papal and anti-Arminian, and his court sermons frequently addressed the contemporary political scene; Fuller thought him a 'perfect Politician' of the utmost cunning (Fuller, *Worthies*, 2.291). At the same time, his works are almost entirely consumed with matters of spiritual experience and practical piety. As an exemplary 'experimental predestinarian' and as a member of the spiritual brotherhood who pursued this approach to piety, Preston was indeed a puritan. In regard to outward conformity, or rather lack of it, he was a moderate or a fully conforming puritan. But this does not imply that he was complacent about the ecclesiastical *status quo*, for in that sense he was a conforming reformer.

JONATHAN D. MOORE

Sources T. Ball, *The life of the renowned Doctor Preston, writ by his pupil, master Thomas Ball, D. D. minister of Northampton, in the year, 1628*, ed. E. W. Harcourt (1885) · J. D. Moore, '"Christ is dead for him": John Preston (1587–1628) and English hypothetical universalism', PhD diss., U. Cam., 2000 · Venn, *Alum. Cant.* · I. Morgan, *Prince Charles's puritan chaplain* (1957) · S. Bendall, C. Brooke, and P. Collinson, *A history of Emmanuel College, Cambridge* (1999) · C. Hill, 'The political sermons of John Preston', *Puritanism and revolution: studies in interpretation of the English Revolution of the 17th century* (1958), 239–74 · B. Donagan, 'The York House conference revisited: laymen, Calvinism and Arminianism', *BIHR*, 64 (1991), 312–30 · P. R. Schaefer, 'The spiritual brotherhood on the habits of the heart: Cambridge Protestants and the doctrine of sanctification from William Perkins to Thomas Shepard', DPhil diss., U. Oxf., 1994 · Y. J. T. Song, *Theology and piety in the Reformed federal thought of William Perkins and John Preston* (1998) · J. F. Veninga, 'Covenant theology and ethics in the thought of John Calvin and John Preston', PhD diss., Rice University, 1974 · 'John Preston, D. D.', B. Brook, *The lives of the Puritans*, 2 (1813), 352–74 · *DNB* · I. Morgan, *Puritan spirituality: illustrated from the life and times of the Rev. Dr. John Preston, master of Emmanuel College, Cambridge; town preacher of Cambridge; preacher at Lincoln's Inn; chaplain to Prince Charles; advisor to George Villiers, duke of Buckingham; leader of the Jacobean puritan movement* (1973) · N. Pettit, *The heart prepared: grace and conversion in Puritan spiritual life* (1966) · R. T. Kendall, *Calvin and English Calvinism to 1649* (1979) · will, PRO, PROB 11/154, fol. 102

Likenesses W. Marshall, line drawing, repro. in J. Preston, *The doctrine of the saints infirmities* (1636) · drawing, repro. in Ball, *Life* · drawing, repro. in Morgan, *Prince Charles's puritan chaplain*, 2 · drawing, repro. in E. Hindson, ed., *Introduction to puritan theology: a reader* (1980), 28 · drawing, repro. in J. Preston, *The golden sceptre held forth to the humble: six sermons on II Chronicles 7:14* (1990), jacket · line drawing, repro. in J. Preston, *The saints qualification* (1633) · line drawing, repro. in J. Preston, *The fulnesse of Christ for us* (1639) · line drawing, repro. in J. Preston, *The onely love of the chiefest of ten thousand* (1640) · line drawing, repro. in J. Preston, *Riches of mercy* (1658) · line engraving, BM, NPG; repro. in J. Preston, *The new covenant* (1629) · line engravings, BM, NPG [*see illus.*] · miniature, oils on panel, Emmanuel College, Cambridge · oils, Emmanuel College, Cambridge; repro. in F. H. Stubbings, *Forty-nine lives: an anthology of portraits of Emmanuel men* (1983), no. 8

Preston, Joseph Henry [Harry] (1911–1985), aeronautical engineer and university teacher, was born on 1 March 1911 at Swinescales, Hutton Soil, Greystoke, near Penrith, Cumberland, the son of William Preston, a farmer, and his wife, Jean Dufton. He was brought up in the small farming community of Bampton, Westmorland, on the edge of the Lake District and was at heart a countryman. He first attended Bampton endowed school, 1916–1921, then the Queen Elizabeth Grammar School in Penrith from 1921 to 1929, after which he moved to London to study aeronautical engineering at Queen Mary College. On graduating in 1932 he spent a brief period of practical training at the famous Short Brothers seaplane works in Rochester, Kent, before returning to his college to study for a PhD which he obtained in 1936.

On 18 April 1938 Preston married a schoolteacher, Ethel (b. 1911/12), daughter of Joseph Noble, a farmer, also from Bampton. They had two children, a boy and a girl, and he is recorded as being a happy family man. With war threatening, and despite having recently secured a position as assistant lecturer at Imperial College, he felt it his duty to move in the same year to the National Physical Laboratory (NPL), Teddington. There he was free to concentrate on refining the aerodynamic methods used then to design aircraft wings. During this period he devised methods to quantify the influence that the growth of the boundary layer (the flow adjacent to the surface that is retarded by viscous forces) has on a wing's performance. He also studied the aerodynamics of control surfaces and pioneered research into applying suction to reduce drag and prevent stall. His approach to this work was intensely pragmatic. Although not quick or flashy, he was an original thinker and he drew inspiration from a sound and physically perceptive understanding of fluid mechanics.

Hostilities over, Preston decided to return to academia. This time it was to the engineering department at Cambridge where, in 1946, he was appointed lecturer in aeronautics. Here he came into contact with a group of talented aerodynamicists who encouraged him in his study of aerofoils. He continued to concentrate on boundary layers and put much effort into devising methods to measure skin friction. One outcome was the ingenious Preston tube probe which was first publicized in 1954, the year of his promotion to reader. Initially this invention was not universally accepted, in particular by his former colleagues at NPL, but this disarmingly simple but effective instrument was the product of a clear-sighted understanding of aerodynamics and it was a brilliant solution to a difficult problem. In 1955, having failed to secure a chair at Cambridge, Preston moved to the University of Liverpool where he was appointed professor of fluid mechanics, a post he held for twenty-one years. Here he widened his interests to water flows studying, for example, the effect of roughness on the resistance of ships' hulls.

Preston was appointed fellow of the Royal Aeronautical Society, and fellow of Queen Mary College in December 1959. He was one of the foremost aerodynamicists of his generation and although remembered principally for the sensing probe that bears his name he left a substantial legacy of discoveries that influenced the development of aircraft throughout the Second World War and the decade that followed. In character he was a reserved, somewhat brisk yet modest, brown suited, gruff man who enjoyed puffing a pipe. He had little time for committees or university politics and whenever possible he would return to his beloved Lake District where, in his younger days, he was an enthusiastic mountaineer. He died suddenly, at Parkside, Askham, Westmorland, on 28 July 1985.

JOHN K. HARVEY

Sources biographical archive, St John Cam. · U. Lpool, D 152 · U. Lpool, subject's curriculum vitae, dated 25/1/1955 · m. cert. · d. cert.

Archives CAC Cam., papers · St John Cam. · U. Lpool L., papers

Wealth at death £75,574: probate, 14 Nov 1985, *CGPLA Eng. & Wales*

Preston [*née* McEwen], **Katherine Mary** (1868–1951), college head, born at School House, Garvock, Kincardine,

Scotland, on 30 April 1868, was the eldest of the two children of Thomas McEwen, parochial schoolmaster, and his wife, Eliza Gray, née Mann. She came from learned Presbyterian stock on both sides, as her maternal grandfather, John Mann, was one of the founders of the Educational Institute of Scotland and headmaster of Baldernock School, prior to her father taking over the post. In 1873, on the death of their mother, Katherine and her sister Euphemia went to Dublin to live with their aunt, and later became pupils of Alexandra School and College. Described as the essence of a Victorian lady, Katherine, or Katie as she was known, became secretary to Miss La Touche, lady principal of Alexandra College. She took an honours degree in modern literature in the Royal University of Ireland in 1892, and was immediately appointed lecturer in Italian at Alexandra College. In 1895 she married the physicist Thomas *Preston (1860–1900), professor of natural philosophy at University College, Dublin. He died in 1900, leaving her a widow with two young children, including the later physicist George Dawson *Preston (another son had died in infancy).

Katherine Preston returned to Alexandra College as a lecturer, librarian, and later assistant principal under Henrietta White, before becoming lady principal of the college in 1932. Known affectionately to her students as Ma P, Mrs Preston took over control of the college at a time of retrenchment and general economic depression. Alexandra had been synonymous with Miss White, who had presided over the college fortunes for forty-two years as lady principal during a period of great intellectual and social brilliance. The college was now facing an uncertain future. It had lost its university classes in the early 1900s, but it still had links with Trinity College, Dublin, through its teacher training department. In the changed economic climate of the 1930s, the future of this department was now in doubt. The school of education at Trinity College tried to end the arrangement in 1933, but Mrs Preston made a strong protest to the board of Trinity and they agreed that the teacher training course at Alexandra would continue to be recognized. This arrangement lasted until 1935 when the secondary training department was finally closed. The Froebel department was then the sole survivor of the teacher training department, and was placed under the control of Alexandra School. Mrs Preston retired in 1940.

Brought up in the humanist tradition, with a deep belief in human excellence, Mrs Preston was renowned for a sympathetic interest in her students which gave them confidence in their own gifts. While there were no dramatic achievements during her short six years in office, her qualities of calmness, serenity, and tact enabled the college to keep going through a very difficult period, both politically and economically. A lover of Italy and its literature, she was a lifelong member of the Dublin Dante Society. Katherine Preston died at her home, Bardowie, 16 Orwell Park, Rathgar, Dublin, on 29 May 1951. She was buried two days later at Whitechapel, Rathfarnham.

A. V. O'CONNOR

Sources *Irish Times* (7 June 1951) · *Alexandra College Magazine* (Dec 1951) · A. V. O'Connor and S. M. Parkes, *Gladly learn and gladly teach: Alexandra College and School, 1866–1966* (1984), 175–81 · K. M. McEwen, 'Presidential address to the students union on the early Renaissance in Italian literature, 1303–1353', *Alexandra College Magazine* (Jan 1893) · 'Memories of Mrs K. M. Preston of the 1890s in Alexandra College', *Alexandra College Magazine* (Dec 1942), 6–8 · lady principal's reports to council, 1933–40, Alexandra College, Milltown, Dublin, archives · b. cert. · d. cert.
Archives Alexandra College, Milltown, Dublin, archives
Likenesses photograph, 1931 · L. Whelan, portrait, 1941, Alexandra College, Milltown, Dublin
Wealth at death £17,063: probate, 27 Nov 1951, *CGPLA Éire*

Preston, Richard (1768–1850), writer, was born at Ashburton in Devon, the only son of John Preston, minister, of Okehampton, also in Devon. He began his career as an attorney, but attracted the notice of Sir Francis Buller by his first work, *An Elementary Treatise on the Quantity of Estates* (1791). On Buller's advice he entered the Inner Temple, in 1793, where, after practising for some years as a certificated conveyancer, he was called to the bar on 20 May 1807, was elected a bencher in 1834, in which year he took silk, and was reader in 1844.

Preston was MP for Ashburton in the parliament of 1812–18, and was one of the earliest and most robust advocates of the imposition of the corn duties. In 1815 he published an *Address to the fundholder, the manufacturer, the mechanic, and the poor on the subject of the corn laws*. Other tracts on the same subject appeared in *The Pamphleteer* between 1816 and 1818. In 1816 he made vigorous attacks in parliament on the government's financial mismanagement. But in the two following sessions his speeches became infrequent. He had invested a large fortune, derived from his conveyancing practice, in land in Devon. In law, as in politics, he was intensely conservative, and thought the Fines and Recoveries Act a dangerous innovation; but his knowledge of the technique of real-property law was considerable and his works on conveyancing were lucid and well researched. He wrote several legal treatises, including *A Treatise on Conveyancing* (1806–9) which ran into a third edition. He was for some time professor of law at King's College, London. He died on 20 June 1850 at his seat, Lee House, Chulmleigh, in north Devon.

J. M. RIGG, rev. ERIC METCALFE

Sources *GM*, 2nd ser., 34 (1850), 328 · *Annual Register* (1850), 236 · S. Warren, *Law studies*, 3rd edn (1863), 1215 · C. Butler, *Reminiscences*, 4th edn, 1 (1824), 62 · D. Lysons and S. Lysons, *Magna Britannia: being a concise topographical account of the several counties of Great Britain*, 4 (1816), 9, 18, 108, 336, 339 · J. G. Marvin, *Legal bibliography, or, A thesaurus of American, English, Irish and Scotch law books* (1847) · Allibone, *Dict.* · HoP, *Commons*

Preston, Roland [name in religion Thomas; pseud. Roger Widdrington] (1567–1647), Benedictine monk, was born in January 1567, probably in Shropshire, though his family are unidentified. He matriculated from Magdalen Hall, Oxford, on 22 December 1576, but he did not take his degree, which may imply that he was a Catholic recusant. In 1586 he went with other students via Allen's English College at Douai (which was temporarily taking wartime shelter in Rheims) to the new English College in Rome. He was already a priest when he entered the Benedictine noviciate at Monte Cassino, where he was professed under the name Thomas on 16 June 1592. Some time later he was transferred to the abbey of Santa Justina at Padua, and may have spent time at San Giorgio, Venice. If so, this helps to explain his later somewhat Gallican view of the church, for there was a good deal of tension between Venice and the papacy at this time. He was well thought of by the superiors of the Cassinese congregation and was employed in teaching theology, being evidently an able man.

In late 1602 the pope agreed, after no little delay, to allow English monks from the Cassinese and Spanish congregations to travel to England as missionaries: the first two Cassinese were Preston and Anselm Beech, who landed at Great Yarmouth in 1603. Here they met, probably by arrangement, Sigebert Buckley, the last survivor of the community of Westminster restored under Queen Mary, who was living with the Woodhouses at Caston, Norfolk. They made arrangements for him to live in London in reasonable comfort. There on 21 November 1607, Buckley was able to aggregate to himself Robert Sadler and Edward Maihew, two newly professed Cassinese monks. They represented (at least in the opinion of the lawyer–monk Augustine Baker, who was present) the entirety of the rights, property, and privileges of the English congregation as it had existed up to the dissolution. It is not clear that Preston was actually present, but he is included in Buckley's list of four monks through whom Buckley extended his handing on of rights to others whom they had received as monks. In fact Preston was the superior for the Cassinese monks working in England for many years.

Preston is known chiefly for his involvement in the disputes about the oath of allegiance, devised in 1606, with the intention of securing a body of Catholics whom the government could consider loyal subjects, and of aiding James I's aspirations towards Christian unity, but opposed by Rome and most Catholic leaders. Preston addressed the issue in his *Apologia cardinalis Bellarmini pro jure principum* (1611), utilizing the probabilism absorbed from his theology teachers in Rome, chiefly the Jesuit Gabriel Vasquez. With Rome slow to make any definite decision he pressed the claim that Catholics could take the oath since there was no definite prohibition or, if there was, there was also a body of theological opinion which would allow the oath, leaving the matter merely 'probable'.

The issue was for many a genuine question, and it generated a European field of publications for several years, in which leading figures like James I and Cardinal Bellarmine took a vigorous part. It is thought that Preston's argument, that the pope's power to depose princes was not *de fide*, and need not be held by every Catholic (though abhorrent to the Jesuit-inspired zeal of the Counter-Reformation), was very convenient to the government, and attractive to James himself in his promotion of conciliarism and European peace. Thus the government was content to keep Preston for over thirty years in relative comfort in the Clink prison, and he was content to be able to write (and operate in some part as a priest), his imprisonment shielding him from direct interference by the Inquisition.

Preston wrote a series of works, mostly in the decade 1611–21, under a pseudonym, Roger Widdrington. The real Widdrington was a keenly recusant minor landlord in Northumberland, a useful front who, because of his remoteness, would not be likely to come to much harm. The general weight of opinion and probability, now as in his own time, is that there was, and is, no real doubt that Preston, not Widdrington, was the author. Widdrington was somewhat unconvincing in this guise as an energetic writer and learned controversialist, but there seems to have been at least friendship, and perhaps co-operation, between the two.

Preston continued to publish on the oath controversy, often as responses to opponents, and in both Latin and English. He was an able and courteous controversialist, and was regarded with considerable respect by Bellarmine, Suarez, and others, who took his position and influence very seriously. Rome several times tried to get him to toe the line, working through people like Panzani, the papal envoy (himself not unsympathetic to Preston's position on the oath), and several of his works finished up on the *Index*, the first in 1614. He responded to his works' condemnation in *A Copy of a Decree* (1614), with an appendix directed against the Jesuit Thomas Fitzherbert. He renewed his appeal to Rome with the lengthy Latin *Rogeri Widdringtoni … supplicatio* (1616), published with a lengthy appendix responding to Bellarmine's accusations, but placed on the *Index*. He continued to publish in English, and in his 'short and plain' *A New-Yeares Gift for English Catholikes* (1620) 'abandoned his uncommitted attitude and told the faithful that they would risk damnation if they refused the oath' since the doctrine of deposition of princes was heretical (Lunn, *English Benedictines*, 50–51). With mounting pressure upon him he appealed to Rome with his 1620 *Appellatio* and his 1621 *Reverendorum partum D. Thomae Prestoni … humillima supplicatio*. He appears to have submitted, and not to have published further. As a forerunner of ecumenism Preston had tried to make accommodation possible.

Preston's later years are unclear. There is in existence a royal warrant which gave him licence to live outside the Clink, being by this time an old man. In 1646 he appealed to parliament after pursuivants had raided his rooms in the Clink and removed all his books and possessions, which on a previous occasion (1634) had amounted to five or six cartloads of books, with many other valuables. For thirty-three years, he said, he had been a prisoner there, writing in the king's service, to his discredit in Rome, and now he was 'not able to cloath and uncloath himself without help'. Indeed shortly afterwards he caught fever and died, either in the Clink or nearby, in the spring of 1647.

ANSELM CRAMER

Sources A. Baker, *Apostolatus Benedictinorum in Anglia, sive, Disceptatio historica*, ed. C. Reyner, trans. Leander [J. Jones] (1626) · A. Allanson, *Biography of the English Benedictines* (1999) · E. L. Taunton, 'Thomas Preston and Roger Widdrington', *EngHR*, 18 (1903), 116–19 · R. H. Connolly, 'The Buckley affair', *Downside Review*, 49

(1931), 49–74 · J. McCann and H. Connolly, eds., *Memorials of Father Augustine Baker and other documents relating to the English Benedictines*, Catholic RS, 33 (1933) · W. K. L. Webb, 'Thomas Preston, OSB, alias Roger Widdrington (1567–1640)', *Biographical Studies*, 2 (1953–4), 216–68 · A. F. Allison and D. M. Rogers, eds., *A catalogue of Catholic books in English printed abroad or secretly in England, 1558–1640*, 2 vols. (1956) · M. Lunn, 'English Benedictines and the oath of allegiance, 1606–1647', *Recusant History*, 10 (1969–70), 146–63 · M. Lunn, 'The Anglo-Gallicanism of Dom Thomas Preston', *Schism, heresy and religious protest*, ed. D. Baker, SCH, 9 (1972), 239–46 · P. Milward, *Religious controversies of the Jacobean age* (1978) · D. Lunn, *The English Benedictines, 1540–1688* (1980) · W. B. Patterson, *King James VI and I and the reunion of Christendom* (1997)

Preston, Sir Simon, of Preston and Craigmillar (*d.* in or before **1575**), administrator and provost of Edinburgh, was the eldest son of George Preston of Preston and his wife, Isabel Hoppringle. His family had possessed the lands of Preston, Midlothian, since the reign of William the Lion, and the lands and castle of Craigmillar, just outside Edinburgh, since 1374. There was a long association between the Prestons and the burgh of Edinburgh. From 1434 members of the family frequently acted as sheriff and lord provost and were among the patrons of the burgh church of St Giles, which had a Preston aisle founded within it in 1455, next to the existing family tomb in the Lady Aisle. The precious relic of the arm bone of St Giles, centrepiece of the annual St Giles's day procession, was presented by the family about 1450.

Simon Preston is mentioned as a bailie of Edinburgh on 24 August 1538. He served as lord provost between 1538 and 1543 and again in 1544–5. In 1538 he was one of the twelve who formed the official reception for Mary of Guise's arrival in Edinburgh. On 25 August 1540 he had a grant from the town of the office of common clerk for life, which was confirmed by a letter of privy seal two days later. On 5 June 1543 he and his second wife, Janet Beaton, a relative of Cardinal David Beaton, were granted the lands of Balgawy in Forfarshire and those of Craigmillar and Preston. In May 1544, when an English army under the earl of Hertford attacked Leith and Edinburgh, Craigmillar Castle was surrendered to the invaders, seemingly to avoid damage to it. The valuables placed in it by Edinburgh inhabitants for safe keeping were plundered, and Preston himself was taken to London as a prisoner. No details survive of his imprisonment and release, and little is known of his activities between then and the summer of 1560, when he travelled via London to France, in order, according to William Maitland of Lethington, who claimed to be a 'near relative', to recover debts owed to him by Mary of Guise (*Salisbury MSS*, 1.250). In January 1561 he was appointed by Queen Mary as one of the four commissioners to convey the news of the death of her husband, François II, to the Scottish privy council.

After her return to Scotland in August 1561 Mary was an occasional visitor to Craigmillar Castle, which lay barely 2 miles to the south of the royal palace of Holyroodhouse. The closeness of the link between her and Preston may be exaggerated: though he was perhaps in an inner circle of trusted friends of the queen, most of whom were minor lords or lairds, few of the royal visits to Craigmillar were

of any length, and it was not until 1565 that Preston, now advanced in years, experienced direct royal patronage. On 23 August 1565, against the background of the failed rebellion by Moray, and after a series of brushes with hardline protestants in the capital the queen dismissed the provost, Archibald Douglas of Kilspindie, who had held office continuously since the Reformation crisis of 1559–60, and replaced him with Preston. At the time of the burgh's annual election five weeks later, the queen imposed a leet on the burgh. Knox's description of those on it as 'a number of papists, the rest not worthy' (*History of the Reformation*, 2.171) was jaundiced and inaccurate. It did include some Roman Catholics, excluded from office since 1560, but it was made up mostly of substantial merchants who were moderate-minded protestants. The effect was that protestant activists were removed from office until after Mary was deposed in 1567.

The role of Preston of Craigmillar in the leet and after was ambiguous. His religious stance is also hard to pin down. It is no surprise that the patron of the burgh's cult of St Giles before the Reformation should have been regarded with suspicion by Knox, who condemned him as a 'right epicurean' for his loyalty to the queen after the Riccio murder. In the earlier crisis which followed the Darnley marriage and Moray conspiracy of 1565, however, Knox admitted that Preston had 'showed himself most willing to set forward religion, to punish vice and to maintain the commonwealth' (*History of the Reformation*, 2.113, 171). Yet Preston also had a number of Roman Catholic connections, and in April 1568 he conferred a free burgess-ship on his kinsman, David Hoppringle, even though two years earlier Hoppringle had fallen foul of the authorities for his marriage by Roman Catholic rites to the daughter of the royal macer Thomas Crichton.

Preston was Catholic in sympathies but probably a nominal protestant, and his concerns, like those of the bulk of the merchant and legal establishment in the capital, were conservative, eirenic, and consensual. As such he served the burgh well, occasionally defending it against heavy-handed action by Mary's administration. Against a background of growing resentment among the burgh's merchants at the crown's spiralling fiscal demands, in September 1565 Preston negotiated the purchase of the superiority of Leith for the burgh, in return for a loan of 10,000 merks to the queen. This was a turning point for the capital in its long efforts to secure control of its port. When the town clerk, Alexander Guthrie, was forfeited for his involvement in the Riccio murder in March 1566, Preston, sensitive to the threat to burgh privilege, opposed his replacement by a royal nominee. His actions during the attempted take-over of the burgh by Moray on 31 August 1565, and again on the night of the Riccio murder on 9 March 1566, showed a concern for order and authority which appealed to the conservative-minded burgh establishment as well as to the queen. Although Preston understandably failed to raise the town to resist Moray's forces entering the burgh, the rebels found little support and retreated on hearing of the approach of the royal army. In 1566 his actions were more decisive: according to Knox, Preston led about five hundred townspeople 'in warlike manner' down the High Street to Holyrood to defend the queen, but retreated on the order of Darnley (*History of the Reformation*, 2.180).

The balancing act continued afterwards. Although Preston continued as provost in October 1566 by means of another royal leet, which was seen as a further example of undesirable interference by the crown in burgh affairs, Preston survived the crisis which brought about the deposing of the queen in July 1567. He remained provost almost to the end of the Moray regency, until replaced by the more overtly Marian figure of William Kirkcaldy of Grange in September 1569. In November 1567 he arranged the gift to the town of the collegiate church of Trinity College, which was intended as a hospital. In the meantime his crucial role in providing stability in the capital as its provost had not prevented his entering royal service. He was appointed to the privy council on 5 November 1565, one of the lesser or professional men who lay behind its reorganization in 1565–6; his attendance was fairly regular. This brought him into association with Bothwell. He was also made keeper of the royal castle at Dunbar, where much of the Royal Artillery was housed, and appointed to a commission to oversee the royal ordnance.

It was during Mary's two-week stay at Craigmillar from 20 November 1566, recuperating from the sudden illness which had struck her at Jedburgh, that plans were discussed among key members of the privy council, including Lethington, Moray, and Argyll, for separating Darnley from the queen. Preston's role in the crisis which brought about the downfall of the queen in June 1567 was largely passive, though he was a party to the bond of 10 June seeking her deliverance from Bothwell. When she was brought into the capital by the confederate lords after Carberry, she was briefly lodged in his house on the north side of the High Street. Preston did not emerge into the open, either before or after Mary's forced imprisonment, as a queen's man. Six days after Mary's escape from Lochleven he entered into a bond with Kirkcaldy of Grange to maintain the cause of the infant king and the regent Moray. By the time Kirkcaldy took over the office of provost of Edinburgh from him in September 1569, Preston was ready to bow out of active politics. In June that year he had arranged formally to resign the lands and barony of Craigmillar to his heir apparent, David, the son of his first marriage, to Elizabeth, daughter of William Menteith of Kerse, Stirlingshire. By 12 June 1570 Preston was in Paris, from where he wrote to Sir William Cecil, informing him of a proposal made by Charles IX on behalf of Queen Mary. After that he fades from the record. He died some time before 8 March 1575.   MICHAEL LYNCH

Sources M. Lynch, *Edinburgh and the Reformation* (1981) · M. Wood and T. B. Whitson, *The lord provosts of Edinburgh, 1296 to 1932* (1932), 28 · T. van Heijnsbergen, 'The interaction between literature and history in Queen Mary's Edinburgh: the Bannatyne manuscript and its prosopographical context', *The Renaissance in Scotland: studies in literature, religion, history, and culture offered to John Durkan*, ed. A. A. MacDonald and others (1994), 183–225, esp. 203, 213, 225 · *Scots peerage*, vol. 3 · M. H. B. Sanderson, *Cardinal of Scotland: David Beaton, c.1494–1546* (1986) · J. D. Maurick, ed., *Extracts from the records of the burgh of Edinburgh, 1528–71*, [3–4], Scottish Burgh RS, 4–5 (1871–4) · J. M. Thomson and others, eds., *Registrum magni sigilli regum Scotorum / The register of the great seal of Scotland*, 11 vols. (1882–1914), vol. 2 · *John Knox's History of the Reformation in Scotland*, ed. W. C. Dickinson, 2 vols. (1949) · *Reg. PCS*, 1st ser. · *CSP Scot., 1547–71* · *CSP for., 1560–61* · *Lettres, instructions et mémoires de Marie Stuart, reine d'Écosse*, ed. A. Labanoff, 7 vols. (1852), vol. 1 · T. Thomson, ed., *A diurnal of remarkable occurrents that have passed within the country of Scotland*, Bannatyne Club, 43 (1833) · *The protocol book of John Foular*, ed. J. Durkan, 4, Scottish RS, new ser., 10 (1985)

Preston, Thomas (*fl.* 1542–1559), composer, is an obscure figure; documentary sources from Oxford, Cambridge, and Windsor omit the first name. He is known as an important composer of organ music for the Catholic liturgy. A Preston was master of the choristers at Magdalen College, Oxford, in 1542–3, and the same name is found in the archives of Trinity College, Cambridge, in the years 1548–59. He originally appears there as a college servant (though probably as organist); later lists show him among the chapel staff, and it is clear that by 1554–5, at least, he was in charge of the newly established choristers and at the head of the singing-men. In 1558 and 1559 he received payments among allowances due to absent fellows. In 1558–9 a man of the same name appears as clerk, organist, and 'instructor choristarum' at St George's, Windsor, where Marbeck was similarly employed as 'magister choristarum' ('supervisor of the choristers') in that period. 'Prestonus, in oppido Vindelisoriensi' is listed, along with Sebastian (Westcote) of St Paul's and Thorne of York, in Nicholas Sander's *De visibili monarchia ecclesiae* (1571) as a musician ejected from office for confessing the papal primacy. Although this assertion requires qualification in Westcote's case, there is indeed no subsequent documentary record of a musician named Preston. The will of a Thomas Preston of Sawston in Cambridgeshire, proved at the consistory court of Ely on 26 April 1564, cannot be shown to be that of the composer.

Apart from the will, none of this documentation is intrinsically unlikely to refer to Thomas Preston the composer. A move from a responsible post at Magdalen to what appears to be the corresponding one at Trinity is not difficult to account for. The evidence from Trinity and Windsor is also easily reconciled, and almost certainly concerns Thomas Preston. It probably does not relate to John Preston, organist of the parish church of St Dunstan-in-the-West, London, in 1544–5, though it may be he, rather than Thomas, who wrote the work attributed to 'Preston' in the earliest section of BL, Add. MS 29996. All the organ music attributed explicitly or implicitly to Thomas Preston survives uniquely in a later section of the same manuscript.

The style of Thomas Preston's organ music is consistent with compositional activity in the reign of Queen Mary. It is all conceived for performance in the Catholic liturgy, unless, as is likely, he also wrote the anonymous non-liturgical piece 'Uppon la mi re' in the same manuscript. Other than this, sixteen works for organ exist, the last incomplete and hence without attribution. Much of it is densely contrapuntal in idiom. Two ensemble pieces survive: an In nomine for strings and a three-part setting of the faburden of the hymn *O lux beata trinitas*. Apart from the intrinsic interest of his music, Preston was an innovator who influenced John Bull and Thomas Tomkins, the latter of whom owned the manuscript in which all of Preston's known keyboard music survives.

JOHN CALDWELL

Sources D. Mateer, 'Further light on Preston and Whyte', *MT*, 115 (1974), 1074–7 · I. Payne, *The provision and practice of sacred music at Cambridge colleges and selected cathedrals, c.1547–c.1646* (1993), esp. 276–8 · E. H. Fellowes, *Organists and masters of the choristers of St George's Chapel in Windsor Castle* (1939), pp. 22–3 and pl. 4 · N. Sanders, *De visibili monarchia ecclesiae* (Louvain, 1571), 702 · T. Morley, *A plaine and easie introduction to practicall musicke* (1597), 96 · F. L. Harrison, *Music in medieval Britain* (1958), 192, 217, 364–6, 394–5 · J. R. Bloxam, *A register of the presidents, fellows … of Saint Mary Magdalen College*, 8 vols. (1853–85), vol. 2, p. 190 · D. Stevens, 'Thomas Preston's organ mass', *Music and Letters*, 39 (1958), 29–34 · J. Caldwell, *English keyboard music before the nineteenth century* (1973), 21–2, 32–7, 49–51 · J. Caldwell, ed., *Early Tudor organ music, 1: Music for the office*, Early English Church Music, 6 (1966) · D. Stevens, ed., *Early Tudor organ music, 2: Music for the mass*, Early English Church Music, 10 (1969) · P. Doe, ed., *Elizabethan consort music*, 1, Musica Britannica, 44 (1979)

Preston, Thomas (1537–1598), playwright and college head, was born at Simpson, Buckinghamshire, of a Lancashire family. He was educated at Eton College and at King's College, Cambridge, where he was elected scholar on 16 August 1553 and fellow on 18 September 1556. He graduated BA in 1557 and MA in 1561. He made a favourable impression on Elizabeth I when she visited Cambridge in 1564 for his performance in the tragedy of *Dido*; for his 'gracefull gesture … and propernesse of person' as a disputant in a philosophy act—despite having the difficult task of refuting the statement 'monarchia est optimus status reipublicæ' ('monarchy is the best form for a state'); and for his oration upon her departure, at which Elizabeth dubbed him 'her scholar' and gave him the not inconsiderable pension of £20 a year (Fuller, 264; Cooper, *Annals*, 2.196). In 1565 he was a proctor in the university. He was directed by his college to study civil law in 1572, and subsequently proceeded to the degree of LLD, possibly in 1576. In 1581 he resigned his fellowship, perhaps in order to marry, since when he was appointed master of Trinity Hall he was the first married man to occupy the post. He was elected to this office by royal mandate in 1585, having been recommended as a man 'void of faction' (Crawley, 66), and on 17 May 1586 his name was entered in the subscription book of the College of Advocates, where, as master of Trinity Hall, he was entitled to lodge. In 1589–90 he served as the university's vice-chancellor. He was admitted an advocate in the court of arches on 17 June 1591.

The best-known work attributed to Preston is the play *Cambises*, which, although licensed to John Allde in 1569–70, could have been written as early as 1560 when it may have been presented at court over Christmas. Comprising thirty-eight parts for eight players, this play is deemed to be innovative both in terms of its staging requirements and as a hybrid dramatic form which marked the transition from the morality play to the tragedies and history plays of Marlowe and Shakespeare. Despite its innovative qualities *Cambises* has also been derogated for its 'gross bombast' and 'absurd ineptitudes' (Wilson, 144), and its plodding couplets in fourteeners, interwoven with unmetrical verse spoken by the character of the Vice. The play was ridiculed by contemporaries, and was notably parodied by Shakespeare in Bottom's play in *A Midsummer Night's Dream* and in *1 Henry IV*, when Falstaff is made to 'speak in passion … in King Cambises' vein' (II.v)—although such parody indirectly suggests the popularity of the play. Perhaps because of the work's more flamboyant qualities Preston's authorship has been questioned, and *Cambises*—together with an anti-Catholic ballad of 1570 entitled 'A Lamentation from Rome' (narrated from the perspective of a fly lodged in the pope's nose) which was also penned by a Thomas Preston—is sometimes attributed to an itinerant actor–playwright rather than the master of Trinity Hall. Two other ballads bear Preston's name, and he was undisputedly the author of Latin verses compiled by the university on the restitution of Bucer and Fagius in 1560, and at the end of Carr's *Demosthenis … orationes* (1571).

Preston died intestate on 1 June 1598, and inventories amounting to more than £450 worth of goods left at his chambers in Doctors' Commons, his house in Barnwell, Cambridge, and in the master's lodging at Trinity Hall, suggest that he died a wealthy man. He was buried in Trinity Hall chapel, where a brass monument commissioned by his widow, Alice, still remains near the altar, commemorating him with an effigy and a Latin inscription.

ALEXANDRA SHEPARD

Sources Cooper, *Ath. Cantab.* · T. Fuller, *The history of the University of Cambridge from the conquest to the year 1634*, ed. M. Prickett and T. Wright (1840) · C. H. Cooper, *Annals of Cambridge*, 2 (1843) · G. D. Squibb, *Doctors' Commons: a history of the College of Advocates and Doctors of Law* (1977) · Arber, *Regs. Stationers* · J. P. Collier, ed., *Old ballads, from early printed copies of the utmost rarity*, Percy Society (1840) · R. C. Johnson, *A critical edition of Thomas Preston's 'Cambises'*, Salzburg Studies in English Literature, 23 (1975) · E. K. Chambers, *The Elizabethan stage*, 4 vols. (1923) · T. W. Craik, *Minor Elizabethan tragedies* (1974) · F. P. Wilson, *English drama, 1485–1585*, ed. G. K. Hunter (1986) · P. Happé, *English drama before Shakespeare* (1999) · university administration bonds, CUL, department of manuscripts and university archives, bundle 2 · inventories, 1598, CUL, department of manuscripts and university archives, bundle 6 · brass monument, Trinity Hall chapel, Cambridge · C. Crawley, *Trinity Hall: the history of a Cambridge college, 1350–1975*, new edn (1992)
Likenesses monumental brass effigy, Trinity Hall, Cambridge
Wealth at death approx. £450: inventory, university inventories, bundle 6, CUL, department of manuscripts and university archives

Preston, Thomas, first Viscount Tara (*b.* in or after **1585**, *d.* **1655**), soldier, was the second son of Christopher Preston, fourth Viscount Gormanstown (1536/7–1600), and his second wife, Catherine Fitzwilliam (*d.* 1602?), daughter of Sir Thomas Fitzwilliam of Baggotsrath, co. Dublin. Preston may have been the brother of the fifth viscount who was reported in December 1600 as receiving his education at the Irish house at Douai (Douai College) alongside other sons of Old English families.

Spanish service As a younger son of a Catholic family, albeit the leading family of the pale, Preston chose military service abroad because it was one of the relatively few careers open to him. In 1605 he recruited a company in Ireland and proceeded to the Spanish Netherlands (later the Southern Netherlands) where he was commissioned in Henry O'Neill's regiment. In 1608 he was pitched into a controversy between Old English captains and their colonel, the son of Hugh O'Neill, earl of Tyrone. The rift over questions of allegiance and to the crown arose 'from a speech of Preston's upon Henry's discourse tending to make war and raise troubles within this kingdom [Ireland]; to which he answered, it was not lawful, neither would he ever bear arms against his sovereign' (Henry, *The Irish Military Community*, 142). Also in 1608 Preston served at the siege of Rheinberg on the German frontier. The regiment was scattered in garrison duties throughout most of the period of the truce with the Dutch (1609–21) apart from Spinola's Palatinate campaign of 1620.

Preston married a daughter of Charles vander Eycken, from one of the most powerful and wealthy families in Brabant, shortly after 1612. They had two sons and a daughter; the sons—Anthony and James, or Diego—were to play an active part in the confederate armies and both fought at the battle of Rathconnell, co. Westmeath, in 1643. Their mother died on 28 October 1621, and Preston married Marguerite de Namur, a widow, about 1623. Though certainly alive two years before Preston's death, she was to predecease him. They had five daughters and a son.

Preston fought with O'Neill's regiment in the initial stages of the siege of Breda (1624–5). By March 1625, three months before the end of the siege, he had left the regiment and recruited a company of Irish cuirassiers. Preston's departure from the Irish regiment probably resulted from tensions with Owen Roe O'Neill, the acting regimental commander. These tensions arose from the outbreak of hostilities between Spain and England in 1625 when English officials tried to persuade Preston and other Old English officers of the Irish regiment to leave the Spanish service. However, the company was disbanded in September 1625, just six months after its inception. Preston was subsequently maintained as an *entretenido*. This status commonly referred to an officer without a command receiving an additional allowance while serving, in effect, as a rank and file soldier. In May 1629 Stadholder Frederick Henry besieged 's-Hertogenbosch, one of the four principal cities of Brabant. Preston served with the Spanish relief force which initially approached the besiegers but then swung eastwards to link up with imperial forces. The joint force then crossed the Ysel to launch a diversionary raid on the more vulnerable eastern flank of the United Provinces. The expedition overran the Veluwe in Gelderland and captured Amersfoort in Utrecht, thereby penetrating to the heart of the United Provinces. However, Frederick Henry was not to be distracted and 's-Hertogenbosch fell in September.

The Anglo-Spanish *rapprochement* of 1629–30 reopened the possibility of large scale recruiting in Ireland and, in January 1632, Preston was promoted major in a new regiment, Tyrconnel's, with instructions to recruit in Ireland. His encouragement to would-be captains to raise companies from the new regiment was the subject of complaints by the lords justices in Ireland who were, apparently, not supportive of the new pro-Spanish foreign policy. However, the arrival of Lord Deputy Wentworth smoothed Preston's path. Wentworth's partiality is evident from his praise of Preston as 'a faithful friend' and 'one of the civilest gentlemen of his nation' (Jennings, 574). In August 1634 Preston was commissioned to form another regiment on his own behalf comprising fifteen companies, each of 200 men. In the event he recruited 2400 men and was back in the Southern Netherlands by April 1635 in time for the long-threatened hostilities with France. The French invaded with an enormous field army of some 26,000 soldiers, their advance being in tandem with Dutch attacks in the north. Preston's regiment played a crucial part in repulsing the French incursion as one of four regiments which held Louvain for eleven days against vastly superior enemy forces. Preston was in charge of two of the city gates against which the French directed their attack and his regiment lost seventy men in counter-attacks. This was the start of a period of heavy attrition for the 7000 or more soldiers in the four Irish *tercios*. The following year, 1636, saw the Cardinal Infante invade northern France and capture Corbie before being forced to withdraw. Preston's regiment probably took part in the invasion; at any rate in November 1636 it was disbanded because it was significantly under-strength and the individual soldiers were transferred to top up Tyrconnel's regiment. Once again Preston was an officer without a field command. In 1641 he was governor of Gennepp, a small city on the eastern borders of the United Provinces. He beat off a storming party after the walls were breached before surrendering in July 'upon honourable terms with no little glory to himself' (Carte, 1.367).

The Irish rising Following the Irish rising of 1641 Preston and Owen Roe O'Neill were chosen to reinforce the insurgents with professional leadership and munitions. In December 1642 Preston was formally commissioned as general of the Leinster provincial army of the Catholic confederates. Preston doubtless owed his appointment partly to the fact that his nephew Nicholas, sixth Viscount Gormanstown, was then the political leader of the Leinster confederates. At any rate he was not picked entirely for his military qualities to judge from the character sketch penned by Hugh de Burgo, the Franciscan mainly responsible for organizing the expedition from the Southern Netherlands. Writing to Luke Wadding at Rome he described Preston as 'very brave, but not a man of much prudence; true it is that he is more popular than the other [O'Neill], but there is absolutely no comparison between the two talents' (*Franciscan MSS*, 145). Traditionally Preston has suffered in comparisons between the two contemporaries and rivals. However, he has not been sufficiently credited for his skill in siege warfare. Admittedly he started inauspiciously after his landing in mid-September when he failed to prevent a relief force from resupplying Ballinakill, a strong protestant garrison a mere 8 miles from the confederate Catholic capital of Kilkenny. After building up his forces he captured Borris, Birr, and Fort Falkland near Banagher, between 30 December 1642 and 27 January 1643, thereby opening a direct route from Kilkenny towards Connaught.

In March 1643 Ormond, the king's representative, marched from Dublin to capture New Ross in order to cut off Kilkenny, and confederate Ireland, from its major ports of Wexford and Waterford. Ormond failed to take New Ross and Preston tried to block his retreat northwards at Ballinvegga. Preston's handling of the battle of Ballinvegga, or Ross, could be faulted in that he deployed his cavalry to attack along a narrow *boreen* lined with hedgerows and covered by enemy artillery. The results were predictably demoralizing. Critics who blamed Preston for not choosing a better blocking position further to the north-west ignored the fact that, had he done so Ormond would have been able to veer north-eastwards and retrace his original line of march. Preston's fault was not in his choice of terrain but his handling of the cavalry. Nor can he be especially blamed for the poor performance of the infantry, who were overwhelmingly poorly trained local militia. Preston redeemed himself by finally capturing Ballinakill in May with the aid of a newly acquired 24-pounder siege gun. He next mobilized a core of 2000 regulars and, supplemented by local militia, spent the early summer trying to eliminate the dense pocket of protestant garrisons—Edenderry, Castlejordan, Portlester, and Athboy—blocking the route from the west, through the midland bogs, towards Dublin. In mid-August, however, he was obliged to disband his army 'for want of means' (Gilbert, 1.48).

The cessation of September 1643 with Ormond left, for the moment, no enemy forces in Leinster. Not until the garrison of Duncannon rejected the cessation and allied themselves with the parliamentarians in Munster did Preston see action again. His siege (20 January – 19 March 1645) of this promontory fort, dominating the approaches to Waterford and New Ross, showed Preston at his best. Duncannon was exceptionally well-fortified yet, despite the rigours of a mid-winter siege, Preston lost remarkably few men through sickness and sustained only 67 killed in action from an army of some 1300 soldiers. The capture involved the innovative use of parallel trenches connecting the saps (the first known parallels were dug by the French at the siege of Gravelines in 1644), plunging mortar fire, direct fire to deter enemy shipping, undermining, and a final assault by the infantry. Later in the campaigning season he was sent by the supreme council to Youghal to assist the earl of Castlehaven in capturing the town. Castlehaven saw Preston's arrival as an implied slight on his conduct of the siege and, moving camp away from the town, he declined to co-operate. Preston eventually abandoned the siege after an assault on the town was beaten back.

The following summer Preston again campaigned outside Leinster. While half his army (by now expanded to 6000 regular infantry and 600 cavalry) was sent to besiege Bunratty in co. Clare he himself led the remainder into Connaught. The object of this campaign was to eliminate the protestant-held garrisons in co. Roscommon which had rejected the cessation. He was then to recapture Sligo, lost the previous year. Preston carried out his initial objectives and beat off a force which tried to relieve Roscommon Castle. However, he declined to move north from Boyle and cross the Curlew Mountains, pleading that the countryside towards Sligo was stripped bare of provisions.

Between Rinuccini and Ormond Meanwhile, the 'Ormond peace' was proclaimed at Kilkenny and Dublin (30 July – 3 August 1646). This treaty referred the repeal of the penal laws against Catholics 'to his Majestie's gracious favour', while the confederates agreed to dissolve their government before the actual granting of such concessions. It was, in short, 'a poor return on almost four years of war' (M. Ó Siochru, *Confederate Ireland, 1642–1649: a Constitutional and Political Analysis*, 1999, 111). Rinuccini, the papal nuncio, rejected the terms on the grounds that they were unfavourable to Catholic interests and threatened to excommunicate all who accepted them. The Leinster army occupied a pivotal role between a clericalist Ulster army and an Ormondist Munster army and Preston was persuaded by the nuncio to join with Owen Roe O'Neill and capture Dublin from Ormond. The importance of their mutual distrust has been exaggerated; at any rate it was not the sole reason why the operation failed. The Dublin hinterland had been stripped of foodstuffs by Ormond, bridges and mills destroyed, while heavy rains had reduced supplies from further afield to a trickle. In the circumstances, campaigning with the largest force ever mustered by the confederation (at least 20,000 soldiers and camp followers) posed insurmountable logistical difficulties. Preston's unauthorized agreement with the earl of Clanricarde, Ormond's intermediary, convinced O'Neill that Preston was plotting against him and a false report that parliamentarian troops had reinforced Dublin precipitated O'Neill's retreat from his camp at Leixlip. In late November Preston withdrew from his camp at Lucan to Naas, complaining that O'Neill's retreat had left him dangerously exposed. He continued to intrigue with Ormond, with the intention, perhaps, of launching a joint attack on the clericalists or sailing with most of his army for France. On the face of it, it seems improbable that he would have sided with France against Spain given his previous service. However, Sir Kenelm Digby later claimed that Preston had secured the agreement of most of the Leinster army while Ormond obtained permission from the parliament to embark the soldiers for France. Moreover Preston's son James, having recently recruited a regiment for the Spanish service, apparently connived at the interception of the troopships and the transfer of the regiment to the French service.

To forestall more intrigues Rinuccini formally threatened Preston and his army with excommunication if the army did not disperse to its assigned winter quarters. Preston complied on 10 December, though even then he allegedly wrote to Ormond urging him to attack the Ulster army. Ormond evidently did not trust Preston because he was 'too much of a bigot in the point of religion and so wavering in his mind, so changeable in his resolutions' (Carte, 1.589). At any rate Clanricarde's agreement had served its main purpose: '… it had saved Dublin and divided the confederates' (ibid., 593). Ormond's army subsequently foraged in the confederate quarters of Westmeath and Cavan, thereby provoking a definitive breakdown in negotiations. Ormond himself handed over Dublin to the parliamentarians and left Ireland shortly afterwards, his army passing to the command of the new commander, Michael Jones. Preston's orders for the campaigning season of 1647 were to constrict Jones to Dublin, and to starve him out by burning the corn and driving off cattle. By late July Preston was encamped near Naas when Jones, with a much smaller army, attacked the camp. After some cannon shot the attackers retreated in some disorder. Preston hesitated about unleashing the cavalry to follow up this success, thereby giving Jones time to escape, conduct which Bellings criticized as 'supine remissness'. By the end of the month Preston had captured Maynooth, co. Kildare, and other outlying garrisons and was besieging Trim, co. Meath. Jones again marched from Dublin but this time hugged the coast until he joined with British forces from Ulster and the Drogheda garrison. With an army almost equal in size to Preston's he then marched to relieve Trim.

Dungan's Hill 'General Preston was much blamed for his conduct in losing that army, for had he stayed within Portlester-pass, as Mac Art [O'Neill] sent him advice … but he did not but thought to do the work himself but his fate was otherwise' (Hogan, 62). The 'British Officer's' criticisms go to the heart of the matter; Preston could have avoided battle. He was faced with an army which now enjoyed numerical parity, if only for the ten days Jones could afford to pay his auxiliaries. Moreover, Jones had the edge in the decisive cavalry arm, both quantitatively and qualitatively. Preston knew all this and could have remained within the impregnable bog-girt confines of Portlester. Instead he tried to steal a march on Jones by making a forced march on Dublin which was thinly garrisoned by a former royalist regiment of apparently doubtful loyalty. He stole away, leaving his tents and colours standing to deceive the enemy and marched some 12 miles to the south-east that day. This was not sufficient to outpace Jones and the following morning, 8 August 1647, he was overtaken. He deployed his forces on Dungan's Hill (about half-way between Trim and Maynooth) to receive the enemy.

The commentator who exulted that Dungan's Hill was 'the greatest victory and most signal victory the English ever had in Ireland' (Borlase, 242) was hardly exaggerating. At least 3000 of the Leinster infantry were slain (out of about 5000 on the battlefield), mainly after the battle, as against the loss of a mere forty, or so, of their enemies. The scale of the slaughter together with the loss of transport, munitions, and arms destroyed what was, arguably, the best organized and equipped of the confederate armies. Defeat, if not annihilation, was predictable given

Preston's relative weakness in cavalry. He compounded this by, as at Ross, deploying his best cavalry troops in a narrow lane where their mobility was fatally constricted.

The long-term effects of the battle may be grasped from the fact that, a year later, Preston's own regiment consisted of a mere 200 soldiers and the Leinster army contained only four under-strength infantry regiments. In 1648, following a truce with Inchiquin, the internal power struggle erupted into open warfare between the clericalists and Ormondists. Preston played a role commensurate with the depleted size of his army, capturing minor garrisons of O'Neill in co. Kildare. When Ormond returned to Ireland to assume command of the new pan-royalist alliance Preston wrote (12 October) pointing out his services in keeping the Leinster army together for the king. In return Ormond, on 28 December 1648, promised him a peerage and a commensurate estate from lands to be forfeited from those opposing the king.

Royalist commander Preston was not given command of a field army, however, and did not play a prominent part in the fighting after Cromwell landed in August 1649. In the spring of 1650 he was appointed governor of Waterford, which had held out against Cromwell the previous December. Increasingly the city was isolated as the royalists were pushed back towards the north and west. The isolation was complete after Hugh *dubh* O'Neill abandoned Clonmel for want of ammunition in May 1650. Apart from his failure to resupply O'Neill, Preston's conduct of the defence cannot be faulted. When Ireton approached the city in June and offered terms Preston replied spiritedly that he had never been asked to surrender a city without a siege, nor had conditions ever been offered to him before he asked for them. He surrendered on good terms in August only on the advice of Ormond and at the insistence of the citizenry, by now suffering from famine and bubonic plague.

During the siege Preston was created Viscount Tara and his next important appointment was as governor of Galway, the last city in Irish hands. Ireton, writing from Clare Castle in November 1651, demanded the surrender of the city and, if this were not forthcoming, threatened 'you may guess whose head shall pay for the trouble and mischief that shall follow' (Hardiman, 134). Preston dismissed Ireton's threats and added that 'such as hazard men's lives without a just cause will one day answer for their blood before God, the just judge, in which (when you reflect on your own actions) you will find yourself as guilty as others' (ibid.).

This acrimonious correspondence was cut short by Ireton's death from the plague. The following month Charles Coote set about shutting off the landward approaches to Galway but made no attempt to storm the city defences, which had recently been strengthened with the addition of an outer curtain and bastions. Preston conducted an active defence, most notably in surprising and wiping out the parliamentarian detachment on Mutton Island. However, his attempts to run the naval blockade failed and civilian morale crumbled with the prospect of famine.

The town surrendered on 5 April 1652 on terms as good as those originally offered by Ireton.

Subsequently Preston was allowed by parliament to embark 4000 or 5000 soldiers for the Spanish service. However, by the autumn of 1653 he had moved to Paris where his offer to serve the exiled Charles II was declined. He then offered his services to the French, apparently to encourage Irish deserters from the Spanish. He died in Paris in October 1655, and was buried there on 21 October.

Assessment Preston's skill in siege warfare was especially useful to the confederates in the early years of their war effort. He was, however, an incompetent battlefield commander. Preston's shortcomings may be attributed to inexperience of cavalry warfare and, more especially, of large-scale command. For most of his career, other than an eighteen-month period (1635–6) as regimental commander, he commanded nothing larger than an infantry company. Nor was he deft at political intrigue. He was 'very cholerick … and broke out, even in Councils of War, into rash expressions, of which he had frequently cause to repent' (Carte, 1.589). Moreover his vacillations between Rinuccini and Ormond were the result of genuine doubts about the religious concessions. Had he thrown his weight unreservedly behind either faction the power struggle might have had a decisive outcome. A definitive victory by either party would have been preferable to the perpetuation of debilitating factionalism. In particular a quick assault on Dublin in 1646 by the combined forces of the Ulster and Leinster armies might very well have taken Dublin from Ormond before he handed the city over to the parliamentarians. In large measure because of Preston's dithering the siege was protracted to the point that the armies used up available supplies and had to retreat. Had the confederates taken Dublin they would have denied Cromwell a convenient beachhead for his landing in 1649. Preston's ill-advised attempt to surprise Dublin the following year led to the destruction of his army at Dungan's Hill. This disaster, and the confederate defeat at Knocknanuss in Munster later in 1647, ultimately brought about the collapse of the Catholic confederates. For all his undoubted skill and courage in siege warfare, both in the Southern Netherlands and Ireland, Preston's record in Ireland is mainly characterized by political and military ineptitude.   PÁDRAIG LENIHAN

Sources B. Jennings, ed., *Wild geese in Spanish Flanders, 1582–1700*, IMC (1964), 78, 81, 194, 195, 199, 259, 260, 261, 272, 282–3, 288, 295, 297, 306, 355, 385, 389, 495, 497, 574, 588–9, 591–3 · T. Carte, *An history of the life of James, duke of Ormonde*, 3 vols. (1735–6), vol. 1, pp. 367, 369, 381–2, 402–7, 428, 449, 587–9, 592–5 · B. O'Ferrall and D. O'Connell, *Commentarius Rinuccinianus de sedis apostolicae legatione ad foederatos Hiberniae Catholicos per annos 1645–1649*, ed. J. Kavanagh, IMC, 1 (1932), 337, 523 · B. O'Ferrall and D. O'Connell, *Commentarius Rinuccinianus de sedis apostolicae legatione ad foederatos Hiberniae Catholicos per annos 1645–1649*, ed. J. Kavanagh, IMC, 2 (1936), 26, 173, 186, 261–5, 357–60, 392, 423–7, 437, 446–8, 450–62, 476–8, 663–77 · B. O'Ferrall and D. O'Connell, *Commentarius Rinuccinianus de sedis apostolicae legatione ad foederatos Hiberniae Catholicos per annos 1645–1649*, ed. J. Kavanagh, IMC, 3 (1939), 57–60, 147–8 · B. O'Ferrall and D. O'Connell, *Commentarius Rinuccinianus de sedis apostolicae legatione ad foederatos Hiberniae Catholicos per annos 1645–1649*, ed. J. Kavanagh, IMC, 4 (1941), 5, 12, 444–7 · B. O'Ferrall and D. O'Connell, *Commentarius Rinuccinianus de sedis apostolicae legatione ad foederatos Hiberniae Catholicos per annos 1645–1649*, ed. J. Kavanagh, IMC, 5 (1944), 102–3 · J. T. Gilbert, *A contemporary history of affairs in Ireland from 1641 to 1652*, 3 vols. (1879–80), vol. 1, pp. 45, 48, 57–8, 60–62, 64–5, 102–4, 124; vol. 2, pp. 79–81, 154–7, 164; vol. 3, pp. 240, 712 · *CSP dom., 1598–1601*, 496 · *CSP Ire., 1633–47*, 374–5, 552–3, 544–5, 557–8, 585, 603–4, 613–15, 627, 688–9 · *History of the Irish confederation and the war in Ireland … by Richard Bellings*, ed. J. T. Gilbert, 7 vols. (1882–91), vol. 1, pp. 90–94; vol. 2, pp. 128–34, 161, 168–9, 191–2; vol. 4, pp. 18, 189, 210–36, 238; vol. 6, pp. 45, 162, 167, 286; vol. 7, pp. 28–33, 171 · J. Touchet, earl of Castlehaven, *The earl of Castlehaven's review, or, His memoirs of his engagement and carriage in the Irish wars, enlarged and corrected* (1684), 53, 77–8, 171 · [E. Hogan], *The history of the warr of Ireland from 1641 to 1653* (1873), 62 · [E. Borlase], *The history of the execrable Irish rebellion* (1652), 242 · J. Hardiman, *The history of the town and county of the town of Galway* (1820), 133–9 · G. Baron, 'The siege of Duncannon', *The Franciscan monasteries and the Irish hierarchy in the seventeenth century*, ed. C. P. Meehan (1872), 272–80 · G. Henry, '"Wild geese" in Spanish Flanders: the first generation, 1586–1610', *Irish Sword*, 17 (1987–9), 189–201, esp. 189 · G. Henry, *The Irish military community in Spanish Flanders, 1586–1621* (1992), 27–8, 40, 49, 63, 72, 88–9, 142–3, 180 · GEC, *Peerage*

Likenesses engraving, 1645 (after unknown portrait), repro. in *History of the Irish confederation*, vol. 4, frontispiece · portrait, Gormanstown Castle, co. Meath, Ireland

Preston, Thomas (1774–1850), radical, was born in London, the son of unknown parents. His father died when he was in his infancy, and when his mother remarried the baby was given to a nurse to look after; at the age of six months an accident left him with a limp for the rest of his life. After a limited education he was apprenticed in turn to a silversmith and a shoemaker, and then spent years tramping around England and Ireland, in Cork leading a successful shoemakers' strike. On returning to London, probably in 1794, he joined the London Corresponding Society, but during Pitt's repression in the mid-1790s he went to Chatham to avoid imprisonment. After a trip to the West Indies he settled again in London and married a widow with three children, details of whom are unknown; they had four children, at least three girls reaching adulthood. The couple ran three shoemaker's shops, employing forty people, and prospered. But in 1807 Preston's wife left him for another man, his business soon failed, and he fell into poverty. A supporter of Sir Francis Burdett in 1810, he was active in several literary and debating clubs, and in 1811 became a supporter of Thomas Spence and his advocacy of common ownership of land. After Spence's death in 1814 his followers formed a regular society of Spencean Philanthropists, with Preston a leading member and known as the Bishop because of his use of the Bible in support of Spenceanism. In 1816 the Spenceans tried to capitalize on the widespread poverty and unemployment in London. Preston joined a society of artisans campaigning for limitations on the use of machinery, not from any agreement with their aims but in the hope of raising an agitation, and as their secretary it was he who called the famous meeting at Spa Fields to petition parliament and the prince regent for relief. The Spenceans James Watson and Arthur Thistlewood played the leading role in organizing this meeting, and Preston organized support among the unemployed silk-weavers of Spitalfields. At the second Spa Fields meeting on 2 December 1816, Thistlewood, Preston, and Watson's son, also James, tried to start an armed rising and led a section of the crowd into the City, where they were soon dispersed. Preston was among those arrested and one of the four charged with high treason, but the acquittal of Watson after the unmasking of an agent provocateur, John Castles, led to the dropping of the charges against the rest.

For the next three years Watson, Thistlewood, and Preston were the leaders of the London group of ultra-radicals and revolutionaries, with Preston the most committed Spencean, although while Watson favoured open mass action the other two preferred secret conspiracies. Late in 1819 they were the leaders of what became known as the Cato Street conspiracy to assassinate members of the government, the inner circle meeting at Preston's house, but he avoided prosecution when the attempt failed in February 1820 [see Cato Street conspirators (act. 1820)].

Preston was not very active in the 1820s, but remained a member of a radical group in the East End of London, and in the early 1830s became a leading figure in the ultra-radical National Union of the Working Classes. At some point he also remarried and had a son. In 1834, in distressed circumstances and embittered, he published a plan, drawing on proposals by Spence and Thomas Paine, for state pensions for the aged, widows, the sick, and orphans, funded by a special tax and death duties (including appropriation of land as the means to ultimate national ownership of all land). In the later 1830s he was an associate of veteran Spenceans and new radical figures such as Julian Harney, and in the 1840s was an occasional lecturer at Chartist meetings. He also published further pamphlets on his plan for state pensions, but none of these have survived. He benefited from relief funds raised by radicals, but died in London on 1 June 1850 in extreme poverty. A collection financed his burial at Bunhill Fields cemetery; the funeral, attended by over 400 people, was led by Harney and Luke Hansard. He was survived by his second wife and son. IORWERTH PROTHERO

Sources T. Preston, *The life and opinions of Thomas Preston, patriot and shoemaker* (1817) · I. J. Prothero, *Artisans and politics in early nineteenth-century London: John Gast and his times* (1979) · M. Chase, *The people's farm: English radical agrarianism, 1775–1840* (1988) · I. McCalman, *Radical underworld: prophets, revolutionaries, and pornographers in London, 1795–1840* (1988) · Home Office MSS, PRO, HO 40/3–9; 42/155–203; 44/1–6; TS 11/197–203 · *Northern Star* (8 June 1850) · *Northern Star* (15 June 1850)
Archives PRO, Home Office MSS
Likenesses W. Holl, group portrait, stipple, pubd 1817 (*Spa Fields rioters*; after G. Scharf), BM, NPG; *see illus. in* Watson, James (1766–1838)
Wealth at death in extreme poverty: *Northern Star* (1850)

Preston, Thomas (1860–1900), physicist, was born on 23 May 1860 in Ballyhagan, Kilmore, co. Armagh, Ireland, the youngest of three sons, the eldest of whom died young, of Abraham Dawson Preston, a gentleman farmer of Mulladry, Kilmore, and his wife, Anne, daughter of John Hall,

quartermaster, and widow of John Ritchie, from which marriage she had a daughter. He was educated at the Royal School, Armagh, and graduated from the Royal University of Ireland in 1884 and from Trinity College, Dublin, in 1885. In Dublin he studied under G. F. Fitzgerald, the mathematical natural philosopher.

In 1886 Preston published *A Treatise in Spherical Trigonometry* with his cousin W. J. McClelland, which ran to several editions. In 1890 he published the first of his two major textbooks, *Theory of Light*, followed by *Theory of Heat* in 1894. These, with many subsequent editions, became standard textbooks for undergraduates until the Second World War. In 1891 he became professor of natural philosophy at University College, Dublin, a position he held until his death, and he was later appointed a fellow of the Royal University of Ireland. In addition to this he held a government post as inspector of science and arts for Irish schools from 1894. In 1895 he married Katherine Mary [see Preston, Katherine Mary], daughter of Thomas McEwen, dominie of Baldernock School. They had one daughter and two sons, one of whom died in infancy; the other, George Dawson *Preston, became a notable physicist. His widow became a pioneer of education for women in Ireland as principal of Alexandra College, Dublin.

Preston's fame rests on his discovery of the anomalous Zeeman effect, which he first reported in a paper presented to the Royal Dublin Society in December 1897. His discovery led to contacts with leading physicists who were investigating the recently discovered Zeeman effect (the way in which atomic spectra are influenced by magnetism), including Joseph John Thomson, William Thomson, Heinrich Hertz, and Albert Michelson. Michelson, using expensive apparatus in Chicago, attempted to disprove the empirical rule discovered by Preston, but Preston publicly disproved him. The Zeeman effect was anomalous whenever it departed from the form predicted by classical theory. Preston's rule helped the Zeeman effect become an important tool in spectrum analysis, and opened up the possibility of quantum physics.

Preston also engaged George Johnstone Stoney, vice-president of the Royal Society and the man responsible for coining the term 'electron', in a public dispute in the *Philosophical Magazine* over a mathematical conclusion, in which the president, J. W. Strutt, intervened on Preston's behalf. Elected FRS in 1898 Preston was also made an honorary DSc by the Royal University of Ireland and awarded the Boyle medal of the Royal Dublin Society. He died at his home, Bardowie, Orwell Park, Rathgar, Dublin, on 7 March 1900. ANNE PIMLOTT BAKER, rev.

Sources *Nature*, 61 (1899–1900), 474–5 · D. Weaire and S. O'Connor, 'Unfulfilled renown: Thomas Preston (1860–1900) and the anomalous Zeeman effect', *Annals of Science*, 44 (1987), 617–44
Wealth at death £1687 13s. 8d.: probate, 9 April 1900, CGPLA Ire. · £434 15s. 7d.—in England: Irish probate sealed in England, 16 May 1900, CGPLA Eng. & Wales

Preston, Walter of (d. 1230). See under Preston, Sir Gilbert of (b. in or before 1209, d. 1274).

Preston, William (1742–1818), printer and writer, was born on 28 July 1742 in Edinburgh, the second son of William Preston (d. 1751), writer to the signet, and Helena, née Cumming, of Edinburgh. He was educated in Edinburgh, first privately and then at the high school, and left the University of Edinburgh, presumably without a degree, in 1757.

Preston then became assistant to the grammarian Thomas Ruddiman (1674–1757), during which time he compiled a catalogue of Ruddiman's books, *Bibliotheca Romana* (1757). After Ruddiman's death in 1757 Preston spent a year as apprentice to Ruddiman's brother Walter (*fl.* 1753–1801), a printer in Edinburgh.

In 1760 Preston went to London with a letter of recommendation to William Strahan (1715–1785), the king's printer. Strahan hired Preston as principal corrector to the press, and Preston was later made superintendent. Strahan's firm was one of the largest and most prosperous printing houses in eighteenth-century London. It printed Johnson's *Dictionary*, Gibbon, Hugh Blair, David Hume, Adam Smith, and other notable authors. As manager and chief corrector of the press, Preston was on friendly terms with these authors, and prospered with Strahan as the business grew. In 1773 Preston married Sarah Couchman Stamp, a widow with one son.

In 1763 a group of Edinburgh men in London, including Preston, formed a masonic lodge (formally constituted as the Caledonian in 1772). His interest in masonic scholarship grew, and he began regularly to meet other masons to discuss masonic practice. This work culminated in an address to a masonic gala in 1772 which was attended by the most prominent freemasons in England. Later in that year Preston published a major work, *Illustrations of Masonry*, which included the text of his address along with descriptions of ceremonies, a historical account of freemasonry, and songs. *Illustrations* was immediately successful and influential; it brought a standardization to masonic practice hitherto lacking. Preston continued to revise the text, seeing nine English, two American (1804, 1816), and three German (1776, 1780, 1786) editions published in his lifetime. It continued to be revised by others after his death, and also exists in several facsimile editions.

After his first public address Preston continued to give numerous lectures on the masonic craft. He wrote for the *Freemason's Calendar* and was a master of the lodge of Antiquity, no. 1, one of England's four oldest lodges. He served as assistant to the secretary of the grand lodge and was appointed official printer to the grand lodge. In 1779 Preston, among others, renounced allegiance to the grand lodge of England and established a rival lodge. The secession did not thrive, however, and Preston was restored to his grand lodge privileges in 1789.

He was made a member of the Stationers' Company in 1794. On his death, William Strahan left Preston an annuity and the firm was inherited by Strahan's son Andrew, who made Preston chief reader and general superintendent, and eventually, a full partner in 1804.

William Preston died after a long illness on 1 April 1818 at his home at Dean Street, Fetter Lane, London, and was buried on 10 April near St Paul's Churchyard. Part of his estate endowed a yearly Prestonian lecture which is administered by the grand lodge of England.

H. R. TEDDER, *rev.* JEFFREY MAKALA

Sources C. Dyer, *William Preston and his work* (1987) • S. Jones, 'William Preston: a biography', *European Magazine*, 59 (May 1811), 323–7 • *GM*, 1st ser., 88/1 (1818), 372 • G. Kloss, *Bibliographie der Freimaurerei und der mit ihr in Verbindung gesetzten geheimen Gesellschaften* (1844), 394–8, 2885 • Allibone, *Dict.* • C. H. Timperley, *Encyclopaedia of literary and typographical anecdote*, 2nd edn (1842); repr. (1977), vol. 2, p. 918 • Nichols, *Illustrations*, 8.490 • A. Mackey, *Encyclopedia of freemasonry and its kindred sciences* (1917), 681–5

Archives United Grand Lodge of England Library, London | BL, Add. MSS 48800–48919

Likenesses J. Thomson, line engraving, pubd 1794 (after S. Drummond), BM • Ridley, engraving (after S. Drummond), repro. in Jones, 'William Preston' • engraving (after S. Drummond, 1794), repro. in *Freemasons Magazine* (1795)

Wealth at death at least £1300 given to masonic charities: Mackey, *Encyclopedia*

Preston, William (1750–1807), poet and playwright, was born in the parish of St Michan's, Dublin, the only son of William Preston, gentleman, who went to India when his son was two years old and was never heard of again. Preston obtained his early education at Dr Campbell's school in Dublin and was admitted a pensioner at Trinity College, Dublin, in 1765. He graduated BA in 1770 and MA in 1773. He entered the Middle Temple in 1775 and was called to the Irish bar in 1777. He assisted in the formation of the Royal Irish Academy, was elected its first secretary in 1786, and was a frequent contributor to its *Transactions*. He wrote occasional verse for various periodicals but a collection of his verse in 1781 proved abortive when the printer went bankrupt. He turned his attention to drama about 1790, and in the space of four years he wrote six plays, predominantly in verse. His chief success in this field was his tragedy *Democratic Rage* (founded on incidents in the French Revolution), which was produced at Dublin in 1793, and in printed form ran through three editions in as many weeks.

In 1793 Preston published a two-volume collection of his verse and plays, with the exception of *Democratic Rage*, already published separately. A further posthumous collection of his verse was published by his widow in 1809. Although he had no small opinion of his abilities as a poet and dramatist, and fancied himself as something of a literary savant wasting his time among 'an unlettered people' ('Preface', *Works*, 1793), in the final analysis posterity has judged him a minor talent.

During the late 1770s and the 1780s Preston was a supporter of Lord Charlemont and the volunteer movement. It was around this time too that he was initiated into the Monks of the Screw, a hard-drinking patriot club which endured until the mid-1790s. These political connections gained him early legal preferment when, in 1784, he was appointed a commissioner of appeals, but further advancement on the bench eluded him. In the 1790s he evinced some sympathy with the ideals of the United Irishmen, for he contributed verse to *The Press*, the journal of that organization, but without apparently becoming a member. He is also believed to have favoured Catholic emancipation.

In 1789 Preston married Frances Dorothea Evans, a daughter of John Evans, who succeeded as the fifth Baron Carbery in 1804; they had seven children. Preston had another son, William, who could not have been the result of his marriage to Frances Evans, for he was killed, aged twenty, at the battle of Delhi in India in 1803. This William was either Preston's natural son or the issue of an earlier marriage, the details of which have not been uncovered.

Preston died in Gloucester Street, Dublin, on 2 February 1807 of miliary fever said to have been brought on by sitting all day in court in wet clothes. He was buried in St Thomas's churchyard, Marlborough Street, Dublin, but during the 1920s a new street was built on the site of this graveyard and in the process Preston's remains were exhumed, with those of some 3500 others, and re-interred in Mount Jerome cemetery, Harold's Cross, Dublin.

PATRICK FAGAN

Sources J. Warburton, J. Whitelaw, and R. Walsh, *History of the city of Dublin*, 2 vols. (1818) · W. Preston, *The posthumous poems of William Preston Esq.* (1809) · T. Ó Raifeartaigh, *The Royal Irish Academy: a bicentennial history, 1785–1985* (1985) · *DNB* [incl. comprehensive work list] · P. Fagan, *A Georgian celebration: Irish poets of the 18th century* (1989) · Burtchaell & Sadleir, *Alum. Dubl.*, 2nd edn · H. A. C. Sturgess, ed., *Register of admissions to the Honourable Society of the Middle Temple, from the fifteenth century to the year 1944*, 3 vols. (1949) · *Journal of Irish Memorials Association*, 12/1 (1926), 66–7 · A. E. Langman, *Marriage entries in the registers of the parishes of S. Marie, S. Luke, S. Catherine and S. Werburgh, 1697–1800* (1915) · E. Keane, P. Beryl Phair, and T. U. Sadleir, eds., *King's Inns admission papers, 1607–1867*, IMC (1982) · *Wilson's Dublin directory* (1779–1807) · Burke, *Peerage* (1975), 473 · 'Diocese of Dublin: index to the act or grant books and original wills', *Report of the Deputy Keeper of the Public Records in Ireland*, 26 (1894), appx · *GM*, 1st ser., 77 (1807), 187 · *Alumni Dublinienses*
Archives NL Scot., letters to Robert Anderson
Likenesses H. Brocas, engraving (after C. Robertson), repro. in Preston, *Posthumous poems*
Wealth at death house, Gloucester Street, Dublin

Prestongrange. For this title name *see* Grant, William, Lord Prestongrange (1700/01–1764).

Prestwich, John [*known as* Sir John Prestwich] (1745–1795), antiquary, was born on 29 or 30 January 1745, the only son of Elias Prestwich (*d.* 1785), of Holme and Prestwich, Lancashire, and his wife, Catherine Lander. As a lineal descendant of Thomas Prestwich, who was created a baronet in 1644, he always claimed the title of baronet, though the claim was not officially allowed. In April 1776 he married Margaret, daughter of Joseph Hall, alderman, and Ruth Drew, in London. His published works were *Dissertation on Mineral, Animal, and Vegetable Poisons* (1775) and a heraldic album entitled *Prestwich's Respublica*, inscribed to Lord Sydney and published in 1787. Illness prevented him from publishing a second volume of this work. He died at Dublin on 15 August 1795 following a long illness, during which he was cared for by his wife. He left unpublished an incomplete *Historical Account of South Wales*, and a *History of Liverpool* which he had deliberately withheld when a similar work was announced by John Holt.

THOMPSON COOPER, *rev.* J. A. MARCHAND

Sources *GM*, 1st ser., 65 (1795), 879, 967 · GEC, *Baronetage* · W. Courthope, *Synopsis of the extinct baronetage of England* (1835), 162 · T. Moule, *Bibliotheca heraldica Magnae Britanniae* (privately printed, London, 1822), 455 · Nichols, *Lit. anecdotes*, 9.23 · *N&Q*, 4th ser., 8 (1871), 47 · *N&Q*, 5th ser., 1 (1874), 269 · *Palatine Note-Book*, 2 (1882), 185, 249

Prestwich, Sir Joseph (1812–1896), geologist, was born on 12 March 1812 at Pensbury, Clapham, the eldest surviving son of Joseph Prestwich, a wine merchant descended from a long line of Lancashire landowners, and his wife, Catherine (*bap.* 1785, *d.* 1850), daughter of Edward Blakeway, one-time porcelain manufacturer at Coalport in Shropshire. The Prestwich family lived in Clapham and later South Lambeth when Joseph was a child, and he attended schools in Wandsworth, Forest Hill, and South Lambeth. In 1823 he was sent to Paris, presumably because of his father's connections with the wine trade in France. He remained at school in Montmartre for two years, becoming fluent in French. On his return to England he went to a school in South Norwood, and then to Richard Valpy's school in Reading, from where he went up to University College, London, in 1828, to study chemistry and natural philosophy. Prestwich became very keen on science, setting up a laboratory at home in Lambeth, and starting a collection of rocks and minerals. He studied oil painting and lithography and became familiar with the British Museum in London. In 1830, at the age of eighteen, he joined the family business in Mark Lane in the City of London.

Geological research was now conducted in Prestwich's spare time; his first independent fieldwork was carried out during holidays with his grandparents at Broseley in the Coalbrookdale coalfield. There he mapped the surface rocks, worked underground in the pits, and collected fossils for later identification. He read accounts of his work to the Geological Society of London in 1834 and 1836, and his paper on the geology of Coalbrookdale was eventually published in the *Transactions of the Geological Society* in 1840. Prestwich made extended visits to Scotland in 1834 and 1835, comparing his Coalbrookdale rocks with their Scottish equivalents, and he read papers on fossil fish from Gamrie and on the elevation of the Banffshire coast to the Geological Society of London which, once again, were published in 1840.

Although Prestwich worked a full week in the wine trade, frequently travelling as the firm's representative, geology became a passion bordering on obsession. Solitary and withdrawn as a young man, he drove himself hard, filling long days with business, study, and self-improvement, while walking great distances on an empty stomach to save money. His health suffered, and throughout his long life Prestwich suffered from stress-related illnesses. It did not help that, in 1842, his business responsibilities were increased when he took control of the family firm, which had been run into difficulties by his father.

In 1840 Prestwich began the systematic study of the Lower Tertiary strata, on which his reputation as a geologist chiefly rests. By meticulous mapping and collecting throughout the Tertiary outcrops of the Thames valley and Hampshire, Prestwich demonstrated that marine sands to the east of London, which he called the Thanet Sands, were the oldest of all the British Tertiaries; that the overlying marine Woolwich Beds were the same age as the terrestrial Reading Beds to the west; and that the London Clay was the same age as the Bognor Beds of Hampshire and therefore older than the Barton and Bracklesham Beds. These results, published in three substantial papers in the *Quarterly Journal of the Geological Society* between 1850 and 1854, laid the foundations for all later studies of the British Tertiary succession. He followed them up in 1855 and 1857 with papers on the correlation of the British succession with strata in France and Belgium. Prestwich was awarded the Geological Society's Wollaston medal in 1849 for his Coalbrookdale and Tertiary researches.

It was about this date that Prestwich first turned his attention to water supply, a subject on which he became recognized as an expert. He published *A Geological Inquiry Respecting the Water-Bearing Strata of the Country around London* in 1851, and served on a royal commission on water supply in 1864. Much later, in the 1880s, Prestwich was instrumental in improving Oxford's water supply. Other practical matters that took his attention, and on which he published, were geological aspects of the proposed channel tunnel (1874) and the prospects for finding coal beneath south-east England (1871, 1872).

At the same time as his Tertiary work Prestwich was also studying the more recent Crag deposits of East Anglia. Between 1845 and 1850 he paid many visits to this area, noting sections and collecting specimens. He published one short paper in 1849, but pressure of other work delayed completion until 1868, when he read three papers to the Geological Society of London. By the time they were published in its *Quarterly Journal* in 1871, much of their novelty had been lost.

Prestwich was a regular visitor to France throughout his life, combining business with geology whenever possible. His papers on the geology of Epernay and Rilly, in the heart of the Champagne region, underline the connection between these two parts of his life. Prestwich became a member of the Société Géologique de France in 1838, and retained close links with French geologists until his death.

In 1858 Prestwich became a member of the committee set up by the Geological Society to oversee the excavation of Brixham cave in south Devon, an untouched site which it was hoped might reveal new information on Pleistocene stratigraphy and on the antiquity of the human race. Although worked flints were found associated with the bones of extinct animals in the cave, Prestwich was not convinced until he and John Evans visited Boucher de Perthes in Abbeville, northern France, where he saw flint implements in bone-bearing gravels, and realized that humans had indeed coexisted with elephants and other Pleistocene mammals. These conclusions, which were accepted by Lyell and others, were published in *Philosophical Transactions of the Royal Society* in 1861. Prestwich was awarded the royal medal of the Royal Society in 1865 in

recognition of the importance of this work. Hugh Falconer, who had been Prestwich's companion throughout the Brixham and Abbeville work, died in 1856, and the task of writing up a report on the Brixham cave excavation devolved to Prestwich. He eventually completed it in 1872, and it was published by the Royal Society in *Philosophical Transactions* in 1873.

On 26 February 1870 Prestwich married Grace Anne McCall (*née* Milne) (d. 1899), the niece of his friend and co-worker Hugh Falconer. In the same year, he was elected president of the Geological Society of London, of which he had already served as secretary and treasurer. Two years later in 1872, at the age of sixty, he retired from his business life to devote himself to science. He and his sister Isabella Civil Prestwich had built a house high on the downs above the village of Shoreham in Kent in 1865, and this, Darent Hulme, now became his home. He took time to organize the great collection of geological specimens he had amassed, and started to write up papers based on the innumerable field excursions of the previous thirty-five years. Not that he ceased or slowed down the pace of his work: he travelled in France in 1872 and again in 1873, in Dorset in 1873, and through the north of England in 1874. Few geologists of his day had seen more rock in the field than Joseph Prestwich.

In 1874 Prestwich was offered and, after some hesitation, accepted, the chair of geology at Oxford, vacant after the death of John Phillips. He held the chair until 1888, working in the museum, leading field excursions, and giving regular courses of lectures. He maintained the pace of his own researches, publishing papers on an astonishing range of subjects including the parallel roads of Glenroy, raised beaches, the causes of volcanic action, regional metamorphism, and on an iguanodon from the Kimmeridge Clay near Oxford. Towards the end of his time in Oxford Prestwich laboured to produce a textbook, and *Geology, Chemical, Physical and Stratigraphical* was published by the Clarendon Press in two volumes in 1886 and 1888. This book was planned as an antidote to the rigidly uniformitarian views which were the legacy of successive editions of Charles Lyell's *Principles of Geology*, and which Prestwich believed were harming the subject. He was prepared to believe that the scale and rate of many geological phenomena had been different in the past from what they are today, and therefore that the earth was not as ancient as postulated by those who insisted on total uniformity. Indeed, towards the end of his life Prestwich found himself backing a number of unfashionable causes. Chief among these was his support for eoliths, supposed human artefacts which had been found by Benjamin Harrison and others in the ancient gravels which cap many plateaus in southern England, and which seemed to take the human race back to the early, or even preglacial period. Papers on this and other topics were published in one of Prestwich's last books, *Collected Papers on some Controverted Questions in Geology* (1895).

Prestwich remained active well into old age. He was president of the International Geological Congress held in London in 1888, regularly visited plateau gravel sites and raised beaches in 1890 and 1891, and wrote a long paper on the great submergence of the land which he detected at the close of the Glacial period, which was published by the Royal Society. However as each year went by he became less and less active, until his health failed in November 1895. He was knighted in the new year's honours list, but never recovered sufficiently to enjoy the honour. Sir Joseph Prestwich died at Darent Hulme on 23 June 1896, aged eighty-four and was buried a few days later at Shoreham. In his will he left money to the Geological Society of London to endow a medal to be awarded for researches into stratigraphical and physical geology.

JOHN C. THACKRAY

Sources G. A. Prestwich, *Life and letters of Sir Joseph Prestwich* (1899) · H. Woodward, 'Eminent living geologists no. 8: Professor Joseph Prestwich', *Geological Magazine*, new ser., 3rd decade, 10 (1893), 241–6 · H. Hicks, *Quarterly Journal of the Geological Society*, 53 (1897), xlix–lii · J. E., *PRS*, 60 (1896–7), xii–xvi · G. Prestwich, *Essays descriptive and biographical* (1901) · H. B. Woodward, *Natural Science, London*, 9 (1896), 89–98
Archives BGS, corresp. and papers · GS Lond., field notebooks and papers · Oxf. U. Mus. NH, Hope Library, corresp., fossil collection daybooks, notebook, and papers | BL, letters to W. E. Gladstone and others, index of MSS, VIII, 1985 · CUL, letters to Sir George Stokes · Falconer Museum, Torres, corresp. with Hugh Falconer · Oxf. U. Mus. NH, corresp., mainly letters to Sir E. B. Poulton · U. Edin. L., special collections division, letters to Sir Archibald Geikie · U. Edin. L., special collections division, corresp. with Charles Lyell
Likenesses oils, c.1875, GS Lond. · Elliott & Fry, photograph, c.1885, repro. in Prestwich, ed., *Life and letters of Sir Joseph Prestwich* · H. R. Hope Pinker, marble bust, exh. RA 1901, Oxf. U. Mus. NH; related bronze medallion, University Museum, Oxford · Morris & Co., lithograph, GS Lond. · P. N., wood-engraving (after photograph by Elliott & Fry), NPG; repro. in *ILN* (11 Jan 1896)
Wealth at death £2596 19s. 8d.: probate, 25 Aug 1896, *CGPLA Eng. & Wales*

Pretender, the. *See* James Francis Edward (1688–1766).

Prevost, Sir George, first baronet (1767–1816), soldier and governor-in-chief of British North America, was born on 19 May 1767 in New Jersey, America, the eldest son of the five children born to Augustin Prévost, a French-speaking Swiss protestant who served in the British army in Canada, and his wife, Nanette (Ann), the daughter of Chevalier George Grand, a wealthy Amsterdam banker. He was educated in England and in continental Europe before in 1779 he entered the army. He became a captain on 9 June 1783, took a company in the 25th foot on 15 October 1784, and was promoted major in the 60th (Royal American) foot on 18 November 1790. On 19 May 1789 he married Catherine Anne, the daughter of Major-General John Phipps, RE; they had four children who survived infancy, including a son, George *Prevost (1804–1893). Shortly afterwards Prevost was sent to the West Indies with his regiment. He became lieutenant-colonel on 6 August 1794. In that and the following year he commanded the troops in St Vincent and saw much active service, in 1796 being twice wounded. On 1 January 1798 he became a colonel, and on 8 March brigadier-general.

In May 1798 Prevost was nominated lieutenant-governor of St Lucia. He spoke fluent French and set himself to conciliate the French population and to reform the disorganized law courts. Following a petition by the local people he was appointed civil governor on 16 May 1801. In the following year poor health compelled his return to England. On 27 September 1802 Prevost was appointed captain-general and governor-in-chief in Dominica. In 1803 he helped retake St Lucia from the French, and in February 1805 prevented their taking Dominica. On 10 May 1805 he again obtained leave to visit England, was placed in command of the Portsmouth district, and on 6 December 1805 was created a baronet. He was now major-general and on 8 September 1806 became colonel commandant in his regiment. In 1808–9 he was second in command when Martinique was captured. In January 1808 he was promoted lieutenant-general.

As relations with the United States deteriorated, the imperial government replaced civilian with military governors in British North America. One such appointment was Prevost's, in 1808, as lieutenant-governor and commander-in-chief of Nova Scotia, where he increased his reputation as a colonial administrator. He helped undermine the American trade embargo by naming customs-free ports in Nova Scotia and New Brunswick, action widely applauded in Anglophile and soon to be neutral New England. In the political arena Prevost's governorship uncannily foreshadowed his later regime in Lower Canada—except for his championing the claims of the Anglican church in Nova Scotia. By avoiding arbitrary positions, he dissociated himself from his predecessor, Sir John Wentworth, whose strident defence of the royal prerogative had antagonized the house of assembly, and he won over the house leader, William Cottnam Tonge, by appointing him assistant commissary for the Martinique expedition. Conciliation produced a useful militia act, generous supply for defence purposes, and, for the most part, placid politics. As in Lower Canada, the assembly voted him money for a testimonial gift.

On 14 February 1811 Prevost was, at a critical juncture, chosen to be governor of Lower Canada, and governor-in-chief of and military commander in British North America, in succession to Sir James Henry Craig.

Craig had imprisoned, without bail or trial, the leaders of the assembly's majority grouping, the *parti canadien*, and had removed their militia commissions. He had treated the Roman Catholic bishop with suspicion and threats. With war against the United States imminent, Prevost wisely adopted the opposite approach of thoroughgoing conciliation. The commissions were restored and *parti canadien* men favoured by patronage, their leader, Pierre-Stanislas Bédard, even being appointed to the bench in 1812. The bishop was promised legal recognition by London (achieved 1817) and had his government stipend raised. The governor distanced himself from the ruling English party, rarely socializing or consulting with its leaders, even when they were executive councillors. Conciliation paid handsome dividends. Senior Roman Catholic clergy were indefatigable in inculcating loyalty among the French-speaking population. Over several legislative sessions Prevost secured legislation strengthening the militia by sanctioning various levels of conscription for active service, granting lavish funds for defence purposes, and authorizing the circulation of up to £1,500,000 in army bills, a form of paper money. The Canadian militia played an important role in repelling the two American invasions of Lower Canada in the battles of Lacolle (November 1812) and Châteauguay (October 1813).

On 18 June the United States declared war; on the 24th the news reached Quebec. Prevost acted promptly, yet showed every consideration to American subjects then within his jurisdiction. When the news of the repeal of the orders in council was received he concluded an armistice with the American general; but it was disavowed by the United States, and the war went on. Through Prevost's influence Canada made it primarily a defensive war. Although he was nominally commander-in-chief, he mostly left the conduct of the war to others, and his own appearance in the field on two occasions was followed by the humiliation of the British arms. With Sir James Yeo he went to Kingston, and on 27 May 1813 concerted the attack on Sacketts harbour. A brilliant attack was made by the British troops—the Americans were already routed—when Prevost, seized with doubt, sounded the retreat. The scheme of invading New York state, in September 1814, was likewise due to Prevost. The Canadian forces had been reinforced by Peninsular War veterans; the army and fleet were together to attack Plattsburg. The attempt ought to have been successful, both by land and sea. But by some error the *Confiance* was sent into action alone, and Prevost, instead of giving her immediate support, suddenly decided to retreat.

Prevost continued his conciliatory policy throughout the war. Despite opposition from the appointed legislative council, he forwarded home articles of impeachment against chief justices James Monk and Jonathan Sewell passed by the assembly early in 1814. When he refused to suspend them, the lower house did complain that its privileges had been violated, but soon made amends by reiterating its belief in the overall 'wisdom of his excellency's administration' (cited in Christie, 2.165).

Prevost's neutrality was the last straw for English party leaders. In the spring of 1814 they attempted to persuade the prince regent to order his recall. Letters attacking the governor's appeasement of 'factious' elements as preparing the way for another Ireland and portraying his military strategy as that of a cowardly fool appeared in the *Montreal Herald* (1814–15), two sets of which, by 'Nerva' (Samuel Gale) and 'Veritas' (unknown), were subsequently published as pamphlets. Much of the military information was supplied by shocked and disgusted Peninsular War veterans.

On 21 January 1815 Provost met the new parliament of Lower Canada, and soon announced that peace had been concluded. The assembly proposed presenting him with a service of plate to the value of £5000, 'in testimony of the country's sense of his distinguished talents, wisdom, and ability'. The legislative council, however, declined to assent to the bill. In closing the session Prevost announced

that he was summoned to England to meet the charges arising out of his conduct before Plattsburg. On 3 April he left amid numerous addresses from the Canadians. The English remained aloof, indeed sullen.

Prevost reached England in September, and, on learning that he had been incidentally condemned by the naval court for his actions at Plattsburgh, he obtained from the duke of York permission to be tried in person by court-martial. But the consequent anxiety ruined his health, and he died of dropsy in London on 5 January 1816, a month before the day fixed for the meeting of the court. He was buried at East Barnet, Hertfordshire. At the urging of Lady Prevost the prince regent publicly expressed his regard for Prevost's services, and granted the family additional armorial bearings, although nothing could be done legally to clear Prevost's name.

Prevost seems to have been cautious to a fault, wanting in decision, always anticipating the worst; but he was straightforward, well-intentioned, and honest. There seems to be little room for questioning his success in civil affairs, and he was an efficient soldier while he filled subordinate rank.

C. A. HARRIS, *rev.* F. MURRAY GREENWOOD

Sources P. Burroughs, 'Prevost, Sir George', *DCB*, vol. 5 · NA Canada, Andrew William Cochran collection, MG24-B16 · *Journals of the House of Assembly of Lower Canada* (1812–15) · minutes of the executive council of Lower Canada, 1812–15, NA Canada, RG1-E1 · correspondence etc. received by the civil secretary, 1812–15, NA Canada, Quebec and Lower Canada S ser., RG4-A1 · dispatches and enclosures to London, 1812–15, NA Canada, Colonial office collection, MG11-CO42 · J. M. Hitsman, *Safeguarding Canada, 1763–1871* (1968), 79–108 · F. Ouellet, *Lower Canada, 1791–1840: social changes and nationalism*, ed. and trans. P. Claxon (Toronto, 1980), 95–115 · R. Christie, *A history of the late province of Lower Canada*, 2 (1849) · *Montreal Herald* (1814–15)
Archives Hunt. L., financial papers · Metropolitan Toronto Reference Library, corresp. and papers | NA Canada, corresp. with Isaac Brock · NA Canada, CO42 series · NL Scot., letters and dispatches to Sir Alexander Cochrane
Likenesses R. Field, oils, 1808, Musée du Séminaire de Quebec, Quebec City · R. Field, oils, McGill University, Montreal, McCord Museum · etching, BM · oils, NA Canada

Prevost, Sir George, second baronet (1804–1893), Church of England clergyman, only son of Sir George *Prevost, first baronet (1767–1816), governor-in-chief of British North America, and Catherine Anne, daughter of Major-General John Phipps, was born at Roseau on the island of Dominica on 20 August 1804. He succeeded to the baronetcy on 5 January 1816. He matriculated at Oxford, from Oriel College, on 23 January 1821, and graduated BA, taking a second class in *literae humaniores* and a first class in mathematics, in 1825. He proceeded MA in 1827 and was ordained deacon in 1828 and priest in 1829.

Prevost was a pupil and disciple of John Keble, whom he frequently visited at Southrop; there he met Isaac Williams whose sister Jane (*d.* 1853) he married on 18 March 1828. He maintained a lifelong friendship with his Oriel contemporary Samuel Wilberforce, successively bishop of Oxford and Winchester. Prevost was curate to Keble's brother Thomas at Bisley, Gloucestershire, from 1828 to September 1834, when he was instituted to the perpetual curacy of Stinchcombe in the same county. He was rural dean of Dursley from 1852 to 1866, proctor of the diocese of Gloucester and Bristol from 1858 to 1865, archdeacon of Gloucester from 1865 to 1881, and honorary canon of Gloucester from 1859 until his death.

Prevost, retiring by nature and profoundly pious, was an ardent supporter of the Tractarian movement from its inception, and despite his attachment to J. H. Newman remained faithful until death to the *via media*. He contributed to Tracts for the Times and translated the *Homilies of St. John Chrysostom on the Gospel of St. Matthew* (1843) for the Library of the Fathers. He edited the *Autobiography of Isaac Williams* (1892), and printed his archidiaconal charges and some sermons.

Prevost and his wife, who died on 17 January 1853, had one daughter and two sons, George Phipps (1830–1885), who held a colonel's commission in the army, and Charles, the third baronet (d. 1902), who married Sarah, daughter of the Revd Thomas Keble. Prevost died at Stinchcombe on 18 March 1893, and was buried in the churchyard there on 23 March.

J. M. RIGG, rev. G. MARTIN MURPHY

Sources *The Guardian* (22 March 1893) · *The Times* (20 March 1893) · Foster, *Alum. Oxon.* · *The letters and diaries of John Henry Newman*, ed. C. S. Dessain and others, [31 vols.] (1961–) · Burke, *Peerage* · *CGPLA Eng. & Wales* (1893)
Archives Glos. RO, corresp. | BL, corresp. with W. E. Gladstone, Add. MSS 44370–44785, *passim* · Bodl. Oxf., corresp. with S. Wilberforce
Wealth at death £2404 8s. 11d.: probate, 14 Aug 1893, *CGPLA Eng. & Wales*

Prévost, Louis Augustin (1796–1858), linguist, the son of a French functionary, was born at Troyes in Champagne on 6 June 1796, and was educated at a college in Versailles. Having come to England in 1823, he was at first tutor in the family of William Young Ottley, afterwards keeper of the prints in the British Museum. From 1823 to 1843 he was a teacher of languages in London, and had Charles Dickens as a pupil. On 30 August 1825 he married Lucy Smith, an Englishwoman. His leisure was spent in the reading-room of the British Museum studying languages. He gradually acquired most of the languages of Europe, many of Asia, especially Chinese, and even some of Polynesia. He was, finally, acquainted more or less perfectly with upwards of forty languages. Like Mezzofanti, who was credited with knowing sixty, he was chiefly interested in their structures. From 1843 to 1855 he was engaged by the trustees of the British Museum in cataloguing the Chinese books. On 25 October 1854 his only son, Frederick William Fraser, who had assumed the name of Melrose, was lost in the charge of the light brigade at Balaklava. Prévost's health gave way, and he died at Great Russell Street, Bloomsbury, London, on 25 April 1858, and was buried in Highgate cemetery on 30 April.   G. C. BOASE, rev. JOHN D. HAIGH

Sources R. Cotwan, *Memories of the British Museum* (1872) · *GM*, 3rd ser., 5 (1858), 87 · Boase, *Mod. Eng. biog.* · IGI

Preyer, Thierry William (1841–1897), physiologist and advocate of Darwinism, was born on 4 July 1841 at Moss Side, Manchester, the son of Thierry Preyer, merchant,

and his wife, Adèle, formerly Kutter (or Kutten). Both parents were originally from Germany and had presumably come to Manchester in connection with the father's business.

Little direct information exists on Preyer's life; what family papers did exist were lost during the Second World War. The problem is compounded by the fact that Preyer's own autobiographical sketches contain false and contradictory information, reversing the order of his names to William Thierry, for example, and so leading a number of writers to believe that Thierry William was his father.

Preyer's education began at home under visiting teachers, native speakers of English and German. After a brief attendance at Clapham grammar school, Clapham, London, he and his family moved to Germany in 1855, settling in Wiesbaden, Prussia. He spent two and a half years at the *Gymnasium* in Duisburg, moved to Bonn where he passed his examinations in the autumn of 1859, and went on to study medicine and natural science at the university there. In the summer of 1860 he made a trip to Iceland, after which he moved to Berlin to prepare for a career in physiology. In the autumn of 1861 he moved to Heidelberg where, among other subjects, he studied chemistry with Bunsen, physiology with Helmholz, and zoology with Bronn. On 13 August 1862 he successfully completed his doctoral examination, submitting the first Darwinian thesis written in Germany. Shortly afterwards he went to Vienna to study physiology with Ludwig for a year, before returning to Berlin to work with Virchow and others. By 1864 he was in Paris studying with Bernard, and in the summer of 1865 he became a *Privatdozent* in zoochemistry and zoophysics at Bonn, where he was given a doctoral degree (and apparently his *Habilitation*) in medicine and surgery. Preyer's educational achievements permitted him in 1869 to accept a position as *ordinarius* professor of physiology in the faculty of medicine at Jena and director of the Physiological Institute.

Preyer is probably best known for his book, *Die Seele des Kindes* (1882), which was published in English as *The Mind of the Child* (1888). It is considered a seminal work in developmental psychology, although Preyer was not associated with the group of psychologists who established the modern discipline. In 1868 he initiated a correspondence with Darwin that continued until shortly before the latter's death. He was an avid Darwinist and protagonist for natural selection. He produced a popularized translation of *On the Origin of Species* and a biography of his idol, *Darwin, sein Leben und Wirken* (1896); in 1891 he published copies of much of his correspondence with Darwin. At Jena he numbered among his friends William Roux, one of the founders of experimental embryology, and E. Ray Lankester, later one of the giants of late nineteenth-century British biology; the older Ernst Haekel apparently was not as close a friend as the younger men.

From a British standpoint, Preyer's greatest significance is his role in popularizing Darwinism in Germany, particularly as one of the few who accepted the ideas in a relatively unqualified form. Most other German proponents of Darwin and British biology used the theses in the furtherance of their own arguments; Haekel, for example, adapted Darwin to the service of his own monistic metaphysics. For Preyer, all his efforts were designed to gather diverse data to support the theory as proposed and demonstrated by the British interpretations. In this particular he stands out from his better-known contemporaries.

In 1888 Preyer resigned the professorship, apparently as a result of personal problems, and moved to Berlin where he lectured as a *Privatdozent* until 1893 when he moved to Wiesbaden where he died after a lengthy illness on 15 July 1897. He was survived by his wife, Erika, and at least one son, Axel Thierry Preyer, who obtained his doctorate at the University of Leipzig on 20 November 1899 with a dissertation in zoology.

J. F. FITZPATRICK JR

Sources H.-D. Schmidt and K.-H. Becker, 'Dokumente über Wilhelm Preyer Beziehungen zu Berlin Universität', *Zeitschrift für Psychologie*, 189 (1981), 247–54 · G. Eckhardt, 'Einleitung', in W. Th. Preyer, *Die Seele des Kindes*, ed. G. Eckhardt (1989), 11–53 · G. Eckhardt, 'Preyer's road to child psychology', *Contributions to a history of psychology*, ed. G. Eckhardt, W. G. Bringmann, and L. Sprung (1985), 77–86 · A. Geus, 'Preyer, Thierry William', *DSB* · J. F. Fitzpatrick and W. G. Bringmann, 'William Preyer and Charles Darwin', *Psychologie im soziokulturellen Wandel: Kontinuitäten und Diskontinuitäten*, ed. S. Jaeger, I. Staeuble, L. Sprung, and H. P. Braunds (1995), 238–44 · b. cert.
Archives Friedrich-Schiller-Universität, Jena · Humboldt University, Berlin
Likenesses photograph, repro. in Eckhardt, ed., *Die Seele des Kindes* · photograph, repro. in Eckhardt, Bringmann, and Sprung, eds., *Contributions*

Price. *See also* Pryce.

Price, Amy Morgan (1878/9–1922), illustrator and jewellery designer, was born in Claremont Road, Handsworth, Birmingham, the fourth child and youngest daughter of the five children of Lorenzo Theodore Candelent Price, a schoolteacher; her mother was a private teacher. Delicate from birth, she was always regarded as the baby of the family, and was educated at home, later attending English literature classes and Monday evening lectures at the Midland Institute with her three sisters. An imaginative and attractive child, she grew up in a bookish atmosphere of 'plain living and high thinking' (Price, 6). Struck down by 'a very serious illness' (ibid., 11), possibly peritonitis, in adolescence, she was first given paints and brushes while convalescing. She continued to suffer poor health throughout her life and remained at the family home for some years after the departure of her siblings, sometimes assisting her father with teaching, but increasingly absorbed by painting.

Price briefly attended the Handsworth School of Art, Birmingham (c.1898–c.1899), but rebelled against the narrowness of the teaching and remained largely self-taught, setting up her first studio on the top floor of her parents' house at 56 Westminster Road at the age of twenty. However, painting soon gave way to illustration (usually in pen and ink), the medium in which she excelled. In 1908 she produced two illustrations—*Mordrac* and *The Trees of Hellac*—for a play with an all-female cast written by one of her elder sisters (who died c.1902); she later illustrated verses and stories written by her two surviving sisters, to whom she always remained close.

Price followed the progress of the women's suffrage movement with great interest, and her work celebrates the women of literature, history, and mythology, often drawing on subjects from her own reading. Early examples include a series of illustrations of the Brontë heroines (1907–8), and *The Five Maries* (original drawing, York Art Gallery). There are also at least nine illustrations of Shakespeare's heroines (reproduction, York Art Gallery), among which *Cleopatra* (ink on paper, Russell-Cotes Gallery, Bournemouth) is one of the finest. However, she never wholly abandoned colour work, and continued to paint watercolours, such as *Night* and *Serniranis* [sic; Semiramis?] (both Russell-Cotes Gallery, Bournemouth) throughout her career. Between 1899 and 1921 she exhibited regularly with the Royal Birmingham Society of Artists, where her exhibits included in 1899 'a painting of a cottage' (Morris and Morris, 4); in 1903 *The Vale of Avalon*—which was 'much admired' (ibid., 46); in 1905 *La Belle Dame sans Merci* (formerly in Worcester Gallery); and in 1909 *The Assumption* (watercolour).

Price's style reflects the influence of the Pre-Raphaelites, particularly of D. G. Rossetti, and has close affinities with the work of the Birmingham Municipal School of Art. She earned her living as a designer to the Birmingham jewellery trade, but no evidence of this seems to have survived. The disappearance of most of her jewellery designs, as well as some of her finest illustrations—*Joan of Arc is Received into Paradise* and *The Death of Clorinda* (both formerly in Derby Art Gallery) among them—has contributed to her loss of reputation, and her work is little known today. Some 125 of her works—including one cameo, a medallion, and the only two known photographs of the artist (c.1898 and c.1908)—are collected in the monograph *Amy Morgan Price and her Drawings*, published by her eldest sister, Maud, in 1928. It includes a brief biographical sketch, and reproductions of many of the works mentioned above. Price never married, and travelled abroad only once—finding herself in France when the First World War was declared in August 1914. She spent the rest of her life in Birmingham, and died of peritonitis on 6 February 1922 at Dudley Road Hospital, Birmingham, aged forty-three. She was buried in the graveyard of the parish church near Heathfield Hall, Handsworth, Birmingham.

SARAH MACDOUGALL

Sources M. A. P. Price, *Amy Morgan Price and her drawings* (1928) · S. Morris and K. Morris, *A catalogue of Birmingham and west midland painters of the nineteenth century* (1974) · J. Johnson and A. Greutzner, eds., *The dictionary of British artists, 1880–1940* (1976), vol. 5 of *Dictionary of British art*; repr. (1994), 410 · private information (2004) · S. MacDougall, catalogue of 127 known works of Amy Morgan Price, priv. coll. · d. cert. · *CGPLA Eng. & Wales* (1922)
Likenesses photograph, c.1898, repro. in Price, *Amy Morgan Price* · photograph, c.1908, repro. in Price, *Amy Morgan Price*
Wealth at death £374 4s. 6d.: administration with will, 27 March 1922, *CGPLA Eng. & Wales*

Price, Arthur (1678/9–1752), Church of Ireland archbishop of Cashel, was the son of Samuel Price, vicar of Straffan in the diocese of Dublin and, from 1672, prebendary of

Kildare. Arthur Price entered Trinity College, Dublin, on 2 April 1696, aged seventeen, and was elected a scholar in 1698; he graduated BA in 1700 and DD on 16 April 1724. After taking holy orders he was successively curate of St Werburgh's Church, Dublin, and vicar of Cellbridge, Feighcullen, and Ballybraine. On 4 April 1705 he was named prebendary of Donadea, Kildare. On 19 June 1715 he became canon and archdeacon of Kildare, and on 31 March 1721 he became dean of Ferns and Leighlin. Two years later he received the benefice of Louth in Armagh.

On 1 May 1724 Price was appointed to the see of Clonfert, a promotion that the Irish chancellor, Lord Middleton, found highly provocative. From Clonfert, Price was translated, on 26 May 1730, to the see of Ferns and Leighlin, and, on 2 February 1734, to that of Meath, the latter on account of his loyalty to George II and his service to the House of Lords. While bishop of Meath he began to build an episcopal residence at Ardbraccan but he left the diocese before it was completed, and the design was abandoned. In May 1744 he succeeded Theophilus Bolton as archbishop of Cashel. Three years later he was made vice-chancellor of Dublin University. At Cashel he initiated the dismantling of the old and rapidly decaying cathedral (proceedings initiated by act of council, 10 July 1749). Price died in 1752 and was buried in the churchyard of St John's, the parish church at Cashel. In 1783 a new cathedral building was completed on the site of St John's.

G. Le G. Norgate, *rev.* Philip Carter

Sources H. Cotton, *Fasti ecclesiae Hibernicae*, 1–5 (1845–60) · Burtchaell & Sadleir, *Alum. Dubl.*
Archives NL Ire., letters to William Smythe
Likenesses B. Wilson, oils, 1749, TCD

Price, Bartholomew (1818–1898), college head, was born on 14 May 1818 at Coln St Dennis in Gloucestershire, the second son of William Price (*d.* 13 April 1860), rector of Coln St Dennis and of Farnborough in Berkshire. He was educated privately and at Northleach School, before matriculating as a scholar from Pembroke College, Oxford, in 1837. He graduated BA in 1840, obtaining a first class in mathematics, and MA in 1843. In 1842 he gained the senior university mathematical scholarship, and two years later was elected a fellow of Pembroke, taking holy orders. In 1845 he became tutor and mathematical lecturer, and in 1847–8 and 1853–5 was a public examiner. He continued to take a large number of private pupils, including C. L. Dodgson, who became a lifelong friend. In 1858 he was a university proctor.

In 1848 Price published his first mathematical work, *A Treatise on the Differential Calculus*, and he then began to prepare his great undertaking, the *Treatise on Infinitesimal Calculus*, which included differential and integral calculus, calculus of variations, applications to algebra and geometry, and analytical mechanics. It was completed in four volumes, the first appearing in 1852 and the last in 1860. A second edition was commenced in 1857, before the completion of the first, and was completed in 1889. Price was elected a fellow of the Royal Society on 3 June 1852 and of the Royal Astronomical Society on 13 June 1856. On 20 August 1857 he married Amy Eliza, eldest daughter of William Cole of Highfield, Exeter. They had several sons and five daughters, the latter befriended by Dodgson.

In 1853 Price was chosen Sedleian professor of natural philosophy at Oxford, a chair which he retained until June 1898. Soon after his appointment he became involved in a controversy over the mathematics examinations at Oxford, complaining that the examiners were placing too much emphasis on pure mathematics as opposed to the 'mixed' mathematics, comprising elements of physics, which Price taught. In 1855 he became a member of the hebdomadal council, and in 1868 he was made an honorary fellow of Queen's College and secretary to the delegates of the university press. At that time he was doing a very large part of the mathematical teaching in the university, but his success in his new position was so great that he became gradually absorbed in its duties. He showed great financial ability in directing the affairs of the press, having assumed overall responsibility for its management in 1873, and increased its business and income enormously before resigning the secretaryship in 1884. He resumed the responsibilities for six months during 1897, his eightieth year.

As time went on the affairs of the university passed more and more into his hands, and 'Bat' Price became a member of nearly every board of council of importance connected with it. His omniscience in university business was hinted at in Lewis Carroll's lines:

> Twinkle, twinkle little bat,
> How I wonder what you're at.

He gave evidence to all the official inquiries touching on Oxford, including the 1867 select committee on university extension, the Devonshire commission on scientific instruction (1870), and the Selborne commission (1877). He was a member of the Cleveland commission, appointed in 1872 to investigate the wealth of the university and colleges. When the university observatory was founded in 1874 he was put on the board of visitors, and in 1878 he was one of a committee of three appointed to consider its outstanding requirements. He was also one of the six representatives of the Royal Society on the board of visitors to the Royal Observatory at Greenwich.

A financial scandal involving his brother, the bursar of Pembroke College, prevented Price from succeeding Francis Jeune as master of Pembroke in 1864. He was eventually elected in 1892, though only by the appointment of the visitor of the college, Lord Salisbury, the votes of the fellows being equally divided. With the mastership went a canonry of Gloucester. Price took the degrees of BD and DD in 1892. He died in Pembroke College on 29 December 1898 and was buried on 3 January 1899 in Holywell cemetery. His wife survived him.

E. I. Carlyle, *rev.* M. C. Curthoys

Sources *The Times* (30 Dec 1898) · *Oxford Magazine* (25 Jan 1899) · *Monthly Notices of the Royal Astronomical Society*, 59 (1898–9), 228–9 · *Yearbook of the Royal Society* (1900), 185–9 · P. Sutcliffe, *The Oxford University Press: an informal history* (1978) · *The diaries of Lewis Carroll*, ed. R. L. Green, 2 vols. (1953) · J. Foster, *Oxford men and their colleges* (1893) · *CGPLA Eng. & Wales* (1899)

Archives Pembroke College, Oxford, corresp. and papers | BL, letters to W. E. Gladstone, Add. MSS 44432–44522, *passim* · CUL, Sir George Stokes MSS · NL Scot., letters to Alexander Campbell Fraser · Oxf. U. Mus. NH, letters to Sir E. B. Poulton
Likenesses M. C. W. Flower, oils, Pembroke College, Oxford · W. Forshaw, photograph, repro. in Foster, *Oxford men*, facing pp. 551–2
Wealth at death £98,981 18s. 7d.: resworn probate, Aug 1899, *CGPLA Eng. & Wales*

Price, Bonamy (1807–1888), economist, eldest son of Frederick Price of St Peter Port, Guernsey, was born there on 22 May 1807. At the age of fourteen he was sent as a private pupil to the Revd Charles Bradley of High Wycombe, Buckinghamshire, where W. Smith O'Brien was one of his fellow pupils. He matriculated at Worcester College, Oxford, in 1825, graduating BA with a double first in classics and mathematics in 1829, and proceeding MA in 1832. While he was an undergraduate at Oxford he was an occasional pupil of Thomas Arnold at Laleham, and formed a friendship with F. W. Newman, his brother John Henry Newman, and other leaders of the Tractarian movement.

In 1830 Arnold, then headmaster of Rugby, offered him the mathematical mastership at that school. In 1832 Price was appointed to a classical mastership, and given charge of a division of the fifth form. Six years later he succeeded Prince Lee in charge of the form known as 'the Twenty'. He retained this post under A. C. Tait, Arnold's successor, but resigned in 1850, shortly after Tait's appointment to the deanery of Carlisle. Like Tait, he was a proponent of university reform: he was one of the movers of a petition in 1847 for a royal commission, and in 1850 published proposals for reorganizing Oxford on German professional lines. He became identified with strong broad-church views, inspired by German theology, and he attacked 'Anglo-Catholic theory' in the *Edinburgh Review* (1851).

An unsuccessful candidate in 1851 for the Greek chair at Edinburgh, Price lived in London from 1850 to 1868, devoting himself to business affairs. He suffered for some months from a cerebral illness, but completely recovered. He served on the royal commissions on Scottish fisheries (1856), which protected the position of herring fishermen on the east coast of Scotland, and on the queen's colleges in Ireland (1857). In 1864 he married Lydia, the daughter of the Revd Joseph Rose, vicar of Rothley, and granddaughter of Thomas Babington of Rothley Temple, Leicestershire. They had five daughters.

When the Drummond professorship of political economy at Oxford, to which elections were made for a term of five years, became vacant in 1868, Price was elected by convocation by a large majority over the former holder of the office, J. E. Thorold Rogers, who offered himself for re-election. Rogers had offended the conservative majority of convocation. Price occupied the chair until his death, being thrice re-elected. He zealously devoted himself to his professorial duties. Master of a clear and incisive style, he lectured with comparative success. Courageous in the expression of his views, fond of controversy, though kindly in his treatment of opponents, he exercised a stimulating influence on his pupils. Prince Leopold

Bonamy Price (1807–1888), by unknown photographer

of Belgium, while resident in Oxford, frequently attended his lectures, and became much attached to him.

Price also lectured in different parts of the country in connection with the movement for the higher education of women, and was a prolific writer for periodicals, contributing nearly fifty articles to *Fraser's Magazine*, *Blackwood's*, and the *Contemporary Review* between 1862 and 1882. He served on the duke of Richmond's commission on agriculture (1879–82) and on Lord Iddesleigh's commission on the depression of trade (1885–6), on which he made a spirited defence of old-style *laissez-faire*. At Cheltenham in 1878, and at Nottingham in 1882, he was president of the economical section of the Social Science Association. He was made an honorary LLD by Edinburgh University in 1881 and in 1883 he was elected honorary fellow of Worcester College. He died at his London home, 29 Michael's Grove, Brompton, on 8 January 1888.

Price possessed in a high degree the qualities of a successful schoolmaster. His power as an economist lay in exposition and criticism, not in original work. He made no important contribution to economic science, though he published *The Principles of Currency* (1869), *Currency and Banking* (1876), and *Chapters on Practical Political Economy* (1878). By the 1880s he seemed a rather old-fashioned exponent of the more simplistic aspects of Ricardian free trade. In his speech on the Land Law (Ireland) Bill on 7 April 1881, W. E. Gladstone referred to him, in connection with the duke of Richmond's commission, as:

> the only man—to his credit be it spoken—who has had the resolution to apply, in all their unmitigated authority, the principles of abstract political economy to the people and circumstances of Ireland, exactly as if he had been proposing to legislate for the inhabitants of Saturn or Jupiter. (*Hansard 3*, 260, 1881, 895)

W. A. S. HEWINS, rev. M. C. CURTHOYS

Sources *The Athenaeum* (14 Jan 1888), 50 · *The Times* (9 Jan 1888) · Foster, *Alum. Oxon.* · Boase, *Mod. Eng. biog.* · R. H. I. Palgrave, ed., *Dictionary of political economy*, [3rd edn], ed. H. Higgs, 3 vols. (1923–6) · *Wellesley index* · A. Kadish, *Historians, economists, and economic history* (1989) · *CGPLA Eng. & Wales* (1888)
Archives BL, corresp. with W. E. Gladstone, Add. MSS 44353–44477, *passim* · LPL, letters to A. C. Tait · NL Scot., letters to Alexander Campbell Fraser
Likenesses pencil drawing on porcelain, Worcester College, Oxford · photograph, NPG [*see illus.*] · wood-engraving, NPG; repro. in *ILN* (21 Jan 1888)
Wealth at death £11,756 4s. 10d.: probate, 27 Feb 1888, *CGPLA Eng. & Wales*

Price, Sir Charles, first baronet (1708–1772), politician in Jamaica, was born on 20 August 1708, probably in St Catherine's parish, Jamaica, the eldest son of the thirteen children of Colonel Charles Price (1677/8–1730), and Sarah (*d.* after 1730), daughter of Philip Edmunds of Jamaica. Price's grandfather Francis was one of the early English settlers in Jamaica following its capture by the English in 1658, and his father extensively developed several plots of land as sugar plantations. Price himself was educated in England; he matriculated at Trinity College, Oxford, on 21 October 1724, and embarked upon a grand tour. He returned to Jamaica in January 1730, shortly before his father's death on 23 May.

Within a few years of his return Price had married Mary Sharpe. They had four sons, the first being born in 1732 or 1733, if his stated age at matriculation is correct. Price was first elected to the Jamaican assembly on 13 March 1732, and aligned himself with the faction headed by Judge Dennis Kelly. When Price and Kelly quarrelled at the end of the 1730s the governor, Edward Trelawny, won over Price to his interest. On 17 April 1745 he was elected temporary speaker of the assembly when the incumbent was ill, and the following year he became speaker. He acted in close alliance with Governor Trelawny in promoting the interests of the planters. In October 1751 he helped to unite the various political factions in the Jamaica Association. Originally the Jamaica Association was pledged to support the governor as long as he had the interests of the colony at heart, and it continued to have good relations with Charles Knowles for about a year after he replaced Trelawny as governor. However, when political conflict broke out again in 1754, Knowles attempted to move the capital from Spanish Town and imprisoned Price and fifteen of his supporters. Price had excellent contacts with the ministry in London and eventually won the resultant power struggle when Knowles was recalled in 1756. The capital returned to Spanish Town.

In October 1763 Price retired from the assembly on grounds of ill health, his son, also Charles [*see below*], taking over as speaker. He made a brief return in 1765, but in 1768 he was nominated to the council by Governor William Trelawny, and on 13 August he was made a baronet. He died at his house, The Decoy, on 26 July 1772, custos of St Catherine's, judge of the supreme court, and a major-general in the militia.

His eldest son, **Sir Charles Price**, second baronet (1732/3–1788), succeeded to an over-extended estate which collapsed as a consequence of the American War of Independence. Having been educated at Trinity College, Oxford (he matriculated 14 May 1752, aged nineteen), he returned to Jamaica, and in 1753 was elected to the Jamaican assembly. He married Elizabeth Hannah (1747/8–1771), daughter of John Hudson Guy, of Berkshire House, chief justice of Jamaica, the widow of John Woodcock. They had no children. Price served as speaker of the assembly from 1763. As speaker in 1765, during the confrontation with Governor William Henry Lyttelton, he refused to apply to the governor to confirm the assembly's privileges, and led the assembly through the crises of repeated dissolutions. He remained speaker until 1775, when he retired to take an extended sojourn in England to try to rescue his near bankrupt estate. He returned to Jamaica in 1779, and by 1786 was forced to appeal to the assembly for assistance. Little was forthcoming and properties had to be sold, including Rose Hall for £18,000. Price died in Spanish Town on 18 October 1788. His widow, Lydia Ann, herself the widow of his brother Rose Price (*d.* 1765), sold The Decoy for a paltry £2500 in 1789. STUART HANDLEY

Sources M. Craton and J. Walvin, *A Jamaican plantation: the history of Worthy Park, 1670–1970* (1970) · GEC, *Baronetage* · G. Metcalf, *Royal government and political conflict in Jamaica, 1729–1783* (1965) · P. Wright, *Monumental inscriptions of Jamaica* (1966), 98, 123–4, 135 · W. A. Feurtado, *Official and other personages of Jamaica from 1655 to 1790* (1896), 125 · GM, 1st ser., 59 (1789), 178 · R. S. Dunn, *Sugar and slaves: the rise of the planter class in the English West Indies, 1624–1713* (1972)

Price, Sir Charles, second baronet (1732/3–1788). *See under* Price, Sir Charles, first baronet (1708–1772).

Price, Daniel (1581–1631), dean of Hereford, was born in Shrewsbury, the eldest son of Thomas Price (*d.* 1620). His father had been admitted as a preacher to the Shearmen's Company in 1578 and was irregularly granted in 1583 by Shrewsbury corporation the crown living of St Chad's, which he served as 'preacher', 'minister', and 'curate' for the rest of his life. Evidently not a university graduate, Thomas Price was a native Welsh speaker, some of whose annotated books survive in the library of Shrewsbury School, which he may have attended; he was a strong godly influence on Daniel Price and his brother Sampson *Price (1585/6–1630). Daniel Price matriculated as a commoner at St Mary Hall, Oxford, on 14 October 1597. Before taking his degree he moved to Exeter College, 'where, by the benefit of a diligent tutor, he became a smart disputant' (Wood, *Ath. Oxon.*, 2.511). He graduated BA on 10 July 1601 and proceeded MA on 22 May 1604.

From 1607 to 1613 Price was rector of Wiston, Sussex, and from 1610 vicar of Old Windsor, in the gift of Lord

Chancellor Egerton. In 1609 he gained admittance to the Middle Temple, and proceeded BD on 6 May 1611 and DD on 21 June 1613. In 1612 he was presented by Prince Henry to the rectory of Lanteglos, Cornwall.

Price was recognized as a frequent and remarkable preacher, 'especially against the papists' (Wood, *Ath. Oxon.*, 2.511), and achieved his greatest fame in this occupation at Prince Henry's court. In 1608 he printed his first sermon preached before the prince, *Recusants Conversion*, with a dedication to Henry seeking appointment as his chaplain. Although not named in the 1610 establishment list of the prince's household, he styled himself in print as Henry's chaplain-in-ordinary in the same year. By chance Price was one of the two chaplains attending in the month of Henry's death, November 1612, and therefore preached half of the routine sermons to the bereaved household before the funeral on 7 December. Early in the new year Price published six of these, all extravagant in their prose, their anti-Catholicism, and their eulogies for the prince. There followed two equally histrionic commemorative tracts on the first and second anniversaries of the prince's death, derived in title and imagery from John Donne's *Anniversary* elegies for Elizabeth Drury (1611, 1612). This body of work drew scorn from two leaders of emergent anti-Calvinism at Oxford, Richard Corbett and Brian Duppa, whose verses satirized Price's humble origins and evangelical Calvinism as much as his literary failings; Price's short verse rejoinder hardly disproves the latter.

In 1620 Price became rector of Worthen, Shropshire. Some time before 1623 he married Isabella (*b*. 1593), youngest child of the wealthy Shrewsbury lawyer Richard Prince and his wife, Dorothy Leighton. On 16 December 1623 Price was instituted dean of Hereford by royal warrant, and in 1624 became a canon residentiary there, and a justice of the peace for Shropshire, Montgomery, and Cornwall. He died at Worthen on 24 September 1631 and was buried in the chancel of the church there on 27 September. A story was circulated in 1633 that he had died a Roman Catholic, but this arises from a confusion of Daniel Price with Theodore *Price, who had died in the same year.   P. E. McCULLOUGH

Sources H. Owen and J. B. Blakeway, *A history of Shrewsbury*, 2 vols. (1825) • P. Collinson and J. Craig, eds., *The Reformation in English towns* (1998) • P. E. McCullough, *Sermons at court: politics and religion in Elizabethan and Jacobean preaching* (1998) [incl. CD-ROM] • Wood, *Ath. Oxon.*, new edn, 2.511 • R. Tresswell and A. Vincent, *The visitation of Shropshire, taken in the year 1623*, ed. G. Grazebrook and J. P. Rylands, 2 vols., Harleian Society, 28–9 (1889) • C. H. Drinkwater and T. R. Horton, eds., *Diocese of Hereford: Worthen registers*, 11, Shropshire Parish Registers (1909) • W. P. W. Phillimore and others, eds., *Diocese of Lichfield: St Chad's, Shrewsbury parish registers*, 1, Shropshire Parish Registers, 29 (1913) • *Poems of Richard Corbett*, ed. J. A. W. Bennett and H. R. Trevor-Roper (1955) • A. J. Smith, *Donne: the critical heritage* (1975) • A. Knafla, 'The "country" chancellor: the patronage of Sir Thomas Egerton', *Patronage in late Renaissance England*, ed. F. R. Fogle and L. A. Knafla (1983) • PRO, E 334/14 • J. H. Morrison, ed., *Letters of administration, 1620–1630* (1935) • C. W. Boase, ed., *Registrum Collegii Exoniensis*, new edn, OHS, 27 (1894)
Archives BL, Lansdowne MSS • PRO, SP 16/204/72 • PRO, E 334

Price, David (1762–1835), orientalist and army officer, was born in Merthyr Cynog, near Brecon, where his father,

also named David Price (*d*. 1775), was curate. The latter soon afterwards became rector of Llanbadarn Fawr, near Aberystwyth, and David Price was brought up until the age of six or seven by his grandfather in Brecknockshire. He then joined his parents in Aberystwyth, and began his classical education under his father. In 1775, however, his father died, leaving a widow and five children, of whom David was the eldest boy. He was then educated at Christ College School, Brecon, until October 1779, when he was awarded a Rustat scholarship and matriculated on 5 November 1779 as a sizar of Jesus College, Cambridge.

By the summer of 1780, however, Price was nearly penniless (partly through his own carelessness) and had to leave Cambridge. Despairing of his prospects in Britain, he volunteered for the army of the East India Company, in which through the influence of friends of his father he obtained a cadetship. He sailed for India in the *Essex* on 15 March 1781, and, after an eventful passage (see Price, 15–26), reached Madras in August. Price was destined for Bombay, but volunteered for temporary service in the south and took part in the siege of Negapatam and the capture of Trincomali in Ceylon as the *Essex* passed those places. The ship completed its voyage to Bombay on 22 April 1782; in November he was appointed to the 2nd battalion of Bombay sepoys, which, under Captain Daniel Carpenter, did service in Malabar against Tippu, sultan of Mysore, up to the peace of 1784. He was promoted lieutenant in February 1788, and in the next war with Tippu (1790–92) he served in Captain Little's battalion at the siege of Dharwar, where he was severely wounded on 7 February 1791 and lost a leg. He was therefore moved to the guard of Sir Charles Malet, political minister at Poona. In 1792 he was transferred by the governor of Bombay, Jonathan Duncan the elder, to a staff appointment at Surat, where he had enough leisure to develop a keen interest in Persian studies, and began to collect Persian manuscripts and study Persian historical classics such as the *Akbar-namah* of Abu'l-Fazl. In 1795, being then brevet captain, he was nominated judge-advocate-general to the Bombay army, a post he retained until his departure from India. He became full captain in September 1797 and served as military secretary and interpreter to Colonel Dow in Malabar (1797–8), where he twice narrowly escaped being cut off. During the last war against Tippu (1799), Price served as Persian translator to the commander of the Bombay army, General James Stuart. He was present at the capture of Seringapatam, and the army appointed him their prize agent to handle the record amount of booty taken; thereafter he was free of financial worries.

After this Price returned to Bombay and resumed his Persian studies. He was promoted major in March 1804, and in February 1805, after twenty-four years' continuous service, he returned to Britain. He finally retired from the East India Company's service on his marriage, to a relative, in October 1807. Thenceforward he lived at Watton House, Brecon, and became a magistrate, and deputy lieutenant of Brecknockshire. He devoted himself to writing long, leisurely works on Arabian, Persian, and Indian history. Of these the best-known and the most important is *Chronological retrospect, or, Memoirs of the principal events of Mahommedan history … from original Persian authorities* (3 vols., 1811, 1812, 1821). This covers the period from the death of Muhammad to the accession of Akbar. The earlier volumes are based chiefly on the Persian chronicles of Mirkhand and Khandamir, and are most detailed and accurate with respect to Persian history; but in the last volume Abu'l-Fazl is largely used. It is written in the over-ornate style of Price's sources, but it is the painstaking work of a genuine scholar anxious to do full justice to his authorities. Without pretending to any striking grasp or generalization, it is nevertheless useful and was for many years almost the only English work of reference for some branches of Eastern history. Price's other main works were his *Essay towards the History of Arabia antecedent to the Birth of Mahommed* (1824, from the Persian text of Et-Tabari); the translation of the unique *Memoirs of the Emperor Jahangueir* (1829; new edn, 1972); *Account of the Siege and Reduction of Chaitur … from the Akbar-namah* (1831); and *The Last Days of Krishna* (1831). These last three were published by the Oriental Translation Fund, of which Price was a committee member, and which awarded him its gold medal in 1830. He also wrote *Memoirs of the early life and service of a field officer on the retired list of the Indian army* (published anonymously in 1839). He was a member of the Royal Asiatic Society, to which he bequeathed over seventy valuable oriental—chiefly Persian—manuscripts (see *Journal of the Royal Asiatic Society*, [1st ser.,] 3, 1836, xii–xiv). He died at Watton House on 16 December 1835. His widow had a memorial inscribed in Brecon parish church paying tribute to his 'unassuming simplicity', 'high moral courage', 'universal benevolence', and 'genuine piety' (Poole, 312–13).

Stanley Lane-Poole, *rev.* R. S. Simpson

Sources [D. Price], *Memoirs of the early life and service of a field officer* (1839) · *Annual Biography and Obituary*, 21 (1837), 1–6 · *Journal of the Royal Asiatic Society of Great Britain and Ireland*, 3 (1836), xii–xiv, lx · E. Poole, *The illustrated history and biography of Brecknockshire* (1886), 312–13 · *DWB* · Dodwell [E. Dodwell] and Miles [J. S. Miles], eds., *Alphabetical list of the officers of the Indian army: with the dates of their respective promotion, retirement, resignation, or death … from the year 1760 to the year … 1837* (1838)

Archives NL Wales, letters to publisher relating to *Chronological retrospect of Mohommedan history*

Price, David (1790–1854), naval officer, entered the navy in January 1801 on board the *Ardent*, with Captain Thomas Bertie, and was present in the battle of Copenhagen on 2 April. He was afterwards in the *Blenheim*, which, on the renewal of the war in 1803, went out to the West Indies. In 1805 he was in the *Centaur* with Sir Samuel Hood, and again in 1806, being present in the action off Rochefort on 25 September, and at the capture of the Russian battleship *Sevolod* on 26 August 1808. In April 1809 he was appointed acting lieutenant of the *Ardent*, and during the following summer was twice captured by the Danes, once while in command of a watering party, and again in a prize which was wrecked; each time, however, he was soon released. The confirmation of his rank as lieutenant was dated 28

September 1809. He continued in the *Ardent* until February 1811, when he was appointed to the brig *Hawk*, with Captain Henry Bourchier, employed on the north coast of France. On 19 August the *Hawk* drove four armed vessels and a convoy of fifteen merchantships on shore near Barfleur. Price, in command of the boats, was sent in to finish the work, and succeeded in bringing out an armed brig and three store-ships; the others were lying over on their sides, completely bilged.

Two months later, on 21 October, Price was severely wounded in an unsuccessful attempt to cut two brigs out of Barfleur harbour. It was nearly a year before he was able to serve again; in September 1812 he was appointed to the *Mulgrave* (74 guns) off Cherbourg. In January 1813 he joined his old captain, Bourchier, in the *San Josef*, carrying the flag of Sir Richard King off Toulon. On 6 December he was promoted to command the bomb-vessel *Volcano*, which he took out in the summer of 1814 to the coast of North America. In the same year he engaged in the operations in the Potomac, against Baltimore, and at New Orleans, where, on 24 December, he was severely wounded in the thigh. On his return to England Price was advanced to post rank on 13 June 1815. From 1834 to 1838 he commanded the *Portland* in the Mediterranean, during which time his services to the Greek government won him the order of the Redeemer of Greece, as well as complimentary letters from Sir Edmund Lyons.

For the next six years Price lived in Brecknockshire, for which county he was a JP. In 1846 he married Elizabeth, daughter of John Taylor, and niece of Admiral William Taylor. In 1846 he was made superintendent of Sheerness Dockyard, where he continued until promoted rear-admiral on 6 November 1850. In August 1853 he was appointed commander-in-chief in the Pacific, and arrived on the station shortly before the declaration of war with Russia. Price proved to be a tactful and courteous joint commander-in-chief, but it appears that the responsibilities of wartime command, and the difficulty of working with his French colleague, weighed heavily on him, and he was susceptible to any advice. The allies moved slowly across the Pacific, spending a considerable period in the Marquesas Islands, and at Honolulu, where they worked to reduce the influence of the Americans. In July 1854 the two squadrons, English and French, met at Honolulu, and on 25 July sailed to search for two Russian frigates, which were reported to be at sea. They found the frigates dismantled at Petropavlovsk; but, on the morning of the attack, 30 August 1854, Price shot himself with a pistol, and died a few hours later. Opinion has long been divided as to whether Price deliberately shot himself, or was the victim of a terrible accident. On balance, the evidence of those closest to him, including the chaplain, to whom he confessed his 'crime', favours the suicide verdict. Sir Frederick Nicolson succeeded to the command, but the attack was postponed until 4 September, when it met with a decisive repulse. On 1 September Price was buried on shore, beneath a tree, on which the letters 'D. P.' were rudely cut with a knife.

Price, a brave and successful junior officer, had suffered

severe wounds. Long years of peacetime service and half pay left him ill prepared for the scale of his task in the Pacific; and, when he was confronted with the problems imposed by an unnecessarily complex command structure, and the prospect of going, once again, under fire while engaging shore batteries, his resolve apparently collapsed. As an isolated incident the suicide of a British admiral on the point of action might seem remarkable; but Price's career had done nothing to prepare him for this situation, while his experience had given him every reason to dread the prospect.

J. K. LAUGHTON, *rev.* ANDREW LAMBERT

Sources I. R. Stone and R. J. Crampton, '"A disastrous affair": the Franco-British attack on Petropavlovsk, 1854', *Polar Record*, 22 (1984–5), 629–41 · B. M. Gough, *The Royal Navy and the north-west coast of North America, 1810–1914* (1971) · M. Lewis, *The navy in transition, 1814–1864: a social history* (1965) · C. I. Hamilton, *Anglo-French naval rivalry, 1840–1870* (1993) · M. Lewis, 'An eye-witness at Petropaulovski, 1854', *Mariner's Mirror*, 49 (1963), 265–72

Price, Dennis [*real name* Dennistoun John Franklin Rose Price] (**1915–1973**), actor, was born on 23 June 1915 in Ruscombe, Berkshire, the younger son and second of the three children of Brigadier-General Thomas Rose Caradoc Price (1875–1949), an army officer descended from a Cornish baronet's family, the Prices of Trengwainton, and his wife, Dorothy Patience, daughter of Sir Henry Verey, official referee of the Supreme Court of Judicature. He was educated at Radley College, Oxfordshire, and read theology at Worcester College, Oxford, where he joined the Oxford University Dramatic Society. On leaving Oxford without a degree he studied for the stage at the Embassy Theatre School, and made his London début at the Queen's Theatre on 6 September 1937 with John Gielgud in Shakespeare's *Richard II*.

In 1939 Price married the actress Joan Schofield, daughter of Major-General Arthur Cecil Temperley of Beaconsfield, Buckinghamshire. They had two daughters. The marriage was soon undermined by Price's homosexuality and alcoholism.

After being invalided out of the Royal Artillery in 1942, Price joined the company of Noël Coward, who was so impressed by his charm that in 1943 he gave him the leading role of Charles Condamine in his play *Blithe Spirit*, at the Duchess Theatre in London. In 1944 he won his first starring role on screen in *A Canterbury Tale*, directed by Michael Powell. Tall, handsome, and urbane, he swiftly became one of Britain's leading international film stars. He played the title role in *The Bad Lord Byron* (1948), was chosen by Ivor Novello for the lead in the Technicolor film of Novello's musical *The Dancing Years* (1949), and reached the peak of his career with *Kind Hearts and Coronets* (1949), in which he was supremely sardonic as the heartless murderer of eight ducal cousins, all played by Alec Guinness.

Joan Schofield divorced Price in 1950, and the British film recession brought a sharp decline in his popularity. On 19 April 1954 he was found unconscious in his gas-filled flat in Egerton Gardens, Kensington, but the dramatic publicity generated by his attempted suicide led to a revival in his fortunes. He starred on the South African

Dennis Price (1915–1973), by Vivienne, 1950–56

stage in *Separate Tables* (1957), made an acclaimed Broadway début as Hector Hushabye in *Heartbreak House* (1959), and had further notable film roles in *Private's Progress* (1955), *The Naked Truth* (1957), *I'm All Right, Jack* (1959), *Tunes of Glory* (1960), and *Tamahine* (1963).

In 1965 Price's nonchalant interpretation of the butler Jeeves in the BBC television series *The World of Wooster* delighted its creator, P. G. Wodehouse, who felt that Price had 'that essential touch of Jeeves mystery'.

Troubles with the Inland Revenue caused Price's strategic withdrawal in 1966 from his London home in Curzon Street, Mayfair, to settle on the channel island of Sark. He was declared bankrupt in 1967. He died from cirrhosis of the liver at the Princess Elizabeth Hospital, St Martin's, Guernsey, on 6 October 1973.

MICHAEL THORNTON, *rev.*

Sources *The Times* (8 Oct 1973) · T. Pettigrew, *British film character actors* (1982) · d. cert. · Burke, *Peerage* (1939) · *The People* (20 March 1966) · H. Baddeley, *The unsinkable Hermione Baddeley* (1984) · H. Tims, *Once a wicked lady* (1989) · D. La Rue and H. Elson, *From drags to riches: my autobiography* (1987) · personal knowledge (1993) · WW
Archives FILM BFI NFTVA, *Those British faces*, Channel 4, 26 Dec 1997 · BFI NFTVA, performance footage |SOUND BL NSA, performance recordings
Likenesses photographs, 1949–63, Hult. Arch. · Vivienne, photograph, 1950–56, NPG [*see illus.*]

Price [Prys], **Ellis** [*called* y Doctor Coch] (*c.*1505–1594), administrator, was the second son of Robert ap Rhys (*d. c.*1534) of Foelas and Plas Iolyn, Denbighshire, chaplain to

Cardinal Wolsey and, as chancellor of St Asaph, the cardinal's principal agent in north Wales. The family had served the Tudors since 1485. As a member of St Nicholas's Hostel, Cambridge, Ellis Price (or Prys) distinguished himself in a disputation with two Oxford students. He graduated BCL in 1533 and DCL in 1535, and was known to his fellow Welshmen as *y Doctor Coch* ('The Red Doctor'), a sobriquet that has been variously explained as denoting either his red hair or his scarlet doctoral gown. He married Ellyw, daughter of Owen Pool, priest, of Llandecwyn, Merioneth; they had two sons and four daughters.

Price was one of the monastic visitors in Wales in 1535. Despite the support of Rowland Lee, president of the council in the marches, he was suspended from his duties when his fellow commissioners complained of the scandal caused by his youthful indiscretions and 'progeny'. He was rehabilitated in 1538, when at Thomas Cromwell's instigation he was appointed commissary-general and chancellor of the diocese of St Asaph. In the meantime he and his brother Richard, abbot of Aberconwy, sought to have the house exempted from the dissolution of the smaller monasteries. Along with his kinsman John Lloyd, Ellis was sued in the court of chancery in 1537 by the vicar of Llanarmon-yn-Iâl, in the newly formed shire of Denbigh, for misappropriation of tithes. Ellis was later ejected from the rectory of Llangwm, but retained the sinecure rectories of Llandrillo-yn-Rhos and Llanuwchllyn.

Price was an assiduous iconoclast in implementing the new laws against the 'superstitious' abuse of images and religious practices. In 1538 he drew Cromwell's attention to the continued veneration by pilgrims of the image of Derfel Gadarn in the diocese of St Asaph. He was careful to inform Cromwell that he had spurned a bribe offered by the incumbent and parishioners of Llandderfel to spare the image. Cromwell used it as kindling for the burning of the Observant friar John Forest, condemned for denying the royal supremacy. An active member of the convocation of 1547, Price was appointed by Archbishop Thomas Cranmer in 1549 to a commission to visit the diocese of St David. But after the Henrician Acts of Union of Wales with England he was mainly involved in civil administration. He was *custos rotulorum* of Merioneth in 1543, and from 1555 until his death, and served as sheriff of Merioneth, Anglesey, Caernarfon, and Denbigh during three reigns. He was elected knight of the shire for Merioneth in Mary's last parliament and in Elizabeth's second.

In 1560 Price became a member of the council in the marches of Wales. After 1564 he assumed the role of chief agent of the earl of Leicester in his lordship of Denbigh and the forest of Snowdon. As steward of Denbigh he was one of the four chief tenants who represented the Welshry of the lordship in negotiations with the earl for the commutation of their customary dues. He also served on the last of three commissions obtained by Leicester to search out concealed lands in the forest of Snowdon (1573). Some of the gentlemen of Llŷn who resisted these inquiries were subsequently imprisoned. The commotion was commemorated in the *cywydd* by Edmund Prys (1544–1623), archdeacon of Merioneth, 'yn erbyn anllywodraeth

y Cedyrn' ('against the unruliness of the great'). In 1560 Price had secured from the crown the manor of Tir Ifan, parcel of the lands of the knights hospitaller at Ysbyty Ifan, Dolgynwal, which became one of the family seats. His younger brother Cadwaladr established another branch of the family with an estate at Rhiwlas, Merioneth. By 1561 Ellis was chancellor of the diocese of Bangor, where he also held the parsonage of Llaniestyn. When in February 1566 the earl of Pembroke nominated Price to the vacant see of Bangor, Archbishop Parker appealed to William Cecil to prevent the appointment, he 'neither being priest nor having any priestly disposition'. Parker would rather run the risk of offending Pembroke than commend a 'doubtful man' to the queen for consecration. In a later letter to Cecil, Parker added another reason for taking pause before filling the vacancy. The 'wise men' he had consulted, some of them from the country there, had advised against appointing a Welshman to Bangor, for the Welsh 'band so much together in kindred, that the bishop can do not as he would for his alliance sake' (*Correspondence*, 257–61).

This objection was overcome with the appointment to the see of the Welshman Nicholas Robinson, with whom Price seems to have co-operated well enough on a commission of 1578 to investigate the recusants of the Llŷn peninsula. He was particularly assiduous in searching Plas-du, Caernarvonshire, the home of Thomas Owen, who maintained regular correspondence with his Catholic exile brothers Hugh and Robert. Price was one of the assistant justices in the trial at Wrexham in October 1584 of the schoolmaster Richard Gwyn (alias Richard White) for denying the queen's supremacy. The anonymous Catholic author of *The Life and Martyrdome of Mr Richard White* doubted whether Ellis, 'who is known to be as prophane a life as any in the world', was a fit man to sit in judgment on 'the servant of God', alleging that he had had children with his own sister (Thomas, 104, 108).

The bard Wiliam Llŷn commended Price as a Hebrew and classical scholar, but he took no discernible role in promoting the contribution of the reformers to consolidating the status of Welsh as a language of learning and worship. During a dispute over property rights in Wrexham in the reign of Henry VIII, Price was arraigned in the court of Star Chamber on a charge of assaulting his brother-in-law William *Salesbury, the humanist scholar and translator. He was present in the Commons when the bill for translating the prayer book and Bible into Welsh was introduced in late February and early March 1563, but was absent from parliament for its final reading. However, Price may well have been responsible for devising the act 8 Eliz. c. 20, passed in this parliament's session of 1566. It repealed the measure of 1534 which provided *inter alia* for the trial in Caernarvonshire and Anglesey of offences committed in Merioneth. Merioneth was in a particularly anomalous position among the Welsh shires: another provision of the act of 1534, authorizing the trial in the border shires of suspects arrested in the marcher lordships, had in the second Act of Union of 1543 been extended to apply to Merioneth as well, so that crimes committed there were also triable in Shropshire as the nearest English shire. As a crown official Price had experienced the difficulties of administering the provision of 1534 in a case involving his own household. In July 1553, at the sessions held at Shrewsbury for trial of offences committed in Wales, five men were indicted for murdering Ellis's servant in Denbighshire. Three of the defendants were executed, one was found guilty of manslaughter, and one acquitted. Price continued to intervene in Merioneth electoral politics after he had ceased to represent the shire in the Commons. He supported the Owens of Llwyn in their feud with the Salesburys of Rug, but his influence declined after Leicester's death in 1588. In an exchequer case of 1590 he and his son and heir were accused of unlawful entry into lands in the county.

Ellis Price's name figures prominently in the royal commission set up by the council in the marches for organizing the eisteddfod at Caerwys in October 1567. His eldest son, Thomas *Price (c.1564–1634), became a bard and buccaneer of renown, and his own patronage kept his reputation sweet among the bards. Wiliam Llŷn, one of the most distinguished poets of the age, lauded him as a 'second Moses' endowed with great attributes of character and wisdom in exercising divinely ordained authority. In the verse of Siôn Tudur, chief apprentice bard at the Caerwys eisteddfod, he is depicted as a protector of the country who was dedicated to imposing the rule of law. In gauging his reputation, the conventional praise of the bards must be weighed in the balance against the colourful accounts of his oppressions and 'indirect dealings' left by his opponents. He was remembered in the community long after his death as a ruthless exploiter of opportunities for his own advancement. Thomas Pennant in his *Tours in Wales* describes him as 'the greatest of our knaves in the period in which he lived; the most dreaded oppressor in his neighbourhood, and a true sycophant' (Pennant, 3.140). Price's devoted service to Leicester is well documented, though the surviving correspondence with his patron does not bear out Pennant's claim that his invariable form of address was 'O Lord, in thee do I put my trust'.

Price died on 8 October 1594, but his will was not proved until 24 May 1596; in it he charged his heir and executor, Thomas Price, to protect the interests of his brothers and sisters, and to 'place my base sons in some service, and not to suffer them to go a begging'. Pennant refers to a portrait of him dated 1605 preserved at Bodysgallen, Conwy, which was presumably a copy, but its present whereabouts have not been traced.   PETER R. ROBERTS

Sources Cooper, *Ath. Cantab.*, 1.397–8, 567 · *DWB*, 805–6 · J. Williams, *The medieval history of Denbighshire*, 1: *The records of Denbigh and its lordship* (1860), 109–13 · H. Sydney and others, *Letters and memorials of state*, ed. A. Collins, 1 (1746), 138–9 · R. Flenley, ed., *Calendar of the register of the queen's majesty's council in the dominion and principality of Wales and the marches of the same* (1916) · P. Williams, *The council in the marches of Wales under Elizabeth I* (1958) · *HoP, Commons, 1509–58*, 3.151–2 · E. Roberts, 'Teulu Plas Iolyn', *Transactions of the Denbighshire Historical Society*, 13 (1964), 38–89 · J. Strype, *Memorials of the most reverend father in God Thomas Cranmer*, new edn, 2 vols. (1840), vol. 1 · *Correspondence of Matthew Parker*, ed. J. Bruce and T. T. Perowne, Parker Society, 42 (1853) · J. E., 'Yspytty Ifan, or, The hospitallers in Wales', *Archaeologia Cambrensis*, 3rd ser., 6 (1860), 107–24, esp. 107–8 · S. Adams, 'Military obligations of leasehold tenants in Leicestrian Denbigh: a footnote', *Transactions of the Denbighshire Historical Society*, 24 (1975), 205–8 · G. Williams, *Wales and the Reformation* (1997) · D. A. Thomas, *The Welsh Elizabethan Catholic martyrs* (1971) · T. Pennant, *Tours in Wales*, 3 (1810), 140

Price, Evadne [*pseud.* Helen Zenna Smith] (1896–1985), novelist, was born at sea of English parents who settled in New South Wales, Australia. She was educated at private and convent schools in New South Wales, Belgium, and England. After her father died she went to London to support herself by becoming an actor, touring the provinces with repertory groups. At fifteen she was understudy to Dorothy Dix in a West End production of *Bird of Paradise* and gained her first leading role in *The Rose and the Ring* at Wyndham's Theatre. She later described herself as 'a real little show-off … I loved reciting, singing, dancing, telling make-believe stories, making people laugh or cry, anything to be the centre of attention' (Marcus, 'Writing the body', 139).

Ill health forced Price to give up the stage and she turned to writing, where her flair for the dramatic soon found an outlet. In 1918 she was a journalist on the *Sunday Chronicle*, and she later wrote for the *Sunday Graphic*. She was married to C. A. Fletcher but was widowed, and in 1929 she married the Australian journalist and writer Kenneth Andrew Attiwill (1906–1983). At the time of their marriage both were working for the *Daily Sketch*, for which she was a feature writer and Attiwill a sub-editor.

As a literary figure Evadne Price is best-known for her First World War novel *Not So Quiet … Stepdaughters of War* (1930), her only book still in print. Her publisher suggested that she should produce a parody of Erich Remarque's *All Quiet on the Western Front*, with the possible title *All Quaint on the Western Front*, but on reading Remarque's novel she feared that a frivolous treatment would be considered tasteless. Instead, Price's novel presented itself as a woman's war memoir of ambulance driving on the western front, drawing on the diary of an ambulance driver, Winifred Young, using a first-person narrator, Helen Z. Smith, and published under the pseudonym Helen Zenna Smith. So convincing was the treatment that many readers took it for a factual work, though Price's own experience of the war seems to have been limited to a stint as a temporary civil servant in the Air Ministry.

Perhaps because she was writing fiction, Price allowed herself to depict a war experience much more graphically brutal than that portrayed in most of the better-known memoirs such as Vera Brittain's *Testament of Youth* (1933) or Irene Rathbone's *We that were Young* (1932). Using what Marcus calls a 'new form of cinematic, dialogic and dramatic interior monologue' (afterword, 265), Price depicts the physical extremes of exhaustion and filth that dominate the young women's existence, as well as the fear and tension that accompany each night of driving. Especially notable is the women's bitter rejection of the older civilian generation's unthinkingly patriotic attitude towards the war, a recurrent theme in much post-war writing by combatants. At the same time Price succeeds in collapsing a conventional trope of much war writing that separates men and women into front and home respectively. Her women definitely belong to the front; they can connect only with each other and their male combatant counterparts; they witness at first hand the wounding and death of each other as well as of the soldiers they drive, and return home as much psychologically destroyed as their combatant brothers and lovers.

Reviewing Price's novel for the *Evening Standard*, Arnold Bennett wrote, 'No war book has appalled me more' (Marcus, afterword, 299). The book won the French prix Severigne as 'the novel most calculated to promote international peace'. Four later novels continue the post-war story of Helen Z. Smith: *Women of the Aftermath* (1931), *Shadow Women* (1932), *Luxury Ladies* (1933), and *They Lived with Me* (1934).

Price was a prolific writer of popular adult and children's fiction. As a children's writer she is best-known for the ten volumes in her Jane Turpin series, about a child heroine who has been described as a less successful female counterpart to Richmal Crompton's William. In addition to the Helen Zenna Smith novels, the 1930s saw the publication of most of her Jane books, and novels for adults including *Diary of a Red-Haired Girl* (1932), *Strip Girl!* (1934), and *Red for Danger* (1936). She also wrote plays and screenplays, the film *The Phantom Light* (1935) being based on her play of the same name (1928), and the film *Once a Crook* (1941) being based on a play which she co-wrote with Kenneth Attiwill.

During the Second World War Attiwill was a prisoner of war in Japan, and for two years Price believed he was dead. He later wrote two books on the fall of Singapore and the war in the Pacific. As a war correspondent for *The People* during 1943–5, she covered the allied liberation of western Europe and was later a correspondent at the post-war Nuremberg trials. After the war she continued to write novels, was a broadcast storyteller on television, and practised astrological prediction, contributing the horoscope page for *She* magazine for twenty-five years. On her retirement to Australia in 1975 she became the horoscope columnist for Australian *Vogue*. She died at Manly, Australia, on 17 April 1985, leaving an unfinished autobiography.

CAROL ACTON

Sources *The Times* (19 April 1985) · M. Cadogan and P. Craig, *You're a brick, Angela: a new look at girl's fiction from 1839–1975* (1976) · J. Marcus, 'Writing the body in/at war', *Arms and the woman: war, gender, and literary representation*, ed. H. Cooper and others (1989) · J. Marcus, afterword, in H. Z. Smith [E. Price], *Not so quiet … stepdaughters of war* (1989) · C. Tylee, *The great war and women's consciousness: images of militarism and womanhood in women's writings, 1914–64* (1990) · G. Wachman, *Lesbian empire: radical crosswriting in the twenties* (2001)

Archives U. Reading L., Bodley Head archive, corresp.

Price, Francis (*bap.* 1704?, *d.* 1753), architectural surveyor and author, was probably the Francis Price who was baptized on 23 June 1704 at Petworth, Sussex, son of Francis and Sarah Price. Nothing is known about his father, but his mother, who is described in his will, married twice, her second marriage being to Thomas Consard of Petworth, a vintner with whom she had at least three children (John, Sarah, and Richard Consard). Little is known about Price's early career or education. He was married (his wife, Elizabeth, outlived him, dying on 25 February 1761 at the age of fifty-seven) but at the time of writing his will in 1750 they had no surviving children. By 1736 he was in Salisbury, possibly at the instigation of Bishop Sherlock; certainly he appears to have lived and worked in the city from that date. A number of accounts survive for works done by him on buildings in the cathedral close, including repairs and additions to the bishop's palace (1736–8), Braybrooke (1746), and the north canonry (1751). He was also responsible for rebuilding the west end of Ellingham Church, Hampshire, in 1747. His most important official post was that of surveyor and clerk of the fabric of Salisbury Cathedral—his gravestone records that he had held this position for seventeen years but, although he seems to have acted in this capacity from around 1737, he was not officially appointed until 1745. As clerk of works he carried out an extensive survey of the cathedral and supervised a number of important repairs and rebuildings of the roof and fabric. His *Series of particular and useful observations … upon … the cathedral church of Salisbury*, published just three months after his death, is one of the first serious architectural studies of a Gothic building. A second enlarged, but anonymous, edition was printed by R. Baldwin in 1774.

Although this book was undoubtedly important, Price's fame chiefly rests on his earlier work, *The British Carpenter*. First published as *A Treatise on Carpentry* in May 1733, it was reprinted under its new title as an expanded second edition in 1735 and it is by the latter title that it has been known ever since. *A Treatise on Carpentry* was the first English book devoted entirely to carpentry and designed specifically for the instruction of craftsmen. The first edition had twenty-eight plates, each labelled alphabetically, with the page of text accompanying that plate beginning with the same letter. In the second edition sixteen plates were added which confused this system further. Through copious drawings Price demonstrated how to construct both timber joints and wooden structures, most of the engravings being devoted to designs for roof trusses for a variety of spans and purposes. In all his books Price drew the plates himself, but had them engraved by others. Many of the structures he showed are complex and may reflect more on the creativity of the artist than the practice of the time, but the popularity of the work meant that his designs were frequently copied by subsequent builders, architects, and writers. From the start the book was well received, running to seven editions by 1768, and this was probably helped by the fact that from the second edition onwards it carried a tribute, dated 28 June 1733, as a 'very Useful and Instructive Piece' from three of the most famous architects of the day, Nicholas Hawksmoor, John James, and James Gibbs.

Price evidently gained some status in his own lifetime in Salisbury but he does not seem to have held any other public office. A portrait of him by George Beare dated 1747 is in the National Portrait Gallery; it shows him holding a drawing of the eastern crossing roofs at Salisbury Cathedral which he himself had designed. At the end of his life he lived in the cathedral close and on his death he was thought sufficiently eminent to warrant an obituary in the *Gentleman's Magazine*. He died in Salisbury on 20 March 1753 and was buried in the cathedral cloister outside the chapter-house door.   J. W. P. CAMPBELL

Sources Colvin, *Archs.* · E. Harris and N. Savage, *British architectural books and writers, 1556–1785* (1990) · J. Harris, *Copies of the epitaphs in Salisbury cathedral, cloisters and cemetery* (1825), 127 · P. Ferridam, 'Francis Price, carpenter: a bicentenary', *ArchR*, 114 (1953), 327–8 · *GM*, 1st ser., 23 (1753), 148 · 'Francis Price, his patrons and his book', *The Builder*, 31 (1873), 765 · D. T. Yeomans, 'Early carpenters manuals, 1592–1820', *Construction History*, 2 (1986), 13–33 · *Salisbury: the houses of the Close*, Royal Commission on Historical Monuments (England) (1993) · will, PRO, 11/802, fols. 40–41 · private information (2004) · J. Kerslake, *National Portrait Gallery: early Georgian portraits*, 2 vols. (1977) · Wilts. & Swindon RO, Price MS D1/31/3 · IGI

Archives Wilts. & Swindon RO, collection of drawings and letters relating to work in Salisbury

Likenesses G. Beare, oils, 1747, NPG; repro. in Kerslake, *National Portrait Gallery*

Price, Harry (1881–1948), writer and psychical researcher, was born at home on 17 January 1881 at 37 Red Lion Square, Holborn, London, the second of two children of Edward Ditcher Price (1834–1906), a commercial traveller for a paper manufacturer, and his wife, Emma Randall, *née* Meech (1860–1902). Price's father was born in Rodington, Shropshire, and the young Harry spent many of his school holidays with relatives in that area. In his autobiography he attributes his lifelong fascination with magical and occult matters to an encounter, at the age of eight, with an itinerant conjuror and purveyor of patent medicines in the market place at Shrewsbury.

Price was educated at the Haberdashers' Aske's Boys' School, Hatcham, in south-east London, and later at Goldsmiths' College, where he studied chemistry, photography, and mechanical and electrical engineering. He evinced an early flair for writing, contributing many articles to the school magazine and to local newspapers. He also carried out some early experiments in wireless communication. Upon leaving school he supported himself by a variety of jobs before joining Edward Saunders & Son, the same paper-making firm as his father. On 1 August 1908 he married Constance Mary Knight (1882–1976), daughter of the deceased Robert Hastings Knight, at St Mary's Church, Pulborough, Sussex. There were no children of the marriage. The Prices continued to live at Arun Bank, Pulborough, until Harry's death.

Price was an enthusiastic collector, and gave lectures and wrote many articles based upon his collections of old coins, tokens, Roman artefacts, and books on conjuring and psychical phenomena. In 1917 he placed about eighty artefacts of the First World War on display in the Eastbourne Home Life Exhibition; these were afterwards donated to the newly formed National War Museum (later the Imperial War Museum).

In 1920 Price joined the Magic Circle and the Society for Psychical Research (SPR). He was initially highly sceptical about allegedly paranormal phenomena, and used his knowledge of conjuring techniques to expose fraud. His exposure of the 'spirit photographer' William Hope brought down upon him the wrath of Sir Arthur Conan Doyle, the great champion of spiritualism ('A case of fraud with the Crewe Circle', *Journal of the Society for Psychical Research*, 20, 1922, 271–83). In the succeeding years Price exposed many fraudulent mediums, including the notorious Helen Duncan, the last woman to be prosecuted in England under the Witchcraft Act of 1735 ('Regurgitation and the Duncan mediumship', *Bulletin of the National Laboratory of Psychical Research*, 1, 1931). However, after a visit to Schrenck-Notzing's laboratory in Munich in 1922, Price was convinced that there are a few phenomena which are genuine and worthy of serious scientific investigation. He spent the rest of his life trying to persuade the academic world of the truth of this conviction.

Price's experimental work was brilliantly conceived and executed. Essentially, he tried to obtain evidence of psychokinetic phenomena (PK) under conditions which left no scope for alternative explanations such as fraud or malobservation. His 'telekinetoscope' was an ingenious device which required the PK force to depress an electrical contact inside a soap bubble, without bursting the latter. At some seances Price wired both the medium and the sitters into an electrical circuit so that any attempt at fraud would be immediately detected, and he made extensive use of photography, including stereoscopic photography, to register the occurrence of phenomena.

Many leading scientists attended these sessions and were impressed with what they saw. Price's meticulously written reports on his work with the mediums Stella Cranshaw and Rudi Schneider were widely read, and are among the great classics of psychical research. Although Price remained a member of the SPR until his death, his relationships with several of its leading members were less than cordial, and he never held any office in the society. However, he was foreign research officer to the American Society for Psychical Research from 1925 to 1931, and in 1937 he was offered an honorary doctorate from Bonn University, and the Red Cross medal, first class, from the German government if he would help to set up a department of parapsychology at Bonn. The onset of the Second World War put a stop to all such plans, and Price never received either his doctorate or his medal.

Price's own organization, the National Laboratory of Psychical Research, was formally opened on 1 January 1926 in a flurry of media attention. On its council were some of the world's leading parapsychologists. Lord Sands, a distinguished Scottish judge, accepted the presidency, and Price took the title of honorary director. In 1934 the management of the laboratory was transferred to a group of academics from London University (the University of London Council for Psychical Investigation), which included the psychologists Cyril Burt, J. C. Flugel, and C. A. Mace, and the popular philosopher C. E. M. Joad. This organization eventually petered out during the Second World War, the books and equipment being transferred to the care of London University. To the general public Price is best-known for his investigation of the allegedly haunted rectory at Borley, Essex, which he conducted intermittently from 1929 until his death. Although Price's conduct of this inquiry has been severely criticized, the case remains the most fully documented example of a haunting in the annals of psychical research.

Price died at Pulborough on 29 March 1948, and was buried in St Mary's churchyard. After his death a number of attacks were made on both his personal integrity and his conduct of psychical investigations, most notably by E. J. Dingwall, K. M. Goldney, and T. H. Hall (1956), T. H. Hall (1978), and A. Gregory (1985). Price's friends and admirers defended his good name, and for a balanced assessment the reader should compare the aforementioned writings with those of M. Coleman (1956), R. J. Hastings (1969), and Ivan Banks (1996).

Price remains a controversial figure in the field of parapsychology. He has been described as 'a man of great ability, great energy and great kindness' but also as very ambitious, and suffering acutely from 'an ingrowing chip on his shoulder about his lack of a university degree' (Haynes, 146). He unquestionably put more time, effort, and money into psychical research than any other Englishman since the founding of the SPR and, despite his personal failings, deserves an honoured place among the ranks of those who have sought to push back the frontiers of the unknown.   JOHN L. RANDALL

Sources I. Banks, *The enigma of Borley rectory* (1996) · M. Coleman, 'The Borley report: some criticisms', *Journal of the Society for Psychical Research*, 38 (1956), 249–58 · E. J. Dingwall, K. M. Goldney, and T. H. Hall, *The haunting of Borley rectory* (1956) · A. Gregory, *The strange case of Rudi Schneider* (1985) · T. H. Hall, *Search for Harry Price* (1978) · R. J. Hastings, 'An examination of the Borley report', *Proceedings of the Society for Psychical Research*, 55 (1966–72), 66–175 · R. Haynes, *The Society for Psychical Research, 1882–1982: a history* (1982) · H. Price, *Stella C: an account of some original experiments in psychical research* (1925) · H. Price, *Rudi Schneider: a scientific examination of his mediumship* (1930) · H. Price, *The most haunted house in England* (1940) · H. Price, *Search for truth* (1942) · H. Price, *The end of Borley rectory* (1946) · P. Tabori, *Harry Price: the biography of a ghost-hunter* (1950) · b. cert. · m. cert. · d. cert.
Archives LUL, corresp. and papers | BL, corresp. with Society of Authors, Add. MS 63317 · Trinity Cam., Society of Psychical Research archives
Likenesses photograph, 1932, Hult. Arch. · J. Dumayne, oils (aged nineteen), LUL, Harry Price collection; repro. in H. Price, *Search for truth* (1942) · photographs, LUL, Harry Price collection
Wealth at death £17,618 12s.: probate, 15 July 1948, *CGPLA Eng. & Wales*

Price, Henry Habberley (1899–1984), philosopher, was born in Neath, Glamorgan, on 17 May 1899, the son of Henry Habberley Price, a mechanical engineer, and his wife, Katherine, *née* Lombard. He was educated at Winchester College and then served in the Royal Flying Corps (later the RAF) during 1917–19. After the war he proceeded to New College, Oxford, as a scholar to read *literae humaniores*. He took a first in 1921. In the following year he was elected a fellow of Magdalen College, Oxford, and he was an assistant lecturer at Liverpool University in 1922 and 1923. During this period he also spent some time at Trinity

Henry Habberley Price (1899–1984), by Ramsey & Muspratt

College, Cambridge, where he acquainted himself with the philosophical approaches of G. E. Moore and C. D. Broad; these he found more congenial than the idealism which still dominated Oxford philosophy. In 1924 he was elected a fellow and lecturer in philosophy at Trinity College, Oxford, where he remained until 1935; in that year he was elected Wykeham professor of logic and moved to New College.

Price specialized in epistemology, particularly the problem of knowledge of the external world. In 1932 he published *Perception*, which attempted to articulate a non-phenomenalist alternative to the causal theory of perception. Phenomenalism regarded objects as 'permanent possibilities of sensation' whereas Price refused to identify families of sense data with the physical objects which cause them. Instead he pursued a phenomenological method to articulate a relation of 'belonging' between sense data and physical objects.

Price continued his research into the philosophy of perception with his *Hume's Theory of the External World* (1940), a sustained and sympathetic reading of a much neglected section of Hume's *Treatise*. Hume had been unable to reconcile sensory experience of an external world with sceptical reason, whereas Price envisaged a resolution of these two faculties through the concept of the imagination which makes perception of the material world possible. According to this interpretation the imagination plays a role akin to Kant's transcendental ego. Hence it sees Hume as somewhat closer to Kant than is usually acknowledged.

Price also explored the philosophy of thinking, and published his findings in *Thinking and Experience* (1953), an analysis of the nature of concepts and their relation to sense experience. He took issue both with the symbolistic theory, which identified conceptual thought with the use of symbols, and with the classical account—attributed to Descartes, Locke, and Kant—which regarded concepts as mental entities. Instead Price proposed that concepts are dispositions rather than entities and that memory is crucial to conceptual cognition.

Price was regarded as an outstanding lecturer and a considerate tutor and supervisor. J. O. Urmson, an undergraduate at Corpus Christi College in the 1930s, remembered Price as the teacher 'who at the time young philosophers wanting to break out a bit went to … a rather left-wing example of the traditional school' (private information). Price retired from the Wykeham chair in 1959. His successor, A. J. Ayer, had earlier attended and been influenced by his lectures. In his inaugural lecture Ayer spoke of Price's influence:

> In the sombre philosophical climate of the Oxford of that time, here was a bold attempt to let in air and light: a theory of perception in which the principles of British empiricism were developed with a rigour and attention to detail which they had in that context never received. (Ayer, 79)

After retiring from his chair Price continued to be philosophically active. He was a visiting professor at the University of California, Los Angeles, in 1962 and pursued his interest in religion. His Gifford lectures given in 1960 (published in 1969 as *Belief*) examined theories of belief and considered the implications of his arguments for propositions on the immortality of the soul and the existence of God. *Contra* the positivist doctrines made popular by Ayer which regarded such propositions as meaningless, Price argued that there is evidence for both the soul and God from the existence of paranormal phenomena.

Price was interested in parapsychology—telepathy, clairvoyance, telekinesis, apparitions, hauntings, mediumship, the psychic ether, and survival after death—throughout his career, but he never attempted to integrate it with his more orthodox philosophical work. He also gave the Sarum lectures in Oxford in 1970 on similar themes, later published as *Essays on the Philosophy of Religion* (1972). A further volume of this work was published posthumously in 1995 as *Philosophical Interactions with Parapsychology*. In 1939 he was president of the Society for Psychical Research.

Price, who never married, lived with his sister, Katy, in Headington, Oxford, where he enjoyed his hobbies of watercolour painting and ornithology. Although a shy man he was a generous host to former pupils and colleagues from abroad, organizing bird-watching expeditions and visits into the woods at night to hear nightingales. He died at the Radcliffe Infirmary, Oxford, on 26 November 1984.   MARK J. SCHOFIELD

Sources R. Wilkinson, 'H. H. Price', *Biographical dictionary of twentieth century philosophers*, ed. S. Brown, D. Collinson, and R. Wilkinson (1996) • *The Times* (1 Dec 1984), 10g • M. Kneale, 'Introduction', *The collected works of Henry H. Price*, 1 (1996) • A. J. Ayer, *Part of my life* (1977) • B. Rogers, *A. J. Ayer: a life* (1999) • private information (2004) [Brian Harrison] • *WWW*, 1981–90 • F. B. Dilley, 'Introduction', *Philosophical interactions with parapsychology: the major writings of H. H. Price on parapsychology and survival*, ed. F. B. Price (1995) • b. cert. • d. cert. • *CGPLA Eng. & Wales* (1985)
Archives CUL, corresp. with Francis John Worsley Roughton
Likenesses Ramsey & Muspratt, photograph, British Academy [*see illus.*]
Wealth at death £69,489: probate, 29 May 1985, *CGPLA Eng. & Wales*

Price, (Frederick George) Hilton (1842–1909), antiquary and banker, born in London on 20 August 1842, was the son of Frederick William Price (d. 1888), for many years partner and eventually chief acting partner in the banking firm of Child & Co. Educated at Crawford College, Maidenhead, in 1860 he entered Child's Bank, where he succeeded his father as chief acting partner. Much of his early leisure was devoted to the history of Child's Bank, and in 1875 he published *Temple Bar, or, Some Account of ye Marygold, No. 1 Fleet Street* (2nd edn, 1902), where Child's Bank had been established in the seventeenth century. In 1877 he brought out a useful *Handbook of London Bankers* (enlarged edn, 1890–91). He was a member of the council of the Bankers' Institute and of the Central Bankers' Association.

Price's life was mainly devoted to archaeology. Always keenly interested in the prehistoric as well as historic annals of London, he formed a fine collection of antiquities of the stone and bronze ages and the Roman period. It also included Samian ware vessels imported during the first and second centuries from the south of France, English pottery ranging from the Norman times to the nineteenth century, tiles, pewter vessels and plates, medieval inkhorns, coins, tokens (many from the burial pits on the site of Christ's Hospital), and other artefacts. His collection was secured to form in 1911 the nucleus of the London Museum at Kensington Palace.

Interested in excavations in Britain and abroad, Price took a leading part in the excavation of the Roman villa at Brading in the Isle of Wight, the remains of which were by his exertions temporarily opened to the public, and on which, in conjunction with J. E. Price, he read a paper before the Royal Institute of British Architects on 13 December 1880. He was treasurer for the research fund for the excavations at Silchester or Calleva Attrebatum, on the subject of which he read a paper at the Society of Antiquaries on 11 February 1886. At the same time he was actively engaged in studying and collecting Egyptian antiquities. In 1886 he described part of his collection in the *Proceedings of the Society of Biblical Archaeology* (of which he was elected member in 1884, vice-president in 1901). A large selection from his collection was exhibited at the Burlington Fine Arts Club in 1895, and two years later he published an elaborate catalogue of his Egyptian antiquities, which was followed in 1908 by a supplement. In 1905 he was elected president of the Egypt Exploration Fund, which he had joined in 1885.

Price was an enthusiastic member of the Society of Antiquaries of London, of which he became a fellow on 19 January 1882. He was elected director on 23 April 1894, and retained the post until his death. A keen numismatist, he joined the Royal Numismatic Society in 1897; he was also elected fellow of the Geological Society in 1872. He was a voluminous contributor to the journals of most of the societies and institutions to which he belonged. A valuable series of illustrated papers on 'Signs of old London' appeared between 1903 and 1908 in consecutive issues of the *London Topographical Record* (2–5).

Price married on 5 November 1867 Christina, daughter of William Bailey of Oaken, Staffordshire, with whom he had one son and one daughter. They lived at 17 Collingham Gardens, South Kensington. He died at Hotel Gallia, Cannes, France, on 14 March 1909, after an operation, and was buried at Finchley in the next grave to his father. His wife survived him. He bequeathed £100 to the Society of Antiquaries for the research fund. His books, coins, old spoons, and miscellaneous objects of art and virtu fetched at auction (1909–11) the sum of £2606 10s. 6d. His Egyptian collection realized £12,040 8s. 6d. at Sothebys on 12–21 July 1911. The same firm sold his coins on 17–19 May 1909 and 7–8 April 1910, 575 lots realizing £2309 9s.

WILLIAM ROBERTS, *rev.* BERNARD NURSE

Sources WWW · *The Times* (18 March 1909) · *Proceedings of the Society of Antiquaries of London*, 2nd ser., 22 (1907–9), 471–2 · *London Topographical Record*, 6 (1909), 107–8 · m. cert.
Archives S. Antiquaries, Lond., corresp. and papers | Salisbury and South Wiltshire Museum, Salisbury, letters to A. H. L. F. Pitt-Rivers
Likenesses photograph, S. Antiquaries, Lond.
Wealth at death £38,878 11s. 3d.: double probate, July 1909, *CGPLA Eng. & Wales*

Price, Hugh (*c.*1495–1574), founder of Jesus College, Oxford, was the son of a Brecon butcher, Rhys ap Rhys. He may have been educated in Brecon, or perhaps at Osney Abbey, and later attended Oxford University; he graduated BCL (probably in 1518), BCnL in 1524, and DCnL in 1526. He was one of a group of judges who tried and condemned James Bainham for heresy in 1532. There is no record of his ordination, but at intervals he held a number of livings: Cranbrook, in Kent (1533–54); St Leonard, Foster Lane, London (1542–8); and Llan-faes, Brecknockshire (1554–74). In 1541 he was appointed treasurer of St David's Cathedral, with dispensation from residing there. When the see of Rochester was re-established in the same year, he was appointed as first prebendary there. He held both preferments until his death. He purchased and retained a house in Brecon, and has been identified as the Hugh Price who was bailiff of the borough in 1572. He died, almost certainly in Brecon, in August 1574, and was buried in St John the Evangelist Priory church; he never married.

Jesus College, Oxford, was founded on Price's initiative in 1571 'for the spread and maintenance of the Christian religion in its sincere form' (Williams, 62). He provided an endowment and petitioned Queen Elizabeth, who established the college, claimed for herself the title of founder, and transferred to it the site, buildings, and property of the former White Hall. Price promised his foundation £60 a year. Only part of the main quadrangle was built before he died. He bequeathed 100 marks and his books, and confirmed the £60 a year to the college on condition 'that I

remaine Founder of the same College' (Jones, 146), but there were long delays before the money was made available. In the eighteenth century Edward Yardley remembered Price, as he would have wished, as 'the worthy promoter or rather the founder of Jesus College'. However, the college did not pay its founder the compliment of adopting his arms. Its familiar arms, originally with a blue field, which can be linked with the arms of the family of Green, were in use by 1590.

DAVID WALKER

Sources E. Yardley, *Menevia sacra*, ed. F. Green (1927), 162–3; 397–8 (will) · G. Williams, 'Hugh Price, founder of Jesus College, Oxford', *Brycheiniog*, 25 (1992–3), 57–66 · T. Jones, *History of Brecknockshire* (1909), 2.144–6 · *DWB*, 785 · *VCH Oxfordshire*, 3.264–79
Likenesses G. Vertue, engraving, 1739 (after oil painting by school of Hans Holbein), repro. in Jones, *History of Brecknockshire*, facing p. 144 · school of H. Holbein, oils, Jesus College, Oxford

Price [*formerly* Higginbotham], **James** (1757/8–1783), chemist, son of James and Margaret Higginbotham, was born in London. He entered Magdalen Hall, Oxford, in 1772, graduating MA in 1777. In 1781 he changed his name to Price, in accordance with the will of a relative who had bequeathed him a fortune. On 10 May 1781 he was elected to the Royal Society, having been described on the certificate of recommendation by Richard Kirwan, who headed the list of proposers, as 'well versed in various branches of Natural Philosophy, and particularly in Chymistry' (Royal Society election certificate, Royal Society Archives, London). On 2 July 1782 the degree of MD was conferred on him by the University of Oxford.

Between 6 May and 25 May 1782 Price performed, at Stoke, near Guildford, experiments which appeared to show that he possessed a white powder and a red powder capable of converting mercury into silver and gold respectively, the substances being heated together in a crucible with a flux of borax. The witnesses included lords Onslow, King, and Palmerston, and other men of social, though not scientific, rank. The gold and silver alleged to be produced were found genuine on assay.

Price related the experiments in detail in *An account of some experiments on mercury, silver and gold, made in Guildford in May, 1782, in the laboratory of James Price, M.D., F.R.S.* (1782). The experiments were the subject of a correspondence between Sir Joseph Banks, president of the Royal Society, and his close friend Charles Blagden, initiated by Banks on 14 July 1782 with a letter telling Blagden of the anger of Richard Kirwan and other chemists caused by 'such an apparent charlatanism' (Royal Society Archives, BLA b.8). A letter written by Blagden, however, shows that he thought it possible that Price had made a genuine discovery. Although alchemy was regarded as discredited by Price's chemist contemporaries, prevailing chemical theories did not preclude the possibility of transmuting metals. Blagden was particularly incensed by the award to Price of the degree of MD by Oxford, assuming like many others that it had been conferred for his apparent success in transmutation. 'Was ever any country more disgraced than ours has been by the conduct of our University?', he wrote. If Price had made the discovery he claimed without revealing it to his colleagues, he continued, he deserved to be excluded from their society, not 'to be adorned [with] extraordinary academical honours' (Fitzwilliam Museum, Cambridge, Archives, H 165). Price later insisted that the award of the degree was for former work in chemistry.

In the preface to his account, Price had declared that his stock of the powders was exhausted, and that the cost of replenishment would be too great in labour and health for him to undertake it. Nevertheless it was made clear to him that he must repeat his experiments in the presence of scientific colleagues, Banks, in particular, reminding him that the honour of the society was at stake as well as his own. Early in 1783, having tried to obtain information in Germany of alchemical processes, Price apparently worked incessantly for six weeks, attempting to verify his claims. In March he prepared a concentrated infusion of laurel leaves (which would contain hydrocyanic acid) and made his will. According to Chambers's *The Book of Days* (1863) he drank this in the presence of the three colleagues who alone came to the laboratory at his invitation on a day in early August which he had appointed for a demonstration. This has usually been repeated in subsequent accounts of Price's suicide. It is, however, difficult to discount the probability of an alternative version in a letter dated 30 September 1783, to an editor of the *Göttingisches Magazin* (3. 886–9) who had earlier published an abstract of Price's book in the journal. The unnamed writer from London, who seemed well informed and went into considerable detail, stated that Price was alone when he drank the poison, no one having accepted his invitation to attend the laboratory that day. Price was buried at St John's Church in the parish of Stoke-next-Guildford, where a memorial gives the date of his death as 31 July.

P. J. HARTOG, rev. E. L. SCOTT

Sources H. C. Cameron, 'The last of the alchemists', *Notes and Records of the Royal Society*, 9 (1951–2), 109–14 · C. Blagden, correspondence with Joseph Banks, RS, Blagden papers, BLA b.8/9 · J. Banks, correspondence with C. Blagden, FM Cam., H 164–6 · *Göttingisches Magazin der Wissenschaften und Litteratur*, 3, 410–52, 579–83, 886–9 · R. Chambers, ed., *The book of days: a miscellany of popular antiquities in connection with the calendar*, 1 (1863), 602–4 · election certificate, RS · memorial, St John's Church, Stoke-next-Guildford, Surrey · *N&Q*, 3rd ser., 8 (1865), 290, 405
Likenesses J. Russell, chalk drawing, NPG · J. Russell, pastel drawing, NPG; repro. in E. L. Scott, 'The Guildford alchemist', *Pharmaceutical Journal*, 257 (1996), 938–9
Wealth at death £10,000–£12,000: *DNB*

Price, John (1602?–1676), classical scholar, was born in London, according to the information transmitted to Anthony Wood by Thomas Lockey, canon of Christ Church, Oxford; he describes himself in his earliest published work as 'Anglo-Britannus'. He was a scholar of Westminster School and went up in 1617 to Christ Church, where he neither matriculated nor graduated, presumably because of his Roman Catholic faith. In this period he apparently composed verses in memory of Queen Anne, who died in 1619. Given the commonness of the names, it is uncertain whether he is the John Price, 'son and heir of John Price of London, Esq., deceased', admitted at Gray's Inn in 1619 (Foster, *Register*, 156). He had apparently acquired a doctorate of law, presumably abroad, some

time before 1640, but nothing in his career suggests an interest in legal practice. His references to his ownership and acquisition of books show that he was a man of some means.

In 1629 Price was in Venice; by 1635 he was in Paris, working on the *Apologia* of Apuleius, his edition of which he published there in that year. It is dedicated to Henry Howard, eldest surviving son of Thomas Howard, earl of Arundel; Price describes himself as having been for three years Arundel's protégé (*cliens*), as a result of the intervention of William Petty. Price had done a great deal of work for this edition before leaving England; while in Paris without his books, he was helped by Jean Bourdelot. His letters to Bourdelot from London in 1635 and 1636 reveal that, before Paris, Price had visited Padua and met Lorenzo Pignoria, perhaps on the same journey as his visit to Venice in 1629; it was presumably in Italy that he had discovered the edition of the *Apologia* by Scipione Gentili (1607), and modified his own plans accordingly. The final outcome is remarkable for the range of classical and medieval texts and earlier scholars cited, and for the use of visual and inscriptional evidence, drawing partly on the Arundel collections and partly on material recorded by Bourdelot. (The Arundel marbles had been collected in Asia Minor by an agent of Nicolas Claude Fabri de Peiresc, diverted by Petty; the inscriptions were published by John Selden in 1628 with the help of Patrick Young and Richard James.) Price describes himself as 'foreign and unknown' to Bourdelot, but his letters show that he was already in touch not only with Pignoria, but also with Cardinal Francesco Barberini, Peiresc, and Selden (Larroque).

It may be that confidence should be placed in the belief that Price went to Ireland during the rule of Thomas Wentworth, earl of Strafford, and met Archbishop Ussher, and even that he served Strafford, but it can only have been for a brief period in 1636, since by February 1637 Price was in Vienna, attracted by the manuscripts brought back from Constantinople by Augerius Busbequius. Price copied manuscripts not only in the Imperial Library, but also in the Tengnagel collection. It was at this stage also that he compiled the index of authors used by Hesychius, printed in his edition of the *Metamorphoses* of Apuleius of 1650. Before the end of the year Price was in Venice copying inscriptions, texts of which passed via Selden and George Harbin to Edmund Chishull. It was presumably from Venice that Price visited Piacenza (a visit to which he refers in a letter of 1658) and that he left for Rome in May 1640.

By late 1640 Price was back in England, writing to Archbishop Ussher from the country house of George Radcliffe, the friend of the earl of Strafford, on 29 August 1640; earlier that month, the dean and chapter of Christ Church had recommended Price to Archbishop Laud for a prebend. The traditions that Price published royalist pamphlets, supported the royalist cause, and was imprisoned by parliament are poorly grounded. By 1644 Price was in Antwerp having his portrait done by Wenceslaus Hollar, a portrait engraved by R. A. Persyn for Price's edition of the *Metamorphoses*. In 1645–6 he was in Paris, where he associated with Claude de Sarrau, leaving with him on 10 February 1646 copies of his notes on the New Testament for G. J. Vossius and Claude de Saumaise. De Sarrau admired Price's learning and fortitude in adversity. An anonymous letter to Ussher from Rouen of 18 May 1647 is probably from Radcliffe, who was at Caen in April 1647; the letter records Price's intention of going to London and recommends him to Ussher. (If the letter is indeed from Radcliffe, he would undoubtedly have known of any earlier visit to Ussher.) Meanwhile, it was in Paris that Price's work on Matthew (1646), Acts (1647), the epistle of James (1646), and Psalms (1647) was published, probably also on five chapters of the gospels and the letter to Philemon (1646). Price's work in this field was in part republished with other New Testament material in London in 1660 as *Joannis Pricaei commentarii in varios novi testamenti librae*, a book to which Price refers in his later correspondence with the Medici. Price's *Apuleii Metamorphoseos libri XI* was published in Gouda in 1650. He had worked on it in England in 1640, using a manuscript he had originally owned, which he had given to Laud, and which Laud had given to Oxford, which Price had borrowed through the good offices of Patrick Young, librarian to James I and Charles I. He had recorded a certain amount of autobiographical data in it, and had also used the notes of Casaubon in his copy of the Leiden edition of 1588 by P. Colvius.

Price had written to Archbishop Ussher from London on 19 August probably of 1649, undertaking to transmit a book of Ussher's to Pierre and Jacques Dupuy. By 1653, when he wrote again to Ussher (also sending greetings to Selden), Price had been for a year in the employ of the Medici as their keeper of coins; he told Ussher that he was working on the epistles of Paul and Aulus Gellius. He was also appointed professor of Greek at Pisa. Tradition has it that he also intended to work on Avienus and further on Hesychius, having resigned his chair in Pisa and gone to Venice for the purpose, only to abandon the project with the publication of the Leiden edition of 1668. This edition, however, includes Price's index, originally published in 1650, and substantial contributions to the commentary. It is in any case certain that Price went to Venice in 1658. In 1661 he moved to Rome and into the patronage of Cardinal Francesco Barberini, and remained there until his death in 1676. He was buried in the Augustinian monastery there. Notes on some of the younger Pliny's *Letters* had by his death perhaps reached proof without being published.

Price was in touch with many of the major European classical scholars of his time, and Colomiès lists many of those who cited him with esteem in their work. Price's scholarship had something of the magpie quality that Peiresc's had, but he did not have Peiresc's birth and wealth that enabled the latter to act as the centre of a European network of scholars. Price's work on classical authors shows judgement and learning, but when he turned to the New Testament he was insufficiently aware of the different nature of its textual tradition and excessively adventurous in emendation.

MICHAEL H. CRAWFORD

Sources P. Tamizey de Larroque, 'Deux lettres inédites de Jean Price à Bourdelot', *Bulletin du Bibliophile*, 1883 [published separately, Paris, 1883] · BL, Add. MS 32096, fols. 336–348v · E. Chishull, *Antiquitates Asiaticae* (1738), 200 · PRO, Roman transcripts 30/9/130 · Vatican Library, Barb Lat. MS 8620, fol. 141 · *CSP dom.*, 1640, 536, 555 · Bodl. Oxf., MS Laud Lat. 55 · R. Parr, ed., *The life of the most reverend father in God, James Usher … with a collection of three hundred letters* (1686), 506, 515, 595, 596 · R. Pennington, *Wenceslaus Hollar* (1982), 1485, 1534 · C. de Sarrau, *Epistolae ex bibliotheca Gudiana auctiores* (Paris, 1654), vol. 144, p. 150; vol. 157, p. 162; vol. 169, p. 173 · Marucelliana Library of Florence, Redi MS (F.) 222, 92–135 · Biblioteca Nazionale Centrale, Florence, Autografi Palatini MS, lettere autografe 1, fols. 75–109 · BL, Add. MS 4385, fol. 62 · Wood, *Ath. Oxon.* · J. Welch, *A list of scholars of St Peter's College, Westminster* (1788) · P. Colomiès, *Bibliothèque choisie* (La Rochelle, 1682), 135 · P. Bayle, *Dictionnaire historique et critique*, 12 (Paris, 1820), 316–17 · E. Chaney, *The grand tour and the Great Rebellion* (1985) · E. Chaney, *The evolution of the grand tour* (1998) · Foster, *Alum. Oxon.* · J. Foster, *The register of admissions to Gray's Inn, 1521–1889, together with the register of marriages in Gray's Inn chapel, 1695–1754* (privately printed, London, 1889)

Likenesses W. Hollar, etching, 1644, BM, NPG · R. de Persyn, line engraving, 1650 (after W. Hollar), BM, NPG; repro. in L. Apuleius, *Metamorphoses* (1650) · W. Hollar, etching (after J. Danckert), BM, NPG

Price, John (1626/7–1691), Church of England clergyman, was born at Gatcombe on the Isle of Wight, the son of Ellis Price, rector of Gatcombe, and his wife, who was probably Ann, *née* Rathborne. John Price went to Eton College as a king's scholar: he and his younger brother William (1631–1684) were so poor that in 1645 they received a grant from the college. On 10 January 1645, aged eighteen, he went to King's College, Cambridge. He graduated BA in 1650, and was elected to a fellowship of the college, a post he held until 1656. He proceeded MA in 1653. His brother William followed him from Eton to King's in 1648 and was also a fellow there, from 1651 to 1666.

Price served General George Monck, who had been a fellow-commoner at King's in 1627, as a chaplain in Scotland from 1654 to 1659, becoming his chosen confidant. In August 1659 he was particularly involved, along with Monck's clerical brother, Nicholas, Dr Thomas Gumble, the Presbyterian chaplain to the Edinburgh council, and Dr Samuel Barrow, a physician, in the plan to send a remonstrance to parliament, 'to complain of the long sitting of Parliament and to call for elections' (Masson, 5.476–7). Indeed Price seems to have been the trusted amanuensis of this Dalkeith letter, which was later burnt once General Lambert had crushed the summer insurrection.

Travelling south with General Monck towards London, Price complained of a long fast sermon he and the general had to endure from Hugh Peters at St Albans in late January 1660. The House of Commons instructed him on 26 April 1660 to preach before them at St Margaret's Church to celebrate the day of solemn thanksgiving for the 'Mercies God has bestowed on the nation through the successful conduct of the Lord General Monk'. In his sermon on 10 May he observed that the Church of England 'could not have fallen but by the heates of its own Ecclesiasticks', that the country would never mean mischief to the court, 'unless the Court first minister occasion of offence, either seeming or real', and that it was to the subjects' advantage 'to keep the prerogative of the Crown inviolable' (J. Price, *Sermon Preached before the Honourable House of Commons at St Margarets*, 1660, epistle dedicatory) and likened the occasion to the annual thanksgiving for the 1605 Gunpowder Plot.

Price was later well rewarded for his loyalty. Nicholas Monck having become provost of Eton, on 12 July 1660 Price became one of the fellows there. He kept rooms at Eton until his death, when he bequeathed the tapestries and fireplace picture in his 'great Roome' to his successor (PRO, PROB 11/404, fol. 188v). Further, Charles II presented him to the prebendal stall of Grimston in Salisbury Cathedral, on 8 October 1660 during the vacancy in see. This was fully three weeks before the house committee on religion was due to meet again to discuss the status of non-episcopally ordained clerics. This followed the rowdy discussions in July for the settling of ministers. Sir Edward Dering fulminated that 'ordination by presbyters without a bishop is … not so much discountenanced, but left equally estimable to the ancient episcopal ordination' (*Diaries and Papers*, 49). Dering's appeals reopened the debate over discipline and nonconformity. In spite of this Price was instituted on 28 November 1660 and later installed. He received Anglican orders as deacon on 23 January, and priest on 31 January the following year, and in the same year the University of Cambridge conferred on him a DD by royal letters patent. (He incorporated this degree at Oxford in 1680.)

In 1669 Price became rector of Petworth, Sussex. Price remained close to Monck and in 1676 wrote 'The designed loyaltie of the renowned Generall George Monck in restoring King Charles', now in the British Library, published in 1680 as *Mystery and Method of his Majesty's Happy Restauration*. In September 1683, following the Rye House plot, he preached against division and backbiting, appealing for unity and, by way of admonition, recalled a time when parliament soldiers 'did Plunder the Houses and take away the Houses of honest country-men' (J. Price, *Sermon Preached at Petworth in Sussex Sept. 9. 1683*, 1683, 9). The sermon was printed at the behest of his patron, the duchess of Somerset.

For many years Price lived at Petworth with his wife, Frances, who suffered from dementia. By his will of 10 October 1690 he provided that she and her sister Margaret Edmonds should be allowed to live in his house in Suffolk Street in London with a lifelong maintenance grant from his estate. He required that at her death a substantial charity be established to support scholars of King's College. He died at Petworth on 17 April 1691 and was buried in the parish church on 20 April. He and his wife had no children.   NICHOLAS W. S. CRANFIELD

Sources Venn, *Alum. Cant.* · T. Skinner, *The life of General Monk, late duke of Albemarle* (1723) · D. Masson, *The life of John Milton*, 7 vols. (1859–94) · J. Gauden, *Slight healings of publique hearts* (1660) · will, PRO, PROB 11/404, fols. 188–9 · patent letter-book, PRO, C 66/2919 · register of bishops of Salisbury, Wilts. & Swindon RO, D 1/2/22 · Salisbury Cathedral chapter act book, 18 · *The diaries and papers of Sir Edward Dering, second baronet, 1644 to 1684*, ed. M. F. Bond (1976) · Foster, *Alum. Oxon.* · IGI · parish register, Petworth, W. Sussex RO, 20 April 1691 [burial]

Price, John (d. 1736), architect of London, of whose parents nothing is known, was a designer of early Georgian churches in an unsophisticated vernacular style derived from Wren. He was the John Price 'of Richmond', who designed Isleworth church, Middlesex, 1705–7, and also architect and builder of the church of St Mary-at-the-Walls, Colchester, Essex, 1713–14. In 1714–16, in conjunction with his son John Price (also of Richmond), he designed and built St George's Chapel, Yarmouth, Norfolk, where in 1715 they also contracted to build a new town hall and assembly room. John Price subsequently designed the church of St George, Southwark, the foundation-stone of which was laid on 23 April 1734 by the deputy of George II, *adjuvante Johanne Price armiger, architecto*. It was completed in 1736.

Price engaged in speculative building in London, and in 1718 took leases on the Harley estate in Holles, Oxford, Margaret, and Prince's streets. In 1720 he was responsible for a project for residential development at Headley in Surrey, near Epsom, then a fashionable watering-place. The design is remarkable as 'the earliest English essay in urban terrace composition' (Hussey, 1539–40) since Inigo Jones's Covent Garden, anticipating Colen Campbell's for Grosvenor Square by five years. This is known from an engraving (found separately, and as plates 96–7 of Badesdale and Rocque's *Vitruvius Brittanicus*, vol. 4, 1739) inscribed 'The Elevation of West Prospect of Part of a Design of Building already began to be Erected on the Lawne at Headly in Surrey/Design'd by John Price, Architect, 1720'. It shows a grand central building with portico and mansard roofs (presumably some sort of assembly rooms) flanked by two identical ranges each of nine houses treated as a uniform composition. It was never completed, but traces of Price's unfinished buildings were still to be seen at Headley in the early nineteenth century.

Price was employed by the duke of Chandos at Cannons House, Middlesex, in 1720–21. By this time the structure was largely complete, and Price's contribution, so far as original designs were concerned, was probably small. However, the elevations of Cannons published by Hulsbergh at this time are inscribed 'John Price Architect, Built Anno 1720', although what they show was largely the work of his three predecessors in the duke's service. The design of the duke's projected mansion in Cavendish Square, owing much to Cannons, is similarly described as 'Design'd by John Price, architect 1720'. It was never built, and by 1723 Price's place as the duke's surveyor had been taken by Edward Shepherd. In 1726–8 Price was among those who made designs for a bridge to be built across the Thames between Fulham and Putney. His designs were not, however, accepted by the Company of Proprietors of Fulham Bridge. In 1735 Price published *Some considerations humbly offered to the House of Commons, for building a stone-bridge over the River Thames from Westminster to Lambeth*, with an engraved design.

John Price died in November 1736. Little is known of the career of his son John, although he appears principally to have been a London surveyor. He was warden of the Carpenters' Company in 1751–2, and was elected master in 1753. He acted as surveyor to the Fishmongers' Company in the 1760s, and died on 17 October 1765.

ALAN MACKLEY

Sources Colvin, *Archs.* · E. Harris and N. Savage, *British architectural books and writers, 1556–1785* (1990) · C. Hussey, 'Surrey's Grosvenor Square', *Country Life*, 143 (1968), 1539–40

Price, John (1735–1813), librarian, was born on 1 March 1735 at Llandegla, Denbighshire, and baptized on 7 March, the son of the Revd Robert Price (*b.* 1705?), rector of the parish, and his wife, Anne (*d.* 1756). In 1737 his father became vicar of Llangollen, Denbighshire, where John was educated before matriculating from Jesus College, Oxford, on 26 March 1754. He graduated BA in 1757 and MA in 1760. In the latter year he was ordained. In 1757 Humphrey Owen, who was Bodley's librarian and a fellow of Jesus College, appointed him janitor of the Bodleian—a position he held until 1760. From 1761 to 1763 he occupied the post of sub-librarian and from 1762 to 1763 also acted as Owen's substitute as curate of Kingston Bagpuize, Berkshire. Owen was elected principal of Jesus College in 1763, and from 1765 to 1767 Price was acting librarian and received Owen's salary. On Owen's death in 1768 Price succeeded him as Bodley's librarian after a close election in which he defeated William Cleaver, afterwards principal of Brasenose College, and, successively, bishop of Chester, Bangor, and St Asaph. Price took the degree of BD in the year of his election and also succeeded Owen as a delegate of Oxford University Press.

Throughout his long period of office in the Bodleian Library, Price also held ecclesiastical appointments. He was curate at Northleigh, Oxfordshire, from 1766 to 1773 and at Wilcote, Oxfordshire, from 1775 to 1810. In 1782 he was presented to the living of Woolaston with Alvington, Gloucestershire, and in 1798 to Llangattock, Brecknockshire, both by Henry Somerset, fifth duke of Beaufort, whom Price frequently visited at Badminton. He was never a fellow at Jesus College, although he drew an annual stipend as a graduate scholar from 1758 until 1783. In June 1789, persuaded by his friend, the poet laureate Thomas Warton, he migrated to Trinity College where he remained until his death.

The advances made by the Bodleian Library during Price's forty-five years as its librarian owed little to his administrative skills. In 1787 Thomas Beddoes, who had just been elected chemical reader at Oxford, addressed a printed *Memorial concerning the state of the Bodleian Library, and the conduct of the principal librarian* to the library's curators. In it he attacked Price for 'a regular and constant neglect of his duty', for non-attendance at the library, and for lending out books before they were catalogued. He also criticized in detail the library's opening hours, its methods of acquisition, its choice of books and serials, and the expenditure of its meagre income on fitting up rooms rather than on acquisitions. The *Memorial* has been called 'a classic of library criticism' (Philip, 107), but it was the curators rather than Price who acted upon it to reform the library's policies and finances. Price's reputation

rested elsewhere. To John Nichols he was the 'able Pioneer in Literature, whose friendly attentions will be recollected by many researchers into the vast treasures of the Bodleian Library' (Nichols, *Illustrations*, 5.514). He was a fellow of the Society of Antiquaries, and shared the interests and enjoyed the friendship and respect of many in the antiquarian and literary worlds. His correspondence reproduced by Nichols shows in particular how much the bequest of Richard Gough's enormous topographical collection to the Bodleian owed to Price's careful cultivation of the benefactor. In these circles he was known as 'honest Johnny Price'.

Price wrote little, although he is acknowledged in the prefaces of many of the works of his friends. His *Short Account of Holyhead in the Isle of Anglesea* was included in Nichols's *Bibliotheca Topographica Britannica* (10, 1783) and an 'Account of a brass image of Roman workmanship found at Cirencester' written in 1767 was published in *Archaeologia* (7, 1785). He amassed a considerable collection of books, prints, maps, and manuscripts (including the benefactors' book from the parish of Northleigh) which were sold, partly at a five-day sale from 17 June 1814 by Thomas King junior, at 125 High Holborn, and partly through a catalogue subsequently issued by King.

Price, who was unmarried, died at his house at 1 St Giles', Oxford, during the night of 11–12 August 1813 and was succeeded as Bodley's librarian by his godson Bulkeley Bandinel. He was buried on 20 August at Wilcote church, where a mural tablet was erected to his memory.

DAVID VAISEY

Sources I. Philip, *The Bodleian Library in the seventeenth and eighteenth centuries* (1983) · W. D. Macray, *Annals of the Bodleian Library, Oxford*, 2nd edn (1890) · Nichols, *Illustrations*, vol. 5 · Nichols, *Illustrations*, vol. 6 · *GM*, 1st ser., 83/2 (1813), 400–01 · D. Womersley, 'Jesus in the eighteenth century', *Jesus College Record* (1996–7), 66–7 · Foster, *Alum. Oxon.* · *Llandegla parish registers*, 3 vols., Clwyd Family History Society (1992–4) · *Llangollen parish registers*, 7 vols., Clwyd Family History Society (1988–94) · *A catalogue of the library of the Revd John Price* (1814) [sale catalogue, Thomas King, London, 17–21 June 1814] · *Bibliotheca curiosa: supplement to Tho. King, junr's catalogue, including the reserved part of the library of the revd John Price* (1814) [sale catalogue, Thomas King, London, 17 June 1814] · *DNB*
Archives Bodl. Oxf., corresp. · Bodl. Oxf., library records · Bodl. Oxf., travel journals · Norfolk RO, travel diary of his Suffolk and Norfolk tour
Likenesses J. C. Bromley, line engraving, pubd 1819 (after H. H. Baber), BM · engraving (after sketch by H. H. Baber, 1798), repro. in Philip, *The Bodleian Library* · line engraving, BM

Price, John (1773–1801), topographer, was born at Leominster, Herefordshire. He gave lessons there in French, Latin, Italian, and Spanish. Subsequently he became a bookseller at Hereford, but finally settled at Worcester. He occasionally made walking tours on the continent. In 1795 he published *An Historical and Topographical Account of Leominster and its Vicinity*. This was followed in 1796 by *An Historical Account of the City of Hereford, with some Remarks on the River Wye*. This 'very respectable performance' was founded on collections given to the writer by John Lodge, author of *Introductory Sketches towards a Topographical History of Herefordshire* (1793). In 1797 Price published *The Ludlow guide, comprising an historical account of the castle and* *town, with a survey of the various seats, views, &c., in that neigh-bourhood.* In 1799 appeared a similar *Worcester Guide.* Price's other publications included *The Seaman's Return, or, The Unexpected Marriage* (1795), an operatic farce, partly trans-lated from German. He died at Worcester on 5 April 1801.

G. LE G. NORGATE, *rev.* ROBIN WHITTAKER

Sources J. Chambers, *Biographical illustrations of Worcestershire* (1820), 575 · J. Allen, *Bibliotheca Herefordiensis, or, A descriptive cata-logue of books, pamphlets, maps, prints, &c. relating to the county of Here-ford* (1821) · D. E. Baker, *Biographia dramatica, or, A companion to the playhouse*, rev. I. Reed, new edn, rev. S. Jones, 1 (1812), 583; 2 (1812), 250 · [D. Rivers], *Literary memoirs of living authors of Great Britain*, 2 vols. (1798) · [J. Watkins and F. Shoberl], *A biographical dictionary of the living authors of Great Britain and Ireland* (1816)

Price, Joseph (*c.*1727–1796), merchant and pamphleteer, described himself as 'Having been born in Wales, suckled with Welch blood' and having 'the Welch devil' in him (Price, 38). It seems that his family came from Monmouth, but other indications of his parentage or upbringing are lacking. He evidently went to India for the first time in 1750, to make his living by the sea as what was known as a 'free merchant', that is, a person not in the service of the East India Company who was permitted to sail ships in Asian waters and trade on his own behalf in the 'country trade' between Asian ports. His first base seems to have been Bombay, but from 1767 he resided in Calcutta, where he became a prominent member of the European com-munity, always known as Captain Price and attracting epi-thets such as 'honest' or 'a man of spirit'.

In his early years in Bengal, Price's commercial activities were very extensive. He evidently took over the business of Robert Gregory, another free merchant, who returned to Britain with a great fortune. Price wrote that he had once had twenty-four ships 'navigating the seas on my own credit'. He made nine voyages as captain or managing agent from India to the Red Sea or the Persian Gulf (Price, 50–51, 71). The extent of his involvement in the China trade is revealed by transactions with Warren Hastings, on whose behalf he shipped cargoes insured for £36,000 to Canton (Guangzhou) in 1774. By then, however, Price's affairs had begun to deteriorate to the point where he could not pay his creditors either in India or in Britain.

In 1778 Hastings gave Price command of two armed mer-chant ships to support the navy in operations against the French. In 1780 Price left India to try to settle with his British creditors and to gain an office from the East India Company for his return. While in Britain he found a new vocation as a pamphleteer. Fourteen tracts have been attributed to him, nearly all published in 1782 or 1783. They were for the most part highly polemical, extolling his friends, above all Hastings, and mercilessly lampoon-ing his enemies, as when he dismissed the pious Charles Grant as 'the most canting, Presbyterian, methodistical, sniveling Oliverian, Scotland ever produced' (Price, 114). Polemic aside, his tracts contain some vivid vignettes of British society in Bengal and his *Letters from a Free Merchant* provides valuable information about the working of the country trade. Price was not sure that Hastings fully appre-ciated his zeal on his behalf, writing 'You will lift up your

Eyes, and express your wish that this Old Fool would be quiet and mind his Own Affairs' (Grier, 351). For a time Price's creditors confined him for debt, but he was able to return to India in 1784 with the promise that he would suc-ceed to the office of marine storekeeper in Bengal. In 1786 he duly assumed that office and also became marine pay-master. Although creditors such as Hastings were never to be paid off, Price's affairs seem to have prospered a little, until he was suspended from office in 1792 and found insane. In 1793 his nephew, also called Joseph Price, was given permission to have him sent to Britain. Price's last years in London were such that his death there 'without a Pang or Struggle' on 3 June 1796 was regarded by his friends as 'a consummation devoutly to be wished' (E. Baber to W. Hastings, 4 June 1796, BL, Add. MS 29174, fol. 317). There is no record of Price's either marrying or having any children. His nephew was his sole heir.

P. J. MARSHALL

Sources J. Price, *Some observations and remarks on a late publication, entitled 'Travels in Europe, Asia and Africa'* (1782) · BL, Warren Hastings MSS · Bengal public proceedings, BL OIOC · will and administra-tion, BL OIOC, L/AG/34/29/10, 1797, no. 16 · *The letters of Warren Hast-ings to his wife*, ed. S. C. Grier [H. C. Gregg] (1905) · K. K. Datta and others, eds., *Fort William–India House correspondence*, 4–10 (1962–72) **Archives** BL, Warren Hastings MSS, Add. MSS 28973–29236, 39871–39904, 63090, 63104 · BL OIOC, MSS Eur. D 1190 · BL OIOC, Bengal public proceedings **Wealth at death** under Rs 100,000 [£11,500]; had long-standing debts: administration, 1797, BL OIOC, L/AG/34/29/10

Price, Joseph (1736?–1807), Church of England clergyman and diarist, was probably born in East Anglia. The nature of his early education is unknown, but he was brought up as a dissenter and maintained contact with several lead-ing dissenters throughout his life. His father had been a successful tradesman in London. Price had two brothers, one of whom became a naval purser, and two sisters. In 1758–9 he served briefly as minister to the small Independ-ent congregation at Southwold in Suffolk, where a local source described him as 'an ingenious young man' (*Kentish Parson*, 2). After one year he conformed to the Church of England, obtaining ordination in the diocese of Norwich as deacon (1759) and priest (1762). In 1762–3 he served as curate of Rumburgh and South Elmham, and in the latter year became curate at Lowestoft. He was tutor to the son of Hill Mussenden, MP for Harwich, and through Mussenden's influence became perpetual curate of Tun-stall, Norfolk, in 1765 and rector of Hellington, some 6 miles away, in 1766.

During the 1760s Price came to the attention of Thomas Secker, archbishop of Canterbury, and, like Price, a for-mer dissenter. Through Secker's patronage Price, in 1767, became vicar of Brabourne in east Kent, the region in which he passed the remainder of his life. In 1776 he added the rectory of Monks' Horton to the vicarage of Brabourne and his two livings in Norfolk. He had already begun to compile an intimate shorthand diary, of which only the manuscript volume 6 (1769–1773) survives, although internal evidence indicates that there were at least twelve volumes altogether. The diary is a remarkably frank, self-critical record of ambition and social climbing, with detailed accounts of the lives (and scandals) of the local clergy and gentry. Price was a correspondent of Charles Yorke (1722–1770), son of the celebrated Lord Chancellor Hardwicke (1690–1764). On Yorke's nomination as lord chancellor in January 1770 Price wrote: 'I must congratulate him and try to get something'; four days later the news of Yorke's sudden death led Price to lament: 'The breaking of a blood vessel discomforts all my glittering hopes and tells me I must die Vicar of Brabourne' (*Kentish Parson*, 9). This prophecy was not fulfilled; he relinquished Brabourne and Monks' Horton in 1786 on his appointment as vicar of Herne, which he exchanged for Littlebourne, his final living, in 1794.

Price never married and one reason for his bachelor status was his unfulfilled hope of acquiring a Cambridge fellowship. His diary reveals much knowledge of the university's politics, since he was enrolled as a 'ten-year man' at Peterhouse and obtained the BD degree in 1776. He refers frequently to the question of subscription to the Thirty-Nine Articles and testifies to the extent of Trinitarian heterodoxy among some of the Cambridge fellows, such as John Jebb. Another reason why he never married, however, was the failure of his pursuit of wealthy matrimonial candidates. He rejected one on the ground that she was a Presbyterian and that such an alliance 'would make an odd figure in this neighbourhood' (*Kentish Parson*, 17), an indication of the distance he had moved from his dissenting origins. His chief target for marriage was Mary Lane, the widow of a London sugar merchant and twelve years Price's senior. Although Mary resisted his proposals of matrimony, she bequeathed her entire estate to him on her death in 1782. Price thus acquired a financial independence rare in a parish clergyman. He could afford to leave most of his duties at Littlebourne to a curate, to visit the hot wells at Bristol, and to lease a house in the Mint Yard, in the precincts of Canterbury Cathedral, where he died on 29 October 1807. He was buried at Littlebourne parish church in the following month.

Price appears never to have published anything, although a manuscript version of a funeral oration written by him for the first earl of Hardwicke (d. 1764) survives among the latter's papers in the British Library. While he lacked the conscientiousness (and literary flow) of his contemporary James Woodforde, the essentially private nature of his diary takes the reader far beyond the printed sermon and the begging letter to a potential patron, which are the only remaining testimonies to the character of so many clergymen of his age.

G. M. DITCHFIELD

Sources *A Kentish parson: selections from the private papers of the Revd Joseph Price, vicar of Brabourne, 1767–1786*, ed. G. M. Ditchfield and B. Keith-Lucas (1991) · Venn, *Alum. Cant.* · T. A. Walker, *Peterhouse* (1935) · E. Hasted, *The history and topographical survey of the county of Kent*, 2nd edn, 12 vols. (1797–1801) · D. Turner, *List of Norfolk benefices, with the names of their respective incumbents and patrons* (1847) · *The autobiography of Thomas Secker, archbishop of Canterbury*, ed. J. S. Macauley and R. W. Greaves (1988) · G. M. Ditchfield and B. Keith-Lucas, 'Reverend William Jones "of Nayland" (1726–1800): some new light on his years in Kent', *N&Q*, 238 (1993), 337–42 · N. Sykes, *Church and state in England in the XVIII century* (1934) · *The speculum of Archbishop Thomas Secker: the diocese of Canterbury, 1758–1768*, ed. J. Gregory (1995) · *Kentish Gazette* (1776) · *Kentish Gazette* (1793) · *Kentish Gazette* (1794) · *Kentish Gazette* (1807) · *GM*, 1st ser., 77 (1807) · will, PRO, PROB 11/1470, fols. 216v–218r · will, PRO, PROB 11/1092, fols. 68–9 · parish registers (burials), Littlebourne parish church, Nov 1807, Canterbury Cathedral Archives

Archives Canterbury Public Library, MS shorthand diary [with typewritten transcript by F. Higenbottam] | BL, Hardwicke MSS, Add. MSS 35612, 35637 · LPL, Archbishop Moore MSS

Wealth at death under £7500; incl. property bequeathed to brother, and 10 guineas left to poor of Littlebourne: will, 28 Nov 1807, PRO PROB 11/1470, fols. 216v–218r; PRO, death duty registers, IR 26/129/160

Price, Joseph Tregelles (1784–1854). *See under* Price, Peter (1739–1821).

Price, Joshua (*bap.* 1672, *d.* 1722). *See under* Price, William, the elder (*d.* 1709).

Price, Laurence (*fl.* 1628–1675), ballad and chapbook writer, is a shadowy figure despite his prolific output. Only three contemporary references to him are known, all from the 1650s and all derogatory. One patronizes his astrological pamphlets, the other two belittle his ballads and verse. In default of information on his origins and life, his bibliography is his biography. However, connections with Bristol have been suggested; and one commentator roundly states that Price was a native of London, adding that 'during the civil war he seems to have occasionally been a hanger-on of the parliamentary army' (*DNB*). Internal evidence from successive publications indicates that Price supported Charles I (*Great Britaines Time of Triumph*, 1641), then at least sympathized with the Commonwealth (*The Quakers Feare*, *The Matchles Sheapard*, both 1656) before in due course welcoming the Restoration (*Win at First, Lose at Last*, 1660?).

Unlike his royalist ballad-writing rival, Martin Parker, Price did not have a strong ideological commitment; rather he sought to write what would sell in order to make a living. (One of his ballads, 'Oh, Gramercy Penny', *c.*1628, deals at length with the predicament of those without money.) He therefore trimmed politically while exploring the traditional staples of the cheap literature trade. His thirty-three 'small books'—in effect, pamphlets of usually eight or twelve pages, roughly 3 inches by 6, illustrated by (sometimes relevant) woodcuts—cover such topics as crime (*Bloody Actions Performed*, 1653), social comment (*Fortune's Lottery*, 1657), sensational news (*The Shepherd's Prognostication Foretelling the Sad and Strange Eclipse of the Sun*, 1652), and fictional tales (*The Famous History of Valentine and Orson*, 1673, Price's version of a tale which originated in fifteenth-century France). Some publications of this kind were miscellanies; for example, he described *Make Roome for Christmas* (1657) as 'A delightful New Book, full of merry Jests, rare Inventions, pretty Conceits, Christmas Carols, pleasant Tales, and witty Verses' (title-page).

Price's broadside ballads, of which sixty-two have been identified (though others may be lost), cover much the same ground as his small books, though with greater emphasis on relations between the sexes, as in 'Two Fervent Lovers' (1632), 'Loves Feirce Desire' (1656), and

'Flora's Farewel' (1675). One may not accept C. H. Firth's judgement that, together with Parker, Price 'perfected' the ballad as a literary form (Firth, 28), but Price's success is clearly demonstrated by the frequent reprintings of his ballads and books not only during his lifetime but in some cases well into the nineteenth century, in both London and the provinces. As was normal with broadsides, his work frequently appeared without acknowledgement; unfortunately, this was also the case in compilations by Thomas Percy, Walter Scott, and F. J. Child. Despite his professed dislike of broadsides Child paid Price a singular compliment by admitting three of his ballads to a collection intended to include only traditional material, *The English and Scottish Popular Ballads* (5 vols., 1882–98). Of one of these, 'Robin Hood's Golden Prize' (1656), Child remarked that his copy 'seems to be signed L. P., probably the initials of the versifier' (Child, no. 147, headnote). The other two, 'The Famous Flower of Serving Men' (1656) and 'A Warning for Married Women' (1657), were not acknowledged. Nevertheless, they remained in popular favour, with versions continuing in oral tradition long into the twentieth century, in both Britain and North America. Price's 'Rocke the Cradle' (1631) enjoyed a similar vogue.

There is no complete and definitive list of Price's publications and their whereabouts; seventeenth-century editions are scattered through a variety of collections such as Douce, Rawlinson, and Wood (Bodl. Oxf.), Euing (Glasgow University), Pepys (Magdalene College, Cambridge), Bagford, Huth, Roxburghe, and Thomason (BL). Selections, sometimes restricted by considerations of perceived indecency, were published in learned volumes by Victorian ballad scholars. A few items resurfaced in anthologies of the late twentieth century. An edition of Price's collected works is long overdue because of their intrinsic qualities, documentary value, and significance in the history of popular culture. ROY PALMER

Sources D. Harker, 'The price you pay: an introduction to the life and songs of Laurence Price', *Lost in music*, ed. A. L. White (1987), 107–63 • C. H. Firth, 'The reign of Charles I', *TRHS*, 3rd ser., 6 (1912), 19–64 • W. C. Hazlitt, *Hand-book to the popular, poetical and dramatic literature of Great Britain* (1867) • W. C. Hazlitt, 'Early Christmas books: an unique volume by Laurence Price', *N&Q*, 4th ser., 2 (1868), 549–51 • F. J. Child, ed., *The English and Scottish popular ballads*, 5 vols. (1882–98) • B. H. Bronson, *The traditional tunes of the child ballads*, 4 vols. (1959–72) • H. E. Rollins, *An analytical index to the ballad-entries in the registers of the Company of Stationers of London* (1924); repr. (1967) • C. M. Simpson, *The British broadside ballad and its music* (1966) • P. Kennedy, ed., *Folk songs of Britain and Ireland* (1975) • W. G. Day, ed., *The Pepys ballads*, 5 vols. (1987) • M. Spufford, *Small books and pleasant histories: popular fiction and its readership in seventeenth-century England* (1981) • H. E. Rollins, *A Pepysian garland* (1922) • J. Ashton, *Humour, wit and satire of the seventeenth century* (1883) • W. Chappell and J. W. Ebsworth, eds., *The Roxburghe ballads*, 9 vols. (1871–99) • R. Palmer, ed., *The Oxford book of sea songs* (1986) • J. Wardroper, ed., *Lovers, rakes and rogues* (1995) • *DNB* • D. Harker, 'A warning [on Price]', *Folk Music Journal*, 6 (1990–94), 299–338

Price [*married name* Maude], **(Lillian) Nancy Bache** (1880–1970), actress and author, was born on 3 February 1880 at Rockmount in the small village of Kinver on the Worcestershire/Staffordshire border, the daughter of William Henry Price and his wife, Sarah Julia Mannix. Her father was 'an aristocrat by birth and choice', a pillar of the local church community, but a remote parent. She had a stronger bond with her mother, who encouraged her artistic talents. Following the death of her elder sister, May, at the age of five from diphtheria, Nancy was brought up as an only child. She sketched, wrote diaries, and played the violin until her father, who was worried about her health and posture, stopped her from doing so, according to one of her several accounts. She attended the village school at the age of nine, before being sent away to a boarding-school, Malvern Wells, which she hated.

Nancy Price had an independent streak in her character. One teacher called her 'not naughty but rather wild' (Price, *Into an Hour Glass*, 16). She liked to think of herself as a vagabond, as in the titles of her later books, such as *Vagabond's Way* (1914) and *The Heart of a Vagabond* (1955). She was thought by her parents to be a sickly child, but she liked riding and walking. Her childhood memories of the midlands landscape delighted her readers, among them Lord Dunsany, who described her tribute to the Lake District, *Shadows on the Hills* (1935), as the 'book of my choice'.

Nancy Price decided to become an actor at the age of fourteen, a choice of profession which her father deplored for moral and economic reasons. She joined F. R. Benson's company in her last term at school and made her non-speaking stage début at the Theatre Royal, Birmingham, in September 1899. Benson staged the summer Shakespeare seasons at Stratford upon Avon, one of the best training grounds for young actors in the United Kingdom. He was also famous for his love of sport and Nancy Price suspected that she was chosen for her skills at golf, tennis, and hockey, as well for her acting. But she was talented enough to attract the attention of the actor–manager Sir Herbert Beerbohm Tree, whose premières at His Majesty's Theatre then provided the high points of London's theatre seasons.

Tree cast Price as Calypso in Stephen Phillips's *Ulysses* (February 1902), a four-hour epic, described in *The Times* as 'a majestic enterprise' (3 Feb 1902). Samuel Coleridge-Taylor composed the incidental music and the sculptor Auguste Rodin designed the sets. Nancy Price was described as 'authentically Homeric', and also as 'the nymph with braided tresses', and her success led to further West End roles. A. W. Pinero wrote for her the part of Hilda Gunning, the shop-girl with airs above her station, in *Letty* (1904), a forerunner of Bernard Shaw's Eliza Doolittle. Max Beerbohm concluded of her performance that 'every sentence rang phonographically true' (*The Times*, 1 April 1970). She played several seasons with Tree's company and Sir Henry Irving wanted her to play Portia to his Shylock, but she had a prior engagement and turned him down. Nancy Price joined the Pioneer Players at the Kingsway Theatre in 1911 in a season which included 'feministic' plays. In 1913 she appeared as India in Sir Edward Elgar's *Crown of India*.

On 17 May 1907 Nancy Price married Charles Raymond Maude (1881/2–1943) at a register office; he was an actor who came from a family distinguished for its army and stage connections. His grandmother was Jenny Lind, the 'Swedish nightingale'. Their marriage lasted until his death in 1943 and they had two daughters, Joan and Elizabeth, who both became actresses. According to her memoirs it was not an easy relationship. She had many 'affairs of the heart' and complained that in art as well as life her husband was a perfectionist. He was a member of Harley Granville Barker's repertory company at the Duke of York's Theatre in 1910, a season distinguished for new-wave drama, including Granville Barker's *The Madras House* and *Waste*. But his acting career was short. In the First World War he applied for a commission and rose to the rank of lieutenant-colonel; but he retired from the stage after the war and never acted again.

During the war Nancy Price continued to act but also raised money for war charities, worked with the blind, and in one bizarre episode, joined a ship's crew off the east coast as a cook, which provided some vivid descriptions for her book, *The Gull's Way* (1937). During the 1920s she was an established leading lady, if not of the first rank, playing in Sutton Vane's *Outward Bound* (1924), Pirandello's *Henry IV* (1925), and opposite Mrs Patrick Campbell in Ibsen's *John Gabriel Borkman* (1928). She lectured on Shakespeare and illustrated her talks with extracts, and led a remarkably active social life in which (from her memoirs) she seems to have met almost every famous person in western Europe from Cork in Ireland (where she had relatives) to Rome, where she met Mussolini. She was committed to many of what were then good causes, among them anti-vivisection and state subsidies for the theatre. 'Even the half-starved Serbian peasant', she wrote in 1940, 'pays tribute to the upkeep of the theatre' (Price, *Nettles and Docks*, 33).

The aim was to establish subsidized repertory companies along the continental lines. Shaw and Granville Barker campaigned for a national theatre, while Lilian Baylis at the Old Vic claimed that hers was the true national theatre. In 1930 Nancy Price joined forces with the playwright–manager J. T. Grein, to found the People's National Theatre, which produced eighty-two plays in various theatres over a period of twenty years. Grein, who died in 1935, soon left the company, but Price became its honorary director. Under her leadership the company presented a worthy repertory of history plays by such writers as Clifford Bax and John Drinkwater, poetic dramas including those of W. B. Yeats, and 'realist' plays in the style of Ibsen and Shaw. Her most popular role was as the grandmother, Adeline, in Mazo de la Roche's *Whiteoaks* (1936), which ran for two years. 'Amazing!', wrote Shaw, 'There has been nothing like it in London since Irving captured it with *The Bells*!' (Price, *Into an Hour Glass*, 183), which she took as a compliment. Her finer performances were held to be as Mrs Jones in Galsworthy's *The Silver Box* (1931) and as Edith Cavell in *Nurse Cavell* (1934).

As Adeline, Nancy Price had an on-stage parrot, Boney, with whom she became very friendly. Her interest in all kinds of birds, mammals, and natural landscapes is a feature of all her books, which numbered over twenty. She was a founder of the Council of Justice to Animals. A talented amateur naturalist, she wrote with equal enthusiasm about the wildlife in London's parks as about the Sussex Downs. At first she disliked the cinema, but appeared in some non-starring film parts, and edited a theatre magazine called *Pedlar's Pack*. In their day, Nancy Price's books were popular and widely read. Through them she scattered names in short but not very revealing anecdotes. She drove with Sir Malcolm Campbell and recalls the 'many delightful hours I spent with Elgar in his studio', without relating what happened in either car or studio. Her style evoked the world of P. G. Wodehouse.

Nancy Price was indisputably what Wooster would have called 'a good egg'. In his foreword to *Nettles and Docks* (1940) Norman Birkett described her as 'a fighter on the side of all things which are honourable and true and of good report amongst men'. She was made a CBE in 1950 for her services to the theatre and died on 31 March 1970 at 145 Rowlands Road, Worthing, Sussex.   JOHN ELSOM

Sources *Who was who in the theatre, 1912–1976*, 4 vols. (1978) · *The Times* (1 April 1970) · *British theatre: a bibliography* (1989) · R. Mander and J. Mitchenson, *The lost theatres of London* (1968) · N. Price, *Nettles and docks* (1940) · N. Price, *Into an hour glass* (1953) · N. Price, *Each in his own way* (1960) · *The Times* (3 Feb 1902) · *The Times* (12 Oct 1932) · *The Times* (15 April 1936) · b. cert. · m. cert. · d. cert. · *CGPLA Eng. & Wales* (1970)

Archives W. Sussex RO, corresp. and working papers | U. Reading L., letters to R. L. Mégroz

Likenesses photographs, *c.*1905–1953, Hult. Arch.

Wealth at death £14,328: probate, 1970, *CGPLA Eng. & Wales*

Price, Owen (d. 1671), schoolmaster, was born in Montgomeryshire. He was made a scholar of Jesus College, Oxford, by the parliamentary visitors in October 1648, and he matriculated on 12 March 1649. He remained at the university for four years before taking a job as a schoolmaster in Wales, where 'he advanced his scholars much in presbyterian principles' (Wood, *Ath. Oxon.*, 3.942). He eventually returned to Oxford to finish his education, graduating BA, and proceeding MA by accumulation from Christ Church on 6 May 1656. In 1657 he succeeded William Wroth as master of Magdalen College School, 'where by his industry and good way of teaching, he drew many youths of the city, whose parents were fanatically given, to be his scholars' (ibid.). He apparently supplemented his income by teaching out-college boys as well as his regular pupils.

On 21 June 1658 Price sent a letter to Henry Scobell, secretary of Oliver Cromwell's council, to complain about the delay in making him master of Westminster School in succession to Richard Busby. The delay 'has disswaded several persons from sending their children to me', he writes, and 'I fear that I shall suffer by it very much' (Peck, 502). He challenges his detractors to 'let any scholars in Oxon be appointed to make a tryall of my boyes here [Magdalen]' (ibid.). His candidacy for Busby's position does not appear to have been successful. At the Restoration Price was ejected from his position at Magdalen for nonconformity, and he taught subsequently in Devon and Besselsleigh, Oxfordshire, where he became 'useful among the brethren, and a noted professor in the art of pedagogy' (Wood, *Ath. Oxon.*, 3.942).

Price's first book, *The Vocal Organ* (1665), comprises a 35-page primer and a 29-page praxis, as well as brief sections on calligraphy, punctuation, and arithmetic. In the primer Price adapts the phonetic system of John Wallis, author of *Grammatica linguae Anglicanae* (1653), to the teaching of spelling. Price's method is to have students master the pronunciation of letters before they are introduced to fifty-six spelling rules. The praxis is a collection of alphabetically arranged verses 'to difference the words of like sound' (p. 47), such as *ant-aunt*, *earn-yarn*, and *sought-soft*. In his preface Price claims that he was not 'guided by our vulgar pronunciation, but by that of London and our Universities', but it has been suggested that some of Price's pronunciations betray the time he spent in Devon. *The Vocal Organ* contains the first illustration of the organs of speech (lips, teeth, palate, tongue, throat) in an English book.

Price's second book, *English Orthography* (1668), is a major revision of *The Vocal Organ*. Price abandons Wallis's phonetic system and presents his spelling rules in a question and answer format; he replaces the verses in the praxis with a table of homophones, or near homophones, and their definitions. In a second edition (1670) he adds a list of frequently misspelt words. His lists are derived largely from earlier spelling books, such as Richard Hodges's *A Special Help to Orthographie* (1643) and Jeremiah Wharton's *The English Grammar* (1654), and they were, in turn, included in many later spelling books, such as George Fox and Ellis Hookes's *Instructions for Right Spelling* (1670).

On 2 July 1657 Price was married in Oxford to Lydia, daughter of John Blagrave of Merton College. Their children included John (*b.* 1659), Samuel (*b.* 1664), and possibly Martha (*b.* 1669). Joseph Foster mentions another son, Thomas, who graduated BA in 1693 and MA in 1695 at Oxford. These dates seem rather late for a son of Price's; however, the register of St Peter-in-the-East does record the baptism of a Thomas Price on 21 May 1672, approximately six months after Owen's death. According to Wood, Price died in his house near Magdalen on 25 November 1671 and was buried two days later in 'the church of S. Peter, in the East, near to the door leading into the belfry' (Wood, *Ath. Oxon.*, 3.943). On 4 December 1671 an Oxford court ordered that no action should be taken on Price's goods, mentioning the name of a possible creditor, Henry Hodges. The administration of Price's effects did not take place until 13 December 1676; his widow Lydia was still living at the time. An inventory of his goods and chattels, dated 15 February 1677, shows his wealth to have been a little more than £298, most of which was derived from a lease granted by the president and fellows of Magdalen College.

EDWARD A. MALONE

Sources Wood, *Ath. Oxon.*, new edn • E. J. Dobson, *English pronunciation, 1500–1700*, 2nd edn (1968) • J. R. Bloxam, *A register of the presidents, fellows … of Saint Mary Magdalen College*, 8 vols. (1853–85) • F. Peck, ed., *Desiderata curiosa*, new edn, 2 vols. in 1 (1779) • Foster, *Alum. Oxon.* • DNB • O. Price, *The vocal organ* (1665); facs. edn (1970) • O. Price, *English orthography, 1668*, ed. R. Alston (1972) • 'Scobell, Henry', *DNB* • M. Burrows, ed., *The register of the visitors of the University of Oxford, from AD 1647 to AD 1658*, CS, new ser., 29 (1881) • private information (2004) [C. Gilliam, Oxon. RO]
Wealth at death £298 9s. 8d.: Bloxam, *Register*, vol. 3, pp. 178–80

Price, Peter (1739–1821), ironmaster, was born at Madeley, Shropshire, the son of Henry Price and his wife, Margaret Habberley. A member of a strong Roman Catholic family, as an infant Price was taken to Derby to see Charles Edward Stuart when he entered the town in 1745. However, at the age of fifteen Price was taken seriously ill and remained unconscious for thirty-two days; this event seriously weakened his interest in religion. This experience made him abandon his faith at about the same time that he entered the famous Coalbrookdale ironworks as an apprentice moulder.

Price became a skilled worker and in 1759 was recruited by Dr John Roebuck for his newly founded Carron Company in Scotland. At Carron, Price became the foreman of the boring mill and worked with James Watt on his early attempts to build an improved steam engine. Watt was later to describe Price to Boulton as 'a man of character and a great deal of knowledge in the foundry way' (J. Watt to M. Boulton, 4 Aug 1781, Boulton and Watt Collection, Birmingham Reference Library).

In 1768 Price left the Carron ironworks for America, where he spent five years putting up blast furnaces in Pennsylvania, Maryland, and Virginia. While in America he dabbled in freemasonry and belonged to the Philadelphia lodge. At this time an injury to his back forced him to give up heavy industrial work. For a brief period he was an officer in the American army but returned to Britain when fighting escalated in the War of Independence. While returning home he was engaged in conversation by a member of the Religious Society of Friends and these discussions on board ship led him to become a Quaker.

On his return to England, Price became an agent for the Coalbrookdale Iron Company in London. Later he became a corn factor in Stourport and then in Cornwall. In 1781 he married Anna (*d.* 1846), the sister of Samuel Tregelles. The couple had one son and two daughters. The Tregelles family were Quaker merchants in Cornwall who were also linked through marriage to the powerful Fox family of Falmouth, who were ships' agents and important adventurers in the Cornish mines. In 1791 the Fox, Price, and Tregelles families were the main investors in the Quaker partnership that founded the Perran foundry near Falmouth. This concern was set up to manufacture engineering parts for the Cornish mines. In 1792 the same partners leased land at Neath Abbey in south Wales. Here an ironworks was built with two furnaces to supply the Perran foundry with pig iron.

In 1801 Price became the resident manager at the Neath Abbey ironworks. Soon the making of machine parts and castings began to be concentrated at Neath Abbey. This soon graduated to the making of complete steam engines. Price with his foundry and engineering expertise was able to develop the Neath Abbey ironworks from a bulk pig-iron producer to a precision engineering establishment. This transition was helped by the partnership's Cornish connections and an illustration of this is that the first engines made at Neath Abbey were of the high pressure design under Richard Trevithick's patent. Price also played an active part in the local Quaker community and he founded a free school for the children of Neath Abbey. He died at Neath Abbey on 13 September 1821.

By the time of his death Price's managerial position at Neath Abbey had been inherited by his son, **Joseph Tregelles Price** (1784–1854). Born at Penryn, Joseph was educated at the Quaker school at Compton. He became a partner in the Neath Abbey Iron Company in 1818 and remained as managing partner until his death in 1854. Under his management the Neath Abbey Iron Company considerably expanded production of steam engines. The 1820s saw the works build its first marine steam engine and in 1829 the building of railway locomotives was commenced. It is no wonder that Joseph Tregelles Price's activities were recorded by one Quaker poet in the following way:

> Joseph Price, Joseph Price,
> Thou are mighty precise,
> Methought t'other night in a dream
> That thou really walked
> Slept, ate, drank and talked,
> And prayed every Sunday by steam.
> (*Diaries of Edward Pease*, 390)

The range of products of the Neath Abbey Iron Company was expanded when in 1842 the works built its first iron ship, which was the first iron vessel launched in Wales. Stationary steam engines continued to be built at the Neath Abbey ironworks and some of the world's largest pumping engines were built for the Cornish mines. The works under the management of Price also exploited the local need for engines in the expanding south Wales coal and iron industries. The Neath Abbey ironworks was a unique engineering establishment for it was the only British works to build marine, stationary, and locomotive engines along with iron ships. Price was not only a manager but also an experienced engineer and during the 1830s he took out two patents for improvements to boilers and steam engines.

Price was more than simply an industrialist for he was well known for humanitarian acts and for the prominent position he took in the affairs of the Society of Friends. One of his well-known acts was his attempt to intervene in the case of Richard Lewis (Dic Penderyn). Lewis had been condemned to death for his part in the Merthyr riots of 1831. Price was convinced of Lewis's innocence and rode to London to talk about the case with the home secretary. A reprieve was granted for a time but Lewis was not saved from the gallows. Price was also active in campaigning for the end of wars of all kinds. With several other Quakers he founded in 1816 the Peace Society in London. In June 1843 the international peace conference was held in London, a conference in which Price played an important part as chairman of one of the sessions. The work of this society broadened out during the 1840s, beyond the propagation of non-resistance on religious grounds, through its involvement with the anti-corn law campaign, which was much supported in nonconformist journals.

Price's sisters were to play an important part in the industrial and religious affairs of the family. Junia Price (1787–1845) was a very active member of the Society of Friends and travelled extensively in England and Ireland as a minister of the gospel. She accompanied her brother to Carmarthen shortly before she died to plead for clemency for those Rebecca rioters that were held there. Christina Abberley Price (1792–1879) was also an active member of the Society of Friends and was involved in the industrial life of the area as a partner in the Neath Abbey Coal Company. Both the Neath Abbey Coal and Iron companies continued to operate in the area until the withdrawal of both the Fox and Price families from business in 1874.

Joseph Tregelles Price died unmarried on 25 December 1854 at Glynyfelin, Cadoxton, Glamorgan. An obituary in a leading south Wales newspaper commented that:

> Mr Price has been familiar to the public of South Wales during very many years as a leading man of business and an indefatigable philanthropist. His character was one of singular energy, cool discrimination and inflexible integrity. Few men could be so greatly missed in his own immediate neighbourhood; but his loss will be felt not only in the religious community of which he was a member, but in various associations for benevolent objects and moral progress.   (*The Cambrian*, 28 Dec 1854)

LAURENCE INCE

Sources priv. coll., Price family MSS · D. Rhys Phillips, *The history of the Vale of Neath* (1925) · L. Ince, *The Neath Abbey Iron Company* (1984) · Birm. CL, Boulton and Watt collection · *The diaries of Edward Pease: the father of English railways*, ed. A. E. Pease (1907), 390 · *The Cambrian* (28 Dec 1854) [Joseph Tregelles Price] · d. cert. [Joseph Tregelles Price]
Archives priv. coll., family MSS
Likenesses photograph (Joseph Tregelles Price), RS Friends, Lond.

Price, Richard. *See* Rice, Richard (1511–1589).

Price, Richard (1723–1791), philosopher, demographer, and political radical, was born on 23 February 1723 at Tynton, in the parish of Llangeinor, in the county of Glamorgan, the only son and eldest of three children of Rice Price (1673–1739) and his second wife, Catherine (1697–1740), daughter of David Richards of Oldcastle, Bridgend. Rice Price was a dissenting minister who officiated at different times in his career at Brynllywarch, Cildeudy, Newcastle, Bridgend, and City, Betws. He also taught for a brief period at the academy founded by Samuel Jones at Brynllywarch. Richard's sister Sarah had eight children, including William *Morgan (1750–1833), the pioneering actuary, and George Cadogan *Morgan (1754–1798).

Early life and ministry Price's education began at home under a Mr Peters, who later became a dissenting minister. At the age of eight or thereabouts he began attending a school run by Joseph Simmons, a dissenting minister at Neath, and in 1735 he went to a school run by Samuel Jones at Pen-twyn in Carmarthenshire. Price then spent a

Richard Price (1723–1791), by Thomas Holloway, pubd 1793 (after Benjamin West, 1788)

short time at an academy run by Vavasor Griffiths (*d.* 1741), located at Chancefield, Talgarth, Brecknockshire.

Rice Price died in 1739, and Catherine and her two daughters left Tyn-ton to live in Bridgend. In the following year Catherine died and, probably on the advice of his uncle Samuel (who was assistant to Isaac Watts at St Mary Axe in Bury Street, London), it was decided that Richard should go to London to attend the academy at Tenter Alley, Moorfields. Here Price remained for four years, being taught by John Eames and Joseph Densham. Eames, a friend and a disciple of Sir Isaac Newton, had won a reputation both as a mathematician and as a teacher, and he gave Price an excellent grounding in mathematics (which was to serve him well in his distinguished career as an adviser to the Society for Equitable Assurances) and in Newtonian physics. One important feature of Price's education is that in the course of it he was weaned away from the theological beliefs of his father and his uncle Samuel, who were both high Calvinists. The home at Tyn-ton had a reputation for a strict puritanical discipline; it was not this, however, that Price rebelled against so much as the orthodox trinitarianism of the older generation. It is likely that it was the teaching of Samuel Jones at Pen-twyn that moved Price towards the rationalism and the libertarianism that in later life he defended with such conviction.

When his stay at Moorfields came to an end in 1744, Price became family chaplain in the household of George Streatfield, a wealthy dissenter, who lived at Stoke Newington. During this period he served as an assistant to Samuel Chandler at Old Jewry Lane, though not to the satisfaction of Chandler, and he also took services at Edmonton and Enfield. Streatfield became involved in a celebrated legal case which proved a landmark in the dissenters' struggle for the full legal recognition of the right to religious freedom. The practice had grown up of appointing dissenters to offices in the City of London. Some dissenters were nevertheless unable to accept them because a precondition was that they should take the sacraments according to the rites of the Church of England, which they could not in conscience do. Those who refused were liable to heavy fines which were unceremoniously exacted.

The dissenters fought the issue through the courts, and their dilemma was not resolved until 4 February 1767 when Mansfield issued his famous judgment that 'Nonconformity was certainly not a crime.' Although Streatfield had been withdrawn from the case at an early stage because he was found not to be within the jurisdiction of the court, Price learned a great deal about the nature of the fight the dissenters would have to wage in order to secure freedom of worship, and the experience had a profound influence on his thought on the subject of toleration. Throughout his career he maintained strongly that everyone has not only the right to worship God according to his conscience but also the right not to be disadvantaged in the way the dissenters had been by the policy of reserving offices under the crown and in municipal authorities to members of the Church of England.

Price's uncle Samuel died in 1756 and his patron George Streatfield died in January 1757. From both he received legacies which enabled him to contemplate marriage. On 16 June 1757 Price married Sarah Blundell (1728–1786), the daughter of a speculator who had been ruined by the South Sea Bubble. In the following year Price accepted the appointment of pastor at the presbyterian chapel at Newington Green, and he and Sarah moved to a house nearby. Not long after their marriage Sarah suffered an attack of the palsy, the first of several which led to her becoming a permanent invalid. There were no children of the marriage.

After the death of Dr George Benson in April 1762 Price became minister at Poor Jewry Lane, retaining the afternoon service at Newington Green. In 1770 he relinquished the appointment at Poor Jewry Lane, and instead became morning preacher at Gravel-Pit Meeting Place at Hackney. He continued to be pastor at Newington Green until 1783, and he remained a preacher at Gravel-Pit until he retired on 20 February 1791, not long before his death the following April. From the accounts that have survived Price does not seem to have been a success as a preacher in the early years of his ministry, and it was after becoming a celebrity that his congregation steadily increased. Notwithstanding his fame in other fields, Price always maintained, as did his friend Joseph Priestley, that his work as a pastor was the most important that he undertook and had the first claim upon his attention and energies.

Publications and patrons Despite his devotion to the pulpit, Price found time for several other occupations. In 1758 he published *A Review of the Principal Questions and Difficulties in Morals*. In 1765 he became a fellow of the Royal Society, Benjamin Franklin being one of his sponsors. This honour was largely due to the work he did editing Thomas Bayes's manuscripts on the theory of probability. In 1767 he published his first theological work, *Four Dissertations*, and in the same year on 7 August he was awarded the degree of doctor of divinity at Marischal College, Aberdeen. In 1766, or thereabouts, he began his influential work with the Society for Equitable Assurances which led to the publication in 1771 of *Observations on Reversionary Payments*. Alongside his actuarial and demographic studies he also became interested in warning the government of the perils of maintaining a large national debt and in advocating the adoption of sinking fund procedures for its reduction.

In 1771 Price's friendship with William Petty, second earl of Shelburne, later the first marquess of Lansdowne, began. Shelburne's first wife died in January 1771 and he found consolation in Price's 'On providence' and 'On the reasons for expecting that virtuous men shall meet after death in a state of happiness', both of which had been published in *Four Dissertations*. Shelburne asked Mrs Montagu to arrange an interview, which eventually took place at Price's home in Newington Green. Price soon entered the Bowood Group, the informal gathering of intellectuals and professional men who met at Shelburne's estate at Bowood in Wiltshire or at his London house in Berkeley Square and advised him on a wide range of subjects. In some ways this circle was an eighteenth-century form of 'think tank' which kept Shelburne abreast of developments in the professions, at the bar, in the armed forces, and in the church, and which kept him well informed as to current opinion on economic and financial matters. This group included Isaac Barré, John Dunning (later Lord Ashburton), Joseph Priestley, Jonathan Shipley, bishop of St Asaph, and, at later periods, Samuel Romilly and Jeremy Bentham.

Price prepared several papers for Shelburne—on toleration and the extension of legal recognition of the freedom of worship, on the relations between Britain and America, but mainly on financial matters, particularly on the most efficacious way of raising government loans and on his favourite project, the revival of sinking fund procedures for the redemption of the national debt. Shelburne helped Price by supplying him with information from official statistics, both when he was in opposition and during the short period when he was in office, and by being his patron—the third and subsequent editions of *Observations on Reversionary Payments* were dedicated to him. Both at Bowood and at Berkeley Square, Price had more opportunities to meet the famous and the learned than might otherwise have fallen to his lot: it was through Shelburne, for example, that he had access to the earl of Chatham, whose support he solicited on behalf of the dissenters' campaign to secure relief from subscription to the Thirty-Nine Articles. Price was instrumental in securing Joseph Priestley's services as Shelburne's librarian.

Another important group which contributed to Price's intellectual development was the Club of Honest Whigs, which met at St Paul's Coffee House and, later, at the London Coffee House on Ludgate Hill. Many of the leading dissenters in London were members, as were Benjamin Franklin (whom Price had first met during Franklin's first visit to England from July 1757 to August 1762) and Jonathan Shipley.

Price's fame increased substantially with the publication of *Observations on the Nature of Civil Liberty* (1776), a pamphlet written in defence of the American patriots. This was followed by *Additional Observations* in 1777, and *Two Tracts* (in which he republished both pamphlets) in 1778. For his work as a political writer Price received two unusual honours. He was elected a freeman of the City of London in 1776 and in 1778 received an invitation from congress to go to America to advise them on financial matters, an invitation conveyed to him by Benjamin Franklin, Arthur Lee, and John Adams, which, however, he declined. In 1780 he published his study on demography, *An Essay on the Population*, which brought him a great deal of notoriety, largely because events proved that his thesis that the population of England and Wales had been and was still declining was false. While Price's support for the rebels made him unpopular in many quarters at home, and made his wife anxious for his safety, in America the opposite was true. His pamphlet *Observations on the Importance of the American Revolution* (1784) was well received in all the regions of the former colonies in which his denunciation of slavery did not make him unpopular.

In 1787 Price published *Sermons on the Christian Doctrine* and *The Evidence for a Future Period of Improvement in the State of Mankind*, which, as the title suggests, shows his optimistic enthusiasm for the doctrine of the indefinite perfectibility of mankind. This address was delivered at the Old Jewry on 25 April 1787 to mark the first anniversary of the founding of what came to be known as New College, Hackney. Price played a part in the founding of the college and it was expected that he would teach there. He did start to take classes but, as his health was declining, he found the strain too much and was glad to hand over his duties to his nephew George Cadogan Morgan.

Reform and revolution Throughout the American War of Independence and afterwards, Price maintained an active interest in domestic political reform. He was engaged in the agitation for the repeal of the Test and Corporation Acts and promoted the cause of parliamentary reform, notably the extension of the franchise, the abolition of corrupt practices, and the redistribution of constituencies to secure a more equitable representation. He was a founder member of the Society for Constitutional Reform (1780) and when the Society for Commemorating the Revolution in Great Britain (known as the Revolution Society) revived its activities, Price played a prominent part in its proceedings. He was invited to address the Revolution Society at the meeting held at Old Jewry on 4 November 1789. His address was published under the title *A Discourse on the Love of our Country* (1789). Price welcomed with great enthusiasm the opening events of the French Revolution, holding that the French were doing for themselves what the British had done in the revolution of 1688 and what the Americans had done in the War of Independence. In the evening of the same day at a dinner held by the society at the London tavern, Price moved a resolution congratulating the French national assembly and welcoming the prospect of a common participation in the blessings of civil and religious liberty by the 'first two kingdoms in the world' (Price, *Discourse on the Love of our Country*, 13). He also drafted the correspondence between the society and the national assembly.

Price's role in these proceedings and the publication of his address to the Revolution Society inflamed the wrath of Edmund Burke, who was provoked to write *Reflections on the Revolution in France* (1790), in which he assailed Price with vitriolic invective of the most uninhibited kind. The ferocity of the attack was thought by some to have contributed to Price's decline and death. This must remain doubtful as Price had been in failing health for some time. He did reply briefly yet effectively in a preface which he attached to the fourth edition of the discourse, and it was left to his friends Joseph Priestley, Mary Wollstonecraft, Joseph Towers (who was morning preacher at the chapel at Newington Green from 1778 until 1799), and Thomas Paine to make lengthier and more studied replies. Price's political sympathies were in any case only one strand of his wide-ranging activities, which covered moral philosophy and theology, as well as probability theory, actuarial science, and demography.

Moral philosophy and theology Price's moral philosophy was firmly grounded in a theistic framework, but although he maintained that it is God's will that we should obey the moral law and that God attaches grave penalties to disobedience, he was quite clear that the obligatoriness of the moral law is founded not in God's will but in the rectitude of the law itself. Following Ralph Cudworth he was able to reconcile this position with God's omnipotence by assuming that the moral law is part of God's nature to which his will is subordinate.

The main controversial purpose of Price's *Review of the Principal Questions and Difficulties in Morals* (1758) was to establish the objectivity of moral judgement against the subjectivism of Francis Hutcheson and David Hume. To secure this position Price tried to show that moral judgement was a function of reason, which apprehends eternal truth, and not a function of feeling or sentiment. Other topics discussed were the universality of moral principles, the indefinability of some simple moral terms, such as 'right' and 'ought', the criteria of moral judgement, a critique of utilitarianism, the principle of subjective rectitude (namely, the principle that everyone ought to do what he thinks he ought to do, provided always that he has done his best to find out what his duty really is), and the principle of candour, that we have a duty to subject our opinions to rational criticism and actively search out the truth. In this work Price adopted a libertarian position, that every man is free in the sense that he has a real choice to do what he thinks is his duty, undetermined by any elements in his character or in the environment. Later in his career he entered into an amicable controversy with Priestley on this last topic, defending a position largely

derived from Samuel Clarke against Priestley's position, which had much in common with that defended by Anthony Collins. The exchange of correspondence was published in 1778 under the title *A Free Discussion of the Doctrines of Materialism and Philosophical Necessity*.

There is an incoherence in Price's moral philosophy which has an important bearing on the interpretation of his political philosophy. On the one hand, as a rationalist he believed that moral principles are instances of necessary truth, parallel to the truths of mathematics, and as such are categorically binding, admitting of no exceptions; on the other hand, he was forced to allow that moral principles do sometimes conflict, and that some, at least, are defeasible. (It will be argued below that Burke was unfair in taking his political thought as operating simply at the level of abstract principles.) Price's claim that we should always do the action that we think is the most fitting does not remove the difficulty, for no generalization of what is most fitting in a particular situation can be represented as the apprehension of a general principle that is necessarily true.

Both in his practical life and in his thought Price lived under the superintending eye of providence. He believed that the existence of God and the nature of his attributes can be rationally demonstrated. The deity superintends the working of the universe, and though he has laid down the laws that govern the working of his creation, he still needs to intervene from time to time to correct any occasional deviations from the rule. Price distinguishes a particular providence from a general one, and in this way presents as divinely ordained both the general rule and the occasional intervention that is needed to correct a deviation. His theology thus accommodates Newtonian cosmology: a happy instance of a harmony between science and religion. It was the feasibility of divine intervention that made it possible for Price to defend the possibility of miracles in his dispute with David Hume.

From the omnipotence and the benevolence of the deity Price draws the conclusion that the deity does not allow anything to happen that ought not to happen. Every seeming calamity is tolerated because it is part of the divine purpose, and what appears to be evil in human life plays a role in the selection of those who are to enter into eternal life—our time on earth being just a period of probation. On the nature of redemption Price took an annihilationist position, which he might have derived from John Locke's *The Reasonableness of Christianity* (1695). He did not think that the doctrine of predestination to eternal punishment was consistent with God's benevolence, and he was reluctant to adopt the doctrine of universal restoration, partly because he thought it unscriptural, and partly because he believed that its adoption would have antinomian tendencies. There are, however, some indications that towards the end of his life he was beginning to move towards universalism. In his early life he believed that the fate of the wicked would not be eternal punishment but oblivion. Price does not make it clear, however, how annihilationism is to be reconciled with the doctrine of the immortality of the human soul.

In his youth Price rebelled against the strictly orthodox Calvinism of his father and his uncle Samuel, and became an Arian. In *Sermons on the Christian Doctrine* he attempts to establish a middle way between the Calvinist orthodoxy of the elder generation and the Socinianism of his friend Joseph Priestley. He allows the pre-existence of Christ, but rejects the doctrine of the consubstantiality of the Father and the Son, as well as the Socinian doctrine of the simple humanity of Christ. The implications of his Arianism for his moral philosophy are that neither the doctrine that man is saved by grace alone nor the doctrine that Christ saves simply through his teaching and his example is valid. For Price a man must contribute to his own salvation in trying to obey the moral law, but no man is worthy by his own efforts alone to merit eternal life. The efforts of the virtuous need to be complemented by the grace that has been made available to mankind by Christ's sacrifice on the cross.

There is a strong millennialist element in Price's theology. Like all good protestants who adopt the doctrine of *sola scriptura* he has to interpret the biblical prophecies, particularly those of Daniel and Revelation. The doctrine that this terrestrial life is primarily a life of probation, testing our worthiness for eternal life, is accompanied by the doctrine that God intervenes in human history to bring about a gradual improvement to make the world fit for the rule of Christ and his saints. Millennialism could thus be reconciled with belief in social progress. There are other unresolved tensions in Price's teaching, not least those that arise from his defence of a rationalist moral philosophy and his adherence at the same time to Christian teaching. If we can discover our duty simply by the exercise of our reason, then revelation is not essential. If we can achieve moral excellence by striving to do what we believe to be our duty, and if we are always free to do what we believe to be our duty, redemption does not of necessity depend upon grace; and if eternal life is the reward due to moral excellence, the interposition of Christ is essential only on the assumption that in practice we will always be found to be wanting in some respect or other.

Probability theory, assurance, and demography When Thomas Bayes, a dissenting minister and a mathematician who gave his name to the theorem of inverse probability, died in 1761, it was found that several of his manuscripts remained unpublished. His relatives asked Price, a friend of Bayes, to examine his papers, and when he did so Price realized their importance. He edited *An Essay towards Solving a Problem in the Doctrine of Chances*, adding an introduction of his own, and submitted it in the form of a letter to John Canton to the Royal Society, where it was read on 23 December 1763. Price submitted a further development of the topic under the title *A Demonstration of the Second Rule* to the Royal Society, where it was read on 6 December 1764. Price believed that this work was important not just for the contribution it made to the development of the theory of probability but also because of the contribution he thought it made to the study of induction, and the support he believed it gave to arguments for the existence of God.

Not long after his election to the Royal Society on 5 December 1765 Price was invited to assist the Society for Equitable Assurances. This society, which had been founded in 1762, sold annuities which were attractive to those who wished to provide for their declining years and for their dependants. The society needed assistance on actuarial matters—the calculation of rates to be paid for reversions, and on demographic trends, particularly those concerning the expectation of life. Price worked hard to provide what was needed on both fronts and the fruits of his work were published in *Observations on Reversionary Payments* in 1771. The book was an immediate success. The second edition appeared in 1772 and the third a year later. A fourth edition, expanded to two volumes, was published in 1783 and Price was working on the fifth edition before he died, this edition and two others being completed by his nephew William Morgan.

The significance of Price's work is much wider than the contribution it made to the success of the Equitable. Many assurance societies were started at this time and Price was able to show that some of the schemes which they operated were ill-founded. Because of defects in their computations or information on the expectation of life, they were likely to promise early annuitants too much, leaving insufficient funds for later claimants. Price criticized the plans of these societies, and in doing so prevented the misery that would have befallen the victims of unsound schemes. On 29 October 1771 the directors of the Friendly Society of Annuitants wrote to Price to say that on receiving his letter of 13 July criticizing their scheme they had decided to dissolve their society. Price helped the Equitable in many other ways, not least in the organization of the office. After some resistance he was able to convince the society that there was no justification for charging women higher premiums, as their expectation of life was longer than that of the men. He suggested introducing medical examinations to avert the dangers of 'bad lives', and he trained his nephew William Morgan, who was appointed actuary to the society in 1775. Thereafter the society thrived, and Morgan, with Price's help, produced the Northampton tables, which remained in use for more than a century.

While he was helping the Equitable, Price also became involved in projects for promoting social insurance. In 1772 Francis Maseres published *A Proposal for Establishing Life-Annuities in Parishes for the Benefit of the Industrious Poor*. The scheme he advocated was a simple one: parishes in town and country would be empowered to sell to persons during their working life annuities which would be paid when they reached the age of retirement. The scheme was designed to encourage people to make provision for their old age, and in doing so help to reduce the increasing burden of providing for the poor. A bill embodying the scheme was presented to parliament, and Price was invited to draw up the actuarial tables that its operation would require. The bill passed its third reading in the Commons on 5 March 1773, but it failed in the Lords, due largely to the intervention of the lord chancellor, Camden, who feared that any failures of the scheme would lay intolerable burdens on parish rates.

Another scheme in which Price became involved was to provide relief for the poor in times of sickness, disablement, and old age, promoted by John Acland, rector of Broad Clyst in Devon. This was not a voluntary scheme: all men and women, with only a few exceptions, would be required during their working lives to subscribe to a scheme that would provide assistance for them when their working lives were over or when they were incapacitated. More ambitious than Maseres's earlier scheme, it was also a pioneering attempt to address the need to provide relief for the poor in times of sickness as well as in old age. Acland published the details of his scheme in *A Plan for Rendering the Poor Independent of Public Contribution* (1786). A bill embodying the scheme was prepared, and once again Price was invited to draw up the actuarial table. The bill, under the title 'A bill for the more effective relief of the poor', was presented to parliament in 1789, but, though it passed the Commons, like its predecessor it failed in the Lords. In his *Reflections on the Revolution in France* Edmund Burke derided Price as 'the calculating divine'; his contempt was misplaced, for in these schemes of private and social insurance Price had given a vivid illustration of the ways in which the skills of the actuary could be brought to bear on social problems, and had shown how well-founded schemes could prevent suffering and meet the needs of those in distress. His involvement in these schemes and other attempts to relieve distress by his fellow dissenters such as Joseph Priestley and Thomas Percival give the lie to the accusation that the dissenters lacked compassion for the poor and the disadvantaged.

One parallel development of Price's interest in financial matters was his advocacy of sinking fund operations to reduce the national debt. In the first edition of *Observations on Reversionary Payments* he drew attention to the dangers that would imperil the financial health of the nation if the debt were not reduced, and he expanded his arguments in a separate publication, *An Appeal to the Public on the Subject of the National Debt* (1774). During his long friendship with the earl of Shelburne, Price wrote many papers dealing mainly with what he regarded as the best way of raising public loans and advocating ways of reducing debt. He also criticized the fashionable policy of raising loans on substantial discounts on the nominal capital. Shelburne was sympathetic to Price's schemes but was not in office long enough to put them into effect. He was able, however, to secure the interest of William Pitt (1759–1806), and Price was summoned to Downing Street to advise. When the Sinking Fund Act was passed in 1786 to much acclaim, William Morgan was incensed that his uncle had not received recognition for the part he had played in the development of the legislation. Price himself does not seem to have been as troubled as his nephew, but he was doubly unfortunate. Although he did not receive applause when the scheme was thought to be beneficial, long after his death, when the mismanagement of the fund became known, much of the blame was laid upon what was thought to be his misleading advocacy.

Another offshoot of Price's interest in demography was his thesis that the population of England and Wales had been and was still declining—in sad contrast to the American colonies, in some of which the population was doubling every twenty-five years or even less. Price turned out to be mistaken, as the census of 1801 made clear, and his reputation suffered. Coming to his defence William Morgan maintained that Price had been in error because he had taken the returns of the window tax on trust. Had these not been corrupt his methods of calculation would have led him to the truth.

Political philosophy In the pamphlet he wrote in defence of the American patriots, Price distinguished four different types of liberty: physical, moral, religious, and civil. Physical liberty is the ability to make one's own decisions and not to be determined by forces over which one has no control; moral liberty is the ability to act in accordance with one's conscience; religious liberty is the ability to worship God according to one's own convictions and not to be disadvantaged in any way in so doing; civil liberty is the enjoyment of the right to govern oneself. Self-government means different things: it includes enjoying one's natural rights, participating in the government of one's own society, and being a member of a community that governs itself and is not subject to the will of another community. Whereas Joseph Priestley made a clear distinction between civil liberty and political liberty, allowing that the former can be enjoyed without the latter, Price was so adamant that political liberty, that is, participation in the government of one's own society, is essential to the enjoyment of civil liberty that he built it into his definition of the term.

The presentation of the different kinds of liberty as different forms of self-government is the basis of Price's strategy for defending the patriots; since every nation has the right to govern itself the American colonies had the right to be independent if they so wished. Price did not want to see the dismemberment of the British empire; on the contrary, he hoped some way could be found of converting it into a confederation of self-governing communities, but this could only be a legitimate solution if the Americans consented. Price expands the notion implicit in the doctrine of the social contract, that a person can be subjected to authority only by his own consent, to embrace the idea that no man is to be subjected to a government in the operation of which he does not in some way participate. To be free is to be subject to no other will than one's own. The main core of the argument is not that a man is more likely to be secure in the enjoyment of his natural rights if he has some part to play in government, nor that democratic government is more efficient and more equitable than other forms, but rather that self-government is required by the demands of moral personality. Morally speaking, a man is not fully a man if he does not enjoy the right and discharge the duty of governing himself.

Price was heavily criticized by Edmund Burke for drawing political prescriptions from abstract ideas and principles and for ignoring the empirical element in political judgement. The charge is unfounded, as a detailed examination of his writings will show, but it has to be conceded that some of Price's expressions can easily give rise to the belief that he thought that political judgement is simply the application of a priori principles. Just as in moral philosophy he admitted that moral principles are defeasible, so in his political writing he allowed that the application of the principle has to be modified to accommodate conflicting considerations. A case in point is to be found in his discussion of the extension of the franchise. In principle, he maintains, every man has the right to participate in the government of his society, but in practice the vote has to be restricted to those capable of independent judgement. There is a danger that some will sell the vote, and to prevent this the vote has to be restricted to those unlikely to fall into temptation. Full participation is always something to be aimed at, but it may not be wise to attempt its realization in all circumstances.

In *A Discourse on the Love of our Country* (1789), his last publication, Price summarized his political credo in a list of what he believed all men have a natural right to enjoy.

> First, the right to liberty of conscience in religious matters; secondly, the right to resist power when abused; and thirdly, the right to chuse our own government, to cashier them for misconduct, and to frame a government for our selves. (Price, *Political Writings*, 89–90)

The most telling implication of Price's defence of self-government in its different forms, is the contribution it made to the assault on imperialism, on the idea that one nation is justified in imposing its will on another, and that there is glory to be found in conquest and domination. Price's enduring legacy is the clarity with which he stated his main thesis: that the true love of country lies in the defence of a system of natural rights, the enjoyment of which promotes the equal status and prosperity of all peoples.

Correspondence and death In addition to his published works, Price's letter writing contributed to his influential position. The last entry Price wrote in his shorthand journal (6 February 1791) reads 'I should be much happier than I am had I no letters to write. They are indeed a burden to me' ('Richard Price's journal', ed. Thomas, 396). This *cri de coeur* reminds us that Price was heavily engaged in correspondence throughout his life. He led a relatively quiet life as a dissenting minister in the seclusion of Newington Green or Hackney. He travelled little, other than visits to his family in south Wales, occasional visits to Shelburne at Bowood, or for 'a recruit of spirits' at Brighthelmstone (Brighton). So it is remarkable that he established such a diverse and wide-ranging set of correspondents.

Through Shelburne, Price had access to Chatham and to William Pitt the younger, who sought his advice on sinking fund matters. His American correspondents included Franklin and Thomas Jefferson, who, when he was in Paris, kept Price up to date with political developments in France. John Adams, who, when he was minister-plenipotentiary at the court of St James, attended Price's chapel at Hackney with his family, was a close friend and sometimes candid correspondent. Other American correspondents included such figures as Benjamin Rush (1745–1813), founder of Dickinson College, Pennsylvania;

Charles Chauncey (1705–1787); Henry Laurens (1724–1792), minister of the First Church at Boston; Joseph Willard (1738–1779), Hollis professor of mathematics and natural philosophy at Harvard; and also Jonathan Trumbull (1710–1785), governor of Connecticut (1768–84). Price's correspondents in France included A. R. J. Turgot, A. B. L. R. Mirabeau (whom Price met when he went to London), and L. A. La Rochefoucauld d'Enville. As might be expected he had close contact with his fellow dissenting ministers: these included not only Joseph Priestley but also Theophilus Lindsey, John Disney, George Walker, and Thomas Belsham. He was also friendly with such Anglicans as William Adams, master of Pembroke College, Oxford, and John Howard, the prison reformer.

Price's sudden death was caused by a chill caught while attending the funeral of a fellow dissenter (and funerals, he had earlier written, had the effect of sending the mourners after the departed). The chill led to the complication of a bladder complaint, from which he died on 19 April 1791. Price was buried at Bunhill Fields burial-ground, London, on 26 April 1791.

Influence In many of the fields of enquiry in which Price was influential in his lifetime his reputation died with him, and interest in his work lay dormant throughout the nineteenth century to be revived only in the twentieth century. With the exception of his work in the actuarial sciences, and the regard in which his memory was held by Unitarians, his work was not republished after his death. There are many reasons for this. Even among Unitarians, the Arianism that he defended yielded ground to the Socinianism espoused by Joseph Priestley: the doctrine of the simple humanity of Christ, though endowing him with miraculous powers, became more attractive than Arianism. In moral philosophy his objectivism and rational intuitionism was seriously challenged by Hutcheson, Hume, and Adam Smith; his rational intuitionism gave way to the doctrines that grounded moral judgement in feelings and sentiments, and the doctrine that a moral system was composed of a plurality of principles of obligation gave way to the kind of utilitarianism advocated by Jeremy Bentham. His reputation as a demographer was marred by his notoriously mistaken thesis that the British population had been and was still declining, and his authority in financial matters suffered after his death, no doubt unjustly, because of the failure of the attempt to reduce the national debt by sinking fund procedures.

The greatest blow, however, came from the hands of Edmund Burke in *Reflections on the Revolution in France*. Burke acquired an immense reputation throughout Europe largely due to his predictions on the course of the French Revolution, and this success lent weight and authority to many other elements in his analysis, including his denunciation of Price, the radicals, and 'the rights of man'. The admiration for Burke in these respects concealed the dangers that lay in his downgrading of human reason. It has to be conceded that Price's rationalism was too optimistic in two respects: he exaggerated the extent to which problems could be solved and difficulties overcome by rational criticism, and he exaggerated the extent to which men were prepared to listen to and be moved by an appeal to rational principles and reasonable considerations. Furthermore, Price was not alive, as Burke certainly was, to the dangers inherent in attempting large-scale comprehensive reforms. He did not appreciate the degree to which habit, custom, prejudice, and inertia governed communities, and the extent to which, when traditional loyalties were destroyed, stability and order could be maintained only by coercion and terror. Yet, despite Burke's views, liberal-democratic societies have enshrined many of the things that Price defended: the idea that the state and social institutions are to be regarded as the servants of the whole people, that all men are entitled to participate to some extent in the government of their society, and that for political purposes the people are not constituted by a relatively small élite.

Interest in Price's moral philosophy revived in the twentieth century, particularly in the work of H. A. Prichard and W. D. Ross, and this was considerably strengthened by the publication in 1948 of D. D. Raphael's edition of *A Review of the Principal Questions in Morals*, which prompted several studies. The first biography of Price was by his nephew William Morgan, *Memoirs of the Life of the Rev. Richard Price, D.D. F.R.S.* (1815). Apart from Fowler's article in the *Dictionary of National Biography*, Price's biography remained virtually untouched until Roland Thomas published *Richard Price, Philosopher and Apostle of Liberty* (1924). This pioneering work was followed in 1952 by Carl B. Cone, *Torchbearer of Freedom: the Influence of Richard Price on Eighteenth Century Thought*, and in 1977 *The Honest Mind* by D. O. Thomas appeared. These works stimulated interest in Price's contributions to a wide range of subjects, including political philosophy, probability theory, insurance, demography, and finance, as well as in his moral philosophy. In 1977 the *Price–Priestley Newsletter* was founded, to be superseded in 1982 by the journal *Enlightenment and Dissent*, which remains a focus for the study of Price's thought.

D. O. THOMAS

Sources D. O. Thomas, J. Stephens, and P. A. L. Jones, *A bibliography of the works of Richard Price* (1993) • W. B. Peach, *The ethical foundations of the American Revolution* (1977) • R. Price, *Four dissertations*, 2nd edn (1768); repr. with a new introduction by J. Stephens (1990) • J. Priestley and R. Price, *A free discussion of the doctrines of materialism and philosophical necessity* (1778); facs. edn with introduction by J. Stephens (1994) • *The correspondence of Richard Price*, ed. W. B. Peach and D. O. Thomas, 3 vols. (1983–94) • 'Richard Price's journal for the period 25 March 1787 to 6 February 1791', ed. D. O. Thomas, *National Library of Wales Journal*, 21 (1979–80), 366–413 [deciphered by B. Thomas] • W. Morgan, *Memoirs of the life of the Rev. Richard Price* (1815) • R. Thomas, *Richard Price: philosopher and apostle of liberty* (1924) • C. B. Cone, *Torchbearer of freedom* (1952) • H. Laboucheix, *Richard Price* (1970) • D. O. Thomas, *The honest mind* (1977) • M. Fitzpatrick, 'Richard Price and the revolution society', *Enlightenment and Dissent*, 10 (1991), 35–50 • J. Fruchtman, jr., *The apocalyptic politics of Richard Price and Joseph Priestley* (1983) • D. V. Glass, *Numbering the people: the eighteenth-century population controversy* (1973) • E. L. Hargreaves, *The national debt* (1930) • A. Lincoln, *Some political and social ideas of English dissent* (1938) • M. E. Ogborn, *Equitable assurances … the Equitable Life Assurance Society, 1762–1962* (1962) • K. Pearson, *The history of statistics in the 17th and 18th centuries* (1978) • M. Thorncroft, *Trust in freedom: the history of Newington Green Unitarian Church, 1708–1958* (1958) • *GM*, 1st ser., 61 (1791), 389–90,

486 • R. Price, *A review of the principal questions in morals*, 3rd edn (1787); repr., ed. D. D. Raphael (1948); repr. (1974) • R. Price, *Political writings*, ed. D. O. Thomas (1991)

Archives American Philosophical Society, Philadelphia, corresp. • Bodl. Oxf., corresp. • DWL, corresp. • NL Wales, journal • NRA, corresp. and papers | American Philosophical Society, Philadelphia, letters to Benjamin Franklin • N. Yorks. CRO, corresp. with Christopher Wyvill • NL Scot., corresp. with Lord Monboddo • NL Wales, letters to Sir William Petty, first marquess of Lansdowne • NL Wales, Shelburne MSS • NRA, priv. coll., letters to Lord Lansdowne

Likenesses J. Sayers, caricature, etching, pubd 1790, NPG • A. Scratch, engraving, pubd 1791, NPG • caricature, etching, pubd 1791, NPG • T. Holloway, line engraving, pubd 1793 (after B. West, 1788), NPG [*see illus.*] • B. West, oils, Equitable Life Assurance Society, London; repro. in Thomas, *Richard Price* • by or after B. West, portrait, RS • caricature, etching, NPG

Wealth at death over £3000; no valuation of entire estate is given in the will; house in Leadenhall Street; Price was comfortably placed

Price, Richard (1790–1833), literary scholar, was the eldest son of Richard Price, merchant. He entered at the Middle Temple on 29 May 1823, and went on to practise on the western circuit.

In 1824 Price superintended an edition of Warton's *History of Poetry*, and provided a long preface, which was reprinted in the editions of R. Taylor (1840) and W. C. Hazlitt (1871). Price incorporated the notes of Ritson, Ashby, Douce, and Park, besides adding some of his own. The edition proved valuable to later editors, although Price retained many of Warton's mistakes, and made some of his own. In 1830, two years after he was called to the bar, he revised and brought up to date, in four volumes, Edward Christian's edition of Blackstone's *Commentaries* of 1809. He also assisted Henry Petrie in his edition of the 'Saxon Chronicle to 1066', in the first volume of *Monumenta historica Britannica* (1848).

Price was a sub-commissioner of the Public Record Commission, a body which sponsored the publication of works tending to advance historical and antiquarian knowledge. He had a wide knowledge of German and Scandinavian literature, to which testimony was later borne by Dr James Grimm, Dr J. J. Thorkelin, and Edgar Taylor, translator of Wace's *Chronicle*. Thorpe, in the preface to his *Ancient Laws and Institutes of England* (published for the Record Commission, 1840), claimed that his labours had been considerably lightened by Price, whom he called 'a good man and highly accomplished scholar' (Warton, 1840). Price died of dropsy on 23 May 1833, at his home at Branch Hill, Hampstead, Middlesex.

G. LE G. NORGATE, rev. P. J. CONNELL

Sources Allibone, *Dict.* • T. Warton, *The history of English poetry*, new edn, 3 vols. (1840) • *GM*, 1st ser., 103/2 (1833), 282, 561 • *The Times* (24 May 1833) • T. Warton, *The history of English poetry*, new edn, ed. W. C. Hazlitt, 4 vols. (1871) • N. H. Nicholas, *Public records: a description of the contents, objects, and uses of the various works printed by authority of the Record Commission* (1831) • H. A. C. Sturgess, ed., *Register of admissions to the Honourable Society of the Middle Temple, from the fifteenth century to the year 1944*, 3 vols. (1949)

Price, Robert (1655–1733), judge and politician, was born in the parish of Cerrigydrudion, Denbighshire, on 14 January 1655, the second son of Thomas Price (*d.* before 1670) of

Robert Price (1655–1733), by George Vertue (after Sir Godfrey Kneller, 1714)

Gilar, Denbighshire, and Margaret (1633/4–1723), daughter and heir of Thomas Wynne of Bwlchybeudy, Denbighshire. He was educated at Ruthin grammar school before entering St John's College, Cambridge, on 28 March 1672, aged seventeen. He entered Lincoln's Inn on 8 May 1673. In 1677 Price joined Lord Lexington on a journey to Europe, which saw him visit Paris in the spring of 1678, and then move on to Florence and Rome. While in Rome one of Price's legal texts was mistaken for an English Bible and he was carried before the pope; on explaining the situation he presented the book to the pope, who placed it in the Vatican Library. Price returned home in 1679 and on 23 September married Lucy (d. 1736), the eldest daughter and coheir of Robert Rodd, of Foxley, Yazor, Herefordshire. They had two sons and a daughter. Price was called to the bar on 28 October 1679. When his wife's father died in 1681 Price bought out the other Rodd coheirs and established himself at Foxley. He also erected and endowed an almshouse for six poor people in the parish of Cerrigydrudion.

Price had a successful legal practice, numbering among his clients such influential figures as the first duke of Beaufort, a leading Welsh territorial magnate. Beaufort was presumably important in obtaining for Price several local offices which became available as the tory reaction set in during Charles II's later years. He became a common councilman at Hereford in 1682, and under the new Hereford charter of 1683 he was named an alderman, and in the following year became recorder of New Radnor and attorney-general for south Wales. At the general election

following the accession of James II, Price was returned as a court supporter on 19 March 1685 at Weobley. Price became steward to Queen Catherine of Braganza. Local office also came his way as he became steward of Shrewsbury and he replaced a Beaufort opponent as town clerk of Gloucester in September 1685. In 1686 he became a member of the council for the Welsh marches. James II's first declaration of indulgence was a turning point in Price's career as his refusal to read it led to his dismissal as town clerk of Gloucester. Both Lord Chancellor Jeffreys and the king were politely rebuffed when they closeted Price in an attempt to persuade him to support repeal of the Test Act. As a result he lost his place as steward of Shrewsbury under the new charter of January 1688, but he kept his other places and was approved by James II's agents as a court candidate for the abortive elections due in 1688.

Price supported the revolution of 1688, subscribing £20 to the Herefordshire loan to the prince of Orange. However, his election campaign for the convention of 1689 was derailed by the discovery that in James II's records he was accounted a supporter of repealing the test and penal laws. He petitioned against his defeat, but with little chance of success he withdrew the petition. There were other distractions, too, at this time as in November 1690 Price received £1500 in damages in a suit against 'Mr Neale, the groom porter's son', for 'enticing' away his wife and 'getting her with child' (Luttrell, *Brief Historical Relation*, 2.131).

Price was re-elected for Weobley in 1690 and retained his seat with one short interruption until 1702. He soon carved out a new career for himself as a tory critic of the government in parliament, which he combined with legal advocacy in the law courts. Thus he spoke on the Treason Trials Bill in 1692; on the Bill of Accounts and the Indemnity Bill in 1693; and acted as defence counsel for Lord Mohun during his trial for the murder of the actor William Mountford in 1693. More famously, he was at the forefront of attempts to prevent the king from granting large estates in Wales to his Dutch favourite the earl of Portland. Price opposed the grant in the Treasury, arguing his case in May 1695. On 14 January 1696 he presented a petition from the freeholders and inhabitants of Denbighshire against the grant, and secured an address to the king which persuaded him to find an alternative means of rewarding Portland. Price's speech on this occasion was subsequently published after the king's death in 1702 under the title *Gloria Cambriae, or, The Speech of a Bold Briton in Parliament Against a Dutch Prince of Wales*. He cited General Monck in support of his opposition to including an abjuration oath in the bill establishing a Board of Trade in January 1696. Price was a notable opponent of proceeding against the Jacobite plotter Sir John Fenwick by parliamentary bill of attainder. He refused the voluntary association in 1696. In 1699 he was one of those members who compiled a blacklist of those voting against the Disbanding Bill which was later published.

The inclusion of some tories in the ministry in 1700 saw Price appointed a Welsh judge, as second justice on the Brecon circuit, an appointment he himself thought due to the influence of Robert Harley. However, it was with the accession of Queen Anne that he achieved important office. In June 1702 he was created a serjeant-at-law, and on 24 June he was named as a baron of the exchequer, and henceforth he had to give up his parliamentary career. However, he retained his interest in politics, helping Harley to lobby against the tack in November 1704. As a judge, Price gave a minority opinion in February 1705 in the *Ashby* v. *White* case, arguing that a writ of error could be refused as it was not a right but an act of grace from the prince. According to Thomas Hearne, Price delivered a charge to a Hampshire grand jury in 1705

> in which he took notice of the slanders and aspersions of the fanatic party in the libels etc cast on the Church of England, and reminded them that the present liberty which they enjoyed was purely the effect of the bounty of the Church of England. (*Remarks*, 2.28)

Given the tone of such public pronouncements, Price's hopes, opined to Harley, of being raised to the court of common pleas in August 1705 were bound to remain unfulfilled. His prospects improved under the ministry headed by Harley from 1710 to 1714 but Harley seems to have used Price as a Welsh parliamentary whip and he was not promoted.

Following the accession of George I, Price was reappointed to office, the result no doubt of his cultivation of the reversionary interest to the throne through his sons. Price was one of the judges sent to Carlisle to preside over the trial of Scottish Jacobites in December 1716; while there he suffered from gout, his fellow judge Tracy reporting that he had a 'little weakness remaining in his feet' (BL, Stowe 750, fol. 226). In 1717 he built a new house at Foxley. Again he was willing to provide a minority opinion from this bench, this time in January 1718 against the king's belief that he could educate his grandchildren. On 20 October 1726 he was promoted to be a justice of common pleas, and he was reappointed following the accession of George II in the following year. Price died at Kensington on 2 February 1733, and was buried at Yazor in Herefordshire. His elder son, Thomas, who had succeeded him as MP for Weobley in 1702, died in Genoa in 1706, leaving the other son, Uvedale Tomkyns Price, as his heir. His daughter, Lucy, married Bampfield Rodd.

STUART HANDLEY

Sources HoP, *Commons, 1690–1715* [draft] · HoP, *Commons, 1660–90*, 1.286 · E. Curll, *The life of the late Hon. Robert Price* (1734) · W. R. Williams, *The history of the great sessions in Wales, 1542–1830* (privately printed, Brecon, 1899), 143–4 · Sainty, *Judges*, 80, 128 · Baker, *Serjeants*, 452, 532 · *The manuscripts of his grace the duke of Portland*, 10 vols., HMC, 29 (1891–1931), vol. 4, pp. 35, 219, 694; vol. 5, p. 553 · N. Luttrell, *A brief historical relation of state affairs from September 1678 to April 1714*, 2 (1857), 131; 5 (1857), 524 · *Remarks and collections of Thomas Hearne*, ed. C. E. Doble and others, 2, OHS, 7 (1886), 28 · *The parliamentary diary of Narcissus Luttrell, 1691–1693*, ed. H. Horwitz (1972), 172, 265, 420, 455, 469 · Cobbett, *Parl. hist.*, 5.1010–11, 1041, 1046 · H. Horwitz, *Parliament, policy and politics in the reign of William III* (1977), 251 · G. S. Holmes, *British politics in the age of Anne*, rev. edn (1987), 310 · *DNB*

Archives St John's College, Oxford, legal commonplace book | BL, Portland MSS · Bodl. Oxf., Carte MS 130

Likenesses King, engraving (after portrait by Dandridge) · G. Kneller, portrait, repro. in *N&Q*, 3rd ser., vol. 9, p. 217; in possession of Sir Charles Price, bt, c.1866 · G. Vertue, line engraving (after G. Kneller, 1714), BM, NPG [*see illus.*]

Price, Robert (1717–1761). *See under* Price, Sir Uvedale, first baronet (1747–1829).

Price, Sampson (1585/6–1630), Church of England clergyman and religious writer, was born in Shrewsbury where his father, Thomas Price (d. 1620), was minister of St Chad's. He followed his elder brother, Daniel *Price (1581–1631), to the stoutly Calvinist Exeter College, Oxford, matriculating aged sixteen on 30 April 1602, but transferred to Hart Hall, from where he graduated BA on 28 February 1605 and proceeded MA on 6 June 1608. Like his brother, he served on the staff of the strongly protestant prince of Wales, and he was almoner of the Chapel Royal at Prince Henry's death in November 1612. In 1609 he had succeeded Daniel as rector of St Martin's, Carfax, Oxford, although he did not receive a preaching licence until 13 May 1615, the year he vacated the living.

By that time Price had already preached at Paul's Cross in London. On 10 October 1613, in a sermon published as *London's Warning by Laodicea's Lukewarmnesse* (1613), he offered Londoners a general warning of the dangers inherent in religious toleration. In his painful homily (Revelation 3: 15, 16) he attacked atheists, papists, and puritans alike. He further claimed that the death, eleven months before, of Prince Henry, 'that sweet Prince, of fresh and bleeding memory, the expectation of all the Christian world' (p. 41), was itself the sinful consequence of lukewarmness. He dedicated 'these rude first-fruits of my paines at the Crosse' (sig. A2) to John King, bishop of London, no doubt hoping for a city benefice since his erstwhile royal master was dead. Initially it was only to a lectureship, that of St Olave (which London parish of that name is unclear), that he was appointed on 24 April 1615.

Price returned to themes of England's jeremiad when he next preached from Revelation at the Cross on 17 March 1616. In this sermon, published as *Ephesus Warning before her Woe* (1616), he denounced the moral decay in London. The city could equal Rome's glory but for the 'byting usurers, inticing Dalilaes, and cozening cheaters' (p. 71) that were not only the sport and subject of plays but were likely to prompt God's judgment. He pointedly dedicated the sermon to Robert Sidney, Viscount L'Isle, who was lord chamberlain to the Catholic Queen Anna of Denmark. Such homilies won for him the sobriquet of 'the Mawl of Hereticks' (Hennessy, lix).

Price proceeded BD from Exeter College on 13 June 1615 and DD on 30 June 1617. On 28 July that year Archbishop George Abbot collated him to the rectory of All Hallows-the-Great in London. On 9 October the mayor and corporation and the governors of St Bartholomew's Hospital appointed him vicar of the former Franciscan royal church of Christchurch, Newgate Street; he took up residence at New Rents in the parish, and published his remaining printed sermons from there. In 1617 he also preached another admonition, at Condover, Shropshire, published as *The Cleansing of the Saints Sight* and on 10 September preached to the corporation of Shrewsbury at the dedication of the town's school chapel by Bishop John Overall. The homily, issued as *The Beauty of Holiness* (1618), continued his attack on atheists who despised 'the calling of the Teachers of our Temples; scorning *Priests*, whose spirituall sacrifice of praier, God accepteth as well as he did incense in the old law' (p. 31). By the spring of 1618 he had become a chaplain-in-ordinary to James VI and I. In 1620 he became vicar of his father's old Shrewsbury church, a post that he held until 1628.

On 8 July 1621 Price preached at Oatlands an anti-Spanish homily. He took as his text Isaiah's prophecy of the Babylonian captivity on learning that Hezekiah had shown his household treasures to the Babylonian ambassadors (2 Kings 20: 13–18) and linked this to Spanish aggression in Germany. This occasioned a short spell of imprisonment in the Tower. According to Joseph Mead, the king threatened to have him hanged for being 'too busy with Rochelle, the Palatinate, and the Spaniard' (Birch, 2.265–6) and it was only Prince Charles who seemingly interceded for his chaplain. A longer term consequence of his intemperate words may have been the forfeiture of his chaplaincy: his name does not appear in the list of those serving in 1621. However, he seems to have been in the household of Prince Charles and was back in harness as royal chaplain by 5 September 1624 when he preached at the funeral of Sir William Byrde, dean of arches, a sermon published as *The Two Twins of Birth and Death* (1624).

In 1622 Price was preacher to Gray's Inn, where his sensitivities to the threat posed by Catholicism to protestant Europe would have been welcome. On 14 July 1626 he was collated by his brother Daniel, by this time dean of Hereford, to the prebendal stall of Church Withington in that cathedral. He died intestate late in 1630 and was buried in the chancel of Christchurch, Newgate Street; administration of his estate was granted on 13 January 1631 to his widow, Elizabeth, of whom nothing else is known.

NICHOLAS W. S. CRANFIELD

Sources M. MacLure, *Register of sermons preached at Paul's Cross, 1534–1642* (Ottawa, 1989) · Foster, *Alum. Oxon.* · 'Chaplains that wait monthly', CCC Oxf., MS E 297, fol. 188 · T. Birch, ed., *The court and times of James the First*, 2 vols. (1848) · Southwark Local Studies Library, YJ 852 ST O, fols. 22r and 30v · G. Hennessy, *Novum repertorium ecclesiasticum parochiale Londinense, or, London diocesan clergy succession from the earliest time to the year 1898* (1898) · GL, MS 9531/14, fol. 228v · B. Willis, *A survey of the cathedrals*, 3 vols. (1742), vol. 2, p. 566 · LMA, DL/C/343: X19/7, fol. 102

Price, Theodore (*c.*1570–1631), Church of England clergyman and reputed Roman Catholic convert, was born at Bron-y-Foel, in the parish of Llanenddwyn, Dyffyn Ardudwy, Merioneth, the son of Rees ap Tudor and Marjory, daughter of Edward Stanley, constable of Harlech Castle. He originally entered All Souls, Oxford, as a chorister and, having probably transferred to Jesus College, graduated BA on 16 February 1588 and proceeded MA on 9 June 1591. He held his first living, the poor rectory of Llanfair, near Harlech, only briefly, from 18 October 1591.

Thereafter his career progressed more swiftly, and he was appointed a prebendary of Winchester in 1596, although he never served as master of the hospital of St Cross, as is sometimes erroneously stated. In 1601 he obtained the rectory of Llanrhaeadr-ym-Mochnant, Denbighshire. It seems likely, however, that Price had remained firmly part of the Oxford scene, and in 1604 he was appointed principal of Hart Hall, a position he held until his resignation in 1622. In 1609 he obtained an Oxfordshire living, the rectory of Launton, and on 5 July 1614 he proceeded DD, as from New College. Price seems to have been well suited to a donnish career: he was later described as of 'untainted Life … of a reverend Presence, liberal, courteous and prudent' as well as 'learned in Scholastical Controversies' (Hacket, 2.97). Although his lectures and a Latin sermon delivered in Oxford were subsequently praised he was not, apparently, a great preacher, a matter which later came back to haunt him. During this period Price evidently took an interest in the fortunes of his old college, Jesus, the Oxford college traditionally favoured by Welshmen. He was one of five commissioners who drew up new statutes for it in 1621, at which time he was also made a fellow.

Price's early patrons are unknown, but his kinsman John Williams, the future archbishop of York, must have been responsible for Price's advancement in mid-career. In 1621 Price was appointed to a prebendal stall at Lincoln Cathedral, where Williams was bishop, and in 1623 Price became a prebendary at Westminster Abbey, where Williams was also the dean. In 1622 Price was one of only two clerics chosen to serve on a commission sent to Ireland to explore various grievances, including a number relating to the parlous state of the Irish church. Price was said to have emerged 'with Praise and with Encouragement from His Majesty' and the promise of further advancement (Hacket, 1.207). Instead, however, there followed a series of disappointments as Bishop Williams's attempts to obtain preferment for Price came to nothing. In 1623 Price was considered for the see of St Asaph, which included his native Merioneth, but he was passed over in favour of John Hanmer. In 1624 the notorious 'Arminian', Richard Mountague, praised Price as one who 'loveth the Church' and saw him as a possible candidate for the vacant see of Gloucester (*Correspondence of John Cosin*, 1.24). In 1625, however, Price apparently broke acrimoniously with Williams over the latter's less than wholehearted support for Price's bid for the archbishopric of Armagh, which went instead to James Ussher. When challenged that Price had virtually ceased preaching for many years and had never preached before the king, Williams 'could give no good Answer and drew of[f] with so much ease upon it' (Hacket, 1.207).

Thereafter, it would appear that Price turned to William Laud, Williams's chief opponent within the Westminster chapter, for further preferment. In 1629, when the see of St Asaph was once again vacant, members of the Durham House group again tipped him for preferment, but ultimately Price found himself passed over once again. By the late 1620s, at the least, Price appears to have aligned himself with Laud's allies, whose strongly ceremonialist leanings he clearly shared. These are confirmed by his will, drawn up in 1631, which included bequests to beautify the chancel of the church in his native parish of Llanenddwyn, and to rail in its altar. In addition Price endowed a sermon at his old college, Jesus, to be preached in support of bowing at the name of Jesus, 'against the Scismaticall opinions of theis times', probably a reference to a recent pamphlet controversy over this practice (Westminster City Archives, PCW, 174v Camden).

In the minds of contemporaries, however, the likelihood that Laudian-style ceremonialism could transmute itself into outright Roman Catholicism seemed to be confirmed by the circumstances of Price's death, which took place at Westminster on 15 December 1631. Following unsuccessful surgery for 'the Torment of the Stone', Price told Roman Catholic visitors of his 'Affection and Devotion' for their church, and received Roman rites. In addition, he emphatically refused to be attended by any Church of England clergyman. The conversion became a *cause célèbre*, with Price's burial at Westminster Abbey on 21 December seemingly delayed by the reluctance of the prebendaries to conduct a burial service (Hacket, 2.97). Peter Heylin, one of the Westminster chapter at the time, later claimed that the story of Price's conversion was merely invented by Williams to blacken the reputation of Laud, who had most recently supported Price. Philip Herbert, earl of Pembroke, certainly sought to use the incident against Laud, reportedly remarking to the king, 'Is this the Orthodoxe man your Majestie would have made a Bishop the last year? Doe but marke him that recommended him unto you in that kinde' (PRO, C115/M35/8387). At Laud's trial William Prynne condemned his familiarity with the 'unpreaching epicure … Arminian' and apostate Price. In reply, Laud did not seek to deny Price's conversion, but merely claimed that Williams 'had laboured … more than I' for Price's preferment (*Works of … William Laud*, 6.495). Price's closeness to Laud, however, is suggested by Price's will, in which the archbishop was referred to as 'my Noble Lord and worthie auntient freind'. Conversely Williams, although a kinsman, was not named. Price's will also included bequests to Hart Hall, Jesus College, and Oriel College as well as moneys for church beautification, and repairs to organs. Others mentioned in Price's will include 'my Noble friend' the Welsh literary figure Hugh Holland, who had previously converted to Catholicism, and two of Price's fellow commissioners in Ireland, Sir William Jones and Sir Thomas Penruddocke. He had apparently never married; his executor was his nephew, Dr William Lewis, the master of St Cross.   J. F. MERRITT

Sources J. Hacket, *Scrinia reserata: a memorial offer'd to the great deservings of John Williams*, 2 pts (1693) • will, City Westm. AC, peculiar court of Westminster, 174–5, Camden, 24 Dec 1631 • John Pory to Viscount Scudamore, PRO, C115/M35/8387 • W. Prynne, *Canterburies doome, or, The first part of a compleat history of the commitment, charge, tryall, condemnation, execution of William Laud, late arch-bishop of Canterbury* (1646), 355 • *The works of the most reverend father in God, William Laud*, 6, ed. J. Bliss (1857), 495 • P. Heylin, *Examen historicum* (1659), 274 • S. G. Hamilton, *Hertford College* (1902), 26–7 • *CSP Ire., 1615–25*, 346–7 • *The correspondence of John Cosin D.D., lord bishop of Durham*, ed. [G. Ornsby], 1, SurtS, 52 (1869), 24 • [T. Birch and R. F. Williams], eds., *The court and times of Charles the First*, 1 (1848), 21 • T. Fuller, *The church history of Britain*, ed. J. S. Brewer, new edn, 6 vols. (1845), vol. 6, pp. 318–20 • C. E. Mallet, *A history of the University of Oxford*, 3 vols. (1924–7); repr. (1968), vol. 2, p. 297

Archives City Westm. AC, peculiar court of Westminster, register Camden, 174–5 • PRO, C 115/M35/8387

Wealth at death £600 p.a.: est. by John Pory: PRO, C115/M35/8387 • will, 1631, City Westm. AC, peculiar court of Westminster, 174–5, Camden

Price, Thomas [Tomos Prys] (*c.*1564–1634), adventurer and Welsh-language poet, was the eldest son of Dr Ellis *Price (*c.*1505–1594), the notorious Red Doctor, and Ellyw Poole. He could trace his lineage to Marchweithan, the head of one of Gwynedd's fifteen tribes. His great-grandfather was Rhys ap Maredudd, who is reputed to have carried Henry Tudor's standard in the battle of Bosworth. Very little is known about Thomas Price's early years, but he is unlikely to have received any formal education.

Despite a lack of firm historical evidence regarding Price's life as a soldier it is possible to conclude a considerable amount from his poems, his *cywyddau* in particular. In 1585 he was a member of the earl of Leicester's force in the Netherlands. He was also present in Tilbury in 1588 as a member of the army assembled there to oppose the armada. He fought in France, probably during the French civil war in 1585–9, and in Ireland, probably during the nine-year war between 1594 and 1603, when Hugh o'Neill, earl of Tyrone, rebelled against the English. It is difficult to ascertain whether he ventured to Spain, although as a privateer he sailed around the Spanish coast and in one of his most famous poems he describes in macaronic language his trials and tribulations as a privateer. Later in life, following the death of his father, in 1595 he returned to live at Plas Iolyn, in the parish of Ysbyty Ifan, Denbighshire, but his adventurous spirit did not diminish, as he continued to plunder and pillage ships from the Isle of Bardsey.

One of Price's contemporaries and colleagues, William Myddleton, was also a privateer, and it is reputed that Price, William Myddleton, and a gentleman named Thomas Koet were the first to smoke tobacco on the streets of London. Price spent much of his time in London and he composed two memorable poems about the city. None the less his time in London was a period of conflicting emotions. In 1613 he was imprisoned in the Fleet prison for allegedly raping his niece, and in one of his poems he sends the nightingale to Wales from his prison cell, bitterly proclaiming his innocence. Price was also involved in a number of other legal wranglings, and his contempt towards the legal profession is frequently expressed in his works.

Price married twice. His first wife was Margaret, daughter of William Gruffydd of Penrhyn, with whom he had three children. His second marriage was with Jane, daughter of Hugh Gwynne of Berth-ddu, with whom he had five sons and five daughters. His heir, Ellis Price, died suddenly in London in 1610, as did his cousin William Gruffydd, son of Pyrs Gruffydd, his brother-in-law, and one of his closest companions, and Price composed an elegy to lament their untimely deaths.

More than 200 of Price's poems have survived, more than 100 each of *cywyddau* and *englynion*, and seven odes. Much of the poetry is conventional, *cywyddau gofyn*, *cywyddau diolch*, eulogies, and *ymryson*, as well as love poems in the style of Dafydd ap Gwilym, which are mainly the products of his early years as their lack of originality and imagination testify.

Price belonged to a group of poets 'a ganai ar eu bwyd eu hunain' ('who sang on their own food'). These composed poems for pleasure rather than for a living, as they did not receive any patronage. As a consequence he often treated traditional themes in an unconventional way, and a great use is made of satire and wit, with Price shifting effortlessly between light-heartedness and pensiveness. One notable element of his work is that he is at his best when he sings about his own personal experiences—his experiences in London, on the sea, or when expressing his frustration with lawyers. Before his time the sea did not figure prominently in Welsh literature.

Lewis Morris, among others, was critical of Price's use of English words, stating that 'his incorrectness and carelessness in his orthography in writing prose, must be attributed to his military & wandring Life in his younger years' (BL, Add. MS 14872, 6r). But it is interesting to note that these English words are much more apparent in those poems which deal with his own adventures, rather than in his more traditional poems. His elegies, in particular those to his sons and Pyrs Gruffydd, are some of his best works.

Until recently there has been a tendency to appraise Thomas Price in the context of his predecessors, poets such as Dafydd ap Gwilym or Tudur Aled. But it is difficult to do this as he is such a unique and original poet. At worst he can be mundane and uninspiring, but at best highly original and memorable. He embodies the traditional and the original, frequently singing on the same subjects as his predecessors but treating them in his own innovative way. Indeed he epitomized all of the characteristics of his period and his personality in his poetry. For the first time the spirit of the sea and the bohemian life of London became a central part of Welsh strict-metre poetry. He stands as a bridge between the professional poets and the more informal and personal poetry that followed. He invigorated a system which was in decline, and although he did not exert a significant influence on those who followed him, with his sparkling personality and his individual muse he left his mark on the poetic tradition in Wales. It is noteworthy that he composed a Welsh grammar (BL, Add. MS 14872, fols. 130v–169v) in which he endeavoured to instruct his fellow gentry in the mysteries of Welsh versecraft. Despite the wealth of his ancestors Price died a comparatively poor man. He had a number of outstanding debts: his legal troubles and extravagance (referred to frequently by Rhys Wyn) were two reasons. Thomas Price

died on 22 August 1634 and was buried the following day in the family's traditional burial place, St John's Church, Ysbyty Ifan.   W. D. ROWLANDS

Sources W. D. Rowlands, 'Cywyddau Tomos Prys o Blas Iolyn', PhD diss., U. Wales, 1998 · W. Rowland, 'Barddoniaeth Tomos Prys o Blas Iolyn', MA diss., U. Wales, 1912 · W. Rowland, *Tomos Prys o Blas Iolyn, 1564?–1634* (1964) · BL, Add. MS 14872 · NL Wales, Mostyn 112 MS, 3031B · NL Wales, MS 279D · E. Roberts, 'Teulu Plas Iolyn', *Trafodion Cymdeithas Hanes Sir Ddinbych*, 13 (1964), 134–51 · W. J. Gruffydd, *Llenyddiaeth Cymru o 1450 hyd 1600* (1992) · N. Lloyd, ed., *Blodeugerdd barddas o'r ail ganrif ar bymtheg* (1993) · J. Fisher, ed., *The Cefn Coch MSS* (1899) · *DNB* · D. H. Evans, 'Cywydd i Ddangos mai Uffern yw Llundain', *Ysgrifau Beirniadol*, 14 (1988) · G. J. Williams and E. J. Jones, eds., *Gramadegau'r penceirddiaid* (1934), lvii–lviii, 189–91, 196–8

Archives BL, Add. MS 14872 · NL Wales, Mostyn MS 112 · NL Wales, MS 279D

Likenesses oils, 1604, priv. coll. · M. Griffith, copy, NMG Wales

Wealth at death not extensive; heir disinherited for marrying without his consent; left estate to first son from second marriage

Price, Thomas (1599–1685), Church of Ireland archbishop of Cashel, was probably born in Wales, although his parents are not known. He was educated in Trinity College, Dublin, graduating BA in 1623 and MA in 1628. He was elected fellow in 1626. Price was ordained deacon in December 1629. After examining him very thoroughly William Bedell, bishop of Kilmore, ordained him priest in 1632, and Price became Bedell's archdeacon. He supported Bedell in 1638 against the disapproval of his archbishop, James Ussher, for convening a diocesan synod. In the rebellion of 1641 the insurgents in co. Cavan imprisoned many civilians, and it was Price who drew up the terms for their release in 1642.

During the interregnum Price became chaplain to the duke of Ormond. After the Restoration he was advanced to the vacant see of Kildare, holding the prebend of Kildare *in commendam*. James Margetson, archbishop of Dublin, consecrated Price in Christ Church in March 1661. His income was to be £400 per annum. At Ormond's recommendation Price was translated to the archbishopric of Cashel and the bishopric of Emly on 20 May 1667, the sees being vacant after the death of Archbishop Thomas Fulwar. When Price vacated Kildare, the diocese owed the king £217, while the preceptory of Tully owed £40. These debts, the result either of Price's parsimony or of his indolence, meant that the manors and estates of the see were forfeit to the crown.

Having been well trained by Bedell, Price as archbishop of Cashel understood the importance of using Irish in preaching the gospel. He ordained one Terence Tierney (or Tiernan) in King Cormac's Chapel on June 1677 to minister to the people in Irish. At a synod held the previous year Price and his clergy agreed that Tierney should preach in Irish in Cashel Cathedral every Sunday afternoon.

The Jesuit Andrew Sall (born in Cashel in 1612) was already friendly with Price by the early 1670s. In 1674, when regular Catholic clergy were proscribed in Ireland, Sall converted to the established church. Price received him into the Church of Ireland, put him up in his house, and acquired benefices for him. Encouraged by Price, Sall was involved in publishing the second edition of William

Daniel's translation of the New Testament into Irish (1681). Sall went to England in 1675 to meet Sir Robert Boyle, who was financing the enterprise. Sall returned to Ireland in 1681 and began with others to prepare Bedell's Irish Old Testament for the press.

Another Catholic convert employed by Price to minister in Irish was Paul Higgins (Pól Ó hUiginn), who was born about 1628. He had been Catholic vicar-general of Connaught and was brought over to the Church of Ireland by Dr Otway, bishop of Killala. Higgins, at the instigation of Narcissus Marsh, was employed in Trinity College to teach Irish, and while in the college transcribed some of Bedell's Old Testament for the printer. When Sall died in April 1682, Price conferred his benefices on Higgins, who left Trinity College shortly thereafter. Higgins's income from his various livings in the diocese of Cashel amounted to about £200 per annum.

Public services in Irish as well as English were apparently customary while Price was archbishop. At synods held in Cashel in 1678 and again in 1682 it was ordered that the practice of saying 'Irish prayers' in the cathedral should be continued. William Daniel's translation of the Book of Common Prayer was the service book used, a copy having been given to Price by Andrew Sall. Price himself had some knowledge of Irish.

It is not known whether Price was married. He died in his archiepiscopal house on 4 August 1685 at the age of eighty-five, and was buried in St John's churchyard in Cashel, where his tombstone still remains.

N. J. A. WILLIAMS

Sources *The works of Sir James Ware*, ed. W. Harris, 1–2 (1749) · H. Cotton, *Fasti ecclesiae Hibernicae*, 1–5 (1845–60) · E. S. Shuckburgh, ed., *Two biographies of William Bedell, bishop of Kilmore, with a selection of his letters and an unpublished treatise* (1902) · N. J. A. Williams, *I bprionta i leabhar* (1987)

Price, Thomas [pseud. Carnhuanawc] (1787–1848), historian, was born on 2 October 1787 at Pencaerelen in the parish of Llanfihangel Brynpabuan, Brecknockshire, second son of Rice Price, vicar of Llanwrthwl, Brecknock (d. 1810), and Mary Bowen, his wife. In 1805 he entered Christ College, Brecon, after having attended local day schools. There he was taught to play the triple harp by a local harpist and attracted the notice of Theophilus Jones (1758–1812), who was then working on the second volume of his history of Brecknockshire. Price's talent for drawing was turned to good account in the illustration of this work, which aroused an enthusiasm for Welsh history. A letter written to Jones in 1811, in which he described some Roman remains near Llandrindod, was printed in *Archaeologia* in 1814.

On 10 March 1811 Price was ordained deacon, and licensed to the curacies of Llanyre and Llanfihangel Helygen in Radnorshire. His ordination as priest on 12 September 1812 was soon followed by a transfer, in April 1813, to Crickhowell, where he served the parishes of Llangenni, Llanbedr Ystrad Yw, and Patrishow as curate-in-charge. To these were added in 1816 the neighbouring parishes of Llangatwg and Llanelli. In 1825 he became vicar of Llanfihangel Cwm Du, to which the curacy of Tretower was

added in 1839. He was appointed rural dean in 1832. Crickhowell, however, continued to be his home until 1841, when he built himself a house on the glebe land at Cwm du.

Price first appeared as a Welsh scholar in 1824, when he contributed a series of papers on 'The Celtic tongue' to *Seren Gomer*, under the name Carnhuanawc, which became his recognized literary title. He was already known as an informed and eloquent speaker on bardism and similar topics at eisteddfods. Inspired by contemporary interests in minority ethnic cultures and pan-national movements throughout Europe, he became an enthusiastic pan-Celticist and laboured to develop Welsh–Breton links, winning a prize at the Welshpool eisteddfod of 1824 for an essay on the relations between Armorica and Britain. He played a key role in persuading the British and Foreign Bible Society to support a Breton translation of the New Testament and began a long correspondence with the Breton scholars Le Godinec and Hersart de la Villemarqué. The Celtic connections of the Welsh interested him greatly, and during the next few years he travelled a good deal in Celtic countries. His account of his tour of Brittany was published in the *Cambrian Quarterly Magazine* in 1830. In 1829 he published *An Essay on the Physiognomy and Physiology of the Present Inhabitants of Britain*, in which he maintained against the Scottish antiquary John Pinkerton the doctrine of the single origin of the human race.

In 1836 Price began his *magnum opus*, the compilation of a history of Wales in Welsh. *Hanes Cymru* appeared in fourteen parts, the first of which was issued in 1836, the last in 1842: the work appeared also as a single volume in that year. Price's desire to secure as great a degree of accuracy as possible led to long delays. A cumbrous and pedantic style and the absence of any constructive treatment of his material detracted from the merits of the work, but it remained for many years the most trustworthy history of Wales.

Price, who had an attractive personality, was an indefatigable worker in all movements which appealed to his fervent patriotism. He was an early advocate of Welsh-language schools and was active in establishing the Welsh Minstrelsy Society and the Welsh Manuscript Society. He participated in the foundation of the Cymreigyddion, or Welsh Society, of Brecon (1823), and that of Abergavenny (1833). His involvement with the annual eisteddfods of the latter society from 1834 drew the support of influential local gentry and antiquarians and they became the means of encouraging the serious study of Welsh literature and history and an important channel for continuing the work of the previous generation of Welsh cultural leaders. Price combined in himself traditional Welsh culture and scholarship and antiquarianism and he was thus able to attract both groups to share their efforts. He was a regular contributor to Welsh periodicals and corresponded widely on Celtic topics. He took a close interest in the Welsh (triple) harp, and through his exertions a school for players of this instrument was for a time maintained at Brecon. He was a regular, though not always successful, competitor at eisteddfods; in October 1845 he won the prize of £80 offered at Abergavenny eisteddfod for the best essay on the comparative merits of Welsh, Irish, and Gaelic literature. Other essays on the history of Welsh literature, the influence of Celtic literature on European literatures, and the Statute of Wales were published in his *Literary Remains*. In 1847 he published a pamphlet on *The Geographical Progress of Empire and Civilisation*, an expansion of Berkeley's theory that 'westward the course of empire takes its way'.

Price died, unmarried, on 7 November 1848 at Llanfihangel Cwm Du and was buried there. In 1854–5 his *Literary Remains* was published at Llandovery, the second volume containing a biography by Jane Williams (Ysgafell).

J. E. LLOYD, rev. BRYNLEY F. ROBERTS

Sources J. Williams, 'Memoir of the life of Thomas Price', in *The literary remains of the Rev. Thomas Price, Carnhuanawc*, ed. [J. Williams], 2 vols. (1854–5), vol. 2 · D. R. Stephen, *Archaeologia Cambrensis*, 4 (1849), 146–50 · M. E. Thomas, *Afiaith yng Ngwent* (1978), 109–18 · S. J. Williams, 'Carnhuanawc, eisteddfodwr ac ysgolhaig', *Transactions of the Honourable Society of Cymmrodorion* (1954), 18–30 · J. Davies, *A history of Wales* (1993), 386–7
Archives NL Wales, corresp. and papers · South Glamorgan Library
Likenesses A. Hall, silhouette, 1833, repro. in Williams, ed., *Literary remains of … Carnhuanawc*, vol. 1, p. 283 · A. Llwyd, pen-and-ink sketch, 1837, NL Wales, MS 781A, 31 · C. A. Mornewick, oils, 1846, NL Wales · W. M. Thomas, plaster bust, c.1848, Llandovery College, Carmarthenshire · L. Dickinson, lithograph (after C. Lucy), NL Wales, MS 12353D, 299 · sketch, repro. in *ILN* (25 Oct 1845), 264

Price, Thomas (1852–1909), politician in Australia, born at Harwd, near Wrexham, Flintshire, on 19 January 1852, was the eldest of the seven children of John Price, a stonemason, and his wife, Jane Morris. In 1853 the family moved to Liverpool, where he was educated at the St George's Church of England penny school, Everton, before being apprenticed at the age of nine to a stonecutter. His father's drinking led Price to temperance and Wesleyanism. After continuing his education at a mechanics institute, he became a teacher and lay preacher at the Boundary Street Sunday school and was active in politics. At St David's Welsh Church of England, Liverpool, on 14 April 1881 he married Anne Elizabeth, the daughter of Edward Lloyd, a timber merchant, of Liverpool. They had four sons and three daughters.

Stonecutting had damaged his lungs, so in 1883 Price and his wife emigrated to Australia and settled in Adelaide at a time when there was much difficulty in getting employment. He lived in suburban Unley, where he resided until his death, and was temporarily employed as clerk of works at the government locomotive shops at Islington. He worked as a stonecutter on many important Adelaide buildings, including the new parliament house, in which he later sat as premier. He was a member and later South Australian secretary and president of the Operative Masons' and Bricklayers' Society of Australia. From 1893 to 1902 he sat in the house of assembly of the colony for the United Labor Party as member for Sturt and from 1902 as member for Torrens. During this time he supported the radical Kingston ministry. In 1899 he became leader of the United Labor Party. In July 1905, after success

at the polls, he formed a coalition with the Liberals and became premier, taking the portfolios of public works and education. He held the office of premier until his death.

Price was a kind man with a strong sense of humour and rugged eloquence. He was one of the few parliamentary speakers who are known to have changed votes and decided the fate of a measure by power of speech. During his premiership he was responsible for the completion of the outer harbour at Adelaide, and for acts creating wages boards, municipalizing the tramway system (which had previously been in the hands of seven companies), reducing the franchise for the upper house, transferring after his death the northern territory to the commonwealth, and tightening control on drinking, gambling, and prostitution. His administration was successful in its own right and paved the way for later Labor administrations. In continuing poor health, he died of phthisis and diabetes at the height of his popularity at Mount Lofty, Adelaide, where he was staying with friends, on 31 May 1909, and was buried on 2 June in Mitcham cemetery at Adelaide.

Price's widow went on to become a JP, perhaps the first in British territories, and was also a Labor Party vice-president. Their eldest son, John Lloyd Price (1882–1941), was also a politician, a member of the Labor Party until 1931 and the United Australia Party thereafter.

C. P. LUCAS, rev. ELIZABETH BAIGENT

Sources S. Weeks, 'Price, Thomas', *AusDB*, vol. 11 · T. H. Smeaton, *From stone-cutter to premier* (1924) · *The Register* [Adelaide] (1 June 1909) · D. Jaensch, ed., *The Flinders history of South Australia*, 2: *Political history* (1986)
Likenesses C. D. Mackenzie, oils, Walker Art Gallery, Liverpool
Wealth at death £2305 15s. 2d.: administration with will, 7 March 1910, *CGPLA Eng. & Wales*

Price, Sir Uvedale, first baronet (1747–1829), writer and rural improver, was born at Foxley, in the parish of Yazor, Herefordshire, where he was baptized on 14 April 1747. He was the eldest son of **Robert Price** (1717–1761), a gentleman artist, and his wife, Sarah (d. 1759), the daughter of John Shute *Barrington, first Viscount Barrington.

Robert Price Robert Price was the son of Uvedale Tomkins Price (1685–1764) and his wife, Anne, the daughter of Lord Arthur Somerset. He made a grand tour in 1738 and was taught to draw in Rome by Giovanni Battista Busiri, one of whose sketchbooks he once owned and which is now in the Fitzwilliam Museum, Cambridge. Of his many sketches, a number are in public collections (Ashmolean Museum, Oxford, and the National Library of Wales, Aberystwyth); his *Castle Mount at Foxley, 1744* showing the 'Ragged Castle', an early example of the Gothic revival, is in Hereford Library. Price was a friend of the artists Thomas Jones and John Baptist Malchair, while Gainsborough was on good terms with three generations of the Price family. With the naturalist Benjamin Stillingfleet, Price made sketching excursions, in search of picturesque scenery, down the Wye valley and into Wales. He drew the plates for Stillingfleet's *Observations on Grasses* (1762) and also 'laid a scheme of improvement … which when executed will make Foxley vye with any place' (Lambin, 252).

He planted ornamental trees, developed new woods, and created 'walks or rather rides … diversify'd with different prospects' (ibid.). In 1824 John Claudius Loudon could still distinguish the oak, beech, and elm, planted by Robert, from the introductions of his son. Robert Price married Sarah Barrington in June 1746. He was buried at Yazor on 1 October 1761.

Uvedale Price: early life and estate management Uvedale Price was educated at Eton College and matriculated from Christ Church, Oxford, in 1763. He became friendly with the whig politician Charles James Fox (1749–1806), and in the autumn of 1767 they travelled to Florence and then to Rome, Venice, Turin, and Geneva. While passing through Perugia, Price purchased six drawings by Salvator Rosa, whose work epitomizes sublime landscape. In August 1768 they paid a visit to Voltaire at Ferney.

Price probably took control of Foxley soon after his return from his grand tour, and in 1772–3 alterations were made to the house on the advice of the fashionable architect Robert Adam. On 28 April 1774 Price married Lady Caroline Carpenter (d. 1826), the youngest daughter of George, first earl of Tyrconnel, whose family were well connected with Herefordshire. They had a son, Robert (d. 1857), and a daughter, Caroline (d. 1853). A survey of Foxley carried out in 1775 by the professional land agent Nathaniel Kent (1737–1810) recorded that it was 3537 acres in extent and provided its owner with an income of £2461. Kent transferred much tenanted woodland to Price, but also recommended, contrary to the current trend, retaining a large number of small-holders and cottagers. Price was a conscientious landowner, farming profitably but at the same time conscious of the aesthetic bonus produced by meticulous management guided by a discriminating eye. Like Joseph Addison and Alexander Pope earlier in the century, he saw no reason why a whole estate should not please the eye, rather than just the pleasure grounds around the house. Indeed, Price had little interest in the picturesque but sterile landscapes of the more rugged parts of Britain, popularized by such tourists as William Gilpin, or the new parklands laid out by Capability Brown. Instead, he celebrated landscapes which were 'flourishing, populous, domesticated and needed to be worked industriously to keep them so' (Daniels and Watkins, 161). Price condemned the improving landowner who, perhaps aided by Capability Brown, lived within a ring-fence of shelter belts, isolated from his tenantry. He believed that Britain could escape the horrors of the French Revolution if the landowning classes espoused the concept of 'connection', maintaining their links, both socially and economically, with the lower classes. These ideas were developed in a pamphlet, *Thoughts on the Defence of Property*, printed in Hereford in 1797, on the occasion of the French landing on the Pembrokeshire coast.

The *Essays* and the picturesque controversy Price's indignation at what he regarded as the 'false taste' purveyed by Capability Brown and his many imitators, such as the 'mechanic improvers' Richard Woods and William Emes, was expressed in the *Essay on the Picturesque* (1794). This

work was long in gestation, and Price sent various drafts to his friends, including Fox and the collector and amateur landscape painter Sir George Beaumont, for their comments. The *Essay* celebrated localism and the diversity of the English landscape in all its forms, epitomized in the phrase 'intricacy and variety'. Price feared that a new uniformity was being imposed upon the countryside because modern improvers were replacing 'intricacy in disposition, and variety of forms, the tints and the lights and shadows of objects' with 'monotony and baldness [which] are the greatest defects of improved places' (Price, 1.22–3). Brown had been consulted at well over 250 estates in Britain, where he had deployed the same elements—belts of trees, clumps, serpentine lakes and drives, and endless acres of lawn—which ignored the singularity of each landscape. Roughness and ruggedness had been banished for acres of smooth turf.

Essentially, the *Essay* promoted in measured terms the more radical view of the picturesque landscape voiced by Richard Payne Knight in *The Landscape: a Didactic Poem, Addressed to Uvedale Price*, also published in 1794. Both authors argued that landscaping was safer in the hands of men of liberal education who understood the character of their own estates. Price, in particular, wished to revive the role of the amateur gardener—such as William Shenstone and Charles Hamilton—who eschewed the borrowed taste of a professional landscaper who, after a brief visit to an estate, in a remote part of the country—such as his native Herefordshire—would make inappropriate improvements. Like Knight, he believed that the sensitivity of the amateur improver was enhanced by a knowledge and understanding of the paintings of Claude, Poussin, and Salvator Rosa. These paintings, set in a rugged classical landscape, where nature was about to engulf the works of man, provided a variety of vignettes, which could be used as a corrective in the late eighteenth-century countryside. Price was conscious that this was being damaged not only by professional landscapers but also by new agricultural practices, industry, and even the turnpike roads. It was this reaffirmation of the role of great art in moulding the countryside which underpinned Price's version of the picturesque. As his taste was more catholic and domestic than Knight's, Price also recommended the paintings of the seventeenth-century Dutch school, such as those of Ruisdael. In every painting there were object lessons for the amateur landscaper, who with sensitivity and imagination could create similar 'pictures' on his estate without sacrificing its productive capacity.

In addition to promoting a more painterly approach to the landscape, Price sought to give greater definition to the much-abused term 'picturesque', which had become a descriptive commonplace in the eighteenth century— *pittoresco* being 'after the manner of painters'. Price believed that the picturesque existed between Edmund Burke's categories of the 'beautiful' and the 'sublime': 'When I first read that original work [*Inquiry into the Origin of our Ideas of the Sublime and Beautiful*, 1756], I felt that there were numberless objects which gave delight to the eye and yet differed as widely from the beautiful as from the sublime' (Price, 1.43). Whereas the beautiful was characterized by smoothness and freshness, the picturesque had the opposite qualities of roughness and decay. Similarly, the sublime, with its characteristics of greatness and infinity, was the antithesis of the picturesque's intricacy and variety. Price was equally unhappy with William Gilpin's category of 'picturesque beauty', which he applied to landscapes that were beautiful and yet would make good pictures. Price expanded the discussion of his theory in *A Dialogue on the Distinct Characters of the Picturesque and the Beautiful* (1801), which was subject to a forthright attack by Knight in *An Analytical Inquiry into the Principles of Taste* (1805). Price's theory, although going beyond Burke, had followed the latter, as well as Hogarth, in believing that the aesthetic categories he described were inherent in objects themselves, whereas Knight, exploiting the views of David Hume, thought that they were simply in the mind of the beholder.

The *Essay* and his letters are an excellent guide to the application of Price's ideas. He admitted to George Beaumont that he spent his time at Foxley 'trying the effect of my own principles'. In another revealing letter he described a moment of picturesque creativity:

> It has been ingeniously said … that in every block of marble a fine statue is enclosed; you have only to clear away the rubbish: so it is with such a place as this; there are pictures in every tangled wood and thicket when the rubbish is removed: but what does, or does not constitute rubbish, is a very nice point: you must not destroy the appearance of intricacy and wildness in the near parts, nor injure the mass and general outline from the distance, and must take special care, while you are clearing, to make one picture, not to sacrifice others in the neighbourhood.

For Price the spade and the axe were the landscaper's tools, and although they were coarse instruments they could be used to picturesque effect 'when working under the eye of a painter, and guided by his potent art'. Like the artist, once the outline of the composition had been achieved, he looked to his palette—'the improver's palet is his nursery' (Allentuck, 73–5).

During the last decade of the eighteenth century and the first of the nineteenth, the picturesque controversy was debated both in writing and in the salons of polite society throughout the country. Several critics, such as George Mason, William Marshall, and Horace Walpole, writing during the climax of the French Revolution, failed to distinguish between Price's practical 'landscape husbandry' and the 'Jacobinical' gardening recommended by Knight (Ballantyne, 'Turbulence and repression', 66). Both Mason and Walpole had aired criticisms of Brown's system at an earlier date, but in the 1790s, perhaps through affection for the memory of Brown, they defended his reputation. Unfortunately for Price, the picturesque ideal was absorbed into the political milieu and taken as a symptom of the social anarchy released in France. The critics claimed that the promoters of the picturesque, by espousing 'undressed nature', were attacking the tastes of the 'folks of high degree' who enjoyed the convenience and obvious charms of the Brownian landscape and,

instead, they were championing a revolution in the countryside. This was a parody of Knight's *The Landscape* and unfair to Price, and yet there was a grain of truth in it. Both Price and Knight were strongly committed whigs. Price supported his friend Fox against the tory prime minister William Pitt, circulating in 1796 several epigrams 'somewhat splenetic' against the government's excessive expenditure (Owen and Brown, 90). This was a traditional whig position, but in the context of the war could be interpreted as radical and unpatriotic.

Jane Austen was also fully conversant with the nuances of the picturesque debate and parodied Gilpin in *Northanger Abbey*, while in *Mansfield Park* her sympathies are certainly with Price. Thomas Love Peacock, in *Headlong Hall* (1816), produced some knockabout scenes between the characters Sir Patrick O'Prism, representing Price, and Mr Milestone, representing the landscape gardener Humphry Repton. The debate clearly impinged upon the professional aspirations of Repton, who quickly went into print with *Sketches and Hints on Landscape Gardening* (1795), in which he denied the affinity between gardening and painting suggested by Price on the premise that the landscape gardener's creativity was much more restricted than the artist's. Repton had also defended the merits of his profession in a 'Letter to Uvedale Price' (1794), where he revealed that he had spent 'pleasant hours' with Price 'amidst the romantic scenery of the Wye' (Price, 3.5). Price replied in a 'Letter to H. Repton' (1795), and both letters were published with a further three essays in 1798. Finally, all the *Essays* were collected in a three-volume edition issued in 1810. An extended edition entitled *Sir Uvedale Price and the Picturesque* was published in 1842 edited by Sir Thomas Dick Lauder.

Price's influence Once the heat of the controversy had faded, Price's original contribution to landscape gardening was generally acknowledged by contemporaries and later generations. Towards the end of his career, even Repton, under pressure from his clients, accommodated picturesque canons in his layouts, as is evident in the Red Books for Hewell, Worcestershire (1811), and Endsleigh, Devon (1814). In his 'Memoir', Repton referred to Price and Knight as those 'ingenious authors' (BL, Add. MS 62112, 'Memoir', 212). The landscape gardener W. S. Gilpin presented himself to his clients as the person who could render Price's *Essays* 'practically useful' (Gilpin, *Practical Hints upon Landscape Gardening*, 1832, vi), while, for John Claudius Loudon, Price was 'the great reformer of landscape gardening' of whom he was a 'profound admirer and disciple' (M. Simo, *Loudon and the Landscape*, 1988, 93). Edward Kemp, writing in 1850, still felt that 'The work of Sir U. Price on the Picturesque is probably the most valuable thing of its kind in our language' (Kemp, *How to Lay Out a Garden*, x). Finally, the American landscape gardener Frederick Olmsted visited Herefordshire in 1850 with the specific intention of soaking up the countryside which nurtured Uvedale Price.

The *Essays* were not only a practical handbook for professional gardeners, but also a manifesto for a new movement in painting—'an ideology for British romanticism'

(J. Murdoch, *David Cox, 1783–1859*, 1983, 12). Thomas Hearne responded in the 1790s to Price's theory by his rejection of prospects and espousal of intimate scenes. David Cox went to live in Herefordshire in 1814 because it was the county of the picturesque, and his adoption of 'the broken tint style' was designed to capture the texture of the countryside admired by Price. Cox painted a *Scene at Foxley Park* which was engraved by G. Hunt in 1823, and one of his pupils, while he was living in Hereford, was Charlotte Price—perhaps Uvedale Price's niece.

The 'Essay on architecture' in volume 2 of the *Essays* was equally influential, especially for its assessment of buildings in the landscape. Lord Aberdeen, who corresponded with Price, made several references to it in *An Inquiry into the Principles of Beauty in Grecian Architecture* (1822), while architects providing designs for *ornée* cottages, such as P. F. Robinson (1776–1858) and Edward Bartell, derived credibility by referring to 'Mr. Price's ingenious *Essay*' (E. Bartell, *Hints for Picturesque Improvements*, 1804, 76).

Aberystwyth and visitors to Foxley In 1794 Price built a seaside house at Aberystwyth—the Castle House—designed by the then relatively unknown architect John Nash. Here Nash was inducted 'into the mystery of the Picturesque' by Price and subsequently carried the style with him into metropolitan improvements in London (J. Summerson, *John Nash*, 1980, 21). Eventually, a synthesis of Nash and Loudon produced the picturesque Victorian suburb, perhaps Price's most abiding legacy. Nash also produced delectable cottages, some of the earliest for Price, which became the essence of Arcadian dreams in the nineteenth century.

The *Essays* and the picturesque controversy brought many visitors to Foxley. Fox came about 1785 and admired Price's planting. The antiquary and topographer John Britton was 'eager and curious to have a personal view of the homes of the literary belligerents' (J. Britton, *Autobiography*, 1850, 150) and visited Foxley on a walking tour in 1798. Writing in 1850, he felt he could detect a 'palpable contrast' (ibid.) between the landscape at Foxley and the pleasure grounds laid out elsewhere by Repton. Perhaps the most flattering reference to Foxley comes from France and occurs in Jacques Delille's much printed work *Les jardins* (1801). Delille recommended Foxley as a model for the improvement of rural estates (*Les jardins*, 12). In 1799 James Plumtre was impressed by the 'Forest Scenery' at Foxley with its under wood of holly, thorns, and brambles. He also noticed some more conventional aspects of Price's pleasure grounds, such as the small flower garden at the back of the house, with its creeping and trailing plants, the conservatory, and rustic alcove. Nearby there was a menagerie and beside a pond a cool grotto (I. Ousby, ed., *James Plumtre's Britain*, 1992). Among other notable visitors to Foxley were the dramatist Richard Sheridan, the poet Samuel Rogers, Sir George Beaumont, and William Combe, the author of *Dr Syntax*. Wordsworth visited Foxley in 1810 but felt that Price had become too 'delicate and fastidious' in his picture making and, notwithstanding the emphasis of its owner upon 'connection', found the estate 'lacked the relish of humanity' (Daniels and Watkins, 163). Price admired Wordsworth's poetry and thought his *Scenery of the Lakes* (1820) should be regarded as 'the manual for improvers in every part of the kingdom' (Owen and Brown, 201). Price and Wordsworth collaborated on the quarry garden at Coleorton, Leicestershire, laid out for Sir George Beaumont. Price gave informal advice on gardening and tree planting to many of his friends. For example, he provided plants and helped with the design of a new walk at Fox's house near Isleworth, on the outskirts of London. It has been suggested by Denis Lambin that Eywood and Whitfield in Herefordshire, Cassiobury in Hertfordshire, Packington Hall and Guy's Cliffe in Warwickshire, and Bentley Priory in Stanmore, London, all received his attention.

Local influence Price's well-publicized association with Knight and his whiggism created a certain detachment from his fellow gentry in Herefordshire. One of them, Dr John Matthews of Belmont, near Hereford, was prepared to challenge the picturesque point of view in print with *A Sketch from the Landscape* (1794). Another neighbour, Thomas Symonds of the Mynde, was very self-conscious about employing a local gardener in 'the county where Mr. U. Price and Mr. Rd. Payne Knight (the first gentlemen professors) reside' (NL Wales, Mynde Park, 2473). Several of Price's neighbours also employed Repton, who expressed his surprise on being consulted by James Hereford of Sufton Court in 1795, in the 'enemy's quarters' (Red Book, Sufton Court). Price could, however, be a generous neighbour. Sarah Harford Jones, newly married, living close to Foxley at Mansel Lacy in 1798, and left alone with difficult servants by her husband, who was travelling in Persia for the East India Company, found Price and his wife very civil and attentive; dancing was provided at Foxley, gardening advice proffered, and a holiday suggested at the Castle House, Aberystwyth.

Friendship with Elizabeth Barrett (Browning) In 1826 Price, nearly eighty years old, struck up a friendship with Elizabeth Barrett (Browning), the twenty-year-old poet of Hope End, near Ledbury. Price was impressed by her *Essay on the Mind, with other Poems* (1826), and a dialogue ensued. Barrett visited Foxley, discussed the poetry of George Crabbe with Price, and found herself being asked to read and criticize the proof sheets for Price's last publication, *An Essay on the Modern Pronunciation of the Greek and Latin Language* (1827), a work which Wordsworth regarded as 'most ingenious … If he be right, we have all been wrong, and I think he is' (Hewlett, 38). Elizabeth Barrett wrote subsequently that 'Mr. Price's friendship has given me more continual happiness than any other single circumstance ever did' (ibid., 39). On Price's death two years later she wrote a poem 'To the Memory of Sir Uvedale Price, Bart' (1829). She recommended reading the *Essay on the Picturesque* for the 'sake of its style … natural, chaste and humorous to a captivating degree' (B. McCarthy, *Elizabeth Barrett to Mr Boyd*, 1955, 44). Price was a compulsive letter-writer, and Edward Henry Barker (1788–1839) began collecting his correspondence with a view to publishing it. He wrote to Elizabeth Barrett asking for her letters, but her father,

Edward, thought that to agree would be 'a dereliction of all I know you to feel towards the memory of Sir U. Price' (M. Forster, *Elizabeth Barrett Browning*, 1988, 54).

Offices, honours, and death Price was elected a member of the Society of Dilettanti in 1784 along with his lifelong friend Sir George Beaumont. He was sheriff of Herefordshire in 1793 and served upon a number of local committees, including the commission for the new county gaol in Hereford, which employed John Nash as architect in 1796. He was the first and only superintendent to the deputy surveyor of the Forest of Dean (1816). On 12 February 1828 he was created a baronet.

Price died at Foxley on 14 September 1829, aged eighty-two, having been predeceased by his wife, on 16 July 1826. His obituary in the *Hereford Journal* (16 September 1829) referred to his 'learning, his sagacity, his exquisite taste, his indefatigable ardour'. He was buried against the east wall of Yazor church, in the churchyard, under a simple table tomb. It survives today, albeit in ruins.

DAVID WHITEHEAD

Sources D. A. Lambin, 'Foxley: the Prices' estate in Herefordshire', *Journal of Garden History*, 7 (1987), 244–70 · S. Daniels and C. Watkins, 'Picturesque landscaping and estate management: Uvedale Price at Foxley, 1770–1829', *Rural History*, 2 (1991), 141–69 · S. Daniels, S. Seymour, and C. Watkins, 'Border country: the politics of the picturesque in the middle Wye valley', *Prospects for the nation: recent essays in the British landscape, 1750–1880*, ed. M. Rosenthal, C. Payne, and S. Wilcox (1997) · F. Owen and D. B. Brown, *Collector of genius: a life of George Beaumont* (1988) · D. Hewlett, *Elizabeth Barrett Browning* (1953) · J. Hutchinson, *Herefordshire biographies* (1860) · A. Ballantyne, *Architecture, landscape and liberty: Richard Payne Knight and the picturesque* (1997) · U. Price, *Essays on the picturesque*, 3 vols. (1810) · D. Jacques, *Georgian gardens* (1983) · A. Ballantyne, 'Genealogy of the picturesque', *British Journal of Aesthetics*, 32 (1992), 320–29 · M. Allentuck, 'Sir Uvedale Price and the picturesque garden: the evidence of the Coleorton papers', *The picturesque garden and its influence outside the British Isles*, ed. N. Pevsner (1974) · B. Hartley, 'Naturalism and sketching: Robert Price at Foxley and on tour', *The picturesque landscape: visions of Georgian Herefordshire*, ed. S. Daniels and C. Watkins (1994), 34–40 [exhibition catalogue, Hereford City Art Gallery and University Art Gallery, Nottingham, 1994] · A. Ballantyne, 'Turbulence and repression: re-reading *The Landscape*', *The picturesque landscape: visions of Georgian Herefordshire*, ed. S. Daniels and C. Watkins (1994), 66–79 [exhibition catalogue, Hereford City Art Gallery and University Art Gallery, Nottingham, 1994] · parish register, Yazor, 14 April 1747, Herefs. RO [baptism]

Archives Herefs. RO, estate MSS, B47 · priv. coll., estate records | BL, Lord Abercorn MSS, Add. MS 43228 · BL, letters to C. J. Fox, Add. MS 47576 · BL, corresp. with Lord Holland and Lady Holland, Add. MS 47576 · Bodl. Oxf., letters to E. H. Barker · Herefs. RO, Knight MSS, T74 · Morgan L., Coleorton MSS · NL Wales, letters to G. Lewis

Likenesses T. Lawrence, oils, *c.*1795, Museum of Fine Arts, Boston · portrait, BM

Price, William (*b.* 1596/7), university professor, was the son of a Denbighshire gentleman. He matriculated from Christ Church, Oxford, on 16 October 1616, aged nineteen, graduating BA on 26 October, and proceeding MA on 21 June 1619. He was appointed White professor of moral philosophy in 1621, with a stipend of £100 a year, and in April 1624 was selected to give the oration in memory of the founder of the post, Thomas White. He proceeded BD

in 1628. The following year he resigned his readership at the end of his allotted five-year span, but must have remained for a time at the university. On 23 April 1630 he and several others signed an appeal to the king against the appointment of William Laud as chancellor of the university, secured illegitimately, as they thought, at the university's convocation eleven days earlier. Price's subsequent movements are obscure, but he may have been the William Price who, also in 1630, acquired the vicarage of Llantilio Pertholey, Denbighshire. The date of his death is unknown. STEPHEN WRIGHT

Sources Foster, *Alum. Oxon.* · Wood, *Ath. Oxon.: Fasti* (1815), 365, 388–9 · *Reg. Oxf.*, 2/2.354 · A. Wood, *The history and antiquities of the University of Oxford*, ed. J. Gutch, 2 vols. in 3 pts (1792–6)

Price, William (*d.* 1666), Reformed minister, was born, according to his own account, in London, but he was later taunted with being a Welshman by one of his congregation, so his family may have come from the principality. His publications reveal that he was educated at Cambridge University and that he gained a BD, but it is not clear if he was either the William Price born in London who was admitted to Sidney Sussex College in 1617, or the namesake who was admitted to Emmanuel College on 28 June 1622, matriculated in 1623, and graduated BA early in 1626. It is possible that it was he who was instituted vicar of Brigstock, Northamptonshire, on 4 January 1633 and who published, as William Price BD, *Janitor animae: the Soules Porter to Cast out Sinne* (1638), dedicated to William Cecil, earl of Salisbury, and his wife from their 'devouted orator and chaplaine'; this man was still resident in Brigstock in 1639, but by 1641 had been replaced as vicar by one Francis Lewis. It is more certain that at some time in or before 1640 William Price (*d.* 1666) married Sybella Geens of London and they had a son, John.

On 13 April 1642 Price, as 'preacher at Covent Garden', delivered before the lord mayor and civic leaders *A Sermon Preached at St Maries Spittle*, published later that year. He was still at Covent Garden when appointed in 1643 to the Westminster assembly, where he spoke often and always supported the presbyterian position, although he opposed the solemn league and covenant. By the time he published *Mans Delinquencie Attended by Divine Justice Intermixt with Mercy* (1646), a fast sermon delivered to the House of Lords, he was pastor of Waltham Abbey. However, as the revolution gathered speed, he became alarmed about religious radicalism and Oliver Cromwell.

On 23 March 1648 the English Reformed church of Amsterdam called Price to serve as co-pastor with Richard Maden; formal induction was on 12 August 1648. Price approved of this church's presbyterial polity, and he supported the larger Dutch Reformed system by joining the Amsterdam classis. He was an active co-pastor but his effectiveness was hampered by family problems. His wife stayed behind in London for over two years, claiming illness and weakness, and this prolonged separation of husband and wife was scandalous. Moreover, Price's own ministerial work was intermittent because of illnesses. On the other hand he translated into English the shorter Dutch catechism, published two Latin works, *Triumphans sapientiae* (1655) and *Ars conciandi* (1657), dedicated respectively to the rulers of Amsterdam and to the University of Cambridge, and was resolute in agitating about political affairs. Price and Maden filled the church with one-sided royalist, anti-Cromwell prayers and sermons. English agents put Price on a list of 'violent incendiaryes' (Thurloe, 2.373–4).

Price's active service in the Amsterdam church ended in 1659, but the following year he published, as from there, *Gods Working and Brittains Wonder*, expressing his 'unspeakable joy' at the Restoration; he remained on the list of pastors until his death in Amsterdam in July 1666. He was survived by his wife, who was buried at the New Church of Amsterdam on 29 July 1687. His son John had become preacher of the English church at The Hague on 22 May 1661.

KEITH L. SPRUNGER

Sources A. C. Carter, *The English Reformed church in Amsterdam in the seventeenth century* (1964) · K. L. Sprunger, *Dutch puritanism: a history of English and Scottish churches of the Netherlands in the sixteenth and seventeenth centuries* (1982) · R. S. Paul, *The assembly of the Lord: politics and religion in the Westminster assembly and the 'Grand debate'* (1985) · W. Steven, *The history of the Scottish church, Rotterdam* (1832, 1833) · S. W. Carruthers, *The everyday work of the Westminster assembly* (1943) · Thurloe, *State papers* · DNB · J. Wagenaar, *Amsterdam in zyne opkomst, aanwas, geschiedenissen* (1760–67), vol. 2, pp.173–5 · Venn, *Alum. Cant.* · H. I. Longden, *Northamptonshire and Rutland clergy from 1500*, ed. P. I. King and others, 16 vols. in 6, Northamptonshire RS (1938–52), vol. 9, p. 85 · *Walker rev.* · *ESTC* · W. Price, *A sermon preached at St Maries Spittle* (1642)
Archives Gemeentearchief, Amsterdam, consistory register of English Reformed Church, Amsterdam, P. A. 318

Price, William, the elder (*d.* 1709), glass painter, of whose parents nothing is known, lived in the parish of St Giles-in-the-Fields, London. He worked in Hatton Garden, and in 1683 was described as being one of only four glass painters in London. His earliest known work (1687) is a royal arms (des.) for the east window of St Andrew's, Holborn, London. In 1696 he supplied a *Nativity* (des.) for Christ Church, Oxford, and in 1701–2 a *Life of Christ* for the east window of Merton College, Oxford. A coat of arms signed by him and dated 1703 is in the Hall of Trinity College, Cambridge. He became an assistant at the Glaziers' Company in 1685, upper warden in 1697, and master in 1699. His wife, Anne (or Ann) Cranley, whom he had married on 9 April 1671 at St Peter-le-Poer, London, received the administration of his estate following his death in the parish of St Giles-in-the-Fields in May 1709.

William Price's son **Joshua Price** (*bap.* 1672, *d.* 1722), glass painter, was baptized on 11 July 1672 at St Andrew's, Holborn, London. The next reference to him appears to be an advertisement of 1705 in which he is mentioned as working with his father in Hatton Garden. In 1715 he reset the seventeenth-century glass in the chapel of Queen's College, Oxford, and supplied an east window in 1717. The following year he painted a *Last Supper* and *Resurrection* (both des.) for the east window of St Andrew's, Holborn. Between 1719 and 1721 he supplied twelve windows for the chapel of Cannons at Lord Chandos's house at Stanmore, Middlesex. Ten of these are now at Great Witley, Worcestershire, and of the other two, a *Conversion of St Paul* and

a *Stoning of St Stephen*, only the former survives (in St Andrew by the Wardrobe, London). His last work, the rose window (1721–2) in the north transept of Westminster Abbey, showing the apostles and evangelists, was based on cartoons by Sir James Thornhill. A contemporary account in the *Northampton Mercury* mentioned 'The great window … glazed with glass curiously painted after the Antique fashion, by Mr Price, who is reckon'd the only artist in England capable of doing it; so that that ornamental art is not so entirely lost as some have alledg'd' (23 Feb 1723). He was buried on 25 September 1722 and his wife, Elizabeth, received the administration of his estate in 1723.

Joshua Price's son **William Price the younger** (1702x7–1765) was also a glass painter. His earliest works of any consequence appear to be the east window (1726) of St Martin-in-the-Fields, London, and the west window (1735–6) of Westminster Abbey. Between 1735 and 1740 he executed five windows for New College, Oxford, followed by the east window (*c.*1742) of Turner's Hospital, Kirkleatham, Yorkshire, and the central window in the great court room of St Bartholomew's Hospital, London. About 1747 he installed the windows that his father, Joshua Price [*see above*], had made for Lord Chandos's house, in St Michael and All Angels, Great Witley, Worcestershire, adding further glass. In 1754 he carried out extensive work for James West of Alscot Park, Warwickshire, both in the house and at St Mary's, Preston-on-Stour, near by. He was almost certainly also responsible for the complete glazing of St John the Evangelist, Shobdon, Herefordshire, from 1750 to 1760, and windows at St Andrew Wimpole, Cambridgeshire. At least nineteen other works may be attributed to him, among them panels for Sir Horace Walpole, whose preferred artist he was. Walpole wrote in his *Anecdotes of Painting in England*:

> William Price the son, now living, whose colours are fine, whose drawing good, and whose taste in ornaments and mosaic is far superior to any of his predecessors, is equal to the antique, to the good Italian masters, and only surpassed by his own singular modesty.   (Walpole, 2.17)

Price retired in 1761 and died in Great Kirby Street, Hatton Garden, London, on 16 July 1765. His obituaries described him as 'a Batchelor, possessed of a large fortune' (*London Chronicle*, 16 July 1765) and 'the most ingenious painter and stainer of glass in Europe' (*GM*, 347). His will, which was proved by his mother, Elizabeth George (who had remarried), his sole executor, left money and interests in mines in Flintshire, Wales.

MICHAEL ARCHER

Sources J. A. Knowles, 'Glass-painters' advertisements', *Journal of the British Society of Master Glass-Painters*, 2 (1927–8), 18–22 · J. A. Knowles, 'The Price family of glass-painters', *Antiquaries Journal*, 33 (1953), 184–92 · M. Archer, 'The case of the superstitious images', *Crown in glory: a celebration of craftsmanship*, ed. P. Moore (1982), 48–57 · M. Archer, 'Stained glass at Erddig and the work of William Price', *Apollo*, 122 (1985), 252–63 [William Price the younger] · *IGI* · H. Walpole, *Anecdotes of painting in England … collected by the late George Vertue, and now digested and published*, 2 (1762), 17 · *Northampton Mercury* (23 Feb 1723) [Joshua Price] · *London Chronicle* (16 July 1765) [William Price the younger] · *GM*, 1st ser., 35 (1765), 347 [William Price the younger] · parish records (baptisms), 1672, London, Holborn, St Andrew's [Joshua Price] · parish records (burials),

1722, London, Holborn, St Andrew's [Joshua Price] • *Lloyds Evening Post*, no. 1251 (15–17 July 1765) [William Price the younger]

Price, William, the younger (1702×7–1765). *See under* Price, William, the elder (*d.* 1709).

Price, William (1780–1830), orientalist, born at Worcester, was said to have been a captain in the East India Company, but this is apparently a confusion with a contemporary William Price who taught oriental languages at Fort William College in Calcutta from about 1815 to 1834.

In 1810 Price was appointed assistant secretary and interpreter to the embassy of Sir Gore Ouseley to Persia in 1811–12. Price kept a diary, and made hundreds of drawings, of both landscapes and buildings. The journal, with its illustrations, was published in 1825. Price deciphered many cuneiform inscriptions. On his return to England he devoted himself to literary pursuits, and taught oriental languages at the seminary of his friend, Alexander Humphreys, at Netherstone House, near Worcester. He set up a private printing press in his house, and became a member of the Royal Society of London and the Asiatic Society of Bengal. He translated from Hindustani and Persian into both French and English and wrote books on the grammar of oriental languages. He died in June 1830.

CHARLOTTE FELL-SMITH, *rev.* PARVIN LOLOI

Sources *Biographie universelle*, suppl. • *Annual Register* (1830), 266 • Allibone, *Dict.*

Archives BL, Persian journal, Add. MS 19270 • BL OIOC, Persian journal, MS Eur. E 332

Price, William (1800–1893), physician, self-styled archdruid, and advocate of cremation, was born on 4 March 1800 at Ty'nycoedcae in the parish of Rudry, Monmouthshire, the third son of an impoverished Anglican clergyman, William Price (1760–1841), and his wife, Mary (*d.* 1844), an illiterate maidservant. After schooling at nearby Machen, Price was apprenticed to Evan Edwards, a surgeon at Caerphilly. His medical education continued in London, at St Bartholomew's Hospital and the London Hospital, and he qualified MRCS LSA in 1821. He returned to south Wales and became a successful general physician practising at Nantgarw, Trefforest, and Pontypridd, where he was the medical officer at the Ynysangharad works.

Price was interested in social and political reform and attempted to establish a national educational and cultural foundation by the ancient rocking-stone at Pontypridd in 1838. He became active in the Chartist movement in south Wales, leading the Pontypridd Chartists and playing a part in planning the Newport rising in 1839 by organizing the supply of arms, although he did not participate in it. He escaped briefly to Paris.

Price returned about March 1840 and continued to be involved in Chartism until the mid-1840s. He was the leader of a Pontypridd Provision Company, the first Welsh co-operative. Thereafter his enthusiasm for druidism and litigation consumed his energies and expressed a mental state which went beyond eccentricity into the realms of schizophrenia. Possibly there was an element of heredity, since his father had been insane from the age of thirty.

William Price (1800–1893), by unknown photographer, pubd 1871

By the late 1840s Price was reported as wearing his famously bizarre 'druidic' clothing of green trousers and fox-skin head-dress, long hair, and beard. He had developed an interest in druidism in the late 1830s, having earlier studied Indian religion and literature. He claimed in 1871, in *Gwyll-llis yn nayd* ('The will of my father'), a privately published pamphlet written in his own version of 'ancient' Welsh, to have discovered an engraved stone in the Louvre in 1839, which supported his extravagant theories and identification with an original 'Primitive Bard'.

Newspapers reported Price's increasingly eccentric public behaviour, culminating in 1884 with the great controversy which brought him national notoriety, when he attempted to burn the remains of his infant son on Cae'r-lan Fields hilltop, overlooking Llantrisant (near Pontypridd), where he had made his home. The boy, the son of Price with his housekeeper, had been proclaimed by him the future messiah and named Iesu Grist Price (Jesus Christ Price). He was tried in Cardiff at the winter assizes of 1884 for the crime of cremation; the jury found him not guilty. The trial and Judge Fitzjames Stephen's judgment established the legality of cremation in Britain.

The judgment was hailed by hygienic promoters of cremation but Price's action was motivated rather by druidic beliefs. Some of his notions on health and hygiene were certainly advanced and unorthodox. He believed that the patient should pay only if his health was restored, rejected conventional medicines as poisonous, and condemned vaccination. Vegetarian from about 1848, he held that Abraham had been a cannibal, and claimed that the pyramids of Egypt had been constructed to destroy this trait. He refused to treat smokers, insisted on the washing of coins, and refused to wear socks.

The cremation and trial consolidated Price's reputation as an arch-eccentric, a reputation elaborated by local anecdotes and press interviews revealing his unorthodox views on marriage and death. He died at Llantrisant on 23 January 1893 in comparative poverty, having made detailed arrangements for his body to be cremated in cast-iron sheeting on Cae'r-lan Fields Hill.

Price had one daughter, Gwenhelion (born c.1841, styled by Price Hiarhles Morganwg, or countess of Glamorgan), with Ann Morgan of Pen-tyrch; his 'druidic' marriage to his housekeeper, Gwenllian Llewllyn of Llanwynno, produced three other children: Penelope Elizabeth, Iesu Grist Price (5 Aug 1883–10 Jan 1884), and a second Iesu Grist Price, born on 9 October 1884.

Price's eccentricity was the result of a combination of mental illness and radicalism. His bizarre behaviour and unwitting role in establishing cremation as a legal alternative means for disposal of the dead secured posthumous fame. The life of the 'archdruid' of Llantrisant has been explored in doctoral research and monographs, and dramatized in stage and radio plays. Fittingly, for a man who was immersed in Welsh culture, whether genuine or self-invented, and whose druidic activity can be seen as an assertion of Welsh identity, his druidic costume and other personalia are preserved at the Museum of Welsh Life in Cardiff.   JAMES GREGORY

Sources J. Cule, 'The eccentric Dr William Price of Llantrisant, 1800–1893', *Morgannwg*, 7 (1963), 98–120 · J. Cule, 'Dr William Price (1800–1892) of Llantrisant: a study of an eccentric and a biography of a pioneer of cremation', MD diss., U. Cam., 1960 · B. Davies, 'Empire and identity: the "case" of Doctor William Price', *A people and a proletariat: essays in the history of Wales, 1780–1980*, ed. D. Smith (1980), 72–93 · 'Ap Id Anfryn', 'Doctor Price of Llantrisant: the famous druid interviewed. Sketch of his life and adventures', *Cardiff Times and South Wales Weekly News* (19 May–23 June 1888) · *DWB*
Archives Museum of Welsh Life, Cardiff, artefacts incl. costume · NL Wales, map collection, photographic albums, and loose photographs · NL Wales, papers
Likenesses A. Steward, oils, c.1820–1821, Museum of Welsh Life, St Fagan's Castle, Cardiff · A. C. Hemming, oils, 1918, Wellcome L. · engraving (after photograph by Forrest, Pontypridd), repro. in *Cardiff Times* (26 May 1888) · photograph, NL Wales; repro. in W. Price, *Gwyll-llis yn nayd* (1871) [*see illus.*] · photographs, NL Wales, department of pictures and maps
Wealth at death £400 5s. 6d.: probate, 20 Feb 1893, *CGPLA Eng. & Wales* · 'comparative poverty': Cule, 'Dr William Price of Llantrisant'

Price, Sir William (1865–1938), milk retailer, was born in Llanwrtyd Wells, Brecknockshire, the sixth of at least nine children born to William Price, a farmer, and his wife, Magdalene. His origins were humble but, like many emigrants from south Wales he was able to turn his rural skills to good effect in the dairy industry of London. Energy and organizational ability hastened Price's promotion until eventually, as Sir William, he dominated the world of milk retailing and wholesaling.

Price first came to London in the early 1880s, and on 23 March 1886 married Sarah Harries (b. 1862), of Llanwrtyd, with whom he had two sons, Ivor and Tudor, and two daughters. Lacking the confidence to approach one of the large companies such as the Aylesbury Dairy Company for employment, he decided instead to set up a small business of his own. He purchased a retail dairy in west London and prospered sufficiently to add a wholesaling function, before joining John Hopkins as a partner in Great Western and Metropolitan Dairies. In 1915 Price was responsible for the formation of the United Dairies wholesale combine (comprising Wiltshire United Dairies, Dairy Supply Company, F. W. Gilbert Ltd, and others) which soon expanded into retailing and very substantially changed the face of the London milk trade.

Price was a networker with a very wide circle of friends and contacts. His confident and determined character, coupled with his remarkable communication skills made him quite formidable. Concerned first and foremost with the broad, strategic, and often controversial issues, he delegated the everyday details to assistants, earning the nickname of 'the General' in the trade. His courage and resourcefulness were tested to the limit during the First World War when the need to supply London with milk had to be balanced against the demand for milk products by the forces overseas. Price's contribution was to organize the collection of liquid milk from an army of small producers all over the country who had hitherto been butter or farmhouse cheese makers, drawing them into the ambit of urban supply for the first time. The geography of dairying was fundamentally restructured as a result. Price was knighted in 1922 for services to the nation's milk industry.

Ironically the wartime shortages later turned to peacetime gluts and precipitated the crisis which eventually required legislation to create the Milk Marketing Board. This might have been avoided if Price's brainchild, the national scheme for the sale and purchase of milk, had been accepted in 1929. The smooth supply of milk to the capital was always Price's prime concern and during the national strike of 1926 he was a combative chairman of the London milk (emergency) committee and London's milk controller. He organized a milk pool in Hyde Park and kept the milk flowing.

Price played a prominent role in the various dairy trade organizations. He was president of the Metropolitan Dairymen's Benevolent Institution, a delegate at the foundation of the National Milk Publicity Council in 1920, an initiator of the United Dairies Benefit Society, president of the National Federation of Dairymen's Associations, and leader of the distributors' side of the permanent joint milk committee. He was also a justice of the peace, treasurer of a small Christian mission in Notting Hill, and for a large part of his life deacon of a Welsh Presbyterian church in Paddington.

In the early 1930s ill health forced Sir William's retirement from active business. He died at the Royal Northern Hospital, Holloway, on 16 April 1938 aged seventy-three, after an operation for an inflamed appendix. He was survived by his wife and sons.   P. J. ATKINS

Sources P. J. Atkins, 'Price, Sir William', *DBB* · B. Davies, 'Sir William Price', *The Milk Industry*, 18 (1938), 35–6 · *The Dairyman, the*

Cowkeeper and Dairyman's Journal, 60 (1938), 312–13 • *The Times* (18 April 1938), 12 • *WWW* • B. Davies, 'Sir William Price', *Our Notebook* [house magazine of United Dairies Ltd], 18 (July 1938) • *Brecon and Radnor Express and County Times* (28 April 1938) • *Dairy World*, 47 (1938) • Burke, *Peerage* • A. G. Enock, *This milk business: a study from 1895 to 1943* (1943) • Kelly, *Handbk* • A. Jenkins, *Drinka pinta: the story of milk and the industry that serves it* (1970) • B. Morgan, *Express journey, 1864–1964* (1964) • P. J. Atkins, 'The milk trade of London, c.1790–1914', PhD diss., U. Cam., 1977 • d. cert. • m. cert.

Likenesses photograph, repro. in Davies, 'Sir William Price', 35

Wealth at death £48,055 18s. 3d.: resworn probate, 27 May 1938, *CGPLA Eng. & Wales*

Price, William Charles (1909–1993), physicist and spectroscopist, was born on 1 April 1909 at 59A King Edward Road, Swansea, Glamorgan, the only son of Richard Price (1878–1970), master baker and grocery shop proprietor, and his wife, Florence Margaret (1876–1950), daughter of Jonas Wade Charles, postmaster at the village of Roch, Pembrokeshire, and his wife, Mary. Price's great-grandfather, John Charles, and Lloyd George's grandmother, Mary, were brother and sister. Price was educated at Swansea grammar school and at the University College of Swansea. He was awarded in 1930 a first-class honours degree in physics. He stayed at the University College for a further two years, and, because of the high promise of two papers he published with his research supervisor, P. M. Davidson, on the spectroscopy of the hydrogen molecule, in 1932 he took up a Commonwealth research fellowship at the Johns Hopkins University in Baltimore, USA. At Johns Hopkins, Price came under the influence of the legendary R. W. Wood. He embarked on a study of the spectra of polyatomic molecules in the vacuum ultraviolet region of the spectrum and was awarded his PhD in 1934.

Price was awarded an 1851 Exhibition scholarship and went to Cambridge in 1935, to the physical chemistry laboratory, to continue his work on the electronic structure of polyatomic molecules. This work afforded a spectroscopic basis for understanding chemical bonding. His discovery that the vacuum ultraviolet spectra could frequently be interpreted in terms of Rydberg series provided, for the first time, an accurate experimental basis against which to test the molecular orbital theories of R. S. Mulliken and Lennard Jones. For this work, in 1937, Price was awarded a Cambridge PhD and was appointed a university demonstrator. In the following year he was awarded the Meldola medal of the Royal Institute of Chemistry and a prize fellowship at Trinity College.

Price married Nest Myra Davies (b. 1910), a junior school teacher, on 12 August 1939; they were to have one son and one daughter. With the outbreak of the Second World War, Price became involved in projects like evaluating the composition, and hence the source, of enemy aviation fuels, and distinguishing true and simulated (decoy) gun flashes. In 1943 he moved from Cambridge to ICI, Billingham, where he established a spectroscopic and analytical section and training centre. Surprisingly, in 1941, he found time to publish with T. M. Sugden and A. D. Walsh a seminal paper on the ionization potentials of polyatomic

William Charles Price (1909–1993), by Godfrey Argent

molecules, containing numerical results of startling accuracy.

Price was delighted to accept an invitation from Mulliken to spend the year 1946–7 at the University of Chicago as a research associate in molecular spectroscopy. On his return from Chicago he accepted, in 1948, a readership at King's College, London, under John Randall. Randall had grafted on to the King's physics department a Medical Research Council biophysics unit and had begun pioneering work in biophysics: he wanted Price's skills in spectroscopy and knowledge of molecular bonding. Randall's success is shown by the sprinkling of biophysical papers in Price's list of publications (151 over his whole career) from 1950 to 1962. Three of the biophysical spectroscopic studies, were, first with one of his own students, R. D. B. Fraser, on the reconciliation of the observed infra-red spectrum for various alpha-proteins and polypeptides with the alpha helix model proposed by Pauling and Corey, then with Randall and his co-workers on the molecular structure of the fibrous protein collagen, and, finally, in a study initiated by Fraser, in association with M. H. F. Wilkins, on the orientation of the hydrogen bonds in DNA. (In 1962, Francis Crick, J. D. Watson, and Wilkins were awarded a Nobel prize for the determination of the helical structure of DNA.) Price also continued with his own developments, especially in the vacuum ultraviolet to which he turned increasingly, for example, to determine first (outer valence electrons) ionization potentials for a range of molecules. He saw immediately the potential of the new method of photoelectron spectroscopy to determine the binding energies of all the electrons in a molecular system, which he developed rapidly, as did D. W. Turner. He was elected Wheatstone professor of physics at King's College in 1955, occupying the chair until his retirement in 1976.

Price was possessed of great personal warmth and kindness and showed genuine care for colleagues, technicians, and students, which was universally reciprocated. He was profligate with his time and ideas to the benefit of others, making use of his unrivalled coverage of spectroscopic methods extending from the vacuum ultraviolet to far infra-red radiation and photoelectron spectroscopy. Price was an all-rounder: he regarded spectroscopy as interdisciplinary and he and his many students made major contributions right across the electromagnetic spectrum to physics, chemistry, and biophysics. Those contributions usually involved a blend of perception of the important problems with a radical revision of any existing experimental consensus by innovative apparatus design and construction, often by his own hands, in the machine shop or at the glass (or more often quartz) blower's bench. He was awarded the Cambridge ScD degree in 1949, was elected FRS in 1959, and in 1972 received the honorary DSc degree of the University of Wales. He died of a heart attack at Orpington Hospital, Orpington, Kent, on 10 March 1993; his remains were cremated at Eltham crematorium on 18 March. He was survived by his wife and two children.

RONALD BURGE

Sources R. N. Dixon, D. M. Agar, and R. E. Burge, *Memoirs FRS*, 43 (1997), 431–42 · private information (2004) · personal knowledge (2004) · *The Times* (16 March 1993) · *The Independent* (16 March 1993) · *The Independent* (22 March 1993) · WWW
Archives Bodl. Oxf., corresp. with C. A. Coulson · CUL, corresp. with and relating to Gordon Sutherland
Likenesses G. Argent, photograph, RS [*see illus.*] · photograph, repro. in *Memoirs FRS*, 430 · photograph, repro. in *The Times* · photograph, repro. in *The Independent* (16 March 1993)
Wealth at death £109,411: probate, 4 Oct 1993, *CGPLA Eng. & Wales*

Prichard [Pritchard], **Caradog** (1904–1980), poet and novelist, was born on 3 November 1904 at 24 Pen-y-bryn, Bethesda, Caernarvonshire, the son of John Pritchard, a slate quarryman who was killed in a quarrying accident when Caradog was only five months old, and Margaret Jane Williams. He was educated at Ysgol Sir Dyffryn Ogwen, Bethesda, but left school to become sub-editor of *Yr Herald Cymraeg* in Caernarfon. By this time his mother's mental health was deteriorating, and her illness left a deep mark on his consciousness for the rest of his life, and was the inspiration of much of his creative work. Bereft of a father, his childhood and adolescence were marked by his emotional dependence on his mother. Another problematic factor in his psychological make-up was his belief that his father had been a blackleg during the great strike at the Penrhyn quarry, a belief now thought to be misplaced. After three years at Caernarfon he moved to Llanrwst, in the Conwy valley, as a representative of the same newspaper. He later took up a post with another newspaper, *Y Faner*, which was also then based at Llanrwst. It was during this period that his mother was taken into the asylum at

Denbigh where she spent the last thirty years of her life. This was the inspiration for his long poem in the free metres, 'Y briodas', which won the crown at the 1927 national eisteddfod. After a period at Llanrwst he joined the staff of the *Western Mail* at Cardiff, and there followed two more eisteddfodic triumphs, in 1928 and 1929, for poems which again allude to the dark recesses of mental illness in various guises.

From Cardiff, Prichard (who published under this spelling of his surname) moved to London to work on the *News Chronicle*, and remained a guilt-ridden exile from Wales for the rest of his life. On 17 June 1933 he married Mattie Adele Gwynne Evans, a Welsh journalist who wrote under the name Mati Wyn. At the onset of the Second World War, Prichard was pushed to the brink of suicide, as he frankly admits in his autobiography. This experience was the inspiration for his long poem 'Terfysgoedd daear', which was submitted to the crown competition at the 1939 national eisteddfod. Although the adjudicators agreed that it was by far the best poem submitted, the prize was withdrawn because in their opinion it didn't adhere closely enough to the set subject. Prichard served in the army for two years during the Second World War, and published his wartime diary as *'R wyf innau 'n filwr bychan* in 1943. On his return he rejoined the *News Chronicle* and later moved to the *Daily Telegraph*. He and his wife, Mati, made their London home a haven for Welsh expatriates. They had one daughter, Mari Christina, who in 1973 married Humphrey Carpenter, the biographer.

It is recognized that Prichard's major literary contribution is his only novel, *Un nos ola leuad* (*One Moonlit Night*, 1961). Most of the raw materials are autobiographical, and the novel, set in a fictitious version of his native Bethesda, depicts the whirlwind reminiscences of the protagonist's childhood and adolescence. He has returned to his home town as a grown man after a presumed period in a mental institution, as if to exorcize the evil spirits of his past. Perversion, madness, the Oedipus complex, and sadism are constant undercurrents, and the novel culminates in a frenzied sexual attack and implied suicide. English and French translations have been published, and a Penguin Modern Classics edition was published in 1999. It has been staged as a play in Welsh and English, and made into a film.

Prichard never achieved the same accomplishment again, although he continued to produce works of merit in both poetry and prose. He won the chair at the Llanelli national eisteddfod in 1962 for his long poem in strict metres 'Llef un yn llefain'. He published three collections of poetry, plus a collected edition in 1979. A collection of his stories, *Y genod yn ein bywyd*, appeared in 1964. Among his strictly autobiographical writings are *Y rhai addfwyn* (1971) and his remarkably candid autobiography, *Afal drwg adda* (1973). Prichard never returned to Wales to live, although he made frequent visits and cut a colourful figure on the national eisteddfod field. He succumbed to bouts of alcoholism, and apocryphal stories about his escapades abound. He died of bronchopneumonia and bronchial carcinoma in St Bartholomew's Hospital, London, on 25 February 1980, survived by his wife, and was buried in his native Bethesda.   JOHN ROWLANDS

Sources C. Prichard, *Afal drwg adda* (1973) · M. Baines, 'Ffaith a dychymyg yng ngwaith Caradog Prichard', MPhil diss., U. Wales, Bangor, 1992 · D. G. Jones, 'Caradog Prichard', *Dyrnaid o awduron cyfoes*, ed. D. B. Rees (1975), 191–222 · J. Rowlands, 'Y fam a'r mab-rhagarweiniad i *Un nos ola leuad*', *Ysgrifau Beirniadol*, 19 (1993), 278–309 · J. Rowlands, 'Caradog Prichard', *Profiles* (1980), 103–6 · b. cert. · d. cert. · personal knowledge (2004) [M. Prichard] · C. Prichard, *One moonlit night / Un nos ola leuad*, ed. M. Baines, trans. P. Mitchell (1999)
Archives NL Wales, corresp., diaries, and papers | NL Wales, letters to Sir Thomas Parry-Williams [in Welsh]

Prichard, Harold Arthur (1871–1947), philosopher, was born in Kilburn, London, on 30 October 1871, the eldest child of Walter Stennett Prichard, solicitor in Bedford Row, and his wife, Lucy Withers. He was educated at Clifton College, and at New College, Oxford, of which he was a mathematical scholar. He was placed in the first class in mathematical moderations (1891) and in *literae humaniores* (1894) and was university mathematical exhibitioner in 1892. In 1894 he was articled to a firm of solicitors in the City of London, but he remained there only a few months. He was a fellow of Hertford College from 1895 to 1898, and of Trinity College from 1898 to 1924. In 1899 he married Mabel Henrietta Ross [see below], with whom he had two sons and one daughter.

After many years of devoted service to Trinity Prichard retired by reason of temporary ill health. In 1928 he was elected White's professor of moral philosophy, which carried with it a fellowship of Corpus Christi College; he retired on reaching the age limit in 1937 and was made an honorary fellow of the college. He was elected FBA in 1932, and received the honorary degree of LLD from Aberdeen University in 1934.

Prichard wrote very little for publication, but much in order to clear his own mind, to elicit the opinions of his friends, and to help them in their own philosophical problems. The only book he published was *Kant's Theory of Knowledge* (1909). He had accepted from John Cook Wilson, for whom he had the greatest admiration, the realistic view which had begun, in Oxford as elsewhere, to prevail over the Kantian and Hegelian views hitherto in the ascendant. He combined with a great respect for Kant the conviction that at bottom Kant's view is an unsuccessful attempt to mediate between realism and idealism. Prichard's book contains, therefore, both a clear and detailed analysis of Kant's view and a vigorous argument against it. Knowledge, he maintained, is an activity entirely *sui generis* and incapable of being interpreted in terms of anything else. Having expressed this view in his book, he did not return to the theory of knowledge in later writings except in his lectures, published in the posthumous volume *Knowledge and Perception* (1950), on the theories of Descartes, Locke, Berkeley, and Hume. With regard to perception, he expressed in his book on Kant the view that the appearing of bodies to minds is, like knowledge, an unanalysable fact, both when it corresponds to reality and when it does not. But his mind remained open on the subject; he dealt with it in four papers published in the posthumous volume, and in the last of them, 'The sense-datum fallacy' (1938), he expressed the view that the unanalysable fact is best stated as 'some-one-seeing-a-colour', 'some-one-hearing-a-sound', and so on, the colour or sound having no separate existence.

In 1912 Prichard published in *Mind* a paper which has had a significant and enduring influence on ethical thought: 'Does moral philosophy rest on a mistake?'. Just as in his book on Kant he had argued in general that there can be no theory of knowledge which supplies an answer to the question 'Is what we have hitherto thought to be knowledge really knowledge?', so he argued here that there is no theory which will prove that what we have thought to be obligations really are so; to attain this certainty we have simply to think harder about the facts. To this he added the thesis that while the rightness of an act depends on the nature of the situation in which we are and on the change the act will originate, the goodness of an act depends on its motive. To this view he supplied an important addendum in a British Academy lecture, 'Duty and ignorance of fact' (1932), by arguing that since being obliged is an attribute of a person, what makes an action right or wrong for the individual is not the objective situation but the agent's opinion about the situation, and, further, that what he is obliged to do is not to produce a certain change, but to set himself to produce it. Prichard was much pressed to state his view at full length, and he made considerable progress with the negative part of the task, the refutation of the most important existing theories; the result is to be found in the long paper called 'Moral obligation' included in the posthumous book of the same name (1949), which includes also several shorter papers dealing with important ethical problems.

Prichard was a great teacher, and he had great influence among his fellow teachers at Oxford and elsewhere. 'A post-prichardian, reading his views for the first time in full, may well be amazed how many of the commonplaces of contemporary Oxford philosophy have their origin in his work', wrote R. M. Hare, reviewing two works by him in 1950 (*Oxford Magazine*, 558). Prichard combined unhesitating conviction of what he considered the fundamentals in philosophy with great readiness to examine over and over again detailed problems both about perception and about obligation. Severe on what he regarded as obvious error in others, he was at least equally critical of himself, modest about his own work in philosophy, and never satisfied with what he had done. In controversy he was formidable, in social intercourse friendly and interested in the interests of his friends. In his work as a tutor, as a professor, and in the Second World War as an air-raid warden, he was conscientious almost to a fault. Physically he was short and slight, but vigorous; as an undergraduate he played lawn tennis for Oxford against Cambridge, and he remained until near the end devoted to golf. He died at his home, 6 Linton Road, Oxford, after a short illness, on 29 December 1947.

He was survived by his wife, **Mabel Henrietta Prichard**

[*née* Ross] (1875–1965), who was born in India on 17 February 1875, the daughter of Surgeon-Major Charles Grant Ross of the Bombay army. She was brought up in England and was educated at Liverpool high school and Royal Holloway College before going to Oxford as a member of the Society of Oxford Home Students, gaining a second in classical moderations followed in 1897 by a first in *literae humaniores*. She spent a year as a lecturer in classics at Westfield College, London, before her marriage in 1899. As well as keeping house for her husband's undergraduate reading parties during vacations and entertaining his pupils, she undertook much unpaid work for women's education at Oxford as honorary treasurer of the Association for the High Education of Women, and, from 1911 to 1948, of the Society of Oxford Home Students (which became in 1942 St Anne's Society and in 1952 St Anne's College, of which she was elected an honorary fellow).

Mabel Prichard was best known for her voluntary welfare work in the city of Oxford. In the early twentieth century she was among a group of dons' wives who pioneered infant welfare work. In 1922 she was elected a university representative on Oxford city council, becoming an alderman in 1932, and she was a city magistrate. She had a particular interest in mental health, and an occupational centre at Littlemore Hospital was named after her. As well as serving on the Oxford Council of Social Service, she was chairman of the Citizens' Advice Bureau and of Skene House, the latter concerned with the moral welfare of young women. For her public services she was appointed OBE; in 1964 she became the first woman to be made an honorary freeman of Oxford. She died in St Luke's Nursing Home, Linton Road, Oxford, on 14 March 1965.

DAVID ROSS, rev. C. A. CREFFIELD

Sources H. H. Price, 'Harold Arthur Prichard', *PBA*, 33 (1947), 331–50 · N. O. Dahl, 'Obligation and moral work: reflections on Prichard and Kant', *Philosophical Studies*, 50 (1986), 369–99 · D. W. Hamlyn, 'Knowing and believing', *Philosophical Review*, 55 (1980), 317–28 · J. Foster, *Oxford men and their colleges* (1893) · *The Times* (16 March 1965) · *The Times* (20 March 1965) · *Oxford Times* (19 March 1965) · *Oxford Magazine* (13 May 1965) · *CGPLA Eng. & Wales* (1948)
Archives Bodl. Oxf., corresp. and papers · Trinity College, Oxford, annotated typescripts of 'Moral obligation'
Likenesses W. Stoneman, two photographs, 1933–45, NPG · Lafayette, photograph, repro. in Price, 'Harold Arthur Prichard'
Wealth at death £26,282 6s.: probate, 26 June 1948, *CGPLA Eng. & Wales* · £18,813; Mabel Henrietta Prichard: probate, 1965, *CGPLA Eng. & Wales*

Prichard, James Cowles (1786–1848), physician and ethnologist, was born on 11 February 1786 in Ross-on-Wye, Herefordshire, the eldest child of Thomas Prichard (1765–1843), a businessman in the iron trade whose ancestors had emigrated from Ireland in 1688, and his wife, Mary Lewis (1763–1794), whose forebears Prichard assumed to be of Welsh descent. Prichard's second Christian name was the family name of his father's mother.

Family background and early education His parents belonged to well-established Herefordshire Quaker families. He had a very wealthy great-uncle. One of Prichard's two sisters died shortly after birth in 1793; the other married a certain Robert Moline. His brother Thomas, born in 1787, emigrated to America, where the family had commercial connections in New York. The youngest son, Edward (1789–1822), became a banker in Ross-on-Wye. Until 1800 Prichard's father kept two houses, one in Ross-on-Wye and one in Park Street, Bristol. He had inherited part of a local iron trade business which brought him into close connection with the influential Harford family of Bristol. In 1793 James Cowles attended Richard Durham's school on College Green, Bristol, as a day scholar. Afterwards his education was entirely private, with an emphasis on languages. According to an apocryphal anecdote, as an eight-year-old he delighted a Greek sailor at Bristol harbour by addressing him in modern Greek. In 1800 Thomas Prichard returned to Ross-on-Wye where he remained until his death on 21 August 1843.

Chooses a career in medicine Despite the religiously motivated reservations of his father, Prichard chose to study medicine. In 1802 he was placed with a Bristol man specializing in anatomical preparations, named Pole; this stay was followed by a period of study of medical pharmacy under the Quaker William Tothill and his partner, Robert Pope, at Staines. In September 1804 Prichard moved to London to study anatomy at the school attached to St Thomas's Hospital, and in 1805 he went to Edinburgh University where he took his MD degree in 1808. Motivated not least by the lectures of Dugald Stewart and thanks to an early fascination with anthropology, he chose the varieties of mankind as the subject of his MD dissertation which, in 1813, appeared in an extended, Anglicized version. Prichard's education was completed by a few terms at Trinity College, Cambridge, in 1809, and, in 1810, short stays at St John's College and Trinity College in Oxford. In the latter year he converted to the Church of England, in part to be able to enter Oxford, and in part, according to his friend, the Quaker Thomas Hodgkin, 'on the grounds of conviction' (Hodgkin, 'Biographical notice', 553). Still, Prichard was exceedingly devout, his faith falling in with contemporary evangelicalism which also influenced his scholarship. In 1810 he took up residence in Bristol in Berkeley Street, set up in private practice and, in 1811, became a physician to St Peter's Hospital, a combined poorhouse and lunatic asylum which he attended until 1832. When, in 1815, a French invasion seemed imminent, Prichard joined a defence corps, priding himself on being 'a tolerable good Match for a Frenchman' (Prichard, letter to J. R. Hale). In 1816, at his third attempt, he was elected to the Bristol Infirmary where he was to serve as physician until 1843.

Marriage and respectability On 28 February 1811 Prichard married Anna Maria Estlin, the daughter of the Unitarian minister John Prior *Estlin (1747–1817) and sister of John Bishop *Estlin (1785–1855), Prichard's student friend in Edinburgh. They had ten children of whom two died in infancy and three others predeceased Prichard. Augustin (1818–1898), the second son, took over his father's Bristol practice. Among the others were James Cowles (*b.* 1818) and Constantine Estlin (*b.* 1820), both of whom were ministers, Albert Hermann (*b.* 1831), a postmaster, and Iltudus

(b. 1825), a soldier in the Bengal army who published *The Mutinies in Rajpootana*. From 1816 the family lived in a house on College Green, Bristol, then in another house in Berkeley Street until, in 1827, they rented the spacious Red Lodge in Park Row. When, in 1837, the Red Lodge was for sale, Prichard bought it at auction for £1800. From the last male member of the Cowles family he also inherited a summer residence in the countryside (its value is not known).

Apart from his medical duties, Prichard took part in the activities of several clubs and societies, figuring prominently in the Bristol Institution for the Advancement of Science, set up in 1822. In 1829 he was one of the leading spirits behind the plan to found a college for classical and scientific education designed to admit religious dissenters. Otherwise his political views, as well as his medicine, were decidedly conservative. He was an adherent of heroic treatment and counter-irritation, including blood letting (which he also practised on himself as a cure for headaches) and trepanning, nicknamed the 'tomahawk practice'. A frightened patient was driven to poetry:

> Dr. Prichard do appear.
> With his attendance & his care,
> He fills his patients full of sorrow
> —You must be bled to day & cupped tomorrow.
> (Smith, 512)

From 1826 to 1828 Prichard acted as a medical visitor to Gloucestershire madhouses, an experience which he used for his publications on insanity. In 1827 he was made a fellow of the Royal Society. In 1835 he received an honorary doctorate from Oxford University. As Prichard's fame grew he became a respected member of the Provincial Medical and Surgical Association and of the British Association for the Advancement of Science (BAAS), though his efforts to have ethnology accepted as an independent section in the BAAS succeeded only partially in 1846 when the subject was made a sub-section. In 1845 Prichard moved to London to take up a well-paid post under Lord Shaftesbury on the lunacy commission—a task for which he had commended himself with his book on legal aspects of mental disorder: *On the Different Forms of Insanity, in Relation to Jurisprudence* (1842).

Character The Reverend William Daniel Conybeare and Francis Newman, as well as the Quaker physicians Thomas Hodgkin and Thomas Hancock were part of Prichard's circle. But his tight schedule and what he called his 'scribbling habit' (Prichard, letter to Hodgkin) did not leave him much time for informal socializing. Despite his keen ethnological interest he travelled little abroad, apart from a few trips to France, Germany, and Switzerland. Prichard was rather bookish. According to a student at the Bristol Infirmary, 'he generally wore a large, loose overcoat, with roomy side-pockets, large enough to hold a quarto or small folio case-book; and he generally carried other books with him on the seat of his carriage' (Alford, 176). Despite his frequent appearance as the chairman of committees, he was a shy and reserved man who was deemed 'too quiet' to be made president of the Bristol meeting of the BAAS in 1836. He was universally praised as 'the scholar, the gentleman, and the Christian', though it did not escape his contemporaries that the wide range of his learning had its limits. His medical colleague, John Addington Symonds (1807–1871) held that:

> Fancy and imagination were not prominent faculties in Dr. Prichard. … I think that he had no decided aesthetical tendency, no such sensibility to the beautiful as would lead him to dwell on the enjoyments of poetry and the fine arts. (Symonds, 48)

Ideas Prichard's various intellectual occupations converge, being all aspects of the science of mankind and the mind. He owed his fame to his ethnological endeavours. Starting with his MD dissertation, *Disputatio inauguralis de generis humani varietate* (1808), he spent his life rewriting the same book some five times. *Researches into the Physical History of Man* was published in 1813; the second edition, *Researches into the Physical History of Mankind*, appeared in two volumes (1826), and the third in five volumes (1836–47), as well as in a German translation: *Naturgeschichte des Menschengeschlechts* (trans. R. Wagner and J. G. F. Will, 4 vols., 1840–48). In 1843 he published a more popular and more biologically oriented version, *The Natural History of Man*, which went through four editions and appeared also in French: *Histoire naturelle du genre humain* (trans. F. Roulin, 1843). Starting from an attempt to refute Lord Kames's polygenism, Prichard's main ethnological aim was to prove the unity of mankind and to vindicate the veracity of the anthropology laid down in Genesis. For this purpose he grappled with problems from all the natural and human sciences: anatomy, physiology, biology, ethnology, palaeontology, archaeology, mythology, and philology. He perceived that traditional accounts of difference in skin colour were flawed: eighteenth-century environmentalism was empirically false. Prichard particularly disdained the notion, put forward by J. B. Lamarck and Erasmus Darwin, that acquired characteristics could become hereditary. To him this seemed to defy the order of creation. Without departing from the notion that external circumstances influenced physiognomy, he offered a new theory of heredity: only those characteristics could be passed on to the offspring that were 'connate', hence his unusual assertion that 'the primitive stock of men were Negroes' (Prichard, *Researches*, 1st edn, 25, 233) who gradually turned white once the process of civilization set in, instilling a better taste in individuals which made them prefer light-skinned spouses over darker ones. Latterly, this argument has been taken for an early form of Darwin's theory of sexual selection. Prichard never came to terms with the question how external influences could engender connate traits. While in the third edition of the *Researches* he did not return to his argument concerning heredity, he still believed, on the one hand, that sudden variations that had sprung up in one individual might over time become characteristics of the entire population, and, on the other, that cultural customs and living standards determined human physiognomy.

Thanks to his great command of literature—in the late 1810s he even learned German—by the 1830s Prichard was appreciated as the main authority on ethnological and anthropological matters. Endeavouring to prove mono-genism, he divided the problem into two propositions: he argued first that all mankind belonged to one species: second, that all human varieties were referable to one single place of origin. The first part of the thesis rested on three arguments: that the 'principal Laws of the Animal Economy' worked uniformly in all human tribes; that all mankind was prone to the same diseases; and that G. L. L. Buffon's criterion of hybridity was valid, that is to say that all those individuals belonged to one species who could engender fertile offspring. To prove the second part of his theory Prichard drew upon a welter of learning. He engaged in bio-geography, arguing that not only mankind but each species came from its own particular centre of creation. Then he ventured into philology to show that all human languages were related, whence he inferred genealogical relationships among human tribes. Finally, he asserted that the myths of all human cultures were so similar that they all necessarily had to share the same primeval history. Prichard had already made this point, concerning Egyptian mythology, in *An Analysis of the Egyptian Mythology, to which is Subjoined a Critical Examination of the Remains of Egyptian Chronology* (1819).

In his philological studies Prichard was one of the very first British scholars to take up the latest methods of comparative historical linguistics from such German scholars as Friedrich Schlegel, Franz Bopp, Jacob Grimm, and Wilhelm von Humboldt. Using their historical comparative approach for his own pious ends, he endeavoured to show in his *The Eastern Origin of the Celtic Nations Proved by a Comparison of their Dialects with the Sanskrit, Greek, Latin, and Teutonic Languages* (1831) that Celtic was the connecting link between the ancient Sanskrit and Hebrew. While not every critic endorsed this fanciful theory, Prichard's other claim, namely, that Celtic was part of the Indo-European language family, was later corroborated independently by continental scholars.

While he always maintained the accuracy of scripture, Prichard never accepted an absolutely literal reading of it. His views adapted smoothly to new findings, since they were so multifarious and eclectic, sometimes collapsing into paradox. Thus he maintained in 1826 that environmental stimuli exerted an effect on physiognomy, while at the same time he rejected the idea that acquired characteristics could become heritable. As he abhorred polygenism he also was a great opponent of racial theories. This attitude was fuelled by his sympathetic attitude towards foreign tribes, many of whom he saw threatened with extinction by European recklessness and an acquisitive selfishness which Prichard called utilitarian: 'It is only by christian nations', he wrote in 1830, 'that such a work of total extermination has ever been thoroughly accomplished' (Prichard, 'Horae Africanae', 738). And as his more secular-minded scientific peers grew intrigued by racial theories, Prichard employed all his knowledge to prove them wrong.

In the third edition of the *Researches*, Prichard emphasized the psychological unity of mankind: common fears of retribution after death and the desire to seek atonement seemed to characterize all human cultures. This evangelical streak of his thought also surfaced in his theory of insanity. Influenced by J. E. D. Esquirol and German somaticists, he developed a new pathological category: moral insanity. Stripped of its religious and anthropological undertones it was to survive until the twentieth century. In *A Treatise on Diseases of the Nervous System* (1822) Prichard toyed with the idea that there might be a mental disease in which 'the active powers are primarily disordered, without any affection of the intellectual faculties' (p. 135). But it was only from the 1830s that he was prepared to shed the Lockian definition of madness and envisage a type of insanity that left the rational faculties unaffected, expressing itself simply in a distortion of the emotive faculties ('Insanity', *The Cyclopaedia of Practical Medicine*, ed. J. Forbes, A. Tweedie, and J. Conolly, 2, 1833, 10–32, 847–75). This notion was further deepened in his comprehensive overview of the state of knowledge concerning mental disorders in *A Treatise on Insanity, and other Disorders Affecting the Mind* (1835).

The pathology of moral insanity Prichard derived from his experiences as a visiting alienist. As the concept stipulated the perversion of the moral, that is, the non-intellectual, faculties, it was rooted in Scottish common-sense philosophy. Unconventional theories such as Philippe Pinel's *manie sans délire* and Esquirol's notion of monomania had paved the way for a departure from received wisdom. Prichard strove to account for insanity in a way that would explain various bodily symptoms, while not infringing on the notion of the inviolable soul. If he was gradually driven towards a somaticist notion of madness, which focused on the entire body rather than the brain alone, this was due to his vehement hostility towards phrenological theory which he, with many others, suspected of attempting to reduce the mind to the cerebral structure. His alternative view of insanity was inspired by a group of German somaticists who contributed to the *Zeitschrift für Anthropologie*, and by the theological ideas of his Quaker friend Thomas Hancock whose theory of an inbred moral sense liable to distortions spelt out the connection between the superior realm and the mundane sphere. Prichard envisaged moral insanity as both a distortion of the emotive faculties and a sign of moral perversion. Yet he was not enough of a religious, or a medical, zealot to believe that the source of corruption could be rooted out. Although he embraced contemporary notions that civilization, commercial worries, and an uprooted lifestyle left their mark on the mind, he none the less believed that the inclination to mental disease was part of the make-up of human nature, common to primitive peoples and refined men alike. Moral insanity became a widely used category, valid well into the twentieth century. But most doctors who adopted it ignored its complex, more or less implicit theological underpinnings. Medical phrenologists appropriated it for their own purposes. Later on, it became linked to notions of the pathological personality.

Death and reputation Prichard fell ill in December 1848. He died of pericarditis in the night of 22–3 December 1848 at his house, 1 Woburn Place, Russell Square, London, and was buried on 30 December in Sellack, Herefordshire, by his son-in-law, William Henry Ley, the local vicar. By the time of his death many perceived that Prichard's anthropological views were tied up too closely with religion. While alienists with a predilection for phrenology took up his nosological category of moral insanity for their own purposes, adherents of racial theory thought that his short time-scale, that left only a few thousand years for the development of mankind, was flawed. His *Researches* remained highly esteemed as a compendium of ethnological detail, yet not for its theoretical frameworks. Prichard became considered as the representative of a bygone age. With the popularization of evolutionism E. B. Tylor thought that his discussion of the races of man as varieties of a single species was rehabilitated. Some historians of anthropology later mistook Prichard for a precursor of Darwin. In fact, his merits lay in his understanding of the problems inherent to eighteenth-century theories of man, in his readiness to grapple with evidence that seemed to contradict his theories, and in his early appreciation of scientific developments on the continent, especially in the fields of linguistics and psychiatry.

H. F. AUGSTEIN

Sources R. Smith, manuscript memoirs, Bristol RO, 35893 (36) k. i. • I. Southall, *Memorials of the Prichards of Almeley and their descendants*, 2nd edn (1901) • J. A. Symonds, *Some account of the life, writings, and character of the late James Cowles Prichard* (1849) • T. Hodgkin, 'Biographical notice of Dr. Prichard', *British Foreign and Medical Review*, 27 (1849), 550–59 • T. Hodgkin, *Journal of the Ethnological Society of London*, 2 (1848–50), 182–207 • R. Cull, 'Short biographical notice of the author', in J. C. Prichard, *The natural history of man*, ed. E. Norris, 4th edn, 2 vols. (1855), xxi–xxiv • H. Alford, 'The Bristol Infirmary in my student days, 1822–1828', *Bristol Medico-Chirurgical Journal*, 8 (1890), 165–91 • G. Munro Smith, *A history of the Bristol Royal Infirmary* (1917) • H. F. Augstein, *James Cowles Prichard's anthropology: remaking the science of man in early nineteenth-century Britain* (1998) • G. W. Stocking, 'From chronology to ethnology: James Cowles Prichard and British anthropology, 1800–1850', in J. C. Prichard, *Researches into the physical history of man*, ed. G. W. Stocking (1973), ix–cx • J. C. Prichard, letter to J. R. Hale, 6 April 1815, National Library, Edinburgh, 15385.f.3 • J. C. Prichard, letter to T. Hodgkin, 23 June 1838, Bodl. RH, Hodgkin MSS, MS Brit. Emp.s.18, press mark C 122/51 • contract concerning the purchase of the Red Lodge, Bristol RO, 5535 (50) • *DNB* • parish register (death and burial), Sellack, Herefordshire, 23 and 30 Dec 1848 • J. C. Prichard, 'Horae Africanae', *The Friends' Monthly Magazine*, 2 (1830), 737–43

Archives Bristol RO, papers • priv. coll. • RGS, letters to Royal Geographical Society | Wellcome L., corresp. with Thomas Hodgkin

Likenesses etching? (aged forty-five to fifty-five), repro. in J. C. Prichard, *Researches into the physical history of man*, ed. G. Stocking (1973)

Prichard, Mabel Henrietta (1875–1965). *See under* Prichard, Harold Arthur (1871–1947).

Prichard, Matthew Stewart (1865–1936), philosopher, was born on 4 January 1865 in Brislington, Keynsham, Somerset, the son of Charles Henry Prichard, merchant, and his wife, Mattie Stewart (*d.* 1881); he claimed Scottish lineage through his mother. Educated at Marlborough College (1883) and at New College, Oxford (1884–7), he practised briefly as a barrister in London. In 1892 he joined a community at Lewes House, Sussex, inspired by the philosophy of Nietzsche and led by Edward Perry Warren, a wealthy American. In 1901, through the influence of the latter's elder brother Samuel Dennis Warren, then president of the Boston Museum of Fine Arts, he was appointed secretary (1902), then assistant director (1904) of the museum. There he met the art collector Isabella Stewart Gardner and the Japanese artist, writer, and museum curator Okakura Kakuzo, who became his lifelong friends. He developed a violent opposition to the traditional concept of a museum and a deep attraction for oriental art. 'The same spirit', he would later say, 'puts objects into museums and men into prisons', whereas, conversely, 'in the East, Art is universal; art is not for the *privilégiés*' (Prichard, notebooks, Boston, Isabella Stewart Gardner Museum Archives).

Dismissed in June 1907 because of conflicts among the trustees, Prichard travelled for a year in Italy, where he became fascinated by Byzantine art. Between December 1908 and June 1914 he lived in Paris: this was to be the most creative period of his life. Through Sarah and Michael Stein, he met Henri Matisse early in 1909. The connection which he enthusiastically drew between Matisse's art and the art of the Orient profoundly influenced the artist, who discovered Byzantine art through Prichard. Prichard was also a fervent admirer of Henri Bergson's philosophy, which he used as a basis for his revolutionary system of aesthetics, denying any value to the Western representational image and conventional ideas of beauty, and celebrating instead the power of decoration. This formed the core of the philosophy which 'the mysterious and mystic Prichard', as Isabella Stewart Gardner called him (*Letters of Bernard Berenson and Isabella Stewart Gardner*, 381), taught to a circle of young Frenchmen, notably Georges Duthuit, the art critic (and Matisse's future son-in-law), and to some of his London acquaintances, such as Roger Fry and T. S. Eliot. Fry, who had first met Prichard in Boston in January 1905, had been impressed by his views about museums and oriental art; on 26 January 1911 he described him to Clive Bell as 'a great friend of the Steins' and 'a great Bergsonite', who would be able to show him 'a good many things' in Paris (*Letters of Roger Fry*, 1.339).

'Art', Prichard would say, 'is formative, not informative', adding that:

> There are certain truths, those which transcend the power of the intellect to grasp, which can only be conveyed by evocation. That is the justification of Byzantine expression or of Matisse's. If the communication is spatial, superficial, something for the intelligence, then spatial terms, the concept, the vision of practical life, suffice for the conveyance, and there is no excuse for an evocative procedure. Reality is one of the truths which exceeds the power of the intelligence to grasp it, but appearance is a simple intellectual fact. (Prichard, notebooks, Paris, Bibliothèque Byzantine, Fonds Thomas Whittemore)

Travelling in Germany in August 1914 Prichard was

interned as an English citizen in the prisoner of war camp of Ruhleben, where he organized the intellectual life of his fellow prisoners, among whom he 'was perhaps the most remarkable character' (Ketchum, 260). Liberated in 1918, he returned to London, worked briefly for the government committee on prisoners, and formed a new circle of disciples at the Gargoyle Club, including David Tennant and John Pope-Hennessy, who was 'introduced to museology' and became 'familiar with Prichard's views' from these 'seminars on aesthetics held by him in the mornings, among shattered glasses, in the Gargoyle nightclub before the *Red Studio* of Matisse' (Pope-Hennessy, 273–4).

In his last years Prichard's moods became increasingly unpredictable. He played a major, though unofficial, role in the writing and publication of the first and second preliminary reports on the rediscovery of Byzantine mosaics in Hagia Sofia, Constantinople, by the Bostonian Thomas Whittemore, one of his pupils (T. Whittemore, *The Mosaics of Haghia Sophia at Istanbul*, 1933 and 1936). He died suddenly, on 15 October 1936, of a coronary thrombosis, in his brother's house at Parslow's Hillock, Great Hampden, Buckinghamshire, and was cremated on 19 October. He never married. Prichard was a Socratic character: his writing mostly took the form of letters. Beyond a few early studies on the museum, his main publication, *Greek and Byzantine Art* (1921), is the text of a conference given at the Taylor Institution, Oxford, in 1919.   RÉMI LABRUSSE

Sources Isabella Stewart Gardner Museum, Boston, Massachusetts, Special Collections, Matthew Stewart Prichard MSS · D. Sox, 'Matt Prichard's story: one bonnet but innumerable bees', *Bachelors of art: Edward Perry Warren and the Lewes House Brotherhood* (1991), 165–208 · W. M. Whitehill, 'Some correspondence of M. S. Prichard and I. Gardner', *Fenway Court* (1974), 14–29 [no vol. no.; journal of the Isabella Stewart Gardner Museum] · M. Luke, *David Tennant and the Gargoyle years* (1991) · Succession Henri Matisse, Paris, Archives Matisse · Collège de France, Paris, Bibliothèque Byzantine, Fonds Thomas Whittemore · J. D. Ketchum, *Ruhleben: a prison camp society* (1965) · G. Duthuit, *Écrits sur Matisse* (1992) · R. Labrusse, 'La pensée de M. S. Prichard et son influence sur Matisse', *Matisse, Byzance et la notion d'orient*, PhD diss., University of Paris I—Sorbonne, 1996, 145–250 · K. E. Haas, 'Henri Matisse: "a magnificent draughtsman"', *Fenway Court* (1985), 36–49 [journal of the Isabella Stewart Gardner Museum; no vol. no.] · J. W. Pope-Hennessy, *Learning to look* (1991) · W. M. Whitehill, 'The battle of the casts', *Museum of Fine Arts, Boston: a centennial history*, 1 (1970), 172–217 · *The letters of T. S. Eliot* (1988) · *The letters of Bernard Berenson and Isabella Stewart Gardner, 1887–1924*, ed. R. van N. Hadley (1987) · *Letters of Roger Fry*, ed. D. Sutton, 2 vols. (1972) · b. cert. · d. cert. · R. Labrusse, 'Byzance, un paradigme (Matisse, Prichard)', *Matisse: la condition de l'image* (1999), 94–115

Archives Isabella Stewart Gardner Museum, Boston, Massachusetts, MSS | Archives Georges Duthuit, Paris · Collège de France, Paris, Bibliothèque Byzantine, Fonds Thomas Whittemore · Succession Henri Matisse, Paris, Archives Matisse

Likenesses photographs, 1892–1936, Isabella Stewart Gardner Museum, Boston · photographs, 1892–1936, Succession Henri Matisse, Paris, Archives Matisse · J. B. Potter, drawing, 1905, Isabella Stewart Gardner Museum, Boston · H. Matisse, engravings, 1914, repro. in M. Duthuit-Matisse and C. Duthuit, *Henri Matisse: catalogue raisonné de l'œuvre gravé*, 2 vols. (Paris, 1983), nos. 43–4

Wealth at death £3901 6s. 9d.: administration, 20 Nov 1936, *CGPLA Eng. & Wales*

Prichard, Rhys [Rice] (*c.*1573×9–1644/5), Church of England clergyman and poet, was born at Llandovery, Carmarthenshire, the eldest son of Dafydd ap Richard of Llandovery, and his wife, Mary. His birth date depends on Anthony Wood's assumption that he was eighteen when he entered Jesus College, Oxford, in 1597, but an exchequer deposition in 1642 described him as 'clerk, 69 years or thereabouts' (Evans, 182), which puts his birth nearer 1573. In 1602 he was ordained priest and appointed as curate of Witham, Essex, on 20 April; he graduated BA on 26 June, and was presented to the living of Llandingad with Llanfair-ar-y-bryn in Llandovery on 6 August.

The date of Prichard's marriage to Gwenllian is not known, and only one child is ever mentioned, Samuel or Sami bach ('dear/little Sami') of the poems (*b. c.*1605), who died before his parents. In his youth Sami vexed his father somewhat, but in a letter from Oxford (5 June 1623) he repented: 'My sinns I doe bewaile and with dayly prayer I will crave the almightie to forgiue' (Jones, 20). These youthful indiscretions gave rise to stories of a louche life and dissolute ways, and he figures in the folklore of the Tywi and Teifi valleys as the lover of various heiresses who met his death by drowning at a young age. In reality Samuel met his future wife, Francis Hardinge, at Oxford, married her and served as his father's curate, before himself becoming rector of Llanynys, Brecknockshire. They had two children, Elizabeth and Rice. Elizabeth, who married Thomas, the son of Bishop Mainwaring of St David's, was anxious to see her grandfather's work published 'provided it be done in the Original Language in which they were wrote and not translated into English or otherwise altered as some have done'.

The only works published during Prichard's lifetime appeared in 1617: *Y catechism nev athrawiaeth Gristianogawl, rhwn y mae pob plentyn y ddyscu, cyn iddo gael y vedydd episcob: neu y dderbyn yr cummûn bendigedig* ('The catechism or Christian doctrine which every child is to learn before he receives confirmation or is received into holy communion'), and a poem, *Cyngor episcob I bob enaid oddi vewn I episcobeth* ('A bishop's advice to every soul within his diocese'). These texts, though on the same theme and bound together, are separate entities, and the poem begins with a direct, personal address to his son, 'F'annwyl blentyn dere nes' ('My dear child come nearer'), but its title, like that of the catechism, encompasses everyone in a diocese. The *Catechism* was inspired by a zeal to educate the illiterate members of his parish, as were his popular little quatrains, and shows that he was well aware of the literary and religious fashions of the day.

Prichard's catechism is the first surviving Welsh printed catechism separate from the prayer book, although there are earlier examples recorded in the Stationers' register, of which no copies have survived. The basic text is that of Archbishop Cranmer's 1552 prayer book, translated by William Salesbury and published in 1567 in an orthographically eccentric version, but Prichard also used Bishop William Morgan's version, published in 1599, which largely eschews the peculiarities of Salesbury. The last part of the catechism provides a good example of Prichard's own translating skills; he incorporates a discussion of the importance of the sacraments of baptism and the eucharist which were added to the prayer book after the Hampton Court conference of 1604, and here Prichard had no earlier translation to guide him. He used vivid phrases, dialect forms, and substantives as he did in his demotic quatrains, and the directness and simplicity of his vocabulary reveal the same sure touch. There is anecdotal evidence that he was a charismatic and successful preacher, although this mostly dates from the post-Methodist revival period which stressed preaching. There is direct evidence from the poems that he himself favoured preaching, even advising people to travel to another parish to hear a sermon if there was none in their parish or if the preacher lacked conviction. This was not acceptable Anglican practice.

Prichard's importance lies in his hundreds of quatrains on all sorts of subjects, from the mysteries of Christian doctrine to the benefits of breast-feeding babies and the nutritional value of vegetables. His biggest concern was to help the poor—first by making good use of the pitifully few resources to which they had access, and second (but more importantly) by helping them to understand the Christian gospel. Despite his love of preaching he realized that few of his listeners would understand or remember theological discourse or the usual homilies of the Anglican church; on the other hand, since they readily picked up songs and ballads heard in fairs and markets, he decided to use these simple forms to teach some of the more abstruse doctrines of the New Testament, in addition to telling vivid stories from the Old Testament over and over again. He stated his intention clearly: it was because people tended to forget a sermon but easily remembered a frivolous song that he turned these verses/lessons into songs, 'for you, the Welsh'. He added, self deprecatingly:

> I sought no intricate work,
> but a smooth, perfect metre,
> Easy to learn in a short time
> by all who hear it thrice.
> (Jones, 34)

Consequently, he was not afraid of repeating himself and many favourite lines were recycled, while characters from the Old Testament or classical antiquity turn up time and again as role models—Daniel and Alexander the Great being particular favourites, the latter sometimes praised as a good man but at other times used as a warning against drunkenness and pride.

Prichard had a successful clerical career and acquired several livings; in 1613 James I appointed him rector of Llanedi, to be held with Llandovery, and in 1614 he became prebendary of the collegiate church at Brecon. In 1626 he was appointed chancellor and a canon of St David's, with the living of Llawhaden. He was diligent in his chapter work, and his distinctive signature occurs frequently in its muniments. Despite his loyalty to the king during the civil war he resented the taxes levied by the commissioners of

array, and a letter of 1642 voices his dismay at his assessment of £200, when his 'Meanes' was in 'Deires or little farmes' from which he received only payment in kind.

The first edition of Prichard's poems predated 1659, and from then on editions came frequently; the first collection of four parts in 1672 by Stephen Hughes was followed by another in 1681 the first to be known as *Canwyll y Cymry* ('The Welshmen's Candle'). Fifty-two editions appeared before 1820. The early printing may have obviated the need to preserve his manuscripts, and only recently are works in his hand being recognized, such as the volume of notes for a sermon found in MS Jesus 145, in the Bodleian Library, and a collection of drafts of poems on eight narrow folios bound into a later manuscript, NL Wales, 15416 E, in Aberystwyth.

Prichard's signature appears in the chapter records of St David's on 2 August 1643. On 2 December 1644 he made his will, leaving bequests to his wife, his daughter-in-law and her children, and others in his family, as well as money to the town of Llandovery to fund a free school. He died at Llandovery—when exactly is not known, nor was his will proved; his burial place is unknown but was probably in the chancel of Llandingad church, where he had served for more than forty years.   NESTA LLOYD

Sources R. B. Jones, *A lanterne to their feete: remembering Rhys Prichard, 1579–1644* (1994) • N. Lloyd, 'Rhys Prichard, c.1579–1644', *Carmarthenshire Antiquary*, 34 (1998), 25–37 • N. Lloyd, 'Sylwadau ar iaith rhai o gerddi Rhys Prichard', *National Library of Wales Journal*, 29 (1995–6), 257–80 • N. Lloyd, 'Catecism y Ficer Prichard, 1617', *Ysgrifau Beirniadol*, 23 (1997), 164–83 • N. Lloyd, *Cerddi'r ficer: detholiad o gerddi Rhys Prichard* (1994) • S. N. Richards, *Y Ficer Prichard* (1994) • E. Rees, ed., *Libri Walliae: a catalogue of Welsh books and books printed in Wales, 1546–1820*, 2 vols. (1987) • G. Evans, *The story of the ancient churches of Llandovery* (1913)
Archives Bodl. Oxf., MS Jesus 145

Pricke, Robert (c.1642–1708), publisher and translator, was born in central London, the son of Robert Pricke (*bap.* 1624) and his wife, Dorothy Mitchell. Little is known of his early life, but Horace Walpole says that he was a student of the etcher Wenceslaus Hollar. His first known publication is an etched map of London showing the damage caused by the great fire, issued about 1667 from an address in Whitecross Street. This was probably his father's house: Robert senior was beadle of the Salters' Company which had, in 1651, granted him the lease of a 'tenement in Whitecross street' (Watson, 45). The fire marks the beginning of Pricke's work as a printseller, and he went on to supply the regenerators of London with a range of practical treatises and pattern books. He had contacts in Amsterdam, probably with the Danckerts family, and imported French, Dutch, and Italian books and prints. Indeed, his greatest contribution was as a popularizer and disseminator of continental ideas and models, which formed the basis for nearly all his own publications.

Pricke's first book was probably *A Booke of Archetecture*, copied from the French artist J. Barbet and issued in the late 1660s from 'the flower pot in Fleete streete'. This was followed by *A New Book of Architecture* and *A New Treatise of Architecture*, both translated by Pricke, from the works of Alexandre Francine and Julien Mauclerc respectively, and published in 1669 from Whitecross Street. At about the same date he married Abigail, and their first child, Robert, was born in 1670, although he seems not to have survived infancy. They had at least six further children: Dorothy (*b.* 1671), Elizabeth (1672–1678), Abigail (*b.* 1673), Mary (*b.* 1676), Anne (*b.* 1678), and Robert (*b.* 1681).

By 1670 Pricke was also publishing from the 'Golden Lion at the corner of New Cheapside'; between 1674 and 1676 he was to be found 'adjoining Cripple Gate within', and in 1677 he moved to the 'Golden Ball' in St Paul's Churchyard. Throughout his life he followed his father's trade of salter (invariably given as his occupation in parish records), and publishing and bookselling were evidently sidelines. However, by 1679 he had issued a dozen books on art and architecture (often in his own translations from French or Dutch), as well as selling maps, games, and ana-tomical, satirical, and biblical prints, and carrying on a secondhand trade. Thereafter his printselling activity was virtually suspended for twenty years, although he repub-lished Edward Cocker's *Penna volans* in 1685. During this period he succeeded his father as beadle of the Salters' Company. In the 1690s the Golden Ball address was used by the printseller and etcher Sutton Nicholls, and in 1695 Pricke, his wife, and his daughter Mary are recorded as Nicholls' lodgers. By 1696, however, Pricke was living 'against Aldermary Church in Bow Lane', and in 1698 he collaborated with Samuel and John Sprint in reissuing three of his books; in 1700 his last publication appeared, a reissue of *The Architect's Store-House* of 1674. He died in late 1708, and was buried at St Mary Aldermary on 10 November.   PAUL W. NASH

Sources E. Harris and N. Savage, *British architectural books and writ-ers, 1556–1785* (1990) · N. Savage and others, eds., *Early printed books, 1478–1840: catalogue of the British Architectural Library early imprints collection,* [5 vols.] (1994–) · L. Rostenberg, *English publishers in the graphic arts, 1599–1700* (1963) · H. R. Plomer and others, *Dictionaries of the printers and booksellers who were at work in England, Scotland and Ire-land, 1577–1775* (1910–32); repr. (1977) · E. Arber, ed., *The term cata-logues, 1668–1709,* 3 vols. (privately printed, London, 1903–6) · H. Walpole, *A catalogue of engravers, who have been born, or resided in England,* 2nd edn (1765); repr. (1786) · R. Pennington, *A descriptive catalogue of the etched work of Wenceslaus Hollar, 1607–1677* (1982) · I. Darlington and J. Howgego, *Printed maps of London, circa 1553–1850* (1964) · S. Tyacke, *London map-sellers, 1660–1720* (1978) · J. S. Watson, *A history of the Salter's Company* (1963)

Pricket, Robert (*fl.* 1603–1645), poet, saw some military service in Elizabeth I's reign and afterwards sought a pre-carious livelihood as a verse-writer and pamphleteer against those holding unorthodox religious and political beliefs. His earliest production, *Times Anotomie,* which he describes as a love song on the death of Queen Elizabeth, does not appear to have been printed. In 1603 he printed two panegyrical celebrations of the accession of James I. *A Souldier's Wish unto his Soveraigne Lord King James* was entered in the Stationers' register in April; it was dedi-cated to the privy council in a passage anticipating James's arrival and emphasizing Pricket's own loyalty. Similarly *Unto the most High and Mightie Prince King James. A Poore Sub-ject Sendeth a Souldiours Resolution* reiterated these themes before panegyrizing Queen Elizabeth, denouncing the

church of Rome, and articulating hopes for sustainable peace and unity. These pledges were made particularly pertinent by Pricket's suspected involvement in the pro-Catholic activities of Philip May, a servant of Lord Huns-don, for which he was examined on 19 April 1603 (*CSP dom.,* 1603, 14/1/31, 33).

In 1604 Pricket secured wider fame by a poetic tribute to the memory of the second earl of Essex, entitled *Honors Fame in Triumph Riding, or, The Life and Death of the Late Hon-ourable Earle of Essex* and dedicated to the earls of South-ampton and Devonshire and to William, Lord Knollys. Pricket referred with satisfaction to the disgrace of Cobham, Grey, and Ralegh, but the praise he bestowed on Essex—

> He doubtles had a sound and faithfull hart.
> To Prince and State, and for the publicke weale,
> The things amisse he alwaies fought to heale.
> (stanza 9)

—led to his imprisonment by order of the privy council and to the recall of copies of the verse (*Gawdy MSS*). He suc-cessfully appealed to Lord Salisbury for release in Septem-ber 1604 and he sought to atone for his offence in *Times Anotomie, Containing: the Poore Man's Plaint, Britton's Trouble and her Triumph* (*Salisbury MSS,* 16.302). Dedicated to the privy council, the first part had been written in 1604 and is a bitter attack on Roman Catholicism and contemporary secular abuses.

Pricket's protestant zeal steadily increased. In 1607 he printed both *The Jesuits Miracles, or, New Popish Wonders,* a critical account of Jesuit activities in England, culminat-ing in a prayer for stability, and a pamphlet entitled *The Lord Coke his Speech and Charge. With a Discoverie of the Abuses and Corruption of Officers.* In the dedication to the latter, signed R. P. and addressed to Coke's father-in-law, Thomas Cecil, earl of Exeter, Pricket described himself as a poor soldier 'unseperably Yoakt with leane-fac't povertie' (sig. A3*v*), willing, once more, to resume his military career to acquire solvency (*Salisbury MSS,* 24.iii, Pricket to the privy council, 1606 or earlier). In a closing request for patronage he represents his text as a verbatim account of a charge given by Coke to the grand jury at Norwich assizes on 4 August 1606: 'So exelent as that it worthyly deserves to be continued in perpetuall memorie which being thus prodused to a publique view, I hope it shall unto our publickeweale remaine a worthy persedent' (sig. A4*r*). On 12 February, however, one day after the text was released, it was suppressed and, in 1608, in the preface to *La sept part des reports S. Edw. Coke Chivaler,* it was repudiated by Coke himself, who condemned its 'palpalde mistakings in the very words of art, and the whole context of that rude and ragged stile, wholly dissonant … from a lawyers dialect' (sig. aV*v*; *Letters of John Chamberlain,* 1.243, Chamberlain to Carleton, 13 Feb 1607).

About the same period Pricket, according to his own account, took holy orders; one 'Robert Pricket, A. M.' was curate of St Botolph, Aldgate, in April 1611 (Newcourt, 1.916). He obtained some preferment in Ireland but, exiled by the rising of 1641, and in great distress, he sought ref-uge in Bath, where in 1645 he wrote *Newes from the King's*

Bath. Printed at his own expense this work catalogues and criticizes examples of political and religious rebellion. In the dedication of the text Pricket retrospectively examines his life of military campaigning, wrangles with the court of high commission, and forty years in God's ministry with dejected cynicism and frustration:

I am alive as buried in my grave
With grief I see the wofull misery
Of honest, poor, dispised poverty.
(p. 3)

SIDNEY LEE, rev. ELIZABETH HARESNAPE

Sources *Calendar of the manuscripts of the most hon. the marquess of Salisbury*, 16, HMC, 9 (1933), 302 (106.157); 24 (1976), iii [petition 445] · *The letters of John Chamberlain*, ed. N. E. McClure, 1 (1939), 243 · *STC, 1475–1640* · A. B. Grosart, ed., *Occasional issues of unique or very rare books*, 16 (1881) · *CSP dom.*, 1608–11 · R. Newcourt, *Repertorium ecclesiasticum parochiale Londinense*, 1 (1708), 916 · E. Brydges, *Restituta, or, Titles, extracts, and characters of old books in English literature*, 4 vols. (1814–16), vol. 3, pp. 445–50 · J. P. Collier, ed., *A bibliographical and critical account of the rarest books in the English language*, 2 (1865), 187–93 · *Report on the manuscripts of the family of Gawdy, formerly of Norfolk*, HMC, 11 (1885), 587 [Francis Morice to Sir B. Gawdy, 7 July 1604] · J. O., 'Lord Coke', *N&Q*, 7 (1853), 376–7 · Broctuna, 'Lord Coke's charge to the jury', *N&Q*, 7 (1853), 433–4 · J. O., 'R. Pricket', *N&Q*, 6th ser., 2 (1880), 235

Pridden, John (1758–1825), antiquary and architect, was born on 3 January 1758 in London, the eldest son of John Pridden (1728–1807), bookseller, and his wife, Anne (d. 1801), daughter of Humphrey Gregory of Twemloves, near Whitchurch, Shropshire. His father was born on 20 July 1728 at Old Martin Hall, near Ellesmere, Shropshire, of wealthy parents and ran away from home to escape a cruel stepfather. In London in 1748 he worked for booksellers John Nourse in the Strand and then Richard Manby, in Ludgate Hill, whom he eventually succeeded, and was friends with many well-known authors and antiquaries.

Pridden entered St Paul's School, London, on 3 August 1764 at the age of six, and matriculated at Queen's College, Oxford, on 15 April 1777 at the age of nineteen. In 1778 he gained the Pauline exhibition which, together with as many other exhibitions as he could obtain from the London livery companies, almost paid for his university education. During vacations he made numerous walking tours, visiting every cathedral and many other historic towns and filling sketchbooks with accurate drawings of what he considered worth preserving. He graduated BA in 1781 and was ordained soon afterwards.

In 1782 Pridden became an afternoon lecturer at Tavistock Chapel, London, and, in November of the same year, a minor canon of St Paul's Cathedral. In Essex, he was vicar of Heybridge, near Maldon, from July 1783, and of Little Wakering from 1788. On 4 September 1787 at St Bride's, Fleet Street, he married Anne (d. 1815), eldest daughter of John *Nichols (1745–1826) [see under Nichols family (per. c.1760–1939)], the compiler and editor, and his first wife, Anne Cradock. He was elected a fellow of the Society of Antiquaries in 1785 and contributed many illustrations, particularly of the Leicestershire collections of his father-in-law, and *An Appendix to the History of Reculver and Herne* (1787) to Nichols's *Bibliotheca Topographica*

Britannica. From 1783 until 1803, he was also curate of St Bride's, Fleet Street, where the vicar was non-resident, and in 1789 was incorporated MA at St John's College, Cambridge, and became chaplain to Earl Paulet. In 1795 he was appointed both priest-in-ordinary of his majesty's Chapel Royal and a minor canon of Westminster Abbey.

With Dr John Coakley Lettsom, the successful Quaker physician and philanthropist, Pridden was co-founder in 1791 and for many years honorary secretary of the Sea-bathing Infirmary at Margate, Kent. He designed the buildings erected in 1796 which included 'provision for patients to sleep on verandahs in the open air, a thing previously unheard of in hospital architecture' (Abraham, 286). He resigned his Essex livings in 1797 on becoming vicar of Caddington, Bedfordshire, where, acting as his own surveyor and architect, he rebuilt the vicarage in 1812 (dem. 1970). He was finally rector of the united parishes of St George's, Botolph Lane, and St Botolph without Bishopsgate, London, from 1812 until his death.

Pridden's extensive knowledge of architecture and interest in civil engineering found expression in a complex scheme which he submitted to the corporation of London to connect the tops of Snow Hill and Holborn Hill by a bridge spanning a projected road linking Blackfriars and the Great North Road. Though considered prohibitively expensive at the time, the project was eventually realized as the Holborn Viaduct. In 1811 he proposed a more effective method for draining the fens at the Bedford Level.

Pridden's greatest antiquarian achievement, assisted by John Calder, was the continuation of the index and glossary, begun by Archdeacon John Strachey, to the *Rolls of Parliament*. 'This laborious task … occupied the last 30 years of his life, broke down his health, and embittered his existence' (Nichols, *Illustrations*, 8.677). It was completed after 1825 by Edward Upham and published in 1832.

Pridden's wife died in 1815; he later married Anne (d. 1847), eldest daughter of Robert Pickwoad of London. He died at the age of sixty-seven on 5 April 1825 at his house in Fleet Street and was buried on 12 April at St Mary's, Islington, beside his first wife. There were no children.

RICHARD RIDDELL

Sources *GM*, 1st ser., 67 (1797), 841 · *GM*, 1st ser., 73 (1803), 450 · *GM*, 1st ser., 77 (1807), 285–6 · *GM*, 1st ser., 81/1 (1811), 84 · *GM*, 1st ser., 86/1 (1816), 17 · *GM*, 1st ser., 94/1 (1824), 237 · *GM*, 1st ser., 95/1 (1825), 467–9 · Nichols, *Illustrations*, 2.683, 849; 5.200, 227, 228, 231, 750, 751; 8.265, 676–7 [esp. 8.676–7] · Nichols, *Lit. anecdotes*, 2.644; 3.421; 9.18, 220n. · J. J. Abraham, *Lettsom, his life, times, friends and descendants* (1933), 282–8 · Colvin, *Archs.* · J. C. Lettsom, *Hints designed to promote beneficence, temperance, and medical science*, 2nd edn (1816), 2.150, 3.238 · Foster, *Alum. Oxon.* · W. Roberts, *The book-hunter in London* (1895), 215 · *IGI* · *DNB*

Archives Bodl. Oxf., corresp. and MSS · Bodl. Oxf., Bedfordshire, Berkshire, Buckinghamshire, and Oxfordshire topographical collections · Col. U., Butler Library, papers · Essex RO, Chelmsford, Essex topographical notebooks · GL, corresp. and papers, incl. many relating to antiquarian researches and incumbency at St George Botolph Lane · Lincs. Arch., topographical collections · Margate Central Library, description of the Isle of Thanet · NL Wales, MS journal of tour in Wales · Northampton Central Library, notebook relating to Northamptonshire buildings and monuments · Suffolk RO, Ipswich, topographical collections relating to Suffolk · Westminster Abbey, topographical collections

Pride, Thomas, appointed Lord Pride under the protectorate (d. **1658**), parliamentarian army officer and regicide, was the son of William Pride, yeoman of Pedwell, near Ashcot, Somerset. On 30 January 1622 he was apprenticed to Thomas Bradway, citizen and haberdasher of London, for seven years. He was duly made free of the company on 24 April 1629. Rather than practise as a haberdasher, however, he took up the lucrative trade of brewing. His business prospered, so that by the 1640s he owned, in partnership with a Maior Yates, two profitable brewhouses in Surrey, and possibly a third in Edinburgh. In August 1647 he affixed his name prominently to a petition of seventy-six brewers to the House of Lords demanding the elimination of the excise tax on beer and ale, on the grounds that they were 'the cheapest food, and cheifest nourishment' of the poor; that the price of malt had reached 'extraordinarie' heights, and that the brewers faced 'utter ruine and destruction' if they continued to be taxed on their product (HLRO, main papers, 24 Aug 1647).

New Model officer When war broke out between king and parliament, Pride was an ensign in the Red regiment of London trained bands. By October 1642 he had been given a captaincy in the new regiment of Colonel Henry Barclay in the earl of Essex's army. By 1644 he had risen to the rank of major, both in the Orange auxiliaries and in Essex's infantry when it was forced to surrender at Lostwithiel in Cornwall. In March 1645, at the foundation of the New Model Army, the House of Lords attempted to alter Sir Thomas Fairfax's proposed list of officers by demoting the radical Major Cowell to captain, and restoring Pride to the rank of major in Barclay's regiment. The Lords' attempt failed; Cowell stayed a major, but Pride none the less soon found himself lieutenant-colonel of the regiment, now under Colonel Edward Harley. Since Harley was absent during the 1645 campaign, Pride was the effective commander of the regiment. At Naseby he played a critical role as leader of one of the three infantry regiments that were held in reserve behind the front line. The king's infantry rolled back their New Model counterparts until they fell behind the reserves. Major-General Philip Skippon had already been gravely wounded; however, thanks to Pride, Hammond, and Rainborowe the reserves did not panic but halted the royalist advance, and helped to save the day for parliament. Pride also distinguished himself at the storming of Bristol, where his regiment was among the first to scale the city walls, and also at the storm of Dartmouth.

When the New Model Army revolted against parliament's attempt to disband it without its arrears in the spring of 1647, Pride was one of the officers most militant in asserting the right of soldiers to petition for redress of their grievances. He drew his regiment to a rendezvous, had the soldiers' petition read at the head of the regiment, threatened a fellow officer that any who declined to sign the soldiers' petition 'should be blotted out of the rolls and excluded and counted as no members of the army'

(*Portland MSS*, 1.418), and extracted 1100 signatures (virtually the whole regiment). His conservative presbyterian colonel, Edward Harley, complained of his activities in parliament, and Pride was summoned to the bar of the House of Commons to explain his conduct. Undeterred and defiant, he next took part in a high-level delegation that laid a *Petition and Vindication of the Officers* before the House of Commons on 27 April. In July he also helped draft the New Model's articles of impeachment against the eleven members who were viewed as its mortal enemies in the House of Commons. When one-quarter of the officers withdrew from the army out of loyalty to parliament Pride replaced Harley as colonel.

Pride's Purge In the second civil war Pride served under Cromwell in the Welsh campaign and at the battle of Preston. His regiment joined with Richard Deane's to present a petition demanding that parliament should proceed against the king 'as an enemy to the kingdom' (*Severall Petitions Presented to his Excellency the Lord Fairfax*, 1648, 8). It was also part of the 7000-strong force that occupied London at the beginning of December 1648. Although David Underdown has questioned whether Pride was 'anything more than the obedient instrument of a policy dictated by others' (Underdown, 141), he was quite possibly a member of the subcommittee of six officers and MPs who, on the night of 5 December, made the arrangements for the purging of the House of Commons of its conservative or presbyterian members. There is no doubt about his enthusiasm for the policy concerted by Ireton and others, for it was Pride who on the morning of the 6th set a guard around the house. He then stood on the stairs leading to the entrance, flourishing his list of members to be secured. Presently Lord Grey of Groby arrived to help him with identifications. About forty-five members were arrested and four times that number were secluded or stayed away. Pride carried out the political cleansing with courtesy except in the case of the lawyer William Prynne. The cantankerous member for Newport tried to force his way past, but Pride with the help of his soldiers pushed him down the stairs and hustled him away to nearby Queen's Court. Prynne is said to have demanded, as he was being carried off, 'By what authority and commission, and for what cause, they did thus violently seize on and pull him down from the House', to which Pride and Sir Hardress Waller pointed to their soldiers with swords drawn, muskets at the ready, and matches alight, answering 'there was their commission' (*The Parliamentary or Constitutional History of England*, 18.449). This violence against the House of Commons became known as Pride's Purge.

In January, Pride was appointed to the high court of justice that was created to try Charles I for treason against the people of England. He attended every sitting of the court except two and signed the death warrant [see also Regicides]. Beside his signature he affixed a seal bearing the impress of a chevron inter three animals' heads erased. His regiment was stationed in London for the rest of the year as a guard for parliament, while Pride himself was elected to the London common council in December.

London and national politics Pride's election to the common council foreshadowed an intense involvement in local politics which lasted for the better part of a decade. A member of John Duppa's separatist church, he had a dense network of personal contacts within the City. In late 1652 he was implicated in a scheme for the overthrow of the oligarchy which controlled the Saddlers' Company, and in another to replace Prideaux's lucrative postal system by a cheaper and more frequent service. In 1653 he was appointed to the committee to look into the Savoy Hospital and Ely House to ensure 'that only such men may be admitted as are proved to be deserving of relief' (*CSP dom.*, 1652–3, 363). In the same year he was one of a group of sequestrators who petitioned for a prolongation of their powers, and for a cure to be provided for St Bartholomew-the-Less. In 1656 he and other MPs were asked by parliament to examine a petition from maimed soldiers in the Savoy. Finally, he got himself named a governor of St Bartholomew's Hospital, in which capacity he became involved in a number of conflicts over the running of the hospital. In 1655–6 he was high sheriff of Surrey, and a commissioner for securing the peace of London, in which posts he continued his campaign, dating back to 1653, for the suppression of cock-fighting, bear- and bull-baiting, and 'playing for prizes by fencers' (*CSP dom.*, 1652–3, 306) in Southwark. After the Restoration he became a figure of fun to royalist wits, who mocked his hostility to these popular entertainments.

From his political base in London, Pride also involved himself in national issues. In August 1649 he presented on behalf of the army's council of officers a petition to parliament calling for the repeal of all statutes and ordinances 'whereby many consciencious people are molested, and the propagation of the gospel hindered', the suppression of 'open acts of prophaneness, as drunkenness, swearing, and uncleanness', the release of political prisoners, and the reform of the law (*Kingdomes Faithfull and Impartial Scout*, 10–17 Aug 1649, 224). Two months later the council of officers, wary of the continuing threat from the religious and Leveller left, decided to meet once a week to work out plans for law reform and the abolition of tithes. Again Pride was prominent in the radical agitation on these questions. Indeed, he stood at the Commons door on 26 December 1651 during the debate on law reform as a mute reminder to MPs of the fate they might expect if they failed to implement desired changes. The vehemence of his feeling towards the legal profession is further reflected in a comment he is reported to have made in Westminster Hall in 1652 'that it would never be well with England until … mercenary lawyers' gownes were hung up by the Scotch-trophies' (*A New Yeers Gift for England*, 1653, 15).

The profits of revolution Satisfaction for the state's financial creditors was another issue in which Pride took a keen interest. As a revolutionary insider he had had no difficulty obtaining redemption of his own debts. In December 1647 he had received £100 towards his arrears of pay, while in 1652 he used his arrears debentures totalling £1418, as well as debentures purchased from the men of his own regiment, to acquire Nonesuch Great Park (also known as Worcester Park) in Surrey for £11,591. In May 1652 parliament further rewarded him with a grant of forfeited Scottish lands worth £500 per annum. He was briefly associated with Samuel Chidley in the latter's agitation for payment of the state's creditors. However, when Chidley, in December 1652, attempted to claim Pride's support for his petition against the Rump's requirement that holders of public faith bills should 'double' (advance the same amount again in cash) in order to be paid off, the colonel issued an angry disclaimer, and the two went their separate ways.

Pride sought profit from the revolution in another way. On 7 November 1654 he and several business associates signed a contract for the victualling of the navy with beer and ale (Bodl. Oxf., MS Rawl. A.216, fol. 257). He had had earlier contracts, and had also been responsible for judging the quality of the provisions and beer supplied by others. In July 1653 he had condemned the beer on two ships at Harwich. Generals Monck and Blake reported that there had been great complaint against the beer, but that 'Col. Pride promises a better supply' (*CSP dom.*, 1653–4, 9). However, the terms of his contract cannot have been as lucrative as Pride expected, since in October 1654 he petitioned for its cancellation and the protector acceded to his request. He also begged to be forgiven his arrears of excise, dating from the years 1643 to 1645, when he was 'absent in the army' (*CSP dom.*, 1654, 426), and amounting to £5580. He claimed also to have lost £1600 for beer delivered to the navy but thrown overboard, presumably because it was unfit to drink. The excise commissioners opposed Pride's petition on account of the precedent it would create for other merchants who were in arrears.

Although he was based mainly in London during the 1650s, Pride did see military action. In 1650 he accompanied Cromwell to Scotland, commanded a brigade at Dunbar, and fought the following year at the battle of Worcester.

Protectorate politics and death Pride was elected to only one parliament during the 1650s, that of 1656, and he never served on the council of state. A committed republican, he was reportedly kept in England in 1654 while his regiment was sent to Scotland because the protector distrusted him. Nevertheless, on 17 January 1656 Cromwell knighted him, performing the ceremony with a faggot stick, according to Ludlow. Little over a year later, however, he played a leading part in the agitation among the officers against making Cromwell king. 'He shall not' (*Memoirs of Edmund Ludlow*, 2.25) was his blunt response to the report that Cromwell was thinking of accepting the crown. He then set about to organize the petition which changed the protector's mind. Yet curiously, after the passing of 'The humble petition and advice', he was pleased to be appointed to Cromwell's other house. 'He hath now changed his principles and his mind with the times' was the sour remark of a republican pamphleteer: 'the noble lawyers will be glad of his company and friendship, for that there is now no fear of his hanging up their gowns by the Scottish colours in Westminster Hall' ('A second narrative', 381). Shortly after the death of Oliver, Pride signed the proclamation of Richard Cromwell as new protector.

Pride died shortly thereafter, on 23 October 1658, and was buried at Nonesuch on 2 November. According to a London newsbook, his last words were 'that he was very sorry for these three nations, whom he saw in a most sad and deplorable condition' (*Weekly Intelligencer*, 1–8 Nov 1659, 212). His will confirmed the picture of a convinced puritan, who bequeathed his soul 'into the hands of my pretious Redeemer, Lord Jesus Christ, being perswaded by the faith he hath wrought in me, that he will wash it thoroughly from all its defilements and present it to his father and my father as his own purchas'. It also revealed a man who by the end of his life had become wealthy, suspicious, and perhaps quarrelsome. He warned his sons William and Samuel not to practise 'fraude, or cousenage' in their stewardship of his major property, Nonesuch Great Park. He named his 'faithfull and loveinge wife', Elizabeth (daughter of Thomas Monck, brother of George Monck, the architect of the Restoration), his executrix, but allowed her 'no more then foure hundred pounds p. annum' out of the park. He threatened to cut her off from all benefits if she disposed of any part of her interest in his estate. Previously he had settled the manor of Great Stoughton, Huntingdonshire, on his first son, Thomas, as well as half the partnership of his two brewhouses at Kingston, Surrey. His son Joseph was to be paid £4000 from the brewhouses when he reached the age of twenty-one, but if Thomas and the other partner tried to block this bequest, the entire ownership of the brewhouses was to be turned over to Joseph. To his daughter Elizabeth and her husband, Robert, son of Colonel Valentine Wauton, he left only £5 each (PRO, PROB 11/283, fols. 213v–214v).

At the Restoration, Pride's estates were confiscated and Nonesuch Great Park was restored to the crown. His carcase, which was voted to be exhumed, drawn to Tyburn, hung up in its coffin, and buried under the gallows, along with those of Cromwell, Ireton, and Bradshaw, seems in the event to have escaped that indignity.

Pride was one of the fearless revolutionaries of the New Model Army who were instrumental in winning the war against the king, bringing him to judgment, and shaping the regime that came after him. No intellectual, he spoke little and wrote even less. But he was a radical puritan who knew his own mind, and did not shrink from imposing his views upon others. Remembered above all for the purge of parliament which bears his name, he also enjoyed a flourishing career as a merchant, in addition to enriching himself from the spoils of revolution.   IAN J. GENTLES

Sources B. Worden, *The Rump Parliament, 1648–1653* (1974) • M. Tolmie, *The triumph of the saints: the separate churches of London, 1616–1649* (1977) • D. Underdown, *Pride's Purge: politics in the puritan revolution* (1971) • I. Gentles, *The New Model Army in England, Ireland, and Scotland, 1645–1653* (1992) • *The parliamentary or constitutional history of England*, 2nd edn, 24 vols. (1751–62), vol. 18 • *DNB* • Haberdashers' Company, apprenticeship bindings, 1610–30, GL, MS 15860/4, fol. 173v • freedom admissions, 1526–1641, GL [unfoliated], 14 April 1629 • PRO, PROB 11/283, fols. 213v–214v •

army pay warrants, PRO, SP28/49, fol. 386 • exchequer, certificates of sale of crown land, PRO, E121/4/8/100 (Nonesuch Great Park) • common pleas, feet of fines, PRO, CP25(2)/560, Huntingdonshire, Easter 1657 (manor of Great Stoughton) • *JHC*, 7 (1651–9), 132 • main papers, 10 March 1645, HLRO, fol. 145v • main papers, 24 Aug 1647, HLRO • J. Rushworth, *Historical collections*, new edn, 6 (1722), 444, 471 • *The manuscripts of his grace the duke of Portland*, 10 vols., HMC, 29 (1891–1931), vol. 1, p. 418 • J. L. Vivian, ed., *The visitations of the county of Devon, comprising the herald's visitations of 1531, 1564, and 1620* (privately printed, Exeter, [1895]), 570 • 'A second narrative of the late parliament (so called)', *The Harleian miscellany*, ed. W. Oldys and T. Park, 10 vols. (1808–13), vol. 3, pp. 470–89 • *The memoirs of Edmund Ludlow*, ed. C. H. Firth, 2 vols. (1894)

Wealth at death £12,015 or more; Nonesuch Great Park, Surrey: exchequer, certificates of sale of crown land, PRO, E121/4/8/100 (Nonesuch Great Park), 3 July 1652; will, PRO, PROB11/283, fols. 213v–214v

Prideaux, Edmond [created Sir Edmond Prideaux, baronet, under the protectorate] (1601–1659), lawyer and politician, was born in September 1601 at Netherton, Devon, and baptized at Farway in the same county on 27 September, the second surviving son of Sir Edmund Prideaux, baronet (c.1555–1629), lawyer, and his second wife, Katherine, daughter of Piers Edgcumbe of Mount Edgcumbe, Cornwall. He was descended from an ancient family originally of Prideaux Castle, Cornwall. He entered the Inner Temple, where his father was an eminent lawyer, in 1615 and was called to the bar on 23 November 1623, where his practice was chiefly in chancery. He lived in Devon during the 1630s serving as a sewer commissioner and a JP. His first wife was Jane (1609/10–1629), daughter and heir of Henry Collins of Ottery St Mary, Devon; shortly after her death he married Margaret (d. 1683), daughter and coheir of William Ivery of Cothay in Somerset.

Prideaux was returned to the Long Parliament for Lyme Regis (which seat he held until his death), and forthwith took sides against the king. His subscription for the defence of parliament, in 1642, was £100. By his own side he was regarded as one of the persons best informed as to the state of feeling in the west of England. He was *custos rotulorum* of Devon from 1646. Retained as a legal counsellor by the corporation of Exeter by 1642, he was recorder there from 1643, serving Bristol in the same capacity from 1647. On the national scene Prideaux attained prominence as a manager of first the 'war' then the independent interests, or parties. For three years, from 10 November 1643 until it was transferred to the custody of the speakers of the two houses, he was one of the commissioners in charge of the great seal of parliament, an office worth £1500 a year; as a mark of respect he was, by order of the House of Commons, called within the bar with precedence next after the solicitor-general. He had also been one of the commissioners appointed to negotiate with the king's commissioners at Uxbridge in January 1645. He fled parliament for the safety of the army in July 1647. On 12 October 1648 he was nominated by the Commons as solicitor-general, the Lords accepting his nomination on 18 October, and an ordinance passed both houses accordingly on 24 November. He avoided acting in the king's trial, but remained busy in the House of Commons throughout December 1648 and January 1649. On 9 April 1649 he was appointed attorney-general, and remained in that office for the rest of his life. He sat on the third and fifth councils of state during the Commonwealth, polling a respectable fifty-three votes in the December 1652 election.

From 1644 to 1653 Prideaux was intimately and profitably connected with the postal service. The question of the validity of patents for the conduct of posts was raised in both houses of parliament in connection with the sequestration, in 1640, of Thomas Witherings's office, granted in 1633. Prideaux served as chairman of the committee appointed in 1642 upon the rates of inland letters. In 1644 he was appointed, by resolution of both houses, 'master of the posts, messengers, and couriers' (*JHC*, 3, 1642–4, 619), and he continued at intervals, as directed by the House of Commons or otherwise, to manage the postal service. He was ordered to arrange a post to Hull and York, and also to Lyme Regis, in 1644; in 1649 to Chester, Holyhead, and Ireland, and also to Bideford; in 1650 to Kendal, and in 1651 to Carlisle. By 1649 he is said to have established a regular weekly service throughout the kingdom. Rumour assigned to his office an income of £15,000 a year—at any rate it was so profitable as to excite rivalry. 'Encouraged by the opinion of the judges given in the House of Lords in the case of the Earl of Warwick *v.* Witherings, 9 July 1646, that the clause in Witherings's patent for restraint of carrying letters was void', Oxenbridge, Thomson, and others endeavoured to carry on a cheap and speedy post of their own, and Prideaux met them by a variety of devices, some in the way of ordinary competition, others in the shape of abuses of power and breaches of the law (*CSP dom.*, 1654, 22). The common council of London endeavoured in 1650 to organize the carriage of letters, but Prideaux brought the matter before parliament, which referred the question to the council of state, on 21 March 1650. On the same day the council made an order that Prideaux should take care of the business of the inland post, and be accountable for the profits quarterly; a committee was appointed to confer with him as to the management of the post. After various claims had been considered, parliament, on 21 March 1652, resolved that the office of postmaster ought to be at the sole disposal of the house, and the Irish and the Scotch committee, to which the question was referred, reported in favour of letting contracts for the carriage of letters. Prideaux contended that the office of postmaster and the carrying of letters were two distinct things, and that the resolution of parliament of 1652 referred to the former only, but eventually all previous grants were held to be set aside by that resolution, and contracts were let for the inland and foreign mails to John Manley in 1653. The loss entailed affected Prideaux little; his legal practice continued to be large and lucrative, being worth £5000 a year. Among several acquisitions of real estate, he bought Forde Abbey, at Thornecombe, on the Devon/Dorset border, and built a large house there. On 31 May 1658 he was made a baronet, ostensibly in reward for voluntarily undertaking the maintenance of thirty foot soldiers in Ireland. He died, leaving a great fortune, on 19 August 1659 and was buried in the chapel of Forde Abbey. He appears to have been a sound chancery lawyer and highly esteemed by his party as a man of religion as well as learning. He was survived by his second wife and a son by that marriage who was to take part in Monmouth's rebellion.

J. A. HAMILTON, *rev.* SEAN KELSEY

Sources GEC, *Baronetage*, 3.6; 1.200 • Keeler, *Long Parliament* • R. E. Shimp, 'Prideaux, Edmund', Greaves & Zaller, *BDBR*, 63–4 • *JHL*, 10 (1647–8), 551, 566, 602 • *JHC*, 2 (1640–42), 500; 3 (1642–4), 619; 4 (1644–6), 51, 86, 182 • *CSP dom.*, 1652–3, 109, 366, 448, 450, 455; 1658–9, 324 • D. Underdown, 'Party management in the recruiter elections, 1645–48', *EngHR*, 83 (1968), 235–64 • Sainty, *King's counsel*, 46, 62 • H. Robinson, *The British Post Office: a history* (1948) • P. Gaunt, 'Interregnum governments and the reform of the Post Office, 1649–1658', *Historical Research*, 60 (1987), 281–98 • S. K. Roberts, *Recovery and restoration in an English county: Devon local administration, 1646–1670* (1985) • *IGI* • C. H. Firth and R. S. Rait, eds., *Acts and ordinances of the interregnum, 1642–1660*, 3 vols. (1911) • will, PRO, PROB 11/296, fol. 315r–v
Archives Dorset RO, commonplace book
Wealth at death real estate in Devon and Dorset; jewellery; mortgage (£1000 plus interest); legacies of several hundred pounds: will, PRO, PROB 11/296, fol. 315r–v; *CSP dom.*, 1658–9

Prideaux, Frederick (1817–1891), lawyer, fifth son of Walter Prideaux of Plymouth, and his wife, Sarah, daughter of Joseph Kingston of Kingsbridge, Devon, was born at 1 Portland Square, Plymouth, on 27 April 1817. His father, a partner in the private bank of Kingston and Prideaux, was a descendant of Humphrey Prideaux, dean of Norwich, but was raised as a Quaker. Frederick Prideaux was educated at the Plymouth grammar school, at a private school at Egloshayle, near Wadebridge, Cornwall, and under a private tutor. He was instructed in law by his elder brother, Walter Prideaux, of the firm of Lane and Prideaux, solicitors, London, and by the eminent Quaker conveyancer John Hodgkin. On 26 May 1834 he was admitted a student at Lincoln's Inn, where he was called to the bar on 27 January 1840. At Clifton on 14 April 1853 he married Fanny Ash, a poet and the second daughter of Richard Ball of Portland House, Kingsdown, Gloucestershire.

After practising for some years in London, Prideaux moved to Bath in 1858. He returned to London in 1865, and in 1866 obtained the post of reader in real and personal property to the inns of court, which he resigned because of ill health in 1875. He afterwards lived successively at Torquay, Gatcombe, and Taunton. In his youth Prideaux abandoned Quakerism for the Church of England, but in later life he became attached to the Baptist society. He was the author of a work on conveyancing that saw a number of subsequent editions. He died in Taunton on 21 November 1891. He was survived by his wife, who died in September 1894.

J. M. RIGG, *rev.* ERIC METCALFE

Sources *The Athenaeum* (18 Sept 1894), 390–91 • F. Prideaux, *In memoriam F.P.* (1891) • W. P. Baildon, ed., *The records of the Honorable Society of Lincoln's Inn: the black books*, 4 (1902) • *CGPLA Eng. & Wales* (1892)

Wealth at death £8350 1s. 4d.: resworn probate, Aug 1892, *CGPLA Eng. & Wales*

Prideaux, Humphrey (1648–1724), dean of Norwich and author, was born on 3 May 1648 at Padstow, Cornwall, third son of Edmund Prideaux (*bap.* 1606, *d.* 1683) of Padstow Place and his wife, Bridget (*bap.* 1620, *d.* 1690), daughter of John Moyle of Bake in St Germans and his wife, Admonition. He was first educated locally at Liskeard and Bodmin schools. On 19 November 1664 his uncle Sir William Morice, then secretary of state, recommended him to Richard Busby at Westminster School with the hope that 'Nature hath in good measure disposed him for Learning, and that his Country-rudiments will be no prejudice to his progresse therein' (BL, Add. MS 28104, fol. 11). He was chosen king's scholar at Westminster in 1665; then on 20 April 1668 commended by the king to the electors of Christ Church, Oxford. He was admitted to Christ Church on 26 October 1668 (matriculating on 11 December) and tutored by Arthur Squibb. He graduated BA on 22 June 1672, MA on 29 April 1675, BD on 15 November 1682, and DD on 8 June 1686; he was praelector in 1673, and in 1680 praelector graecae. In 1676 Lord Chancellor Finch asked him to tutor his undergraduate son Charles, and through Finch's patronage Prideaux became sinecure rector of Llandewi Felffre, Pembrokeshire (1677), rector of St Clement's, Oxford (1679), and prebend of Norwich (installed 15 August 1681); also, thanks to Finch's successor, Lord Guilford, rector of Bladon-cum-Woodstock, Oxfordshire (1683).

Dean Fell employed Prideaux as an editor. On 27 September 1674 he complained to his student friend and correspondent John Ellis, 'I am now groaneing under the oppression of two or three heavy burdens which Mr. Dean hath layed upon me.' One was completion of Edmund Chilmead's edition of John Malalas—'a horrid musty foolish booke'—eventually published in 1691. Another was a catalogue of the Arundel, Selden, and other marbles, from which (in particular the Parian marble) Prideaux designed an annotated 'table of all Greek chronology … the most methodicall and correct of any that have yet been set forth' (*Letters*, 22–3). But *Marmora Oxoniensia* (1676), hastily completed and depending largely on earlier scholarship, was, as Hearne noted in 1719, 'wonderfully defective, and what the D^r. was now asham'd of, at least as to the transcribing part' (T. Hearne, *Remarks and Collections*, vol. 7, 1906, 6). Like Busby at Westminster, Fell valued the Near Eastern languages, and Prideaux was further encouraged in those studies by 'the more than ordinary helpe' he hoped to receive from Edward Pococke (*Letters*, 43). In 1677 a letter described Prideaux as 'Hebrew reader in our college' (Bill, 206), and in 1679 he published Moses Maimonides' *De jure pauperis et peregrini*, with Latin translation and notes. Prideaux's dedication to Finch links the lord chancellor with Maimonides by supposing English municipal law to have Mosaic origins.

On 9 July 1685 Prideaux announced his resolution to leave Oxford and marry: 'I little thought I should ever come to this; but abundance of motives have overpowred me' (*Letters*, 144). On 16 February 1686 he married Bridget,

the only child of Anthony and Mary Bockenham of Helmingham, Suffolk, who brought him £3000. Having exchanged his Bladon rectory for Saham Toney, Norfolk, and settled there 'in great content', he refused the Hebrew professorship offered him on Pococke's death in 1691—'I nauseate that learning,' he wrote, 'and I nauseate Christ Church'—but later regretted his decision (ibid., 147, 150).

Prideaux was not a retiring man: his correspondence shows him concerned with his preferment and with church and local politics. He was active against Catholics (and later Jacobites) and in mid-1688 published letters he had written to dissuade a Norfolk convert—*The Validity of the Orders of the Church of England*. He preached against the Catholic mass, frustrated the reading of James II's declaration of indulgence, and armed his servants in support of William of Orange's landing. As archdeacon of Suffolk, installed on 21 December 1688, he used his visitation the following May to urge subscription to the new oaths, only three incumbents refusing. He advocated the prayer-book changes for dissenters that were never brought forward when convocation met on 21 November 1689; but he feared a misunderstanding of the Toleration Act would 'turn halfe the nation into downe right atheisme' (*Letters*, 154). Among other questions, he took up that of clandestine marriage and wrote for Bishop Richard Kidder of Bath and Wells *The Case of Clandestine Marriages* (1691), which argued that the bill before parliament was needlessly severe and the existing canons, if enforced, quite sufficient.

In 1694 Prideaux gave up Saham, which he found unhealthy, to live in Norwich; in 1697 he acquired the neighbouring vicarage of Trowse and held it until 1709. His superiors in Norwich were uncongenial: the 'close designeing' Bishop John Moore and the 'horrid sot' Dean Henry Fairfax (*Letters*, 148, 160). However, he succeeded Fairfax as dean in 1702 (installed on 8 June) and might have succeeded Moore in 1707, except that he thought himself too old and supported Charles Trimnell's elevation instead.

Prideaux's practical churchmanship led him to write *The Original and Right of Tithes*, first published at Norwich in 1710. His main fame as a writer has rested on two frequently reprinted works, his *Life of Mahomet* (1697) and his *Connection* (1716–18). The former's title states its purpose—*The True Nature of Imposture Fully Displayed in the Life of Mahomet*—and the life itself is followed by a long 'Letter to the *Deists*' identifying seven marks of imposture chargeable on 'Mahometism' but not on Christianity. Prideaux's learned footnotes and bibliography of thirty-six Arabic authorities imply original research in manuscript sources; but, as P. M. Holt shows, everything derives from printed editions (with Latin translations) or citations and references in Christian writers. '[Edward] Pococke above all provided a mine of information in his *Specimen historiae Arabum* [1650]. … An impressive array of Arabic authorities in a footnote usually implies the incorporation of material from Pococke's notes in the *Specimen*' (Holt, 293–4). Prideaux's *Old and New Testament Connected* is a much larger work, covering the history of the Jews from 747 BC to AD 33 in two parts, divided at 292 BC, when the Old Testament canon was complete. Here too Prideaux had, as his preface acknowledges, one of the great seventeenth-century scholars to guide him, James Ussher in his *Annales veteris et novi testamenti* (1650–54). However, unlike Ussher (or Pococke), Prideaux aimed to make things easy for the general reader by writing clearly and fully in English, with translated quotations and without exotic words; so the *Connection*, while outdated in execution and perhaps conception, continued to be printed into the mid-nineteenth century. Two Gaudy orations on Prideaux at Christ Church, in 1790 and 1863, are evidence of his work's continuing currency.

In his preface to the *Connection* Prideaux describes himself as disabled from preaching. In 1710, when seriously afflicted with the stone, he was told 'I cannot bear that operation, but that in all likelyhood I must dy under it' (*Letters*, 205). In fact he was operated upon successfully, but afterwards his case was unfortunately managed. Although ill and depending on an amanuensis, his last letter to Ellis, of 29 September 1722, shows him concerned with the usual matters: an unconscientious clergyman, a local election, a Jacobite, and a new session of parliament (*Letters*, 206–7). Prideaux died in the deanery, Norwich, on 1 November 1724 and was buried in the nave of Norwich Cathedral. In his will, dated 4 August 1714, he left his whole estate to his first child, Edmund. He had already given his oriental books to Clare College, Cambridge, in 1721.   HUGH DE QUEHEN

Sources *Letters of Humphrey Prideaux … to John Ellis*, ed. E. M. Thompson, CS, new ser., 15 (1875) • *The life of the Reverend Humphrey Prideaux* (1748) • Boase & Courtney, *Bibl. Corn.*, 2.527–33, 3.1319 • F. Madan, *Oxford literature, 1651–1680* (1931), vol. 3 of *Oxford books: a bibliography of printed works* (1895–1931); repr. (1964) • P. M. Holt, 'The treatment of Arab history by Prideaux, Ockley, and Sale', *Historians of the Middle East*, ed. B. Lewis and P. M. Holt (1962), 290–302 • *Hist. U. Oxf. 4: 17th-cent. Oxf.* • *Fasti Angl., 1541–1857*, [Ely] • *Old Westminsters*, vol. 2 • E. G. W. Bill, *Education at Christ Church, Oxford, 1660–1800* (1988) • *CSP dom., 1667–8*, 350 • will, 1725, Norfolk RO, MF 432

Archives JRL, notes relating to medieval ecclesiastical law • Norfolk RO, corresp., collections and transcriptions, diaries | BL, letters to John Ellis, Add. MS 58929 • Bodl. Oxf., corresp. with William Sancroft and others • Devon RO, Pine-Coffin corresp.

Likenesses E. Seeman, oils, Christ Church Oxf. • J. Simon, mezzotint (after unknown artist), BM, NPG • G. Vertue, line engraving (after E. Seeman junior), BM, NPG; repro. in H. Prideaux, *The Old and New Testaments connected*, 1 (1716)

Prideaux, John (1578–1650), bishop of Worcester, was born at Stowford, Devon, on 17 September 1578, one of twelve children and the fourth son of John Prideaux, farmer, and his wife, Agnes (*d.* 1625/6). The death of his father in 1592 or 1593 left resources stretched and the latter part of Prideaux's early education, probably at Ashburton grammar school, was subsidized by Lady Fowell. After failing to become parish clerk of Ugborough, Prideaux walked to Oxford and entered Exeter College as a servant. He matriculated on 14 October 1596 and was tutored by William Helme.

John Prideaux (1578–1650), by Claude Warin, 1638

Education and rectorship of Exeter College Prideaux graduated BA on 31 January 1600, became fellow of Exeter College in June 1601, and proceeded MA on 11 May 1603. Subsequently he was appointed chaplain to Henry, prince of Wales, and was thereby dispensed from some requirements in taking his BD on 6 May 1611. Shortly before Prince Henry died he secured Prideaux's election on 4 April 1612 to the rectorship of Exeter. As a result Prideaux took his DD early, on 30 June 1612. In his theses he denied that grace sufficient for salvation was granted to all; that those reborn to grace might lose it; and that sacraments confer grace *ex opere operato*. In the same year Prideaux became chaplain to King James, a post in which he continued under Charles I.

Prideaux shortly after married Anne, daughter of Dean William *Goodwin of Christ Church, and granddaughter through her mother of the Marian martyr Rowland Taylor. Of their nine children, two daughters survived their father. Anne Prideaux died on 11 August 1627 and in August the next year Prideaux entered a childless marriage with Mary (*d.* 1666), daughter of Sir Thomas Reynell of Ogwel, Devon.

Fuller calls Prideaux a generous almsgiver, but it was ecclesiastical pluralism which made this possible: with his headship of Exeter College came the vicarage of Kidlington, Oxfordshire; in 1614 he obtained the vicarage of Bampton, Oxfordshire, which he resigned to his son-in-law, William Hodges, in 1634; in 1617 he received a Christ Church canonry in reversion and in 1620 the vicarage of Chalgrove, Oxfordshire, which he resigned to a miscreant brother-in-law in 1625; also in 1620 he became a canon of Salisbury. Nine years later he became rector of Ewelme, and soon after of Bladon-cum-Woodstock.

Prideaux was famed as tutor and theologian before his rectorship, during which he enhanced the college's appeal to Calvinists at home and abroad, and numbers in residence increased. Some came after a period in the household of Bishop John Williams. There were distinguished Scots, such as James Hamilton, marquess of Hamilton from 1624, and Richard Spottiswood. Prideaux attracted John Sigismund Cluverius, James Casaubon, Sixtinus Amama, and other continental scholars. Archbishop Ussher dispatched a kinsman reclaimed from popery, James Dillon, who later returned to Catholicism. Wood noted that Exeter produced besides sound men 'many that did great mischief' (Wood, *Ath. Oxon.*, 3.271). Anthony Ashley Cooper, later first earl of Shaftesbury, was there from 1637. Prideaux had a pedagogue's penchant for punning and wordplay, in part mnemonic technique; Thomas Fuller spoke of his 'becoming festivity' (*Worthies*, 1.279). He kept the well-born, some of whom were accommodated in his lodgings, on a loose rein and tolerated some indiscipline. Exeter men were prominent in 'coursing' or baiting rival colleges at academic exercises, and Laud induced Charles I to threaten implicated heads in 1631.

By-products of Prideaux's arts tutoring were his widely used manuscript notes and published textbooks, notably *Tabulae ad grammaticam Graecam introductoriae* (1607), *Tyrocinium ad syllogismum legitimum contexendum* (1629), and *Heptades logicae* (1639). John Aubrey was taught with Prideaux's logic at Trinity College in the early 1640s, and also used his notes on moral philosophy; he later praised these easy-to-memorize manuals. To improve college tuition Prideaux obtained from his kinsman Sir John Maynard endowment of a theological readership, and established another in Hebrew.

Effective fund-raising enabled major building work, and even the hostile Peter Heylyn allowed that the college was transformed. Sir John Acton funded a new hall, Sir John Peryam new rector's lodgings, and George Hakewill a new chapel. Prideaux's sermon at the chapel consecration was published in 1625 and in 1631 he produced a survey of the altered college. Ever intolerant of opposition, he accepted in 1630 forged documentation of birthplace for a tied fellowship and expelled dissenting fellows. Petitions and appeals drew in Laud (as chancellor), the Star Chamber, and the king. The visitor, Bishop Joseph Hall of Exeter, censured Prideaux and reinstated the fellows.

Prideaux was active in the university at large. William Herbert, earl of Pembroke, and chancellor, 1616–30, whom Prideaux called his 'Maecenas', nominated him vice-chancellor during four years, 1619–21 and 1624–6. In 1620 Prideaux high-handedly imposed a kinsman of the chancellor as principal of Jesus College over fellows' objections. In January 1626 he declared Sir Thomas Edmonds, recommended by Pembroke and Archbishop Abbot, MP for the university despite opposition at the election by supporters of Sir Francis Stewart. The latter appealed, and despite a skilful rebuttal, the vice-chancellor was summonsed by the committee of privilege and the election quashed. Prideaux vigorously asserted academic privileges against the city. When free to do so he courted popularity, backing in 1620 a demand by young masters to wear caps in congregation and convocation and securing Pembroke's assent.

Laud's ascendancy banished Prideaux to sterile opposition. In a 1627 dispute at Wadham College the enemies of Laud, then bishop of Bath and Wells, sought unsuccessfully to undermine his visitatorial jurisdiction in the secular courts, and Prideaux, a member of Gray's Inn from 1625, was implicated. In 1630 he worked to elect as chancellor the deceased Pembroke's brother, Philip, instead of the victorious Laud.

Regius professor of divinity Since December 1615, however, Prideaux had been regius professor of divinity and he remained in control of theological teaching. Peter Heylyn observed that James I's 'Directions' for uprooting puritanism of 1617 had been thwarted because the then vicechancellor was Prideaux's father-in-law (*Cyprianus Anglicus*, 1668, 72). Prideaux responded to the 'Directions' by debating anti-Arminian points at Exeter College.

Prideaux had a deep knowledge of continental writers, medieval and modern, protestant and Catholic. An eclectic rather than an original theologian, he was a skilful dialectician. He was a competent Hebrew scholar and always a promoter both of that language and of Arabic. Placing great emphasis on the Synod of Dort, and a consistent proponent of the absolute decree of reprobation, he was esteemed by non-Arminians and opponents of liberal or rational theology. Affirmation of the pope as Antichrist was central to his creed and he rejected the alternatives of Mohammed or the Turk, but he had reservations about extreme apocalyptic approaches. He assailed Richard Montague's *Appello Caesarem* in 1625 and told students, contrary to the 'Directions', to apply themselves first to systematic catechism and only then to the fathers. Although prominent in collecting for distressed Calvinist ministers abroad, he rejected being labelled as a Calvinist. Always hard to pin down, he supported episcopacy but excused foreigners unable to enjoy it. He believed in visible pre-Reformation congregations of protestant hue but claimed that they had remained under legitimate bishops and pastors.

Prideaux used less measured expressions in the heat of public disputations: mature opponents were flayed by sarcasm—his rebuke of Christopher Potter at his doctoral disputation in 1627 rankled ever after with the provost of Queen's College. When Gilbert Sheldon, later warden of All Souls, denied in his 1628 DD disputation that the pope was Antichrist, he was assailed by Prideaux who said the pontiff was his debtor and likely to award him a cardinal's hat. Prideaux's most celebrated opponent was Peter Heylyn, a dialectically sharp protégé of Laud, who provoked him and then reported incautious expressions. At his BD exercises in 1627 Heylyn examined the visibility of the church. Prideaux, addressing jibes to the youthful gallery, spoke sufficiently loosely to be represented as asserting pre-Reformation visibility in conventicles. In considering church authority at his 1633 DD disputation, Heylyn drove Prideaux to speak as if deprecating church authority.

1631 was a black year for Prideaux. Laud rebuked him for failing to deliver the statutory number of lectures, and again in the king's name for allowing an inconvenient Act question. Charles I considered dismissing him for his implication in efforts to thwart new statutes, entangled with court intrigue and anti-Arminian sermons by young men who flouted the vice-chancellor's jurisdiction. Laud, however, after vigorous prosecution, unexpectedly sought leniency and Prideaux escaped with a reprimand, probably after intervention by Philip, earl of Pembroke. Harassment by his ascendant enemies continued in 1634 when Heylyn published a translation of his 1622 Act lecture, *The Doctrine of the Sabbath*, to embarrass the professor with puritanical supporters and Vice-Chancellor Brian Duppa had a sermon by Francis Mason on church authority reprinted to undermine Prideaux's influence in lectures. Meanwhile Prideaux had published nothing new since collections of his lectures and Act orations in 1625/6. He had complained to Ussher in 1628 that supervision hindered printing sound theology. For fear of Laud's spies Prideaux refused open support to John Dury's promotion of international protestant unity. The content of a set of sermons he published in 1637 got him into trouble and he must have been under considerable pressure from the archbishop when he tamely approved in that year Chillingworth's *Religion of Protestants*, the tenor of which was hateful to him. However, there were occasional flashes of spirit as when in 1636 he criticized adulatory language in the university's letter thanking Laud for new statutes. In 1640 he backed Laud's enemy, Sir Nathaniel Brent, to be a university MP.

Prideaux's career revived with the fall of Laud, and the new chancellor, Philip Herbert, nominated him vice-chancellor in 1641. He struggled to balance loyalties to king and chancellor. Obeying royal directions, and raising money for Charles, he seems none the less to have acquiesced in the protestation oath in early 1642. He accepted Pembroke's imposition in March 1642 of a lay lawyer, Giles Sweit, as commissary to exercise judicial functions from which parliament had seemingly debarred a clerical vice-chancellor. Infuriated fellow heads later censured his accounts for unwarranted spending, especially on Sweit's commission.

Bishop of Worcester On 22 November 1641 the king, at the marquess of Hamilton's urging, made Prideaux bishop of Worcester to assuage religious opposition. Consecrated at Westminster in December, he seems to have been absent when most of the bishops incurred impeachment and, despite voting against removing bishops from the Lords, he had sufficient credit with the Commons to be approved Worcestershire representative to the assembly of divines. His fund-raising for the king as vice-chancellor, however, provoked parliament to order his arrest on 12 July 1642. By then Prideaux had left Oxford for Worcester. Although 'almost grown to the Chair, he had sate so long and close therein' (Lloyd, 536) he was replaced as professor by Robert Sanderson on 19 July. Prideaux resigned as rector of Exeter College on 3 August.

According to Wood, the royalist Bishop Prideaux excommunicated the king's enemies. In 1643 he headed a parliamentary list of Worcestershire delinquents to be sequestrated and the following year his eldest son, William, died

a colonel at Marston Moor. At the surrender of Worcester, Prideaux helped calm military hotheads. Petitioning the Lords on 24 September 1646 he claimed that he had no private means on which to survive the sequestration of his bishopric. On 25 December the Commons allowed bail to Prideaux, then in custody of the serjeant-at-arms, and granted him his books and manuscripts providing he stayed within 20 miles of London. Later he was permitted to live with his son-in-law, Henry Sutton, at Bredon rectory in Worcestershire, where he was allowed 4s. 6d. a week for his support. He visited Oxford about 1648, probably to publish *Viginti-duae lectiones de totidem religionis capitibus*, a collection of his Latin theological works. His important *Fasciculus controversiarum theologicarum* appeared in 1649.

Death and reputation Prideaux died of a fever at Bredon on 29 July 1650. 'Such was the number and quality of persons attending his funeral' there on 16 August that 'such as deny *Bishops* to be *Peers*, would have conceived this *Bishop* a *Prince*' (Fuller, *Worthies*, 1.280). An ornate and adulatory Latin sermon was delivered. In his will of 20 June, Prideaux declared that he died 'firmely beleevinge and houldinge the Doctrine Worship and Discipline established and professed in the Church of England, in the raigne of Queene Elizabeth King James and the beginninge of the raigne of the late Kinge Charles' (Butcher, 24). He bequeathed his wife bonds for £1000 owed by her family and £100 in gold, as well as other goods. To Henry Sutton he left leasehold property adjoining Exeter College. He divided his library between his two sons-in-law, Sutton and William Hodges, joint executors and residuary legatees. Stories that he sold his library to support himself are evidently exaggerated: more than 600 of his books survive in Worcester Cathedral Library.

A number of Prideaux's works were published posthumously during the interregnum. In 1651 there appeared his *Scholasticae theologiae syntagma mnemonicum* and his *Conciliorum synopsis*. Notes left to his daughters on the use of common prayer were printed as *Euchologia* (1655), and a work on conscience written for his wife appeared in 1656. His collected *Hypomnemata logica, rhetorica, physica, metaphysica, pneumatica, ethica, politica, oeconomica*, tutorial notes for undergraduates, reached the press in 1656, and *Manuductio ad theologiam polemicam* the following year.

Matthias Prideaux (c.1625–1646?), author, was son of John Prideaux and his first wife, Anne. He matriculated from Exeter College on 3 July 1640 and was elected fellow on 30 June 1641. Graduating BA on 2 November 1644, he entered the king's army and his captaincy obtained him an accelerated MA on 3 December 1645. Following the surrender of Oxford in 1646 he moved to London where he died from smallpox shortly after. His father edited from his papers for publication at Oxford in 1648 the popular *An Easy and Compendious Introduction for Reading All Sorts of Histories*.

A. J. HEGARTY

Sources V. Butcher, 'Dr John Prideaux (1578–1650)', 1979, Exeter College, Oxford · V. Butcher, 'Dr John Prideaux (1578–1650)', 1979,

Worcester Cathedral library · R. M. Prideaux, *Prideaux: a west-country clan* (1989) · S. P. T. Prideaux, *John Prideaux, in piam memoriam* (1938) · Foster, *Alum. Oxon.* · J. Prince, *Danmonii orientales illustres, or, The worthies of Devon* (1701), 510–16 · *The works of the most reverend father in God, William Laud*, 5, ed. J. Bliss (1853), 15, 27–8, 48–71, 87–91; 165–6, 191 · PRO, SP 14/93, fol. 237r; 16/22, fol. 59r; 16/86, fols. 63r–64r; 16/171, fol. 92r; 16/198, fol. 72r–v; 16/199, fol. 50r–v; 16/245, fols. 18r–21v; 16/277, fols. 136r–139v; 16/344, fol. 35r–36r; 16/348, fol. 115r; 16/349, fol. 86r; 16/369, fol. 226r; 16/406, fols. 167r–168r; 16/488, fol. 115v · Bodl. Oxf., MS Jones 17; MS Jones 56, fols. 21r–22v · A. Wood, *The history and antiquities of the University of Oxford*, ed. J. Gutch, 2 (1796), 316–442 · T. Nash, *Collections for the history of Worcestershire*, 2 vols. (1781–2) · *Hist. U. Oxf.* 4: *17th-cent. Oxf.* · D. Lloyd, *Memoires of the lives … of those … personages that suffered … for the protestant religion* (1668), 536–8 · Fuller, *Worthies* (1811), 1.279

Archives Worcester Cathedral library, books, some with MS notes

Likenesses C. Jansen?, portrait, *c*.1612, Laycock Abbey, Wiltshire · C. Warin, medal, 1638, BM [*see illus.*] · C. Warin, plaster medallion?, 1638, Worcester Cathedral library · J. Smith, oils, *c*.1832 (after C. Jansen?), Christ Church Oxf. · W. Faithorne, line engraving, BM, NPG; repro. in J. Prideaux, *Doctrine of practical praying* (1655) · C. Jansen?, portrait, priv. coll. · J. Smith, oils (after C. Jansen?, *c*.1612), Exeter College, Oxford; repro. in Prideaux, *Prideaux: a westcountry clan*, jacket · D. Wise, monument (after C. Warin), Worcester Cathedral · engraving (after C. Jansen?), repro. in Nash, *Collections for the history of Worcestershire*, vol. 1, facing p. 132 · engraving, repro. in J. Prideaux, *Euchologia* (1655)

Wealth at death £1000 in bonds; £100 in gold; leasehold property; valuable library; plus other goods: Butcher, 'Dr John Prideaux'

Prideaux, John (*bap.* 1720?, *d.* 1759), army officer, was the second son of Sir John Prideaux, sixth baronet (1695–1766), of Netherton Hall, near Honiton, Devon, and his wife, Anne (*d.* 1767), the eldest daughter of John Vaughan, first Viscount Lisburne. He was probably the John Prideaux baptized at Sutcombe, Devon, on 21 September 1720. On 17 July 1739 he was appointed ensign in the 3rd foot guards (later the Scots Guards); he was adjutant of his battalion at Dettingen (27 July 1743), and became lieutenant-colonel of his regiment on 24 February 1748. On 24 November 1746, at St George's, Mayfair, Westminster, he married Elizabeth, the daughter of Colonel Edward Rolt and the sister of Sir Edward Baytum-Rolt, bt, of Spy Park, Wiltshire; they had three sons and two daughters. She was described by a nineteenth-century descendant as 'a worldly, heartless, extravagant woman' (*N&Q*, 8th ser., 9, 1896, 85) who played little part in her children's upbringing.

On 20 October 1758 Prideaux was appointed colonel of the 55th foot, in succession to George Augustus Howe, third Viscount Howe (1725?–1758), killed at Ticonderoga. In 1759, during the Seven Years' War, William Pitt, the secretary of state, instructed General Jeffrey Amherst (later Baron Amherst; 1717–1797), commander in America, that, while Wolfe attacked Quebec, attempts should be made to invade Canada via Ticonderoga and Crown Point, and that at the same time he should undertake any other operations to weaken the enemy without detriment to the main task of the expedition. Amherst decided to attempt the capture of Fort Niagara, and entrusted the task to Prideaux, then brigadier-general, who had just arrived, appointing Sir William Johnson (1715–1774) his second in

command. Prideaux was to ascend the Mohawk River with 5000 troops, regulars and New York provincials, together with Native Americans drawn from the Five Nations under Johnson, to leave a strong garrison at Fort Stanwix, the great portage, descend the Onondega, leaving part of his force under Colonel Frederick Haldimand (1718–1791) at Oswego, and to attack Niagara with the rest. Prideaux reached Oswego by the middle of June, rebuilt the fort, and on 1 July started for Niagara. Fort Niagara, on the site of a former post, was a strong modern fort, recently rebuilt by the French, commanded by Captain Pouchot, and garrisoned by part of the French regiment of Béarn. Prideaux arrived before it on 6 July 1759 and began siege operations. The British engineers were so incompetent— a highland officer called them 'fools and blockheads' (Parkman, 448)—that, to Prideaux's disgust, the first approaches were completely swept by the French fire and had to be constructed anew. On 19 July 1759 the batteries were ready. That morning Prideaux's force repelled a French vessel which attempted to land reinforcements, but in the afternoon Prideaux was struck on the head by a fragment of shell, which burst prematurely at the mouth of a British cohorn and instantly killed him. He was described by some writers as an unpopular officer. Colonel Eyre Massey (later first Baron Clarina; 1719–1804), 46th regiment, the next senior regular officer, waived any claim to command in favour of Sir William Johnson, to whom the fort surrendered on 24 July 1759.

Since his elder brother, Sanderson Prideaux, a lieutenant in Colonel Moreton's marines, had died at Cartagena, Spain, in 1741, Prideaux's elder son, John Wilmot Prideaux (1748–1826), became heir to the baronetcy, to which he succeeded, as seventh baronet, on his grandfather's death in August 1766; he was father (with his third wife) of the last two holders of the baronetcy, which became extinct in 1875 on the death of Sir Edward Prideaux, ninth baronet.

Prideaux had two daughters, Maria Constantia (*d.* in or before 1793) and Georgina Frances Anne, one of whom (although which is unknown) became an actress. She appeared first at Bath in October 1787, and played several times at the Haymarket or Drury Lane in London between 1788 and 1790, although never to any acclaim, and was discharged from the Drury Lane company in the 1791–2 season.　　　H. M. CHICHESTER, *rev.* ROGER T. STEARN

Sources Burke, *Peerage* (1871) · home office military entry books, PRO, HO 51 · F. Parkman, *Montcalm and Wolfe*, 2 vols. (1884); repr. (1984) · Fortescue, *Brit. army*, vol. 2 · J. Holland Rose and others, eds., *Canada and Newfoundland* (1930), vol. 6 of *The Cambridge history of the British empire* (1929–59) · J. Black, *Britain as a military power, 1688–1815* (1999) · C. B. Balfour, *The Scots guards* (1929) · Highfill, Burnim & Langhans, *BDA* · *N&Q*, 8th ser., 9 (1896), 85 · GEC, *Baronetage* · *IGI*

Prideaux, Matthias (*c*.1625–1646?). *See under* Prideaux, John (1578–1650).

Prideaux, William (1604/5–1660), diplomat, was the son of William Prideaux of Tavistock, Devon. On 13 December 1622 he matriculated at Exeter College, Oxford, aged seventeen, graduating BA on 25 November 1626. He then became a merchant involved in foreign trade, based in London and acquiring links with the Muscovy, Levant, and East India companies. After Charles I's execution Tsar Alexis restricted English traders in Russia to Archangel and threatened to expel them altogether, incited by royalist officers in Russian service who persuaded him not to recognize the Commonwealth. The Muscovy Company petitioned Cromwell in May 1654 to send an ambassador, and on 8 June his council ordered that 'some fit person' be sent (*CSP dom.*, *1654*, 202–3). The company selected Prideaux, and Cromwell entrusted him with an official letter justifying his assumption of power and enquiring reasons for the Russian attack on Poland.

Prideaux left Tilbury in July for Archangel, where his presence served to deter the authorities from harassing English traders. He secured permission for them to export all goods except contraband, and to trade upriver to Kholmogory. Unimpressed with the locals, he informed Thurloe that they were 'subtle and crafty but … very pusillanimous', superstitious, and addicted to sodomy (Thurloe, *State papers*, 2.607–8). When he arrived in Moscow on 5 February 1655 his attempts to obtain an audience with Alexis were hindered by his letter of accreditation not being properly addressed, but he was received on 16 February. As Cromwell was not a king the Russians refused to grant his representative royal honours, but Alexis condescended to refer to him as 'Vladitela, that is sole commander or director' (ibid., 3.255–7). Prideaux assured him that English power was undiminished, despite royalist claims, and astutely compared Cromwell's 'election' in place of an older dynasty with that of Alexis's father, Michael, in 1613. On 6 March he delivered Cromwell's complaint at the merchants' restrictions of movement to Chancellor Morozov, and queried motives for the Polish war. His determination on minor points, such as wearing a sword at audiences, impressed the Russians, and he received more respectful treatment at his second audience on 11 March, when Alexis even got up from his throne.

However, the Russians stalled on a treaty, and Prideaux blamed royalist intrigue and even suspected the loyalties of his interpreter, John Hebden. Minor slights and refusal of permission to travel home via the theatre of war (probably due to security) were followed by Morozov sending a list of reasons for the restrictions on movement, mostly vague, unprovable allegations of past malpractice by Englishmen. Complaining that the well-meaning young ruler had been corrupted by ministers, particularly his father-in-law, Miloslavsky, and Patriarch Nikon, and was 'much given to avarice, cruelty and self-wilfulness' (Thurloe, *State papers*, 3.711–14), Prideaux heard that Alexis had been informed of the recent royalist rising in England by English officers and would not sign a treaty with Cromwell until his hopes of Charles II's restoration had been ended. He had to leave without agreement, and noted when he reached Archangel and had Alexis's letter translated that it omitted Cromwell's full titles. The restrictions on English movement were lifted after his departure, but Alexis remained hostile and in 1657 refused to receive Cromwell's next ambassador, Richard Bradshawe.

Back in London, Prideaux's reputation as a reliable diplomat had risen and in January 1658 he unsuccessfully stood for election as the Levant Company's consul in the Peloponnese. He was however chosen on 26 April to succeed the East India Company's consul at Bantam, Quarles Browne, on the latter's recommendation. He soon pulled out of the mission, but was chosen instead on 15 October for the difficult, dangerous, and prestigious post of the company's first resident at Macao and ambassador to China, where only one company trading expedition had previously ventured. He had the confidence and the reputation to haggle over terms, but on friends' advice accepted £150 p.a., or £200 if a factory was set up at Macao. He duly requested an official commission and state letters to the governor and the 'King of China', but political uncertainty cancelled the mission. On 10 March 1659 he was appointed as the Levant Company's consul at Smyrna as 'a man of much prudence and of some repute as well' (*CSP Venice*, *1659–61*, 5), succeeding Spencer Bretton. He was criticized on his arrival by Sir Thomas Bendish, ambassador at Constantinople, for punishing illegal coiners without consulting him, and he died some time in 1660, unmarried, at Smyrna. A capable and adventurous diplomat trusted by three separate mercantile companies and given two important embassies to far-flung countries ruled by unpredictable autocrats, his qualities nearly made him the first English ambassador to visit both Russia and China.
TIMOTHY VENNING

Sources Thurloe, *State papers*, vols. 2–3 • *CSP dom.*, *1654*; *1657–60* • PRO, SP 25/121 [council of state committee bk] • PRO, SP 105/151 [Levant Company court bk] • *CSP Venice*, *1659–61* • E. B. Sainsbury, ed., *A calendar of the court minutes … of the East India Company*, [5]: *1655–1659* (1916) • Foster, *Alum. Oxon.* • C. H. Rigby, ed., *P. C. C. administrations*, *1655–1660* (1952) • A. C. Wood, *A history of the Levant Company* (1935)

Priest, Josias (*d.* 1734/5), dancer and boarding-school proprietor, was almost certainly a performer on the London stage from at least 1667, when Mr Priest danced a 'Tony', or fool, in act v of Dryden's comedy *Sir Martin Mar-All* and the end of the play was 'Crown'd with an Excellent Entry … by Mr. *Priest* and Madam *Davies*' (Downes, 62–3). John Downes, the theatre prompter, named 'Mr. Joseph Preist' as choreographer, with Luke Channell, for the spectacular 1673 production of *Macbeth*. When writing of the great dramatic operas of the early 1690s he credited 'Mr. Jo. Priest' with the dances for *King Arthur*, and then 'Mr. Priest' with those for *Dioclesian* and *The Fairy Queen*, seeing the dances as second in importance only to Henry Purcell's music. Thomas Bray's *Country Dances* (1699) includes a tune from act II of *The Fairy Queen*, headed 'An Entry by the late Mr. *Henry Purcell*, the Dance compos'd by Mr. *Josias Preist*', as well as dances from Purcell's last dramatic opera, *The Indian Queen* (1695), and the operatic version of Fletcher's *The Island Princess* (1699), created by 'Mr. *Preist*'. *The Second Book of Theatre Musick* (1699) tells us that 'Mr Prist' was the performer of the first of Bray's *Island Princess* dances, and it seems likely that he also performed the second, the dance for the Old Miser in the final masque. It was Priest's skill in 'Grotesque Dancing' that John Weaver remembered in

1712: 'Mr. *Joseph Priest* of *Chelsey*, I take to have been the greatest Master of this kind of *Dancing*, that has appear'd on our Stage' (Weaver, 166–7). In 1711 'Mr. Preist Sen., of Chelsea' subscribed to Edmund Pemberton's collection of notated dances and contributed his minuet for twelve ladies. Josias's son Thomas (*b*. 1671), who also lived in Chelsea, wrote four dance tunes for Bray's *Country Dances*.

In June 1669 a warrant had been issued to arrest Josiah Priest and others for teaching and performing music without a licence, and in 1675 Joseph Priest was paid £100 for work on dances for the court masque *Calisto*. It is likely, though not certain, that Josias, Josiah, and Joseph Priest were all the same person. The registers of St Mary-le-Bow record the baptism of Frances, daughter of Josiah Preist, in 1665 and the burial of Frances, daughter of Joseph Priest, a year later. The dancing-master husband of Frances (or Frank) Preist (*d*. 1733) was variously called Josias and Josiah in the baptismal registers of St Andrew's, Holborn, between 1668 and 1675. The organist of Bath Abbey was referred to as Joseph Priest and Josias Priest in two subscription lists in 1724 but his relationship to the dancer is unknown.

On 25 November 1680 the *London Gazette* announced: 'Josias Priest, Dancing Master, who kept a Boarding-School of Gentlewomen in *Leicester-fields*, is removed to the great School-House at *Chelsey*, that was Mr. *Portman's*'. This was Gorges House, where the violinist Jeffrey Bannister and the singer James Hart had been running a girls' school. *The Antiquities of Middlesex* (1705) described the 'large spacious House … in which for many Years past has been kept a famous Boarding School for young Ladies, by Mr. *Jonas Priest*' (Bowack, 13). Priest appears to have had twelve children before he moved to Chelsea, and seven more were baptized there between 1682 and 1693, where he is named as Joseph Priest in the registers. Early in May 1684 'Mrs Priest the Schoolmistress … had a little girl (one of her daughters) drowned in a Tub of Water' (Thorp, 202–4), presumably Susanna, who was buried on 12 May, aged two.

Priest is best known for having staged John Blow's *Venus and Adonis* in 1684 and Purcell's *Dido and Aeneas* in 1689, at his boarding-school in Chelsea. Both operas were performed by Priest's pupils, but the role of Adonis in Blow's opera was taken by 'Mr. Priest's daughter' (Luckett, 76), probably Katherine, baptized at St Mary-le-Bow in 1666. In May 1691 Mrs A. Buck, who was investigating girls' schools for a friend, expressed her disapproval: 'Preists att Little Chelsey was one which was much commended; but he hath lately had an Opera, which I'me sure hath done him a great injurey; & the Parents of the Childern not satisfied with so Publick a show' (Goldie, 392). By contrast when John Verney's niece Mary became a pupil at 'Mrs. Priest's' (Verney, 220) in 1683, aged eight, the family was pleased with the progress that she made there. She appeared in balls at the school and in *Venus and Adonis* (of which her affectionate uncle preserved the libretto), and, as an extra, learned to japan boxes. When Priest staged *Dido and Aeneas* his friend the playwright Thomas Durfey supplied the epilogue, which was 'Spoken by the Lady Dorothy Burk'

(Durfey, *New Poems*, 81). Durfey's successful comedy *Love for Money, or, The Boarding School*, performed in January 1691, was set in a Chelsea girls' school, with a sub-plot involving two hoydenish pupils who elope with the dancing-master and the singing-master. Some members of the audience hissed, 'especially the Dancing-Masters, and other Friends to the Boarding-Schools, who supposed themselves, and their Livelihood expos'd' (Gildon, 51). In his preface to the play Durfey denied that he had portrayed any particular school and was particularly indignant at rumours that he had accepted the Priests' hospitality the previous summer and then 'writ this Play ungratefully to expose 'em' (Durfey, *Love for Money*, preface).

Rate books show that the Priests' school had closed by January 1712, and Chelsea parish registers record the burials, at St Luke's, of Mrs Frank Priest on 20 April 1733 and of Mr Josias Priest on 3 January 1735.

OLIVE BALDWIN and THELMA WILSON

Sources J. Downes, *Roscius Anglicanus*, ed. J. Milhous and R. D. Hume, new edn (1987) · *LondG* (22–5 Nov 1680) · M. Goldie, 'The earliest notice of Purcell's *Dido and Aeneas*', *Early Music*, 20 (1992), 392–400 · R. Luckett, 'A new source for *Venus and Adonis*', *MT*, 130 (1989), 76–9 · J. Thorp, 'Dance in late 17th-century London: Priestly muddles', *Early music*, 26 (1998), 198–210 · M. M. Verney, *Memoirs of the Verney family*, 4 (1889) · T. Durfey, *Love for money, or, The boarding school* (1691) · T. Durfey, *New poems* (1690) · [C. Gildon], *The lives and characters of the English dramatick poets … first begun by Mr Langbain* [1699] · T. Bray, *Country dances* (1699) · J. Bowack, *The antiquities of Middlesex* (1705) · J. Weaver, *An essay towards an history of dancing* (1712) · P. Motteux, *The island princess* (1985), ser. C, vol. 2 of *Music for London entertainment* [with introduction by C. A. Price and R. D. Hume] · E. Pemberton, *An essay for the further improvement of dancing* (1711) · W. Van Lennep and others, eds., *The London stage, 1660–1800*, pt 1: *1660–1700* (1965) · E. Boswell, *The Restoration court stage (1660–1702): with a particular account of the production of 'Calisto'* (1932) · A. Ashbee, ed., *Records of English court music*, 1 (1986) · R. Neale, *A pocket companion for gentlemen and ladies* (1724), list of subscribers · W. Croft, *Musica sacra* (1724), list of subscribers · D. Falconer, 'The two Mr Priests of Chelsea', *MT*, 128 (1987), 263 · parish register, Chelsea, St Luke, 3 Jan 1735 [burial] · parish register, Chelsea, St Luke, 20 April 1733 [burial: Frank Priest, wife]

Priestland, Gerald Francis (1927–1991), radio and television broadcaster and writer, was born on 26 February 1927 at Meadow Cottage, Berkhamsted, Hertfordshire, the son of Francis Edwin Priestland (1884–*c*.1962), sales manager for Cooper, McDougall, and Robertson, agricultural chemists, of Berkhamsted, and his wife, Ellen Julianna (Nelly), *née* Renny (1900–1964). He was educated at Charterhouse School, from where he won an open history scholarship to New College, Oxford. There he read politics, philosophy, and economics, graduated with a second-class degree in 1948, and met his future wife, (Helen) Sylvia Rhodes (*b*. 1924/5), daughter of Edward Hugh Rhodes and a student at the Ruskin School of Drawing. They married on 14 May 1949, and had two sons and two daughters.

In 1948 Priestland became one of the first six graduates recruited for training by the BBC news division. His career in the news division began with six months as an obituarist and then five years as a sub-editor. He then had a few months' experience working under Thomas Cadett in

Paris before being posted in south-east Asia from 1954 to 1958. Then followed postings in the United States (1958–61 and 1965–9) and in the Middle East (1961–5). During his second period in Washington, Priestland interviewed Martin Luther King shortly before the civil rights leader's assassination. From Washington he also covered the Vietnam War. Priestland and his wife, Sylvia, tried hard, and succeeded, in combining his postings with family life for their four children, but in the autumn of 1969 they decided that the children should finish their schooling at home. Priestland persuaded Desmond Taylor, who was then editing BBC television news, to let him provide for the main evening bulletin a short commentary on the lines of the text provided at that time by Eric Sevareid for the CBS evening news in the United States. In the autumn of 1969 Priestland experimented with this format. Charles Curran, the director-general of the BBC, complimented him on the result, but pressure from the television news managers was too strong, and the experiment was discontinued at the end of that year. At the beginning of 1970 he became the anchorman of *Newsdesk* on BBC Radio 4, part of the attempt made between 1970 and 1974 to revive that station's fortunes. He also presented radio series such as *Analysis*.

In the mid-1970s Priestland suffered a nervous breakdown, which he attributed to the violence he had seen while covering the Vietnam War as well as to the race riots he had witnessed during the civil rights campaigns in the American south. He recovered with the help of his wife, Sylvia, by now a psychiatrist, but also through discovering within himself a belief in the love of God and the reality of forgiveness. He had already developed an engagement with religion at school, where he was known as the school atheist and had thought it important 'to emphasize the meaninglessness and boredom of divine worship, which I did by refusing to bow my head during the Creed and by annotating any hymnbook with scornful comments during the sermon' (Priestland, 52). Having been a nominal Anglican for most of his life, he became a Quaker, partly because of his friendship with Gerard Hoffnung, in 1976. In 1977 he was appointed the BBC's religious affairs correspondent in succession to Douglas Brown. Here he was in his element in bringing religious ideas to a mass audience. *Priestland's Progress*, which he described as a plain man's guide to religious faith, was heard by millions and it attracted a postbag of 20,000 letters, an unprecedented response for a religious programme. At the end of 1981 listeners to Radio 4's early morning *Today* programme voted him ahead of the pope and second only to the prince of Wales as their man of the year. His Saturday morning talks, *Yours Faithfully*, on the same programme brought him more letters in a week, he said, than he used to receive in Washington in a year. After retiring from the BBC in 1982 Priestland continued to present television series on TV South—*Priestland Right and Wrong*—and a weekly spot on Terry Wogan's Radio 2 show, as well as continuing to write books mainly concerned with the exposition of a religious view of life. He died at the Royal Free Hospital, Camden, London, on 20 June 1991, after suffering a stroke while returning from a shopping trip. His wife, two daughters, and two sons survived him.

GEORGE WEDELL

Sources *The Times* (22 June 1991) · *The Independent* (22 June 1991) · G. Priestland, *Something understood* (1986) · private information (2004) [Dr M. Bond] · *WWW*, 1991–5 · b. cert. · m. cert. · d. cert. **Archives** FILM BFI NFTVA, *Time to talk*, Channel 4, 1 Aug 1987 · BFI NFTVA, current affairs footage | SOUND BL NSA, current affairs recording · BL NSA, performance recordings **Likenesses** photograph, repro. in *The Times* · photograph, repro. in *The Independent*

Priestley, (Jessie) Jacquetta. *See* Hawkes, (Jessie) Jacquetta (1910–1996).

Priestley, John Boynton (1894–1984), writer, was born on 13 September 1894 at 34 Mannheim Road, Bradford, Yorkshire, the only child of Jonathan Priestley (1868–1924), schoolmaster, and his first wife, Emma Holt (1865–1896). His father was one of several children of an illiterate mill worker, while little is known of his mother except that she might have been a mill worker, and she had a brother, Tom, who kept one of Bradford's most popular public houses. She died when Priestley was two years old, and in 1898 his father married Amy Fletcher, whom Priestley described as a loving stepmother; his stepsister, Winifred, was born in 1903.

Education and war service The young John Priestley (the middle name, Boynton, was added mysteriously in later years) was educated at Whetley Lane primary school, Belle Vue preparatory school, and then, on a scholarship, Belle Vue high school. His father wanted him to go on to college but he left at sixteen, complaining that school had become tedious, and so went to work as a clerk for Helm & Co., a wool firm with offices in Bradford's Swan Arcade. It was during this period that he first began writing for publication and had his own column in the Labour Party weekly, the *Bradford Pioneer*, under the title 'Round the hearth'. Later he described his pontificating as sounding as if it had been written by 'a retired clergyman about 150 years old' (Priestley, *Margin Released*, 70). He was to return to that period throughout his life, his nostalgic writings recalling a golden age before the First World War.

In later life Priestley was continually referred to as Jolly Jack Priestley, the somewhat rotund, bluff, pipe-smoking, archetypal Yorkshireman, but he was far more complex than that, and the roots of the dark side of his character go back to his service on the western front in the First World War. He enlisted as a private soldier in the duke of Wellington's West Riding regiment early in September 1914, and went through almost the entire war in the trenches, being wounded twice. He finally accepted a commission in 1917. Unlike many of his contemporaries, such as Robert Graves, he did not write of his experiences until nearly half a century later, but his letters home make bitter reading, not least his last to his stepmother, which enclosed dried flowers found 'growing out of dead men'. In the book of essays *Margin Released* (1962) he wrote:

> I felt as indeed I still feel today and must go on feeling until I die, the open wound, never to be healed, of my generation's fate, the best sorted out and then slaughtered, not by hard necessity but by huge, murderous public folly. (Priestley, *Margin Released*, 136)

After Priestley's death his fellow Bradfordian John Braine said of him: 'I think the real Jack Priestley died in August 1914 somewhere on the Western Front ... and what all those millions and millions of words were really written for was so that he wouldn't remember the 1914–1918 War' (Braine).

After the war Priestley took advantage of a grant enabling former officers to go to university, and in 1919 he went up to Trinity Hall, Cambridge, to read English and history, later switching to history and political science. Like many of his contemporaries who had fought in the war, he was unhappy at Cambridge, surrounded by 'immature' eighteen-year-olds. He also felt self-conscious about his accent and background. However, he made one lifelong friend in the poet Edward Davison, a friendship which survived Davison's permanent move to the USA, for the two wrote constantly to each other until Davison's death in 1970.

Marriage and affairs On 29 June 1921, eight days after acquiring his BA, Priestley married Pat Emily Tempest (1896–1925), a librarian and his long-time girlfriend, in the Westgate Baptist Chapel, Bradford, where his father was a lay preacher. He remained at Cambridge for a further year after his marriage. During this time his first two books, *Brief Diversions* (1922) and *Papers from Lilliput* (1922), were published; the first is a collection of epigrams, anecdotes, and stories, the second a series of essays on personalities past and present. In 1922, after turning down a teaching post, he moved to London, determined to succeed as a writer, and he and his wife set up home in Walham Green. Here he worked as a freelance for, among others, J. C. Squire's *London Mercury*, *The Bookman*, *The Spectator*, the *Saturday Review*, and the *Times Literary Supplement*, and as a reader for the Bodley Head, as a result of which he found himself mixing for the first time in the literary circles of the day.

In March 1923 Priestley's wife gave birth to their first child, Barbara, to be followed prematurely in April 1924 by a second daughter, Sylvia, when it was discovered that Pat was suffering from the cancer which was to prove terminal. Priestley then suffered another blow, with the death of his father in June 1924. Priestley moved his family to Buckinghamshire, where he struggled to survive and pay the medical bills by writing freelance pieces for a variety of publications. He also published several books, the most notable being *English Comic Characters* (1924) and a biography, *George Meredith* (1926). The latter, he said, was written because he was 'so deep in despair I didn't know what to do with myself' (J. Cook, *Priestley*, 1997).

During this period Priestley met Jane Mary Wyndham Lewis, *née* Holland (1892–1984), a graduate of Bedford College, London, who was to become his second wife. Her marriage to the journalist Bevan Wyndham Lewis was not

a success, and was to end in divorce in 1926; she and Priestley began an affair which resulted in the birth of a daughter, Mary, in March 1925. Priestley had a number of affairs and in later life in *Over the Long High Wall* (1972), he described himself as 'lusty' and as one who has 'enjoyed the physical relations with the sexes ... without the feelings of guilt which seems to disturb some of my distinguished colleagues' (Priestley, *Long High Wall*, 13). In autumn 1925 Priestley moved back to London to be near Guy's Hospital, and on 25 November 1925 Pat Priestley died. On 9 September 1926 Priestley married Jane Wyndham Lewis, combining the two families, for as well as Mary, Jane had also had a daughter, Angela, with Wyndham Lewis. Priestley and Jane were to have two more children, Rachel (*b.* 1930) and Thomas (*b.* 1932). The marriage, in spite of Priestley's infidelities, was to last nearly thirty years before it ended in divorce, although it nearly foundered in 1931 when he had a serious relationship with the actress Peggy Ashcroft.

Literary career Priestley's literary output between 1926 and 1929 was immense and covered almost every field: collections of essays, including *Open House* (1927) and *The Balconinny* (1929); a biography of Thomas Love Peacock (1927); literary criticism, *The English Novel* (1927) and *English Humour* (1929); and his first attempts at fiction, *Adam in Moonshine* (1927), and a gothic novel, *Benighted* (1928). During this period A. D. Peters, who had been at Cambridge with Priestley, became first his agent and later his business partner.

Shortly before Pat's death Priestley formed a deep and lasting friendship with the best-selling novelist Hugh Walpole. To no other person was he able to reveal his feelings and insecurities as he did in his letters to Walpole and Walpole reciprocated with tremendous warmth, affection, and constant support. In 1927 Walpole suggested they write the joint novel *Farthing Hall* (1929). Because of his own popularity Walpole could command a substantial advance, and this he gave entirely to Priestley, thus enabling him to write the book that was to make his name and fortune. *The Good Companions*, a picaresque novel 250,000 words long, was completed in March 1929, and published in July. Sales started slowly, but by Christmas the publishers Heinemann had to use taxis to rush copies to bookshops, so great was the demand; it became one of the best-sellers of the century. He followed this with what some consider his best novel, *Angel Pavement* (1930).

Although Priestley was to continue writing almost until the end of his life, the 1930s were particularly fruitful, with lesser-known novels such as *Faraway* (1932) and *The Doomsday Men* (1937); the autobiographical essays printed in *Rain upon Godshill* (1939); his biography *Charles Dickens* (1936); and the remarkable book of social commentary, *English Journey* (1933). In *English Journey* he travelled from the south to the north of England, brilliantly describing in bitter prose the poverty and unemployment of the time. Nothing becomes Priestley's humanity and social conscience better than his comments on the horrors of Rusty

Lane, West Bromwich, when he suggests that future economic conferences in Britain should be held not 'in Mayfair in the season but West Bromwich out of season. Out of all seasons except the winter of our discontent' (Priestley, *English Journey*, 115).

Priestley had always had a love affair with the theatre, and during the thirties he wrote fourteen plays, the best-known of which are *Dangerous Corner* (1932), *Eden End* (1934), *I Have Been Here Before* (1937), *Time and the Conways* (1937), *When we are Married* (1938), and *Johnson over Jordan* (1939). He put his own money into *Dangerous Corner* when his backers took fright, and it was a tremendous success. Later he described it as 'merely an ingenious box of tricks' (Priestley, *Margin Released*, 199), but, like the classic comedy *When we are Married*, it has rarely been out of repertory since. *I Have Been Here Before* and *Time and the Conways* show his growing fascination with J. W. Dunne and P. D. Ouspensky's theories of time, while *Johnson over Jordan* was a brave experimental piece of work starring his friend Ralph Richardson, with music by the young Benjamin Britten and design by Gordon Craig.

Throughout the thirties Priestley was a regular visitor to the United States, spending family holidays in Arizona, going on lecture tours, and writing film scripts, most of which are unknown, except for *Sing as we Go*, a vehicle for the Lancashire entertainer Gracie Fields. As a result he numbered among his friends most of the great names of the Hollywood of the day, including Charlie Chaplin and Groucho Marx.

At the outbreak of the Second World War, Priestley approached the BBC and asked if he could do some broadcasting. The result was the famous *Postscripts*, broadcast on Sunday nights after the 9 p.m. news. The series ran from June to October 1940, and quickly became not only a national but an international institution, his deep, resonant voice proving compulsive listening. The segments varied from the comic to the deeply serious, the latter including a reminder to listeners of what had happened to the men of the First World War who had returned from the trenches only to be faced with unemployment and poverty, and demanding that it did not happen again. A critical minority, led by the MP Brendan Bracken and a section of the media, demanded that the broadcasts be stopped on political grounds; although letters were running 300:1 in Priestley's favour, the BBC dropped him, possibly on the orders of Winston Churchill. During the war he also wrote several topical novels, a number of information booklets such as *Britain at War* (1942), and three plays, the best-known of which is *They Came to a City* (1943).

Later work and assessment Although never a member of a political party, in 1945 Priestley stood as an independent candidate for the Cambridge University seat on a broadly socialist agenda, but was defeated. This was probably just as well, as he could never have borne the life of a backbencher. In 1946 he wrote one of his best-known plays, *An Inspector Calls* and, unable to find a venue for it in London, sent it to his Russian translator, as a result of which it had its première later that year jointly in Moscow and Leningrad. In 1949 it was made into a film starring Alistair Sim.

While Priestley's plays have always been popular outside London and abroad, it became fashionable over the years to consider them too old-fashioned for metropolitan audiences, a view which took a severe knock when Stephen Daldry's production of the play for the National Theatre in the 1990s became a critical and box-office smash hit not only in London, but in major cities all over the world. Over the years he wrote several more plays, including *The Linden Tree* (1947) and, with Iris Murdoch, *A Severed Head* (1963), but one feels that the main impetus had gone.

Priestley was to write only five more novels, of which by far the best are *Bright Day* (1946) and *Lost Empires* (1965), both with autobiographical overtones, although his own favourite was the two-volume *The Image Makers* (1968). However, he continued writing non-fiction right up until 1977, his most remarkable achievement being a *tour de force*, *Literature and Western Man* in 1960.

Priestley never enjoyed belonging to any movement or society, and was notorious for resigning from them when he had joined, but he was persuaded to represent literature and the arts at the setting up of UNESCO (United Nations Educational, Scientific and Cultural Organization) in Mexico at the end of 1947. At a preliminary meeting held in Paris he met Jacquetta *Hawkes, née Hopkins (1910–1996), archaeologist and writer, the wife of the archaeologist Professor Christopher Hawkes. They began an affair which was to last until both were divorced. The Hawkes divorce was contested, and the judge's subsequent scathing remarks about Priestley made headlines in the national press. On 23 July 1953 he married Jacquetta, and settled into what he and his friends described as an idyllic marriage. He also moved from the Isle of Wight, where he had been living since before the war, to Kissing Tree House on the outskirts of Stratford upon Avon. The two wrote one memorable book together, *Journey Down a Rainbow* (1955).

Priestley's critical essays continued to range over a host of subjects and on occasion could be prophetic, such as his coining of the word 'admass' in *Journey Down a Rainbow* to describe what he feared would become a rampantly consumerist society. For many years he had contributed to the *New Statesman*, and in 1957 he wrote an article which led directly to the founding of the Campaign for Nuclear Disarmament, with which his name will always be associated. He never sought honours and over the years turned down a knighthood and two offers of peerages, but was proud to accept the Order of Merit when it was offered to him in 1977.

J. B. Priestley was a big man in every respect, in bulk, in his prodigious appetite for work, and in his generosity of spirit. He was a man of many loves; he loved women and women loved him, not only his wives and those with whom he had affairs, but also those who became his friends. He loved the old music-hall, theatre, music, particularly the great German composers (he was a good pianist), classic literature, and the English countryside, especially the Yorkshire dales. In his later years he also became an accomplished painter in watercolour and gouache. He was a confirmed grumbler, could be extremely difficult when the mood took him, and never suffered fools gladly, even when it might have been politic to do so. The darker side of his nature never left him, however, and in later years he increasingly fell prey to depression.

Priestley suffered throughout his life from the metropolitan literary attitude towards writers from the provinces in general, and towards those who are successful in particular. The fact that he had written an international best-seller often led to unfair disparagement. 'I was outside the fashionable literary movement even before I began', he said, which was true (Priestley, *Margin Released*, 188). He also often said that he never claimed genius but 'had a hell of a lot of talent'. Paul Johnson rightly described him as 'a shrewd, thoughtful, subtle, and sceptical seer, a great craftsman' (*DNB*); John Atkins, in his 1981 book on Priestley's work, dubbed him 'the last of the sages'. Having travelled widely, Priestley spent the last years of his life in Warwickshire. He remained forever sceptical of Christianity but wrote that he hoped that at death the human spirit was not entirely extinguished, 'snuffed out like guttering candles' (*Over the Long High Wall*, 119). He died of pneumonia at Kissing Tree House on 13 August 1984, surrounded by his family, and his ashes were buried in Hubberholme church, at the head of Wharfedale in Yorkshire. His memorial in the church reads: 'Remember J. B. Priestley O.M. 1894–1984. He loved the Dales and found "Hubberholme one of the smallest and pleasantest places in the World"'.   JUDITH COOK

Sources priv. coll., family papers · Davison–Priestley correspondence, Yale U. · letters, Ransom HRC · J. B. Priestley, *Margin released: a writer's reminiscences and reflections* (1962) · J. B. Priestley, *English journey* (1933) · J. B. Priestley, *Rain upon Godshill: a further chapter of autobiography* (1939) · J. B. Priestley, *Over the long high wall: some reflections and speculations on life, death and time* (1972) · J. B. Priestley, *Instead of the trees: a final chapter of autobiography* (1977) · J. Braine, *J. B. Priestley: a workmanlike man*, BBC, IWM SA [sound recording] · personal knowledge (2004) · private information (2004) [family]
Archives Ransom HRC, corresp. and literary papers · University of Bradford, J. B. Priestley Library, corresp. and literary papers | Bodl. Oxf., letters to Jack W. Lambert, with Lambert's notes · Ransom HRC, corresp. with John Lane · U. Lpool, letters to Olaf Stapledon · U. Reading, letters to Bodley Head Ltd · U. Sussex, letters to Kingsley Martin · U. Sussex, corresp. with *New Statesman* magazine · Yale U., corresp. with Davison | SOUND IWM SA
Likenesses H. Coster, photograph, 1926, NPG · J. Kramer, charcoal drawing, 1930, NPG · P. Evans, ink drawing, 1930–34, NPG · J. Epstein, bronze bust, 1931, U. Texas · J. P. Barraclough, oils, 1932, Bradford City Art Gallery · W. Lewis, pencil drawing, 1932, Graves Art Gallery, Sheffield · photographs, c.1932–1979, Hult. Arch. · H. Coster, photograph, 1937, NPG · E. Kapp, drawing, 1947, Barber Institute of Fine Arts, Birmingham · M. Lambert, bronze cast of bust, 1948, NPG · M. Lambert, bronze head, 1948, U. Texas · Y. Karsh, bromide print, 1949, NPG · H. Carr, oils, 1950, U. Texas · H. Coster, photograph, 1950–59, NPG · M. Gerson, photograph, 1960, NPG · G. Argent, photograph, 1968, NPG · M. Noakes, oils, 1970, Bradford City Art Gallery · M. Noakes, oils, 1970, NPG · D. Hockney, ink drawing, 1973, Bradford City Art Gallery · A. Newman, bromide print, 1978, NPG · D. Low, caricatures, pencil sketches, NPG · Snowdon, photograph, Camerapress · F. Topolski, portrait, NPG
Wealth at death £117,501: probate, 7 Dec 1984, *CGPLA Eng. & Wales* · £113,570: family papers

Priestley, Joseph (1733–1804), theologian and natural philosopher, was born on 13 March 1733 at Birstall Fieldhead, West Riding of Yorkshire, about 6 miles south-west of Leeds. He was the first of six children of Jonas Priestley (1700–1779), cloth dresser, and his first wife, Mary (*d.* 1739), daughter of Joseph Swift, farmer and maltster of Shafton near Wakefield. Priestley was a major figure of the British Enlightenment and a notable polymath, and his publications number, in first editions, more than 150 books, pamphlets, and papers in journals. An early nineteenth-century edition of his collected works, minus the science, filled twenty-six octavo volumes and the science would have added at least five more. Remembered today primarily for his isolation and identification of seven gases, including oxygen, in his own day he was known also as a vigorous advocate of unitarianism and of liberal reform of government, education, and theology.

Early life and education, 1733–1755 Priestley's independence of thought and authority was a partial consequence of virtual estrangement from his family. His 'mother having children so fast', as he says in his memoirs, Joseph was taken from home to live with his maternal grandfather and there he was to stay, 'with little interruption till my mother's death'. Even then he was not to live long at the family home, for his father remarried in 1741 and Joseph was sent to the father's older sister and her husband, Sarah and John Keighley, at Old Hall, Heckmondwike, about 3 miles from Fieldhead. The Keighleys were childless, and possessors of considerable property. When John Keighley died in 1745 young Joseph became Sarah's presumptive heir. Though Old Hall and the Independent chapel of Heckmondwike provided a centre for Priestley family social life, Joseph was already on a path diverging from that of his cloth-working family.

Sarah Keighley, impressed with the intelligence of her ward, determined that he should be educated to become a dissenting minister. He learned to read and write probably at a local dame-school, but was then sent to Batley grammar school, where he learned Latin and some Greek, and began his facility in shorthand—Peter Annet's, for whom he wrote some commendatory verses published in an edition of Annet's *Expeditious Penmanship* (c.1750). From 1746 to 1749 he went to a small school kept by John Kirkby, minister at Heckmondwike Upper Chapel, where he began his study of Hebrew and (probably from a polyglot Bible) the rudiments of Chaldee, Syriac, and Arabic. When, at sixteen, it was thought he might have to go to Lisbon for his health, he taught himself French and High Dutch (German) for service in a counting house. Health recovered, he resumed his plan to become a minister and continued his studies independently with the occasional aid of George Haggerstone, a former student of Colin Maclaurin and Calvinist minister of nearby Hopton.

Some thirty-five years later, when he commenced writing his memoirs, Priestley cited only three books, Isaac Watts's *Logic*, John Locke's *Essay Concerning Human Understanding*, and W. James 'sGravesande's *Mathematical Elements of Natural Philosophy*, as those he read during this period of self-education. His career suggests that they

Joseph Priestley (1733–1804), by or after Ellen Sharples [original, c.1797]

were primarily influential for their treatment of language, of the nature of history, and of Sir Isaac Newton's 'mechanical philosophy'. Together with his earlier studies, his learning from these works was sufficient to excuse him from the first and most of the second year of the curriculum of his dissenting academy.

As an Independent it was not possible for Joseph to go to Oxford or Cambridge, while the alternatives of Scotland or the continent were excluded by expense. As the eighteenth-century English universities were in the doldrums, certain of the academies established by English dissenters for the education of their ministers and sons could be eminently worthy competitors. That initially selected for Priestley, Zephaniah Marryat's in Stepney, was not one of these, but Joseph, with the support of John Kirkby, refused to go there. And, in any event, he could not have done so. The extended Priestley family in Birstall parish, father, stepmother, aunts, uncles, sisters, brothers, cousins, were all fervent dissenting Calvinists. Joseph's memoirs report the importance of religion in family activities. His mother, 'the little time I was at home', taught him the shorter Westminster catechism; he could repeat all its 107 questions and answers 'without missing a word' by the time he was four. There were family prayers, morning and evening, at Fieldhead and Heckmondwike. Priestley led those at Old Hall when he became seventeen. He attended weekly prayer meetings, attended chapel twice each Sunday, committing the sermons to memory and writing them down at home. But his serious illness, at sixteen, had brought on a religious crisis. Thinking he might die, he lived months in a state of terror, for he could not persuade himself that he had experienced the 'new birth', that religious experience produced by the immediate agency of the spirit of God he had been taught was necessary for his salvation. Fortunately Sarah Keighley entertained the candidates to succeed the superannuated Kirkby as guests at Old Hall and some of these were Baxterians, or even Arminians, and did not believe in the necessity of a new birth. They eased Priestley's mind and even persuaded him that the sin of Adam had not condemned all mankind forever to the wrath of God. A consequence of this liberation, however, was his rejection by the elders when he applied for membership of Heckmondwike Upper Chapel. And without the recommendation of his church he could not attend Marryat's academy, even had he wanted to. His family was forced to choose another.

Priestley's stepmother had been housekeeper for Philip Doddridge, and she and Kirkby recommended his academy at Northampton. Doddridge died in 1751, but his academy was moved to Daventry under the auspices of Caleb Ashworth, a Priestley family connection, and Joseph was sent there, in September 1752, one of the earliest to enrol in the new academy. Daventry Academy continued the liberal practices that had earned Northampton its reputation as one of the finest of the dissenting academies. Priestley was happy there in its spirit of intellectual freedom and though he was later (somewhat unfairly) critical of its curriculum, he was solidly grounded in the classical languages, ancient history, and biblical studies. There he was also schooled in the classics of English literature and in rhetoric and sermon making, though he never quite lost his Yorkshire accent nor his tendency to stammer. He also studied mathematics, anatomy, medical chemistry in the work of Herman Boerhaave, and Newtonian natural philosophy, including the dynamic particle matter theory of John Rowning and the physico-theologians.

Priestley was introduced to metaphysics in a set of lectures by Doddridge, later published as *A Course of Lectures on the Principal Subjects in Pneumatology, Ethics, and Divinity* (1763). Doddridge's *Lectures* contained references to many of the early eighteenth-century religious and philosophical controversialists, including the Cambridge Platonists and Samuel Clarke, Anthony Collins, and John Toland. Most important, it referred Priestley to the *Observations on Man* (1740) by David Hartley, which was to be of enormous influence throughout Joseph's life. Doddridge's teaching practices, begun at Northampton and continued at Daventry and other major dissenting academies, involved the study and comparison of opposing views before reaching a final conclusion. This introduced Priestley to the dialectic process of obtaining truth which made him one of the most contentious theologians of eighteenth-century England, for he came to believe that truth was always ultimately to emerge from the conflict of contending ideas.

Theological debate at Daventry also persuaded Joseph to

become an Arian. This partial denial of the doctrine of the Trinity completed the break with his family, for while Joseph was adopting the liberal radical adjustment of eighteenth-century dissent, his family had adopted the conservative evangelical. During the process of finding a new minister for Heckmondwike Chapel they had become evangelical Calvinist Methodists. Timothy *Priestley, Joseph's brother, became a minister in the Countess of Huntingdon's Connexion and it was he who engineered Priestley's disownment, revealing to Sarah Keighley the liberal direction of Joseph's theology. She eventually transferred her financial support to the building of a new chapel at Heckmondwike. From this time, though there were occasional references to family (including, oddly enough, Timothy), Priestley essentially lived without association with the Fieldhead Priestleys or their Leeds and London relations.

Needham Market and Nantwich, 1755–1761 Upon graduation from Daventry Academy in 1755 Priestley accepted the call to assist the ageing minister of the dissenting chapel of Needham Market, Suffolk. Although he had preached at Needham and been interviewed by the congregation, his appointment there was a mistake. The senior minister, the Revd John Meadows, resented his coming, neither his stammer nor his Yorkshire accent was welcome, and no one seemed aware, initially, that he was an Arian. The congregation was poor and Priestley could not qualify for assistance from the Independent fund established to promote the denomination's cause, while the allowance his aunt had promised him should he become a minister was not now forthcoming. Without the aid of Andrew Kippis and George Benson, London ministers with access to various charitable funds, he might have suffered severely and, as it was, the stress increased his stammer, his congregation dwindled, and no one enrolled in the school that he proposed to open.

Rejected by the local dissenting community and in desperate material circumstances, Joseph maintained his spirits by referring to David Hartley's determinism—a wise providence disposed all things for the best—and by concentrating on theological studies. Besides writing a sermon a week, he produced a treatise, *The Scriptural Doctrine of Remission*, which challenged the orthodox view of atonement by an analysis of relevant texts in the Old and New testaments, to be understood in the cultural and historical context in which they were written. This treatise, published in 1761 with the encouragement of Samuel Clark, his former tutor at Daventry and by Caleb Fleming and Nathaniel Lardner, London leaders of liberal dissenting thought, was Priestley's first use of a method of biblical analysis which was to be taken up in the nineteenth century as 'the higher criticism'.

It was clear to Priestley's friends that his position at Needham Market was untenable. Benson, Kippis, and Samuel Clark recommended Priestley for a position as tutor of languages and *belles-lettres* at the newly opening (1757–8) dissenting academy at Warrington, Lancashire, but the trustees were apprehensive about his youth and the report of a 'hesitation' in his manner of speaking.

They chose, instead, John Aikin, former pupil and assistant of Doddridge and tutor at Kibworth Academy. Thomas Haynes, a distant relation of Priestley's mother, then arranged an appointment for him as minister to the dissenting chapel at Nantwich, Cheshire, where he moved in September 1758.

Priestley's congregation at Nantwich was no larger than that at Needham, but was less obsessed with Priestley's heterodoxies; members were from the same midlands dialect region as his West Riding accent, and sufficiently sympathetic to his stammer as to allow him to learn its control. They also encouraged him to open a school in a building opposite the chapel yard. The school was very successful and lasted, with various vicissitudes, through at least four succeeding ministers and until 1846. Priestley taught both boys and girls (in a separate room) for three years. He taught Latin and some Greek, English grammar, geography, natural and civil history, some mathematics, and natural philosophy, for which he purchased apparatus—an air-pump and electrical machine, among others—that his older pupils operated.

Warrington, 1761–1767 The success of his school at Nantwich prompted the trustees of Warrington Academy to offer Priestley the tutorship in languages and *belles-lettres* vacated when Aikin was transferred to that in divinity. He accepted the offer, moved to Warrington in September 1761, and immediately fitted happily into the academic community. He made friends with other academy faculty, soon became deputy to John Seddon, resident agent of the academy's committee of managers, was a member of the governors of Warrington's subscription library, and, in May 1762, moved into a new house provided by the trustees. Later in May he was ordained minister at the Warrington Provincial Meeting of the ministers of the county of Lancaster and on 23 June he married Mary Wilkinson (1743–1796), daughter of ironmaster Isaac *Wilkinson, sister of John *Wilkinson and of William *Wilkinson, who had been one of Priestley's students at Nantwich and who followed him to Warrington. Their first child, a daughter, Sarah, was born in April 1763.

At the academy Priestley gave his immediate attention to the languages and *belles-lettres* for which he had been employed. He taught the classical languages and antiquities, French, and English grammar and composition for which he used the text he had prepared for his Nantwich students. Printed and published in Warrington in 1761, *The Rudiments of English Grammar* and a companion work, *A Course of Lectures on the Theory of Language and Universal Grammar*, printed in 1762, had a long and influential history. The *Rudiments* went through nine English editions and the lectures, though not published, were distributed for use in other dissenting academies. Together these books have earned Priestley the reputation as a major grammarian of his time. His insistence that usage was the only viable standard for correct English and his detailed descriptions of the structure and vocabulary of his day are noted in most modern histories of the English language. His *Course of Lectures on Oratory and Criticism* (1777) has also won attention from modern students of rhetorical theory.

Not himself a gifted speaker, he avoided the subject of elocution, concentrating instead on the other offices of rhetorical theory. There his use of Hartleyan associationism led him to a psychological rationale for topical analysis and for aesthetic taste. *Oratory and Criticism* was less generally influential than the *Rudiments*, as the delay in its publication let George Campbell's *Philosophy of Rhetoric* take precedence in basing rhetoric on human nature, but it is still regarded as one of the classics of modern rhetoric.

Priestley's greatest contribution in making Warrington the most notable of dissenting academies was, however, in his restructuring of its curriculum. In his *Essay on a Course of Liberal Education* (1765) he argued that the standard course of studies had been designed for pupils entering the learned professions. Most of the students at Warrington and other dissenting academies were intended, instead, for civil, active, and commercial life. A different plan should be adopted and that plan, outlined in the *Essay* and later developed in his *Miscellaneous Observations Relating to Education* (1778), showed Priestley as an innovative educational philosopher. Probably the most important of his innovations was the minimizing of language study, except for English, and an emphasis on that of natural history, natural philosophy, and modern history. He had a broad conception of history as involving the social, cultural, and economic aspects of a society as well as its government and laws. A syllabus of his lectures on history was printed in 1765, but the *Lectures on History and General Policy* were not to be published until 1788.

To supplement his history teaching Priestley prepared and had published two aids to study: a *Chart of Biography* (1765) and a *New Chart of History* (1769) with accompanying *Descriptions*. These graphic time line representations of the span of life of major historical figures or of empires were popular for the rest of the century in England and the United States, and the *Descriptions*, at least, went through several editions. The time line form of biography was adopted, with acknowledgement to Priestley as late as 1853, by J. C. Pogendorff and that of history by Francis Baily in 1813. More important to Priestley the forthcoming publication of the *Chart of Biography* was instrumental in his being awarded the LLD degree of Edinburgh University on 4 December 1764 and the *Chart* is the only publication explicitly cited in his certificate for fellowship in the Royal Society of London.

Although Priestley's interests in science had been growing since his days at Daventry, he had little opportunity of exploring them before going to Warrington and there, because John Holt was tutor in mathematics and natural philosophy, he was, at first, confined to lecturing in anatomy and aiding in the organization of some lectures in chemistry by Matthew Turner. Examples drawn from the sciences in his *Oratory and Criticism* and in the *Description* of the *Chart of Biography* show that he had not lost interest and when, in 1765, he could finally find some time, he commenced writing a didactic history of electricity. Associationist theory maintained that history and geometry were the best approaches to teaching and he could prevail on Seddon to introduce him to John Canton and, through

Canton, to Benjamin Franklin, then the foremost authority on electricity in Britain. After going to London he obtained the assistance of Canton, Franklin, William Watson, and Richard Price for his enterprise. They also became his friends and supported his bid to become a fellow of the Royal Society, even before his history was published. After 12 June 1766 Priestley could, and usually would, style himself J. Priestley LLD FRS.

When published, in 1767, *The History and Present State of Electricity, with Original Experiments* was to be one of Priestley's most successful non-theological publications. The historical part was based, whenever possible, on primary sources and the 'present state' on papers in scientific journals and on interviews with his new London friends. The friends also insisted that he perform the experiments that he wrote about. What he had intended as a Baconian *histoire* became also a manual of competently described experiments and an example of independent work and analysis on his subject. The work went through five English editions and was translated into French and German. A primary source for eighteenth-century understanding of electricity it is credited for the first statement of the inverse square law of electrical force based on reasonable deduction from experiment.

Leeds, 1767–1773 Hardly had the *History of Electricity* been published when Priestley received an invitation to be minister to the dissenting congregation of Mill Hill Chapel in Leeds. He accepted the call and moved in September 1767. His memoirs cite Mary Priestley's bad health to explain the move and one can add that the financing of Warrington was always uncertain and there was little prospect for an increase in salary to match a possibly increasing family. Additionally, Priestley was always to regard the role of dissenting minister as the most important of any in the world and he was here invited to return to it for a major congregation and one within the cognizance of his family. He was, that is, returning a success to the 'home' that had rejected him.

The Mill Hill congregation was a liberal one and supported Priestley's move from Arianism to complete anti-Trinitarianism. This probably occurred in 1769 after he re-read Nathaniel Lardner's *Letter … [on] the Logos* (1759). The Priestleys were happy in Leeds, though there is no record of visits to or from Fieldhead. Joseph junior was born there in July 1768 and William in May 1771. Priestley took a minor part in community activities. He helped organize the Leeds proprietary circulating library and preached annual charity sermons for the charity school and general infirmary. And it was there that he began his long career in religious and polemical publication.

Anxious to succeed as a minister Priestley exploited his major talent, that of teacher, by organizing religious classes within his congregation. He wrote catechisms for two younger groups and a text, *Institutes of Natural and Revealed Religion* (1772, 1773, 1774), to teach the principles of rational dissent. He had begun the *Institutes* while a student at Daventry, and its publication was not completed until after he had left Leeds, but it soon became a standard exposition of Unitarian beliefs. He also attacked the sacramental nature of the Lord's supper, recommended family religious exercises and a renewal of some kind of church discipline, and supported the practice of infant baptism. His pamphlets *An Appeal to the Serious and Candid Professors of Christianity* (1770) and *Familiar Illustration of Certain Passages of Scripture* (1772) went through multiple editions—30,000 copies of the *Appeal* being circulated by 1787. And he established the first English scholarly journal for speculative theology, the *Theological Repository*, published in three annual volumes (1769–71) and then suspended for lack of support from any contributors but Arians or Unitarians. Priestley himself contributed about one third (fifteen articles) of the early *Repository*'s contents.

Each of his religious publications elicited attacks and, to most of these attacks, Priestley published at least one answer. This was partly because he sincerely believed that controversy was the best avenue towards truth, but also, it is clear from his polemical works, because he enjoyed debate. He developed a style of patient condescension and irony which, from this provincial schoolmaster and dissenting minister, infuriated his opponents, usually university graduates. Although not conducive to convincing his opponents, his polemics were to make of Priestley the most prominent English spokesman for rational theology in the later eighteenth century.

They were also to make Priestley a major spokesman for liberal political reform. In his *Liberal Education* he had objected, partially on political grounds, to a scheme for national education. His friends encouraged him to develop these ideas further in his *Essay on the First Principles of Government* (1768), which separated the concepts of civil and political liberty and used a principle of utility which Jeremy Bentham was to claim, in his 'Short history of utilitarianism' (1829), was the source of his own normative greater happiness principle. Priestley's *Remarks on some Paragraphs in … Blackstone's Commentaries* (1769) objected to William Blackstone's description of dissenters as tolerated criminals and succeeded in making Blackstone retract some of his statements and moderate his language in others. In the same year Priestley's anonymous *Present State of Liberty in Great Britain and her Colonies* reflects his, and his congregation's, concern over the economic and political consequences of government action toward Britain's American colonies. This plea for liberal reform in politics led, in turn, to pamphlets on liberal reform in church establishment.

None of his Leeds activities precluded Priestley's scientific investigations. Indeed, he regarded both the politics and the science as aspects of his theological work. He sent five papers of electrical experiments to the Royal Society between 1768 and 1770 in which he explored aspects of electrical spark discharge, including an early reference to oscillatory discharge of Leyden jars, and a study of comparative conductivities / impedances. He also prepared *Familiar Introductions*, teaching manuals for electricity (1768) and perspective (1770), and commenced preparations for a series of volumes on the history of experimental philosophy to follow his *History of Electricity*.

For the first of these volumes Priestley chose the history of optics, on which there was abundant information. He had to publish by subscription and the *History and Present State of Discoveries Relating to Vision, Light and Colours* (1772) was a disappointment. The subject required mathematics, which he had determined not to use, and the excess of information called for a nicety of judgement that Priestley was unable to supply. Though it was favourably reviewed many of the subscribers defaulted payment and the only advantage Priestley gained was his reintroduction to a dynamic particle theory of matter in the detailed form proposed by the Abbé Roger Joseph Boscovich in his *Philosophiae naturalis theoria* (1763).

As he had not received an adequate financial return for his labours on the *Optics*, Priestley declared that he would not continue his histories. He had, however, already become intrigued by 'taking up some of Dr. [Stephen] Hales's inquiries concerning air', as he wrote to his friend Theophilus Lindsey in 1770, and doubtless would not have continued writing about other people's discoveries anyway. He had been doing some chemical experiments as early as his work on electricity. When living next to a brewery the ready supply of by-produced carbon dioxide led him to seek applications for what was then termed fixed air. His first explicitly chemical publication *Directions for Impregnating Water with Fixed Air* (1772) developed out of a contemporary mistaken view that scurvy was a putrefactive disease associated with the loss of carbon dioxide from the body tissues. The publication elicited much favourable attention and ultimately led to the establishment of the carbonated beverage industry.

Priestley's study of airs (gases) took a more significant form in his long paper, 'Observations on different kinds of air', published in the *Philosophical Transactions of the Royal Society* for 1772. Seldom has a first paper been so important: it announced the isolation and identification of nitric oxide and anhydrous hydrochloride acid gases, introduced the notions of eudiometry and of photosynthesis, and described simple apparatus and manipulative techniques that enabled others to extend his work. The paper richly deserved the Copley medal conferred by the Royal Society for 1773.

Calne, 1773–1780 By the time he received the medal Priestley had moved from Leeds and Mill Hill Chapel to Calne, Wiltshire, and the service of William Petty, second earl of Shelburne. The combined failures of the *Theological Repository* and the *History of Light* had brought financial problems and Priestley's friends also agreed that Leeds was too small a niche for a man of his abilities. There had been one abortive effort to extract him when Joseph Banks, planning to go on James Cook's second voyage to the south seas as supernumary botanist, invited Priestley to accompany him as an astronomer. The invitation, in December 1771, had to be withdrawn when Banks realized that he had exceeded his authority in offering the appointment and that Priestley lacked the astronomical expertise demanded by the board of longitude and the Royal Society. Franklin failed to locate an academic post for him in the colonies and, finally, Richard Price came to the rescue by recommending him to Lord Shelburne for a post of companion at a salary of £250 and a house. The Priestleys moved to Calne, near Shelburne's estate of Bowood, in June 1773.

Shelburne was a major figure in the Chathamite faction in opposition to the North ministry and Priestley was a vigorous representative of the most vocal part of dissenting interests. Priestley and Shelburne were too unlike to become the kind of companions that Shelburne had wanted, but Priestley could provide political information and intellectual consequence. He performed experiments for Shelburne's guests, supervised the education of his children, and acted as librarian, buying books and cataloguing the library and manuscript collections. The Calne years were good ones for Priestley. During them he became an important political voice among British dissenters, as well as developing a metaphysical position and continuing his theological and pneumatic studies. His third son, named Henry at Shelburne's request, was born there in May 1777.

Priestley's first political chore for Shelburne was to summarize dissenting opinion respecting the attempted repeal, in 1773, of the Test Act. Failure of that attempt led to a pamphlet advising dissenters on conducting the next appeal, including suggestions on reform of the established church. It also led to his *Address to Protestant Dissenters on the Approaching Election* (1774) attacking the parliamentary majority for its failure to repeal and for its activities relating to the colonies. The *Address* was the most extreme political tract Priestley had written and attracted the most national attention of any appeal favouring the Americans. Continuation of the North ministry dampened overt political activity though Priestley continued to act as intermediary between Shelburne and dissenters and, as an impartial agent, between the allies of the marquess of Rockingham and the Chathamites. His only visit to the continent was during August to October 1774, in the company of Shelburne.

Not having a congregation in Calne, Priestley's religious activities were confined to occasional preaching and publications such as his homily advocating premarital celibacy. He supported Theophilus Lindsey in establishing Essex Street Chapel, the first avowedly Unitarian place of worship in England and he again directed his attention to formal theology. He attempted a chronological arrangement of passages in the four gospels in a *Harmony of the Gospels, in Greek* (1777), and in English (1780). Though a somewhat conventional approach to biblical study prior to synoptic analysis, his *Harmony* inevitably led to a pamphlet argument. He also published the first of a continuing series of letters answering atheistic arguments, this one addressed to Holbach and Hume. His most singular activity of this period was the writing of five metaphysical works, starting with an acerbic attack on several leading Scottish philosophers, *An Examination of Dr. Reid's Inquiry … Dr. Beattie's Essay … and Dr. Oswald's Appeal* (1774), presenting an alternative to their doctrine of common sense. He followed this with an edition of that part of David Hartley's *Observations on Man* which provided an associationist alternative to the common-sense philosophers. His *Hartley's Theory of the Human Mind* (1775) provided an influential source for Hartley's ideas into the next century.

One of the introductory essays to the *Hartley* announced Priestley's adoption of monism, which he was then obliged to defend in his *Disquisitions on Matter and Spirit* (1777), followed by his *Doctrine of Philosophical Necessity* (1777), which supported a type of mechanistic determinism. Together these books started a flood of criticism which Priestley attempted to answer in a *Free Discussion of the Doctrines of Materialism and Philosophical Necessity* (1778) with his good friend Richard Price. Price was never to understand, nor did the majority of Priestley's contemporaries, that Priestley saw matter as the manifestation of spiritual force and determinism as an active acceptance of causality in the will of God.

During the period of his metaphysical writing Priestley was also continuing his pneumatic investigations. Except for occasional *Philosophical Transactions* papers, such as that of 1776 which inspired Lavoisier's oxidation theory of respiration, these appeared as books. The papers, and the volumes of experiments and observations—*Experiments and Observations on Different Kinds of Air* (1774, 1775, 1777) and *Experiments and Observations Relating to Various Branches of Natural Philosophy* (1779)—were eagerly awaited for their new discoveries and new techniques. In them, he announced his discovery of ammonia gas, nitrous oxide, nitrogen dioxide, sulphur dioxide, and, most important, of oxygen. The latter, for which he is most famous, was first mentioned in *Transactions* letters (1775) and was described in detail in the book of that year. He also wrote a vigorous defence again a charge of scientific plagiarism and expanded his pneumatic studies beyond chemistry into investigations of heat expansion, indices of refraction, and sound transmission of gases and continued his study of photosynthesis.

Birmingham, 1780–1791 Lack of real companionship between Priestley and Shelburne was amplified by the latter's becoming head of the Chathamite whigs on Lord Chatham's death (1778) and his remarriage in 1779. The Priestleys had become political and social impediments. By mid-1780 the association was broken and Priestley retired to Birmingham, retaining an annual pension of £150. By December he accepted an invitation to be senior minister of New Meeting, one of the largest and most affluent dissenting congregations in England, at a salary of £100 and he was, once again, happy in his real vocation. He retained his scientific avocation, particularly in becoming a member of the Lunar Society, comprising entrepreneurs and scientists such as Matthew Boulton, Erasmus Darwin, James Watt, Josiah Wedgwood, and William Withering. Most of his Birmingham science was in the area of applied science, in service of the interests of that group or of his brother-in-law, the ironmaster John Wilkinson. Priestley advised Wedgwood on the airs entrapped in ceramic clays, Boulton on the cost and elasticity of the new gases, Watt and Wilkinson on steam interaction with iron, and Withering on the inexpensive generation of hydrogen for balloon flight. Priestley continued sending occasional papers to the Royal Society for publication, including a confusing set ultimately revealing the diffusion of gases through unglazed ceramic walls. His volumes of *Experiments and Observations Relating to ... Natural Philosophy* were continued (1781, 1786) and in 1790 he published an 'abridged and methodized' version of the six-volume *Experiments and Observations*. The originality in the earlier volumes had, however, chiefly disappeared and the major theme of his published science during the remainder of his life was his conflict with Antoine Lavoisier, who had used his discovery of oxygen and the work of Watt and Cavendish on the composition of water (started by hints from Priestley) to attack the doctrine of phlogiston. Priestley never accepted Lavoisier's interpretation of oxygen, nor the composite nature of water and his criticisms of Lavoisier's experiments, though frequently correct, could not succeed in face of the systematization and pedagogic usefulness of the Lavoisian taxonomic revolution of chemistry.

Most of Priestley's time was devoted to the role of minister, which he happily resumed. During the Birmingham years he was to publish thirty-eight pamphlets or books, some of the latter in several volumes, on religious and educational issues, including sermons, prayers, exhortations to Jews, an edition of hymns, annotations for an edition of the Bible, and the resumed publication of the *Theological Repository* (1784, 1786, 1788). He preached regularly and, as in Leeds, conducted religious classes for children and young adults in the New Meeting congregation. Priestley's Sunday class had a total membership of nearly 150, of whom 80 were aged between seventeen and thirty. He also joined members of Old and New Meeting in establishing Sunday schools at which nominees of the congregations could learn reading, writing, sums, and basic job skills and that led to the Birmingham Sunday Society—open to any former pupil of a basic Sunday school in town—at which were taught natural and revealed religion and a range of philosophical subjects.

In 1788, Priestley's *Lectures on History and General Policy*, first delivered at Warrington Academy, were finally published. They did not have the influence they warranted, though there were to be seven English editions and translations into German and French, but they were adopted for use in dissenting academies throughout England, in universities in the United States, and even, it is said, were used by John Symonds at Cambridge and Thomas Arnold at Oxford. More historiographic than narrative, and in the exemplary rather than the nineteenth-century historicism mode, still the *Lectures* supported a doctrine of progress and recommended a wide variety of sources for research into a broadly defined social, economic, and cultural as well as political and diplomatic history.

Priestley's major historical work of the period was also theological, in that he wrote some five historio-theological works dedicated to the single purpose of establishing an uncompromising monotheism. In Priestley's opinion both Arianism and Trinitarianism were compromises between the monotheism of Judaism and the early Christian church and the polytheism of Hellenistic gnosticism and neo-Platonism. To prove this he wrote *An History of the Corruptions of Christianity* (1782) in two volumes, and, in response to the arguments that caused, *An History of Early Opinions Concerning Jesus Christ* (1786), in four. Positions adopted in these works—insistence that the early Christian church had been unitarian, denial of the virgin birth of Christ, and supporting Nazareth as his birthplace—led to increasingly intemperate argument, especially with Samuel, soon to be Bishop, Horsley, who attacked Priestley's scholarship without addressing the substance of his arguments. Soon there were annual volumes in defence of Unitarianism, and, in 1790, a two-volume *General History of the Christian Church to the Fall of Empires*. Altogether, counting the pamphlet war, Priestley wrote nearly 4800 pages in this cause and many of his arguments have been sustained by modern, liberal scholarship.

Anger of many clergymen at their inability to silence Priestley's theological arguments was increased by his support of attempts to repeal the Corporation and Test Acts, represented, for example, in his *Letter to the Rt. Honourable William Pitt* (1787) and his sermon of 1789 (for he regarded repeal to be a religious issue), *The Conduct to be Observed ... to Procure the Repeal of the Corporation and Test Acts*. Priestley's enthusiastic welcoming of the French Revolution, evidenced in his *Letters to the Rt. Hon. Edmund Burke* (1791), convinced many people that he was a revolutionary, bent on destruction of church and crown. Untrue though these suspicions were they encouraged members of the Birmingham establishment to acquiesce, at least, in those acts of mob violence variously known as the Birmingham, church and king, or Priestley riots of 1791. The immediate excuse for the riots was a dinner in celebration of Bastille day, held by the Constitutional Society of Birmingham, a dinner which Priestley did not attend though he had assisted in the organization of the society. The riots raged from the evening of the 14th of July to that of the 16th, and were put down only at the arrival of dragoons sent from Nottingham. Damage was extensive: Old and New Meeting houses and seven residences were destroyed, other houses were wrecked. Priestley's house, his library, laboratory, and papers were ruined and his life was saved only because he had fled. English authorities generally approved of the riots, but they were denounced by many persons and organizations in England, Europe, and the United States and remain a blot on the history of British toleration.

Hackney, 1791–1794 Priestley found temporary refuge with friends and then, in November, settled in Clapton, near Hackney, and accepted the invitation to succeed Richard Price, whose funeral sermon he had preached six months earlier, as morning preacher at Gravel Pit meeting. He was discouraged from returning to Birmingham with a sermon—'Forgive them Father, they know not what they do'—guaranteed to incite the establishment to blind fury.

Only seventeen of the rioters were ever tried and, of these, only notorious criminals were convicted. Compensation paid the victims by assessment on Hemlingford hundred was woefully inadequate, but John Wilkinson made Priestley an annual allowance of £200, and settled on him an (unproductive) £10,000 in French funds. He was elected a citizen of France, which he accepted, and a representative to the National Convention, which he declined.

Priestley's polemical and theological work continued, as in his *An Appeal to the Public on … the Riots in Birmingham* (1791), which went through four printings in a year. He continued his series pamphlet war on atheists, this time attacking Gibbon's *Decline and Fall*; Gibbon declined to respond publicly. Priestley lectured on history and on natural philosophy at Hackney New College, publishing his only general statement on the latter in his *Heads of Lectures on a Course of Experimental Philosophy* (1794). Hackney was not, however, a satisfactory solution to his problems. He missed his friends of the Lunar Society, associates of the Royal Society avoided him, and he ceased attending meetings, publishing his continued attack on Lavoisian chemistry, *Experiments on the Generation of Air from Water* (1793) as a separate pamphlet. His sons were unable to find employment and attempts of the younger Pitt's administration to silence all criticism were coming closer and closer to him. Finally, in 1794, he resolved to emigrate to the United States.

Pennsylvania, 1794–1804 After obtaining official notice that he was not fleeing arrest Priestley sailed with his wife, on 8 April 1794, for the United States. They arrived at New York city on the evening of 4 June, to be met by Joseph junior and his wife and, the following day, by official greetings from Governor Clinton, and deputations from merchants and various patriotic societies all expressing delight at their arrival. A fortnight later the Priestleys went to Philadelphia where, again, they were warmly welcomed. In mid-July they began their five-day journey, 130 miles, to Northumberland, Pennsylvania, where they were to stay while a community of emigrating English liberal dissenters and reformers was to be established on the nearby 700,000 acres of land optioned to Priestley's sons and Thomas Cooper. The projected community was never realized as the expected flood of refugees from the younger Pitt's liberal witchhunt failed to materialize after the acquittals in the high treason trials of Thomas Hardy, Horne Tooke, and John Thelwall late in 1794. Nevertheless the Priestleys remained at Northumberland. Experiences of the Birmingham riots had given Mary Priestley a distaste for cities, and the location in central Pennsylvania, at the junction of two branches of the Susquehanna River, was an attractive one. There they were to build their home, though Harry, who died in late 1795, and Mary, who died on 17 September 1796, never saw the completed house. Priestley moved into it, along with the family of Joseph junior, and there he was to stay, with occasional visits to Philadelphia, until his death.

When the Priestleys had left England they were recipients of many public statements of sorrow and support. In New York and Philadelphia, Priestley was welcomed as a friend of liberty and a distinguished philosopher who had been badly treated in England. He visited President Washington several times and was befriended by Thomas Jefferson as 'one of the few lives precious to mankind'. Not everyone was as welcoming and Priestley was to discover that bias and bigotry were as evident in the United States as in England. William Cobbett, just embarked on his career as reactionary radical journalist, was incensed at the criticism of England implied in the reception given Priestley and, under the name Peter Porcupine, crudely attacked him as a friend of anarchy and godlessness. Many ministers preached against him in their pulpits and he was unable to establish himself as a minister in any church, though he preached occasionally in Philadelphia, where he assisted the formation of a small Unitarian society, and regularly at services held in his home in Northumberland.

It was the summer of 1795 before Priestley could return to his experiments and though he was to build a laboratory and publish more scientific papers (at least forty), in the *Transactions of the American Philosophical Society* and the *New York Medical Repository*, as well as two pamphlets affirming his continued belief in phlogiston, his scientific work was essentially an anticlimax. He inspired a number of young chemists in the United States to experiment, had an indirect influence in the identification of carbon monoxide as a new gas, and extended his interests to opposing Erasmus Darwin's belief in spontaneous generation and writing an essay on hearing and another on dreams. In essential isolation he kept up as well as he could with the news in science, experimenting, for example, with the newly discovered voltaic cell. But most of his work was a repetition of experiments he had done before, inadvertently illustrating Priestley's own complaint that he frequently forgot things he had done in the past. His futile opposition to Lavoisian chemistry was a solitary one.

Priestley retained his political interests. In February 1798 he wrote an anonymous article, 'Maxims of political arithmetic', published in the Republican newspaper, *Aurora*, which John Adams, elected president in 1797, regarded as attacks on his policies. Reacting to French interference in American politics, and to suppress criticism, the Adams administration had passed the Aliens and Sedition Acts, which Timothy Pickering, secretary of state, wanted to apply to Priestley. Responding to federalist attacks, Priestley wrote *Letters to the Inhabitants of Northumberland* (1799) to defend himself. Adams rejected Pickering's suggestion—Priestley's influence was too weak to take that seriously—but Priestley was not to feel completely secure until the election to the presidency of Jefferson, to whom he wrote, in dedicating the second part of his church history (1802), 'Tho' I am arrived at the usual term of human life, it is now only that I can say I see nothing to fear from the hand of power, the government under which I live being for the first time truly favourable to me.'

Priestley's most effective activities in exile were in education and theology. He had an extensive correspondence with Jefferson on the establishment of the latter's new college for the state of Virginia, including a lengthy 'Hints concerning public education', which echoed his Warrington recommendations, but with some specifics such as the number of professors (nine) that would be needed for a fledgeling college and the value of a good library, though students should not be encouraged to read while 'under tuition'. He delivered two sets of discourses on the evidences of revealed religion, continued his series of attacks on atheistic ideas—this time those of Tom Paine and those of Constantin Volney, and completed his *General History of the Christian Church* (1802–3). He wrote notes on the scriptures and prepared his *Index to the Bible* (1804). Of more than twenty theological publications while in America the most noteworthy is perhaps *Socrates and Jesus Compared* (1803), which was among Jefferson's favourite religious reading. His last works, corrected on his deathbed, were theological, particularly the *Doctrines of Heathen Philosophy Compared with those of Revelation*.

Priestley died on 6 February 1804 in his Pennsylvania home. He was buried beside his wife and son, Henry, in the Friends' burial-ground in Northumberland. His daughter, Sarah Priestley Finch, predeceased him (1803). His eldest son, Joseph Priestley, returned to England in 1812 and died there (1863). The younger Joseph's first son remained in the United States and continued the Priestley line there, but his eldest daughter married a Birmingham politician, Joseph Parkes. Their daughter Bessie married Louis Belloc, and their children included Hilaire Belloc and Marie Belloc Lowndes. Of Priestley's other children, William Priestley was a disappointment to his father. Though he had married a Miss Peggy Foulke in February 1796, he was unable to settle down. In 1800 he created a scandal by putting tartar emetic in the family flour before departing to become a sugar planter in Louisiana. His daughter Catherine married another sugar planter named Richardson and their son, Henry Hobson Richardson, became a towering figure in the history of American architecture.

When most of the reforms he had advocated were achieved in the nineteenth century, and then superseded, Priestley was forgotten, except as a name occasionally cited in dispersed topical histories. Even in theology, to which he had devoted most of his efforts, he became a remote historical figure. German theologians surpassed him in revisionary scholarship and the sentimental ecumenism of W. E. Channing and James Martineau replaced his militancy in unitarianism. Only in science, usually the least historical of areas, has his memory remained bright—as the discoverer of oxygen, who never quite recognized his own discovery, and as the persistent critic of Lavoisian chemistry who, with the advent of physical chemistry, was shown to be not entirely wrong. His house and laboratory at Northumberland became a museum and the American Chemical Society was planned by men meeting on its porch on 1 August 1874. Memorials and brief biographies of Priestley have been published since his death, but only during the last years of the twentieth century was the full range of his accomplishments recognized.   ROBERT E. SCHOFIELD

Sources R. E. Schofield, *The enlightenment of Joseph Priestley: a study of his life and works from 1733 to 1773* (1997) · R. E. Schofield, *The enlightened Joseph Priestley* (2001) · *The theological and miscellaneous works of Joseph Priestley*, ed. J. T. Rutt, 25 vols. in 26 (1817–32); repr. (1972), esp. vol. 1 · R. E. Crook, *A bibliography of Joseph Priestley, 1733–1804* (1966) · C. C. Sellers, ed., 'The Priestley family collection, Dickinson College', *Genealogy* (1965), 13–19 · minute books, *Senatus Academicus*, U. Edin. · election certificate, RS · *Memoirs of Dr Joseph Priestley*, ed. J. Priestley, T. Cooper, and W. Christie, 2 vols. (1806) · D. R. N. Lester, *History of Batley grammar school, 1612–1962* [1962]

Archives American Philosophical Society, Philadelphia, corresp. and papers · Beds. & Luton ARS, biographical chart of the world · Birm. CA, letters and sermons · Birm. CA, papers relating to damages claimed after 'Priestley riots' · Dickinson College Library, Carlisle, Pennsylvania, corresp. and papers · DWL, corresp. and papers · Harris Man. Oxf., notebooks and sermons · Leeds Central Library, Leeds Leisure Services, MS address and sermon relating to Birmingham riot · RS, Priestleyana · U. Birm. L., letters · University of Pennsylvania, Philadelphia, Van Pelt Library, corresp. and papers | American Philosophical Society, Philadelphia, corresp. with Benjamin Franklin · American Philosophical Society, Philadelphia, letters to John Vaughan · Birm. CA, letters to Matthew Boulton · Birm. CA, letters to James Watt · BL, letters to William Russell, Add. MS 44992 · Bodl. Oxf., Bowood papers · Bodl. Oxf., letters to Richard Price · DWL, letters to Theophilus Lindsey · Hist. Soc. Penn., letters to Benjamin Barton, etc. · N. Yorks. CRO, corresp. with Christopher Wyvill · NRA, corresp. with Sir Joseph Banks · NRA, priv. coll., letters to Lord Lansdowne · RS, corresp. with J. Canton · RS, letters to Josiah Wedgwood · Warrington Library, Cheshire, corresp. with John Wilkinson

Likenesses oils, *c.*1760, Unitarian Memorial Church, Cambridge · oils, 1763–5, RS · G. Ceracchi, Wedgwood medallion, 1779, Brooklyn Museum, New York · J. Opie, oils, *c.*1781, Harris Man. Oxf. · H. Fuseli, oils, *c.*1783, DWL · J. G. Hancock, medal sculpture, 1783, NPG · J. Millar, oils, 1789, RS · J. Gillray, caricature, etching, pubd 1791, BM · T. Holloway, mezzotint, pubd 1792 (after his earlier work), NPG · J. Sayers, etching, pubd 1792 (after his earlier work), NPG · W. Artaud, oils, exh. RA 1794, DWL · Phipson, medallion, *c.*1795 (after G. Ceracchi), NPG · R. Peale, oils, *c.*1800, New York Historical Society; copies, American Philosophical Society, Philadelphia · G. Stuart, oils, *c.*1803, Smithsonian Institution, Washington, DC, National Portrait Gallery · C. Turner, mezzotint, pubd 1836 (after H. Fuseli), NPG · E. B. Stephens, statue, 1860, New Museum, Oxford · J. F. Wilkinson, statue, 1874, Birmingham · G. Bayes, statue, 20th cent., Russell Square, London · T. Halliday, medallion (after Hollins), NPG · M. Haughton junior, wash over pencil and chalk drawing, BM · Hollins, plaster medallion, DWL · J. Opie, oils, Brompton Hospital, London · J. Sayers, etchings, NPG · by or after E. Sharples, drawing (original, *c.*1797), NPG [see illus.] · J. Sharples, pastel drawing, NPG; related drawings, NPG · bronze medal, NPG · oils (after G. Stuart), Birmingham Museums and Art Gallery · oils, RS · portraits, repro. in J. McLachlan, *Joseph Priestley, man of science, 1733–1804: an iconography of a great Yorkshireman* (1983) · statue, Leeds · statue, Warrington · statue, Birstall, West Yorkshire

Wealth at death house and lot in Northumberland, Pennsylvania; large library; virtually nothing else: Priestly, Cooper, and Christie, eds., *Memoirs*

Priestley, Sir Raymond Edward (1886–1974), geologist and academic administrator, was born in Tewkesbury, Gloucestershire, on 20 July 1886, the second son and second of eight children of Joseph Edward Priestley, headmaster of Tewkesbury grammar school, and his wife, Henrietta Rice. Priestley was educated in his father's school and taught there for a year before reading geology at University College, Bristol (1905–7), where he was captain of hockey and in the cricket eleven. At the end of his second year in the university a chance contact led to his joining the British Antarctic expedition of 1907–9 led by Sir Ernest Shackleton.

Although from a staunch Methodist background, Priestley adapted well to expedition life with sailors, adventurers, and two outstanding university geologists—T. W. Edgeworth David and Douglas Mawson. Because of a knee injury Priestley spent more time caring for ponies and less on geological fieldwork than expected. The achievements of Shackleton, who reached a position 97 miles from the south pole, and David, who attained the south magnetic pole, brought fame to the expedition on its return. Priestley spent four months in England and contributed to the geological sections of Shackleton's classic book, *The Heart of the Antarctic* (1909), before returning to Sydney, Australia, in October to work with Edgeworth David on volume 1 of the geological report which was published in 1914.

Captain R. F. Scott recruited Priestley when passing through Sydney to the Antarctic in 1910. He joined the northern party under Victor Campbell. After spending 1911 at Cape Adare the six-man party was landed 200 miles further south for summer fieldwork with provisions for eight weeks. The ship was stopped by pack-ice from returning and the epic story of how the party survived and then sledged 250 miles to the main party early in the following summer is told in Priestley's book *Antarctic Adventure* (1914; repr., 1974). They survived the fierce winds by digging a cave in a snow-drift. A line across the middle of the 12 foot by 9 foot floor separated the wardroom from the mess deck of three petty officers. By agreement, nothing said on one side of the line could be 'heard' or answered by those on the other side. Priestley considered this splendid training for dealing with unreasonable, irascible professors in later life without loss of temper. His responsibility for the commissariat in the ice cave in these circumstances shows an early reputation for fairness and reliability.

On return, Priestley matriculated as a pensioner in Christ's College, Cambridge, for a course of research study. The First World War intervened and he served as adjutant at the Wireless Training Centre (1914–17), and then with the 46th divisional signal company in France. He won the MC. During the war he married, on 10 April 1915, Phyllis Mary (d. 1961), daughter of William Boyle Boyd, from Dunedin, New Zealand, the master of a barquentine; they had two daughters. After the armistice he wrote the official record, *The Work of the Royal Engineers, 1914–19: the Signal Service* (1921), and *Breaking the Hindenburg Line* (1919). After return to Cambridge he completed sections of *British (Terra Nova) Antarctic Expedition, 1910–13: Glaciology* (1922), written jointly with Charles S. Wright, a classic of early glaciological literature. A thesis on this subject brought him a BA in 1920, after which he studied agriculture (diploma, 1922) before becoming a fellow of Clare College, Cambridge, in 1923 (fellow, 1923–34; honorary fellow, 1956).

Priestley's career then turned to academic administration. He was secretary to the board of research studies as assistant registrary (1924–7), first assistant registrary and

secretary to the general board (1927–34), and secretary-general of the faculties (1934–5). His keen interest in the British Commonwealth led him to become first vice-chancellor of Melbourne University (1935–8) before returning to Britain as vice-chancellor of Birmingham University (1938–52). In these posts he took a deep interest in students, their sport, and student unions. Although he felt a lack of support from industry and government in Melbourne, he left a fine students' union building. In Birmingham, thanks to public support and despite the Second World War, the university doubled in size, started new departments, and recruited some outstanding professors. In the wider field Priestley helped found the University College of the West Indies and was chairman of the Imperial College of Tropical Agriculture, Trinidad (1949–53).

After his retirement to Bredon's Norton near Tewkesbury in 1952, Priestley continued his public service, first as chairman of the royal commission on the civil service (1953–5). The Priestley commission accepted the principle and set out guidelines to link pay throughout the civil service with equivalent posts in industry—a concept which helped maintain the flow of first-class people to the civil service, possibly to the detriment of industry.

Priestley never lost his love of the Antarctic and often lectured on his experiences to undergraduates in Cambridge, to servicemen in the Second World War, and to many others. He helped his expedition colleague Frank Debenham to found the Scott Polar Research Institute in the University of Cambridge in 1920, but his academic activities gave him little time for polar affairs until retirement. From 1955 to 1958 he deputized as acting director, London headquarters of the Falkland Islands dependencies survey (later the British Antarctic survey) for Vivian Fuchs during his absence on the trans-Antarctic expedition. His presidential address to the British Association for the Advancement of Science in 1956 was titled 'Twentieth-century man against the Antarctic'. He twice visited the Antarctic again, with the duke of Edinburgh to the Falkland Islands dependencies in 1956 and to Victoria Land with the US Navy in 1959, when he visited his early expedition area. During the former trip on the *Britannia*, his fondness for talking about polar subjects led the ornithologists and the duke to call him the 'Lesser Polar Backchat' but this was soon upgraded to 'Greater Polar Backchat'. *Antarctic Research* (1964), edited by Priestley, R. J. Adie, and G. de Q. Robin, reflected the recognition and consolidation of British research activities in the Antarctic following the International Geophysical Year (1957–8), Fuchs's success, and Priestley's influence as acting director.

Priestley's last considerable public office was as president of the Royal Geographical Society (1961–3). Thereafter the effects of old war injuries kept him increasingly in Bredon's Norton, where he enjoyed family life and visitors while remaining mentally alert and active to the end. He was a patient man of modest tastes and a sense of humour whose sympathetic and realistic judgements left their mark on twentieth-century education and research.

He was knighted in 1949, and held the Polar medal and bar and the Founder's medal of the Royal Geographical Society. He held honorary doctorates from Melbourne, New Zealand, St Andrews, Natal, Dalhousie, Birmingham, Malaya, Sheffield, and the West Indies. He died in the Nuffield Nursing Home, Cheltenham, on 24 June 1974.

G. DE Q. ROBIN, rev.

Sources R. E. Priestley, autobiographical notes of his early years, priv. coll. · personal knowledge (1986) · private information (1986) [Margaret Hubert, daughter] · *Antarctic* [NZ] · Central Office of Information obituary · *The Times* (27 June 1974) · CUL, department of manuscripts and university archives · *AusDB* · *CGPLA Eng. & Wales* (1974)

Archives PRO, corresp., BW90 · Scott Polar RI, corresp., journals, and papers · U. Birm., corresp. and papers · U. Birm., additional papers · University of Melbourne, letters, diaries, etc. · Wellcome L., natural history notes | TCD, corresp. with Thomas Bodkin

Likenesses H. G. Ponting, photographs, c.1910–1912, U. Cam. · A. R. Middleton Todd, oils, c.1950, U. Birm. · W. Stoneman, photograph, 1952, NPG · W. Bird, photograph, 1962, NPG · S. Buchan, photograph, 1972, NPG

Wealth at death £1415: probate, 31 July 1974, *CGPLA Eng. & Wales*

Priestley, Timothy (1734–1814), Independent minister, was born on 19 June 1734 at Owler Lane, Birstall Fieldhead, West Riding of Yorkshire, the second of the six children of Jonas Priestley (1700–1779), cloth-dresser, and his first wife, Mary Swift (1706–1739), daughter of Joseph Swift, maltster and farmer of Shafton, near Wakefield. He was brought up by his maternal grandfather after his mother's death in childbed in December 1739 and was sent to school at Batley, Yorkshire. For some time he followed his father's trade. His elder brother, Joseph *Priestley, the scientist and theologian, who thought him frivolous, related how he snatched from his brother 'a book of knight-errantry' and flung it away. Timothy recalled kneeling down with Joseph 'while he prayed' at the age of six and his brother's growing interest and delight in scientific experiments (*Autobiography of Joseph Priestley*, 140). Whenever his brother made a new discovery Timothy was 'soon acquainted with it', and he remembered that when Joseph 'was making much progress in electricity' he showed him 'how to melt steel' (ibid., 12). None the less, Timothy was far more practical than his brother and later used his self-taught skills in brass- and wood-working to make 'electrifying machines' to his brother's designs (ibid., 20). Their strong Calvinistic family background encouraged both brothers to train for the dissenting ministry, and Timothy became only the second student to enrol at the academy established in 1756 by James Scott (1710–1783), the recently appointed minister of Upper Chapel, Heckmondwike, Yorkshire. Joseph Priestley regarded the course of studies as 'an imperfect education', but it strengthened Timothy's Calvinist theology. Joseph subsequently embraced unitarian doctrines, which placed an increasing strain on the relationship between the two brothers. Timothy distinguished himself as an assiduous pupil; he got into trouble, however, by going out to preach without leave. His preaching was popular, and he was employed in mission work at Ilkeston, Derbyshire, and elsewhere.

In 1760 Priestley was ordained pastor of the congregation at Kipping, Thornton, near Bradford. It was a difficult pastorate, for the owner of the Kipping estate had ceased to be in sympathy with nonconformity. He also faced difficulties when he became minister of Hunter's Croft Congregational Church, Manchester, in 1766. Although the chapel was enlarged during his ministry, he had frequent quarrels with his deacons. Described by Dr Alexander Mackennal as 'a strong preacher, careless of personal dignity, and of abounding audacity both in his pulpit utterances and in private speech', many stories were told of his eccentricities: his deacons criticized him for irreverently ascending the pulpit with his hat on his head and for making packing cases for the liquor trade on Sunday nights (Nightingale, 5.117). He retorted that he never began work until the clock struck twelve and that his ministerial stipend of £60 was inadequate to support his wife and family. Priestley had married some time before 1768 when his son William was born, and referred to his 'small family … having a child added to my number every year' (*Autobiography of Joseph Priestley*, 20). His wife may have been Margaret Brodie, whose marriage to a Timothy Priestley on 26 April 1764 is recorded in the parish register of Manchester parish church.

Priestley's unsolicited and ultimately unsuccessful attempts to persuade the congregation at Hale Chapel, near Altrincham, Cheshire, to resist the appointment of an Arian or Socinian minister when a vacancy arose at the chapel after 1767 confirm his uncompromising adherence to Calvinist orthodoxy. A letter written to William Whitelegg at Hale Barns Green (c.1767–1769) reveals his concern for 'the decay of the Dissenting cause in general' as a result of the advance of theological liberalism (Kenworthy, 131). Priestley refused to join the petitions of 1772–3 for relaxation of the Toleration Act unless concealment of heresy should be made a capital offence. His relationship with his brother deteriorated further after 1774 when Timothy received an invitation to preach at George Whitefield's Tabernacle, Moorfields; Joseph told him that it mortified him to hear people say 'Here is a brother of yours preaching at the Tabernacle.' In August 1782 the two Priestleys were appointed to preach the 'double lecture' at Oldbury, Worcestershire; Joseph wished his brother to decline, and, on Timothy's refusal to give way, withdrew himself, his place being taken by Habakkuk Crabb.

Priestley's Manchester ministry terminated in his formal dismissal on 14 April 1784, only two hands being held up in his favour. He moved to Dublin, where he remained for some two years. He then received a call to succeed Richard Woodgate, who had died in 1787, as minister of the Jewin Street Independent Church, London. He issued a periodical, the *Christian's Magazine, or, Gospel Repository*, designed to counteract unitarianism, under the patronage of Selina, countess of Huntingdon, to whom he dedicated the first volume in 1790 and whose friendship he enjoyed. It contains a biography of his tutor, Scott, which was reprinted separately in 1791. On his brother's death he preached at Jewin Street on 29 April 1803 and printed a funeral sermon, with an appendix of 'authentic anecdotes', the authenticity of some of which has been disputed. He was more imaginative than his brother and probably shared his defects of memory. His advertised *Animadversions* on his brother's theological views does not seem to have been printed. He did, however, publish *The Christian's Looking Glass* (1790–92), *Family Exercises* (1792), an annotated *Family Bible* (1793), and a few single sermons. He died at Islington on 23 April 1814 'in great peace and tranquillity', and was buried at Bunhill Fields on 29 April (Nightingale, 5.117). The Revd Joseph Cockin of Halifax delivered the funeral address and the Revd George Burder preached a funeral sermon at Jewin Street 'to a very crowded congregation'. The inscription on his tomb recorded that 'for more than half a century he preached with fidelity and success the unsearchable riches of Christ' (ibid., 5.119). His son William (1768–1827) was Independent minister at Fordingbridge, Hampshire.

JOHN A. HARGREAVES

Sources *Autobiography of Joseph Priestley*, ed. J. Lindsay (1970) · B. Nightingale, *Lancashire nonconformity*, 6 vols. [1890–93], vol. 5 · R. Halley, *Lancashire, its puritanism and nonconformity*, 2nd edn (1872) · J. G. Miall, *Congregationalism in Yorkshire* (1868) · F. Peel, *Nonconformity in the Spen valley* (1891) · D. R. N. Lester, *History of Batley grammar school, 1612–1962* [1962] · J. G. Gillam, *The crucible: the life of Dr Joseph Priestley* (1954) · A. D. Orange, *Joseph Priestley* (1974) · A. Holt, *Life of Joseph Priestley* (1931) · F. Kenworthy, 'Heresy at Hale Chapel', *Transactions of the Unitarian Historical Society*, 12 (1959–62), 131–2 · R. E. Schofield, *The enlightenment of Joseph Priestley: a study of his life and works from 1733 to 1773* (1997) · DNB · IGI · parish register (burial), Dec 1739, Birstall parish church, West Riding of Yorkshire [Mary Priestley] · parish register (marriage), 26 April 1764, Manchester parish church

Archives JRL, Acc. no. R117106

Likenesses T. Holloway, mezzotint, pubd 1792 (after his portrait), BM, NPG · engraving, repro. in Nightingale, *Lancashire nonconformity*, vol. 5, p. 118

Priestley, Sir William Overend (1829–1900), obstetric physician, was born at Morley Hall, near Leeds, on 24 June 1829, the eldest son of Joseph Priestley and Mary, daughter of James Overend of Morley. He was a great-nephew of Joseph Priestley. Priestley was educated at Leeds, King's College, London, Paris, and the University of Edinburgh. In 1852 he became a member of the Royal College of Surgeons and in 1853 he graduated MD from Edinburgh with a thesis entitled 'The development of the gravid uterus', which was awarded Professor Simpson's gold medal and the senate gold medal for excellence in original work. After graduating Priestley acted as private assistant of Sir James Young Simpson, then went to London and lectured at the Grosvenor Place school of medicine, where he was one of the pioneers of the new science of gynaecology. Following his master, Simpson, he was among the first to convert midwifery into obstetric medicine by attempting to use scientific methods. On 17 April 1856 Priestley married Eliza, the fourth daughter of publisher Robert *Chambers (1802–1871); they had two sons and two daughters. Through his wife Priestley came into connection with the Edinburgh intelligentsia and made many influential contacts. His close friends included Louis Pasteur and Oliver Wendell Holmes.

In 1858 Priestley was appointed lecturer in midwifery at the Middlesex Hospital, and in 1862 he was elected professor of midwifery at King's College, London, and obstetric physician to King's College Hospital in the place of Arthur Farre. Priestley suffered a severe attack of diphtheria soon after his election and was absent from his posts for some months. Despite this set-back his future appeared to be brilliant and Priestley's reputation and connections enabled him to build up the largest maternity and gynaecological practice in London. This prevented him from giving sufficient time to his scientific work and in 1872 he resigned from his hospital appointments. As a result, he fell into the background in the London medical establishment. He was appointed consulting obstetric physician to King's College Hospital and became an honorary fellow of King's College and a member of the council but this did not compensate for his loss of clinical status. Though personally respected and liked, Priestley came to be regarded as somewhat reactionary and out-of-date in his own subject. In 1896 he gave evidence in the famous libel case in which his successor at King's, William Playfair, was sued by a patient for breaching medical confidence. Priestley, like other medical witnesses, thought it was in order for a doctor to breach a patient's confidence to protect his own family from contact with an 'immoral' woman.

Priestley became a member of the Royal College of Physicians of London in 1859 and a fellow in 1864. He was a member of the council from 1878 to 1880, Lumleian lecturer in 1887, and censor in 1891–2. He became a member of the Royal College of Physicians of Edinburgh in 1858, and from 1866 to 1876 he was an examiner in midwifery at the Royal College of Surgeons of England. He was also at different times an examiner at the Royal College of Physicians of London and at the universities of Cambridge, London, and Victoria. He was president of the Obstetrical Society of London in 1875–6 and was a vice-president of the Medical Society of Paris. Priestley was a physician accoucheur to Princess Louis of Hesse (Alice of England), and to Princess Christian of Schleswig-Holstein. He received the honorary degree of LLD at the University of Edinburgh in 1884 and was knighted in 1893.

In 1895, in an address to the British Medical Association, Priestley deplored the current craze for 'over-operating' in gynaecology. A Conservative and Unionist, in 1896 he was elected to parliament, where he represented the universities of Edinburgh and St Andrews for the rest of his life. He had long been interested in politics but entered parliament too late in his life to have much influence there. He was especially interested in the remodelling of London University from an examining to a teaching body. He also wished to restore the library of the University of Edinburgh but the government refused to give a grant for this. Priestley was taken in ill in December 1899 and in January was moved from his country house in Sussex to London. He died at his home at 17 Hertford Street, Mayfair, London, on 11 April 1900 and was buried on 14 April at St Margaret's, Warnham, near Westbrook Hall, his estate in Sussex. He was survived by his wife.

ANN DALLY

Sources *The Lancet* (21 April 1900) · *BMJ* (21 April 1900) · *DNB* · Burke, *Peerage* · *WWBMP*, vol. 2 · *CGPLA Eng. & Wales* (1900)
Archives RCP Lond., corresp. · U. Birm., corresp.
Likenesses R. Lehmann, oils, *c*.1901, RCP Lond.; replica of portrait, exh. RA 1885 · G. Jerrard, photograph (after portrait), Wellcome L. · Silvy, photograph, Wellcome L. · B. Stone, photographs, NPG · Swan, photogravure (after R. Lehmann), Wellcome L. · photograph, repro. in *The Lancet* · photograph, repro. in *BMJ*
Wealth at death £141,094 10*s*. 2*d*.: probate, 9 May 1900, *CGPLA Eng. & Wales*

Priestman, Anna Maria (1828–1914), social reformer and campaigner for women's rights, was born on 23 March 1828, the seventh of the nine children of Jonathan Priestman (*d.* 1863), a prosperous Quaker tanner of Newcastle, and Rachel Bragg (1791–1854), a travelling minister in the Society of Friends, the daughter of Margaret Wilson Bragg, another noted Quaker minister. Her family home was Summerhill, in Newcastle.

During Anna Maria Priestman's childhood her family took an active part in the temperance movement, the campaign to abolish slavery, the Reform Bill agitation, and the Anti-Corn Law League. Her eldest sister, Elizabeth, became the first wife of the radical statesman John Bright, and lifetime friendships were formed between the Priestman and Bright sisters that survived Elizabeth Bright's early death and were further strengthened in the shared care of the infant child of this marriage, Helen Priestman Bright. This circle was to prove of considerable importance in the formation of an ongoing national women's rights movement from the 1860s.

As a young woman Anna Maria Priestman lived largely the life of a daughter at home, caring for her father in his widowhood. After his death she and her younger sister, Mary, eventually moved to Clifton, Bristol, in 1869. Here they settled for the remainder of their lives—near to both their eldest surviving sister, Margaret Tanner, and their niece Helen, who had married the shoe manufacturer William Stephens Clark—moving in circles of like-minded radicals that included their close friend the abolitionist Mary Estlin.

The mid-1860s saw the beginnings of an organized demand for women's suffrage, and Anna Maria Priestman, together with other members of the Bright kinship circle, helped form some of the first women's suffrage societies, in London, Bristol, and Bath. She also supported the Ladies' National Association for the Repeal of the Contagious Diseases Acts, formed by Josephine Butler in 1870 to protest legislation that undermined the civil rights of those designated prostitutes by the authorities in specified naval and military towns. Mary Priestman acted as the secretary of this organization and Margaret Tanner as its treasurer. All three sisters also supported the international campaigns against state regulation of prostitution, and maintained their family's close association with the cause of temperance.

In the early 1870s Anna Maria Priestman helped form the National Union of Women Workers in Bristol, a trade union and benefit society for women workers that became part of the Women's Protective and Provident Union. She was especially concerned with the effect of protective labour legislation on limiting economic opportunities for women, and gave evidence as to these concerns to the royal commission on the Factory and Workshop Acts (1876). In 1881 she helped establish the Bristol Women's Liberal Association, which was then emulated in other towns and cities, resulting in 1887 in the establishment of a national organization, the Women's Liberal Federation (WLF). One of her motives appears to have been a certain frustration with the central leadership of the suffrage movement, and a wish more effectively to mobilize Liberal rank-and-file support for the demand for the vote. She also advocated a closer alliance between women's suffragists and working-class radicals like Joseph Arch. Renewing her friendship with the Priestman sisters after forty years, the visiting United States suffragist Elizabeth Cady Stanton commented on her pleasure at finding 'three women on the shady side of sixty, so bright, so liberal, so ready for new thought on all subjects' (Stanton to Priestman sisters, 13 Oct [1890], Priestman MSS).

In the 1890s Anna Maria Priestman became increasingly dissatisfied by the refusal of the Liberal Party to make women's suffrage part of its programme, and of the WLF to make it a test question for Liberal candidates seeking support in elections. She established the Union of Practical Suffragists (UPS) with the support of other disaffected women Liberals to act as a ginger group within the WLF. Her strategy appeared to have met with success in 1903, when the WLF at last made votes for women a test question, and the UPS was, in consequence, wound up. Her opponents regained the upper hand, however, and the WLF policy was subsequently reversed. Perhaps not surprisingly, then, in their last active years Anna Maria and Mary Priestman became vocal supporters of the militant Women's Social and Political Union. This suffrage body, under the leadership of Emmeline and Christabel Pankhurst, sought to pressure the Liberal government into adopting women's suffrage by campaigning against its candidates in parliamentary elections.

Anna Maria Priestman upheld the peace testimony of her religious society throughout her life. The outbreak of the First World War was said to have been too much for either herself or Mary Priestman to bear; she died at their Bristol home, 37 Durdham Park, on 9 October 1914 within five days of her sister.   SANDRA STANLEY HOLTON

Sources S. J. Tanner, *How the women's suffrage movement began in Bristol 50 years ago* (1918) · K. Robbins, *John Bright* (1979) · S. S. Holton, *Suffrage days: stories from the women's suffrage movement* (1996) · J. T. Mills, *John Bright and the Quakers*, 2 vols. (1935) · H. Blackburn, *Women's suffrage: a record of the women's suffrage movement in the British Isles* (1902) · G. M. Trevelyan, *The life of John Bright* (1913) · R. S. Benson, *Photographic pedigree of the descendants of Isaac and Rachel Wilson* (1912) · J. Somervell, *Isaac and Rachel Wilson, Quakers, of Kendal, 1714–1785* [1924] · 'Dictionary of Quaker biography', RS Friends, Lond. [card index] · d. cert. · Priestman MSS, C. and J. Clark Ltd, Street, Somerset, Clark family archive
Archives C. and J. Clark Ltd, Street, Somerset, Clark family archive | Women's Library, London, Butler MSS · Women's Library, London, McIlquham MSS
Likenesses group portrait, photograph (with her sisters), repro. in P. Lovell, *Quaker inheritance: a portrait of Roger Clark of Street...*

(1970), facing p. 32 · photograph, repro. in Tanner, *How the women's suffrage movement began*, facing p. 10
Wealth at death £10,675 19*s*. 5*d*.: probate, 5 May 1915, *CGPLA Eng. & Wales*

Priestman, John (1805–1866), manufacturer of worsted goods and peace campaigner, son of Joshua and Hannah Priestman, was born at Thornton, near Pickering, Yorkshire, where his ancestors had lived for more than 200 years. He is believed to have been educated at the Society of Friends' school at Ackworth, Yorkshire, and apprenticed to an uncle, a tanner at York, but at nineteen he joined his brother-in-law James Ellis in the Old Corn Mill, Bradford. Together they founded the first ragged school in Bradford, in a room at the top of one of their mills. Priestman was one of the founders in 1832 of the Friends' Provident Institution, a society whose conspicuous success was due to economic management and the temperate habits of the members, and he remained on the board of directors until his death.

In early life Priestman became a free-trader, and he represented Bradford at many of the conferences called by the Anti-Corn Law League. A staunch Liberal, he was twice invited, and twice declined, to stand as a parliamentary candidate for Bradford. Priestman and his partner Ellis actively resisted the collection of church rates. For refusal to pay the rate for 1835 they were summoned before the magistrates; and, partly because of the publicity surrounding their case, the rate was not levied again in their parish.

Chiefly from a desire to utilize the surplus power of machinery in his mills, Priestman in 1838 commenced manufacturing worsted goods in an upper room. He removed to larger premises in Preston Place in 1845, and in 1855 he abandoned corn milling altogether. His treatment of the millhands, chiefly women and girls, was sympathetic and enlightened, and they grew so refined that his works became known as 'Lady Mills'. He successfully introduced a system of profit sharing with part of his workforce.

Much of Priestman's time and money was devoted to the causes of peace and temperance. From 1834, when the Preston 'teetotallers' first visited Bradford, he adopted total abstinence. At the same time he and his partner relinquished malt crushing, a process in the manufacture of beer, which was the most profitable part of their milling business. He was one of the few supporters of Richard Cobden in his condemnation of the Crimean War and he seconded the unpopular anti-war resolution proposed by Cobden at a great meeting at Leeds in 1854. In 1855 he was elected a town councillor, but resigned before taking his seat.

Priestman married on 28 November 1833 Sarah, daughter of Joseph Burgess of Beaumont Lodge, Leicester, who died in 1849, leaving two sons and a daughter. In 1852 he married Mary, daughter of Thomas Smith, miller, of Uxbridge, Middlesex, who survived him; they had two sons.

A stern adherent to Quaker principles through life, after three months of illness Priestman died suddenly while dressing at his home at Whetley Hill, Bradford, on 29 October 1866; he was buried on 2 November in the Undercliffe cemetery, Bradford; 1100 of his workpeople attended the funeral. CHARLOTTE FELL-SMITH, rev. K. D. REYNOLDS

Sources *Biographical catalogue: being an account of the lives of Friends and others whose portraits are in the London Friends' Institute*, Society of Friends (1888) · Boase, *Mod. Eng. biog.* · *Friends' Quarterly Examiner*, 1 (1867), 344–56 · *Annual Monitor* (1868), 198 · *Bradford Observer* (1 Nov 1866) · *CGPLA Eng. & Wales* (1866)
Likenesses photograph, 1868, RS Friends, Lond.
Wealth at death under £100,000: resworn probate, Jan 1867, *CGPLA Eng. & Wales* (1866)

Priestman, William Dent (1847–1936), engineer, was born on 23 August 1847 at East Mount, Sutton, near Hull, the second son of eleven children of Samuel Priestman (1800–1872), corn miller and railway company director, and his wife, Mary Anne (1807–1899), daughter of William Dent, farmer, of Marr, near Doncaster.

Raised a Quaker, Priestman was educated from 1860 at Bootham School, York, where he won the school mechanical drawing prize for Joseph Rowntree's works steam engine. He left school in 1864 and became an engineering apprentice at Martin Samuelson & Co., owners of the Humber Iron Works in Hull. Within eighteen months the business had failed, and he completed his apprenticeship in the locomotive shops of the North Eastern Railway Company, Gateshead. In 1869 he joined the firm of Sir William Armstrong & Co. in the hydraulics department in Newcastle. An opportunity arose for him to become a partner in B. & W. Hawthorne, locomotive builders of Newcastle, but his father was opposed to the idea and wanted him to set up his own business in Hull. Without consulting his son he paid £3000 for a small, run-down engineering works there, known as the Holderness Foundry. By the time of his death in 1872 serious financial problems had already beset the business.

The partnership was dissolved in 1873, and Priestman was joined by his younger brother Samuel. For the next two years they concentrated on repair work for ships in the docks and general engineering. In 1874 Thomas Christy, a London company promoter and brother of the well-known hatter, ordered a winch capable of operating a grab that he bought in the USA. The purpose was to dredge for gold in Vigo harbour, north-west Spain, where a vessel sunk in the Spanish Civil War of 1702 was believed to contain treasure. The winch performed well, and although no treasure was found the order had put the brothers unwittingly into the grab business. The first grab crane mounted on a rail bogie was supplied to James Pearson & Son, contractors, whose descendants, the Cowdrays, were to own the *Financial Times*.

On 18 April 1878 Priestman married Marion (1849–1945), the daughter of Samuel Bewley of Bray, Ireland, at the Hull Friends' meeting-house. In Paris, where the couple were on honeymoon, a silver medal was awarded to the firm at the Paris Exhibition for its first steam crane and self-acting bucket, and the prince of Wales paid a visit to their stand.

In 1879 Priestman lectured at the Hull Mechanics' Institute on a project to use liquid fuel directly in the engine cylinder instead of steam or gas, so producing a great increase in efficiency. In 1883 he spotted, in a London office window, an Étève model engine of the internal combustion type. The Étève–Hume patents purchased in 1884 applied only to petroleum spirit (gasoline) powered engines, so in 1886 he decided to patent his own design for a two-stroke-cycle engine running on paraffin fuel oil. For two years he experimented on ways of spraying the paraffin (benzoline) mixture into a chamber warmed by the exhaust, mixing it with oil, and exploding the mixture with an electric spark. Eventually success was achieved. Sir William Thomson (later Lord Kelvin) was asked and gave a favourable report on the new engine, which was first patented on 30 January 1886 and given a second, and more precise, patent on 11 October 1886. Three silver medals were awarded at the Royal Agricultural Society shows for the engine at Nottingham (1888), Windsor (1889), and Plymouth (1890). Being portable and safe it was particularly suitable for use in lighthouses, pumping stations, coal mines, and on country estates.

In 1889 Priestman was badly hurt in his legs and arms when a vessel exploded at the works during testing; he recovered on a trip to Tasmania. In 1890 it was decided to enter the marine market, and a series of twin-cylinder vertical engines of 30 and 65 bhp were introduced. These included a reversible gear box for the propeller, which was successfully patented. Many of these were fitted to canal barges and private launches. For demonstration purposes one launch was moored opposite the houses of parliament in London and another belonging to the French agent plied the River Seine in Paris.

From 1891 the competition which was eventually to prove fatal for the business began to emerge. Although by 1894 one of the major difficulties of the Priestman engine—the problem of carbonization—had been overcome, larger concerns were now selling engines at substantially lower prices, which the Priestman company could not match. The business went into receivership in January 1895. A board of management was appointed after attempts to sell the designs failed, and it was decided to return to the manufacture of grabs and cranes only. From this point Priestman was excluded from the board and had no official voice in the company he founded, though both his son Philip and his grandson James subsequently became managing directors. He died at his home, 81 Village Road, Garden Village, Hull, on 7 September 1936, of pneumonia, and was buried at the eastern cemetery, Hull.

From 1885 to 1901 Priestman had obtained forty-five patents covering designs of grabs, grab cranes, winches, and engines. His firm designed, manufactured, and sold over 1000 engines during its fifteen years of manufacture; some of its engines were still working after the Second World War. Priestman was a steadfast believer in Quaker faith and principles. His abhorrence of backhanders, in what he felt amounted to bribery, encouraged him to seek out Sir Edward Fry, the eminent barrister, who he helped to draft the Bribery and Illicit Commissions Bill, which became law in 1907. A Quaker obituary in *The Friend* described him as combining 'Something of the steadfastness of Peter and the flaming enthusiasm of Paul' in his character.

JAMES DENT PRIESTMAN

Sources S. H. Priestman, *The Priestmans of Thornton-Le-Dale*, rev. [S. Doncaster and J. Priestman], 2nd edn (privately printed, Sutton-on-Hull, 1978) · C. L. Cummins, J. R. Priestman, and J. D. Priestman, 'William Dent Priestman, oil engine pioneer and inventor: his engine patents, 1885–1901', *Proceedings*, 199/133 (1985) [IMechE/ Newcomen Society Joint Lecture, 20 Nov 1985] · W. D. Priestman, handwritten recollections, unpublished biography, Goathland notes, 1921, Sci. Mus. · S. H. Priestman, 'William Dent Priestman: memorial lecture', *Journal of Hull Association of Engineers*, new ser., 28 (1960–61) · J. D. Priestman, *William Dent Priestman of Hull and the first oil engine* (1994) · *The Friend* (18 Sept 1936), 862–3 · b. cert. · d. cert. · personal knowledge (2004)
Archives Sci. Mus.
Wealth at death £1309 19s.: probate, 23 March 1937, CGPLA Eng. & Wales

Prim, John George Augustus (1821–1875), antiquary and newspaper proprietor, was born in Kilkenny, the eldest son of John H. Prim. He was probably educated in Kilkenny. He was a general printer and stationer in the city and in the mid-1850s became proprietor of the *Kilkenny Moderator*, a Conservative newspaper founded in 1814. In 1849, with James Graves, Prim founded the Kilkenny and South East of Ireland Archaeological Society and acted as its honorary secretary. The society's object was to publish articles on local history and archaeology, but Prim and Graves did not stop there, regarding themselves as the guardians of their antiquities, and as their interpreters. They tackled local landowners who were neglecting and destroying monuments: in 1848 they physically intervened in the case of the Dunbell ogham stones, which they rescued when their site was being destroyed (the stones are now in the National Museum of Ireland in Dublin). They also published the collections held in the muniment room in Kilkenny Castle. This was particularly fortunate as much of this material was subsequently sent to the Public Record Office in Dublin, where it was destroyed in the fire of 1922.

Prim saw the *Moderator* as more than a reporter of local news, and used it to widen understanding of the history of Kilkenny and the county. When the society was unable to issue a journal of its own, he used the newspaper to publish articles on local history and archaeology. The society became the Historical and Archaeological Association of Ireland in 1868, and Prim was one of its founding fellows. Prim and Graves wrote the history of the architecture and antiquities of St Canice's Cathedral, Kilkenny (1857). It was first intended to be a history of the see and bishops of Ossory, and of the corporation of Kilkenny, but the material proved to be so large that this plan had to be abandoned and they confined themselves to the cathedral. They had hoped to publish a second volume to include the rest of their material, but this never happened. Prim also planned to write a series of articles on the most important families of Kilkenny as part of a history of the county— one of the original objects of the society. His *Memorials of the Family of Langton of Kilkenny* (1864) was part of this project.

Prim was married—to a woman of whom nothing is known but that her name was Mary—and had a family. He died on 2 November 1875 at Nore Cottage, Kilkenny, his brother's house, and was buried in the churchyard of St Canice's, Kilkenny. His kindness and generosity, and his work on the history and culture of Ireland, were widely recognized. MARIE-LOUISE LEGG

Sources *Kilkenny Moderator* (3 Nov 1875) · *Kilkenny Moderator* (10 Nov 1875) · *Journal of the Royal Historical and Archaeological Association of Ireland*, 4th ser., 4 (1876–8), 5
Wealth at death under £6000: administration, 16 Dec 1875, CGPLA Ire.

Primatt, Humphry (*bap.* 1735, *d.* 1776/7), Church of England clergyman and writer on animal welfare, was born in London and was baptized on 24 April 1735 at St Andrew's, Holborn, the second son of the Revd William Primat (*bap.* 1702, *d.* 1770), rector of West Walton, Norfolk, and his wife, Elizabeth. Little is known of Primatt's life. He became a pensioner at Clare College, Cambridge, on 11 July 1752, matriculating in Michaelmas the same year, graduating BA in 1757, and proceeding MA in 1764. He was vicar of Higham in Suffolk and of Swardeston in Norfolk from 1766 to 1774, and rector of Brampton, Norfolk, from 1771. On 2 November 1769, at St Katharine Cree, Leadenhall Street, London, he married Sarah Gullifer, daughter of John Wood. On his father's death in 1770 he inherited half of his estate, the remainder passing to his elder brother, William. He resigned his living in 1774 and, being then described by an anonymous contemporary source as 'a man of means', he lived 'in some style' at Kingston upon Thames 'for the honour of Aberdeen' (Venn, *Alum. Cant.*). (Marischal College in Aberdeen, had appointed him DD on 3 September 1773.)

Primatt's only known work is *A Dissertation on the Duty of Mercy and the Sin of Cruelty to Brute Animals*, first published in 1776. The book was one of the first ever devoted entirely to an attack upon cruelty to animals. The last two-thirds consist of quotations from scripture to support his case. In the earlier pages, however, Primatt expresses himself with clarity, arguing that 'pain is pain, whether it be inflicted on man or on beast; and the creature that suffers it, whether man or beast, being sensible of the misery of it while it lasts, suffers evil' (*Duty of Mercy*, 7–8). Primatt points out that if animals lack the hope of an afterlife their earthly miseries are made worse. He draws the parallel between what were later called racism and speciesism: the white man 'can have no right, by virtue of his colour, to enslave and tyrannise over a black man' (ibid., 11), so, similarly, 'the difference of shape between a man and a brute, cannot give to a man any right to abuse and torment a brute' (ibid., 15). Primatt chides mankind for its arrogance and injustice towards animals. 'A brute is an animal no less sensible of pain than a man. He has similar nerves and organs of sensation' (ibid., 13). Physical differences are morally irrelevant:

> whether we walk upon two legs or four; whether our heads are prone or erect; whether we are naked or covered in hair; whether we have tails or no tails, horns or no horns, long ears or round ears; or whether we bray like an ass, speak like a man, whistle like a bird, or are mute as a fish—nature never intended these distinctions as foundations for right of tyranny and oppression. (ibid., 18)

The book's arguments also circulated in a summary appended to a sermon by a Dorset clergyman, John Toogood, which reached its third edition in 1790, and a fourth edition, published in Boston, Massachusetts, in 1802. A new edition of Primatt's book, edited by Arthur Broome, appeared in 1822. Further editions appeared in 1831, 1834, and 1992. The book was an inspiration to Broome who helped Richard Martin, William Wilberforce, and others to found in 1824 the society that was to become the Royal Society for the Prevention of Cruelty to Animals (RSPCA). It was also cited by Henry Salt, the intellectual leader of the animal rights movement in the late nineteenth century.

Primatt's emphasis upon the moral importance of pain has stood the test of time and it anticipated by several years Jeremy Bentham's much-quoted comment about the moral status of animals: 'The question is not can they *reason*? Nor, can they *talk*? But can they *suffer*?' (Ryder, *Animal Revolution*, rev. edn, 71).

Primatt died in late 1776 or early 1777; his will, proved on 29 March 1777, left most of his estate to his wife, Sarah. No children are mentioned, although it refers to his relatives named Primatt, Kennedy, Maud, and Blackall, and to relatives of his wife, who were then living around Boston, Massachusetts. He left his books in Latin, Greek, and Hebrew to Marischal College, Aberdeen. His widow remarried on 24 July 1780. RICHARD D. RYDER

Sources H. Primatt, *The duty of mercy and the sin of cruelty to brute animals*, ed. R. D. Ryder (1992) [incl. introduction by R. D. Ryder, 11–13] · R. D. Ryder, *Animal revolution: changing attitudes towards speciesism* (1989); rev. edn (2000) · will, PRO, PROB 11/1029, sig. 127 · H. Primatt, *A dissertation on the duty of mercy and sin of cruelty to brute animals* (1776) · Venn, *Alum. Cant.* · P. J. Anderson and J. F. K. Johnstone, eds., *Fasti academiae Mariscallanae Aberdonensis: selections from the records of the Marischal College and University, MDXCIII–MDCCCLX*, 3 vols., New Spalding Club, 4, 18–19 (1889–98), vol. 1, p. 454; vol. 2, p. 85

Prime, John (1549/50–1596), Church of England clergyman and preacher, was born in Holywell parish, Oxford—according to Anthony Wood, son of Robert Prime, a fletcher. Scholar of Winchester College from 1564 and then of New College, Oxford, from 1569, he became fellow there in 1571, gaining his BA in 1572 and his MA in 1576. Ordained in 1575, he then proceeded to supplicate successfully for a university preaching licence in 1581, and for the degrees of BTh and DTh in 1584 and 1588 respectively. He established a reputation for aggressively protestant preaching, and fittingly dedicated to Sir Francis Walsingham in 1583 *A Short Treatise of the Sacraments* and a longer *Fruitefull and Briefe Discourse … of Nature … [and] of Grace*, especially directed against the Rheims edition of the New Testament, both insisting on the indefectibility of election. Between 1586 and 1590 Prime delivered the Oxford city lecture at Carfax. His longest work, *An Exposition and*

Observations upon St Paul to the Galatians (1587), was dedicated to John Piers, bishop of Salisbury (possibly also the recipient of a paper by Prime two years before on the question of Christ's descent into hell), and was professedly based upon sermons that Prime had been preaching at Abingdon 'every other week'.

Prime made something of a speciality of sermons in the university church, St Mary the Virgin, for Elizabeth's accession day, 17 November. In 1585 he delivered and then rapidly published *Sermon Briefly Comparing the Estate of King Salomon and his Subjects with Queene Elizabeth and her People*, in which he seemed to consider himself as compensating for the popish past of New College (perhaps hinting at tensions that he might have experienced there); in 1588 there followed *The Consolations of David Briefly Applied to Queen Elizabeth*. This last was dedicated to Thomas Cooper, bishop of Winchester, with expressions of dismay at the attack on him by Martin Marprelate. 'Were all thinges amisse, is this the way to reforme … ?' (sig. A2). Calvinist theology did not presuppose presbyterian sympathies, and Prime was certainly concerned to dissociate himself from Marprelate. The latter retorted in *Hay any Worke for Cooper* (1589), calling Prime 'Wynken de Worde', an otherwise obscure allusion to a printing pioneer which may refer to Prime as having been one of the signatories of the foreword to John Case's *Moral Questions* (1585), the first book from Oxford University's press, which soon afterwards printed books by Prime himself. *Hay any Worke* threatened, 'I'll bepistle you, Dr Prime, when I am at more leisure; though, indeed, I tell you true, that as yet I do disdain to deal with a contemptible trencher-chaplain' (Pierce, 267).

In 1589 Prime was presented to the New College vicarage of Adderbury, Oxfordshire, being instituted early the following year and soon afterwards quitting his fellowship and lectureships. Perhaps he fulfilled the stern views of parochial duties he had expressed earlier; at any rate he seems to have distracted himself no further with publication. In April 1596 he made his will in 'sickness of body', but with 'full hope for a better resurrection' (Oxfordshire Archives, MS Wills Oxon. 190, 167), leaving his books to his old college and most of his money to his nieces. He died on 11 or 12 April at Adderbury, and was buried there.

JULIAN LOCK

Sources Wood, *Ath. Oxon.*, new edn, 1.652–3 · J. Prime, will, 1596, Oxfordshire Archives, MS Wills, Oxon. 190, fol. 167 · *The Marprelate tracts, 1588–1589*, ed. W. Pierce (1911) · Foster, *Alum. Oxon.* · T. F. Kirby, *Winchester scholars: a list of the wardens, fellows, and scholars of … Winchester College* (1888), 139 · H. E. Salter, ed., *Oxford council acts, 1583–1626*, OHS, 87 (1928), 23, 53 · LPL, Carte Miscellanee 12, no. 3, fol. 27r · composition books, PRO, exchequer, first fruits, E334/11, fol. 85r · *VCH Oxfordshire*, 9.32 · D. D. Wallace, *Puritans and predestination: grace in English protestant theology, 1525–1695* (1982) · B. T. Whitehead, *Brags and boasts: propaganda in the year of the Armada* (1994) · J. Strype, *Annals of the Reformation and establishment of religion … during Queen Elizabeth's happy reign*, new edn, 3/1 (1824), 519

Archives Bodl. Oxf., copy of letter (to Bishop Piers, 1585?) about Christ's descent into hell, MS Rawl. C.167, fol. 19

Wealth at death £296 17s. 3d.; Adderbury vicarage valued at £66 13s. 4d.: inventory, Oxon. RO, Oxfordshire Archives, MS Wills,

Oxon. 190, fol. 167; J. Howard-Drake, ed., *Oxford church court depositions, 1589–1593* (1997), 30; PRO, E334/11, fol. 85r.

Prime, Sir Samuel (1701–1777), serjeant-at-law, was born on 21 August 1701, the second son of Thomas Prime, a grocer at Bury St Edmunds, Suffolk, and his wife, Elizabeth, and attended the grammar school there before going up to St John's College, Cambridge, in 1718. Two years later he was admitted to the Middle Temple, where he was called to the bar in 1724. Numerous surviving opinions under his name show that he had an extensive chambers practice, and he distinguished himself sufficiently at the bar to be given the coif at the last general call of serjeants, in 1736, and a patent as one of the king's serjeants in 1738. Together with Serjeant Birch he was knighted in 1745. On 23 August 1748 he married Hannah, daughter of E. Wilmot of Banstead, Surrey, and widow of John Sheppard of Campsey Ash.

By dint of seniority as a king's serjeant Prime became in 1749 the king's prime serjeant-at-law, and as such leader of the bar of England until his retirement in Trinity term 1758. The reason for his retirement, according to Lord Thurlow, was a chance remark by the latter on the affront to his rank by the government in entrusting the prosecution of the French spy Florence Hensey, for high treason, to Sir Fletcher Norton. He was treasurer of Serjeants' Inn, Chancery Lane, from 1749 until the same year. His office of king's serjeant was not renewed after the demise of the crown in 1760. Professional anecdotes of him, handed down into the following century, suggested that he was a dry and long-winded advocate with little or no sense of humour. Nevertheless, the *Gentleman's Magazine* perhaps intended a compliment when it said, after his death: 'He was the Sir Fletcher Norton of his time.' Serjeant Prime lived nearly twenty years in retirement. He died on 24 February 1777 and was buried in the Temple Church, where there is an inscription. His only son, Samuel Prime (d. 1813), followed him to St John's College and the Middle Temple, where he was called in 1773.   J. H. BAKER

Sources Baker, *Serjeants* · Sainty, *King's counsel* · Venn, *Alum. Cant.* · H. A. C. Sturgess, ed., *Register of admissions to the Honourable Society of the Middle Temple, from the fifteenth century to the year 1944*, 3 vols. (1949) · S. H. A. H. [S. H. A. Hervey], *Biographical list of boys educated at King Edward VI Free Grammar School, Bury St Edmunds, from 1550 to 1900* (1908), 316 · W. Musgrave, *Obituary prior to 1800*, ed. G. J. Armytage, 1, Harleian Society, 44 (1899) · H. W. Woolrych, *Lives of eminent serjeants-at-law of the English bar*, 2 vols. (1869) · *GM*, 1st ser., 47 (1777), 96 · monumental inscription, Temple Church, London · A. Polson, *Law and lawyers, or, Sketches and illustrations of legal history and biography*, 2 vols. (1840)

Likenesses drawing, NPG

Primmer, Jacob (1842–1914), Church of Scotland minister and religious controversialist, was born on 6 October 1842 at 9 Broad Wynd, Leith, the second of the four children of John Primmer (1815–1846), merchant seaman, and his wife, Louisa (1810–1891), daughter of Commodore Jacob White RN. Primmer was educated at St John's Free Church Infant School (c.1848–1850), where he also attended a Sunday school held in the same building, and Kay's Commercial School (c.1850–1855). Here, in recollection at least, Primmer's enthusiasm was confined to scripture lessons and devotional exercises; by his own account his most formative religious experience as a child was gloating over the illustrations to Foxe's book of martyrs. After leaving school he was apprenticed as a compositor, but continued to educate himself by independent study and attendance at Christian Fellowship meetings, and, significantly, at the anti-popery classes instituted by John Hope. He studied divinity at the University of Edinburgh from 1865 and, by 1872, the year of his graduation, Primmer's views were fully formed. He believed in total abstinence and sabbatarianism, and was committed to defending the principles, and often the forms and practices, of the original protestant reformers.

Primmer's first charge, which he took up in 1872, was at Gardenstown Mission, Banff. At Gardenstown he met Jessie Munro (1848–1912), the village schoolmistress, who became his wife on 12 July 1876; they had two sons. In the year of his marriage he was given charge of Townhill Mission, in a mining village near the town of Dunfermline, Fife; in 1903 he moved to Kingseathill in Dunfermline. Immediately on his arrival at Townhill he courted controversy. In defiance of the presbytery of Dunfermline he administered unfermented wine to communicants in his church and successfully took his case to the general assembly in 1879. This experience gave him a taste for litigation and many of his causes were pursued through civil and church courts. He relished direct confrontation and, in his campaign against ritual and vestments, visited other churches and denounced offending ministers as they preached in their own pulpits. In Primmer's own estimation, his major achievement was the series of open-air meetings, or 'historic conventicles', held throughout Scotland between 1888 and 1908. These were impressive, rowdy occasions, where Primmer's simple, pugnacious preaching style and bearded, prophet-like appearance were used to powerful and provocative effect.

Primmer wrote at least fifty pamphlets and was a tireless correspondent, both in the press and with public figures. In 1897 the curious *Jacob Primmer in Rome*, a comprehensive tourist account of the Italian capital, as seen through the eyes of a primitive protestant zealot, was published. Ultimately, though contemporaries testified to his sincerity and energy, his antics were an irrelevant and eccentric sideshow in the religious life of Scotland. Primmer died from a stroke on 14 August 1914 at the manse, Kingseathill, Dunfermline, and was buried four days later at Warriston cemetery in Edinburgh. CHRIS NEALE

Sources J. B. Primmer, ed., *Life of Jacob Primmer* (1916) · J. B. Primmer, *A church of truth* (1962) · *Fasti Scot.* · *Church of Scotland Assembly Papers* (1902) · *Dunfermline Journal* (15 Aug 1914) · *Dunfermline Press* (22 Aug 1914) · D. Jamie, *John Hope: philanthropist and reformer* (1900) · 'Pastor Jacob Primmer's semi-jubilee', *Dunfermline Journal* (23 March 1901)
Archives Dunfermline Central Library
Likenesses Turnbull & Sons, photograph, c.1880, repro. in Primmer, ed., *Life of Jacob Primmer*, frontispiece · W. Y. C., pencil drawing, 1890, repro. in *The Bailie*, 924 (2 July 1890) · two photographs, c.1900–1910, repro. in Primmer, ed., *Life of Jacob Primmer*, facing p. 303, 313 · caricatures, repro. in *Dundee Evening Post* (1900–02) [v.d.]
Wealth at death £610 16s. 10d.: confirmation, 21 Oct 1914, CCI

Primrose, Sir Archibald, first baronet, Lord Carrington (1616–1679), legal official and judge, was born on 16 May 1616, son of James *Primrose (d. 1640), clerk to the privy council of Scotland (1599–1640), and his second wife, Catherine (d. 1651), daughter of Richard Lawson (fl. 1603–1622) of Boghall, Lanarkshire, presbyterian bookseller of Edinburgh. Little is known of Primrose's early life and education but he clearly studied law before he succeeded his late father as clerk to the privy council in September 1641.

Primrose's career was split into two halves by the Cromwellian interregnum. At first he acted as clerk to the convention of estates in 1643 and 1644. However, after the royalist victory at Kilsyth he joined the army of Montrose, persuading others to switch sides. He was taken prisoner as Montrose was defeated at the battle of Philiphaugh on 13 September 1645, and found guilty of treason at the covenanting parliament of St Andrews in 1646, yet suffered only a spell in prison. Having taken part in the failed engagement of 1648, that last attempt to unite moderate Scottish royalists with the interests of Charles I, he was on 10 March 1649 deprived of the office of clerk of the privy council by the Act of Classes. However, he was absolved by the commission of the kirk on 4 January 1651, pardoned by the committee of estates on 10 January, and fully reinstated on 6 June 1651. Primrose went on to accompany Charles II on his march into England and was created a baronet in August 1651 just after being knighted. But after the disastrous defeat of the Scottish army at the battle of Worcester, Primrose had his estates sequestrated and remained out of office during the protectorate.

At the Restoration, Primrose was appointed lord clerk register on 7 August 1660. It was necessary for him to buy off Sir William Fleming to whom Charles II had granted the post during his exile. On 15 February 1661 he was appointed a lord of session under the title Lord Carrington, and also a lord of exchequer and member of the Scottish privy council. As clerk register he was instructed to draft legislation reasserting royal authority and especially the Rescissory Act, by which all the acts of the Scottish parliament since 1633 were rescinded. Gilbert Burnet's idea that Carrington suggested this sweeping act 'half in jest' is incredible (*Bishop Burnet's History*, 1.213). Although associated with the Clarendonian party in England and a follower of the party of the royal commissioner John, earl of Middleton, in opposition to John Maitland, earl of Lauderdale, secretary of state, Carrington was astute enough to oppose the 1662 Act of Billeting which was designed to destroy Lauderdale. He, therefore, retained his offices after Middleton's fall from power in 1663–4, his position apparently 'right and fixed' in Lauderdale's interest (Airy, 1.180).

Unfortunately, Carrington fell foul of Lauderdale's second wife, Elizabeth, countess of Dysart, whom Lauderdale had married in 1672. Intrigues attributed to her led to his resignation from the office of clerk register by 11 June 1676. The position passed in November 1677 to the duchess's kinsman Sir Thomas Murray of Glendook. As

Sir Archibald Primrose, first baronet, Lord Carrington (1616–1679), by John Scougall

merks (£106,000 Scots); in due course this became the seat of the Rosebery family. He died on 27 November 1679 with an estate valued at £58,000 Scots, including £27,000 of cash and gold, and was buried at the parish church of Dalmeny. He was well read and died with a library valued at £200. He was a born conservative, an astute politician, and a believer in compromise. Burnet, Carrington's contemporary, describes a conscientious public servant, 'dexterous ... in business ... he had always expedients ready at every difficulty [and] ... was always for soft councils and slow methods' (*Bishop Burnet's History*, 1.192). His long tenure as clerk register is testament to these qualities.

A. J. MANN

Sources *Bishop Burnet's History of his own time*, ed. M. J. Routh, 1, 72, 192, 213, 214 · *Reg. PCS*, 3rd ser., vols. 1–5 · *The Lauderdale papers*, ed. O. Airy, 1, CS, new ser., 34 (1884), 16, 180 · *APS*, 1643–51; 1661–9 · A. F. Mitchell and J. Christie, eds., *The records of the commissions of the general assemblies of the Church of Scotland*, 3, Scottish History Society, 58 (1909), 190–91 · parliamentary records, committee of estates, NA Scot., PA.11.10, fol. 18 · Register House, old parish registers, NA Scot., 681.1.44 · NA Scot., Clerk of Penicuik MSS, GD.18.5167 · register of testaments, Edinburgh, NA Scot., CC.8/8/78 · *Scots peerage* · G. Brunton and D. Haig, *An historical account of the senators of the college of justice, from its institution in MDXXXII* (1832), 352–5 · J. Buckroyd, *Church and state in Scotland, 1660–1681* (1980), 118–28
Archives NL Scot., corresp. [transcripts] | BL, letters to Lauderdale and Charles II, Add. MSS 23115–23137 · Buckminster Park, Grantham, corresp. with duke of Lauderdale · NA Scot., letters to John Clerk · U. Edin. L., letters to duke of Lauderdale
Likenesses J. Scougall, oils, Penicuik House, Midlothian · J. Scougall, oils, second version, Scot. NPG [*see illus.*]
Wealth at death £58,000 Scots, incl. £27,000 in cash and gold: register of testaments, Edinburgh, NA Scot., CC. 8/8/78, proved 21 Dec 1686

compensation Carrington was granted the office of justice-general with its inferior emoluments. He then had an important role in the trial of the covenanter James Mitchell. Mitchell had been arrested in 1674 for an attempt in 1668 to murder Archbishop James Sharp and had been promised his life by Lauderdale and the privy council provided he confessed. After his confession Mitchell was left in prison. However, he was brought to trial again in January 1678, the indemnity conveniently forgotten. No doubt for reasons both of revenge and of justice, Carrington made known the extract of the privy council register to embarrass Lauderdale who hid behind a lapse of memory. This made not the slightest difference to the outcome and Mitchell was executed. In October, Carrington was, not unexpectedly, deprived of the office of justice-general.

Carrington married, first, in or before 1641, Elizabeth, daughter and coheir of Sir James Keith of Benholm, and second, in or before 1657, Agnes, daughter of Sir William Gray of Pittendrum and widow of Sir James Dundas of Newlinston. William, his eldest son from his first marriage, succeeded to the baronetcy. His youngest son of the same marriage, Gilbert (1654–1731), served on the Rhine and in the Low Countries under Marlborough and by 1710 had risen to the rank of major-general. The only son by the second marriage, Archibald *Primrose, became the first earl of Rosebery in 1703.

Carrington became extremely wealthy. In 1662 he acquired the lands and barony of Barnbougle in Dalmeny, Linlithgowshire, from the earl of Haddington for 160,000

Primrose, Archibald, of Dalmeny, first earl of Rosebery (1664–1723), politician, was born on 18 December 1664 at Edinburgh. He was the only son of Archibald *Primrose, Lord Carrington (1616–1679), lord justice-general, and his second wife, Agnes, daughter of Sir William Gray of Pittendrum, and widow of Sir James Dundas. In his youth he travelled abroad and served in the imperial army of Hungary, returning to Scotland in 1687. On 26 June 1688 he was summoned before the privy council on the charge of spreading discord among the officers of state opposed, like him, to James II's policies in Scotland. Through the intervention of the duke of Berwick, however, the investigation was suspended.

After the revolution of 1688 Primrose was appointed one of the gentlemen of the bedchamber to Prince George of Denmark, on whose death in 1708 the salary of £600 a year attached to the office was continued to him for life. He married on 3 February 1691 Dorothy Cressy (b. 1672/3?, d. after 1724), daughter of Everingham and Anne Cressy of Birkin, Yorkshire; they had six sons and six daughters. In 1695 he was chosen to represent the county of Edinburgh in the Scottish parliament, and, on account of his consistent support of the government, he was in April 1700 created Viscount Rosebery, Lord Primrose and Dalmeny. On the accession of Queen Anne in 1702 he was sworn of the privy council, and in April 1703 created earl of Rosebery, viscount of Inverkeithing, and Lord Dalmeny and Primrose in the Scottish peerage. He was one of the commissioners for the Union with England, and after its accomplishment was chosen as a Scottish representative peer in 1707, 1708, 1710, and 1713. Between 1703 and 1714 he also served as chamberlain of Fife and Strathearn. Rosebery died on 20 October 1723, and was succeeded by his eldest son, James Primrose, second earl of Rosebery (1691–1755), who on the death in 1741 of his kinsman Hugh, Viscount Primrose, inherited the family estate and baronetcy of the elder branch of the family.

T. F. HENDERSON, *rev.* PHILIP CARTER

Sources GEC, *Peerage*
Archives NRA Scotland, priv. coll., papers
Likenesses J. B. Medina, oils, Scot. NPG · P. Vanderbank, line engraving (after J. Riley), BM
Wealth at death presumed wealthy

Primrose, Archibald John, fourth earl of Rosebery (1783–1868), politician, eldest son of Neil, third earl of Rosebery (*d.* 25 Jan 1814), and his second wife, Mary, only daughter of Sir Francis Vincent of Stoke d'Abernon, Surrey, was born at Barnbougle Castle, Dalmeny, near Edinburgh, on 14 October 1783. He was educated at Pembroke College, Cambridge, graduating MA in 1804; he was made an honorary DCL by the university in 1819. He sat in parliament for Helston, Cornwall (1805–6), and for Cashel (1806–7), for which he paid 4000 guineas. He succeeded his father on 25 January 1814; for several parliaments he was chosen a representative peer, until the parliament of 1828 when, on Goderich's advice, he was created a peer of the United Kingdom with the title Baron Rosebery of Rosebery, Midlothian. In 1819 he moved the family seat from the medieval Barnbougle Castle to the neo-Gothic Dalmeny House, newly built near by. He was well liked in the Forth valley as a public-spirited, reforming landowner.

Rosebery took an active interest as a whig in the passing of the Reform Bill of 1832. In 1831 he was sworn of the privy council, and in 1840 was made a knight of the Thistle. From 1843 to 1863 he was lord lieutenant of Linlithgowshire. He was a fellow of the Royal Society, and a member of other learned institutions.

With his first wife, Harriet, second daughter of the Hon. Bartholomew Bouverie (afterwards earl of Radnor) and his wife, Mary, Rosebery had two sons and a daughter. The marriage was dissolved in 1815 after her adultery with Sir Henry Mildmay, bt, from whom Rosebery obtained £15,000 in damages. Harriet married Mildmay the same year and died in 1834. Rosebery married as his second wife the Hon. Anne Margaret Anson, eldest daughter of Thomas, first Viscount Anson (afterwards earl of Lichfield), and his wife, Anne Margaret, with whom he had two sons. His eldest son from the first marriage, Archibald, Lord Dalmeny (1809–1851), represented the Stirling burghs in parliament from 1833 to 1847, and from April 1835 to August 1841 was a lord of the Admiralty. He was the author of *An Address to the Middle Classes on the Subject of Gymnastic Exercises* (1848), and was the father of Archibald

Philip *Primrose, fifth earl of Rosebery, the prime minister.

Rosebery died at his London residence, 139 Piccadilly, on 4 March 1868, and was buried at Dalmeny.

T. F. HENDERSON, *rev.* H. C. G. MATTHEW

Sources GEC, *Peerage* · R. R. James, *Rosebery: a biography of Archibald Philip, fifth earl of Rosebery* (1963) · HoP, *Commons*
Archives Dalmeny House, Dalmeny, near Edinburgh, Rosebery MSS · NRA, priv. coll., corresp. and papers · Surrey HC, corresp. and papers relating to trusts, etc. | BL, corresp. with Sir Robert Peel, Add. MSS 40345–40605, *passim* · NA Scot., letters to James Loch · NA Scot., corresp. with R. B. W. Ramsay · NA Scot., letters to eighth earl of Stair · NL Scot., letters to J. P. Wood · U. Durham L., letter to Charles, second Earl Grey · W. Sussex RO, letters to duke of Richmond
Likenesses E. Burton, mezzotint (after J. R. Swinton), BM · G. Hayter, group portrait, oils (*The trial of Queen Caroline, 1820*), NPG
Wealth at death under £25,000 in England: probate, 15 June 1868, CGPLA Eng. & Wales

Primrose, Archibald Philip, fifth earl of Rosebery and first earl of Midlothian (1847–1929), prime minister and author, was born at 20 Charles Street, Berkeley Square, London, on 7 May 1847, the third child and first son of Archibald Primrose, Lord Dalmeny (1809–1851), and Catherine Lucy Wilhemina Stanhope (1819–1901), daughter of Philip Henry *Stanhope, fourth Earl Stanhope [*see under* Stanhope, Philip Henry].

Education Primrose became Lord Dalmeny on the death of his father in January 1851; his mother married Harry Vane, fourth duke of Cleveland, in August 1854. In 1855 Dalmeny was sent to his first school, Bayford House, near Hertford; five years later he entered Eton College. There he became a protégé of William Johnson (later William Cory), whose letters to the duchess of Cleveland on her son's progress provide a vivid account of Dalmeny's Etonian idyll. Johnson's letters to Dalmeny's mother show an initial enthusiasm for his pupil's intellect yielding to frustration at his laziness: he 'could not give him a good character for industry' (Rhodes James, 32). He feared that the 'fashionable triflers, gamblers, loungers, and cricketers' at Christ Church, which the thirteen-year-old Dalmeny had precociously selected as his Oxford college in 1861, would encourage his idleness. Dalmeny none the less matriculated at Christ Church in January 1866, surrounding himself with Etonians. In the event his examination performance was impressive, but he was noted more for his involvement in horse-racing—his extravagantly unsuccessful bets and his purchase of a racehorse, Ladas, in 1868. The college authorities held racehorse ownership to be incompatible with undergraduate status and requested him to dispose of his acquisition. Misguidedly calling their bluff, he was sent down, without a degree, at Easter 1869.

Peerage and early political life Dalmeny had already succeeded to the earldom of Rosebery on the death of his grandfather Archibald John *Primrose, fourth earl of Rosebery, in March 1868. With the title came 21,000 acres of land in Midlothian and Linlithgow, the medieval Barnbougle Castle, and the Gothic-revival Dalmeny House, built by his grandfather in 1819 (Rosebery later purchased

Archibald Philip Primrose, fifth earl of Rosebery and first earl of Midlothian (1847–1929), by Sir John Everett Millais, 1886

The Durdans, near Epsom, in 1872, and spent much of his life at the Rothschild house at Mentmore, near Aylesbury, after his marriage to Hannah de Rothschild in 1878). A total income probably above £30,000 p.a. gave Rosebery enormous wealth; the peerage assigned him to the House of Lords. This elevated him effortlessly to a political stage which had always attracted him, but it confined him to a 'gilded dungeon', in his words, which would become increasingly constricting. Though courted as a possible parliamentary candidate by the Darlington Conservatives in 1867, Rosebery had inherited his father's Liberalism, and he found himself in the first generation of Liberal peers for whom a position in the Lords was a political drawback, even before the mass defection of Liberal peers over Irish home rule in 1886. After a quarter of a century in the Lords, Rosebery claimed that he could remember once voting in the majority, though not, he thought, on a vital question. In 1890 he considered 'unfrocking' himself as a peer and running for a parliamentary seat in order to test at law the barriers assumed to stop peers standing for the Commons. For most of his political career he advocated the reform of the Lords to produce a more balanced and more plausible second chamber. The recurrent crises triggered by the Lords' anomalous position gave Rosebery a platform: his first reform proposal, the motion for a select committee to examine the house's composition, coincided with the Lords' resistance to franchise extension in the summer of 1884; his last, the motions in 1910 to reduce the representation of the hereditary peerage and introduce *ex officio* and nominated peers, were mooted during

the constitutional battle over the 1909 budget, but such crises, while illustrating the case for Lords reform, provided the worst moments to propose it. Twenty-five years of sporadic devotion to this cause yielded nothing, and Rosebery spent his entire career in what he once described as the political equivalent of the Tower of London.

In common with most of the peerage in this period, Rosebery mixed eclectically with the leaders of both parties. Disraeli fascinated him, and in later life, disenchanted with the Liberal Party, Rosebery expressed his regret at not having followed him, but if he was attracted to toryism at all in his youth it was to the evanescent Young England idealism of Disraeli, or the quixotic tory democracy of Lord Randolph Churchill, an Eton contemporary whose biographical sketch Rosebery published in 1906. His earliest political expressions—his concern that the French Revolution had resulted from the estrangement of classes, his interest in working-class political organizations, his exposure of the condition of children in the Glasgow brickfields, and his presidency of the Edinburgh United Industrial School from 1871—reflect something of this paternalist spirit, as does his call in 1871 for 'a union of classes without which power is a phantom and freedom a farce' (Lord Rosebery, *The Union of England and Scotland: an Inaugural Address to the Edinburgh Philosophical Institution*, 1871). The emergent toryism of resistance and the protection of property—the toryism of Salisbury and Balfour—appeared to him ungenerous and short-sighted, at least until his embittered twilight years. Burke he thought 'completely, though naturally and accountably, in the wrong' (ibid., 1.189). Rosebery came from a whig background, was said by his sister to have 'taken a very strong Radical turn' by 1867, and affirmed his commitment to Liberalism in 1869 even in declining Granville's invitation to second the address on behalf of the Gladstone government in the Lords. His acceptance of a further invitation in 1871 made public his allegiance and brought his maiden speech in the Lords.

Subsequent interventions in Lords debates were, though, infrequent and largely inconsequential in the 1870s. Rosebery preferred to develop his public career by means of platform speeches, mostly in Scotland, where he gained an enthusiastic public following. His growing political stature north of the border was confirmed by his leading role in the overhaul of Scottish Liberalism in the mid-1870s. Alongside the then Liberal leader, Hartington, he attended the birth of the two federal associations created in 1877, becoming president of the Edinburgh-based East and North of Scotland Liberal Association (ENSLA). The aim of the leadership in sponsoring these bodies was to improve the organizational efficiency of the Scottish party without creating vehicles for the critics of party policy. Rosebery was suited to this delicate task: a whig aristocrat who could sway a public meeting, he had voiced radical views on social reform and foreign policy (he had supported Gladstone's campaign against Ottoman atrocities in Bulgaria in 1876) but was at best agnostic on—and apparently uninterested in—church disestablishment, the most divisive issue in Scottish Liberal politics. Chairing the inaugural meeting of the ENSLA he stressed that the new body should not become 'a sickly and despotic society [demanding] an exact profession of faith from every member that enters it'. He defined Liberalism whiggishly as 'the principle in politics that neither class nor creed nor privilege shall hinder the progress of our national development' and cited corn law repeal, Catholic emancipation, and the Reform Act as the party's defining moments (*The Scotsman*, 7 Nov 1877). The Scottish radical press remained unconvinced by such archaisms, and doubted that the 'blank shield' of policy could be maintained for long (*Scottish Reformer and Weekly Review*, 10 Nov 1877), but the Scottish caucuses remained more tolerant of whiggery than their English equivalents. Rosebery went on to become the first president of the newly united Scottish Liberal Association in 1881, and the Scottish leadership succeeded in containing radicalism until the damaging battles over disestablishment in 1885.

Rosebery's reputation as Scottish Liberalism's leading crowd-puller was confirmed by his speeches in support of Gladstone's Midlothian campaign of 1879–80, when Dalmeny became the base for Gladstone's operations and Rosebery, in effect, his manager. The campaign's success underlined Rosebery's claim to office in the subsequent Liberal government which Gladstone formed. It was less clear, though, what sort of preferment Rosebery was entitled to expect. He had been a peer for more than a decade and had become a regional magnate within the party, but Gladstone did not consider these attributes to exempt a man still in his early thirties from the normal apprenticeship of junior office. The next five years saw a succession of efforts to tempt Rosebery into offices which he clearly considered inadequate. In 1880 he declined an under-secretaryship at the India Office for characteristically fastidious reasons: publicly because the appointment would be seen as a political reward for his work and money in the election campaign, privately from annoyance that he had not been offered a cabinet post. Such self-denial would become a familiar feature of his later career, but he did agree to become under-secretary at the Home Office in August 1881, attracted by a brief to handle Scottish business. His reasons for resigning from this office in June 1883 combined the principled and the petty: his belief that London habitually neglected Scottish business and his fear that this neglect would spawn a Scottish home-rule movement; his overreaction to criticism of the Home Office in the Commons; his difficult relationship with the home secretary, Sir William Harcourt; and the fact that he was bored with the work. It is a sign of the general belief that Rosebery was the 'man of the future' that neither the difficulty in inducing him to accept office nor the speed with which he had left it prevented his being offered the projected post of minister for Scotland under the Local Government Board (Scotland) Bill of 1883. Again he refused on the two grounds, uncomfortably conjoined, that he had lobbied for the ministry himself and that the post was not in the cabinet, and stilled all argument by departing in September 1883 on an Australian tour. The eventual offer of a cabinet post as commissioner of works in November 1884 brought another display of reluctance, attributable either to Rosebery's disapproval of the government's Egyptian policy or to the unglamorous nature of the post. Gladstone, still sceptical about Rosebery's administrative capacity and reluctant to allow any cabinet newcomer to dictate his terms, stood firm, ensuring a stalemate which lasted until February 1885, when the death of Gordon at Khartoum allowed Rosebery to swallow his misgivings at a moment of national crisis. The pill was sugared by his concurrent appointment as lord privy seal, which he held until June 1885.

Foreign secretary Rosebery thus assumed a position of limited importance only four months before the second Gladstone ministry fell, but his inexperience did not prevent his being seen as the natural successor to the failing Granville at the Foreign Office when the Liberals returned to power in January 1886. His first period of office lasted until June 1886. His appointment as foreign secretary allowed him to demonstrate an executive talent which validated the hopes long vested in him. Entrusted with policy making for the first time, he acclimatized himself rapidly to the mores of a department more aristocratic in tone than most of Whitehall and better insulated from party politics. As foreign secretary the former critic of Beaconsfieldism became an advocate of bipartisanship in foreign policy. Over time he would elevate the doctrine of continuity to the level of principle—'the second rate foreign policy which is continuous', he asserted in 1905, 'is better than the first rate foreign policy which is not' (Matthew, 196)—but he had not entered office in 1886 with a clear determination to perpetuate second-rate tory diplomacy. Rosebery was anxious that the complex problem of protecting Britain's interests should not be complicated further by deference to a separate radical ethical standard in foreign policy. This determination was reinforced by the inclinations of a predominantly tory set of officials and ambassadors, but the continuity evident in Rosebery's treatment of the problem which dominated his brief first tenure of the Foreign Office, the Bulgarian crisis, was facilitated by Salisbury's earlier revision of British Near Eastern policy when the crisis erupted in September 1885.

Salisbury's decision to support moves for the union of Bulgaria and Eastern Roumelia, thereby endorsing another blow to the authority of the Porte, reflected his growing realization that the enfeebled Ottoman empire no longer provided the best guarantee of British interests in the region. It meant that *raison d'état* no longer required Britain to turn a blind eye to Ottoman misbehaviour, and consequently allowed Rosebery to cope with the ramifications of the Bulgarian revolt undistracted by radical pressure. He was also undistracted by Gladstone, now preoccupied by Irish home rule, though in fact the new Foreign Office orthodoxy, favouring the yoking of Bulgaria and Eastern Roumelia under Prince Alexander, was consistent with Gladstone's earlier advocacy of a united Bulgaria and with traditional Liberal support for nationalist movements. It may be that an inherited Liberal belief in the robustness of free peoples induced Rosebery to leave the new Bulgaria with fewer safeguards against Russian designs than Salisbury would have allowed: Russian agreement to Turkish military guarantees to Bulgaria was bought at the cost of preventing the eventual agreement from naming Alexander personally as governor-general of Eastern Roumelia (leaving open the possibility that he could be supplanted by a Russian puppet) and limiting his initial appointment to five years. With these concessions, though, Rosebery was able to engineer a great power agreement in Europe's most volatile region which proved acceptable to domestic opinion, and to do so within weeks of his appointment. Gladstone could not 'remember an instance of such an achievement carried through in the *first quarter* of a Foreign Secretaryship' (Gladstone to Rosebery, 28 April 1886, Gladstone, *Diaries*, 11.541). Two subsequent measures arising from the crisis, the co-ordination of a naval blockade of Greece to deter her from exploiting the situation and a stern dispatch to Russia to dissuade her from abrogating the free port status (under the 1878 Berlin treaty) of Batum on the Black Sea, demonstrated that Liberal diplomacy would not be distorted by the party's previous pan-Hellenism or its Russophilia. Rosebery was aware that his success in defusing the crisis owed much to the fact that the issue had not been the subject of partisan debate within the cabinet or within the country at large. His subsequent anxiety to take foreign policy out of party politics, which later prompted idiosyncratic musings that the foreign secretary and the service ministers should be made fixed-term appointments to shield them from electoral disfavour, was rooted in the events of 1886. So, by extension, was his eventual disenchantment with party politics.

Gladstonian Liberal Crucially, Rosebery remained loyal to his party and its leader during the crisis over Irish home rule. To the Conservative Lord Birkenhead, surveying Rosebery's career in the 1920s, it was clear that Rosebery, bemused by Gladstone's magnetism, had imprisoned himself in the wrong party in 1886. If wealth and membership of the peerage are taken as predictors, Rosebery might indeed have been expected to join the whig secession over home rule. A whig by background and upbringing, his intellectual make-up was that of educated whiggery—a concern for the nation's literature, history, and constitutional traditions; a lack of interest in abstract philosophy, in mathematics, or in economics. He had inherited the whig faith in a measured progress towards democracy at a pace which did not threaten property or the social order, but he did not—in the 1880s at least—share whig anxieties about the direction of Liberalism. The weakness of toryism north of the border served generally to limit the number of defections from the Scottish Liberal peerage, and Rosebery was more of a Gladstonian than most of his colleagues. He displayed something of the populism that most whigs abhorred in Gladstone, and he was skilled in the platform oratory which most of them shunned. His speeches were characterized by an elegance of phrase and a refinement of construction that guarded him from appearing demagogic, but also by a scepticism

towards irresponsible privilege that had been sharpened by criticism of the House of Lords and advocacy of Scottish land reform. In 1880 Dilke and Chamberlain had seen him as a potential recruit for radicalism. Rosebery never was a radical; the hope that he might be one derived rather from the fact that his whiggism was more elevated and idealistic than that which most of the 1886 defectors carried into alliance with the tories. His anxiety in 1888 that 'if in the future there should again be encroachments of the Crown, the aristocracy would all be found on the side of the Crown; so unlike their forefathers' (*Diary, 1885–1906*, 26 Feb 1888, 77) shows a Macaulayan concern for constitutional liberty that was at best dormant in most whig minds by the 1880s. Similarly, Rosebery's views on empire were drawn from an earlier whig tradition. His Australian visit of 1883–4 had imparted an enthusiasm for empire that he never shed, but it was at heart an enthusiasm for self-government in the white settler colonies, formed at a time when other whigs were citing the unicameral colonial parliaments to demonstrate the dangers of unfettered democracy. Rosebery argued for the voluntary confederation of largely self-governing colonial democracies—he became the first president of the Imperial Federation League in 1884—at a time when much whig and Conservative thought was moving towards imperial centralization. This determined his response to the home rule question in 1886. He shared whig distaste for concessions to militant nationalism, and resented the fact that Irish violence appeared to bring rewards while London continued to neglect the law-abiding Scots. He might have resigned from the government over Gladstone's dealings with Parnell in 1882 had he occupied a more exalted position. He none the less shared Gladstone's view that Irish grievances could be assuaged by statesmanlike devolution. Home rule was probably not his preferred option: in one of his earliest public speeches he had stressed the benefits brought to Scotland by the 1707 union—'like nothing so much as a poor man marrying an heiress' (*The Union between England and Scotland, Address to Edinburgh Philosophical Institution*, 1871)—and while fighting the Scottish corner in the 1880–85 government he had considered administrative devolution preferable to a Scottish parliament. He had inclined towards Chamberlain's scheme for enhanced local government in Ireland, but when Gladstone's home rule proposals killed the Chamberlain scheme Rosebery accepted that a Dublin parliament offered the only alternative to coercion, which, again faithful to the whig tradition, he rejected entirely. His later disenchantment with home rule developed *pari passu* with his disenchantment with the Liberal Party; in 1886 there is no sign that he contemplated joining the whig revolt.

In the wake of the Liberal split Rosebery convinced himself that the whole cathartic episode had given the party a clarity of purpose previously lacking. The years after 1886, however, saw Rosebery, like most Liberal leaders, reassessing the future of a party clearly substantially damaged. For the first time he began seriously to question

Gladstone's judgement, and in 1889 he attempted unsuccessfully to induce him to establish a small front-bench committee to reassess the 1886 Home Rule Bill. By the summer of 1887 he had concluded that a major party realignment was almost inevitable—a view which he would hold for the next twenty years. Whatever the future of the policy, the departure of so many of the party's ruling cadre left Rosebery—still young but with a successful foreign secretaryship behind him—by some way the most plausible contender for high office among the next generation of Liberals. Having spent much of 1880–85 anxious not to lose ground in the scramble for preferment, Rosebery now had public prominence thrust upon him as a duty to his party.

The London county council and the Newcastle programme The process began early in 1889 when Rosebery was urged by Harcourt and others to accept the chairmanship of the newly formed London county council. Despite the usual professions of incapacity, he was attracted by the challenge. His belief in local self-government as a means by which social politics could be pursued without state socialism had grown during the 1880s in parallel with his faith in imperial devolution. Initially anxious to stand for a division like Whitechapel 'in order to show community of feeling between the lower classes and the aristocracy' (*Diary, 1885–1906*, 6 Jan 1889), he was persuaded to run in the City of London, where a peer might be more acceptable. Deference duly carried him to the top of the poll, despite the weakness of Liberalism in the City, and to the chairmanship of the first council, despite a muted radical protest. The principal ground for opposition to Rosebery was his refusal to commit himself to support the taxation of land values—a prudent course in the City but one which many radicals found suspicious in a landed aristocrat. In reality the council lacked legal power to impose land taxes or any other innovations in local taxation, and while the question retained much totemic significance, it did not come before the council in any concrete form during Rosebery's chairmanship. Whatever his views on the issue, which are unclear at this point, it is unlikely that he would have sought to use the largely formal powers of the chair to restrain the council's (radical) Progressive majority. As chairman Rosebery was punctiliously impartial in his regulation of debates, and was not normally called upon to vote. Formal pronouncements such as the chairman's review of the first year's work were couched in magisterial terms, endorsing the LCC's programme of urban improvement and treating it, despite the council's increasingly partisan atmosphere, as the fruit of shared objectives. In fact his formal impartiality overlaid a broad sympathy with the council's social objectives which was clear from his public speeches at the time, with the result that the Progressive majority on the council felt more comfortable with his chairmanship than with that of his Liberal Unionist successor, Sir John Lubbock.

Rosebery, too, remained more comfortable with London's municipal 'new Liberals' than with the traditional radicals who dominated provincial Liberalism. Though he spoke at one time or another in support of most of the items in the Newcastle programme (the radical shopping list adopted at the National Liberal Federation's Newcastle conference in 1891) and would make the implementation of the programme his first commitment to the party as prime minister in 1894, he believed that programmatic politics encouraged axe grinding and the proliferation of minority causes. In particular Rosebery had little affinity for the representatives of political nonconformity, whose stock had risen in the party with the departure of the Anglican whigs. He did not share their evangelical temper or their sectarian outlook. His own religious attitude was eclectic: brought up in an Episcopalian household, he defined himself as an Anglican, but would attend kirk services on occasion when in Scotland and go to mass when abroad in a Catholic country. He married a Jewish woman. Ever fearful that the Christian ideal would be obscured by 'the dust of warring faiths', he contemplated optimistically the reunion of the Scottish church (Lord Rosebery, *Dr Chalmers: an Address*, 1915, 20). His son-in-law and biographer, Lord Crewe, believed that the kirk made 'particular appeal to one side of his character'; John Buchan claimed in an obituary that 'while to the world he seemed like some polished eighteenth-century grandee, at heart he was the Calvinist of seventeenth-century Scotland' (Crewe-Milnes, 1.65; *Glasgow Herald*, 22 May 1929).

Marriage and bereavement Buchan's simile was intended to depict Rosebery's cast of mind rather than to label him doctrinally. If Rosebery was a Scottish Calvinist he was an unusual one, who collected pornography and ran a racing stable. The former was a private hobby, the latter necessarily a public one, which aroused nonconformist disapproval in proportion to Rosebery's success. This was considerable: Rosebery twice won the Derby as prime minister, in 1894 and 1895 (with Ladas II and Sir Visto), and again in 1905 (with Cicero). His involvement in the turf was a committed and professional one—between 1875 and 1928 he won every major English race except the Ascot Gold Cup—but the sport still carried overtones of aristocratic debauchery. Rosebery's association with it was a sign that he lacked the moral earnestness that liberal nonconformity sought in its leaders, distinguishing him pointedly from Gladstone when he succeeded him as prime minister.

What Buchan had in mind was rather Rosebery's pervasive melancholia, his 'haunting sense of transience' and of the futility of human action, perhaps even the preoccupation with death that impelled him to inspect the corpses of deceased friends before burial. He was prone to depression throughout his life, but particularly during his lugubrious old age, when Crewe and Buchan knew him best. His was, indeed, a life scarred by many personal tragedies—the loss of his father when Rosebery was three and the deaths of his younger brother, Everard, in the Sudan in 1885, of his nephew in 1895, of his second son, Neil (b. 1882), killed in action in 1917, and above all of his wife in 1890.

Rosebery had been introduced to Hannah de Rothschild (1851–1890), only child of Baron and Baroness Mayer de

Rothschild, by Disraeli in 1868. The couple married on 20 March 1878, despite the reservations of his antisemitic mother and those of Britain's Jewish community, reluctant to see the most prominent Jewish heiress marry out of the faith. 'I do not know the young lady personally', commented Rosebery's stepfather, the duke of Cleveland, caustically after the engagement, 'but I am told that the family is well-to-do in the City' (F. E. Smith, 'Men of the hour: Lord Rosebery', *Sunday Times*, n.d., Rosebery MSS); marriage into the Rothschilds augmented Rosebery's personal fortune. Hannah, tory-leaning but little interested in politics, accepted the role of statesman's wife without demur, though she disliked the official functions that were Rosebery's lot as foreign secretary. She provided Rosebery with the adulation that always reassured him and submitted uncomplainingly to his recurrent public teasing. Her death from typhoid fever in November 1890, at the age of thirty-nine, devastated him. Out of office at the time, he withdrew completely from public life for about eighteen months. He continued to use black-edged writing paper for his correspondence for four or five years after her death. During his protracted bereavement his innate melancholia deepened, and the misanthropy that was a part of his nature developed into a profound craving for solitude. This coloured his attitude towards public life and public office in a critical period when others looked to him to renovate post-Gladstonian Liberalism. Refusal of honours and appointments was habitual for him throughout his life, but before 1890 his refusals either reflected a contempt for the office on offer or were founded in an elaborate sense of etiquette which his colleagues found wearisome if they understood it at all; after Hannah's death, when he found the highest positions in the land being pressed upon him, Rosebery was genuinely reluctant to return to public life. In these years he was a better judge of his own incapacity than those who started from the premise that only he could restore the credibility of Liberalism. Bereavement exacerbated his insomnia, 'the curse of his life' that had afflicted him since his twenties, impairing his judgement and his patience. During the protracted effort to tempt him back to the Foreign Office when the Liberals regained power in 1892, John Morley found him 'haggard-looking and distressed', insisting that his political ambitions had been buried with his wife (*Diary, 1885–1906*, 6 Aug 1892).

Return to the Foreign Office: imperial problems Morley considered Rosebery's reluctance to serve 'a downright act of desertion of Mr G and his colleagues'. Hamilton believed that a Gladstone government without Rosebery would immediately fall to pieces, but that his joining the government would reassure the commercial classes and steady the markets. Harcourt maintained that 'without him we should have been simply ridiculous … with him we are only impossible' (*Diary, 1885–1906*, 6, 11, 15, 17 Aug 1892). Rosebery's prominence and the reputation derived from his previous Foreign Office term and his chairmanship of the London county council meant that his absence from a Liberal cabinet already low in ministerial experience would indeed have been conspicuous, making it morally

difficult for him to abstain. Denied the private life he sought, Rosebery may have found the Foreign Office a substitute, accepting the office in August 1892. It remained an insular and independent department—'we did not send too much information from the FO to the other side of the street', Ronald Munro Ferguson recalled (Ferguson to Crewe, 22 Oct 1929, Crewe MS 10195)—staffed by solicitous permanent officials who had briefed him privately since 1886 in anticipation of his return. Rosebery's sense that he had been bullied into office reinforced his own determination to claim complete freedom of action, unaffected by the scruples of cabinet colleagues or radical back-benchers. The doctrine of continuity, developed pragmatically during his first Foreign Office term, now became more a dogma, invoked to justify overriding Liberal qualms about empire, than a guide to policy. In his handling of the inherited crisis over Uganda, Rosebery in fact adopted a stance more imperialistic than that of his Conservative predecessor.

The crisis was rooted in the bankruptcy of the Imperial British East Africa Company, the chartered company through which the outgoing Salisbury government had sought to exercise a vicarious British control over the upper Nile. This region was taken to be crucial to the security of Egypt, itself vital to the freedom of the Suez Canal and the short route to British India. Rosebery was doubtless as ready as most imperial enthusiasts in the 1890s to accept the alarmist argument a foreign power on the upper Nile might dam the river or otherwise imperil Egypt, but Salisbury had not seen this possibility as justification for bailing out a speculative venture, let alone asserting a permanent British claim to a region which was, in itself, of little value. In fact Rosebery was virtually the only member of the Gladstone cabinet to advocate retention with any fervour, but his actions throughout the episode were founded on the premise that withdrawal was not an option. The compromise solution of placing Uganda under the control of the friendly sultan of Zanzibar appealed to him as a means of retaining British influence which did not require the trappings of formal rule, especially as this solution appeared to satisfy Harcourt, the chief opponent of retention, and Gladstone himself. The appointment of Gerald Portal, progenitor of the Zanzibar option, as special commissioner to report on the Uganda question, was apparently intended to lead to this solution. That Portal, generally taken to be a fervent retentionist, should be so impressed by the unpromising nature of the territory itself as to return reports which weakened the case for continued British influence was not anticipated. Faced with this outcome, Rosebery suppressed Portal's findings, aided by his unexpected death in January 1894, and in February presented the cabinet with a demand for a protectorate. Uganda was eventually annexed in April 1894, a month after Rosebery's accession to the premiership.

Rosebery's stance over Uganda was, in fact, an incongruous gesture towards expansionism on the part of one who was at heart a consolidationist rather than an expansionist. It sprang in part from his desire to make a point to his colleagues, affirming that he would be his own man at the Foreign Office and would not allow foreign policy to become the plaything of a fractious cabinet, as he believed it to have been during Granville's final foreign secretaryship in 1880–85. This carried the risk of antagonizing colleagues, and the risk became a certainty when Portal failed to endorse the anticipated compromise, leaving the cabinet with a stark choice between retention and withdrawal. Whether or not cabinet divisions disturbed Rosebery, they carried an ulterior benefit. Rosebery's policy towards the wider world was conducted with an eye to the European implications. In 1892 he was concerned to distance himself from the Francophilia of Gladstone and much of the Liberal cabinet. He shared Salisbury's view that French hostility towards Britain was inescapable, implying a need to cultivate Germany and her partners in the triple alliance, Austria–Hungary and Italy. At the same time Rosebery, like every nineteenth-century foreign secretary, was 'anxious to obtain the full advantage of the insular position with which Providence has endowed us' (Martel, 121), and determined that Britain should not become so dependent upon Germany as to be effectively drawn into the European alliance system, with attendant continental obligations. By taking a robust line on Uganda, Rosebery hoped to show Germany that British policy was not set by its largely Francophile cabinet, but at the same time that Britain could defend her position in Egypt without German aid. Similar arguments applied to Egypt itself, where Rosebery resisted Gladstone's attempts to end the quarrel with France which had simmered since the unilateral British occupation of 1882, arguing that concessions to France in that strategically sensitive area would only increase British dependence upon Germany.

Rosebery believed that Britain's foreign policy had necessarily become a colonial policy since the 1860s. He was very conscious of the extended and ultimately indefensible nature of Britain's empire and aware that any substantial military commitment in defence of one part of the empire might leave other parts open to attack. He considered the Crimean War to have been a mistake because it advertised the limits to British military power; during the Panjdeh crisis in 1885 he had warned that 'if we have one hand tied down in Central Asia and another in Central Africa we may be practically danced upon in every other part of the world' (Martel, 232). While refusing to acknowledge French claims to Siam during the crisis there in 1893, as possession of Siam would bring France to the borders of British Burma, Rosebery was careful that his rebuttal should not be so bellicose as to allow the Siamese to take British military support for granted. Rosebery's carefully weighted blend of tact and firmness secured a French withdrawal without necessitating a military commitment.

Crewe believed that no statesman of his generation was so reluctant to risk war. In a jingoistic age Rosebery was a cautious diplomat. His loose talk during the Uganda crisis of 'pegging out claims' for the future by acquiring barren territory was out of character; Rosebery considered imperial adventurism to be provocative and dangerous. Britain was a satisfied power, whose main concern should be to maintain her possessions within existing limits. Diplomacy was the means to that end, but Rosebery shunned the obvious diplomatic strategy, to be followed by his successors in the 1900s, of protecting the empire by reaching agreements with the powers most likely to threaten it. He saw formal alliances as a threat to Britain's freedom of action, carrying the danger of drawing Britain into conflicts irrelevant to her own interests. In many ways his diplomacy was Bismarckian in its suppleness, its attention to detail, and its lack of ideological preconceptions, but Rosebery never enjoyed the freedom of diplomatic invention central to the Bismarck system. To some extent he constrained himself with his reluctance to make any arrangements which depended upon 'Gallic good faith'; his unvarying assumption of French enmity made negotiations with France over areas of potential tension—notably the upper Nile—more difficult and threatened to conflict with his objective of avoiding war. The provocative declaration of Edward Grey, under-secretary at the Foreign Office, in March 1895 that any French move into the Nile valley would be seen as an 'unfriendly act' was consistent with Rosebery's attitude; Rosebery might have inspired it and would endorse it three years later when the Fashoda crisis threatened to drag Britain and France into war. At that point, indeed, Rosebery, no longer in office, suggested privately that 'a war with France now would simplify difficulties in the future' (R. Brett, journal, 28 Oct 1898, Stansky, 260). The real obstacle to an unfettered foreign policy was, however, the polarization of the powers that had taken place since Bismarck's departure. Since 1890 the growth of Franco-Russian co-operation had divided Europe into two clear camps. France and Russia were the two powers which most directly threatened Britain's overseas possessions; the limited extra-European interests of the triple alliance powers posed little direct threat to the British empire. Rosebery's Francophobia and his aversion to dealing with the empire's potential enemies underlined his inclination towards the triple alliance; denied a completely free hand, his intellectual dexterity was devoted to maintaining friendly relations with the alliance without becoming a tool of German policy.

The alliance system Rosebery's policy of, in effect, seeking the protection offered by the alliance system without making the commitments which it required of the other powers was an attempt to preserve the tradition of 'splendid isolation' in the altered circumstances of the 1890s. It was not cost-free. Britain's status as a naval power obliged her to offer something more than moral support to the triple alliance in view of Franco-Russian strength in the Mediterranean. Without a stronger British naval presence in the Mediterranean to bolster the alliance Italy might be tempted to deal with France, and Austria–Hungary with Russia. Where Gladstone had seen the chance to scale down Britain's Mediterranean Fleet as one of the benefits of an accommodation with France (it would later be an effect of the 1904 entente), Rosebery's policy entailed naval expansion, and was the principal reason for the £4 million programme which Spencer, first lord of the Admiralty, presented to an alarmed Liberal cabinet in 1894. The consequences were to be considerable: the navy programme entailed Gladstone's resignation as prime minister; Harcourt's redistributionary 1894 budget, which alarmed Rosebery; and in due course the imitative German naval build-up of 1897, which, by turning Germany into a maritime rival, would eventually undermine the Rosebery system.

Its essential fragility had been exposed before then, however. Rosebery's foreign policy was indeed a colonial policy, but it was always unclear how valuable was the understanding with the triple alliance in extra-European matters. Rosebery assumed that the existence of the alliance would act as a deterrent inhibiting France and Russia from extra-European adventurism. To some extent it may have done so, but it was equally true that the alliance members would not jeopardize European peace to defend British colonial interests while Britain remained no more than an associate member of the alliance. Britain remained obliged to make her own arrangements to protect her territory. Her greatest security lay in the fact that the Russians, at least, did not consider the Franco-Russian understanding relevant outside Europe. This became clear when Russia failed to endorse French objections to Rosebery's Anglo-Congolese agreement of 1894, by which territory on the upper Nile was leased to King Leopold of the Belgians in order to forestall any French advance into the area; it was rather unanticipated German objections to the implications of the arrangement for the future of German East Africa which necessitated its abandonment. Rosebery had, in fact, few inhibitions about antagonizing France; Russia was more problematic because a Russo-German rapprochement—increasing the likelihood of Russian interference in India—was feasible, where a Franco-German rapprochement was not. The question of Britain's attitude towards Russia became critical with the sudden emergence of Japan as a military power following her intervention to suppress the Tonghak rebellion in Korea in the summer of 1894. Rosebery had become prime minister three months before the crisis emerged, strengthening his ability to determine foreign policy, but his replacement as foreign secretary, Kimberley, was not simply a mouthpiece for the new premier. Kimberley in fact saw Japan as a 'natural ally' against Russia. Rosebery, who had worked to improve relations with St Petersburg since 1892, in the hope of limiting the Russian threat to India and dissuading Russia from supporting French expansion, could not agree, but nor could he offer the tsar much practical help in his efforts to coerce Japan to moderate its demands in Korea. Fearful that military escalation might lead to a European war in China, Rosebery ruled out British intervention where no British interest was at stake. Russia was left to ask what benefits could be derived from Britain's friendship. Seven years after Rosebery left office, the 1902 Anglo-Japanese alliance would begin the process by which his successors reversed his policy of relying upon reactive diplomacy to defuse threats to

Britain's extended empire, and looked instead to agreements with potential imperial predators. Rosebery feared the consequences of this reversal: he warned that the 1902 alliance 'may be the first Treaty of the kind for many years past, but having been made it cannot be the last' (Rhodes James, 449), and advised Edward Grey in 1905 that the previous year's entente with France would lead to war. Events may have vindicated him, but the fact remained that his own sinuous diplomacy had been unsuited to the polarized power relations developing after 1890.

Prime minister, 1894–1895 Gladstone's retirement in March 1894 left Rosebery the leading contender for the succession, and he resisted this preferment less strenuously than usual. His only plausible rival, Harcourt, had the advantages of seniority and greater ministerial experience, but the drawback of being personally unacceptable to almost the entire cabinet. Harcourt's efforts in February to dictate the terms on which he could work, as Liberal leader in the Commons, with a prime minister in the Lords—freedom to act and speak on all issues, the right to be consulted on foreign policy and patronage questions—indicated his recognition of the inevitable even before Gladstone stepped down. They also presaged troubles to come. The position of a Liberal peer-premier was inevitably less comfortable than that of a Conservative one, and Rosebery's personal relations with Harcourt were far less secure than Salisbury's had been with his leader in the Commons, his nephew Arthur Balfour. The situation did require the terms of Harcourt's role to be spelled out, but given Harcourt's opposition to the principle of a peer as prime minister his demands implied that Rosebery held his position on sufferance. Rosebery, characteristically ready to feel slighted, claimed that the terms would make him 'a dummy prime minister' (Rhodes James, 313). Fractious relations with Harcourt blighted Rosebery's premiership, partly because of Harcourt's ungenerous behaviour, but partly because his performance as prime minister was open to real criticism. Rosebery had once likened the office to 'a "dunghill", on which the other ministers threw everything that was disagreeable' (*Diary, 1885–1906*, 17 April 1887); he regretted losing the real power he had enjoyed at the Foreign Office. He complained repeatedly of his 'inherited programme and … inherited Cabinet' but did little to change either (ibid., 21 May 1894).

The succession question had been decided on the basis of the personal merits of the main candidates and their acceptability to their cabinet colleagues. It had not been necessary for Rosebery to promulgate anything resembling a manifesto and he entered office without giving any clear indication of his policy intentions. He had contributed little to the Liberal debates on future policy after the home rule débâcle; in the seclusion of the Foreign Office after 1892 he had done little to shape the domestic programme of the Gladstone cabinet. He kissed hands on 5 March 1894. On the previous day he was urged by G. E. Buckle, editor of *The Times*, to modify his party's domestic policy as he had modified its foreign policy. The task of educating his party appealed to him. He had already, in September 1893, voiced ostentatiously tepid support for

Irish home rule when Gladstone's second bill was obliterated in the upper house, and his first speech in the Lords as prime minister reinforced that impression by maladroitly implying that home rule required the approval of a majority of MPs from England, as 'the predominant member of the Three Kingdoms' (Rhodes James, 338). He was now convinced of the depth of the damage done to the party in 1886. Three speeches in the City of London, in Birmingham, and in Manchester in April and May 1894 were interpreted as appeals to rank-and-file Liberal Unionists to return to the fold.

It was none the less unclear what Rosebery could offer to those Liberal Unionists who were worried less by home rule than by the Liberals' drift towards social radicalism. He was not anxious to reverse social policies either passed or pledged, such as hours limitation for government employees or the eight-hour day for miners, and was anyway powerless to do so. His impotence was emphasized by his failure significantly to modify the redistributionary budget proposed by Harcourt in 1894. In a pattern that would be repeated in 1909, a budgetary crisis largely due to increased naval expenditure became the occasion for a radical fiscal experiment, conducted with an eye to electoral benefit. Harcourt proposed to meet the largest ever peacetime army and navy estimates by raising duties on beer and spirits, increasing the basic rate of income tax while raising allowances for the poorest taxpayers, and above all overhauling the death duties. Higher death duties hit the wealthy, while the increased tax allowances were designed to benefit higher-paid workmen, clerks, struggling professionals, small shopkeepers, and agriculturalists. Rosebery, who continued to hope that Gladstone's retirement might encourage some Liberal Unionists to rejoin the party, believed that the budget would alienate the Liberals' few remaining wealthy supporters. He expressed his fears in a private memorandum to Harcourt in April 1894, receiving a dismissive and combative reply, after which the prime minister and the chancellor of the exchequer hardly spoke to each other for six months. He achieved only a limited modification of the scale of death duty graduation.

At the heart of the broader battle between Rosebery and Harcourt was the question of whether the Liberal Party should extend its electoral base by moving to the centre or to the left. This was a major strategic dilemma, not easily resolved, but Rosebery was unwise to pick a fight over the 1894 budget. Its redistributionary benefits were limited to the income-tax-paying classes; the beneficiaries were an electorally significant group whose disenchantment with unionism in 1892 was believed to have helped the Liberals regain office. The losers by the budget were wealthy but numerically insignificant; Harcourt was probably right to suggest that the few among them who contributed to Liberal Party funds could be appeased with honours. The surplus produced by the tax changes went not towards the free breakfast table, old age pensions, or any other social objective, as some Liberal back-benchers had urged, but to defray the increased naval estimates, largely a product of Rosebery's foreign policy. Rosebery himself offered no alternative means of funding naval expansion. None the less, his failure to defeat the cabinet's senior prize-fighter reinforced the sense of inadequacy which had clouded his accession to the premiership, and drove him into a seclusion which lasted for most of his first summer as prime minister.

This seclusion ended with Rosebery's re-emergence in October to revive his pet subject of House of Lords reform, proposing in a speech at Bradford to introduce a Commons resolution asserting the legislative supremacy of the lower house. Some kind of gesture against the Lords was necessary to reassure the Liberals' Irish nationalist allies after the peers had contemptuously disposed of home rule in 1893 and the Evicted Tenants (Ireland) Bill in 1894, but Rosebery had not discussed his proposal with the cabinet, most of whom preferred in principle to abolish rather than reform the Lords, and saw limitation of the Lords' veto as a more practical way of clipping their wings. In November this option was adopted in place of Rosebery's resolution, but no measure of Lords reform appeared in the 1895 queen's speech.

The failure of this initiative marked the end of Rosebery's serious efforts to shape the domestic policy of his own government. Without a dominant legislative aim, the government fell back upon the agenda of radical objectives such as Welsh church disestablishment, liquor licensing reform, and the abolition of plural voting. The simultaneous launch of measures of this sort—contentious and intricate and therefore vulnerable in parliament—by a government with a slender and dwindling majority indicated that most were being aired to encourage their supporters, with little prospect of success: the unionist Goschen depicted the 1895 agenda as a programme of 'first nights'. Only the Welsh church measure made any substantial progress, but it had not passed the Commons when the government was defeated on a snap vote criticizing the War Office for shortages in army cordite in June 1895. Resignation, though constitutionally unnecessary, was grasped by ministers anxious to escape the 'nightmare' that government had become.

Breakdown and scandal Rosebery himself was a distant figure for most of the 1895 session, victim of a comprehensive nervous and physical breakdown. Its outward symptoms—a severe influenza attack in February, followed by general debilitation and what his physician, Sir William Broadbent, described as a 'long-continued derangement of the digestive organs' (Crewe-Milnes, 2.501)—were probably induced by the recurrence of chronic insomnia over the preceding months, which Rosebery eventually contained by resort to the patent tranquillizer Sulfonell. Insomnia was doubtless prompted by the strain of presiding over a warring cabinet and a failing government, but also, almost certainly, by an emerging scandal.

On re-entering the Foreign Office in 1892 Rosebery had appointed Francis Douglas, Lord Drumlanrig, heir to the marquess of Queensberry, as his assistant private secretary, drawing himself thereby into the affairs of an eccentric and feud-ridden family. When Rosebery persuaded Gladstone to appoint Drumlanrig as lord-in-waiting to the queen, entailing his elevation to the English peerage, Queensberry, himself a former Scottish elective peer, objected not merely to the honour but also to Rosebery's 'evil influence' on his son. Queensberry pursued Rosebery on his rest-cure at Homburg in August 1893, seeking to dog-whip the foreign secretary, but was thwarted in this purpose by the local police, apparently in response to a request from the prince of Wales. Farce turned to tragedy in October 1894 when Drumlanrig shot himself on a shooting party in Somerset. The inquest recorded a verdict of accidental death; society rumour alleged suicide, prompted by fear of blackmail over homosexual relations with Rosebery.

Rosebery would doubtless have absorbed the easy toleration of male love prevalent at Eton, as at other major public schools, but in that he was hardly alone among the British governing class of the period; the nature of his relations with his tutor William Johnson, later dismissed on suspicion of homosexuality, cannot be determined. That Rosebery retained in adulthood an emotional attachment to young men is suggested by the highly charged tone of a note in one of his jottings books on the anniversary of the death of Frederick Vyner, 'a pale, tall, beautiful English boy' murdered by Greek brigands in 1870:

I locked the door and looked on it with dry sobs. Why had he gone? His life was beautiful and pleasant. He lived in an atmosphere of love … I can believe in no future state where we can be divided. I hardly think that death divides us now. (jotting books, 12 April 1871, Rosebery MS 10188, fols. 25–6)

Accusations of homosexual promiscuity appear all to relate to the years after Hannah's death: his 'considerable fancy' for Drumlanrig, his affection for the homosexual British consul in southern Italy, Eustace Neville-Rolfe, his reclusive holidays in the midst of the colony of homosexual English expatriates around Naples, and his purchase (with Neville-Rolfe) of the Villa Delahante at Posilippo in 1897. References to Rosebery in the diaries of the homosexual proselytizer George Ives and, however spuriously, in those of the fantasist Sir Edmund Backhouse suggest that Rosebery's homosexuality was taken for granted in homosexual circles. Queensberry took little convincing. His son's death made Queensberry much more dangerous to Rosebery than he had been in 1893. In the first place, convinced that Rosebery's high office made him immune to punishment—Ives later claimed that 'Hyde Park Police had orders never to arrest Lord R. on the principle that too big a fish often breaks the line' (Ives's journal, 21 May 1929, Ransom HRC)—and that 'the Snob Queers' would cover up the circumstances of Drumlanrig's death, he became still freer with charges which, even if false, Rosebery could not easily refute. Second, Queensberry became all the more determined to detach his youngest son, Lord Alfred Douglas, from his relationship with the playwright Oscar Wilde. Wilde was no more than an acquaintance of Rosebery, but the danger of collateral damage from any exposure of the Douglas family's sexual adventures was considerable. Exposure became more likely when Wilde responded to Queensberry's attacks with an ill-advised criminal libel suit. Rosebery's name was mentioned in the grand jury hearing preceding the main trial and leaked into the French press. The collapse of Wilde's libel action was followed by the prosecution of Wilde himself on the strength of the evidence of homosexuality adduced by Queensberry in his own defence. When the jury failed to agree upon a verdict the solicitor-general, Sir Frank *Lockwood, insisted upon a retrial for fear that any leniency towards Wilde would fuel rumours about Rosebery. Only when Wilde was convicted and imprisoned in May 1895 was Rosebery relieved of the daily fear that sexual allegations against him would surface in court, protected by privilege and guaranteed publicity.

The tension that built up steadily from the day of Drumlanrig's death virtually paralysed Rosebery during his last few months as prime minister. His memory of those months remained vivid eight years later:

I cannot forget 1895. To lie night after night, staring wide awake, hopeless of sleep, tormented in nerves, and to realise all that was going on, at which I was present, so to speak, like a disembodied spirit, to watch one's own corpse as it were, day after day, is an experience which no sane man with a conscience would repeat.   (Crewe-Milnes, 2.586–7)

This breakdown, following his failure to alter the 1894 budget, the collapse of his initiative for Lords reform, and the unravelling of his foreign policy completed an ineffective premiership. Always afraid of failure, Rosebery reassured himself by acerbic denunciations of disloyal colleagues, particularly Harcourt, and of his own party. He became the sharpest critic of the 'faddist' programme of 1895 and welcomed the electoral catastrophe that arrived a month after his government's resignation. Gladstone's political re-emergence in September 1896 to advocate European action against the Turks following massacres in Armenia provided the occasion for Rosebery's resignation as Liberal leader in October. A week later he expressed to Hamilton his impatience with the role of 'Mr G's political executor': 'the real fact was that he had been too tied to Gladstonian chains ever since he had taken a prominent part in politics' (*Diary, 1885–1906*, 16 Oct 1896). Thus disavowing his party's household god, he began a nine-year effort to rescue Liberalism from the Liberal Party.

Liberal Imperialist Another period of solitude ended with Rosebery's re-emergence in February 1898 with an effective intervention in support of the Progressive Party in the London county council elections. Over the next five years he developed a role better suited to his abilities and in some ways reminiscent of his successful period on the council—that of patron to a group of younger Liberals aiming to modernize their party. He cultivated the group of 'Liberal Imperialists', prominently H. H. Asquith, Sir Edward Grey, R. B. Haldane, Ronald Munro Ferguson, and Sidney Buxton—more cerebral, more metropolitan, and less sectarian than most of the party's rank and file, and untouched by 'little Englander' hostility to the spirit of empire. How far this group shared Rosebery's conviction that a party realignment was inevitable remains unclear, but they did display an independence of thought which Rosebery found refreshing. Their differences with the party mainstream were emphasized by the outbreak of the Second South African War in October 1899. Though Rosebery and his acolytes had misgivings about the provocative British diplomacy which hastened the conflict, they supported the war once it was under way and relished the embarrassment of the Liberal Party, with its substantial anti-war minority. Public reaction to early British reverses made fashionable the belief that Britain's liberal institutions were unfit for an age of competing empires. The vogue for 'national efficiency' which moved the nation in the wake of reverses in the Second South African War promised to rehabilitate Rosebery, a long-term iconoclast towards the House of Lords and now a vocal critic of party dogma and discipline. In 1900–01 he gained a renewed prominence, campaigning for Britain's political rejuvenation in a series of platform speeches, notably in his address as rector of Glasgow University, when he warned 'It is beginning to be hinted at that we are a nation of amateurs' (*The Times*, 17 Nov 1900).

Rosebery's broad objectives were clear enough: to 'restore efficiency to our parliament, our administration and our people', to attain 'a condition of national fitness equal to the demands of our empire', and to mobilize that 'great volume of opinion not very expressive … which does not greatly sympathise with the extreme men of either party' (Lord Rosebery, *National Policy*, 1902, 16; Lord Rosebery, *Liberal Principles and Prospects*, 1902, 31). How his objectives were to be achieved was less clear. At times his distaste for conventional politics inclined him towards some of the anti-democratic proposals which gave the national efficiency movement its illiberal aspect: in 1901 he advocated a cabinet of businessmen and was, indeed, said to 'have the "business man" fad on his brain' (Northbrook to Curzon, 12 Dec 1901, G. R. Searle, *The Quest for National Efficiency*, 1971, 88). At other times, notably in his much-trailed Chesterfield speech of December 1901, he appeared rather to be urging the Liberal Party to mend its ways—to drop Irish home rule, to love the empire, and to redraw policy on a 'clean slate'. He continued to hanker after the return of the Liberal Unionists to the party. He was, moreover, tempted by press speculation that he might lead a coalition government, formed of the best men of both parties, though he could not ignore the scars left by his premiership. His characteristic response to this dilemma was to wait to be called, but it soon became clear even to the sympathetic Hamilton that there was 'no great flocking of persons to the Rosebery standard' (*Diary, 1885–1906*, 3 March 1902). His Gaullist stance annoyed his supporters—Grey warned him that there was no such thing as a political conscript, and although the Liberal League, formed by the Liberal Imperialist group in February 1902, served in part as a Rosebery vehicle, it emerged as a ginger group on the right of the Liberal Party rather than the independent political organization that Rosebery had wished to create. Rosebery's eclipse began with the revival of partisanship over the 1902 Education Bill. Initially sympathetic to the bill as an 'efficiency' measure of modernization, he was persuaded not to separate himself from Liberal criticism of it. His platform speeches concentrated upon the threat to the best urban school boards, while his speech in the House of Lords reiterated nonconformist objections to subsidizing Anglican education.

Free-trader The launch of Joseph Chamberlain's campaign for tariff reform in May 1903—advocating a departure from Britain's free-trade tradition in order to confer tariff preference upon imperial goods—did subtler but deeper damage to Rosebery's claim to embody a modern, streamlined, and undogmatic politics. An awareness that his own enthusiasm for empire was shared by the mass of the British people had given Rosebery the confidence that his whiggish views were not unpopular. Liberal embarrassment over empire during the Second South African War had justified his claim that a party in hock to its activists had grown out of touch with the wider public. After 1903, though, Britain's imperial visionaries aligned themselves with a protectionist policy which Rosebery could not support. He was, like most whigs, a free-trader by habit. Uninterested in economics, he was impervious to protectionist arguments founded upon Britain's relative economic decline. He had attacked the protectionist groundswell for some years before Chamberlain's policy emerged, arguing that a British imperial customs union would weaken the empire internally by encouraging disputes over duty levels, that it would antagonize the rest of the world, and that food duties would turn the working classes against empire. After an initial hesitation he reiterated these arguments in 1903, intensified by his personal dislike of Chamberlain. In his defence of free trade he found himself at one with his party for the first time for a decade. Indeed he believed that 'for the first time since 1886 the deliberate intellect and the highest intellect of the country … is beginning to turn slowly but surely in the direction of Liberalism' (*A Supreme Contest: a Speech*, n.d. [1904?], 8), raising the possibility that Liberalism could recapture the centre ground lost by Gladstone, as he had hoped in 1894. In the event the Liberals probably did win the argument over free trade, but the number of tory defectors was small, and the effect of the debate was rather to polarize British politics around the free-trade issue. Rosebery was only one of many Liberal defenders of free trade, and neither the most original nor the most distinctive.

Rosebery's redundancy was demonstrated by the events of 1905. The 'Relugas compact' of September—the arrangement by which Asquith, Grey, and Haldane agreed to serve in a future Liberal government if Campbell-Bannerman could be removed to the Lords—made no reference to Rosebery and was not communicated to him. Nor was Asquith's agreement with Campbell-Bannerman on a step-by-step approach to home rule. Accustomed throughout his career to turning down offers of office, Rosebery did not take kindly to being ignored, and saw Relugas as a betrayal. Unaware of Asquith's steps towards a compromise over home rule, he called at Stourbridge in October for a clear statement of the party's Irish policy. When Campbell-Bannerman unfurled the step-by-step policy in November Rosebery responded with unexpected asperity at Bodmin, rejecting home rule for impairing the Liberals' hard-won unity and declining 'emphatically and explicitly' to serve in a government pledged to home rule. He was no longer likely to be asked. Campbell-Bannerman thought him 'off his head'; even Hamilton thought Rosebery had 'put his foot in it' at Bodmin.

Last years The last years of his political life saw Rosebery become a purely negative critic of the Liberal governments of Campbell-Bannerman and Asquith. His crusade 'for freedom as against bureaucracy, for freedom as against democratic tyranny, for freedom as against class legislation, and … for freedom as against Socialism' (*The Times*, 16 Feb 1910) was a lonely one, conducted from the cross-benches in the Lords. He did join the die-hard unionist peers in attacking Lloyd George's redistributive budget in 1909, but stopped short of voting against the measure for fear of bringing retribution upon the Lords. The crisis provoked by the Lords' rejection of the budget encouraged him to reintroduce his resolutions for Lords reform, but they were lost with the dissolution of parliament in December 1910. After assaulting the 'ill-judged, revolutionary and partisan' terms of the 1911 Parliament Bill (Rhodes James, 469), which proposed to curb the Lords' veto, he voted with the government in what proved to be his last appearance in the House of Lords. This was effectively the end of his public life, though he made several public appearances to support the war effort after 1914 and sponsored a 'bantam battalion' in 1915. Though Lloyd George offered him 'a high post not involving departmental labour' to augment his 1916 coalition, Rosebery declined to serve (Crewe-Milnes, 2.51).

The last year of the war was clouded by two personal tragedies—his son Neil's death in Palestine in November 1917 and Rosebery's own stroke a few days before the armistice. He regained his mental powers, but his movement, hearing, and sight remained impaired for the rest of his life. His sister, Constance, described his last years as a 'life of weariness, of total inactivity, & at the last of almost blindness'; John Buchan remembered him in his last month of life, 'crushed by bodily weakness' and 'sunk in sad and silent meditations' (Rhodes James, 485). Rosebery died at The Durdans, Epsom, Surrey, on 21 May 1929, to the accompaniment—as he had requested—of a gramophone recording of the Eton boating song. He was buried in the small church at Dalmeny. Rosebery was survived by three of his four children: Lady Sybil Myra Caroline Primrose, later Lady Sybil Grant (1879–1955); Lady Margaret Primrose, later the marchioness of Crewe (1881–1967); and (Albert Edward) Harry Mayer Archibald *Primrose (1882–1974), who became the sixth earl.

Author and historical biographer Rosebery wrote a number of literary and historical essays, many of which were edited by John Buchan and published in his *Miscellanies* (2 vols., 1921). He published two essay-length lives—*Sir Robert Peel* (1899) and *Oliver Cromwell* (1899)—and four books. The first was a study of William Pitt the younger—a distant relative on his mother's side whose standard life was by

Rosebery's grandfather Lord Stanhope; it was commissioned by John Morley for Macmillan's Twelve English Statesmen series and published in 1891. Three other biographical studies—*Napoleon: the Last Phase* (1900), *Lord Randolph Churchill* (1906), and *Chatham: his Early Life and Connections* (1910)—punctuated his semi-retirement. Each displays its author's wit and verbal fluency, though each has its *longueurs*, suggesting that Rosebery was ideally a miniaturist in prose. Frederic Harrison recalled that Macaulay was the model for Rosebery's character studies, which may account for their sometimes dated tone. Technically Rosebery's work certainly compares uncomfortably with the best professional history of the time. He did, though, enjoy the advantage conferred by his status of access to aristocratic houses and to collections of private papers not then generally available, an advantage conspicuous in the Chatham study and in his edition of *The Windham Papers* (1913). Reviewers enjoyed spotting parallels between Rosebery's subjects' careers and his own. His choice of subject for the two larger works was certainly revealing. *Chatham* and *Napoleon* both avoid their subjects' periods of high office and provide deeper character studies than *Pitt*. Chatham emerges as a 'haughty, impossible, anomalous character … difficult to calculate and comprehend', who 'retires, distempered if not mad, into a cell' after his premiership (*Chatham: his Early Life and Connections*, 1910, viii, 25). The anonymous *Times Literary Supplement* reviewer noted unkindly that Rosebery's Chatham owed his ascent to little more than his eloquence. Napoleon, like Cromwell, represented a type always appealing to Rosebery—'the man of destiny, whose spirit attracts and unites and inspires'—but it is the defeated, exiled Napoleon that Rosebery portrays, a lost leader in premature retirement enduring 'the monotony of a suppressed life' (*Napoleon: the Last Phase*, 1900, 162). Even Churchill, personally unlike Rosebery, was depicted as victim of a party machine, 'now so developed that no individual, however gifted, can fight against it' (*Lord Randolph Churchill*, 1906, 119–20). In general the professional reception of Rosebery's books was reserved, but lay reviewers were enthusiastic, and the books sold well. *Pitt*, which disappointed Morley, went through twenty-seven printings between 1891 and 1962.

Assessment Few politicians have been the subject of such high hopes on the strength of so little political experience, and though Rosebery's career clearly was an unsuccessful one if success is measured by accomplishment—he was identified with no major legislative achievement except, indirectly, the creation of the Scottish Office, and his foreign policy was unravelled within a few years of his resignation—the impression of failure is enhanced by the unusually demanding expectations vested in him. The assumption of future greatness—'there is perhaps no man of his age in either House whose political future is so assured', Gladstone wrote in 1883 to James Donaldson (Gladstone, *Diaries*, 10.458)—hung over him from the start of his career. Even when he was prime minister his junior acolytes in the Liberal Imperialist circle discussed 'how to make Rosebery *great*, which is really rather funny when you come to think about it' (E. Grey to Lady Grey, 21 March 1894, Stansky, 174).

Most who lived to be disappointed in Rosebery put his failings down to an inscrutable personality—'was there ever such a complex person?', Crewe asked, in compiling the official biography (Crewe to the marquess of Huntly, 25 July 1929, Crewe MS 10195). Early in his career his closest political friend had feared that his 'over-sensitive, thin-skinned nature will sadly stand in the way of a really successful political future' (Hamilton to Ponsonby, 5 June 1883, *Diary, 1880–1885*, 1.xxvii). It certainly did not help him. During the second Gladstone government his conviction that first Granville then Gladstone himself had taken against him threatened to become self-fulfilling. His fear that any delay in his attaining offices for which he had been tipped in the press would be taken as a sign that he had been tried and found wanting led him to put himself forward in a manner which won him few friends. Gladstone 'thought it marvellous how so clever a man as Rosebery could be so silly' (ibid., 22 Nov 1882). His everyday actions were guided by a dated etiquette which some found charming, others frustrating. This was most evidently true of his ritual refusal, amid professions of inadequacy, of virtually every preferment offered him. The list of appointments initially declined by Rosebery is formidable: minister at the board of rating (1872), lord lieutenant of Linlithgow (1873), under-secretary at the India Office (1880), member of the Order of the Thistle (1881), trustee of the British Museum (1883), projected minister for Scotland (1883), lord lieutenant of Midlothian (1884), commissioner of works (1884), foreign secretary (1892), Liberal leader in the House of Lords (1892), chairman of the London county council for the second time (1892), high commissioner of the Church of Scotland (1915), unspecified high office in the Lloyd George war coalition (1916). There was generally a reason for refusal, but the fact that he eventually accepted all the more substantial offers except the last led colleagues to see the initial refusal as a tiresome and precious affectation—'pretty Fanny's way' in Harcourt's uncharitable phrase. That this 'way' was rooted in a genuine fear of inadequacy and of failure appears incontestable; a telling passage in *Pitt* describes how men wearied by office none the less dreaded the process of leaving it—'the triumph of enemies and the discomfiture of friends'—as men weary of life still feared death (*Pitt*, 1891, 286).

Personal insecurity probably does explain the paradox that one clearly possessing immense personal magnetism and an easy ability to attract admirers could appear tetchy and defensive to those unready to defer to him. A. H. D. Acland found Rosebery 'intolerable as head of the Cabinet, shy, huffy and giving himself the airs of a little German king' (Rhodes James, 357), while his insensitive chairmanship of the Lords select committee on the reform of the upper house in 1907 helped thwart one of his lifelong projects. With hindsight the chairmanship of the London county council, in which he was a success, can be seen as a position ideal for him—raised somewhat above the party battle yet not merely ornamental, allowing him to act as a public advocate for a body in which his work was generally admired. It was a position with no equivalent in national politics.

There are identifiable moments in Rosebery's political career at which his personal shortcomings proved damaging—most obviously in the prolongation of his quarrel with Harcourt during and after his premiership. But the Victorian political world was crowded with complex and difficult individuals, many of whom enjoyed successful careers. That Rosebery did not, owed something to his personality but more to the problems facing a Liberal peer in a rapidly evolving democracy. Rosebery believed that by the extension of the urban franchise in 1867 'English public life received a shock from which it has scarcely recovered' (Rosebery, 'Sir Robert Peel, review of C. S. Parker's *Peel*', *Anglo-Saxon Review*, 1899, 92). Like most of his contemporaries in the British political élite, he sought to comprehend democracy and to guide it. He admired Gladstone for a political style which was popular without being demagogic, and discovered in himself a skill in platform oratory virtually unique among Liberal peers. Yet the high point of Weberian charismatic leadership in Britain had been reached in the era of Gladstone and Disraeli; rhetorical skills remained valuable after 1880, but political leadership required also a mastery of the more modern democratic arts of party management and a sensitivity to the demands of the electorate. As a peer Rosebery was disadvantaged in these respects. He never had to 'nurse' a constituency, for instance: his only real experience of electoral work derived from his involvement with Gladstone's Midlothian campaign in 1879–80. This campaign was, of course, a pivotal episode in the democratization of late Victorian politics, but Rosebery's principal contribution to it—the expenditure of £50,000 to buy up property in the constituency in the hope of generating faggot votes—was a tactic from an earlier electoral age. Growing electorates and legal restrictions upon election expenditure gave greater prominence to the volunteer activist, who demanded in return, particularly in the Liberal Party, the opportunity to promote his own policy concerns. Political activity became, in the 1880s, less dependent upon the stump oratory at which Rosebery excelled and more dependent upon electoral organization.

Rosebery had little understanding of the mechanics of modern party organization and was irritated by his colleagues' readiness to defer to the party's rank and file. He believed that party politics worked to obscure the popular will and that 'the great difficulty of the age as regards politics is the impossibility of ascertaining the real feeling of the country' (Rosebery to Haldane, 1 April 1896, Hamer, 252). Never losing his ability to sway an audience—even the rancorous Bodmin speech of 1905 was punctuated by 'wild applause'—he became convinced that he understood *demos* better than Liberal 'faddists'. He was perhaps right, but his awareness of the weakness of his party's programme sometimes blinded him to the limitations of his own. Though lionized as a 'modern' politician by the Webbs and others on the strength of his detachment from party dogmas, his outlook was in fact rather dated by the

1900s. His Macaulayan ideals of enlightened aristocratic government, constitutional reform, and free-trade imperialism had bound him to the Gladstonian Liberal Party whatever his reservations about the Gladstonian style of politics, but he had little contact with the thinkers who refashioned Liberalism in the 1890s and 1900s, and was largely unreceptive to their doctrines of social and fiscal reform. He could support the social measures of the LCC as the fruits of local self-government, but proved resolutely hostile to the statist social reforms of the 1905–14 Liberal governments. As a peer—and a very wealthy one—Rosebery was also vulnerable to the revival of the fiscal debate. In 1894 he had been insensitive to the electoral dangers of loading the naval programme onto the existing fiscal system and the electoral advantages of a redistributive budget. After 1903 he was slow to appreciate that fiscal controversy would intensify partisanship, destroying his hope that in his detachment from party he could speak for a silent majority. He himself remained too much of a Gladstonian to stomach either the protectionist remedies of the Unionist tariff reformers or the wealth taxes enacted by the Liberals, but his agnosticism condemned him to political isolation. 'Those who are neither Tariff Reformers nor Socialists nor Home Rulers have no refuge to look to,' he complained in 1907 (Rosebery to Ernest Pretyman, 7 June 1907, Rosebery MS 10202, fol. 171). In the event he found refuge only in his long-promised retirement from politics.   JOHN DAVIS

Sources R. R. James, *Rosebery: a biography of Archibald Philip, fifth earl of Rosebery* (1963) · R. O. A. Crewe-Milnes, *Lord Rosebery*, 2 vols. (1931) · NL Scot., Rosebery MSS · *The diary of Sir Edward Walter Hamilton, 1880–1885*, ed. D. W. R. Bahlman, 2 vols. (1972) · *The diary of Sir Edward Walter Hamilton, 1885–1906*, ed. D. W. R. Bahlman, 2 vols. (1993) · G. Martel, *Imperial diplomacy: Rosebery and the failure of foreign policy* (1986) · P. Stansky, *Ambitions and strategies: the struggle for the leadership of the liberal party in the 1890s* (1964) · D. A. Hamer, *Liberal politics in the age of Gladstone and Rosebery* (1972) · Gladstone, *Diaries* · H. C. G. Matthew, *The liberal imperialists: the ideas and politics of a post-Gladstonian élite* (1973) · A. Adonis, *Making aristocracy work: the peerage and the political system in Britain, 1884–1914* (1993) · NL Scot., Crewe MSS · R. Ellmann, *Oscar Wilde* (1987) · B. Roberts, *The mad, bad line: the family of Lord Alfred Douglas* (1981) · J. O. Baylen and R. L. McBath, 'A note on Oscar Wilde, Alfred Douglas and Lord Rosebery, 1897', *English Language Notes*, 23/1 (1985), 42–8 · *The destruction of Lord Rosebery: from the diary of Sir Edward Hamilton, 1894–1895*, ed. D. Brooks (1987)

Archives Dalmeny House, Queensferry · NL Scot., corresp., literary MSS, and papers · NL Wales, letters · NRA, priv. coll., corresp. and papers | Balliol Oxf., corresp. with Sir Robert Morier · BL, Add. MS 16926 · BL, corresp. with Arthur James Balfour, Add. MS 49692 · BL, letters to Lord Battersea and Lady Battersea, Add. MS 47909 · BL, corresp. with Sir Henry Campbell-Bannerman, Add. MS 41226 · BL, letters to Sir Charles Dilke, Add. MS 43876 · BL, letters to T. H. S. Escott, Add. MS 58790 · BL, corresp. with Lord Gladstone, Add. MS 45986 · BL, corresp. with Mary Gladstone and Catherine Gladstone, Add. MSS 46226, 46237 · BL, corresp. with W. E. Gladstone, Add. MSS 44288–44290 · BL, corresp. with Sir Edward Walter Hamilton, Add. MS 48612 · BL, corresp. with Lord Kilbracken, Add. MS 44902 · BL, corresp. with Lord Northcliffe, Add. MS 62154 · BL, corresp. with Lord Ripon, Add. MS 43516 · BL, corresp. with J. A. Spender · BL OIOC, letters to Lord Morley, MS Eur. D 573 · BLPES, letters to Henry Broadhurst · Bodl. Oxf., corresp. with Margot Asquith [some copies] · Bodl. Oxf., letters to H. A. L. Fisher · Bodl. Oxf., corresp. with Sir William Harcourt and Lord Harcourt · Bodl. Oxf., letters to Lord Kimberley · Bodl. Oxf., letters to Sir Henry Miers · CAC Cam., corresp. with Lord Randolph Churchill · CAC Cam., corresp. with Lord Esher · CAC Cam., corresp. with Lord Fisher · CAC Cam., corresp. with David Saunders · CAC Cam., letters to W. T. Stead · Chatsworth House, Derbyshire, letters to duke of Devonshire · CKS, letters to Stanhope family · CKS, letters to Edward Stanhope · CUL, letters to Lord Acton · CUL, corresp. with Lord Hardinge · Durham RO, letters to Cuthbert Headlam · Glos. RO, letters to Lord St Aldwyn · HLRO, letters to Herbert Samuel · HLRO, corresp. with John St Loe Strachey · Hove Central Library, Sussex, letters to Lord Wolseley and Lady Wolseley · ICL, letters to Lord Playfair · King's AC Cam., letters to Oscar Browning · King's Lond., Liddell Hart C., corresp. with General Grant · Lincs. Arch., letters to Lord Monson · LMA, corresp. with Sir Willoughby Maycock · Lpool RO, letters to Sir Edward Evans · Mitchell L., Glas., Glasgow City Archives, letters to Arthur Jamieson · NA Canada, corresp. with Sir George Parkin · NAM, letters to Lord Roberts · News Int. RO, letters to Moberly Bell · NL Scot., letters to J. S. Blackie · NL Scot., letters to John Buchan · NL Scot., letters to W. M. Conway · NL Scot., corresp. with John Gribbel · NL Scot., corresp. with Lord Haldane · NL Scot., letters to Lord Kimberley · NL Scot., corresp. with H. P. Macmillan · NL Wales, letters to T. E. Ellis · NPG, letters to George Frederick Watts · NRA, priv. coll., letters to Lord Aberdeen · NRA, priv. coll., letters to ninth duke of Argyll · NRA, priv. coll., letters to Lord Elgin · NRA, priv. coll., corresp. with Sir John Ewart · NRA, priv. coll., letters to Lady Leconfield · Nuffield Oxf., corresp. with Lord Emmott · PRO, corresp. with Lord Cromer, vols. 6–7, 18, 23–4 · PRO, corresp. with Lord Granville, PRO 30/29 · PRO, corresp. with Sire Edward Malet, FO 343 · PRO NIre., corresp. with Lord Dufferin, D 1071 · Queen's University, Kingston, Ontario, corresp. with John Buchan · St Deiniol's Library, letters to Catherine Gladstone · Surrey HC, corresp. with James Andrews · U. Birm. L., corresp. with Joseph Chamberlain · U. Birm. L., corresp. with Norris & Son, solicitors, relating to Matacong Island · U. Lpool L., letters to Sir Edward Russell · U. Nott. L., corresp. with Lord Galway · University of Bristol Library, letters to Charles Geake · Wilts. & Swindon RO, corresp. with Sir Michael Herbert | FILM BFI NFTVA, news footage

Likenesses H. Weigall, oils, 1866, Christ Church Oxf. · A. E. Emslie, group portrait, oils, 1884 (*Dinner at Haddo House, 1884*), NPG · G. Jerrard, photograph, c.1884, NPG · J. E. Millais, oils, 1886, priv. coll. [*see illus.*] · Elliott & Fry, photograph, 1890–99, NPG · M. Beerbohm, drawings, c.1901–1912, AM Oxf., V&A · M. Beerbohm, drawings, c.1901–1912, Indiana University, Bloomington · M. Beerbohm, drawings, c.1901–1912, U. Texas · H. Furniss, pen and ink sketches, NPG · F. C. Gould, three pencil, pen, and ink sketches, NPG · J. H. Lorimer, oils (after J. E. Millais), Eton · B. Partridge, two caricature drawings, NPG; repro. in *Punch* · Spy [L. Ward], caricature, chromolithograph, NPG; repro. in *VF* (3 June 1876) · Spy [L. Ward], caricature, chromolithograph, NPG; repro. in *VF* (14 March 1901) · ink drawing, Scot. NPG · woodburytype photograph, NPG; repro. in *University Magazine* (1878)

Wealth at death £1,396,577 4s. 11d.—in England: probate, 27 Aug 1929, CGPLA Eng. & Wales

Primrose, Eleanor. See Dalrymple, Eleanor (d. 1759).

Primrose, Gilbert (1566/7–1642), Reformed minister, was born in Edinburgh in late November 1566 or 1567, the son of Gilbert Primrose (c.1535–1615) of Culross, Perthshire, principal surgeon to James VI, and his wife, Alison Graham. In 1587 he entered St Andrews University, where he graduated MA. He then went to France, and in August 1596 was received as a minister of the French Reformed church. His first charge was at St Jean d'Angély, Mirambeau, in the province of Saintonge, where he married Elizabeth Brenin (c.1567–1637) and where his first two children, James (or Jacques) *Primrose (1600–1659) and David, were born. In February 1603 he was transferred to the large and important church of Bordeaux.

However, Primrose maintained his contacts with Scotland and its ministers, and it was mainly through his influence that John Cameron (d. 1625) was made regent in the new college of Bergerac. The national synod of the Reformed church, which met at La Rochelle in March 1607, appointed Primrose to wait upon John Welsh and other Scots ministers who had been banished, and to inquire into their financial needs. At this synod Primrose presented letters from King James and from the magistrates and ministers of Edinburgh recalling him home to serve the church in that city. The synod entreated him to consider the interests of his present charge, 'which, by his most fruitful preaching and exemplary godly conversation, had been exceedingly edified' (Quick, 1.290), and he was induced to remain at Bordeaux. In the latter part of the same year he visited Britain, when he was commissioned by the Reformed congregation at La Rochelle to ask King James to set at liberty Andrew Melville, who was then a prisoner in the Tower of London, and to allow him to accept a professorship in their college. The request was refused, and the application gave offence to the French court. On his return Primrose was called before the king of France, and the people of La Rochelle were reprimanded for communicating with a foreign sovereign without the knowledge or consent of their own. In 1608 John Cameron became Primrose's colleague at Bordeaux, and they 'lived on the most cordial terms and governed the church with the greatest concord for ten years' (Wodrow, MS Gen 1207), after which Cameron left for a professorship at Saumur.

Throughout his ministry at Bordeaux, Primrose was an active theological controversialist, publishing a number of works, including Le voeu de Jacob opposé aux voeux de moines (4 vols., 1610), which was later translated into English by John Bulteel as Jacob's Vow, Opposed to the Vows of Monks and Friers (1617); La trompette de Sion (1610); and La défense de la religion reformée (1619).

In 1623 an act was passed forbidding ministers of other nations to officiate in France, and at the national synod which met at Charenton in September of that year the royal commissioner presented letters from the French king intimating that Primrose and Cameron were no longer to be employed, 'not so much because of their birth as foreigners as for reasons of state' (Quick, 2.101). Primrose was obliged to quit the country, and, according to an account of his own life which he wrote in 1626, his banishment was mainly due to the machinations of the Jesuits, to whom he had given special offence.

On his return to London in the autumn of 1623, Primrose was chosen one of the ministers of the French and Walloon refugee church, an appointment which he held for the rest of his life. On 18 January 1625 his degree was incorporated at the University of Oxford, and he received the degree of DD on the same day on the recommendation of James I. Charles I appointed him chaplain, probably some time after October 1626, and in July 1628 preferred

him to a canonry of Windsor. During his career in England, Primrose continued to maintain his contacts with the Huguenot churches. He corresponded frequently with André Rivet, professor of theology at Leiden, to whom he relayed news of their French and Scottish colleagues and of the education in the French church of London of Rivet's nephew, Pierre du Moulin the younger (whom Primrose considered talented but lazy).

Primrose's writings of this period equally evince a continuing concern for the Huguenots. The Panégyrique à très grand et très puissant Prince Charles, prince de Galles (1624) and the collection of sermons Reconciliation de l'homme avec Dieu (1624) were both published in French for a French audience. In The Righteous Man's Evil, and the Lord's Deliverance (1625), Primrose places the recent military campaign by the French crown against the Huguenots firmly in the long history of Christian martyrdom and persecution, and advocates continuing support from England for those brethren suffering abroad. His friend Bishop Joseph Hall of Exeter dedicated his response to Urban VIII's vituperative attack on the Huguenots, An Answer to Pope Urban his Inurbanity (1629), to Primrose, who in return wrote a grateful letter of commendation (printed as an appendix to the same work). Primrose's other major works include The Christian Man's Tears and Christ's Comforts (1625), Three Sermons of the Table of the Lord (1627), and an English translation of his son David's work, A Treatise of the Sabbath and the Lords-Day (1636).

After the death of his first wife, Elizabeth, in July 1637, Primrose married twice more—on 14 December 1637 to Jeanne, née Hersent, widow of Abraham *Aurelius, and (Jeanne having died on 8 June 1641) on 21 September 1641 to Louise de Lobel, widow of Jacob *Cool. At his death in early December 1642, 'att my house in Chiswell streete neare to Finsbury house' (PRO, PROB 11/190, fols. 351v–352v), Primrose was survived by his sons James, David, Stephen, and John and by his married daughter Louise Blakal.   CHARLES G. D. LITTLETON

Sources D. C. A. Agnew, Protestant exiles from France, chiefly in the reign of Louis XIV, or, The Huguenot refugees and their descendants in Great Britain and Ireland, 3rd edn, 1 (1886), 144–6 · Primrose's 'relation' of his own life, dated 14 Oct 1626, SPD 16/37/75 [repr. in Proceedings of the Huguenot Society of London, 2 (1887–8), 450–53] · F. de Schickler, Les églises du réfuge en Angleterre, 3 vols. (Paris, 1892) · Wood, Ath. Oxon.: Fasti (1815), 419–20 · U. Glas., Robert Wodrow biographical collections, vol. XIII, Gen 1207, item 49 · J. Pannier, 'Quelques lettres inédites de pasteurs écossais ayant exercé leur ministère en France au XVIIᵉ siècle', Bulletin [Société de l'Histoire du Protestantisme Français], 60 (1911), 410–41 · J. Quick, Synodicon in Gallia Reformata, 2 vols. (1692) · H. Wagner, pedigree of Primrose family, UCL, Huguenot Library · PRO, PROB 11/190, fols. 351v–352v [Primrose's will] · 'Actes du consistoire', 1615–80, French Protestant Church of London, Soho Square, MS 5 · Gheschiedenissen ende Handelingen die Voornemelick aengaen de Nederduytsche Natie ende Gemeynten, wonende in Engelant ende in Bysonder tot Londen, vergadert door Symeon Ruytinck, Cesar Calandrinus ende Aemilius van Culenburgh, ed. J. J. van Toorenenbergen, Werken der Marnix-Vereeniging, ser. 3, pt 1 (1873) · Foster, Alum. Oxon.
Likenesses engraving
Wealth at death £32 monetary bequests; also pictures; silver plate (five pieces); 'suite' for a table of damask work containing

two table cloths, one towel, and twenty-four napkins; plus long table made of walnut: will, PRO, PROB 11/190. fols. 351ᵛ–325ᵛ

Primrose, (Albert Edward) Harry Mayer Archibald, sixth earl of Rosebery and second earl of Midlothian (1882–1974), landowner and racehorse breeder, was born at Dalmeny House, near Edinburgh, on 8 January 1882, the elder son (there were also two daughters) of Archibald Philip *Primrose, fifth earl of Rosebery (1847–1929), Liberal prime minister. His mother was Hannah (1851–1890), only daughter of Baron Mayer Amschel de *Rothschild [see under Rothschild, Nathan Mayer], of Mentmore, Buckinghamshire. The prince of Wales (later Edward VII) was one of his godfathers. Harry, Lord Dalmeny—his courtesy title as heir to the earldom—was educated at Eton College, from where he passed top into the Royal Military College, Sandhurst, and was commissioned in the Grenadier Guards.

At the age of twenty-one, at the insistence of his father, Lord Rosebery, Dalmeny very reluctantly resigned his commission to stand as Liberal candidate for the county of Edinburgh, which he represented from 1906 to 1910. At twenty-four he thus became the youngest MP. The prime minister, Campbell-Bannerman, in an attempt to heal an old feud with Dalmeny's father, invited the former to second the motion for the royal address in the Commons. He told his father of the proffered honour, but his father replied: 'If you accept Campbell-Bannerman's invitation you are no son of mine.' It was, said Harry Rosebery many years later, 'very embarrassing'. It effectively quenched whatever political prospects he had. His maiden speech in March 1906 was on army expenditure and reorganization, but after that he spoke very little and confined his interventions to local issues. This was regrettable, for Dalmeny was a loss to English politics because he had both political ambition and political interest. He also possessed political skill, as was shown many years later, in 1941, when he became regional commissioner for Scotland. He combined his father's intelligence with common sense and an ability to get on with very different sorts of people, which his father never had.

Meanwhile, Dalmeny was making a name for himself as a cricketer. While still at school he had distinguished himself in the Eton v. Harrow match at Lord's in 1900. He played for Buckinghamshire in 1901, twice for Middlesex in 1902, and finally in 1905 became captain of Surrey, the youngest captain the county had ever had. In 1906 he played for Scotland against the Australians. In 1907 he resigned the captaincy because of conflicting duties in the House of Commons. But in December 1908 he wrote to his constituency agent:

It is with great regret that I write to inform you that I do not propose to stand for Parliament at the next General Election. It is being forced upon me more and more that my politics are not far enough advanced to meet the views of the Liberal Party as at present constituted.

Dalmeny insisted to the end of his life that he was a Liberal; in fact, he was a Conservative, or perhaps a Liberal of so old a vintage as to merit the designation whig. Later, in the stress of a major economic crisis, he became a National Liberal, and ultimately the party's president. But he never took the final step of joining the Conservatives. In 1914, shortly after the outbreak of war on 4 August, Dalmeny rejoined the Grenadier Guards and, after a short spell at general headquarters in France, became an aide-de-camp to General E. H. H. Allenby. In June 1917 he joined Allenby in Palestine as assistant military secretary. This was a remarkable and happy relationship. Each had the reputation of being difficult to get on with; each was outspoken, did not suffer fools gladly, and possessed great common sense. Dalmeny was mentioned in dispatches, was awarded the MC (1916), was admitted to the French Légion d'honneur (1917), and was appointed DSO (1918). His younger brother, Neil Primrose, MP for Wisbech, was also in Palestine serving with the Buckinghamshire yeomanry. On 18 November 1917 he was killed in the last shot of a battle with the Turks at Gaza. Their father, Lord Rosebery, never got over this blow and in 1919 suffered a severe stroke from which he did not recover. Thus Dalmeny became in fact head of the family, although his father did not die until 1929. Then he entered the House of Lords as second earl of Midlothian, a title bestowed on his father in 1911 but never used. Nevertheless, he continued to be known as the sixth earl of Rosebery.

On 15 April 1909 Dalmeny married Dorothy Alice Margaret Augusta (d. 1966), daughter of Lord Henry George Grosvenor and sister of the third duke of Westminster. The marriage was brief and unhappy, but produced a son and daughter, to whom Dalmeny was devoted. In 1919 the marriage was dissolved and on 24 June 1924 Dalmeny married Eva Isabel Marian (d. 1987), daughter of Henry Campbell Bruce, second Baron Aberdare, and former wife of Algernon Henry Strutt, third Baron Belper. She was appointed DBE in 1955. They had a son and a daughter, the latter of whom died at birth. In 1931 Rosebery's son and heir by his first marriage, Archibald Ronald, Lord Dalmeny, died suddenly at the age of twenty-one from blood poisoning contracted during a dental operation at Oxford. By all accounts a golden boy, modest, charming, and intelligent, he was, to his father's delight, an excellent cricketer and it had been prophesied that he would have a glittering future as a batsman and bowler.

Between the wars, apart from managing his great estates, Rosebery established himself as a racehorse breeder and owner and won most of the famous races. Perhaps his best-known horse was Blue Peter, foaled at Mentmore, which won not only the Two Thousand Guineas, the Blue Riband at Epsom, and the Eclipse stakes, but also—Rosebery's proudest racing moment—the Derby in 1939. Ocean Swell, sired by Blue Peter, later won the Derby (1944) and the Ascot gold cup. Rosebery was elected to the Jockey Club in 1924. He became president of the Thoroughbred Breeders' Association and remained so until 1955.

From 1941 until the beginning of 1945 Rosebery was regional commissioner for Scotland. Like his father, he had a passionate love for Scotland and he worked indefatigably at his difficult task. He never courted popularity; but this did him no harm in the long run, either with the prime minister or the Scottish people. In 1945 he became secretary of state for Scotland in the brief caretaker government and, after its defeat, he led the National Liberals in the Lords. In 1947 he was created a knight of the Order of the Thistle. He was sworn of the privy council in 1945. Henceforth his public interests were varied but nonpolitical. He was chairman of the Royal Fine Art Commission for Scotland (1952–7) and president of the Royal Scottish Corporation. He was president of the Surrey County Cricket Club (1947–50) and of the MCC (1953–4). He was a member of the royal commission on justices of the peace (1946–8) and was himself a JP for many years. He was lord lieutenant for Midlothian (1929–64). In 1949 the Labour government asked him to preside over a committee of inquiry into the export and slaughter of horses, and from 1955 to 1965 he was chairman of the Scottish Tourist Board. He was one of the original supporters of the Edinburgh Festival, in which his wife, Eva, played a notable part.

Rosebery had fantastic energy and was interested in and curious about everything, down to the minutest detail. These characteristics, combined with a marvellous memory, enabled him to sift, analyse, and digest information at a speed which made his opinions seem intuitive. He was an excellent judge of character. This was coupled with the ability to form personal relationships equally well with soldiers, stockmen, the young and the very young, financiers, policemen, and politicians. He died at his home, Mentmore Towers, on 30 May 1974, aged ninety-two. Having handed his Dalmeny estates to his son and heir, Neil Archibald Primrose (who was born in 1929 and succeeded to the earldom on his father's death), he was delighted that the birth of a grandson in 1967 ensured the continuation of the family name.   ROTHSCHILD, *rev.*

Sources C. K. Young, *Harry, Lord Rosebery* (1974) • personal knowledge (1986) • Burke, *Peerage* (1999) • d. cert.
Archives HLRO, corresp. with Lord Beaverbrook | FILM BFI NFTVA, news footage
Wealth at death £9,941,699: probate, 5 July 1974, *CGPLA Eng. & Wales*

Primrose, Sir Henry William (1846–1923), civil servant, was born in Edinburgh on 22 August 1846, the second of the six sons of the Hon. Bouverie Francis Primrose and his wife, Frederica Sophia, daughter of Thomas Anson, first Viscount Anson, and sister of Thomas William Anson, first earl of Lichfield. Primrose, whose father was the second son of Archibald John *Primrose, fourth earl of Rosebery, was the cousin of Archibald Philip Primrose, fifth earl of Rosebery, the prime minister. Henry Primrose was educated at Trinity College, Glenalmond, and Balliol College, Oxford. He obtained second classes in classical moderations (1867) and in the final honour school of law and modern history (1869). From Oxford he passed into the home civil service, entering the Treasury in 1869.

Primrose was one of W. E. Gladstone's secretaries from April to June 1880, but then went to India as secretary to Lord Ripon, the viceroy. In 1884 he returned to Gladstone's service, serving until the fall of the ministry in 1885. In

Gladstone's government of 1886 he was head of the Downing Street secretariat. He was the least admiring of Gladstone's secretaries, and was a useful conduit of information to his cousin, Rosebery (then foreign secretary). In 1887 Primrose was appointed secretary to the office of works. In 1888 he married Helen Mary (*d.* 1919), eldest daughter of Gilbert McMicking of Miltonise, Wigtownshire, and formerly the wife of James Montgomery Walker; they had one son. In 1895 Primrose was appointed chairman of the board of customs, and in 1899 of the Board of Inland Revenue, which post he held until he retired from the civil service in 1907, aged sixty-one. As a financier Primrose was a strict Gladstonian at a time when Treasury attitudes were fast changing. His evidence to the select committee on income tax in 1906 vigorously defended Victorian precepts.

After retirement Primrose continued active in public life. He chaired the Pacific Cable company from 1907 until 1914. In 1911 he chaired a special committee on the financial clauses of the Irish Home Rule Bill, a subject with which he had had experience since 1886. He boldly proposed that an Irish government should have full control over its revenue, with the imperial government providing some additional funds to meet the deficit. His plan was thought to offer excessive financial autonomy and was not included in the Home Rule Bill of 1912, the financial clauses of which were drawn up by Herbert Samuel. In 1912 he was a member of the MacDonnell royal commission on the civil service and in 1913 of the Loreburn royal commission on railways. In 1914 Primrose became chairman of the Welsh church commission consequent on Welsh disestablishment. In the First World War he was chairman of the sugar commission and in 1918 he was a member of the Bradbury committee on staff retrenchment in government offices. Primrose was thus a distinguished and valuable public servant, especially known for the clarity of his minutes and reports. He was created KCB in 1899 and was sworn of the privy council in 1912, an unusual honour for a civil servant. Primrose was, like his cousin Lord Rosebery, a chronic insomniac, and suffered from depression as a result. On the morning of 17 June 1923 he was found to have shot himself in Kensington Gardens (he lived nearby at 44 Ennismore Gardens); he was taken to St George's Hospital, where he died almost immediately.   H. C. G. MATTHEW

Sources DNB • *The Times* (19 June 1923) • Gladstone, *Diaries* • P. Jalland, *The liberals and Ireland* (1980) • *The diary of Sir Edward Walter Hamilton, 1880–1885*, ed. D. W. R. Bahlman, 2 vols. (1972) • *The diary of Sir Edward Walter Hamilton, 1885–1906*, ed. D. W. R. Bahlman (1993)
Archives Duke U., Perkins L., corresp. and papers | BL, corresp. with Herbert Gladstone, Add. MS 45991 • BL, minutes and corresp. with W. E. Gladstone, Add. MSS 44442–44680 • BL, letters to Sir Edward Walter Hamilton, Add. MS 48610 • BL, corresp. with D. Panioty and Lord Ripon, Add. MSS 43523–43635 • BL, corresp. and papers as secretary to Lord Ripon, Add. MSS 43627–43635 • BL OIOC, corresp. with Sir Alfred Lyall, MSS Eur. F 132 • BL OIOC, letters to lords Ripon and Dufferin, viceroys of India, MSS Eur. F 102 • Bodl. Oxf., corresp. with Lord Kimberley • NL Scot., corresp. with Lord Rosebery
Likenesses E. E. Gostowski, plaster bust, 1891, Somerset House, London • photograph, NPG

Wealth at death £9212 13s. 1d.: probate, 21 July 1923, *CGPLA Eng. & Wales*

Primrose, James (d. 1640), government official, was the second son of Archibald Primrose, of Culross, Perthshire, a law agent, and Margaret Bleau, of Castlehill. Nothing is known of his early life. He was appointed clerk to the privy council of Scotland for life on 1 February 1599. He was twice married: his first marriage was to Sibylla Miller, with whom he had a son, Gilbert, and six daughters; by 1616 he had married Catherine (d. 1651), daughter of Richard Lawson of Boghall, Lanarkshire, with whom he had a son, Archibald [see Primrose, Sir Archibald, Lord Carrington (1616–1679)], and six daughters.

On 13 June 1616 Primrose was granted a monopoly of printing and selling the catechism entitled *God and the King*, a work that emphasized the supremacy of royal prerogative over the kirk. James VI intended that it should supplant John Craig's *Examination before the Communione*, which had served as the 'official' catechism of the kirk since 1592. In entrusting the monopoly to Primrose, the king sought to employ the authority of the privy council to enforce its use in schools, universities, and kirks, and to disseminate a copy in every household in Scotland. Presbyterian opponents of royal policy, however, were quick to broadcast that the new 'catechisme' contained 'little of God and much for the king' (NL Scot., Calderwood, 'Ane answere', fol. 49r). Thus the work was never widely popular, and Primrose appears to have made little effort regarding recovery of payment and distribution of stock following the king's death in 1625.

Although Primrose courted royal favour, he and his wife were not unsympathetic to the plight of presbyterianism in Scotland. In 1617 Primrose drew up the Act of Caution by which the nonconformist minister David Calderwood was released from 'ward' pending his appeal against the sentence of banishment. Subsequently, Calderwood received a letter, 'penned by James Primrois … informing me that [meanwhile] it was his majesties will that I should forbear to preach', which clause had been omitted from the act. Primrose, noted the minister, beseeched him 'to bewarr that I involve myself not in a new trouble' (Calderwood, 'A trew relatioun', fols. 5v–6r). Catherine Lawson (a prominent presbyterian matron) shared her husband's concern for Calderwood, and was entrusted with the care of 'twa kist full of [the minister's] books' during his enforced exile (Wells, 132). The discovery of such material in the house of a trusted servant of the crown would almost certainly have led to Primrose's dismissal.

Almost nothing is recorded of Primrose's private activities during the reign of Charles I. He was a man of moderate means, leaving possessions worth £700 Scots to his second wife, Catherine, who died in 1651. Primrose continued as a trusted servant of the crown until his death at Edinburgh, on 21 January 1640, of causes unknown.

VAUGHAN T. WELLS

Sources D. Calderwood, *The history of the Kirk of Scotland*, ed. T. Thomson and D. Laing, 8 vols., Wodrow Society, 7 (1842–9), vols. 7–8 · *Reg. PCS*, 1st ser., vols. 5–10 · Edinburgh testaments, NA Scot., CC 8/8/59 · D. Calderwood, 'A trew relatioun of my trall before the high commissioun and my troubles following thereupon', 1617, NL Scot., Wodrow MS Qto 76.1 · D. Calderwood, 'Ane Answere … to the tripartite discourse entituled Calderwods Recantation', NL Scot., Wodrow MS Qto 76.5 · V. T. Wells, *The origins of covenanting thought and resistance: c.1580–1638* (1997) · A. J. Mann, *The Scottish book trade, 1500–1720* (2000) · *DNB*

Archives NL Scot., corresp.

Wealth at death £800 Scots: Edinburgh testaments, NA Scot., CC 8/8/59

Primrose, James (1600–1659), physician, the eldest of four sons of Gilbert *Primrose (1566/7–1642), a Scottish minister in the French Reformed church, and his wife, Elizabeth Brenin (c.1567–1637), was born at Mirambeau, Saintonge. Much of his youth was spent in Bordeaux, to whose Reformed church his father had been called in 1603. He attended the University of Bordeaux and graduated there MA. After a period of medical study in Paris he matriculated at the University of Montpellier in 1615 and in short order gained an MB, a medical licence, and in 1617 an MD. At least part of his studies were paid for by James I of England.

The Primroses had a strong connection to the house of Stuart. Primrose's grandfather was Gilbert Primrose, principal surgeon to James VI and I and his wife, Queen Anne. On the surgeon's death in 1615, his place was taken by Duncan Primrose, probably his son. In 1623 James Primrose's father was forced to leave France and took a position as minister of the French Reformed church in London. He continued in that position until his death in 1641. Gilbert Primrose was made a royal chaplain and in 1625, on the king's personal recommendation, he was created a DD by the University of Oxford.

James Primrose incorporated on his Montpellier MD at Oxford in 1628, doubtlessly as a prelude to applying for a medical licence from the London College of Physicians. On 9 December 1629 he was successfully examined for the licence at the home of the college president, John Argent. On 11, 12, and 14 December Primrose attended the lectures of Helkiah Crooke on morbid anatomy, held in the college house. Much of the discussion among the fellows centred on William Harvey's book on the circulation of the blood, which had been published only recently. Primrose became concerned over the lack of criticism of the new theory and subsequently was able to gain the support of Charles I, a family patron and ally, for delivering a series of public medical lectures in London. The college was aghast that a new licentiate, and not even a fellow of their company, should be allowed the right of any public lectures. The matter was dropped, but Primrose, in a very short time, according to his later reckoning, published in London in 1630 the first serious rebuttal of Harvey's discovery: *Exercitationes et animadversiones in librum Gulielmi Harvaei de motu cordis et circulatione sanguinis*. Primrose's stay in the capital was a brief one. He first appeared before the college in 1629; was listed among foreign doctors in the City in 1632; but was not named among licentiates living in London in 1635.

In his appearance before the college, Primrose stated among his qualifications that he had studied medicine with Professor Jean Riolan at the University of Paris. This may have occurred just after his Montpellier MD of 1617, but much of the time from that date was spent in actual medical practice, probably in Yorkshire, and possibly in Hull, where he was to spend a large part of his medical life. In one of his last books before his death in 1659 he mentioned having seen a case of rickets, before the illness even had a name, in Yorkshire in 1628. The ten years of medical practice, to which he referred in his book against Harvey, were likely therefore to have been spent in England not France. His return to Hull by no later than 1634 has better documentation, for he was charged with being a Roman Catholic recusant there in 1637 and 1640. He returned briefly to London again in the latter year to marry Louise (Lucie) de Haukmont (d. 1653) at his father's Reformed church. They had several children. The marriages of Roman Catholics in protestant churches for legal reasons was not unknown. Primrose's religion is not easy to tease from his many books, but there are indications in them that he remained a Roman Catholic after the charges of 1637 and 1640.

In 1638 Primrose had published in London what would turn out to be his most popular book: *De vulgi in medicina erroribus*. The book was a systematic attack on the non-professional practice of medicine, folk medicine, quackery, and malpractice. In 1640 a young physician from Hull, Robert Wittie, published an English version of a separate work by Primrose on part of the same subject, *The Antimonial Cup Twice Cast*. It was the beginning of a long and fruitful friendship and professional partnership. Though Wittie was strongly Presbyterian in religious sympathies and a Harveian on the circulation of the blood, a fierce dedication to the medical profession, shared by Primrose, made possible an unlikely alliance. In 1651 Wittie published his translation of a revised edition of Primrose's *De vulgi*: *Popular Errours, or, The Errours of the People in Physick*. Some of the common errors refuted by Primrose were that the linen of the sick ought not to be changed; that remedies ought not to be rejected for their unpleasantness; and that gold boiled in broth will cure consumption, to name but a few. The book featured some dedicatory poetry by another Hull resident and native, Andrew Marvell. Primrose remarried in 1653 and with his second wife, Elizabeth, had two children: James, baptized in 1654, and Maria, baptized at Holy Trinity, Hull, in 1656.

Despite writing many books on many medical topics, Primrose is best known as the orthodox Galenic opponent of Harvey's discovery of the circulation. Using some contemporary anatomists as well, including Vesalius, Primrose questioned the truth of any doctrine based on vivisection, which was an unnatural intrusion into the ordinary functioning of the body that could yield only unnatural conclusions. Such discoveries had absolutely no utility to the actual practice of medicine, an art that was best learned from the well-established authority of Hippocrates and Galen, and traditional commentators. More than that, these discoveries threatened to undermine fundamental therapeutic techniques like phlebotomy, based on ancient physiology and which would be rendered nonsensical if the blood actually circulated through the body as Harvey maintained. Primrose did allow that in systole, or contraction, some blood left the heart, but this was not the heart's primary function which was rather as a receptacle for the heating of the blood. Primrose was by no means a slave to books and his own medical practice was tempered by experience, which he thought essential for a doctor. He was suspicious of academic medicine because it inevitably produced useless novelties, like that of the circulation, but he was very capable of independent thought which led him to accept in his last years the lesser or pulmonary circulation. He was also open to the benefits of chemical medicine, while his work throughout showed him flexible in modifying his traditional method with original thought and observation.

Primrose was a prolific and highly regarded medical author, enjoying a wide European audience and numerous reprints of his many books. In addition to the *Exercitationes* of 1630, he wrote at least four other books against Harveian professors of medicine: one against Walaeus of Leiden in 1639; two against Regius of Utrecht in 1640; and a fourth against the converted Harveian, Plempius of Louvain, in 1657. Like his idol Galen, there was scarcely a field of medicine on which he did not write. These included two handbooks on the main principles and practice of medicine, *Aphorismi necessarii ad doctrinam medicinae acquirendam perutiles*, published at Leiden in 1647, and *Enchiridion medicum*, at Amsterdam in 1650; another on pharmacy and the compounding of medicines, *Ars pharmaceutica*, appeared in Amsterdam in 1651. Three of his later books were published at Rotterdam: one on gynaecology, *De mulierum morbis* (1655); a second on fevers, *De febribus* (1658); and his final book, on childhood illnesses, *Partes duae de morbis puerorum*, which was published in the year of his death, 1659. The last was still much respected by British physicians in the late eighteenth century. Primrose was also the author of a short Latin history of Montpellier, *Academia Monspelienses descripta*, published at Oxford in 1631 and dedicated to the regius professor of physic, Thomas Clayton. Primrose died in Hull in December 1659 and was buried in the parish church of the Holy Trinity, a parish in which he had lived and worked for most of his medical life. He was buried near his first wife. At least six of their children had been baptized in the church between 1642 and 1651. Primrose left his surviving sons under the guardianship of Robert Wittie, who is known to have seen Caesar and Isaac, the sons of Primrose and his first wife, through Cambridge. Primrose's widow married John Smithson, vicar of Paghill on 18 January 1664.   WILLIAM BIRKEN

Sources Holderness D./Prog., Dec 1664, Borth. Inst. • J. A. R. Bickford and M. E. Bickford, *The medical profession in Hull* (1983) • private information (2004) • G. Clark and A. M. Cooke, *A history of the Royal College of Physicians of London*, 3 vols. (1964–72) • A. C. Germain, 'Jacques Primerose: historien de l'École Médecine de Montpellier', *Memoires de la Société Archéologique de Montpellier* (1882), 280–92 • R. French, *William Harvey's natural philosophy* (1994) • H. Aveling, *Post Reformation Catholicism in east Yorkshire, 1558–1790* (1960) • J. Lawson, *A town grammar school through six centuries: a history of Hull grammar school against its local background* (1963) • Wood, *Ath. Oxon.* • G. Whitteridge, *William Harvey and the circulation of the blood* (1971) •

G. Keynes, *The life of William Harvey* (1966) · Venn, *Alum. Cant.* · A. Ross, *Arcana microcosmi* (1652) · A. J. L. Jourdan, ed., *Biographie médicale*, 7 vols. (1820–25) · *DNB* · private information (2004) [J. A. R. Bickford, M. E. Bickford]

Primrose, William (1904–1982), viola player, was born on 23 August 1904 at 18 Wilton Drive, Glasgow, the elder son and the first of the three children of John Primrose, an orchestral violinist, and his wife, Margaret McInnis Whiteside (1872/3–1962). His parents, lowland Scots of modest means, sent him to local council schools, but the focus of his education was musical. Given a quarter-sized violin when he was four, the boy had promptly played a melody at perfect pitch. For ten years Willie Primrose took violin lessons from Camillo Ritter, an expatriate Austrian who had studied with Otakar Ševčík and Joseph Joachim. He appeared in a few Congregational church concerts, but nobody let him know that his talent was prodigious (though Ritter did persuade him to give up boxing for the sake of his hands).

In 1919 Primrose performed before Landon Ronald, who helped him to a scholarship at the Guildhall School of Music in London. Max Mossel's tuition left him cold, but he emulated violinists heard at concerts: Fritz Kreisler inspired the sweetness of tone for which Primrose was later famous. These years saw him polishing his manners too. Sharp-nosed, straight-backed, and well-groomed, the young Scot assumed a gentlemanly persona (and wore a pencil moustache when fashionable). Following his début at Queen's Hall in 1923, he left the Guildhall with a gold medal in 1924.

Despite fair success as a soloist, Primrose grew worried that his playing had ceased to improve. He consulted Eugène Ysaÿe in 1926 and spent many months at Le Zoute sur Mer during the next three years, deriving fresh motivation and technical refinement from the ageing Belgian virtuoso, to whom he admitted that he really preferred the sound of the viola to that of the violin. Chamber-music performance gave him most pleasure, he explained, and the weakest member of the ensemble was usually the viola player. By 1928 he was contemplating a change: instead of being one fine violinist among very many, might he not become a uniquely fine violist? Ysaÿe told him to follow his inclination; others said that to switch would be professional suicide, as the viola was a secondary instrument without prestige.

Primrose joined the London String Quartet on viola in March 1930—to the furious despair of his father. John Primrose, rather an Anglophobe, had already taken exception to William's marriage on 2 October 1928 to Dorothy Fanny Friend (1899/1900–1951), an English-woman, and he found this musical apostasy unforgivable. The estrangement lasted many years, despite the high reputation of the London String Quartet, which toured Europe and America until it disbanded in 1935.

For a while Primrose struggled to find employment. Orchestras hired him for major viola works, but only Berlioz's *Harold in Italy* and Mozart's *Sinfonia concertante* (K364) were programmed with any frequency. Regardless of the efforts of Lionel Tertis (1876–1975), the viola was not recognized as a solo instrument. In 1937 Primrose went to the USA to join the new NBC Symphony Orchestra under Arturo Toscanini, and NBC had him head the subsidiary Primrose Quartet (1939–41). He condemned diffidence in chamber music: a virtuoso quartet should mean four virtuosos. Later he recorded with Jascha Heifetz and Gregor Piatigorsky and performed with the Festival Piano Quartet (1954–62).

Colleagues found Bill Primrose a no-nonsense character of equable temperament who did not romanticize his calling. His mode of life was methodical, and he relaxed by watching soccer and boxing and playing golf and chess. Yet he had his sensitivities, such as an aversion to performing in casual surroundings and a preference that an orchestra should never engage him rather than do so just the once (lest people wonder why he was not asked back). His recordings for Columbia and RCA Victor rarely satisfied him.

On the mistaken assumption that Toscanini was retiring, Primrose resigned from the NBC Symphony Orchestra in 1941 and relaunched his career as a soloist. Concert promoters remained disappointingly sceptical of the viola's appeal until a chance encounter on 57th Street, New York, provided a breakthrough. The popular tenor Richard Crooks asked Primrose to tour the USA as his supporting act, and they ended up working together for four years. Once the big-name singer had drawn the audiences, the violist used his outstanding technique to win them over to his instrument (even if this meant resorting to hackneyed crowd-pleasers such as Ethelbert Nevin's *The Rosary*). He played Amati, Stradivari, and Guarneri violas without a shoulder rest and eschewed heavy vibrato. By 1945 Primrose had become a star in his own right: 'The world's greatest violist'.

Although he made many arrangements and transcriptions of pieces written for other instruments, Primrose insisted that the viola had a distinct 'personality': it was not just a low-tuned violin. He commissioned viola concertos from Quincy Porter (1948), Béla Bartók (1949), Edmund Rubbra (1952), Peter Fricker (1952), and Darius Milhaud (1955), and performed the Bartók over a hundred times once he had overcome the phobia of flying which threatened his international career around 1950.

Widowed in 1951, Primrose married Alice Virginia French from Iowa in 1952, in which year he was appointed CBE and took US citizenship. He had two daughters from his first marriage and one son from the second. World-class orchestras competed to book him, but he began to suffer from whistling in his ears. Chronic tinnitus curtailed his recording career in 1958 and a heart attack precipitated his retirement from the platform in 1963.

Primrose latterly devoted his time to teaching, basing himself first at the University of Southern California (1961–5) and then at Indiana University (1965–72), while making visits to New York and Tokyo. Three books outline his approach. His last decade was transformed by Hiroko Sawa, a Japanese violin teacher, whom he married in 1978 during two years spent in Australia. Although ailing, he was guest lecturer at Brigham Young University from 1979 until his death from cancer at Provo, Utah, USA, on 1 May 1982.

William Primrose was the foremost viola player of the twentieth century. His influence on the technique, repertoire, and status of the instrument seemed certain to endure. JASON TOMES

Sources W. Primrose, *Walk on the north side* (1978) · M. Riley, *The history of the viola* (1980) · D. Dalton, *Playing the viola: conversations with William Primrose* (1988) · *New Grove*, 2nd edn · D. Dalton, 'The first star of the viola', *The Strad*, 105 (1994), 148–55 · T. Potter, 'William Primrose on the record', *The Strad* (1994), 157–9 · m. cert. [Dorothy Friend]
Archives Brigham Young University, Utah, music MSS and papers | FILM Brigham Young University, Utah, Primrose International Viola Archive
Likenesses group photograph, 1947, Hult. Arch. · photographs, Brigham Young University, Utah, Primrose International Viola Archive; repro. in Primrose, *Walk on the north side*

Prince, Gilbert (*d.* 1396), painter, first appears in a minor capacity in 1350/51, working for 9*d.* a day under Hugh St Albans (*d.* 1368) on the decorations of St Stephen's Chapel in the palace of Westminster. He witnessed Hugh's purchase of a house on Fore Street, London, in 1353, and also a further transaction relating to his estate in 1374. In 1376 he was warden of the guild of painters, and in the period 1384–8 a member of the common council of the city of London. He was also eventually exempted from jury and assize service. Prince was wealthy. In 1393 he drew an exceptionally large payment of £650 from the exchequer. He purchased properties in the parishes of St Giles Cripplegate and St Dionis Backchurch between the 1360s and 1395, and his will, enrolled in 1396 (and suggesting that he died in that year, in London), points to a substantial estate with a private chapel, to judge from the bequest of his missal, chalice, and vestments to St Giles. It also states that his equipment was to be sold off, so his business was apparently closed. He was married twice, first to Isolde and second to Elizabeth, and had at least three children. The best-established painter working for the crown in the later fourteenth century, Prince was employed steadily throughout the reigns of Edward III and Richard II and his employers also included John of Gaunt. Much of his documented work was on the decorative paraphernalia for tournaments and 'disguisings', such as banners and other painted textiles administered by the wardrobe, or for funerals like that of Joan, queen of Scotland, in 1364. It is unclear if any extant wall or panel paintings should be attributed to him: the tester over the tomb of Edward, the Black Prince (after 1376), at Canterbury might be his work, since Edward had earlier employed Prince's mentor, Hugh St Albans.

Thomas Lytlington (*fl.* 1390–1401), painter, is named as Gilbert Prince's clerk and as a beneficiary in Prince's will of 1395 or 1396; he appears to have taken Prince's tradename after his death. He first appears in 1390 in danger of arrest at the suit of John Wesenham for employing threats. In 1393 he appeared at the exchequer to draw the payment to his master of £650 noted above. In 1394–6 he was engaged upon important decorations at Richard II's manor at Windsor (costing £290 and including work on

five chambers for the use of the king) and on three chapels decorated with Richard's emblems. In June 1399 he was granted protection to cover his going to Ireland in the retinue of John Holland, duke of Exeter (*d.* 1400), on Richard's expedition there; and in 1401 he is recorded as vendor of part of a shop on Cripplegate, perhaps Prince's. The kind of work for which Lytlington was responsible may be judged by the large chained and couched white hart painted on a dividing wall in the muniment room at Westminster Abbey; but there is no positive evidence for attributing any extant work to him, least of all the Wilton diptych. PAUL BINSKI

Sources F. Devon, ed. and trans., *Issues of the exchequer: being payments made out of his majesty's revenue, from King Henry III to King Henry VI inclusive*, RC (1837), 207, 252, 258 · Tout, *Admin. hist.*, 4.391, n.8 · R. R. Sharpe, ed., *Calendar of wills proved and enrolled in the court of husting, London, AD 1258 – AD 1688*, 2 (1890), 319–20 · W. A. Shaw, 'The early English school of portraiture', *Burlington Magazine*, 65 (1934), 171–84 · J. H. Harvey, 'Some London painters of the 14th and 15th centuries', *Burlington Magazine*, 89 (1947), 303–5 · E. W. Tristram, *English wall painting of the fourteenth century* (1955), 288, 291 · J. H. Harvey, 'The Wilton diptych, a re-examination', *Archaeologia*, 98 (1961), 1–28, esp. 7 · R. Brown, H. M. Colvin, and A. J. Taylor, eds., *The history of the king's works*, 2 (1963), 1008 · Chancery records

Prince, Henry James (1811–1899), founder of the Agapemonites, was the youngest son of Thomas Prince (1745–1816), a West Indian plantation owner, formerly of Liverpool, and his wife, Mary Ann, *née* Stevens (1775–1847). Henry was born on 13 January 1811 at 5 Widcombe Crescent, Bath, Somerset, and was brought up by his widowed mother and her elderly Roman Catholic lodger, Martha Freeman, the daughter of a business associate of Henry's father. He was educated at a school in Corsham. In September 1827 he was articled to John Nicholls, an apothecary in Wells, moving to London in 1831 to study at Guy's Hospital and the Webb Street medical school. Having qualified on 16 February 1832, he was appointed in May as medical officer to the General Hospital in Bath, but after an abdominal operation in London in April 1835 he resigned. A year earlier he had experienced an evangelical conversion, and he was now encouraged to consider ordination when, as a convalescent, he visited his half-brother John Prince of Shincliffe Hall, co. Durham. With this object he entered St David's College, Lampeter, in March 1836. Further ill health caused him to miss a term in September 1837. Devout and earnest by temperament, he gathered about him a small group of Welsh students, known as the Lampeter Brethren, who fasted, prayed, and studied with him. On 10 July 1838 he married his mother's lodger, Martha Freeman (*d.* 1842), who was considerably older than him. In 1839 he completed the course at Lampeter and was ordained.

In June 1840 Prince became curate of Charlinch, near Bridgwater, Somerset, where his initially absent rector, Samuel Starky, soon joined in the popular enthusiasm for his ministry, which Prince later described in *The Charlinch Revival* (1842). Shocked by his unconventional methods, the bishop of Bath and Wells revoked Prince's licence to preach on 4 May 1842. There was further adverse comment when, only months after his wife's death in April

1842, Prince married Starky's sister Julia on 16 September. Meanwhile he engaged in open-air preaching near Charlinch before taking up a temporary curacy at Stoke by Clare, Suffolk, but in November the parochial discord sown by Prince led the bishop of Ely also to prohibit him from preaching.

Adopting typically messianic language Prince proclaimed the imminent 'Day of the Lord'. He referred to himself as Elijah, and to Starky and himself as the 'two witnesses' of Revelation 11, also privately claiming that he was the incarnation of the Holy Ghost. In 1843 he preached in Adullam Chapel in Brighton, but when in 1844 some former colleagues denounced him as heterodox, Prince joined Starky in Weymouth, gathering there an entourage of devoted followers. Meanwhile, near Bridgwater, some of his admirers, known as Princites, were engaged in energetic revivalism, but in early 1846 their leader decided that the days of evangelism were over and the elect should wait in isolation for the imminent return of Christ. In December 1846 the community moved to more spacious accommodation in a purpose-built settlement in Spaxton, barely a mile from Charlinch. The purchase of this Agapemone, or 'abode of love', was made possible when his followers sold their lands, allowing Prince (known in the community as Beloved) to dispose of the proceeds. Particularly controversial was the way in which he had persuaded three wealthy sisters to marry three of his clerical followers.

In 1856 Prince announced that he was the chosen means of reconciling God's spirit with the sinful flesh of humanity. In a ceremony called the Great Manifestation, Prince was 'spiritually married' to a young member of the community, Anne Willet (or Zoë) Paterson. He sought to justify his action in one of his characteristically tortuous books, *The Little Book Open* (1856), but several of his scandalized followers abandoned him when Paterson gave birth to a daughter, Eve, whose father was almost certainly Prince.

The wealthier members of the community lived in some comfort, but rumours of general profligacy, as opposed to Prince's special privileges, were unfounded. In 1860 Prince was publicly discredited in the case of *Nottidge v. Prince*, heard in chancery, when the relatives of a deceased member of the community successfully contested her will, revealing how Prince had secured control of his followers' assets. The movement survived quietly in Prince's later years, gaining more publicity when its members held a campaign at Clapton, London, in the 1890s. The preacher, approved by Prince, was a lapsed Anglican curate, John Hugh Smyth-Pigott. When Prince died at the Agapemone in Spaxton on 8 January 1899 and was buried in its grounds, Smyth-Pigott was soon recognized as his successor.

TIMOTHY C. F. STUNT

Sources [H. J. Prince], *Br. Prince's journal, or, An account of the destruction of the works of the devil in the human soul by the Lord Jesus Christ through the gospel* (1859) · H. J. Prince, *The Charlinch revival, or, An account of the remarkable work of grace which has lately taken place at Charlinch, in Somersetshire* (1842) · J. J. Schwieso, 'The founding of the Agapemone at Spaxton, 1845–6', *Proceedings of the Somersetshire Archaeological and Natural History Society*, 135 (1991), 113–21 · J. J. Schwieso, '"This frightful and Blasphemous Sect": apocalyptic millenarians in Victorian Dorset', *Dorset Natural History and Archaeology Society*, 114 (1992), 13–18 · J. J. Schwieso, 'Deluded inmates, frantic ravers and communists: a sociological study of the Agapemone, a sect of Victorian apocalyptic millenarians', PhD diss., U. Reading, 1994 · O. W. Jones, 'Prince and the Lampeter Brethren', *Trivium* (1970), 10–20 · C. Mander, *The Reverend Prince and his abode of love* (1976)

Archives Taunton Library, Somerset, Agapemonite collection

Likenesses photograph, c.1890, repro. in Mander, *Reverend Prince*

Prince, John (1643–1723), Church of England clergyman and author, was born at Newenham Abbey farmhouse in Axminster, Devon, on the site of the Cistercian abbey, and probably baptized at Uffculme on 4 February 1644, the eldest son of Bernard Prince (d. 1689) and his first wife, Mary, daughter of John Crocker of Lyneham, Yealmpton, Devon. His kinsman Sir John Drake, maternal uncle to John Churchill, later duke of Marlborough, was his godfather. Prince matriculated from Brasenose College, Oxford, on 13 July 1660, and graduated BA on 23 April 1664. The same year Lord Petre nominated him to one of the fellowships on the foundation at Exeter College vacated by ejected nonconformists, but the right of patronage was not acknowledged by the college.

Prince was ordained as curate to Arthur Giffard, rector of Bideford, north Devon, and he remained there until the rector's death in March 1669. His next post was at St Martin's, Exeter, where he seems to have been curate and minister until 1675. While there he published, in 1674, *A Humble Defence of the Exeter Bill in Parliament for Uniting the Parishes* and *A Sermon Preached … at the Visitation of the Bishop of Exon*. It was probably also at Exeter that he met and married Gertrude (1644–1725), youngest daughter of Anthony Salter, physician at Exeter, and his wife, Gertrude, daughter of John Acland.

In 1675 Prince was incorporated at Cambridge, and proceeded MA from Gonville and Caius College. From 25 December 1675 until 1681, according to articles of agreement between the corporation and himself, he received a stipend of £50 from the vicarage of Totnes, Devon, being instituted on 4 April 1676. On 21 April 1681 he was instituted, on the presentation of Sir Edward Seymour, to the neighbouring vicarage of Berry Pomeroy.

Prince published a few other religious tracts and several unpublished sermons and tracts by him are mentioned by Anthony Wood, some of them withheld because they were too intemperate in their opposition to dissenters. His great work was the chatty and entertaining *Danmonii orientales illustres*, better known by its subtitle, *The Worthies of Devon*. The first edition came out in 1701, with a dedication 'from my study, Aug. 6 1697'. The manuscript materials on which it is based were a transcript by Prince of the work of Sir William Pole (BL, Add. MS 28649) and a similar transcript of Thomas Westcote's 'View of Devonshire' (Bodl. Oxf., MSS Top Devon b 1–6, c 6–19, e 7–8). The insertions between brackets in the 1845 published text of Westcote's work were from Prince's notes, and are described in the introduction as containing many errors. Prince also owned in the 1680s the manuscript of John Hooker's 'Synopsis chorographical of Devonshire' (Devon RO). His own library was very small, but he had the free use of the very good library of Robert Burscough, his successor at Totnes.

A long letter from Prince to Sir Philip Sydenham dated 5 August 1712 (BL, Egerton MS 2035) details the problems faced in the publication (by subscription) of *The Worthies of Devon*, a task made more difficult by a sentence given against him for misconduct, which deprived him of his living in 1700. During the appeal he incurred the wrath of Bishop Trelawny, who described him as 'impudent' and as having 'as little truth as modesty' (Smith). The result of Prince's appeal is uncertain, but in 1701 he resumed his duties at Berry Pomeroy, where he remained for the rest of his life. Prince died intestate on 9 September 1723 and was buried in the chancel of the church at Berry Pomeroy. Letters of administration were granted to his widow, who was herself buried there on 4 February 1725.

IAN MAXTED

Sources W. Jones, 'The author of *The worthies of Devon*, and the Prince family', *Report and Transactions of the Devonshire Association*, 25 (1893), 416–30 · M. Smith, 'John Prince and the publication of *The worthies of Devon*', *Devon and Cornwall Notes and Queries*, 34 (1978–81), 301–7 · E. Windeatt, 'John Prince, author of *The worthies of Devon*', *Transactions of the Plymouth Institution*, 6 (1875), 340–72 · E. Windeatt, 'John Prince, author of *The worthies of Devon*', *Western Antiquary*, 4th ser., 3 (Aug 1884), 45–6; 4th ser., 8 (Jan 1885), 158–60 · Wood, *Ath. Oxon.*, new edn, 4.608–9 · *Fasti Angl.* (Hardy), 2.277 · W. H. H. Rogers, *Memorials of the west* (1888), 26–9 · J. Davidson, *The history of Newenham Abbey* (1843), 217–24 · G. P. R. Pulman, *The book of the Axe*, 4th edn (1875), 403, 666, 707 · Foster, *Alum. Oxon.* · J. Prince, *Danmonii orientales illustres, or, The worthies of Devon*, 2nd edn (1810), 632–3 · W. Cotton, 'Oliver's notes on Prince's *Worthies of Devon*', *Notes and Gleanings*, 4/47 (16 Nov 1891), 179–80 · G. J. Wolseley, *The life of John, duke of Marlborough* (1894), 1.2–6 · *DNB* · T. Gray, *The curious sexual adventure of the Reverend John Prince* (2001)
Archives Plymouth and West Devon RO, MSS of *Danmonii orientales illustres* · Westcountry Studies Library, Exeter, MSS of *Danmonii orientales illustres* | Bodl. Oxf., letters to Anthony Wood

Prince, John Critchley (1808–1866), poet, was born on 21 June 1808 at Wigan, Lancashire, and baptized on 11 August 1808 at Ebenezer Methodist New Connexion Chapel, Bolton-le-Moors, the eldest among eight or more children of Joseph Prince (1788/9–1854) and his wife, Nancy Critchley (1787/8–1868). Joseph Prince was a maker of 'reeds' (instruments of lath and wire used by hand-loom weavers for separating threads); he was also a drunkard and a wanderer. John Prince learned to read and write at a Baptist Sunday school, but at nine he started reed-making for fourteen to sixteen hours a day with his father; his few hours of leisure were spent reading. He improvidently married Ann Orme (*bap.* 1808, *d.* 1858) of Hyde, near Manchester, when they were both eighteen, and by 1830 they had two daughters and a son. From 1828 Prince earned tiny sums from verses contributed to *The Phoenix* and many other local periodicals.

In 1830 Prince spent seven fruitless months seeking work in northern France, at St Quentin in Picardy, and Paris, and underwent extraordinary hardships on his homeward journey; meanwhile his wife and children were in Wigan poorhouse. Reunited, they slept on straw in an unfurnished garret in a court off Long Millgate, Manchester, and would have starved if Ann had not worked as a power-loom weaver while Prince was unemployed; even so, their youngest baby died and its flesh was putrid before they could raise money for a funeral. Prince found work as a reed-maker for a while at Ashton under Lyne, then returned to Hyde. There, at 'Flowery Field' in 1836, he established a small club of working-class poets, the 'Literary Twelve', and in Hyde in 1837 he was prosaically employed in a cotton mill, twelve hours a day for 18s. a week (when fully employed). Between 1838 and 1840 he worked as a yarn warehouseman.

Prince's *Hours with the Muses*, printed for and sold by the author, ran into three successively enlarged editions in 1841–2 and attracted attention in London as well as Manchester, giving Prince hopes of making money by poetry. He now had a small shop in Long Millgate, Manchester, and was secretary of a short-lived Lancashire Literary Association which met at The Sun inn, opposite the shop, and where it seems he drank the profits of trade and verse. Promised a government post, he wrote on 22 June 1842 of being 'feasted, flattered, lionized, and promise-crammed for twelve months' (Procter, *Memorials*, 180), but the 'post' was a postman's job at 15s. a week in Southampton which he left after a few days. Robert Peel refused his application for a librarianship but sent him £50 from the royal bounty in October 1842 and in the same year *Bradshaw's Manchester Journal* paid him for cheerful articles describing the 'rambles of a rhymester' in search of work.

The shop failed and was relinquished at the end of 1842. Prince resumed work as a reed-maker, at 20s. a week if fully employed, and found intermittent employment in Manchester, Blackburn, and Ashton under Lyne. His wife was disabled with rheumatism but worked in factories when she could. For six years from 1845 he earned £12 p.a. as editor of the *Ancient Shepherds' Quarterly Magazine*, the journal of an Ashton under Lyne friendly society; he was awarded £40 from the Royal Literary Fund in 1844 and another £20 in 1846. A 'Prince testimonial' was established by well-wishers in 1846 to give financial help, 'but the committee found that intemperance was his weakness' (Lithgow, 187), despite his taking the pledge more than once and writing verses for temperance journals.

Prince's *Dreams and Realities in Verse and Prose* (1847), *The Poetic Rosary* (1850), *Autumn Leaves* (1856), and *Miscellaneous Poems* (1861), were printed for the author, and were sold by him from his home through what were little better than begging letters to friends, acquaintances, and strangers. Reed-making was in decline as machinery supplanted manual labour, Prince's addiction to poetry and/or drink deterred potential employers, and his income from poetry was at best precarious. Rent on a succession of cottages in Ashton was often in arrears until in 1851 the Princes were 'sold up, dish and spoon, goods, working tools, everything' (Lithgow, 212), and moved in with their married daughter Elizabeth in Hyde and later in Ashton under Lyne. In 1855 another daughter died, leaving two infants in the Princes' care. Prince tramped widely and usually fruitlessly in search of work and was often disabled by inflamed eyes, severe rheumatism, or drink. He tried to live by his pen but survived only by scrounging.

Prince's wife died in September 1858; one of his daughters took care of the orphaned grandchildren and, after a spell of wandering, Prince married Ann Taylor (b. 1813/14) on 30 March 1862 at St Mary's parish church, Mottram in Longdendale, Lancashire. Ann was illiterate, so perhaps to save her from humiliation, or perhaps as a joke, Prince too signed the marriage register with a mark. Fortunately, she was more careful, thrifty, and tidy than Prince's first wife—soon after the wedding Prince had a stroke from which he never fully recovered and they were both out of work during the cotton famine. By autumn 1865 Prince was dependent on tobacco and drink, almost blind, and partially paralysed. He died on 5 May 1866 at Brook Street, Hyde, and was buried in St George's churchyard, Hyde.

Prince was about 5 feet 10 inches tall, 'of slight physique, but wiry', his head unusually large, his neck narrow (Lithgow, 109, 120). He disapproved of socialism and Chartism and his verse rarely touches on social issues; it consists mostly of anodyne lyrics on religion and nature, and, considering the circumstances of his life, is astonishingly sunny and optimistic.   JAMES SAMBROOK

Sources letters to John Fowler, Man. CL, Manchester Archives and Local Studies, MS Q.928.21.P3 · letters to John Harland, Man. CL, Manchester Archives and Local Studies, MS FO91 H15 · G. F. Mandley, 'Sketch of the author's life', in J. C. Prince, *Hours with the muses* (1841), v–xv · R. A. D. Lithgow, *The life of John Critchley Prince* (1880) · B. E. Maidment, *A descriptive catalogue of records relating to John Critchley Prince in the possession of Abel Heywood & Co.* (1975) · R. W. Procter, *Memorials of bygone Manchester* (1880), 146, 151, 167–92, 253, 344, 395 · B. E. Maidment, ed., *The poorhouse fugitives* (1987), 111–12, 338–44 · R. W. Procter, *Literary reminiscences and gleanings* (1860), 117–21 · parish register, St Peter's Church, Ashton under Lyne, Lancashire · parish register, St George's Church, Hyde, Cheshire · J. Evans, *Lancashire authors and orators* (1850), 208–12 · W. E. A. Axon, ed., *The annals of Manchester: a chronological record from the earliest times to the end of 1885* (1886), 250, 303 · *The letters of Charles Dickens*, ed. M. House, G. Storey, and others, 2 (1969), 245–6; 3 (1974), 494, 569, 592; 5 (1981), 149; 7 (1993), 753, 830–31, and nn. · G. H. Whittaker, *The reed-maker poet: John Critchley Prince, 1808–1866* (1936) · *The festive wreath … contributions read at a literary meeting held in Manchester, March 24th 1842, at The Sun inn, Long Millgate* [1842] · m. cert. · d. cert.
Archives BL, letters, Add. MSS 40596, fol. 326, 29960, fol. 26 · Man. CL, Manchester Archives and Local Studies, letters and poems, Brothers 33; MS 136/2/3/2618; MS 524/13; MS 524/11/1/5 · Wigan Archives Service, Leigh, letters and poems, MMP 22/5 | Man. CL, Manchester Archives and Local Studies, letters to John Fowler, MS Q.928.21.P3 · Man. CL, Manchester Archives and Local Studies, letters to John Harland, MS FO91 H15 · W. Sussex RO, letters with verse, Cobden papers 2, 4
Likenesses T. Gillett of Chorley, oils, exh. Whittle Springs Inn 1856 · J. Macdiarmid, portrait, 1901; known to be in Hyde Public Library in 1937 · engraving, repro. in Lithgow, *Life* · portrait; known to be in Wigan Library in 1937 · portrait (after drawing by W. Morton, 1852), repro. in Procter, *Memorials* · woodcut (after drawing by W. Morton), repro. in Procter, *Literary reminiscences and gleanings*

Prince, John Henry (b. 1770, d. in or after 1818), writer, was born on 21 May 1770 in the parish of St Mary, Whitechapel, the son of George Prince (d. 1773), originally of Dursley, Gloucestershire, and his wife, Dorothy, née Dixon (1735/6–1791). He was educated in the charity school of St Mary's, Whitechapel; he started life as errand-boy to a tallow chandler, and eventually, about 1790, became clerk to an attorney in Carey Street, Lincoln's Inn. Dismissed after three years' service, Prince entered another office, and a year later became secretary to a retired solicitor, who gave him access to an excellent library. His weekly salary was only half a guinea, but he deemed it sufficient to maintain a wife, and was married on 29 May 1794; he and his wife had one daughter.

From 1796, when Prince's essay 'On detraction and calumny' appeared in the *Lady's Magazine*, he began to turn out articles and pamphlets on the most varied subjects. He left his patron in 1797, and served with several firms of solicitors. Besides his literary and legal work, he found time to act for a while as minister of Bethesda Chapel—a Methodist congregation—and was prominent in debating societies, such as the London and Westminster forums. A religious organization of his own, of a methodistical type, had a short-lived existence.

Besides ephemeral tracts including three letters (1801–2) attacking Joseph Proud, Prince wrote *A Defence of the People Denominated Methodists* (1797), *Original Letters and Essays on Moral and Entertaining Subjects* (1797), *The Christian's Duty to God and the Constitution at all Times, but Especially at this Critical Juncture* (1804, 3rd edn), and *Remarks on the Best Method of Barring Dower* (1805; republished, with additions, 1807). His *Life, Pedestrian Excursions, and Singular Opinions of J. H. P., Bookseller … written by Himself* (1806) is a lively and entertaining work, dedicated to the Society of Eccentrics, of which he declared himself a worthy and enthusiastic member.

In 1813 Prince was living at Islington, and in 1818 he published a small legal treatise on conveyancing. The date of his death is unknown.

E. G. HAWKE, rev. M. CLARE LOUGHLIN-CHOW

Sources J. H. Prince, *The life, adventures, pedestrian excursions, and singular opinions of J. H. Prince, bookseller …*, 2nd edn (1807) · [J. Watkins and F. Shoberl], *A biographical dictionary of the living authors of Great Britain and Ireland* (1816)

Prince, Mary (d. 1679), Quaker preacher, of unknown parentage, was probably born in Bristol. A signed letter in the manuscript collection at Friends' House, London, indicates that she received at least some level of primary education. Her husband, Edward Prince, does not feature in the main sources of Quaker biography; of him little is known. The marriage produced at least three daughters, known from their marriages in the 1660s; Edward was dead by the time their daughter Mary married in May 1661.

Mary Prince travelled extensively in the 1650s during the period of Quaker expansion. In 1656 she accompanied Sarah Bennett to Cornwall. Contemporary letters indicate that the two women distributed books and preached to local sympathizers. Their contacts included Coroner Bennett, Hannah (Anna) Trapnell, and Thomas Mount.

In the summer of 1656, after the attempt by Mary Fisher and Ann Austin to 'propagate' Quaker opinion in Massachusetts had resulted in banishment, Prince arrived in Boston. Her companions were Christopher Holder, Thomas Thrifton, William Brend, John Copeland, Sarah Gibbons, Mary Weatherhead, and Dorothy Waugh. They were taken, almost immediately, to the governor. In court the governor threatened to cure their disorder with a noose. They were subsequently banished, but suffered eleven weeks' imprisonment before they could secure a passage home. The ship's captain was ordered to land them 'no where but in England' (Norton, 9).

Mary Prince also evangelized in Islamic countries. She was part of the mission designed for the court of Sultan Mohammed IV of Turkey, though she played a comparatively small part in this complicated and largely abortive trip. Of the six Quakers who set out, only Mary Fisher definitely reached the sultan, probably in May or June 1658 (though Beatrice Beckley possibly accompanied her). Meanwhile, in Venice in March 1658, John Luffe and John Perrot were imprisoned; the former was eventually hanged. The activities of John Buckley and Mary Prince, being less notorious, are also more difficult to trace. Prince seems to have abandoned the mission earlier than the others. Though she landed in Smyrna, Turkey, by November 1657, she had certainly begun the journey back to England by June 1658. She has, consequently, been erased from all but the most thorough historical accounts—a notable exception is William Braithwaite's *The Beginnings of Quakerism* (420–28).

Little is known of the last twenty years of Prince's life. Several incidents link her to Bristol. She was arrested at a Quaker meeting in the city in 1663–4; she was also a witness to the Bristol marriage of Margaret Fell and George Fox in 1669. Clearly an admirer of Fox since the 1650s, Prince termed him the 'cheaf' of ten thousand and 'prince' of wisdom (Swarthmore MS 4.58). In June 1674 Mary Prince and Mary Gouldney approached the Bristol men's meeting on behalf of the women's meeting for money towards the relief of the poor, as demand had recently out-stripped what the contributions to their meeting could provide. Barbara Blaugdone's *An Account of the Travels* (1691) recounts an incident in which she and Prince were attacked in Bristol by a 'Rude Man'. Blaugdone suffered the worse abuse—she took a knife wound to the side of her stomach—but the assailant also struck off Prince's hat. Mary Prince died in 1679.   CATIE GILL

Sources M. Bell, G. Parfitt, and S. Shepherd, *A biographical dictionary of English women writers, 1580–1720* (1990) · 'Dictionary of Quaker biography', RS Friends, Lond. [card index] · H. Norton, *New Englands ensigne* (1659) · M. Prince and S. Bennett, letter to G. Fox, 1656, RS Friends, Lond., Swarthmore MS 3.116, trans. 1.163 · W. C. Braithwaite, *The beginnings of Quakerism*, ed. H. J. Cadbury, 2nd edn (1955); repr. (1981) · J. Besse, *A collection of the sufferings of the people called Quakers*, 2 vols. (1753) · M. Prince, letter to G. Fox, 1656, RS Friends, Lond., Swarthmore MS 4.58 · B. Blaugdone, *An account of the travels* (1691) · M. R. Brailsford, *Quaker women, 1650–1690* (1915) · R. Mortimer, ed., *Minute book of the men's meeting of the Society of Friends in Bristol*, Bristol RS, 26 (1971)
Archives RS Friends, Lond., Swarthmore MSS

Prince [*married name* James], **Mary** (*b. c.*1788), freed slave, was born at Brackish Pond, Devonshire parish, Bermuda. She was the daughter of slaves: her mother was a house-servant, her father, named Prince, was a sawyer. Mary (or Molly) Prince was the first black British woman to 'walk away' from slavery, claim her freedom, and chronicle her experiences. Her narrative, entitled *The History of Mary Prince, a West Indian Slave*, was published in London in 1831. The book catalogues Mary Prince's struggle to survive in Bermuda, Turks Island, Antigua, and finally in England.

Sold in front of her mother and siblings at the age of ten, Mary Prince was passed around a succession of sadistic masters, beginning with Captain and Mrs I—. On Turks Island she worked up to her waist in salt ponds all day, plagued by boils; she endured sexual abuse at the whim of another master, Mr D—. She returned to Bermuda in 1810 and then was sold at her own request to Mr and Mrs John Wood. They ill-treated her in Bermuda, Antigua, and London, but perversely refused to sell her or to allow her to purchase her own freedom. She was converted to Moravianism in Antigua, where she also married a free black carpenter, Daniel James, about December 1826. She remained in slavery in Antigua until the Woods took her to England in 1828.

Slavery was outlawed in Britain (although not her colonies) by this time, and in London, Mary Prince decided not to endure the cruelty of the Woods any longer, and walked quietly to freedom. She made her way to the headquarters of the Anti-Slavery Society, and ended up working for Mary and Thomas Pringle. Thomas Pringle was secretary of the society, and it was he who submitted her unsuccessful petition to parliament to be emancipated in 1829. (Formal manumission was essential if a former slave wished to return to the West Indies without reverting to slavery.) Effectively trapped in England, Mary Prince narrated her experiences as a slave to Susannah Moodie, a sister of the historian Agnes Strickland; this was published as *The History of Mary Prince* (1831). Edited by Thomas Pringle, it ran to three editions in the first year, later editions additionally containing testimonials on her behalf and an appendix describing 'the marks of former ill-usage on Mary Prince's body'.

The *History* was highly controversial: an attack by the pro-slavery editor, James MacQueen, of *Blackwood's Magazine* (November 1831) led Pringle to sue the publisher, Thomas Cadell, and the Woods to counter-sue Pringle. On both occasions Mary Prince appeared in court to give evidence. The *History of Mary Prince* became a valuable document in the struggle for the abolition of slavery; the fate of its author remains unknown. After 1833 Mary Prince disappears from the record, and it is not known whether she died or succeeded in rejoining her husband in Antigua.

                                    MOIRA FERGUSON

Sources *The history of Mary Prince, a West Indian slave*, ed. [T. Pringle] (1831) · T. Pringle, 'Supplement to the history of Mary Prince', in *The history of Mary Prince, a West Indian slave*, ed. [T. Pringle] (1831) · Mary Prince's petition to parliament, 1829 · T. Pringle, postscript, in *The history of Mary Prince, a West Indian slave*, ed. [T. Pringle], 2nd edn (1831) · T. Pringle, appendix, in *The history of Mary Prince, a West Indian slave*, ed. [T. Pringle], 3rd edn (1831) · *Reports of cases determined at nisi prius* (1837), 277 · R. v. *Pringle* (1840), 2 Moody and Robinson 276, 174 ER 287 · *The Times* (22 Feb 1833), 4 · J. MacQueen, 'The colonial empire', *Blackwood*, 30 (1831), 744–64 · Devonshire parish assessment books, Bermuda, 1667–1799, Bermudan archives · H. C. Wilkinson, *Bermuda from sail to steam*, 2 vols. (1973) · C. O. Packwood, *Chained on the rock: slavery in Bermuda* (1975) · C. Midgley, *Women against slavery: the British campaigns, 1780–1870* (1992) ·

F. Shyllon, *Black people in Britain, 1555–1833* (1977) • P. Edwards and D. Dabydeen, eds., *Black writers in Britain, 1760–1890* (1991)
Archives Bermudan Archives, Devonshire parish assessment books

Prince, Thomas (*fl.* **1630–1657**), Leveller, was a son of John Prince (*d.* in or after 1634), yeoman of West Garforth, Yorkshire. He was apprenticed in the London Clothworkers' Company in February 1630, gaining his freedom in April 1639 and joining the company's livery in August 1645. Prince remained a liveryman until 1652 and was the only Leveller to attain that status in a London company.

By 1640 Prince was a householder in the London parish of St Martin Orgar. Two children of Thomas and his wife, Elizabeth, were baptized in the parish, but seemingly only one survived infancy. Although a religious Independent, Prince remained a member of his parish church, a rare exception among the predominately nonconforming Levellers, while supportive of more extreme views; on 30 January 1649 he presented a petition to the Commons defending the anti-Trinitarian John Fry. He took the protestation in 1641 and supported parliament in the civil war, taking the vow and covenant and serving in the Blue regiment of London's trained bands until he was seriously wounded in 1643 at the battle of Newbury. Elected to the petty jury of Bridge Within ward in 1646 he rose through various local offices to the level of common councilman by 1654.

Although a freeman of the Clothworkers' Company, Prince was a cheesemonger by trade. From the early 1640s he secured a number of wholesale contracts with parliament, supplying its troops with both cheese and butter. Perhaps this initially brought him a certain amount of wealth as in 1642 he invested over £100 in the Irish Adventure. However, by 1647 he was petitioning parliament for arrears of pay and still claimed to be owed over £1000 in 1649.

Prince first became prominent as a Leveller in November 1647, when he was one of five men imprisoned by the Commons for presenting a petition supporting the *Agreement of the People*. Having regained his liberty by December, he was arrested and detained for disrupting the annual wardmote meeting of Bridge Within ward. He attempted to sue his captors for wrongful imprisonment, but it was ordered that they had acted in obedience to an ordinance excluding supporters of the *Agreement of the People* from local elections.

From 1648 Prince became a more prominent Leveller figure. In January he was appointed as one of the Levellers' treasurers and in December he was among those who petitioned Sir Thomas Fairfax with the Levellers' objections to the conduct of discussions over the second *Agreement of the People*. When in March 1649 the Levellers published *The Second Part of Englands New Chaines Discovered*, a hostile attack on the new military regime in which he may have had a hand, Prince was arrested alongside the Leveller leaders, John Lilburne, Richard Overton, and William Walwyn. During his interrogation by the council of state, he followed his fellow Levellers in refusing to acknowledge the authority of his accusers, arguing that to do so would be a betrayal of his own and the people's liberties. As a result all four men were committed to the Tower of London on suspicion of high treason. Nevertheless, collaborative Leveller works continued to appear, including *The Picture of the Council of State*, which contained Prince's account of his arrest and examination, *A Manifestation*, and the third *Agreement of the People*.

Prince wrote the only publication of which he appears as sole author from the Tower in June 1649. *The Silken Independents Snare Broken* was a reply to an attack upon the Levellers by leading London Independents. Refuting the charge that he was a simple fellow, blindly following the Leveller leaders, Prince called for the nation to be settled on foundations of equity. He affirmed that all parliament's actions should be to the supreme end, the safety of the people, and that man should live by the golden rule of 'do as ye would be done unto'. The tract also expressed opposition to the military reconquest of Ireland, although Prince actually retained his shares in the Irish Adventure until 1653 when he assigned them to his brother.

In September 1649 Prince and his fellow prisoners took part in ill-fated discussions to establish a reconciliation between the Levellers, the Commons, and the army. Lilburne was finally brought to trial in the following month, but was acquitted of high treason against the state; as a result all four Leveller prisoners were released in November 1649. Prince was probably forced to take the engagement and returned to his former trade. However, when Lilburne sought to end his exile in 1653, he named Prince among those who would provide grounds of security and confidence for his return. Later that same year Prince appeared as a prominent and outspoken supporter of Lilburne during his trial at the Old Bailey. Resident in London until at least 1657, the Leveller is possibly the Thomas Prince of Woolwich, Kent, whose administration was granted in 1665.

P. R. S. BAKER

Sources P. R. S. Baker, 'The origins and early history of the Levellers, *c.*1636–*c.*1647', PhD diss., U. Cam. [in preparation] • T. Prince, *The silken Independents snare broken* (1649) • J. Lilburne, R. Overton, and T. Prince, *The picture of the council of state* (1649) • [J. Price], *Walwins wiles* (1649) • K. Lindley, *Popular politics and religion in civil war London* (1997) • *JHC*, 4 (1644–6), 269; 5 (1646–8), 308, 367–8; 6 (1648–51), 125, 183–4, 189–90, 196, 205, 208, 210 • *JHL*, 6 (1643–4), 153, 155–6; 9 (1646–7), 440, 444, 467–8 • *CSP dom.*, 1640–41, 109; 1649–50, 57–9, 121, 129, 527–8, 540, 552 • Clothworkers' Company, register of apprentices, 1606–41, Clothworkers' Hall, London, unfoliated entry for Feb 1630 • Clothworkers' Company, orders of courts, 1639–49, Clothworkers' Hall, London, fols. 124, 130 • A. W. Hughes Clarke, ed., *The register of St Clement, Eastcheap, and St Martin Orgar*, Harleian Society, 68 (1938), 60, 62, 112 • PRO, PROB 6/40

Pring, Isaac (1777–1799). *See under* Pring, Jacob Cubitt (*bap.* 1770, *d.* 1799).

Pring, Jacob Cubitt (*bap.* **1770**, *d.* **1799**), composer and organist, was baptized at St Mary's, Lewisham, on 3 November 1770, the eldest son of Martha Cubitt (*d.* in or after 1796) and Jacob Pring (*d.* in or before 1795). He and two of his brothers all trained as choristers at St Paul's Cathedral, have been credited with taking music degrees at Oxford, and pursued musical careers. The 'Master Pring' who sang in concerts at Drury Lane in 1786 was almost certainly Jacob. Appointed organist jointly with Elizabeth Goadby at St Botolph, Aldersgate, in January 1786, he became sole organist in 1790. On 16 December of the latter year he married Mary Shuckburgh, a widow.

Pring is listed as 'Composer, organ, tenor clarion' (Doane, 52), and his participation in oratorios at Drury Lane, in Handel concerts at Westminster Abbey, and in performances at the Academy of Ancient Music is noted. He was a founder member of the music club Concentores Sodales (1798–1847), devoted to the encouragement and performance of English music. His most substantial publication, *Eight Anthems as Performed at St Paul's Cathedral* (1791), presents well-crafted, contrapuntally motivated works in an idiom reminiscent of the early Georgian era. Pring also produced glees, 'at once graceful, pleasing and brilliant' (Baptie, 81), vocal canons, solo songs, and some polished keyboard music for amateurs requiring limited technical facility in a backward-looking early classical style. Pring was elected in 1793 to the Royal Society of Musicians, in whose annual benefit concerts he played as a violinist, and later became a governor. On 27 June 1797 he matriculated at Magdalen Hall, Oxford, and he took his BMus the next day with his anthem 'Let God arise'. He died at his home in Low Layton, Essex, before 10 July 1799, the date on which his employers at St Botolph, Aldersgate, learned of his death; he was survived by his wife.

Jacob Cubitt Pring was soon followed to the grave by his youngest brother **Isaac Pring** (1777–1799), organist and singer, who was born in Kensington Gravel Pits, London, to the north-east of Kensington Gardens, to which the family had moved in the early 1770s. At St Paul's (1784–93) he was notable for his remarkably fine treble voice. Isaac may be identified with the 'Master Pring' who deputized successfully for Mrs Clendining at Covent Garden in 1793 (*Public Advertiser*, 21 March) singing Galatea's 'As when the dove' from Handel's *Acis*. Besides participating in other London concerts he performed at Oxford in 1793. He moved there in 1794, becoming assistant to Philip Hayes, organist at New College. On Hayes's death in 1797 Pring succeeded him at New College, matriculating there on 1 March 1799. He appears to have taken his BMus later that year (Abdy Williams, 97), but it is not listed in the university records, nor is his exercise preserved in the Bodleian Library. He composed anthems and chants, two of the latter being printed in the collection of Bennett and Marshall (1829). At Oxford he became a friend of William Crotch, successor to Hayes as professor of music. He died from consumption and was buried in the cloister at New College, Oxford, on 23 September 1799.

Joseph Pring (1773–1842), organist and composer, was baptized on 27 December 1775 at St Mary Abbots, Kensington, aged two and a half years. After his training at St Paul's he sang as a tenor in the same range of London concerts as his brother Jacob. Though appointed organist at Bangor Cathedral in April 1793, he was not formally elected until 1810. He matriculated at Magdalen Hall, Oxford, on 21 January 1808, and accumulated the degrees of BMus and DMus at Oxford on 27 January. Pring's major publication, *Twenty Anthems …* (1805), attracted a large number of subscribers. Critical opinion, however, has been divided: one commentator claims, 'There is much excellent music in these compositions, the boldness of many of the subjects being strongly reminiscent of Boyce' (Bumpus, 438), while another finds the music 'agreeably mellifluous but not very memorable' (Watkins Shaw, 'Church music', 719).

The three Pring brothers were once described as 'amiable', but Joseph proved also to be astute and resolute. In 1811 he became aware of a scheme devised by the chapter at Bangor to divert for other purposes funds (the tithes of Llandinam) that had by an act of parliament of 1685 hitherto been used partly for the benefit of the cathedral choir and organist. A protracted dispute arose which was eventually resolved by the lord chancellor with a compromise ruling that delivered at least a partial victory for Pring and his choristers. Pring published a full account of the affair in *Papers, documents, law proceedings … respecting the maintenance of the choir of the cathedral church of Bangor* (1819). He died on 13 February 1842 at Bangor, and was buried at Bangor Cathedral. He was succeeded in his post at Bangor by one of his sons, James S. Pring. Another son, Joseph Charles Pring (1799/1800–1876), maintained the family's Oxford connections, becoming chaplain of New College and vicar of Headington.   IAN BARTLETT

Sources Highfill, Burnim & Langhans, *BDA* · D. Gedge, 'In quires and places (iii): the Bangor affair', *Musical Opinion*, 105 (1981–2), 18–25, 32 · J. Doane, ed., *A musical directory for the year 1794* [1794] · O. W. Jones, 'Dr Pring and the tithes of Llandinam', *MT*, 114 (1973), 529–31 · H. W. Shaw, 'Church music in England from the Reformation to the present day', *Protestant church music*, ed. F. Blume (1975), 691–732 · D. Baptie, *Sketches of the English glee composers: historical, biographical and critical (from about 1735–1866)* [1896] · M. L. Clarke, *Bangor Cathedral* (1969) · L. D. Paul, 'Music at Bangor Cathedral church: some historical notes', *Welsh Music*, 3/9 (1971), 11–33 · H. W. Shaw, *The succession of organists of the Chapel Royal and the cathedrals of England and Wales from c.1538* (1991) · J. S. Bumpus, *A history of English cathedral music, 1549–1889*, 2 vols. [1908]; repr. (1972) · D. Dawe, *Organists of the City of London, 1666–1850* (1983) · B. Matthews, ed., *The Royal Society of Musicians of Great Britain: list of members, 1738–1984* (1985) · Foster, *Alum. Oxon.* · J. Rennert, *William Crotch (1775–1847): composer, artist, teacher* (1975) · C. F. Abdy Williams, *A short historical account of the degrees in music at Oxford and Cambridge* [1893] · parish register, Lewisham, St Mary, Lewisham Local History Library [baptism] · parish register, Kensington, St Mary Abbots, Kensington Reference Library [Joseph Pring; baptism] · will, PRO, PROB 11/1327 · [J. S. Sainsbury], ed., *A dictionary of musicians*, 2 vols. (1825) · Grove, *Dict. mus.* (1954) · records of St Paul's choir school, London

Archives Bodl. Oxf., DMus, exercise of Joseph Pring [Joseph Pring] · Bodl. Oxf., MusBac, exercises submitted by Jacob and Joseph Pring

Likenesses oils (Joseph Pring), repro. in '"Dotted crotchet", Bangor and its cathedral', *MT*, 44 (1903), 728

Wealth at death left money, instruments, music, furniture and clothes to wife: will, PRO, PROB 11/1327

Pring, Joseph (1773–1842). *See under* Pring, Jacob Cubitt (*bap.* 1770, *d.* 1799).

Pring, Martin (*bap.* 1580, *d.* 1626), naval officer and explorer, was baptized on 23 April 1580 at Feniton, Devon, the son of John Pring of Awliscombe. His early life is obscure, but by 1603 he had gained the confidence of Richard Hakluyt and the patronage of the Society of Merchant

Venturers of Bristol, especially of John Whitson, the local MP.

Pring was put in charge of a voyage to Virginia to make a more intensive study of the area covered by Gosnold and Bartholomew Gilbert (1602). With a licence from Ralegh, the Virginia patentee, he set out with the 50 ton *Speedwell* (possibly Drake's ship of 1587–8) and the 26 ton *Discoverer*, and sailed from Milford Haven (10 April 1603) via the Azores to the coast of Maine. He established a camp on the shore of Massachusetts Bay which he called Whitson Bay. Most commentators place the site at Plymouth harbour, but Quinn suggests it was near modern Provincetown on Cape Cod (Quinn, 359–62). Having protected his camp with a palisade and two mastiffs to keep the curious natives at bay, Pring stayed there for seven weeks, loading his ships with cedar and sassafras, a tree whose dried root was considered good for flavouring and a cure for plague and the pox. He commented on the fertile soil, the abundance of fish, and the great variety of trees. He arrived home on 2 October 1603, having clarified available knowledge about the region; his descriptions, printed by Purchas, were a great encouragement to future settlers.

Pring is almost certainly identifiable with the Martin Prinx who sailed from Woolwich in March 1604 as master of the *Phoenix* (or *Olive Branch*) in Charles Leigh's ill-fated expedition to Guiana. He seems to have led a mutiny against Leigh, who was determined to colonize the area, despite the climate and lack of food, and finally Pring sailed home in a Dutch ship, leaving those who remained to die of disease and hunger or to linger in Spanish prisons.

In 1606 Pring was employed by Sir John Popham to link up with Challons in choosing a site for a new colony in north Virginia. Challons failed to reach the rendezvous (his ship was seized by the Spanish authorities) but Pring's exploration of the coast of Maine produced a chart and report that Sir Ferdinando Gorges later pronounced 'the most exact discovery of that coast that ever came to my hands since' (Gorges, repr. in Baxter, 1.73). Pring's encouraging report led to Popham's attempt to establish two colonies in the area (1607).

Pring then entered the East India Company's service, probably in 1607–8. In 1610 he was employed in surveying the Bristol Channel, but the first mention of him in the East Indies is in 1613–14, when he was master of a new 550 ton vessel, the *New Year's Gift*, the flagship of a squadron of four ships engaged in the first voyage of the newly formed joint-stock company. The fleet defeated a far larger Portuguese armada off Surat (January–February 1615), and the *New Year's Gift* proceeded to Bantam to load spices. On Pring's return to England the dividend on the voyage proved to be 120 per cent.

The East India Company's regard for Pring can be seen from his appointment in 1617 to command the fifth joint-stock voyage, with the 1000 ton *James Royal* as his flagship. After confiscating two interlopers outfitted by Lord Robert Rich, Pring formed a close relationship with Sir Thomas Roe, the English ambassador to the Mughal empire, and with him planned the expulsion of the Portuguese, the extension of British trade in the Red Sea, the Persian Gulf, and Persia, and keener rivalry with the Dutch. Pring joined his ships to those of Sir Thomas Dale off Bantam and in 1618–19 engaged the Dutch fleet in Jacatra Bay, Java, and at Masulipatam, where Dale died in August 1619, leaving Pring in overall command.

The poor condition of the fleet and news of peace made with the Dutch at home persuaded Pring to favour an alliance with the Dutch in the East to overthrow Spain and Portugal there, and in March 1620 he entered into friendly relations with Coen, the Dutch commander. Pring then voyaged to Japan (July) and after a stay of five months, in which his ships were repaired, he arrived back in the Downs on 16 September 1621 with a rich cargo on board. On the voyage home Pring had contributed the largest amount (£6 13 *s*. 4 *d*.) towards a collection for the building of a free school in Virginia; he became a freeman of the Virginia Company, and was granted 200 acres of Virginian land. After his return the company censured Pring for his lack of vigour in opposing the Dutch following Dale's death, for his friendship with them after the signature of peace (which the Dutch had not kept), for his diversion to Japan, and for indulging in private trade to his own profit. Pring narrowly escaped a privy council trial and eventually cleared himself, but when he left the company's service in 1623 the customary gratuity was withheld.

In the same year Pring was elected a member of the Society of Merchant Venturers of Bristol, and in 1625 he was one of its wardens. He commanded the 300 ton privateer *Charles*, authorized by the government to prey on French and Spanish shipping, and was very successful in capturing prizes. He may have sailed to Virginia again in 1626, the year of his death. He was buried in St Stephen's Church, Bristol, where his monument bears a long epitaph, the arms of the Society of Merchant Venturers, and four carved ships. His will mentions his wife, Elizabeth, and six children.

BASIL MORGAN

Sources A. L. P. Dennis, 'Captain Martin Pring, last of the Elizabethan seamen', *Collections of the Maine Historical Society*, 3rd ser., 2 (1906), 2E–50 · *CSP col.* · C. K. Shipton, 'Pring, Martin', *DAB* · H. S. Burrage, ed., *Early English and French voyages, 1534–1608* (1906), 343–52 · D. B. Quinn, A. M. Quinn, and S. Hillier, eds., *New American world: a documentary history of North America to 1612*, 3 (1979), 359–62 · W. P. Cumming, R. A. Skelton, and D. B. Quinn, *The discovery of North America* (1971) · J. H. Pring, *Captain Martin Pringe* (1888) · A. L. Rowse, *The Elizabethans and America* (1959) · A. Farrington, *The English factory in Japan, 1613–1623*, 2 (1991) · J. Latimer, *The history of the Society of Merchant Venturers of the city of Bristol* (1903) · F. Gorges, *A briefe narration of the originall undertakings of the advancement of plantations into the parts of America* (1658); repr. in J. P. Baxter, *Sir Fernando Gorges and his province of Maine*, 2 (1890) · will, PRO, PROB 11/151, sig. 26
Wealth at death will exists: Shipton, 'Pring, Martin'

Pringle, Andrew, **Lord Alemoor** (d. 1776), judge, was the eldest son of John Pringle, Lord Haining, a lord of session, and his wife, Anne, eldest daughter of Sir John Murray of Philiphaugh. He was admitted advocate at the Scottish bar in 1740, appointed sheriff of Wigtown in 1750, and in the following year named sheriff of Selkirk. Pringle first came to notice as counsel for the crown in the claims on the forfeited estates, earning a good name and much money. In contrast to many of his contemporaries, his language was plain and straightforward, his gestures restrained, his success at the bar being entirely due to his legal ability. The historian Thomas Somerville described him as 'the most admired speaker at the bar in the middle of the last century' (Somerville, 108).

On 5 July 1755 Pringle was named solicitor-general, and on 14 June 1759 he was raised to the bench as Lord Alemoor, taking his title from a property he owned in Selkirkshire. At the same time he was appointed a lord of justiciary, retiring in 1769. Pringle was a lay elder of the general assembly of the kirk in 1757 when that assembly, opposed to the theatre, expressed outrage at the staging in Edinburgh of *Douglas*, a play written by John Home, himself a minister. His speech on behalf of Alexander Carlyle, who had been criticized by the synod for attending the performance, led Carlyle to judge him 'the most eloquent of all the Scottish bar' (*Autobiography*, ed. Burton, 321).

Alemoor built himself a beautiful villa at Hawkhill, near Edinburgh, where he erected the first grape-house in Scotland. He died at Hawkhill on 14 January 1776. As he was unmarried his estates passed to his brother John Pringle of Haining.   T. F. HENDERSON, rev. ANITA McCONNELL

Sources *Scotland and Scotsmen in the eighteenth century: from the MSS of John Ramsay, esq., of Ochtertyre*, ed. A. Allardyce, 1 (1888), 322–7 · *Autobiography of the Rev. Dr. Alexander Carlyle … containing memorials of the men and events of his time*, ed. J. H. Burton (1860) · G. Brunton and D. Haig, *An historical account of the senators of the college of justice, from its institution in MDXXXII* (1832), 523 · T. Somerville, *My own life and times, 1741–1814*, ed. W. Lee (1861); repr. with new introduction by R. B. Sher (1996) · T. Craig-Brown, *The history of Selkirkshire, or, The chronicles of Ettrick Forest*, 2 vols. (1886), 2.309–10
Likenesses attrib. W. Millar, oils, Faculty of Advocates, Parliament Hall, Edinburgh

Pringle, George (1631–1689), politician, was born on 3 March 1631, the eldest son of James Pringle (1596–1658), of Torwoodlee, Selkirkshire, and his second wife, Janet (*b.* 1614), daughter of Sir Lewis *Craig of Riccarton. He may have been the Georgius Pringle who attended Glasgow University in 1646. On 22 June 1654 he married Janet (*c.*1626–*c.*1690), daughter of Alexander Brodie of Lethen, Moray. They had one son and four daughters. Like his brother-in-law, Walter Pringle of Greenknowe, he was a zealous covenanter. He fought against Cromwell at the battle of Dunbar on 3 September 1650. He made his peace with the Cromwellian regime and both he and his father were made commissioners for the cess in 1655. Pringle succeeded his father in 1658 and was named as sheriff of Selkirkshire by Richard Cromwell in 1659 and a commissioner of cess in 1660.

Following the Restoration, Pringle was excepted from the Act of Indemnity of 1662, but allowed a royal pardon upon payment of a fine of between £1600 and £2000. 'Though he did not conform to prelacy', according to Wodrow, 'he had no share in those struggles for religion and liberty at Pentland and Bothwell.' Rather, while Pringle lived in quiet retirement, 'his home was a sanctuary for all the oppressed that came to him, and these were neither few nor of the meanest quality' (Wodrow, 4.228).

Pringle became active in politics once more in the late 1670s, being named a commissioner of supply in 1678. He was involved in the escape of Archibald Campbell, ninth earl of Argyll, on 20 December 1681, meeting him at an alehouse near Torwoodlee and ensuring his safe escape into England and thence to the Netherlands. To the government he was a dangerous man, being described as 'a great fanatic and of anti-monarchical, republican principles, from his infancy' (Willcock, 285). In 1684 Pringle was fined 5000 merks for church offences, and in September, William Carstares, under torture, implicated him in the Rye House plot of the previous year, when he revealed that meetings had been held at his house. Pringle escaped arrest in September 1684 and fled to the Netherlands. He was summoned to appear at the Scottish parliament on 26 March 1685 but did not do so. His estate was then declared forfeit for treason and granted in May 1686 to Lieutenant-General Drummond. Meanwhile in Amsterdam on 7 April 1685 he was one of twelve exiles who constituted the council 'for the recovery of the religion, rights and liberties of the kingdom of Scotland'. He was sent by Argyll to the south of Scotland in preparation for Argyll's expedition, but upon its failure he escaped again to the Netherlands.

Pringle returned to Scotland at the revolution of 1688, and he was elected a commissioner for Selkirkshire to the convention of estates in 1689, which was later turned into a parliament. He served as a commissioner of supply and the militia, but he was clearly ailing, and was excused attendance at the parliament on 22 July 1689, being 'very sick'. He died soon afterwards. His son, James, was able to secure the reversal of his attainder in 1690.

STUART HANDLEY

Sources Burke, *Gen. GB* · M. D. Young, ed., *The parliaments of Scotland: burgh and shire commissioners*, 2 (1993), 574 · *IGI* · *Historical notices of Scotish affairs, selected from the manuscripts of Sir John Lauder of Fountainhall*, ed. D. Laing, 2, Bannatyne Club, 87 (1848), 555–643 · E. W. M. Balfour-Melville, ed., *An account of the proceedings of the estates in Scotland, 1689–1690*, 1, Scottish History Society, 3rd ser., 46 (1954), 175 · C. Innes, ed., *Munimenta alme Universitatis Glasguensis / Records of the University of Glasgow from its foundation till 1727*, 3, Maitland Club, 72 (1854), 100–01 · T. M'Crie, ed., *Memoirs of Mr. William Veitch and George Brysson* (1825), 147–8, 311 · A. Pringle, *The records of the Pringles or Hoppringles of the Scottish border* (1933), 216–20 · R. Wodrow, *The history of the sufferings of the Church of Scotland from the Restoration to the revolution*, ed. R. Burns, 4 (1830), 224–9 · J. Willcock, *A Scots earl in covenanting times: being life and times of Archibald, 9th earl of Argyll (1629–1685)* (1907), 285

Pringle, Sir John, first baronet (1707–1782), military physician, was born on 10 April 1707 at Stichill House, in the Scottish border county of Roxburghshire, the youngest son of Sir John Pringle, baronet, and his wife, Magdalen, sister of Sir Gilbert Elliott, baronet, of Stobs. Robert *Pringle and Sir Walter *Pringle were his uncles. After receiving private tuition at home Pringle attended St Andrews, Scotland's oldest university, where his uncle Francis was professor of Greek. Pringle matriculated in 1722 in St

Sir John Pringle, first baronet (1707–1782), by Sir Joshua Reynolds, 1774

Leonard's College, and in 1727 entered Edinburgh University.

It appears that Pringle was intending to pursue a career in commerce and was sent to Amsterdam to gain some knowledge of business. During his stay there he paid a visit to Leiden and heard a lecture by the renowned physician Hermann Boerhaave, which made him decide to follow a career in medicine. He then went to Leiden to take his studies further. From student age Pringle maintained contact with Flanders and Holland, where he would later return to earn his great reputation as a military physician and epidemiologist. Pringle graduated MD at Leiden in 1730, his thesis diploma, 'De marcore senili', being signed by Boerhaave, C. B. Albinus, and W. J. Gravesande. He then completed his medical studies in Paris. Four years after graduating MD and starting practice in Edinburgh, Pringle was appointed joint professor of pneumatics (metaphysics) and moral philosophy in Edinburgh University. The appointment did not stop him from practising medicine. Pringle's move into military medicine was probably because of local connections. The earl of Stair, a nobleman whose lands lay only a short way north of Roxburgh, and who knew the Pringle family, appointed him his physician. Lord Stair was then general officer commanding the British army on the continent. Dr Stevenson, a prominent Edinburgh physician, also advanced Pringle's career. Again through the good offices of the earl of Stair, in 1742 Pringle was appointed physician to the army in Flanders. He achieved further advancement after the retirement of the earl of Stair, when the duke of Cumberland appointed him physician-general in 1744. He now resigned his professorship in Edinburgh. His service ran from the fall of

Walpole, through the campaign launched by the French into the Austrian Netherlands, to the peace of Aix-la-Chapelle in 1748. Pringle's great innovations encompassed both administration and epidemiology. It was probably owing to his efforts that military hospitals were first recognized as neutral territory and safely set up near a battlefield. At the battle of Dettingen in 1743, the last in which a British king led his army into battle, British and French hospitals under a temporary red cross and with the agreement of the duc de Noailles, the French commander, were set up side by side, each taking wounded from the other army if the occasion arose.

Although Pringle left the physician-general's post in 1748—he had been posted back to Britain during the 1745 Jacobite rising and was present at the battle of Culloden in 1746—he did not publish his *Observations on the Diseases of the Army* until 1752. This watershed work has probably not received the credit it deserves. Like his countryman James Lind, Pringle had quickly recognized hospitals as the chief causes of sickness and death in the army. His special contributions were the first scientific account of epidemiology in the field and prevention of cross-infection. In his own words, as expressed in the fourth edition of his *Observations*:

in the camp, the contagion (of dysentery) passes from one who is ill to his companion in the same tent, and from them perhaps to the next. The foul straw becomes very infectious. But of what nature is this infection? In the former editions of this work, I considered the spreading of the distemper as owing to putrid exhalations of the humours of those who first fell ill of it; and that when this *miasma* is received into the blood, I conceived it to act upon the whole mass as a ferment, disposing it to putrefaction … But having since perused the curious dissertation, published by *Linnaeus*, in favour of *Kircher's* system of contagion by animalcula, it seems reasonable to suspend all *hypotheses*, till the matter is further enquired into.   (*Observations*, 4th edn, 24–5)

In his thinking he was influenced by the great men of Leiden: 'Leeuwenhoeck had shown "small insects" in the pustules of scabies, under the microscope … So the frequency of the itch is not to be ascribed to change of air or diet, but to the infection propagated by a few such.' Pringle also began to think in terms of 'septic' and 'antiseptic': 'The faeces are rendered less, if at all infectious, by means of a strong acid combined with the parts that are really septic—especially, in the dysentery, where the faeces are highly corrupted and contagious' (ibid., 103–4). He even considered the systemic use of such 'antiseptics': 'were putrefaction the only change made in the body by contagion, it would be easy to cure such fevers, at any period, by the use of acids, or other antiseptics' (ibid., 258).

From 1748 Pringle settled in London and continued in medical practice. He entered into the period of his life when he published a series of papers and received a succession of honours. In 1749 he became physician-in-ordinary to the duke of Cumberland. In 1750 he published *Observations on the Nature and Cure of Hospital and Jayl Fevers*, and, in the *Philosophical Transactions of the Royal Society*, 'Experiments upon septic and antiseptic substances, with remarks relating to their use in the theory of medicine'. For the latter he received the Copley gold medal in 1752 from the society, of which he had been admitted a fellow in 1745. His 'Account of persons seized with the gaol fever while working in Newgate' appeared in the *Philosophical Transactions* in 1753. Pringle became a council member of the Royal Society in 1753, LRCP in 1758, FRCP in 1763, *speciali gratia*, physician to the queen in 1761, president of the Royal Society in 1772, and in 1766 was created a baronet. He was gazetted physician-in-ordinary to the king in 1774. On 14 April 1752 Pringle had married Charlotte, the second daughter of William *Oliver, an eminent physician of Bath; they had no children. In 1778 Pringle resigned as president of the Royal Society. His resignation has usually been ascribed to his ill health, as it preceded his return to Scotland, where he was soon known to have been failing. However, recent evidence shows that Pringle may have been forced to resign following his difference of opinion with George III on the best shape of lightning conductors. Carl van Doren, in his *Life of Benjamin Franklin*, writes that 'because Pringle would not sustain the king in this prejudice [that blunt lightning conductors were superior] he was forced to resign as president of the Royal Society and dismissed from his post as royal physician'. He returned briefly to Edinburgh, but Edinburgh did not cheer his spirits. While there he presented a manuscript collection of his 'Medical and physical observations' in ten volumes to the Royal College of Physicians of Edinburgh and to St Andrews. Pringle was also the author of the first biography of General James Wolfe, published in 1760. In 1781 he was back in London, and soon after, on 14 January 1782 had a probable stroke while at his club, Watson's in the Strand. He died on 18 January 1782, aged seventy-four. He was buried in St James's Church, Piccadilly. A monument was erected in his memory at Westminster Abbey; his name was celebrated in eulogies by Vicq d'Azyr and Condorcet at the French Academy. Through his life his religious belief varied—he was a Unitarian for a time—but he became 'very diligent in reading sermons and Scripture in his later life'. In politics he was a strong whig. While he loved music, he had no liking for poetry. His portrait by Sir Joshua Reynolds shows him to look somewhat severe, with a high cheek colour. His letters and writings, however, show him a pleasantly civil person. J. S. G. BLAIR

Sources [W. MacMichael and others], *Lives of British physicians* (1830), 172–82 • D. Dow, ed., *The influence of Scottish medicine* (1988) • D. Guthrie, *A history of medicine* (1945) • G. M. Fraser, *The steel bonnets: the story of the Anglo-Scottish border reivers* (1971) • *DNB* • Munk, *Roll* • *GM*, 1st ser., 22 (1752), 191 [marriage] • private information (2004) [Michael Atiyah; Royal Society Library]
Archives Niedersächsische Staats- und Universitätsbibliothek, Göttingen, letters • RCP Lond., annotated book • Royal College of Physicians of Edinburgh, corresp. and papers • RS, papers • U. Edin. L., lecture notes • U. St Andr. | Bürgerbibliothek, Bern, letters to Albrecht von Haller • NA Scot., letters to Sir John Hall • NA Scot., letters to the Hall family • NL Scot., letters to Sir William Forbes • NL Scot., letters to Lord Hailes • NL Scot., corresp. with Lord Monboddo • U. St Andr., Boswell MSS • University of York, Boswell MSS • Yale U., Beinecke L., corresp. with James Boswell

Likenesses W. H. Mote, stipple, 1774 (after J. Reynolds), NPG • J. Reynolds, oils, 1774, RS [*see illus.*] • J. Reynolds, portrait, Royal Army Medical Corps, Camberley, Surrey

Pringle, John Christian (1872–1938), Church of England clergyman and social work administrator, was born on 27 August 1872 at 1 Melville Street, Edinburgh, the second son of Robert Pringle (1845–1930), writer to the signet, and his wife, Katherine (d. 1908), the daughter of Robert Jameson, writer to the signet, and sister of Leander Starr Jameson (1853–1917), who was to lead the 'Jameson raid' into the Transvaal in 1895. He had at least three sisters. He was educated at Cargil Field, Edinburgh, and at Winchester College, where he was a scholar, before winning a scholarship to Exeter College, Oxford, in 1892; he took a first class in honour moderations (1893) and a second class in *literae humaniores* (1895).

Pringle entered the Indian Civil Service in 1896, but while serving in Sind he decided to go into the church, and returned to England in 1901 to train at Ripon Clergy College, Oxfordshire. He was ordained in 1902 and worked in London as a curate at All Saints', Poplar, from 1902 to 1905. He married on 22 August 1905 a Charity Organization Society social worker in Poplar, Constance Mary (1875/6–1937), daughter of Howgate Greaves Warburton, a merchant; they had no children. He was a curate at St John's, Hackney, from 1905 to 1909, when he went to Japan for three years as professor of English at the Hiroshima Higher Normal College.

It was Charles Loch (1849–1923) who persuaded Pringle to return to England in 1912 to help him at the headquarters of the Charity Organization Society (COS) in London as assistant secretary, responsible for the districts subcommittee; when Loch retired in 1914 Pringle became secretary to the council of the COS until May 1918. He had already been involved for some years in the activities of the society, as a member of the Hackney district committee, and he had served as an expert investigator for the royal commission on the poor law from 1906 to 1907. After spending the last few months of the First World War as chaplain to the Royal Garrison Artillery, he did not return immediately to the COS, but became rector of St George-in-the-East, Stepney, where he was involved in social work and a member of the board of guardians. In 1925 he returned to the COS as secretary, and from 1936 to 1938 he was director and consulting secretary.

The Charity Organization Society (from 1946 the Family Welfare Association), founded in 1869, concentrated on work with individuals; it aimed to co-ordinate voluntary charitable work, first of all in London through committees in every London borough, and later throughout the country, working alongside the poor law guardians. The COS confined its help to the 'deserving poor', those who with its help would be restored to self-sufficiency. The rest, after investigation by caseworkers, were referred to the poor law, and ended up in the workhouse. It was not enough just to give people money; they had to be helped to change their behaviour and attitudes, and so help was based on family casework, with each family assigned a professional social worker. The COS, with its belief in individual responsibility, resisted the growing view that the state should take on responsibility for the poor, reflected in the welfare legislation passed by the Liberal government of 1906–14.

When he returned to the COS in 1925 Pringle tried to return to the principles of Loch: 'as the spirit of Elijah rested on Elisha so Mr Pringle carried on the work of Sir Charles Loch', recorded the annual report of the Islington district committee of 1937–8 (Rooff, 133). But between the wars these principles seemed increasingly outdated, and the COS was losing its pre-war influence on social questions. Its role was increasingly being taken over by the National Council of Social Service. Pringle refused to accept the increasing role of the state in social provision, speaking out against socialists, trade unionists, Bolshevists, the Fabian Society, the London School of Economics, Sidney and Beatrice Webb, and William Beveridge. In turn, in the many Labour-controlled boroughs unsympathetic to the idea of voluntary work, the district committees came to an end. In *The Nation's Appeal to the Housewife* (1933) Pringle described the social worker standing aghast before

the serried ranks of the official hierarchies, tens of thousands of highly organised public servants, … the vast mountains of bricks, mortar, girders, and reinforced concrete, the hundreds of thousands of beds in the public institutions constituting a financial liability of a magnitude at which the imagination boggles.   (pp. 166–7)

He edited the *Charity Organization Quarterly* from 1927, and a few weeks before his death he finished *Social Work of the London Churches* (1938), a plea to the church to train the clergy to do family casework. He travelled widely, visiting the United States on several occasions. Pringle was a less able administrator than Loch, and his greatest contribution to the work of the Charity Organization Society was at a personal level, in his day-to-day work in the districts. The obituaries stressed his genius for friendship.

To the end Pringle opposed state involvement in social welfare provision, describing the advocates of social reform as making inroads into the field of social service like 'the barbarous Goths upon the civilized, elegant, philosophical Graeco-Roman world' (J. C. Pringle, *Social Work of the London Churches*, 209–10). Pringle died after many years of illness on 11 April 1938 at his home, 104 Manor Way, Blackheath, London, and was buried at Shooters Hill cemetery on 14 April. After his death the Pringle memorial fund was set up to encourage the study of family casework.   ANNE PIMLOTT BAKER

Sources J. Lewis, *The voluntary sector, the state, and social work in Britain* (1995), 88–91 · M. Rooff, *A hundred years of family welfare* (1972), 123–34 · C. L. Mowat, *The Charity Organization Society, 1869–1913* (1961) · 'In memoriam: John Christian Pringle', *Charity Organization Quarterly* (July 1938), 121–58 · H. A. Mess, *Voluntary social services since 1918* (1947) · *The Times* (13 April 1938) · *WWW* · b. cert. · m. cert. · *The Society of Writers to His Majesty's Signet with a list of the members* (1936) · *CGPLA Eng. & Wales* (1938)
Archives Bodl. Oxf., corresp. with Sir Henry Burdett
Likenesses pencil drawing, Family Welfare Association, London · photograph, repro. in 'In memoriam: John Christian Pringle'

Wealth at death £13,004 7s. 10d.: probate, 16 June 1938, *CGPLA Eng. & Wales*

Pringle, John Quinton (1864–1925), painter, was born in Glasgow on 13 December 1864, the second son and second child in the family of seven sons and one daughter of James Christie Pringle (1837–1896), a railway employee, and his wife, Jane Bowie, *née* Davidson (1840–1893). He lived in Glasgow all his life except during the years 1869 to 1874 when the family lived at Langbank on the River Clyde, near Port Glasgow, where his father was stationmaster. He left school in 1876 and was apprenticed to an optician until 1878. In 1896 he set up his own business as an optician and repairer of small items of domestic equipment at 90 Saltmarket, Glasgow.

In 1883–5 Pringle attended evening classes in art organized by the Glasgow schools board and was awarded a bursary to attend evening classes at the Glasgow School of Art, which he did from 1885 to 1895, supplemented by some early morning classes. Among his fellow students was Charles Rennie Mackintosh. His final session at the school was in 1899–1900. He won the South Kensington national competition gold medal for life drawing in 1901.

As the subjects for his oils and watercolours Pringle took themes from his home and near by, his family and one or two friends, old buildings and back courts, and the street near the tenement where he lived; his portraits at that period have an intensity rare in Scottish painting and recall the work of William Dyce and the Pre-Raphaelites. He was a pioneer in depicting townscapes and back courts seen unromantically, rendering them with a detached viewpoint and restrained affection. He adopted the technique of applying paint using the square brushstroke which derived from the French *plein-air* painter Jules Bastien-Lepage, whose work was shown at the Glasgow Institute of the Fine Arts in 1883 and 1886. For the rest of his life he used the square brushstroke, later diluting the oil paint with turpentine to get a consistency almost like watercolour.

Pringle began to paint fanciful pictures in the late 1880s. *Children at the Burn* (1889, Tate collection), for example, is a landscape painting to which figures of children were later added. Girls and young women featured frequently in his landscapes. In the mid-1890s he began to paint miniatures, usually commissioned portraits. Some paintings of the period 1895 to 1905 have something of the flavour of Glasgow art nouveau. After opening his own shop he seems to have painted less, though his keenness to make pictorial experiments increased. From about 1906 he heightened his palette and his brushstrokes became looser and sometimes smaller, akin to the technique of the French neo-impressionists: he would not have seen work by Georges Seurat or Paul Signac but probably saw examples of Henri Le Sidaner's paintings, similar to neo-impressionism, shown at the Glasgow Institute between 1903 and 1906.

In 1910 Pringle made his only visit to the continent, staying at Caudebec in Normandy for ten days painting landscapes. His output was probably less than 100 oils, mainly small in scale. On only three occasions was his work shown outside Scotland during his lifetime: some miniatures were on view at the fifteenth secessionist exhibition in Vienna in 1902 and three works were shown in 'Twentieth century art: a review of modern movements', an exhibition at the Whitechapel Art Gallery, London, in 1914, probably on the initiative of Fra Newbery, director of the Glasgow School of Art, who had a high regard for Pringle's art and greatly regretted that he did not paint full-time. Pringle's sister died in 1911 and he did not paint again in oils until 1921. In 1922 sixty-eight of his works were shown in an exhibition which was highly praised at the Glasgow School of Art, and one, *Muslin Street* (1895–6, City Art Centre, Edinburgh), was bought for presentation to a public gallery. Later, also in his lifetime, a landscape, *Caudebec*, was presented to the Glasgow Art Gallery and Museum. His other notable paintings include *Back Court (Bartholomew Street), Glasgow* (watercolour, 1887, British Museum, London), *Two Figures at a Fence* (1904, Glasgow Art Gallery and Museum), *Poultry Yard Gartcosh* (1906, Scottish National Gallery of Modern Art, Edinburgh), *Children at Play* (1906) and *Tollcross, Glasgow* (1908, both Hunterian Art Gallery, University of Glasgow), and *The Window* (1924, Tate collection). There is a miniature by him in the Victoria and Albert Museum, London.

Pringle gave up his optician's business in 1923 but had only a short time left to paint, as he died, unmarried, in East Kilbride, near Glasgow, of liver cancer on 21 April 1925. He was buried in Sandymount cemetery, Shettleston, Glasgow. The Glasgow Art Gallery and Museum has a large collection of his works, and there are works by him in most major art galleries in Scotland.

DAVID BROWN

Sources J. Meldrum and A. Auld, *John Q. Pringle, 1864–1925: a centenary exhibition* (1964), Glasgow Art Gallery and Museum exhibition catalogue · J. Meldrum and D. Brown (1981), Scottish Arts Council exhibition catalogue · private information (2004) · *CCI* (1925)
Archives NL Scot., notes and press cuttings of and about him
Likenesses J. Q. Pringle, self-portrait, oils, c.1886, Glasgow Art Gallery and Museum
Wealth at death £1355 19s. 0d.: confirmation, 21 Aug 1925, *CCI*

Pringle, John William Sutton (1912–1982), biologist, was born in Manchester on 22 July 1912, the eldest of four sons (there were no daughters) of John Pringle, a medical practitioner of Rochdale and then of Manchester, and his wife, Dorothy Emily Beney, of Huguenot extraction. He won a scholarship to Winchester College in 1926 where in the sixth form he took science subjects and also Greek. He was awarded a major scholarship at King's College, Cambridge, in 1931, and then went on to gain a first in both parts of the natural sciences tripos (1933 and 1934). He held a research studentship at King's in 1934–7 under R. J. Pumphrey. He was made a university demonstrator in 1937 and was elected to a fellowship at King's College in 1938. His gift for rigorous analysis and immense skill in experimental design were soon in evidence and he produced important papers on the function of campaniform sensilla in 1938–9.

When the Second World War broke out Pringle joined the RAF and was assigned to research on airborne radar

with the Telecommunications Research Establishment. He headed a research team which made many valuable contributions to the war effort, particularly during the invasion of Europe. For this service he was appointed MBE and awarded the American medal of freedom (both 1945). He returned to the Cambridge department of zoology in 1945. The following year he married Beatrice Laura, a widow with one daughter of Captain Martin Wilson and daughter of Humphrey Gilbert-Carter, a well-known Cambridge botanist. They had a son and two daughters.

Pringle remained at Cambridge until 1961, acting as lecturer, administrative officer, and finally as reader in experimental cytology. In 1959 he was made a member of the general board of the university. He was appointed to a fellowship at Peterhouse in 1945, where successively he became tutor, senior tutor (1948–57), senior bursar (1957–9), and librarian (1959–61). In 1954 he was made FRS, and in 1955 was awarded his ScD in recognition of his outstanding contributions to arthropod biology.

In 1961 Pringle accepted the Linacre chair of zoology at Oxford together with a fellowship at Merton College. He was offered the challenge of designing the promised new zoology department (opened in 1971). He planned the building, going into every detail with characteristic thoroughness and imagination. The result, if somewhat unlovely on the outside, was exceptionally well planned within. While at Oxford he gave the Royal Society Croonian lecture in 1978, was made president of the Society for Experimental Biology in 1977, and gave the Bidder lecture to that society in 1980. He retired in 1979.

Pringle's contributions to research were in insect physiology and muscle biophysics. He made a full analysis of the haltere mechanisms of flies and investigated the skeletal and muscular mechanisms of insect flight. At Oxford he directed an Agricultural Research Council unit which through the use of insect material made many fundamental contributions to the understanding of muscular contraction. Penetrating analysis combined with skill in experimental design were the hallmarks of his research. He made imaginative use of engineering principles, incorporating them into sophisticated models of mechanisms. His book *Insect Flight* (1957) and numerous papers set high standards. In addition Pringle was able to sustain a productive interest in many other biological fields. He made original contributions to such topics as the origins of life, the two biological cultures, biological responsibility and education, world population, and conservation.

Pringle's vision of the central unifying role of biology bore fruit when Oxford launched a new honour school in human sciences whose first undergraduates arrived in 1970. He was also much concerned with the development of science in 'third-world' countries and with forming links with tropical universities. He was visiting professor at Nairobi University in 1973 and gave strong support to a new international centre for insect physiology and ecology, later acting as chairman of its governing board.

In the laboratory Pringle's honesty, sincerity, and clear-minded approach to problems were paramount, while at home he could be a genial host. At times, however, these qualities were concealed below a cold and formidable exterior. He was once compared to a *bombe surprise* turned inside out, the thin cold layer of austerity being spread over a warm and generous humanity. He was deeply religious and found no incompatibility between his science and his faith. Throughout his life he pursued many other interests, which included gardening, bee-keeping, painting, embroidery, winemaking, woodwork, canals, and gliding (for which he won a gold medal in 1960). He died in Oxford on 2 November 1982.   P. L. MILLER, *rev.*

Sources V. B. Wigglesworth, *Memoirs FRS*, 29 (1983), 525–51 · personal knowledge (1990) · *The Times* (3 Nov 1982)
Archives Bodl. Oxf., corresp. and MSS | CAC Cam., corresp. with A. V. Hill · CUL, corresp. with Torkel Weis-Fogh · Rice University, Houston, Texas, Woodson Research Center, corresp. with Sir Julian Huxley · Wolfson College, Oxford, corresp. with H. B. D. Kettlewell
Wealth at death £133,320: administration with will, 7 Jan 1983, *CGPLA Eng. & Wales*

Pringle, Mia Lilly Kellmer (1920–1983), psychologist and first director of the National Children's Bureau, was born in Vienna on 20 June 1920, the elder child and only daughter of Samuel Kellmer, a prosperous wholesale timber merchant, and his wife, Sophie Sobel. Her younger brother, Chanan Kella, emigrated to Israel. She attended the State Humanistic Gymnasium at VI Rahlgasse, Vienna, where she matriculated with distinction. She went to Britain with her mother as a refugee in 1938. They arrived virtually penniless, speaking no English, and Mia worked as a primary school teacher to support herself and her mother, while studying at Birkbeck College, London. She was awarded a first-class honours BA in psychology in 1944. She then qualified as an educational and clinical psychologist at the London Child Guidance Training Centre in 1945. Between 1945 and 1950 she worked as an educational psychologist in Hertfordshire while studying at the University of London for a PhD, which she was awarded in 1950. On 18 April 1946 she married William Joseph Somerville Pringle (1916/17–1962), an analytical chemist, son of William Mather Rutherford *Pringle, barrister and MP.

From 1950 to 1963 Pringle taught in the University of Birmingham, first as a lecturer, then senior lecturer and deputy head of the remedial education centre (later the department of child study). During this time she did much to develop the department as a research and postgraduate training centre, and published a large number of research articles concerned with disabled children, remedial education, and children in care.

In 1963 Pringle was invited to become the first director of the National Children's Bureau, then known as the National Bureau for Co-operation in Child Care. The eighteen years she spent there until her retirement in 1981 were her most productive. Initially the bureau consisted of herself, two researchers, and a secretary. When she retired she left a staff of sixty-five in a large purpose-built building. She started the bureau with the four aims of bringing together the different professions concerned with children; publicizing research knowledge about children; improving services for children and pioneering new ones; and carrying out policy related research about children.

The most important of the bureau's research projects was the national child development study, a longitudinal study of 17,000 children born in 1958. As well as the major findings on this cohort, published in such books as *Birth to Seven* (1972, by R. Davie and others) and *Britain's Sixteen Year Olds* (1976, by K. Fogelman), there were important studies of special groups within the cohort, such as children in care, one-parent families, and gifted children. Many researchers were involved in this research programme, but its inception, continuation, and success owed much to Mia Pringle's drive. While at the bureau she wrote or edited twenty books, as well as many articles. One of her most influential and best-selling books, *The Needs of Children* (1974), was translated into German, Swedish, and French, but some researchers preferred her annotated research summaries on policy issues, including *Adoption: Facts and Fallacies* (1967) and *Foster Home Care: Facts and Fallacies* (1967).

Although a considerable scholar, with an almost obsessive concern for detail, Mia Pringle was only interested in research that had a direct bearing on a practical problem. She was not only, or perhaps essentially, an academic. She was also a great administrator and publicist, tirelessly working to bring different professions together to influence policy on children. She regarded herself above all as a campaigner for children's rights, and to this end wrote widely in the popular as well as the academic press, appeared frequently on television and radio, and served on many government committees. At times she aroused hostility, as when she argued against nursery provision, and the employment of women with under-fives. However, she was listened to with respect by cabinet ministers and senior civil servants.

Pringle was appointed CBE in 1975. In 1970 she was given the Henrietta Szold award for services to children. She also received honorary doctorates from the universities of Bradford (1972), Aston (1979), and Hull (1982). She was made an honorary fellow of Manchester Polytechnic (1972), of the College of Preceptors (1976), and of Birkbeck College, London (1980). After her retirement she acted as a consultant to UNICEF.

Mia Pringle was a very hard-working person who needed little sleep. In personality she was somewhat authoritarian, finding it difficult to share power. At the same time she had great charm, and part of her effectiveness came from a combination of charm, diplomacy, and quick-wittedness. About personal matters she was unusually reserved, and some who knew her well spoke of an underlying melancholy.

On 25 April 1969 Pringle had married William Leonard Hooper (d. 1980), assistant director-general of the Greater London Council, son of Alfred Albert Edward Hooper, insurance inspector. There were no children from either marriage. She died by her own hand in her London flat, Flat 5, 68 Wimpole Street, on 21 February 1983.

BARBARA TIZARD, *rev.*

Sources *The Times* (25 Feb 1983) · *Newsletter* [of the Association of Child Psychologists and Psychiatrists] (summer 1983) · personal knowledge (1990) · private information (1990) · m. certs. · *CGPLA Eng. & Wales* (1983)
Wealth at death £145,051: probate, 16 Dec 1983, *CGPLA Eng. & Wales*

Pringle, Robert (d. **1736**), politician, was the third son among nineteen children of Sir Robert Pringle, first baronet (c.1630–1692), of Stichill, Roxburghshire, and his wife, Margaret, the daughter of Sir John Hope, Lord Craighall. After studying at the University of Leiden, which he entered on 19 November 1687, he served with William III in the invasion of 1688. He was called from his advocate's practice to become under-secretary of state for Scotland on 29 April 1695. He attended William on his later campaigns abroad as his man of business for Scotland, and kept office under Anne without becoming embroiled in the union controversy. He was promoted to under-secretary for the southern department in June 1710. Pringle married a Miss Law and had one son, Robert; the date of the marriage is unknown, but it ended with his wife's death before 1736. On 18 May 1718 he was appointed secretary at war on a salary of £1000, plus £500 rent for a London house at the king's desire following William's grant. He presented the annual army estimates to the Treasury in November, but was replaced on 24 December. Later he became registrar-general of shipping. Pringle resided at Hampstead, but kept up his Dutch links. He died at Rotterdam on 13 September 1736. TIMOTHY VENNING

Sources C. Donn, ed., *Records of the court baron of Stitchel, 1655–1807* (1905) · *An honest diplomat at The Hague: the private letters of Horatio Walpole, 1715–1716*, ed. J. J. Murray [1955] · *London Magazine*, 5 (1736), 581 · *GM*, 1st ser., 6 (1736), 620
Archives NRA, priv. coll., letters relating to political matters | BL, letters to George Bubb, Egerton MSS 2170–2171 · NA Scot., letters to duke of Montrose · NL Scot., corresp. with first and second marquesses of Tweeddale

Pringle, Robert (**1795–1859**), knitwear manufacturer, was born on 16 August 1795 in Hawick, Scotland, the second of the four children of Walter Pringle (b. 1748), a merchant of Hawick descent, and his second wife, Anne (Anny) Scott. In 1810 he was apprenticed to Dixon and Laings in Hawick to learn stocking making. At the end of his apprenticeship in 1815 he set up a business with local spinner John Waldie, and Peter Wilson, stocking maker, in a factory called Whiskyhouse in Slitrig Crescent, Hawick. Waldie, Pringle, and Wilson produced cloth, stockings, and spun yarn. The partnership was successful until 1819, when for reasons not known Wilson left to set up a separate business. Shortly afterwards Pringle moved with his stocking makers into premises at Cross Wynd, Hawick. Although Pringle continued to trade under the original company name, the partnership was effectively dissolved.

Now free to establish a business in his own name, Pringle utilized the introduction in 1827 of the 'broad frame' and new yarn carrier designs to develop fine, high quality yarns from imported merino wools and local cheviot fleeces. He was also able to put into practice his strongly held beliefs in the importance of staff welfare to the growth of a company. By the 1830s the company was firmly established as producers of fine quality knitted underwear and hosiery. In 1824 Robert Pringle married Charlotte Patterson and they had nine children. It was a happy and devoted marriage. Pringle involved himself in many local civic and religious duties, becoming a member of the town council and the parochial board of Hawick, and a police commissioner; he also sat on the Hawick kirk sessions. In addition to his staunch support of the Liberal Party, Pringle passed down this strong sense of political, religious, and civic responsibility to his children. In 1846, when his son Walter had completed his apprenticeship in stocking making, Pringle renamed the company Robert Pringle & Son Hosiery Manufacturers. During the 1850s it was Walter who developed the intarsia method of producing Argyle patterned socks by which the characteristic two-coloured design was incorporated.

Robert Pringle died on 11 December 1859 at 18 Buccleuch Street, Hawick, and was buried in the new burying-ground, Hawick. His wife survived him. His son Walter took over the full running of the company. He married Mary Sutton in 1860; their son, named Robert after his grandfather, was born on 11 June 1862. This Robert Pringle joined the company as an apprentice and became an equal partner in 1885 at the age of twenty-three. At this time the company turned from wholesale to retail and developed a unique method of inserting cable stitches into ladies' jackets. Other patents followed and the company's knitwear designs were market leaders. After his father's death in 1895 overall control of the company went to Robert Pringle. His only son, Walter Pringle (b. 1892), was groomed for succession but was killed at Passchendaele in 1917. The company continued to prosper and became a limited company in 1922. Robert Pringle retired in 1940 and died in 1953. CATHERINE HORWOOD

Sources S. Edgar, *A history of Pringle of Scotland* [n.d.] · J. Wilson, 'Register of deaths', *Transactions of the Hawick Archaeological Society* (1915) · private information (2004) [family] · NA Scot., SC 62/44/32/646 · d. cert.
Wealth at death £1143 19s. 2d.: confirmation, 6 Oct 1860, NA Scot., SC 62/44/32/646

Pringle, Thomas (**1789–1834**), poet, journalist, and philanthropist, was born on Blaiklaw Farm near Kelso, Roxburghshire, on 5 January 1789, the third son of Robert Pringle, farmer, and Catherine Haitlie, daughter of a Berwickshire farmer. Thomas seemed destined for a farming life until an accident at the age of three months, which left him permanently disabled and unable to walk without the aid of crutches. Barred from outdoor activities, he was encouraged to develop an interest in learning and literature, which he retained even after his mother's death in 1795. After attending a local parish school he was enrolled in Kelso grammar school in 1802, the former school of Walter Scott. In November 1805 he matriculated at the University of Edinburgh, where he studied classics. His early academic promise was not realized during his three years at university. By all accounts his was an undistinguished scholarly record, due in part to his outside literary interests, which included a weekly literary club he started to discuss poetry and read original work and compositions by club members.

In February 1808 Pringle left university to take up a post as clerk in Edinburgh's General Register House. When not copying old records he spent time writing poetry and engaging in fledgeling literary work. His first major publication, in 1811, was 'The Institute', a satirical poem lampooning the Edinburgh Philomatic Society, and co-written with his schoolboy friend Robert Story. It was not until 1816, however, with publications in *Albyn's Anthology* and the featuring of the lyrical verses 'The Autumnal Excursion' in the *Poetic Mirror*, edited by James Hogg, that Pringle began making a literary mark for himself. 'The Autumnal Excursion', set in Kelso and a clear imitation of Walter Scott, was read and admired by Scott, who knew the area described and remarked upon receiving it from Pringle that he wished his own notes on the subject 'had always been as fine as their echo' (Doyle, 184). It led to a close friendship between the two authors, and Scott was to prove significant in advancing Pringle's career in future years.

Pringle quit his clerical post to concentrate on literary activity. In 1817 he was invited to co-edit with James Cleghorn the newly established *Edinburgh Monthly Magazine*. Envisaged by its publisher, William Blackwood, as a tory alternative to the whig-influenced *Edinburgh Review*, as well as a riposte to his rival Constable's *Scots Magazine*, the magazine was launched in April 1817 to lacklustre reception. Pringle's energies were not in the enterprise, as he was simultaneously occupied with editing the Edinburgh *Star*, described by Pringle's first biographer, Josiah Conder, as 'almost the only Liberal paper in Scotland' (Doyle, 23). Disappointed with his editors' lack of inspiration and commissioning zeal, Blackwood dismissed them and set about recruiting a more dynamic team to run the journal. Calling on James Hogg, John Wilson, and John Gibson Lockhart, he relaunched *Blackwood's Edinburgh Magazine* in October 1817 to great success. In the same month Pringle took on the editorship of Constable's rival publication, the *Edinburgh Magazine*. By now he was also married, having wed Margaret Brown (1780–1854) on 18 July 1817 in St Cuthbert's Church in Edinburgh.

By 1819, however, Pringle's editorial activities were at an end. Despite publication that year of his first volume of poetry, *'The Autumnal Excursion' and Other Poems*, the dissolution of the *Star* and the *Edinburgh Magazine* saw him return to clerical duties at the register house. Soon after, with his extended family in similar reduced circumstances, Pringle decided to emigrate to southern Africa. With the help of Sir Walter Scott he secured free passage to and a grant of land in southern Africa for the Pringles. On 15 February 1820, with Pringle as their leader, what became known as the 'Scottish party' of twenty-four Scots emigrants set sail from Gravesend for the Cape on the brig *Brilliant*. The group arrived at their new southern African landholding in late June 1820. Over the next two years, Pringle worked hard to secure the future of the new settlement of Glen-Lynden. He was also to undertake several journeys round southern Africa, which were to form the basis for his ground breaking *Narrative of a Residency in South Africa* (1834), one of the first published travel accounts of pioneering life in the Cape.

In September 1822 Pringle took up a post in Cape Town as librarian of the South African Public Library, a position secured through the influence of Sir Walter Scott and Sir John MacPherson. Sixteen months later, in December 1823, joined by his long-time friend John Fairbairn, he founded the Classical and Commercial Academy, which enrolled fifty pupils within a month of its launch. Not content with this, Pringle also launched a newspaper in January 1824, the *South African Commercial Advertiser*, and in March of the same year started South Africa's first literary journal, the bilingual Dutch–English monthly *South African Journal*.

During this period Pringle also assisted in raising funds for the relief of settlers in Albany, who as a result of crop failures and floods between 1820 and 1823, had been left destitute. Through determined letter writing, journal publications, and his account of their plight, *Some Account of the Present State of the English Settlers in Albany, South Africa*, published in London in 1824, he helped raise more than £10,000 by the end of 1825.

Pringle's activities were not always welcomed, though. His uncompromising championing of freedom of the press brought him into conflict with the autocratic Cape governor Lord Charles Somerset, who in May 1824 suppressed both Pringle's periodical publications and launched a campaign against him. By October, with his school struggling for support and no further outlets for income, Pringle and his wife returned to the Pringle homestead at Glen-Lynden to prepare for the long voyage back to Britain. In July 1826, 'Ruined in circumstances and in prospects but sound in conscience and character', Pringle arrived in London with his wife and sister-in-law, and resumed his journalistic career (Meiring, 109). An article in the *New Monthly Magazine* in October 1826 on the horrors of slavery led to his appointment in 1827 as secretary of the powerful Anti-Slavery Society. Working with the abolitionists William Wilberforce and Sir Thomas Fowell Buxton, he was reputedly responsible for producing more than half the organization's multi-varied publications. Pringle's energetic political activism bore fruit. On 23 August 1833 parliament passed the bill which abolished slavery. On 27 June 1834 the document proclaiming the Act of Abolition was published, with Pringle its signatory.

In addition to political work Pringle found time to publish several collections of prose and poetry, including *Ephemerides, or, Occasional Poems Written in Scotland and South Africa* (1828), *Glen-Lynden: a Tale of Teviotdale* (1828), and *African Sketches* (1834). His best known poem, 'Afar in the Desert' (1832), a romantic description of the southern African bush, was admired by Samuel Taylor Coleridge, who declared it 'among the three most perfect lyric poems in our language' (Meiring, 163). Pringle's poems were the first to represent southern African life and incorporate local dialect and phraseology, leading him to be dubbed the father of south African poetry, a view still held at the end of the nineteenth century by Rudyard Kipling who, when asked what southern African poetry there was, replied: 'As to South African verse, it is a case of there's Pringle and there's Pringle' (Meiring, 163). According to a South African critic, A. M. Lewin Robinson, Pringle was 'the first poet of any acknowledged ability to attempt to describe the South African scene in English' (Meiring, 163).

Pringle's political and literary successes came too late in his life for him to enjoy the benefits. The day following publication of the Act of Abolition, Pringle was taken seriously ill with tuberculosis, eventually dying at his home in London on 5 December 1834. Buried at Bunhill Fields, London, he was reinterred on 5 December 1970 at Eildon church, on the grounds of the Pringle family estate in South Africa's Baviaans river valley.

DAVID FINKELSTEIN

Sources DSAB, 656–8 · J. R. Doyle jun., Thomas Pringle (1972) · S. J. Kunitz and H. Haycraft, eds., British authors of the nineteenth century (1936), 505–6 · J. Meiring, Thomas Pringle: his life and times (1968) · E. Pringle, ed., Scottish party day celebrations, 5 Dec. 1970 (1971) · D. H. Thomson, The life and works of Thomas Pringle (1961) · African poems of Thomas Pringle, ed. M. Chapman and E. Pereira (1989)
Archives Bodl. RH, corresp. as secretary to the Anti-Slavery Society · Surrey History Society, Woking, corresp. relating to pamphlet entitled 'Opposition to Henry Goulburn's candidature for parliament on grounds of being a slave owner' | Library of Parliament, South Africa, Fairbairn MSS · NL Scot., letters to Blackwoods · NL Scot., letters to James Hogg · NL Scot., letters to D. M. Moir · NL Scot., letters to Sir Walter Scott · NL Scot., Hugh Walpole collection · Sheff. Arch., letters to James Montgomery
Likenesses W. Findler, stipple and line engraving, pubd 1837 (after unknown artist), NPG · portrait, repro. in Kunitz, ed., British authors, 505

Pringle, Walter, of Greenknowe (1625–1667), covenanter, was born in Bartinbush, Dumfriesshire, the second son of Robert Pringle (1581?–1649), first laird of Stitchel, Roxburghshire, and his first wife, Catherine Hamilton of Silverton Hill. Robert Pringle, second son of George Pringle of Craiglatch, was originally of Bartinbush but, making his fortune as a writer to the signet in Edinburgh, in 1628 he purchased the lands and barony of Stitchel from Sir John Gordon of Lochinvar, later first Viscount Kenmure. Robert continued to acquire various lands in Berwickshire, including in 1637 the lands of Wester Gordon from James Seton of Touch which were granted to Robert and his wife, but on his death to pass to his second surviving son, Walter, including 'the manor place called Greenknowe' (Thomson and others, 6/2.374–5). Robert Pringle represented Roxburghshire as a commissioner to parliament from 1639 to 1641 and became a regular on the parliamentary commissions and committees of the covenanter regime, including the commission for manufactories (1641), the commission for loans and tax (1643), and the committee of war (1643–9).

Walter Pringle was apparently educated at Edinburgh University but seems not to have graduated. As a boy he and his elder brother John were put in the care of James Leckie, an ejected minister of Stirling. This attempt at a 'godly' education was abandoned after Leckie's death in the 1630s, and the youthful Pringle began, in his own words, 'years of darkness, deadness and sinfulness'

including a year in Leith and two years in France ('Memoirs', 1.424). On the death of his father in 1649 he succeeded to the estate of Greenknowe, his father's grandson Sir Robert Pringle of Stitchel succeeding to the Stitchel estate. He married Janet Pringle, daughter of James Pringle of Torwoodlie, Selkirkshire, in November 1649. Their marriage took place at Stow and the officiating minister was James Guthrie of Lauder, and later of Stirling, the covenanting martyr who was executed in 1661. Walter Pringle had his father's enthusiasm for the covenanting regime and, according to his own memoirs, spent five years in the 1640s as a volunteer soldier. On the invasion of Scotland by Cromwell in 1650 Walter, along with his younger brother-in-law George Pringle of Torwoodlie (1631–1689), who was later part of the disastrous Argyll rebellion of 1685, joined the covenanting army in its defeat at the battle of Dunbar in September 1650. Cromwell's victory over covenanting forced Walter and George Pringle to take refuge at Torwoodlie. In November, however, when Walter was returning from a visit to his wife at Stitchel where she had just given birth to Catherine, their first child, an incident occurred whereby he killed an English trooper. This led him to take more distant refuge in Northumberland where he stayed with his cousin, a certain Major Pringle, although before long he was arrested and brought to trial at Selkirk. Fortunately, his plea of self-defence was accepted and he was allowed liberty on a bond of £2000 sterling. He lived peaceably for the remainder of the 1650s.

After the Restoration, Pringle's covenanting beliefs became the target of official displeasure and he was cast into prison in Edinburgh Castle in September 1660 for 'ayding, assisting and pairtaking with the Remonstrators and uther seditious persones' (Nicoll, 302). Although not detained long, in July 1664 his nonconformity led to his trial and examination before Archbishop Sharp and the court of high commission, created that year. Finding difficulty in taking the oath of allegiance, and especially that part referring to royal supremacy over the church, Pringle incurred the wrath of the episcopate when attempting to take the oath according to Bishop James Ussher's old formula as approved by James VI. He was heavily fined and subsequently, in November, imprisoned in the Tolbooth of Edinburgh for defaulting on the fine. After confinement for several months he was in the summer of 1665 banished to the burgh of Elgin, and his exile continued until February 1666 when a group of his friends, without his knowledge, obtained from the high commission a transfer to 'open prison' at his own home of Greenknowe and 3 miles around. The government conceded this on payment of £200 sterling and his agreement to peaceable behaviour.

Little detail of Pringle's private life is known, other than that provided by his autobiography, *The memoirs of Walter Pringle of Greenknowe, or, Some of the few mercies of God to him, and his will to his children, left them under his own hand*, written in those years of intermittent captivity from 1662 to 1666, first printed posthumously in 1723 and republished by the Wodrow Society in 1845. It is a pious 'life' full of fatherly advice, Christian virtue, and awe at the godliness of the ministry, yet tinged with doubt and fallibility. Pringle and his wife had a large family of five sons and three daughters; he was succeeded by his sons Robert and, in 1677, James, who transcribed the 'Memoirs', then by his grandson George, son of James (1694), and after him his own ageing son John (1724). Walter Pringle died at Greenknowe on 12 December 1667. He was survived by his wife. His will and testament have not survived.   A. J. MANN

Sources W. Pringle, 'The memoirs of Walter Pringle of Greenknowe', *Select biographies*, ed. W. K. Tweedie, 1, Wodrow Society, 7/1 (1845), 419–94 · A. Pringle, *The records of the Pringles or Hoppringills of the Scottish border* (1933), 200–19 · M. D. Young, ed., *The parliaments of Scotland: burgh and shire commissioners*, 2 (1993), 573 · R. Wodrow, *The history of the sufferings of the Church of Scotland from the Restoration to the revolution*, ed. R. Burns, 1 (1828), 394 · J. Nicoll, *A diary of public transactions and other occurrences, chiefly in Scotland, from January 1650 to June 1667*, ed. D. Laing, Bannatyne Club, 52 (1836), 302 · *The historical works of Sir James Balfour*, ed. J. Haig, 2 (1824), 22, 61 · J. M. Thomson and others, eds., *Registrum magni sigilli regum Scotorum / The register of the great seal of Scotland*, 11 vols. (1882–1914), vol 8, pp. 473, 1304 · *APS*, 1625–41; 1648–60 · *Reg. PCS*, 3rd ser., 2.141 · *Memoirs of Walter Pringle of Greenknow* (1751)
Archives NL Scot., diary

Pringle, Sir Walter, Lord Newhall (1664?–1736), judge, was the second son among the nineteen children born to Sir Robert Pringle, first baronet (*c*.1630–1692), of Stichill, and his wife, Margaret, daughter of Sir John Hope, Lord Craighall. Thirteen children survived infancy; Thomas Pringle and Robert *Pringle (*d*. 1736) were distinguished in law and politics. Walter Pringle graduated at Edinburgh in 1682 and at Leiden in 1684, and was admitted advocate on 10 December 1687. He married first in 1698 Helen, daughter of Sir John Ayton, and secondly a daughter of Johnston of Hilton, Berwickshire, with whom he had three sons: Robert, his heir, Joseph, who was a captain in the earl of Drumlanrig's regiment when he died in Holland in 1753, Walter, who was a captain in Holmes's foot when he died at Aberdeen in 1756, and a daughter, Margaret (*d*. 1742), married to Andrew Handyside.

Although he became a leading Scottish barrister, Pringle was not made a judge until 6 June 1718, taking his seat as Lord Newhall, from the family estate of that name, and being knighted at the same time. On 24 June 1725 the hated malt tax led to an insurrection in Glasgow; the leaders were taken to Edinburgh for trial, and sentenced to whipping or transportation. Concerning this trial, the president wrote to the secretary of state:

> I find four of the Judges inclined to do all they can, and more than there is any shadow of law to warrant, to screen the criminals from justice. Those I mean are Lord Newhall, who is a Whig, and the best lawyer among them, and consequently does most harm, so far as to influence lords Polton and Pencaitland, both Whigs; the other is Lord Dun. (Pringle, 313)

Newhall died on 14 December 1736; at his funeral, his judicial colleagues paid him the unique tribute of attending in their robes of office, while a special eulogy, written by Sir Robert Dundas of Arniston, then dean, was included in the minutes of the Faculty of Advocates. The estate of Lochton, Berwickshire, which had come to Newhall in 1726, passed to a nephew.

A. H. MILLAR, *rev.* ANITA McCONNELL

Sources G. Brunton and D. Haig, *An historical account of the senators of the college of justice, from its institution in MDXXXII* (1832), 495 · A. F. Tytler, *Memoirs of the life and writings of the Honourable Henry Home of Kames*, 2nd edn, 3 vols. (1814), vol. 1, p. 31 · J. Grant, *Cassell's old and new Edinburgh*, 3 vols. [1880–83], vol. 1, p. 169 · A. Pringle, *The records of the Pringles or Hoppringills of the Scottish border* (1933)
Likenesses attrib. A. Allan, oils, Scot. NPG · R. Cooper, line engraving (after portrait attrib. A. Allan), BM · J. B. Medina, oils, Parliament Hall, Edinburgh

Pringle, William Mather Rutherford (1874–1928), politician, was born at Gordon, Berwickshire, on 22 January 1874, the third and youngest son of George Pringle, farm steward, of Gordon, and his wife, Elizabeth Mather. He was educated at Garnethill School, Glasgow, and at Glasgow University, where he graduated with honours in classics and history. In 1904 he was called to the bar by the Middle Temple. On 4 June 1906 he married Lilias Patrick (*b*. 1877/8), who survived him, daughter of Joseph Somerville, timber salesman, of Glasgow. They had four sons and one daughter.

At the 1906 general election Pringle unsuccessfully contested the Camlachie division of Glasgow as the Liberal candidate. He entered parliament as the member for North-West Lanarkshire at the general election of January 1910, and quickly gained a reputation for his skill in the use of parliamentary procedure and tactics, which he later used to great effect. On 3 August 1914 he made an important speech in the House of Commons in support of the decision to go to war with Germany over the violation of Belgian neutrality: 'We who hold to the Liberal tradition, and still honour Mr Gladstone's ideas, are bound in a conflict of this kind to range ourselves on the side of international morality against the forces of blood and iron' (*Hansard 5C*, 66, 1880). But he subsequently objected to what he regarded as the oppressive methods used to carry out the war, opposing conscription and other aspects of the Military Service Acts.

After the Liberal split which saw Lloyd George become leader of a new coalition government in late 1916, Pringle became one of the most determined and vocal critics of the new prime minister, whom he personally 'detested' (Wilson, 332). He and James Myles Hogge became known as the 'terrible twins' who kept up the attack on the Lloyd George government in defence, as they saw it, of true Liberal beliefs and individual liberty. Pringle strongly condemned Lloyd George's manipulation of his 'Kept Press' (Owen, 467).

Pringle lost his seat in the 1918 'coupon' election, when he came third behind a coalition Conservative and a Labour candidate at Glasgow Springburn, and he was again third in a by-election at Manchester Rusholme in October 1919. After coming second in a by-election at Yorkshire Penistone in March 1921, he was returned for that seat in the 1922 general election and held it in the following year. He had developed—after earlier being a critic—a fierce loyalty to Asquith, and he maintained this throughout his second period in the house, alongside his peculiar ability to annoy and distract ministers through his use of parliamentary tactics. *The Times* noted that it 'was said that Labour Ministers dreaded nothing more than the guerrilla warfare of Mr Pringle on the Liberal benches' (*The Times*, 2 April 1928, 19). Asquith wrote of parliament in 1924 that 'This would be the dullest place in Europe but for Pringle … he is far the most resourceful Parliamentarian in the House' (Asquith, 211).

In 1924 Pringle was invited to join the Liberal 'shadow cabinet' under Asquith, but in the general election of October 1924 lost his seat. Following the election, an 'angry meeting' (Owen, 684) of around one hundred defeated Liberal candidates was held, with Pringle in the chair. Much of the blame for their defeat they attributed to Lloyd George's failure to direct sufficiently the resources of his 'Lloyd George Fund' towards the general benefit of the party in the election. At this meeting the Liberal and Radical Candidates' Association was formed and Pringle, as its first chairman, sought to have this body gain a formal say in the choice of the parliamentary leadership.

Pringle also played a significant role in the formation of the Liberal Council in 1927 and was largely responsible for its monthly publication, *Burdens on Industry*. He attempted to return to parliament, and at the time of his death he was the prospective candidate for Paisley, which had previously been held by Asquith. His loyalty, in his later years, to Asquith was unquestioned, and his ability to keep ministers of whatever party on their toes, sometimes almost as a lone voice, was widely respected. Although not in office he played an influential role in the parliaments of his period. He died of heart failure at his home, Hampton, 10 Sutherland Grove, Southfields, Surrey, on 1 April 1928, and was buried on 5 April. MARC BRODIE

Sources *The Times* (2 April 1928) · *The Times* (5 April 1928) · H. H. Asquith, *Memories and reflections, 1852–1927*, ed. A. Mackintosh, 2 vols. (1928) · F. Owen, *Tempestuous journey: Lloyd George, his life and times* (1954) · T. Wilson, *The downfall of the liberal party, 1914–1935* (1966) · J. Turner, *British politics and the Great War: coalition and conflict, 1915–1918* (1992) · M. Bentley, *The liberal mind, 1914–1929* (1977) · WWBMP · b. cert. · m. cert.
Archives HLRO, corresp. and papers | Bodl. Oxf., corresp. with H. H. Asquith and others
Likenesses photograph, repro. in *The Times* (2 April 1928), 18
Wealth at death £2575 7s. 4d.: administration, 6 July 1928, CGPLA *Eng. & Wales*

Prinsep, Charles Robert (1789–1864). *See under* Prinsep, Henry Thoby (1792–1878).

Prinsep, Henry Thoby (1792–1878), East India Company servant, was the fourth son of **John Prinsep** (1746–1830) and his wife, Sophia Elizabeth Auriol (1760–1850), sister of James Peter Auriol, secretary to the government of Warren Hastings, whom he married in Calcutta in 1782. Having gone out to India as a military cadet in 1771, John Prinsep had resigned the military service immediately and made a considerable fortune in trade. He trafficked chiefly in indigo, of which industry he may be regarded as the

Henry Thoby Prinsep (1792–1878), by Julia Margaret Cameron, 1866

founder, and introduced into Bengal the printing of cotton fabrics. He returned to England in 1787 and settled at Thoby Priory in Essex; he was MP for Queenborough (1802–6) and an alderman of the city of London. He published in 1789 *A Review of the Trade of the East India Company*, and this was followed by pamphlets on the cultivation of sugar cane in Bengal and on other East Indian topics. In his later life, after considerable losses in trade, his city influence procured his appointment as bailiff to the court of the borough of Southwark, with a salary of £1500 a year.

Henry Thoby Prinsep was born at Thoby Priory on 15 July 1792. At the age of thirteen he went to Mr Knox's school at Tonbridge, and in 1807, having obtained a writership to Bengal, he entered the East India College, then recently established at Hertford Castle. He left the college in December 1808, and arrived at Calcutta on 20 July 1809, at the age of seventeen. After spending two years in Calcutta, first as a student in Fort William College, where he came to know Holt Mackenzie, and afterwards as an assistant in the office of the court of *sadr adalat*, he was sent in 1811 to Murshidabad, where he was employed as assistant to the magistrate, and also as registrar, a judicial office for the disposal of petty suits. After serving in the jungle mahals and in Bakarganj, Prinsep was appointed, in 1814, assistant to the secretary to the governor-general, Lord Moira (afterwards marquess of Hastings), whom he accompanied on his tour through Oudh and the North-Western Provinces (1814–15). He was subsequently (1816) the first holder of the office of superintendent and remembrancer of legal affairs—an office established for the protection of the interests of the government in the courts in the provinces. His tenure of the post was interrupted by summonses to join the governor-general's camp during Lord Hastings's second tour (1817–18), which embraced the period of the Pindari wars and the third war with the Marathas; the governor-general, who was also commander-in-chief, exercised the chief command. At the close of the Anglo-Maratha War, Prinsep obtained the permission of the governor-general to write *A Narrative of the Political and Military Transactions of British India under the Administration of the Marquis of Hastings, 1813 to 1818*. He sent the completed manuscript to his elder brother, Charles Robert Prinsep [*see below*]. A letter to George Canning, president of the Board of Control, from Lord Hastings recommended that the publication of the work should be sanctioned, but, without reading the manuscript, Canning prohibited it. Charles Prinsep, however, decided to publish on his own responsibility, and placed the manuscript in the hands of John Murray, who brought out the book in 1820. The proofs were sent to the Board of Control, where they were seen by Canning, who, on reading them, approved of the work. The book is generally considered to be the best and most trustworthy narrative of the events of that time. The original edition was revised, extended to 1823, and republished in two volumes, when the author was in England on leave, in 1825.

In 1819 and 1820, while still holding, as his permanent appointment, the office of superintendent and remembrancer of legal affairs, Prinsep was employed upon more than one special inquiry. The most important was an investigation into the condition of the land tenures in the district of Burdwan and the adjoining country. The principal landowner in these districts was the raja of Burdwan, who paid over 40 lakhs of rupees, representing in Prinsep's time over £400,000 sterling, as annual revenue to the government. The raja had introduced the system of letting his estates in large blocks, called *patni taluks*, to tenants who were called *patnidars*, on payment of large sums of money as bonus; these again sublet them to under-tenants called *darpatnidars*, by whom they were again further sublet; so that there were sometimes five or six middlemen between the raja and the cultivating ryot. The tenure of the *patnidars* was, by stipulation, perpetual and hereditary, and gave to them all the rights and authority of the raja over the subtenants; the result was much confusion and litigation, difficulty in collecting the raja's dues, and risk to the government revenue. Prinsep, after a thorough inquiry, came to the conclusion that there was no security for the government revenue, and no remedy for the existing confusion, unless a law were passed that, on default of the *patnidar*, all the middlemen who derived their rights from him should fall with him. He accordingly drafted a regulation, which was passed into law as regulation 8 of 1819, which remained in force in Bengal for the rest of the century.

From that time Prinsep was recognized as one of the ablest men in the service, and his promotion to high office was assured. On 16 December 1820, before he had been twelve years in India, he was appointed Persian secretary to the government on a salary of 3000 rupees a month; and except on two occasions (1824–6, 1832–4), when he was compelled by the state of his health to leave India for a time, he never left the secretariat until he was appointed a member of council, first during a temporary vacancy in 1835, and five years later, when he was permanently appointed to the office. He finally retired from the service and left India in 1843.

During his long service Prinsep was brought into close contact with a succession of governors-general, including lords Hastings, Amherst, William Bentinck, Auckland, and Ellenborough. Many years afterwards, in 1865, he wrote a valuable but unpublished autobiographical sketch of his official life, in which he recorded his impressions of each of these men. Of Lord Minto, whom he saw only from a distance, Prinsep had a poor opinion, although he gives him credit for the firmness he displayed in the operations against Java. He regarded Lord Hastings's nine-year administration as 'a glorious one', which had 'nearly doubled the revenues and territories of the East India Company, and established its diplomatic influence over the whole peninsula of India'. Lord Amherst he describes as a courteous gentleman, and a ready and fluent speaker, but he 'lacked confidence in his own judgment and was by no means prompt in decision', and 'had extraordinary notions of the importance of a very punctilious ceremonial'. He had a high admiration for John Adam, who was acting governor-general for seven months in 1823, and on his death in 1825 wrote a memoir of Adam at the request of his family, which was published in the *Asiatic Journal* for 1825.

The governor-general upon whom Prinsep is most severe is Lord William Bentinck. He regarded him as addicted to change for the mere sake of change, as unduly suspicious of those who worked under him, and too much given to meddling with details; but he gives him credit for honesty of intention, especially in the distribution of his patronage. The two men differed essentially in character. Lord William was a strong liberal, while Prinsep was a conservative to the backbone. On the education question Prinsep was strongly opposed to the policy, initiated by Macaulay and supported by Bentinck, of imposing English as the language of instruction. The policy ultimately adopted was a compromise in deference to Prinsep's opposition. Later on, during the interregnum in which Sir Charles Metcalfe officiated as governor-general, Prinsep, while not opposing the act to give freedom to the press of India, predicted gloomily, and without any real justification in his lifetime, that 'the native press might become an engine for destroying the respect in which the government is held'.

Prinsep appears to have been on very friendly terms with Lord Auckland throughout his administration, but he regarded him as slow to take decisions, and timid of his responsibilities. He entirely disapproved of Auckland's Afghan policy, and foretold the failure of the policy of supporting Shah Shuja.

On his return to England in 1843 Prinsep settled in London. His ambition at that time was to enter the House of

Commons, and he contested no less than four constituencies as a Conservative candidate, the Kilmarnock burghs (1844), Dartmouth (1845), Dover (1847), and Harwich (1851, twice). At the last of these places he was returned, but was unseated by petition on technical grounds. He then canvassed for a seat in the court of directors of the East India Company, to which he was elected in 1850. He took a prominent part in the discussions at the India House, and when the number of directors was reduced from twenty-four to eighteen (six being crown nominees) under the act of 1853, he was one of those elected by ballot to retain their seats. In 1858, after the East India Company's rule was superseded by that of the crown, and the Council of India was established, he was one of the seven directors appointed to the new council.

Prinsep served in the Council of India until 1874, displaying the same activity and conservatism which had characterized his whole official life. He recorded frequent dissents from the decisions of the secretary of state. He was much opposed to some of the measures adopted after the mutiny. He emphatically disapproved of the transfer of the East India Company's European regiments to the British army, and joined on that occasion with thirteen other members of the council in a written protest against the course taken by the cabinet in deciding this question before the Council of India had been consulted on it. He also disapproved of the original scheme for the establishment of staff corps for India, and especially of that part of it which provided for the appointment of officers from the line for Indian service. He was much opposed to the re-establishment of the maharaja of Mysore after the state had been administered since 1831 by British officers; the rendition of Mysore finally took place in 1881. On financial grounds he opposed the works undertaken to improve the navigation of the Godavari River, which subsequently, owing to their enormous cost, had to be abandoned. In his last year of office he recorded a protest against the adoption of the narrow, or metre, gauge for Indian railways.

Busy as was Prinsep's official life, he found time to write a number of works on Indian subjects, including *Origin of the Sikh Power in the Punjab* (1834), *Tibet, Tartary, and Mongolia: their Social and Political Condition* (1851), and an exhaustive pamphlet, *The India Question in 1853*, when the Charter Act of that year was under discussion. He also brought out the work of Ramchunder Doss (Ramachandra Dasa) entitled *Register of the Bengal Civil Servants, 1790–1842, Accompanied by Actuarial Tables* (1844), a subject to which he had given a good deal of attention. He also wrote verses; in his old age he printed for private circulation *Specimens of Ballad Poetry Applied to the Tales and Traditions of the East* (1862). He kept up his classical studies to the end of his life. When failing health brought him sleepless nights, he often whiled away the time by translating the odes of Horace into English verse. He was a keen mathematician. Only a few days before his death he worked out a new method of proving the forty-seventh proposition of the first book of Euclid.

Prinsep's domestic life involved him in a very different circle from that of his official career. On 14 May 1835 he married Sara Monckton (1816–1887), daughter of James

Pattle of the Bengal civil service; she was one of seven sisters known for their beauty and talents, including the photographer Julia Margaret Cameron and Virginia, Countess Somers. The Prinseps had a daughter and three sons. Through his sister-in-law Virginia he met the artist G. F. Watts, and when the Prinseps set up their home at Little Holland House, Kensington, Watts joined them and remained an inmate of their house and a recipient of their patronage for some twenty-one years. Under the guidance of Sara Prinsep, Little Holland House became one of the artistic and literary centres of London, where Tennyson, Browning, and Thackeray mingled with Du Maurier, Ruskin, and Burne-Jones. The Prinseps' second son, Valentine Cameron *Prinsep, became an artist of the aesthetic movement. It was at Watts's house at Freshwater on the Isle of Wight that Henry Thoby Prinsep died on 11 February 1878.

Of Prinsep's numerous brothers one, James *Prinsep, is separately noticed. Another, **Charles Robert Prinsep** (1789–1864), was admitted a pensioner of St John's College, Cambridge, on 23 May 1806, and proceeded BA in 1811 and MA in 1814. He was called to the bar by the Inner Temple in Trinity term 1817. He was the author of *An Essay on Money* (1818) and a translation of J. B. Say's *Political Economy, with Notes*, 2 vols. (1811). He was created LLD in 1824, practised at the Calcutta bar from 1824, and was advocate-general of Bengal (1852–5). He died at his home, Rothbury House, Chiswick Mall, Chiswick, Middlesex, on 8 June 1864.

A. J. ARBUTHNOT, *rev.* R. J. BINGLE

Sources H. T. Prinsep, 'Autobiographical memoir' (c.1865), vol. 2 of *Three generations in India*, 3 vols. (1912), BL OIOC, MS Eur. C 97 · HoP, *Commons* · *The pantheon of the age, or, Memoirs of 3000 contemporary public characters, British and foreign*, 2nd edn, 2 (1825), 187 · GM, 3rd ser., 17 (1864), 124 [Charles Robert Prinsep] · Venn, *Alum. Cant.* · *CGPLA Eng. & Wales* (1878) · *CGPLA Eng. & Wales* (1864) [Charles Robert Prinsep] · P. Fitzgerald, *Edward Burne-Jones* (1975) · R. B. Martin, *Tennyson: the unquiet heart* (1980) · D. S. Macleod, *Art and the Victorian middle class: money and the making of cultural identity* (1996) · BL OIOC
Archives BL OIOC, corresp. relating to Burma, MS Eur. D 662 | BL OIOC, letters to Lord Amherst, MS Eur. F 140 · Bodl. Oxf., corresp. with Lord Kimberley · PRO, corresp. with Lord Ellenborough, PRO 30/12
Likenesses H. Weekes, bust, 1844, Victoria Memorial Hall, Calcutta · G. F. Watts, portrait, c.1852; Sotheby Belgravia, 28 November 1972, lot 71 · G. F. Watts, portrait, c.1865; Christies, 21 November 1977, lot 113 · J. M. Cameron, photographs, 1866, NPG [*see illus.*] · D. W. Wynfield, photograph, RA
Wealth at death under £4000: probate, 26 Feb 1878, *CGPLA Eng. & Wales* · under £3000—Charles Robert Prinsep: probate, 13 July 1864, *CGPLA Eng. & Wales*

Prinsep, James (1799–1840), Indologist and scientist, was born on 20 August 1799 at 147 Leadenhall Street, London, the seventh son and tenth child of John *Prinsep (1746–1830) [*see under* Prinsep, Henry Thoby (1792–1878)], merchant and MP, and his wife, Sophia Elizabeth Auriol (1760–1850). John Prinsep went penniless to India in 1771. He was successful as an indigo planter and entrepreneur, and returned to England in 1787 with a fortune of £40,000. He established himself in the City in 1793 as a general merchant and India agent, but business losses and the expenses of contested elections and of his large family (eight surviving sons and three daughters) caused him to move to Clifton, Bristol, in 1809. Prinsep's connections, however, secured places for his sons: all but one made their careers in India. They included Charles Robert *Prinsep [see under Prinsep, Henry Thoby], economist and advocate-general of Bengal, and Henry Thoby *Prinsep, a civil servant and commentator on Indian affairs, whose son, Valentine Cameron *Prinsep, was a noted painter.

James Prinsep's only formal early education was two years at the school of a Mr Bullock in Clifton. He was educated mostly at home, with help from his talented siblings. He excelled from an early age at drawing, music, and mechanical invention. Such skills destined him for architecture but a temporary weakness of the eyes developed and his father therefore sought for him an opening in the assay department of the government of India. After studying chemistry at Guy's Hospital and assaying at the Royal Mint in London (1818–19), Prinsep was appointed assistant assay master at the Calcutta mint and arrived in Calcutta on 15 September 1819. Within a year he had been sent by the assay master, Horace Hayman Wilson, to be assay master at the Benares mint, where he remained until its abolition in 1830. He returned to Calcutta as deputy assay master, and upon Wilson's resignation in 1832 he was (despite Wilson's favouring his own protégé James Atkinson) appointed to succeed him at the newly built Greek revival mint on the Strand with its adjacent house for the assay master. He married in the cathedral of Calcutta on 25 April 1835 Harriet Sophia Aubert, daughter of Lieutenant-Colonel Jeremiah Aubert and his wife, Hannah. There was only one surviving child, a daughter, Eliza, born in 1837.

Prinsep's early death prompted many eulogies from his contemporaries. He was one of the 'most talented and useful' Englishmen ever to work in India (Malconer, Colonial Magazine, December 1840).

> Of his intellectual character, the most prominent feature was enthusiasm, a burning, irrepressible enthusiasm, to which nothing could set bounds [which led him] to apply his powers to a greater range of subjects than any human mind can master or excel in. To this enthusiasm was fortunately united a habitude of order, and power of generalization, which enabled him to grasp and comprehend the greatest variety of details.   (ibid.)

His official duties as assay master drew him first to scientific research, and to the means for more accurate measurement of very high temperatures. He invented the first practical pyrometer utilizing the expansion of gases for such measurements; his research was communicated to the Royal Society in London and published in the Philosophical Transactions for 1828. He was shortly afterwards elected FRS. In Calcutta he organized the reform of Indian weights and measures in 1833, and advocated the introduction of a uniform coinage based on a new, East India Company's, silver rupee. This was introduced in 1835.

Prinsep's major contributions, however, fell outside his official duties. His enthusiasm for the communication of scientific knowledge led him to collaborate with Major James Herbert in a new monthly journal Gleanings in Science in 1829. He was himself a principal contributor, and became sole editor in 1831. In 1832 he succeeded Wilson

also as secretary of the Asiatic Society of Bengal, and he brought new vigour to the society's meetings and publications. In the same year he became editor of a new monthly title, The Journal of the Asiatic Society, which absorbed the earlier Gleanings. To this new journal Prinsep contributed articles on chemistry and mineralogy, and above all on Indian antiquities, into the study of which he now wholeheartedly threw himself.

As a result of both his own labours and his encouragement of others, Prinsep's seven years as editor of the Journal was one of the most fruitful periods of ancient Indian studies. Coins and copies of inscriptions were transmitted to him from all over India, to be deciphered, translated, and published. He reduced to order the complex dynasties and dating systems of pre-Islamic India. His Useful Tables, published in 1834, stands as a monument to his labours in this field. Prinsep's greatest achievement was to decipher the hitherto unreadable scripts of the most ancient of Indian inscriptions: the results were published in a series of papers in the Journal in 1837–8. These scripts were the Brahmi used on the pillars at Delhi and Allahabad and on rock inscriptions from both sides of India, and also the Kharosthi script in the coins and inscriptions of the northwest. He demonstrated that the pillar and rock inscriptions were put up by the emperor Asoka Maurya, whose dates could be approximately fixed through his references to contemporary kings of western Asia in the third century BC. They allowed the first verified correlation of Indian history and archaeology with those of the Western world. In consequence of these discoveries Prinsep was elected a corresponding member of many of the learned societies of Europe.

Both in Gleanings in Science and in the Journal Prinsep undertook much of the drawing and lithography of the accompanying plates. In 1822 he had applied his talents in draughtsmanship to a thorough survey of Benares. A complete map at 8 inches to the mile was prepared, and lithographed in England. A series of exquisite watercolours of the monuments and festivals of Benares was sent to London in 1829 to be lithographed. These were published in Calcutta and London between 1830 and 1834 as Benares Illustrated, in a Series of Views. Nor did he confine his interest in Benares to recording it: he designed and built several public buildings. He improved the sanitation of Benares by constructing underneath the most densely populated part of the city an arched tunnel down to the river, thereby draining various stagnant lakes and pools. The high and graceful minarets of Aurangzeb's mosque were in danger of collapse, so he had them taken down and rebuilt. And so that pilgrims approaching Benares by road from the east should not have to set foot in the polluting waters of the River Karamnasa, he built a stone bridge over this stream of ill repute. In Calcutta one of his first duties, self-imposed but accepted by government, was to complete his brother Thomas's canal linking the River Hooghly at Calcutta with more easterly branches of the Ganges, work on which had been interrupted by his brother's sudden death in 1830.

He was a man who had to fill every waking moment

with intense activity. Victor Jacquemont calls him 'the wittiest man in India' (*Letters from India*, 1834, 1.166) and describes him in Benares devoting his mornings to his own manifold projects, his days to work at the mint, and his evenings to musical entertainments (Jacquemont, *Voyage dans l'Inde*, 1.341–5). From the recollections of his brother William he emerges as a charming and gracious individual who 'carried everything we did together to perfection, whether in writing, drawing, music or invention of any kind' (W. Prinsep, 1.126). His enthusiasm emerges from his memorial bust, executed with William's help, with its round, open, and generous face, and wild tufts of hair emerging from the crown.

The heavy labours to which Prinsep subjected himself began to tell on his health, and in 1838 he fell severely ill. He suffered from recurrent headaches and sickness, and eventually from a deterioration in mental functioning. A sea voyage to England afforded no relief. He arrived in England in a very poor condition which did not improve. He died in London on 22 April 1840 in the house of his sister Sophia Haldimand, at 31 Belgrave Square. The news of his death was greeted with the greatest dismay in Calcutta, and subscriptions for memorials immediately opened among both the European and Indian communities. The former commissioned a bust from Francis Chantrey, finished by Henry Weekes, for the Asiatic Society's rooms in Calcutta; the latter subscribed to an elegant Palladian porch on the river, built by W. Fitzgerald in 1843 and still known as Prinsep's Ghat.   J. P. LOSTY

Valentine Cameron Prinsep (1838–1904), self-portrait, 1883

Sources H. T. Prinsep, 'Memoir of the author', *Essays on Indian antiquities of the late James Princep, F. R. S.*, ed. E. Thomas (1858), 1.i–xvi • H. T. Prinsep, *Three generations in India*, BL OIOC, MSS Eur. C 97, vv1–2 • W. Prinsep, 'Memoirs', and other Prinsep family documents, BL OIOC, MSS Eur. D 1160 • I. E. Cottington, 'High temperature gas thermometry and the platinum metals: some aspects of nineteenth-century developments', *Platinum Metals Review*, 31/4 (1987), 196–207 • C. R. Markham, *A memoir on the Indian surveys*, 2nd edn (1878), 242–6 • R. H. Phillimore, ed., *Historical records of the survey of India*, 3 (1954), 495 • V. Jacquemont, *Voyage dans l'Inde pendant les années 1828 à 1832*, 6 vols. (Paris, 1841), vol. 1, pp. 341–5
Archives BL OIOC, corresp. relating to Asiatic Society of Bengal, MSS Eur. C 351 | RS, corresp. with Sir John Herschel
Likenesses G. Chinnery, chalk drawing, *c.*1820, priv. coll. • H. Weekes, marble bust, 1843, Victoria Memorial Hall, Calcutta, India • C. G., lithograph, BM • C. Grant, lithograph (after his earlier work), repro. in *Public characters* (1838) • plaster bust (after H. Weekes), BL OIOC
Wealth at death see will, BL OIOC, Bengal wills, 1840, pt 3, L/AG/34/29/62

Prinsep, John (1746–1830). *See under* Prinsep, Henry Thoby (1792–1878).

Prinsep, Valentine Cameron (1838–1904), artist and writer, was born on St Valentine's day (14 February), 1838, at Calcutta, the second of the four children of Henry Thoby *Prinsep (1792–1878), Indian civil servant and author, and his wife, Sara Monckton (1816–1887), one of seven 'singularly handsome' daughters of James Pattle. Prinsep's parents retired to London in 1843, living first at 9 Chesterfield Street, and then from 1851 at Little Holland House on the Holland estate in Kensington, where they were joined the following year by the artist George

Frederic Watts. Prinsep was educated at Haileybury College, with the expectation of joining the Indian Civil Service. However, even before leaving school in 1856 he had decided to become an artist. He was influenced by the salon his mother had established at Little Holland House around Watts. The guests, almost all of whom became Prinsep's friends, included Tennyson, Thackeray, Browning, Holman Hunt, Millais, Leighton, D. G. Rossetti, and Burne-Jones; Sara Prinsep's sister, Julia Margaret Cameron, took photographs of the group.

With financial support from his father and tuition from Watts, Prinsep embarked on a career which brought him recognition by his peers as a dedicated artist, though never of the first rank: 'well known in Art and highly esteemed in Society … a thorough artist in his aspirations, a fine painter, and a right good honest man' (*VF*, 23). His engaging personality made him welcome in the country houses of the aristocracy and newly rich industrialists, in London clubs and theatres; his large build and shock of hair earned him the nickname Buzz. In 1857 he came under the influence of Pre-Raphaelitism when invited by Rossetti to help decorate the Union debating hall in Oxford with scenes from Sir Thomas Malory's *Morte d'Arthur*. He chose the story of *Sir Pelleas and the Lady Etarde*. In 1859 he took a studio in Charlotte Street, London, close to Burne-Jones, travelled in Italy with him, and exhibited, for the first time, *The Queen was in the Parlour Eating Bread and Honey* at the Hogarth Club (Manchester City Art Galleries). The first of his paintings to be exhibited at the Royal Academy, *How Bianco Capello Sought to Poison her Brother-in-Law the Cardinal de Medici* (1862), was still influenced by the movement and shortly before his death he wrote, for the

Magazine of Art (1904), an entertaining account of his early experiences with Rossetti.

Prinsep studied at Gleyre's atelier in Paris from 1859 to 1860. Shortly after returning to London he became friends with George Du Maurier, who had also attended the atelier and used Prinsep as a model for Taffy in his novel *Trilby* (1894). Du Maurier introduced Prinsep to the artists of the St John's Wood clique, who became the next major influence on his work. *Home from the Gleaning* (exh. RA, 1875) and *The Linen Gatherers* (exh. RA, 1876) are strongly influenced by two members of this eclectic group, Frederick Walker and George Heming Mason. Prinsep's closest friend was Frederic Leighton, whom he first met at Little Holland House about 1856. In 1860 both joined the 38th Middlesex (Artists') rifle volunteer corps, from which Prinsep retired as major in 1885; four years later they acquired neighbouring plots of land in Holland Park Road on which to build studio-houses. Prinsep's costs were paid by his father; Philip Webb, who had recently completed the Red House for William Morris, was his architect. Though considerably altered, the house survives (14 Holland Park Road).

Through his father's Indian connections Prinsep was commissioned by Lord Lytton, viceroy of India, to paint the Delhi imperial assemblage to celebrate Queen Victoria's accession to the title empress of India in 1877 (Royal Collection). The 27 foot-long painting received a mixed reception when it was exhibited at the Royal Academy in 1880. *Vanity Fair* referred to it as 'that Eastern monstrosity'. However, the commission resulted in Prinsep's election as an associate of the Royal Academy in 1878 and in a number of fine paintings based on his Indian travels: *A Nautch Girl* (exh. RA, 1878) and *The Roum-i-Sultana* (exh. RA, 1879) were bought by the prince of Wales (Royal Collection). Prinsep wrote a lively account of the visit, *Imperial India: an Artist's Journals* (1879). He also tried his hand at writing plays while completing the durbar painting. He was a friend of the actor John Hare, painting his portrait in 1879. The same year Hare produced and acted in Prinsep's two plays: *Cousin Dick*, at the Court Theatre, and *Monsieur le duc*, at the St James's. Later Prinsep wrote two novels: *Virginie: a Tale of one Hundred Years Ago* (1890) and *The Story of Abibal the Tsourian* (1893).

On 28 July 1884 Prinsep married Florence (*b.* 1859), daughter of Frederick Richard Leyland (1831–1892), a Liverpool shipping millionaire and patron of Rossetti, Burne-Jones, and Whistler. Florence's annual income was reputed to be £10,000, and Prinsep was now a wealthy man (Leighton had given him financial support after his father's death). Prinsep joined the boards of shipping and investment companies, he extended his London house, bought property by the sea at Pevensey, and acquired an apartment on the Grand Canal in Venice.

Prinsep continued to paint, exhibiting at the Royal Academy every year until his death. He was elected a royal academician in 1894 and was appointed professor of painting in 1901 (his lectures were privately published in 1901 and 1902). Of his later works, *At the Golden Gate* (exh. RA, 1882; Manchester City Art Galleries) and *Ayesha* (exh. RA, 1887; Tate Collection) are orientalist in style: his diploma work, *La révolution* (exh. RA, 1896), is a historical piece, set during the French Revolution. He also painted his wife and their three sons, Thoby, Anthony, and Nicholas, as well as commissioned portraits. A number of his works are in the South London Art Gallery. Prinsep died on 11 November 1904 at Welbeck House, Welbeck Street, London, after a prostate operation and was buried in the Brompton cemetery. He was survived by his wife.

CAROLINE DAKERS

Sources P. Saville, 'Valentine Cameron Prinsep in relation to the practice and theory of academic painting in late 19th century', BLitt diss., U. Oxf., 1970 • N. Jarrah, 'Valentine Cameron Prinsep', MA diss., Courtauld Inst., 1983 • C. Dakers, *The Holland Park circle* (1999) • F. Steelcroft, 'Mr Val C. Prinsep RA', *Strand Magazine*, 12 (1896), 603–15 • Graves, *RA exhibitors* • V. Prinsep, 'A chapter from a painter's reminiscence', *Magazine of Art*, 28 (1903–4), 281–4, 338–42 • V. Prinsep, *Imperial India: an artist's journals* (1879) • *Morning Post* (14 Nov 1904) • *The Times* (14 Nov 1904) • *VF* (1880) • *Financial Times* (14 Nov 1904) • private information (2004) • *CGPLA Eng. & Wales* (1905) • *DNB*

Archives Herts. ALS • priv. coll., papers | priv. coll., Philip Webb MSS • RIBA, Philip Webb designs

Likenesses D. W. Wynfield, photograph, *c.*1860–1869, National Museum of Photography, Film and Television, Bradford, Royal Photographic Society collection • D. W. Wynfield, photograph, *c.*1862, NPG • H. N. O'Neil, group portrait, oils, 1869 (*The Billiard Room of the Garrick Club*), Garr. Club • G. F. Watts, oils, 1872, priv. coll. • J. M. Cameron, photograph, 1874, National Museum of Photography, Film and Television, Bradford, Royal Photographic Society collection • V. C. Prinsep, self-portrait, oils, 1883, Aberdeen Art Gallery [*see illus.*] • J. P. Mayall, photograph, 1884, repro. in F. G. Stephens, ed., 'Artists at home', 1884 • A. Legros, etching, U. Hull • London Stereoscopic Co., cabinet photograph, NPG • R. W. Robinson, photograph, NPG; repro. in *Members and Associates of the Royal Academy of Arts* (1891) • Spy [L. Ward], chromolithograph caricature, NPG; repro. in *VF* (13 Jan 1877) • wood-engraving, NPG; repro. in *ILN* (3 May 1879)

Wealth at death £13,636 2*s.* 9*d.*: resworn probate, 7 Feb 1905, *CGPLA Eng. & Wales*

Prior, Arthur Norman (1914–1969), philosopher, was born on 4 December 1914 in Masterton, New Zealand, the only child of Norman Henry Prior, physician, and his wife, Elizabeth Munton Rothesay Teague, who died two weeks after giving birth. He grew up with two brothers and a sister from his father's second marriage. Educated at Wairarapa high school in Masterton, he took a BA in philosophy and psychology (1935) and an MA in philosophy (1936) at Otago University, Dunedin. The grandson of two Methodist missionaries in Australia, he became a Presbyterian at university and was active in the Student Christian Movement (SCM) as a Christian socialist. In 1937 he married an SCM colleague, Claire Hunter, and sailed to Europe. For three years the couple lived a bohemian existence, supported principally by religious journalism. In 1940 Prior returned to New Zealand and worked as a railwayman, dock labourer, and hotel bellman before joining the Royal New Zealand Air Force in 1942. In 1943 his first marriage was dissolved and he married Mary Laura Wilkinson, daughter of Frank Howitt Wilkinson, a Presbyterian minister of Timaru, New Zealand. She was then a zoology undergraduate at Otago and was later to become a historian. One son and one daughter were born to this happy marriage.

On demobilization Prior resumed the academic career he had begun at Otago as assistant lecturer under John Findlay in 1937. From 1946 to 1958 he taught philosophy at the University of Canterbury at Christchurch, as lecturer, senior lecturer, and (from 1952) professor. Initially isolated as a philosopher, he frequented the literary group around Charles Brasch which ran the journal *Landfall*. His earliest philosophical publications concerned religion and ethics; his first book, *Logic and the Basis of Ethics* (1949), combined historical erudition with contemporary relevance in a manner typical of him throughout his life.

The logic of that title was very informal, but soon Prior began to take an interest in logic which, if at first traditional, was much more formal. In 1951 he completed a 220,000 word textbook entitled 'The craft of formal logic'; it was never published in his lifetime, but a shorter and almost totally rewritten version was published in 1955 as *Formal Logic*. By now Prior had shifted his attention from traditional logic to the mathematical logic in which henceforth he worked; this change was largely due to the Polish logician Jan Lukasiewicz, in homage to whom he used, throughout his life, the unfashionable Polish logical notation.

In 1954, taking cues from the modal logic of the Stoics and from some remarks on time by Findlay, Prior conceived the idea that the logical relationships between sentences in past, present, and future tenses could be set out as a self-standing branch of logic. In the same year he hosted a visit to New Zealand by Gilbert Ryle, and impressed him with the clarity and independence of his thought. He received, and accepted, an invitation to visit Oxford to give the John Locke lectures.

In these lectures, delivered in the first six months of 1956, Prior presented his new ideas on the relationship between modal logic and the grammar of tense. Their publication in 1957 as *Time and Modality* launched the tense-logic that he was to pursue until 1968 and that was to be developed by many other logicians before and after his death. Tense-logic is significant for metaphysics as showing the coherence of the thesis that tense belongs to the real and not just to the mental world; but it also has importance for linguistics and computer science.

In Oxford in 1956 Prior met many British logicians, helped to organize logic colloquia, and lectured in many universities. He quickly made his name in the British philosophical community, and he accepted an invitation to hold a newly created chair of philosophy in Manchester. At the end of 1958 he and his family left New Zealand for good. While at Christchurch he had been ordained as a church elder. On arrival in England in 1959 he severed his links with Presbyterianism, though he retained an expert knowledge of Scottish Calvinism until his death.

Prior held the Manchester chair for six years. During this time he published many insightful, and often provocative, papers on metaphysics. His researches into tense-logic led him to reflect on the nature of time and on traditional problems about foreknowledge and determinism, the persistence of substances through time, and the criteria for identity and the reidentification of individuals. The papers he published on these topics were original contributions to ongoing philosophical debates; but in all of them he was able to draw on an extraordinary reservoir of knowledge of medieval logic as well as post-Reformation theology. Most of his papers on these topics were collected in the volume *Papers on Time and Tense*, published in 1968 just before his death.

In 1962 Prior spent a quarter at Chicago as a visiting professor. In 1963 he was elected as a fellow of the British Academy, and in 1965–6 he held the Flint professorship of philosophy at the University of California at Los Angeles. There he was surrounded, for the first time, by enthusiasts for tense-logic. With the aid of colleagues and pupils he worked out a new and mathematically much more sophisticated presentation of his system, published in 1967 as *Past, Present and Future*, a book which surveyed the whole field which had developed from the initial enrichment of classical logical calculi with symbols for forming past and future tenses. It presented different formal systems corresponding to different traditional positions about time, fate, and chance.

On his return to Manchester in January 1966 Prior received an invitation from Balliol College, Oxford, to take up a tutorial fellowship recently vacated by R. M. Hare. Though the transition involved an increased teaching load and a loss of salary and status, Prior accepted the invitation and quickly became one of the most valued members of Balliol's governing body. His college fellowship went with a university lecturership, which was upgraded to a readership in 1969.

Throughout his life, whether at Christchurch, Manchester, or Oxford, Prior was an inspiring and selfless teacher. He and his wife kept open house for his pupils at all hours. They never set up defences to keep private life separate from academic. They were generous hosts, happy to allow friends to use their Shropshire cottage or to join them in cruises on the canals which they loved. Prior had a special gift for making friends with children, entering into their games and sharing their fantasies. Throughout life he himself preserved the virtues of childhood in the open frankness of his friendship and the wide-eyed enthusiasm of his curiosity. He was quite free of pretence or pomp, and could never be persuaded to take trouble over the appearance of his clothes or his hair.

When following a new line in research, Prior could write at enormous speed and in the most adverse circumstances; *Formal Logic* was largely completed in nine weeks, and the first version of tense-logic was worked out during horrible months while he was nursing his two children through tuberculosis and his wife was hospitalized with the same disease.

In 1969 Prior's first Balliol sabbatical fell due: he arranged to spend it at the University of Oslo. But during the previous year he had suffered from both rheumatism and angina pectoris, and though he obtained initial relief from cortisone in Norway he suffered a lethal heart attack on 7 October 1969. He was cremated in Trondheim, where he had died, and a memorial ceremony was held in Balliol. Between 1971 and 1976 three volumes of his writings were published posthumously (*Objects of Thought*, *The Doctrine of Propositions and Terms*, and *Papers in Logic and Ethics*, all edited by Peter Geach and Anthony Kenny). An unfinished work was completed by K. Fine and published as *Worlds, Times and Selves* in 1979. Prior's papers were deposited in the Bodleian Library in Oxford.   ANTHONY KENNY

Sources A. Kenny, 'Arthur Norman Prior, 1914–1969', *PBA*, 56 (1970), 321–49 • O. Flo, 'Bibliography of the philosophical writings of A. N. Prior', *Logic and reality: essays on the legacy of Arthur Prior*, ed. B. J. Copeland (1996), 519–32 • I. Thomas, 'In memoriam A. N. Prior (1914–69)', *Notre Dame Journal of Formal Logic*, 12 (1971), 129–30 • *DNB* • personal knowledge (2004) • private information (2004)
Archives Bodl. Oxf., philosophical MSS
Likenesses photograph, Balliol Oxf.; repro. in *PBA*, 61, pl. xxii
Wealth at death £8866: probate, 13 Nov 1969, *CGPLA Eng. & Wales*

Prior, Edward Schroder (1852–1932), architect and writer on architecture, was born on 4 January 1852 at Croom's Hill, Greenwich, Kent, the sixth of eleven children of John Venn Prior (1812–1855), barrister, and his wife, Hebe Catherine Templer (*d.* 1887), headmistress, the daughter of James Templer (1787–1858), solicitor, and his first wife, Catherine (*d.* 1845). After his father's early death, his mother moved to Roxeth Mead, Harrow on the Hill, to take advantage of the residents' right to reduced tuition at Harrow School, which Prior attended from 1863 to 1870. A scholar–athlete, Prior won a Sayer scholarship to Gonville and Caius College, Cambridge (1870–1874), where he was a blue and amateur high-jump champion (1872). A disappointing third class in the classical tripos, however, reflected his growing preoccupation with Gothic architecture.

Articled to the architect Norman Shaw from 1874 to 1879, Prior absorbed the office styles of Old English and Queen Anne and made sketching tours of Belgium, France, and England. His leading role in the arts and crafts movement began with fellow pupils and assistants, including W. R. Lethaby, who with him founded in 1884 the Art Workers' Guild, the central metropolitan organization of the movement, and its forerunner, the St George's Art Society (1883–6). As Shaw's clerk of works at Ilkley, Yorkshire (1877–9), he gained a respect for the process of building and the importance of building craftsmen, which profoundly marked his architecture.

In 1885 Prior married Louisa Maunsell (*d.* 1942), second daughter of the Revd F. W. Maunsell of Symondsbury, and they lived at 6 Bloomsbury Square, London, where his daughters Laura and Christobel were born. At 17 Southampton Street, London, he developed a small but well-tended practice, which concentrated on domestic and ecclesiastical work, but also featured school and university buildings. In the 1880s he built mainly in Bridport, Dorset, notably Quay Terrace, West Bay (1884–5), in Cambridge (Henry Martyn Hall, 1885–7), and at Harrow School (for example, the music school, 1888–9), where he had strong family and personal connections. In the 1880s he made additions to Caius College and laid out estates on college building land and later designed a medical school

Edward Schroder Prior (1852–1932), by Elliott & Fry

for the university in a simplified, mannered classicism (1899–1902; now the zoology department).

Both tradition and invention are represented in Prior's influential Edwardian houses: The Barn, Exmouth, Devon (1895–7), and Home Place, Holt, Norfolk (1903–5), which were, in part, stimulated by C. F. A. Voysey, his neighbour in St John's Wood. While exploring the surface effects of pattern, colour, and texture in local vernacular materials, he took an experimental approach to form and planning using, for example, an X-shaped 'butterfly' plan, materials such as reinforced concrete, and methods which involved reorganization of the building process. His later houses, such as Greystones, Highcliffe, Dorset (1911–12), were mellower, though like the others, indivisible from their gardens. Although Prior was pronounced 'biologically incapable of the *via media*' (Blomfield, 90), his true measure can be found in these gardens, where he demonstrated his preference for practice over theory, building with feeling and direct knowledge of working conditions.

Prior is most lastingly known as the author of *A History of Gothic Art in England* (1900), which argued for the English origins of Gothic architecture, based on regional differences of materials and craft techniques. He also wrote numerous articles and four other books on medieval and contemporary architecture, best combined in *The Cathedral Builders of England* (1905). He patented Prior's Early English Glass, employed most extensively in his restoration of St Michael's, Framlingham, Suffolk (1889), and designed three outstanding arts and crafts churches: Holy Trinity, Bothenhampton, Dorset (1884–9), St Andrew,

Roker, co. Durham (1905–7; with Randall Wells), and St Osmund, Parkstone, Dorset (1913–16; with Arthur Grove).

Appointed Slade professor of fine art at Cambridge University (1912–32) and fellow of Caius College (1912–20), he retired from practice, continued writing, lectured badly on architectural studies, and established the school of architecture. He died of cancer at Westgate, Chichester, on 19 August 1932 and was buried in an unmarked grave at St Mary's Church, Apuldram, Sussex.

LYNNE WALKER

Sources L. Walker, 'E. S. Prior, 1852–1932', PhD diss., U. Lond., 1978 · RIBA BAL, manuscripts and archives collection · private information (2004) · The Caian, 41 (1932–3), 1–7 · R. Blomfield, Richard Norman Shaw RA (1940) · Venn, Alum. Cant.
Archives CUL, archive · Gon. & Caius Cam., archives · NRA, priv. coll., family MSS
Likenesses W. Strang, lithograph, 1907, probably priv. coll. · Elliott & Fry, photograph, NPG [see illus.]

Prior, Sir James (c.1790–1869), writer, son of Matthew Prior, was born at Lisburn, co. Antrim, about 1790. He entered the navy as a surgeon, and sailed from Plymouth in the *Nisus* frigate on 22 June 1810 for the Cape of Good Hope, Mauritius, the Seychelles Islands, Madras, and Java (at the capture of which by the British in September 1811 he was present). This journey he described in a *Voyage in the Indian Seas* (1820). His next expedition (1812–13), in the same frigate, was to South Africa, Brazil, and other areas, and was described in a *Voyage Along the Eastern Coast of Africa* (1819).

Prior was present at the surrender of Heligoland and, in 1815, at the surrender of Napoleon. He then became staff surgeon to the Chatham division of the Royal Marines, and to three of the royal yachts. In 1817 he married Dorothea, widow of E. James. She died at Oxford Terrace, Hyde Park, London, on 28 November 1841.

Prior was appointed assistant to the director-general of the medical department of the navy, and on 1 August 1843 he was created deputy inspector of hospitals. In 1847 he married Caroline, widow of Charles H. Watson. He was knighted at St James's Palace on 11 June 1858. In 1830 he had been elected to the Royal Irish Academy, the Athenaeum, and the Society of Antiquaries. For many years before his death he lived at 20 Norfolk Crescent, Hyde Park, London; but he died at Brighton on 14 November 1869, survived by his widow who died on 14 December 1881 aged eighty-five.

Prior's chief works were biographies. His *Memoir of the Life and Character of Edmund Burke* (1824) ran to several editions and was quite well regarded. His *Life of Oliver Goldsmith* (2 vols., 1837) and his *Miscellaneous Works of Goldsmith* (4 vols., 1837) were assiduously compiled. When John Forster (1812–1876) brought out *The Life and Adventures of Oliver Goldsmith* (1848) he was accused by Prior of wholesale plagiarism, an accusation which Forster consistently denied. Washington Irving, in his *Life of Goldsmith* (1849), admitted his obligations to 'the indefatigable Prior', who none the less denounced him in *Goldsmith's Statue*.

W. P. COURTNEY, rev. ELIZABETH BAIGENT

Sources Men of the time (1868) · GM, 2nd ser., 17 (1842), 112 [death notice of Dorothea Prior] · Allibone, Dict. · CGPLA Eng. & Wales (1869) · Proceedings of the Society of Antiquaries of London, 2nd ser., 4 (1867–70), 472, 475–6
Likenesses W. Brockedon, black and red chalk drawing, 1832, NPG · W. Drummond, lithograph (after E. U. Eddis), BM, NPG; repro. in Athenaeum portraits (1835) · E. U. Eddis, portrait · D. Turner, lithograph (after E. U. Eddis)
Wealth at death under £25,000: administration, 9 Dec 1869, CGPLA Eng. & Wales

Prior, Matthew (1664–1721), poet and diplomat, was born in Stephen's Alley, Westminster, on either 21 or 23 July 1664, the son of Elizabeth (probably *née* Pennefather) and George Prior (d. c.1675), a London joiner. The fifth of six children, he was the only one to survive early childhood.

Early years and education, 1664–1687 Prior's father had left Dorset to practise his joiner's trade in Westminster, where two of his brothers were already keeping taverns—Arthur, The Rhenish tavern on Channel Row, Samuel, The Rummer tavern between Whitehall and Charing Cross. Prior's mother appears to have married below her class—she was probably Elizabeth Pennefather, from a good Dorset family. His father George, however, appears to have prospered in his carpenter's trade, and could afford to send young Matthew to nearby Westminster School, which was presided over by the formidable Dr Richard Busby. Dr Busby emphasized strict discipline, the traditional classical curriculum, extemporaneous composition in both prose and verse, and oratory. Prior was later to praise what Thomas Sprat, bishop of Rochester, had called 'the genius of that Place'—that even very young boys there were made to compose extemporaneous verses and declamations in a very short space of time.

His father's death—when Prior was about eleven—had forced the family to withdraw him from Westminster School and put him to work at his uncle Arthur's Rhenish tavern. A year later Charles Sackville, sixth earl of Dorset, came into The Rhenish tavern and found the twelve-year-old Matthew behind the bar, reading Horace. Dorset asked Matthew to construe a passage or two of Horace, then to turn a Horatian ode into English. He did so with such skill that on subsequent visits to the tavern Dorset often asked him to entertain his friends and himself by turning Horace or Ovid into English verse. Finally, the earl of Dorset offered to pay Prior's tuition to return to Westminster School, if his uncle Arthur would pay for his clothing and other necessities. The Priors gratefully accepted this offer, and Matthew returned to Westminster School about 1676, becoming a king's scholar there in 1681, an award based on his distinction in classical languages.

Westminster king's scholars usually went to Christ Church, Oxford, and Dr Busby and the earl of Dorset expected Prior to do the same. Instead, he defied them and chose to attend Cambridge, where three of his best friends (Charles and James Montagu and George Stepney) were already in attendance or planned to be. Prior applied for and in the spring of 1683 received one of the first five duchess of Somerset scholarships to St John's College, Cambridge. By the terms of this scholarship Prior was exempted from paying tuition and received an allowance

Matthew Prior (1664–1721), by Sir Godfrey Kneller, 1700

of 5s. a week for living expenses, a bedroom that he shared with four other young men, and a private study. During his four years at St John's College, Prior followed a curriculum still heavy in logic and divinity, one that he later felt had turned him away from poetry and in the direction of politics and prose. Yet while he was an undergraduate at St John's he wrote more than thirty Latin pieces and a dozen poems in English. None would have made his reputation as a poet, but he thought highly enough of them to preserve them carefully for the rest of his life. They show the direction in which his writing of poetry in English was moving: they are particularly concerned with royal or aristocratic occasions, and in them he utilizes pastoral or mythological machinery to advance his own causes.

On 9 February 1687 Prior graduated BA, eleventh in the *orde senioritatis*. He produced a thirty-four-line Latin hexameter poem in honour of the occasion, arguing against Thomas Hobbes that 'Fuit justum et injustum ante Leges Civiles'.

Years in London, Cambridge, and Burleigh, 1687–1690 Soon after graduating from Cambridge, Prior returned to London, probably largely because of the death of his uncle Arthur, who died there in May 1687, leaving Prior £100. For the next three years Prior was reaching out for a professional role he had not yet defined, but which he was increasingly convinced he might find in politics rather than poetry. On 3 April 1688 he was entered as a Keyton fellow at St John's and moved into the fellows' quarters there, assigned to one of its two medical fellowships, and was later required to lecture on Galen as Linacre lecturer (1706–10).

Prior seems to have spent most of this period (1687–90) as tutor to the two sons of the earl of Exeter at Burleigh and as a fellow at St John's College. In his poems of these years there is an increasing sense that poetry is not his métier and that politics might be, if he were given an opportunity to serve in that sphere. *The Hind and the Panther Transvers'd* (1687), written in collaboration with Charles Montagu, was a satiric attack on Dryden's *The Hind and the Panther*, out less than two months earlier, and won instant public acclaim for both Montagu and Prior. 'On Exodus Iii. 14' was an irregular ode in the style of Cowley, later to be echoed frequently in the fideistic sections of Alexander Pope's *Essay on Man*. Apparently one of Prior's favourite serious pieces, he was to use the Exodus ode as the lead poem in both his collected editions of *Poems on Several Occasions*. 'Journey to Copt-Hall', written in this period but not printed until 1907, is interesting chiefly as a predecessor, in content, method, and tone, thirty years earlier, of Prior's now famous 'Down-Hall: a Ballad'. A group of four poems addressed to Fleetwood Shepherd, the wit and poet who served as intermediary between the earl of Dorset and the many poets whose patron he became, show two of the other directions in which Prior was moving in his light verse: the mock heroic and the familiar verse epistle.

Years at The Hague, 1690–1697 Prior's opportunity to enter politics came on 1 November 1690, when he was appointed as secretary to Charles Berkeley, Viscount Dursley, British ambassador to The Hague. Prior's responsibilities included issuing or refusing passports, forwarding newspapers with details relevant to England, sending on with his own comments newsletters arriving from various important towns in the League of Augsburg, and reporting details of battles in the war and of local diplomatic gossip. For three of his seven years at The Hague (1692–5) there was no English ambassador in residence there and Prior fulfilled those duties, acting as chief minister with skill, diligence, and good sense while receiving the pay only of a secretary. The Hague was at this time an important listening post and relay station in the Nine Years' War, which had already been going on for two years when Prior was appointed to The Hague and was to continue for almost seven more. Finally, Edward, Viscount Villiers, later earl of Jersey, assumed office as ambassador to The Hague in September 1695. For Prior it was a fortunate appointment. Both men were alumni of St John's College, and Prior's favourite cousin, Katharine, had married Colonel George Villiers, Edward's cousin. The earl of Jersey requested that Prior remain at The Hague and that his salary be doubled. When the peace negotiations of the treaty of Ryswick were beginning, Prior received the appointment he requested to be secretary to the embassy at The Hague, beginning on 10 March 1697. In the subsequent drawing up of the treaty of Ryswick (9 May – 20/21 September 1697), it was Prior's function to check the French and Latin versions of the negotiations.

Prior's poems during his seven years at The Hague assumed a much more laureate bent, celebrating British war victories and events in the life of the royal family.

From this period dates his most famous and successful such poem, 'An English Ballad, on the Taking of Namur by the King of Great Britain, 1695', in which Prior takes Nicolas Boileau's earlier 'Ode sur la prise de Namur, par les armes du roy, l'année 1692', in a stanza by stanza refutation and demythologizing. Boileau had referred to himself (or Pindar) as an audacious eagle; Prior reduces him to a handsomely paid vulture. Boileau had described Louis XIV's plume as a leading star; Prior retorts that it was more like a short-lived meteor.

Prior wrote two other equally successful poems in two very different veins during this same seven-year Hague period. In 'Written in the Year 1696' Prior describes his unusual Saturday and Sunday activities at The Hague and hence, by indirection, his usual daily activities there. 'To the Honourable Charles Montague, Esq.' strikes the note of melancholy which was to characterize Prior's treatment of a favourite moral insistence that mankind can console itself with imagined pleasures, for the truth, if seen, is bleak.

Prior was physically much the same figure when he first went to The Hague at twenty-six as he was thirty years later: thin, wooden-faced, red-cheeked, already somewhat easy prey to the lung and intestinal disorders that were to mark his remaining thirty years and eventually claim his life.

By the year he went to The Hague, Prior had also established an intimate relationship with Jane, or Jinny, Ansley (also known as Jane Flanders), and while helping to draw up the treaty of Ryswick in 1697 he had met at the Congress of Ryswick a man who was to become his friend, amanuensis, transcriber, and preserver of his manuscript poems after his death, Adrian Drift. Like Prior, Drift was London-born and came to the Congress of Ryswick in the service of the earl of Jersey.

First years in Paris, 1698–1699 On his return to England in November 1697 Prior expected to be sent to Dublin to assume his duties as secretary to the lords justices. Instead, he was sent to the reopened British embassy in Paris as secretary to the new ambassador, William Bentinck, first earl of Portland. Prior's appointment was announced by 11 December 1697; he and Portland left for Paris one month later, on 21 January 1698. During his brief sojourn in London, Prior had been nominated as a fellow of the Royal Society. He was elected to membership in his absence, possibly on 23 March 1698. Meanwhile in Paris, Prior had his first private audience with Louis XIV on 4 February 1698; in mid-August of the same year he saw the exiled James II and his queen; still later he glimpsed the young Stuart prince. Prior had few official duties during his early stay in France, his main responsibility being to report to his superiors in England the activities of those in power in France and of the Jacobites there. When the earl of Portland left France in June 1698, the earl of Jersey was appointed to succeed him, arriving in September of that year.

In his initial nineteen-month stay in Paris, Prior found his expenses painfully greater than his pay, so when in April 1699 the fourth earl and first duke of Manchester was appointed to replace Jersey in Paris and Jersey was appointed secretary of state for the southern department, Prior at his own request was sent back to London as under-secretary of state, leaving Paris on 27 August 1699. In these nineteen months in Paris he had produced no poems, but had established a network of friendships and favourable recognitions from such political figures as the duc de Villeroy, the marquis de Torcy, and Louis XIV himself, and such literary figures as Boileau, Dacier, and Fontenelle.

Further London years, 1699–1711 From Paris, Prior travelled first to Loo in Holland to report to William III. Through William's intercession, Prior was permitted to keep his Irish post, *in absentia*, and was given an allowance of £600 per year as well, to continue until he received a new government post. From Loo, Prior journeyed to The Hague and returned from there to London with William III and the earl of Jersey. For the remaining two years of William's life, Prior acted mainly as a peripatetic diplomatic agent, going on repeated journeys to Paris and Marly, in secret negotiations with Louis XIV on the second partition treaty. On 28 June 1700 he was appointed a commissioner of the Board of Trade and Plantations, succeeding John Locke, who had resigned because of poor health. The Board of Trade and Plantations oversaw the governing of all the American colonies and supervised all international English trade.

Although Prior was frequently ill during this twelve-year sojourn in London, it was also a significant social period for him. By 1700 he had become a member of the Kit-Cat Club, the gathering of whig wits that included Charles Montagu, Jacob Tonson, Joseph Addison, Richard Steele, William Congreve, and the earl of Dorset. But Prior, like his friend Jonathan Swift a few years later, found himself moving away from the whig political positions to the tory ones, especially in his belief that England needed a strong king, unhampered by the majority opposition in parliament.

In 1700 Prior decided to run for the position of member of parliament from Cambridge, presenting himself as an independent. When it became apparent that he had neither the funds nor the time to run for this position, he accepted instead, from the earl of Dorset, membership in parliament from the pocket borough of East Grinstead, a position that he held for five months (February–June 1701). The last surviving child of Queen Anne had just died, and the whigs feared that on Anne's death a Stuart would be brought in from France to rule. The issue came to a climax during Prior's brief term in parliament in a vote of censure on the partition treaty, which Prior himself had had some hand in drawing up. The treaty had never been popular in England, had never been signed by the Austrian emperor, and was later repudiated by Louis XIV. Prior voted with the tories to impeach the four leading whigs involved in drawing up the treaty—barons Somers and Halifax (Prior's old friend Charles Montagu) and the earls of Orford and Portland.

Prior explained later that *not* to vote to impeach these lords would have been to blame William himself for the unpopular treaty, but by his vote he had estranged himself from any further whig patronage and from the whig party itself. The earl of Dorset did not award him again the pocket borough seat in parliament; the earl of Portland and Charles Montagu were no longer his friends; his membership in the Kit-Cat Club was abruptly terminated. Yet Prior avoided much of the bitterness often attendant on political shifts in party; he later patched up his friendship with the Montagus, and Horace Walpole, son of the greatest whig of the eighteenth century, later wrote that 'Prior is much a favourite with me, *though a Tory*, nor did I ever hear anything ill of him. He left his party, but not his friends, and seems to me to have been very amiable' (letter to William Cole, 10 June 1778, in Walpole, *Corr.*, 2.90).

Even in this period of his relative prosperity, Prior often found himself in financial distress. He was not paid his salary as one of the commissioners of trade and plantations from 29 September 1700 to 8 March 1702. Yet in 1700 he had increased his expenses by buying 'Matt's Palace', a Westminster house on the west side of Duke Street, overlooking St James's Park to the rear. A source of great pleasure to Prior, the palatial house was his chief home for the remaining twenty years of his life. During the last three years of William's life, Prior had written a wide-ranging variety of original poems: political poems and laureate verse, love songs, poems to and about children, two more Horatian nostalgic requests for the simple life. But Anne's succession to the throne in 1702 limited Prior's political activities for two reasons—she disapproved of appointing to public political office those of 'meane extraction' (as she described Prior), and Sarah, duchess of Marlborough, her trusted friend, considered herself Prior's implacable enemy.

During this same period in London, Prior courted Elizabeth Singer (later Elizabeth Rowe), the poet, whom he met at Longleat, the country seat of Viscount Weymouth, in the autumn of 1703. He wrote her nine extant letters and two poems, but neither of the participants seems to have taken the courtship very seriously. Slightly later during this same period (between 1706 and 1708), Jane Ansley was replaced in Prior's affections by Anne Durham, who remained his mistress for perhaps a decade, until she was at least twenty-six. When he returned to Paris she accompanied him. When the two finally parted, Prior set her up in business, apparently as proprietor of a small shop, and left her £300 in his will at his death three years afterwards. Less demanding than his other two mistresses, she seemed genuinely grieved at his death and satisfied with her legacy.

In 1709 Prior published *Poems on Several Occasions*, the first of two so-named collections of his poetry that he was to supervise and bring out during his lifetime. Prior himself spoke of the poetry contained in this collection as divided into four categories—'Public Panegyrics', 'Amorous Odes', 'Idle Tales', and 'Serious Reflections'—but some of its most famous poems (*Henry and Emma*, 'An English Padlock', and 'Jinny the Just') do not fit easily into any one of these four categories.

Another equally significant result for Prior of these dozen years when he was based in London was the cementing of his friendship with Swift and the Tory Brothers Club, which ranged from seventeen to twenty-two members, and met weekly during the last years of Queen Anne's reign. Swift's *Journal to Stella* records at least thirteen occasions when Prior dined with Swift, often with all the Brothers but sometimes with only two or three of them. On 21 February 1711 Swift records that he and Prior often walked together in St James's Park (behind Prior's 'Duke Street Palace'). 'This walking is a strange remedy', he wrote to Stella; 'Mr. Prior walks to make himself fat, and I to bring myself down' (J. Swift, *Journal to Stella*, ed. H. Williams, 2 vols., 1948, 1.198). On another occasion he wrote that 'Prior and I stayed on, where we complimented one another for an hour or two upon our mutual wit and poetry' (ibid., 1.98). Several of Swift's anonymous political writings were attributed by their readers to Prior, and Swift reported to Stella that a whig newspaper had called Prior and him 'the two Sosias' (ibid., 2.422).

Negotiations with France, 1712–1715 During the latter part of June 1711 Robert Harley, now earl of Oxford and lord treasurer, asked that Prior be sent to France along with Abbé François Gaultier, the French priest who was serving similarly as a secret negotiator for the opposite side. On 12 July 1711 Prior and Gaultier left London and eventually crossed the channel incognito and journeyed to Fontainebleau. There Prior entered into negotiations with Jean Baptiste Colbert, marquis de Torcy, his friendly acquaintance from his previous mission in Paris over a decade before. After ten days of negotiation and an audience with Louis XIV, Prior (still travelling under a false passport) set out once more for England, this time accompanied by Nicholas Mesnager, who was empowered to carry out further negotiations on behalf of France in England. However, Prior was apprehended and briefly gaoled by an overzealous English customs official. The secret negotiations were secret no longer, and when Swift attempted to divert attention by an imaginative satiric spoof, a pamphlet called *A New Journey to Paris: together with some Secret Transactions between the Fr—h K—g, and an Eng— Gentleman*, he probably made matters worse, for his 'pure inventions' came uncomfortably close at several points to the fiercely guarded truth.

Prior was annoyed, but the peace negotiations continued through August and September 1711, often at Prior's Duke Street house, where Mesnager was sequestered. On 8 October 1711 three documents were signed as preliminary treaties between England and France. Prior's share in drawing up these documents, to become the basis of the treaty of Utrecht, was so conspicuous that the whigs derisively called the preliminary treaties 'Matt's peace'. Yet although the English government wished to name Prior as plenipotentiary to protect Britain's commercial interests, Queen Anne did so only grudgingly, and Lord Strafford, ambassador at The Hague (described by Swift as 'proud as hell'), flatly refused to serve with Prior. Prior nevertheless continued to function behind the scenes during the final negotiations, in both London and Paris. His comings and goings across the channel were at this period of sufficient importance in the mind of the English populace that Swift could write to Stella 'Prior is just come over from France for a few days; I suppose, upon some important affair. I saw him last night, but had no private talk with him. Stocks rise upon his coming' (J. Swift, *Journal to Stella*, ed. H. Williams, 2 vols., 1948, 2.566).

Finally, on 11 April 1713, the treaty of Utrecht was signed between England, Holland, Portugal, Prussia, Savoy, and France, ending the War of the Spanish Succession for these nations. The duke of Shrewsbury wrote to the earl of Oxford, on 8 March 1713, of Prior's role in the treaty of Utrecht:

> I think I may congratulate your Lordship that the peace is made, in which if by good fortune I have any share, I must do Mr. Prior the justice to inform you, that I have been in so particular a manner assisted by his zeal, diligence and ability that I hope he will be immediately encouraged and countenanced by some mark of your Lordship's favour. (*Bath MSS*, 230)

However, in the celebrations that followed the signing of the treaty of Utrecht, Prior fell ill of cholera morbus, recurring fits of vomiting to which he was subject all his mature life, complicated this time by pleurisy as well. Though he remained in Paris, his commission had really expired with the signing of the treaty. He served in the absence of the duke of Shrewsbury as an acting ambassador to France and stayed at Fontainebleau during September and October 1713 at the particular request of Louis XIV. His main role during this period was, at the request of Henry St John, Viscount Bolingbroke, to draw France into a closer military, political, and commercial alliance with England.

Arrest and confinement in London, 1715–1716 After Anne's death on 1 August 1714, Prior continued his duties in Paris, negotiating with Louis XIV about the destruction of Dunkirk. Prior had already incurred a £5000 debt while serving as unofficial and poorly allowanced ambassador in Paris, and his financial condition worsened when he was removed from his post as commissioner of customs. In January 1715 John Dalrymple, earl of Stair, came to Paris to serve as English ambassador to France and to relieve Prior of his duties there. The whig ministry finally agreed to pay off Prior's ambassadorial debts there, chiefly in order to return him to London for questioning.

The House of Commons had set up a secret committee to investigate corruption and treason in the tory party, particularly as related to the negotiations for the treaty of Utrecht, and Prior and Thomas Harley were arrested and confined in their own homes on Duke Street on 9 June 1715. As Prior later noted in his *History of his Own Time*, the secret committee intended to support charges of treason against the earl of Oxford by having Prior verify that the earl had been present at a meeting with Mesnager and Gaultier at Prior's Duke Street house, but Prior replied that either the duke of Shrewsbury or the earl of Oxford had been present, with the other absent, but that he could not recollect, four years later, which man had attended—an answer, Prior recorded, that 'had this Effect, that it was the same Thing as if they were both absent, since they

could not determine which of them was present' (M. Prior, *The History of his Own Time*, 1740, 417–35). Despite repeated questioning, Prior kept to his story. He was confined in the home of the serjeant-at-arms of the House of Commons for more than a year thereafter, and unable to receive guests without permission of the speaker of the House of Commons or to write or receive letters from friends. But he had managed to protect his tory friends while saving his own neck, the most delicate diplomatic manoeuvring of his whole political career.

Prior was released on 26 June 1716, when parliament was prorogued. Even a year later his name, along with Thomas Harley's and the earl of Oxford's, was omitted from the list of those pardoned by the royal Act of Grace in July 1717. The injustice of the whole episode rankled with many tories; Prior's name became synonymous with undeserved political ill treatment. Yet it was during the spring months in London, when his life and those of his friends hung in the balance, that Prior wrote one of his most successful poems in domesticating the myth, his 'Daphne and Apollo', and while under house arrest that he wrote the first draft of one of his equally successful longer poems, a favourite of Alexander Pope's, *Alma, or, The Progress of the Mind*.

Last years, 1716–1721 After he was released, his political career irrevocably ended by the whig–Hanoverian ascent into power, Prior returned to his Duke Street home without any immediate source of funds. To assist him, Bathurst and Lord Harley conceived the scheme of bringing out his poems in a subscription edition. Details of the plan were worked out at a meeting in January 1717, at which Bathurst, Harley, Prior, Pope, Gay, Arbuthnot, and Erasmus Lewis were present. Jacob Tonson, who was much experienced in subscription publication, was to be its publisher, and Alexander Pope, who had himself recently brought out his *Iliad* in a very successful subscription, would be a valuable adviser. When the volume finally appeared in mid-March 1719, it was a large, handsome folio, 1 foot across and 1 yard tall, 500 pages long, with a list of 1445 persons who had subscribed for 1786 books. The book reprinted and reordered all the poems from the 1709 edition of *Poems on Several Occasions* and added a number of poems written since that time, notably *Solomon* and *Alma*. Though he probably did not make as much money as is commonly cited (4000 guineas), Prior undeniably made a small fortune by this publication and found himself comfortably off for the rest of his life, independently wealthy and no longer dependent on repayments from a remiss and recalcitrant government.

Prior thus found himself free to devote himself to his chief interests beyond politics: women, collecting, friends, a country estate, and writing. By 1715 or 1716 he had met Elizabeth Cox, wife of John Cox, a Long Acre tavern keeper, and by 1718 Betty (Lisetta) had apparently replaced Anne Durham (Cloe) as Prior's mistress. Shortly after Prior's death, Dr Arbuthnot wrote that 'PRIOR has had a narrow escape by dying; for, if he had lived, he had married a brimstone bitch, one Bessy Cox, that keeps an alehouse in Long Acre. Her husband died about a month ago' (*European Magazine and London Review*, 13, January 1788, 8).

But an affluent Prior was collecting more than mistresses. A virtuoso, he filled 'Matt's Palace' with treasures: coins, medals, jewels, antique bronzes, prints, drawings, and sculptures. Almost a hundred paintings covered the walls of his drawing-room and its adjacent 'closet'; his bookshelves were lined with several thousand volumes.

Always a gifted and winning public letter-writer when abroad, Prior displayed the same abilities as a private correspondent at home in retirement. Through his correspondence he kept up his friendship with Swift, whom he never saw again, and in person he strengthened his friendship with Adrian Drift, who moved into the Duke Street house at the latest by the end of 1717 to serve as amanuensis, companion, and friend. Drift wrote after Prior's death that Prior had honoured him with 'Esteem and Affection full Five & Twenty Years, without One harsh word ever falling from his Tongue' (Rippy, *Prior*, 38). Finally, the brightest new friendship which Prior made during his last years was with Edward Harley, son of the earl of Oxford, his wife, Lady Harriett, and his daughter, Margaret Cavendish Harley, later duchess of Portland. The Harleys and Prior became close friends; three solemn poems of Prior's last years are responses to the parents, and a charming poem ('My Noble, Lovely, Little Peggy') and the coda to another ('The Turtle and the Sparrow') are directed to young Peggy Harley, these last notable in a century that showed little interest in children's poems.

It was partly through Harley that Prior was able to realize his wish to own a country estate—Down Hall near Hatfield Broad Oak in Essex. Harley provided Prior with half the amount necessary for its purchase in return for an agreement that the property would revert to Harley at Prior's death. Prior engaged James Gibbs to draw up plans and specifications for the new house and Charles Bridgeman to plan its gardens—and wrote a long, colloquial poem, 'Down Hall: a Ballad', about his mixed anticipations and disillusionments connected with its first viewing. But his sudden death put an end to all this estate planning. Down Hall, with a number of improvements already made, reverted to Harley. Two other financial arrangements that Prior had worked out with Harley—with Prior's paying a large lump sum to begin with and Harley then paying Prior an annuity for every year he lived—would have had to exist for ten years for Prior to break even (excluding any calculation of interest). Prior lived only four years after the first and two years after the second. Harley, as Drift wrote, 'was a Gainer by Mr. Prior's Death by the sum of £2058. 6s. 8d.'

During the two years after the appearance of his subscription edition and before his sudden death, Prior continued to write poems, the most notable three being 'The Conversation: a Tale', 'The Turtle and the Sparrow', and ten fragments of 'Predestination, a Poem'.

In August 1721 Prior went to visit Wimpole as a guest of the Harleys. On 11 September he once again fell violently ill of cholera morbus. On 13 September he seemed somewhat better, but the attacks resumed that evening, and he died at one in the afternoon on 18 September 1721. On Friday 22 September his body was carried to Westminster Abbey in a hearse accompanied by a mourning coach, each drawn by six horses and escorted by an outrider. The body lay in state in the historic Jerusalem chamber for three days. The funeral, held on 25 September, was attended by, among others, Richard Shelton (probably Prior's closest personal friend), Dr Arbuthnot, Erasmus Lewis, forty king's scholars from Westminster School, carrying white tapers, seventy men in mourning with branchlights, and a dozen almsmen with torches. A few weeks after the funeral, all those who had been present, and forty-two persons who had not, received gold mourning rings engraved 'M. Prior. Ob: 18.Sep:1721 Aetat 57'. James Gibbs, who had drawn up the plans for Prior's new country estate at Down Hall, instead designed his 'stately Monument', the most sumptuous in the Poets' Corner of Westminster Abbey, planned by Prior himself and wryly described by him as 'this last piece of human vanity'.

Prior, famous British diplomatist, was arguably the most important poet writing in English between the death of Dryden (1700) and the poetic majority of Pope in 1712. To his friend Jonathan Swift he gave specific lines and, more significantly and pervasively, an elegant courtliness and ease of familiar verse that Swift had not hitherto mastered. In 1723, as his prospective editor, Pope read almost everything extant of Prior's, looking closely at Prior as he did at Dryden, as a literary figure whose unusual merit both he and the English reading public conceded without question. His own work displays a lasting awareness of Prior's example. Prior likewise influenced Samuel Johnson in two of Johnson's works that shared Prior's Christian pessimism: *The Vanity of Human Wishes* (1749) and *Rasselas* (1755). Among lesser eighteenth-century writers influenced by the poetry of Prior were William Cowper, Anne Finch, countess of Winchilsea, and John, Charles, and Samuel Wesley the younger in England, Allan Ramsay in Scotland, and Christoph Martin Wieland and Friedrich von Hagedorn in Germany.

As the eighteenth century moved into heavy use of the heroic couplet form, Prior continued to practise other forms commoner in the Restoration—anapaests, tetrameter, lyrical lyrics, *vers de société*—and helped to keep these feet and syllables and tones alive through eighteenth-century English verse, as minor streams within a major current of heroic couplet versification. Finally, his very successful 1717–19 subscription edition of his *Poems on Several Occasions* made a useful point: that a popular poet might make a small fortune from a subscription edition of his original poems, not just as a translator but as a practising poet, without dependence on one particular titled patron.

FRANCES MAYHEW RIPPY

Sources *Calendar of the manuscripts of the marquis of Bath preserved at Longleat, Wiltshire*, 5 vols., HMC, 58 (1904–80) • *The literary works of Matthew Prior*, ed. H. B. Wright and M. K. Spears, 2 vols. (1959) • *The literary works of Matthew Prior*, ed. H. B. Wright and M. K. Spears, 2nd edn, 2 vols. (1971) • F. M. Rippy, *Matthew Prior*, Twayne's English Authors Series, 418 (1986) • F. M. Rippy, 'Matthew Prior', *Eighteenth-century British poets: first series*, ed. J. Sitter, DLitB, 95 (1990), 210–39 • F. M. Rippy, 'Matthew Prior as the last Renaissance man', *Studies in* medieval, Renaissance, American literature: a Festschrift, ed. B. F. Colquitt (1971), 120–31, 203 · C. K. Eves, Matthew Prior: poet and diplomatist (1939) · F. Bickley, The life of Matthew Prior (1914) · L. G. W. Legg, Matthew Prior: a study of his public career and correspondence (1921) · The works of the English poets, with prefaces, biographical and critical, by Samuel Johnson, 13 (1779), 1–63 · H. B. Wright, 'Matthew Prior: a supplement to his biography', PhD diss., Northwestern University, 1937 · H. Ransom, 'The rewards of authorship in the eighteenth century', University of Texas Studies in English, 18 (1938), 47–66 · H. B. Wright, 'Ideal copy and authoritative text: the problem of Prior's Poems on several occasions (1718)', Modern Philology, 49 (1951–2), 234–41 · H. B. Wright, 'Matthew Prior and Elizabeth Singer', Philological Quarterly, 24 (1945), 71–82 · H. B. Wright, 'Matthew Prior's Cloe and Lisetta', Modern Philology, 36 (1938–9), 9–23 · H. B. Wright, 'Matthew Prior's funeral', Modern Language Notes, 57 (1942), 341–5 · H. B. Wright, 'Matthew Prior's last manuscript: "Predestination"', British Library Journal, 11 (autumn 1985), 99–112 · H. B. Wright, 'Matthew Prior's "Wellbeloved and dear cossen"', Review of English Studies, 15 (1939), 318–23 · H. B. Wright and H. C. Montgomery, 'The art collection of a virtuoso in eighteenth-century England', Art Bulletin, 27 (1945), 195–204 · R. W. Ketton-Cremer, Matthew Prior (1957) · M. Mack, 'Matthew Prior: et multa prior arte', Sewanee Review, 68 (winter 1960), 165–76

Archives BL, corresp., journals, and literary MSS · BL, corresp., literary MSS, and papers, Add. MSS 70358–70371 · BL, financial papers relating to Paris, Add. MS 15947 · BL, journal of a journey to Paris, Add. MS 70028 · Longleat House, Wiltshire, papers · Miami University, Walter Havighurst Special Collections Library, papers | BL, letters to William Blathwayt, Add. MSS 12112, 21508, 46537 · BL, letters to John Ellis, Add. MS 28928 · BL, corresp. with Lord Lexington, Add. MS 46539 · BL, letters to Lord Oxford, Add. MS 70253 · BL, letters to Jonathan Swift, Add. MSS 4804–4805 · BL, corresp. with James Vernon, Add. MSS 40771–40774 · LMA, letters to Lord Jersey and others · St John Cam., letters to Lord Dorset

Likenesses oils, 1699 (after H. Rignaud), Mapledurham House, Oxfordshire · G. Kneller, oils, 1700, Trinity Cam. [see illus.] · attrib. M. Dahl, oils, 1713, NPG · A.-S. Belle, oils, c.1713–1714, St John Cam. · A. Coysevox, bust on monument, 1714, Westminster Abbey · M. Dahl, oils, c.1718, Knole, Kent · T. Wright, oils, c.1718 (after J. Richardson), NPG · J. Faber junior, mezzotint, 1750 (after F. Hayman), BM, NPG · bust, c.1775–1779 (after A. Coysevox), NPG · F. Kyte, mezzotint (after J. Richardson), BM, NPG · J. Simon, mezzotints (after J. Richardson), BM, NPG

Wealth at death left handsomely furnished Duke Street home and collection; Essex country estate, Down Hall; after expenses and debts, £9875 17s. 6d. remained for legacies

Prior, Melton (1845–1910), artist reporter, was born on 12 September 1845 in London, the son of William Henry Prior (1812–1882), draughtsman and landscape painter, and his wife, Amelia. Educated at St Clement Danes Grammar School, London, where he attended art classes, and at Blériot College, Boulogne, France, he helped his father, and so developed his artistic ability. From 1868 he was one of the 'special artists', employed by the illustrated press, who preceded press photographers. They were sent to sketch newsworthy events; their sketches were worked on by the illustrated paper's studio artists and then engraved on wood or sometimes, from the 1880s, reproduced as photomechanical facsimiles. Prior worked throughout his career for the world's leading weekly illustrated paper, the *Illustrated London News*, which gained an extensive circulation and large profits for its proprietor, Sir William Ingram.

For five years Prior sketched events in Britain, then in 1873 Ingram sent him as a special war artist on Wolseley's Asante campaign. War artists were an élite: their work was well paid, adventurous, and dangerous. Prior's success in the Second Anglo-Asante War brought him fame and established his career. For the following thirty years he worked primarily as a special war artist, on numerous wars including the 1874 Carlist War, Russo-Turkish War, 1878 Cape Frontier War, Anglo-Zulu War, First South African War, 1882 Egyptian campaign, eastern Sudan campaigns, Gordon relief expedition, and pacification of Burma (1886–7). From 1889 to 1892 he was in South America, sketching revolutions in Brazil, Argentina, and Venezuela. In 1895, invited by Barney Barnato, he went to Johannesburg and drew mine scenes. He then drew the Jameson raid and its aftermath, and the Matabele (Ndebele) uprising (1896). He went through the brief Graeco-Turkish War (1896), the Afridi campaign (1897) on the north-west frontier of India, and the Cretan rising (1898). In the Second South African War he witnessed the battle of Elandslaagte, was besieged with White's force in Ladysmith (November 1899 to February 1900), reported Roberts's advance to Pretoria, and returned to England in July 1900, 'the *doyen* of war artists' (*ILN*, 21 July 1900). In 1903 he was on the Somaliland campaign. In 1904 he went to draw the Russo-Japanese War, but the Japanese prevented reporters going to the front, which Prior bitterly resented: he wrote they were 'smiling, deceitful liars' (Prior, 335). Frustrated and disappointed, he returned to England.

Prior's war reporting had been interspersed with peaceful assignments overseas, including the visit to Athens by the prince of Wales in 1875 and the 1903 Delhi durbar. He went twice round the world, and travelled much in America. He claimed he had experienced twenty-six wars and had between 1873 and 1904 spent only one full year, 1883, at home. He did some work for *The Sketch*, also owned by Ingram. He occasionally fought in battle, was repeatedly under fire, and had, he claimed, numerous narrow escapes from death by shooting, spearing, drowning, or disease. Short (5 feet 6½ inches), bald, and with a high-pitched voice and very shrill laugh, he was nicknamed 'the screeching billiard ball' (Furniss, 128). A member of the Savage Club, he was energetic, genial, convivial, 'a Rabelaisian humorist [with] a certain roughness of metaphor in his own speech' (*The Times*).

A competent but not great artist, Prior worked very quickly, usually in pencil or ink. His sketches were lively, pleasing, and often dramatic, with skilful use of chiaroscuro, and the published engravings were often inferior to the sketches. An imperialist, Prior identified with the British forces, especially their officers, and British settlers, and his portrayal of their enemies was unflattering. Well paid and with generous expenses—Ingram called him the 'Illustrated Luxury' (Prior, 209)—Prior travelled well provided with whisky and Moyer's tinned Irish stew. He repeatedly drew himself in action. Boosted by the *Illustrated London News*, he enjoyed his celebrity. He belonged to the adventurous, self-advertising school of war correspondents of whom Archibald Forbes was a leading figure.

He was awarded foreign decorations and, like his colleagues, resented the War Office's refusal to award campaign medals to war correspondents. However, he wore the campaign ribbons to which he believed himself entitled.

Prior married in 1873 Mary, daughter of John Greeves, a surgeon. Except for accompanying him to Turkey in 1877, she stayed at home while he travelled, and reportedly his long absences contributed to the breakdown of the marriage. She was killed in 1907 in a tramway accident at Lewisham, London, where they lived. In 1908 Prior married Georgina Catherine, daughter of George MacIntosh Douglas; she survived him. He had no children from either marriage. In his last years Prior's health deteriorated, and he wrote his memoirs which—edited, expurgated, and cut by about half by his *ILN* colleague S. L. Bensusan—were published after his death. Following heart weakness, asthma, and in February 1910 a serious attack of pleurisy, he died at his home, 12A Carlyle Mansions, Cheyne Walk, Chelsea, on 2 November 1910, and was buried at Hither Green cemetery, London. A memorial tablet was placed in St Paul's Cathedral crypt.

Through his work in the *Illustrated London News*, Prior helped shape the Victorian public's perceptions of the empire and of war. His pictures remain useful historical sources and have been much reproduced, particularly in works of military history.   ROGER T. STEARN

Sources M. Prior, *Campaigns of a war correspondent*, ed. S. L. Bensusan (1912) · *The Times* (3 Nov 1910) · *ILN* (21 July 1900), 87 · *ILN* (5 Nov 1910) · J. Carruthers, *Melton Prior: war artist in southern Africa, 1895–1900* (1987) · H. Furniss, *My bohemian days* (1919) · P. Hodgson, *The war illustrators* (1977) · P. Johnson, *Front line artists* (1978) · P. Hogarth, *The artist as reporter* (1986) · R. T. Stearn, 'War correspondents and colonial war, c.1870–1900', *Popular imperialism and the military, 1850–1950*, ed. J. M. Mackenzie (1992) · *WWW, 1897–1915* · *Men and women of the time* (1899) · A. Watson, *The Savage Club* (1907) · *CGPLA Eng. & Wales* (1910)

Likenesses M. Prior, self-portrait, wood-engraving, NPG; repro. in *ILN* (3 Feb 1877) · M. Prior, self-portrait, wood-engraving, NPG; repro. in *ILN* (28 July 1877) · M. Prior, self-portrait, wood-engraving, NPG; repro. in *ILN* (18 Nov 1879) · F. Whiting, oils, Savage Club, London

Wealth at death £2265 10s. 3d.: resworn probate, 1 Dec 1910, *CGPLA Eng. & Wales*

Prior, Thomas (1681–1751), author and a founder of the Dublin Society, was born at Garriston, near Rathdowney, Queen's county, the second son of Colonel Thomas Prior (d. 1700) and grandson of Captain Thomas Prior of Ely, who settled in Ireland with his regiment in 1636. He was educated at the public school at Kilkenny between January 1697 and April 1699; there he formed what became a lifelong friendship with George Berkeley, subsequently bishop of Cloyne, to whom he later served as legal adviser and Dublin agent. Prior entered Trinity College, Dublin, obtained a scholarship in 1701, and graduated BA in 1703. He subsequently devoted himself to the promotion of trade and industry among the protestant population in Ireland.

In 1729 Prior published his *List of the Absentees of Ireland*, which contained details of estates and incomes from rents. In this popular and often reprinted pamphlet he estimated that up to £600,000 went overseas in remitted rents, a figure which has since been identified as an overestimate (Cullen, 172). In 1730 there appeared his *Observations on Coin*. In the following year Prior and twelve other associates including Samuel Madden, philanthropist, Sir Thomas Molyneux, physician, Francis Bindon, architect and portrait painter, and Patrick Delany, dean of Down, succeeded in establishing the Dublin Society for the Promotion of Agriculture, Manufactures, Arts and Sciences. It was duly incorporated, and in 1749 received a grant of £500 per annum from parliament; it subsequently became the Royal Dublin Society. Prior dedicated his *Authentic Narrative of the Success of Tar-Water in Curing a Great Number and Variety of Distempers* (1746) to Lord Chesterfield, with whom he had corresponded during the latter's spell as viceroy to Ireland (1745–6). An essay by Prior, advocating the encouragement of the linen manufacture in Ireland, was also published at Dublin in 1749.

After a long illness Prior died, unmarried, on 21 October 1751 at Rathdowney, where he was buried on 25 October. A monument erected by subscription to his memory in Christ Church, Dublin, carried an inscription by Bishop Berkeley, who styled him 'Societatis Dubliniensis auctor, institutor, curator'.   J. T. GILBERT, rev. PHILIP CARTER

Sources J. T. Gilbert, *History of Dublin*, new edn (1903) · G. A. Chamberlain, *Thomas Prior: founder of the Royal Dublin Society* (1946) · D. Clarke, *Thomas Prior, 1681–1751: founder of the Royal Dublin Society* (1951) · L. M. Cullen, 'Economic development, 1750–1800', *A new history of Ireland*, ed. T. W. Moody and others, 4: *Eighteenth-century Ireland, 1691–1800* (1986), 159–95

Likenesses J. van Nost, marble bust, 1751, Royal Dublin Society · C. Spooner, mezzotint, 1752 (after J. Van Nost), NG Ire.; repro. in Clarke, *Thomas Prior* · I. Taylor, line engraving, pubd 1779 (after R. Pool and J. Cash), NG Ire. · J. Hall, line engraving, BM, NPG; repro. in Maty, *Memoirs of Chesterfield* (1777) · J. van Nost, bust? on monument, Christ Church, Dublin

Prior, Thomas Abiel (1809–1886), line engraver, was born on 5 November 1809. His early work was done for the publishers Henry Fisher and George Vertue and consisted of landscapes of Britain, the Mediterranean region, China, and America. He first distinguished himself with a print, *Heidelberg Castle and Town* (1844), engraved on copper from one of Turner's drawings that he had bought, and executed under Turner's supervision. It was published by subscription, and its success led to its re-engraving on steel for the *Art Journal* (1864). After one plate in mezzotint, *More Frightened than Hurt*, after James Bateman, Prior returned to line engraving, executing several more plates after Turner, including *Zurich* (1852), *Dido Building Carthage* (1863), *Apollo and the Sibyl* (1873)—the latter two were exhibited at the Royal Academy in 1864 and 1874 respectively—and *The Sun Rising in a Mist* (begun by William Chapman; 1874). Other plates were engraved for the Turner Gallery and the Vernon Gallery. He produced *Crossing the Bridge* after Sir Edwin Landseer, and fourteen plates on steel for the *Art Journal* between 1850 and 1871, notably several pictures from the Royal Collection, among them *The Windmill*, after Ruysdael; *The Village Fête*, after David Teniers; *Dover*, after George Chambers; *The Opening of the New*

London Bridge, after Clarkson Stanfield; and *Constantinople: the Golden Horn*, after Jacobus Jacobs.

Prior married on 18 November 1837 Emma Sharrow; she may have died about 1860, for at this time he went to live in Calais to be near his son, Thomas William Prior (*b.* 1838). He taught drawing at one or two of the schools in Calais, which considerably slowed down the rate of his own work. The large plates of his *Dido* and *Apollo*, produced during these years, were considered to be his best works. It was Prior's custom to visit England annually, to oversee the proving of his plates. In September 1886 he completed his large engraving of *The Fighting Téméraire*. Its publication drew admiring comments in *The Times*, which noted that Prior was 'one of the last surviving masters of the now obsolete method of line engraving' (*The Times*, 2 Nov 1886, 8a). A few days later the same newspaper reported his death at Calais on 8 November 1886.

ANITA McCONNELL

Sources B. Hunnisett, 'Prior, Thomas Abiel', *The dictionary of art*, ed. J. Turner (1996) · *The Times* (2 Nov 1886), 8a · *The Times* (11 Nov 1886), 3d · *The Athenaeum*, 2 (1886), 677–8 · Bryan, *Painters* (1886–9), 2.323 · B. Hunnisett, *An illustrated dictionary of British steel engravers*, new edn (1989), 71–2
Likenesses E. Carpot, carte-de-visite, NPG · R. T., wood-engraving, NPG; repro. in *ILN* (27 Nov 1886) · portrait, repro. in Hunnisett, *Illustrated dictionary*, 71

Prise, Sir John [Syr Siôn ap Rhys] (1501/2–1555), administrator and scholar, was born between 12 October 1501 and 11 October 1502, the son of Rhys ap Gwilym ap Llywelyn of Brecon and Gwenllian, daughter of Hywel ap Madog. After study at Oxford University and practice in the court of arches he graduated BCL at Cambridge in 1535/6. However, the crucial step in his career had been taken by 1530, when he is found in the service of Thomas Cromwell. Appointed registrar-general in ecclesiastical causes on 1 September 1534, Prise played a direct role in the dissolution of the monasteries, both as visitor in 1535—when he urged the virtues of a moderate approach in the face of the arrogant, even violent, behaviour of his fellow visitor, Thomas Lee—and as a commissioner for the surrender of monasteries in Hampshire, Wiltshire, and Gloucestershire in late 1539 and early 1540. He also participated in other aspects of the turbulent politics of the 1530s, being involved in the search for incriminating documents in the bishop of Durham's palace in 1532; recording, as a public notary, the interrogations of various rebels and traitors in the Tower of London, including Bishop John Fisher and Sir Thomas More, as well as of participants in Hallam's rebellion at Kingston upon Hull early in 1537; and drawing up documents relating to Henry VIII's divorces of Anne Boleyn (at whose marriage in 1533 Prise had been a servitor) and Anne of Cleves.

On 11 October 1534 Prise, aged thirty-two, married Joan Williamson (*b.* 1515/16), aged eighteen, niece by marriage to Cromwell, at the latter's house in Islington. This may not have been Prise's first marriage, for his will refers to a married daughter apparently older than any of the eleven children he had with Joan. The first four of those children were born in London, and the godparents after whom

they were named reflect their father's connections in the city: the eldest son, Gregory, was named after Thomas Cromwell's son, the second surviving son, Richard, after Cromwell's nephew, Richard Williams, and the eldest daughter, Eleanor, after the wife of Christopher Barker, Garter king of arms.

Although Prise retained royal favour following Cromwell's execution in July 1540 he was never again to play such a central role in public affairs as he had in the 1530s. Instead his public career entered a new phase, focused mainly on Wales and its borders. From 8 June 1540 he had the lease, and from 13 November 1542 the grant in fee, of the dissolved Benedictine priory of St Guthlac at Hereford, which he seems to have made his principal residence, for it was the birthplace of his fifth and subsequent children from 1542 onwards. He was also granted Brecon Priory in fee in 1542, though he never resided there. In the meantime, on 27 September 1540 Prise was appointed secretary for life of the council of Wales and the marches, subsequently serving the crown in a variety of capacities, for example, as sheriff of Brecknockshire (1542–3) and justice of the peace in Herefordshire and numerous other counties.

Prise was knighted two days after Edward VI's coronation, on 22 February 1547, and was elected MP for Brecknockshire in the same year: the poet Lewys Morgannwg aptly likened his progress to 'a long summer's day' in 1548 (Gruffydd, 'The earliest Welsh printed book', 106). In 1552 he was admitted at Doctors' Commons. Nor was Prise's success clouded by the accession of Queen Mary, for he sat in the first three Marian parliaments without opposing measures to restore Catholicism, and also dedicated a treatise on the coinage to the queen. He died at St Guthlac's Priory, Hereford, on 15 October 1555, survived by his wife and ten of their children, leaving lands worth about £135 per annum together with numerous bequests, including 1000 marks for the dowries of his daughters. His will, made nine days earlier, was essentially Catholic in character, bequeathing his soul to God, to 'owre blessede ladie Sainte Marye And to all the blessed cumpanie of heavin' (Morgan, 255), and requesting prayers on its behalf. He asked to be buried in Hereford Cathedral.

Although critical of the monasteries he helped to dissolve, Prise also played an important role, which has been compared to that of Bale and Leland, in collecting and studying monastic manuscripts, of which he owned or annotated more than a hundred; in his will he urged his son Richard to arrange for the publication of the works of William of Malmesbury and other medieval historians in his collection. His familiarity with medieval texts informed his two best-known works, the *Historiae Brytannicae defensio* (probably completed by 1547 though not published until 1573), a measured refutation of Polydore Vergil's attack on Geoffrey of Monmouth's account of early British history, and *Yny lhyvyr hwnn* … ('In this book …'), attributed to Prise by Richard Davies, bishop of St David's in 1567, a compilation of religious texts in Welsh, including the creed and Lord's prayer, published in

1546 and the earliest known printed book in Welsh. Drawing extensively on medieval Welsh religious texts, the latter compilation reveals not only a deep dissatisfaction with the failure of the clergy to provide elementary religious instruction but also an awareness, shared by other contemporary Welsh humanists, of the potential of print as a means of preserving and disseminating the vernacular literary heritage of Wales. Though he certainly carved a successful public career through his prudently supple commitment to the Tudor regime, it is as 'a lover of antiquity', to quote Leland's tribute (Gruffydd, 'The earliest Welsh printed book', 109), that Prise enjoys his greatest reputation.   HUW PRYCE

Sources LP Henry VIII, vols. 4–20 • T. Phillipps, 'Welsh MSS', *Cambrian Journal*, 4 (1857), 39–47 • F. C. Morgan, 'The will of Sir John Prise of Hereford, 1555', *National Library of Wales Journal*, 9 (1955–6), 255–61 • [J. Prise], *Yny lhyvyr hwnn a ban o gyfreith Howel*, ed. J. H. Davies (1902) • P. S. Edwards, 'Price, Sir John (1501/2–55) of Brecon and Hereford', HoP, *Commons, 1509–58*, 3.154–6 • N. R. Ker, 'Sir John Prise', *The Library*, 5th ser., 10 (1955), 1–24; rev. in N. R. Ker, *Books, collectors, and libraries*, ed. A. G. Watson (1985), 471–96 • G. Williams, 'Sir John Pryse of Brecon', *Brycheiniog*, 31 (1998–9), 49–63 • R. G. Gruffydd, 'Yny lhyvyr hwnn (1546): the earliest Welsh printed book', *BBCS*, 23 (1968–70), 105–16 • R. G. Gruffydd, 'Y print yn dwyn ffrwyth i'r Cymro: Yny lhyvyr hwnn, 1546' ['Print bearing fruit for the Welshman: Yny lhyvyr hwnn, 1546'], *Y Llyfr yng Nghymru / Welsh Book Studies*, 1 (1998), 1–20 • *DWB* • T. D. Kendrick, *British antiquity* (1950) • E. D. Jones, 'Llyfr amrywiaeth Syr Siôn Prys' ['Sir John Prise's commonplace book'], *Brycheiniog*, 8 (1962), 97–104 • W. A. J. Archbold, 'A manuscript treatise on the coinage by John Pryse, 1553', *EngHR*, 13 (1898), 709–10 • Emden, *Oxf.*
Archives Balliol Oxf., commonplace book • Hereford Cathedral Library, MSS • Jesus College, Oxford, MSS
Wealth at death approx. £135 p.a.: inquisition post mortem, PRO, C142/105/83; E[dwards], 'Price', 155–6 • 1000 marks for marriages of daughters; other smaller bequests of money: 6 Oct 1555, Morgan, 'The will'

Prisot, Sir John. *See* Prysot, Sir John (d. 1461).

Pritchard, Andrew (1804–1882), microscopist, eldest son of John Pritchard of Hackney, and his wife, Ann, daughter of John Fleetwood, was born in London on 14 December 1804. He was educated at St Saviour's Grammar School, Southwark, and was afterwards apprenticed to his cousin, Cornelius Varley, a patent agent and brother to the artist John Varley. On the expiration of his apprenticeship he started in business as an optician, from 1827 to 1835 at 18 Pickett Street, Strand (on the corner of 312 Strand), from 1836 to 1838 both there and at 263 Strand, and from 1839 to 1858 at 162 Fleet Street. Afterwards he had a business address at 49 Coleman Street in the City, shared with one of his sons, Andrew Goring Pritchard, a solicitor. On 16 July 1829 he married Caroline Isabella Straker.

Pritchard was brought up as an Independent. Later in life he associated with, though never actually became a member of, the sect known as Sandemanians, and it was in connection with that body he first made the acquaintance of Michael Faraday. Pritchard finally became a Unitarian, and in 1840 joined the congregation at Newington Green, a connection which lasted throughout his life. He was greatly interested in all the institutions of his religion, and was treasurer of the chapel from 1850 to 1872.

Pritchard early turned his attention to microscopy, and in 1824, while still with Varley, at the instigation of Dr C. R. Goring, he ground a single lens out of a diamond. He also fashioned simple lenses of sapphire, ruby, garnet, and spinel, but later sold rather old-fashioned microscopes. He is much better known for his microscope slides, which had their edges filled with red sealing wax. He mounted some of his specimens in a gum and isinglass mixture, a very early and innovative use of such a medium. His practical work on the microscope, however, was less important than his books on the applications of the instrument. His *List of 2000 Microscopic Objects* (1835) is very important in the history of microscopy, as it described the use of Canada balsam for mounting for the first time; his *History of the Infusoria* (1841) was long a standard work, and the impetus it gave to the study of biological science cannot be overestimated.

Pritchard wrote several other books on aspects of natural history as seen through the microscope, on optical instruments, and on patents. He also wrote four papers on microscopical optics between 1827 and 1833 in the *Quarterly Journal of Science*, the *Edinburgh Philosophical Magazine*, and the *Philosophical Magazine*. He was elected fellow of the Royal Society of Edinburgh in 1873. He retired from business about 1852, and died at 87 St Paul's Road, Islington, on 24 November 1882. Profits from his writing contributed to the nearly £40,000 left at his death.

Henry Baden Pritchard (1841–1884), chemist and writer, the third son of Andrew Pritchard, was born in Canonbury on 30 November 1841, and sent to Eisenach and University College School, going afterwards to Switzerland to complete his education. In 1861 he obtained an appointment in the chemical department at the Royal Arsenal, Woolwich, and for some years before his death conducted the photographic department there. He was also proprietor and editor of the *Photographic News* from 1878 to 1884. On 25 March 1873 he married Mary, daughter of Matthew Evans of Shropshire.

A prolific author, Pritchard wrote travel books illustrated with his photographs and works of fiction. He died at Charlton, Kent, on 11 May 1884.

B. B. WOODWARD, *rev.* BRIAN BRACEGIRDLE

Sources B. Bracegirdle, *A history of microtechnique* (1978) • d. cert. • private information (1896)
Archives Temple University, Philadelphia, corresp. and papers
Likenesses portrait (Henry Baden Pritchard), repro. in *British Journal of Photography* (1884) • portrait (Henry Baden Pritchard), repro. in *Year Book of Photography* (1885)
Wealth at death £39,290 15s. 3d.: probate, 9 Jan 1883, CGPLA Eng. & Wales

Pritchard, Charles (1808–1893), headmaster and astronomer, the fourth son of William Pritchard (d. 1859), a hatter of Shrewsbury, and his wife, Elizabeth, née Lloyd, was born at Alberbury, Shropshire, on 28 February 1808. He and his brothers were baptized on 18 December 1808 at Christchurch, Southwark, after the family moved to Brixton in south London. Pritchard went to school first near Uxbridge, then as a day boy at Merchant Taylors' School (1818–19), and for a year he walked to Suffolk Lane in the

Charles Pritchard (1808–1893), by Henry John Whitlock

City of London, a distance of 4 miles, every morning before seven. In 1822 he was sent to John Stock's academy at Poplar, where he benefited from Stock's inspired teaching of mathematics and learned to use surveying and astronomical instruments. His last school was Christ's Hospital, Newgate Street, in the City, and for twelve months there he utilized the long walk in learning by rote passages from classical authors. Financial difficulties at home, however, compelled his removal, and for two years he worked alone, chiefly at mathematics, though he also attended some lectures on chemistry. In 1825, when only seventeen, he published an *Introduction to Arithmetic*, and in 1826 he was enabled, by the help of friends and relatives, to enter St John's College, Cambridge, whence he graduated as fourth wrangler in 1830. He proceeded MA in 1833, having been elected a fellow of his college in March 1832.

Headmasterships In 1833 Pritchard accepted the headmastership of Stockwell proprietary grammar school, but his relations with the proprietors were always strained, as they opposed his desire to include science in the curriculum, and he left in June 1834. The parents of many of his pupils did, however, wish him to teach their sons in a modern manner, and the Clapham grammar school was founded to give him a freer hand in carrying out much-

needed educational reforms. In the interim he had married, on 18 December 1834, Emily, the daughter of J. Newton; they had several children, including Sir Charles Bradley *Pritchard, before her early death.

Pritchard packed the Clapham school with scientific apparatus and equipped it with an observatory and, eventually, a swimming pool. He presided over this establishment with remarkable success from 1834 to 1862. His system of teaching was wide and accommodating, his zeal indefatigable. Many of the boys who followed him from Stockwell achieved fame in later life. In 1866 nearly 100 men turned up for a banquet given in Pritchard's honour by the old boys of Clapham; a further 100 apologized for absence—a unique tribute to the manner of his rule there.

Retirement interlude Pritchard married second, on 10 August 1858, Rosalind (*d.* 1892), the daughter of Alexander Campbell; they also had children. On leaving Clapham in 1862 he retired with his family to Freshwater, on the Isle of Wight. He had been ordained in 1834, and earnestly desired to devote himself to pastoral duties, but failed to obtain a curacy. He nevertheless delivered addresses, generally on the harmony between science and scripture, at various church congresses, and preached so often before the British Association that he came to be known as its 'chaplain'. His discourse at the Nottingham meeting in 1866 led to his appointment as Hulsean lecturer at Cambridge in 1867. He was, besides, one of the select preachers at Cambridge in 1869 and 1881 and at Oxford in 1876 and 1877.

Pritchard joined the Royal Astronomical Society on 13 April 1849. He contributed to their proceedings, made some photometrical experiments on the annular solar eclipse of 15 March 1858, and joined the expedition in SS *Himalaya* which sailed to Spain for the total eclipse of 18 July 1860. He served continuously on the council of the society from 1856 to 1877, and again from 1883 to 1887, and came under fire for championing the aged Sir George Airy against the reformers seeking to end Airy's domination of the council. As president in 1866, Pritchard delivered two admirable addresses when presenting gold medals to Huggins and Leverrier in 1867 and 1868 respectively.

Savilian professorship Early in 1870 Pritchard succeeded William Fishburn Donkin as Savilian professor of astronomy at the University of Oxford, where it was hoped that his teaching would revitalize the post. The family moved into 8 Keble Road, Pritchard's home for the remainder of his life. Although just sixty-two, he entered upon his new duties with the ardour of youth. A new observatory was erected in the university parks; a 12 inch refractor was purchased from Sir Howard Grubb, and Warren De La Rue gave other instruments, including a 13 inch reflecting equatorial telescope that he had constructed. The 'New Savilian Observatory for Astronomical Physics' was completed in 1875.

Pritchard was well aware of the advantages of photography, and adopted De La Rue's suggestion of investigating in this way the moon's libration. He next undertook the micrometric determination of forty stars in the Pleiades, with a view to ascertain their relative displacements since F. W. Bessel had measured them more than fifty years earlier; his results, however, were later questioned. To standardize the various estimates of the brightness of these stars, Pritchard adapted the wedge photometer, designed by W. R. Dawes, and vigorously defended it against all criticism. With it, he determined, in 1881–5, the relative magnitudes of 2784 stars from the pole to 10 degrees south of the equator. Early in 1883 he travelled to Egypt, where he hoped to obtain a better value for atmospheric absorption. He was accompanied by his wife and his assistant, Jenkins. After completing the observations from the khedive's observatory for the resulting photometric catalogue, entitled *Uranometria nova Oxoniensis* (1885), he received in 1886 jointly with the American astronomer Edward Charles Pickering, whose catalogue had been produced using the rival method of photometry, the Astronomical Society's gold medal.

Stellar photography Pritchard was a pioneer in the photographic measurement of stellar parallax. From 200 plates of the star 61 Cygni exposed in 1886 he derived a parallax of 0.438 inches. Later measurements of twenty-eight stars, mostly of the second magnitude, yielded an average parallax of 0.56 inches, corresponding to a distance of 58 light years, a project which earned him, in 1892, the Royal Society's royal medal.

In 1886 Pritchard contributed to the Royal Society lengthy descriptions of his researches in stellar photography, and a second account was published by the Royal Astronomical Society in 1891. He never observed at Oxford; all the observations were undertaken by his able and loyal assistants Plummer and Jenkins, to whom he always gave full credit. In 1887 he committed his observatory to participate in the Carte du ciel, the first large international co-operative programme in astronomy. De La Rue donated the regulation 13 inch astrograph, and in 1890–91 Pritchard made lengthy experiments and tests and cajoled Sir Howard Grubb in order to ensure that the overseas observatories received satisfactory and standardized apparatus, a task for which his mathematical abilities were ideally suited. At the time of his death some progress had been made in photographing the zone of sky assigned to the Oxford observatory.

Pritchard was elected FRS on 6 February 1840, and was a member of the council in 1885–7. He was also a fellow of the Cambridge Philosophical Society and, from 1852, of the Geological Society. He proceeded MA by decree from New College, Oxford, on 11 March 1870, and DD in 1880, and, as Savilian professor, became a fellow in 1883. To his great delight, he was elected to an honorary fellowship of St John's College, Cambridge, in 1886. He was placed on the Solar Physics Committee in 1885.

Pritchard's enthusiasm for teaching never left him. He would instruct up to fifteen students at a time in practical matters in the subsidiary observatory fitted up for their use. Taking full advantage of De La Rue's benefactions, he made Oxford's the most active university observatory in the country, and the gold medals established it among the first rank in Europe. In his later years his eyesight failed and he was unable to walk, but he was conveyed to the observatory in a bath chair. He was full of plans for future work, and had, at the time of his death, fully prepared for a further photographic investigation of the Pleiades. He died at his home on 28 May 1893 and was buried in Holywell cemetery.

During the last twenty years of his life Pritchard sent fifty astronomical papers to learned societies; wrote many excellent popular essays, including a series in *Good Words*; and contributed several articles to the ninth edition of the *Encyclopaedia Britannica*, and to Smith's *Dictionary of the Bible*. His *Occasional Thoughts of an Astronomer on Nature and Revelation* (1889) gathered his miscellaneous addresses and discourses, though many of his sermons were printed separately. Next to the stars, Pritchard loved flowers. He practised floriculture as a fine art, and had at Clapham one of the finest ferneries in England. Yet he would have preferred parish work to his scientific accomplishments. 'Providence', he used to say, 'made me an astronomer, but gave me the heart of a divine.'

A. M. CLERKE, rev. ANITA McCONNELL

Sources A. Pritchard, *Charles Pritchard … memoirs of his life* (1897) • C. Pritchard, *Annals of our school life* (1886) • D. Leinster-Mackay, 'Pioneers in progressive education: some little-known proprietary and private school exemplars', *History of Education*, 9 (1980), 213–17 • G. G. Bradley, 'My schooldays from 1830–40', *Nineteenth Century*, 15 (1884), 455–74 • E. D., *PRS*, 54 (1893), iii–xii • H. H. T. [H. H. Turner], *Monthly Notices of the Royal Astronomical Society*, 54 (1893–4), 198–204 • W. E. P. [W. E. Plummer], 'Rev. Charles Pritchard', *The Observatory*, 16 (1893), 256–9 • *Journal of the British Astronomical Association*, 3 (1892–3), 434 • *Daily Graphic* (31 May 1893), 4 • *The Times* (30 May 1893) • Mrs E. P. Hart, ed., *Merchant Taylors' School register, 1561–1934*, 2 (1936) • Foster, *Alum. Oxon.* • Boase, *Mod. Eng. biog.* • *DSB* • m. cert. • parish register (birth), 28 Feb 1808, Alberbury, Shropshire • parish register (baptism), 18 Dec 1808, Christchurch, Southwark

Archives MHS Oxf. | CUL, letters to Sir George Stokes • RAS, letters to Royal Astronomical Society • RS, corresp. with Sir John Herschel

Likenesses H. W. Taunt, photograph, repro. in Pritchard, *Charles Pritchard*, frontispiece • H. J. Whitlock, photograph, NPG [*see illus.*] • portrait, repro. in Plummer, 'Rev. Charles Prichard', 256 • woodengraving (after photograph by Taunt & Co. of Oxford), NPG; repro. in *ILN* (3 June 1893)

Wealth at death £10,741 2s. 7d.: resworn probate, March 1908, *CGPLA Eng. & Wales* (1893)

Pritchard, Sir Charles Bradley (1837–1903), administrator in India, born at Clapham on 5 May 1837, was the eldest son of Charles *Pritchard (1808–1893), headmaster and astronomer, and his first wife, Emily, daughter of J. Newton. After early education by his father he entered Rugby School in 1849, and was transferred to Sherborne School in 1852. He obtained a nomination to the Indian army, and went to Addiscombe College in 1854, but secured a writership in the Indian Civil Service and completed his education at Haileybury College. In 1862 he married Emily Dorothea, daughter of Hamerton John Williams; they had two sons and two daughters.

On his arrival at Bombay in January 1858 Pritchard first served as assistant magistrate and collector at Belgaum, and was active in suppressing banditry in the district. In

1865 he was put in charge of Thana, and carried on a successful campaign to extend the control of the forest department over the forests of the district. Nominated to the province of Khandesh in 1867, he was active in trying to check the exploitation of the Bhils by moneylenders, and in organizing relief measures during the famine of 1868. The trenchant manner in which he dealt with fraud in the public departments led to his appointment as first collector of salt revenue in the Bombay presidency. In this capacity he reformed the administration, suppressed smuggling, and established a large salt factory at Kharaghoda. Considerable opposition was excited by the system of private licences, which he introduced with a view to ensuring that the salt was properly weighed, but owing to his perseverance the controversial tax on salt became gradually easier to collect. The stability of the Bombay salt revenue was henceforth assured, and when in 1876 a commission was appointed to reform the abuses of the Madras salt revenue, Pritchard was nominated its president.

In 1875 Pritchard put forward a plan to reform the system of excise (*abkari*) on Indian-made liquor and toddy (the fermented sap of palm trees) in the Bombay presidency. At the time the manufacture and sale of these drinks was highly localized, which made it hard for the government to collect the excise. Pritchard's plan was to centralize the manufacture of liquor in central distilleries, to discourage toddy-drinking by placing a steep tax on toddy trees, and to require all liquor shopkeepers to be licensed and to buy their supplies from the central distilleries. These proposals were accepted by the government of Bombay and formed the basis for Act V of 1878. Pritchard was appointed first *abkari* commissioner in the same year so that he could personally supervise the implementation of the act. Raising as it did the price of liquor and toddy, the new system proved very unpopular, and there was widespread protest as well as evasion of the law. Although a few concessions had to be made, Pritchard refused to compromise on the fundamental principles. Between 1874 and 1888, excise revenue rose in consequence by 145 per cent.

Pritchard, who had been made CSI in 1886, held the post of commissioner of Sind from 1887 to 1889, and there he did much to develop harbour works and railway communications. He revived the idea of the Jamrao canal, which was completed in 1901, and he set on foot the scheme for the construction of a line linking up Karachi with the railway system of Rajputana which was carried out by his successor, Sir Arthur Trevor.

In November 1890 Pritchard was promoted to be revenue member of the government of Bombay, and in 1891 was created KCIE. In the following year he took his seat on the central legislative council as member for the public works department. During his tenure of office he frequently found himself at variance with Lord Elgin, the viceroy, and with the majority of his colleagues on questions of high policy. He disapproved of the 'forward' policy, and he joined Sir Antony MacDonnell and Sir James Westland in protesting against the high expenditure and casualties involved in military expeditions to Waziristan,

Swat, Chitral, and Tirah. In 1896 his health showed signs of failure, and he resigned his seat on the council. He returned to England and settled in London. He died at his home, 2 Charles Street, Berkeley Square, London, on 23 November 1903, and was buried at Norwood. A memorial tablet to him was placed in the crypt of St Paul's Cathedral, London.   G. S. WOODS, *rev.* DAVID HARDIMAN

Sources The Times (25 Nov 1903) · *Times of India* (29 Nov 1896) · H. Birdwood, 'A great civilian: a personal appreciation of Sir Charles Pritchard', *National Review*, 42 (1903–4), 771 · A. Pritchard, *Memoirs of Prof. Pritchard* (1897) · C. E. Buckland, *Dictionary of Indian biography* (1906) · private information (1912) · D. Hardiman, 'From custom to crime: the politics of drinking in colonial south Gujarat', *Subaltern Studies*, ed. R. Guha, 4 (1985) · CGPLA Eng. & Wales (1904)

Likenesses G. Reid, portrait, Karachi, Pakistan

Wealth at death £11,749 15s. 2d.: probate, 5 Jan 1904, CGPLA Eng. & Wales

Pritchard, Sir Edward Evan Evans- (1902–1973), social anthropologist, was born on 21 September 1902 at Crowborough, Sussex, the younger of two sons, the only children of the Revd Thomas John Evans-Pritchard (d. 1929), a Welsh-speaking Church of England clergyman from Caernarfon, and his wife, Dorothea, daughter of John Edwards of Liverpool. 'Evans' came into the name from his maternal grandmother, daughter of Eyre Dixon Evans JP, merchant of Liverpool. Evans-Pritchard was educated at Winchester College (1916–21) and at Exeter College, Oxford (1921–4), where he took a second class in modern history.

Though Evans-Pritchard never lost the values and sentiments of his upbringing there was a non-conforming side to him, which was attracted to the unconventional, the Bohemian, even the raffish. When at Oxford he was a member of the privileged artistic coterie the Hypocrites Club, and is described at that time by a fellow member, Anthony Powell, the novelist, as 'Evans-Pritchard the anthropologist, grave, withdrawn, somewhat exotic of dress'. In middle and later life his conviviality and sometimes mischievous humour often concealed a deeper reclusiveness, while in dress he became notably careless, though formal enough for formal occasions.

At Exeter College, with anthropologist R. R. Marett as a fellow and later rector, Evans-Pritchard read works on primitive cultures by Sir Edward B. Tylor and Sir James G. Frazer. The immense variety of the forms of social life they described, with all that remained to be discovered, caught his imagination; and—Celt that he was—people who held to their own customs and beliefs in the face of powerful foreign interference had his sympathy. In their direction he saw a future that would satisfy both his appetite for adventure and his intellectual curiosity. So it was that he chose an anthropological career, for which he was well endowed by physical stamina, self-reliance, sociability, and a subtle understanding of human relationships.

Since no teacher in Oxford at that time had experience of anthropological field research, in 1924 Evans-Pritchard moved to the London School of Economics, where C. G. Seligman and B. Malinowski were gathering around them young anthropologists with aspirations similar to his own. Malinowski (though Evans-Pritchard came to dislike him personally and sometimes to depreciate his work) set an outstanding example of thorough field research conducted through the native language. Seligman, who, with his wife B. Z. Seligman, had earlier made surveys in the (then Anglo-Egyptian) Sudan, arranged with the Sudan government for Evans-Pritchard to undertake more intensive research there. He chose eventually to study the Azande of the southern Sudan, among whom he lived on and off between 1926 and 1930. With characteristic industry, in 1927 he gained the PhD of the University of London for a preliminary thesis on the Azande.

Evans-Pritchard's first book, *Witchcraft, Oracles and Magic among the Azande* (1937), a brilliant analysis of Zande mystical belief and practices, implicitly raised general questions of the relationship between faith and reasoning, and impressed not only anthropologists but philosophers (for example, R. G. Collingwood and Michael Polanyi) and social historians (for example, Keith Thomas). In this book Evans-Pritchard already shows two characteristics of his own style of social anthropology: the development of general ideas through detailed ethnography rather than by abstract argument, and unusual insight into the intellectual and moral coherence of apparently disparate social phenomena. As in his other writings, sociological analysis never deprives the reader of a living and sympathetic impression of the people themselves. In later life he regretted that, in their formalism, some of his successors in the subject were losing this touch and making of the study of man what the scholastics had made of the study of God.

Between 1930 and 1940 Evans-Pritchard was a wandering scholar with part-time lectureships in London and Oxford, and three years (1932–4) as professor of sociology at King Fuad I University in Cairo, where he began to learn Arabic. His field research continued for a while, mostly in the southern Sudan. In 1930 he started twelve months' difficult and interrupted work among the warlike, pastoral Nuer tribes of the upper Nile swamps, where he arrived shortly after a punitive government expedition; but though, as he wrote, he 'entered [the Nuers'] cattle-camps not only as a stranger but as an enemy', he respected their recalcitrance and eventually gained their confidence. The research produced many articles and three books: *The Nuer: a Description of the Modes of Livelihood and Political Institutions of a Nilotic people* (1940), *Kinship and Marriage among the Nuer* (1951), and *Nuer Religion* (1956). The first provided a model for much subsequent anthropological analysis of political institutions, showing as it did the structural principles of political order among peoples without any centralized authority. *African Political Systems* (1940), a symposium which he co-edited with his friend Meyer Fortes, extended that discussion.

Nuer Religion (unusually, for a social anthropologist, written from an explicitly theistic viewpoint) again brought Evans-Pritchard readers among psychologists, theologians, and philosophers, and he was wryly pleased that the meaning of Nuer expressions should add to British philosophical speculations. He had become a Roman Catholic in 1944 and though he was not, as some were led

to suppose, a zealous convert, he advocated religious faith, which for him was an answer to his own inveterate scepticism. This religious stance and his dismissive attitude to claims then being made for social anthropology as 'a natural science of society' raised controversy and some polemic among professional colleagues.

In 1939 Evans-Pritchard married Ioma Gladys (d. 1959), daughter of George Heaton-Nicholls, later South African high commissioner in London; they had three sons and two daughters. He was commissioned in the Sudan defence force in 1940 and for some time returned to the Sudan–Ethiopian border to fight against the Italians alongside irregular troops of the Anuak, whom he knew from his brief researches there in 1935 (published as *The Political System of the Anuak of the Anglo-Egyptian Sudan* in 1940). Later he spent some time among the Alawites in Syria, and ended the war as a political officer of the British administration among the Bedouin of Cyrenaica. His book *The Sanusi of Cyrenaica* (1949) shows the effect on an acute anthropological observer of close personal involvement in practical affairs. But though he never wished, as he wrote later, 'to become just, I almost said, an intellectual', and had many friends outside intellectual circles he remained by temperament a scholar and in some measure a contemplative.

Evans-Pritchard was appointed reader in social anthropology at Cambridge University in 1945 and professor of social anthropology at Oxford University in 1946. There he built up a large and lively postgraduate school at the Institute of Social Anthropology. His energies, diverted from field research, were then directed towards promoting and consolidating the position of his subject within the academic world and beyond it as, for example, in his course of lectures for the BBC, published as *Social Anthropology* (1951). He was president of the Royal Anthropological Institute (1949–51), a founder and first life president of the Association of Social Anthropologists of the British Commonwealth, fellow of the British Academy (1956), foreign honorary member of the American Academy of Arts and Sciences (1958), and honorary fellow of the School of Oriental and African Studies (1963). Among other distinctions were honorary doctorates of the universities of Chicago (1967), Bristol (1969), and Manchester (1969), at the last in company with the sculptor Henry Moore and with Lord Sieff, who became a friend. He was knighted in 1971 and became a chevalier of the Légion d'honneur in 1972.

Meanwhile Evans-Pritchard continued to teach and to write prolifically (his bibliography has nearly 400 entries), he co-edited the Oxford Library of African Literature, promoted the translation of French anthropological classics, and gave numerous foundation lectures. He retired in 1970 and died suddenly, on 11 September 1973, at his home in Oxford, The Ark, Jack Straw's Lane, where he had continued to bring up his family after his wife's early death in 1959. He never got over that loss, which is commemorated by a junior fellowship in her name at her Oxford college, St Anne's.

Evans-Pritchard's international academic reputation, wide range of friendships, and sharp intelligence, at once pragmatic and intuitive, gave him a central position in his profession and on his retirement he could not relinquish it. Even in his last few years, when intermittent illness, deafness, and a sometimes factitious, or nostalgic, conservatism might have reduced his circle of friends or admirers, they remained with him, whether in All Souls or gathered, regardless of age or status, in his favourite Oxford pubs. Disarming though he was he could make enemies; nevertheless the many Festschriften and dedications in his honour affectionately acknowledge the debt which so many owed to his example, encouragement, and personal generosity.

In ease of manner, literary and artistic taste, and love of the wild and the natural world, Evans-Pritchard preferred to remain in some ways an Edwardian country gentleman; but he had a free, inventive imagination uniquely his own, which undermined—and from within—the bastions of Edwardian prejudice alienating modern from primitive man.   R. G. LIENHARDT, *rev.*

Sources personal knowledge (1986) · *The Times* (14 Sept 1973) · J. A. Barnes, 'Edward Evan Evans-Pritchard, 1902–1973', *PBA*, 73 (1987), 447–90 · T. O. Beidelman, *A bibliography of the writings of E. E. Evans-Pritchard* (1974) · *CGPLA Eng. & Wales* (1973)
Archives U. Oxf., Institute of Social and Cultural Anthropology, ethnographic and professional corresp. and papers | CUL, corresp. with Meyer Fortes | FILM BFI NFTVA, 'Strangers abroad', Central Independent Television, 5 Nov 1986
Likenesses photograph, repro. in Barnes, 'Edward Evan Evans-Pritchard', facing p. 447
Wealth at death £52,793: probate, 5 Nov 1973, *CGPLA Eng. & Wales*

Pritchard, Edward William (1825–1865), surgeon and poisoner, son of Captain John White Pritchard RN, was born at Southsea, Hampshire, on 6 December 1825. He was educated in London and Paris, and apprenticed in September 1840 to Edward and Charles Scott, surgeons, in Portsmouth. On completing his apprenticeship he entered King's College as a hospital student of surgery in October 1843, although this was later denied by the hospital authorities. Much of the information about his medical career derives from an entry supplied by himself in the *Medical Directory* of 1865; the dates are variously given by several writers on his life and should all be viewed with some scepticism.

Pritchard was admitted a member of the College of Surgeons on 29 May 1846 and was at once gazetted assistant surgeon serving on board the *Collingwood*, the *Calypso*, and the *Asia*, going to Egypt and other countries bordering the Mediterranean, as well as to the Pitcairn Islands on the steam-sloop *Hecate*. He resigned from the navy in 1847 and became private physician to a gentleman traveller with whom he visited the Holy Land. He passed the examinations for licentiate of the Society of Apothecaries in the same year. Pritchard decided to settle in England, and on 19 September 1850 married Mary Jane, daughter of Michael Taylor, a retired silk and lace merchant of Edinburgh, whom he met at a ball in Portsmouth. They had five children. With his father-in-law's help he established

himself in a general practice in Hunmanby, Yorkshire, in 1851, and moved to Filey in 1854. In 1857 he purchased the degree of MD from the University of Erlangen in Germany, and moved to Edinburgh in 1859. In 1860 he moved to Glasgow, where he lived at 11 Berkeley Terrace, applying unsuccessfully for the chair of surgery at the Andersonian University in October of that year. He was not popular with his medical colleagues and was considered 'ignorant, daring and reckless'. Nevertheless, he published articles in reputable medical journals, and became a director of the Glasgow Athenaeum and an examiner in physiology under the Society of Arts.

Late on the night of 5 May 1863 there was a fire at Pritchard's house in which a servant, Elizabeth McGirn, perished. The fire insurance was unpaid, and Pritchard was suspected of raising the fire to cause McGirn's death as it was likely that she was pregnant, but the matter was not pursued. In May 1864 he purchased the practice of Dr Corbett and his house in Clarence Place, 131 Sauchiehall Street, Glasgow, with a loan of £500 from his mother-in-law, Mrs Jane Cowper Taylor. He had by now seduced a fifteen-year-old servant, Mary McLeod, and procured an abortion for her. In November 1864 his wife became ill and went to stay with her mother in Edinburgh to recover, but became ill again on her return. Her mother came to Glasgow to nurse her. In December of that year, and in January, February, and March 1865, Pritchard bought Fleming's tincture of aconite. Mrs Taylor died on 25 February 1865 after eating a tapioca pudding; Pritchard signed a death certificate attributing the death to a stroke. Mrs Pritchard died on 17/18 March, and Pritchard registered the death as caused by gastric fever. The procurator fiscal received an anonymous letter accusing Pritchard of causing the two deaths, and he was arrested on a charge of murder soon afterwards.

The trial began on 3 July 1865 at the high court of justiciary in Edinburgh before John Inglis and lasted for five days. Both bodies were exhumed and autopsies showed that both contained large quantities of antimony. The defence suggested that the murders had been committed by Mary McLeod, who testified that Pritchard had promised to marry her on the death of his wife. It was proved that Pritchard was in debt and expected a large sum of money on the death of the two women, and that he administered antimony to his wife over some months and aconite to Mrs Taylor in a sedative which she took regularly. Pritchard confessed to his guilt on the day of sentencing, exonerating Mary McLeod, and was sentenced to death. He was hanged by William Calcraft in front of Glasgow gaol on 28 July 1865; 100,000 people attended what was the last public execution in Glasgow.

Pritchard had some reputation as a lecturer on such subjects as 'Egypt and its climate' and, in addition to his medical papers, published works including *A Visit to Pitcairn Island* (1847), *Observations on Filey as a Watering Place* (1853), which ran to three editions, and *Coast Lodgings for the Poorer Cities* (1854). He was described as being a plausible liar, vain to a degree, 5 feet 11 inches tall, well proportioned, with a pleasing face, regular features, and aquiline nose, bald but with a lock of light brown hair adjusted to cover his head, and with a flowing beard.

A. H. MILLAR, rev. J. GILLILAND

Sources *A complete report of the trial of Dr. G. W. Pritchard* (1865) · H. L. Adam, *Pritchard the poisoner* (1913) · W. Roughead, ed., *The trial of Dr. Pritchard* (1906) · G. L. Browne and C. G. Stewart, *Reports of trials* (1883), 397–448 · *Annual Register* (1865), 107, 221–7 · A. Vincent, *A gallery of poisoners* (1993) · M. Farrell, *Poison and poisoners* (1994) · Allibone, *Dict.* · Boase, *Mod. Eng. biog.* · *Illustrated Times* (15 July 1865), 24

Likenesses photograph, repro. in Roughead, ed., *The trial of Dr. Pritchard* · photograph, repro. in *Complete report* · photograph, repro. in Adam, *Pritchard the poisoner* · woodcut, repro. in *Harper's Weekly*, 9 (1865), 509

Pritchard [Richards], **Evan** [*pseud.* Ieuan Lleyn] (**1769–1832**), Welsh-language poet, was the son of Richard Thomas, a stonecutter, of Tŷ-mawr in the parish of Bryn-croes, Caernarvonshire, and his wife, Mary Charles (Mari Siarl). Both his mother and her father, Siarl Marc, were writers of Welsh verse. Evan Pritchard began life as a schoolmaster at Llangïan, near his home; he afterwards kept school at Llanddeiniolen in the same county. In 1795 his parents emigrated to America, and he lived at Tŷ-mawr, first with his grandfather, and then with his uncle, Lewis Charles. In 1800 he went to England as an excise officer, and returned to Tŷ-mawr in 1812; for the rest of his life he conducted a travelling school in the neigh-bouring parishes. In 1816 he married his cousin, Mary Roberts of Hen-dŷ, Bryncroes, and they had two sons and a daughter.

Pritchard was a versatile writer in all forms of Welsh verse. He wrote much for the periodicals of his time, and edited *Yr Eurgrawn*, of which some numbers appeared at Caernarfon in 1800. He was a frequent competitor at eisteddfods, and his best-known poems are the 'Ode on Belshazzar's Feast', that on the massacre of the bards, and the translation of 'The Cottar's Saturday Night'. He died on 14 August 1832, and a collected edition of his verse was published under the title *Caniadau Ieuan Lleyn* at Pwllheli in 1878.

J. E. LLOYD, rev. M. CLARE LOUGHLIN-CHOW

Sources *DWB* · R. Williams, *Enwogion Cymru: a biographical dictionary of eminent Welshmen* (1852)

Pritchard, George (1796–1883), missionary and diploma-tist, born in Birmingham on 1 August 1796, worked from childhood with his father, a journeyman brass-founder, and showed great mechanical skill. In his youth he and his family attended the Congregational chapel in Carr's Lane, and he became a local preacher in villages around Bir-mingham. He entered a boarding-school in Stafford in 1820, to prepare for further study at the mission seminary at Gosport, from 1820 to 1824. He was ordained as a Con-gregational minister in 1824, and on 25 July of the same year he married Elizabeth Ayllen (*d.* 1871), of West Meon, Hampshire. Two days later, on 27 July, they left on a cargo ship bound for Tahiti, in the Society Islands of the Pacific Ocean, where Pritchard was to undertake missionary work for the London Missionary Society.

Pritchard and his wife were welcomed on their arrival

George Pritchard (1796–1883), by George Baxter, pubd 1845

by Queen Pomare. On 21 November 1836 the queen refused to admit two French priests, Laval and Carret, from the Gambia Island, into her territories, and there fol-lowed a long quarrel with the French government, which ended in the islands being placed under French protection in 1842, and temporarily annexed by France in 1843. Prit-chard, appointed in 1837 as British consul for the Geor-gian, Society, Navigator's, and Friendly islands, advised the queen throughout this critical period, and he helped to pay an indemnity of 2000 Spanish dollars summarily demanded by the French admiral, Du Petit-Thouars, in 1838. In 1841 Pritchard went to England to lay the case of the dispossessed queen before the British government, and to describe the outrages which the invaders had allegedly inflicted on British subjects; but he returned in February 1843 without obtaining any genuine guarantee of security. On 5 March 1844 he was seized by the French authorities on the pretence that he encouraged disaffec-tion among the islanders. Captain Gordon, of HMS *Cor-morant*, negotiated his release, on condition that he should leave the islands and never return.

Pritchard sailed in the *Cormorant* to Valparaiso, and then on to London. The British government demanded that the French apologize and make financial reparations: Prit-chard claimed that his property had suffered damage to the amount of £4000. Eventually, in the queen's speech of 1845, an announcement was made that the difficulty had been satisfactorily adjusted.

Pritchard returned to the south Pacific in 1845, as Brit-ain's first consul in Samoa. His term of office was marked by controversy about his commercial activities and by quarrels with Samoan chiefs. Even during his missionary days in Tahiti, Pritchard had been involved in private trading ventures, and now, from his consulate at the port of Apia, he began dealing openly in alcoholic liquor and in weapons. The area around Apia was embroiled in civil war for most of Pritchard's tenure, creating a demand for firearms and ammunition, and occasionally leading to the destruction of buildings or livestock. Pritchard forwarded a deluge of complaints to London from British traders and Samoans demanding redress for property damage, while pursuing his own escalating compensation claims. His dispatches also demanded better support from the Royal Navy: visiting captains tended to sympathize more with the Samoans than with Pritchard and the Europeans. A series of these captains, seconded by missionaries and Samoan chiefs, complained to the Foreign Office about Pritchard's unsuitability, and requested the appointment of a consul more sympathetic to Samoan culture, along with instructions to forbid consular trade. Accepting the inevitable, Pritchard resigned his post and returned to England in 1856.

Pritchard subsequently lived in retirement in England. His first wife died in 1871; his second wife, Charlotte Annie, and several of his children survived him. He died from bronchitis at his home, 1 St Andrews Terrace, Hove, Sussex, on 6 May 1883. His son William had become Britain's first consul in Fiji in 1857. Pritchard published *Queen Pomare and her Country* (1878), and left in manuscript an account of French activities in the south Pacific, which was published in 1983.

SAMUEL TIMMINS, *rev.* JANE SAMSON

Sources P. Dekker, ed., *The aggressions of the French at Tahiti* (1983) · C. Haldane, *Tempest over Tahiti* (1963) · N. Gunson, *Messengers of grace: evangelical missionaries in the south seas, 1797–1860* (1978) · R. P. Gilson, *Samoa, 1830 to 1900* (1970) · C. W. Newbury, *Tahiti nui: change and survival in French Polynesia, 1767–1945* (1980) · J. Sampson, *Imperial benevolence: making British authority in the Pacific islands* (1998) · R. Lovett, *The history of the London Missionary Society, 1795–1895*, 2 vols. (1899) · *CGPLA Eng. & Wales* (1883) · d. cert. · candidates' papers, SOAS, Archives of the Council for World Mission (incorporating the London Missionary Society)

Archives Mitchell L., NSW, Tahiti consulate MSS · PRO, FO MSS, Pacific islands · SOAS, LMS

Likenesses G. Baxter, engraving, pubd 1845; Christies, 13 June 1973, lot 147 [*see illus.*] · C. Baugniet, lithograph, BM, NPG · G. Baxter, portrait, NL NZ, Turnbull L. · G. Baxter, print, BM

Wealth at death £127: probate, 24 May 1883, *CGPLA Eng. & Wales*

Pritchard [*née* Vaughan], **Hannah** (1709–1768), actress and singer, was born in London on 28 October 1709, the second of the five children of Edward Vaughan (*b. c.*1680, *d.* before 1736) and his wife, Judith Dun (*b. c.*1680, *d.* after 1758). She was baptized on 15 November at St Martin-in-the-Fields, and grew up in Holford's Alley, in the close vicinity of Drury Lane theatre. Her father was a staymaker and may have supplied stays and related accessories to the theatres.

On 4 October 1730 Hannah married William Pritchard (1708–1763), then an 'Ingraver in prints', at The Globe tavern, Hatton Garden. William later became, briefly, an actor and then undertook a variety of administrative jobs in the theatre. Hannah and William had three daughters:

Hannah Pritchard (1709–1768), by Francis Hayman, 1750

Judith, baptized on 13 July 1731 at St Martin-in-the-Fields; Tamara (or Tamary) Elizabeth, baptized at St Clement Danes on 24 January 1738; and Hannah Mary, baptized on 13 April 1739, also at St Clement Danes. Eleven years later Hannah gave birth to a son, John (baptized on 17 June 1750), who appears to have died in infancy. By the time of his birth the Pritchards were living at 67 Great Queen Street, Lincoln's Inn Fields (before that they had lived at 8 Craven Buildings in the parish of St Clement Danes, 56 Great Queen Street, Lincoln's Inn Fields, and Duke's Court, where they leased a house from the duke of Bedford). Little is known about Hannah Pritchard's private life except that she seems to have been a devoted wife and mother. In addition to their stage careers, the Pritchards ran a thriving dressmaking business which included the provision of theatrical costumes.

The date of Hannah Pritchard's first theatrical engagement is uncertain. Benjamin Victor claimed, in his *The History of the Theatres*, that she was engaged by the managers of Drury Lane theatre in 1732. Thomas Davies, however, in his *Memoirs of the Life of David Garrick*, states that her first appearance was at the Haymarket Theatre in one of Fielding's farces. Her first recorded role was the First Phillis in Edward Philips's ballad opera *The Livery Rake*, at Drury Lane on 5 May 1733 (though it is possible, according to *The London Stage*, that the cast list could be for a revival later that year). On 23 August 1733 she played Loveit in a ballad opera, *A Cure for Covetousness*, at Fielding and Hippisley's booth at Bartholomew fair. The company performed at the fair until 4 September, on which date the management responded to the public's enthusiasm for a duet entitled 'Sweet, if you love me, smiling turn', sung by Mrs Pritchard and the actor and tenor Salway, by providing free copies of the song to be given away daily at the booth. A contributor to the September issue of the *Gentleman's Magazine*, one 'R. S.' (possibly the poet Richard Savage), praised her grace and wit in verse and looked forward to her translation to 'some nobler stage' where she would her 'rival actresses outshine' (*GM*, 3, 1733, 490).

Shortly after her appearance at Bartholomew fair Mrs Pritchard joined Theophilus Cibber's new company, the Comedians of his Majesty's Revels, at the Haymarket Theatre. Over the next few seasons she appeared, mostly at the Haymarket and Drury Lane, in a variety of roles. In 1740 she achieved her first major triumph, when, on 20 December, at Drury Lane, she played Rosalind in a revival of *As You Like It*, a play 'Not Acted these Forty Years' (Scouten, 2.875). In *The Actor*, John Hill wrote that 'the first speech that ever obtained Mrs Pritchard a loud applause' was Rosalind's 'Take the cork out of thy mouth, that I may drink thy tidings'. She was 'applauded throughout [the speech] and for ever after'. If it had not been for this performance of Rosalind, Hill suggests, it is possible that 'the best actress of the British stage would have perished in oblivion' (Hill, 195). Her other roles that season included Nerissa in *The Merchant of Venice*. It was in this production that Charles Macklin first enacted his legendary portrayal of Shylock.

On 5 October 1742 Mrs Pritchard acted for the first time with the young David Garrick, then a rapidly rising star. The venue was the Drury Lane theatre, and Garrick and Mrs Pritchard played Chamont and Monima in Thomas Otway's *The Orphan*. In the same season, on 16 November, Mrs Pritchard was Gertrude to Garrick's Hamlet. The two actors continued to appear together in a variety of roles over the next few seasons. Then, in 1747, the Pritchards joined Garrick and James Lacy, who had bought the patent of the Drury Lane theatre. Hannah was engaged as a leading actress and William as treasurer.

On 19 March 1748 Garrick and Mrs Pritchard appeared together in *Macbeth* for the first time, and the excellence of their performances was the subject of immediate acclaim. In the opinion of Thomas Davies their portrayal of events immediately before and after Duncan's murder could not be equalled. The 'merits of both were transcendent' (Davies, *Dramatic Miscellanies*, 2.148). Johann Zoffany's portrait of David Garrick and Hannah Pritchard in *Macbeth* (now at the Garrick Club), in which the tall, statuesque figure of Hannah Pritchard—particularly in contrast to the smaller, slighter Garrick—holds the dagger in one hand while pointing towards Duncan's chamber with the other, captures something of the physical power of her performance. Its thrilling intensity is suggested by Henry Fuseli's more atmospheric version of the scene. Mrs Pritchard was generally recognized as the greatest Lady Macbeth of her day. After her retirement Garrick acted the role of Macbeth only once (on 22 September 1768 before the king of Denmark, with Mrs Barry as Lady Macbeth), out of

respect, it was believed, for the brilliance of Mrs Pritchard's performance.

Mrs Pritchard was a gifted actress, excelling in both tragedy and comedy, though, for a number of her contemporaries, her greatest skills were in comedy. Her performance of Beatrice in *Much Ado about Nothing*, when teamed with Garrick's Benedick, was highly acclaimed. She was slender and attractive as a young woman, though later in life she became very stout. She had a good voice and excellent timing. Her greatest strength, on the evidence of a number of her contemporaries, was her versatility. Whereas other actors, John Hill wrote, were immediately recognizable in every role they played because of one overriding characteristic (Garrick's 'spirit', Mr Barry's 'softness', Mrs Cibber's 'melancholy'), 'Mrs Pritchard, having no distinguishing mark of this kind, carries with her nothing that is peculiar to herself into the character' (Hill, 60–61). Her focus was primarily on the part she played, rather than on herself.

The fact that Mrs Pritchard identified strongly with the characters she played (occasionally to their detriment) is evident from her performance of the eponymous character in John Delap's *Hecuba* on 11 December 1761, in the course of which, according to the play's author, she sobbed so much that she spoiled the play. She had other detractors too. Samuel Johnson told Sarah Siddons, who asked his opinion of Mrs Pritchard's acting (which she had never seen), that she 'was a vulgar idiot' (Manvell, 95), and claimed that she had read only her own part in *Macbeth*. Johnson appears, however, to have blamed Mrs Pritchard for the hostile reception of his play *Mahomet and Irene*, in which she played Irene, and this probably clouded his view. This was the opinion of Mrs Thrale, who considered Mrs Pritchard 'incomparable', and noted that 'her Intelligence pervaded every Sense' (*Thraliana*, 2.726).

By the 1764–5 season Mrs Pritchard's health had begun to suffer. On 25 April 1768 she gave her final performance, in the role of Lady Macbeth. Garrick, who played Macbeth, wrote a farewell epilogue for her to speak, which Davies writes that she delivered 'with many sobs and tears' (Davies, *Life of David Garrick*, 2.190). Following this she retired and moved to Bath, where she died on 20 August 1768, 'of a mortification in her foot' (ibid.). She was buried on 28 August at St Mary's, Twickenham. In 1772 a white marble memorial tablet was erected in Westminster Abbey, next to Shakespeare's monument in Poets' Corner. O'Keeffe, who often saw Hannah Pritchard act, noted in his *Recollections* that she 'well deserve[d]' this recognition (O'Keeffe, 1.107). The memorial was later moved to the triforium.

The chief beneficiaries of Hannah Pritchard's will were her daughters. Her property in Twickenham (Ragman's Castle) was left, in common, to the three of them, and Tamara Elizabeth and Hannah Mary inherited the lease of her house in Tavistock Street, London (with thirty years still to run). Tamara Elizabeth received, in addition, £700, in stocks or a house purchased with that sum, along with a variety of household and personal effects belonging to her late mother. Judith received a mourning ring (which had originally been her mother's wedding ring and which Hannah had had transformed into a mourning ring on the death of her husband), and Hannah's two portraits by Francis Hayman. GERALDINE COUSIN

Sources A. Vaughan, *Born to please: Hannah Pritchard, actress, 1711–1768* (1979) • A. Vaughan, note, *Theatre Notebook*, 36 (1982), 126–7 • Highfill, Burnim & Langhans, *BDA* • [J. Hill], *The actor, or, A treatise on the art of playing* (1755); repr. (New York, 1972) • T. Davies, *Dramatic miscellanies*, 2 (1784); repr. (1971) • T. Davies, *Memoirs of the life of David Garrick*, 2 vols. (1808), vol. 2 • *Thraliana: the diary of Mrs. Hester Lynch Thrale (later Mrs. Piozzi), 1776–1809*, ed. K. C. Balderston, 2nd edn, 2 (1951) • R. Manvell, *Sarah Siddons* (1970) • J. O'Keeffe, *Recollections of the life of John O'Keeffe, written by himself*, 1 (1826); repr. (1969) • A. H. Scouten, ed., *The London stage, 1660–1800*, pt 3: *1729–1747* (1961) • PRO, Fleet marriages MSS, MS RG7.573
Likenesses F. Hayman, 1747, Yale U. CBA; version, Museum of London • F. Hayman, oils, 1750, Garr. Club [*see illus.*] • J. Macardell, mezzotint, pubd 1762 (after F. Hayman), BM, NPG • J. Zoffany, oils, 1768, Garr. Club
Wealth at death see will, PRO, PROB 11/942; Vaughan, *Born to please*

Pritchard, Henry Baden (1841–1884). *See under* Pritchard, Andrew (1804–1882).

Pritchard, John Langford (1799–1850), actor, the son of a captain in the navy, was born, it is said, at sea, in February 1799, and, adopting his father's profession, became a midshipman. Inspired by the performances of Edmund Kean and other actors, he took to the stage, and after some practice as an amateur joined a small company in Wales. In May 1820, as 'Pritchard from Cheltenham', he made his first appearance in Bath, when he took the part of Captain Absolute in *The Rivals*. In August he played Lord Trinket, Sir Benjamin Backbite, and other parts under Alfred Bunn at the New Theatre, Birmingham. He reappeared in Bath in October as Irwin in Elizabeth Inchbald's *Everyone has his Fault*. In the summer of 1821 he joined the York circuit under Mansell and made his first appearance as Romeo. Parts such as Jaffier, Pythias, Iago, Edmund in *King Lear*, and Richmond were assigned him.

Pritchard then joined W. H. Murray's company in Edinburgh, where he remained for eleven years. He played a variety of Scottish characters, including Edward Waverley in a new version of *Waverley* and Rob Roy, a difficult part in Edinburgh for an Englishman. He also took on historical characters such as Richard I in *The Talisman*, George Douglas in *Mary Stuart* (*The Abbot*), and Oliver Cromwell in *Woodstock, or, The Cavalier*. In 1830–31 Pritchard went with Murray to the Adelphi Theatre. He appeared there through the summer season of 1832 and then left Edinburgh. While he was there he won very favourable recognition, both artistic and social, and took a prominent part in establishing the Edinburgh Shakespeare Club, at the first anniversary dinner of which Scott owned himself the author of *Waverley*. During his vacations he had played in Glasgow, Perth, Aberdeen, and other leading Scottish towns.

In October 1833 Pritchard made his first appearance in Dublin, playing Bassanio and Petruchio, followed by Wellborn to the Sir Giles Overreach of Charles Kean. He was hospitably entertained in Ireland, where he also appeared as Jeremy Diddler, Mark Antony, and Meg Merrilees, and established a club similar to that in Edinburgh. He made his début in London on 16 November 1835 at Covent Garden, as Alonzo in *Pizarro*. He played Macduff, and was popular as Lindsay, an original part in Edward Fitzball's *The Inheritance*. During W. C. Macready's tenure of Covent Garden in 1838 he reappeared as Don Pedro in Susannah Centlivre's *The Wonder*; Macready himself played Don Felix, which was held to be Pritchard's great part. He took a secondary role in the performance of Bulwer-Lytton's *The Lady of Lyons*, and was the original Felton in Sheridan Knowles's *Woman's Wit, or, Love's Disguises*. Macready, justifiably it seems, was charged with keeping him back. Pritchard retired ultimately to the provinces and became the manager of the York circuit, where he continued to act. He died on 5 August 1850. He was a sound, careful, and judicious actor, but only just reached the second rank; his best parts appear to have been Don Felix and Mercutio.

JOSEPH KNIGHT, *rev.* NILANJANA BANERJI

Sources *Actors by Daylight* (30 June 1838) • Hall, *Dramatic ports.* • *The history of the Theatre Royal, Dublin, from its foundation in 1821 to the present time* (1870) • J. C. Dibdin, *The annals of the Edinburgh stage* (1888) • *The Idler* (1838)
Likenesses W. H. Nightingale, pencil drawing, 1836, NPG • caricature, repro. in *Actors by Daylight* • prints, BM, NPG • prints, Harvard TC

Pritchard, Sir John Michael (1918–1989), conductor, was born on 5 February 1918 at 17 Cromwell Road, Walthamstow, London, the younger son (there were no daughters) of Albert Edward Pritchard, violinist, and his wife, Amy Edith Shaylor. He was educated at Sir George Monoux School in London, and he studied privately with his father and other music teachers. In his teenage years he visited Italy to listen to opera. When the Second World War broke out Pritchard registered as a conscientious objector, to his father's dismay. He therefore underwent an army medical examination, but, because of an earlier attack of pleurisy, was registered unfit to serve. In 1943 he took over the Derby String Orchestra and was its principal conductor until 1951. Meanwhile he joined the music staff of Glyndebourne Opera (1947) and was appointed chorus master there (1949). He succeeded Reginald Jacques as conductor of the Jacques Orchestra (1950–52). By 1951 he was sharing with Fritz Busch major Mozart productions at Glyndebourne and at the Edinburgh Festival.

Important opportunities came Pritchard's way in 1952: at Edinburgh he appeared with the Royal Philharmonic Orchestra, replacing Ernest Ansermet, who was ill; and he made his débuts at the Royal Opera House in Covent Garden, and at the Vienna State Opera. He appeared regularly with the Vienna Symphony Orchestra (1953–5). He continued to work at Glyndebourne, conducting their productions of Mozart's *Idomeneo* and Richard Strauss's *Ariadne auf Naxos* at the Edinburgh festivals of 1953 and 1954. After the latter he conducted the Glyndebourne production of Rossini's *La Cenerentola* at the Berlin Festival. The performance was a triumph.

At home, Pritchard was appointed principal conductor

Sir John Michael Pritchard (1918–1989), by Derek Allen

of the Royal Liverpool Philharmonic Orchestra (1957–63) and within a year had launched the Musica Viva series at which contemporary music was introduced, illustrated, performed, and then discussed. During five seasons, unfamiliar music by many living composers was heard for the first time in Britain. Pritchard's success in Liverpool led to his appointment as musical director of the London Philharmonic Orchestra (1962–6). At Glyndebourne he became music counsellor (1963), principal conductor (1968), and musical director (1969–77). In 1969 he took the London Philharmonic to the Far East and made his American début, at the Chicago Lyric Opera. Appearances at the San Francisco Opera (1970) and the Metropolitan Opera (1971) followed. In 1973 he conducted the London Philharmonic in China—the first visit by a Western orchestra.

By 1980 Pritchard had conducted many of the world's greatest orchestras, including the Berlin Philharmonic, the Leipzig Gewandhaus, the Dresden Staatskapelle, and the Philadelphia Orchestra; he had appeared at the Salzburg festival, the Maggio Musicale in Florence, and the Munich State Opera. In London he was a regular guest at the Royal Opera House, Covent Garden, at the Proms, and with the BBC Symphony Orchestra, whose chief conductor he became in 1982. Overlapping posts included at that time the musical directorships of the Cologne Opera (1978), the Théâtre de la Monnaie, Brussels (1981), and the San Francisco Opera (1986).

Pritchard's innate musicality, his quick grasp, his range of sympathies, and his gift for getting the best out of the musicians (with whom he was very popular) combined to bring him a career of astonishing concentration and variety. No conductor can have had a fuller diary. Although this sometimes led to a perfunctoriness bordering upon indolence, he was, at his best, an interpreter of lasting distinction. His Mozart and Strauss were superbly idiomatic, but he also excelled in nineteenth-century Italian opera. And he could surprise his public with, for example, some tough Shostakovich. He was not, however, a great star; he did not make enough recordings to achieve that status. But he was appointed CBE in 1962 and was knighted in 1983. The coveted Shakespeare prize (Hamburg) was awarded him in 1975.

Pritchard's much imitated manner of speech—bland, almost epicene—was an outward sign of his unabashed homosexuality, but there was nothing effeminate about his music-making. He had friends in every walk and style of life and was loyal and generous to them. Witty and well-informed, he lived in some style (in a number of homes, including an elegant house near Glyndebourne and a villa in the Alpes-Maritimes above Nice). Indeed his enjoyment of good food and wine became a problem when he needed to lose weight for a hip replacement operation not long before his death. It was a problem he observed with rueful detachment. Though already ill, with lung cancer, he conducted the last night of the Proms on 16 September 1989 and made a touchingly prescient and self-deprecating speech. He died on 5 December 1989 in Daly City, California. He left a large part of his estate to Terry MacInnes, his partner. ROBERT PONSONBY, rev.

Sources S. Hughes, *Glyndebourne* (1965) · N. Kenyon, *The BBC Symphony Orchestra … 1930–1980* (1981) · J. Higgins, ed., *Glyndebourne: a celebration* (1984) · *The Independent* (6 Dec 1989) · *The Times* (6 Dec 1989) · b. cert.

Likenesses D. Allen, bromide print, NPG [*see illus.*]

Pritchard, Thomas Farnolls (*bap.* 1723, *d.* 1777), architect, was baptized on 11 May 1723 at St Julian's Church, Shrewsbury, the eldest in the family of four sons and one daughter of John Pritchard (*d.* 1747), a joiner of Shrewsbury, and his wife, Hannah Farnolls. His own background was also as a joiner, but from the late 1740s onwards he developed a quite extensive professional practice in both Shropshire and the neighbouring counties. A speciality of his was the supply of chimney-pieces and other elements of interior decoration, and of funerary monuments; and an album of his designs of this type, later acquired by the library of the American Institute of Architects in Washington, indicates that he employed a number of carvers on a regular basis—the two principal names are Alexander van der Hagen and John Nelson of Shrewsbury—to execute them. Overall, his churches and houses are no more than pleasant provincial work—examples are the rebuilding of St Julian's Church in Shrewsbury (1749–50) and Hatton Grange, Shropshire (1764–8)—but his decorative and funerary designs reveal him as a highly competent exponent of both the rococo style and the Gothic manner of Batty Langley. Examples of his interior decoration are at Croft Castle, Herefordshire (1765), Gaines in Whitbourne, Herefordshire (*c.*1765), and Shipton Hall, Shropshire. Among his monuments, in the Gothic and rococo modes respectively, are those to Sir Whitmore Acton in Acton Round church, Shropshire (1763), and to Mary Morhall (d. 1765) in St Mary's, Shrewsbury.

Pritchard's chief claim to fame, however, lies in his role in connection with a structure of a quite different type which he did not live to see executed—the famous iron bridge across the River Severn in Coalbrookdale, Shropshire. His involvement with bridge building started in 1767, when he was appointed surveyor to direct the widening of the English bridge in Shrewsbury to a design by Robert Mylne; when that project was abandoned, he submitted a design for the new bridge which was rejected in favour of that by John Gwynn. Then in 1773–4 he made two designs for a bridge to cross the Severn in Stourport, Worcestershire, the first to be of timber with stone abutments and the second a single arch of brick but resting on a cast-iron centre. Neither of these was adopted—the executed bridge was a conventional masonry structure of three arches—but in his design for the Coalbrookdale Bridge, made in 1775, he adapted some of the principles of the timber proposal to a structure wholly of cast iron. It was a modified version of this design which was executed by the Coalbrookdale ironworks in 1777–9, the first iron bridge in the world.

In 1751 Pritchard married Eleanor Russell (d. 1768); three of their children died young. Their surviving daughter married the surveyor John White, whose son John White junior published an illustrated account of Pritchard's bridge designs in a pamphlet entitled *On Cementitious Architecture as Applicable to the Construction of Bridges* (1832). In his later years Pritchard lived in a house called Eyton Turret in Eyton-on-Severn, Shropshire, which he had formed from one of a pair of Jacobean garden buildings in the former grounds of a demolished mansion. He died on 23 December 1777 and was buried at St Julian's, Shrewsbury.

PETER LEACH

Sources Colvin, *Archs.* · R. Gunnis, *Dictionary of British sculptors, 1660–1851* (1953) · J. F. Harris, 'Pritchard redivivus', *Architectural History*, 11 (1968), 17–24 · J. Harris, *A catalogue of British drawings for architecture, decoration, sculpture and landscape gardening, 1550–1900, in American collections* (1972) · T. Ruddock, *Arch bridges and their builders, 1735–1835* (1979) · J. L. Hobbs, 'Thomas Farnolls Pritchard', *Shropshire Magazine*, 10/4 (Aug–Sept 1959), 29–30, 34
Likenesses portrait, Ironbridge Gorge Museum, Shropshire

Pritchard [Prichard], **Sir William** (1631/2–1705), politician, was probably born in Horsleydown, Surrey, the second son of Francis Prichard, rope maker, and his wife, Mary, daughter of Edward Eggleston. Apprenticed to a Southwark merchant tailor in 1647, Pritchard became free of the Merchant Taylors' Company in 1655. By the time of the Restoration he had succeeded to his father's trade, which he continued at Eltham, Kent; and after 1663 he was the supplier of rope and match to the Ordnance office. The diarist Samuel Pepys encountered him in 1662 and again in 1668, mistaking him on the first occasion for a theatre musician and demanding a song from him. About 1669 Pritchard married Sarah (d. 1718), daughter of Francis Cook of Kingsthorpe, Northamptonshire.

By the late 1670s Pritchard had made a fortune supplying cordage and match to the navy during the second and third Dutch wars. In 1671 he sold the manor house of Tower Place in Woolwich to the king, receiving royal wharves and storehouses in exchange, properties that he subsequently leased back to the crown. After relocating his business to Heydon Yard in the Minories, near the Tower of London, he quickly became prominent in the corporation of London. Knighted and chosen alderman of Broad Street in 1672, he was also elected sheriff of London and Middlesex in 1672–3 and master of the Merchant Taylors' Company in 1673–4. He served as a London assessment commissioner in 1673–80 and 1689–90, as a London militia colonel in 1676–87, 1690–94, and 1702–5, as a London lieutenancy commissioner in 1677–87, 1688–94, and 1702–5, and as president of the Honourable Artillery Company in 1681–90 and 1703–5. In 1678 he purchased the manor of Great Linford, Buckinghamshire, from Richard Napier for £19,500. He also established an additional London residence in Highgate.

In September 1679, in the midst of the Popish Plot furore, Pritchard was reportedly among the aldermen who refused to kiss the hand of James, duke of York. But as the contest over the royal succession spawned whig and tory parties in London, his Anglican loyalist convictions and his business interests aligned him with the court. Pritchard was a steward for a feast for loyalist apprentices in August 1682; and as the senior alderman beneath the chair, he was the loyalist candidate for lord mayor for 1682–3. The mayoral election of 1682 was overshadowed by the protracted contest for the shrievalty that preceded it; but Pritchard's election was just as much a part of Charles II's campaign to recover London from the whigs, and his mayoralty was memorable. The court-sponsored tory sheriffs for 1682–3, who were sworn just before the mayoral election of 29 September and who were the presiding officers in common hall, declared that a majority of the electors preferred Pritchard. But this result was contested on behalf of two whig candidates by Thomas Papillon and John Dubois, whose claim to the shrievalty was recognized by the London whigs and who had also attempted to preside. When both whigs topped Pritchard in the ensuing poll, the loyalist-dominated court of aldermen adjusted a scrutiny in favour of Pritchard. But the aldermen's declaration of Pritchard as lord mayor was rejected by the whigs, who boycotted the mayoral show and sued for the offices of sheriff and lord mayor in the court of king's bench. In Pritchard's first days as lord mayor, whig crowds commemorating the Gunpowder Plot mobbed him when he sought to disperse them with the trained bands, and broke his windows.

Pritchard laboured throughout his mayoralty to reduce whig influence in the corporation and to enforce the Conventicle Acts. When he and the tory aldermen ignored a mandamus the whigs had secured from king's bench to show why they should not invest Papillon and Dubois with the shrievalty, the lord mayor was threatened with impeachment by William Williams, former speaker and chief whig legal adviser. When king's bench accepted the aldermen's eventual reply to the mandamus, the whigs brought individual suits against Pritchard and his predecessor for accepting false sheriffs. Legal and extra-legal whig strategies converged in April 1683, when Pritchard and several aldermen were arrested by the city coroner for their failure to respond to writs on behalf of Papillon and Dubois that were taken out by Richard Goodenough, one of their counsel. Goodenough and some of the coroner's associates were already involved in a plot to assassinate the king, and they also planned to murder the lord mayor in their intended insurrection.

What exactly was intended in Pritchard's arrest is unclear; but after the subsequent disclosures about whig plotting, the government claimed that it was intended to provide cover for an uprising. While the privy council panicked, Pritchard outmanoeuvred his captors, eventually suing Papillon and Dubois for false arrest, and winning £10,000 in damages from Papillon. Pritchard's mayoralty nevertheless ended in personal embarrassment. When the crown, which had won its *quo warranto* suit against the corporation charter, gave the corporation the opportunity to surrender its charter voluntarily, the whigs managed to carry a common council vote against the surrender, and Pritchard was said not to have 'answered expectations' (*Dartmouth MSS*, 3.125). The charter was declared forfeit, but Pritchard continued as lord mayor, by royal commission, until the end of the customary term. He transferred as alderman to Bridge at this time and became a JP for Kent (1683–8).

Pritchard was among the Anglican loyalists chosen in 1685 to represent London in James II's parliament, but he became uneasy in 1687 as James reconstructed his regime on the basis of toleration. When James sought to mend fences with his former enemies, Pritchard agreed to legal relief for Papillon, who had fled the country; but the king discharged him from all his London offices when he refused to support an address on behalf of liberty for conscience. In October 1688, when James restored the London charter upon news of an impending invasion from the Netherlands, Pritchard turned 'Knave', in royal eyes, by declining to reaccept office as lord mayor without a writ of error in the *quo warranto* case (DWL, Morrice, Ent'ring book, Q. 303). After some hesitation, he did resume his aldermanic position, returning to Broad Street; and he was among the city representatives who presented an address to the arriving prince of Orange in December. He was also chosen president of St Bartholomew's Hospital at this time, serving for the remainder of his life.

As the whigs gained the initiative in civic affairs during the revolution of 1688, Pritchard became politically vulnerable as one of those who had co-operated in the crown's take-over and suppression of the corporation in 1682–3. He had 'but a very few hands' when put up in common hall for city MP for the convention in January 1689; and his political behaviour, as well as that of the other leading civic tories, was investigated in the House of Lords in May 1690 (DWL, Morrice, Ent'ring book, Q. 419). By that time, however, William III had broken with the whig leadership in parliament and signalled his new favour for the

church party in an alteration of the London lieutenancy, which promptly reappointed Pritchard and other tories as militia colonels. Pritchard and three tory colleagues were also chosen city MPs for a new parliament in March 1690. They promoted passage of a Commons bill to require fresh civic elections as part of a statutory reversal of the *quo warranto*. When the court of aldermen, now dominated by the whigs, responded by continuing the sitting whig lord mayor, despite a slight common hall majority for a tory opponent, Pritchard borrowed a legal leaf from the whigs. He took out a king's bench mandamus for the office himself, claiming that he should return to the position he held when the charter was forfeited.

Although this device failed, Pritchard remained involved in party wrangling for the remainder of William's reign. He was defeated as a church tory candidate for city MP in 1695 and January 1701; but he returned to his seat in July 1702, after the succession of Queen Anne. Although a marginal figure in parliamentary affairs, Pritchard became a leading investor in the Royal African Company and (after initial association with its critics) in the 'old' East India Company, in which he eventually owned £15,000 in shares. He served on the governing court of committees of the East India Company in 1696–7 and 1698–1703 and as a Royal African Company assistant in 1699–1700 and 1704–5. In 1698–1701 he acted as a delegate of the East India Company in negotiations with the 'new' company that had been launched in 1698. Pritchard also served as a commissioner for the construction of Greenwich Hospital and for the national land bank scheme of 1696. In 1701 he was a founding member of the Society for the Propagation of the Gospel.

Pritchard died on 20 February 1705 at his Heydon Yard residence, aged seventy-three. He was buried in the church at Great Linford, Buckinghamshire, after a procession from Highgate. Lewis Atterbury, Highgate parson and brother of the high-flying Francis Atterbury, preached his funeral sermon. Because his only son had died twenty years earlier, Pritchard left most of his estate to two kinsmen, after first providing a £1200 annuity for his wife, who died in 1718. He also endowed almshouses at Great Linford and provided for a charity school there.

GARY S. DE KREY

Sources 'Pritchard, Sir William', HoP, *Commons, 1690–1715* [draft] • E. Cruickshanks, 'Pritchard, Sir William', HoP, *Commons, 1660–90* • J. R. Woodhead, *The rulers of London, 1660–1689* (1965), 133 • R. Morrice, 'Ent'ring book', DWL, P. 644, Q. 154, 163, 302–3, 309, 350, 419; R. 129, 132, 142, 153–4 • *CSP dom.*, 1682, 441–2, 453, 462, 487, 497, 512, 548, 550, 562, 580, 583–4; *Jan–June 1683*, 16–17, 41, 49, 82, 113, 204–6, 210, 214–15, 260, 329, 330; *July–Sept 1683*, 433; *1683–4*, 11, 13, 16, 284, 391–2; *1684–5*, 200; *1685*, 56, 86; *1687–9*, 300; *1689–90*, 487, 501; *1690–91*, 70; *1693*, 360; *1694–5*, 21 • N. Luttrell, *A brief historical relation of state affairs from September 1678 to April 1714*, 6 vols. (1857), vol. 1, pp. 32, 212, 225–7, 231–3, 283, 319, 397, 410–11, 466, 471; vol. 2, pp. 13, 19, 25, 49; vol. 3, pp. 538, 540; vol. 4, pp. 495, 721; vol. 5, pp. 193, 521 • L. Cong., manuscript division, London newsletters collection, vol. 7, pp. 297, 303 (12, 19 Dec 1682); vol. 8, pp.123–4, 127, 129–30, 132 (30 Sept and 5, 12, 17, 19, 26 Oct 1682); 252–5, 257 (26, 28, 31 Oct and 2, 7 Nov 1682); 322 (16 April 1683); 391–2, 403 (2, 4, 6 Oct 1683) • Newdigate newsletters, Folger, L.c. 838 (20 Sept 1679); 1283, 1291–4 (5, 24, 26, 28, 31 Oct 1682); 1312–15 (14, 16, 19, 21 Dec

1682); 1368 (26 April 1683); 1445–7 (4 [bis], 6 Oct 1683) · W. A. Shaw, ed., *Calendar of treasury books*, 3, PRO (1908), 757, 800; 5 (1911), 11, 79, 222; 7 (1916), 50, 205; 9 (1931), 682, 2002; 10 (1935), 797 · G. S. De Krey, *A fractured society: the politics of London in the first age of party, 1688–1715* (1985), 28, 63–7, 155–6 · *State trials*, 10.319–72 · *Memoirs of Thomas Papillon, of London, merchant*, ed. A. F. W. Papillon (1887), 228–32, 237–50 · Home misc. ser., vols. 2–3 (lists of adventurers, 1699, 1701–2), BL OIOC, East India Company court minute books, 41.364; 43.383 · *The manuscripts of the earl of Dartmouth*, 3 vols., HMC, 20 (1887–96), vol. 1, pp. 143–4; vol. 3, p. 125 · Pepys, *Diary*, 3.36; 9.37 · *An exact account of the proceedings at Guild-hall upon the election of … Sir William Prichard* (1682) · *Daily Courant* (5 March 1705) · PRO, PROB 11/483, sig. 155

Likenesses T. Althow, wash drawing, AM Oxf. · portrait, Merchant Taylors' Hall, London

Wealth at death over £35,000 (1678 purchase price of Great Linford Manor and East India stock)

Pritchett, James Pigott (1789–1868), architect, was born at St Petrox, Pembrokeshire, on 14 October 1789, and baptized there on 4 January 1790. He was the fourth son of Charles Pigott Pritchett, fellow of King's College, Cambridge, rector of St Petrox and Stackpole Elidor, Pembrokeshire, prebendary of St David's, and domestic chaplain to the earl of Cawdor, and his wife, Anne, daughter of Roger Rogers of Westerton in Ludchurch, Pembrokeshire; Delabere Pritchett, sub-chanter of St David's Cathedral, was his grandfather. He first married, at Beckenham, Kent, on 22 October 1813, Peggy Maria, daughter of Robert Terry, with whom he had three sons and one daughter, Maria Margaret. The latter married John Middleton (1846–1896), her father's pupil. Pritchett was articled to James Medland, an architect in Southwark, and in 1809 he submitted at the Royal Academy a design for a villa. After completing his articles he worked for two years in the office of Daniel Asher Alexander, architect of the London Dock Company. During this time he was engaged on the construction of Maidstone county gaol.

Pritchett set up independently in London in 1812, but in the following year he moved to York, where he entered into partnership with Charles Watson (c.1770–1836). Watson, who had been a pupil, and from 1792 to 1800 a partner, in the Doncaster office of William Lindley, had first set up in practice on his own account in Wakefield about 1800. He was, for a time, the leading architect in Yorkshire, working in a neat Grecian style, as in the court houses in Beverley (1804–14), Wakefield (1807–10), Pontefract (1807–8), and Sheffield (1807–8). With Lindley he designed St John's Church, Wakefield (1791–5), and the square and terrace related to it. In 1807 Watson moved to York, and in 1813 he took Pritchett into partnership. Their first joint major work was the Pauper Lunatic Asylum, Wakefield, which was designed according to the reforming ideas of Samuel Tuke as well as paying attention to heating, air circulation, and fire precautions. In York they built Lendal Chapel and the Friends' meeting-house (both started in 1816); these were neo-classical in style, but the later Ramsden Street Chapel, Huddersfield (1824), marked a change to a Gothic style which they developed in the Nether Chapel, Sheffield (1827), and in the deanery, York, which was designed in the same year. After the death of

his first wife, Pritchett married, on 6 January 1829, Caroline, daughter of John Benson, solicitor, of Thorne, near York; they had three sons and two daughters, of whom the eldest son, James Pigott Pritchett (1830–1911), adopted his father's profession at Darlington.

In their public buildings Watson and Pritchett continued to be faithful to a neo-classical taste. In 1828 they completed a new elevation to Lord Burlington's famous assembly rooms in York, and in the same city they built the savings bank in St Helen's Square (1829). By this time Watson was taking less part in the firm's affairs, and the partnership was dissolved in 1831. On his own account, Pritchett designed the cemetery chapel (1836–7) and Salem Chapel (1838–9), both in York and Grecian in style, but he also used a Gothic design for other churches, such as that at Meltham Mills (1845).

Pritchett's most important work is at Huddersfield, where he built one of the great monuments of railway architecture. The station was designed to serve two companies, and it is a symmetrical classical composition in which the central pedimented block contains offices, meeting-rooms, and refreshment rooms, while the flanking wings and pavilions were intended originally to serve the two companies. It is a noble design, bold and sculptural in its massing. It was completed in 1850. Another of his additions to the town is the Lion Arcade (1852–4).

Pritchett had various professional interests. For a while he was architect to the dean and chapter of York Minster, and for fifty years he was surveyor and architect to three successive earls Fitzwilliam at Wentworth Woodhouse. He was a prominent Congregationalist in York and he played an active role in the affairs of the York Cemetery Company. He died at York on 23 May 1868, and was buried in the cemetery there on 27 May. His second wife survived him.   DEREK LINSTRUM

Sources G. H. Broadbent, 'The life and work of Pritchett of York', *Studies in architectural history*, ed. W. A. Singleton, 2 (1956), 102–24 · D. Linstrum, *West Yorkshire: architects and architecture* (1978), 383, 386 · *CGPLA Eng. & Wales* (1868) · DNB

Archives Borth. Inst., MS history of nonconformist churches in York from 1662

Likenesses photograph, repro. in Broadbent, 'The life and work of Pritchett of York', fig. 1

Wealth at death under £3000: probate, 3 July 1868, *CGPLA Eng. & Wales*

Pritchett, Robert Taylor (1828–1907), gun maker and landscape painter, was born, probably in London, on 24 February 1828, the son of Richard Ellis Pritchett (c.1782–1866), and his wife, Ann Dumbleton. His father was head of the firm of Enfield gun makers, which supplied arms to the East India Company and to the Board of Ordnance. Educated at King's College School, London, he entered his father's firm, taking charge—at an early age—of the royal small arms factory at Enfield. He was made free of the Gunmakers' Company by patrimony and took livery in 1849, and he was gun maker at 86 St James's St, London, from 1856 to 1862. By 1852 Pritchett was working with William Ellis Metford; they invented the Pritchett rifle bullet with 'a hollow and unplugged base which did much to counteract the eccentricity of the Enfield Rifle' (*The Times*,

20 June 1907). The invention brought Pritchett fame, the nickname the Father of the Enfield Rifle, and an award of £1000 from the government on its adoption by the small-arms committee. He married Louisa Kezia McRae (d. 1899) on 22 September 1857; they had a son and a daughter. His wife and both children predeceased him.

With the abolition of the East India Company in 1858, Pritchett's firm lost its principal customer and he made a new career for himself as an artist. However, he continued to lecture on gunlocks and rifles, remaining a lifelong liveryman of the Gunmakers' Company; he was also an original member of the Victoria Rifles. As an artist he retained, as his device, an ancient harquebusier and his gun—an allusion to his early trade—and he drew the illustrations for Sir Sibbald Scott's The British Army (1868). Pritchett helped to establish the London Working Men's College, and in 1851, 1852, 1869, and 1871 he exhibited at the Royal Academy. In the 1860s, probably through his friendship with John Tenniel, Pritchett joined the staff of Punch, made some twenty-six drawings for publication, and became a close friend of Charles Keene, John Leech, and Myles Birket Foster. He travelled in Britain and abroad and exhibited views of the continent. In 1868, while in the Netherlands, he met the painter Jozef Israëls and dined at the palace of Het Loo with the Belgian king Leopold II. In the same year and in 1870 he exhibited views of Scheveningen at the Royal Academy and in 1871 he published Brush Notes in Holland; other publications included Smokiana: Historical and Ethnographical, etc, published in facsimile by photochromolithography in 1890. In 1874–5 he visited Norway and subsequently published Gamle Norge (1878), and he illustrated twenty-four articles on Norway in the Art Journal in 1877–8.

In March 1868 Queen Victoria bought two of Pritchett's watercolours of Scotland, perhaps through the duchess of Atholl. This signalled the beginning of sustained royal patronage of the artist. A sketch of Skye was shown at Agnew's in 1868 and two exhibitions of Pritchett's views of the Netherlands were held there in 1869; more were shown in later years. Princess Louise visited an exhibition in 1869 and, in 1870, she and Lord Lorne visited the artist's house, the New Lodge, at Esher, Surrey. In June 1868 Pritchett had requested permission to sketch at Claremont near by, and in 1870 he showed his work to Queen Victoria, who acquired sketches of Esher. The prince of Wales bought two views of Denmark; in November 1871 he saw Pritchett's drawings of Paris during the Franco-Prussian War, published as Paris 1871: under the Reign of the Commune.

A keen and expert yachtsman, by 1899 Pritchett had been made marine painter to the Royal Thames yacht club. Between 1880 and 1882 he went round the world with Joseph Lambert and his wife on their yacht and illustrated their book The Voyage of the 'Wanderer' (1883). In 1883 and 1885 he travelled as artist on the journeys of Sir Thomas and Lady Brassey on the Sunbeam. His illustrations appear in Lady Brassey's In the Trades, the Tropics and the Roaring Forties (1885) and The Last Voyage of the 'Sunbeam' (1889). Pritchett lectured about his travels and exhibited

his work in London between 1884 and 1890. His illustrations appear in the 1890 edition of Charles Darwin's Voyage of the 'Beagle' and in the Badminton Volumes on Yachting (1894) and Sea Fishing (1895). He also published Pen and Pencil Sketches: Shipping and Craft All Round the World (1899).

From 1872 Queen Victoria commissioned from Pritchett over eighty watercolours of ceremonies relating to her golden and diamond jubilees and scenes of family events; these are now in the Royal Collection. She was delighted to have found an artist able to record on a small scale, and at small expense, the many events of her later years. Pritchett was also prepared to accept criticism and, at her request, to make corrections to his watercolours. He attended many ceremonies, anxious to be commissioned to paint the scenes for his royal patron. On 7 September 1898 he suggested publishing a book containing thirty sketches made for the queen, for 'without the Queen's favour the Sketches are things of the past, with it they will be Kings of the Future' (Windsor Castle, Royal Archives, PP Vic 1209), but the scheme was never carried out. Queen Victoria's death in 1901 was a great blow to Pritchett, 'depriving him as it did of a quasi right of entrée on grand occasions' and 'closing one of the principal sources of his slender income' (Catalogue, 7).

Pritchett died, after months of illness, on 16 June 1907 at Burghfield, Berkshire, the village where he lived. He was buried in the churchyard at Burghfield. The sale of his memorabilia, books, and watercolours, held by Haslam & Son at Reading on 30–31 October 1907, contained many of his own versions of watercolours painted for the queen; some were purchased by Edward VII. Pritchett's works fetched low prices; his obituarist in The Times (20 June 1907) rightly described him as 'a man of strangely varied talent who had in some measure outlived his fame'.

DELIA MILLAR

Sources The Times (20 June 1907) · Catalogue of the possessions of R. T. Pritchett, deceased (1907), 3–8 [Haslam & Son, Reading, sales catalogue] · D. Millar, 'Artist of the grand occasion', Country Life, 180 (1986), 210–13 · H. L. Blackmore, A dictionary of London gunmakers, 1350–1850 (1986) · Royal Arch. · Encyclopaedia Britannica, 11th edn (1910–11), vol. 23, pp. 325–36 · D. Millar, The Victorian watercolours and drawings in the collection of her majesty the queen, 2 (1995) · DNB · Graves, RA exhibitors

Archives Royal Arch.

Likenesses photograph, repro. in M. H. Spielmann, The History of 'Punch' (1895), 520

Wealth at death £590 4s. 10d.: resworn probate, 10 July 1907, CGPLA Eng. & Wales

Pritchett, Sir Victor Sawdon (1900–1997), writer and critic, was born on 16 December 1900 at 41 St Nicholas Street, Ipswich, Suffolk, the son of Walter Sawdon Pritchett, who at the time of Victor's birth was unsuccessfully running a stationery business, and his wife, Beatrice Helena, née Martin. His first name was a mark of respect for the reigning monarch but he preferred not to be called Victor (as a child he was nearly mauled by a dog with the same name), and was known to his friends as VSP. Walter and Beatrice were living in a small flat above a toyshop, but within weeks they moved on to London in search of

Sir Victor Sawdon Pritchett (1900–1997), by Howard Coster, 1942

the brighter prospects after which Walter, like Mr Micawber, was constantly hankering. Walter became an itinerant salesman, but seldom earned enough to cover the rent. The Pritchett family—there were two more sons and a daughter—moved from Woodford, then to Palmers Green, Balham, Uxbridge, Acton, Ealing, Hammersmith, and Camberwell, among other places in and around London. Beatrice, worn down by poverty and childbearing, cried each time a cab arrived at the door to transport them and their potted plants and ornaments (with mottoes such as 'Dinna trouble trouble till trouble troubles you', and 'Don't worry it may never happen') to yet another rented home. Each time Beatrice, quite understandably, lamented her fate, Walter, buoyed up by his faith in Christian Science, sang a chirpy song:

Oh dry those tears
Oh calm those fears
Life will be brighter tomorrow.

Early life and education It was while briefly at Alleyn's School in Dulwich that Victor Pritchett first experienced the urge to write. The First World War had just begun and Walter was away, so he—as eldest son—had to look after his increasingly discontented mother. One night there was a Zeppelin raid. At school the following morning, the boys could talk of nothing else, but Victor had written an account of it, expressing the fear that Beatrice had undergone:

I hit by this accident on the first duty of the novelist, to become someone else. I pretended to be my mother and in her person told her what she felt as she called her children down and hysterically thought of her husband.

Victor's schooldays ended when he was fifteen. His parents decided it was time he earned a living, and a job was found for him as a clerk in a tannery in Bermondsey, the centre of London's leather trade. Pritchett revelled in the sulphurous atmosphere of the tannery where he worked for two years: almost unconsciously he was learning his craft as a writer through listening to the lively speech of the men who surrounded him. He recalled how he discovered the City of London during his lunch breaks, gazing at the newspaper buildings in Fleet Street, and listening to Bach in the churches on Ludgate Hill and even venturing into the exotic streets of Soho. 'It was a foreign country as strange as India. Often I longed to be in love, but I already was in love. London was seeping into me without my knowing it' (Pritchett, *Cab at the Door*).

Living by the eye: France and Spain In *Midnight Oil*, V. S. Pritchett revealed that his first serious ambition was to be an artist. John Ruskin's *Modern Painters*, which he had read in his teens, had fuelled his desire to paint, or so he imagined. 'Well smoked and kippered' by Bermondsey, Pritchett left England aged nineteen and was living in a cheap room in a modest house in Auteuil, a fashionable quarter of Paris, when he decided to put his early ambition into practice. He owed his survival to his landlady, Madame Chapin, a forbidding woman and strict Catholic whose husband had been killed in the First World War, who fed and tended him when sick and impoverished. There were paintings all around him—in the galleries, where he spent whole afternoons, and in the shops, which were full of the work of the post-impressionists. The virginal young man gazed helplessly at the various nudes:

The attraction of painting was that a work could be instantly seen—no turning of the page—and each brush stroke 'told' to the eye. I lived by the eye: the miles I walked in Paris fed the appetite of the eye above all, so that I could imagine that everything in the city was printed or painted on me.

But he soon realized, sitting in St Cloud surrounded by artists, that he was an 'incompetent' painter: 'Other painters, stout men with beards, were painting Cézanne-like pictures of Prussian blue avenues. I squeezed and dabbed my paints and after a couple of hours got up to study the running muddle I had made.' He caught a heavy cold from sitting on the damp grass and after he had recovered his 'career as a painter was over; but, all the more, pictures seemed to tell me how I ought to write'.

Meanwhile Pritchett found work as a commercial traveller, selling shellac, glue, and ostrich feathers from shop to shop. He learned to speak French fluently by conversing with the people he met as he went about his business. He now had another language to read in, which he did avidly. Inspired by the ease with which he acquired French, he went on to teach himself Spanish and German. He left France in 1922, after two years in the capital. He had not even heard of Gertrude Stein, Scott Fitzgerald, Sylvia Beach, and Ernest Hemingway, who were noted residents in the Latin quarter. News reached him almost by accident of the publication of Joyce's *Ulysses*, which he read in England when the furore had died down. Apart from a brief meeting with the sculptor Zadkine, he met no one famous or especially talented during his stay. This served his artistic purpose, making him a connoisseur of the eccentricities of otherwise ordinary human beings—men and women who perform their own versions of themselves by way of fending off boredom or the harsh truths they are unable to confront. What he acquired from France was of enduring value, as he acknowledges in *Midnight Oil*:

> What I gained, lastingly, was a sense of the importance of the *way* in which things are done, a thrift of the mind. I also began to see my own country—a very powerful one at that time—from abroad; and I felt the beginning of a passion, hopeless in the long run, but very nourishing, for identifying myself with people who were not my own and whose lives were governed by ideas alien to mine.

On returning to London, Pritchett answered an advertisement for the post of foreign correspondent on the *Christian Science Monitor*. He was dispatched to Ireland during the troubles, and there met his first wife, Evelyn Maude Vigors, of an upper-middle-class Anglo-Irish family. Her mother, a D'Arcy of Clifden Park, Galway, was an enthusiastic Christian Scientist. Her father was a retired army officer who had fought in the South African War. They were married in Dublin on 3 January 1924. Immediately following the wedding the couple travelled to Spain, Pritchett having been sent to Madrid by the *Christian Science Monitor*. He was in Spain from 1924 to 1925. This was the beginning of his fascination with the country, the subject of his first book, *Marching Spain* (1928), which describes his journey through Estremadura. To read this work of travel writing is to register the accuracy of his pronouncement of 'living by the eye'. No one, not even George Borrow, has described the barren, sun-soaked sierras of rural Spain with such vividness, while his pen portraits of unlettered Spaniards 'place' them with bemused admiration, with no trace of condescension. His first collection of short stories, *The Spanish Virgin*, followed two years later. His thoughts returned to Spain again in 1954 with another highly acclaimed travel book, *The Spanish Temper*.

Finding a voice   Pritchett's first novel, *Clare Drummer* (1929), dedicated to his wife, Evelyn, shows what he learned as a painter. The pleasures to be encountered in this novel are almost entirely physical—people, objects, and landscapes (in this case, Irish), vividly and minutely observed. The reader can absorb them at leisure, delighting in the word-pictures, but the complicated plot, involving in part the marriage of Colonel and Mrs Drummer, often goes astray (Pritchett's marriage was unhappy at the time). It was not until he freed himself from the constraints of a long narrative that he found his true voice both as story-teller and as critic. His earliest published writing was a series of vignettes, which he had managed to sell to the *Saturday Westminster*, *Time and Tide*, and the *Christian Science Monitor*.

The *New York Herald* also bought his humorous sketches of everyday life in Paris for a time, accompanying them with appropriate drawings.

In 1928 Pritchett accepted a job reviewing books for the *New Statesman* at the invitation of the literary editor, Raymond Mortimer. The advances he had received for the novels *Shirley Sanz* (1932), about Anglo-Hispanic relations, and *Nothing Like Leather* (1935), which drew on his experiences in the tanning factory in Bermondsey, were meagre even by the standards of the time, and they sold only 300 or 400 copies. Pritchett regarded journalism as a means to boost his income. He reviewed for the *New Statesman* for half a century, gracing its pages with some of the finest criticism of the age. His spacious essays, under the title 'Books in General', illuminate works too often summarily regarded as masterpieces. Time and again Pritchett reveals, sometimes in a single phrase, why a novel or story has a claim on readers' attention. He shakes off the dust that has gathered on Samuel Richardson, for example, in order to say precisely why Lovelace in *Clarissa* is the most vibrant villain in English fiction. His tone is invariably one of enthusiastic discovery. Pritchett makes his presence felt without ever employing the personal pronoun. He achieves the rare feat of being both disinterested and passionately involved, whether the subject is Edward Gibbon or D. H. Lawrence, whose 'phallic cult was a disaster to descriptive writing. The ecstasies of sexual sensations are no more to be described than the ecstasies of music which they resemble.'

On Guy Fawkes' night in 1934 Pritchett met and fell instantly in love with Dorothy Rudge Roberts. She was nineteen and from Welshpool, the daughter of Richard Samuel Roberts, a master butcher, and worked in London in the office of a literary and theatrical agent, where Evelyn Pritchett was also employed. Pritchett's first marriage officially lasted twelve years, and his novel *Shirley Sanz* is dedicated to Evelyn, but the relationship had been over for some time. Evelyn was having an affair with a younger man with whom she became pregnant during the time Pritchett and Dorothy became lovers. Pritchett's second wedding took place, after his first marriage was dissolved, on 2 October 1936. Dorothy was indispensable to him. His handwriting was legendarily ugly and difficult to decipher, but she typed his manuscripts, corrected his spelling mistakes, and made clean copies on which he could scrawl his endless revisions. She then retyped the revised version, to the delight of his publishers. Every book he produced after 1934 is dedicated to her. They had a daughter and a son, Oliver, who became a well-known medical correspondent for the *Daily Telegraph*. His grandson Matthew Pritchett became, as Matt, a well-known cartoonist, also for the *Daily Telegraph*.

A life at the desk   During the Second World War, V. S. Pritchett worked for the government writing pamphlets on his survey of factories, mines, and shipyards. He was one of those writers who do all their adventurous living when young, and then settle down to a life at the desk. It was there that he honed and polished his art. A novel, *Dead Man Leading*, was published in 1937, and a collection of short stories, *You Make your Own Life*, in 1938. His one moderately successful novel, *Mr Beluncle* (1951), is concerned with the kind of self-creating individuals he had met while in France, and similar characters populate his stories from the 1930s to the 1980s: con-men, crooked antique dealers, adept or unskilled adulterers of both sexes—performers forever trapped in their own performances. Pritchett needed the constrictions of the short-story form: they contained his exuberance, which runs away with itself in the novels, leaving him out of fictional breath. A few well-chosen examples of colloquial speech are enough to establish character. With his self-deluded father in mind he created a series of men and women who are trapped in duplicity, frequently unaware of their own hypocrisy. Pritchett's people are from the toiling middle classes. He views them from a discreet distance, a glancing quality that has been mistaken for coldness. His stories are not burdened with plot, but rather take off on the instant, as Chekhov's do, with a single telling incident, usually understated. These subtle excursions into everyday madness and eccentricity, in 'The Sailor', 'Many are Disappointed', 'Handsome is as Handsome Does', 'You Make your own Life', 'A Camberwell Beauty', and 'On the Edge of the Cliff', have a timelessness about them; for all that they are rooted in a particular time and place. Pritchett's sense of the human comedy ensures their likely survival. He is never concerned with the topical: he knew, and said so, that nothing dates quicker than the up-to-date.

From the 1960s Pritchett wrote books on the writers dearest to him: *George Meredith and English Comedy* (1970), *The Gentle Barbarian: the Life and Work of Turgenev* (1977), *Chekhov: a Spirit Set Free* (1988), and *Balzac* (1993). Of Chekhov he observes:

> In his later work he had been alert to the false image or sentence. The danger—as we know from Henry James's revisions—lay in the temptation to elaborate, but Chekhov was a cutter, sensitive to the musicality of simple language.

He might be commenting on himself.

Pritchett also wrote on the cities that he loved, collaborating with the photographer Evelyn Hofer on *London Perceived* (1962), *New York Proclaimed* (1965), and *Dublin: a Portrait* (1969). His texts are as evocative of the peculiar qualities of these cities as are Hofer's photographs. He saw London's eccentrics as 'withdrawn deeply into private life', much like the characters in his stories. He returned to the London of his childhood, among other places, in his first volume of autobiography, *A Cab at the Door* (1968). *Midnight Oil* (1971) takes up the story in later life.

Public life The self-educated Pritchett had become a university lecturer in the 1950s. Invited to conduct a seminar at Princeton in 1953 as Christian Gauss lecturer, he remarked, 'I didn't even know what a seminar was.' Nine years on, he was Beckman professor at Berkeley. He was writer-in-residence at Smith College, Massachusetts, and at Vanderbilt University in Tennessee, and visiting professor at Brandeis and Columbia. These posts brought him more money than he had ever earned from his writing—

an irony he was probably the first to appreciate. Small, with twinkling eyes discernible from behind thick spectacles, and rarely far from his pipe, Pritchett appealed to his American students. They may not have been accustomed to meeting a lecturer who spoke about the art of fiction from the very source. He, in turn, was enchanted by their use of the vernacular. At last he felt secure financially, and purchased a large house near Regent's Park.

Receiving many honours in old age, beginning with the CBE in 1968, Pritchett was knighted in 1975, and was made a Companion of Honour in 1993. In that year he was also awarded a PEN Golden Pen award for long service to literature. He stopped writing for the *New Statesman* in 1978, but contributed reviews of contemporary fiction to the *New York Review of Books*. These pieces are generous in spirit and detached, but he was less assured in his criticism of modern writers. He saw merits in the purveyors of magical realism that are now being seriously questioned and scrutinized, and he tended to overpraise the novels of his old friend Graham Greene (they had collaborated with Elizabeth Bowen on *Why do I Write?* originally published in the *Partisan Review* in 1948). His finest criticism is founded on the perspective of history, of reputations lost and regained, and takes the long view. He was not afraid of generalizations. Writing of George Eliot he states, confidently, that there is no real madness in Victorian fiction. And yet madness also attracted him: he wrote of it in Shakespeare, Dostoevsky, Gogol, Balzac, and even in the exquisitely reasonable Chekhov. Pritchett had witnessed a certain kind of madness all about him in his youth, not least in his father's terrible optimism. Victor had watched as his slender father ballooned into a massive 18 stone as he ate and ate to compensate for the privations of his young manhood. Pritchett understood that madness functions outside institutions, in the kitchen and the sitting-room, in every ordinary circumstance. This understanding was Walter Pritchett's great aesthetic gift to his son, and it made him a story-teller.

The term 'man of letters' has an old-world ring to it now, but V. S. Pritchett was happy to have it applied to him. For over sixty years he lived by the pen—producing novels, travel books, literary journalism, biographies, and a generous number of incomparable short stories. He was at home in, and in love with, the art of writing, which he practised every day, well into old age. It was a process that brought him despair, but also delight:

> I had my first experience of the depression and sense of nothingness that come when a piece of work is done. The satisfaction is in the act itself; when it is over there is relief, but the satisfaction is gone. After fifty years I still find this to be so and that with every new piece of writing I have to make that terrifying break with my real life and learn to write again, from the beginning.

V. S. Pritchett died in the Whittington Hospital, Islington, on 20 March 1997, following a stroke.

Even though Pritchett's fictional subject matter was based in the ordinary, it has often been remarked since his death that he is a writerly writer, not having achieved the fame of lesser talents such as H. E. Bates or Somerset

Maugham. This may have something to do with his preferred anonymity, his quiet and constant dedication to the act of writing itself. His prose is clean and clear and his phrase-making always apropos. There are no digressions into philosophizing or moralizing. He never takes the easy route of advising the reader what to think or feel. He knew, as an unlettered boy, that reading is an art in itself, and that it commands respect from the writer. Although secure in his talent, he was modest in the face of unruly genius. He was not, and could not afford to be, unruly himself, yet it is safe to predict that his carefully structured stories will outlive many of the overvalued 'baggy monsters' of the twentieth century. He could sympathize with grandiose literary ambition in the writers of the past—or find reasons for countenancing it, at least—but such ruthlessness was unknown to him. The task of writing well was enough for V. S. Pritchett. That task, honourably and lovingly undertaken, will constitute his lasting triumph.

PAUL BAILEY

Denis Nowell Pritt (1887–1972), by Howard Coster, 1944

Sources V. S. Pritchett, *The cab at the door* (1968) · V. S. Pritchett, *Midnight oil* (1971) · *The Times* (22 March 1997) · *The Independent* (22 March 1997) · J. Treglown, 'The logical foreigner in love', *TLS* (12 July 2002) · b. cert. · m. cert. [Dorothy Rudge Roberts] · d. cert.
Archives Ransom HRC, corresp. and literary papers | U. Reading L., letters to Bodley Head Ltd | FILM *Bookmark*, BBC 2, 7 May 1997 | SOUND BL NSA, documentary recordings · BL NSA, performance recordings
Likenesses H. Coster, photographs, 1942, NPG [*see illus.*] · G. Argent, photograph, 1970, NPG · photograph, 1974, Hult. Arch. · C. Corr, drawing, 1980, News International, London · C. Beaton, photograph, NPG
Wealth at death £60,328: probate, 27 June 1997, *CGPLA Eng. & Wales*

Pritt, Denis Nowell (1887–1972), lawyer and political activist, was born at Fern Bank, Greenhill Park, Harlesden, Middlesex, on 22 September 1887, the younger of two children of Harry Walter Pritt, metal merchant, and his wife, Mary Owen Wilson. Educated at Winchester College (1901–5), and Geneva, where he went in 1905 to study French, Pritt joined the Middle Temple in furtherance of his father's wishes in 1906. As a pupil of R. F. Colam, he was called to the bar in November 1909 and the following year obtained a pass degree in law from the University of London. On 27 July 1914 he married Marie Frances (Mollie; *b.* 1895/6), daughter of Walter Maurice Gough, an accountant.

Except for a brief wartime interruption working in postal censorship at the War Office, Pritt's junior practice grew steadily, bearing witness to his industry, his appetite for study, and his sharp forensic intelligence. About 1924 he joined the chambers of R. A. Wright, an outstanding specialist in commercial work, and in 1927 became king's counsel. Although a member of the Labour Party since shortly after the First World War, his extensive practice had to this point betrayed no strong political convictions. Nor, until adopted as Labour candidate for Sunderland in June 1931, was he in any public way a political figure.

At that year's general election Pritt, like the Labour Party nationally, was comprehensively defeated. Nevertheless, the encounter with working-class deprivation in

the constituency had already begun to work its political effects. By the time of his next and successful contest, at North Hammersmith in 1935, Pritt was now well advanced in his remarkable transformation into one of Britain's sturdiest fellow-travellers. Evidently the decisive moment of awakening occurred on a New Fabian Research Bureau visit to the USSR in 1932. According to another of the party, Margaret Cole, Pritt while there had simply 'fallen in love' with Soviet socialism. 'The eminent K.C. swallows it *all*,' she noted privately. 'He'll be some Communist before he's done' (Cole MSS, July 1932). That prediction turned out to come all but true, although formally Pritt seems never to have joined the Communist Party.

The moment of Pritt's enchantment coincided with a more sophisticated appreciation in communist circles of the utility of such middle-class contacts, and Pritt's legal talents were rapidly harnessed for a variety of progressive causes. Earliest of them was his presidency of an international enquiry into the Reichstag fire trial in September 1933. Masterminded by the legendary Comintern fixer Willi Münzenberg, this did much to establish both the innocence of the trial's communist defendants and the likely culpability of their accusers, and for the first time brought Pritt to international notice. Domestically, he successfully defended the veteran agitator Tom Mann, on trial for sedition with Communist leader Harry Pollitt in 1934, and the same year won damages against the police for the organizers of the National Unemployed Workers' Movement. Pritt also lent his services to the newly formed National Council for Civil Liberties, and was to maintain this identification with left-wing causes for the rest of his professional life. Consistent at least in his own mind, in August 1936 he attended the first Moscow show trial as a singularly complaisant expert observer. His seemingly authoritative endorsement of the proceedings, published as *The Zinoviev Trial*, was translated into some seven or eight languages as Pritt willingly lent himself to Stalin's international propaganda machine.

Having so fully committed himself to the communists' world-view, Pritt's political fortunes were now to ebb and flow exactly as theirs did. At the time of the show trials, in 1937, his pro-Sovietism was unexceptional enough on the left for him to be elected to the constituencies' section of Labour's national executive committee. That can be taken as a sure mark of his popularity with Labour Party activists. Three years later, amid the disillusionments of the Nazi-Soviet pact and Russo-Finnish war, his elaborate apologias for these episodes proved far more controversial. Circulating widely as Penguin Specials, his outspoken views led in March 1940 to his summary expulsion from the Labour Party, to which, unlike other rebels like Bevan and Cripps, he was never to be readmitted. Isolated in parliament, Pritt now collaborated ever more closely with the Communist Party and its lone MP, William Gallacher. By the time he headed the guardedly anti-war People's Convention, organized by the Communist Party in January 1941, he should probably be counted with the communists in all but name. Like them, his fortunes were once again revived by the mood of Russophilia which followed the Soviet entry into the war in June 1941. George Orwell thought him in this period 'perhaps the most effective pro-Soviet publicist in this country' and Pritt even pondered his course of action should he be invited to join the government (Collected Essays, 224; diary, 15 Jan 1942, D. N. Pritt MSS). If that says more about his considerable vanity and political ingenuousness than any real demand for his services, the general leftward trend did at the 1945 election bring him one memorable moment of vindication. Defending his North Hammersmith seat as an independent, and supported by such celebrities as Bernard Shaw and J. B. Priestley, Pritt secured almost two-thirds of the poll and that rarest of twentieth-century phenomena, a triumph over the big party machines. The official Labour candidate, a mere footnote to his party's landslide, lost his deposit.

That was to be Pritt's political swansong. Inevitably, the cold war dealt him further setbacks, and this time they proved irreversible. In February 1950 he lost his seat in parliament and henceforth was little regarded in Britain outside obvious communist front organizations. Internationally, he retained a more considerable reputation: in 1954 he was awarded the Stalin peace prize, while his standing with anti-colonial movements was confirmed by his defence of Jomo Kenyatta and five other defendants in the Mau Mau case that began in 1952. Pritt's commitment to such political cases had long since meant the shrinkage of his general practice, and this was now reinforced by the fiercer anathemas of the cold war. Pritt retired from the bar in 1960, honoured far more in other countries than his own.

Physically ample and attached to life's good things, Pritt was politically a lightweight figure. Always the lawyer, he was ingenious in point-scoring but one vainly scours his writings for any breath of profundity or imagination. Nevertheless, if incorrigible as a Stalinist, he should be remembered too for diverting his career from more lucrative legal pastures to a mostly exemplary body of work for the labour and anti-colonial movements. If his plaudits from the people's democracies were fulsome, he also knew the less pleasant experience of professional and social ostracism at home. His wife, less political than her husband, apparently found their moments of isolation especially trying (Edwards, 327–8). The couple had a son and a daughter and experienced the further distress, at a difficult political time, of the former's death from cancer early in the Second World War. From this period if not before, Pritt's closest friendships as well as political contacts were with leading communists like Robin Page Arnot and Ivor Montagu. Fittingly, it was they who paid him the warmest tributes when he died at his home, Barn End, Pamber Heath, near Silchester, Hampshire, on 23 May 1972.   KEVIN MORGAN

Sources D. N. Pritt, *The autobiography of D. N. Pritt*, 3 vols. (1965–6) · BLPES, Pritt MSS · letters to G. D. H. Cole, 1932, Nuffield Oxf., M. Cole MSS · *The collected essays, journalism, and letters of George Orwell*, ed. S. Orwell and I. Angus, 3: *As I please, 1943–1945* (1968) · J. R. D. Edwards, *Victor Gollancz: a biography* (1987) · D. N. Pritt, 'Recollections of William Gallacher in Parliament', *Essays in honour of William Gallacher*, ed. P. M. Kemp-Ashrat and J. Mitchell (1966) · b. cert. · m. cert.
Archives BLPES, corresp. and papers | Bodl. Oxf., corresp. with Lord Monckton · JRL, letters to the *Manchester Guardian* · Labour History Archive and Study Centre, Manchester, Communist Party archives, corresp. with R. Palme Dutt · NL Wales, corresp. with Leo Abse · U. Hull, Brynmor Jones L., corresp. with R. Page Arnot
Likenesses H. Coster, photographs, 1930–44, NPG [*see illus.*] · W. Stoneman, photograph, 1949, NPG · two photographs, *c.*1960–1969, BLPES · photographs, People's History Museum, Manchester
Wealth at death £16,173: probate, 31 July 1972, CGPLA Eng. & Wales

Prittie, Terence Cornelius Farmer (1913–1985), journalist and author, was born in London on 15 December 1913, the younger son (there were no daughters) of Henry Cornelius O'Callaghan Prittie, fifth Baron Dunalley in the Irish peerage (1877–1948), and his wife, Beatrix Evelyn (*c.*1878–1967), daughter of James Noble Graham of Carfin, Lanarkshire. His parents led a peripatetic life, partly in France, until they moved back to the rebuilt family seat at Kilboy in co. Tipperary. Prittie had indifferent health as a child and remained short of stature, but he became an excellent player of ball games in adult life and was a first-class shot. He was educated at home until 1923, when he was sent to Cheam School, where he was not happy, and then on to Stowe School in 1927. There he blossomed, partly under the influence of an outstanding history master, and made many friends. Having left Stowe at Christmas 1932 he spent some months in Germany and began to acquire his mastery of German. In 1933 he entered Christ Church, Oxford, and widely extended his circle of friends; he read modern history, gained a good second class in 1936, and in his last year was awarded a Boulter exhibition. He narrowly missed blues in both real tennis and lawn tennis; in 1935 he was the lawn tennis open champion of his native province of Munster.

In 1937 Prittie joined Child's Bank in Fleet Street but, not finding banking congenial, he moved to a firm of stockbrokers. In 1938 he had joined the reserve of the rifle brigade; after episodic training in England and Northern Ireland he embarked in May 1940 for Calais, where on 26 May, after the stubborn defence, he was taken prisoner. He was mentioned in dispatches (1940). An attempt to escape in France miscarried, and thereafter he succeeded in breaking out of prison on six occasions (described in *South to Freedom*, 1946). One escape brought him within sight of the Swiss frontier, and on his final evasion he joined a unit of the advancing Americans in April 1945. While within walls he was agile at goading his captors and also invented a form of cricket in the moat at Spangenberg. On his return to England in 1945 he was appointed MBE (military). On 29 August 1946 he married Laura (*d.* 1988), only daughter of Gustave Dreyfus-Dundas, an oil engineer, of Colombia, South America; they had two sons.

Prittie's knowledge of cricket and his memory of obscure statistics were already outstanding; he joined the staff of the *Manchester Guardian* in February 1946 as sports correspondent, in succession to Neville Cardus, and was to publish four books on cricket past and present. But in October 1946 he was sent to Germany as the paper's chief correspondent and there he made his home with his new wife in Düsseldorf after three difficult years in occupied Berlin. His alert intelligence and potent memory, coupled with a slightly detached viewpoint furnished by his Cromwellian-Irish ancestry, enabled him to become a superb commentator on the German scene. In addition to his lively and well-informed reports he produced biographies of two of the German chancellors whom he had met. The true affection that he developed for the country comes out in *My Germans* (1983); an interest in local wine inspired *Moselle* (with Otto Loeb, 1972). When he left Germany in 1963 his industry and his experience rendered him an outstanding and influential figure in press and diplomatic circles.

In London, Prittie became the diplomatic correspondent of *The Guardian* and held this post until 1970. In December 1971 the German authorities awarded him the officer's cross (civil) of their Order of Merit. His wife had been so ill that he had contemplated retirement to Malta, when a new career opened up. He had been interested in the cause of Zionism and Jewry since his early days in Germany, and now he became an official advocate of the Israeli cause; he had already published *Israel: Miracle in the Desert* (1967) and a biography of Eshkol (1969) and had contributed to the Israeli paper *Ha'aretz*. From a series of small offices he issued a monthly broadsheet, 'Britain and Israel', commenting on contemporary problems and expounding the Jewish case. His research was meticulous and his language clear and convincing; his dedication was entire. Frequent visits to Israel and journeys to the United States and elsewhere enlarged his audience. Meanwhile he was frequently at Lord's to watch cricket and play tennis.

Prittie's wonderfully retentive memory enriched his public and his private life. A sleepless night could be alleviated by naming an eleven of left-handed clergy in first-class cricket. His public manner embodied a robust natural courtesy but among intimates he loved a private, and occasionally a practical, joke; pomposity he abhorred. Many friends from each facet of his varied career enjoyed his natural gaiety. Relations between Britain and Germany, and between Britain and Israel, were enriched and enhanced by his career and writings. He died in a London hospital on 28 May 1985.   MICHAEL MACLAGAN, *rev.*

Sources T. Prittie, *Through Irish eyes* (1977) · *The Times* (29 May 1985) · Burke, *Peerage* · G. Taylor, *Changing faces: a history of The Guardian, 1956–1988* (1993) · WWW · CGPLA Eng. & Wales (1985) · personal knowledge (1990)
Archives JRL, letters to *Manchester Guardian* · U. Southampton L., corresp. with James Parkes | SOUND BL NSA, documentary recording
Likenesses photographs, repro. in Prittie, *Through Irish eyes*
Wealth at death £179,686: probate, 30 Oct 1985, CGPLA Eng. & Wales

Pritzler, Sir Theophilus (*d.* 1839), army officer, was in 1793 appointed ensign in an independent company in the British army, and on 18 March 1794 he became a lieutenant in the 85th foot. He exchanged, on 27 August 1794, into the 5th dragoon guards, went to the Netherlands, and served through the two unsuccessful campaigns of 1794 and 1795, in the Netherlands and Germany. He then took part in an expedition to San Domingo (1796–8). On 21 September 1796 he transferred to the 21st light dragoons, in which regiment he remained until 21 September 1804, when he was appointed major in the Royal Fusiliers. He acted as major of brigade at Portsmouth from 1800 to 1804, and from 1807 to 1809 held the post of assistant adjutant-general at the Horse Guards. He received the brevet of lieutenant-colonel on 16 April 1807, and on 4 June 1813 was appointed lieutenant-colonel of the 22nd light dragoons. He had the brevet of colonel in the army on 4 June 1814.

Pritzler then went to India with his regiment. On the outbreak of the Third Anglo-Maratha War in 1817, he was given the rank of brigadier-general, and ordered to pursue the peshwa on the latter's flight from Poona on 16 November 1817. On 8 January 1818, with a force partly European and partly Indian, he came upon a large enemy force close to Satara, where they had been left to cover the peshwa's retreat. Pritzler attacked and dispersed them, and continued his pursuit, marching rapidly southwards in co-operation with Brigadier-General Smith. He came up with the peshwa's rearguard on 17 January, near Meritch, and severely defeated them.

Pritzler was for a time employed in the movement against the smaller fortresses in the southern Maratha districts. He was ordered to press the siege of Sinhgarh, which surrendered, after a short resistance, on 2 March 1818. He was then ordered to reduce to obedience the country in the vicinity of Satara. His chief achievement in this district was the capture of Vasota, a fort situated in an almost impregnable position of the Western Ghats. The siege began on 11 March, and ended in unconditional surrender on 5 April. Pritzler then marched south and joined

Colonel Thomas Munro on 22 April at Nagar-Manawali. The united British force now moved across the Sena River to the siege of Sholapur, the peshwa's last great stronghold in the southern districts. On 10 May two columns, under Colonel Hewitt, advanced to the assault. Pritzler, with a reserve force, stood by to offer support. The Maratha commander, Ganpat Rao, moved round to the east side of the town with the object of taking the assailants in flank. The Marathas were checked and driven back in disorder by Pritzler, which contributed to the speedy capture of the town that day. The Maratha garrison, about 7000 strong, tried to escape. Pritzler, however, pursued, came up with them on the banks of the Sena, and inflicted upon them so crushing a defeat that they ceased to exist as an organized force. Pritzler was made a KCB on 3 December 1822. He died suddenly at Boulogne on 12 April 1839.

G. P. MORIARTY, rev. JAMES LUNT

Sources Fortescue, *Brit. army*, vol. 11 · J. Bradshaw, *Sir Thomas Munro and the British settlements of the Madras presidency* (1894) · J. Philippart, ed., *The royal military calendar*, 3 vols. (1815–16) · *GM*, 1st ser., 88/2 (1818) · *Annual Register* (1839) · *Army List* · J. G. Duff, *History of the Mahrattas*, 3rd edn (1873) · G. R. Gleig, *The life of Sir Thomas Munro*, 3 vols. (1831)
Archives BL OIOC, letters to Mountstuart Elphinstone, MSS Eur. F 87–89

Proast, Jonas (c.1642–1710), Church of England clergyman and religious controversialist, was the son of Jonas Proost (1572–1668), pastor successively of the Dutch Calvinist congregations in Colchester and London. Oxford weaned Proast from puritanism: he matriculated at Queen's College in 1659, graduated BA in 1663, and MA, from Gloucester Hall, in 1666. He incorporated MA of Cambridge in 1670. Thereafter he remained in Oxford as chaplain of Queen's and, from 1677, of All Souls.

In 1688 occurred the signal event of his career, his expulsion from All Souls. The warden, Leopold Finch, was one of James II's tory collaborators. In April 1688 he stood for election to the Camden chair of history, but was beaten by his high-church rival Henry Dodwell, for whom Proast was a canvasser. Enraged at his chaplain's disloyalty, Finch peremptorily sacked him. Proast turned to Archbishop William Sancroft, the college's visitor. Sancroft would willingly have challenged the crown on Proast's behalf, but the revolution of 1688 intervened. Proast meanwhile stoutly defended the church against popery in two unpublished tracts, 'A brief defence of the society of St Mary Magdalen College' and 'The case of reading the declaration for liberty of conscience'. Proast dithered over accepting the oaths of allegiance to William and Mary. More importantly, he hated the Toleration Act and he attacked John Locke's *Letter Concerning Toleration*. It became imperative for the new latitudinarian archbishops to avoid countenancing the view that the revolution was a victory for the type of intolerant Anglicanism of Sancroft and Proast. Archbishop John Tillotson was, complained the Jacobite antiquary Thomas Hearne, 'very dilatory in doing [Proast] justice' (*Remarks*, 1.97). Proast was restored in 1692, but he did not secure arrears of stipend,

and the case dragged on until 1698, in the reign of Archbishop Thomas Tenison. Proast's friends found preferment for him: in 1692 as ecclesiastical law officer for Berkshire, and in 1698 as archdeacon of Berkshire, which he remained until his death.

Proast's only published works were three tracts against Locke: *The Argument of the 'Letter Concerning Toleration' Briefly Considered* (1690), *A Third Letter Concerning Toleration* (1691), and (confusingly) *A Second Letter to the Author of the Three Letters Concerning Toleration* (1704). Locke's second (1690), enormous third (1692), and unfinished fourth (1704) letters are replies. In them Locke buttressed Tillotson's position and assaulted the Oxonian high-church citadel. The debate concerned the efficacy of coercion on behalf of 'true religion'. Proast argued astutely, drawing upon St Augustine's arguments against the Donatists. He conceded that the mind cannot directly be forced to assent to a proposition, but held that penal laws can break the weight of intellectual prepossession. Thus coercion is indirectly efficacious in altering people's disposition to search for truth, and consequently the godly magistrate should use force. Locke's friends commended him for demolishing Proast's ecclesiastical regime as effectively as he had the absolutist civil polity of Sir Robert Filmer.

Proast died in St Mary Magdalen parish, Oxford, unmarried, on 18 April 1710, and he was buried in St Mary Magdalen Church the next day. Hearne thought him 'a truly honest, wise man, and a good scholar, but reserved in his conversation' (*Remarks*, 2.374). Tenison judged him 'full of an evil spirit'—understandably, since Proast had told him that 'justice forsook Lambeth when Archbishop Sancroft removed from thence' (Goldie, 153).

MARK GOLDIE, rev.

Sources M. Goldie, 'John Locke, Jonas Proast, and religious toleration, 1688–1692', *The Church of England, c.1689–c.1833*, ed. J. Walsh and others (1993), 143–71 · *Remarks and collections of Thomas Hearne*, ed. C. E. Doble and others, 11 vols., OHS, 2, 7, 13, 34, 42–3, 48, 50, 65, 67, 72 (1885–1921) · R. Vernon, *The career of toleration: John Locke, Jonas Proast and after* (1997) · LPL, MS 688 · Bodl. Oxf., MSS Tanner 28, 338 · *The case of Jonas Proast* [1690]
Archives Bodl. Oxf., Tanner MSS 28, 338 · LPL, MS 688
Wealth at death under £1000: *Remarks and collections*, ed. Doble and others, vol. 2, p. 337

Probert, Lewis (1837–1908), Congregational minister and college head, third son of Evan Probert, a miner, and his wife, Mary, was born at Llanelli, Brecknockshire, on 22 September 1837. He was baptized on 15 October 1837. He became a Congregational church member during a revival in 1860, and began to preach in 1862. After a short preparatory course at the Revd Henry Oliver's school at Pontypridd, Probert entered Brecon Independent college in 1863. In July 1867 he was ordained to the Congregational ministry at Bodringallt, in the Rhondda valley, where he was active in establishing new churches among a rapidly growing colliery population, particularly in the villages of Ystrad, Cwm-parc, Tonypandy, and Pentre. In October 1874 he moved to Porthmadog, Caernarvonshire, where he spent twelve years again leading the effort to expand and build Congregational chapels.

In 1886 Probert returned to Pentre. Here he added to his

renown as a preacher an increasing reputation as an essentially conservative theologian. Accordingly, upon the death of Evan Herber Evans in 1896, Probert was chosen to succeed him as principal of the Congregational college at Bangor, a post which he held until his death. At the time, Congregational students at Bangor were being prepared in co-operation with the Baptist denomination, and Probert's skill and diplomacy in maintaining the unity of the college was renowned. In 1891 he received the degree of DD from Ohio University, and was chairman of the Welsh Congregational Union for 1901. Among his most notable publications were *Y weinidogaeth ymneillduol yng Nghymru* (The nonconformist ministry in Wales) (1882) and a commentary on the Romans, *Esboniad ar y Rhufeiniaid* (1890). *Nerth y goruchaf* (1906), a treatise on the work of the spirit, sheds important light on the nature of religious revivals in Wales.

Probert was twice married: first, on 14 September 1870, to Annie (1844/5–1874), daughter of Edward Watkins, a miner from Blaenau, Monmouthshire, and second, on 20 May 1886, to Martha(b. 1845/6), only daughter of Benjamin Probert, a boot manufacturer from Builth. Probert died suddenly on 29 December 1908 at Henfryn, Bangor, Caernarvonshire, and was buried at Llanelli.

J. E. LLOYD, rev. ROBERT V. SMITH

Sources *DWB* · T. Stephens, *Album Aberhondda* (1898), 232 · *Congregational Year Book* (1910), 185–6 · *CGPLA Eng. & Wales* (1909) · m. certs. · *IGI*
Likenesses W. Williams, oils, 1886, NMG Wales
Wealth at death £4534 7s. 11d.: administration, 5 April 1909, *CGPLA Eng. & Wales*

Probert, William (1790–1870), Unitarian minister, was born on 11 August 1790 at Painscastle, Radnorshire, where his parents farmed a small freehold. He was brought up by two bachelor uncles who intended that he take orders in the Church of England, but he became a Wesleyan Methodist, serving as a local preacher in Bolton, Leeds, and Liverpool, and in Staffordshire. In 1814 he married Margaret Carr (1790/91–1866) of Broxton, Cheshire, with whom he had six children.

In 1815, while stationed at Alnwick in Northumberland, through the influence of William Turner (1761–1859), minister at Newcastle, Probert adopted Unitarian views. He was appointed in 1821 to the Unitarian chapel at Walmsley, near Bolton, Lancashire. Probert found the place encumbered with debt and the people disheartened and scattered. He succeeded in gathering around him a loyal congregation, to which he ministered for nearly fifty years; Walmsley Chapel was commonly known in the district as 'old Probert's chapel'. He often went on foot to conduct Sunday evening services at other chapels in the neighbourhood.

Probert was a man with a good sense of humour and eccentric habits. He noted that, for reasons of conscience, he had sacrificed the prospect of attending Oxford and proudly avowed that he was self-educated. His knowledge of Hebrew was extensive: he published a favourably noticed grammar (1832), a lexicon (1850), and *The Laws of Hebrew Poetry* (1860). But his greatest interest and mastery lay in the Welsh language. He published *The Godolin, being Translations from the Welsh* (1820) and *The Ancient Laws of Cambria* (1823), and his historical essay on Flintshire castles was awarded a medal at the Denbigh Eisteddfod in 1828. He also wrote a history of Walmsley Chapel, which appeared in the *Christian Reformer* in 1834. He died at Dimple, Turton, on 1 April 1870 and was buried on 7 April in the graveyard attached to his chapel.

T. B. JOHNSTONE, rev. R. K. WEBB

Sources J. Worthington, *The Inquirer* (9 April 1870) · *Bolton Evening News* (7 April 1870) [partly incorporating *The Inquirer* article] · obituary index, Harris Man. Oxf. · *DWB* · d. cert.
Wealth at death under £450: resworn probate, Aug 1872, *CGPLA Eng. & Wales* (1870)

Probus (*fl.* **9th–11th cent.**), writer, was the author of a life of St Patrick, which has been attributed to various dates in the period between the mid-ninth century and the eleventh. About eighty per cent of the text of the life is based on that by Muirchú, plus material from Patrick's own *Confessio* and the *Collectanea* of Tírechán (though neither of these works was necessarily known to Probus). The author names himself as Probus in the final chapter of the life, in which he also mentions a *frater*, Paulinus, who seems to have requested the writing of the work. Although long known only through the sixteenth-century edition by Johann Herwagen of Basel (based on a lost manuscript), two copies have more recently come to light: an Italian manuscript of the eleventh or twelfth century in the Capitular Archives of the cathedral of Pistoia, near Florence; and the Passional of Böddeken in Westphalia, dated to between about 1454 and 1459, now known only through later copies. Also, some eleventh-century glosses on Muirchú's life in Vienna, Nationalbibliothek, MS ser. nov. 3642, seem to attest to an indirect tradition of parts of that by Probus.

The identity, date, and context for Probus have all been matters of uncertainty. Father John Colgan (d. 1658) suggested that Probus was an Irishman; and, having identified his friend Paulinus with Máel Póil mac Ailella (d. 922), abbot of Int Ednén, near Slane in Meath, he suggested that Probus himself was Cóenechair (Coinecán), lector at Slane, who was killed by vikings in 950. However, the manuscript tradition of the life may suggest that the author was based on the continent, and Jean Mabillon, the seventeenth-century founder of modern diplomatic, identified Probus with the Irish monk Probus Scottus of Mainz (and perhaps previously at Rheims), whose death is recorded for 25 June 859. This Probus is addressed in a poem by Walahfrid Strabo of Reichenau, from whom he had requested various Latin texts via an intermediary called 'Chronmal' (or Crónmáel in Irish), and his scholarly pursuits (including a liking for Virgil and Cicero) are mentioned in two letters by Lupus, abbot of Ferrières. However, the number of errors in the life may indicate that the Mainz scholar could not have been the author, and the relative ignorance of Irish topography may indicate that the author was not an Irishman. Indeed, the change of Muirchú's phrase 'our sea' for the Irish Sea into 'the western sea' suggests that he was from Britain, either a Briton or an Anglo-Saxon; and the apparent use of the name Scotia for Scotland, not attested before *c*.975, may indicate a date in the late tenth or, probably, the eleventh century for the work, if the relevant passage is not a later interpolation. Accordingly, it has even been suggested that Probus and his friend Paulinus were English monks associated with Glastonbury Abbey, which had a strong interest in the cult of St Patrick. However, the matter remains uncertain.   DAVID E. THORNTON

Sources *Four Latin lives of St Patrick: Colgan's 'Vita secunda, quarta, tertia and quinta'*, ed. L. Bieler (1971) • M. Esposito, 'Notes on a Latin life of St Patrick', *Classica et Mediaevalia*, 13 (1953), 59–72 • J. Colgan, *Acta sanctorum veteris et maioris Scotiae seu Hiberniae*, 2 (1647) • L. d'Archery and J. Mabillon, eds., *Acta sanctorum ordinis sancti Benedicti*, 9 vols. (Paris, 1668–1701), vol. 2 • G. W. Regenos, *The letters of Lupus of Ferrières* (1966) • Strabo, 'Carmina', *Poetae Latini aevi Carolini*, ed. E. Dümmler, MGH Poetae Latini Medii Aevi, 2 (Berlin, 1884), 393–4

Proby, Granville Leveson, third earl of Carysfort (1781–1868), naval officer, was the third son of John Joshua *Proby, first earl of Carysfort (1751–1828), and his first wife, Elizabeth (d. 1783), only daughter of Sir William Osborne, bt, of Newtown, co. Tipperary. He was educated at Rugby School (1792–8), and was aged seventeen, somewhat older than was usual, when he entered the navy in March 1798 on the *Vanguard*, with Captain Edward Berry, and Rear-Admiral Sir Horatio Nelson. He was at the battle of the Nile, and following Berry to the *Foudroyant*, took part in the blockade of Malta and in the capture of the *Généreux* on 18 February 1800, and of the *Guillaume Tell* on 31 March 1800. In 1801, still in the *Foudroyant*, then the flagship of Lord Keith, he was at the operations on the Egyptian coast. He afterwards served in the frigates *Santa Teresa* and *Resistance*, and in 1803–4 in the *Victory*, Nelson's flagship in the Mediterranean. On 24 October 1804 he was promoted lieutenant of the frigate *Narcissus* and in May 1805 was appointed to the *Neptune* and took part in the battle of Trafalgar. On 15 August 1806, through his father's friends' influence, he was promoted to command the sloop *Bergère*, and on 28 November 1806 was posted to the *Madras* (54 guns). In 1807 he commanded the frigate *Juno* (32 guns) in the Mediterranean; in 1808–9 the *Iris* (32 guns) in the North Sea and the Baltic; in 1813–14 the *Laurel* (38 guns), at the Cape of Good Hope; and in 1815–16 the *Amelia* (38 guns) in the Mediterranean.

On 5 April 1818 Proby married Isabella (d. 1836), daughter of Hugh Howard, a younger son of the first countess of Wicklow. They had four sons and four daughters. From February 1816 to June 1829 he was whig MP for co. Wicklow, where his family had a significant interest. Supported by the dominant interest of William, fourth Earl Fitzwilliam, Proby was elected *in absentia* and unopposed, while at sea. He reportedly did not speak in the house and voted with the Grenvillite opposition and for Roman Catholic relief.

Proby had no further service afloat, but became in due course rear-admiral on 23 November 1841, vice-admiral on 16 June 1851, and admiral on 9 July 1857. He succeeded as third earl of Carysfort on the death, on 11 June 1855, of his brother John, second earl (b. 1780). Proby died on 3 November 1868 at his seat, Elton Hall, Huntingdonshire.

J. K. LAUGHTON, rev. ANDREW LAMBERT

Sources D. Syrett and R. L. DiNardo, *The commissioned sea officers of the Royal Navy, 1660–1815*, rev. edn, Occasional Publications of the Navy RS, 1 (1994) • *The Times* (6 Nov 1868) • O'Byrne, *Naval biog. dict.* • R. G. Thorne, 'Proby, Hon. Granville Leveson', HoP, *Commons* • GEC, *Peerage* • Burke, *Peerage*
Archives NL Ire.
Wealth at death under £60,000: probate, 1869, *CGPLA Eng. & Wales* • £140,000—in Ireland: GEC, *Peerage*

Proby, John, first Baron Carysfort (1720–1772), politician, was born on 25 November 1720 in Stamford, Lincolnshire, the eldest son of the six children of John Proby (d. 1762), politician, of Elton Hall, Huntingdonshire, and his wife, the Hon. Jane Leveson-Gower (d. 1726), the younger daughter of John Leveson-Gower, first Baron Gower. He was educated at Westminster School in 1736 and the following year entered Jesus College, Cambridge, where he graduated BA in 1741 and MA in 1742. At the general election in June 1747 he was returned on the Sandwich interest to the House of Commons for Stamford. He married, on 27 August 1750, the Hon. Elizabeth Allen (bap. 1722, d. 1783), the elder daughter and coheir of Joshua, second Viscount Allen, and his wife, Margaret Du Pass; they had two children. On 23 January 1752 he was created Baron Carysfort of Carysfort in the county of Wicklow, in the Irish peerage.

In May 1754 Carysfort was elected MP for Huntingdonshire, and he continued to represent that county until the dissolution in March 1768. He was also the grand master of freemasons from 1752 to 1754. He took his seat in the Irish House of Lords on 7 October 1755 and was subsequently admitted to the Irish privy council. He was one of the lords of the Admiralty from April to July 1757. In 1758 he was chosen chairman of the two select committees appointed to inquire into the laws relating to the standards of weights and measures. He was invested a knight of the Bath on 23 March 1761, and was installed on 26 May following. He moved the address in the House of Commons at the opening in November 1762, and on 1 January 1763 was reappointed a lord of the Admiralty, a post which he resigned in August 1765.

Carysfort's final years were tainted by rumours of debts and sexual philandering. It was reported that he had wasted an 'enormous expense in kept women' (*Mrs Montagu*, 1.150). He died at Lille, France, on 18 October 1772, aged fifty-one, and was buried at Elton, Huntingdonshire. His widow died in March 1783. They were survived by both their children: John Joshua *Proby (1751–1828) also pursued a political career and was created earl of Carysfort in August 1789; and Elizabeth (1752–1808) married Thomas James Storer (d. 1792).   G. F. R. BARKER, rev. J.-M. ALTER

Sources L. Namier, 'Proby, John', HoP, *Commons* • GEC, *Peerage* • *Mrs Montagu, 'Queen of the Blues': her letters and friendships from 1762 to 1800*, ed. R. Blunt, 1 (1923), 150 • Burke, *Gen. GB* • Venn, *Alum. Cant.* • *GM*, 1st ser., 20 (1750), 380 • *GM*, 1st ser., 78 (1808), 368 • *The Grenville papers: being the correspondence of Richard Grenville … and … George Grenville*, ed. W. J. Smith, 2 (1852), 5
Likenesses J. Reynolds, oils

Proby, John Joshua, first earl of Carysfort (1751–1828), politician, was born on 12 August 1751, the only son of John *Proby, first Baron Carysfort in the peerage of Ireland (1720–1772), politician, and his wife, the Hon. Elizabeth Allen (*bap.* 1722, *d.* 1783), elder daughter of Joshua Allen, second Viscount Allen, and Margaret Du Pass. He was educated at Westminster School (*c*.1764–*c*.1767) and Trinity College, Cambridge, where he graduated MA in 1770. He succeeded his father as second Baron Carysfort on 18 October 1772, and took his seat on 12 October 1773 in the Irish House of Lords, where he soon became a prominent debater. On 19 March 1774 he married Elizabeth Osborne (*d.* 1783), daughter of Sir William Osborne, eighth baronet, MP, of Newtown, co. Tipperary, and Elizabeth Christmas. They had three sons and two daughters.

On 2 March 1780 Carysfort joined Lord Charlemont and others in protesting against the address, and in February 1780 he wrote a letter 'to the gentlemen of the Huntingdonshire committee', which was subsequently printed and distributed by the Society of Constitutional Information, advocating the shortening of parliaments, a fuller representation of the people, and 'a strict œconomy of the public treasure'. He intended to contest the University of Cambridge at the general election in that year, but he did not go to the poll. He was elected a knight of St Patrick on 5 February 1784, and installed in St Patrick's Cathedral, Dublin, on 11 August 1800. Carysfort opposed the Fox–North coalition in 1783, even though he had previously been leader of the administration in the Irish House of Lords. He rejected a peerage from the Foxite whigs, but accepted an offer from the duke of Rutland, Pitt's viceroy in Ireland. His political allegiance was confirmed by his second marriage, on 12 April 1787, to Elizabeth Grenville (1756–1842), daughter of George *Grenville and Elizabeth Wyndham (*d.* 1769) and sister of the marquess of Buckingham, the new lord lieutenant, and of William Grenville, Pitt's foreign secretary. Henceforward, he was a steadfast supporter of Pitt and Grenville. On 16 February 1789 he protested against the opposition address to the prince of Wales requesting him to exercise the royal authority in Ireland during the king's illness. As a reward for his support of the lord lieutenant's policy he was appointed, on 15 July, joint guardian and keeper of the rolls in Ireland, and was sworn a member of the Irish privy council. On 20 August 1789, in fulfilment of an engagement by the previous viceroy, the duke of Rutland, he was created earl of Carysfort in the peerage of Ireland at his wife's insistence, after Buckingham had persuaded him to withdraw his pretensions.

Carysfort was ambitious to follow his father as member for Huntingdonshire, but the representation of the county was monopolized by Lord Sandwich and the duke of Manchester and he had to settle for the purchase of a seat at East Looe, Cornwall, in 1790 on the recommendation of Buckingham. When parliament was dissolved at the end of the session, he was nominated by Lord Exeter for the borough of Stamford as a compensation for not 'disturbing the peace' of Huntingdonshire by challenging the predominant interests (HoP, *Commons*). He continued to represent Stamford until he was made a peer of the United Kingdom. In April 1791 he supported Wilberforce's motion for the abolition of the slave trade, and he opposed Fox's amendment to the address on 14 December 1792, declaring that, though a friend to moderate reform, he would have no truck with French extremism. He warmly advocated the claims of the Irish Roman Catholics, who had 'the same interests as the protestants, and ought to have the same privileges', as a reward for their loyalty to the existing orders (Cobbett, *Parl. hist.*, 30.78–9). He supported the address to the king in November 1797, and maintained that the French government was founded on a system of 'monstrous ambition and exorbitant pretensions' which were 'hostile to the re-establishment of tranquillity' (ibid., 33.1017–18).

Carysfort was in Ireland when the rising broke out in 1798. He declared that the time was ripe for a union of Great Britain and Ireland, and on 21 April 1800 he described Pitt's measure as 'wise, politic, and advantageous to the two countries' (Cobbett, *Parl. hist.*, 35.83). He expected a British peerage in return for his support, and he duly received a United Kingdom barony as Baron Carysfort of Norman Cross, Huntingdonshire, on 21 January 1801. He took his seat in the Lords on 27 November 1802. Meanwhile, Grenville had sent him as envoy-extraordinary and minister-plenipotentiary to Berlin on 24 May 1800, a post which he retained until October 1802. He supported Grenville after the latter's resignation from office with Pitt and continued to do so for the remainder of his career. On 20 January 1805 he attacked the foreign policy of Pitt's second ministry, and moved an amendment to the address, but was defeated by fifty-three votes.

On the formation of the 'ministry of all the talents' in February 1806 Carysfort was sworn of the privy council (12 February) and became joint postmaster-general (20 February). On 18 June he was further appointed a member of the Board of Trade, and on 16 July, a commissioner of the board of control. He resigned these three offices on the accession of the duke of Portland to power in the spring of the following year. He signed a protest against the bombardment of Copenhagen on 3 March 1808. He retained his interest in Ireland and on 31 January 1812 he spoke in favour of Lord Fitzwilliam's motion for the consideration of the state of Irish affairs. He supported the second reading of the Preservation of the Peace in Ireland Bill, but spoke at length against the Irish Seditious Meetings Bill in July 1814. He spoke for the last time in the House of Lords on 23 November 1819.

Carysfort, who wrote a pamphlet on parliamentary reform, published in 1783, and a collection of poems and dramatic works, was 'esteemed a good and elegant scholar', but as a speaker 'his utterance is disagreeably slow, tedious and hesitating, perpetually interrupted by the interjections Ah! Ah!' (GEC, *Peerage*, 3.71). He died at his house in Upper Grosvenor Street, London, on 7 April 1828, aged seventy-six. He was buried in Elton church, Huntingdonshire, where a tablet was erected to his memory. His second wife survived him and died at Huntercombe, near Maidenhead, on 21 December 1842, aged eighty-six. Of the five children from his first marriage, his eldest son, William Allen, Viscount Proby, MP for Buckingham from 1802 to 1804, was a naval captain and died of yellow fever at Surinam on 6 August 1804 while commanding the frigate *Amelia*. His second son, John Proby, a general in the army, succeeded as second earl of Carysfort, and died unmarried and insane on 11 June 1855, when the title passed to his younger brother, Granville Leveson *Proby, third earl of Carysfort (1781–1868), a naval officer.

G. F. R. BARKER, *rev.* E. A. SMITH

Sources R. G. Thorne, 'Proby, John Joshua', HoP, *Commons, 1790–1820* · Cobbett, *Parl. hist.*, 29.333–4; 30.78–9; 33.1017–18; 35.83 · *Hansard 1* (1803–20) · GEC, *Peerage* · *The manuscripts of J. B. Fortescue*, 10 vols., HMC, 30 (1892–1927) · *Journals of the House of Lords of the kingdom of Ireland*, 8 vols. (1783–1800) · N. H. Nicolas, *History of the orders of knighthood of the British empire*, 4 vols. (1842) · GM, 1st ser., 61 (1791), 586 · GM, 1st ser., 75 (1805), 84 · GM, 2nd ser., 19 (1843), 218 · GM, 2nd ser., 44 (1855), 313–14 · GEC, *Baronetage*
Archives priv. coll., corresp. and papers · PRO, corresp. and letter-books, FO353 | BL, corresp. with Lord Grenville, Add. MSS 58891–58893 · BL, letters to Lord Hardwicke, Add. MSS 35645–35733, *passim* · BL, corresp. with first earl of Liverpool, Add. MSS 38235, 38310, 38570–38571, *passim* · Hunt. L., letters to Grenville family · NL Scot., letters to first earl of Minto · NMM, corresp. with Lord Grenville [copies] · PRO, letters to William Pitt, PRO30/8 · Sheff. Arch., corresp. with Earl Fitzwilliam
Likenesses J. Downman, chalk and watercolour drawing, 1799, FM Cam. · J. Reynolds, oils · C. Tomkins, mezzotint (after J. Reynolds), BM, NPG

Probyn, Sir Dighton Macnaghten (1833–1924), army officer and courtier, was born in London on 21 January 1833, third of six sons of Captain G. Probyn RN, and his wife, Alicia, the daughter of Sir Francis Workman-Macnaghten. Her brother was Sir William *Macnaghten (1793–1841), and this family connection enabled Probyn, following schooling at the Revd C. Worsley's at Finchley, to obtain a cornet's commission in the 6th Bengal light cavalry in 1849, when only sixteen. In 1852 he transferred to the 2nd Punjab cavalry in the Punjab frontier force, then commanded by Samuel James Browne, inventor of the sword belt.

Probyn served with his regiment during the siege of Delhi in 1857, repeatedly distinguishing himself. He later accompanied his regiment in the force dispatched for the relief of Agra, where he captured an enemy standard and was recommended for the VC, awarded to him in 1857. The citation by General Hope Grant, commanding the force, described Probyn as: 'skilful in the use of his sword and spear and an excellent horseman, his active courage and coolness in conflict have borne him safely through many combats' (dispatch, 10 Jan 1858). He transferred to the 1st Sikh irregular cavalry, with which he served throughout the operations to relieve Cawnpore and Lucknow and to drive the rebels out of Oudh, first as second in command, and then as commanding officer in 1858. The regiment soon became known as Probyn's Horse. Probyn was made CB in 1858.

In 1860 a joint Anglo-French expedition was mounted in response to the Chinese refusal to abide by the treaty of Tientsin (Tianjin) (June 1858), whereby China had agreed to accept a resident minister from each of the two countries at Peking (Beijing). However, when the two ministers designate arrived at the mouth of the Peiho (Beihe) River in the Gulf of Pecheli (Beizhili), escorted by a fleet commanded by Admiral Hope, their way upriver was barred by the Taku (Dagu) forts on 17 June 1859. Permission to proceed further was refused, and eventually it was decided by the French and British governments to enforce the terms of the treaty.

Lieutenant-General Hope Grant was made the overall commander. The British contingent, of both British and Indian troops, included only three cavalry regiments, two of them Indian and irregular—Probyn's and Fane's Horse. All were required to volunteer, which Probyn's, mostly Sikhs, did to a man. They then marched to Calcutta from Lucknow to embark, covering 600 miles in eighteen days. They sailed for China in May 1860. Reporting back to the duke of Cambridge, Hope Grant praised the two irregular cavalry regiments and their commanders, 'two excellent officers, Major Fane and Major Probyn' (H. Knollys, *Incidents in the China War of 1860*, 1875).

Probyn and his regiment added to their laurels in China. The cavalry showed to advantage during the advance to Peking, both in reconnaissance and in shock action, which the Chinese Tartar cavalry tried to avoid. Probyn's regiment returned to India in November 1860, after what had been a very well-conducted campaign, Probyn receiving the brevet of lieutenant-colonel and being mentioned in dispatches.

Probyn's reputation, already high in the Indian army, was enhanced by his conduct in China. He had led several charges on his horse Clear-the-Line. In 1861 he was rewarded by his regiment's being taken onto the regular establishment as the 11th Bengal cavalry, remaining known unofficially as Probyn's Horse. Shortly after its return from China the regiment was informed that it had been paid twice. This was disputed, but until the matter was settled the duplicate pay was lodged in the regimental treasure chest. Nothing more was heard from the army pay department, and after two years the money was used to establish a regimental stud farm in the Punjab, which came to be known as Probynabad. The first Arab stallion at the stud was Probyn's Clear-the-Line.

Probyn commanded his regiment in the Ambela campaign in 1863, his last active service. In 1870, as a colonel, he was chosen as equerry to Prince Alfred, duke of Edinburgh, Queen Victoria's second son, during the prince's tour of India, and in 1872 he was appointed equerry to the prince of Wales, whom he accompanied on his tour of India in 1875. Probyn had been promoted major-general (15 July 1870), but his career as a soldier had ended, and that of courtier had begun. In 1901, on Edward VII's accession, he was made privy councillor and keeper of the privy purse. After the king's death in 1910 Probyn became comptroller of Queen Alexandra's household. In his biography of Edward VII, Sir Sidney Lee comments on Probyn's competence, fidelity, and faculty for rigorous finance. He took a prominent part in advising the king over the development of the Sandringham estate. In 1872 he married his first cousin, Letitia Thelusson. They had no children and she died on 17 January 1900. After his wife's death it was believed that he was on the verge of marrying Charlotte Knollys (Queen Alexandra's principal lady in waiting), who was deeply attached to him, but he did not marry again.

Probyn was promoted full general on the half-pay list on 1 December 1888. He was made KCSI in 1876, KCB in 1887, GCVO in 1896, GCB (civil) in 1902, GCB (military) in 1910 and GCSI in 1911. He was awarded the ISO in 1903, and in 1904 was appointed honorary colonel of Probyn's Horse, an appointment he held until his death aged ninety-one. He died on 20 June 1924, at Sandringham, Norfolk, where he was buried. He left no memoirs or papers, but his extensive correspondence with Field Marshal Lord Birdwood, who served many years in Probyn's Horse, survived in the British Library oriental and India Office collections. JAMES LUNT

Sources V. Birdwood, 'General the Rt Hon. Sir Dighton Probyn', *Journal of the Society for Army Historical Research*, 55 (1977), 32–4 · Lord Roberts [F. S. Roberts], *Forty-one years in India*, 1 (1897) · C. A. Boyle, *The history of Probyn's horse* (1929) · *The Times* (21 June 1924) · M. Mann, *China* (1989) · S. Lee, *King Edward VII*, 1 (1925) · G. Battiscombe, *Queen Alexandra* (1969) · Lord Birdwood, *In my time: khaki and gown* (1941) · P. Mason, *A matter of honour: an account of the Indian army, its officers and men* (1974) · P. Magnus, *King Edward the Seventh* (1964) · *WWW* · NAM, Hodson MSS · Burke, *Peerage* · *CGPLA Eng. & Wales* (1924)

Archives BL, letters to Sir C. W. Dilke and others · BL OIOC, letters to Sir W. R. Birdwood, MSS Eur. D 686 · BL OIOC, letters to Sir F. E. Younghusband, MSS Eur. F 197 · Bodl. Oxf., corresp. with Sir Henry Burdett · Bodl. Oxf., corresp. with Lord Kimberley · CUL, letters to Lord Hardinge · NAM, letters to Lord Roberts

Likenesses photograph, 1860 · portrait (as an old man), repro. in Birdwood, 'General the Rt Hon. Sir Dighton Probyn'

Wealth at death £6679 9s.: probate, 25 July 1924, *CGPLA Eng. & Wales*

Probyn, Sir Edmund (1678–1742), judge, was born at Newland, in the Forest of Dean, Gloucestershire, and was baptized there on 16 July 1678. He was the elder of the two sons of William Probyn of Newland and his wife, Elizabeth, eldest daughter of Edmund Bond of Walford, Herefordshire, and widow of William Hopton of Huntley, Gloucestershire. He matriculated at Christ Church, Oxford, on 23 April 1695, entered the Middle Temple on 27 November 1695, and was called to the bar on 15 May 1702. In 1720 he married Elizabeth (d. 1749), daughter of Sir John Blencowe, justice of the common pleas. They had no children.

Probyn was appointed second justice of the Brecon, Glamorgan, and Radnor circuit in 1721, and became a serjeant-at-law on 27 January 1724. It was he who defended the lord chancellor, Thomas Parker, first earl of Macclesfield, when he was impeached for embezzling chancery funds, but despite his able defence, Macclesfield was found guilty and sent to the Tower until he paid his £30,000 fine. Probyn succeeded Sir Littleton Powys as judge of the king's bench on 3 November 1726, was knighted on 8 November, and succeeded Sir John Comyns

Sir Edmund Probyn (1678–1742), by John Faber junior

as lord chief baron of the exchequer on 24 November 1740.

Probyn died on 17 May 1742, and was buried in Newland church. He left his estates in Gloucestershire to his nephew, John Hopkins, of Lincoln's Inn, provided that he took the name of Probyn.

J. M. RIGG, *rev.* ANNE PIMLOTT BAKER

Sources W. R. Williams, *The history of the great sessions in Wales, 1542–1830* (privately printed, Brecon, 1899), 146–7 · Foss, *Judges*, 8.154 · Baker, *Serjeants*, 532 · Foster, *Alum. Oxon.* · *GM*, 1st ser., 12 (1742), 275 · *IGI*

Archives NL Wales | NL Wales, accounts and memoranda

Likenesses J. Faber junior, mezzotint, BM · J. Faber junior, mezzotint, second version, NPG [*see illus.*] · monument with bust, Newland church, Gloucestershire

Procter, Adelaide Anne [*pseud.* Mary Berwick] (1825–1864), poet and women's activist, the eldest daughter and first child of the poet Bryan Waller *Procter (1787–1874) and his wife, Ann, *née* Skepper (1799–1888), was born on 30 October 1825 at 25 Bedford Square, London, where her parents lived with Basil Montagu and his wife, Ann, Ann's stepfather and mother. She grew up in a household where 'everybody of any literary pretension whatever seemed to flow in and out' of her mother's literary salon (Belloc, 162). She was close to her father; Jane Brookfield wrote of Bryan Procter's attachment to his 'bright, enthusiastic daughter', and of father and daughter 'with critical approbation' admiring each other's work (Brookfield and Brookfield, 460–61). According to Charles Dickens, Adelaide Procter showed an early appreciation of poetry, and also a great facility for learning languages (French, Italian, and German), and for Euclidean geometry, music, and drawing.

Adelaide Anne Procter (1825–1864), by Emma Gaggiotti Richards

Nathaniel P. Willis described her as 'a beautiful girl, delicate, gentle, and pensive', looking as if she 'knew she was a poet's child' (*Pencillings by the Way*, 1835).

Adelaide Procter's first published poem was 'Ministering Angels', which appeared in *Heath's Book of Beauty* in 1843, but her poetical career was established in 1853 when she began a long connection with Charles Dickens's periodical *Household Words*. She submitted her poems under the pseudonym Mary Berwick, lest Dickens, who was a friend of her father's, print them 'for papa's sake, and not for their own' (Dickens). Dickens, however, admired the poems, and in December 1854, after he had shown Adelaide's mother a proof of the poem 'The Sailor Boy', Adelaide revealed her true identity. She became Dickens's most published poet, with seventy-three poems published in *Household Words* and seven in *All the Year Round*. In 1858 a first series of her *Legends and Lyrics* was published by Bell and Daldy, and was followed in 1861 by a second series. Both series were posthumously published in a single volume in 1866, with an introduction by Dickens. According to Coventry Patmore, demand for her poetry was greater than for any other English poet with the exception of Tennyson. Some of her poems were widely sung as hymns in the latter half of the nineteenth century; undoubtedly the most famous of her lyrics was 'A Lost Chord', set to music by Sir Arthur Sullivan in 1877. Her poetry was translated into German and published in America. Individual poems appeared in the *Cornhill Magazine*, *Good Words*, and the *English Woman's Journal*.

The first series of *Legends and Lyrics* was dedicated to Matilda Hays (1820–1897), at this time living in a 'female marriage' with the American actress Charlotte Cushman

and for whom Adelaide Procter cherished an intense friendship. The friendship with Hays reflected Procter's involvement with the Langham Place circle which was dedicated to improving conditions for women. Procter had been one of the original students at Queen's College in Harley Street in 1850, and had been a childhood friend of Bessie Rayner Parkes, a leading figure among the Langham Place group. At the end of the decade she was involved in the foundation of both the *English Woman's Journal* (1858) and the Society for the Promotion of the Employment of Women (1859). Her work for the society, which sought to create employment for middle-class women, involved visiting work places, including a watchmaking factory in Christchurch, Dorset, where women dominated the workforce. In 1861 she edited *Victoria regia*, a collection of poetry and prose intended to demonstrate the work and skills of the Victoria Press, which was run by Emily Faithfull to provide work for women as compositors. In the following year her collection of religious lyrics, *A Chaplet of Verses*, was published for the benefit of the Providence Row night refuge for women and children, a Catholic organization in east London founded by Daniel Gilbert; Procter had converted to Roman Catholicism about 1851, and Gilbert was her confessor. Adelaide Procter had always been delicate, and in 1862 her health began to fail as tuberculosis developed. She tried the cure at Malvern, but after some fifteen months bedridden she died on 2 February 1864 at 32 Weymouth Street, London, and was buried in Kensal Green cemetery.

Dickens wrote in his tribute in the 1866 edition of her poetry that 'she was a finely sympathetic woman, with a great accordant heart and a sterling noble nature', also noting that 'she was exceedingly humorous, and had a great delight in humour'. Procter's poetry, which often reflected the concerns of the Langham Place circle with the position of the single woman, was much neglected in the twentieth century until the 1980s, when her work began to receive critical attention, and several of her poems were anthologized. Isobel Armstrong drew attention to her 'magnificently humane lyrics on the Crimean War', and to some of her finest verses, including 'Unexpressed', 'Words', and 'A Lost Chord'. Commentators have applauded the originality of Adelaide Procter's poetry, while some have noted her unconventional treatment of women's sexuality in lyrics such as 'Three Roses' and in 'A Legend of Provence', a narrative poem concerning a nun who leaves her convent with a knight, but who is totally absolved of her sins and received back into her religious community. Some of the narrative poems, for example 'The Angel's Story', 'A Legend of Bregenz', 'A Tomb in Ghent', and 'The Story of a Faithful Soul', provide poignant, dramatic, and disturbing accounts of homelessness, exile, and displacement. She also wrote 'Adventures of your Own Correspondents in Search of Solitude', a humorous and ironic account of a journey to the Lake District made by herself and a woman friend identified as 'A' (possibly Annie Leigh Smith), and a life of the French *salonière* Juliette Récamier (*English Woman's Journal*, 4–6, 1859–61). GILL GREGORY

Sources C. Dickens, 'Introduction', in A. A. Procter, *Legends and lyrics together with a chaplet of verses* (1914) • B. R. Belloc, *In a walled garden* (1895) • [B. Parkes], 'The poems of Adelaide Anne Procter', *The Month*, 5 (1866), 79–88 • *B. W. Procter (Barry Cornwall): an autobiographical fragment*, ed. C. P. [C. Patmore] (1877) • I. Armstrong, '"A music of thine own": women's poetry', *Victorian poetry: poetry, poetics, and politics* (1993), 318–77 • G. Gregory, 'Adelaide Procter's "A legend of Provence"', *Victorian women poets: a critical reader*, ed. A. Leighton (1996), 88–96 • J. Julian, ed., *A dictionary of hymnology* (1892), 913 • C. H. E. Brookfield and F. M. Brookfield, *Mrs Brookfield and her circle*, 2 vols. (1905) • A. Leighton and M. Reynolds, eds., *Victorian women poets: an anthology* (1995) • O. Banks, *The biographical dictionary of British feminists*, 1 (1985) • private information (2004)
Archives U. Reading L., corresp. relating to copyright of her poems • University of Iowa Libraries, Iowa City, corresp. and poems | Girton Cam., letters, mainly to Bessie Rayner Parkes
Likenesses C. H. Jeens, engraving, repro. in A. A. Procter, *Legends and lyrics* (1866) • E. G. Richards, oils, NPG [*see illus.*] • H. Watkins, carte-de-visite, NPG

Procter, Bryan Waller (1787–1874), poet and lawyer, the eldest child of Nicholas Procter (*d.* 1816) and his wife, Amelia (*d.* 1837), was born on 21 November 1787 and named after a great-uncle from whom an inheritance was expected. His ancestors were small farmers in Yorkshire or Cumberland, but his father moved to London and set up in trade. He may have been the Nicholas Procter who dealt in wine and brandy at 241 Piccadilly between 1799 and 1804; he was certainly a man of leisure and property when he died in 1816 at Gloucester Place, Camden Town. The Procters' other children were Margaret (*d.* in or before 1867) and Nicholas (*b.* 1802), who inherited the landed estate in Yorkshire of their great-uncle Bryan Waller and changed his surname from Procter to Waller in 1816.

Procter was educated at, successively, a dame-school in Finchley, a small boarding-school perhaps at Acton, and Harrow School. He entered Harrow in Lent term 1801, spent about three years there, and acquired some skill at football, cricket, fives, and marbles alongside a modicum of classical education. He was then articled for about three years to a solicitor, Nathaniel Atherton of Calne, Wiltshire, before moving to London about 1807 and concluding his law studies. He was admitted to chancery as a solicitor in summer 1811 and practised in various partnerships in Brunswick Square (1812–19) and in Gray's Inn Place (1819–23). By his father's will, proved on 23 February 1816, he obtained about £500 per annum as a share of the rentals of four houses in Jermyn Street, whereupon he briefly became a dandy; he also took boxing lessons from Tom Cribb, though a lightweight. Procter had a 'slight neat figure, vigorous for his size' and a 'fine genially rugged little face' (Carlyle, 1.223).

From 1815 Procter contributed poems to many journals using various pen-names but eventually fixing upon Barry Cornwall. He became a close friend of Leigh Hunt, Charles Lamb, and William Hazlitt, and over the years became acquainted with most of the best writers in London. He had a genius for friendship, being a man of great kindness and generous appreciation, 'a man whom everybody loves' (*Henry Crabb Robinson*, 2.548), and an excellent host. He was a good talker, but in five volumes published over four years he never found a poetic voice of his own. His

Bryan Waller Procter (1787–1874), by John Henry Foley

pseudo-Jacobean playlets in *Dramatic Scenes and other Poems* (1819) are modelled on Lamb's *Specimens of the English Dramatic Poets*. In *A Sicilian Story, with Diego de Montilla, and other Poems* (1820) the first title-poem imitates Hunt and the second unwisely attempts to imitate Procter's old Harrovian schoolfellow Lord Byron. *Marcian Colonna, an Italian Tale, with Three Dramatic Scenes, and other Poems* (1820) mostly echoes Hunt. Procter's only full-length play, the blank-verse tragedy of *Mirandola*, is Jacobean pastiche again, but it ran for sixteen nights at Covent Garden in 1821, and, with three printed editions that year, earned £630 for the author. A third volume of mostly Huntian narrative verse, *The Flood of Thessaly, The Girl of Provence, and other Poems* (1823) was damned by *Blackwood's* as Greekish cockney.

Marriage and financial need, probably more than bad reviews, stemmed the flood of poetry. On 7 October 1824 Procter married Ann Benson Skepper (1799–1888), the daughter of Thomas Skepper of York (deceased), and his wife, Ann Dorothea, *née* Benson, now married to the distinguished lawyer and legal writer Basil Montagu (1770–1851) and hostess to a brilliant literary salon at 25 Bedford Square. The newly-weds had a cheese-paring honeymoon, lived for some months at 14 Southampton Row, and then moved in with the Montagus at Bedford Square; they remained there for seven years with their growing family (four daughters and two sons) while Procter, with Montagu's help, cultivated a practice in conveyancing and read for the bar. He entered Gray's Inn on 5 May 1826 and was admitted barrister on 4 May 1831. He continued to write occasional poems and prose essays for journals and published *English Songs, and other Small Poems* (1832), a collection of melodious but trite lyrics mostly written ten or more years earlier, but otherwise was 'altogether abandoned to law', as he complained to Leigh Hunt in 1826 (Mayer, 561). In 1832 he was appointed a metropolitan commissioner of lunacy with a stipend of £800 per annum (increased to £1500 with a greater workload in 1845), and removed his family from the Montagus' grand house to a little Gothic cottage at 5 Grove End Road, St John's Wood. His young son Edward died of scarlet fever in 1836 and his mother died in 1837, leaving Procter nearly £800 in bank annuities.

Apart from revised and enlarged editions of *English Songs* and *Dramatic Scenes*, Procter's new books after the creative burst between 1819 and 1823 were all in prose, some of them little better than hack work. They included letterpress for engraved portraits in *Effigies poeticae* (1824) and *Tableaux of National Character* (1837), a preface to *Melanie and other Poems* (1835) by the flamboyant American Nathaniel Parker Willis, and memoirs of Ben Jonson and Shakespeare in editions of their works (1838 and 1843). Procter's longest prose work, *The Life of Edmund Kean* (1835), was justifiably damned in *Blackwood's* and the *Quarterly Review*. His circle of friends expanded to embrace many younger writers, notably Thomas Lovell Beddoes, Charles Dickens, William Makepeace Thackeray, Coventry Patmore, and, especially, Robert Browning and John Forster. Among the dedications he received were those of Browning's *Columbe's Birthday* (1844) and Thackeray's *Vanity Fair* (1848).

Procter continued his conveyancing business at 4 Gray's Inn Square, where Alexander Kinglake, Patmore, and Eliot Warburton were among his pupils, and as lunacy commissioner expended much time and energy inspecting asylums all over England, attending meetings, and making reports. Mary Lamb, the sister of his dear, dead friend, was one of the patients he helped. He wrote to Leigh Hunt in 1840 of 'being stupid and exhausted, as I am nine nights out of ten, owing to my sitting up (at work) till three or four o'clock in the morning' (Mayer, 562), and it was during journeys between asylums that he acquired the habit of sleeping in company.

In 1843 the Procters moved to 13 Upper Harley Street and in 1853 to 32 Weymouth Street. At both houses Procter's sociable and talented wife's 'tremendous energy and genius for gossip made her a hostess of distinction' (*Letters and Private Papers of … Thackeray*, 1.cliii), so that the Procters' parties became a long-lived institution of literary London. Procter received a legacy of £6500 from his friend John Kenyon (*d.* 1856), but it seems that he lost heavily on some American state loan that was repudiated at the time of the civil war and had to sell a much admired collection of Italian masters. In February 1861 he relinquished office as lunacy commissioner and was awarded a pension of £625 per annum. His close friend John Forster succeeded him as commissioner and helped him complete two last tributes to literary friendships, *Selections from Robert Browning* (1863) and *Charles Lamb: a Memoir* (1866).

Procter was now in the 'dark desert' of old age (Chorley,

2.241). His eldest child, Adelaide Anne *Procter, died in 1864, having eclipsed his poetical reputation with her *Legends and Lyrics*, and his only surviving son, Montagu, was an army officer in India. By 1867 Procter was suffering from the prostate gland; by 1868 his speech was impaired, he was partly paralysed by a stroke, and could venture out only in an invalid's chair, but he could still read without spectacles. He died of 'paralysis' (presumably a stroke) on 4 October 1874 (three days short of his golden wedding anniversary) at 32 Weymouth Street and was buried two days later in St Marylebone cemetery, East Finchley.

Procter's widow continued the literary salon until she died in 1888, having survived all her children but one daughter. With Coventry Patmore she edited Procter's *An Autobiographical Fragment and Biographical Notes* (1877). It was prefaced by verse tributes from Walter Savage Landor (*b.* 1775) and Algernon Swinburne (*d.* 1909), testifying to the range and endurance of Procter's friendships.

JAMES SAMBROOK

Sources R. W. Armour, *Barry Cornwall: a biography* (1935) · [C. Patmore], *Bryan Waller Procter (Barry Cornwall): an autobiographical fragment and biographical notes* (1877) · *The complete works of Thomas Lovell Beddoes*, ed. E. Gosse (1928), vol.1, pp. 4–108 · T. Carlyle, *Reminiscences*, ed. J. A. Froude (1881), vol. 1, pp. 223–4 · [B. W. Procter], 'My recollections of the late William Hazlitt', *New Monthly Magazine*, 29 (1830), 469–82 · *Byron's letters and journals*, ed. L. A. Marchand, 12 vols. (1973–82), 7 (1977), 113, 225; 8 (1978), 56, 207; 9 (1979), 83–4; 10 (1980), 115–16 · *The Brownings' correspondence: a checklist*, ed. P. Kelley and R. Hudson (1978), 416 · *The letters of William Hazlitt*, ed. H. M. Sikes and others (1978), 200, 255, 382 · *The letters and private papers of William Makepeace Thackeray*, ed. G. N. Ray, 1 (1945), cliii–cliv · *The letters of Charles Dickens*, ed. M. House, G. Storey, and others, 12 vols. (1965–2002) · *The letters of John Keats, 1814–1821*, ed. H. E. Rollins (1958), vol. 2, pp. 266–7, 271, 278 · J. Foster, *The register of admissions to Gray's Inn, 1521–1889, together with the register of marriages in Gray's Inn chapel, 1695–1754* (privately printed, London, 1889), 432 · M. G. Dauglish and P. K. Stephenson, eds., *The Harrow School register, 1800–1911*, 3rd edn (1911), 16, 33 · S. R. T. Mayer, '"Barry Cornwall": unpublished letters, personal recollections, and contemporary notes', *GM*, 5th ser., 13 (1874), 555–68 · *Henry Crabb Robinson on books and their writers*, ed. E. J. Morley (1938), vol. 1, pp. 238, 294; vol. 2, pp. 548, 597, 755 · H. G. Hewlett, 'Barry Cornwall's life and poems', *EdinR*, 147 (1878), 333–53 · J. T. Fields, 'Barry Cornwall and some of his friends', *Yesterdays with authors* (1900), 355–419 · W. Jerdan, *The autobiography of William Jerdan: with his literary, political, and social reminiscences and correspondence during the last fifty years*, 4 vols. (1852–3), vol. 3, p. 230 · *The complete works of William Hazlitt*, ed. P. P. Howe, 21 vols. (1930–34), vol. 8, p. 203 · parish register, St Olave's, York, 30 Sept 1800 [baptism: Ann Benson Skepper, wife] · *GM*, 1st ser., 94/2 (1824), 560 · W. Allingham, *A diary*, ed. H. Allingham and D. Radford (1907), 178, 265, 310, 323, 368 · H. Martineau, *Biographical sketches, 1852–1875*, 4th edn (1876), 457–87 · H. T. Chorley, *Autobiography, memoir, and letters*, ed. H. G. Hewlett (1873), vol. 1, p. 161; vol. 2, pp. 107–8, 241 · *N&Q*, 5th ser., 2 (1874), 339–40 · *GM*, 2nd ser., 6 (1836), 423 · d. cert.

Archives BL, letters, with related papers, Add. MSS 28511, fol. 314; 34624, fols. 523, 543; 36717, fol. 394; 38109, 38523–38524, 45680; 52343, fols. 46–9 · Bodl. Oxf., letters and poems · Holborn Library, Camden, London, Camden Local Studies and Archives Centre, essay, poem, and letters · JRL, poems and letters · Keats House, Hampstead, London, letters and a poem · NL Scot., letters · Trinity Cam., letters, Cullum P56 · Trinity Cam., letters to Lord Houghton and Lady Houghton · UCL, letters · University of Iowa Libraries, corresp. and poems · V&A NAL, letters and notes, mainly to John Forster but six to W. S. Landor | BL, letters written as sponsor to Royal Literary Fund, loan 96 · Blackburn Central Library, letters to

Charles Dickens • Brown University, Providence, Rhode Island, letters to Robert Browning • Harvard U., Houghton L., letters to Taylor and Hessey • Hunt. L., letters to Robert Browning • NL Scot., letters to John Scott • University of Chicago Library, corresp. with Elizabeth Browning and Robert Browning • University of Iowa Libraries, letters to Robert Browning and poems • W. Yorks. AS, Leeds, letters, Symington collection, box 13

Likenesses W. Brockedon, black and red chalk drawing, 1830, NPG • R. Holl, print, pubd 1832 (after A. Wivell), Harvard TC • D. Maclise, group portrait, lithograph, pubd 1835 (*The Fraserians*), BM • A. D'Orsay, pencil and chalk drawing, 1841, NPG • C. Martin, pencil sketch, 1844?, BM; repro. in Armour, *Barry Cornwall*, 64 • R. Lehmann, drawing, 1869, BM • J. H. Foley, marble bust, NPG [*see illus.*] • D. Maclise, group portrait, pencil sketches, V&A • engraving, BL; repro. in Armour, *Barry Cornwall* • engraving, JRL, English MS 725, vol. 2 • portrait, repro. in *The Graphic*, 10 (1874), 367 • portrait (aged eighty-two; after a pencil sketch by R. Lehmann), repro. in Armour, *Barry Cornwall*, 120 • wood-engraving (after photograph by H. Watkins), repro. in *ILN*, 65 (10 Oct 1874), 353

Wealth at death under £16,000: probate, 3 Nov 1874, *CGPLA Eng. & Wales*

Procter, Chrystabel Prudence Goldsmith (1894–1982), horticulturist, was born on 11 March 1894 at 11 Kensington Square, London, the elder daughter of Joseph Procter (1865–1945), a member of the London stock exchange, and his wife, Elizabeth Harriet (1862–1925), the daughter of William Brockbank and his wife, Jane, *née* Benson. Brought up as an Anglican, she moved towards the Catholic church in her early thirties, but was also associated with the Society of Friends, of which her mother had been a member until 1893. Procter had a metropolitan childhood, but each of her homes possessed a large garden and allowed her to indulge a love of plants and animals. After attending Norland Place School (1904–8) she spent four years at St Paul's Girls' School, Hammersmith, which she found 'a very happy school' ('Flora and fauna', 10). She was proud to be a Paulina. Both parents, keen educationists, assumed that Chrystabel and her sister Joan would proceed to Cambridge. By the age of fifteen, however, Chrystabel had lost her hearing. Both she and her father thought that attendance at university would be impossible. She turned, therefore, but with delight, to gardening.

After a spell of war service in the voluntary aid detachment Procter attended (1915) the Glynde College of Lady Gardeners, founded in 1902 by Viscountess Wolseley. Glynde made intense demands on its students and offered only one afternoon off from Monday to Saturday, a privilege readily revoked for a small mistake. After Glynde, Procter accepted the invitation of Frances Gray, the high mistress of St Paul's, to become the gardener of Bute House, Luxemburg Gardens, where the school had its playing field and an orchard. At first paid merely as 'gardener's boy', she joined the teaching staff and received the title lady gardener once she had passed the Royal Horticultural Society's teachers' honours examination (1919). An immense success both as a teacher and a gardener, she transformed the 5 acres of Bute from an overgrown and weed-covered area into a flourishing vegetable, flower, and fruit garden and also maintained there a small piggery.

Keen to develop her career, Procter moved on in 1925 to a similar post at Bingley Training College in Yorkshire, where she learned to cope with land that was stony and exposed compared with the enclosed clay grounds of Bute. After seven years at Bingley she returned south and took up the post of garden steward at Girton College, Cambridge, in January 1933. There she was successful in developing spectacular flower beds in the courtyards and, during the Second World War, growing vegetables for the war effort. In autumn 1939, for example, her staff picked a complete ton of damsons, which was then sent to the Cambridge canteens for evacuated children; 13 cwt of potatoes were produced in 1937–8 but 19 tons in 1941–2. Her garden reports in the *Girton Review* convey her professional ebullience. Cloisters Court, she wrote in the autumn 1934 issue, 'will have in it Red Hot Pokers, late Michaelmas Daisies, Chrysanthemums. It is hoped it will then shout a welcome to Freshers on the day that they arrive.' An emergency appeal to college members and alumni for crocuses in the late 1930s produced 11,000 corms, and 'Girton then became a serious rival of Trinity in March' ('Flora and fauna', 116).

Though devoted to Girton, Procter was tempted away in 1945, when she was offered the post of estate steward at Bryanston School, Dorset. She adjusted easily to her new responsibilities. The governors expressed concern that she might be offended by the school's tradition of nude bathing, but she told them by telegram: 'Stop worrying about my modesty I have none.' For clearing weeds and brush, she let the boys deploy a flame-thrower, which, she noticed, they loved to use.

By the time she was fifty-five Procter could afford to retire (1950). She spent the next few years travelling in Australia and east Africa, and living in Kenya (1957–61) with her great friend Helen Neatby, a principal at Kaimosi training college. She returned to England in 1961 and occupied the ensuing twenty-one years with her correspondence, meeting old acquaintances, attending horticultural and Paulina events, and writing.

Throughout her life, Procter had combined work as a gardener and teacher with writing and publishing. From childhood she developed the habit of sending essays, letters, and poems to newspapers and journals, especially to the *Daily Express*, *Everyman*, and *Time and Tide*. As a teacher, she contributed to periodicals such as *Education*, *Mother and Child*, and the *Practical Senior Teacher*. Many of her poems or occasional pieces were used by the Tanganyika schools broadcasts in the late 1950s. Her autobiography, 'Flora and fauna', she vainly sought to have published before she died. *Helen Neatby: a Quaker in Africa* she had printed in 1973. She was a fellow of both the Linnean Society and the Royal Horticultural Society and a freeman of the Worshipful Company of Gardeners.

Although she lived during her last years in a nursing home at Weston-super-Mare, Procter remained alert and active to within a few days of her death on 21 June 1982. She should be remembered as a remarkable gardener who developed beautiful and useful grounds at Bute, Bingley, Girton, and Bryanston and whose writings and teaching influenced and trained hundreds of pupils. For her, as she explained in an article for the *Practical Senior Teacher* (1934), gardening was an introduction to natural science, a preparation for life, an outdoor laboratory, and an aesthetic training ground. HOWARD BAILES

Sources Girton Cam., Procter MSS · C. Procter, 'Flora and fauna', Girton Cam., Procter MS · *Paulina* (1908–82) · J. Brown, *A garden of our own: a history of Girton College garden* (1999) · b. cert. · d. cert.
Archives Girton Cam., papers · St Paul's Girls' School, London, file
Likenesses photograph, St Paul's Girls' School Archives, London
Wealth at death £56,424: probate, 13 Aug 1982, *CGPLA Eng. & Wales*

Procter [*née* Shaw], **Doris Margaret** [Dod] (1892–1972), painter, was born on 21 April 1892 in London, the only daughter of Frederick C. Shaw, a ship's doctor, and his wife, Eunice Mary, *née* Richards, an artist who had studied at the Slade School of Fine Art, London. When Doris was young the family moved to Tavistock, Devon, where Dr Shaw died. They moved again in 1907 to Myrtle Cottage, Newlyn, Cornwall, and Doris studied painting under Stanhope Forbes at his Meadow Studios in the town during 1907–8. Fellow students there were Ernest Procter, her future husband, and Laura Knight, a lifelong friend, who described Doris as 'a charming young thing, with a brilliant complexion, enormous dark eyes and long slender legs—swift and active as a gazelle' (L. Knight, *Oil Paint and Grease Paint*, 1936, 161–2).

In 1910–11 Doris Shaw studied painting at the Atelier Colarossi in Paris, following the advice of **Ernest Procter** (1886–1935), who was already there. Ernest was born on 22 May 1886 at Tynemouth, Northumberland, the son of Henry Richardson Procter, a professor at Leeds University. After attending the Quaker school, Bootham, at York he enrolled at Leeds Art School about 1905–6 and then studied at the Stanhope Forbes Art School, Newlyn, before entering the Atelier Colarossi. Doris and Ernest returned to Newlyn in 1912 and married on 9 April at Paul parish church; they travelled to Paris and Versailles for their honeymoon. On their return to Newlyn they rented Dunton House, where their only child, Bill, was born in February 1913. Also in 1913 they had their first joint exhibition of watercolours at the Fine Art Society in London. By 1923 they had moved to North Corner, Newlyn, an old fisherman's cottage. Here, in unlikely circumstances, they created a magical garden, with grottoes and brilliant patches of coloured planting, all surrounded and protected by a high granite wall. Doris lived here until her death in 1972, and the garden was the subject of many of her paintings.

In 1919 both painters were invited to paint murals for the Kokine Palace in Rangoon, Burma, belonging to the Chinese millionaire Lim Ching Tsong. They travelled to Rangoon in December 1919 and worked at the palace for a year, assisted by Burmese, Indian, and Chinese craftsmen. Shortly after her return to England, Doris began a series of portraits of young women, depicted in simplified, rather sculptural forms. She sent her work to mixed exhibitions at the Leicester Galleries, London, from 1913 to 1935. She first sent a painting to the Royal Academy Summer Exhibition in 1913, a Versailles subject inspired by her honeymoon visit. In 1916 and 1917 she sent flower paintings and in 1922 a Burmese scene. But from 1923 she sent paintings of women. She also began exhibiting under the androgynous name of Dod rather than Doris.

In 1926 Dod and Ernest Procter had their second joint exhibition, this time at the Leicester Galleries. In 1927 Dod's painting *Morning* (Tate collection), which depicted Cissie Barnes, the daughter of a Newlyn fisherman, asleep on a bed, was voted the picture of the year at the Royal Academy Summer Exhibition. It was bought for the nation by the *Daily Mail* newspaper. On Dod's return to Newlyn from visiting the opening of the exhibition at the Royal Academy, flags were hung in celebration of her success and she was led home from the station by a silver band. *Morning* was so popular with the public that it was toured round regional galleries in Britain, being seen by 60,638 visitors at Birmingham City Art Gallery during February 1928. It was sent to New York on the ship *Queen Elizabeth*, and on its return it was given to the Tate Gallery. A two-page illustrated article entitled 'Painting the picture of the year' describes the artist thus:

> Not very tall, slight and dark, modern looking and extremely feminine … [with] her shingled head, her pearl stud earrings, slim, silk-stockinged legs and neat feet … her legs crossed, her large dark eyes reflective, a long, thin, black cigarette holder in her extremely sensitive, slender hand … surround an outstanding personality illuminated brilliantly from within when art, which is the real business of her being, is under discussion. Then there is clarity and conviction in everything she says. (Tate collection, archives)

As a result of Dod's successes at the Royal Academy summer exhibitions during the second half of the 1920s, the Procters rented a flat in London, first at 26 Stanley Gardens, Belsize Park, then at 32 Elsworthy Road, Primrose Hill. In 1929 the Royal Academy Summer Exhibition jury rejected Dod's painting *Virginal*, a full-length nude figure of a young woman, and she sent it instead to the Leicester Galleries. The genitals of the young woman were visible, and this was probably the reason for its rejection. However, she was elected an associate of the Royal Academy in 1934, a rare distinction for a woman painter, and only the third woman in the academy's history. She was made a Royal Academician in 1942.

In the 1930s Dod Procter continued to paint her favourite subject of women, but her style became softer and more painterly. She joined the New English Art Club and showed with them between 1929 and 1932. Two paintings were bought for the nation under the terms of the Chantrey Bequest during the 1930s (*The Orchard*, 1934, and *Kitchen at Myrtle Cottage*, 1935; Tate collection) and one by the Contemporary Art Society in 1931. Procter contributed regularly to the prestigious Carnegie Institute's international exhibitions at Pittsburgh, and in May 1935 she was given a show at the Carl Fischer Gallery in New York. Ernest Procter died on 21 October 1935 in North Shields, Northumberland, and after his death Dod started to travel, both for work and for pleasure. She visited Canada and America in 1936; the Canary Islands in 1938 and 1946; Tenerife in 1938 and 1939; and Jamaica four times in the 1950s. On many of these travels she was accompanied by the painter Alethea Garstin, a close friend. She painted in Ireland during the Second World War, and her subjects at this time included flower pieces. Dod died in Newlyn on 31 July 1972, and was buried alongside her husband, Ernest, in the churchyard of St Hilary nearby. Her work is in Oldham Art Gallery; the Laing Art Gallery, Newcastle upon Tyne; the Atkinson Art Gallery, Southport; the City Museum and Art Gallery, Stoke-on-Trent; Penlee House Gallery, near St Ives, Cornwall; and the Tate collection.

JUDITH COLLINS

Sources E. Knowles, *Dod Procter, RA, 1892–1972* (1990) [exhibition catalogue, Laing Art Gallery, Newcastle upon Tyne, 1990] • A. Bertram, 'Dod Procter', *Studio*, 97 (Jan–June 1929), 92–7 • D. Gaze, ed., *Dictionary of women artists* (1997) • C. Fox, *Painting in Newlyn, 1900–1930* (1985) [exhibition catalogue, Newlyn Orion Galleries, 1985] • m. cert. • 'Painting the picture of the year', *c.*1927–1928, Tate collection • *CGPLA Eng. & Wales* (1935)
Archives Tate collection, corresp., mainly with family, and papers
Likenesses photographs, *c.*1919–1949, repro. in Gaze, ed., *Dictionary of women artists*
Wealth at death £7992 8s. 1d.—Ernest Procter: probate, 16 Dec 1935, *CGPLA Eng. & Wales*

Procter, Ernest (1886–1935). *See under* Procter, Doris Margaret (1892–1972).

Procter, Francis (1812–1905), Church of England clergyman and liturgical scholar, born at Hackney on 21 June 1812, was the only son of Francis Procter, a warehouseman in Gracechurch Street, Manchester, and his wife, Mary. He was of delicate health, and spent the early years of his life at Newland vicarage, Gloucestershire, under the care of an uncle, Payler Procter, who was vicar there. In 1825 he was sent to Shrewsbury School under Samuel Butler, and thence passed in 1831 to St Catharine's College, Cambridge, where another uncle, Dr Joseph Procter, was master. In 1835 he graduated BA as thirtieth wrangler and eleventh in the second class of the classical tripos. In the following year he was ordained deacon in the diocese of Lincoln, and in 1838 priest in the diocese of Ely. He served curacies at Streatley, Bedfordshire, from 1836 to 1840, and at Romsey from 1840 to 1842, when he gave up for a time parochial work in order to become fellow and assistant tutor of his college. In 1847 he left the university for the vicarage of Witton, Norfolk. There the rest of his long life was spent. In 1848 he married Margaret, daughter of Thomas Meryon of Rye, Sussex; they had five sons and three daughters. Procter died at Witton on 24 August 1905 and was buried in its churchyard.

Procter was author of *A History of the Book of Common Prayer, with a Rationale of its Offices*, first published in 1855. In many subsequent editions Procter kept the work abreast of the liturgical studies of the day. Further revised with Procter's concurrence in 1901 by W. H. Frere, it remained of value for many years. Later he edited the Sarum breviary, for which he transcribed the text of the great breviary printed at Paris in 1531. The first volume,

with Christopher Wordsworth as joint editor (and with the assistance of Henry Bradshaw and others), was published in 1875, the second in 1882, and the third in 1886. Procter's liturgical work was careful and scholarly; his text book followed the lines of sound exposition laid down by Charles Wheatley (1686–1742) and his followers, and his edition of the Sarum breviary was the most notable achievement of an era which was first developing the systematic study of medieval service books.

W. H. FRERE, *rev.* H. C. G. MATTHEW

Sources Crockford (1903) • *Clergy List* (1904) • Venn, *Alum. Cant.* • private information (1912)
Archives Lincoln Cathedral, transcripts of MSS at Lincoln and Cambridge
Likenesses B. Rogers, oils, 1891, St Catharine's College, Cambridge • portrait; in family possession, 1912

Procter, Jane (1810–1882), headmistress and temperance campaigner, was born on 2 November 1810 in Worsell in the parish of Kirklevington in Yorkshire, the first of the four children of James Procter (1766–1816), merchant, and his second wife, Elizabeth, daughter of John Thurnam of Osbaldwick in the North Riding of Yorkshire and his wife, Elizabeth. Both her parents were members of the Religious Society of Friends and on her father's side she could trace her Quaker ancestry back to the last quarter of the seventeenth century.

As a child, Jane lived initially in the Yorkshire town of Yarm, near Stockton-on-Tees, before her family moved to Blackburn in Lancashire. After her father's death in 1816, her mother took her and her three younger sisters back to Yorkshire where they went to live with her father's cousins in the small town of Selby. Here she enjoyed a relatively comfortable existence and in 1821 was sent to Ackworth School, a co-educational boarding-school near Pontefract in the West Riding of Yorkshire, which had been founded in 1779 on the initiative of the Quaker physician, John Fothergill.

Jane Procter could have stayed on at Ackworth to train as a teacher, but after four years she decided to go and work in a private Quaker school in Doncaster. She returned to Selby after the death of her mother in 1828. Although only eighteen at the time, she automatically assumed responsibility for the welfare of her sisters but was apparently given considerable assistance by the Quaker meeting in Selby which arranged for a couple to live with the girls until Jane was able to prove her competence in running a household. She decided to establish a girls' school of her own and with her sisters' help set up a modest institution under the shadow of the abbey. This proved a successful venture which lasted for twenty years. But as the prosperity of Selby declined with the collapse of the cottage linen industry, Jane and her two unmarried sisters, Barbara and Elizabeth, eventually decided to move to the expanding town of Darlington in co. Durham to set up a new school. A property was duly purchased in July 1848 and a new boarding-school was opened shortly afterwards at 11 Houndgate under the name of Selby House.

At Selby House, Jane Procter offered the daughters of the more prosperous Quaker families a 'liberal and useful education' which emphasized the 'practical utility of literary and scientific pursuits' and thus included such varied subjects as astronomy, botany, Latin, and Greek. Despite the rather daring nature of the venture, the school proved a success and after six years was moved to larger premises on a nearby estate where it became known as Polam Hall. As a headmistress, she showed herself to be a woman of commanding presence who, although not physically imposing, was able to inspire great respect and devotion from her pupils. An enthusiastic and skilful teacher, she had the capacity to make learning enjoyable and, despite her own rather austere lifestyle, was renowned for her kindness and generosity. Indeed, it was said of her that she possessed the rare quality of commanding respect without severity and of influencing and guiding her pupils to aspire to the highest ideals without apparent effort on her part.

As a member of the governing committee of the British and Foreign School Society's Training College for Mistresses in Darlington, Jane Procter helped to promote teaching as a profession among working-class women in the north of England following the introduction of compulsory elementary education under the Education Act of 1870. But Polam Hall nevertheless remained the focus of her existence and under her direction it became a thriving educational institution, as well as a meeting place for the local Friends' Essay Society. It also became a centre for temperance activity: Jane and her sister Elizabeth had established the Darlington Women's Temperance Association in 1850 and over the years the school played host to a series of fund-raising activities, while its pupils were entertained by a steady stream of visiting temperance lecturers who came to enjoy the sisters' hospitality.

Jane Procter remained headmistress of Polam Hall for thirty-four years, running the school with the help of her sister Elizabeth following the death of Barbara Procter in 1859. Although a strong, independent-minded woman, she relied heavily on Elizabeth for support and was greatly shocked by her sudden death during a holiday in Frankfurt in 1881. Jane Procter herself died suddenly while on a visit to Rome, on 5 January 1882, less than five months after the loss of her sister. She was buried in the city's protestant cemetery, where a group of her former pupils had a marble monument erected to mark her grave.

MARGARET A. E. HAMMER

Sources K. Davies, *Polam Hall: story of a school* (1981) [held at the library, Friends' House, Euston Rd, London] · R. A. Mounsey, 'Misty memories of Polam', *By Kent and Skerne* [school magazine of Polam Hall], 3 (1903–4), 77–84 [held at the Centre for Local Studies, Darlington Branch Library, Crown St, Darlington] · digest registers of births, marriages, and burials, RS Friends, Lond. [for Yorkshire, Lancashire] · digest registers (burials, 1837 on), RS Friends, Lond. [microfilm] · *The Darlington and Stockton Times* (8 Sept 1883), 5 [held at The Centre for Local Studies, Darlington Branch Library, Crown St, Darlington] · CGPLA Eng. & Wales (1882)
Likenesses photograph, repro. in Mounsey, 'Misty memories of Polam', 76

Wealth at death £1324 18s. 4d.: administration with will, 13 June 1882, CGPLA Eng. & Wales

Procter, Joan Beauchamp (1897–1931), herpetologist, was born on 5 August 1897 at 11 Kensington Square, London, the younger daughter and child of Joseph Procter (1865–1945), member of the London stock exchange, and his wife, Elizabeth Harriet (1862–1925), daughter of William Brockbank and his wife, Jane, née Benson. She was brought up as an Anglican, but, as an adult, called herself an agnostic. She attended Norland Place School from 1904 to 1908 and St Paul's Girls' School, 1908–16. As a child Joan showed a precocious fascination with reptiles and batrachians. Though she and her sister, Chrystabel *Procter, had many pets, Joan was especially fond of her Dalmatian green lizard. Ignoring her dolls she played with her lizard and also took it to school. At the age of sixteen she acquired a baby crocodile, which she also took to school, until it caused consternation in a mathematics lesson. On holiday she took the crocodile for walks with a mauve ribbon tied about its waist. A brilliant pupil at St Paul's, Joan hoped to read natural sciences at Cambridge. Chronic intestinal illness, however, convinced her that she would not be able to cope with life in college. Fortunately, a professional opening was found through the inadvertent agency of her crocodile. She had taken it to the British Museum (Natural History) to seek advice on its care from the celebrated zoologist Dr G. A. Boulenger. Under his guidance, she began work in 1917 as an unpaid research assistant. In 1920 she was appointed a curator on a small stipend.

Work at the Natural History Museum gave Procter a scholarly training, allowed her to develop an expert knowledge of reptiles, and secured her fellowships of the Zoological Society (1917) and Linnean Society (1923), and, ultimately, an honorary DSc from the Intercollegiate University, Chicago. Once at the museum she began to publish. Perhaps her most significant article was 'A study of the remarkable tortoise *Testudo Loveridgii Blgr.*, and the morphology of the Chelonian carapace' (*Proceedings of the Zoological Society*, September 1922, no. 34) which showed how the animal's flexible shell enabled it to hide in crevices. During her last few years she moved into popular science, writing for the *Manchester Guardian* and for J. A. Hammerton's *Wonders of Animal Life* (1928).

In 1923 Procter was invited to succeed Boulenger as curator of reptiles. This appointment caused a sensation in the press because the new curator was a woman, only twenty-five, and striking in appearance: slender, with dark hair and an intense gaze. The newspapers liked to compare her size with some of her charges, such as a 14-foot anaconda or two 7-foot Komodo dragons. Press attention, however, she largely ignored. Procter's eight years at the Zoological Society were packed with achievements. During her first two years, she designed rockwork for the new aquarium and the layout of the monkey hill. Meeting Sir Compton Mackenzie, she managed to persuade him to supply tons of shell sand for the aquarium from his Channel Island of Herm. She developed new techniques in the care of reptiles, such as operations for mouth infections and occluded sight. The reptile house, considered the most sophisticated building of its kind in the world, was completed in 1927 to her design. Fighting against constant intestinal pain she continued to work and to write and, in her last year, was involved in the design of Whipsnade Zoo. Procter died in her sleep on 20 September 1931 at her home, 10 St Mark's Square, Regent's Park, London. After a service at Golders Green crematorium on 23 September a second service was held at All Saints' Church, Leighton Buzzard, three days later, when the urn containing her ashes was placed in the family vault. HOWARD BAILES

Sources Girton Cam., Procter MSS · Wolfson College, Oxford, J. Procter MSS · Royal Zoological Society, London, J. Procter MSS · P. Chalmers Mitchell, *Centenary history of the Zoological Society of London* (1929) · J. Procter file, St Paul's Girls' School Archives · *CGPLA Eng. & Wales* (1931) · d. cert.
Archives Royal Zoological Society, London, papers | Girton Cam., C. Procter papers
Likenesses G. Alexander, bust, London Zoo · photograph, repro. in Chalmers Mitchell, *Centenary history* · photograph, Girton Cam.
Wealth at death £6474 6s. 1d.: probate, 16 Dec 1931, *CGPLA Eng. & Wales*

Procter, Richard Wright (*bap.* 1816, *d.* 1881), author, son of Thomas Procter (*d.* 1823), of Paradise Vale, Salford, and his wife, Isabella Wright (*d.* 1825), was born at Paradise Vale and baptized in Salford on 19 December 1816. His parents were poor and his education sporadic. After his father's death in 1823 his mother made a vain attempt to gain him entrance to Chetham Hospital school. Shortly afterwards he was orphaned at the age of nine. He was apprenticed to a barber, David Dodd of Angel Meadow, and later set up in business as a barber at 133 Long Millgate, Manchester, where he was to remain for the rest of his life. In 1845 he purchased a circulating library which he ran from his shop. In 1840 he married Eliza Waddington; they had five sons.

During his youth Procter acquired a great hunger for literature and bought many books in spite of his poverty. His early attempts at poetry were published in the *Manchester and Salford Advertiser*. He adopted the *non de plume* of Sylvan. In 1842 he was associated with Samuel Bamford, J. C. Prince, J. B. Rogerson, and other local poets in meetings held at an inn, afterwards called the 'Poet's Corner'; he contributed to a volume of verse entitled *The Festive Wreath*, which was based on these gatherings. Several of his poems were also published in *City Muse* (1853), edited by William Reid. His other contributions to poetry include a volume of poetical selections published in 1855, of which the first and last poems are by himself, and *Literary Reminiscences and Gleanings* (1860), devoted mainly to Lancashire poets. He published two works based on his own experiences at work, *The Barber's Shop* (1856) and *Our Turf, our Stage and our Ring* (1862), written from knowledge gained from his customers during his apprenticeship. His most important works were, however, historical in nature: *Memorials of Manchester Streets* (1874) and *Memorials*

of *Bygone Manchester* (1880), which were originally published as serials in the *Manchester Guardian*.

By nature a shy man, in later years Procter became a literary recluse, yet he was said, when his shyness was overcome, to be full of geniality, curious information, and gentle humour. He died at home at 133 Long Millgate, Manchester, on 11 September 1881, and was buried at St Luke's, Cheetham Hill. C. W. SUTTON, *rev.* ZOË LAWSON

Sources W. E. A. Axon, 'Memoriam', in R. W. Procter, *The barber's shop*, rev. edn (1883) · *Palatine Note-Book*, 8 (1888), 165 · B. A. Redfern, 'Procter's barber's shop', *Papers of the Manchester Literary Club*, 10 (1884), 184–8 · *CGPLA Eng. & Wales* (1881)
Likenesses Langton, portrait, repro. in *Palatine Note-book*
Wealth at death £156 2s. 8d.: probate, 14 Oct 1881, *CGPLA Eng. & Wales*

Procter, Sir Stephen (*bap.* 1562, *d.* 1619), courtier and revenue official, eldest son of Thomas Procter (*c.*1535–1621), ironmaster and entrepreneur, of Friar Head, Winterburn, in the parish of Gargrave, Yorkshire, and later of Warsill near Ripon, and his first wife, Mary, daughter, according to the heraldic window in Fountains Hall, of Thomas Procter of Winterburn, was baptized at Gargrave on 4 May 1562. On 12 September 1582 he married Honor (*c.*1565–1625), daughter of Ralph Green, sackbut player to the queen, and from about 1588 to 1598 he shared his father-in-law's house in Westminster.

In June 1598 Procter completed the purchase of the residue of the Fountains Abbey Yorkshire estates from William and Thomas Gresham, and by early 1604 had built Fountains Hall. He now came into conflict with neighbouring gentry through his claims to former abbey lands which had passed to other people, his conduct as a justice of the peace, his searches for Roman Catholic priests, and his later involvement on recusancy commissions in Yorkshire. He became an esquire of the body to James I, was knighted on 14 March 1604, and entertained the future Charles I at Fountains in August 1604. On 1 November 1605 he was admitted to Gray's Inn. Soon after, he was investigating the Gunpowder Plot in London and Yorkshire.

Procter prepared a book of projects showing how revenue was lost to the crown through the conduct of officials. He was employed in collecting debts to the crown, first in 1607 and more widely after Salisbury became lord treasurer in 1608. By letters patent of 1 August 1609 he was made 'particular receiver and collector' (PRO, C66/1820) of fines on penal statutes, with responsibility for prosecutions brought by informers. Procter was energetic in raising money—£4456 in Michaelmas term 1608—but his career ended after an attack on him in parliament in 1610, led by his neighbour Sir John Mallory. A punitive bill against him did not pass the Lords, but he was excluded by name from the general pardon of 23 July 1610. In 1614 he was almost convicted of slandering the earl of Northampton, a consequence of his attempts to have two neighbouring gentry charged with complicity in the Gunpowder Plot.

Procter spent his last years heavily in debt and at odds with former associates, including his closest friend, Sir Timothy Whittingham. He died intestate on 30 May 1619, survived by his wife and four daughters, of whom Honor was the mother of Sir Charles Lloyd (1608–1661), and Sir Godfrey Lloyd. Fountains Hall was sold three years later.

CATHERINE COLLINSON

Sources C. Howard, *Sir John Yorke of Nidderdale* (1939) · E. R. Foster, ed., *Proceedings in parliament, 1610*, 2 vols. (1966) · BL, Lansdowne MSS, vol. 167 · PRO, STAC5/P14/21 · BL, Lansdowne MSS, vol. 811, fols. 103–32 · PRO, C24/297, C24/455, C24/456, C66/1820, C142/708/92 · W. Yorks. AS, Leeds, Vyner papers, esp. 1016–19, 1046–50 · L. M. Hill, *Bench and bureaucracy: the public career of Sir Julius Caesar, 1580–1636* (1988), 147–8 · *Yorkshire Parish Register Society*, 28 [baptism] · J. Foster, *The register of admissions to Gray's Inn, 1521–1889, together with the register of marriages in Gray's Inn chapel, 1695–1754* (privately printed, London, 1889) · W. B. Bannerman and W. B. Bannerman, jun., eds., *The registers of St Stephen's, Walbrook, and of St Benet Sherehog, London*, 1, Harleian Society, register section, 49 (1919) [marriage]
Archives W. Yorks. AS, Leeds, deeds, etc., of Fountains estate
Wealth at death goods valued at approx. £300; plus lands: PRO, C2/JAS1/D8/56, 1625, answer of Lady Proctor to a chancery bill

Proctor, Sir (Philip) Dennis (1905–1983), civil servant, was born at Foxley Hatch, Godstone Road, Purley, Surrey, on 1 September 1905, the son of Sir Philip Bridger Proctor KBE (1870–1940), a businessman and a senior civil servant during the First World War, and his wife, Nellie Eliza Shaul. He was educated at Harrow School (where he was a noted cricketer) and at King's College, Cambridge (1924–8), achieving a first in both parts of the classics tripos. He was made an honorary fellow of the college in 1968.

In 1929, after a year at the University of Marburg, Proctor entered the civil service, serving first in the Ministry of Health, but soon switching to the Treasury, where he spent twenty years (1930–50). For a short time he was assistant private secretary to Stanley Baldwin, then lord president of the council, but was transferred out of Baldwin's office because it was feared that Mrs Baldwin would not approve of his imminent appearance as co-respondent in a divorce case involving the woman who became his first wife, Dorothy Vardas (1900/01–1951), whom he married on 4 July 1936. She was divorced from Gerald Roberts *Reitlinger, the art connoisseur, and the daughter of John Edward Stewart, mechanical and electrical engineer. There were no children.

During the Second World War, Proctor's work in the Treasury brought him into close contact with the Ministry of War Transport (he acquired a great interest in and knowledge of shipping), and he also served as principal private secretary to the chancellor of the exchequer, Kingsley Wood. He knew Keynes well during this time. From 1948 to 1950, as a Treasury third secretary, he had responsibility for dealing with the arts and science.

Proctor suddenly resigned from the civil service in 1950 to take a job with a shipping company in Copenhagen, but though he intended a permanent break with Whitehall this foray into the business world did not work out, and he was fortunate that in 1953 Sir Edward Bridges invited him to rejoin the civil service as deputy secretary in the Ministry of Transport. The suicide of his wife in 1951 was a shocking blow. On 29 August 1953 he married Barbara Forbes, daughter of General Sir Ronald Forbes Adam,

chairman of the British Council; the couple later adopted two sons and a daughter.

In 1958 Proctor was appointed permanent secretary at the Ministry of Power, a post he held until 1965. Having been appointed CB in 1946, he was created KCB in 1959. As a civil servant, in the words of his *Times* obituary:

> he was an effective and popular colleague in a style all his own: practical sense and good judgment battled continuously with strong views and natural impatience. The only jobs he could not do were those … which involved suppressing his personality. Where force, originality and disregard of convention were required, he was first-rate. (*The Times*, 31 Aug 1983)

As permanent secretary he saw his main task as putting the right people into every job and then keeping them on their toes, the Ministry of Power winning a reputation as something of a centre of excellence in mid-1960s Whitehall. Under his supervision was developed the country's first explicit energy policy (he wrote a pioneering paper in his own hand in the late 1950s), and the framework for early North Sea oil exploration. In great secrecy, he prepared a plan for steel nationalization in the run-up to the 1964 election which he was able to present to the new Labour minister of power, Fred Lee, as he came out of no. 10.

Unusually, Proctor was chairman of the Tate Gallery, 1953–9, while still a civil servant, having become a trustee of the gallery in 1952. A connoisseur of the arts, with many friendships in the art world, he was always passionate about painting. But he came into a difficult situation at the Tate, and there were huge battles with the then director which left their scars. He also served on the governing body of the Courtauld Institute and on a number of Gulbenkian Foundation arts committees.

Proctor believed strongly in the traditional values of a non-political civil service, but his own politics were firmly left-wing. He once said that at Cambridge he had been a Marxist, but he was never a member of the Communist Party. As a Cambridge Apostle, and a close personal friend of Guy Burgess and Anthony Blunt, he inevitably came under suspicion as a Soviet agent and was investigated by MI5 in 1966. Blunt told his interrogators that Proctor had been one of Burgess's best sources, and Proctor himself admitted that he had no secrets from Burgess (adding he had 'no real secrets to give'). The authorities seem to have concluded that there was no evidence of treason or other wrongdoing, and that while Proctor may have been indiscreet he was not an intentional or committed spy.

In retirement Proctor took a directorship at William Hudson Ltd, a shipping and fuel firm (1966–71). His interest in the Vaucluse region of France (where he had a second home) inspired his book *Hannibal's March in History* (1971), praised as a piece of scholarly detective work about Hannibal's route through Gaul and over the Alps. *The Experience of Thucydides*, published in 1980, was the product of a lifelong interest in the subject. At Cambridge he had been profoundly influenced by Goldsworthy Lowes Dickinson (and had indeed been Dickinson's last love). He took over Dickinson's papers from E. M. Forster and in 1973 published, with a sensitive introduction, the unexpurgated version of his *Autobiography*. Proctor's intellectual curiosity and appetite for new experience never let up. Having a family late in life kept him young. He took up horse-riding in his fifties, studied A-level maths in his seventies, and began work on a layman's guide to astronomy. Diagnosed with cancer of the lung in 1982, he died at his home, 102 High Street, Lewes, Sussex, on 30 August 1983. His funeral was held on 9 September.

KEVIN THEAKSTON

Sources *Annual Report of the Council* [King's College, Cambridge] (1984) • *The Times* (31 Aug 1983) • R. Mountfield, funeral address, 9 Sept 1983 • private information (2004) • P. Wright, *Spycatcher* (1987) • *The Observer* (8 Nov 1981) • b. cert. • m. certs. • d. cert. • B. Penrose and S. Freeman, *A conspiracy of silence* (1987) • *WWW*
Archives King's AC Cam., letters to G. H. W. Rylands | SOUND BL NSA, documentary recording
Wealth at death £33,293: probate, 30 Jan 1984, *CGPLA Eng. & Wales*

Proctor, John (1521–1558), schoolmaster and author, was born in Somerset and matriculated as of that county at Corpus Christi College, Oxford, in January 1537, being described as sixteen years and nine months old. He graduated BA on 20 October 1540 and was immediately elected to a fellowship at All Souls College, suggesting a successful undergraduate career. He proceeded MA on 9 February 1545 and resigned his fellowship in 1546. This may have been on account of a reluctance to take orders, connected with a desire to marry. It is not known what Proctor did after leaving Oxford. He would have found the regime of Edward VI distasteful, and may well have served as tutor in some conservative household. In 1549 he published an attack on certain aspects of the protestant programme, entitled *The Fall of the Late Arrian*.

In 1553 Proctor was appointed as the first master of the newly founded Tonbridge School, and he continued to hold that post until his death in October or early November 1558. His will, which is dated 23 October, is a most interesting document. In it he requested burial in the chancel 'dyrectly where I use to sytt', and bequeathed vestments, a crucifix, and a corporas case to the church. At the same time the preamble bequeathed his soul 'unto almightie god thorough the passyon of whose deare sonne Jesus Chryst I do assuredly beleve that I shall enioye the merittes of heaven'—which would normally be described as a protestant formula (CKS, MS DR6/pwr 12, fols. 328–9). His wife, Elizabeth, was named as sole executrix and residual legatee, and he made modest bequests to his sister, his brother William, and his godchildren. Twenty shillings were also set aside for a dole at his funeral, in the traditional manner. He was buried in the parish church at Tonbridge, probably on 3 November. According to the parish register, Elizabeth married Henry Stubberfield on 12 July 1559, two days before John's will was proved. There is no mention of children, but perhaps Elizabeth was pregnant at the time of his death, thereby accounting for the delay of probate. The poet Thomas *Proctor is usually identified as his son. The John Proctor

who was presented to the rectory of St Andrew's, Holborn, in 1578, and who died in the autumn of 1584, was clearly a different man.

Proctor's chief claim to notice is his authorship of *The Historie of Wyates Rebellion* (1554; 2nd edn, 1555). He was hostile to the rebels, representing them as covert heretics masquerading under a concern about the Spanish marriage. He was also very close to the events which he described, and his work has always been accepted as an informed source about the events of late January and early February 1554, particularly in Kent. If he wrote with any expectation of reward from the government, however, he seems to have been disappointed. In 1554 he also published a work of Catholic piety, entitled *The Way Home to Christ and Truth*, but this was not an original composition, being a translation of the fifth-century *Liber de catholicae fidei antiquitate* by Vincent of Lérins. Although this is described as 'by the Queenes highnes authorised to be sette forthe', he seems to have received no reward for this work either.

DAVID LOADES

Sources Emden, *Oxf.*, 4.465 • S. Rivington, *The history of Tonbridge School*, 4th edn (1925) • CKS, MS DR6/pwr 12, fols. 328–9
Wealth at death approx. £10 in bequests: will, 1559

Proctor, John (*d.* 1692). *See under* Salem witches and their accusers (*act.* 1692).

Proctor, Mary (1862–1957). *See under* Proctor, Richard Anthony (1837–1888).

Proctor, Richard Anthony (1837–1888), astronomer and science writer, was born on 23 March 1837 in Cheyne Row, Chelsea, London, the youngest of two sons and two daughters of William Proctor (*d.* 1850), a successful solicitor, and his wife, Mary (*d. c.*1857). A delicate child, Richard was educated by his mother and 'lived much in his father's library' until his father's death when he was thirteen (Willard, 319). Proctor spent 1855 at King's College, London, graduating in 1856 with a BA in theology. He entered St John's College, Cambridge, as a pensioner in 1856, won a scholarship in 1857, and read mathematics and theology. Shortly after his mother's death during his second year there he met Mary Mills (*d.* 1879), from near Dublin, and on 26 March 1860 they married in the parish church of St Mary Magdalene, Richmond. This was held responsible for his graduating below prediction as twenty-third wrangler that year.

From soon after his marriage, for some years Proctor practised Roman Catholicism, but in 1875 he publicly declared that religion was irreconcilable with scientific facts. Meanwhile he was admitted to Lincoln's Inn. However, it was the life (and death) of his eldest son that shaped Proctor's career. J. P. Nichols's *Architecture of the Heavens* and O. M. Mitchell's *Popular Astronomy* had inspired him to equip himself to teach his son mathematics and astronomy and, in 1863, distraught at his son's death, Proctor abandoned law and immersed himself in astronomy. He made his own 3.5 inch refracting telescope, and in 1865 his first article was published. At his own expense he published *Saturn and its System*, an exhaustive monograph that had taken four years' work. Although commercially unsuccessful, those publications immediately established his reputation in astronomy. Then in 1866 he lost all his savings and incurred £13,000 of debt in the failure of a New Zealand bank, which left him dependent upon writing and teaching mathematics to support his family of three children. It took five years of grim struggle and entrepreneurial publishing risks to establish himself as a writer.

Proctor had concluded that the only way to interest the public in astronomical research was to link the latter to their curiosity regarding the broader religious and intellectual debate about the plurality of life upon other worlds. His first major success was *Other Worlds than Ours* (1870) which went to twenty-nine editions by 1909. This and subsequent works discussed the probability that the mixture of familiar and unfamiliar conditions and temperatures revealed by spectroscopic observations of planets and stars, and hence upon myriad unseen worlds, could support many forms of life. By 1875 he believed that life was much scarcer, as worlds evolved or depleted with time. Two lecture tours in America consolidated his success and influence.

The death of Proctor's wife in 1879 left him with six children. Returning through America from a lecture tour of Australia and New Zealand, in 1881 Proctor met and married Sallie Duffield Crawley, *née* Thompson (1856–1941), the widow of Robert J. Crawley of Missouri, and keenly interested in astronomy, who had two young daughters. They lived at Kew until 1884, but lost their two infant sons. While living in Kew, in 1881 Proctor established a scientific weekly periodical, *Knowledge and Illustrated Scientific News*.

A man of unbounded energy and wide interests, Proctor's gifts of vivid clarity, lecturing style, and scientific exactness in writing on many subjects gained him renown. He wrote at least 500 essays, 83 technical astronomy papers, and 57 books. His *Old and New Astronomy*, a systematic work embodying his studies over a quarter century, was completed by his friend Arthur Cowper Ranyard in 1892. Between 1870 and 1914 'the impact of his publications was immense; thousands were introduced to astronomy by them' (Crowe, 548).

Proctor was held in high esteem by contemporaries as an original investigator. He was elected a fellow of the Royal Astronomical Society in 1866, to its council in 1868, was a secretary in 1872, and was a prolific contributor to its *Monthly Notices*. Among papers on the distribution of stars and nebulae, perhaps his greatest scientific work resulted from the 400 hours copying Argelander's 324,198 stars on to an equal surface chart. By this, and well illustrated papers in *Monthly Notices*, contemporaries credited him with demolishing Sir William Herschel's theory of the stellar universe. Proctor showed that the aggregation of stars in the Milky Way was real, not merely optical. He urged others to study structure by observing small areas

to fainter magnitudes, a precursor of Jacob Kapteyn's later work. In 1869 he was among the first to advocate the theory of the solar corona and inner solar envelope, although the trajectory of prominences which he explained by a resisting medium or ether is now known to be due to magnetic fields. His research deriving the rotation period of Mars within an error of 0.005 seconds was highly regarded, and is within 0.25 seconds of what later became the accepted value. Adept at charting, in 1870 he discovered the phenomenon of star drift. Proctor rightly dismissed the canals of Mars as an optical effect. Although prone to speculate, his wide knowledge and exact investigations gained him influence.

Contemporary obituarists barely hinted that Proctor was one of several activists seeking reform of the Royal Astronomical Society council. He could not abide dogmatists, and was 'determined to oppose all cliquery and jobbery' (*Astronomical Register*, 1873, 98). He made bitter enemies of Colonel Alexander Strange and J. Norman Lockyer by siding in 1872 with the astronomer royal George Airy in opposing their manoeuvres for a solar observatory at government expense. In November Lockyer resigned from council rather than sit at the same table as Proctor, who constantly attacked him in journals. Proctor had no hand in his own nomination in December 1873 for the society's gold medal, perhaps made partly to block Lockyer's third nomination. Despite his having obtained a simple majority of six to four council votes, Proctor bore Airy no animosity for vetoing him in January. In 1869 Proctor had questioned arrangements for the December 1874 transit of Venus. Lacking Airy's reply, in February 1873 Proctor used an article in the *Spectator* and a letter in *The Times* to criticize arrangements. Airy's reply to the Admiralty, printed in *Monthly Notices* (1873), conceded nothing. In the same issue Proctor's exact calculations and clear charts in *Monthly Notices* exposed errors, omissions, and neglect by Airy, the new KCB and president of the Royal Society, in planning for the transit. The Admiralty hydrographer supported Airy in *The Times*. Unfortunately Proctor responded witheringly in a supplementary *Monthly Notices*—of which he was temporarily editor. Airy criticized him, and council viewed it as misuse of office. Proctor resigned his secretaryship in order to lecture in America. Through zeal and politics he had overreached himself. On his return, in May 1874, Proctor read a semi-apology to the society while Airy was in the chair. Proctor took no further active part in the society, but in 1880 did not hesitate to support the group led by William Noble in opposing Airy's nomination of William Huggins for the society medal; he ended a scathing attack in the *Newcastle Weekly Chronicle* with 'to do the bidding of the Astronomer Royal is not the purpose for which the Astronomical Society has been established' (*Newcastle Weekly Chronicle*, 28 Feb 1880). In 1887 Proctor predicted that the 36 inch Lick refractor was likely to prove a disappointment. Unwisely, the new director, E. S. Holden, extended his defence to a personal attack. Proctor exposed Holden's observing mistakes in Washington, with lasting damage to his reputation.

A family man with many friends, Proctor in 1884 moved to Orange Lake, Florida, but isolation motivated the family's return to London. While travelling from Florida to England to give a lecture tour, on 10 September 1888 Proctor booked into a New York hotel. Suddenly taken violently ill, he was diagnosed as having yellow fever, then epidemic in Florida, and for fear of contagion he was removed on a windy and wet night. Twelve hours later, on the evening of 12 September 1888, Proctor died alone and unconscious at the Willard Parker Hospital. His friends later asserted that he had received little attention and had died of malarial fever compounded by a cold. Proctor was buried in an unmarked and unkept part of the undertaker's lot in Greenwood cemetery, Brooklyn. He had been unable to leave provision for his family. In 1893 a benefactor helped the family re-inter Proctor in the same cemetery, with a memorial.

On hearing of her husband's death Sallie Proctor hurried to New York. She courageously fulfilled his English tour by reading his lectures to such effect that by the influence of many scientists she was awarded a civil-list pension of £100. Proctor was survived by two daughters and three sons.

Mary Proctor (1862–1957) was born on 1 April 1862 at Dublin. As a teenager she was a constant companion of her father, fascinated by the mythology of the stars; she arranged his library and proof-read for him. After his second marriage he taught her the craft of commercial writing. After her graduation from Columbia University and his death in 1888 she made a career popularizing astronomy. Mary Proctor was elected a member of the American Association of Astronomical Societies in 1898, and was a member of several American, Mexican, and British astronomical societies. She visited observatories, and was supplied with material and illustrations by leading astronomers. She attended the total solar eclipses at Bodo, Norway (1896); Virginia (1900); Burgos (1905), where she drew the corona; from an aeroplane in England (1927); in Canada (1932); and in the Mediterranean (1936). Her articles were published in *Science*, her father's magazine *Knowledge*, *Scientific American*, and after 1897 in *Popular Astronomy*. An acclaimed lecture in 1893 at the World's Columbian Exposition in Chicago led to popular engagements, a contract with the New York board of education, and lecture tours in the USA, Canada, England (1908–9), Australia, and New Zealand; she was equally comfortable addressing children, working men's institutes, or literary and scientific societies.

Sometimes known as the children's astronomer, Mary Proctor did little observing, but gained lasting reputation by her books (Creese, 238). From 1894 until about 1920 she lived in New York. Her first book, *Stories of Starland* (1898), was used as a reader in New York schools; two more books followed in 1906 and 1911. Living in London after the First World War, she lectured and published thirteen books between 1922 and 1939. From January 1916 women were eligible for election as fellows of the RAS. Proctor was elected in February and her stepmother Sallie in May 1916.

Proctor was also a fellow of the Royal Meteorological Society. She died at Nazareth House, East End Road, Finchley, Middlesex, on 11 September 1957 aged ninety-six; a crater on the moon bears her name.   ROGER HUTCHINS

Sources A. C. R. [A. C. Ranyard], *Monthly Notices of the Royal Astronomical Society*, 49 (1888–9), 164–7 · M. J. Crowe, *The extraterrestrial life debate, 1750–1900* (1986) · W. Noble, 'Richard A. Proctor', *The Observatory*, 11 (1888), 366–8 · J. D. North, 'Proctor, Richard Anthony', *DSB* · 'Richard A. Proctor', *Sidereal Messenger*, 7 (1888), 362–4 · *History of the Royal Astronomical Society*, [1]: 1820–1920, ed. J. L. E. Dreyer and H. H. Turner (1923) · C. R. Willard, 'Richard A. Proctor', *Popular Astronomy*, 1 (1894), 319–21 · M. R. S. Creese, *Ladies in the laboratory? American and British women in science, 1800–1900* (1998) · British Astronomical Association, Historical Section, *Who's who in the moon* (1938) · R. A. Proctor, 'Autobiographical notes', *New Science Review*, 1 (1895), 393–7 · R. A. Proctor, 'Proctor's chart of 324,198 stars', *Astronomical Register*, 115 (1872), 187–8 · A. Chapman, 'An historian of the constellations', *Astronomy Now* (Aug 1999), 46–9 · R. A. Proctor, 'The transit of Venus in 1874', *Monthly Notices of the Royal Astronomical Society*, 33 (1872–3), 278–93 · A. M. Clerke, *A popular history of astronomy during the nineteenth century*, 3rd edn (1893) · W. Sheehan, *The immortal fire within* (1995) · *DNB* · *Nature*, 38 (1888), 499 · 'Circular to fellows [RAS]', 25 March 1873, CUL, Royal Greenwich Observatory papers, RGO 6 241, 96 · R. A. Proctor, 'The annual meeting of the Astronomical Society, and what took place thereat', *Astronomical Register*, 11 (1873), 97–100 · 'The Holden–Proctor unpleasantness', *Sidereal Messenger*, 6 (1887), 192 · E. S. Holden, 'President Holden's reply to Professor Proctor', *Sidereal Messenger*, 6 (1887), 210–12; 259–62 · J. M. Wheeler, *A biographical dictionary of freethinkers of all ages and nations* (1889) · Venn, *Alum. Cant.* · *Newcastle Weekly Chronicle* (28 Feb 1880) · M. Proctor, 'Sallie Duffield Proctor-Smyth', *Monthly Notices of the Royal Astronomical Society*, 102 (1942), 73–4 · M. B. B. Heath, 'Proctor's altazimuth telescope', *Journal of the British Astronomical Association*, 39 (1928–9), 83–5, 256 · J. C. Poggendorff and others, eds., *Biographisch-literarisches Handwörterbuch zur Geschichte der exacten Wissenschaften*, 2 vols. (Leipzig, 1863) · d. cert. [Mary Proctor]

Archives RAS, letters to Royal Astronomical Society · RAS, MSS 29 (1869), 31 (1870), 32 (1871), 34 (1878) | RS, corresp. with Sir J. F. W. Herschel

Likenesses Spy [L. Ward], watercolour, before 1883, NPG · W. Notman, carte-de-visite, NPG · R. T., wood-engraving, NPG; repro. in *ILN* (29 Sept 1888) · Spy [L. Ward], chromolithograph caricature, NPG; repro. in *VF* (3 March 1883) · R. & E. Taylor, woodcut, NPG; repro. in *Illustrated Review* (28 Aug 1873) · photograph, RAS · photograph, repro. in Willard, 'Richard A. Proctor', 318

Wealth at death £3257 16s. 5d.: resworn administration, Aug 1889, CGPLA Eng. & Wales (1888) · £673 5s. 5d.—Mary Proctor: probate, 16 Oct 1957, CGPLA Eng. & Wales

Proctor, Robert George Collier (1868–1903), bibliographer, was born at Budleigh Salterton, Devon, on 13 May 1868, the only child of Robert Proctor (1821–1880) and his wife, Anne Tate. His father was a good classical scholar, while his grandfather Robert Proctor (1798–1875) published in 1825 a description of a journey in South America, and married Mary, sister of John Payne Collier, who was thus the bibliographer's great-uncle. A sister of Proctor's father, Mariquita, was first wife of George Edmund Street, the architect.

Proctor, who early developed a precocious love of study, went from a preparatory school at Reading to Marlborough College at the age of ten. But his father died on 5 March 1880, and soon afterwards Proctor was taken away from Marlborough, it is said partly owing to eye trouble. The family had settled at Bath as early as January 1878, and in January 1881 the boy entered Bath College. In 1886 he won an open classical scholarship at Corpus Christi College, Oxford, and he matriculated at the university in October. His mother lived at Oxford during his academic course. He won a first class in classical moderations in Hilary term 1888, and graduated BA in 1890. While an undergraduate, Proctor engaged in antiquarian research; a visit to Greece stimulated his archaeological interests. As a schoolboy he had collected books, and at Oxford he spent much time in his college library. A love of bibliographical study developed, and he prepared a catalogue of the Corpus incunabula and printed books up to 1600.

Proctor remained at Oxford after taking his degree in order to continue his study of early printed books. Between 23 February 1891 and September 1893 he catalogued some 3000 incunabula in the Bodleian Library, continuing the work begun by E. Gordon Duff, and he did similar work at New College and at Brasenose. On 16 October 1893 he is first found in the house lists of the British Museum, having competed successfully (after a first failure) for entry into the library. He remained as assistant in the printed books department until his death. He lived at Wimbledon from the autumn of 1893 to the summer of 1897, when he and his mother moved to a new house at Oxshott. At the British Museum he soon became a leading expert on early typography. He rearranged the incunabula at the museum and revised their entries in the catalogue, in which he was also responsible for the heading 'Liturgies'. He soon set himself to describe every fount of type used in Europe up to 1520, and first read through the whole of the British Museum catalogue. His reputation was finally established by his 'Index of early printed books from the invention of printing to the year MD', issued in four parts in 1898, the result of four years' labour. He then worked on a similar index for the period 1501–20, but of four projected sections only the German one was completed in his lifetime (1903).

Proctor's earliest contribution to bibliographical research was an article on Jan van Doesborgh, the sixteenth-century printer of Antwerp, which appeared in *The Library* in 1892 and was expanded into a monograph for the Bibliographical Society in 1894. Proctor soon read other papers before that society, for which he also prepared 'A classified index to the Serapeum' (1897) and 'The printing of Greek in the fifteenth century' (1900). He likewise printed for private circulation three pamphlets on early printing, published in 1895 and 1897.

Proctor subsequently experimented in Greek printing, adapting a beautiful type from the sixteenth-century Spanish fount used in the New Testament of the Complutensian polyglot Bible. With his new type Proctor had printed at the Chiswick Press an edition of Aeschylus' *Oresteia*, which Frederic Kenyon completed for publication in 1904. Homer's *Odyssey* was subsequently printed in the same type in 1909.

Interest in the work of William Morris's Kelmscott Press led to an acquaintance with Morris, with whose socialist opinions Proctor was in sympathy. On F. S. Ellis's death in 1901 Proctor became one of the trustees under Morris's will. Morris's influence developed in Proctor an enthusiasm for Icelandic literature. His first rendering of an Icelandic saga, *A Tale of the Weapon Firthers*, was printed privately in 1902 as a wedding gift for his friend Francis Jenkinson of Cambridge University Library. He later published a version of the *Laxdæla saga* (1903).

From boyhood Proctor, who never married, often went on long walking tours, usually with his mother, in Great Britain and on the continent and in Scandinavia. On 29 August 1903 he left London for a solitary walking tour in the Austrian Tyrol. He reached the Taschach hut in the Pitzthal on 5 September and left to cross a glacier pass without a guide. Nothing more was heard of him; he doubtless perished in a crevasse. Some have thought that suicide was a possible explanation, caused by a knowledge of his oncoming blindness. At the end of the month, when his disappearance was realized in Britain, the weather had broken and no search was possible.

A memorial fund was formed for the purpose of issuing his scattered *Bibliographical Essays*: the collection appeared in 1905, with a memoir by A. W. Pollard. The memorial fund also provided for the compilation and publication of the three remaining parts of Proctor's *Index of Early Printed Books from 1501 to 1520*, of which Frank Isaac published the section on Italy, Switzerland, and eastern Europe as late as 1938.

For the major collections of the world today 'Proctor order' is still followed. This means that the books are arranged and described in order of country of origin, then of town, then of printer, in chronological order. Proctor order is used in the incunabula catalogues of the British Library (beginning in 1908 and still incomplete), Cambridge University Library (J. C. T. Oates, 1954), and Harvard University (James E. Walsh, beginning in 1991). Smaller collections find it more appropriate to arrange their incunabula in alphabetical order according to authors and anonymous headings.   DENNIS E. RHODES

Sources A. W. Pollard, 'Memoir', in R. Proctor, *Bibliographical essays* (1905) • A. W. Pollard, 'A great bibliographer', *Wimbledon and Merton Annual* (1903), 26–31 • V. Scholderer, 'The private diary of Robert Proctor', *The Library*, 5th ser., 5 (1950–51), 261–9 • B. C. Johnson, *Lost in the Alps* (1985) • *The Athenaeum* (10 Oct 1903), 483 • *CGPLA Eng. & Wales* (1903) • J. Foster, *Oxford men and their colleges* (1893)
Archives BL, corresp. and diaries, Add. MSS 50190–50196, 60742 • BL, translation of Vatnsdaela Saga, Add. MS 60742 • CUL, letters and papers on Greek type | BL, corresp. with Sir Sydney Cockerell, Add. MS 52743 • CUL, corresp. with G. Dunn
Wealth at death £6116 1s. 3d.: administration, 4 Feb 1904, *CGPLA Eng. & Wales*

Proctor, Thomas (*fl.* 1578–1584), poet, has usually been identified as the son of John *Proctor, first master of Tonbridge School. But all that can be proved definitely about him is that he became apprenticed to John Allde, the printer, and was made a freeman of the Stationers' Company on 17 August 1584.

The most important publication with which Proctor was involved is *A gorgious gallery of gallant inventions … first framed and fashioned in sundry forms by divers worthy workemen of late dayes, and now joyned together and builded up by T.P., a* quarto printed by Richard Jones in 1578. Jones's entries in the Stationers' register show that this project had a complicated gestation, since 'R. Williams' was seemingly named as the compiler in an entry of 5 June 1577, and the book's title was changed from 'A Handful of Hidden Secrets' to 'Delicate Dainties to Sweeten a Lover's Lips Withal', before taking on its final form. As it is, the anthology begins with an address and a poem by Owen Roydon, an experienced compiler of miscellanies, and Hyder E. Rollins has plausibly argued that Proctor was called in to take over the project after Owen Roydon's death during the period when the book was being developed. The miscellany continues with unsigned poems from several hands, including Thomas Churchyard and Jasper Heywood, until page 100. The heading 'Proctor's Precepts' introduces another fifty-two pages of poems, of which ten are signed 'T. P.' As a poetical miscellany, it takes its place in the line that starts with Richard Tottell's in 1557: to modern readers, its most interesting individual item is 'The History of Pyramus and Thisbie Truly Translated', a translation which may possibly have given Shakespeare material for *A Midsummer Night's Dream*.

Anthony Munday, who like Proctor was an apprentice of John Allde, wrote commendatory verses for *A Gorgious Gallery*, and in the following year, 1579, Proctor repaid the compliment in contributing commendatory verses to Munday's *The Mirror of Mutability*. In the same year, both writers also provided commendatory verses for *Newes from the North*, by 'T. F.'

Also probably by Proctor is a poem entitled *The Triumph of Trueth, Manifesting the Advancement of Virtue and the Overthrow of Vice*, published by T. P. This publication is not dated, and survives only in one incomplete fragment now in the Bodleian Library, Oxford. A 'T. P.' also wrote a prose tract *Of the Knowledge and Conduct of Warres, Two Bookes, Latelie Written and Sett Foorthe*, licensed to Tottell in 1578. The tract is a collection of general and rather abstract advice on military matters, and once again it seems possible that its author was Proctor.

Strangely, apart from the records above, there is no trace of Proctor having been involved in the printing of books. His career after 1584 remains obscure. It is possible, but unlikely, that he was the Thomas Proctor who wrote three Jacobean pamphlets, *A Profitable Worke to the Whole Kingdome* (1610) and *The Right of Kings* and *The Righteous Man's Way* (both 1621).   MATTHEW STEGGLE

Sources T. Proctor, *A gorgious gallery of gallant inventions* (1578), ed. H. E. Rollins (1926)

Proctor, Thomas (1753–1794), history painter and sculptor, was born at Settle, Yorkshire, on 22 April 1753. His impoverished father apprenticed him to a tobacconist in Manchester, but he afterwards moved to London, and for a time worked in a merchant's counting-house. In 1777 he enrolled as a student at the Royal Academy Schools. Inspired by the works of James Barry, he painted a large picture, *Adam and Eve*, and in 1780 began to exhibit, sending a portrait to the Royal Academy, and another to the Incorporated Society of Artists. In 1782 he gained a premium at the Society of Arts, and a medal at the Royal Academy for life drawing. This early success continued when in 1783 he was awarded a silver medal at the Royal Academy for a model from life, and in 1784 the gold medal for history painting, the subject being a scene from Shakespeare's *Tempest*. He then turned to modelling, and produced a statue, *Ixion*, which was exhibited at the Royal Academy in 1785, and was so highly praised by Benjamin West that it was bought by the art patron Sir Abraham Hume. He next modelled a group entitled *The Death of Diomedes, King of Thrace*, which was greatly admired at the academy in 1786, but not purchased. Bitterly disappointed, Proctor broke his work in pieces and abandoned sculpture.

Proctor reverted to painting, but did not again exhibit until 1789, and then sent only a portrait; but in 1790 he contributed to the exhibition of the Society of Artists *Coronis*, a subject from Ovid's *Metamorphoses*, and to the Royal Academy *Elisha and the Son of the Shunammite*, and *The Restoration of Day after the Fall of Phaethon*, a sketch. In 1791 he exhibited at the academy *Hannah Declines Accompanying her Husband to the Yearly Sacrifice*, and in 1792 two portraits and a group in plaster, *Peirithous, the Son of Ixion, Destroyed by Cerberus*. Three portraits and *The Final Separation of Jason and Medea* were his exhibited works in 1793, and *Venus Approaching the Island of Cyprus* in 1794. After 1790 Proctor exhibited without giving an address, and his abode was unknown to his contemporaries. West, then president of the Royal Academy, discovered that he had been living in London in miserable circumstances at Clare Market. West brought his case to the notice of the council of the Royal Academy, and in 1793 it was resolved that he should be sent to Italy as the travelling student, with a grant of £50 for preliminary expenses. Unfortunately the generous help came too late. Before he could leave England he was found dead in his bed, worn out by mental anguish and privation. He was buried in Hampstead churchyard on 13 July 1794.   R. E. GRAVES, *rev.* J. DESMARAIS

Sources Redgrave, *Artists* • Bryan, *Painters* (1886–9) • W. Sandby, *The history of the Royal Academy of Arts*, 1 (1862), 251 • exhibition catalogues (1780–94) [RA, Incorporated Society of Artists, and Free Society of Artists] • private information (1896) [S. B. Burnaby, vicar, Hampstead church] • Waterhouse, *18c painters* • E. Hailstone, *Portraits of Yorkshire worthies*, 2 vols. (1869) • R. N. James, *Painters and their works*, 3 vols. (1896–7) • J. T. Smith, *Nollekens and his times*, 2 vols. (1828) • G. Hamilton, *The English school* (1831) • A. Pasquin [J. Williams], *An authentic history of the professors of painting, sculpture, and architecture who have practiced in Ireland … to which are added, Memoirs of the royal academicians* [1796]

Progers, Edward (1621–1713), courtier, was born on 16 June 1621 in the parish of St Martin-in-the-Fields, Westminster, the third son of Philip Progers (*d.* 1644), equerry to the king, originally of Gwernvale, Brecknockshire, and his wife, Mary Brightmer, of Caister St Edmund, Norfolk. It was said in 1678 that Progers had been 'not born to a farthing' (Marvell, 29), but from an early age he was in the service of Charles I as a page of honour. He spent the civil war with the court at Oxford. On joining Henrietta Maria in Paris in 1646 he was sent to Jersey, where the prince of

Wales appointed him in late November 1646 as one of the grooms of his bedchamber.

To Charles II, Progers was always Poge, and throughout the years of exile he relied on him to undertake missions of particular sensitivity. Progers accompanied him in Scotland in 1650, but was among those servants banished for negotiating with the engagers. He was arrested in England in late 1652 and, after a brief period of imprisonment, was released on bail in January 1653. A further spell in prison followed in June 1655. He was in London again in December 1657, but was soon back in Brussels, whence he was dispatched to remove the king's eight-year-old bastard, the future duke of Monmouth, from the custody of his mother, Lucy Walters. (Later gossip suggested that it was Progers who had been Monmouth's real father.) He crossed the channel several times in the spring of 1660 carrying confidential correspondence on behalf of the king.

Progers was confirmed as a groom of the bedchamber on 3 February 1661. In February 1664 his friend Samuel Pepys complained that he was one of those around the king who were manipulating him, although, in reality, he was probably a rather lightweight figure. Andrew Marvell's description of him as the 'Gentlest of men' was, no doubt, ironic (A. Marvell, *The Poems & Letters of Andrew Marvell*, ed. H. M. Margoliouth, 2 vols., 1927, 1.145) and he was among the most importunate of Charles II's servants, repeatedly petitioning for benefits for himself or his family. By 1663 Progers was deputy to George Monck, duke of Albemarle, as ranger of Bushy Park at Hampton Court, and, having been granted the reversion in 1667, he succeeded as ranger after the duke's death in January 1670. He preferred to use the house he had built for himself in Bushy Park as his main residence, rather than West Stow Hall in Suffolk, which he was bequeathed about 1670 by one of his debtors, Lady Crofts, widow of Sir John Crofts. Progers had been the MP for Brecknockshire since March 1662, in which capacity he seems usually to have supported the court. He used his royal duties as the excuse against standing again in either of the 1679 elections. He ceased to hold his bedchamber position at the accession of James II in 1685 and retired to Hampton where he continued to manage the royal park. He and his wife, Elizabeth Wells, whom he had married at some stage before 1668, produced two sons (neither of whom survived him) and five daughters. He died on 31 December 1713 from the improbable cause of inflammation of the gums and was buried in the parish church at Hampton, Middlesex.

ANDREW BARCLAY

Sources *West Stow parish registers, 1558 to 1850*, ed. S. H. A. H[ervey] (1903) · *The manuscripts of the earl of Westmorland*, HMC, 13 (1885); repr. (1906), 146–52 · L. Naylor, 'Progers, Edward', HoP, *Commons, 1660–90* · *Calendar of the Clarendon state papers preserved in the Bodleian Library*, ed. O. Ogle and others, 5 vols. (1869–1970) · Pepys, *Diary* · W. A. Shaw, ed., *Calendar of treasury books*, 1–8, PRO (1904–23) · *CSP dom.*, 1641–80 · T. Brown, *Miscellanea aulica* (1702) · *The Nicholas papers*, ed. G. F. Warner, 4 vols., CS, new ser., 40, 50, 57, 3rd ser., 31 (1886–1920) · *The manuscripts of his grace the duke of Portland*, 10 vols., HMC, 29 (1891–1931), vol. 4, pp. 301–4 · *Report on the Pepys manuscripts*, HMC, 70 (1911), 238, 255 · *Fifth report*, HMC, 4 (1876), 194 · [A. Marvell], *Flagellum parliamentarium*, ed. N. H. Nicolas (1827) · memorial, Hampton parish church, Middlesex

Archives Yale U., Osborn collection, papers

Likenesses oils, repro. in H[ervey], ed., *West Stow parish registers*; formerly at Rushbrooke Hall, Norfolk

Proops [*née* Israel], **(Rebecca) Marjorie** (1911–1996), advice columnist, was born at 55 Eastbourne Road, Tottenham, Middlesex, on 10 August 1911, elder daughter of Abraham Israel, who later changed his name to Alfred Rayle, and his wife, Martha Flatau. At that time her father was a van traveller in mineral water, but he soon gave that up and bought a series of pubs, moving restlessly from one district to another. Marje, as she was always known (having been mocked as 'Bekky the Jew girl' as a child), went to a series of London schools; she left her last, Dalston secondary school, just before she was sixteen and had three terms at Hackney Technical School. Considered 'the brainy one' beside her pretty sister Josephine, she also had a powerful contralto voice which won her talent competitions and an offer to join the D'Oyly Carte opera company, which her mother made her turn down. And she could draw: when she left art school her father paid a premium (unknown to her) to get her taken on by a commercial art studio in London's Smithfield meat market, where she was given mainly dogsbody tasks but was taught by her friendly seniors to dress more smartly, thin her eyebrows, and paint red with nail varnish the heavy glasses she always wore.

At seventeen Marje set up as a freelance fashion artist, managing to sell drawings to several papers and magazines. On 21 November 1935 she married Sidney Joseph Proops (1908–1988), a builder, and had a son, Robert, nine months later; but, unusually for those days, she went on working. In 1939 she was appointed resident fashion artist at the *Daily Mirror*, but when the war came, Sidney (Proopsie) joined the Royal Engineers and was posted to the midlands and then abroad; Marje and her son moved to Stoke Poges in Buckinghamshire to be near her parents in Windsor. She was able to go on selling fashion sketches, particularly of knitwear, as a freelance; and on the strength of her captions to these, the editor of *Good Taste* magazine asked her to write an article on the problems of mothers coping on their own in wartime. A pamphlet on venereal disease for female servicewomen and other commissions followed, and at the end of the war she joined the *Daily Herald* as fashion editor, later graduating to woman's editor. And when the existing advice columnist, writing as May Marshall, left, Proops, unable to find a replacement, started answering the letters herself.

So began her career as an 'agony aunt', which gave her 'Dear Marje' column iconic status in journalism and the country, a role she continued when she moved back to the *Woman's Mirror* under Hugh Cudlipp in 1954. He had been impressed by the witty, forthright replies of American columnists Abigail van Buren and Amy Landers, and reckoned Marje could emulate them, and more. At first she was alarmed by how little she knew, but her friend the psychiatrist Dr Eustace Chesser let her bring round the letters in his lunch hour and gradually schooled her in their

(Rebecca) Marjorie Proops (1911–1996), by Dezo Hoffmann

interpretation. She built up over the years not only increasing experience but a vast knowledge of the organizations and agencies where her troubled readers could go for help. She answered, or caused to be answered by her team of trained helpers, every one of the 50,000 letters she received each year; other readers telephoned her, and occasionally she was compelled to take practical action, for example when one girl rang from a call box to say she had taken suicide pills; Marje kept her in conversation for long enough for her staff and the police to locate and rescue her.

Her columns were distinguished from the more conventional and moralistic work of previous advice columnists by their frankness about forbidden areas such as homosexuality, impotence, divorce, and incest; she claimed to be the first person to mention masturbation in a family newspaper. She was compassionate but could be tough with her correspondents: her journalist colleague Felicity Green described her answers as being 'brutally frank, sexually aware, liberal to the point of illegality' (private information). Her writing bridged in its fifty years a change in public attitudes from that in which wives wrote about 'submitting' to their husbands to one in which, in her own words, 'questions about orgasms are as common as questions about mothers-in-law'. She and those who followed her were even reproached for having accelerated the process, though she saw herself as struggling against hypocrisy and repression and cruelty.

In her own life Marje appeared to be happily married to Sidney Proops, living in London first in Golders Green, then St John's Wood, and finally Barnes, and becoming a model grandmother to her son's two children. Not until 1992 did her authorized biography, *Marje: the Guilt and the Gingerbread* by Angela Patmore, reveal that her marriage to Proopsie had been a disaster from the start, her wedded bliss a sham. Her appreciation of sex, however, was not; for many years (from about 1967) her real love was Philip Levy, the *Mirror*'s company lawyer, though there were other lovers as well. Though *jolie laide* rather than pretty,

she had an excellent figure, dressed with flair and suitability, and was popular—with women as well as with men. She was not a good judge of people, being inclined to like anyone who liked her (even Robert Maxwell, the *Mirror*'s maverick proprietor, who put her briefly on the Mirror board). She enjoyed the grand style, and the procession of editors for whom she worked made a point of courting her and ensuring her the chauffeur-driven luxury she expected and—in terms of her value to the *Mirror*—deserved.

She wrote features and interviews as well as 'Dear Marje', and her talents were widely recognized. She was woman journalist of the year 1969, and was appointed OBE in the same year. She served on Sir Morris Finer's committee on one-parent families from 1976 to 1978, and on Lord Rothschild's royal commission on betting, lotteries and gaming 1976–8. She wrote two books, *Pride, Prejudice and Proops* (1975) and *Dear Marje* (1976). A rose was named after her, and in 1977 she went on display at Madame Tussaud's waxworks.

Both Philip and Sidney died before her in the 1980s and Marje missed them both. In her last years she was increasingly frail, having survived an early hysterectomy and breast cancer, and moving with two false hips; she died of pneumonia at Cromwell Hospital, Kensington, on 10 November 1996, having concealed her age to the last. She was following Hugh Cudlipp's advice given long before: 'One day', he said, 'your name will be in the record books and you'll want to go on working. If you let them know your age, you won't be able to.' Marje reckoned that during her working life she had corresponded with 3 per cent of the British population, and had influenced countless more; in a friend's words 'she saved more souls than the Salvation Army'. And she embodied the best of the liberal spirit of the second half of her century.

KATHARINE WHITEHORN

Sources M. Proops, *Dear Marje* (1976) · *The Times* (12 Nov 1996) · *The Guardian* (11 Nov 1996) · *Daily Mirror* (11 Nov 1996) · private information (2004) [Felicity Green] · *WW* · *Debrett's People of today* (1996) · A. Patmore, *Marje: the guilt and the gingerbread* (1992) · b. cert. · *The Independent* (12 Nov 1996) · m. cert. · d. cert. · d. cert. [Sidney Proops]

Archives FILM BFI NFTVA, documentary footage

Likenesses D. Hoffmann, photograph, Rex Features Ltd, London [*see illus.*]

Wealth at death £1,095,996: probate, 13 March 1997, *CGPLA Eng. & Wales*

Propert, John Lumsden (1834–1902), physician and art critic, was born on 9 April 1834, the son of John Propert (1792–1867), surgeon, and his wife, Juliana Ross. His father founded in 1855 the Royal Medical Benevolent College, Epsom, and served as its treasurer. Propert was educated at Marlborough College (August 1843 – December 1847), and at King's College Hospital. He obtained the diploma of the Royal College of Surgeons of England and the licence of the Society of Apothecaries in 1855, and in 1857 he graduated MB with honours in medicine at the University of London. He then joined his father in general practice in New Cavendish Street, London, and became highly successful. On 21 April 1864 he married Mary Jessica (*bap.*

1835), daughter of William and Caroline Hughes of Worcester, with whom he had three sons and three daughters.

Propert was widely known in artistic circles as a good etcher. He favoured landscapes, particularly river or marine views, and exhibited his work frequently at the Royal Academy from 1870 to 1882. Later in life he also took up landscape painting in oils. He was a connoisseur, as well as a practitioner, of art in the broadest sense, and his home, 112 Gloucester Place, Portman Square, London, was filled with beautiful specimens of Wedgwood, bronzes, and jewelled work. His deepest fascination was reserved for portrait miniatures and he accrued one of the most significant private collections of miniatures in existence in the late nineteenth century. A contemporary, G. C. Williamson, doubted that there had ever been: 'a private collection so numerous in examples of the finest work of each of the great masters' (Williamson, *Portrait Miniatures*, 2.141) and it was certainly an exceptional, balanced collection containing many signed examples of work by miniaturists of the first order. Today miniatures with a Propert provenance grace collections such as the Victoria and Albert Museum, London (Nicholas Hilliard, *Mrs Holland*), the Fitzwilliam Museum, Cambridge (Samuel Cooper, *Robert Lilburne*), and the Huntington Library and Art Collections, San Marino (Andrew Plimer, *The Three Graces*). A privately printed catalogue was issued prior to the collection's dispersal, following an exhibition at the Fine Art Society, London, in May 1897.

It was, however, as a scholar rather than a collector that Propert made his greatest contribution to the subject. His *History of Miniature Art with Notes on Collectors and Collections* (1887) presented the public with the first scholarly and comprehensive treatment of the history of portrait miniatures, setting their development in England in the early sixteenth century in the context of early illuminated manuscripts. He also compiled in 1889 the catalogue of the Exhibition of Portrait Miniatures at the Burlington Fine Arts Club. Propert died from pneumonia at his home, 112 Gloucester Place, London, on 7 March 1902 and was buried at Brookwood cemetery. He was survived by his wife.   D'A. POWER, rev. V. REMINGTON

Sources J. L. Propert, *Catalogue of miniatures* (privately printed, 1896) [exhibition catalogue, 112 Gloucester Place, Portman Square, 1896] · *Catalogue of the historic collection of miniatures formed by Mr J. Lumsden Propert* (1897) [exhibition catalogue, Fine Art Society, May 1897] · *The Times* (10 March 1902), 10 · *The Lancet* (15 March 1902), 782 · *The Connoisseur*, 3 (1902), 48 · *BMJ* (15 March 1902), 689 · G. C. Williamson, *The history of portrait miniatures*, 2 (1904), 140–41 · G. C. Williamson, *Andrew and Nathaniel Plimer: miniature painters* (1903), 4–6 · Graves, *RA exhibitors* · IGI · F. E. Thompson, ed., *Marlborough College register from 1843 to 1909 inclusive*, 6th edn (1910), 12 · m. cert.

Likenesses A. Praga, oils, exh. Royal Society of Portrait Painters, Grafton Gallery 1897 · A. Praga, drawing, 1899, repro. in *The connoisseur*

Wealth at death £54,589 8s. 2d.: probate, 10 May 1902, CGPLA Eng. & Wales

Prophete, John (c.1350–1416), dean of York and administrator, was Welsh by birth, from the diocese of St David's, and probably from Carmarthenshire, but he had family ties across the border, especially with the Prophetes, Plowfields, and Hores around Hereford and the Felds of Ombersley, Worcestershire, all in the lower strata of county society. His nephew, Thomas Feld DCL, lived and worked with his uncle and aspired shamelessly to his cast-off offices and preferments. Their wills catalogue the family.

Prophete was a chief trustee to the heretic and rebel Sir John Oldcastle (d. 1417) and also his kinsman, probably through Katherine ferch Richard ab Ieuan, Oldcastle's first wife. He also did business with another heretic, Sir John Cheyne of Beckford (d. 1414), but no suspicion ever fell upon himself. Probably educated at Oxford, he had become a notary public by July 1376, and in that capacity he followed William Courtenay, bishop of Hereford (1369–75), to London (1375–81), where he recorded the controversial 'confession' of the rebel John Ball in 1381, and to Canterbury, where he served as registrar of the provincial court from 19 February 1382 to 18 November 1384, and thereafter as secretary, trusted adjutant, and friend until Courtenay died in 1396. When the archbishop, by rank rather than enthusiasm, headed the reform commission imposed on Richard II in 1386, Prophete was seconded to the king's household as a watchdog. After Richard's critics moved against the king and his friends in 1387–8, Prophete was assigned to service the proceedings of the council through which Richard II was now obliged to work. Although formally designated as a clerk of the privy seal (1389) and the holder of the office of secondary there (1394), his status and duties had only nominal connections with that place of drudgery. By 1392 he was formally 'clerk of the council' and had, by shrewd organization of its records, contributed greatly to its claims to political authority. Richard II recognized this by his brusque dismissal of Prophete in 1395.

Prophete spent his exile in and around his deanery of Hereford until, after the revolution of 1399, he was recalled at once to become one of the most active attenders on the royal council, doubtless to contribute bureaucratic flair to a government badly needing to prove its administrative competence. In 1402 he even acted briefly as secretary to Henry IV. On 4 October 1406, when Henry's government was at its nadir, he finally became keeper of the privy seal. There he remained through nearly nine years of sharp ministerial changes, an unprecedented term, perhaps indicative of a unique standing in the civil service, but also of lack of personal political influence.

To his nephew's bitterness and despair, Prophete never gained the bishopric that customarily ended the keeper's term. By Prophete's own analysis this was because he would not stoop to intriguing for one on his own account. Possibly his several masters thought him indispensable or, less graciously, simply a workhorse. But he held such a plurality of rich benefices already (reckoned at £750–£900 p.a.) that, with his £100 salary on top, only certain bishoprics were worth considering: by chance, next to none of these fell vacant in his time, and those that did were too politically important to fall to him.

Between 1378 and 1407 Prophete enjoyed thirty-five

benefices (although never more than twelve at once). In his heartlands of Hereford (where he was dean) and Wales, he was Trollopian in touch, and a generous kinsman. A letter-book (BL, MS Harley 431) may not be his compilation, but is the memorial to his intrigues. Yet, after becoming dean of York in 1406 he did one more reshuffle of his holdings, then never changed them again. Did such brokerage seem ill-becoming to one in great office? On 3 June 1415 (as Henry V was leaving for France) he resigned, just when his licence for absenteeism from his deanship of York ran out. None the less, it was in London that he made his will on 8 April 1416, characteristically dedicated to his kin, staff, and domestic servants. To them he gave detailed care, now as always: most had been with him for many years. At some point affection had crept in on both sides. Similarly, Prophete still had a shrewd and not unaffectionate eye on his several scattered preferments. He had always been willing to spend on them. With Archbishop Courtenay long dead there was no one from a greater world to consider. He died before the end of April 1416 and was buried in Ringwood, Hampshire, in accordance with his directions to be buried there should he die within the province of Canterbury.   R. G. DAVIES, *rev.*

Sources A. L. Brown, 'The privy seal clerks in the early fifteenth century', *The study of medieval records: essays in honour of Kathleen Major*, ed. D. A. Bullough and R. L. Storey (1971), 260–81 · Tout, *Admin. hist.*, chaps. 3, 5 · [J. W. Clay], ed., *North country wills*, 1, SurtS, 116 (1908), 10–11 · E. F. Jacob, ed., *The register of Henry Chichele, archbishop of Canterbury, 1414–1443*, 2, CYS, 42 (1937), 652 · BL, Harley MS 431 · Emden, *Oxf.*, 3.1521–3
Archives BL, Harley MS 431
Wealth at death est. £1000 p.a.; ecclesiastical livings: Emden, *Oxf.*

Prosser, Richard (*bap.* **1747**, *d.* **1839**), Church of England clergyman and tutor, was baptized on 26 July 1747 at Market Drayton, Shropshire, the third son and fourth child of Humphrey Prosser (1694–1781), gentleman, and Eleanor Witherston (1708–1779), his wife, who both have prominent gravestones in the floor of the church at St Margarets, Herefordshire.

Prosser was admitted to Balliol College, Oxford, as a commoner in 1767, graduated BA in 1770, and proceeded MA (1773), BD (1784), and DD (1797). He was elected a chaplain-fellow in 1773, having been ordained deacon in London in 1771. He took his full share of the various college offices, was a university proctor in 1783–4, and earned a reputation as a painstaking tutor. The anatomist Matthew Baillie was one of his pupils. In his time there was a series of fellowship election disputes in which he was consistently for ability against interest. Later, as one of Balliol's elder statesmen with Baillie, he promoted the same principle, and, by a testamentary codicil made in 1828, established six exhibitions to encourage 'the Intellectual Improvement of the Undergraduates of Balliol College', prescribing 'that no Exhibition shall ever be given to any Undergraduate whose literary and scientific attainments are not respectable and worthy of distinction'. He was the first of the tory disciplinarians who in such ways laid the foundations of Benjamin Jowett's Balliol.

Prosser was nominated curate of Spelsbury, Oxfordshire, in 1790, and in 1792 took the Balliol living of All Saints, Colchester, where he was an active resident incumbent. After the customary year of grace he resigned his Balliol fellowship. He married Sarah (1753–1824), daughter of the wealthy barrister Samuel Wegg FRS (1723–1802), of Colchester and Acton, on 20 June 1796. Soon after his marriage Prosser was preferred to the rectory of Gateshead by Shute Barrington, bishop of Durham, and in 1804 was collated to the third prebendal stall of Durham Cathedral. In 1808 he was appointed archdeacon of Durham, to which the rectory of Easington was annexed until 1832. He became very attached to Easington, to which he gave communion plate in 1817, and he also built (1814) and endowed (1833) a parochial charity school there. Sarah Prosser died on 4 March 1824 and was buried in Durham Cathedral, with a memorial; their only child, Richard Samuel (1797–1809), was also buried there. In 1826 Prosser bought the mansion of Belmont, designed by James Wyatt, in the parish of Clehonger, Herefordshire, and associated lands. He lived mainly at Belmont thereafter, and resigned the archdeaconry in 1831, but continued to reside as a canon at Durham for three months every year until he was ninety.

A scholarly man with an extensive library, from which he bequeathed to Balliol an illuminated fifteenth-century translation of the letters of Ovid into Norman French, and a Vulgate Bible printed in 1521, Prosser left instructions that his own manuscript writings were to be burned. His only publications were sermons preached at a visitation at Newcastle (1797), to the House of Commons (1801), and at the consecration of Henry Bathurst, bishop of Norwich (1805).

Prosser died at Belmont on 8 October 1839 and was buried in Clehonger church, where there is a memorial. Thirty-five years as a golden canon of Durham had made him a very wealthy man. His principal heir was Francis Richard Haggit MP (1824–1911), only son of Lucy Haggit, daughter of Prosser's sister Frances Parry; he changed his name to Francis Richard Wegg-Prosser by royal licence in 1849. Ironically much of the wealth accumulated by Prosser out of the unreformed Church of England assisted the recovery of English Roman Catholicism, because Wegg-Prosser, a convert in 1852, used much of it to establish and endow the Benedictine community which became Belmont Abbey.   JOHN JONES

Sources J. Jones, *Balliol College: a history*, 2nd edn (1997) · J. Jones, 'The life and benefaction of Richard Prosser', *Balliol College Annual Record* (1980), 58–61 · Balliol Oxf., archives, MISC 5.13 [extensive source of diverse information] · *IGI* · gravestones, St Margaret's church, Herefordshire [Humphrey Prosser and Eleanor Witherston] · memorial, Durham Cathedral [Sarah Wegg] · memorial, Clehonger church, Herefordshire
Archives Herefs. RO, Belmont collection, legal and estate papers, C38
Likenesses W. Owen, oils, 1816, Balliol Oxf. · W. B., oils, 1820, Durham Cath. CL · oils, 1833, U. Durham
Wealth at death over £250,000 (?)

Prothero, Sir George Walter (1848–1922), historian, was born on 14 October 1848 at Charlton, Wiltshire, the eldest

Sir George Walter Prothero (1848–1922), by Sir William Rothenstein, 1904

of the four sons of the Revd George Prothero, vicar of Clifton upon Teme, Worcestershire, later rector of Whippingham, Isle of Wight, chaplain-in-ordinary to Queen Victoria, and canon of Westminster, and his wife, Emma, daughter of the Revd William Money Kyrle of Homme House, Herefordshire, and Whetham House, Wiltshire. His brother Rowland Edmund *Prothero was president of the Board of Agriculture and Fisheries from 1916 to 1919.

Prothero was educated on the foundation at Eton College and became head of the school. In 1868 he went to King's College, Cambridge, as a scholar; he was awarded the Bell scholarship in 1869, and in 1872 was sixth in the classical tripos. He was elected a fellow of King's in 1872; he also captained his college boat (1870–71). After a short time as assistant master at Eton, he studied at Bonn University, from 1873 to 1874, under von Sybel; there he became familiar with the work of the great German historians of the time. It was at Bonn that Prothero began to develop a strong commitment to what C. H. Firth called 'the historical teaching of history'—the view that the distinct, objective, methodological techniques developed by historians had a unique educational value and should therefore be taught as an intrinsic component of every university history course. When Prothero returned to Cambridge in 1875 he persuaded John Seeley, regius professor of history, to allow him to lecture on the newly created history tripos. Seeley agreed on condition that Prothero did so, not on the German history he so admired but on the middle ages, for which the board of historical studies was finding it difficult to find a reliable teacher. Prothero complied, and his *Life and Times of Simon de Montfort* (1877) was written as a text to support his lectures. After a

year of trying he then succeeded in persuading the King's College educational council to support the new tripos by establishing a college lectureship in history, to which he himself was elected in 1876. His wife, whom he married in 1882, was Mary Frances, daughter of Samuel Butcher, bishop of Meath, and sister of Samuel Henry Butcher and of John George Butcher, later Lord Danesfort. There were no children of the marriage.

In May 1884 Prothero was one of five college lecturers to be appointed to the first university lectureships in history, and a year later he was one of a small group who campaigned successfully for the addition to the history tripos of a special subject, which, based on the detailed study of historical source material, was intended to teach students historical techniques. Prothero's chief and most enduring work of scholarship is a compilation, *Select Statutes and other Documents Illustrative of the Reigns of Elizabeth and James I* (1894), which was intended for teachers and students of history; it went into four influential editions.

In 1894 Prothero was appointed to the newly created chair of modern history at Edinburgh University. In 1899 he accepted the editorship of the *Quarterly Review*, resigned by his brother Rowland, which he held until his death. The *Quarterly* was a digest of articles on politics, literature, art, archaeology, philosophy, and religion, but rarely published historical material. Indeed of the eighteen articles written by Prothero himself during his editorship none was on history. No longer a specialist teacher or writer of history, he now took on a new role as a high-profile spokesman for British historical scholarship. He was elected president of the Royal Historical Society (1901–5), fellow of the British Academy (1903), Rede lecturer at Cambridge (1903), Lowell lecturer at Boston University and Schouler lecturer at Johns Hopkins University, USA (1910), Chichele lecturer at Oxford (1915, lectures delivered 1920). He was co-editor of the *Cambridge Modern History* (1901–12) and general editor of the Cambridge Historical Series. He used his standing in the social and intellectual life of the London of his time to promote ideas of community and co-operation in British historical scholarship, and to help to define a growing sense among historians that they were part of a profession with a clearly defined set of skills and duties, and a career structure. Prothero acted as historical adviser to the Foreign Office between 1917 and 1919, where, working with the intelligence division of the Admiralty, the geographical section of the general staff of the War Office, the war trade intelligence department, and a specially created historical section of the Foreign Office, he edited the handbooks containing the relevant historical, geographical, and economic data supplied to British delegates at the Peace Conference at Versailles in 1919. These 162 handbooks were published in 25 volumes, by HMSO, in 1920. Prothero himself was invited to attend the peace conference in November 1918 but a severe attack of influenza delayed his arrival until February 1919. As a result he was not asked to serve on any of the committees and was rarely consulted. The two historical memoranda he did produce went unread, prompting him to reflect that he felt he was 'the fifth wheel in the coach'. In 1920 Prothero was created KBE for his services to the peace effort. He died at his home, 24 Bedford Square, London, on 10 July 1922.

ALGERNON CECIL, *rev.* PETER R. H. SLEE

Sources *The Times* (12 July 1922) · A. C., 'Sir George Prothero', *QR*, 238 (1922), 213–18 · C. W. Crawley, 'Sir George Prothero and his circle', *TRHS*, 5th ser., 20 (1970), 101–28 · P. R. H. Slee, *Learning and a liberal education: the study of modern history in the universities of Oxford, Cambridge and Manchester, 1800–1914* (1986), 68–86 · U. Lond., Institute of Historical Research, J. R. Seeley MSS · Royal Historical Society, G. W. Prothero MSS · King's College educational council, minutes, 1861–2, 1882–1901, King's Cam. · *CGPLA Eng. & Wales* (1922)

Archives King's AC Cam., corresp. and papers mainly relating to his biography of Henry Bradshaw · King's AC Cam., journals and notebooks · NL Scot., corresp. · Royal Historical Society, London, corresp., diaries, and papers · U. Edin. L., lecture notes and papers · UCL, corresp., diaries and MSS | BL, corresp. with Sir Charles Dilke, Add. MS 43921 · CUL, letters to Lord Acton · CUL, letters to Oscar Browning · Derbys. RO, letters to Peveril Turnbull · Institute of Historical Research, London, J. R. Seeley MSS · King's AC Cam., letters to Oscar Browning · King's Cam., King's College educational council, minutes, 1861–1901 · Mitchell L., NSW, letters to G. E. Morrison · U. Birm. L., corresp. with H. Dawson · U. Edin. L., corresp. with Charles Sarolea · U. Edin. L., corresp. with A. B. Keith · UCL, letters to Karl Pearson

Likenesses W. Rothenstein, portrait, 1904, NPG [*see illus.*]

Wealth at death £18,324 8s. 7d.: probate, 22 Sept 1922, *CGPLA Eng. & Wales*

Prothero, Rowland Edmund, first Baron Ernle (1851–1937), author, land agent, and politician, was the third son of Canon George Prothero and Emma, daughter of the Revd William Money Kyrle of Homme House, Herefordshire; he was born at Clifton upon Teme, Worcestershire, on 6 September 1851. His father was the rector of Whippingham in the Isle of Wight, and the proximity of the church to Osborne, Queen Victoria's summer residence, brought the Prothero family into close contact with the royal family and their many distinguished guests. Educated first at home by his mother, who gave him a grounding in English, Latin, French, and German, the young Prothero also learned arithmetic and writing from the village schoolmaster. At the age of ten he was sent to Temple Grove at East Sheen, London, a well-known private school; but a prolonged illness kept him at home until he was well enough to go to Marlborough in 1864. From there he entered Balliol College, Oxford, to read law and history, took a first class in modern history in 1875, and shortly afterwards was elected a fellow of All Souls.

After a year spent at Darmstadt improving his German, Prothero trained as a barrister and practised briefly on the Oxford circuit until, in 1881, the weakening of his eyesight obliged him to give up a career in the law. In an effort to improve his eyes he took up an outdoor life, walking the length and breadth of France. His time there, spent following the paths of Jeanne d'Arc, Agnès Sorel, and Rabelais, and staying in primitive village inns, gave him a lasting love for that country, and led eventually to a collection of his essays on French poetry and related topics in *The Pleasant Land of France*, published in 1908.

His choice of career still limited by his improved but frail eyesight, Prothero was a proctor at Oxford in 1883–4, and then, at the age of thirty-three, embarked on gaining

Rowland Edmund Prothero, first Baron Ernle (1851–1937), by Walter Stoneman, 1931

a livelihood by his pen, a profession which gave him some latitude in the hours he chose to devote daily to reading and writing. He was, nevertheless, remarkably prolific, publishing as many as fifty-four unsigned articles in seven years, mainly in the *Quarterly Review* and the *Edinburgh Review*. He developed an attractively simple, pellucid style, writing on a variety of biographical, historical, topographical, political, and literary subjects, as well as producing obituaries of leading figures of the day, and contributing signed articles to *Blackwood's Edinburgh Magazine* and other periodicals. Having some knowledge of farming (some farmland was attached to the rectory at Whippingham), he wrote in 1887–8 for *The Guardian* on the effect of the great depression in agriculture on the glebe lands of the clergy, and on the anti-tithe agitation in Wales. A long-standing interest in the history of agriculture led in 1888 to a book on *The Pioneers and Progress of English Farming*, which was subsequently developed into his well-known *English Farming Past and Present*, a work hailed as a 'classic' on its appearance in 1912, and which went through five editions in the author's lifetime.

Prothero's literary career advanced as he became assistant editor of *The Nineteenth Century*, and in 1893 editor of the *Quarterly Review*. His position had become financially secure and in August 1891 he married Mary Beatrice, third daughter of John Bailward of Horsington Manor, Somerset, and the sister of an old undergraduate friend at Balliol. They were married by Canon Prothero in the

Henry VII chapel of Westminster Abbey, and settled down to live at 3 Cheyne Walk, Chelsea, a house which remained Prothero's London home for the rest of his life. His wife, a gifted artist in water-colours and a lover of horses and dogs, gave him a son, and they enjoyed a brief seven and a half years of 'perfect happiness' until her untimely death in 1899.

Meanwhile, a steady flow of major works ran from Prothero's pen—a life of A. P. Stanley in 1893, and in 1896 his edition of the previously unpublished *Letters of Edward Gibbon, 1753–94*, followed in 1898–1901 by the six volumes of the *Letters and Journals of Lord Byron*. Queen Victoria commissioned from him for private circulation a *Life of Prince Henry of Battenberg* (1897). A familiar figure at literary gatherings of the period, Prothero rubbed shoulders with such celebrities as Gladstone, Tennyson, Browning, Huxley, and Oscar Wilde. Through visits home to Whippingham his acquaintances also included Crown Prince Frederick of Germany and his wife, and Princess Alice, the second daughter of Queen Victoria who had married Prince Louis of Hesse (with whom he frequently dined while at Darmstadt), as well as many other distinguished members of the European aristocracy.

Suddenly, in 1898, Prothero decided to give up his now established literary career and turn to estate management, accepting the handsome offer of the duke of Bedford to become his chief agent. Prothero was then aged forty-seven and, as he remarked, if he were to make a new career this was the time. He was succeeded as editor of the *Quarterly Review* by his eldest brother, George Walter *Prothero.

Prothero's change of course was not quite so abrupt or so unlikely as some contemporaries supposed, for he had already some experience in managing estates for an uncle and for All Souls. His move to Bedfordshire was marred by a great personal loss—the death of his wife—but three years later, in April 1902, he married Barbara Jane, the only daughter of Lieutenant-Colonel Charles Hamley, who after her father's early death had spent much of her life with her uncle, General Sir Edward Hamley, MP for Stockport. She was an early supporter of the cause of women's suffrage, and also a talented miniature painter, and a writer of short stories, which were published in *Blackwood's Magazine*. She died in 1930, predeceasing her husband by seven years.

While serving as chief agent for the duke of Bedford, Prothero still managed to put aside two or three hours a day for reading and writing, and continued to publish books and articles. In 1903 began the third phase of his life, a career in public life. He became chairman of the higher education committee of Bedfordshire county council, and in 1907 stood unsuccessfully as Unionist candidate for the parliamentary seat of Biggleswade. The introduction of the 1911 National Insurance Act encouraged him to put forward a scheme for associating village benefit clubs into large groups, and for long he was president of the newly formed National Federation of Rural Approved Societies, an organization always close to his heart and for which he was widely remembered by farm workers. In 1914 he was chosen to stand unopposed as member of parliament for the University of Oxford, though at the age of sixty-three he found life in the House of Commons somewhat strange and lonely. However, he served on two highly important inquiries, the Milner and Selborne committees on agriculture, whose proposals he was to put into effect when asked by Lloyd George in December 1916 to become president of the board of agriculture.

As president Prothero undertook a demanding role at a time of crisis, when as a result of the German submarine warfare the nation's food supplies were under severe threat and it was becoming evident that the expansion of agricultural production at home was vital for sustaining the war effort. In promoting his 'plough campaign' to expand production of grains and potatoes on suitable grasslands, Prothero found it difficult at first to convince farmers and the public of the need for urgent and drastic measures. His plans for higher production had to meet the problems of shortages of farm equipment, inadequate supplies of fertilizers, and, not least, a critical lack of labour as many skilled farm workers had joined the armed forces. In addition to obtaining the services of British troops, German prisoners of war, and public schoolboys to help get in the crops, he also established a women's branch of the board of agriculture to recruit village women and to organize the Women's Land Army, as well as to foster the infant Women's Institute movement. The success of the plough campaign in adding nearly 3 million acres to the arable acreage, together with the passing of the 1917 Corn Production Act (designed to win over farmers to the policy of expanding corn production after many years of converting to more profitable grass) played a key part in sustaining the country through the final stages of the First World War. The Corn Production Act also promised to put British agriculture on a new post-war course of government-supported high production, thereby ending the long depression which had affected grain farming before the war. The failure of government to follow Prothero's policies after his resignation in 1919 was a prime cause of the agricultural problems that arose in the 1920s.

Prothero's retirement from government was probably hastened by the news near the end of the war of the death of his only son in Mesopotamia. He had been created Baron Ernle in 1919, and lived on in retirement, still battling with weakening eyesight, for a further eighteen years. Two more books appeared in the 1920s, *The Land and its People* (1925) and *The Light Reading of our Ancestors* (1927), the latter reflecting an early interest in the history of the novel, which he had long postponed fulfilling. His delightful volume of reminiscences, *Whippingham to Westminster*, was left almost complete at his death and appeared in 1938. He was the recipient of many honours, not the least to him the presidency of the MCC in 1924–5, a testimony to his lifelong support of cricket. As a great wartime administrator of agriculture Ernle's reputation remains undiminished, and many of the measures which he introduced for the control and expansion of farming to meet the food crisis of the First World War were reinstituted in the Second. Of his many books, *English Farming Past and Present* best survived the test of time, reaching a sixth edition in 1961, and continuing to serve as a major source for the history of agriculture.

Physically Ernle was an impressively tall, thin, and erect figure, very active in his habits and one inclined to walk rather than take a cab. In his earlier years he was an enthusiastic cricketer, playing at Oxford and later for I Zingari and the Harlequins. He was also a lifelong collector of portrait busts and figures in china and brass. He was always assiduous at attending to his responsibilities and was widely admired for his good judgement and great integrity, as well as for his unfailing wit and charm. He died on 1 July 1937, in his eighty-seventh year, at his country home, Ginge Manor, near Wantage, Berkshire, close to the garden he always loved.

G. E. MINGAY

Sources R. E. Prothero, *Whippingham to Westminster: the reminiscences of Lord Ernle* (1938) · *The Times* (8 July 1937) · J. Thirsk, ed., *The agrarian history of England and Wales*, 8, ed. E. H. Whetham (1978) · *WWW* · *Wellesley index*
Archives NRA, priv. coll., papers | All Souls Oxf., letters to Sir William Anson · Bodl. Oxf., corresp. with Lord Lovelace and Lady Lovelace · Bodl. Oxf., corresp. with Lord Selborne · HLRO, corresp. with David Lloyd George, etc. · HLRO, corresp. with Andrew Bonar Law · Wilts. & Swindon RO, corresp. with Viscount Long
Likenesses W. Stoneman, photograph, 1920, NPG · W. Stoneman, photograph, 1931, NPG [*see illus.*] · photographs, repro. in Prothero, *Whippingham to Westminster*
Wealth at death £23,791 7s. 3d.: probate, 30 July 1937, CGPLA Eng. & Wales

Proud, Joseph (1745–1826), Swedenborgian preacher and hymn writer, was born at Beaconsfield, Buckinghamshire, on 22 March 1745, the son of John Proud (d. 1784), a General Baptist minister, and his wife. He quickly entered the ministry, assisting his father at Wisbech, Cambridgeshire, in 1767, then at General Baptist churches at Knipton, Leicestershire (1772–5), and Fleet, Lincolnshire (1775–86). In 1786 he was called to a chapel in Ber Street, Norwich. By conviction a universalist, he was hostile to the growing evangelical New Connexion. Perhaps in search of a belief structure as appealing as the new Calvinism, he swung dramatically when he heard a Swedenborgian, J. W. Salmon, preach.

Proud was expelled from the General Baptist conference in 1791, but in June 1790 he had moved to Birmingham to commence a Swedenborgian congregation there, occupying himself in the meantime by writing the first Swedenborgian hymnbook. In May 1791 he was ordained into the ministry of the New Jerusalem church, and in June a grand temple was opened with a flourish and some puzzled attention from Priestley and the Unitarians, but it was saved from burning in the church and king riots a month later only when Proud insisted on the patriotism of the congregation. This indeed was Proud's view; he was far from the radical experimentation of other early Swedenborgians, lacking the interest in the intricacies of Swedenborgian thought of other devoted followers, and feeling uneasy enough to abandon extemporaneous preaching on joining the sect. He wore robes to officiate as minister, but the grand temple had to be abandoned a year later when the society's sponsor defaulted. He was on friendly terms with the Unitarians and preached at their chapel in Warwick in 1792. After a brief ministry in Manchester in 1793–4 and a period of ministry in a humbler chapel in Paradise Street, Birmingham, he was invited by the 'high-church' Swedenborgians to form a London congregation for them in a chapel erected in Cross Street, Hatton Gardens, and then, after a dispute with the proprietors, moved to York Street, St James, drawing large and fashionable crowds with his blend of evangelical rhetoric, high-church ritual, and simplified Swedenborgian ideas. After 1813 his success faded. A much humbler chapel was hired in Lisle Street, Leicester Square, but soon after this in 1814 Proud retired to Birmingham.

Proud was married twice; first on 3 February 1769, from which marriage he had eleven children, only two of whom survived, and second in 1785 to Susannah, a widow, who died on 21 November 1827; none of the three children from his second marriage lived beyond childhood. Proud died at Handsworth, Birmingham, on 3 August 1826, and was buried in St George's churchyard, Birmingham, on 20 August, when his funeral sermon was preached by Edward Madeley. Proud's success was typical of idiosyncratic preachers in the protestant world of London, the equivalent of the contemporary televangelists.

PETER J. LINEHAM

Sources 'Memoirs of Joseph Proud', New Church General Conference, London, c.1830 · E. Madeley, 'Memoir', in J. Proud, *The aged minister's last legacy*, 2nd edn (1854) · E. A. Payne, 'Joseph Proud: General Baptist, Swedenborgian and hymn writer', *Baptist Quarterly*, 23 (1969–70), 280–82 · P. J. Lineham, 'The English Swedenborgians, 1770–1840: a study in the social dimensions of religious sectarianism', DPhil diss., U. Sussex, 1978 · *DNB* · D. M. Lewis, ed., *The Blackwell dictionary of evangelical biography, 1730–1860*, 2 vols. (1995) · *Intellectual Repository*, ns, 2 (1827), 433

Proudman, Joseph (1888–1975), mathematician and oceanographer, was born on 30 December 1888 at Thurston Fold Farm, Unsworth, near Bury in Lancashire, the eldest child of John Proudman (d. 1943), farm bailiff and later tenant farmer at Bold, near Widnes, Lancashire, and his wife, Nancy Blease. He attended primary schools at Unsworth and Bold. From 1902 to 1907 he was a pupil teacher at Farnworth primary school. During the winters of 1902–4 he attended evening classes at the Widnes Technical School; from 1903 to 1907 he taught for only half of each week, and during the other half he attended classes at the Widnes secondary school. In 1907 he was awarded the Tate technical science entrance scholarship at Liverpool University, where in 1910 he received a BSc (first class) with honours in mathematics. He was also awarded the Derby scholarship for mathematics and an entrance exhibition to Trinity College, Cambridge, where he became a senior scholar in 1911. The following year he received a first class in schedule A and a distinction in schedule B of part two of the mathematical tripos.

Following a suggestion by Professor Horace Lamb of Manchester, Proudman started research on a problem in the theory of ocean tides which set the course for his entire subsequent career. In 1913 he became a lecturer in mathematics at Liverpool University. During the first year he had no time for research except during vacations, but he did find time to direct the postgraduate work of A. T. Doodson for the MSc degree and thus began a collaboration which continued until Doodson's death. In 1915 he also became a fellow of Trinity College, Cambridge, and thus received an additional salary without any prescribed duties. He always said that this was of the greatest help to him. When the First World War broke out he was placed in a low medical category and did not serve in the armed forces. He spent the war years in Liverpool, except for the second half of 1918 when he worked in the research department of Woolwich arsenal. In 1916 he married, in Manchester, Rubina (d. 1958), daughter of Thomas Ormrod, insurance company manager. They had a daughter and two sons, one of whom later became professor of applied mathematics at Essex University.

In 1919 Proudman was instrumental in persuading two shipowners, C. Booth, chairman of Booth Steamship Company, and his brother, Sir Alfred Booth, chairman of Cunard, to endow the foundation of a tidal institute which was later amalgamated with the Liverpool observatory. He served as its director until 1945. Also in 1919 he was appointed professor of applied mathematics at the University of Liverpool, a post which was created for him. In 1933 he was transferred at his own request to the chair of oceanography from which he retired in 1954, when he was made professor emeritus. He took a full share in the administration of the university, serving as pro-vice-chancellor and deputy chairman of senate from 1940 to 1946 during the difficult war and post-war years. After his transfer to the oceanography chair he was chiefly responsible for shifting the emphasis of his department from marine biology to marine physics, at a time when the latter was not well catered for in Britain. He was thus responsible for giving the Liverpool school of oceanography its distinctive role.

Proudman's scientific work was concerned mainly with tidal theory, almost every aspect of which was treated by him during his scientific career, including large-scale oceanic tides, problems relating to smaller seas, and the tidal elastic yielding of the earth's crust. With Doodson he made significant improvements in tidal predictions for British ports and in charts for tidal streams and elevations in British waters. When he became professor of oceanography he widened his range of marine studies. He studied surface temperatures and salinities in the Irish Sea, and deduced from them the main patterns of circulation. His membership of the Waverley committee, set up to report on the disastrous floods of 1953, led to his important work on storm surge equations. He worked on the interaction of storm surges and tides in an estuary, and wrote an influential textbook, *Dynamical Oceanography* (1953), which for many years had few rivals. Nevertheless, tides remained his prime interest throughout his long career. He solved practically all the remaining tidal problems soluble within the framework of classical hydrodynamics and analytical mathematics.

Proudman was awarded the Adams prize in mathematics by the University of Cambridge in 1923 and was elected a fellow of the Royal Society in 1925. He was appointed CBE in 1952 and was made an honorary LLD of Liverpool University in 1956. As chairman of the British National Committee for Geodesy and Geophysics he took a leading part in the negotiations of 1943 which led to the foundation of the National Institute of Oceanography. His work also received recognition from the international scientific community. In 1951–6 he was president of the International Association of Physical Oceanography, after serving as its vice-president from 1948 to 1951 and its general secretary for the preceding fifteen years. In 1944 he was the George Darwin lecturer of the Royal Astronomical Society, in 1946 he received the Alexander Agassiz medal for oceanography of the National Academy of Sciences of the United States, and he was also elected a foreign member of the Norwegian Academy of Science and Letters. He received the Hughes medal of the Royal Society in 1957.

In 1958 Proudman's wife died. In 1961 he married, at Poole, Mrs Beryl Gladys Waugh Gould (*née* Barker), who survived him. Proudman died on 26 June 1975 at a nursing home in Fordingbridge, Hampshire, near his home at Verwood, Dorset. F. URSELL, *rev.*

Sources D. E. Cartwright and F. Ursell, *Memoirs FRS*, 22 (1976), 319–33 · personal knowledge (1986) · RS, Proudman MSS
Archives RS
Likenesses W. Stoneman, photograph, 1931, NPG · Burrell & Hardman, photograph, RS; repro. in Cartwright and Ursell, *Memoirs FRS*, facing p. 319
Wealth at death £45,682: probate, 28 Aug 1975, *CGPLA Eng. & Wales*

Prout, Father. See Mahony, Francis Sylvester (1804–1866).

Prout, Ebenezer (1835–1909), music theorist and journal editor, was born on 1 March 1835 at Oundle, Northamptonshire, the son of the Revd Ebenezer Prout, a Congregational minister, from a Devon family, and nephew of the water-colour painter Samuel Prout. He was taught music by his father, and was educated at Denmark Hill grammar school, London (1848–51). He was a lay student at New College, St John's Wood, for a year, and in 1852 he became an usher at Priory House School, Clapton. He graduated BA from London University in 1854. After teaching at Joseph Payne's School, Leatherhead, Surrey, from 1856 to 1859, he decided to enter the music profession, despite strong opposition from his father. Although Prout received some piano lessons from Charles Kensington Salaman, he was almost entirely self-taught. He began by teaching singing at a girls' school in Hackney, and from 1860 to 1884 he was a professor of piano at the Crystal Palace School of Art. He was organist at Union Chapel, Islington, from 1861 to 1873. In 1862 he won the first prize in a competition for a new string quartet, instituted by the Society of British Musicians, and in 1865 their prize for a piano quartet.

In 1871 Prout was appointed the first editor of the *Monthly Musical Record*. He at once introduced a new element into music criticism, which he made the prominent feature of his journal. He wrote detailed analyses of the

Ebenezer Prout (1835–1909), by Elliott & Fry

the National Training School for Music in 1876 he became professor of harmony, a post he held until 1882, and from 1879 until his death he taught at the Royal Academy of Music, where his pupils included Henry Wood and Edward German. He also became professor at the Guildhall School of Music in 1884. The reputation of his textbooks secured him in 1894 the professorship of music at Trinity College, Dublin, a non-resident post, in succession to Sir Robert Prescott Stewart, and he was awarded the honorary degree of MusD in 1895.

Prout was a leading Handel scholar, and he wrote additional accompaniments for a performance of *Samson* at the Leeds festival in 1880. In 1891 he carried on a long controversy in print over Franz's edition of *Messiah*, and in 1902 brought out his own edition of the work, still often used by choirs, eliminating textual errors and adding accompaniments. In his later years he concentrated mainly on Bach. Large selections of airs from Handel's operas and Bach's cantatas, translated and edited by him, appeared between 1905 and 1909. He invented words for all the fugue subjects of Bach's '48' to help students to see where the fugue subject ends, and these mottoes were widely circulated.

Prout married Julia West, the daughter of a nonconformist minister. They had one son, Louis Beethoven Prout, and three daughters. He lived at 246 Richmond Road, Hackney, always spending the summer vacation at Vik, Norway. He died suddenly at home, on 5 December 1909, and was buried at Abney Park cemetery.

HENRY DAVEY, rev. ANNE PIMLOTT BAKER

Sources J. A. Westrup, 'Ebenezer Prout', *Monthly Musical Record*, 65 (1935) · *MT*, 40 (1899), 225–30 · E. Lomax, 'Dr Ebenezer Prout—and Bach', *Music in Education*, 23 (July–Aug 1959), 76 · *Monthly Musical Record*, 40 (1910), 1–2 · *New Grove* · *CGPLA Eng. & Wales* (1910)
Archives TCD, letters to N. Kilburn
Likenesses E. B. Walker, portrait, 1904, Incorporated Society of Musicians, London; repro. in *MT* (Jan 1910), 13 · Elliott & Fry, photograph, NPG [*see illus.*] · cartoon, repro. in *Musical Herald* (June 1891), 168 · photograph, repro. in *MT* (April 1899), 225
Wealth at death £4749 6s. 10d.: probate, 1 Jan 1910, *CGPLA Eng. & Wales*

less known works of Schubert, of Schumann's symphonies, and of some of the later works of Wagner, all of which were practically unknown in England, and led the way for the introduction of Wagner's operas. In 1875 he was forced to resign the editorship, and after a period as music critic of *The Academy* he wrote for *The Athenaeum* from 1879 to 1889.

Prout continued to compose, and in 1871 produced an organ concerto in E minor which was performed by John Stainer at a Crystal Palace concert. This was followed by a duet sonata in A major for piano and harmonium, which became very popular. He wrote several cantatas, including *Hereward* (1878), *Alfred* (1882), *Queen Aimée* (for female voices, 1885), and *Damon and Phintias* (for male voices, 1889), as well as three symphonies, overtures, chamber music, and sonatas. He also published many arrangements of classical pieces for the organ.

In 1877 Prout contributed a valuable text on instrumentation to Novello's series of music primers. He began a series of treatises in 1889 with *Harmony, its Theory and Practice*, which reached a twenty-fourth edition. *Counterpoint, Strict and Free* (1890; 9th edn, 1910), *Fugue* (1891), and *The Orchestra* (1897) were among many of his works which became standard textbooks.

From 1876 to 1890 Prout was conductor of the Borough of Hackney Choral Association. At the establishment of

Prout, Elizabeth [*name in religion* Mary Joseph of Jesus] (1820–1864), Roman Catholic nun, was born on 2 September 1820 in Coleham, Shrewsbury, the only child of Edward Prout, a cooper, and his wife, Ann Yates. She was baptized on 17 September 1820 in St Julian's church, Shrewsbury. By 1841 she and her parents were living in New Brewery Yard, at Stone, Staffordshire. After the arrival of the Passionist priest Dominic Barberi in nearby Aston Hall in 1842, Elizabeth became a Catholic under his influence. In July 1848, on the recommendation of another Passionist, Father Gaudentius Rossi, she entered the convent of the Sisters of the Infant Jesus in Northampton. By 1849, however, she had contracted tuberculosis in her knee and had to leave the noviciate.

Back at Stone, Elizabeth Prout recovered her health, but met with so much opposition to her Catholicism from her mother that she decided to leave home. With the help of Father Rossi she found a teaching post in St Chad's, Manchester. She was then invited by him and her parish priest,

Father Robert Croskell, to co-operate with them in founding a new religious order. Then aged only twenty-nine, she was the youngest and the first Catholic Englishwoman to found a religious order in nineteenth-century England. Her congregation marked a break with tradition, offering a consecrated religious life, with choir observance for all, no dowry, and no class distinctions, to women of the working and lower middle classes who could not afford the dowries required by the established orders. With the approval of Bishop William Turner of Salford, Elizabeth and five companions professed their simple vows of poverty, chastity, and obedience on 21 November 1854. From then she was known as Mother Mary Joseph of Jesus. Both contemplative and active, Mother Mary Joseph's congregation was distinguished, like the Passionist congregation, by the spirituality of St Paul of the Cross. The congregation helped to provide Catholic education in the working-class districts of Manchester, the inhabitants of which included the poorest Irish immigrants, many of them refugees from the famine of the late 1840s. The sisters also visited the poor in their own homes, instructed converts, provided retreats for women, and worked at vestment making and other forms of church needlework.

In 1853, with the exception of Mother Mary Joseph, all the sisters caught fever. After a period of recuperation at Newton Heath, they moved to Levenshulme in April 1854. There, as well as opening a school for the poor children of the locality, Mother Mary Joseph kept a boarding-school for lower-middle-class girls. She made other foundations in Ashton under Lyne and in Sutton and Blackbrook near St Helens, Lancashire, in 1855. She had to close her convent in Ashton in 1857 when one of her sisters plunged the congregation into debt, but returned in 1862 to conduct sewing classes and night schools for the unemployed girls and women during the Lancashire cotton famine. She hoped to open a home for factory girls in Ashton but was unable to acquire the land.

Although lively and enterprising, Mother Mary Joseph was small in stature and physically delicate. She died of tuberculosis at the Holy Cross Convent, Sutton, on 11 January 1864 and was buried in St Anne's Monastery cemetery in Sutton three days later. During the next century her congregation opened new houses throughout the British Isles and in North and South America, Botswana, Sweden, and Papua New Guinea, totalling sixty-three houses in 1964. In 1973 her remains were exhumed from the monastery cemetery and reinterred in the adjacent church of St Anne and Blessed Dominic, Sutton, beside those of Father Dominic Barberi and Father Ignatius Spencer. The cause for her canonization was opened by Archbishop Worlock of Liverpool on 18 May 1994.   E. HAMER

Sources E. Hamer [Sister Dominic Savio], *Elizabeth Prout, 1820–1864: a religious life for industrial England* (1994) • Sisters of the Cross and Passion, Salford, General Archives • d. cert. • Shrops. RRC, 2711/Rg/6
Archives Sisters of the Cross and Passion, Salford, General Archives
Likenesses photograph, *c.*1855, Sisters of the Cross and Passion, Salford, General Archives • photograph, 1864, Sisters of the Cross and Passion, Salford, General Archives • photograph, 1973, Sisters of the Cross and Passion, Salford, General Archives

Prout, John (1810–1894), agriculturist, was born on 1 October 1810 at South Petherwin, near Launceston, Cornwall, the son of William Prout, farmer, and his wife (also his cousin), Tomazin Prout. John was educated at a school in Launceston. He gained practical experience of farming by working for his father. Dissatisfied with the position of a tenant farmer on the smallholdings of his native land, and with the antiquated restrictions of land tenure, he emigrated to Canada and purchased land at Pickering, Ontario, which he farmed from 1832 to 1842. Having married, about 1841, Sophia (*d.* 1893), niece of Colonel Thomson of Aikenshaw, Toronto, Prout returned to England, and joined his uncle, Thomas Prout, a medicine vendor and performer, in business at 229 Strand, London. On the death of his uncle, Prout carried on the business. In 1861 he bought Blount's Farm, Sawbridgeworth, Hertfordshire, which he cultivated until June 1894.

Prout helped to pioneer the adoption of scientific farming by his thirty-three years' successful cultivation of Blount's Farm, and his experience was valuable to agriculturists not only in Britain but also in other countries. His system was based on his Canadian experience and his study of Sir John Lawes's experimental plots at Rothamsted, Hertfordshire. He demonstrated that successive crops of cereals could be produced on land of heavy clay with the use of artificial fertilizer, if the soil was adequately drained and cultivated. In 1881 he published a report of his methods, entitled *Profitable Clay Farming under a Just System of Tenant Right*, which ran to several editions and was translated into French and German. His text helped to popularize the adoption of a more scientific approach to the problems of arable farming, particularly on heavy soils.

Prout died while living with his married daughter at Wimbish vicarage, Saffron Walden, Essex, on 7 December 1894. His wife had died the previous year.

B. B. WOODWARD, *rev.* JOHN MARTIN

Sources *The Times* (11 Dec 1894) • *The Field* (15 Dec 1894) • *Agricultural Gazette* (10 Dec 1894) • *Hertfordshire and Essex Observer* (15 Dec 1894) • J. Prout, *Profitable clay farming under a just system of tenant right* (1881) • *CGPLA Eng. & Wales* (1895) • d. cert.
Likenesses portrait, repro. in *Cable* (Aug 1893), 313
Wealth at death £10,040 17s. 2d.: probate, June 1895, *CGPLA Eng. & Wales*

Prout, John Skinner (1806–1876), watercolour painter, was born at Plymouth in 1806, perhaps the son of Thomas Prout. Although a nephew of Samuel *Prout (1783–1852), whose style he began by emulating, he was largely self-taught, perhaps because his uncle was then building his career in London. He was educated at Plymouth grammar school. In early life Prout moved to Bristol and produced topographical watercolours and architectural lithographs, notably the sets of the *Antiquities of Chester* and *Castles and Abbeys of Monmouthshire* (1838). In June and July 1833 he toured Wales and visited Dublin with Samuel Jackson and William James Muller, fellow members of the newly founded Bristol sketching club. Towards the end of the 1830s, however, he found himself in 'continued difficulties and harassment of mind' (Bonyhady, 44). He was elected to the New Society of Painters in Water Colours in 1838, but his membership lapsed after his departure for Sydney two years later.

In Australia Prout shone as a painter, printmaker, teacher, and promoter of the fine arts, his greatest success coming after his move to Hobart, Tasmania, in 1843. There he built up a considerable teaching practice, and was on friendly terms with John Glover and his family: his sketch of the older artist asleep in a chair was used in Glover's obituary in the *Art Journal* in July 1850. He also produced three volumes of lithographs of scenery around Sydney, Melbourne, Geelong, and Hobart, and he gave lectures and mounted exhibitions. In April 1848, after a farewell concert attended by the governor, he left Hobart for England.

Prout was re-elected associate and member of the New Society of Painters in Water Colours in 1849 and 1862 respectively, and he lived off Australian subject matter for a number of years. In 1850 his *Dioramic Views Illustrative of Convict and Emigrant Life*, accompanied by a publication with the same title, was shown in London, and two years later he produced a panorama, *A Voyage to Australia and a Visit to the Gold Fields*. He had not himself visited the goldfields, and his two collaborators on the project had never even been to Australia. Probably his most notable works, in Tasmania and later, were of tree ferns, especially in the Valley of Ferns, near Hobart, which for picturesque effect he peopled with the Aborigines who had already been exiled to Flinders Island. His later style perhaps owes more to J. M. W. Turner, J. D. Harding, and his fellow members of the Bristol school, than to his uncle.

Prout returned to Bristol, but later moved permanently to London, where he died of kidney disease on 29 August 1876 at his home, 4 Leighton Crescent, Kentish Town; his brother Thomas, who lived in Plymouth, was with him. The date of his marriage and wife's name are unknown, but they had two daughters, Agnes and Mary, who each exhibited a sea-shore subject at the Society of British Artists in 1869. There was a studio sale at Christies on 26 February 1877. Sixty-three of Prout's paintings were used in E. C. Booth's *Australia Illustrated* (1873–6), and in 1893 some of his Bristol drawings with letterpress descriptions were published as *Picturesque Antiquities of Bristol*. In Australia the New South Wales and Tasmanian state galleries, the Mitchell Library and Dixson Gallery, Sydney, and the National Library, Canberra, have examples of his work. In Britain there are watercolours in the British and Victoria and Albert museums, and in provincial galleries at Bristol, Cambridge, Chester, Exeter, Leeds, Leicester, Newport, and Reading.
HUON MALLALIEU

Sources *Art Journal*, 38 (1876) · A. V. Brown, 'John Skinner Prout: his Tasmanian sojourn, 1844–48', *Art Bulletin of Tasmania* (1984), 20–51 · T. Brown, 'John Skinner Prout: a colonial artist', *Art and Australia*, 22, 516–22 · T. Bonyhady, *The colonial image. Australian painting, 1800–1880* (1987) · will, principal registry of the family division
Likenesses wood-engraving, NPG; repro. in *ILN* (9 Sept 1876)
Wealth at death £1500: probate, 5 May 1877, *CGPLA Eng. & Wales*

Prout, Samuel (1783–1852), watercolour painter, was born on 17 September 1783 at Trevil Street, Plymouth, Devon, the fourth of the fourteen children of Samuel Prout (1747–1823), a shopkeeper and naval outfitter, and his wife, Mary Cater. He was baptized at the Old Tabernacle in Plymouth but by 1810 had joined the Church of England, and he is recorded as a devout attender at St Mary's, Hastings, in the 1840s. Prout was educated at Plymouth grammar school, where he and the painter Benjamin Robert Haydon were encouraged to sketch by the headmaster, Dr Bidlake. He had some drawing lessons at this time from T. H. Williams, who anticipated an early speciality of west country cottage and village scenes. Thereafter he received no formal artistic training.

Early career, marriage, and friendships In 1802 Prout moved to London, where he learned his trade in the circle of the antiquarian publisher John Britton. As one of Britton's team of illustrators, Prout contributed to the first volume of *Architectural Antiquities of Great Britain* (4 vols., 1807–18). He formed his earliest drawing and tinted-wash style in the ambience of his fellow illustrators J. C. Smith, Frederick Nash, T. R. Underwood, Frederick Mackenzie, and George Shepherd. Britton stated that, from about 1803, he also employed Prout to copy sketches by Thomas Hearne, William Alexander, J. M. W. Turner, J. S. Cotman, and Mackenzie. Prout was particularly indebted to Hearne and never abandoned the picturesque, antiquarian tradition. His characteristic, mature, broken-line drawing technique can be traced back through Thomas Girtin and Joseph Farington to Canaletto. Henry Edridge was a later influence, and around 1820 Prout's drawings are sometimes indistinguishable from those of Edridge.

Prout married Elizabeth Gillespie (1788–1863) in Brixton, London, on 27 December 1810; they had four children, born between 1813 and 1822. From 1811 to 1835 the Prouts lived in Brixton, though their last years in London were spent at 5 De Crespigny Terrace, Camberwell. Ill health twice drove Prout from the city, first back to Plymouth from 1805 to 1808 and then to Hastings between 1836 and 1844. He suffered from disabling headaches and from congestion of the lungs throughout his life; the headaches have been linked to an attack of sunstroke in childhood.

Among Prout's west country artist friends were Haydon, John Jackson—who depicted Prout at his most confident in an oil portrait of 1823 (NPG)—Francis Chantrey, Charles Eastlake (a pupil), and William Brockedon—whose 1826 portrait drawing (NPG) suggests a more brittle personality. At least from 1828 to 1833 Prout regularly attended the Artists' Conversazione, an evening social gathering in London to which young artists brought recent work. There he met friends such as Clarkson Stanfield, David Roberts, Cotman (who exhibited some of Prout's watercolours at the Norwich Society of Artists in 1831), David Cox, and T. S. Boys. R. P. Bonington and Prout sketched together at St Omer in northern France about 1822, as recorded by an oil painting by Bonington (Nottingham Castle Museum) and two fine drawings of the ruined abbey church by Prout (V&A). Prout's connections with the Paris art world were with the dealers John Arrowsmith, Claude Schroth, and Baron Taylor, through whom he showed watercolours of Augsburg, Cologne, and Utrecht at the Salon of 1824. He also contributed some lithograph views to the third volume (1825) of Nodier and Taylor's *Voyages pittoresques et romantiques dans l'ancienne France*.

Among Prout's London friends were art collectors such as John Allnutt and Francis Broderip and aristocratic patrons such as the dukes of Bedford and Newcastle and the marquess of Stafford, to whose families he gave drawing lessons at a guinea a time. From 1809 to 1821 Prout also taught at Dr Glennie's school, Dulwich Grove; two of his pupils, the Revd J. D. Glennie and W. H. Harriott, later became amateur artists and travel writers. J. D. Harding, the only artist with whom Prout had a serious professional disagreement, is said to have been a private pupil about 1811.

Prout and the print trade For most of his career a significant proportion of Prout's income came from the print trade; among his publisher friends were Rudolph Ackermann—whose son Richard travelled with him in Germany in 1821—George Cooke, E. W. Cooke, and Charles Turner. Prout's account book for 1811–16 (North Devon Athenaeum, Barnstaple) lists more than 1330 watercolours and sepia wash drawings bought for a total of £800 by Thomas Palser (his first important client after John Britton) and Rudolph Ackermann. Prout was a prominent author of 'teach yourself' watercolour painting books. *Rudiments of Landscape in Progressive Studies* (1813) demonstrated how to draw and to add sepia wash, lessons illustrated through soft-ground etching and aquatint; the colour for the final lessons in *A Series of Easy Lessons in Landscape Drawing* (1820) was added by hand. Later art manuals such as *Hints on Light and Shadow, Composition etc.* (1836) and *Prout's Microcosm: the Artist's Sketchbook* (1841) were illustrated in the new technique of lithography, of which Prout was a pioneer. His first lithograph was published by Ackermann in 1817, and he contributed to Alois Senefelder's *A Complete Course of Lithography* in 1819. He used this technique for a volume of sixteen *Marine Sketches* (1820) and for the first of his next and celebrated speciality, the old towns of Europe, *Picturesque Buildings in Normandy* (1821), printed by Charles Hullmandel. He made his first foreign tour, to Normandy, in 1819, following in the footsteps of Edridge and Cotman and, by a small margin, was the first to publish his Normandy views in print form and the first to make a substantial show of them, exhibiting ten such subjects at the Society of Painters in Water Colours in 1821. In the same fashion Prout can be said to have explored the old towns of France (Loire), the Netherlands, Belgium, Germany (Rhineland, Saxony, Bavaria, Bohemia), and Italy, all of which he toured between 1819 and 1829. From these visits came often repeated views of Rouen, Tours, Ghent, Strasbourg, Cologne, Nuremberg, Dresden, and Verona, to name but a few.

Prout's finest work in lithograph, *Illustrations of the Rhine* (1822–6), displaying wide and spacious river landscapes, was untypical and was followed by more restricted and characteristic urban 'close-ups' in his nevertheless splendid *Facsimiles of Sketches Made in Flanders and Germany* (fifty plates, 1833), executed in tinted (two-toned) lithograph. This ambitious book was published independently by subscription and from it Prout made some £2000 over three years. *Facsimiles of Sketches Made in France, Switzerland and Italy* (twenty-six tinted lithographs) was published by Hodson and Graves in 1839 in the usual way.

Among Prout's most impressive early landscapes of panoramic coastal and cottage scenes were the *Picturesque Delineations in the Counties of Devon and Cornwall*, published by Palser in 1812. The breadth and freedom of these etchings was matched only by the *Illustrations of the Rhine*. Both are a far cry from the small-scale copper- or steel-engravings after Prout that appeared in Britton's antiquarian publications such as the *Beauties of England and Wales* (1803–15) or later in the new, popular travel books and annuals. The *Landscape Annual*, for which Prout provided all the illustrations in 1830 and 1831 following a tour to the Alps and Italy in 1824, was printed in large numbers and reached a very wide audience.

Prout and Ruskin The sight of *Flanders and Germany* prompted John Ruskin's father to make a tour of the Rhine in 1833 and to buy a watercolour of Lisieux, Normandy, in 1834. Ruskin's critical championing of Prout began in the 1846 edition of *Modern Painters*, where he wrote: 'There is *no* stone drawing, *no* vitality of architecture like Prout's' (*Works of John Ruskin*, 3.217). Ruskin wrote an appreciation of Prout for the *Art Journal* in 1849 and further praised the artist in *The Stones of Venice* in 1851–3, in which he coined the term 'Proutism'. In 1879 he arranged an exhibition of Prout's drawings, alongside those of their mutual friend W. H. Hunt, 'to illustrate the outgoing course of an old-fashioned Continental tour, beginning at Calais, and ending at Rome' (*Notes by Mr. Ruskin*, 39). These *Notes* contain Ruskin's most detailed analysis of Prout as a draughtsman, and the autotype illustrations to the catalogue, mostly of drawings made on site on tour, demonstrate not only his broken line but also a vigorous use of the lead pencil, with tone added with the finger or stump (an implement for spreading pencil or chalk) and touches of white highlights, both emphasizing lights and shadows, a subject much dwelt on in his drawing manuals.

Ruskin was less admiring of Prout's watercolours, which he criticized for occasional patches of strong or hot colour, probably executed with non-transparent gouache or bodycolour, creating an imbalance often exaggerated by the fading of the more transparent pigments. Prout never took on the more fluid and highly charged style developed by Cotman and the younger generation of Harding, Boys, and William Callow, and his use of warmer colouring was never fully absorbed into his otherwise picturesque manner. His general method, unchanged from his early maturity, was to establish a warm, brown tone in the foreground set off against the blue and white of naturalistic skies. Prout's characteristic drawing with the reed pen, which he used to emphasize structure in finished watercolours, also remained as a survival of the antiquarian picturesque and was regarded by some critics, other than Ruskin, as mannered.

Later career Prout's contemporary reputation was at its height by 1830. His first major notice, in the *Magazine of the Fine Arts* in 1821, featured a seascape (25½ in. x 38½ in.), *A Man-of-War Ashore*, similar perhaps to a smaller watercolour now in the Whitworth Art Gallery, Manchester. This was the first major subject in watercolour that Prout developed after his cottage scenes. Large trading ships or naval relics in harbour or on the beach also go back to his west country origins. For his most characteristic subject, the old towns and streets of Europe, Prout broke new and foreign ground which first gained critical notice in 1824:

> There are some views of towns, and some river scenes, of large dimensions, by Mr Prout, which, for pictorial character, originality of effect, depth of tone, and general energy of style, excel all his former works, and may be regarded as wonders in water-colours.   (E. Hardcastle [W. H. Pyne], *Somerset House Gazette*, 2, 1824, 477–8)

Prout was appointed 'Painter in Water-Colours in Ordinary to His Majesty' in 1829, an honour renewed by William IV and Queen Victoria. In 1830 he became a fellow of the Society of Antiquaries. He was then among the top half-dozen watercolour painters exhibiting in London, and known to a wider public as an illustrator of drawing manuals and travel books.

After 1830 ill health prevented Prout from making more than the occasional foreign or home tour, and his subject matter therefore became highly repetitive. *Porch of Ratisbon Cathedral*, for example, was exhibited at the Society of Painters in Water Colours in 1824, 1826, 1828, 1844, and 1849, and perhaps more often, since a fine version of the same view (V&A) was listed in 1832 as *At Ratisbonne*. Sometimes a watercolour is based so loosely upon the original site-drawing as to be a capriccio or imaginary landscape and can be regarded as a response to Prout's inability to add to his stock. Friends and rivals such as Roberts out-travelled him, visiting destinations such as Spain and the Holy Land, and the novelty of Prout's subject matter faded. He lost the commission in 1832 for a third Italian volume of the *Landscape Annual* to Harding.

The focus of Prout's professional activity from 1815 to 1851 was the annual exhibition of the Society of Painters in Water Colours. Prices for his leading exhibits there rose from £42 for *Malines, Flanders* and *Louvain* in 1823 to £52. 10s. for *Indiaman Dismasted* and *Munich* in 1824, to a maximum £63 for *Ponte di Rialto, Venice* in 1827. Half of Prout's most expensive exhibits from the 1820s to the 1840s featured Venice. However, his income fell from a high point in 1833–4 as he became more dependent on dealers and publishers, and by the end of his career he was selling much of his work to dealers outside London, such as John Hewett in Leamington and J. C. Grundy in Manchester.

Death and posthumous reputation Prout died at his home in Camberwell, London, on 10 February 1852 from an apoplectic fit, after a birthday party given for John Ruskin by his parents, neighbours in Denmark Hill. He was buried in Norwood cemetery. His widow and family moved to Ilfracombe, Devon. Later that year a sale of his drawings at Sotheby and Wilkinson raised £1788. The contents of his studio and drawings that failed to sell later, in 1880 at Christies, were given after the death of Prout's only son and last surviving child to the North Devon Athenaeum, Barnstaple. Samuel Gillespie Prout (1822–1911) painted in his father's manner but by the 1870s was occupied primarily as a popular religious writer and philanthropist at home and abroad. John Skinner *Prout (1806–1876), Samuel's nephew, a professional watercolour painter, like many other amateur and professional artists of the time, was also influenced by his uncle's style.

Ruskin's critical support raised Prout's posthumous reputation to a peak by the 1880s, and it is symptomatic that twenty-one of Prout's watercolours were included in the Manchester Royal Jubilee Exhibition of 1887. Thereafter Prout's reputation as a watercolour painter declined, and it reached a low point in the mid-twentieth century. A partial recovery, based upon greater recognition of his importance in introducing the subject of the European picturesque, took place in the last quarter of that century. The qualities of Prout's best work in watercolour remain obscured by his numerous repetitions of subject and by the large body of work by imitators or contemporaries influenced by his style. He has not yet been recognized as the principal English promoter of lithography as a reproductive method for landscapes in the 1820s, although notice has increasingly been given to his etchings, lithographs, and drawings. His watercolours are well represented in the Victoria and Albert Museum, London, the City Museum and Art Gallery, Birmingham, and the City Art Gallery and Whitworth Art Gallery, Manchester. Sketchbooks by Prout are in the National Maritime Museum and the Victoria and Albert Museum, London, the North Devon Athenaeum, Barnstaple, and the Cleveland Museum of Art, Ohio.   RICHARD LOCKETT

Sources R. Lockett, *Samuel Prout, 1783–1852* (1985) · M. Hardie, *Watercolour painting in Britain*, 2–3 (1967–8) · J. Britton, 'The late Samuel Prout', *The Builder*, 10 (1852), 339–40 · J. Ruskin, 'Samuel Prout', *Art Journal*, 11 (1849), 76–7 · *Notes by Mr. Ruskin on Samuel Prout and William Hunt*, 5th edn (1880) [exhibition catalogue, Fine Art Society, London] · *The works of John Ruskin*, ed. E. T. Cooke and A. Wedderburn, 39 vols. (1903–12) · J. L. Roget, *A history of the 'Old Water-Colour' Society*, 2 vols. (1891) · C. E. Hughes, 'Samuel Prout (1783–1851)', *Old Water-Colour Society's Club*, 6 (1928–9), 1–22 · *Catalogue of the very beautiful works of the Late Samuel Prout, Esq., F.S.A.* (1852) [sale catalogue, Sotheby and Wilkinson, London, 19–22 May 1852] · *The work of Samuel Prout: 1783–1852* (1951) [exhibition catalogue, Plymouth City Museum and Art Gallery, 1951] · J. Hine, 'Samuel Prout, artist', *Transactions of the Plymouth Institution*, 7 (1878–81), 261–92 · E. G. Halton, 'Sketches by Samuel Prout in France, Belgium, Germany, Italy and Switzerland', *The Studio* (1915) · J. R. Abbey, *Travel in aquatint and lithography*, 1 (1956); repr. (1972) · J. R. Abbey, *Life in England in aquatint and lithography* (1953); repr. (1972) · B. S. Long, 'The Salon of 1824', *The Connoisseur*, 68 (1924), 66–76

Archives BL, corresp., Add. MS 42523 · BL, letters to J. H. Maw, Add. MS 45883 · FM Cam., letters · North Devon Athenaeum, Barnstaple, account books · Plymouth City Museum and Art Gallery, transcripts of letters and diary · Plymouth City Museum and Art Gallery, corresp. and papers | Cleveland Museum of Art, Ohio, sketchbooks • NMM, sketchbooks • North Devon Athenaeum, Barnstaple, sketchbooks • Royal Watercolour Society, London, J. J. J. Jenkins papers, letters, MSS 167/175–1949 • V&A, sketchbooks

Likenesses J. Jackson, oils, 1823, NPG • W. Brockedon, chalk drawing, 1826, NPG • W. Brockedon, pencil and chalk drawing, 1826, NPG • S. M. Smith, chalk drawing, 1828, North Devon Athenaeum, Barnstaple • watercolour drawing, 1830?–1839, Plymouth City Museum and Art Gallery; repro. in *Painters of Plymouth* (1971), 57 • watercolour drawing, 1830?–1839, repro. in S. Baring-Gould, *Devonshire characters and strange events* (1926), 564; priv. coll. • C. Turner, chalk drawing, c.1836, NPG • photograph, c.1840, North Devon Athenaeum, Barnstaple • woodcut, 1849 (after W. C. Ross), BM, NPG • W. H. Hunt, chalk drawing, 1879, repro. in *Notes by Mr. Ruskin*, no. 177 • W. Boxall, wood-engraving (after chalk drawing), repro. in *Art Journal*, 129 (1849), 76 • W. Hunt, watercolour drawing, Plymouth City Museum and Art Gallery • S. Prout, self-portrait, pencil drawing, Scot. NPG • miniature, Royal Collection • oils, Plymouth City Museum and Art Gallery

Wealth at death see will, proved 29 April 1852, and made 3 Aug 1811

Prout, William (1785–1850), physician and chemist, was born on 15 January 1785 at Horton, Gloucestershire, the youngest son of John Prout (1745–1820), a farmer and copyholder of Horton, and Hannah Limbrick (*b*. 1756). Although he learned to read and write at a dame-school at Wickwar, attended a charity school at Badminton, and probably had access to the fine library formerly belonging to the Paton family at Horton Manor, his early teenage years appear to have been occupied in farming. In 1802, however, he joined the Sherston Academy managed by the Revd John Turner, vicar of Horton, in order to master Latin and Greek. In 1805 he advertised locally for advice on the further educational prospects for a man of twenty. When a helpful reply came from the Revd Thomas Jones (1758–1812), Prout joined Jones's classical seminary at Redland, Bristol, where, between 1805 and 1807, he taught pupils in exchange for private tuition. A pupil's inquiry concerning Humphry Davy's electrochemical work stimulated Prout's interest in chemistry. In 1808, on Jones's recommendation, he began medical studies at the University of Edinburgh, boarding with Jones's friend, Dr Alexander Adam, rector of Edinburgh high school, whose daughter he was to marry; Prout graduated MD on 24 June 1811 with a thesis on intermittent fevers.

After failing to establish a medical practice in the west country, Prout moved to London in 1812, walking the wards of St Thomas's and Guy's hospitals before being admitted LRCP on 22 December 1812. (Fellowship of the Royal College of Physicians came on 28 June 1829.) Ambitious to gain the summit of the medical profession, Prout set up practice in Arundel Street, near the Strand, where he delivered a course of advertised lectures on animal chemistry between February and April 1814. These lectures, which contained speculations on the nature of matter and metabolism, as well as a remarkable observation on the distinction between taste and flavour, ensured his election to the Medical and Chirurgical Society on 10 May 1814 and brought him the friendship of Astley Cooper, John Elliotson, and Alexander Marcet. The latter reported favourably on Prout's researches to the great Swedish chemist Jöns Berzelius, and ensured Prout's election as FRS in March 1819.

On 22 September 1814 Prout married Agnes Adam (1793–1863); their honeymoon was spent in Paris. There were six children: John William (1817–81), a lawyer; Alexander Adam (1818–54), an army doctor; Walter Robert (1820–57), a soldier; Thomas Jones (named after his father's former teacher, 1823–1909), who took holy orders and taught classics at Christ Church, Oxford; and two daughters, Elizabeth (1825–1918) and Agnes (1826–78). From 1815 to 1821 Prout practised as a specialist in stomach and urinary diseases from his home at Southampton Street, Bloomsbury, and from 1821 until his death from 40 Sackville Street, Piccadilly. The fruits of his clinical studies of private patients were first published in *An inquiry into the nature and treatment of gravel, calculus and other affections of the urinary organs* (1821; 2nd edn, 1825). This was revised and enlarged as *On the Nature and Treatment of Stomach and Urinary Diseases* (1840; 5th edn, 1848).

In 1815 and 1816, in two anonymous articles on the 'relation between the specific gravities of bodies in their gaseous state and the weights of their atoms', Prout suggested that there were grounds for believing that the atomic weights of all the elements were whole number multiples of the atomic weight of hydrogen; and he tentatively identified hydrogen with the *prōtē hylē*, or basic matter, of the ancient Greeks. Prout was influenced towards these views both by Humphry Davy's speculations that the so-called elements were probably undecompounded bodies, and by his reading while a student in Edinburgh of the *Philosophical Arrangements* (1775), a commentary on Aristotle by James Harris. 'Prout's hypothesis', as it was labelled by Berzelius, was supported by Thomas Thomson and others, but dismissed on experimental grounds by Berzelius, and later J. B. Stas. In 1831 Prout suggested privately that hydrogen itself might be formed from 'some body lower in the scale' (Daubeny, *Atomic Theory*, 129). The hypothesis remained an experimental and theoretical stimulus to chemists and physicists throughout the century, and, following the concept of isotopes, it received a justification from Francis Aston in 1920.

Prout was a consummate analytical chemist. He published elaborate self-experiments on carbon dioxide output in 1813–14 and a pioneering study of the chemical changes in an incubating egg (1822). He spent years attempting to perfect an accurate method of analysing organic compounds. Although he developed a technique in 1827, it was costly and difficult, and could not compare with the cheap and easy method introduced by Liebig in 1830. Between 1815 and 1827, however, he published a series of important papers on urine and digestion that began to open up questions about metabolism. In 1824 he showed brilliantly, but controversially, that the gastric juices of animals contain hydrochloric acid. The point demonstrated, contemporaries were quick to adopt his 1827 classification of the components of food into water, saccharinous (carbohydrates), oleaginous (fats), and nitrogenous (proteins), a balanced diet containing all of these foodstuffs. Prout, who was not a reductionist, was firmly convinced that the four aliments (food groups) were transformed into blood and tissues ('primary assimilation') by a vital principle that also organized and controlled the destruction and removal of unwanted parts from the system ('secondary assimilation'). Full details of his highly speculative metabolic theory were expounded in *Chemistry, Meteorology, and the Function of Digestion* (1834), the most curious of the eight Bridgewater Treatises intended to demonstrate the existence of God from design that had been sponsored by the will of the earl of Bridgewater in 1829. The meteorological section is notable for his coinage of the word 'convection' to describe one method of heat dissemination.

Although he was a brilliant experimentalist and stimulating theoretician, Prout's later life was marred by deafness that led him to avoid contact with the scientific and medical communities. Significantly he did not join the Chemical Society on its foundation in 1841. He died at his home in Sackville Street, Piccadilly, London, on 9 April 1850 from gangrene of the lung following a burst abscess. He was buried in Kensal Green cemetery. A simple memorial tablet was laid in Horton church.

W. H. BROCK

Sources W. H. Brock, *From protyle to proton: William Prout and the nature of matter, 1785–1985* (1985) • *Medical Times*, 1 (1850), 15–17 • *Edinburgh Medical and Surgical Journal*, 76 (1851), 126–83 • C. Daubeny, *Edinburgh New Philosophical Journal*, 53 (1852), 98–102 • Munk, *Roll* • C. Daubeny, *An introduction to the atomic theory* (1831) • *Gloucestershire Notes and Queries*, 3 (1887), 4
Archives NRA Scotland, priv. coll., corresp., family papers, and notes • RS, corresp. and papers • Wellcome L., notebooks and papers
Likenesses J. Hayes, oils, *c*.1830–1839; in family possession, 1896; photographic copies, *c*.1904, Royal Society of Chemistry, London • H. M. Paget, oils (after type by J. Hayes, *c*.1835–1840), RCP Lond.; version, U. Edin. • H. W. Phillips, oils (after miniature, *c*.1855), RCP Lond.

Provost, John (*fl.* 1595–1604). *See under* American Indians in England (*act. c*.1500–1609).

Prowse, William (1751/2–1826), naval officer, was born in Stonehouse, Devon, and was probably raised as a child on a trading vessel. From November 1771 to February 1776 he was an able seaman in the *Dublin*, guardship in Hamoaze; and from November 1776 to August 1778 he was in the *Albion*, one of the ships which sailed for North America in June 1778, under the command of Vice-Admiral John Byron. Early in 1778 Captain George Bowyer was appointed to the *Albion*, and on 31 August he rated Prowse a midshipman, in which capacity, or as master's mate, he was present at the actions off Grenada on 6 July 1779, and near Martinique in April and May 1781. On 17 January 1782 he passed his examination; afterwards he served in the *Atlas* and *Cyclops*, and on 6 December 1782 he was promoted lieutenant.

Prowse continued in the *Cyclops* on the coast of North America until March 1784, after which, for several years, his service was intermittent, much of the time being probably spent in command of merchant ships. During the armament of 1787 he served for a couple of months in the

Bellona with George Bowyer, and in 1790 he was in the *Barfleur* and *Stately* with Captain Robert Calder. From August 1791 to January 1793 he was in the *Duke*, carrying the flag of Lord Hood at Portsmouth; in March 1793 he joined the *Prince* with Bowyer, now a vice-admiral, and Captain Cuthbert Collingwood, whom in December he followed to the *Barfleur*. With them Prowse took part in the action of 1 June 1794. From July 1794 to October 1795 he was with Calder in the *Theseus*, and later he went to the Mediterranean with him in the *Lively*. From her he joined the *Victory*, carrying the flag of Sir John Jervis. On 20 October 1796 Prowse was promoted to the command of the *Raven*, in which he was present in the action off Cape St Vincent on 14 February 1797. On 6 March he was promoted by Jervis to the command of the *Salvador del Mundo*, one of the prizes, which he paid off in the following November.

From August 1800 to April 1802 Prowse was flag-captain to Calder in the *Prince of Wales*, and in August 1802 he commissioned the frigate *Sirius*. For the next three years he was attached to the fleet off Brest and in the Bay of Biscay, and especially during 1804 and 1805 with Calder off Rochefort and Ferrol. After involvement in the action off Cape Finisterre on 22 July 1805, the *Sirius*, with Calder, joined the fleet off Cadiz, and, remaining there on Calder's return to England, was present at the battle of Trafalgar. The *Sirius* continued in the Mediterranean under Collingwood's command, and on 17 April 1806 attacked a flotilla of French armed vessels near Civita Vecchia, capturing the corvette *Bergère*. For his conduct on this occasion the patriotic fund voted Prowse a sword of the value of £100. The *Sirius* was paid off in May 1808, and from March 1810 to December 1813 Prowse commanded the *Theseus* in the North Sea; in 1813 he brought the East India Company's fleet home from St Helena, for which he received a piece of plate from the commanders. He had no further service afloat, but was nominated a CB on 4 June 1815, made colonel of marines on 12 August 1819, and promoted rear-admiral on 19 July 1821; he died on 23 March 1826, aged seventy-four, at his home, 3 Tonbridge Place, New Road, London.

Prowse was considered a worthy man, and his career offers a good example of how it was possible for someone of humble origins to rise to flag-rank through consistent, if not remarkable, service. He was apparently unmarried, and was able to leave his five sisters £2000 each.

J. K. LAUGHTON, rev. A. W. H. PEARSALL

Sources J. Leyland, ed., *Dispatches and letters relating to the blockade of Brest, 1803–1805*, 2 vols., Navy RS, 14, 21 (1899–1902) • *Recollections of James Anthony Gardner*, ed. R. V. Hamilton and J. K. Laughton, Navy RS, 31 (1906) • T. S. Jackson, ed., *Logs of the great sea fights, 1794–1805*, 2 vols., Navy RS, 16, 18 (1899–1900), vol. 1, p. 199; vol. 2, p. 144 • *Private papers of George, second Earl Spencer*, ed. J. S. Corbett and H. W. Richmond, 2, Navy RS, 48 (1924), 91 • J. Marshall, *Royal naval biography*, 4/2 (1835), 182 • *GM*, 1st ser., 96/1 (1826), 380 • PRO, ADM 1/2344, 36/7594, 107/8, p.196
Archives PRO
Wealth at death over £10,000; bequeathed £2000 to each of five sisters

Prowse, William Jeffery (1836–1870), humorist, was born at Torquay, Devon, on 6 May 1836, the son of Isaac Prowse

(d. 1844) and his wife, Marianne Jeffery, who had known Keats and who had a volume of her poems published. Upon the death of his father in 1844, he was taken charge of by an uncle, John Sparke Prowse, a notary public and shipbroker, of Greenwich. At Greenwich he attended the school of Nicholas Wanostrocht, a well-known writer on cricket under the pseudonym of Nicholas Felix, who inspired him with his own enthusiasm for the game.

Prowse was from youth deeply interested in all forms of sport and was devoted to the sea. Before he was twenty he developed a talent for humorous verse, and soon drifted into journalism. About 1856 he obtained a position on the *Aylesbury News*, and in subsequent years he contributed tales, descriptive articles, and verses to *Chambers's Journal*, the *Lady's Companion*, the *National Magazine*, and *The Porcupine*. In 1861 he was appointed a leader writer on the *Daily Telegraph*, writing mainly on sporting topics. In 1865 his friend, Tom Hood the younger, became editor of *Fun*. Prowse contributed each week, under the signature of 'Nicholas', a rambling article on horse-racing, into which he introduced much good-humoured satire on other subjects.

In 1865 Prowse's health began to fail. He returned to Torquay, and passed the winters of 1867, 1868, and 1869 at Cimiez, near Nice. He died of tuberculosis at Cimiez on Easter Sunday 17 April 1870 and was buried in the protestant cemetery there. Prowse was known for his witty verse, the most famous example of which is his satire on Coleridge's 'The Rime of the Ancient Mariner'. His 'The City of Prague' has been described as 'a clever defense of Bohemianism' (Kunitz and Haycraft, 509), and his 'My Lost Old Age, by a Young Invalid', written in 1865, has been anthologized in collections of Victorian verse (Burnham, 10). SIDNEY LEE, *rev.* MEGAN A. STEPHAN

Sources Nicholas [W. J. Prowse], 'Memoir', *Nicholas's notes and sporting prophecies, with some miscellaneous poems, serious and humorous*, ed. T. Hood [1870] [with brief biographical notice by T. Hood] · S. J. Kunitz and H. Haycraft, eds., *British authors of the nineteenth century* (1936), 509 · Lord Burnham [E. F. L. Burnham], *Peterborough Court: the story of the Daily Telegraph* (1955), 9–10 · C. R. Cheney, *Handbook of dates for students of English history* (1945)
Likenesses T. Scott, drawing, *c*.1870 (after photograph by C. Watkins), repro. in Nicholas, 'Memoir', frontispiece · Dalziel, woodcut, BM

Prudde, John (*d.* 1460/61), glass painter, was probably the foremost practitioner of his craft in Henry VI's reign. Although his work is well documented, only one extant monument can be attributed to him for certain. He first occurs in 1426/7, when he was working at Westminster Abbey. He remained a resident of Westminster until his death in 1460 or 1461; he was termed esquire and enjoyed high standing in his community, where he served as chief constable. In 1440 he was appointed king's glazier, on the usual terms of 12*d.* per day, plus a gown at Christmas and the occupancy of the glazing shed in Westminster Palace. For the extensive new works undertaken in the 1440s by Henry VI at Shene Palace and Eton College, Prudde received additional payments. His office gave him access

to patrons in Lancastrian ruling circles. In 1441 his servants were working at Archbishop Henry Chichele's foundation of All Souls College, Oxford, and two years later they occur at Fromond's chantry in Winchester College.

Prudde's best documented and principal masterpiece is the glazing of the mausoleum of Richard Beauchamp, earl of Warwick at St Mary's Church, Warwick. The glazing contract of 1447 with the earl's executors, known from a seventeenth-century transcript, is revealing about the relationship between late medieval craftsmen and patrons and the processes of production. The executors devised the iconographical scheme, which was supplied as a design to Prudde, who was to employ another painter to make the cartoons. The executors were concerned with quality of craftsmanship and splendour; Prudde was to undertake the glazing and use the richest and best-quality coloured glasses available. The surviving glazing of the Beauchamp Chapel explains the cost of 2*s.* per square foot, a rate for late medieval glazing only exceeded in 1401 at Eltham Palace. The lavish and varied colours and technical virtuosity exhibited by the Marian imagery, by the saints and prophets, and by the tracery angels, make a major contribution to the chapel's reliquary-like impression, and seem to have influenced subsequent glass painting in the midlands. The heraldic glass at Ockwells Manor, Berkshire, also makes extensive use of 'jewels' and is probably to be attributed to Prudde. It provides an indication of the lost works he executed at Eton and in the royal palaces, which from the costs must have been less sumptuous.

After Prudde's death, which took place in 1460 or 1461, his widow, Elizabeth, gave two altar-cloths to St Margaret's Church, Westminster, in her husband's memory, before taking the veil at Haliwell nunnery, Shoreditch. RICHARD MARKS

Sources R. Marks, *Stained glass in England during the middle ages* (1993), 44–51, 189–90, 194 · G. M. White, 'The iconography of the stained glass of the Beauchamp Chapel, St Mary's, Warwick', *Journal of Stained Glass*, 19/2 (1991–3), 133–57 · H. C. [H. Chitty], 'John Prudde, king's glazier', *N&Q*, 12th ser., 3 (1917), 419–21 · F. E. Hutchinson, *Medieval glass at All Souls College* (1949) · G. Rosser, *Medieval Westminster, 1200–1540* (1989), 153, 395

Prujean, Sir Francis (*bap.* 1597, *d.* 1666), physician, was the eldest of at least four children of the Revd Francis Prujean (*d.* 1624), curate of Widford by Chelmsford, Essex, in 1596, and rector of Boothby, Lincolnshire, from 1596 to 1622, and his first wife. The younger Prujean was baptized at Bury St Edmunds, Suffolk, on 21 February 1597, and educated at home by his father. He matriculated in 1610 as a sizar at Gonville and Caius College, Cambridge, his father's former college. The family seems to have been under some financial constraints, as Prujean's father took out three episcopal licences in 1605: to teach as a schoolmaster; to preach; and to practise medicine. He was, in addition, a writing clerk and notary. Some of the financial burden was eased in 1613, when Francis gained a scholarship at Caius. Prujean gained his BA in 1614 and MA in 1617. By 22 December 1621 he was a licentiate of the College of Physicians, but his movements between 1617 and

1621 are unclear. He met and married Margaret Legatt (d. 1661), daughter of Thomas Legatt of Hornchurch, Essex, probably towards the end of this period; they had a son, Thomas (c.1622–1662). Prujean may possibly have still been at Cambridge at the time of his marriage, as he received a grace for an MD in 1621, though he did not receive the degree until 1625. The puritan John Gee suggested in 1624 that popish sympathies caused this delay.

Prujean was clearly in London, practising medicine, from 1621 to 1626, when he was elected to a fellowship in the College of Physicians. Soon after his election he returned to Lincolnshire, where he practised until 1638, gaining a great reputation among his patients.

In 1639 Prujean returned to London, took up residence in the parish of St Martin Ludgate and was elected censor at the College of Physicians. He was re-elected in 1642 and held the office until 1647, also serving as college registrar from 1641 to 1647. A stalwart of the college, Prujean was its president from 1650 to 1653. In 1654 the college elected William Harvey president, but he declined and Prujean was re-elected on Harvey's recommendation. It was through Prujean in 1651 that Harvey first conveyed a proposal to build a library for the college; it was finally completed and opened on 2 February 1654, the last year of Prujean's presidency. Prujean continued to serve the college as its treasurer from 1655 to 1663, and as consiliarius from 1656 to his death in 1666. He was knighted by Charles II on 1 April 1661 and was credited with curing his queen of typhus in 1663.

Prujean was a man of many talents and interests. John Evelyn described a visit to Prujean's London home on 9 August 1661:

> I went to that famous Physitian Sir Fr: Prujean who showed me his Laboratorie, his other Workhouse for turning and other Mechanics, also many excellent Pictures, especially the Magdalen of Carrachio: some incomparable paisages don in distemper: He plaied to me likewise on the Polyphone, an instrument having something of the Harp, Lute, Theorb & c: it was a sweete Instrument, by none known in England, or described by any Author, nor used but by this skillful & learned Doctor. (Evelyn, 294)

It was perhaps Prujean's talent, tastes, and keen appreciation of art and beauty that led to recurring suspicions that he was a papist. In 1643 his house in London was ransacked, with a loss of goods valued at £500. In 1658 he was brought before a London quarter-sessions court, charged that he was 'a Papist or popishly affected', a charge he repeatedly denied.

Prujean married for a second time on 13 February 1664. His second wife, also named Margaret, was the widow of Sir Thomas Fleming and the wealthy daughter of Edward, Lord Gorges. Prujean died in London on 23 June 1666 and was buried with his first wife and son at Hornchurch, Essex. Samuel Pepys noted his death in his diary:

> Sir Francis Prujean is dead, after being married to a widow about a year or thereabouts. He died very rich, and had, for the last yeare lived very handsomely, his lady bringing him to it. He was no great painstaker in person, yet died very rich; and, as Dr. Clerke says, was of very great judgment, but hath writ nothing to leave his name to posterity. (Diary, 318–19)

In accordance with Prujean's wishes, Baldwin Hamey composed an epitaph for Prujean, his wife, and son. Prujean disbursed a great deal of money in his will and named his grandson, Robert, as his principal heir (PRO, PROB 11/321/122). Prujean's home was near the Old Bailey, and the place where he lived was named after him Prujean Square.   WILLIAM BIRKEN

Sources J. J. Keevil, *The stranger's son* (1953), 160 • *The diary of Samuel Pepys*, ed. H. B. Wheatley and others, 10 vols. (1893–9), vol. 5, pp. 318–19; repr. (1924) • Evelyn, *Diary*, 3.294 • Venn, *Alum. Cant.* • Munk, *Roll* • annals, RCP Lond. • B. Hamey, 'Bustorum aliquot reliquiae …', RCP Lond. • *N&Q*, 8th ser., 5 (1894), 28, 71, 152 • LCC wills, Lincs. Arch., 1624/110 • will, PRO, PROB 11/321, sig. 122 • *Lincolnshire Notes and Queries*, 13 (1914–15) • *Lincolnshire Notes and Queries*, 16 (1920–21), 247 • *Lincolnshire wills: second series, AD 1600–1617*, ed. A. R. Maddison (1891) • L. Hutchinson, *Memoirs of the life of Colonel Hutchinson*, ed. J. Sutherland (1973) • G. Holles, *Memorials of the Holles family, 1493–1656*, ed. A. C. Wood, CS, 3rd ser., 55 (1937) • H. Bowler, ed., *London sessions records, 1605–1685*, Catholic RS, 34 (1934) • H. Foley, ed., *Records of the English province of the Society of Jesus*, 7/2 (1883)

Likenesses attrib. R. Streater, oils, 1662?, RCP Lond. • Beynon & Co., coloured lithograph, Wellcome L.; repro. in *Buildings and famous alumni of St Thomas's Hospital*

Prujean, John (c.1630–1706), maker of mathematical instruments, was first apprenticed for eight years to Thomas Alcock in the Clockmakers' Company on 6 May 1646, then turned over to Elias Allen, the foremost London instrument maker of the period. There is no record that Prujean took his freedom, but on 11 March 1664 he matriculated as a *privilegiatus* (a non-academic member of the University of Oxford), thus acquiring the right to trade in the city as a mathematical instrument maker. He remained there for the rest of his life, living in New College Lane in the parish of St Peter-in-the-East, an area which was particularly favoured by craftsmen and tradesmen with strong university connections. From there he worked both for the university, its colleges and buildings, and for the mathematics tutors in the colleges. Publications by Oxford mathematicians such as Richard Holland and Thomas Edwards carried advertisements for Prujean, and the small number of surviving instruments by him include several made of printed paper pasted on wood, suggesting that they were designed to appeal to the undergraduate and 'poor scholar' market.

In 1685 Prujean prepared a plan of the duke of Monmouth's march at Sedgemoor which he presented to Arthur Charlett. In 1688 he was paid 8s. for his part in the restoration of the dial of the church of St Mary the Virgin, and in 1689, with Henry Wildgoose, he repaired 'gratis' the dial of his parish church. To accompany the instruments he sold, Prujean printed a number of instruction sheets, of which the few surviving examples have been listed by Bryden (266), and in 1701 he issued a *Catalogue* of his production. This very short, slightly old-fashioned list is historically important as the earliest example of such a record known from outside London. Despite this gently innovative activity, the instruments Prujean offered related strictly to the traditional mathematical arts and he does not seem to have prospered from them. He died in Oxford in 1706, being at that time, according to Hearne

(3.347), 'very poor, wanting bread'. His nameless widow, despite the efforts of Edmond Halley and others, was refused a place in Crosse's Hospital, Ampthill, Bedfordshire. He was buried in Oxford on 10 September 1706.

A. J. TURNER

Sources D. J. Bryden, 'Made in Oxford: John Prujean's 1701 catalogue of mathematical instruments', *Oxoniensia*, 58 (1993), 263–85 · R. W. T. Gunther, *The astrolabes of the world*, 2 vols. (1932); repr. (1976) · C. E. Atkins, ed., *Register of apprentices of the Worshipful Company of Clockmakers of the City of London* (privately printed, London, 1931) · church wardens' accounts, 1688–9, St Mary the Virgin, Oxford · *Remarks and collections of Thomas Hearne*, ed. C. E. Doble and others, 3, OHS, 13 (1889) · parish register (burial), 1706, St Peter-in-the-East, Oxford
Archives MHS Oxf.
Wealth at death poor: *Remarks*, ed. Doble and others, vol. 3, p. 347

Pry, Paul. *See* Heath, William (1794/5–1840).

Pryce, George (1799–1868), historian and librarian, born on 2 October 1799, was largely self-educated. He was at first a schoolmaster, but subsequently became an accountant at Bristol. He devoted his leisure to the study of archaeology and the early history of Bristol. In April 1856 he was appointed city librarian in Bristol. The city library, founded in 1613, was possibly the oldest municipal library in the country, but was run by a private library society, which severely restricted public access. Its premises were taken over and the holdings reformed by the city council. It reopened in 1856 with Pryce as its first librarian. Through his efforts the collection of local literature in the library was assembled: some 4000 volumes were added during his term of office.

Pryce was elected fellow of the Society of Antiquaries on 30 April 1857. He published many papers on archaeology and local history. His chief work, the *Popular History of Bristol* (1861), is, like his earlier *Fact versus Fiction* (1858), very severe on Bristol historians, especially William Barrett, Samuel Seyer, and John Corry; yet it draws heavily on their work, and has not lasted as well as they have. Pryce was described as 'cocksure' (Wells) for his dismissiveness of other historians. His other works include *Notes on the ecclesiastical and monumental architecture and sculpture of the middle ages in Bristol* (1850) and *Memorials of the Canynges' Family* (1854). His unpublished works relating to Bristol history are in the Bristol Municipal Library collection in the central library.

Pryce died of paralysis on 15 March 1868, at the city library, leaving a widow, Elizabeth.

GORDON GOODWIN, *rev.* ELIZABETH BAIGENT

Sources *Daily Bristol Times and Mirror* (18 March 1868) · *Bristol Daily Post* (17 March 1868) · *Bristol Mercury* (21 March 1868) · private information (1896) · H. E. Meller, *Leisure and the changing city, 1870–1914* (1976) · C. R. J. Currie and C. P. Lewis, eds., *English county histories: a guide* (1994) · J. Latimer, *The annals of Bristol in the nineteenth century*, [1] (1887) · C. Wells, 'Written in a library', *c*.1929, Bristol Central Library · *Public libraries in Bristol, 1613–1974*, City and County of Bristol Arts and Leisure Committee (1974) · *CGPLA Eng. & Wales* (1868)
Likenesses portrait, Free Library, Bristol
Wealth at death under £300: probate, 29 April 1868, *CGPLA Eng. & Wales*

Pryce, William (*bap.* 1735, *d.* 1790), surgeon, mineralogist, and antiquary, was born at Redruth, Cornwall, and baptized there on 14 June 1735. He was the only son (there was also a daughter, who died in infancy) of surgeon Samuel Pryce (*d.* 1741) and his wife, Catherine (*d.* 1744), daughter of William Hill and his wife, also Catherine, who was sister of the antiquary William Borlase (1695–1772). Orphaned at an early age, Pryce was cared for by the prominent Falmouth attorney Philip Webber, a kinsman who became a lifelong friend.

In 1751 Pryce was apprenticed to the Redruth surgeon Philip Tingcombe. Following an additional period studying dissection under a Dr Hunter (probably either John or William Hunter of London), Pryce himself set up as a surgeon in Redruth. About this time, he also bought shares in local mines (and managed some small-scale mining operations). On 17 August 1758 he married Catherine Michell (*bap.* 1733, *d.* 1813) in Redruth. The couple had two sons, Samuel Vincent (1761–1817), who became a surgeon and banker, and William, a surgeon, and a daughter, Catherine (1764–1765), who died in infancy.

With commercial interests in local mining, Pryce appreciated the advantage of bringing coal more cheaply to the local tin and copper mines. As a result, he initiated a scheme to build a quay at Portreath in 1763 but failed to meet his part of the costs; his shares were sold in 1767. Some time thereafter Borlase encouraged Pryce to develop his notes on mining into a book. He drew on manuscripts on the history of mining in Cornwall, adding information obtained from his own observations and from local experts, as well as from such diverse characters as Cookworthy (on the divining rod) and Matthew Boulton (on Watt's improvements to the steam engine). Pryce's *Mineralogia Cornubiensis* was published by subscription in 1778.

A freemason, in 1773 Pryce proposed that the Redruth lodge should be known as the Druids Lodge of Love and Liberality. It proved an inappropriate name, as in 1779 relations between the brethren became far from loving and he set up an irregular lodge.

Pryce was awarded the degree of MD by the University of St Andrews in 1781. Two years later, on 26 June 1783, Pryce was elected a fellow of the Society of Antiquaries. The society's vice-president, Barrington Daines, knew that Pryce was the owner of a manuscript on Cornish by Tonkin and that he intended to publish a Cornish grammar and dictionary. *Archaeologia Cornu-Britannica* was finally published in 1790. In it, Pryce collated the manuscripts of Tonkin, Hals, and others and added information gained by interviewing old people who claimed to speak Cornish. Although accused at the time of plagiarism, he referred to himself as editor and fully acknowledged his sources in the work's preface. He died at Redruth in December 1790 and was buried there on the 20th of that month.

ALAN PEARSON

Sources W. Pryce, *The plan of a work, entituled Mineralogia Cornubiensis et leges stannariæ* [1774] · W. Pryce, *Mineralogia Cornubiensis* (1778); repr. (1972) · J. G. Osborn, *History of freemasonry in* west Cornwall (1901) • Medical Register (1779) • Boase & Courtney, Bibl. Corn. • G. C. Boase, Collectanea Cornubiensia: a collection of biographical and topographical notes relating to the county of Cornwall (1890) • R. Polwhele, The history of Cornwall, 7 vols. (1803–8), vol. 5 • W. Pryce, account book, Cornwall RO, TEM/58 • W. Pryce, corresp., Royal Institution of Cornwall, Truro, MEN/82/A–N • W. Pryce, letters to Matthew Boulton, April 1778, etc., Birm. CL, Boulton and Watt collection • W. Pryce, letters to Lt Henderson, March 1777, etc., Birm. CL, Matthew Boulton MSS • Penzance Library, Cornwall, Borlase Collection, vol. 15 • parish register, Redruth, Cornwall [baptism, marriage, burial], 14 June 1735, 17 Aug 1758, 20 Dec 1790 • parish register, Falmouth, Cornwall [burial], 22 Aug 1741, 5 March 1743 • MS index to apprentices of Great Britain, GL

Archives BL, papers relating to Cornish language, Add. MS 43409 • Royal Institution of Cornwall, Truro | Birm. CL, Boulton and Watt collection, letters to Matthew Boulton; letters to Lieutenant Henderson • Cornwall RO, corresp. relating to Portreath quay **Likenesses** J. Basire, line engraving (after Clifford), BM, NPG; repro. in Pryce, Mineralogia Cornubiensis **Wealth at death** medical practice considered successful

Pryde, James Ferrier (1866–1941), artist and designer, was born at 23 London Street, Edinburgh, on 30 March 1866, the only son of six children of David Pryde (1834–1907), headmaster of Edinburgh Ladies' College (1870–91), and his wife, Barbara (b. c.1833/4), daughter of William Lauder and niece of the painters Robert Scott and James Eckford Lauder.

In 1872 the family moved to a Georgian townhouse at 10 Fettes Row in Edinburgh's New Town. Pryde was educated at George Watson's Boys' College and he developed a lifelong interest in the theatre through his parents, who were close friends of the actors Sir Henry Irving and John Lawrence Toole. He was a student of the Royal Scottish Academy life school from 1885 to 1888, and first exhibited at the Royal Scottish Academy in 1884. Pryde's early work consisted mostly of portraits, and he received encouragement from the Glasgow school painters James Guthrie and Edward Arthur Walton. He then studied in Paris for three months at the Académie Julian, under W.-A. Bouguereau. He returned to Edinburgh in 1889, but moved to London in 1890.

Pryde's memories of Edinburgh profoundly influenced his art: the family house with its tall windows, high ceilings, and stone staircase; the slum tenements of the Old Town, with their narrow closes and archways, and washing draped from windows; and the ornate four-poster bed at Holyrood Palace, said to have belonged to Mary, queen of Scots. Pryde was first noticed in London as a pastellist when he exhibited *Little Girl in Black* (*Miss Mutton*) (1890; priv. coll.) at the Grosvenor Gallery. The sitter was the daughter of his landlady at Bushey, Hertfordshire, where he shared lodgings with his sister Mabel. She was studying at Hubert von Herkomer's school, and another student was William Nicholson (1872–1949). In 1893 Nicholson married Mabel Pryde, and the couple moved to an old inn, the Eight Bells, at Denham, Buckinghamshire. During these years James Pryde became a close friend of Nicholson, and he moved in with them.

British poster design underwent significant changes in the 1890s. The old-fashioned bills with dense wording

James Ferrier Pryde (1866–1941), by Sir James Gunn, exh. Royal Glasgow Institute of the Fine Arts 1924

gave way to posters with a greater pictorial input, showing the influence of Toulouse-Lautrec and Japanese prints. In 1894 Pryde and Nicholson prepared several designs for an exhibition at the Westminster aquarium. Using paper cut-outs on rolls of brown paper their designs relied on striking, uncluttered silhouettes. They employed flat colours, strong outlines, and the spare use of lettering to create apparently easy yet memorable designs. They named themselves the Beggarstaff Brothers, and their posters include *Kassama Corn Flour* (1894; Kunstgewerbemuseum, Cologne) and *Rowntree's Elect Cocoa* (1896; V&A). Other designs were never put into production—for example, *Becket* (1894; Ellen Terry Memorial Museum, Tenterden) and *Don Quixote* (1895; V&A), both designed for Henry Irving. The partnership lasted until 1899. Although it was never a financial success it had a profound influence on graphic art world-wide for many decades.

After the breakup of the Beggarstaff partnership Pryde supplemented his earnings with occasional stage appearances. His acting abilities were limited, and his roles were mostly confined to walk-on parts. In 1899 he married Marian Symons (c.1877–1945), a talented singer and pianist. In 1903 they had a daughter, Betty, who was a talented dancer but died of consumption in 1932. Marriage provided an early stimulus to Pryde's work as a painter but was short-lived, and Pryde and his wife separated in 1914.

In the early 1900s Pryde continued to produce graphic work, but he also painted studies of grotesque characters. Culminating in *The Celebrated Criminals* (c.1902; BM) and *Sir Henry Irving as Dubosc in The Lyons Mail* (1906; Scottish

National Gallery of Modern Art, Edinburgh), these have a larger-than-life, theatrical quality and are painted with a vigour reminiscent of Henri Daumier. About this time Pryde began painting imaginative landscapes and architectural subjects. Often melancholic, they show a knowledge of the work of Velázquez as well as memories of the architecture of Edinburgh, for example *The Slum* (1910; Musée National d'Art Moderne, Paris). The purchase of his *Guildhall with Figures* (1905) by J. S. Sargent was a landmark in Pryde's career, and henceforth he exhibited regularly at the International Society, of which he eventually became vice-president, and at the Goupil Gallery. The first painting of his series called The human comedy, *The Doctor* (c.1909; Tate collection), introduces the motif of the four-poster bed. This grows in stature, culminating in the painting *The Death of the Great Bed*, which remained unfinished at Pryde's death (c.1929–41; Royal Pavilion Art Gallery and Museums, Brighton). Here the bed has become a stage set, back-lit, before which the human drama of life takes place. In 1911 Pryde visited Venice and shortly afterwards began *La casa rosa* (1911–12; priv. coll.), another dramatic architectural subject relying on the contrasts between strong, flat colours and deep, dark shadows. Again, the building is not specific but is a memory of both Venice and Edinburgh. From 1912 onwards Pryde found a generous patron in Viscountess Cowdray, for whose library at Dunecht House, Aberdeenshire, he was commissioned to paint a large series of decorative canvases. This provided useful income, for Pryde's spendthrift habits resulted in serious cash-flow problems.

One important commission towards the end of Pryde's career was to design the sets for a production of *Othello* at the Savoy Theatre in 1930. Despite his lifelong love of the theatre and the influence of the stage on his paintings, this was his only foray into theatre design. The set was based around a flight of steps behind which ran a massively scaled colonnade. Other scenes used painted sets and a huge four-poster bed as a prop. The scenery proved unwieldy, and his desire for dramatic lighting resulted in the cast being plunged into darkness. At the time his designs were not well received, although their visual effects look forward to such artists as Giorgio de Chirico and Graham Sutherland. Pryde received recognition towards the end of his life. He had a one-man show at the Leicester Galleries in 1933, and in 1937 he received a civil-list pension in recognition of his services to art. In 1939 his health declined and he was admitted to St Mary Abbots Hospital, Kensington. He died there on 24 February 1941, and was cremated at Golders Green.

James Pryde was tall and handsome. He was a witty and engaging companion but could also be lazy, extravagant, and unproductive for long periods. He often taxed the patience of his friends. Pryde's output was small but he influenced his contemporaries such as William Nicholson and William Orpen. Although his paintings are well represented in public collections, there have been few exhibitions. The Arts Council of Great Britain organized a memorial exhibition in 1949. Thereafter his work has had little re-evaluation, apart from his role as one of the Beggarstaff Brothers, until an exhibition mounted by the Scottish National Gallery of Modern Art in 1992.

DEREK HUDSON, *rev.* JOANNA SODEN

Sources D. Hudson, *James Pryde, 1866–1941* (1949) • R. Calvocoressi and others, *James Pryde* (1990) • C. Campbell, *The Beggarstaff posters: the work of James Pryde and William Nicholson* (1990) • D. Hudson, *James Pryde, 1866–1941: memorial exhibition* (1949) [exhibition catalogue, Arts Council, Edinburgh and London] • J. Rothenstein, *Modern English painters*, [3rd edn], 1: *Sickert to Lowry* (1984), 86–93 • F. Rutter, *Some contemporary artists* (1922), 59–65 • C. B. de Laperriere, ed., *The Royal Scottish Academy exhibitors, 1826–1990*, 4 vols. (1991), vol. 3, pp. 498–9 • birth record, 30 March 1866, NA Scot.
Archives Scottish National Gallery of Modern Art, Edinburgh, James Pryde: Derek Hudson papers, GMA.A15 | Royal Scot. Acad., life class records
Likenesses W. Nicholson, chalk or crayon drawing, pubd 1897, Scot. NPG • W. Orpen, group portrait, oils, c.1911–1912, Musée d'Art Moderne, Paris; copy, Café Royal, London • J. Gunn, oils, exh. Royal Glasgow Institute of the Fine Arts 1924, City of Edinburgh Museums and Galleries [*see illus.*] • J. Simpson, etching, c.1928, NPG • J. Gunn, oils, c.1931, Scot. NPG • J. Davidson, bronze head, c.1938, Savage Club, London • J. W. Brooke, miniature, watercolour on ivory, NPG • W. O. Hutchison, charcoal drawing, Scot. NPG • W. Nicholson, pen and black ink drawing, AM Oxf. • J. Pryde, self-portrait, oils, Castle Museum, Nottingham

Pryme, Abraham (1671–1704), antiquary, was born on 15 January 1671 in the parish of Hatfield, in the East Riding of Yorkshire, the eldest child of Mathias Pryme (1645–1694), yeoman, and Sara (1649–1729), daughter of Peter Smagge or Smaque, a Parisian Huguenot. Born in a house on the broad levels that had been drained by Dutch engineers in the early part of the century, Abraham Pryme descended from a family that had come over from Ypres to take part in the enterprise. He was baptized in the Dutch congregation at Sandtoft in Lincolnshire on 15 or 22 January. In 1680 the family moved a short distance to Crowtrees Hall, a large house built by one of the Valkenburgh brothers who had been prominent in the drainage scheme.

Despite the dissenting inclinations of the Dutch settlers and his own family, Pryme received schooling from William Eratt, the Church of England incumbent at Hatfield and a friend of his father. In childhood he began to keep, albeit inconsistently, a diary in which he recorded contemporary political chatter and his own antiquarian activities. In adult life this became a more regular activity, supplemented by letters received and sent, with other freestanding insertions, but there are large gaps in the early years and parts of it were clearly written up later. Published by the Surtees Society in 1870, it constitutes an interesting record of his studies, with much entertaining anecdotal detail, although it is not greatly informative about his major projects.

His father hoped he would go to Glasgow University but on 2 May 1690 Pryme was admitted pensioner at St John's College, Cambridge, becoming Cardinal Morton scholar on 7 November following. In addition to his prescribed work he pursued, in his first year, private botanical studies, and in February 1692 his diary discloses a practical interest in magic. In this Pryme was not, apparently, alone; esoteric pursuits may have contributed, at any rate, to the suicide of his friend Humphrey Bohun later that year, which affected him deeply. He none the less continued the study of magic until, the following January, he received a severely worded letter from Bohun's father dissuading him. Thereafter he reverted to botany and natural sciences, which remained an interest all his life.

Pryme graduated BA in January 1694. In July his father died, leaving most of his property to Abraham's younger brother Peter, though Abraham received £100 and certain occupied copyhold tenements near Epworth in Lincolnshire. He was ordained deacon in September 1694, and the following June was appointed curate of Broughton near Brigg, in Lincolnshire, due east across the Trent from his native area. Situated near the northern terminus of Ermine Street, this region is rich in Roman remains, particularly coin hoards and the traces of rural settlements. Chance finds of this sort—such as the mosaic floor of a villa at Roxby—and the documentary and architectural remains of the area's medieval past focused Pryme's antiquarianism. Apart from a rather weak history of the nearby parish of Winterton, dated 1703 (and published in 1866), he produced several papers on the antiquities and natural phenomena of the area that later appeared in the Royal Society's *Philosophical Transactions*.

Pryme resigned his curacy in November 1697 and returned to Hatfield, 'the better to carry on my history of that place', as he says in his diary. The resulting 'Historia universalis oppidi et parochiae Hatfieldensis', a substantial work in thematic sections, survives in Lansdowne MS 897 in the British Library. Section 7 ('Belgicus') is doubtless the history of the Dutch drainage of Hatfield Chase referred to in a letter of March 1703 as begun more than six years earlier. Probably in connection with the section entitled 'Ecclesiasticus', he discovered that some of his land had belonged to a religious house before the dissolution. Genuinely distressed, he made it over to the parish of Hatfield.

In September 1698 Pryme was ordained priest and appointed curate and reader at Holy Trinity Church, Kingston upon Hull, at the invitation of the rector. It was to Hull's history that he now turned his attention, compiling a detailed analytical index of the records of the city corporation and applying the method already used for Hatfield to produce the 'History, antiquities and description of the town and county of Kingston upon Hull'. This work, surviving in various manuscript copies both in Hull and in the British Library, is thorough and intelligently done, displaying a close and laborious application to the documentary evidence. It is still of great value for those writing on Hull. Again, he made an unwelcome discovery, namely that his appointment as curate was irregular, leave not having been given by the corporation. The mayor and aldermen, themselves previously unaware of the technical requirement, were happy to confirm him in the position.

In his years at Hull, Pryme built up a wide correspondence with other antiquaries including Nathaniel Johnston, Thomas Gale, Ralph Thoresby, and Hans Sloane. On 18 March 1702, proposed by Sloane, he was elected a fellow of the Royal Society. He also used his contacts to collect manuscripts, coins, and other antiquities, which placed his income under severe strain and required him to seek a benefice. On 1 September 1701 he was presented to the living of Thorne, near Hatfield, by the duke of Devonshire. Visiting the sick in his parish, however, he caught a fever and died, unmarried, on 12 or 13 June 1704; he was buried near his father in Hatfield church on 14 June. On 18 October his brother Peter was admitted heir to his copyhold lands in the manorial court of Epworth. From Peter descended the family who later regularly called themselves de la Pryme, a form which was in retrospect firmly attributed to the antiquary, but was only rarely used by him. His collections were dispersed, many manuscripts passing to the herald John Warburton, thence being subsumed in the Lansdowne collections now in the British Library.

C. E. A. CHEESMAN

Sources The diary of Abraham de la Pryme, the Yorkshire antiquary, ed. C. Jackson, SurtS, 54 (1870) • A. Pryme, diary, CUL, Add. MS 7519 • A. Pryme, letters to Hans Sloane, BL, Sloane MSS 4025, 4038–4039, 4060 • A. Pryme, 'Historia universalis oppidi et parochiae Hatfieldensis', BL, Lansdowne MS 897 • A. Pryme, collections for the 'History of Hull', BL, Lansdowne MS 890 • A. Pryme, 'History, antiquities and description of the town and county of Kingston upon Hull', BL, Add. MS 8936 and Lansdowne MS 890 • A. Pryme, A history of Kingston upon Hull, ed. J. Meadley (1986) • C. Jackson, 'The Stovin manuscript', Yorkshire Archaeological and Topographical Journal, 7 (1881–2), 194–238 • J. Hunter, 'Yorkshire biography', BL, Add. MS 24475 • W. T. Lancaster, ed., Letters addressed to Ralph Thoresby FRS, Thoresby Society, 21 (1912), 134 • Venn, Alum. Cant.
Archives BL, Yorkshire collections, Lansdowne MSS 890–891, 894, 897–898, 972 • CUL, diary • Hull City Archives, MS accounts of history of Hull • JRL, History and antiquities of Winterton, Eng. MS 128 | BL, Add. MS 8936 • Bodl. Oxf., Nathaniel Johnston's Antiquities of Yorkshire, incl. an account of Doncaster annotated by Pryme
Wealth at death income from two copyhold tenements and 49 acres; interest in property on Hatfield chase: Diary of Abraham de la Pryme, ed. Jackson

Pryme, George (1781–1868), economist, was born at Cottingham, Yorkshire, on 4 April 1781, the only surviving child (an elder brother had died in infancy) of Christopher Pryme, merchant of Hull, and Alice, daughter of George Dinsdale of Nappa Hall, Wensleydale. He was a descendant of Peter, the younger brother of Abraham Pryme, an antiquary. After his father's early death, George Pryme and his mother moved to Nottinghamshire, where he attended several private schools. In 1796 he went to Hull grammar school, where the headmaster was the Revd Joseph Milner, and he was later tutored by John Dawson.

In October 1799 Pryme entered Trinity College, Cambridge, where he won a scholarship in the following year; he became sixth wrangler and graduated BA in 1803. Before 1805, when he was elected a fellow of his college, he won no fewer than five prizes for Latin, Greek, and English, and earned himself the nickname of Prize Pryme. Having already begun studying law in Lincoln's Inn in October 1804, he was called to the bar in 1806. He practised in London until his health broke down, and on medical advice he returned two years later to Cambridge, where he won a prize in 1809 for an English poem. He then worked as a provincial barrister, being dubbed Counsellor

Pryme. On 30 August 1813 he married Jane Townley (1788–1871), daughter of Thomas Thackeray (1736–1806), a Cambridge surgeon. A son and a daughter were born to them.

In 1816 Pryme began to lecture on political economy in Cambridge, the first lectures specifically on that subject to be delivered in any British university. Requiring from his audience no prior knowledge, these were elementary and eclectic, a popularization—in the best sense—of a subject that could then be mastered only with great perseverance. Although he gained the vice-chancellor's permission, the college heads, suspicious of such innovations, would not allow his lectures to begin before midday, so as not to interfere with college teaching. That year he turned his lectures into a book, *Syllabus of a Course of Lectures on Political Economy*, which reached its fourth (revised) edition in 1859. The courses were well attended, and in 1828 the senate granted him the title of professor.

Unusually for a don, Pryme involved himself in town affairs. He was appointed a paving commissioner and, as a reforming whig, in the 1820s he opposed the parliamentary candidates sponsored by the duke of Rutland. After the Reform Bill was passed, the duke's nominees faded away, and Pryme stood for Cambridge in the general election of 1832 as a whig and headed the poll. In the House of Commons his speeches were heard with respect and attention, and he was soon a member of several committees. Later he was entrusted with steering through minor but useful bills, for example, one that enabled a sect called separatists to affirm. In 1836 he took an active part in the discussion of the Tithe Commutation Act. He favoured shorter parliaments and the admission of dissenters to Oxford and Cambridge universities.

Pryme's efforts to become a university reformer were not all that successful. In 1834 he spoke in favour of a petition to the house for abolishing subscription on graduation, and three years later (on 4 May 1837) introduced a motion to appoint a commission of inquiry into the state of Oxford and Cambridge universities. The chancellor of the exchequer, Thomas Spring-Rice, stymied him with the reply that that was a matter for the crown, and university reform languished for another decade and a half. Characteristically, he very seldom left the house until it rose, and he voted in practically every division of importance. He so ran down his health that his family compelled him to retire from parliament in 1841.

Back in Cambridge, Pryme continued to deliver his lectures and practised from time to time as a barrister. He became interested in the Norfolk estuary scheme and other local improvements. In 1847 he and his family moved to Wistow in Huntingdonshire, where he had bought a 500 acre estate; having absorbed the elements of chemistry, he applied them to the cultivation of his land, which made a profit in most years, except just after the repeal of the corn laws, a measure which he supported. He gave up his Cambridge lectures in 1863, when the senate voted to continue his chair. He died in Wistow on 2 December 1868 and was buried there a week later.

Pryme crammed a great amount into his long life, but the range of his interests denied him the chance of becoming as celebrated as his abilities warranted. An early riser, he never wasted a moment of the day. When not writing at his desk, he was reading; he often held a book in his hand while driving himself in his open carriage. He helped to nourish his retentive memory by meditating on a book for some time after closing it. He bequeathed his books and pamphlets on political economy to the University of Cambridge.   T. A. B. CORLEY

Sources DNB · G. Pryme, *Autobiographic recollections of George Pryme*, ed. A. Bayne (1870) · Venn, *Alum. Cant.* · *Hansard 3* (1830), 22.597; (1837), 38.509–12 · Boase, *Mod. Eng. biog.* · IGI
Archives LPL, lecture notes | Hull City Archives, letters to John Richardson · NL Ire., corresp. with J. E. Cairnes · U. Hull, Brynmor Jones L., letters from T. P. Thompson · U. Leeds, Brotherton L., letters to T. P. Thompson
Wealth at death under £12,000: probate, 21 Jan 1869, CGPLA Eng. & Wales

Prynne [Prynn], **George Rundle** (1818–1903), Church of England clergyman and writer, was born at West Looe, Cornwall, on 23 August 1818, the younger son among the eight children of John Allen Prynn (whose form of the surname was abandoned later by his son) and his wife, Susanna, daughter of John and Mary Rundle of Looe, Cornwall. John Prynn, who claimed descent from William Prynne (1600–1669), the puritan, was a native of Newlyn, Cornwall.

After education at a school run by his sister at Looe and at the private Devonport Classical and Mathematical School, Prynne matriculated at St John's College, Cambridge, in October 1836, but migrated to St Catharine's College. He graduated BA on 18 January 1840 (MA in 1861, and MA *ad eundem* at Oxford on 30 May 1861). Ordained deacon on 19 September 1841 and priest on 25 September 1842, he was licensed as curate first to the parish of Tywardreath, Cornwall, and on 18 December 1843 to St Andrew's, Clifton, Bristol. There he first came in contact with E. B. Pusey, who was the greatest influence on his adoption of Tractarian ideas and practices, especially the hearing of confessions, which he began at this time. However, Prynne declined Pusey's suggestion to join St Saviour's, Leeds, on account of an implied obligation of celibacy, as he was already contemplating marriage. On the nomination of the prime minister, Sir Robert Peel, Prynne became vicar of the parish of Par, Cornwall, newly formed from that of Tywardreath, from October 1846 to August 1847, when he took by exchange the living of St Levan and St Sennen in the same county. From 16 August 1848 until his death he was incumbent of the newly constituted parish of St Peter, formerly Eldad Chapel, which contained many of the poorest districts in Plymouth. On 17 April 1849 he married Emily (d. 1901), daughter of Admiral Sir Thomas Fellowes; they had four sons and six daughters.

At Plymouth, a town then predominantly nonconformist and evangelical in sympathy, Prynne's strenuous advocacy of Tractarianism involved him in heated controversy. The conflict was largely fostered by John Hatchard, vicar of Plymouth. In 1850 Prynne brought a charge of criminal libel against Isaac Latimer, the editor, publisher, and proprietor of the *Plymouth and Devonport Weekly Journal*, for an article, prompted by religious differences, that seemed to reflect on his moral character (24 January 1850). The trial took place at Exeter, before Sir John Taylor Coleridge, on 6 and 7 August 1850. The defendant alleged that the English Church Union was responsible for the prosecution and was supplying the necessary funds: the jury found Latimer not guilty and the heavy costs of the case almost ruined Prynne.

In 1852 Prynne was once again at the centre of controversy, this time as a result of his support of Priscilla Lydia Sellon (1821–1878) and her Devonport community of Sisters of Mercy. Despite the heroic endeavours of Prynne, Sellon, and the sisters during a cholera epidemic in 1849, this support, together with Prynne's advocacy of auricular confession and penance, especially his hearing the confessions of young girls from the sisters' orphanage, provoked a pamphlet war with the Revd James Spurrell and the Revd Michael Hobart Seymour. On 22 September 1852 an inquiry by Henry Phillpotts, bishop of Exeter, into allegations against Prynne's doctrine and practice found in Prynne's favour, but a riot took place when Phillpotts held a confirmation at Prynne's church the next month. In 1860 Prynne 'conditionally' baptized Joseph Leycester Lyne, known as Father Ignatius, and employed him as an unpaid curate. Prynne joined the Society of the Holy Cross in 1860 and the English Church Union in 1862, becoming vice-president of the latter body in 1901.

Meanwhile opposition diminished, and Prynne's local reputation improved as his pastoral work expanded. He built schools, established guilds, and conducted missions. His church was rebuilt and consecrated in 1882 without disturbance. (The architectural design was carried out by his second son, George, while his third son, Edward, executed the Prynne memorial mural after their father's death.) Although Prynne always remained a staunch Tractarian, he was chosen with prebendary M. F. Sadler proctor in convocation for the clergy of the Exeter diocese from 1885 to 1892, and he was on friendly terms with his diocesans, Frederick Temple and E. H. Bickersteth. Contrary to the views of many of his party, Prynne submitted to the first Lambeth opinion of 1899, which condemned the liturgical use of incense, until the death of Bishop Bickersteth in 1901.

Prynne acquired a considerable reputation as a compiler and author of hymns. His first published hymnal was produced as early as 1854, and contained 177 hymns; the 1866 edition grew to include 433, of which nearly 200 were eventually included in *Hymns Ancient and Modern*, a collection he subsequently helped to revise in 1875. His own collected hymns were published in *The Soldier's Dying Visions, and other Poems and Hymns* (1881), the best-known being 'Jesu, meek and gentle', written in 1856. In addition Prynne's writings about the eucharist were also significant, especially *The Eucharistic Manual*, designed for the non-academic reader: the ten editions through which it passed from 1865 to 1895 attest to its popularity in late Victorian high-church circles. Prynne also wrote *Truth and Reality of the Eucharistic Sacrifice* (1894) and *Devotional Instructions on the Eucharistic Office* (1903), as well as a number of sermons and controversial pamphlets.

After a short illness, Prynne died at his vicarage, 28 Wyndham Square, Plymouth, on 25 March 1903, and was buried at Plympton St Mary, near Plymouth, on 30 March.

E. S. HOOPER, *rev.* GEORGE HERRING

Sources A. Clifton Kelway, *George Rundle Prynne: a chapter in the early history of the Catholic revival* (1905) · G. Rowell, *The vision glorious: themes and personalities of the Catholic revival in Anglicanism* (1983) · *CGPLA Eng. & Wales* (1903) · J. S. Reed, *Glorious battle: the cultural politics of Victorian Anglo-Catholicism* (1996)

Likenesses Talford, chalk drawing, c.1853; in family possession, 1912 · E. Prynne, oils, 1885; in family possession, 1912 · photographs, repro. in Clifton Kelway, *George Rundle Prynne*

Wealth at death £967 5s. 2d.: probate, 18 April 1903, *CGPLA Eng. & Wales*

Prynne, William (1600–1669), pamphleteer and lawyer, was born in Upper Swainswick, near Bath, Somerset, the son of Thomas Prynne, farmer, and his second wife, Marie, daughter of William Sherston (the first mayor of Bath under Elizabeth I's charter). He attended Bath grammar school from 1612, and from 1616 Oriel College, Oxford, owners of the land which his father farmed. He graduated BA on 22 January 1621 and was admitted a student of Lincoln's Inn in the same year. He was called to the bar in 1628, and by then had produced the first of his more than two hundred pamphlets.

Early writings, 1628–1641 Prynne was tried twice, in 1633 and 1637, in Star Chamber for sedition. In his pamphlet against stage plays, *Histriomastix* of 1633, he had indeed denounced female actors at the same time as Queen Henrietta Maria was participating in a court masque. But Prynne's defence was that this huge work had been long in gestation (which was true), and even then it had been published a month before the queen's performance. This defence is not as impressive as it might seem. Prynne had inserted additional criticisms of female actors in an appendix while Henrietta Maria was rehearsing for the event. But, to the main charge, Prynne was not guilty. He had not attacked the crown, even if he had been rude about amusements patronized by it. *Histriomastix* is a crime against literature, not against the state. Samuel Butler rightly said that Prynne's real weakness was to cast holy things, not unto dogs, but into doggerel (S. Butler, *Posthumous Works*, 1732, 84). Another contemporary also had the wit to see that soured misanthropy on so generalized a scale robbed the attack of particular application: 'it was fitter to be called *Anthropomastix* than *Histriomastix*, the scourge of mankind rather than the Kings sacred person' (Bodl. Oxf., MS Douce 173, fol. 14). He was nevertheless found guilty of sedition, sentenced to have his ears cut off, fined £5000, and sentenced to life imprisonment. With the connivance of a friendly gaoler, he continued to smuggle pamphlets out of the Tower of London. Four years later, in 1637, he came for a second time before Star Chamber. Once more he was accused (and found guilty) of sedition, along with a divine (Henry Burton) and a doctor

Mr: William Prynne, for writing a booke
against Stage-players called Histrio-mastix
was first censured in the Starr-Chamber to loose both his eares in the pillorie, fined 5000# & perpetuall imprisonment in the Towre of London
After this, on a meer suspition of writing other
bookes, but nothing at all proved against him,
hee was again censured in the Starr-chamber to
loose the small remainder of both his eares in
the pillorie, to be Stigmatized on both his Cheekes
with a firey-iron, was fined again 5000# and banished into ye Isle of Iersey, there to suffer perpetuall Close-imprisonm: no freinds being permitted to see him, on pain of imprisonment,

William Prynne (1600–1669), by Wenceslaus Hollar

(John Bastwick). His ears, lightly cropped in 1633, now received the full treatment, his nose was slit, and the initials 'S. L.' burnt into his cheeks. They stood for 'Seditious Libeller'; to Prynne they stood for 'Stigma of Laud'. He described his sufferings in a pamphlet in 1641. The executioner had heated the iron very hot, and burnt one of his cheeks twice. After this he cut one of Prynne's ears so close that he cut off a piece of cheek, and cut him deep in the neck near the jugular vein. Then, hacking the other ear until it was almost off, he left it hanging and went down from the scaffold. He was called back by the surgeon, who made him perform a complete amputation. Smiling up to heaven, said Prynne, he responded with 'this heavenly sentence' (his own evaluation): 'The more I am beat down, the more am I lift up' (W. Prynne, *A New Discovery of the Prelates Tyranny*, 1641, no pagination). The events of 1637 made an impact upon public opinion that those of 1633 had failed to do: Prynne's exile to the Channel Islands became a triumphant progress, as no less was the return journey in 1640 when the Long Parliament was called.

Throughout his writings in the 1630s, Prynne assailed Laudianism as a betrayal of his sentimentalized (but sincerely held) perception of what the Elizabethan church had been. The answer to the take-over of the church by semi-papists, led by Archbishop Laud, was not therefore separatism (which he abhorred) nor even presbyterianism (in which he showed no interest before 1641, and which he actively opposed after August 1645). What he advocated instead was a return to the Elizabethan principles of another archbishop, Whitgift, whom Prynne quaintly saw as a 'Puritane' (W. Prynne, *A Breviate of the Prelates Intollerable Usurpations*, 1637, 123), while Whitgift's presbyterian opponent, Cartwright, was on the other hand now viewed by Prynne as an 'Opposite' (W. Prynne, *A Vindication of Four Serious Questions*, 1645, 7). Until 1641 Prynne had not lost faith in those episcopalians who were seemingly untarnished with the Laudian brush: bishops like Joseph Hall and John Williams, who were seen by him as custodians of Elizabethan values. But in 1641 he lost his faith in these non-Laudian bishops. Hall's defence of divine right episcopacy aligned him with Laud, not Whitgift. The pamphlet which Prynne wrote in 1641, *The Antipathie*, is a watershed in his career. For the first time in his writing he attacked all bishops, and argued for a 'root and branch' destruction of episcopacy. This did not make him, or his fellow 'root and branchers' for the most part, necessarily card-carrying presbyterians. But he was won to their view that a 'New Jerusalem' was possible, and the millenarian views of Thomas Brightman carried more weight with him and his fellows than the more conservative readings of the book of Revelation by John Foxe. In 1641 Prynne had presented Foxe's *Acts and Monuments* to his Swainswick parish church (Bodl. Oxf., MS Tanner 69, fol. 1). But by then he had already implicitly rejected Foxe's legacy by his conversion to a belief in 'root and branch' destruction of all bishops (and that included even Foxe's martyrs).

Civil war reappraisals Central for Prynne, as for many fellow puritans explaining the origins of the civil war, was the suspicion that Charles I had secretly commissioned the Irish rebels of October 1641. Prynne defended Sir John Hotham's refusal to yield Hull to the king in 1642, not on Calvinist resistance grounds (with which he had no sympathy) but on the self-preservative grounds which he had learned from the anti-Calvinist Hugo Grotius: 'That a King who aliens and would actually deliver up possession of all or any part of his Realm to another forraign power without the peoples consent, may lawfully be resisted with force by his subjects' (W. Prynne, *The Soveraigne Powers of Parliaments*, 1643, 1.103).

Prynne opposed both Calvinist Independency and presbyterianism in the civil war. The Presbyterian Scot, Robert Baillie, knew the contingent nature of Prynne's interest in their cause when he instructed his London agent in 1640 to 'try the present estate' of Prynne (*Letters and Journals of Robert Baillie*, 226). The Presbyterians' alibi for the subsequent delay in reform in the 1640s was that they had been thwarted by Independents. In 1644 Prynne went along with this explanation. He attacked Independency as an anti-social force which denied man's dependence upon his neighbours, church, and country for the fulfilment of his nature. Against such ideas he quoted Aristotle's view of man as a social animal. But a year later (in common with other English puritans from an Erastian tradition) he saw the enemy no longer as Laudian crypto-popery but presbyterian theocracy. 'A speedy reformation in our Church', he now recognized, could not by its nature come from that 'strict discipline which really reforms very few or none' (W. Prynne, *A Vindication of Four Serious Questions*, 1645, 57–8). An exasperated Presbyterian, Robert Baillie, on 5 September 1645 conceded that 'Mr. Prin and the Erastian lawyers are now our *remora*' (*Letters and Journals of Robert Baillie*, 315).

The sovereignty of parliament Although Prynne's was the officially commissioned defence by parliament of its sovereignty (and he had read, and quoted, Jean Bodin on sovereignty), it is no landmark in political theory. Rather, *The Soveraigne Powers of Parliaments* is a series of *post hoc* justifications of actions taken by the parliamentary army during the campaign itself. The full title of the work reflects Prynne's priorities: *The Treachery and Disloyalty of Papists to their Soveraignes, in Doctrine and Practise*. Charles I had been deceived by his advisers (principally Laud and Henrietta Maria) into the betrayal of his own royal supremacy. Prynne's *The Popish Royall Favourite* of 1643 is the most bitter personal attack upon Charles I; only Charles's martyrdom in 1649 wiped out his previous faults, and that crime too had been perpetrated by papists. After 1649, and until the end of his life, Prynne reverted to the royalism of his earlier years, maintaining that he had been consistent even in the period from 1642 to 1649, since (in his view) it was Charles I, not himself, who had lapsed from his imperial principles. Prynne's record of Archbishop Laud's trial, *Canterburies Doome* (1646), was constructed with one end in view: to show that Laud's crime lay not in advancing royal absolutism, but in subverting it. He was impenitent about rigging the record to fit the conclusion: 'no indifferent person can justly taxe me with partiality or injustice for inserting into the History, [materials] for the fuller discovery of his Popish intentions in this kinde' (*Canterburies Doome*, dedicatory epistle). In 1647 he looked back upon the lessons of the archbishop's trial and execution: 'the late Archbishops familiarity, correspondence and confederacy with Priests and Jesuits to introduce Popish Superstitions, and subvert the established Protestant Religion, was charged against him by the whole House of Commons, as a Treasonable and Capitall Offence' (W. Prynne, *The Sword of Christian Magistracy*, 1647, 68). By 1647 the papist menace had taken a different form, however. The Jesuits by then had given up working through the monarchy by a fifth column in the church, and now (according to Prynne) were working directly against the monarchy through Leveller soldiers. Pride's Purge, Charles I's trial, and then his execution were all seen by Prynne as part of an orchestrated 'popish plot'. Hence the important symbolism to him of Henrietta Maria's Jesuit confessor waving his sword in triumph as the king's head was cut off (W. Prynne, *A True and Perfect Narrative*, 1659, 60–63)—a canard with wide currency in the literature of

the 1650s. The 'Popish Royall Favourite' of 1643 had metamorphosed into the royal martyr of 1649. No wonder the Independent minister, John Goodwin, accused Prynne of 'melting down' the 'mountain' which he had first set up in 1643 (*Right and Might well Met*, 1649, 4, 8, 9). Prynne *had* changed his mind about Charles I (whatever he protested to the contrary), but he had not—in this he was correct—changed his mind about monarchy. Nevertheless he had changed his mind about another institution (the House of Commons) by 1648, and he did so for scholarly reasons. Sir Robert Filmer published his *The Freeholders Grand Inquest* in January 1648. A contemporary wrote across his copy of Filmer's work this shrewd observation: 'in a considerable degree an answer to the exceptionable doctrines in Prynne's *Sovereignty of Parliament*'. So it was, and this makes it all the more remarkable how Prynne responded to it. In two works in 1648 Prynne answered Filmer (in February and March respectively): *The Levellers Levelled to the Very Ground* and *A Plea for the Lords*. Up to that point, Prynne's mentor on constitutional matters had been Sir Edward Coke. But Filmer—drawing upon antiquarian researches—revealed the sketchiness of Coke's history. He drew upon election writs to show that the Commons had not been historically part of the common council. He denied the antiquity of the Commons: 1265 was the first extant summons of knights by the sheriff's writs. Filmer used these points to make a royalist case; Prynne did not go quite that far, but he accepted the main findings of Filmer's scholarship. However, he fashioned them to a different end from Filmer's: to subordinate the Commons not to the king merely (as Filmer had done), but to subordinate it to the ancient law of England, which required the co-operation of king and Lords. He was wholly receptive, however, to Filmer's means of reaching his conclusion, and this would fashion Prynne's career for the rest of his life. Coke had put his trust in commentaries on the records, not upon a study of the records themselves. This was the lesson that Prynne drew in *A Plea for the Lords*. Henceforth ancient parliamentary rolls and journals should be transcribed and published to preserve them from the threat of fire or war (*A Plea for the Lords*, dedicatory epistle). His conviction of the need to study the primary sources made him quarrel with contemporaries who still lived in the land of historical make-believe, and who still saw Sir Edward Coke as an oracle (W. Prynne, *The First Part of a Brief Register*, 1659, 422).

The cavalier hero? From February 1644 Prynne had been a member of the committee of accounts; on 1 May 1647 he had been appointed one of the commissioners for the visitation of the University of Oxford; in November 1648 he was MP, for the first time, for Newport in Cornwall. He emerged as the great champion of a negotiated settlement with Charles I, and vigorously opposed Pride's Purge and the trial and the execution of the king. For nearly three years after these events he was imprisoned without trial for opposing the Commonwealth. It was a cavalier who now called him 'the Cato of his Age'; Clarendon's papers abound with testimonies to Prynne's contribution to the royalist cause in the interregnum; Charles II himself recognized Prynne's worth. He subsequently served both in the Convention Parliament and the Cavalier Parliament as MP for Bath, and from 1660 onwards as recorder of Bath. Bath council formally thanked him 'for his readiness to promote the advantage of this City' as its recorder (Bath council minutes, vol. 2, fol. 89).

It was a master stroke for Charles II to appoint Prynne as keeper of the records in the Tower of London after the Restoration: he called it 'most suitable to my Genius'. This is how he described the work in a letter to Sir Harbottle Grimston:

> whilst you are sucking in the fresh country air, I have been almost choked with the dust of neglected records (interred in their own rubbish for sundry years) in the White Tower; their rust eating out the tops of my gloves with their touch, and their dust rendering me, twice a day, as black as a chimney sweeper. (*Verulam MSS*, 58)

F. W. Maitland called this aspect of Prynne's career 'heroic' (Holdsworth, *Eng. law*, 5.407). There was a double heroism: the physical labour that Prynne described, but also the intellectual rescue of a historical feudal law from the myth of an ancient constitution (to which Prynne in the 1630s, as a disciple of Coke, had himself subscribed). The Commons' claim to sovereignty could not stand up to the scrutiny of sources; the king's imperial powers, on the other hand, were given a heightened vindication. Prynne called his *Aurum reginae* of 1668 a minor contribution to the defence and assistance of 'all Jurisdiction, Priviledges, Preheminencies and Authorities granted to or belonging to the IMPERIALL CROWN of the REALM' (BL, Add. MS 71534, fol. 14). The major contribution, he believed, were the volumes which he published after the Restoration under the title, *An Exact Chronologicall Vindication … of our Kings Supreme Ecclesiastical Jurisdiction*. In the introduction to the fourth volume, he argued that the king embodied the patriarchal authority of Adam; the king was God's viceroy to implement his rule on earth; the distinction between church and state is a popish invention; all church power derived its authority from the crown (W. Prynne, *The First Tome of the Exact Chronologicall Vindication*, 1666, 4.1, 2, 7, 77). These were the four principles, it could be argued, not of his dotage, but of his entire career.

Not all royalists appreciated that fact. They remembered the man twice convicted for sedition in the 1630s, and who had built a 'mountain' (in John Goodwin's words) of invective against Charles I between 1643 and 1648. Sir Thomas Bridges, for instance, wrote to Secretary Nicholas on 20 March 1661 to argue that Prynne should at all costs be prevented from continuing to serve as MP for Bath in the Cavalier Parliament (*CSP dom.*, Charles II, *1660–61*, 564). The minutes of Bath council record the lengths to which opponents would go to silence Prynne. In September 1661 Prynne's supporters were even kidnapped in a mayoral election to prevent them from voting (Bath council minutes, vol. 2, fol. 68; Peach, 43–5). At Archbishop Juxon's funeral in 1663, Robert South delivered a gratuitous swipe at the 'famous and Scurrillous' Prynne (Wood, *Ath. Oxon.*, 3rd edn, 1.481). As late as 18 March 1668, when Prynne

pressed for the exemption of an opponent from the royal pardon, Sir Thomas Littleton sourly reminded him that 'if Prynne had not had his, he might have been in the same predicament' (A. Grey, ed., *Debates of the House of Commons from the year 1667 to the year 1694*, 1769, 118).

If unforgiving royalism was one problem for Prynne in his life after the Restoration, another surely ought to have been the gap between Prynne and the unpuritan court which he now served. He has even been accused of cowardice in not emphasizing that gap (Murch, 31–2). The criticism is not fair. Prynne went on attacking his enemies of the 1630s—duels, taverns, and the drinking of healths (*The Second Part of the Signal Loyalty and Devotion of Gods True Saints*, 1660, dedicatory epistle; *Letter and Proposals to our Gracious Lord and Sovereign King Charles*, 1660). He even had his pamphlet, *Healthes Sicknesse* (1628), reprinted after the Restoration. Always, though, his criticisms went in tandem with professions of loyalty to Charles II; the Baptist, Henry Jessey, borrowed the criticisms but left out their royalist accompaniment (H. Jessey, *The Lords Loud Call to England*, 1660, 32). Moreover, Prynne attacked the Corporation Act of 1661, not only legally and futilely in the Commons (*JHC*, 8.282, 291) but by an extra-constitutional anonymous printed plea to the Lords (*Summary Reasons, Humbly Tendred to the most Honourable House of Peeres*). When his cover was blown, he apologized, unexpectedly abjectly. This was hailed as a 'conquest' by an opponent (*Beaufort MSS*, 50–51). But his standing in the Commons did not seem to have been diminished. Certainly a fortnight later he was managing a conference with the Lords on restraining unlicensed printing (of which he was now something of an expert). He described himself, in another context, in February 1661 as 'quite tyred out' (W. Prynne, *Brevia parliamentum rediviva*, 1661, 515). Was this the explanation for his 'conquest' in that year? At times he could seem a more mellow figure after the Restoration. Anthony Wood recalls how, in 1667, as a young historian furnished with letters of commendation from the provost of Prynne's old college, Oriel, he went to Prynne in the Tower of London to be introduced to the study of historical records. Wood says that Prynne 'received him with old fashion compliments, such as were used in the raigne of King James I'. He seemed 'to be glad that such a young man as he was (for so he called him) should have inclinations towards venerable antiquity' (Wood, *Ath. Oxon.*, 3rd edn, 1.lix). Wood has left an unforgettable picture of the aged antiquarian scholar, with his 'black taffaty-cloak, edg'd with black lace at the bottom' (ibid.), conducting his young pupil through the smoking ruins of London after the great fire, and unable to resist the chance of a yarn on the way with acquaintances before getting down to the documents. This later Prynne must not, however, be sentimentalized. He had opposed the readmission of Jews into England; he saw the Quakers as masked papists; he blamed the great fire of London on the papists; he commented upon impeachment proceedings against Clarendon: 'I pray God this be not a foreigner's plot' (A. Grey, ed., *Debates of the House of Commons*, 1765, 65). Pepys was no prude, but recorded his discomfiture at being seated next to Prynne at a dinner table:

> who, in discourse with me, fell upon what records he hath of the lust and wicked lives of the nuns heretofore in England, and showed me out of his pocket one wherein 30 nuns for their lust were ejected out of the house. (Pepys, *Diary*, 3.93)

At the time of the great fire one public servant complained about receiving a long and tiresome letter from a person called William Prynne, 'a stranger to him speaking of fears and jealousies, of plots and designs of Jesuits and Romanists against the Church and Religion' (*CSP dom.*, Charles II, *1660–67*, 318). He feared that it would 'stir up hornets'. Prynne would go on stirring up hornets until his death on 24 December 1669 at Lincoln's Inn, where, according to Wood, he was buried 'in the walk under the chapel' (Wood, *Ath. Oxon.*, 3rd edn, 3.876).

Reputation and sources John Aubrey records that Prynne worked to a set routine. He wore a long quilt cap, 2 or 3 inches over his eyes, to protect them from the light. A servant would bring him a roll and pot of ale every three hours to revive his spirits, and he would study and drink into the early hours (*Brief Lives*, 413). Prynne's profuse citations of sources in the margins of the text earned him his contemporary nickname, 'Marginal' Prynne. Contemporaries did not rate him highly. One critic thought it a pity that his parents were not German, since he then 'might have outdone the reputation of the greatest of their Authors, who are commonly valued at the rate of their boldnesse and prolixity' (*A Serious Epistle to Mr. William Prynne*, 1649, 6–7). But a fellow critic, while deploring their superficiality, conceded that his arguments 'take with the people' (H. Woodward, *Inquiries into the Cause of our Miseries*, 1644, 11). Indeed parliament would not have commissioned Prynne to write its official defence in the civil war, nor its official record of the trial of Archbishop Laud, without a similar belief that his words would 'take with the people'. Prynne has a claim to scholarly attention not through the originality of his writings or the depth of his insight (although he made a significant contribution to the study of the past), but because he was involved in most of the great events of the time, and his public writings offer a continuous commentary upon them. Ideally there would be a private archive to complement this public history, but this is not the case. Prynne never married: waggishly he remarked in the Commons in November 1660, on his support for measures to punish women who refused to cohabit with their husbands, that he himself had 'never had a good or bad wife in his life' (Cobbett, *Parl. hist.*, 4, 1660, 145). The executors of his will were a brother (Thomas) and a sister (Kathleen Clarke). The importance of gaining access to his private papers was grasped by two fellow antiquarian scholars, Anthony Wood and Sir William Dugdale. They lamented the obstacles placed in their way by Prynne's executors (W. Hamper, ed., *The Life, Diary, and Correspondence of Sir William Dugdale*, 1827, 390–91). Gilbert Sheldon, then archbishop of Canterbury, wanted Prynne's papers for another reason: to get his hands upon the papers relevant to Prynne's prosecution of Archbishop Laud. Jonas Moore suggested to Sheldon that the

ideal middleman in the quest was the husband of one of Prynne's executors, George Clarke, who had once been a contact link with Charles II in the interregnum (*Portland MSS*, 1.594). This too drew a blank. His private papers have never been recovered. In their absence, historians as much as contemporaries have been over-reliant on the message seemingly conveyed by the violence of the language of his pamphlets. Thus the great twentieth-century historian of puritanism, William Haller, offers the picture of Prynne as a Bakunin-like anarchist (*The Rise of Puritanism*, 1938, 393, 219), which is not very different from what opponents of the time had said about him: 'a constant opponent of all governments' (*Mercurius Democritus*, no. 5, 31 May – 7 June 1659); 'the Spirit of Contradiction' (*Democritus Turned Statesman*, 1659, 6).

When the spectre of a 'Laudian' revival (without Laud) appeared a real possibility at the Restoration, Prynne's response was to revert to his moderate episcopalianism of 1628–40, and not to champion his 'root and branch' principles of 1641–5. The appointment in 1663 as preacher to his own Lincoln's Inn of John Tillotson was a hopeful sign; to this future archbishop of Canterbury, Prynne later bequeathed one of his unreadable tomes in his will. Tillotson was seen by Prynne as the heir to Whitgift's legacy, not Laud's. What Prynne admired in both Whitgift and Tillotson was their defence of the royal supremacy: a recognition that bishops owed their office to the king (which was incompatible with Laudian claims for divine right sanction). Recent researches on Prynne, and many of his fellow puritans, have corrected the 'fanatic' stereotype. His claim in his last will and testament to have had as his aim 'to doe my God King and Country all the best publick service I could' is one that is now taken more seriously than it once was, and one which was wholly compatible, in his mind at least, with loyalty to the Church of England.

The violence of Prynne's language misled contemporaries, as it misled historians later. He was in truth no more an egalitarian than he was a separatist. He had proudly flourished his grandfather's sword when he entered the recalled Long Parliament of February 1660. Farce mingled with triumph—it usually did with Prynne—even at such a high point in his career. The sword got entangled with the short fat legs of Sir William Waller 'and threw him down which caused laughter' (*Brief Lives*, 414). The very fact that the sword in question had belonged to an Elizabethan mayor of Bath, his grandfather, was a source of intense pride to Prynne. An opponent hit a shrewd blow at Prynne's social pretensions when he claimed the real motive for Prynne's hostility to the readmission of Jews into England in 1656: 'surely the party who writ so furiously against the Jews coming in, was afraid his chamber in Lincolnes-Inn should have been for their habitation, or else his Mannour of Swainswicke, or Swainswick, of which he writes himself Esquire' (D. L., *Israels Condition and Cause Pleaded*, 1656, 70). Similarly, for an acute observer like Henry Parker in 1641, it was the authorities' paranoid failure to see how 'moderate' a puritan like Prynne really was (and he could equally well have added the epithets 'snobbish', 'hierarchical', 'conservative'), which would seal their subsequent doom (*A Discourse Concerning Puritans*, 7).

WILLIAM LAMONT

Sources M. I. Fay and G. Davies, 'Notes and documents', *Huntington Library Quarterly*, 20 (1956–7), 53–93 • W. Lamont, *Marginal Prynne* (1963) • E. W. Kirby, *William Prynne: a study in puritanism* (1931) • R. E. M. Peach, *History of Swainswick* (1890) • J. Murch, *William Prynne* (1878) • S. R. Gardiner, ed., *Documents relating to the proceedings against William Prynne*, CS, new ser., 18 (1877), 101–18 • *The life and times of Anthony Wood*, ed. A. Clark, 1, OHS, 19 (1891) • *Aubrey's Brief lives*, ed. O. L. Dick (1949) • Bath RO, Bath council minutes, vol. 2 • *The letters and journals of Robert Baillie*, ed. D. Laing, 3 vols. (1841–2) • Wood, *Ath. Oxon.*, new edn • PRO, PROB 11/331, fols. 300v–301v • *Calendar of the Clarendon state papers preserved in the Bodleian Library*, 4: *1657–1660*, ed. F. J. Routledge (1932), 591–615 • J. G. A. Pocock, *The ancient constitution and the feudal law* (1957) • DNB **Archives** BL, papers relating to clergy's encroachments on royal prerogative, Lansdowne MS 228 • Bristol Baptist College, papers • Canterbury Cathedral, archive, articles against Archbishop Laud, incl. Prynne's marginal notes • Inner Temple, London, cases, arguments, notes • U. Nott. L., MS volume relating to star chamber jurisdiction | BL, Add. MSS 11308, 11764 • Bodl. Oxf., Tanner MS 69 • Bath, council minutes **Likenesses** line engraving, 1641, BM, NPG; repro. in [W. Prynne], *A new discovery of the prelates tyranny* (1641) • R. Dunkarton, mezzotint, pubd 1811 (after S. Woodforde), BM, NPG • W. Hollar, etching, BM, NPG [*see illus.*] • line engraving, BM, NPG • portrait, Courtauld Inst.; repro. in Lamont, *Marginal Prynne* • portrait (Prynne's homage to Charles II), BL; repro. in Lamont, *Marginal Prynne* • portrait (Laud on trial, Prynne as prosecutor), BL; repro. in Lamont, *Marginal Prynne* **Wealth at death** substantial bequests to executors and families: will, PRO, PROB 11/331, fols. 300v–301v

Pryor, Alfred Reginald (1839–1881), botanist, was born at Hatfield, Hertfordshire, on 24 April 1839, the eldest son of Alfred Pryor, brewer, and Jane Anne (*née* Pryor). He was educated at Tonbridge School and at University College, Oxford, whence he graduated BA on 26 June 1862. While at Oxford, in 1858, he converted to Catholicism. He was interested in botany by 1873 when the first of his papers appeared in *The Journal of Botany, British and Foreign*. In the following year he began work, with R. H. Webb, on a supplement to Coleman's *Flora Hertfordiensis* (1849), but this soon gave way to a plan for a new county flora. He worked on this for several years, before being compelled by bad health to winter abroad in 1879–80. His health never really recovered and he died, unmarried, at Baldock, Hertfordshire, on 18 February 1881. He left his herbarium, books, and manuscript flora to the Hertfordshire Natural History Society, with a small sum of money to enable the society to print the manuscript, which appeared as *A Flora of Hertfordshire, edited … by B. Daydon Jackson, with an introduction … by John Hopkinson and the editor*, in 1887. However, the residue of his estate was to go (after supporting his mother until her death) to Cardinal Manning.

B. D. JACKSON, rev. PETER OSBORNE

Sources Foster, *Alum. Oxon.* • *Journal of Botany, British and Foreign*, 19 (1881), 276–8 • A. R. Pryor, *A flora of Hertfordshire*, ed. B. D. Jackson (1887), xliv–xlvi • *Proceedings of the Linnean Society of London* (1880–82), 19 **Archives** Hertfordshire Natural History Society **Likenesses** portrait, Carnegie Mellon University, Pittsburgh, Hunt Botanical Library

Wealth at death under £30,000: probate, 20 May 1881, CGPLA Eng. & Wales

Prys, Edmwnd (1542/3–1623), Church of England clergyman and Welsh poet, was the son of Siôn ap Rhys ap Gruffudd ap Rhys and Siân, daughter of Owain ap Llywelyn ab Ieuan. Long thought to have been a native of Merioneth, he is now known to have hailed from Llanrwst, Denbighshire: both his father and grandfather feature among Llanrwst taxpayers in a 1543–4 subsidy roll, and genealogies place his mother's family also in the locality. His Llanrwst kinsmen included the humanist William Salesbury, a possible early influence. It is not certain where Prys received his early education, but an association with the Wynn family of Gwydir, Llanrwst, seems likely. Sir John Wynn of Gwydir claimed that William Morgan, translator of the Bible into Welsh, received his early education at Gwydir, where there is evidence that the family employed a tutor. In 1565 both Prys and Morgan enrolled in St John's College, Cambridge; significantly perhaps, John Gwynn, Sir John Wynn's uncle, had served as fellow there from 1548 to 1555.

Prys graduated BA from St John's in 1568, and MA in 1571. Elected fellow there in 1570, he was later elected college preacher (1574) and chaplain (1575); in 1575–6 he served as university preacher. His prominence in university circles led to his inclusion in the 'Cockolds Kallender', a scurrilous Cambridge satire by Stephen Valenger. Prys's long stay at St John's familiarized him with humanist culture and provided him with a formidable linguistic armoury. He claimed to know eight languages: these would have included the three classical languages in addition to his native Welsh and acquired English, and probably also some of the modern continental vernaculars. His friend William Morgan is credited with a knowledge of French; it may be significant that the Frenchman Antoine Chevallier, said to have been Princess Elizabeth's French tutor, was Hebrew lecturer at St John's during the two Welshmen's time there.

Prys was ordained deacon in 1567 and priest in 1568 and was licensed to preach by John Whitgift in 1570. Having served a curacy at Harlton near Cambridge from 1568, he obtained his first living—the rectory of Ffestiniog and Maentwrog in Merioneth—in 1573, being at first an absentee incumbent. Appointed both rector of Ludlow and archdeacon of Merioneth in 1576, he probably still resided to some extent at Cambridge until 1577. He relinquished Ludlow in 1579, settling in Merioneth, at Tyddyn Du, Maentwrog (his popular association with Gerddi Bluog in nearby Llanfair is spurious). He served as archdeacon of Merioneth and rector of Ffestiniog and Maentwrog for the remainder of his life, serving also from 1580 as rector of Llanenddwyn and Llanddwywe. By virtue of his office as archdeacon he held the sinecure rectory of Llandudno. He also served as a canon and prebend at Bangor Cathedral, and in 1602 was appointed a canon at St Asaph's Cathedral by Bishop William Morgan, another indication of their close association.

Prys combined his clerical duties with the life of a country gentleman—he acquired land in Ffestiniog and Maentwrog—and he served as a justice of the peace for some thirty years. Charges of illegal acquisition of land, cattle stealing, assault, bribery, and perjury were brought against him in the court of Star Chamber (1594, 1607), but their outcome is unknown. It is credible, however, that Prys—a man of very large physical stature who sometimes displayed an arrogant disposition in his poetry—could have been capable of overbearing and aggressive behaviour. Prys married twice. His first wife, Elin, daughter of Siôn (John) ap Lewis of Pengwern, Ffestiniog, bore him three children, John, Robert, and Jane. His second wife, whom he had married by 1588, was Elin's cousin Gwen, daughter of Morgan ap Lewis and widow of Rhys ap Robert of Llanfair Talhaearn. She bore him three sons, Ffowc, Morgan, and Edmwnd. Like their father, both John and Ffowc Prys wrote poetry.

Prys, the finest Welsh amateur poet of his day, produced a considerable body of strict-metre poetry (i.e. featuring *cynghanedd*). Much of it consisted of debates with other poets, Siôn Phylip, Huw Machno, Thomas Prys, and Wiliam Cynwal. Of these, the debate with Cynwal, extending to some fifty-four poems (1581–7), was easily the most significant. In this exchange Prys voiced a humanist critique of professional bards such as Cynwal, drawing on a wide range of reference derived from both classical and Welsh learning. Prys pursued a dual line of attack. First, he criticized Cynwal and his ilk for the mendacity of their eulogies—the staple product of professional bardism— echoing the criticism of the fifteenth-century poet Siôn Cent. In Prys's view this mendacity was compounded by an attachment to discredited medieval lore, exemplified by Cynwal's references to Mandeville's travels and the story of Merlin. Second, he attacked Cynwal for his poetry's lack of substance, a fault Prys attributed to a lack of learning. Dismissing Cynwal's bardic degrees and training, he urged the bards to resort to the universities, asserting that a poet should be both a philosopher and a linguist. As alternatives to eulogy Prys championed both divine poetry based on the Bible and scientific poetry, genres popular in contemporary humanist circles; a passage advocating scientific poetry suggests that he knew the then much admired *La Sepmaine* (1578) of Guillaume Du Bartas.

Prys's other poetry included elegies to his friends Richard Vaughan, bishop of London (a contemporary at St John's), and the poet Siôn Phylip, religious and moral poems such as 'An Ode on our Redemption' and 'A Carol on Conscience', an allegorical poem of social criticism, 'The Misgovernment of the Mighty', and a satire on football. His poem employing the English song-metre 'About the Bank of Helicon' anticipated the seventeenth-century vogue of deploying *cynghanedd* in metres other than the canonical ones of classical bardism. Prys wrote in Latin as well as Welsh. Latin quatrains by him occur in manuscripts, and a Latin hexameter poem he composed in praise of the author was prefaced to Dr John Davies's grammar, *Antiquae linguae Britannicae … rudimenta* (1621).

In a prefatory epistle to his 1588 Bible William Morgan cited Prys, with Dr David Powell and Richard Vaughan, as ones who had given him aid which was 'not to be discounted'. The extent of this contribution is unknown, but modern scholars doubt if it amounted to actual translation. Interestingly, Prys, in an elegy to Cynwal which concluded their debate, claimed that he chose him as an adversary in order to become acquainted with bardic linguistic usage and thus facilitate the provision of scripture in Welsh. Morgan may have sought his advice concerning the classical literary language of the bards, the medium adopted for the translation.

Prys's masterpiece, his Welsh metrical psalms, was composed in old age. The London stationer Thomas Salisbury referred as early as 1610 to Prys's promise to produce them, but they did not appear until 1621 when they were published as a supplement to an edition of the Welsh Book of Common Prayer. In a preface Prys justified his decision to compose the work in free metre, citing the danger of distorting scripture had he used the restrictive medium of *cynghanedd*. Although Prys knew Hebrew, modern scholarship has demonstrated—contrary to earlier claims—that he was more indebted to the earlier Welsh translations of the psalms by William Salesbury and William Morgan than to the Hebrew originals. This does not diminish his achievement, however, for his work is noteworthy for its felicitous phrasing and copious Welsh and for its versatility in conveying the psalms' wide range of emotions. Prys's psalms were the staple of Welsh congregational praise until a more subjective hymnody evolved in the wake of the eighteenth-century evangelical revival. Over 100 editions of them have been published; some have continued to feature in Welsh hymn collections in the early twenty-first century.

Prys died aged eighty in September 1623 and was probably buried in Maentwrog parish church. His wife survived him, Ffowc Prys inheriting Tyddyn Du.

GRUFFYDD ALED WILLIAMS

Sources A. O. Evans, 'Edmund Prys: archdeacon of Merioneth, priest, preacher, poet', *Transactions of the Honourable Society of Cymmrodorion* (1922–3), 112–68 · G. A. Williams, *Ymryson Edmwnd Prys a Wiliam Cynwal: fersiwn llawysgrif Llanstephan 43 gyda rhagymadrodd, nodiadau a geirfa* (1986) · G. A. Williams, 'Edmwnd Prys, un arall o enwogion Llanrwst', *Denbighshire Historical Society Transactions*, 23 (1974), 294–8 · G. A. Williams, 'Edmwnd Prys ac Ardudwy', *National Library of Wales Journal*, 22 (1981–2), 282–303 · G. A. Williams, 'William Morgan ac Edmwnd Prys yng Nghaergrawnt', *BBCS*, 29 (1980–82), 296–300 · R. Hughey, ed., *The Arundel Harington manuscript of Tudor poetry* (1960) · I. Thomas, 'Salmau cân Edmwnd Prys: eu perthynas â'r testun Hebraeg ac â'r fersiynau blaenorol', *Efrydiau Beiblaidd Bangor*, 4, ed. E. W. Davies (1988), 191–215 · G. A. Williams, 'Mydryddu'r Salmau yn Gymraeg', *Llên Cymru*, 16 (1989–91), 114–32 · J. E. Griffith, *Pedigrees of Anglesey and Carnarvonshire families* (privately printed, Horncastle, 1914) · R. G. Gruffydd, *'The translating of the Bible into the Welsh tongue' by William Morgan in 1588* (1988) · W. P. Griffith, *Learning, law and religion* (1996) · T. Baker, *History of the college of St John the Evangelist, Cambridge*, ed. J. E. B. Mayor, 2 vols. (1869) · NL Wales, Tanybwlch MS, 563

Wealth at death lent £200 to Richard Nanney of Llanfair in 1622: PRO plea rolls, Merionethshire, 22 James I (Wales: class 23, roll 23); translation of document in Evans, 'Edmund Prys', 161–2

Prys, Tomos. *See* Price, Thomas (c.1564–1634).

Pryse [Price], **Sir Carbery**, **fourth baronet** (d. 1694), mine owner and landowner, was the son of Carbery Pryse (Price), landowner, and his wife, Hester, daughter of Sir Bulstrode Whitelocke. His family owned Gogerddan, one of the major estates in north Cardiganshire, close to the county town of Aberystwyth, and had jealously guarded their mineral rights throughout the seventeenth century. Pryse succeeded to the estate and baronetcy in 1682, following the death, without issue, of his two uncles, Richard and Thomas. He was elected as knight of the shire for Cardiganshire in March 1690 (and held the seat until 1694), but the controversy over his election did not endear him to many members of parliament and may help to account for the lengthy proceedings against him during his battle to secure his mineral rights.

Although British landowners had previously enjoyed the right to minerals on their estates, the crown in the sixteenth century sought to encourage mining in Britain by bringing over various German mining experts and granting chartered status in 1568 to two monopoly companies, the Company of Mines Royal and the Society of Mineral and Battery Works. The former was granted the right to minerals containing gold and silver, but since these metals were frequently found mixed with other metals, landowners found their mining rights severely compromised. This was especially true in Cardiganshire, where the lead which was mined all over the county was often very rich in silver. Lessees of the mines royal challenged various landowners over their mines, particularly after one of the lessees, Thomas Bushell, gained the establishment of a mint in Aberystwyth in 1638.

In the late 1680s a shepherd discovered a rich vein of lead ore at Bwlch-yr-esgair-hir on the eastern boundary of the Gogerddan estate. Pryse decided to work the vein himself, and on 1 January 1690 established a company, dividing the capital required into twenty-four shares. Of these, he kept twelve himself and sold the other twelve to shareholders who included the earl of Danby. He was then challenged by Anthony Shepherd, lessee of the mines royal in Cardiganshire, who claimed that the lead ore at Esgair Hir was argentiferous and therefore came within the mines royal monopoly. Pryse refused to surrender his mines, and eventually the case was tried before the House of Lords. Samples of the ore were assayed, and whereas that brought by Shepherd was rich in silver, the specimen submitted by Pryse himself was not. Moses Stringer, a noted mineralogist, believed that the sample came from Derbyshire and was provided by William Waller, Pryse's notorious mine manager, in a deliberate attempt to mislead the court. However, many members of parliament, as landowners themselves, were sympathetic to Pryse's case and the verdict was finally delivered in his favour. The outcome was an Act to Prevent Disputes and Controversies concerning the Royal Mines, which received royal assent in February 1693 (Shiers, 3), and thereafter landowners could work their own mines, even if they contained gold or silver, so long as the crown could purchase the ore from the mine owner—a right that was rarely exercised. A contemporary report noted that 'upon the passing of this Bill, Sir Carbery Pryse, anxious to communicate the glad intelligence to his mining friends, rode from London to Esgair Hir in forty eight hours' (Hunt, 646).

Sir Carbery did not live long to enjoy his victory. The cost of draining the mines proved beyond the slender resources of the company he had set up, and in 1693 the capital was redivided into 4008 shares, Pryse retaining half and the remainder divided among the original members of the company. He had already engaged William Waller, a mine agent from the north of England, to run the company, though he remained chairman. To promote investment at Esgair Hir, Waller drew up an encouraging estimate of the profit of the mines at £70,500 and later likened the mines to the rich silver mine of Potosi in Bolivia—hence its name of Welsh Potosi. Pryse had intended to be an active chairman, but after his death in 1694 his heir, Edward Pryse, did not pursue the same policy and the company suffered from weak management. Waller eventually persuaded Sir Humphrey Mackworth, an industrialist from south Wales, to take over the company, and it was eventually worked by the Company of Mines Adventurers, founded in 1698.

Pryse, like his immediate predecessors, died unmarried, and the baronetcy, which had been created in 1641, expired with him. His vigour in pursuing his right to work his mines at Esgair Hir had, however, guaranteed the freedom of the British landowner to exploit the mineral resources on his estates, which was an important factor in Britain's early lead in industrialization.

MARILYN PALMER

Sources D. Jenkins, 'The Pryse family of Gogerddan', National Library of Wales Journal, 8 (1953–4), 176–98, 353–68 · W. Rees, Industry before the industrial revolution, 2 vols. (1968) · R. Hunt, 'Notices of the lead mines of Cardiganshire', Memoirs of the Geological Survey, 2/2 (1848) · W. R. Scott, The constitution and finance of English, Scottish and Irish joint-stock companies to 1720, 2 (1910) · M. Palmer, 'The richest in all Wales': the Welsh Potosi, or, Esgair Hir and Esgair Fraith lead and copper mines of Cardiganshire (1983) · M. Stringer, Opera mineralia explicata (1713) · W. Waller, 'A short account of Sir Carbery Pryse's lead work', 1693, BL, MS Cup. 645. b11 (14) · W. Waller, An essay on the value of the mines, late of Sir Carbery Price (1698) · W. Shiers [H. Hackworth], 'A familiar discourse, or, Dialogue concerning the mine adventure', 1709, BL, MS 444.a.3 · W. J. Lewis, Lead mining in Wales (1967)
Archives NL Wales, Gogerddan MSS

Prysot [Prisot], **Sir John** (d. 1461), justice, was the son of John Prisot of Haslingfield, Cambridgeshire; suggestions that his family came from Kent appear to be unfounded. The early stages of his career are unknown, but from the late 1430s he is recorded as active in Cambridgeshire and Hertfordshire—his marriage brought him the manor of Wallington in the latter county. He was a JP in Cambridgeshire from 1437, escheator in that county and Huntingdonshire in 1438, and a JP in Hertfordshire from 1443 (presumably in consequence of his marriage), as well as in other counties in the south midlands and East Anglia from the late 1440s. In July 1443 he became a serjeant-at-law, and he was promoted king's serjeant at the following Michaelmas. His contributions to courtroom debate at once begin to be recorded in the year-books. Between 1445 and 1447 he was retained by the duchy of Lancaster, while in 1448 he was a justice of assize and gaol delivery for the liberty of Ely.

On 16 January 1449 Prysot was appointed chief justice of the court of common pleas, even though he had not previously been a puisne justice, and was granted £93 6s. 8d. per annum and additional sums for his robes. He was soon active away from Westminster in the service of the crown, as a commissioner of oyer and terminer in Kent in 1451, after Jack Cade's uprising, in the same capacity in Lincolnshire in 1452, in the aftermath of the duke of York's demonstration at Dartford, and at York in 1454 'for execution of justice uppon such as hafe offended yn cause creminall' (Paston Letters, 1.290). He was a trier of petitions from Gascony and overseas territories in the parliaments of 1453 and 1455. In the latter year he was a member of the Hertfordshire commission for raising funds for the defence of Calais, while in 1459 he became a feoffee to the use by the crown of various duchy of Lancaster estates. He appears to have been knighted in that year. He was frequently employed as a commissioner by the king, and was also engaged in private business as a feoffee and arbitrator.

Prysot was known as a learned judge—he is recorded as citing a law book of Edward I's time which was probably Britton. His opinions are frequently recorded in the law reports, for instance in his argument for statute as the only 'positive' law, taking precedence over prescription. He was said to have assisted Sir Thomas Littleton (d. 1481) in the preparation of the latter's Tenures, and his opinions were still being referred to over a century after his death. Ordinances issued on 1 July 1457 for the behaviour and fees of the officials of the court of common pleas are described as having been drawn up under his direction. A complaint of his partiality in the conduct of business at Norwich in July 1451 should be regarded with scepticism, as emanating from a disappointed litigant. Prysot died early in 1461, probably shortly before 17 May, when the parson of Clothall, Hertfordshire, near Wallington, was granted administration of his will. He may have been buried in the north chapel of St Mary's Church, Wallington, where stained glass survives bearing his arms. He was outlived by his wife, Margaret, who was still living in 1475, and by their daughter, Anne, who married George Dallyson.

R. J. SCHOECK

Sources Chancery records · VCH Cambridgeshire and the Isle of Ely, vols. 4–5 · Baker, Serjeants · Sainty, Judges, 47 · [Paston], The Paston letters, 1422–1509 AD, ed. J. Gairdner, new edn, 1 (1872); repr. (1900), 211–13, 290 · H. Chauncy, The historical antiquities of Hertfordshire (1700); repr. in 2 vols., 1 (1826), 96, 357 · M. Hemmant, ed., Select cases in the exchequer chamber, [1], SeldS, 51 (1933), 137 · Reports from the lost notebooks of Sir James Dyer, ed. J. H. Baker, 1, SeldS, 109 (1994), 186, 210 · N. Doe, Fundamental authority in late medieval English law (1990), 25 · M. Hastings, The court of common pleas in fifteenth century England (1947) · Registrum Thomae Bourgchier ... 1454–1486, ed. F. R. H. Du Boulay, CYS, 54 (1957), 197 · R. Barnewal, ed., Les reports de les cases conteinus in les ans vint primer et apres in temps del roy Henry le siz (1601) · Hertfordshire, Pevsner (1977), 374 · R. Somerville, History of the duchy of Lancaster, 1265–1603 (1953), 451 · N. H. Nicolas, ed., Proceedings and ordinances of the privy council of England, 7 vols., RC, 26 (1834–7), 6.239 · RotP, 5.227, 279; 6.355

Psalmanazar, George (1679–1763), impostor and author, was born in southern France under a name that is now unknown and to parents whose names, like that of his place of birth, he does not mention in his Memoirs (published posthumously in 1764), the only source of information about his early life. For an important and lengthy period of his life he claimed to be a native of Formosa (now Taiwan), but his confessional Memoirs make it clear that he was born of Roman Catholic parents in southern France. This is affirmed in the advertisement to the first edition of the Memoirs in the testimony of an acquaintance of twenty years: 'He was a Frenchman. His pronunciation had a spice of the Gascoin accent, and in that provincial dialect, he was so masterly, that none but those born in the country could equal, none though born there could excel him' (Memoirs, i–ii). The little Psalmanazar says about his background in the Memoirs indicates that his was a family of slender means, and that his 'father was of an ancient, but decayed family, and had been obliged to leave my mother before I was five years old, and to live near five hundred miles from her' in Germany (ibid., 71). Psalmanazar left his mother's house to visit his father at the age of sixteen, but the visit was brief, and there is no indication that he ever saw either of his parents in later life.

Education and early career By his own account, Psalmanazar's 'more than common readiness at learning' (Memoirs, 73) in childhood gained him admiration and special treatment from teachers. At six he went to a 'free-school taught by two Franciscan monks' (ibid.), where he immediately started Latin. He then attended a Jesuit college, where he proceeded through the forms to 'Humanity', rhetoric, and philosophy. In the Memoirs Psalmanazar makes much of his precocity, especially in learning languages, and of the over-indulgent treatment he received from his teachers. After the Jesuit college, he went on to study philosophy and theology in a Dominican university in a nearby town, 'too young quite, in all appearance, to herd among the rest of the students, some of whom were twice my age, and none by many years so young as I' (ibid., 98). Finally, disenchanted with the Dominican teachers' Thomism and with his studies in general, he left his university and went to nearby Avignon as a tutor. By this time, aged about sixteen, he was fluent in Latin and knew a good deal of philosophy and theology. Because of one teacher's special interest, he was also knowledgeable about military fortification, but otherwise his education was not very broad.

In his first professional appointment, Psalmanazar was undone by his attractiveness to his superiors. The mother of his tutees, he says, made sexual overtures to him, and when he did not respond he was dismissed. In poverty in Avignon, he explained his ragged appearance and soothed his pride by pretending he was 'a sufferer for religion for too great attachment to the church' (Memoirs, 113). Finally out of funds, he resolved to return home, and as a 'means of facilitating [his] long journey' he obtained a certificate signifying that he was a 'student in theology, of Irish extract', a religious exile on a pilgrimage to Rome (ibid., 117). He stole a cloak and staff for the purpose and

George Psalmanazar (1679–1763), by unknown engraver

set off first to his mother and then to his estranged father.

Becoming Formosan Finding his father's circumstances very uninviting and the neighbouring towns and universities inaccessible, Psalmanazar decided to return home but was persuaded by his father to tour northern Germany and the Netherlands first. In order to gain alms on this journey, Psalmanazar decided to make his identity more exotic, and posed as a Japanese convert to Christianity. To facilitate the project, he revised the certificate that he had had drawn up to prove that he was Irish, and devised an alphabet and many words of a language that he thought might be taken for Japanese. Aware that Hebrew was written from right to left, he imagined that other 'oriental' languages would follow that pattern. He invented twenty letters with shapes, names, and pronunciations that resemble some Greek and Hebrew letters. By his own account, he also added 'many other particulars equally difficult, such as a considerable piece of a new language and grammar, a new division of the year into twenty months, a new religion, &c. and all out of my own head' (*Memoirs*, 137).

Destitute and scabrous after travelling, Psalmanazar enlisted in a military regiment camped near Bonn. Taking to swearing and profligacy, he pretended then to be an 'unconverted or heathenish' Japanese (*Memoirs*, 162). He soon joined another regiment (under the duke of Mecklenburg) in Cologne, and this time used the name of Salmanazar (ibid., 169), which he took from the name of a biblical king of Assyria and captor of the Israelites, Shalmaneser (2 Kings 17). Later he began spelling the name with an initial P to make it more exotic, and he began claiming he was from the island of Formosa, a place he described as politically and culturally dependent upon Japan.

Changing regiments once again, Psalmanazar enlisted at Sluys, Holland, and there met the British chaplain Alexander Innes, who saw in him an opportunity for his own advancement. First, Innes revealed the fraud. 'His stratagem', wrote Psalmanazar:

> was to make me translate a passage of Cicero de natura deorum, of some length, into my (pretended) Formosan language, and give it to him in writing; and this I easily did … But, after he had made me construe it, and desired me to write another version of it on another paper, his proposal, and the manner of his exacting it, threw me into such visible confusion, having had so little time to excogitate the first, and less to commit it to memory, that there were not above one half of the words in the second that were in the first. (*Memoirs*, 184–5)

To his great shame in later life, Psalmanazar then allowed Innes to baptize him in the Church of England with the name of George Lauder, the governor of the regiment. For this deed Innes received commendation from the bishop of London, Henry Compton, and Psalmanazar received an invitation to come to England with the hope that he would teach Formosan at Oxford to Christian missionaries (ibid., 192).

Psalmanazar earned fame in England within a year of his arrival when he published *An Historical and Geographical Description of Formosa* (1704). He dedicated the work to Henry Compton, to whom he had earlier given drafts of 'Formosan' material: a translation of the Lord's prayer, a table of the alphabet, and drawings of the dress of the Formosans. The history, which Psalmanazar wrote in Latin over several months, was concurrently translated into English. (Judging from the French translation of 1705, R. M. Swiderski suggests that Psalmanazar may have written originally in French.) The fulsome dedication to Compton, the description of his conversion, and his high praise of the Church of England as a 'true Apostolical Church' helped Psalmanazar earn a loyal following. However, his fanciful account of Formosa, which occupies little more than half of the book's 327 pages, raised doubts about his veracity in several quarters at the same time as it excited many readers. Among his entertaining but suspicious claims were that Formosa was Japanese rather than Chinese; that the state religion, founded by an avatar named Psalmanaazaar, required the annual sacrifice of 18,000 boys under the age of nine; and that the production of children was facilitated by the encouragement of polygamy, although adultery was absolutely forbidden.

Although Psalmanazar took a few descriptions out of Bernhardus Varenius's *Descriptio regni Japoniae et Siam* (1649), his work is mostly pure fiction. In his *Memoirs* he claimed to have borrowed more than he had done from

Varenius and also from the fabulous account of Formosa by George Candidius in his *Collection of Voyages and Travels* (1704). Despite the paper-thinness of its research, Psalmanazar's book was an instant success, and Henry Compton sent him to Christ Church, Oxford, where he remained in residence for three months. There he wrote an expanded and more daring second edition, which included sensational new claims about cannibalism and the subordination of Formosan women. In fact the two topics are sometimes conflated, as when Psalmanazar describes men devouring sinful women or discarded wives. It appears from some of the letters from Richard Gwinnet to Elizabeth Thomas (1731) that Psalmanazar claimed to have eaten human flesh himself (Foley, appendix C).

At Oxford Psalmanazar was fortunate to have as his tutor the sympathetic (or gullible) Samuel Reynolds (father of the painter Joshua Reynolds and principal addressee in Psalmanazar's extant correspondence). The admiration of Reynolds notwithstanding, much of the learned community knew of Psalmanazar's fraud even before his book was published, as evidenced in the correspondence of John Locke, Anthony Collins, and Thomas Hearne, as well as in Samuel Parker's journal *History of the Works of the Learned*. On 2 February 1704 Psalmanazar was invited to attend a meeting of the Royal Society along with Father Jean de Fontenay, a French Jesuit who had spent time in China. According to Psalmanazar's account in his *Description*, he defeated Fontenay's arguments that Formosa was Chinese rather than Japanese. Psalmanazar did not mention until the second edition (1705) the probing enquiry by Edmond Halley about the duration of twilight in Formosa, which revealed the fraud, according to a note on the flyleaf of a second edition of the *Description* in the British Library (Foley, 19). Further notes in the *Journal of the Royal Society* show that fellows were convinced of the fraud by 13 June 1705, when they received letters concerning Formosa from a traveller there (ibid., 20). But the society made no pronouncement against Psalmanazar, and to the extent that its opposition was known it helped Psalmanazar to portray himself as a defender of revealed religion hounded by the rationalistic freethinkers of the Royal Society. In a lengthy review of his *Memoirs*, the *Monthly Review* confirmed that he profited from the Royal Society's opposition (p. 447).

Psalmanazar received 10 guineas for the first and 12 guineas for the second edition of the *Description*, 'besides such presents as were made me by the generous few to whom I presented them' (*Memoirs*, 220–21). With the support of these 'few', in 1706 and again in 1707 Psalmanazar published defences of himself that emphasize his allegiance to revealed religion. About 1710 he made a final attempt to defend himself in print with the publication of two more pamphlets. Nevertheless, credulity was growing thin. By 16 March 1711 Psalmanazar's fraud was well enough known for *The Spectator* to make a joke at his expense by printing a false advertisement, claiming that

On the first of April will be performed at the playhouse in the Hay- market an Opera call'd The Cruelty of Atreus. N. B. The scene

wherein Thyestes eats his own children, is to be performed by the famous Mr. Psalmanazar, lately arrived from Formosa: The whole Supper being set to Kettle-drums. (*The Spectator*, ed. D. Bond, 5 vols., 1965, 1.65)

Final deception and later career After five or six years in England, Psalmanazar made his last public attempt to capitalize on his feigned origins: he conspired with a man named Pattenden to promote a kind of lacquer called white Formosan work. The project failed, and until 1715 Psalmanazar lived on the small income he earned as a tutor. In that year he became clerk to a regiment of dragoons fighting against the Jacobites, and after the defeat of the rising he stayed for a time in Lancashire, where he advised the newly established Manchester College Library on the expenditure of its gift funds for books.

Back in London about 1717, Psalmanazar began painting ladies' fans for a living, until friends took up a subscription for him to study divinity. Feeling guilty about this generosity, however, he earned an income as a translator.

It was then I began to perceive, with no small joy, how God blessed my endeavours in proportion to my diligence and honesty … From translating of other people's works, I came at length to print some of my own, and … bless the Divine mercy, for the wonderful and undeserved success I have since met with. (*Memoirs*, 249)

For the rest of his life Psalmanazar was a pious and productive member of Grub Street. The principal works to which he made significant contributions are Samuel Palmer's *The General History of Printing* (1732), which he took over after the death of the first author; Emanuel Bowen's *A Complete System of Geography* (2 vols., 1744), to which he contributed articles on thirty countries including a confessional piece on Formosa; and *An Universal History from the Earliest Account of Time* (8 vols., 1736–50). To this last, immense folio work and its twenty-volume octavo second edition (1747–54) Psalmanazar contributed articles on at least twelve vast subjects, including a history of the Jews to the present, as well as on ancient Greece, the ancient Spaniards, the Gauls, and the Germans. The quality of Psalmanazar's known work is less impressive than the indomitable energy and considerable linguistic skill he displayed to complete it.

Confession Soon after becoming a writer, Psalmanazar resolved to overcome his vanity and confess his impostures. Several books of practical divinity were important to his salvation, he said, but the decisive experience was his reading of William Law's *A Serious Call to a Devout and Holy Life* (1728), which was also read at this time, and with similar effect, by the future lexicographer Samuel Johnson. Later Johnson identified Psalmanazar's devotion as one of the reasons why he 'sought after' him 'the most' of any of his London acquaintance (Boswell, *Life*, 3.314). According to Sir John Hawkins, Johnson:

was very well acquainted with Psalmanaazar, the pretended Formosan, and said, he had never seen the close of the life of any one that he wished so much his own to resemble, as that of him, for its purity and devotion … asked whether he ever contradicted Psalmanaazar;—'I should as soon', said he, 'have thought of contradicting a bishop'; so high did he hold his character in the latter part of his life. When he was asked whether he had ever mentioned Formosa before him, he said, he was afraid to mention even China. (*Johnsonian Miscellanies*, ed. G. B. Hill, 2 vols., 1897, reprinted 1970, 2.12–13)

In 1753 Psalmanazar published anonymously his *Essays on the Following Subjects*, which purport to offer a defence of revealed religion from the attacks of Viscount Bolingbroke, Anthony Collins, and especially David Hume, whose essay on miracles had recently been published. For the most part, Psalmanazar relies here on the old argument of Lactantius and others that human ignorance disqualifies man from passing judgement on the miracles of revelation. However, his engagement with the details of his opponents' thinking is minimal.

In 1752 Psalmanazar wrote to Thomas Birch of his failing health. In the same year he also made his will and named his executor and residuary legatee as Sarah Rewalling, 'my pious and worthy friend … of this parish of St. Luke, in Middlesex' (*Memoirs*, 3–4). She is named as the publisher of the *Memoirs*, but nothing further is known of her or of their relationship. In the preface to his *Memoirs* Psalmanazar provided 'some account of that vast quantity of laudanum I have been known to take for above these forty years' to which he attributed his good health (ibid., 57). Although 'quite sound in mind', Psalmanazar described himself as 'weak in my body' when he ratified his will on 1 January 1762 (ibid., 9). He died on 3 May 1763 at Ironmonger Row, St Luke's parish, London. Then, according to the *Gentleman's Magazine*, aged eighty-four, Psalmanazar was 'known for many ingenious performances in different parts of literature' (*GM*, 33.257). His will was printed in several magazines, and also in his *Memoirs*. Perhaps most striking in this document are his directions for a humble burial 'without any kind of coffin … but only a shell of lowest value, and without lid or other covering which may hinder the natural earth from covering it all around' (*Memoirs*, 4).

The obvious cultural milieu in which to place Psalmanazar is the impostors and forgers of the eighteenth century, including William Lauder, Thomas Chatterton, James MacPherson, and Richard Savage. In these and many other cases of forgery and assumed identity in the period, the impostor imagined he had access to hidden information and that he himself was in touch with a deeper or older, often more 'natural', tradition of knowledge than that accepted by the current establishment. The flourishing of such forgers at this time may have been a response to the increased professionalization of knowledge during the period. Psalmanazar's quarrel with the Royal Society, his defence of revelation in religion, and his immersion in ancient Hebrew may be all regarded as a rebellion against modern forms of knowledge. Unlike his fellow impostors, Psalmanazar outlived his impersonation by several decades and became an admired penitent and an industrious, if not brilliant, contributor to the productions of Grub Street. ROBERT DEMARIA, JUN.

Sources DNB · *Memoirs of ****, commonly known by the name of George Psalmanazar* (1764) · F. J. Foley, *The great Formosan impostor* (1968) · R. M. Swiderski, *The false Formosan: George Psalmanazar and the eighteenth-century experiment of identity* (1991) · Boswell, *Life* · R. Gwinnett and E. Thomas, *Pylades and Corinna*, 2 vols. (1731–2) · Allibone, *Dict.* · abstract of *Memoirs* with commentary, *Monthly Review*, 31 (1764), 364–85, 441–54 · *GM*, 1st ser., 33 (1763), 257

Archives BL · LPL · Yale U., Beinecke L. | Four Oaks Farm, Somerville, New Jersey, Hyde collection

Likenesses line engraving, BM, NPG [*see illus.*] · portrait, repro. in *Memoirs*, frontispiece

Wealth at death very little: will, repr. in Psalmanazar, *Memoirs*

Pucci, Francesco (1543–1597), theological writer, was born on 11 February 1543 in the via Ghibellina, Florence, the eldest son of Antonio Pucci (*b.* 1496) and Lisabetta Giambonelli (*d.* 1590). He came from the junior branch of a patrician Florentine family. He was educated in the Accademia dei Lucidi in Florence, and took minor orders. His uncle, Mariotto Giambonelli, a rich Roman jeweller, made him his heir and decided in 1564 that he should be apprenticed to a Florentine banker in Lyons. The death of his uncle in 1570 enabled Pucci to leave the bank and recommence his education, and he enrolled in 1571 as a student of theology at the University of Paris. He witnessed the massacre of St Bartholomew's day there in 1572, and this persuaded him to leave Paris and become an undergraduate at the University of Oxford. He graduated MA on 18 May 1574. His quarrelsome and enquiring disposition led him into theological difficulties at Oxford and by 1575 he had been expelled from the university. He spent two years in London, where he became a member of the Huguenot church and quarrelled with its leading figures, arguing that each individual had the authority to decide on theological matters for himself. He left England in 1576, and went by way of Paris to Basel, where he began the first of his debates with the Unitarian theologian Fausto Sozzini. Pucci developed the idea that Adam before the fall was immortal. After just over a year Pucci was expelled from Basel for publishing a provocative list of his beliefs, and he returned to London, where he is to be found by early 1579.

While on this second visit to London, Pucci wrote two important theological pamphlets. In the *Informazione della religione Christiana*, which was printed in London in 1580, he outlined his humanist theology, called for a general council to reunite Christendom, and launched a vigorous attack on the Roman Catholic church. The following year Pucci produced his most ambitious and fanciful work, which seems to have circulated only in manuscript, the 'Forma d'una republica catholica'. He advocated the creation of an underground secret society uniting those of goodwill throughout Christendom to prepare the way for the hoped-for general council. He described the structure of his secret utopia: it would consist of cells or 'colleges' each run by a provost, chancellor, and censor elected for four years by universal manhood suffrage, who would regulate the marriage, education, and morals of its members, and tax them. Discipline would also be maintained by the use of spies and informers. The colleges dispersed throughout Europe would send delegates to a central diet, which would have supreme legislative and judicial authority. The members of this 'republic' would, until the general council had pronounced, be Nicodemites, attending the local religious services enforced by law to a sufficient degree to avoid punishment, and then at home would practise a simple religion based on those beliefs which were accepted by all Christians. In June 1582 Pucci left London for Antwerp and then in 1583 he migrated to Cracow, partly to resume his debates with Sozzini who was presently ensconced in that city. Two years later (1585) he had removed to Prague, to meet the English alchemists John Dee and Edward Kelley. Pucci's thought was already increasingly millenarian and occultist, and in Dee and Kelley he found kindred spirits. He made the mistake of lending Kelley money at a time when his own financial position was increasingly precarious since he had nearly exhausted his inheritance.

By 1585 Pucci was trying to arrange for a return to Florence, negotiating through Florentine and Roman channels, although the Inquisition had already taken an interest in him. He wrote penitent letters to the pope and formally abjured his heresy at Prague. However, at the same time he continued to write and distribute as widely as possible works of speculative theology which were certainly heretical. All his works were placed on the Index in 1592, after the publication in that year at Gouda of *De Christi servatoris efficacitate*, dedicated to the pope, in which he maintained that Christ had saved the whole of humanity. He continued to drift from European city to city until at last in 1593 at Salzburg, where he was confined to bed having broken a leg in a carriage accident, he was arrested by agents of the Roman Inquisition who took him in chains to Rome. Here he was imprisoned, stripped of his property, and forced (at the insistence of his relatives) to change his surname. He was a relapsed heretic and hence liable to suffer the supreme penalty. He was saved from the stake by a second abjuration, but was killed instead by being beheaded at the Tor di Nona prison on 5 July 1597. His remains were burnt in the campo dei Fiori.

PETER HOLMES

Sources E. Barnavi and M. Eliav-Feldon, *Le périple de Francesco Pucci* (Paris, 1988) · L. Firpo, *Gli scritti di Francesco Pucci* (Turin, 1957) · L. Firpo and R. Piattoli, eds., *Francesco Pucci: lettere, documenti e testimonianze*, 2 vols. (Florence, 1955); (1959) · DNB · M. Eliav-Feldon, 'Secret societies, utopias, and peace plans: the case of Francesco Pucci', *Journal of Medieval and Renaissance Studies*, 14 (1984), 139–58 · A. Rotondo, 'Il premio soggiorno in Inghilterra e i primi scritti teologici di Francesco Pucci', *Studi e Ricerche* [Turin] (1974), 225–71, 514–27 · L. Firpo, 'Francesco Pucci in Inghilterra', *Revue Internationale de Philosophie* [Brussels] (1951), 158–73 · D. Cantimori and E. Feist, *Per la storia degli eretici Italiani del secolo XVI in Europa* (Rome, 1937) · L. Firpo, 'Processo e morte di Francesco Pucci', *Rivista di Filosofia*, 40 (1949), 371–405 · L. Firpo, 'Nuovo ricerche su Francesco Pucci', *Rivista Storica Italiana*, 79 (1967), 1051–74 · Wood, *Ath. Oxon.*, new edn, 1.587–9
Wealth at death confiscated by inquisition: Barnavi and Eliav-Feldon, *Le périple de Francesco Pucci*

Pucelle, Gerard (d. 1184), canonist and bishop of Coventry, is of unknown origins, though his surname suggests French or Norman provenance. He was a teacher before 1156, lecturing in canon law, perhaps also in theology and civil law, in the schools of Paris, and he came to enjoy the special favour of Louis VII (r. 1137–80).

Gerard Pucelle received his first orders and benefice from Archbishop Thomas Becket (d. 1170) before the latter left England in November 1164. He was with Becket in the early days of the latter's exile, but by the first months of 1166 had gone to Germany. It was a time of schism in the church, and the German emperor, Frederick Barbarossa (r. 1152–90) was supporting a rival pope against Alexander III (r. 1159–81). Pucelle was received with great acclaim in Cologne, whose schismatic archbishop, Rainald von Dassel, was Frederick Barbarossa's chancellor. Pucelle's friend John of Salisbury (d. 1180) protested, and refused Pucelle's invitation to join him in Germany, but Pucelle stayed on. He seems to have been master of the cathedral school of Cologne in this period, and to have played a significant role in the brief efflorescence of a Colognese school of canon law. Writing to Becket in 1167 Pucelle affirmed his loyalty to the archbishop and informed him of events in Germany.

Gerard Pucelle distanced himself from Becket's cause in 1168 by returning to England and taking an oath to Henry II. Later in that year, however, Pucelle was reconciled with the archbishop. At Becket's request Alexander III absolved Pucelle of his association with the schism, on condition that he renounce the benefice that he had obtained in Germany, and take an oath denying the validity of schismatic orders. Becket and Alexander also interceded with Louis VII for Pucelle. Pucelle was still involved with the supporters of Henry II in 1170, when he tried to arrange for Becket to meet Geoffrey Ridel, the archdeacon of Canterbury, and Froger, bishop of Sées. John of Salisbury chastised Pucelle for having associated with the excommunicated Ridel and bluntly warned him that he would find it difficult to be reconciled with the church a second time. At about this time Pucelle may have resumed teaching in France.

Between 1174 and 1183 Gerard Pucelle witnessed at least fifty-six—approximately a quarter—of the surviving *acta* of Archbishop Richard of Dover (d. 1184); normally he heads the list of witnesses. He was not with Richard for the entire period, however. In the early months of 1178 he was with Peter of Blois in Rome, representing the archbishop in a dispute with St Augustine's Abbey, Canterbury. In February Alexander III, praising Pucelle's *litteratura* and *scientia*, granted him the privilege of retaining the income from his English benefices for four years while he was teaching. In March Alexander permitted Pucelle to recover the revenues of his German benefices. At about the same time Cardinal Pietro da Pavia, the papal legate in France, commended Pucelle to the pope. Attending the Third Lateran Council in March 1179, as Richard of Dover's representative, Pucelle pleaded the cause of Master Bertram, a distinguished lawyer who may have been Pucelle's pupil at Cologne, and who had been elected bishop of Bremen. Pucelle probably taught again in Cologne in 1180, before returning to England some time before September 1181.

Gerard Pucelle was elected bishop of Coventry, probably in May or June 1183, and was consecrated at Canterbury on 25 September. However, he died at Coventry on the following 13 January, under circumstances that led some to suspect that he had been poisoned, and was buried in Coventry Cathedral. The monks of Canterbury celebrated his obit with the rites usual for an archbishop.

According to Herbert of Bosham (*d. c.*1194), Gerard Pucelle was celebrated in his day, both as a lawyer and a teacher, though the reasons for his fame are not entirely clear. He was associated with canonistic activity at Paris and Cologne, but none of the known products of those schools is likely to have been his work. He may have written a lost *Summa super decretalia*. Various canonistic glosses and *summae* refer to his opinions, and there is at least one reference to his theological opinions. Pucelle was one of only two twelfth-century authors to claim a knowledge of Cresconius, an obscure African canonist of the sixth or seventh century; the other author may have been Pucelle's pupil. To characterize Pucelle as a polymath of wide reading would fit well with John of Salisbury's lighthearted description of him rifling the bookshelves of Rheims for manuscripts to take with him to Cologne. Another generation of canonic studies may reveal more.

Pucelle's character is difficult to assess. He may have been—like many lawyers before and after him—a person who thought that he could do good while doing well. His association with the schismatics was, at best, impolitic, and his reconciliation with Henry II was disloyal to Becket, but in both instances Pucelle may have thought that he could act as a mediator. The fact that he was reconciled with both Becket and Alexander III suggests that he was not a man with whom one could remain angry for long. In his later years Pucelle advanced his own career while remaining loyal and of service to his patron, Archbishop Richard. He seems to have incurred no opprobrium when he argued successfully on behalf of Battle Abbey that one of his patron's early *acta* was invalid, and his argument may well have been correct. If he died the victim of foul play, then that should probably be attributed to local politics, rather than to any personal failing.

CHARLES DONAHUE JUN.

Sources S. Kuttner and E. Rathbone, 'Anglo-Norman canonists of the twelfth century', *Traditio*, 7 (1949–51), 279–358, esp. 296–303 · J. Fried, 'Gerard Pucelle und Köln', *Zeitschrift für Rechtsgeschichte (Kanonistische Abteilung)*, 99 (68) (1982), 122–35 · C. R. Cheney and B. E. A. Jones, eds., *Canterbury, 1162–1190*, English Episcopal Acta, 2 (1986) · M. J. Franklin, 'The bishops of Coventry and Lichfield, c.1072–1208', *Coventry's first cathedral: the cathedral and priory of St Mary* [Coventry 1993], ed. G. Demidowicz (1994), 118–38, esp. 132–4 · *The letters of John of Salisbury*, ed. and trans. H. E. Butler and W. J. Millor, rev. C. N. L. Brooke, 2 vols., OMT (1979–86) [Lat. orig. with parallel Eng. text] · *The historical works of Gervase of Canterbury*, ed. W. Stubbs, 2 vols., Rolls Series, 73 (1879–80) · P. R. Coss, *Early records of medieval Coventry* (1986) · BL, Cotton MS Cleopatra D. ix · BL, Cotton MS Vespasian E. xvi · C. Donahue, 'Gerard Pucelle as a canon lawyer: life and the Battle Abbey case', *Grundlagen des Rechts: Festschrift für Peter Landau zum 65. Geburtstag*, ed. R. Helmholz, P. Mikat, J. Müller, and M. Stolleis (Paderborn, 2000), 333–48

Puckering [*formerly* Newton], **Sir Henry, third baronet** (*bap.* **1618**, *d.* **1701**), royalist army officer and local politician, was baptized on 13 April 1618 at St Dunstan-in-the-West, London, the son of Sir Adam *Newton, first baronet

(*d.* 1630), a Scot, and his wife, Katherine Puckering, daughter of Sir John *Puckering of Weston, Hertfordshire, the Elizabethan lord keeper. His mother died shortly after his birth and his father on 13 January 1630. On the death of his brother in the early 1630s, he inherited the baronetcy. He attended Eton College in 1630–31 and was admitted to the Inner Temple the following year. In 1635 he travelled abroad to complete an education which was designed to fit him for a life of royal service consonant with his background and by 1640 he had entered the service of Charles I. He married, probably about 1640, Elizabeth Murray, daughter of the late Thomas *Murray, provost of Eton, and his wife, Jane Drummond. His wife's family had also come from Scotland in the service of the Stuarts. In 1641 he became a justice in Kent.

At the outbreak of the civil war Newton raised a troop of horse for the king and was a commissioner of array in Kent. He was present at Edgehill and served with the king's forces as a captain of horse in 1643 and as a major from 1644 to 1646. He was allowed to go into exile after the fall of Truro. His wife subsequently negotiated with parliament on his behalf and in 1646 his composition was set at £1273, reduced from £1910 as being within the Exeter articles. While officially pardoned for his 'delinquency', Newton remained suspect and in June 1648 was apprehended on parliament's orders to prevent his joining the king's forces in Essex. Despite his continued royalism he is not known to have played any part in cavalier plotting. In 1649 his cousin Jane, the daughter and heir of Sir Thomas Puckering of The Priory, Warwick, was kidnapped and taken to Flanders in an attempt to force her into marriage. Crossing the channel in pursuit of Jane he encountered Colonel Joseph Bampfield, the married suitor of his sister-in-law Anne Murray [*see* Halkett, Anne], whom he challenged to a duel in which he was wounded in the hand. Jane Puckering was returned to England and married Sir John Bale of Carlton, Leicestershire, but died childless in 1652, leaving Newton as her heir male. He subsequently assumed the name of Puckering. Although Sir Thomas Puckering had died in 1637, the Puckering estate had been sequestrated in 1646 on the grounds that he would have been a royalist had he lived. The sequestration was lifted only in 1651 and its reimposition was threatened following Jane's death. John Evelyn, a close friend and neighbour of Newton at Greenwich, visited The Priory in August 1654 and adjudged it 'a melancholy old Seate' compared to Charlton House with its 'noble' prospect over the Thames, which would have been a 'princely seat' had the house had running water (Evelyn, 3.85, 120). Unfortunately his losses in the king's cause, extravagant housekeeping, and generosity obliged Puckering to sell Charlton and to take up permanent residence in Warwick in 1656. His generosity included a gift of £300 to his sister-in-law before her marriage to Sir James Halkett. Thomas Fuller dedicated a section of his *Church History* (1655) to Newton's son and heir apparent Henry, stressing the royal connections of his family.

Puckering has been described as managing the election

for the Warwickshire county seats to the Convention Parliament in the royalist interest, but his activity seems to have been less directed than this would imply. At the Restoration he became a justice and deputy lieutenant in Warwickshire and in 1661 he was elected to one of the county seats. He was a moderately active member of the Cavalier Parliament, in which his son sat for Warwick. He continued to be known for his good housekeeping and liberality to the poor and was 'distinguished throughout the kingdom for being a generous benefactor to the poor cavaliers, whose services were not rewarded by King Charles II' (Burke, 385). He was a committed Anglican and a strong opponent of dissent. In 1666, following a dispute between him and the townsmen of Warwick, 'scandalous reports' circulated concerning his Catholic sympathies and it was alleged that he had attended a mass at Weston Hall, home of the Sheldon family (*CSP dom.*, *1666–7*, 168). This was a particularly damaging accusation for Puckering, whose father had certainly passed himself off as a priest during his early life in France and may have taken Catholic orders. Puckering was appointed paymaster to the forces in 1676 and held the post until 1679, when he was elected to parliament for Warwick. He retired from the Warwickshire bench and as a deputy lieutenant in 1681, although he reassumed the latter responsibility briefly in the reign of James II.

Following his wife's death in 1689 Puckering appears to have retired from public life; in 1691 he gave the bulk of his library to Trinity College, Cambridge, and spent some time in residence there. He also forgave his wife's sister Anne all her debts to him. He died intestate on 22 January 1701 and was buried at St Mary's, Warwick. His four sons, all childless, had predeceased him so the baronetcy became extinct; his estate was settled on his wife's niece Jane, daughter of Henry Murray, esquire, groom of the bedchamber to Charles II, and widow of Sir John Bowyer of Knippersley, Staffordshire.   JAN BROADWAY

Sources A. M. Mimardière, 'Puckering (formerly Newton), Sir Henry', HoP, *Commons, 1660–90*, 3.299–301 • Evelyn, *Diary*, vol. 3 • F. L. Colvile, *The worthies of Warwickshire who lived between 1500 and 1800* [1870], 596–9 • J. Burke and J. B. Burke, *A genealogical and heraldic history of the extinct and dormant baronetcies of England, Ireland and Scotland*, 2nd edn (1841); repr. (1844), 385 • GEC, *Baronetage* • *The autobiography of Anne Lady Halkett*, ed. J. G. Nichols, CS, new ser., 13 (1875) • A. Hughes, *Politics, society and civil war in Warwickshire, 1620–1660* (1987), 335–6, 338 • P. Styles, *Studies in seventeenth century west midlands history* (1978), 39–40 • M. A. E. Green, ed., *Calendar of the proceedings of the committee for advance of money, 1642–1656*, 3 vols., PRO (1888), 693, 1433 • M. A. E. Green, ed., *Calendar of the proceedings of the committee for compounding … 1643–1660*, 2, PRO (1890), 1200–01 • *CSP dom.*, 1648, 106, 120, 124, 127; 1666–7, 117, 168 • E. Hasted, *The history and topographical survey of the county of Kent*, 2nd edn, 1 (1797), 35

Likenesses oils, Trinity Cam.

Wealth at death sold Charlton estate for £8500, 1656; Puckering estate value £2000–£3000 p.a. in 1640s; The Priory

Puckering, Sir John (1543/4–1596), administrator and speaker of the House of Commons, was the eldest son of William Puckering of Flamborough, Yorkshire, and his wife, Anne, daughter of John Ashton of Great Lever Hall, near Bolton, Lancashire. Admitted to Lincoln's Inn on 10 April 1559, he was called to the bar in 1567. On 21 February 1569 he married Jane (*d*. after 1599), daughter of Nicholas Chowne of Aldenham, Hertfordshire, and Fairlawn, near Wrotham, Kent, and his second wife, Elizabeth Scott. They had a son, Thomas [*see below*], and four daughters.

Under-treasurer of Lincoln's Inn in 1569, Puckering was a governor of the inn by 1575, and in that year became a justice of the peace in Hertfordshire. He was Lent reader of Lincoln's Inn in 1577, and became in the same year a member of the council of Wales and the marches and a justice of the peace in Welsh and border counties. On 7 September 1577 he was appointed justice of the Carmarthen circuit, becoming chief justice when Richard Atkyns was associated with him on 15 September 1578. Puckering retained his London practice, though his letters patent to act by deputy in Wales caused discord with Atkyns. A close ally of Robert Devereux, earl of Essex, in building up Essex's influence in south-west Wales, Puckering was created serjeant-at-law in October 1580. In 1582 he bought the priory of St Sepulchre, Warwick, from Edward Fisher, whose fraud necessitated an act of parliament confirming Puckering's title.

Of the *quorum* of the commission of the peace in Hertfordshire in 1583, on 19 November 1584 Puckering was returned to parliament for Carmarthen, but chose instead to sit for Bedford, where the government had had him returned on 2 November. The parliament was relatively inexperienced, and as a newcomer Puckering was chosen as speaker. A 'very able member of the … House' (D'Ewes, 333), he acted as the government's agent, relying upon Burghley for assistance. In the parliament of 1586–7 he was returned for the borough of Gatton, near Reigate, Surrey, and again elected speaker. He had been appointed queen's serjeant-at-law on 3 July 1585, and in 1586 he prosecuted at the trial of Edward Abington and other Babington plot conspirators. In 1587 he resigned his place as counsel to the town of St Albans, and appeared for the crown at the trial of Secretary Davison for his conduct in sending off the death warrant for Mary, queen of Scots. In 1589 came the trials of Philip Howard, earl of Arundel, for treason, and of Sir Richard Knightley and others for sedition. In the following year, in which he became recorder of Warwick, Puckering presided with Mr Baron Clarke over the trial for sedition at the Surrey assizes of the puritan minister John Udall. Puckering's last appearance at a state trial was at the prosecution for treason in 1592 of Sir John Perrott, late lord deputy of Ireland.

On 28 May 1592 Puckering was knighted, sworn of the privy council, and appointed lord keeper of the great seal, succeeding Sir Christopher Hatton since whose death in November 1591 the seal had been in commission. Lacking Hatton's accomplishments, and despite his reputedly extraordinary knowledge of the real actions, Puckering was not an automatic choice for the lord keepership. Almost all his chancery orders date from after Sir Thomas Egerton's appointment as master of the rolls in April 1594, though Puckering launched a broad offensive against lesser equity courts, much in keeping with his hostility towards the earls of Pembroke and Huntingdon, presidents respectively of the councils in Wales and in the north. Never certain of royal favour, Puckering solicited reassurance from the court, and entertained Elizabeth lavishly when she visited him at Kew in Surrey in 1595. Despite such expenditure, and while petitioning the queen for a grant of land in 1595, Puckering complained that as speaker he had lost £2000 from his practice, and that the lord keepership cost him £1000 a year. But like lord keepers Bacon and Egerton, Puckering bought land on a large scale, acquiring the manor of Weston, Hertfordshire, in 1593, and further Warwickshire lands in 1596. It was said that he had abused the lord keeper's ecclesiastical patronage, though Camden assigned the responsibility to his servants. He died intestate of apoplexy on 30 April 1596, aged fifty-two, according to his memorial inscription, leaving 'no regret of him' (BL, Lansdowne MS 982, fol. 194); he was buried in St Paul's Chapel, Westminster Abbey where his widow erected a substantial monument.

His son, **Sir Thomas Puckering**, baronet (1591/2–1637), was aged four at his father's death. Educated at the King's School, Warwick, under John Owen the epigrammatist, and admitted to the Middle Temple in 1605, he was for some years a companion to Henry, prince of Wales, before completing his education in Paris, having left England in September 1610 in the company of Thomas Lorkin with whom he was to maintain a regular correspondence. Created baronet on 25 November 1611 and knighted on 3 June 1612, on 2 July 1616 he married Elizabeth (*d.* 1652), daughter of Sir John Morley of Halnaker, Sussex, and his wife, Cicely Carryll. They had three daughters, of whom two died as children. A member of the North West Passage Company, he was admitted to Lincoln's Inn on 20 February 1621; represented the borough of Tamworth, Staffordshire, in the parliaments of 1621, 1625, 1626, and 1628; and was sheriff of Warwickshire in 1625. Living mainly in Warwick, he founded there a hospital for poor women and a charity to provide houses for tradesmen. He died on 20 March 1637 and was buried in St Mary's, Warwick. Jane, his surviving daughter, died childless in 1652, the Puckering estates passing to Sir Henry Newton, son of Sir Thomas's sister Katherine. N. G. JONES

Sources HoP, Commons, 1558–1603 · W. J. Jones, The Elizabethan court of chancery (1967) · R. Clutterbuck, ed., The history and antiquities of the county of Hertford, 2 (1821) · J. Campbell, Lives of the lord chancellors, 3rd edn, 7 vols. (1848–50), vol. 2 · J. E. Neale, The Elizabethan House of Commons (1949) · State trials, vol. 1 · W. P. Baildon, ed., The records of the Honorable Society of Lincoln's Inn: admissions, 1 (1896) · W. P. Baildon, ed., The records of the Honorable Society of Lincoln's Inn: the black books, 1 (1897) · P. Williams, The council in the marches of Wales under Elizabeth I (1958) · J. E. Cussans, History of Hertfordshire, 3 (1881) · J. Nichols, The progresses and public processions of Queen Elizabeth, new edn, 3 (1823) · BL, Lansdowne MS 982 · E. W. Brayley and J. P. Neale, The history and antiquities of the abbey church of St Peter, Westminster, 2 (1823) · S. D'Ewes, ed., The journals of all the parliaments during the reign of Queen Elizabeth, both of the House of Lords and House of Commons (1682) · W. Dugdale, The antiquities of Warwickshire illustrated, rev. T. Thomas, 2nd edn, 1 (1730) · GEC, Baronetage, vol. 1 · Herald and Genealogist, 3 (1866) · Members of parliament: return to two orders of the honorable the House of Commons, House of Commons, 1 (1878) · A. F. Leach, History of Warwick School (1906) · T. Birch, ed., The life of Henry, prince of Wales (1760) · VCH Warwickshire, vols. 5–6 · E. Hasted, The history and topographical survey of the county of Kent, 1 (1778) · A. Brown, ed., The genesis of the United States, 2 (1890) · H. A. C. Sturgess, ed., Register of admissions to the Honourable Society of the Middle Temple, from the fifteenth century to the year 1944, 1 (1949) · H. Chauncy, The historical antiquities of Hertfordshire (1700); repr. in 2 vols., 2 (1826)

Archives BL, corresp., Add. MS 34727 · BL, corresp. and MSS, Harley MSS 6994–6997, 7000, 7002 · BL, corresp, Lansdowne MS 174 · Trinity Cam., commonplace books

Likenesses J. Cole, engraving (after tomb effigy), repro. in J. Dart, Westmonasterium, or, The history and antiquities of the abbey church of St Peters, Westminster, vol. 1 [1723], p. 176 · tomb effigy (with his wife), Westminster Abbey

Puckering, Sir Thomas, baronet (1591/2–1637). *See under* Puckering, Sir John (1543/4–1596).

Puckle, James (*b.* in or before **1667**, *d.* **1724**), writer and inventor, was the son of James Puckle (*bap.* 1633, *d.* 1690), a merchant trading with Amsterdam, whose brother Thomas (1638–1724), a London merchant, took out patents in 1693 for plastic wood and for a screw-wheel device for lifting heavy weights, thus perhaps encouraging his nephew's bent for invention. His mother's name is unknown and nothing is known of the younger James Puckle's life until he was married to Mary Francis at St Vedast, Foster Lane, on 22 January 1688. They had at least eight children before Mary died at some time between 1702 and 1714.

By 16 June 1690, when he obtained letters of administration for the estate of his father, who had died a widower overseas, Puckle was a notary public in partnership with one Jenkins in Pope's Head Alley, Cornhill. Puckle was also a stockjobber. Between 1696 and 1700 he published three pamphlets demonstrating the importance of the English fishing industry and advocating the purchase of shares in the company of the Royal Fishery of England (incorporated 1676), which it seems he was selling on commission. About 1707 he attempted to float a joint-stock company to be called 'The Merchant Adventurers of Great Britain' which would trade on the Pacific coast of South America, and which sank with little trace.

In 1711 Puckle published *The Club*, a series of prose dialogues in which a young man describes members of his club to his father, who follows each description with appropriate moralisms. This device provides an alphabetical sequence of Theophrastian characters, from Antiquary and Buffoon to Youth and Zany. *The Club* was dedicated to two London tobacco importers, Micajah Perry and Richard Perry, and to the memory of a third, Thomas Lane, who had married Puckle's cousin Mary. Its third edition (1713) included a portrait of Puckle engraved by George Vertue after J. B. Closterman.

On 21 February 1715 Puckle was married at New Brentford to Elizabeth Fownes, *née* Cabell (*b.* 1675), widow of Richard Fownes, apothecary. Puckle and his new wife lived in the parish of St Stephen, Coleman Street, and had no children. There was apparently a family quarrel because Puckle signed a will on 30 June 1715 leaving 1s. to each of the four surviving children, aged thirteen to twenty-five, of his first marriage. The rest of his estate went to his new wife, who was named sole executrix.

On 15 May 1718 Puckle took out a patent for a portable breech-loading machine-gun that could be swivelled and elevated on a collapsible tripod, while its six-chambered breech could be turned by hand and replaced by others which enabled it to fire grenades, or either round or square bullets according to whether the enemy was Christian or Turk. Puckle's flotation of a joint-stock company to market this invention was satirized (along with many other 'bubbles') in prints and on playing cards. Prints and playing cards at this time also satirized the Royal Fishery. Undeterred, Puckle invented a patent sword, which, he wrote to James, first Earl Stanhope, on 11 April 1720, 'was worth a victory to the army first has it' (PRO, SP 35/21/10). Though the *London Journal* on 31 March 1722 reported a successful trial of the machine-gun, asserting that 'one man discharged it 63 times in seven minutes' despite continuous rain, though two of Puckle's guns were included in the armament of the second duke of Montagu's disastrous expedition to St Lucia that year, and though shares offered at £4 rose at one point to £8, the satirists were correct in saying that 'Puckle's Machine' was dangerous only to investors. More reliably, Puckle revised *The Club*, now subtitled *a grey-cap for a green-head*, for a subscription edition in 1723, with a re-engraving of the Closterman portrait by J. Cole.

Puckle was interred in the burial-ground of St Stephen, Coleman Street, on 26 July 1724, the day after his contentious will was proved. *The Club* was reprinted in London, Dublin, and Philadelphia several times between 1733 and 1795, and came to wider notice in 1817 when it was republished with wood-engravings by John Thurston, John Thompson, and others, and became one of the works that significantly raised the prestige of wood-engraving in the early nineteenth century. The last reprint of the illustrated edition appeared in 1900 with an introduction by Austin Dobson, shortly after Sidney Lee observed that *The Club's* 'long lease of popularity seems to exceed its literary merits' (*DNB*). There is a Puckle machine-gun in the Royal Armouries, Leeds.

JAMES SAMBROOK

Sources G. S. Steinman, *The author of 'The club' identified* (1872) · patent 418, 15 May 1718, BL · F. G. Stephens and M. D. George, eds., *Catalogue of prints and drawings in the British Museum, division 1: political and personal satires*, 2 (1873), 427–30, 438–43 (nos. 1620, 1625) · Puckle to Lord Stanhope, 11 April 1720, PRO, SP 35/21/10 · W. A. Littledale, ed., *The registers of St Vedast, Foster Lane, and of St Michael le Quern, London*, 2, Harleian Society, register section, 30 (1903), 31 · IGI · [begins] 'In the name of God, amen. Whereas the coasts of Chiley, Peru … ', 1707 [a proposal for a joint-stock company to be called ' The Merchant Adventurers of Great Britain'] · patent 311, 17 Jan 1693; patent 317, 7 March 1693, BL · J. E. Hodgkin, 'Anticipations of modern inventions: Puckle's "defence"', *N&Q*, 7th ser., 8 (1889), 365 · *N&Q*, 8th ser., 9 (1896), 368, 450 · signet warrant for inventor's patent, BL, Eg Ch 7546 · *GM*, 1st ser., 92/1 (1822), 204–7 · A. Dobson, 'Puckle's "Club"', *Eighteenth century vignettes: third series* (1896), 270–92

Archives PRO, letter to Lord Stanhope, SP 35/21/10

Likenesses G. Vertue, engraving (after J. B. Closterman), BM, NPG; repro. in J. Puckle, *The club*, 3rd edn (1713), frontispiece

Wealth at death everything to second wife, except 1 shilling each to four surviving children of first marriage: will, 30 June 1715

Puddicombe [*née* Evans], **Anne Adalisa** [*pseud.* Allen Raine] (**1836–1908**), novelist, was born on 6 October 1836 in Bridge Street, Newcastle Emlyn, Carmarthenshire, the eldest child of the two sons and two daughters of Benjamin Evans (1809–1884), solicitor of that town, and his wife, Letitia Grace Morgan (*b.* 1814, *d.* after 1871), daughter of Thomas Morgan, surgeon, also of Newcastle Emlyn. Both parents came from families noteworthy in the cultural history of Wales: Benjamin Evans was the grandson of the Revd David Davis (1745–1827) of Castellhywel, Cardiganshire, a leading figure in the Unitarian movement and translator into Welsh of Gray's 'Elegy', and Letitia Evans was the granddaughter of the religious reformer Daniel Rowland (1711?–1790). Anne Adalisa herself (known as Ada to her family) went to school in Carmarthen (1846–9) before being sent to Cheltenham to be educated with the family of the Revd Henry Solly, Unitarian minister, pioneer of the movement for working men's institutes and friend of literary figures such as Charles Dickens, George Eliot, Mrs Henry Wood, and Bulwer-Lytton. In 1851 the Sollys moved to Southfields, near Wimbledon; Ada, who had now been joined by her sister, Lettie, went with them and the two girls stayed at Southfields until 1856, when they returned to Newcastle Emlyn.

Once home, Ada led the conventional life of a young lady of the period, but she maintained her intellectual interests, learning French and Italian and studying botany. She also edited a short-lived magazine called *Home Sunshine* with a group of friends (in particular the Leslie family of Adpar, Cardiganshire, through whom she was to meet her future husband). She remained at Newcastle Emlyn for the next sixteen years until, on 10 April 1872, she married Beynon Puddicombe (1839–1906) at Penbryn church, Cardiganshire. Puddicombe was foreign correspondent at Smith Payne's Bank, London, and the couple settled at Elgin Villas, Addiscombe, near Croydon, where they stayed for the next eight years, a period during which Ada suffered from serious, but unspecified, ill health. This improved when the Puddicombes moved to Winchmore Hill, Middlesex. Despite her poor health, Ada learned to play the violin during these years, becoming a capable musician.

There is also evidence to suggest that Ada's earliest attempts at novel writing also date from this period in the 1880s, though her official career as Allen Raine, novelist, did not begin until 1894, when she was fifty-eight. In that year she shared a prize given at the national eisteddfod for a story descriptive of Welsh life; 'Ynysoer' was then serialized in the *North Wales Observer* and finally published posthumously in book form as *Where Billows Roll* (1909). *A Welsh Singer*, her first full-length novel, was published in 1897. Originally entitled *Mifanwy*, it had been rejected by six publishers before Hutchinson & Co. accepted it, but it became an immediate best-seller on publication. *A Welsh Singer* was followed by ten more novels, of which *Torn Sails*

(1898), *Garthowen* (1900), *A Welsh Witch* (1902), and *Queen of the Rushes* (1906) are the most accomplished; she also published a collection of short stories, *All in a Month* (1908), and an *Allen Raine Birthday Book* appeared in 1907. The novels sold worldwide and in April 1908 *The Bookman* ranked her as one of the four best-selling novelists of the day, along with Marie Corelli, Hall Caine, and Silas Hocking. Her books eventually went out of print at the beginning of the Second World War, though three appeared in Welsh translations in the 1960s and a fourth, *Garthowen*, was published in 1983. However, the late twentieth-century growth of women's studies led to a new interest in her work and *Queen of the Rushes*, perhaps her most completely achieved work, set in west Wales during the religious revival of 1904, was republished by Honno, the Welsh women's press, in 1998, with a new critical introduction.

Although based in London, the Puddicombes had kept their links with west Wales, building a house, Bronmôr, at Tre-saith, Cardiganshire, in 1897. In 1900 Beynon Puddicombe retired from the bank, due to mental illness, and the couple moved permanently to Tre-saith. Beynon Puddicombe died on 29 May 1906 and Ada herself died of cancer at Bronmôr on 21 June 1908; they were both buried in nearby Penbryn churchyard. They had no children.

The pseudonym Allen Raine appeared to Ada in a dream, and it is unlikely that she deliberately chose a masculine pen-name. Whether this affected the earliest critical response to her novels is not clear, but in his obituaries in 1908 (when she was known to be a woman) Ernest Rhys was typical in categorizing her novels as unsophisticated potboilers with cardboard characters. As he said, 'She wrote love-stories, in short' (*Manchester Guardian*, 27 June 1908). Ironically, in view of the way in which she is so often contrasted with Caradoc Evans, her work too was stigmatized as a caricature of Welsh life. Rhys commented that 'Welsh readers who wish to see Wales pictured as it really is were not satisfied to accept her as a genuine Welsh novelist' (*Manchester Guardian*, 24 June 1908), while H. Elvet Lewis asserted that 'the dialect she has used in her stories … distressed those who know Wales from within and love its everyday speech' (*British Weekly*, 25 June 1908). However, the appearance of a volume on Allen Raine in the Writers of Wales series led to the beginnings of a critical reappraisal which rejects her easy categorization as a popular novelist of romance, with little realism or depth of analysis.   SALLY ROBERTS JONES

Sources S. Jones, *Allen Raine* (1979) · Carmarthenshire RO, Allen Raine/Anne Adalisa Puddicombe archive · private information (2004) [Mrs M. S. Beckingsale] · J. Harris, 'Queen of the rushes', *The Planet*, 97 (1993), 64–72 · K. Gramich, 'Introduction', in A. Raine [A. A. Puddicombe], *Queen of the rushes* (1998), 1–23 · M. Stephens, 'Books', *Western Mail Magazine* (28 Nov 1998) · DWB · tombstone, Penbryn church, Cardiganshire
Archives Carmarthenshire RO, corresp. and papers; journals
Likenesses photograph, c.1900, NL Wales
Wealth at death £8573 3s. 6d.: probate, 1 Sept 1908, CGPLA Eng. & Wales

Pudney, John Sleigh (1909–1977), poet and journalist, was born on 19 January 1909 at Homewood Farm, Langley, Buckinghamshire, the only child of Henry William

Pudney, a tenant farmer, and his wife, Mabel Elizabeth, daughter of H. C. Sleigh, who had spent her early life nursing in Dublin and Australia. His father abandoned farming in 1907 but continued to live a rural life at Langley, and there John grew up. He was sent to boarding-school at Westerham Hill, and later even further away, to Gresham's School, Holt. Soon after he went there his mother died, and thus much of Pudney's holidays were spent as a solitary boy in the countryside. Later in life he looked back to a happy childhood and stimulating schooldays—among his friends at Gresham's were W. H. Auden, Benjamin Britten, and Humphrey Spender—but already he was aware of being something of a loner, a countryman at heart, with an inner withdrawal which needed to find expression in poetry.

Pudney's father persuaded him to leave school at sixteen, and to go to work for an estate agent in London. For several years he worked towards a surveyor's qualification, but meanwhile was also writing—short stories, articles, verse—frequenting David Archer's bookshop, and soon achieving publication. In 1933 his first volume of verse, *Spring Encounter*, was published by Methuen, and this swiftly brought Pudney into the literary circle of Lady Ottoline Morrell. On 30 October 1934 he married Crystal Selwyn (b. 1915/16), the eldest child of A. P. Herbert, and they had two daughters and a son, Jeremy Peter Pudney. Supported by his new connections, he decided to give up the property business for the more precarious trade of writing.

Spring Encounter contained some lines that already struck a distinctive note which Pudney would maintain in all his verse—incisive rhythm, simple diction, and a courageous, if occasionally mawkish, effort to celebrate man's place in nature and the importance of nature's influence on man's imagination:

> here avenues, ways begin,
> April to June, river to tidal basin,
> this summer's crop and new stock on the farm.
> This is where I, abashed to hesitate,
> in eagerness must pause, and O my love,
> certain that I must gather strength, with you
> tidal become, the traffic way for ships.
> ('Source', *Spring Encounter*, 1933, 1)

In those early years of married life, Pudney took jobs on *The Listener*, and as a writer and producer in the BBC (1934–7), incidentally becoming concerned with the first broadcasting of music by Britten. He was able to move back into the country, first near Thaxted, Essex, and later at Chipstead in Kent. In 1937 he became a journalist with the *News Chronicle*, and the following year his first novel, *Jacobson's Ladder*, appeared. In August 1940 he was commissioned into the RAF as an intelligence officer, and later, with H. E. Bates and Patrick Balfour (third Baron Kinross), joined the Air Ministry's Creative Writers Unit, formed by Hilary St George Saunders, and for it wrote the anonymously published *The Air Battle of Malta* (1944) and *Atlantic Bridge* (1945, about RAF transport command).

After flying over the beaches during the invasion of France, Pudney accompanied General Leclerc's victorious troops into Paris, and was the first member of allied forces to visit Pablo Picasso in his studio. He had never fired a gun during his brief training, but an involvement in street fighting at Billancourt, and some hazardous scrapes during the many flying sorties which he accompanied, gave rise to his claim to have been the only wartime officer who 'never fired a shot except in anger'.

It was while he was serving as squadron intelligence officer at St Eval in Cornwall that Pudney wrote one of the best-known poems of the war. First published over initials by the *News Chronicle* in 1941, it was broadcast on radio by Laurence Olivier, and spoken by Michael Redgrave in *The Way to the Stars* (1945), a film directed by Anthony Asquith. After that it almost attained the status of a ballad, and was often quoted without permission or attribution:

> Do not despair
> For Johnny-head-in-air;
> He sleeps as sound
> As Johnny underground.
>
> Fetch out no shroud
> For Johnny-in-the-cloud;
> And keep your tears
> For him in after years.
>
> Better by far
> For Johnny-the-bright-star,
> To keep your head,
> And see his children fed.
> (J. S. Pudney, *Collected Poems*, 1957, 35)

Pudney wrote more considerable war poems, and more deeply felt ones—for example, 'Elegy for Tom Roding', or 'Missing'—but 'For Johnny' became the most renowned.

After the war Pudney returned to freelance journalism and book reviewing, and to fight (unsuccessfully) the 1945 general election for Labour at Sevenoaks. During the next few years he published a novel and a children's book (the *Fred and I* adventure stories) every year, as well as regular features in *Illustrated* and *News Review*, short stories, television and radio plays, and his first volume of collected verse in 1957. Of Pudney's ten published novels, probably the most successful was *The Net* (1952), a romantic thriller about an aeronautical research station. He also worked as a resourceful literary adviser first to Evans Bros. and then to Putnam & Co. This versatile energy, and his talent for turning out effective prose to order, may have tended to discourage critical appreciation of his more serious work.

In those years, like many others in the London literary world, Pudney was often rather drunk. His first marriage had been dissolved in 1955, and he had unhappily moved out of the country into the town. He had been used to create around himself a vigorous social life at home with his family and friends, enlivened by music, acting, dancing, singing—and, naturally, a cheering flow of good drink. This enthusiastic conviviality started to turn into 'over-drinking' (as he later described it) and then led to an alcoholic addiction which began to wreck his work, his relationships, and himself. In 1965 he made up his own mind to tackle his problem by therapy, and then described his successful cure in periodicals and a later book. This public confession was deliberately made, for Pudney believed

that medical efforts to treat alcoholism were being handicapped by the general reluctance to discuss it as a normal medical problem. Unlike many converts to abstinence, he lost neither his creative energy nor his sociability—drink still flowed for his thirstier guests.

By 1967 Pudney had made a complete recovery from addiction, with the tireless support of his second wife, Monica Ethel Curtis (b. 1916/17). She was the daughter of J. Grant Forbes and they had married on 7 July 1955. He became enthusiastically involved in a new activity, poetry reading, for which he wrote prolifically—verses often to be accompanied by jazz music.

In 1976 Pudney developed cancer of the throat, and after a year of pain and fearsome surgery, he died in his London home, 4 Macartney House, Chesterfield Walk, Greenwich, on 10 November 1977. Author to the last, he wrote of this final agonizing phase of his life in a courageous and remarkable book, *Thank Goodness for Cake*, published posthumously by Michael Joseph in 1978. His two last poems appeared in the *Times Literary Supplement* a few days after his death. ROGER LUBBOCK, rev.

Sources J. S. Pudney, *Home and away* (1960) · J. S. Pudney, *Thank goodness for cake* (1978) · personal knowledge (1986) · b. cert. · m. certs. · d. cert. · *The Times* (11 Nov 1977)
Archives Ransom HRC, corresp. and literary papers | BBC WAC, corresp. with BBC staff · BL, letters to Alida Monro, Add. MS 57752 · U. Reading L., letters to Bodley Head Ltd
Wealth at death £13,447: probate, 10 Feb 1978, *CGPLA Eng. & Wales*

Pudsey, Edward (*bap.* 1573, *d.* 1612/13), keeper of a commonplace book, was baptized on 13 January 1573 in Longford, Derbyshire, the eldest of nine children of Thomas Pudsey of Derby (b. 1544). No record of his education has been found, though his cousin Richard Pudsey (b. 1562) received a BA (1580) and an MA (1583) from St John's College, Oxford. Another cousin's son, George Pudsey, was at Oxford in 1613 and Gray's Inn in 1616.

Pudsey's claim to fame is the commonplace book he kept during the first decade of the seventeenth century, which contains some of the earliest manuscript excerpts from Shakespeare's plays. The bulk of the book is now preserved as Bodleian MS Eng. poet.d.3, but four leaves (two containing Shakespeare extracts) were taken from the mid-point of the manuscript in the late nineteenth century, and are now at the Shakespeare Birthplace Trust Record Office as ER 82/1/21. Three other leaves were taken out at the same time, but are now bound at the end of the original book. Most of the notebook is in Pudsey's hand, but two other hands have transcribed a genealogy of English kings near the beginning of the book, and two later hands have added various notes and marginalia.

The first page contains the title 'Edward Pudseys Booke. 1600', and most of the volume was apparently written within the next two years, since it contains extracts from books published no later than 1602. However, six leaves toward the end were written later, possibly over a period of years, and contain extracts from books published as late as 1612. Pudsey used the book as a repository of wisdom and wit gleaned from his reading, and it is more wide-ranging and neatly organized than most common-place books of the time. The subjects of the extracts tend toward history and philosophy, but current events and controversies are also well represented.

Modern interest, however, centres on the extracts from contemporary printed plays which Pudsey transcribed. The early portion of the manuscript contains extracts from four plays by Ben Jonson, three by John Marston, two by Thomas Dekker, two by John Lyly, one each by Thomas Nashe, George Chapman, and Thomas Heywood, and six by Shakespeare—*The Merchant of Venice*, *Titus Andronicus*, *Romeo and Juliet*, *Richard II*, *Richard III*, and *Much Ado about Nothing*. The later portion of the manuscript has extracts from the second quarto of Shakespeare's *Hamlet*, as well as plays by Dekker, Jonson, Marston, Cyril Tourneur, and John Webster. For the most part, these extracts are so accurate and well-organized that Pudsey must have taken them from the printed quartos. However, after the extracts from *Richard III* is a short series of passages which appear to echo Shakespeare's *Othello*, though not very accurately. Since *Othello* was not printed until 1622, these may be Pudsey's recollections from a trip to the theatre.

On 15 February 1605 Pudsey married Edith Faban at St Andrew by the Wardrobe in London. By 1610 the couple had moved to Tewkesbury, Gloucestershire, and that year in Tewkesbury Abbey they baptized twin daughters, Amy and Anna, the latter of whom died in infancy. At some point they also had a son, Edward, who grew up to be a travelling actor in Germany between 1628 and 1640. Pudsey made his will in 1610, adding a codicil on 13 September 1612, and died some time before 17 November 1613, when the will was proved. The will, which divides up an estate of nearly £1000, has strongly religious overtones and asks that Pudsey's son be trained in divinity. It specifically bequeaths Pudsey's notebooks to his son, but the surviving notebook apparently passed to his executor John Daighton, who jotted some business records on folio 84 for his brother-in-law Edward Bassett in 1615–16.

DAVID KATHMAN

Sources J. M. Gowan, 'An edition of Edward Pudsey's common-place book (c.1600–1615) from the manuscript in the Bodleian Library', MPhil diss., U. Lond., 1967 · four leaves from 'Edward Pudsey's Booke', Shakespeare Birthplace Trust RO, Stratford upon Avon, ER 82/1/21 · J. Rees, 'Shakespeare and "Edward Pudsey's Booke", 1600', *N&Q*, 237 (1992), 330–31 · E. A. J. Honigmann and S. Brock, eds., *Playhouse wills, 1558–1642: an edition of wills by Shakespeare and his contemporaries in the London theatre* (1993), 92–4 · R. Savage, *Shakespearean extracts from 'Edward Pudsey's Booke'* (1887) · IGI · will, PRO, PROB 10/307

Archives Bodl. Oxf., notebook, MS Eng. poet.d.3 · Shakespeare Birthplace Trust RO, Stratford upon Avon, missing four leaves from notebook, ER 82/1/21

Wealth at death approx. £1000: will, PRO, PROB 10/307

Pugh, Sir Arthur (1870–1955), trade unionist, was born on 19 January 1870 at Ross, Herefordshire, the fifth child of William Thomas Valentine Pugh, a civil engineer, and his wife, Amelia Rose Adlington. His circumstances and prospects clearly suffered from the death of both his parents in his infancy. Arthur received his education at the local elementary school, and at thirteen was apprenticed to a

farmer–butcher. In 1894 he moved to south Wales, close to his father's birthplace of Neath, obtaining a series of short-term jobs as a subordinate hand in the steel industry. He probably remained in Wales until his marriage, on 7 April 1901, to Elisabeth (1879/80–1939), daughter of David Morris of Port Talbot. Shortly afterwards, evidently in search of promotion to the senior grade of smelter, he moved to the Frodingham iron works in Lincolnshire. He had already been active in the British Steel Smelters' Association, and now became a branch secretary. As administrator and negotiator he was manifestly successful, and in 1906 the smelters' executive appointed him as assistant secretary.

The smelters' union had, from its origins in Glasgow in 1885, developed into a national organization with ambitions to dominate the labour force of the industry. Pugh readily acceded to the conciliatory strategy of its full-time president, John Hodge, designed to secure recognition of the union by the employers, the equalization of working conditions among the different tiers of labour, and thereby the eventual displacement of smaller, rival unions. Pugh's main sphere of responsibility was the conduct of the smelters' finances, and under him its central office became, in the view of the Webbs, the most efficient in the union movement. Pugh's elevation had coincided with Hodge's election as a Labour MP. In December 1916 the latter became a minister in the war-time coalition government, and Pugh again received promotion, to central office secretary. As the *de facto* chief of the premier steel union he took the lead in the negotiations to create a single organization for all steel workers. He may well have devised the ingenious scheme which, in 1917, gave birth to the Iron and Steel Trades Confederation and to the British Iron, Steel and Kindred Trades Association—which was intended ultimately to absorb all the existing unions.

In 1920 Pugh was elected to the parliamentary committee of the TUC, and he remained on the general council, its successor, until 1936, retiring as secretary of the Iron and Steel Trades Confederation a year later. His widening sphere of activity reflected the expanding role of the union movement in government. He was Labour representative on several public inquiries into industrial disputes, and on others considering the application of 'safeguarding' duties. He joined the British delegates on the economic consultative committee of the League of Nations, and in 1939, in retirement, served on the Central Appeal Tribunal under the Military Service Acts. On behalf of the TUC he oversaw the educational facilities provided for union members, and for many years helped to administer the *Daily Herald*. It was these various services which earned him a knighthood in 1935. The role he played in the general strike of 1926 was, by contrast, relatively unimpressive. Though acting *ex officio* as the chief public spokesman of the general council he was almost certainly a reluctant participant in this conflict. 'I have never heard him say that he was in favour of it', remarked Hodge in the aftermath, 'but I have never heard him say that he was against it' (J. Hodge, *Workman's Cottage to Windsor Castle*, 1931, 363). He made little contribution to the organization of the strike, though he was more heavily involved in the discussions with Viscount Samuel which brought it to an end. He was similarly supportive, over the next two or three years, of the TUC's attempts to launch negotiations with national employers' organizations.

Although Pugh gained public prominence mainly as the chairman of the TUC during the general strike, he achieved far more in the quieter arena of the iron and steel industry. He was praised by his obituarists as a 'born conciliator' and a 'brilliant negotiator'. He was certainly not a born orator, and the committee room appeared his natural milieu. 'One great difficulty', complained his president, 'was to get Mr Pugh to go out into the country' (*Workman's Cottage*, 359). To another observer he had the qualities of a chartered accountant, his competence in financial matters being of like value to his union and to the general council. He was described as 'a man of temperate habits, medium height, and wiry build, of fresh complexion, with greying hair and moustache, and a high bald forehead' (*DNB*). He was steadfastly loyal to the union movement and looked for the same virtue in his members. He belonged to that genre of labour leader for whom central co-ordination of policy, internal discipline, and strict adherence to collective agreements were articles of faith. He was not attracted to a political career, and though never questioning his union's association with the Labour Party, gave precedence to the former's interests, notably in championing industrial protection against the party's free-trade line. His history of the metal unions, *Men of Steel*, was published in 1951, and was characteristically painstaking, restrained, and self-effacing. It marked his continued interest in union affairs after his retirement. He died at the General Hospital, Bedford, on 2 August 1955, leaving a son and three daughters.

G. A. PHILLIPS

Sources J. C. Carr and W. Taplin, *History of the British steel industry* (1962) · H. A. Clegg, A. Fox, and A. F. Thompson, *A history of British trade unions since 1889*, 1–2 (1964–85) · W. H. Fyfe, *Behind the scenes of the great strike* (1926) · *Man and Metal* (Aug 1955) · G. A. Phillips, *The general strike: the politics of industrial conflict* (1976) · A. Pugh, *Men of steel, by one of them: a chronicle of eighty-eight years of trade unionism in the British iron and steel industry* (1951) · *The Times* (3 Aug 1955) · *Annual Report* [Trades Union Congress] (1928) · *DNB* · m. cert.
Likenesses photographs, Trades Union Congress, London
Wealth at death £6481 17s. 4d.: probate, 25 Nov 1955, CGPLA Eng. & Wales

Pugh, Edward (*bap.* 1763, *d.* 1813), miniature painter and topographer, was baptized in June 1763 at Ruthin in Denbighshire, the son of David and Dorothy Pugh. His father was a barber and presumably, therefore, of moderate means, and nothing is known of how his son acquired a training in art. By 1793 Pugh was exhibiting miniatures at the Royal Academy where he continued to show both portraits and landscapes until 1808. He lived in London, although he spent a considerable amount of time in Wales, and was in Chester in 1799. He cut a minor figure in the London art world, possessed, as he himself conceded, only of a 'moderate talent' (Pugh, vii), but, nevertheless, provided drawings for *Modern London* (1804), and was known to individuals of note including the magistrate,

amateur painter, and Sir Richard Phillips's caricaturist Henry Wigstead, by whom he is credited with drawing for his *Remarks on a Tour to North and South Wales* (1800). Pugh's miniature practice drew on both Welsh and English patronage, notably among the literati in Chester and London, where he painted William Owen Pughe (*c*.1802). In its engraved form his miniature of the playwright Thomas Edwards, *Twm o'r Nant* (1799), became his most celebrated portrait.

It was Pugh's association with John Boydell, the publisher of prints, which led him in 1804 to commence his most important work, *Cambria depicta*. Over the next nine years Pugh travelled extensively on foot through north Wales, and both wrote the substantial text and provided the original drawings for seventy-two aquatints. Although the biographical details of Pugh's life are sketchy, a great deal can be said of his character, since *Cambria depicta* was written in the first person and in a lively and entertaining style. It presents Wales from the perspective of a native Welsh-speaker, rather than of an English traveller, on which grounds the author particularly commended the work to his audience for the insights it offered. Pugh regaled his readers with interesting incidents, gossip, and his idiosyncratic opinions on aesthetics and the general state of the world. Although working broadly within the eighteenth-century tradition of topographical and antiquarian descriptive writing, his was a fresh and democratic voice, expressing ambitions for the improvement of contemporary Welsh culture, as well as relating its history and myths. For instance, he proposed the establishment of a national academy on the Scottish model. Pugh died, apparently unmarried, in his home town of Ruthin where he was buried (at Well Street) on 20 July 1813, and did not see his masterpiece in printed form; it was published by Evan Williams in London three years later. Examples of his work are in the National Library of Wales, Aberystwyth, the National Museum and Gallery of Wales, Cardiff, and the Victoria and Albert Museum, London.

PETER LORD

Sources E. Pugh, *Cambria depicta* (1816) · bishop's transcripts, St Asaph, Ruthin parish, NL Wales · NL Wales, MS 13224B, item 203 · T. M. Rees, *Welsh painters, engravers, sculptors (1527–1911)* (1912)

Pugh, Edwin William (1874–1930), novelist, short-story writer, and critic, was born on 22 January 1874 at 47 Foley Street, Marylebone, London, the second of four children of David Walter Pugh (1843–1887), a theatrical property maker, Covent Garden orchestra player, and sometime member of the Moore and Burgess Minstrels, and his wife, Emily, *née* Harris (1845–1925), a Covent Garden wardrobe mistress. Pugh attended a local board school, leaving aged thirteen in 1887 to work in an iron factory, where he worked fourteen hours a day for three months. He then worked in a lawyer's office for eight years and later drew on his experiences in his writings.

Pugh began his writing career by publishing a short story when he was twelve. His first collection was *A Street in Suburbia* (1895), a series of sketches of London working-class life, closely followed by his first novel, *The Man of*

Straw, in the following year. The former, though rather sentimental, was similar in style to the work of Arthur Morrison, the latter to that of Dickens. Both books were favourably reviewed and Pugh turned to full-time writing as a result. His early work dealt with the life and times of the London East End cockney, and he established himself as a member of the 'cockney school' of writers, which included William Pett Ridge (1860–1930) and Henry Nevinson (1856–1941). Pugh's enthusiasm for the East End and its inhabitants was a reflection of his own early background and his ability to better himself.

Pugh's depiction of working-class life is oversentimental and unrealistic. Unlike Morrison he fights shy of the vicious, criminal life of the East End, writing rather of the unkind circumstances and ugliness of life, of poverty, and of the problems caused by personal relationships. A good example is the novel *Tony Drum: a Cockney Boy* (1898), a story of the trials and tribulations of a very untypical cockney. He is physically deformed and an innocent; all that is good in his life is destroyed, including in the end his own life itself. This is the essence of Pugh's attitude towards the working class; his characters are frequently untypical and he portrays a rather false picture. In his essay 'Real realism' in *Slings and Arrows* (1916) Pugh was critical of writers who painted a one-sided picture of East End life, emphasizing the brutal and criminal aspects, and neglecting much that was good in the everyday. Pugh himself, however, was guilty of such bias.

Autobiographical elements appear in a number of Pugh's books, especially in *The Eyes of a Child* (1917) and *The Secret Years* (1923). In these two novels the character Tobias Morgan relates the trials and tribulations of his early life and his working in a factory at the age of thirteen and then, after a breakdown, finding employment in a lawyer's office.

In his essay 'The decay of the short story' Pugh wrote that 'the short story has fallen into decay, not because we lack living authors capable of excelling in that form of literature, but because we deceive ourselves with false notions of what the public needs' (*Slings and Arrows: a Book of Essays*, 1916, 199). Here Pugh, to a certain extent, must include himself, not only as a short-story writer but also as a novelist. At the turn of the nineteenth century the vogue for working-class novels of the cockney school was in decline and by the end of the first decade interest had virtually ceased. Despite this Pugh continued to write of the East End, publishing *Harry the Cockney* (1912) and *The Cockney at Home* (1914).

Apart from his cockney novels Pugh produced two novels on alcoholism: *The Heritage* (1901), in collaboration with Godfrey Burchett, and *The Fruits of the Vine* (1904). Pugh greatly admired Dickens, publishing *Charles Dickens: the Apostle of the People* in 1908, and he saw Sam Weller as 'the typical Cockney' of the late Victorian period (*The Charles Dickens Originals*, 1912, 206). If Pugh is remembered today it is for his cockney novels and stories, but he also wrote a mystery novel, *The Purple Head* (1905), and various books about London including *The City of the World* (1912).

Pugh always had to struggle to make a living and he supplemented his novel writing by his many contributions to journals and newspapers including the *Sun*, *Morning Leader*, *New Review*, *Idler*, *To-Day*, *English Illustrated Magazine*, *Chapman's Grand Magazine*, the *Bookman* (where he was a reviewer for many years), and the *New Age*. In the last of these Pugh expounded his socialist views in articles with such titles as 'Why I joined the Fabian Society' (*New Age*, 1, 1907, 40) and 'Socialism and suburbia' (*New Age*, 3, 1908, 330). He also contributed 'The Mere Clerk', a series of articles in volume 1.

Pugh suffered from financial problems from the beginning of the twentieth century and applied on four occasions to the Royal Literary Fund between 1902 and 1916. He received a civil-list pension of £100 in 1929.

Thomas Burke described Pugh as 'short, stocky in build, with a high colour, and hair, before it went white, of jet-black—altogether Welsh' (Burke, 187). He also had a beard in later life. Pugh died in sad circumstances. According to Burke he was found in Putney unconscious, battered, and bruised, and died a few days later in hospital on 5 February 1930, aged fifty-six. Yet the death certificate records that Pugh died of alcoholism at 164 St John's Hill, the address of the Lambeth, Battersea, and Wandsworth public assistance committee local offices: the hospital was next door. Pugh was saved from a pauper's burial through a subscription raised by the writer Arthur St John Adcock and was buried at Magdalen Road cemetery, Wandsworth, on 8 February 1930.   DAMIAN ATKINSON

Sources W. B. Thesing, ed., *British short-fiction writers, 1880–1914: the realist tradition*, DLitB, 135 (1994) · *The Times* (7 Feb 1930) · *Daily Telegraph* (7 Feb 1930) · WWW · T. Burke, *Son of London* (1946) · b. cert. · d. cert. · civil list pensions, *The Times* (18 July 1929) · J. Sutherland, *The Longman companion to Victorian fiction* (1971) · census returns, 1881 · P. J. Keating, *The working classes in Victorian fiction* (1971) · V. Brome, *Four realist novelists* (1965) · S. Kemp, C. Mitchell, and D. Trotter, *Edwardian fiction: an Oxford companion* (1997) · M. Gaipa, 'Pugh, Edwin William (1874–1930)', www.modjourn. brown.edu/mjp/Bios/Pugh.html · St J. Adcock, *The glory that was Grub Street* (1928)
Archives NYPL, letters to Thomas Burke · NYPL, letters to Pinker & Sons
Likenesses photograph, repro. in *The Bookman* (April 1897) · photograph, repro. in *Daily Telegraph* · photograph, repro. in *The Bookman* (March 1930) · photograph, repro. in DLitB

Pugh, Ellis (1656–1718), Quaker minister in America, was born in August 1656 at Penrhos, near Tyddyn-y-garreg, Dolgellau, in Merioneth, to unknown parents. His father died before his birth, and his mother a few days after he was born. He received only a limited education and became a stonemason at Brithdir. In his early years Pugh was inclined to indulge in 'the heedless haste of youth, in the paths of folly' ('Biographical sketches', 28.284), but in 1674, under the ministration of the Quaker itinerant preacher John ap John, he became a convinced Friend, and in 1680 he became a minister.

Pugh married Sina, a widow with nine small children, but there is no further information relating to this marriage. In 1686 Pugh and his family emigrated to America, but before he set sail Pugh caught a fever. During this period he received a visitation from God whereby he was warned that he would 'meet with trouble and exercises … and that he had work for him in that country (Great Britain), and that he must return, after a time, to his native land' (Evans and Evans, 4.338). The winter voyage to the West Indies was particularly turbulent, and Pugh was grateful to reach Barbados in March 1687. The following summer Pugh continued his journey to America, and at first settled at Schuylkill, near Haverford, where he was 'a faithful and zealous labourer of the gospel, preaching fervently in his native tongue' ('Biographical sketches', 28.284). He later bought land near Plymouth township, Montgomery county, Pennsylvania. There he was 'a serviceable instrument in the Lord's hand, to cherish and instruct many, in meekness and tenderness' (Evans and Evans, 4.339), and his missionary endeavours drew many converts to Quakerism.

In 1706 Pugh returned to Wales and conducted a missionary tour around the country 'to the benefit and acceptance of many' ('Biographical sketches', 28.292). On 29 December 1706 John Kelsall, a Montgomeryshire Friend, noted Pugh's visit to the Dolobran meeting: 'he was concerned wholly in Welsh, there was much innocency with him & he had many pretty openings and advice to Friends' (RS Friends, Lond., MS 193/4). In 1708, shortly after his return to America, three of his children died within a month. This naturally caused him severe anguish, but with divine help he was able to overcome this tragedy and stated that 'If he could bear his affliction acceptably in the sight of God, it would be marrow to his bones' (Evans and Evans, 4.339). During the last fifteen months of his life Pugh suffered from a prolonged illness, but did not neglect his missionary work for Friends. During the last Quaker meeting for worship he attended, the following was said of him:

> he was weak of body, but fervent in spirit, as one taking his last leave in a great deal of love and tenderness. … He was fitted to counsel others, because his life and conversation were answerable to his testimony; and amongst his family he was tender, and careful to counsel them to live in the fear of God. (ibid., 4.340)

On 3 December 1718 Ellis Pugh died in Pennsylvania aged sixty-two. According to Friends he was 'of a meek and quiet spirit, considerate and solid in his judgement, of few words, honest and careful in his calling, honourable among his Friends, and of a good report among people generally' (Bowden, 2.259).

In 1721 Pennsylvania Friends posthumously published Pugh's *Annerch ir Cymru*, which was subsequently translated by Rowland Ellis and David Lloyd as *A Salutation to the Britains*, published in Pennsylvania in 1727 and reprinted in London in 1739. The first version, it has been suggested, was the first Welsh printed book in America. The preface to this edition encouraged 'craftsmen, labourers and shepherds, men of low degree, of my own quality', and sought that they would become 'wiser than their teachers' (*DNB*). This text offered 'encouragement and instruction of them that were seeking the way to Sion, the New

Jerusalem' (Pugh, *A Salutation*, xi). During his life Pugh also wrote *On Baptism and the Lord's Supper*, which offered an insight into his theological beliefs.

RICHARD C. ALLEN

Sources E. Pugh, *Annerch ir Cymru iw galw oddiwrth y llawer o bethau at yr un peth angenrheidiol er mwyn cadwedigaeth euheneidiau* (Philadelphia, PA, 1721); repr. (1782); repr. (1801) • E. Pugh, *A salutation to the Britains, to call them from the many things to the one thing needful for the saving of their souls*, trans. R. Ellis, rev. D. Lloyd (1727) [see also later edns, 1732, 1739, 1793] • 'Dictionary of Quaker biography', RS Friends, Lond. [card index] • an account of Friends who have visited Dolobran meetings, RS Friends, Lond., MS 193/4 • H. Blackwell, notes for the *DWB*, NL Wales, MS 9270 • Swarthmore College Library, Swarthmore, Pennsylvania, Sw. BX 7614 • *DNB* • *DWB* • W. Evans and T. Evans, eds., *Piety promoted*, 4 vols. (1854), 4.338–40 • T. M. Rees, *A history of the Quakers in Wales* (1925), 20, 153, 161, 166, 230 • R. Jones, *Crynwyr Bore Cymru, 1653–1699* (1931), 84, 129, 130, 131 • 'Biographical sketches of ministers and elders, and other concerned members of the Yearly Meeting of Philadelphia: Ellis Pugh', *The Friend* [Philadelphia, PA], 28 (1844–5), 284, 292–3 • F. J. Gibbins, 'An early American Welsh book', *Friends' Quarterly Examiner*, 36 (1902), 517–23 • C. H. Browning, *The Welsh settlement of Pennsylvania* (1912), 213, 215, 218, 224, 243, 267, 302, 317, 487, 498, 505, 526 • T. A. Glenn, *The Welsh founders of Pennsylvania*, 2 vols. (1911–13), 1.204 • H. G. Jones, 'John Kelsall: a study in religious and economic history', MA diss., U. Wales, Bangor, 1938, 134–46, 155 • J. Comly and I. Comly, eds., *Friends Miscellany*, 12 vols. (1834–9), 11.371 • J. Bowden, *The history of the Society of Friends in America*, 2 (1854), 259 • 'Extracts from Friends' meetings accounts', *Pennsylvania Magazine of History and Biography*, 41 (1917), 486 [cost of printing Ellis Pugh's 'Welch Book' (42-01-06), entry dated Philadelphia 19 Sept 1721] • G. H. Jenkins, 'Quaker and anti-Quaker literature in Wales from the Restoration to Methodism', *Welsh History Review / Cylchgrawn Hanes Cymru*, 7 (1974–5), 403–26 • G. H. Jenkins, *Literature, religion and society in Wales, 1660–1730* (1978), 209 • G. H. Jenkins, 'The early peace testimony in Wales', *Llafur*, 4 (1985), 10–19 • J. G. Williams, 'The Quakers of Merioneth during the seventeenth century', *Journal of the Merioneth Historical and Record Society*, 8 (1977–80), 122–56, esp. 135–6; 312–39, esp. 322 • J. Lloyd, *The Quakers in Wales* (1947) • E. S. Whiting, E. R. Morris, and J. R. Hughes, *The background of Quakerism in Wales and the border* (1952)

Archives RS Friends, Lond., letters and papers relating to his *Salutation*

Pugh, (Lewis) Griffith Cresswell Evans (1909–1994), physiologist and mountaineer, was born on 29 October 1909 at Coton Manor, Berwick Road, Shrewsbury, the son of Lewis Pugh Evans Pugh (1865–1940), a Calcutta barrister, and his wife, Adah Emily Sophia, daughter of Thomas Chaplin, medical practitioner. He had four sisters. He was educated at Harrow School (1924–7), where he won a trophy for marksmanship, and at New College, Oxford (1927–30), where he achieved third-class honours in law in 1930 and took his BA in 1931. He returned to Oxford to study natural sciences during 1931–3, and medicine until 1938, when he received his BM along with an MA. As a student he climbed in the Alps and became an expert skier. He competed in the world downhill championships and was selected for the 1936 winter Olympic team as a cross-country skier, but an injury kept him off the slopes. He qualified as a doctor at St Thomas's Hospital in 1938. On 5 September 1939 at the parish church in Lilly, near Hitchin, he married Josephine Helen Cassel (b. 1916/17), daughter of Sir Felix Cassel, first baronet (1869–1953), barrister. They had three sons and one daughter.

In 1939 Pugh entered the army as a medical officer in the Bedfordshire yeomanry, and he later joined the 26th General Field Hospital at the Radcliffe Infirmary, Oxford. He served in Greece, Palestine, Crete, Egypt, Iraq, Iran, and the Lebanon. In 1942 W. J. Riddell, a Harrow classmate, recruited him for the 'Cedars School', the mountain warfare training centre in the Lebanon, which trained troops in ski-mountaineering and mountain warfare at 2100 metres. Pugh was allowed to study every aspect of the school, from tests to select trainees to tests on diet, fitness, clothing, and equipment, and he analysed his results in papers for the army. In 1944 he was briefly medical officer to the 44th Royal Tank regiment in Sicily, before being posted to Whitehall to write training manuals on snow and mountain warfare, based on his earlier research. This research also was the basis for his appointment after the war as a scientist at the medical school at Hammersmith Hospital, where he worked for five years and published papers on rheumatism. In 1950 he joined the Medical Research Council's department of human physiology, founded after the outbreak of the Korean War, and spent the rest of his career in their laboratory at Holly Hill, Hampstead.

In 1951 the organizers of a Mount Everest reconnaissance approached Pugh for advice on high-altitude physiology, and his research was important to the ascent of Everest. In 1952 Eric Shipton invited him to join a training expedition in Nepal to climb Cho Oyu (8153 metres). Though the climbers failed to reach their objective, Pugh's research was productive. With a grant from the Royal Society he camped at Nangaon (4720 metres) and Menlung La (6100 metres) to study acclimatization, respiration, haemoglobin, nutrition, and thermal properties of clothing. Pugh recommended doubling the flow of oxygen to counter the effects of hypoxia—the reduced pressure of oxygen at higher elevations that leads to extreme fatigue—and increasing the consumption of fluids and carbohydrates to prevent dehydration and weight loss. Pugh also criticized Shipton's leadership of the expedition. After Colonel John Hunt was appointed Everest leader, he adopted many of Pugh's suggestions and included him on the team. The film *The Conquest of Everest* (1953) shows Pugh before the trip testing himself in a pressure chamber. As a result of Pugh's advice and Hunt's planning, Edmund Hillary and Tenzing Norgay had the supplies of oxygen, food, and fluid that enabled them to make the first ascent of Everest (8848 metres). When the Everest expedition returned to Katmandu, Pugh was still wearing his pyjamas as part of an eccentric experiment. His research appeared in many articles and a film, *Physiology on Mount Everest* (1954).

In 1956–7 Pugh joined a research team at Scott Base affiliated with Hillary's transantarctic expedition. He researched solar radiation, carbon monoxide poisoning, and human tolerance to cold. While in Antarctica he and Hillary hatched a plan to spend the winter in the Himalayas carrying out research. In 1960–61 Hillary and Pugh led the 'silver hut' expedition to Nepal. Funded by an American encyclopaedia, the expedition combined mountaineering and a search for the yeti with physiological research on hypoxia in a prefabricated hut. Observations on exercise, pulmonary functions, metabolic rates, and electrocardiograms were made at base camp on the Mingbo glacier (4650 metres) and in the hut just below the Ama Dablam col (5800 metres). Pugh stayed at the hut while other researchers measured oxygen consumption as high as 7830 metres during an attempt on Makalu (8481 metres). The ascent was abandoned below the summit after Peter Mulgrew and Edmund Hillary became severely ill.

Pugh later studied the role of body fat in preventing hypothermia among cross-channel swimmers. After Kurt Hahn asked him to investigate deaths from 'exposure' during outdoor sports in 1964, he published a series of articles on hypothermia that led to improvements in outdoor clothing, increased awareness of risks, and a reduction in the incidence of hypothermia among outdoor enthusiasts. At the 1968 Olympics in Mexico City, Pugh examined the influence of the altitude (2300 metres) on athletic performance. Colleagues said he worked best on his own or with a small team. Pugh's many professional publications were listed in a collection of essays dedicated to him in 1993 (*Hypoxia and Molecular Medicine*, 175–7). His work on high-altitude physiology contributed to the ascent of the world's highest peaks, and his research on hypothermia probably saved lives.

Pugh was tall, with angular features and red hair. His absent-mindedness was legendary. When he forgot, as he frequently did, where he had parked his car in London, he would take the train home, report the car stolen to the police, and wait for them to recover it. The story that he once did this with his children in the car is considered apocryphal. He enjoyed sailing and was a ferocious driver. A series of automobile accidents later in life left him crippled with arthritis. He died of a heart attack and dementia on 22 December 1994 at his home, Hatching Green House, Harpenden, Hertfordshire. His wife survived him.

PETER H. HANSEN

Sources *The Times* (7 Jan 1995) · *The Independent* (27 Jan 1995) · *Alpine Journal*, 100 (1995) · J. R. Sutton, C. S. Hourton, and C. S. Coates, eds., *Hypoxia and molecular medicine* (1993), essays by J. S. Milledge, M. Ward, and J. B. West · J. B. West, *High life: a history of high-altitude physiology and medicine* (1998) · J. Hunt, *The ascent of Everest* (1953) · E. Hillary and D. Doig, *In the thin cold air* (1962) · register, New College, Oxford · private information (2004) [J. B. West] · b. cert. · m. cert. [Josephine Helen Cassell] · d. cert.

Archives U. Cal., San Diego, Mandeville Special Collections Library, high-altitude medicine and physiology collection | FILM BBC, newsfootage · BFI NFTVA · NL Aus., 'Physiology on Mount Everest'

Likenesses photographs, 1953, RGS

Wealth at death £454,107: probate, 21 April 1995, *CGPLA Eng. & Wales*

Pugh, Herbert (*fl.* 1758–1788), landscape painter, was born in Ireland, and moved to London about 1758. He contributed to the first exhibition of the Society of Artists in 1760, sending *Landscape with Cattle*. In 1765 he gained a premium at the Society of Arts, and in 1766 was a member of the newly incorporated Society of Artists. He continued exhibiting with them up to 1776. He tried his hand at some pictures in the manner of Hogarth, but without success, although some of these pictures were engraved. Pugh lived in The Piazza, Covent Garden, London. His death in London soon after 1788 was hastened by intemperate habits. Two views of London Bridge by Pugh were contributed to the 'Century of British art' exhibition at the Grosvenor Gallery in 1888. L. H. CUST, rev. J. DESMARAIS

Sources Redgrave, *Artists* · Bryan, *Painters* (1886–9) · Graves, *Artists* · Waterhouse, *18c painters* · Mallalieu, *Watercolour artists*, vol. 1 · E. Edwards, *Anecdotes of painters* (1808); facs. edn (1970) · R. N. James, *Painters and their works*, 3 vols. (1896–7) · M. Pilkington, *A general dictionary of painters: containing memoirs of the lives and works*, ed. A. Cunningham and R. A. Davenport, new edn (1857) · W. G. Strickland, *A dictionary of Irish artists*, 2 vols. (1913) · Graves, *Soc. Artists* · Walpole Society, 9 (1920–21), 53

Pugh, Hugh (1613/14–1683), Church of England clergyman, was born in Tal-y-llyn, Merioneth, the son of Hugh Pugh and brother of Maurice Pugh. On 6 June 1634 he matriculated from All Souls College, Oxford, graduated BA on 8 December 1635, and proceeded MA on 31 June 1640.

It is thought that in 1648 Pugh was appointed as the vicar of Shrivenham, Berkshire, before returning to Wales the following year to serve as the minister of Trefeglwys, Montgomeryshire. There is evidence that he was among those clergymen endorsed by the commissioners for the propagation of the gospel in Wales during the early 1650s, and in an exchequer return for Trefeglwys in 1654 Pugh is recorded as 'the minister that now is' (Richards, *Religious Developments*, 37). On 5 May 1654 he was presented to the commission for the approbation of public preachers, more commonly known as the Triers, and on 15 June was appointed rector of Llanbedr Dyffryn Clwyd, Denbighshire.

In 1666 Pugh, along with other clergymen and gentry in north Wales, assisted Dr Robert Morgan in his aim to become the bishop of Bangor upon the death of Dr William Roberts. In 1668 he was appointed as the rector of Llanfwrog, Denbighshire. This was a position he held until 1675, as well as accepting the appointment as rector of Llandudno, Caernarvonshire, and the office of warden of Ruthin school and hospital in Denbighshire between 1668 and 1672.

On 7 April 1676 Pugh, along with the domestic chaplain to Bishop Humphrey Lloyd of Bangor, provided a report about the Anglican free schools in north Wales. This may have been in response to the dearth of Anglican scholars and clergymen in north Wales as well as to the growth of 'puritan seminaries' throughout Wales. In 1665 there were only five schools with licensed teachers in the diocese of St Asaph, while in 1678 Bishop Isaac Barrow of St Asaph complained that the clergy in the same diocese were 'illiterate and contemptible' (Richards, *Penal Code*, 142). Pugh wrote that the development of scholastic learning was a worthy enterprise as it would leave a record for future generations and 'perpetuate the memory of the generous founders and bountifull benefactors, of their respective schooles, and encourage others to imitate their

good examples' (Vincent, 30). Furthermore, he believed that every free school should be accountable for its existence and income, and avoid apathy and covetousness, which could 'devour and destroy' these institutions (ibid., 30).

In 1680 Pugh accepted appointment as archdeacon of Merioneth, a position which he held until his death. He died in Wales on 22 March 1683 and was buried soon afterwards at Llanbedr parish church, aged sixty-nine.

RICHARD C. ALLEN

Sources Foster, *Alum. Oxon.* · T. Richards, *Religious developments in Wales, 1654–1662* (1923), 22, 37, 173, 456 · W. A. L. Vincent, *The grammar schools: their continuing traditions, 1660–1714* (1969), 30–31 · T. Richards, *A history of the puritan movement in Wales* (1920), 65 · T. Richards, *Wales under the penal code, 1662–1687* (1925), 38–9, 138–43, 161–70 · D. R. Thomas, *Esgobaeth Llanelwy: the history of the diocese of St Asaph*, rev. edn, 2 (1911), 88 · 1657, PRO, London MS exchequer misc. slip. 116 · LPL, MS 997, lib, i, fol. 244 · Bodl. Oxf., MS CCC Oxon 390/3, fol. 201v · Bodl. Oxf., MSS Christopher Wase, MS Add. C. 302, fol. 153 [Dolben MSS]

Pugh, Philip (1679–1760), Independent minister, was born at Hendre, Blaenpennal, Cardiganshire, the eldest son of Philip Pugh and Ann, daughter of David Jones of Coedmor Fawr, Llanbedr. Unusually for a Welsh nonconformist minister, he was the scion of a landed family. He was educated for the ministry at Samuel Jones's academy at Brynllywarch and, after Jones's death in 1697, at that of Roger Griffiths at Abergavenny. He was received as a church member at Cilgwyn, Cardiganshire, in 1704, and in October 1709 was ordained joint minister, with David Edwards and Jenkin Jones, of several churches in the area. He married about 1705 Elizabeth Morris, daughter of John Morris of Carrog, Llanddeiniol; she brought further property to augment Pugh's inherited estate. They lived at Blaengwern, in the parish of Llanfair Clydogau, and had two sons.

Pugh's power as a preacher and his piety, together with his social status, gave him widespread influence, and he became the leading Independent in north Cardiganshire. His success was such that, according to the John Evans list, the churches could claim 1000 'hearers' by 1715. Between 1709 and 1760 he baptized 680 children. At his own expense he built a chapel at Llwynpiod, and paid Morgan Williams to keep school at three separate places.

Pugh remained a staunch Calvinist, and though he avoided controversy he was greatly perturbed by the spread of Arminian and Arian doctrines in his churches. However, he and other Independents longed for a revival, and he sympathized with the Calvinistic Methodist movement under Daniel Rowland of Llangeitho, to whom he was a friend and counsellor. After Pugh's death, some of his former churches went over to either Arianism or Methodism. Pugh published *Darluniad y gwir Gristion* (1748), being a translation of John Shower's work, and a collection of his own communion hymns. He died at Blaen-gwern on 12 July 1760, aged eighty-one, and was buried on 15 July in the parish churchyard of Llanddewibrefi.

D. R. L. JONES

Sources D. Morgan, *Hanes ymneilltuaeth* (1855) · B. Williams [Gwynionydd], *Enwogion Ceredigion* (1869) · T. Rees and J. Thomas,

Hanes eglwysi annibynol Cymru, 4 (1875) · T. E. Davies, 'Philip Pugh a'i Lafur yn y Cilgwyn', *Y Cofiadur*, 14 (1937), 16–36 · J. H. Davies, 'The Abermeurig family and its connections', ed. F. Green, *West Wales Historical Records*, 2 (1911–12), 149–60 · *DWB* · R. T. Jones, *Hanes Annibynwyr Cymru* (1966)

Archives NL Wales, journal
Wealth at death substantial; left considerable real estate: will, PRO, PROB 11/861, sig. 478

Pugh, Ralph Bernard (1910–1982), historian and editor of the *Victoria History of the Counties of England*, was born on 1 August 1910 in Sutton, Surrey, the only child of Bernard Carr Pugh (1859–1940), journalist, and his wife, Mabel Elizabeth (or Elizabeth Mabel) Pugh (1869?–1943). His grandfather Samuel Pugh was a Baptist minister in Devizes, Wiltshire (PRO, RG 9/1293, fol. 190v, p. 22); (*VCH Wiltshire*, 10.306), and he was probably unbaptized until becoming much later a firm High Anglican. Ralph's visits to Devizes, where his uncles Clarence Woodburn Pugh and Cyril S. Pugh ran the grammar school until 1917 (*VCH Wiltshire*, 10.306), gave him a lasting devotion to Wiltshire history. After Homefield preparatory school, five years at St Paul's School from 1924 were immediately followed by three reading modern history at Queen's College, Oxford, where he obtained a first in 1932. He abandoned after two years a doctoral thesis on early-nineteenth-century European academic historiography, a failure of completion which, with failure to marry and to learn to drive a car, he always regretted.

In 1934 Pugh became an assistant keeper (second class) at the Public Record Office (PRO). The late-Victorian curatorial culture that gave priority to the production of scholarly calendars of archives, and to the necessary editorial skills, still flourished, and Pugh soon used for Wiltshire tools acquired in Chancery Lane. He was the chief founder in 1937 of the records branch of the Wiltshire Archaeological and Natural History Society, and edited its first volume. A spinal deformity precluded military service, and from 1940 to 1946 he was seconded to the Dominions Office, an experience later reflected in *Records of the Colonial and Dominions Offices* (PRO handbook no. 3, 1964) and in a history of the Colonial Office in the *Cambridge History of the British Empire*, vol. 3 (1959). The civil service gave him enthusiasm for systematic administration and record-keeping, besides pedantic precision.

Pugh returned to the PRO in 1946, but his work on Wiltshire continued with the *Calendar of Antrobus Deeds* (1947), whose introduction remained for forty years the standard short guide to English conveyancing instruments. When Swindon corporation, seeking to sponsor local history, contacted him in 1945, he encouraged a partnership between London University and a committee of local authorities to finance the Wiltshire volumes of the *Victoria History of the Counties of England* (*VCH*). Since no Wiltshire *VCH* volumes had appeared, Pugh in 1946 proposed a new scheme. He became joint honorary editor for Wiltshire in May 1949. The Wiltshire financial model was soon followed in other counties, reviving the *VCH*.

In autumn 1949 Pugh succeeded Louis Francis Salzman as general editor of the *VCH*. While improving the project's finances through partnerships with local authorities, which by 1977 funded work in eleven counties, he sought to modernize its content without changing its structure. Apart from reducing the architectural emphasis, he achieved that by addition rather than subtraction. General articles were much expanded, those written for Wiltshire forming a model. From the early 1950s the topographical articles also acquired new topics, and the treatment of others became more thorough. Pugh set out his views in *How to Write a Parish History* (1954), and wrote extensively to guide contributors.

Pugh's *VCH* work in the 1950s and 1960s did not preclude extensive reviewing, teaching palaeography in London, occasional teaching from 1959 as supernumerary fellow of the recently independent St Edmund Hall, Oxford (whose principal John Kelly was a close friend), and continued work for the Wiltshire records branch (from 1967 Record Society), as chairman from 1953 and president from 1967. He became expert in medieval penology, publishing articles from the 1950s, *Imprisonment in Medieval England* in 1968, and in the 1970s editions of trailbaston trials. He also enjoyed four American sabbaticals from 1963 to 1978, the first two at Princeton. London University made him professor of English history in 1968 and awarded the honorary degree of DLitt.

An intimidatingly tall man despite his stoop, and with manners so correct as to arouse distrust, Pugh made enemies especially by lobbying for the preservation of and access to records, and by the pains taken in selecting and managing *VCH* staff, which sometimes put him at loggerheads with county grandees. His paternal concern for his subordinates' welfare often irritated the recipients. From 1966 Pugh sought unsuccessfully to prevent new *VCH* alliances with local authorities, which made editorial control more difficult, and to expand his central staff.

Some sixty *VCH* volumes appeared during Pugh's editorship. By the 1970s academic reviewers were criticizing the enlarged content as too fragmented, and as neglecting much of local history, though the utility of Pugh's redesign later attracted growing public support. After retirement in 1977 Pugh continued to work on London's penal history, but increased spinal curvature and the effects of pipe-smoking undermined his health. Entering University College Hospital, Gower Street, London, with diverticulitis late in 1982, he contracted pneumonia, died on 3 December 1982, and was cremated at Golders Green on 10 December. C. R. J. CURRIE

Sources *The Times* (6 Dec 1982) · *WWW*, 1981–90 · *VCH General introduction* · C. R. Elrington, 'Ralph Bernard Pugh: an appreciation', and S. M. Keeling, 'Bibliography', *Coroners' bills, 1752–1796*, Wilts RS, 36 (1980), xiii–xxvi · VCH correspondence files from 1951, U. Lond., Institute of Historical Research · VCH subcommittee minutes, 1943–78, U. Lond., Institute of Historical Research · A. H. Mead and others, eds., *St Paul's School registers* (1990) · will, 3 Oct 1971, probate granted, 8 April 1983 · C. R. Elrington, diaries, 1968, 1982, 34 Lloyd Baker Street, London WC1 · personal knowledge (2004) · private information (2004) [C. R. Elrington]
Archives Institute of Historical Research, London, Victoria County History records

Likenesses K. R., oils, *c.*1950, Institute of Historical Research, London · A. P. Baggs, photograph, 1970–79, Institute of Historical Research, VCH records; repro. in C. R. J. Currie and C. P. Lewis, eds., *English county histories: a guide* (1994), 25 · C. K. Roise and P. D. Rushing, photograph, 1980, repro. in Elrington, 'Ralph Bernard Hugh', frontispiece

Wealth at death £110,373: probate, 8 April 1983, *CGPLA Eng. & Wales*

Pugh, Robert (*c.*1610–1679), Roman Catholic controversialist, was born in Wales; Wood claimed that he had been born at Penrhyn in the parish of 'Eglos-Rosse' (Llan-rhos) Caernarvonshire. In 1628 he entered the noviciate at the English College at Watten and by his ordination, on 20 March 1638, he was in Liège. In 1639 he returned to Watten and after two years at the English Jesuit college at St Omer in 1641–2—where he entered under the name of Robert Phillips—he returned to England, where he is said to have served in Charles I's army taking the rank of captain. However, this led to his dismissal by the Jesuits on 8 May 1645 for, according to Wood, accompanying the royalist army 'without the consent of the superiors of his order' (Wood, *Ath. Oxon.*, 3.829). He bore the Jesuits no ill will following his dismissal and is said to have desired to be readmitted to the society when on his deathbed.

Following his dismissal from the society Pugh went on to study civil and canon law (probably at Paris) and became a doctor of both disciplines. He apparently acted as tutor to Henry, duke of Gloucester, the fourth son of Charles I. Pugh's reputation as a theologian grew rapidly, and in 1655 he was created *protonotarius publicus apostolicus* by Pope Alexander VII. He was known to Walter Montagu, the secret agent and friend of Henrietta Maria, who was later made abbot of the Benedictine monastery of Nanteuil by the queen-dowager of France. Pugh was a prominent opponent of Blackloism and with Montagu's aid he attacked the philosophical views of Thomas White (alias Blacklo) in a pamphlet entitled *De Anglicani cleri retinenda in apostolicam sedem observantia* (1659). In this he claimed, in opposition to White, that the regular clergy should be exempt from the jurisdiction of the Catholic chapter in England. White's views on purgatory, hell, and the infallibility of the pope were seen by many of the Catholic clergy as unsound and exception was also taken to his politico-religious views, especially his teaching in favour of passive obedience to any established government. Several of White's theses were censured by the inquisition in decrees of May 1655 and September 1657, and many of his friends and former students publicly rejected his principles. Eventually he withdrew those opinions which had been censured and submitted himself and his writings to the Holy See. White's reply to Pugh's repudiation, *Monumentum excantatus* (1660) was in turn answered by Pugh in *Excantationis amuletum* (1661). Using another alias, Petrus Hoburgus (an anagram of Robertus Pughus), which he had used in a letter to Cardinal Francesco Barberini in November 1661, Pugh published another attack on White in 1662 as *Animadversiones in Thomae Albii*. Pugh is also said to have written a life of White, which is not known to be extant.

Following the Restoration Pugh settled for part of the year in London and the rest in Redcastle, Wales, with the family of the marquess of Powis. In 1664 there appeared from the pen of 'a royal veteran' *Elenchus elenchi, sive, Animadversiones*, a response to George Bates' *Elenchus motuum* (1650; *Elenchus elenchi*, title-page). It was initially credited to Pugh, but it has since been accepted that although it was not his work he probably had a hand in its production. With Roger Palmer, earl of Castlemaine, with whom he was closely connected, Pugh wrote *The Catholic Apologie* (1666). This text was answered by William Lloyd, later bishop of Lichfield, and was later defended in *A Reply to the Answer of the 'Catholic Apologie'* (1668). Pugh's *Bathoniensium et aquisgranensium thermarum comparatio* (1676) was dedicated to his patron, Palmer. A series of manuscripts, reputedly by Pugh, entitled 'Unpublished works', from the Gillow Library, are to be found in the library of Downside Abbey. Pugh is also credited with the authorship of a Latin ode to the memory of Sidney Montagu, who died in the sea battle with the Dutch in June 1672, entitled *In nobilissimi juvenis Sidnaei Montacuti* (1672).

During the furore of the Popish Plot from 1678 onwards Pugh, 'having been betrayed by a wicked miscreant when paying a visit of charity to the Catholic gentry confined in a London prison' (Foley, ser. 7, 5.34), was himself committed to Newgate. Pugh died, while still incarcerated, on 22 January 1679. He was buried in Christ Church churchyard, Newgate, the next day. The following year the Jesuit John Warner published a cache of letters by White and several of White's associates (including Sir Kenelm Digby and Henry Holden) that Pugh had collected through the agency of Walter Montagu and had deposited at the English Jesuit college at Ghent; the work accused White of opposition to the regulars and to episcopal authority, and of disloyalty to the pope.

Wood, who appears to have known Pugh personally, described him as a 'person of a most comely port, well favour'd, and of excellent parts, and therefore he deserved a better end'; however, Wood seems to confuse him with Robert Philips, the oratorian, who was confessor to Henrietta Maria (Wood, *Ath. Oxon.*, 3.830).

ROBERTA ANDERSON

Sources T. M. McCoog, *English and Welsh Jesuits, 1555–1650*, 2 vols., Catholic RS, 74–5 (1994–5), vol. 5, p. 34 · H. Foley, ed., *Records of the English province of the Society of Jesus*, 7 vols. in 8 (1875–83), vol. 5, p. 34; vol. 7, pp. 596, 635; vol. 8, p. 34 · Wood, *Ath. Oxon.*, new edn, 3.697, 828–30; 4.716 · M. V. Hay, *The Jesuits and the Popish Plot* (1934) · Wing, *STC* · R. Pugh, 'Unpublished works', 12 vols., Downside Abbey Library, F72B, 79480 · Gillow, *Lit. biog. hist.* · R. Pugh, *Blacklo's cabal* (1680), repr. with introduction by T. A. Birrell (1970) · T. H. Clancy, *English Catholic books, 1641–1700: a bibliography*, rev. edn (1996)

Archives Downside Abbey, near Bath, Somerset, unpublished MSS, F72B/79480

Pughe, William Owen [*pseud.* Idrison] (1759–1835), antiquary and lexicographer, was born William Owen at Tyny-bryn in the parish of Llanfihangel-y-Pennant, Merioneth, on 7 August 1759. He was the son of John Owen (1712–1800) of Rhiwywerfa, near Abergynolwyn, and his wife, Anne Owen (1733–1811). His father was a skilled singer to the harp, and he thus acquired at an early age an interest in Welsh poetry, which was deepened by the study of *Gorchestion beirdd Cymru*, when that collection appeared in 1773. Some biographers claim that he received his education at Altrincham, Cheshire, but there is no definite proof to support this. In 1776 he went to live in London. About 1782 he made the acquaintance of Robert Hughes (Robin Ddu yr Ail o Fôn) and Owen Jones (Owain Myfyr), through whom he became in 1783 a member of the Gwyneddigion, a society of London Welshmen founded in 1770. Owen thereupon began to collect materials for a Welsh–English dictionary. The first section appeared ten years later, on 27 June 1793. Its publication proceeded slowly until 1803, when it was completed and issued in two volumes, with a grammar prefixed to the first. It contained about 100,000 words, with English equivalents, and, in a large number of cases, illustrative quotations from early Welsh literature. Its erroneous etymology is based on the assumption that all Welsh words can be resolved into monosyllabic elements of abstract signification, a notion first put forward with regard to English and other languages by Rowland Jones in his *Philosophy of Words* (1769). An abridgement of Owen's dictionary appeared in 1806, a new edition (revised by the author) in 1832, and a further edition, extended by Robert John Pryse, in 1866.

Meanwhile in 1789 Owen, together with Owain Myfyr, edited the poetry of Dafydd ap Gwilym (reprinted 1873), adding in English a sketch of the life and writings of the poet. On 9 August 1790 he married Sarah Elizabeth Harper (1771–1816), with whom he had a son, Aneurin *Owen (1792–1851), and two daughters, Isabella and Ellen. Ellen later married John, the son of the antiquary Richard Fenton. In 1792 Owen published *The Heroic Elegies and other Pieces of Llywarc Hen*, with a translation and a prefatory sketch on bardism, probably written by Edward Williams (Iolo Morganwg). Owen had become dissatisfied with the orthography of the Welsh language, and throughout this work uses 'ç' for the sound usually written 'ch', and 'v' for Welsh 'f'. In his dictionary a third innovation appeared— the use of 'z' for 'dd'. In 1800 Owen translated into Welsh *A Cardiganshire Landlord's Advice to his Tenants*, a treatise on agriculture, by Thomas Johnes of Hafoduchtryd. The next year saw the publication of a far more important work, the first volume of the *Myvyrian Archaiology of Wales*, an enterprise for which Owen, Owain Myfyr, and Iolo Morganwg were all nominally responsible, though the main literary work was probably done by Owen, while the cost (above £1000 for the three volumes) was defrayed by Owain Myfyr. The first volume was an attempt to give from the manuscripts the text of all Welsh poetry to 1370 (excluding that of Dafydd ap Gwilym, already printed). The design of supplementing this with a selection of later poetry (general advertisement of 1 January 1801) was never carried out. Volume two, which also appeared in 1801, contains the text of the Trioedd, the Brutiau, and other prose documents of a historical nature; volume three (didactic literature, laws, and music) followed in 1807. The three were reprinted, with some additions, in one volume at Denbigh in 1870. Owen was the editor of the *Cambrian Register*, a periodical devoted to Welsh history and literature, of which three volumes appeared, in 1795, 1799, and 1818. In June 1805, together with Thomas Jones (Y Bardd Cloff), Owen started the *Greal*, a Welsh quarterly of a similar character, which was issued under the patronage of the Gwyneddigion and Cymreigyddion societies of London. Its orthographical peculiarities proved an obstacle to its success, and it was discontinued in June 1807. *Cadwedigaeth yr iaith Gymraeg*, a Welsh grammar published by Owen in 1808, was printed at London in the same orthography, but an edition in ordinary spelling also came from a Bala press. Owen's concise *Cambrian Biography* appeared in 1803.

About 1803 Owen became a follower of Joanna Southcott, the religious fanatic. He remained a member of her intimate circle and often acted as her amanuensis until her death in 1814. In 1806 he inherited an estate at Nantglyn, near Denbigh, from a distant relative, Rice Pughe, whereupon he assumed the surname of Pughe. During the rest of his life he spent much of his time in Wales, and his literary activity diminished. Pughe's wife died on 28 January 1816, and to divert his mind from the loss he undertook to translate *Paradise Lost* into Welsh. *Coll gwynfa* appeared in 1819: its ponderous and artificial diction made it unintelligible to the ordinary Welsh reader. Pughe was no doubt the anonymous translator of Dodsley's *Life of Man* (*Einioes dyn*, 1821). In 1822 he published a Welsh poem in three cantos about Hu Gadarn, and in the same year he issued a volume of translations from English, which included Gray's 'Bard' and Heber's 'Palestine'. Most of his poetry appeared under the pseudonym Idrison. During his later years Pughe was chiefly occupied in preparing an edition of the *Mabinogi*, the Welsh romances; but although the Cymmrodorion Society in 1831 voted £50 for the publication of this work at Denbigh, it never appeared.

Pughe died of apoplexy on 3 June 1835 in a cottage near Dôl-y-cae, in the neighbourhood of his birthplace, where he had gone for the sake of his health, and was buried that month at Nantglyn. He had been elected a fellow of the Society of Antiquaries in 1793, and on 19 June 1822 received from the University of Oxford the degree of DCL. Pughe's contribution to scholarship must be regarded as a product of its own age, and it was the Romanticism of that age which clouded his linguistic approach. Many of his idiosyncrasies remained in the Welsh orthography and vocabulary until the early years of the twentieth century, when Sir John Morris Jones did much to rid the language of his influence. However, Owen did lay the foundations for later scholars, and his dictionary shows a very profound knowledge of early Welsh texts. His main faults were his fanciful orthographical experiments and his lack of critical power.

J. E. LLOYD, rev. GLENDA CARR

Sources G. Carr, *William Owen Pughe* (1983) · G. Carr, *William Owen Pughe* (1993) · W. Owen, introduction, *Geiriadur Cynmraeg a Saesoneg | A Welsh and English dictionary* (1793) · W. D. Leathart, *The origin and progress of the Gwyneddigion Society of London* (1831) · R. Williams, *A biographical sketch* (1836) · I. Foulkes, *Enwogion Cymru* (1870) · T. M.

Pierce, *Dr W. Owen Pughe* (1914) • bishop's transcripts, Bangor diocese, parish of Llanfihangel-y-Pennant, NL Wales • *Y Dysgedydd* (July 1835), 228 • NL Wales, MS 13248

Archives BL, papers, Add. MSS 14956, 15003 • NL Wales, corresp., diaries, and literary papers • NL Wales, papers | BL, Cymmrodorion School MSS, Add. MSS 14866–15089 • BL, Gwyneddigion MSS, Add. MSS 9848–9850

Likenesses T. George, portrait, repro. in W. O. Pughe, *A dictionary of the Welsh language*, 2nd edn (1832), frontispiece • D. Maclise, portrait, NL Wales; repro. in Carr, *William Owen Pughe* (1983), 85 • C. Picart, stipple (after E. Jones), BM, NPG • line engraving, BM • portrait, NL Wales • woodcut, NPG

Pugin, Auguste Charles (1768/9–1832), artist and architectural draughtsman, was born in the parish of St Sulpice, Paris, one of the seven children of François Joseph Pugin (*fl.* 1765–1794), who was probably in the service of a German aristocrat resident in Paris, and of Marguérite Duchêne (*fl.* 1768–*c.*1800). Most of what is known of Pugin's French origins is in the form of uncorroborated notes collected from Madame Antonia Molineux, Pugin's only niece, by Benjamin Ferrey, in preparation for his biography of Pugin and his son, A. W. N. Pugin.

Family background and education Pugin's father was apparently the youngest of a large family in Switzerland, probably Fribourg. He came to France *c.*1765 and was, according to Madame Molineux, 'first gentleman to the Prince de Selm', who was probably Frederick John Otto, prince de Salm-Kyrbourg (1745–1794), who served in the French army. Pugin is described as 'fils de labroureur' on the certificate of his first marriage, but the family's claim to nobility relates to their presumed descent from a noble medieval Fribourg family, one of whom, Louis De Corbières, fought at the battle of Morat in 1477, an incident recounted by Ferrey and corroborated in the *Dictionnaire historique et biographique de la Suisse* (2, 1924, 579). His father's second marriage, to Pugin's mother, seems to have brought some prosperity, which was lost under the French Revolution, during which period he appears to have died and the prince de Salm-Kyrbourg was guillotined. How many of Pugin's six brothers and sisters survived is unknown, but only two sisters, Jeanne Adélaïde Lafitte and Sophie Bernard, are mentioned in family papers. The family clearly prospered in France under the restoration and by 1827 was reusing the family coat of arms, which had been taken from that of the De Corbières family. The arms also appear as Pugin in the early nineteenth-century *Armorial combaz* (Bibliothèque cantonale et universitaire de Fribourg, fol. 43). Pugin does not appear to have used the arms but his son, A. W. N. Pugin, made them widely known in his publications, with slight changes and the addition of the motto 'en avant', which he no doubt intended to be provocative. It seems clear that Pugin believed himself to be a gentleman, though always an impecunious one.

Also nothing is known of Pugin's education, but among his lifelong friends were Louis Lafitte (1770–1828), a neoclassical painter who became his brother-in-law, and C. P. J. Normand (1765–1840), a neo-classical architect, both of whom studied at the Académie Royale. It has been suggested that he may have been the artist of illustrations

Auguste Charles Pugin (1768/9–1832), by unknown artist

signed 'Pugin' which appeared in the magazine *Le Cabinet des Modes* between April 1776 and November 1789 (Hill, 12–13). This seems a reasonable conjecture, suggesting a struggling young artist seeking to make a little money in such a way.

On 27 March 1792 Pugin entered the Royal Academy Schools in London, when his age was given in the register as twenty-four. His reasons for leaving France have not been established although various glamorous stories circulated among his pupils. He did not remain in London long, however, but soon had a position as a draughtsman to the architect John Nash. Nash was then working in Wales, where he developed his picturesque style. Pugin acknowledged his debt to Nash in the dedication of his first volume of *Specimens of Gothic Architecture* (1821), where he wrote: 'Soon after my arrival in this country, I was fortunately introduced to you, and prosecuted my architectural studies in your office with much gratification and advantage to myself'. Signed drawings of this period show Pugin's style to be typical of late eighteenth-century topography, with a heavy outline and a somewhat naïve approach.

Early career Nash returned to London *c.*1796 and it must be presumed that Pugin came with him and continued to work for him. By this time Pugin felt himself to be a qualified architect and in 1799 he exhibited at the Royal Academy an *Intended Villa in the North of England*, but in the same year he was also listed as a member of the Royal Academy life class. It seems that he quickly gave up the attempt to establish himself as an architect, unlike the eldest son of Humphry Repton, J. A. Repton (1775–1860), who had also been with Nash in Wales, and concentrated on improving his artistic skills. In London Pugin found companions among the artistic émigré community, such as J. Merigot,

Pierre Condé, and J. C. Nattes. During this period his style and technique, in particular his handling of watercolour, developed a long way from its previous stiffness. As importantly, on 2 February 1802 he married Catherine Welby (c.1772–1833), an interesting and intelligent lady who was related to a prominent landowning family in Lincolnshire. She set about the organization and promotion of her easy-going husband, which proved to be a slow process at first. They began their married life in her father's house, 3 Pullens Row, Islington.

The turning point in Pugin's career was the forming of a connection with Rudolph Ackermann, the German publisher who played such an important role in the formation of the taste of the Regency period, particularly with his shop on the Strand and his magazine, both called the *Repository of the Arts*. The most famous joint production of Pugin and Ackermann, *The Microcosm of London*, appeared between 1808 and 1810. The project seems to have originated in an idea of the Pugins (Hill, 16): a draft prospectus survives for a publication entitled 'Views of London and Westminster', which was to contain plates combining 'the most interesting public edifices … with the characteristics peculiar to each part of the town' (Yale Center for British Art, Pugin 176). Perhaps they intended the text to be by Catherine Pugin, but the work was realized in all its editorial and technical complexity by Ackermann, who used professional writers for the text and for the coloured aquatints crucially brought in the artist Thomas Rowlandson, whose rumbustious figures were the perfect foil to Pugin's clear and accurate architectural settings. The result was an acknowledged masterpiece and was followed by Ackermann's *History of Westminster Abbey* (1812), to which Pugin contributed eighteen plates, the *History of the University of Oxford* (1814), with thirty plates by Pugin, the *History of the University of Cambridge* (1815), with twenty-two plates by Pugin, and finally the *History of the Colleges of Winchester etc.* (1816), with fourteen plates by Pugin. These books, widely held to be among the most beautiful illustrated books of the first half of the nineteenth century, established Pugin's reputation and in 1809, helped by a bequest from Catherine's father, they were established at 39 Keppel Street, Bloomsbury, where, in March 1812, their only child, Augustus Welby Northmore *Pugin, was born.

This period marks the high point of Pugin's skill as an artist. He had been elected an associate of the Society of Painters in Water Colours in 1807 and had a great mastery of that medium, in which he liked to explore the effects of light. He became a full member in 1812 and was a regular contributor to their exhibitions. He also continued to exhibit occasionally at the Royal Academy. Among his best pictures are the *View of Louth* (c.1817, Louth Naturalists' Antiquarian and Literary Society, Lincolnshire) and *View from the Excavated Ground of the Highgate Archway* (1812, Highgate Literary and Scientific Institute, London). His architectural interests at this period seem to have been concentrated on helping friends, particularly with Gothic details, in which he was by then considered an expert. An important example, which may be attributed to Pugin in 1817, was the gothicizing of a garden building at Claremont, Surrey, as a mausoleum to Princess Charlotte, a work which was executed by J. B. Papworth, the acknowledged architect.

As well as these two activities, Pugin carried out a number of miscellaneous commissions, no doubt to make ends meet, including in 1810 the supervising of the erection of a Coade stone statue of George III at Nocton, Lincolnshire. From 1814 his French connections were revived: immediately following the peace treaty with France, Louis Lafitte, his wife, and daughter, joined the Pugins in London. Lafitte had been a court painter to the Empress Josephine and then to Napoleon, and no doubt felt that a period of absence from France would benefit his career. Pugin was able, principally through Nash, to help Lafitte obtain commissions to provide decorations for the victory celebrations. The family stayed in England until the battle of Waterloo had clarified the political situation, and 'the visit established a pattern of mutual assistance and co-operation between the brothers-in-law which continued until Lafitte's death' (Hill, 18). It is not known whether Lafitte ever returned to England, but from that time onwards the Pugins made regular visits to Paris, where Lafitte soon held another court position under Louis XVIII. This connection must have helped him set up a minor cross-channel business dealing in prints, books, and probably antiques.

Major works Pugin continued to work for Ackermann, for whom in the *Repository of the Arts* he produced a series of remarkable designs for Gothic furniture, first published between 1825 and 1827, and then gathered into a book, *Gothic Furniture*, published by Ackermann with no date but presumably 1828. Pugin's major occupation became his production of illustrated architectural books, which were overwhelmingly devoted to medieval architecture. In his obituary in *Arnold's Library of the Fine Arts* it was acknowledged that he had 'performed for gothic architecture services similar to those which [James] Stuart and his fellow-labourers effected for that of Greece' (*Arnold's Library*, 323).

It is not surprising that with all his experience Pugin soon attracted the attention of the antiquary and topographer John Britton (1771–1857) in his enormous publishing enterprises, and in 1818 Pugin was in Lincoln making illustrations for Britton's fifth volume of the *Architectural Antiquities of Great Britain* (1826). Pugin went to Lincoln often, perhaps to visit Welby relations, and frequently exhibited paintings of the city and its surroundings. Here he was approached by a local Catholic architect, E. J. Willson (1787–1854), with the idea of producing a book useful to builders and architects, with measured drawings of details of the different parts of Gothic architecture. The scheme was taken up swiftly and the two volumes of *Specimens of Gothic Architecture* were published in 1821 and 1823, with the text by Willson. Britton said: 'I declined to place my name in the title-page' but 'I soon found that nearly the whole of the business department devolved on me' (*The Builder*, 13, 1855, 5). These volumes were successful and widely recognized as a new departure. In contrast to

Britton's earlier enterprises, which were illustrated with densely hatched etchings, this one used steel-engravings. This new technique, combined with an emphasis on practical construction, by showing a large number of mouldings and other details, and with Pugin's own genius for creating an attractive plate, produced architectural drawings of unrivalled elegance, clarity, and accuracy. The absence of picturesque views and dedicated plates must have added to the impression of modernity. The publication was not a commercial success, and in order to undertake *Specimens* Pugin took on pupils and established a flourishing school of architectural drawing in his own house at 105 Great Russell Street. Among his first pupils were Charles Moore (*fl.* 1820s) and Charles James Mathews (1803–1878), who left an affectionate account of his time in Pugin's office. His father, the actor Charles Mathews, who had met Pugin in Wales, is supposed to have based his character of M. Mallet on his knowledge of Pugin and his experiences as a newly arrived foreigner in England. Pugin and his pupils made extended tours in Britain, and also to Paris and in Normandy to find the material for his books. After *Specimens*, Pugin and Britton used the same formula to produce *Specimens of the Architectural Antiquities of Normandy* (1827), with text by Britton. At the same time they were working on *Illustrations of the Public Buildings of London*, which appeared in two volumes in 1825 and 1828. The books were modelled on a French prototype, *Description de Paris et de ses édifices* (1806–9), by J. G. Legrand and C. P. Landon. They are not pretty books in the sense that the *Microcosm* volumes were, but they are invaluable to architectural historians and 'nearly one and a half centuries later, Britton and Pugin are still our most reliable guides to Regency London' (Crook, 117). Sadly, the collaboration came to an unhappy conclusion and Pugin and Taylor (the printer) involved Britton in a lawsuit. Britton wrote to Soane:

> I am now endeavouring to seperate [*sic*] all accounts and connection with Pugin and Taylor, both of whom have acted meanly and dishonourably towards me. The Normandy and London Buildings being finished, I shall never again have connection with either. (John Britton to John Soane, 22 Nov 1828, London, Soane Museum, III B.1.68)

An alternative point of view is hinted at in Pugin's obituary (*Arnold's Library*, 324).

The *London* volumes actually recorded a loss of £460, but Pugin and his pupils continued with his schemes undaunted. The next books to appear were *Paris and its Environs*, in two volumes (1829 and 1831), with the text by L. T. Ventouillac, and a series of attractive books, aimed for a different market, which imaginatively explored the new medium of lithography. These were: *A Series of Views Illustrative of Pugin's Examples of Gothic Architecture* (1830), with the text by W. H. Leeds and lithography by Joseph Nash; *Gothic Ornaments from Ancient Buildings in England and France* (1828–31), with lithographs by J. D. Harding; and *A series of ornamental timber gables from existing examples in England and France of the sixteenth century* (1831), with text by E. J. Willson and lithographs by B. Ferrey. These works were brought out with the second wave of Pugin's pupils, who were approximately the same age as Pugin's son. Among the best-known are T. T. Bury, Benjamin Ferrey, Joseph Nash, and James Pennethorne. In his account of Pugin's drawing school, Ferrey gave a particularly unfair description of Mrs Pugin's management of the household.

Later works Of other important commissions that came Pugin's way during this period, one was from John Nash for the splendid plates for his book, *The Royal Pavilion at Brighton* (1826), on which Pugin worked between 1819 and 1824. He also continued to practise occasionally as an architect: in 1823 he designed the interior of the Diorama in Regent's Park, together with James Morgan (*fl.* 1806–1834). Between 1826 and 1827 he exhibited three designs for cemeteries, and early in 1830 he was associated with Sir Marc Isambard Brunel in the layout of the cemetery at Kensal Green. Pugin's knowledge and advocacy of the Gothic styles were continued in his final publication, the first volume of *Examples of Gothic Architecture* (1831), in which the examples were taken from 'habitable' buildings, 'civil architecture being much less understood than ecclesiastical'. The text was once more by E. J. Willson, whose late delivery delayed the publication. Pugin was working on the second volume at the time of his death in his home at 105 Great Russell Street on 19 December 1832. He was buried on 27 December in St Mary's Church, Islington.

Pugin's character was clearly delightful, charming, and relaxed, appealing to all kinds of people, from his pupils to his aristocratic patrons. He also seems to have enjoyed a happy family life with his clever wife and precocious son, whose spectacular early successes and failures must have caused him considerable uneasiness from time to time. A. W. N. Pugin paid an affectionate tribute to his father in the frontispiece to the second volume of *Examples* which, again greatly delayed by Willson, eventually appeared in 1836, although it was one of his pupils, Thomas Larkins Walker, that Pugin made his literary executor, and it was he who wrote the text and supervised the third volume of *Examples*. Pugin was never affluent at any period of his life and always had to husband his income. After his death his extensive library of architectural books was sold at Wheatleys on 4 June 1833. ALEXANDRA WEDGWOOD

Sources B. Ferrey, *The recollections of A. N. Welby Pugin, and his father Augustus Pugin* (1861) · HLRO, Pugin family papers, PUG/3 [microfilm] · Yale U. CBA, Pugin correspondence, MS/Pugin · *Arnold's Library of the Fine Arts*, new ser., 1 (1833), 320–27 · R. Hill, *Burlington Magazine*, 138 (1996), 11–19 · A. Wedgwood, *Catalogue of the drawings collection of the Royal Institute of British Architects: the Pugin family* (1977) · A. Wedgwood, *A. W. N. Pugin and the Pugin family* (1985) · J. M. Crook, 'John Britton and the genesis of the Gothic revival', *Concerning architecture*, ed. J. Summerson (1968) · GM, 1st ser., 103/1 (1833), 278–9 · [W. Papworth], ed., *The dictionary of architecture*, 11 vols. (1853–92) · DNB · Colvin, *Archs.* · A. Wedgwood, 'Pugin (1) A. C. Pugin', *The dictionary of art*, ed. J. Turner (1996) · *The life of Charles James Mathews*, ed. C. Dickens, 2 vols. (1879) · J. L. Roget, *A history of the 'Old Water-Colour' Society*, 2 vols. (1891) · A. K. Placzek, ed., *Macmillan encyclopedia of architects*, 4 vols. (1982) · *The Royal Watercolour Society: the first fifty years, 1805–1855* (1992) · *Almanach de Gotha* (1775) · *Almanach de Gotha* (1798) · J. Ford, *Ackermann, 1783–1983: the business of art* (1983) · *Dictionnaire historique et biographique de la Suisse*, 2 (1924) · L. M. Prudhomme, *Dictionnaire de la Révolution Française*

(1797) • *Schweizerische Heraldische Gesellschaft* • S. C. Hutchison, 'The Royal Academy Schools, 1768–1830', *Walpole Society*, 38 (1960–62), 123–91, esp. 153

Archives priv. coll., MSS [microfilm in HLRO] • RIBA, corresp. and drawings • V&A, notes and drawings • Yale U. CBA, MSS, MS/Pugin | Bibliothèque Cantonale et Universitaire, Fribourg, Armorial Combaz, cote L 462

Likenesses J. Green, oils, *c*.1810, RIBA • A. F. R.?, etching, 1844, NPG • J. Nash, lithograph, repro. in Ferrey, *Recollections of A. N. Welby Pugin* • A. J. Oliver?, oils, priv. coll. • E. Scriven, stipple (after J. Green), repro. in *Arnold's Library of the Fine Arts* • portrait, priv. coll. [*see illus.*]

Wealth at death impecunious throughout life • architectural library, engravings, objets d'art: Wheatleys sale catalogue

Pugin, Augustus Welby Northmore (1812–1852), architect, writer, and designer, was born on 1 March 1812 at 39 Keppel Street, Russell Square, London, the only child of Auguste Charles *Pugin (1768/9–1832), architect, and Catherine Welby (*c*.1772–1833).

Early years Pugin was a precocious child and grew up in a household full of pupils attending the school of architectural draughtsmanship run by his father. His formal education was minimal; he attended school at Christ's Hospital, London, briefly, but from an early age he was fascinated by medieval architecture and drawing. These interests he must have inherited from his father; from his mother he gained his energy and his ability with words. From 1819 the family made several visits to Paris and Normandy, both to see their French relations and to gather material for his father's books. The young Pugin's career as an independent designer began in 1827 with two grand commissions. Benjamin Ferrey (1810–1880), a pupil of A. C. Pugin, who wrote the first biography of A. W. N. Pugin, tells the story of how he was discovered by a member of the firm of royal goldsmiths Rundell and Bridge in the print room of the British Museum, where he was copying the prints of Dürer. This connection resulted in the production for George IV of a Gothic standing cup now in the Royal Collection and known as the Coronation Cup, and unexecuted designs for a set of church plate, probably intended for St George's Chapel, Windsor. His next commission was also for George IV, as one of the craftsmen engaged by the upholsterers Morel and Seddon to furnish the new apartments at Windsor Castle. A considerable amount of Gothic furniture, very much in his father's style, survives in the castle.

After this glamorous start there followed a restless period for this lively and highly talented youth. As well as medieval architecture, Pugin was passionate about both the sea and the stage. He had his own boat, and began to make theatrical friends, one of whom was George Dayes, son of the artist Edward Dayes (1763–1804), and it was through him, Pugin wrote, 'that I first imbibed the taste for stage machinery and scenic representation to which I afterwards applied myself so closely' ('Autobiography', fol. 20, V&A, National Art Library).

In 1829 Pugin became a stage carpenter at Covent Garden, and he later designed stage sets for William Grieve (1800–1844) at the King's Theatre, including one for the ballet *Kenilworth* in 1831, which was much praised. Also in

Augustus Welby Northmore Pugin (1812–1852), by John Rogers Herbert, 1845

1829 he set up his own business, designing and making interior decorations and furniture, but, as a result of his inexperience and impracticality, it failed in 1831. At the same period he was introduced to James Gillespie Graham (1776–1855), the Scottish architect, and began to help him with his work. Pugin married in 1831 Anne Garnet (*c*.1811–1832), a connection of George Dayes, whom his parents thought to be socially beneath him and who died on 27 May 1832, a week after the birth of a daughter, Anne (1832–1897). This was the first of a number of personal tragedies: Pugin's father died in December the same year, followed a few months later by his mother, and finally his aunt Selina Welby, who left him a legacy which gave him some independence. He seems always to have needed female companionship and married in 1833 Louisa Burton (*c*.1813–1844), who also seems to have had theatrical connections.

These events encouraged Pugin to concentrate on becoming an architect, though his training for the profession was highly unusual. His knowledge of architecture was based on his detailed sketches and observation of many medieval buildings, both in Britain and in northern Europe. This study, which he continued throughout his life, was for him an essential activity and gave authority to his style. He also designed a series of imaginary Gothic buildings, all with medieval themes, in the form of little books with titles such as *The Hospital of St John* (1833), *The Deanery*, and *St Marie's College* (both 1834). These ideal schemes were presented fully furnished. During these years he continued to produce designs for furniture and metalwork and this aspect of his work culminated in three books that were published by Ackermann in 1835 and 1836.

In 1835 Pugin became a Roman Catholic, a turning point in his life. From then on he devoted himself to the further-ance of his faith and of Gothic architecture. His father, nominally a Catholic, was uninterested in religion but his mother, who fell under the influence of the preacher and theologian Edward Irving (1792–1834) and took her son to listen to Irving's lengthy sermons in the 1820s, brought him up a protestant. It seems clear that Pugin was drawn to Catholicism originally by the beauty of medieval archi-tecture. The principal human influence was probably that of E. J. Willson (1787–1854), a Catholic architect in Lincoln and a collaborator of his father, to whom he wrote on 6 November 1834:

> I have long seen the fallacy of the new sects, and trust ere long I shall be united in the original true and apostolick church which suffers no variation. I trust no man will attribute my motives *solely* to my love for antient architecture. For although I will allow the change has been brought about in me owing to my *studies of antient art* yet I have still higher reasons which I can satisfactorily account for if required for my belief. (A. W. N. Pugin to E. J. Willson, Fowler collection, Johns Hopkins University)

From 1835 Pugin's diaries survive, which give much information about his life. In that year he built himself a house, St Marie's Grange, Alderbury, near Salisbury, and was working for the established architects James Gillespie Graham and Charles Barry (1795–1860), both of whom found Pugin useful in providing Gothic internal decor-ation and furnishing for their buildings. In the autumn of that year he drew for both men their competition entries for the new houses of parliament. His draughtsmanship, with its flowing lines and sureness of touch, always impressive, was then at its height. At the end of January 1836 Barry was declared the winner. Pugin continued to help him for a further year with the drawings needed for the preparation of the estimate.

In August 1836 Pugin published his most famous book, *Contrasts, or, A parallel between the noble edifices of the four-teenth and fifteenth centuries, and similar buildings of the present day; shewing the present decay of taste: accompanied by appro-priate text.* The text explains the 'decline' of architecture following the Reformation and was influenced by the work of the sixteenth- and seventeenth-century English historians, particularly William Dugdale (1605–1686), and also by the more recent Roman Catholic bishop John Milner (1752–1826). The major interest of the book lies in the 'contrasts', drawings of satirical comparisons between splendid types of medieval buildings such as par-ish churches, chapels, episcopal residences, town halls, public inns, and so on, and their meagre early nineteenth-century counterparts. In his championship of Gothic and his criticism of Regency architecture, Pugin was in many ways following the ideas recently expressed with equal force by the writer and antiquary John Carter (1748–1817). The book stirred up considerable interest and controversy and contributed greatly to Pugin's growing reputation, particularly among Roman Catholics.

1837–1844 Pugin's career as an independent architect began in 1837 and expanded rapidly. His first commission was for Charles Scarisbrick (1801–1860) at Scarisbrick Hall, Lancashire, where he made substantial alterations between 1837 and 1845 to the existing sixteenth-century manor house, including the addition of a clock tower. Here he was able to draw together his knowledge of medi-eval architecture and decorative arts with ideas from his own ideal schemes, to create splendid and inventive inter-iors. In the same year of 1837 he had an introduction to St Mary's College, Oscott, Warwickshire, the Roman Cath-olic school and seminary, which became a centre for his influence in the Roman Catholic church. He provided the college, particularly the chapel, with fittings and furnish-ings, established a museum for medieval religious arte-facts, and gave lectures to students on the history of medi-eval architecture. At the same time, and probably in the same place, he met John Hardman (1811–1867), the Bir-mingham button maker and medallist, who became his closest friend and colleague, manufacturing metalwork to his designs from 1838 and stained glass from 1845. Finally, in this year he made his first visit to Alton Towers, Staffordshire, the seat of John Talbot, sixteenth earl of Shrewsbury (1791–1852), who became his chief patron. His work at Alton Towers, an immense early nineteenth-century house around an earlier core, has been demon-strated to be much greater than originally thought (see Fisher).

Pugin quickly became a leading architect for new Roman Catholic churches. He found Salisbury inconveni-ent for his work and in 1837 moved to London, where he took lodgings in Chelsea. His first important commissions were for St Mary's Church, Derby (1837–9), and St Alban's, Macclesfield (1839–41). Both of these are in a Perpendicu-lar style with good fittings and stained glass. The church at Macclesfield also contains a rood screen, separating the nave and chancel, which became an essential feature in all Pugin's churches. In 1840 he began the hospital of St John, Alton, for the earl of Shrewsbury, which was intended as an ideal religious community, modelled on medieval examples. Built gradually around three sides of a quadran-gle, it has principally been used as a parish church, priest's house, convent, and school.

The Roman Catholic cathedral of St Chad, Birmingham (1839–41), was unusual in Pugin's *œuvre* both in style (that of the fourteenth-century Baltic churches) and in material (the red brick of industrial Birmingham), but it is a most successful building. In the interior, space is handled very effectively under the steeply pitched roof, which has a continuous slope over both nave and aisles. Opposite the cathedral stood the bishop's house (1840–41), now des-troyed but an influential red-brick courtyard house. The builder was George Myers (1804–1875), who from 1838 erected most of Pugin's buildings. Pugin never had an office, unlike most successful nineteenth-century archi-tects, but worked by himself, relying on a close group of colleagues who understood his swiftly drawn designs.

In 1841, when he published *The True Principles of Pointed or Christian Architecture*, Pugin felt confident about both the progress of the Gothic revival and the growth of the Roman Catholic church in England. In *True Principles* his message is directed at the architect. He begins by stating his two great principles for design: '1st, that there should be no features about a building which are not necessary for convenience, construction or propriety; 2nd, that all ornament should consist of enrichment of the essential construction of the building' (*True Principles*, 1). This theory closely follows that expounded by the Abbé Laugier (1713–1769) in his *Essai sur l'architecture* (1753), and later French rationalist writers, who, however, interpreted it in classical terms. It has also led some to consider Pugin as a forerunner of twentieth-century functionalism. He strongly believed in his own principles, and the clarity of his style, where ornament never overwhelms the essential construction, is an important characteristic. In the rest of the book Pugin demonstrates practical examples of good medieval architecture, and ridicules both the symbolism and the methods of construction of neo-classical architecture in a Christian northern country. He also considers the decorative arts with many forceful remarks in favour of appropriate Gothic patterns. As usual, he reinforces his argument with attractive and witty illustrations. In the same year he published a second edition of *Contrasts* with a substantially revised text in which he altered his admiration for late Gothic architecture to that of the fourteenth-century Decorated period and his blame for the 'decline' from the Reformation to the Renaissance. He also emphasized the social context of the superiority of the medieval Catholic world with two new contrasts, of towns and poorhouses. He had probably been influenced in this direction by a leading French liberal Catholic, Charles-Forbes-René, comte de Montalembert (1810–1870), whom he met in 1839, and who added a long appendix in French to this edition. It was titled 'Account of the destructive and revived pagan principle in France'.

The early 1840s was a period of great activity and success for Pugin. During this time he met the two other men who became his close colleagues, Herbert Minton (1793–1858), the Staffordshire pottery manufacturer, and J. G. Crace (1809–1889), the London interior decorator. He worked with great energy and speed, and was inundated with commissions for Roman Catholic churches throughout the United Kingdom, including Ireland. Among the most important were the Roman Catholic cathedrals of St George, Southwark, London (1841–8), St Barnabas, Nottingham (1841–4), and St Mary, Newcastle upon Tyne (1841–4), and Mount St Bernard's Abbey, Leicestershire (1839–c.1844), the first monastery in England since the Reformation. These cathedrals, along with twenty-two other ecclesiastical buildings by Pugin then under construction or already built, are shown in the frontispiece to *An Apology for the Revival of Christian Architecture in England* (1843). It is an immensely impressive display, shown as the new Jerusalem against the rising sun, but it illustrates Pugin's most sanguine hopes rather than facts. The great towers and spires with which Pugin hoped to crown his buildings, for example that of St George's, Southwark, in the centre of his picture, were often not built, or built only

after years of struggle. Moreover, Pugin's churches frequently suffered from a lack of funds, or were built for poor urban communities in unattractive settings, such as the Roman Catholic churches of St Mary, Stockton, co. Durham (1840–42), St Wilfrid, Hulme, Manchester (1838–42), and St Oswald, Old Swan, Liverpool (1839–42).

In 1843 Pugin started to build his own house, St Augustine's (now The Grange), on the edge of a cliff looking out to sea at Ramsgate, Kent. In the same year he experienced his first major reverse when his designs for rebuilding Balliol College, Oxford, were rejected, principally because he was a Roman Catholic. At the beginning of 1844 he completed his most magnificent and scholarly book, the *Glossary of Ecclesiastical Ornament and Costume*, which explained the symbolism and use of vestments and church furnishings with a scholarly text and beautiful illustrations, including seventy-three chromolithographs (then a new technique). Many of the objects which Pugin described were no longer in common use, but after the publication of this book they were frequently revived by both Anglican and Roman Catholic communions. On 22 August 1844 Louisa, his second wife, with whom he had had five children, died suddenly. Following this personal tragedy Pugin received a letter from Charles Barry on 3 September, asking for his help with the fittings for the House of Lords. He therefore returned to work at the houses of parliament, which became one of his major occupations until his death.

1844–1852 From the end of 1844 the character of Pugin's work started to change. He received far fewer architectural commissions and his position as the leading architect to the Roman Catholic church was challenged by others such as M. E. Hadfield (1812–1885) and Charles Hansom (1816–1888). He was also attacked by critics, for example in *The Ecclesiologist* in January 1846, and some prominent priests, such as Nicholas Wiseman (1802–1865) and John Henry Newman (1801–1890), questioned his exclusive attachment to Gothic architecture and his devotion to rood screens in particular. He was, however, commissioned by the government in 1845 to build the Roman Catholic college of St Patrick, Maynooth, Ireland. His time was taken by work for the houses of parliament, and supplying endless designs for ecclesiastical plate, memorial brasses, and stained glass for John Hardman and of furniture, wallpaper, and textiles for J. G. Crace. By the beginning of 1845 John Hardman Powell (1827–1895), John Hardman's nephew, came to stay at Ramsgate to help Pugin with designs for stained glass and metalwork. He became Pugin's only pupil and in 1850 married his eldest daughter, Anne. Throughout this last period Pugin continued to write, mostly on polemical themes, but he also produced *Floriated Ornament* (1849), with its enchanting plates.

Pugin's collaboration with Barry at the houses of parliament produced some of his best-known and greatest achievements. Barry realized that he needed Pugin's knowledge of medieval detail and his ability to work swiftly and to make rich and vivid designs to give life to the interior of his great building. Barry retained control and Pugin would revise his designs to meet Barry's ideas.

Barry protected Pugin's position by preventing the Treasury from putting the decorative work out to tender. He thus enabled Pugin to work with his friends who could interpret his hasty sketches: Hardman, who manufactured the metalwork and stained glass, Crace, whose firm executed the decorative painting and supplied wallpapers plus some furniture, and Minton, who manufactured the encaustic tiles. Barry and Pugin started with the interior of the House of Lords, which was planned as the climax of the building and forms their masterpiece. Here all the fittings, with the exception of the frescoes and statues, are Pugin's work and survive largely unaltered except for the stained glass, which was destroyed in the Second World War. The setting for the throne is particularly magnificent: the immense amount of ornament is always secondary to the construction, a triumph for Pugin's *True Principles*. The House of Lords was opened in 1847, after which Pugin continued to work on other interiors, including the House of Commons (which was finally opened in 1852), the libraries, and committee rooms. He designed great numbers of objects, both large and small, drawing on his experience to create a whole range of items, such as umbrella stands and gas lamps, which had no medieval precedent. For once Pugin was able to work with sufficient funds at his disposal to produce sumptuous results.

Although Pugin's work, other than the metalwork, was limited to the interiors, it seems probable that Barry habitually asked his advice and in this way he suggested his clock tower at Scarisbrick Hall, with its projecting clock storey and ornate steeply sloping roof, as the prototype for the clock tower at Westminster. Barry valued Pugin greatly and the two men worked together in harmony, a splendid combination of Barry's judgement and Pugin's imagination. After the deaths of both men the sons Alfred Barry (1826–1910) and E. W. Pugin (1834–1875) quarrelled over their fathers' respective contributions.

From 1845 Pugin built lovingly and slowly, at his own expense and next to his own house, the Roman Catholic church of St Augustine, Ramsgate, one of his most successful and individual churches. It lies beyond a cloister, with the east range of which building began. The plan is unusual, with nave and chancel of almost equal length, divided by a central tower, a south aisle almost as wide as the nave, south-east lady chapel, a south transept (the Pugin chantry), and a south porch. The exterior is of knapped flints and narrow bands of Whitby stone, the interior of Whitby stone with excellent woodwork, all in a strong early fourteenth-century style. Pugin also fitted it out generously. In 1846 there opened another of the few buildings with which Pugin himself was really satisfied, his beloved Roman Catholic church of St Giles, Cheadle, Staffordshire. It was built at the expense of the earl of Shrewsbury, who agreed with Pugin's aim to make it a model parish church in the Decorated style. Started in 1840, it is built of the local red sandstone with a magnificent west tower and spire, which dominates the town and surroundings. The interior is amazing: J. H. Newman described it shortly before it opened as

the most splendid building I ever saw. It is coloured inside every inch in the most sumptuous way. … the windows are all beautifully stained. The Chapel of the Blessed Sacrament is, on entering, a blaze of light—and I could not help saying to myself 'Porta Coeli'. (*Letters and Diaries*, 11.210)

Pugin's private life remained troubled after the death of his second wife. In November 1844 he proposed to Mary Amherst (1824–1860), the sister of the future Roman Catholic bishop of Nottingham and a relation of the earl of Shrewsbury. Mary accepted him, though her family disapproved, feeling that Pugin was socially inferior, but in May 1846 she entered the convent of the Sisters of Providence at Loughborough. Following this rebuff he met Helen Lumsdaine, the daughter of the rector of Upper Hardres-with-Stelling, Kent, at a neighbour's house. He proposed to her in November 1847 and they became engaged in January 1848, but this attempt also ended in disaster in April, following her father's implacable opposition to her becoming a Roman Catholic. Amid this personal turmoil Pugin's friends persuaded him to make a longer than usual continental sketching tour: he left London on 27 March 1847 and made his only visit to Italy, going to Rome, Florence, Venice, and Milan before arriving home on 17 June. Fortunately, in July 1848 he became engaged to Jane Knill (1825–1909), the youngest daughter of Thomas Knill, and they were married on 10 August. She brought order and tranquillity to his final years and they had two children. Pugin spent more time at home, conducting much of his work by post.

Pugin had both an entrepreneurial spirit for business and a propagandist zeal for promoting the Gothic style. In 1849 he wrote to Crace:

I am so anxious to introduce a sensible style of furniture of good oak and constructively put together that shall compete with the vile trash made and sold. These things are very simple and I am certain that with a little practice can be made to pay and sell well. (A. W. N. Pugin to J. G. Crace, PUG 6/19, RIBA)

It must have become obvious, however, that the greatest publicity would come from participation in the Great Exhibition of 1851. His close colleagues combined to produce striking examples of their work, designed by Pugin, for an exhibition stand which they called 'The mediæval court'. Hardman showed much metalwork, both domestic and ecclesiastic, and stained glass; Myers's display included the tomb of Bishop Thomas Walsh, furniture and the font, tabernacle, and statue which Pugin subsequently placed in his own church at Ramsgate; Minton showed ceramics and encaustic tiles, and Crace showed textiles, wallpaper, and furniture. These pieces formed an excellent demonstration of the high quality of craftsmanship, the understanding of medieval techniques, and the strength and clarity of Pugin's designs and his 'true principles', and they stood out among the many fussily ornate objects in the exhibition and were generally acclaimed. Pugin's desire, however, to improve the general standard of interior design was prevented by illness. After his death Hardman, Minton, and Crace all continued to use and adapt his designs.

Aggravated by constant overwork and the application of mercury, Pugin's health finally broke down by the end of February 1852 and he was certified insane. He was first placed in a private establishment in Kensington and then moved to the Bethlehem Pauper Hospital for the Insane. He returned to Ramsgate a few days before his death there on 14 September 1852; he was buried on 21 September in the Pugin chantry in St Augustine's Church. The cause of death was recorded on his death certificate as 'insane 6 months: convulsions followed by coma' (d. cert.). He left a young widow and eight children. His eldest son, Edward Welby *Pugin, took over some of his practice. His estate was valued at £10,000, but his widow received a government pension and sold his library and fine collection of medieval artefacts in 1853.

The best-known portrait of the mature Pugin is that by J. R. Herbert (1810–1890) in the Palace of Westminster collection, but he has been vividly described by J. H. Powell:

Pugin was only just middle height but very strong, broad chest, large hands, massive forehead, nose and chin, well curved flexible mouth, and restless grey eyes, the expression of which turned inwards when in deep thought. His hair was darkest brown, thick, not crisp, and he shaved clean like a sailor. All his movements were rapid, full of mental and bodily energy, shewing a nervous and choleric temperament. His sight was 'like a hawk's': he never used or needed glasses either in making sketches from clerestory stained glass or working minutely, and most of his early designs were on a very fine scale, probably from having etched much.

His memory was the marvel of all who knew him for long; the mind seemed to receive its impressions without a particle of mist or shadow, keen, definite and lasting, to be recalled at will unchanged. He was thorough and earnest in doing all he undertook with all his might, and not resting till it was accomplished. He was passionate, but believed his anger was always another's fault, honest rages with no malice in them, blowing over without leaving resentment. (Wedgwood, 'Pugin in his home', 176)

Pugin's open and direct character were defining qualities, as Rosemary Hill has described:

Pugin was no respecter of persons. He used very nearly the same tone to everyone and was often tactless, but he had no spite or rancor. This directness made his friends and workmen love him, his opponents dread him, and more subtle temperaments, such as John Henry Newman, shudder with embarrassment.   (Atterbury, 33)

Pugin was completely uninterested in London society, enjoying his quiet family life at Ramsgate. In this he was the opposite of Barry, and his one attempt to become a member of the Royal Academy was unsuccessful. He was very methodical in his ways: as J. H. Powell put it, 'a rare thing for a genius to be orderly, but he was' (Wedgwood, 'Pugin in his home', 178). As a result there exists a large amount of documentation about him. His immediacy and his humour are evident in all his writing, most particularly his letters, many of which have survived and an edition of them, *The Collected Letters of A. W. N. Pugin, Volume 1: 1830–1842*, by Margaret Belcher, was published in 2001.

Pugin's influence on the course of the Gothic revival throughout northern Europe and the English-speaking world was great, spread principally by his writing. His central idea, the equation of Christianity with Gothic, triumphed, so that the visible symbol of church architecture for the rest of the nineteenth century became the pointed arch. He always had bitter critics, however, one of the first of whom was John Ruskin, who might have been expected to be in sympathy with many of his aims. It seems, however, that Ruskin's early hatred of Catholicism blinded him to Pugin's importance; he denied his influence and famously criticized St George's Cathedral, Southwark, for its 'eruption of diseased crockets' (J. Ruskin, *The Stones of Venice*, 1, 1851, 373). At the end of the nineteenth century, with a return to fourteenth- and fifteenth-century styles in the work of such architects as G. F. Bodley (1827–1907) and Thomas Garner (1839–1906) and such decorative artists as the stained-glass designer C. E. Kempe (1837–1907), there was renewed interest in Pugin's work. This lapsed again for the first half of the twentieth century, but in the 1960s there began a renewed appreciation of Victorian architecture which has grown steadily and, in Pugin's case, has led to several important books, the designation of a 'Pugin room' in the houses of parliament in 1981, an exhibition in the Victoria and Albert Museum in 1994, and the foundation in 1995 at Ramsgate of the Pugin Society, which has a newsletter entitled *True Principles*.

ALEXANDRA WEDGWOOD

Sources A. Wedgwood, *A. W. N. Pugin and the Pugin family* (1985) [incl. transcriptions of diaries and letters] · B. Ferrey, *Recollections of A. N. Welby Pugin, and his father, Augustus Pugin* (1861) · M. Belcher, *A. W. N. Pugin: an annotated critical biography* (1987) · J. H. Powell, 'Pugin in his home: a memoir', *Architectural History*, 31 (1988), 171–205 · E. W. Pugin, *Who was the art architect of the Houses of Parliament: a statement of facts, founded on the letters of Sir Charles Barry and the diaries of Augustus Welby Pugin* (1867) · A. Barry, *The architect of the new palace at Westminster: a reply to a pamphlet by E. Pugin, esq*, 2nd edn (1868) · P. Stanton, *Pugin* (1971) · J. Macaulay, 'The architectural collaboration between J. Gillespie Graham and A. W. N. Pugin', *Architectural History*, 27 (1984), 406–20 · M. J. Fisher, *Alton Towers: a Gothic wonderland* (1999) · P. Atterbury and C. Wainwright, eds., *Pugin: a Gothic passion* (1994) · R. Hill, 'Reformation to millennium: Pugin's "Contrasts" in the history of English thought', *Journal of the Society of Architectural Historians*, 58 (1999), 26–41 · P. Atterbury, ed., *A. W. N. Pugin: master of Gothic revival* (1995) · A. Wedgwood, *Catalogue of the drawings collection of the Royal Institute of British Architects: the Pugin family* (1977) · [A. J. B. Beresford-Hope], 'The artistic merit of Mr. Pugin', *The Ecclesiologist*, 5 (1846), 10–16 · *The letters and diaries of John Henry Newman*, ed. C. S. Dessain and others, [31 vols.] (1961–), vol. 11 · letters, RIBA BAL · *The collected letters of A. W. N. Pugin*, ed. M. Belcher, 1–2 (2001–3) · PRO, PROB 6/228, fol. 413*v* [will] · d. cert. · private information (2004) [M. Egan]

Archives East Riding of Yorkshire Archives Service, Beverley, corresp. and papers relating to St Mary's, Beverley · priv. colls., corresp. and family MSS [microfilms in HLRO, PUG/1 and 3] · RIBA BAL, corresp. · Ushaw College, Durham, corresp. and drawings relating to Ushaw College · V&A NAL, diaries, juvenile autobiography, corresp., and MSS · Yale U. CBA, corresp. and family MSS | Alnwick Castle, Northumberland, letters to Henry Drummond · Johns Hopkins University, Baltimore, Fowler collection, corresp. · Surrey HC, letters to Lord Midleton

Likenesses A. J. Oliver, oils, 1819, priv. coll. · oils, *c*.1840, NPG · J. R. Herbert, oils, 1845, RIBA BAL [*see illus.*] · photograph, *c*.1847, priv. coll. · E. W. Pugin? and G. Myers, stone effigy on tomb, *c*.1853,

R.C. Church of St Augustine, Ramsgate · J. Nash, lithograph, c.1860, repro. in Ferrey, *Recollections of A. N. Welby Pugin*, frontispiece · marble podium relief, Albert Memorial, Kensington Gardens

Wealth at death £10,000: administration, PRO, PROB 6/228, fol. 413v

Pugin, Edward Welby (1834–1875), architect, was born on 11 March 1834 at Ramsgate, the eldest son of Augustus Welby Northmore *Pugin (1812–1852) and his second wife, Louisa Burton (c.1813–1844). He was trained by his father and at the age of eighteen found himself in charge of his father's practice, which he developed with many pupils and various partnerships, most importantly with his brother-in-law George Coppinger *Ashlin in Ireland (1859–69) and his brother Peter Paul Pugin (1851–1904).

Edward Pugin's practice was overwhelmingly Roman Catholic. He worked initially in his father's preferred Decorated Gothic style, at St Mary's, Crook, co. Durham (1853), Oulton Abbey, Staffordshire, for Benedictine nuns (1853), and Belmont Abbey church, Herefordshire (1854–85). From 1856 his style became more elaborate but his church plans simpler by widening the span of the arcades, diminishing chancel arches, and abolishing rood screens, so as to achieve ample sightlines to his elaborate altars with towering reredoses set in shallow apses. Examples are St Vincent de Paul, Liverpool (1856–7), St Hubert's, Great Harwood, Lancashire (1858–9), Our Lady, Eldon Street, Liverpool (1859–60), All Saints', Barton upon Irwell, Lancashire (1863–8), his richest English church, Stanbrook Abbey church, Worcestershire (1869–71), and English Martyrs, Prescott Street, Tower Hamlets, London (1873–5). His most important churches are Our Lady, Dadizeele, Belgium (designed 1857; built 1857–67 in partnership with Baron Jean Baptiste Bethune), and, in Ireland, Sts Peter and Paul, Cork (1859–66), Sts Augustine and John, Dublin (1862–93), and St Colman's Cathedral, Cove, co. Cork (1859–1916), all with Ashlin. He designed much school, monastery, and convent architecture, notably the Franciscan Recollect Priory (1863) and the church of St Francis of Assisi (1866–72; completed 1878–85), Gorton, Manchester. E. W. Pugin was a talented draughtsman and watercolourist; his drawings are characterized by a frenetic, nervous line and his attenuation is reminiscent of his father's early work. He is at his most characteristic in the elaborate architectural carving, sculpture, and varied materials of his altars and chantry chapels such as the Knill chantry, St George's Cathedral, Southwark (1856), and the de Trafford chantry, Barton-on-Irwell, Lancashire (1863). He failed to keep up his father's close relationship with George Crace, John Hardman, and George Myers, instead commissioning his designs for metalwork and stained glass from Hardman & Co. (but he was not the chief designer); for architectural sculpture he preferred Farmer and Brindley. He set up a furniture manufacturing business for the large speculation the Granville Hotel, Ramsgate (1869–73); earlier domestic furniture also survives. Important interiors and additions are at Scarisbrick Hall, Lancashire (after 1866), and the castle of Loppem,

Edward Welby Pugin (1834–1875), by W. B. M. Measor, exh. RA 1862

Belgium (designed 1856; built from 1859 by Pugin and Bethune).

Reconciling the Roman Catholic clergy to the use of the Gothic style in the wake of the 'rood screen controversy' provoked by A. W. N. Pugin, E. W. Pugin yearned for his father's commanding position in architectural matters for the Roman Catholic church in England. His claims were taken very seriously in Belgium, and in Ireland, where he was made a papal knight in 1858. He visited the USA in 1873, and at least one church was begun there.

The Pugin family moved back to The Grange, Ramsgate, in 1862, where Edward made extensive additions to his father's house and to St Augustine's Church, where he had designed his father's tomb in the Pugin chantry (1853). He added the Digby chantry (1857) and the north (1857) and west (1859) cloisters, and fitted out the lady chapel (1862). He also built St Augustine's Monastery, Ramsgate (1859–60), for the Benedictines. Although he inherited his father's papers, he did not authorize a biography (certainly not B. Ferrey's *Recollections of A. N. Welby Pugin, and his Father, Augustus Pugin*, 1861). Having earlier claimed that Sir Charles Barry refused to give him a pupilship, he subsequently initiated a pamphlet war with *Who was the art architect of the houses of parliament: a statement of facts, founded on the letters of Sir Charles Barry and the diaries of Augustus Welby Pugin* (1867).

Edward Pugin died unmarried, at his home, Victoria House, 111 Victoria Street, Westminster, of syncope of the heart, on 5 June 1875. He was buried in St Augustine's Church, Ramsgate, Kent, five days later. As an architect, he was less important than his father; however, his style and plans became normative for Roman Catholic churches in the British Isles in the second half of the nineteenth century. The firm continued as Pugin and Pugin.

RODERICK O'DONNELL

Sources R. O'Donnell, 'The later Pugins', *Pugin: a Gothic passion*, ed. P. Atterbury and C. Wainwright (1994), 258–71 • R. O'Donnell, 'The Pugins in Ireland', *A. W. N. Pugin: master of the Gothic revival*, ed. P. Atterbury (1995), 136–59 • R. O'Donnell, 'E. W. Pugin', *The dictionary of art*, ed. J. Turner (1996) • M. Belcher, *A. W. N. Pugin: an annotated critical bibliography* (1987), D 499–D 522, D 573–8 • A. Wedgwood, *Catalogue of the drawings collection of the Royal Institute of British Architects: the Pugin family* (1977), 113–19 • A. Wedgwood, *A. W. N. Pugin and the Pugin family* (1985), 312–15 [Catalogue of architectural drawings in the Victoria and Albert Museum] • S. Welsh, 'Biographical notes and list of principal works', RIBA BAL • *DNB* • *The Builder*, 33 (1875), 522–3 • *The Tablet* (19 June 1875), 792 • E. W. Pugin, *Who was the art architect of the Houses of Parliament: a statement of facts, founded on the letters of Sir Charles Barry and the diaries of Augustus Welby Pugin* (1867) • *CGPLA Eng. & Wales* (1875)

Archives Hardman & Co., Birmingham, letters • HLRO, diary [microfilm] • RIBA, corresp. • RIBA BAL • Sheffield City Libraries • Ushaw College, Durham • V&A, diary | Archives of the bishop of Brugge, Belgium • BL, corresp. with second earl of Hardwicke, Add. MS 45030 • HLRO, corresp. with earls of Shrewsbury • Irish Architectural Archive, Dublin, Ashlin and Coleman collection • Lancs. RO, letters to archbishops of Liverpool • priv. coll., John Hardman Powell MSS • Scottish Catholic Archives, Edinburgh, Gillis corresp. • Kourtrik, Belgium, Archife de Bethune, [Kastel de] Marke

Likenesses A. W. Pugin?, stained glass, c.1843, chapel, The Grange, Ramsgate; repro. in Atterbury and Wainwright, eds., *Pugin: a Gothic passion* • G. Myers, stone figure, c.1852, St Augustine's Church, Ramsgate • W. B. M. Measor, oils, exh. RA 1862, RIBA [*see illus.*] • J. H. Powell?, stained glass, c.1866, Scarisbrick Hall, Lancashire; repro. in *Catalogue of the drawings collection of the Royal Institute of British Architects*, Royal Institute of British Architects, 20 vols. (1969–89) • A. Pippet, wall-painting, c.1868, All Saints' Church, Barton upon Irwell, chancel; repro. in Atterbury and Wainwright, eds., *Pugin: a Gothic passion* • O. Hall, marble bust, 1879, Victoria Parade, Ramsgate

Wealth at death under £600: probate, 2 Nov 1875, *CGPLA Eng. & Wales*

Puiset, Hugh du, earl of Northumberland (c.1125–1195),

bishop of Durham, was the younger son of Hugues, lord of Le Puiset, and his wife, Agnes, daughter of Stephen, count of Blois, and Adela (d. 1137), a daughter of *William I.

Family background and early advancement Le Puiset, 38 kilometres south-east of Chartres, was the site of a strong castle, first built in the eleventh century, which enjoyed a strategic position covering the route from the Île-de-France to Orléans. Its lords had over several generations acquired a reputation as violent and aggressive exploiters of feudal power. Hugues seems to have gone to the Holy Land in 1129, following what had become a family tradition of crusading activity. In the same year Hugh's brother-in-law Henry de Blois (d. 1171), one of the younger brothers of Count Theobald (son and successor of Count Stephen), was given the rich bishopric of Winchester by Henry I, having already been abbot of Glastonbury for three years. It was natural that a younger son of the Le Puiset family, directly descended from William the Conqueror, should look for preferment in the English church. And when Count Theobald's next youngest brother, Stephen, count of Mortain, gained the English throne at the end of 1135, the prospects for a nephew of the new king must have seemed bright indeed.

By 1139 Hugh du Puiset had become archdeacon of Winchester, the right-hand man of his uncle Henry. The archbishop of York, Thurstan, died in 1140 and the Blois family interest was mobilized to secure the archbishopric and as much influence as possible in the northern province. In this Blois campaign, Hugh du Puiset co-operated with William Fitzherbert (d. 1154), the treasurer of York and a leading figure in the chapter there, whom, despite what many regarded as his personal unsuitability, the king wished to make archbishop. Before Fitzherbert was driven from his see by the party of church reform, he had obtained for du Puiset (c.1143) the important offices of cathedral treasurer and archdeacon of the East Riding. The period from 1147 to 1153 was occupied by open hostilities or uneasy truces between Archdeacon Hugh and the Cistercian Henry Murdac, abbot of Fountains, who through the influence of Abbot Bernard of Clairvaux and Pope Eugenius III (r. 1145–53) was consecrated archbishop of York at Trier in December 1147. During most of Murdac's troubled pontificate Blois influence in northern England waned, but it recovered strongly, though briefly, before the death of King Stephen in October 1154. In November 1152 the bishop of Durham, William de Ste Barbe, died. Partly because the two strongest local aspirants for the succession, the prior and the archdeacon, were evenly poised, the clergy and people of the diocese (that is, the monks of the cathedral priory and the leading barons of the bishopric) on 22 January 1153 chose Hugh du Puiset, although he was still not twenty-eight years of age, and as such under the canonical age for becoming a bishop.

Bishop of Durham For some nine months Archbishop Murdac bitterly opposed the election, declaring it null because it was carried out without his consent, as metropolitan, and also because of the elect's youth and scandalous lifestyle. He excommunicated the electors, who appealed to the papal curia, to which they dispatched a delegation accompanied by the bishop-elect himself. Luckily for du Puiset Pope Eugenius died in July 1153 and his more sympathetic successor Anastasius IV (r. 1153–4) consecrated du Puiset on 21 December. Meanwhile Archbishop Murdac had died (14 October), and the way was clear for the new bishop of Durham to return to his diocese and be enthroned in his cathedral on 2 May 1154. He was supported by the now restored Archbishop Fitzherbert who, however, died a month later. The window of opportunity for the Blois family interest had been opened barely long enough for Hugh du Puiset to become established in his see. It closed decisively with King Stephen's death on 25 October and the accession of Henry of Anjou (Henry II) on 19 December 1154. Already the see of York had been refilled: Roger de Pont l'Évêque, a clerk and protégé of Archbishop Theobald of Canterbury, was consecrated in October 1154. Since Bishop Æthelwold of Carlisle died c.1156 and his see was not filled again until 1204, the north of England was dominated ecclesiastically for nearly thirty years by two prelates bent on self-aggrandizement and the exploitation of both spiritual and secular authority. And since York had no consecrated archbishop for a decade after Roger's death in 1181, du Puiset enjoyed a virtual monopoly of episcopal and palatine power in northern England until his own death in 1195.

The diocese of Durham comprised what became in the twelfth century the counties of Northumberland and Durham, with the addition of the district of Alston at the head of the south Tyne and (just north of the Tweed and therefore in Scotland) the tiny parish of Wester Upsettlington. Within certain parts of this extensive area the bishop, inheriting a long series of grants of privileges and immunities by kings of the eleventh century and earlier, enjoyed a wholly exceptional position of quasi-royal authority and military power. The rationale behind this 'palatine' liberty was defence of England against the Scots, but the real roots of St Cuthbert's Land (or Haliwerfolc—'the Saint's people'—as it was known) derived from Durham's jealously guarded possession of the body and relics of St Cuthbert, the most renowned and venerated of all English saints. Since the time of Bishop Ranulf Flambard (d. 1128) the actual custody of these relics and the responsibility for serving the great cathedral church, begun in 1093 and by 1154 well on the way to completion, lay with the Benedictine monks of the cathedral priory. Nevertheless the bishop as successor of Cuthbert was recognized as effectively abbot of the monastery, and the position into which du Puiset stepped in 1154 was one of the grandest, richest, and most magnificent in the English kingdom.

Episcopal splendour Hugh du Puiset was determined not to allow the grandeur, wealth, or magnificence to be abated one jot. Untouched by either the clerical zeal of the Gregorian reformers or the humility beloved of the Cistercians and their admirers, he pursued the life of an old-fashioned late-Frankish aristocrat. His relationship with the most prominent of his mistresses, Alice de Percy, was so public and of such long duration that it almost amounted to a marriage. With Alice Bishop Hugh had at least two children, Henry the knight and Hugh, who rose to become chancellor of Philip Augustus, king of France, and perhaps two others, William, archdeacon of Northumberland, and Burchard, archdeacon of Durham and treasurer of York. Hugh du Puiset lived in great style, maintaining a large household, taking with him wherever he went a private chapel richly furnished with liturgical ornaments and vessels of gold and silver. Surviving inventories show that his vestments were of velvet and other expensive cloth, profusely embroidered with pearls and other precious gems and elaborately worked with birds, animals, and motifs drawn from romance and chivalry. At Stanhope in Weardale the bishop's hunting lodge was provided with a new kitchen and larder every year by the local peasantry. When he proposed to undertake a crusading expedition in 1189 a great ship was built, stuffed with so many furnishings and utensils that a house had to be hired to contain them all when the ship was laid up.

Du Puiset was an indefatigable builder, carrying out large-scale work at the castles of Durham, Northallerton, and Norham. He undertook the erection of Elvet Bridge in

Durham (some remains of its chapel came to light in 1995) and co-operated with the king of Scots in building the earliest known bridge over the tidal Tweed at Berwick. He founded one hospital, Sherburn, and refounded another, Flambard's hospital of Kepier, both of them near to Durham itself. The crowning glory of his building activity is the Galilee Chapel which in the 1170s he caused to be built against the west front of the cathedral. Although now sadly altered and damaged, it is still possible to appreciate how splendid the chapel must have been originally, consisting of five parallel aisles supported on freestone shafts each provided with a pair of columns of black Purbeck marble. The interior was evidently richly painted and decorated, and the centrepiece was a magnificent altar to the Blessed Virgin. As well as being a great patron of masons and craftsmen, du Puiset, although not himself learned or even especially well educated, formed a considerable library and commissioned the making of two great bibles, one of which, in four large volumes still treasured at Durham (Durham Cathedral Library, MS A. II. 1), is one of the masterpieces of twelfth-century English book production. The bishop was lord of one of England's most extensive estates, reaching from the Tweed to Lincolnshire, and including a palace in London. In 1183 du Puiset caused a detailed survey to be made of much of this lordship, especially the vills in what later became co. Durham and in Northumberland (Bedlingtonshire and Norhamshire), recording the numbers of unfree tenants with their rents and services, the universal royal tributes, such as cornage, which the bishop levied in place of the king, and the obligations of a handful of boroughs and freeholders, for example thegns and drengs. This important record is known as Boldon Buke, from a manor on the episcopal demesne taken to be typical, and survives in several manuscripts ranging in date from the thirteenth to the fifteenth century.

Ecclesiastical disputes and secular politics It was entirely in character that du Puiset was engaged over many years in disputes with his own cathedral chapter, where his success in litigation stimulated the production by the priory's monks of numerous forgeries designed to demonstrate that earlier bishops had given them immunity from many episcopal demands. The bishop also quarrelled, from the later 1160s, with his own metropolitan, Roger de Pont l'Évêque. A fruitful source of conflict was the existence in York diocese of privileged estates such as Northallerton and Howden, which belonged to the bishops of Durham, and in Durham diocese of a similar estate (Hexhamshire) belonging to the archbishops of York. Such long-drawn-out disputes were a commonplace of twelfth-century ecclesiastical politics and in no way inhibited du Puiset from serving as a judge or investigator in numerous other legal conflicts, including the notoriously never-ending argument between Canterbury and York over the limits of their primatial and metropolitan privileges.

Another *cause célèbre* in which du Puiset was involved arose from the unwise action of the cathedral chapter of St Andrews in electing Master John the Scot (d. 1203) as their bishop in 1178 in succession to Bishop Richard. Master John was a nephew of an earlier bishop, and as an experienced and educated clergyman might have been judged a suitable candidate. But William the Lion was determined to appoint his chaplain Hugh, and drove John the Scot and his supporter, the bishop of Aberdeen, into exile. The canons of St Andrews appealed to the papal curia, and since Bishop Hugh attended the Third Lateran Council in 1179 it was natural that he, along with Archbishop Roger of York, should have been commanded by the pope to bring the king of Scots to heel, if necessary by means of excommunication and interdict. Neither of the northern English prelates was allowed into Scotland, although Bishop Hugh met the king of Scots at Redden in August, 1181, and vainly argued the case for John the Scot. The dispute was settled in 1183, inevitably by a compromise. The bishop of Durham must have been well known to the officials of the papal curia, for apart from figuring frequently in litigation he had attended Alexander III's Council of Tours in 1163, the sole suffragan of York to be present in person.

The kings of Scots, Malcolm IV (r. 1153–65) and especially William the Lion (r. 1165–1214), were almost hereditary enemies, ever since the Scots had favoured Anjou against Blois in 1136. The building of Berwick Bridge is almost the sole instance of du Puiset's co-operation with the Scots, who saw his massive rebuilding of Norham Castle on the border in the 1160s as an act of provocation. Yet in the great rebellion instigated by Henry II's eldest son, Henry, the Young King, in 1173, the bishop of Durham displayed such caution in the face of King William's invasions of Northumbria in support of the rebels as to incur a suspicion of collusion and certainly the wrath of the English king. Not only did du Puiset enter into truces with the Scots that allowed their armies safe passage through the bishopric and were obviously designed to minimize the damage which Scottish raids might do to St Cuthbert's Land; but at one point, in the summer of 1174, the bishop's nephew and namesake, Hugues du Puiset, count of Bar, landed at Hartlepool at the head of a sizeable military force, ostensibly to defend the bishopric against rebel attacks but widely suspected of being du Puiset's contribution to the hoped-for overthrow of Henry II. Only the prompt surrender of the castles of Norham, Durham, and Northallerton and the payment of heavy fines could, after some interval of time, bring about a reconciliation between bishop and king. The same inclination to be neutral at times of major crisis had shown itself in the Becket dispute, where it has been said by David Knowles that for reasons that do not appear du Puiset kept entirely clear of the controversy, although he had collaborated with Archbishop Roger in the fatal coronation of the Young King on 14 June 1170. Between 1175 and the end of Henry II's reign relations between du Puiset and the king seem to have been reasonably harmonious. The bishop helped to settle the Galloway dispute in 1186, and two years later went to the Scottish border to demand that the Scots contribute to the 'Saladin tithe' raised by Henry II throughout his dominions as his contribution to the campaign to recover Jerusalem for the Christians. Although the bishop negotiated with the Scots, King William's reply was that his barons flatly refused to pay the tithe; the Scottish contribution towards the third crusade came only after Richard I had succeeded his father, and was willing to give William the Lion his independence for a payment of 10,000 marks of silver.

Last conflicts and death Du Puiset's greatest show of loyalty to the house of Anjou came in the first five years of Richard I's reign, and even there it may be argued that the bishop's motivation was essentially the enhancement of his own power and authority. Taking advantage of his own wealth and of the king's need for money, he was able to buy from Richard the wapentake of Sadberge—the largest territory between Tees and Tyne not yet in episcopal hands—and also the much prized earldom of Northumberland, hankered after for many years by the king of Scots. He also became joint justiciar of England, though this was reduced to a justiciarship of the north in 1190. Du Puiset was completely outmanoeuvred by the king's chancellor, William de Longchamp (d. 1197), who put the bishop under virtual house arrest at Howden in the summer of 1190 and stripped him of his offices. On Longchamp's fall the next year du Puiset made some recovery, but although he retained the earldom of Northumberland until 1194, he was now too elderly to get the better of such astute and persistent opponents as the king's brother and heir, John, count of Mortain, and their half-brother Geoffrey Plantagenet (d. 1212), who to the fury of du Puiset had been given the archbishopric of York in September 1189, following an election to which du Puiset formally objected. There ensued a most unseemly dispute, which involved not only the clergy and people of York but also the papacy and the regents governing for the king, now absent on his crusade. Eventually in the autumn of 1192 the bishop and his metropolitan (consecrated in August of the previous year) were formally reconciled. Nevertheless du Puiset's last two years were hardly peaceful. From the end of 1192 until early in 1194 the king was a prisoner in Austria and Germany. Against a background of John's treachery and the unremitting enmity of Philip of France, a huge ransom had to be raised in England to secure the king's release. Du Puiset's share in the events of this difficult time included a successful siege of John's castle at Tickhill and a payment of £2000 towards Richard's ransom to escape having his cathedral plate and ornaments confiscated. The return of the king in March 1194 should have meant peace for the north of England and rewards for the bishop of Durham. But even in the atmosphere of rejoicing the bishop could not resist the temptation to insult King William of Scotland, gravely displeasing King Richard who was William's friend. Du Puiset was prompted to surrender the earldom of Northumberland, and although he had the satisfaction of seeing King William's demand for it refused, he never recovered it for himself. He died at Howden on 3 March 1195 aged about seventy.

The combination of a royal and princely family background and a position of immense wealth and potential power made this imperious and quarrelsome nobleman a major figure of the English, and indeed of the European, twelfth century. Tall, handsome, and—when he chose to be—affable, Hugh du Puiset was clearly capable of impressing his contemporaries with his personality. To judge from the witness lists of Henry II's *acta* he was often at court, especially at meetings of what may be called the great council. He took part in many weighty decisions affecting both secular and ecclesiastical politics. He was no scholar, still less a spiritual leader. For fifty years he was a force to be reckoned with in the life of northern England. Yet he is chiefly remembered in the great castles of Norham and Durham, and above all in the splendid Galilee Chapel which still adorns his cathedral.

G. W. S. BARROW

Sources G. V. Scammell, *Hugh du Puiset, bishop of Durham* (1956) · D. Knowles, *The episcopal colleagues of Archbishop Thomas Becket* (1951) · J. Morris, ed., *Domesday Book: a survey of the counties of England*, 38 vols. (1983–92), vol. 35 [*Boldon Book*, Northumberland and Durham] · D. W. Rollason, M. Harvey, and M. Prestwich, eds., *Anglo-Norman Durham* (1994) · *Gir. Camb. opera*, vol. 4 · W. Stubbs, ed., *Gesta regis Henrici secundi Benedicti abbatis: the chronicle of the reigns of Henry II and Richard I, AD 1169–1192*, 2 vols., Rolls Series, 49 (1867) · *Chronica magistri Rogeri de Hovedene*, ed. W. Stubbs, 4 vols., Rolls Series, 51 (1868–71) · *Radulfi de Diceto … opera historica*, ed. W. Stubbs, 2 vols., Rolls Series, 68 (1876) · R. Howlett, ed., *Chronicles of the reigns of Stephen, Henry II, and Richard I*, 4 vols., Rolls Series, 82 (1884–9) · M. Snape, ed., *Durham, 1071–1195*, English Episcopal Acta [forthcoming] · Gaufridus de Coldingham [Geoffrey of Coldingham], 'De statu ecclesiae Dunhelmensis', in *Historiae Dunelmensis scriptores tres: Gaufridus de Coldingham, Robertus de Graystanes, et Willielmus de Chambre*, ed. J. Raine, SurtS, 9 (1839), 3–31

Archives U. Durham

Likenesses seals, repro. in W. Greenwell and C. H. Blair, *Durham seals*, 2 vols. (1911–12), 2.443

Pujol, Juan Garcia (1912–1988), spy, was born in Barcelona on 14 February 1912, the third child of Juan Pujol (*d.* 1931), a Catalan who owned a dye factory in Barcelona, and his wife, Mercedes Garcia. He was educated at the La Salle Brothers School, Barcelona, and the Royal School of Poultry. After compulsory military service, he was appointed manager of a chicken farm north of Barcelona. However, when the Spanish Civil War broke out Pujol was called up by the republicans as a reservist and, when he went into hiding, was listed as a deserter. He was arrested just before Christmas 1937 but managed to gain his release a week later, going straight back into hiding. Early the following year he managed a union farm in northern Catalonia until it failed, and he then joined an infantry battalion in the hope of deserting to the nationalists at the first opportunity. This he did, only to be imprisoned in northern Spain. There one of his father's friends, a priest, negotiated his release and he was commissioned in the nationalist army. By the time Madrid fell he had not fired a shot for either side, and had found a job managing the Hotel Majestic there.

When the Second World War started Pujol had developed a hatred of political extremism, and in January 1941 he volunteered his services to the British embassy. Abruptly rejected, he decided to enhance his value before making a second approach, and accordingly contacted the German military attaché, to whom he masqueraded as an enthusiastic fascist willing to work for the Nazis.

Pujol's apparent willingness to undertake a secret mission to England evidently impressed the Germans, who trained him in wireless techniques and in July 1941 dispatched him to Portugal, *en route* for London, with $3000. However, unable to obtain the necessary entry visa, Pujol started to manufacture reports for the *Abwehr*, and pretended that he had indeed succeeded in travelling to Britain. Once the Germans had accepted this ruse he visited the British embassy, only to be rebuffed for a second time. It was only after he had made another approach, this time to the Americans in February 1942, that an explanation was found for the mysterious messages from an elusive spy code-named Arabel that had been intercepted by MI5. Security Service analysts had expressed considerable doubt about Arabel's veracity, his reports making bizarre claims for expenses and being full of patently untrue information.

When MI5 realized that Arabel was nothing more than an enthusiastic amateur agent who had successfully duped his *Abwehr* handler, the decision was taken to allow Pujol to come to London and operate under strict supervision. His assigned case officer was a brilliant half-Spanish artist, Tomas Harris, and together they were to form an astonishing partnership, inventing a completely notional network of twenty-six subagents, all of whom drew their expenses. MI5 were able to monitor the *Abwehr*'s growing admiration for their star agent, and when he correctly forecast the date of the allied invasion in Normandy, they rewarded him with an Iron Cross. However, Pujol, now code-named Garbo by MI5 because he was considered such an inspired actor, had been authorized to tip off the enemy to the D-day landings, insisting that they were only a diversionary feint, the true assault being scheduled for the Pas-de-Calais a fortnight later. This key contribution to a carefully orchestrated deception campaign helped persuade the *Wehrmacht* high command not to launch an immediate counter-attack, while the troops were at their most vulnerable, thus ensuring D-day's success.

Pujol was made an MBE in September 1944, although the award was made in conditions of great secrecy by the director-general of the Security Service and the decoration was never officially gazetted. At the end of the war, the Germans never having discovered his true role as a double agent, he was given a new identity in Venezuela and worked as a language teacher for Shell oil. Eventually his wife tired of Maracaibo and returned to Madrid with their two children, and he remarried, fathering another two sons. Pujol died in Caracas, aged seventy-six, on 15 October 1988; he was undoubtedly the most successful double agent of the Second World War. NIGEL WEST

Sources J. Pujol and N. West, *Garbo* (1985) · J. C. Masterman, *The double-cross system in the war of 1939 to 1945* (1972) · S. Delmer, *The counterfeit spy* (1973) · F. H. Hinsley and C. A. G. Simkins, *British intelligence in the Second World War, 4: Security and counter-intelligence* (1990), vol. 4 · M. Howard, *British intelligence in the Second World War, 5: Strategic deception* (1990) · R. Hesketh, *Fortitude* (1998) · T. Harris, *Garbo: the spy who saved D-day* (2000)

Archives PRO, KV 2/39–42, KV 2/63–71

Puleston, Hamlet (1632–1662), writer, was born at Old Alresford, Hampshire, in 1632, the son of Richard Puleston (*b.* 1591), and Mary Marshall (*fl.* 1622–1632), and nephew of John *Puleston. Hamlet's father was born at Burcott in Oxfordshire, but was descended from a Flintshire family. He graduated from Hart Hall, Oxford, BA in 1611, MA in 1613, BD in 1620, and DD in 1627. He obtained a fellowship at Wadham College, Oxford, which he resigned in 1619, and was a prebendary of Winchester in 1611–16 and rector successively of Leckford, Hampshire (1616), Kingsworthy (1618), and Abbotsworthy. He was moderator of philosophy in 1614, and humanity lecturer in 1616 at Oxford.

Hamlet, admitted a scholar of Wadham on 20 August 1647, graduated BA on 23 May 1650 and proceeded MA on 25 April 1653. He at first declined to subscribe to the ordinances of the parliamentary visitors, but subsequently became a fellow of Jesus College, and was nominated *moderator dialecticae* on 19 May 1656. Wood says also that he became 'a preacher in those parts', presumably Oxfordshire (Wood, *Ath. Oxon.*, 3.544). He ultimately settled in London. He published in 1661 *Monarchiae Britannicae singularis protectio, or, A brief historical essay tending to prove God's especial providence over the British monarchy*. A slight piece, its ambitions confined to a brief history of the monarchies of England, Scotland, Ireland, and Wales and the conjunction of the royal lines in the person of Charles II, it was reissued as the *Epitome monarchiae Britannicae* in 1663.

Puleston died in London at the beginning of 1662 'in a poor condition and in an obscure house' (Wood, *Ath. Oxon.*, 3.544). The administration of his estate was granted on 27 April. G. Le G. Norgate, rev. Sean Kelsey

Sources A. Wood, *The history and antiquities of the University of Oxford*, ed. J. Gutch, 2 vols. in 3 pts (1792–6), vol. 2., pt. 2, p. 703 · Wood, *Ath. Oxon.*, new edn · Wood, *Ath. Oxon.: Fasti* (1820), 160, 176 · M. Burrows, ed., *The register of the visitors of the University of Oxford, from AD 1647 to AD 1658*, CS, new ser., 29 (1881), 505, 560 · PRO, PROB 12/39, fol. 35r

Puleston, John (1583?–1659), lawyer, was born at Kingsworthy, Hampshire, eldest son of Richard Puleston (*b.* 1548), a clergyman from Emral in Flintshire who was later rector of Kingsworthy, and his wife, Alice, daughter of David Lewis of Burcot, Oxfordshire; his younger brother was Richard Puleston (*b.* 1591), later also rector of Kingsworthy and father of the political writer Hamlet Puleston (1632–1662). On 22 May 1601 he matriculated from Oriel College, Oxford, from where he went to Clifford's Inn before being admitted to the Middle Temple on 24 May 1606. He was called to the bar on 8 July 1614 and confirmed on 3 February 1616. A 'devout Puritan' (Prest, 386), in 1619 he was fined for serving flesh on St Matthew's day in the Middle Temple hall. At an unknown date he married Elizabeth (*d.* 1658), daughter of Sir John Woolrych of Dudmaston, Shropshire, 'an earnest Presbyterian' (*DWB*); they had two sons, Roger and John.

In 1634 Puleston became a reader and bencher of his inn. The same year, his religious stance notwithstanding, he accompanied Richard Cartwright on a visit to advise Archbishop Laud on ecclesiastical law. Also about this time he inherited from his childless uncle, George Puleston, the family estate at Emral. In 1641 Puleston petitioned parliament against the chief justice of Chester, accusing him of 'taking of the presents money'. About September 1642 his wife and children were evicted from Emral by royalist troops under the command of Sir John Hammer. The Commons recommended him in February 1643 for the post of baron of the exchequer, but the king declined to appoint him. Puleston became treasurer of his inn in 1646 and was created serjeant-at-law by parliament on 12 October 1648. After seven of the existing fifteen common law judges had declined to continue under the Commonwealth, in 1649 parliament made Puleston a judge of common pleas, in which capacity he rode the home, midland, Oxford, and northern circuits. He served on the commissions that tried and convicted the governor of Pontefract Castle, Colonel John Morris, at York in August 1649 and that acquitted the Leveller leader John Lilburne at the Guildhall later that year. He was named under a proposed act for the establishment of a new high court of justice in April 1650 and to a commission for trying offenders at Norfolk in December 1650. He also served on the north Wales composition committee (1649), on the commission for the propagation of the gospel in Wales (1650), and, between 1647 and 1657, on numerous parliamentary commissions for Denbighshire and Flintshire.

Oliver Cromwell did not reappoint Puleston to the bench in 1653. At about this time his family re-occupied the Emral estate and, on 30 September 1653, Philip Henry, later an eminent nonconformist minister, was appointed tutor to Puleston's two sons there, accompanying them to Oxford the following year. His wife died in 1658, and Puleston died at Emral on 5 September 1659, and was buried there three days later. D. A. Orr

Sources DNB · DWB · Foss, *Judges* · S. F. Black, 'The courts and judges of Westminster Hall during the great rebellion, 1640–1660', *Journal of Legal History*, 7 (1986), 23–52 · S. F. Black, '*Coram protectore*: the judges of Westminster Hall under the protectorate of Oliver Cromwell', *American Journal of Legal History*, 20 (1976), 33–64 · W. R. Prest, *The rise of the barristers: a social history of the English bar, 1590–1640* (1986), 307, 386 · Baker, *Serjeants*, 532 · J. S. Cockburn, *A history of English assizes, 1558–1714* (1972), 219–45, 262–93 · A. Cromartie, *Sir Matthew Hale, 1609–1676* (1995), 58, 73 · H. A. C. Sturgess, ed., *Register of admissions to the Honourable Society of the Middle Temple, from the fifteenth century to the year 1944*, 1 (1949), 86

Pulford, Conway Walter Heath (1892–1942), air force officer, was born at Agra in India on 26 January 1892, the son of Colonel Russell Richard Pulford (1845–1920), chief engineer of the India public works department, and his wife, Lucie Annie. He was educated at the Royal Naval College at Osborne and Dartmouth, where he became a keen sportsman, playing rugby, cricket, and golf. He joined the Royal Navy as a midshipman in 1910, and was commissioned in 1912. He was transferred to the Royal Naval Air Service as a flight lieutenant in December 1914, and embarked on his flying training at the Central Flying School, graduating with his pilot's wings in March 1915. In

June 1915 he was sent to the Dardanelles to join HMS *Ark Royal*, whose seaplanes had been providing reconnaissance support for the fleet's shelling of Turkish ports. In May 1916 he survived a serious aircraft crash and, after convalescence, he was sent back to London to serve as a liaison officer between the Royal Naval Air Service and the Royal Flying Corps. He married, on 20 September 1916, Elinore Mildred (b. 1890/91), daughter of George Henry Norman, gentleman, of Park Lodge, Budleigh Salterton, Devon. He then spent a year in the Mediterranean on a seaplane squadron.

During the last year of the war Pulford was an instructor at the Torpedo Training School, RAF Gosport, and, a few weeks before the armistice, served on Britain's first true aircraft-carrier, HMS *Argus*. He was appointed OBE and awarded the Air Force Cross for his wartime service, in addition to a Croix de Guerre given by the French in April 1918. After the war, and by now a squadron leader in the RAF, he was engaged in further torpedo tactics development at Gosport. In 1919 he won first prize (the Dunning cup) in a torpedo dropping competition against decommissioned naval ships. He then attended RAF Staff College, and went on to serve as a staff officer in the Air Ministry.

In November 1925 Pulford was sent to the Middle East to take command of the Cairo to Cape flight, which ultimately paved the way for commercial air routes in Africa. His experience in naval aviation led him to be transferred next to HMS *Furious* as the senior air force officer. Between 1929 and 1931 he attended the Imperial Defence College and took a higher commander's course. After making group captain in mid-1932, he was sent to Egypt to command RAF station Heliopolis, just outside Cairo, which formed a vital link in the establishment of Britain's air routes in both Africa and the Middle East.

Pulford was promoted to air commodore in mid-1936, after being transferred back to Britain to serve in the new Training Command. This had the vital role of manning the rapidly expanding Royal Air Force. He played a key role in harmonizing the syllabus and output of civilian flying training schools with service demands, which, literally, saved Britain in 1940. The greatest constraint on the RAF's operations in the first two years of the war was a shortage of pilots, and had Training Command not geared up its output of aircrew in the late 1930s, the battle of Britain would have been won by the Germans. Pulford took over as air officer commanding volunteer reserves in August 1938, and much of the credit for the volunteer reserve training over 10,000 aircrew personnel by 1939 must go to Pulford, a prime mover in the expansion of volunteer reserve training. In recognition of his work he was promoted to air vice-marshal in April 1939. In March 1940 he became air officer commanding 20 group, which was responsible for technical training in the RAF.

In 1941 Pulford was sent to Singapore as air officer commanding-in-chief, Far East. In a service that was already ill-equipped, the RAF units in the Far East were the worst off, as this theatre was last on the list of strategic priorities. The handful of squadrons under Pulford's command were equipped with aircraft belonging to the previous generation (aircraft such as the Vildebeest biplane). Exacerbating this problem was a chronic shortage of pilots, and Pulford had to be content with mostly inexperienced aircrews coming directly from flying training schools in Australia and New Zealand. When the Japanese launched their attacks on 7 December 1941, the aircraft defending Malaya and Hong Kong were quickly beaten. After only two days of combat, the RAF strength over northern Malaya had been cut in half, from 110 aircraft to fifty. Losses among the bomber units were so heavy that Pulford made the decision to limit their operations to night-time. By February 1942 the Japanese land forces had advanced to the southern end of the Malayan peninsula and were assaulting Singapore. On 10 February 1942 Pulford ensured that the RAF aircraft still intact were withdrawn to Sumatra, and the following day he ordered those who remained in his air headquarters to make their way to the docks and take one of the many boats escaping to the Indonesian islands. He himself stayed on in Singapore for another two days, and was seen boarding a speedboat along with Admiral Ernest John Spooner (rear-admiral, Malaya) in an attempt to escape to Palembang in Sumatra. Shortly after leaving Singapore the speedboat was strafed by Japanese seaplanes, and the party of forty-five was driven ashore on Chubia Island, just off the east coast of Sumatra, on 15 February.

Over the next three months eighteen of the party died of various causes, and most of the remainder were taken prisoner by the Japanese, including Lieutenant-General Arthur Ernest Percival, who had commanded the Malayan garrison. Pulford was one of those who died on Chubia Island, on or about 10 March 1942. The cause of his death remains uncertain, but records suggest that he was wounded in the enemy attack on the speedboat and, because of malnutrition on the island, never recovered from his wounds. He was not in a robust condition, having suffered from dengue fever since his arrival in the Far East. Among the others who died was Rear-Admiral Spooner, and the decision was made by the Commonwealth War Graves Commission to leave his and Pulford's remains on the island, rather than re-interring their bodies at Singapore.

CHRISTINA J. M. GOULTER

Sources records, air historical branch (RAF) · record of service file, ministry of defence · casualty file, ministry of defence · H. Probert, *The forgotten air force: the Royal Air Force in the war against Japan, 1941–1945* (1995) · Bengal baptisms, BL OIOC, N/1/219/120 · m. cert. · *WWW*

Wealth at death £735 15s. 9d.: probate, 28 May 1946, *CGPLA Eng. & Wales*

Pullain, John. *See* Pulleyne, John (c.1517–1565).

Pullan, Richard Popplewell (1825–1888), architect and archaeologist, was born on 27 March 1825 at Knaresborough in Yorkshire, the son of Samuel Popplewell Pullan (b. 1796), solicitor, and his wife, Eliza, *née* Dewes. He was educated at Christ's Hospital, became a Grecian, and was afterwards a pupil of Richard Lane, architect and sur-veyor, of Manchester, along with Alfred Waterhouse. At Manchester, Pullan studied old missals and illuminated manuscripts in Chetham's Library, and became interested in medievalism. He developed a passion for heraldry, and amused himself by producing coloured pedigrees. In 1844 he submitted a design for the royal robing-room of Queen Victoria at the House of Lords. This was praised for its rich-ness of colour, though Pullan was considered too young to be awarded the commission. Subsequently he produced stained glass designs and retained a lifelong interest in the study and practice of polychromy. He wrote extensively on architectural matters and read a number of papers at meetings of the Royal Institute of British Architects.

On 24 February 1859 Pullan married Mary Leschallas Burges, the sister of William Burges, the architect. They had no children. Mary Pullan later travelled throughout Asia Minor with her husband, and on the death of her brother, William Burges, in 1881 she and Pullan moved to the house Burges had built for himself in Melbury Road, London. During a visit to Italy Pullan studied church archi-tecture. On his return he helped Sir Digby Wyatt with the polychrome decoration of the Byzantine and medieval courts of the Crystal Palace, which were opened by Queen Victoria on 10 June 1854. In October of that year Pullan went to Sevastopol and made sketches and models of the contours of the district which was under siege. When he returned home he exhibited a model of the country and the fortifications about Sevastopol.

In 1856, in conjunction with (Charles Emmanuel?) Evans, he entered the Lille Cathedral competition and won a silver medal. In 1857 the Foreign Office appointed him as architect to the expedition which was being sent to survey the mausoleum at Halicarnassus, which Charles Newton had excavated in 1856. Pullan arrived at Bodrum on 25 August 1857. He not only measured the architectural remains, but attempted a restoration of the mausoleum, in accordance with the descriptions of Pliny the elder, Hyginus, and Guichard.

On Newton's instructions Pullan then went to Cnidus, where he discovered a gigantic figure of a lion, 10 feet long and 6 feet high, weighing, with its case, 11 tons. This he sent to Britain, and it is now in the Elgin room of the British Museum. He made a restoration of the tomb which the lion had crowned, a survey of the principal sites in the island of Kos, and drawings of the remains. All these res-torations are recorded in *A History of Discoveries at Halicar-nassus, Cnidus, and Branchidae, by C. T. Newton, M.A., Assisted by R. P. Pullan* (1862–3).

After this the Society of Dilettanti employed Pullan on further similar investigations. In April 1862 he began excavations on the site of the Temple of Bacchus at Teos, where he found the temple to be hexastyle (as described by Vitruvius in *De architectura*, vol. 3, chap. 3), with eleven columns on the flanks, rather than pseudodipteral, and so proved that it was not the one built by Hermogenes. Instead he believed that it had been erected in Roman times.

In 1862 Pullan visited the remains of the Temple of Apollo Smintheus, or the 'mouse-queller', near Kulakli, in the Troad, which had been discovered by Thomas Spratt in 1853. In 1864 he published, with Charles F. Texier, *Byzan-tine architecture, illustrated by examples, with historical and archaeological descriptions* and in 1865 they published *The Principal Ruins of Asia Minor Illustrated and Described*. He returned to Smyrna on 5 August 1866, and completed the excavation and drawings on 22 November 1866. He found sufficient remains to show that it was an octastyle pseudodipteral temple, with only fourteen columns on the flank, being superior to the Temple of Minerva Polias at Priene, and probably of about the same date. In 1869 Pullan, under an order from the society, excavated the site of the Temple of Minerva Polias at Priene, which had hith-erto been encumbered with ruins. Accounts of Pullan's work on the three temples were published in the fourth part of *The Antiquities of Ionia* (1881).

At the same time Pullan visited most of the Byzantine churches in Greece and Asia Minor, and published an account of the examples of Byzantine and classical work that had been accumulated by himself and Charles Texier in two volumes, entitled respectively *Byzantine Architecture* (1864), and *Principal Ruins of Asia Minor* (1865). On Pullan's advice Lord Savile, the British ambassador at Rome, undertook excavations on his property at Civita Lavinia, on the Alban hills (Lanuvium), where the ruins of the imp-erial villa of Antoninus Pius were discovered, and magnifi-cent fragments of sculpture, as well as some archaic terra-cottas. Pullan's other publications include: *The Altar, its Bal-dachin and Reredos* (1873); *Eastern Cities and Italian Towns: with Notes of their Architecture* (1879); *Studies in Architectural Style* (1883); and *Studies in Cathedral Design* (1888).

Pullan managed to combine a good London-based archi-tectural practice with his archaeological explorations. He became a fellow of the RIBA in 1861. He competed for the memorial churches at St Petersburg and Constantinople, for Truro and Lille cathedrals, the War and Foreign offices, the Liverpool exchange buildings, the Natural History Museum (South Kensington), the Glasgow municipal buildings, the Dublin Museum, and the Hamburg town hall. His principal executed works were churches at Pon-tresina and Baveno in Italy, and the conversion of Castel Aleggio, between Lake Maggiore and Lake Orta, into an English Gothic mansion. The church at Baveno is octago-nal in plan, and of the Lombard type, and was built for the numismatist Henry William Henfrey in the grounds of his villa. The whole of the coloured decoration was designed by Pullan—much of it was also executed by him—and a drawing of it was exhibited at the Royal Academy in 1882. On the death of Pullan's brother-in-law William Burges, in 1881, he completed all Burges's unfinished works, and edited his posthumously published works.

Pullan was a fellow of the Society of Antiquaries and a member of the Royal Archaeological Institute. A long-term sufferer from bronchitis, he died at 1 Oriental Place, Brighton, on 30 April 1888.

GEORGE AITCHISON, *rev.* JOHN ELLIOTT

Sources *The Builder*, 54 (1888), 319, 341 · G. Aitchison, 'A notice of the late Mr Pullan', *Transactions of the Royal Institute of British Architects*, new ser., 6 (1889–90), 249–54 · *Dir. Brit. archs.* · IGI · *CGPLA Eng. & Wales* (1888)
Archives RIBA, drawings collection · RIBA, nomination papers · RIBA, photographs collection
Wealth at death £6598 10s. 1½d.: probate, 16 June 1888, *CGPLA Eng. & Wales*

Pullar, John (1803–1878). *See under* Pullar, Sir Robert (1828–1912).

Pullar, Sir Robert (1828–1912), dyer, was born on 18 February 1828 at Burt's Close, Perth, the first of nine children of **John Pullar** (1803–1878), dyer, of Perth, and his wife, Mary Walker. John Pullar, born 22 April 1803 at Pomarium, Perth, was the son of Robert Pullar (1782–1835), a cloth manufacturer, and his wife, Elizabeth Black (*d.* 1857). He was educated locally, and served an apprenticeship from 1816 to 1822 as a dyer with the Perth firm of Peter Campbell. On 23 February 1824 he established his own dyeworks with six employees in Burt's Close, dyeing materials for his father, a well-established cloth manufacturer, and providing a dyeing and cleaning service to the public for clothing, furniture, and carpets. On 5 August 1826 he married Mary Walker (1805–1891) of Brahan, Ross-shire. They had nine children.

In 1828 neighbours' complaints about noxious vapours from the dyeworks forced John Pullar into an ultimately advantageous move across the Lade to Mill Street. Water from the Lade was a source of power and facilitated cleaning processes, while land for business expansion was more readily available. The firm grew steadily, assisted by the arrival of the railway in 1847 and the patronage of Queen Victoria in 1852. By 1856 Pullars had approximately a hundred employees and a chain of thirty agencies.

As a radical Liberal John Pullar became a town councillor in 1847, and lord provost of Perth (1867–73). In this role he promoted railway development, city improvement schemes, and legislation favourable to his business. He was a director of the Bank of Scotland, the Caledonian Railway Company, and Perth Royal Infirmary, and a leading figure with numerous local charity organizations. A man with strong religious beliefs, he became a deacon of the Baptist church, applying its teaching to family life by imposing a regime of austerity and strict discipline. He fostered harmony in the workplace, but opposed trade unionism, and unsuccessfully attempted to impose habits of temperance on employees. He died of heart failure in his spacious home at 3 St Leonard's Bank on 16 December 1878. Five days later his coffin was paraded through the streets of Perth before being interred at Wellshill cemetery.

Robert Pullar was educated in Perth at Stewart's academy, Atholl Street, and Greig's academy, Stormont Street, followed by a short spell at Perth Academy and continuation classes in French and German. In 1841, aged thirteen, he was apprenticed as a dyer to his father; he became a partner in 1848. In 1859 he married Ellen Mary Daniell

(1830–1904) of Wantage, Berkshire. They had two sons, Rufus Daniell (1861–1917) and Albert Evans (1865–1945).

John Pullar's political ambitions meant that Robert Pullar was left to run the business, which received a major boost in 1856 with the discovery, by the chemist William Perkin, of a purple aniline dye extracted from coal tar. Perkin approached Robert Pullar, who doubted the commercial viability of the discovery, but when a suitable mordant was found and the new colour became fashionable it was quickly introduced. Demand increased and the firm expanded, and by 1865 it employed 500 workers. Subsequent experimentation in the new organic chemistry led to an increasing variety of colours and shades for supply to the dyeing trade.

The other major development in the industry was dry cleaning, involving the use of benzine to release dirt from cloth without distorting the fibres. The Pullar family learned of this process from the German firm of Wilhelm Spindler, with whom they had had a long association, consolidated in 1867 with the marriage of Robert Pullar's younger brother and business partner James F. Pullar (1836–1912), to Adelgunde Spindler. By 1869 Pullars had pioneered the use of machinery which tumbled garments in dry-cleaning solvent. These developments ensured success, but expansion in the city centre was approaching its limits, and benzine was dangerously volatile. In 1882 Robert Pullar solved this problem by purchasing a 110 acre site at Tulloch, then on the outskirts of Perth, for the firm's dry-cleaning plant and benzine storage depot.

As expansion continued, Pullar's sons Rufus and Albert and his nephew Herbert became partners, and in 1895, the year Pullar was knighted for his entrepreneurial activities and services to science education, there were 2061 employees. In 1909, three years before his death, the workforce peaked at 2818. His achievements were also marked by his election to the Royal Society of Edinburgh in 1880, an honorary LLD from St Andrews University in 1905, and the freedom of the City of Perth in 1911. In a portrait by Sir John E. Millais he appears as a dignified and dapper figure.

Pullar's efforts to provide employees with a healthy and safe working environment are well documented and, compared with many, the firm was progressive. However, some work processes were hazardous. Employees suffered burns from fires while treating items of clothing, benzine inhalation caused nausea and giddiness, and hard-pressed sewing machine operatives frequently pierced their fingers with needles. Some of the extensive welfare schemes failed through employees' lack of enthusiasm, while others were conditional upon loyalty and good behaviour. Nevertheless, in 1899, to commemorate his commercial jubilee and in recognition of his generosity, the employees presented Pullar with a bronze plaque, erected outside the firm's offices in Kinnoull Street, Perth.

Labour relations at Pullars have been described as harmonious, and until the twentieth century strikes were rare, but the workforce was controlled by individualized negotiating procedures that discouraged trade unionism. In 1912 the system broke down irretrievably as workers went on strike and joined trade unions in protest at Pullars's refusal to discuss wage advances.

Pullar became an influential figure in Liberal politics as a supporter of free trade and Irish home rule, and as a major source of party finance. By the 1890s he had become an executive member of the Scottish Liberal Association. When he was seventy-eight he became Perth's Liberal MP for two years (1907–9), but seldom, if ever, spoke in House of Commons debates. Moreover, his failure to support legislation designed to assist the unemployed served to distance Perth's trade union movement from the Liberal Party.

Pullar's philanthropic activities were extensive. As a justice of the peace and an eminent member of the United Free Church he appeared on the boards of all leading charitable, religious, and philanthropic organizations, making large donations to these and numerous civic schemes. His desire to relieve poverty and distress was accompanied by a belief in the need to promote the values necessary for industrial society, such as discipline, temperance, industry, and household economy.

As the business matured, Robert Pullar began to enjoy travel, including trips to Scandinavia, Russia, America, and the Middle East. He was widely, and justifiably, regarded as Scotland's leading dyer; a man of simple habits, a great entrepreneur, important employer of labour, Liberal leader, and philanthropist.

Equally, Pullar's career had started from a position of privilege, and Perth had been the means to great wealth for his family. Sir Robert died of a seizure at his home, Tayside, Isla Road, on 9 September 1912. More than two thousand people attended the funeral two days later, at St Leonard's United Free Church, and Wellshill cemetery, Perth, of 'an advanced Liberal' and a 'model employer' (*Perthshire Constitutional*, 10 Sept 1912).

JOHN McG. DAVIES

Sources Perth and Kinross council archive, John Pullar & Sons Ltd MSS · *Perthshire Advertiser* (11 Sept 1912) · *Perthshire Advertiser* (19 Dec 1878) [John Pullar] · 'Sir Robert Pullar's commercial jubilee, 1848–1898', *Perthshire Constitutional* (13 Feb 1899) · *Perthshire Constitutional* (10 Sept 1912) · *Perthshire Constitutional* (18 Dec 1878) [John Pullar] · J. McG. Davies, 'Social and labour relations at Pullars of Perth, 1882–1924', PhD diss., University of Dundee, 1991 · L. Pullar, *Lengthening shadows* (privately printed, Perth, 1910) · Town council minutes, 1826–73, Perth and Kinross council archive · 'The story of Pullars, 1824–1924', *Perthshire Advertiser* (29 March 1924) · 'Pullars of Perth: history of the great enterprise and a tour of the establishment', *People's Journal* (23 May 1903) · *CCI* (1912) · *CCI* (1879) [John Pullar] · Perth directories, 1837–1912, A. K. Bell Library, Perth · Perth trades council minute book, Perth and Kinross council archive, MS 41/2 [18 March 1908] · Perth trades council minute book, Perth and Kinross council archive, MS 41/3 [5 June 1912] · Register of burials, Perth cemeteries, Perth and Kinross council archive, 11 Sept 1912 · Register of burials, Perth cemeteries, Perth and Kinross council archive, 18 Dec 1878 [John Pullar] · *Perthshire Courier* (10 Sept 1912)

Archives A. K. Bell Library, Perth, Perth and Kinross council archive

Likenesses J. M. Barclay, oils, 1875 (John Pullar), Perth Museum and Art Gallery · J. E. Millais, oils, 1896, Perth Museum and Art Gallery · J. Tweed, bronze plaque, 1898, Kinnoull Street, Perth · photograph, repro. in *Perthshire Constitutional* (9 Sept 1912)

Wealth at death £505,909 8s. 2d.: Scottish probate sealed in London, 8 Nov 1912, *CGPLA Eng & Wales*

Pullen, Henry William (1836–1903), Church of England clergyman and writer, was born at Little Gidding, Huntingdonshire, on 29 February 1836, the elder son of the four children of William Pullen, rector of Little Gidding, and his wife, Amelia, daughter of Henry Wright. Pullen was educated at Marlborough College from 1845 to 1848, in which year his family moved to Babbacombe, Devon, owing to his father's poor health. In the same year his father published a volume of young Pullen's verses and rhymes, called *Affection's Offering*.

Pullen went to Clare College, Cambridge, where he graduated BA in 1859 and MA in 1862. In 1859 he was ordained deacon on appointment to an assistant mastership at St Andrew's College, Bradfield, and became priest in 1860. Deeply interested in music, he was elected vicar-choral of York Minster in 1862 and was transferred in 1863 to a similar post at Salisbury Cathedral. Pullen did his chief literary work while at Salisbury. He published several pamphlets (1869–72) on reform of cathedral organization and clerical unbelief, which were often viewed as pugnacious.

Near the end of 1870 Pullen published a pamphlet on the Franco-Prussian War entitled *The Fight at Dame Europa's School*. Here he presented the European situation as a simple parable, in which John, the head of the school (and representing England), refuses to separate Louis (France) and William (Germany), though he sees that Louis is beaten and that the prolongation of the fight is mere cruelty. John is reproached by Dame Europa for cowardice: he is told that he has grown 'a sloven and a screw', and is threatened with loss of his position.

The pamphlet was enormously successful. The first edition of 500 copies was printed at Salisbury on 21 October 1870. By 1 February 1871 29,000 copies had been issued. The Salisbury resources then became overstrained, and the publisher, Spottiswoode of London, printed 50,000 copies (1–9 February). By 18 April 192,000 had appeared, and the final thousand were printed in April 1874. The pamphlet was translated into French, German, Italian, Danish, Dutch, Frisian, Swedish, Portuguese, and Jersey French. A dramatized version by George T. Ferneyhough was acted on 17 March 1871 by amateurs at Derby in aid of a fund for French sufferers. *The Fight*, which brought Pullen £3000, evoked a host of replies, especially ones justifying Britain's non-involvement in the conflict. Pullen's further pamphleteering critical of the 1868–74 Gladstone government was less successful.

In 1875 Pullen retired from Salisbury. During that year and 1876 he served in Sir George Nares's Arctic expedition as chaplain on the ship *Alert* and received on his return the Arctic medal. For the next twelve years he travelled widely on the continent, making Perugia his headquarters. The publisher John Murray, to whom he had sent useful notes of travel, appointed him editor of his popular travel guides. Fluent in five or six languages, Pullen successively revised nearly the whole of the series, beginning with north Germany. His writing continued throughout his life, focusing on political and religious pamphleteering.

Pullen resettled in England in 1898, and held successively the curacy of Rockbeare, Devon (1898–9), and several locum tenencies. In May 1903 he became rector of Thorpe Mandeville, Northamptonshire, but died, unmarried, in a nursing home at 70 Newhall Street, Birmingham, seven months later, on 15 December 1903. He was buried at Birdingbury, Warwickshire, and a brass tablet to his memory was put up on the chancel wall of the parish church at Thorpe Mandeville.

H. C. MINCHIN, rev. JOSEPH COOHILL

Sources *The Times* (18 Dec 1903) · *WWW, 1897–1915* · W. Pullen, 'Preface', in H. W. Pullen, *Affection's offering* (1848) · H. W. Pullen, *The fight at Dame Europa's school* (1870) · G. Nares, *Narrative of a voyage to the polar sea* (1878) · Allibone, *Dict.* · Brown & Stratton, *Brit. mus.* · private information (1912) · *CGPLA Eng. & Wales* (1904)
Likenesses W. T. & R. Gowland, carte-de-visite, NPG · E. Rogers, carte-de-visite, NPG
Wealth at death £196: administration with will, 5 Jan 1904, *CGPLA Eng. & Wales*

Pullen, Josiah (1631–1714), Church of England clergyman and university teacher, was possibly the son of John Pulleyn. He matriculated at Magdalen Hall on 15 November 1650, graduated BA on 26 May 1654, and proceeded MA in 1657. His MA was incorporated at Cambridge in 1659. In 1657 he was elected vice-principal of Magdalen Hall, a position he held until his death. Among his pupils were Robert Plot, the Oxfordshire naturalist, Richard Stafford, a Jacobite pamphleteer, and Thomas Yalden the poet. Under Henry Wilkinson (principal from 1648 to 1662), Magdalen Hall was renowned as a puritan house; in 1661 Clarendon refused an invitation to dine in hall, acknowledging Pullen alone as an 'honest man' among 'a company of factious people' (*Life and Times of Anthony Wood*, 1.415).

Pullen was ordained priest at Lincoln Cathedral in September 1662, and became domestic chaplain to Bishop Robert Sanderson. He gave the sermon at Sanderson's funeral in 1663. In 1675 he was appointed minister of St Peter-in-the-East, Oxford, and in 1684 rector of Blunsdon St Andrew in Wiltshire. Also in that year Pullen became one of the original members, and signatories to the rules, of the Philosophical Society of Oxford.

In the company of Alexander Padsey, a fellow of Magdalen, or Richard Steele, the essayist, Joe Pullen was often out walking, an activity which, according to Hearne, kept him 'very healthy and vigorous' (*Remarks*, 5.8). An elm tree which he planted at the top of Headington Hill, and which in 1832 came to mark the limit of the parliamentary borough of Oxford, carried his name even after it was cut down to a stump in 1894. Pullen's Lane in Headington continued his memory.

Pullen officiated at services until his death, refusing to wear his spectacles, which made him 'guilty of great Blunders at Divine service' (*Remarks*, 5.8). He died, unmarried, at Oxford on 31 December 1714, aged eighty-three, and was

Josiah Pullen (1631–1714), by unknown engraver

buried, on 7 January 1715, in the lady chapel of St Peter-in-the-East, where a slab with an epitaph by Thomas Wagstaff was erected. In his will, proved in the chancellor's court at Oxford on 11 May, Pullen bequeathed his estate to his nephew, John, for the education of John's son, James.

H. E. D. BLAKISTON, rev. J. H. CURTHOYS

Sources *Remarks and collections of Thomas Hearne*, ed. C. E. Doble and others, 5, OHS, 42 (1901) · *VCH Oxfordshire*, vol. 5 · *The life and times of Anthony Wood*, ed. A. Clark, 1, OHS, 19 (1891) · R. T. Gunther, *Early science in Oxford*, 1: *Chemistry, mathematics, physics and surveying*, OHS, 77 (1923) · Foster, *Alum. Oxon.* · Venn, *Alum. Cant.*
Likenesses R. Byng, oils, Bodl. Oxf. · mezzotint, BM · mezzotint, second version, NPG [*see illus.*]

Pullen, Robert (*d.* in or after **1146**), theologian and cardinal, derived his surname from Latin *pullus*, meaning either 'dingy' or 'small animal'. It is very unlikely that he is the Master Robert called Amiclas ('Poor Man') who appears in the contemporary poem *Metamorphosis Goliae episcopi*, as well as in the *History* written by William of Tyre. Pullen may have come from Sherborne in Dorset and he may also have studied in a school for clerks in northern France, perhaps at Laon or Paris, in the early years of the twelfth century. He should not be confused with Robert, archdeacon of Exeter, who studied at Laon and became bishop of Exeter in 1138. But he probably taught for a time in Exeter before 1133, where he may have had Gilbert Foliot (*d.* 1187) among his pupils. He then moved to Oxford, and from 1133 to 1138 (in the words of the Osney annalist) 'he began to lecture at Oxford on the holy scriptures, which had been neglected in England' (*Ann. mon.*, 4.19). Several of his sermons of this period have survived, and he must also in these years have begun work on his

Sentences, which systematically treat of the main areas of theology. He was not, as has been suggested, a canon of Osney Abbey.

According to the chronicler John of Hexham, Pullen refused a bishopric offered him by Henry I; he would seem an unlikely choice, and anyway in his lectures he expressed his belief in free elections. He soon moved to Paris where he taught, supported by the revenues of the archdeaconry of Rochester which he obtained possibly before 1137. John of Salisbury (*d.* 1180) describes him as a man 'of joyful memory', and as 'commendable alike in his life and his learning' (*Ioannis Saresberiensis Metalogicon*, 21, 72), who taught him theology at the cathedral school of Paris as the successor of Gilbert de la Porrée, who had left to be bishop of Poitiers in 1142. Bernard of Clairvaux wrote, probably in 1142, to apologize to Ascelin, bishop of Rochester, for detaining Pullen at Paris 'on account of the wholesome doctrine that is in him' (*Sancti Bernardi opera*, 64). The revenues that supported Pullen were hotly disputed by the monks of Rochester. Ascelin tried to force Pullen to return and appealed to Rome. He obtained a judgment from Celestine II allowing him to appoint a new archdeacon unless Pullen were to successfully appeal by 14 May (Pentecost) 1144. Pullen did appeal and Bernard reproached Ascelin for 'stretching out his hand upon the goods of the appellant after his appeal was made' (ibid.). Bernard also mentioned that Master Robert had many friends in the curia.

This action must have brought Pullen to Rome. His creation as cardinal-priest of St Martin, certainly by 4 January 1145, represents an unusual promotion, for no Englishman had hitherto become a cardinal, and Pullen was a teacher apparently lacking administrative experience. Gilbert Foliot wrote to congratulate his 'dearest master' (*Letters and Charters*, 84) but did not quite conceal his surprise before going on to beg for favours. John of Salisbury, too, gives a hint of surprise in writing that the pope 'made a chancellor out of a scholastic doctor' (*Ioannis Saresberiensis Metalogicon*, 22): Pope Lucius II, who succeeded Celestine II in March 1144, appointed Pullen chancellor of the Roman church, in which post he appears between 31 January 1145 and 22 September 1146. Lucius allowed Pullen to nominate his successor at Rochester; the bishop recorded his disappointments in a letter. Pullen appointed his nephew. This was Paris (Parisius), who is found as archdeacon between 1145 and 1190; he also held a prebend in London.

On the accession to the papacy in 1145 of Bernard's friend, Eugenius III, Bernard wrote to Pullen warmly commending the new pontiff to him, and inviting him to become 'our Eugenius's consoler and counsellor' (*Sancti Bernardi opera*, 309–10). Pullen disappears from papal documents after 22 September 1146, probably through death or ill health. He had probably been responsible for an increase in the number of Englishmen working in the curia, including his pupil John of Salisbury, Nicholas Breakspear (who later became Pope Adrian IV in 1154), and (perhaps) Boso, who became Adrian's biographer. He illustrates the growing interaction between scholastic and administrative activity during the second quarter of the twelfth century. He used his position in Rome to promote the interests of his relatives, including his cousin Joseph, prior of Sherborne Abbey, who brought a complaint against the bishop of Salisbury to Rome by June 1145, and obtained thereby confirmation of a substantial list of privileges and rights for his abbey.

Pullen's *Sentences* are a synthesis of theology in eight books, beginning with God's existence and the work of creation, and closing with the last judgement and the final state. They are characteristic of the early scholastic period, being comprehensive in scope but not as long as later collections were to become. They were presumably finished before 1144, as they arise from classroom teaching, which included carefully structured discussions of questions and of varying opinions about the teachings of the Bible. They are not as systematic as Peter Lombard's, which were completed by 1158, but they left a mark on the latter work. Pullen was remembered, and his opinions recorded, to the end of the twelfth century.

Nineteen sermons ascribed to Pullen are found in Lambeth Palace Library, MS 458, and Hereford Cathedral Library, MS O.viii.2. They were evidently addresses delivered to clerical scholars (*fratres carissimi*) as an integral part of Pullen's teaching of the Bible. The line of division between theology lectures and sermons was thin, but the link between both and the exposition of the Bible was strong: a selection of biblical books and of passages within them underlies Pullen's teaching of both the Old and New testaments. His style in both his *Sentences* and his sermons is discursive and homiletic, and also moralizing and admonitory. He also left an ascetical treatise on conversion and amendment of life entitled *Sermo de contemptu mundi* or *De omnibus humane vite necessariis*. A further twenty-six sermons ascribed to one Master Robert Pulo in Paris, Bibliothèque Nationale, MS Lat. 2945, are not in fact Pullen's.

DAVID LUSCOMBE

Sources F. Courtney, *Cardinal Robert Pullen: an English theologian of the twelfth century* (1954), section A, n. 10 • F. Courtney, 'An unpublished treatise of Cardinal Robert Pullen (†1146), *Sermo de omnibus humane vite necessariis* or *De contemptu mundi*', *Gregorianum*, 31 (1950), 192–223 • B. Smalley, *The Becket conflict and the schools* (1973), 40–45, 242–6 • Emden, *Oxf.*, 3.1525 • *Hist. U. Oxf.* 1: *Early Oxf. schools*, 6–8, 27 • *Ann. mon.*, 4.19–20 • John of Hexham, 'Historia regum continuata', Symeon of Durham, *Opera*, 2.319 • *Fasti Angl., 1066–1300*, [Monastic cathedrals], 81 • J. Thorpe, ed., *Registrum Roffense, or, A collection of antient records, charters and instruments … illustrating the ecclesiastical history and antiquities of the diocese and cathedral church of Rochester* (1769), 8–10, 39–40, 370, 413 • *Ioannis Saresberiensis Metalogicon*, ed. J. B. Hall and K. S. B. Keats-Rohan (Turnhout, Belgium, 1991), bk 1, chap. 5; bk 2, chap. 10 • *Letters and charters of Gilbert Foliot*, ed. A. Morey and others (1967), 84–5 • *Sancti Bernardi opera*, ed. J. Leclercq and others, 8 (Rome, 1977), 64, 309–10 [letters 205, 362] • R. Pullen, *Sententiarum libri VIII*, ed. H. Mathoud (Paris, 1655); repr. in *Patrologia Latina*, 186 [n.d., 1892?]
Archives Hereford Cathedral, MS O.viii.2 • LPL, MS 458

Pullen, Samuel (*bap.* 1598, *d.* 1667), archbishop of Tuam, was baptized on 2 July 1598 at Ripley, Yorkshire, the first child, in a family of five sons and one daughter, of William Pullen (*d.* 1631), rector of Ripley, and his second wife,

Johan (*d.* 1622), daughter of George Sheffield. He matriculated as a sizar from Pembroke College, Cambridge, in 1615, graduated BA in 1620 and proceeded MA in 1623, and was ordained deacon in York in December 1624 and priest in March 1625. In 1624 he was appointed the first headmaster of the re-endowed Leeds grammar school, minister of the New Chapel, and lecturer in St Peter's parish church, of which his father was a trustee. He married Ann (*d.* 1631), daughter of the Revd Robert Cooke, vicar of Leeds, in Leeds parish church on 8 June 1624, and they had three children—Samuel (1625–1656), Alexander (*b.* 1626), and William (1629–1668). His wife died on 17 November 1631 and he married second, on 20 December 1632 in Pontefract parish church, Elizabeth (*d.* in or after 1667), daughter of Peter Bramhall of Carlton near Pontefract, the sister of John Bramhall, later bishop of Derry and archbishop of Armagh.

In 1632 Pullen accompanied the marquess (later James, first duke) of Ormond, as his private chaplain, to Ireland and there he gained preferment in the Church of Ireland. On 5 June 1634 he was installed as prebendary of Killamery in St Canice's Cathedral, Kilkenny, where in 1636 he was appointed to the chancellorship which he held with the rectory of Knockgraffon in co. Tipperary. To these preferments, in 1638 he added the deanery of Clonfert, co. Galway. He was residing in Cashel, co. Tipperary, at the outbreak of the Irish rising of 1641, in the course of which he lost goods and property to the value of £4652, escaping to England only after a period of three months during which he was sheltered by a Jesuit, James Saul (or Sall) 'who had received from the Dean several favours which caused James Saul to preserve the Dean from being murthered' (Nalson and Ware, 2.98). While in England Pullen was chaplain to Aubrey de Vere, earl of Oxford, whose wife, a Roman Catholic, introduced him to a shoemaker who was a much admired preacher. Pullen recognized the preacher as James Saul, whom he thanked 'for preserving his life in Ireland … and as you saved mine, I shall save yours' (ibid., 2.100). He prevailed on the earl and countess of Oxford to do Saul no harm providing he left Oxfordshire, and thereby the countess was said to have returned to the Church of England.

After returning to Ireland, in 1642 Pullen was awarded the degree of DD by the University of Dublin, and in October of the same year was collated to the prebend of Swords in St Patrick's Cathedral, Dublin, which he held until the Restoration when, on the recommendation of the duke of Ormond, he was appointed archbishop of Tuam and bishop of Kilfenora. Pullen was one of twelve bishops who were consecrated by his brother-in-law, the archbishop of Armagh, John Bramhall, in St Patrick's Cathedral, Dublin, on 27 January 1661. His sojourn as archbishop of Tuam was unremarkable and short, for he died on 24 January 1667 at about five or six in the evening and was buried on 27 January in St Mary's Cathedral, Tuam, 'iuxta thronum archiepiscopalem' ('next to the archiepiscopal throne') under an inscribed stone which was subsequently removed from the cathedral and inserted in a

boundary wall. Under the terms of his will, dated 10 January 1667, in which the principal legatees were his wife and son, William, he left houses in Patrick Street, Dublin, leased from the dean and chapter, rents of lands in co. Galway, furniture, coaches, and £600 to buy land, while his books were left to his nephew Tobias, later bishop of Cloyne and bishop of Dromore. Despite his pedagogical background and his ownership of books, he left no writings. Likewise as priest and bishop he left no permanent mark on the life of the Church of Ireland.

RAYMOND REFAUSSÉ

Sources C. Pullein, *The Pulleyns of Yorkshire* (1915) • Venn, *Alum. Cant.* • [J. Nalson and R. Ware], *Foxes and firebrands*, 2 pts (1682) • H. Cotton, *Fasti ecclesiae Hibernicae*, 1–4 (1845–51) • J. B. Leslie, *Ossory clergy and parishes* (1933) • H. J. Lawlor, *The fasti of St Patrick's, Dublin* (1930) • J. Higgins and A. Parsons, *St Mary's Cathedral … Tuam* (1995) • depositions, co. Tipperary, 1641, TCD, MS 821 • Tuam diocesan register, 1665–98, Representative Church Body Library, Dublin • F. E. Ball, 'Some notes on the households of the duke of Ormonde', *Proceedings of the Royal Irish Academy*, 38C (1928–9), 1–20
Archives Hunt. L., corresp.
Wealth at death see Pullein, *The Pulleyns*

Pullen, Samuel (1713–1784?), Church of England clergyman and writer, was born at Dromore, co. Down, Ireland, the son of the Revd William Pullen (*c.*1655–1726). He was educated at Newry, then obtained a scholarship at Trinity College, Dublin, in 1730; he graduated BA in 1734 and MA of Trinity in 1738. He translated from the Latin of Marcus Hieronymus Vida, bishop of Alba (*d.* 1566), *The Silkworm: a Poem in Two Books* (1750), for which the Royal Dublin Society awarded him the Madden prize of £50 as the best-written book of the year.

Pullen's father had been born in Jamaica, and a relative, William Pullen, was governor of Jamaica, which fuelled Pullen's interest in the introduction of silk cultivation into the American colonies. He wrote *The Culture of Silk, or, An Essay on its Rational Practice and Improvement* (1758), and two papers on the same subject were published by the Royal Society. Pullen was rector of Skryne, co. Meath, in 1765–84 and vicar of St Catherine's, Dublin. He probably died in the early part of 1784; administration of his estate was granted to his sister on 13 July 1784.

CHARLOTTE FELL-SMITH, *rev.* ANITA MCCONNELL

Sources Burtchaell & Sadleir, *Alum. Dubl.* • D. J. O'Donoghue, *The poets of Ireland: a biographical dictionary with bibliographical particulars*, 1 vol. in 3 pts (1892–3) • J. S. Crone, *A concise dictionary of Irish biography* (1928) • *Clergy of Down and Dromore* (1996), 62

Pullen, Tobias (1648–1713), Church of Ireland bishop of Dromore, was born at Middleham, Yorkshire, the son of Joshua Pullen (*d.* 1657), dean of Middleham, and Hester Stannicliffe, and was the fourth child in a family of four boys and one girl. Owing, it is said, to the interest of his uncle, Samuel *Pullen (*bap.* 1598, *d.* 1667), archbishop of Tuam, he entered Trinity College, Dublin, on 11 March 1664 at the age of sixteen and was elected to a scholarship in 1668. While still a student he was appointed in 1666, by his uncle, as a vicar-choral of St Mary's Cathedral, Tuam, and while he was permitted to enjoy the emoluments of the post he was granted leave of absence for six years to continue his studies in Dublin. It is uncertain if he was ordained at this time as he was below the canonical age, but he had been ordained by 1671, when he was elected a fellow of Trinity College. In May 1667 he was appointed to the college living of Tullyaughnish in the diocese of Raphoe, to which he added, in September of the same year, the treasurership of Armagh Cathedral and the appropriated rectory of Creggan. Having resigned his fellowship in May of the previous year on 16 May 1678 he married Elizabeth (d. 1691), daughter of alderman Robert Leigh of Drogheda, co. Louth, with whom he had five children: Thomas (b. 1679), Samuel (b. 1682), Isabella (b. 1683), Elizabeth (b. 1684), and Joshua (1687–1767), who became chancellor of Dromore Cathedral in 1727. Pullen resigned his Raphoe and Armagh livings in 1682 when he was appointed dean of Ferns, but retained an interest in Armagh with his appointment as rector of Louth and Bewley and vicar of St Peter's, Drogheda, where he resided. He also retained his links with Trinity College, Dublin, from which he graduated BD and DD in 1688.

In January 1689 Pullen fled to England before the advancing Jacobites, abandoning in Drogheda his books and manuscripts, which were seized by an Irish Roman Catholic, Nicholas Fitzgerald. He was attainted of treason by the Irish parliament in 1689, but, following the accession of William and Mary, Pullen returned to Ireland, where by February 1691 he was attempting to recover his stolen property. Later in the same year his wife died and was buried in St Peter's Church, Drogheda, on 4 October 1691. On the recommendation of Thomas Tenison, bishop of Lincoln, Pullen was appointed by letters patent of 13 November 1694 to the bishopric of Cloyne, with which he was permitted to continue to hold the rectories of Louth and Bewley. However, in the following year he was translated to the see of Dromore, where he built an episcopal residence at Magheralin.

In 1695 Pullen published, anonymously, *An Answer to the Case of the Protestant Dissenters of Ireland*, which sought to refute the arguments of Joseph Boyce, a presbyterian minister, who advocated toleration for dissenters in Ireland. Pullen was one of twenty-one bishops in the Irish House of Lords who in the same year voted down a bill which would have eased the position of dissenters, and his loyalty to the establishment was further demonstrated in November 1695 when he preached in Christ Church, Dublin, on 'the happy deliverance of James I from the gunpowder plot and the happy accession of his present majesty King William' (*A Sermon Preached in Christ Church*). He returned to the theme of religious toleration in 1697 when he published, again anonymously, a defence of his *Answer*. To him also is attributed the anonymous publication *A vindication of Sir Robert King's designs and actions in relation to the late and present Lord Kingston*, which appeared in 1699. That his time as bishop of Dromore was not devoted solely to politics is suggested by the gift in 1703 of a silver flagon to Dromore Cathedral, where it is still used. Pullen died on 22 January 1713 and was buried on 18 April in St Peter's Church, Drogheda, where he is memorialized as 'an able and faithful minister of Christ … honoured and beloved in every station' (Leslie, 239).   RAYMOND REFAUSSÉ

Sources C. Pullein, *The Pulleyns of Yorkshire* (1915) • H. Cotton, *Fasti ecclesiae Hibernica* (1848–51) • J. B. Leslie, *Armagh clergy and parishes* (1911) • W. M. Brady, *Clerical and parochial records of Cork, Cloyne, and Ross*, 3 (1864) • Burtchaell & Sadleir, *Alum. Dubl.*, 2nd edn • Tuam diocesan register, 1665–98, Representative Church Body Library, Dublin • *A list of … names … who are … attainted of high treason* (1690)
Wealth at death £1500 to daughter Jane; £1000 to daughter Elizabeth; £100 to sister-in-law; £5 p.a. for life to Alexandra Pullein; tithes worth £20 p.a. to clergy widows: will (destroyed 1922), repr. in Pullein, *The Pulleyns*

Pullen, William John Samuel (1813–1887), naval officer, was the son of Lieutenant W. Pullen RN. After serving for some years in the navy he left it in 1836, and went out under the auspices of the South Australia Company to assist in the establishment of the colony, afterwards becoming marine surveyor under the colonial administration. Returning to the navy in 1844, he was appointed to the paddle surveying vessel *Columbia*, working on the Atlantic coast of Canada under Lieutenant P. F. Shortland. He was promoted lieutenant on 9 November 1846, but continued in the *Columbia* until she was paid off in 1848. He was then appointed to the *Plover* with Captain Thomas Moore for a voyage to the Pacific and the Arctic through the Bering Strait. In the summer of 1849 he and Hooper were ordered by Captain Kellett of the *Herald* to search the coast from Point Barrow to the mouth of the Mackenzie by boat, for signs of Sir John Franklin's expedition. After wintering on the Mackenzie, at Fort Simpson, in the following summer they searched the coast as far as Cape Bathurst, before returning to winter at Fort Simpson. They travelled overland to New York, and arrived in England in October 1851. Pullen had been promoted to the rank of commander, on 24 January 1850, and in February 1852 was appointed to the *North Star* for service in the Franklin search expedition under the orders of Sir Edward Belcher. The *North Star* spent the next two winters at Beechey Island, and returned to England in October 1854, having brought out Kellett and the crew of the *Resolute*. In the following January Pullen was appointed to the *Falcon*, attached to the fleet in the Baltic during the summer of 1855. On 10 May 1856 he was advanced to post rank, and in September 1857 was appointed to the *Cyclops* paddle steamer on the East India station. In 1858 he bombarded Jiddah and ran soundings down the Red Sea, with a view to laying telegraph cable from Suez to Aden; and throughout 1859 and 1860 he was employed on the survey of the south and east coasts of Ceylon. The *Cyclops* returned to England early in 1861, and from 1863 to 1865 Pullen was stationed at Bermuda, where he carried out a detailed survey of the island. From 1867 to 1869 he commanded the *Revenge* coastguard ship at Pembroke, and on 1 April 1870 was retired. He became rear-admiral on 11 June 1874, vice-admiral on 1 February 1879, and was granted a Greenwich Hospital pension on 19 February 1886. He had married a daughter of G. D. Berton, sheriff of Fredericton, Scotland; she predeceased him. He died at his residence, Vue Charmante, Torquay, Devon, on 11 January 1887.   J. K. LAUGHTON, rev. R. O. MORRIS

Sources *The Times* (19 Jan 1887) • L. S. Dawson, *Memoirs of hydrography* (1885); repr. (1969) • E. Belcher, *Last of the Arctic voyages* (1855) •

The journal of Rochfort Maguire, 1852–1854, ed. J. Bostocke, 2 (1988) • Boase, *Mod. Eng. biog.* • Kelly, *Handbk* • *CGPLA Eng. & Wales* (1887)
Archives Maritime Museum of British Columbia Society, log-book and papers, incl. HMS *Falcon* and HMS *Cyclops* • State Library of South Australia, Adelaide, papers
Wealth at death £248 8s. 4d.: probate, 1 March 1887, *CGPLA Eng. & Wales*

Puller, Sir Christopher (1774–1824), lawyer, was the grandson of Christopher Puller (*d.* 1789), and the son of Richard Puller (1747–1826), merchant, of London and afterwards of Painswick Court, Gloucestershire. Puller was educated at Eton College and Oxford University, where he matriculated from Christ Church on 4 February 1792; he gained the Latin verse prize in 1794. He graduated BA in 1795, and was subsequently elected fellow of Oriel College. In 1800 he was called to the bar at the Inner Temple. On 9 August 1804 Puller married Louisa (1772–1857), daughter of Joseph King of Taplow and niece of Daniel Giles of Youngsbury, Hertfordshire, to which estate she succeeded in 1840. They had one son, Christopher William Giles Puller (1807–1864).

In 1812 Puller transferred to Lincoln's Inn, where he was elected a bencher in 1822. He was associated as a law reporter with Sir John Bernard Bosanquet, with whom he wrote five volumes of common pleas cases (1796–1807), which were highly regarded and influential. In 1823 he was knighted on succeeding Sir R. H. Blossett as chief justice of Bengal. He died on 25 May 1824 in Calcutta, five weeks after arriving in India.

J. M. RIGG, rev. JOANNE POTIER

Sources *GM*, 1st ser., 95/1 (1825), 273–4 • Foster, *Alum. Oxon.* • *GM*, 1st ser., 59 (1789), 1211 • *GM*, 1st ser., 56 (1786), 349 • H. E. C. Stapylton, *The Eton School lists, from 1791 to 1850* (1863) • D. E. C. Y. [D. E. C. Yale], 'Puller, Sir Christopher', *Biographical dictionary of the common law*, ed. A. W. B. Simpson (1984) • W. P. Baildon, ed., *The records of the Honorable Society of Lincoln's Inn: admissions*, 2 vols. (1896) • Burke, *Gen. GB*
Archives Herts. ALS, corresp.
Likenesses F. C. Lewis, stipple (after J. Slater), BM, NPG • oils, Eton

Puller, Timothy (*bap.* 1637/8, *d.* 1693), Church of England clergyman, was baptized on 17 January 1637 or 1638 at the parish of All Saints, Hertford, the eldest of five children of Isaac Puller (*bap.* 1612, *d.* in or before 1693) and his wife, Elizabeth Barber, daughter of Gabriel Barber of Hertford. He came from a family with puritan and parliamentarian sympathies. The conformist vicar of All Saints was deprived of his living by the House of Commons in 1642 because he had refused to admit Timothy's grandfather Abraham as lecturer there. Timothy's father was joint author of the account sent to the Derby House committee of the taking of the earl of Holland at St Neots after the failure of his attempt to raise a force for the king, and served as JP and trier in Hertfordshire and as MP for Hertford in all three protectorate parliaments.

Timothy Puller was admitted pensioner and matriculated at Jesus College, Cambridge, in 1653, graduating BA in 1657 and MA in 1660 (in which degree he was incorporated at Oxford on 9 July 1661); he proceeded BD in 1667 and DD in 1673. On 12 February 1658 he was admitted student

of Gray's Inn, but any intention he may have had to take up the law was soon abandoned: elected a fellow of his college in that year, he remained on the fellowship until 1673. He was ordained priest by the bishop of Ely on 24 September 1664; he is recorded as preaching a funeral sermon at All Saints', Cambridge, in April 1668. On 11 July 1671 he was presented to the rectory of Sacombe, Hertfordshire, to which was added on 23 September 1679 the rectory of St Mary-le-Bow, London: both these livings he held to his death. On 23 December 1676 he took out a licence to marry Alice Codrington (*bap.* 1646, *d.* 1723?), spinster, then of Kingston, Surrey, the daughter of William Codrington, citizen and draper of London. They were married in King Henry VII's chapel at Westminster Abbey five days later.

Puller was the author of *The Moderation of the Church of England* (1679). In this work he argued that no further measures to comprehend dissenters within the Church of England were necessary as the Anglican church already offered a middle way between popery and puritanism. He believed that royal indulgences had been offered to dissenters not because the constitution of the church was oppressive but out of consideration 'of the weakness of the people' (T. Puller, 29). In fact, because of the intransigence of the dissenters he felt that the censures of the church should be imposed 'in full and free vigour for their seasonable reduction and emendation' (ibid., 520). None the less the work remained a popular statement of Anglican theology and was reprinted several times in the nineteenth century. A book whose frontispiece showed the Church of England as the mother church threatened by popish traitors (Guy Fawkes guided by a Jesuit), by puritans who tore and trampled upon the liturgy and Thirty-Nine Articles, and by Jesuit wolves in sheep's clothing was appropriated by a rather different tradition of what constituted the Anglican *via media* as 'a calm and argumentative statement of the views of the church as conclusively set forth in her liturgy, articles and homilies' (*DNB*).

Puller died in his parish of St Mary-le-Bow, where he was buried on 27 November 1693. His will, made on 9 October 1693 and proved by his widow on 23 January 1694, made provision for her and their two sons, William and Timothy, and two daughters, Elizabeth and Mary. Puller bequeathed property in Rugeley, Staffordshire, Tottenham High Cross, Middlesex, and Shrewsbury which was to pass to his sons after the death of their mother, while the daughters were to be provided with marriage portions of £400 apiece. His parishes of Sacombe and St Mary-le-Bow each received 40s. for their poor. Puller's widow is probably the Alice Puller whose body was taken from St Paul's, Shadwell, to be buried at St Mary-le-Bow on 25 September 1723. His younger son, Timothy, followed him to the grave four years later; his elder son, William, graduated BCL from Hart Hall, Oxford, on 29 November 1704, aged eighteen, and was presented to the rectory of Yattendon, Berkshire, which he held until his death.

EDWARD VALLANCE

Sources Foster, *Alum. Oxon.* • Venn, *Alum. Cant.* • *DNB* • T. Puller, *The moderation of the Church of England* (1679) • J. L. Chester, ed., *The* *marriage, baptismal, and burial registers of the collegiate church or abbey of St Peter, Westminster*, Harleian Society, 10 (1876) • will, PRO, PROB 11/418, sig. 15, fols. 119r–121r • *CSP dom.*, 1654, 227; 1655–6, 305 • W. Urwick, *Nonconformity in Hertfordshire* (1884) • J. L. Chester and J. Foster, eds., *London marriage licences, 1521–1869* (1887) • will of Abraham Puller, PRO, PROB 11/204, sig. 91, fol. 297r–v • W. B. Bannerman, ed., *The registers of St Mary le Bowe, Cheapside, All Hallows, Honey Lane, and of St Pancras, Soper Lane, London*, 2 vols., Harleian Society, register section, 44–5 (1914–15), vol. 1 • *IGI* • *The diary of Samuel Newton, alderman of Cambridge (1662–1717)*, ed. J. E. Foster, Cambridge Antiquarian RS, 23 (1890)

Wealth at death see will, PRO, PROB 11/418, sig. 15

Pulleyne [Pullain], **John** (*c*.1517–1565), preacher and Church of England clergyman, was reputedly born in Yorkshire. He was educated at Oxford, graduating in 1540 and proceeding MA in 1544, and ordained successively deacon on 20 November 1550 and priest on 29 March 1551 to the title of Christ Church. His evident enthusiasm for protestantism won him patronage at the heart of the Edwardian regime: in 1553 he was appointed rector of St Peter Cornhill, an important posting in an influential London city church. He was also at some point serving as chaplain to the duchess of Suffolk, a stalwart of the protestant inner circle during Edward's reign who would become a beacon of constancy during the Marian reaction.

After the accession of Mary, Pulleyne remained in England. He was forced to vacate his living at St Peter Cornhill early in 1554 (though formally deprived only in February 1555), but departed only as far as Essex. Here, it was reported to Edmund Bonner, bishop of London, a considerable congregation of protestants had gathered, served by a number of ministers including 'Master Pulleyne, otherwise called Smith' (Byford, 29). It was alleged that Pulleyne and another minister, 'William, the Scot' (probably Pulleyne's former curate at St Peter Cornhill), often travelled to the continent to see the duchess of Suffolk. No doubt assisted by such strategic intervals abroad Pulleyne was able to maintain his clandestine ministry for much of Mary's reign, both in Colchester and in London, where he is recorded as conducting Easter communion at his house in Cornhill using the Edwardian prayer book in both 1555 and 1556. But soon the dangers of such high-profile service to the protestant community became too great, and in 1557 Pulleyne was forced to withdraw abroad more permanently; the arrival of a child may also have played a part in this decision. With his wife, Joan (*née* Wilbore), and their daughter Faith he made for Geneva, where he arrived, via Strasbourg and Basel, in June. He received a warm welcome in Knox's congregation, which elected him in December a deacon of the church—a sure sign of the high respect in which he was held even in this distinguished company. In Geneva Pulleyne became heavily involved in the project to develop an English metrical psalter, and the eleven new psalms added for the second edition of the *Psalms in English* (1558) contained two by Pulleyne. He was also reputed to have been a collaborator on the English Geneva Bible.

On Mary's death Pulleyne lingered in Geneva long enough to sign the letter of December 1558 urging the exiles to avoid contention over superfluous ornaments. By spring 1559, though, he was back in Colchester: there, with local encouragement, he soon began to preach. His sermons were outspoken and uncompromising, and at a time when unauthorized preaching was still forbidden, and he himself was unbeneficed, they soon attracted official disapproval. In April 1559 Pulleyne was arrested and brought to face the privy council in London. The charge revealed that his sermons had included an inflammatory denunciation of those who compromised with Catholicism under Mary, and had taken a tough Calvinist line on swearing, fornication, and other moral offences. Notwithstanding this unhelpful precipitancy, Pulleyne had friends both locally and at court, and this assured him an important role in the new Elizabethan regime. He was sufficiently well thought of for Cecil to have included him on a list of those marked for high office in July 1559: that this was only weeks after his arrest and appearance before the privy council indicates the radicalism of Cecil's thinking in these months. Equally important, local Colchester opinion was firmly behind him. In August 1559 the electors of Colchester's north ward voted for Pulleyne to be their headsman—an important gesture of support, given that the Yorkshire-born Pulleyne was technically not qualified for the post. These expressions of local opinion may have been decisive in the decision to name Pulleyne as archdeacon of Colchester, rather than the episcopal rank for which he had first been considered. Pulleyne was, in effect, to be the superintendent of a region known for its precocious loyalty to protestantism. This was a decision in which the new bishop of London, Edmund Grindal, seems heartily to have concurred, although the initiative was probably Cecil's: Pulleyne was instituted by royal visitors before Grindal's formal enthronement.

In Colchester Pulleyne proved an enthusiastic leader of the town's reformation, though apparently somewhat to the detriment of his wider responsibilities in the deanery. In 1561 thirteen of the fifteen livings in the deanery were vacant, a position substantially unaltered two years later. His outspoken sermons continued to inspire and provoke in equal measure. He was not afraid either to address mundane moral issues (one complainant grumbled 'he did love to make many sermons of beerpots') or to publicly shame individual offenders; a meeting in the house of the apothecary Simon Smyth in January 1562 heard their host complain that Pulleyne 'made his last sermon … against him and none other' (Byford, 41). But Pulleyne was also an innovator. Colchester's livings were poor, and it proved difficult to replenish the ranks of the parochial ministry after the last of the Marian incumbents had resigned in September 1559. To make good this deficiency Pulleyne appointed 'readers' from among the ranks of the protestant godly. From this beginning he harassed the mainly conservative town aldermen into voting funds for the maintenance of the preaching ministry. A further reflection of his experiences in Geneva was the institution of twenty-five overseers of church attendance, charged with keeping the streets free of unlawful work or play on the Sabbath. Pulleyne died in 1565, some time before 16 July, and was survived by his wife, Joan. In addition to his arch-deaconry he was also a prebendary of Wenlocksbarn in St Paul's (12 September 1561) and rector of Copford, Essex (8 March 1560), a valuable crown living to which he had been advanced on the recommendation of Grindal. His wife was granted letters of administration in the archdeaconry on 16 May 1566; these she renounced, so on 6 February 1568 letters were regranted to her brother Nicolas Wilbore (a prominent Colchester citizen) during the minority of her children.   ANDREW PETTEGREE

Sources M. Byford, 'The birth of a protestant town: the process of reformation in Tudor Colchester, 1530–1580', *The Reformation in English towns*, ed. P. Collinson and J. Craig (1998), 23–47 • P. Collinson, *Archbishop Grindal, 1519–1583: the struggle for a reformed church* (1979) • B. Usher, *William Cecil and episcopacy* [forthcoming] • R. A. Leaver, *Goostly psalmes and spirituall songes* (1991) • C. H. Garrett, *The Marian exiles: a study in the origins of Elizabethan puritanism* (1938) • J. W. Martin, *Religious radicals in Tudor England* (1989), 135–7 • Emden, *Oxf.*, 4.466 • *Fasti Angl., 1541–1857*, [St Paul's, London]

Pullin, Alfred William [*pseud.* Old Ebor] (1860–1934), sporting journalist, was born at Abergwili, Carmarthenshire, on 30 July 1860, the son of Alfred Trask Pullin, schoolmaster, and his wife, Adelaide Evans. His father was ordained in 1875, and held curacies in Yorkshire, where Pullin began his journalistic career in 1880 as Castleford district reporter for the *Wakefield Express*, before joining the *Yorkshire Post* as Bradford reporter. In the early 1880s he played rugby football for Cleckheaton, and he subsequently became a referee for the Yorkshire union. During the early 1890s, when newspapers were developing sports pages, he became cricket and football correspondent for both the *Yorkshire Post* and the *Yorkshire Evening Post*. He covered Yorkshire and England at his two sports, and for forty years wrote a daily column under the pseudonym Old Ebor.

Pullin's greatest achievement was to define the role of the journalist in sport as the critic, popularizer, and interpreter of a particular team to its public. His career coincided with the rise of Yorkshire county cricket. He followed the club round the country, becoming, in the words of the captain, Lord Hawke, 'the non-playing member of the county team' (*Wisden*, 272). He wrote the *History of Yorkshire County Cricket, 1903–23* (1924). The biographer of Alfred Shaw (1902), Pullin was a sound judge of cricketers and his criticisms were valued. His close and sympathetic relationship with the players underlay his best-known book, *Talks with Old English Cricketers* (1900). A pioneering work, *Old English Cricketers* (as it is often referred to) was based on interviews and helped to establish the idea that life after a career in professional sport could often be unhappy.

Pullin, who retired in 1931, had a wife, Alice, daughter of C. W. Ramsden of Wakefield, and three sons. He died, as he had wished, 'with his boots on': he collapsed on a bus in Upper Street, Islington, on 23 June 1934, while on his way to a test match at Lord's, and was found dead on arrival at the Royal Free Hospital, Gray's Inn Road, London. He was buried five days later at Wakefield cemetery after a service at Holy Trinity Church. In the 1920s recognition was paid to his position by his inclusion as one of the game's immortals in *Wisden Cricketer's Almanack*, but the florid prose of Neville Cardus and other later writers on cricket has perhaps put Old Ebor unduly in the shade.

LINCOLN ALLISON

Sources *Yorkshire Post* (25 June 1934) • *The Times* (25 June 1934) • *Wisden* (1935), 271–2 • G. Howat, *Cricket's second golden age* (1989) • b. cert. • d. cert.
Likenesses photograph, repro. in *Yorkshire Post*
Wealth at death £968 17s. 10d.: probate, 27 July 1934, *CGPLA Eng. & Wales*

Pulling, Alexander (1813–1895), serjeant-at-law and legal writer, was born on 1 December 1813 at the Court House, St Arvans, Monmouthshire, the fourth son of George Christopher Pulling, a naval officer, and his wife, Elizabeth, daughter of Robert Moser of Kendal, Westmorland. He was educated at a private school at Llandaff before entering the Merchant Taylors' School in April 1829. On 30 October 1838 he was admitted to the Inner Temple, where he was called to the bar on 9 June 1843. He practised first on the western and afterwards on the south Wales circuit, where he became a leader. While still in his pupillage he published *A Practical Treatise on the Laws, Customs, and Regulations of the City and Port of London* (1842), in which he concentrated a vast amount of previously inaccessible legal and antiquarian lore and sketched a bold scheme of metropolitan municipal reform, which in essence anticipated the Local Government Act of 1888. In November 1853 he gave evidence before the royal commission on the state of the corporation of London (*Parl. papers*, 1854, 26); and in 1855 he was appointed senior commissioner under the Metropolitan Management Act of that year. He frequently represented the city both in court and before parliamentary committees. On 30 August 1855 he married Elizabeth, fourth daughter of Luke Hopkinson of Bedford Row, Middlesex; they had two sons.

Pulling was an energetic member of the Society for Promoting the Amendment of the Law and of the National Association for the Promotion of Social Science, and a principal promoter and original member of the Incorporated Council of Law Reporting. He advocated the payment of jurors. He called for the relief of parliament by the transference of private-bill business to local authorities, writing an article on that subject in the *Edinburgh Review* in January 1855 and publishing *Private Bill Legislation* in 1859 and a *Proposal for Amendment of the Procedure in Private Bill Legislation* in 1862. He favoured the supersession of election petitions by a system of routine scrutiny. In 1857 he was appointed revising barrister for Glamorgan, and in 1864 was made a serjeant-at-law. From 1867 to 1874 he resided at Newark Park, near Wotton under Edge, was in the commission of the peace for Gloucestershire, and took an active part in local administration, acting frequently as deputy county court judge and commissioner of assize under the Welsh circuit commission. He died on 15 January 1895 at home at 68 Redcliffe Gardens, South Kensington, London. He was survived by his wife.

Pulling was one of the last surviving members of the

ancient order of serjeants-at-law, of which he wrote a history. He was an active writer on a broad range of legal concerns, including law reporting, mercantile law, and parliamentary procedure.   J. M. RIGG, *rev.* ERIC METCALFE

Sources *The Times* (17 Jan 1895), 6 · J. Foster, *Men-at-the-bar: a biographical hand-list of the members of the various inns of court*, 2nd edn (1885) · private information (1896) · J. Haydn, *The book of dignities: containing lists of the official personages of the British empire*, ed. H. Ockerby, 3rd edn (1894) · W. T. S. Daniel, *The history and origin of the law reports* (1884) · *CGPLA Eng. & Wales* (1895)
Wealth at death £1664 0s. 3d.: probate, 21 Feb 1895, *CGPLA Eng. & Wales*

Pullinger [*married name* Martin]**, Dorothée Aurélie Marianne** (1894–1986), automobile engineer and businesswoman, was born on 13 January 1894 at St Aubin-sur-Scie, Seine Inférieure, France, the eldest of the eleven children of Thomas Charles Pullinger (1867–1945), engineer, and his wife, Aurélie Berenice, *née* Sitwell (1871–1956). She moved to England with her family at the age of eight and attended Loughborough high school, Leicestershire, where she passed the Oxford local examination as a junior candidate in 1909.

Pullinger was of the generation of women who grew up in the years of the women's militant suffrage campaigns, and reached maturity during the First World War. For many of those women organized political campaigns, or the notion of a sex war between women and men, were not appealing, and they were inclined to conceive of women's advancement in terms of opportunities to achieve economic and professional equality; these, women could quietly exploit rather than publicly demand. The desire to become an engineer was one such feminist aspiration, and was first expressed by some middle-class women in the years leading up to the First World War. It received a tremendous boost during the war from the mass production of armaments in factories where women supplied a large part of the labour force. The Women's Engineering Society, of which Pullinger was a founding and lifelong member, was established in 1919 to maintain and develop women's inroads into engineering during those years.

Like those of many women who were able to enter the profession at that time, Pullinger's father was an engineer, and helped to secure her first job in the field. She began in 1910 as a junior in the drawing office of the Scottish car manufacturer, Arrol-Johnson, where her father had just been taken on as the manager of their Paisley works. He had extensive workshop and management experience in the early cycle and automobile manufacturing industry in England and France, and had travelled to the United States to observe car factory design and the mass production methods in Detroit. A multi-storeyed glass and ferroconcrete factory was built under his direction for Arrol-Johnson at Heathhall, Dumfries. It was the first such factory in the United Kingdom, and embodied some of those new principles. The First World War began before the factory was in full production, and the company switched from manufacturing automobiles to producing aero engines for the Ministry of Munitions.

Dorothée Pullinger worked for approximately four years at the Paisley works, becoming familiar with all aspects of manufacturing, including foundry work, and she was for a time forewoman of the core shop. When the war broke out she was appointed manager of women newly employed by Vickers at Barrow in Furness, making high explosive shells, eventually becoming responsible for 7000 female munitions workers there. She was appointed MBE in recognition of that work in 1920.

Pullinger's father oversaw the construction of a second modern 'daylight' factory for the Arrol-Johnson company near Kirkcudbright in 1916. The factory was conceived of not just as a munitions factory staffed by women for the duration of the war, but as an engineering college for ladies. The company aimed to attract educated young women, and set up a structured apprenticeship system to train women who wished to take up engineering as a profession while producing aero engine components for the Heathhall works. After the war, as Galloway Motors Ltd, and with Dorothée Pullinger as one of the directors and managers, the factory produced a light car for Arrol-Johnson, the Galloway, with a largely female workforce. The venture failed, and the factory closed in 1923; production of the Galloway was transferred to the Heathhall works until the demise of Arrol-Johnson in 1928. Dorothée Pullinger remained with the company and was a sales representative for southern England in 1925–6. She drove Galloway roadsters in the Scottish Six Day Car Trials in the early 1920s, winning the cup in 1924. On 9 October 1924, in Dumfries, she married Edward Marshall Martin (1895–1951), at that time a ship's purser on SS *Naldera*, and son of Edwin Lewis Martin, naval architect, and his wife, Althea Lillywhite, *née* Beagent. They had two children, Yvette (*b.* 1926) and Lewis (*b.* 1931).

By the mid-1920s, in addition to the poor showing of the Scottish motor industry, Pullinger was encountering considerable opposition to a woman's remaining in the engineering side of the car industry. With her husband in the late 1920s she therefore set up the White Service Laundries Ltd at Croydon, with new American steam laundry machinery, claiming that 'I thought washing should not be doing men out of a job' (unpublished family biography). At its height the business had seventeen shops in the London area for receiving laundry. The business was sold in 1946. During the Second World War Pullinger worked with the Nuffield Group in Birmingham, advising them on women's wartime employment issues. She was the only woman appointed to the Ministry of Production's industrial panel. She was part of the wartime committee on post-war problems of the Conservative and Unionist Party which produced the report *Looking Ahead: Work and the Future of British Industry*.

Pullinger settled in Guernsey in 1947, where she built and established Normandy Laundries in 1950. Her husband died in 1951. In later years she travelled extensively, visiting relatives in Australia, Canada, and the United States. She died of old age at la Borne Milliaire, rue à l'Or, St Peter Port, Guernsey, on 28 January 1986. She was survived by her two children.   GEORGINE CLARSEN

Sources private information (2004) [family] · unpublished family biography, written by subject, priv. coll. · m. cert. · d. cert. **Archives** priv. coll., family **Likenesses** photographs, priv. coll.

Pulman, George Philip Rigney (1819–1880), antiquary, was born at Axminster, Devon, on 21 February 1819, the son of Philip Pulman (1791–1871) and his wife, Anne Rigney (1788–1855). In early life he was organist at Axminster parish church and wrote for local newspapers. On 12 December 1848 he married at Cattistock, Dorset, Jane, third daughter of George Davys Ewens of Axminster.

In 1848 Pulman bought a printing and bookselling business at Crewkerne, Somerset, where he settled. For some years he was editor of the *Yeovil Times*, and on 10 March 1857 he instituted *Pulman's Weekly News and Advertiser*, which for over twenty years he owned and edited. It was the first paper to be established at Crewkerne and soon attained a large local circulation.

In June 1878 Pulman sold his newspaper and business and retired to The Hermitage at Uplyme, between Axminster and Lyme Regis. He died there on 3 February 1880, and was buried at Axminster cemetery on 7 February. His wife and his son, G. B. Pulman, a solicitor at Lutterworth, both survived him.

Pulman was a keen fisherman. At the Great Exhibition of 1851 he won a bronze medal for artificial flies. He wrote the popular work *The Vade-mecum of Fly-Fishing for Trout* (1841; 2nd edn, 1846; 3rd edn, 1851), and *The Book of the Axe*, published initially in numbers and later, in 1841, as a book. Other editions followed in 1844, 1853, and 1875, the last being 'rewritten and greatly enlarged'. It was a piscatorial description of the district along the course of the Axe, and contained histories of the towns and houses on the river's banks. Pulman's interest in language and dialect was reflected in *Rustic Sketches, Being Poems on Angling in the Dialect of East Devon* (1842; repr. 1853 and 1871), *Local Nomenclature: a Lecture on the Names of Places, Chiefly in the West of England* (1857), and a version of *The 'Song of Solomon' in the East Devonshire Dialect* (1860). Under the name John Trotandot he published *Rambles, Roamings, and Recollections* (1870), which described the country around Crewkerne, and *Roamings Abroad* (1878). He used the pseudonym Tickler for *Devonshire Sketches* (1869), and also wrote under the pseudonym Elias Tozer.

In the 1840s Pulman published *The Western Agriculturist*, a magazine for west-country farmers; he also published *United Counties Miscellany* from 1849 to July 1851. He supplied the music for songs entitled 'The Battle of Alma' (1854) and 'I'll love my love in the winter', with words by W. D. Glyde, and composed a 'Masonic Hymn' and 'Psalms, Hymn-Tunes, and Twelve Chants' (1855).

W. P. COURTNEY, rev. IAN MAXTED

Sources *Pulman's Weekly News* (10 Feb 1880) · W. P. Courtney, *The Academy* (14 Feb 1880), 120 · J. Davidson, *Bibliotheca Devoniensis* (1852), 14 · J. Davidson, *Bibliotheca Devoniensis. Supplement* (1861), 3, 25 · W. H. H. Rogers, *Memorials of the west* (1888), 32 · Collection of correspondence relative to the election of an organist for Axminster Church (1849) · CGPLA Eng. & Wales (1880) **Archives** Leics. RO, letter-book **Likenesses** Dalziel, woodcut, BM

Wealth at death under £7000: probate, 19 Feb 1880, *CGPLA Eng. & Wales*

Pulman, (Herbert) John (1923–1998), snooker player, was born on 12 December 1923 at 13 Lower Brook Street, Teignmouth, Devon, the son of Ernest Charles Pulman (*d.* in or before 1953), master baker and confectioner, and his wife, Gertrude Mary Kent. The family moved to Plymouth in 1929, when his father bought a billiards club, and later to Exeter. John Pulman served for three months in the army during the Second World War before receiving a medical discharge. In 1946 he won his first and, he maintained, his most satisfying title by beating Albert Brown in the English amateur snooker championship. He turned professional in the same year, and soon became heir apparent to Fred Davis's crown. After losing to Davis in the finals of the world professional snooker championships in 1954 and 1956, he finally won the title in 1957 by defeating Jackie Rea, one of only three other competitors. Pulman and Davis greatly admired each other's play, and their contrasting characters added spice to their competition: Davis rotund, genial, and ever smiling, Pulman looming over the table from his height of 6 feet 2 inches, and prone to displays of temperament. He was also *News of the World* champion in 1954 and 1957, and runner-up in 1958. On 25 April 1953 he married Frances Anne Hayes (*b.* 1931/2), with whom he had three children before the marriage ended in divorce after twenty-five years.

Unfortunately for Pulman he arrived on the snooker scene when interest in the sport was in decline and, although the televising of certain sports had been very lucrative, snooker was not considered suitable. In consequence, there was very little money to be made in competitions, even for a player as talented as Pulman, and he was obliged to make his regular money in the clubs and on the holiday camp exhibition circuit. Introduced to an audience as the man 'who wasn't world champion for eleven years for nothing', he quipped, 'Next to nothing' (*The Guardian*). When the world championships were resumed in 1964 after a period in abeyance, Pulman defeated Davis 19–16 under the new challenge format, and retained the title against a number of challengers until the competition resumed the knock-out format in 1969. He was narrowly defeated in the final (37–33) by Ray Reardon in 1970, but found the new breed of player too much for him, and—despite a huge effort which took him to the semi-finals at the Crucible in Sheffield in 1977—he never again reached the heights of the previous decades.

It was television that saved Pulman from an ignominious decline. He was knocked down by a London bus and hospitalized for six months. His leg was seriously damaged and provided him with an excuse to retire gracefully from the game. Invited to become a television commentator on the sport, Pulman, who had always been a raconteur and natural wit, moved seamlessly into his new career. He commentated for ITV, the BBC, and for RTE in Ireland. His mellow Devonian tones made him a favourite with the viewers and sound engineers alike, and his encyclopaedic knowledge of snooker was put to good use. He was presented with an award for services to snooker by the Snooker Writers' Association in 1993. When not in the commentary box, Pulman spent much of his time fishing on the River Exe, talking snooker with friends, 'accompanied by a tumbler or two of whisky' (*Daily Telegraph*, 28 Dec 1998). In 1965 he published *Tackle Snooker this Way*, reissued in 1974 as *Tackle Snooker*. In December 1998 John Pulman broke his hip in a fall at his home in Northampton; he died in Northampton General Hospital on 22 December 1998. His body was cremated.

RACHEL CUTLER

Sources *The Independent* (26 Jan 1999) · *Daily Telegraph* (31 Dec 1998) · *The Guardian* (28 Dec 1998) · *The Times* (31 Dec 1998) · b. cert. · m. cert. · d. cert.
Archives SOUND BL NSA, Commentary—Davis v. Pulman, World Championship Final 1955
Likenesses photograph, 1964, Hult. Arch. · photograph, repro. in *The Times* · photograph, repro. in *The Independent* · photograph, repro. in *Daily Telegraph* · photograph, repro. in *The Guardian*

Pulteney, Daniel (*bap.* 1682, *d.* 1731), politician, the son of John Pulteney (*d.* 1726), commissioner of customs and MP, and his wife, Lucy, *née* Colville, was baptized on 26 September 1682 at St Martin-in-the-Fields, London. His grandfather Sir William Pulteney represented Westminster for many parliaments, and his first cousin was William *Pulteney, later earl of Bath. He was educated at Westminster School and matriculated at Christ Church, Oxford, on 15 July 1699 but left without a degree. In 1700 he contributed a series of Latin verses to the university collection commemorating the death of the young duke of Gloucester. Between 1704 and 1706 he toured the Dutch Republic and the German states, and was then appointed envoy-extraordinary to Denmark, a position he held until 1715. From 1717 until 1720 he served as a commissioner of trade in France, and produced notably informative reports for the Board of Trade in England. Pulteney married, on 1 December 1717, Margaret (1699–1763), daughter and coheir of Benjamin Tichbourne, and sister-in-law of Charles Spencer, third earl of Sunderland. The earl was a leading opponent of Robert Walpole, and proved a significant influence on the development of Pulteney's political views.

On 23 March 1721 Pulteney was elected MP for the Cornish borough of Tregony, and in October was appointed a lord of the Admiralty. At a by-election the following month he was returned in the interest of his cousin William Pulteney as a member for Hedon, near Hull. In the following year he exchanged this seat for that of Preston borough, where he remained for the rest of his political career. Sunderland's death on 19 April 1722 came as a severe blow to Pulteney who now, according to Arthur Onslow, intensified his criticism of Walpole 'who had been the chief opponent of his friend and patron' (HoP, *Commons*). At first covertly, and then openly after relinquishing his government office, Pulteney became a leading figure in the emerging country whig opposition to the Walpole ministry. According to Onslow it was Daniel who did most to encourage William Pulteney to oppose the administration.

On the death of his father in 1726 Pulteney inherited a considerable fortune and the clerkship to the council in Ireland under a reversion granted by Queen Anne. From this date he had no further need of patronage and was unimpeded in his opposition to Walpole, against whose ministry he made his first recorded speech on 9 February 1726. Other strategies included his provision of financial support, along with his cousin and Lord Bolingbroke, for *The Craftsman* journal, to which Pulteney was also an occasional contributor. Ultimately his failure to bring down the ministry had a deep impact; in Onslow's view 'he fell at last a martyr … for his not succeeding preyed upon his spirits'. Otherwise he was a 'very worthy man, very knowing and laborious in business, especially in foreign affairs, of strong but not lively parts, a clear and weighty speaker' (HoP, *Commons*).

Pulteney's private life was also blighted by the early deaths of six of the couple's children, two of whom were commemorated in odes by Ambrose Phillips. Only one daughter, Frances (1728–1782), reached maturity; she later married William Johnstone [*see* Pulteney, Sir William, fifth baronet], politician and property developer. In 1767 Frances inherited the Pulteney estate belonging to her great-grandfather Sir William Pulteney and the considerable wealth accrued by her father's cousin William, and she and her husband adopted the Pulteney surname. Daniel Pulteney died on 7 September 1731 and was buried at St James's, Westminster, on 14 September 1731. His remains were moved on 17 May 1732 to the east end of the south cloister at Westminster Abbey, where a fine monument by James Leoni, lauding his independent spirit, was erected.

M. J. ROWE and W. H. McBRYDE

Sources DNB · E. Cruickshanks, 'Pulteney, Daniel', HoP, *Commons* · Foster, *Alum. Oxon.* · W. Coxe, *Memoirs of the life and administration of Sir Robert Walpole, earl of Orford*, 3 vols. (1798) · Lord Bolingbroke [Henry St John], *Contributions to The Craftsman*, ed. S. Varey (1982)
Archives BL, letters to C. Townshend and R. Walpole, Add. MSS 38500–38501 · Bodl. Oxf., letters to R. Walpole and C. Townshend
Likenesses G. Kneller, oils, NPG

Pulteney, Sir James Murray-, seventh baronet (*c.*1755–1811), army officer, born James Murray, was the son of Sir Robert Murray, sixth baronet (*d.* 1771), and his first wife, Janet (*d.* 1759), the daughter of Alexander Murray, fourth Baron Elibank. His parents had been married on 22 June 1750. Educated at Westminster School under William Markham, he was commissioned lieutenant in the army on 25 December 1762 and appointed to a lieutenancy in the 19th foot on 2 March 1770. He progressed to captain in the 57th foot on 30 April 1771 and succeeded to his father's baronetcy the same year. In February 1776 the 57th foot sailed from Cork as part of the Charles Town expedition under Major-General Charles Cornwallis, but following the expedition's failure the troops joined instead the main British army off Staten Island, New York. Murray served throughout the New York campaign of 1776 and in New Jersey the following year. He was wounded at the battle of Brandywine.

Having been promoted major in the 4th foot on 31 January 1778, Murray continued to serve in New York and New

Jersey until the end of 1778, when his regiment was sent to the West Indies as part of the expedition commanded by Major-General James Grant. On 12 December 1778 a landing was made on French-held St Lucia. The fortified naval base was immediately captured, but two French counter-attacks on 18 December had to be repelled before the island capitulated. The 4th foot did not participate in this action, but Murray commanded a provisional battalion of light companies during the battle.

The 4th foot returned home in 1780 and Murray was promoted lieutenant-colonel in the army on 6 February that year before transferring to the newly raised 94th foot on 2 March. He was placed on half pay when the 94th was disbanded in 1783 and was promoted colonel in the army and aide-de-camp to the king on 18 November 1789. He entered parliament as MP for the Weymouth and Melcombe Regis constituency in 1790 and continued to serve in this capacity until his death, acting primarily as a supporter of the government.

Murray was sent on diplomatic missions on several occasions, notably to the allied headquarters at Koblenz in 1792, and to the Prussian headquarters at Frankfurt an der Oder between January and March 1793. It was probably this experience which led to his appointment on 24 March 1793 (back-dated to 25 February) as adjutant-general to the expeditionary force sent to Belgium under the duke of York, since the British troops were acting in close co-operation with Austrian and Prussian forces. Indeed, aside from his duties as adjutant-general, Murray was used by York on a number of occasions to co-ordinate strategy with the Austrian army commander, the prince of Coburg. However, Murray did not prove a success and was sacked by the duke of York, who informed the king that he 'is without doubt a perfectly good man, and has very good military talents, but unfortunately is not endowed with that spirit of exactness and order which are absolutely necessary in an Adjutant General' (*Later Correspondence of George III*, 2.131). This blow was softened by Murray's promotion to major-general on 20 December 1793 and his appointment as colonel of the 18th foot on 26 February 1794.

Murray made a very advantageous marriage, on 24 July 1794, to (Henrietta) Laura *Pulteney (1766–1808), the only child of William Pulteney, fifth Baron Johnstone, and his first wife, Frances Pulteney, the niece of William Pulteney, earl of Bath. She had been created baroness of Bath in her own right on 26 July 1792 and countess of Bath on 26 October 1803. Murray assumed the surname and arms of Pulteney on his marriage, and so became Murray-Pulteney. His wife died on 14 August 1808, leaving the Pulteney estates to her family in her will.

Murray-Pulteney served in Ireland in 1798 and was promoted lieutenant-general on 26 June 1799. He then participated in the ill-fated expedition to The Helder in the Netherlands and commanded the first wave of troops landed in the face of the enemy on 27 August 1799. He served as a divisional commander during the campaign and returned home only after supervising the provisions

of the peace treaty at its close. The following year he commanded an expedition to attack Spanish naval assets at Ferrol and Vigo. The force arrived off Ferrol on 25 August 1800 and disembarked the same day. However, after examining the fortifications with his senior officers Murray-Pulteney decided that they were too strong and the garrison too large. The troops were therefore re-embarked, despite strong protests from the naval officers with the expedition. After leaving Ferrol, and deciding that no profit could be gained from attacking Vigo, Murray-Pulteney proceeded to Gibraltar, where he arrived on 19 September as second-in-command to General Sir Ralph Abercromby in the Mediterranean. He briefly occupied Lisbon with a small military force before returning home at the end of 1800.

Murray-Pulteney survived a censure motion in the House of Commons relating to Ferrol on 19 February 1801 and later commanded the troops in Sussex during the invasion scare of 1803–4. His next appointment was as secretary at war in the Portland administration, from March 1807 until his resignation in June 1809. While in office he concentrated on army recruitment, introducing legislation to increase the militia and easing the transfer of men from these formations to the regular army. He was a supporter of the duke of York and favoured the inquiry into his administration of the army, believing that it would lead to the duke's exoneration. He was promoted general on 25 April 1808.

There are several descriptions of Murray-Pulteney by contemporaries. A conversation with him in November 1793 led Lieutenant Thomas Fenwick to write: 'He is a strange kind of man, and seldom knows what he is saying' (Leslie, 31). While admiring his courage and intelligence, Henry Bunbury (an aide-de-camp to the duke of York in 1799) stated that he was indecisive and a dreamer. Bunbury added that:

> Pulteney had awkward manners; received officers uncouthly; did not know, or seem to care, how to put them at their ease; and till one came to know him in intimacy … the kindness of his nature, the extent of his knowledge, and the largeness of his views remained hidden under a grotesque and somewhat repulsive exterior.   (Bunbury, 30–31)

This notwithstanding, Murray-Pulteney was generally regarded as being able and active.

Murray-Pulteney died on 26 April 1811 as a result of injuries received from the explosion of the powder in a copper flask while out shooting on his rented estate at Buckenham, Norfolk. He was buried at Buckenham. Since he had no children, his estates and title devolved on his half-brother John *Murray (1768?–1827), who became eighth baronet, and although he was not in possession of his wife's fortune after her death, he was still able to leave £600,000 to his brother John and £200,000 to his other younger brother, the Revd William Murray.

R. N. W. THOMAS

Sources GEC, *Baronetage*, vol. 2 · *GM*, 1st ser., 81/1 (1811), 499 · Burke, *Peerage* · Fortescue, *Brit. army* · R. G. Thorne, 'Murray (afterwards Pulteney), Sir James', HoP, *Commons, 1790–1820* · *Army List* (1762–1811) · *An accurate account and impartial narrative of the war by an officer of the guards*, 3rd edn, 2 vols. (1796) · *The later correspondence* of George III, ed. A. Aspinall, 5 vols. (1962–70), vol. 2 • *The correspondence of George, prince of Wales, 1770–1812*, ed. A. Aspinall, 7: 1810–1811 (1970) • *Old Westminsters*, vols. 1–2 • H. Bunbury, *Narratives of some passages in the great war with France (1799–1810)*, [new edn] (1927) • J. H. Leslie, 'Campaigning in 1793: Flanders', *Journal of the Society for Army Historical Research*, 8 (1928), 2–32 • *The Taylor papers, being a record of certain reminiscences, letters and journals in the life of Lieut.-Gen. Sir Herbert Taylor*, ed. E. Taylor (1913)

Archives Morgan L., corresp. and MSS, MA487, MA297, MA1260–1290 • NL Scot., legal corresp. and MSS, MSS 1410–1412 | BL, Auckland MSS, Add. MSS 34447–34448 • PRO, Chatham MSS, PRO 30/8/162 • PRO, commander-in-chief in-letters, WO 1/166, 167 • PRO, letters to William Pitt, PRO 30/8

Wealth at death £800,000: *GM*, 499

Pulteney [Neale], **Sir John** (*d.* 1349), merchant and mayor of London, was probably the son of Adam Neale, or Neel, of Clipston in Leicestershire, rather than of Clipston in west Sussex, as has been suggested. His mother was Matilda Napton, daughter of a Warwickshire landowner. Pulteney was probably married twice, on both occasions to a wife called Margaret. He had married first by 1333, when he was granted permission to choose a confessor for himself and his wife, of whom little is otherwise known. He had married his second wife by 1341, when their son William was born. The second Margaret was the daughter of John St John of Lageham; within a year of being widowed she had married Sir Nicholas Loveyn. It is possible that Pulteney had a son of his first marriage, also named William, who predeceased him. He had a brother and a sister; the latter, Ellen, married William Owen and their son, Robert, inherited the family lands. Both his brother and sister predeceased him.

Pulteney was not a Londoner. Although the extent of the family lands suggests that the Pulteneys were among the substantial minor landowners of Leicestershire, he moved to the city from his family lands, probably in search of higher social status through the opportunities that trade afforded for enrichment and land purchase. He was established in London by 1316, when he was appointed attorney with Simon Swanlond, mayor from 1324 to 1330, for Ralph Walecote, a London merchant who was travelling overseas on pilgrimage; and he stood surety for Richard Bluntesham and William Flete, merchants of London, who were supplying corn to the royal fortresses of Berwick and Newcastle. He had achieved citizenship by May 1322.

Pulteney became a wealthy merchant who dealt in wool and wine and traded overseas. He was a draper and moneylender with extensive business dealings among the foreign merchants in London. He supplied the king's wardrobe and the royal army overseas in 1338. He lent money to merchants, clerics, minor gentry, knights, and nobles, including Sir William Zouche, the earl of Huntingdon, the earl of Kent, and the prior of the hospital of St John of Jerusalem in England. Throughout the 1330s and 1340s, moreover, Pulteney had a close financial involvement with the crown, making twenty-six loans between 1332 and 1347 to the exchequer of receipt. Many of these loans, which ranged from a few pounds to £1100, were termed 'for the King's secret affairs'. Often he acted as a guarantor for royal repayment of debts. It is not surprising that these close links with the crown benefited him. He was knighted in February 1337, and granted an annuity of 100 marks to support this knighthood. After 1326 he was regularly granted exemption from taxation and from royal and civic offices, and in 1341 he obtained a licence to crenellate his manor houses in Cambridgeshire, Kent, and London. Such closeness also had its dangers. In 1341 he was arrested when Edward III returned from France, and his conduct investigated for corruption or mismanagement. He was imprisoned in Somerton Castle, Lincolnshire, and only released in 1343.

Pulteney was alderman of Coleman Street ward (1327–34), of Candlewick Street ward (1334), and of Vintry ward (1335–8), and he may have been alderman of Farringdon ward in 1334 also. Mayor in 1331, 1332, 1334, and 1337, he represented the city at royal councils in 1328 and 1345; and in January 1329 he was appointed by the city to meet the king to assure him of London's loyalty in the aftermath of the rebellion of Henry, duke of Lancaster. In 1335, 1336, and 1340 he acted on behalf of the city in its dealings with the crown. He was appointed to array troops for the campaign in Scotland in 1335, and for the campaign in France in 1337, and in 1338 he was one of those entrusted with the organization of the city's defences. Pulteney was also frequently employed by the crown. Thus he was commissioned in 1332 to investigate the establishment of a wool staple at Bruges, in 1339 to investigate complaints concerning taxation and the decline in business at Westminster, and in 1343–4 to audit the accounts of Italian merchant houses in England. For almost every year between 1332 and 1345 he was a commissioner of oyer and terminer. He was a royal envoy overseas in 1334, 1336, and 1338, and collector of customs and subsidies in London in 1343–4.

At his death Pulteney held land in Cambridgeshire, Hertfordshire, Kent, Leicestershire, Middlesex, Northamptonshire, Suffolk, and Warwickshire. The great hall of his manor house at Penshurst Place in Kent is arguably the finest surviving example of mid-fourteenth-century domestic architecture. In London he held a number of small properties and two major ones: Pulteney's Inn, later called the Manor of the Rose, in St Lawrence's parish, which his wife and son inherited; and The Coldharbour in the parish of All Hallows-the-Great, which was sold at his death and became the residence of Edward, prince of Wales, until 1359. Pulteney died during the black death on 8 June 1349, although the cause of his death is unknown. Nor is it certain where he was buried, although Stow states that he was buried in the chantry chapel that he had endowed in St Paul's Cathedral. C. L. Kingsford argues that Pulteney was buried at St Lawrence's, Candlewick Street, as he requested in his will, and which the dean and chapter of St Paul's confirmed in 1439. Both in his will and during his lifetime Pulteney made many religious benefactions; these included the establishment of the chapel of Corpus Christi in St Lawrence's Church, Candlewick Street, the building of the church of All Hallows-the-Less, Thames Street, and his chantry at St Paul's Cathedral. The

supervisors of his will were the earl of Huntingdon and the bishop of London. His son having died in 1367 without heir, the family property passed to his sister's family from whom William Pulteney, earl of Bath (*d.* 1764), the earls of Harborough, and the barons and earls of Crewe, were descended.
ROGER L. AXWORTHY

Sources M. Livingstone, 'Sir John de Pulteney's landed estates: the acquisition and management of land by a London merchant', MA diss., Royal Holloway College, Egham, Surrey, 1990 · exchequer documents, PRO · chancery documents, PRO · R. R. Sharpe, ed., *Calendar of letter-books preserved in the archives of the corporation of the City of London*, [12 vols.] (1899–1912), vols. F, G · A. H. Thomas and P. E. Jones, eds., *Calendar of plea and memoranda rolls preserved among the archives of the corporation of the City of London at the Guildhall*, 6 vols. (1926–61) · CLRO, Husting rolls · CKS · J. Stow, *A survey of London*, rev. edn (1603); repr. with introduction by C. L. Kingsford as *A survey of London*, 2 vols. (1908); repr. with addns (1971) · DNB · Rymer, *Foedera*, new edn · C. L. Kingsford, 'Historical notes on medieval London houses', *London Topographical Record*, 10 (1916), 44–144 · P. Norman, 'Sir John Pulteney and his two residences in London … with a few remarks on the parish of St. Laurence Poultney', *Archaeologia*, 57 (1900–01), 257–84 · S. L. Thrupp, *The merchant class of medieval London, 1300–1500* (1948) · J. Alexander and P. Binski, eds., *Age of chivalry: art in Plantagenet England, 1200–1400* (1987), 271–2 [exhibition catalogue, RA]

Pulteney [*formerly* Johnstone], (**Henrietta**) **Laura**, *suo jure* **countess of Bath** (**1766–1808**), heiress, was born on 26 December 1766 in Cleveland Row, St James's, Westminster, the only child of William Johnstone (1729–1805), from 1794 fifth baronet [*see* Pulteney, Sir William], and his wife, Frances (1728?–1782), daughter of Daniel *Pulteney. In 1767 her mother inherited the estates of her kinsman General Harry Pulteney, who had in turn inherited them from his brother, the politician William Pulteney, earl of Bath; her parents took the name Pulteney and moved to Bath House, Piccadilly, where Laura (as she was known) spent her childhood. On her mother's death, she inherited the vast Pulteney fortune and properties, subject to a partial life interest to her father.

Initially educated at home under the supervision of her father's cousin, Miss Murray, Laura completed her education at the convent of Montparnasse in Paris in 1783. Her letters to her father show that she responded well to the nuns' instruction. They also show that her social education was not neglected. She mentions visits from her kinswoman Elizabeth Hope, countess of Hopetoun; her friend Henrietta Lowry-Corry, Lady Belmore; and Anne Cochrane, countess of Dundonald, who introduced her to Parisian society. Although her education by a female relation and then at a convent seemed to follow an orthodox pattern, at a later date her education was reported by the *European Magazine* as having been 'after the manner of Jean Jacques Rousseau; with what success this manner has here been adopted does not belong to me to say'.

Laura took a lively interest in her father's development of her estates in London, Bath, Shropshire, Northamptonshire, Staffordshire, and Wales. His success and his entrepreneurial development of his own Scottish, West Indian, and huge American estates, and her increasingly direct involvement, contributed to her reputation both as the richest heiress in England, and as a cautious and shrewd

(Henrietta) Laura Pulteney, *suo jure* countess of Bath (1766–1808), by Angelica Kauffman, *c.*1777

businesswoman. Letters from her father in 1791 and 1802, for example, refer to sending receipts for American debentures and endorsing bills, and a letter from her father to her husband chides them for their tardiness in responding on matters relating to the upkeep of the Pulteney Bridge in Bath. After her death she was described as having gained 'much useful knowledge, and in those affairs which may be called business, she was considered an expert, and was certainly persevering when she did apply them' (*Bath Herald*). Her wealth allowed her a wide scope for philanthropy, and she endowed schools at Sudborough in Northamptonshire and at Clewer in Berkshire, and also supported nuns who had fled France following the revolution.

Laura's health was always a cause for concern; in a reply to a letter from her father early in 1782, she assured him that she was obeying instructions that she take plenty of exercise while she was in Paris. As a young woman she spent time living in the country at Sudborough with the Revd Archibald Alison, writer on taste, and his wife. Sudborough was a Pulteney living and the Alisons were close friends. She was godmother to their son, the physician and social reformer William Pulteney Alison. Laura continued to move in aristocratic circles although she was never a leader of fashion. She seems particularly to have enjoyed music and dancing, and a piece of dance music, 'Miss Pulteney's Fancy', by an anonymous composer, was published by Longmans in 1791.

The Pulteney family's wealth made them independent of the government, and although Laura's father never sought office he did procure a peerage for his daughter, who in 1792 was created baroness of Bath. Although the family had held the earldom of Bath earlier in the century a marquessate of Bath had been created for Thomas Thynne, third Viscount Weymouth, in 1789, and some lords attempted to have the creation cancelled on the grounds that the use of the same place name in two separate peerages was unprecedented and that Laura's title implicitly disinherited the Thynnes. Their protest was rejected, and in 1803 Laura was promoted to countess of Bath.

Laura should have been attractive to noble suitors on the basis of her fortune alone, but in 1791 a newspaper asked whether it was 'from the reluctance of our unmarried gentlemen to ask *too much*, or the extreme nicety of the lady, that Miss Pulteney, perhaps the richest spinster in Europe, has at present no ostensible suitor?' (*Gazetteer and New Daily Advertiser*, 25 Feb 1791, quoted Walpole, *Corr.*, 11.238n.). In the event, she married on 17 July 1794, by special licence at Bath House, General Sir James Murray of Claremont, seventh baronet (*c*.1755–1811) [*see* Pulteney, Sir James Murray-], a first cousin of her father. He took the additional surname Pulteney. The marriage was childless. They made the grand tour in 1795 and her increasingly unpredictable temperament was the subject of comment by Emma, Lady Hamilton, in Naples.

> She is very shy … she envited all the Neapolitan ladies of the first distinction, and I was to present them, and she took a nervous fit and wou'd not come out of her room for three hours. … Sir William [Hamilton] says he would not have her with all her money. (Ingamells, 60)

Lady Bath was deeply religious, but she did not condemn friends who broke society's moral conventions. When her cousin and close companion Elizabeth Evelyn Markham (*née* Sutton) was divorced in 1802 by the Revd George Markham, son of William Markham, archbishop of York, and later himself dean of York, on the grounds of adultery with John Fawcett, Mrs Markham married Fawcett and they remained under the protection of Lady Bath. The condoning of this divorce and, earlier, that of her friend Lady Belmore, who in 1793 divorced her husband to marry William Kerr, earl of Ancram, indicates a remarkably liberal attitude in sexual matters.

In 1805 Sir William Pulteney died intestate and his personal estate passed to his second wife and to his only daughter. Lady Bath paid duty of £6000 which was at the time the largest single payment ever recorded. She inherited two-thirds of his estimated £600,000 personal estate together with his landed property in England and America. Unfortunately she controlled the entire Pulteney fortune for only three years before she died on 14 July 1808, at The Steyne, Brighton, Sussex. Her death may have been caused by tuberculosis. To the end, contemporaries regarded her as eccentric: 'Of her peculiarities she was herself very sensible, and more than once observed, that she believed that people thought her very odd and to sometimes use a harsher term' (*Bath Herald*). She was buried on 23 July in the south cloister of Westminster Abbey under the large stone known as Great Meg. Surprisingly no monument was ever erected. Her will left her personal estate, amounting to £500,000, apart from some minor legacies and subject to her husband's customary rights, to her cousin Elizabeth Evelyn Fawcett, whose husband then adopted the Pulteney name. Her immense landed estates passed under family settlements to William Henry *Vane, third earl of Darlington (later first duke of Cleveland) and Sir Richard Sutton bt. She was survived by her husband, who died on 26 April 1811. As they had no children, her titles, limited to heirs male of her body, became extinct.

M. J. ROWE and W. H. MCBRYDE

Sources GEC, *Peerage*, new edn · *European Magazine*, 22 (1792), 15 · J. Ingamells, ed., *A dictionary of British and Irish travellers in Italy, 1701–1800* (1997) · *The letters of Horace Walpole, fourth earl of Orford*, ed. P. Toynbee, 16 vols. (1903–5) · *The Phoenix and Patriot, or, Blagdon's Weekly Chronicler* (24 June 1808) · *Bath Herald* (24 June 1809) · RIBA BAL, Cotterel collection, box 22 · JHL, 39 (1790–93), 561–4 · Walpole, *Corr.*, 11.238 · Westminster Abbey archives
Archives Hunt. L., letters · priv. coll.
Likenesses A. Kauffman, oils, *c*.1777, Holburne Museum of Art, Bath [*see illus.*] · Cosway, miniature (Pulteney?), V&A · pencil sketch, Hunt. L.
Wealth at death £500,000—plus enormous settled landed estates: PRO, PROB 11/1483, sig. 626

Pulteney, Richard (1730–1801), botanist and physician, was born on 17 February 1730 at Loughborough, Leicestershire, the sole survivor of the eleven children of Samuel Pulteney (1674–1754), a prosperous tailor, and Mary Tomlinson (1692–1759), a native of the nearby village of Hathern. The family belonged to a sect known as Old Anabaptists. As a pupil at the Old Free School, Loughborough, he already displayed an enthusiasm for botany and natural history, encouraged by the example of his uncle George Tomlinson. At the age of fifteen he was apprenticed for seven years to an apothecary of Loughborough. In 1752 he settled as a surgeon and apothecary in Leicester, but as a dissenter he met with a degree of hostility and prejudice which compromised the success of his practice.

More encouraging was Pulteney's increasing acceptance as a respected botanist by a widening circle of friends and correspondents. Prominent among these was William Watson, who became an influential friend and mentor, and by the loan of books such as the *Flora Anglica* of Linnaeus enabled the young apothecary to further his study of botany. In 1750 Pulteney began to publish articles in the *Gentleman's Magazine*, mainly on botanical topics such as the new Linnaean system of botanical classification. With typical modesty he left these early writings unsigned or merely initialled. These papers were sent for correction and comment to Watson who then passed them on to the *Gentleman's Magazine* or to the Royal Society for publication in the *Philosophical Transactions*. In 1756 Pulteney was thanked by Lord Macclesfield, president of the Royal Society, for his *Account of the More Rare Plants Observed in Leicestershire*.

A turning point in Pulteney's career came in 1764, when, in spite of his natural diffidence, he was persuaded to take a medical degree at Edinburgh University. Although he had already been elected FRS in 1762, he realized that a medical qualification was vital to his advancement.

Richard Pulteney (1730–1801), by P. Roberts, pubd 1805 (after Thomas Beach, 1788)

Accompanied by his friend Maxwell Garthshore he took the necessary examinations and graduated in May 1764. His inaugural dissertation, on the medicinal properties of Peruvian bark (*Cinchona officinalis*) enabled him to display both his medical and botanical knowledge. The graduation of Pulteney and Garthshore after barely three months' residence aroused deep resentment among less favoured students, particularly Americans and fellow botanists. Their protest caused Pulteney much anguish, but friends rallied round, notably John Hope, professor of medicine and botany at Edinburgh University. That same year also brought disappointment to hopes of aristocratic patronage with the death of Lord Macclesfield, to whom Pulteney had intended to dedicate his thesis. A further setback came with the death in July of William Pulteney, earl of Bath, who had acknowledged Pulteney as a relative and appointed him as his domestic physician; Pulteney then had the task of finding a new situation, for absence had destroyed his prospects in Leicester. Financial considerations made his ambition to live in London and travel to Leiden or Paris impossible, but in 1765, assisted by letters of recommendation from Watson and George Baker, he secured the practice of physician in Blandford, Dorset, a position he vainly hoped would be temporary.

After initial difficulties, Pulteney established himself as a successful and popular physician but he regretted that he could not devote himself wholly to the study of botany. In an undated letter to John Hope written shortly after the move he commented bitterly on the low esteem in which botany was held; display of any knowledge of it, he claimed, would harm his reputation as a medical man. In spite of this intellectual exile, however, he found it possible, through an expanding network of correspondents such as Thomas Martyn and William Withering, to keep up with developments in medicine and natural science. In 1767 he became acquainted with Margaret Cavendish Bentinck, dowager duchess of Portland, an enthusiastic conchologist, who would visit him on her way to collect shells at Weymouth. He sent the duchess plants and she provided him with shells for his own collection, some brought over in 1771 from New Zealand on Captain James Cook's ship *Endeavour*.

In 1779 Pulteney married Elizabeth Galton of Blandford (1739–1820); they had no children. Three years later he published his most significant work, *A General View of the Writings of Linnaeus*, which contained the first biography of Linnaeus in English. In his memoir of Pulteney in Rees's *Cyclopaedia* (vol. 23, 1813) Sir James Edward Smith stated that this book 'has contributed more than any work, except perhaps the *Tracts of Stillingfleet*, to diffuse a taste for Linnaean knowledge in this country'. The Royal Academy of Sciences of Stockholm presented Pulteney with two medals struck in honour of Linnaeus as a mark of appreciation and a French translation of the book by L. A. Millin de Grandmaison (1789) drew favourable comments on the continent. His second book, *Historical and Biographical Sketches of the Progress of Botany in England* (1790), was less popular, but it was still valued by historians two centuries later.

In 1790 Pulteney was elected a fellow of the Linnean Society which had been instituted by Smith, its first president, in 1788. He published several papers in the *Transactions* and bequeathed his herbarium and collections of shells and minerals to the society.

Pulteney is remembered as a zealous promoter of the methods and nomenclature of Linnaeus and as a historian of botany in Britain. His benevolence, integrity, and tolerance endeared him to his contemporaries. His papers, preserved in the archives of the Linnean Society library, incorporate a lifetime's correspondence with most of the eminent botanists and physicians of his day and provide an important and fascinating commentary on the history of natural science in the latter half of the eighteenth century. He died of pneumonia at Langton near Blandford on 13 October 1801 and was buried in Langton churchyard. His wife placed a memorial tablet to him in Blandford church engraved with a sprig of *Pultenaea stipularis*, an Australian shrub named by J. E. Smith in his honour.

I. D. HUGHES

Sources Linn. Soc., Pulteney papers · W. G. Maton, 'Introduction', in R. Pulteney, *General view of the writings of Linnaeus*, 2nd edn (1805) · J. E. Smith, 'Memoir of Pulteney', in A. Rees and others, *The cyclopaedia, or, Universal dictionary of arts, sciences, and literature*, 45 vols. (1819–20), vol. 23 · J. Nichols, *The history and antiquities of the county of Leicester*, 3 (1800–04) · R. Jeffers, *Richard Pulteney and his correspondence* (1960) [unique copy in Linn. Soc. library; incl. bibliography]
Archives Leics. RO, catalogue of Loughborough plants · Linn. Soc., corresp. and papers · MHS Oxf., drawings · NHM, letters and catalogue · RS, papers | BL, corresp. with E. M. da Costa, Add. MS 28541 · BM, herbarium · Linn. Soc., letters to Sir James Smith

Likenesses T. Beach, oils, 1788, Linn. Soc. · T. Beach, oils, 1788, Leicester City Art Gallery · J. Basire, engraving (after T. Beach, 1804), repro. in Nichols, *History and antiquities* · J. Basire, engraving (after T. Beach), repro. in Nichols, *Lit. anecdotes*, 8 (1814), 196 · F. Mackenzie, engraving (after drawing by R. Hancock, 1798), repro. in *Philosophical Magazine* (1802) · P. Roberts, engraving (after T. Beach, 1788), NPG; repro. in Pulteney, *General view of the writings of Linnaeus* [*see illus.*]

Wealth at death over £10,000; incl. stocks, books, and scientific collections plus property at Langton, Dorset, and Loughborough and Hathern, Leicestershire: will, PRO, PROB 11/1366

Pulteney, William, earl of Bath (1684–1764), politician, was born on 22 March 1684 and baptized in London on 28 or 29 March 1684, at St Martin-in-the-Fields, Trafalgar Square, the eldest son of Colonel William Pulteney (*b.* in or after 1655, *d.* 1715) and his first wife, Mary Floyd. His grandfather Sir William Pulteney (1624–1691), a descendant of the Pulteneys of Misterton, in Leicestershire, was a substantial London landowner and MP for Westminster (1679–81 and 1689–91); his aunt Anne married Charles Fitzroy, second duke of Cleveland, natural son of Charles II and Barbara Villiers. Pulteney was educated at Westminster School and at Christ Church, Oxford, where he matriculated on 31 October 1700. He was a noted classical scholar and was chosen to deliver the congratulatory speech to Queen Anne on her visit in 1702. In parallel to his classical scholarship he developed a skill in sports, excelling particularly at horse riding and fencing. The earliest known portrait of him depicts him as a boy with a hawk on his arm.

Following Oxford, Pulteney made the grand tour in 1704–5, his presence recorded in Padua in October 1704, Rome in 1705, and Venice and Augsburg in August 1705. While visiting Hanover in the summer of 1705 he was called home to take his seat as MP for Hedon, in Yorkshire, which he had won in the 1705 general election, at the age of twenty-one. He owed this seat to the patronage of Henry Guy, former secretary to the Treasury, who was a close friend of the family and a trustee of the will of Sir William Pulteney. On the death of his sister in 1692 Guy had settled his estates for the ultimate benefit of Pulteney.

Early political career From the outset of his parliamentary career Pulteney was a whig, and voted in October 1705 for John Smith, the whig candidate for the speakership of the House of Commons. The presence of his uncle John Pulteney in the Commons makes identification difficult for Pulteney's early years in the House. However, he supported the court in February 1706 over the place clause promoted by the country whigs as an amendment to the Regency Bill. Pulteney's political gifts saw him earmarked as a rising whig star; Thomas Wharton, first earl of Wharton, had him in mind in 1708 as his secretary following his appointment as lord lieutenant of Ireland. About this date Pulteney fell into the orbit of another rising whig, Robert Walpole, with whom he was to be associated for most of his political career, first as an ally, then as a deadly political foe. It may have been Walpole who introduced Pulteney to the Kit-Cat Club, the centre of the whig élite's social

William Pulteney, earl of Bath (1684–1764), by Allan Ramsay, 1762

activities. Pulteney's active social life occasionally caused him trouble; in January 1709 it was reported that:

> the Pulteney which is distinguished as Henry Guy's heir—he had a quarrel with a gentleman at the Playhouse, and they went outside to decide it, but before he got out of the passage there came two more and drew their swords upon him, but the footmen and chairmen prevented any mischief that night. (*Wentworth Papers*, 71)

However, the next morning Pulteney met the man again and knocked him down with his cane, leading to another fracas and to fears of a vendetta. In parliament Pulteney continued to toe the whig line, voting in February 1709 for the naturalization of the Palatines and in March 1710 for the impeachment of Dr Henry Sacheverell.

Following the installation of a tory ministry under Robert Harley (later earl of Oxford) in autumn 1710 Pulteney faced a rare challenge at Hedon in the ensuing general election, held in October. He defeated his tory rival with ease and survived a subsequent petition against his return. The death of Henry Guy, in February 1711, left him independently rich. He inherited from Guy an estate at Stoke Newington, Middlesex, another at Muswell Hill, and money and other property, eventually realizing some £20,000, which was to be invested in land. Guy also left Pulteney his property at Hedon, which included the town hall, where portraits of both of them hang and which formed the basis for his political control of the borough. In parliament Pulteney continued to support the whigs, possibly with sufficient effect to ensure that his uncle John lost his government post on the Board of Trade in June 1711. On 7 December 1711 he voted for the 'No peace without Spain' motion. In January 1712 he defended first

Walpole and then John Churchill, duke of Marlborough, against charges of corruption relating to government army contracts. Pulteney kept in close touch with Walpole when the latter was incarcerated in the Tower, although intemperate language in a debate on 28 May 1712 on the restraining orders issued to James Butler, second duke of Ormond, in which he described the ministry as 'weak and treacherous' (Hanham), angered the tories so much that he was in danger of being sent to join him. At the opening of the 1713 session Pulteney spoke and voted against the address, and was soon a key debater in the campaign against the peace made at Utrecht and the commercial treaty with France. Nor was Pulteney's opposition confined to the debating chamber; in 1713 he penned the satirical dedication to Lord Treasurer Oxford affixed to Walpole's *Short History of a Parliament* and he was a subscriber to a fund designed to enable Emperor Charles VI to continue the war following the Utrecht settlement. In the parliamentary session of 1714 Pulteney was again at the forefront of whig critics of the ministry, particularly their attempt to expel Richard Steele from the Commons in March. Pulteney was also one of the first to allude publicly to the widening fissure in the tory ministry between Oxford and Bolingbroke in June 1714, noting that 'he did not know who the ministry was, or whether we had any, or how such as are reckoned can be relied on, seeing they cannot trust one another' (ibid.). Not surprisingly Pulteney was one of those whigs courted by Bolingbroke in late July 1714 in a desperate attempt to shore up his crumbling political position.

Office The short parliamentary session following the accession of George I, in August 1714, saw Pulteney support provision of a reward of £100,000 for the capture of the Pretender. Pulteney's own prize for his steadfast support of the whig cause in the latter years of Queen Anne's reign was his appointment as secretary-at-war in October 1714. One account has Pulteney taking the post at the old salary—£1000 less than usual—'that his majesty might have £1,000 a year to gratify somebody else', adding that 'this story he [Pulteney] tells himself' (*Wentworth Papers*, 425). On 27 December 1714 Pulteney married Anna Maria (1694–1758), one of three daughters and coheirs of John Gumley (d. 1728) of Isleworth, a mirror-glass- and cabinet-maker, who provided her with a portion of £6000. Through his son-in-law's influence Gumley became deputy commissary-general of the army in 1716, MP for Steyning in 1722, and commissary-general in 1724. The new couple set up house in Arlington Street, Piccadilly. Pulteney's wife was acknowledged as very good-looking but she had attracted a reputation for having been free with her favours, at least before their marriage, and this was later to be used to punishing effect by satirists intent upon attacking her husband. Thus she appears in one print with her bare backside being used as a desk by a secretary and later she was branded 'Mrs Pony' and 'Bath's ennobled Doxy'. Like Pulteney she was also perceived to be interested in the accumulation of wealth, and she was notable for successfully managing her own separate fortune. Both Pulteneys were reputed to have sharp tongues, Horace

Walpole later referring to 'my Lord and Lady Bath who live in a vinegar bottle' (*Letters*, 16). A son and a daughter lived beyond infancy, but neither survived their father.

The death of his father, in 1715, saw Pulteney inherit a life interest in the London estates settled by the will of his grandfather. This property primarily comprised part of Cleveland Row opposite St James's Palace, together with a large part of the western side of Soho and two pieces of land on the northern side of Piccadilly, at that time undeveloped. Pulteney immediately began to plan developments and improvements across the whole estate. The development in Soho is today represented by the area bounded by Wardour Street and Carnaby Street, with Great Pulteney Street at its heart. In Piccadilly the eastern portion extends from Piccadilly Circus to Sackville Street, and the western area covers Bolton Street to Down Street. It was on this portion that Pulteney built his London home—known after his elevation to the peerage as Bath House—to the designs of Giacomo Leoni in 1735. Surviving records show that in spite of the Pulteneys' reputation for parsimony the house was furnished and equipped expensively and in the fashionable taste of the period. The house was demolished and rebuilt in 1821.

In April 1715 Pulteney served on the committee of secrecy appointed to investigate the conduct of the recent peace negotiations that had led to the peace of Utrecht and to the impeachment of the earl of Oxford. On 9 January 1716 he moved the impeachment of Lord Widdrington for his involvement in the 1715 rising, and later opposed a motion to the king requesting clemency for Jacobite recantors. He was sworn of the privy council on 6 July 1716. In the split in whig ranks in 1717 he sided with Charles, second Viscount Townshend, and with Walpole, and, following the dismissal of the first and the resignation of the second, he and Sir Paul Methuen resigned on 11 April 1717. For the next three years Pulteney was a whig in opposition to the whig ministry. As early as 4 June 1717 he made a long speech attacking William, first Baron Cadogan, a mainstay of the Sunderland–Stanhope ministry, charging him with fraud and embezzlement over the costs of transporting troops. However, Pulteney was not an unthinking follower of Walpole, and refused to join him in January 1718 in voting with the tories to reduce the standing army. Pulteney voted against the repeal of the occasional conformity and schism bills in January 1719 and opposed the Peerage Bill in December 1719.

Pulteney's first real cause for disagreement with Walpole followed the negotiations in April 1720 that saw Walpole return to political favour with a leading role at the Treasury and a promise that those whigs who had resigned with him would be brought back into office. When the other whigs were given office at the end of the session all Pulteney was offered was a peerage, which he refused with some indignation. His reasons for declining this offer were probably political because his estate could certainly bear the burdens of a peerage and he may have felt that Walpole was deliberately sidelining him as a dangerous rival for power. Pulteney's recent foray into the South Sea Company had increased his wealth, as he had sold out before the 'bubble' burst and incidentally enhanced his reputation for understanding public finance. Further, from the resultant profits he purchased the Bathwick estate, comprising 600 acres of agricultural and nursery-garden land on the east side of the River Avon opposite Bath. Although he improved the management of this estate he did not develop it beyond providing land for the creation of pleasure gardens for visitors to the increasingly fashionable spa. It was left to another generation to build the major extension to Bath known as the Pulteney estate and exploit its valuable sources of pure spring water. Concurrently Pulteney used his own and his wife's money to purchase the Wrington estate, of about 4000 acres, in north Somerset. This completed his major acquisition of income-producing land.

Pulteney showed his resentment at his omission from the ministry through a series of speeches in the Commons criticizing Walpole, most notably on 14 July 1721, when he accused him of changing his mind according to whether he was in or out of office, and again, on 16 February 1722, when he spoke of Walpole's attitude to financial questions being influenced by his investments in the Bank of England. Nevertheless he was given the prestigious lord lieutenancy of the East Riding of Yorkshire in December 1721, and the Pulteney estates in London were converted from a lease from the crown into a freehold. Pulteney remained a whig, taking charge of, and reporting from, the committee appointed to examine the relevant papers, and leading the examination of Christopher Layer and other Jacobite conspirators. His extensive parliamentary work on the Layer case between January and March 1723 was rewarded in May 1723, when he was appointed cofferer of the household. These favours may have helped to keep Pulteney loyal to the ministry but they were inconsiderable when compared to a major office of state. When John, second Baron Carteret, was replaced as secretary of state in April 1724 Pulteney expected to be given the office, which instead went to Thomas Pelham-Holles, duke of Newcastle. In the following parliamentary session Pulteney openly opposed Walpole's proposal for discharging a civil list debt in April 1725, even accusing Walpole of increasing his fortune 'by indirect means and corruption' and of squandering public money on bribing MPs. After criticizing the proposal at every stage Pulteney eventually voted for the bill, claiming that he did so at the personal request of the king. However, this did not prevent his dismissal from the cofferer's post at the end of the parliamentary session in May 1725.

Opposition Pulteney may have led only a small group into opposition, possibly as few as seventeen, but he was soon to make clear his opposition to the Walpole ministry, speaking on the address on 20 January 1726 'not to oppose it, only to show in what a sad condition we were in to go to war' (Sedgwick, 'Introductory survey', 35). This was a precursor of the motion of 9 February 1726 for a committee of investigation into the management of the public debts. Although this initiative was defeated it did allow an opposition group to begin to coalesce around Pulteney,

and this included some tories, such as Sir William Wyndham. Foreign policy proved to be another fruitful area of co-operation for the opposition, and on 16 February 1726 Pulteney attacked the treaty of Hanover (1725) for having been solely intended to serve the interests of Hanover and for reversing Britain's traditional alliance with Austria. Pulteney continued his opposition in the following session, asking on 21 February 1727 for an account of the money spent on secret service payments. However, he resisted the intrigues of Charles VI, who hoped that a change of foreign policy could be effected by a change of ministry, even going so far as to back the address of 13 March 1727 supporting the treaty of Hanover.

As a vehicle for their burgeoning campaign against the Walpole ministry, on 5 December 1726 Pulteney, his cousin Daniel (son of his uncle John Pulteney), and the recently returned exile Henry St John, Viscount Bolingbroke, launched *The Craftsman*, initially as a weekly single-sheet publication. It soon developed into a twice-weekly paper that achieved a circulation estimated at 13,000 at its peak, in 1731. The anonymous articles were collated by Nicholas Amherst, and not all the authors were identified, so that some pieces remain unattributable. Pulteney was a major contributor, and his scholarship, literary background, and journalistic versatility set him apart from other contributors, so that it is probable that the majority of his articles have been correctly attributed. Most of Pulteney's literary output was in the form of anonymous pamphlets that were attributed to him at the time on the grounds of a recognizable style. His ability to communicate in an approachable manner, however complex the matters of state under discussion, allowed him to win a wide range of public support and understanding. He was considered a humorous writer but his attacks on his enemies in parliament and at court were sometimes vicious, lacking in subtlety, and over-fond of intemperate language. He was able to slip quickly from the reasoned argument into the heights of passion, and in speeches he was sometimes openly abusive. No doubt his wit in particular benefited from the friendship of Jonathan Swift, John Gay, and Alexander Pope, all of whom penned anti-ministerial material. Indeed, together with Pulteney, all of them seemed to have been involved in the good-humoured banter that arose from the publication of a series of satirical verses to be sung to the tune of 'Molly Mogg', which ran for several weeks in *Mist's Weekly Journal* in 1726. To such a well-qualified commentator on literary merit as Philip Dormer Stanhope, fourth earl of Chesterfield, Pulteney had:

> lively and shining parts; a surprising quickness of wit; and a happy turn to the most amusing and entertaining kinds of poetry, epigrams, ballads, odes, etc, in all which he had an uncommon facility. His compositions were sometimes satirical, often licentious, but always full of wit.
> (*Miscellaneous Works*, 25)

The death of George I, on 10 June 1727, provided Pulteney with a significant chance of displacing Walpole, because he had been careful to cultivate the prince of Wales, now George II. However, the new queen, Caroline, was a strong supporter of Walpole, and this defeated Pulteney's attempts to undermine him by pressing for an increase in the civil list to £800,000 per annum, which Walpole was able to obtain from parliament in any case. Pulteney was even rebuffed when he was refused leave to stand for Westminster on the court interest, which when added to being 'never consulted in the closet and always very coldly received in the drawing room' (Sedgwick, 'Pulteney', 1.375) led him back into opposition. He duly renewed his attack on the government's financial policy in a pamphlet entitled *A State of the National Debt* (1727), in which he examined the worsening situation between 1716 and 1725. This challenge to Walpole's financial competency led to a debate on 22 February 1728 in which the workings of the sinking fund were laid before the Commons. On 29 February Pulteney undertook to prove the allegations contained in his pamphlet, but in the resultant debate on 8 March he was defeated by a large majority. After the end of the session, in July 1728, he was even replaced as lord lieutenant of the East Riding.

At the beginning of the 1729 session Pulteney refused to vote against the address on 21 January in case it was seen as 'a want of respect to his Majesty' (Colley, 209). This had the added advantage of allowing Pulteney to exploit any openings at court caused by the growing rift between Walpole and Viscount Townshend. Indeed on 31 January 1729, when Pulteney was disparaged in the Commons for opposing the ministry merely to return to office, he responded that:

> he was so far from desiring employments that he took pains to get rid of that he had, and, should any be offered him again, his refusal would show that he did not accuse the administration out of any such view.   (Sedgwick, 'Pulteney', 1.375)

In November 1729 Richard Franklin, the publisher of *The Craftsman*, was prosecuted by the government, but a sympathetic jury acquitted him. The public rejoicing following this verdict no doubt prompted Pulteney to celebrate in print himself with the ballad *The Honest Jury, or, Caleb's Triumphant*.

Pulteney continued to harass the Walpole ministry, particularly its foreign policy. In the debate on the address on 13 January 1730 he attacked the treaty of Seville, and on 6 February he criticized the continued employment for a further year of 12,000 Hessian troops, although his public pronouncements were considerably less inflammatory than his private comments. Further criticism followed on 10 February, over allegations that the ministry had allowed the fortifications at Dunkirk to be rebuilt by the French in contravention of the treaty of Utrecht. Pulteney was true to his word about not taking office when, following Townshend's dismissal in May 1730, Walpole offered him the vacant secretaryship coupled with a peerage. His refusal led to an ever more bitter pamphlet exchange between ministerial supporters and their opponents. One of the government's leading protagonists was Pulteney's erstwhile ally John, Lord Hervey, who penned an anonymous preface to an unsigned pamphlet entitled *Sedition and Defamation Display'd: in a Letter to the Author of The Craftsman*.

Later, in January 1731, Pulteney replied with *A Proper Reply to a Late Scurrilous Libel Intitled Sedition and Defamation Display'd*, in which, under the mistaken belief that Hervey had written the whole pamphlet, he launched a virulent and openly offensive attack on Hervey, which included scarcely veiled accusations of homosexuality. The result of this exchange was a duel on 25 January 1731 in what later became Green Park, in which both combatants were slightly wounded. The duel was commemorated in a series of prints that show a smirking Walpole in the background. Pulteney and Walpole continued to attack each other in pamphlets in 1731, most notably following a piece by Bolingbroke in *The Craftsman* that defended his own and Pulteney's political conduct. This prompted a ministerial riposte, *Remarks on the Craftsman's Vindication of his Two Honourable Patrons*, which heaped personal abuse on Pulteney. In response Pulteney published *An Answer to One Part of a Late Infamous Libel*, which dealt with the years of the Pulteney–Walpole co-operation. So bitter had the exchanges become that an enraged Walpole had the printer of the tract arrested, and George II personally struck Pulteney's name off the list of privy councillors on 1 July 1731. He was also removed from the commission of the peace. Neither could Pulteney expect much succour from the church, Bishop Gibson informing Newcastle in July 1731 that 'the clergy look upon Mr P[ultene]y and his friends to be their greatest enemies' (Sykes, 145), following opposition whig support for the Tithe Bill.

Pulteney was a leading opponent of Walpole's excise scheme, which was introduced into parliament in 1733. He took part in a formal consultation at Cassiobury House at Christmas 1732 with Sir William Wyndham, lords Bolingbroke and Gower, and others to plan the opposition's tactics. However Pulteney was less comfortable with the use of 'instructions' and popular political devices for pressurizing MPs. In debate he branded the excise as a plan for arbitrary power, noting that 'this scheme is absolutely inconsistent with a free election of members of parliament' (Langford, 74) and coining the phrase 'that monster the Excise' (Wright, 21). This sobriquet was perfect for the pamphleteers and the cartoonists, who weighed into the debate against the government. With Walpole forced to withdraw his proposal and his hold on power seemingly weakening, one opposition plan for a new ministry made Pulteney both first lord of the Treasury and chancellor of the exchequer, a sure sign of his pre-eminence among the opposition. However, Walpole recovered his political poise, purged his enemies within the court, and retained power with a convincing majority following the 1734 general election. Pulteney had taken this opportunity to stand, and gain election, for Middlesex in a joint candidature with a tory, Sir Francis Child, and incidentally thereby freeing a seat at Hedon. The disappointment of the election defeat and the prospect of more years in opposition led to some recrimination among the leaders of the opposition, which Lord Hervey gleefully recorded: Pulteney and Lord Bolingbroke 'hated one another; Lord Carteret and Pulteney were jealous of one another; Wyndham and Pulteney the same; whilst Lord Chesterfield had a little correspondence with all, but was confided in by none of them' (Hervey, 1.305).

Pulteney was involved in the litigation following the death, in December 1734, of Henry Newport, third earl of Bradford, an old travelling companion during his years on the grand tour. Bradford had disinherited his brother Thomas (d. 1762) as heir of his unentailed estate in favour of his mistress Ann Smyth, whose illegitimate son, known as John Newport, he acknowledged as his own. It is said that Ann Smyth was contemporaneously the mistress of Pulteney, who acted as guardian of John Newport in the litigation between Ann Smyth and the Newport family after Bradford's death, in which she successfully defended her inheritance. On her death, in 1742, she left the reversion of her inherited estates to Pulteney in the event that her son died without lawful issue. John Newport was a lunatic but lived in Chelsea until his death, in 1783, whereupon Pulteney's heirs inherited the property. After Ann Smyth's death Pulteney was a supporter of the successful bill to prevent the marriage of lunatics, which thereby safeguarded his family's future inheritance. Such stories gave credence to Pulteney's reputation for being fascinated by money, which was characterized by Chesterfield: 'his breast was the seat of all those passions which degrade our nature' and 'avarice, the meanest of them all, generally triumphed' (*Miscellaneous Works*, 25).

In November 1734 Pulteney had suffered another political blow, with the retirement of his main ally at court, Henrietta Howard, countess of Suffolk, who had been groom of the stole to the queen. Exhausted and depressed, Pulteney was absent from the parliamentary session of 1735, spending most of the time in the Netherlands attempting to recover his zest for politics. New opportunities for the opposition arose when Pulteney began to exploit the reversionary interest to the throne centred on Frederick, prince of Wales, who was on bad terms with his father. In this, however, he faced stiff opposition from the young 'patriots' grouped around Richard Temple, first Viscount Cobham, and distrust between these elements of the opposition constantly bedevilled their attempts to dislodge Walpole from power. Following the marriage of Prince Frederick, on 29 April 1736 Pulteney moved an address of congratulation in the Commons. On 22 February 1737 he moved the Commons for an address to settle £100,000 out of the civil list on Prince Frederick, backing it up with a host of precedents, but it failed to win much support from the tories and was defeated. However, Pulteney did not support the prince in his quarrel with the king that led to his expulsion from St James's in September 1737.

Pulteney returned to the fray with renewed vigour in 1738 in support of British merchant interests in their dispute with Spain. He exploited the affair of Captain Robert Jenkins's ear, which led to clamours for war with Spain, beginning in October of the following year. In February 1739 Cobham was again worrying that Pulteney and Carteret were working 'to get the Prince of Wales into their hands, by which they might make a property out of him' (Gerrard, 43). The opposition again found itself in disarray

when they decided to secede from the Commons *en bloc* following the debate of 9 March 1739 on the convention of Pardo. When the new parliamentary session opened on 15 November 1739 Pulteney gave his full support to the war effort, in effect reminding the tories that he was an indispensable part of the opposition. However, on 21 November he moved for an address in which the king was not to enter into negotiations with Spain unless the rights of British ships in the American seas were recognized. On 21 February 1740 Pulteney signalled an attack on Walpole by asking for the papers relating to the convention of Pardo to be presented to the Commons, preparatory to an investigation that he hoped would launch impeachment proceedings, as had occurred in 1715. The government's conduct of the war saw a rise in support for the opposition and a rise in Pulteney's popularity. In January 1741 Walpole sent a perceptive missive to George II on the need to destroy Pulteney's popularity by inviting him to court and persuading him to accept a peerage as a mark of royal appreciation, for then 'the bee will have lost his sting, and become an idle drone, whose buzzing nobody heeds' (Graves and Cronin, 27). Pulteney supported Samuel Sandys's motion on 13 February 1741 for an address to the crown for the removal of Walpole from office. However, Pulteney was determined to be seen as supportive of the war effort, approving of the address of 8 April 1741 that provided a vote of credit to allow British obligations to be fulfilled towards Austria. At the fiercely contested general election of May 1741 Pulteney again secured election for Middlesex, but two Walpolian whigs captured Hedon, although they were later unseated on petition, for bribery. The general election was followed by an extensive progress by Pulteney from July to October in England and Wales aiming at a united opposition in the new parliament. In September Lord Chesterfield bemoaned Pulteney's preference for a negotiated entry into power and peculiar power as a party politician: Pulteney 'has a personal influence over many, and an interested influence over more. The silly, half-witted, zealous Whigs consider him as the only support of Whiggism, and look upon us as running headlong into Bolingbroke and the Tories' (Owen, 17).

Walpole's parliamentary majority in the new house was now precarious, and Pulteney pressed home his advantage by moving for a secret committee on the proceedings surrounding the convention of Pardo, which suggested that the war with Spain was being mismanaged and which the ministry defeated by only three votes, on 21 January 1742. During this debate Pulteney 'declared very explicitly and peremptorily, that he never would accept of any share in any administration but would always employ his influence in parliament to support the present royal family and constitution' (*Tory and Whig*, 175). The defeat of the government on an election petition for Chippenham, on 2 February 1742, heralding as it did the ministry's imminent loss of control of the lower house, saw parliament adjourned on 3 February to facilitate a change of ministry. Walpole accepted a peerage on 6 February 1742.

Office again Even before Walpole's resignation pressure had been building up on Pulteney regarding the future composition of the ministry. A particularly heated meeting took place at the Fountain tavern on 12 February 1742, in which Pulteney faced severe questioning as to his negotiating stance with John Campbell, second duke of Argyll, arguing for a 'broad-bottom' administration. With Walpole out of office George II instructed Newcastle and Philip Yorke, first Baron Hardwicke, lord chancellor, to invite Pulteney to form an administration, with the condition that Walpole be shielded from any inquiry into his conduct. Pulteney declined at first, in order to have the condition removed, and then, on accepting, declined major office in favour of a seat in the cabinet and readmission to the privy council, which was effected on 20 February 1742. Pulteney also played a key role in reconciling Prince Frederick to the new administration, acting as a messenger between the opposition assembled at Carlton House and the ministers meeting at Lord Wilmington's. Having played the patriot country whig for so long Pulteney no doubt feared an adverse reaction should he take a position at the head of the Treasury. Instead Pulteney put his long-term ally Lord Carteret forward for that post, but the king declined to follow his suggestion and made Spencer Compton, earl of Wilmington, first lord. Pulteney's absence from court and the Commons following the death of his fourteen-year-old daughter, Anne, in March 1742 further weakened his influence in the new ministry, packed as it was with colleagues of Walpole. When he returned to the Commons he supported, on 23 March 1742, the establishment of a committee of inquiry into the last ten years of the Walpole administration (a motion for a twenty-year inquiry having been lost in his absence) but refused to serve on it and spoke little thereafter in the chamber. He successfully opposed the repeal of the Septennial Act on 31 March, a long-time objective of the opposition, and on 15 April he introduced a limited place bill, dismissed by one tory as 'a sham bill and of no use' (*Tory and Whig*, 58), which was the only reform measure to pass into law.

On 13 July 1742 Pulteney was created earl of Bath. According to Chesterfield his acceptance was a deliberate act and not an error of judgement, as some have suggested. Nevertheless it did unleash a torrent of hostile commentaries and satire, as, far from heralding a new dawn in which political reform would be achieved and Walpole's corruption punished, the ex-minister went unpunished and the new Lord Bath looked on benignly from the Lords. In particular the anonymous cartoon and vindictive writings of Sir Charles Hanbury Williams did more damage to Bath's reputation than twenty years of *The Craftsman* had done to his enemies. Bath revealed his anger and distress in letters to his close friend Zachary Pearce, dean of Westminster, and he became enraged when the pamphlet justifying his position—*Faction Detected*, now believed to have been written by John Perceval, first earl of Egmont—was falsely attributed to Bath himself by Hanbury Williams. Nevertheless Pulteney's defence, that he was pushed into a deal with the old corps

whigs because patriot politicians like George Lyttelton, William Pitt, and the Grenvilles had entered into negotiations before Walpole had resigned, appears to have had some basis in fact. This was little consolation for what Thomas Birch described as 'the abuse of my Lord of Bath both in prose and verse fills our daily as well as our weekly papers' (Harris, *Patriot Press*, 60).

Bath spoke infrequently in the Lords, but the death of Wilmington, on 2 July 1743, saw him make an attempt to become head of the Treasury. He sent a message to Lord Carteret, who was in Hanau with George II, but despite Carteret's support the king preferred the Pelhams, and Bath seems to have acquiesced in the decision. He served as a lord justice in 1743 and 1745, and on 15 November 1744 he was elected a fellow of the Royal Society. When George II attempted to escape from the domination of his government by the Pelhams he turned to Bath, who accepted the Treasury, received the seals of office, and kissed hands on 10 February 1746. Such was the parliamentary strength of the Pelhams that within two days Bath had relinquished the seals on finding insufficient support to carry an administration. The anonymous satirist of the *History of the Long Administration* referred to him as, 'the minister having to the astonishment of all wise men, never transacted one rash thing, and what is more marvellous, left as much money in the Treasury as he found in it' (Speck, 248). He now left the cabinet. In November 1746 his brother-in-law Samuel Gumley was returned in a by-election for Hedon, but he was unseated on petition in February 1747 because it was said that the ministers 'wanted to show the king that Lord Bath had not the interest he boasted' of in the House of Commons (Sedgwick, 'Introductory survey', 1.358).

Declining years Bath continued to attend the Lords, although with declining vigour in debate, which he explained as a desire not to rock the boat. His most important contribution probably lay behind the scenes as an adviser to John Stuart, third earl of Bute, and the Leicester House court of the young Prince George. Bath's wife died on 14 September 1758, apparently leaving her estate to her husband. Lady Mary Wortley Montagu, commenting on the recent demise of both Lady Bath and Lady Burlington, thought that 'they have long been burdens (not to say nuisances) on the face of the earth' (Jenkins, 165) and Horace Walpole pictured the two countesses making 'such an uproar that … St. Peter himself turned the key [of the gates of heaven] and hid himself' (ibid.). In his widowhood Bath spent much time in the company of such bluestockings as Elizabeth Carter (1717–1806), daughter of the Revd Nicholas Carter, and Elizabeth Montagu (1720–1780), wife of Edward Montagu. He continued to travel with such respectable and cultured women, including a trip to Spa, in the Austrian Netherlands, and the Rhine in June–September 1763, when he was described as being the life and soul of a party of very fashionable people. Bath made his last recorded speech in the Lords in 1760. Following the accession of George III he was made lord lieutenant of Shropshire on 13 March 1761. His son and heir, William, Viscount Pulteney, a soldier and MP, predeceased him, having died of an infectious enteritis while returning from a campaign in Spain in 1763.

Bath died at Bath House, Piccadilly, at 10 p.m. on 7 July 1764, following the effects of a chill. His body was taken in grand procession from Bath House to Westminster Abbey, where it lay in the Jerusalem Chamber before being buried on the night of 17 July in the Islip Chapel, in the north aisle. The remains of his immediate family had already been removed from St Martin-in-the-Fields to be interred with Viscount Pulteney under a slab of blue stone finely cut with the family arms. Public rioting attended the funeral, resulting in damage to neighbouring tombs. Later Bath's brother caused to be erected close by a substantial monument designed by Joseph Wilton.

It is difficult to be sure of Hanbury Williams's statement that written on the door of Bath House was an epitaph, 'Here, dead to fame, lives patriot Will; his grave a lordly seat; his title proves his Epitaph; his robes his winding sheet' (Wheatley, 30). Horace Walpole wrote that 'grass grows before my Lord Bath's door who nobody will visit' (*Letters*, 16). Such venomous shafts may have reflected Pulteney's lack of political friends in later years or the fact that the domestic arrangements were poor in Bath House, then occupied by two elderly gentlemen. Such friends as Pulteney did have at the end he largely offended by the terms of his will, in which he made no provision for those in financial difficulties and made only very modest gifts to those most close, such as the jewellery he left to Elizabeth Montagu.

The London estate of the Pulteneys was entailed in the absence of issue on his brother, General Harry Pulteney (1686–1767). Bath left the remainder of his landed and personal estate to his brother as well. This consisted of his estates at Bathwick and Wrington, Burrington and Ubley, in Somerset, and the reversion of the Bradford–Newport property in Shropshire, Monmouthshire, Staffordshire, and Northamptonshire. His personal estate in the form of cash and investments was estimated variously at between £600,000 and £1.2 million at the time. He was certainly one of the richest men in Britain at his death, so far as disposable capital was concerned. The fortune remained intact by inheritance until the death of his kinswoman Henrietta Laura Pulteney, *suo jure* countess of Bath, in 1808, when it was dispersed for lack of Pulteney heirs.

Assessment Bath ordered the destruction of his personal papers after his death, which denied posterity a full text of his speeches, but they are often described as brilliant both in reasoning and in wit and playing heavily upon members' emotions. Contemporaneous transcripts of some of them, particularly about the time of Walpole's fall, show them to be of great length, and for years Bath was by far the most frequent speaker in parliament. His resort to vulgarity was an unattractive weakness that manifestly represents a character flaw. He was clearly hurt by unfounded attacks on him in the press, but was unwavering in his support of its freedom—in a letter to Zachary Pearce he wrote: 'all our liberties depend on preserving the liberties of the press' (Zachery Pearce papers).

Pulteney's personal relationships were soured from

time to time and he seems to have had only a handful of long-term friendships. The rift with Lord Hervey exemplifies his loss of good friends through his lack of self-control in matters relating to his parliamentary struggles. Hervey's desertion to Walpole was punished by Pulteney with public humiliation in outrageous personal terms, impugning Hervey's sexual habits and laying him open to prosecution for libel.

In contrast letters to Zachary Pearce show Pulteney as a tender, caring man capable of sustaining a long and successful marriage undoubtedly founded on love and a deep respect for his wife, the end of which caused him deep distress (his first letter on her death being penned to Pearce). Despite the relish with which Horace Walpole reported on family disagreements Pulteney's concern for his children is apparent, although they seemed to have lived in some awe of him. His refusal to countenance the marriage of his son to Frances Catherine, daughter and heir of Sir Charles Gunther Nichol, reputedly because of arguments about marriage settlements, caused some estrangement with his son and ultimately left Pulteney with no direct heirs, and hence somewhat isolated in later life as his political friends died or drifted away. His only close relative, his brother Harry, latterly lived with him at Bath House.

Pulteney was, however, an intensely sociable man given to enjoying being at centre stage. In his early days he raked around London with Swift, Gay, and other literary friends. Later accounts survive of some grand entertainments at Bath House when his fine collection of plate, recorded in an inventory on his brother's death, was clearly a source of great pride. He was not a collector of pictures on the scale of some of his contemporaries but, to judge by the quality of those surviving at Raby Castle, the seat of Lord Barnard, whose family ultimately inherited many of the Pulteney heirlooms, he was well advised in his modest purchases. Pulteney's library was of a significant scale but was broken up at auction in 1811. He particularly treasured two volumes of Cicero's works given to him by Pearce, which appear in the portrait of Bath now at Yale University.

Pulteney sat for portraits on at least seven occasions—always in formal pose, increasingly overweight, and latterly appearing somewhat unapproachable and disgruntled, leaning heavily on his walking-stick, which he needed because of increasing lameness following a fall. On one occasion he returned to Reynolds's studio, after sitting for the portrait given to Mrs Montagu, to have him 'mend my sickly looks', although Mrs Montagu does say that the artist had captured the great intensity of Pulteney's dark brown eyes (*Correspondence*, 28).

Pulteney was also a man of broad interests. He was a director of the Royal Academy of Music and a patron of his wife's nephew George Colman in promoting that playwright's first works in the early 1760s. His interest in the designs for his own London residence was matched by his role in chairing the committee for designing the new London Bridge. Philanthropic gestures included donating funds for the construction of a hospital at Bath, which now houses the Royal National Hospital for Rheumatic Diseases, and the provision of a market cross at Hedon. The latter was of course his original parliamentary constituency, making the point that above all Pulteney was a political figure.

STUART HANDLEY, M. J. ROWE, and W. H. McBRYDE

Sources A. A. Hanham, 'Pulteney, William', HoP, *Commons, 1690–1715* · R. R. Sedgwick, 'Pulteney, William', HoP, *Commons, 1715–54* · R. R. Sedgwick, 'Introductory survey', HoP, *Commons, 1715–54*, 1.1–114 · GEC, *Peerage* · J. Ingamells, ed., *A dictionary of British and Irish travellers in Italy, 1701–1800* (1997) · C. Gerrard, *The patriot opposition to Walpole: politics, poetry, and national myth, 1725–1742* (1994) · P. Langford, *The excise crisis: society and politics in the age of Walpole* (1975) · R. Harris, *A patriot press: national politics and the London press in the 1740s* (1993) · L. Colley, *In defiance of oligarchy: the tory party, 1714–60* (1982) · H. T. Dickinson, *Bolingbroke* (1970) · *The Wentworth papers, 1705–1739*, ed. J. J. Cartwright (1883) · R. Halsband, *Lord Hervey: eighteenth-century courtier* (1973) · J. B. Owen, *The rise of the Pelhams* (1957) · *Tory and whig: the parliamentary papers of Edward Harley, third earl of Oxford, and William Hay, MP for Seaford, 1716–1753*, ed. S. Taylor and C. Jones (1998) · J. H. Plumb, *Sir Robert Walpole: the king's minister* (1960) · R. Harris, ed., 'A Leicester House political diary, 1742–3', *Camden miscellany, XXXI*, CS, 4th ser., 44 (1992), 375–411 · S. Jenkins, 'Lady Burlington at court', *Lord Burlington: the man and his politics*, ed. E. Corp (1998), 149–79 · N. Sykes, *Edmund Gibson, bishop of London, 1669–1748* (1926) · J. C. Sainty and R. O. Bucholz, *Officials of the royal household, 1660–1837*, pt 2 (1998) · J. C. Sainty, ed., *List of lieutenants of counties of England and Wales, 1660–1974* (1979) · *Lord Bolingbroke, contributions to The Craftsman*, ed. S. Varey (1982) · John, Lord Hervey, *Some materials towards memoirs of the reign of King George II*, ed. R. Sedgwick, 3 vols. (1931) · archives, Westminster Abbey, Zachary Pearce papers · *Miscellaneous works of Philip Dormer Stanhope, earl of Chesterfield*, ed. M. Maty, 3 vols. (1777) · A. Graves and W. V. Cronin, *A history of the works of Sir Joshua Reynolds* (1899) · *The correspondence of Mrs Elizabeth Montagu, 1720–1761*, ed. E. J. Climenson, 2 vols. (1906) · H. B. Wheatley, *Round about Piccadilly and Pall Mall* (1870) · T. Wright, *Caricature history of the Georges* (1904) · *Letters of Horace Walpole* (1906) · *Survey of London*, vols. 24, 30–33 · W. A. Speck, *Stability and strife in England, 1714–1760* (1977) · DNB

Archives Bath City Library, estate papers · Raby Castle, co. Durham, MSS [on loan] | BL, corresp. with George Colman and Francis Colman, Add. MS 18915 · BL, corresp. with Lord Hardwicke, Add. MSS 35584–35603, *passim* · BL, corresp. with Lord Loudon, Add. MSS 44068–44079, *passim* · BL, corresp. with duke of Newcastle, Add. MSS 32697–32900, *passim* · Glos. RO, letters to Brudenell Rooke · Hunt. L., letters to Elizabeth Montagu · NA Scot., letters to Sir Archibald Grant · NMM, corresp. with Edward Vernon · U. Nott. L., letters to Henry Pelham, etc. · Westminster Abbey Muniments, corresp. with Z. Pearce

Likenesses oils, 1695, Raby Castle, co. Durham · oils, *c*.1705, Heddon town hall, Yorkshire · G. Kneller, oils, 1717, NPG · attrib. C. Jervas, oils, *c*.1720, Guildhall, Bath · J. Simon, mezzotint, *c*.1720 (after G. Kneller), BM, NPG · C. Philips, group portrait, oils, 1730–34, Yale U. CBA · J. Faber, engraving, 1732 (after Kneller) · T. Buckram, engraving, 1741 (*The motley team of state*), BM · engraving, 1741 (*The acquittal*), BM · J. A. Dassier, copper medal, 1744, BM · W. Hoare, oils, *c*.1745, Harvard U., law school · attrib. A. Ramsay, oils, *c*.1750, Raby Castle, co. Durham · S. F. Ravenet, engraving, *c*.1750 · W. Hoare, oils, *c*.1755, Holburne Museum of Art, Bath · J. Reynolds, oils, 1755, NPG · J. Mc. Ardell, mezzotint, 1758 (after J. Reynolds), BM, NPG · W. Hoare, oils, *c*.1760, Raby Castle, co. Durham · oils, *c*.1760, Raby Castle, co. Durham · A. Ramsay, oils, 1762, priv. coll. [*see illus.*] · D. Martin, engraving, 1763 (after Ramsay) · J. Wilton, marble plaque, 1764, Westminster Abbey · S. W. Reynolds, engraving, *c*.1820 (after J. Reynolds) · W. H. Mote, line and stipple engraving, 1835 (after C. Jervas), NPG · J. Scott, mezzotint,

1874 (after J. Reynolds), NPG · Broughton, engraving (*A political battle royal*), BM · T. Cooper, engraving (*The motion*), BM · J. Wilton, portrait medallion, Westminster Abbey · caricature (*The three courtiers*), BM · caricature (*The London merchants triumph*), BM · caricature (*Britannic excise*), BM · caricature (*The state juggler*), BM · caricature (*Political vomit*), BM · caricature (*The promotion*), BM · caricature (*From one house to another*), BM · caricature (*The wheel of fortune*), BM · caricature (*The treacherous patriot unmasked*), BM · caricature (*The craftsman unmasked*), BM · caricature (*The antcraftsman unmasked*), BM · caricature (*Lord Hervey's duel with Mr. Pulteney*), BM · double portrait (with W. Stanhope); at Stowe before 1848–9 · engraving (*The political libertines, or, Motion upon motion*), BM · engraving (*The H—r T—p man*), BM · engraving (*The wheel of fortune, or, The Scot's step completed*), BM

Wealth at death one of richest men in England; est. £600,000–£1.2 million; excl. land (some of which was entailed)

Pulteney [*formerly* Johnstone], **Sir William**, **fifth baronet** (**1729–1805**), politician and property developer, was born William Johnstone on 19 October 1729 at Westerhall, Dumfriesshire, the third son of Sir James Johnstone MP, third baronet (1697–1772), and the Hon. Barbara Murray (d. 1773), daughter of the fourth Lord Elibank. Little is known of his childhood or early education until he attended prelections on history and Roman antiquities with Dr Charles Mackie at Edinburgh University in 1746–7. He was admitted to the Scottish bar on 16 July 1751. From references in the correspondence of contemporaries such as Adam Smith and Sir John Sinclair it seems that he lived the life of an intelligent, if impoverished, young lawyer in literary and intellectual circles in Edinburgh. As a younger son he was dependent upon the patronage of senior members of the family to obtain appointments but surviving correspondence reveals that at an early stage he was developing a reputation as a sound political and financial adviser. He remained close to his family, particularly to his brothers George and John and his unmarried sister Betty, who cared for their, often difficult, parents.

Johnstone left Edinburgh for London in 1759 when he was appointed to a post worth £400 a year in customs and excise. He was now in possession of a secure income and on 10 November 1760 married Frances (1728?–1782), daughter and heir of Daniel *Pulteney MP, whose means were then similar to his own. Johnstone's employment allowed him to return to Edinburgh and the couple lived comparatively modestly until the unexpected deaths in quick succession of Frances Johnstone's cousin, Viscount Pulteney, in 1763, and his father, William Pulteney, earl of Bath, in 1764. Lord Bath's immense fortune was entailed upon his 79-year-old bachelor brother General Harry Pulteney but on his death in 1767 it passed to Frances Johnstone. The Johnstones, who had returned to live in London, immediately adopted the Pulteney name and moved to General Pulteney's home, Bath House, Piccadilly, from Cleveland Row, St James's. Their only child to survive infancy, (Henrietta) Laura *Pulteney, had been born the previous year, on 26 December 1766.

His developing interest in politics led to Pulteney's return to parliament for Cromarty in 1768, following an unsuccessful attempt at Shrewsbury, in which the Pulteney family had an interest, in the same year. In 1775 he was successful at Shrewsbury and represented the borough until his death. Pulteney remained independent and there is no evidence that he actively sought office. His principal interests were in financial and economic matters, which encompassed American and East Indian affairs, agriculture, fisheries, and transport throughout Great Britain. In all of these he had, or developed, a personal financial interest.

> He possessed a sound understanding and his opinion was always received in the House with respect for full attention. As a public man, no commoner understood the Constitution of a country better, or more uniformly supported it by his conduct. (*GM*)

During a period of great parliamentary turbulence in 1797–8 a proposal was mooted for the establishment of a third party to form a government and Pulteney was identified, by others, as a likely chancellor of the exchequer. James Gillray recorded the episode in a caricature entitled *Le trésorier* on 21 May 1798.

Pulteney's American interests appear to have stemmed from the appointment of his brother George Johnstone as governor of West Florida in 1763 and existing Johnstone family interests in the West Indies. On the outbreak of the American War of Independence in 1776 he and his brother George, by then also an MP, became involved in attempts at reconciliation. George Johnstone joined the earl of Carlisle's peace mission to America while Pulteney undertook a secret mission, under the alias of Mr Williams, to Paris to attempt negotiations with Benjamin Franklin, the American ambassador to France. Neither initiative bore fruit but subsequently Pulteney made his views known in pamphlets criticizing government policy, pointing out the cost of the American war, and supporting a more generous treatment of the rebellious colonists.

Pulteney applied a similar approach to Indian affairs. His brother John Johnstone held a post with the East India Company, and the brothers corresponded regularly on Indian affairs. In 1783 Pulteney wrote a pamphlet entitled *The Effects to be Expected from the East India Bill upon the Constitution of Great Britain* criticizing Fox's policies and setting out his views on a proper relationship with the subcontinent.

While pursuing his political interests, Pulteney was engaged in schemes for the management and development of his wife's extensive estates in London and Bath. The Bath estate offered the greatest potential for building development and to exploit this he promoted an act of parliament in 1769 allowing the bridging of the Avon between the old city and the parish of Bathwick on the east bank. Robert Adam, an Edinburgh contemporary and friend, was commissioned to design the estate but in the event only the Pulteney Bridge was built according to his plans. The bridge and the Great Pulteney Street development, which took place over the next thirty years, remain the greatest visible monuments to Pulteney's endeavours.

Frances Pulteney died in 1782 and Pulteney was then responsible for managing the estates on behalf of his daughter, Henrietta Laura, as her mother's heir. His role diminished on her marriage in 1794 to Sir James Murray,

seventh baronet (1751–1811), his first cousin, who changed his name to Pulteney on marriage. Pulteney had earlier used his influence to have his daughter created Baroness Bath in her own right in 1792. She was advanced to the rank of countess of Bath in 1803.

Pulteney had always been interested in agricultural improvements and originally experimented at Solway Bank, his own small estate near Lockerbie in Dumfriesshire. He subsequently applied the same principles to his wife's estates in Staffordshire, Shropshire, Montgomeryshire, Northamptonshire, and Somerset. At Solway Bank there were also fisheries which he developed and improved and his experience here was later applied nationally in Scotland through his role in the British Fisheries Society, of which he was director from 1790 to 1805. He was particularly concerned with highland fisheries and he is commemorated in the nineteenth century development of Wick, known as Pulteney Town.

The opening up and development of the highlands was made possible by road construction in which Thomas Telford, a native of Westerhall and a protégé of Pulteney's, was much involved, as he was in earlier road and canal construction on the Pulteneys' other estates. Because of his modest nature the true extent of Pulteney's patronage is largely unrecorded, but although careful he was not ungenerous. When Andrew Stuart, a close friend and political associate, became financially embarrassed Pulteney granted him an annuity of £400. He encouraged not only Thomas Telford but the children of friends and protégés, including William Pulteney Allison, sometime president of the Royal College of Physicians of Edinburgh, and Admiral Sir Pulteney Malcolm who served under Lord Nelson and whose father came from Westerhall. His public benefactions included the endowment of the chair of agriculture in the University of Edinburgh.

From 1791, as part of the *rapprochement* with the USA, Pulteney invested heavily in American stock and then began his greatest speculation of all by buying 1 million acres in upper New York state, of which a new town of Bath became the centre. Largely through the work of his agent Colonel Charles Williamson, the scheme was so successful that by 1802 the whole area was opened up and the initial investment of £250,000 was valued at £2 million.

Always a frugal man, with few personal social aspirations and of unpretentious appearance and demeanour, Pulteney lived quietly between Bath House and Shrewsbury, where with Telford's assistance he adapted the ruinous castle as a house. The only doubts recorded about his conduct relate to his apparent failure to attend appropriately to the early social needs of his daughter, who was noted as the richest heiress of her day, but who appears to have been somewhat eccentric and who eventually married a professional soldier many years her senior.

In 1794, on the death of his older brother James Johnstone, Pulteney became fifth baronet and inherited the Westerhall estate together with plantations and slaves in the West Indies. On 3 January 1804 Pulteney married his second wife, Margaret, daughter of Sir William Stirling, bt, of Ardoch and widow of his old friend Andrew Stuart.

Pulteney died on 30 May 1805 at Bath House, Piccadilly, London, and was buried in the south cloister of Westminster Abbey on 11 June 1805 next to his first wife, Frances, and at the foot of the monument to her father, Daniel Pulteney. No monument to him or his wife or his daughter, who died in 1808, was ever erected. Surprisingly, for such a rich and careful man, he died intestate. His personal estate in England passed to his widow and daughter and was valued at over £600,000. The landed estates in England and the overseas properties passed to the countess of Bath and his Scottish properties passed to his nephew Sir George Johnstone of Westerhall, sixth baronet. M. J. ROWE and W. H. McBRYDE

Sources HoP, *Commons* · GEC, *Peerage* · Burke, *Peerage* · *GM*, 1st ser., 75 (1805), 587 · W. H. McBryde and M. J. Rowe, *Beyond Mr. Pulteney's bridge* (1987) · H. I. Cowan, *Charles Williamson*, ed. D. Perkins (1941) · I. J. Fleming and N. F. Robertson, *Britain's first chair of agriculture* (1990) · L. T. C. Rolt, *Thomas Telford* (1958) · J. Dunlop, *The British Fisheries Society, 1786–1893* (1978) · M. Cormack, *The paintings of Thomas Gainsborough* (1991) · *The papers of Benjamin Franklin*, 26, ed. W. B. Willcox and others (1987) · *The letters of Horace Walpole, earl of Orford*, ed. P. Cunningham, 9 vols. (1857–9); repr. (1906)
Archives Bath City Library, estate papers · Hunt. L., corresp. · NA Scot., letters · priv. coll. · Rochester Museum and Science Center Library, legal papers | BL, letters to Lord Grenville, Add. MS 58974 · Devon RO, corresp. with Henry Addington · NL Scot., corresp. with Henry Dundas · NL Scot., corresp. with John Lee · PRO, letters to William Pitt the younger, PRO 30/8/169 · RIBA, Cotterel collection, Box 22 · U. Edin., class lists · Westminster Abbey, muniments, burial accounts
Likenesses J. Gillray, three etchings, 1798–1800, BM · T. Gainsborough, oils, Yale U. CBA · H. Raeburn, oils, priv. coll. · photograph (after oil painting by H. Raeburn), Scot. NPG
Wealth at death approx. £600,000—personal wealth in England: *GM* · approx. £2,000,000—value of estate in USA in 1802: Cowan, *Charles Williamson*

Pulter [*née* Ley], **Lady Hester** (1595/6–1678), poet, was born probably at Westbury, Wiltshire, the daughter of James *Ley (1550–1629), judge and politician, who was created first earl of Marlborough in 1626. Her mother was his first wife, Mary (*d.* 1613), daughter of John Pettie (or Pettey) of Stoke Talmage, Oxfordshire.

It is only relatively recently that Lady Hester has come to public attention, and until the emergence of a manuscript held by the Brotherton Collection at the University of Leeds, she was not the most famous of Ley's daughters. Notably, her father is the subject of a sonnet by John Milton which is addressed to her sister, Lady Margaret Ley (Sonnet 10, 'Daughter to that good earl'). In 1623 Lady Hester married Arthur Pulter (1603–1689) of Broadfield (or Bradfield) in Hertfordshire. The couple had seven sons (Jacob, James, William, Arthur, Edward, Charles, and John) and eight daughters (Margaret, Mary, Jane, Hester, Penelope, Ann, Elizabeth, and Mary). The Pulter manuscript includes comments to the effect that she wrote during her periods of confinement. Her husband was born at Hadham Hall, Hertfordshire, in August 1603, the son of Lytton Pulter (1575–1626) and Penelope Capel (1581–1611). He was a justice of the peace, a captain in the militia, and, in 1641, high sheriff of Hertfordshire. He apparently withdrew from public life during the civil war period, dedicating himself to the building of a house at Broadfield, which

no longer stands. Details of the Pulters are contained in Sir Henry Chauncy's *The Historical Antiquities of Hertfordshire* (1700), and clearly Chauncy was a family friend.

The Leeds manuscript contains about 120 poems under the title 'Poems Breathed Forth by the Noble Hadassas' (Hadassas being a biblical synonym for Esther), and a prose romance, 'The Unfortunate Florinda', in two parts, the second of which is incomplete. From the dates given in the manuscript, this material appears to have been brought together between 1645 and 1665. Pulter's writings were produced by an educated and highly literate woman. The connection that her sister Margaret had to the London literary world through Milton might have been a route for Hester to keep in touch with the poetry of the period, and her connection to this milieu is marked in the subject matter of some of the poems. She also writes about and for members of her family, and there are many devotional poems in a meditative, metaphysical mode. The poetry reveals a strong involvement in public affairs, including a substantial number of polemical poems on the events of the civil war, all of which are characterized by her commitment to the royalist cause.

Pulter's work seems set to attain a prominent place within the canon of seventeenth-century women writers, and the volume and variety of her output makes her a figure of importance comparable only to Lady Mary Wroth. That she did not publish in her lifetime, and that her work does not appear to have circulated widely, is not an indication of the texts' quality. While it is inevitable that the standard is various, the best of her work will assure her continued presence in considerations of the literature of the period.

Pulter outlived all but two of her fifteen children, and the records of Cottered in Hertfordshire show that she was buried on 9 April 1678, at the age of eighty-two. Arthur Pulter died, having outlived his wife and all his children, on 27 January 1689. Their only grandson and sole heir was James Forester (1660–1696). MARK ROBSON

Sources U. Leeds, Brotherton L., MS Lt q 32 · H. Chauncy, *The historical antiquities of Hertfordshire* (1700) · H. Pulter, *Poems breathed forth by the noble Hadassas*, ed. M. Robson [forthcoming] · parish register, Hertfordshire, Cottered, 9 April 1678 [burial]
Archives U. Leeds, Brotherton L., MS Lt q 32

Pulton [Poulton], **Andrew** (1654–1710), Jesuit, was born on 20 January 1654 in Northamptonshire, the second son of Ferdinand or Ferdinando Pulton of Desborough and his wife, Mary Giffard. His younger brother, Thomas (*b.* 1668), also became a Jesuit, and the legal writer Ferdinando *Pulton was probably related. He was educated at St Omer in 1669–74 and entered the Society of Jesus on 31 October 1674. He studied at Watten (1674–5), Liège (1676–9), and St Omer (1680–83), and again at Liège (1684–6), and was ordained priest on 3 May 1685. In 1682 he apparently converted Charles, the son of John Manners, the first duke of Rutland, to Catholicism.

Pulton was sent to London at Whitsuntide 1687 to teach at the college the Jesuits had established in the Savoy. On 29 September he held a debate with the rector of St Martin-in-the-Fields (and later archbishop of Canterbury),

Dr Thomas Tenison. According to *A true and full account of a conference held about religion between Dr Tho. Tenison and A. Pulton* (1687) Pulton had not intended to publish an account, but was forced to do so when Tenison printed his own favourable description of the event. Tenison had mocked Pulton's poor command of English; Pulton responded by claiming that:

> having been Eighteen years out of his own Country, pretends not yet to any Perfection of the *English* Expression or Orthography; wherefore for the future he will crave the favour of treating with the *Dr.* in *Latine* or *Greek*, since the *Dr.* finds fault with his *English*.   (*A True and Full Account*, sig. A1v)

('Send Pulton to be lashed at Busby's school / That he in print no longer play the fool' declared a contemporary satire over Pulton's linguistic errors; Gillow, *Lit. biog. hist.*, 5.351.) Further printed exchanges followed over the following months, drawing in Edward Meredith in support of Pulton as well as a number of others taking Tenison's part. During this time Pulton also published *A Full and Clear Exposition of the Protestant Rule of Faith*, a critique of the Anglican church.

Following the destruction of the college by a protestant mob during the events of late 1688 Pulton fled London but was arrested at Canterbury on 11 December *en route* for the continent. He was released the following year, and was at the college at St Omer in 1689. He rejoined the exiled Stuart court at St Germain and became socius to John Warner, confessor to James II. Pulton accompanied James to Ireland in 1690 as an army chaplain. After his return Pulton remained at St Germain until his death there on 5 August 1710. A court sermon of his was included in *A Select Collection of Catholick Sermons, Preach'd before their Majesties King James II* (1741).   THOMAS H. CLANCY

Sources T. H. Clancy, *English Catholic books, 1641–1700: a bibliography*, rev. edn (1996) • H. Foley, ed., *Records of the English province of the Society of Jesus*, 7 vols. in 8 (1875–83) • A. F. Allison and D. M. Rogers, eds., *The contemporary printed literature of the English Counter-Reformation between 1558 and 1640*, 2 vols. (1989–94) • T. M. McCoog, ed., *Monumenta Angliae*, 1–2 (1992) • G. Holt, *St Omers and Bruges colleges, 1593–1773: a biographical dictionary*, Catholic RS, 69 (1979), 212 • G. Holt, *The English Jesuits, 1650–1829: a biographical dictionary*, Catholic RS, 70 (1984), 202 • Gillow, *Lit. biog. hist.*, 5.351–2 • *DNB*

Pulton, Ferdinando (1536–1618), legal writer, was born in Desborough, Northamptonshire, the son of Giles Pulton of Desborough. The Pulton family was well established in the county. Pulton matriculated at Christ's College, Cambridge, on 23 November 1552, graduated BA in 1556, and was a fellow from 25 March 1556 to 25 March 1557.

On 28 June 1556 Pulton was admitted a commoner at Brasenose College, Oxford. He was admitted to Lincoln's Inn on 5 June 1559 and, although a Roman Catholic, he was called to the bar in May 1609. A legal researcher and compiler, he lived at Desborough and had a house at Bourton, near Buckingham, in addition to his quarters at Lincoln's Inn. He married Katherine (*d.* in or after 1618), with whom he had four sons—Francis, Giles, Thomas, and Ferdinando—and two daughters.

A Catholic who supported Elizabeth I and James I, his interest in theology, Roman and biblical law, and the strict execution of the criminal law allowed him to retain the critical support of James and Thomas Egerton, Baron Ellesmere, the lord chancellor. He wrote in his prefaces that the purpose of publishing the law was to educate the people in it. He believed that the criminal law must be firmly implemented and that knowledge of it would deter unlawful acts. His Catholicism affected his posthumous reputation. Two of his sons became Catholic priests, and Thomas Pulton, using the alias Underhill, was among the Jesuits discovered in March 1628 at the house of George Talbot, earl of Shrewsbury and earl of Waterford, in Clerkenwell.

Pulton's chief occupation was producing an edition of the statutes for publication. Robert Bowyer, clerk of parliament, and Henry Elsing, keeper of the records in the Tower of London, contracted him as the first private person to research the records of parliament. His patrons Sir William Cordell and Ellesmere gave him further assistance. Bowyer and Elsing were unhappy at seeing an outsider producing a comprehensive edition that gave the full text of statutes still in force and an abridged text of the remainder, pointing out that these had been published in their original language before. They did not believe he had the technical skill to read the old documents without their assistance and were concerned that he could disclose deficiencies in the state of the archive, including the fact that some important statutes were no longer extant. Both men were also concerned that Pulton would make money, while they went without. The situation was resolved when it was agreed that the proceeds be shared. Pulton's compilation of statute law consisted of five major works: *An Abstract of All the Penal Statutes which be General* (1577), *A kalender, or table, comprehending the effect of all the statutes that have been made and put in print* (1606), *Collection of Statutes Repealed and Not Repealed* (1608), *A Collection of Sundry Statutes Frequent in Use* (1618), and *The Statutes at Large* (1618). He was also the author of *De pace regis et regni* (1609), a major treatise on criminal offences. His literary interests included theology and medieval history, works on which were prominent in his extensive library. Shortly before his death he presented to Christ's College a copy of Robert of Gloucester's chronicle.

Catholicism did not curtail Pulton's life in the community. Living in both Desborough and Bourton, he acquired additional land, orchards, and mills in Buckingham, Maidstreet, and Stowe. His eldest son, Francis, was admitted to his father's inn as a gentleman in 1569, and called to the bar, but died young. Francis Pulton's sons were raised by Katherine Pulton. Ferdinando Pulton was considered a very compassionate man by the Catholic playwright and poet John Beaumont. Pulton's will provided generous allowances and bequests for his servants, for the poor of the parishes in which he held land, and to various hospitals in Buckinghamshire and Northamptonshire. He made his wife his sole executor, and warned his sons to leave her in completely peaceful possession of the Bourton estate for the remainder of her life. Pulton died on 20 January 1618 in his house at Bourton. He was buried in Desborough parish church, and had a brass plate memorial erected at Bourton church.   LOUIS A. KNAFLA

Sources Foster, *Alum. Oxon.*, *1500–1714*, 2.214 • W. P. Baildon, ed., *The records of the Honorable Society of Lincoln's Inn: the black books*, 1–4 (1897–1902), 364, 366 • W. P. Baildon, ed., *The records of the Honorable Society of Lincoln's Inn: admissions*, 1 (1896) • J. Bridges and P. Whalley, *The history and antiquities of Northamptonshire*, rev. edn, 2 vols (1812), vol. 2, pp. 26–8 • G. Lipscomb, *The history and antiquities of the county of Buckingham*, 4 vols. (1831–47), vol. 2, p. 588 • V. B. Heltzel, ed., 'Ferdinando Pulton, Elizabethan legal editor', *Huntington Library Quarterly*, 11 (1947–8), 77–9 • L. A. Knafla, '"Such a rural chancellor": the patronage of Sir Thomas Egerton, Lord Ellesmere', in F. R. Fogle and L. A. Knafla, *Patronage in late Renaissance England* (1983) • PRO, PROB 11/131, sig. 5 • BL, Ayscough MS 4572, fols. 85r, 261r • BL, Cotton MS Vespasian F.ix, fols. 279r–280r • Inner Temple Library, London, Petyt MSS 512, 537 • J. G. Nichols, ed., 'The discovery of the Jesuits' college at Clerkenwell in March 1627–8', *Camden miscellany*, *II*, CS, 55 (1853) [see also J. G. Nichols, 'Supplementary note', *Camden miscellany, IV* (1859)]

Pumphrey, Richard Julius (1906–1967), zoologist, was born at 30 Wynnstay Gardens, Kensington, London, on 3 September 1906, the only child of Julius Pumphrey, a manufacturer of umbrellas, and his wife, Alice Lilian, the daughter of Edward Towgood of Hawkes Bay, New Zealand. His father came from a well-known Quaker family in Worcestershire; his mother had moved to Kent as a child. Pumphrey was educated at Arnold House School, London, and at Marlborough College (1920–25). There H. L. O. Fletcher imbued him with an abiding interest in the English language, and the biologist A. G. Lowndes encouraged him to explore the Wiltshire countryside. Pumphrey won an entrance scholarship to Trinity Hall, Cambridge, where he took part one of the natural sciences tripos in 1927, gaining second-class honours. He went on to finish with first-class honours in part two in 1929 (in zoology and comparative anatomy) and was awarded the Frank Smart prize as the best zoologist of the year.

Pumphrey now began research in experimental cytology at Cambridge, working on the physical chemistry of the surface membranes of trout eggs. In 1931 he was appointed Amy Mary Preston Read scholar, and the following year he was awarded his PhD. In 1934 he was a Rockefeller fellow at the Eldridge Reeves Johnson Foundation at the University of Pennsylvania, where he gained experience in electrophysiology that set a pattern for his future work. He held a Beit fellowship in the University of Cambridge from 1936 to 1939. At Cambridge Pumphrey met Sylvia Margaret Mills, a research student in the department of zoology, and daughter of the chemist W. H. *Mills (1873–1959); they were married at Chesterton, near Cambridge, in 1933. A daughter, Alison Margaret, and two sons, Nicholas and Richard, were born.

In October 1939 Pumphrey joined the Admiralty Surface Weapons Research Establishment at Ports Down, transferring in 1941 to the Admiralty Signal Establishment at Witley. There he became an important contributor to electronics and radar development, gaining admiration for both his hard work and ingenuity as an experimenter. He developed the accurate radar ranging apparatus, for which he was granted £400 from the Admiralty Awards Council. In 1945 he returned to Cambridge, where he collaborated with Professor T. Gold on the biophysics of hearing, both in man and the higher vertebrates, and at the fourth symposium of the Society for Experimental Biology in 1949 (the year he was awarded the degree of ScD by the University of Cambridge) he presented one of the most definitive publications on the subject of hearing. Between 1947 and 1949 he was assistant director of research in zoology.

In 1949 Pumphrey was appointed Derby professor of zoology at the University of Liverpool, where he became recognized as a shrewd, wise defender of his department who acquired the best possible facilities for his staff and students. During his tenure he served terms as both dean and chairman of the faculty of science and was also active on national bodies (serving on the councils of both the Marine Biological Association and the Society for Experimental Biology). He was also recognized as a gifted lecturer who could explain a complicated subject with clarity; he was a master of the stimulating phrase and sentence.

Despite his teaching and administrative loads Pumphrey continued his own research into the sense organs and central nervous systems of animals. He greatly clarified knowledge of the intermediate zone between touch and hearing, and produced a theory of frequency modulation in the hearing and vision of birds and insects which explained the ability of grasshoppers and crickets to recognize the sounds of their own species. Much of this research was conducted on equipment which Pumphrey had constructed himself. (He later collaborated with A. F. Rawdon-Smith in the design of more advanced equipment which became widely used in electrophysiology.) Pumphrey extended his bird and insect studies much further by investigating human hearing and demonstrating the high sensitivity of resonant elements in the ear. His continuing study of vision resulted in an important article published in the Festschrift for Sir James Gay.

Pumphrey had been interested in languages since his Marlborough days and his inaugural lecture at Liverpool on 'The origin of language' was published by the university press. His work was published in Norwegian, and through his love of Snowdon he also came to appreciate the Welsh language. In his university days he had been a formidable athlete, rowing in the Trinity Hall first boat and playing in the University of Cambridge hockey first eleven, and he never lost his love of country pursuits such as fishing and rock climbing. Pumphrey died following a short illness, at Clatterbridge Hospital, Bebington, on the Wirral, on 25 August 1967. He was survived by his wife.

D. BEN REES

Sources J. W. S. Pringle, *Memoirs FRS*, 14 (1968), 435–42 • *University of Liverpool Recorder*, 45 (Oct 1967), 18 • *DNB* • d. cert.
Archives Rice University, Houston, Texas, Woodson Research Center, corresp. with Sir Julian Huxley
Wealth at death £10,036: probate, 8 Jan 1968, *CGPLA Eng. & Wales*

Punch [Ponce], **John** (1599–1672/3), theologian, was born in Cork. Nothing is known of his parents. At an early age he went to study in the Irish college at Louvain, where he entered the Franciscan order. After studying philosophy at Cologne he moved to Rome to join the newly established Irish college at St Isidore's on 7 September 1625. Upon graduating, he taught philosophy and later theology at St Isidore's. By 1630 he was rector of St Isidore's, and on 8 June that year became governor of the Ludovisian college at Rome for the education of Irish secular priests.

During the 1640s Punch was an active agent at Rome for the Catholic confederation of Ireland. He did not trust the royalists and strongly supported the stance taken by Giovanni Rinuccini, papal nuncio to Ireland from 1645 to 1649. After the defeat of the confederates several Irish exiles established themselves in Paris, where they engaged in bitter recriminations; Punch himself was based mainly in Paris from 1648, lecturing there and at Lyons. Taking exception to Richard Bellings's criticisms of Rinuccini, Punch published his *D. R. Bellingi vindiciae eversae* in 1653. This defended the nuncio's rather questionable 1648 excommunication of those confederates who supported a truce with protestant forces commanded by Murrough O'Brien, Lord Inchiquin. Punch also attacked John Callaghan, an associate of Bellings, for his Jansenist views. In a withering riposte Bellings characterized Punch as having spent too long abroad in academia to appreciate the realities of Irish politics. Throughout the 1650s Irish Franciscan refugees continued to arrive in Paris, arousing the ire of the local friars. In September 1657 Punch was given jurisdiction over the Irish Franciscans to investigate accusations made against them.

Punch is best remembered for being foremost among the Irish scholars under Luke Wadding at St Isidore's who contributed hugely to the seventeenth-century revival of Scotism. From 1634 he assisted Wadding in the laborious task of producing the first complete edition of the works of John Duns Scotus. Wadding describes him as combining a subtle intellect with the capacity to communicate knowledge. Punch's first major work, *Philosophiae cursus integer*, was published at Rome in three volumes in 1642–3. The celebrated Scotist theologian Mastrius challenged Punch's conclusions, leading the latter to reply in 1648 with the *Appendix apologetica*. In the *Appendix* Punch declared that while he accepted Scotus's conclusions, he did not agree with all his proofs. Mastrius subsequently accepted the force of Punch's reasoning. In 1652 Punch published a textbook on Scotism, derived mainly from his *Cursus*. This was a hugely significant contribution to the study of Scotism, as it was the first time a complete course of Scotist theology, as opposed to the traditional commentaries, had been written. He continued to publish books related to this subject during the 1650s and early 1660s, the most significant being his magnum opus, *Commentarii theologici*, in 1661. He died between early 1672 and early 1673, presumably at Paris.   TERRY CLAVIN

Sources G. Cleary, *Father Luke Wadding and St Isidore's College, Rome* (1925), 83–7 · B. Millet, *The Irish Franciscans, 1651–66* (1964), 365, 384–7, 474–8 · P. J. Corish, 'John Callaghan and the controversies among the Irish in Paris, 1648–54', *Irish Theological Quarterly*, 21 (1954), 32–50 · *Father Luke Wadding: commemorative volume*, ed. Franciscan Fathers dún Mhuire, Killiney (1957), 60–61, 290, 487, 572–3 · *Report on Franciscan manuscripts preserved at the convent, Merchants' Quay, Dublin*, HMC, 65 (1906), 5, 21, 32 · T. W. Moody and others, eds., *A new history of Ireland*, 3: *Early modern Ireland, 1534–1691* (1976); repr. with corrections (1991)
Likenesses E. di Como, fresco, 1672, St Isidore's College, Rome

Punnett, Reginald Crundall (1875–1967), geneticist, was born in Tonbridge on 20 June 1875, the son of George Punnett, builder and architect, and his wife, Emily Crundall. (A strawberry growing ancestor devised the wooden basket known as a 'punnet'.) He went to Clifton College, where he was taught by W. A. Shenstone, the first schoolteacher to be elected FRS. He won a scholarship to Gonville and Caius College, Cambridge, where, after years of athletic inactivity on medical advice, he became an accomplished cricketer. He obtained a second class in part one (1896) and a first in part two (1898) of the natural sciences tripos.

In 1898 Punnett worked for some months in Naples on the evolution of small sharks before becoming a demonstrator in the natural history department of St Andrews University. In 1901 he was elected to a fellowship at Caius. Among his colleagues there was Ronald Fisher, who was to succeed him in the chair of genetics. A common interest in cricket brought Punnett in touch with William Bateson, with whom he began to collaborate on inheritance in 1903, first in mice and later in peas, fowls, and rabbits. Bateson had already published a defence of Gregor Mendel's principles of heredity; in 1905 Punnett published his influential *Mendelism*, in both small and large versions. The book was a popular success; its sales at one time were said to compete with those of Marie Corelli. It contained 'Punnett's diagram', a geometric representation of the consequences of fertilization. In 1908, following discussions at the cricket nets after a lecture on Mendelism to the Royal Society of Medicine, Punnett consulted with G. H. Hardy, his fellow cricketer and co-secretary of the committee for the retention of Greek in the previous examination. The result was Hardy's law, a cornerstone of mathematical genetics.

Bateson and Punnett worked together for nearly seven years; they were the founders of experimental genetics in Britain, and the main exponents of Mendel's models of inheritance. Both started as marine biologists, and in Cambridge both worked on animals and plants. Each had a robust approach to mathematical exuberance, a deep respect for farmers and seedsmen, and an interest in the broader implications of Mendelism. Their joint experimental work ended when Bateson was appointed director of the newly founded John Innes Horticultural Institute in south London in 1910. In 1911 Bateson and Punnett founded the *Journal of Genetics*, which they edited jointly until Bateson's death in 1926. In 1912 Punnett was appointed to the Balfour professorship of biology at Cambridge—effectively the first chair of genetics to be established anywhere—after Bateson had declined it. In the same year Punnett was elected FRS.

During the First World War, Punnett served in the food production department of the Board of Agriculture and Fisheries, where he developed sex-linked plumage variants as a means of sexing chicks; this led to many of the

Reginald Crundall Punnett (1875–1967), by Walter Stoneman, 1931

commercial self-sexing breeds. In 1923 he published *Heredity in Poultry*, and produced a map of the X chromosome of the chicken.

In 1913 Punnett married a widow, Eveline Maude Froude Nutcombe-Quicke (*d.* 1965), daughter of John Froude Bellew of Stockleigh English, Devon; they had no children. After his marriage Punnett diverted his formidable athletic activities from cricket to tennis. In 1943 he retired to Somerset, where he maintained his wide interests, which included Japanese prints, Chinese porcelain, biologists of the seventeenth and eighteenth centuries, and wine: he retained a personal cellar at Caius, which he visited annually. At seventy-four he published humorous verse in Latin. He died on 3 January 1967 while playing bridge at his home, Bilbrook Lodge, Bilbrook, Washford, near Minehead in Somerset.   J. H. EDWARDS, *rev.*

Sources F. A. E. Crew, *Memoirs FRS*, 13 (1967), 309–326 · J. Needham, *The Caian* (1966–7), 43–4 · Venn, *Alum. Cant.* · *CGPLA Eng. & Wales* (1967)
Archives RS, corresp., MSS · U. Cam., department of genetics, experimental record of books · U. Cam., department of zoology, lecture notes | Bodl. Oxf., corresp. with C. D. Darlington · CUL, corresp. with Charles C. Hurst
Likenesses W. Stoneman, photograph, 1931, NPG [*see illus.*]
Wealth at death £8618: probate, 8 May 1967, *CGPLA Eng. & Wales*

Punshon, William Morley (1824–1881), Wesleyan Methodist minister and public lecturer, born at Doncaster on 29 May 1824, was the only child of John Punshon (1793–1840) and his wife, Elizabeth (1800–1838), who married in 1823 at Cantley, near Doncaster. His father was a member of the firm of Wilton and Punshon, mercers, at Doncaster. His mother was the eldest daughter of William Morley, a freeman of the same town. His maternal uncle Isaac was knighted in 1841, and was twice mayor of Doncaster. William Punshon was taught at Doncaster grammar school, and afterwards at a boarding-school at Tadcaster. In 1837 he entered his grandfather Morley's counting-house in Hull, and began to learn the business of a timber merchant. He employed his leisure time in reading.

His mother's death, and the influence of the Revd Samuel Romilly Hall, led Punshon to consider religious questions; he was converted and joined the Methodist society in Hull in May 1839. At the age of sixteen he began to preach, his first sermon being at Ellerby, near Hull. With like-minded friends he formed a society for mutual improvement, and soon displayed remarkable powers of oratory. In 1840 he moved to Sunderland, the place of origin of his father, where he had work with an uncle by marriage and became an accredited local preacher. Abandoning business pursuits, he prepared for the work of the Wesleyan Methodist ministry under his uncle the Revd Benjamin Clough, in Woolwich. After spending four months at the theological college at Richmond, he was sent into circuit work early in 1845; two years of probation were passed in Whitehaven and two more in Carlisle. Ordained at the Manchester conference of 1849, he spent three years in each of Newcastle upon Tyne, Sheffield, and Leeds. From 1858 to 1864 he was stationed in London (Hinde Street and Islington circuits); subsequently, until 1867, he was in Bristol.

After his ordination Punshon married, on 22 August 1849, Maria Ann Vickers of Gateshead. She died in 1858, leaving him in a depressed state of health. This, and his decision to marry her sister Fanny, occasioned a removal from Britain to Canada, where such a marriage was legally possible, turning his back, it seemed, on a promising career in British Methodism. They were married on 15 August 1868, but Fanny died in 1870. In the five years Punshon spent in Canada, he presided over each annual conference, and helped to consolidate the Methodists of the dominion in the wake of confederation. He was fraternal delegate of the British conference to the General Conference of the Methodist Episcopal church in the United States in 1868 and 1872. In June 1872 the Victoria University of Cobourg, Canada, conferred on him the degree of LLD.

Punshon returned to England in 1873, and was married a third time, on 17 June of that year, to Mary, daughter of William Foster of Sheffield. He lived in London until his death—for two years as superintendent of Kensington circuit, and from 1875 as one of the general secretaries of the Wesleyan Methodist Missionary Society.

Punshon's refinement and eloquence gained for him a reputation, not only among the Methodists but with the general public, as one of the greatest pulpit orators of his age. His lectures covered the prophet of Horeb; John Bunyan; the Huguenots; Wilberforce; science, religion, and literature; and Daniel in Babylon. Delivered with a powerful voice, animated action, and rich rhetoric to crowds at the Exeter, St James's, and other halls in London, and to delighted audiences in the provinces, they greatly enhanced his popularity. Through his efforts he raised more than £10,000 to support the building of churches in watering places such as Bournemouth, where a memorial chapel bearing his name was erected, and in London. His lecture on the Huguenots raised more than £1000 for the chapel at Spitalfields. After his death the lectures were published.

Punshon also developed a great administrative talent. At the Manchester conference, July 1859, he was elected into the legal hundred, a rare distinction for one so young. Despite his absence in Canada he was elected president of conference on his return in 1874. To the mission cause at home and overseas Punshon devoted great energy throughout his life. He took a prominent part in the jubilee celebrations of missions in 1863. He also published a popular imitation of Keble's *Christian Year* entitled *Sabbath Chimes, or, Meditations in Verse*, in 1867. His last years were spent in presenting and enforcing the claims of the work of the Wesleyan Methodist Missionary Society, in superintending the society's missions, in administering its funds, and in directing its agents. He died at Tranby, Brixton Rise, London, on 14 April 1881, and was buried in Norwood cemetery five days later. Punshon had four children, and was survived by his third wife.

W. B. LOWTHER, rev. TIM MACQUIBAN

Sources W. Hill, *An alphabetical arrangement of all the Wesleyan-Methodist ministers, missionaries, and preachers*, rev. J. P. Haswell, 10th edn (1866) · minutes of the Methodist Conference, 1872–81 · N. B. Harmon, ed., *The encyclopedia of world Methodism*, 2 vols. (1974) · G. G. Findlay and W. W. Holdsworth, *The history of the Wesleyan Methodist Missionary Society*, 5 vols. (1921–4) · T. McCullagh, *The Rev. W. Morley Punshon: a memorial sermon* (1881) · F. W. Macdonald, *The life of William Morley Punshon* (1887)
Archives John Wesley's Chapel, London, letters and sermon notes · JRL, Methodist Archives and Research Centre, corresp. · Queens University, Kingston, Canada, Archives, journals of tours in Europe and Canada · Rhodes University, Grahamstown, South Africa, Cory Library for Historical Research, corresp. with W. M. Impey [copies]
Likenesses Appleton & Co., carte-de-visite, NPG · H. C. Balding, etching, NPG · W. Holl, stipple and line engraving (after photograph), NPG · Manesse, etching, repro. in Macdonald, *Life of William Morley Punshon* · Maull & Co., carte-de-visite, NPG · D. J. Pound, stipple and line engraving (after photograph by Mayall), NPG; repro. in D. J. Pound, *Drawing room portrait gallery of eminent personages* (1859–60) · chromolithograph, NPG · wood-engraving (after photograph by Notman & Fraser), NPG; repro. in *ILN* (8 Aug 1874)
Wealth at death under £14,000: probate, 12 May 1881, *CGPLA Eng. & Wales*

Punt, William (*fl.* 1548–1563), polemicist and book smuggler, emerged from obscurity in 1548 as the author of *A New Dialoge called the Endightment agaynste Mother Messe*. This work proved to be popular (three editions were published in two months), perhaps because it skilfully drew on the work of major evangelical writers such as William Turner and John Bale. Punt's links to Bale went beyond imitation; some time between 1549 and 1552, Punt loaned the great bibliophile two books of Latin poetry. In Mary's reign Punt demonstrated the extent of his devotion to the protestant cause. Throughout the years 1554 and 1555, he ran considerable risks acting as a courier for imprisoned protestant leaders, a task which included smuggling letters, documents, and treatises in and out of various English prisons. In 1554 Punt made the first (or at least the first known) of numerous trips to the continent, carrying a letter John Hooper wrote to his wife, Anna, in Frankfurt. Punt, however, seems to have been particularly close to John Bradford, and he was almost certainly the 'W. P.' whom Bradford made co-executor of his books and to whom the martyr bequeathed two shirts.

Some time during this period Punt married Dorothy Rawlins, the daughter of Erkenwald Rawlins, an affluent London merchant and correspondent of Bradford. Rawlins fled into exile in Mary's reign, arriving in Frankfurt by the autumn of 1555 and settling in Geneva by October 1558. His daughter initially remained in England with her husband. Some time after Bradford's execution on 1 July 1555, Punt seems to have gone abroad, very probably taking his wife with him. This, however, was only a respite. In the spring of 1556, an informer wrote to Bishop Edmund Bonner of London, describing Punt as one of the 'principal teachers of heretical doctrine in London' and as one of those who 'do most harm in persuading the people' (Foxe, 1605). The informant also reported that Punt was a bachelor; this probably indicates that Punt left his wife on the continent and returned to England alone. Most particularly, Bonner's informant reported that Punt was 'a great writer of devilish and erroneous books' and that he smuggled heretical books printed on the continent into England. On Palm Sunday 1556 Punt, smuggling a barrel-load of books into London, publicly read from one of them, an attack on the Anabaptists.

The two major concerns of Punt's life, books and the Marian martyrs, were combined in Elizabeth's reign, when he assisted John Foxe in the research for Foxe's great martyrology, the *Actes and Monuments*. Punt's role in aiding Foxe is revealed in a letter he wrote to Foxe from Ipswich on 23 April 1563. The accuracy of one of the stories Foxe had related in the first edition had been challenged. Punt, in his letter to Foxe, revealed that he had helped Foxe interview the sources for the disputed story. Now he travelled back to Ipswich to gather depositions from various witnesses to verify the story. After this, Punt vanishes back into obscurity. He was very probably the William Punt who was licensed by Bishop John Parkhurst of Norwich to read the proscribed *Admonition to Parliament*. The William Punt of Heacham, Norfolk, whose undated will was proved in 1582 may have been the protestant writer and activist; if so, he had a new wife named Elizabeth and a daughter named Mary.

THOMAS S. FREEMAN

Sources J. Foxe, *Actes and monuments* (1563), 1295, 1605 · Emmanuel College, Cambridge, MS 260, fols. 114r–v, 144v, 203v, 224r, 276r–v · Emmanuel College, Cambridge, MS 262, fol. 71v · BL, Harley MS 416, fol. 122r–v · W. Punt, *A new dialogue called the endightment agaynste mother Messe* (1548) · T. S. Freeman, 'Fate, faction and fiction in Foxe's *Book of martyrs*', *HJ*, 43 (2000), 601–23 · C. H. Garrett, *The Marian exiles: a study in the origins of Elizabethan puritanism* (1938), 263–4,

268 • Bale, *Index*, 207 • *The letter book of John Parkhurst, bishop of Norwich*, ed. R. A. Houlbrooke, Norfolk RS, 43 (1974–5), 60 • Norfolk RO, Norwich consistory court will register, Moyse, fols. 414*r*–415*r*

Purbeck. For this title name *see* Villiers, John, Viscount Purbeck (1591?–1658); Danvers, Robert, styled second Viscount Purbeck (1624–1674).

Purcell, Albert Arthur [Alf] (1872–1935), trade unionist and socialist, was born on 3 November 1872 at 29 Britannia Street, Hoxton, London, the son of Albert Duncan Purcell and his wife, Charlotte (*née* Alleway), who were both Irish. Purcell spent much of his childhood in Keighley, where he received an elementary education and began his first job, as a half-timer in a woollen mill, at the age of nine. In 1890, back in Hoxton, Purcell was apprenticed to his father's and brothers' trade as a French polisher. In 1895 he married Sarah Elizabeth, daughter of George Thomas Fidler, an engine driver of Edmonton; they had three daughters. An active member of the London French Polishers' Union, Purcell was elected first treasurer and then, in 1898, general secretary of the Amalgamated Society of French Polishers, into which the London union had merged. In 1900 he moved with his union's central office to Manchester and made his home in Salford. With the merger of his union into the newly formed National Amalgamated Furnishing Trades Association in 1910, Purcell became its Manchester organizer. He was by this time a familiar figure at meetings of Manchester and Salford Trades Council, serving the first of several stints as president and vice-president from 1905 to 1907.

In 1895 Purcell had begun lecturing for the temperance movement, only to recoil from its leaders' narrow-mindedness some two years later. Instead he was drawn by the Eight Hours Movement into the avowedly Marxist Social Democratic Federation (SDF), forerunner of the British Socialist Party (BSP). While he shared the SDF's disdain for the compromising attachments of Labour pragmatists, Purcell's was an ecumenical socialism and in Salford he held both SDF and Independent Labour Party (ILP) memberships. With their support he won a seat on the borough council in 1906, held, with a year's interruption, until 1912. In the parliamentary election of January 1910, he fought West Salford as an independent socialist, backed by Victor Grayson, the countess of Warwick, and a self-consciously exclusive Socialist Representation Committee. Some Labour MPs responded by supporting his Liberal opponent and Purcell came bottom of the poll. This débâcle may help to explain the greater attractiveness to him of notions of direct action based on the workplace. In November 1910 he chaired the Manchester conference on industrial unionism initiated by Tom Mann, and helped to establish Mann's Industrial Syndicalist Education League. Purcell told the conference that he looked upon industrial unionism as a movement which was far more important than the political labour movement, and observed that 'This force [is] what [is] required to emancipate the workers, if they [are] to be emancipated at all'

(*Industrial Syndicalist*). It is a measure of the period's complexities that he had, that same month, sought and regained election as a Salford borough councillor.

During the war years Purcell remained identified with the BSP left and in 1920, representing South Salford BSP, he moved the formation of the British Communist Party at its founding congress. Like many early converts, he left the party soon afterwards but without distancing himself from his left-wing past. He sat in parliament for Coventry (1923–4) and then the Forest of Dean (1925–9), but according to his colleague George Hicks he felt penned up in its clubby precincts. Instead, his true métier was as one of the 'Communistic trade union leaders' noted by Beatrice Webb, assured and assertive in the early 1920s but inevitably somewhat deflated by the failure of the general strike. In 1919 he was elected to the TUC parliamentary committee and remained on its successor body, the TUC general council, until 1927. His was a robust militancy and heartfelt internationalism, exemplified by the journal he founded in 1925, *Trade Union Unity*. In particular he was identified with the cause of Soviet Russia. A stalwart of the Hands Off Russia movement and its successor, the Anglo-Russian parliamentary committee, he had been enthused by visits to the new workers' state in 1920 and 1924. He was, with Mikhail Tomsky, the main force behind the Anglo-Russian committee of the British and Soviet trade union centres, conceived at the euphoric Scarborough TUC of 1925 and buried amid mutual recriminations two years later. As president of the International Federation of Trade Unions (IFTU) from 1924, he found that his pro-Soviet attitudes were not always palatable to the continental unions and in 1927 they failed to re-elect him to the IFTU's executive.

At the 1929 general election, Purcell returned to Manchester to contest Moss Side but lost by some 2000 votes. He remained in the city and that September was elected secretary of Manchester and Salford Trades Council. He devoted his final years of undiminished vigour to its activities, organizing a notable People's Congress in May 1931 and helping set up a local tenants' association. Purcell died suddenly at his Manchester home, 24 Kendall Road, Crumpsall, on 24 December 1935. He was survived by his wife, for whom a trades council appeal raised just over £1200.

Powerful and stockily built, Purcell was as combative in debate as he had at one time proved in east London boxing rings. S. G. Hobson, with whom he had set up the short-lived Furnishing Guild in 1922, remembered him to have been 'as ready with his fists as with his tongue'. Joe Toole, a Salford Labour MP, recalled him on his arrival in Salford as 'a man of fine physique, a first-class speaker, and possessed of a good knowledge of working-class life, [who] threw himself into our propaganda work and rallied thousands to our standard'.   KEVIN MORGAN

Sources R. Hagburn, D. Martin, and J. Saville, 'Purcell, Albert Arthur', *DLB*, vol. 1 • J. Toole, *Fighting through life* (1935) • S. G. Hobson, *Pilgrim to the left: memoirs of a modern revolutionist* (1938) • D. Morris, 'Labour as socialism: opposition and dissent within the independent labour party 1906–14 with special reference to the

Lancashire division', PhD diss., University of Manchester, 1982 · E. Frow and R. Frow, *To make that future — now! A history of Manchester and Salford Trades Council* (1976) · D. F. Calhoun, *The united front: the TUC and the Russians, 1923–1928* (1976) · *Salford Reporter* (8 June 1907) · J. Mahon, 'A. A. Purcell: a champion of working class unity', *Labour Monthly* (Feb 1936) · G. Hicks, 'The passing of A. A. Purcell', *Tailor and Garment Worker* (Feb 1936) · *Industrial Syndicalist*, 1/6 (1910), 3–43 · *The diary of Beatrice Webb*, ed. N. MacKenzie and J. MacKenzie, 4 vols. (1982–5), vol. 4 · d. cert.

Archives U. Warwick Mod. RC, Trade Union Congress MSS **Likenesses** photographs, Trade Union Congress, London **Wealth at death** £775 6s. 8d.: administration, 24 Jan 1936, *CGPLA Eng. & Wales*

Purcell, Daniel (*c*.1670–1717), organist and composer, was long thought to be the son of Henry the elder (*d*. 1664) and his wife, Elizabeth (*d*. 1699), but was in fact probably the youngest son of Thomas Purcell (*d*. 1682), Henry's brother, and his wife, Katherine. Born probably in London, he was a chorister in the choir of the Chapel Royal, where payments are recorded for his attendance at Windsor from 14 August to 26 September 1678, 22 April to 30 June 1682, and 8 July to 10 September 1682, after which his whereabouts and the source of his musical training are unknown. He was appointed organist of Magdalen College, Oxford, at some time about 1689–90, and was well known as a musician and socialite. Although his earliest published compositions predate this appointment, it was while in this post that he wrote most of his early music, including an ode for Oxford's St Cecilia's day celebrations in 1693, *Begin and Strike th'Harmonious Lyre*, and a number of anthems.

When Henry Purcell fell ill in 1695, Daniel seems to have moved to London and taken over most of his work in the theatre. Here he wrote music for Cibber's *Love's Last Shift*, Behn's *The Younger Brother*, the anonymous *Neglected Virtue*, the unfinished *The Indian Queen*, and Manley's *The Lost Lover* before finally resigning his post at Magdalen College (probably at Easter 1696) and moving to London permanently. He kept his Oxford connections, though, writing music for St Cecilia's day odes in 1698, 1699, and 1707. However, it was in the London theatre that Purcell worked most during this hectic period, contributing music to over forty plays between 1696 and 1707, the bulk of them (over thirty) being in the first five years. The largest of these productions were Nahum Tate's *Brutus of Alba* and Thomas D'Urfey's *Cynthia and Endymion* (1696), Elkanah Settle's *The World in the Moon* (1697), and Peter Anthony Motteux's immensely popular *The Island Princess* (1699), on which he collaborated with Jeremiah Clarke and Richard Leveridge. Of his large-scale productions, only John Oldmixon's *The Grove* (1700) and an adapted version of Nathaniel Lee's *The Rival Queens* (1701) date from the eighteenth century, as Purcell suffered because of the growing vogue for Italianate opera. His only contribution towards this genre, the advertised setting of an adaptation of Philippe Quinault's *Orlando Furioso* (1707), was never produced and possibly never even written.

Purcell's setting of William Congreve's Musick Prize masque *The Judgment of Paris* (1701) was awarded third prize, behind John Weldon and Jeremiah Clarke, although Gottfried Finger (who finished fourth) claimed it was the best work after his own. In London, he also wrote odes for the return of William III from Flanders (1697), a St Cecilia ode (*Cecilia, Charming Saint*) for 1698, and two odes for the celebration of Queen Anne's birthday, *Welcome, Welcome, Glorious Day* (1698) and *Again the Glorious Morn* (1700). His collection of Italian-style cantatas with English words, published in 1713, was one of the first of its type.

Soon after Purcell moved to London he became organist at St Dunstan-in-the-East. The surviving records suggest that he played for no pay from 1696, but he was certainly in the post by November 1698, where the churchwardens' accounts record the first payment: 'Mr Purcell 1/2 years salary £10'. He seems to have kept this job throughout all of his time in London, as his final payment is dated 11 November 1717, only days before his death. He was also organist at St Andrew's, Holborn, where in 1713 Dr Henry Sacheverell (formerly his colleague at Magdalen College) was appointed to the living. Sacheverell found the organ shut up and unpaid for, and so arranged for the money to be raised and appointed Daniel as organist. This may have been an unpopular move, as future organists were democratically elected, comments being recorded about the previous appointment procedures at these subsequent elections. Purcell's association with Sacheverell and the high-church party contributed to the suspicion that he had nonjuring sympathies. He also wrote instrumental music, his numerous sonatas for one or two flutes being published in 1708–10 and performed in a number of concerts at the York Buildings and at Stationers' Hall. *The Psalms Set Full*, which demonstrates the genre of psalm organ interludes, was published posthumously in 1718. Autograph manuscripts of his anthems can be found in the British Library (Add. MSS 17841, 31461) and in the Bodleian, Oxford (T 310).

Daniel Purcell was also famous as a punster and socialite. While at Magdalen College, he was threatened with summons to the university court owing to non-payment of debt, and his payments of college battels were sporadic, to say the least. *Joe Miller*, the collection of jokes and puns first published in 1738, contains many examples of his celebrated wit, some of which were reproduced by Sir John Hawkins.

On 9 May 1705, at St Anne Blackfriars, a Daniel Purcell married Elizabeth Tozer. In the vicar-general's marriage licence application, the couple are described as from the parish of St Paul's, Covent Garden, and are stated to be aged 'about 35 years' and '27 years' respectively. If this was Daniel Purcell the composer, then a birth date of *c*.1670 must follow. This places his birth considerably after the death of his supposed father, Henry the elder, in 1664. It appears that Franklin B. Zimmerman, in his major biography of Henry Purcell, suppressed this information for some reason, transcribing the entire document apart from the reference to Daniel's age. While some doubt may be cast on this person's identity, as Daniel Purcell the composer is described as 'Celibis' in a record relating to his will, the existence of a wife would explain the appearance of a portrait miniature depicting a female in a portrait putatively thought to be of Daniel.

The date of Purcell's death is unknown, but he was buried at St Andrew's, Holborn, on 26 November 1717. Although some of his music was performed throughout the eighteenth century, he has remained in the shadow of his illustrious relative ever since.   MARK HUMPHREYS

Sources A. Ashbee, ed., *Records of English court music*, 9 vols. (1986–96) · F. B. Zimmerman, *Henry Purcell, 1659–1695: his life and times*, rev. edn (1983) · J. Hawkins, *A general history of the science and practice of music*, 5 vols. (1776) · parish register, London, St Ann Blackfriars, 9 May 1705 [marriage] · parish register, London, St Andrew's, Holborn, 26 Nov 1717 [burial]
Likenesses J. B. Closterman?, oils, NPG · oils, Worcester Cathedral · oils, Royal Society of Musicians, London · oils, Christ Church Oxf.

Purcell, Edmund Sheridan (1823–1899), journalist and biographer, was born on 1 December 1823 at 28 Montagu Square, London, one of the ten children of Richard Purcell (*d.* 1836), an estate owner in Granada and Trinidad, and Calia Catherine, *née* Lyndsey, daughter and heir of Thomas Lyndsey, an estate owner in Granada. The family were of Roman Catholic Anglo-Irish origins, though settled in the West Indies. In 1837 Purcell's widowed mother took her children to Bonn, where Edmund attended the university and was tutored by his historian uncle Dr James Burton *Robertson (1800–1877). He afterwards graduated from Würzburg University. On returning to England in 1844, he took a post in the Bank of England, and in 1848 married Jane Desanges, daughter of the later bankrupted Sir Francis Desanges, sometime sheriff of Oxfordshire. They had five children, including Edmund Desanges Purcell, barrister of the Middle Temple.

Purcell's first attempt at biography began when, at the wish of A. W. N. Pugin's relatives, he supplied an appendix on Pugin as a Roman Catholic to the non-Catholic Benjamin Ferrey's *Recollections* of Pugin in 1861. In 1866 Purcell became founding editor of the *Westminster Gazette*, reputedly financed by Archbishop Henry Edward Manning. The first issue of the *Gazette* contained a report, allegedly inspired by Manning, that Newman had abandoned his plan of returning to Oxford. Purcell also contributed an essay on church and state to Manning's publication *Essays on Religion and Literature* (1867) for the Academia of the Catholic Religion. Manning, along with other members of the Catholic hierarchy, afterwards withdrew his support from the *Gazette*, which took a very moderate line on the contentious issue of papal infallibility that was being debated at the First Vatican Council (1869–70). After several more years of struggle, the journal folded in 1879. In 1880 Purcell approached William Ewart Gladstone for help in getting a post on the Liberal *Daily News*. Purcell's sketch of Newman in *Celebrities of the Day* (1881) distressed Newman by denigrating his Catholic opponents as 'fanatical', among them, by implication, Manning.

In 1887, perhaps in order to compensate Purcell for his losses on the *Gazette*, Manning authorized him to write a brief outline of his own public career, but lent him only his rather impersonal diary of his travels to Italy in 1847–8 as material. It was on this understanding that Purcell approached Manning's former friend Gladstone for his side of their correspondence, claiming that Manning had offered him the other. Manning and Gladstone both took alarm at this: Manning intended his friend J. E. C. Bodley to be his biographer, and Gladstone forbade Purcell the right to publish his letters. But after Manning's death in 1892, Purcell used his vague and verbal invitation of 1887 as the excuse to carry off a large part of Manning's papers at St Mary of the Angels in Bayswater, securing the permission of at least two of Manning's four trustees, both oblates of St Charles Borromeo. The material taken included the highly sensitive correspondence between Manning and the papal chamberlain Monsignor George Talbot, charting the rise of the often contentious ultramontane party to its ascendancy within the Roman Catholic church in England.

Despite attempts by Friedrich von Hügel, Wilfrid Ward, and Cardinal Herbert Vaughan to persuade Purcell to accept some degree of censorship or not to publish at all, the biography appeared very late in 1895. Its consistent two-fold theme of Manning's devouring ambition and his high holiness, under the heading of what Purcell described as a 'double voice', made a powerfully destructive case. Gladstone, who had granted Purcell several interviews to discuss Manning's Anglican days, told the author: 'You have so pierced into Manning's innermost interior that it really seems as if little more remained for disclosure in the last day' (W. E. Gladstone, *Correspondence on Church and Religion of William Ewart Gladstone*, ed. D. C. Lathbury, 2, 1910, 341).

By its none too subtle denigration of its subject, Purcell's portrayal of Manning, which was eagerly seized upon by Lytton Strachey to provide the damning portrait given in his *Eminent Victorians* of 1918, did lasting damage to Manning's reputation. Yet despite Purcell's biases and inaccuracies as a biographer, which included the misdating of letters and journal passages, inaccurate transcriptions, conjecture, and factual errors (even Manning's birth date was wrong), Purcell's revelations made a critical history of Victorian Catholicism possible. Because some of the Manning papers taken by Purcell were never returned and others, apparently neglected and deteriorating in the Bayswater archives, were removed in the twentieth century by the Abbé Alphonse Chapeau (and, after his death, still inaccessible), reassessments of Manning's life have been piecemeal, leaving Purcell's judgement largely undisturbed. After the success of his *Life of Cardinal Manning*, Purcell began the *Life and Letters* of his friend Ambrose Phillipps De Lisle which was completed by De Lisle's son Edwin (1900). Purcell died at Hillsdown Cottages, Eastbourne, on 12 April 1899, and was buried in Ocklynge cemetery.   SHERIDAN GILLEY

Sources Gillow, *Lit. biog. hist.* · S. Gilley, 'New light on an old scandal: Purcell's *Life of Cardinal Manning*', *Opening the scrolls: essays in Catholic history in honour of Godfrey Anstruther*, ed. D. A. Bellenger (1987), 166–98 · *The Times* (20 April 1899) · *The Tablet* (29 April 1899) · C. Butler, *The life and times of Bishop Ullathorne, 1806–1889*, 2 vols. (1926) · Boase, *Mod. Eng. biog.* · Gladstone, *Diaries* · *The letters and diaries of John Henry Newman*, ed. C. S. Dessain and others, [31 vols.]

(1961–), vol. 29, pp. 388–9; vol. 30, p. 4 • D. Newsome, *The convert cardinals: John Henry Newman and Henry Edward Manning* (1993)
Archives Birmingham Oratory, corresp., mainly with William Neville • BL, letters to W. E. Gladstone, Add. MSS 44494–44525 • U. St Andr. L., von Hügel MSS • U. St Andr. L., letters to duke of Norfolk; corresp. with W. P. Ward

Purcell, Henry (1659–1695), organist and composer, was born in London or Westminster, possibly on 10 September 1659, the third or fourth of six children of Henry Purcell (*d.* 1664), musician, and his wife, Elizabeth (*d.* 1699), and perhaps a cousin of Daniel *Purcell. No record survives of his baptism, and his year of birth is inferred from the ages given on his memorial tablet in Westminster Abbey and the frontispiece portrait of his *Sonnata's of III Parts* of 1683. Both memorial and portrait incorporate a coat of arms used in the seventeenth century by the Purcell family of Shropshire and Staffordshire, but any relationship must have been distant.

Henry Purcell the elder established himself as a leading musician in London during the Commonwealth, being named as a performer in the 1656 edition of William Davenant's musical drama *The Siege of Rhodes*. At the Restoration he became a gentleman of the Chapel Royal; on 16 February 1661 he was installed as a singing man and master of the choristers at Westminster Abbey, moving into a house in the Great Almonry which had been occupied before the civil war by the singing man James Try. His daughter Katherine was baptized in the abbey in March 1662. He died on 11 August 1664, and the administration of his estate, which amounted to £32 3*s.*, was granted to his widow, Elizabeth, in the court of the dean and chapter of Westminster on 7 October. A few months later she left the Great Almonry, perhaps for a house in Tothill Street in which she certainly lived from 1666 until 1680. Some part in the upbringing of her six children may have been played by their uncle Thomas Purcell (*d.* 1682), who held a number of musical and other appointments at court and was in a position to exercise influence on their behalf. A letter written by Thomas to the singer John Gostling in 1679 which refers to 'my sonne Henry' has led to speculation that the composer's parents were really Thomas and his wife, Katherine, though other evidence, such as Thomas Ford's manuscript history of music (*c.*1710) and the will of Purcell's godfather John Hingeston (*d.* 1683), unequivocally points towards the elder Henry and Elizabeth.

Musical training At the age of eight or nine Purcell must have been admitted as a child of the Chapel Royal under Henry Cooke, who was master of the children until his death in 1672. Cooke's successor was Pelham Humfrey (1647–1674), and an early Purcell autograph, a score of Humfrey's 'By the waters of Babylon' with the string sections abbreviated and clumsily arranged for keyboard, may have been copied while Purcell was still a choirboy. On 10 June 1673 he was appointed unpaid assistant to John Hingeston, keeper of the 'regals, organs, virginals, flutes and recorders and all other kind of wind instruments whatsoever', to take up the salaried position when Hingeston died or retired. Warrants dated 17 December the same

Henry Purcell (1659–1695), attrib. John Closterman, 1695?

year provide for the issue of clothing and annual maintenance of £30 customary after a chorister's voice had broken (Ashbee, 1.126, 131–2).

The musicians named in early sources as Purcell's teachers, with whom he probably studied after he left the choir, are John Blow (1649–1708), master of the children from 1674, and Christopher Gibbons (1615–1676), son of the great Orlando Gibbons and a distinguished keyboard player and composer in his own right. Matthew Locke (*d.* 1677) is not known to have taught Purcell formally but was undoubtedly a significant influence: there is some evidence that Purcell inherited Locke's consort music scorebook (BL, Add. MS 17801) and 'What hope for us remains now he is gone', Purcell's elegy for Locke published in John Playford's *Choice Ayres* of 1679, is one of the most striking of his early works.

Early works, c.1675–1680 Purcell composed more music before 1680 than was once thought, and a number of surviving autographs date from the 1670s. Some instrumental bass parts (Yale University, Beinecke Rare Book and Manuscript Library, Osborn MS 515) include a movement entitled 'The Stairre Case Overture', featuring hurrying scale passages, which may have been inspired by Locke's famous 'Curtain Tune' for *The Tempest* (1674), and the earliest version of Purcell's funeral sentences (BL, Add. MS 30931, fol. 81*v*) may have been composed in 1674 for the interment of Pelham Humfrey in the cloisters of Westminster Abbey. A payment at the abbey of £10 'To Mr Tucker for Coppying out some Musick bookes for the use of the Church' in the year ending at Michaelmas 1677

(WAM 33712, fol. 5v) almost certainly refers to the part-books of Triforium set I, which include six Purcell anthems: a few notes of 'Let God arise' are corrected in Purcell's own hand (alto cantoris book, fol. 58v). In the mid-1670s Purcell seems to have been closely involved with the abbey, where his teacher Blow was organist, as he received a number of payments for tuning the organ and, in 1676, for writing out organ parts. About Michaelmas 1679 he took over from Blow, receiving an annual payment of £10, equivalent to that of a singing man, and an additional £8 for house rent.

On 10 September 1677 Purcell succeeded Matthew Locke in his first adult court appointment, that of 'composer in ordinary … for the violin' (Ashbee, 1.173). It is likely that this was simply a vacancy available on (or shortly after) Purcell's eighteenth birthday, and he does not seem to have had to write the music for the royal violin band which the post nominally required. Two incomplete violin suites which may have been composed for this purpose (BL, Add. MS 30930; BL, Royal Music MS 20.h.9; Yale University, Filmer MS 8) date from the early 1680s, after he had acquired other interests, and the theatre suites later published in *A Collection of Ayres, Compos'd for the Theatre* (1697) were in fact drawn from stage works written towards the end of his life. The main focus of Purcell's work in the late 1670s seems, instead, to have been sacred music in a variety of forms, including the elaborate symphony anthem for antiphonally spaced solo and chorus voices and a solo string group. By December 1677 three such anthems, which were performed in the king's presence, had been copied by William Tucker in the Chapel Royal bass partbook (BL, Add. MS 50860): one, 'My beloved spake', survives complete in autograph score (BL, Add. MS 30932, fol. 87) and is a highly accomplished work. Despite this achievement, however, Purcell drew back from the most prestigious forms of composition for the next two or three years, instead subjecting himself to a rigorous course of advanced musical study and carrying out some editorial tasks in the existing repertory of the Chapel Royal.

In September 1677 Purcell took possession of a major scorebook (Cambridge, Fitzwilliam Museum, MU MS 88) from its previous custodian, John Blow, who had made beautiful calligraphic copies of symphony anthems by Pelham Humfrey and himself. At the reverse of the book Purcell now began to copy full and verse anthems without strings, not only by his contemporaries but also by earlier composers including Thomas Tallis, William Byrd, and Orlando Gibbons. He worked from separate partbooks, sometimes demonstrably the printed parts of John Barnard's *First Book of Selected Church Musick* (1641), and his objective was apparently to arrive at corrected, edited scores with regular barring and properly underlaid texts. Purcell later added some works of his own, extended the original series of symphony anthems with a few more works by Blow and Locke, and wrote on the reverse flyleaf the inscriptions 'God bless Mr Henry Purcell 1682' and 'September the 10th 1682', an entry which suggests this as a date for his birthday. Towards the end of the 1670s Purcell also composed most or all of the devotional partsongs (such as *Jehova quam multi sunt hostes*) found in his autograph score BL, Add. MS 30930; most of the extant partsong autographs are revisions of earlier versions transcribed by John Blow in Christ Church, Oxford, Mus. 628.

The sacred partsongs are vocal chamber music rather than anthems, and whereas Fitzwilliam MS 88 is essentially a document of Purcell's working life, Add. MS 30930 contains mainly music composed at least to some extent for his own interest or self-improvement. The most remarkable aspect of the latter manuscript is its inclusion of a series of fantasias for three to seven instruments, music in an old-fashioned polyphonic genre which Purcell re-created rather than slavishly imitated. Twelve four-part works bear dates showing that they were written in a short period over the summer of 1680, and most of the remaining fantasias are more or less contemporary. The two works in six or seven parts are In nomines, employing a slow-moving *cantus fermus* derived from a plainchant, and the five-part 'Fantazia upon One Note', as its title suggests, carries the same compositional principle to its logical extreme, the second tenor part consisting simply of a middle C breve repeated forty times. Add. MS 30930 also contains seven complete sonatas for two violins, bass, and organ: probably composed at different times between about 1677 and about 1685, they were eventually published by Purcell's widow in 1697. Like the sacred partsongs, the sonatas were substantially revised by Purcell and the surviving autograph does not necessarily represent their original version.

Later works for Charles II, 1680–1685 Although the next official change in Purcell's status at court, his appointment as an organist of the Chapel Royal, did not take place until 1682, he seems to have been accepted as a fully-fledged royal composer about the time of his twenty-first birthday in the late summer or autumn of 1680. In that year he wrote *Welcome Vicegerent of the Mighty King*, which was not only his own first royal ode but also the first of a series of 'welcome songs' to be performed on the king's return to Whitehall from his summer progress. The late summer or autumn welcome song appears to have been an innovation intended to provide a showcase for Purcell's talents without disadvantaging Blow and other senior composers, and Purcell provided one each year until 1687. A second indication of Purcell's changed status at court was his acquisition of the great scorebook (BL, Royal Music MS 20.h.8) in which he copied symphony anthems from one end and secular court music from the other, beginning with the 1681 welcome song, *Swifter Isis Swifter Flow*. Between 1680 and 1685 Purcell had few musical interests outside the court and Westminster Abbey: after his music for Nathaniel Lee's *Theodosius*, performed at the Dorset Garden Theatre in the first half of 1680, he wrote no more extended works for the public stage until 1690.

Some time in 1680 Purcell married Frances Peters (d. 1706), daughter of John Baptist Peters (d. 1675), a naturalized Flemish immigrant, and his wife, Amy. No record of the marriage or documentary evidence of Frances's maiden name exists, but members of the Peters family were closely involved with the Purcells in later years and on Purcell's memorial his own arms impale those used by the Peters family. Amy Peters appears to have kept a tavern in Thames Street in the City of London parish of All Hallows, and there can be little doubt that a child named Henry, son of Henry and Frances Purcell, baptized at All Hallows-the-Less on 9 July 1681 and buried there on 18 July, was the composer's son. Purcell's mother, Elizabeth, paid poor rates on the Tothill Street house only until midsummer 1680 and perhaps left on the marriage of Henry and Frances, with whom she may thereafter have lived. The years 1680 to 1682 form the first of two short periods in Purcell's adult life in which his place of residence is unknown. It would not have been unusual for Frances to return to her own mother's home in Thames Street for her first confinement, but Purcell could hardly have lived permanently so far from Whitehall. By Easter 1682 he had taken a house in Great St Ann's Lane, Westminster, where his son John Baptista, baptized on 9 August and buried on 17 October 1682, must have been born.

Further advancement in Purcell's career came on 14 July 1682 when he was admitted as a gentleman of the Chapel Royal to serve as one of the three organists in place of Edward Lowe. Close examination of his handwriting in one of his scorebooks (BL, Royal Music MS 20.h.8) suggests that several of the symphony anthems in it were composed fairly soon after this new appointment, and Purcell's new status was proudly announced in 1683 in his first major publication, *Sonnata's of III parts … composed by Henry Purcell, composer in ordinary to his most sacred majesty, and organist of his Chappell Royall*. The parts of the twelve trio sonatas were printed 'for the Author', at Purcell's own risk, and beautifully engraved by Thomas Cross rather than set in the moveable type normally employed for English music publications of this period. They were first available to subscribers from Purcell's house in Great St Ann's Lane and thereafter were sold by John Playford, John Carr, and Henry Rogers. Purcell's intention was to consolidate his reputation as a serious composer. Written, according to his introduction, in 'just imitation of the most fam'd Italian masters', the sonatas are related to the complex Italian instrumental music exemplified by the sonatas of Colista and Lonati and reveal a strong native influence in their harmony and counterpoint.

Earlier in 1683 Purcell had obtained a sacrament certificate, signed on 4 February 1683 by the minister and a churchwarden of St Margaret's, Westminster, and witnessed by two fellow musicians, Moses Snow and Robert Tanner. As Snow and Tanner received the sacrament on the same occasion, along with another court musician, John Goodwin, the certificate is more likely to represent fulfilment of the requirements of the 1673 Test Act—that all office-holders under the crown possess one—than to reflect any official suspicion about Purcell's Anglican conformity. He finally succeeded to the court post of instrument keeper after John Hingeston died in December 1683, and the following year his 1683 St Cecilia's day ode, *Welcome to All the Pleasures*, was published by John Playford. In

the summer of 1684 Purcell became involved in a competition to select a new organ for the Temple Church, demonstrating the instrument built by Bernard Smith, the court 'organ maker'.

Despite the publication of the sonatas, and the performance and printing of *Welcome to All the Pleasures*, Purcell's creative life between 1680 and 1685 was essentially dedicated to the court of Charles II, providing anthems for the king's worship in the Chapel Royal, odes for formal occasions, and smaller-scale works for private entertainment in the royal apartments. Although a number of songs appeared in John Playford's publications during the early 1680s, none of the music composed for the court and copied in MS 20.h.8 was printed until after 1685, and the manuscript's contents suggest that, contrary to the impression given by Roger North, the king was an enlightened and sophisticated musical patron. It is possible that Purcell's opera *Dido and Aeneas*, performed in 1689 at Josias Priest's boarding-school for girls at Gorges House in Chelsea, also had its origins at court. Its immediate model, John Blow's *Venus and Adonis*, was certainly presented at Whitehall in the early 1680s and later revived at Priest's school, and *Dido* fits in well not only with Charles II's interests but also with a court tradition of masques and musical dramas which included, as well as *Venus and Adonis*, Crowne's masque *Calisto* of 1675 and Rochester's *Valentinian* of early 1684.

Charles II's death in February 1685 seems to have taken Purcell completely by surprise: he had apparently begun transcribing a group of anthems into MS 20.h.8, and had listed their titles in the table of contents, but left 'They that go down to the sea in ships' unfinished and did not copy the two following works. At the secular music end of MS 20.h.8 he wrote the solo song 'If pray'rs and tears', headed 'Sighs for our Late Sovereign King Charles the Second', and Fitzwilliam MS 88 contains the opening section of a full anthem, 'Hear my prayer O Lord', which appears from its handwriting to have been copied about 1685, much later than previously recognized. Quite possibly this powerful work is Purcell's funeral anthem for Charles II, for although according to John Evelyn the late king's burial was carried out quietly (Evelyn, 4.415), the *London Gazette* for 12–16 February 1685 states that the abbey choir was present. The winter of 1684–5 must have involved some disturbance in Purcell's family as well as his working life, as about the beginning of 1685 he moved from his house in Great St Ann's Lane to Bowling Alley East.

The court of James II, 1685–1688 The accession of the Catholic James II inevitably affected Purcell's musical career, though one change in his terms of employment must have been more apparent than real: James reorganized his private musick to form a properly-constituted baroque orchestra of string and wind instruments together with the vocal soloists required to perform a court ode, and Purcell is listed in this ensemble not as composer but as 'harpsicall' (Ashbee, 2.3). He retained his post as organist of the Chapel Royal, but the status of the Anglican chapel was diminished by the fact that the king and queen attended Catholic services and his function as instrument keeper appears for a time to have been forgotten. Early in 1688 he successfully petitioned for back payments and the restoration of his salary for this position, the Chapel Royal organ being then 'so out of repair that to cleanse, tune and put in good order will cost £40' (Ashbee, 8.275–6).

Purcell's treatment of his scorebook MS 20.h.8 suggests that he did not feel the same commitment to James II as he had to his brother Charles. He composed 'My heart is inditing' for the coronation of James II and Queen Mary of Modena on 23 April 1685 but thereafter no sacred music was added to MS 20.h.8 until about 1689, even though Purcell continued to write symphony anthems during this period. The fact that he did not transcribe the new works into his scorebook, or even complete the series of fair copies he was making at the time of Charles II's death, points to a conviction that a permanent repertory of Anglican symphony anthems was no longer required. Even the secular contents of MS 20.h.8 show signs of changing circumstances, the welcome songs for 1685 and 1686 being substantially in the hand of an assistant. Possibly this copyist was Purcell's pupil Robert Hodge from Exeter, about whose debts to local tradesmen he had to complain to the dean of Exeter in November 1686. The dedicated character of the Whitehall repertory began to be lost, and a number of songs and vocal ensembles from MS 20.h.8 appeared in print between 1685 and 1688. Purcell seems also to have accepted other kinds of work beyond the court, and on 30 September 1686 was one of a panel of experts who first examined a new organ built by Bernard Smith for the church of St Katharine Cree and then auditioned candidates for the post of organist.

Meanwhile, the years 1686 and 1687 were also difficult ones for the Purcell family. A son, Thomas, whose baptism is unrecorded, was buried at Westminster Abbey on 3 August 1686 and a second child named Henry, baptized at St Margaret's on 9 June 1687, died in September. However, on 30 May 1688 the Purcells' daughter Frances, the first of their children to survive to adulthood, was baptized at Westminster Abbey.

Revolution, 1688–1689 With the accession of William and Mary, Purcell's career as a composer primarily dedicated to the court ended. His appointments were perpetuated, and his birthday odes for Queen Mary include some of his finest works, but Whitehall itself was no longer to be the self-contained and cohesive centre of musical excellence it had been under Charles II. As early as 23 February 1689 the use of stringed instruments in the Chapel Royal was forbidden (Holman, 140 n.), and in 1691 it was again decreed that 'the King's Chapel shall be all the year through kept both morning and evening with solemn musick like a collegiate church' (Ashbee, 2.43). There was no prospect of the revival of the elaborate Anglican symphony anthem, although MS 20.h.8 contains evidence that for a time Purcell continued to hope that the chapel would be restored to its former glory. About 1689 an assistant, possibly the Temple Church organist Francis Pigott, added three new symphony anthems, but the third, 'Praise the Lord O my soul', was left incomplete, petering out as though the copyist realized it was never again likely to be performed with stringed instruments, and most of Purcell's late anthems exist only in versions accompanied by organ alone.

A misunderstanding over incidental proceeds from the coronation of William and Mary on 11 April 1689 may have caused some friction at Westminster Abbey, though its significance has almost certainly been exaggerated. The organist and choirmen were permitted to sell places for spectators to view the coronation from the organ loft or from scaffolds erected at the choir's own expense within the church, but on 25 March 1689 it had been decreed that all money raised in this way at the forthcoming coronation should be paid to the treasurer and redistributed by the dean and chapter. For some reason Purcell had not handed over his takings by 18 April and was peremptorily ordered to do so within two days on pain of dismissal. He complied promptly with the chapter's instruction, being allowed to deduct 'his poundage & other things' before passing on the sum of £78 4s. 6d., and in the distribution received £35, much more than the £24 received by the precentor, Stephen Crespion, and almost twice the sum of £18 paid to each of the minor canons. There is no evidence that this incident sullied Purcell's reputation or caused any lasting ill feeling between himself and his colleagues or superiors.

Quite apart from the coronation, 1689 appears to have been a very busy year for Purcell. He contributed several pieces to Playford's *The Second Part of Musick's Hand-Maid*, a collection of easy keyboard music of which he was also the editor, and the opera *Dido and Aeneas* was presented at Josias Priest's boarding-school for girls in Chelsea. Purcell composed two odes influenced by the up-to-date Italian style recently exemplified in *From Harmony, from Heavenly Harmony*, Draghi's ode for St Cecilia's day performed on 22 November 1687. *Now Does the Glorious Day Appear* (30 April 1689) was the first of a series of annual 'birthday songs' for Queen Mary which culminated in *Come Ye Sons of Art Away* of 1694, and *Celestial Music* (5 August) was written for Lewis Maidwell's progressive academy in King Street, Westminster. The year also saw the baptism at the abbey on 6 September of the second of Purcell's children to survive to adulthood, his son Edward.

Composer for the theatre, 1690–1695 After 1690 the public theatre assumed the place previously occupied by Whitehall at the centre of Purcell's creative life. Between 1690 and 1695 he contributed music to over forty theatrical works produced by the United Company, until 1695 the only company licensed to perform plays in London. Often the music consisted of a single song or a suite of incidental instrumental movements, but some plays, such as *Oedipus*, involved long and elaborate passages of music as part of the action. The 'dramatic operas' *Dioclesian* (1690), *King Arthur* (1691), *The Fairy Queen* (1692, revived 1693), and *The Indian Queen* (1695) consist of a succession of musical scenes linked together by dialogue spoken by actors who did not normally sing even though they might nominally be central characters. The annual sequence of dramatic operas was broken in 1694 by the first two parts of Thomas D'Urfey's trilogy *The Comical History of Don Quixote*, a less extravagant production with songs by Purcell and John Eccles.

Although Purcell was mainly concerned with theatre music in the last five years of his life, he had other important commitments. On 27 March 1690 the 'Yorkshire Feast Song', *Of Old when Heroes Thought it Base*, was presented at the annual festival of the Yorkshire Society in London at Merchant Taylors' Hall, in 1692 Purcell produced his second St Cecilia's day ode, *Hail Bright Cecilia*, and in 1693 he edited and contributed to a second book of *Harmonia sacra* issued by Henry Playford. In 1694 he revised the twelfth edition of John Playford's *Introduction to the Skill of Music*, the standard musical instruction book of the time, updating the section on composition, 'The art of descant'; on 20 July he was one of three Westminster Abbey officials who signed a contract with Bernard Smith for a major overhaul and extension of the abbey organ, and for the Cecilian celebrations in November he composed the Te Deum and Jubilate in D. Considering the number of major works he produced in this period together with his other activities it is little wonder that he did not manage to compile orderly fair-copy autographs of his theatre music and late odes comparable to the anthem scores in MS 20.h.8.

In addition Purcell had several pupils. In 1693 and 1694 his former Chapel Royal colleague John Walter, now master of the choristers at Eton College, sent the talented John Weldon to study with Purcell, and aristocratic female pupils included Annabella Howard, fourth wife of the elderly Sir Robert Howard, Sir Robert's granddaughter Diana, and Rhoda Cavendish. Two of Purcell's late autograph manuscripts, a keyboard book (BL, MS Mus.1) and the 'Gresham' songbook (Guildhall Library, London), seem to have been compiled for teaching or coaching, in the case of the Gresham book for an advanced performer rather than a young pupil, and are thus quite different in character from his archival volumes of earlier years. Other late autographs show that Purcell sometimes worked in great haste: the score of *The Fairy Queen* (Royal Academy of Music, MS 3) is largely the work of a very competent professional scribe but contains a few sections in Purcell's own hand, as though he did not finish composing them until the last minute.

The Westminster poor rate assessments suggest that in 1691 Purcell acquired a second property adjoining his house in Bowling Alley, but in 1692 and 1693 he disappears from the Westminster rate books, his name being replaced by 'Ann Peters'. The highway rate for Christmas 1693 correctly identifies this householder as Amy Peters, Purcell's mother-in-law, and in 1694 the rates were paid by Frances's sister Amy Howlett. Purcell's absence is difficult to explain, as he still held his court offices and his post as organist of Westminster Abbey. Possibly he lived temporarily outside London in some location more convenient for the palaces of Hampton Court and Kensington, preferred by William and Mary, as well as for Windsor and Eton, or perhaps he wanted to move his family to a healthier location. At least one of the Bowling Alley houses was let to tenants, and when the Purcells returned to Westminster about Christmas 1693 they moved into a house in

Marsham Street. Their youngest child, Mary-Peters, who does not appear to have been living when her mother made her will in 1706, was baptized at Westminster Abbey on 10 December 1693.

The beginning of 1695 was overshadowed by the death of Queen Mary from smallpox on 28 December 1694. For her state funeral on 5 March 1695 Purcell provided a march and canzona for 'flat trumpets', instruments with slides to permit them to play in minor keys, and an old-fashioned setting of one of the Anglican funeral sentences, 'Thou knowest Lord the secrets of our hearts'. The service to be sung was that by Thomas Morley, used at the funeral of James I, from which this section had been found to be missing. After the period of mourning, however, Purcell's life seems to have proceeded normally. As well as *The Indian Queen* he wrote music for several other dramas, including *Timon of Athens* and *Bonduca*, and for 24 July 1695 he composed his last court ode, *Who Can from Joy Refrain*, for the sixth birthday of Princess Anne's son the duke of Gloucester.

In the London theatre 1695 was a year of upheaval. A group of experienced actors led by Thomas Betterton deserted the United Company to set up a rival theatre of their own and Purcell's *The Indian Queen* was therefore performed by the remnant of the company, 'for the most part Learners, Boys and Girls, a very unequal match for them who revolted' (Wells, 7). Fortunately the 'remnant' included Jemmy Bowen, Letitia Cross, and other talented singers, and a successful production apparently took place in the early summer of 1695. For subsequent revivals an 'Additional Act' for a concluding masque was provided by Daniel Purcell, 'Mr Henery Purcell being dead' (BL, Add. MS 31453, fol. 69).

'From rosy bowers', 'the last Song that Mr. Purcell Sett, it being in his Sickness' (*Orpheus Britannicus*, 1, 1698, 90), was Purcell's only contribution to the third part of D'Urfey's *Don Quixote*, performed in November 1695. The fact that Purcell wrote no more music for this production may indicate that he was unwell for some weeks before his death, but there is no evidence in his working life up to September 1695 to indicate a more protracted illness. 'Lovely Albina', 'The last Song Mr Henry Purcell set before his Sickness' (ibid., 133), alludes to the reconciliation of a quarrel between Princess Anne and King William, and cannot have been composed before William's return to London from the continent on 12 October 1695. The story referred to by Hawkins (Hawkins, 2.748) that Purcell caught a cold which suddenly turned to something much more serious is probably essentially correct, though Hawkins himself questions the further detail, lacking any independent corroboration, that Purcell was taken ill after Frances locked him out when he came home late and drunk from a tavern. Purcell seems not to have realized the seriousness of his condition until the day he died, on 21 November 1695 at his home in Marsham Street, when he made his will bequeathing all his possessions to his 'Loving Wife Frances Purcell'. The witnesses were his Marsham Street neighbour John Capelin, William Eeles, an apothecary from Bowling Alley who had perhaps been attending him, and his brother-in-law John Baptist Peters, whose signet ring was used to seal the will. Arrangements for the funeral, which took place in Westminster Abbey on the evening of 26 November, were described in that day's issue of the *Flying Post*: Purcell was to be buried near the organ without charge to his widow, the entire chapter attending along with the choirs of Westminster Abbey and the Chapel Royal. According to the *Post Boy* of 28 November 1695 the funeral was conducted 'in a magnificent manner' and the composer Thomas Tudway states that Purcell's new setting of 'Thou knowest Lord' was performed with its accompaniment of 'flat Mournfull Trumpets' (BL, Harleian MS 7340, fol. 264*v*).

Posthumous events Purcell died at the height of his powers, and his music was evidently in great demand. Frances Purcell herself published *A Choice Collection of Lessons for the Harpsichord or Spinnet* in 1696 and three works in 1697—the *Ayres, Compos'd for the Theatre*, *Ten Sonata's in Four Parts*, and the *Te Deum & Jubilate for Voices and Instruments Made for St Caecilia's Day, 1694*. The two books of *Orpheus Britannicus*, which contained songs and vocal ensembles by Purcell, including movements extracted from longer works, were issued in 1698 and 1702 by Henry Playford: further editions of books 1 and 2, with altered contents, were issued in 1706 and 1711 respectively, and a third edition of both books in 1721. Frances Purcell's dedication of book 1 of *Orpheus Britannicus* to Annabella, Lady Howard, discloses that Lady Howard was responsible for Purcell's monument in Westminster Abbey and for 'gracing it with an inscription which may perpetuate both the Marble and his Memory'. Some of the verses printed in the two volumes seem to pass beyond the conventional to express sincere affection, and surviving musical tributes include two outstanding works—John Blow's *Mark how the Lark and Linnet Sing* and Jeremiah Clarke's *Come, Come Along for a Dance and a Song*, in which celebration turns to despair at the news of the composer's death.

Frances Purcell left Marsham Street for a house in Dean's Yard, Westminster, at which address the third edition of *A Choice Collection* (1699) was advertised for sale, and in 1705 she moved to Richmond, where she died in February 1706. Her nuncupative will, witnessed by her sister Amy Howlett, Ann Eeles, probably the wife of William Eeles, the Bowling Alley apothecary, and Ann Pendleton, refers to an organ and two spinets left to her son Edward along with 'the books of music in general'. These certainly included the scorebook Royal Music MS 20.h.8, inscribed on the reverse flyleaf 'Anthems and Welcome Songs and other Songs all by my father'. Frances was buried near her husband in Westminster Abbey on 14 February 1706. Their son Edward (*d*. 1740) became organist of St Clement, Eastcheap, and St Margaret's, Westminster; his sister Frances, who administered her mother's will, married the writer Leonard Welstead and died in 1724 at the age of thirty-six.

Historical significance Although Purcell was one of the greatest and most individual of English composers, his music was as much a product of the age in which he lived as of his nationality. He belonged to a vigorous but by no means insular English musical tradition and himself responded both to the French influence favoured by Charles II and to Italian music. His musical knowledge demonstrably extended from English polyphony of the sixteenth and early seventeenth centuries to contemporary Italian vocal and instrumental writing, and his works draw upon a wide variety of stylistic resources. He excelled in the setting of English words, in his last years coming close to establishing a form of music drama distinct from Italian opera and acceptable to English audiences.

Purcell has never been without admirers, but the exalted reputation he enjoyed in the two decades following his death did not last, and many mid-eighteenth-century musicians compared his works unfavourably to those of Corelli and Handel. His gradual recovery of the classical status earlier implied by *Orpheus Britannicus* began towards the end of the eighteenth century, and in the 1780s Benjamin Goodison unsuccessfully attempted to bring out a complete edition, a project finally carried out over many years by the Purcell Society, founded in 1876. By the mid-twentieth century Purcell's independent part-writing and sometimes astringent harmony had perhaps become more congenial to performers and listeners than they had been for more than 200 years. Developing interest in early music and historically informed performance of music and drama means that Purcell's work can again be judged in its proper context as the culmination of almost a century of baroque music in England rather than merely as part of the background to the international baroque style of the eighteenth century.

ROBERT THOMPSON

Sources Westminster Abbey precentor's book, 1660–72, Westminster Abbey Archives, 61228A · Westminster Abbey rental, *c.*1662, Westminster Abbey Archives, 44034 · Westminster Abbey treasurers' books, 1660–94, Westminster Abbey Archives, 33694–33710, 33712–33728 · Westminster Abbey chapter act book 5, 1683–1714 · Westminster Abbey miscellaneous coronation documents, 1689, Westminster Abbey Archives, 51226, 51137 · T. Ford, 'An account of Musicians and their works', Bodl. Oxf., MS Mus e 17 · St Margaret's Westminster accounts of the overseers of the poor, 1656–90, City Westm. AC, E170–E202 · St Margaret's Westminster poor rate assessments, 1684–96, City Westm. AC, E299–E311 · St Margaret's Westminster highway rate assessments, 1666–95, City Westm. AC, E850–E875 · St Margaret's Westminster poll tax, 1692, City Westm. AC, E2415 · administration, prerogative court of the dean and chapter of Westminster, City Westm. AC [the elder Henry Purcell, act book 3, 1645–66, fol. 55; Elizabeth Purcell, act book 8, 1687/1688–99, fol. 93] · Purcell's will, PRO, PROB 1/8 · PROB 11/429, fol. 317 [register copy] · PRO, PROB 11/489, fol. 157 [Frances Purcell] · PRO, PROB 11/375, fols. 134–5 [John Hingeston] · F. B. Zimmerman, *Henry Purcell, 1659–1695: his life and times* (1967); rev. edn (1983) · F. B. Zimmerman, *Henry Purcell, 1659–1695: an analytical catalogue of his music* (1963) · *The works of Henry Purcell*, 32 vols. (1878–1965) · J. A. Westrup, *Purcell* (1937); rev. edn, rev. N. Fortune (1980); repr. with foreword by C. Price (1995) · P. Holman, *Henry Purcell* (1994) · M. Duffy, *Henry Purcell* (1994) · A. Ashbee, ed., *Records of English court music*, 9 vols. (1986–96), vols. 1–2, 5, 8 · R. Shay and R. Thompson, *Purcell manuscripts: the principal musical sources* (2000) · J. Hawkins, *A general history of the science and practice of music*, new edn, 3 vols. (1853); repr. in 2 vols. (1963) · R. Luckett, '"Or rather our musical Shakespeare": Charles Burney's Purcell', *Music in eighteenth-century England: essays in honour of Charles Cudworth*, ed. C. Hogwood and R. Luckett (1983), 59–77 · P. A. Scholes, *The Oxford companion to music*, ed. J. O. Ward, 10th edn (1970) · M. Tilmouth, 'A calendar of references to music in newspapers published in London and the provinces (1660–1719)', *Royal Musical Association Research Chronicle*, 1 (1961) • M. Tilmouth, 'A calendar of references to music in newspapers published in London and the provinces (1660–1719) [pt 2]', *Royal Musical Association Research Chronicle*, 2 (1962), 2–15 • Evelyn, *Diary* • B. Wood and A. Pinnock, '"Unscarr'd by turning times"? The dating of Purcell's *Dido and Aeneas*', *Early Music*, 20 (1992), 372–90 • B. Wood, 'The first performance of Purcell's funeral music for Queen Mary', *Performing the music of Henry Purcell* [Oxford 1993], ed. M. Burden (1996), 61–81 • N. Luttrell, *A brief historical relation of state affairs from September 1678 to April 1714*, 6 vols. (1857) • A. Browning, 'Purcell's *Stairre case overture*', *MT*, 121 (1980), 768–9 • S. B. Wells, ed., *A comparison between the two stages: a late Restoration book of the theatre* (1942)

Archives Exeter Cathedral, dean and chapter library, letter, MS 6077/1

Likenesses J. Closterman, chalk drawing, 1695?, NPG [*see illus.*] • after J. Closterman, oils, 1695?, NPG • attrib. J. Closterman, oils, 1695?, NPG • T. Cross junior, line engraving (aged 23), BM, NPG; repro. in H. Purcell, *Sonnatas of III parts* (1683), frontispiece • R. White, line engraving (after painting by or after J. B. Closterman, 1695), BM, NPG; repro. in H. Purcell, *Orpheus Britannicus* (1698) • G. Zobel, mezzotint (after J. B. Closterman), BM, NPG • charcoal sketch, BM • oils, NPG

Purcell, John (c.1674–1730), physician, was born in Shropshire. In 1696 he became a student of medicine in the University of Montpellier; there he attended the lectures of Pierre Chirac, then professor of medicine, for whom he retained a great respect throughout his life (Purcell, 48). After taking the degrees of bachelor and licentiate, he graduated MD on 29 May 1699.

Purcell practised in London, and in 1702 published *A Treatise of Vapours or Hysteric Fits*, a second edition of which appeared in 1707. The book is dedicated to 'the Honourable Sir John Talbott, his near relation' and gives a detailed clinical account of the symptoms of hysteria, mixed with pathology drawn from the ideas of Thomas Willis. Purcell moved away from traditional humoralism and wrote that

> Raving is produc'd by a Mixture of Hetrogeneous Particles with the Spirits, which fermenting with them, make their Motion violent and irregular in the Emporium of the Brain, where they do at once irritate a great many Nervous Fibres, and renew many confus'd Ideas of things past.   (Porter, 47)

Purcell makes a number of original comments, and points out that there are no grounds for the ancient belief that the movement of the uterus is related to the symptoms of hysteria. He supports Sydenham's statement that similar symptoms are observable in men, while recognizing that the malady had a particular 'gusto for the tender sex' (Porter, 84). Its greater frequency in women Purcell attributes to their menses being more likely to cause an obstruction to digestion. He recommends crayfish broth and Tunbridge Wells waters, among a variety of prescriptions, including seeing plays, merry company, and airing in the parks.

In 1714 Purcell published *A Treatise of the Cholick*, dedicated to his relative, Charles, duke of Shrewsbury; a second edition appeared in 1715. This work shows less observation than his former book, but contains the description of an autopsy which he witnessed at Montpellier, giving

the earliest observation in any English book of the irritation produced by the exudation in peritonitis on the hands of the morbid anatomist.

On 3 April 1721 Purcell was admitted a licentiate of the Royal College of Physicians, London. He died on 19 December 1730.   NORMAN MOORE, *rev.* PATRICK WALLIS

Sources Munk, *Roll* • J. Astruc, *Mémoires pour servir à l'histoire de la faculté de médecine de Montpellier* (1767) • J. Purcell, *A treatise of vapours*, 2nd edn (1707) • R. Porter, *Mind-forg'd manacles: a history of madness in England from the Restoration to the Regency* (1987)

Purcell, Richard (*fl.* 1746–1766), engraver, was born in Dublin and was a pupil of John Brooks. After Brooks went to London in 1746, Purcell remained in Dublin working for the printsellers and probably assisting Andrew Miller. Twelve mezzotints of portraits, signed R. Purcelle or R. P., date from the years 1748–55, at which point he moved to London, following in the footsteps of his fellow pupil James Macardell.

Purcell displayed some talent, but he had a marked weakness for drink and never established an independent career. He worked for the printsellers—chiefly for Robert Sayer—and a large part of his output consisted of copies of prints by other artists, notably his more reliable and successful compatriots Macardell and James Watson. Many of his prints are signed with the aliases Chas. Corbutt and C. Corbutt. Five prints are signed Philip Corbutt, which Strickland has tentatively identified as a son, but is more probably just another alias. Many unsigned plates published by Sayer are probably by him. Purcell probably died about 1766.

TIMOTHY CLAYTON and ANITA MCCONNELL

Sources W. G. Strickland, *A dictionary of Irish artists*, 2 vols. (1913); repr. with introduction by T. J. Snoddy (1989), vol. 2, pp. 264–70 • J. C. Smith, *British mezzotinto portraits*, 4 vols. in 5 (1878–84)

Purchas, John (1823–1872), Church of England clergyman and religious controversialist, eldest son of Captain William Jardine Purchas RN (1779–1848), sometime mayor of Cambridge, and his wife, Jane Hills, a niece of the novelist Frederick Marryat (1792–1848), was born at Cambridge on 14 July 1823, and educated at Rugby School from 1836. He was admitted to Christ's College, Cambridge, on 8 July 1840, and graduated BA in 1844. He served as curate at Elsworth, Cambridgeshire, from 1851 to 1853, at Orwell in the same county from 1856 to 1859, and at St Paul's, West Street, Brighton, from 1861 to 1866. He was appointed perpetual curate of St James's Chapel, Brighton, in 1866, and there he introduced practices that were denounced as ritualistic. On 27 November 1869 he was charged before Sir Robert Phillimore, dean of the court of arches at Canterbury, with infringing the law of the established church by using a cope (otherwise than during the communion service), chasubles, albs, stoles, tunicles, dalmatics, birettas, wafer bread, lighted candles on the altar, crucifixes, images, and holy water. He was also accused of standing with his back to the people when consecrating the elements, mixing water with the wine, censing the minister, leaving the holy table uncovered during the service, directing processions round the church, and giving notice of unauthorized holidays. Purchas did not appear, claiming that he was too poor to pay for legal assistance and too infirm to defend the case in person. On 3 February 1870 Phillimore ruled against him on eight points. This decision was not satisfactory to the promoter of the suit, Colonel Charles James Elphinstone, who appealed for a fuller condemnation of Purchas to the queen in council, but died on 30 March 1870 before the case was heard. Henry Hebbert of Brighton, a retired judge of the high court at Bombay, was then permitted to revive the appeal. The privy council decided against Purchas on 16 May 1871, declaring that eucharistic vestments, the eastward position, the mixed chalice, and wafer bread were all illegal. Purchas, however, had made over all his property to his wife, and he neither paid the costs, amounting to over £2096, nor discontinued the illegal practices. On 7 February 1872 the privy council consequently suspended him from the discharge of his clerical office for twelve months.

The 'Purchas judgment' gave rise to much controversy but proved virtually impossible to enforce, since most bishops were reluctant to take the ritualists to court. Although a copy of the order of suspension was affixed to the door of St James's Chapel on 18 February 1872, Purchas continued his services as usual for the last months of his life. He died at his home in Montpellier Villas, Brighton, on 18 October 1872, and was buried in the churchyard of St James's on 23 October. He left a widow and five sons.

Purchas's best-known work was the *Directorium Anglicanum* (1858), a standard manual on Anglican ritual. In his youth he had published a comedy, *The Miser's Daughter* (1839), and several volumes of poetry, but his later works were exclusively ecclesiastical.

G. C. BOASE, *rev.* G. MARTIN MURPHY

Sources L. E. Ellsworth, *Charles Lowder and the ritualist movement* (1982) · Venn, *Alum. Cant.* · *The Times* (19 Oct 1872), 5 · *Annual Register* (1871), 187–210 · *Law reports: admiralty and ecclesiastical cases*, 3 (1872), 66–113 · *Law reports: privy council appeals*, 3 (1871), 605–72
Archives LPL, corresp. and papers on the Purchas judgment
Likenesses W. & A. H. Fry, cartes-de-visite, NPG

Purchas, Samuel (*bap.* 1577, *d.* 1626), geographical editor and compiler and Church of England clergyman, was baptized on 20 November 1577 at Thaxted, Essex, the sixth of the ten children of George Purcas (*c.*1549–1625), who was in the cloth trade, and his wife, Anne (*c.*1544–1619). He matriculated from St John's College, Cambridge, in 1594 (probably December), and graduated BA by 1597 and MA in 1600; he received a Lambeth BD on 14 March 1615 and was incorporated as an Oxford BD on 11 July 1615. He sought a bishop's licence to marry Jane Lease (*bap.* 1573) of Westhall, Suffolk, on 2 December 1601. They had three children: Mary (1603/4–1619); Samuel (1605/6–1658/9), author of *A Theatre of Politicall Flying-Insects* (1657); and Martha.

Purchas spent his professional life in the Church of England. He was ordained deacon (1 May 1598) and then priest (25 January 1601) in Witham church, Essex. In Essex he became successively curate of Purleigh (before 23 April 1601), vicar of Eastwood (24 August 1604), and rector of Snoreham (1615); then in London he was appointed chaplain to Archbishop George Abbot in 1613 or 1614, rector of St Martin Ludgate (1614), and finally rector of All Hallows, Bread Street (22 April 1626). From 1621 to 1624 he was also a fellow of King James's College at Chelsea, the major arsenal of anti-Catholic polemic, where he composed his one published sermon, *The Kings Towre* (preached at Paul's Cross on 5 August 1622), and compiled much of his major work, *Hakluytus Posthumus, or, Purchas his Pilgrimes* (1624–5).

Purchas was admitted to the Virginia Company on 22 May 1622, and attended six meetings of the company court in 1622–4 (Kingsbury, 2.20, 26, 103, 485, 498, 512, 518, 533). His first published compilation of travel literature was *Purchas, his Pilgrimage* (1613); he dedicated the second, expanded edition (1614) to his ecclesiastical patron Archbishop Abbot. By this time Purchas had already become acquainted with Richard Hakluyt, his great predecessor in the memorializing of English travel narratives, who lent books and some manuscripts for the second edition of the *Pilgrimage*. Two further editions appeared in 1617 and 1626. His only independent original works, *Purchas his Pilgrim: Microcosmus, or, The Historie of Man* (1619) and *The Kings Towre* (1623), referred to travel accounts, but were primarily works of speculative theology characteristic of the Calvinist consensus of their time. Purchas was no traveller himself: as he confessed, 'Even I, which have written so much of travellers & travells, never travelled 200. miles from

Samuel Purchas (*bap.* 1577, *d.* 1626), by unknown engraver, pubd 1624

Thaxted in *Essex*, where I was borne' (Purchas, *Pilgrimes*, I. i. 74).

The *Pilgrimes* (as it is usually known) was the culmination of almost twenty years' collecting oral and written accounts of travels in Europe, Asia, Africa, and the Americas. It was based in part on Hakluyt's remaining manuscripts, which Purchas had acquired in 1620. (Their subsequent history is unknown.) The result was a four-volume folio that took more than three years to print; at the time of its publication it was the largest book ever seen through the English press. The *Pilgrimes* combined editing with editorializing to comprise the bulkiest anti-Catholic tract of the age and the last great English work of geographical editing for almost a century. Its four volumes traversed the world from the ancient Near East to the latest English colonies. The first volume comprised the travels of ancient kings, patriarchs, apostles, and others; comparative histories of languages, religion, church government, and 'letters'; circumnavigations of the globe; and English voyages to Africa, Persia, India, and Asia. The second volume extended the collection of travel narratives to encompass Africa and the Near East, while the third covered China, Russia, 'Tartary', Iceland, Greenland, the north-west passage, and the Arctic. Purchas's coverage of European exploration and settlement in the Americas began at the end of the third volume, but made up the bulk of the fourth, which treated South and North America, and ended with English settlements in Bermuda, Virginia, New England, and Newfoundland. Purchas edited oral accounts and manuscripts (many from Hakluyt's papers), translated texts in classical and foreign languages, and reprinted previously published works. His only original contributions came in the form of various editorials scattered through the volumes on, among other things, Solomon's voyage to Ophir, Pope Alexander's bulls of donation of 1493, the 'iniquitie' of papal power, the history of Europe, and 'Virginia's Verger', an ideological justification for English settlement in Virginia in the wake of the Powhatan uprising of 1622 (*Pilgrimes*, 4.1809–26).

Since the nineteenth century Purchas's editorial methods have always been contrasted unfavourably with Hakluyt's, though his influence (and the European dissemination of his works) were arguably much greater. Unlike Hakluyt, Purchas attempted to construct an argument upon geographical and historical evidence that was cosmopolitan, pan-European, global, and transhistorical. The militantly theological purpose of his works may partly account for the contempt and neglect into which he largely fell in the centuries after John Locke evenhandedly advised in 1703 that for 'books of travel ... the collections made by our countrymen, Hakluyt and Purchas, are very good' (Locke, 353). Purchas made final alterations to his will (originally composed on 31 May 1625) on 9 September 1626. His exact death date is unknown, though it was before 29 September 1626, when the rectory of All Hallows, Bread Street, fell vacant. His burial at St Martin Ludgate was recorded on 30 September 1626, and his will was proved on 21 October 1626.

DAVID ARMITAGE

Sources D. R. Ransome, 'A Purchas chronology', *The Purchas handbook: studies of the life, times and writings of Samual Purchas*, ed. L. E. Pennington, 1, Hakluyt Society, 2nd ser., 185 (1997), 329–80 · H. W. King, 'Ancient wills (no. 7)', *Transactions of the Essex Archaeological Society*, 4 (1869), 164–83 · J. MacLehose, 'Publisher's note', in S. Purchas, *Hakluytus Posthumus, or, Purchas his pilgrimes*, bk 1, Hakluyt Society, extra ser., 14 (1905), xxi–xxvii · Venn, *Alum. Cant.* · Foster, *Alum. Oxon.* · J. L. Chester and J. Foster, eds., *London marriage licences, 1521–1869* (1887) · S. M. Kingsbury, ed., *The records of the Virginia Company of London*, 4 vols. (1906–35) · D. Armitage, *The ideological origins of the British empire* (2000) · J. Locke, *Political essays*, ed. M. Goldie (1997)
Archives Chatsworth House, Derbyshire, 'Virginia's verger', Hardwick MS 56
Likenesses engraving, pubd 1624, BM [*see illus.*] · J. Benajamin, print (copy of line engraving, 1625), NPG · line engraving, BL; repro. in S. Purchas, *Hakluytus Posthumus, or, Purchas his pilgrimes*, 4 vols. (1625), vol. 1 · line engraving, NPG

Purdeator, Ann (*d.* 1692). *See under* Salem witches and their accusers (*act.* 1692).

Purdey, James (1784–1863), gun maker, was born in August 1784 in Whitechapel, London, the third son of James Purdey, blacksmith, and his wife, Anne. Of their three sons and five daughters, only James and his sister Martha (1774–1853) survived infancy. Martha married in 1793 Thomas Keck Hutchinson, a gun maker of Whitechapel, and, despite having eight children of their own, Thomas accepted James Purdey as his apprentice in 1798. Purdey lived with the Hutchinsons in Moorfield, from 1800 in the Minories, then, near the shop, in Southwark.

Shortly after completing his apprenticeship in 1805, Purdey married; the exact date and the former name of his wife, Mary (1790–1860), are unknown. Four daughters were born before a son, James [*see below*], was born on 19 March 1828. In 1805 Purdey went to work for Joseph Manton (1766–1835) of Oxford Street, the leading gun maker of the day. There Purdey honed his craft skills and established good relationships with Manton's customers. In 1808 Purdey moved to join Alexander John Forsyth (1789–1843), inventor of the percussion lock. Forsyth, an Aberdonian, had moved to London in 1806 and through influential contacts had been given premises in the Tower, workmen, and materials to perfect his device for the benefit of the armed forces. When he was obliged to leave the Tower, Forsyth set up shop at 10 Piccadilly, with his former mechanic, Joseph Vicars, in charge and with James Purdey employed to make stocks and locks.

Purdey took his freedom in the Gunsmiths' Company in 1812 and in 1814 opened his own shop at 4 Princes Street, off Leicester Square, where he manufactured single and double flintlock guns, duelling pistols, flintlock rifles, and the new percussion locks. By this time he was well known in shooting circles, his reputation second only to that of Manton. Besides constructing new guns, Purdey fitted percussion locks to customers' old flintlock guns, undertook repairs and maintenance, and sold shooting accessories, even supplying favoured clients with gun dogs and live birds for pigeon shoots. His customers included aristocrats and high-ranking military men, numerous clergymen, and from 1823 a steadily growing list of European, Indian, and British royalty. In 1826 Purdey acquired

James Purdey (1784–1863), by unknown artist

Manton's Oxford Street shop and workshop, and from these enlarged premises he began to manufacture and sell guns of a lower quality to the trade. In 1838 he supplied Queen Victoria with a lavishly cased pair of pistols for presentation to the imam of Muscat, the first of several commissions from the queen and Prince Albert, and in 1857 the firm received the royal warrant as gun makers to the prince of Wales.

The opening up of trade with India, together with the fashion for rifle clubs, brought a vastly increased volume of business but Purdey, like other tradesmen, was often let down by impecunious worthies who delayed or defaulted on their payments. This drain on his cash flow eventually brought Purdey perilously close to bankruptcy himself but he was saved in 1847 by the influence of Lord Henry Bentinck who in some discreet fashion (never disclosed to other members of the family) managed to keep Purdey in business and with a full order book.

James Purdey junior (1828–1909), gun maker, on 19 March 1851 married Caroline (c.1832–1870), eldest daughter of George Thomas of Bolton Row, Mayfair. They lived first at 17 Warwick Crescent, Paddington, where their seven children were born, before moving to 28 Devonshire Place. Trained in his father's workshops, James Purdey junior was a skilful gun maker and competent businessman. When he formally took charge of the firm

on 1 January 1858 the premises included, in addition to the shop and workshop, shotgun-testing fields at Hornsey Wood and a 6 acre shooting ground and rifle-testing site known as Foxholes, near Harrow. The growing number of live-pigeon shooting clubs, enthusiasm for shooting on British estates, and, increasingly, pursuing big game overseas, helped to keep sales buoyant.

The elder Purdey spent his closing years in Rifle House, Margate, Kent, where his sister Martha had died in 1853, and in Rifle Cottage, Bayswater. He died in Margate on 6 November 1863, leaving to his heirs, besides the business and its various premises, property in Bayswater, Hendon, Margate, and Yorkshire. He was buried at Paddington old cemetery.

Caroline Purdey died suddenly in 1870; on 12 August 1873 Purdey married Julia Haverson (d. 1911), who, at nineteen years old, was the same age as her eldest stepson. Another six children were born, of whom four died young. James Purdey (1854–1890), the eldest son of James and Caroline, followed his father into the trade but was to die of consumption at thirty-five; it was the second son, Athol Stuart (1858–1939), who succeeded to the business. In 1877 the name of the firm was amended to Purdey & Sons, to include Athol and James, but without bestowing any partnership rights. Both sons spent some time in France. Purdeys showed its wares at the 1878 Paris Exhibition, and, with less success, in the Sydney and Calcutta exhibitions. Foreseeing the expiry of his shop lease in 1882, Purdey began to buy up leases at 57–60 South Audley Street, Westminster, where in 1881–2 he built Audley House, a vast and stylish establishment with workshops below ground, lavish showrooms, and accommodation for the many clerks. Subsequently he added the nearby 84 Mount Street.

James Purdey continued to oversee his sons until his mind began to fail. Dividing his time between London and Margate, he gradually became weaker and died after a short illness on 13 March 1909 at 28 Devonshire Place, London. He was buried in the family vault in Paddington old cemetery, alongside his parents, his first wife, and several of his own children. Julia Purdey died in 1911 and was also buried there.   ANITA McCONNELL

Sources R. Beaumont, *Purdey's: the guns and the family* (1984) · *CGPLA Eng. & Wales* (1864) · *CGPLA Eng. & Wales* (1909) [James Purdey jun.]
Archives priv. coll.
Likenesses portrait, James Purdey & Sons, London [*see illus.*] · portraits, repro. in Beaumont, *Purdey's*
Wealth at death under £7000: probate, 14 July 1864, *CGPLA Eng. & Wales* · £206,013 13s. 8d.—James Purdey jun.: resworn probate, 27 Aug 1909, *CGPLA Eng. & Wales*

Purdey, James, junior (1828–1909). *See under* Purdey, James (1784–1863).

Purdon, Edward (*bap.* 1729, *d.* 1767), writer, the son of the Revd Edward Purdon and his wife, Elizabeth, was baptized at St Mary's Cathedral, Limerick, on 17 September 1729. In 1744 he entered Trinity College, Dublin, where he became friends with Oliver Goldsmith. After dissipating his inheritance he enlisted. Subsequently Purdon settled in London and became a 'scribbler in the newspapers'. While working for Ralph Griffiths he translated for him Voltaire's *Henriade*, which appeared in the *British Ladies' Magazine*. Probably Purdon had a share also in the 'Memoirs of M. de Voltaire', by Goldsmith, which accompanied the poem. In 1759 Purdon was compelled to publish an apology in the *London Chronicle* for an abusive pamphlet, in the form of a letter to David Garrick, against Henry Mossop and other Drury Lane performers (Lowe, 140, 273). Purdon fell dead in Smithfield on 27 March 1767. Goldsmith's epitaph on him, for the Wednesday Club, has preserved his memory:

> Here lies Poor Ned Purdon, from misery freed,
> Who long was a bookseller's hack;
> He led such a damnable life in this world,
> I don't think he'll wish to come back.
> (*Goldsmith: Interviews*, 29)

E. I. CARLYLE, rev. MICHAEL BEVAN

Sources *GM*, 1st ser., 37 (1767), 192 · *N&Q*, 4th ser., 8 (1871), 453, 558–9 · J. Forster, *The life and times of Oliver Goldsmith*, 2nd edn, 2 vols. (1854), vol. 1, pp. 25, 168; vol. 2, p. 60 · D. J. O'Donoghue, *The poets of Ireland: a biographical dictionary with bibliographical particulars*, 1 vol. in 3 pts (1892–3) · *London Chronicle* (13–15 Oct 1759) · *Public Advertiser* (7 Feb 1759) · R. W. Lowe, *A bibliographical account of English theatrical literature* (1888) · *IGI* · *Goldsmith: interviews and recollections*, ed. E. H. Mikhail (1993)

Purdy, John (1773–1843), hydrographer, was born on 14 August 1773 at Norwich, the eldest of four known children of John Purdy, a tailor and freeman of the city, and his wife, Sarah Cady. While John was still young the family moved to London, where in 1795 he entered an apprenticeship with David Steel, nautical publisher and bookseller, of Little Tower Hill. In 1806 he drew his first known charts; these were of English Channel harbours, published by Steel's widow and successor, Penelope Mason, and of the North Sea, published by Laurie and Whittle of 53 Fleet Street. Within a few years he was working exclusively for Laurie and Whittle and by 1812 had become its principal hydrographer. He compiled charts and wrote the accompanying sailing directions for Laurie and Whittle and its successor, R. H. Laurie, until his death.

Purdy's greatest contribution was to the knowledge of the Atlantic Ocean and the Caribbean Sea. In his *Memoir … to Accompany the New Chart of the Atlantic Ocean* (1812, with eight editions in his lifetime) he made available to ordinary navigators James Rennell's work on ocean currents. Rennell had 'a high opinion of his talents', and in 1832 his daughter, Lady Rodd, entrusted Purdy with editing her father's *Wind and Current Charts*. Purdy's other works included *Tables of the Positions …* (1816), to accompany Laurie and Whittle's *Oriental Navigator*; *The Columbian Navigator* (1817); and works on the south Atlantic, northern European waters, and the Mediterranean. Most of these went through several editions in his lifetime and continued in print after his death under the editorship of his successor, Alexander George Findlay.

Purdy exchanged information with leading hydrographers of the day, both British and foreign. He was respected as the foremost authority in private chart publishing, where he was exceptional for the care with which he acknowledged the many varied sources on which his work was based. His work and letters give the impression of a meticulous, modest, and industrious man; however, nothing is known of his private life. He died of gangrene of the leg at his home at 29 Gloucester Street, Clerkenwell, London, on 29 January 1843.

A. F. POLLARD, rev. SUSANNA FISHER

Sources BL cat. · *British Library map library catalogue* (1998) [CD-ROM] · J. Rennell, *An investigation of the currents …* (1832) · Hydrographic Office Archives, Taunton, Incoming Letters P (397–406) · Hydrographic Office Archives, Taunton, Misc 23/1 · Hydrographic Office Archives, Taunton, Letterbooks 2–5 · parish register (baptism), 15 Aug 1773, Norwich, St Andrew's · parish register (marriage), 13 Sept 1792, Paddington, St James's · parish register, Holborn, St Andrew's, 1808 [baptism] · D. F. McKenzie, ed., *Stationers' Company apprentices*, [3]: 1701–1800 (1978) · d. cert.

Purefoy, William (*c*.1580–1659), politician and regicide, was born at Caldecote, Warwickshire, the son of Francis Purefoy (*d*. 1613), and his wife, Eleanor, daughter of John Baskerville of Curdworth, Warwickshire. He was briefly at Emmanuel College, Cambridge, in 1598 and Gray's Inn in 1599; in 1622 he was granted leave to travel abroad for three years.

The Purefoys were a long-established family from the Warwickshire–Leicestershire border with branches also in Lincolnshire and Berkshire; kinsmen still co-operated over political and financial affairs in the seventeenth century. The marriage of William's grandfather to an heir of the Wigstons of Wolston, Warwickshire, had added to the family's status and wealth, while his aunt Magdalen Purefoy (1572/3–1653) was the wife of Anthony Grey, earl of Kent (1556/7–1643). The Purefoys of Caldecote were none the less on the fringes of the county élite; William served as sheriff of Warwickshire in 1630–31 and was an active justice of the peace from 1632. He was added to the quorum only in 1649, however, by which time he was among the most influential politicians in England.

William Purefoy was a consistent and early opponent of Charles I's policies. He was summoned before the privy council for his refusal of the forced loan in February 1627, and his election, in a disputed contest, to the parliament of 1628 as member for the nearby city of Coventry was attributed by some newsletter writers to his status as a loan refuser. In 1630 he gave the defiant answer 'that he believeth himself not legally liable to be fined' (PRO, E 178/7154/186) to the commissioners for distraint of knighthood, but he paid up in the following year (during his shrievalty). Purefoy was already close to Robert Greville, second Lord Brooke (and was indeed credited by some with an undue influence on the younger man) and a patron of godly clergy in Warwickshire, especially Richard Vines, rector of Caldecote and the adjacent parish of Weddington. Through Brooke Purefoy was elected as MP for Warwick in both the Short and the Long parliaments, having failed to become knight of the shire. He was an active and determined opponent of the personal rule. He argued for the removal of popish commanders from the English army, and in a famous and stormy session on 15 December 1641 moved that the grand remonstrance be printed, 'that so we might satisfy the whole kingdom' (*The

Journal of Sir Symonds D'Ewes, ed. W. H. Coates, New Haven, 1942, 294–5).

From the start of the civil war Purefoy worked tirelessly to defeat the royalists, both as a military leader and administrator in Warwickshire and as a conscientious MP in Westminster. With Brooke he raised troops in the summer of 1642 under the authority of parliament's militia ordinance; the two men were indicted at the Warwickshire assizes by a royalist gentleman for opposing the king's commission of array. Purefoy had married, in 1609, Joan, the daughter of Aleyn Penkeston and widow of George Abbott—both minor Yorkshire gentlemen. There were apparently no children of the Purefoy marriage, but her son George Abbott the younger was a close political associate of his stepfather in Warwickshire's civil war administration. Joan Purefoy was a plucky woman, praised in the London press in the autumn of 1642 for defending Caldecote from Prince Rupert's forces.

Purefoy held command in the association army of Staffordshire and Warwickshire under Lord Brooke in 1642–3; when these forces were dispersed on their commander's death Purefoy was commissioned by the earl of Essex as colonel of a regiment of cavalry to be raised in Warwickshire. Despite his advanced age, Purefoy did see some military service in 1643–4, contributing to the relief of Gloucester, and for the rest of his life was known as Colonel Purefoy. More broadly, however, he cemented a position as the archetypal 'county boss', with a tight political and administrative hold on Warwickshire parliamentarianism. He was named to every parliamentary committee established for Warwickshire from 1642 until 1659; throughout the 1640s his stepson Abbott, his cousin Gamaliel Purefoy, and three of the latter's sons were also prominent in Warwickshire's war effort. Purefoy's dominance was not popular with the more moderate, established county gentry, who in 1644 mobilized behind the attempt of Basil Feilding, second earl of Denbigh, to establish a military association independent of the Warwickshire county forces. An ally of the earl claimed Purefoy's 'estate being inconsiderable, his actions so harsh and resolutions so disconsonant to the welfare of the country that he hath wholly lost himself in his reputation there' (HLRO, Main papers, 8 Nov 1644). None the less, Purefoy's national political connections and his military and financial dominance in Warwickshire sabotaged Denbigh's association, and he survived also the later challenges to his local administration by moderates on the local subcommittee of accounts.

Purefoy lost his military command with the self-denying ordinance and in the summer of 1645 he resided with the unpopular Scottish army while it was in the midlands. In parliament he supported a determined prosecution of the war and a stern peace settlement. He was hostile alike to 'prelacy' and to sectarianism. He led local iconoclasm, tearing down Warwick's market cross and offensive monuments in the Beauchamp chapel in 1642; but unlike many of his closest associates he favoured a strict presbyterian church settlement. In October 1647, for example, he was on the opposite side to Cromwell as he

attempted (unsuccessfully) to have a permanent presbyterian settlement written in to the peace propositions to be sent to the king.

In January 1649 Purefoy was named to the commission to try Charles I and signed the death warrant with no apparent hesitation, but he was clearly unhappy about the military purge of the Commons and the abolition of the House of Lords [*see also* Regicides]. It was as an indefatigable MP during the Rump or Commonwealth regime (1649–53) that Purefoy reached the apex of his political power. He served on the council of state throughout and was on all the important committees of the Rump, particularly concerned with religious affairs. Purefoy was predictably opposed to the dissolution of the Rump and to Cromwell's assumption of rule as a 'single person', but he was not an irreconcilable enemy of the protectorate. He continued to be active in local government and as member for Coventry in the first protectorate parliament he acquiesced in the demand that all MPs recognize Cromwell's authority. Purefoy's close links with Coventry were emphasized when he turned down the more prestigious Warwickshire county seat, to which he had also been elected. He sat on several committees, including, characteristically, one charged with revising the religious liberty granted under the 'Instrument of government' and enumerating 'damnable heresies' (*JHC*, 7.399).

Purefoy was also elected for Coventry in 1656 and protested, unsuccessfully, against the council of state's exclusion of republican MPs. He played a full role in the parliament himself, however, sitting on the crucial committee for privileges, a committee to reform alehouses, and the committee that oversaw the trial and punishment of the Quaker James Nayler. He turned up in a thin house on 25 December 1656 for a debate on the decimation tax and sat on several heavyweight committees concerned with the *Humble Petition and Advice*. Purefoy was clearly hostile to the offer of the crown to Cromwell, and his sympathies were vividly revealed when he was one of the few members willing to take the oath of the provocative Commonwealthman Arthur Hesilrige, who attempted to enter the Commons in January 1658 despite being nominated to the upper house by the protector.

Purefoy was elected yet again for Coventry for Richard Cromwell's parliament, but his health was clearly failing, as he was one of the elderly MPs excused at the end of a long debate on the 'other house' in March 1659. His status as an elder statesman ensured his nomination to important committees such as that for elections. The old man rallied quickly to the restored Rump in May 1659, but he was not active after August when he made his will. His wife was dead by then and his lands were settled, apparently reluctantly, on his nephew and namesake who had married a distant relative, Dorothy, daughter of George Purefoy of Wadley, Berkshire. Those with whom Purefoy had the closest ties—his trustees, executors, and witnesses to his will—were all veterans of Warwickshire's civil-war administration, minor gentlemen and tradesmen of Coventry. The veteran parliamentarian and puritan trusted to 'be taken into those blessed mansions of everlasting happiness prepared for and predestined to the elect' (will). At the very end of his life William Purefoy kept Coventry secure during the scare of Sir George Booth's presbyterian–royalist rising in the August in which he made his will, and died in Warwickshire shortly afterwards, spared the collapse of his political hopes in the restoration of Charles II. His unloved nephew seems to have recovered the estates confiscated for regicide. ANN HUGHES

Sources A. Hughes, *Politics, society and civil war in Warwickshire, 1620–1660* (1987) · D. Underdown, *Pride's Purge: politics in the puritan revolution* (1971) · B. Worden, *The Rump Parliament, 1648–1653* (1974) · Keeler, *Long Parliament* · Commonwealth exchequer papers, PRO, SP28 · State papers Charles I, PRO, SP16 · Council of state records, PRO, SP25 · HLRO, Main papers collection, HL · *JHC*, 1–8 (1547–1667) · *Diary of Thomas Burton*, ed. J. T. Rutt, 4 vols. (1828) · *DNB* · J. Fetherston, ed., *The visitation of the county of Warwick in the year 1619* · will, PRO, PROB 11/304, fol. 77
Archives Birm. CL, Land settlement
Wealth at death approx. £500 p.a.: 1659, will, PRO, PROB 11/304, fol. 77

Purnell, Robert (1606–1666), Baptist leader and author, was born on 15 October 1606, probably in Bristol. He was a carpet weaver and freeman of the city, and lived with his wife in St James's Back; their son John (d. 1686) was an ironmonger in Maryport Street, Bristol.

Purnell was a member of the separatist Broadmead congregation, known as 'a Church of Christ', in Bristol from its inception in 1640. Baptism was first considered by the congregation when it migrated to All Hallows, London, in 1643 following the capture of Bristol by the royalists but was not formally adopted. 'I lost mine estate by siding with them [parliament]', commented Purnell in 1651, 'I was in a banished condition one hundred and forty miles from home, for the space of two full years' (*No Power but of God*, 166–7). In a brief pamphlet, *Englands Remonstrance* (1649), which he later expanded, Purnell vigorously complains that parliament, with all the power in its own hands, neglected those who supported it and feathered their own nests.

Purnell's works, written between 1649 and 1663, confirm he came to a Baptist position only slowly. In 1649 he commended Baptists for performing 'a right ordinance to right subjects', their 'sin' was 'idolizing it', but disagreed with those who made

> Baptisme a ground of your communion and so disorder what God hath ordered; for the ground of communion should arise first from that union you have with Christ your head; and secondly from that near relation you have to each other, as being one in the same Spirit.

He believed a time would soon come when all Christians will be

> ashamed to own one another by their fleshly titles but look upon and love one another as Christians, members of the same body … [whose] love of each other shall arise from union in the Spirit. Against this church-state the gates of hell shall not prevail. (*Good Tydings for Sinners*, 57–8)

His books advocate religious toleration on the basis of a common love of Christ, and he shared Cromwell's dismay at parliament's desire to enforce religious uniformity. In 1653 Purnell, not yet a Baptist, considered contemporary

disputes 'about the garment of religion' while 'the power thereof is much abated' futile: 'a true communion of saints according to the Gospel institution' comes about when 'a saint comes to see that everyone in whom the Lord Jesus appeareth, is a member together with him in the same body whereof Christ is Head' (*The Way to Heaven Discovered*, sig. B4r, p. 156).

Purnell's move towards baptism was paralleled by developments in the Broadmead congregation. In 1651 the first questions about 'Sprinkleing of Children' arose and the following year 'the Lord awakened some … to consider there was noe ground for Baptizing children, much less for Sprinkleing them' and they joined 'the other Church in Bristol that were all Baptized' (Hayden, 103, 105). In 1653 a member of Broadmead, Thomas Cattle, was sent to London for baptism by the Baptist minister Henry Jessey, and in 1654 when Purnell, already a deacon, was elected 'Eldest Ruleing Elder', he also sought baptism from Jessey, having for sometime been 'convinced of his duty therein, but omitted ye practice thereof' (Hayden, 111, 122). By now, Broadmead had become an open communion baptized congregation.

Purnell advocated toleration between all Christian communities, pleading for a third way as advocated by Henry Jessey, John Bunyan, and others between particular and general baptist beliefs; and in his own congregation Purnell never allowed believers' baptism to create a barrier between Christians of a different persuasion. However, he faced the opposition of another founding member of Broadmead, Dennis Hollister, who had served as MP for Somerset in Cromwell's nominated parliament of 1653 and, while in London, had begun to espouse Quaker views. Hollister ridiculed the 'Baptized-Independent people' of Broadmead for becoming 'imitators of water baptism … a practice disowned by those I joined' (Hollister, 2). Thomas Ewins, 'an open professed Dipper', spoke for Purnell and Broadmead when he claimed many supported him in administering the Lord's Supper to all:

> though some of them mis-baptised, yet none of them deny the ordinance of Christ, onely some of them have not the light to see the right administration of it, but reckon that infant baptism is sufficient; yet as further light comes in, they are prepared to walk up to it, in the mean time we can bear with them in love, as we desire them and others to bear with us in other things. (Purnell and others, 59)

However, Purnell found himself on the same side as Hollister in voting for John Haggatt, one of two unsuccessful Independent candidates who stood against presbyterian and royalist sympathisers in the controversial 1654 parliamentary election in the city.

By 1657 Purnell was asserting baptism was

> an ordinance of the New Testament by the washing of water … representing the powerful washing of the blood of Christ … and so sealing our regeneration or new birth, and entrance into the covenant of grace, our grafting into Christ and into the Body of his Church. (*A Little Cabinet Richly Stored*, 255)

But he still warned his co-religionists: 'You that have taken up this ordinance, beware of laying a greater stress upon it than ever God appointed you, viz, it was never appointed to break love and communion, and to quench the Spirit, and to jostle out some other ordinances, nor to shut out the weak in Faith' (ibid., 261).

Purnell published only one work, *A Serious Exhortation to an Holy Life, or Conversation* (1663), after the Restoration, and died in Bristol in November 1666.

ROGER HAYDEN

Sources R. Hayden, ed., *The records of a church in Christ in Bristol, 1640–1687*, Bristol RS, 27 (1974), 19–27, 111, 113, 117, 127 • H. E. Nott and E. Ralph, eds., *The deposition books of Bristol*, 2, Bristol RS, 13 (1948), 37, 180 • E. Ralph, ed., *Marriage bond licences for the diocese of Bristol*, 1 (1952), 95 • E. B. Underhill, *The records of a Church of Christ, 1640–1687* (1842) • *DNB* • [R. Purnell and others], *The church of Christ in Bristol recovering her vail* (1657) • D. Hollister, *The skirts of the whore discovered* (1656)

Purnell, Thomas [*pseud.* Q] (1834–1889), theatre critic and writer, was born in Tenby, Pembrokeshire, the son of Robert Purnell and his wife, Ann, and was baptized on 13 March 1834 at Narberth, Pembrokeshire. He matriculated at Trinity College, Dublin, in 1852 and afterwards went to London and began a career in journalism. In 1862 he was, on the recommendation of Thomas Duffus Hardy, appointed assistant secretary and librarian of the Archaeological Institute of Great Britain and Ireland, and retained the post until 1866. In 1870–71 he contributed to *The Athenaeum*, under the signature Q, a series of severe and incisive dramatic criticisms to which Charles Reade and Tom Taylor published aggrieved replies.

Purnell was popular in literary society and founded a club known as the Decemviri, of which A. C. Swinburne, J. A. M. Whistler, R. E. Francillon, and Joseph Knight were members. He also came to know Giuseppe Mazzini, to whom he introduced Swinburne and others. In 1871 he edited Lamb's *Correspondence and Works* and organized the Charles Lamb centenary dinner. Purnell's collected *Athenaeum* theatre reviews were reprinted in *Dramatists of the Present Day* (1871). He also wrote literary essays and *The Lady Drusilla: a Psychological Romance* (1886), and edited (1868) Dr John Herd's *Historia quatuor regum Angliae* for the Roxburghe Club.

After a long illness Thomas Purnell died on 17 December 1889 at Lloyd Square, Pentonville, London, where his sister kept house for him.

MEGAN A. STEPHAN

Sources *The Athenaeum* (21 Dec 1889), 860 • *Archaeological Journal*, 19–23 (1862–6) • Allibone, *Dict.* • Q [T. Purnell], *Dramatists of the present day* (1871) • *IGI* • private information (1896)

Purney, Thomas (1695–1730?), poet and prison chaplain, was born on 1 August 1695. His parents have not been identified. Perhaps he was related to a family of Purneys in Buckinghamshire, but his poems hint that he spent his childhood in Kent. After two years at Merchant Taylors' School, London, he was admitted as a pensioner to Clare College, Cambridge, on 2 July 1711. He graduated BA in 1715–16.

Purney's two volumes of *Pastorals* (November 1716 and February 1717) purport to be written 'after the simple manner of Theocritus', but their closer model is the anti-classical, faintly Spenserian eclogues of Ambrose Philips, featuring English rural scenery, folklore, and dialect. Purney's critical theory is developed in his prose *Full Enquiry into the True Nature of Pastoral* (1717), greatly indebted to the *Guardian* papers on pastoral by Thomas Tickell. A long anti-Jacobite mock-heroic poem, *The Chevalier de St. George* (published in October 1718), is attributed to Purney by Giles Jacob, who notes justly that it is written in an extraordinary style (*Poetical Register*, 1723, 2.304). Outlandish diction is a feature of *The Last Day*, a long poem by a deceased college friend, John Bulkeley, which Purney prepared for the press in 1719. Purney advertised in 1717 a poem in fifteen books on Edward, the Black Prince, but it never appeared.

Purney was ordained priest (London diocese) on 24 May 1719 and in November of that year, as 'a young suckling divine of twenty-four years of age' (*Orphan Reviv'd*), was appointed ordinary (full-time chaplain) of Newgate prison on the recommendation of the bishop of Peterborough. Purney's salary was £35 p.a. but the great profit of his much sought-after post was in writing accounts of the behaviour, confessions, and dying words of hanged malefactors: his predecessor, Paul Lorrain (*d.* 1719), is said to have left £5000 after twenty years as ordinary of Newgate. Purney's accounts were particularly colourful because he harried condemned men to confess to more crimes than they had committed. He also tried unsuccessfully to reduce disorder at religious services in prison.

Purney's health declined from 1724, perhaps owing to typhus, endemic in Newgate. He withdrew from most duties two years before he resigned as ordinary in November 1727. His last *Ordinary's Account* appeared in May 1725, when one of the malefactors hanged was Jonathan Wild. However, Fielding's satire of the Newgate ordinary in his *History* of Wild (*Miscellanies*, vol. 3, 1743) is probably directed against Purney's successor James Guthrie (cf. *Craftsman*, 460, 26 April 1735). Purney is portrayed sympathetically in Harrison Ainsworth's *Jack Sheppard* (1839). It is thought he died in Kent in 1730.

JAMES SAMBROOK

Sources H. O. White, 'Thomas Purney: forgotten poet and critic of the eighteenth century', *Essays and Studies by Members of the English Association*, 15 (1929) • *The works of Thomas Purney*, ed. H. O. White (1933) • T. Purney, *A full enquiry into the true nature of pastoral* (1717); repr. with introduction by E. Wasserman (1948) • P. Linebaugh, 'The ordinary of Newgate and his *Account*', *Crime in England, 1550–1800*, ed. J. S. Cockburn (1977), 246–69 • H. Fielding, *Miscellanies*, ed. B. A. Goldgar and H. Amory, 3 (1997), 135–6 n. • C. J. Robinson, ed., *A register of the scholars admitted into Merchant Taylors' School, from AD 1562 to 1874*, 2 (1883), 26 • Venn, *Alum. Cant.* • *Orphan Reviv'd* [Powell's Weekly Journal] (21 Nov 1719) • 'Lorrain, Paul', *DNB* • D. F. Foxon, ed., *English verse, 1701–1750: a catalogue of separately printed poems with notes on contemporary collected editions*, 2 vols. (1975) • *DNB*

Purse, Benjamin Ormond (1874–1950), social worker and expert on blind welfare, was born on 29 August 1874 at Salford, Lancashire, the son of Edward Purse, general labourer, and his wife, Matilda, *née* Clavering. His sight became defective in early life, but it was not until he was thirteen, when it had become extremely poor, that he was sent to school at Henshaw's Institution for the Blind, Manchester.

Purse was trained as a piano-tuner, took the certificate, and struggled for more than two years to build up a tuning practice. However, his inclinations were towards a career of professional or public service, and to prepare himself he devoured every book he could lay hands on. His first step in this direction was taken when he became the first paid secretary (at 8*s*. a week) of the National League of the Blind, a small body which voiced the unsatisfactory conditions prevalent among blind people. He used a legacy of £60 left to him in 1898 to launch a journal, the *Blind Advocate*, as the organ of the league, and in 1901 he devoted himself full-time to the organization at a weekly salary of £1 3*s*. 0*d*. In 1902 the league was affiliated to the Trades Union Congress.

The next few years were crowded with activity for Purse—writing, lecturing, expending all his efforts for blind people. In 1905 he was a delegate at an international conference of blind welfare workers; between 1904 and 1910 he visited forty-eight municipal authorities and secured travel concessions from thirty-seven of them; in 1907 he was the only witness to give evidence concerning the blind before the royal commission on the poor laws, and he took an active part in the movement which led in 1914 to the compulsory notification of ophthalmia neonatorum, a foremost measure in sight-saving. He was responsible for preparing the preliminary matter, and subsequently helped to frame the recommendations which resulted in the setting up in 1917 of the government's advisory committee for the welfare of the blind, of which he was a member until 1942.

In 1916 Purse was persuaded by Sir Arthur Pearson to join the staff of the National Institute for the Blind, as director of the aftercare department, which helped to train, and to find employment for, blind persons. Although by so doing he signified his approval of voluntary organizations, he by no means relinquished his efforts to secure a degree of state aid for blind people, and no blind person contributed more than he to the movement which led to the passing of the Blind Persons' Act in 1920.

From 1920 until 1943 Purse superintended the administration of relief, training, and general employment at the National Institute for the Blind. In 1921 he played a prominent part in forming what later became the National Association of Blind Workers, and he edited its official journal, the *Tribune*, until 1942. In that year he was elected a vice-president of his old school, Henshaw's Institution, an honour no blind person had ever received before; and in 1944 his work for blind people was recognized by his appointment as OBE.

Ben Purse's massive intelligence, amazing statistical memory, power of debate, and grim courage left their mark for all time on the British blind community. He published a number of works, which mainly concerned his campaign to improve the position of blind people in work. His publications include *The Blind in Industry* (1925), *The British Blind* (1928), and a book of verse, *Moods and Melodies* (1931).

Purse had married in 1899 Mary Elizabeth, daughter of John Alcock, a collier, of Oldham. She and their two children had predeceased him. Purse himself died at Wembdon, Bridgwater, on 31 March 1950.

J. DE LA MARE ROWLEY, rev. PATRICK WALLIS

Sources Beacon (Aug 1925) · New Beacon (April 1950) · personal knowledge (1959) · M. G. Thomas, *The Royal National Institute for the Blind, 1868–1956* (1957)

Likenesses photograph, repro. in B. Purse, *The British blind* (1928)

Purser, John (*fl.* 1728–1747), printer and Jacobite sympathizer, of Whitefriars and then Red Lyon Court, London, was of unknown parentage. He was involved in the production of at least four Jacobite or anti-government newspapers, and was arrested and questioned for these activities on many occasions. Purser may have begun his career printing the *Daily Journal* from 14 March 1728 until perhaps 1731. In 1731 he began printing the most notorious and long-running anti-Hanoverian newspaper, *Fog's Weekly Journal*. Purser was arrested on numerous occasions for the publication of this paper, including in 1732, 1733, and 1734. He was taken into custody on the evening of 19 July 1737 for the paper of 16 July, described in Lord Harrington's warrant as 'a false, scandalous, & seditious Libel' (PRO, SP 36/41/200). On this occasion Purser seems to have been fairly co-operative with his interrogators, naming John Kelly as the author of the offending opening letter, going with the messengers to arrest Kelly, and handing over a manuscript in the author's handwriting to establish his identity. The newspaper then collapsed.

The motive for Purser's actions was probably one of personal survival, as his involvement in printing opposition newspapers continued unabated. In November 1737 Charles Molloy, another notorious Jacobite projector and author, formerly involved with Purser in *Fog's Weekly Journal*, switched the printing of his new newspaper *Common Sense* from a rival, James Purser in Bartholomew Close, to John Purser in Whitefriars. A sustained quarrel developed in which James Purser continued to publish his own newspaper as *Old Common Sense*, while Molloy and John Purser claimed that their paper had all of the original authors working for them. It is possible that John and James Purser were related (Duncan Eaves and Kimpel, 242–7).

John Purser was again taken in for questioning by the government on 2 July 1739, regarding issue number 125 of *Common Sense* for 23 June. On this occasion his behaviour was far less co-operative, his answers displaying all the obtuseness of a recalcitrant schoolboy malefactor. He refused to say whether he had printed the paper, and would not give the author's name or identify the handwriting of the manuscripts found in his drawer, begging 'to be excused from making any Answer thereto' (PRO, SP 36/48/1). He went so far as to claim that the name 'J. Purser' appearing on the newspaper might mean someone else. He was bailed for £200 on the same day, one of his sureties being Thomas Read, another printer. *Common Sense* continued until 1743, though Purser's involvement remains obscure.

Between 1742 and 1746 Purser was involved in printing *Old England, or, The Constitutional Journal*, the leading anti-

Hanoverian paper of those years. His name appears directly on the editions printed between 18 June and 5 November 1743, and again from 6 to 27 September 1746. A series of warrants for his arrest and questioning were issued, in March 1743 and again in January and May 1745. It is claimed that, from late 1744, the paper's joint editors, William Guthrie and James Ralph, were bought off by government pensions (R. Harris, 40–46).

In 1746, with government sensibilities heightened by a Jacobite rising and invasion, Purser was arrested and held in Newgate prison for printing the *National Journal, or, The Country Gazette*, organized by George Gordon. He was charged with treason for the publication of a clearly Jacobite letter on the birthday of the Old Pretender (James Francis Edward Stuart) on 10 June. The newspaper's early issues had confined themselves to criticism of the brutal treatment of the Jacobites at and after the battle of Culloden, and to praising the heroic Charles Edward Stuart. However, its final issue not only lamented the fate of a monarch in exile but also referred to the 'fatal issue of the late glorious, but unsuccessful struggle in the present Rebellion' (*National Journal*, 35, 10 June 1746). Purser was discharged from prison on 26 February 1747 following the end of the emergency act to suspend habeas corpus, and his agreement to stop printing the *National Journal*.

John Purser's chequered career, as an opposition printer in London over perhaps twenty years, shows both the possibilities and limitations of such a role. Government harassment repeatedly shut down opposition journals. However, the state was constrained by the rule of law and the nature of the evidence available. A resourceful printer determined to make his point, and prepared to suffer for it, could, like Purser, prove an irritating thorn in the side of George II's ministers.   PAUL CHAPMAN

Sources PRO, SP 36/41 and 48 · PRO, SP 44/82 and 83 · R. Harris, *A patriot press: national politics and the London press in the 1740s* (1993) · M. Harris, *London newspapers in the age of Walpole* (1987) · T. C. Duncan Eaves and B. D. Kimpel, 'Two notes on Samuel Richardson', *The Library*, 5th ser., 23 (1969), 242–7 · P. K. Monod, *Jacobitism and the English people, 1688–1788* (1989) · H. R. Plomer and others, *A dictionary of the printers and booksellers who were at work in England, Scotland, and Ireland from 1726 to 1775* (1932)
Archives Bodl. Oxf., Burney newspapers · Bodl. Oxf., Nichols newspapers

Purser, Louis Claude (1854–1932), classical scholar, was born at Dungarvan, co. Waterford, on 28 September 1854, the youngest son of Benjamin Purser, grain merchant, of Dungarvan, and his wife, Anne, daughter of John Mallet, iron, brass, and copper founder, of Dublin (but originally from Devon), and sister of the engineer Robert *Mallet. He was educated first at Midleton College, co. Cork, then at Portora Royal School, Enniskillen, before entering Trinity College, Dublin, in 1871. There he was influenced by that brilliant group of fellows, J. P. Mahaffy, Arthur Palmer, and R. Y. Tyrrell, who were then winning high repute for Dublin classical scholarship. Oscar Wilde was among his university contemporaries. A reverse in the family fortunes drove him into teaching before he graduated as senior moderator in classics in 1875, and between then and his election as a fellow in 1881 habits of industry and

self-denial became second nature to him. By this time he had been attracted to the main interest of his life. In 1882 he collaborated with Tyrrell in the second volume of *The Correspondence of Cicero* (1886) and during the preparation of the subsequent volumes (1890, 1894, 1897, 1899) his contribution became predominant. In 1898 he was appointed professor of Latin at Trinity College but his modesty led him to resign in 1904 despite protests from his colleagues, and he thenceforth confined himself to administrative duties in the college. He was appointed vice-provost in 1924, but with the ill health of the provost, J. H. Bernard, Purser found himself burdened with quasi-public duties and, daunted perhaps by the pressures of the post, was driven once again by his anxious nature to resign after three years. In 1927 he also resigned his fellowship, but he lived long enough to complete the revision of *The Correspondence of Cicero* for its second edition. A private man, Purser clung to his rather cheerless rooms in the college and made his study his hearthstone. He died, unmarried, at Elpis Hospital, Lower Mount Street, Dublin, on 20 March 1932.

Purser's scholarship was marked by a literary gift and historical grasp as well as by minute and exhaustive criticism of text and language, and he will be remembered by *The Correspondence of Cicero*. His output is impossible to quantify precisely, for besides a critical text of Cicero's letters in the Oxford Classical Texts series (*Ad familiares*, 1901, and *Ad Atticum*, 1903), an edition of Apuleius's *Story of Cupid and Psyche* (1910), work on Sidonius Apollinaris and Prudentius in later years, and contributions to *Hermathena* and the *Proceedings* of the Royal Irish Academy, much of his work was inextricably involved with that of other scholars, whose books he completed and revised when they were stricken by illness. His completion of the edition of Ovid's *Heroides* by his colleague Arthur Palmer was praised with uncharacteristic warmth by A. E. Housman. Purser was elected a fellow of the British Academy in 1923, and received honorary degrees from the universities of Glasgow (1914), Oxford (1923), and Durham (1931). He refused the presidency of the Royal Irish Academy, of which he was secretary from 1902 to 1914 and vice-president in 1916, 1922, and 1927–8.

OLIVE PURSER, rev. RICHARD SMAIL

Sources A. C. Clark, 'Louis Claude Purser, 1844–1932', *PBA*, 18 (1932), 407–21 · R. B. McDowell and D. A. Webb, *Trinity College, Dublin, 1592–1952: an academic history* (1982) · A. E. Housman, review of Arthur Palmer's *P. Ovidi Nasonis Heroides, with the Greek translation of Planudes*, *Classical Review*, 13 (1899), 172–8
Archives TCD, scholarly corresp.
Likenesses L. Whelan, oils, 1926, TCD · W. Stoneman, photograph, 1930, NPG
Wealth at death £547 10s. od.: probate, 11 June 1932, CGPLA Eng. & Wales

Pursglove, Robert [*name in religion* Silvester] (1503/4–1580), prior of Guisborough and bishop-suffragan of Hull, was the son of Adam and Mudwina Pursglove of Tideswell in the Peak District of Derbyshire; he was said to be forty-four years old in 1548. His mother dispatched her son at a young age to her brother, William Bradshawe, a London merchant who lived in the parish of St Michael, Cornhill. Bradshawe placed his nephew at St Paul's School, founded by Dean Colet in 1509, where he was one of the earliest pupils of William Lily, the first headmaster. After studying at St Paul's for nine years Pursglove entered the neighbouring Augustinian priory of St Mary Overie, which after a short time sent him to continue his humanist education at Corpus Christi College, Oxford. He remained at the university for fourteen years.

Until the mid-1530s Pursglove (who on entering religion had taken the name Silvester) had not been directly involved in religious politics but in 1536 everything changed. In February of that year Cromwell's officials visited Guisborough Priory, the richest Augustinian house in the north of England, where they discovered sufficient evidence of immorality to justify the enforced resignation of the prior, James Cockerill. As his replacement Cromwell imposed Pursglove upon the community, which had no choice but to elect him prior on 25 April 1536, when his disgruntled predecessor retired to a mansion in Guisborough called Bishop's Place. During the Pilgrimage of Grace Sir Francis Bigod attempted to restore Cockerill, who publicly commended Bigod's book condemning the royal supremacy. In December Pursglove was very concerned about discontent among his canons, but he succeeded in retaining control, and Cockerill's subsequent imprisonment in London on a charge of treason in the spring of 1537 removed his chief opponent from the scene.

Used by Cromwell in 1538 to oversee the election of a candidate acceptable to the government as abbot of Whitby, Pursglove accepted Archbishop Lee's nomination to become suffragan bishop of Hull in 1538 only after he had secured the vicegerent's approval. In 1539 and 1540 he was particularly active in conducting ordination ceremonies, mainly at York Minster, but on two occasions in September and December 1539 in Guisborough Priory church. On 1 October 1538 he was also collated to the prebend of Langtoft in York Minster, which he exchanged for the more valuable prebend of Wistow on 2 May 1541.

By the autumn of 1539 Pursglove must have realized that the dissolution of his priory could no longer be delayed. On 22 December 1539 he and his convent surrendered Guisborough Priory, one of the last of the Yorkshire monasteries to be suppressed, receiving the very large sum of £166 13s. 4d. as his pension. Pursglove also accumulated a considerable amount of church preferment at this period. On 26 June 1544 he became provost of Jesus College, Rotherham, and held this office until the suppression of the college at the beginning of Edward VI's reign. In 1548, besides his stipend of £13 6s. 8d. and other perquisites as provost, he was reported to have his pension of 250 marks and a prebend in York Minster worth £58 a year. In September 1549 he acquired the living of his home village of Tideswell, and on 29 January 1550 he was installed archdeacon of Nottingham in succession to Cuthbert Marshall.

Pursglove's tenure of the bishopric of Hull continued without interruption during the protestant regime of Archbishop Holgate and the Catholic restoration of Archbishop Heath, the successors of Archbishop Lee. As a former Augustinian canon he was reconciled to the Catholic church on 18 March 1555, and in September 1558 received the prebend of Oxton in Southwell Minster. In 1559, however, he felt called to make a stand, and lost all his offices for refusing to take the oath of supremacy. Commissioners in 1561 informed the privy council that he was 'very wealthy, stiff in papistry and of estimation in the country', and confined him to within a 20 mile radius of his manor house at Ugthorpe near Whitby (*CSP dom.*, 1601–3, 521).

In November 1559, the year of his deprivation, Pursglove obtained letters patent from Elizabeth to found a grammar school at Tideswell, dedicated to the child Jesus, with lands to the yearly value of £20. Some of his statutes contain provisions resembling those devised by Colet for St Paul's. Then on 5 June 1563 he gained permission from the crown to found a similar school, bearing the same name, and also a hospital, or almshouse, for six poor men and six poor women at Guisborough. In his deed of foundation, probably in his own hand, dated 11 August 1563, he placed both institutions under the visitatorial power of the archbishop of York.

Pursglove lived in his last years partly at Tideswell and partly at Dunston in Derbyshire, from which he made a number of further donations to his school and hospital at Guisborough, including a gift of Greek grammars, the works of Plutarch, Sallust, Cicero, Horace, Ovid, Juvenal, and Erasmus, and other books for the school library. He made his will on 31 March 1580, setting aside the huge sum of £40 to be distributed to the poor at his funeral. He left his plate, his half year's pension from Guisborough due at Lady day, and most of the rest of his possessions to various members of the Eyre family of Dunston, into which his sister Alice Pursglove had married. He died on 2 May 1580 and was buried in Tideswell church, where a fine brass of a bishop in eucharistic vestments (noteworthy as one of the last of its kind), together with a long verse inscription, marks his resting place. CLAIRE CROSS

Sources J. C. Cox, *Notes on the churches of Derbyshire*, 2: *The hundreds of the High Peak and Wirksworth* (1877), 303–4 · will, PRO, PROB 11/62, sig. 32 [summarized in J. W. Clay, ed., *North country wills*, II, SurtS, 121 (1912), 226] · PRO, SP 1/102, fol. 89r · PRO, E 101/76/24 · PRO, E 164/31, fol. 57 · PRO, LR 6/122/8, m. 24 · T. M. Fallows, 'Names of Yorkshire ex-religious, 1573; their pensions and subsidies to the queen thereon', *Yorkshire Archaeological Journal*, 19 (1906–7), 100–04 · Borth. Inst., abp. reg. 28, fols. 197v–201v · Borth. Inst., abp. reg. 29, fol. 32r · W. Page, ed., *The certificates of the commissioners appointed to survey the chantries, guilds, hospitals, etc., in the county of York. Part II*, SurtS, 92 (1895) · *CSP dom.*, 1601–3 · *CPR*, 1558–60, 138–9, 289–90; 1560–63, 83 · D. O'Sullivan, *Robert Pursglove of Guisborough and his hospital* (1990) · Emden, *Oxf.*, 4.467–8 · C. Cross and N. Vickers, eds., *Monks, friars and nuns in sixteenth century Yorkshire*, Yorkshire Archaeological Society, 150 (1995) · A. G. Dickens, *Lollards and protestants in the diocese of York, 1509–1558* (1959) · H. Aveling, *Northern Catholics: the Catholic recusants of the North Riding of Yorkshire, 1558–1790* (1966) · J. C. H. Aveling, *Catholic recusancy in the city of York, 1558–1791*, Catholic RS, monograph ser., 2 (1970) · J. M. Fletcher, 'Bishop Pursglove of Tideswell', *Journal of the Derbyshire Archaeological and Natural History Society*, 32 (1910), 1–32 • *LP Henry VIII*, 13/1, no. 1045 **Likenesses** brass sculpture, Tideswell church, Derbyshire; repro. in Cox, *Notes*

Purton, William (1784–1825), schoolmaster and teacher of stenography, is of unknown parentage and education. At the time of his death, about Christmas 1825, he was married to Mary Gimler Purton and resided at Pleasant Row, Winchester Street, Pentonville, London. He was buried at Elim (Baptist) Chapel, Fetter Lane, Holborn.

At his school near Pentonville, Purton taught to a few selected students a system of shorthand, possibly of his own invention, that, as later practised by two of those students and their own pupils, became one of seven systems used in parliament and the Supreme Court of Judicature in the nineteenth century. Purton's system, unmentioned in nineteenth-century histories or bibliographies of shorthand and unpublished until 1888, should perhaps be called 'the Purton system as improved by Oxford and Hodges' (Hodges, 26), after the two students who developed it for their own use in the law courts, Thomas Oxford and John George Hodges. Apparently Hodges never divulged the name of their teacher; his son, also John George Hodges, himself an adept practitioner of the Purton system in the law courts, gave credit to Alexander Tremaine Wright for 'extracting' this information from the elderly Thomas Oxford (Hodges, 25).

On 16 October 1843 the elder John George Hodges, aged thirty-six, was sent to Dublin as a government shorthand writer during the repeal agitation, to record meetings of and speeches made by members of the Loyal National Repeal Association. He also recorded the trials of Daniel O'Connell, William Smith O'Brien, Thomas Francis Meagher, and John Mitchel. The accuracy of his transcribed notes was praised by both sides of the bench. The facility and accuracy with which John George Hodges senior employed the Purton system were also displayed by his son, who recorded the celebrated cases *Small* v. *Attwood* and *Swinfen* v. *Lord Chelmsford*, as well as complicated cases involving patent infringements and the Metropolitan Board of Works. PAGE LIFE

Sources J. G. Hodges, *Some Irish notes, 1843–1848, and other work with the Purton system of shorthand, as practised since 1825* (1888) • A. Paterson, 'The Purton system of shorthand', *Phonetic Journal*, 62 (1903), 956 • PRO, PROB 11/1707, sig. 34 • *DNB*
Wealth at death freehold estates, property, household goods, and proceeds of stock bequeathed to wife; £100 from stock sale bequeathed to wife's sister: will, 1825, PRO, PROB 11/1707, sig. 34

Purver, Anthony (1702–1777), biblical translator and Quaker preacher, was the son of a farmer at Hurstbourne Tarrant, Hampshire. He was a promising pupil at the village school. While apprenticed to a shoemaker, he read *Rusticus ad academicos* by the Quaker Samuel Fisher. Fisher's argument that scripture is 'corrupted, vitiated, altered and adulterated in all translations' (S. Fisher, *Rusticus ad academicos*, 1660, fol. A4v), contributed to Purver's belief 'that he was called and commanded' by the divine spirit to translate the scriptures (Coleridge, 717). At twenty he opened a school. Three or four years later he went to London. He became a Quaker, and preached at meetings in London, Essex, and elsewhere. John Wesley, who met him several times in 1739, described him as 'one of much experience in the ways of God' (*Works of John Wesley*, 25.637). About 1739 he married Rachell Cotterel, mistress of a girls' boarding-school at Frenchay, Bristol. There he lived, taught, and was clerk to the meeting until returning to Hampshire in 1758. Besides his Bible, he published *Youth's Delight* (1727), a popular verse broadside, *Counsel to Friends' Children* (6th edn, 1785), and *Poem to the Praise of God* (1748).

Purver studied Hebrew during his apprenticeship, and also learnt Aramaic, Syriac, Greek, and Latin. He read voluminously in biblical criticism (including rabbinic commentary), in the earlier English translations and in literature. All this finds its way into his translation and the accompanying notes. He began the Old Testament about 1733, often shutting himself up for days seeking inspiration for difficult passages. About 1742, when 'Ester', 'the Poem of Solomon' and some of the minor prophets were complete, the Bristol printer, Felix Farley, issued the work in parts as *Opus in sacra Biblia elaboratum*. Dr John Fothergill recommended it in an advertisement in the *Gentleman's Magazine* (1746), but the venture was unsuccessful and only a few numbers appeared. Wesley was much disappointed in his 'old friend's' work, finding 'the text flat and dead—much altered indeed, but commonly for the worse—and the notes merely critical, dull, and dry, without any unction, or spirit, or life' (*Works of John Wesley*, 20.81–2). In 1763 the work, including important 'introductory remarks' and appendices criticizing the scholarship and English of the King James Bible, was complete. Fothergill paid Purver £1000 for the copyright and published it at his own expense as *A new and literal translation of all the books of the Old and New Testament; with notes, critical and explanatory* (2 vols., 1764).

In its renderings and its language, the 'Quaker's Bible' sometimes anticipates later versions, but it was rarely appreciated. Not only was the language constantly unlike that of the King James Bible but it was often decidedly colloquial. However, the *Monthly Review* did note 'no small share of erudition. This is a work to which we should have thought very few individuals equal, however great and extensive their abilities; and we cannot help admiring the man who hath intrepidity enough to attempt it' (*Monthly Review*, 1st ser., 32, 1765, 194).

Purver died at Andover in July 1777, and is buried in the Quaker burial-ground there. DAVID NORTON

Sources *DNB* • H. Coleridge, *Biographia borealis* (1833) • *The works of John Wesley*, 25, ed. F. Baker (1980) • *The works of John Wesley*, ed. F. Baker and others, 19–20 (1990–91) • Nichols, *Lit. anecdotes* • *GM*, 1st ser., 87/1 (1817), 510 • D. Norton, 'The Bible as a reviver of words: the evidence of Anthony Purver, a mid-eighteenth-century critic of the English of the King James Bible', *Neuphilologische Mitteilungen*, 4/86 (1985), 515–33 • D. Norton, *A history of the Bible as literature*, 2 vols. (1993), 2.73–85 • J. Spence, *Observations, anecdotes, and characters, of books and men*, ed. J. M. Osborn, new edn, 2 vols. (1966) •

R. Southey and S. T. Coleridge, *Omniana*, ed. R. Gittings (1969) · www.aida.demon.co.uk/Friends/Frenchay.html

Purves, James (1734–1795), Universalist preacher, was born on 23 September 1734 at Blackadder, Identown (Edington), Berwickshire, the son of a shepherd who died in 1754. After only a quarter of a year at school he was taught writing and arithmetic by his parents. In 1756 he apprenticed himself to his uncle, a wheelwright at Duns. According to his own, now lost, account he was raised in the Church of Scotland. Then from reading the books of seceders he 'discovered that the revolution settlement was erroneous in doctrine and government'. In 1755 he joined a covenanting society at Chirnside connected with the minority Reformed Presbytery. The minority in 1753 had sided with the theory of universal atonement in James Fraser Brea's *Treatise on Justifying Faith* (1749) and split off when the majority condemned it. In 1755 the minority presbytery itself divided when some members relaxed their loyalty to the Scottish covenants. The Chirnside society remained loyal. In spring 1756, after reading Isaac Watt's *Dissertation on the Logos* (1726), Purves adopted an Arian position that Christ, with a pre-existent human soul, was first born of all creation. By 1763 he had achieved sufficient prominence for the society to send him to Coleraine, Ireland, to consult with Irish dissenters of similar doctrine. Then, six years later, on 27 July 1769, the society chose him by lot to become a preacher among them. The society sent him to Glasgow to gain competence in the biblical languages but he proved unable to disengage himself from secular affairs because of 'an increase in disastrous occurrences'. Purves later interpreted these disastrous occurrences as the start of the final half day of the apocalyptic three and one half days (Revelation, 11: 11) which ended when the American War of Independence began.

In the spring of 1771 the Universalist societies published an account of their faith. No copy survives, but it was denounced by other members of the minority Reformed Presbytery for following the Socinian doctrine of John Taylor of Norwich. The denunciation occasioned some correspondence between Purves and Alexander Fortune, and members of the Reformed Presbytery, and in 1778 Purves published the Arian side of the correspondence in his *Observations on the Conduct of … the Reformed Presbytery*.

In 1776 some members moved from the Merse to Edinburgh and, according to their minute book, 'formed a new society, with a member who was there before'. Having consulted with their friends in the Merse, they asked James Purves to join them, and on 15 November of that year invited him to take pastoral charge. He had special responsibility for administering the sacraments, but leading worship was shared with others who were inclined to do so, and who were encouraged to pray and give exhortation in public meetings. The society may have strayed from Westminster orthodoxy, but these Universalist Arian dissenters remained faithful to the covenanting tradition of the Reformed Presbytery for their original minute begins: 'The successors of the Remnant who testified against the corruption of the Revolution Constitution of the Church of Scotland as settled about the year 1689' (NA Scot., CH 15/1/1).

The society consisted of eight or nine families, mainly tradesmen and craftsmen, who met in the Broughton area of the city. Purves had correspondence addressed to him in Broughton Loan and was described as a teacher. From 1777 he was living at Wright's Houses, Bruntsfield, Edinburgh. Between 1785 and 1787 he exchanged letters and books with the Unitarian Thomas Fyshe Palmer, who hoped to move Purves on from a pre-existent Arian christology to a fully humanitarian Unitarian (Socinian) one by lending him books by Nathaniel Lardner, Joseph Priestley, and Theophilus Lindsey. But neither Palmer nor Purves would move from their respective positions. Purves set out his views in *Some Observations on Socinian Arguments* (1790), which on its title page bears the text from Colossians 1: 17 'he is before all things, and by him all things consist'.

On 21 June 1792, after the society had moved into the Barber's Hall, Todrig's Wynd, High Street, Edinburgh, they resolved to publish a *Declaration of Religious Opinions of the Universalist Dissenters*, written by Purves, in which they adopted the name Universalist dissenters. The *Declaration*'s christology accords with Purves's high Arianism. Christ the first created of God was born of a virgin, died on the cross for the sins of humankind, rose on the third day and is seated on the right hand of the Father, 'angels authority and powers, being made subject to him' (Purves, section 2.4). Humankind is in a state of rebellion but God's kingdom is universal and 'all things shall be finally reconciled and gathered together' (Purves, section 4.4). Copies were sent to friends in Dalkeith, Dunbar, Chirnside, and Dundee.

Purves, according to a descendant who possessed copies of his works, was a prolific writer of some twenty titles, many of which he typeset himself and sold at his bookshop in St Patrick's Square on Edinburgh's south side. Several of these titles can no longer be traced. Among the lost works were two treatises on civil government, a Hebrew grammar, and *Observations on the Visions of the Apostle John* (1789), where Purves predicted that Christ would manifest his priestly and kingly power about 1811. Among works which have survived is *An humble attempt to investigate the scripture doctrine concerning the Father, the Son and the Holy Spirit* (1784) which was reprinted by American Universalists in 1819. This upholds the doctrine of universal restoration and defends the Arian remodelling of the Trinity against Socinian Unitarianism.

Purves was married three times: first to Isabel Blair about 1765, second, on her death, to Sarah Brown, about whom no details are known, and finally to Lilias Scott. For many years Purves suffered from asthma. He became seriously ill in the autumn of 1794 and died on 1 February 1795. He was buried in the old Calton cemetery, his remains being removed to its new site when Regent Road was built. His widow continued his book-selling business before emigrating to America. His daughter Elizabeth (1766–1839), by his first marriage, married Hamilton

Dunn and this family remained associated with the Universalist society which in 1813 changed its name to Unitarian. In 1835 Purves's society became St Mark's Unitarian Church, Castle Terrace, Edinburgh.

ANDREW M. HILL

Sources *Monthly Repository*, 15 (1820), 77–80 · St Mark's Unitarian Church, Edinburgh, minutes, 1, NA Scot., CH15/1/1 · A. M. Hill, 'The successors of the remnant: a bicentenary account of St Mark's Unitarian Church, Edinburgh [pt 1]', *Transactions of the Unitarian Historical Society*, 16/3 (1975–8), 101–23 · W. J. Couper, 'A breach in the Reformed Presbytery 1753', *Records of the Scottish Church History Society*, 1 (1923–5), 1–28 · JRL, Unitarian College MSS · J. Purves, *Declaration of religious opinions of the Universalist dissenters* (1792)
Archives JRL · NA Scot. | DWL, corresp. with Thomas Fyshe Palmer

Purvey, John (*c*.1354–1414), Wycliffite heretic, is usually identified with the John Purvey of Lathbury, Buckinghamshire, who was permitted to enter all priestly ranks on 13 March 1377 or 1378 (Lincoln reg. 12, fol. 161); he may have been a member of the Buckinghamshire family of Purefoy. No direct contemporary evidence establishes his education, though it is possible (and has usually been assumed) that he gained his acquaintance with Wyclif's ideas in Oxford. Purvey's name appears with those of Nicholas Hereford, John Aston, William Swinderby, and John Parker in the mandate of 10 August 1387 issued by Henry Wakefield, bishop of Worcester, to prevent their preaching. A commission of 1388–9 apparently sent to all bishops, some copies of which are recorded in the patent rolls, ordered a search for heretical books by Purvey himself, by Hereford, Aston, and the late John Wyclif.

Purvey, according to Knighton, about this time preached heresy in Bristol. The next firm record is of Archbishop Arundel's investigation of Purvey on seven heretical views between 28 February and 5 March 1401; on 6 March Purvey recanted at Paul's Cross in London. The articles follow the main outline of Wyclif's teaching on the eucharist, sacerdotal absolution after confession, the preaching obligations of the clergy, the invalidity of wrongful excommunication, the ineffectuality of papal law, including that of clerical celibacy, unless founded expressly in scripture, and proclaim the priesthood of all believers. The number and rank of the clerics and lay persons assembled for the trial and for the recantation suggest that Purvey was viewed as an important suspect. On 11 August 1401 he was admitted as rector of West Hythe in Kent, close to the archbishop's residence at Saltwood Castle; the living was vacant by October 1403. Immediately preceding the list of the six errors abjured by Purvey in March 1401, *Fasciculi zizaniorum* lists eleven subdivided errors headed 'libelli Purvey Lollardi, collecti per reverendum magistrum fratrem Ricardum Lavynham Carmelitam' (*Fasciculi zizaniorum*, 399). Their proximity with the errors of 1401 may not be significant, since some undoubtedly heretical views concerning clerical temporalities and the pope are not replicated in the charges before Arundel.

Purvey's whereabouts, and his theological opinions, are then unknown for a further period of years; in 1407 William Thorpe stated that he 'schewith now himsilf to be

neithir hoot ne coold' (Hudson, 363). Purvey, though not described as a local man, was named as one of the instigators of the Oldcastle rebellion in Derbyshire and Warwickshire. He was present at the confrontation between the king's forces and the rebels at St Giles's Field on 9 January 1414, evaded capture for a few days, but by 12 January had been arrested. He was held in Newgate prison until his death, apparently from natural causes, on 16 May of that year. By the time of his arrest Purvey was resident in London, and a list survives of the property that had been confiscated by the escheator from his residence following his imprisonment. It was valued at £12 18*s*. 8*d*. This list contains among other effects nineteen books; though the details given do not establish any as certainly Wycliffite in origin, they include biblical and patristic texts, canon law, and sermons.

Knighton in his *Chronicon* under 1382 described Purvey as the *quartus haeresiarcha* ('fourth arch-heretic') following Wyclif, Hereford, and Aston, and claimed that Purvey lived in the same house as Wyclif (probably after the latter's retirement in 1381 to Lutterworth), and that he worked tirelessly to forward the master's views. Thomas Netter in his *Doctrinale*, written between 1421 and 1427, mentions Purvey a number of times. He quotes from a *De compendiis scripturarum, paternarum doctrinarum et canonum*, a copy of which he claims was taken from Purvey in prison; the book defended the right of all priests, laymen, and laywomen to preach, alleging support from canon law, Augustine, and Gregory. The second work, his *Libellus de oratione*, seems to have used the same method in regard to the length of prayers and the reason for them; this second is, however, slightly dubious, since it resembles in title and opinions a work elsewhere ascribed by Netter to William Taylor (correctly, to judge by parallel quotations given in the record of Taylor's 1423 trial before Archbishop Chichele). Netter's descriptions of Purvey as *doctor eximius* ('excellent doctor'), *glossator Wicleffi* ('commentator on Wyclif'), and *librarius Lollardorum* ('librarian of the Lollards') encouraged extensive later speculation about Purvey's writing. Purvey is listed, along with William Swinderby, William Taylor, Sir John Oldcastle, and the Londoner John Claydon, as known to the Lollard suspect John Walcote, shepherd of Hasleton, Gloucestershire, when questioned in 1425.

Nothing that can firmly be attributed to Purvey survives. John Bale lists nineteen works in all, most of whose titles were extracted by Bale from the 1401 and Lavenham's listings of Purvey's views in the *Fasciculi zizaniorum* and from Netter. To this was added *Commentarius in Apocalypsim*, with the incipit of the work printed at Wittenberg in 1528 with a preface attributed to Luther; this was an abbreviated version of the *Opus arduum*, a work written in England between Christmas 1389 and Easter 1390 by an imprisoned Lollard, but there is no evidence before Bale to connect it with Purvey. In 1729 Daniel Waterland conjectured that Purvey was the writer of the so-called general prologue to the Wycliffite Bible and, through the contents of that, deduced that Purvey had a hand in the entire translation; John Lewis, who published

Waterland's suggestion without indication of its conjectural nature, associated Purvey particularly with the later, more idiomatic version. This attribution has been repeated as established fact without question almost to the present day. To Purvey, following this, was also assigned a large number of other English Wycliffite texts, again without medieval supporting evidence.

ANNE HUDSON

Sources A. Hudson, 'John Purvey: a reconsideration of the evidence for his life and writings', *Viator*, 12 (1981), 355–80 · M. Jurkowski, 'New light on John Purvey', *EngHR*, 110 (1995), 1180–90 · PRO, KB 9/204/1, mm. 60, 61, 63 · PRO, KB 9/991, mm. 12, 14 · PRO, KB 27/611, m. 23 · PRO, E 153/1066, mm. 5–6 · PRO, E 357/24, m. 49 · PRO, E 368/186, m. 190 · PRO, E 368/187, m. 300 · [T. Netter], *Fasciculi zizaniorum magistri Johannis Wyclif cum tritico*, ed. W. W. Shirley, Rolls Series, 5 (1858), 383–407 · *Knighton's chronicle, 1337–1396*, ed. and trans. G. H. Martin, OMT (1995), 290–93 [Lat. orig., *Chronica de eventibus Angliae a tempore regis Edgari usque mortem regis Ricardi Secundi*, with parallel Eng. text] · *Thomæ Waldensis … doctrinale antiquitatum fidei Catholicæ ecclesiæ*, ed. B. Blanciotti, 3 vols. (Venice, 1757–9), bks 2.70, 2.73, 5.145, 6.13, 6.117 · Bale, *Cat.*, 1.541–3 · Arundel reg. 2, LPL, fols. 179v–85 · Arundel reg. 1, LPL, fols. 278, 290v · Worcester reg. Morgan, 168–9 · *The works of the Rev. Daniel Waterland*, ed. W. van Mildert, 10 vols. (1823), vol. 10. pp. 359–63 · J. Lewis, preface, in *The New Testament, translated out of the Latin Vulgat by John Wiclif … to which is praefixt a history of the several translations* (1731), 218–21 · Lincoln reg. 12 (Buckingham), fol. 161
Wealth at death £12 18s. 8d.: PRO, E 153/1066 mm. 5–6

Purvis, Arthur Blaikie (1890–1941), industrialist and buyer of war supplies, was born in London on 31 March 1890, the son of William Blaikie Purvis, a commercial clerk, of Perth, Scotland, and his wife, Annie Maria Baker. He was educated at Tottenham grammar school and won a scholarship, but owing to the death of his father began work at thirteen. In 1905 he joined the firm of Lynch Brothers in London, and in 1910 went to Glasgow to the Nobel Explosives Company Ltd, where his ability was quickly recognized by Harry Duncan McGowan. He represented the firm in South America and South Africa and, despite his youth, by 1914 was in charge of the New York office. On the outbreak of war he made one of the largest war purchases, $25 million of acetone, which was in acute shortage in the United Kingdom; he remained responsible for the purchase in America of materials for explosives throughout the war. In 1918 he married Margaret, daughter of Cyrus Emory Jones, of Jamestown, New York; they had one son.

The strain of Purvis's wartime duties resulted in a prolonged breakdown in health. He went to the Adirondacks where, by sheer will-power, he made a recovery so complete that in 1925 he was able to go to Canada as president of Canadian Explosives Ltd, which he reorganized into Canadian Industries Ltd. He was eager to encourage chemical research in its application to Canada's natural resources and urged manufacturers to take risks in the adoption of scientific ideas. By 1939 he had become one of the foremost figures in Canadian industry and director of eleven important Canadian concerns. During these years he also devoted much time to community work, especially in Montreal where he was a governor of McGill University; as the remarkably successful chairman of the national employment commission (1936–8), he also contributed services of a national character.

'A man of the highest integrity with no enemies and, indeed, no critics', as the governor-general of Canada, Lord Tweedsmuir, described him, Purvis became director-general of British purchasing in the United States in November 1939, and in the following January chairman of the Anglo-French purchasing board 'with a high degree of effective authority', which on the British side did not, however, at first extend beyond making contracts for the Ministry of Supply. Purvis soon found his work hampered by the 'uncontrolled' purchases of other missions, which, as he pointed out, 'destroyed his background' with American industry and the United States government. Not until mid-1940 did he succeed in extending his own direct responsibility for purchase to machine tools and iron and steel, or in receiving, as of right, complete and detailed information from all other purchasing bodies.

From the outset, however, all doors in Washington were thrown open to Purvis. He conceived his task as far wider than the mere purchase of American supplies. He entered at once with President Roosevelt and Henry Morgenthau, secretary of the United States treasury, into the economic planning of the war and the denial of supplies, especially of strategic metals, to the enemy. 'From the first', said Morgenthau, 'Purvis impressed me tremendously.' It was essential, he counselled Purvis, to have a complete statement of all allied requirements lest they be swept aside when a still neutral United States turned to war expansion on its own account. Purvis, in his persuasive turn, pressed this lesson upon a British government not yet imaginatively ready, as Purvis was himself, to 'talk big', or, to Purvis, big enough.

It was Purvis who took immediate action in Washington during the fall of France, initially by negotiating the swift transfer of American arms to replace in part those lost by the British at Dunkirk. In one week he signed both the $37.5 million contract for this transaction and, on 17 June 1940, a document committing the British government to the payment of $600 million for the French contracts in America. 'Never', said Lord Woolton in the House of Lords a month later, 'have wider powers to commit this country been delegated to any mission.'

In the next six months Purvis played the leading part in carrying through the decision to empty the British war chest by both financing massive British war contracts in the United States and, by a series of capital investments, laying the foundations of the American munitions industry. In July 1940 he was joined in Washington by M. Jean Monnet, who, like himself, recognized the vital importance of the British striking a proper balance between their own competing claims. Without explicit authority Purvis set about the necessary co-ordination at a time when there were a number of separate British missions in the United States, some *ad hoc* and some representing different departments in Whitehall; of these the air commission was especially independent. Until December 1940 Purvis achieved such co-ordination as was attained by his personal efforts and persuasion and the especial confidence of Morgenthau. After visiting the United Kingdom in the closing weeks of that year for discussions on the strategy of British supply in the United States, on his return Purvis was given explicit status by his appointment as chairman of the British supply council in North America and thus, on the civilian side, director of the entire British war organization there.

If his authority was now assured, to Purvis the basic issue remained unchanged: 'it was a cardinal feature of the Purvis–Monnet programme to get the Americans to raise their sights all round'. The president resumed with Purvis the discussions which had already borne fruit in the idea of the Lend-Lease Bill and were now shaping the range and scope of the act. Purvis now went into action with 'a well-tried weapon from Monnet's armoury', the balance sheet technique. Largely on his own initiative, in January 1941 he boldly translated into dollars British requirements which he had gathered from departments in Whitehall, and produced his estimate of British production and of the resultant deficiency which American production could alone make good. The president took his estimate of $15 billion, Purvis reported, in his stride. It was held in official circles at the time that Purvis's balance sheet powerfully influenced the first appropriation under the Lend-Lease Act. British policy in Washington at this period 'formulated in large measure by Monnet's planning mind and propagated by the persistence and persuasiveness of Purvis' was making demands on American industry greatly in advance of contemporary American opinion. Purvis himself was by now the most powerful British influence in the United States. To Morgenthau he was not only 'the ablest British representative in Washington but one of the rarest persons I have ever known'. He was nominated to the privy council in December 1940 but did not live to be sworn.

At the time of his death Purvis was planning to secure from President Roosevelt the greatest directive yet issued, to place all American production on a full war basis. He was killed when the aircraft in which he was returning from Britain to Washington crashed on taking off from Prestwick on 14 August 1941. 'Purvis was a grievous loss', wrote Winston Churchill (*Second World War*, 3, 1950), 'as he held so many British, American, and Canadian threads in his hands, and had hitherto been the directing mind in their harmonious combination.' The Anglo-American consolidated statement that month represented the climax of Purvis's work and the effective beginning of that Victory programme which thereafter took the central place in the wartime economic planning of the Western allies. Purvis saw—was perhaps the first to see—the size of the problem.   H. D. HALL, *rev.*

Sources H. D. Hall, *North American supply* (1955) · W. K. Hancock and M. M. Gowing, *British war economy* (1949) · E. R. Stettinius, jun., *Lend-lease* (1944) · H. Morgenthau, *Collier's Magazine* (Oct 1947) · *New York Times* (24 Jan 1946) · *Toronto Star Weekly* (10 Feb 1940) · *Fortune* (April 1940) · *The Times* (16 Aug 1941) · *The Times* (18 Aug 1941) · b. cert. · *CGPLA Eng. & Wales* (1942)

Wealth at death £481 2s. 0d. — effects in England: administration with will, 25 June 1942, *CGPLA Eng. & Wales*

Pury, Thomas (1589/90–1666), politician, was born in Gloucester, the only son of Walter Pury, a Gloucester clothier and minor landowner, and Anne Clutterbuck. He was the scion of a long-established city family. According to a newsletter, he studied at Oxford, then worked as a cashier to a Gloucester clothier, setting up in business with the £600 savings he had made when his employer died about 1611. At an unknown date he married Mary Alye (d. 1668), with whom he had one son, Thomas [see below], and two daughters.

Pury became sheriff of Gloucester in 1626 and an alderman in 1638. By then he was a practising attorney, though he had not attended an inn of court—hence the jibes labelling him 'first a weaver in Gloucester, then an ignorant Countrey Solicitor' (*A List of the Names of the Members of the House of Commons*, 1648). He was a leading figure in the faction that made Gloucester a centre of civic puritanism in the 1630s. He failed to gain election for Gloucester to the Short Parliament in March 1640, but in November he was elected to the Long Parliament. His published speech against episcopacy in the Commons in February 1641 catalogued many grievances against the dean and chapter of Gloucester, but also some well-thought-out alternative uses for its wealth.

Upon the outbreak of civil war Pury was one of the most zealous early parliamentarians in Gloucestershire, serving in arms, and was exempted from pardon in the king's first declaration. He was in Gloucester during the siege in the summer of 1643, when the governor, Colonel Edward Massey, described him as one of very few to remain 'cordiall' to the cause, and remained there for most of 1644. He served on many parliamentary committees, mainly on local, Irish, and religious matters, becoming chairman of the committee of Gloucester from October 1643, and was on most county and city committees between 1642 and 1660, as well as becoming a JP. By November 1644 he and Massey were bitterly at odds, in what was mainly a personality clash. On 17 March 1645 Massey called Pury and Isaac Bromwich the 'guides at a distance' to the committeemen who were obstructing him.

From 1645 to 1651 Pury was mostly in London. He served as clerk of the petty bag from 18 December 1643 to 11 March 1661 and, on 2 January 1647, was rewarded out of the earl of Worcester's estates for his services. Royalist diatribes alleged that the clerkship was worth £400 per annum and the lands £3000; Pury's defenders said that they were worth much less and not enough to compensate for his losses in the cause. However, he did acquire at least three estates near Gloucester during the period. He was assaulted by troops in 1647, probably in London. In the same year he founded a charity to provide £8 per annum to feed the poor of two parishes and prisoners in Gloucester from the proceeds of confiscated church lands.

Although inclined to the Independent party in the Commons, Pury was not a regicide—his son allegedly 'blessed God that his father and he had no hand in that … action of

Killing the King' (G. Bishop, *A Modest Check to Part of a Scandalous Libell*, 1650, 5). However, he returned to the Rump on 1 February 1649, two days after the king's execution. He was fairly active at first but appeared only once after February 1652, partly because he was mayor of Gloucester in 1653 and spent much time fighting attempts by the shire gentry to overthrow Gloucester's jurisdiction. On 12 July 1654 he was again elected MP for Gloucester in the first protectorate parliament and was named to several committees. However, on 11 January 1659 he was defeated in Gloucester's election for Richard Cromwell's parliament, two other candidates standing against him on a moderate ticket. In July 1659 he and his son raised 300 volunteer foot to foil Massey's attempted uprising on Gloucester. Facing certain removal from the corporation as a purge of old puritans approached, Pury resigned his gown in 1662, ostensibly on the grounds of his advanced age and residence in London. He died in Gloucester, aged seventy-six, on 13 August 1666 and was buried in St Mary de Crypt, Gloucester. Although his will contained bequests of less than £10, he left a number of properties in Gloucestershire and London.

Pury was survived by his wife and his son, **Thomas Pury** (1618/19–1693), army officer and politician, who matriculated at Magdalen College, Oxford, on 18 November 1635 and entered Gray's Inn on 25 January 1641. He married Barbara Kyrle (1623–1688), with whom he had a son, Thomas (1654/5–1709). He worked for an attorney of Staple's Inn in London in 1642 and was a parliamentarian captain, first in Colonel Stephens's regiment and later in the New Model Army. He acted as receiver of the king's rents in Gloucestershire and Wiltshire from 20 October 1643 to 12 July 1652, a post allegedly worth £200 per annum, as well as being the local clerk of the peace between 1646 and 1660. In December 1646 he was elected recruiter MP for Monmouth. In 1648 he helped to re-establish Bishop Goodman's library in Gloucester Cathedral. More strongly opposed to the regicide than his father, Pury stayed away from the Rump until 2 June 1649. He was also involved in managing the ironworks of the Forest of Dean until their suppression in 1650, after his servants had committed numerous abuses. In 1650 his regiment went with Sir William Constable's regiment to Bristol and may have served in Ireland.

Pury sat for Gloucester in the second protectorate parliament in 1656, but was not very active. At the suppression of Massey's uprising in 1659 he became a colonel of a foot regiment and was a pivotal figure in the region in the events leading up to the Restoration. In January 1660 he restored order in Gloucester after the departure of Sir Brice Cochrane's mutinous troops. A close adherent of General Monck, he spent the next few months holding the city and the local counties against dissident republican elements, and proclaimed Charles II at Hereford before 17 May. After the Restoration he was named lieutenant-colonel to his old regiment under Lord Herbert and continued to enjoy certain fee farm rents by the king's order for some time. He retired to Taynton, near Gloucester, and rebuilt the church, which had burned down in the civil

war. In June 1670, he was an attorney of the court of common pleas. He died aged seventy-four on 26 August 1693 at Taynton, where he was later buried.

ANDREW WARMINGTON

Sources *JHC*, 2–6 (1640–51) · W. R. Williams, *The parliamentary history of the county of Gloucester* (privately printed, Hereford, 1898) · A. R. Warmington, *Civil war, interregnum and Restoration in Gloucestershire, 1640–1672* (1997) · *CSP dom., 1641–5; 1649–51* · *VCH Gloucestershire*, vol. 4 · C. H. Firth and R. S. Rait, eds., *Acts and ordinances of the interregnum, 1642–1660*, 3 vols. (1911) · *Packets of Letters*, no. 29 (3 Oct 1648) · D. Underdown, *Pride's Purge: politics in the puritan revolution* (1971) · B. Worden, *The Rump Parliament, 1648–1653* (1974) · P. Clark, '"The Ramoth-Gilead of the good": urban change and political radicalism at Gloucester, 1540–1640', *The English Commonwealth 1547–1640*, ed. P. Clark, A. G. R. Smith, and N. Tyacke (1979), 167–87 · *Mr Thomas Pury Alderman of Glocester his speech…* (1641) · R. Austin, 'The city of Gloucester and the regulation of corporations', *Transactions of the Bristol and Gloucestershire Archaeological Society*, 58 (1936), 257–274 · Glos. RO, Gloucester borough records, B2–3 · T. F. Fenwick and W. C. Metcalfe, eds., *The visitation of the county of Gloucester* (privately printed, Exeter, 1884) · PRO, PROB 11/326, fols. 176*v*–177*r*

Archives BL, speech and MSS relating to petition in parliament, E 198 (21)

Wealth at death said to have inherited lands valued at £100 and accumulated £600 in savings by 1611; held paid offices in civil war; acquired three manors during 1640s but only one remained in family: will, PRO, PROB 11/326, fols. 176*v*–177*r*

Pury, Thomas (1618/19–1693). *See under* Pury, Thomas (1589/90–1666).

Puseley, Daniel [*pseud.* Frank Foster] (1814–1882), writer, was born at Bideford, Devon, on 9 February 1814, the son of Henry Puseley, maltster, and was educated at Bideford grammar school until the age of fifteen, when, having been left 'without parental protection and guidance' (Puseley, *Faith, Hope, and Charity*, 1863, 21), he took up a clerkship at a large wholesale establishment in London. For several years thereafter he attended evening classes at a literary and scientific institute near the General Post Office in order to supplement his elementary education.

On 27 July 1844, after a period as a commercial traveller, Puseley married Mary Anne, daughter of John Darlington, a London builder, and in the same year he set up as a hosier and silk merchant in Gutter Lane. He was soon, however, 'compelled to close his shutters' (Puseley, *Dependence or Independence*, 16), finding that a successful business career was incompatible with literary ambition. His first book, a moralistic novella entitled *Harry Mustifer* (1847), sold only twelve copies in its first year and Puseley thereafter interspersed creative projects (such as *Five Dramas*, 1854, a forlorn attempt to purge the English stage of foreign influence) with the compilation of solidly factual handbooks such as *The Commercial Companion for the United Kingdom* (1858; 3rd edn, 1860), and *The Traveller's Assistant* (1867). He also produced, often using the pseudonym Frank Foster and, later, An Old Author, a long succession of pamphlets on a wide range of topical themes and, encouraged by the success of his acquaintance Albert Smith, he established a reputation as a comic lecturer at the Royal Polytechnic Institution and elsewhere. By these means, Puseley contrived to build up a modest competence with which to support his growing family (he and his wife had four sons: Herbert John; Berkeley Edward, a journalist who assisted his father in some of his later work; Percy Daniel; and Sydney George).

In 1854 Puseley travelled to Australia and New Zealand for his health, making a second trip in 1857. These journeys resulted both in his most interesting poem, a narrative of high society entitled *The Wave of Life* (1857), and in his most commercially successful book, *The Rise and Progress of Australia, Tasmania, and New Zealand* (1857), which quickly went through five editions. In addition to the usual barrage of practical information, Puseley provided an opinionated account of his own reactions. He found New Zealand 'the finest colony in the world' (p. 232), but Australia he pronounced 'the most objectionable of all British dependencies' (p. 231) and he took especial exception to Melbourne ('a little hell upon earth'; p. 4).

After his second return to England, Puseley's industry continued unabated, but his career as a lecturer was cut short by failing health and his attempts at fiction; *Our Premier* (1867), for example, a would-be sensation novel, and the rambling *All Round the World* (1876), met with scant success. In 1866 he lost a large part of his savings through injudicious investments, but efforts to procure a civil-list pension failed with the resignation of Lord Derby in 1868. He died on 18 January 1882 at 21 Rochester Road, Camden Town, London, where he had lived for many years and from which he had published much of his own work; he was buried in Highgate cemetery. He was survived by his wife.

Puseley devoted much of his time to charitable causes and was a lifelong champion of education for the poor. His greatest practical achievement in this field occurred on 18 December 1868, when he co-ordinated a ragged schools festival in St James's Hall, at which 600 selected children were presented with prizes. Although Puseley's writings seldom rise above the level of hack work, he exemplifies, in his industry and independence, the virtues of self-help he so strenuously championed.   ROBERT DINGLEY

Sources *DNB* · D. Puseley [F. Foster], *Who'd be an author? With the answer* [1869] · *The Academy* (28 Jan 1882), 63 · *The Athenaeum* (28 Jan 1882), 127 · *CGPLA Eng. & Wales* (1882)

Likenesses engraving, repro. in D. Puseley, *The age we live in, or, Doings of the day* (1863), frontispiece

Wealth at death £265 19s. 5d.: probate, 14 Feb 1882, *CGPLA Eng. & Wales*

Pusey, Edward Bouverie (1800–1882), Church of England clergyman and university professor, was the second child of Philip Pusey (1746–1828), landowner, the youngest son of Jacob Bouverie, first Viscount Folkestone, who took the name Pusey when he inherited extensive property at Pusey, a small village in Berkshire, and Lady Lucy Sherard (1770–1858), the daughter of the earl of Harborough and widow of Sir Thomas Cave.

Early life and education Pusey was born at Pusey House, Pusey, on 22 August 1800 and attended a preparatory school at Mitcham in Surrey run by a clergyman, Richard Roberts, who grounded him well in the classics. In 1812 he went to Eton College under 'Flogger' Keate. A shy, rather weakly boy, not much interested in sport though a good

Edward Bouverie Pusey (1800–1882), by George Richmond, *c.*1890

chess player, he made few close friends there. Then, after fifteen months with a private tutor, Edward Maltby, later bishop of Durham, in January 1819 he went up to Christ Church, Oxford, where he was tutored by Thomas Vowler Short (later bishop of St Asaph). He graduated with a first class in 1822, and in 1823 successfully competed for an Oriel fellowship, then one of the most coveted distinctions in the university.

Further studies and first publication Aspiring to ordination, Pusey attended the lectures of Dr Charles Lloyd, regius professor of divinity and later bishop of Oxford, whom he described as 'a second father' to him. Lloyd, conscious of the disturbing developments in German biblical scholarship and theology, urged Pusey to learn the language and to study in Germany. Pusey responded willingly, as he was already aware of the threat of rationalism to the Christian faith through his attempts to counter the scepticism of Julian Hibbert, a friend from Eton. He spent the long vacation of 1825 and a whole year, 1826–7, in Germany at the universities of Berlin, Bonn, and Göttingen studying theology, most notably under Schleiermacher. Realizing that the Old Testament was the most vulnerable area to attack, he also learned Hebrew, Arabic, and other cognate languages, with Freytag and Kosegarten.

Already he showed the immense capacity for work which was characteristic of him throughout his life, studying from fourteen to sixteen hours a day. Soon after his return to England, in May 1828, he published his first book, *An historical enquiry into the probable causes of the rationalist character lately predominant in the theology of Germany*. He was encouraged to do this by his German friends who were very critical of the recently published lectures by Hugh James Rose on the same subject. Pusey consequently wrote more sympathetically. This, coupled with his rather obscure style, led to his being widely misunderstood. Whereas Rose had attributed the condition of German theology to the lack of credal formularies and episcopal government which protected the English church, Pusey attributed it to what he confusingly called 'dead orthodoxism', the aridity of Lutheran scholasticism, a phenomenon which he also detected in the Church of England. He consulted Newman and produced a 'Second part' in 1830, defending himself against suspicions of rationalism. Dissatisfied with the work himself, he withdrew it from sale a few years later. This did not prevent charges of early liberalism being made from time to time in his later life, and in his will he directed that the book should never be reprinted. It did not, however, damage his prospects.

Hebrew professorship On 1 June 1828 Pusey was made deacon, and the following November he was appointed by the prime minister, the duke of Wellington, regius professor of Hebrew at Oxford; to the chair was attached a Christ Church canonry, so Pusey had to be ordained to the priesthood. On 12 June 1828 he had married Maria Catharine Barker (1801–1839), the daughter of Raymond Barker of Fairford Park, with whom he had fallen in love at their first meeting ten years earlier. Neither father had approved of the match; Pusey's consequent unhappiness and frustration partly accounted for his burying himself in work. They had one son, Philip Edward (1830–1880), and three daughters: only his youngest daughter, Mary Amelia (Mrs Brine), survived him. His wife died of consumption, aged thirty-eight, on 26 May 1839. On 23 November 1828 he was ordained priest by Bishop Lloyd at Cuddesdon and on 9 December was installed canon of Christ Church.

As Pusey understood it, his work was as much theological as linguistic. All cathedrals, indeed, had a responsibility for the education of those intending to be ordained, as he argued in his pamphlet *Remarks on the Prospective and Past Benefits of Cathedral Institutions* (1833). The German system of clerical education provided a model which cathedrals could adopt. Meantime the two ancient universities were the only institutions for such education in England and Pusey intended to use his position to improve it. The university statutes envisaged only one lecture twice a week, but, with the help of a deputy, he provided three courses of lectures, three times a week. He treated the study of Hebrew as a religious subject and aimed to impart a full idiomatic knowledge so that students might 'enter more fully into the simple meaning of God's Word' (*DNB*). Arthur Penrhyn Stanley, who attended his lectures in 1845, said 'the whole atmosphere of [them] breathed the spirit of Germany to a degree' (E. G. W. Bill, *University Reform*, 1973, 252). In 1832 Pusey, together with his elder brother, Philip, and a friend, Dr Ellerton, founded the three Pusey and Ellerton Hebrew scholarships. For some years he gave board and lodging to students in his house so that they could study theology and, when his wife was

ill, rented a house nearby for them. Later he accommodated non-graduates to help prepare them for ordination. He also founded a Theological Society, mostly for young fellows, which met in his lodgings, where papers were presented and discussed. He supported the establishment of theological colleges, giving, for example, £2500 towards the founding of Salisbury Theological College (1861).

Pusey felt obliged to complete the catalogue of the oriental manuscripts in the Bodleian Library begun by his predecessor, Alexander Nicoll. The laborious task took him nearly six years. The only work he published in direct connection with his chair was *Lectures on Daniel the Prophet* (1864). He chose the subject because 'disbelief in Daniel has become an axiom in the unbelieving critical school' (p. vi). It is usually dismissed as a monument of conservatism but his successor, Dr S. R. Driver, who was far from sharing Pusey's views, acknowledged it as 'extremely learned and thorough' (Butler, *Pusey Rediscovered*, 111). His *Minor prophets, with a commentary, explanatory and practical and introduction to the several books*, which appeared in parts between 1860 and 1877, was the only published part of a projected popular commentary on the whole Bible planned by Pusey.

Pusey's Hebrew scholarship was widely acknowledged and is also attested by his astute purchases of Hebrew manuscripts for the Bodleian, of which he was a curator. He was invited to take part in the revision of the Authorized Version of the Bible in 1870 but, although he had himself made an abortive attempt at a revision of the Old Testament on his return from Germany, he declined.

Adherence to the Oxford Movement and contribution to the Tracts Pusey occupied the chair of theology for over fifty years and faithfully fulfilled the duties of his office, but his name will always be associated with the Oxford Movement, the Catholic revival in the Church of England. His election to a fellowship at Oriel had brought him into close contact with John Keble and John Henry Newman who, together with Richard Hurrell Froude, were the real originators of the movement, but he had not immediately joined them. His other commitments, to his work on the catalogue of manuscripts, to his growing family (four children between 1829 and 1833), and a period of ill health diverted his energies. His political liberalism, too, had led him to support Peel and Catholic emancipation in 1829, which they had opposed. Initially he had wondered whether he 'could not best aid the plan by separate action with the same end' (Trench, 80). Eventually, however, he threw himself into the movement, to use his own words,

as an effective means of bringing to the vivid consciousness of members of the Church of England, Catholic truths, taught of old within her, presupposed in her formularies, but unhappily overlaid or watered down in the meagre practical teaching of the 18th century

in order to realize the ideal God had set her, 'to represent in life and in doctrine the teaching of the undivided Church' (*University Sermons, 1859–72*, 1872, v–vi). He agreed to write a tract on the value of fasting, which was published at the end of 1833 as Tract 18, on condition that his initials were attached to it. Since the earlier tracts were anonymous the unintended result was that his name became synonymous with Tractarianism and the movement was popularly known as Puseyism. As Newman acknowledged in his *Apologia*, 'he at once gave to us a position and a name'. This was due as much to his character as to his status.

> He had a vast influence in consequence of his deep religious seriousness, the munificence of his charities, his Professorship, his family connexions, and his easy relations with University authorities. … He was a man of large designs, he had a hopeful sanguine mind; he had no fear of others; he was haunted by no intellectual perplexities.
> (*Apologia*, ed. M. Svagelic, 1967, 646)

Pusey's adherence to the movement changed the character of the Tracts. They became weighty theological treatises, none more than his own. In 1835 he contributed a major study, *Scriptural Views of Holy Baptism*, which was published in three parts as Tracts 67, 68, and 69. In it he sought to demonstrate the biblical and patristic basis of the doctrine of baptismal regeneration. In 1839 he produced an enlarged edition of the first part, Tract 67, expanding it from 48 pages to 400, incorporating in it material from some very original lectures he had given on types and prophecies. He also wrote a tract, 81, on the other great sacrament, the eucharist, *Testimony of writers of the later English church to the doctrine of the eucharistic sacrifice, with an historical account of the changes made in the liturgy as to the expression of that doctrine* (1837). Pusey wrote the historical account, although the catena of quotations was largely the work of Benjamin Harrison. The doctrine was widely forgotten in the Church of England and Pusey's exposition of it was much vaguer than his later teaching.

Tract 81 shows the importance Pusey attached to the Caroline divines as witnesses to the teaching of the Church of England. One of the great projects of the Oxford Movement was the Library of Anglo-Catholic Theology (1841–63), which republished many of their works, but, according to Newman, neither he nor Pusey was 'warm' about it. Pusey, however, was the driving force behind the other great literary project, the Library of Fathers of the Holy Catholic Church, Anterior to the Division of East and West (1838–85). This made available in translation the works of thirteen writers, mostly of the fourth century, notably Athanasius, Chrysostom, and Augustine. The burden of organizing the translators, revising their work, negotiating with the publishers, and raising subscriptions fell on Pusey. He provided the first volume, a revised translation of St Augustine's *Confessions*, with a preface on the need and value of patristic study. There were forty-eight volumes in all, the last ones appearing after his death.

Apologist for the Tractarians Pusey's position in Oxford made him the obvious spokesman and apologist for the Tractarians. In 1836 he wrote *An Earnest Remonstrance*, published as Tract 77, in response to an anonymous attack on their teaching on prayers for the dead. Three years later Richard Bagot, the bishop of Oxford, puzzled by the refusal of Pusey and the other Tractarians to subscribe to a

memorial to the protestant martyrs, asked him to explain their attitude to the Reformation. This he did in an open *Letter to the Bishop of Oxford* (1839). It was Pusey's most explicit exposition of his understanding of the Church of England as the *via media*, treading 'a broad and tangible line, not verging towards, or losing itself in Romanism', and 'distinct from the bye-ways of Ultra Protestantism' (4th edn, 1840, 22), a line which was moreover 'the "old path" of the Primitive Church' (ibid.). In 1841 he defended Newman when he was attacked for trying, in Tract 90, to demonstrate that the Thirty-Nine Articles were patent of a Catholic interpretation. He persuaded the bishop not to censure the tract and published another open letter, this time to his Etonian friend and fellow canon of Christ Church Dr R. W. Jelf, in which he claimed significantly that Newman's interpretation was not 'only *an* admissible, but *the* most legitimate interpretation of them' (*Letter to Jelf*, 1841, 148f.). In the autumn Archbishop Howley sent for Pusey to ascertain the state of things in Oxford and, at the suggestion of his chaplain, Pusey wrote an open letter to the archbishop defending the movement against the criticisms levelled at it in many bishops' charges and urging that the church 'be what she is in theory and in her prayer book' (*Letter to the Archbishop*, 3rd edn, 1842, 119).

Leadership of the movement Pusey was becoming increasingly prominent in the leadership of the movement. Newman was on his Anglican 'deathbed' and retired to live at Littlemore in 1842, while Keble was resident in his country parish and no longer professor of poetry. In 1843 Pusey was attacked for his teaching in a university sermon, *The Holy Eucharist: a Comfort to the Penitent*. Six doctors of divinity were appointed to examine it and, without his being allowed to speak in his own defence, he was condemned for preaching unspecified doctrines 'dissona et contraria' to those of the Church of England and suspended from preaching before the university for two years. Many sprang to Pusey's defence, including W. E. Gladstone and Lord Coleridge. Pusey took the advice of Newman, whom he feared would be further unsettled by the condemnation, and published the sermon with supporting quotations from the Caroline divines and notes from the fathers.

Newman's submission to Rome on 9 October 1845, 'one of the deep sorrows of my life' (letter to *The Guardian*, 9 Oct 1865) as Pusey described it, left him exposed as the reluctant leader of the party. Almost immediately he had to face a storm of hostility over the consecration of St Saviour's, Leeds, on 28 October. He had built the church anonymously after the death of his wife to further the work of his friend W. F. Hook in evangelizing the city and as an act of penitence. Hook was fearful and did not even want him to come to Leeds, and the bishop of the diocese, C. J. Longley, raised repeated objections to its furnishings, even, most hurtfully to Pusey, to the inscription on the communion plate given by Pusey's daughter, Lucy, on her deathbed the previous year. Pusey wished the octave of the consecration to be kept as a kind of retreat, and there were sermons every day, mostly preached, though not all written, by him, which were subsequently published. The early death of Maria Pusey in 1839 after only eleven years of marriage was but one of the tragedies in Pusey's private life. Of their four children, one died in infancy, one, the only son, Philip, became deaf and lame after an illness in 1838, and a third, the eldest, Lucy, who was particularly close to him because she shared his hopes for the revival of the religious life, died, like her mother of consumption, in 1844. He outlived most of his closest friends, even some of the younger ones such as Bishop Forbes, news of whose death in 1875 caused him to go deaf, and Miss Sellon in 1876. Affectionate and sensitive by nature, he felt these losses deeply. He retired from society after his wife's death and became reclusive. He was also wounded by the misrepresentations and criticisms of his theological position and the questioning of his loyalty to the Church of England. He regarded his personal losses and the obloquy he endured as chastenings, or even punishment, by God for his sins. He lived the life of a penitent, rather like a desert father and, in his private papers, expressed self-loathing. He had practised systematic fasting from about 1835 but after 1839 he adopted other traditional ascetic practices, such as wearing hair cloth and using the discipline, the extent of which are revealed in the rule of life he showed Keble, whom he asked to be his confessor and director (Liddon, 3.104–8). Rumours of his own asceticism and the advice he gave to others, particularly nuns, both fascinated and repelled people. By some he was regarded as a saint, by others as unbalanced or worse. For those who agreed with his beliefs, his sufferings and reputation for holiness gave him great moral authority.

For the rest of his long life Pusey acted as the stabilizing force of the Catholic revival, steadfast in his loyalty to the Church of England, quietly persistent in his teaching about the meaning of the sacraments and their value in practice, dogged in his fight against rationalism and liberalism.

Eucharistic teaching Pusey's personal spirituality increasingly centred on the eucharist. He urged more frequent celebrations, and himself, in middle age, used to celebrate every day in his own house at four in the morning. He was concerned, however, that increased communions should be accompanied by more disciplined lives. In 1853 he preached another university sermon, *The Presence of Christ in the Holy Eucharist*, 'to set forth to young men the greatness of the mystery, that they should be more careful to live as they should, to whom such gifts are vouchsafed' (Liddon, 3.424). The prosecution of Archdeacon Denison for preaching the same doctrine, though rather unwisely expressed, led Pusey to produce notes to his sermon setting out the patristic evidence. They constituted a volume of 724 pages, published in 1855. The following year he drew up a declaration in protest against a church court's condemnation of Denison, which was signed by most of the leading high-churchmen. In 1857 he wrote another volume of minute scholarship, *The real presence of the body and blood of our Lord Jesus Christ, the doctrine of the English church*, defending their teaching from the Anglican formularies. The prosecution of another friend, W. J. E. Bennett,

vicar of Frome, for his eucharistic teaching, expressed in an open *Letter to Pusey* in 1868, drew Pusey once more into the defence of eucharistic doctrine. He felt himself to be on trial as, except for two careless expressions which he persuaded Bennett to retract, the language of the letter was largely his. He even tried to get the Church Association to prosecute him instead. The court of arches acquitted Bennett in 1870 and its judgment was upheld by the privy council in 1872. In the interval Pusey published his last statement on the eucharist, a university sermon, *This is my Body* (1871). He always claimed to have no interest in eucharistic ceremonial, although he invariably used a mixed chalice and even wore vestments in places where it was the custom, but when 'ritualist' priests were prosecuted under the Public Worship Regulation Act of 1874 he came to their defence on the grounds that they were 'setting before the eyes', giving outward expression to what he believed. It was in response to the bishops' first attempt to restrain the ritualists that he declared that

> if it should be decided by competent authority, that either the real Objective Presence, or the Eucharistic Sacrifice, or the worship of Christ there present … were contrary to the doctrine held by the Church of England, I would resign my office. (E. B. Pusey, 'Will ye also go away', 1867, 28, *University Sermons, 1864–1879*, 1880)

Practice of confession Pusey's name will always be associated with the revival of auricular confession: he became a kind of confessor extraordinary to the Church of England. In a letter to *The Times* on 13 November 1866 he said, 'I have been applied to to receive confessions from persons in every rank, of every age, old as well as young, in every profession, even those which you would think least accessible to it—army, navy, medicine, law'. His first university sermon after his suspension, in 1846, was on the spiritual and practical value of confession, *The Entire Absolution of the Penitent*. He followed it up with a second sermon, defending his interpretation of the Anglican formularies which had been questioned, and two days later made his own first confession to Keble. In 1850, having been criticized for hearing confessions outside his home diocese, he defended his practice in an open letter to W. U. Richards, *The Church of England Leaves her Children Free to whom to Open their Griefs*. He was also criticized for hearing confessions of young persons without parental knowledge and consent. For this and other practices which, it was alleged, 'tended to the spread of Romanism amongst us' (Liddon, 3.302), his own bishop, Samuel Wilberforce, secretly inhibited him from preaching in the diocese of Oxford. The unwise petition of 483 clergymen to convocation for the 'licensing of qualified confessors' in 1873 roused a furore. Pusey, T. T. Carter, and one or two others drafted a *Declaration on Confession and Absolution, as Set Forth by the Church of England*, a concise and careful statement of their understanding. In 1878 he published an edition of a French *Manual for Confessors*, by the Abbé Gaume, adapted for the use of Anglicans, with a lengthy historical and apologetic preface. Later that year the second Lambeth conference passed a resolution which appeared to condemn detailed confessions and the practice of habitual confession. Pusey responded by publishing a letter to the archbishop, *Habitual Confession not Discouraged by the Resolution Accepted by the Lambeth Conference*, minimizing the resolution and asking whether he should consider himself censured by the resolution.

Revival of the religious life Pusey first began thinking about the revival of the religious life in 1834, partly for practical reasons (for evangelism and for relief and educational work among the poor) and partly for spiritual reasons (to meet the desire for a more devout life on the part of some who might otherwise have become Roman Catholics). He collected information about the rules, work, devotions, and discipline of Roman Catholic communities, and even visited several convents in Ireland in 1841. Independently of him a group of laymen led by Lord John Manners decided to establish a sisterhood in memory of the poet Southey, and a house was opened in Park Village, London, on 26 March 1845. The external work was under the direction of the parish priest, William Dodsworth, but Pusey was the spiritual superintendent, and in fact had to take on more and more responsibility for its direction and finances. A similar experiment was started in 1848 in Plymouth by Priscilla Lydia Sellon, and after a few years the two communities joined together to form the Society of the Most Holy Trinity. Pusey had no official connection with the society, although he became adviser to, and intimate friend as well as spiritual director of, Miss Sellon. He also heard the confessions of many of the sisters and was a great benefactor of the community. He gave most of the money he inherited from his mother in 1858 towards the building of a priory for the sisters and a convalescent hospital at Ascot. He often spent part of the long vacation there with Miss Sellon and went abroad with her on more than one occasion. Their relationship caused much gossip and her brother eventually published a formal denial of any engagement between them. In 1841 Pusey had received the vows of Marian Rebecca Hughes, who eventually started the Society of the Holy and Undivided Trinity in Oxford some ten years later, after what she called 'a sort of novitiate', in Pusey's house in Christ Church. He also influenced another early community, the Sisters of Bethany, through its founder and first superior, Ethel Benett, who was one of his penitents. Pusey had hoped to establish a college of celibate priests living under a rule at St Saviour's, Leeds, but this ambition was never realized. Father Ignatius (Joseph Leycester Lyne) claimed the support of Pusey in reviving the Benedictine life in the Church of England but, although Pusey initially encouraged him, he had little to do with his later experiments. Pusey presided at the first meeting which led to the foundation of the Cowley Fathers, the Society of St John the Evangelist, in 1866, but his influence on the community was only indirect, through Father Benson, the first superior, who owed much to him both intellectually and spiritually.

Ecumenical endeavours Pusey must also be regarded as one of the leading ecumenists of the nineteenth century. He early appreciated that unity was of the essence to the church and that reunion involved not only the search for truth but also prayer and penitence and the pursuit of holiness. In 1844 he published the first of a series of Roman Catholic devotional books mostly by the French affective writers Jean Baptiste Avrillon and Jean Joseph Surin, adapted for use in the Church of England, in order to encourage and deepen holiness of life. He was much criticized for the project, although there were precedents for such adaptations. He justified it on the grounds that 'whatever the Holy Spirit has anywhere given to the Church, He has given to the whole Church. It belongs to us as a portion of that Church' (J. B. Avrillon, *Lent*, 2nd edn, 1844, xiii).

Newman's secession to the Roman Catholic church was a crushing blow to Pusey, but within a few days he published his prophetic view that it might help to bring about reunion between Roman Catholics and Anglicans:

> If anything could open their eyes as to what is good in us, or soften in us any wrong prejudices against them, it would be the presence of such an one, nurtured and grown to such ripeness in our Church and now removed to theirs. (Liddon, 2.461)

Henceforth he adopted a neutral position towards the Roman Catholic church. In 1850, in the face of mounting hostility towards Rome in the wake of further defections over the Gorham judgment and rumours of the establishment of a Roman hierarchy in England, he resolutely resisted the attempts of some in the Catholic movement to make any formal anti-Roman declaration to defend themselves against the accusation of being a fifth column. He spoke powerfully at meetings of the Church Unions in both Bristol and London and carried the day.

In 1865, stung by a taunt of Manning and perhaps stimulated by a reunion with Newman and Keble at Keble's vicarage in Hursley, Pusey published what was to be the first part of an *Eirenicon*, an open *Letter to Keble*. There were two further parts, in the form of *Letters to Newman*, published in 1869 and 1870, on the eve of the meeting of the first Vatican Council. Pusey was motivated by the belief that the two communions could be reconciled by mutual explanations of their formularies. From the Anglican side, he was convinced they were 'kept apart much more by that vast practical system which lies beyond the letter of the Council of Trent, things which are taught with quasi-authority in the Roman Church, than by what is actually defined' (*Eirenicon*, 1, 1865, 98). In the *Letter to Keble* he set out the difficulties of Anglicans over the cult of the Virgin Mary, particularly the doctrine of the immaculate conception, and over the position of the papacy. The fact that he did not make his purpose clear led to Newman's accusing him of 'discharging his olive branch as if from a catapult' (*Letter to Pusey*, 1866, 9).

Pusey also tried to explain the Thirty-Nine Articles which, he admitted, 'made negative statements to show against what she [the Church of England] protested, but set down no positive statement to explain what on the same subjects she accepted' (*Eirenicon*, 1, 1865, 267). First, in 1865, he reprinted Newman's Tract 90 together with a historical preface by himself, and an essay by Keble, which had only been privately circulated earlier, *Catholic Subscription to the 39 Articles*. All through 1867 he worked closely with his friend Alexander Forbes, bishop of Brechin, on a lengthy volume entitled *Explanation of the 39 Articles*. Although it was published under Forbes's name alone in 1867, parts of it are by Pusey.

Spurred on by rumours of an imminent council, Pusey went to France in the autumn and again in the winter of 1865 to meet bishops and theologians, to get a hearing with 'the non-extreme party' as he put it. He was greatly encouraged, particularly by the response of the archbishop of Paris, Darboy, and the bishop of Orléans, Dupanloup. Both offered to lay any propositions he might make before the council. Pusey and Forbes also entered into a correspondence with a Belgian Jesuit, Victor De Buck, who suggested that Forbes should go in person to the council with Pusey as his theologian. Pusey was cautious. He preferred his own idea of written propositions and actually drafted some in Latin which he sent to Newman for comment. In the end, no propositions were submitted. The climate of opinion at Rome became increasingly unfavourable, and any interest in the question of reunion was overwhelmed by the mounting pressure to define the infallibility of the pope. The definition crushed his hopes. 'I have done what I could', he told Newman, 'and now have done with controversy and Eirenica' (Liddon, 4.193).

Pusey was not solely concerned with the possibility of reunion with Rome, although he came to think of it as a priority. He had, in fact, originally looked to Orthodoxy. He withdrew his initial support for the proposal in 1841 to establish a bishopric in Jerusalem for Anglicans and Lutherans when he discovered that Anglican and Lutheran missionaries were proselytizing among the Orthodox. He joined the Eastern Church Association at its foundation in 1864 and had discussions with various Orthodox dignitaries when they visited England. In 1867 he was largely responsible for altering the draft of a memorial on reunion, which was to be presented to the First Lambeth conference, so that it commended attempts to approach both the Orthodox and Roman Catholics. However, 1870 saw the dashing of his hopes for reunion with the Orthodox as well as with the Roman Catholics. Conversation with a visiting bishop, Archbishop Lycurgos of Syria and Temos, convinced him that the filioque controversy was insoluble. He subsequently elaborated his views in a long historical essay in the form of a letter to H. P. Liddon, *On the Clause 'and the Son'*, in 1876. He was convinced that the Orthodox view that it involves heresy was 'invincible prejudice', although he was willing that the Western church should anathematize that heresy so long as it had the right to retain the clause in the creed. Dr Döllinger, the leader of the Old Catholics, claimed that 'the mischief' done by Dr Pusey in the line which he took on the filioque was one of the reasons for there being no third Bonn conference on reunion between Anglicans, Orthodox, and Old Catholics. Pusey, convinced that he was being eirenic, characteristically ended his essay hopefully, speaking of it

as his 'last contribution to a future which I shall not see' (*On the Clause*, 1876, 181).

Pusey had little to do with protestantism, although he was always charitable in his dealings with individual protestants. In the preface to the volume *Essays on the Reunion of Christendom* edited by F. G. Lee in 1867, however, he wrote against a proposal for reunion with the Lutherans in Scandinavia on the grounds that they had a 'radically different' doctrine of the fall and redemption, were 'in error' as regards the eucharist, and that for them to receive Episcopal consecration or ordination would only be 'a concession to our supposed prejudices'. With Lord Ashley (later Shaftesbury), 'a Protestant of the Protestants' (Hodder, 325), he had a fluctuating relationship. They were cousins and Christ Church contemporaries, disagreed over the Jerusalem bishopric and other religious issues, but were reconciled in 1864 in opposition to 'neology'. After Pusey's death Shaftesbury wrote that, despite their disagreements, 'I … reverenced his profound piety' (ibid., 735).

Fight against rationalism   Another of Pusey's lifelong interests was his fight against rationalism and secularism, liberalism as he and Newman called it, or the 'strong tide of half-belief, misbelief, unbelief, which so largely occupied every sort of literature' as he once characterized it in a sermon (Liddon, 4.77). The experience of failing to win back to Christianity his sceptical Eton friend Julian Hibbert haunted him. He referred to it at the last meeting which he attended of the governing body of Christ Church in 1882. His opposition to Dr Hampden's being made regius professor of divinity in 1836 was motivated by his fear of rationalism, 'the assumption that uncontrolled human reason in its present degraded form is the primary interpreter of God's Word' (ibid., 1.373). When a royal commission revealed its plans for the reform of Oxford University in 1852, Pusey was foremost in defending it as a place of moral and religious education rather than as 'a forcing house for intellect'. His lengthy evidence, informed by his first-hand knowledge of university education in Germany on which the commissioners' proposals were modelled, was the largest contribution to the volume produced by the university authorities in opposition to them. He backed it up in 1854 by a pamphlet entitled *Collegiate and Professorial Teaching and Discipline*. When, in spite of the opposition, an act reforming the university on the basis of the commission's report was passed, Pusey was elected to the new hebdomadal council and proved a hardworking and effective member. His influence softened the impact of the reforms, slowing down the process of change so that the ethos of the university remained predominantly Anglican in spite of the abolition of subscription to the articles and the admission of nonconformists.

One of the most influential liberals was Benjamin Jowett, the master of Balliol and regius professor of Greek. He was one of the contributors to *Essays and Reviews*, a volume published in 1860 which became a *cause célèbre* for its perceived heterodoxy. Pusey opposed a very reasonable proposal to increase Jowett's salary on the grounds that it would express the university's approval of his theological views. He even went to the lengths of prosecuting him for those views before the court of the vice-chancellor of the university, although he eventually had to drop the case as there was doubt about the court's jurisdiction. The attempt outraged the liberals, and Pusey's subsequent support for increasing the endowment of the Greek chair in a different way alienated some of his friends.

Meanwhile two other contributors to *Essays and Reviews* had been prosecuted for heresy in the church courts. In 1864, however, the judicial committee of the privy council, the then final court of appeal, reversed the lower court judgment and ruled their statements were not contrary to the formularies of the Church of England. Pusey was prominent in trying to neutralize the effects of this. He was one of a group that drew up a declaration on the inspiration of scripture which was eventually signed by 11,000 clergymen. He published a pamphlet, *Case as to the Legal Force of the Judgment of the Privy Council* (1864), and preached a series of powerful university sermons countering the essayists' views on the atonement, prophecy, everlasting punishment, and the ground of faith. His lectures on Daniel also come from this period.

In 1869 an attempt was made to drop the use of the Athanasian creed in accordance with the rubrics of the Book of Common Prayer, largely because of the misunderstanding of the damnatory clauses. Much of Pusey's correspondence, both public and private, over the next few years was occupied in agitating against this attempt and in defending and explaining the creed. He also delivered a fine university sermon in Advent 1872, *The Responsibility of the Intellect in Matters of Faith*, expounding its teaching. His public threat to retire from his teaching office if the use or the wording of the creed were altered led to the abandonment of the project, although he agreed to the publication of an explanatory note and, indeed, suggested various versions of it. A few years later his views on everlasting punishment were attacked by Dr Farrar in a series of sermons in Westminster Abbey, subsequently published in 1887 under the title *Eternal Hope*. After a delay of two years, largely due to his prostration after the death of his only son, Philip, Pusey answered this in a book which was very influential at the time: *What is of Faith as to Everlasting Punishment?*

Pusey was rigid in his stance on doctrinal orthodoxy and very conservative in biblical criticism, but he encouraged the introduction of natural science into the university and supported the setting up of the University Museum. In a paper to the church congress in Norwich in 1865, he tried to reconcile the supposed antagonism between the Bible and the physical sciences, claiming that there was no need to fear scientific research and asserting that 'the right interpretation of God's Word will never be found in contradiction to the right interpretation of His works' (Liddon, 4.80). In his penultimate sermon to the university in 1878, *Unscience, not Science Adverse to Faith*, which had to be read by his disciple and biographer H. P. Liddon, he reaffirmed his view that Christianity need have no fear of true science. He even allowed a place for evolutionary theories. 'Theology does not hold them excluded by Holy Scripture, so that they spare the soul of man' (ibid., 334).

As a preacher The list of Pusey's published writings occupies over forty pages in an appendix to Liddon's biography. Most are works occasioned by some controversy, some, such as the incomplete *The Royal Supremacy not an Arbitrary Authority* (1850) and *The Councils of the Church* (1857), so substantial as to be works of reference. The most widely read were his collections of sermons, nine in all. He preached not only in the university and cathedral but also in London and Bristol, and places where he holidayed. He was no orator. He spoke 'in a low, deep, rather monotonous voice, which in his later years was thick and husky'. His style was crabbed and quaint, his sentences long and involved, full of neologisms and archaic words. His sermons were packed with references to the fathers and Anglican divines, but he delivered them with intense earnestness 'as from a man inhabiting his message', and conveyed an 'overwhelming impression of personal saintliness'. He preached ecstatically on the joys of heaven and the union of God and man, but he was also outspoken on the social evils of the day and the hypocrisy of the rich. He taught a very practical form of holiness, especially to the country people of Pusey, 'in short pithy sayings which stuck in their minds'. At the end of his weighty university sermons, his manner would change:

> He would lift his eyes from his manuscript to the Undergraduates' Gallery and, addressing us as 'My Sons' would give us a quarter of an hour of directly personal appeal; searching the hearts' secrets, urging repentance, and exhorting to a way of life more consistent with our Divine vocation. (Russell, 97, 170f.)

Appearance and death Pusey would never sit for his portrait or allow a photograph to be taken of him, probably because he had refused his wife's request but also out of humility. He told Newman it was 'utterly unfitting that any likeness should be taken of me, who have so sorely injured the likeness of God in me' (*The Letters and Diaries of John Henry Newman*, ed. C. S. Dessain and others, 31 vols., 11-31, 1961-77, 11.36). After his death a death mask was taken. George Richmond sculpted a bust of him, and also painted a portrait, as did Rosa Corder. The personal feature most often remarked on was 'his gentle winning smile'. Pusey died at The Hermitage, Ascot Priory, Berkshire, on 16 September 1882, and was buried, in the same grave as his wife and two eldest daughters, at Christ Church Cathedral, Oxford, on St Matthew's day, 21 September. After his death his friends purchased his theological library and endowed the Dr Pusey Memorial Library (the 'Puseum'), later Pusey House, St Giles', Oxford, both a library and a 'house of sacred learning', providing pastoral care and theological instruction to members of the university. Pusey Street, Pusey Lane, and Pusey Place, Oxford, were later named after him.

Significance Pusey devoted his life to the recovery and reaffirmation of the Catholic inheritance of the Church of England. To this end he threw in his lot with the Oxford Movement, seeing himself as one strand in the 'triple-cord', together with Newman and Keble. When Newman seceded to Rome he kept the movement on a steady course, in spite of the defections to Rome. Frederick Oakeley, one of the converts, described him as the 'St Barnabas of the movement' (*Historical Notes*, 1865, 49). His role was to reconcile and explain, which he did with singular reasonableness and charity. His last public intervention in controversy, the publication of the pamphlet *Unlaw in Judgements of the Judicial Committee and its Remedies* (1881), was a plea for peace in the church and the reform of the court of appeal. Pusey was a man of great learning and patient scholarship, so that it was appropriate that his library was preserved as his memorial in Pusey House. He was also a man of profound spirituality, the 'doctor mysticus' of the Tractarians, as Brilioth called him (*The Anglican Revival*, 1925, 296). This is apparent in his *Spiritual Letters* and published prayers, but above all in his sermons, where his theology and scholarship, his personal sufferings and wrestlings in prayer, his eucharistic devotion and love of God come together.

PETER G. COBB

Sources H. P. Liddon, *The life of Edward Bouverie Pusey*, ed. J. O. Johnston and others, 4 vols. (1893–7) · P. Butler, ed., *Pusey rediscovered* (1983) · D. Forrester, *Young Dr Pusey* (1989) · [M. Trench], *The story of Dr Pusey's life* (1900) · G. W. E. Russell, *Dr Pusey* (1907) · G. L. Prestige, *Pusey* (1933) · E. Hodder, *The life and work of the seventh earl of Shaftesbury*, [new edn] (1890) · P. Butler, *Gladstone: church, state and Tractarianism* (1982) · C. Hibbert, ed., *The encyclopaedia of Oxford* (1988) · H. C. G. Matthew, 'Edward Bouverie Pusey: from scholar to Tractarian', *Journal of Theological Studies*, new ser., 32 (1981), 101–24
Archives Bodl. Oxf., corresp. with his wife and children · Pusey Oxf., corresp. and papers · U. Leeds, Brotherton L., notebooks | Berks. RO, corresp. with brother, Philip · BL, corresp. with W. E. Gladstone, Add. MS 44281 · Bodl. Oxf., letters to the Aclands · Bodl. Oxf., letters to Francis Jeune · Bodl. Oxf., letters to Friedrich Max Müller · Bodl. Oxf., letters to Benjamin Webb · Bodl. Oxf., letters to R. I. Wilberforce · Bodl. Oxf., corresp. with Samuel Wilberforce · Borth. Inst., corresp. with Lord Halifax · Exeter Cathedral, letters to Henry Phillpotts · Keble College, Oxford, letters to John Keble · LPL, corresp. with Charles Golightly · LPL, letters to A. C. Tait · LPL, letters to Henry Woodgate · LPL, corresp. with Christopher Wordsworth · NL Scot., corresp. with J. R. Hope-Scott · Oriel College, Oxford, letters to Edward Hawkins · Pusey Oxf., letters to William Gresley · Pusey Oxf., letters to Thomas Henderson · Pusey Oxf., letters to F. Heurtley and family · Pusey Oxf., letters to Robert Scott · Pusey Oxf., letters to H. A. Woodgate [transcripts] · Society of the Most Holy Trinity, Ascot, letters to Sister Clara (Clarissa Powell) · Society of the Most Holy Trinity, Ascot, letters to William Stubbs · University of Dundee, archives, letters to Alexander Forbes
Likenesses engravings, c.1826–1834, Pusey Oxf.; repro. in Forrester, *Young Dr Pusey* · M. S. Morgan, engraving, pubd 1831, NPG · E. Kilvert, sketch, c.1843, Pusey Oxf. · C. Pusey, drawing, 1853, Pusey Oxf. · C. Pusey, sketches, c.1856 (with family members), NPG · A. Macdonald, drawing, 1882, repro. in Liddon, *Life of Edward Bouverie Pusey*, vol. 4 · G. Richmond, marble bust, 1883, Pusey Oxf.; plaster cast, Keble College, Oxford · G. Richmond, black and white chalk drawing, c.1890, NPG [see illus.] · G. Richmond, oils, c.1890, Christ Church Oxf. · Ape [C. Pellegrini], caricature, watercolour study, NPG; repro. in *VF* (2 Jan 1875) · R. Corder, oils, Pusey Oxf.; copy, Christ Church Oxf. · G. Richmond, chalk study, NPG · Touchstone, caricatures, lithographs, NPG · engravings, NPG · etching, BM, NPG; repro. in *Oxford Theologians* · oils, Christ Church Oxf. · pen-and-ink drawing, Christ Church Oxf.
Wealth at death £16,416 7s. 4d.: administration with will, 17 March 1883, *CGPLA Eng. & Wales*

Pusey, Philip (1799–1855), agriculturist, was born at Pusey, Berkshire, on 25 June 1799, the eldest of the three sons of Philip Bouverie Pusey (1724–1828) and his wife, Lucy (1772–1858), daughter of Robert Sherard, fourth earl of Harborough, and widow of Sir Thomas Cave. His father was the youngest son of Jacob Bouverie, first Viscount Folkestone, whose sister married the last male member of the Pusey family; the Pusey sisters bequeathed the Pusey estates to their brother's nephew by marriage, Philip Bouverie, on condition that Bouverie took the name of Pusey, which he did in 1784, inheriting the estates of some 5000 acres in Berkshire in 1789. Philip Pusey's next brother was Edward Bouverie *Pusey, and a sister, Charlotte, married Richard Lynch Cotton, provost of Worcester College, Oxford. Philip was educated at Eton College and Christ Church, Oxford (where he matriculated in 1817, though he left without taking a degree), becoming great friends with Henry John George Herbert, Lord Porchester and later third earl of Carnarvon, to whose sister Lady Emily Herbert he became engaged in 1818. The marriage took place on 4 October 1822, no doubt postponed because of the youth of the couple, and in the interval Pusey went on tour with Porchester, both tourists being captured by rebel guerrillas near Montserrat in Catalonia, who temporarily mistook them for constitutionalists or soldiers in the army of the Cortes. Pusey and his wife settled for six years in Rome, at the Palazzo Aldobrandini, and became friendly with Chevalier Christian Bunsen (later German ambassador in London). In memory of his time in Rome, Pusey presented a pedestal for the font in the German chapel at Rome, with groups in relief by Thorwaldsen.

In 1828 Pusey inherited the family estate and at once began to build a reputation as a progressive and practical farmer, taking the management of the home farm of between 300 and 400 acres into his own hands. The rise in reputation was meteoric, and in 1830 he was elected FRS. The development of his farming was more measured, and it was not until the late 1840s that he laid out the water meadows at the Faringdon farm which secured him a permanent place in agricultural history through the detailed and laudatory notice by James Caird in *English Agriculture in 1850 and 1851* (1852). Pusey's fully developed farming system, hinging on the lush, and early, feed furnished by the water meadows in order to support a very large flock of ewes and early-maturing lambs, was similar to the Hampshire and Wiltshire sheep-and-barley farming with water meadows (somewhat oddly, Pusey apparently brought in experts from Devon to level his fields and construct the irrigation works), and the system was notable for close attention to detail rather than for radical innovation. His own farm had a 'fine dry easy-working soil ... excellent corn and turnip land' (Caird, 107–8), and was naturally well-drained. Pusey kept himself fully informed of all the latest developments in agriculture, however, and was an early enthusiast for the advantages of field drainage using the recently invented earthenware drainpipes. Convinced that the future prosperity and efficiency of

Philip Pusey (1799–1855), by George Richmond, 1842

agriculture depended on effective dissemination of information on good farming practice and reliable developments in technology, he played a prominent part in the formation in 1838 of what became, from 1840, the Royal Agricultural Society of England. He was a member of the original committee of management, and chairman of the committee for establishing a journal for the diffusion of agricultural information. He was thus the first editor of the *Journal of the Royal Agricultural Society of England*, until 1854, and contributed forty-seven articles to the *Journal* on such subjects as drainage, fertilizers, the breeding and feeding of sheep, water meadows, and agricultural machinery, as well as on surveys of the state of agriculture and the progress of agricultural knowledge. His contributions were informed by practical experience: the first trial of Cyrus Hall McCormick's reaping machine, for instance, was held on his farm in August 1851. He was president of the society in 1840–41, and was again elected president in 1853. He was unable to attend the annual meeting and show at Lincoln in 1854 because of his wife's last illness; she died on 13 November 1854, only eight months before her husband.

An obituary of Pusey in 1855 justly noted that 'by a rare union of endowments he did much to win for agriculture a worthy place among the intellectual pursuits of the present day' (Acland, 608). By virtue of his social and political position he was also well placed to become one of the leading agricultural authorities in parliament. Already in 1828 he had published two political pamphlets on public finance, and in 1830 he was elected as MP for the Treasury borough of Rye, but was unseated on petition. Later in 1830 he was elected as one of the two members for Chippenham, but he lost that seat in the general election of April 1831, whereupon he migrated to Cashel. In 1832 he was an unsuccessful candidate for one of the two Berkshire county seats; he became one of the Berkshire MPs in 1835, and continued to be one until the 1852 election, when he withdrew after his re-election was opposed by George Henry Vansittart, an ultra-protestant protectionist; Pusey recorded, 'I hear that, among electioneering tricks, some call me a Puseyite. I am no more than Lord Shaftesbury is; but I will not consent to find fault with my brother in public'.

As an MP Pusey spoke sparingly, but he was active on committees concerned with agriculture and in the 1840s was an adviser on agricultural matters to Peel and Gladstone, with whom he had a close political relationship. He provided Gladstone with a long memorandum in the early 1840s containing a programme of what needed to be done for agriculture (Spring, 140), and he stayed at Drayton in 1844 to talk to Peel's tenantry about scientific farming. In February 1846 Peel wrote to Pusey, 'I know of no one who has done more than yourself to enable the Country to enter into successful competition with other Countries in respect to agricultural produce' (ibid., 140). Pusey, however, who had come to the conclusion that the corn laws could not be retained, broadly on Caird's grounds that high farming was the best substitute for protection, voted against repeal on the first reading later that month, in deference to the strong feelings of his county constituents. He then absented himself from parliament so as not to obstruct Peel's policy—conduct which caused Peel to take a more jaundiced view of his character, noting, 'Mr Pusey's letter is a good specimen of an agricultural leader—I never saw such an avowal under a Senator's own handwriting' (Gash, 614).

Pusey's parliamentary services to agricultural interests centred on his conviction that the productivity, and hence the international competitiveness, of British farming could be vastly improved by more intensive capital investment, especially in field drainage, and that investment was being significantly held back by the legal inability of many of the larger landowners to find the money. This was because strict settlements, which governed the estates of most of the aristocracy and gentry, normally prevented the owner for the time being, or the life tenant, from mortgaging the family estate in order to invest in its improvement. Accordingly Pusey's chief aim was to obtain legislation that would enable these 'limited owners' to borrow in order to invest in improvements, and his efforts became the origin of a whole strand of Victorian land-law reforms designed to raise the economic efficiency of land ownership without undermining or destroying its social and family structure. His direct legislative achievement was modest. In 1840 he piloted a bill 'to enable Owners of Settled Estates to defray the Expenses of draining the same', which became 3 and 4 Vict. c. 55, known as Pusey's Act, which was very little used because it required resort to the great delays and expense of chancery. As he later explained, he regarded his Act as tactical rather than practical; its scope was restricted to drainage, to the exclusion of other types of investment: 'because of the extreme difficulty of carrying it in the House of Commons I had to be content with just the principle, for it was so much guarded as to make it too expensive for persons to use' ('Select committee … entailed estates', 12.1372). The crucial point was that Pusey had carried onto the statute book the principle of overruling family settlements in the interests of encouraging borrowing to make productive investments; thereafter other hands devised less costly and more efficient administrative machinery for the practical application of this principle.

Pusey soon extended his concern about the adequacy of the supply of capital to agriculture so as to embrace tenant farmers as well as landowners, arguing that tenants would not invest in the latest developments in farming techniques, such as the use of artificial fertilizers or feeding stuffs, unless they could be certain of reaping the full returns on their outlays. Thus was initiated the campaign to provide outgoing tenants with compensation for unexhausted improvements, a concept which Pusey called 'tenant right', much to the alarm of many landowners, who resented the interference with their property rights and anticipated the later cry of 'tenant right' becoming 'landlord wrong'. For this reason he achieved even less on this front, obtaining a select committee on agricultural customs in 1848, which he chaired, but being humiliated by having his chairman's conclusions and recommendations rejected by his committee in favour of the less radical version proposed by Edward Pleydell-Bouverie; this roundly repudiated any idea of compelling landlords to compensate their tenants and relied instead simply on voluntary agreements. Bills did pass the Commons in 1849 and 1850, but were rejected by the Lords: there the matter was left, until the first Agricultural Holdings Act was passed in 1875 (itself a largely ineffectual measure). Nevertheless, as Disraeli observed when moving the second reading of the 1875 bill, 'Mr Pusey was the first person to introduce into this House the term "tenant rights"' (*DNB*).

Pusey's friend Bunsen called him 'a most unique union of a practical Englishman and an intellectual German, so that when speaking in one capacity one might think he had lost sight of the other' (Bunsen, 1.522). Pusey was that rare being, a country gentleman who understood ideas and mingled with the leading thinkers of the time. He breakfasted with Samuel Rogers and Monckton Milnes, and he entertained Lord Spencer, Sir Robert Peel, Gladstone, Carlyle, Whewell, Grote, Galley Knight, Bishop Wilberforce, and Lord Stanhope. In 1840 he became a member of the original committee of the London Library, and in 1851 he was chairman of the agricultural implement section of the Great Exhibition; he brought 500 of his labourers to London to see the exhibition, a visit commemorated by the presentation to him of a silver snuffbox. Thereafter in almost every cottage on the Pusey estate there hung an engraving of Pusey's portrait with a picture of the snuffbox underneath. Many of these cottages had been improved or rebuilt, to designs by the architect George Edmund Street; and as a model landlord Pusey provided his labourers with allotments, and organized works to keep them in constant employ. He was fond of sport, and was one of the best whips in England, once driving a four-in-hand over the Alps.

Pusey and his wife Emily had three children: an only son, Sidney Edward Bouverie-Pusey (1839–1911), who succeeded to the family estate, and two daughters; the elder, Edith Lucy, died unmarried in 1904, whereas the second daughter, Clara, married Francis Charteris Fletcher in 1862, and their son, Philip Francis Bouverie-Pusey (whose name was changed from Fletcher), inherited the Pusey estate when her brother died in 1911 without children. After the death of his wife in 1854 Philip Pusey went to live with his brother at Christ Church, Oxford, and within a week he was paralysed by a stroke; after a second stroke he died there on 9 July 1855.   F. M. L. THOMPSON

Sources *DNB* · D. Spring, *The English landed estate in the nineteenth century: its administration* (1963) · N. Gash, *Sir Robert Peel: the life of Sir Robert Peel after 1830* (1972) · 'Select committee of the House of Lords on entailed estates', *Parl. papers* (1845), vol. 12, no. 490 [charges for drainage] · 'Select committee on agricultural customs', *Parl. papers* (1847–8), vol. 7, no. 461 · A. D. M. Phillips, *The underdraining of farmland in England during the nineteenth century* (1989) · T. Acland, *Journal of the Royal Agricultural Society of England*, 16 (1855), 608 · J. Caird, *English agriculture in 1850–51* (1852), 107–13 · F. Bunsen, ed., *A memoir of Baron Bunsen*, 1 (1868), 522

Archives Berks. RO, corresp. and papers | Berks. RO, letters to E. W. Gray of Newbury · BL, Add. MSS 44362, fol. 299; 40585, fol. 297 · BL, letters to William Buckland, Add. MSS 40428, 40554–40555, 40562 · BL, corresp. with W. E. Gladstone, Add. MSS 44355–44527 · BL, corresp. with Sir Robert Peel, Add. MSS 40485, 40499–40500, 40503, 40563, 40584–40585, 40602 · Bodl. Oxf., letters to his brother, Edward Bouverie Pusey · CKS, letters to Lord Stanhope · UCL, corresp. with Edwin Chadwick · W. Sussex RO, letters to duke of Richmond

Likenesses S. W. Reynolds, engraving, 1842 (after R. Ansdell) · G. Richmond, photogravure photograph, 1842 (after Walker and Boutall), NPG [*see illus.*] · J. Fewell Penstone, engraving, 1851 · R. Ansdell, study; at 13 Hanover Square, London, 1896 · F. C. Lewis, stipple (after G. Richmond; Grillion's Club series), BM, NPG · G. Richmond, crayon drawing; at Pusey, 1896 · miniature (as young man); in family possession, 1896 · portrait; at Pusey, 1896

Putnam, Ann (b. 1662). *See under* Salem witches and their accusers (*act.* 1692).

Putnam, Ann (b. 1679). *See under* Salem witches and their accusers (*act.* 1692).

Putnam, Israel (1718–1790), revolutionary army officer in America, was born on 7 January 1718 in Salem village, Massachusetts, the twelfth of thirteen children of Joseph Putnam (1670–1723), farmer, and Elizabeth Porter (b. 1674), daughter of Israel Porter. Although his parents were well-to-do, his education consisted of only a few years' schooling. Applying himself to hard farm work, he grew into adulthood as a stocky, courageous, exuberant, fearless, and tenacious citizen. Many stories later were told about his exploits as a youth, all emphasizing his image as a rustic, self-reliant citizen of the soil. In 1739 he inherited from his father's estate £2500 in Massachusetts currency, and on 19 July he married Hannah Pope (1721–1765). In the following year the couple moved to Pomfret, Connecticut, and settled on a farm of 500 acres. There they prospered and had ten children. Hannah Putnam died on 4 June 1765, and Putnam, having also just lost a daughter, sought consolation in Christianity.

In 1755 Putnam joined the Connecticut militia as a volunteer, and in August was commissioned a second lieutenant. During the Seven Years' War he fought at Crown Point, then joined Robert Rogers's rangers. He was promoted captain in 1755 and major in 1758. Having been captured by the Native Americans in 1758, he was rescued just before being burned alive. He was promoted lieutenant-colonel in 1759, and led troops in further military operations. In 1762 he was shipwrecked by a hurricane on the Cuban coast while campaigning against Havana, and almost died of hunger and disease. During the Pontiac War in 1764 he soldiered as a major, then a lieutenant-colonel, under Colonel John Bradstreet. Settling into farming and tavern-keeping, he held various local offices, became active in the Sons of Liberty, and served two terms (1766–7) in the general assembly. On 3 June 1767 he married Deborah Lothrop Avery Gardner, a prosperous widow; they had no children. She died on 14 October 1777. In 1772–3 he was employed by speculators in exploring the Mississippi River. He was chairman of the local committee of correspondence in 1774, and in October was appointed lieutenant-colonel in the Connecticut militia.

In April 1775, upon the outbreak of the American War of Independence, Putnam was appointed brigadier-general of Connecticut militia. He joined the American army besieging Boston, and soon was promoted major-general in the continental line. Popular and energetic, he prepared for and fought vigorously in the battle of Bunker Hill (17 June 1775). In 1776 he served at New York as second in command under George Washington. In the battle of Long Island on 27 August, he was outwitted by General William Howe, who overwhelmed his left wing. In late 1776 Washington gave Putnam command at Philadelphia, and in May 1777 sent him to command the Hudson highlands. By then Washington had come to distrust Putnam's military skills and judgement. On a number of occasions Putnam misunderstood Washington's orders and thereby inadvertently irked the commander-in-chief. Then in October 1777 Putnam again was outmanoeuvred when General Sir Henry Clinton captured American forts on the Hudson River. Court-martialled for negligence, Putnam was exonerated; but when he requested leave in March 1778 to go home on recruiting service Washington willingly complied. He rejoined the army in 1779 as commander at White Plains, but his military career was ended in December by a paralytic stroke.

Putnam returned to Pomfret and spent the remainder of his days running a tavern and telling stories. In the 1780s his part of Pomfret was renamed Brooklyn. He died at his home on 29 May 1790 of an inflammatory disease, and was buried in Brooklyn cemetery on 1 June 1790. He left an estate of 1000 acres of land and £1350 Connecticut currency. His reputation among early Americans was based more upon his image as the quintessential New World citizen than upon his actual exploits. Celebrated as a rough-hewn Cincinnatus, he was ranked second only to Washington in the pantheon of revolutionary heroes.

PAUL DAVID NELSON

Sources W. F. Livingston, *Israel Putnam: pioneer, ranger, and major general, 1718–1790* (1905) · A. Bates, ed., *The two Putnams, Israel and Rufus, in the Havana expedition, 1762, and the Mississippi river exploration, 1772–1773* (1931) · I. N. Tarbox, *Life of Israel Putnam ('Old Put'), major-general in the continental army* (1876) · J. Niven, *Connecticut hero: Israel Putnam* (1977) · B. C. Daniels, 'Putnam, Israel', *ANB* · D. Humphreys, *An essay on the life of the Honorable Major General Israel Putnam* (1788) · E. Putnam, *History of the Putnam family in England and America*, 2 vols. (1891–1908) · E. D. Larned, *History of Windham county, Connecticut*, 2 vols. (1874–80) · F. S. Luther, 'General Israel Putnam', *Worcester Historical Society Proceedings*, 20 (1904), 204–14 · W. C. Ford, ed., *General orders issued by Major-General Israel Putnam when in command of the highlands in the summer and fall of 1777* (1972) · W. F. Livingston, 'The homes and haunts of Israel Putnam', *New England Magazine*, new ser., 17 (1897), 193–212

Archives New Hampshire Historical Society, Concord, papers | Connecticut State Library, Hartford, Connecticut colonial war archives · L. Cong., Washington papers

Likenesses H. J. Thompson, oils, State House, Hartford, Connecticut; repro. in Livingston, *Israel Putnam*, frontispiece

Wealth at death £1350 (probably Connecticut currency); plus 1000 acres of land: Livingston, *Israel Putnam*, 4, 5

Putta (*d. c.*688), bishop, appears as the first bishop in the Anglo-Saxon episcopal lists for Hereford. It is uncertain whether the see serving the Anglo-Saxons west of the Severn (the kingdom of the Magonsæte) was already at Hereford in Putta's day; Lidebiri (either Ledbury or Lydbury North) is mentioned as a former site by Gilbert Foliot (*d.* 1187), bishop of Hereford. This western Putta should not be identified with Putta, bishop of Rochester, who, according to Bede, resigned in 676 and found refuge with Seaxwulf, bishop of Lichfield, as a peripatetic music teacher. It must be the western Putta, on his first known appearance, who attests as 'Putta gratia Dei episcopus' in an authentic charter, to be dated to 680, in the Bath cartulary (*AS chart.*, S 1167). Here he attests alongside Bosel, bishop of Worcester, and together with their spiritual and temporal overlords, Theodore, archbishop of Canterbury, and Æthelred, king of the Mercians. Putta's see, like Bosel's, was then a very recent creation by Theodore, who had divided up Seaxwulf's greater Mercian diocese after the Synod of Hertford (672 or 673) and probably by 679. Bosel and Putta head the Anglo-Saxon episcopal lists for their respective sees 'after Seaxwulf'; the theory that Putta's name is an interpolation inspired by Bede's account of Putta of Rochester is possible but unnecessary. The next bishop in the 'Hereford' list, Tyrhtil (*fl.* 688?–*c.*709), succeeded Putta in 688, according to John of Worcester. Putta's fourth successor, Bishop Cuthbert (736–40), composed an epitaph on a tomb which he constructed for his three immediate predecessors, but Putta's name is absent from the epitaph. The inference should probably be, not that Putta was never bishop, but that he had been buried at another site. His see may have moved more than once before reaching Hereford, and perhaps had not got there even in Cuthbert's time.

PATRICK SIMS-WILLIAMS

Sources P. Sims-Williams, *Religion and literature in western England, 600–800* (1990) • *AS chart.*, S 1167 • J. G. Hillaby, 'The origins of the diocese of Hereford', *Transactions of the Woolhope Naturalists' Field Club*, 42 (1976–8), 16–52

Puttenham, George (1529–1590/91), writer and literary critic, was the second son of Robert Puttenham of Sherfield upon Lodon, Hampshire, and his wife, Margery, daughter of Sir Richard Elyot and sister of Sir Thomas *Elyot. He matriculated from Christ's College, Cambridge, in November 1546, aged seventeen, but took no degree. He was admitted to the Middle Temple on 11 August 1556. In late 1559 or early 1560 Puttenham married Elizabeth, Lady Windsor (1520–1588/9). She was the daughter and coheir of Peter Cowdray of Herriard, Hampshire, and widow of Richard Paulet (will proved on 6 February 1552) and William, second Baron Windsor (d. 20 Aug 1558). Most of what is known about Puttenham's subsequent career derives from court records centring on the dissolution of his marriage with Lady Windsor and his efforts to wrest ownership of Sherfield from Francis Morris and his wife, Anne, the daughter of George's elder brother, Richard Puttenham [see below].

Early legal wranglings Puttenham deposed in 1578 that he made his first trip abroad about 1562–3 to purchase Sherfield from Richard, who had fled to the continent in 1560. George certainly resided at the manor house during the autumn of 1562 when he charged Lady Windsor's brother-in-law Thomas Paulet with inciting others to steal a goshawk from his mew at Sherfield. Paulet admitted that he confronted Puttenham at his home, wounded him in the head with his dagger, and 'then agayne with the blade of the said dagger gave unto the said complainant one other little Stroke' (PRO, STAC 5, P66/2). Puttenham continued to occupy Sherfield until 1567, when his brother returned secretly to England and gave the property to Anne and Francis Morris. Thereafter, Morris seized the house from Puttenham by force, initiating the quarrel with George that lasted nearly a decade.

Meanwhile, one Richard Hartilpoole had secured a ruling against Puttenham in the court of requests on charges that Puttenham withheld bedding and other furnishings that Hartilpoole had conveyed to Puttenham's house in Trinity Lane, London, in autumn 1565. Puttenham ignored this judgment, and on 24 July 1569, the court ordered the sheriffs of London and Middlesex to arrest Puttenham on sight 'to Aunswere not only unto his said contemptes' against Hartilpoole but for other crimes as well (PRO, REQ 2 219/25). At about the time of Hartilpoole's suit, John Bardolph, parson of Shalden, just 3 miles south and east of Herriard, sued Puttenham, Richard Aprice, clerk, John Marriner, and others in Star Chamber. Bardolph charged that he was assaulted in the church and again in his parsonage in July and August of 1566 at Puttenham's instigation. In July 1565 Puttenham had obtained a lease to the parsonage from the former parson, Giles More. But More

was then deprived of the living on a charge of non-residence, after which Bardolph apparently occupied the parsonage despite Puttenham's claim to it. No outcome to this case is recorded, but in conjunction with the Hartilpoole business it probably influenced Richard Horne, bishop of Winchester, to react with alarm early in 1569 on learning that Puttenham was to be appointed a justice of the peace. Horne wrote to Secretary Cecil praying 'that it be not true for his evil life is well known, and also that he is a "notorious enemye to God's Truthe"' (*Salisbury MSS*, 1.392–3, Horne to Cecil, 21 Jan 1569).

By June 1570 Puttenham was lodged in the Fleet prison, apparently in response to one Julio Mantuano's deposition of 7 April that Puttenham had both slandered the queen and incited him to murder the bishop of London. The divorce records mention that George 'was comytted to the Flete upon matter of highe Treason' (Hants. RO, 44M69/F2/14/1). He was released from prison on 15 June on £200 bail and under guard to attend to his other legal problems at the Winchester assizes. Thereafter he must have thoroughly exonerated himself from Mantuano's charges, for he not only regained his freedom but in 1574 won a court judgment of £20 against Brian Annesley, warden of the Fleet, the sum Annesley had failed to disburse in payment of Puttenham's debts during his imprisonment.

Neither the court cases nor this imprisonment caused Puttenham lasting inconvenience. Early in 1571 he resumed his efforts to regain control of the family home. In April, Puttenham's men seized the mill at Sherfield which Morris reclaimed by force. Puttenham was by this time residing in Sherfield at the house of a Margaret Marriner, probably the widow or mother of the John Marriner who had joined Puttenham in the assault on Parson Bardolph. For her pains, Margaret claimed that Morris's men evicted her and pulled down the house, which she and Puttenham rebuilt only to have Morris and his cronies pull it down again.

Domestic disputes Meanwhile, Puttenham's conflict with his wife served to widen his circle of opponents. According to Lady Windsor's son John Paulet, his mother had sued Puttenham for divorce within five or six years of the marriage; she may have separated from him as early as 1566. George was bound to provide £100 annually to support his estranged wife but his failure to make the required quarterly instalments after 1572 led to his confinement in the Wood Street compter in the autumn of 1575 when the court of arches ordered him to begin paying Lady Windsor £3 weekly. By this time the privy council was involved on Lady Windsor's behalf. The council ordered George to resume the payments in so far as all of his income derived from resources she had brought to the marriage. On 24 June 1576 the privy council accused him of unlawfully conveying the manor of Herriard to his brother-in-law Sir John Throckmorton. In July, Puttenham was served with a writ of *excommunicatio capiendo*, formally excommunicating him from the Anglican church for non-payment of his wife's alimony.

On 9 June 1578 the sentence of divorce became final,

whereon Lady Windsor resumed her appeals for redress to the council which issued an order for George's arrest on 23 June. As late as October, however, Puttenham wrote to the council that he would not appear before them for fear of his wife's children, and he accused Thomas Paulet and Katherine Paulet of twice assaulting him. On 26 October the council issued letters of protection for George's appearance before them and they ordered Throckmorton to ensure that Puttenham did not manage his affairs to the detriment of Lady Windsor's interests. On 20 December George was arrested 'with some difficulty' (*Salisbury MSS*, 2.222), sent to the court the next day to answer to the privy council, but was released by mistake from the Gatehouse at Westminster on 23 December.

The Paulets had, in fact, taken matters into their own hands for on 3 February 1578 John Paulet's son Richard, with his mother, Katherine, and other members of the family confronted Puttenham at his lodgings in the Whitefriars, London, in search of legal documents. According to George's suit in Star Chamber, the Paulets broke open the doors to his rooms, allowing one John Hall to serve him with another writ of excommunication. They then carried 'away the said Puttenham by force without any cappe, hatt or carchiffe bare heded' to a prison in Middlesex, after rifling his chests and desks where bonds and indentures to the value of £11,000 or £12,000 were allegedly deposited (PRO, STAC 5 P9/4, P3/3). Whether or not the privy council succeeded in returning Puttenham to prison, he had by 13 July 1579 agreed to provide his former wife with six servants, four suits, a coach, and £20 yearly. By November, however, he had again defaulted and the council was pressuring Throckmorton to make George comply with the terms of the settlement.

Puttenham's contention with Lady Windsor plagued him for the next eight years. His conflict with Francis Morris over Sherfield ended in 1581 when Morris was arrested for harbouring the Jesuit Edmund Campion. Francis died in prison in 1584, but Puttenham did not gain title to the property. In the same year, Lady Windsor sued George again in the court of arches, an action that earned him another confinement in the Wood Street compter. He was served with a third writ of excommunication in November 1586, and was once more imprisoned for failing to honour the court's decree in favour of Lady Windsor. A fourth writ was sworn out in November 1588, followed by yet another imprisonment, but this is the final episode in his dispute with his former wife. Puttenham's 1589 bill associated with these matters refers to Lady Windsor as 'deceased' (PRO, STAC 5 P33/22).

Literary works George Puttenham the fugitive excommunicant is not easily reconciled with Puttenham the author, whose writings in prose and verse secure his place in English literary history. His rhetorical skills were attested by witnesses for Morris in 1571 who deposed that George was 'full of brables of subtyll practyses and slanderous devyses … overconnynge in defacing of truthe by wordes & speache eloquente and in invencon of myscheiffe verie perfytte' (PRO, STAC 5 P5/10). A single autograph leaf of his translation of Suetonius's *Lives of the Caesars* ('in vita Tiberii', chaps. 58–61, PRO, SP 12/126/67) bears faint witness to his literary interests. More persuasive is the autograph 'inventory of all my bookes and library' for 10 November 1576 (Hants. RO, 44M69/E19/4, fol. 16v). This list of more than ninety titles is weighted toward law, rhetoric (including Aristotle, Erasmus, and Ramus), French history, and politics (from Aristotle to Machiavelli). The Latin poets are well represented (among them Ovid, Catullus, Juvenal, Tibullus, and Horace), along with a few vernacular authors, notably Pierre Ronsard, Luigi Alemanni, and two copies of Jacopo Sannazarro's *Arcadia*. What Puttenham's catalogue omits is any reference to English poetry such as Richard Tottel's *Songs and Sonnets* or the works of George Gascoigne and George Turberville, all drawn on heavily in the *Arte*, and all in print by 1576. Puttenham's inventory does, however, reinforce his claim to 'A justificacion of Queene Elizabeth in relacion to the affaire of Mary queene of Scottes'. This prose defence of Mary's execution presents sophisticated legal and political arguments in support of the government's decision to condemn Mary to death. The tract, edited for the Camden Society in 1867, is assigned to Puttenham in two contemporary manuscripts (BL, Add. MS 48027, Harley 831), and there are no conflicting attributions. To reward Puttenham for this work, which circulated widely in manuscript, Thomas Windebank, Lord Burghley's protégé and a clerk of the signet, secured the queen's signature to a gift of two leases in reversion for Puttenham in May 1588.

On 9 November 1588 *The Arte of English Poesie* was entered in the Stationers' register for the first time. It was published anonymously in 1589 with a dedication to Burghley subscribed 'R. F.' by the printer, Richard Field. Although *The Arte* has been claimed for both Richard Puttenham and John, Baron Lumley, the case for George Puttenham's authorship of this important work of literary criticism is strong if not indisputable. About 1590 John Harington requested that Field set forth portions of Harington's translation of Ariosto 'in the same printe that Putnams book ys' (BL, Add. MS 18920, fol. 336). In his 'Hypercritica' (1610), Edmund Bolton cited the rumour that one Puttenham, gentleman pensioner to Queen Elizabeth, wrote *The Arte*. Neither George nor Richard served as pensioners or in any other capacity under Elizabeth, yet clearly someone named Puttenham wrote *The Arte*. Its author claimed to have written at the age of eighteen the lost *Elpine*, dedicated to Edward VI. Richard Puttenham was eighteen in 1538, but George turned eighteen about 1547 just as Edward came to the throne. Moreover, the praise of Sir John Throckmorton in *The Arte*, including a verse elegy in his honour, also points to George rather than Richard. Throckmorton was very much involved with George's affairs, especially during the 1570s, but there is no record of Richard's connection with him. Other aspects of *The Arte*, such as its author's claim to have studied at Oxford and to have been brought up in foreign courts, fit neither of the Puttenhams. On balance, however, George Puttenham's claim trumps that of any other candidate.

The Arte is an ambitious work of literary history and criticism as well as a rhetorical handbook for the practising poet; Ben Jonson carefully annotated his copy of the book. Yet no second edition appeared, perhaps because *The Arte* was somewhat out of fashion by 1589, drawing most of its examples from early to mid-sixteenth-century writers. In his 'Brief apology for poetrie' prefixed to his translation of *Orlando Furioso* (1591), Harington asserted that poetry was a divine gift rather than an art to be learned, and he ridiculed Puttenham's own poetic talent.

In *The Arte* Puttenham refers to at least eleven of his works in prose and verse, only one of which can now be identified. More than a dozen verse quotations in *The Arte* can be traced to his 'Partheniades', a collection of seventeen poems dedicated to Queen Elizabeth which exists in a single manuscript text, BL, Cotton Vesp. MS E.8, fols. 169–78. While some or all of the 'Partheniades' were supposedly written as a new year's gift for the queen, about 1579–81, the work's absence among the Royal manuscripts in the British Library argues that it was either not delivered or not accepted, for that collection preserves new year's gifts addressed to the queen by such poets as George Gascoigne and Thomas Churchyard. In addition, Puttenham mentions in *The Arte* his interludes 'Lustie London' and 'The Woer', his comedy 'Ginecocratia', a verse romance entitled the 'Isle of Great Britain', and the prose tracts 'De decoro', 'Ierotekni', and 'Originals and pedigree of the English tongue'. In September 1590 Puttenham made out his will leaving all his goods (unspecified) to widow Mary Symmes, his servant. He was buried at St Bride's, Fleet Street, London, on 6 January 1591.

Richard Puttenham (b. 1520, d. in or after 1597) neither attended university nor can be certainly connected with any work of a literary nature. He inherited the property of his uncle Sir Thomas Elyot in 1546, while his father conveyed Sherfield upon Lodon to him in 1550. He married Mary, daughter of Sir William Warham and his wife, Elizabeth; Lady Warham lived in Sherfield during her widowhood and is mentioned several times in George's lawsuits. Richard was convicted of rape in April 1561, a crime that had probably motivated his flight to the continent the year before. He may have returned to England on occasions other than that of 1567, but he was certainly abroad in 1572–3. He apparently was back in England towards the end of 1578 and in February 1579 petitioned to receive certain payments that Francis Morris was making annually to the exchequer in connection with his tenure of Sherfield.

Richard enjoyed little more matrimonial success than his brother George. He termed Mary a 'clamorous strumpet' who demanded exorbitant maintenance from him although she had brought nothing to their marriage (Stretton, 191–2, 220). He had been imprisoned for debt in the king's bench for four years by May 1587 when he petitioned the masters of requests to reduce the £20 to £30 he had paid his wife annually for more than twenty years. Richard is almost certainly not the Richard Puttenham of Amersham, Buckinghamshire, yeoman of the queen's guard, who was buried at St Clement Danes on 2 July 1601, leaving a widow, Mary. George's brother was more likely the Richard Puttenham, prisoner in the king's bench, who signed his will on 22 April 1597. In it he designated as his executor and sole heir 'my verilie reported and reputed daughter Katherin Puttinham' (PRO, PROB 11/89/39). Richard's uncertainty about his relationship to Katherine suggests that she is his illegitimate daughter, perhaps an outcome of the rape of 1560.   STEVEN W. MAY

Sources G. Puttenham, *The arte of English poesie*, ed. G. D. Willcock and A. Walker (1936); repr. (1970) [rpt. 1970] · M. Eccles, *Brief lives: Tudor and Stuart authors* (1982) · PRO, SP 12/127/26–30; STAC 5 B31/14; M3/35; P5/10; M14/32; P65/27; P35/10; REQ2 219/25; STAC 7 14/1; STAC 5 P1/8; P26/3; P3/3; P9/4; P33/22; P66/2.Y; PROB 11/89, sig. 39 [Richard Puttenham]; SP 12/127/25; SO 3/1, fol. 153v · APC, 1558–91 · VCH Hampshire and the Isle of Wight · GEC, Peerage · Calendar of the manuscripts of the most hon. the marquis of Salisbury, 1–2, HMC, 9 (1883–8) · CSP for., 1569–71, no. 795 · BL, Add. MS 18920 · T. Stretton, *Women waging law in Elizabethan England* (1998) · J. Peile, *Biographical register of Christ's College, 1505–1905, and of the earlier foundation, God's House, 1448–1505*, ed. [J. A. Venn], 1 (1910) · Hants. RO, Jervoise of Herriard papers, 44M69: E4/122/1; E4/122/3; E19/14; F2/14/1; F2/14/27/1
Archives Hants. RO, Jervoise of Herriard papers, 44M69
Wealth at death see will, PRO, PROB 11/84, sig. 69

Puttenham, Richard (b. 1520, d. in or after 1597). *See under* Puttenham, George (1529–1590/91).

Pycroft, James (1813–1895), writer on cricket, was born at Geyers House, Pickwick, Wiltshire, the second son of Thomas Pycroft, barrister, and his wife, Mary. His elder brother was Thomas *Pycroft. He was educated at King Edward VI Grammar School in Bath, matriculated from Trinity College, Oxford, in 1831, and graduated BA in 1836. After four years (1836–40) studying law at Lincoln's Inn he was ordained into the Church of England in 1840. On 8 July 1843 he married Ann, the widow of F. P. Alleyn; she later predeceased him. He taught at the collegiate school, Leicester, for five years, held a curacy (1845) at Chardstock, Dorset, and was perpetual curate—a technicality giving him freehold—of St Mary Magdalen, Barnstaple, Devon, from 1845 to 1856. He held no other clerical preferments, and lived for the rest of his life at Bathwick, Bath, and then Brighton.

At Oxford, Pycroft was partly responsible for the revival in 1836 after a lapse of seven years of the cricket match between Oxford and Cambridge, and opened the batting at Lord's himself. A month earlier he had made his own highest recorded score, 85 not out, for Non-Wykehamists against Wykehamists at Oxford. He made one further appearance at Lord's, in 1838, for Left-Handed Batsmen against the MCC. He described himself as having as much right 'as anyone' to be a founder of the Lansdown club in Bath, and in his last match for them he countered some gentle barracking from the fielders for his slow batting by remarking 'I'll tell you what, gentlemen; I am here to guard three stumps and claim to play accordingly'.

Pycroft's career as a writer began while still an undergraduate at Oxford. In 1835 he published anonymously *The Principles of Scientific Batting*. This contained a formal set of rules on how to bat, together with some dietary advice for cricketers: 'Ale and porter render the eye dull'. But it was through his *The Cricket Field* (1851) that his reputation as a cricket writer became established. It ran to nine editions (1851–1887), including one published in Boston (1859) to coincide with the game's period of popularity in the United States in the ante-bellum era. The book was both a historical essay on the game's origins and a manual of instruction. Soon after leaving Oxford, Pycroft had visited the Surrey and Hampshire villages associated with cricket in the eighteenth century, such as Hambledon. He had met William Beldham, the last survivor of that era; and John Mitford had given him his own notes, containing the reminiscences of William Fennex, another Hambledon player, while Pycroft himself had 'man and boy played and watched the game'. The instructional pages were a development of his earlier book.

Pycroft's other cricket writing consisted in his regular contributions to the journal *Cricket* and to the *Cricketers' Companion* and *Cricketers' Annual*, issued regularly by the publishing family of Lillywhite. There was some repetition of material from the earlier years, a feature of his conversation as well. Nevertheless, to the end of his life people, especially the young, were attracted to hear what he might have to say while attending some match at Lord's or Brighton.

Pycroft also wrote five novels, of which *Twenty Years in the Church* (1859) and *Elkington Rectory* (1860) are semi-autobiographical. Where cricket is mentioned, it is seen as a vehicle of social cohesion 'to encourage sympathy between man and man however wide their ranks might be set asunder'. The novels illustrate Anglican optimism and clerical paternalism, and contain parallels with the novels of Anthony Trollope. They were well received by reviewers but had no lasting appeal. During his schoolmastering years he also published textbooks on Greek and Latin grammar and the reading of English. His *Oxford Memories* (2 vols., 1886) provide a fascinating—even colloquial—account of the university in his day and of his later cricketing associations.

Pycroft saw cricket 'as a standing panegyric on the English character' and a test of mental ability and manly fibre. In this he was at one with Charles Wordsworth, one of the early exponents of the concept of muscular Christianity, who established the first university cricket match in 1827. The essayist E. V. Lucas remembered seeing Pycroft in old age, 'a tall, erect and clerical figure, clad always in black, with a cape and a silk hat, pure white hair and a fringe of white whisker' (*The Hambledon Men*, 1907, xvii). Pycroft died of influenza at his home, Dudley Mansions, Lansdown Place, Brighton, on 10 March 1895.

GERALD M. D. HOWAT

Sources *Wisden* (1896) · J. Pycroft, *The cricket field*, ed. F. S. Ashley-Cooper (1922) · G. M. D. Howat, 'Cricket and the Victorian church', *Cricket Society Journal*, 9 (1979), 7–11 · *Cricket*, 14 (1895), 382
Likenesses Blanche, photograph, *c*.1890, repro. in Pycroft, *The cricket field*
Wealth at death £9236 6s. 10d.: probate, 30 March 1895, *CGPLA Eng. & Wales*

Pycroft, Sir Thomas (1807–1892), East India Company servant, was born on 4 December 1807, probably in the parish of St John, Hampstead, Middlesex, the eldest son of Thomas Pycroft, of Pickwick, Wiltshire, a barrister practising at Bath, and his wife, Mary. James *Pycroft, the

writer on cricket, was his brother. Educated first at Bath grammar school, and then under private tutors, he matriculated at Trinity College, Oxford, on 13 May 1826. In early 1829 he competed successfully for an East India Company writership presented to the university in the previous year by Charles Wynn, president of the Board of Control, and thus thirty years before it became the norm was the first of the 'competition wallahs', men appointed to the Indian Civil Service as the result of competitive examination. On his success the honorary degree of MA was conferred upon him by the university.

Pycroft arrived in Madras in August 1829 and served in that presidency in various subordinate posts in the revenue and judicial administration of the *mofussil*, principally in South Arcot, until 1839, when he returned to England on three years' furlough. While in England he married in 1841 Frances Susannah, second daughter of Major H. Bates RA, with whom he had two sons and four daughters.

On his return to India in 1843 Pycroft was transferred to the secretariat, or headquarters, of the Madras government and never again returned to district appointments. He was first appointed sub-secretary, and then in 1845 secretary, to the board of revenue. His Tamil was sufficiently good for him also to be appointed in 1845 acting Tamil translator to the government. In 1850 he was appointed secretary to the Madras government in the revenue and judicial departments and finally in 1855 chief secretary to the government. The governor of the time, Lord Harris, praised him (as had Harris's predecessors) as an able man, careful and painstaking, but did not think him brilliant or comprehensive in his views.

In October 1862 Pycroft was appointed a member of the legislative council of Madras, in which post he remained for the standard term of five years, before taking his retirement in October 1867. He had been made a KCSI in 1866. With thirty-eight years' experience behind him, he was viewed by Madras civilians as one of the gentleman officials of the old pre-1857 school of company servants, skilled in the art of genial and expansive hospitality. At the time of his retirement he was an *ex officio* fellow of Madras University and a member of the faculties of arts and medicine, chairman of the managing committee of the Madras Literary Society, and, by virtue of his membership of the Madras council, one of the governors of the Military Male Orphan Asylum at Egmore, Madras. Lady Pycroft was a vice-patroness of the Military Female Orphan Asylum. After his departure Pycroft's memory survived in Madras, for thirty years at least, in the name both of his palatial residence and of a road in the suburb of Nungumbaukum, where he had lived.

Upon his return to England, Pycroft settled in west London and devoted considerable time to philanthropic ventures. In particular he took a leading role in the government of St Mary's Hospital at Paddington. He died from influenza at 13 Eversfield Place, St Leonards, Sussex, on 29 January 1892, and was survived by his widow and their six children.   A. J. ARBUTHNOT, *rev.* KATHERINE PRIOR

Sources *The Times* (1 Feb 1892) · *Madras Mail* (1 Feb 1892) · W. Thomas, *The Asylum Press almanac and compendium of intelligence, 1867* (1866) · BL OIOC, Haileybury MSS · Lord Harris to Sir Charles Wood, 28 Feb 1855, BL OIOC, Wood MSS
Wealth at death £18,548 16s. 8d.: probate, 23 March 1892, *CGPLA Eng. & Wales*

Pye, Charles (1777–1864). *See under* Pye, John (1782–1874).

Pye, Sir David Randall (1886–1960), mechanical engineer and academic administrator, was born on 29 April 1886 in Hampstead, London, the sixth of the seven children of William Arthur Pye, wine merchant, and his wife, Margaret Thompson, daughter of James Burns Kidston, writer to the signet, of Glasgow. Edith Mary *Pye was his sister. A scholar of Tonbridge School and Trinity College, Cambridge, he was placed in the first class of the mechanical sciences tripos in 1908; he also won his half blue for rifle shooting. In 1909 C. F. Jenkin, who had just been appointed the first professor of engineering science at Oxford, invited Pye to join him there. He was elected a fellow of New College in 1911.

During the First World War, Pye taught at Winchester College (1915–16), then worked as an experimental officer in the Royal Flying Corps on design and testing, and learned to fly as a pilot. In 1919 he returned to Cambridge as a lecturer, and became a fellow of Trinity. There he met Henry Tizard and Harry Ricardo, his association with whom led to important pioneer work on the internal combustion engine. In 1926 Pye married Virginia Frances, daughter of Charles Moore Kennedy, barrister. The couple had two sons and a daughter. She became a well-known writer of books for children under the name of Virginia Pye and was a younger sister of the writer Margaret Kennedy. Pye's outstanding exposition, *The Internal Combustion Engine* (2 vols., 1931–4) was published in the Oxford Engineering Science series, of which he became an editor. In 1925 he was appointed deputy director of scientific research at the Air Ministry under H. E. Wimperis. He succeeded him as director in 1937 and in the same year was appointed CB and elected FRS. During the early war years he became closely associated with the development of the new jet propulsion aircraft engine which he did much to encourage.

In 1943 Pye accepted the provostship of University College, London. He entered upon his new duties with enthusiasm and determination to make a real contribution to the college and to post-war education. Before serious illness caused his resignation in 1951, he had seen the college through an extremely difficult period of rebuilding, following war damage, and of reorganization: probably the greatest achievement of his career. He was knighted in 1952 and in the same year became president of the Institution of Mechanical Engineers, to which he gave a memorable presidential address on the higher education of engineers, stressing the importance of the artistic or design aspects of engineering.

Pye was fastidious and had the charm of a man of taste and intelligence who preferred to convince others by persuasion rather than by asserting the superiority of his own ideas. Believing in the highest standards, he was never arrogant or certain that he was right. Partly perhaps because he appeared to have no ambitions to leadership he was trusted and followed by his many colleagues in all his working life.

An enthusiastic climber, Pye led the first ascent of the severe Crack of Doom in Skye; in 1922 he was elected to the Alpine Club of which he became vice-president in 1956. He was a friend of G. L. Mallory (whose notice he contributed to the *Dictionary of National Biography*) and in writing of his loss on Everest, with his companion A. C. Irvine, Pye perhaps best revealed his own character and sensitivity: 'Those two black specks, scarcely visible among the vast eccentricities of nature, but moving up slowly, intelligently, into regions of unknown striving, remain for us a symbol of the invincibility of the human spirit' (*Memoirs FRS*, 204). Pye died at his home, Cuttmill Cottage, Shackleford, Godalming, Surrey, on 20 February 1960.

O. A. SAUNDERS, rev. JOHN BOSNELL

Sources O. A. Saunders, *Memoirs FRS*, 7 (1961), 199–205 · *Nature*, 186 (1960), 433 · *The Engineer* (26 Feb 1960), 330 · *Alpine Journal*, 65 (1960) · personal knowledge (1971) · *CGPLA Eng. & Wales* (1960)
Archives IWM, corresp. with Sir Henry Tizard · Nuffield Oxf., corresp. with Lord Cherwell
Likenesses photograph, *c.*1952, Institution of Mechanical Engineers, London · W. Stoneman, photograph, 1953, NPG · drawing, UCL
Wealth at death £10,112 6s. 1d.: probate, 3 May 1960, *CGPLA Eng. & Wales*

Pye, David William (1914–1993), woodworker and writer, was born on 18 November 1914 at 66 Glade Croft, Kingswood Road, Betchworth, Surrey, the second of two children of Edmund Burns Pye, wine merchant, and his wife, Gwendolen, daughter of the painter John *Brett.

Pye was born into the arts and crafts tradition of which he was to become such a constructive, astringent critic. His maternal grandfather was the Pre-Raphaelite artist John Brett, one of whose best-known works is *The Stonebreaker*, a Ruskinian vision of nature. Pye's aunt, Sybil Pye, was an accomplished bookbinder of the William Morris/Sidney Cockerell school. His father, too, preferred jewellery making and boat building to running the family business.

Pye recalled that at the age of four he had been deeply impressed by a piece of wood his brother brought home, 'I thought … [it] absolutely marvellous because of its surface quality' (*Crafts*, 20, 36). In his teens he saw two eighteenth-century country chairs and thought 'that's what I want to do' (ibid.). Yet despite these early insights he did not at once become a craftsman.

Educated at Winchester College, Pye went on to train at the Architectural Association. He reacted immediately and strongly against the doctrinaire modernism he found there. He chose to work in wood rather than concrete, designing more boats than buildings. He soon came to believe 'functionalism is a phoney' (*Crafts*, 100, 46), a point he was to argue persuasively all his life.

Pye had little time to practise as an architect before the outbreak of the Second World War. His few buildings were designed in wood. The war, when it came, was a kind of release. His six years in the navy not only fed his love of boats but gave him 'time to think a bit' (*Crafts*, 20, 36).

On 17 May 1944 Pye married at Christ Church, Kensington, Pamela Agnes Mary (1913–1992), daughter of David Grierson Waller, knight bachelor, of Frimley Green, Surrey. When the war ended, realizing there would be little opportunity to build in wood, he decided to 'stick to wood and ditch buildings' (*Crafts*, 20, 36). After a short period teaching at the Architectural Association he was offered a post at the Royal College of Art by the architect R. D. (Dick) Russell, brother of the designer Gordon Russell. The college was then being transformed by Robin Darwin and Pye's role in the furniture department contributed to its post-war revival.

The pattern of Pye's life was now set. He and his wife settled in Wadhurst, Sussex. Pye taught, designed and made furniture, and created his own refined style as a carver. His first significant exhibition was in 1951, in the Lion and Unicorn pavilion at the festival of Britain. Designed by R. D. Russell and Robert Goodden to illustrate the British character, the pavilion made an illuminating setting for Pye's work. His fluted bowls and boxes spoke of a humane, northern European modernism. The arts and crafts love of materials, the respect for skill were there but purified in Pye's hands of sentimentality and revivalism.

Pye occasionally ventured into abstract sculpture but his most successful pieces were functional; the distinctive yet endlessly varied bowls and boxes. Like his Pre-Raphaelite grandfather he saw the point at which design and nature met. Shells and gourds as well as architectural elements, domes and minarets, were echoed but never imitated in his forms.

Modernism and Ruskinism influenced Pye's carving. In his writings, however, he was trenchantly critical of both. His earliest publications were part of the post-war drive for design reform, including, in 1950, *Ships* in the Penguin series Things We See. In 1964 he published *The Nature of Design*. Its sequel, *The Nature and Art of Workmanship*, came in 1968. *The Nature and Aesthetics of Design*, published in 1978, was a revised and extended version of the earlier books. Pye's prose was tough and aphoristic: 'Little is ever said which touches on the fundamental principles of useful design, and what is said is often nonsense' (Pye, 11).

Dismissing arts and crafts anti-industrialism as 'paranoia' Pye coined the terms 'workmanship of risk' and 'workmanship of certainty' to distinguish between mechanical and hand work (*David Pye, Woodcarver and Turner*, 21–2). Neither, he argued, was intrinsically superior. Indeed he saw all design and production as a continuum, from the predictable mass-produced object at one extreme to the free work of the basket maker at the other. He was as hard on the myth of form following function as on medievalism, arguing that 'function' was itself subjective and changeable and that it had no necessary formal consequences. By 1951 Pye had invented his 'fluting engine', on which he made his own work. It was a tool in argument as well as craftsmanship, the practical demonstration of his theoretical position, allowing him to introduce varying degrees of regularity, of 'risk' and 'certainty', to his own

work. Pye's writings raised the level of critical debate and helped to brighten the 'sadly tarnished term "crafts"' in the 1960s and 1970s, when handwork seemed to many to have lost itself in a sea of brown mugs and hippy culture (*David Pye, Woodcarver and Turner*, 21).

As a teacher too Pye was influential. His abrupt, sometimes testy, manner never stopped him from sympathizing with serious endeavour, even if the results differed widely from his own aesthetic. From 1963 to 1974 he was professor of furniture design at the Royal College of Art where he gave his students 'a solid and serious foundation' on which they could experiment. He seemed to them an old-fashioned if compelling figure, 'this most curious combination of shy intellect and gentleman craftsman' (Van den Broecke, 14).

Of his own work Pye was reluctant to talk. Pressed for a statement he wrote: 'What I seek to achieve is to do it a bit better ... in the hope that in time to come someone's eye will light' (*The Maker's Eye*, 56). It was a view that showed how close, for all his quarrels with it, Pye remained to the arts and crafts ideal.

Appointed OBE in 1985 Pye continued to work until, in his last years, he became crippled by Parkinsonism. His wife died in November 1992. He then declined rapidly. He died on 1 January 1993 at the Beaumont Nursing Home, Boars Hill, Oxford, and was cremated in Oxford. Examples of Pye's work are in the Victoria and Albert Museum, London; the Crafts Council Collection, London; the Cecil Higgins Art Gallery, Bedford; the Southern Arts Association, Winchester; North West Arts Collection; Parnham House, Dorset, and the Drapers' Company, London.

ROSEMARY HILL

Sources *David Pye, woodcarver and turner* (1986) · D. Pye, *The nature and aesthetics of design* (New York, 1978) · M. Coleman, 'Wood and workmanship', *Crafts*, 20 (1976), 36–9 · F. MacCarthy, 'Sources of inspiration', *Crafts*, 100 (1989), 46–7 · *The maker's eye* (1981) [exhibition catalogue, Crafts Council, London] · F. van den Broecke, *Furniture*, 3 (1993), 14–15 · J. Houston, ed., *Craft classics since the 1940s* (1988) [exhibition catalogue, Crafts Council Gallery, London, 19 Oct 1988 – 8 Jan 1989] · D. W. Pye and R. Hill, interview, *The Guardian* (30 Jan 1986) · personal knowledge (2004) · private information (2004) · b. cert. · m. cert. · d. cert.

Archives West Surrey College of Art and Design, Farnham, Craft Study collection, papers and artefacts

Likenesses photographs, Crafts Council, London; repro. in *David Pye* (1986)

Wealth at death £389,435: probate, 1 March 1993, *CGPLA Eng. & Wales*

Pye, Edith Mary (1876–1965), midwife and international relief organizer, was born on 20 October 1876 in London, the eldest daughter in the family of three daughters and four sons of William Arthur Pye JP, wine merchant, and his wife, Margaret Thompson Kidston, daughter of James Burns Kidston, writer to the signet, of Glasgow. The sister of Sir David Randall *Pye (1886–1960), and niece of an eminent surgeon, Edith Pye trained as a nurse (SRN) and midwife (SCM) and by 1907 was superintendent of district nurses in London. In 1908 she joined the Society of Friends.

In December 1914 Edith Pye went to Châlons-sur-Marne to set up a maternity hospital for women refugees from

Rheims in what had been an insane asylum, without hot water or electricity, 15 miles from the fighting line. One thousand babies later, in April 1919, Edith Pye departed, one of very few women to have been made a chevalier of the Légion d'honneur.

From March 1921 until October 1922 Edith Pye joined her lifelong friend Dr Hilda *Clark (1881–1955), granddaughter of John Bright, to try to feed all the severely undernourished children under the age of four in Vienna. Together they successfully masterminded the acquisition and distribution of British and American hard currency, with which they bought Croatian fodder to feed the Swiss cows donated to Austria, which in turn provided free milk. Edith Pye privately published Hilda Clark's letters from France, Austria, and the Near East, 1914–24, in a book called *War and its Aftermath* (n.d., c.1956), which documents their joint relief operations at that time.

In May 1923 the Quakers sent Edith Pye to report on conditions in the French-occupied Ruhr. She found 'a complete absence of civil justice' and the seeds of implacable future enmity. Throughout the 1920s and 1930s her moderate and conciliatory personality worked to mediate between the revolutionary and the gradualist wings of the Women's International League as she served on its international executive. 'She was not the sort who enjoyed a scrap' (private information). In May 1928 the league sent Edith Pye on a three-month goodwill mission to India, Indo-China, and China to study the status of women.

In 1929 Edith Pye became president of the British Midwives' Institute, later called the Royal College of Midwives, a post she occupied for twenty years. It was during her period of office and with her strong encouragement that the chloroform capsule was developed that first enabled midwives to administer pain relief to women in childbirth in their own homes. In July 1932 Edith Pye published an article on this subject entitled 'Anaesthetics in labour from the midwife's point of view' in the *Newsletter of the Medical Women's Federation*. Between 1934 and 1936 Edith Pye was accorded the honour of being made president of the International Confederation of Midwives.

In addition to this high-profile commitment to midwifery, Edith Pye never ceased her efforts at international rescue work. In 1934 she became vice-chairman of the Friends' Germany emergency committee that she had helped found to succour German and German Jewish refugees from Hitler. During the Spanish Civil War Edith Pye instigated the formation in Geneva of the international commission for the assistance of child refugees in Spain. Between January 1939 and June 1940 she worked on the French–Spanish border to alleviate the wretchedness of the defeated Spanish republicans, only leaving on the last boat to sail for Britain from Bordeaux. Between 1940 and 1945 she worked as honorary secretary to the famine relief committee (chaired by G. K. A. Bell, bishop of Chichester) which tried, via the Red Cross, to send food, vitamins, and medical aid to children in German-occupied Europe, against the wishes of the British Ministry of Economic Warfare. Immediately after the Normandy landings in 1944 Edith Pye toured liberated France with the Friends'

relief service to arrange bulk food supplies for the children she found suffering from malnutrition. It was said of her in the *Manchester Guardian*—on the occasion of her seventieth birthday—that her 'activities for refugees and humanitarian causes have in their own way been as assiduous as those of the late Eleanor Rathbone' (*Manchester Guardian*, 10 Oct 1946).

In 1952 Edith Pye and Hilda Clark retired to Street, Somerset. Edith Pye complemented her friend's daring breadth of vision with her own genius for detailed organization. Both women were exceptionally free from egotism, always drawing out the talents of their co-workers and being very willing to delegate authority. Both believed that 'there is something that is contagious other than hate', as Edith Pye said in her Lister lecture to the Quaker Medical Society in 1934. Both women were a credit to what Edith Pye called 'the secular arm' of the Society of Friends. Edith Pye died at her home, 4 Overleigh, Street, Somerset, on 16 December 1965 and was buried in the Quaker burial-ground under the same headstone as Hilda Clark. SYBIL OLDFIELD

Sources E. Pye, ed., *War and its aftermath* (c.1956) • O. A. Saunders, *Memoirs FRS*, 7 (1961), 199–205 [obit. of David Randall Pye] • 'Miss Edith Pye', *Manchester Guardian* (10 Oct 1946) • *The Friend* (31 Dec 1965) • *The Guardian* (20 Dec 1965) • *The Times* (21 Dec 1965) • private information (2004) • d. cert.
Archives RS Friends, Lond., papers relating to relief work in Spain
Likenesses photograph, c.1919, repro. in Pye, ed., *War and its aftermath* • photograph, c.1952, Institution of Mechanical Engineers, London • W. Stoneman, photograph, 1953, NPG • drawing, UCL
Wealth at death £9385: probate, 8 March 1966, *CGPLA Eng. & Wales*

Pye, Harold John (1901–1986). *See under* Pye, William George (1869–1949).

Pye, Henry James (1745–1813), poet, was born on 20 February 1745 in London and baptized on 24 February at St Anne's, Soho, the eldest of four children of Henry Pye (1709–1766), MP for Berkshire from 1746 to 1766, and Mary (1717/18–1806), daughter of the Revd David James. His father's ancestors included Sir Robert Pye (1585–1662) and John Hampden (1594–1643). Henry James Pye was educated at Magdalen College, Oxford, from 1762 to 1766 (honorary MA 1766, DCL 1772). In 1766 he married Mary (d. 1796), daughter of Colonel William Hook(e) (d. 1761). There were two daughters from this marriage: Mary Elizabeth (d. 1834), later the wife of Captain Jones, 35th regiment, and Matilda Catherine (d. 1851), later the wife of Samuel James Arnold (1774–1852), playwright and portrait painter.

When his father died in 1766 Pye inherited large debts; he was obliged to sell ancestral estates at Knotting, Bedfordshire, and at Great Faringdon, Berkshire. He was a keen field sportsman, and a Berkshire magistrate and militia officer. Nathaniel Hone painted him (1775) in militia uniform, holding helmet and musket with fixed bayonet. Pye's election as MP for Berkshire in 1784 was assisted by the unusually large disbursement of £2500

Henry James Pye (1745–1813), by Samuel James Arnold, c.1800

from the government's secret service fund, and consequently he always supported Pitt in the Commons, but he retired from parliament at the dissolution in 1790. His residences after Faringdon were in Queen Square, Westminster, and Pinner, Middlesex, but he maintained an interest in field sports: his 'improved and enlarged' edition of *The Sportsman's Dictionary* appeared in 1807. From 1792 he was a police magistrate for Westminster; he wrote a useful *Summary of the Duties of a Justice of the Peace* (1808; 4th edn, 1827).

Pye said he was 'a rhymer for life'. His earliest publication was an ode in an Oxford congratulatory volume on the birth of the prince of Wales (1762); it was followed by a stream of descriptive and didactic poems in heroic couplets: *Beauty, a Poetical Essay* (1766), *The Triumph of Fashion, a Vision* (1771), *The Art of War* (1778, translated from the French of Frederick the Great when Pye was at militia camp), *The Progress of Refinement: a Poem in Three Parts* (1783), *Faringdon Hill: a Poem in Two Books* (1774, a 'local poem'), *Shooting* (1784, a georgic), and *Amusement: a Poetical Essay* (1790). These poems conventionally praise the pleasures of gentlemanly rural life, but Pye extended the range of didactic verse with his *Aerophorion* (1784) on hot-air ballooning. There were lyrics too: most of Pye's *Elegies on Different Occasions* (1768) are love-sick effusions addressed to 'Delia' but one refreshingly hails the opening of the partridge-shooting season. Some of the above, with songs, odes, pseudo-Spenserian stanzas, translations, and other new pieces, reappeared in *Poems on Various Subjects* (2 vols., 1787).

On Pye's retirement from the Commons, his support of Pitt was rewarded on 28 July 1790 with the award of the poet laureateship, vacant on the death of Thomas Warton. As well as his annual salary of £100, a laureate received a pension of £27 in lieu of the tierce (42 gallons) of canary wine which had once been part of the stipend; this exchange was made well before Pye's time, though Pye has often mistakenly been blamed for it. The laureateship was an office of little profit (Pye badgered Pitt unsuccessfully for other posts) and in Pye's hands it became one of little credit too. Of the odes that he conscientiously wrote, year by year, for the new year and for the king's birthday (4 June), the best that can be said is that their rhymes and regular stanzas made them easier to set to music by the master of the king's band, Sir William Parsons, than the irregular odes of Pye's successor Robert Southey.

Pye's term of office coincided with a long war against France, so his odes dwell on 'Gallic perfidy', 'Peace by Victory led', the 'golden beams of Freedom', the benefits of commerce, and Britannia's rule of the waves. The same unreflective patriotism fills Pye's longer wartime poems, such as *Naucratica, or, Naval Dominion* (1798), dedicated to George III, *Carmen seculare for the Year 1800* (with a preface arguing that the new century really begins on 1 January 1801), and the ambitious *Alfred, an Epic Poem in Six Books* (1801). In quieter vein Pye celebrated his friendship with the writer John Penn (1760–1834) in *Verses on Several Subjects, Written in the Vicinity of Stoke Park* (1802).

Laureate odes were sometimes sung as entr'actes in London theatres, but Pye, like his sister-in-law Henrietta Pye (author of a farce *The Capricious Lady*, 1771), had a more sustained flirtation with the stage. His solemn blank-verse historical tragedies on medieval subjects, *The Siege of Meaux* (1794) and *Adelaide* (1800), were printed and were given enough performances (three nights) to secure an author's benefit for each. Pye was also joint author of *The Inquisitor, a Tragedy* (from the German, 1798) and *A Prior Claim, a Comedy* (1805). A prologue he was persuaded to write for the 1796 production of *Vortigern*, a Shakespeare forgery by William Henry Ireland, was so dubious in tone that, happily for Pye, it was not used. Pye also tried his hand at prose fiction: his epistolary novel *The Spectre* (1789) is conventionally sentimental and sensational; his two later anti-Jacobin novels, *The Democrat* (1795) and *The Aristocrat* (1799) mildly satirize sentimentality. His *Sketches on Various Subjects: Moral, Literary, and Political* (1796) collected miscellaneous thoughts on novels, the army, gardening, Shakespeare, field sports, and many other topics. He enlarged his Shakespeare 'sketch' into a nit-picking volume, *Comments on the Commentators on Shakespeare* (1807), attacking the editorial labours of George Steevens, Edmund Malone, Francis Douce, and others. Douce hit back in the *Gentleman's Magazine* (October 1807, 921–7) and in the heavily annotated copy of *Comments* now in the Bodleian Library, in which Douce has altered the author's name to 'Goose-Pye'.

In addition to all the above Pye translated verse from French, Italian, German, Latin, and Greek. His translation in 1775 of six Olympic odes of Pindar and his revision in 1812 of Philip Francis's version of Horace's *Odes* found a place in standard English reprints of those authors, but his translations of the *War Elegies* of Tyrtaeus (1795), and the hymns and epigrams of Homer (1810), were less durable. His version, in 1796, of Bürger's *Lenore* was eclipsed by those of William Taylor and Sir Walter Scott. His most interesting piece of intertextual scholarship is a bulky *Commentary* (1792) on a translation of Aristotle's *Poetics* he had published four years earlier: his illustration of Aristotle by examples from modern literature is often original, shrewd, and learned.

Pye's original verse is never distinctive enough to be really bad: his odes, elegies, and seemingly interminable heroic couplets are mechanically competent, but he rarely has anything interesting to say. His novels, plays, miscellaneous prose, and even his somewhat more highly regarded translations soon sank, like his poems, without trace. However, his conspicuous public position as poet laureate exposed his meagre talents to the gaze of satirists, especially those such as John Wolcot (Peter Pindar) and Lord Byron who wanted to attack George III through his laureate.

Pye wisely did not reply to the wits who attacked him, but he greatly curtailed his writing, so that after 1802 he published no original new verse other than twice-yearly laureate odes. In November 1801 he married his second wife, Martha Corbett (1769/70–1861); their children were Henry John (1802–1884) and Jane Ann, who married Francis Willington of Tamworth. In May 1813 an edition of Pye's *Select Writings* in six volumes was announced in the press, but it never appeared. Pye died at Pinner on 11 August 1813.

Pye's portrait, painted about 1800 by his son-in-law S. J. Arnold, shows a bullet-head, firm mouth, large nose, hazel eyes, ruddy complexion, and sparse white hair: more sportsman than poet. Henry Crabb Robinson wrote in his diary (13 October 1812) that Pye had 'a singular diseased affection: the sight of any extended plain, either the sea, or a heath, throws him into a nervous disorder amounting to convulsion'. William Thomas Fitzgerald (like Pye a butt of Byron's) was

> once with him when they were crossing Blackfriars Bridge by moonlight. Pye caught a glimpse of the water with the reflection of the moon upon it, and sank down into the carriage pretending to look for his glove in order to conceal the trouble the sight gave him. (*Henry Crabb Robinson*, 110–11)

JAMES SAMBROOK

Sources DNB · J. Nichols, 'Memoir of the late Henry James Pye, esq., poet laureat', *GM*, 1st ser., 83/2 (1813), 293–6 · Burke, *Gen. GB* (1871) · IGI · *VCH Berkshire*, 4.490, 493 · *VCH Middlesex*, 4.179 · R. Walker, *National Portrait Gallery: Regency portraits*, 1 (1985), 404 · *Henry Crabb Robinson on books and their writers*, ed. E. J. Morley, 1 (1938), 110–11 · *The later correspondence of George III*, ed. A. Aspinall, 5 vols. (1962–70), vol. 1, p. 116 · *The life and correspondence of Robert Southey*, ed. C. C. Southey, 6 vols. (1849–50), vol. 4, p. 49 · *The letters of Sir Walter Scott*, ed. H. J. C. Grierson and others, centenary edn, 12 vols. (1932–79), vol. 1, pp. 59–60n.; vol. 3, pp. 335, 338, 348 · *The correspondence of Thomas Warton*, ed. D. Fairer (1995), 629–30 · HoP, *Commons, 1754–90*, 2.344 · C. B. Hogan, ed., *The London stage, 1660–*

1800, pt 5: 1776–1800 (1968) · R. Southey, *Poetical works* (1837), preface to vol. 3 · *New letters of Robert Southey*, ed. K. Curry, 1 (1965), 214 · A. H. Ehrenpreis, 'Introduction', in C. Smith, *Emmeline* (1971), ix–x **Archives** Bodl. Oxf., MS Montagu d.3; MS Bland Burges 22–4 · Bodl. Oxf., letters to Mark Noble · PRO, 30/8/169 **Likenesses** N. Hone, oils, 1775, priv. coll. · pastel, *c.*1785; sold in 1938 · J. Chapman, stipple, pubd 1796 (after portrait by S. Drummond), AM Oxf., Hope collection, WAHP 32448; repro. in *European Magazine* (1796) · S. J. Arnold, oils, *c.*1800, NPG [*see illus.*] · B. Pym, mezzotint, pubd 1801 (after portrait by S. J. Arnold), AM Oxf., Hope collection, WAHP7005 · stipple, pubd 1803 (after portrait by S. J. Arnold) · J. Cundee, engraving, 1807 (after portrait by S. J. Arnold) · stipple, *c.*1810 (after drawing by Miss Pye)

Pye [*née* Mendez, *other married name* Campbell], **Jael Henrietta** (1737?–1782), writer, was born in London. Little is known of her background or upbringing, though the family name of Mendez identifies a Jewish family of Portuguese or Spanish origins. Her father was a wealthy merchant who lived or worked in Red Lion Square, Holborn; her uncle Moses *Mendez was a banker and poet, the last of the family to belong to the Bevis Marks Synagogue. It would appear that, like many Sephardi Jews at this period, the Mendez family assimilated into mainstream English society.

In 1762 Mendez married John Neil Campbell of Milton Ernest, Bedfordshire, who had been admitted to Lincoln's Inn in 1755. It is not known how this marriage ended. In 1766 she married Robert Hampden Pye in Faringdon, Berkshire; Pye was an ensign in the fashionable 1st foot guards. His father, Henry Pye, had been MP for Berkshire, and had died leaving debts of £50,000. Her new brother-in-law was Henry James Pye (1745–1813), poet laureate from 1790 until his death; some of his poems are dedicated to him. Together Jael and Robert Pye had at least one son and one daughter, but it seems the marriage was difficult. By 1774 she was impoverished and living in France with her young daughter. Here, Pye advised Le Tourneur on his translations of Shakespeare, corresponded frequently with Garrick, and pursued her own writing. She stayed in France for five years, during which time her husband was ordered to America. She hoped to be reunited with him in later life, but died before this could happen. In 1777 Pye was slandered in the British papers, apparently in reprisal for something she had written. The same year, in a word portrait, Pye described herself 'at forty years as above middle height with a small head, penetrating black eyes, pretty jet-black hair, a well-formed chest, good legs, and a noble walk' (Todd, 261).

An outsider, Pye tried to be accepted into mainstream British society not only through her marriages but also through her writing. Her first published work was *A Short Account of the Principal Seats and Gardens in and about Richmond and Kew* (1760). Her first husband had come from Twickenham and therefore Pye knew the area well. In this account she describes twenty homes situated along the River Thames, owned by members of the aristocracy and gentry, including Pope, Garrick, Horace Walpole, Mrs Clive, the dukes of Argyll and Newcastle, and the earls of Radnor and Portmore. Pye is generally traditional in her tastes. However, not surprisingly, given her own background, Pye is keen to embrace influences from other cultures, hence her admiration for the chinoiserie in the duke of Argyll's house. But hers is not merely a factual account: there is poetic writing here. The countess of Suffolk's house is as 'white as snow' and the barges on the river reflected in the looking-glasses of Mrs Pritchard's home present 'the most beautiful moving pictures imaginable'. Pye also comments on the position of women whom she laments as having so few opportunities to travel and therefore having to acquire their aesthetic education through visiting such homes.

Pye's book was reprinted twice, once in 1767 along with a volume, *Poems*, and renamed *A Short View of the Principal Seats and Gardens in Twickenham*, and then in 1775 as *A Peep into the Principal Seats and Gardens at and about Twickenham*. These volumes were privately printed and circulated. In 1771 Garrick produced, at Drury Lane, her farce about a bossy mother, 'The Capricious Lady', but it was never published. In 1771 Pye brought out *Poems. By a Lady*, with a second edition in 1772, which was praised in the *Critical Review*. In 1786 her husband published posthumously, in two volumes, *Theodosius and Arabella. A Novel. In a Series of Letters. By the Late Mrs Hampden Pye*, but the *Critical Review* was not so forthcoming in its praise this time.

In her poetry Pye is aware of the restrictions that money, gender, and social standing can place on the individual. In particular, she constantly draws attention to the plight of women. *A Picture Taken from the Life* (1760) celebrates the life of Lady Clive as, Pye argues, everyone knows about her husband but not about her. In *To Love* (1771) she asks why women are always praised for their beauty and not for their other qualities. In *To David Garrick, Esq.* (1769) she feels that she has to decline an invitation to a masked ball because she is a woman of a certain age. Another woman warns her:

> Your sex in narrow circle placed,
> If once they pass it are disgraced.

Much of Pye's poetry is humorous but she also enjoyed retelling classic tales. Her modernized version of Walpole's *Childe Waters*, which she named *Earl Walter*, was much praised. She wrote a poetic version of the letter which Elgiva might have sent Edwy when she was banished by Archbishop Odo.

Through her description of the Twickenham homes and through her poetry, it was clear that Pye longed to be accepted into the mainstream gentrified society from which her origins excluded her. From derisive comments such as Walpole's, that she was 'a Jewess, who has married twice and turned Christian, poetess and authoress' (Todd, 261), and from the slander against her in the British newspapers in 1777, one suspects it was a battle that she ultimately lost. Pye died in France in 1782. **TAMAR HODES**

Sources A. M. Hyamson, *The Sephardic England* (1951) · J. H. Pye, *A short account of the principal seats and gardens in and about Richmond and Kew* (privately printed, 1760) · J. Todd, ed., *A dictionary of British and American women writers, 1660–1800* (1984)
Archives BL, letters | V&A NAL, letters to David Garrick

Pye, John (*b.* 1746, *d.* after 1789). *See under* Boydell, John, engravers (*act.* 1760–1804).

Pye, John (1782–1874), engraver, was born in Birmingham on 7 November 1782, the second of two sons of Charles Pye, writer, and Ann, daughter of William Radclyffe. Charles Pye had, in expectation of a sizeable inheritance, seen no need to practise any trade. A lawsuit, however, dashed his hopes, and obliged him to support his family by writing works on local history and antiquities—subjects he had already explored as a gentleman amateur. His son did not receive any extensive schooling beyond basic instruction in engraving gained from his father, who had engraved illustrations for his works himself.

Pye moved to London in 1801 to become a paid assistant of James Heath ARA, to whom his brother Charles Pye [*see below*] was already apprenticed. In 1808 he married Mary, daughter of the engraver Samuel Middiman; they had an only child, Mary. Much of Pye's work at this period consisted of engravings of historical buildings and landscapes for topographical works such as Thomas Dunham Whitaker's *History of Richmondshire* (1823). He also produced vignettes for various pocket-sized ladies' annuals such as *The Amulet*. Throughout his career Pye remained fiercely loyal to the line engraving medium.

J. M. W. Turner had praised Pye's skill in rendering subtle light effects when the latter engraved *Pope's Villa* in 1809 (Rawlinson, 1.xxv–xxvi, lxvi); in later years Pye engraved several other Turner landscapes. Despite Pye's strong reciprocal admiration for Turner, his large engraving of the latter's *Ehrenbreitstein* (1845) was the only instance in which the painter and engraver entered into a direct contractual relationship to engrave, print, and publish a specific work. In contrast to the eagerness with which younger engravers courted popular painters such as Edwin Landseer for engraving contracts in the 1840s, Pye remained largely aloof. He produced only one engraving after a work of Landseer, *All that Remains of the Glory of William Smith* (1836). This is surprising given Landseer's respect for Pye, whom he was to call in 1854 'the head of a particular school of art which had taught all who followed him' (Dyson, 'Images interpreted', 33). Although Pye had his admirers, his position as leader of and spokesman for his fellow engravers was not justified by any superior quality appreciable in his work. It was rather his organizational skills and seniority relative to his somewhat younger colleagues that gained him their respect.

Pye hoped to raise the fortunes, status, and public profile of engravers by means of professional association and co-operation. He was active at the birth of the Artist's Joint Stock Fund in 1819. Despite much internal wrangling, the fund grew and was chartered in 1827, when Pye was its president. It was at the fund's annual dinner on 23 January 1823 that Pye made an address urging engravers to associate and publish their own prints. In this way, he argued, engravers would cut out manipulative printsellers and receive a larger proportion of the revenue from prints. Pye's friend the painter William Mulready offered the copyright of his popular playground scene, *The Wolf and*

John Pye (1782–1874), by Henry Behnes, 1831

the Lamb, to facilitate this endeavour. The print (1824) realized a profit of over £1000 for the associated engravers.

Emboldened by this success, Pye went on in 1827 to propose a series of engravings after paintings in the National Gallery, which had opened to the public in 1824. He gathered together a group of engravers including George Doo, William Finden, and others for this purpose. Pye found his hopes for the project, which he believed could have been 'a monument honourable to the country', shared by the well-known collector of contemporary British art John Sheepshanks (Pye Papers, National Art Library, fol. 50). Sheepshanks advanced £3000 towards the venture, which, largely owing to Pye's efforts, had 870 subscribers by the end of 1831. Difficulties financing loans and the dilatory progress of several engravers, however, eventually terminated the project. Seven instalments in all appeared between 1832 and 1840; among them was Pye's engraving (1834) of Gaspar Dughet's *Abraham and Isaac*. Despite its failure, Pye's *Engravings from Pictures in the National Gallery* is noteworthy for being one of the earliest attempts to engrave paintings from a European public art gallery.

Parliamentary select committees on the arts and manufactures (1835–6) and on art unions (1844) both questioned Pye in his capacity as the outspoken advocate of the engravers. In the 1844 art union select committee Pye was at pains to point out as 'a fact … not generally known, that the arts of this country have risen principally on engraving' (*Select Committee on Art Unions*, 224). The Royal Academy should, he argued, recognize the debt they owed to

engravers as the creators of an open art market. Pye had been leading efforts to end the Royal Academy exclusion of engravers for election to full membership of the academy by means of petitions since 1812, when a memorial was sent to the prince regent. Although engravers could be elected to associate membership of the Royal Academy, Pye believed that to stand for election under these terms was both personally and professionally demeaning. In 1826 he and other leading engravers vowed never to do so; further petitions were to follow in 1836 and 1837. In 1836 and 1859 Pye was to publish pamphlets attacking the Royal Academy.

Pye's pamphlets echoed earlier jeremiads by other engravers, such as Robert Strange's *Conduct of the Academicians* (1771) and John Landseer's *Lectures on the Art of Engraving* (1807). The Royal Academy had insisted in 1812 that engravers were beyond the pale of art; even if they gained election, engraver associates were not allowed to vote on academy business or hold any office. To Pye this exclusion was conclusive evidence that the academy's principles were diametrically opposed to those of engraving, 'whose very essence is expansion and diffusion' (Pye, *Patronage*, 296). The Royal Academy's stance contrasted sharply with the compliments paid to Pye by foreign academies: he received a gold medal from the French government in 1846 and was elected to membership of the Paris and St Petersburg academies in 1862 and 1863 respectively.

Pye's most important publication was a history of the relationship between the visual arts and the state in Britain: his book *Patronage of British Art* (1845). This well-researched book traces the development of public, rather than noble, patronage from the middle of the eighteenth century onwards. Pye's history describes how Hogarth and other eighteenth-century figures made engraving into the profitable catalyst of a public sphere for art:

> the mass of the people became the first source of patronage open to native talent; hence, too, a new and vast channel of enterprise was opened to the commercial speculator; and the various powers of the painter's mind were applied, through the art of engraving, to advance the interests of trade, by cultivating and feeding the taste of the million, both at home and abroad. (ibid., 141)

A profile drawing of Pye by William Mulready engraved by J. H. Robinson and reproduced in his *Patronage of British Art* records his high forehead, furrowed brow, and slightly ironic smile, which together evoke a probably characteristic expression of wry amusement.

Although he was uninvolved with the project, Pye was an important collector of rare states and proofs of Turner's engraved *Liber Studiorum*, which he held an indispensable resource to training the eye of professional artists and amateurs alike. Pye sold his collection to the British Museum in 1869. His death at his home, 17 Gloucester Crescent, Regent's Park, London, on 6 February 1874 deprived engravers of an individual who had been their best spokesman, albeit one whose faith in public taste and belief that commercial and aesthetic considerations could coexist in harmony often seem more at home in the late eighteenth-century world of Josiah Boydell. His leadership, however, was instrumental in encouraging engravers to associate for their mutual benefit and in forwarding projects which sought to make the relationship between engravers and their public closer and more aesthetically improving.

Charles Pye (1777–1864), engraver, elder brother of John, was born in Birmingham. He was apprenticed to James Heath ARA by 1801, becoming specialized in line engraved illustrations for books and pocket annuals. Typical of these is his *Luxembourg Palace* (after a drawing by Frederick Nash) in J. Scott and P. B. de la Boissière, *Picturesque Views of the City of Paris and its Environs* (London, 1823). Charles Pye died at Leamington Spa on 14 December 1864.   JONATHAN CONLIN

Sources C. Fox, 'The engraver's battle for professional recognition in early nineteenth-century London', *London Journal*, 2 (1976), 3–31 • A. Dyson, *Pictures to print: the nineteenth-century engraving trade* (1984) • J. Pye, *Patronage of British art* (1845) • J. Pye, *Evidence relating to the art of engraving* (1836) • J. Pye, *A glance at the rise and constitution of the Royal Academy* (1859) • A. Dyson, 'Images interpreted: Landseer and the engraving trade', *Print Quarterly*, 1 (1984), 29–43 • W. G. Rawlinson, *The engraved work of J. M. W. Turner, RA*, 2 vols. (1908) • Redgrave, *Artists* • CGPLA Eng. & Wales (1874) • Pye MSS, V&A NAL • DNB
Archives BL, notebooks, Add. MSS 36934–36935 • V&A NAL, corresp. and MSS | BL, John Pye II folders
Likenesses H. Behnes, plaster cast of bust, 1831, NPG [*see illus.*] • J. H. Robinson, etching (after W. Mulready), BM; repro. in Pye, *Patronage* • J. Watkins, photograph, NPG • wood-engraving (after photograph), BM, NPG; repro. in *ILN* (1874)
Wealth at death under £7000: resworn probate, July 1874, CGPLA Eng. & Wales

Pye, Sir Robert (*bap.* 1585, *d.* 1662), exchequer official and politician, was baptized on 24 March 1585 at Much Dewchurch, Herefordshire, the fourth and youngest son of Roger Pye (*d.* 1591) of the Mynde (which lay in the parish) and his wife, Bridget (*d.* 1624), daughter of Thomas Kyrle of Walford, Herefordshire. Pye did not attend university but was admitted to the Middle Temple in June 1607.

At some date between 1615 and 1618, together with his eldest brother Walter *Pye, Robert joined the service of George Villiers (later first duke of Buckingham). In March 1617 he was granted the profit on the extra import duty levied on the goods of foreign merchants entering the country (a kind of revenue farm), in place of Sir Lionel Cranfield, who was moving on to higher things. Their paths were to cross and recross in the years ahead. In April 1618 Pye became co-grantee of a minor but potentially profitable office in chancery—presumably granted by the lord chancellor, Sir Francis Bacon (later Viscount St Albans) to gratify Buckingham. But the decisive advance in Pye's prospects came with the disgrace and dismissal in 1619 of the lord treasurer, Thomas Howard, first earl of Suffolk, and his henchman Sir John Bingley. He succeeded the latter as auditor of the exchequer of receipt and writer of tallies. Successive holders of this post and of the clerkship of the pells, which had overlapping duties, had been at odds during the previous reign. Their relative importance was partly a matter of administrative procedures, but perhaps even more of the personality and political

connections of their respective holders. In any case the auditorship was a lucrative office.

Pye was knighted in 1621. In the early 1620s he was able to acquire an estate at Faringdon in Berkshire, the manor house then comprising the castle. By then he had married Mary Croker, daughter of John Croker of Battisford, Gloucestershire; by 1623 they had a one-year-old son, Robert *Pye, and three daughters, and at least one more son and a daughter followed. Pye proved able to arrange advantageous matches for the three daughters who survived to adulthood: in 1632 Anne married Edward, son and heir of Sir Robert *Phelips of Montacute, Somerset, carrying with her a portion of £3000; Dorothy married Edward Poole of Kemble, Wiltshire, in 1638; and Mary married in 1641 George *Speke of White Lackington, Somerset, whose wardship Pye had earlier bought for £1800 [*see* Speke, Mary]. His youngest son, who died in 1660, Pye set up in business as a Levant merchant.

Pye sat in the parliaments of 1621 and 1624 as MP for Bath. The potential conflict between his financial responsibilities as a royal office-holder and his obligations as servant or client of the Villiers interest emerged openly in the parliaments of 1624–6. In the last parliament of King James's reign, that of 1624, he turned against his old colleague and now chief, the lord treasurer, the earl of Middlesex (as Cranfield had become), who was the victim of the new alliance between Buckingham and the Commons' majority in favour of war against Spain. The auditor appeared as one of the witnesses in the lord treasurer's impeachment. In 1625 Pye was elected MP for Ludgershall and in 1626 for Westminster (where Buckingham was steward). In these first two parliaments of Charles I he defended his master, as in turn relations deteriorated between the Commons and Buckingham, although in 1627 Sir James Whitelocke privately praised Pye's conduct in connection with his disapproval of the then lord treasurer. In September of that year Pye, appalled by the disastrous financial and political consequences of the forced loan, advised his patron that the regime should make 'some speedy accommodation of this loan, for nothing pleaseth so long as this is on foot' (Cust, 71). In the election of 1628 Buckingham was unable to place Pye as MP for Westminster for a second time. In a tumultuous election, one newsletter reported, 'when Sir Robert Pye's party cried, "A Pye, a Pye! a Pye!" the adverse party would cry "A pudding! a pudding! a pudding!" and others "A lie! a lie! a lie!"', and he was beaten by over 1000 votes by his 'patriot' opponents and forced to find a seat in the small Cornish borough of Grampound (T. Birch, ed., *The Court and Times of Charles the First*, 2 vols., 1848, 1.327). In the parliament of 1628—when his colleague, the senior revenue auditor of the upper exchequer, was savagely attacked, expelled from the house and committed to the Tower of London—Pye's defence of Buckingham was limited to assuring the Commons that it was the favourite's mother and not his wife who was a recusant Catholic. Otherwise he tended to speak on financial technicalities. He was, however, extremely active in his capacity as an executor after Buckingham's assassination. Indeed, as late as 1638, the lord deputy of Ireland, Sir Thomas Wentworth (later first earl of Strafford) was strongly critical of him for putting the interests of the Villiers family before those of the crown, in connection with the Irish customs revenues.

As against this, Pye seems to have worked hard—or got others to do so—in preparing the revenue and expenditure balances and averages of 1635 (covering the years from 1631) and of 1636–9; and he appears to have set about the same process for the reconstructed administration of 1641. Pye's very lukewarm support for the parliamentarian side may have owed more to his determination to retain his office than to any principled convictions. More than once he was saved from serious trouble only by his connections by marriage with John Hampden, whose daughter Anne had married his son Robert. None the less the king did summon the officers of the exchequer to join him in Oxford; Pye's colleague, who was also his 'comptroller' and administrative rival, the clerk of the pells, obeyed this call. So there were two lower exchequers of receipt, in Westminster and in Oxford, during 1643–6, although a large proportion of parliament's revenues came in through various *ad hoc* treasuries in the City of London, bypassing the exchequer altogether.

Pye's own estate lay in disputed territory which changed hands at least twice. Having been captured by the cavaliers, Faringdon Castle was virtually destroyed in a siege by Pye's own party. More positive evidence for his religious commitment is found in his membership (with his boyhood friend Sir Robert Harley) of a small committee to oversee the destruction of crucifixes and images in the captured royal regalia.

Pye was elected to the Long Parliament in December 1640 in a by-election at Woodstock. Not surprisingly he was among those members secluded at Pride's Purge in December 1648. His record as an MP, especially in the Long Parliament, suggests someone extremely active, and useful to the house, but not of major political importance. He seems to have taken no part in public life under the Commonwealth, but when the exchequer was re-established under the protectorate he failed to regain his old post as auditor, having to wait for this until the Restoration, when he protested, perhaps predictably, that he had never really been a parliamentarian at all. Pye's career epitomizes the interactions between the obligations of patron and client and the public service under the old administrative system. He died at Westminster on 20 May 1662. His will suggests considerable wealth but not vast affluence. The Berkshire estate went to the elder surviving son, Robert. The younger, John, inherited properties that Pye had bought in Staffordshire and Derbyshire which formed an estate substantial enough to support the baronetcy that he acquired in 1665.   G. E. AYLMER

Sources G. E. Aylmer, *The king's servants: the civil service of Charles I, 1625–1642* (1961); rev. edn (1974) • G. E. Aylmer, 'The officers of the exchequer, 1625–1642', *Essays in the economic and social history of Tudor and Stuart England in honour of R. H. Tawney*, ed. P. J. Fisher (1961), 164–81 • G. E. Aylmer, *The state's servants: the civil service of the English republic, 1649–1660* (1973) • HoP, *Commons, 1604–29* [draft] • HoP, *Commons, 1640–60* [draft] • C. J. R. [C. J. Robinson], 'Some memorials of the family of Pye', *Herald and Genealogist*, 5 (1870), 130–39 • J. Maclean and W. C. Heane, eds., *The visitation of the county of Gloucester taken in the year 1623*, Harleian Society, 21 (1885), 48 • W. H. Rylands, ed., *The four visitations of Berkshire*, 1, Harleian Society, 56 (1907), 270 • H. A. C. Sturgess, ed., *Register of admissions to the Honourable Society of the Middle Temple, from the fifteenth century to the year 1944*, 1 (1949) • Keeler, *Long Parliament* • will, PRO, PROB 11/308, sig. 70 • M. W. Helms, L. Naylor, and G. Jagger, 'Pye, Sir Robert', HoP, *Commons, 1660–90* • J. P. Ferris and B. D. Henning, 'Phelips (Phillips), Edward I', HoP, *Commons, 1660–90* • B. D. Henning, 'Poole, Edward', HoP, *Commons, 1660–90* • I. Cassidy and B. D. Henning, 'Speke, Sir George', HoP, *Commons, 1660–90* • R. P. Cust, *The forced loan and English politics, 1626–1628* (1987) • G. E. Aylmer, 'Studies in the institutions and personnel of the English central administration, 1625–42', DPhil diss., U. Oxf., 1954, 849–70

Archives Sheff. Arch., papers relating to affairs of fourth earl of Pembroke

Wealth at death considerable affluence but not vast wealth: will, PRO, PROB 11/308, sig. 70

Pye, Sir Robert (*c*.1622–1701), army officer, was the son of Sir Robert *Pye (*bap.* 1585, *d.* 1662) of Faringdon Manor, Berkshire, and his wife, Mary Croker. His father was a remembrancer of the exchequer from 1618, MP for Woodstock in the Long Parliament, and a parliamentary advocate of peace with the king at the beginning of the civil war. At that juncture, his son, who had married Anne Hampden (*b.* 1625), daughter of John Hampden, raised a troop of horse for the earl of Essex, and his parliamentarian military career began: he was wounded when Cirencester was captured in September 1643. In the February 1644 reorganization of Essex's army Pye's was designated one of the six cavalry regiments, and in June of the same year he was in command of the surrender of Taunton Castle to parliament. In February 1645 he was sent to Buckinghamshire to suppress expected disorder, and by March he was commanding three troops under Cromwell to march on Coventry and assist Sir William Brereton. In that month, however, Pye's military career began to run into the political shoals of intra-parliamentarian conflict. Despite his bellicose record, he was politically associated with moderate and Presbyterian parliamentarianism, and his father attached to the peace party. Hence the action of parliament, during debates over the formation of the New Model Army, of securing a regimental command for Pye in place of the radical Nathaniel Rich was a setback for the party of all-out war with the king.

In May 1645 the committee of both kingdoms regrouped 900 troops in Buckinghamshire under Pye's command. The recipient of warm commendations from the committee ('very ready to go upon the service … very great readiness and much affection to prefer the public service to any particular interest of his own' (*CSP dom.*, 1644–5, 503, 504), he was ordered northwards, with a group of cavalry commanders, to assist the Scots against the king. That was how he became involved, displaying 'great valour' (*VCH Leicestershire*, 2.115) in a parliamentarian disaster, the failed defence of Leicester, which fell to crown forces in May 1645. Pye was captured on 31 May, though subsequently paroled, on 4 June, and exchanged for a royalist officer on the 20th. His reputation with the committee of both kingdoms reached new heights, arrangements were made to reimburse him for losses, he was entrusted with the conveyance of money and recruits to Portsmouth, and brought reinforcements from Reading to assist Fairfax in the siege of Sherborne in August 1645. He led his regiment in the siege of Bristol in September, and in May 1646 was sent by Fairfax to command the siege of Faringdon, Berkshire, which fell on 24 June.

In 1646 with peacetime legal conditions returning, soldiers such as Pye were losing immunity from prosecutions for damages done during the hostilities and he was sued for a horse he had commandeered in Reading. However, a further high point in his career came in 1647, when a section of his regiment kept guard on Charles I at Holdenby House. If a malicious story from Edmund Ludlow has any credit, the full extent of Pye's political conservatism became evident when he 'supplied the place of a querry, riding bare before [Charles I] when he rode abroad' (*Memoirs of Edmund Ludlow*, 1.151). Given his conservative political profile as a 'moderate Presbyterian' (Kishlansky, 162–3), it is not surprising that Pye was targeted as an ally in the programme of the Presbyterian politician Denzil Holles to disband the regiments not needed for service in Ireland, thereby neutralizing the army radicals. Creating division in his own regiment, the bulk of which mutinied and joined the main body of the army, Pye was vilified by the majority of the forces for willingness to accept, without redress of grievances, the proposed package of large-scale demobilization, with Irish service. Pye's personal regimental following were the first units to arrive in Westminster in June 1647, having resolved to volunteer for Ireland. In August they were instructed to prepare the defence of the capital against the threatened army takeover. When the army took possession of the capital, involving the deaths of seven of Pye's men at Deptford, he secured a pass from Fairfax to go into exile, probably in Holland. This, for Pye, was the low point of a career in which the complexities of politics tended to prove his downfall. The pamphlet *A Speedy Hue and Crie* of 1647, attacking him and other refugee officers as renegades, added vilification to his defeat.

Nevertheless, with the gradual return of civilian government in the 1650s, Pye represented his native Berkshire in the parliaments of 1654 and 1658. When, on 25 January 1660, he presented a petition, which arose out of a Berkshire county meeting, for the return of the 1648 'secluded members' (of whom his father was one) who were thought likely to favour a royal restoration, his political judgement was faulty in moving too far ahead of events. He was imprisoned, and his case awoke a constitutional issue over parliament's refusal to dispute the judgement of a lower court, the upper bench, in favour of his habeas corpus. By February, however, as George Monck's ascendancy nudged developments towards a restoration and with the secluded members admitted on 21 February, Pye was freed, and on 2 March his prosecution was expunged from the record. He was a member of the convention and, although he can be classed with the 'Presbyterian' grouping, he played no recorded active role.

Although his contribution to the Restoration was courageous rather than creative, Pye won royal gratitude for his role. By August 1661 he was an auditor of the exchequer under the lord treasurer Southampton, and on 22 December 1662 a royal warrant was issued to give him a baronetcy, though this does not seem to have resulted in the assumption of that honour. Further evidence of Charles II's favour, however, came on 22 June 1670, when, 'of assured loyalty and faithfulness', he was exempted from the order of 10 June expelling all officers 'of the late usurped power' from London (*CSP dom.*, 1670, 267, 292). Pye was otherwise out of public life until the revolution, when, in December 1688, he accompanied William of Orange on his way to London. Recognition came towards the end of his life when, in 1700, he acted as deputy lieutenant for Berkshire. He and his wife, Anne, had two sons, Hampden and Edmund. Pye died in 1701 at Faringdon. He was a brave and able soldier, a military man passionately, even rashly, attached to civilian government but sometimes out of his depth in politics and for the last forty years of his life generally keeping clear of their currents.

C. H. FIRTH, *rev.* MICHAEL MULLETT

Sources *CSP dom.*, 1644–7; 1661–2; 1690–91 · C. H. Firth and G. Davies, *The regimental history of Cromwell's army*, 2 vols. (1940) · M. A. Kishlansky, *The rise of the New Model Army* (1979) · I. Gentles, *The New Model Army in England, Ireland, and Scotland, 1645–1653* (1992) · J. H. Plumb, 'Political history, 1530–1885', *VCH Leicestershire*, 2.102–34 · *The memoirs of Edmund Ludlow*, ed. C. H. Firth, 2 vols. (1894) · G. F. T. Jones, 'The composition and leadership of the Presbyterian party in the convention', *EngHR*, 79 (1964), 307–54 · M. A. Mullett, 'Pye, Sir Robert', Greaves & Zaller, *BDBR*, 3.69–70
Archives BL, letters etc.
Likenesses W. Hogarth, oils, *c*.1700–1799, Marble Hill House, London

Pye, Thomas (*d.* **1609/10**), Church of England clergyman, was born at Darlaston near Wednesbury in Staffordshire. According to Anthony Wood, Pye was 'educated for the most part in logicals and philosophicals in Merton college, [Oxford], of which he became one of the chaplains in 1581, being then esteemed among the learned to be one of them'; he graduated BTh on 21 June 1585, winning a reputation as 'an eminent linguist, excellent in sacred chronology, in ecclesiastical histories and polemical divinity' (Wood, *Ath. Oxon.*, 59). He translated as *Solomons Sermon* (1586) a work by the catechist Antonio del Corro, whom he praised highly.

From 1577 until 1589 Pye was rector of Newton Toney in Wiltshire, from where evidence emerged of his sympathy with puritan positions; in 1584–5 it was reported that he did not wear a surplice and refused to baptize with the sign of the cross. In 1586 he was instituted as rector of Earnley-with-Almodington, Sussex. On 5 December 1587 he was collated to the prebend of Selsey in the diocese of Chichester. About 1590 he became vicar and schoolmaster of Bexhill near Hastings in Sussex. For many years during his mastership, Pye was also rector of nearby Brightling, from where he reported in 1603, that 'there is no man or woman recusant or backwards in religion and there is none that doth not receive the communion orderly' (*VCH Sussex*, 9.228). Pye was sufficiently reconciled to the establishment to preface his book *An Hourglasse Containing a Computation from the Beginning of Time to Christ by X Articles*

(1597) to Archbishop Whitgift, but advised the primate of his alarm at the prospects for godly protestantism, during the 'very dogdaies of the church and religion, which now lie together in a desperate paroxism and most dangerous fitte, jointly shaken and assaulted by popery and atheism'.

In 1602–3 Pye became engaged in a controversy with Bishop John Howson of Oxford. Pye thought it lawful for a man to divorce an adulterous wife, and then to remarry, and in January 1603 he signed *Epistola ad ornatissimum virum D. Johannem Housonum*, a short refutation of theses on such matters which Howson had published the previous year. Pye also prepared a much fuller statement of his position and sent it to John Rainolds, president of Corpus Christi College, who in 1597 had set down similar views on the issue (issued posthumously in 1609). Rainolds replied that he liked Pye's work and wished it could be published, but pointed out that when he had sought permission to publish his own views on the same subject, Archbishop Whitgift had given his opinion that this was inappropriate owing to the dangerous freedoms they encouraged. Rainolds counselled against Pye's explicit defence of his 1597 views, and advised against the violence of some of his strictures against Howson. He proffered detailed and sympathetic suggestions for toning down the book for publication. Whether or not Pye took the advice, his work was refused a licence. A Latin account of the controversy appears, with Rainolds's letter appended, in *Uxore dissmissa … tertia thesis Johannis Howsoni* (1606).

In 1606, when Pye returned to Darlaston to visit his family, 'some of his servants went to ring in the old steeple, which was of wood, and much decayed, so that their lives were in danger'; Pye therefore 'proffered the town, that in case they would be at the charge of bringing stone, he would find workmanship, and build them a tower, which accordingly he did' (Plot, 297). On the outside of the tower an inscription was cut—'Pietati et Priis. Vive pius, et moriere pius'—a pun on the benefactor's name, which may be translated 'By piety and pious deeds, Pious live and pious die'. Pye died three years later at Bexhill. In his will dated 20 December 1609 he desired that his body might be buried in the schoolhouse at Bexhill, which he had recently had repaired and repaved. He mentioned three sons, Nicholas, George, and Hennege, all under age, and a brother, Richard Pye of Porlaston, Staffordshire. The inclusion of Sir Nicholas Parker and Thomas Pelham esquire among his overseers hints at his patrons. The will was proved by his widow and executor, Ellynor or Elianore (*née* Hennege?) on 20 March 1610.   STEPHEN WRIGHT

Sources Foster, *Alum. Oxon.* · Wood, *Ath. Oxon.*, new edn, 2.59 · *Uxore dissmissa … tertia thesis Johannis Howsoni* (1606) · *VCH Sussex*, vol. 9 · *VCH Wiltshire*, vol. 15 · S. Shaw, *The history and antiquities of Staffordshire*, ed. M. W. Greenslade and G. C. Baugh, 3/2 (1976) · R. Plot, *The natural history of Stafford-shire* (1686) · *Fasti Angl., 1541–1857*, [Chichester] · L. Stone, *Road to divorce: England, 1530–1987*, new edn (1992) · J. Rainolds, *A defence of the judgement of the reformed churches: that a man may lawfullie not onlie put awaie his wife for her adulterie, but also marrie another* (1609) · W. Hackwood, *A history of Darlaston* (1887) · will, PRO, PROB 11/115, fol. 164

Wealth at death no value given: will, PRO, PROB 11/115, fol. 164

Pye, Sir Thomas (1708/9–1785), naval officer, was the son of Henry Pye (1683–1749) and his wife, Anne, *née* Bathurst. Through his mother he was related to Allen, first Earl Bathurst, a political strength which ensured peacetime commands and steady promotion during a long and undistinguished career. Pye passed his lieutenant's examination on 12 June 1734, his age then being given as twenty-five (PRO, ADM 107/3, p. 252), and on 18 April 1735 he was promoted third lieutenant of the *Preston* (48 guns, Captain Charles Cotterell), cruising in home waters. He transferred with his captain to the *Ripon* (60 guns), based at the Tagus. For the next three years he served in the *Warwick* (60 guns) in the Mediterranean before, on 13 April 1741, he was given command of the newly built *Seaford* (24 guns). Stationed in home waters for a year, the ship then went to the Mediterranean under Admiral Thomas Mathews, who sent her to the Adriatic to disrupt supplies going to the Spanish army in Italy. In August 1744 Mathews appointed Pye to the *Norfolk* (80 guns), which remained on the station under Vice-Admiral Henry Medley, supporting the Austrian army off the south of France. Pye brought the ship home in March 1748. At the peace he was given the *Norwich* (50 guns), going to North America, and in the following year he commissioned the *Humber* (44 guns), cruising to the west coast of Africa. He sailed for Nova Scotia in the *Gosport* (44 guns) in June 1751, returned the same year, and in February 1752 was appointed to the *Advice* (50 guns), with a broad pennant as commander-in-chief in the Leeward Islands.

It was at this point that Pye's hasty temperament caused a dispute which nearly ended his career. In October 1755 he was superseded by Commodore Thomas Frankland but Pye, according to Frankland, 'excessively angry', kept his broad pennant flying (PRO, ADM 1/306, Frankland to John Clevland, 8 Oct 1755). Frankland, reprimanding Pye for not obeying a senior officer, also charged him with financial irregularities, interfering with the purchase of naval stores, and with damaging the *Advice* by removing parts of her timbers for an unnecessary survey. Pye returned home, claiming that he would not receive a fair hearing in the Leeward Islands. Since he should have been tried there, the Admiralty at first did nothing, though Pye was eventually tried by court martial in the first four days of March 1758. He was reprimanded for the lesser charges and was lucky to escape the charge of disobeying a senior officer. Lord Anson and Edward Boscawen were at sea at the time, and Pye was able to ensure leniency by bringing political pressure to bear on the civilian members of the Admiralty board (NMM, papers of Sir Gilbert Elliot, ELL/9, Thomas Pye, 'An account of my conduct'). On 5 July 1758 he was promoted rear-admiral, but he saw no active service during the Seven Years' War.

In 1762 Pye was made commander-in-chief at Plymouth and promoted vice-admiral (21 October). From 1766 to 1769 he was again made commander-in-chief of the Leeward Islands, flying his flag first in the *Lark* (32 guns) and then the *Chatham* (50 guns). On his return Pye made a short and unremarkable foray into politics, being elected as government candidate for Rochester on 9 May 1771. He appears never to have spoken in the Commons and was defeated at the election on 7 October 1774. Philip Stephens, the secretary to the Admiralty, remarked to Lord Hardwicke that the voters of Rochester 'had conceived an utter aversion to our Admiral Sir Thomas Pye, and I find they would have taken anybody who offered himself in preference to him' (BL, Add. MS 35612, fol. 114). From 9 May 1771 to 18 May 1774 he had been commander-in-chief at Portsmouth, during which time the king had reviewed the fleet at Spithead. On 24 June 1773 he had knighted Pye on the quarterdeck of the *Barfleur* (98 guns) and at the same time ordered his promotion to admiral.

Pye served as commander-in-chief at Portsmouth for most of the American War of Independence, taking up his command on 27 May 1777. He presided at the celebrated court martial of Admiral Augustus Keppel in Portsmouth, in January 1779, which he tried to avoid by pleading ill health. He was made lieutenant-general of marines on 26 September 1780 and retired on 31 March 1783. Pye died on 26 December 1785 at his house on Suffolk Street, London. His wife, details of whom are unknown, had died in 1762; the couple had one daughter, Mary. Pye's will also reveals that for seventeen years he had a mistress, Anna Maria *Bennett, wife of Thomas Bennett, customs officer. At his death Pye left his Suffolk Street residence to Anna Maria and forgave the sizeable debt owed to him by her husband; this relationship produced at least two children, including Harriet [*see* Esten, Harriet Pye].

Contemporary opinion of Pye's abilities (he was known by junior officers as Goose Pye) is uniformly harsh, while he has been described by a modern authority as 'something of a naval grotesque who aroused mingled amusement and contempt' (Rodger, 76). He was unable to express himself clearly on paper and his handwriting was awkward: when a vice-admiral he wrote to Lord Sandwich, enjoining the first lord

> not to scrutinize too close either to the spelling or the grammatical part as I allow myself to be no proficient in either. I had the mortification to be neglected in my education, went to sea at 14 without any, and a man of war was my university. (*Private Papers*, 1.36)

In this and in many other ways Pye was not a typical mid-eighteenth-century naval officer. ROGER KNIGHT

Sources DNB · N. A. M. Rodger, *The wooden world: an anatomy of the Georgian navy* (1986) · J. Brooke, 'Pye, Thomas', HoP, *Commons, 1754–90* · *The private papers of John, earl of Sandwich*, ed. G. R. Barnes and J. H. Owen, 4 vols., Navy RS, 69, 71, 75, 78 (1932–8) · Pitcairn-Jones, 'Ship histories', NMM [card file] · D. Syrett and R. L. DiNardo, *The commissioned sea officers of the Royal Navy, 1660–1815*, rev. edn, Occasional Publications of the Navy RS, 1 (1994) · NMM, Elliot papers, ELL/9 · admiralty secretary in-letters, PRO, ADM 1/306 · P. Mackesy, *The war for America, 1775–1783* (1964) · will, PRO, PROB 11/1136, fol. 321 · PRO, ADM 107/3, 252
Archives City Westm. AC, account books, corresp. with his mistress | NMM, letters to Lord Sandwich · PRO, admiralty secretary in-letters, ADM 1 · Warks. CRO, corresp. with Lord Denbigh
Wealth at death residence on Suffolk Street, London: will, PRO, PROB 11/1136, fol. 321

Pye, Sir Walter (bap. **1571**, d. **1635**), lawyer, was born at The Mynde in Much Dewchurch, Herefordshire, and baptized there on 1 October 1571, the first child of Roger Pye (d.

1591) and his wife, Bridget (d. 1624), daughter of Thomas Kyrle of Walford, Herefordshire. He was admitted a commoner at St John's College, Oxford, in 1585, and entered New Inn in 1589. Transferring to the Middle Temple the following year, he was called to the bar in 1597, was Lent reader in 1618, and treasurer in 1626–7. On 22 July 1602 he married Joan, daughter of William Rudhall of Rudhall, Herefordshire, and his wife, Margaret; they had fifteen children. She died on 10 September 1625 and on 31 October 1628 he married Hester (d. *c*.1643), daughter of John Ireland and widow of Ellis Crispe, alderman of London; she died about 1643.

The family of Pye or Apie (that is ap Hugh) had been minor gentry in Herefordshire from at least the fifteenth century, but Walter Pye's fortune was small and no match for his appetite for land purchases. He seems first to have sought advancement by attaching himself to Charles Howard, earl of Nottingham: it was probably through his influence as high steward of the borough that he was elected MP for Scarborough in 1597. Afterwards he built up his practice as a lawyer, and it was another twenty years before his next preferment. He and his younger brother Robert *Pye (bap. 1585, d. 1662) attached themselves to George Villiers, marquess of Buckingham, probably as legal and financial adviser respectively, and through the favourite Walter Pye was made chief justice in Glamorgan, Brecknockshire, and Radnorshire in February 1617. In February 1621 he was knighted and made attorney of the court of wards and liveries. He sat in parliament for Brecon borough in 1621, 1624, and 1625, and for Herefordshire in 1626 and 1628–9. In both 1626 and 1628 he was also elected for Brecon; on the latter occasion he surrendered his seat to his eldest son, also Walter (1610–1659).

Pye was recognized by his contemporaries as a learned and ingenious but unscrupulous lawyer, which made his talents both feared and much demanded. In 1607 there were complaints in Herefordshire of his 'underhand dealing' (BL, Add. MS 11042, fols. 11–12) and in 1631 a Welsh victim of one of his judgments tried to run him through with a sword. Criticism of his attorneyship of the court of wards mounted towards the end of his life. In 1633 it was said that he 'does now what he pleaseth' and that a new master of the court was needed to restrain his power (Birch, 2.229). Later there were allegations that he suppressed the evidence of witnesses and overruled and directed juries. Sir Richard Hutton called him 'more than ordinarily covetous' and reckoned that he 'advanced the profit' of the court of wards 'excessively', getting thereby a great estate and preferring his children 'in ample manner' (CUL, MS 6863, fol. 81*r*). Nevertheless, his income was probably never more than £2000 per annum. Pye died on 25 December 1635 and was buried in Much Dewchurch on 9 January 1636; at his death he was mocked as 'the devil's Christmas Pye' (Bodl. Oxf., MS Tanner 465, fol. 62*r*).

IAN ATHERTON

Sources Pye estate book, Sheff. Arch., Elmhirst MS, 1331 · parish register, Much Dewchurch, 1558–1745, Herefs. RO, AJ25/1 · C. J. R. [C. J. Robinson], 'Some memorials of the family of Pye', *Herald and*

Genealogist, 5 (1870), 130–39 • G. E. Aylmer, *The king's servants: the civil service of Charles I, 1625–1642*, rev. edn (1974), 308–10 • C. J. Robinson, *A history of the mansions and manors of Herefordshire* (1873), 87–8 • C. T. Martin, ed., *Minutes of parliament of the Middle Temple*, 4 vols. (1904–5) • H. E. Bell, *An introduction to the history and records of the court of wards and liveries* (1953) • BL, Add. MS 11042, fols. 11–12 • *Diary of John Rous*, ed. M. A. E. Green, CS, 66 (1856), 62 • [T. Birch and R. F. Williams], eds., *The court and times of Charles the First*, 2 vols. (1848) • *CSP dom.*, addenda, 1625–49, 496 • CUL, MS 6863, fol. 81r • G. Radcliffe, *The earl of Strafforde's letters and dispatches, with an essay towards his life*, ed. W. Knowler, 2 vols. (1739) • Bodl. Oxf., MS Tanner 465, fol. 62r • Bodl. Oxf., MSS Bankes 14/8, 62/18 • *Liber famelicus of Sir James Whitelocke, a judge of the court of king's bench in the reigns of James I and Charles I*, ed. J. Bruce, CS, old ser., 70 (1858), 54

Archives NL Wales, Mynde Park deeds and documents • Sheff. Arch., Elmhirst papers

Likenesses tomb effigy, *c*.1625, Much Dewchurch church, Herefordshire

Wealth at death approx. £1500 p.a. from land (possibly £2000 p.a.): Aylmer, *King's servants*; Garrard to Wentworth, 8 Jan 1636, in {earl of Strafford}, *Earl of Strafforde's letters and dispatches*, vol. 1, p. 506

Pye, William George (1869–1949), scientific instrument and radio manufacturer, was born at Battersea, London, on 27 October 1869, the eldest son and the third of the eight children of William Thomas Pye and his wife, Elizabeth. Trained as a scientific instrument maker by his father, who was associated with the Cambridge Scientific Instrument Company, he joined the staff of the Cavendish Laboratory at Cambridge University at the age of twenty-three. In the same year, 1892, he married Annie Eliza, the daughter of John Atkins, a joiner. They had four children: William John (who died in infancy), Donald Walter, Marjorie Irene, and Harold John [*see below*], who later assisted in his father's business.

Pye started his own company in 1896. He worked at first on a part-time basis assisted by his wife, his father, and his brothers Henry and Frederick. In 1899 he left the Cavendish Laboratory to devote himself full-time to the business, by then known as W. G. Pye & Co. The company prospered, moving into larger premises in 1899 and again in 1913.

The outbreak of war in 1914 brought a sudden large demand for optical and electrical instruments for the armed services. In addition to its normal ranges of equipment, the company produced such specialized items as precision gunsights and the first Aldis signalling lamps. Pye's staff more than doubled to meet these orders during the war years.

After the war the market contracted almost as quickly as it had grown. In 1922 the company sought new business, and produced panels which could be connected together to make various items of radio apparatus. Intended as teaching aids for schools and colleges, they were soon popular with radio hobbyists as well. After the formation of the BBC at the end of the year, the company decided to produce complete radio receivers. However, its sets of the '500' series, though well made, were less sensitive than those of its competitors, and consequently unpopular.

William's son, **Harold John Pye** (1901–1986), born at 19 Humberstone Road, Chesterton, Cambridgeshire, on 27 November 1901, joined the company after graduating from St John's College, Cambridge, in 1923, and was made a partner in 1924. He was an energetic salesman and a skilled engineer. His receivers of the '700' series, designed to meet customers' needs, were the first really successful Pye sets. With careful attention to the styling of the receivers' cabinets, demand increased rapidly. The radio side of the company expanded to occupy the whole of the original factory site by 1927; the instrument business was again obliged to move into new premises. Harold's former tutor, Sir Edward Appleton, was technical adviser to the company at this period.

Apparently disturbed by the dominance of what he had intended to be no more than a subsidiary, William Pye sold the radio business to Charles Orr Stanley in 1929. It continued to trade under the name of Pye Radio Ltd at first, then in 1937 changed to Pye Ltd. The original company, W. G. Pye & Co., continued under William's leadership, successfully surviving the depression of the 1930s.

William Pye retired and sold his interest in the business to Harold in 1936. He moved to Bexhill, Sussex, where he was able to indulge his interest in sailing. He died at his home, Stepaside, 5 Beaulieu Road, on 13 October 1949.

Harold Pye ran the company from 1936 to 1947, concentrating again on the design and manufacture of military equipment during the Second World War. He then agreed to sell the company to Pye Ltd. The radio and instrumentation businesses were reunited but no longer controlled by the Pye family. Having ensured that his employees' careers were adequately protected, Pye retired at the early age of forty-six.

Pye had married Jennie, the daughter of Clowes Garner Milson, on 1 March 1927. They had no children. After Jennie's death in 1948 he moved to Burnham-on-Crouch in Essex and started a second career as a farmer. He remarried on 20 December 1955; his second wife was Edith Pinney, *née* Flight, a widow, who brought him two stepchildren, Janet and John. Edith died in 1969; Harold then sold his farm and, like his father, devoted his time to sailing. He died at 40 Westerfield Road, Ipswich, Suffolk, on 20 January 1986.   ROWLAND F. POCOCK

Sources G. Bussey, 'Pye, William George', *DBB* • G. Bussey, 'Pye, Harold John', *DBB* • K. Geddes and G. Bussey, *The setmakers: a history of the radio and television industry* (1991) • G. Bussey, *The story of Pye wireless* (1979) • *CGPLA Eng. & Wales* (1950) • *CGPLA Eng. & Wales* (1986) [Harold John Pye] • b. cert. [Harold John Pye] • m. certs. [Harold John Pye] • d. cert. • d. cert. [Harold John Pye]

Archives priv. coll.

Likenesses photographs, priv. coll.

Wealth at death £46,049 19s. 6d.: probate, 9 Jan 1950, *CGPLA Eng. & Wales* • £145,313; Harold John Pye: probate, 7 Oct 1986, *CGPLA Eng. & Wales*

Pyel, John (*c*.1315–1382), mayor of London, was probably born in Irthlingborough, Northamptonshire, in the second decade of the fourteenth century. He was descended from a family of bondsmen of Peterborough Abbey, and his father, also John, was a minor landholder in the area.

His younger brother, Henry, was educated at Oxford and went on to a career in the church, becoming archdeacon of Northampton. John the younger, however, was sent to London to be apprenticed to trade. He was evidently successful, and his first appearance in the records, in 1345, shows him lending the sum of £40. The following year he was a commissioner appointed to sell off or lease the property of non-resident alien clergy in the diocese of London, for whose profits he was to account to the king.

Pyel was a supporter of the syndicate of customs farmers headed by Walter Chiriton, which ultimately collapsed in 1349, and Pyel's involvement in questionable practices before the collapse led to his trial and imprisonment for debt. He was bailed by his friends and associates, John Wesenham and Adam Fraunceys, in the spring of 1350, and shortly afterwards appears to have undertaken some diplomatic service for the king in Spain. Besides dealing in wool Pyel seems to have been specifically concerned with trade in the east midlands. He was connected with John Garlekmongere, member of a prominent mercantile family of Northampton, and in 1370 was appointed to a commission which had been established to inquire into the construction of new mills and ponds which were blocking the passage of merchandise along the River Ouse between Huntingdon and St Ives. In the same year he was granted a licence to buy and ship cereals from the east midlands and Sussex to London.

Pyel was also a financier, but apparently not on the same scale as some of his contemporaries. He lent to religious houses, fellow Londoners, and the rural gentry, but only much later in his career to the crown. Many of his loans to the gentry, especially those living in Northamptonshire, were made with the intention of, or at least in the hope of, acquiring land. Some landholders, like Sir Thomas Wake of Blisworth, became indebted at the time of the Calais expedition of 1346–7, when large sums had to be spent on equipment for the campaign. Sir Thomas died while on service, and his manor of Cransley was evidently insufficient to redeem his debts, for it passed to Pyel on the eve of the black death in July 1348. Cransley was the first substantial estate in Northamptonshire which Pyel obtained, and its acquisition may well have been fortuitous. His other lands, principally the two fees of Irthlingborough and the manors of Sudborough, Cranford, and Woodford, were acquired during the following two decades from landlords who found themselves impoverished in the aftermath of the black death, or at least unable to keep up estates in which they themselves were not resident. By 1370 Pyel had carved out for himself a coherent landed estate in Northamptonshire centred on Irthlingborough, his birthplace.

It was about this date that Pyel turned his attention back to London. Despite his relative affluence and status he had held no major office in the city. He had been a common councilman and MP in 1361, but it was not until 1369 that he was elected alderman of Castle Baynard and sheriff, and he became mayor in 1372. He bought a house in Broad Street from Adam Fraunceys in 1374. His connection with the court party also dates from this period. He was involved in diplomatic activities in Flanders between 1371 and 1375, and was associated with John of Gaunt. In 1372 and 1374 he made two large loans to the crown, the second of them with Richard Lyons, a London merchant with close court connections. This loan of 20,000 marks was repaid as £20,000, a profit to the creditors of 10,000 marks, or 50 per cent interest. During the Good Parliament it was cited as an example of the corruption of Lyons, who with other members of the court faction was being impeached by the Commons. Pyel, who by foresight or good fortune was sitting in this parliament, successfully managed to distance himself from Lyons and so escaped censure. Nevertheless he was forced to resign his aldermanry in 1376 under the new regulations governing the election of aldermen in London, and although re-elected in 1378, he apparently left the city shortly afterwards and retired to Irthlingborough. In his will, dated 1379, he gave orders for a college to be established at St Peter's Church in Irthlingborough (where he was later buried), an act of piety which his widow successfully completed. He died in 1382 and was survived by his wife, Joan (d. 1412), and his second son, Nicholas (d. 1406).　　　　　　　STEPHEN O'CONNOR

Sources S. J. O'Connor, ed., *A calendar of the cartularies of John Pyel and Adam Fraunceys*, CS, 5th ser., 2 (1993) · S. J. O'Connor, 'Finance, diplomacy and politics: royal service by two London merchants in the reign of Edward III', *Historical Research*, 67 (1994), 18–39 · S. J. O'Connor, 'Adam Fraunceys and John Pyel: perceptions of status among merchants in fourteenth-century London', *Trade, devotion and governance: papers in later medieval history* [Manchester 1989], ed. D. J. Clayton and others (1994), 17–35 · S. J. O'Connor, 'Joan Pyel', *Medieval London widows, 1300–1500*, ed. C. M. Barron and A. F. Sutton (1994), 71–6 · CLRO, Husting rolls, 110/117 · episcopal register 12, Lincs. Arch., Lincoln diocesan archives, fols. 244v–245v
Archives Coll. Arms, cartulary, Vincent 64
Wealth at death see wills, register of John Buckingham, Lincs. Arch., Episcopal register XII, fols. 244v–245v; CLRO, HR 110/117

Pygott, Richard (d. 1549), composer and church musician, is of unknown parentage and background. He spent more than thirty years in two of the foremost choral foundations of early Tudor England, first as master of Cardinal Wolsey's household chapel choir and later as a gentleman of Henry VIII's royal household chapel. He was in Wolsey's employment by January 1517, when a royal pardon for unauthorized possession of a crossbow and handgun describes him as a servant of the cardinal of York living in Westminster. His position in the household is not specified; presumably he was either a singer in the choir or already its director; an inventory of Wolsey's goods compiled during the 1520s mentions 'a fedderbedde bought for Pygoote maister of the children' in December 1517. Wolsey's choir so prospered under Pygott's direction that it aroused the king's envy. In March 1518 Henry's secretary Richard Pace wrote requisitioning one of Wolsey's choristers on the grounds that the cardinal's choir was better than the king's. Shortly afterwards Pace thanked Wolsey for the chorister and remarked that 'Cornyshe [the master of the king's chapel] doies gretly laude & prayse the chylde … and doies in lyke maner extolle mr pygote for the techynge of hym' (PRO, SP 1/16, fol. 206v). Pygott continued to direct the choir until it was disbanded on Wolsey's death in 1530; he and the singers accompanied their master on embassies to France in 1521 and 1527, and must also have been among his retinue at the Field of Cloth of Gold in 1520.

Pygott's work with Wolsey's choir must have recommended him to the king; after the cardinal's demise he seems quickly to have found employment as a gentleman or singer in the royal household chapel. He first appears in this guise in an undated wages list assignable to about 1533–4, but he may have been appointed earlier: in October 1532 he received a corrody in Coggeshall Priory surrendered by another gentleman, and in April 1533 he obtained a canonry in the collegiate church of St Editha at Tamworth, whose prebends were habitually awarded to members of the king's chapel. Other grants during the 1530s and 1540s show that he continued to enjoy royal favour.

By 1545 Pygott may have been contemplating retirement: in November the cathedral authorities at Wells were instructed to allow him to reside upon his prebend there, and in the lay subsidy roll of April 1546 the £40 on which he was assessed is for the first time described as 'lands' rather than 'fee'. He seems, however, to have carried on living in London. His very informative will, dated 24 August 1549, details money gifts amounting to more than £120 (including a legacy of £2 to Thomas Tallis) and bequests of horses, clothes, and jewels. On 2 October he added a codicil mentioning 'the time of my sickness', and by 12 November, when the will was proved, he had died; payments to him from the court of augmentations ceased after November 1549. Thus he cannot be the Richard Pigot or Pigott to whom Princess Elizabeth made payments in December 1551 and January 1552.

Pygott's few extant compositions, most of which lack one or more voice parts, are polished, imaginative, and virtuosic enough to test even the first-rate choirs with which he worked. They include a *Missa veni sancte spiritus* for Whitsunday (one of the chief days in the royal court's liturgical calendar) and a huge and very elaborate setting of *Salve regina* (a Marian motive antiphon, used particularly during Lent). Single voices of several other works remain, among them an antiphon *Gaude pastore* to St Thomas of Canterbury, probably intended as a compliment to Wolsey. The only composition to survive complete is a devotional partsong *Quid petis O fili*, which continues a tradition established during Henry VII's reign. In *A Plaine and Easie Introduction to Practicall Musicke* (1597) Thomas Morley lists Pygott among the 'practicioners' consulted, and prints an extract from an unidentified composition by him.

NICK SANDON

Sources R. Pygott, *Missa veni sancte spiritus*, ed. N. Sandon (1993), ii–vii · R. Bowers, 'The cultivation and promotion of music in the household and orbit of Thomas Wolsey', *Cardinal Wolsey: church, state, and art*, ed. S. J. Gunn and P. G. Lindley (1991), 178–218 · A. Ashbee, ed., *Records of English court music*, 7 (1993) · F. L. Kisby, 'The royal household chapel in early Tudor London, 1485–1547', PhD diss., U. Lond., 1996 · PRO, SP 1/16, fol. 206v

Archives BL, Add. MS 31922 · BL, Add. MS 34191 · BL, Harley MS 1709 · CUL, Peterhouse MSS, 471–474
Wealth at death £120; plus horses, clothes, and jewels: will, 12 Nov 1549, PRO, PROB 11/32/42

Pyke, Magnus Alfred (1908–1992), food scientist, author, and broadcaster, was born on 29 December 1908 at 209 Gloucester Terrace, Paddington, London, the son of Robert Bond Pyke (d. 1924), wholesale confectionery manager, and his wife, Clara Hannah (*née* Lewis). He was educated at St Paul's School, London, and Macdonald College of McGill University in Montreal, where he studied agriculture. After seven years in Canada he graduated BSc in 1933 and returned to England where in 1934 he became chief chemist at Vitamins Ltd in Hammersmith, London. He remained with the firm until 1941, at the same time collaborating with Professor J. C. Drummond at University College, London, on vitamin research. This earned him a PhD in biochemistry in 1936. His marriage to Dorothea Mina Vaughan (1906/1907–1986), an accountant, on 23 August 1937 brought them a daughter, Bessie, and a son, John.

In 1941 Pyke joined Drummond, by then scientific adviser to the Ministry of Food, to study the nutritional effects of wartime food restrictions. His lectures on practical nutrition for those working in institutional catering were published as *The Manual of Nutrition* (1945) under the auspices of the Ministry of Food. This book was revised frequently by his successors and reprinted many times during his lifetime. After a brief sojourn during 1945–6 as nutritional adviser to the allied commission for Austria in Vienna, Pyke returned to the Ministry of Food as a principal scientific officer, continuing to work on institutional diets and to take an active interest in nutrition education.

Early in 1949 he joined the Distillers Company as deputy manager of its yeast research outstation, and he gained promotion to the position of manager of the Glenochil research station at Menstrie in Clackmannanshire in 1955. He held this position until he retired in 1973. Throughout his time in industry Pyke continued as an active member of a number of specialist scientific societies. These included the Society for Analytical Chemistry (vice-president 1959–61), the Society of Chemical Industry (council member 1967–9), the Nutrition Society (chairman of Scottish section 1954–5), the Institute of Biology (member of the council of the Scottish section 1959–62), and the Institute of Food Science and Technology of the UK (president 1969–71). He became a fellow of the Royal Society of Edinburgh in 1956 and was also active in the British Association for the Advancement of Science (BAAS), joining its council in 1968.

This involvement with the BAAS reflected a longstanding commitment to communicating science to non-specialist audiences which Pyke had pursued through extensive writing and occasional media appearances. He produced many books on food and nutrition during this period, including *Townsman's Food* (1952), *The Boundaries of Science* (1961), *Food and Society* (1968), *Synthetic Food* (1970), and *Technological Eating* (1972). These sought to explain developments in food technology to the general reader

Magnus Alfred Pyke (1908–1992), by Kyffin Williams, 1966

and stressed the links between technological and social change. He frequently emphasized the difficulties of feeding modern urban populations and defended food manufacturers against those who accused them of tampering with food in ways that made it deleterious to health, by claiming that they in fact provided a valuable social service. After retiring from Distillers, Pyke continued to pursue this aspect of his work, initially in the role of secretary and chairman of the BAAS, a position he held until 1977. One of his earliest projects was to convene a committee to consider the relationship between science and the media. He also continued to write. It was during this period that he received in 1974 from the University of Stirling the first of three honorary degrees; this was followed by awards from Lancaster (1976) and McGill (1981).

Pyke's national fame was, however, based on a further role which he took on shortly after moving to the BAAS. In 1974 he began his appearances on Yorkshire Television's *Don't Ask Me*, which was followed by *Don't Just Sit There*. In the first of these a studio audience asked Pyke and his co-presenters questions about physics, medicine, zoology, and botany. Pyke, tall, white-haired, and bespectacled, became famous for his enthusiastic and effusive responses. These frequently involved much arm waving as he unselfconsciously sought to provide (often using extensive props including his pipe) a clear explanation of complex scientific phenomena. Seen by many as the archetypical scientist on account of his apparent eccentricities, Pyke had an on-screen image that belied the seriousness of his efforts to bring science alive to a mass audience. This new career brought a host of distinctions, notably the Pye colour television award for the most promising male newcomer to television in 1975 and the Multi-Coloured Swap Shop star award (expert of the year, 1977–8). In 1978 he was appointed OBE.

After *Don't Just Sit There* ended in 1980 he retired from broadcasting, apart from occasional appearances. He continued to write and to find himself bombarded with scientific questions when he appeared in public. He nursed his wife, who died in 1986, through her final illness. He was living at the Elmbank Nursing Home, 38 Carlton Drive, Wandsworth, at the time of his death on 19 October 1992.

SALLY M. HORROCKS

Sources *The Independent* (22 Oct 1992) · *The Times* (21 Oct 1992) · *The Guardian* (21 Oct 1992) · *The Guardian* (1 Nov 1992) · *Daily Telegraph* (21 Oct 1992) · *Daily Mail* (21 Oct 1992) · *Chemistry in Britain*, 19 (1993), 340 · WWW · WW (1992) · M. Pyke, *Technological eating* (1972) [jacket] · M. Pyke, *The six lives of Pyke* (1981) · 'TV scientist Magnus Pyke dies', *The Independent* (21 Oct 1992) · b. cert. · m. cert. · d. cert.
Archives FILM BFI NFTVA, performance footage | SOUND BL NSA, performance recording · BL NSA, recorded lecture
Likenesses K. Williams, portrait, 1966, priv. coll. [*see illus.*] · photograph, repro. in *The Independent* · photograph, repro. in *The Times* · photograph, repro. in www.stuart.cann.freeuk.com/magnus_pyke.html, 4 Oct 2002
Wealth at death £524,981: probate, 6 May 1993, *CGPLA Eng. & Wales*

Pyke [*née* Chubb], **Margaret Amy** (1893–1966), campaigner for family planning, the eldest child of William Lindsay Chubb (1856–1937), a medical practitioner, and his wife, Isabel Margaret Pringle, was born on 8 January 1893 at Darenth House, Sandgate, Kent, where she spent most of her first two decades. She attended Conamur School, Sandgate, to 1911 as a day girl and was happy there. In 1912 Margaret Chubb went to Oxford to read modern history at Somerville College, a period which she also enjoyed. She made many friends at Oxford, some of whom remained close to her for the rest of her life. She went down in 1915 with a second-class honours degree and, as war service, joined the Queen Mary's Army Auxiliary Corps (QMAAC). From 1916 to 1917 she worked in the recruiting department of the War Office doing higher grade secretarial work. From 1917 to 1919 she was deputy assistant to the chief controller of the QMAAC and from 1919 to 1920 she was head of the employment department of the London Society for Women's Service.

In 1918 Chubb married Geoffrey Nathaniel Pyke (1893–1948), the elder son of Lionel Pyke QC. Their only child, David (b. 1926), became a doctor and for twenty-seven years was a consultant physician at King's College Hospital, London, and registrar of the Royal College of Physicians. Geoffrey Pyke had achieved fame in 1915 by escaping from Germany. He had been sent there as correspondent to the *Daily Chronicle* but had soon been arrested and interned at Ruhleben camp outside Berlin. A few months later he escaped from the camp and made his way on foot to the Dutch frontier. After that he divided his time between lecturing on his experiences and founding, with others, the *Cambridge Magazine*, a critical review.

In 1923 the Pykes moved to Cambridge, largely to found an infant school, the Malting House School. Geoffrey Pyke had original ideas about the education of very young children, encouraging them to learn, as far as possible, for themselves, adults being there to help and guide them and to answer questions rather than instruct them. These ideas gained influence through the writings of Susan Isaacs, whom the Pykes engaged as head of the school staff. In all this Margaret Pyke was a strong supporter of the school and its ideas. The school depended financially on Geoffrey Pyke's speculations on the stock exchange. In 1929 he went bankrupt, the school closed and the Pykes separated. For the next year, needing to support herself and her son, Margaret Pyke worked as secretary to the headmistress of a girls' school, Hayes Court, at Hayes, Kent.

In 1930 her life's course was set when Pyke was appointed secretary to the National Birth Control Council (NBCC), a newly created group of previously independent birth control clinics and bodies. At that time the subject of birth control was virtually taboo and, opposed by both Roman Catholic and Anglican churches, was not discussed in public. However, under the presidency of the celebrated physician, Lord Horder, and the chairmanship of Lady Denman, supported by the energy and ability of Margaret Pyke, swift progress was made. New branches were formed all over the country to meet the considerable but largely unmet need for advice on all aspects of sex and marriage, not only contraception. Mrs Pyke was tireless in creating and sustaining these branches, which were staffed entirely by volunteers (except for the doctors) and worked in borrowed premises.

In 1931 the NBCC changed the word 'council' in its title to 'association' and in 1939, to reflect the changing scope of its activities, it became the Family Planning Association (FPA). The need for its services was considerable, especially in depressed areas such as south Wales and the north and north-east of England. One small paragraph advertising the existence of an FPA leaflet led to 5300 enquiries. After five years there were sixty-six municipal and forty-seven voluntary clinics, the office had enlarged, doctors were increasingly supportive, and the Ministry of Health was helpful. Yet the organization still depended entirely on voluntary contributions.

In 1939 Margaret Pyke became honorary secretary of the Family Planning Association, which was greatly reduced in size and activity during the Second World War. After the death of Lady Denman in 1954, Margaret Pyke became chairman, a post she held until her death in 1966. The great event in the history of the FPA, and indeed of the whole family planning movement, came in 1955 when the minister of health, Iain Macleod, at Margaret Pyke's instigation (helped by Lady Monckton), paid an official visit to the FPA national office and one of its clinics. This changed the climate and from then on publicity for birth control was widespread and respectable.

Margaret Pyke's contribution to the family planning movement was considerable, particularly in Britain, though she was also involved in the foundation of the International Planned Parenthood Federation. The earlier pioneers, such as Marie Stopes, had been, and perhaps needed to be, highly outspoken, courageous people who found pioneering more to their taste than organizing, persuading, and conciliating, which were the qualities of Margaret Pyke. She was calm, patient, determined, and always friendly. She never lost her temper, she never lost a friend and so she got her way amid agreement and affection. She was appointed OBE in 1963, which at that time and for her particular kind of work was a triumph of official recognition, given openly and specifically for her work in family planning.

Margaret Pyke had other interests. She was a governor of St Clement Danes School in London. During the Second World War she edited the *Journal* of the Women's Land Army. In her younger days she was a county hockey player and later she was a keen (though not particularly expert) golfer and an enthusiastic bridge player.

Margaret Pyke died suddenly from a cerebral haemorrhage on 19 June 1966 at Ardchattan Priory, Argyll, while staying with friends in Scotland. Her body was cremated at Glasgow. ANN DALLY

Sources *Family Planning* (Oct 1966), 66–73 · private information (2004) · d. cert. · b. cert.
Wealth at death £20,786: probate, 18 Jan 1967, *CGPLA Eng. & Wales*

Pyle, Thomas (1674–1756), Church of England clergyman and religious controversialist, was born at Stody, Norfolk, the son of John Pyle (*d.* 1709), rector of Stody. He was educated at Gresham's grammar school at Holt, Norfolk, under Mr Bainbrigg, and then at Gonville and Caius College, Cambridge, where he was admitted sizar on 17 May 1692, aged seventeen, and elected scholar the following Michaelmas. He graduated BA in 1696 and MA in 1699. He was ordained deacon on 30 May 1697 and priest on 25 September 1698 by Dr Moore, bishop of Norwich; the bishop's chaplain, William Whiston, noted that Pyle was one of the two best scholars that he had ever examined. He was appointed vicar of Thorpe Market in 1698. Following his marriage to Mary Rolfe (1681/2–1748), of King's Lynn, in 1701 he was appointed minister of St Nicholas's Chapel in King's Lynn. He served as lecturer and curate of St Margaret's from 1711, and also held the neighbouring rectories of Outwell (1709–18), Bexwell (1708–9), and Watlington (1710–26).

Pyle was an eloquent preacher and a strong whig. The accession of the house of Hanover and the representation of King's Lynn in parliament by the prime minister, Robert Walpole, gave him hope of preferment in the church. He was not slow to take advantage of the Bangorian controversy, writing *A Vindication of the Bishop of Bangor, in Answer to the Exceptions of Mr Law* and *A Second Vindication* in 1718. He also published two tracts in reply to Henry Stebbing's tracts on the controversy. This flurry of pamphlets proved his talent as a disputant and gained him the friendship of Benjamin Hoadly. After Hoadly became bishop of

Salisbury he collated Pyle to the living of Durnford, in that diocese. Pyle had begun to be noticed as a preacher in London, and his *Paraphrase of the Acts and Epistles, in the Manner of Dr Clarke* (1725) attracted favourable attention from the low-church party and from dissenters such as Samuel Chandler, and John Rastrick of King's Lynn. A further volume of paraphrases helped to strengthen his position with notable latitudinarians such as Samuel Clarke, Arthur Ashley Sykes, and Thomas Herring. But Pyle never received additional preferment, even after Herring became archbishop of Canterbury. Herring explained some of his reservations about Pyle in a letter to William Duncombe of 29 July 1745: 'That very impetuosity of spirit, which under proper government, renders him the agreeable creature he is, has, in some circumstance of life got the better of him, and hurt his views' (Herring, 81). Pyle made no secret of his views on the Trinity, in which he adopted an Arian position, and revelled in 'the glorious prerogative of private judgement, the birth-right of Protestants' (Richards, 1017). His heterodoxy probably cost him advancement in the church. In 1732 he exchanged his old livings for the vicarage of St Margaret's, King's Lynn, which he retained until 1755.

Despairing of promotion for himself Pyle used his influence with Hoadly and others on behalf of his three sons. The eldest, Edmund (1702–1776), succeeded his father as lecturer at St Nicholas's, King's Lynn, in 1732, became archdeacon of York in 1751, and acted as chaplain to the king and to Hoadly; he left some piquant memoirs of Matthew Hutton, archbishop of York and then of Canterbury. Pyle's second son, Thomas (1713–1807), became canon of Salisbury in 1741 and of Winchester in 1760. Philip, the third son (1724–1799), was appointed rector of North Lynn in 1756. Mary Pyle died on 14 March 1748, aged sixty-six.

Thomas Pyle retired to Swaffham in 1755, where he died on 31 December 1756. He was buried in All Saints', King's Lynn. Three collections of his religious discourses were published by Philip Pyle, in 1773, 1777, and 1783.

E. G. HAWKE, rev. ANDREW ROBINSON

Sources Venn, *Alum. Cant.* · W. Richards, *The history of Lynn*, 2 vols. (1813), 1012–23 [through paginated] · B. Mackerell, *The history and antiquities of King's Lynn* (1738), 89 · Nichols, *Lit. anecdotes*, 9.433 · *Fasti Angl.* (Hardy), 2.668 · J. W. Legg, *English church life from the Restoration to the Tractarian movement* (1914), 7 · T. Herring, *Letters to William Duncombe, from the year 1728 to 1757* (1777) · E. Pyle, *Memoirs of a royal chaplain, 1729–1736*, ed. A. Hartshorne (1905)

Pym, Barbara Mary Crampton (1913–1980), novelist, was born on 2 June 1913 at 72 Willow Street, Oswestry, Shropshire, the elder daughter of Frederic Crampton Pym (1879–1966), solicitor, of Oswestry, and his wife, Irena Spenser, *née* Thomas (1886–1945). Frederic Pym had been born at Pitminster, Somerset, the illegitimate son of a domestic servant, Phoebe Pym; it seems likely that his father was Fiennes Henry Crampton, of a landowning family. The family of Irena Thomas had originally farmed in the Welsh border country, and her father had founded an ironmongery business in Oswestry in 1865.

The Pym family, augmented by the birth of Hilary in

Barbara Mary Crampton Pym (1913–1980), by Mark Gerson, 1979

1916, moved into Morda Lodge, a substantial Edwardian house in Oswestry, where the sisters grew up in loving and easy circumstances. Barbara Pym was educated at a girls' boarding-school, Liverpool College, Huyton (later Huyton College, Liverpool). She went up to St Hilda's College, Oxford, in 1931 to read English, with the twin devotions of her life—to English poetry and the rituals of the Church of England—already formed. While at Oxford, her third emotional strand, the tendency to develop unrequited attachments to unresponsive men, often younger than herself, sometimes homosexual, first became manifest, in her passion for a fellow undergraduate, Henry Harvey. He served as the model for one of her best comic characters, Henry Hoccleve, the archdeacon in *Some Tame Gazelle*. She began writing this *roman-à-clef*, based on herself, her sister, and their circle of friends, imagined as middle-aged, almost immediately upon going down from Oxford with a second-class degree in 1934.

Barbara Pym lived mainly at home with her parents for much of the 1930s, following no profession, but developing her talents as a novelist, and diversifying her life with nostalgic returns to Oxford (where, in 1937, she became attached to the young Julian Amery), and with several trips to Germany, Hungary, Czechoslovakia, and Poland, in which last country she was briefly a governess. In 1936 *Some Tame Gazelle* was offered to several publishers, all of whom turned it down, including Jonathan Cape, who was to publish it, in substantially revised form, fourteen years later. In late 1938 she and her sister, who was taking a secretarial course in preparation for entry to the BBC, moved into adjacent bed-sitters in London, and from that point on they were generally to share accommodation and a large part of their lives.

When war broke out Barbara Pym first undertook voluntary work in Oswestry; then in 1941 became a postal censor in Bristol; then, from 1943 to 1946, served in the Women's Royal Naval Service, reaching the rank of third officer, and being posted to Naples in 1944 and 1945. While in Bristol she experienced the most painful of her infatuations, that for the writer and broadcaster C. Gordon Glover; in the second half of her life, what she had once given to the heart was to be devoted to writing her books.

On demobilization in 1946 Barbara Pym joined the International African Institute, where she passed the whole of her working life, first as a research assistant, then, from 1958, as editorial secretary and assistant editor of the institute's journal *Africa*. She had little interest in Africa as such but enjoyed editorial work, and was fascinated by the manners of anthropologists. In 1950 she was joined on the staff by Hazel Holt, with whom she shared an office, and who was to be her literary executor and the friend to whom she first showed her writing. Meanwhile, she and her sister Hilary lived successively in Pimlico, Barnes, and Kilburn, where they passed much time in parish work and keen social observations.

Some Tame Gazelle was published in 1950; this was the first of six novels which appeared until 1961, and which constitute the first phase of Barbara Pym's work. They are largely high-spirited pictures of the 'excellent women' and ambiguous males who populate Anglican parishes in London. They have great humour, leavened with sadness, each quiet sentence seeming to tremble with a smile. The second novel, *Excellent Women* (1952), is perhaps the most typical of the books; the fifth, *A Glass of Blessings* (1958), the most subtle. In the sixth, *No Fond Return of Love*, which is over-long, there are perhaps signs that this vein was beginning to be worked out. These novels appealed chiefly to the Boots library public and made a steady, unspectacular impact. By the early 1960s Jonathan Cape was insisting more on profit and fashion, a trend associated with a new senior editor, Tom Maschler. In 1963, when Barbara Pym submitted her new novel, *An Unsuitable Attachment*, to Cape, it was summarily rejected.

Thus began fourteen years in the wilderness, during which Barbara Pym offered her work to twenty-one publishers, sometimes in her desperation going so far as to adopt an assumed name or to plead with those who might conceivably have influence. The mid-1960s saw the last of her romantic attachments, to the young Bahamian antique dealer Richard Roberts, and the situation was quickly transmuted into the most atypical but one of the best of her books, *The Sweet Dove Died*, eventually published in 1978. In 1971 she was diagnosed with breast cancer and underwent a mastectomy. In 1972 Hilary bought a retirement cottage for them both in the Oxfordshire village of Finstock, and when in 1974 a stroke led to a temporary period of dyslexia Barbara Pym was advised to retire from the institute. Domestic comforts beckoned, and she had never stopped writing, but her career as a novelist must have seemed long over.

Early in 1977, however, the *Times Literary Supplement* published a symposium on the most over- and underrated writers of the twentieth century, and Barbara Pym was the only writer to be named twice in the latter category—by Philip Larkin (long a friend and encourager) and Lord David Cecil. On 14 February the publishers Macmillan told her they were accepting the novel they had currently under consideration, *Quartet in Autumn*. This fine work, by general consent her best, tells of four people on the verge of retirement. It is more sombre than her earlier books, with a blacker humour, but in its final uplift confirms the voice that had always been hers. It was shortlisted for the Booker prize, and a period began of a limelight she had not known before, including her election as a fellow of the Royal Society of Literature in 1979. This success was cruelly brief. In early 1979 it became evident that her remission of cancer was over. She struggled to complete her last book, the elegiac *A Few Green Leaves*, and bore her last illness with the stoicism and good humour that had marked her life. She died in Michael Sobell House, a hospice attached to the Churchill Hospital in Oxford, on 11 January 1980 and she was buried at Finstock church. Several novels, an autobiography in letters and diaries, a compilation of early work, and a biography were posthumously published, although it is doubtful whether at least two of these novels, and the compilation, really merited print.

Barbara Pym was tall, and stooped in later life; pretty and bouncing in youth, she later became in appearance the epitome of the sensible English spinsters, cherishing their cats, whom she celebrated; an early ebullience gave way to what Philip Larkin called the 'gentle watchfulness of her conversation' (*DNB*). She will be remembered not for any impact on the society of her time but for the luminous works which she contributed to literature.

C. A. R. HILLS

Sources *DNB* · H. Holt, *A lot to ask: a life of Barbara Pym* (1990) · *A very private eye: the diaries, letters and notebooks of Barbara Pym*, ed. H. Holt and H. Pym (1984) · Bodl. Oxf., MSS Barbara Pym · private information (2004)
Archives Bodl. Oxf., corresp., diaries, and papers | Bodl. Oxf., Larkin MSS
Likenesses M. Gerson, photograph, 1979, NPG [*see illus.*] · photographs, repro. in Holt and Pym, eds., *A very private eye* · photographs, repro. in Holt, *A lot to ask*
Wealth at death £48,488: probate, 14 April 1980, *CGPLA Eng. & Wales*

Pym, John (1584–1643), politician, was born on 20 May 1584, the son of Alexander Pym (*c.*1547–1585) and his wife, Philippa Colles (*d.* 1620), and was baptized at St Giles Cripplegate, London, on 18 June.

The Pym family and its estates Pym came from an old Somerset family on the fringe of the magisterial class. He was not a man born to a place in county or parliamentary politics. On the other hand, people from backgrounds much more obscure than his, such as his fellow Somerset man Sir Francis Cottington, could achieve political careers by clinging to a career ladder and cultivating possible patrons as they went up it. It was perhaps Pym's difficulty that he fell rather heavily between these two stools.

The Pym family appear to have been established in the

Reade in this Image him, whose dearest blood
Is thought noe price to buy his Countryes good,
Whose name shall flourish, till the blast of ffame
Shall want a Trumpet, or true Worth, a name.
Edw: Bower pinxit   G: Glover fecit

John Pym (1584–1643), by George Glover, pubd 1644 (after Edward Bower, *c*.1640–41)

manor of Brymore, Somerset, since the thirteenth century, but had not had a particularly distinguished sixteenth century. The family entered it under a cloud. In October 1498 Alexander Pym was made to take out a recognizance of £10,000 for aiding Perkin Warbeck. The dissolution of the monasteries passed them by and, in a fluid land market, their holdings remained almost static. It did not help, either, that the family experienced three wardships during the century. The first of these, in 1507, produced the highest valuation of the three, at £56 5s. 7d. per annum. In 1528 Pym's grandfather Erasmus in turn became a ward, and the wardship was sold to Sir Thomas Elyot, author of *The Boke Named the Governour*, who was a distant cousin. The estate was then valued at £41 9s. 8d. per annum. Erasmus Pym lived an unremarkable life on the fringe of the magisterial class.

In 1575 Erasmus Pym was succeeded by John's father, Alexander, under whom the family fortunes began to look up. He was a JP, a commissioner for musters, and a significant figure in the Middle Temple. In 1584 he was elected MP for Taunton, though there is no evidence that he had taken his seat before he died in January 1585. He seems to have brought enhanced economic status to the family. He was responsible for the family's one substantial purchase of the sixteenth century, Wollavington Throckmorton,

sold by Francis Throckmorton of Feckenham, Worcestershire, for £1700 in 1581. The money was to be paid 'in and upon the Fante Stone in the Temple Church in the suburbs of London, or in and upon the place where the Fante now standeth' (Pym MSS, Somerset Archive and Record Service, DD/BW, no. 113). The Middle Temple network was widespread and powerful, and it worked for Alexander. The manor adjoined, and consolidated, the existing manor of Wollavington Pym, and when Burghley gave the accolade of arrival to the Pyms by marking them on his political atlas he put them at Wollavington.

Alexander's first marriage, in 1576—which cannot have lasted more than three or four years—continued one habit which limited the Pyms' county strength, which was that of marrying outside the county. It was to Elizabeth, daughter of John Conyers of St Botolph Aldgate in London. It was a Middle Temple marriage: Alexander had shared a chamber with her brother. They had one daughter, Catherine, who subsequently married William Cholmeley, foreign apposer of the exchequer.

Alexander's second marriage was to John Pym's mother, Philippa Colles, daughter of Humphrey Colles of Pitminster, Somerset. She was the sister of John Colles, JP, deputy lieutenant and, crucially for the history of John Pym, county feodary. She had two children: Jane, who subsequently married Richard Rous of Wotton, Cornwall, with whom she had at least seventeen children, and John. On 5 January 1585, seven months after John's birth, Alexander Pym died, and plunged the family into its third wardship of the century.

The wardship appears not to have attracted the attention of any big speculators. There were two serious contenders for it: John's mother and his uncle William Pym. Since John Colles as feodary acted consistently in the interests of his sister, the wardship in effect became a duel between John's two uncles. That was no contest: John Colles was far the abler operator of the two. The friendship between the families lasted, and John Colles may have been a more important influence in the development of Pym's political sense than is normally recognized. The Colleses were not ideologues: they had made their fortune by favourable leases from Bishop Gilbert Bourne during the reign of Mary, but John Colles put his name to the bond of association in defence of Queen Elizabeth against her Catholic enemies in 1584. The religious clause of John Colles's will, which is unique among all Pym's contacts in its eschewal of hot protestantism, strikes the key note. He expresses belief in the resurrection of the flesh, the life everlasting, 'and all other articles of my faithe whiche a Christyane man oughte to beleeve' (PRO, PROB 11/111, sig. 63). Unlike many other neutral wills, this one was so by studied choice.

The wardship was duly granted to Pym's mother, Philippa. It was valued at the inquisition post mortem at £52 15s. 10d., and reduced in the feodary's survey to £51 13s. 10d. This is a valuation below that arrived at by Henry VII in 1507. There is no reason to suppose that these figures had any resemblance to what the estate was worth. First, the valuation concealed the newly purchased manor of Wol-lavington Throckmorton, by lumping the two Wollaving-ton manors, Wollavington Throckmorton and Wollaving-ton Pym, together under the conflated name of Wol-lavington. If the price had been set at the rate of twenty years' purchase, the value of the suppressed manor would have been £85. The other reason why a rental income was not a credible estimate of the value of the property was the habit of taking much of the income in entry fines in return for long leases. In 1614, in a document designed to be produced in the event of a wardship, Pym estimated his rental at £100 6s. 8d. per annum. His recorded income from entry fines, in a very incomplete collection of estate documents, comes to £158 per annum for the reign of James and £293 per annum for the reign of Charles up to 1640, when the series stops until well after both the war and John Pym's life were over. The late Miss Evelyn Gore, who had access to surveys which do not now survive, esti-mated Pym's median income from land at the beginning of James's reign at between £400 and £500 per annum, with the mean inflated above the median by occasional very large fines.

The Rous circle It was a status on which magistracy was possible, but one at which being out of sight very quickly became out of mind. Pym never had the chance to get to know his Somerset contemporaries, since before he reached the age of four his mother married Anthony Rous of Halton St Dominic in Cornwall, and took the boy to live on the Cornish shore of Plymouth Sound. The Rouses were a very large and affectionate family, in which kin counted for even more than it did with the Pyms. John Pym adopted them as his own, and from then on, his car-eer would be more easily understood if he were known as John Rous, younger son of Anthony Rous.

Anthony Rous, originally from the borders of Sussex and Hampshire, was a rare character who made a success of being an expatriate in another county. In Cornwall he became JP and vice-warden of the stannaries. He was sher-iff in the two crucial years of 1588 and 1603 and was knight of the shire in 1604, sitting on the committee to draft an act of thanksgiving for deliverance from the Gunpowder Plot. His committee service was regular, at least for the first session of the parliament, but he was not a frequent speaker. He was executor to Sir Francis Drake, who seems to have been a close personal friend. He was knighted in 1604.

Both the children of Alexander Pym and Philippa mar-ried into the inner Rous circle. Jane married Anthony Rous's son from his first marriage, Robert. John, on 28 May 1604, married Anne Hooke (bap. 1586, d. c.1620), of Bram-shott in Hampshire, daughter of John Hooke and Anthony Rous's sister Barbara. This marriage both cemented Pym into the Rous circle and began his connection with Hamp-shire.

Among Rous's other children, Francis *Rous was to be John Pym's regular parliamentary colleague, and one of the very few people who ever made Pym's hatred of Armi-nianism look half-hearted. Philippa married Humphrey Nicoll of Penvose, Cornwall, and their son Anthony

*Nicoll was an active member of the Long Parliament. Dorothy Rous married John Upton of Brixham, who was repeatedly MP for Dartmouth. John Upton was an active JP in Devon, and an active member of the Providence Island Company. He also created the connection between John Pym and John *Clotworthy, since his brother married Clotworthy's sister. This connection was to be vital to rela-tions between the Long Parliament and Ireland.

Two other people, Charles Fitz-Geffrey, later vicar of Halton St Dominic, and Diagory Wheare, later Pym's tutor at Oxford, are firmly embedded in this circle. On 6 July 1593 Francis, Richard, and Robert Rous, Charles Fitz-Geffrey, and Diagory Wheare all matriculated at Broad-gates Hall, Oxford (now Pembroke College), on the same day. Wheare was later named by William Camden as reader of his history lecture in Oxford. He remained in close contact with Pym, and was probably his source for much of his information on Oxford matters.

According to Anthony Rous's funeral sermon, preached by Fitz-Geffrey in 1622, he showed evident signs of saving grace in his religious course. It was in the Rous circle that Pym imbibed a protestantism far hotter than the conven-tional Calvinism of his Somerset background. Anthony Rous sustained distressed ministers from Scotland, Ire-land, and the Netherlands, and in 1584–5 employed as his domestic chaplain John Cowper, a Scottish minister in exile from the Black Acts. Rous was thought to have died by catching a cold going up the Tamar by boat on a frosty morning to attend the weekly lecture at Saltash. On the sabbath, he made religious notes in a book. The praise in his funeral sermon for his generosity to the poor is on the whole sustained by his administration of John Pym's estates during the wardship.

Yet trying to make too clear a distinction about 1600 between puritans and Calvinist conformists carries the risk of creating an anachronism: this was a fault line the Laudians had not yet cracked open. Calvinist ideas of pre-destination and assurance, which Whitgift and Cart-wright shared and which members of the Rous circle expressed at every possible opportunity, were, in Dr N. Tyacke's phrase, 'a common and ameliorating bond' between conformist and nonconformist ('Puritanism, Arminianism and counter-revolution', The Origins of the English Civil War, ed. C. Russell, 1973, 121). The fact is nowhere clearer than in Pym's circle. The only exception seems to have been Pym's mother, who appears to have been one of those tragic Calvinists who believed they were predestined to damnation.

In 1599 Pym followed the rest of the Rous tribe to Broad-gates Hall. His Oxford loyalty, together with his loyalty to Diagory Wheare his tutor, appears to have been strong. In 1623 he contributed 44s. to a Broadgates appeal for enlar-ging the hall, for meeting at disputations, and lodgings for students. He was more munificent in 1630 in reply to a per-sonal appeal from Wheare for subscriptions to Gloucester Hall, of which Wheare had become principal. The total yield of the appeal was £88, of which John Pym contrib-uted £20, and his eldest surviving son, Alexander, another £20. Much the clearest statement of his Oxford loyalties is in his parliamentary diary for 1621. In reporting the debate on whether Oxford or Cambridge should be mentioned first in the subsidy bill, he said:

> All those which had been of either Universitie inclined to that place of which they were. But such as had been of neither remained indifferent and were only swayed by reason. Soe that upon the question the precedence was appointed to Oxford.   (Notestein, Relf, and Simpson, 4.144–5)

That is the true faith.

Pym also followed the family path to the Middle Temple, where he was admitted on 5 February 1602, and bound with Francis Rous and William Whitaker of Westbury, later to be his regular lawyer, a parliamentary colleague, and a member of the Rous circle. However, the Middle Temple appears not to have taken as Oxford did, and the records show a succession of absences during readings, for which he was fined. The Middle Temple did, however, produce a friendship with Benjamin Rudyerd which lasted the rest of his life.

In his thirty-eight years from coming of age to death, Pym had at least five different addresses. Up to the death of his wife about 1620, he lived at his ancestral home at the manor of Brymore, in the parish of Cannington, outside Taunton in Somerset. During most of the 1620s he divided his time between Sir William Boswell's house in the parish of St Clement Danes in London, which he rented jointly with his brother-in-law William Cholmeley, and a house in the parish of Wherwell (or Horwell) in Hampshire, where he tried to turn himself into a Hampshire country gentleman. From 1630 onwards he was usually found in London, in the parish of St Andrew's, Holborn. From about 1636 onwards until parliament met, he was normally living in the house of Richard Knightley in Fawsley in Northamptonshire, in what Clarendon called 'a kind of classis' (Clarendon, 1.145).

Early adulthood After livery of his estate in 1605, Pym returned home to Somerset with his new bride. He apparently intended to get re-established there, since he had plans to install a new water supply at Brymore. Up to about 1620, when his wife, his mother, his stepfather, and his eldest son, John, all died within a short space of time, Pym seems to have been set on planting himself on the Somerset stage. He was resident reasonably regularly and paid serious attention to the management of his property. What he did not achieve was any entry into Somerset county society. In all this period, only two Somerset gentlemen so much as appear on documents with him. One is Sir John Mallett of Penvose, who was one of his sureties for the office of receiver of crown lands for Hampshire, Wiltshire, and Gloucestershire. The other sureties were Thomas Conyers of East Barnet, his father's old Middle Temple chamberfellow and brother of his father's first wife, and William Cholmeley, husband of his elder sister. It is a clear example of the tendency of the Pyms to rely on kin rather than on neighbourhood, and underlines the point that Sir John Mallett was the son of Philippa Pym's sister.

The other Somerset gentleman associated with Pym was William Frauncis of Combe Florey, an established but not particularly important JP. He appears in several minor documents, and in the complex uses of 1614, by which Pym attempted to protect his property against wardship in the event of his death. These documents attempted the complex, and legally dubious, arrangement of a use upon a use. The feoffees to the first were William Frauncis, Humphrey Nicoll of Penvose, Cornwall, Robert Rous of Wotton, Cornwall, another of Pym's stepbrothers, and Diagory Wheare. The feoffees for the second were William Cholmeley his brother-in-law, William Whitaker of the Middle Temple, his lawyer, and one new arrival, Sir Edward Wardour of the parish of St Giles-in-the-Fields, clerk of the pells in the exchequer. Wardour was also an active Middlesex and Westminster JP, and a friend of Francis Russell, fourth earl of Bedford. He may possibly have been the man who established contact between Pym and Bedford. Wardour was a parliamentary colleague during the 1620s, and involved in the draft plans for Pym and Bedford's revenue settlement in 1641. Along with Ralph Brownrigg, master of St Catharine's College, Cambridge, and bishop of Exeter from November 1641, who married William Cholmeley's daughter, he was one of only two people in Pym's circle who became royalists in the civil war.

The enfeoffments to use secured a descent to three of Pym's sons in order. John, eldest son and heir apparent, was born in 1609, matriculated at Gloucester Hall in 1623 aged fourteen, and appears to have died very shortly afterwards. The second son, Alexander, followed his father into the Middle Temple in 1629, spent time abroad in the service of the states general of the United Provinces in the early 1630s, became a recruiter member of the Long Parliament, and was associated with the radical faction in county politics during the civil war. He died childless and unmarried some time before the Restoration. The third son, Anthony, is known only from a letter he wrote on 29 July 1633, saying: 'Let my miserable example make thee avoid all wicked and prodigal courses. I am now going out of England and doubtful I am whether ever I shall see any of you again' (C. J. Sawyer & Co., catalogue no. 155, no. 71). The striking point about this letter is its recipient. It is not John Pym, but his youngest son, Charles, not yet born in 1614, and therefore still under nineteen in 1633. As their father grew more deeply embedded in the affairs of Providence Island and of parliament, Charles Pym appears to have become the human cement which held the family together. He was the recipient of aching letters from his sister Dorothy, suffering for about two months from toothache, or begging letters from his sister Katherine, who died unmarried in 1649, about the chances of buying second-hand virginals cheap. It was to Charles Pym that she wrote: 'Speake to my father to send me some money … for I want it very much you know there is no living without it' (ibid., no. 69). Such letters may help to understand why Charles Pym was so much more successful in Somerset county society than his father or his elder brother.

Philippa Pym, the eldest daughter, in 1625 married Thomas Symons of Whittlesford in Cambridgeshire, a cheerful man who ordered his tobacco pipes by the gross. He had a small adventure in the Providence Island Company, and was a member of the Cambridgeshire county committee at the beginning of the civil war, presumably to provide a link with his father-in-law. Dorothy, the middle daughter, was not married until 1641, when she married back into the Rous circle; her husband was Sir Francis Drake of Werrington. Pym, trying to keep up a new-found status, committed himself to paying a dowry of £2300, but in the encumbered state to which Providence reduced him he did not pay it. Alexander Pym later had to mortgage Wollavington for it.

Estate manager and receiver of crown lands As Pym's financial difficulties increased during the 1630s, a slow change occurred in the management of the estate. At the beginning of Pym's ownership his manors were still recognizable village communities. The lessees normally lived on their tenements, and appeared at the manorial court with at least reasonable regularity. They might pay high fines and low rents, but they took manageable plots of land for a single occupier, and the level of rents made them still recognizably tenants.

In the upland manors of Cutcombe Mohun and Cutcombe Raleigh, on the edge of Exmoor, this pattern on the whole persisted. In the lowland country around Wollavington, on the edge of the levels and in cattle country, there was a tendency for some leases to be of very large plots of land, with an enormous fine and derisory rent. These leases necessarily implied subtenants, and the leases confined themselves to insisting that subtenancies must be registered with the manorial court. In return for the high fines, there was bargaining over the identity of the lessees, and one lease bears a note, probably by Pym's steward, 'all three lessees are children' (Pym MSS, Somerset Archive and Record Service, DD/BW, no. 212). In these cases, leases stress with increasing stridency a need to attend the manorial court, and to accept its decisions and pay fines imposed by it. The requirement to notify deaths of lessees to the manorial court is stated in increasingly draconian terms. One of them even invents a manorial version of the doctrine of *praemunire*, in that taking any case to any other court which ought to go to the manorial court leads to forfeiture of the tenement.

In this high-fine economy, a very fine line separates the lease from the mortgage. A lease of much of Wollavington to James Hayward, yeoman, for a fine of £460 and a rent of 29s. 6d., with a special clause forbidding Hayward to carry away the manure, comes close to this line. Hayward, presumably a grazier, was an up-and-coming man, and in the civil war he was a captain in the parliamentarian army alongside Pym's sons Charles and Alexander. A lease of 1626 to John Grabham, grazier, illiterate but employing counsel, for a fine of £240 and a rent of 15s. for three lives, all of them children, is another out of the same stable. By 1634, when John Grabham took a much bigger lease for a fine of £300, he is styled gent., but still illiterate. Such leases are still a minority, but they are the ones which financed Pym's political career, and made the fortunes of his leading tenants. If there was a 'rise of the middle classes' going on during Pym's lifetime, he was not its beneficiary: he was its victim.

'One Pym, a Receiver' When Pym first came to the attention of the newsletter writer John Chamberlain, in the parliament of 1621, he was characterized as 'one Pym, a Receiver' (*The Letters of John Chamberlain*, ed. N. E. MacClure, 2 vols., Memoirs of the American Philosophical Society, vol. 12, pts 1–2, 1939, 2.412). His office as receiver of crown lands for Hampshire, Wiltshire, and Gloucestershire was his only office in the gift of the crown. He was originally granted the reversion to the office on 17 June 1605. Henry Audley, his predecessor, died on 18 November 1606 owing £2000 of arrears to the crown, and Pym took up the office shortly afterwards. He held it until 16 July 1638, when he surrendered it to Bedford's former servant Robert Scawen. Attorney-General Bankes wrote a note on the dorse of the docket: 'Mr Pym hath surrendered his office' (Birmingham Central Library, Birmingham City Archives, Coventry MS, grants of offices, no. 596. What is notable about the placing of Bankes's comment on the dorse, and revealing a note of triumph, is that it was left where a messenger could read it.). As receiver Pym received a fee of £100 per annum, supplemented by portage and poundage at 1 per cent of the money he handled. His income from office was supplemented, from 1608, by appointment as the queen's receiver, at a fee of £149 without portage or poundage, and later by a similar appointment for the prince of Wales, and subsequently for Queen Henrietta Maria. Since this merely required him to collect rents from some of the manors for which he was already responsible, and to pay them to the queen instead of the king, it was a useful device for increasing salaries. His income from office, including occasional windfall payments such as £400 for attending twenty-two meetings of the commission for disafforesting Blackmore and Pewsham Forest, and for keeping all its accounts, may have come to over £300 per annum.

Pym's main duty was to collect the king's rents. In this task he unusually employed a printed form with blanks, on which he filled in the times at which people were to appear before him (NRA, catalogue of Kingsmill MSS). He was occasionally employed on embarrassing business, as in 1621, when Cranfield sent him to dun William Herbert, earl of Pembroke, to his face for unpaid rent. Pym was regularly employed in delivering timber for the repair of the coastal forts, and knew at first hand what a parlous state of repair they were in. He was frequently employed in special commissions out of the exchequer, and investigated, for example, a remarkable story of waste of wood from Chute Forest and the New Forest. Pym made £133 6s. 8d. out of delivering in to the crown the receipts from massive wood sales conducted by the notorious patentee Sir Giles Mompesson, and exchanged rival memos with Mompesson about exchequer practice. Mompesson wanted to abolish receivers and give the business back to the exchequer, a view with which Pym of course disagreed. Pym had already encountered Mompesson through his patent for the licensing of inns, under which he had given a licence to the Unicorn at Wollavington.

After the parliament of 1621, Pym took home one of Mompesson's inn licences, and kept it among his papers as a souvenir.

By far the most significant business for Pym's own career was the clearance and disafforestation of Blackmore and Pewsham Forest, in Wiltshire. This probably accounted for his first two elections to parliament, at Calne in 1621 and at Chippenham in 1624. Both boroughs had closed corporation franchises. At Chippenham, there were twelve members of the corporation, of whom seven voted for Pym and five for Sir Francis Popham. Of the twelve, six and the father of a seventh had recently taken leases from Pym of disafforested grounds in Blackmore and Pewsham. Moreover, Pym was vehemently defending the tenants in a magnificent row with Lionel Cranfield about terms of their leases. In the absence of a list of members of the Calne corporation, it is impossible to prove that the same thing happened there, but the probability is considerable. At Chippenham, which gave rise to an election dispute, the commoners were unanimously for Sir Francis Popham. They had the usual grievance about loss of rights of common, they had been restrained from taking wood from the forest, and the conversion to arable had closed the old line of the road from Chippenham to Devizes. For the commoners, involvement in the forest clearance is unlikely to have been an electoral asset. The project won Pym his only substantial patron in the government service, Lionel Cranfield, who was responsible for getting him out of prison after the parliament of 1621. In spite of the quarrel over the lease the relationship seems to have lasted until Cranfield's fall.

The row with Cranfield resulted from the fact that the terms of the leases had been agreed before the agricultural depression of 1620–21, but the leases themselves were not to be signed until after it. On 22 August 1622 the commissioners advised Cranfield that the level of rents in the area had fallen by a fifth, and the ground was less good for agriculture than had been hoped. Robert Treswell, the king's woodward, one of the most active commissioners, wrote a private letter to Cranfield in support of this argument. Cranfield and Weston replied in typical treasury tones that they had been 'over-easy … to his Majesty's great disadvantage' (Sackville MSS, CKS, U269). Pym and Treswell replied that the leases had not been concluded since the treasurer and chancellor of the exchequer had not approved them before the depression, and that the tenants were unwilling to take them on these terms and could not be forced to do so. Cranfield recognized the inevitable and, having evicted one tenant to save face, reached compromises with the others.

At this stage, immediately after this hectic emphasis on the king's service, the king chose to grant the whole forest, at a rent below its rental excluding fines, to Christopher Villiers, earl of Anglesey. The conversion of what had been supposed to be a major project for increasing crown revenue into a Villiers relief project in favour of the duke of Buckingham's brother enabled Pym to make a substantial personal input into the impeachment of Buckingham.

To Pym the need to preserve the king's revenue came second only to the need to combat popery. Indeed, since he regularly thought of combating popery in terms of powder and shot, as befitted one brought up by one of Drake's executors, the two needs were very closely related in his mind. Presenting the eleventh and twelfth articles of the duke's impeachment to the Lords in 1626, dealing with his enrichment of his kindred at the public expense, he said:

> This makes the Duke's offence the greater that in this weaknes and consumcon of the comon wealth he hath not byn content alone to consume the publique comon wealth treasure, wch is the bloode and nourishmt. of the state, but hath brought in others to help him in this worke of distruccion. And that they might do it more eagerly, by enlarging theire [sic] honor, he hath likewise enlarged theire necessities and therie appetites. (Hants. RO, Winchester, Jervoise MS O 7)

As a comment on the evidence known to have been in Pym's possession, this cannot be called inaccurate.

Pym of Hampshire During the 1620s Pym appears to have been trying to establish himself in Hampshire. He was assessed for the second subsidy of 1621 at Whitchurch, in Kingsclere division, at £15 in lands. From 1621 to 1626 he responded to Hampshire assessments for subsidy with a certificate saying he was assessed in the parish of St Clement Danes in London where he ordinarily dwelt. His assessment was £10 6s. 8d. For the forced loan in 1626 he was assessed for two payments of £10 each in the hundred and village of Wherwell, which was the address he gave on the marriage licence for the marriage of Philippa to Thomas Symonds, in February 1626.

Pym was previously thought to have paid the forced loan. What happened is rather more interesting. On 11 December 1626, his brother-in-law Henry Hooke sent to Sir Thomas Jervoise the money required of 'my brother Pym', and asked Jervoise to send Pym a receipt for it (Hants. RO, Winchester, Jervoise MS O 21). On 26 December Pym wrote to Jervoise from Wherwell: 'though I conceive my brother Hooke payed this mony out of his desire of my safety, yet I fynde my selfe very hartely greved that he should write that I had sent it'. He said he had returned Hooke his receipt, and begged Jervoise, if it was not too late, to get the record of his payment off the file. This letter has the unmistakable note of a seasoned man of business trying to combine the maximum possible troublemaking with the minimum possible discourtesy (Hants. RO, Winchester, Jervoise MS O 12). In 1628 he was reported as defaulting for one horse for the musters at Whitchurch, where he probably no longer lived, and this is the last mention of him in Hampshire save for his work as receiver.

The certificates showing Pym to be living in St Clement Danes were perfectly genuine. He and William Cholmeley paid the surveyor's rates for Boswell's house in the duchy liberty of the Savoy from 1619–20 until the account of 12 April 1626. In 1627–8 there is a blank against their names, and thereafter they do not appear in the accounts. This lease predates his election to parliament, and it is possible that, being left with young children on the death of his wife, Pym relied on his sister Catherine to help to care for them. From 1621 to 1623 Pym also contributed to the churchwardens' rate and pew rate, and this provides an interesting sidelight on the level of his ecclesiastical tolerance before the rise of Arminianism. He worshipped at a church which kept two surplices. Where churches kept accounts for washing the surplice, the date for which it was washed is something of a thermometer between high and low. St Clement Danes washed the surplice for 5 November, which was about the lowest possible choice of date for which to wash it. The annual bellringings were for 5 November and for the king's delivery from the Gowrie conspiracy, which should have caused no trouble for a protestant conscience. However, the parish beat the bounds and tolled the passing bell for deaths, a habit rejected at neighbouring St Margaret's, Westminster. All this may have been rather high for Pym's tastes, and it does not appear to be the way things were done at Cannington or at Wherwell, but it does suggest, like much other evidence, that the central thrusts of Pym's religious passion were directed at the twin issues of predestination and anti-popery. It tends to lend credence to the report in the Commons journals of a sentence in his maiden speech, saying 'the exception against ceremonies now almost worn out, and scarce appeareth'. It is not something Pym would have said a few years later, and he left it out of the report of the speech in his own diary, but it may for all that be a genuine statement of his mood of the moment (*JHC*, *1547–1628*, 524).

Parliaments under James I Pym was perhaps the first Englishman who acquired a national reputation based on what he did in parliament. Yet like some others of equal stature in parliamentary history (Gladstone and Churchill, for example) he was not a particularly good politician according to conventional criteria. He once dried in a crucial speech at the close of the trial of the earl of Strafford, to the amusement of Robert Baillie. For every major performance he relied heavily on a written script, carefully altered and interlineated to the point where it becomes astonishing that he could read it. He could not respond to a debate, and adjust his position to its ebb and flow: his arguments emerged, like a regiment of tanks, fully armoured from his own head. Where he did not have a script, he usually confined himself to very brief procedural interventions. He was destitute of humour, and lacked the politician's crucial ability to read the mood of the house. On one occasion, unable to accept his failure to do so, he walked out in a huff. On another occasion, speaking on the bill against adultery in 1628, he raised what may have been the biggest belly-laugh of the decade at his expense by concluding his speech with the motion 'that we commit it' (Johnson and others, 3.26, 30).

What made Pym a successful parliamentary politician was his total inner certainty, and the emotional force this gave to his performances. He benefited from a curious incongruity which combined the meticulous attention to unemotional detail of a skilled accountant with the driving passion of a religious enthusiast. With this, he combined an Aristotelian tendency to philosophize which often enabled him to see far more general implications in

a misdemeanour than others could do. It is the classic political ability to see all hell in a grain of sand. He also enjoyed a considerable intelligence, and an exceptional personal force. All this was backed up by a prodigious capacity for hard work. By 1626 his colleagues had learned that he was the man who could be left to write the report, and when he did, it usually contained passages taken verbatim from his own speeches. He also had a serious interest in parliamentary procedure, and put a lot of effort into being on the right side of successive speakers.

At first Pym was unknown to many of his parliamentary colleagues, and Sir Thomas Barrington once referred to him under the inappropriate name 'Mr Pope' (Notestein, Relf, and Simpson, 3.190). The first sign that he was acquiring a patron came with his return for Tavistock in 1624, the constituency for which he sat for the rest of his career. Since there is no evidence that he ever set foot in the constituency, Bedford's patronage is the only sensible interpretation of that return. What is striking is the effort he put in 1624 in trying to secure the disputed seat at Chippenham, to which he had been elected by his own efforts.

In 1628 Pym became an executor for Bedford's draft will, and he retained that position so long as there was a risk of Bedford's leaving minor heirs. His patron was not Edward, third earl of Bedford, but Francis, second Lord Russell of Thornhaugh, who had bought his predecessor out of the estates in 1617 and succeeded to the Bedford title in 1627. Pym also attracted the patronage of Robert Rich, earl of Warwick, possibly through Sir Nathaniel Rich, who became a close parliamentary collaborator. In November 1626 he became a feoffee to uses to Warwick, taking on a share of responsibility for managing Warwick's estate during his voyage of 1627, and for payment of his debts, which Warwick calculated at £13,000. To put these debts in proportion Warwick's calculation of his income for 1634 should be considered. His certain rents he put at £6447 17s. 6d., and casualties at £318 7s., giving a total income from land of £6766 5s. 6d. This puts his income from land, which was almost certainly smaller than Bedford's, at thirteen times a high estimate of Pym's.

Early seventeenth-century patrons did not normally operate a political whip, except on personal matters such as private bills or on highly sensitive matters such as the impeachment of Buckingham, where the only possible safety was in numbers. For people such as Pym the usual service was work, and the management of Warwick's estate during his absence, using his special skill as a receiver, was typical of what was wanted. His later post as treasurer of the Providence Island Company grew out of this tradition. It was the connection with Warwick which led Pym into his colonial interests; the beginning of the connection cannot be dated, but was certainly after 18 April 1621, when he proposed a total ban on tobacco (*JHC*, *1547–1628*, 543).

Bedford, if he had left a wardship, would have drawn on Pym's same skills of land management. Meanwhile, his chief use for Pym seems to have been to satisfy his voracious appetite for information. Pym's parliamentary diaries for 1621, 1624, and 1625 were all in his possession, and he annotated them. Some of his comments, especially on the treatment of nonconforming ministers and impropriations in 1625, indicate strong disagreement with the line Pym was taking, but there is no evidence that he tried to restrain him.

In his first parliament, in 1621, Pym was only an occasional speaker, and many of his early speeches were on matters in which he was personally interested. Sir John Bennet had admitted his uncle William Pym's will to probate, and he had crossed swords with Sir Giles Mompesson. In that case, he put his accountancy skills to such good use that he helped to manage the charge, though William Hakewill, whom he was assisting, complained that he was 'no lawyer'. His interest in the parliamentary representation of Ilchester and Minehead must have been obvious, and the case of Morgan, Bowdler, and Meggs was one in which his feoffee Sir Edward Wardour, also a member, was personally concerned.

The fact that Pym was 'no lawyer', and not attuned to the constitutional concerns, or the sense of honour, of many of the house, accounts for many of the occasions when he hit the wrong note. On 18 April, on the case of Sir John Bennet, he suggested that they should investigate whether he had taken bribes to do justice or to do injustice; Sir Edward Coke bluntly reminded him that it was a bribe in any case. On 21 April he again clashed with Coke and Edward Alford, who were calling for an act of parliament for suppression of a monopoly. Pym said the proclamation against it was good, 'which was not denyed, all the House sayth' (Notestein, Relf, and Simpson, 3.44). He learned, but there is truth in the remark that Pym's attachment to the law always had a certain intermittency about it (Hexter, 194–5).

Pym also made some remarkably significant contributions. In a speech of 20 April against Sir John Bennet he set out in full what was to become the procedure of impeachment. He said, in a characteristic phrase, 'the high court of Parliament is the great eye of the kingdom, to find out offences and punish them' (Notestein, Relf, and Simpson, 2.303). In his vision, the Commons were to keep control of the prosecution, the Lords of judgment, and the king of execution. On 15 May, in a remarkable anticipation of Rousseau, he said: 'Men accused heear cannot be condemned but by him selfe, all voyces being included heeard' (ibid., 3.264). It took him twenty years to make this vision a reality, but he succeeded.

Pym gained most notice for his speeches of 27 and 28 November on the foreign policy issue. He favoured war, but thought that without raids on the king of Spain's treasure in the West Indies it could not be financed. Characteristically, he was more interested in the home front, and thought that 'we are not secure enough at home in respect of the enemy at home which groes by the suspence of the lawes at home'. The king received 'no redress by the subordinate ministers that he trusts'. He proposed that every man take an oath of association 'or not be admitted into the commonwealth'. He said papists broke the 'independency upon others' which loyal subjects owed, and that the king, by mistaken lenity towards them, was hazarding the state. He offered a proposal, which looked far into his political future, for the execution of the recusancy laws to be entrusted to a commission including members of both houses of parliament (Notestein, Relf, and Simpson, 3.461–2; Nicholas, 2.238; Notestein, Relf, and Simpson, 4.448). The attitude to the king echoes the remark of Simon de Montfort during the battle of Saintes in 1242: 'The King must be locked up until the battle is over, or we will lose'. Neither king took the attitude kindly. The attitude to Rome might have been more in place in the year of Pym's birth, when Roman Catholics could be legitimately suspected of wanting to put Mary, queen of Scots on the throne, than it was in the year when the speech was delivered. Pym seems not to have seen the peace of 1604 as anything but a temporary truce. It was in this context that he placed his hatred of attacks on 'Puritans', which he thought alienated the king from his only loyal subjects. It was this Manichaean view of the world, concealed under the practicality of a man of business, which made him such a potentially dangerous enemy. In his proposal for a commission to execute the recusancy laws, he showed what was to be his driving conviction twenty years later, that it was the executive power which was in the supreme position, and no amount of parliamentary power could change the situation without getting a handle on it. He was in immediate trouble for this speech, and no doubt made things worse the next day by bravely saying he would ignore 'the whisperings of his own fortune' (ibid., 6.206). The imprisonment which followed the dissolution made him more careful, but more determined.

In 1624, the year of his quietest parliament, Pym gave full support to the breach of the treaties with Spain, saying that 'we have made one step from the greatest danger that ever threatened us, God grant that we relapse not again'. He supported, almost alone, the king's full request for six subsidies and twelve fifteenths (diary of Sir William Spring, Harvard U., Houghton L., 19 March 1624). He continued his hunt for recusants, including 'those who by their practice show what they are, as well as those that are convicted' (BL, Add. MS 18597, fol. 109b). Legal rights were not for fifth columns. He also began, in attacks on Richard Mountague and Samuel Harsnett, the attack on Arminian clergy which was to become his major theme of the 1620s.

Parliaments under Charles I In the parliament of 1625 Pym gave priority to this religious business. He kept his head down about most of the contentious secular business, and confined himself to supporting Fleetwood's final move for compromise, on 8 August. Much of his time went on the preparation of the petition on religion, managed jointly by him and Sir Edwin Sandys. One of his phrases about the papists, from his offending speech of 27 November 1621, has passed almost unaltered into the petition: 'if they gayne but a connivencye, they will presse for a toleration; then strive for an equallitie, and lastly aspire to such a superioritye as may worke the extermination both of us and of our religion' (Gardiner, 19). He was responsible for most of the work of the committee on Richard

Mountague and, though Heneage Finch delivered its report, it is easy to hear Pym's voice in the drafting of it. Unusually, this committee delivered a further report, which was delivered by Pym, to the next parliament, on 17 April 1626. In that, he directly charged Mountague with discouraging the well affected in religion, 'and to incline them, and as much as he can, to reconcile them, to popery'. The two key points in this charge were Mountague's maintaining that Rome was a true church, and that it was possible to fall from grace (ibid., 180). It is likely that Pym meant the charge of popery against the Arminians entirely literally. They were the fifth column in the pulpit.

For Pym the chief attraction of the rule of law was always that it guaranteed England's true protestant status. The area in which he most wanted to control the executive was always that of religion, to prevent it from either corrupting the doctrine of the Church of England, or subverting it by too much leniency to the popish enemy. When parliament met again, in 1626, Buckingham had just given his support to the Arminians at the York House conference. Pym therefore knew that attempts to subvert the religion of England were continuing with the consent of the chief minister, and the connivance, possibly unwitting, of the king.

Together with both his patrons, Bedford and Warwick, Pym committed himself wholeheartedly to the impeachment of Buckingham. From the beginning he linked this issue with that of the royal revenue. He supported Sir Nathaniel Rich's motion of 24 February to consider the king's revenue. He asked to consider 'confusion' (no doubt a euphemism) by the king's officers (Bidwell and Jansson, 2.116). Typically, he took the first chance to link the issues of protecting the revenue and of fighting the popish danger. On 1 March he used his accountant's skill to cut through a fog in the debate on the duke's alleged embezzlement of the goods from the captured French ship the St Peter. The issue was in danger of being lost in a difficult dispute about whether the St Peter was a lawful prize. Pym saw that that issue was irrelevant, and asked for the commissioners to be sent for to ask by what warrant they delivered the money of the king or the Frenchmen to the duke. It was the parliamentary question at its best: a straightforward request for information and lethally unanswerable. On 4 March he co-operated with Bedford to avoid a row between the houses about an unwise order of the Commons to send for Buckingham, made without the consent of the Lords. The Commons pretended, with the clerk's consent, that the order had been mistakenly entered, and altered it before there could be an official complaint.

Pym continued to show awareness of the need to limit executive power. On 14 April he reminded the king of James's promise in 1624 that he would not end the war by making peace without the advice of parliament. On the same day he gave strong support to Digges's proposal for a West India Company. Like the proposal for a commission to execute the recusancy laws, which he had offered in 1621, this was designed to delegate executive power to safe

hands. It was in effect a proposal which looked towards the privatization of war, by allowing it to be conducted by a private company for prizes, rather than by the state out of inadequate taxation. The immediate model was clearly the Dutch West India Company, but some of the activities of Wallenstein in Germany, and the move towards funding war by *asiento*, or contract, in Spain, looked in the same direction. War was not merely too important to be left to the generals: it was too expensive to be left to the king. This was becoming an increasingly common note in Pym's thinking.

Pym's main business continued to be the committee for religion, from which he made fourteen reports. Most of these were part of a drive, on which Sandys had started him in 1625, to hunt down and exclude from teaching all the popish schoolmasters he could find. He also carried on the task of listing office-holders who were recusant, were married to recusants, or had recusants in their households. On 3 May he showed how utterly unpolitical his hatred of popery was by trying unsuccessfully to insist on including Thomas Howard, earl of Arundel, in the list of popish office-holders because he had two recusant servants. Arundel was not merely too big for this sort of treatment; he was also, along with Pembroke, one of the two principal backers of the impeachment of the duke within the privy council. Any attack on Arundel would have unravelled the uneasy coalition which made the impeachment of Buckingham possible, between Arundel's supporters who wanted to impeach Buckingham for being at war with Spain, and Pembroke's who wanted to impeach him for not doing it properly. Pym was overruled.

Pym's anxieties ratcheted up when the king reacted to the beginning of impeachment proceedings by trying to have Buckingham elected as chancellor of Cambridge University. Pym was clearly well informed on this issue, and probably got his information from his niece's husband Ralph Brownrigg, who was one of the organizers of the Cambridge Calvinists. On 3 June he drew the house's attention to the fact that the duke's campaign was being organized by men such as John Cosin, 'who have bene agents to utter Montagues book', and suggested that 'it may be to perfect a conspiracy to bring in Arminianism' (Eaton Hall, Cheshire, diary of Sir Richard Grosvenor, fol. 148; Bidwell and Jansson, 3.352, 356). From then on, Pym knew that a creed which he regarded as popish was being promoted from within the heart of government, with the full knowledge of the king.

Among the speeches given in 1628, and to a lesser extent in 1625 and 1626, there is a difficulty in distinguishing Pym's from those of John Pyne, MP for Poole, who too was from Somerset. Even if Pyne is given the benefit of every doubt, 1628 was still Pym's most active session to date, and he made more speeches then than in all of his first three parliaments put together. For the first time he was thoroughly converted to the Cokeian version of the rule of law. On 25 March, right at the beginning, he acknowledged Coke as his source, and added a commitment to the Cokeian doctrine of the ancient constitution. On 25 April he committed himself to the theory of liberty as a birth-right. On 26 April he opposed the Lords' proposed amendments to the petition of right, saying that 'for reason of state I desire it may never come amongst laws', and that bare confirmation would not suffice, because 'we have our liberties, but they have been broken by martial law' (Johnson and others, 3.107, 102, 111, 118). He joined in the specific condemnations of arbitrary imprisonment, forced loans, martial law, billeting, and the use of soldiers in England.

At the same time Pym tried not to block off avenues to any satisfactory compromise. He refused to make an issue of the king's demand that the house sit on Good Friday. As in 1625 he seconded the final motion for a compromise, in this case Rudyerd's motion that the king be asked for a second answer, but this time he was successful. He was not, however, prepared to take an inadequate compromise for form's sake. On 6 May he replied to a request that they should rely on the king's word by saying he was entirely willing to rely on the king's word, but the king had not said the right word. 'If he understood the laws he would not err' (Johnson and others, 3.282, 271, 276, 281–2).

In a large report of 11 June Pym continued his attack on Richard Mountague. He repeated his charge that Mountague was 'drawing the subjects to popery and reconciling them to the see of Rome'. He accused him of dividing the church in foreign parts from the Church of England, and complained of the rapidly widening meaning he and his allies were giving to the word 'Puritan':

> he layes the name of Puritans upon the King's subjects that are dutifull and honest subjects in trueth at first this word was given to them that severed themselves from the church but he sayes there are Puritans in heart and Puritanes in doctrine and under this name he comprehends some of our bpps.

The house resolved to send the case to the Lords, but adjournment prevented them (Johnson and others, 4.262, 238–240).

Pym's biggest new contribution was in the attack on Roger Manwaring, vicar of St Giles-in-the-Fields, who had preached in the most arbitrary terms in defence of the forced loan. Pym summarized the case to the house on 14 May, and officially presented it to the Lords on 4 June. He said he 'strikes at the root of all government' by supporting 'an absolute power not bounded by law'. He brought 'spiritual poison offered to the ear of the King, appropriating omnipotency to princes'. This was, more or less fully fledged, the concept of alteration of government which was to be the staple of Pym's Long Parliament impeachments. He said:

> First, that no alteracon of the forme of government in a state can be made without danger of ruyne of the state. Secondly, that these lawes did not growe by graunt of princes, nor by pragmatique sanction, but are fundamentall from the very originall of this kingdome, and are part of the essentiall constitution thereof.

He charged him with 'conspiring with the Jesuits and the Church of Rome, to disturb the government'. There is no extant proof that Manwaring was an Arminian, but it appears that Pym believed he was, and that he intended to sweep aside law and parliaments because they stood in the way of the introduction of Arminianism (Johnson and others, 3.407–10; HLRO, Braye MS I, fols. 63b, 60b).

For Pym 1629 was probably his least successful session in parliament. The house's proceedings were dominated by two issues. One was the issue of tonnage and poundage and the customs farmers. The customs farmers had arrested John Rolle, a member of parliament, for not paying tonnage and poundage, which parliament had not yet confirmed, in spite of Pym's attempt to get them to do so before they rose in 1628. The group led by Pym, Rich, and Rous accepted that the king could not be made to punish the customs farmers for obeying his commands, thought that sooner or later he would have to be legally allowed tonnage and poundage, and wanted to give priority to the attack on Arminianism and popery. Sir John Eliot and John Selden, who led the demand for a fight on the question of punishing the customs farmers, had the better of it, and the house slid inexorably towards dissolution.

At the end of 1629 Pym was definitely not a leader of parliament. He was, perhaps, one of the twenty or so most important members, but he had staked his authority on a course the house would not accept, and shown the same fatal capacity to misjudge the mood of the house as he had shown in his first session, in 1621. His speech of 19 February, saying that 'the liberties of this House are inferior to the liberties of the kingdome, to determine the previledge of this House is but a meane matter, and the mayne end is to establishe possession of the subjects', may have been intellectually perfectly sound, but the phrase 'a meane matter' showed the inability of the bad politician to suffer fools gladly. Rich tried to rescue him, but he was roundly damned by Eliot and Sir Francis Seymour, and comprehensively defeated (Notestein and Relf, 156–7).

One would not expect, looking at these exchanges, that when the house met again eleven years later this man would be unambiguously recognized as its spokesman and leading figure. It was not a position Pym had come anywhere near during the 1620s. The conclusion seems to follow inexorably that his rise to supremacy inside the house was the result of events which took place outside it.

Pym without a parliament Among these events, the founding and development of the Providence Island Company must be one. There has been a long-standing belief that Pym contemplated emigration during the 1630s. The solid evidence on which this rests is Oliver St John's obituary tribute to Pym in the House of Commons. St John referred to him:

> having about 10 or 12 years since gotten up his estate about the town, fearing lest popery would overgrow this kingdom, intending to make some plantation in foreign parts where the profession of the Gospel might have a free course; in wch designe, and in using his best endeavours for the service of the Parlt.; both before the Parlt and since, he hath wasted his estate and his person. (BL, Add. MS 31116, fol. 99b)

Coming from one of Pym's executors, the statement is authoritative in what it says, but it is somewhat lacking in precision. It does not actually say that Pym himself intended to emigrate. He did not sell his estate, though he certainly borrowed heavily on it. Moreover, the statement is self-interested, since it ends with a motion for money for Pym's heir, for whose debts most of St John's friends were bound.

During most of the early 1630s Pym was living in High Holborn, in the parish of St Andrew, alongside Sir Nathaniel Rich, William Fiennes, Viscount Saye and Sele, Robert Greville, Lord Brooke, Sir John Clotworthy, William Jessop, and, later, Samuel Hartlib. Informal meetings for planning must have been very easy. The Providence Island Company, formed in 1630, involved most of the key figures of the parliamentary leadership of 1640: Saye, Brooke, Warwick, Edward Montagu, Lord Mandeville, Henry Rich, earl of Holland, Sir Thomas Barrington, Sir Gilbert Gerrard, Sir Benjamin Rudyerd, Oliver St John, and Henry Darley. William Jessop, Warwick's servant, was secretary and Pym was treasurer. The conspicuous absentee was Bedford, whether because he was never quite of that political group, or because he was too careful of his money.

In this group Pym was socially and financially outclassed. He had to make a big effort to distinguish his status from that of William Jessop, Warwick's servant and the other working officer, and underlined the point by writing to him as 'Good Will' (Lancs. RO, Preston, Hulton MS 46/21). In 1630 Sir Thomas Barrington turned down a proposal to allow Pym to stay in Barrington Hall for the summer. By 1633, when he was better established, the Barringtons were using Pym as a feoffee to uses. In 1635 he was bound, along with Sir Gilbert Gerrard, Sir Benjamin Rudyerd, and Henry Darley, for Lord Brooke's debt to Lord Saye and Sele.

Such bonds became steadily more frequent. Early reports from Providence were encouraging, talking optimistically of fruit and tobacco, and calling it an island 'like the Eden of God'. By 20 March 1637 the company was being told that it had already spent £10,000 on defence, and another £20,000 was urgently needed. The company was under-capitalized for this sort of debt. Most of its members had borrowed the money for their initial adventures, at £1025 each, and borrowed further for the additional costs. Since they were all sureties for each other's debts, when the bonds were forfeit their debts all redoubled on each other, turning them into a collection of merchants of Venice. In September 1641 the Spanish capture of Providence deprived them of any hope of recovering this money.

The cat's cradle of debts which resulted can probably never be fully reconstructed. William Jessop in summer 1642 tried to calculate debts owed to the company. He brought out Pym's at £1739 19s. 3d., second only to the debt owed by Lord Brooke, who could better afford to pay it. This was very far from the total debt owed by Pym, for which the estimate of £10,000 offered to the House of Commons may well have been accurate. Since he no longer enjoyed any earnings from office, this means that he owed something in the region of twenty years' income.

By any standard that is an unsustainable debt, and many of those who pressed for the House of Commons to undertake these debts were themselves bound for them. As late as 1652 Katherine Brooke reported that her brother William Greville still feared arrest for Pym's debts.

Landowners who run up debts of this order tend to quarrel with their heirs, and John Pym was no exception. In November 1634 he discovered that his heir, Alexander, had been borrowing money from Henry Darley, Richard Knightley, and others without telling his father. He instructed Alexander, who was with the English regiments in the service of the states general, not to come home, and not to reveal that they were reconciled, 'for if they ever take notice you are reconciled to me, I shall bring them to no reason'. Alexander had shown his father up before his rich friends, and the resulting fury was to be expected. Alexander, who never married, may have remained angry for longer (BL, Add. MS 11692, fol. 1).

Other business continued as usual. In July 1632 Pym wrote to the provost of King's College, Cambridge, casually dropping the information that he had just returned from staying with the earl of Warwick at Leighs, Essex and asking for a fellowship for Francis Rous (which he did not get). In 1632 he and Sir Dudley Digges jointly bought the wardship of Dudley Palmer, heir of Sir Anthony Palmer, an old friend and distant relation, for £750. In 1638 Pym's children took refuge from the plague with one of his new friends, Sir Arthur Hesilrige. In 1637 he again enfeoffed his estates to use: his feoffees were Rudyerd, Richard Knightley, John Upton (a member of the Providence Island Company as well as of the Rous circle), Oliver St John, and John Graunt, clerk of the cheque, who combined membership of the company with running the king's messenger service.

In 1635 Gerrard credited Pym and Sir Nathaniel Rich with influencing the younger Vane towards emigration to New England. This is credible, if uncertain, and if Pym himself contemplated emigration, Saybrooke, where he was a patentee, is as likely to have been a destination as Providence. He was left a ring by Richard Sibbes, and it may have been admiration for Sibbes's preaching which induced him to send his younger son Charles to Lincoln's Inn instead of to the Middle Temple. Pym defaulted on his ship money assessments in Middlesex in 1636–7 and 1637–8, and appears on a list of people selected for distraint, alongside Sir Nathaniel Rich, who was over a year dead, as well as Sir Gilbert Gerrard and Lord Brooke.

Pym's relationship with Bedford was evidently undisturbed by all these developments. In 1633 Robert Scawen, who had been acting as lawyer for Bedford, drew up a chancery bill describing a massive quarrel with Bedford about the pay the latter had not given him. In a long description of the quarrel he records 'one Mr John Pym' as being repeatedly called in to signify the earl's pleasure to him and to act as go-between in the resulting disputes. Pym, in his attempts to smooth things over, seems to have been acting in something very close to a menial capacity (Alnwick Castle, Northumberland, MS Y III 2(4), envelope 7). It is tempting, but no more, to connect Pym's resigning his receivership in favour of Scawen with a belated conclusion of these negotiations.

It is easy to underestimate how difficult the requirement to attend church could become during the 1630s for a godly worshipper who did not own his own advowson. Pym is not recorded as ever having been associated with nonconformity, but the conformity he practised seems to have been what one of John Winthrop's correspondents called 'the old conformity', not the newer and more rigorous version required by the Laudians. At Cannington in Somerset the Elizabethan Pyms had had leave to build a pew on the site of the old high altar. That pew seems not to have survived disturbances whose basis was social jealousy, but it was not replaced by an altar. At Wollavington, where Pym probably more often resided, he became involved in 1639 in a chancery lawsuit with his vicar, Richard Prigge, about a glebe terrier and a tithe commutation agreement from the reign of Henry VIII. There is no record of any dispute involving worship, but Prigge had been appointed in 1626 by Sir John Sydenham, a pugnacious ceremonialist highly unlikely to appoint anyone congenial to Pym. Perhaps most ominously for Pym, in the tithe lawsuit the churchwardens, both Pym's tenants, sided with the vicar. At Wherwell, Matthew Nicholas, Sir Edward Nicholas's brother, got the prebend in 1634, and moved in and took the service. He reported trouble about the surplice, which some refractory persons took as the mark of the beast, and about coming to the rails. The vicar, he said, covertly supported the nonconformists, but after 1634 Wherwell was unlikely to remain a safe place for Pym to worship. At St Andrew's, Holborn, there was a lecturership. The previous lecturer had been suspected of seditious preaching, but cleared by Bishop George Mountain. John Wood, the lecturer in 1637, was described by Laud as 'a wild turbulent preacher, and formerly censured in the High Commission Court' (P. Seaver, *The Puritan Lectureships*, 1970, 258). The lights were going out here too.

This may be why, from about 1636, Pym spent much of his time with Richard Knightley (1593–1639) of Fawsley in Northamptonshire. Fawsley was an ecclesiastical peculiar, wholly owned by Knightley, and the vicar was largely funded by a donation from Knightley which was voluntary and therefore capable of diversion. From about 1626 the vicar was the great Elizabethan veteran John Dod, a survivor of the classical movement who had been deprived by Bancroft as long ago as 1606. In 1630 Knightley entrusted Dod's private endowment to feoffees, who were Saye and Sele, Nathaniel Rich, John Crew, John Pym 'of London', and Christopher Sherland, recorder of Northampton.

After 1636, when Pym reported that he had been in the country or was going there, Fawsley was, apparently, usually the place involved. In September 1639 he reported to Samuel Hartlib that he intended to stay at Fawsley all term. Much of what is known of him in this period comes from the Hartlib papers. They contain many impressions of sympathy from Pym and, while these are no doubt genuine, Pym's correspondence with Hartlib shows that there were two things he badly wanted from him. One was continental political intelligence: Hartlib wrote a regular newsletter, for which Pym on 30 September 1639 paid Ralph Brownrigg's subscription as well as his own. The other thing Pym wanted desperately was the service of Christopher de Bergh, a Moravian drainage engineer who was a friend of Hartlib: the coalmine, at Bedworth near Coventry, run by Knightley, Pym, and others, was costing £1500 a year or more for drainage, with twelve horses working day and night. Once again Pym had shown skill in making influential friends, and a genius for losing money. That is the story of Pym in the 1630s.

Scots and parliaments When parliament reassembled in April 1640 Edmund Rossingham the newsletter writer was asked for a copy of the grievances of the parliament, and replied by sending a text of Pym's opening speech. This is an immediate recognition of a status Pym had been nowhere near on 2 March 1629, when parliament had last sat. There were three important reasons for this change. The first was that there was a remarkably low survival rate among those who had been the most prominent members of the Commons in the 1620s. Sir Edward Coke, Sir Edwin Sandys, Sir Robert Phelips, Sir Dudley Digges, Sir John Eliot, William Noy, and Sir Nathaniel Rich were dead. Thomas Wentworth and Edward Littleton had been promoted in the king's service, the former now earl of Strafford, and William Hakewill had ceased to sit. Of the top twenty of 1629, only Pym and Sir Francis Seymour still sat.

In 1629 Seymour had probably been the more influential of the two. In the Short Parliament of 1640 this picture was reversed. This is partly because Pym spoke throughout for the group Sir Edward Nicholas described as 'Pym's junto' (PRO, SP 16/472/45), who were roughly those identified here, with the important addition of Robert Devereux, earl of Essex. The energy devoted to copying Pym's set speeches and distributing copies around the country has left traces in many archives. The third reason was a change in the mood of the house. Pym was always most influential in a house which was thoroughly alarmed, and he experienced this from 1640 in a way in which he had rarely experienced it in the 1620s.

The opening speech, of 17 April, was made in tandem with Francis Rous. Rous, who came first, made the key charge that 'the roote of all or grievances I thinke to be an intended union betwist us and Rome', and Pym undertook the charge of pulling all the miscellaneous grievances of the 1630s together under this heading (Cope, 146). It was almost certainly the object of Pym's group, as Oliver St John later told the earl of Clarendon, to ensure that the parliament should fail. The king's object was to secure supply to fight the Scottish covenanters. For Pym the prospect of armed foreign help was the only thing which gave him any hope of success against a king he knew to be implacably opposed to everything he wanted. He thus had to prevent an agreement while appearing to be working for one. This meant always introducing a new demand when agreement seemed possible. On 2 May he added a new issue by demanding that any settlement must require an act of parliament giving legal authority to the militia and military charges. Since the Marian Militia Act had lapsed in 1604 the need was a real one, and Pym had addressed it constructively in 1628. However, since Charles was known to believe that the prerogative was a sufficient basis for the militia, the issue was an obstacle to agreement. To make certain, Pym may have been responsible for encouraging a story which spread at the very end of the parliament, that the Commons were about to investigate the grievances of the Scots, which was *ultra vires* as well as offensive to the king. This may explain the disorderly haste of the king's dissolution on 5 May.

During the summer of 1640, when there was no parliament in session, the junto seem to have kept communication with the Scots open. Their next public move was the drafting of the petition of the twelve peers, calling for the summons of a parliament and 'uniting of both your realms against the common enemies of the reformed religion'. The petition was drawn up at Bedford House in the Strand, closely watched by the secretary of state, Sir Francis Windebank, who was a near neighbour and Bedford's tenant in Drury Lane. Windebank observed the presence of Pym and Hampden, and the petition is believed to have been written by Pym and Oliver St John. It immediately went to the Scots, who had crossed the Tyne and defeated the English army on the same day. With it went a good deal of political advice from 'N. F.', probably Saye's son Nathaniel Fiennes. The Scottish petition of 4 September, their response to this advice, which survives in a copy in Pym's papers, indicates a close working relationship. That relationship was founded on common interest, and lasted through the winter of 1640–41. The Scottish covenanters had defeated the English twice, and occupied Northumberland and Durham. Yet they knew they could not count on winning a third time, and they needed the English parliament as guarantors of any Scottish peace settlement. Equally, the English knew that without a Scottish army in the field, there would not be a parliament at all. Mutual need could not be much greater.

This commitment to the Scottish alliance lasted for the rest of Pym's life. He had understood by November 1621 that success in any parliamentary enterprise lay not in the raising of a parliamentary majority, but in persuading the king. The more reluctant the king proved, the bigger the inverted commas needed round the word 'persuading'. By 1640 it was clear that Charles was as reluctant to accept Pym's religion as Mary, queen of Scots, had been to accept the religion of John Knox. The help Scottish protestants had then had from the English, English protestants now needed from the Scots.

Before the Long Parliament met on 3 November 1640 Pym had also cemented an alliance with the French ambassador, who observed that this parliament would be different from all previous ones, because the king could not dissolve it without risking losing England. It was the Scots' success in depriving Charles of the trump card of the power of dissolution which was the centre of Pym's strategy up to the king's treaty with the Scots of 7 September 1641. On 7 November 1640 Pym again opened serious proceedings with a speech two hours long, claiming there

was a design of papists to alter law and religion, which were so necessarily joined, 'that with the one, the other falls' (Bodl. Oxf., MS Clarendon 19, no. 1448).

Up to January 1641 the main objective was to bring the king, still punch-drunk after the English defeat at Newburn, to realize that he needed to undertake serious negotiations before he could get the Scottish army to leave England. Between the junto and the Scottish commissioners, who were in London to negotiate the treaty, there was regular social contact. The Scots, even more than the English, were determined to get rid of Strafford as part of a settlement. He was known to want Scotland to be annexed as a province of England, and he was the only councillor who had publicly argued for continuing the war after Newburn. His disappearance from office was necessary as a mark of the king's abandonment of the policies for which he had stood. When impeachment proceedings were begun against him, it was in response to demands from all three kingdoms, with Pym acting as co-ordinator between them. Because they wanted frequent English parliaments as a guarantee of Anglo-Scottish peace, the Scots also joined with Pym in wanting a triennial act for England.

In terms of serious politics it was necessary to mark time until the middle of January 1641, when the king realized that it was necessary to start serious negotiation if he was ever to change his situation. From the middle of January to the first week of March 1641 politics were dominated by the need to try to negotiate a settlement. For the king it was an obvious chance to try to divide the Anglo-Scottish alliance. For the Scots the two essentials were the abolition of bishops in England, so that pressure for harmonization should no longer lead Charles to press for a Laudian church in Scotland, and a long-term place in the sun for parliaments in England, which would enable them to be guarantors of Anglo-Scottish peace. For the king the essentials were an adequate revenue, the survival of bishops, who were his machinery for governing the church, and the life of Strafford. For Pym the essentials were the abolition of Arminianism and popery, an adequate revenue, and security against a comeback by an angry king some years later. His essentials probably did not include the abolition of bishops if it were possible to ensure that Charles did not appoint them.

Granted willingness to compromise, there was a serious possibility of a low-level settlement between Charles and the Scots, or of one between Charles and the junto. The chance of a settlement involving all three was always going to be slender because the issues of Strafford and bishops stood in the way. The terms on which Charles negotiated from the middle of January onwards might have been designed to divide the junto from the Scots.

On money, a good deal of progress was made on paper. The plan was for Bedford to be made lord treasurer, with Pym as chancellor of the exchequer. The plans worked out became the nucleus of the Restoration financial settlement, where they proved to be adequate for a generation. The big problem would have been getting the assent of the House of Commons, and the rest of the settlement never became far enough advanced for that task to be seriously attempted.

On religion, Charles began negotiations with James Ussher, archbishop of Armagh, who happened to be in London giving a series of lectures in Bedford's parish church at St Paul's, Covent Garden. With Ussher came Richard Holdsworth, vice-chancellor of Cambridge University, and Ralph Brownrigg, Pym's relative and ally. These people could have run a church in which Pym a few years earlier would have been perfectly happy. They were the core of the Calvinist episcopalian cause. They were, on the other hand, utterly unacceptable to the Scots. A deal of this sort could have been had only by giving up the Scottish security which would have made Pym feel safe to adopt it. It would also have alienated the network of London ministers who were the third leg of the junto's political organization.

During February 1641 many of the Londoners who were lending to finance the Scottish army's stay in England refused to lend further until they had justice on the earl of Strafford. Pym, in desperation, proposed on 20 February to compel them to lend. This was followed by the Scots' paper of 24 February which insisted on abolition of episcopacy in England and the death of Strafford. These were non-negotiable terms for Charles, and the Scottish commissioners in London grew less bold when advised that the Scottish army in Newcastle had not enough money to march south.

The settlement was probably dead from this moment. If there had been any doubt, it would have been removed by the issue of the queen's Catholic servants. Pym had already been in trouble for the proposal that Catholics should be forced to wear a distinctive mark of dress, which the French ambassador said was rejected by 'tout le monde' (Russell, *Fall*, 177). He and the Commons then proposed that the queen, marriage treaty notwithstanding, should be deprived of all her Catholic servants. Bedford, from the Lords, told them they could not do this. Pym refused to back down, saying 'that we ought to obey God rather than man, and that if we doe not prefer God before man, he will refuse us, with many other good notions' (ibid., 267). This was something with which neither Charles nor Henrietta Maria could live.

The issue of Strafford became as divisive. As Strafford himself appreciated, the debate became so heated because the king would not let him leave office, and therefore refused to signal his renunciation of the policies associated with him. For the Scots Strafford's survival was incompatible with a secure peace. Pym may have been encouraged to feel the same because he had come into possession of Strafford's letter to Olivares of 18 July 1640, asking for Spanish help to Charles in the second bishops' war. It is interesting that he never used this letter in public. He was also facing strong pressure from behind him in the House of Commons. The switch from impeachment to attainder was introduced against his opposition, and was designed to block the royal power of pardon by specifying the penalty of death in the bill, which the king could not amend. Even more tension was created when, in the last few days before Strafford's condemnation, it emerged that the king had entered into the army plot, designed to rescue Strafford by force and possibly to bring about a forcible dissolution of parliament. It is possible that it was this revelation of the king's readiness to fight rather than settle which finally made Pym irreconcilable. There is no evidence of serious negotiation between Pym and the king after this date.

The failure of the plans for settlement revealed the intellectual limitations of the junto. Their basic outlook was in line with previous baronial leaderships from Simon de Montfort onwards. They planned to have authority exercised in the king's name by a series of commissions given to people the parliament would have cause to confide in. They freely used precedents taken from royal minorities, but they could not envisage any authority which was not exercised in the king's name. They never contemplated government being carried on by a parliament as a force independent of the king. They were right, since no parliament could sit except by royal writ. They could not turn to the regular recourse of a pretender, since there was none available. Their only hope was, in Lord Brooke's words, 'to reduce the King to a necessity of granting' (Russell, *Fall*, 274–5).

Without the Scots, whose departure was foreseeable from May 1641 onwards, this was going to be extremely difficult. Pym, as always, was prepared to use money to buy concessions in religion. The two bills he kept linked during the summer of 1641 were for tonnage and poundage and 'root and branch'. The Root and Branch Bill would have abolished bishops, not in order to set up a Scottish church, but to set up one governed by lay commissioners very much along the lines of the triers and ejectors of the protectorate. It would have achieved the key objective of taking control of the church out of Charles's hands, but not the key Scottish objective of a church governed by an assembly of elected ministers. Tonnage and poundage was granted through the summer in temporary bills for a few weeks at a time. It was to be made permanent when they had perfected a new book of rates. The sum at stake was no less than £482,000 per annum. The need for a book of rates was genuine, but it was understood that action would not be taken until the king accepted root and branch. It was a powerful strategy, but Pym did not understand that Charles's religion was no more for sale than his own. In the ten propositions of June 1641 Pym proposed to anticipate the militia ordinance by having lords lieutenant and deputy lieutenants nominated by the parliament, though his own allies refused to back him in this. He also wanted great officers chosen with the approval of the parliament, and the queen to be attended by nobles appointed by the parliament, with 'competent guards'. Not since the insanity of Henry VI had an adult king been so restricted. Yet the dissolution of the parliament, which could not be put off indefinitely, could make all these measures vanish in a puff of smoke. On 10 August 1641 the king's departure for Edinburgh to conclude the treaty with the Scots behind the parliament's back made that event look uncomfortably near. It is true that since the army plot there was an act of parliament requiring parliament's consent to dissolve it. After so long a sitting that was not likely to be difficult to get, and if there had been any doubt, the appearance of plague in London would have removed it. Sir Edward Nicholas was realistic in his expectation that as soon as the Scots returned home, 'those that have depended upon them will … fall flat' (Russell, *Fall*, 304).

Meanwhile Pym tried to use the moment to change as much as possible. He was largely responsible for the Commons' order of 8 September ordering the destruction of altars, rails, crucifixes, and other monuments of superstition. This put the Commons on a collision course with the Lords, who issued a contrary order to observe the law as it stood. It also involved treating an order of the Commons as if it were an act passed by king, Lords, and Commons. This order did a great deal to export the crisis atmosphere of Westminster to the parishes.

From 8 September to 20 October the Commons adjourned for an overdue recess, while adopting an innovation Pym had proposed in 1621, that of leaving a standing committee in session during the recess. This was more important than many more headline measures, since it ended the situation whereby parliaments ceased to have any part in politics on the day they adjourned.

When the houses returned the king, to Nicholas's despair, was still away in Scotland, and no date was fixed for his return. He seems to have overreached himself in the 'incident', a plot to kidnap Archibald Campbell, earl of Argyll, and James Hamilton, marquess of Hamilton. Charles gave his English servants no account of the 'incident', perhaps because there was none he could honourably give. Pym had no such inhibitions. He persuaded the Lords that the 'incident' was likely to be part of a design involving both kingdoms, and that this justified the parliament at Westminster in having a guard. It is easy to underrate how far Pym's policy after the army plot and the death of Strafford was driven by simple physical fear of royal retaliation. He also persuaded the Lords that the peace of the kingdoms was indivisible, and that they should offer their support to suppress any who tried to break the peace of Scotland or the recent treaty between the kingdoms. He was offering to the covenanters to return the favour of 1640, and already looking towards the solemn league and covenant of 1643.

On 1 November, well before the king returned, dissolution or adjournment ceased to be a practical possibility on the arrival of news of a major uprising in Ireland. This raised the stakes significantly by introducing the issue of raising armed force. This was dangerous not merely because no unquestionably legal method of raising armed force existed, but also because many members, and Pym most of all, were afraid to put armed force into the hands of a king they thought likely to use it to kill them. On 9 November he told the Lords at a conference that the Irish rising was the result of a popish conspiracy, that that conspiracy was favoured by some 'who have been admitted into very near places of counsel and authority' about the king, and that he feared some such attempt by the papists

in England. He added that 'diseases which proceed from the inward parts, as the liver, the heart or the brains, the more noble parts, it is a hard thing to apply cure to such diseases' (Russell, *Fall*, 419). The reference to diseases of the brain was not accidental: he repeated it on 25 January 1642. The casting of suspicion on the king was obvious, but impossible to reply to. From then on his objective was to ensure that any forces sent to Ireland should be under either Scottish or parliamentary control. This was pursued first through the additional instruction to the parliament's committee in Scotland, and then through the militia ordinance. Pym's key Irish objective, that popery should never be tolerated there, showed a lack of realism reminiscent of Charles's attempts to enforce the prayer book in Scotland.

With the drive for the militia ordinance came a drive to win a majority in the House of Lords by excluding the popish lords and the bishops. There was never, all the way through the civil war, any possibility of the Lords' excluding the popish lords: they might be popish, but they were peers. The bishops were a more doubtful case, and over Christmas 1641 the Lords were surrounded by crowds demonstrating against the bishops. When, in February 1642, the king finally agreed to their exclusion, the Commons asked the London ministers to restrain the crowds, and they disappeared immediately. The passing of the grand remonstrance, timed to come immediately before the king's belated return on 25 November, was designed very largely to help in raising the temperature on the London streets.

The king's response to these escalating threats was to publish articles accusing Pym, John Hampden, Sir Arthur Hesilrige, Denzil Holles, and William Strode, and with them Lord Mandeville, of high treason. Mandeville faced out the accusation in the Lords and offered to stand trial, but the five members of the Commons went to ground. On 4 January 1642 they took their seats in the Commons, and the king, as he was perhaps meant to do, went to the house with an armed guard to arrest them. He had omitted to guard the river, by which the members made a last-minute escape. By a brilliant exercise in propaganda, the Commons turned this attempt on the five members into an armed assault on the whole of the Commons, and Charles's reputation never recovered. Almost at the same moment, the newly elected common council took office in the City, and delivered control of the City trained bands into hands favourable to Pym. Charles had lost military control of his capital, and did not return until he was brought back to stand trial for his life.

For Pym the victory was pyrrhic, and had led him only into a new stage of deadlock. If he showed any willingness to fight the king, all the support he was enjoying would evaporate, and if he did not, he could only enjoy stalemate until the wheel of fortune turned, as it was almost bound to do. Serious negotiation, which had been unlikely ever since the army plot, was unthinkable now. Pym was not the sort to trust his life to a man he believed intended to kill him if he could. Clarendon is clearly right that after the attempt on the five members he had no thought of moderation.

The war, the Scottish alliance, and death What then were Pym's objectives after January 1642? He appears to have had two. One was to provoke Charles further into over-reacting, giving Pym himself the excuse of claiming he was fighting in self-defence. This was the only reason for fighting the king a respectable protestant could afford to give in public. Pym almost certainly knew the alternative tradition of protestant resistance theory, but he was far too good a politician to reveal what he thought of it; like adultery, this was something to which no wise man admitted in public. Fortunately, the strategy of provoking Charles into overreacting was one in which Charles could be counted on to co-operate. In his attempt to seize the arsenal at Hull in April, and in raising his standard at Nottingham in August, Charles duly obliged.

There was still no chance of a pretender. Charles had taken the elector palatine Charles Lewis with him into the Commons to arrest the five members, and took him with him to the gates of Hull. These actions would have made him unacceptable as a pretender, even if he had been willing. There remained outside help. Pym could usually count on discreet sympathy from the French ambassador, who had warned the five members the king was coming to arrest them. Yet at the crisis of the Thirty Years' War, serious help from France or anywhere else on the continent was unthinkable: the crisis of manpower was too serious. There remained only Scotland.

When Charles had concluded the treaty with Scotland, he had exacted from John Campbell, earl of Loudoun, from Argyll, and probably from others also, promises not to meddle in the internal affairs of England. Almost immediately on his departure from London, Charles wrote to Loudoun, now lord chancellor of Scotland, to remind him of his promise. Loudoun, in reply, reminded Charles that he had already broken the Scottish peace treaty. When he charged the five members with treasonable correspondence with the Scots, Charles had forgotten that he was breaking the Act of Oblivion, which had been a key part of the treaty. Loudoun had not. It was impossible to open up that correspondence without threatening those at its Scottish end as much as at the English end. There were already Scottish commissioners in London, involved in the suppression of the Irish rising. Pym, Hampden, and Rous pursued friendship with these commissioners with a dedication they had not shown since the winter of 1640.

Through the spring and summer of 1642 Pym's efforts were devoted to the measures for further reformation of religion whose absence had dismayed the Scots in the spring of 1641. Francis Rous took up the Scottish proposal for an English general assembly, which was to produce a common confession of faith for the two kingdoms. It was to settle church government, get rid of the Book of Common Prayer, ensure discipline, and do all those things which warmed the hearts of Scottish ministers and chilled those of English gentry. It was a risky strategy, for every increase in Pym's Scottish friends was also an increase in his English enemies. It was not until his two declarations of 10 September 1642, after Charles had raised his standard, that Pym burnt his boats for this strategy, assuring the Scottish privy council he agreed with them about prelacy, and the Scottish general assembly that some of their number would be appointed to the Westminster assembly. The Scots had already burnt their fingers trusting English promises, and it took a long time to secure their final agreement to the solemn league and covenant, which arguably turned the course of the English civil war.

In creating an administrative machine to run the parliamentarian war effort, Pym was at his best. He built up a system of standing committees at Westminster, and of county committees in the country, which worked. He and others succeeded, as he had not in 1641, in introducing the excise. In the politics of war he showed a firm allegiance to the earl of Essex as parliamentarian commander-in-chief. Essex was a man whose political advantages matched his military disadvantages, and the support for him was what might have been expected, not only of a servant of the junto, now much damaged by the strains of war, but of a political ally of the Scots.

Pym died, presumably in London, on 8 December 1643, before the times which sorted the Scottish sheep from the New England goats among the parliamentarian ranks, but the evidence, such as it is, suggests that his sympathies might have gone with Essex and Holles rather than with St John and Saye. This is thin ice, and no weight should be placed on it. His death, which was attributed to a 'large abcesse or impostume', may have been from cancer of the bowel (*Narrative*, 3).

In being led into civil war, Pym had suffered a defeat. He had bargained for a coercive settlement with Charles I which was not available. There is no reason to think he was any better provided with a strategy for handling victory than his colleagues were. His vision of authority, like that of Saye or the earl of Manchester (the former Lord Mandeville), always depended on the existence of a lawful king as a name in which power could be put into commission. In his crucial failure to appreciate that the king's dedication to his religion was as strong as his own, Pym failed to achieve policies for the situation in which he actually found himself. Longer life could only have exposed this limitation more cruelly than during his life.

Pym's funeral sermon was preached by Stephen Marshall, who claimed that his mastery of his papers was achieved by regularly beginning work at three in the morning. Pym left a will, which does not appear to survive, but it is known from many other sources that his executors were: Oliver St John, Sir Benjamin Rudyerd, John Crew (who had been Richard Knightley's executor), Francis Rous, Anthony Nicoll, and his heir, Alexander Pym. Their struggle to collect some of the money the House of Commons voted to pay Pym's debts is a story too long to tell here. They saved the estate from major sales, but not from mortgages. By 1670 it was approaching recovery from its former owner's political exploits. Pym was given a ceremonial funeral and was buried in the Henry VII chapel in Westminster Abbey on 15 December 1643. After the Restoration, it was decided that the burial was unauthorized, and the body was dug up and flung into the ditch.

CONRAD RUSSELL

Sources E. Gore, incomplete biography of John Pym, priv. coll. · C. Russell, 'The wardship of John Pym', *EngHR*, 84 (1969), 304–17 · E. Gore and C. Russell, 'John Pym and the queen's receivership', *BIHR*, 46 (1973), 106–7 · estate documents, Som. ARS, Pym MSS, DD/BW · *The manuscripts of the marquess of Abergavenny, Lord Braye*, G. F. Luttrell, HMC, 15 (1887) [Pleydell Bouverie MSS] · BL, Pym corresp., Add. MS 11692 · sale catalogue no. 155, C. J. Sawyer & Co. (1940) [sale catalogue of Pym's papers] · Yale U., Beinecke L. [copies in BL, reserve photocopies] · Pym's parliamentary diary, 1621, BL, Add. MS 26637 [annotated by the earl of Bedford] · Pym's parliamentary diary, 1624, BL, Add. MS 26639 · J. Pym, parliamentary diary, 1624, Northants. RO, Finch-Hatton papers, MS 50 [full text] · Pym's parliamentary diary, 1625, and Trustees of the Bedford Settled Estates, Woburn Abbey, Bedford MS 197 [annotated by earl of Bedford] · C. Russell, 'The parliamentary career of John Pym, 1621–9', *The English Commonwealth, 1547–1640: essays in politics and society presented to Joel Hurstfield*, ed. P. Clark, A. G. R. Smith, and N. Tyacke (1979), 147–65 · N. Tyacke, *Anti-Calvinists: the rise of English Arminianism, c.1590–1640* (1987) · C. Russell, *Parliaments and English politics, 1621–1629* (1979) · A. P. Newton, *Colonizing activities of the English puritans* (1914) · C. Russell, *The fall of the British monarchies, 1637–1642* (1991) · W. Notestein, F. H. Relf, and H. Simpson, eds., *Commons debates, 1621*, 7 vols. (1935) · S. R. Gardiner, ed., *Debates in the House of Commons in 1625*, CS, new ser., 6 (1873) · M. Jansson and W. B. Bidwell, eds., *Proceedings in parliament, 1625* (1987) · W. B. Bidwell and M. Jansson, eds., *Proceedings in parliament, 1626*, 4 vols. (1991–6) · [E. Nicholas], *Proceedings and debates of the House of Commons, in 1620 and 1621*, ed. [T. Tyrwhitt], 2 vols. (1766) · R. C. Johnson and others, eds., *Proceedings in parliament, 1628*, 6 vols. (1977–83) · W. Notestein and F. H. Relf, eds., *Commons debates for 1629* (1921) · E. S. Cope and W. H. Coates, eds., *Proceedings of the Short Parliament of 1640*, CS, 4th ser., 19 (1977) · City Westm. AC, St Clement Danes, B 2 and B 10 (1) · Hants. RO, Jervoise of Herriard papers, O 12, O 21, O 7 · PRO, Ward 7/59/48 · E. Hyde, earl of Clarendon, *The history of the rebellion and civil wars in England*, 3 vols. (1702–4) · PRO, C 66/1255, mm. 28–9 · *JHC*, 1–3 (1547–1644) · PRO, C 2/Charles.I/ P 51/17 · *Reg. Oxf.*, 2/2.234 · PRO, E 159/430, m. 56 · PRO, SP 46/68/1 · PRO, E 101/536/40 · PRO, LR 7/116, fol. 33 and LR 7/55/6 · PRO, E 178/3097 · BL, Add. MS 12504, fols. 168–74 · PRO, E 179/175/492 · PRO, E 115/295/136 · A. J. Willis, ed., *Hampshire marriage licences, 1607–1640* (1960), 54 · P. Hembry, *The bishops of Bath and Wells, 1540–1640* (1967), 91–9, 134 · *IGI* · M. R. Pickering, 'Pym, Alexander', HoP, *Commons, 1558–1603* · I. Cassidy, 'Rous, Anthony', HoP, *Commons, 1558–1603* · parish register, Bramshott, Hants. RO, 23 May 1586 [baptism: Anne Hooke, wife] · *A narrative of the disease and death of the noble gentleman John Pym esquire* (1643) · DNB · J. Hexter, *The reign of King Pym* (1941) · J. Morrill, 'The unweariableness of Mr Pym: influence eloquence in the Long Parliament', *Political culture and cultural politics in early modern England*, ed. S. D. Amussen and M. A. Kishlansky (1995), 19–54 · A. Fletcher, *The outbreak of the English civil war* (1981) · L. Glow, 'The committee of safety', *EngHR*, 80 (1965), 289–313 · J. S. A. Adamson, 'Pym as draftsman: an unpublished declaration of March 1643', *Parliamentary History*, 6 (1987), 133–140 · J. S. A. Adamson, 'Parliamentary management, men-of-business and the House of Lords, 1640–1649', *A pillar of the constitution: the House of Lords in British politics, 1640–1784*, ed. C. Jones (1989), 21–50

Archives Beds. & Luton ARS, tracts and speeches · BL, corresp. and papers, Add. MS 11692; Egerton MSS; Harley MSS; Stowe MSS · Yale U., Beinecke L., letters and state papers

Likenesses woodcut, 1641 (after E. Bower), NPG; repro. in pamphlet, 'Master Pym his speech in parliament' · G. Glover, line engraving (after E. Bower, c.1640–1641), BM, NPG; repro. in S. Marshall, *Funeral sermon* (1644) [see illus.]

Pym, Sir Samuel (1778–1855), naval officer, was the son of Joseph Pym of Pinley, near Henley in Arden, Warwickshire, and his wife, a daughter of Thomas Arnott MD, of Cupar, Fife; his brother was Sir William *Pym. In June 1788 Samuel Pym was entered on the books of the frigate *Eurydice* as captain's servant. After service on the home station, in the Mediterranean, and the West Indies, on 7 March 1795 he was promoted lieutenant of the sloop *Martin* with Captain William Grenville Lobb, whom he followed to the *Babet* and the *Aimable* in the West Indies. In January 1798, in one of *Babet*'s boats, he took *La Désirée*, of 6 guns and 46 men, in a bloody struggle, won at the cost of one man killed, another drowned, and Pym and all the rest wounded. In November 1798 he joined the *Ethalion*, one of four frigates which on 16–17 October 1799, near Cape Finisterre, captured the Spanish treasure ships *Thetis* and *Santa-Brígida*, with specie worth nearly £700,000. As one of the lieutenants, Pym received over £5,000 in prize money. On Christmas day the *Ethalion* was wrecked on the Penmarks, off the south-west point of Brittany. On 10 February 1801 Pym was made commander of the *Swan* on the Portsmouth station, and was posted captain on 29 April 1802. On 25 May he married a daughter of Edward Lockyer of Plymouth: they had at least one child. In April 1804 he was appointed to the *Mars* in the Bay of Biscay, and in June to the *Atlas*, one of the squadron with Sir John Thomas Duckworth in the battle of San Domingo on 6 February 1806; for this, with the other captains, Pym received the gold medal.

In October 1808 Pym was appointed to the *Sirius*, in which, under Commodore Josias Rowley, he had an important share in the capture of St Paul's in the island of Bourbon in September 1809, and of the island itself in July 1810.

Pym was then sent to blockade Mauritius as senior officer of a frigate squadron consisting of the *Sirius*, *Iphigenia*, *Néréide*, and *Magicienne*, with the brig *Staunch*, and suffered the worst British naval defeat of the entire 1793–1815 wars (and the only French naval victory recorded on the Arc de Triomphe, albeit wrongly inscribed as Port Louis). Facing a French squadron of five more powerful frigates, Pym began well by seizing the fortified Isle de la Passe, commanding the approach to Grand Port. Going on to blockade Port Louis, he learned that two enemy frigates and a sloop, with a prize, had been lured into Grand Port, and he snatched at the chance of destroying them before they reunited with their squadron. Haste, however, led to disaster. Trying to attack with *Néréide* on 22 August, he ran *Sirius* aground. When the whole squadron attacked next day, *Sirius* and *Magicienne* grounded through failing to follow *Néréide*, whose captain alone knew the reef-strewn channel. *Néréide*, isolated, was battered into surrender; *Sirius* and *Magicienne*, stuck fast, had to be burnt on 25 August; and *Iphigenia* was captured on 27 August, when the rest of the French squadron arrived. His squadron annihilated, Pym and the survivors were taken prisoner. He was freed when Mauritius was captured in the following December, and a court martial acquitted him of blame for the catastrophe. He was appointed in February 1812 to the *Hannibal*, off Cherbourg, and in May to the *Niemen*, which he commanded for the next three years on the West Indian station.

Pym was nominated a CB on 4 June 1815; in 1830–31 he commanded the *Kent* in the Mediterranean. Promoted rear-admiral on 10 January 1837, he was made a KCB on 25 October 1839. From 1841 to 1846 he was admiral-superintendent at Devonport, and in the autumn of 1845 commanded the experimental squadron in the channel. He became a vice-admiral on 12 February 1847 and admiral on 17 December 1852; he died at the Royal Hotel, Southampton, on 2 October 1855.

J. K. LAUGHTON, *rev.* MICHAEL DUFFY

Sources O'Byrne, *Naval biog. dict.* · J. Marshall, *Royal naval biography*, 2/2 (1825), 715–19 · *GM*, 2nd ser., 44 (1855), 537 · C. N. Parkinson, *War in the eastern seas, 1793–1815* (1954) · E. Chevalier, *Histoire de la marine française sous le consulat et l'empire* (1886), 373–9 · W. James, *The naval history of Great Britain, from the declaration of war by France, in February 1793, to the accession of George IV in January 1820*, 5 vols. (1822–4)

Pym, Sir William (1772–1861), military surgeon, son of Joseph Pym of Pinley, Warwickshire, and his wife, daughter of Thomas Arnott MD, of Cupar, Fife, was born in Edinburgh in January 1772. He was the elder brother of Sir Samuel *Pym. William was educated at Edinburgh University and then entered the medical department of the army. He served with the 35th and 70th regiments of foot, and from 1794 to 1796 was in medical charge during an epidemic of yellow fever in Martinique, when it is estimated that nearly 16,000 troops died. Pym thus obtained an unparalleled knowledge of yellow fever. He also served in Sicily, Malta, and in Gibraltar, where he acted as medical adviser to the governor, the duke of Kent. He became deputy inspector-general of army hospitals in 1810, and in 1811 was president of the board of health in Malta.

Pym returned to England in 1812 and lived in London, but in 1813 returned to Malta, where plague was raging. In September 1816 he became inspector-general of army hospitals. In 1815 he published *Observations upon the Bulam Fever*, one of the first comprehensive accounts of the disease now known as yellow fever. In this work Pym maintained: that it was a disease *sui generis* known by the name of African, yellow, or bulam fever, and was the *vómito prieto* of the Spaniards, being attended with that peculiar and fatal symptom the 'black vomit'; that it was highly infectious; that its infectious powers were increased by heat and destroyed by cold; that it attacked natives of warm climates in a comparatively mild form; and that it had also a singular and peculiar character, attacking, as in a case of smallpox, the human frame only once. The work attracted considerable criticism, and the ensuing debate was illustrative of the confusion over the nature of tropical diseases at the time.

In 1826 Pym was appointed superintendent-general of quarantine, and in 1831 he was made a knight commander of the Hanoverian order. During the cholera epidemic of 1832 he served as chairman of the central board of health. In 1845 the ship *Eclair*, paralysed by an outbreak of yellow fever, was refused permission to land at Haslar by the quarantine officer, on the grounds that yellow fever was contagious. This was contested by Sir William Burnett and Alexander Bryson of the navy, who perceived the disease to be non-infectious. In 1848 Pym published an enlarged edition of his book on yellow fever, in which he reviewed Burnett and Bryson's *Report on the Climate and Principal Diseases of the African Station* (1847), and reiterated his belief in the contagious nature of the disease.

Pym died of a stroke on 18 March 1861 at his house in Upper Harley Street, London.

D'A. POWER, *rev.* CLAIRE E. J. HERRICK

Sources A. Peterkin and W. Johnston, *Commissioned officers in the medical services of the British army, 1660–1960*, 1 (1968), 78 · J. J. Keevil and others, *Medicine and the navy, 1200–1900*, 4 vols. (1957–63), 3.342–3; 4.168–9, 176, 184–8 · N. Cantlie, *A history of the army medical department*, 1 (1974), 286; 2 (1974), 392 · *The Lancet* (23 March 1861), 304 · *BMJ* (23 March 1861), 320 · *Proceedings of the Royal Medical and Chirurgical Society*, 4 (1861–4), 76 · Walford, *County families*

Pyncebeke [Pyncebeck, Pinchbeck], **Walter** (*fl.* 1330–1339), Benedictine monk and archivist, presumably came from Pinchbeck in Lincolnshire. Nothing is known about his early career in Bury St Edmunds Abbey. However, on 2 July 1330 Edward III confirmed the abbey's liberties at his suit. He appears as a visiting monk in the accounts of the chamberlain's manor of Hildeclay (1329–30), and as the receiver in the accounts of the abbot's manors of Worlingworth and Palgrave. Finally in 1338–9 he occurs in a document as infirmarer. His reputation rests on his work on the abbey's muniments. The immediate incentive was undoubtedly the violent revolt of the town against the abbey in 1327, when the rebels seized many of the monks' registers, charters, and other records: as Pyncebeke explains, without such evidences the monks could not protect their rights in the lawcourts. To remedy the loss he compiled a survey of the abbey's rights over the town, in St Edmunds' liberty of the eight and a half hundreds, and in each of the abbey's manors. An early fourteenth-century copy of the survey is in the composite volume, now Harley MS 230 (fols. 158–69) in the British Library.

Pyncebeke next produced his principal work, the great register which bears his name, a handsome, arguably partly holograph, volume, now MS Ee 3.60 in Cambridge University Library. Pyncebeke states in a colophon that he began composition in 1333, and lists the contents of the proposed five sections: all pleas between the abbey and the town 'from the beginning of the world until the present' (Hervey, 1.57); the abbey's feudal fees; churches in the abbot's collation and their assessments for taxation; all liberties granted to Bury St Edmunds Abbey by various kings; and a register of the eight and a half hundreds and all the abbey's lands. He never wrote the last item, whose subject was covered by his earlier survey, but he added a preliminary section, comprising copies of the abbey's papal privileges. The register's usefulness was recognized in its own time—its length was more than doubled by later fourteenth-century additions. By *c*.1400 it was kept in the vestry, and is therefore sometimes called the Vestry register. It remains an invaluable source for the history of Bury St Edmunds Abbey.

ANTONIA GRANSDEN

Sources F. Hervey, ed., *The Pinchbeck Register*, 2 vols. (1925) · Harley MS, BL, 230, fols. 158–169 · CUL, MS Ee 3.60 · R. M. Thomson, *The archives of the abbey of Bury St Edmunds*, Suffolk RS, 21 (1980), 123–6, 132–3 · M. D. Lobel, *The borough of Bury St Edmunds* (1935) · T. Arnold, ed., *Memorials of St Edmund's Abbey*, 2, Rolls Series, 96 (1892), 327–54, 357–61; 3 (1896), 38–47 · Lansdowne MS, BL, 416 fol. 31ᵛ · manorial account of Worlingworth, 1335–6, Suffolk RO, Ipswich, S1/2/9.9 [microfilm] · Bacon MS, University of Chicago, 457 [microfilm, CUL. Manorial accounts of Hildeclay] · Bacon MS, University of Chicago, 458 [microfilm, CUL. Manorial accounts of Hildeclay] · private information (2004) [Mr N. Poynder and Dr P. Schofield]
Archives BL, Harley MS 230, fols. 158–169 · CUL, MS Ee 3.60

Pynchon, William (1590–1662), public official and pamphleteer in America, was born on 26 December 1590 at Springfield, Essex, the son of John Pynchon (*d.* 1610) and Frances Brett (*bap.* 1590). As the child of a wealthy gentry family he was taught Latin, Greek, and Hebrew, but there is no evidence that he attended university. In 1624 he married Anne Andrew (*d.* 1630/31), with whom he had at least four children. Active in the Massachusetts Bay Company since its planning, Pynchon sailed to New England in the Winthrop fleet in 1630, and was the leading citizen of Roxbury at its founding in the same year. His wife died during the winter of 1630–31 and by 1632 he had married Frances Sanford (*d.* 1657), widow successively of men named Smith and Sanford. There were no children from his second marriage. Pynchon had been elected to the office of assistant prior to his arrival in the colony and continued in the post until 1636 and served again from 1642 to 1650. He was also treasurer from 1632 to 1633.

In 1636, at a time when hundreds of residents of Massachusetts Bay were moving to the Connecticut River valley, Pynchon headed a group of residents of Roxbury and other Bay communities to the site of what would become the town of Springfield. The town was initially considered to be part of the new colony of Connecticut, but in 1641 Pynchon was able to switch Springfield's allegiance back to Massachusetts Bay. As Springfield was the most westerly Massachusetts Bay town, Pynchon could count on little regular oversight from the Bay authorities, and so had far more power in his settlement than did other magistrates in closer proximity to Boston. Active in the fur trade along the rivers near Boston since his time in Roxbury, and with Springfield the northernmost settlement on the Connecticut River for the better part of two decades, Pynchon was able to obtain complete control over the fur trade over a wide swath of northern New England. The account books maintained by his son John are of central importance for our knowledge of the early history of western Massachusetts. Pynchon also acted as magistrate in the courts in this part of Massachusetts, and again the court records kept by William and his son are extremely valuable. In addition to his powerful position in political and economic affairs, Pynchon held very strong religious opinions of the puritan strain, but not in complete agreement with what had become the orthodoxy of New England. In 1650 he published *The Meritorious Price of our Redemption*, a work which controverted the Calvinistic view of the atonement. The general court declared the

William Pynchon (1590–1662), by unknown artist, 1657

book heretical and ordered it to be burnt, and Pynchon was made to recant:

> It hath pleased God to let me see that I have not spoken in my book so fully of the prize and merit of Christ's sufferings as I should have done … But now at present I am inclined to think that His sufferings were appointed by God for a farther end, namely as the due punishment for our sins by way of satisfaction to divine justice for man's redemption. (*ANB*)

Not surprisingly, he was not elected assistant in 1651, and in 1652 he returned to England, settling in Wraysbury, Buckinghamshire. Making his contribution to the political and religious atmosphere of 1650s England, Pynchon continued his pamphleteering throughout the decade, his next work, published almost immediately upon his arrival in England, being *The Jewes Synagogue*. In 1654 he wrote a detailed work on the sabbath, describing its ordination and true limits. He died in Wraysbury on 29 October 1662 leaving a substantial estate, which he distributed among family and friends in both old and New England.

ROBERT CHARLES ANDERSON

Sources R. C. Anderson, *The great migration begins: immigrants to New England, 1620–1633*, 3 (1995) · M. P. Winship, 'Contesting control of orthodoxy among the godly: William Pynchon revisited', *William & Mary Quarterly*, 3rd ser., 54 (1997), 795–822 · M. P. Winship, 'William Pynchon's *The Jewes synagogue*', *New England Quarterly*, 71 (1998), 290–97 · J. H. Smith, ed., *Colonial justice in western Massachusetts (1639–1702): the Pynchon court record* (1961) · R. A. McIntyre, *William Pynchon: merchant and colonizer* (1961) · S. E. Morison, *Builders of the Bay Colony* (1930) · D. L. Jacobs and E. F. Waterman, *Hale House and related families mainly of the Connecticut River valley* (1952) · W. Penack, 'Pynchon, William', *ANB* · PRO, PROB 11/309/156
Likenesses portrait, 1657, Essex Institute, Salem, Massachusetts [*see illus.*]

Pyne, James Baker (1800–1870), landscape painter, was born on 5 December 1800 in Bristol. Following his parents' wishes he entered a solicitor's office but, at the age of twenty-one, abandoned the law and took up painting, which he reputedly taught himself. In 1824 he first exhibited in Bristol and is said to have undertaken picture restoration as well as to have taught. In 1827 W. J. Müller was apprenticed to Pyne. In 1828 Pyne is first recorded as a drawing-master, living at 6 Dove Street, Kingsdown, Bristol; a year later he briefly shared a studio with Samuel Jackson, a fellow landscape painter. However, he enjoyed little of the social life of Bristol's other artists, though their influence upon him was profound. The idyllic *Imaginary Scene* (1828, Anglesey Abbey), for instance, is an original response to Francis Danby's poetic landscapes, and *View of the Avon from Durdham Down* of 1829 (City of Bristol Museum and Art Gallery) reflects the intensity of observation of Danby's Bristol scenes.

Pyne probably moved to London in 1835, and in 1837 his *Clifton, Near Bristol, from the Avon* (City of Bristol Museum and Art Gallery) was shown at the Royal Academy. It was considered 'disagreeably white' by a reviewer in *Blackwood's Edinburgh Magazine* for September of that year (p. 341), who wondered 'in what sick fit' (ibid.) it had been painted; such comments as these reflect Pyne's increasingly restricted and light-toned palette which was influenced by J. M. W. Turner, of whose more conventional works Pyne was a rare and sympathetic follower. Pyne exhibited regularly at the British Institution from 1833 until 1844 and almost annually at the Royal Academy from 1836 to 1841, but thereafter his loyalty was to the Society of British Artists, whose vice-president he became. In 1846 he travelled through Germany, Switzerland, and Italy. He returned to Italy in 1851, travelling with the watercolourist William Evans of Bristol (1805–1858) for three years.

Between 1838 and 1840 Pyne published *Windsor and its Surrounding Scenery*, a volume of lithographs. With the patronage of the picture dealer William Agnew there followed *The English Lake District* in 1853 and *The Lake Scenery of England* in 1859. Pyne occasionally collaborated with other artists, including T. S. Cooper and William Shayer who painted the foreground figures and animals in his pictures. From 1840 to 1868 he numbered his paintings and kept related notebooks recording their details. These two volumes are in the Victoria and Albert Museum, London, where there is also a small but representative collection of his later oils and watercolours. Pyne died on 29 July 1870 at his home, 203 Camden Road, London, and was buried in Highgate cemetery. His sons James Baker Pyne, a photographer, and Charles Pyne, an artist, survived him. His studio sale was at Christies on 25 February 1871.

FRANCIS GREENACRE

Sources *Men of the time* (1857), 620 · *Art Journal*, 32 (1870), 276 · *Art Journal*, 18 (1856), 205–8 · F. Greenacre, *The Bristol school of artists: Francis Danby and painting in Bristol, 1810–1840* [1973] [exhibition catalogue, City Museum and Art Gallery, Bristol, 4 Sept – 10 Nov 1973] · M. H. Grant, *A chronological history of the old English landscape painters*, rev. edn, 8 (1961), 708–10 · Redgrave, *Artists* · Graves, *RA exhibitors* · Graves, *Brit. Inst.* · W. H. Dunman, *Ten Bristol artists* (1934) [exhibition catalogue, City of Bristol Museum and Art Gallery] ·

N. Neal Solly, *Memoir of the life of William James Müller* (1875) · F. Greenacre, introduction, *William Evans of Bristol* (1987) [exhibition catalogue, Martyn Gregory Gallery, London, 10–28 Nov 1987] · 'Exhibitions—the Royal Academy', *Blackwood*, 42 (1837), 330–41 · R. Parkinson, ed., *Catalogue of British oil paintings, 1820–1860* (1990) [catalogue of V&A] · *CGPLA Eng. & Wales* (1870) · directories, Bristol, 1828–30 · d. cert.

Archives V&A NAL, details of pictures sold and exhibited · V&A NAL, MS *Picture memoranda*

Likenesses woodcut, 1849 (after J. J. Hill), BM, NPG; repro. in *Art Journal* (1849) · wood-engraving, 1870 (after photograph by J. B. Pyne junior), BM, NPG; repro. in *ILN* (20 Aug 1870) · J. B. Pyne junior, photograph, Bristol City Museum and Art Gallery · J. Watkins, carte-de-visite, NPG

Wealth at death under £1500: resworn probate, Aug 1871, *CGPLA Eng. & Wales* (1870)

Pyne, John (*bap.* 1600, *d.* 1678), politician, was baptized on 21 February 1600 at East Down near Barnstaple, Devon, the eldest son of Thomas Pyne (*d.* in or before 1609), gentleman, of Merriott in Somerset, and his wife, Amy, daughter of Thomas Hanham of Wimborne Minster, Dorset. He was heir to his grandfather, John Pyne of Curry Mallet, Somerset, who died in 1609. He matriculated from Hart Hall, Oxford, in February 1610, graduated BA in 1612, and proceeded MA in 1615. He entered the Middle Temple in 1619 and was called to the bar in 1629; he kept chambers until 1637. The influence of his mother's family secured Pyne's election for Poole in Dorset to the parliaments of 1625, 1626, and 1628, but he did little in Westminster. Most of the speeches by 'Mr Pyne' in 1628 were almost certainly made by his uncle, Hugh Pyne. John may have spoken on the Marriage Bill on 22 April, however; he would have been especially interested, because of difficulties over his intended marriage to his cousin, Eleanor Hanham, with whom he eloped in 1629 and married on 23 April.

In the 1630s Pyne held minor offices in Somerset, but he was not a JP until 1646. He obstructed collection of ship money in 1638 and Poole returned him to both 1640 parliaments. He was regarded as one of the 'rigid party' against the king. Named one of parliament's deputy lieutenants in March 1642, he subsequently had an undistinguished military record. Moderately wealthy, he claimed wartime losses of £1000. By 1645 he headed an extreme parliamentarian faction in Somerset, which in the recruiter elections assisted radical candidates. Under his leadership the Somerset county committee became notorious for its vindictiveness. Pyne used it ruthlessly to pursue royalists, harass political opponents, and bully witnesses and minor officials. He promoted county petitions supporting the vote of no addresses, Pride's Purge, and the trial of Charles I. But although named to the high court of justice in January 1649, he stayed away and returned to parliament only after the king's execution. He occasionally attended the Rump Parliament, but his main achievement during the Commonwealth was to govern Somerset successfully. He survived the abolition of the county committee in 1650, and sat in the nominated assembly of 1653, though he was largely inactive as a member. Presbyterian in religion, he was tolerant of other sects, and supported proposals to abolish tithes and remodel the universities. As he was an outspoken critic of the 'Instrument of government' the protectorate brought an end to his parliamentary career. He appeared against John Penruddock and his rebels in 1655, but refused any office under Oliver Cromwell, and was badly beaten in the 1656 elections. Nevertheless, he sat in the restored Rump in 1659, and retained his position as a JP throughout the 1650s.

At the Restoration, Pyne took the oath of allegiance but was debarred from holding public office. He was several times imprisoned on suspicion of plotting, but otherwise lived quietly in Curry Mallet. His first wife died some time in or after 1654, and he later married Amy White. He died in 1678, having asked to be buried silently at night. Two sons survived him (Pyne disinherited John, the elder, making the younger, Charles, his heir); a daughter Susannah (Pitts) died in 1676. DAVID UNDERDOWN, *rev.*

Sources S. W. Bates Harbin, *Members of parliament for the county of Somerset* (1939), 156–7 · Keeler, *Long Parliament*, 319–20 · R. C. Johnson and others, eds., *Proceedings in parliament, 1628*, 1–4 (1977–8) · *Ninth report*, 2, HMC, 8 (1884), 494 · D. Underdown, *Somerset in the civil war and interregnum* (1973) · D. Underdown, *Pride's Purge: politics in the puritan revolution* (1971) · A. Woolrych, *Commonwealth to protectorate* (1982)

Pyne [*married name* Boddy], **Louisa Fanny** (1828?–1904), singer, born in London, probably on 27 August 1828, was the youngest daughter of George Pyne (1790–1877), an alto singer, and niece of the tenor James Kendrick Pyne (*d.* 1857). She studied singing under George Smart, and in 1842, at the age of ten, made a successful appearance in public with her elder sister Susannah (*d.* 1886) at the Queen's Concert Rooms, Hanover Square. In 1847 the sisters performed in Paris, and in August 1849 Louisa made her operatic début at Boulogne as Amina in *La sonnambula*, a role she repeated that autumn at the Princess's Theatre, where she also sang Zerlina in *Don Giovanni* and created the role of Fanny in Sir George Macfarren's *Charles the Second*, to considerable acclaim. She declined several engagements abroad because of her strong objection to singing on Sundays. On 14 August 1851, at short notice, she performed the Queen of Night in Mozart's *The Magic Flute* at Covent Garden before the queen; she was so successful that the grateful director, Frederick Gye, presented her with a diamond brooch. She subsequently performed for the queen at Windsor Castle and Buckingham Palace.

In August 1854 Louisa Pyne went to America with her sister and the tenor William Harrison (1813–1868), where her flexible and expressive soprano voice was greatly appreciated, and stayed through three seasons. On her return to England in 1857 she went into partnership with Harrison, who was the lessee of the Lyceum and Drury Lane theatres, for the performance of opera in English. The Harrison–Pyne enterprise was successfully inaugurated at the Lyceum on 21 September 1857 and was transferred the following year to Covent Garden, where the performances continued each winter until 1863—one of the longest running undertakings of the kind. Nearly a dozen new operas, by Balfe, Benedict, Glover, Mellon, and Wallace, were produced, but their success was short-lived. Pungent, not to say derisive, notices in the *Musical World* finally

assisted in killing the enterprise. The partnership was dissolved and Louisa Pyne transferred to Her Majesty's Opera House and the Haymarket.

On 12 October 1868 she married the baritone Francis Henry Boddy, known professionally as Frank Bodda. She then retired from public life and successfully engaged in teaching in London. Her husband died on 14 March 1892, aged sixty-nine. She received a civil-list pension of £70 in 1896, and died at 85 Cambridge Gardens, London, on 20 March 1904. She had no children.

FREDERICK CORDER, *rev.* J. GILLILAND

Sources *The Athenaeum* (26 March 1904), 411 · *Musical World* [various] · F. Hays, *Women of the day: a biographical dictionary of notable contemporaries* (1885) · D. Hyde, *New-found voices: women in nineteenth-century English music* (1984) · J. N. Ireland, *Records of the New York stage, from 1750 to 1860*, 2 vols. (1866–7) · *MT*, 45 (1904), 260 · Brown & Stratton, *Brit. mus.* · *New Grove* · D. Baptie, *A handbook of musical biography*, 2nd edn (1887) · N. Temperley, ed., *The romantic age* (1988), vol. 5 of *The Blackwell history of music* · *Baltzell's dictionary of musicians* (1911) · m. cert. · d. cert.
Likenesses C. Banquiet, lithograph, BM · Southwell Bros., carte-de-visite, NPG · engraving, repro. in *Gleason's Pictorial*, 7 (1854), 400 · engraving, repro. in *Gleason's Pictorial*, 13 (1857), 380 · portrait, repro. in *Century*, 2 (1882), 196 · prints, BM, NPG · prints, Harvard TC
Wealth at death £1783 4*s.* 11*d.*: probate, 12 April 1904, *CGPLA Eng. & Wales*

Pyne, Valentine (1603–1677), naval officer and soldier, the second son of George Pyne, an ordnance officer of Curry Mallet, Somerset, was the first cousin of John Pyne, the revolutionary MP who was to be notably absent from Valentine's will. A lesser landed family claiming ancient lineage, the Pynes had become established in Tudor times. Valentine's uncle Hugh Pyne had a record of political dissent under Charles I.

Valentine Pyne served with his father as an officer of the ordnance in the expedition to Cadiz in 1625, and in 1627 in the expedition to the Île de Ré. He was almost certainly the Valentine Pyne serving in the navy in the 1630s, master of the *Jonas* in 1637, and connected with Sir John Pennington who apparently brought him to the notice of Sir Edward Nicholas. He served with Charles I during the civil war but his activities during the interregnum are unknown. He received royal favour after 1660, probably owing to his loyalty, expertise, and royalist connections, being appointed a gunner in the Ordnance office in 1661 and master gunner of England in 1666. He was praised by Pepys for his conduct in keeping his post at Chatham during the Dutch attack on the Medway in 1667.

Pyne died, unmarried, on 30 April 1677. His will, made six years before his death, disposed of £2000 among his extended family while recognizing approximately the same amount in debts, reflecting the fact that ordnance gunnery was a genteel but middling occupation. A mural tablet was erected to his memory in the chapel of the Tower of London.

Pyne's life was one of service and modest profit within the naval–military interface of his time. Loyalty, courage, and humour were his discernible characteristics. He left £40 to his cousin George 'to be spent in idle company in drink and tobacco' and £50 to his cousin Grace 'to be cast away upon the first idle fellow that makes a suit unto her' (PRO, PROB 11/354/52). Pyne has been confused with his naval cousin Captain Valentine Pyne (referred to in the former's will as 'being much at sea') who served in Rupert's fleet during the interregnum, commanded various vessels in the Restoration navy, and fought in the Second Anglo-Dutch War.   L. J. REEVE

Sources DNB · CSP dom., 1630–35, 213, 234, 438; 1636–7, 506; 1638–9, 125; 1640, 59; 1667–8, 103, 158, 485 · PRO, WO 54/20, 22–5 · will of Valentine Pyne, PRO, PROB 11/354/52 [dated 20 Dec 1670, with codicil 22 Jan 1671] · Pepys, Diary, 8.307–8 · personal information (2004) [Somerset RO] · D. Underdown, Pride's Purge: politics in the puritan revolution (1971) · H. C. Tomlinson, Guns and government: the ordnance office under the later Stuarts, Royal Historical Society Studies in History, 15 (1979) · D. Brunton and D. H. Pennington, Members of the Long Parliament (1954) · F. Kitson, Prince Rupert: admiral and general-at-sea (1998) · R. Ollard, Man of war: Sir Robert Holmes and the Restoration navy (1969) · The journals of Sir Thomas Allin, 1660–1678, ed. R. C. Anderson, 1, Navy RS, 79 (1939), 55 n. 2
Wealth at death debts of £3000 · £2000 cash assets disposed: will, PRO, PROB 11/354/52

Pyne, William Henry [pseud. Ephraim Hardcastle] (1770–1843), artist and writer, was born at 9 Exeter Court, Strand, London, on 21 April 1770, the second son of John Pyne (1727–1794), a leather dresser in Holborn, and Mary Craze (d. 1819). He was baptized on 10 May and lived in London throughout his life. His early interest in drawing induced his father to send him for instruction at the drawing school of Henry Pars but he refused to be apprenticed to him and left at the age of fourteen.

Pyne developed quickly a great facility for drawing and at the age of sixteen was inspired by Philippe Jacques de Loutherbourg to introduce into his works realistic groups of figures and animals following some characteristic occupation. Two of his earliest drawings, published as aquatints in 1790, entitled A Country Theatre and A Country Church, are similar in style to those of Thomas Rowlandson, while subsequent works were principally landscapes in watercolours in the early tinted style, progressing later to full colour. He was married on 24 July 1792 at St George's Church, Hanover Square, London, to Dorothy Pearse (b. 1770), a spinster of the same parish. One of their sons, George, married Esther, daughter of John Varley, and also practised in watercolours.

Pyne first exhibited at the Royal Academy in 1790, sending three watercolours, Travelling Comedians, Bartholomew Fair, and A Puppet Show. Altogether he exhibited twenty-two works, two of which included animals painted by Robert Hills; his final exhibits in 1811 were portraits. In 1804 he was one of the four artists who originated the idea of founding the Society of Painters in Water Colours; he contributed twenty-six works to its first exhibition in 1805, followed by a further twenty-eight until 1815, despite having resigned in 1809 in protest at the society's exclusivity.

As a skilful etcher Pyne often made prints of his drawings; he was also among the first artists to draw on stone for lithographic reproduction. He recognized the needs of amateurs to copy and began a long collaboration with Rudolph Ackermann to publish several books for this purpose, the first in 1798 entitled Book with Groups of Figures by Pyne for Decorating Landscapes. He pursued the objective further with a substantial undertaking entitled Microcosm that depicts 'a Series of above Six Hundred Groups of Small Figures for the Embellishment of Landscape' involving 120 plates, which he drew and etched from 1802 until 1807. These plates were published in parts by W. H. Pyne and John Claude Nattes until 1803, when sixty plates were collected together to form the first edition of the work. The completed project was published in 1808 in two volumes with the addition of text by C. Gray. In 1803 Pyne designed and etched the title-page and rustic vignettes for Sébastian Le Clerc's Nattes's Practical Geometry, or, Introduction to Perspective, and in 1805 wrote the text to and designed and etched the plates for The Costume of Great Britain. He also contributed the text for the first two volumes of Ackermann's Microcosm of London (from 1808). Thereafter, Pyne's collaboration with Ackermann was considerable, with the publication of Rudiments of Landscape Drawing in a Series of Easy Examples (1812); W. H. Pyne on Rustic Figures in Imitation of Chalk (1813); and Etchings of Rustic Figures for the Embellishment of Landscape by W. H. Pyne (1815), first published in Ackermann's Repository. He also supplied the figures for some of the plates in Ackermann's A History of the University of Oxford (1814) and one drawing to A History of the University of Cambridge (1815).

Pyne's next major project was a sumptuously illustrated work entitled The History of the Royal Residences, for which he wrote the text and commissioned artists and engravers to provide 100 aquatints. He published the first part in 1816 but was forced to dispose of the work at a loss before its completion although he remained its editor. Writing became his principal means of earning a living. Pyne enjoyed gossip and took advantage of his knowledge of fellow artists and their techniques to become an energetic art critic under the pseudonym Ephraim Hardcastle. He supplied a long and historically valuable series of anecdotes to the Literary Gazette and in 1823 the collected papers were published in two volumes entitled Wine and Walnuts. He interrupted his writings in 1822 to provide twelve satirical drawings for The Social Club, returning to them a year later when he launched a weekly journal (later renamed Somerset House Gazette), edited under his pseudonym; it was discontinued after just one year. He also contributed many articles to Arnold's Magazine of the Fine Arts, the Library of the Fine Arts, and Fraser's Magazine.

Pyne's last book, The Twenty-Ninth of May, a novel published in 1825, was not successful. He edited the last four volumes of Ackermann's The World in Miniature, completed in 1827, before serious financial difficulties caused him to be confined, in 1828, in the king's bench prison for debtors until his friends obtained his release. Afterwards he painted a few watercolours and in 1831 contributed to a work entitled Lancashire Illustrated before being confined again in the debtors' prison in 1835. Though long popular, Pyne had become an obscure, almost forgotten figure at the time of his death from apoplexy at 2 a.m. on 29 May 1843 at Pickering Place, Paddington, Middlesex, after a long illness. It was the very day he had chosen for the title of his last book. He was survived by his wife. Many of Pyne's watercolours, drawings, and books are held by the British Museum and Victoria and Albert Museum, London.

HARRIS MYERS

Sources H. Myers, *William Henry Pyne and his 'Microcosm'* (1996) • pedigree of Pyne family of Bishop's Nympton, Society of Genealogists, London • M. T. Pyne, *Memorials of the family of Pyne*, 1917, Society of Genealogists, London, vol. 1 • *Art Union*, 5 (1843), 265–6 • *Literary Gazette* (3 June 1843), 371–2 • parish register (birth and baptism), St Mary le Strand, London, 1770 • marriage licence application, GL, MS 10091, vol. 168 • Graves, *Brit. Inst.*, 220 • A. Bury, 'William Henry Pyne, 1769–1843', *Old Water-Colour Society's Club*, 28 (1950), 1–9 • J. L. Roget, *A history of the 'Old Water-Colour' Society*, 1 (1891), 240–42 • St Mary-le-Strand poll books, 1780, 1790, Greater London Council Archive • records of King's Bench prison, abstract book of commitments, PRO, PRIS 10/25

Pynnar, Nicholas (*d.* 1644?), military engineer, is of unknown parents and background. Nothing is known of his early life, but he fought in the Low Countries before arriving in Ireland in May 1600 as captain of a regiment of foot to serve as part of the Lough Foyle garrison. His company was disbanded in 1604 and he received a pension. In September 1606 he appears in Venice, probably on government business, and remained in Italy working as a military engineer before returning to London in December 1607. By May 1609 he was in Sweden with Irish troops raised to help the Swedes in their war with Poland, probably having been in Ireland to arrange the levying and transportation of the Irish forces. He was back in Ireland by 1611 to assist the plantation of Ulster and was granted 1000 acres in co. Cavan. However, he appears to have later sold his portion. The same year he appears as a tenant of Sir Richard Boyle in Munster. He left Ireland in 1612 for France and may also have gone again to Venice.

By March 1617 Pynnar had returned to Ireland. On 27 February 1618 he was appointed director-general and overseer of fortifications and buildings along with Sir Thomas Rotherham, and also became muster-master of the undertakers in Ulster and Connaught in the same year. From 1 December 1618 to 25 March 1619 he surveyed the progress of the plantation in the six counties of Armagh, Donegal, Tyrone, Cavan, Fermanagh, and Londonderry. He also executed surveys on the plantations in Longford, Ely O'Carroll, Leitrim, and King's and Queen's counties. During the early to mid-1620s he was active surveying, repairing, and designing military fortifications across the country. In 1630 he travelled to London to complain that his official salary had been cut since 1624. Four years later the government agreed to pay him half his arrears (£2000) in return for reducing his salary by half. Up to the late 1630s Pynnar was still engaged in various official surveys. He was appointed surveyor-general of the lands, plantations, and mines in 1643. He probably died in 1644.

TERRY CLAVIN

Sources R. Loeber, 'Biographical dictionary of engineers in Ireland, 1600–1730', *Irish Sword*, 13 (1979), 284–7 • W. P. Pakenham-Walsh, 'Captains Sir Thomas Rotherham and Nicolas Pinnar, director-generals of fortifications in Ireland, 1617–44', *Royal Engineers Journal*, new ser., 10 (1909), 125–34; new ser., 40 (1926), 664–8 • *CSP Venice*, 1603–10 • G. Hill, *Plantation in Ulster* (1877), 338, 445ff. • J. S. Brewer and W. Bullen, eds., *Calendar of the Carew manuscripts*, 5: 1603–1623, PRO (1871), 91, 342ff. • *Report on the manuscripts of the marquis of Downshire*, 6 vols. in 7, HMC, 75 (1924–95), vol. 2, pp. 79, 435–6 • *Report on the manuscripts of the late Reginald Rawdon Hastings*, 4 vols., HMC, 78 (1928–47), vol. 4, pp. 165 • *Calendar of the Irish patent rolls of James I* (before 1830), 539 • F. W. Steer and others, *Dictionary of land surveyors and local map-makers of Great Britain and Ireland, 1530–1850*, ed. P. Eden, 2nd edn, 2, ed. S. Bendall (1997), 419

Pynson, Richard (*c.*1449–1529/30), printer, was Norman by birth, as attested by a patent in the Rolls Chapel (now lost) describing him as 'in partibus Normand. oriund'. Citing this same patent, Joseph Ames claims that Pynson became a naturalized English citizen about 1493 (Ames, 2.iii). The earliest known reference to Pynson is in 1464, when he appears among a list of students enrolled at the University of Paris (Duff, 55). By 1482 he was working in London, first as a glover (Plomer, 'Richard Pynson'), then, by 1490, as a bookseller, in which year he commissioned Guillaume Le Talleur in Rouen to print two books, both legal texts, for sale in England. In the plea rolls of 1496 Pynson is described as a 'pouchemaker' and 'bokeprynter' in the parish of St Clement Danes (Plomer, 'Some notices'). Pynson was also a bookbinder; bindings featuring a panel stamp with his device have survived.

It is not known where Pynson learned the art of printing. Over the years scholars have variously speculated that he was apprenticed to Guillaume Le Talleur in Rouen, Jean du Pré in Paris, John Lettou and William de Machlinia in London, or William Caxton in Westminster. The fact that printer's waste from Machlinia's shop has been found in Pynson's bindings suggests he may have taken over his predecessor's equipment, stock, and possibly clientele. Pynson's first dated publication, a grammatical text, appeared on 13 November 1492. However, typographical evidence suggests that among his earliest surviving publications are two yearbooks.

Pynson moved from St Clement Danes, and by 10 July 1502 was established in his premises at 'the sign of the George' on the north side of Fleet Street, west of the church of St Dunstan-in-the-West. This location, within the Temple Bar, served him well, for legal printing was always to be a mainstay of his trade, and here he remained until his death. Among his early patrons were the lord privy seal, Bishop Richard Fox, who entrusted his edition of the *Sarum processionale* to Pynson's press in 1501, and Archbishop John Morton and Henry VII, both of whom commissioned from Pynson lavish missals in 1500 and 1504, respectively.

Pynson's experience in legal printing, as well as his connections at court, made him well qualified to be king's printer, a post which he held from as early as 6 January 1506, when he first styles himself *regius impressor*. He had already received several government commissions, including *Ordenaunces of Warre* in 1492 and, in 1500, *Traduction & Mariage of the Princesse*, issued in preparation for Prince Arthur's marriage to Katherine of Aragon. Henry VII had created the post of king's printer in 1504 apparently to coincide with the last parliament of his reign. The crown's first appointee, William Faques, printed the statutes for that parliament as well as the first extant printed proclamation, regarding coinage. The earliest opportunity Pynson had, in his official capacity, to print the original edition of the sessional statutes came with the opening parliament of Henry VIII's reign, in 1510. However, it was not until 1512, when Pynson—always the shrewd businessman—secured the exclusive right to print all statutes and proclamations, that the king's printer became the true precursor of HMSO.

In view of the political agenda for 1512–13, it seems likely that Thomas Wolsey had a hand in consolidating and strengthening the role of king's printer. Wolsey was at this time promoting a war between the holy league and France. Pynson, at Wolsey's instigation, produced a number of publications to justify this 'holy war', including a papal bull declaring Louis XII of France an enemy of the church. Henry VIII and Wolsey continued to use Pynson's office to advance the crown's interests, whether in times of war or peace. Their most sophisticated press campaign centred on religious orthodoxy and Henry's bid for the title 'defender of the faith'. The carefully planned offensive against Martin Luther began in 1521 with the *Assertio septem sacramentorum*, composed in part by Henry VIII.

Little is known of Pynson's character. He was involved in numerous legal wrangles, either suing or being sued for broken contracts and debts, but this was common in the book trade (Plomer, 'Some notices'). Certainly, he was a pious and respected member of the community. He belonged to the Corpus Christi Guild at Coventry (A. W. Reed, *Early Tudor Drama*, 1926, 8); he was elected churchwarden of St Dunstan-in-the-West; and he was the first printer known to have received commissions from the city of London, in 1517. Through his links with churchmen sympathetic to evangelical humanism, such as John Colet and Christopher Urswick, Pynson published reforming texts, including a Latin sermon by Savonarola. The sermon was one of three books from Pynson's press in 1509 to feature roman type, marking its first appearance in England. But it is in the—sometimes haphazard—development of printing as an instrument of state policy that Pynson's importance lies.

By 17 December 1529, the close of the parliament of 21 Henry VIII, Richard Pynson was either dead or incapacitated. His will, dated 17 November 1529, was probated on 23 February 1530. John Rastell stepped in to print the statutes for that session, and by 15 February 1530 Thomas Berthelet had been appointed king's printer. Pynson was survived by his daughter, Margaret Warde; his son Richard had died in September 1520. Pynson's first wife, whose name is not known, had been dead for nearly thirty years; in his will, Pynson asked to be buried beside her in the churchyard of St Clement Danes. He had buried another wife, Joan, in St Dunstan-in-the-West, Fleet Street, in 1528. Margaret's third husband, John Hawkins, finished the last book off Pynson's press on 18 July 1530. Robert Redman, Pynson's chief rival in the publication of legal texts, eventually took over his printing house and materials.

PAMELA NEVILLE-SINGTON

Sources P. Neville, 'Richard Pynson, king's printer (1506–1529): printing and propaganda in early Tudor England', PhD diss., U. Lond., 1990 • P. Neville-Sington, 'Press, politics and religion', *The Cambridge history of the book in Britain*, 3: *1400–1557*, ed. L. Hellinga and J. B. Trapp (1999), 576–607 • S. H. Johnston, 'A study of the career and literary publications of Richard Pynson', PhD diss., University of Western Ontario, 1977 • *STC, 1475–1640* • E. G. Duff, *The printers, stationers, and bookbinders of Westminster and London from 1476 to 1535* (1906) • H. R. Plomer, 'Notices of English stationers in the archives of the City of London', *Transactions of the Bibliographical Society*, 6 (1900–02), 13–27 • H. R. Plomer, 'Some notices of men connected with the English book trade from the plea rolls of Henry VII', *The Library*, 3rd ser., 1 (1910), 289–301 • H. R. Plomer, 'Richard Pynson, glover and printer', *The Library*, 4th ser., 3 (1922–3), 49–51 • J. Ames, T. F. Dibdin, and W. Herbert, eds., *Typographical antiquities, or, The history of printing in England, Scotland and Ireland*, 4 vols. (1810–19) • LP *Henry VIII* • GL, MS 2968/1, fols. 1–6 • will, PRO, PROB 11/23, sig. 15
Likenesses woodcut, NPG
Wealth at death prosperous: will, PRO, PROB 11/23, sig. 15

Pyott, Edward (*d.* 1670), parliamentarian army officer, lived in Lower Easton, near Bristol. He and his wife, Elizabeth (*d.* 1672), formerly married to Richard Dittie, were Quakers. They had two sons, Edward, cited as a 'young lad' in 1680, and Alexander (*d.* 1696), of Warminster, Wiltshire, who co-authored a *Brief Apology in Behalf of … the Quakers* (1693).

A merchant and influential member of his community, Pyott sided with parliament during the civil wars, taking part in the battle of Naseby in June 1645. Dissatisfied with parliament's restructuring of the church along presbyterian lines Pyott, like numerous Bristolians, joined the Quaker movement following the visit of the preachers John Audland and John Camm in September 1654. The early Quakers' 'metaphorical sign performances', such as wearing sackcloth and ashes, or going naked in public to demonstrate the humble nature of divine truth, frequently provoked violence and arrest. In response Pyott and four brethren wrote *The Cry of Blood* (1656), appropriating the growing radical press to represent the Quakers as friends of the Commonwealth who adhered to the principles of the early church, and to document the violence they encountered. *The Cry of Blood* remains an essential source for understanding the establishment of early Bristol Quakerism.

However, it is Pyott's efforts to secure the safety of the growing Quaker movement that makes him significant. When founding Quaker George Fox met Pyott in 1654 or 1655, he recognized in him the organizational skills needed for advocating liberty of conscience and publicizing the movement's peaceful intentions. The most memorable of Pyott's journeys with Fox occurred in Cornwall during 1655–6 in the wake of orders raised in several counties to check Quaker disturbances and control their expansion. Detained at several locales, including Marazion and St Ives, Pyott and Thomas Salt of London were with Fox in January 1656 when he publicly read a paper that local magistrates regarded as a threat to law and order. During his eight-month confinement at Launceton, and undoubtedly at Fox's behest, Pyott orchestrated a propaganda effort, circulating letters, testimonies, and documents to Oliver Cromwell, Major-General John Desborough, and local justices and magistrates to rehabilitate the Quakers' image.

Many of the writings from Launceton were included in *The West Answering to the North* (1657), in which Pyott and his co-authors denounced the disregard for their rights as freeborn Englishmen and contended that although liberty of conscience was a natural right, rights and law were being subverted by lawyers, and scripture was being 'mangled' by the clergy. While the tract advocated liberty of conscience and served as a testimony that contrasted the Quakers' peaceful intentions with the persecution they experienced, it was also a document with an important subtext that warned their brethren away from conspicuous behaviour and legal entanglements. Pyott was released in September 1656, months after he, Fox, and Salt had declined Cromwell's offer to set them free if they discontinued their preaching.

Pyott was an ardent advocate for republican ideals who warned Cromwell away from taking the crown in 1657. When the Commonwealth was faltering in 1659, he served as a militia commissioner for Bristol to counter the rebellion staged by George Booth and other 'new royalists'. In 1661 he and Fox argued for the Quakers' loyalty to the restored king before the House of Commons, which was debating the bill that would become the Quaker Act of 1662. After Restoration legislation made subject to arrest those who refused to take an oath or who met in groups of five or more, Pyott was arrested and fined on several occasions. In 1663 he challenged the Bristol court that was trying him, contending that matters concerning the worship and service of God exceeded their authority. He further developed his position regarding the metaphysical nature of conscience in *The Quaker Vindicated* (1667).

A signatory of the Margaret Fell–George Fox marriage certificate in 1669, Pyott remained active in Bristol Quaker affairs until the end of his life. He became ill and died in London on 3 May 1670, perhaps while preparing another appeal for religious liberty and the Quaker right to worship.   MARYANN S. FEOLA

Sources R. Mortimer, ed., *Minute book of the men's meeting of the Society of Friends in Bristol*, Bristol RS, 26 (1971) · C. Horle, ed., records of sufferings, RS Friends, Lond. [transcription], fols. 1–3 · G. Fox, *The west answering to the north* (1657) · *The journal of George Fox*, ed. N. Penney, 2 vols. (1911) · Greaves & Zaller, *BDBR* · J. Besse, *A collection of the sufferings of the people called Quakers*, 1 (1753) · 'Dictionary of Quaker biography', RS Friends, Lond. [card index], fol. P · 'Booth, George (1622–1684)', *DNB* · R. Bauman, *Let your words be few: symbolism of speaking and silence amongst seventeenth-century Quakers* (1983) · G. Bishop, T. Goldney, and others, *The cry of blood* (1656)
Archives RS Friends, Lond., Original Records of Sufferings

Pyper, William (1797–1861), classical scholar, was born of poor parents in the parish of Rathen, Aberdeenshire. After matriculating at Marischal College, Aberdeen, he completed his course there with distinction. From 1815 to 1817 he was parochial schoolmaster at Laurence Kirk; he afterwards held a similar position at Maybole, and was a teacher at Glasgow grammar school in 1820. Two years later he succeeded James Gray as headmaster in the High School of Edinburgh, and retained that post for twenty-two years.

On 22 October 1844 Pyper was appointed professor of humanity at St Andrews University, in succession to Dr Gillespie. He obtained the degree of LLD from Aberdeen University. He died on 7 January 1861 and his assistant, John Shairp (afterwards principal of St Andrews), succeeded him in the humanity chair.

Pyper was an excellent Latinist and a thorough classical scholar. He proved an admirable professor. He helped to organize and improve the university library, and by a bequest of £500 he founded a bursary. He published a school text book, *Gradus ad Parnassum* (1843), and *Horace, with Quantities* (1843).

A. H. MILLAR, *rev.* C. A. CREFFIELD

Sources M. F. Connolly, *Eminent men of Fife* (1866) · Boase, *Mod. Eng. biog.* · Irving, *Scots.*
Wealth at death £4982 18*s.* 2*d.*: inventory, 27 April 1867, NA Scot., SC 20/50/32/647

Pytheas (*fl.* 4th cent. BC), explorer, was the first Greek author to describe Britain. He is an authority rather than a personality but seems to have come from Massalia (Marseilles). Not mentioned, as far as is known, by Aristotle, he was treated with suspicion by his pupil, the polymath Dikaiarkhos of Messana (*fl. c.*320–300 BC). At more or less that date, or a little later, he was quoted with more approval by the Sicilian Greek historian Timaios of Tauromenion. Timaios wrote in radical isolation in exile in Athens in the early third century BC. It is not safe to conclude either that Dikaiarkhos was appraising a recently published work, or that Timaios recognized the intellectual merits of a contemporary narrative. The work of Pytheas, as it is known from attributed quotations, mainly in the *Geography* of Strabo and the *Natural History* of the elder Pliny, claimed to detail the Atlantic coast northwards from Gades (Cadiz). It contained genuine toponyms: apart from 'Prettania' (Britain) and 'Ierne' (Ireland), it included 'Kantion' (the land of the Cantii, Kent), 'Ouxisame' (probably Ouissant), and the land of the Ostimii (probably the later Osismi) of Brittany. Its estimate of the circumference of Britain was, however, about double the correct value. Further allusions to a great gulf, an amber-producing island, and the famous sluggish sea beyond the northern island of Thoule (Thule), have provoked copious debate but little agreement. Thoule itself, though identified by Tacitus and Ptolemy as Shetland, was apparently beyond Britain. It was possibly Iceland, and (as far as written sources go) would seem not to have been known to Greek or Roman voyagers after Pytheas. The book identified Pytheas as a private citizen (as distinct from a state-sponsored voyager) and a poor man (a term which fits, but does not prove, the idea that he was a commercial captain). It also made use of astronomical observations, and seems to have been the first work to propound the idea of an Arctic circle. A number of passages in Diodorus Siculus's *Universal History* may also be derived from Pytheas through Timaios. Some of their ethnographic details have become well known: a description of the mining and sale of tin, and picturesque glimpses of life on Thoule. Diodorus's account adds the toponyms 'Orkadion' (on the coast of Scotland facing Orkney, probably Dunnet Head, Caithness), and Belerion (in the Cornish peninsula, either

Land's End or the Lizard). These were the promontories which, with Kantion, became the angles of the standard triangular representation of Britain. He also mentions the island 'Iktis', which should be Vectis (Wight), though the (probably imaginative) description is more reminiscent of St Michael's Mount.

The literary genre in which such a voyage was presented cannot be reliably deduced from these snippets. Timaios's interest may indicate that it shed light on the geography of myth, and it was certainly soon classified as marvel literature. It is not very likely that the work had (as it was once normal to argue) a primarily utilitarian aim, to be compared to the accounts of post-classical explorers or fitted into a context of commercial rivalry between the Greeks of the western Mediterranean and the Carthaginian communities which dominated the Strait of Gibraltar. On the other hand, the vilification which it received later, especially from Strabo, may equally derive from the wrong expectations; and the evidence of the toponyms suggests that Pytheas had (as would not be surprising at Massalia in the late fourth century) some contact with people who (by whatever means) had genuine experience of travelling in the Atlantic seaboard and the narrow seas. It remains possible that the first-person narration which seems to have underlain the exposition of the coasts in order (which was a normal way of presenting geographical material) was more than a commonplace.

NICHOLAS PURCELL

Sources C. H. Roseman, *Pytheas of Massalia: on the ocean* (1994) • C. F. C. Hawkes, *Pytheas: Europe and the Greek explorers, a lecture delivered at New College, Oxford on 20th May 1975, revised and amplified with ten maps* (1977) • V. Manfredi and L. Braccesi, *Mare Greco: eroi ed esploratori nel Mediterraneo antico* (1992) • A. L. F. Rivet and C. Smith, *The place-names of Roman Britain* (1979)

Quadal, Martin Ferdinand (1736–1808), animal and portrait painter, was born at Niemtschitz, Moravia, on 28 October 1736. He studied first at the Akademie der Bildenden Künste, in Vienna, before moving to Paris, where he undertook further study in 1768. While there he painted a number of horse subjects for Louis-Joseph, prince de Condé. Continuing his peripatetic life, in 1772 he moved to London, where he stayed with the painter E. F. Cunningham. He exhibited a number of animal paintings at the Royal Academy in 1772 and enrolled in the Royal Academy Schools on 6 December 1773, when he gave his age as twenty-eight. In 1776 he painted a pair of half-length portraits, of John Mathews and Anna Mathews, both signed and dated (ex Christies, East New York, April 1988, lot 99). He may have been in Yorkshire from *c.*1777 to 1779, after which date he moved to Dublin. Again he met with considerable success; the Dublin Society purchased a number of his animal studies for use by its students.

Quadal was in Italy in 1784, when he visited Rome and Naples. On returning to Vienna in 1787 he painted one of his most ambitious works, *The Nude Room at the Vienna Academy with the Academy Members* (Akademie der Bildenden Künste, Vienna). This work is rather uncharacteristic, his usual output being a combination of hunting scenes, animal paintings, and portraits. He returned to England and in 1791 is recorded in Bath, from where he exhibited *Two Italian Lazzaroni Boys Reposing with a Group of Dogs* and *A Boy Teaching a Dog to Count* at the Royal Academy. He was in London again by 1793, where he exhibited once more at the academy and published, from 6 George Street, Hanover Square, *A Variety of Tame and Wild Animals … for the Use … of the Young Practitioner … of Design*, a series of engraved animal studies. By 1794 he was in the Netherlands, in 1796 in Hamburg, and finally, in 1797, he was in St Petersburg, where he was appointed master of the Academy of Arts. He remained in St Petersburg until his death there on 11 January 1808.   DEBORAH GRAHAM-VERNON

Sources J. Turner, ed., *The dictionary of art*, 34 vols. (1996) • Waterhouse, *18c painters* • Graves, *RA exhibitors* • W. G. Strickland, *A dictionary of Irish artists*, 2 vols. (1913); repr. with introduction by T. J. Snoddy (1989) • Thieme & Becker, *Allgemeines Lexikon*

Quain, Sir John Richard (1816–1876), judge, was born at Ratheahy, co. Cork, the youngest son of Richard Quain of Ratheahy and his second wife, Margaret, daughter of Andrew Mahoney. Two half-brothers, Jones *Quain and Richard *Quain, became prominent figures in the medical profession. Quain was educated at Göttingen, and at University College, London, where he won many prizes, graduated LLB in 1839, and was elected to the university law scholarship. He became a fellow of University College in 1843, was for several years an examiner in law to the University of London, and in June 1860 became a member of the senate. Admitted to the Middle Temple on 18 November 1837, he was in the chambers of Thomas Chitty and practised as a special pleader from 1841 until his call on 30 May 1851. He then joined the northern circuit, wrote a book on the Common Law Procedure Acts with Holroyd (1853), and soon obtained a considerable practice. On 23 July 1866 he became a queen's counsel, and later the same year, a bencher of the Middle Temple. In 1868 he was made attorney-general for the county palatine of Durham and he also served on the judicature commission.

Quain was appointed a judge of the queen's bench in December 1871, took his seat and was made a serjeant on 5 January 1872, and was knighted on 22 April. Adolphus Liddell, author and fellow lawyer, described him as: 'An odd man, outwardly and inwardly. He was short and round, with a large forehead, protruding eyes, and no chin' (Liddell, 130). Rather mercurial in temperament, he was touchy and sensitive of his dignity. Before he could make much of an impression as a judge, his health failed and, after some months of intermittent illness, he died at his house, 22A Cavendish Square, on 12 September 1876, and was buried at Marylebone cemetery, Finchley, on 18 September. He was unmarried. His interest in legal education was attested by a substantial bequest for that purpose and his law library was presented to University College, London, by his half-brother, Professor Richard Quain MD.

J. A. HAMILTON, *rev.* PATRICK POLDEN

Sources Boase, *Mod. Eng. biog.* • [W. D. I. Foulkes], *A generation of judges* (1886) • *Law Times* (23 Sept 1876) • *Law Journal* (16 Sept 1876), 521–2 • *Solicitors' Journal*, 20 (1875–6), 884 • A. G. C. Liddell, *Notes from the life of an ordinary mortal* (1911) • Sainty, *King's counsel* • Sainty, *Judges* • J. M. Collinge, *Officials of royal commissions of enquiry, 1815–70*

(1984) · Baker, *Serjeants* · Allibone, *Dict.* · H. A. C. Sturgess, ed., *Register of admissions to the Honourable Society of the Middle Temple, from the fifteenth century to the year 1944*, 2 (1949)
Likenesses F. Lockwood, group portrait, sketch, repro. in A. Burrell, *Sir Frank Lockwood: a biographical sketch*, 2nd edn (1898), 58 · T. Woolner, bust, Middle Temple, London
Wealth at death under £70,000: probate, 22 Sept 1876, *CGPLA Eng. & Wales*

Quain, Jones (1796–1865), anatomist, born in November 1796, was the eldest son of Richard Quain of Ratheahy, co. Cork, and his first wife, whose maiden name was Jones. His grandfather was David Quain of Carrigoon, co. Cork. He received the name of Jones from his mother's family. Richard *Quain (1800–1887) was his full brother, and Sir John Richard *Quain (1816–1876) his half-brother. Sir Richard *Quain bt, FRS (1816–1898), was his first cousin. He commenced his education in Adair's school at Fermoy. He subsequently entered Trinity College, Dublin, where, in 1814, he obtained a scholarship, then the highest classical distinction. He graduated in arts, and in 1820 he took the degree of bachelor of medicine, though he did not proceed MD until 1833. At the end of his college career he visited the continental schools and spent some time in Paris working on *Manual of Pathology* (1826), a translation of the work by Louis Martinet.

Quain went to London in 1825 and joined, as one of its anatomical teachers, the school of medicine founded by Mr Tyrell in Aldersgate Street. The other teacher of anatomy was William Lawrence. While working here Quain prepared and published the *Elements of Descriptive and Practical Anatomy: for the Use of Students* (1828), which he introduced 'with a Paean of praise for the new French approach' (Desmond, 99). It became the standard textbook on the subject in all English speaking countries. It was also translated into German (1870–72). An attack of haemoptysis occurring while he suffered from a dissection wound forced Quain to take a rest for two years.

In 1831 Quain accepted the post of professor of general anatomy at University College, then vacant by the resignation of Granville Sharp Pattison; Richard Quain, his brother, acted as senior demonstrator and lecturer on descriptive anatomy, while Erasmus Wilson was his prosecutor. He was also invited to lecture upon physiology. He resigned his post at University College in 1836, and in the same year he was appointed a member of the senate of the University of London. He lived in retirement during the last twenty years of his life, chiefly in Paris, devoting himself to literary and scientific pursuits. Quain died, unmarried, at his home, 103 Stanhope Street, Mornington Crescent, London, on 31 January 1865, and was buried in Highgate cemetery. Quain was an elegant and accomplished scholar, and he was deeply interested in literature as well as science.   D'A. POWER, *rev.* MICHAEL BEVAN

Sources R. Partridge, *Proceedings of the Royal Medical and Chirurgical Society*, 5 (1864–7), 49 · *Medical Circular*, 26 (1865), 87 · private information (1896) · *CGPLA Eng. & Wales* (1865) · A. Desmond, *The politics of evolution: morphology, medicine and reform in radical London* (1989)
Wealth at death under £450: administration, 1865, *CGPLA Eng. & Wales*

Quain, Richard (1800–1887), anatomist and surgeon, was born in July 1800 at Fermoy, co. Cork, Ireland, the third son of Richard Quain, of Ratheahy, co. Cork, a gentleman farmer, and his first wife, whose maiden name of Jones became the Christian name of their eldest son, also an anatomist. The subject of this biography (henceforth, Quain) is occasionally mistaken for his half-brother, Sir John Richard *Quain, a judge, and very frequently confused (even in contemporary historical literature) with his cousin, Sir Richard *Quain, a physician. All four Quains had intimate associations with University College.

Quain was educated locally at Adairs School, Fermoy, and underwent an apprenticeship with a surgeon in Ireland. He then followed his brother Jones *Quain to London, where the latter was associated with the Aldersgate School of Anatomy, one of the private anatomy schools that flourished in London until the late 1820s. Quain then spent some time studying in Paris, where a friend of his father, Richard Bennett, was an extramural lecturer in anatomy. When in 1828 Bennett became demonstrator in anatomy at the new University of London (now University College, London), Quain followed to assist. There was much jockeying for power and position in the new medical school, and Bennett (who had applied for the chair in anatomy) quarrelled from the beginning with the anatomy professor, Granville Sharp Pattison. The students, whose fees counted for much, preferred Bennett's teaching, and Charles Bell, professor of surgery, also gave surgical anatomy lectures. By 1831 the air had cleared somewhat, following Bell's departure to the Middlesex Hospital, Pattison's forced resignation, and Bennett's death. Jones Quain was appointed professor of anatomy, and his brother became (in 1832) professor of descriptive anatomy. By then, relations between the brothers were not cordial.

Quain held this chair until 1850, during which period he had a number of able demonstrators, including Erasmus Wilson, Viner Ellis, and John Marshall. Quain also produced his major work, *The Anatomy of the Arteries of the Human Body* (3 vols., 1841–4), a handsome folio, the drawings for which were done by surgeon–artist Joseph Maclise, brother of the Royal Academician. The work was based on more than 1000 dissections, and although essentially descriptive, it dealt with arterial diseases and anomalies as well as normal structure and distribution. Quain also edited (with William Sharpey) the fifth edition (1848) of *Elements of Anatomy*, the earlier edition of which had been written by Jones Quain. Quain had been instrumental in luring William Sharpey to London from Edinburgh, to take over Jones Quain's general anatomy (physiology) teaching when the latter left University College in 1836.

Quain was also appointed assistant surgeon to the North London Hospital (subsequently University College Hospital) shortly after it opened in 1834. He was promoted to full surgeon in 1850, but was deeply disappointed not to obtain the vacant chair in surgery, which went to Eric Erichsen. Quain was a conservative, even timid surgeon whose active career was over by the time antiseptic techniques revolutionized the discipline. He was methodical in all details of patient care and demanding of his students. Of short stature, he was pompous and authoritarian, quick to attribute bad motives to anyone who disagreed with him.

Quain's clinical publications were not of lasting importance. *The Diseases of the Rectum* (1854) was based largely on his own experience with rectal diseases; his *Clinical Lectures* (1884) gathered together material, much of which had been published in journals long before. Its appearance late in Quain's life probably owed more to vanity than consumer demand.

A member of the Royal College of Surgeons from 1828, Quain was one of the original fellows when that rank was created in 1843. He sat on the college's council and its court of examiners, represented it on the General Medical Council and served (1868) as its president. He was elected FRS in 1844, and was surgeon-extraordinary to Queen Victoria.

One of the most attractive aspects of this irascible man was Quain's advocacy of a more liberal education for medical students. The subject of his 1869 Hunterian lecture at the Royal College of Surgeons was defects in the current system of educating doctors, and he had published a variety of pamphlets and articles on the same general theme over many years. True to his principles, he left the bulk of his estate, valued at about £78,000, to University College, London, for the promotion and encouragement of 'general education in modern languages (especially in English language and composition in that language) and in natural science'. The present Quain chairs at University College, London, derive from this bequest. Quain used to list speaking correct English as one of his hobbies.

Some of Quain's estate had been left to him by his half-brother, Sir John Richard Quain, whose name Quain also wished to be perpetuated. Quain's late marriage, in 1859, to Ellen Brodrick, (*d.* 1886), Viscountess Midleton, widow of the fifth viscount, had produced no children. He died on 15 September 1887 at his last residence, 32 Cavendish Square, London, of cystitis and urinary retention, having refused Sir Henry Thompson permission to attempt to crush the obstructing bladder stone, an operation he had performed successfully on Quain a decade earlier. He was buried in Marylebone cemetery, Finchley, Middlesex, on 21 September. Confusion of the two medical Richard Quains had already begun, his cousin's wife receiving a number of letters of condolence on the putative death of her husband.   W. F. BYNUM

Sources 'Richard Quain, FRS', *BMJ* (24 Sept 1887), 694–5 · 'Richard Quain, FRCS, FRS', *The Lancet*, 2 (1887), 687–8 · V. G. Plarr, *Plarr's Lives of the fellows of the Royal College of Surgeons of England*, rev. D'A. Power, 2 (1930), 207–8 · J. F. Clarke, *Autobiographical recollections of the medical profession* (1874), 295ff · H. H. Bellot, *University College, London, 1826–1926* (1929) · W. R. Merrington, *University College Hospital and its medical school: a history* (1976) · F. L. M. Pattison, *Granville Sharp Pattison, anatomist and antagonist, 1791–1851* (1987) · *CGPLA Eng. & Wales* (1887) · m. cert.

Archives RCP Lond., letters · UCL, corresp.; notes of his lectures · Wellcome L., lecture notes

Likenesses G. Richmond, oils, exh. RA 1872, RCS Eng. · T. Woolner, marble bust, 1884, RCS Eng. · R. T., wood-engraving, NPG; repro. in *ILN* (24 Sept 1887)

Wealth at death £78,886 10s. 4d.: will, 28 Oct 1887, *CGPLA Eng. & Wales*

Quain, Sir Richard, baronet (1816–1898), physician, was born at Mallow, on the Blackwater, near Cork, while the clocks were striking midnight on 30 October 1816. He was the eldest surviving child of John Quain, a small landowner at Carrigoon, and his wife, Mary Burke. He was educated at a local dame-school before attending the diocesan school at Cloyne. His apprenticeship to Dr Fraser, a surgeon–apothecary at Limerick, was terminated by the general distress in Ireland. He was set to work in the tannery business of his maternal uncle before resuming his medical studies at University College, London, where his cousins Jones Quain (1796–1865) and Richard Quain (1800–1887) were both established in medical practice. In 1840 he graduated as bachelor of medicine, obtaining a scholarship and gold medals, as well as honours in surgery and midwifery. He proceeded to MD (1842) and FRCP (1851).

Working as a house surgeon in University College Hospital, Quain's high capacities were widely recognized. From 1845 he was a leader writer for *The Lancet*, and afterwards a contributor to the *Saturday Review*. He was one of the founders of the Pathological Society in 1846 (secretary, 1852; president, 1869). In 1849 he published two papers on cerebral apoplexy. However, his paper of 1850 on fatty degeneration of the heart established him as an authority on the disease; he later declared that if he had been physician to a great general hospital, fatty degeneration would have been known as Quain's disease. He also wrote on cognate subjects including angina pectoris and heart aneurysms. On 31 January 1854 he married Isabella Agnes (1828–1891), daughter of George Wray, captain in the Bengal army. They had four daughters.

Quain was assistant physician (1848–55) and physician (1855–75) at Brompton Hospital for Diseases of the Chest. He was also consulting physician to the Royal Naval Hospital at Greenwich and the Royal Hospital for Consumption at Ventnor. But from the 1850s his great success was as a general physician and society doctor practising in Harley Street. Politicians (including Benjamin Disraeli) as well as distinguished authors, painters, and officials consulted him. Such patients introduced him to equally eminent men who became his friends and treated him as a representative exponent of professional opinion. He became the repository of many high professional confidences. A chance remark by Quain at the Athenaeum led to the premature leaking of Lord Northbrook's appointment to the viceroyalty of India in 1872.

Quain's superior connections ensured many public appointments. In 1860 he was nominated by the queen in council to the senate of the University of London. As such he was a leading figure in establishing the university's pathological research centre called the Brown Institution. Quain gave steadfast support to his friend and patient Robert Lowe, afterwards Viscount Sherbrooke, in his successful campaign of 1868 to become first member for the new University of London parliamentary constituency. Quain's influential friends obtained his appointment to

Sir Richard Quain, baronet (1816–1898), by Sir John Everett Millais, 1895–6

the General Medical Council in 1863. He remained a member continuously for thirty-five years until his death. Active on the council's pharmacopoeia committee (initially as secretary and from 1874 as chairman), he was closely involved with the publication of four new editions of the *British Pharmacopoeia* between 1867 and 1898. He served as treasurer of the General Medical Council for nearly thirty years before his election in 1891 as president; he was re-elected in 1896. Throughout this presidency Quain was active in the council's business, and somewhat despotic in his methods. He curbed prolixity at meetings by a reminder that speeches cost the council 13*s.* per minute. From 1896 younger physicians such as Victor Horsley publicly criticized the anachronistic organization of the council under Quain.

A few bullocks imported from Reval, which were infected with rinderpest and sold in London, caused a national epidemic in 1865. Quain was just leaving on a holiday when he was persuaded to join the royal commission on cattle plague chaired by Earl Spencer. He was convinced that the only way to stop the terrible mortality among herds was the absolute prohibition of moving cattle from infected districts together with the slaughter of all infected beasts, all healthy bovine animals with which they had contact, and all imported animals at their port of

debarkation. Through his friendship with John Delane he contributed a series of letters to *The Times* signed 'Q', which were widely copied in provincial newspapers. Quain's campaign dispelled popular, parliamentary, and journalistic doubts, and overcame the resistance of railway companies and cattle-jobbing interests to the drastic measures that he advocated. In total, 300,000 animals were killed. Quain more than anyone contributed to ridding Britain of rinderpest. (In 1886 he sat on a government committee reporting on Pasteur's treatment for rabies.)

In 1871 Quain was elected a fellow of the Royal Society, and he later received several honorary degrees. His connection with the discovery of the nature of fatty degeneration was beginning to be forgotten by the late 1870s when he accepted the editorship of a *Dictionary of Medicine.* He toiled ferociously on this project, sometimes through the night after a full day's work, recruiting distinguished contributors and assiduously scrutinizing their efforts. The dictionary, which sold 33,000 copies in its first edition of 1882, revived his professional standing. Having narrowly failed in 1888 to achieve his great ambition, the presidency of the Royal College of Physicians, he was consoled with its vice-presidency in 1889. Appointed physician-extraordinary to Queen Victoria in 1890, he was elevated to a baronetcy in 1891.

He fell ill in 1897 with a painful and exhausting cancer of the rectum, which required three operations. His herculean constitution astounded his friends: he roused himself to work on council business until his last days. He died on 13 March 1898 at his home, 67 Harley Street, St Marylebone, when his baronetcy became extinct. On 16 March he was buried in Hampstead cemetery.

'An Irishman of the best type, always genial, always kindly, always amusing, an admirable *raconteur* and afterdinner speaker, Quain frequented most societies and was welcome in all' (*The Times*, 14 March 1898). He had a great power of making and keeping friends. Although never brilliant in medicine, he was endowed with excellent sense. As a diagnostician he was quick and intuitive. He was ready and practical in recommending cures. With patients he was cheerful, sympathetic, and considerate. He worked very hard, and used his time with ruthless efficiency. Though many colleagues relished 'his intense, jovial, pugnacious attitude towards life' it riled those who suspected him of 'selfish designs and motives' (*The Lancet*, 19 March 1898). RICHARD DAVENPORT-HINES

Sources *The Times* (14 March 1898) · *BMJ* (19 March 1898), 793–5 · *The Lancet* (5 Feb–19 March 1898), 798, 816–20 · *Annual Register* (1898), 149–50 · R. Quain, *Dictionary of medicine* (1882) · R. Quain, *The healing art* (1885) · A. Patchett Martin, *Life and letters of the Right Honourable Robert Lowe, Viscount Sherbrooke*, 2 vols. (1893) · E. Cook, *Delane of The Times* (1915) · m. cert. · d. cert. · Burke, *Peerage* (1894) · *London and Provincial Medical Directory* (1848–98)
Archives RCP Lond., letters · UCL, corresp.; notes of his lectures · Wellcome L., lecture notes | probably ICL, Lord Playfair MSS
Likenesses D. Maclise, oils, *c.*1866 · photograph, 1880–89, repro. in *BMJ*, 793 · T. Barlow, mezzotint, pubd 1883 (after D. Maclise), NPG · photograph, 1890–98, repro. in *The Lancet* (19 March 1898), 817 · J. E. Millais, oils, 1895–6, RCP Lond. [*see illus.*] · R. T., wood-

engraving, NPG; repro. in *ILN* (17 Jan 1891) • Spy [L. Ward], chromo-lithograph caricature, NPG; repro. in *VF* (15 Dec 1883)
Wealth at death £118,121 13s. 2d.: probate, 10 May 1898, *CGPLA Eng. & Wales*

Quaque [Kweku], **Philip** (1741–1816), first African Church of England clergyman and missionary, was born at Cape Coast and named Kweku, the name to indicate born on Wednesdays. A Fante, he was reputedly the son, but more likely a remoter relative, of Birempong Cudjo, the inter-mediary between the local Fante and the African Com-pany, which administered the British trading fort, Cape Coast Castle. In 1751 the London based Society for the Propagation of the Gospel (SPG) sent a missionary to Cape Coast, Thomas Thompson, who in 1754 sent three Fante boys, one of them Quaque, to London to be educated. Two died, but Quaque, baptized Philip in 1759, spent the next seven years there under the tuition of the Revd John Moore in Charterhouse Square (he is sometimes said, wrongly, to have studied at Oxford University). In 1765 he became the first African to be ordained a priest of the Church of England. The SPG then appointed him a mis-sionary with a £50 salary. Before leaving London he mar-ried, on 2 May 1765, an English wife, Catherine Blunt, and returned with her to Cape Coast in 1766.

Quaque was also appointed by the African Company chaplain at Cape Coast Castle with a £60 salary, plus a £13 allowance for his wife, who died soon after in November 1766. On arrival he wrote at once to the SPG committee in London with his news, and from then on regularly sent them detailed and lucid letters recording his views and activities. The society, however, took little interest in them and he received only three letters in return. In his first letter he lamented that all the company's employees, whose spiritual welfare he was responsible for, lived unmarried with African women. Moreover, over the suc-ceeding fifty years of his ministry he was to find that most of them not only ignored the company's regulation that they attend prayers, but lived wholly unchristian lives. Many even refused to send their children to the school he opened for their use. Sometimes the governors were hos-tile: one openly ridiculed religion. But the company sup-ported Quaque and eventually raised his salary to £150. Though rarely more than half a dozen children, almost all Eurafricans, ever attended his school, he provided them with a basic, useful schooling (some became clerks in the company's service), and has thus been counted a pioneer of European education in Ghana.

Quaque's other role, as a missionary, was even less fruit-ful. During his years in London he had lost his fluency in Fante and found it difficult to explain the Christian gospel in what he called a 'vile jargon' (Priestley, 123n.). He per-formed a few baptisms, but made not one convert. He lived in the style of his European colleagues. To avoid the accusation that he was copying their morals (so he wrote to the SPG), after his wife died he married her Fante wait-ing maid in September 1769. When she died a few months later, in April 1770, he married another Fante woman, in March 1772. With his substantial salary he could afford to live in comfort, and so moved out of the dilapidated old fort and built himself a house in the adjoining town, with mahogany furniture and a library. From time to time he would visit the other trading forts along the coast and in 1784 he took his son and daughter to London to be edu-cated. His latter years seem to have been unhappy. His last surviving letter, of 1811, reported severe ill health and included a long diatribe against his family. During his last five years he refrained from drawing his SPG salary and when he died at Cape Coast Castle on 17 October 1816 there was a balance of £369 which, with another £100, he had bequeathed to his successor as missionary. But as he too had died by the time the SPG received the news, the money was sent to Quaque's heirs. Quaque, who was bur-ied at Cape Coast Castle, seems to have taken no part in local political affairs, nor, unsurprisingly, given that he was the employee of a company principally concerned with the slave trade, any part in the campaign to abolish it.   CHRISTOPHER FYFE

Sources M. Priestley, 'Philip Quaque of Cape Coast', *Africa remem-bered: narratives by west Africans from the era of the slave trade*, ed. P. D. Curtin (1967), 99–139 • F. L. Bartels, 'Philip Quaque, 1741–1816', *Transactions of the Gold Coast and Togoland Historical Society*, 1 (1952–5), 153–77 • Bodl. RH, United Society for the Propagation of the Gospel MSS, C/AFW/1, west Africa • C. F. Pascoe, *Two hundred years of the SPG*, rev. edn, 2 vols. (1901)
Archives Bodl. RH, Society for the Propagation of the Gospel archives
Wealth at death over £469: Pascoe, *Two hundred years*, 258

Quare, Daniel (1648/9–1724), maker of clocks, watches, and barometers, is presumed to have been of a strict Quaker family, but nothing is known of his parentage. It has been suggested he was a native of Somerset, perhaps on account of the former existence of a manor named Quarre in that county, coupled with the fact that Besse records a John Quire of Misterton, Somerset, who was fined in the 1660s for his Quaker beliefs. Nor is anything known of his apprenticeship, the earliest record of Quare appearing in the minutes of a Clockmakers' Company quarter court held in London on 3 April 1671 when he was 'admitted and Sworne a Brother of the Company', paying £3. He was also ordered to abandon an illegally recruited and unidentified apprentice; he enrolled the first of his fif-teen authorized pupils in June 1673.

Quare's premises were subjected to a Clockmakers' 'search' in March 1675 when he was working in the 'Mid-dle or Cittie' precinct—one of three company divisions at that date. He was probably in St Martin's-le-Grand, which was his address when he married Mary, daughter of Jere-miah Stevens, maltster, of High Wycombe, Buckingham-shire, on 18 April 1676; the ceremony took place at a Friends' meeting at Devonshire House, Bishopsgate, where Quare was one of the early members. A clock by him is recorded signed with a more precise address—'in Martins Neare Alders Gate Londini',—where he was still living in August 1680. One authority reports, without veri-fiable reference, that he next had a business at the Plough and Harrow in Cornhill, but by June 1682 he was in the par-ish of All Hallows, Lombard Street, where, in 1683, he was lodging with one Edward Hoult. By 1686 he was established in Exchange Alley in the parish of St Mary Woolnoth in the heart of the City. Many renowned watchmakers flourished there, and Quare took over the premises vacated by Robert Seignior, who had been appointed in 1682 to succeed Edward East as the king's chief clockmaker, though in the event East outlived him. No business association between Seignior and Quare has been discovered but doubtless Quare inherited a measure of goodwill. Seignior named the shop The Dial but Quare used the King's Arms as his address. The adjoining shops were occupied by a confectioner and a vintner.

Quare, it may be presumed of one of his faith, was a peace-loving and honest member of the community but he came into conflict with authorities by refusing, in accordance with his beliefs, to pay tithes or to swear an oath; either action could have brought about his disownment. Consequently, goods to the value of £5 were seized from him in 1678 to offset his rate of £2 12s. 6d. 'for the maintenance of the Parochial Priests in London', two clocks and two watches worth £11 5s. were taken from him in 1679 when he refused to contribute towards the militia, and in 1682–3 Quare and five other Friends had goods to the value of £145 17s. 6d. seized for attending a proscribed meeting at White Hart Court. On 4 June 1686 Quare was summoned, with about fifty other Friends, to appear before the commissioners appointed by James II to hear their grievances. Matters were eased by the Toleration Act of 1689 but plate worth just over £3 was taken from him that year for tithes and priests' maintenance. He subsequently served the parliamentary committee of the meeting for sufferings, disbursing over £350 in expenses in 1700–02.

Quare's religious leanings did not exclude him from election to parish duties, though he was not keen to serve and twice paid fines to be excused. Nevertheless, he was a member of the vestry committee of St Mary Woolnoth in 1693, a sidesman in 1694, and one of two collectors for the poor in 1696. In September 1698, while away in Flanders, he was chosen to be a member of the court of assistants of the Clockmakers' Company. He later served them in higher office: in September 1705 he was elected junior warden, and he rose through the ranks of renter and senior warden to become master in September 1708.

In 1695 an ambitious lottery, the proceeds of which were to finance two colleges of science and art, offered 2000 winners the opportunity to learn a chosen trade. Quare and his former apprentice John Marshall, by then working 'against the Royal Exchange', volunteered to teach the art of watch making. The scheme failed through lack of interest but in the following year Quare assisted John Bellers in drawing up his *Proposals for Raising a College of Industry of All Useful Trades* (1695); although the bill did not succeed before parliament, it led to the establishment of the Quaker workhouse at Clerkenwell, where Quare was said to have been 'responsible for some boys there for many years'.

Quare worked in relative obscurity until the 1680s and he may well have spent most of the 1670s in the employment of others. His early work is rare and displays no significant contribution to the improvement of mechanical designs. Two events brought him to the fore: first, his move to Exchange Alley between 1683 and 1686 placed him in the centre of London's business quarter (where he was said to have successfully speculated in the shares and funds with which it abounded); second, in 1687, he played a major part in the Clockmakers' Company's opposition to Edward Barlow's patent application for 'pulling or repeating clocks and watches'. James II judged that Barlow's watch, made by Tompion, was inferior to one submitted by Quare because it required two buttons to be pushed instead of Quare's one. This was a tremendous boost to Quare's reputation and secured his place in horological history. The Ashmolean Museum, Oxford, holds a watch believed to be that proffered by Quare and supposedly retained by James. It has been claimed that Quare adapted the concentric minute hand, but examples by several other makers are now recorded to show this was not the case. In the first decade of the eighteenth century he was, however, among the first to use jewel endstones in watches to improve the action and durability of escapements, and to use dust caps to help keep movements clean.

In August 1695 Quare was granted a fourteen-year patent for 'the sole use and benefit of a Portable Weather Glass or Barometer, by him invented', which could 'be removed and carried to any place, though turned upside down, without spilling one drop of the quicksilver, or letting any air into the tube'. The Clockmakers' Company opposed this application too, and it is questionable whether or not Quare deserved priority; a similar design had already been published in Holland in 1688 and Robert Hooke reported that Thomas Tompion had made an example a year earlier. When William Derham carried out barometric experiments at the Monument in 1696 he used two of Quare's 'best portable barometers'. Several examples have survived but it is unlikely that any has its original tube.

Quare's influential standing came to be of use to Friends when appealing to the throne. On his petition two Friends imprisoned in Westmorland were released and on 2 May 1695 he introduced four Friends, including George Whitehead and Gilbert Latey, to a private interview with William III when a statement on the sufferings of Friends was presented to the king. Quare and nineteen other Quakers signed a petition to the Commons, presented by Edmond Waller on 7 February 1696. When in Flanders in 1698 upon business Quare distributed Latin copies of Robert Barclay's *Apologies*, reporting upon his return that it was 'much more desired' in French. Such an edition was published in 1702.

Though Quare was never a clock- or watchmaker to the crown, he certainly enjoyed royal patronage. At Hampton Court an enormous 10 foot-high year-going burr walnut timepiece he made for William III was still standing in his bedchamber at the end of the twentieth century. It has dials to show the times of sunrise and sunset, and the latitude, and it was able to display either solar time or mean time until 1836 when it was altered by Vulliamy. In 1691–2 Quare supplied William with a repeating watch costing £69 17s. 6d. which was reported to be 'still in a good state of preservation' in 1866, though its later whereabouts are unknown. At Windsor Castle a small travelling clock with gilded brass case survives, the movement of which originally provided a choice of balance or pendulum control, a mechanism previously seen only in two clocks by Tompion, also of royal provenance, from whom Quare may have acquired the movement of this clock. It lacks any personal cipher but could have been made between about 1705 and 1715 for either Anne or George I. Quare also supplied at least three barometers, of which two were at Hampton Court in the 1990s. He was held in especially high regard by George I, and at Friends' House is a copy of his paper dated 4 February 1715 refusing George's invitation to be the king's watchmaker for £300 per annum. He declined because he could not swear an oath but begged the king not to appoint anyone else. The king told Quare, then aged about sixty-seven, that he could call to see him at any time and, accordingly, the yeoman of the guard at the back stairs let him 'frequently go up without calling any body for leave as otherwise is usual, tho Persons of Quality'. Quare also mentioned in passing that in forty years he had served 'men of the Greatest Rank of most other Nations in Europe, as well as this Nation'.

Of Quare's children who survived infancy (and seven did not), Jeremiah was a 'merchant', Anna married John Falconer in 1705, Sarah married Jacob Wyan in 1712, and Elizabeth married Silvanus Bevan, 'citizen and apothecary', in 1715. The weddings were lavish affairs attended by nobility, foreign ambassadors and envoys, and leading Quakers including William Penn and George Whitehead.

About 1721 or 1722 Quare took into partnership his former apprentice, Stephen Horseman, who was bound in January 1701 and made free in September 1709. Horseman, also a Quaker, in 1712 married Quare's niece Mary Savage, who lived in Exchange Alley with her uncle, who consented to the marriage. Towards the end of his life Quare retired to the country, acquiring a property at Croydon where he died, aged seventy-five, on 21 March 1724; he was buried at the Quaker burial-ground, Bunhill Fields, on the 27th. The *Daily Post* of 26 March reported: 'Last week dy'd Mr. Daniel Quare, watch and clock maker in Exchange Alley, who was famous both here and at foreign courts for the great improvements he made in that art and we hear he is succeeded in his shop and trade by his partner Mr. Horseman'. Quare's will, dated 3 May 1723, named his son Jeremiah executor and was proved on 26 March 1724. He left £2800 and all his household goods in London and Croydon to his wife, Mary, along with 'the two gold watches she usually wears, one of them being a repeater and the other a plain watch'; six grandchildren received £400 each and Jeremiah inherited £2000 and the residue of the estate. Mary spent her last years with Jeremiah in the parish of St Dionis Backchurch, Lime Street; she died, aged seventy-seven, on 4 November 1728. Jeremiah died in

the following year. Horseman continued the Exchange Alley business until he was declared bankrupt, a notice appearing in the *London Gazette*, 1 December 1730; Richard Peckover, present in the alley from at least March 1731, is believed to have then taken over the goodwill.

Between about 1680 and 1685 Quare began numbering watches in series, and between then and 1724 his business retailed nearly 6500—roughly 5000 timepieces, 1150 repeating watches, and 300 clockwatches and alarm watches. He numbered them in two series, the first accommodating all types of watch, the second, begun about 1688, being exclusively for repeating watches. It was not until between 1705 and 1710 that he began to number his clocks in a series which exceeded 300 items, though it is probable the business sold twice that number. These series were continued by Horseman, and Peckover then continued the watch series. Quare also numbered his barometers, that series reaching about 150. Many forgeries of Quare's work were produced both in England and on the continent.

Aesthetically, much of Quare's seventeenth-century work is indistinguishable from that of many of his contemporaries—he did not sell standard models with recognizable features as did Tompion and Knibb—and it was not until the turn of the century that his characteristic designs of clock case and dial developed. He made or retailed most types of clock and watch (though there is no evidence that he ever worked on turret clocks) and the wide range of styles of workmanship found in their movements reflects not only the extent of his employment of others but also the lack of rigid implementation of workshop practices. Quare's own hand is unrecognizable. The daybook of Richard Wright of Warrington, Lancashire, reveals that Quare's business did not rely solely upon London outworkers because in 1721–2 Horseman sent Wright fourteen watches, one at a time, in different stages of production, for finishing. Quare also retailed several table clocks whose movements, far superior to any others bearing his name, were made by Tompion's workmen. In 1720 the London clockmaker Joseph Williamson claimed, probably legitimately, to have made Quare's equation clocks including a 400-day clock showing true and mean time which Quare, 'for whom I wrought mostly', supplied to Charles II of Spain about 1700. Thomas Grignion worked for Quare as a finisher, probably of watches, and John Penkethman also appears to have been associated with him; in 1720 Penkethman advertised from his shop in Exchange Alley for the recovery of a lost, almost new, Quare watch, and a poor tax assessment of 1725 locates him 'under Mr Quares'. Daniel Quare is also likely to have employed the watchmaker Robert Quare, who in 1695 lived with his family a short distance away in Lothbury, lodging with a Thomas Paul, possibly the clockmaker. Robert Quare's relationship to Daniel has not been established. Watches by Robert are recorded, and his son, also named Daniel, was the last of Quare's apprentices. Among Quare's other pupils were Richard Vick, appointed watch- and clockmaker to George I in 1722 and master of the Clockmakers' Company in 1729, Joshua Appleby, who served as master in 1745, and John Marshall, who is recorded as the inventor of the 'Magic Night Watch'.

E. L. RADFORD, *rev.* JEREMY LANCELOTTE EVANS

Sources C. Jagger, *Royal clocks* (1983) · J. Besse, *A collection of the sufferings of the people called Quakers*, 2 vols. (1753) · Clockmakers' Company court minutes, GL · renter wardens' accounts, GL · St Mary Woolnoth parish assessments: returns of names of lodgers, poor tax · S. E. Atkins and W. H. Overall, *Some account of the Worshipful Company of Clockmakers of the City of London* (privately printed, London, 1881) · A. Smith, 'An early 18th century watchmaker's notebook', *Antiquarian Horology and the Proceedings of the Antiquarian Horological Society*, 15 (1984–5), 605–25 · F. Buckley, *Old watchmakers*, 5 vols. (1929–30), vol. 4 · marriage registers, Friends House · C. E. Atkins, ed., *Register of apprentices of the Worshipful Company of Clockmakers of the City of London* (privately printed, London, 1931) · J. Francis, *Chronicles and characters of the stock exchange*, new edn (1855) · W. D. [W. Derham], *The artificial clockmaker* (1696) · G. C. Williamson, *Behind my library door* (1921) · E. J. Wood, *Curiosities of clocks and watches* (1866) · *Antiquarian Horology and the Proceedings of the Antiquarian Horological Society*, 7 (1970–72), 741 · F. J. Britten, *Old clocks and watches and their makers*, ed. F. W. Britten, 6th edn (1933) · H. A. Lloyd, *Some outstanding clocks over seven hundred years* (1958) · A. Raistrick, *Quakers in science and industry* (1950); repr. (1968) · N. Goodison, *English barometers, 1680–1860*, rev. edn (1985) · *DNB* · E. H. Milligan and M. J. Thomas, *My ancestors were Quakers: how can I find out more about them?* (1983); repr. (1990)

Archives AM Oxf. · BM · GL, Clockmakers' Company Museum · Kensington Palace, London · MHS Oxf. · RS Friends, Lond., paper explaining refusal of royal warrant, 4 Feb 1715 [copy] · Sci. Mus. · V&A · Windsor Castle | RS Friends, Lond., letter to Thomas Aldam

Wealth at death approx. £10,000; incl. £ 2800 to his wife, £2000 to his son, and £400 each to his six grandchildren: will, 1724

Quaritch, Bernard Alexander Christian (1819–1899), bookseller and publisher, was born on 23 April 1819 at Worbis, a village in Thuringia, Germany. He was the eldest of five children of Karl Gottfried Bernhard Quaritsch (1795–1828), a man probably of Croatian extraction who was a fusilier in the Prussian army and a veteran of Waterloo, latterly an officer of justice at Worbis and Heiligenstadt, and his wife, Eleanore Henriette Amalie, *née* Rhan (1795–1875), the daughter of a Nordhausen merchant. Karl is said to have squandered his wife's fortune; he died at Heiligenstadt when Bernard was nine, and in 1831 the widow returned to Nordhausen, where Bernard completed his *Gymnasium* education, learning Greek, Latin, and French.

From the age of fifteen to nineteen Quaritch served an apprenticeship with a local bookseller, Koehne, and in 1839 set off for Berlin. There he found work at the publishing firm of Klemann, and in the bookshop of Adrien Oehmigke, mastering various bibliographical manuals, and acquainting himself with the English book world from literary and trade periodicals. Early in 1842 he moved to London, where he persuaded Henry George Bohn, the leading bookseller–publisher of his day, to hire him as cataloguer and general assistant. In 1844–5 he put in a year's stint with Théophile Barrois at Paris, crossing paths with the legendary bibliographer Jacques-Charles Brunet, but returned to London and Bohn for two final years of employment. In April 1847, announcing his ambition to be 'the first bookseller in Europe' (Quaritch), he set up on

Bernard Alexander Christian Quaritch (1819–1899), by unknown photographer

his own, with a capital of just £70 saved from his earnings, and an income eked out with piece-work for Marx and Engels as correspondent for their *Neue Rheinische Zeitung*—an improbable assignment, but one through which he briefly explored English politics, meeting Richard Cobden, Joseph Hume, and the rising bibliophile statesman W. E. Gladstone.

From 16 Castle Street, Leicester Square, London, Quaritch issued his first catalogue—a two-page, three-column 'Cheap book circular'—in October 1847. His first season's sales amounted to no more than £168 10s., rising to £766 10s. in 1848, but hard work and tenacity rewarded him, and by 1855 his turnover was up nearly tenfold. His early specialities included literature, theology, law, mathematics, natural history and geography, music, fine arts, and architecture, from the outset distinguished by the linguistic scope of his stock. Catalogues 25 and 26, for instance (1851), listed books in no fewer than twenty-seven tongues, with particular emphasis on the oriental, which few English booksellers of the day could assess, let alone catalogue.

Most of Quaritch's early stock was, and remained, usefully 'learned'—second-hand scholarly books at moderate prices—but the pursuit of fine, rare, and costly materials, for which he became famous, began in the mid-1850s, through connections with private collectors like Alexander, Lord Lindsay, later twenty-fifth earl of Crawford, who initially patronized him for the range of his academic wares. For Lindsay he purchased, in the 1858 Daly sale, a

Gutenberg Bible for £595, characteristically exceeding his commission of £525 in his determination to vanquish his rival agents; but Lindsay cheerfully forgave him, and a pattern was established. Over the next forty years Quaritch increasingly dominated the salerooms in London, and often elsewhere, like no other bookseller in history: armed with generous commissions and auction-house credit (which he began to demand, when his non-participation could seriously depress auction results), and counting on rapid turnover, he bought substantially at every major sale from the late 1850s to his death, taking the lion's share of such glamorous dispersals as Perkins (1873), Tite (1874), Didot (1878–9), Sunderland (1881–3), Beckford-Hamilton (1882–4), Syston Park (1884), Osterley Park (1885), Gaisford (1890), Salva-Heredia (1892–3), Ashburnham (1897–8), and William Morris (1898). On several occasions his bids accounted for nearly half the results, though it must be remembered that he sometimes shared purchases with colleagues like Morgand and Techener of Paris and F. S. Ellis of London, and participated, like most of his contemporaries, in post-sale 'settlements'. Commissions from a host of institutions and private collectors also swelled his figures, but in bidding for stock he set individual price records again and again, famously paying £3900 for the Gutenberg Bible in the Syston Park sale (breaking the single-lot benchmark which had stood since 1812) and £4950, four days later, for a 1459 Mainz psalter printed on vellum. By then he had earned his nickname in the press, the Napoleon of Booksellers—although he himself, perhaps with a thought for his father, held Bonaparte 'in horror and contempt' for 'his extreme selfishness and his cruelty' and 'possess[ed] no books or objects concerning him' (letter to Miss Kett of Bedford, 28 Jan 1893, priv. coll.).

Quaritch's ever-expanding inventory was housed in London, successively, in shops at 61 Great Russell Street (a false start in 1847), 16 Castle Street (1847–60, retained until 1909 as a warehouse), and 15 Piccadilly (1860–1907, premises reaching back to Vine Street). Although visitors were many and welcome, especially in Piccadilly, the principal method of distribution was by posted catalogues, and for these Quaritch soon became known all over the world. The earliest broadsheets gave way to octavo pamphlets (disguised between 1855 and 1864 as a low-postal-rate periodical, *The Museum*), then plump miscellaneous and specialist catalogues, and finally the massive 'General catalogues' of 1874 (with supplement, 1877), 1880, and 1887–8 (with index and supplements, 1892–7). The double-decker of 1874–7 contained 44,324 entries, representing about 200,000 volumes, while the 1880 catalogue ran to 2395 pages, measured over 6 inches thick, and weighed nearly 10 pounds—deliberately surpassing in bulk the 5 inch 'guinea pig' of Quaritch's old master Bohn (1841), and even Bohn's 'enlarged' catalogue of 1847–67, upon which Quaritch himself had once laboured. The final 'General catalogue', long esteemed as a bibliographical reference, extends to seventeen grand volumes, but of course the books listed in such compendia were not always available: the point of Quaritch's enterprise was to set guideline prices for standard copies of antiquarian and out-of-print books, appropriate to his policy in re-purchasing them, and to his customers' expectations.

Side by side with his more than 400 numbered and unnumbered catalogues (1848–86), Quaritch issued between 1867 and 1899 nearly 200 'rough lists', aimed at clearing new purchases—often from recent named auctions—rapidly; he also revived the practice of marketing directly at auction himself, by trade sales at home and abroad of rare books and general stock, including his own publications, and remainders with new 'Quaritch' imprints. The last involved him in 1879 in a dispute with the United States customs authorities, whom he addressed in an aggressively autobiographical essay, *A Letter to General Starring* (1880); America did not back down, but Quaritch's trade-sale venues at one time spanned the globe from Australasia to Japan, Shanghai to Singapore to Calcutta, Amoy (Xiamen), and Rangoon, Cape Town to Leipzig, Dublin to Valparaiso.

As a publisher and distributor of books and periodicals, and agent for learned societies, Quaritch at first followed his forte in orientalia, with grammars and dictionaries in Turkish, Arabic, Persian, and Chinese. From 1854 onwards he concentrated almost exclusively on unpopular but meritorious scholarly works, preferring to buy titles outright from their authors, who would have been hard put to find an alternative; and although his manner in negotiating was peremptory, he took genuine interest in the projects he backed, and regarded 'his' writers as feathers in his own cap. He encouraged bibliographers like Charles Sayle, F. C. Bigmore, and C. W. H. Wyman (who prefaced their *Bibliography of Printing* (1880) with a portrait of Quaritch), J. G. Gray, and H. Buxton Forman, and sponsored W. C. Hazlitt's multi-volume *Collections and Notes* on English popular literature, as well as the standard *Works of William Blake*, edited by E. J. Ellis and W. B. Yeats (3 vols., 1893), translations by his friends Sir Richard Burton (*The Lusiads*, 1880–81) and Gladstone's cousin Lord Lyttelton (*Translations from the Greek*, 1861), and numerous facsimiles and reprints. His most celebrated publication was Edward FitzGerald's *Rubáiyát of Omar Khayyam*, the first four editions of which (1859, 1868, 1872, and 1879) name Quaritch as publisher, although FitzGerald himself paid for the printing of the earlier two. The history of the rediscovery of the poem in a Castle Street remainder tray, and its subsequent celebrity, is well known, but the later, unedifying struggle over copyright between Quaritch and FitzGerald's estate casts Quaritch himself in a harsh light. His dispute with William Morris, however, whose Kelmscott Press books he contracted to subsidize and distribute in 1890, found him, if anything, the abused party.

In later life Quaritch was as proud of his clientele as his stock, boasting personal acquaintance with Disraeli and Gladstone, John Ruskin, William Morris, Edward FitzGerald, Sir Richard Burton, Sir Henry Irving, and Ellen Terry, as well as most of the noble and wealthy British collectors of the day. Although he never visited America, he represented and corresponded extensively with New York's

James Lenox (falling out with him over a conflict at auction with Lord Crawford) and New England's briefly meteoric William Gibbons Medlicott (1816–1883), whose cause he adopted with uncustomary fervour in 1866. Institutional librarians at home and abroad flocked to his saleroom banner, notably Bodley's E. W. B. Nicolson, Cambridge University's Henry Bradshaw, Harvard's Justin Windsor, and George Bullen and Edward Maunde Thompson of the British Museum, whose agent Quaritch became on the retirement of F. S. Ellis in 1885; while from Athens John Gennadius showered Quaritch with commissions (1885–91), and, in New Zealand, Alexander H. Turnbull began his intensive collecting career with offers and parcels from Quaritch. Literary and press recognition, which Quaritch relished and courted, came in periodical notices, interviews, episodes in Richard Jefferies' *Amaryllis at the Fair* (1887) and C. J. Wills's three-decker novel of 1891, *John Squire's Secret*, and in recollections by A. C. Swinburne, W. C. Hazlitt, and Oliver Wendell Holmes. Many books and booklets bear Quaritch's own name as compiler or author, but most were largely ghost-written, like the useful *Dictionary of Book-Collectors* (1892) and various tracts and 'opuscula' of the Sette of Odd Volumes, a dining-club he co-founded in 1878.

Bernard Quaritch married, in 1863 or 1864, Charlotte (Helen) Rimes (1831/2–1899), with whom he had three children: Charlotte, Gertrude Annie, and Bernard Alfred (1871–1913), who succeeded his father as head of the bookselling firm. Quaritch died of bronchial pneumonia at his home, 34 Belsize Grove, London, on 17 December 1899, in his eighty-first year; he was buried in Highgate cemetery. Physically and mentally he was a powerful man, short but wiry and barrel-chested, irrepressibly forthright, and given to bluff sardonic humour, but convivial and loyal, with a streak of unabashed sentimentality towards friends, and a patriotic devotion to his adopted country. His influence upon the international book trade in his fifty-year career can hardly be overestimated, and he was perhaps the last individual bookseller to unite under one roof major stocks of scholarly and rare works in virtually all fields of knowledge and imagination. In that achievement he was ably seconded by an intelligent staff, long led by the mercurial, multilingual, and polymath Irishman Michael Kerney (c.1832–1901), who joined Quaritch in 1857 and spent forty years as his chief assistant, 'literary adviser', and *éminence grise*. In later years Kerney was joined by Frederic S. Ferguson (1878–1967), the bibliographer whose speciality of early English literature helped to ensure Quaritch's pre-eminence in that field, and Edmund H. Dring (1864–1928), who, with his son Edmund (1906–1990), directed the firm in the century after Quaritch's death, and between them served it for 113 years. The shop moved from Piccadilly to 11 Grafton Street in 1907, and 'Bernard Quaritch' became a private limited company in 1917, remaining in the Quaritch family until 1971. Under new proprietorship, and after one more removal—to Lower John Street, Golden Square, in 1970—it continued into the twenty-first century.

ARTHUR FREEMAN

Sources C. Q. Wrentmore, foreword, in *A catalogue of books and manuscripts issued to commemorate the one hundredth anniversary of the firm*, Bernard Quaritch Ltd (1947), v–xvii · A. Brauer, 'Bernard Quaritch 125 Jahre', *Börsenblatt für den Deutschen Buchhandel* (27 Feb 1973), A64–A67 · A. Brauer, 'Der bedeutendste Antiquariatsbuchhändler des 19. Jahrhunderts und seine Familie', *Archiv für Sippenforschung*, 52 (1973), 262–85 · B. Quaritch, *Bernard Quaritch's letter to General Starring* (1880) · N. Barker, *Bibliotheca Lindesiana* (1978) · N. Barker, 'Bernard Quaritch', *Book Collector* (1997), 3–34 [special number for the 150th anniversary of Bernard Quaritch] · F. Herrmann, *Sotheby's: portrait of an auction house* (1980) · A. Freeman and J. I. Freeman, *Anatomy of an auction* (1990) · A. Freeman, 'Bernard Quaritch and "My Omar": the struggle for FitzGerald *Rubáiyát*', *Book Collector* (1997), 60–75 [special number for the 150th anniversary of Bernard Quaritch] · N. Kelvin, 'Bernard Quaritch and William Morris', *Book Collector* (1997), 118–33 [special number for the 150th anniversary of Bernard Quaritch] · E. M. Dring, 'Michael Kerney', *Book Collector* (1997), 160–66 [special number for the 150th anniversary of Bernard Quaritch] · *CGPLA Eng. & Wales* (1900) · obit. [B. A. Quaritch — son]

Archives Bernard Quaritch Ltd, London, company archives · Bodl. Oxf., corresp. and papers | Auckland Public Library, letters to Sir George Grey · BL, corresp. with W. E. Gladstone, Add. MSS 44389–44524, *passim* · Bodl. Oxf., bills and letters to Sir Thomas Phillipps · NHM, letters to members of the Sowerby family · University of Toronto, Thomas Fisher Rare Book Library, corresp. with Lord Amherst of Hackney

Likenesses photograph, c.1849, repro. in Barker, 'Bernard Quaritch' · J. Mayall, photograph, c.1880, repro. in *A catalogue of books and manuscripts*, Bernard Quaritch Ltd · photograph, 1899, repro. in *A catalogue of books and manuscripts*, Bernard Quaritch Ltd · J. Brown, engraving (after photograph by J. Mayall), BM; repro. in Barker, 'Bernard Quaritch' · J. Brown, stipple, BM · oils (after photograph by J. Mayall), Bernard Quaritch Ltd, London · photograph, Bernard Quaritch Ltd, London [see illus.]

Wealth at death £38,782 4s.: probate, 23 Feb 1900, *CGPLA Eng. & Wales*

Quarles, Charles (*d.* 1727), organist, is of unknown parentage and background, though it is assumed, on account of his profession and unusual name, that he was the son of Charles Quarles (*d.* 1717), organist of Trinity College, Cambridge. He was appointed organist of York Minster on 30 June 1722 with an annual salary of £40 and during his brief period of office was paid on several occasions for copying music into the minster organ books and partbooks. Given that the last (and indirect) payment to Quarles in the York Minster accounts was made on 7 October 1727 and that a Charles Quarles was buried in All Saints', Cambridge, on 21 October 1727, it is probable that the death of the York organist occurred at Cambridge. A sonata for unspecified treble instrument (probably a flute) and basso continuo, attributed to Carlo Quarlesi, can be found in a manuscript in the library of Durham Cathedral. This was copied by Edward Finch, a canon of York Minster, who also copied 'Mr Quarles way of Fingering in Gamut natural', which survives in a manuscript in Glasgow University Library. An anthem, 'Out of the deep', remains in manuscript in the library of Worcester Cathedral; it was printed in 1775 in the *Cathedral Magazine*, where it is ascribed to 'Mr Quarles, late Organist at York'.

DAVID GRIFFITHS

Sources W. Shaw, 'Quarles, Charles (ii)', *New Grove* · H. W. Shaw, *The succession of organists of the Chapel Royal and the cathedrals of England and Wales from c.1538* (1991) · York Minster Library, Dean and Chapter archives · parish register, All Saints', Cambridge, Cambs. AS, 1727 [burial]

Quarles, Francis (1592–1644), poet, was born at the family's manor house of Stewards in Romford, Essex, the son of James Quarles (*d.* 1599) and Joan Dalton (*d.* 1606). He was baptized on 8 May 1592 at St Edward's Church, Romford.

Family, education, and early career Quarles's godfather was Sir Francis Barrington, head of a prominent Essex puritan family. His father, James, made his fortune by accumulating the posts of clerk of the royal kitchen, clerk of the green cloth, and surveyor-general of victualling for the navy. Francis, who alludes to himself as an 'Essex Quill' (*Threnodes*, 1641, sig. A3*v*), was proud of his native county, the ancient lineage of his family, and his father's work for Queen Elizabeth.

The family lineage is complicated, and Grosart's introduction to Quarles's works requires some correction (Höltgen, 'Two Francis Quarleses', 132–4; also papers deposited by Daisy Quarles in the Library of Congress, no. CS 71. Q 17 1952a). The family originated in the village of Quarles, Norfolk, where Nicholas de Wharfles in 1258 owned the advowson of the church. About 1400, after the black death, the Quarleses withdrew to nearby Gresham. The earliest recorded ancestor of the poet is Thomas Quarles, of Gresham, whose will was proved in 1462 (Norwich consistory court, 75 Betyns). His grandson George, auditor to Henry VIII, settled at Ufford, Northamptonshire. The auditor's son Francis purchased the manor of Ufford in 1555. The eldest son of this Francis with his second wife, Bridget Brampton, was James, the surveyor-general of victualling. The state papers and other records offer glimpses of his important and lucrative activities as purveyor. He was probably a protégé of Lord Burghley, a distant kinsman. In 1588 he bought Stewards. Several years before he had substantially increased his wealth by marrying an heiress, Joan, the daughter of Eldred Dalton, of Moor Place, Much Hadham, Hertfordshire. The marriage took place in 1571 at Farnham, Essex (parish register). For a time he was tenant of the crown manor of Farnham (P. Morant, *History of Essex*, 1768, 2.623; Essex RO, crown grant, D/D/Tw/T15, T16). Legal papers submitted by his son Arthur, however, mention Moor Place as 'Mr. Quarles chief seat' in 1580 (Hunt. L., Ellesmere MS 6063). In her will of 1606 (Quarles, *Works*, 1.xv), Joan Quarles left 'my Mansion house' and other possessions at Much Hadham to Robert, her eldest, and Arthur, her youngest son.

The family at Romford numbered four sons, Francis being the third, and four daughters. Sir Robert Quarles (1580–1639), the heir, became MP for Colchester and married three prosperous ladies in succession. Quarles's mother was a puritan. In 1589 the archdeaconry court dealt with the illegal burial of the family's maidservant, 'without any seremony, and not according to the communion booke', for which Mrs Quarles and John Leech, a schoolmaster and conventicler of Hornchurch, had been responsible (Essex RO, act book 1588–90, fol. 148, D/AEA/13). An account of discussions at the Hampton Court conference between 'Puritanes' and 'Antipuritanes' in 1604 was addressed to Sir Edward Lewkenor, an MP of

Pictor adumbravit Vultum quem cernimus, aft hic
  Non valet egregias pingere mentis Opes .
Has si scire cupis, sua consule Carmina , in illis
  Dotes percipies pectoris eximias .

What heere wee see is but a Graven face ,
Onely the fhaddow of that brittle cafe
Wherin were treafur'd up those Gemms, which he
  Hath loft behind him to Pofteritie . *Al: Roſs.*
W:M: *ſculp*.

Francis Quarles (1592–1644), by William Marshall, pubd 1645

puritan sympathies, 'att Mistress Quarles in Rumford' (Townshend MSS, BL, Add. MS 38492, fol. 81).

Quarles was educated initially at a 'schoole in the Countrey' and afterwards at Christ's College, Cambridge (U. Quarles, sig. A3*r*). James and Francis remained at the college from 1605 until their graduation in January 1609 (Cambridge University Archives, liber gratiarum, 1598–1620, p. 112). At Christ's College, Ramism and puritanism were widespread, but government pressure gradually reduced the strength of the latter. In 1610, to complete the education considered necessary for a gentleman, Francis entered Lincoln's Inn. He studied law for some years without aiming at a legal career.

Quarles very likely took part in the *Maske of the Middle Temple and Lincolns Inne* arranged by George Chapman and Inigo Jones for the wedding of Princess Elizabeth, the future queen of Bohemia, and Frederick, the elector palatine, in February 1613. The marriage of the Thames and the Rhine had been designed to promote the great protestant anti-papal and anti-Habsburg alliance. On their triumphal progress to Heidelberg the young couple were escorted by four noblemen and a large number of gentlemen. Quarles and Inigo Jones travelled in the entourage of the earl of Arundel, the celebrated art collector. Quarles did not hold the office of cup-bearer to the princess, as his widow suggests, but may have performed this duty on occasion. Three of the four surviving lists show 'Mr. Quarles' in an unspecified honorary position, directly after the earl's steward, Mr Dixe (Höltgen, *Quarles*, 319–23; see also PRO, declared accounts, E 351/2801–2). Like most of the English gentlemen in the bridal party, Quarles returned from Heidelberg to England in the summer of 1613. As Arundel and his countess went on to Italy, Quarles probably travelled home with Viscount Lisle (Robert Sidney, later earl of Leicester), who, on 12 August, was at Flushing, waiting for passage to England. In 1620 Quarles dedicated his first book to him, a paraphrase of the story of Jonah under the unpromising title *A Feast for Wormes*. Here he acknowledged 'the love you did beare to my (long since) deceased Father' and the 'undeserved Favours, and Honourable Countenance towards me in your passage thorow *Germany*, where you have left in the hearts of men, a *Pyramis* of your Worth' (Quarles, *Works*, 2.5). Perhaps he found Lisle, a brother of Philip Sidney, and an experienced diplomat and a poet, more congenial than the aloof Arundel, whom he never mentions. The courtly interlude no doubt led to a deeper understanding of the political and religious cross-currents in Europe on the eve of the Thirty Years' War, but not to any preferment or patronage. In September 1615 he obtained a licence to travel abroad, but whether he made use of it is unknown.

In the spring of 1617 Quarles bought a house in the parish of St Vedast, near St Paul's Cathedral, and on 26 May 1618 a marriage licence was issued to 'Francis Quarles, Gent. of Romford, about 26, and Ursely [Ursula] Woodgate, of St Andrew's, Holborn, Spinster, 17, daughter of John Woodgate, Gent.' (*Marriage Licences Issued by the Bishop of London*, 1887, 2.60). Two days later Quarles married his young bride at St Andrew's. They had eighteen children including the poet John *Quarles. In 1620 he bought land in Much Hadham from his brother Sir Robert. With an annuity of £50 and, presumably, further income from the family estates, he could, at least for the moment, settle down in London to the life of a cultivated gentleman of scholarly and literary interests 'to which he devoted himself late and early, usually by three a clock in the morning' (U. Quarles, sig. A3r). The fruits of these labours were a succession of biblical verse paraphrases published from 1620 onwards, and in a revised collection entitled *Divine Poems*, from 1630 onwards. Quarles tried to solve the problem inherited from Du Bartas, the French pioneer of a new type of Christian epic, of how to combine narration and devotion, by breaking up the text into sections of 'History' and of 'Meditation'. This crude method and the Ramist habit of exploiting the rhetorical 'places of invention' account for the inordinate length and diffuseness of most of the poems. Despite these shortcomings there was a real demand for such pious light reading in the vernacular. Quarles's insistence, throughout his works, on the need for meditation derives (unacknowledged) from Joseph Hall, who had attempted to reconcile Calvinism with the Catholic meditative tradition (J. Hall, *The Arte of Divine Meditation*, 1606). About 1625 Quarles presented *The Workes of King James* (1616) to Christ's College, Cambridge. On the flyleaf he wrote in neat calligraphy a flattering poem to the king and the university, 'Rex pater est patriae, mihi clara academia mater'. This is one of the two surviving autographs of the poet. He had read the royal works and in meditation 19 of *Hadassa* (1621) he seems to echo James's claims for the divine right of kings. His gift was recorded by an elaborate Latin eulogy in the *liber donationum* (Bb.3.8), a document of Quarles's early reputation (photographs of the poem and the eulogy in Höltgen, 'Two Francis Quarleses', plates 1 and 2).

At this time Quarles is found in the unlikely role of company promoter seeking, together with Sir William Luckyn and Sir Gamaliel Capell (both prominent in Essex) and one William Lyde, an act of parliament giving them a monopoly in a new method of producing saltpetre, an ingredient of gunpowder. Nothing seems to have come out of this venture. Instead, Quarles became secretary to James Ussher, the great church historian and newly appointed archbishop of Armagh. In 1625 Ussher stayed with 'Sir Gerard Harvy and his lady' in Moor Place, Much Hadham, the former house of Quarles's mother. The archbishop was looking for a qualified research assistant, and it seems that the poet was recommended to him by his godfather, Sir Francis Barrington, and by his friend, Dr Ailmer, rector of Much Hadham, whose death Quarles mourned in *An Alphabet of Elegies* (*Works*, 3.3). When Ussher set out for Ireland in July 1626 he was probably joined by his secretary with his wife and two children who were to live with him in the palace at Drogheda. Quarles returned to London before 20 March 1630 when he addressed a letter to Ussher (Bodl. Oxf., MS Rawl. lett. 89, fol. 69). The men remained on cordial terms. Quarles shared Ussher's anti-Catholicism and anti-Arminianism, his insistence on conformity to the established church, and his royalism. *Argalus and Parthenia*, a long verse romance written in Ireland, dated from Dublin, 4 March 1629 and published in London in that year, marks Quarles's systematic extension of his literary repertoire. The poem is based on a story from the *Arcadia*, a scion 'taken out of the Orchard of Sir *Philip Sidney*, of precious memory' (Quarles, *Works*, 3.240). Its blend of heroic, erotic, and comic elements remained popular throughout the century. A critical edition was published by David Freeman in 1986. Edmund Malone, in a note in his copy of Langbaine's *English Dramatick Poets* (Bodl. Oxf., Malone 131, s. v. Quarles), observes: 'The original M.S. of his *Argalus and Parthenia* is in the Library of the College of Dublin, and is dated from his house in Cole Alley in Castle Street in that City, where he kept a School'. This statement lacks confirmation as does another one by John Aubrey, who says that the poet 'lived at Bath at the Katherine-wheele inne (opposite to the market-house), and wrote there, a yeare or two' (*Brief Lives*, ed. A. Clark, 1898, 2.176). After petitioning Charles I in May 1631, Quarles received 'a lease in reversion of the impositions on Tobacco and Tobacco pipes to be imported into the Kingdom of Ireland' (*Fourth Report*, HMC, 369). This attempt to augment his income failed; the reversion never came his way. About this time he composed the epigrams of *Divine Fancies* (1632) in which he established his religious and political stance as an Anglican and royalist, vigorously attacking both puritans and papists. He also presented himself as a critic of social and moral abuses.

The time of achievement: *Emblemes* and *Hieroglyphikes* By 1632 Quarles and his family were living at Roxwell in his native Essex, perhaps in or near Skreens, a large house then occupied by his friend, Sir William Luckyn. An epitaph for Lady Luckyn in the shape of an hourglass, part of the elegy *Mildreiados* (*Works*, 3.26), survives in the church of Abbess Roding nearby. The years 1632–8 at Roxwell were the most creative and perhaps the happiest period of Quarles's life; his literary reputation and his circle of friends continued to grow. In April 1636 his eldest daughter, Frances, aged seventeen, married Eusebey Marbury, apparently a son of the rector of St James Garlickhythe, London (*Marriage Licences Issued by the Bishop of London*, 1887, 2.226). During the 1630s he composed *The Shepheards Oracles* (published later, in 1646), which deals with autobiographical, political, and religious matters under the thin guise of pastoral allegory. The poem includes satirical attacks on the radical fringe of the anti-episcopal 'Root and Branch' party, also allegorical portraits of his friend, Phineas Fletcher, and an Arminian 'Master Shepheard' who is severely criticized and must be Archbishop Laud (Quarles, *Works*, 3.218–19).

Emblemes (1635), the work which secured Quarles's fame, was dedicated to his young friend Edward Benlowes, a would-be-poet, wealthy virtuoso, patron, and Essex neighbour: 'You have put the *Theorboe* into my hand; and I have play'd'. On the frontispiece, the theorbo, a type of lute, appears as a symbol of divine poetry (and Quarles was himself a lutenist). What Benlowes put into Quarles's hand were the two Jesuit models for *Emblemes* which he had brought home from the grand tour, *Pia desideria* (1624) by Herman Hugo and *Typus mundi* (1627), compiled by nine clever schoolboys at the Antwerp Jesuit college under the direction of their master. The frontispiece of *Emblemes* shows a globe in which are inscribed the names of Finchingfield and Roxwell, while an additional name, Hilgay, appears on a globe in emblem V.6. These are the villages inhabited by the three friends Benlowes, Quarles, and Fletcher. All three were involved in attempts to create new forms of allegorical divine poetry. It is Quarles's historical achievement to have established in protestant England the dominant type of the Catholic baroque emblems representing the encounters of Amor Divinus or Divine Love and the Soul. These books were acceptable to moderate Catholics and protestants because they promoted the general tenets of the Christian life, not controversial doctrines. The main figure has sometimes been misunderstood as the infant Jesus, but it is an allegory of Divine Love, God or Christ: 'Let not the tender Eye checke, to see the allusion to our blessed SAVIOUR figured, in these Types' (*Emblemes*, 'To the reader'). Quarles uses the forty-five emblems from *Pia desideria* in the original order, though he draws selectively from *Typus mundi*. Occasional alterations to individual plates are of no major doctrinal or sectarian significance. His poems are largely independent and new. They exploit the mimetic quality of the pictures and transform them into allegories of spiritual truth. They speak in the different voices of dramatic dialogue, meditative soliloquy, spiritual love song, irony, or flippancy. Conceits, sometimes derived from patristic texts, are often elaborated with semantic precision and dense intertextuality and repay close study. The overall structure of the work preserves patterns of the spiritual pilgrimage and the Ignatian meditation. The plates copied by William Marshall, William Simpson, and two other engravers are mostly accurate and refined but fall short of the artistry of the Antwerp originals.

When John Marriot, a major literary publisher at St Dunstan-in-the-West, Fleet Street, brought out the first edition of *Emblemes*, it proved such a success that a second edition was called for. The two editions, which can be distinguished by textual variants, are both dated 1635 on the title-page. But there is evidence (*inter alia* from dated emblematic decorations at Caerlaverock Castle, near Dumfries) that the first edition actually appeared in 1634. Four years later Quarles produced what he called 'a second service' of the same dish, *Hieroglyphikes of the Life of Man* (1638), a shorter book of fifteen emblems. It is the most notable English version of the theme of the ages of man. In 1639 the two works were reprinted and issued in one volume as *Emblemes and Hieroglyphikes*, and it is in this form that they have commonly appeared since. There are about sixty editions or issues, more than thirty of them after 1800. Christopher Harvey's *School of the Heart* was mistakenly attributed to Quarles and, from the late eighteenth century onward, from time to time included in editions of *Emblemes and Hieroglyphikes*.

Quarles's association with New England is recorded by an Essex neighbour, the traveller John Josselyn, who in July 1639 delivered to Governor Winthrop and John Cotton in Boston six metrical psalms (nos. 16, 25, 51, 88, 113 and 137) from 'Mr. *Francis Quarles* the poet' for Cotton's approbation (Höltgen, 'New verse', 118–41). If there was a chance of a handsome fee for supplying the full number of psalms for the proposed *Bay Psalm Book*, Quarles lost it. His versions would have lacked puritan plainness and were not included in the book. However, scribal manuscripts of hitherto unknown versions of psalms 1 to 8 by Quarles and of his *Threnode on Lady Masham* of 1641 were published in 1998 (ibid.). Manuscript PwV 358 in Nottingham University surely represents a portion of the 'Psalmes of David' left unpublished at the poet's death and mentioned by his widow in a chancery suit (PRO, C.2 Chas. I/Q1/23). She also mentions a lost 'Chronicle of the Citty of London', which was written after Quarles's appointment in February 1640, as city chronologer, at the request of the earl of Dorset with an annual stipend of 100 nobles, or just over £33 (CLRO, repertory 54, fol. 86v.) For this favour Quarles owed thanks to Lady Dorset to whom he had dedicated two books. In *Quarlëis* (1634), Benlowes had already requested financial support for Quarles from the city fathers.

Later years: financial troubles and political conflicts Entries in the parish registers suggest that Quarles must have moved from Roxwell to Terling, another Essex village, between May 1638 and January 1640. Here he lived at Ridley Hall, a house which still stands and at the time was owned by the five Frank sisters, to whom he dedicated *Observations Concerning Princes and States upon Peace and Warre* (1642): 'Sweete Ladies, *When the* Drum *beates loud, soft language is not heard*' (*Works*, 1.52; Höltgen, *Quarles*, 269). Under the impact of constitutional conflicts and civil war and with an eye to the market, he turned to prose writing and became a literary apologist for Charles I. The years at Terling until his death in 1644 were overshadowed by poverty and the hostility of radical puritans and sectaries. In February 1640, with the help of Marbury, his son-in-law, he obtained a loan of £30 upon handing over the plates and copy of *Emblemes and Hieroglyphikes* to the stationers Eglesfield and Williams as security. When the loan was not redeemed they attempted to reimburse themselves by preparing a new edition. In a chancery petition Quarles tried to regain the copyright but the court found against him (PRO, C.2 Chas. I, Q1/84, Q1/10; C.33/182, fols. 235v, 263v). The suit provides useful bibliographical information: Quarles's books were printed in large editions (3000 copies or more) and, as a popular author, he could retain far more control over his copyright than might have been supposed (F. Kellendonk, *John and Richard Marriott*, 1978, 31).

Enchiridion (1640, augmented 1641), a book of aphorisms, rivalled *Emblemes* in popular appeal and the number of editions. Borrowing from Machiavelli and Bacon, Quarles brings together timeless wisdom tersely expressed, and political advice for a king threatened by civil war. Large portions of these maxims reappeared under the name of King James in a royalist publication, *Regales aphorismi* (1650); others were translated into Latin by Constantijn Huygens. There were Dutch, Danish, Swedish, and German translations (Höltgen, 'Quarles and the Low Countries', *Anglo-Dutch Relations in the Field of the Emblem*, ed. B. Westerweel, 1997, 148). The main interest in Quarles's posthumous comedy *The Virgin Widow* (1649), which at times turns into a real romp, arises from its topical allusions. The political and ecclesiastical allegory is somewhat obscure, but the heroine, Kettreena, clearly represents the Christian church and the Church of England as the widowed bride of Christ. It can be argued that the play was originally written and performed in 1640 for the Barrington household at Hatfield Broad Oak, and that further topical allusions and a second personification of the church, Lady Temple, were added about February 1641, when the Long Parliament was negotiating with the Scots. It tells that Lady Temple three years ago suffered from a surfeit of '*Canterbury Duck*' (Dr Arthur Duck was one of Laud's officials), and is now beset by 'a rude rabble of unsanctified Mechanicks' (Quarles, *Works*, 3.309). Comedies were a regular feature in the puritan and parliamentary Barrington family; a 'Messenger that came from Mr Quarles concerneing the Comody' is noted in their household accounts in August 1640 (Essex RO, D/D Ba A2, fol. 57v.) Although Quarles was not of a mind with the Barringtons' brand of puritanism he stayed on friendly terms with them. He and Sir Thomas Barrington took an interest in Comenius's plans for educational reform and Ussher's scheme of a moderate or 'reduced' episcopacy acceptable to the puritans; the archbishop had returned from Ireland in 1640 (Höltgen, *Quarles*, 274–6).

In three anonymous civil war tracts partly written in Oxford and published 1644–5 Quarles sought to create for himself the persona of a moderate protestant patriot and arbitrator. In *The Loyall Convert* he blames England's troubles on 'a *viperous* Generation' of 'desperate enemies of all *Order* and *Discipline*'. He affirms his loyalty to the king, the '*Lords Anointed*' who had by then accepted the reforms of 1641 and the system of mixed monarchy and would defend this constitutional monarchist position against '*undetermined alteration*' (*Works*, 1.142–5). David Lloyd claims that Quarles suffered much 'in his Peace and Name for writing the *Loyal Convert*, and for going to his Majesty to *Oxford*' (*Memoirs of those that Suffered for the Protestant Religion*, 1668, 621). In *The New Distemper* Quarles alludes to his troubles in Terling where he suffered from the hostility of John Stalham, the fanatical puritan vicar and his followers, who had preferred a petition against him and spread a malicious rumour that he was a papist. Such circumstances suggest that he left Terling to join the king's court at Oxford in 1643 or 1644. Remarks in *The New Distemper* on the activities of royalist writers in Oxford (Quarles, *Works*, 1.156), and the fact that his son John served in the Oxford garrison, support this conclusion. Quarles's defence in *The Whipper Whipt* of the controversial Dr Cornelius Burges, who was a puritan and a royalist, prompted Anthony Wood's false, but much repeated description of Quarles as 'an old puritanical poet' (Wood, *Ath. Oxon.*, 3rd edn, 3.648). A posthumous Oxford edition of the three tracts entitled *The Profest Royalist* appeared in 1645. The poet's last book, *Barnabas and Boanerges* (1644), which appeared in several versions and in Dutch and German translations, was an ingenious combination of meditation and character essay, and was much in demand.

Death and reputation Little is known about the last phase of Quarles's life. By May 1644 all unauthorized strangers had to leave Oxford. Quarles died on 8 September 1644, aged fifty-three, in the presence of his wife and friends, probably in Terling or in London and was buried on 11 September at St Olave's Church, Silver Street, London. He died intestate, and is noted as 'pauper' in the entry of the administration granted to his widow (PRO, PROB 6/20, fol. 29, 4 Feb 1645). Ursula Quarles tried to recover copyrights and unpublished manuscripts from the stationers, but did not succeed and was left in great want. The reasons for Quarles's persisting poverty from the late 1630s onward are not quite clear. It may be that his occasional criticism of abuses in the monarchy prevented the court patronage for which he strove so hard in his numerous dedications. Contemporaries acknowledged the essential goodness of his character and his engaging personality. Quarles was not a puritan but a moderate protestant and royalist with a reverence for the divine institution of the monarchy and who, after 1641, accepted constitutional royalism (I. M. Smart, 'Francis Quarles: professed royalist and "Puritanical Poet"', *Durham University Journal*, 70, 1978, 187–92). He was probably the most successful English poet of his age. His six major works owed their appeal until about 1700 mainly to the mixture of 'competent Wit with Piety' (Richard Baxter, *Poetical Fragments*, 1681, preface). The change of taste about that time caused all of them except *Emblemes and Hieroglyphikes* to fall into neglect. This book proved a cultural achievement and a durable success. It brought to protestant England, suitably adapted, the spiritual and emotional qualities of the Catholic meditation on pictures. It survived as a work of edification when the emblem tradition itself had declined and it played an important role in the Victorian emblematic revival. It has been found especially rewarding in recent studies of the interaction of word and image. Nearly all of Quarles's works stand in an interesting relationship to public affairs and serve to enrich the picture of Stuart England.

KARL JOSEF HÖLTGEN

Sources F. Quarles, *Works*, ed. A. B. Grosart, 3 vols. (1880–81) · F. Quarles, *Hosanna, or, Divine poems on the passion of Christ, and Threnodes*, ed. J. Horden (1960) · K. J. Höltgen, 'New verse by Francis Quarles: the Portland manuscripts, metrical psalms, and *The Bay psalm book* (with text)', *English Literary Renaissance*, 28 (1998), 118–41 · U. Quarles, 'A short relation of the life and death of Mr. Francis Quarles', in F. Quarles, *Solomons recantation* (1645), A3r–A4v · K. J. Höltgen, *Francis Quarles 1592–1644: meditativer Dichter, Emblematiker, Royalist* (1978) [incl. Eng. summary, descriptive list of 95 emblem pl., and lists of uncollected verse and unpubd documents] · K. J. Höltgen, *Aspects of the emblem* (1986) · J. Horden, *Bibliography of Francis Quarles to 1800* (1953) · P. M. Daly and M. V. Silcox, *The English emblem: bibliography of secondary literature* (1990) · F. Quarles, *Emblemes* (1635), *Hieroglyphikes of the life of man* (1638), and E. Benlowes, *Quarlёis* (1634); facs. edn with introduction by K. J. Höltgen and J. Horden (New York, 1993) · M. Bath, *Speaking pictures: English emblem books and Renaissance culture* (1994) · P. M. Daly, *Literature in the light of the emblem*, 2 edn (1998) · C. Hill, 'Francis Quarles and Edward Benlowes', *Writing and revolution in 17th century England: collected essays*, 1 (1985), 188–209 · B. K. Lewalski, *Protestant poetics and the seventeenth-century religious lyric* (1979) · E. Gilman, *Iconoclasm and poetry in the English renaissance* (1986) · K. J. Höltgen, 'Catholic pictures versus protestant words? The adaptation of the Jesuit sources in Quarles's *Emblemes*', *Emblematica*, 9 (1995), 221–38 · K. J. Höltgen, '*Religious emblems* (1809) by John Thurston and Joseph Thomas and its links with Francis Quarles and William Blake', *Emblematica*, 10 (1996), 107–43 · K. J. Höltgen, 'Two Francis Quarleses: the emblem poet and the Suffolk parson', *English Manuscript Studies, 1100–1700*, 7 (1998), 131–61 · M. Bath and B. Willsher, 'Emblems from Quarles on Scottish gravestones', *Emblems and art history*, ed. A. Adams (1996), 169–201 · G. S. Haight, 'The publication of Quarles' *Emblems*', *The Library*, 4th ser., 15 (1934–5), 94–109 · J. Horden, '*The Christian pilgrim*, 1652, and Francis Quarles's *Emblemes and hieroglyphikes*, 1643', *Emblematica*, 4 (1989), 63–90 · A. H. Nethercot, 'The literary legend of Francis Quarles', *Modern Philology*, 20 (1922–3), 225–40 · parish register, Romford, Essex [baptism] · U. Nott. L., Portland MSS, PwV 357, PwV 358 · *Report on the manuscripts of his grace the duke of Buccleuch and Queensberry … preserved at Montagu House*, 3 vols. in 4, HMC, 45 (1899–1926), vol. 3, pp. 41, 50 · *Liber Gratiarum, 1589–1620*, CUL, department of manuscripts and university archives, p. 112 · W. P. Baildon, ed., *The records of the Honorable Society of Lincoln's Inn: admissions*, 1 (1896), 154 · parish register, St Olave's Church, Silver Street, London [burial] · parish register, St Andrew, Holborn, London [marriage] · administration, PRO, PROB 6/20, fol. 29, 4 Feb 1645 · *Fourth report*, HMC, 3 (1874)

Likenesses T. Cross, line engraving (after W. Marshall), BM; repro. in F. Quarles, *Boanerges and Barnabas* (1646) · W. Marshall, line engraving, BM, NPG; repro. in F. Quarles, *Solomons recantation entitled Ecclesiastes* (1645) [*see illus.*]

Wealth at death pauper: administration, PRO, PROB 6/20, fol. 29

Quarles, John (1624/5–1665), poet, was the son of Francis *Quarles (1592–1644), author of the celebrated *Emblemes* (1635), and his wife, Ursula Woodgate (b. 1601). Of the eighteen children born to them, John was the eldest son to survive infancy. Francis Quarles belonged to an Essex family that was prosperous and well connected. At the time of John Quarles's birth his parents were apparently still living in Foster Lane, London, where they had resided since their marriage in 1618. About 1626 Francis Quarles became secretary to James Ussher, archbishop of Armagh, primate of Ireland. Archbishop Ussher preferred to reside at Drogheda, rather than in his palace at Armagh, and it is clear that the Quarles family lived with him. In an elegy on Ussher which John Quarles wrote in 1656 he recalls that he received his education from Ussher alone and that:

the example of his life did every day
Afford me Lectures.
(J. Quarles, *An Elegie on … James Usher*, 1656, 21)

By 1633 the Quarles family had returned to England and were living at Roxwell in Essex, although, within six years, Francis Quarles, no longer prosperous, had moved to a different part of the county and was residing at Ridley Hall, Terling. On 9 February 1643 John Quarles matriculated from Exeter College, Oxford, where, according to Anthony Wood, he was a batteler. By 1643 the king had made Oxford his headquarters, and Quarles is believed to have been a captain in one of his armies and to have served in the Oxford garrison. Presumably military duties curtailed Quarles's university career, and there is no record of his taking a degree.

Quarles was launched on his career as poet at a comparatively early age. He produced twelve or more works—broadsides, pamphlets, and books—which appeared in at least twenty-seven editions and reissues over a period of nearly thirty years. His first substantial publication was *Fons lachrymarum* (1648). When it appeared, Quarles was living in Flanders whither he had been banished, and his 'Farewell to England' of the following year perhaps suggests that he anticipated a lengthy stay. Neither his movements over the next few years nor the date of his eventual return to London have been established. His next considerable work, *Regale lectum miseriae* (1649), which included his 'Farewell', was principally a lament for Charles I. It was his most successful publication, and had reappeared a further six times by 1679. Perhaps only his *God's Love and Mans Unworthiness* (1651), *Divine Meditations* (published with *God's Love* in 1655), and *The Historie of the most Vile Dimagoras* (1658), a continuation of his father's immensely popular heroic romance, *Argalus and Parthenia*, have comparable merit.

In common with a number of writers of the time, Francis Quarles freely acknowledged his indebtedness to Edward Benlowes (1602–1676); John Quarles was to follow in his father's footsteps by dedicating to Benlowes, as his 'much-honoured and Esteemed Friend', *Gods Love and Mans Unworthiness*. Inevitably John Quarles's work was compared with that of his father. In the lines appended to William Marshall's portrait frontispiece to *Fons lachrymarum* it is declared that but for the portrait the work would clearly have been taken for that of '*old smooth* Quarles *himself*'. While Richard Love, who, as vice-chancellor of Cambridge University, had written an imprimatur in verse for *Emblemes* (1635), remarked in the commendatory verse he contributed to *Fons lachrymarum* that:

> The Son *begins to rise, the* Father's *set:*
> *Heav'n took away one* light, *and pleas'd to let*
> *Another rise.*
> (J. Quarles, *Fons lachrymarum*, sig. A8r)

Love's sentiments were to be echoed even by those personally unacquainted with John Quarles. Samuel Sheppard, for instance 'consecrated' an epigram to him, hailing him as heir to his father's genius (S. Sheppard, *Epigrams*, 1651, 161).

Quarles died in London of the plague in 1665. Winstanley believed that he might have been saved had he gone to live with his kinsman William Holgate at Saffron Walden, Essex. Quarles's place of burial has not been traced. He has been confused with John Quarles (1631–1674), fellow of Peterhouse, Cambridge, and John Quarles (1596–1647), merchant of Delft and Rotterdam.   JOHN HORDEN

Sources Wing, *STC*, no. 1503.5 · Foster, *Alum. Oxon.* · Venn, *Alum. Cant.*, 1/3 · A. M. Hind, *Engraving in England in the sixteenth and seventeenth centuries*, 1–2 (1952–5) · A. M. Hind, *Engraving in England in the sixteenth and seventeenth centuries*, 3, ed. M. Corbett and M. Norton (1964) · K. J. Höltgen, *Francis Quarles 1592–1644: meditativer Dichter, Emblematiker, Royalist* (1978) · J. Horden, *John Quarles (1625–1665): an analytical bibliography of his works* (1960) · Wood, *Ath. Oxon.*, new edn, 3.697–9 · W. Winstanley, *The lives of the most famous English poets* (1687) · J. Hall, *Emblems with elegant figures*, ed. J. Horden (1970)
Likenesses T. Cross, engraving, repro. in J. Quarles, *Divine meditations* (1671), frontispiece · attrib. W. Faithorne, line engraving, BM, NPG · W. Marshall, line engraving, BM; repro. in J. Quarles, *Fons lachrymarum* (1648), frontispiece

Quarrier, William (1829–1903), philanthropist, was born in Greenock on 16 September 1829, the only son and second of three children of William Quarrier, a ship's carpenter, and his wife, Annie Booklass. When William was three years old his father died of cholera and was buried in Quebec. Shortly afterwards the family moved to Glasgow where his mother provided for her children by doing fine sewing and laundry work. At the age of six years Quarrier started work in a pin factory, where, for ten hours a day, working a hand-machine, he put heads on ladies' hat pins. He was paid 1*s.* a week. His mother realized that this was a job with very little future, and at the age of eight years he began an apprenticeship as a boot and shoemaker, becoming a qualified journeyman by the age of twelve. In his first Orphan Homes annual report Quarrier recorded the thoughts he had at the end of the first week of his apprenticeship, recalling how, bareheaded and barefoot, cold and hungry, he had stood in the high street of Glasgow, wondering at the lack of compassion shown by passers-by.

William Quarrier (1829–1903), by unknown engraver (after J. A. Brock & Co.)

Eventually Quarrier found employment with a Mrs Hunter, who owned a shoe shop in Argyle Street, Glasgow. She was a member of Blackfriars Baptist Church, which she encouraged Quarrier to attend. He soon became very active in church life and was soon appointed church officer. At the age of twenty-three he established his own shoemaking business, and on 2 December 1856 married Isabella, the daughter of Mrs Hunter. By 1864 Quarrier and his wife had a family of four (three girls and one boy) and his business was prospering. He was, in fact, one of the first multiple shoe-shop owners in Glasgow, with shops in Argyle Street, Anderston, and Cowcaddens. During this period his younger sister, who had been widowed, died, leaving three children. The Quarriers took them in and cared for them as part of their family.

Quarrier had not forgotten the hardships of his early life, and when, travelling home one night, he met a young boy crying over the theft of his matchbox stock by an older boy, he determined to do something to alleviate the plight of street children like him. After discussions with friends, he decided to establish a Shoeblack Brigade, a self-help group. The boys wore a simple uniform consisting of a cap, navy blue jacket trimmed with red, a red badge on the arm, and dark trousers. Each was provided with a box of brushes, blacking, and all that was required for the job. The aim was that they would be united in their work and would respect each other. Each boy kept 8*d.* out of every shilling, and 4*d.* was paid into a common fund from which all the shoeblacks' needs were to be met. In addition, they were required to attend a night class which Quarrier set up and they were expected to attend a Sunday school.

Soon Quarrier turned his attention to another section of Glasgow's underprivileged young, the children hawking newspapers in the streets. They, too, were turned into a brigade with school lessons during the morning. Within a year of the formation of the Shoeblack Brigade, the third of the groups came into being. This was the Parcel Brigade. Wearing a canvas tunic, black belt, and a special badge, they carried parcels for citizens at a rate of 2*d.* per half mile, 3*d.* a mile. The parcels carried had their delivery guaranteed by the brigade. Quarrier was one of the prime movers in getting the town council to take responsibility for the young vendors. They, however, were slow to move and for some years the brigades worked in the face of continuing difficulties. Eventually, with changes in education, social conditions, and the organization of labour, the brigades were dissolved. Quarrier's initial vision had led to a major philanthropic endeavour in Scotland's largest city, which had met with considerable success. After the dissolution of the brigades, he turned his attention to another project. While working with the brigades, he had met Annie MacPherson, a Quaker working in the East End of London who was involved in Canadian immigration work. She convinced Quarrier that this might be a way forward. In September 1871 he wrote a letter which appeared in the *Glasgow Herald* and *North British Daily Mail* pleading the cause of the destitute children of Glasgow. Thomas Corbett, on reading this letter, forwarded £2000 to allow William Quarrier to open the first of his homes for orphaned children at 10 Renfrew Lane in 1871. Within six months he had thirty-five children ready to emigrate to Canada. The home at Renfrew Lane soon proved too small and the girls were transferred to a rented house in Renfield Street. During this time a night refuge and mission hall were established in Dovehill. In 1872, with the need for expansion, the boys moved to Cessnock House—a mansion in the suburbs of Govan. Later the girls moved to Newstead and Elmpark homes which were in the same neighbourhood as Cessnock House. The premises at Dovehill were bought by the Glasgow school board but the need for a night refuge remained. In 1875 a new building was erected in James Morrison Street to provide accommodation and a mission hall. This building became known as the City Orphan Home, and eventually provided accommodation for working boys and girls and served as a receiving home for children who were subsequently transferred to Quarrier's Village at Bridge of Weir.

In Quarrier's first annual report, which he entitled *A Narrative of Facts Relative to the Work Done for Christ*, Quarrier developed his concept of cottage homes, which represented a new departure in the care of dependent children. In this document he discussed the establishment of an orphanage near Glasgow, open to children from any part of Scotland, which would consist of adjacent cottages, each able to accommodate twenty or thirty children. A 'father' and 'mother' would head each household, and a playground would be attached to each cottage. A central school and workshop would be established, and the fathers of the households would each be able to teach a different trade, while the mothers would cook for the households, with assistance if necessary. Each boy would learn the trade to which he was best suited, and all the children would meet together at school and church, and, on special occasions, in the common playground. Quarrier hoped, by these new arrangements, to keep up 'the family and home feeling' among the children; he criticized the traditional institutions for orphans, where the 'strict uniformity' necessary for the management of large numbers of children destroyed any domestic attachment.

The village at Bridge of Weir was the realization of Quarrier's ideal. In 1876 he purchased 40 acres of farmland at this site, which was 16 miles west of Glasgow, and in September 1878 the first buildings of what was to become known as Orphan Homes of Scotland were officially opened. The houses were built chiefly through the gifts of individual friends. Quarrier's Village grew, with more than fifty houses, a school, church, and dairy, poultry farms and workshops. From 1872, when the first thirty-five children went to Canada through Annie MacPherson's immigration scheme, until 1932, Quarrier and his successors continued to send boys and girls to Canada.

In 1887 Quarrier established his own distribution home at Brockville, Ontario. As he did for the children who remained in Scotland, Quarrier fought for and defended the members of his large family. In 1897 he fell out with the Canadian authorities over proposed legislation which would 'mark' all children entering the country through schemes such as his. Each distribution home was to be licensed and a dossier kept on each child, classified until they were eighteen years of age. Quarrier felt that since the regulations were to apply only to children such as those he brought to Canada, it amounted to unjust treatment. As he was in Canada at the time, he discussed the legislation with the Canadian premier and members of the Ontario legislature, who had nothing but praise for his work and for the children he sent. But he did not receive a satisfactory answer to his queries concerning the act, which was passed in 1897; Quarrier immediately stopped his scheme. Immigration was later restarted in the year following Quarrier's death by his son-in-law, who had satisfied himself that all was in order.

In 1896 another of Quarrier's initiatives, a consumption sanatorium, was opened, and in 1906, three years after his death, his daughter opened a centre for epileptics, which was Quarrier's third area of concern. He died on 16 October 1903 at Quarrier's Homes at Bridge of Weir and was buried in Quarrier's Village. His wife, Isabella, died on 22 June 1904. The administration of the homes was continued by members of the family, together with elected trustees. In 1948 the consumption sanatorium was brought under the management of the local health board. At the end of the twentieth century Quarrier's homes were administered by a council of management and a team of senior managers, who were jointly responsible for the continuing and diverse work of this organization, which remained as a living memorial to the energy and achievement of nineteenth-century Scottish philanthropy.

WILLIAM MacLEAN DUNBAR

Sources J. Urquhart, *The life-story of William Quarrier* (1900) · J. Climie, *William Quarrier, the orphans' friend* (1902) · A. Gammie, *A romance of faith: the story of the Orphan Homes of Scotland, and the founder, William Quarrier* (1942?) · J. Ross, *The power I pledge* (1971) · A. Magnusson, *The village: a history of Quarrier's* (1984) · *Annual Reports* [Quarrier's Orphan Homes] (1872–1993) · Register of births and baptisms, parish of Greenock West · Quarriers Homes records of deaths and burials
Archives Quarrier's Homes, Bridge of Weir, near Glasgow | FILM Scottish Film Library, Glasgow
Likenesses engraving (after J. A. Brock & Co.), NPG [*see illus.*] · five photographs, repro. in Magnusson, *The village*
Wealth at death £3548 7s. 7d.: confirmation, 18 Nov 1903, CCI

Quaye, Cab. *See* Kaye, Cab (1921–2000).

Quayle, Sir (John) Anthony (1913–1989), actor and theatre director, was born on 7 September 1913 at 2 Delamere Road, Ainsdale, Southport, Lancashire, the only child of Arthur Quayle, solicitor, and his wife, Esther Kate Overton. The Quayle family had Manx roots. During a rather lonely youth Anthony's interest in the theatre was encouraged by his lively and imaginative mother. He was educated at Rugby School and at the Royal Academy of Dramatic Art, where he stayed only a year. His first appearance on the professional stage, unpaid, was in *The Ghost Train* at the Q Theatre while on holiday from RADA. He began his career in earnest playing both Richard Coeur de Lion and Will Scarlett in *Robin Hood* at the same theatre in 1931.

In the following year, after touring as feed to a music-hall comic, Quayle found his feet in classical theatre and met two men whose influence was to be an important factor in his career, Tyrone Guthrie and John Gielgud. By 1939 he had appeared in many supporting roles, with Old Vic seasons in 1932 and 1937–8, had appeared in New York, and had played Laertes in the famous Guthrie production of *Hamlet* at Elsinore. Strongly drawn to the classics and especially to Shakespeare, he took over the lead from Laurence Olivier in *Henry V* during an Old Vic tour of Europe and Egypt just before the Second World War. Though not yet at the top of his profession, he was known and liked by many who were.

Quayle spent the war in the Royal Artillery, reaching the rank of major. Characteristically, he gave up an administrative job in Gibraltar, learned to parachute, and joined Albanian partisans behind German lines. He later wrote two slight novels suggested by his wartime experiences.

After the war Quayle returned to the stage and as Enobarbus in *Antony and Cleopatra* (1946) was a great success in the first of the many supporting roles he was to make his own. He also turned to directing, and in 1946 his *Crime and Punishment*, starring John Gielgud, was considered outstanding.

In 1948, through Guthrie, he joined the Shakespeare Memorial Theatre in Stratford upon Avon as actor and stage director. He was soon promoted to run the whole memorial theatre. In eight years he transformed it from an unfashionable provincial theatre to a world-famous centre of classical drama. Because of his many contacts, he was able to attract illustrious players and directors to Stratford, as well as encourage such major new talents as

Sir (John) Anthony Quayle (1913–1989), by Godfrey Argent, 1970

Richard Burton and Peter Hall. He took companies on tours of Australasia in 1949 and 1953 and tried, although without success, to secure the kind of London shop window for the company which was later obtained by the Royal Shakespeare Company. With his 'Cycle of the Histories' for the Festival of Britain in 1951 he foreshadowed the later practice of staging Shakespeare's historical plays in chronological order. Among his own parts during these strenuous years were Henry VIII, Falstaff, and Othello. His work was not entirely confined to Stratford, but his enthusiastic leadership and hard work at the memorial theatre, proudly unsubsidized, put it on the map. He paved the way for the subsequent achievements of Peter Hall, Trevor Nunn, and the Royal Shakespeare Company.

In 1956 Quayle resigned from Stratford and returned to mainstream theatre. For over twenty more years he continued to act and direct in the West End, having a steady if unspectacular career, occasionally taking the lead, as in *Tamburlaine* in 1956, but more often in highly praised supporting parts. He also appeared in over thirty films, most of them British, again in strong supporting roles. His portrayal of stiff-upper-lip Englishmen was much admired in films, especially in *The Battle of the River Plate* (1956), *The Guns of Navarone* (1961), and *Lawrence of Arabia* (1962). The first of his many television appearances was in 1961.

In 1978, at sixty-five, Quayle's career took a different course and he toured with the Prospect Theatre Company, playing leading roles in *The Rivals* and *King Lear*. The company closed, however, when its Arts Council subsidy was withdrawn. Several years later, in 1983, he formed his own Compass Theatre, which bravely stumped the country without subsidy, dedicated to bringing major plays to people who could otherwise never see them.

Quayle had a big physique, a vigorous personality, and a steadfast—even romantic—devotion to great plays and classical traditions. Despite his fine technique he had neither the personality nor the face for a great actor. As he grew older his face became more rugged but there was something about his amiable blue eyes which suggested a warm and pleasant person and deprived his acting of some of its emotional impact. However, as a man of great courage and integrity he was a natural leader and a major influence on the theatre in Britain.

Quayle was appointed CBE in 1952 and knighted in 1985. He had honorary DLitt degrees from Hull (1987) and St Andrews (1989). He was guest professor of drama at the University of Tennessee in 1974, and was nominated for an Oscar as best supporting player for his performance as Cardinal Wolsey in the 1969 film about Anne Boleyn, *Anne of the Thousand Days*.

On 3 March 1935 Quayle married Hermione (*d.* 1983), actress daughter of the actor Nicholas James Hannen, but the marriage was dissolved in 1943. On 3 June 1947 he married another actress, Dorothy Wardell Hyson [*see below*], divorced wife of Robert Douglas Finlayson and daughter of another actress, Dorothy Dickson (1897?–1995), and Carl Constantine Hyson, of independent means. They had a son and two daughters. He was still touring until two months before his death from cancer at his London home, 49B Elystan Place, Chelsea, on 20 October 1989.

Quayle's second wife, Dorothy Wardell Hyson (or Heissen) [**Dorothy Wardell Quayle** (1914–1996)], was born on 24 December 1914 in Chicago into a theatre family, which moved to London in 1921. She appeared on the London stage as a child actress in Barry's *Quality Street* (1927) and Daisy Ashford's *The Young Visiters* (1928) and made her adult début in Novello's *Flies in the Sun* (1933). A series of successful roles followed, but in 1934 overwork caused a nervous breakdown. She recovered to return in comedy roles, marrying Robert Douglas Finlayson, the actor, in 1935, 'a failure from the start' (*The Times*, 25 May 1996). She met Anthony Quayle in 1936, who was at once dazzled by her beauty; misunderstanding and complications on both sides deferred romance, but they were eventually married in 1947. Hyson had continued to play a variety of comedy roles, but after her second marriage retired from the stage. It was her dislike of Hollywood that caused Quayle to reject the offer of a contract with MGM in favour of the Stratford directorship. During Quayle's years at Stratford, Hyson became a noted hostess there. A striking beauty, her 'perfect heart-shaped face, vivid cornflower-blue eyes and translucent halo of blond hair' (*The Times*, 25 May 1996) inspired the Rodgers and Hart song, 'The Most Beautiful Girl in the World'. RACHAEL LOW, *rev.*

Sources *Daily Telegraph* (21 Oct 1989) · *The Times* (21 Oct 1989) · *The Times* (25 May 1996) · *The Independent* (21 Oct 1989) · *The Independent* (25 May 1996) · A. Quayle, *A time to speak* (1990) · b. cert. · m. certs. · d. cert.
Likenesses photographs, 1935–78, Hult. Arch. · G. Argent, photograph, 1970, NPG [*see illus.*]
Wealth at death £626,664: probate, 11 May 1990, *CGPLA Eng. & Wales*

Quayle, Dorothy Wardell (1914–1996). *See under* Quayle, Sir (John) Anthony (1913–1989).

Queally, Malachy [Maolseachlain Ó Caollaidhe] (1586–1645), vicar apostolic of Killaloe and Roman Catholic archbishop of Tuam, was born of aristocratic landowning stock at Drinagh, barony of Inchiquin, co. Clare, the son of Donagh Queally (Donnchadh Ó Caoillaidhe) and his wife,

Sive. After studies in local schools he went to Paris, apparently in 1613, for he took his MA degree, usually awarded after two years' study, in 1615. This was the year in which the French clergy adopted the Council of Trent as the pattern for church reform. He went on to study theology, and it was probably at this time that he was ordained priest. He took his baccalaureate in 1617, and taught philosophy at the Collège de Boncourt while residing in the Collège de Navarre and studying for his licentiate, which he took in 1622. An academic career was opening up for him, but he had already decided to return to Ireland. There the Roman Catholic church was being reorganized by the appointment to the historic dioceses of vicars apostolic (priests in charge by virtue of papal delegation) or, more cautiously, by the appointment of bishops. Queally had been appointed vicar apostolic of his native diocese of Killaloe on 20 August 1619 and he returned to Ireland shortly after taking his licentiate.

Queally was a man of commanding presence and of great energy and commitment, and he vigorously promoted church reform as laid down by the Council of Trent. Soon there were requests from many quarters that he be promoted to the episcopate. However, the Roman authorities were slow to multiply bishops, and another candidate, John O'Molony, had the powerful advocacy of the French queen mother, Marie de' Medici. In 1629 Archbishop Conry of Tuam died in exile. Queally was appointed his successor on 12 April 1630 and O'Molony was appointed to Killaloe on 2 August. Queally was consecrated in Galway on 10 October by Archbishop Walsh of Cashel. As archbishop of Tuam he was also metropolitan of the western ecclesiastical province, hitherto only superficially touched by either Roman Catholic or protestant reform. He embarked on a forceful programme, recorded in the provincial synods held in 1632 and 1640, and in his reports to the Roman authorities in 1634 and 1637. He even attempted to extend his authority over his suffragans further than the Council of Trent envisaged, but in this he did not obtain Roman support. He failed too in his attempt to reassert control over the warden of the collegiate church of St Nicholas in Galway, exempted from archiepiscopal jurisdiction since 1488. He opposed the unbridled attacks on the regular clergy made by an extreme faction of the seculars, in this possibly influenced by his close links with the Franciscan order. The wide range of his interests appears from his efforts in 1639 to find priests to replace those who had gone to St Kitt's when it was first settled in 1623 and had since died. Four surviving chalices are associated with him (the existing church plate had passed to the established church). His Gaelic and Franciscan links appear in his formal approbation of the martyrology of Donegal and the annals of the four masters, completed in 1630 and 1636 respectively, and in his list of the churches and antiquities of the Aran Islands, printed by John Colgan in *Acta sanctorum Hiberniae* (1645).

An account written by a protestant in 1641 indicates that in Tuam and in the western province generally the Roman Catholic church had prevailed almost to the exclusion of protestantism, but the tensions inherent in this situation were coming to a head. There had been confrontation in 1635, when the refusal of a Galway jury to find land titles for the king had been punished by fines and imprisonments. In consequence there was widespread support in Connaught for the insurrection of 1641. When the principal Catholic nobleman, the marquess of Clanricarde, was reluctant to give active support, leadership devolved on the forceful archbishop of Tuam. In the summer of 1642 Queally raised a troop of 200 foot at his own expense, primarily indeed to maintain order, for though there was no enemy in Connaught there had been a massacre of protestant refugees at Shrule on 13 February. By the end of the year, however, he had gone to Kilkenny, first as a member of the general assembly of the Irish confederates and then of their supreme council or executive. The tortuous negotiations conducted by the confederates with Charles I came to a head in a secret treaty with his representative, the earl of Glamorgan, concluded on 25 August 1645. By now, however, Connaught was threatened because parliamentarian forces under Sir Charles Coote had captured Sligo on 7 July. Queally returned to rally a counter-attack. He did succeed in mustering a sizeable force, but he was killed at Ballysadare near Sligo on 25 October, in a skirmish according to one account, surprised in his tent according to another. A copy of the Glamorgan treaty was found among his effects, and revelation of the great concessions Glamorgan was prepared to make to the Irish confederates on the king's behalf did great damage to his cause in England. Archbishop Queally's mutilated body was ransomed and taken to Tuam Cathedral for burial.

PATRICK J. CORISH

Sources P. F. Moran, ed., *Spicilegium Ossoriense*, 3 vols. (1874–84) · J. Hagan, ed., 'Miscellanea Vaticano-Hibernica', *Archivium Hibernicum*, 5 (1916), 74–185, esp. 97–100; 6 (1917), 94–155, esp. 141–3 · C. Giblin, 'Vatican library MSS Barberini Latini: a guide to the material of Irish interest on microfilm in the National Library, Dublin', *Archivium Hibernicum*, 18 (1955), 67–144, esp. 79–89 · B. Jennings, ed., 'Acta sacrae congregationes de Propaganda Fide, 1622–50', *Archivium Hibernicum*, 22 (1959), 28–139 · *Collectanea Hibernica*, 6–7 (1963–4) · *Collectanea Hibernica*, 8 (1965) · *Collectanea Hibernica*, 10 (1967) · *Collectanea Hibernica*, 12–13 (1969–70) · *Collectanea Hibernica*, 36–7 (1994–5) · *Report on Franciscan manuscripts preserved at the convent, Merchants' Quay, Dublin*, HMC, 65 (1906) · B. Jennings, ed., *Wadding papers, 1614–38*, IMC (1953) · C. Giblin, 'The Processus datariae and the appointment of Irish bishops in the 17th century', *Father Luke Wadding: commemorative volume*, ed. Franciscan Fathers dún Mhuire, Killiney (1957), 508–616 · A. Bruodinus, *Propugnaculum Catholicae veritatis* (Prague, 1669) · J. Linchaeo [J. Lynch], *De praesulibus Hiberniae*, ed. J. F. O'Doherty, 2 vols., IMC (1944) · L. W. B. Brockliss and P. Ferté, 'Irish clerics in France in the seventeenth and eighteenth centuries: a statistical study', *Proceedings of the Royal Irish Academy*, 87C (1987), 527–72 · J. Lannoi, *Regii Navarrae Collegii historia* (1667) · L. F. Renehan, *Collections on Irish church history*, ed. D. McCarthy, 2 vols. (1861–74) · O. J. Burke, *The history of the Catholic archbishops of Tuam* (1882)

Archives Franciscan Library, Killiney, co. Dublin, Franciscan archives, MSS · Sacra Congregazione di Propaganda Fide, Rome, MSS

Queen's Maries (*act.* 1548–1567) were four small girls chosen to be maids of honour to five-year-old *Mary, queen of Scots, when she was sent to France in 1548 as the fiancée of the dauphin François. All four came from well-known Scottish families with royal connections. The mother of **Mary Fleming** (1542–*c.*1600) was both the young queen's governess and her aunt, for Lady Fleming was an illegitimate daughter of *James IV. **Mary Seton** (*b. c.*1541, *d.* after 1615) and **Mary Beaton** (*c.*1543–1597) were daughters of French ladies-in-waiting to the queen's mother, Mary of Guise. Marie Pieris, mother of Mary Seton, married George *Seton, fourth Lord Seton, as his second wife; Jeanne de la Reinville, mother of Mary Beaton, married Robert Beaton of Creich, himself a page of honour from a family with a long tradition of royal service. Alexander, fifth Lord Livingston, and his wife, Lady Agnes Douglas, guardians of the queen, were the parents of **Mary Livingston** (*d.* 1585). Contemporaries frequently commented upon the coincidence of all four girls sharing the same first name, but Alexander Jamieson, the nineteenth-century lexicographer, linked the term 'Maries' to the Icelandic word 'maer', meaning a virgin or maid.

When Mary, queen of Scots, arrived at the French court Henri II, though delighted with her, was dismayed that she did not speak French. Believing that she would forget her own country more quickly if she were surrounded by French ladies, he sent the Maries to Poissy to be educated under the supervision of the Dominican abbess Françoise de Vieuxpont, but their separation from the queen seems to have been brief. On their return to Scotland with her in 1561 the Maries were obviously her close friends and confidantes, often sleeping in her bedchamber, as was the custom of the time. Elegant, sophisticated, and sumptuously dressed, they attracted admiring attention wherever they went. The English ambassador Thomas Randolph thought Mary Beaton the most beautiful, but Mary Fleming dazzled him at the twelfth night festivities of 1564, when she took the principal role, wearing diamonds and cloth of silver.

In 1565 Mary, queen of Scots, said that she was marrying off her Maries and had a mind to take another husband herself. On 6 March Mary Livingston became the wife of John (*d.* 1583), son of Robert, third Lord Sempill, the queen having provided not only the dowry and the wedding dress but a magnificent scarlet bed; on 29 July she herself married Henry *Stewart, Lord Darnley (1545/6–1567). The following April the court celebrated Mary Beaton's marriage to Alexander Ogilvy of Boyne. Mary Seton showed no interest in matrimony, but the vivacious Mary Fleming had a string of suitors, and on 6 January 1568, after a long courtship, she married William *Maitland of Lethington, the queen's secretary of state, a widower eighteen years older than she.

A month later Darnley was murdered at Kirk o' Field and the queen married James, earl of Bothwell. Mary Seton was with her when she surrendered to her rebellious lords at Carberry Hill. She and Mary Livingston accompanied the queen on her ignominious return to Edinburgh and they attended her during her imprisonment in Lochleven Castle. When the queen tried to escape, disguised as a washerwoman, she gave her long black dress to Mary

Seton, who put it on and prepared to impersonate her until she could get safely away. The attempt failed, but after the queen's eventual escape, defeat at Langside, and imprisonment in England, Mary Seton once more became her companion and won praise for her skill at daily devising new hairstyles for her. The other Maries remained in Scotland.

Mary Seton had at least two suitors during her time in England. During her stay at Wingfield Manor, Sir Richard Norton's son Christopher wanted to marry her but was executed after his involvement in the northern rising. The master of the queen's household, Andrew Beaton, had also fallen in love with Mary Seton but she was reluctant, telling him that she had taken a vow of chastity; he died just as it seemed that she was changing her mind. In poor health Mary retired to Rheims in 1583 to spend the rest of her life in the abbey of St Pierre aux Dames, where the abbess, Renée de Lorraine, was an aunt of the Scottish queen. The longest lived of the four Maries, she eventually died there some time after 1615.

Mary Livingston died in 1585, two years before Mary's execution. Her eldest son, Sir James *Sempill, was James VI's ambassador to the English court. Mary Beaton lived until 1597. It has been suggested that either she, or Mary Fleming and her husband, Maitland of Lethington, may have forged the notorious casket letters, but that is pure speculation. Mary Fleming was with her husband during his long illness and when he finally died, in 1573, after the fall of Edinburgh Castle to English and Scottish forces, she successfully pleaded with William Cecil for her husband's body to be given a decent burial instead of being put on display at his trial for treason, as would otherwise have happened. A month later she was refusing to give up a diamond and ruby chain belonging to Queen Mary, which was now being claimed by the representatives of King James. She devoted herself to bringing up her son and daughter and, having outlived her husband by many years, and having at some stage married, secondly, George Meldrum of Fyvie, she died about 1600.

The identity of the four Maries has been the subject of much confusion, thanks to a ballad entitled 'Marie Hamilton', which arguably dates from the eighteenth century. It tells the apocryphal tale of one of Queen Mary's ladies-in-waiting having an affair with Lord Darnley, drowning her illegitimate child, and going to the gallows with the poignant words:

> Yestreen the queen had four Maries
> This night she'll ha'e but three
> There was Marie Seaton and Marie Beaton
> And Marie Carmichael and me.

In 1802–3 Sir Walter Scott published this ballad in his *Minstrelsy of the Scottish Border*. Realizing that there had been no such person as Marie Hamilton in Mary's retinue he believed that the tale derived from an incident related in John Knox's *History of the Reformation*, in which one of the queen's waiting women was executed for murdering her illegitimate child by the royal apothecary. C. K. Sharpe, the antiquarian who had collected the ballad and given it to Scott in the first place, more plausibly linked it with

Mary Hamilton, a Scotswoman at the court of Peter the Great, who had an affair with the tsar, killed the resulting infant (and her two other illegitimate children), and was executed on 14 March 1719.

In the nineteenth century the final section of the ballad, beginning with the famous verse quoted above, was lifted from it and published separately as 'The Four Maries'. It became very popular, and ever since then the fictitious Mary Hamilton and Mary Carmichael have displaced the real Mary Fleming and Mary Livingston in the minds of many people, despite the publication of Thomas Duncan's authoritative article in the *Scottish Historical Review* for 1905, pointing out that the ballad has nothing to do with the historical four Maries. However even without this highly-coloured and irrelevant tale of adultery and infanticide the notion of the four small childhood companions of Scotland's tragic queen has caught the public imagination, and they are still remembered as romantic figures after more than four centuries.

ROSALIND K. MARSHALL

Sources G. Seton, *A history of the family of Seton*, 2 vols. (1896), 1 · T. Duncan, 'The queen's Maries', *SHR*, 2 (1904–5), 362–71 · *Scots peerage*, vols. 5, 8 · T. Thomson, ed., *A collection of inventories and other records of the royal wardrobe … in some of the royal castles* (1815) · A. de Ruble, *La première jeunesse de Marie Stuart* (1891) · J. Maitland, *Maitland's narrative* (1833) · A. Strickland, *Life of Mary, queen of Scots* (1873) · A. Fraser, *Mary, queen of Scots* (1969) · G. Donaldson and R. Morpeth, *A dictionary of Scottish history* (1977) · G. Eyre-Todd, ed., *Scottish ballad poetry* (1893), 318–23

Queensberry. For this title name *see* Douglas, William, first earl of Queensberry (*d.* 1640); Douglas, James, second earl of Queensberry (*d.* 1671); Douglas, William, first duke of Queensberry (1637–1695); Douglas, James, second duke of Queensberry and first duke of Dover (1662–1711); Douglas, Charles, third duke of Queensberry and second duke of Dover (1698–1778); Douglas, Catherine, duchess of Queensberry and Dover (1701–1777); Douglas, William, fourth duke of Queensberry (1725–1810); Scott, Henry, third duke of Buccleuch and fifth duke of Queensberry (1746–1812); Scott, Walter Francis Montagu-Douglas-, fifth duke of Buccleuch and seventh duke of Queensberry (1806–1884); Scott, Charlotte Anne Montagu-Douglas-, duchess of Buccleuch and Queensberry (1811–1895) [*see under* Scott, Walter Francis Montagu-Douglas-, fifth duke of Buccleuch and seventh duke of Queensberry (1806–1884)]; Douglas, John Sholto, ninth marquess of Queensberry (1844–1900); Mann, Cathleen Sabine [Catherine Sabine Douglas, marchioness of Queensberry] (1896–1959).

Quekett, Edwin John (1808–1847). *See under* Quekett, John Thomas (1815–1861).

Quekett, John Thomas (1815–1861), histologist, was born at Langport, Somerset, on 11 August 1815, the youngest son of William Quekett, master of Langport grammar school, and his wife, Mary, daughter of John Bartlett. His elder brothers were William Quekett (1802–1888) and Edwin John Quekett (1808–1847) [*see below*].

Quekett was educated by his father at home, where an emphasis was placed on natural history; when only sixteen, John gave lectures on microscopical subjects with the aid of a home-made microscope. He was then apprenticed to a local surgeon, and subsequently to his brother Edwin in London. He entered King's College and worked at the London Hospital medical school, qualifying at Apothecaries' Hall and the Royal College of Surgeons in 1840. He won a competitive three-year studentship in human and comparative anatomy at the latter in the same year, and on its completion in 1843 was appointed assistant conservator to the Hunterian Museum of the College of Surgeons, under Richard Owen, becoming demonstrator of minute anatomy in 1844. He made a collection of 2500 plant and animal microscopical preparations, including many injections, which was bought by the college in 1846. In 1841, on Owen's recommendation, he had been appointed secretary of the recently founded Microscopical Society of London. He retained the post until 1860, when he became president, but by that time he was too ill to contribute anything except his presidential address.

In 1846 Quekett married Isabella Mary Anne (d. 1872), daughter of Robert Scott of the Bengal civil service; they had four children. In 1852 he became the Royal College of Surgeons' professor of histology and resident conservator at the Hunterian Museum, Owen having moved out to reside at Richmond. On Owen's appointment as director of the natural history collections of the British Museum in 1856, the post of conservator was at once offered to Quekett, at £500 per year.

Quekett's work as a histologist, both practical and literary, was original and prolific. His *Practical Treatise on the Use of the Microscope* (1848) was the first such work, and gave much encouragement to individual workers at this fruitful period in the use of the instrument in histology. He was a well-connected man of considerable scientific stature (the prince consort was among those who came to him for instruction). He was working with the microscope during the period in which it was becoming established as a serious scientific tool. He applied this tool with vigour, in one of the few places in Europe where his potential could have been realized.

In addition to his handbook, Quekett wrote two volumes of a catalogue of the histological preparations in the college (1850 and 1853), two volumes of lectures on histology (1852 and 1854), a joint work on fossil plants in the college (1859), and a catalogue of plants and invertebrates (1860). He wrote twenty-two papers, the majority of which were published in the *Transactions of the Microscopical Society*. In the early 1840s, while still a student and an assistant to Benjamin Travers (1783–1858), he carried out highly original experimental work on the healing of wounds, which was published in Travers's *The Physiology of Inflammation and the Healing Process* (1844). In this the very eminent Travers pays most fulsome tribute to his young partner.

Quekett was elected to fellowship of the Linnean Society in 1857, and of the Royal Society in 1860. He had gone to Pangbourne to recover from an illness, and died there on 20 August 1861, of a seizure consequent on chronic Bright's disease. After his death his possessions were auctioned over several days from 10 December 1861. He had a large variety of scientific apparatus, including some important microscopes and scientific books, but also arms and armour, pottery, minerals, and machine tools. The auction realized some £681, but did not include most of his ordinary household effects. The College of Surgeons paid an annuity to his widow, and the microscopical world set up a fund to assist his family. The Quekett Microscopical Club was established in 1865, and named so in his memory.

Edwin John Quekett (1808–1847), surgeon and microscopist, was born at Langport. He underwent medical training at University College Hospital, becoming a member of the Royal College of Surgeons in 1830. He practised as a surgeon from 50 Wellclose Square, Whitechapel, and in 1835 he became lecturer on botany at the London Hospital medical college. He was elected a fellow of the Linnean Society in 1836. A meeting, held in his house in 1839, resulted in the foundation of the Microscopical Society of London (later the Royal Microscopical Society), which was to exert so great an influence on the development of the instrument. He wrote fifteen papers, and had his name commemorated by Lindley in a genus of Brazilian orchids, *Quekettia*. He died in London on 28 June 1847 of diphtheria contracted during his duties, and was buried at Seasalter, Kent, near the grave of a Miss Hyder to whom he had been engaged before she had died of consumption.

William Quekett (1802–1888), Church of England clergyman, was born at Langport on 3 October 1802; he was the eldest of the three brothers. He entered St John's College, Cambridge, in 1822, and in 1825 was ordained curate of South Cadbury, Somerset. In 1830 he became curate of St George-in-the-East, where he remained until 1841 and was instrumental in establishing Christ Church, Watney Street, of which he was the incumbent from 1841 to 1854. On 2 July 1851 he married Mary Bennett, widow of the Revd E. V. Williams. His energy attracted the attention of Charles Dickens, who based his articles 'What a London curate can do if he tries' (*Household Words*, 16 Nov 1850) and 'Emigration' (ibid., 24 Jan 1852) on Quekett's work. In 1849 Quekett and Sidney Herbert established the Female Emigration Society. In 1854 Quekett was presented by the crown to the rectory of Warrington, where he restored the parish church, and died on 30 March 1888, just after the publication of his autobiography, *My Sayings and Doings* (1888). BRIAN BRACEGIRDLE

Sources B. Bracegirdle, 'Famous microscopists: John Thomas Quekett, 1815–1861', *Proceedings of the Royal Microscopical Society*, 23 (1988), 149–69 · B. Bracegirdle, 'John Thomas Quekett and his work on the healing of wounds', *Quekett Journal of Microscopy*, 36 (1988), 1–13 · Venn, *Alum. Cant.* · Desmond, *Botanists*, rev. edn · *CGPLA Eng. & Wales* (1861)
Archives RCS Eng., diaries, notebooks, and papers
Likenesses lithograph, 1851, repro. in *Maguire's series of national portraits* · W. Walker, mezzotint (after E. Walker), BM · print, repro. in *ILN*, 39 (1861)
Wealth at death £600: administration, 28 Oct 1861, *CGPLA Eng. & Wales* · £2786 14s. 6d.—William Quekett: probate, 29 Nov 1888, *CGPLA Eng. & Wales*

Quekett, William (1802–1888). *See under* Quekett, John Thomas (1815–1861).

Quelch, Henry [Harry] (1858–1913), socialist and journalist, was born at Park Street, Hungerford, Berkshire, on 30 January 1858, son of James Quelch, a village blacksmith, who was an invalid for the last twenty years of his life, and his wife, Mary Ann Wooldridge, the daughter of an agricultural labourer. He had at least one brother, Lorenzo. The family was poor and the young Quelch began full-time work at the age of ten, migrating to London when he was fourteen. On 19 May 1878 he married Sarah (*b.* 1856/7), daughter of Thomas Fisher, a labourer. In 1881 they were living in Bermondsey with their two daughters. He had a variety of unskilled jobs, and at the beginning of the 1880s, when he first became involved in radical politics, he was working in a wallpaper warehouse.

Always known as Harry, Quelch first joined the Bermondsey Radical Club and soon became known in London left-wing politics. He became a member of the Democratic Federation, later the Social Democratic Federation (SDF), and was one of its few proletarian activists in the early days of the newly emerging socialist movement. Quelch was entirely self-educated: one of the great autodidacts of the modern labour period. He taught himself French in order to read Karl Marx's *Capital*, and later learned German. He began writing for *Justice*, the weekly paper of the SDF which first appeared in January 1884, and two years later he took over the editor's position from H. M. Hyndman. Quelch resigned from the editorship in 1889 in order to work full-time for the new unionism, but he returned to the editor's chair in 1891 and remained editor until his death. In 1891 he also became manager of the newly established Twentieth Century Press. He was a competent and careful administrator, and retired in 1909, with unfortunate results for the publishing company for the next few years.

Quelch produced in *Justice* a lively and well-informed paper which remains invaluable for the history, especially the grass roots history, of the modern labour movement. In politics he was usually to the left of H. M. Hyndman, whom he much admired, but he accepted the latter's scepticism towards trade unionism and its place in the socialist movement. Quelch was inevitably involved in most of the many disputes and debates of the decades before 1914, and not only in Britain, for he was a constant attender at international conferences of the European left. He was a vigorous opponent of the 'impossibilities' in Scotland and London, anti-syndicalist in general, hostile to the Pankhursts, and only lukewarm on women's suffrage. He was a wholehearted supporter of Indian independence, and gave unstinted assistance to the Russian revolutionaries. When *Iskra* had to be printed in London, Quelch put all the resources of the Twentieth Century Press at the disposal of the Russians, who for a time included Lenin. On the issue of Germany in the years before 1914 Quelch was not as xenophobic as Hyndman, but he supported the idea of a 'citizen' army and an 'adequate' navy to counter German expansionist aims. It was an issue that sharply divided the Marxist left.

Quelch married twice. There was one son, Tom, but it is unknown whether Quelch's first or second wife was his

Henry [Harry] **Quelch** (1858–1913), by unknown photographer

mother. Henry Quelch died on 17 September 1913 at his home, 35 Limesford Road, Peckham, London, having been in increasing ill health for a number of years. He was survived by his second wife, M. C. E. Quelch.

JOHN SAVILLE, *rev.*

Sources DLB · C. Tsuzuki, *H. M. Hyndman and British socialism* (1961) · b. cert. · d. cert. · m. cert. [Sarah Fisher] · census returns, 1881
Likenesses photograph, People's History Museum, Manchester [*see illus.*]

Quennell, Sir Peter Courtney (1905–1993), writer and editor, was born on 9 March 1905 at 9 The Avenue, Bickley, Bromley, Kent, the eldest of the three children of Charles Henry Bourne Quennell (1872–1935), architect, author, and social historian, and his wife, Marjorie (1885?–1972), painter, illustrator, and social historian, and eldest daughter of Alan and Clara Courtney. Together his parents wrote *A History of everyday Things in England*. A sister, Gillian, was born in September 1909; a brother, Paul, born in June 1915, was killed in Belgium in 1940. Quennell began his education at St Alfred's School in Chislehurst, staying there until the family moved to Berkhamsted in 1917. He continued his studies at Berkhamsted School under the care of headmaster Charles Greene, father of his boyhood friend and classmate Graham Greene. Early attempts at writing poetry resulted in Quennell's publication in *Public School Verse: an Anthology, Volume 2, 1920–1921* (1922) and *Masques and Poems* (1922). His piece for Richard Hughes's *Public School Verse* was mistakenly interpreted by certain newspapers as a witty satire on modern literature and made him famous in some circles. Through Hughes, Quennell was introduced to Edith Sitwell, the start of a long friendship with the Sitwell family. Quennell received a scholarship in English at Balliol College, Oxford, in 1922, but on advice from his father postponed entry until October 1923. He arrived at Oxford to considerable acclaim after Edward Marsh published his early poems in *Georgian*

Poetry 1920–1921 (1923). While at Oxford he formed friendships with Evelyn Waugh, Edward Sackville-West, Anthony Powell, Harold Acton, and Cyril Connolly. Although his relationship with Waugh later soured, he maintained a lifelong friendship with Connolly. Quennell was asked to leave Oxford in October 1925 for not complying with 'the University's standards' (Quennell, Marble Foot, 140) and never resumed his formal studies there. Evelyn Waugh commented that he had been reputedly 'Consorting with a woman called Cara who [threatened] to bring an action against the proctors' (The Diaries of Evelyn Waugh, 1976, 228). Quennell joined Sacheverell Sitwell, who was honeymooning in Amalfi, where he learned from artistic guests the value of a daily writing discipline as well as the delights of an evening's social banter.

On his return to London Quennell made ends meet by reviewing books. He also abandoned writing poetry and began developing a prose style characterized by elegance, clarity, concreteness, and precision. He is perhaps best known as a biographer and readily admitted T. S. Eliot's influence on his long career examining others' lives. Eliot, he noted, encouraged him to write a biography of Baudelaire. Quennell threw himself into the project and produced the impressive Baudelaire and the Symbolists: Five Essays (1929). On 2 July 1928 Quennell married Nancy Marianne (b. 1904/5), the daughter of Edward Stallibrass, a civil engineer. In 1930 Quennell accepted a three-year teaching post in the English department at Tokyo Bunrika Daigaku University. On arrival, however, he immediately realized that the department head despaired of his youth and lack of experience. Dealing with adjustments to marriage, intense culture shock, and his employer's lack of confidence in him, Quennell endured only one year in Tokyo—including a side trip to China—before resigning his post to return to London. His dismal experience in Asia is recounted in A Superficial Journey through Tokyo and Peking (1932). After divorce from his first wife, on 11 July 1935 he married Marcelle Marie José (b. 1914/15), the daughter of Hadelin Pierre Rothé, a diplomat. This marriage too soon ended in divorce, and on 22 February 1938 he married Joyce Frances Glur (b. 1917/18), the daughter of Charles Warwick-Evans, a musician. Shortly after this he became involved with the writer Barbara Skelton and shared a flat with her.

In the 1930s Quennell returned to biography with the first of four studies of Byron, Byron: the Years of Fame (1935). These are considered fine examples of his authority as a historian and stylist. Quennell's biographies—which also included those of Shakespeare, Pope, Johnson, Ruskin, Hogarth, and Caroline of Ansbach—display an uncanny gift for recreating the period in which a subject lived and worked, and for connecting past with present in a lively, sophisticated style that appealed to both scholar and general reader.

The Second World War brought a series of dull administrative posts with the Ministry of Information, Ministry of Economic Warfare, fire service, and Radio News Reel. Still, he managed to enjoy a convivial bohemian existence in London, attending parties, writing, and cultivating personal and professional relationships. After the war Quennell worked as an advertising copywriter, handling his agency's account with Elizabeth Arden in New York. Although he made good money, he left the agency to review books for the Daily Mail (1943–56) and eventually secured a position as editor of Cornhill Magazine (1944–51). Quennell is well known for his co-editorship—along with historian Alan Hodge—of History Today (1951–79); the magazine's reputation for sound scholarship, engaging style, and fine illustrations owes much to Quennell's leadership.

Following a third divorce Quennell married Sonia Geraldine Leon (b. 1928/9) on 23 May 1956; they had a daughter, Sarah. When this relationship ended he was married lastly, on 26 April 1967, to (Joan) Marilyn Peek, née Kerr (b. 1928/9), with whom he had a son, Alexander. He guarded his wives' privacy and that of his children zealously. This devotion to protecting his private life is evident in his critically and popularly praised volumes of autobiography: The Marble Foot: an Autobiography, 1905–1938 (1977) and The Wanton Chase: an Autobiography from 1939 (1980). A tall, trim man with closely cropped dark hair combed back from his forehead, Quennell exuded elegance and charm. He was a willing and perceptive conversationalist and devoted enormous energy and considerable intellect to his many different writing and editorial tasks. Despite an active social and travel schedule, Quennell wrote some thirty books and edited thirty-seven more. He was made a commander of the Order of the British Empire in 1973 and was knighted in 1992. He died in University College Hospital, Camden, London, on 27 October 1993; his funeral was held at St Mark's Church, Regent's Park.

JAMES B. DENIGAN

Sources P. Quennell, The marble foot: an autobiography, 1905–1938 (1977) · P. Quennell, The wanton chase: an autobiography from 1939 (1980) · S. Serafin, ed., Twentieth-century British literary biographers, DLitB, 155 (1995) · 'Quennell, Peter (Courtney)', Current Biography Yearbook (1984), 334–7 · B. Brothers and G. M. Gergits, eds., British travel writers, 1910–1939, DLitB, 195 (1998) · D. Fallowell, 'Mr and Mrs Peter Quennell at home', American Scholar, 61 (1992), 598–601 · B. Lambert, 'Peter Quennell, a man of letters and man about town, dies at 88', New York Times (31 Oct 1993) [final edition] · M. Grant, 'Sir Peter Quennell, 1905–1993: an appreciation', History Today, 43 (Dec 1993), 50 · b. cert. · m. cert. [Joyce Frances Glur] · m. cert. [Sonia Geraldine Leon] · m. cert. [Joan Marilyn Peek] · m. cert. [Nancy Marianne Stallibrass] · m. cert. [Marcelle Marie José Rothé] · d. cert.

Archives Ransom HRC, corresp. and literary MSS | King's AC Cam., letters to Clive Bell

Quesnel [Quesuel], **Peter** (fl. c.1320), Franciscan friar and canonist pastoral theologian, is known only through his popular handbook, Directorium iuris in foro conscientiae et juridiciali, where he is referred to in at least one early manuscript as a Franciscan friar. Bale states that a copy of his work was in the library of Norwich Cathedral priory, on the basis of which he was later believed to be a Franciscan of Norwich, but without supporting evidence. The identification of Quesnel with John the Canon (Juan Marbres, canon of Tortosa), made in the colophons of the first and second books of the first edition of the Quaestiones *super physica* of Canonicus (Padua, 1475), is without foundation. The facts that he used the *Summa confessorum* of Johann von Freiburg, written about 1300, and that his book was in circulation in England by about 1350, when Master Simon Bredon (*d.* 1372) had a copy (now MS 223 in the library of Merton College, Oxford), show that he must have been at work about 1320. The work was intended to be a practical guide to the administration of the sacraments in the light of up-to-date canon law, and in most manuscripts was accompanied by a full index. Besides Johann von Freiburg's work, Quesnel made extensive use of that of the thirteenth-century canonist Ramón de Peñafort. In the fifteenth century, his work became popular throughout Europe; it survives in at least sixteen manuscripts, and was known to the Franciscan bibliographers in five more in Spain, Italy, France, Germany, and Bohemia.   JEREMY CATTO

Sources *Directorium iuris in foro conscientiae et juridiciali*, Bibliothèque Royale, Brussels, MSS 225–226 (2549), 152–154 (2550) • *Directorium iuris in foro conscientiae et juridiciali*, Merton Oxf., MS 223 • Bale, *Index*, 323 • L. Waddingus [L. Wadding], *Scriptores ordinis minorum*, [new edn] (1806), 195, 604 • Johannes a Sancto Antonio, ed., *Bibliotheca universa Franciscana*, 2 (1732), 467 • Tanner, *Bibl. Brit.-Hib.*, 610–11 • A. Teetaert, 'Quesvel, Pierre', *Dictionnaire de théologie catholique*, ed. A. Vacant and others (Paris, 1903–72)
Archives Merton Oxf., MS 223 • Royal Library of Belgium, Brussels, MSS 225–226

Quick, Henry (1792–1857), poet, was born on 4 December 1792 in Zennor, Cornwall, the son of Henry Quick (1754–1805), a miner, and his wife, Margery, *née* George (1759–1834). Quick spent his life in Zennor, and from an early age wrote rugged verses for the countryside. He attended school until about the age of eight, and his first work was printed in 1826. From 1830 until his death he commemorated in verse all the local calamities and crimes, usually closing each poem with a religious exhortation. Most of his works were printed as broadsides, which he distributed along with the popular journals procured monthly from Penzance which supplied his income. On 25 October 1835 he married Jane Rowe (*c.*1767–1855), a widow much older than himself, because he 'needed someone to care for him' (Pool, 3).

In 1836 Quick wrote his *Life and Progress* in eighty-nine verses. He also printed *A New Copy, &c., on the Glorious Coronation of Queen Victoria* (1838), *A New Copy of Verses on the Scarcity of the Present Season and Dreadful Famine in Ireland* (1848), and similar minor works both in verse and prose.

An engraving by R. T. Pentreath depicts Quick in curious costume, with a printed sheet in his hand and a basket under his arm, distributing his poems and pamphlets. (Millett, 36). He died of tuberculosis at his home, Mill Hill Down, Zennor, on 9 October 1857, and was buried in the local churchyard three days later.

G. LE G. NORGATE, rev. MEGAN A. STEPHAN

Sources P. A. S. Pool, ed., *The life and progress of Henry Quick of Zennor* (1963); rev. edn (1984) • G. B. Millett, *Penzance, past and present* (1876) • Boase, *Mod. Eng. biog.*, 2.1688 • *Cornish Telegraph* (21 Oct 1857)

Likenesses R. T. Pentreath, wood-engraving, repro. in Millett, *Penzance, past and present*, 36 • photograph (after print by R. T. Pentreath, 1833), repro. in Pool, *Life and progress of Henry Quick*, frontispiece

Quick, John (*bap.* 1636, *d.* 1706), clergyman and ejected minister, was born at Plymouth and baptized at St Andrew's Church, Plymouth, on 19 June 1636, the son of Thomas Quick and his wife, Ann (*bap.* 1608), who was probably the daughter of John Hunt. He had one brother, Philip, who died at the age of twenty-five. John entered Exeter College, Oxford, as a servitor in 1653, matriculating on 20 July 1654. Both the rector of Exeter College, John Conant, and Quick's tutor, John Saunders, were strong puritans and Quick was undoubtedly influenced by the prevailing climate in the university and the country. He graduated BA in 1657 and began preaching shortly afterwards at Ermington, Devon. He was ordained on 2 February 1659 at Plymouth, having been already presented by the corporation of Exeter on 3 November 1658 to the vicarage of Kingsbridge-with-Churchstow, Devon, for which he undertook to pay £4 yearly to the sequestered vicar Robert Sparke.

Following the Restoration in 1660, Quick was ejected; he then acquired the curacy of Brixton, Devon, but was again ejected when the Act of Uniformity came into force in August 1662. He resumed preaching, however, when no one was appointed in his place, and on Sunday 13 December 1663, while preaching his morning sermon, he was arrested following action by Bishop Seth Ward. As Ward wrote on 19 December:

> my diocese had not one outed presbyter who dared to preach publicly for these 12 months past (at least wch I have heard of). Till a while since, one Quick, ejected out of Brixton, undertook boldly to preach there. I did what I was obliged to do, and he is now prisoner … in the Castle of Exon, to wch he was brought this week … He saith that after his removal, he stayed some months, to see whether any other would supply his place, but at length finding that no man was put in his stead and that the people went off, some to atheism and debauchery, others to Sectarism (for he is a Presbyterian) he resolved to adventure to gather his flock again … And he had gathered as I am told a flock of 1500 or 2000 upon Sunday last when … he was taken from the pulpit and brought away. (*Calamy rev.*)

The justices accepted Quick's counsel's contention that the indictment was flawed and of no legal force, but Quick would not enter into sureties for good behaviour, nor promise to give up preaching. He was sentenced to gaol for three months and a day. Ward then had him prosecuted for preaching to his fellow prisoners, but he was acquitted. At Devon assizes in March 1664 Quick was released and bound in £40 and two sureties to prosecute his traverse; according to Edmund Calamy, though suffering from consumption at the time of his imprisonment he had 'perfectly recovered when he came out' (Calamy, *Abridgement*, 2.247). At an unknown date Quick married Elizabeth (*d.* 1708), daughter of Colonel George Cook, of Essex, and Mary Glover, descended from Robert Glover, the Marian martyr; they had at least three daughters.

On 11 April 1672 Quick was licensed to preach in Plymouth but the following year he was imprisoned with other nonconformist preachers there. On release he moved to London and took charge of a congregation in Bridge Street, Covent Garden, but on 16 October 1680 he was appointed pastor of the English church at Middleburg in the Netherlands, where he settled on 5 January 1681. However, he ran into trouble with the Zeeland authorities for his refusal to administer the sacraments according to Dutch forms. On 27 April he announced to the consistory that he intended to accept a position as chaplain to the countess of Donegal, and on 23 May he gave them leave to elect his successor. Quick left Middleburg on 6 July 1681 and was back in London by 22 July. There he gathered a presbyterian congregation in a small meeting-house in Middlesex Court, Smithfield, which abutted the church of St Bartholomew-the-Great, and even afforded a view into it. Quick was fined and imprisoned in 1682, but in 1687 he was one of those who took advantage of James I's declaration of indulgence, and was apparently not further troubled in his ministry at Smithfield. He was certified as a preacher there in 1689.

Quick also maintained contact with the west country for many years. On 10 August 1681 he preached the funeral sermon for Philip Harris of Alston in Devon, and in May 1699 he was present at the Exeter assembly of ministers. His west-country connections may explain his interest in French protestantism, Plymouth being home to an important Huguenot community after 1680; he wrote a substantial two-volume work on French protestantism, *Synodicon in Gallia reformata* (1692), and in 1700 made arrangements to publish a three-volume work, 'Icones sacrae Anglicanae', containing accounts of many French and English divines, but was too ill to collect the necessary subscriptions. From about this time onwards 'His bodily pains by the stone were frequent for six years, and scarce tolerable for the last three' (Williams, 34).

John Quick died on 29 April 1706 in London. Funeral sermons were preached by his successor, Thomas Freke, and by Daniel Williams, who recalled that 'Though his temper was sudden, he was a very tender relation, exceeding compassionate to the distressed' (Williams, 36). Quick left money to two French refugee ministers and to the poor of the French church in London, but his most important bequest was the manuscript of 'Icones', now at Dr Williams's Library, Gordon Square, London, a valuable source for west-country nonconformity and used by Calamy for seven of his lives of ejected ministers. Quick was survived by his wife, who died in 1708, and one of his daughters, Elizabeth.

ALEXANDER GORDON, rev. STEPHEN WRIGHT

Sources Calamy rev. • D. Williams, *A funeral-sermon occasioned by the death of the Reverend Mr John Quick, minister of the gospel, preached May the 7th, 1706* (1706) • E. Calamy, ed., *An abridgement of Mr. Baxter's history of his life and times, with an account of the ministers, &c., who were ejected after the Restauration of King Charles II*, 2nd edn, 2 vols. (1713) • C. Whiting, *Studies in English puritanism* (1931) • Wood, *Ath. Oxon.*, new edn • M. Burrows, ed., *The register of the visitors of the University of Oxford, from AD 1647 to AD 1658*, CS, new ser., 29 (1881) • Foster, *Alum. Oxon.* • J. Quick, *The triumph of faith: a funeral sermon preached to a church of Christ, at the meeting-house in Bartholomew-Close, London, January 16, 1697* (1698) • A. Brockett, ed., *The Exeter assembly: the minutes of the assemblies of the United Brethren of Devon and Cornwall, 1691–1717*, Devon and Cornwall RS, new ser., 6 (1963) • IGI

Archives DWL, icones sacrae Anglicanae

Likenesses J. Sturt, line engraving, BM, NPG; repro. in J. Quick, *Synodicon in Gallia reformata*, 2 vols. (1692), frontispiece

Quick, John (1748–1831), actor, was born in Whitechapel, London, the son of a brewer. He allegedly left home when he was about fourteen to become an actor and joined a strolling company run by Oliver Carr. Before he was eighteen he supposedly played Altamont in Nicholas Rowe's *The Fair Penitent* at Fulham or Croydon and Hamlet, Richard III, Romeo, George Barnwell, Jaffeir, and Tancred.

Quick's versatility as an actor recommended him to Samuel Foote at the Haymarket, where he made his first appearance on 18 June 1766, as Folly in Henry Fielding's *The Miser* and as Jasper in David Garrick's *Miss in her Teens*. He also acted that season in Barry's company at the King's Theatre, first appearing there on 13 August 1766. Although he returned to Foote's company in the summer of 1767, he came more prominently to notice when he played Beau Mordecai in *Love à la Mode* for Edward Shuter's benefit at Covent Garden on 9 June 1767. Charles Macklin, who wrote the play, instructed Quick in the part. Subsequently recommended to George Colman, then a patentee of Covent Garden Theatre, Quick commenced an engagement there by playing James, in Fielding's *The Mock Doctor*, on 14 September 1767. A further boost to his career occurred when, on the recommendation of Joseph Younger, he was cast as Mungo, in Isaac Bickerstaff's *The Padlock*, on 23 October 1770. Although he was reluctant to play the part so soon after Dibdin, Quick's success paved the way to future laurels. He subsequently created Tony Lumpkin in *She Stoops to Conquer* (14 March 1773), winning the praises of both the public and of Goldsmith, and two Sheridan characters, Bob Acres in *The Rivals* (17 January 1775) and Isaac Mendoza in *The Duenna* (9 November 1776). Quick became one of the leading performers at Covent Garden, able to choose the characters he played, and a great favourite of George III.

Quick also appeared in Bristol in 1768 and 1769, playing relatively minor roles, and from 1775 to 1778 he was a shareholder and joint manager of the Bristol theatre. At Bristol, on 16 November 1772, Quick married Anna Parker (*c.*1751–1819), a clergyman's daughter. For his Bristol benefit in September 1776 he played Richard III; although he commenced the role seriously, he soon succumbed to burlesque when he found his audience inclined to mirth. After he had disposed of his share in the theatre he played summer engagements at Liverpool, Richmond, Weymouth, Southampton, Portsmouth, Brighton, Windsor, Cheltenham, and Gloucester, although he frequently revisited Bristol, partly to visit the Hotwells for health reasons.

When Quick's articles expired at the end of the 1797–8 Covent Garden season, he stipulated that the following season he should not play in both the comedy and the farce on the same night because of poor health. Harris, the manager, objecting to Quick's demand, gave his line of parts to Joseph Shepherd Munden. Thus, says Genest,

Quick 'seems to have thrown himself out of a good engagement rather foolishly' (Genest, 7.378). When he later undertook an engagement at Bath and Bristol, where he played in both play and farce, he made sure the bills stated that he was acting by permission of the manager of Covent Garden. Gilliland states that Quick subsequently undertook a number of lucrative engagements in the provinces, visiting Edinburgh, York, Hull, Birmingham, and Liverpool. On 9 May 1799 he made his first appearance on the Drury Lane stage for Elizabeth Leake's benefit. The remainder of his professional career consisted of sporadic appearances in the patent theatres and a number of provincial tours. Quick would, adds Gilliland in 1808, return to the London stage if an adequate offer was made. In fact a manuscript letter to the *Monthly Mirror* from its Edinburgh correspondent in March 1800 forbears detailing Quick's recent engagement there on the grounds that 'he is still I hope to be considered a London Performer'. His last appearance was at the Haymarket Theatre for Mrs Mattocks's benefit, on 24 May 1813.

Quick, says Hazlitt, made 'an excellent, self-important, busy, strutting, money-getting citizen; or crusty old guardian, in a brown suit and a bob wig' (*London Magazine*, January 1820). He was widely praised for his performances as old men. 'There was a peculiarity in his voice which rendered his old characters exceedingly whimsical' (Jenkins, 2.91). He was also successful in Shakespearian roles, such as the First Gravedigger, Dromio of Ephesus, Launce, and Launcelot Gobbo. For his Covent Garden benefit on 6 April 1790 he again attempted Richard III, in earnest, with slightly more success than at Bristol, but his audience evidently hoped for a comic performance.

Boaden saw Quick as an actor 'of very great and peculiar merits' (Russell, 211). His squat figure seemed perfect for many of the parts he played: 'The person of Mr Quick', wrote Gilliland, 'is happily formed for a comedian; with features beaming with good humour, he has eyes particularly expressive of mirth, and a facetiousness of disposition' (Gilliland, 2.926). The author of the *Candid and Impartial Strictures* remembered Quick as:

> long and deservedly a favourite of the town—his comic talents were purely original—they were not richly fraught with a mellowness of humour, but still they possessed a certain quaintness and whimsicality which proved an irresistible incentive to laughter … he had not much variety, but his entrances were always the signal for hearty merriment. (*Strictures*, 52)

Pasquin refers to Quick

> With his gibes and his quiddities, cranks and his wiles, His croak and his halt, and his smirks and his smiles (Pasquin, 51)

while Bellamy declares him the 'prince of low comedians' (Bellamy, 23) and a natural successor to Parsons.

Yet aspects of Quick's acting were also criticized. The *Strictures* felt his voice, deportment, and action were always the same, whatever the part. Early in his career he was accused of grimacing: 'he is now too apt … to screw the muscles of his face into many ridiculous forms' (Hawkins, 50). That his acting was viewed ambivalently and that his departure from Covent Garden might also have

been hastened by changes in fashion is implicit in *Records of a Stage Veteran*: 'his acting went out of fashion when a more intellectual school appeared. Munden knew little, but Quick knew less; noise and extravagance were with him substituted for nature and humour.' (Russell, 210) He was unfavourably compared with William Dowton, 'who rounded off the square corners of Quick's old men, and brought them nearer if not quite to the standard of nature and truth'. As a result he 'quitted the stage in disgust', while still at the height of his powers. According to the same account he was extremely vain:

> He believed in no living actor but himself. The dead he lauded indiscriminately (except Foote of whom he equally disliked to speak or hear), and the mere mention of the name of a new performer playing one of his original characters would make him silent for the evening. (ibid.)

Most accounts of Quick paint a kinder portrait. 'In private life', said Richard Jenkins, he 'was much esteemed; though not extravagant, he was generous; and, though partial to a domestic life, was occasionally a cheerful and facetious companion abroad' (Jenkins, 2.92). John O'Keeffe recalled 'many instances of good will and kindness' (O'Keeffe, 2.333) from him. Ann Mathews, who called him 'Little Quick (the retired Dioclesian of Islington), with his squeak like a Bart'lemew fiddle', refers to him as 'a pleasant little fellow', who had not 'an atom of improper consequence in his composition' (Russell, 210). Fond of punch, he had been warned by his doctors while still at Covent Garden to give it up or it would be the death of him, but he continued drinking it until the end of his life. He was reputedly an early riser and a great walker. Up until the last day of his life he regularly visited the King's Head opposite Islington church, although a newspaper clipping in the Billy Rose collection describes him visiting the Mail Coach.

Quick died at his home, 122 Upper Street, Islington, on 4 April 1831, at the age of eighty-four. The *Gentleman's Magazine* referred to him as 'the [John] Liston of his day' and as 'one of the last of the Garrick school' (GM, 1st ser., 101, 1831, 474). He was buried in the old chapel of ease at Islington church, Lower Holloway Road, beside his wife, who had died in 1819. He had reputedly retired with a fortune of £10,000 and was able to leave significant amounts to both offspring. His will, which was in a very tattered condition—according to an affidavit from his servant, he had constantly carried it about with him in a side pocket of his coat—was proved at Doctor's Commons. JIM DAVIS

Sources Genest, *Eng. stage* · T. Gilliland, *The dramatic mirror, containing the history of the stage from the earliest period, to the present time*, 2 vols. (1808) · R. Jenkins, *Memoirs of the Bristol stage*, 2 vols. (1826) · GM, 1st ser., 101/1 (1831), 474 · W. C. Russell, *Representative actors* [1888] · *Le Beau Monde Magazine* (March 1809) · *The thespian dictionary, or, Dramatic biography of the present age*, 2nd edn (1805) · *Candid and impartial strictures on the performers* (1795) · A. Pasquin [J. Williams], *The children of Thespis*, 13th edn (1792) · T. Bellamy, 'The London theatres: a poem', *Miscellanies in prose and verse*, 2 vols. (1794–5) · W. Hazlitt, 'On play-going and on some of our old actors', *London Magazine*, 1 (1820) · T. Davies, *Dramatic miscellanies*, new edn, 3 vols. (1785) · J. O'Keeffe, *Recollections of the life of John O'Keeffe, written by himself*, 2 vols. (1826) · *Bristol Gazette* (23 Nov 1775) · *Felix Farley's Bristol Journal* (14 Sept 1776) · clippings, Theatre Museum, London ·

clippings, Harvard TC · clippings, NYPL · Highfill, Burnim & Langhans, *BDA* · *London Chronicle* (26 Nov 1772) · W. Hawkins, *Miscellanies in prose and verse, containing candid and impartial observations on the principal performers belonging to the two Theatres-Royal, from January 1773 to May 1775* (1775)

Archives Harvard TC, letters · Theatre Museum, London, letters **Likenesses** T. Parkinson, oils, 1774, University of Victoria, British Columbia, Robertson Davies collection · J. Zoffany, oils, *c.*1777, Garr. Club · mezzotint, pubd 1777 (after unknown portrait), NPG · S. Harding, drawing, *c.*1789, Harvard U., Widener Library · T. Lawranson, oils, *c.*1789, NPG · G. Dupont, oils, exh. RA 1794, Garr. Club · S. De Wilde, oils, 1796, Yale U. CBA · S. De Wilde, oils, 1805, Garr. Club · J. Hopwood, stipple, pubd 1807 (after S. De Wilde), BM, NPG · S. De Wilde, watercolour drawing, Harvard TC · R. Dighton, pen, brown ink, and watercolour drawing (as Isaac Mendoza in *The Duenna*), Garr. Club · J. Nixon, pencil, pen, black ink, and wash drawing, Garr. Club · J. Roberts, coloured drawing (as Judge Gripus in Dryden's *Amphytrion*), BM · J. Zoffany, group portrait, oils (in *Speculation*), Garr. Club · engravings, Theatre Museum, London · engravings, Harvard TC · oils (as Isaac Mendoza in *The Duenna*), Garr. Club · prints, BM, NPG

Wealth at death personal estate, sworn at under £6000, divided between son and daughter, apart from an annuity of £25 to a friend and £20 to a maid: *GM*; unidentified clipping, Theatre Museum, London

Quick, Sir John (1852–1932), lawyer and politician in Australia, was born at Trevega, Towednack, near St Ives, Cornwall, on 22 April 1852, the only child of John Quick, a farmer, and his wife, Mary, the daughter of James Quick, of Trevega. The family arrived in Victoria in October 1854 to search for gold, but the father died at Bendigo shortly after their arrival, leaving his wife and child badly off. Quick attended various schools until he was ten, and then, to help support his mother, worked successively in a foundry, a goldmine (above ground), and a printing press. Eventually, when he was seventeen, he became a reporter on the Bendigo *Independent* and, later, on the *Bendigo Advertiser*.

Quick decided to study law, and in 1874 entered the University of Melbourne. He graduated LLB in April 1877, and was admitted to the Victorian bar in June 1878. While studying law he had worked as a reporter with *The Age*; he now became leader of its parliamentary staff, and so entered political circles. He became a strong supporter of the 'liberal' party of Graham Berry, advocating protection and land reform. Encouraged by Berry, he stood for the Victorian parliament in July 1880, and was returned as one of the members for Sandhurst (Bendigo). He began practice as a barrister at Bendigo, and in April 1882 was admitted to the degree of LLD by the University of Melbourne. On 24 December 1883 he married Catherine (*d.* 1938), the daughter of Joseph Harris from Liskeard, Cornwall, a mine manager and former mayor of nearby Eaglehawk; they had no children of their own, but brought up a niece of Catherine Quick as their daughter. Quick built up a good legal practice in Bendigo, becoming senior partner of Quick, Hyett and Rymer there, while also, as an independent member, playing an active part in Victorian politics until he lost his seat in 1889.

Quick was keenly interested in Australian federation. The federal movement received popular impetus after

Sir John Quick (1852–1932), by Portia Geach, *c.*1910

July 1893, when a conference was held at Corowa of delegates from many voluntary organizations including the Australian Natives' Association, which Quick represented, despite not being Australian born. At Corowa Quick was chiefly responsible for the formulation and adoption of the idea that each colony should pass an act for the election of representatives to a federal convention; the draft constitution would then be submitted to a popular referendum. Quick drafted a model bill for submission to the six colonial parliaments, and for the next few years was tireless in getting these ideas adopted. He also proposed at an unofficial 'People's Federal Convention', held at Bathurst in November 1896, that the senate in the federal constitution be elected democratically by the people, not by state legislatures. In 1897 he was one of the ten Victorian delegates elected to the constitutional convention, and his work for federation was recognized by his being knighted on 1 January 1901.

In 1901 Quick was returned unopposed to the commonwealth parliament for Bendigo, and held the seat until 1913. From December 1904 to July 1907 he was chairman of a royal commission on commonwealth tariffs, whose rather inconclusive reports were ignored when in 1908 the government decided to impose higher duties, with preferential rates to Great Britain. Quick helped to bring about the Deakin–Cook (anti-Labor) 'fusion' government of 1909–10, in which he gained ministerial office as postmaster-general. On his defeat in 1913 he retired from politics, and he devoted himself to his legal practice and business interests until June 1922, when he became deputy president of the commonwealth arbitration court. Here, until his retirement in 1930, his even-handed judgments won him wide respect.

Throughout his life Quick retained his interest in literature, from his presidency of the Shakespeare and Pickwick societies in Bendigo to his membership of the Author's Society in Melbourne, where he was also patron of the Australian Literary Society and began to compile a bibliography of Australian literature (completed and published in 1940). His other chief publications were *The History of Land Tenure in the Colony of Victoria* (1883), *The Annotated Constitution of the Australian Commonwealth* (with Sir Robert Garran, 1901), *The Judicial Power of the Commonwealth* (with Sir Littleton Groom, 1904), and *Legislative Powers of the Commonwealth and the States of Australia* (1919). They show his unmatched grasp of constitutional matters and his desire that the public of the new commonwealth be well informed on such matters.

Quick died on 17 June 1932 at his home in the Melbourne suburb of Camberwell, survived by his wife. He was buried on 20 June in Back Creek cemetery, Bendigo. His colleague Garran likened himself to the 'junior partner of a steam-roller', but undoubtedly Quick's painstaking, meticulous, and determined work enabled the federal movement to achieve success earlier than it would otherwise have done.

HERBERT BURTON, rev. ELIZABETH BAIGENT

Sources J. Quick, *Sir John Quick's notebook*, ed. L. E. Fredman (1965) · *AusDB* · A. Deakin, *The federal story: the inner history of the federal cause*, ed. J. A. La Nauze, 2nd edn (1963) · *The Times* (18 June 1932) · *The Age* [Melbourne] (18 June 1932) · J. A. La Nauze, *The making of the Australian constitution* (1972) · R. R. Garran, *Prosper the commonwealth* (1958) · C. Daley, 'Sir John Quick: a distinguished Australian', *Victorian Historical Magazine*, 15 (1934), 33–52 · *The Argus* [Melbourne] (18 June 1932) · *The Argus* [Melbourne] (20 June 1932)
Archives NL Aus., corresp. with Alfred Deakin
Likenesses P. Geach, portrait, *c*.1910, NL Aus. [*see illus.*] · W. B. McInnes, oils, Bendigo Art Gallery, Victoria, Australia; repro. in Daley, 'Sir John Quick'
Wealth at death A£10,706 8*s.* 6*d.*—in Australia, estate sworn for probate: Supreme Court of Victoria, probate division

Quick, Oliver Chase (1885–1944), theologian, was born on 21 June 1885 at Sedbergh vicarage, Yorkshire, the only son of Robert Hebert *Quick (1831–1891), educationist, and Bertha, daughter of General Chase Parr of the Indian army. He was Anderson scholar and head of school at Harrow School, winning a scholarship to Corpus Christi College, Oxford, in 1904. He gained a first class in classical moderations, but, partly because of intellectual differences with his tutor, F. C. S. Schiller, was placed in the third class in Greats in 1908. Turning to theology, he won the Ellerton prize in 1911 for an essay on mysticism. After a year at Bishop's Hostel, Farnham, he was ordained deacon in 1911 and priest in 1913, serving curacies in Beckenham and Wolverhampton. He became a friend of H. R. L. (Dick) Sheppard and member of the so-called Clique associated with Oxford House, Bethnal Green. After two years as vice-principal of Leeds Clergy School from 1913, he served as Sheppard's curate at St Martin-in-the-Fields until his appointment as domestic chaplain to Randall Davidson, archbishop of Canterbury, in 1915. He published his *Essays in Orthodoxy*, much influenced by Charles Gore, in 1916. In 1917 he married Davidson's secretary, Frances Winifred,

daughter of Hugh William Pearson, of Malton, Yorkshire. They had two sons and two daughters.

After a year as army chaplain, where Quick was associated with his former principal, B. K. Cunningham, at the chaplains' school at St Omer, he became vicar of Kenley, Surrey, in 1918. A series of residentiary canonries followed, beginning with Newcastle in 1920 and Carlisle in 1923, which gave him the opportunity to lecture widely. He published several volumes of lectures and addresses, including his 1922 Paddock lectures, *Liberalism, Modernism and Tradition*, delivered at the General Theological Seminary, New York. His powers of synthesis made him an obvious choice for membership of the archbishops' commission on doctrine set up in 1922. He made a considerable contribution, forming a close friendship with the chairman, William Temple.

In 1927 Quick published *The Christian Sacraments* which became an important part of the debate over Anglican orders. He was a keen ecumenist, taking part in the Missionary Conference in Jerusalem in 1928, and the Faith and Order conferences in Lausanne in 1927 and Edinburgh in 1937, where he contributed an influential paper. In 1930 he became a canon of St Paul's, an institution he found backward-looking, but where he wrote his apologetic works, *The Ground of Faith and the Chaos of Thought* (1931) and *The Gospel of Divine Action* (1933), which sought to 'soften the lines at present dividing our "schools of thought"' (*The Gospel of Divine Action*, viii). In 1934 Hensley Henson, the bishop of Durham, offered him the professorship at Durham which carried a canonry, where he wrote *Doctrines of the Creeds* (1938), 'one of the outstanding books on Christian doctrine of our generation' (Robinson, 62).

In 1939 he was appointed regius professor of divinity and canon of Christ Church, Oxford, where, although hampered by illness and producing no substantial writings, he made an impact through his lectures on the atonement (published posthumously as *The Gospel of the New World*, 1944), which attempted to reconcile competing theories. He was awarded honorary DDs from St Andrews in 1928, Oxford in 1939, and Durham in 1941, and became chaplain to the king in 1933. In August 1943 he collapsed in the cathedral and was forced into retirement in December of that year. He died at his home at Larch Hill, Longborough, Gloucestershire, on 21 January 1944 and was buried four days later in Lonborough churchyard; he was survived by his wife.

Quick, who possessed a personal humility and a sense of humour 'both lively and dry, like good champagne' (Mozley, 'Quick as a theologian', 8), was primarily a philosophical theologian with a theological temper both 'catholic and evangelical, and at the same time inherently Anglican' (Mozley, *Tendencies*, 87). Although he was criticized for lacking an acute historical sense and for being 'tone-deaf' to religious experience (Robinson, 62), his 'liberal orthodoxy' (Ramsey, 107), which listened to all opinions, was influential on the post-war generation of Anglican theologians.

MARK D. CHAPMAN

Sources W. Temple, 'Memoir', in O. C. Quick, *The gospel of the new world* (1944), ix–xiv · D. M. MacKinnon, 'Oliver Chase Quick as a theologian', *Theology*, 96 (1993), 101–17 • J. K. Mozley, *Some tendencies in British theology* (1951) • *The Times* (24 Jan 1944) • *Church Times* (28 Jan 1944) • R. Ellis Roberts, *H. R. L. Sheppard* (1942) • A. M. Ramsey, *From Gore to Temple* (1960) • J. K. Mozley, 'Oliver Quick as a theologian', *Theology*, 48 (1945), 6–11, 30–36 • J. A. T. Robinson, *Honest to God* (1963) • *CGPLA Eng. & Wales* (1944)

Archives LPL, letters to H. R. L. Sheppard

Wealth at death £18,574 3s. 3d.: probate, 21 July 1944, *CGPLA Eng. & Wales*

Quick, Robert Hebert (1831–1891), educationist, was born on 20 September 1831 in London, the eldest son of James Carthew Quick, a prosperous merchant. He had a brother, Frederick James Quick (1837–1902), a tea and coffee importer, who endowed the Quick chair of biology at Cambridge. Delicate health, the result of a childhood attack of measles, interrupted his education. He attended schools conducted by Miss Gutty and by Miss Burrows, and then a private school at Weybridge, before entering Harrow School in 1846. Poor health forced his removal, and he was taught by private tutors before his admission to Trinity College, Cambridge, in 1849. Graduating as senior optime in the mathematical tripos in 1854, he was ordained in the following year, becoming unpaid curate to his lifelong friend, J. Llewelyn Davies, at St Mark, Whitechapel, until 1856, and afterwards at Christ Church, Marylebone. Travels in Germany stimulated an interest in modern languages. He returned to England in 1858 and accepted a mastership at Lancaster grammar school, where he taught classics and mathematics. Subsequently he held appointments at Guildford grammar school, at the recently founded Woodard Society school, St John's Hurstpierpoint, and at the Surrey county school, which opened at Cranleigh in 1865, where he gave important assistance to the first headmaster, Joseph Merriman.

In 1868 Quick published *Essays on Educational Reformers*, which was to prove a classic work of pedagogic theory. Based on practical experience of teaching, it provided a readable approach to the educational ideas of earlier writers, including Locke, Milton, Rousseau, and Pestalozzi, in a way that was relevant to current educational practice. In 1890, after several pirated American editions, a second English edition was published.

In 1869 Quick's former schoolfriend H. M. Butler offered him a mastership in modern languages at Harrow, which he held until 1874, when severe headaches, depression, and the laborious school routine caused his resignation. From 1876 to 1883 he ran a small preparatory school, at Orme Square, London, and then at Guildford. In 1876 he married Harriet Bertha (d. in or after 1891), daughter of General Chase Parr of the Bombay army. They had a daughter, Dora, and a son, Oliver Chase *Quick, who became regius professor of divinity at Oxford.

A strong supporter of training for teachers in secondary schools at a time when the need for this was far from generally accepted, Quick was appointed in 1879 by the newly formed teachers' training syndicate at Cambridge University to give a series of lectures on the history of education. He repeated the lectures in 1881 and 1883, but became dispirited and resigned in 1883. He returned to the ministry and was presented in 1883 by Trinity College to the living

Robert Hebert Quick (1831–1891), by unknown engraver, pubd 1899

of Sedbergh, Yorkshire. The strain of this position proved too much for his sensitive temperament, and he resigned in January 1887. He retired to Earlswood Cottage, Redhill, in Surrey, where he continued his literary activities, writing for *The Spectator* and the *Journal of Education*, and contributing articles on educational subjects to the *Encyclopaedia Britannica*. While visiting J. R. Seeley at Cambridge, Quick was stricken with apoplexy, and died there, at 7 St Peter's Terrace, on 9 March 1891. Shortly after his death the educational portion of his library was given to the Teachers' Guild, and later formed the Quick Memorial Library at the University of London. C. E. LINDGREN

Sources *Life and remains of Rev. R. H. Quick*, ed. F. Storr (1899) • J. Llewelyn Davies, H. M. Butler, J. R. Seeley, and others, memoirs, *Journal of Education*, new ser., 13 (1891), 221–7 • *The Athenaeum* (28 March 1891), 409 • Venn, *Alum. Cant.* • *CGPLA Eng. & Wales* (1891)

Archives King's AC Cam., letters to Oscar Browning

Likenesses engraving, repro. in *Life and remains of Rev. R. H. Quick*, frontispiece [see illus.] • photograph, repro. in *Life and remains of Rev. R. H. Quick* (1899)

Wealth at death £21,172 14s. 8d.: probate, 9 June 1891, *CGPLA Eng. & Wales*

Quickswood. For this title name *see* Cecil, Hugh Richard Heathcote Gascoyne-, Baron Quickswood (1869–1956).

Quig, Alexander Johnstone (1892–1962), industrialist, was born on 5 January 1892 in Glasgow, the son of Alexander Quig, mechanical engineer. He was educated at Glasgow high school, leaving in 1908 at the age of sixteen to go into Nobel's Explosives Company Ltd. During the First World War he joined first the Glasgow highlanders and London Scottish regiments to serve in France, followed by a period in India with the Highland light infantry. After five years' service he rejoined Nobel's, which later expanded into Nobel Industries Ltd. In 1925 Quig transferred to Nobel Chemical Finishes Ltd, a company jointly owned with Du Pont, and rose rapidly from general manager to managing director; in 1936 he became chairman. In 1926 Nobel Industries Ltd was one of the four major chemical companies in Britain which merged to form the giant Imperial Chemical Industries.

Quig's managerial experience stood him in good stead and at the beginning of 1939 he was made one of five new executive managers of ICI in a reorganization aimed at alleviating the workload of the hard-pressed board of directors. A year later he joined the full board as commercial director. He was instrumental in moving ICI away from the defensive alliances—such as that with Distillers—which had made it more secure but at the same time limited its scope in the 1930s, and proved himself more forceful and commercially aggressive than other ICI directors. By 1948, he was one of three deputy chairmen, from which position he retired in 1956.

Quig's background in the cut and thrust environment of the paints and lacquers industry had provided him with ample opportunity to develop a shrewd commercial expertise and in 1944 he was made a director of British Nylon Spinners Ltd, a company jointly set up in 1940 by ICI and Courtaulds. He was largely responsible for the development of BNS and the establishment during the late 1940s of spinning factories near Pontypool in Wales and close to ICI's Billingham works on Teesside. Quig felt that ICI's group chairmen tended to be involved in the chemical and technical aspects of their various businesses at the expense of the commercial side. He strongly backed the creation, after the Second World War, of a staff college for the training of incoming managerial staff.

Quig's reputation for expert management, developed during his Nobel and ICI years, was recognized outside the industry. He acted as chairman of the Industrial Management Research Association from 1946 to 1949, as well as being one of the founder members of the British Institute of Management. In 1948–9 he acted as chairman of a committee set up by the secretary of state for air to review the structure and management of the Air Ministry. In 1952, four years before his retirement, Quig married Joan Leason, the director of a box-manufacturing company, a widow and the daughter of Ernest Johns, a shipbuilder; they had no children. His Scottish roots were maintained in his membership of the Caledonian Club in London which boasted a large Scottish membership. He was also a member of the East India Club and the Royal Thames Yacht Club.

Quig, who listed farming as one of his hobbies, lived at and managed Combe Farm, near Bramley, Surrey, with its herd of Ayrshire cattle, for many years until his death. He died at the age of seventy in the Hospital of St John and St Elizabeth, Marylebone, London, on 13 December 1962, and was cremated at Golders Green crematorium on 18 December.   ANN K. NEWMARK

Sources WWW · *The Times* (14 Dec 1962) · W. J. Reader, *Imperial Chemical Industries, a history*, 2 (1975) · m. cert. · d. cert. · *Surrey Advertiser*

Wealth at death £240,041 9s.: probate, 28 Feb 1963, *CGPLA Eng. & Wales*

Quigley, Janet Muriel Alexander (1902–1987), radio broadcaster, was born on 10 May 1902 at 38 Mount Charles, Belfast, only daughter of Harold Harfager Quigley, a commercial traveller and later a company director, and his wife, Louisa Dobie. She was educated at Richmond Lodge (a Belfast girls' school) and Lady Margaret Hall, Oxford (1920–23), where she took a second in English. She worked in publishing and on the Empire Marketing Board before joining the BBC in 1930 in the foreign department; in 1936 she moved to the talks department where her main task was assessing what kind of talks might appeal to women. One of its first fruits was her production (helped by Guy Burgess, who also joined the talks department in 1936 and was already working as a clandestine Soviet spy) of *Towards National Health*, a twelve-part series in 1937 covering fitness and nutrition and an early example of social action broadcasting which combined self-help with an appeal to collectivism.

Quigley thereafter took charge of morning talks and those for women. Particularly influential was *The Kitchen Front*, a series of weekday morning 'talks to housewives' beginning in 1940 on the Home Service. With its hints on how to eke out rations, homilies on cod liver oil, and recipes for eggless pasta, this was regarded as a vital part of the war effort at a critical point in the nation's fortunes. The Ministry of Food (one of whose liaison officials with the BBC was Emily Blair, George Orwell's wife) decided what was said, vetoed the scripts, and sometimes picked the speakers. Inevitably this caused friction. When, from 1943, the slot also began to offer advice on clothes, mending, and fuel on a similar basis, Quigley urged that 'every precaution should be taken to prevent the other Ministries concerned from getting into anything like the same position of would-be dictators that the Ministry of Food has achieved over the years' (BBC WAC, memo to director of talks, 5 Aug 1943).

For her work on wartime radio talks, Quigley was appointed MBE in 1944. In 1945 she suggested 'a series of very simple talks on bringing-up children' (BBC WAC, memo to director of talks, 2 Jan 1945), saying the idea arose from a conference at the Ministry of Health which was starting a drive for 'better parentcraft' (ibid.): once again, she was showing how radio could assist public policy while remaining free of direct government control. She left the BBC in 1945 to marry, on 24 October 1945 in London, Kevin Columba Fitzgerald (d. 1993), an Irish businessman and writer. They went to live in Dublin. Each was forty-three years old and they produced no children, though he had a daughter from an earlier marriage.

Quigley returned to the BBC in 1950 as editor of *Woman's Hour* and accelerated the process, under way since the arrival of the first woman editor in 1947, of making it less staid. She introduced items on child guidance, loneliness, divorce, and marital difficulties (prompting the *Daily Mirror* in 1952 to label one woman's reference to the 'intimate' side of wedlock as the programme's 'frankest ever talk'). Items on the menopause, however, were not broadcast during school holidays. In one of her last memos as editor, seeking permission to cover a conference on prostitution, she outlined her editorial philosophy:

> This would be in accordance with the policy which we try to follow in *Woman's Hour* of bringing 'hush-hush' topics into the open, so that the less-educated amongst our listeners may get used to the idea that no subject which concerns them as citizens need be taboo.   (BBC WAC, memo to controller of talks, 16 March 1956)

In 1956 Quigley was promoted to talks department management. As chief assistant (1956–60) she played a significant role in launching the *Today* programme and as assistant head (1960–62) helped to create *In Touch*, the world's first national radio series for blind listeners. She sat on the executive committee of the Keep Britain Tidy group and in 1962 urged *Today* to mention its latest anti-litter campaign. Writing on the same subject in 1955, she told three senior managers:

> I said that so far as Talks were concerned experience had shown that indirect propaganda was the most effective [type] and that in talks addressed to women and children references were made to litter whenever the subject (e.g. picnics) made it appropriate.   (BBC WAC, memo to controller of talks, 25 April 1955)

Quigley was formidable but charming, her steely wit coupled to genuine warmth. Invariably well groomed and coiffured, she also had a pronounced limp, though never discussed it with colleagues. A transforming editor, she spent nearly thirty years developing radio's capacity for 'indirect propaganda', as she herself called it, in which it could convey useful social messages.

After she had retired from the BBC in 1962, Quigley serialized more than twenty books for her old programme, *Woman's Hour*, despite increasingly severe arthritis. She continued to live in a cottage in Chinnor, Oxfordshire, which was the main marital home and from where she and Fitzgerald had daily commuted to London. She died of peritonitis on 7 February 1987 in the John Radcliffe Hospital, Oxford; her husband died in 1993.

PAUL DONOVAN

Sources controller interview, 25 April 1955, BBC WAC, broadcasting files, R34/1085 · director interview, 5 Aug 1943, BBC WAC, broadcasting files · director interview, 2 Jan 1945, BBC WAC, broadcasting files · controller interview, 16 March 1956, BBC WAC, broadcasting files · J. Cain, 'Dealing with deprivation: the origins of social action broadcasting in Britain between 1923 and 1973', PhD diss., Open University, 1996 · *Woman's hour*, 40th anniversary edition, 3 Oct 1986 · Oxf. UA · *Belfast News-Letter* (5 Jan 1944) · *Irish Times* (12 Jan 1944) · *The Times* (12 Feb 1987) · A. Boyle, *The climate of treason*, rev. edn (1980) · private information (2004) · P. Donovan, *All our todays: forty years of Radio 4's 'Today' programme* (1997) · b. cert. · m. cert. · d. cert.

Archives BBC WAC |SOUND BBC WAC

Likenesses photograph, repro. in Donovan, *All our todays*, facing p. 84

Quill, Jeffrey Kindersley (1913–1996), aviator and military aircraft marketing executive, was born on 1 February 1913 at Belle Croft, 72 South Terrace, Littlehampton, Sussex, the third son and fifth of the five children of Arthur Maxwell Quill (1864/5–1925), civil engineer, and his wife, Emily Molesworth (1870–1938), daughter of Captain Edward Molesworth Kindersley JP. His father was Irish and his mother English.

Inspired by flying from the age of five after seeing aeroplanes land near his birthplace, Quill was educated at Lancing College before entering the Royal Air Force in 1931 as a pilot officer on a short service commission. He went solo after only five hours twenty minutes' dual instruction at 3 flying training school, Grantham, and passed out the following year as a flying officer with the rating of 'exceptional'. He then served with the crack 17 (fighter) squadron at Upavon.

In November 1934, aged only twenty-one, Quill was posted to command the RAF meteorological flight at Duxford, near Cambridge. He was rated 'exceptional' again; and in the ensuing thirteen months made two flights a day in all weathers (in open-cockpit, unheated Siskin IIIAs) with 100 per cent reliability. For this achievement he was awarded the Air Force Cross in 1936.

Hearing that Joseph (Mutt) Summers, chief test pilot at Vickers (Aviation), needed help with the demanding flight test programme at Weybridge and at Vickers Supermarine, Eastleigh—in particular with Reginald Mitchell's new type 300 fighter, later named 'Spitfire'—Quill applied for release from the RAF, and on 6 January 1936 became Summers's principal assistant.

After Summers had made the maiden flight of this prototype fighter K5054 at Eastleigh on 6 March 1936 Quill first flew it himself on 26 March 1936. Sadly this was the only example of the 22,749 Spitfires and Seafires subsequently built that Mitchell saw: he died only three months after Summers and Quill had pronounced it an unqualified success. On 9 October 1937 Quill married Patricia Ann (*b.* 1915), daughter of Colonel John Stuart Campbell; the marriage was dissolved in 1945.

After transferring full time to Vickers Supermarine in 1938 Quill took complete charge of Spitfire test flying; but with the outbreak of war and the fall of France he felt it his duty to return to a fighter squadron. Forestalling opposition from his employers, he successfully argued the need to gain frontline operational experience, and returned to the Royal Air Force during the battle of Britain in 1940, serving with 65 (Spitfire) squadron. He shot down two enemy aircraft before returning to his own hazardous job. In the same year he became chief test pilot for Vickers-Armstrongs (Supermarine Works). In January 1943 he was awarded the OBE, and he served for five months of that year with the Fleet Air Arm as a lieutenant-commander, Royal Naval Volunteer Reserve, helping to develop better carrier-deck-landing with the Seafire, the naval version of the Spitfire.

Quill made the first flights and masterminded the development and production test flying of all fifty-two variants of the Spitfire—the only allied fighter to remain in full production and frontline service throughout the Second World War. He also made the first flights of the Dumbo, an experimental variable-incidence wing torpedo bomber; the Spiteful; the Seafang; and ultimately, in July 1946, the Attacker, the Royal Navy's first jet fighter. Quill's second marriage—to (Eirene) Pamela Acland Allen (1921–1969), daughter of Captain Cecil Charles Acland Allen RN, on 24 February 1945—produced two daughters, Sarah (*b.* 1946) and Virginia (*b.* 1948). The marriage was dissolved on 21 March 1967.

In 1947, after sixteen years of arduous flying had taken their toll on his health, Quill had to retire from active flight testing, having logged more than 5000 flying hours in ninety aircraft types. Undaunted, he stepped immediately into another demanding career, initially as sales manager of Vickers-Armstrongs (Supermarine Works) in 1948 during the pioneering transition into the jet age; he returned to Weybridge in 1957 as head of the military aircraft office of Vickers-Armstrongs (Aircraft). As military aircraft sales manager of British Aircraft Corporation (formed in 1960) he became deeply involved in development of the TSR2 supersonic bomber until its cancellation by the Labour government in 1965. Meanwhile he kept his aerobatics well honed, flying the aptly registered Spitfire QJ-J at air displays, and he made his last Spitfire flight in June 1966, thirty years after his first flight in the prototype in 1936.

In 1966 Quill was appointed sales director of the Anglo-French company set up to develop the Jaguar supersonic combat aircraft. Later he became marketing director of Panavia, the Anglo-German-Italian consortium developing the Tornado swing-wing fighter. His third marriage, on 3 October 1969, was to (Theodora) Claire (1918–2000), daughter of Alfred Reginald Legge. She was a retired WRAF wing commander. Quill retired in 1978 after forty-seven years in the aviation industry, and was elected a fellow of the Royal Aeronautical Society in 1980. He also served as president of the Spitfire Society, and was a distinguished member of the Royal Air Force Club in London for sixty-four years.

A keen sportsman, Quill had interests that included sailing (he was shortlisted for the British Olympic-class sailing team) and in 1962 he won the Daily Express offshore powerboat race in 'Tramontana', designed by Peter Du Cane. Passionately interested in English literature, he spent his initial retirement in north Wales reading and writing, and published two highly regarded books: *Spitfire: a Test Pilot's Story* (1983) and *Birth of a Legend: the Spitfire* (1986). Later he and his wife, Claire, moved to the Isle of Man. He died at his home there, Reayrt House, Andreas, near Ramsey, on 20 February 1996, and was buried on 27 February at Andreas church.

One of the finest British test pilots of his era, whose name will remain forever linked with the Spitfire, Jeffrey Quill showed outstanding professionalism and a courteous manner in everything he did. Sir George Edwards OM said of him: 'Jeffrey Quill was one of the most articulate test pilots I ever encountered; and to him goes much of the credit for turning Mitchell's brilliant concept into a great fighting machine'.   NORMAN BARFIELD

Sources *The Times* (29 Feb 1996) · *Daily Telegraph* (21 Feb 1996) · [N. Barfield], *The Guardian* (24 Feb 1996) · *The Independent* (5 March 1996) · IWM SA · BBC film and television archive · BL NSA · British Movietone news archive · British Pathé film archive · ITN archive · Royal Air Force Museum, Hendon, film archive · PRO, DEFE 2 · Royal Aeronautical Society · Smithsonian Institution, Washington, DC, National Air and Space Museum Archives, Record Unit 330, ser. 2, box 43, folder 8 · b. cert. · m. certs. · private information (2004) [Sarah Quill, daughter]

Archives Cabinet Office, London · General RO · IWM, papers · Lancing College, West Sussex · priv. coll., family Bible with entries of births, deaths, and marriages · priv. coll., family papers · priv. coll., papers, photographs, tape recordings, memorabilia · Royal Aeronautical Society, London, articles, lectures, photographs · Royal Air Force, RAF Innsworth, Gloucester · W. Sussex RO | civil registry, Douglas, Isle of Man · Family Division, London, principal registry · PRO, 'Operation Airthief'; papers relating to 12 Commando and the proposed capture of a German aircraft, Ref. DEFE 2 · Quadrant House, Sutton, Surrey, *Flight* collection, photographs relating to career in aviation · Smithsonian Institution, Washington, DC, papers relating to Charles Lindbergh memorial lecture, 17 May 1984, Record Unit 330, series 2, box 43, folder 8 | FILM BFI NFTVA · British Movietone News Archive, news footage · British Pathé, film archive, news footage, 22 June 1936, 36/50 [incl. footage of JKQ flying prototype Spitfire] · ITN Archive, 'Spitfires being built', 2 Feb 1939, P.8188, tape V617(3), issue 828 · Royal Air Force Museum, Hendon, film archive · Uden Associates, London, *Equinox*, Channel 4, 9 Sept 1990, 09300 | SOUND BL NSA, 'Farnborough international', BBC, 5 Sept 1974, LP36158 · BL NSA, 'Test pilot', BBC, 1 Sept 1970, LP332376 · IWM SA, oral history interviews, 10687

Likenesses photograph, 1942, priv. coll. · A. Mason, pencil drawing, 1944, priv. coll. · photograph, 1966, Royal Aeronautical Society, London · R. Steel, oils, 1986, Brooklands Museum, Weybridge, Surrey · W. Jenkins, bronze bust, 1994, R. J. Mitchell Memorial Museum, Southampton Hall of Aviation · photographs, Quadrant House, Sutton, Surrey, 'Flight' collection

Quilliam, William Henry [*known as* Sheikh Abdullah Quilliam; Haroon Mustapha Leon] (1856–1932), lawyer and Muslim leader, was born on 10 April 1856 at 22 Elliot Street, Liverpool, the son of Robert Quilliam, watch manufacturer, and his wife, Harriet, *née* Burrows. He was of Manx descent (and at one point active in the Liverpool Manx Society), and among his ancestors was John Quilliam, first lieutenant on HMS *Victory* at the battle of Trafalgar and one of the pallbearers at Nelson's funeral.

Quilliam's parents were Wesleyan Methodists, and he was brought up in that denomination. He was educated at the Liverpool Institute, and there were early signs not only of a brilliant academic mind but also of an interest in theology. As a teenager he met and came under the influence of Charles Beard, a well-known Unitarian pastor, who may have sown the seeds of Quilliam's later attitude to Christianity. After leaving the Liverpool Institute he was articled to a solicitor in the city, and qualified as a solicitor himself in 1878. He then built up one of the largest and most successful legal practices in the north of England at his chambers at 15 Manchester Street, Liverpool. It is clear from an entry in B. Guinness Orchard's *Liverpool's Legion of Honour* (1893) that Quilliam was a highly regarded member of Liverpool society. On 2 July 1879 he married Hannah Johnstone (*b.* 1857/8), daughter of William Johnstone, provision merchant; they had at least one son. He is also thought to have married, in Liverpool, Ethel Mary

Burrows, an Irishwoman with whom he had further children.

In 1882 Quilliam became ill, and was advised to recuperate in north Africa. It was while travelling in Morocco that he developed an interest in Islam, though it was not until 1887 that he publicly renounced Christianity and declared himself a Muslim, taking the name Abdullah Quilliam. He gave his first lecture on the Muslim faith to the Temperance League at their premises in Mount Vernon Street, Liverpool, and the lecture was so well received that he began to hold weekly meetings there. Converts to the faith grew to such an extent that in 1891 Quilliam was able to purchase a large Georgian terraced house at 8 Brougham Terrace, West Derby Road, as premises for his 'Muslim Institute'. With gifts from the Ottoman sultan and the shah of Afghanistan, the institute soon expanded to include a mosque, library, lecture hall, boys' day and boarding-school, girls' day school, the Medina Home for Children (for illegitimate children from the Liverpool area), and a printing press. The latter was used to print numerous pamphlets and lectures, and also two periodicals, the weekly *Crescent* and monthly *Islamic World*, which were soon circulated throughout the Muslim world. The existence of the institute excited considerable local hostility, and fireworks and other missiles were thrown at the new mosque in 1891, in a near riot. Quilliam also faced hostility from several prominent Muslims abroad, who criticized him for diluting the Islamic faith and rituals in his attempts to proselytize.

Quilliam continued to travel extensively throughout the Middle East. In 1893 he was recognized by the Islamic University of Fez as an *Alim* (qualified to offer opinions as an Islamic jurist), and in 1894 the Ottoman sultan honoured him as sheikh-ul-Islam (leader of the Muslims) of the British Isles. In 1899 he was appointed Persian consul in Liverpool. His writings on Islam were widely circulated: one pamphlet, *Fanatics and Fanaticism* (1890), was translated into thirteen languages. He also published numerous articles on geology, palaeontology, philology, and Manx history, sometimes under the pseudonyms Haroon Mustapha Leon or Henri Marcel Léon. He described himself as 'a loyal British subject by birth, and a sincere Muslim from conviction' (Beckerlegge, 262), but he frequently encountered difficulties in reconciling the two identities. His defence of Turkish policy and of the legitimacy of the Turkish caliphate provoked controversy at the height of the Armenian crisis, and in 1896 his *fatwa* against the Sudanese campaign led to further local demonstrations and his vilification in some parts of the national press.

In 1908 Quilliam was struck off the roll of solicitors, for falsifying evidence in a divorce case. He left Liverpool, and the Brougham Street mosque and Muslim Institute went into rapid decline and closed shortly afterwards. Little is known of his activities over the next few years, though some versions of his life claim that he spent the First World War in Turkey, spying for the allied cause. In 1919 he resurfaced in the Isle of Man, where in 1903 he had bought a substantial property, Woodland Towers, in Onchan. He became well known around the village and

island, where he was never seen without his scarlet fez; local society was frequently scandalized by tales of orgies and multiple marriages, and it seemed that Quilliam could hardly step outside the front door of Woodland Towers without starting another colourful story. He continued to live at Woodland Towers while also retaining a base in London, where (as Henri Marcel Léon) he worked as secretary-general of the Société Internationale de Philologie, Sciences, et Beaux-Arts, and editor of its journal, *The Philomath*. He also (as Haroon Mustapha or Mustafa Leon) was closely involved in the running of the Shah Jehan mosque in Woking. He died at 23 Wellbeck Street, London, on 23 April 1932, after an operation for intestinal obstruction and an enlarged prostate, and was survived by his third wife, Miriam. He was buried with full Muslim rites at Brookwood cemetery, Woking. In October 1997 his granddaughter Patricia Gordon unveiled a plaque at the former site of the Muslim mosque and institute, 8 Brougham Terrace, Liverpool, to commemorate his achievements, in a ceremony organized by members of the local Abdullah Quilliam Society. JOHN GUILFORD

Sources 'Spotlight on topics, personalities and places', *Ramsey Courier* (Aug 1967) [Isle of Man] · *Isle of Man Examiner* (14 April 1978) · *Liverpool Review* (13 Dec 1902) · B. Guinness Orchard, *Liverpool's legion of honour* [privately published, 1893] · 'The unveiling of an historic mosque', *Muslim News* (31 Oct 1997) · G. Beckerlegge, 'Followers of "Mohammed, Kalee and Dada Nanuk": the presence of Islam and south Asian religions in Victorian Britain', *Religion in Victorian England*, ed. I. Wolffe, 5 (1997), 222–67 · 'Men who are talked about', *Islamic World*, 4/43 (Nov 1896), 212–15 · 'Sheik Abdullah Quilliam', *Porcupine* (7 April 1900) · 'A man of many parts: Mr W. H. Quilliam and his varied life', *Liverpool Freeman* (8 July 1905) · M. A. Khan-Cheema, 'Islam and the Muslims in Liverpool', MA diss., U. Lpool, 1979 · www.media.isnet.org/off/Islam/New/leon.html, March 2002 · www.hizmetbooks.org/Why_Become_Muslims/3.htm, March 2002 · private information, 2004 [Abdullah Quilliam Society; William Kerruish, grandson] · b. cert. · m. cert. [Hannah Johnstone] · d. cert.
Likenesses photograph, repro. in Wolffe, ed., *Religion*, 221
Wealth at death £501 17s. 5d.: probate, 23 Aug 1932, *CGPLA Eng. & Wales*

Quillinan, Dorothy (1804–1847). *See under* Quillinan, Edward (1791–1851).

Quillinan, Edward (1791–1851), poet, was born on 12 August 1791 at Oporto, Portugal, the son of John Quillinan, wine merchant, and his wife, Mary, *née* Ryan. Both his parents were Irish and his father, of good but impoverished family, had become a prosperous wine merchant in Portugal.

Education, army career, and first publications Edward was sent to Catholic schools in England: first, unhappily, to Sedgley Park, Staffordshire; second, happily, to a Dominican school at Bornheim House, Carshalton, near London, where he first wrote poems. 'Being a catholic, I was unfortunately not sent to either of the universities, which I have ever since lamented' (Johnston, 6). From 1807 he worked for some months in Oporto—not happily—for his father, who by this time had remarried: 'I was heartily sick of the counting-house, for my passion was for books very unlike ledgers' (ibid.).

The French invasion under Junot of Portugal in 1807

forced the family to leave for England, and Quillinan entered the army, becoming a cornet 'by purchase in the Queen's Bays' (2nd dragoon guards) stationed at Hastings, then at Canterbury: 'the life suited me extremely well, and I had plenty of time to read' (Johnston, 7). In 1809 he went on the Walcheren expedition, watching with the rest of his regiment the British bombardment of Flushing from boats mustered on the River Scheld. In 1810 he published satirical verses, *The Ball Room Votaries* ('two editions in a month'), and the periodical *The Whim* (his responsibilities being editorial)—insults led to duels, and a necessity for Quillinan's transfer to another regiment. He first purchased a lieutenancy in the 23rd light dragoons and then exchanged the commission for one in the 3rd dragoon guards, with whom in 1813 he first saw service at St Sebastian in Spain, and was a part of Wellington's pursuit of the enemy from Spain into France. His diary records his march from Toulouse to Calais, from 13 March to 17 July 1814, and contains notes about a proposed novel, ultimately published as *The Conspirators* (1841).

In 1814 Quillinan published *Dunluce Castle, a Poem*, the first of several of his works to be issued by the private and prestigious Lee Priory Press of Sir Egerton Brydges, who, in the same year (15 December) dedicated his *Occasional Poems* (written 1811): 'To Edward Quillinan Esq these fugitive poems are dedicated as a sincere but unworthy tribute to his pure genius, his brilliant wit, and noble disposition'. Quillinan was abroad when *Dunluce Castle*, an elegant volume with sixty-eight handmade sheets of wove paper, set as large type, well spaced, with only eighteen lines per page, appeared. Quillinan, perhaps through his friendship with his fellow soldier Brydges' elder son, Thomas Brydges Barrett (the last name assumed to inherit the Lee Priory estate from his maternal uncle), came into Brydges' circle in 1813; Brydges had been persuaded in 1813 by John Johnson and John Warwick, formerly compositor and printer, respectively, for Bensley, to set up under his aegis the Lee Priory Press. Colonel Thomas Brydges Barrett provided the premises, Egerton Brydges found the copy, and Johnson and Warwick the equipment and the labour; the press continued until 1823, even though Johnson left in 1817. Typically, the works are printed on cream wove paper, ideal for finely cut engravings; a greyish white Chinese paper was often used for blocks. There were never more than 100 copies of a work printed. Quillinan's contributions continued throughout: *Stanzas by the Author of 'Dunluce Castle'* (1814) was twenty-six pages of rather more closely spaced text; *Consolation* (1815) was a five-page poem addressed to Lady Brydges in memory of her son, Grey Matthew Brydges, who had died in Minorca, a midshipman aged fourteen years and four months. Quillinan published *Elegiac Verses* (1817), again addressed to Lady Brydges, on the loss of another child, Edward William George, in 1816. By this date Johnson had left the press, but for Warwick, Quillinan provided verses for the remarkable *Woodcuts and verses* (1820) which included all the woodblocks which had been engraved for use at the Lee Priory Press (ninety-eight in all, including forty-one small armorial initials). In his introduction Quillinan commented,

with appropriate modesty: 'the embellishments in most books are secondary to the printed composition: in this, with very few exceptions, the reverse is the fact'. Quillinan had also printed with other publishers: Longman brought out *Monthermer* (1815), a substantial verse romance, and with Bensley *The Sacrifice of Isobel* (1816); these two were his most substantial poems to date.

Marriage, retirement from the army, and Jemima's illness In 1817 Quillinan married his first wife, Jemima Anne Deborah Brydges (1793–1822), the second daughter of Sir Egerton. Not for the first or last time, Quillinan involved himself in controversy. In 1819 *Blackwood's Magazine* had published an attack on *Dunluce Castle* by Captain Thomas Hamilton, the original Morgan O'Doherty of *Blackwood's* who ridiculed the poem in a long review entitled 'Poems by a Heavy Dragoon'. In his *Retort Courteous* (1821) Quillinan, stationed at Hamilton, Edinburgh, and not knowing the true author of the attack, turned on the editors of *Blackwood's*, John Wilson and J. G. Lockhart, coining most of his satire by extracting passages from Lockhart's *Peter's Letters to his Kinsfolk* (1819). Ultimately, Quillinan and Captain Hamilton were reconciled by Robert Pearse Gillies, a friend and correspondent of Wordsworth, and it was Gillies who encouraged Quillinan, indeed armed him with a letter of recommendation, to visit Wordsworth at Rydal Mount. Quillinan made three journeys to Rydal, but it was only on the third that he summoned up enough courage to meet the poet; and then he was frigidly received because he had forgotten the letter, and was admitted into friendship only through the intervention of the poet's sister-in-law Sara Hutchinson. In that year, 1821, Quillinan retired from the army:

> I was settled with poor Jemima & her little baby name-sake at Spring Cottage, Loughrigg. John Reeves & his Wife whom I took with me out of the 3rd [Dragoon Guards], he having obtained his discharge, were my groom & cook—the old Irish Nurse and her young assistant Eliza Cooke, with Flora the pet spaniel and my two horses completed my rustic establishment; and never did I pass so happy & satisfactory a summer. De Quinsey [*sic*], the Opium-Eater, was my nearest neighbour, and lent me his coach-house and stables; but I saw very little of him, for he remained in bed, I understood, all day, and only took the air at night, and then was more shy than an owl.

Quillinan's happy manuscript reminiscence does not mention an event recorded in the 'Lancaster lunatic asylum admissions and discharge book' for 1816–24 (Lancs. RO), which suggests that the marriage had a difficulty: Jemima, aged twenty-five, of the parish of Ambleside, was admitted on 17 October 1821 and discharged on 13 February 1822: the entry concludes: 'Cured'. The diagnosis was 'Mania 2nd attack', followed by the mysterious word 'Lactœa'. Dorothy Wordsworth records in a letter of 13 June 1822: 'She was afflicted with mental derangement after the birth of her last child' (*Letters of William and Dorothy Wordsworth*, 4.140). The Quillinans by 1822 had moved to Ivy Cottage (now Glen Rothay), not five minutes' walk from Rydal Mount, Wordsworth's home, and it was there, while Quillinan was away on business in London, that his wife, who had been ill, was badly burnt when her dress caught fire. Dorothy Wordsworth nursed her until her death on 25 May 1822, aged twenty-eight, and then arranged the funeral and superintended the nurse and the two motherless children. Wordsworth, godfather of the younger daughter, Rotha (1821–1876), helped Quillinan to write an epigraph that celebrated his wife:

> the tender virtues of her blameless life,
> Bright in the daughter, brighter in the wife,
> And in the cheerful mother brightest shone.

The monument, in Grasmere church, was designed by Chantrey.

Thereafter, Quillinan's life, though based at his London house, 12 Bryanstone Street, Portland Square, or at Lee Priory in Kent, involved travel and writing, and ultimately hopes of marrying Dora Wordsworth. From time to time poems appeared. Some of his elegies to the Brydges family were collected in *Carmina Brugesiana: Domestic Poems* (1822). Sir Egerton had been based at Geneva since 1818, and Quillinan, in his grief, visited him there in August 1822. *Shamrock Leaves, or, The Wicklow Excursion*, a series of poems celebrating his Irish tour with the Brydges family in 1820, was published by Longman in 1823. In 1829 Quillinan published *The King: the Lay of 'a Papist'*—on the relation of church and state; interestingly, though always remaining a Roman Catholic, Quillinan brought up his own children in the Church of England, and attended English services. In 1831 Edward Moxon published the first section of *Mischief*, influenced by Byron's *Beppo* and J. H. Frere's *Monks and Giants* (1818), but written in Spenserian stanzas; its light tone is more social amusement than true satire. A second section was published in 1834 with a preface defending himself from the charge of plagiarism from Byron; Wordsworth commented to Quillinan: 'It is written with great spirit and a variety of talent which does the author no small credit' (11 June 1834, *Letters of William and Dorothy Wordsworth*, 5.719). Perhaps Wordsworth's most positive comment on Quillinan came on 20 September 1837:

> it is in your power to attain a permanent place among the poets of England, your thoughts, feelings, knowledge, and judgement in style, and skill in metre entitle you to it; if you have not yet succeeded in gaining it the cause appears to me merely to lie in the subjects wh. you have chosen.
> (ibid., 6.464)

Marriage to Dora Wordsworth Quillinan was becoming more than a Wordsworth family friend. The relationship was built on a mutual concern for Quillinan's two daughters. Wordsworth, however, from 1837, when the matter was raised, refused to encourage Quillinan in his hopes of marrying Dora [*see below*]. Wordsworth's reluctance was neither on the grounds of Quillinan's religion, nor a simple unwillingness to let Dora marry.

Quillinan was entangled in the disastrous financial affairs of his brother-in-law and friend, Colonel Thomas Brydges Barrett, and his father-in-law, Sir Egerton Brydges; trust monies had been mishandled, and the colonel was ruined and died in a fisherman's hut at Boulogne in July 1834; Anthony, a younger son, was thrown in a debtors' prison, from which he was to be discharged only as a lunatic. Quillinan was not finally acquitted of fraud until March 1842, almost a year after he had married Dora on 11 May 1841, at St James's Church, Bath, in the presence of her mother, her two brothers, John, who performed the service, and William, who gave her away, and Quillinan's half-brother John Thomas. Wordsworth, like his sister in 1802 at his own marriage, was too overcome to attend. Quillinan wrote to his daughter: 'we all, Miss F[enwick] & Mrs W[ordsworth] & Dora herself seeing how much he was moved, requested him *not* to come; for we had all we wanted from him in the kind & amiable manner in which he had behaved towards us' (MS, Wordsworth Library). The Wordsworths were visiting Isabella Fenwick at Bath, and it was she who had persuaded the poet to set aside his objection that Quillinan had no fortune. John Thomas, who had successfully maintained their father's business in Oporto, gave him some support; according to Crabb Robinson, Quillinan was indeed to be completely dependent on Dora in financial matters. The whole party then went on a visit to Somerset, where Wordsworth and Coleridge had, famously, written *Lyrical Ballads* (1798).

Later writings and final years Quillinan continued to publish. His three-volume novel *The Conspirators* (1841), a series of tales centring on Philadelphian plots against Napoleon, based on his military services in Spain and Portugal, received some praise from reviewers. He wrote a rhymed defence against the attack on Wordsworth in Walter Savage Landor's 'Imaginary conversation' between Porson and Southey (*Blackwood's Magazine*, April 1843). Landor mockingly responded by speaking of Quillinan's writings as 'Quill-inanities', though Quillinan claimed that he himself had given the pun to Landor some thirty years before in Bath. Wordsworth, again, was not impressed and thought the defence indiscreet. Quillinan proved an assiduous husband, and the couple were at their happiest in 1843 and 1844 when they spent their summers on Belle Isle in Windermere, the 'Borow-Me-An Island', as Wordsworth punned, borrowed from the Curwens, but Dora's health grew worse, and, writing and sketching, they travelled in search of health, wandering through Portugal and Spain in 1845–6. On their return via Marseilles and Paris, they moved into a newly built section of Loughrigg Holme, thus sharing the property with John Carter, Wordsworth's man of business. In her final illness, Dora returned to Rydal Mount and died there on 9 July 1847. Wordsworth felt he could not visit Quillinan's house after Dora's death: 'I cannot bear to cross the Bridge and Field that leads to his Abode', Wordsworth wrote to Isabella Fenwick on 6 December 1847, 'and he does not come hither' (*Letters of William and Dorothy Wordsworth*, 7.859). Both men, though courteous, were essentially fixed into separate grief. William Johnston does record walking with Quillinan and Wordsworth in the autumn of 1849, with Wordsworth's thoughts that they would not meet again. On 2 January 1850 Wordsworth did visit the other guests, including Matthew Arnold and his bride, but in his depression declared the prospect 'a trial which I feel that I am unable to bear as with due submission to God's Will I ought to do. May He have mercy upon me, and upon the Mother of Her whom we have lost' (ibid., 7.914).

Even so Quillinan continued to write and translate to the last. Importantly, before Dora's death, it was Quillinan who drafted Wordsworth's one laureate ode, 'Ode on the Installation of His Royal Highness Prince Albert as Chancellor of the University of Cambridge', of 6 July 1847 (two imprints, Cambridge, University Press, 1847, and London, George Bell, undated):

> the plan and composition of this ode was chiefly prepared by Mr. Quillinan, but carefully revised in MS. by Mr. Wordsworth, who, being in a state of deep domestic affliction, could not otherwise have been able to fulfil the engagement with Prince Albert.   (MS note by Mary Wordsworth)

Wordsworth had expressed to Miss Fenwick on 19 September 1844 his mortification that Quillinan did so little 'because his talents are greatly superior to those of most men who earn a handsome livelihood by Literature' (*Letters of William and Dorothy Wordsworth*, 7.597). Wordsworth was perhaps unfair. In 1845 Quillinan contributed to the first volume of *The Edinburgh Tales* his fiction 'The Rangers of Connaught'; in 1846 he wrote for *Tait's Magazine* 'The Bell: Adventures at a Portuguese Watering-Place' (about Oporto); and again in 1846 *The Quarterly* published Quillinan's article on Gil Vicente, the Portuguese dramatic poet (Wordsworth read the proof and told J. G. Lockhart: 'It is well done and I think it will be a pleasing variety in the Quarterly' (ibid., 7.817)). His latest literary activity involved his beginning a translation in *ottava rima* of the first half (or five cantos) of Camoens's *Lusiad*, published posthumously in 1853 by John Adamson, another and admiring translator of Camoens; and he also began a translation (unpublished) of Herculano's history of Portugal.

Edward Quillinan died at Rydal on 8 July 1851 after a cold caught when fishing. He was buried at Grasmere.

A memoir by his friend William Johnston was published by Moxon in 1853 with a selection of Quillinan's poems. Johnston rather suppressed Quillinan's social and humorous verses; some of his lyrics are gently sentimental; his letters and diaries supplement an understanding of the literary circle of which he was a part. Matthew Arnold's epitaph of 27 December 1851, 'Stanzas in Memory of Edward Quillinan', speaks of him as 'a man unspoil'd, Sweet, generous, and humane'. Quillinan's friend Johnston, however, twice suggested that Quillinan could be irritable. In his obituary of Quillinan (*Inverness Courier*, 21 April 1853) he quotes an exchange of letters between them in which Johnston suggests that 'small men were more irritable than those of larger growth', and Quillinan, in denying it, confirms he was indeed small: 'taller, physically speaking than Tom Moore, and not so tall as Tom Campbell: consequently he is no giant'. In his memoir Johnston quotes John Carter:

> Mrs Wordsworth was much attached to him, and indeed he was a favourite with everyone who knew him, and his society was much courted by every one in this neighbourhood. Probably his failing was an excitability and restlessness which indicated that Irish blood was in his

veins. But I believe, upon the whole, that a more noble, generous, and high-minded creature never breathed. (Johnston, 32)

Dorothy [Dora] **Quillinan** (1804–1847), writer, the second child of William Wordsworth and Mary Hutchinson, was born on 16 August 1804 at Dove Cottage, Grasmere. She was educated primarily at home and at Miss Dowling's boarding-school at Ambleside, 2 miles from home. She had a gift for friendship and this is revealed in her correspondence: her letters to the Crumps, the Cooksons, to the daughters of Southey and Coleridge, to Mary Stanger, to Maria Jane Jewsbury, and to her own family are lively. Wordsworth celebrated Dora, along with Edith Southey and Sara Coleridge, in his poem 'The Triad', first drafted in 1817. Dora acted as amanuensis for her father, and often travelled with him: in 1828 (21 June–5 August) they travelled with Coleridge into Germany, Dora keeping a journal; in 1831 they visited Walter Scott for the last time; in 1838 they travelled to Northumberland and Durham, when Wordsworth received an honorary degree from Durham University. In 1841 she married Edward Quillinan after surmounting several years of her father's disapproval. In search of health for Dora, the Quillinans travelled in Portugal and Spain. Her one book, published just before her death on 9 July 1847, was dedicated to her parents: *A Journal of a Few Months Residence in Portugal, and Glimpses of the South of Spain* (2 vols., 1847). It received a complimentary review in *The Quarterly*. 'It comes too late to give pleasure', wrote Crabb Robinson. Her letters are numerous, and can give valuable insight into the life of her father and their whole circle. Dora was skilful in her pencil drawings and small watercolours (in the manner of Amos Green), and numbers of these (together with a few by Quillinan) survive in the Wordsworth Library, Grasmere. She had a central place in her parents' affections, but was often in ill health, and ultimately died of tuberculosis. Her death was catastrophic to Wordsworth's last years. When he died, Quillinan wrote to Sara, Coleridge's daughter, 'He has, no doubt, now a higher reward: he is gone to Dora' (MS, Wordsworth Library).

PAMELA WOOF and ROBERT WOOF

Sources letters, manuscripts, diaries, Wordsworth Trust, Dove Cottage, Grasmere • R. P. Gillies, *Memoirs of a literary veteran*, 2 vols. (1851) • W. Johnston, memoir, in E. Quillinan, *Poems* (1853) [republished with slight notes, 1891] • *Diary, reminiscences, and correspondence of Henry Crabb Robinson*, ed. T. Sadler, 3 vols. (1869) • H. Taylor, *Autobiography*, 2 vols. (1885) • P. W. Clayden, *Samuel Rogers and his contemporaries*, 2 vols. (1889) • F. W. Morley, *Dora Wordsworth, her book* (1924) • *Maria Jane Jewsbury: occasional papers, selected with a memoir*, ed. E. Gillett (1932) • M. Woodworth, *The literary career of Sir Samuel Egerton Brydges* (1935) • H. Crabb Robinson, *Books and their writers*, ed. E. J. Morley, 3 vols. (1938) • H. P. Vincent, *Dora Wordsworth: the letters* (1944) • *The letters of Sara Hutchinson, 1800–1835*, ed. K. Coburn (1954) • *The letters of Mary Wordsworth, 1800–1855*, ed. M. E. Burton (1958) • M. Arnold, *Poems*, ed. K. Allott (1965) • *New letters of Robert Southey*, ed. K. Curry, 2 vols. (1965) • *The letters of William and Dorothy Wordsworth*, ed. E. De Selincourt, rev. C. Shaver and A. Hill, 8 vols. (1967–93) • S. Gill, *William Wordsworth: a life* (1989) • *Sara Coleridge: a Victorian daughter*, ed. B. K. Mudge (1989) • J. W. Page, *Wordsworth and the cultivation of women* (1994) • K. Jones, *A passionate sisterhood* (1997) • J. Barker, *Wordsworth: a life* (2000) • d. cert.

Archives Wordsworth Trust, Dove Cottage, Grasmere, letters, MSS, diaries | BL, letters to Catherine Clarkson, Add. MS 41186 [Dorothy Quillinan] · BL, letters to William Jackson, M/534 [copies] [Dorothy Quillinan] · U. Edin. L., letters to Mary Laing [Dorothy Quillinan] · Wordsworth Trust, Dove Cottage, Grasmere, letters to Mary Stanger [Dorothy Quillinan]

Quilter, Harry (1851–1907), art critic, was born at Knight Hill Road, Lower Norwood, Surrey, on 24 January 1851 to William *Quilter (1808–1888) and his wife, Elizabeth Harriot Cuthbert (d. 1874). William Quilter was first president of the Institute of Accountants and a collector of British watercolours, and his eldest son, Sir William *Quilter, first baronet (1841–1911), was also a collector, as well as a politician. Harry was privately educated and entered Cambridge University in 1870. He graduated BA in 1874 and MA in 1877. Abandoning his original intention, which was to pursue a career in business, Quilter opted to travel abroad instead, informally studying art in Italy.

After returning to England, Quilter began preparing for the bar as a student of the Inner Temple, which he had entered in 1872. Meanwhile he continued to study art, enrolling at the Slade School of Fine Art. In 1876 he began writing art criticism for *The Spectator*, and he continued until 1887. He was called to the bar in 1878, but an attack of smallpox and a restless temperament made it difficult for him to concentrate his energies. He subsequently abandoned his career in law and devoted his time to art and journalism. From 1879 to 1887 he lectured on art and literature around England. In 1880–01 he worked for a short time as art critic for *The Times*, taking over from Tom Taylor. Between 1884 and 1893 he exhibited at the Institute of Painters in Oil Colours and in 1885 he studied landscape painting at Van Hove's studio in Bruges. Despite his efforts he never succeeded as an artist, but rather became known for his art criticism. In 1886 he applied for the Slade professorship at Cambridge, but failed. Tired of being edited, he started his own periodical in 1888, entitled *The Universal Review*, which only lasted a year. On 16 June 1890 he married Mary Constance (b. 1869/70), daughter of a gentleman, Charles Hall; they had six children.

Quilter was a prolific writer and contributed to numerous newspapers and periodicals, including the *Contemporary Review*, the *Cornhill Magazine*, the *Fortnightly Review*, *Fraser's Magazine*, *MacMillan's Magazine*, the *National Review*, the *New Review*, and the *Nineteenth Century*. In addition to art he wrote about theatre, literature, and women's rights (as an opponent). He was renowned for his outspokenness, which often resulted in controversy. He was a conservative art critic whose views reflected those of the 'philistine'. He opposed avant-garde movements, such as aestheticism and impressionism. Ideologically opposed, he was an enemy of James McNeill Whistler, siding in the press with John Ruskin during the famous Ruskin versus Whistler trial of 1878. In 1879 he infuriated Whistler by purchasing the artist's former home, the White House, in Chelsea, and replacing the painter's interior design with his own conservative style. Whistler sought vengeance on 'Arry (Whistler's nickname for Quilter) after he castigated

the artist's Venetian etchings in *The Times*. Quilter's criticism, along with Whistler's rebuttal, appeared in the artist's book, *The Gentle Art of Making Enemies*, in 1890. He found himself at the centre of yet another dispute between the philistine and the avant-garde regarding Edgar Degas's *L'absinthe* (1875–6), which was displayed at the Grafton Gallery, London, in 1893. The controversy began when the art critic D. S. MacColl maintained in *The Spectator* that the painting set a standard for art. Quilter, writing for the *Westminster Gazette*, joined a band of philistine art critics who retaliated against MacColl's assertion.

Quilter also wrote several books, including *Sententiae artis* (1886), *Preferences in Art, Life, and Literature* (1892), and *Opinions on Men, Women and Things* (1909). The climax of his career as an artist was his one-man show held in January 1894 at the Dudley Gallery. Between 1894 and 1896 he managed two boarding-schools using a system he formulated and wrote about in the *Nineteenth Century* in 1895. He continued to write up until his death on 10 July 1907 at 42 Queen's Gate Gardens, London, and was buried at Norwood; his wife survived him. Most of his collections were sold at Christies in April 1906.

WILLIAM ROBERTS, rev. KIMBERLY MORSE JONES

Sources H. Quilter, *Opinions on men, women and things* (1909) · *WW* (1906) · *The Times* (13 July 1907) · *Morning Post* (12 July 1907) · C. W. Earle, *Memoirs and memories* (1911) · private information (1912) [Mrs Mary MacNalty, widow; S. E. Muter, sister-in-law] · *Wellesley index*, vol. 1 · J. A. M. Whistler, *The gentle art of making enemies* (1890) · A. Anderson, '"Woman's aesthetic mission": the aesthetic obsession with "things", or, The dangers of beautiful carpets, wallpapers and curtains', 'The high art maiden: Burne-Jones and the girls on the golden stairs', PhD diss., Exeter University, 2001 · K. Flint, *Impressionists in England: the critical reception* (1984) · C. Harrison, ed., *The essence of art: Victorian advice on the practice of painting* (1999), 127–45 · L. Bell, 'Fact or fiction: James McNeill Whistler's critical reputation in England, 1880–1892', PhD diss., University of East Anglia, 1987 · A. Heywood, 'The gospel of intensity: 'Arry, William Morris and the aesthetic movement', *Journal of the William Morris Society*, 13 (1999), 14–25

Archives NL Scot., corresp. | BL, corresp. with S. Butler, Add. MSS 44034–44042

Wealth at death £6898 8s. 8d.: probate, 29 July 1907, CGPLA Eng. & Wales

Quilter, Roger Cuthbert (1877–1953), composer, was born on 1 November 1877 at 4 Brunswick Square, Hove, Sussex, the fifth of the seven surviving children and the third son of Sir William Cuthbert *Quilter (1841–1911) and his wife, Mary Ann Bevington (1842–1927). His family was extremely wealthy: his father, the first baronet, was a shrewd businessman, and his mother was strong-minded, energetic, and devoted to her family. He grew up in an atmosphere appreciative of the arts, but one which, following Victorian social mores, saw music as a diversion, not an occupation.

Quilter was happy at Pinewood, his preparatory school in Farnborough, Hampshire, where his musical abilities were nurtured; in contrast, his period at Eton College was one of utter misery. A family friend suggested he continue his musical studies abroad, still a common route at that time, and he began at the Hoch'sche Konservatorium in

Roger Cuthbert Quilter (1877–1953), by Wilfred Gabriel de Glehn, 1920

Frankfurt am Main in 1896. He stayed in Frankfurt for four and a half years, initially studying the piano with Ernst Engesser but later taking composition lessons with Ivan Knorr, who had a remarkable ability to develop individuality in his students. Knorr's pupils also included Balfour Gardiner, Norman O'Neill, Cyril Scott, and Percy Grainger, and the five were together known as the Frankfurt group: though not collectively influential, they nevertheless made significant contributions to the contemporary musical scene. Back in England in 1901, Quilter eventually settled in London, first at 27 Welbeck Street, and then from 1912 at 7 Montagu Street, Portland Square. Two short-term addresses preceded the move in 1938 to his final home, 23 Acacia Road, St John's Wood, and over several decades he held open house to many artists, musicians, and writers. He was well read and well travelled, with an eye for beautiful things, but he was not ostentatious, preferring to use his substantial private means to give young musicians discreet financial support—support which also enabled Jewish friends to flee Vienna in the 1930s: his mother, of Quaker stock, had bequeathed him a warm, humanitarian outlook.

Quilter first achieved public acclaim when Denham Price sang his *Four Songs of the Sea* at the Crystal Palace in March 1901. His songs were performed frequently by the major singers of the day: John Coates, Harry Plunket

Greene, Ada Crossley, Dame Nellie Melba, and, most especially, the tenor Gervase Elwes, whose great lyrical refinement, integrity, and artistry matched his own. He freely acknowledged Elwes as 'the greatest inspiration to me always' (Quilter to Lady Winefride Elwes, 16 Jan 1921, Lincolnshire County Archives), claiming that he owed 'more to G Elwes than anyone, for the popularity of my songs' (Quilter Papers, priv. coll.). Quilter became a founder member and benefactor of the memorial fund (later the Musicians' Benevolent Fund) set up in Elwes's memory after his tragic death in 1921 at Boston, Massachusetts, and he dedicated many of his songs to him, including the song cycle *To Julia*, which they premièred together in 1905. In 1923 Quilter met the young baritone Mark Raphael, who took up Elwes's mantle, though never to the same degree; however, the performances in their 1934 recording of seventeen of Quilter's songs are definitive, and he was evidently a fine, sensitive pianist and accompanist.

Quilter loved the theatre: he wrote music for it from 1909 onwards, and his delightful incidental music to the children's play *Where the Rainbow Ends*, produced by Charles Hawtrey at the Savoy Theatre, London, in December 1911, proved immensely popular. He collaborated with Rodney Bennett on *The Blue Boar*, a light opera broadcast by the BBC in 1933; extensively revised, it was renamed *Julia* and performed at Covent Garden in 1936, but, though it received moderately favourable reviews, it was not performed in that version again. However, it produced a glorious waltz song, 'Love calls through the summer night', which stands comparison with the music of Edward German or Eric Coates. His orchestral piece *A Children's Overture* (1919), a sparkling and felicitously woven medley of nursery rhymes inspired by Walter Crane's illustrated children's book *The Baby's Opera*, was already well known by the time the BBC transmitted it in its first broadcast concert in 1922.

Quilter's tastes in music ranged from Bach to Stravinsky and ragtime, but his sensibilities did not lie with mainstream musical developments, and he was content—notwithstanding his German training—with his own inimitably English sound, untouched by the folk-song revival movement. His songs were broadcast frequently for many years, but despite his fame he remained shy, with a slight stammer. He was more at ease with fellow artists than with those of his own class, unless they too were artistic, and he was relaxed in the non-threatening company of children (though they sometimes found his great height a little daunting): his children's parties at the end of each *Rainbow* season were famous.

Quilter's friends were many and very dear to him. He dedicated his choral work *Non nobis, domine*, first performed at the pageant of parliament in 1934, to his friend Walter Creighton, who produced it; he also dedicated the first set of Shakespeare songs (1905) and three other Shakespeare songs to him. Other close friends, from before the First World War, were Major Benton Fletcher and the American millionaire philanthropist Robert Allerton, and although he never had a lifelong partner, relationships with them have been presumed. Creighton's cousin Wilfrid Gabriel de Glehn painted the oil portrait of Quilter now held by the National Portrait Gallery.

Quilter was never well (he was exempted from service during the First World War on medical grounds) and was a chronic depressive. An operation in 1945 coupled with the shattering news of the execution by a German officer of his favourite nephew, Arnold Vivian, during the Second World War triggered a mental breakdown and he was twice admitted to St Andrew's, Northampton, a private mental hospital. It was alleged after his death that he had been blackmailed for his homosexuality, and while the allegations have never been substantiated they are certainly plausible—a sad coda to his life.

Quilter knew where his strengths lay and never attempted music on a grand scale. He wrote orchestral works, partsongs, some fine piano pieces, and theatre music, much of it in light vein, but he is best-known for his songs—exquisite gems, showing a love of lyricism and language—which mirrored his personal elegance. They are bathed in Edwardian wistfulness, but rise well above the banality of the drawing-room ballad and make a significant contribution to the art-song repertory. Quilter crafted every phrase, every note, and the graceful beauty of the finished product belies the effort that went into its making. Shakespeare and Robert Herrick were his favourite poets among an eclectic selection: three of his most famous songs were settings of Tennyson ('Now sleeps the crimson petal'), Shelley ('Love's Philosophy') and Edmund Waller ('Go, lovely rose').

In November 1952 the BBC celebrated Quilter's seventy-fifth birthday with a concert conducted by the chorus-master of the BBC, Leslie Woodgate, Quilter's personal secretary during the 1920s. For the last few weeks of his life he was completely bedridden; he died at his home in St John's Wood on 21 September 1953 of heart failure and pneumonia, and was buried on 25 September in the family vault at St Mary's Church, Bawdsey, Suffolk. A memorial service at St Sepulchre's Church, Holborn Viaduct, was attended by family, musicians, and ordinary members of the public who loved the music of this gentle and gentlemanly composer. VALERIE LANGFIELD

Sources BL, Quilter papers, Add. MSS 70595–70607 · Quilter–Grainger correspondence, University of Melbourne, Grainger Museum · private information (2004) · S. Banfield, *Sensibility and English song* (1985) · T. Hold, *The walled-in garden: a study of the songs of Roger Quilter*, 2nd edn (1996) · P. Cahn, 'Percy Grainger's Frankfurt years', *Studies in Music*, 12, 101–13 · L. East, 'Roger Quilter (1877–1953)', *Music and Musicians*, 26 (Nov 1977), 28–30 · *DNB* · T. Armstrong, 'The Frankfort Group', *Proceedings of the Royal Musical Association*, 85 (1958–9), 1–16 · Eton · *CGPLA Eng. & Wales* (1953) · R. C. Quilter, letter to Lady W. Elwes, 16 Jan 1921, Lincs. Arch., 2 ELWES 1/13 L–Q · *The Times* (26 Sept 1953), 8

Archives BBC WAC, files, R 27/58 · BL, corresp. and MSS, Add. MSS 70595–70607 · priv. coll. | BL, corresp. with Society of Authors, Add. MS 63318 · University of Melbourne, Grainger Museum, Quilter–Grainger corresp. | SOUND BL NSA, performance recordings

Likenesses Gabelli, photograph, c.1899, University of Melbourne, Grainger Museum · Beresford, photograph, c.1904, University of Melbourne, Grainger Museum · W. G. de Glehn, oils, 1920, NPG [*see illus.*] · H. Lambert, photogravure, 1922, NPG ·

H. Coster, photograph, c.1925, priv. coll. · H. Coster, photograph, c.1925, Gov. Art Coll., London
Wealth at death £28,548 3s. 0d.: probate, 9 Dec 1953, *CGPLA Eng. & Wales*

Quilter, William (1808–1888), accountant, was born on 7 August 1808, the youngest of four sons of Samuel Sacker Quilter, a farmer, and his wife, Sarah May Chapman. Little is known of his early life other than that he went to London at the age of seventeen and joined the office of one of the leading public accountants of the day, Peter Harriss Abbott. Abbott was one of the first accountants whose value was recognized by the government, being appointed a commissioner inquiring into the method of keeping public accounts in 1829. Four years later he was appointed an official assignee in bankruptcy, leaving Quilter to enter into partnership with another of his former clerks, John Ball. The new firm benefited from a continued connection with Abbott who, in his new position, was able to commission the partnership to prepare financial statements for debtors prior to their appearance in court. Quilter married Elizabeth Harriot, *née* Cuthbert (d. 1874), in 1834 and they had three sons, including the art collector and politician Sir William Cuthbert *Quilter and the art critic Harry *Quilter, and two daughters.

A major stimulus for an already well-established practice was the collapse of the railway mania in 1847, resulting in shareholder committees engaging public accountants to help them to investigate the machinations of failed companies. The most famous revelations were contained in the report Quilter, Ball & Co. was called in to prepare on the affairs of the Eastern Counties Railway Company, whose chairman was George Hudson, the Railway King. The report showed that profit had been overstated by well over £400,000: £318,144 was wrongly omitted from the debit of the revenue account, £35,315 was wrongly credited to the revenue account, and interest amounting to £84,591 was charged to capital instead of revenue. Indications of the prominent role played by the firm in the handling of insolvency work are estimates that they were responsible for 8 of the 43 cases chronicled by D. M. Evans as arising out of the commercial crisis of 1847–8 and 31 of the 147 cases arising during a corresponding crisis ten years later (*DBB*, 792). As organizations increasingly took advantage of the option for companies to register with limited liability under the Companies Act of 1862, Quilter began to develop in addition a substantial audit practice. This may have compensated for a diminishing involvement in liquidations, with his firm placed sixth in an analysis made of the number and value of liquidations in the hands of leading London practices in 1866 (*DBB*). Quilter was invited to give evidence to the government select committee on the audit of railway accounts appointed in 1849 where he expressed the belief that his practice was the most extensive in England. A particular feature of Quilter's evidence was his opposition to any requirement that the auditors of railway companies should be shareholders, based on the belief that this compromised their independence. The gradual replacement of the shareholders as auditor by the professional is a notable feature of the history of auditing during the second half of the nineteenth century.

Further evidence of government recognition was the appointment of Quilter's firm to undertake a large-scale investigation of the army clothing store in Weedon in 1859 while, together with William Turquand, he was appointed by the Board of Trade as an investigating inspector under the Joint Stock Companies Act 1856.

It may well be that Quilter's heavy personal investment in railway shares—he owned shares valued at more than £276,000 at the time of his death—explains the fact that his firm were never permanent auditors of any of the major British railways. It is known, however, that he did hold shares in railways where his partners were auditors. Quilter also benefited from family links with some of the companies of which he was auditor. His son Sir William Cuthbert Quilter was a director of several of these companies including the National Telephone Company and Swan United Electric Light. There was also Eley Brothers, the cartridge makers, of which the young Quilter was also a shareholder and director. Important audits undertaken by the firm included that of the Hudson Bay Company from 1863, the Birmingham Joint Stock Bank from 1866, the Alliance Bank (jointly with John Sutherland Harmood-Banner) from 1869, the London Joint Stock and the Eastern Telegraph (each jointly with Deloittes) and the Bank of Australia. At the time of his death Quilter's firm audited more than seventy quoted companies.

In addition to being a successful practitioner, Quilter may be seen as a leading architect of the British accounting profession. It was he who called a meeting at his office of nine leading practitioners in 1870 to propose the formation of an institute of accountants in London. This action was part of an endeavour to achieve chartered status and so distinguish 'chartered accountants' from others who were seen to be bringing the practice of accountancy into disrepute. The new institute was formed in December 1870 with Quilter elected its first president. It was an élitist organization, insisting on high entrance fees and demanding entrance requirements. The resulting slow rate of growth and continued failure to obtain a royal charter, together with the more rapid expansion of rival professional associations, led to growing criticism of the institute's performance and, accordingly, Quilter's leadership. He resigned his position as president in January 1877 and both his seat on the council and membership of the institute the following May. Thus, when the Institute of Chartered Accountants in England and Wales was established in 1880 and a royal charter obtained, Quilter was no longer a member.

Many leaders of the profession passed through the office of Quilter, Ball & Co.: they included the founders of Cooper Brothers, William and Arthur; and three of Quilter's clerks became president of the institute—Thomas Abercrombie Welton, Arthur Cooper, and J. B. Ball. However, perhaps his best-known employee in the world of business was John Reeve Ellerman who, after refusing an offer of partnership, left in 1886 to found his shipping empire.

Some fascinating insights into the man were provided by Ernest Cooper in an obituary. Quilter is described as:

> accountant, art collector, and something of a financier. I remember attending a meeting of creditors, when Mr. Quilter walked about the room, distributing copies of the statement of affairs. He had more the appearance of a farmer than a professional man. He sold his great collection to Christie's some years before his death for a very large sum, and left one of the largest professional fortunes, if not the largest, I have ever noticed, but not, it was said, mainly earned directly from our profession.　(Cooper, 555)

His notable collection of watercolours fetched £58,000 at Christies in 1875; and the value of the remaining pictures at the time of his death was £31,486. Quilter died on 12 November 1888 at his home, 28 Norfolk Street, Park Lane, London, leaving well over half a million pounds, one of the largest known estates of any Victorian accountant.

JOHN RICHARD EDWARDS

Sources M. Bywater, 'Quilter, William', *DBB* · J. R. Edwards, *A history of financial accounting* (1989) · H. Howitt and others, eds., *The history of the Institute of Chartered Accountants in England and Wales, 1880–1965, and of its founder accountancy bodies, 1870–1880* (1966); repr. (1984) · E. Cooper, 'Fifty-seven years in an accountant's office', *The Accountant* (22 Oct 1921), 553–63 · *The Accountant* (17 Nov 1888) · d. cert.

Wealth at death £580,934 0s. 8d.: resworn probate, Sept 1889, *CGPLA Eng. & Wales* (1888)

Quilter, Sir William Cuthbert, first baronet (1841–1911), art collector and politician, was born at South Audley Place, London, on 29 January 1841, the eldest son of William *Quilter (1808–1888), the first president of the Institute of Accountants and a prominent art collector, and his wife, Elizabeth Harriot Cuthbert (d. 1874), and brother of Harry *Quilter (1851–1907), an art critic. Following his private education, Quilter spent five years (1858–63) working for his father's accountancy business. He married Mary Ann, daughter of John Wheeley Bevington of Brighton, on 7 May 1867. Together they had five sons and two daughters. After working for his father, Quilter started his own business, eventually founded as the firm Quilter, Balfour & Co. in 1885. He was one of the founding directors of the National Telephone Company (registered on 10 March 1881) and continued as a director and large shareholder for the remainder of his life. In 1883 Quilter purchased the Bawdsey estate near Felixstowe in Suffolk. He spent vast sums of money on the estate, which totalled 9000 acres, in the form of sea defences, a manor house, and an alpine garden. He was an agriculturist and was particularly adept at cattle breeding. Quilter, an enthusiastic yachtsman, owned a number of famous boats, including the 40 ton cutter *Britannia*, and was vice-commodore of the Royal Harwich Yacht Club from 1875 to 1909. He was also president of the Suffolk Horse Society. In December 1885 Quilter was elected as the Liberal Party member of parliament for Sudbury. He was re-elected as a Liberal Unionist in 1886 and continued as a representative of his constituency until he was defeated at the beginning of 1906. He rarely spoke in the House of Commons. Quilter was made a baronet on 13 September 1897. He was also a justice of the peace and a deputy lieutenant for Suffolk, as well as an alderman of the West Suffolk county council.

Quilter shared his father's interest in art collecting, although he cultivated his own unique, albeit catholic, taste. His collection included works by modern English artists, such as the Pre-Raphaelite painters D. G. Rossetti, Millais, and Holman Hunt; Royal Academicians including Sir Frederic Leighton, Sir Edwin Landseer, and Sir Hubert von Herkomer; nineteenth-century French masters, for example Corot, Daubigny, and Millet; and old masters such as Frans Hals and Velázquez. His collection was well respected. The art critic F. G. Stephens praised Quilter's collection in a series of articles written for *Cassell's Magazine of Art* in 1896–7, wherein he claimed it 'possesses a number of modern masterpieces the merits of which form a whole inferior to none in England' (Stephens, 121). In his reminiscences the artist William Rothenstein made note of the opportunity afforded him to view Quilter's collection. Quilter was generous in loaning his acquisitions to public exhibitions; he lent Sir Joshua Reynolds's *Nymph* and *Piping Boy* (Tate Collection) and Hals's *Pieter Tjarck* to the Royal Academy's winter exhibition in 1891. The whole of his collection was displayed at Lawrie's Galleries, Bond Street, in 1902 in aid of King Edward's Hospital Fund for London. He presented Herkomer's portrait of Spencer Compton Cavendish, eighth duke of Devonshire, to the National Portrait Gallery in 1909. Quilter's assemblage of paintings at his London house, 28 South Street, Park Lane, was sold at Christies on 9 July 1909, realizing £87,780. He died suddenly at Bawdsey Manor on 18 November 1911 and was buried in the parish churchyard.

KIMBERLY MORSE JONES

Sources DNB · F. G. Stephens, 'The collection of Mr W. Cuthbert Quilter, MP', *Cassell's Magazine of Art*, 20 (1896), 121–8; 21 (1897), 316–20 · WWBMP, 2.295 · W. Rothenstein, *Man and memories* (1931), 97 · b. cert. · d. cert. · CGPLA Eng. & Wales (1912) · D. S. Macleod, *Art and the Victorian middle class: money and the making of cultural identity* (1996)
Likenesses B. Stone, photograph, 1901, NPG · Lib [L. Prosperi], chromolithograph caricature, NPG; repro. in VF (9 Feb 1889)
Wealth at death £1,220,639 8s.: probate, 11 Jan 1912, CGPLA Eng. & Wales

Quin [*née* Marshall], **Anne** (*fl.* 1660–1682), actress, was possibly the daughter of Mr Marshall, chaplain to Lord Gerard, and Elizabeth Dutton, illegitimate daughter of John Dutton of Cheshire. She was thought to have been 'educated by godly parents' (Fane, 352). Her sister Rebecca *Marshall also became an actress. Anne was one of the first female performers on the London stage, with the King's Company on 26 March 1661 (PRO, LC 3/73, p. 113). Manuscript casts suggest that Richard Flecknoe intended her to play a breeches role, Aurindo, in his *Erminia* in the 1660–61 season, and she was possibly cast, with her younger sister Rebecca, in Thomas Heywood's *The Royall King* the following year.

Anne was a flexible performer, playing comedic roles such as Margareta in Fletcher's *Rule a Wife and have a Wife*, Celia in his *The Humorous Lieutenant* (which opened the Bridges Street theatre), and Mrs Diligence in John Wilson's *The Cheats*. She was also popular in John Dryden's and Robert Howard's *The Indian Queen*, when Pepys thought 'the eldest Marshall did do her part most excellently well as ever I heard woman in my life; but her voice is not so sweet as Ianthe's [Mrs Betterton]' (Pepys, 25 Jan 1664). She had several supporting tragic roles, such as Almeria in Dryden's *The Indian Emperor*, and another breeches role as the battling Florio in William Killigrew's *The Siege of Urbin*.

Anne Marshall became Mrs Quin or Guin in 1666/7 (causing much confusion with Nell Gwyn), when she married, probably, the actor Peter Quyn, who only appears in records when arrested for acting without a warrant on 28 January 1668 (PRO, LC 5/186, p. 193; Wilson, 169). Anne seems to have suffered a setback in 1667, recorded only in the minor role of Candiope in Dryden's *Secret Love* in February. In May of that year she used the lord chamberlain to order the King's Company to return her larger roles to her, and to allot her 'a dressing roome with a chymney in it to be only for her use & whome she shall admit' (PRO, LC 5/138, p. 376). This indicates her significance to the company, and although Pepys thought less of her acting by 1668, he acknowledged that she was increasingly popular. Of her performance as Zempoalla in *The Indian Queen*, he muses 'do not doat upon Nan Marshall's acting therein, as the world talks of her excellence therein' (Pepys, 27 June 1668).

After 1668 Mrs Quin disappeared from the London stage until 27 November 1675, when she was listed again at the King's Company. However, no named roles are recorded for her until 24 March 1677, by which time she is acting for the rival, more successful, Duke's Company at Dorset Garden. Although we have no record of her earnings, financial considerations may well have played a part in her movement between companies. At Dorset Garden she excelled in comedy, playing the feisty Angelica in Aphra Behn's *The Rover*, Lady Knowell in her *Sir Patient Fancy*, to which she also spoke the epilogue, Lady Squeamish in Otway's *Friendship in Fashion*, as well as an unrecorded part and the epilogue to John Banks's *The Destruction of Troy* (1679). In these troubled years records of Anne's performances are patchy and she does not appear again until May 1681 when she has returned to the King's Company to perform Queen Elizabeth in Banks's *The Unhappy Favourite*. She stayed with the troupe, creating one final role as Sunamire in Thomas Southerne's *The Loyal Brother* in February 1682. It seems that Anne did not perform with the United Company after its formation in 1682.

Anne's celebrity as a performer, in part linked to her attractive figure and dark-haired beauty, is suggested by the commercial representations of her, such as an engraving of her delivering the epilogue to *Sir Patient Fancy*. There is also a record of a remarkable miniature portrait on copper, misidentified as Nell Gwyn, with 'some thirty mica covers … upon which various head-dresses and costumes are painted', which can be overlaid to show Quin in a variety of her roles (Highfill, Burnim & Langhans, *BDA*).

J. MILLING

Sources Highfill, Burnim & Langhans, *BDA* · W. Van Lennep and others, eds., *The London stage, 1660–1800*, pt 1: *1660–1700* (1965) · J. H.

Wilson, *All the king's ladies: actresses of the Restoration* (1958) · J. Downes, *Roscius Anglicanus*, ed. M. Summers, [new edn] (1928) · F. Fane, 'Commonplace book', Shakespeare Memorial Library, Stratford upon Avon [cited in Wilson] · Pepys, *Diary* · lord chamberlain's papers, PRO, LC 3, LC 5
Likenesses engraving, V&A; repro. in M. Summers, ed., *The Restoration theatre* (1934), 88 · engraving, repro. in M. Summers, ed., *The works of Aphra Behn* (1915), vol. 4, p. 115 · portrait, on copper

Quin, Edward (1794–1828), cartographer, son of Edward Turnly *Quin (1762–1823), a newspaper editor of Irish protestant descent, and his wife, Ann Delhoste, matriculated from Magdalen Hall, Oxford, on 26 November 1812, graduated BA in 1817, and proceeded MA in 1820. He was admitted to King's Inns on 13 June 1817 and was called to the bar at Lincoln's Inn in 1823.

Quin practised as a barrister but is remembered chiefly for his *Atlas in a Series of Maps of the World as Known in Different Periods*, published posthumously in 1830. It consists of an unremarkable text by Quin and twenty-one maps, engraved by Sidney Hall. The maps begin with one of 2248 BC, 'The deluge', and end with one of 1828, 'At the general peace' (after the Napoleonic era). The first map shows the garden of Eden sited in Mesopotamia, and occupies little more than a square inch, geographically isolated near the middle of the plate. It is surrounded by clouds that darken away from the small map to the four edges, making nine-tenths of the plate black. In each successive subsequent map the geographical area gradually extends and the clouds roll slowly back as knowledge of the world increases until at last they disappear. The maps are line-engraved on copper, but the clouds themselves are aquatint. The effect of both the individual maps and of the succession of maps is striking and dramatic, and credit for the innovation, widely attributed to the engraver Sidney Hall, lies in fact with Quin himself. An important technical attribute is Quin's use of the same scale for each map. His aim thereby was to represent the world as known in earlier periods but always in comparison with the world as known in his day. In the revealed portion of the world each empire was differently coloured so that:

> every successive map thus combines, at a single glance, both the Geography and History of the age to which it refers; exhibiting by its *extent* the boundaries of the known world and by its *colour* the respective empires into which that world was distributed. (preface)

It is his artistic device of the clouds, however, which marks out the atlas.

The critical reception of Quin's work was narrow but positive. Later commentators have noticed that his idea of the world's gradual revelation had a forerunner in two atlases by the Prussian Friedrich Benicken. There is no evidence that Quin knew of Benicken's atlas, though a German connection is possible, as his father is said in some sources to have served in the army in Germany. Whatever the origin of the idea, Quin's execution was far superior to Benicken's and the succession of maps is compelling, though the text plods. Quin has rather simplistically been accused of Eurocentrism (Black), but Goffart points out that his clouds have no moral quality. They do not

re-advance if an area is lost to civilization, for example in the dark ages that followed the fall of the Roman empire.

A second edition with Hall's plates was issued in 1836, and a third edition published in 1846 has plates by William Hughes. This edition contains the atlas only, without the text. Hughes redrew the maps on a hemispherical projection which somewhat undermines the dramatic effect. Fourth and fifth editions (1850 and 1856) also have Hughes's plates. The text was also published separately. Quin's work was copied by the American educator Emma Willard in her educational works but was not directly taken up by any British successor.

The atlas was Quin's only known cartographic work, and why a barrister should have produced such a striking work is unclear. Quin died, unmarried, at Hare Court, Inner Temple, London, on 4 May 1828.

ELIZABETH BAIGENT

Sources Foster, *Alum. Oxon.* · W. A. Goffart, 'Breaking the Ortelian pattern: historical atlases with a new program, 1747–1830', *Editing early and historical atlases*, ed. J. Winearls (1995), 49–81 · private information (2004) [Roger Mason] · *GM*, 1st ser, 98/2 (1828), 91 · *IGI* · J. Black, *Maps and history: constructing images of the past* (1997) · administration, PRO, PROB 6/204, fol. 274r

Quin, Edward Turnly (1762–1823), journalist, the son of Henry Turnly Quin of Roscommon, was born in Ireland and entered Trinity College, Dublin, as a pensioner in June 1779, proceeding BA in 1787. On leaving Dublin, according to one account he 'embraced a military life, and distinguished himself in the German service' (Gilliland, 1.511), while another version has it that he went to France 'to teach the pugilistic art' (*A Biographical Dictionary of the Living Authors of Great Britain and Ireland*, 285). He married Ann Delhoste at St Pancras old church on 18 September 1793; they had a son, Edward *Quin (1794–1828). Having settled in London as a journalist and reporter of debates, in 1803 he became editor of *The Traveller* (incorporated in 1822 with *The Globe*), an evening paper which, though intended primarily for commercial travellers, attracted a wider readership and was noted for its advocacy of political reform. As editor, Quin published the earliest of Leigh Hunt's essays (1804). In 1805 he was elected to the common council of the City of London as deputy for the ward of Farringdon Without. Though a protestant himself, Quin was an eloquent defender of civil rights for Catholics, and a speech he delivered in the common council in 1807 against a motion opposing the admission of Roman Catholics into the army was published that year under the title *Catholic Vindicator*. By 1808 he was also the proprietor of three weekly papers, the *Mirror of the Times*, *The Englishman*, and the *British Mercury*. Financial difficulties forced him into temporary retreat, but he later returned to journalism as editor of *The Day*, the auctioneers' paper, until its amalgamation with the *New Times* in 1817. He died at his home in Sheerness, Kent, on 7 July 1823.

G. MARTIN MURPHY

Sources T. Gilliland, *The dramatic mirror, containing the history of the stage from the earliest period, to the present time*, 1 (1808) · [J. Watkins and F. Shoberl], *A biographical dictionary of the living authors of Great*

Britain and Ireland (1816) • H. R. Fox Bourne, *English newspapers: chapters in the history of journalism*, 1 (1887), 288 • *A new biographical dictionary of 3000 cotemporary [sic] public characters, British and foreign, of all ranks and professions*, 2nd edn, 3 vols. in 6 pts (1825) • *The new Cambridge bibliography of English literature*, [2nd edn], 3, ed. G. Watson (1969) • L. Hunt, *The autobiography of Leigh Hunt*, ed. J. E. Morpurgo (1949), 139 • Burtchaell & Sadleir, *Alum. Dubl.* • *DNB*
Archives BL, letter to Thomas Sheridan

Quin, Edwin Richard Windham Wyndham-, third earl of Dunraven and Mount Earl (1812–1871), landowner and archaeologist, was born on 19 May 1812 in London. He was the only son of Windham Henry Wyndham-Quin, second earl of Dunraven and Mount Earl (1782–1850), and his wife, Caroline, *née* Wyndham (1790/91–1870). Their son, known from 1824 as Viscount Adare, graduated BA at Trinity College, Dublin, in the spring of 1833, and represented Glamorgan in parliament as a Conservative from 1837 to 1851. As a member of the House of Commons, his political activity was largely taken up with the attempt to safeguard religious education in Ireland. He became subsequently one of the commissioners of education in Ireland. He was twice married. First, on 18 August 1836, he married Augusta (*d.* 1866), the third daughter of Thomas Goold, master in chancery in Ireland. They had a son and three daughters. He married secondly, on 27 January 1870, Anne (*d.* 1917), daughter of Henry Lambert of Carnagh, Wexford, who, after his death, married the second Lord Hylton.

Adare succeeded his father as third earl in the Irish peerage in 1850, and retired from the House of Commons in the following year. In 1855 he converted to Roman Catholicism. In 1866 he was created a peer of the United Kingdom, with the title Baron Kenry, of Kenry, co. Limerick. He acted as lord lieutenant of county Limerick from 1864 until his death in 1871.

Dunraven had a number of intellectual interests. For three years he studied astronomy under Sir William Hamilton at the Dublin observatory, and acquired a thorough knowledge both of the practical and theoretical sides of the science. He became interested in the claims of spiritualism and was convinced of the genuineness of the phenomena which he investigated. His son, the fourth earl, prepared for him minute reports of séances which the fashionable medium Daniel Dunglas Home had conducted with Dunraven's help in 1867–8. The reports were privately printed in 1869 as *Experiences in Spiritualism with Mr. D. D. Home*, to which Dunraven contributed an introduction. But he was best-known for his zealous interest in archaeology. He was associated with George Petrie, William Stokes, and other Irish archaeologists in the foundation of the Irish Archaeological Society in 1840, and of the Celtic Society in 1845. In 1849 and 1869 he presided over the meetings of the Cambrian Society held at Cardiff and Bridgend, and in 1871 was president of a section of the Royal Archaeological Institute. In 1862 he accompanied the French liberal Catholic Montalembert on a tour of Scotland, and five years later he travelled through France and Italy in order to study churches, and particularly campaniles. But his main interest was in Irish archaeology. He was said to have visited every barony in Ireland, and

nearly every island off the coast, usually in the company of a photographer. Dr William Stokes and his daughter Margaret McNair Stokes frequently accompanied him on his archaeological expeditions.

The chief results of Dunraven's studies, which were meant to continue the work of his friend Petrie, were assembled in *Notes on Irish Architecture*, edited and published in two volumes after his death by Margaret Stokes. The work was illustrated with 161 wood-engravings of drawings by Petrie, W. F. Wakeman, Gordon Hills, Margaret Stokes, Lord Dunraven, and others, as well as with 125 plates. The first volume (1875) dealt with stone buildings and the second (1877) with belfries and with Irish Romanesque architecture.

In 1865 Dunraven compiled, as an appendix to his mother's *Memorials of Adare*, an exhaustive treatise on architectural remains to be found in the immediate vicinity of Adare. The section of this work which discussed the round tower and church of Dysart was reprinted in the second volume of the *Notes*. Dunraven also contributed generously to the restoration of these buildings for the use of religious services. He also contributed some valuable papers to the Royal Irish Academy. He was elected a fellow of the Royal Archaeological Society in 1831, FSA in 1836, FRGS in 1837, and on 10 April 1834 became FRS. Dunraven died at the Imperial Hotel, Great Malvern, Worcestershire, on 6 October 1871, and was buried at Adare. He was a man of quick perceptions and great power of application, an ardent Roman Catholic and admirer of Montalembert, and a highly popular landlord. His son Windham Thomas Wyndham-*Quin, the fourth earl, was an active Irish politician and yachtsman.

G. LE G. NORGATE, *rev.* MICHAEL HERITY

Sources W. T. Wyndham-Quin, 'Preface', in E. R. W. Wyndham-Quin, *Notes on Irish architecture*, ed. M. Stokes, 2 vols. (1875–7) • *The Times* (10 Oct 1871) • *ILN* (21 Oct 1871) • *Limerick Reporter* (10 Oct 1871) • GEC, *Peerage* • Boase, *Mod. Eng. biog.* • Burke, *Peerage* • W. G. Gorman, *Converts to Rome* (1910) • A. Owen, *The darkened room: women, power and spiritualism in late Victorian England*, pbk edn (1989)
Archives Limerick University Library, corresp. and papers • NL Ire., department of manuscripts • NL Ire. • NRA, priv. coll., family corresp. • PRO NIre. | BL, corresp. with W. E. Gladstone, Add. MSS 44358–44364 • BL, corresp. with Sir Robert Peel, Add. MSS 40425–40554 • Bodl. Oxf., corresp. with Lord Kimberley • JRL, letters to E. A. Freeman • NL Ire., corresp. with Lord Emly
Likenesses portraits, NMG Wales
Wealth at death under £100,000: probate, 11 Jan 1872, *CGPLA Eng. & Wales* • £25,783 10*s*. 3*d*.: resealed probate, 16 March 1872, *CGPLA Ire.*

Quin, Frederic Hervey Foster (1799–1878), homoeopathic physician, was born on 12 February 1799, probably in Ireland. Because of his forenames he was incorrectly regarded as the son of Lady Elizabeth Foster, *née* Hervey, mistress and later second wife of the fifth duke of Devonshire; he may have been her godson. He attended a school in Putney run by a Mr Carmalt at what is now Carmalt Gardens. In 1815, after the Napoleonic wars ended, he was sent to France, where he became fluent in French. He attended Edinburgh University from 1817 to 1820 and graduated MD. He was immediately offered, by the prime minister, the post of physician to Napoleon on St Helena. Instead he went to Italy in December 1820 as physician to Elizabeth, by then duchess of Devonshire, and he attended her during her fatal illness in March 1824. Lord Byron invited him to accompany him on his (last) expedition to Greece, but to his regret Quin had to refuse on grounds of ill health. In July 1821 he commenced practice at Naples, and his social gifts made him popular with all the English residents there, who included Sir William Gell, Sir William Drummond, and the countess of Blessington, and with the Comte d'Orsay, upon whom Quin is said to have modelled himself.

At Naples, Quin met Dr Neckar, a disciple of Hahnemann, the founder of homoeopathy, and was impressed favourably enough to visit Leipzig in 1826, in order to study the system. He returned seriously interested if not converted. On the journey he met in Rome Prince Leopold of Saxe-Coburg-Saalfeld, afterwards king of the Belgians, and soon left Naples to become his family physician in England. Quin continued a member of the prince's household until May 1829, either at Marlborough House, London, or at Claremont, Surrey, and he extended his acquaintance in aristocratic circles. From May 1829 to September 1831 he practised in Paris, chiefly but not entirely in homoeopathy. In September 1831, after consulting with Hahnemann as to the treatment of cholera, he proceeded to Tischnowitz in Moravia, where the disease was raging. He contracted the disease himself, but recovered, though he never regained perfect health. He returned to work and under his treatment there were no deaths.

At length, in July 1832, Quin settled in London and introduced the homoeopathic system into England. He lived first at 19 King Street, St James's, and then removed in 1833 to 13 Stratford Place. His practice rapidly grew, owing as much to his attractive personality as to his medical skill. In 1844 he founded the British Homoeopathic Society (later the Faculty of Homoeopathy) which he served as president until his death. Chiefly through his efforts the London Homoeopathic Hospital (later the Royal London Homoeopathic Hospital) was founded in 1849 in Golden Square, Soho; it moved to Great Ormond Street in 1859.

Quin was popular in London society. He was an essential dinner guest of Edward, prince of Wales, and his friends included Dickens, Thackeray, the Bulwers, Macready, Landseer, and Charles Mathews. His contribution to homoeopathic literature was not of major importance. His value lay in the social and medico-political fields. His patients included the duchess of Cambridge, to whom he was physician-in-ordinary, the duke of Edinburgh, and many other members of the aristocracy. From these he was able to obtain the funds to endow the hospital. Their support was always available when homoeopathy was threatened by the medical establishment. Quin was frequently referred to as 'the little doctor', but Thomas Uwins's portrait shows him to have been a handsome man. A brilliant wit and a mine of information, he was also gifted with an unusual memory for past events. His welcome in society was not just due to his medical skill, nor his unusual wit; for though aware of the scandals and

the secrets, he could also be relied upon as a true friend who kept confidences.

Throughout Quin's career homoeopathy was repeatedly attacked by the medical institutions and journals and Quin himself was denounced as a quack. In February 1838, when he was a candidate for election at the Athenaeum, he was blackballed by a clique of physicians led by John Ayrton Paris, who publicly attacked Quin with a virulence for which he had to apologize under threat of a duel. Despite chronic severe asthma and arthritis which necessitated his early retirement from practice, Quin ensured that these battles were won. Homoeopathy spread throughout the country and many of its remedies were appropriated by the conventional establishment.

Unfortunately Quin tended to regard the British Homoeopathic Society and the hospital as his personal property. He showed little patience with homoeopathic colleagues who had different views on policy, but recognizing his merit they tolerated his attitude.

Quin died of bronchitis at the Garden Mansions, Queen Anne's Gate, Westminster, on 24 November 1878, and was buried four days later at Kensal Green cemetery.

G. C. BOASE, rev. BERNARD LEARY

Sources E. Hamilton, *A memoir of F. H. F. Quin* (privately printed, [London], 1879) • S. Uwins, *A memoir of Thomas Uwins*, 2 vols. (1858) • D. M. Stuart, *Dearest Bess: the life and times of Lady Elizabeth Foster* (1955) • journal and correspondence of the sixth duke of Devonshire, Chatsworth House, Derbyshire • Minutes of the British Homoeopathic Society, 1849, 1853, 1854, 1855 • Minutes of the board of governors of the London Homoeopathic Hospital, May–Sept 1876 • M. Sadlier, *Blessington–D'Orsay: a masquerade*, 2nd edn (1947) • R. Gower, *My reminiscences*, 2 vols. (1883) • personal information (2004) • R. R. Madden, *The literary life and correspondence of the countess of Blessington*, 3 vols. (1855), vol. 1, p. 191; vol. 2, pp. 26, 27, 111–14, 448–54; vol. 3, p. 201 • *Morning Post* (29 Nov 1878), 5 • *Memoirs, journal and correspondence of Thomas Moore*, ed. J. Russell, 6 (1854), 318 • [C. J. Mathews], *The life of Charles James Mathews*, ed. C. Dickens, 1 (1879), 102 • d. cert. • *Pioneers of Homeopathy*

Archives Royal Arch., corresp. • Royal Sandringham Library, letters | U. Durham L., archives and special collections, letters to Viscount Ponsonby

Likenesses A. Cecioni, coloured lithograph, 1872, Wellcome L. • duke of Cambridge, sketches, Royal Collection • Count D'Orsay, lithograph, BM • E. Morton, lithograph, Wellcome L. • E. Taylor, sketches, Royal Collection • T. Uwins, oils (as a young man), Faculty of Homoeopathy, London; copy, 1850, Hahnemann House Trust, London

Wealth at death under £14,000: resworn probate, Jan 1881, CGPLA Eng. & Wales (1879)

Quin, James (1620/21–1659). *See under* Quin, Walter (c.1575–1641).

Quin, James (1693–1766), actor, was born in King Street, Covent Garden, London, on 24 February 1693, in circumstances that have embarrassed some biographers and confused others. His paternal grandfather was lord mayor of Dublin in 1667; evidently worried about money, he committed suicide in 1674. His son, James Quin, studied at Trinity College, Dublin, and then at London's Lincoln's Inn. It was in England that he met and married Elizabeth Grindzell about 1690. This James Quin, an unusually unworldly lawyer, seems to have accepted Mrs Grindzell's word that her first husband, formerly a soldier but now

James Quin (1693–1766), by William Hogarth, *c.*1739

working as a shoemaker in Shrewsbury, was dead. It was not until about 1701 that the news of the bigamy broke, and even then the Quins agreed to maintain their marriage. The young James Quin was their only child, and had hopes of inheriting a considerable estate when his father died in May 1710, but the will was successfully contested by his Irish uncle John Quin and a first cousin called William Whitehead. Quin did not abandon the fight, nor did he lose touch with his Irish roots. His parents had sent him to school in Dublin from about 1700, and he may have attended Trinity College, Dublin, with a view to a legal career, but he enjoyed the company of actors and quite early aspired to the stage. His first appearances probably occurred in Dublin in 1713 or 1714, and by early 1715 he was a member of the company at Drury Lane in London. He made his English début as Vulture in Charles Johnson's derivative *The Country Lasses* on 4 February 1715, and followed it with a number of supporting roles in the season's repertory.

Quin's rise was not a meteoric one. Even as a young man he was stately rather than handsome. His weight would increase with his years, his face grow fat, and his chin double. It was intelligence of phrasing and vocal musicality that distinguished him, placing him in direct descent from Thomas Betterton. It was to these qualities that the Drury Lane audience responded on 7 November 1716, when John Mills was taken ill and Quin stepped in to read the part of Bajazet in Nicholas Rowe's *Tamerlane*. Despite the warmth of the reception, he had to be satisfied with supporting roles in the well-established Drury Lane company. It was probably financial necessity that led him to perform at Southwark fair in September 1717, and at the

end of that year he transferred from Drury Lane to John Rich's company at the Lincoln's Inn Fields playhouse. He would remain with Rich for the next sixteen years, during which he climbed to the head of his profession.

Witty and socially at ease, Quin did not lack self-belief. To the unknown writer who rushed a racy biography through the presses immediately after Quin's death in 1766, his subject was:

> one of the best actors and most facetious men of his time; who was at once the gentleman and the scholar—the philosopher and the critic—the humourist and the moral man, the scourge of knaves and fools, and the admiration of the sensible and good. (*Life*, 7)

The portrait was recognizable by those who had known Quin in his maturity, but probably not by those who knew him only in his youth. There was much gossip, then, about drinking bouts, philandering, and intrigue. Things came to a head towards the end of Quin's first season at Lincoln's Inn Fields. On the afternoon of 17 April 1718, during a chance meeting at a Cornhill tavern, he had a fierce quarrel with William Bowen, a notoriously hot-headed member of the Drury Lane company twice Quin's age. It culminated in a scrappy duel in which Bowen was fatally wounded. At his trial Quin was found guilty of manslaughter, but seems not to have been branded on the hand, exonerated perhaps by Bowen's reputation. The theatrical public welcomed him back, but the fiery temper remained. Although Quin had many friendships, including a lifelong one with the actor Lacy Ryan, it was his enmities that made news. Actors were so much in the public eye by the middle of the century that they were hard-pressed to conceal their private quarrels. Given their common sensitivity to provocation, it is hardly surprising that Quin, at various stages of his long career, had noisy spats with Charles Macklin and Theophilus Cibber. His dislike of Peg Woffington and Kitty Clive led him to make cutting observations about both in the semi-public forum of the green room, but this was out of character with his normal chivalry towards women. He never married, perhaps burdened by a fear of his sexual unattractiveness. Lady Mary Coke reported an occasion when the duchess of Queensberry, observing that he rarely played lovers, asked him, 'Pray, Mr Quin, do you ever make love?', to which the actor replied, 'No, Madam, I always buy it ready made' (Nash, 196). His habitual overeating may, of course, have been Quin's compensating response to loneliness. His protective concern for actresses he admired, Susannah Cibber and George Anne Bellamy, for example, was sentimental rather than sexual. They, like the poet James Thomson, benefited from his generosity at crucial periods in their lives.

During his years at Lincoln's Inn Fields, Quin played leading roles in both tragedy and comedy: Othello, Macbeth, King Lear (in the Nahum Tate version), Brutus in *Julius Caesar*, the title role in Jonson's *Volpone*, Pinchwife in Wycherley's *The Country Wife*, once (for his own benefit performance in 1730) Macheath in Gay's *The Beggar's Opera*: the stately Quin letting his hair down in a singing role. He was, though, generally careful in his choice of parts, knowing himself unsuited to romance and heroism. His comic preference was for the sourer, scowling edges, and he was probably at his finest as the debauched Sir John Brute in Vanbrugh's *The Provoked Wife*. But it was memories of his Falstaff that endured longest, monumentalized in china statuettes put out by Bow, Derby, and Staffordshire and widely sold. This was a part in which he had no rivals. Indeed, between the death of Robert Wilks in 1732 and Garrick's London début in 1741, Quin was England's leading actor, able to command high salaries wherever he went. Dublin's theatres vied for his favours during the summer closure of London's patent houses, and he seems to have used his visits to the Irish capital to pursue his claims on his patrimony. Given the prosperity in which he lived his last years, it is possible that he reached a settlement with his Irish relations.

It was a sign of Quin's status that Drury Lane petitioned for his return at the beginning of the season in 1734. Charles Fleetwood, the new patentee, needed help with the management of his troublesome company, and Quin was one of the very few people with sufficient authority to take on the job. He remained at Drury Lane until the early summer of 1741. Despite his brushes with Macklin and Cibber, he merited and earned the respect of his fellows. Whether or not he recognized it, he was the guardian of an old theatrical tradition. But times were about to change. The first major sign came with the Drury Lane revival of *The Merchant of Venice* on 14 February 1741. Quin played Antonio, just as he had played such parts before, but the Shylock of his old adversary Macklin was revolutionary, no longer a comic villain but a feeling, suffering human being. Beside Quin's measured cadences, Macklin's speaking style was startlingly natural. Audiences, a little bemused, were stirred. Not so Quin. At the end of the season he undertook the longest of his Irish tours, playing mostly at the Aungier Street theatre from June 1741 to February 1742. He was not in London in October 1741, when Garrick's début at Goodman's Fields carried the Macklin revolution a significant step further. For the rest of his life Quin would always, and generally unfavourably, be compared with Garrick.

Despite the clamour of the theatrical public, it was some years before the two men acted together. Garrick was still at Goodman's Fields when Quin marked his return to Rich's company at Covent Garden on 25 March 1742 by playing one of his favourite Roman characters, Joseph Addison's Cato. His arrangement with Rich allowed him, now that he had passed fifty, to appear less regularly, and it was in the 1740s that he began to develop his fashionable contacts in Bath. Finally, for the 1746–7 season at Covent Garden, Rich succeeded in bringing Garrick and Quin together. It was a curious misjudgement of Quin's to open his campaign as Richard III, a part which Garrick had made his own, and it was not until 14 November 1746 that the two appeared together, Quin as Horatio and Garrick as Lothario in Rowe's *The Fair Penitent*. For the fourteen-year-old future playwright Richard Cumberland, the contrast was thrilling: Lothario, 'young and light and alive in every muscle and in every feature', bounding onto the stage to confront a 'heavy-paced Horatio'. 'It seemed as if a whole century had been stept over in the transition of a single scene' (Cumberland, 59–60). Quin measured up better when playing Falstaff to Garrick's Hotspur in *I Henry IV* on 6 December 1746, but was again at risk on 2 January 1747 when playing Gloster to Garrick's Hastings in Rowe's *Jane Shore*. Quin had his loyal defenders, but he knew he was outgunned. It is to his credit, as well as Garrick's, that, although they never again acted together, the two men remained friends. Garrick seems even to have envisaged a managerial partnership with Quin when first contemplating a bid for the Drury Lane patent. Susannah Cibber applauded the idea, writing of Quin, 'He is an honest, worthy man, and besides being a great actor he is a very useful one and will make the under actors mind their business' (Nash, 217–18).

There is no evidence that Quin was interested in so heavy a commitment. He was in Bath when the Covent Garden season opened in September 1747, and there was a widely rumoured correspondence between him and his manager, John Rich. 'I am at Bath', wrote Quin. 'Stay there, and be damned', replied Rich. But if there was a quarrel, it was a short-lived one. Quin remained a regular member of the Covent Garden company from 1748 until his formal retirement on 15 May 1751, when he appeared in the inauspicious role of Horatio in *The Fair Penitent*. If, as has been claimed, Rich paid Quin £1000 for his final season, it was the highest salary any actor had yet received. Later appearances at Covent Garden were confined to the benefit performances of his old friend Lacy Ryan in 1752 and 1753. But for the loss of front teeth, he would have been there again in 1754. His note to Ryan has appeared in various versions, but it was along the lines of 'There is no person on earth, whom I would sooner serve than Ryan, but by G—, I will whistle Falstaff for no man' (Highfill, Burnim & Langhans, *BDA*).

In retirement, Quin was a familiar figure, carrying his vast bulk (he weighed as much as 20 stone) into the assembly rooms. There were even rumours that he aspired to succeed Beau Nash as master of ceremonies, though that seems unlikely. He was content to hobnob with the nobility and to gourmandize. Most summers he would travel north as a house guest of the aristocracy. In June 1762, for example, he amused Garrick and other guests of the duke of Devonshire at Chatsworth House by driving himself about the Peak district in a one-horse chaise, carrying always an umbrella, rain or shine (Oman, 226). It was during a visit to the Garricks' villa in Hampton in January 1766 that one of Quin's hands became seriously inflamed. He returned to Bath in great anxiety, and died there on the 21st. He was buried in Bath Abbey on 25 January, and Garrick composed an epitaph for his monument there.

Quin's will, drawn up in July 1765, is, in some ways, a surprising document. There were no theatrical beneficiaries, and the only familiar name is that of Thomas Gainsborough, 'limner, now living at Bath'. Bequests to relatives are outnumbered by those to tradesmen—a London oilman, a publican, a wine merchant (these were his executors). Always a valetudinarian, Quin left £200 to his London doctor and his gold-headed crutch cane to a Bath surgeon, perhaps the one who treated ineffectively his infected hand in January 1766. Particularly touching is the gift of £100 to Mrs Mary Sampson, landlady, with whom Quin may have boarded at Centre House in Bath's Pierpont Street, 'to be paid by my executors into her own hands, independent of all her creditors whatsoever' (*Life*, 63–4). It is noteworthy, since Quin's detractors accused him of obsequiousness, that there are no bequests to the nobility.

Quin was the first actor to be well treated by painters, though surviving portraits all date from his maturity. Most fascinating is a pencil sketch by Hogarth, now in the Royal Collection, comparing the physical proportions of Quin and Garrick. Quin and Hogarth were fellow members of the freemasons' lodge at the Bear and Harrow in London's Butcher Row, and the artist painted the actor at least three times. Gainsborough's portrait of Quin in old age expresses more of the gourmand than the player, but the greatest damage to Quin's standing was committed by the unknown artist who sketched him in ink and wash as Coriolanus. The often reproduced engraving of this sketch shows a mountainous Quin, sporting a ludicrously plumed helmet and a suit of armour rimmed by a flared miniskirt beneath which his knee-breeches are just visible. There were, to be sure, people who accused Quin of walking in blank verse, but he was never as risible as this drawing makes him.   PETER THOMSON

Sources Highfill, Burnim & Langhans, *BDA* · *The life of Mr James Quin, comedian* (1766); repr. (1887) · M. Nash, *The provoked wife: the life and times of Susannah Cibber* (1977) · J. Dunbar, *Peg Woffington and her world* (1968) · W. W. Appleton, *Charles Macklin: an actor's life* (1961) · C. Oman, *David Garrick* (1958) · G. W. Stone and G. M. Kahrl, *David Garrick: a critical biography* (1979) · K. A. Burnim, *David Garrick, director* [1961] · R. Cumberland, *Memoirs of Richard Cumberland written by himself*, 2 vols. (1806–7)

Likenesses attrib. W. Hogarth, oils, *c.*1730, Garr. Club · W. Hogarth, oils, *c.*1739, Tate collection [*see illus.*] · J. Highmore?, oils, *c.*1740, Garr. Club · J. Faber junior, mezzotint, 1744 (after T. Hudson), BM, NPG · T. Hudson, oils, 1744 · ink and wash drawing, *c.*1745 (as Coriolanus), priv. coll. · W. Hogarth, pencil sketch, *c.*1747, Royal Collection · T. Hudson?, oils, *c.*1750, Stafford House, collection of Sir Philip Grey Egerton · F. Hayman, oils, 1754 (as Falstaff), NG Ire. · T. Gainsborough, oils, 1763, NG Ire.; version, Royal Collection · T. King, relief portrait medallion on monument, Bath Abbey, Somerset · J. Macardell, mezzotint (as Falstaff), BM, NG Ire. · J. Macardell, oils, Folger · S. Rogers, engraving (after T. Hudson, 1744), repro. in *Life of Mr. James Quin*, frontispiece · J. Vanderbank, oils; Christies, 22 Sept 1978 · china statuette (as Falstaff)

Wealth at death £2371 named bequests plus residue: will · possibly property in Bath, London, Dublin

Quin, Michael Joseph (1796–1843), journalist and travel writer, was born in Thurles, co. Tipperary, the third son of Morty Quin, distiller. He entered Trinity College, Dublin, as a pensioner on 4 November 1811, was admitted to Lincoln's Inn on 26 January 1818, and was subsequently called to the bar. He made a name for himself as a writer on foreign affairs with *A Visit to Spain* (1823), first published as a series of letters to the *Morning Herald*, which gave an impartial and vivid account of the state of the country at the end of the liberal triennium (1820–23). It was favourably reviewed by Blanco White in the *Quarterly Review* of 1823 (vol. 29, 240–41). While defending the cause of constitutional liberty, Quin accurately reported the reactionary trend of popular opinion, provoked by anti-clerical extremists. A firm opponent of the Holy Alliance, he published in the same year a *Secret History of the Council of Verona*, exposing the part played by Don Carlos, the comte de Jouffroy, and the duc de Montmorency in plotting French armed intervention against the Spanish constitutional government. His translation, entitled *Memoirs of Ferdinand VII*, of the work by José Joaquín de Mora (1823), provided further evidence against the king whom the French restored to absolute power.

In 1824 Quin took up the cause of the former emperor of Mexico, Agustín de Iturbide, then in London planning a return to power. He tried unsuccessfully to win Canning's backing for Iturbide, and translated the latter's apologia, *A Statement of some of the Principal Events in the Public Life of Agustín de Iturbide*, published by John Murray in June 1824. When Iturbide left for Mexico in May, Quin was entrusted with the care of his elder children's education and was responsible for placing his son at Ampleforth College. Iturbide was executed on 19 July, five days after reaching Mexico.

Quin contributed many articles on foreign affairs to the *Morning Chronicle* and *Morning Herald*, and for seven years (1825–32) was editor of the *Monthly Review*. He was a loyal supporter of Daniel O'Connell and of the campaign for Catholic emancipation, and from March 1828 to March 1829 edited the *Catholic Journal*, which represented the English Catholic Cisalpines who advocated the policy of making some concessions to the government in return for the grant of emancipation. He defended this policy at a heated meeting of the Catholic Association which was reported in the *Catholic Miscellany* of February 1829 (2.69). The author described Quin as 'eminently conciliatory; his forehead is good; a ruddy freshness is diffused over his face, and his eye is quick and good-natured', even though he lacked the power to move an audience. 'There is more of the lawyer than the orator about him. In his moments apparently the most impassioned you can see the man of prudent calculation.' In 1835 he approached Nicholas Wiseman, then on a visit to London, with a view to the establishment of a Catholic periodical comparable with the *Edinburgh Review* and *Quarterly Review*. Quin, Wiseman, and O'Connell were co-proprietors of the new journal, entitled the *Dublin Review*, though it had no financial backing other than an indemnity fund of £500. Quin edited the first two issues (May and July 1836) but in October 1836, on being offered a post in the Spanish colonial service in Cuba, he precipitately resigned, leaving the trustees to find a new editor in the absence of Wiseman and O'Connell. The Cuban venture fell through, and when Quin returned from Madrid, O'Connell refused to reinstate him as editor and regarded his co-proprietorship as having lapsed. Though Quin continued to contribute articles to the review, the episode created a rift in his relations with O'Connell. In February 1842 the printers of *The*

Tablet, after a dispute with Frederick Lucas, appointed Quin to succeed him as editor and he held the post for the remainder of the year, during which time Lucas produced a rival publication, the *True Tablet*. O'Connell swayed opinion in favour of Lucas, who resumed full control in January 1843.

In addition to the titles already listed, Quin published *The Trade of Banking in England* (1833), summarizing the evidence submitted to the parliamentary committee appointed to examine the renewal of the Bank of England's charter, and an 'oriental romance', *Nourmahal* (1838). He enjoyed his greatest success, however, as a travel writer, and was one of the first to exploit the opportunities of steam. His *Steam Voyage Down the Danube: with Sketches of Hungary, Wallachia, Servia and Turkey* (1835) explored territory unfamiliar to the reading public, and this was followed by *Steam Voyages on the Seine, the Moselle and the Rhine* (1843). He was elected a fellow of the Royal Society of Literature about 1823.

In his last years Quin was beset by poverty and ill health. For reasons of economy he moved to Boulogne, where he died of lung disease on 19 February 1843 and was buried in the English cemetery. He was survived by his widow, the daughter of Edward Wallis of Burton Grange, York, and three daughters. His brother-in-law, John Edward Wallis, succeeded Frederick Lucas as editor of *The Tablet* in 1855.

G. MARTIN MURPHY

Sources *GM*, 2nd ser., 19 (1843), 438 · Gillow, *Lit. biog. hist.* · J. L. Altholz, 'Early proprietorship of the *Dublin Review*', *Victorian Periodicals Review*, 23 (1990), 54–6 · *The correspondence of Daniel O'Connell*, ed. M. R. O'Connell, 5–7, IMC (1977–80) · W. M. Robertson, *Iturbide of Mexico* (1952) · Burtchaell & Sadleir, *Alum. Dubl.*, 2nd edn · W. P. Baildon, ed., *The records of the Honorable Society of Lincoln's Inn: admissions*, 2 (1896), 74 · *Wellesley index* · *The Oscotian*, new ser. (April 1887), 102
Archives PRO, FO 50/5, fols. 146–71 · PRO, FO 50/8, fols. 149–51, 161 | Ushaw College, Durham, Wiseman papers 154, 247, 270

Quin, Walter (*c*.1575–1641), poet and royal tutor, was born in Dublin. He was apparently studying at Edinburgh University when, in 1595, he was presented to James VI, who was charmed with his manner. He further recommended himself to the king by giving him some poetic anagrams of his own composition on James's name in Latin, Italian, English, and French, together with a poetical composition in French entitled 'Discours sur le mesme anagramme en forme de dialogue entre un Zelateur du bien public, et une Dame laquelle represente le royaume d'Angleterre'. The good impression which Quin made was confirmed by his presenting the king, on new year's day 1596, with an oration about his title to the English throne. The Edinburgh printer Waldegrave refused, however, to print a book on the subject which Quin prepared in February 1598. Quin was at the time reported to be writing a response to the fourth book of Edmund Spenser's *Faerie Queene*, where the king's mother, Mary, queen of Scots, was denounced under the name of Duessa.

Meanwhile Quin had been taken into the service of James VI as tutor to his sons, and he gave abundant proof of his loyalty by publishing *Sertum poeticum in honorem Jacobi sexti serenissimi ac potentissimi Scotorum regis* (1600).

The volume consists of some of Quin's early anagrams on the king's names, some Latin odes and epigrams, and some English sonnets, addressed either to members of the royal family or to frequenters of the court who interested themselves in literature. In 1604 Quin celebrated the marriage of his friend Sir William Alexander in a poem that was to remain unprinted among the Hawthornden manuscripts at Edinburgh University.

Quin migrated with the Scottish king to England in 1603 on his accession to the English throne, and was employed as music teacher in the household of Prince Henry at a salary of £50 per annum. He lamented the prince's death in 1612 in two sonnets, respectively in English and Italian, in Latin verse, and in some stanzas in French; these elegies were printed in Joshua Sylvester's *Lachrymae lachrymarum* (1612), and the two in English and Latin were reissued in *Mausoleum* (1613). In 1611 he contributed Italian verses in praise of the author to Thomas Coryat's *Odcombian Banquet*.

Quin became, after Prince Henry's death, preceptor to his brother Charles. For Charles's use he compiled *Corona virtutum principe dignarum ex variis philosophorum, historicorum, oratorum, et poetarum floribus contexta et concinnata*, with accounts of the lives and virtues of Antoninus Pius and Marcus Aurelius (1613); this was reissued at Leiden in 1634, and in Stephen de Melle's *Syntagma philosophicum* (1670, 5.336–481). A more ambitious literary venture followed in *The memorie of the most worthy and renowned Bernard Stuart, Lord D'Aubigni, renewed, whereunto are added wishes presented to the prince at his creation* (1619); 'A short collection of the most notable places of histories' in prose is appended, together with a series of poems, entitled 'Wishes', and addressed to Prince Charles.

On Charles I's marriage in 1625 Quin published a congratulatory poem in four languages—Latin, English, French, and Italian. It bore the title *In nuptiis principum incomparabilium, Caroli Britannici imperii monarchae … et Henriettae Mariae gratulatio quadrilinguis* (1625). Ten Latin lines signed 'Walt. O—Quin Armig.' are prefixed to Sir Thomas Herbert's *Travels* in 1634. An undated petition, assigned to 1635, from Quin's son John describes both Quin and his wife as ancient servants of the royal family, and prays that the pension of £100 per annum granted to Quin may be continued during life to the petitioner. Nothing more is heard of Quin until 1641, when notification of his death in London was lodged by his widow, Anne.

Another son, **James Quin** (1620/21–1659), was born in Middlesex, obtained a scholarship at Westminster School, and was elected aged eighteen to Christ Church, Oxford, in 1639. He graduated BA in 1642 and MA in 1646, and was elected a senior student. He contributed to the Oxford University collections of Latin verse issued on the return of the king from Scotland in 1641, and on the peace with the Netherlands in 1654.

As an avowed royalist Quin was ejected from his studentship by the parliamentary visitors in 1648. Anthony Wood, who was acquainted with him, often heard him 'sing with great admiration'. His voice was a bass, 'the best … in England', but 'he wanted skill and could scarce sing in consort'. He contrived to obtain an introduction to Cromwell, who was so delighted with his musical talent that, 'liquored by him with sack', he restored him to his place at Christ Church (*Life and Times of Anthony Wood*, 1.287). In 1651 he was reported to be 'non compos'. He died in October 1659, in a crazed condition, in his bedmaker's house in Penny Farthing Street in Oxford, and was buried in the cathedral of Christ Church.

SIDNEY LEE, *rev.* J. K. MᶜGINLEY

Sources *CSP Scot. ser., 1589–1603* · E. Brydges, *Restituta, or, Titles, extracts, and characters of old books in English literature*, 4 vols. (1814–16), vol. 1, p. 520; vol. 3, p. 431 · C. Cornwallis, *A discourse of the most illustrious prince, Henry, late prince of Wales* (1641), sig. C7 · Society of Antiquaries of Scotland, *Archaeologica Scotica*, 4 (1831) · J. P. Collier and F. Egerton, *Catalogue, bibliographical and critical, of early English literature* (1837) · *CSP dom., 1625–49*, 2 · T. Birch, ed., *The life of Henry, prince of Wales* (1760), 51 · J. Welch, *The list of the queen's scholars of St Peter's College, Westminster*, ed. [C. B. Phillimore], new edn (1852), 114 · Foster, *Alum. Oxon., 1500–1714* [James Quin] · M. Burrows, ed., *The register of the visitors of the University of Oxford, from AD 1647 to AD 1658*, CS, new ser., 29 (1881) · *The life and times of Anthony Wood*, ed. A. Clark, 5 vols., OHS, 19, 21, 26, 30, 40 (1891–1900) · will

Quin, Windham Thomas Wyndham-, fourth earl of **Dunraven and Mount Earl** (1841–1926), politician and yachtsman, was born at Adare Manor, co. Limerick, on 12 February 1841. He was the only son of Edwin Richard Windham Wyndham-*Quin, third earl (1812–1871), and his first wife, Augusta (*d.* 1866), daughter of Thomas *Goold, master in chancery in Ireland. During his boyhood his father, who had been under the influence of the Tractarian movement, joined the Roman Catholic church. Lady Dunraven, however, remained strongly protestant; the boy was sent to Rome for education, and forbidden to communicate with his mother. This produced an obstinate resistance. Lord Adare, as he then was, after some tuition in Paris, went to Christ Church, Oxford, in 1858.

After three idle years at Oxford, Adare entered the army in 1862, as cornet in the first Life Guards, and with his troop saw the 'battle of Hyde Park' on 23 July 1866, when the crowd threw down the railings as a protest against the cabinet's prohibition of a meeting of the Reform League. He rode steeplechases, being a very light weight, and raced a little; but already the passion of his life was sailing, and his leaves were mostly spent on a yacht. In 1867, when the military expedition to Abyssinia was announced, Adare contrived to get the post of war correspondent for the *Daily Telegraph*, and was present at the capture of Magdala. He again acted for the *Daily Telegraph* in the war of 1870 between France and Prussia, and witnessed the earlier battles from the Prussian crown prince's headquarters. He spent the winter of 1870–71 at Versailles, and was present when the king of Prussia was proclaimed German emperor. There, in 1919, he saw the signing of the peace between the allies and defeated Germany: he was the only person who was present on both occasions.

Adare married on 29 April 1869 Florence Elizabeth (1841–1916), second daughter of Lord Charles Lennox Kerr; they had three daughters, two of whom predeceased him. In 1871 he succeeded to the peerage, taking his seat in the House of Lords as second Baron Kenry, a United Kingdom

Windham Thomas Wyndham-Quin, fourth earl of Dunraven and Mount Earl (1841–1926), by F. A. Swaine

title granted to his father in 1866; he inherited estates in county Limerick, but his wealth was mostly derived from his lands in south Wales. He went to America (which he had visited with his wife in 1869) for big game shooting. He was introduced by General Sheridan to Buffalo Bill (William Cody) and Texas Jack, and with these famous scouts he shot buffalo and wapiti about the Platte River during the Indian wars. He purchased a ranch in Colorado, which was later neglected and a troublesome incubus to its owner. In 1874 he again went to the United States, accompanied Dr George Henry Kingsley, and explored the Yellowstone region. His observations were published as *The Great Divide* (1876). From this time on for sixteen years he yearly crossed to North America for sport, especially in Canada and Newfoundland.

Unlike his predecessors, who had lived chiefly at Dunraven Castle, Glamorgan, Dunraven made his home at Adare, co. Limerick. In 1880 he wrote to the American press in defence of Irish landlords, and published the first of his many pamphlets on Irish public affairs, *The Irish Question*. In politics, Dunraven became closely associated with Lord Randolph Churchill. He was president of the Fair Trade League (whose views he represented in the royal commission on the depression of trade in 1885) and in April 1883 published in the *Nineteenth Century* a tory-democratic manifesto with Churchill's support. This document called for the reorganization of the Conservative Party along Chamberlainite lines, denounced radicalism as essentially 'communistic', and advocated protectionism and imperialism. In 1885–6 and again in 1886–7 he was under-secretary for the colonies in Lord Salisbury's administration but resigned, ostensibly because he thought the government unfair to Newfoundland in the controversy with France over the fishery question, but really in support of Lord Randolph Churchill. In 1889 he was offered but declined the governorship of the Cape Colony.

Turning his attention to social subjects, Dunraven moved in the House of Lords for the appointment of a committee on sweated labour, carried his motion, and was appointed chairman (1888–90). He considered that much later legislation sprang from its recommendations. In 1895 he was elected a London county councillor for Wandsworth, and took a particular interest in the provision of working-class housing. A different task was the chairmanship in 1896 of the commission on Irish horse breeding. His stud at Adare was famous and successful. He raced a good deal, but his interest lay chiefly in breeding: Desmond was the most famous of his sires.

In the years before 1900, however, Dunraven was chiefly known to the public as a yachtsman and faced criticism for neglecting his political duty for this sport. He competed for the America's Cup in 1893 and 1895 with two specially built yachts, *Valkyrie II* and *Valkyrie III*—both times unsuccessfully. In the second contest against the American *Defender* he withdrew from the third race, being dissatisfied with the keeping of the course. His subsequent protest in a pamphlet created much acrimony, and he was struck off the membership of the New York yacht club. Dunraven took out his certificate as master and extra master, and in 1900 published *Self-Instruction in the Practice and Theory of Navigation*, primarily for the use of yachtsmen. This training enabled him in the First World War to take command of the steam yacht *Grianaig* (bought and run at his own expense) for service as a hospital ship.

Dunraven's interest in Ireland revived in the early 1900s. In 1902 George Wyndham, as chief secretary, was contending with a renewed outburst of land agitation, when the idea of a conference between representatives of landlords and tenants was suggested in a public letter by Captain John Shawe-Taylor, a young Galway squire. Wyndham recognized the political usefulness of the idea and gave it official endorsement. It was also accepted by the nationalist leaders, but repudiated by the Irish Landlords' Convention. However, a group of landlords, of whom Dunraven was chief, set up an organization which polled the lieutenants and deputy lieutenants of Ireland on the question and secured 103 votes for conference against 33 opposing. After further proceedings, the landlords' convention having renewed its refusal, a poll of individual landlords nominated four representatives, Lord Mayo, Colonel Sir Hutcheson Poe, Colonel Nugent Everard, and Lord Dunraven. When the conference of eight assembled, Dunraven was named chairman on the motion of John Redmond. After long and difficult negotiation a unanimous report recommended a general policy of land purchase, and specified terms. This became the basis of the Wyndham Land Act (1903), which settled the policy that Irish landlords should, without exception, be bought out and the occupier become the owner. The actual terms

agreed at the conference were less important to Dunraven than the opportunity it provided for presenting the bill as a 'final solution' to the land question, reached by conciliatory means.

This achievement was the great success of Dunraven's life, and naturally led him to attempt more. However, his hopes received a setback when William O'Brien, the foremost nationalist advocate of 'conciliation', resigned from the party in November 1903. In 1904 the Land Conference was revived as the Irish Reform Association, which advocated the policy of 'devolution', a partial transfer of Irish administration and legislation to an Irish assembly. Dunraven hoped that such self-government within the UK would restore the landlords to their natural place as architects of Irish social regeneration. Sir Antony MacDonnell, the under-secretary, helped to draft the proposals which, when published in 1905, were denounced by extreme nationalists and unionists alike, with the result that the scheme broke down and Wyndham was forced into resigning the chief secretaryship. Dunraven did not abandon his hopes for conciliation, and when O'Brien returned to active political life and launched a new organization, the All-for-Ireland League, in 1909, he gave it public support.

In the struggle over the Home Rule Bill and the Parliament Act, Dunraven played a cross-bench part. His last opportunity to forward what he always believed in, a settlement of the Irish difficulty by conciliation between different sections of the Irish community, came with the Irish Convention in 1917, in which he advocated a solution on federal lines. But there, as elsewhere, he lacked one of the main qualifications of a political leader: he had neither the equipment nor the temperament of an orator. Dunraven was saddened by partition and by the violence of 1919–21, but he supported the Anglo-Irish treaty of 1921. In January 1922 he urged southern unionists to recognize the Irish provisional government and support its efforts to restore order. He was among the members nominated by President Cosgrave to serve on the first senate of the Irish Free State in June 1921.

Physically, Dunraven was a small, sturdy man with a weathered face. Few of his contemporaries touched life at more points, and although he experimented in many directions, he dropped nothing that interested him, while his physical endurance permitted. A large experiment in tobacco-growing at Adare was checked by the accidental burning of his factory in 1916; but even so he continued to grow as much Turkish leaf as would supply the cigarette factory that he had established. He also constantly advocated the serious development of fish supply by hatcheries, both freshwater and marine, for the British Isles. Politically, his career was eccentric and unsuccessful. His early adherence to Lord Randolph Churchill ruled out any significant role in British politics after 1887. In Ireland the 'Dunravenites' were always a small minority of protestant landowners, dependent on the sympathetic ear of Dublin Castle for success. Their weakness was compounded particularly in 1904–5 by ineptitude in political tactics and their limited strategic vision. The failure to resolve the contradiction between unionism and devolution had disastrous political consequences for the advocates of 'constructive unionism'. In the course of his life Dunraven published a number of pamphlets defending his political opinions. His memoirs were published in 1922 as *Past Times and Pastimes*. He died at his home, 22 Norfolk Street, Park Lane, London, on 14 June 1926, and was succeeded by his cousin Windham Henry Wyndham-Quin.

S. L. GWYNN, *rev.* PETER GRAY

Sources R. F. Foster, *Lord Randolph Churchill: a political life* (1981); repr. (1988) · A. Gailey, *Ireland and the death of kindness* (1987) · P. Bew, *Conflict and conciliation in Ireland, 1880–1910* (1987) · P. Buckland, *Irish unionism*, 1: *The Anglo-Irish and the new Ireland* (1972) · *The Times* (15 June 1926) · A. T. C. Pratt, ed., *People of the period: being a collection of the biographies of upwards of six thousand living celebrities*, 2 vols. (1897)

Archives Limerick University Library, corresp. and papers · NRA, priv. coll., corresp. and papers, incl. diaries · PRO NIre. | CAC Cam., corresp. with Lord Randolph Churchill · Herts. ALS, Grenfell MSS, letters to Lady Desborough · NL Ire., corresp. with Lord Emly · NL Ire., letters to T. C. Harrington · NL Ire., corresp. with W. O'Brien · NL Ire., corresp. with James O'Mara · NL Ire., letters to John Redmond · Plunkett Foundation, Long Hanborough, Oxfordshire, corresp. with Sir Horace Plunkett · priv. coll., Meath MSS

Likenesses W. Roffe, stipple and line engraving, pubd 1893 (after photograph by Debenham), NPG · A. S. Cope, oils, exh. RA 1921, Adare Manor, co. Limerick, Ireland · J. Lavery, oils, exh. 1923, Hugh Lane Gallery, Dublin · Ape [C. Pellegrini], chromolithograph caricature, NPG; repro. in *VF* (4 May 1878) · Spy [L. Ward], chromolithograph caricature, NPG; repro. in *VF* (6 Dec 1894) · F. A. Swaine, photographs, NPG [*see illus.*]

Wealth at death £722,971 7s. 10d.: probate, 3 Aug 1926, *CGPLA Eng. & Wales* · £1,240,000: further grant, 23 Oct 1926, *CGPLA Eng. & Wales* · £55,308 2s. 8d.: probate, 14 Jan 1927, *CGPLA Éire*

Thomas Penson De Quincey (1785–1859), by Sir John Watson-Gordon, *c*.1845

Quincey, Thomas Penson De (1785–1859), essayist, was born in Manchester on 15 August 1785, the fourth of the eight children of Thomas Quincey (1753–1793), a textile importer from Lincolnshire, and his wife, Elizabeth Penson (*c*.1756–1846). A cultured man of liberal views, the elder Quincey was the author of a *Short Tour in the Midland Counties of England* (1774), an opponent of the slave trade, and a founder member of the Manchester Literary and Philosophical Society. Thomas was probably born at his house in Cromford Court, Market Street Lane.

Childhood and schooling, 1785–1802 The family moved after a few months to The Farm, in the rural district of Moss Side, where Thomas, a small and rather sickly child, suffered severely from ague and whooping cough. In 1791 the Quinceys moved to their newly built mansion, Greenhay, also in Moss Side. Thomas saw little thereafter of his father, who had contracted tuberculosis and sought to recover his health by living mainly in Jamaica (where he had business interests), in Madeira, and in Portugal, visiting England only occasionally.

In his father's absence, Thomas's early life was dominated by his mother, a strict and somewhat austere disciplinarian, and by his eldest sister Elizabeth (*b*. 1783), with whom he formed an intense emotional bond. Her death, probably from meningitis, in the summer of 1792 affected him deeply, and in *Suspiria de profundis* (*Blackwood's Magazine*, 1845) he recalled, as a profound spiritual experience, his solitary visit a few days after her death to the room

where her body lay. The following year his father returned home acutely ill and died on 18 July 1793.

Thomas and his boisterous elder brother William (*b*. 1781/2) were sent to be tutored by Samuel Hall, curate of St Anne's Church, Manchester, the most active of five guardians appointed under Thomas Quincey's will. Thomas, an omnivorous reader, revealed a gift for classical studies. When his mother moved to North Parade, Bath, in 1796 he was transferred to Bath grammar school, where he made rapid progress in Latin and Greek, the headmaster (according to De Quincey's *Confessions of an English Opium-Eater*, 1821) telling a visitor that Thomas 'could harangue an Athenian mob, better than you or I could address an English one' (*Works*, 2.14).

At Bath Mrs Quincey, always fervently religious, entered the evangelical circle of Hannah More. She also changed the family name to De Quincey, an affectation which she soon abandoned but which her son always retained thereafter. (The question of upper- or lower-case 'd' was never settled: De Quincey himself wrote it in both ways and, although in old age he asserted that the 'd' should be lower-case and the name alphabetized under Q (Hogg, 220n.), the consensus has generally been the reverse on both points.)

In autumn 1799 De Quincey was transferred for obscure reasons to Wingfield (Winkfield) School in Wiltshire, which he regarded as an inferior school. In this year he first read and was deeply impressed by the anonymous *Lyrical Ballads* of Wordsworth and Coleridge. The summer of 1800 was spent as companion to the young Peter Howe Brown, Lord Westport, visiting London, Windsor (where he met George III), Dublin (where he was in the Irish House of Lords to witness the passing of the Act of Union), and the co. Mayo estate of Westport's father, the earl of Altamont. On his return to England in September he visited Lady Susan Carbery at Laxton, Northamptonshire, and on 9 November 1800, despite his pleas for a return to the Bath grammar school, was enrolled at the Manchester grammar school, where his guardians expected him to stay for the three years required to qualify for a scholarship to Brasenose College, Oxford.

A formerly excellent school then stagnating under the failing hand of its superannuated high master Charles Lawson, the Manchester grammar school increasingly stimulated De Quincey's sense of boredom and resentment. A visit to family friends at Liverpool in summer 1801 brought him into contact with the intellectual circle of William Roscoe, William Shepherd, and James Currie, the biographer of Burns. All were correspondents of Coleridge, and although in 'A literary novitiate' (*Tait's Magazine*, February 1837) De Quincey was to travesty their politics as a snobbish pretence of radicalism and their literary taste as 'blind servility to the narrowest of conventional usages', he presumably learned much from them about the authors of *Lyrical Ballads*.

De Quincey's discontent with the Manchester grammar school continued to grow, and having failed to persuade his mother and guardians to allow him to transfer prematurely to Oxford, on 20 July 1802 he absconded from the school and walked to Chester, where he presented himself the following day at his mother's new residence, St John's Priory. Accepting this *fait accompli*, his mother and guardians granted him an allowance of 1 guinea a week, and he set off on an indefinite walking tour of north Wales, sleeping by turns at inns and cottages and in the open air.

Vagrancy, Oxford, and early opium use, 1802–1808 Tiring of these conditions and reluctant to return home, late in November De Quincey broke off communication with his family and travelled to London. For his experiences there no record survives apart from his own later *Confessions of an English Opium-Eater*, but surviving letters confirm the facts of a loss of contact with his guardians and a return some months later. According to *Confessions*, De Quincey applied to moneylenders (prominent among them a certain Dell) hoping to borrow money against the £2600 he expected to inherit under his father's will upon coming of age. During the ensuing delays he spent his remaining funds and became destitute, living in the streets by day and sleeping at night in an unfurnished house in Greek Street, Soho, made available by an attorney, one Brunell or Brown, who acted for Dell. It was during this period of destitution that De Quincey later claimed to have been innocently protected and comforted by the young prostitute celebrated in *Confessions* as 'Anne of Oxford-street'.

After failing to obtain the expected loan, De Quincey effected a reconciliation with his mother and returned to Chester, apparently in March 1803. Later the same month he was sent to stay with family friends at Everton, near Liverpool, where he remained until 3 August. While there he kept a diary which notes his sexual encounters with local prostitutes, offers scathing observations on the trivialities of provincial life, details his extensive literary interests (including enthusiasm for Gothic fiction and the poetry of Wordsworth, Coleridge, and Southey), and states his aspiration to write poetic drama.

The diary also contains drafts of a letter, sent on 31 May, to William Wordsworth, in which De Quincey introduces himself as a worshipper of nature, expresses his 'admiration and love' for the *Lyrical Ballads* and 'earnestly and humbly' begs for Wordsworth's friendship. Wordsworth's cautious but encouraging reply, written at Grasmere on 29 July, pointed out that 'My friendship it is not in my power to give: this … is the gift of time and circumstance' (*The Letters of William and Dorothy Wordsworth: the Early Years, 1787–1805*, ed. E. De Selincourt, rev. C. L. Shaver, 1967, 400–01), but invited the young man to visit him at Grasmere.

In December 1803 De Quincey entered Worcester College, Oxford. He made few friends and in March 1804 moved from the college to lodgings at the nearby village of Littlemore. He read widely, though not within the syllabus, and resumed his study of German (begun, he claimed, during his period of wandering in Wales). He continued to correspond with Wordsworth.

It was during a visit to London in the autumn of 1804, according to his own account in *Confessions*, that De Quincey first took opium, initially as a remedy for toothache but afterwards for the sake of the 'abyss of divine enjoyment … suddenly revealed' by ingestion of the drug. Cheaply and legally available from any druggist's shop, opium became a repeated occasional pleasure for De Quincey, who would indulge in it while exploring the city or attending the opera during his frequent visits to London. On one such visit early in 1805 he met Charles and Mary Lamb, but took offence at Charles Lamb's mockery of Coleridge's *Rime of the Ancient Mariner* and failed to pursue the relationship.

Correspondence with Wordsworth continued sporadically, and in the summer of 1805 De Quincey visited Coniston in the Lake District, intending to make his way to Grasmere and call on Wordsworth, but was too nervous to make the approach. A year later, again at Coniston, he once more failed to make a planned visit to the poet, but spent his twenty-first birthday (15 August 1806) in drawing up a document (now in the Wordsworth Library, Grasmere) on 'the constituents of Happiness', listing (among other desiderata) 'A capacity of thinking—i.e., of abstraction and reverie … Books … some great intellectual project' and 'the education of a child'. On his coming of age he received the expected patrimony of £2600, of which £600 was at once swallowed by debts contracted since his entrance at Oxford.

In July 1807 De Quincey, then visiting his mother at Wrington, Somerset, obtained an introduction to Coleridge. A friendship immediately developed, and in October De Quincey, aware of Coleridge's financial difficulties, offered (through the mediation of Joseph Cottle) a gift of £300, which Coleridge accepted as a 'loan'. Later the same month De Quincey escorted Coleridge's wife, Sara, and their children, who were returning to their home at Keswick, as far as Grasmere, where he at last met William, Dorothy, and Mary Wordsworth. He stayed at Grasmere for two nights before travelling north with Wordsworth to Penrith and Keswick, where he was introduced to Robert Southey.

De Quincey returned to Oxford and set himself to study intensively for his degree examinations, contending for honours and offering the whole corpus of Greek tragedy as his field of study. Having performed brilliantly in the first day's examination, he suffered a loss of nerve and failed to present himself for the second and final day, 16 May 1808, instead fleeing to London.

The lake poets and marriage, 1808–1818 In October 1808 De Quincey rejoined the Wordsworths, now at Allan Bank, Grasmere, where Coleridge was also visiting. Wordsworth was drafting his pamphlet criticizing the convention of Cintra, and in February De Quincey travelled to London to see the pamphlet through the press. This arrangement caused some resentment on the part of Coleridge, who seems to have felt his collaborative relationship with Wordsworth threatened.

On 21 October 1809 De Quincey moved into the Grasmere cottage formerly rented by the Wordsworths, later known as Dove Cottage. He remained on good terms with the Wordsworth family and developed friendships with neighbours, among them the poets Charles Lloyd and John Wilson (later famous as Christopher North of *Blackwood's Magazine*). His time was spent in studying German literature, reading political economy, and planning an ambitious philosophical work. There were annual visits lasting several months to London and to his mother, now at Westhay in Somerset. In 1814 and 1815 De Quincey was in Edinburgh with John Wilson and was introduced to several of the city's leading literary figures, including J. G. Lockhart, Sir William Hamilton, and James Hogg (the Ettrick Shepherd).

De Quincey, however, was overspending his meagre income. In June 1812 he had entered the Middle Temple with the intention of reading for the bar; he kept terms until the early 1820s but failed to pursue his legal studies. The death of three-year-old Catherine, his favourite among the Wordsworth children, on 11 June 1812, plunged him into depression. He returned to Grasmere in late June and later claimed ('Society of the lakes', *Tait's Magazine*, Aug 1840) that there he 'often passed the night upon [Catherine's] grave'. His opium use, hitherto sporadic, became daily, and within a year he was fully addicted.

By 1814 De Quincey was also conducting a love affair with Margaret (1796–1837), the eighteen-year-old daughter of John Simpson, a 'statesman' (independent farmer) of The Nab, a small farmhouse on the shores of Rydal Water. Their son William was born on 15 November 1816, and on 15 February 1817 the couple were married at Grasmere church. The relationship, together with De Quincey's increasingly obvious opium addiction, did much to sour his relationship with the Wordsworth family. The marriage was none the less a happy one, and there were

eventually seven more children: Margaret (*b.* 1817), Horatio (*b.* 1820), Francis John (*b.* 1823), Florence and Paul Frederick (both *b.* 1827), Julius (*b.* 1829, who died in infancy), and Emily (*b.* 1833).

Entrance into journalism, 1818–1821 As the general election of 1818 approached, the tory ascendancy of the Lowther family in Westmorland was threatened by the popular whig candidate Henry Brougham. Wordsworth, sympathetic to the tory cause, proved willing to recommend to the election committee a pamphlet by De Quincey, *Close Comments upon a Straggling Speech*, attacking Brougham's speech at Kendal on 23 March. The anonymous pamphlet's effective polemic marked De Quincey out as a possible editor for the *Westmorland Gazette*, a weekly paper established in May 1818 to support the tory interest. When the first editor failed to satisfy the proprietors and was dismissed after seven issues the post was offered to De Quincey, who produced his first issue on 11 July.

De Quincey was on the whole a successful editor who increased his paper's circulation. His readership included the educated gentry of the district, and besides combative political leaders and general news he was able to include articles on political economy and German philosophy as well as more sensational material on murder trials and breach of promise cases. He was unreliable, however, in meeting deadlines; he lived 18 miles from the press; and May 1818 and June 1819 are the dates subsequently assigned in his *Confessions* to the 'Pains of Opium' with their hideous nightmares. The paper was often saved from disaster by its subeditor, John Kilner. Late in June 1819 the proprietors were warning De Quincey of their dissatisfaction with the lack of 'regular communication between the Editor and the Printer', and on 5 November he resigned the editorship to Kilner.

Despite a regular allowance from his mother De Quincey was again in debt. John Wilson, now associated with the recently established *Blackwood's Edinburgh Magazine*, was pressing him to write for it, and in December 1820 De Quincey travelled to Edinburgh expecting to become a regular contributor. He began work on several essays, including an 'Opium article' which may have been an early draft of the *Confessions*. Soon, however, he quarrelled with the proprietor and editor, William Blackwood, over the magazine's editorial policy and in January returned to the Lake District having published only one item, 'The Sport of Fortune' (a translation from Schiller), in the magazine.

After spending the spring with his family at Fox Ghyll, Rydal, De Quincey visited London in June 1821 with a letter of introduction from Thomas Noon Talfourd to Taylor and Hessey, publishers of the *London Magazine*. Engaged as a contributor, he took lodgings over the premises of the German bookseller R. H. Bohte at 4 York Street (now Tavistock Street), Covent Garden, and early in August resumed work on *Confessions of an English Opium-Eater*, an account of his early life and opium addiction. Despite persecution by creditors he finished the work in time for it to appear in the September and October numbers of the magazine. A highly selective memoir tracing its author's progress from innocent waif to seasoned addict, *Confessions* impressed its readers equally by the pathos of its account of 'Anne of Oxford-street' and by the intricate orientalism of the opium nightmares it recounted:

> I was stared at, hooted at, grinned at, chattered at, by monkeys, by paroquets, by cockatoos. I ran into pagodas: and was fixed, for centuries, at the summit, or in secret rooms; I was the idol; I was the priest; I was worshipped; I was sacrificed … I was buried, for a thousand years, in stone coffins, with mummies and sphynxes, in narrow chambers at the heart of eternal pyramids. I was kissed, with cancerous kisses, by crocodiles; and laid, confounded with all unutterable slimy things, amongst reeds and Nilotic mud. (*Works*, 2.71)

It was an immediate critical success, attracting nationwide attention. Republished in book form in 1822, *Confessions* went through seven British and at least nine American editions during De Quincey's lifetime and remained in print into the twenty-first century.

The *London Magazine* period, 1821–1825 De Quincey was now a leading contributor to a monthly magazine of modest circulation but high and generally admired literary standards. His fellow contributors included Lamb (with whom he now formed a warm friendship), Hazlitt, Hood, T. N. Talfourd, B. W. Proctor, Thomas Carlyle, H. F. Cary, John Clare, and Allan Cunningham. By the end of 1822 De Quincey was close enough to the editorial circle to draft an article outlining the magazine's policy for the following year, and between 1821 and 1826 the *London Magazine* published more than twenty of his essays, including notable translations from German writers (in particular 'Jean Paul' Richter and Kant), articles on political economy, the 'Letters to a young man whose education has been neglected', and a miscellaneous series of 'Notes from the pocket-book of a late opium-eater' which included short essays on Malthus and on suicide, and his most famous critical essay, 'On the knocking at the gate in Macbeth', which appeared in 1823.

De Quincey produced few contributions to the magazine in 1824 and the year was a difficult one for him. He was now sufficiently well known to be brutally attacked in the first (July) issue of a satirical magazine, *John Bull*, as one of the 'Humbugs of the Age'. The article, by William Maginn, a regular contributor to *Blackwood's*, mocked his physical appearance, publicized the illegitimate birth of his first child, and claimed that De Quincey had married his household servant. De Quincey considered challenging the author to a duel but thought better of it. A possible flight to Boulogne to escape creditors is indicated by a letter of 26 October in which De Quincey states that he has just returned from a visit to this favourite refuge of English debtors.

In 1825, having reviewed the German pseudo-Waverley novel *Walladmor*, a fake concocted to satisfy demand at the Leipzig book fair for a new novel by Scott, De Quincey produced a witty, parodic translation of the novel for publication by Taylor and Hessey. It was among his last pieces of work for them, for the *London Magazine* was failing and De Quincey was in any case becoming unhappy at the exigencies of spending alternate periods in London, far from his family, and in Westmorland, where he lost contact with his editors and found it difficult to write.

Blackwood's and the Edinburgh Post, 1826–1833 During summer 1825 De Quincey's wife and children were evicted, in his absence, from their rented house, Fox Ghyll. They moved in with Margaret's parents at The Nab. The farm was already heavily mortgaged to the Rydal estate, and De Quincey, despite his own continuing debts, tried to save the property by taking over the mortgage. This precarious arrangement held until 1829. For unknown reasons, but perhaps partly because of financial complications involving The Nab, De Quincey seems to have written and published nothing between January 1825 and the end of 1826. In October of that year, however, he travelled to Edinburgh, where he resumed contact with John Wilson and began writing for *Blackwood's*, to which he was to remain a prominent contributor until 1849.

De Quincey's work for *Blackwood's*, which includes much of his most original and admired writing, initially took the form of translations from the German. His 'Gallery of the German prose classics' opened in November 1826 and January 1827 with an abridged translation of Lessing's *Laokoon*, the first version of that important aesthetic treatise to appear in English. The February 1827 *Blackwood's* continued the 'Gallery' with 'The last days of Kant' and also contained the first essay 'On murder considered as one of the fine arts', a complex exercise in sinister irony to which he was to return in 1839 and 1854 and which has remained, after *Confessions*, his most famous work.

In July 1827 De Quincey began to supplement his income by regular work for the tory *Edinburgh Saturday Post* (from May 1828 the *Edinburgh Evening Post*). His position at the *Post*, held for about a year, has never been entirely clarified, but it was evidently a senior post with staff responsibilities, since he not only contributed reviews and compiled news reports from the national papers, but also wrote regular political editorials. When for a few weeks, early in 1829, he returned to the *Post* for a second stint, he apparently edited the newspaper himself. De Quincey's contributions take a decidedly 'metropolitan' line, at times subtly satirizing what he sees as the Edinburgh provincialism of his colleagues and audience. They also develop his theory of British politics, whereby whig and tory represent two permanent principles from whose conflict and balance good government emerges.

In November 1827 De Quincey met Thomas Carlyle, a tense encounter since De Quincey had given Carlyle's translation of Goethe's *Wilhelm Meister* a hostile review in 1824. The two men, however, soon formed a friendship, and by the end of 1828 Carlyle was proposing that De Quincey join him at Craigenputtoch to form a 'bog school' to rival the 'lake school' of poets. Instead, De Quincey retreated to Rydal in the spring of 1829, and though his articles continued to appear in *Blackwood's* they were mostly pieces written during the previous year and little new work was done until June 1830, when De Quincey returned to Edinburgh, where he lodged in John Wilson's house. There he began to concoct new *Blackwood's* articles, including 'Kant in his miscellaneous essays' and 'Bentley'.

At the end of the year threats of suicide from the lonely and exhausted Margaret, isolated at The Nab with six children, persuaded De Quincey to end his divided existence and unite his family in Edinburgh, initially at 7 Great King Street, where Margaret and the children joined him in December 1830. Although De Quincey remained nominal owner of The Nab until September 1833 and continued to rent Dove Cottage until 1835, the family henceforth lived together in Edinburgh.

With the prospect of parliamentary reform, De Quincey's political journalism was welcomed by the tory *Blackwood's*, but debts were constantly accumulating and on 2 October 1831 he was briefly imprisoned for debt in the Canongate toll-booth, being released the same day on grounds of ill health. Henceforth the threat of imprisonment for debt hung constantly over him and his existence became a complex and fugitive one. He was a frequent denizen in the Holyrood debtors' sanctuary; false addresses and assumed names were regular features of his daily life. His articles were often delivered clandestinely to editors by his children, who became expert at avoiding pursuit by creditors. Continued writing, however, was a necessity and April 1832 saw publication of his only original novel, *Klosterheim, or, The Masque*, a Gothic romance set in Germany during the Thirty Years' War, followed in the October and November *Blackwood's* by the first two episodes of *The Caesars*, a brilliantly stylish and humorous recasting of material from Suetonius and the *Augustan History*.

Blackwood's and Tait's, 1833–1850 During 1833 the firm of Blackwood came increasingly into the hands of William Blackwood's son Alexander, who was far less tolerant than his father of De Quincey's irregularities and inability to meet deadlines. Friction between author and editor led De Quincey to turn to the liberal *Tait's Edinburgh Magazine* as a market for his work. A few miscellaneous pieces ('Kant on the age of the earth', 'Mrs Hannah More', and others) were followed, far more significantly, by 'Sketches of life and manners; from the autobiography of an English opium-eater', which began to appear in February 1834. Collectively these recollections, which were to appear sporadically under varying titles until 1839, constitute one of the great nineteenth-century autobiographies. At times frustratingly digressive, they none the less offer an incomparably detailed, thoughtful, and imaginative account of a late eighteenth-century childhood, an upper-class English adolescence, and rich encounters with the literary world of the early nineteenth century. The circulation of *Tait's Magazine* soared as the series became known.

When Coleridge died in July 1834 it was natural that De Quincey, already well embarked on reminiscence, should turn his long relationship with his fellow opium addict to account, and in September *Tait's* published the first instalment of a four-part series, 'Samuel Taylor Coleridge'. The first paper opened memorably with the revelation that Coleridge was a 'plagiary', most notably in *Biographia literaria*, where several pages of literal translation from Schelling had been claimed by Coleridge as original work.

De Quincey presented this and other instances of 'barefaced plagiarism' as amiable eccentricities on the part of Coleridge, who 'spun daily and at all hours, for mere amusement of his own activities, and from the loom of his own magical brain, theories more gorgeous by far [than] Schelling ... could have emulated in his dreams'. Despite this genial tone, the essay and its sequels, published in November, December, and January, which revealed details about Coleridge's opium addiction and the failure of his marriage, aroused intense indignation among Coleridge's family and friends. The poet's daughter Sara declared herself 'much hurt' and his son Hartley, with Southey's encouragement, stated his intention of giving De Quincey a beating. None the less subsequent scholarship has on the whole vindicated De Quincey's account, which remains an essential source for Coleridge's biography. Through the late summer and autumn of 1834, as he completed the essays on Coleridge, De Quincey witnessed the rapid decline and painful death from chloroleukaemia of his eldest son, William, who died on 25 November.

Financial troubles continued as usual, hardly mitigated by a small inheritance from his maternal uncle Thomas Penson, and by May 1836 De Quincey and his family were living in the debtors' sanctuary at Holyrood. Autobiographical essays continued to appear sporadically in *Tait's*, and in July 1837 De Quincey resumed contribution to *Blackwood's* with 'Revolt of the Tartars', an oriental fantasy loosely based on historical sources. A pattern was thus established whereby autobiographical pieces appeared in *Tait's* while political articles and miscellaneous essays, often ornately written and involving a vein of fantasy, went to *Blackwood's*—a situation which continued until 1841. His position as contributor simultaneously to both the tory *Blackwood's* and the Liberal *Tait's* was remarkable for the period and made both proprietors uneasy. De Quincey's range of interests and his need for money, however, dictated it, and his reputation as a writer now gave him the power to bring editors, however grudgingly, into line. In addition, articles on Pope, Schiller, Shakespeare, and Goethe were contributed to the *Encyclopaedia Britannica*. None is notable, and the Goethe article is strikingly inadequate, being based solely on Goethe's early autobiography, *Dichtung und Wahrheit*. The poor quality of the *Encyclopaedia* pieces may reflect the fact that for much of 1837 Margaret De Quincey was ill with typhus, from which she died on 7 August. De Quincey, a notably affectionate husband, was profoundly saddened by her death and when in 1839 his autobiographical reminiscences reached his Grasmere years, his treatment of Wordsworth was shot through with bitterness at what he believed to have been Wordsworth's snobbish disapproval of his relationship with her.

In January 1840 De Quincey's eldest daughter, Margaret, now twenty-two, began to take charge of her father's affairs and moved the family to Mavis Bush Cottage, Lasswade, 7 miles from Edinburgh. Under Margaret's management the family finances improved and there were no further prosecutions for debt. From this time De Quincey also developed increasingly close friendships with members of both Edinburgh and Glasgow universities. In 1841 he came to know John Pringle Nichol, professor of astronomy at Glasgow, and visited him at the Glasgow observatory. From the conversation of Nichol and others, scientific imagery began increasingly to enter De Quincey's works. Meanwhile, although his historical and political essays continued to appear in *Blackwood's*, De Quincey quarrelled with Tait over the latter's mode of editing his articles and between February 1841 and September 1845 contributed nothing to *Tait's Magazine*. In 1842 his second son, Horatio, a lieutenant in the British army, died near Canton (Guangzhou), China, probably of fever.

The mid-1840s produced a group of important works. *The Logic of Political Economy*, an exposition of Ricardian economics, was published as a separate volume by Blackwood in 1844 and won an admiring review from John Stuart Mill; in 1845 an essay 'On Wordsworth's poetry' appeared in *Tait's*; and *Blackwood's* published 'Coleridge and opium-eating' and *Suspiria de profundis*, a 'sequel' to *Confessions of an English Opium-Eater*; and 'System of the heavens as revealed by Lord Rosse's telescopes', a speculative essay inspired by Nichol's work on the nebulae, appeared in *Tait's* in 1846. *Suspiria de profundis*, to which he attributed great importance and which he claimed had cost him 'seven months of severe labour' (Japp, *Life*, 253–4), is a sequence of visionary prose poems on themes of time, memory, and suffering. It centres partly on painful childhood memories (notably of Elizabeth's death in 1792) and partly on psychologically charged symbols (such as the palimpsest, a multi-layered text which De Quincey uses as a figure for the processes of memory). In *Suspiria de profundis* De Quincey calls such evocative images 'involutes': images which carry emotion and meaning folded within them, to be explicated only by efforts of reflection and introspection.

Dissatisfied, however, with the share of *Blackwood's Magazine* made available for *Suspiria*, and irritated by editorial interventions, De Quincey terminated the series abruptly in July 1845, *Tait's* becoming his main outlet until 1849 when one more major essay, 'The English mailcoach', appeared in *Blackwood's*. Blending grim humour, horror, and suspense with political vision and nostalgic reminiscence, and written in intricately ornate prose, the work has generally been regarded as one of his finest and most characteristic achievements.

Hogg's *Instructor* and *Titan*, the collected editions, and death, 1850–1859 Early in 1850 De Quincey introduced himself to James Hogg, editor and publisher of a cheap and poorly regarded magazine, *The Instructor*. The move, though its motives remain obscure, is likely to have been prompted by long-standing discontent with the editing of both Blackwood and Tait. Hogg now became De Quincey's principal publisher. Between 1850 and 1858 *The Instructor* (known from 1856 as *Titan*) published more than thirty articles on an immense range of topics, and from 1852 Hogg became the publisher of the first British collected edition of De Quincey's writings.

Despite his substantial reputation in Britain and, still more, in the United States as a periodical writer, by 1850 no attempt had been made to retrieve and reprint De Quincey's very numerous essays, and he himself dismissed the task as impossible. In 1850, however, the firm of Ticknor and Fields of Boston, Massachusetts, undertook a collected edition (*De Quincey's Writings*) with De Quincey's agreement, salvaging whatever they could find from files of periodicals to which he had contributed, and also drawing (in the case of *Confessions* and perhaps other works) on unauthorized American reprints.

The Boston edition, which eventually extended to twenty-two volumes, lacked systematic arrangement and was textually inaccurate. It provided the opportunity, however, for Hogg to propose that De Quincey take it as the basis for a revised edition of his writings. Work on such an edition, under the title *Selections Grave and Gay, from Writings Published and Unpublished by Thomas De Quincey*, began in 1852, and the last years of De Quincey's life were spent mainly on its preparation, sometimes at Lasswade and sometimes in lodgings at 42 Lothian Street, Edinburgh. Hogg patiently coaxed De Quincey through volume after volume, and a formidable amount of work was done in stylistic revision and expansion of a large selection (perhaps three-quarters) of his previously published output.

The most important recasting concerned *Confessions of an English Opium-Eater*, which was enlarged to more than twice its previous length, mainly by the elaboration of its early pages dealing with De Quincey's childhood. De Quincey himself seems to have regarded the revision partly as a practical necessity to turn the *Confessions* into a volume of uniform size with the rest of the edition and partly as an opportunity to supplement the earlier short text with explanatory and commentarial material; there is no evidence that he intended it to replace the original text, as it had first reached book form in 1822, and that version was still in print both in Britain and America. In the event, the enlarged version soon became the only text available, eclipsing the shorter, livelier, and more accessible 1822 version for a century thereafter.

Late in October 1859, in the course of revising the fourteenth and final volume of *Selections Grave and Gay*, De Quincey (who had for some years suffered intermittently from erysipelas, purpurea, and arthritis) became seriously ill, though apart from persistent 'fever' his symptoms are not recorded. He remained bedridden and over the next six weeks became steadily weaker, experiencing some mental confusion at times. He died peacefully in the presence of his daughters Margaret and Emily at 42 Lothian Street on 8 December 1859 and was buried five days later in St Cuthbert's churchyard, a short distance from Prince's Street. A large ornamental headstone marks his grave.

Literary and historical significance During his lifetime and subsequently, De Quincey was best-known for *Confessions of an English Opium-Eater*, which gave him both a reputation and a pseudonym which he continued to exploit. Throughout the nineteenth century the work was viewed as having medical authority as a case history, and De Quincey was widely read in British and American medical circles. Highly regarded by the American reading public, he was extravagantly praised by Edgar Allan Poe, who emulated his treatment of the macabre and grotesque in his own fiction and drew on his presentation of crime and mystery in his detective stories. The translation of *Confessions* with extracts from *Suspiria de profundis* by Baudelaire in *Les paradis artificiels* stimulated interest in his work in France during the later nineteenth century and De Quincey became a significant figure for the *symbolistes* and subsequently the surrealists. Thus during the twentieth century his reputation consistently stood higher in France than in Britain.

The appearance of an enlarged collected edition, *De Quincey's Writings*, edited by David Masson (14 vols., 1889–90), supplemented by A. H. Japp's editions *De Quincey Memorials* and *Posthumous Works* (both 2 vols., 1891), reaffirmed De Quincey's importance at the end of the nineteenth century. Both underrepresented De Quincey's humour, fiction, and political writing; Japp's texts were unreliable, often silently revised, and chosen to emphasize the veins of religious speculation and visionary fantasy in De Quincey's work. They helped to establish De Quincey as a stylistic model for elaborate prose, and where contemporaries had valued him as a polymath and philosopher, he was regarded between the 1890s and 1920s as important chiefly for his style, selections from his essays being routinely reprinted as school texts. Wilde, Chesterton, and Kenneth Grahame all admired his work and show clear signs of his influence. Virginia Woolf wrote three essays on De Quincey and read his works during her composition of *To the Lighthouse*.

After 1920, however, De Quincey began to lose favour as part of a general critical rejection of elaborate nineteenth-century prose. Two biographies, Horace A. Eaton's massive documentary *Thomas De Quincey* and Edward Sackville-West's lighter, more populist *A Flame in Sunlight* (both 1936), failed to rekindle interest. De Quincey was generally neglected by the English-speaking world until the 1960s, when a renewal of interest in the literary presentation of mind-altering drugs led to the reissuing of *Confessions* in its original, terse form. Literary reassessment followed, with a gradual acceleration in the publication of biographical and critical monographs and articles. By the end of the twentieth century a new and comprehensive edition of his works was in progress.

De Quincey's work has been influential in many fields. Pre-eminently he is regarded as the prototype of the writer as visionary drug user. His fiction and his essays 'On murder considered as one of the fine arts' have proved formative influences on modern crime-writing, both documentary and fictional. His translations and his essays on Kant, as well as many incidental passages of commentary scattered throughout his works, make him an important figure (alongside Coleridge and Henry Crabb Robinson) in the dissemination of German literature and Kantian philosophy in nineteenth-century Britain. His essays in autobiography and his speculations about the nature of

memory, transmitted initially by Baudelaire, had important European repercussions and contributed to the thinking of both Freud and Proust. In Britain and America his biographical accounts of Wordsworth and Coleridge, together with his commentary on their writings, helped to shape the reception of these poets in the later nineteenth century and to establish them as the dominant figures in what came to be seen as Romanticism, while his development of their insights and attitudes in his own work led him to be viewed as in some respects their heir. This is to some extent, however, a misconception, in that De Quincey's scepticism and inclination to the comic and the grotesque align him more fundamentally with the German Romantics, and in particular with 'Jean Paul' Richter, from whom his aesthetic of contrast, incongruity, and sentimental pathos is avowedly derived.

De Quincey remains hard to classify, partly because of his immense range of subject matter and the variety of genres in which he wrote. Moreover, although he wrote almost exclusively for periodicals and so seems most readily approached as an essayist, the length and elaboration of many of his works entirely contradict the usual associations of the essay with the brief and the tentative. His highly finished exercises in non-fictional prose derive their effectiveness precisely from their ability to evade generic boundaries and offer the reader the unexpected.

GREVEL LINDOP

Sources H. A. Eaton, *Thomas De Quincey: a biography* (1936) • A. H. Japp, *De Quincey memorials*, 2 vols. (1891) • G. Lindop, *The opium-eater: a life of Thomas De Quincey* (1981) • S. M. Tave, *New essays by De Quincey: his contributions to the Edinburgh Saturday Post and the Edinburgh Evening Post, 1827–8* (1966) • *The works of Thomas De Quincey*, ed. G. Lindop and others, 21 vols. (2000–02) • J. Hogg, *De Quincey and his friends* (1895) • A. H. Japp [H. A. Page], *Thomas de Quincey: his life and writings*, new edn (1890) • J. E. Jordan, *De Quincey to Wordsworth: a biography of a relationship* (1960) • parish register, Edinburgh, St Cuthbert's, 13 Dec 1859 [burial] • m. cert.

Archives Bodl. Oxf., 'Sketches from childhood' • Harvard U., Houghton L., papers • Hunt. L., family letters and literary MSS • Lpool RO, diary • Man. CL, Manchester Archives and Local Studies, MSS • NL Scot., corresp. and papers • NL Scot., essays • NL Scot., letters • Worcester College, Oxford, corresp. and papers • Wordsworth Trust, Dove Cottage, Grasmere, papers | BL, letters to *London Magazine*, Add. MS 37215 • Bodl. Oxf., papers relating to resignation of Huskisson • NL Scot., corresp. with *Blackwood's* and articles • NYPL, Berg collection

Likenesses F. Schenck, lithograph, 1845 (after 'WHD'), Scot. NPG • J. Watson-Gordon, oils, *c.*1845, NPG [*see illus.*] • J. Watson-Gordon, oils, 1846, Scot. NPG • daguerreotype, *c.*1850, Dove Cottage, Grasmere • J. Archer, chalk drawing, 1855, Dove Cottage, Grasmere • J. Archer, oils, 1859, Man. City Gall. • J. R. Steell, marble bust, 1875, Scot. NPG; related plaster bust, NPG • J. Cassidy, bust, Moss Side Public Library, Glasgow • F. Croll, stipple (after daguerreotype by Howie junior), BM, NPG; repro. in *Portrait gallery of Hogg's instructor* • J. Watson-Gordon, oils on millboard, Scot. NPG • S. Wood, plaster medallion, Scot. NPG • photographs, Dove Cottage, Grasmere

Wealth at death under £3000: administration, 19 Sept 1860, *CGPLA Eng. & Wales*

Quincy, John (d. 1722), apothecary and physician, was apprenticed to an apothecary, and afterwards practised as an apothecary in London. He was a dissenter and a whig, a friend of Richard Mead, and an enemy of John Woodward. In 1717 he published a *Lexicon physico-medicum*, dedicated to John, duke of Montagu, who had just been admitted a fellow of the College of Physicians. It is based on the medical lexicon of Bartholomew Castellus, published at Basel in 1628, and went through eleven editions, of which the last two appeared respectively in 1794 and 1811 (greatly revised). Quincy's *English Dispensatory* (1721), which had run to twelve editions by 1749, contains a complete account of the materia medica and of therapeutics, and many of the prescriptions contained in it had long-lasting popularity.

Quincy studied mathematics and the philosophy of Newton, and received the degree of MD from the University of Edinburgh for his *Medicina statica Britannica* (1712), a translation of the *Aphorisms* of Sanctorius, a second edition of which appeared in 1720. In 1719 he published a scurrilous *Examination* of Woodward's *State of Physick and Diseases*. A reply, entitled *An Account of Dr Quincy's Examination, by N. N. of the Middle Temple* (1719), speaks of him as a bankrupt apothecary, a charge to which he made no reply in the second edition of his *Examination*, published, with a further 'letter to Dr Woodward', in 1720. In the same year he published an edition of the *Loimologia; of an historical account of the plague in London*, by Nathaniel Hodges, and a collection of *Medico-Physical Essays* (1720) on ague, fevers, gout, leprosy, king's evil, and other diseases, which show that his main skill was as an apothecary. He considered dried millipedes good for tuberculous lymphatic glands, but considered the royal touch a method 'that can take place only on a deluded imagination', which had been 'justly banished with the superstition and bigotry that introduced it'. Joseph Collet, governor of Fort St George, was one of his patrons, and Quincy printed in 1713 a laudatory poem on their mutual friend, the Revd Joseph Stennett (1663–1713).

Quincy died in 1722, and in 1723 his *Praelectiones pharmaceuticae*, lectures which had been delivered at his own house, were published with a preface by Peter Shaw.

NORMAN MOORE, *rev.* MICHAEL BEVAN

Sources P. Shaw, preface, in J. Quincy, *Praelectiones pharmaceuticae* (1723) · *An account of Dr Quincy's Examination, by N. N. of the Middle Temple* (1719) · J. Quincy, *Medico-physical essays* (1720)

Quincy, Roger de, earl of Winchester (c.1195–1264), constable of Scotland, was the second son of Saer de *Quincy, earl of Winchester (d. 1219), and Margaret de Breteuil, younger daughter of Robert de *Breteuil, earl of Leicester (d. 1190). Roger had four brothers and three sisters. His elder brother, Robert, died in 1217; with his wife, Hawise, sister of Ranulf (III), earl of Chester (d. 1232), he had one daughter, Margaret, who was passed over in the succession to the earldom of Winchester in favour of Roger. His younger brother, also named Robert, married Helen, daughter of Llewelyn ab Iorwerth, prince of Gwynedd (d. 1240), and widow of John the Scot, earl of Chester and Huntingdon. Of his sisters, Hawise married Hugh de Vere,

earl of Oxford, and Arabella married Sir Richard de Harcourt. Roger himself married three times: first Helen, eldest daughter of *Alan, lord of Galloway and constable of Scotland; second Maud, daughter of Humphrey (IV) de *Bohun, earl of Hereford (d. 1275); and third Eleanor, daughter by his first marriage of William de Ferrers, earl of Derby, by whom he was survived. According to Matthew Paris, he contracted his third marriage in haste, hoping for a male heir, but his only children were the three daughters of his first marriage: the eldest, Margaret, married William de Ferrers, sixth earl of Derby, as his second wife [*see* Ferrers family (*per.* c.1240–1445)]; the second, Elizabeth (or Isabella), married Alexander Comyn, earl of Buchan (d. 1289); and the youngest, Helen, married Alan de la Zouche (d. 1270).

Little is known of Roger de Quincy before 1219. He was probably the son whom Saer delivered to King John in 1213 as a Scottish hostage for the security of the Anglo-Scottish treaty of 1212. He emerged onto the political stage in 1215 when, along with Saer and the leaders of the baronial rebellion against John, he was excommunicated by Innocent III (*r.* 1198–1216), but did not figure prominently in the civil war that followed the king's death. He perhaps accompanied his father on crusade in 1219, and apparently did not return to England until some considerable time after Saer's death at the siege of Damietta in that year, for it was not until 1221 that Roger did homage to Henry III and received his father's lands. He did not receive the title of earl until after his mother's death in 1235.

The death in 1234 of his father-in-law, Alan of Galloway, led to a considerable expansion of Roger de Quincy's already substantial estates in both Scotland and England. Galloway and Alan's extensive Scottish properties were divided in right of their wives between Quincy, who as husband of the eldest daughter received also the office of constable of Scotland, John de Balliol of Barnard Castle (d. 1269), and William de Forz, future earl of Aumale (d. 1260). The refusal of Alexander II, king of Scots (*r.* 1214–49), to accede to Galwegian requests that he allow instead the lordship to pass intact to Thomas, bastard son of Alan, or to another male relative, or himself assume direct lordship over Galloway, provoked a rebellion in 1235 in support of Thomas. On its suppression by Alexander, partition among the husbands of Alan's daughters was enforced. Further disturbances in Galloway followed the death in 1246 of Quincy's sister-in-law, the childless Christina, countess of Aumale, and division of her lands among her surviving sisters. A rebellion in 1247, which Matthew Paris attributed to Quincy's oppressiveness, trapped him in one of his Galloway castles, probably Cruggleton in Wigtownshire which belonged to his Comyn heirs later in the century, but he succeeded in escaping to the Scottish court. There he was successful in soliciting Alexander's aid in crushing the rebellion.

Notices of his involvement in Galloway apart, there is no evidence for Roger de Quincy's fulfilling a role in Scotland commensurate with his landed position. Despite his holding the office of constable he played no part in Alexander II's campaign in Argyll in 1249, nor in the crisis of 1263 when Haakon IV of Norway mounted his expedition to the Hebrides in response to Scottish threats to the Norwegian possessions there. The survival of a considerable body of his *acta* and confirmations of his grants by the Scottish crown, however, demonstrate that he was frequently resident in Scotland. His appointment in 1257 by Henry III of England as a commissioner to arbitrate between Alexander III and the leaders of the Comyn and Durward factions in Scotland on the one hand underscores his lack of active involvement in Scottish politics, while on the other it stresses his influential position as a major Anglo-Scottish nobleman.

Roger de Quincy did not hold the prominence in politics that his father had commanded in England either, but his wealth secured him an important role. In 1239 and 1246 he joined in written remonstrances from the English nobility to Gregory IX (*r.* 1227–41) and Innocent IV (*r.* 1243–54) concerning papal interference in English affairs. Association with the stirrings of dissatisfaction with the government of Henry III expressed in the parliaments of 1248 and 1254 led to identification with the baronial opposition in 1258. At the Oxford parliament Quincy was elected by the barons to the twelve-member commission charged with attendance at the three annual parliaments provided for under the provisions of Oxford, and was appointed also to the committee that arranged the financial aid promised to Henry. In 1259 he led a delegation to St Omer to intercept Richard, earl of Cornwall (*d.* 1272), and forbid him to return to England until he had sworn to observe the provisions of Oxford. This appears to have been Roger de Quincy's last major act, for he played little part in subsequent events which culminated in open conflict between the king and his baronial opponents, and died on 25 April 1264, eighteen days after Henry had precipitated the country into civil war. At his death he was probably the greatest Anglo-Scottish landowner of his day, holding not only one of the largest agglomerations of land in baronial hands, but one with estates spread from Perthshire in the north to the channel coast in the south. With only daughters to succeed him, however, these extensive lands were ultimately divided among their husbands, and the title of earl of Winchester lapsed.   RICHARD D. ORAM

Sources G. G. Simpson, 'An Anglo-Scottish baron of the thirteenth century: the acts of Roger de Quincy, earl of Winchester and constable of Scotland', PhD diss., U. Edin., 1965 · G. G. Simpson, 'The "familia" of Roger de Quincy, earl of Winchester and constable of Scotland', *Essays on the nobility of medieval Scotland*, ed. K. J. Stringer (1985) · A. A. M. Duncan, *Scotland: the making of the kingdom* (1975), vol. 1 of *The Edinburgh history of Scotland*, ed. G. Donaldson (1965–75), 359–60, 532, 571, 575, 586 · A. Young, 'The earls and earldom of Buchan in the thirteenth century', *Medieval Scotland: crown, lordship and community: essays presented to G. W. S. Barrow*, ed. A. Grant and K. J. Stringer (1993), 174–202, esp. 194–5, 197 · A. Young, 'Noble families and political factions in the reign of Alexander III', *Scotland in the reign of Alexander III, 1249–1286*, ed. N. H. Reid (1990), 1–30, 14, 17 · N. Mayhew, 'Alexander III – a silver age? an essay in Scottish medieval economic history', *Scotland in the reign of Alexander III, 1249–1286*, ed. N. H. Reid (1990), 53–73, 57 · *Scots peerage*, 4.142 · *CIPM*, 1, nos. 587, 732, 776

Wealth at death estates from Perthshire to Channel coast, esp. north-east Fife, Lothian, Galloway, Ayrshire, and English Midlands

Quincy, Saer de, earl of Winchester (*d.* 1219), magnate, was the son of Robert de Quincy (*d.* 1197) and his wife, Orabile, daughter of Ness, son of William, lord of Leuchars in Fife. About 1190 he married Margaret (*d.* 1235), daughter of Robert de Breteuil, earl of Leicester (*d.* 1190), with whom he had five sons and three daughters. His eldest son, Robert, predeceased him in 1217, leaving only a daughter with his wife, Hawise, daughter of Hugh, earl of Chester, who was passed over in the succession to the earldom of Winchester in favour of her uncle, Saer's second son, Roger de *Quincy.

Quincy's career before *c.*1190 is obscure. In the 1180s and 1190s he witnessed several Scottish royal *acta* and confirmed his parents' grants to Newbattle Abbey, near Edinburgh, also making new gifts to the abbeys of Dunfermline and Cambuskenneth. Most English references to Saer de Quincy between *c.*1160 and 1192 relate to his uncle, who was one of Henry II's *familiares*, served him as castellan of Nonancourt in 1180–84, and died in 1190, and his son, also named Saer, who accompanied Henry, the Young King, to the court of Louis VII of France and joined his rebellion against Henry II in 1173. This younger Saer was dead by 1192, whereupon his estates in six English counties passed to his uncle, Robert.

It was following his father's inheritance of these properties that Quincy entered English public life. In 1197 he was in France, and was present with Richard I at Roche d'Orval in August 1198. On Richard's death in April 1199 Quincy acknowledged John's succession. In October 1200 he was sent to escort William the Lion, king of Scots, to Lincoln, and was present at the ceremony on 22 November when William renewed his homage for his English estates. In 1202 Quincy accompanied the king's army to Normandy to confront Arthur, duke of Brittany, and his ally, Philip Augustus of France. Quittances in 1202 and 1203 of debts due to the king and to Jewish moneylenders may represent rewards for service. Quincy was appointed joint castellan with Robert Fitzwalter of the strategic Norman stronghold of Vaudreuil. In the spring of 1203 they offered no resistance to Philip and surrendered Vaudreuil, an action which earned universal contempt. John displayed his disgust by refusing to contribute to their ransom.

The death in 1204 of Quincy's brother-in-law, Robert de Breteuil, earl of Leicester, brought a dramatic change of fortune. Robert's heirs were his sisters Amice, wife of Simon de Montfort (*d.* by 1188), and Margaret, Quincy's wife, and until the partition of the inheritance was settled Quincy was given custody of the earldom and appears also to have exercised the office of steward of England which had been held by the earls. An equal division of the lands, ratified in 1207, was made between Quincy and Montfort. The settlement awarded the title of earl of Leicester and the office of steward to Montfort, but Quincy's enhanced status was given formal recognition by his creation as earl of Winchester. Quincy's new social position brought added political importance. In the summer of 1209 he

Saer de Quincy, earl of Winchester (*d*. 1219), seal [obverse]

Quincy was named as one of the twenty-five barons chosen to enforce John's observance of the rights conceded in Magna Carta, and when civil war erupted in October 1215 he and Henry de Bohun, earl of Hereford, headed a baronial embassy to France to seek French assistance and to offer the crown to Philip's son, the dauphin Louis. On 9 January 1216 he returned to England with a force of French knights, followed in May by the dauphin and his army.

John's unexpected death in October 1216 opened an opportunity for reconciliation between the rebels and the royalists, but Quincy maintained his allegiance to Louis. In spring 1217 Quincy learned that Ranulf, earl of Chester, was besieging Mountsorrel, and on 30 April prevailed upon Louis to send an army commanded jointly by him, Robert Fitzwalter, and Thomas, count of Perche, to its relief. They arrived at Mountsorrel to find the siege abandoned, so turned to attack the royalist-held castle at Lincoln, unaware that the royalist army was marching north in pursuit. On 20 May at Lincoln they were defeated and Quincy was taken prisoner. He played no further part in the civil war and was released only after the end of hostilities in September 1217, when letters were issued to the sheriffs of eleven counties instructing restoration of his lands. Moves were made to include former rebels in Henry III's government, and Quincy attended the Westminster council of November 1217 which conceded a new version of Magna Carta and granted the charter of the forest. Although he was held in high regard at the council, Quincy did not recover possession of Mountsorrel, but was compensated by the grant of the farm of Chesterton, another manor to which he had a claim. In March 1218 at Worcester he attested the settlement agreed with the rebels' former ally, Llywelyn ab Iorwerth.

Towards the end of December 1218 Quincy was fitting out a vessel in Galloway in preparation for his departure on crusade, and in spring 1219 he sailed for the Holy Land, in the company of his son Roger, Robert Fitzwalter, and William d'Aubigny, earl of Arundel. Soon after his arrival at the siege of Damietta he became ill, and died on 3 November 1219. In accordance with his wishes he was buried at Acre and the ashes of his internal organs returned to England for burial in Garendon Abbey, of which he was patron. His son, Roger, did homage to Henry III in 1221 and received his father's lands, but did not gain the title of earl of Winchester until his mother's death in 1235. At the time of his death Quincy was one of the most significant Anglo-Scottish landholders of his day, and possessed properties in eleven English sheriffdoms and substantial estates in Perthshire, Fife, and Lothian in Scotland. He was a noted benefactor of the church, especially the monks of Garendon Abbey and Brackley Hospital, and his generosity was further evidenced by *acta* in favour of several Scottish monasteries and a large corpus of charters to private individuals.   RICHARD D. ORAM

Sources G. G. Simpson, 'An Anglo-Scottish baron of the thirteenth century: the acts of Roger de Quincy, earl of Winchester and constable of Scotland', PhD diss., U. Edin., 1965 • S. Painter, 'The house of Quency', *Feudalism and liberty: articles and addresses of*

accompanied the embassy sent to resolve the diplomatic crisis that had resulted from the Scots' demolition of the English fortification at Tweedmouth. It was probably at this time that his long-running dispute with St Andrews Cathedral priory over the patronage of the church of Leuchars was resolved. Certainly he appears to have been at his castle of Leuchars in April 1209, when he received John's protection for a vessel that he was taking from there to Lynn. In the summer of 1210 Quincy served in John's Ulster campaign. He was possibly the unnamed commander of a force sent in 1211 to assist the Scots to crush the rising of Guthred mac William in Ross. He was again in Scotland on John's business in March 1212. This period saw the peak of his career in royal service: between 1211 and 1214 he acted as a justiciar, sat as an auditor in the exchequer in 1212, and in the same year was an ambassador to John's nephew, the emperor Otto IV, whose assistance was sought against France and the papacy. On 15 May 1213 at Dover, Quincy attested John's surrender of his crown to Innocent III. Some of his men may have been involved in the naval victory at Damme on 30 May, as John later instructed delivery to Quincy of a galley captured by them in Flanders. In January 1215 he witnessed the reissue of the king's charter of ecclesiastical liberties, and on 4 March was one of the nobles who took the cross with John.

Despite this apparent closeness to John, Quincy had unresolved grievances concerning property of which he felt he had been unjustly deprived, most notably Mountsorrel Castle in Leicestershire, and was associated closely with the first stirrings of rebellion. He travelled to Scotland and in early April 1215 was at the court of Alexander II, where he joined an influential group urging Scottish intervention in England. Before the end of April he joined the dissident barons at his principal residence, Brackley in Northamptonshire, and marched with them to London.

Sidney Painter, ed. F. A. Cazel (1961), 1135–1264 · D. A. Carpenter, *The minority of Henry III* (1990) · W. L. Warren, *King John* (1961) · F. M. Powicke, *The thirteenth century* (1962), vol. 4 of *The Oxford history of England*, ed. G. M. Clarke, 2nd edn · G. W. S. Barrow, ed., *Regesta regum Scottorum*, 2 (1971) · *CDS* · A. A. M. Duncan, *Scotland: the making of the kingdom* (1975), vol. 1 of *The Edinburgh history of Scotland*, ed. G. Donaldson (1965–75) · K. J. Stringer, 'Periphery and core in thirteenth-century Scotland: Alan, son of Roland, lord of Galloway and constable of Scotland', *Medieval Scotland: crown, lordship and community: essays presented to G. W. S. Barrow*, ed. A. Grant and K. J. Stringer (1993), 82–113 · *The cartulary of Cambuskenneth* (1872) · *Registrum S. Marie de Neubotle* (1849) · *Registrum de Dunfermeleyn* (1842) · D. Crouch, *William Marshall: court, career and chivalry in the Angevin empire* (1990) · *Ann. mon.* · Annals of Waverley **Likenesses** seal, BL; Birch, *Seals*, 6355 [*see illus.*]
Wealth at death £1600 in debt to English crown · estates in eleven English counties; also three Scottish sheriffdoms

Quinil [Quivil], **Peter** (*c*.1230–1291), bishop of Exeter, was the son of Peter Quinil, provost of Exeter, and his wife, Helewis. Until recently the surname was interpreted as Quivil, but it appears to be a variant of the modern name Quen(n)ell or Quin(n)ell. Peter was also called 'de Exonia' during his lifetime. The fact that he was styled master in 1262 when he resigned his first known benefice, the rectory of Mullion in Cornwall, may imply that he received a university education. He became archdeacon of St David's in 1263 and was made a canon of Exeter Cathedral by Bishop Walter of Branscombe in 1276. After Walter's death on 22 July 1280, Quinil was elected bishop of Exeter by his fellow canons between 4 August and 7 October; he was consecrated in Canterbury Cathedral by Richard of Gravesend, bishop of London (*d.* 1303), on 10 November.

Quinil did not hold major royal offices while bishop, and spent most of his episcopate in Devon and Cornwall, undertaking only short visits to London. He continued the work of previous bishops rather than making significant new departures. His most notable achievement in the diocese was to hold a synod in April 1287, which enacted fifty-six canons in the tradition of thirteenth-century ecclesiastical legislation. These regulated the sacraments, duties of the clergy, functioning of parish churches, and behaviour of the laity, and were copied, kept, and referred to in the diocese until the fifteenth century. In Exeter he joined together some of the small city parishes to make more viable units, but he was later accused of obstructing the attempts of the local Franciscan friars to move to a better site. His episcopal register—the second to survive in Exeter diocese—is partly extant in a volume of twenty-four folios but these are chiefly limited to the years 1281–4. The state of the diocese in his day is also well illustrated by the lists of ecclesiastical revenues contained in the *Taxatio* of Pope Nicholas IV conducted in 1291.

Quinil gave much attention to his cathedral. In 1281 and 1283 he issued statutes regulating its liturgy, commemorative anniversaries (obits), finances, and its clergy's dress and behaviour. He completed its administrative structure on national lines by ordering the chancellor in 1283 to lecture on theology or canon law and by instituting the office of subdean in 1284. He also gave the cathedral the tithes of nine churches in the diocese, either for specific dignitaries or for the chapter as a whole. In 1281, one of the

canons, John Pycot, was elected dean in dubious circumstances. Quinil refused to recognize him, inaugurating a struggle between his own supporters, led by the precentor Walter of Lechlade, and those of Pycot. The latter had the backing of Archbishop John Pecham, whose relations with Quinil were generally poor. On 10 November 1283 Lechlade was murdered outside the cathedral on his way to matins. Nineteen local clergy and laity were implicated in the deed, and Edward I visited Exeter in December 1285 to see that justice was done. The mayor and four other laymen were hanged; Pycot, deprived of the deanery, retired to a monastery. On 1 January 1286 the king gave permission for the cathedral close to be surrounded by walls and gates to protect the clergy at night. The gates remained until the nineteenth century, symbolizing the uneasy relationship between the city and the cathedral.

Quinil's other legacy to the cathedral was architectural. His predecessor Walter of Branscombe had begun to transform the Norman building into a Gothic structure by building a new lady chapel. Quinil continued this work, and although it is not clear who conceived the idea of rebuilding the main church on Gothic lines, he was regarded after his death as 'first founder of the new work' and was said to have contributed to it at his own expense (Erskine, 1.xiii). During his episcopate, the lady chapel was finished and work began on the presbytery, the choir aisles, and two double chapels, following a plan similar to that of Salisbury Cathedral but on a smaller scale. Further west, the two Norman towers of the cathedral were opened to the interior and made into transepts with chapels on their eastern sides to accommodate altars. This work caused the cathedral to grow larger and more complex, reflecting a growth in the number of clergy and their liturgical functions.

Quinil died on 1 October 1291, choking on syrup according to a local story, which attributed his death to his hostility towards the friars. He was buried before the altar of the new lady chapel under an incised marble slab bearing a foliated cross and the inscription 'Petra tegit Petrum: nichil officiat sibi tetrum' ('The stone covers Peter; may nothing do you [Peter] harm'). The tomb is modest and the bishop founded no chantry, but the cathedral chapter later endowed an anniversary mass in his honour.

NICHOLAS ORME

Sources F. C. Hingeston-Randolph, ed., *The registers of Walter Bronescombe (AD 1257–1280) and Peter Quivil (AD 1280–1291), bishops of Exeter* (1889) · F. M. Powicke and C. R. Cheney, eds., *Councils and synods with other documents relating to the English church, 1205–1313*, 2 (1964), 982–1077 · A. M. Erskine, ed. and trans., *The accounts of the fabric of Exeter Cathedral, 1279–1353*, 2 vols., Devon and Cornwall RS, new ser., 24, 26 (1981–3) · G. R. Oliver, *Monasticon dioecesis Exoniensis* (1846–54) · F. Rose-Troup, *Exeter vignettes* (1942) · N. Orme, *Exeter Cathedral as it was, 1050–1550* (1986) · W. J. Harte, 'List of civic officials of Exeter in the 12th and 13th centuries ... by Miss Easterling', *Report and Transactions of the Devonshire Association*, 70 (1938), 435–44 · A. G. Little and R. C. Easterling, *The Franciscans and Dominicans of Exeter* (1927), 15–16 · *Registrum epistolarum fratris Johannis Peckham, archiepiscopi Cantuariensis*, ed. C. T. Martin, 3 vols., Rolls Series, 77 (1882–5) · T. Astle, S. Ayscough, and J. Caley, eds., *Taxatio ecclesiastica Angliae et Walliae auctoritate P. Nicholai IV*, RC (1802)

Archives BL, Harley MS 1027, fols. 21v–26r, 28r–30v · Devon RO, Chanter I · Exeter Cathedral, archives

Quinn, William (b. c.1911). See under Knoydart, Seven Men of (act. 1948).

Quinton, James Wallace (1834–1891), administrator in India, was born on 7 October 1834 in Enniskillen, the son of William Quinton, a wine merchant in the town. Richard Frith Quinton (1849–1934), criminologist and governor of Holloway prison, was his younger brother. Quinton was educated at Enniskillen Royal School and Trinity College, Dublin, where he graduated BA in 1853. In 1856 he joined the Bengal civil service.

Quinton spent most of his career in the North-Western Provinces and Oudh. On 20 March 1865, while stationed at Meerut, he married Pauline May, daughter of Francis Drummond, with whom he had two children, Francis William Drummond (b. 1865) and Anna Henrietta Drummond (b. 1867). In April 1875 he was appointed officiating judicial commissioner of British Burma, but returned to the North-Western Provinces and Oudh in March 1877 to become magistrate of Allahabad. In November 1878, after three months on the North-Western Provinces famine commission, he became officiating commissioner of Jhansi division, an appointment which was confirmed in April 1880. A supporter of Lord Ripon's plans for local self-government, he readily accepted an appointment in 1883 to the governor-general's legislative council, a position he again held in 1889. In June 1885 he became junior member of the North-Western Provinces and Oudh board of revenue and thereafter twice served, in 1886 and 1889, on the lieutenant-governor's council. He was a member of the public service commission of 1886 and in 1889 chaired an inquiry into the administrative structure of the North-Western Provinces and Oudh. In 1887 he was gazetted CSI and in October 1889, after thirty-three years' service, he was appointed chief commissioner of Assam.

Quinton knew little of Assam and was given its top job purely on the basis of his seniority in the service, a fact which provoked much criticism in the wake of the disaster which overtook him in the state of Manipur. Manipur's ruling family was loyal to the British, but in return expected military aid to help them repel rivals for the throne. When, in the 1880s, British aid dried up, Tikendrajit, the state's commander-in-chief and most able brother of Raja Sura Chandra, began to doubt the value of the alliance. Instead of openly opposing the British, however, Tikendrajit befriended the young political agent Frank St Clair Grimwood. Thus, in September 1880, when Tikendrajit staged a palace coup, Grimwood obligingly hurried Sura Chandra into exile and persuaded Quinton to leave Tikendrajit and his new regent, Kula Chandra, in power.

In March 1891, after six months of dithering, the governor-general's council in Calcutta dispatched Quinton to Manipur with instructions to recognize Kula Chandra as raja in return for greater submission to the British. Tikendrajit was to be banished. Accompanied by Colonel Skene and 400 Gurkhas, Quinton arrived at the Manipur residency on 22 March 1891 and immediately called a durbar, at which it was his intention to have Tikendrajit seized. Not surprisingly, Tikendrajit refused the bait and on 24 March Quinton ordered his men to attack the fort and seize him. The battle was horribly lopsided and within hours the British were besieged within the residency. Rejecting the option of retreat, Quinton decided to negotiate for peace and that evening, along with Grimwood, Skene, and two other British officers, he entered the fort. The talks failed, however, and on attempting to return to the residency Quinton and his companions were set upon by an angry crowd. Grimwood was speared to death almost immediately, but the others managed to scramble back into the fort. Tikendrajit apparently gave orders for them to be protected, but the crowd continued to clamour for blood and during the night they were led out to their execution.

British revenge was thorough. A month later 8000 soldiers entered Manipur and seized the fort. Quinton's body, along with those of his companions, was recovered and buried with military honours in the residency cemetery on 30 April. In the following months Tikendrajit and his leading general, Thangal, were tried and hanged and an infant raja from a rival family was installed on the throne.

In Britain the affair provoked popular outrage reminiscent of 1857, but although in public official criticism of Quinton was muted, in private many old India hands believed that he had paid the price of diplomatic inexperience. His widow and mother were awarded pensions.

KATHERINE PRIOR

Sources J. Roy, History of Manipur (1958) · E. St C. Grimwood, My three years in Manipur and escape from the recent mutiny (1891) · History of services of gazetted officers … of the North-Western Provinces and Oudh (1890) · J. Johnstone, My experiences in Manipur and the Naga hills (1896) · The Times (31 March 1891) · The Times (April–May 1891) · The Times (8 Sept 1891) · ecclesiastical records, BL OIOC · Manipur: compiled from the columns of 'The Pioneer' (1891) · DNB · appointment lists, BL OIOC, L/F/10/245
Archives BL, Ripon MSS, letters
Likenesses portrait, repro. in The Graphic (18 April 1891), 428
Wealth at death £266: probate, 21 Jan 1892, CGPLA Eng. & Wales

Quivil, Peter de. See Quinil, Peter (c.1230–1291).

Raban, Edward (d. 1658), printer, was born in England, possibly in Worcestershire. He was in London in 1600, awaiting embarkation to the Low Countries to serve in the armies fighting against Spanish occupation. Remaining on the continent he was in Leiden about 1617–19; there he learned to print, probably at the press of the Pilgrim Fathers. The details of his early life are gleaned from two of his publications, Raban's Resolution Against Drunkennesse and The Popes New Years Gifts, both 1622.

On his arrival in Edinburgh in 1620 Raban set up a printing press at the Cowgate Port, at the sign of the ABC. That same year he moved to St Andrews and took up residence in South Street, again at the sign of the ABC. Why Raban moved to Aberdeen in 1622 is unknown, though Robert Baron, professor of divinity at Marischal College, Aberdeen, Bishop Patrick Forbes, and Sir Paul Menzies, provost, are said to have been instrumental in his travelling north. But given the presence of both King's and Marischal colleges in Aberdeen, and the educated groups associated with these institutions, the arrival of a printer can be seen as a natural development. Raban fulfilled the role of semi-official printer to the two colleges and to the town council but his enterprise was not limited to such work. Shortly after having arrived in Aberdeen he became associated with David Melvill, burgess and bookseller. Melvill initially paid the rent on the premises (in the Castlegate, at the sign of the Townes Armes) offered to Raban by the council. Many books (particularly grammars, almanacs, and editions of the Psalms) printed by Raban between 1622 and 1633 carry Melvill's name on the imprint.

Some time before 1624 Raban married Janet Johnston, with whom he had at least one child, a daughter, baptized Constanzia. Janet died in 1627 and by 1637 Raban had married Janet Ailhous. In 1643 (the year of Melvill's death) Raban moved to accommodation in the Broadgate. Six years later he retired, and in 1650 he was succeeded by James Brown, son of the minister of Innernochty.

Over 150 publications (excluding jobbing printing) emanated from Raban's Aberdeen press. This output included graduation theses and some of the writings of the local professoriate, such as William Guild, principal of King's College, and Robert Baron, who was responsible, as one of the six Aberdeen doctors, for the *Generall Demands Concerning the Late Covenant* (1638). The instabilities of the times are further reflected in Raban's printing of *A Solemn League and Covenant* (1643) and *A Declaration of … James, Marquess of Montrose* (1644). His initiative as printer can be seen in his production in 1622 of *A New Prognostication*, which was brought out probably annually. Such was the work's success and reliability that it was subsequently ruthlessly pirated. And Raban's 1625 edition of the Psalms is the first in Scotland to incorporate harmonized tunes. Raban died in Aberdeen in 1658 and was buried in the west wall of St Nicholas churchyard, Aberdeen, on 6 December.

IAIN BEAVAN

Sources J. P. Edmond, *The Aberdeen printers: Edward Raban to James Nicol, 1620–1736* (1886) [esp. annotated copy, priv. coll.] · J. P. Edmond, *Last notes on the Aberdeen printers* (1888) · W. R. Macdonald, 'Devices used by Raban in Guild's *Limbo's batterie*, 1630', *The Biblotheck*, 4 (1963–6), 77–9 · W. R. Macdonald, 'Some aspects of printing and the book trade in Aberdeen', *The hero as printer*, ed. C. A. McLaren (1976), 27–36 · I. Beavan, 'Raban and his successors: local printing (1622–1800) in Aberdeen University', *Northern Scotland*, 18 (1998), 97–104 · H. G. Aldis, *A list of books printed in Scotland before 1700*, [rev. edn] (1970) · J. F. Kellas Johnstone and A. W. Robertson, *Bibliographia Aberdonensis*, ed. W. D. Simpson, 2 vols., Third Spalding Club (1929–30) · *Record of the celebration of the tercentenary of the introduction of the art of printing into Aberdeen by Edward Raban in the year 1622* (1922)

Rabin, Samuel [Sam; *formerly* Samuel Rabinovitch] (1903–1991), artist and art teacher, was born on 20 June 1903 at 20 Dewhurst Street, Cheetham, north Manchester, the son of Jacob Rabinovitch (1872–1962), a cap cutter, later a cap manufacturer and wholesale milliner, and his wife, Sarah, *née* Kraselschikow (1879–1961), a jewellery assembler. His parents were both Jewish Russian exiles from Vitebsk who later moved to Salford, where he grew up. His family

encouraged his drawing talent early on and he won a scholarship, aged eleven, to the Manchester Municipal School of Art in 1914, becoming the youngest pupil ever to attend that institution. He was taught there by the French painter Adolphe Valette, who instilled in him a lifelong belief in proficiency at drawing as a basis for all pictorial representation. From 1921 to 1924 he studied under Henry Tonks at the Slade School of Fine Art in London.

In 1926 Rabin visited the sculptor Charles Despiau in Paris, which he later described as one of the greatest experiences of his life (private information). Little is known of Rabin's work as a sculptor in the late 1920s. In 1928 he was commissioned by the architect Charles Holden, probably at Jacob Epstein's suggestion, to carve a large stone sculpture personifying the west wind, part of a modernist sculptural scheme for the new London Underground headquarters. Epstein, Henry Moore, and Eric Gill also worked on the exterior. In 1930 he produced two stone heads, *Past* and *Future*, for the exterior of the new *Daily Telegraph* building in London.

Unable to make a living from sculpture, much of which he destroyed, or to find a teaching post, Rabin became a wrestler to finance his art. A man of awesome physical strength, he had wrestled as an amateur and had won a bronze medal at the Amsterdam Olympics in 1928. He turned professional in 1932 and quickly became a favourite with the press and public, fighting all over Britain as Rabin the Cat and Sam Radnor the Hebrew Jew. He came to the attention of the film producer Alexander Korda, who cast him as the champion wrestler in *The Private Life of Henry VIII* (1933) and as the Jewish prize-fighter, Mendoza, in *The Scarlet Pimpernel* (1934). Rabin was also highly gifted musically and, despite a lack of formal musical education and unable to read music, worked as a professional singer (using the name Samuel Rabin) throughout the 1940s. A bass baritone, he was coached by Dinh Gilly and Albert Garcia. During the Second World War he joined Freddie Frinton's Stars in Battledress and sang operatic arias with the prestigious Army Classical Music Group. In 1946 he was auditioned at the Albert Hall in London by Victor de Sabata of the Milan Opera.

In 1949 Rabin went to teach at Goldsmiths' College of Art in New Cross, south London. He was an outstanding teacher of drawing, renowned among his students and colleagues for his commanding presence and disciplined classes and for demonstrating the principles of drawing. His students included the designer Mary Quant, the abstract painter Bridget Riley, who became a great admirer and friend, and the notorious painter of fakes, Tom Keating.

Few pictures by Rabin pre-dating this period have survived, because of their accidental destruction by his Hampstead landlady during the war and owing to his lifelong habit of destroying works he considered imperfect. His extant pictures fall into two categories: figure studies, many of which were demonstration drawings for students; and coloured boxing scenes, with related action studies first exhibited at Wildenstein & Co. Ltd, London, in 1951. The boxing scenes, often mistaken for oil paintings, are heavily worked with thick home-made wax crayons packed with pigment. Pictures such as *Knockdown* (reproduced in Sheeran, 31), *Knockout* (reproduced in Sheeran, front cover), and *Prelude* (Gov. Art Coll.) are characterized by dramatic compositions and lighting, simplified forms, decisive line, rhythmic movement, and bold but selective colour. The visual harmony of Rabin's work relies on a careful balance of all these elements so that none is allowed to dominate. Underlying all is a sureness of drawing which brilliantly eliminates the superfluous so that weight, mass, and balance are perfectly expressed, no matter how awkward the pose or movement of the figure.

Little is known of Rabin's first marriage to Ida Lily Shuster about 1935, which ended in divorce. On 11 June 1956 he married Frances Kaye, formerly known as Lucienne Karpeles (1917–1988), a journalist and schoolteacher, who predeceased him; they had one son, David, born in 1960. Rabin left Goldsmiths' in 1965, dissatisfied because teaching was moving away from the figurative tradition. Thereafter he taught drawing at Bournemouth College of Art (1965–85) and, after retirement, at the Poole Art Centre until shortly before his death on 20 December 1991.

Rabin never used an agent or sought to promote himself. His own severest critic, he regarded his work as an intense personal struggle for perfection. He never joined an artistic group or movement and rarely exhibited; hence the artist's obscurity until a retrospective touring exhibition, organized by the Dulwich Picture Gallery, London, in 1985–6, attracted widespread publicity. Rabin won the drawing prize at the 1969 and 1977 International Biennale of Sport in Fine Art, and is represented in the British Museum, London, the Government Art Collection, and the Musée de Sport, near Paris.   JOHN SHEERAN

Sources J. Sheeran, *Introducing Sam Rabin* (1985) [exhibition catalogue, London, Southampton, and Salford] • *Sam Rabin*, Granada Television, *Celebration* ser. broadcast (16 May 1986) [video documentary] • *Daily Telegraph* (24 Dec 1991) • *The Guardian* (30 Dec 1991) • *The Times* (24 Dec 1991) • personal knowledge (2004) • private information (2004) • b. cert. • m. cert. [Sam Rabin and Frances Kaye] • b. certs. [Jacob Rabinovitch and Sarah Kraselschikow]
Archives priv. coll. | FILM BFI NFTVA
Likenesses P. Drury, soft ground etching, *c.*1951, Goldsmiths' College collection; repro. in Sheeran, *Introducing Sam Rabin* • photographs, repro. in Sheeran, *Introducing Sam Rabin*

Rabisha, William (*fl.* 1625–1661), cook and author, may have been of a Yorkshire family: his surname appears to be a variant of the West Riding name Robertshaw or Robertshay. In the preface to his *The Whole Body of Cookery Dissected* (1661), he states that he had worked as a cook in aristocratic and ambassadorial households in England and abroad since before the civil war. The book claims to be written 'for the instruction of young Practitioners' (A sig. 4*v*) rather than for private householders. It begins with bills of fare for very grand dinners, of between forty and seventy separate dishes, and continues with recipes on an equally lavish scale, for instance for caviar, baked swan, and roast porpoise. It concludes with a modernized text (perhaps taken from John Murrell's *Two Bookes of Cookerie and Carving*, published in 1631) of the *Boke of Keruynge*, which had originally been printed by Wynkyn de Worde in 1508; and with a description of George Neville's vast installation feast of 1468, which was purportedly taken from 'the Records of the *Tower*' (Rabisha, 159) but which was possibly taken from the text printed as *The Great Feast at the Intronization of … George Neuell* (*c.*1570).

The tone of Rabisha's book is not only antiquarian but pointedly royalist. It is dedicated to five women with royalist connections and refers to the author's experience as a cook 'in the late Kings Court, of ever blessed memory' (A sig. 3*r*). It is therefore unclear whether Rabisha the cook was also the Captain William Rabisha who brought the news of the fall of Wexford from Cromwell to parliament in 1649 and who wrote the heterodox *Adam Unvailed, and Seen with Open Face* (1649) and a tract on Christopher Love's plot of 1651. The royalism of the cookery book must have been meant either to distance the author from his parliamentarian past, or to distance him from a parliamentarian namesake.   JOHN CONSIDINE

Sources *CSP dom.*, 1649–50 • N. Smith, *Literature and revolution in England, 1640–1660* (1994) • W. Rabisha, preface, *The whole body of cookery dissected, taught, and fully manifested* (1661)

Race, Ernest Dawson (1914–1964), furniture and industrial designer, was born on 16 October 1914 in Newcastle upon Tyne, the third of the three sons of Joseph Dawson Race (1880–1966), a banker, and May Tweddle (1882–1950). Joseph Race was born in Hankow (Hankou), China, a month after the death of his father, a Methodist minister. He returned to Weardale with his mother and was brought up there. Race moved with his family from Northumbria to Hammersmith when he was small. He was educated at St Paul's School in London, which he left in 1932, before moving on to be trained as an interior designer at the Bartlett school of architecture at London University where he followed a three-year course. On completing his studies he began making his living as a model maker but very soon, about 1936, turned to lighting design for the manufacturing company Troughton and Young, under the lead of its distinguished in-house designer, A. B. Read. The company was among the very few creating modern lighting designs in these years and the short apprenticeship that Race undertook there was undoubtedly very important for his later development. He left in 1937 to form his own firm, Race Fabrics, in London's Motcomb Street, through which he sold designs of his own which were hand-woven in India. The fact that he had a missionary aunt based in India, who ran a weaving workshop in Madras and whom he had visited for four months immediately after leaving Troughton and Young, made this possible.

The wartime years were important ones for Race, who worked through them as a member of the Auxiliary Fire Service. It was during that time that he married Sara Hope Blower (known as Sally), who was born on 14 September 1912. Sally had also studied interior design at the Bartlett school. The couple married in 1941. At the end of the war Race was employed by the architects Colcutt and Hemp, but most of his creativity was dedicated to designing unit furniture at home. It was in this context that he met his future business partner, an engineer named J. W. Noel Jordan, who was trying to move into the area of furniture at the end of the war. After he put an advertisement in *The Times*, to which Race responded, Race and Jordan founded Ernest Race Ltd together. The former became the director and chief designer while the latter took on the role of managing director of the new venture. They began to manufacture furniture from aluminium alloy, having received a licence from the Board of Trade which made it impossible for them to use wood.

Race's little 'BA' dining chair of 1945, the tapering T-section legs and seat and back structures of which were made of sand-cast aluminium, featured in the exhibition entitled 'Britain can make it', held in London's Victoria and Albert Museum in that year. It was visible in a number of room settings but also provided the seating in the tearoom at the exhibition. The chair was part of a complete dining-room set which included a table, a little coffee-table, and a sideboard. All of them were made from aluminium but had tops made of holoplast, a laminated plastic with a mahogany veneer. The manufacturing company produced more than 250,000 BA chairs between 1945 and 1969 and they became familiar objects in many of Britain's public buildings and commercial areas through this period. Combining lightness with elegance, the chair won Race a gold medal at the prestigious Milan triennale exhibition of 1954.

In 1948 Race designed and manufactured a metal-frame wing chair and set of storage units which were included in the exhibition linked to the international competition for low cost furniture design which was held in New York's Museum of Modern Art. The success of the BA chair was repeated by two more designs that Race produced for the Festival of Britain, a large exhibition located on the south bank of the River Thames in London in 1951. Intended as outdoor seating, both Antelope and Springbok were made out of thin steel rod and presented a delicate, spindly form to their viewers. Their silhouettes conformed perfectly to the need for lightness and modernity that was 'in the air' at that time and they provided a level of visual and technological sophistication which was then more apparent in designs emanating from the USA, Scandinavia, and Italy. Race succeeded in putting British design on the international map in the early 1950s and his two chairs of 1951 were among the festival's lasting icons. Soon they could be found in pub gardens and outdoor public areas across Britain. Their small ball feet, made of cast aluminium and said to have been inspired by molecular structures, were both stylistically evocative and practical as they ensured that the thin steel legs of the chairs did not force their way into the flooring on which they sat. The bent ply seat of Antelope was a result of another spin-off from wartime technological developments.

In 1953 Race designed the Neptune lounge chair for the P. & O. shipping line. For this design he abandoned his use of metal and used plywood which became much more widely available after the war with the lifting of post-war restrictions upon its use. It was a striking chair made of two identical curved plywood forms which could be folded into each other.

Race was a director of Ernest Race Ltd (from 1961 Race Furniture Ltd) until 1954, after which date he worked as a freelance designer for the company. During the last ten years of his life he continued to design furniture pieces but never achieved the same level of success as he did in the first decade after the war. Items he designed included the Flamingo chair of 1959 and the Sheppey sofa of 1963. His designs were well received abroad and he showed pieces at the Milan triennales of 1951, 1954, 1957, and 1960, winning a number of gold and silver medals over that time period. In 1953 he was made a royal designer for industry, an award made to important and influential designers by the Royal Society of Arts. Professionally he was one of the small number of highly innovatory British designers who embraced the potential of new materials and the modern idiom in design without reservation, and whose creations made a significant impact in the mass environment and were recognized internationally. This impact was made all the more significant by the fact that he and a partner formed their own manufacturing company to produce Race's designs. He played a key role in the formulation of what came to be called the 'contemporary' style, a softened version of its more austere pre-war predecessor, modernism. The former became extremely popular in Britain in the 1950s, both in the decor of private dwellings and in the interiors of public buildings. With a strong sense of humour, Race remained a quiet, private and hard-working man throughout his career and he died prematurely in London on 22 January 1964 at the relatively young age of forty-nine, survived by his wife. The 1990s saw a revival of interest in Race's early designs and a number of them were put back into production.

PENNY SPARKE

Sources H. Conway, *Ernest Race* (1982) · E. Race, 'Trends in factory made furniture', *ArchR*, 103 (1948), 218–20 · G. Naylor, 'Ernest Race', *Design* [London], 101 (May 1957), 18–21 · *CGPLA Eng. & Wales* (1964)
Wealth at death £6313: probate, 23 March 1964, *CGPLA Eng. & Wales*

Race, Robert Russell (1907–1984), geneticist and serologist, was born on 28 November 1907 at Hull, the eldest of the three sons (there were no daughters) of Joseph Dawson Race, a banker, and his wife, May, daughter of Robert Tweddle, a sanitary engineer of West Hartlepool. He was educated in London at St Paul's School and then, from 1926, at St Bartholomew's Hospital, where he qualified MRCS (Eng.) and LRCP (Lond.) in 1933.

In 1937, after four years in a junior post in pathology, Race became assistant serologist at the Galton Laboratory. His job was to assist in the laboratory's serum unit which had been set up by R. A. Fisher with a grant from the Rockefeller Foundation. The following year Race married Margaret Monica (1909–1955), daughter of John Richard Charles Rotton, a solicitor. They later had three daughters (the first was adopted).

At the outbreak of the Second World War Race moved with the serum unit to Cambridge. At first work was confined to the ABO and MN blood group systems but in 1942 the unit began to study the Rh antigen and antibody which had recently been described in the USA. It soon became clear that there were several different Rh antigens, but Fisher suggested a scheme which brought immediate understanding of the interrelationships. So far, Race's role had been to produce entirely reliable serological results and Fisher's to supply the ideas. Very soon, however, Race showed that he had his own powerful contribution to make.

In 1946 Race moved with his small team to the Lister Institute in London and the enterprise became the Medical Research Council's blood group unit. As a result of his growing fame and owing largely to his open, friendly, and cheerful manner, he now started to receive blood samples from all over the world, containing antibodies to be identified. When there was no obvious solution he showed a great flair for developing and testing hypotheses. He introduced the application of simple statistical tests to distinguish between real and chance associations and as each new antigen was identified he was able to show whether or not it was related to existing antigens. In this way he played a leading role in establishing knowledge of the various blood group systems. His unit soon gained an international reputation. One of its most important discoveries was of an antigen carried on the X chromosome. The potential of this discovery was immediately recognized and in the next few years understanding of the numerous clinical syndromes stemming from abnormal arrangements of the X and Y chromosomes was greatly increased.

From 1942 to the time of his retirement in 1973 Race's work was immensely influential not only in determining the rapid and orderly development of knowledge of human blood group systems but also in initiating the mapping of the human genome.

After the death of his first wife in 1955, Race married in 1956 Ruth Ann, daughter of the Revd Hubert (Tom) Sanger, headmaster of Armidale School, New South Wales. There were no children of the marriage. Ruth Sanger had come to work at the blood group unit in 1946 and stayed there until her retirement. From 1948 onwards she was a co-author of virtually every important paper which Race wrote, and their separate contributions became hard to disentangle. Together they produced six editions (1950–75) of a notable book, *Blood Groups in Man*. This work was not only the best source of information in its field for twenty-five years but was written with great clarity, reflecting Race's love of literature, and humour, reflecting his exceptionally amusing personality.

Race was elected FRS in 1952, and became FRCP (Lond.) in 1959 and FRCPath in 1972. He was appointed CBE in 1970. He received honorary degrees from the universities of Paris (1965) and Turku (1970), and many awards, including the Oehlecker medal of the Deutsche Gesellschaft für Bluttransfusion in 1970. In 1973 he was made a member of the Deutsche Akademie der Naturforscher Leopoldina. Jointly with Ruth Sanger he was given the Karl Landsteiner award of the American Association of Blood Banks in 1957 and Gairdner Foundation award in 1972. He was a member of many foreign societies. He died on 15 April 1984 in Putney Hospital, London.   P. L. MOLLISON, *rev.*

Sources C. Clarke, *Memoirs FRS*, 31 (1985), 453–92 · personal knowledge (1990) · *The Times* (1 May 1984) · *CGPLA Eng. & Wales* (1984) · private information (2004) [family]
Archives Wellcome L., corresp. and papers
Likenesses photograph, repro. in Clarke, *Memoirs FRS* · photographs, Wellcome L.
Wealth at death £59,600: probate, 6 June 1984, *CGPLA Eng. & Wales*

Rachel. *See* Félix, Elisa (1820/21–1858).

Rachman, Peter [Perec] (1920?–1962), racketeer, was born at Lwów, Poland, son of David Rachman, a dental surgeon, who, together with his wife, vanished in the Holocaust. After the Nazi invasion of Poland, Rachman was forced onto a road-building chain-gang and later captured by Russians, who starved him. He arrived in Britain as a stateless person about 1945–6. He endured menial jobs (including dishwashing at Bloom's kosher restaurant in Whitechapel) before setting up as a flat-letting agent.

During the 1950s Rachman built a slum empire (chiefly in Paddington and North Kensington) by methods which, when they were exposed after his death, gave the ugly epithet of Rachmanism to the English language. At a time of severe housing shortages he bought properties occupied by tenants paying statutorily controlled rents pegged at 1939 levels. Knowing that rents became decontrolled once tenants vacated their homes, Rachman's technique with a property was to 'put in the Schwartzes and de-stat it' (*Sunday Times*, 7 July 1963). He hired black hooligans to intimidate white tenants or white thugs against black tenants and forcibly obtained vacant possession. His profiteering from racial tension contributed to the Notting Hill race riots of 1958. Bullies with alsatians would wrench the doors of communal lavatories off their hinges, cut off gas, water, and electricity, break into flats, destroy furniture, rip up floorboards, and throw out tenants' possessions. Tenants who publicized their grievances were driven into hiding. Once empty, a property's value massively increased. Rachman would then 'sweat' the property, either by overcrowding it with Caribbean immigrants, or by leasing it at exorbitant rents to brothel-keepers or club-owners. Typically he was able to collect £10,000 a year in rent for a house which cost him £1500. Later the property could be sold to shady associates. Rachman exploited flaws that existed until 1961–2 in the Companies Act, the Rent Act of 1957, and housing regulations. He controlled a proliferation of interlocking companies (fronted by nominee directors) so that sanitary notices, certificates of disrepair, and compulsory acquisitions were frustrated by the impossibility of identifying the beneficial owner of the property. Companies were wound up, and the properties reassigned to other companies, in order to keep a

Peter Rachman (1920?–1962), by unknown photographer, 1960

defective drain festering and drive out the statutory tenants. The Metropolitan Police, Ministry of Housing, borough councils, public health authorities, and rent tribunals all tried to catch him in legal nets but their mesh was too wide. In five years he made a million pounds, tax-free; with the relaxation of exchange control he was able to squirrel his fortune abroad.

In 1959, when Rachman controlled about eighty houses, ten cases of intimidation were submitted to the director of public prosecutions, who judged there was insufficient evidence to prosecute. Rachman's application for British nationality was, however, rejected after a police investigation. As he desired the security of a British passport he began dealing in better-class flats, hotels, and offices in south Kensington after 1959, although in 1962 he still held the head leases of some dozen basement clubs. He became the principal shareholder in Streatham Hill Playhouse Ltd which sold the Streatham Hill Theatre for £200,000 and contracted to buy the Golders Green Hippodrome for £130,000.

After his failure to obtain British nationality Rachman, on 7 March 1960, married Audrey, daughter of Frank O'Donnell, a tailor's designer, of Lancashire; her role in his business was described under cover of parliamentary privilege in the House of Commons on 22 July 1963 (Hansard 5C, 681, 1963, 1104). Rachman's satyriasis was relieved by a daily routine of mistresses. 'Sex to Peter Rachman was like cleaning his teeth, and I was the toothpaste', remembered Christine Keeler, whom he came to hate (Keeler, 58). By contrast Mandy Rice-Davies was devoted to Rachman, who kept her in 1961–2; the two-way mirror installed in their bedroom was often pruriently mentioned at the much-publicized and controversial trial of his friend Stephen Ward (1963).

Rachman was short, chubby-faced, plump, and balding. He habitually wore dark glasses and a gold bracelet which was locked to his wrist and inscribed with serial numbers of his Swiss bank accounts and safe-combinations. The huge stakes in his inveterate gambling laundered his cash

income. He used a sunlamp daily, and dressed in silk shirts, cashmere suits, and crocodile shoes. He sported big cigars, employed a bodyguard, and kept a gun in the glove compartment of his Rolls-Royce. Despite his sinister appearance, 'Rachman, socially, was … courteous, intelligent, witty, and almost excessively generous' (Irving, Hall, and Wallington, 35). After seeing a flamboyant American limousine while in Russian captivity Rachman had vowed to become rich enough to buy similar status symbols. In his prosperity his fleet of motor cars included a red Rolls-Royce saloon and a blue Rolls-Royce convertible; he gave a Cadillac to his favourite rent collector as a birthday present. In the 1960s he still hoarded bread-crusts under his bed as security against starvation and stockpiled his homes with food. 'He was freaky about cleanliness, took several baths a day using gallons of Dettol … He suffered appalling nightmares and he would wake, screaming and sweating with fear, crying for his mother' (Rice-Davies, Mandy, 72).

Rachman died after a coronary thrombosis, on 29 November 1962, at Edgware General Hospital, Edgware, Middlesex, and was buried at the Jewish cemetery in Bushey. His wife survived him. Rumours abounded in 1963 that he had assumed a new identity and was living off his Swiss fortune. Journalists had previously been deterred from publicizing his activities by fear of libel actions; his posthumous exposure was set against the resignation of John Profumo as secretary for war, and Ward's suicide. The techniques of Rachmanism were used in provincial cities like Nottingham and Newcastle, and by other London racketeers in Southwark, Lambeth, and Deptford, but in 1963 the blame was heaped 'on this particular, unhappy, dead, foreign Jew' (Hansard 5C, 681, 1963, 1114).

RICHARD DAVENPORT-HINES

Sources Sunday Times (7 July 1963) · Sunday Times (14 July 1963) · Sunday Times (21 July 1963) · Hansard 5C (1963), 681.1058–1186 · M. Rice-Davies, The Mandy report (1964) · M. Rice-Davies, Mandy (1980) · C. Keeler, Scandal! (1989), 53–61 · C. Irving, R. Hall, and J. Wallington, Scandal '63 (1963) · P. Knightley and C. Kennedy, An affair of state: the Profumo case and the framing of Stephen Ward (1987) · 'The significance of Peter Rachman', New Statesman (12 July 1963) · m. cert. · d. cert. · CGPLA Eng. & Wales (1963)

Likenesses photograph, 1960, Popperfoto, Northampton [see illus.] · photograph, c.1961, repro. in Sunday Times (14 July 1963) · photograph, c.1962, repro. in Rice-Davies, Mandy report

Wealth at death £72,830 9s.: administration, 29 April 1963, CGPLA Eng. & Wales

Rack, Edmund [pseud. Eusebius] (c.1735–1787), writer on agriculture, was born in Attleborough, Norfolk, the son of Edmund Rack, weaver, and his wife, Elizabeth, a Quaker preacher. He was brought up as a Quaker, and was apprenticed to a shopkeeper in Wymondham. At the end of his apprenticeship he moved to Bardfield in Essex, and was employed as a shopkeeper by a Miss Agnes Smith, whom he later married. He became interested in literature, and at the age of thirty began to write in magazines such as the Monthly Ledger and the Monthly Miscellany under the name Eusebius.

About 1775 Rack settled in Bath. While still living in Norfolk he had taken an interest in agriculture, and in 1777 he published a scheme for an agricultural society in the *Farmer's Magazine* and the *Bath Chronicle*, which was to encourage agriculture in the counties of Somerset, Wiltshire, Dorset, and Gloucestershire. The society was founded in 1778 with Rack as secretary, and it later became the Bath and West of England Agricultural Society.

Rack edited three volumes of papers contributed to the Agricultural Society, including several of his own articles. His papers 'On the origin and progress of agriculture' and 'The natural history of the cock-chafer' were reprinted in volume 3 of Alexander Hunter's *Georgical Essays* (1803), and that on the cockchafer also appeared in the *Annual Register* for 1784–5. He edited the second edition of *Caspipina's Letters* (1777) by the Revd Jacob Duché, to which he added an appendix on William Penn. Rack spent the final years of his life making a topographical survey of Somerset as part of a history of the county of Somerset. This work was published by the Revd John Collinson in 1791 in three volumes.

In 1779 Rack helped to found the Bath Philosophical Society, and he became its first secretary. His literary works included *Poems on Several Subjects* (1775), *Mentor's Letters Addressed to Youth* (1777)—written five years previously for a few of his young friends—which ran to four editions, and *Essays, Letters, and Poems* (1781). Philip Thicknesse accused him of writing *A Letter Addressed to Philip Thickskull, Esq.*, and responded with the satirical *Letter from Philip Thickskull, Esq, to Edmund Rack* (1780). Rack was in poor health for many years. He died on 22 February 1787 in Bath. Richard Polwhele wrote an elegy in his memory.

W. P. COURTNEY, rev. ANNE PIMLOTT BAKER

Sources J. Collinson, *The history and antiquities of the county of Somerset*, 1 (1791), 77–82 • *GM*, 1st ser., 57 (1787), 276 • R. Polwhele, *Traditions and recollections; domestic, clerical and literary*, 2 vols. (1826) • P. Thicknesse, *The valetudinarian's Bath guide* (1780)
Archives Bath Central Library, journal
Wealth at death lost savings c.1780: DNB

Rackam, John [nicknamed Calico Jack] (d. **1720**), pirate, was quartermaster under Charles Vane, one of the leaders of the New Providence 'pirate republic', when, in November 1718, he challenged Vane's decision not to attack a French frigate in the Windward passage, and was elected captain in his place. Essentially a small-time and not particularly bloodthirsty pirate, who preyed mostly on fishing boats and small coastal vessels, his main claim to fame is that his ship was the one in which two female pirates, Anne *Bonny and Mary *Read, pursued their scandalous careers. Rackam was supposedly a tall, dark-eyed, handsome man whose swashbuckling manner was matched and supported by his theatrical dress: striped calico shirt, jacket, and trousers.

In May 1719 Rackam, like many of his profession, took advantage of the pardon being offered by the governor of the Bahamas, Captain Woodes Rogers, and while ashore in Nassau he met Anne Bonny (1698–1782), who became his mistress, and joined his crew when he again took up piracy. Mary Read joined them later when Rackam captured the ship on which she was travelling. On 22 August 1720, Rackam and his twelve crew stole the 12 ton sloop

William from Nassau harbour, hoisted Rackam's distinctive skull and crossed cutlasses, and attacked several small vessels on a cruise from the Bahamas to Jamaica. On 5 September Woodes Rogers issued a proclamation naming 'Rackum' and his crew, including Bonny and Read, as pirates, and sent out vessels to hunt them down. In early November they were captured by 'a brisk fellow, one Jonathan Barnet' in the well-armed 90 ton *Tyger*, one of ten vessels commissioned in 1715 by the then governor of Jamaica, Lord Hamilton, to hunt pirates.

On 16 November 1720, Rackam along with his sailing master George Fetherston, his quartermaster Richard Corner, and most of his crew were tried for piracy before a vice-admiralty court at Spanish Town, Jamaica, under the presidency of the governor, Sir Nicholas Lawes. All eleven were condemned and sentenced to hang. In a separate trial, held ten days after Rackam's execution, Mary Read and Anne Bonny were also sentenced to hang, but were reprieved when they informed the court that they were both 'quick with child'.

Rackam and his ten male accomplices were hanged at Gallows Point, Port Royal, Jamaica on 18 November 1720. His body was afterwards hung in irons from a gibbet on Deadman's Cay at the entrance to the harbour, as a deterrent to others. This sandy islet is today named Rackam's Cay.

W. R. MEYER, rev.

Sources PRO, transcript of trial, CO 137/14 • PRO, Barnet's commission, CO 137/12 • *The tryals of Captain John Rackam and other pirates* (1721) • D. Cordingly, *Life among the pirates* (1995) • *CSP col.*, vol. 32 • C. Johnson, *A general history of the robberies and murders of the most notorious pyrates* (1724) • J. Stanley, *Bold in her breeches: women pirates across the ages* (1995)

Rackett, Thomas (1755–1840), Church of England clergyman and antiquary, was the son of Thomas Rackett of Wandsworth, Surrey, and Marie Caillouel. His mother belonged to a Huguenot family who settled in England in 1685. From an early age he displayed a remarkable talent in natural history, music, and drawing. At fourteen he impressed David Garrick with his ability to recite in public, and received from him a folio copy of Shakespeare with a laudatory inscription. George Romney's full-length portrait shows the youthful Rackett declaiming his ode on stage. He matriculated from University College, Oxford, on 16 November 1773, graduated BA in 1777, and proceeded MA in 1780. On 26 December 1780 he became rector of Spetisbury with Charlton-Marshall, near Blandford Forum in Dorset, and held the living for sixty years. On 31 July 1781 he married Dorothy (d. 1835), daughter of the Revd Thomas Tattersall, rector of St Paul's, Covent Garden, and Streatham.

Spetisbury provided Rackett with a handsome living worth £750 per annum and a splendid parsonage house built in 1716 at a cost of £1000. His parochial duties were not onerous, and he was able to pursue his many interests with zeal. He travelled widely throughout the western counties studying burial-mounds, and was often accompanied by his daughter Dorothea. In 1794 and 1796 he toured the west country collecting minerals with Thomas

Hatchett FRS and Dr Maton MD, physician to Queen Charlotte. He was an active member of the Linnean Society, the Society of Antiquaries, and the Royal Society, and a corresponding member of the Société Statistique Universelle. He contributed several very fine drawings to the second edition of John Hutchins's *History of Dorset*. Rackett was an avid collector throughout his life and the county record office in Dorchester contains a large collection of his documents, while the county museum houses his splendid collection of Greek coins found in the British Isles. His manuscripts reveal his interest in subjects as diverse as electricity and magnetism, gas lighting, perpetual motion, genealogy, heraldry, agriculture, botany, trigonometry, overseas trade, French politics, salt manufacture, and dry rot in ships. He corresponded with a wide range of people, among them Mrs Garrick, Sir Richard Colt Hoare, Tiberius Cavallo, Richard Gough, and Mrs Siddons, and wrote to people as far afield as India, Moscow, Nova Scotia, Boston, and Cape Town.

Rackett's many activities and lengthy periods in London led to the accusation by the marquess of Lansdowne in the House of Lords in a debate on Roman Catholic emancipation in 1829 that his parish was being neglected. Rackett admitted that his absence had occasionally been longer than the period 'allowed by Law' (letter to bishop of Bristol, Rackett MSS, D/RAC bundle 66), but claimed that he had resided in Spetisbury 'for a considerable part of every year for the last 40 years' (Dorset RO, photocopy 267), and his curate lived only 1½ miles away. The bishop of Bristol accepted his explanation and wrote to Lansdowne in Rackett's defence. The accusation was subsequently dropped.

Dorothy Rackett died, aged eighty-one, in June 1835 and was buried in Spetisbury churchyard on 17 June. Thomas Rackett died at Spetisbury on 29 November 1840, aged nearly eighty-five, and was buried with his wife on 5 December. They are commemorated with a large pyramidical monument in Spetisbury churchyard, though the dates inscribed do not correspond with the parish register entries.

M. G. WATKINS, rev. GLANVILLE J. DAVIES

Sources The Thomas Rackett papers, ed. H. S. L. Dewar (1965) · J. Hutchins, *The history and antiquities of the county of Dorset*, 3rd edn, ed. W. Shipp and J. W. Hodson, 3 (1868); facs. edn (1973), 528–31 · *An inventory of historical monuments in the county of Dorset*, Royal Commission on Historical Monuments (England), 3/2 (1970), 242–6 · register, Spetisbury, 1813–1904, Dorset RO, PE/SPY RE 4/1 [burial] · charges against Rackett, 1829, Dorset RO, photocopy 267 · family affairs, science, French politics etc, Dorset RO, photocopy 604/1–8 · *GM*, 2nd ser., 15 (1841), 428–31 · Foster, *Alum. Oxon.* · Dorset RO, Rackett papers, D/RAC bundles 66, 81, 85, 107, 139; D/RAC NU 113
Archives Dorset RO, antiquarian and scientific corresp. and papers · Linn. Soc., conchological papers | Bodl. Oxf., letters to Richard Gough, J. B. Nichols, and John Nichols relating to second edition of Hutchins's *History of Dorset*
Likenesses G. Romney, oils, c.1771, repro. in Dewar, *Thomas Rackett papers*; priv. coll.; on loan to Walker Art Gallery, Liverpool

Rackham, Arthur (1867–1939), painter and illustrator, was born on 19 September 1867 at 2 St James's Terrace, Lambeth, London, the fourth of the twelve children of Alfred Thomas Rackham (1829–1912), a legal clerk, and his

Arthur Rackham (1867–1939), self-portrait, 1924

wife, Anne Stevenson (1833–1920), the daughter of a Nottingham draper. Bernard *Rackham (1876–1964) was his younger brother. His father became chief clerk at the Admiralty registry in 1875 and Admiralty marshal at the High Court in 1896. Rackham grew up with his many siblings at 210 South Lambeth Road in a busy part of south London, directly opposite the evocative remains of the large garden set out in the seventeenth century by John Tradescant the elder and younger. He was encouraged to paint as a child, and his first paintbox became the 'modest silent convenient companion' from which he was rarely parted (A. Rackham, 'In praise of watercolour', *Old Water-Colour Society's Club*, 1933–4, 51–2). He attended the City of London School (1879–83), where he won prizes for drawing, and made many visits to the British Museum and the Natural History Museum, where he painted from the exhibits. His health, however, was indifferent, and at the age of sixteen he left school on medical advice to take a return sea voyage to Australia. This journey, extending from January to July 1884, and the six weeks he spent painting landscapes and plants in and around Sydney, renewed his health and became his informal apprenticeship to art.

On his return Rackham enrolled in evening classes at Lambeth School of Art, where he studied under the landscape painter William Llewellyn. His fellow students included Charles Shannon, Charles Ricketts, and Thomas Sturge Moore, and, with others, they encouraged his talents as a painter and a black and white illustrator. Their example urged him to submit illustrations to magazines, but to earn a secure living Rackham became a junior clerk in the Westminster fire office in 1885, a post he held until 1892. He resigned to join the staff of the *Pall Mall Budget* as a news and features illustrator, and the following year he moved to the *Westminster Budget* and the *Westminster Gazette*. By now he was living in Buckingham Chambers, Strand, and was widening his practice by illustrating books for publishers. His name and reliability for delivery and content became known to publishers and public alike, and he was increasingly in demand. Rackham's first notable successes, which coincided with the beginnings of the fashion for lavishly produced gift books, were illustrations to *The Ingoldsby Legends* (1898), *Gulliver's Travels* (1900), and *Grimm's Fairy Tales* (1900). These were followed by *The Greek Heroes* (1903), *Rip Van Winkle* (1905), *Peter Pan in Kensington Gardens* (1906), and *Alice in Wonderland* (1907).

In the earlier books Rackham's style tended to take on the appearance of woodcuts, with the main features being drawn in thick pen and brush. From 1905 to 1910, as printing techniques improved, his line became sharper and likewise his detail more intense. In *Rip Van Winkle* and *A Midsummer Night's Dream* (1908) he developed his gift for drawing witches, gnomes, fairies, and anthropomorphized trees and brought them to a pitch of vivid characterization, sometimes with an unsettling frisson of horror. Trees with human limbs and faces became one of his trademarks, and may have been throwbacks to childhood memories of the Tradescants' garden. Despite the fantasy of his subjects, however, Rackham always maintained a strict sense of reality by giving his figures human traits and foibles and naturalistic, even recognizable, settings— illustrations in *A Midsummer Night's Dream* are variously set in Wimbledon Park, Ruislip churchyard, and Walberswick, Suffolk.

Rackham embarked on his new edition of *Alice in Wonderland*, with illustrations to rival John Tenniel's, when the book came out of copyright in 1907. Rackham's advantage over Tenniel was that he now could introduce colour; also his pen line would not be reproduced by wood-engraving. This gave him some new freedoms for invention, but his amendments to the ingrained image of Alice were not only technical. Rackham's Alice was very much a fleshly Edwardian child who would question the status quo of Wonderland. Her courtesy carried an undercurrent of insistent argument. A contemporary critic observed 'a tender, flickering light of imagination in [Alice's] eyes' (*Daily Telegraph*, 27 Nov 1907).

Rackham travelled extensively in Europe, particularly to Germany, the Alps, and Italy, and he painted in watercolour on these journeys. As a direct result European landscape and architectural subjects peppered his illustrations, and he developed a particular fondness for German literature and language. This came to the fore in his two illustrated volumes of Wagner's *Ring* cycle, *The Rhinegold and the Valkyrie* (1910) and *Siegfried* (1911).

Unlike his contemporary Edmund Dulac, Rackham was not a bold colourist. He tended to restrict his palette to soft blues, greens, and reds, in local highlights or in several layers of transparent watercolour wash, over a yellowy-buff tone which gives to the whole a quality of vellum, or age. This was a practical as well as an artistic decision, as colour handled in this way could be faithfully reproduced

by the three-colour separation printing process which was a new feature of pre-First World War book production.

On 16 July 1903 Rackham married the painter Edyth Harriet Gertrude Gabrielle Starkie (1867–1941) in St Saviour's, Hampstead. She had been born and brought up in Ireland, where her father, William Robert Starkie JP, was an Anglo-Irish resident magistrate in co. Galway. At the age of sixteen she had been taken by her mother, Frances Starkie, on a tour of Europe which included a period in Paris (1884), where she studied painting at the Académie Julian. On William Starkie's death Edyth and her mother settled in London, and moved in 1897 to 3 Wynchcombe Studios, Hampstead, next door to Rackham. Edyth and Arthur met over the garden wall. At the height of Arthur's success (1905–20) the Rackhams lived in a house designed in 1881 by Charles Voysey, 16 Chalcot Gardens, Hampstead. Each had a studio there in which to pursue their individual artistic enterprises. Although the pattern of her career was undermined by ill health and motherhood—the Rackhams' only surviving child, Barbara, was born in 1908— Edyth Rackham, who worked under her maiden name, became a considerable portrait painter in her own right.

The steady flow of commissions that Rackham received settled, from 1905 to 1913, into a pattern in which late-autumn publication of the year's book coincided with an exhibition at the Leicester Galleries, London, of its original illustrations for sale. Rackham was by now in great demand socially and artistically, and delighted in entertaining and in his celebrity. His tastes, however, remained simple, and because of the frugality of his earlier professional years he found it hard to spend money on pleasure or to waste it on unnecessary expense. Recalling her father as she remembered him during her childhood, Barbara Rackham later wrote:

> He seemed to me always to look much the same, small and thin, with a deeply grooved but clear-cut face, and smooth pepper-and-salt hair at the sides of his bald head. If he grew slightly balder, more wrinkled and silvery during the years, it hardly altered his general appearance. (Hamilton, *Rackham*, 1990, 82)

Rackham was active and precise in all he did, and, having introduced his own self-portrait into his work because it was the most convenient and ever-ready face to draw, he continued during the period before the First World War to establish the image of himself that was to precede him for the rest of his life. His nephew the writer Walter Starkie confessed to thinking Rackham *was* a goblin 'in his shabby blue suit and carpet slippers, hopping about the studio with a palette on one arm, waving a paintbrush in his hand' (W. Starkie, *Scholars and Gypsies*, 1963, 18). Eleanor Farjeon remembered: 'He watches you from behind Spectacles of Cunning, and there's a whimsical line on his face that can translate itself into the kindliest of smiles. He is light and spare and alert' ('Arthur Rackham—the wizard at home', *St Nicholas*, March 1914, 385–9).

Rackham's milieu was the London artistic and literary circles of the day. Among his friends were George Bernard

Shaw, Charles Holroyd (the director of the National Gallery), and fellow artists Edmund Sullivan, Walter Bayes, and Lewis Baumer. Although characteristically apart from it, he also enjoyed the roistering element of the bohemian London art world. Walter Starkie remembers Augustus John remarking with 'a Homeric roar of laughter … "Don't shock little Arthur too much, ladies and gentlemen: he is learning about life from you and he must not advance too quickly"' (W. Starkie, *Scholars and Gypsies*, 167). He did not develop a friendship with Edmund Dulac, but he did keep a file of cuttings of press reviews of his rival's work.

The First World War effectively destroyed the illustrated gift-book market, and this brought Rackham a financial and professional reverse. He was, however, enough of a celebrity to be asked to create compilations such as *Arthur Rackham's Book of Pictures* (1913) and *The Allies' Fairy Book* (1916), and he contributed readily to war charity publications. Determined to continue his work despite the war, Rackham also produced editions of Dickens's *A Christmas Carol* (1915) and Thomas Malory's *Romance of King Arthur* (1917). 'In addition to his detachment', Walter Starkie recalled, 'he possessed an innate stoicism which made him endure austerity without complaining' (W. Starkie, *Scholars and Gypsies*, 166).

In 1920 the Rackhams moved from London to Houghton House, Amberley, Sussex, where they lived until 1930. This gave Edyth the country air she needed for her failing health, while for the working week Rackham kept a London studio at Primrose Hill. The principal market for Rackham's work was now the United States. Fashions in England had shifted away from Rackham's fanciful subject matter, and this caused his income to shrink. In America, however, his illustrations remained in demand both for books and advertising. To maintain markets on both sides of the Atlantic, American and English publishers continued to co-operate on books such as *The Sleeping Beauty* (1920), Milton's *Comus* (1921), and Shakespeare's *The Tempest* (1926), and Rackham also accepted contracts for illustrations to books published solely in America, such as A. F. Brown's *The Lonesomest Doll* (1928). In 1927 he travelled to New York, Boston, and Philadelphia, returning with an important commission from the New York Public Library to illustrate a unique copy of *A Midsummer Night's Dream*, to be written out by the calligrapher Graily Hewitt (completed in 1930).

In tune with the changing times, Rackham's style during the 1920s began to adopt hints of art deco, even of syncopation. This was a manner in which he was perhaps uneasy, but nevertheless his natural sense of design, of characterization, and his lyrical handling of line and wash did not leave him. Nor was there any perceptible change in the sympathetic approach he had always adopted to the reading of the texts he had chosen to illustrate. He had a keen ear for the moods his authors evoked and a natural understanding of the subtleties of human expression. This was the mature grounding which he drew upon throughout his career in his narrative evocations of evil, redemption, and fancy. In landscape watercolours and oil paintings, and in the handful of portraits he painted, Rackham emerges as a considerable artist whose gifts had been circumscribed by the needs of commercial book illustration. This reflection had struck Rackham himself, and, writing in the 1930s, he appears to have bitterly regretted having compromised and having followed what was, he believed, a 'lesser aim' (Hamilton, *Rackham*, 1990, 149).

Among Rackham's last books—made after the family moved in 1930 to Stiegate, the house they had built near Limpsfield, Surrey—are E. A. Poe's *Tales of Mystery and Imagination* (1935), *Peer Gynt* (1936), and a third version of *A Midsummer Night's Dream* (1939). His illustrations to Poe's *Tales* have a sharp edge of true horror, a re-emergent strain from the earlier Grimm and Wagner subjects. The last few years of Rackham's life were interrupted by spells in hospital for both him and Edyth. During his last illness he worked on illustrations to Kenneth Grahame's *The Wind in the Willows*, a book for which he had a strong affection, and which he had longed for years to illustrate. The resulting pictures (the edition was published posthumously in 1940) are among his most affecting works, replete with wit, invention, and carefully controlled emotion. Rackham died at Stilegate on 6 September 1939 and was cremated in Croydon. There is a memorial in Amberley churchyard lettered by Bettina Furnée which was installed in 1992.

Rackham brought a renewed sense of excitement to book illustration that coincided with the rapid developments in printing technology in the early twentieth century. Working with subtle colour and wiry line, he exploited the growing strengths of commercial printing to create imagery and characterizations that reinvigorated children's literature, electrified young readers, and dominated the art of book illustration at the start of a new century. A memorial exhibition of his work was held at the Leicester Galleries in December 1939, and a touring exhibition was shown in Sheffield, Bristol, and the Victoria and Albert Museum, London, in 1979–80. Principal collections of original watercolours for Rackham's illustrations in the United Kingdom are in the Victoria and Albert Museum, the British Museum, the Tate collection, and museums and libraries in Cambridge, Leeds, and Sheffield. Original works and papers are in the National Art Library at the Victoria and Albert Museum; the Harry Ransom Humanities Research Center at the University of Texas, Austin; the Butler Library of the Columbia University, New York; the Free Library of Philadelphia; and the University of Louisville, Kentucky.   JAMES HAMILTON

Sources J. Hamilton, *Arthur Rackham: a life with illustration* (1990) · D. Hudson, *Arthur Rackham: his life and work*, 2nd edn 1974 (1960) · J. Hamilton, 'Edyth Starkie', *Irish Arts Review Yearbook*, 8 (1991–2), 155–63 · J. Hamilton, '"The Americans have done great things for me": Arthur Rackham and his American friends', *Columbia Library Columns* (Dec 1991) · private information (2004) [B. Edwards] · B. Edwards, 'Try to look like a witch!', *Columbia Library Columns* (May 1968) · J. Hamilton, *Arthur Rackham, 1867–1939* (1979) [exhibition catalogue, Graves Art Gallery, Sheffield, 1 Dec 1979 – 6 Jan 1980] · G. McWhorter, *The Arthur Rackham memorial collection* (1988) · F. Gettings, *Arthur Rackham* (1975) · R. Baughman, *The centenary of*

Arthur Rackham's birth (1967) · A. S. Hartrick, 'Arthur Rackham (1867–1940): an appreciation', *Old Water-Colour Society's Club* (1940), 53–6 · b. cert. · m. cert. · d. cert.
Archives Col. U., Butler Library, MSS and works · Free Library of Philadelphia, corresp., drawings, and papers · Ransom HRC, MSS and works · University of Louisville, Kentucky, MSS and works · V&A NAL, MSS | BL, corresp. with Macmillans, Add. MS 55235
Likenesses A. Rackham, self-portrait, oils, 1924, Art Workers' Guild, London [*see illus.*] · A. Rackham, self-portrait, oils, 1934, NPG
Wealth at death £24,782 9s. 10d.: probate, 15 Nov 1939, CGPLA Eng. & Wales

Rackham, Bernard (1876–1964), museum curator and expert on ceramics, was born in London on 26 July 1876, the third son of Alfred Thomas Rackham (1829–1912), later Admiralty marshal of the High Court of Justice, and his wife, Anne (1833–1920), daughter of William Stevenson, draper, of Leicester and Nottingham. His eldest brother was Arthur *Rackham (1867–1939), the illustrator. Rackham was educated at the City of London School and went with an exhibition in 1895 to Pembroke College, Cambridge, where he took a first in the classical tripos in 1898. He then entered a competition for an assistant keepership at the South Kensington Museum (later the Victoria and Albert Museum) under a scheme whereby the government aimed to attract Oxford and Cambridge graduates to the museum service. Successful, he was posted to the department of ceramics, where he was destined to remain for forty years, during the last twenty-four of which he was its head. In 1909 he married Ruth (1880/81–1963), daughter of Francis Adams, of Clapham, a colonial merchant; they had one son and one daughter.

To Rackham belongs the credit of putting ceramic studies in England on a firm footing, a service which in many fields was also of international significance. Before his time the study of English ceramics was based on facts, assumptions masquerading as facts, and vague traditions. Rackham, by his intellectual vigour and grasp of essentials, reduced this formless mass to order, eliminating baseless assumptions and calling in aid only verifiable and relevant information. The same strict method was applied in other fields. With this disciplined approach he combined a real enthusiasm for art in all its manifestations, ancient and modern, oriental and Western. For him the aesthetic quality of an object was its ultimate justification.

Shortly after appointment to the museum, Rackham was detailed to register the vast mixed ceramic collection (some 5000 objects) acquired from the Museum of Practical Geology on its dissolution. This experience underlay his subsequent great and diverse knowledge of ceramics.

Rackham's first publications lay in the field of English ceramics, partly because the main emphasis of the practical geology collection lay there, partly because he was charged with reworking the catalogue of the Lady Charlotte Schreiber collection of English pottery, porcelain, and enamels, the greatest of its kind. The three volumes appeared in 1924–30, only the first volume of the revision having been published previously, in 1915. In 1917 there

appeared a complementary catalogue of the English porcelain in the Herbert Allen collection. These works established the basic categories of English porcelain.

After the First World War it fell to Rackham to rearrange the enormous collections of his department. As a fitting complement to this work he undertook the translation from Danish of Emil Hannover's encyclopaedic *Keramisk haandbog* (which appeared in three volumes in 1925 as *Pottery and Porcelain*). The previous year he had returned to English studies in *English Pottery*, written with Herbert Read. This work represented the first modern classification of all branches of English pottery, and was succeeded by his catalogue (2 vols., 1935) of the vast Glaisher collection at the Fitzwilliam Museum, Cambridge, which has remained one of the most useful reference works on English pottery.

In 1918 Rackham had turned to an entirely fresh theme in the *Catalogue of the Le Blond Collection of Corean Pottery*, and although he never explored oriental subjects in great depth, he was perennially interested and stimulated by them, and became a founder member of the Oriental Ceramic Society. By then he was devoting himself increasingly to the European middle ages and Renaissance, particularly tin-glazed earthenware and stained glass. About 1900 he had been invited to help catalogue the works of art inherited by Francis Wyndham Cook, and in 1903 he published his *Catalogue of Italian Maiolica and other Pottery, 8 Cadogan Square*. This experience was the beginning of his special interest and mastery in this field. In 1926 he published a pioneer work on the tin-glazed pottery made in the Low Countries (*Early Netherlands Maiolica*). He contributed important articles on Italian maiolica to learned periodicals, and in 1933 brought out a *Guide to Italian Maiolica* in the museum, a masterly work of compression and lucid exposition. The true fruit of his work in this field, however, was seen in his monumental *Catalogue of Italian Maiolica* (1940) in the museum, a two-volume catalogue raisonné of the more than 1400 items in that great collection, and the essential tool in all maiolica studies. Rackham's vast erudition in this branch of ceramics was later distilled into the more popular *Italian Maiolica* (1952).

In 1936 a series of articles on stained glass culminated in a *Guide to the Collections of Stained Glass* in the museum, one of the best short summaries of the whole subject in any language. The summit of his work in this field, however, was reached with his *Ancient Glass of Canterbury Cathedral* (1949). This was more than ten years after his retirement, and he continued to publish on various ceramic themes— *A Key to Pottery and Glass* in 1940, *Medieval English Pottery* in 1948, and *Early Staffordshire Pottery* in 1951. He also published important articles on English and continental glassware, on Limoges enamels, and on continental porcelain.

Rackham, who was a fellow of the Society of Antiquaries, was appointed CB in 1937. He was honorary remembrancer of Guildford, and president of the English Ceramic Circle and of the Guildford Art Society. Apart from his scholarly work, Rackham was also a civil servant, charged with the administration of a department. These duties he conscientiously fulfilled, requiring of his subordinates the same high standards which he imposed upon himself. Personally, he was highly strung and eager, overflowing with enthusiasm, and endowed with a keen sense of humour. He was tall and lean, with a bright eye and a strikingly erect carriage even in old age. He died at the Hillbrow Nursing Home, Liss, Hampshire, on 13 February 1964.   R. J. CHARLESTON, *rev.*

Sources *The Times* (15 Feb 1964) · *WWW* · *Burlington Magazine*, 106 (1964), 424–5 · personal knowledge (1981) · private information (1981) · *CGPLA Eng. & Wales* (1964) · d. cert. [Ruth Rackham]
Archives V&A NAL, corresp. and papers | V&A, letters to Derek Hudson
Wealth at death £9990: probate, 2 July 1964, *CGPLA Eng. & Wales*

Rackham [*née* Tabor], **Clara Dorothea** (1875–1966), suffragist and political activist, was born at 44 Lansdowne Road, Notting Hill, London, on 3 December 1875, the fifth and youngest child and second daughter of Henry Samuel Tabor, a nervous, pessimistic, and shy member of a Congregationalist and public-spirited farming family long settled in the Braintree area. Her mother, Emma Frances Woodcock, came from a family in Wigan which had also been active in public life. Brought up on a regime of plain food, missionary meetings, and Sunday observance, Clara (always known within the family as Dorothea) was tormented when reading *Black Beauty* as a young child by the suffering of horses, and became a lifelong supporter of the Royal Society for the Prevention of Cruelty to Animals. She displayed a lifelong anger at cruelty and insensitivity to suffering. She accompanied her mother in performing good works and her father in sampling selected London preachers, but in 1886 she did not follow her parents into Liberal Unionism, though her earliest political activity was to canvass with her mother on the Progressive side in the London county council election of 1889.

After being educated at Notting Hill high school and then spending two happy years (1892–3) at St Leonard's College, St Andrews, Clara Tabor was a pioneer cyclist from the age of seventeen. Her ambitious cycle tours took her to many parts of England and then in 1899 to Belgium and in 1900 to Normandy; she was a cyclist for seventy years. In 1894 she attended lectures twice weekly at Bedford College, London, and in the subsequent year followed her elder sister Margaret to Newnham College, Cambridge. She led a full social life, made many friends, and captained the university women's hockey team. She was Liberal leader in Newnham College undergraduate debates, and in 1898 she was not immediately told of Gladstone's death, which occurred the day before her examination for part one of the classical tripos, for fear that her examination performance would suffer; she obtained a third. Her connection with the college persisted: she was on its governing body from 1920 to 1940 and on its council from 1924 to 1931.

On 16 March 1901 Clara married the classical scholar Harris Rackham (1868–1944), fellow of Christ's College, Cambridge, and brother of Arthur Rackham, the book illustrator. They had no children, but her marriage exempted her from the role of daughter-at-home, which

was assumed by her sister Margaret in her place. She was a poor-law guardian in Cambridge from 1904 to 1915, joint honorary secretary of the Charity Organization Society's Cambridge branch, president of the Women's Co-operative Guild's Cambridge branch, which she founded in 1902, and contributed chapters on co-operation to Eglantyne Jebb's *Cambridge: a Social Study* (1906). By 1908 she was active in the Cambridge branch of the National Union of Women's Suffrage Societies and was holding open-air meetings in the villages near Cambridge to promote women's suffrage; in the following year she was organizing motor tours round the villages, and was seen as 'an excellent speaker, being remarkably clear and direct in style' with 'the faculty of putting herself on a level with people of little education' (*Queen*, 17 April 1909). In 1910 she was elected president of the Eastern Federation of Suffrage Societies, and she soon revealed that she had other skills valuable to British feminism. She was on the National Union of Women's Suffrage Societies executive committee from 1909 to 1915, and Mary Stocks recalled that when she chaired union meetings 'she possessed a masterly capacity for guiding a large conference through a maze of resolutions and amendments without expressing personal bias, getting in a muddle herself, or allowing delegates to do so' (Stocks, 77). She backed Millicent Fawcett in 1915 against secessionists despite supporting the Union of Democratic Control and diverging from Fawcett's support for the war.

In 1915–19 Clara Rackham was a government factory inspector while her husband taught (1915–17) at Winchester College. She was a member of the departmental committee on medical examination of young persons for factory employment in 1924 and of the departmental committee on the factory inspectorate in 1925. In 1930 she was the sole woman member of the royal commission on unemployment insurance. In the public controversy over factory legislation in 1929 between a libertarian 'me-too feminism' and a socialist interventionism, she opted for the latter, and argued (alongside Beatrice Webb, R. H. Tawney, and other Labour leaders) that women—less organized and more vulnerable in the labour market than men—needed special protection in factory legislation. Rather than relax the restrictions specific to women she wanted to approach equality by tightening the restrictions on men. Her short book *Factory Law* (1938) was businesslike, detailed, and very practical in its purpose: to summarize and explain the Factory Act of 1937, with which she was in complete sympathy.

As soon as women got the vote in 1918, Clara Rackham joined the Labour Party, which henceforth became her main preoccupation. Relieved from domestic worries by her childlessness and by her devoted housekeeper Mrs Jones—whose labours she did her best to relieve by rationalizing her domestic arrangements—she was free for such public work as a Labour activist in Cambridge could undertake. In 1919 she had been the first woman Labour councillor on Cambridge city council, on which she remained almost continuously for thirty-eight years; from

1926 to 1957 she was also on the county council, and among her many causes she included welfare issues, nursery schools, Cambridgeshire village colleges, and swimming pools. She chaired the county education committee from 1945 to 1957. From 1920 to 1950 she was a JP, retiring on reaching the age limit. In 1928 she said that if she got into parliament she would make penal reform her speciality. She stood unsuccessfully as Labour candidate for parliament twice: she came bottom of the poll at Chelmsford in 1922 in a three-cornered contest, and was soundly defeated by R. A. Butler in a straight fight at Saffron Walden in 1935. Her intense commitment to an ethic of localized community service could not readily be combined with a career in national Labour politics, for Labour was not electorally powerful in her part of England. However, with her determined chin and formidable intellect, she tenaciously championed the local labour movement. She did her best to strengthen it by holding for many years a summer school at Newnham for working women, and by lecturing widely on social history and local government for the Workers' Educational Association, whose meetings she also attended as a student; for a time she chaired the association's eastern district.

Harris Rackham died in 1944, but Clara's old age was decidedly active. Sociable, intellectually alert, with a good sense of humour and physically fit, she got on well with young people, and enjoyed taking in students as lodgers during the Second World War. Her nieces were deeply influenced by 'Aunt Dorothea', and vividly recalled how beautifully she read aloud to them when young, and how interested she became in their choice of career. She was disappointed that so few women took up the opportunities her feminist generation had created. She keenly supported humanism in Cambridge, and as a member of the inter-war League of Nations Union she gravitated naturally into the Campaign for Nuclear Disarmament; by 1961, at the age of eighty-five, she was participating in her fourth Ban the Bomb march, though she supported the Gaitskellite Campaign for Democratic Socialism. She hated being ill, but responded rationally to her deafness in later life by resigning from her many committees. She cycled about to read aloud to blind people, or (as she put it) to her 'old ladies', when very much an old lady herself, and was an enthusiastic swimmer in the Cam almost to the end. She died at home at Langdon House, 1 Scotland Road, Cambridge, on 11 March 1966.

Clara Rackham's career demonstrates how readily nonconformist energies could transfer to secularized humanitarian causes, effecting an easy transition from Liberal to Labour. Yet it also illustrates the limits to what consistent, courageous, and intelligent Labour Party energy and commitment over many years could achieve in rural parts. For the transition to Labour weakened anti-Conservative forces in those parts of England where the two progressive parties were forced into mutual competition, and where Labour lacked the breadth of local appeal that the Liberals had earlier enjoyed. Rackham's career also illustrates, however, the broad scope that local government offered to a feminist whose democratic instincts and methods had been nourished within the non-militant suffragist tradition.   BRIAN HARRISON

Sources J. Bellamy and E. Price, 'Rackham, Clara Dorothea', *DLB*, vol. 9 · private information (1975, 1976) [Mary Tabor, Lucy Tabor] · priv. coll., Rackham family papers · M. Stocks, *My commonplace book* (1970) · *The Queen* (17 April 1909) · *Cambridge News* (12 March 1966) · *The Times* (16 March 1966) · b. cert.
Likenesses bust, Guildhall, Cambridge
Wealth at death £9815: probate, 19 April 1966, *CGPLA Eng. & Wales*

Rackstraw, Marjorie (1888–1981), educationist and social worker, was born in Highgate, Middlesex, on 24 June 1888, the second of five daughters of Matthew Rackstraw and his wife, Fanny (*née* Blofeld). The early death of his father obliged Matthew Rackstraw to abandon professional ambitions and enter trade. The Blofeld family were dealers in Smithfield; several of them became liverymen of the Butchers' Company. Matthew Rackstraw bought two small shops in Upper Street, Islington, then a fashionable neighbourhood, and with his sister in charge of staff welfare built up a thriving department store. He sold it when trade began to move westwards to new stores such as Selfridge's. The family lived in a handsome house in Cholmondeley Park on Highgate Hill, moving as the girls left home to a smaller but still substantial house in North Grove, Highgate village. Matthew had been a paternalistic employer. He was also a good father of daughters, giving each educational opportunities and a share of his fortune, enabling her to choose her way of life.

During her schooldays at the Grove School, Highgate, Marjorie Rackstraw developed spinal trouble, possibly undiagnosed polio. She was sent to a school for invalids at Margate and spent long periods on her back. A spinal disability remained throughout life but she never accepted it as an impediment to service. Her elder sister Frances (Nancy) went from the Grove School to Somerville College, Oxford. Marjorie, it is said, was offered a place at Somerville on returning from a year in France, but her parents judged that Birmingham was a healthier place than Oxford. In Birmingham, Margery Fry, fourteen years older than Marjorie, was warden of University House, a fine purpose-built residence for women: they became lifelong friends. After studying history, Marjorie in 1912 took the undifferentiated arts degree then available and went for a year to Bryn Mawr College, Pennsylvania. She returned to Birmingham to assist her friend at University House, but when the older woman left to work with the Friends' War Victims Relief Committee among refugees on the Marne, Marjorie soon followed her. 'She is champing to be off', wrote Margery Fry in July 1915. In 1920 Marjorie volunteered for relief work in Russia and remained there through the famine, beloved, it was said, by both colleagues and Russian peasants.

From 1924 to 1937 Marjorie was warden of Masson Hall, Edinburgh University, and adviser to the women students. She gave advice on accommodation and future careers, and took a close interest in the social life of the women students. It seems that she was hoping to plan a new hall.

Proposals for this appear as early as 1931 but the new hall was not opened until 1965, long after she had left. She was a generous contributor: a part of the hall and a bursary bear her name. She had while in Edinburgh joined the Fabian Society.

In 1937 Marjorie bought 1 Keats Grove, Hampstead, her home for the rest of her life. Spare rooms were soon occupied for long or short periods by former students, refugees, and friends from a wide circle. She became involved in voluntary and public work, much of it linked with her local Labour Party. In 1944 she volunteered for work abroad with the United Nations Relief and Rehabilitation Administration, and was in the first team to enter Germany from France. But in the following year she was back in Hampstead, having been elected during her absence as a Labour councillor. She served on many committees before she retired from the council in 1951.

Marjorie's special concern for elderly people who, during the war, had lost their homes through bombing in eastern and southern parts of London and had been rehoused in makeshift accommodation in an unfamiliar district, led in 1947 to the foundation of the Hampstead Old People's Housing Trust, of which she remained chair until her eightieth year. Large houses, standing empty, were bought and converted into homes for elderly people. Marjorie, who valued her own garden, insisted that the gardens should be brought back into cultivation, often by the residents themselves. One house was a bequest from a lady who wished it to accommodate 'gentlefolk'. The historian of the association says, 'No difficulty arose over the interpretation of that phrase.'

After visiting a former housemaid in the newly furbished attic which she had once shared as a bleak bedroom with other servants, Marjorie remarked, 'You could hardly find anyone gentler.' The association's first purpose-built block of flats, occupied in 1968, was called Rackstraw House; Marjorie, who had resisted the idea of naming it after her, finally agreed because the family name would die out with her.

Marjorie Rackstraw was tall, and angular in her movements because of her disability. 'She peeps out of her house like a good kind witch,' said a child. Her strong features bore a habitual expression of happy benevolence, and she had a memorable ringing laugh. Though she had worked with Quakers, she did not attend their religious meetings. She remained an Anglican, though not a regular churchgoer. She died at home, in her sleep, on 28 April 1981, and was cremated at Golders Green on 5 May.

ENID HUWS JONES

Sources J. Bellamy and M. Bucke, 'Rackstraw, Marjorie', *DLB*, vol. 8 • W. R. Page, *The first thirty years: the story of the Hampstead Old People's Housing Trust, 1947–1977* • E. H. Jones, *Margery Fry: the essential amateur* (1966) • RS Friends, Lond. • U. Edin. L., special collections division • private information • personal knowledge (2004) • C. Dyhouse, *No distinction of sex? Women in British universities, 1870–1939* (1995)

Archives U. Edin. L., special collections division

Likenesses double portrait, photograph (with Arthur Greenwood), Rackstraw House, Primrose Hill, London • photograph, repro. in Page, *The first thirty years* • photograph, Central and Cecil Housing Trust, Camden, London

Wealth at death £188,694: probate, 28 Aug 1981, *CGPLA Eng. & Wales*

Raczyński, Count Edward Bernard Andrzej Maria (1891–1993), Polish diplomatist and president-in-exile, was born on 19 December 1891 at Zakopane, Galicia, Austria–Hungary, the younger son of Edward Aleksander Raczyński, third Count Raczyński-Raczyński (1847–1926), landowner and patron of the arts, and his second wife, Countess Róża Krasińska, née Potocka (1849–1937). He derived his Polish patriotism from his strong-willed mother. The family's principal home was the Raczyński Palace, set in a 25,000 acre estate at Rogalin, near Posen, Prussia.

Raczyński attended school in Cracow and university at Leipzig before entering the London School of Economics in 1912. He was conscripted into the Austro-Hungarian army two years later, but poor eyesight soon led to his discharge. After completing a law doctorate at the Jagiełłonian University, Cracow (1915–18), he briefly trained as an officer in a Polish division attached to the German army. His only memorable duty, however, was to disarm German soldiers in Warsaw in November 1918, when Poland regained its independence after 123 years.

The new Polish foreign service engaged Count Raczyński in 1919, posting him to Bern and then Copenhagen. From 1922 to 1926 he was first secretary of the Polish legation in London. On 24 July 1925 he married Joyous Markham (1902–1931), only daughter of Sir Arthur Basil Markham, first baronet, Liberal MP for Mansfield from 1900 to 1916. She died in Warsaw in February 1931 from a complication during pregnancy. Raczyński, now head of the eastern department of the Polish foreign ministry, on 25 August 1932 married Cecilia (Cesia) Maria Jaroszyńska (1906–1962), with whom he had three daughters between 1933 and 1939.

After representing his country at the League of Nations and the world disarmament conference in Geneva (1932–4), Raczyński was initially disappointed at being made Polish ambassador to Great Britain from 1 November 1934, despite his fondness for English culture. Anglo-Polish relations had hitherto been distant at best. Many British people imagined the Poles to be militaristic hotheads. Raczyński helped weaken this stereotype with his habitual air of cool reason. Tall and slender, with brown hair parted in the middle and a monocle, he was highly articulate in accented English. In his spare time, he translated poetry.

Raczyński tried to convince the British government that Poland was the only country in east central Europe capable of pursuing an independent policy vis-à-vis Germany. He rebutted Nazi claims about persecution of German minorities and worked to convert the British guarantee of Polish independence (of 31 March 1939) into an alliance. The Anglo-Polish treaty of mutual assistance was signed by him on 25 August 1939; one week later he had to invoke it. Relief at the Anglo-French declaration of war turned to dismay at the passivity of allied strategy, as Germany and the USSR effected a fresh partition of Poland.

Late in September 1939 Raczyński visited Paris to help form the Polish government-in-exile (PGIE), which settled in London in June 1940. As few of its members spoke English, he interpreted for the premier, Władysław Sikorski, in meetings with Churchill. The PGIE divided over the Sikorski–Maisky treaty of 30 July 1941, whereby Poland reopened diplomatic relations with the USSR without first obtaining a commitment to restore the pre-war frontier. Raczyński backed Sikorski and found himself promoted to acting minister for foreign affairs on 22 August 1941. This title changed to minister of state in charge of foreign affairs in 1942, the qualifications reflecting the fact that he also remained ambassador. Not a very forceful character himself, Raczyński worked harmoniously with the more abrasive Sikorski, though disgruntled Poles accused them of giving in to British pressure to appease the Russians. Efforts to secure the release of Polish prisoners of war and deportees held in the USSR still left 15,000 missing. Britain and the United States would not endorse Polish territorial integrity.

When the PGIE asked the Red Cross to investigate mass graves of Polish officers at Katyn, the USSR broke off relations in April 1943. Raczyński knew that the power of the PGIE was ebbing away, but his bleakly realistic prognosis was not what his colleagues wanted to hear. After Sikorski's death, he was dropped from the cabinet on 13 July 1943. As ambassador still, he spent the next two years issuing ever stronger yet vainer protests against the allied abandonment of Poland to Soviet domination. Informed on 5 July 1945 that Britain recognized the government of national unity in Warsaw—at root a puppet regime installed by the Red Army—the count insisted that the PGIE was the sole legitimate authority. The Poles in London declined to acknowledge the post-war European order.

A member of the interim Treasury committee for Polish questions and the Anglo-Polish resettlement committee, Raczyński arranged terms for some 160,000 Polish servicemen and refugees to remain in Britain after 1945, and from 1952 to 1956 advised the Ministry of Labour on their employment. He chaired the Polish Research Centre (1940–67), which tried to reunite families divided by the iron curtain, spoke for free Poland in the liberal international and European movement, and chaired the Polish Institute and Sikorski Museum (1966–77). Though too dignified ever to manifest rancour, he could not accept that Britain had treated its ally justly or very honourably, yet he praised it as a haven of freedom.

Polish émigré politics were notoriously fractious. The PGIE split in 1954, when President August Zaleski refused to step down after completing his seven-year term. Raczyński, having failed to reach a compromise, set up the 'council of three'—an alternative PGIE in effect—in a bid to preserve constitutional legitimacy. Unity returned after twenty years, and in April 1979 the 87-year-old Raczyński assumed the presidency himself. The Polish cabinet still met every fortnight at 43 Eaton Place—though without any real power or foreign recognition. Raczyński perceived the absurd aspect of this but believed in the PGIE as

a symbol of defiance. Communism was sure to fail, he argued; as Poland had reasserted itself before, so it would again.

Polish dissidents who visited London in the 1980s nearly all made their way up the dilapidated stairs of 8 Lennox Gardens, Knightsbridge, to the old-fashioned flat where Raczyński lived in impoverished gentility (while keeping his address in Who's Who as 5 Krakowskie Przedmieście, Warsaw). They found him blind and hard of hearing yet mentally alert, kept up to date by relays of friends who read to him. After his retirement on 8 April 1986, sheer longevity meant that he remained a figurehead. The collapse of communism in Poland elated him. The PGIE dissolved itself on 22 December 1990.

Too frail to return to his homeland after more than fifty years, on 18 May 1991 Raczyński married Aniela Maria Mieczysławska, née Lilpop (1910–1998), who had looked after him since the 1960s. He received an honorary knighthood (GBE) on his hundredth birthday. Count Raczyński, who left several volumes of memoirs, died of old age at 8 Lennox Gardens, London, on 30 July 1993. His body was buried with full honours on 9 August 1993 in the family chapel at Rogalin, Poland.   JASON TOMES

Sources Daily Telegraph (31 July 1993) · The Independent (31 July 1993) · The Times (2 Aug 1993) · The Guardian (2 Aug 1993) · New York Times (2 Aug 1993) · E. Raczyński, In allied London (1962) · T. Lenczewski, ed., Genealogie rodów utytułowanych w Polsce (1995) · C. Tyler, 'An aristocrat who survived history', Financial Times (14 Dec 1991) · S. Cranshaw, 'Voice of pre-war Poland lives to hail a miracle', The Independent (19 Dec 1991) · E. Hoffman, 'The government of memory: Poland's exiled President Raczyński', Atlantic (Feb 1986), 18–23 · P. Lannin, 'Polish count survives turbulent century', Los Angeles Times (26 Jan 1992) · A. McEwen, 'Frail count hangs on for Polish democracy', The Times (18 April 1990) · Documents on Polish–Soviet relations, 1939–1945, General Sikorski Historical Institute, 2 vols. (1961–7) · E. Raczyński, Pani Róża (1969) · WWW · m. cert. [Aniela Maria Mieczysławska] · m. cert. [Joyous Markham] · d. cert.
Archives Polish Institute and Sikorski Museum, London, papers
Likenesses photograph, c.1935 (with Josef Beck), Hult. Arch. · photograph, 1939, repro. in The Times · photograph, 1941 (with Rabbi J. H. Hertz), Hult. Arch. · photograph, 1990, repro. in The Independent · photographs, repro. in Raczyński, In allied London
Wealth at death £662,785: probate, 7 Feb 1994, CGPLA Eng. & Wales

Radcliffe, Alexander (b. c.1653, d. in or before 1696), poet, was probably born in the Southern Netherlands, the only son of the exiled royalist Alexander Radcliffe (1633–1682), later of Hampstead, Middlesex. His father and grandfather both fought with the royalist forces during the civil war and the family estate was much reduced by sequestration. Radcliffe's father remained in exile between 1651 and 1660.

Radcliffe was admitted to Gray's Inn on 12 November 1669 but, like a number of gentlemen at the inns of court, never practised law. His association with Gray's Inn continued at least until 1681, when he was one of the selfstyled 'truely loyall gentlemen' of Gray's Inn who, 'in a tumultuous manner', climbing on tables and throwing their hats in the air, sought to move a declaration in support of Charles II's dissolution of parliament (Luttrell,

1.99; *Works*, vii). Radcliffe treats this incident in his poem 'The Lawyers Demurrer Argued', where he characterizes his opponents as:

> a parcell of *Whiggs*,
> The Spawn of some *Rebells*

who had the 'Impudence' to claim that 'Giving Thanks to the King was judg'd an affray' (A. Radcliffe, *The Ramble*, 1682, 110–15).

In March 1672 Radcliffe acquired a captaincy in Colonel John Fitzgerald's regiment of foot, and was generally known thereafter as Captain Radcliffe. He had a reputation as *bon viveur* and rake, and his poems 'The Ramble' and 'A Call to the Guard by a Drum' were included in Rochester's *Poems on Several Occasions* (1680). A substantial number of his poems are parodies and lampoons, including *Ovid Travestie* (1680, 2nd edn, expanded from five to fifteen poems, 1681), with its parodied versions of translations of the *Heroides* by Dryden and others in *Ovid's Epistles, Translated by Several Hands* (1680). *The Ramble: an Anti-Heroick Poem. Together with some Terrestrial Hymns and Carnal Ejaculations* (including among its contents several 'songs burlesqued and varied') was published in 1682 and reprinted, together with *Ovid Travestie*, in *Works* (1696). *Bacchinalia coelestia: a Poem in Praise of Punch* was published as a broadside in 1680. Radcliffe is primarily a comic poet, whose poems are crude, energetic, and conventional in their attitudes, with none of the complexity of Rochester; 'The Ramble' contains some sharp touches of social satire. The date of Radcliffe's death is unknown, but in 1696 he is described as 'late of Grayes Inn' (*Works*, viii).

WARREN CHERNAIK

Sources *The works of Alexander Radcliffe* (1696), ed. K. Robinson (1981) · D. Vieth, *Attribution in Restoration poetry* (1963) · J. Foster, *The register of admissions to Gray's Inn, 1521–1889, together with the register of marriages in Gray's Inn chapel, 1695–1754* (privately printed, London, 1889) · Burke, *Gen. GB* (1972) · N. Luttrell, *A brief historical relation of state affairs from September 1678 to April 1714*, 6 vols. (1857) · R. J. Fletcher, ed., *The pension book of Gray's Inn*, 2 vols. (1901–10)

Radcliffe [*née* Ward], **Ann** (1764–1823), novelist, was born on 9 July 1764 in London, where she was baptized on 5 August 1764 in St Andrew's, Holborn, the only child of William Ward (1737–1798), a haberdasher with premises at 19 Holborn Street, and Ann Oates (1726–1800) of Chesterfield.

Early life and marriage In 1772 the family moved to Bath, where William Ward managed a showroom for the firm of Wedgwood and Bentley in the Westgate buildings before moving to the more fashionable Milsom Street in 1774. Thomas Bentley was Ann Ward's uncle, having married Ann Oates's sister Hannah in 1754, and played an important role in her upbringing. After Hannah's death in 1759 her elder sister Elizabeth kept house for Bentley until he was married a second time, to Mary Stamford, in 1772. From 1768 until his death in 1780 Bentley was a partner in Joseph Wedgwood's pottery business. He moved to Little Cheyne Row, Chelsea, in 1769, to 13 Greek Street, Soho, in 1774, and to Turnham Green in the summer of 1777. After William Ward's haberdashery business collapsed at the beginning of the 1770s Ann appears to have spent long periods with the Bentleys, where her playfellow was Susannah Wedgwood, the future mother of Charles Darwin.

Ann Ward married William Radcliffe (1763–1830) on 15 January 1787, at St Michael's Church, Bath. A graduate of Oxford, and for a time a student at the Middle Temple, William Radcliffe was primarily a journalist, an occupation he pursued for most of the 1790s. A brilliant linguist with a formidable memory and a flair for reporting parliamentary business, William Radcliffe was much in demand during a period in which there was a keen appetite for news from, and debates about, France. William survived his wife, and it is from him that most of the information about Radcliffe derives. In the obituary he wrote of his wife William Radcliffe omits reference to the Wards, 'nearly the only persons of their two families not living in handsome, or at least easy independence' (*Annual Biography*, 98), in order to concentrate on his wife's illustrious maternal relatives, such as the famous de Witts of Holland, William Cheselden, surgeon to George II, and her maternal grandmother, Ann Oates, the sister of Dr Samuel Jebb of Stratford, who included among her nephews Samuel's son Sir Richard Jebb, the king's physician, and Dr Samuel Hallifax, the bishop of Gloucester. However, he does not mention Hallifax's cousin Dr John Jebb, the radical Unitarian and distinguished theologian, who for much of Ann Radcliffe's childhood lived nearby in London.

The omission is of a piece with another of William Radcliffe's economies. In the obituary notice he describes himself as the proprietor of the *English Chronicle*, with which he was associated from 1796. Before that, he was a journalist working for, and then editor of, the *Gazetteer and New Daily Advertiser*, the most radical of the London newspapers, from 1790 to 1793. Apart from enthusiastically welcoming the French Revolution, the *Gazetteer* staunchly supported the impeachment of Warren Hastings, the campaign to free dissenters from the Toleration Act, the freedom of the press, and the illegality of duelling. According to Ann Radcliffe, her husband was responsible for the political sentiments expressed in her travel book; if so, the Radcliffes were still supporting the *Gazetteer's* politics in 1794, as can be seen from the following response to a monument celebrating the revolution of 1688 in Kendal:

> At a time, when the memory of that revolution is reviled, and the praises of liberty itself endeavoured to be suppressed by the artifice of imputing to it the crimes of anarchy, it was impossible to omit any act of veneration to the blessings of this event. (A. Radcliffe, *A Journey Made in the Summer of 1794*, 1795, 389)

In a notebook entry from 1797, Joseph Farington relates how Giuseppe Marchi had recently dined with the Radcliffes, noting that William was 'democratically inclined' (Rogers, *Bio-Bibliography*, 43).

Thomas Noon Talfourd reports that Radcliffe regularly attended the Anglican church. Although there is no reason to disbelieve Talfourd, the statement misleads as much as it informs. While it is probably true that Radcliffe attended the Anglican church in the last decades of her life, it is not at all certain that she did so in the 1790s. Even if she did throughout her lifetime, this is not the same as saying that she was Anglican in belief, outlook, or family background. Like the 150 Anglican clergyman who subscribed to John Jebb's collected works, dissenting sympathizers who stopped short of breaking cover, she appears to have taken a liberal view of doctrinal matters. Similarly, both the *Annual Biography* and Talfourd relate that the years she spent visiting Thomas Bentley were the future novelist's most formative period. Besides her uncle's improving company, she encountered such luminaries as Elizabeth Montagu, Hester Piozzi, Mrs Ord, and Athenian Stuart. However, both sources neglect to mention that Bentley was one of the country's most prominent dissenters, who as a founder and trustee of the dissenting academy at Warrington included among his friends and acquaintances Joseph Priestley, Dr John Aikin, and his sister Anna Laetitia, later Mrs Barbauld. The appointment of Talfourd as Ann Radcliffe's biographer may signify the enduring nature of the Radcliffes' dissenting affiliations, as Talfourd was a Unitarian, a fringe member of Leigh Hunt's 'cockney school', and a passionate advocate of William Godwin.

Writing and achievement According to her husband, Ann Radcliffe began writing as a means of amusing herself during the long evenings when William was away reporting parliament. She published five novels in her lifetime, though she always called them 'romances'. They were *The Castles of Athlin and Dunbayne* (1789); *A Sicilian Romance* (1790); *The Romance of the Forest* (1791); *The Mysteries of Udolpho* (1794); and *The Italian* (1797). Her travel book, *A Journey Made in the Summer of 1794*, appeared in 1795. A final novel, *Gaston de Blondeville*, was published posthumously in 1826. Her first romance was barely noticed; the second caused a stir; the third made her famous. At the time of her death in 1823, she was hailed as the 'great enchantress' and the 'Shakespeare of Romance writers' (Miles, 7, 10), and was generally esteemed as one of the pre-eminent novelists of her generation (*GM*, 1st ser., 93.87). Several volumes of poetry appeared under her name during her lifetime, but these were pirated collations of the verse she had published interspersed with her romances.

Radcliffe's historical settings vary considerably, from pre-Reformation (*The Castles of Athlin and Dunbayne*), to the recent past (*The Italian*), with the rest falling somewhere in between. Despite these differences all her romances contain a heroine with a modern sensibility who finds herself imperilled by the forces of feudalism. Generally speaking, her plots turn on the inheritance of property. Her first romance, set in Scotland, features a heroine who is nearly blackmailed into marrying the murderer of her father and the usurper of the family castle, a threat she prosecutes by holding the heroine's brother at knife-point. Predictably, the comely peasant youth who rescues the heroine himself turns out to be a usurped nobleman. The melodramatic plot and hectic pace is continued in *A Sicilian Romance*. The Marquis Mazzini wishes to trade his daughter, Julia, to a friend. Escaping, Julia wanders

through the scenic landscape of Sicily, thus creating the opportunity for a form of graphic travelogue that Radcliffe was to make famous in her subsequent romances. Featuring rocky crags and precipitous cliffs interspersed with Arcadian retreats, her style was repeatedly characterized as a verbal equivalent of Salvator Rosa and Claude Lorraine. Julia eventually stumbles on her mother, who had been buried alive in an abandoned wing of the family palazzo after the marquis had faked her death, a piece of marital brutality that comes to loom large in the imagination of Catherine Morland, the heroine from Jane Austen's *Northanger Abbey*, who suffers from having read too much Radcliffe. *The Romance of the Forest* features an incest theme that appeared again in *The Italian*. In these romances a heroine is menaced by an uncle who has dispossessed her of both family and property. In *The Mysteries of Udolpho* Emily is held prisoner in a castle in the Apennine mountains by Montoni, who has already murdered her aunt, and threatens her with much the same unless she surrenders the rights to her estates. The heroine escapes once again to embark on her picturesque and sublime travels. In *The Italian* Radcliffe broke new ground by featuring the Roman Inquisition, until then an untried source of Gothic horror.

Although Radcliffe was studiously apolitical as a novelist, her works are permeated with the progressive Enlightenment values that were commonplace before the terror in France, and which were staunchly held by her uncle Bentley and by her husband William. All her novels, save the first, are set in periods transitional between feudalism and modernity; and while her happy couples are themselves well born, their attitudes are distinctly bourgeois, especially as regards companionate marriage. The religious attitudes displayed in her romances are also deistical. Her heroines evince a deep interest in natural religion, in the hand of creator that lurks behind the veil of nature, and no enthusiasm whatsoever for revealed or codified religion. These values are most pronounced in *The Romance of the Forest*, which, in the figure of La Luc, also pays warm homage to the vicar of Savoyard in Rousseau's *Émile*.

Radcliffe's romances contain numerous innovations. She was understood to have brought landscape description to a new peak of perfection, an expertise particularly evident in the way in which she interweaves the sublime and picturesque into the fabric of her narratives. Her style of romance was understood to be 'poetic', by which reviewers meant, apart from the beauty of her scenery, her ability to evoke moods of melancholic introspection and enchantment. Her earlier romances are interspersed with poetry, while her chapters bear epigraphs, principally from Shakespeare and the pre-Romantics, itself an innovative practice. Perhaps the innovation with which she was most associated was the so-called 'explained supernatural'. While she was universally admired for the ingenuity with which she escaped the guesses of the reader, before revealing the sublunary causes of her supernatural mysteries, the device was understood to be subject to the law of diminishing returns, and she was criticized for using it, especially by Sir Walter Scott. The criticisms were certainly unfair, as the device is integral to Radcliffe's narrative practice of balancing symbolic and literal meanings, where the symbolism generated by supernatural appearance takes on its significance precisely because it is fantasized, rather than 'real'. Despite being attacked for working in a formulaic genre, Radcliffe rarely repeats herself but attempts something new in each succeeding romance, often in response to her critics. Thus her penultimate novel, *The Italian*, makes very sparing use of the explained natural, while her final, posthumous one, *Gaston de Blondeville* (1826), dispenses with it altogether, a fact which may partially explain the lack of critical interest in it.

Radcliffe was unquestionably the dominant romance writer of the 1790s. Her influence on the fiction of the decade, and on what has subsequently come to be known as the Gothic novel, was formative and deep. Her position is reflected in the unprecedented sums she received for her last two novels: £500 for *Udolpho*, and £800 for *The Italian*. To put these figures in perspective, £80 was the average payment for the surrender of copyright, a figure including Radcliffe's distorting remuneration, while her nearest competitor was Frances Burney, whose highest figure, before 1797, was the £250 she received from Payne and Cadell for the copyright of *Cecilia* (Raven and others, 52). Radcliffe's rising stock is also reflected in her publishing career: from Hookham, who was associated with a circulating library, to Cadell and Davies, who were at the prestigious end of the publishing market. Before *The Castles of Athlin and Dunbayne* only a handful of Gothic novels had been published; by the time *Udolpho* appeared, the genre accounted for roughly a third of all new novels. Although Horace Walpole's *The Castle of Otranto* (1764), Clara Reeve's *The Old English Baron* (1777), and Sophia Lee's *The Recess* (1783–5) were Radcliffe's acknowledged models, critics were united in saying that Radcliffe had transformed her 'meagre' materials into a new, powerful and 'enchanting' form. Among her critics there was virtual unanimity that she stood at the head of her own school of romance. At the peak of her career, much imitated, much lauded, and very richly rewarded, Ann Radcliffe suddenly stopped publishing. She had produced five romances and a travelogue in eight years and had become one of the country's most famous novelists and was still only thirty-three.

Radcliffe's contemporaries were mystified by her silence. In the absence of any hard information wild rumours circulated about her, some alleging her death, others arguing that she had been driven mad by her propensity for terror. According to one story, she was confined, insane, at Haddon Hall in Derbyshire, while in 1810 the anonymous 'Ode to Horror' represented Radcliffe as 'having died in that species of derangement called "the horrors"' (Talfourd, 95; Norton, 211). Radcliffe declined the opportunity of correcting these exaggerations.

William Radcliffe advanced reasons for the abandonment of his wife's career. According to Talfourd, Ann Radcliffe was so much the gentlewoman that nothing other than the direst necessity could force her to assume the indecorous mantle of woman author. Her husband claimed that an inheritance relieved her from the burden of writing, an apparent reference to the legacy left her by her father after his death, on 4 July 1798, of 'interests in the rents of property in Houghton-on-the-hill, near Leicester' (Rogers, *Bio-Bibliography*, 11). There was also property left to her after her mother's death on 14 March 1800. Given that the same sources indicate that Ann Radcliffe began writing for pleasure, it hardly seems credible that she stopped because of her wealth. Nor is there any evidence from early on in her career that she was shy about publicity. After the success of *The Romance of the Forest*, she broke the anonymity that was still customary for novelists by appending her name to the third edition.

Ann Radcliffe's sensitivity to criticism appears to provide a more likely explanation. When her third romance was published in 1791, her style of writing was still relatively novel; by the mid-1790s, the market was awash with Radcliffe's imitators. Although Radcliffe herself was untouchable, those who followed her were subject to a great deal of derision. Moreover, the reviewers began to undermine Radcliffe herself, through insinuation, innuendos, and faint praise. While they did not attack her on political grounds, apart from the Jacobinical smear of being at the head of 'terrorist novel writing', critics did accuse her of subverting norms of gender and genre and of making such basic errors as suspending tripods from ceilings (*Spirit of the Public Journals*, 223).

Although Radcliffe ceased to publish after the appearance of *The Italian* she did not stop writing. As can be seen from the book she based on her journey down the Rhine with her husband in the summer of 1794—the only occasion on which she left Britain—she was an inveterate travel writer. With the Napoleonic wars making foreign expeditions difficult, the Radcliffes confined their journeys to Britain, largely to the south coast. It is from the notebooks she kept to record her travels that Talfourd extracted material for his memoir.

Ann Radcliffe died at her home, 5 Stafford Row, Pimlico, at 2 a.m. on 7 February 1823, attended by her physician, Charles Scudamore, who cited as the cause of death the inflammation of the cerebral membranes, which he in turn linked to the asthma Radcliffe periodically suffered during the last twelve years of her life. On the basis of her commonplace book Rogers and Norton both infer that Radcliffe died of a bronchial infection exacerbated by Scudamore's prescriptions. She was buried at St George's Church, Hanover Square. No will survives, but Norton claims that William Radcliffe left a fortune of £8000 on his death in 1830 at Versailles. He was attended by his second wife, formerly the Radcliffe's housekeeper, who he married in 1826.

Afterlife and reputation There were several posthumous works: *Gaston de Blondeville* (1826), with a prefatory memoir by Talfourd; *St Albans's Abbey*, a 'metrical romance' (1826); and the important 'On the supernatural in poetry' (1826). Written in dialogue form, and originally intended as an introduction to *Gaston de Blondeville*, 'On the supernatural in poetry' is Radcliffe's fullest statement on her aesthetic practices.

It was only with Radcliffe's death that more information began to emerge about her, but for her modern biographers, this is where the problems begin. Two biographical sketches appeared: Talfourd's 'Memoir', and another in the *Annual Biography and Obituary, for the Year 1824*. The latter includes material written by William Radcliffe, while the former was produced under his close supervision, to such an extent that Talfourd complained to Mary Russell Mitford that his trouble 'exceeds anything that can be imagined' (Norton, 248). Both sources contain William's recollection of his wife's appearance:

> This admirable writer, whom I remember from about the time of her twentieth year, was, in her youth, of figure exquisitely proportioned; while she resembled her father, and his brother and sister, in being low of stature. Her complexion was beautiful, as was her whole countenance, especially her eyes, eyebrows, and mouth.   (*Annual Biography and Obituary*, 99)

The accounts report that Radcliffe's old-fashioned education, although good, did not include the classics, and that she delighted in having Latin and Greek works read out to her before being translated. They also relate that she was passionately fond of music and that she liked to attend the opera; she preferred to sit in the pit, where she enjoyed protection from draughts as well as from the gaze of curious onlookers. Her morbid fear of being thought forward, as regards her literary fame, preoccupies both memoirs. Indeed, the greater portion of William Radcliffe's contribution to his wife's obituary notice concerns two slights on her character that preyed on her mind throughout her life. The first was that she was thought to have claimed authorship of Joanna Baillie's *Plays on the Passions*, when these works were still anonymous; the other was that Mrs Carter, the famous bluestocking, had snubbed her. Apart from rectifying these slights, the main consequence of William Radcliffe's intervention was to protect his wife's fame by tightly controlling the information that appeared about her.

It is unclear whether William's management of his wife's reputation extended to the destruction of her papers. As the excerpts in Talfourd's memoir show, Radcliffe was an inveterate journal writer, yet none of her private papers survived, apart from a commonplace book covering the last period of her life, and the contract for *The Mysteries of Udolpho*. In the 1880s Christina Rossetti abandoned her attempts to write Radcliffe's life for want of material. The scarcity of information has hindered all subsequent biographies of Radcliffe. Adeline Grant wrote a substantial life of Radcliffe in the 1950s, but as it was unsupported by any evidence, its claims must be viewed with caution. Deborah D. Rogers's *Ann Radcliffe: a Bio-Bibliography* (1996) keeps scrupulously to the known facts, and is correspondingly brief. Only with the publication of Rictor Norton's *Mistress of Udolpho* has any new light been shed on Ann Radcliffe. Norton's discoveries about Radcliffe have been limited, but he has produced additional information on the career of her husband, William, and on the relatives William had omitted from his wife's biography.   ROBERT MILES

Sources *Annual Biography and Obituary* (1824) · *GM*, 1st ser., 93 (1823), 87–8 · A. Grant, *Ann Radcliffe: a biography* (1951) · R. Miles, *Ann Radcliffe: the great enchantress* (1995) · R. Norton, *Mistress of Udolpho: the life of Ann Radcliffe* (1999) · D. D. Rogers, *The critical response to Ann Radcliffe* (1994) · D. D. Rogers, *Ann Radcliffe: a bio-bibliography* (1996) · J. Raven and A. Foster, eds., *The English novel, 1770–1829: a bibliographical survey of prose fiction published in the British Isles*, 1: 1770–1799 (2000) · *Spirit of the Public Journals for 1797* [London], 1 (1798), 223–5 · T. N. Talfourd, 'Memoir of the life and writings of Mrs Radcliffe', in A. Radcliffe, *Gaston de Blondeville*, 1 (1826), 3–132

Radcliffe, Anne, countess of Sussex (*d.* 1579x82). *See under* Radcliffe, Robert, first earl of Sussex (1482/3–1542).

Radcliffe, Charles, styled fifth earl of Derwentwater (1693–1746). *See under* Radcliffe, James, styled third earl of Derwentwater (1689–1716).

Radcliffe, Charles Bland (1822–1889), physician, born at Brigg, Lincolnshire, on 2 June 1822, was the eldest son of Charles Radcliffe, a Wesleyan Methodist minister. John Netten *Radcliffe (1826–1884) was his younger brother. He completed his education, begun at home, in the grammar school at Batley, near Leeds, and was subsequently apprenticed to Mr Hall, a general practitioner, at Wortley. He finished his medical training in Leeds, Paris (where he studied under Claude Bernard), and London. He graduated MB at London University in 1845, when he is said to have been the first student from a provincial medical school to have been awarded a gold medal, and graduated MD in 1851. In the same year he married Mary Reece Urling, daughter of George Frederick Urling, lace manufacturer; there were no children. He became a licentiate of the Royal College of Physicians in 1848, and was elected a fellow in 1858. He was Goulstonian lecturer in 1860 and Croonian lecturer in 1873. He subsequently became a councillor of the College of Physicians, and in 1875–6 he acted as censor.

In 1853 Radcliffe was appointed assistant physician to the Westminster Hospital, where he became full physician in 1857, and was elected to the consulting staff in 1873. He lectured on botany and materia medica in the medical school attached to the hospital. In 1863 he was appointed physician to the National Hospital for the Paralysed and Epileptic in Queen Square, London, in succession to Charles Brown-Séquard, and it was in connection with this institution, and the diseases of the nervous system, that Radcliffe's name was best known. He was a prolific writer, publishing works on vital motion, epilepsy, and disorders of the nervous system. Between 1845 and 1873 he was also joint editor with W. H. Ranking of Ranking's *Abstract of Medical Sciences*.

Radcliffe was one of the earliest investigators in Britain of the electrical physiology of muscle and nerve, but he was more a theorist than an experimentalist. Sir John Burdon-Sanderson claimed that Radcliffe was essentially a vitalist, but in his doctrine electricity took the place of the vital principle. Radcliffe had a great interest in music, architecture, and theology, and was a devout if unorthodox Christian. He was a friend of Frederick Denison Maurice, the founder of Christian socialism. He died suddenly at his home, 25 Cavendish Square, London, on 18 June 1889 and was buried in Highgate cemetery.

D'A. POWER, *rev.* CAROLINE OVERY

Sources *Westminster Hospital reports* (1889) · *Proceedings of the Royal Medical and Chirurgical Society*, 3rd ser., 3 (1890–91), 9–11 [pt 1] · *The Lancet* (29 June 1889) · *BMJ* (22 June 1889), 1416 · personal knowledge (1896) · private information (1896) · Munk, *Roll* · m. cert. · *CGPLA Eng. & Wales* (1889)
Likenesses W. Boxall, portrait (unfinished); in possession of Mary Reece Radcliffe, 1896
Wealth at death £11,071 6s. 11d.: probate, 20 July 1889, *CGPLA Eng. & Wales*

Radcliffe [Radclyffe], **Charles Edward** (1774–1827), army officer, was the third son of Edward Radclyffe of Barnsley (*b.* 1728) and his second wife, Elizabeth, daughter of William Adamson of Milton, Yorkshire. He received his first commission as adjutant of the 1st dragoons (Royals) on 11 October 1797, having previously served under the duke of York in the campaign of 1794. He was made cornet on 12 April 1799, lieutenant on 4 May 1800, and captain on 1 December 1804. He embarked for the Peninsula with the Royals in September 1809, and in the following June he was appointed brigade-major to General Slade's brigade, which consisted at that time of the Royals and the 14th dragoons. He continued in this position up to the battle of Toulouse in 1814, being present at Busaco, Fuentes d'Oñoro, Vitoria, and various minor engagements. After the action at Maquilla on 11 June 1812, in which Slade's brigade (Royals and 3rd dragoon guards) was routed by Lallemand and driven in confusion for 6 miles with a loss of 150 men, Slade reported that he was particularly indebted to Radcliffe for his assistance in rallying the men. As a result of his experience in the war Radcliffe submitted a strong recommendation that British troopers should be taught to use the point instead of the edge of their swords, and published a small work on the subject.

Radcliffe was employed as assistant adjutant-general of cavalry after the Peninsular War. He became a brevet major on 4 June 1814, and on 25 September was made brigade-major to the inspector-general of cavalry. In 1815 he went to Belgium with his regiment, which formed part of the famous Union brigade. His squadron constituted the rearguard of the brigade in the retreat from Quatre Bras on 17 June, and he was thanked for his conduct by Sir William Ponsonby. He was specially praised by Ponsonby's successor, Colonel Clifton, for his part in the great cavalry charge at Waterloo the following day. He was severely wounded by a bullet in the knee, which could not be extracted and caused him much pain for the rest of his life. He was given a brevet lieutenant-colonelcy, dating from the day of the battle.

Radcliffe was placed on half pay on 20 April 1820, and was appointed brigade-major to the inspector-general of cavalry. 'He was a dexterous swordsman, an accomplished officer, and an able tactician … a warm and sincere friend,

a conscientious Christian, and a brave man', wrote General de Ainslie, historian of the Royals.

Radcliffe married in 1800 Mary, eldest daughter of Henry Crockett, of Littleton Hall, Staffordshire, who died a week before him. He died at Connaught Square, London, on 24 February 1827. His only son, the Revd Charles Edward Radclyffe (*c.*1801–1862), had a son, also Charles Edward Radclyffe, of Little Park, Hampshire.

E. M. LLOYD, *rev.* DAVID GATES

Sources *GM*, 1st ser., 85/2 (1815), 81 · *GM*, 1st ser., 97/1 (1827), 365 · C. P. de Ainslie, *Historical record of the first or the royal regiment of dragoons* (1887) · *Supplementary despatches (correspondence) and memoranda of Field Marshal Arthur, duke of Wellington*, ed. A. R. Wellesley, second duke of Wellington, 15 vols. (1858–72), vol. 10, p. 569 · Foster, *Alum. Oxon.* · Burke, *Gen. GB* (1937) · D. Gates, *The Spanish ulcer: a history of the Peninsular War* (1986) · R. Muir, *Britain and the defeat of Napoleon, 1807–1815* (1996)

Radcliffe, Charlotte Maria, *suo jure* **countess of Newburgh** (1694–1755). *See under* Radcliffe, James, styled third earl of Derwentwater (1689–1716).

Radcliffe, Cyril John, **Viscount Radcliffe** (1899–1977), lawyer and public servant, was born at Plas Gwyn, Llanychan, Denbighshire, on 30 March 1899, the third in the family of four sons of Captain Alfred Ernest Radcliffe, of the Royal Lancashire regiment, and his wife, Sybil Harriet, daughter of Robert Cunliffe, a London solicitor, who was president of the Law Society in 1890–91.

Radcliffe was at school at Haileybury College. After service in the labour corps—because of his poor eyesight the only form of war service open to him—he entered New College, Oxford, as a scholar in 1919, and took first-class honours in *literae humaniores* in 1921. He was a fellow of All Souls from 1922 to 1937. In 1923 he became Eldon law scholar and was called to the bar by the Inner Temple in 1924. He went into the chambers of Wilfrid Greene. He took silk in 1935, and by 1938, after Greene and Sir Gavin Simonds were appointed to the bench, he had become the outstanding figure at the chancery bar.

This meteoric legal career was interrupted by the Second World War. Radcliffe joined the Ministry of Information, and by 1941 had become its director-general. His gifts and skills complemented those of his minister, Brendan Bracken, in an unlikely but effective partnership. In May 1945 he resumed his practice at the bar; and in 1949 he was appointed a lord of appeal in ordinary, the first man (other than former law officers) for over sixty years to be appointed to the House of Lords direct from the bar.

In 1947 Radcliffe was appointed chairman of the two boundary commissions set up with the passing of the Indian Independence Act of that year. The time he spent in India, and his eldest brother's death there while serving in the army, left him with a lifelong feeling for the country, and an intense admiration for the achievements, courage, and dedication of the early generations of British administrators there.

Over the next thirty years Radcliffe was the chairman of a series of public inquiries, including the royal commission on taxation of profits and income (1951–5); the constitutional commission for Cyprus (1956); committees on the

Cyril John Radcliffe, Viscount Radcliffe (1899–1977), by Walter Stoneman, 1949

working of the monetary system (1957–9) and on security procedures and practices in the public service (1961); the tribunal of inquiry into the Vassall case (1962); and committees of privy councillors on the *Daily Express* and D notices (1967) and on ministerial memoirs (1975–6). Though he continued to carry out judicial duties when he was not fully engaged on an inquiry, the law was no longer enough to satisfy his intellectual appetite; he enjoyed the succession of challenges provided by these public inquiries, whose reports reflected his own thoroughness, lucidity, and wisdom of judgement. The frequency with which his skill as a chairman was pressed into service led Sir A. P. Herbert to comment on 'Government by Radcliffery', but it is perhaps the fact that his achievements covered so diverse a range of activities that partly accounts for a sense that his outstanding gifts were never really put to full use.

Radcliffe retired from judicial work in 1964. He became a trustee of the British Museum in 1957, and was chairman of the trustees from 1963 to 1968. He was chairman of the governors of the School of Oriental and African Studies from 1960 to 1975. He became the first chancellor of the University of Warwick in 1966. In his last ten years he withdrew increasingly into private life, partly in order to care for his wife but also because of his increasing disenchantment with the quality of public life.

Radcliffe was much in demand as a speaker and lecturer. He spoke, as he wrote, with exceptional lucidity and power, and with a sense of style well characterized as intellectual eloquence. He had an abiding interest in the arts, and assembled—but eventually disposed of—a small but distinguished collection of impressionist paintings. For many years a trusted friend of Calouste Gulbenkian, he was disappointed not to be able to fulfil Gulbenkian's hope, and indeed his own, that he might become the first chairman of the Gulbenkian trustees.

Radcliffe was by common consent one of the outstanding intelligences of his generation. He had a capacious and powerful mind, disciplined by his academic and legal training, and nurtured by extensive reading, particularly in English history and literature. He cherished freedom and the liberal values, and order and the rule of law as the condition of freedom. He believed in the power of reason as a determinant of human conduct, and measured the foibles and follies of men with a detached and unsparing perceptiveness. He was a reserved and fastidious man. All this made him for some people unapproachable, and he had relatively few close friends; but their devotion was rewarded by the discovery of a keen sense of humour, a dry wit, and a warm and steadfast affection.

Radcliffe was a man of middle height, with a large, square head: a high forehead, with crinkly brown—later silvery grey—hair brushed tight back from his forehead; a blunt mouth and a firm chin; and blue-grey eyes behind thick spectacles.

Radcliffe's principal publications were *The Problem of Power* (1951 Reith lectures, 1952; reissued with new preface, 1958), *The Law and its Compass* (1960 Rosenthal lectures, 1961), *Mountstuart Elphinstone* (Romanes lecture, 1962), *Government by Contempt: Whitehall's Way with Parliament and People* (1968), and *Not in Feather Beds* (a collection of speeches, lectures, and articles, 1968).

Radcliffe was appointed KBE in 1944 and GBE in 1948. As a law lord, he became a life peer and a privy councillor in 1949; and he was created viscount in 1962. He was elected FBA in 1968 and had many honorary degrees, including an Oxford DCL (1961).

Radcliffe married on 11 December 1939 Antonia Mary Roby (1903–1982), the daughter of Godfrey Rathbone Benson, first Baron Charnwood, politician and man of letters. She was the former wife of John Tennant. There were no children of the marriage. Radcliffe died of cancer at his home, Hampton Lucy House, Hampton Lucy, Warwickshire, on 1 April 1977, and was buried in Hampton Lucy churchyard. The viscountcy became extinct on his death.

ROBERT ARMSTRONG, *rev.*

Sources *The Times* (4 April 1977) · R. Stevens, 'Four interpretations', *Law and politics: the House of Lords as a judicial body, 1800–1976* (1979) · personal knowledge (1986) · private information (1986) · E. Heward, *The great and the good: a life of Lord Radcliffe* (1994) · Burke, *Peerage* (1967)
Likenesses W. Stoneman, photograph, 1949, NPG [*see illus.*] · photograph, *c.*1952, repro. in Heward, *The great and the good*, pl. 12
Wealth at death £362,184: probate, 2 June 1977, *CGPLA Eng. & Wales*

Radcliffe, Egremont (*d.* 1578), rebel and alleged assassin, was the son of Henry *Radcliffe, second earl of Sussex (*c*.1507–1557) [*see under* Radcliffe, Robert], magnate, among whose titles was Lord Egremont, and his second wife, Anne (*d.* 1579x82), daughter of Sir Philip Calthorpe of Burnham Thorpe, Norfolk, and his second wife, Jane. He had two sisters, one of whom, Frances (1552–1602), married Sir Thomas Mildmay. His half-brothers included Thomas *Radcliffe and Henry *Radcliffe, third and fourth earls of Sussex respectively. His parents were married at some point between 1534 and 1538, but were divorced by private act of parliament on 13 November 1555, after which his mother married Andrew Wise, vice-treasurer of Ireland. The third earl of Sussex was embittered by the divorce and later described Egremont Radcliffe as 'a wicked bastarde, taken for my brother' (Sharp, 75).

Radcliffe was educated in the household of Robert Horne, bishop of Winchester, who told Sussex in 1563 that he had sent him from Bishop's Waltham to 'your L[ordship's] Stuarde' to avoid plague but would have him back 'untill your L[ordship] shall thinke good otherwise to provide for him' (BL, Cotton MS Titus Bxiii, fol. 95r). Later he lived in York, as did Thomas Jenye, with whom he joined the northern uprising in 1569. His residence in York is unusual, considering his family was based in Norfolk and Somerset, unless he was serving Sussex, who was lord president of the queen's council of the north. He was a notable Catholic and felt alienated from Elizabeth I's protestant and centralizing regime. Jenye claimed to have met Radcliffe near Topcliffe, North Riding of Yorkshire, going north. Radcliffe persuaded him to join the enterprise by producing assurances and a ring that he had received from Charles Neville, sixth earl of Westmorland. Later, Radcliffe specified Westmorland as having been the 'onelie cause of his wicked revolte' (PRO, SP 70/133, fol. 101r).

Sussex excepted Radcliffe and Jenye from the pardon offered on 19 November, the only two not named in the list of original rebels earlier in the proclamation. It is, however, quite likely that they had joined as early as 15 November—according to Christopher Norton, their arrival between Durham and Darlington 'comfortyd the coman sorte' and embarrassed Sussex (Sharp, 285). The earl wanted to be 'revenged' before 'the worlde' for 'the trayterous doings of an unnatural brother' (PRO, SP 15/15/46). On the collapse of the rising Radcliffe fled into Liddesdale on the Anglo-Scottish border, remaining with Westmorland rather than the ill-fated Thomas Percy, seventh earl of Northumberland. A ship was arranged, which English officials plotted to secure by bribing the captain or by interception. Probably Radcliffe postponed his departure, as Sussex was still seeking his extradition from the borderers in August 1570. However, in October Sir Henry Norris found him in Paris. Radcliffe then went to the Spanish Netherlands, where he met Catholic exiles, and Philip II gave him a pension of 30 crowns per month. He became close to Henry Parker, eleventh Baron Morley, stepson of his aunt Elizabeth Calthorpe.

In April 1571 Radcliffe was said to have killed George Breame, an Englishman living in Antwerp, 'with a pistolet for that he wold len[d] him no silver' (*CSP Scot.*, 1569–71,

527). He was subsequently alleged to have gone to Spain in 1572 to get a royal pardon, but seemed in no hurry. In May he was sent with Jenye to represent the English exiles at Madrid. In September he went to Milan, but (according to a hostile source), 'having killed there two other … was compelled to retourne from thence' (Knox, *Diaries*, 300). In December 1573 he was said to be in prison for debt in Madrid and in May 1574, passing through France *en route* for Flanders, to be again in prison for debt and (inevitably) for 'disorders' (PRO, SP 15/23/58). By August Philip had spent 800 ducats on him.

Radcliffe apparently changed his attitude in Spain from the hard-core dissidence formerly attributed to him. He made overtures, asking for a pardon, to William Cecil, first Baron Burghley, the lord treasurer, from Bruges in August 1574. By February 1575 he claimed to have left 'the entertaynement I had of the kinge of Spayne', referred to 'the injuries I have suffred in Spayne for defending according to my duty her magestie's honnore against Stuclye [Sir Thomas Stucley] and othare of greatar credit', but darkly said that, being 'indetted', he might 'be forced to take wher I have bine prayed … which I wolde be loathe to doe yf I might choose' (PRO, SP 15/24/4). He defended Morley and Westmorland as also opposing Stucley's invasion plans. Personal disputes may have loomed large in his desire to return to England. He described his previous behaviour as 'a yonge man's first faulte, for which the gates of reconciliation is not clene to be cutt awaye' and hoped for subsidy, especially if willing to serve in Ireland (Sharp, 72). He had returned to London by November. Sir Francis Walsingham, principal secretary, warned Burghley that were Radcliffe to 'lynger in this realme', Elizabeth might 'be dryven for example's sake to extende that punishment towardes him, that to his former offences is dewe' (BL, Harley MS 6992, fol. 32r). Radcliffe was sent to the Tower of London—it was reported to Spain that he was about to make false statements against Philip and would claim that the latter planned to retaliate for English provocations. He carved his name in the Beauchamp Tower, and wrote *Politique Discourses Translated out of French* (1578), which he dedicated to Walsingham. It was a personal volte-face, advocating acceptance of the social and political order. He might well ask, 'who ever sawe so many discontented persons … so many controllers of princes and their procedinges: and so fewe imbracing obedience?' (E. Radcliffe, *Politique Discourses*, 1578, sig. A3v).

In May 1578 Radcliffe was 'secretly released and exiled'; the Spanish ambassador in London, Bernardino de Mendoza, reported that he was going to serve Don John of Austria in the Spanish Netherlands. 'He is a rash and daring man, ready for anything, and his sudden liberation and decision to serve us may well engender suspicion' (*CSP Spain*, 1568–79, 584). He claimed to Sir Amias Paulet, the English ambassador in Paris, that Elizabeth would be his preferred source for 'his maintenaunce as maye be mete for a gentleman', failing which he would 'seeke his lyving where he maye finde it' (PRO, SP 78/2/42). Catholic suspicion intensified. Anselmo Dandino, the papal nuncio in France, heard that Radcliffe was going to Italy—with the musician and probable spy Alfonso Ferrabosco—at Elizabeth's behest, although he made a pretence of being angry with the queen. Cardinal William Allen, founder of the English seminary at Rheims, welcomed him there, though he had been warned of Radcliffe's murderous potential. Radcliffe was arrested, with a man called Gray, when he arrived in Flanders. The details are unclear, reflecting confusion over the facts at the time. Radcliffe was suspected of foul play towards Don John, who died shortly after meeting him. It is unlikely that Radcliffe and Gray were charged with Don John's death, though the Catholic exile, Sir Francis Englefield, put forward the argument that Philip should not meet an English envoy because 'some intimates of Don John' observed 'that his highness was never well after Ratclyf the Englishman gave a letter into his hands' (BL, Add. MS 28702, fol. 4r). Poison was suspected. The decision to execute Radcliffe and Gray was probably taken by Alessandro Farnese, duke of Parma. They were beheaded in the market-place of Namur on either 19 or 26 December 1578.

Walsingham heard that Radcliffe blamed him for the supposed plot. Disingenuously dismissing the reliability of confessions obtained by torture, he asked William Davison, the English envoy to the Netherlands, to investigate 'so villainous a slaunder', considering Radcliffe not 'so develishe but that at the houre of his deathe he wolde revoke that which before he had untruely uttered' (PRO, SP 83/11/23). Accounts conflicted, but the Spaniards continued to allege Walsingham's complicity. Sir Lewis Lewknor believed that Radcliffe and Gray had been 'most faithfully affected both in religion and service to the Spanish king', yet 'though there never was, nor ever coulde bee anie thing proved against them, and they at their deaths protested themselves to be innocent … yet theyr heads were stricken off' (Lewknor, sig. A3r). However, an anonymous correspondent of 1581 reminded Walsingham about a dangerous security breach when an informer 'sawe good Mr Egmonde Radlyffe goinge up to Hampton Court unto you, and afterward mayde him lose his heade for it' (PRO, SP 78/6/37). In 1599 Thomas Harrison, among other doubtful alleged services, claimed: 'If I had not cunningly escaped I had died with Egrammond Ratclif and his man, from whom I was to receive notice for Mr Secretary' (Salisbury MSS, 9.86). It does seem likely that the English government made some use of Radcliffe's proffered services because he was eminently expendable. His picaresque career makes it probable that he died poor and unmarried—'A ballett of the deathe of Ratlyffe w.ch rosse w.th the earle of Northumberland Lorde Pearse whiche he made a lytle spaice before he was hanged' (BL, Cotton MS Vespasian A. xxv, fol. 158v) seems to be entirely generic, implying that he was executed in England, and the alleged farewell to his 'wedded wiffe' it recounts hardly signifies.

JULIAN LOCK

Sources State papers, domestic additional, PRO, SP 15 · State papers, foreign, Elizabeth I, PRO, SP 70 · State papers, Holland and Netherlands, PRO, SP 83 · State papers, France, PRO, SP 78 · BL, Lansdowne MSS 18, 19, 25, 102 · BL, Add. MS 28702, fols. 1–4 · BL, Harley MS 6992, fol. 32r · BL, Cotton MS Titus Bxiii, fol. 95r ·

C. Sharp, ed., *Memorials of the rebellion of 1569* (1840); repr. with foreword by R. Wood as *The rising in the north: the 1569 rebellion* (1975), 51n, 71–5, 122, 138–9, 230, 264, 285 · *CSP Spain, 1568–79* · *CSP Rome, 1558–78* · [A. Dandino], *Correspondance du nonce en France Anselmo Dandino, 1578–81*, ed. I. Cloulas, Acta Nuntiaturae Gallicae, 8 (1970) · *CSP Scot., 1569–71* · [L. Lewknor], *Estate of English fugitives under the king of Spaine and his ministers* (1595), sig. A3r · T. F. Knox and others, eds., *The first and second diaries of the English College, Douay* (1878), appx 7 · *The letters and memorials of William, Cardinal Allen (1532–1594)*, ed. T. F. Knox (1882), vol. 2 of *Records of the English Catholics under the penal laws* (1878–82), 14–15 · GEC, *Peerage* · *Calendar of the manuscripts of the most hon. the marquis of Salisbury*, 24 vols., HMC, 9 (1883–1976), vol. 2, p. 100; vol. 9, p. 86 · G. Pollini, *L'historia ecclesiastica della rivoluzion d'Inghilterra* (1594), 449–50 · A. Haynes, *Invisible power: the Elizabethan secret services, 1570–1603* (1992), 84 · S. E. Taylor, 'The crown and the north of England, 1559–70: a study of the rebellion of the northern earls, 1569–70, and its causes', PhD diss., University of Manchester, 1981 · S. Doran, 'The political career of Thomas Radcliffe, third earl of Sussex (1526?–83)', PhD diss., U. Lond., 1977 · T. Wright, *Queen Elizabeth and her times: a series of original letters*, 2 vols. (1838), vol. 1, pp. 500–04 · P. O. de Törne, *Don Juan d'Autriche et les projets de conquête de l'Angleterre, 1568–78*, 2 vols. (1915–28), vol. 1, p. 150 · W. E. F., 'The Beauchamp Tower', *GM*, 3rd ser., 2 (1857), 196–9 · R. Kelso, *The doctrine of the English gentleman in the sixteenth century*, University of Illinois Studies in Language and Literature, 14 (1929)

Archives BL, letters to Lord Burghley, Lansdowne MSS 19, 25 · PRO, letters to Lord Burghley, SP 12/112, SP 15/24, SP 70/132

Radcliffe [*née* Sidney], **Frances**, countess of Sussex (1531?–1589), benefactor of Sidney Sussex College, Cambridge, was reputedly born in 1531, the fourth daughter of Sir William *Sidney (c.1482–1554) [*see under* Sidney, Sir Henry (1529–1586)] and his wife, Anne (d. 1543), daughter of Sir Hugh Pagenham and widow of Thomas Fitzwilliam. The family moved in the highest court circles. Her brother Sir Henry *Sidney married the sister of the queen's favourite, the earl of Leicester; Sir Philip *Sidney was her nephew; Mary *Herbert, countess of Pembroke, was her niece. She married Thomas *Radcliffe, Lord Fitzwalter (1526/7–1583), at Hampton Court by licence, between 26 and 29 April 1555, and the marriage was celebrated by a tournament honoured by the king's participation. She was Fitzwalter's second wife; his first, Elizabeth Wriothesley, had died about three months previously, without surviving children. Her successor was barren. Frances now all but disappears from the public record for many years. Nevertheless she was with her husband in Ireland (1556–64) when he was lord deputy, and later lord lieutenant. In 1557 he became third earl of Sussex. She was with him at Berwick when he was lord president of the north. Here in 1571 she caught smallpox. When he was allowed to visit her, Sussex wrote 'she took greater comfort from my visit to her than with all they [the doctors] did besides' (*CSP dom.*, addenda, 1566–79, 343). She was a loved and loyal wife, but how the open enmity between her husband and Leicester affected her is unknown.

In 1571 the queen favoured Frances and her husband with two visits to their house in Bermondsey; in 1572 she made Sussex lord chamberlain of the household, and in 1574 granted him New Hall in Essex and various Essex manors. Life now revolved around the court, but only after 1578 does Lady Sussex begin to appear in the record.

Frances Radcliffe, countess of Sussex (1531?–1589), by unknown artist, 1570–75

Perhaps it was then that she became a lady of the bedchamber. She exchanged new year gifts with the queen in 1578 and 1579. Books were dedicated to Frances in 1581, 1582, and 1583. *The Faith of the Church Militant* (1581), a translation by Thomas Rogers of a work by the Dane Nicholas Hemmingius, had two dedications. Rogers, addressing the countess, advocated education as a bulwark against papacy and heresy, and ended with pious wishes for the peace and felicity of husband and wife. Hemmingius's dedication to Peter Oxe, master of the palace in Denmark, praised his support of students in Denmark and abroad. Sussex, chamberlain of the household, did not take the hint.

Sussex became seriously ill in September 1582 and died on 9 June 1583. In his last months the countess's enemies (unspecified) alienated his affections from her, and turned the queen against her. In her distress Frances turned to Sir Christopher Hatton to ask him to deliver a letter to the queen, expressing loyalty to Elizabeth, and to her 'dear Lord'. Sussex's will was equitable, chilling, and legalistic,

but made her rich. In her bitterness she adopted the motto that appears on her seal: *Dieu me garde de calomnie*. Widowhood brought other problems. In or about 1586 the disreputable MP Arthur Hall wooed her. She was affronted and repulsed him. He attacked her in a scurrilous book, which was burnt by her Sidney nephews, the Harringtons. He continued to hound her, and in 1588 was committed to the Marshalsea.

Lady Sussex made her will on 6 December 1588, died at Bermondsey on 9 March 1589, and was buried on 15 April with due ceremony in the chapel of St Paul in Westminster Abbey. By her will she left quantities of lovingly described possessions and money to over a hundred persons, including Sidney kin. Puritan sympathies appear in bequests to poor preachers of London, and the funding and founding of a lectureship at the abbey. Her true memorial, however, is her college at Cambridge. Since her husband's death, she wrote, she had yearly set aside from her revenues 'so much money as she conveniently could'. The sum, £5000, was to be augmented by plate and 'other things', and the college erected as a 'good and godly monument for the mayntenance of good learning'. It was to be called Lady Sidney Sussex College. The will was contested unsuccessfully by certain Sidney relatives.

MARY PRIOR

Sources will of Frances Radcliffe, Lady Sussex, PRO, PROB 11/74, sig. 82; sentence, PROB 11/76, sig. 52 · will of Thomas Radcliffe, earl of Sussex, PRO, PROB 11/68, sig. 52 · 'Radcliffe, Thomas, third earl of Sussex', *DNB* · 'Sidney, Sir Henry', *DNB* · 'Fitzwilliam, Sir William', *DNB* · GEC, *Peerage*, new edn, 12/1.522–5 · N. H. Nicolas, *Memoirs of the life and times of Sir Christopher Hatton* (1847), 271, 344–8, 416–17 · H. G. Wright, *Life and works of Arthur Hall* (1919), 80–87, 194–201 · N. Hemmingius, *The faith of the church militant*, trans. T. Rogers (1581) · J. Nichols, *The progresses and public processions of Queen Elizabeth*, new edn, 3 vols. (1823) · *CSP dom., addenda, 1566–79*, 343 · *CSP Ire., 1509–73*, 152, 170, 236 · *CPR, 1560–63*, 20; *1569–72*, 361–2 · G. M. Edwards, *Sidney Sussex College* (1899), 8–14 · B. Burke, *A genealogical history of the dormant, abeyant, forfeited and extinct peerages of the British empire*, new edn (1866), 450

Likenesses portrait, 1570–75, Sidney Sussex College, Cambridge [*see illus.*] · G. Gower, portrait, *c.*1575, Sidney Sussex College, Cambridge · statue, Sidney Sussex College, Cambridge · tomb effigy, Westminster Abbey, chapel of St Paul

Wealth at death over £5000: will, PRO, PROB 11/74, sig. 82; PRO, PROB 11/76, sig. 52

Radcliffe, Sir George (bap. 1593, d. 1657), lawyer and politician, was baptized in Thornhill on 21 April 1593, the son of Nicholas Radcliffe (d. 1599) of Overthorpe in the parish of Thornhill, Yorkshire, and Margaret (d. 1628), eldest daughter and coheir of Robert Marsh of Darton, Yorkshire, and widow of John Baylie of Honley in the same county. In 1607 he attended Mr Hunt's school at Oldham, where he proved himself a good scholar; in November 1609 he matriculated at University College, Oxford, and graduated BA on 24 May 1612. Earlier in the year, on 5 February, he entered Gray's Inn, where he was called to the bar in 1618. About this time he contracted what proved a brief first marriage to a daughter of John *Finch, later Baron Finch.

Early association with Wentworth, 1618–1633 Radcliffe's early career appears to have been successful, but his prospects were improved by his association with Sir Thomas Wentworth, later earl of Strafford. He was introduced to Wentworth at Christmas 1618 by his former tutor, Charles Greenwood, who had accompanied Wentworth on his tour of France. During the next few years Radcliffe acted as counsel for Wentworth and his sister on a number of matters, and by 1629 he was also handling work for Wentworth's father-in-law, John Holles, earl of Clare. Together with Greenwood (later replaced by Christopher Wandesford), Richard Marris, Wentworth's steward, and Peter Man, his solicitor, Radcliffe oversaw the management of Wentworth's estate from the early 1620s onwards. His second wife, Anne (1600/01–1659), eldest daughter of Sir Francis Trappes of Harrogate and of Nidd, both in Yorkshire, whom he married on 21 February 1622, was Wentworth's first cousin.

By the mid-1620s Radcliffe's practice kept him in London for at least the law terms, and he was in the capital in 1627 during the early period of the forced loan. By April he had decided to refuse, and he was imprisoned in the Marshalsea on the orders of the privy council on 24 April. He answered his wife's concerns with assurances of 'exceeding good company, pleasant and sweet walkes, and every kind usage, beyond expectation in a prison', and explained his resolve not to follow the example of two fellow prisoners who had attracted derision by subsequently conforming (Whitaker, 107, 148). In June he was joined by Wentworth, and together they were moved to Dartford, Kent, in late July. Radcliffe spent the next few months in confinement, apart from a brief trip to London on the dowager countess of Leicester's business. He appears to have announced his freedom a little prematurely, which prompted Wandesford to warn Wentworth not to do likewise. Radcliffe's correspondence with his wife shows him to have sat in the 1628 parliament, but his name is not listed in the register.

Wentworth's promotion to the offices of president of the council of the north and later lord deputy of Ireland brought benefits for Radcliffe. In December 1628 he informed his wife that Wentworth aimed to secure him the office of king's attorney at York, and he was certainly in office by the summer of 1629. He was not immediately added to the commission of the peace, nor was he placed on the northern commission for compounding with recusants, despite the close connection between that commission and the council of the north. In November 1632, however, he was preferred to the office of one of the king's council learned in the law; that year he also became a bencher of his inn.

Service in Ireland, 1633–1640 In January 1633 Radcliffe preceded Wentworth to Ireland on 'special service' (*CSP Ire., 1625–32*, 675), armed with the king's directions that the lords justices Richard Boyle, earl of Cork, and Adam, Viscount Loftus, support him in his work. Wentworth's first dispatch to Secretary Sir John Coke of 3 August 1633 reported on Radcliffe's work in the case against the bishop of Kilfenora, and ended with the request that Radcliffe be sworn of the council, 'ther being many of them allready at this Bord almost beneath him as farr in estate as they are in Partes and understanding' (Strafford papers, 5/10). The king granted the request immediately and Radcliffe was knighted by the lord deputy on 1 November of that year. In October 1632, in an attempt to ingratiate himself with Wentworth, Cork had suggested Radcliffe for the mastership of the rolls, an office that was filled instead by Christopher Wandesford. Unlike Wandesford, Radcliffe was not given a key office in Ireland, although suitable posts did become vacant: in 1636 the post of attorney-general went to another member of Wentworth's team of Yorkshiremen, Richard Osbaldeston, also a bencher of Gray's Inn. Wentworth seems to have preferred to employ Radcliffe in a more flexible manner, ensuring that he was well rewarded for his efforts by his membership of the Irish customs farm from 1632. In 1636–7, following Wentworth's reorganization of the farm, Radcliffe's eighth part of the profits earned him £2800. The king had also granted him £500 per annum in compensation for the loss of his legal practice. His income enabled him to invest in land in the Connaught plantation, and he also acquired property in co. Wicklow.

It has been noted that 'None of his servants in Ireland was more important to Wentworth, or more trusted, than Sir George Radcliffe, his legal expert, whose ingenious legal trickery was vital in enabling the crown to regain the political initiative in Ireland' (Merritt, 140). He worked on a very broad range of business, including legal work, the customs farm—of which he controlled the accounts—and church affairs, on which he advised Archbishop William Laud and Bishop John Bramhall. In addition he handled the private landed and commercial interests of Wentworth's friends and political allies. Radcliffe made several visits to England to further and protect the lord deputy's concerns, and he accompanied Wentworth in the summer of 1636 when he was added to the commissions of the peace for all three ridings of Yorkshire. In the parliament of 1634 he sat for the city of Armagh, following Cork's refusal to place him in a seat under his control, and he was an active government member. It was Radcliffe who informed the council of Sir Piers Crosby's opposition to a government bill, prompting his removal from the board. In 1639 Radcliffe and Wandesford both contributed £500 towards the king's war effort against the Scots. In the Irish parliament of 1640 he was knight of the shire for Sligo, his son Thomas (*b.* 1623?) sitting for the borough, but he travelled to England in June to attend his patron, now earl of Strafford, who was seriously ill. Staying until August, he stood surety with Francis Cottington, Lord Cottington, chancellor of the exchequer, and another individual, possibly Wentworth, for the cost of the pepper cargo. His service earned him the lord deputy's praise, but it also ensured that he would be implicated in the charge of high treason brought against Strafford.

Imprisonment and exile On 13 November the English House of Commons resolved that Radcliffe's membership of the Irish parliament did not protect him against a possible charge of high treason, and he was ordered to appear before the house. On 9 December 1640 he was committed to the gatehouse and articles of impeachment against him were read in the Commons and presented to the Lords at the end of that month. On 27 February 1641 the Irish House of Commons began impeachment proceedings against Radcliffe, Bramhall, Lord Chancellor Richard Bolton, and Lord Chief Justice Gerard Lowther, all potential witnesses in Strafford's defence. Radcliffe was not brought to trial in either country, but during the trial of Strafford in March 1641 he was alleged to have threatened MPs Sir John Clotworthy and Nicholas Barnewall following their opposition to the government. His role in the prosecution of Sir Piers Crosby was raised, and Crosby and Lord Baltinglass presented petitions against him. When Strafford pointed out that he had not been in Ireland when the alleged intimidation of Barnewall took place, Pym observed that 'the Spirit of my lord of Strafford could move in Sir George Radcliffe, whensoever it was spoken' (Rushworth, 112). The earl of Clarendon noted that the purpose of the impeachment of Radcliffe was to render him incapable of giving evidence on Strafford's behalf and he was barred from assisting Strafford in preparing his response to the Irish remonstrance. On the king's order, however, a copy of the Irish remonstrance was sent to Radcliffe in January 1641 and later that month his answer was delivered to Strafford, 'who sent his Majesty word that he had perused it and did avow and would humbly abide by it' (CSP dom., 1640–41, 433).

In his last letter to Strafford, Radcliffe promised his faithful service to the earl's family, and in July 1641 he was acknowledged by the earl's brother, Sir George Wentworth, as the only person in England acquainted with Strafford's estate business. In 1641–2 correspondence passed between Radcliffe and Strafford's heir, William Wentworth, Lord Raby, later second earl; later on Radcliffe wrote to William telling him of his intention to write a life of Strafford, and sending him a plan of the work (Radcliffe, *Earl of Strafforde's Letters*, 2.429–36). He appears to have drafted further sections that can be read in Cooper's edition of the earl's early correspondence (Wentworth, 319–26), and these two pieces provide important information on some aspects of Strafford's private life, and on the origins and nature of Radcliffe's relationship with the earl. It was, no doubt, a source of much regret to Radcliffe that by the 1650s, if not before, the second earl appears to have lost interest in him.

Radcliffe was released from prison in June 1642 but his whereabouts during the rest of that year are not known. In 1643 he joined the king at Oxford, and was created a doctor of law by the university in October. His correspondence with James Butler, marquess of Ormond, in 1643–4 shows him still to have been handling some Irish matters. He was refused a pardon by parliament in both the Uxbridge and the Newcastle propositions, and following the surrender of Oxford he took charge of James, duke of York. Lacking an order from the king, he chose not to take the duke abroad but handed him over to the earl of Northumberland. From 1647 onwards he lived mainly in France. In June 1648 he sailed with Edward Hyde and Cottington

to join the prince of Wales's fleet, but their ship was captured by an Ostend corsair, who robbed Radcliffe and a member of the Wandesford family of money and jewellery. Having reached Paris, Radcliffe attached himself to the duke of York, alleging the instruction of the late king. In October 1650, according to Clarendon, he encouraged James to visit the duke of Lorraine in Brussels and then to travel to The Hague, both against the wishes of Queen Henrietta Maria. While in Brussels Radcliffe took control of the duke's household, and upon hearing rumours of Charles II's death, allegedly began to direct the duke's affairs as though he were now king. He seems to have regained Charles II's favour to some extent in 1654 following his key role in preventing the attempted conversion of the duke of Gloucester to the Roman Catholic faith. This incident, however, added to the queen's hostility towards him.

By early 1655 Radcliffe was very weary of his situation, complaining to Secretary Sir Edward Nicholas that the duke of York no longer consulted him and that the queen continued to speak ill of him: he was, he claimed, 'an eysore to some and useless to all' (*Nicholas Papers*, 2.265). His letters to his wife, written the following year and intercepted by John Thurloe, contain similar sentiments. By this time he appears to have had difficulty in paying for much-needed new clothes, although he refused his wife's offer of money. In September 1656 he left Paris and joined the exiled court in the Low Countries. He died at Flushing on 22 May 1657 and was buried there three days later. According to an intelligence report 'all the cavaliers were at his burial, except the chancellor and two more that was at Bruges. They are generally sorry for him; for they say he was the best counsellor their master had' (Thurloe, 6.325), a comment that does not fully reflect the general view of Radcliffe held by some of his fellow exiles. Clarendon portrayed him as 'a man very capable of business; and if the prosperity of his former fortunes had not raised in him some fumes of vanity and self-conceitedness, very fit to be advised with, being of a nature constant and sincere' (*Life of … Clarendon*, 1.244). Christopher Hatton, Lord Hatton, sent Nicholas a similarly mixed assessment, claiming that Radcliffe's 'vanity in blabbing and feare to offend heere is able to spoile all his honest endeavors'; Nicholas himself described Radcliffe as 'a very busy and meddling person and none of the most secret or the most discreet' (*Nicholas Papers*, 1.292; 2.134). It is perhaps not surprising that Radcliffe was not on good terms with Hyde, whom he no doubt regarded as partly responsible for the destruction of the council of the north. His bitter relationship with Henry Jermyn, Lord Jermyn, was also caused at least in part by old animosities between Strafford and the queen's circle. With Ormond, however, he seems to have remained on very good terms. Radcliffe was survived by his second wife, who died 'aged fifty-eight' on 13 May 1659, and was buried in the north choir aisle of Westminster Abbey. Their son Thomas held a seat on the Irish council and died unmarried and childless in Dublin in 1679.

FIONA POGSON

Sources T. D. Whitaker, ed., *The life and original correspondence of Sir George Radcliffe* (1810) · Strafford papers, Sheff. Arch., Wentworth Woodhouse muniments, 5, 12–13, 22 · J. P. Cooper, ed., *Wentworth papers, 1597–1628*, CS, 4th ser., 12 (1973) · G. Radcliffe, *The earl of Strafforde's letters and dispatches, with an essay towards his life*, ed. W. Knowler, 2 vols. (1739) · J. Rushworth, *The tryal of Thomas earl of Strafford* (1700) · *A collection of original letters and papers, concerning the affairs of England from the year 1641 to 1660. Found among the duke of Ormonde's papers*, ed. T. Carte, 1 (1739) · [T. Carte], *The life of James, duke of Ormond*, new edn, 6 vols. (1851), vols. 5–6 · *Calendar of the manuscripts of the marquess of Ormonde*, new ser., 8 vols., HMC, 36 (1902–20), vol. 1 · E. Berwick, ed., *The Rawdon papers* (1819) · CSP *dom.*, 1640–41; 1650 · CSP *Ire.*, 1625–47 · Clarendon, *Hist. rebellion*, vols. 1, 5 · *The life of Edward, earl of Clarendon ... written by himself*, 2 vols. (1857), vol. 1 · Foster, *Alum. Oxon.* · J. Foster, *The register of admissions to Gray's Inn, 1521–1889, together with the register of marriages in Gray's Inn chapel, 1695–1754* (privately printed, London, 1889) · W. A. Shaw, *The knights of England*, 2 (1906) · J. L. Chester, ed., *The marriage, baptismal, and burial registers of the collegiate church or abbey of St Peter, Westminster*, Harleian Society, 10 (1876) · *The Nicholas papers*, ed. G. F. Warner, 4 vols., CS, new ser., 40, 50, 57, 3rd ser., 31 (1886–1920), vols. 1–3 · Thurloe, *State papers*, vols. 4–6 · *Calendar of the manuscripts of the marquis of Bath preserved at Longleat, Wiltshire*, 5 vols., HMC, 58 (1904–80), vol. 2 · H. Kearney, *Strafford in Ireland*, 2nd edn (1989) · M. A. E. Green, ed., *Calendar of the proceedings of the committee for advance of money, 1642–1656*, 1, PRO (1888) · R. P. Cust, *The forced loan and English politics, 1626–1628* (1987) · *The journals of the House of Commons of the kingdom of Ireland*, 1 (1796) · J. F. Merritt, 'Power and communication: Thomas Wentworth and government at a distance during the personal rule, 1629–1635', *The political world of Thomas Wentworth, earl of Strafford, 1621–1641*, ed. J. F. Merritt (1996), 109–32, 140 · *Report on manuscripts in various collections*, 8 vols., HMC, 55 (1901–14), vols. 3, 8 · *Report on the manuscripts of the late Reginald Rawdon Hastings*, 4 vols., HMC, 78 (1928–47), vol. 4 · PRO, C 231/5, and SO 3/10 · APC, 1627–8 · *The manuscripts of the Earl Cowper*, 3 vols., HMC, 23 (1888–9), vol. 2 · *Fourth report*, HMC, 3 (1874) · *Sixth report*, HMC, 5 (1877–8) · *Report on the manuscripts of the earl of Egmont*, 2 vols. in 3, HMC, 63 (1905–9), vol. 1

Archives BL, letters to E. Nicholas, Egerton MSS 2534–2535 · Sheff. Arch., Wentworth Woodhouse muniments, Strafford papers, corresp. with T. Wentworth

Radcliffe, Henry, second earl of Sussex (*c.*1507–1557). *See under* Radcliffe, Robert, first earl of Sussex (1482/3–1542).

Radcliffe, Henry, fourth earl of Sussex (1533–1593), soldier and administrator, was the second son of Henry *Radcliffe, second earl of Sussex (*c.*1507–1557) [*see under* Radcliffe, Robert], landowner and administrator, and Elizabeth (*d.* 1534), daughter of Thomas *Howard, second duke of Norfolk. He was brother to Thomas *Radcliffe, third earl of Sussex. There is no record of his early years. He was married to Honor, daughter and coheir of Anthony Pound of Drayton in Farlington, Hampshire, in February 1549.

Radcliffe's public career began when he and his father declared their support for Mary I in July 1553. He was knighted on 2 October at her coronation. He accompanied his brother to Ireland on the latter's appointment as lord deputy in 1557. He was appointed to the Irish privy council and sat in the Irish parliament as MP for Carlingford in 1559. In the same year he was sent on a mission to Elizabeth I in order to ascertain her resolution regarding Ulster. Also in that year, he corresponded several times with Sir William Cecil, the secretary of state, giving a general account of the state of Ireland. In 1561 he was appointed lieutenant of the colony established in King's and Queen's counties, where he commanded a band of some 200 soldiers, foot and horse, and in 1564 he was employed in putting down the O'Mores. He also defended Maryborough in King's county against an O'Connor attack.

When the third earl of Sussex was discharged from his office in 1564 Sir Nicholas Arnold was appointed head of a commission to investigate alleged corruption in the Irish government. Radcliffe was one of several officers charged by the commission of misuse of some £8000 of soldiers' pay funds. Feeling he was treated with undue harshness, Radcliffe refused to hand over certain records; thereupon he was imprisoned. The English privy council frowned on this action and ordered his release on bond. He left Ireland after this although his offices were not filled until 1566.

On his return Radcliffe settled down on the Hampshire estate inherited by his wife. He had sat in parliament for Maldon in 1555, presumably by family interest, then for Chichester in 1559, when his patron was probably his wife's relative, the twelfth earl of Arundel. However, he may have been absent in this session. By 1571 his influence in Hampshire was enough to gain him election as county MP. In 1572 he sat for Portsmouth, where he had just been appointed (May 1571) warden and captain of the town and castle. He did not speak in this session but served on some half-dozen committees.

Radcliffe spent the rest of his life busy in the affairs of Portsmouth and of the county. He had been constable of Portchester Castle and lieutenant of Southbere Forest in Hampshire since 1560. He was also steward of various crown possessions in Essex. From 1573 he was a JP in Hampshire, commissioner of musters for the county by 1576, and joint lord lieutenant with the third marquess of Winchester from 1585.

The governorship of Portsmouth entailed heavy and diverse responsibilities since it was a major naval base and an important fortress. Radcliffe was in constant correspondence with Cecil and the privy council over details of maintenance of new work. Besides these administrative responsibilities, he gathered and passed on intelligence brought by ships from abroad. He sent out vessels specifically to bring back information from the French or Spanish coasts, and was on a constant outlook for spies and smugglers. In times of war he was the commander of a garrison of several hundred men. During the Armada he dispatched four ships to join Sir Francis Drake. In 1589 he was responsible for supplies and shipping for 1000 men sent to France.

In his county offices Radcliffe was equally busy, examining suspects and grilling recusants (with the assistance of the bishop of Winchester), including one of the Babington plotters. He was responsible, with the marquess of Winchester and the bishop, for the county musters, including their training and equipment. He was of course especially busy in the late 1580s. Although there were disputes with his partner in the lieutenancy, he seems to have won the confidence of the privy council. In 1589 he was awarded the Order of the Garter.

Radcliffe had succeeded his brother, as fourth earl of

Sussex, in 1583. The estates were heavily burdened with accumulated debts to the crown, especially those incurred by his brother. In 1587 he wrote a piteous letter to the queen. His income from the inheritance was £450 a year; the annual instalment on debt repayment to the crown was £500. He had to borrow in order to make the payment. He begged the queen to allow him to reduce the payment to the exchequer to £250 a year. He emphasized that since he could not obtain private access to the queen, his request made publicly might well be impeded by his enemies. Whether his petition was granted is not known. This letter plays up the wholly provincial and local character of the earl's public career. His only court office was that of sewer to Mary. The lack of entrée or of a patron (after his brother's death) denied him the rewards which public service brought to those who frequented the court. His career is a good example of the conscientious, hardworked, poorly rewarded servants of the Elizabethan regime on whom the smooth operation of government rested.

Sussex, active to the last, died on 14 December 1593. He was buried with his predecessors in the church at Borham, Essex. He was succeeded by his son, Robert *Radcliffe, fifth earl of Sussex. WALLACE T. MacCAFFREY

Sources CSP dom., 1547–94 · J. S. Brewer and W. Bullen, eds., Calendar of the Carew manuscripts, 1: 1515–1574, PRO (1867) · CPR, 1553; 1555–7 · J. G. Nichols, ed., The chronicle of Queen Jane, and of two years of Queen Mary, CS, old ser., 48 (1850) · JHC, 1 (1547–1628) · CSP Ire., 1509–73 · HoP, Commons, 1558–1603

Radcliffe, Sir Humphrey (1508/9–1566), landowner and member of parliament, was the third son of Robert *Radcliffe, first earl of Sussex, and his first wife, Elizabeth Stafford, daughter of Henry Stafford, second duke of Buckingham. He was contracted to marry Katherine, daughter of John, second Baron Marney, when she was still a child, but she eventually married his brother George, while Humphrey married Isabel, or Elisabeth, the daughter of Edmund Harvey and his wife, Margaret Wentworth. They had six children: Thomas, Edward (who became the last Radcliffe earl of Sussex and married three times), Mary (lady-in-waiting to Queen Elizabeth I), Frances, Elizabeth, and Martha. From 1537 he received an annuity of £100 from the estates of the sixth earl of Northumberland, but his lands seem to have come from his marriage.

As a young nobleman Radcliffe took part in the life of the court, though he does not appear to have held office there in the 1530s. A vivid letter survives from William London to Viscount Lisle describing a mock naval battle held on the Thames, in which Radcliffe captained the 'carrack' (built on a forty-ton lighter), against the 'Turks'. As real ordnance was used, there were casualties—two gunners sustained broken legs and one heavily armoured soldier was drowned jumping from boat to boat. Otherwise Radcliffe's experience at court was ceremonial rather than military: he was knighted at the marriage of Henry VIII to Jane Seymour in 1536, was present at the baptism of Prince Edward, and acted as a pallbearer at Queen Jane's funeral. In 1539 he headed the list of Henry VIII's new bodyguard of 'spears'—the gentlemen pensioners—and

as such received Anne of Cleves, as well as being present on other state occasions in the 1540s. At the coronation joust for Edward VI he acted as a defender. He was paid £46 13s. 4d. p.a. as a gentleman pensioner, rising to 100 marks when he became the lieutenant in 1552/3. During the French campaign of 1544 he was listed as supplying five horsemen to 'the battle' and took part in the siege of Boulogne. For his services he was awarded estates in Cumberland and Westmorland but rapidly resold them, perhaps because they were too remote for his attention.

After his marriage, Radcliffe settled in his wife's home at Beddington in Surrey, where from 1539 his father-in-law was keeper of the property of Sir Nicholas Carew, executed in that year. He was returned as MP for Bedfordshire in the parliament of March 1553, apparently against the wishes of the privy council, who favoured Sir John St John, who had sat for the county at least twice before. His noble blood and position at court apparently outweighed his inexperience. His lack of a Bedfordshire residence was remedied in July 1553 when his wife's father made over to him the manor of Elstow, which was to remain his home until his death. He does not appear to have been prominent as an MP, though he was re-elected for Bedfordshire in April and November 1554, in 1555, and in 1558, and in 1559 for Maldon, Essex, where his family had influence. He attended the Commons fairly regularly (37 per cent of the days in 1554), voted against a government bill in 1555, and almost certainly took a personal interest in the private bill punishing the alleged adultery of his sister-in-law Anne, wife of the second earl of Sussex. Meanwhile his career as a gentleman pensioner had come to an end, though he remained active in local government, as a JP for Bedfordshire, where he was a member of the quorum in 1561–6, and sheriff of that county and of Buckinghamshire in 1558–9.

It is possible that Mary ensured that Radcliffe stayed away from court because of his protestant sympathies, though the evidence on this is not straightforward. He was one of the gentlemen pensioners loyal to Northumberland in 1553, but though he wept as he escorted Princess Elizabeth to the Tower in 1554, this may have owed as much to loyalty to the Tudors as to religious sentiment. Edward Underhill, the so-called 'hot gospeller', claimed that Radcliffe always favoured the gospel, but this seems to have been because Radcliffe protected him on two occasions, and the latter may have acted from *esprit de corps* (Underhill was a fellow gentleman pensioner) rather than protestantism. In the 1564 inquiry he was rated 'indifferent' in religion. Radcliffe died at Elstow on 13 August 1566 and there is certainly nothing evangelical about his funerary monument: an alabaster Renaissance monument of the Doric order, it is positioned above the altar at the east end of Elstow church and consists of kneeling effigies of himself and his wife, surmounted by their coat of arms and with those of their fathers to left and right.

CATHARINE DAVIES

Sources HoP, Commons, 1509–58, 3.169–70 · LP Henry VIII, vols. 4–21 · F. A. Blaydes, ed., The visitations of Bedfordshire, annis Domini 1566, 1582, and 1634, Harleian Society, 19 (1884) · VCH Bedfordshire ·

J. Loach, *Parliament and the crown in the reign of Mary Tudor* (1986) · J. G. Nichols, ed., *Narratives of the days of the Reformation*, CS, old ser., 77 (1859) · CPR, 1547–53, 7 vols. · W. J. Tighe, 'The gentlemen pensioners, the duke of Northumberland, and the attempted coup of July 1553', *Albion*, 19 (1987), 1–11
Archives PRO, state papers, Henry VIII, Edward VI, SP1, SP10
Likenesses funeral effigy, Elstowchurch, Bedfordshire

Radcliffe, James, styled third earl of Derwentwater (1689–1716), Jacobite army officer, was born in Arlington Street, London, on 28 June 1689, the eldest son of Edward, second earl of Derwentwater (1655–1705), and Lady Mary Tudor (1673–1726), the daughter of *Charles II and the actress Mary (Moll) Davies. He descended from a long Roman Catholic and royalist ancestry. His grandfather, Sir Francis Radcliffe, third baronet (1625–1696), was raised to the earldom of Derwentwater in March 1688, one of the few peerages created by James II. With five adult sons in 1689, he was feared as the most dangerous Jacobite in the north-east; he refused the oaths to William and Mary and was briefly imprisoned in 1691. James Radcliffe's parents parted in 1700 because the countess remained implacably opposed to becoming a Roman Catholic. In 1702, together with his younger brothers Francis (1691–1715) and Charles Radcliffe (1693–1746) [see below], James was sent to the Stuart court at St Germain at the request of Queen Mary, widow of James II, to be a companion and fellow pupil of Prince James Francis Edward, his kinsman.

His personal attachment to Prince James, his ancestry, and his religion coalesced to make Radcliffe a fervent Jacobite. He succeeded to the earldom in April 1705 and appears to have undertaken a grand tour before engaging in the disastrous Jacobite expedition of 1708; he was captured on board the French prize *Le Salisbury* but released, presumably because he was under age. In November 1709 he and his brothers obtained a licence to return to England. In 1710 he travelled throughout the north to establish contact with his kinsfolk and to inspect his numerous estates, which included agricultural properties in the border counties, collieries in Northumberland and Durham, and extensive lead-mining interests on Alston Moor. He also began to form a circle of friends, mostly Roman Catholics and Jacobites, of whom he soon became the natural leader. He was described as personable, slim, fair, and an accomplished singer and guitarist; he enjoyed field sports and was hospitable and generous to his friends and charitable towards his tenants and employees, with whom he became popular. On 10 July 1712 Derwentwater married a childhood friend, Anna Maria Webb (1692/3–1723), eldest daughter of Sir John Webb, third baronet, of Odstock, Wiltshire, and Barbara Belasyse, daughter and coheir of John, first Baron Belasyse; they had two children, John (d. 1731) and Anna Maria Barbara (1716–1760)—Anna Maria Barbara *Petre [see under Petre family]—who married Robert James *Petre, eighth Baron Petre in 1732.

Derwentwater was one of the leaders to whom the execution of the northern contribution to the rising of 1715 was entrusted, though he was not given formal command because he was a Roman Catholic. He rose with his brother Charles and seventy men but he was bitterly disappointed that, despite many promises of support, only 200 Northumbrians joined them. Derwentwater showed considerable leadership and courage in action at Preston; he deplored Thomas Forster's capitulation, although the position was hopeless, and accepted it only to save further unnecessary bloodshed. He was impeached for treason and arraigned at the bar of the House of Lords on 19 January 1716. He pleaded guilty but said in mitigation that he had had no foreknowledge of the plot; that he had risen impulsively and without any military accoutrements; that he had acted with decent restraint while in arms; and that he had surrendered at the first opportunity. He protested his future loyalty and asked that his innocent young family's predicament be considered. Lord Chancellor Cowper scorned the arguments and condemned him to death; by an act of attainder his titles and estates were forfeited. Considerable efforts to obtain a reprieve were made: the House of Lords petitioned the king; various individual peers and peeresses made representations; and the pregnant countess even approached the king in person. It was said that Derwentwater contemptuously rejected a reprieve in return for his abjuring Jacobitism and renouncing his faith. It was also rumoured that Robert Walpole was offered a bribe to save him and that an armed party was ready to rescue him.

King and government were determined on his execution, however, fearing that his Stuart blood, his wealth, and his popularity would make further rebellion a continuing threat. On the scaffold Derwentwater regretted having pleaded guilty, declared his adherence to Roman Catholicism, and said that he had never owned any other but James III as his rightful king, whom he loved as a person and whom he had desired to serve since infancy. He was beheaded on Tower Hill on 24 February 1716 and immediately became a romantic martyr figure. A display of the aurora borealis coincided with the arrival in co. Durham of the hearse bearing his body for interment in the family vault in the chapel at Dilston; the phenomenon was thereafter known locally as Derwentwater's Lights. He was in addition portrayed as a tragic hero in a number of folk-songs or ballads; some Catholics treasured his relics and miracles were attributed to his intercession, and there were those who wanted him proclaimed a confessor for the faith. In 1874 the bodies of the three earls of Derwentwater were reinterred in the Petre family vault at Thorndon, Essex. In 1721, to prevent Lady Mary Tudor securing the guardianship of John Radcliffe, the countess and her father fled with both children to Brussels; she died, aged thirty, two years later and was buried in the convent of St Monica's, Louvain, where two Radcliffe aunts were professed. John, regarded by Jacobites and other sympathizers as the rightful fourth earl of Derwentwater, always a sickly boy, remained on the continent to complete his education. He returned to England for a medical consultation in August 1731 but his condition was hopeless and he died on 31 December, aged eighteen and unmarried, and was buried at Louvain.

Charles Radcliffe, styled fifth earl of Derwentwater

(1693–1746), Jacobite conspirator, was born at Little Parndon, Essex, on 3 September 1693. Along with his elder brother James he participated in the Jacobite rising of 1715 and surrendered at Preston. He was tried on 18 May 1716, found guilty, and sentenced to death, but his execution was deferred until July, and he obtained a further stay because of a changed public mood in favour of clemency. With several other Jacobite prisoners he escaped from Newgate on 11 December and fled to Urbino, where he lived in poverty, though he was later appointed the chevalier's agent in Paris. In 1723 he made his addresses to Charlotte Livingston [**Charlotte Maria Radcliffe**, *suo jure* countess of Newburgh (1694–1755)], Jacobite sympathizer, posthumous daughter of Charles, second earl of Newburgh (*c*.1662x6–1694) and Frances Brudenell (*c*.1672–1736). At the time of Charles Radcliffe's advances she was a widow, having been married to Thomas Clifford (1687–1719), second son of Lord Clifford of Chudleigh. She refused Radcliffe on fifteen occasions and submitted only when he climbed down the chimney of her boudoir on the sixteenth; they were married at Brussels on 24 June 1724. He took a commission in Fitzjames's regiment of the French army; he was active in freemasonry and became grand master of France, but he resigned in 1738 when the church proscribed the society. He later moved to Rome, where the Jacobite court had settled and where he had inherited a house in the Lingaria from his bachelor uncle William.

The forfeiture of the Radcliffe estates was prevented initially when it was shown that they were properly entailed on Derwentwater's son, John, but if he died under age they would be forfeited because his heir, Charles Radcliffe, was debarred as a convicted rebel, although the latter and his wife visited England incognito on several occasions to protect their children's rights of succession. At John's death in 1731 the estates fell to the crown during the lifetime of Charles Radcliffe who became titular fifth earl on his nephew's death and, to prevent their recovery by his sons at his death, the act 4 Geo. II c. 21 was passed, prohibiting foreign-born issue of convicted traitors inheriting English titles or landed estates. By 8 Geo. II c. 29 the revenue of the estates, some £9000 p.a., was allocated to the completion of the Seamen's Hospital at Greenwich and for the maintenance of the seamen thereafter, although grants for the relief of Radcliffe's children were made and other entailed annuities and encumbrances were honoured. In 1745 Charles Radcliffe and his son James were taken by the British ship *Sheerness* while in the French privateer *Esperance*, bound for Scotland with arms for the Jacobites, and imprisoned in the Tower. They repudiated British jurisdiction and Charles claimed misidentification; James was freed and banished because he was a French citizen, but Charles was easily identified and condemned to death on his previous conviction for his part in the rising of 1715. He was beheaded on Tower Hill on 8 December 1746 and was buried in St Giles-in-the-Fields. His widow, who died on 4 August 1755, aged sixty-one, was buried with him. Their son James Bartholomew Radcliffe (1725–1786) became third earl of Newburgh and

was granted £30,000 from the Derwentwater estates; his son Anthony James (1757–1814), the fourth earl, died without issue and the earldom devolved upon the descendants of Thomas Clifford.   LEO GOOCH

Sources L. Gooch, *The desperate faction? The Jacobites of north-east England, 1688–1745* (1995) · GEC, *Peerage* · S. Hibbert Ware, *Lancashire memorials of the rebellion*, 2 pts in 1, Chetham Society, 5 (1845) · F. J. A. Skeet, *The life of the Right Honourable James Radcliffe, third earl of Derwentwater* (1929) · *Calendar of the Stuart papers belonging to his majesty the king, preserved at Windsor Castle*, 7 vols., HMC, 56 (1902–23) · P. Hampson, *The book of the Radclyffes* (1940) · R. Patten, *The history of the late rebellion*, 2nd edn (1717) · R. Arnold, *Northern lights* (1959) · T. Stephens, 'Radcliffe papers and letters', *Proceedings of the Society of Antiquaries of Newcastle upon Tyne*, 3rd ser., 6–8 (1913–18) · W. S. Gibson, *Dilston Hall, or, Memoirs of the Rt. Hon. James Radcliffe* (1850)
Likenesses W. Sykes, oils, 1715, Ingatestone Hall, Essex · G. Vertue, line engraving (after G. Kneller), BM, NPG · engraving (after G. Kneller), repro. in Gooch, *Desperate faction*
Wealth at death £93,000 capital value, incl. £6372 p.a.: Stephens, 'Radcliffe papers and letters'

Radcliffe, John. *See* Ratcliffe, John, sixth Baron Fitzwalter (1452–1496).

Radcliffe, John (*bap.* 1650, *d.* 1714), physician and philanthropist, was born in Wakefield, Yorkshire, the son of George Radcliffe, governor of the Wakefield house of correction (1647–61) and a man of strong republican principles, and Sarah, daughter of Mr Louder, a prosperous Wakefield resident. He was baptized at All Saints, Wakefield, on 1 May 1650. Radcliffe claimed that he was a kinsman of the Catholic earl of Derwentwater. As Radcliffe's father had numerous children he initially intended that his son pursue trade or agriculture; however, members of the neighbouring gentry and clergy noticed John's cleverness and persuaded the father to send him to the local grammar school, where he proved an apt pupil. He matriculated at University College, Oxford, on 23 March 1666 as a batteler, or exhibitioner, on the freestone foundation, and in 1667 was made senior scholar on account of his success in the logic school. He graduated BA on 26 October 1669 and became a fellow (until 1677) of Lincoln College as no vacant fellowship was available in University College. He then pursued courses in botany, chemistry, and anatomy, receiving an MA with 'uncommon applause' (*Biographia Britannica*) on 7 June 1672. During his time at Lincoln he was supported in part by his mother, his father having died. He then enrolled for degrees in physic and received his BM on 1 July 1675, after which he promptly began a medical practice from his college rooms. He possessed few books and disparaged those who relied on old medical treatises, preferring instead contemporary texts, particularly those of Thomas Willis, then England's most influential medical authority. When visited in his rooms as a medical student by Ralph Bathurst, master of Trinity College and a former experimental collaborator of William Harvey and Willis, who asked Radcliffe the location of his study, he supposedly pointed to a few vials, a skeleton, and a herbal. University contemporaries valued his wit and vitality rather than his scholarship, observing that he had little interest in contemplative pursuits.

Throughout his career Radcliffe expressed himself with

John Radcliffe (*bap.* 1650, *d.* 1714), by Sir Godfrey Kneller, *c.*1710–12

a candour that at times verged on rudeness. As a bachelor of medicine he offended James Lydall, an eminent Oxford practitioner (and early colleague of Willis), as well as John Luffe, later regius professor of physic, and two apothecaries. None the less, Radcliffe's early success with patients soon persuaded the apothecaries to keep his prescriptions in their files. Radcliffe gained a reputation early on for success in treating smallpox, which was epidemic in Oxfordshire in the late 1670s. In contrast to most other practitioners, who used external heat in their treatment, Radcliffe adopted Sydenham's 'cooling treatment' for the disease, which was then unorthodox. Rapid recovery of some smallpox patients who Radcliffe had treated by this means enhanced his reputation. More significant, however, was his success with Lady Spencer, a well-connected but chronically ill woman then living near Oxford at Yarnton. She had been under Dr Lydall's and Mr Musgrave's care with little success and had not been ambulatory for years when she first saw Radcliffe. However she started walking within three weeks of his first consultation, and her recommendation of Radcliffe to her numerous noble relatives established him as a pre-eminent local practitioner within two years of his taking the bachelor's degree. He graduated DM on 5 July 1682 as a 'grand compounder', a designation that referred to his accumulation of substantial wealth. In 1684 he moved to Bow Street, Covent Garden, London, where he soon established a lucrative practice, earning, his apothecary Francis Dandridge said, 20 guineas a day within his first year. His timing was propitious, for the court reputation of Richard Lower,

a well-known Covent Garden physician who had succeeded to Willis's practice upon the latter's death in 1675, was declining owing to his outspoken support of whig principles. In 1686, two years after arriving in London, Radcliffe succeeded in being appointed principal physician to James II's daughter, Princess Anne of Denmark. He became a fellow of the Royal College of Physicians on 12 April 1687, where he opposed physician, poet, and whig notable Samuel Garth in his successful campaign to have the college sponsor the first English dispensary for the deserving poor.

Radcliffe's eighteenth-century biographers noted that his appealing and often witty conversation attracted patients as much as his clinical skill. A frequenter of fashionable coffee houses, Radcliffe was known to love wine. At times his wit could be coarse. For example, a hypochondriacal nobleman who had befriended Radcliffe sent him repeated requests for a consultation, only to receive the reply eventually that 'his Lordship did not know when he was well, for he was in perfect health, if he would but think himself so'. Finally, though, Radcliffe visited the man, who told him he had a 'strange singing' in his head. 'If it be so', Radcliffe reportedly replied, 'I can prescribe to your Lordship no other remedy than that of swiping your a— with a ballad', a response that 'perfectly cured his Lordship's malady' (*Biographia Britannica*, 3453). At other times Radcliffe's intended jests crossed the boundary of acceptable levity. Having successfully treated William III for symptoms of dropsy, including leg swelling, in 1697, Radcliffe was called by the king for advice on a recurrence of the illness in 1699. Apparently the monarch had not followed Radcliffe's earlier advice for temperance, and the physician found him with an emaciated body but swollen lower legs. When William III asked him his opinion of the legs Radcliffe reportedly replied: 'Why truly, I would not have your magesty's two legs for your three kingdoms', a jest that terminated his presence at William's court (*Biographia Britannica*). However, despite his occasional conversational blunders with social superiors Radcliffe, who was 'a confirmed Jacobite and violent tory' (Sakula, 256), was capable of political caution. When James II's daughter and son-in-law, Princess Anne and Prince George of Denmark, abandoned her father's cause and joined the prince of Orange (later William III) in Nottingham in 1688, Radcliffe was encouraged by the bishop of London to visit her there as she was in an advanced stage of pregnancy. Radcliffe demurred, citing a need to attend his critically ill patients in London. However, his contemporary biographer, William Pittis, attributed this behaviour to Radcliffe's reluctance to declare himself at a politically unstable moment. Radcliffe was elected MP for Bramber in Sussex and sat for the borough until the dissolution in 1695.

Even though William III appointed his countryman, Bidloo, as his chief physician, Radcliffe's court practice continued to prosper after the departure of James II. When two of William's foreign attendants, William Bentinck, afterwards earl of Portland, and William Zulestein, earl of Rochford, became seriously ill and recovered after Radcliffe's ministrations, William rewarded him with 500 guineas and an appointment as one of his physicians at a salary of £200 p.a. Aware that William's tenure was new and, perhaps, not secure, Radcliffe declined the appointment. None the less he continued to be called to court and stated that he received £600 per year for the period 1688–99 from the king alone. In 1691 William, duke of Gloucester, the two-year-old son and heir of Princess Anne and Prince George, experienced 'fainting fits' (seizures), a malady that had proved fatal to some of their other children. Radcliffe agreed to care for him provided that Princess Anne and her sister, Queen Mary, rely on him exclusively for medical advice. The child recovered and did not experience additional fits, an outcome that brought Radcliffe a reward of 1000 guineas. In 1695 William III directed Radcliffe to attend the earl of Albemarle, one of the king's favourite commanders, who had then been ill on the continent for two months with fever. When the patient recovered within a week the king gave Radcliffe £1200 and the offer of a baronetcy, while Albemarle gave him 400 guineas and a diamond ring. (Radcliffe declined the title.) Although he experienced some investment losses, notably £5000 on a failed East Indies shipping venture in 1692, Radcliffe calculated his remaining wealth in 1692 at £30,000 and at £80,000 in 1707. He acquired estates in Buckinghamshire, Yorkshire, and Northamptonshire, and had paintings by Rembrandt and Rubens in his house in Bloomsbury Square, London.

Part of Radcliffe's medical reputation rested on his ability to make accurate prognoses, which he often delivered bluntly. When Queen Mary developed smallpox in December 1694 the privy council called for Radcliffe. Reviewing her treatment regime before seeing her Radcliffe pronounced her 'a dead woman', saying that it was impossible to save her because the treatments she had received from others assured her demise. She died soon after. Late in 1697 he told William III that he would live a maximum of four more years regardless of his medical regime. William died in 1702. In 1699 the duke of Gloucester became ill with what his physicians, Edward Hannes and Bidloo, judged to be smallpox. When the youth's condition worsened Radcliffe was called. He despaired of the duke's recovery and accurately predicted the time of his death to the hour, but not before indulging in his custom of disparaging the skill of the other physicians. Radcliffe's impolitic manner lost him a position as Princess Anne's principal physician. Reportedly he accepted a summons to see her in 1695 but then failed to appear, justifying his behaviour by saying that her illness was 'nothing but the vapours, and that she was in as good a state of health as any woman breathing, could she but give into the belief of it'. A contemporary said he did not appear because he 'was too addicted to the bottle' (*Biographia Britannica*, 3457). None the less, when Anne became queen and seemed critically ill her physicians consulted secretly with Radcliffe and used his prescriptions, for which he was paid handsomely by the government.

A lifelong bachelor, Radcliffe acknowledged one marriage proposal. It failed, however, for though the woman brought a dowry of £15,000 and the balance of her parents' estate on their deaths, she was pregnant by a family bookkeeper. In breaking the engagement Radcliffe's letter to her father of 19 May 1693 expresses his characteristic sauciness:

> The hounour of being ally'd to so good and wealthy a person as Mr. S—d has push'd me upon a discovery that may be fatal to your quiet, and your daughter's reputation, if not timely prevented. Mrs. Mary is a very deserving gentlewoman, but you must pardon me, if I think her by no means fit to be my wife, since she is another man's already, or ought to be. In a word, she is … actually quick with child, which makes it necessary that she be disposed of to him that has the best claim to her affections. … Hanging and marrying, I find, go by destiny; and I might have been guilty of the first, had I not so narrowly escaped the last. (*Biographia Britannica*, 3456)

At the age of fifty-nine Radcliffe became enamoured of a patient, Miss Tempest, on whose account he refurbished his coach and servants' liveries. Addison, writing under the name Aesculapius, ridiculed him for this in the *Tatler* of 21 and 28 July, and 13 September 1709.

In 1713 Radcliffe was elected MP for Buckingham and began recommending the physician Richard Mead to his patients. In the same year he purchased a mansion at Carshalton, Surrey, which later became St Philomena's Convent School. Radcliffe died in semi-disgrace, his final three months shadowed by a recurrence of contentious behaviour toward his most venerable royal patient, Queen Anne, who died on 31 July 1714. During her final hours one of her intimates, Lady Masham, sent for Radcliffe. Suffering from a severe episode of gout and learning beforehand from Mead that the queen's case was hopeless, Radcliffe declined to attend. Also, he said that in view of the queen's antipathy to him his presence might worsen her final moments, adding later in a letter that he would have come if the request had come from the proper authorities. Subsequently an old friend, Sir John Pakington MP, moved that Radcliffe be censured by the House of Commons for his failure to serve the queen, but the matter dropped. Radcliffe suffered an apoplexy while at church and died at Carshalton on 1 November 1714, having accurately predicted the date of his demise in a letter of 15 October 1714. His body lay in state at Carshalton until the 27th, and was then moved to Oxford, where it was buried on 3 December in St Mary's Church.

Although Radcliffe described himself as avaricious and was known to be a slow payer of debts and not above cadging drinks, he was also known for his generosity to those in need, particularly members of the clergy. His will, dated 13 September 1714, provided substantial annuities to his sisters and other relatives. He left the bulk of his estate to University College in trust for building and operating a library (completed 1747), enlargement of college buildings, two medical travelling fellowships, and faculty annuities. Executors of additional trusts used the funds to build the Radcliffe Infirmary, the Radcliffe Observatory, and the Lunatic Asylum, Oxford. Additional substantial contributions were made to the building of the Royal College of Physicians (in Pall Mall East), and St John's Church,

Wakefield. He also bequeathed £500 a year to St Bartholomew's Hospital, London. In 1811 it was decided that the Radcliffe Camera should be limited to books on medicine and natural science. A larger library was eventually needed, and in 1901 the Radcliffe Science Library was opened and extended in 1934 with the aid of a Rockefeller grant. In 1715 Jean Gagnier published an elegy on Radcliffe's death, *Exequiae clarissimo viro Johanni Radcliffe MD* (1715). A gold headed cane, said to have been Radcliffe's, was given to the Royal College of Physicians by Mrs Baillie.

John Radcliffe (1690–1729), physician, seems to have been no relative of his namesake. He was the son of John Radcliffe of London, gentleman, and his wife, Ann, and was born on 10 May 1690; he was admitted to Merchant Taylors' School in 1703. He matriculated at St John's College, Oxford, on 17 October 1707, and became BA on 2 June 1711, MA on 23 April 1714, and DM on 30 June 1721. On 25 June 1724 he was chosen a fellow of the Royal College of Physicians; he was physician to St Bartholomew's Hospital. He died on 16 August 1729.

ROBERT L. MARTENSEN

Sources W. Pittis, *Some memoirs of the life of John Radcliffe* (1715) · A. Kippis and others, eds., *Biographia Britannica, or, The lives of the most eminent persons who have flourished in Great Britain and Ireland*, 2nd edn, 5 vols. (1778–93) · Munk, *Roll* · Wood, *Ath. Oxon.*, new edn · [W. MacMichael and others], *Lives of British physicians* (1830) · *DNB* · N. Moore, *The physician in English history* (1913) · A. Sakula, 'Dr John Radcliffe, court physician, and the death of Queen Anne', *Journal of the Royal College of Physicians of London*, 19 (1985), 255–60 · K. Dewhurst, 'Dr John Radcliffe', *Oxford medicine: essays on the evolution of the Oxford Clinical School to commemorate the bicentary [sic] of the Radcliffe Infirmary*, ed. K. Dewhurst [1970], 32–9 · *Hist. U. Oxf.* 5: *18th-cent. Oxf.* · *IGI* · Munk, *Roll*, 2.86 [John Radcliffe (1690–1729)] · Foster, *Alum. Oxon.*

Archives Bodl. Oxf., Radcliffe Science Library, papers | Badminton House, Gloucestershire, papers of Lord Charles Somerset as his trustee

Likenesses G. Kneller, oils, *c.*1710–1712, Radcliffe Camera, Oxford [*see illus.*] · F. Bird, statue, *c.*1719, University College, Oxford · G. Kneller, oils, second version, RCP Lond. · J. M. Rysbrack, statue, Radcliffe Camera, Oxford · statue, University College, Oxford

Wealth at death £129,822—personal estate and real estate; excl. debts owing from the estate £29,021, legacies, incl. £5000 to University College, plus further £600 p.a.; funeral charges and mourning £13,042: Bodl. Oxf. MS DD Radcl. c.65, 'Abstract of the General Acct to 1718 St Mich to be pass'd 1720 in Augst'

Radcliffe, John (1690–1729). *See under* Radcliffe, John (*bap.* 1650, *d.* 1714).

Radcliffe, John Netten (1826–1884), epidemiologist and public health activist, the son of Charles Radcliffe, Wesleyan minister, and younger brother of Charles Bland *Radcliffe (1822–1889), was born in Yorkshire on 20 April 1826. Educated at the Leeds school of medicine, he gained a diploma and immediately undertook service in the Crimea as a surgeon attached to the headquarters of Omar Pasha. This proved a decisive experience. Although after returning from the war he was appointed medical superintendent of the Hospital for the Paralysed and Epileptic in Queen Square, London, Radcliffe had already developed an intense interest in 'exotic' diseases. Each of the classic research papers and reports that he wrote between the early 1860s and the late 1870s described the manner in which infections are spread from their 'natural' habitats to environments in which they sustain an 'artificial' and hence potentially eradicable existence.

Elected to membership of the Epidemiological Society of London at the age of twenty-four, Radcliffe served as honorary secretary from 1862 to 1871 and president from 1875 to 1877. Here he met John Simon, who was at that time eager to recruit young medical men and epidemiologists to undertake studies for the medical office of the privy council. Radcliffe was appointed a public health inspector in 1869 and assistant medical officer at the Local Government Board in 1871. On 5 July 1870, at the mature age of forty-four, he married Anne Martha Billing, daughter of John Turner Billing, a London solicitor; they had three sons and four daughters. Radcliffe shunned major administrative responsibilities, preferring to concentrate on the temporal and spatial minutiae of the disease process. Simon described him as a perfectionist who immersed himself in the 'time, place and dynamics of … epidemic and endemic disease', and displayed 'the familiar knowledge which a Charing-cross policeman is supposed to have of the ominibuses which pass his beat'. A reticent man, Radcliffe possessed 'a somewhat unpunctuated and unaccentuated mode of speech' and a 'frequent preference for semi-sarcastic (though never ill intended) forms of expression' (*Lancet*, 562–3). Overwork was said to have played a role in triggering the terminal neurological illness which forced him to resign from the Local Government Board in 1879.

Adding empirical substantiation to the theoretical insights associated with the discoveries of John Snow and William Budd, Radcliffe's research into cholera, typhoid, water supply, and the disposal of sewage convinced large numbers of public health activists during the 1860s and 1870s that infection was unlikely to be exclusively propagated by a foul atmosphere, climatic variation, or the condition of the soil. His work on the diffusion of cholera in the Mediterranean region in 1865 was complemented by a scathing attack on the East London River Company, in 'On cholera in London' (1867), which, together with an equally damning investigation by William Farr and Edward Frankland, confirmed that failure to maintain consistent waterworks procedures had led to traumatic mortality from the pandemic infection in the poorest districts of the capital. Three years later Radcliffe returned to the fray and argued, in 'On the turbidity of water' (1870), that the private London water companies had failed to regulate themselves or conform to minimal safety requirements. Insisting that choice of raw river water and the state of filtering equipment must now be subject to rigorous scientific control, Radcliffe canvassed public ownership of London's water supply system.

Radcliffe was equally radical in his attitude towards the monitoring of milk. In 1873, in collaboration with W. H. Power, he produced a masterly analysis of a large-scale outbreak of enteric fever in Marylebone. Noting that incidence and mortality were heavily concentrated among the well-to-do, Radcliffe and Power excluded both miasmatic processes and the pollution of local water supplies. Discovering that 'nursery milk' had been 'collected from three or four cows selected and set apart from the general herd' (*Parl. papers*, 1874, 31), the two epidemiologists located the origins of the outbreak deep in the Buckinghamshire countryside, and thereby drew public attention in their 'Report on an outbreak of enteric fever' (1874) to the central role played by tainted water in small and remote dairies.

Returning in the same year to an earlier preoccupation, Radcliffe visited nearly fifty communities to evaluate the rival claims of the midden, pail, water, earth, and charcoal systems of excrement disposal. Rejecting Edwin Chadwick's obsession with the water closet, Radcliffe nevertheless urged public authorities to ensure that the appliance should be made as readily available to the working as to the middle classes. As his health began to fail, Radcliffe also worked long and hard on papers on hospital hygiene and measures to be taken to prevent any possibility of a recrudescence of bubonic plague in north-western Europe.

Together with William Farr and Edward Frankland, Radcliffe successfully combined the roles of disinterested scientist and social critic. Convinced of the frailty of explanations of disease behaviour which depended on non-quantifiable variations in atmospheric and meteorological conditions, he was converted early in his career to the idea that individual infections were transmitted by specific and potentially detectable 'germs'. However, the precise chemical and, or, biological components of these entities, and their mode of reproduction in the environment, defied explanation. Thus Radcliffe drew on an increasingly reliable body of data collected by local medical officers of health and sought through exclusion and controlled statistical observation to infer the presence of the germs associated with cholera, typhoid, and gastroenteritis. Radcliffe and William Farr's ideal—a standardized procedure to predict future outbreaks of disease through detailed knowledge of previous episodes—remained theoretically and empirically unattainable. But during the interregnum which separated the supremacy of the atmospheric theory and the application of new bacteriological insights in the 1880s and 1890s, Radcliffe's methodology was central to a redefinition of epidemiological practice and the environmental processes with which it was concerned.

Radcliffe died of 'chronic cerebritis' on 11 September 1884 at 43 Fitzroy Road, London, and was buried in Highgate cemetery.   BILL LUCKIN

Sources R. Lambert, *Sir John Simon, 1816–1904, and English social administration* (1963) · B. Luckin, *Pollution and control: a social history of the Thames in the nineteenth century* (1986) · *The Lancet* (27 Sept 1884), 562–3 · *BMJ* (20 Sept 1884), 588 · m. cert. · d. cert. · *DNB*
Archives RIBA BAL, MS report (with P. Gordon Smith) on housing in Yorkshire
Likenesses G. Jerrard, photograph, 1881, Wellcome L.

Radcliffe, Margaret [*name in religion* Margaret Paul] (1582x5–1654), abbess, was the second daughter of Sir

Francis Radcliffe (1563–1622) of Dilston, Northumberland, and Derwentwater, Cumberland, and his wife, Isabel, daughter of Sir Ralph Grey of Chillingham, Northumberland. She was the first of Sir Francis's four daughters to enter the English Poor Clare convent at Gravelines in the Spanish Netherlands, making her religious profession on 3 July 1612 aged, according to one source, twenty-seven, and taking the name Margaret Paul. Her sister Elizabeth was professed in 1617, with Dorothy and Ann taking their vows in 1619.

In 1622 Margaret was sent to assist as abbess at a newly established English cloister in Brussels, accompanied by her sister Elizabeth as her deputy, the vicaress. During this secondment Margaret presided over the profession of twenty-three nuns and oversaw the implementation of the monastery's governmental and spiritual structures. The Brussels convent followed a different, and less rigorous, Franciscan rule (that of the third order of St Francis) to her own Poor Clare training. Margaret nevertheless established a strict observance of the religious life there, which she later worried might have proven 'more strickt then your Rule and constitutions doe require' (Franciscan MS 16, fol. 5). However, the Brussels nuns were so successfully grounded in their order's traditions that within four years it was deemed possible for one of them to assume sole governance, and Margaret and Elizabeth returned to Gravelines. The esteem with which the Radcliffe sisters were held by the Franciscan nuns can be seen in continued correspondence between Margaret and her former charges when years later she was asked for advice about the duties of the vicaress. Moreover, the English translation of the life of Franciscan visionary Joan of the Cross was dedicated to them in 1625 by Francis Bell, the convent's confessor.

Margaret's return to Gravelines in September 1626 was mired in controversy. Abbess Elizabeth (Sister Clare Mary Ann) Tyldesley was deposed by a Franciscan official who appointed Margaret in her place, causing considerable dissension. A week later part of the convent burnt to the ground in a devastating fire, attributed by the traumatized nuns to divine providence. An inquiry into the monastery's troubles reinstated the former abbess, and in January 1627 Margaret Radcliffe and her supporters were sent to a Poor Clare house in Dunkirk. However, the fracas at Gravelines continued until 1629 when twenty-four nuns, novices, and lay sisters, including those who had gone to Dunkirk, founded a separate cloister at Aire in Artois, with Margaret as abbess. As in many other English convents the Gravelines conflict was about clerical jurisdiction, with a minority favouring the continuing control of the English Franciscan fathers and the majority desiring to be placed under the authority of the bishop, which would allow greater spiritual diversity, namely access to Jesuit confessors. Margaret apparently led the pro-Franciscan faction. Significantly her sisters all joined the Aire filiation, suggesting a family adherence to the order, although subsequent generations joined Benedictine and Augustinian cloisters.

Margaret Radcliffe was abbess at Aire for seven years.

She died there on 26 July or in August 1654 aged seventy-one according to two sources, and was buried there. Her modest obituary noted that she had governed with 'prudence, charitye, and Regular observance [of the Poor Clare rule]' (MS Aire Register). Significantly a notice of her death at Gravelines did not mention her former positions of authority, rather commending her for 'the well Spending of her time, and in gitting of humble work' ('Registers', 40). Margaret Radcliffe is typical of the many post-Reformation English abbesses who achieved the respect of their contemporaries but whose achievements have been lost in the public memory as a consequence of strict monastic enclosure, their geographic isolation from England, and their gender.

CLAIRE WALKER

Sources W. M. Hunnybun, 'Registers of the English Poor Clare Nuns at Gravelines … 1608–1837', *Miscellanea, IX*, Catholic RS, 14 (1914), 25–173, esp. 26–7, 39–40, 46–7, 50–51 · MS Gravelines Chronicles, St Clare's Abbey, Darlington, fols. 31, 33, 37, 144–63 · MS Aire Register, St Clare's Abbey, Darlington [unfoliated] · R. Trappes-Lomax, ed., *The English Franciscan nuns, 1619–1821, and the Friars Minor of the same province, 1618–1761*, Catholic RS, 24 (1922), 9, 12–14, 125–30 · A. Hamilton, ed., *The chronicle of the English Augustinian canonesses regular of the Lateran at St. Monica's in Louvain*, 2: 1625–44 (1906), 203–5, pedigree · P. Guilday, *The English Catholic refugees on the continent, 1558–1795* (1914), 297–300, 302–3 · 'Account of the duties of the vicaress by Rev. M. Margaret Paul Radcliffe', Poor Clare Convent, Arundel, Franciscan MS 16 Miscellanea, vol. 1, fol. 5 · Anthony of Aca, *Historie, life and miracles extasies and revelations of the blessed virgin, sister Joane of the Crosse of the third order of our holy father S. Francis*, trans. F. Bell (St Omer, 1625), dedication

Archives Poor Clare Community, Arundel, West Sussex, Franciscan MSS · St Clare's Abbey, Darlington, Gravelines and Aire MSS

Radcliffe, Mary Ann (*b. c.*1746, *d.* in or after **1810**), writer, was the only child and heir of an Anglican retired merchant, already past seventy years old when she was born, and his thirty-year-old Roman Catholic wife. Her father, whose forename was James, died when she was two. Mary was educated at the Bar Convent in York, after which she was courted, aged fourteen, by the 35-year-old Joseph Radcliffe: 'poor, little me! … like a bird in a cage, I fluttered to be at liberty' (Radcliffe, 16). She eloped while visiting London, 'And from these transactions … have I to date the area of my misfortunes' (ibid., 30). She and Radcliffe married in 1761, and she bore the first of her eight children at fifteen; the last two died young.

After Radcliffe's fortune was withheld by law and her husband's business ventures in London and elsewhere failed, she ran a coffee house, took in lodgers, and chaperoned a pregnant unmarried young lady. Her last spell of living with her husband ended when she sought work as a governess in London. Other jobs included sewing, shopkeeping, and housekeeping from 1781 to 1783 for Mary Stewart, countess of Traquair, an old school friend at whose home Radcliffe met the liberal Catholic theologian and translator of the Bible Alexander Geddes.

Radcliffe's *Memoirs* (1810) mentions obliquely the writing of fiction ('was I soaring into the airy regions of fiction, I would quickly change the theme'), but does not mention any of the novels ascribed to her. Although she wanted to remain anonymous, her publisher set her name to her polemic *The Female Advocate* (1799), out of 'a view to extend

the sale, from the same name at that period standing high amongst the novel readers' (ibid., 387). Sales strategy and the fame of Ann Radcliffe probably account for other ascriptions and half-ascriptions to Mary Ann Radcliffe, first made in 1802 though some refer to 1790. *Radcliffe's New Novelist's Pocket Magazine* published its two numbers as hers in 1802 (giving her current address correctly); the second number credits her with *The Secret Oath*, also 1802, a chapbook. The same year a Minerva Press catalogue listed 'Mrs. Radcliffe' as author of *The Fate of Velina de Guidova* (1790), an epistolary novel; in 1814 another of its catalogues listed 'Mrs. Ann Radcliffe' as author of *Radzivil, a Romance*, 'translated from the Russian of the celebrated M. Wocklow' (1790), whose text speaks of its author, translator (a 'young gentleman'), and editor–reviser as all male. In 1809 J. F. Hughes published *Manfroné, or, The One-Handed Monk* as by 'Mary Anne Radcliffe', and switched authorship of *The Mysterious Baron* (1808) to her from Eliza Ratcliffe. *Manfroné*, reprinted in 1819, 1825, 1839, [1878], and 1971 as either hers or Ann Radcliffe's, was claimed in a letter to the Royal Literary Fund by Louisa Theresa Bellenden Ker. An extremely gory, high-flown Gothic novel, it is nothing like *Velina* or *Radzivil*, and none of these novels resembles Mary Ann Radcliffe's known work.

If not a novelist, Radcliffe remains an unusual writer. *The Female Advocate, or, An Attempt to Recover the Rights of Women from Male Usurpation* (1799) which, despite advice from Arthur Murphy, led to 'an unlucky circumstance … between the bookseller [Vernor and Hood] and myself' (Radcliffe, 387), discusses the shrinking female job market and the snare of prostitution; its feeling but down-to-earth tone reflects harsh experience: 'All women possess not the Amazonian spirit of a Wolstonecraft; but, indeed, unremitted oppression is sometimes a sufficient apology for their throwing off the gentle garb of a female' (ibid., 399). The *Critical Review* (December 1799) was unwarrantably hostile. Radcliffe's *Memoirs … in Familiar Letters to her Female Friend* (which reprints her earlier book) was begun at Portobello near Edinburgh in 1807, finished in dire poverty after five years housebound with rheumatism, and published by subscription in 1810.

ISOBEL GRUNDY

Sources University of York, Bar Convent MSS · *Critical Review*, [new ser.], 27 (1799) · D. A. McLeod, 'The Minerva Press', PhD diss., University of Alberta, 1997 · London, Royal Literary Fund MSS · letters, BL, 4/33418, 9, 11 · letters, Edinburgh, Scottish Catholic Archives · Lady Traquair's diary, Traquair House, Peebles · *Memoirs of Mrs. Mary Ann Radcliffe* (1810) · M. Summers, *A Gothic bibliography* (1940) · D. Blakey, *The Minerva Press, 1790–1820* (1939) · G. Luria, 'Introduction', in M. A. Radcliffe, *The female advocate*, facs. edn (1974) · R. C. Fuller, *Alexander Geddes, 1737–1802: a pioneer of biblical criticism* (1984)

Archives Scottish Catholic Archives, Edinburgh, letters | University of York, Bar Convent MSS

Radcliffe, Nicholas (*d.* **1396×1401**), prior of Wymondham and theologian, entered St Albans Abbey in the 1350s and studied at Gloucester College, Oxford, from *c.*1360. A contemporary of Wyclif in the theology faculty, he was a bachelor of theology by 1365, and incepted as doctor in

1368. In the same year he was appointed prior of Wymondham, a cell of St Albans, and shortly afterwards was drawn into a dispute with Henry Despenser, bishop of Norwich (d. 1406), over the collection of a clerical subsidy. He returned to St Albans in 1380, and in 1382 played a leading role in the council at Blackfriars that secured a condemnation of Wyclif's works. At the same time he was credited with persuading a notorious Wycliffite, John Aston, to renounce his errors. He served as archdeacon of the abbey at least until the death of Abbot Thomas De la Mare in 1396, and may for a short time have become prior. He was appointed diffinitor (an officer responsible for pronouncing upon issues of discipline) for the provincial chapter for the year 1393–4.

As a theologian Radcliffe was distinguished for his opposition to the work of John Wyclif (d. 1384). His contemporary at the abbey, Thomas Walsingham, included his name in a list of illustrious monks, and recalled that he had 'written many books against the opinions of the heretic' (Riley, 2.305). He was the author of a sequence of six dialogues with the Carmelite theologian Peter Stokes (d. 1399): *De immortalitate primi hominis*, *De dominio naturali*, *De obedienciali dominio*, *De dominio regali et judiciali*, *De potestate Petri apostoli successorum*, *De eodem argumento*. (BL, Royal MS 6 D.x, fols. 1–283r). These were probably written at the request of the abbot, Thomas De la Mare, and not only tackle many of the theological questions raised by Wyclif but also reflect De la Mare's concern to counter Lollardy in the local community. Radcliffe also wrote a separate treatise *De viatico salutari animae*, two *quaestiones*, *De voto religionis*, and *De imaginum cultu*, and an *Invectio contra errores Wyclif*, all of which were known outside St Albans. Several of his academic exercises dating from his time as a bachelor respondent, including some disputations with the celebrated Benedictine master, later cardinal, Adam Easton (d. 1397), also survive in fragments recorded in the lecture notes of a monk of Worcester. Radcliffe was still alive when John Moot was elected abbot in 1396, but was dead by the time of the election of William Heyworth in 1401. At his death he left 20 marks for the completion of the private dormitory, and this benefaction, together with a record of his achievements and a portrait, was inserted in the abbey's book of benefactors. JAMES G. CLARK

Sources *Gesta abbatum monasterii Sancti Albani, a Thoma Walsingham*, ed. H. T. Riley, 3 vols., pt 4 of *Chronica monasterii S. Albani*, Rolls Series, 28 (1867–9), vol. 3, pp. 282–3, 425–8 • [T. Netter], *Fasciculi zizaniorum magistri Johannis Wyclif cum tritico*, ed. W. W. Shirley, Rolls Series, 5 (1858) • H. T. Riley, ed., *Registra quorundam abbatum monasterii S. Albani*, 2, Rolls Series, 28/6 (1873), 305 • Bale, *Index*, 307 • Worcester Cathedral Chapter Library, MS F 65, fols. 1v; 8v; 20v • CUL, MS Ee.4.20 • W. A. Pantin, ed., *Documents illustrating the activities of ... the English black monks, 1215–1540*, 3 vols., CS, 3rd ser., 45, 47, 54 (1931–7), vol. 2, p. 94 • BL, Royal MS, 6 D.x, fols. 1–283r • S. L. Forte, 'Some Oxford schoolmen of the middle of the fourteenth century with special reference to Worcester Cathedral MS F65', 2 vols., BLitt diss., U. Oxf., 1947, 54–7
Archives BL, MS Harley 635 • BL, Royal MSS 6 D.x, 10 D.x • Worcester Cathedral, MS F 65
Likenesses portrait, BL, Cotton Nero MS D vii (*Liber Benefactorum*, fol. 85r

Radcliffe, Ralph (1518/19–1559), schoolmaster and playwright, is of uncertain origins. The Radcliffe monument in St Mary's Church, Hitchin, Hertfordshire, declares that in the reign of Henry VIII Ralph 'came out of Lancashire where his Ancestours were antiently seated one of whom was Richard Radcliffe of Radcliffe Tower'. According to Hine's *Worthies*, he was descended from a younger brother branch of this noble Lancashire stock, and his father was Thomas Radcliffe of Ordsall. He was a poor but talented scholar, and by 1533 was installed in the Carmelite house in Cambridge, being drawn to Thomas Cromwell's notice as 'an excellent scholar in Greek and Latin' suitable for the post of grammar master at Jesus College. As this letter of recommendation reveals, he was considered particularly worthy because of the accomplished polemical works he had penned 'against our school men in Cambridge' (*LP Henry VIII*, addenda, 1/2, no. 624). Radcliffe secured the post, and financed his studies both through his teaching at Jesus, and through tutoring the children of the marquess of Dorset. He graduated BA at Cambridge in 1535–6, and MA in 1538–9, having sparked controversy there by challenging John Cheke's pronunciation of Greek.

Radcliffe's radical protestant credentials meant that, following the dissolution of the monasteries, he was granted permission to establish a school for boys in the dismantled Carmelite priory at Hitchin where he took up residence about 1539. He married Elizabeth Marshall of Mitcham, and they had four children: Ralph, Jeremy, Edward, and Elizabeth. The eldest, Ralph, was educated by Radcliffe's close friend Roger Ascham.

Radcliffe became a celebrity in Hitchin and beyond largely because of the plays that he wrote for his pupils to perform, at least once a year, for public audiences on a stage erected in the lower part of the priory. Along with noted reformers like John Bale and John Foxe, he clearly believed in the important role of the popular stage in the war against the Roman Catholic 'Antichrist'. Besides tragedies and comedies in Latin and English, Radcliffe wrote dramatic dialogues in the vernacular. Three of these survive, confirming his flair for penning entertaining polemics. The dialogues are bound together in a presentation volume (c.1540) for Henry VIII, and the contents are prefaced as:

> iii dialogues: the firste concernyng a governance of the Chyrche (the Interspekers ... be these. The Chyrche. The two bysshoppes. The iii dyssemblars. The foole. The harlotte, and the Ryche man). The seconde is bytwen the power [poor] man, and fortune. The thirde, bytwen deth, and the goer by the waye. (*Second Report*, HMC, 85)

None of Radcliffe's other works has survived, and what is known of his theatre and library is mostly reliant on Bale's favourable account of his stay at Hitchin School. Bale waxed enthusiastic about the 'theatrum ... longe pulcherrimum' which the schoolmaster had constructed there (Bale, *Cat.*, 700). In the extensive library Bale found pedagogical and grammar treatises as well as Radcliffe's plays, which he admired, urging Radcliffe to publish. Among Radcliffe's plays as listed by Bale are *De patientia*

Griseldis, *De Melibaeo Chauceriano*, *De Sodomae incendio*, *De Jo.Hussi damnatione*, and *De Judith fortitudine*.

By 1553 the school had so flourished that Radcliffe was in a position to purchase the priory estate. A portrait (*c*.1559) of this frank and genial-looking schoolmaster clutching a scroll of 'letters' hung in Hitchin Priory well into the twentieth century; a reproduction of it can be found in Hine's *Worthies*. When Radcliffe made his will in 1558 he described himself as 'in hoole mynde … but sick in body'; he died the next year, aged forty, and was buried in St Mary's Church, Hitchin.   MARGARET HEALY

Sources R. Radcliffe, 'Three dramatic dialogues', *c*.1540, NL Wales, Ser. II.10. Brogyntyn MS 24 · *First report*, HMC, 1/1 (1870); repr. (1874) · *Second report*, HMC, 1/2 (1871); repr. (1874) · *LP Henry VIII*, addenda 1/2, p. 624 · will, Herts. ALS, D/ERF2 · R. L. Hine, *Hitchin worthies: four centuries of English life* (1932) · Bale, *Cat.* · J. E. Cussans, *History of Hertfordshire*, 1 (1870) · Emden, *Oxf.*, vol. 4 · Radcliffe family monument inscription, St Mary's Church, Hitchin, Hertfordshire · Bale, *Index* · C. H. Herford, *Studies in the literary relations of England and Germany in the sixteenth century* (1886) · J. W. Harris, *John Bale: a study in the minor literature of the Reformation* (1940)
Likenesses portrait, *c*.1559, repro. in Hine, *Hitchin worthies*
Wealth at death several houses; a mill; tenements and fields; a library: will, Herts. ALS, D/ERF2

Radcliffe, Sir Richard. *See* Ratcliffe, Sir Richard (*d*. 1485).

Radcliffe, Robert, first earl of Sussex (1482/3–1542), soldier and courtier, was the son and heir of John *Ratcliffe, sixth Baron Fitzwalter (1452–1496), and his wife, Margaret. The sixth baron was attainted and executed in 1496 for his part in the Perkin Warbeck conspiracy and it was not until November 1505 that the attainder was reversed. His son was first summoned to parliament as Baron Fitzwalter on 28 November 1511, following an act of parliament in 1509 confirming his right to the title (1 Hen. VIII c. 19), but his rehabilitation had already been confirmed on 23 June 1509 when he was made a knight of the Bath, while on the following day he was lord sewer at Henry VIII's coronation.

Radcliffe prospered in the early years of Henry VIII's reign through friendship with and proximity to the young king. In 1513 he served in the vanguard of the army in France under the earl of Shrewsbury. In 1521 he served at sea, and in the following year campaigned under the earl of Surrey at Morlaix and in Picardy. In 1515 he took part in the ceremony at which Wolsey received his cardinal's hat; he was at the Field of Cloth of Gold in 1520; on 7 May 1524 he was installed as a knight of the Garter; by February 1526 he was a member of the king's council. On 18 July 1525, at the creation of Henry Fitzroy as duke of Richmond, he was raised to the dignity of Viscount Fitzwalter.

Fitzwalter was above all a loyal servant of Henry VIII, and as such he supported the king's divorce from Katherine of Aragon. In June 1529, aged forty-six, he gave evidence concerning the latter's marriage to Prince Arthur and its consummation. It was his loyalty which led to his being created earl of Sussex on 8 December that year. On 7 May 1531 he became lieutenant of the Order of the Garter

and on 31 May 1532 was appointed one of the chamberlains of the exchequer. He served as lord sewer at the coronation of Anne Boleyn and was appointed to carry the king's demands to Katherine of Aragon in December 1533. On 23 June 1537 he was granted the reversion of stewardship of the royal household, once held by his father and now by the fourth earl of Shrewsbury, but when Shrewsbury died the following year he was succeeded, apparently without letters patent, by the duke of Suffolk. This turn of events shows the limitations of Sussex's power, though he was compensated by being made chief steward of the duchy of Lancaster in the north on 5 December 1539, a position formerly held by Suffolk. He exchanged his new office for the duchy's southern stewardship on 17 November 1540 and held that until his death. He had previously played an important role in quelling the disturbances in the north of England in 1536–7: he was appointed, along with the earl of Derby, to quell unrest in Lancashire and between February and April 1537 suppressed the abbeys of Whalley and Furness. On 9 May 1540 he was sent to Calais to head a commission to inquire into charges of misgovernment and sacramentarianism there, having already reached the pinnacle of his career in royal service when he was made lord great chamberlain of England for life on 3 May.

Despite this impressive *cursus honorum* Sussex seems to have been only a second-rate politician and statesman. In 1538 he was described as being 'of small power and little discretion and many words' (*LP Henry VIII*, vol. 13/2, no. 732). His military resources were small and he rarely attended meetings of the council. He had, however, close links with Thomas Howard, third duke of Norfolk, from whom he held the manor of Wrentham, Suffolk, for half a knight's fee. Cromwell, wary of his close links with Norfolk, may for that reason have prevented him from becoming lord steward. Conversely, his siding with Norfolk against Cromwell probably explains his elevation to the chamberlaincy and his dispatch to Calais in May 1540 following the chief minister's fall from power in the previous month.

Sussex married three times. His first wife was Lady Elizabeth Stafford, daughter of the second duke of Buckingham, whom he married before 1507 and with whom he had Henry, the second earl, and Sir Humphrey Radcliffe of Elnestow. Elizabeth died some time before 11 May 1532, and by 1 September following Sussex married Lady Margaret Stanley, daughter of the second earl of Derby. A special dispensation was needed as the two were within the prohibited degrees of consanguinity. They had a son, Sir John Radcliffe, who died without children in 1568, and a daughter, Anne, who married Thomas, second Baron Wharton. Margaret probably died in February 1534, and on 14 January 1537 her husband married Mary, daughter of Sir John Arundell of Lanherne, Cornwall. They had no children. Sussex died on 26 or 27 November 1542 and was buried in the church of St Laurence Pountney, London, but his remains were later removed to Boreham, Essex. In 1545 his widow married Henry Fitzalan, twelfth earl of Arundel, and died childless on 20 October 1557. The claims once made for her literary attainments have proved to be unfounded; the translations of classical texts surviving among the royal manuscripts in the British Library, once attributed to her, are children's exercises written by her stepdaughter Mary, later duchess of Norfolk.

Henry Radcliffe, second earl of Sussex (*c*.1507–1557), was aged about thirty-five when his father died. He combined service to the crown with a regional interest in East Anglia and a close affinity to the Howard family. He accompanied Henry VIII to Calais and Boulogne to meet the French king François I in 1532 and was made a knight of the Bath at the coronation of Anne Boleyn. In 1539 he was one of the commissioners given responsibility for the defence of the Norfolk coast and in the 1544 invasion of France commanded 100 footmen in the vanguard under Norfolk. He survived the disgrace of the Howards in 1547 and exercised his hereditary office of lord sewer at the coronation of Edward VI. In April 1551 he was made joint lord lieutenant of Norfolk, and was reappointed in May 1552 and May 1553.

Sussex gave important support to the coup which brought Princess Mary to the throne. At the time of Edward VI's death he was at Atleburgh in Suffolk. According to Robert Wingfield, the earl (who was conservative in religion) was immediately inclined to support the princess's claims, but was deterred by Lord Robert Dudley's telling him that Edward was still alive. He was persuaded to throw in his lot with Mary when his son Henry was captured by Sir John Huddleston with letters from his father to the council at Westminster. To protect his son Sussex now joined the princess at Kenninghall and raised a substantial body of men on her behalf. Presumably on the strength of his military experience he was made her commander-in-chief, 'the queen's lieutenant and, as the proverb goes, her mouth and chin' (MacCulloch, 261). On 17 May he was made a privy councillor, and in November he served as a commissioner at the trial of Lady Jane Grey. His rewards included the wardenship of the royal forests south of Trent and annuities worth about £300. In 1554 he was elected a knight of the Garter, and in 1556 lord lieutenant of Norfolk and Suffolk. But although Sussex was active in pursuing heretics in Norfolk, he did not always support royal policy. He opposed Mary's marriage to Philip (but later accepted a Habsburg pension) and upheld the position of Princess Elizabeth as the queen's heir presumptive. One of the councillors who escorted Elizabeth to the Tower in 1554, he is reported to have wept and warned his colleagues, 'What will ye doe, my Lordes … She was a kinges daughter and is the queenes syster, and ye have no sufficient commyssyon so to do' (Loach, 92).

Sussex married twice. His first wife, married before 21 May 1524, was Elizabeth, daughter of Thomas Howard, second duke of Norfolk. They had three sons, Thomas *Radcliffe and Henry *Radcliffe, successively third and fourth earls, and Robert who predeceased his father. One of Anne Boleyn's attendants when Henry VIII met François I at Calais in 1532, Elizabeth died on 18 September 1534, and by 21 November 1538 her husband had remarried. **Anne Radcliffe**, countess of Sussex (*d.* 1579x82), was the daughter of Sir Philip Calthorp, a Norfolk landowner, and his second wife, Jane Blennerhassett. She and Sussex had three children: Egremont *Radcliffe; Maud, who died young; and Frances, who married Sir Thomas Mildmay. But the relationship proved stormy, at least partly because of religious differences. Sussex's conservatism was not shared by his wife, who had a position in Queen Katherine Parr's household and shared the latter's evangelicalism—she was one of the queen's ladies whom Anne Askew was pressed to incriminate in 1546. But there seem to have been other differences. In 1552 the countess was in the Tower, charged with sorcery, and when she fled abroad after Mary's accession her husband divorced her; in November 1553 a bill was introduced into parliament 'against the adulterous living of the late countess of Sussex' (Loach, 71). The bill did not pass, nor did another in 1555 which would have deprived her of her jointure unless she came back to England and underwent purgation before a bishop. But she may have returned, for in the following year she acted as intermediary between the French ambassador and Princess Elizabeth, when the latter was contemplating flight abroad. In April 1557 she was in the Fleet prison, but the bill which finally passed in 1558 was somewhat more generous over her jointure than the abortive previous ones had been.

By then Sussex was dead, having described Anne in his will as 'my unnaturall and unkynde devorsyd wiff' (GEC, *Peerage*, 12/1.521 n. k). He died at Cannon Row, Westminster, on 17 February 1557 and was buried nine days later at St Laurence Pountney; but his remains, like those of his father, were later removed to Boreham. By 23 June 1559 his second countess had married Andrew Wyse, formerly vice-treasurer of Ireland, who was then in prison following his dismissal for maladministration in 1554. Her plea for his release may have been heeded, since Wyse returned to Ireland in 1564 as secretary to a commission of inquiry, and they had several children. He had died by 26 January 1568; his widow died between 22 August 1579 and 28 March 1582. DAVID GRUMMITT

Sources will, PRO, PROB 11/39/39 · PRO, E 150, Exchequer, king's remembrancer, inquisitions *post mortem*, series 2, 643 · *LP Henry VIII* · GEC, *Peerage*, new edn, 12/1.517–22 · H. Miller, *Henry VIII and the English nobility* (1986) · S. J. Gunn, *Charles Brandon, duke of Suffolk, c.1484–1545* (1988) · D. Starkey, *The reign of Henry VII: personalities and politics* (1985) · *DNB* · W. G. Davies, 'Whetehill of Calais', *The New England Historical and Genealogical Register*, 102 (1948), 241–53; 103 (1949), 5–19 · J. L. Vivian and H. H. Drake, eds., *The visitation of the county of Cornwall in the year 1620*, Harleian Society, 9 (1874), 9 · E. A. Fry, ed., *Inquisitions post mortem for Cornwall and Devon, 1216–1649*, Devon and Cornwall RS, 1 (1906) · J. Loach, *Parliament and the crown in the reign of Mary Tudor* (1986) · D. Loader, *The reign of Mary Tudor*, 2nd edn (1991) · D. Starkey, *Elizabeth: apprenticeship* (2000) · D. MacCulloch, 'The *Vita Mariae Angliae Reginae* of Robert Wingfield of Brantham', *Camden miscellany, XXVIII*, CS, 4th ser., 29 (1984), 181–301 · M. A. R. Graves, *The House of Lords in the parliaments of Edward VI and Mary I* (1981) · C. Brady, *The chief governor: the rise and fall of reform government in Tudor Ireland, 1536–1588* (1994)

Radcliffe, Robert, fifth earl of Sussex (1573–1629), soldier and courtier, was born on 12 June 1573, the son of Henry *Radcliffe, fourth earl of Sussex (1533–1593), and his wife,

Honor (d. 1593), daughter of Anthony Pound of Farlington, Hampshire. His birthplace is unknown, though it may well have been Hampshire, where his father was lord lieutenant and governor of Portsmouth. The details of his education are also unknown. His family had Cambridge connections—his aunt, Frances *Radcliffe (née Sidney), countess of Sussex, had founded Sidney Sussex College, and he later sent one of his sons to Trinity College. There is, however, no evidence that he attended the university. From 1583 to 1593 Radcliffe bore the courtesy title Lord Fitzwalter.

In or before 1592 Fitzwalter married Bridget (bap. 1575, d. 1623), the eldest daughter of Sir Charles Morison of Cassiobury, Hertfordshire. Their two sons and two daughters all died before both of them. The couple gained a reputation as literary patrons in the 1590s. In 1592 Robert Greene dedicated to Lord Fitzwalter Thomas Lodge's *Euphues Shadow* and to his wife *Philomena*, which he subtitled *The Lady Fitzwater's Nightingale*. She also received the dedication of a music-book, *The New Book of Tabliture* (1596). Henry Lok addressed a sonnet to the earl of Sussex (as he was by then) in *Sundry Christian Passions* (1597) and Emanuel Ford dedicated his romance *Parismus* to him the following year.

Radcliffe succeeded his father on 14 December 1593 and quickly assumed a modest role at court despite a straitened income—in addition to large private debts, he owed £12,000 to the crown. In August 1594 Queen Elizabeth sent him to Scotland as her ambassador for the baptism of Prince Henry. But peaceful pursuits bored him, and in 1595 he asked the queen's permission to serve in the imperial army against the Turks. In the end, however, a less speculative project emerged and in 1596 he took command of a regiment in the earl of Essex's assault on Cadiz. Sussex's place in Essex's circle was confirmed when the general knighted him in the field on 27 June 1596. Sussex served as earl marshal from October to December 1597, and in 1599 he received the Garter. The same year, in August, Elizabeth named him colonel-general of foot, leading a London-based army charged with repelling an expected Spanish invasion. The attack never materialized, however, and Sussex's army remained a paper one. In 1601 his close relations with Essex endangered him; Essex claimed that Sussex was committed to his rebellion, and the privy council confined him in London at Sir John Stanhope's house. But Essex's claim was probably no more than wishful thinking, for no hard evidence emerged against Sussex and he was restored to favour by his re-appointment as earl marshal later the same year.

James I's accession offered Sussex new scope for action. In August 1603 James appointed him lord lieutenant of Essex, a position he filled conscientiously until his death. But a lieutenancy offered no relief from his increasingly desperate financial plight—by 1601 he had sold lands worth £20,000, and he continued to sell his patrimony in succeeding years. In 1614 Lionel Cranfield bought his manor of Shering, Essex, and in 1621 Sussex sold New Hall, his principal seat, the impressive pile enlarged by his uncle the third earl, to Buckingham for £21,000. King James occasionally offered Sussex some help: remitting debts to the crown, a grant of lands worth 100 marks per year in 1603, and a £400 pension in 1609, but these did nothing to halt Sussex's financial decline. His problems were probably exacerbated by the breakdown of his marriage. By 1602 he was keeping as his mistress one of his wife's former gentlewomen, Sylvester Morgan. His wife lived separately on £1700 a year charged on his estate. The illicit relationship scandalized some contemporaries; the diarist John Manningham recorded how the earl called his mistress his 'countess', even though his wife lived, and dressed her in her velvet gown. He recorded the comment of a friend that, 'I would be loath to come after him [the earl] to a wench for feare of the pox' (*Diary of John Manningham*, 97–8). George Chapman in 1609 felt it appropriate to include a verse dedicated to Sussex, 'with dutie, alwaies profest to his most Honor'd Countesse' in his translation of the Iliad, hinting perhaps at a rapprochement between the earl and his wife, but if any such existed it was soon over (G. Chapman, *Homer Prince of Poets*, 1609, sig. EC2v). In September the following year Jane, ostensibly the daughter of Edward Shute but in fact Sussex's, was baptized at St Clement Danes. Sussex lived with her mother, Frances (d. 1627), daughter of Hercules Meautys, Shute's wife and in due course widow, for many years. Their relationship came before the privy council in 1618, when the earl obstructed their attempt to summon his mistress. The countess of Sussex died in 1623 and Sussex married Frances within days of her burial on 11 December—or even sooner. According to John Chamberlain, Sussex forestalled his wife's deathbed efforts to prevent the marriage taking place by wedding Frances the very day after the countess died, before the pursuivants could deliver a warrant to stop it. Frances died on 18 November 1627, having borne no legitimate children with Sussex.

In 1625 Sussex played a significant part in the defence of Essex from an expected French attack. He organized preparations, strengthening local fortifications and leading 3000 militiamen to Harwich. Although Sussex seems to have performed this task well, Charles I alienated him by sending the earl of Warwick to Harwich with a commission appointing him joint lord lieutenant of the county. Sussex took the slight badly, claiming that his reputation was 'a-bleeding' (*CSP dom.*, 1625–6, 150). Charles then restored him to sole command—thereby alienating Warwick. Sussex later refused Warwick's offer of £2000 for his lieutenancy. Although he bore the orb at Charles I's coronation and retained his lieutenancy, Sussex never occupied a very important place in the new reign. He died at his house in Clerkenwell, London, on 22 September 1629, and was buried at St Andrew's Church, Boreham, Essex, near his former home, New Hall, on 23 October. He was succeeded as sixth earl by his cousin, Edward Radcliffe. He devised the ancient Radcliffe estate of Attleborough in Norfolk to his illegitimate daughter Jane and her husband.   VICTOR STATER

Sources GEC, *Peerage* · *CSP dom.*, 1595–1601; 1611–18; 1625–6; addenda, 1580–1625 · *The diary of John Manningham of the Middle Temple, 1602–1603*, ed. R. P. Sorlien (Hanover, NH, 1976) · L. Stone, *The*

crisis of the aristocracy, 1558–1641 (1965) · M. Prestwich, Cranfield: politics and profits under the early Stuarts (1966) · A. Mee, Essex (1940) · APC, 1618–19 · IGI

Archives Bodl. Oxf., Essex lieutenancy book, E. Jas I–Chzs I
Likenesses attrib. M. Gheeraerts, oils, c.1593, Tower of London armouries · attrib. M. Gheeraerts, oils, c.1599, Woburn Abbey, Bedfordshire · R. Peake, double portrait, c.1601 (with Elizabeth I; of Radcliffe?)
Wealth at death fortune was in rapid decline: Stone, Crisis, 484, 760

Radcliffe, Thomas, third earl of Sussex (1526/7–1583),

lord lieutenant of Ireland and courtier, was the eldest son of Henry *Radcliffe, second earl of Sussex (d. 1557) [see under Radcliffe, Robert, first earl of Sussex], and his first wife, Lady Elizabeth (d. 1534), daughter of Thomas *Howard, second duke of Norfolk. From his father's accession to the earldom in 1542, he was styled Lord Fitzwalter until he succeeded to the earldom in 1557. Possibly educated in the household of Bishop Steven Gardiner of Winchester, he was at home in Latin and later acquired Italian and perhaps Spanish. There is no evidence he was educated at Cambridge or was admitted to Gray's Inn as sometimes alleged.

Early career Fitzwalter's public career began with his participation in the French campaign of 1544, during which he was knighted by the king at Boulogne on 30 September. In the last years of Henry VIII's reign he figured in court ceremonial occasions and in the lists, and he was a canopy bearer at Henry's funeral. In 1546 he had attended Gardiner on a mission to Brussels and John Dudley on another to France. Probably in 1545 he married Elizabeth (d. 1555), daughter of Thomas Wriothesley, a match arranged in 1543.

In the new reign the eclipse of Gardiner may have checked Fitzwalter's advance, although he fought at Pinkie Cleugh, narrowly escaping with his life. In 1549 he was appointed captain of Portsmouth, possibly through his father-in-law's temporary influence. He held this post to 1561 when he handed it over to his brother Henry *Radcliffe, the future fourth earl. In 1549 he was one of the notables accompanying Northampton's French embassy to discuss a possible royal match. In 1553 he sat as MP for Norfolk (the other knight was Robert Dudley). With his father he witnessed Edward VI's will in behalf of Lady Jane; but they were not among the notables assigned by Northumberland to rally support in the counties. Father and son were among the first to join Mary at Framlingham, where the earl took command of her forces. Fitzwalter was rewarded with a land grant worth £50 p.a. During Wyatt's rebellion he was among those fighting the rebels at the gates of London. Almost immediately thereafter he was sent to Brussels with a suite of ten men to inform the emperor on recent events. He went with the strong recommendation of the imperial ambassador, Renard, and was warmly received, being detained by Charles so that he might familiarize himself with the Habsburg court. On his return he was employed jointly with the earl of Bedford in a mission to Spain to secure Philip's ratification of

Thomas Radcliffe, third earl of Sussex (1526/7–1583), attrib. Steven van der Meulen [original, c.1565]

the marriage treaty. Warmly entertained, they preceded Philip in their return to England, reaching Southampton in time to greet him on his arrival.

Fitzwalter, who had been summoned to sit in the Lords, was now appointed gentleman of the privy chamber to Philip, a role in which he essayed to learn Spanish. He became a favourite with the king who not only attended his second marriage, to Frances (1531?–1589) [see Radcliffe, Frances], daughter of Sir William Sidney, on 24 April 1555, but participated in the jousts. (His first wife had died in January of that year.) He accumulated posts of dignity, becoming captain of the gentlemen pensioners and chief justice of the forests south of the Trent, and was awarded the honour of the Garter. He also went on a mission to Brussels, probably to urge Philip's return, and he was there again in January 1558 to solicit aid for Calais.

Service in Ireland In 1556 Fitzwalter had received his first appointment to a place of power as governor of Ireland and in February 1557 he succeeded to the earldom of Sussex. He went to Dublin, accompanied by his new brother-in-law, Henry *Sidney, appointed under-treasurer and effectively as second in command. Sidney, and later Sir William Fitzwilliam, would serve as Sussex's alter ego, substituting for the earl in the latter's frequent absences in England, totalling some thirty-five months out of his eight years' term.

Sussex's appointment as governor, the first English earl to have held the post since Surrey in 1520, was a token of a new and widened political horizon which now included

Ireland as an area of primary concern to the rulers of England—and a land of opportunity for ambitious Englishmen. In the decades since Surrey's sojourn, English policy had come to focus on new and far-reaching aims—nothing less than the establishment of effective royal supremacy throughout the island. This was to be achieved through the full Anglicization of the ruling classes and the duplication of English legal, social, and economic institutions. The options of military conquest had been ruled out in favour of a carrot-and-stick strategy: persuasion backed by force only under necessity. For the several decades preceding Sussex's arrival, it was the former persuasion which had prevailed. The new deputy came, as he wrote in 1560, aiming at a continuation of existing policy but favouring a shift towards stronger measures designed to speed up the process, and for this purpose the English garrison was doubled to 2000. His was to be a new broom, sweeping away the lax habits and congestion of the past decades, imparting new vigour to the commands of royal authority and exacting obedience of them.

On his arrival the new deputy found urgent problems awaiting his attention. His first move was an expedition to expel Gaelic Scots intruders in Antrim, chiefly MacDonalds, a perennial problem in that corner of the island where they were seen as possible agents of Franco-Scottish intrusion. He then turned his attentions to the garrisons in Laois and Offaly, nuclei of a protected colony of English settlers established by his predecessors. The ungenerous terms which he offered those local inhabitants who were to be allowed to remain led them to revolt under their chiefs, O'More and O'Connor. Sussex crushed the revolt and hanged O'More, but continuing resistance in the bogs and woods made any settlement impossible. Not until 1563 were grants, belatedly and vainly, made to an assortment of English, Gaels, and palesmen. Laois and Offaly remained a running sore.

In 1558 Sussex took six months' leave in England, returning to launch a summer expedition against the Scottish isles which left a trail of desolation but failed to assail the MacDonald base of Islay. On Mary's death he returned to London and served as chief sewer at Elizabeth's coronation. Then in February 1559 he made a desperate plea to the queen to allow him to resign the governorship. He argued among other things that the reduced forces she allowed him prevented his carrying out a programme of strong government. He proposed Henry Sidney as his replacement. But the queen was adamant, and in August 1560 Sussex returned. He was now promoted to the full dignity of lord lieutenant.

Sussex soon had to deal with the greatest of the Gaelic lords, Shane O'Neill of Ulster, younger son of the earl of Tyrone. O'Neill was already pushing his claims to succeed to the title, alleging his half-brother illegitimate. In 1557 Sussex had chastised him, ravaging Armagh and forcing him to recognize his father's authority and his brother's rights. When the father died in 1559, O'Neill pressed his claim. Elizabeth was disposed to grant him the earldom but Sussex, who had taken a great dislike to O'Neill, dissuaded her and won consent to an armed expedition

against the recalcitrant chief. In the operation which followed in 1561 the lord lieutenant failed to engage his foe and, provisions dwindling, retired to Dublin. Between 1560 and 1563, after a failed attempt to assassinate O'Neill, Sussex launched further expeditions in which he ravaged Tyrone and reclaimed Loch Foyle, but did not catch his elusive prey. Thereupon the queen sent the recently rehabilitated earl of Kildare, a protégé of Dudley towards whom Sussex entertained a deep antipathy, to deal with O'Neill. The latter was invited to court, made his peace, and returned to Ulster under a provisional agreement which soon crumbled. The story then repeated itself. Sussex resumed hostilities in 1562 and 1563 without success and in the end Kildare, helped by the palesman lawyer, Sir Thomas Cusack, signed a treaty which gave Shane O'Neill full recognition as the O'Neill.

Sussex had, of course, to deal with the problems raised by the successive religious changes of these years. Under Edward VI enforcement of the new order had been uneven and had been unsuccessful in building a reformed party in the island. Consequently the Marian reversal was welcomed. It was not even thought necessary to undo the dead letter of the Edwardian legislation until Sussex summoned a parliament in 1557. There the Henrician and Edwardian laws were erased and provision made for re-establishing the old order. Hence when Sussex was commanded in 1559 to undo what he had done two years earlier, he faced a recalcitrant community. He did his best to pack the upper chamber, but it was beyond his power to do the same in the lower. The four-week session which ensued is veiled in utmost obscurity, but the government's bills were enacted; immediate dissolution followed while the governor departed for England in obedience to royal command. Later Irish tradition held that the enactment was achieved in the face of strong opposition by trickery. The houses were told they would not be sitting on the day the bills were pushed through. More recent research seems to show there was no irregularity.

Sussex had little success on other fronts. In Mary's reign he had been criticized by the Geraldine earls and primate Dowdall for his harsh action in Laois and Offaly, and in Armagh. While there were protests to Westminster from the palesmen against heavy taxation and debasement of the coinage, Sussex's position at court was strong enough to fend off his critics.

Recall Under Elizabeth, Sussex was more vulnerable. When petitions from a group of law students in the pale and later from the pale gentry reached court, they got a hearing thanks to the intercession of Robert Dudley. Then an agent of the pale gentry, William Bermingham, enlarged the charges, alleging corruption and negligence in the army with the wastage of large sums. For a queen obsessed with the need for economy, these were grave matters. A special commissioner, Sir Nicholas Arnold, a protégé of Dudley, was dispatched to investigate and his findings led to a further commission of two with a very large remit, including the handling of religion and an alleged plot to poison O'Neill. This was a direct challenge to Sussex's authority. When his attempt to dispatch another army against O'Neill was disallowed and the treaty mentioned above approved, Sussex's humiliation was complete. From December 1563 he was seriously ill; his friends urged his recall on grounds of health and in May 1564 he left Ireland for good.

Sussex had little cause for satisfaction in the record of his administration. Not only had his hostility to O'Neill wrecked the chance of an accommodation with the Ulster chief, but his policy in the pale had aroused the discontent of a community hitherto loyal to the English crown. Pushing aside the local élite accustomed to the confidence of the governor and employment in the crown's business, Sussex brought in a retinue of Englishmen, eager to advance their fortunes in this new area of politics. Insulated from local opinion, Sussex went far to arouse the resentment of a community which was the pillar of English authority in the island. They were also offended by the unaccustomed burden of taxation which he levied on the pale in order to support his frequent military campaigns. Another important bloc, the Anglo-Irish earls, was alienated by his hostility to Kildare and Desmond. Lastly, Sussex's forthright, single-minded, and impatient style was ill-suited to the infinite complexities and ambiguities of Irish affairs.

Nevertheless Sussex had learned from experience. In 1562 he presented the queen with a detailed set of recommendations for the governance of Ireland, proposing the establishment of provincial councils, modelled on the council of Wales and the marches and the council of the north, each headed by an English president with local associates and each backed by a small contingent of armed men. The Ulster president was to have increased powers and more armed force. He proposed law codes which would blend Brehon (Gaelic) and common law. Overall there was to be more effort at patient and peaceful persuasion. None of the ideas was individually new but he set forward a coherent, clearly articulated programme, much of which would be adopted by his successor, Sidney. What it revealed about Sussex was a capacity for understanding some of his own errors and in the process advancing a considered plan for long-term policy. In spite of his blunders he had learned something about Ireland. His influence on English policy in Ireland would last well beyond his term of office there.

Sussex's recall was in no small part due to his own failures, but there were powerful forces in the English court working to achieve his downfall. Robert Dudley had backed the rehabilitation of Kildare, had entertained O'Neill on his English visit, and patronized the discontented palesmen. The commissioner sent to investigate complaints, Sir Nicholas Arnold, was his nominee. Dudley's motives seem not to have been personal but wholly political. Seeing the new opportunities for influence and patronage which Ireland offered, he moved to stake out a claim.

The Austrian match Although Sussex left Ireland under a cloud, he had no difficulty in re-entering the court world. He had always seen the Irish adventure as a short-term enterprise whence, having won a reputation, he could return to the main stage of English politics. By virtue of his rank, his past experience, and his family connection with Norfolk, he found easy readmission to the court political scene. There he quickly identified with the circle clustered around the duke of Norfolk, and soon found a role which satisfied both his public and private concerns—campaigning for Elizabeth's marriage to the Austrian Archduke Charles. He was convinced of the necessity of a royal husband to provide for the succession and stabilize domestic politics. An Austrian match, the best possible, would also stabilize England's international situation by renewing the traditional Burgundian connection without incurring the problems posed by a match with another sovereign.

This position, of course, conflicted with the marital ambitions of Dudley, a man Sussex now cordially detested. In 1560 Sussex had expressed approval of the Austrian match to a disapproving Cecil, but in 1561 and again in 1562 had urged the assembled Garter knights to petition the queen to marry Lord Robert. The latter's attack on his Irish government had altered his view. In any case the personal animosities of the two earls (Dudley was now earl of Leicester) were soon intertwined with the marriage issue. Hostility between them would flare up intermittently until Sussex's death, although it would be an error to see a long-term factional division in the court between their respective partisans. The two would sit together in council and on committees and not infrequently join forces on a particular issue.

When an imperial envoy arrived in London in 1565 Sussex worked hard lobbying him, seeking to convince the Austrian that Elizabeth was serious in her intentions to entice the archduke to a visit to England, but nothing definite was arrived at. Pressure on Elizabeth to marry continued from council, court, and parliament, while the rivalry between Leicester and his opponents convulsed the court. In summer 1565 and again a year later there were open confrontations between the earls; royal intervention was required when Leicester accused Sussex of dealings with the Irish rebel, O'Neill. Sussex on his part was harassing his replacement at Dublin, Henry Sidney, Leicester's brother-in-law and protégé. A public reconciliation enforced by the queen papered over the quarrel, but in the winter of 1565–6 adherents of the two rivals sported coloured badges, purple for the Norfolk and Sussex followers, yellow for Leicester's; and the courtiers went about armed. The continued pressure on the queen to marry, focused in the 1566 parliament, pushed her to act and in November of that year she appointed Sussex to a mission to Vienna to discuss marriage. Royal vacillation delayed his departure to June 1567. He went still apprehensive as to Elizabeth's intentions, conscious of the strong opposition and royal irresolution. How far could he risk his own credit in the cause? He was accompanied by Lord North, allegedly placed there by the opposition to checkmate him.

The emperor and his brother proved amenable to the match but reserved the latter's right to exercise his own religion. Henry Cobham was dispatched to London with this information. While waiting for the queen's response Sussex worked out a compromise with Charles by which the latter would have a private mass in his own quarters but attend the queen in public religious ceremonial. Cobham's letter was debated by a divided council, Norfolk ill and absent. The queen's reply fudged the issues, but a refusal to make exceptions for the archduke's religion effectively ended negotiations. Sussex, bitterly disappointed, condemned those who used religion as a cloak for their real aims, particularly 'the party'—probably North—who, he believed, had persuaded both courts that agreement was impossible. Sussex's persistence in pressing Elizabeth to a decision she was unwilling to make did not halt further employment in her service, but it did identify him as one of the Norfolk circle, a band of nobles conservative in religion. He did in fact go so far as to vote against the bill to secure the bishops' legal authority.

President of the north Back at court, Sussex directed his energy to the pursuit of office. He aimed first at the presidency of Wales and the marches held by Henry Sidney, now Irish governor. Allegedly the queen promised him the post, but Leicester defeated his efforts and secured his brother-in-law's continuance in office. The queen, however, found Sussex a consolation appointment in the presidency of the council of the north, opportunely vacant. He took up the office in July 1568. Almost immediately he found himself involved in another highly sensitive mission. Mary Stuart had fled to England in May. She sought support for her restoration; the regent Moray adamantly opposed it, alleging her involvement in Darnley's murder. In October Elizabeth appointed a commission to hear both sides. Norfolk was chairman, his colleagues Sussex and the veteran councillor Sir Ralph Sadler. They were to listen to the evidence presented and report what they heard for the queen's future judgment.

Sussex had in 1565 been thought too favourable to the Scottish queen to be sent on a mission during the Darnley marriage crisis. At that time he had bluntly expressed his views on the troubled relations between the queens. Mary should yield her claims to present possession, marry an Englishman, and in return receive recognition of her place in the succession. The commission, having held its hearing and reported, was summoned to London to join the privy council and the other earls in hearing the evidence. Sussex joined in approving Elizabeth's decision not to make a judgment, but to send Mary to Tutbury, where, he wrote, she would be a 'nearer guest'. Sussex had already in early October given his own judgment: Mary must at all costs be kept in England; a trial would be unwise for all concerned. She should be persuaded to abdicate on the promise that there would be no trial. If she refused she should then be simply detained; Moray should be backed while Elizabeth became the arbiter of Scottish affairs.

The next chapter of Mary's history touched Sussex sorely. In spring 1569 a scheme was set afoot, backed by a surprisingly wide range of supporters, to marry Norfolk to Mary and to overthrow Secretary Cecil. The latter effort fizzled out, but the marriage was actively pursued. Norfolk's agent approached Sussex for support. The latter dodged a direct answer, pleading his distance from the political scene, expressing surprise at the proposal, and warning the duke against false advisers (Leicester was party to the plot). He did not inform Cecil of the approach. When the plot unravelled, this contact was revealed. It led to a letter from Cecil to Sussex, now lost, the contents of which are clear from the latter's reply. Cecil had expressed belief in Sussex's loyalty but he had also uttered a warning: Sussex must deal plainly with him or not at all. The earl replied defensively, asserting his plain dealing in relationships: 'I know no cunning nor will learn one' (Wright, 1.320–27). Sussex went on to lament Norfolk's fall from grace, wishing he had been present to give better counsel and urging leniency and forbearance towards the duke.

Hard upon the Norfolk marriage affair—triggered by it—came the rising of the northern earls. Sussex's past associations placed him under suspicion. His enemies at court were quick to stoke the fire. His brother Sir Henry wrote anxiously from court, wishing the earl could be present to defend himself. Suspicion grew when Sussex's half-brother, Egremont *Radcliffe, joined the rebels. The situation was worsened by the course of events. Sussex had met the council's warning of unrest in the north with optimistic reassurances. When the storm broke, he acted with vigour, but the initial response of the country was sluggish. Complaints came from London about his slowness, and the queen rebuked him for allowing Northumberland's escape. She now sent Sir Henry Sadler, the privy councillor, and her cousin Lord Hunsdon, to assist Sussex. On arrival, both, after preliminary queries, wrote strongly affirmative reports on the president, justifying his slowness to act by the inadequacy of the force at his disposal. Within a couple of weeks, the country rallied to Sussex's call while additional forces came from the south, commanded by Warwick and Clinton. The rising fizzled out before Christmas without bloodshed as the earls fled to Scotland. Sussex's vigorous leadership had in fact counted heavily in rallying a somewhat wavering countryside to the crown's support.

Sussex's position was much improved, although the queen could still complain about the clemency shown the meaner prisoners while the earl, writing grumpily of Warwick and Clinton's intrusion on his authority, could talk of retirement. As late as February 1570 the vice-president and other council members were writing to deny that the earl had pressured them into accepting the Norfolk match. In January Sussex had leave to attend at court, where he defended his actions before the queen and council and received a clean bill of health. He had an interview with the queen about which he wrote to Cecil. She had shown her favour and confidence by continuing him in office, but Sussex complained the world would see this as mere approval of his services, not as evidence of her good affection towards him. She had declared she would deal with him so that the world would know, although nothing specific was mentioned. Then—a broad hint—he listed his personal expenses in the twelve years of service to the crown: leases sold worth £12,700. He had had no benefit other than ordinary fees. The lack of reward for his service had aroused comment elsewhere, Lord Hunsdon, among others, expressing his surprise.

Sussex's services were now required on the border, where he returned in March 1570. The assassination of Moray had thrown Scottish affairs into disarray; civil war raged between the king's party and the Marians; the latter sheltered English fugitives, who spawned border disorder. Sussex had in January prepared a raid into Scotland, but the queen refused to allow it and reduced his forces. However, by March she was convinced of the necessity for action and authorized a campaign which Sussex carried out in later April, ravaging the eastern Borders while Lord Scrope swept through the western. Sussex was convinced the queen must assist the king's party, which was weaker, importuned her to act, and fumed at her indecision. On his own he opened negotiations with regent Morton's supporters and helped restore their morale. The queen finally agreed to send money and lend aid in mid-May. An English force commanded by Sir William Drury drove the Marians back to Glasgow, but a proposed siege of Dumbarton was halted by Elizabeth.

She was now eager to demobilize, but Sussex dragged his feet while negotiating with the Marians for general disarmament. This engaged him in an exchange with Maitland of Lethington on the subject of loyalty. (Maitland had changed sides.) Sussex displayed both learning and intellectual verve in letters well laced with Latin quotations. This won a letter of royal praise which must have warmed his heart. She praised him for a sufficiency of wisdom mixed with good learning 'as would over match Maitland, the flower of Scottish wit'. She added, 'truly, cousin, we have always judged you wise and we know you sufficient for the place you hold but we have not seen at any time a more absolute proof of your wit and learning' (Wright, 1.369–70). Elizabeth throughout these operations had expressed approval of his actions and confidence in him. Sussex's intellectual skills did not achieve the pacification he hoped for, and the queen authorized a third raid in August and September. Scotland, although by no means settled, no longer constituted a danger to the Borders and in late December Sussex was back in London.

Privy councillor The last trace of suspicion wiped away by his service, Sussex received the public display of royal confidence he longed for with his appointment as privy councillor on 30 December 1570. He remained an absentee president until 1572. In that year Elizabeth appointed him lord chamberlain of the household in succession to Howard of Effingham. Material benefits followed. In 1572 there was a grant of lands in Somerset, part of the Glastonbury Abbey estate. In 1574 he received the honour of Beaulieu in Essex, a cluster of manors, and the mansion of New Hall, a residence of Henry VIII, to which Sussex made extensive alterations. In the same year he had licence to export £2000 worth of woollen cloth free of custom, which he sold for £3200. For the remainder of his career

Sussex was a diligent member of the council, a regular attender, and an active participant in the central business of state. He now sat at the same board as Leicester, a colleague not only there, but also very frequently on special committees. There were occasional flare-ups, as in 1581 and again the next year. Although the causes are obscure, the first of the two required Elizabeth's intervention. In 1578 there had also been a row with Lord North, who had disparaged Sussex's handling of his duties as chamberlain. Sussex saw the episode as a deliberate attack by Leicester's followers.

If Sussex had an enemy in Leicester, he had a firm friend in Cecil. The secretary had been a sympathetic supporter as early as Sussex's Irish days, giving helpful advice, warning of critics at court, and playing down his failures. Cecil shared Sussex's views on the Habsburg marriage and the queen of Scots. He stood by Sussex in 1569–70 and must have welcomed a councillor who shared so many of his own goals. In the years which followed they almost always stood together on major issues. How close and personal the relationship was is revealed in two letters from Sussex to the lord treasurer. In 1578 he wrote that he would on all occasions 'stick as near to you as your shirt on your back' (*Salisbury MSS*, 2.224–5). Two years later he declared that he and his wife 'love, honour and obey as a father and will do all service to you' (ibid., 2.326–7).

Sussex's role in council business can to some degree be gauged by his membership on special committees, charged with important and sensitive tasks. Three names recur regularly on such committees: Burghley, Leicester, and Sussex; more variably appear Hatton and Walsingham. In 1576 the trio were to deal with the prince of Orange, in 1578 to receive a special French embassy, in 1581 to negotiate on marriage with Simier, Anjou's agent, or to deal with the Terceira caravel problem in the same year. In the Simier negotiations they reported back to the full council and in turn conveyed council opinion to the queen. These assignments are testimony to Sussex's role as a member of a trio (himself, Burghley, and Leicester) who formed an inner core within the council (joined frequently by Walsingham and Hatton) in whom rested the centre of power in that body.

Two great problems engaged the council's attention in the 1570s, the successive marriage negotiations with France and the gathering crisis in the Low Countries. In the exchanges of 1570–71 over a match with Henry, duke of Anjou, Sussex as a newcomer on the council played a slight role, voting for it along with Burghley. It is just possible that his name had cropped up in the unfolding Ridolfi plot, reawakening old doubts. In the prolonged on-again, off-again negotiations for the hand of Henry's younger brother, Francis, duke of Alençon, Sussex played a significant part. In the first 1572 phase he backed Cecil in supporting the match until the St Bartholomew's day massacre put a stop to proceedings. When in 1576 a league was proposed to include Anjou (as Francis now was), the elector Palatine, and the Huguenots, to force Henri III to accept a toleration edict, Sussex firmly rejected it, doubting the Huguenots could win; more probably they would be utterly ruined. The queen, he argued, could not procure peace by war. She should look at the marriage scheme again. Events foreclosed the proposed league.

Sussex's initial attitude towards the Dutch revolt was shaped by his anxiety to avoid war and he steadily backed proposals for Elizabeth's mediation, but when, for a moment in 1576, the seventeen provinces were united in revolt, he favoured financial aid and even armed intervention. However, he soon returned to his previous views. Then in 1578 news arrived that Anjou was treating for leadership of the state's forces. Sussex's comment on this development was that the queen's case (and England's) would be hard 'if either the French possess or the Spanish tyrannise in the Low Countries' (PRO, SP 63/8, no. 13). There must be a balance so that neither Spain nor France should triumph over the other.

Sussex now, with the queen's backing, took the initiative (without Cecil's knowledge), when he contacted the resident French ambassador, Mauvissière, to propose reopening the marriage question. He was convinced that only marriage could divert Anjou's search for a role in the Low Countries on one side or the other. For Sussex the overriding concern was to avoid war with Philip, and that could be done only by joint Anglo-French pressure. Here was the chance to achieve that goal. Anjou's marriage to Elizabeth would cement their co-operation and pressure Philip into accepting a compromise in the Low Countries. Lastly, the earl still had a lingering hope that Elizabeth might yet bear a child and resolve the succession problem.

Sussex, steadfast in this policy, found an ally in Burghley (previously opposed to the marriage) during the prolonged council debate in spring 1579. Temporarily successful, they persuaded Elizabeth to invite Anjou to England. In October both were members of a committee to debate the marriage, but they failed to carry the full council in recommending it. In 1580, when anarchy in France seemed to leave England no option but intervention in the Low Countries, Sussex continued to oppose such a move. In 1582 he served on another committee, ostensibly to revive the match, but actually to seek alliance in lieu of her hand. This ended Sussex's co-operation with Leicester, who favoured the war. He had throughout the 1570s supported a clearly conceived policy, pivoting on his determination to avoid war through a marital alliance with France and joint pressure on Philip. When Sussex died, hopes for peace were fast fading. In failing health in 1582, Sussex died on 9 June 1583 in his house at Bermondsey, where his bowels were buried in the church; his body was interred at Boreham in Essex in the red brick building adjoining the church he had built. A large altar tomb features recumbent figures in memory of the first three earls of Sussex.

Assessment In a public career of nearly forty years Sussex had held office under three monarchs. He had enjoyed highly favourable circumstances in pursuit of that career. Among his colleagues on the council he was one of the few who inherited free entry into the world of high politics.

This advantage had opened the way to the Irish viceroyalty and also insured that after a poor record there he could effortlessly re-enter the public arena. A second advantage of great importance was his relationship with Cecil, who supported him even in the Irish years and sustained him in the difficulties of 1569–70. The relationship was, however, as much one of association as dependence. Usually in agreement with Cecil, Sussex did not hesitate to differ. The royal confidence was won more slowly. Only after the testing time of the northern uprising was it fully accorded. Thus, even though he had the advantage of birth, it was merit which won him the trust of those two demanding judges, Elizabeth and Cecil.

What sets Sussex apart from most of his contemporaries was his independence, both in judgement and in action. He had no visible ideological commitment, in spite of his intimacy with a group of noblemen regarded as Catholic sympathizers, and he displayed no confessional bias. He found it easy to contemplate a Catholic consort if that concession guaranteed English security. Void of strong religious commitment, he was insensitive to the protestant outcry against a Catholic husband. This left him free to formulate a wholly pragmatic view of English foreign relations. Sussex's analysis of problems showed him a shrewd diagnostician, but when it came to prescribing remedies he was less perceptive. Solutions for him were straightforward, the alternatives black and white. He was apt to brush aside the nuances, the complexities, the ambiguities surrounding any decision. The queen's hesitation only aroused his impatience. He was curiously indifferent to the religious passions of the age and deaf to the clamours of the anti-papists.

Sussex did not share the driving ambition of most of his fellow councillors. Two prizes he had inherited: title and estate; the latter yielded somewhere between £1000 and £2000 p.a., not a grand figure but a substantial base. Childless, he had no need to provide for his posterity and was content to leave an estate ruinously indebted to the crown. In his early years he sought power, first in Ireland and then in the north, but after accession to the council, he was content to be a participant, saying his say, but eschewing any desire to impose his will or dominate decision making. This left him free to advocate what seemed to him to be best for the realm. This independence meant that he could press on the queen courses of action unpalatable to her, from which the more politic Burghley would shy.

Of Sussex outside his public life there is not much to be said. He patronized a company of players, the Lord Chamberlain's Men, but showed no interest in their productions. He counted no dedications by hopeful authors. His religious views were coolly neutral although he took care to fill the livings in his grant with men of learning and integrity. His personal character, so far as it comes across, is that of a downright man, firm and articulate in his opinions but able to work in a team with fellow politicians, even with the 'Gypsy', Leicester, his life-long foe.

WALLACE T. MacCAFFREY

Sources S. M. Doran, 'The political career of Thomas Radcliffe, third earl of Sussex (1526?–1583)', PhD diss., UCL, 1977 · *The diary of Henry Machyn, citizen and merchant-taylor of London, from AD 1550 to AD 1563*, ed. J. G. Nichols, CS, 42 (1848) · E. Lodge, *Illustrations of British history, biography, and manners*, 1, 2 (1791) · T. Wright, *Queen Elizabeth and her times*, 2 vols. (1838), vol.1 · W. Camden, *The historie of the most renowned and victorious princesse Elizabeth*, trans. R. N. [R. Norton] (1630), 79 · *A collection of state papers ... left by William Cecil, Lord Burghley*, ed. W. Murdin, 2 (1759) · P. Morant, *The history and antiquities of the county of Essex*, 2 (1768) · *Calendar of the manuscripts of the most hon. the marquis of Salisbury*, 1–2, HMC, 9 (1883–8) · Cooper, *Ath. Cantab.*, vol. 1 · *CSP for.*, 1553–83 · *CSP dom., addenda*, 1566–79 · *CSP Spain*, 1554–86 · *CPR*, 1556–82 · *LP Henry VIII* · HoP, *Commons, 1509–58*, vol. 3 · C. Brady, *The chief governors: the rise and fall of reform government in Tudor Ireland, 1536–1588* (1994) · C. Read, *Mr Secretary Cecil and Queen Elizabeth* (1955) · C. Read, *Lord Burghley and Queen Elizabeth* (1960) · N. Canny, *From Reformation to Restoration: Ireland 1534–1660* (1987) · S. G. Ellis, *Ireland in the age of the Tudors* (1998) · PRO, PROB 11/68, fols.414v–418r

Archives BL, corresp. and papers · Essex RO, Chelmsford, inventory | NRA, priv. coll., letters to Sir George Bowes

Likenesses oils on panel, c.1565 (after unknown artist), NPG · oils on panel, c.1565 (after unknown artist), NPG · R. Stevens, alabaster tomb effigy, 1589, St Andrew's Church, Boreham, Essex · M. Gheeraerts senior, group portrait, etching (*Procession of garter knights, 1576*), BM · attrib. S. van der Meulen, portrait, priv. coll. [*see illus.*]

Radcliffe, William (1761?–1842), improver of cotton machinery, was born probably in 1761, and baptized on 14 November 1761, at Mellor, Derbyshire, the son of William Radcliffe, a weaver, and his wife, Mary. His early life is obscure, but in 1785 he married Sarah Jackson, the daughter of Oliver Jackson, a farmer at Mellor, and four years later began business at Mellor as a spinner and weaver. He produced warps for the hand-loom weavers employed by Samuel Oldknow and also gave out some work to muslin weavers on his own account. In 1794, concurrent with the sudden collapse of Oldknow's integrated cotton-manufacturing empire, Radcliffe decided to add weaving to his capitalist activities. With wartime needs for textile products, and with the spread of the new cotton-spinning technologies (waterframe, jenny, and mule), demand pushed up weaving rates and expanded hand-loom weaving, but probably not by as much as Radcliffe claimed. He evidently profited from adding weaving to spinning: he claimed to employ more than 1000 weavers across three counties in the late 1790s, exporting the plain and fancy goods they made. To support expansion, in 1799 Radcliffe took as partner Thomas Ross of Montrose, the son of a rich Scottish merchant, who brought £6000 to the business. Ross had charge of the sales side, and travelled to the continent. Around this time the firm also moved its headquarters to the Muslin Hall at Stockport. In 1801 Radcliffe settled his family at Stockport; he became captain in the Stockport Loyal Volunteers in 1803 and was elected manorial mayor of the town in 1804.

Radcliffe's espousal of weaving pursued political and technological directions as well as a commercial route. In April 1800, in response to a trade depression and the prospect of the export of British yarns to rival manufacturers abroad (especially the German states), Radcliffe proposed to a meeting of Stockport manufacturers held at The Castle inn that Britain's weaving capacity could be increased by mechanization, providing export of yarns was prohibited. He canvassed his mercantilist views and in 1811 wrote a pamphlet entitled *Exportation of cotton yarns: the real cause of the distress that has fallen upon the cotton trade for a series of years past*.

A technological breakthrough in weaving was adumbrated in the late 1780s by the primitive power-loom of Edmund Cartwright, and Radcliffe publicly committed himself to the goal of mechanizing weaving. He and his partner used their combined resources of £11,000 to buy the empty factory built by Samuel Oldknow in the Hillgate, Stockport. Here they concentrated production and recruited Thomas Johnson of Bredbury, near Stockport, an ingenious weaver, to work on the problem, Radcliffe specifying objectives and Johnson designing mechanical solutions. Modifications were recorded in four patents, taken out in Johnson's name (to conceal their source and value), between 1803 and 1807. The most important, dated 2 June 1804, was for the dressing-frame which starched the warp before it was put into the loom. With Johnson's aid Radcliffe also added mechanical movements to the loom, chiefly the taking up of the cloth by the motion of the lathe. Built with an iron frame, this superior hand-loom was known as the 'dandyloom'. Together with Robert Miller's cam-driven shedding principle (1796) and William Horrocks's variable batten speed motion (1813), Radcliffe's take-up motion formed the basis of the first truly practical power-loom, built by Richard Roberts (1822).

By 1806 Radcliffe's profits from hand-loom weaving, now concentrated mostly in workshops, amounted to £90 to £100 a week, and his patent royalties (sold only to British manufacturers) to about £50 a week. These increases in scale and investment overstretched him, however. By now he had separated from his partner and was raising capital by mortgaging his Mellor estate, his Stockport premises, and his patents. He raised a loan of £5000 from four 'gentlemen', but still his credit contracted, and in March 1807 he was declared bankrupt. The loan of £2000 from four friends enabled him to resume business soon afterwards, but he was unable to pay off all his debts and gain a discharge from bankruptcy until 1817. Meanwhile his patented ideas were freely borrowed by rivals, and his fellow manufacturers never kept their promise to fight for restrictions on yarn exports.

The Luddites on 14 March 1812 broke into Radcliffe's mill and residence (as well as those of other manufacturers) and destroyed both his machinery and furniture. His wife was so alarmed and injured by the rioters that she died a few weeks later, on 18 May 1812, aged forty-seven. In old age, and embittered by his struggles, Radcliffe published *Origin of the New System of Manufacture, Commonly called Power-Loom Weaving* (1828), a rambling set of recollections, and blamed the 'Foreign Anglo Junto' centred on Manchester for all his troubles.

Radcliffe gave evidence in 1808 in the inquiry which resulted in a parliamentary grant of £10,000 to Edmund Cartwright for his inventions. Efforts in 1825, 1834, and 1836 to obtain public recognition of Radcliffe's services were in vain until, in the last year of his life, the government awarded him a small grant of £150. He died at Mill Gate Hall, Stockport, on 20 May 1842 and was buried in Mellor churchyard on 24 May. Ten children predeceased him; he was survived by four sons and three daughters.

DAVID J. JEREMY

Sources A. M. Ashworth and T. F. Oldham, *Mellor heritage* (1985) · D. Bythell, *The handloom weavers: a study in the English cotton industry during the industrial revolution* (1969) · R. A. Glen, 'The working classes of Stockport during the industrial revolution', PhD diss., U. Cal., 1978 · H. Heginbotham, *Stockport: ancient and modern*, 2 vols. (1882–92) · D. J. Jeremy, *Transatlantic industrial revolution: the diffusion of textile technologies between Britain and America, 1790–1830s* (1981) · J. de L. Mann, 'The textile industry: machinery for cotton, flax, wool, 1760–1850', *A history of technology*, ed. C. Singer and others, 4: *The industrial revolution, c. 1750 to c. 1850* (1958), 277–307 · W. Radcliffe, *Origin of the new system of manufacture, commonly called 'power-loom weaving'* (1828) · G. Unwin and others, *Samuel Oldknow and the Arkwrights*, 2nd edn (1968) · *DNB* · d. cert. · *Stockport Advertiser* (3 June 1842)

Likenesses T. O. Barlow, mezzotint, pubd 1862 (after Huquaire), BM

Radclyffe, Charles Walter (*bap.* 1817, *d.* 1903). *See under* Radclyffe, William (1783–1855).

Radclyffe, Edward (*bap.* 1810, *d.* 1863). *See under* Radclyffe, William (1783–1855).

Radclyffe, William (1783–1855), engraver, was born on 20 October 1783 at Birmingham, and was self-educated. Nothing is known of his parents, but he was a relative of John Pye (1782–1874), and both were apprenticed to W. Tolley, a writing engraver, of 17 New Meeting Street, Birmingham. They also attended drawing classes under J. V. Barber (1788–1838). At the end of their indentures in 1801 Radclyffe and Pye decided to try their fortunes in London, where Pye's brother was already working. However, Radclyffe's resources ran out, and he returned from Stratford upon Avon, leaving Pye to go on alone. On 30 October 1804 Radclyffe married Elizabeth Hemming at Aston Juxta, Cheshire. He was probably the William Radcliffe, engraver, at Gough Street, Birmingham, in 1810, but William Radclyffe was an engraver and copperplate printer by 1814 at 21 Edmund Street, and in 1817 he had taken in Thomas Radclyffe (possibly a younger brother, whose major work was engraving forty-seven plates for William West's *Picturesque Views … in Staffordshire and Shropshire*, 1830–31). During this period J. T. Willmore and S. Fisher were taken on as pupils, and Joseph Goodyear, Thomas Jeavons, and Thomas Garner were his assistants.

Among Radclyffe's earliest important engravings was a portrait of Bishop Milner after Barber, followed by a portrait of Lord Nelson in 1805. Both demonstrated his technical abilities. He engraved some plates for Oliver Goldsmith's *Animated Nature* (1813), thus attracting the attention of Charles Heath, which later resulted in commissions for London publications. Six plates after J. Roe were done for *A Historical … Account of … Warwickshire* (1815), and for John Britton's *History … of … the Cathedral Church of Norwich* (1816) he engraved Plate 2 after Frederick Mackenzie. Four plates of Kenilworth Castle were exhibited at W. B. Cooke's exhibition of engravings in London in

1821. Radclyffe used steel-engraving from about 1823, notably for thirty-two plates for A. Blair's *Graphic Illustrations of Warwickshire* (1823–9), after Barber, David Cox, William Westall, and Peter DeWint. This was followed by fifty plates for *Jones' Views of the Seats of Noblemen and Gentlemen* (1829–31), all after J. P. Neale. About 1825 Radclyffe expanded the printing and engraving business and moved his residence to George Street, Edgbaston, leaving the joint business at 18 Edmund Street and 34 New Street, Birmingham. His reputation as a landscape engraver was enhanced by the ninety-seven plates done for Thomas Roscoe's *Wanderings and Excursions in North Wales and … South Wales* (1836), for which David Cox the elder was originally intended to provide all the drawings, since Radclyffe was almost alone in appreciating his talent. Wrightson and Webb the publishers, however, insisted that about half the total should be done by George Cattermole, Thomas Creswick, Copley Fielding, J. D. Harding, and others. He had worked earlier for Roscoe in his *Tourist* series (1832–3), with four plates after Harding. He engraved four plates after J. M. W. Turner for *Turner's Annual Tours* (1833–6), and George Virtue employed him from 1836 to 1840 for landscape plates in some of his works. From 1840 to 1855 he provided a series of plates for the *Oxford Almanack*, and in 1842–3 he engraved five plates for *London Interiors*; he may have done six more signed only 'Radclyffe'. His plates were usually signed 'W. Radclyffe', 'W. Radcliffe' or 'W. Radcliff'. *Prayer in the Desert*, after W. Muller, and *Crossing the Sands*, after William Collins, appeared in the *Art Union* in 1847–8. Radclyffe did much to encourage the group of engravers emanating from and working in Birmingham and from 1814 took an active part in the promotion of the local artistic community, by whom he was much respected, culminating in 1842, when what is now the Royal Birmingham Society of Artists was formed. He was affectionately regarded by his many friends and pupils. His great skill in landscape engraving was well known nationally and enhanced the reputation of those associated with him. He died in Birmingham on 29 December 1855.

Edward Radclyffe (*bap.* 1810, *d.* 1863), engraver, the eldest son of William Radclyffe, was baptized on 1 August 1810 at St Phillip's, Birmingham. Taught engraving by his father and drawing by J. V. Barber, he showed early promise by some etchings done at Hazlewood School in 1823, and in 1824 he was awarded the Society of Arts silver Isis medal presented by the duke of Sussex for an etching of animals. The following year he was given the society's silver palette for an engraving of cattle. At the end of his apprenticeship he moved to London about 1831, and immediately set up on his own. One of his earliest steel plates was for Roscoe's *Wanderings in … North Wales* (1836). He was primarily a landscape and figure engraver, and worked extensively for Charles Heath in *The Keepsake* (1836–47), *Heath's Book of Beauty* (1839–47), *Heath's Versailles* (1836), and *Heath's Picturesque Annuals*. By 1838 he was sufficiently well established to marry Maria, the daughter of Major Revell of Round Oak, Englefield Green, Surrey. He contributed often a single plate to George Virtue's and

H. Fisher's topographical volumes, although he engraved seven plates for Christopher Wordsworth's *Greece* (1839), eleven for E. W. Brayley's *Topographical History of Surrey* (1841–8), and nineteen for John D'Alton's *History of Drogheda* (1844). He engraved after contemporary artists, including Thomas Allom, W. H. Bartlett, Cattermole and Creswick. For the *Art Journal* he engraved seven plates published between 1848 and 1866, among them *The Homeward Bound* and *Morning on the Sea Coast*, both after F. R. Lee, and his last, *Hay Time*, after Cox. He engraved a number of plates after his brother Charles [*see below*], eighteen of which were brought together in Robert Bell's compilation *Golden Leaves* (1863). He engraved views on Admiralty charts, of which *The Persian Gulf* was exhibited at the Paris Universal Exhibition of 1862. After 1859 he returned to etching for eleven designs after Cox, 300 sets of which were given as prizes by the Art Union of London in 1862. He began a *Liber Studiorum* of Cox's work, but completed only three before his death. These were published in 1876 by the Liverpool Art Club in connection with their Cox exhibition by the print publishers. Radclyffe used mezzotint especially for four plates after Cox, two of castles and two of Welsh scenery. He exhibited six engravings at the Royal Academy between 1859 and 1863. He died on 25 November 1863 at his home in Camden Town, London, and was buried in Highgate cemetery. His plates were variously signed, probably on account of mistakes by writing engravers; variants were 'E. Radcliffe', 'E. Ratcliffe' and 'E. Ratclyffe'.

William Radclyffe junior (*bap.* 1813, *d.* 1846), painter, was baptized on 21 January 1813 at St Phillip's, Birmingham, the second son of William Radclyffe. Although his mezzotint of *The Serenade*, after H. Liverseege, showed his promise as an engraver, he became a portrait painter and worked mainly in London. He exhibited two portraits at the Royal Academy and two still lifes at Suffolk Street. His portraits of David Cox (1830; National Portrait Gallery, London) and his elder brother Edward were quite highly regarded. He died in London on 11 April 1846 of paralysis.

Charles Walter Radclyffe (*bap.* 1817, *d.* 1903), painter, the youngest son of William Radclyffe, was baptized on 11 March 1817 at St Phillip's, Birmingham, in which city he lived all his life. He became a landscape painter and exhibited three paintings at the Royal Academy between 1849 and 1881. He also exhibited elsewhere in London, and *The Path through the Wood* is among his best work. Credited with lithographing some views of Rugby School about 1840, Radclyffe also proposed the exhibition of engravings of Birmingham men in 1877. In 1863 he lived at 268 Hagley Road, Birmingham. He died at King's Norton, Birmingham, in the first quarter of 1903, aged eighty-six.

B. HUNNISETT

Sources Art Journal, 18 (1856), 72 · Art Journal, 24 (1862), 144 · Art Journal, 26 (1864), 40 · J. Thackray Bunce, introduction and biographical notes, Exhibition of engravings by 19 Birmingham men (1877), 16–18, 29–30, 39–41 [exhibition catalogue, Royal Birmingham Society of Artists, Birmingham, 1877] · Working papers for … book trade to 1850, Birmingham Bibliographical Society, 3–7 (1977–87), vol. 3, p. 15; vol. 4, p. 11; vol. 5, p. 18; vol. 6, p. 30; vol. 7, pp. 40–41 · Transactions of the Society of Arts, 42/84 (1823–4) · Transactions of the Society of Arts, 44 (1825–6), xliii · W. Upcott, A bibliographical account of the principal work relating to English topography, 3 vols. (1818), nos. 1265–6; 1483 · J. Hill and W. Midgley, History of the Royal Birmingham Society of Artists (c.1928), 33 · Wood, Vic. painters, 3rd edn · R. K. Engen, Dictionary of Victorian engravers, print publishers and their works (1979), 159–60 · B. Hunnisett, An illustrated dictionary of British steel engravers, new edn (1989), 72–3 · J. H. Slater, Engravings and their value, rev. F. W. Maxwell-Barbour, 6th edn (1929) · IGI · CGPLA Eng. & Wales (1864) [Edward Radclyffe] · index of deaths, Family Records Centre, London [C. W. Radclyffe]

Archives Birmingham Museums and Art Gallery, proofs and watercolours

Likenesses W. Radclyffe junior, portrait, exh. 1877 (E. Radclyffe) · portrait (C. W. Radclyffe), repro. in Hill and Midgley, History of the Royal Birmingham Society of Artists, 57

Wealth at death under £4000—Edward Radclyffe: will, 5 Jan 1864, CGPLA Eng. & Wales · £295 16s. 6d.—Charles Walter Radclyffe: probate, 2 April 1903, CGPLA Eng. & Wales

Radclyffe, William, junior (*bap.* 1813, *d.* 1846). See under Radclyffe, William (1783–1855).

Radford [*alias* Tanfield], **John** (*c.*1562–1630), Jesuit, was born in the diocese of Lichfield, probably in Derbyshire because of his subsequent association with the Peak District. He stayed at the English College, Rome, from 20 until 24 December 1584, when he entered the Society of Jesus. He left some time later and on 1 June 1586 he arrived at the English College then situated in Rheims. Ordained priest on 14 March 1587 he was sent to England on 17 January 1589. In 1593 Henry Garnet informed Father General Acquaviva that Radford regretted leaving the society and asked to be re-admitted. His trip to the continent to enter the noviciate in Tournai in the summer of 1594 was cancelled at the last minute because of unspecified dangers. Radford ministered to Catholics in the Peak District. On 3 February 1595 a spy reported that Radford dwelt at Mr Williamson's at Sawly until he kicked Mrs Williamson's dog down the stairs for making noise during mass. The same spy also reported Radford (under the alias of Tanfield), who was 'a fine handsome man, having no hair on his face', at a house owned by Mr Jenison, brother-in-law of the Jesuit John Gerard, at Rowsley near Bakewell (Morris, 12–13). In August 1599 he was staying with Humphrey Alsop at Butterley, Derbyshire.

Radford's *A directorie teaching the way to the truth in a briefe and plaine discourse against the heresies of this time* (1605) was apparently written over ten years: his preface was dated 10 April 1594 and the *Epistola dedicatoria* to the archpriest George Blackwell 27 March 1599. The treatise asserted that, contrary to the 'Adiaphorists' and 'Neuters', there was only one sure path to salvation and he provided proof that the Roman Catholic church was that path. Written 'plainly for the simple sorte' (sig. A2v), the book expounded orthodox Catholic teaching on all controverted matters from the four marks of the true church through justification, predestination, papal primacy, purgatory, and the sacraments to images, prayers, and devotional practices. In 1608, Thomas Manly (alias Rogers) attributed his conversion to Parsons's *Christian Directory* and Radford's *Directorie*. Indeed, he was later reconciled to the Roman church by Radford himself.

On 30 October 1606 Father Robert Jones (alias North)

recommended that Radford be accepted into the society and remain on the mission. Radford accordingly entered the Jesuits in England in 1607. He pronounced his final vows as a spiritual coadjutor in London on 20 January 1619. Jesuit catalogues list him in Northamptonshire from 1621 until 1623 and at the house of probation of St Ignatius, London, from 1623 until 1629. He died at the residence of Blessed Stanislaus in Devon on 9 January 1630.

THOMAS M. MCCOOG

Sources T. M. McCoog, *English and Welsh Jesuits, 1555–1650*, 2 vols., Catholic RS, 74–5 (1994–5) · T. M. McCoog, ed., *Monumenta Angliae*, 1–2 (1992) · H. Foley, ed., *Records of the English province of the Society of Jesus*, 7 vols. in 8 (1875–83) · G. Anstruther, *The seminary priests*, 1 (1969) · T. F. Knox and others, eds., *The first and second diaries of the English College, Douay* (1878) · A. F. Allison and D. M. Rogers, eds., *The contemporary printed literature of the English Counter-Reformation between 1558 and 1640*, 2 vols. (1989–94) · J. Morris, *The life of John Gerard of the Society of Jesus*, 3rd edn (1881) · A. Kenny, ed., *The responsa scholarum of the English College, Rome*, 1, Catholic RS, 54 (1962)

Archives Archives of the British Province of the Society of Jesus, Stonyhurst College, Lancashire · Archivum Romanum Societatis Iesu, Rome

Radford, Nicholas (d. 1455), lawyer, was the son of Robert Radford of Okeford, Devon. Radford first appeared on the scene in 1420 when he stood as surety for the lessees of two Somerset manors, was appointed a feoffee for a London goldsmith, and attended the shire elections at Exeter Castle. In 1421 he was elected MP for Lyme Regis; his only other election to parliament was in 1435 for the county of Devon. A justice of the peace in Devon from 1424 until his death, Radford also served as escheator of Devon and Cornwall in 1435–6, and on numerous royal commissions of inquiry in Devon, Cornwall, Somerset, and Wiltshire. Married by 1431, he became a wealthy man and purchased lands in Devon at Grantland, North Yeo, Babbadon, and Cheriton Fitzpaine along with the manors of Cadeleigh, Poughill, and Ford. At his death he had goods worth well over £1337 and a minimum of £780 in cash.

Described at his death as 'one of the most notable and famous' apprentices-at-law (Radford, 'Nicholas Radford', 274), Radford's legal skill and reputation are evident in his wide client base. He was retained by several Devon boroughs, especially Exeter which he served in the office of city recorder from 1442 until his death, at a salary of £3 per annum plus other fees. During the mayoralty of John Shillingford in 1447–50 Radford was Exeter's chief representative in London, and its legal adviser in a suit brought against the city by the dean and chapter of Exeter Cathedral and by Edmund Lacy, bishop of Exeter, over their jurisdictional claims in Exeter. Many prominent members of the gentry, especially in Devon, also sought Radford's legal advice. Cardinal Henry Beaufort, John Holland, earl of Huntingdon, Humphrey Stafford, earl of Stafford, the duchy of Lancaster, members of the Carew family, and the Courtenay earls of Devon were among his more notable clients.

Radford's contact with the Courtenays began in 1423, when he was appointed joint steward of the estates of the earldom of Devon until the heir, Thomas Courtenay (d. 1458), came of age c.1435. Radford became close enough to the family to act as godfather to the earl's second son, Henry. Radford's relations with the Courtenays later soured, however, as he came more and more to be associated with Sir William Bonville (d. 1461), Lord Bonville from 1449, a Devon landowner who, with the support of William de la Pole, earl of Suffolk (d. 1450), from the 1430s contested the pre-eminence in south-west England hitherto enjoyed by the earls of Devon. An increasingly bitter struggle led to serious disorders, and Bonville's success in avoiding their consequences probably owed much to Radford's counsel.

Whether the earl authorized the killing of Radford is uncertain, but he certainly sheltered the murderers and participated in the ensuing cover-up. The murder and subsequent events are related in several contemporary accounts. Late on the night of 23 October 1455, Sir Thomas Courtenay (d. 1461), the eldest son of Earl Thomas, arrived at Radford's manor house in Upcott Barton (about 11 miles north of Exeter) at the head of an armed band of some ninety men. Woken by the noise, Radford agreed to come down and talk only after Sir Thomas had promised as a knight and gentleman that no harm would come to him or his goods. But once inside the house Courtenay distracted Radford while his men broke open Radford's coffers and stole valuable goods worth 1000 marks along with a good deal of cash; they even rolled Radford's invalid wife, Thomasina, out of her bed to take the very sheets on which she lay to bundle up some of their loot. Courtenay then lured Radford out of the house by telling him that the earl wished to see him; only a stone's throw away, however, Courtenay rode off saying 'Farewell, Radford' and leaving behind several followers who then stabbed Radford to death.

The Courtenays' injuries against Radford did not stop there. Four days later Henry Courtenay, the earl's second son and Radford's godson, came to the chapel at Upcott where Radford's body lay, and held a farcical coroner's inquest which declared Radford a suicide. Henry Courtenay then ordered servants to bear Radford's body to the nearby churchyard of Cheriton Fitzpaine, where Courtenay's men cast the naked corpse into a pit and threw stones Radford had purchased for his own grave onto the body, crushing it beyond recognition. A few days later on 1 November the earl and his two sons marched at the head of some 1000 armed men from Tiverton to Exeter where they seized the gates of the city, set their own watch, and quartered in the city until 21 December. On 22 November the earl compelled the dean and treasurer of Exeter Cathedral to hand over goods worth £600, and £700 in money, which Radford had deposited with them. Two days later over a hundred of the earl's followers raided a house formerly belonging to Radford in Exeter and carried away more valuable plate, jewels, and money. Whether these actions of the Courtenays indicate that financial gain had been a motive for Radford's murder, or only show that they needed such plunder to pay their followers, is unclear.

News of Radford's murder and of the Courtenays' subsequent actions quickly reached London where they gave considerable strength to a petition to the lords by a group of MPs that Richard, duke of York, should be appointed protector of the realm for a second time. York duly became protector, but the Courtenays and the three murderers nevertheless eventually secured royal pardons for their actions, in spite of the complaints of Radford's heir and cousin, John Radford. MARYANNE KOWALESKI

Sources Mrs G. H. Radford, 'Nicholas Radford, 1385(?)–1455', *Report and Transactions of the Devonshire Association*, 35 (1903), 251–78 [incl. transcriptions of the most important contemporary accounts of Radford's murder and subsequent events] · *Chancery records* · Ancient petition, PRO, SC8 · Ancient indictments, PRO, KB9 · Devon RO, Exeter city archives · *Letters and papers of John Shillingford, Mayor of Exeter, 1447–50*, ed. S. A. Moore, CS, new ser., 2 (1872) · J. R. Lander, 'Henry VI and the duke of York's second protectorate, 1455 to 1456', *Bulletin of the John Rylands University Library*, 43 (1960–61), 46–69 · R. L. Storey, *The end of the house of Lancaster* (1966) · Mrs G. H. Radford, 'The fight at Clyst in 1455', *Report and Transactions of the Devonshire Association*, 44 (1912), 252–65 · N. Davis, ed., *Paston letters and papers of the fifteenth century*, 2 vols. (1971–6) · HoP, *Commons* · *Itineraries [of] William Worcestre*, ed. J. H. Harvey, OMT (1969) · *English historical documents*, 4, ed. A. R. Myers (1969) · H. R. Watkin, *The history of Totnes priory and medieval town*, 3 vols. (1914–17) · J. R. Chanter and T. Wainwright, eds., *Reprint of Barnstaple records*, 2 vols. (1900) · M. Cherry, 'The struggle for power in mid-fifteenth century Devonshire', *Patronage, the crown and the provinces in late medieval England*, ed. R. A. Griffiths (1981), 123–44 · *CCIR, 1429–35*, 164, 301 · J. Benson, 'Nicholas Radford', *Devon and Cornwall Notes and Queries*, 25 (1952–3), 25–6, 142–3; 26 (1954–5), 117–18

Wealth at death over £780, excl. value of lands; plus over £1337 in goods: PRO, SC8/138/6864; PRO, KB9/15/50; Radford, 'Nicholas Radford'

Radford, (Courtenay Arthur) Ralegh (1900–1998), archaeologist, was born on 8 November 1900 at the Cedar House, Hillingdon, Middlesex, the only son of Arthur Lock Radford, antiquary and medieval scholar, and his wife, Ada Minnie, *née* Bruton. He was educated at St George's School, Harpenden, and Exeter College, Oxford, where he graduated with a second-class degree in modern history in 1921. Born into a wealthy Devon-based family, he could rely upon a private income to pursue his interest in archaeology at a time when paid posts were rare. He helped to excavate Whitby Abbey in the early 1920s and, after travels in central Europe and the Balkans, held scholarships at the British Schools at both Athens and Rome. After work at Richborough (Kent), he became the inspector of ancient monuments for Wales and Monmouthshire in 1929; in this capacity he surveyed many sites and produced guidebooks which remained standard texts for thirty years. Not all his work won acclaim, however: his reconstruction of Tretower Court (Brecknockshire) attracted much adverse comment.

In 1936 Radford was appointed director of the British School at Rome, a post for which he was excellently suited at that time. His political views were well to the right of centre throughout his life, but his work in Italy was limited by the fascist government's ban on excavation by foreigners. He was able, however, to raise the funds required to complete the south wing of Lutyens's building, and witnessed its opening by King Victor Emmanuel III. By 1939 he was seeking a post in Britain, but failed to be appointed to the Disney chair of archaeology at Cambridge. Shortly afterwards the British School at Rome was closed, but not before Radford had prudently destroyed many of its records in the courtyard.

Radford returned to Britain and took up war work, first with the European service of the BBC, then with the Air Ministry, and finally with the psychological warfare board in Algiers. Secrecy still surrounds much of Radford's war service. He himself revealed little about it, though it is known that he attained the rank of staff colonel and ended the war as assistant deputy director of the psychological warfare board, based in Rome. In 1947 he was appointed OBE.

After resuming his archaeological career, from 1946 to 1948 Radford acted as the secretary of the Royal Commission on the Ancient and Historical Monuments of Wales and Monmouthshire (which he had served as member from 1935 to 1946). He then embarked on excavations at Glastonbury (Somerset), Whithorn (Argyll), and Birsay (Orkney), all major early medieval sites. The next years saw his most important fieldwork, never published in full. He had already, in the months before the outbreak of war, taken part in Mortimer Wheeler's exploration of the prehistoric hillforts of northern France, though he made no secret of his fastidious aversion to the prickly undergrowth which covered several of the Breton sites. His own fieldwork in south-west England centred on Glastonbury and Tintagel (Cornwall), which he identified as an early Christian monastery. His interpretation of both was subsequently challenged, and more recent work has overturned his conclusions.

Despite his modest record of publication, Radford retained his position as a leading figure in the field of early medieval studies, not least because of his wide knowledge and striking powers of exposition in lectures and meetings. His lecturing style was distinctive and almost mesmeric, as he rocked back and spoke with closed eyes in a high-pitched clerical drawl. His powers of recall were phenomenal and were retained into his tenth decade.

Radford was much in demand in the counsels of the leading archaeological bodies in Britain. He was elected a fellow of the Society of Antiquaries in 1928, a fellow of the Royal Historical Society in 1930, and a fellow of the British Academy in 1956. He was a member of the Royal Commission on Historical Monuments (England) from 1953 to 1976 and served as president of the Prehistoric Society (1954–8), the Royal Archaeological Institute (1960–63), and the Society for Medieval Archaeology (1969–71). The Society of Antiquaries gave him its highest award, its gold medal, in 1972. No fewer than three Festschriften were dedicated to him, but he received little public recognition, nor did he seek it.

In the latter stages of his life Radford was a rather solitary figure, with little contact with colleagues. The increasing influence of quangos in determining policy towards the national heritage he viewed with disdain. In retirement at Uffculme, Devon, surrounded by his splendid private library, later bequeathed to the University of

Exeter, he kept in touch with developments in the fields he loved, though he resisted most reinterpretations of his work. It did not help that he usually refused access to his material evidence and records. He was also very selective among the younger scholars whom he chose to help. Increasingly frail in his last years, he was supported by a few friends and died peacefully at the Old Vicarage Nursing Home, Gravel Walk, Cullompton, Devon, on 27 December 1998. He was unmarried.   MALCOLM TODD

Sources archives, S. Antiquaries, Lond. · archives, University of Exeter · *The Times* (27 Jan 1999) · *The Independent* (8 Jan 1999) · *WWW* · personal knowledge (2004) · b. cert. · d. cert.
Archives Derbys. RO, notes relating to Derbyshire parish of St Alkmunds · S. Antiquaries, Lond. · University of Exeter, archives | Bodl. Oxf., letters to O. G. S. Crawford · Bodl. Oxf., corresp. with Sir J. L. Myres · Devon RO, corresp., mainly relating to membership of Exeter Diocesan Advisory Committee · NL Wales, corresp. with Thomas Jones
Likenesses group portrait, photograph, 1938, S. Antiquaries, Lond.; repro. in *The Independent* · photograph, repro. in *The Times*
Wealth at death £1,329,883: probate, 4 March 1999, *CGPLA Eng. & Wales*

Radford, Thomas (1793–1881), obstetric physician, was born at Hulme Fields, Salford, on 2 November 1793, the son of John Radford, dyer and bleacher. After early education at a private school at Chester, at the age of seventeen he was apprenticed to his uncle William Wood, surgeon, who was attached to the Manchester and Salford Lying-in Institution. Radford studied medicine at Guy's and St Thomas's hospitals, qualifying LSA and MRCS in 1817. In 1818 he was elected surgeon to the Manchester and Salford Lying-in Hospital. He continued his connection with the hospital as well as with St Mary's Hospital, which was associated with it, in various capacities to the end of his life. He was man-midwife-in-ordinary in 1821; surgeon-extraordinary in 1834; consulting physician from 1841 to 1881; and chairman of the board of management of St Mary's Hospital from 1874 to 1881. Radford graduated MD at Heidelberg in 1839, and later that year he was elected fellow of the Royal College of Physicians of Edinburgh. He married in 1821 Elizabeth Newton, daughter of John Newton, incumbent of Didsbury, near Manchester. She died in 1874. Their only child died young.

The interests of St Mary's Hospital were always Radford's special concern. A new building for the hospital, opened in 1856, was built mainly through the exertions of Radford and his wife. He gave to the hospital, in 1853, his valuable library, rich in obstetrical works, and his museum of surgical objects, afterwards making many important additions to both collections. Some time before his death he put the sum of £3670 into a trust. Of this sum, £2670 was set aside for the provision of medical care to the poor residents in Hulme Fields; the remaining £1000 was intended for the maintenance of the library. A catalogue of the Radford Library, compiled by C. J. Cullingworth, was published in 1877.

Radford was a pioneer of medical education in Manchester. Between 1825 and 1826 he lectured at Mr Jordan's school of anatomy on the theory and practice of midwifery. In 1829 he gave lectures on midwifery and the diseases of women and children at the theatre of anatomy and medicine at 9 Marsden Street. In 1832, in conjunction with Mr R. T. Hunt, also of the Lying-in Hospital, he lectured on the same subject at Hunt's rooms at 90 King Street. In 1833 he taught midwifery at Mr Turner's medical school in Pine Street, the first complete provincial medical school. Radford was elected president of the Manchester Medical Society in 1848.

Radford delivered the first address on obstetrics before the Provincial (now British) Medical Association at its meeting in 1854, and was the author of many papers and communications on midwifery, and of *Observations on Cæsarean Section, Craniotomy and other Obstetric Operations* (1865), besides several pamphlets. Radford was a notable link in the chain of able and well-known Manchester gynaecologists, starting with Charles White and including John Roberton, James Whitehead, and others. Influenced by John Hull, Radford campaigned for the replacement of craniotomy by caesarean section at a time when the procedure was strongly condemned by the British obstetrical establishment. He defended the operation in a short treatise entitled *The Value of Embryonic and Foetal Life, Socially and Obstetrically Considered* (1848). Radford was also one of the first in Britain to advocate the removal of cystic ovaries by abdominal section, a controversial procedure that provoked fierce debate in Britain. He gave much advice and support to Charles Clay in his early operations for the removal of diseased ovaries, helping to justify the claim of Manchester to have been the cradle of abdominal surgery in Britain. Radford was also the inventor of two types of forceps.

Radford died at his residence at Higher Broughton, Manchester, on 29 May 1881 and was buried in the neighbouring church of St Paul, Kersal.

C. W. SUTTON, *rev.* ORNELLA MOSCUCCI

Sources J. W. Bride, *A short history of St Mary's Hospital, Manchester, and the honorary medical staff, from the foundation in 1790 to 1922* (1922) · C. J. Cullingworth, *Catalogue of the Radford Library, St Mary's Hospital* (1877) · *The Lancet*, 2 (1881), 32 · personal knowledge (1896) · private information (1896) [D. Lloyd-Roberts] · *The Lancet* (11 Feb 1882), 218 · *Manchester newspapers* (30 May 1881)
Archives St Mary's Hospital, Manchester, library; museum
Likenesses oils, St Mary's Hospital, Manchester; repro. in Bride, *A short history*, facing p. 75
Wealth at death £20,851 17s. 9d.: probate, 4 July 1881, *CGPLA Eng. & Wales*

Radhakanta Sarman (d. 1803), pandit, was born in the early eighteenth century in a Bengali Brahman family of modest means. His father died at the age of 100, his mother at eighty on the funeral pyre of her husband. Radhakanta received a traditional Sanskrit education as a student of the famed Jagannatha Tarkapancanana, who conferred upon him the title Tarkavagisa ('master of dialectics'). His first apparent work was an undated *Vastutattva*, a Vaisnava text part of which was already lost by 1805. Although he may have been first patronized by traditional rulers such as the raja of Krishnagar, as his teacher and his father were, his career flourished under new forms of patronage in the new town of Calcutta. Along with Jagannatha and others, he was patronized by, and helped legitimize, the *nouveau riche* friend of the British, Maharaja Nabakrishna (Nobkissen) of Sobha Bazar, Calcutta, who gave him a grant of land and had the Mughal emperor confer upon him the title panditapradhana ('foremost among pandits').

Radhakanta became involved with the British in 1783 when, at the request of Governor-General Warren Hastings, he composed and supervised a Persian translation of the *Puranarthaprakasa*, a digest of Indian antiquities (BL, Or. MS 1124; Add. MS 5655) which was Sir William Jones's primary source on ancient Indian chronology. An English translation by N. B. Halhed was published in 1809 (Hindley, 109–17). Although he accepted a traditional reward of land, Radhakanta declined an offer to join the civil service as a pandit assistant to the supreme court in 1785. He personally guided John Shore in collecting Persian translations of Sanskrit texts in 1783–5, and again after Shore's return to India in 1787, and, in financial straits, became Jones's primary mentor in Sanskrit literature and antiquities. He first made Jones aware of Sanskrit theatre and pointed to *Sakuntala*, which Jones translated in 1789, as the best play. Among other contributions to Jones's enquiries, he interpreted the inscriptions on the Delhi-Topra pillar which Jones presented to the Asiatic Society, and was his primary source of information on Indian chess. In 1788 he accepted becoming a household pandit to Krishna Kanta Nandy (Cantoo Babu), Hastings's erstwhile banian, and formal employment with the British regime when Jones chose him as 'a Brahmen of distinguished abilities, and, highly revered by the Hindus in Bengal for his erudition and virtue' to direct the project which he viewed as his foremost legacy, a digest of Hindu law on the model of Justinian's pandects (*Letters of Sir William Jones*, 802). Although his teacher, the venerable Jagannatha, was also recruited and made the eponymous author of the *Vivadabhangarnava*, Radhakanta effectively headed the group of pandits who worked on the project for the law of Bengal, which was still incomplete at Jones's death in March 1794, while Sarvoru Tiwari, as the lone pandit for Bihar, produced the *Vivadasararnava* (1789). All the while, Radhakanta and Sarvoru were recurrently called upon to give opinions on Hindu law for the superior court, the *sadr diwani adalat*, when the pandit assistants to the court rendered contradictory opinions or were distrusted, which was increasingly the case. This culminated in their formal appointment in 1794 when Governor-General Sir John Shore and the council wished 'to render the digest the book of authority for determining legal questions and consequently to attain the desirable object of introducing uniformity in the Decisions of the Court' (BL OIOC, P/28/15, 10 Oct 1794, civil nos. 15–16). Although 'old and infirm' (*Letters of Sir William Jones*, 928), Radhakanta was concurrently retained to supervise the preparation, for the use of the court, of a copy of the digest which, in Henry Thomas Colebrooke's translation (1797–8), became the standard source for administering law to Hindus in Bengal. Radhakanta died, still in British employ, on 8 March 1803. Pursuing what had become a family tradition of British employment, his son Srikanta sought in vain to

succeed him in his position with the *sadr* court; Ghanasyama, another pandit who had worked on the law digest and a grandson of Radhakanta's teacher Jagannatha, was appointed his successor. ROSANE ROCHER

Sources R. Rocher, 'The career of Rādhākānta Tarkavāgīśa, an eighteenth-century pandit in British employ', *Journal of the American Oriental Society*, 109 (1989), 627–33 · R. Rocher, 'Weaving knowledge: Sir William Jones and the pandits', *Objects of enquiry: the life, contributions, and influences of Sir William Jones*, ed. G. Cannon and K. R. Brine (1995), 51–79 · L. Rocher and R. Rocher, 'The Purānārthaprakāśa: Jones's primary source on Indian chronology', *Bulletin of the Deccan College Postgraduate and Research Institute*, 54–5 (1994–5), 47–53 · civil and criminal records, BL OIOC · H. T. Colebrooke, *A digest of Hindu law on contracts and successions*, 4 vols. (1797–8) · [J. H. Hindley], ed. and trans., *Antient Indian literature* (1809) · W. Jones, 'Inscriptions on the staff of Fīrūz Shah, translated from the Sanskrit, as explained by Rādhācānta Sarman', *Asiatic Researches*, 1 (1788), 379–82 · W. Jones, 'On the Indian game of chess', *Asiatic Researches*, 2 (1790), 159–65 [1790, repr. 1799] · *The letters of Sir William Jones*, ed. G. Cannon, 2 vols. (1970) · N. N. Ghose, *Memoirs of Maharaja Nubkissen Bahadur* (1901) · S. C. Nandy, *Life and times of Cantoo Baboo* (*Krisna Kanta Nandy*), *the banian of Warren Hastings*, 2 vols. (1978–81)
Archives BL, Or MS 1124

Radhakrishnan, Sir Sarvepalli (1888–1975), philosopher and president of India, was born on 5 September 1888, in the pilgrimage centre village of Tiruttani, in the then undivided presidency of Madras. He was the second son of middle-class but poor parents, Sarvepalli Veeraswami, a *tahsildar*, a minor revenue official, and his wife, Sitamma. At least, this is the official version. More probably, he was the illegitimate son of a visiting Vaishnavite official: certainly he was physically quite different from his four brothers and sister. His capacity to absorb both the anti-Brahman prejudice that clearly slowed down his early academic career, and the Bengali hostility to southerners which isolated him in his early years at the University of Calcutta, might well have acted as a screen for coming to terms with the deeper pain of illegitimacy. Veeraswami, whom Radhakrishnan accepted as a father, was orthodox and would have preferred his son not to learn English and to become a priest. But scholarships were to take Radhakrishnan from the age of nine into Christian missionary institutions, his secondary education at Hermansburg Evangelical Lutheran Mission High School at Tirupati (1896–1900), and Voorhee's College, Vellore (1900–04), his university education at Madras Christian College (1904–8), and into a quite different career. It was an education which bred a defensive reaction in favour of Hindu religious culture, and significantly his choice of subject for his MA dissertation was on an area always derided by Christian missionaries, the ethics of the Vedanta. His later philosophical work, however, was to be largely on metaphysics rather than ethics. Through a sense of his life being guided by some higher power, he was, between 1918 and 1929, to shift the axis of his thought from philosophy to religion. But his study of European philosophy (absurdly he could not study Indian philosophy at the University of Madras at that time) had also bred scepticism and prompted his lifelong search for a synthesis between

Sir Sarvepalli Radhakrishnan (1888–1975), by Derek Hill, 1967

the European scientific and humanist tradition and that of Eastern religions.

Radhakrishnan began his academic career at Madras Presidency College, 1909–16, and thence went to Rajahmundry and Mysore, until Sir Asutosh Mookerjee, vicechancellor of the University of Calcutta, invited him in 1921 to succeed Brajendra Nath Seal to India's most distinguished post in philosophy, the King George V chair of mental and moral philosophy. His twenty years in Calcutta were to lay the foundations of his Indian and international reputation. Professor J. H. Muirhead had in 1917 invited him to write an account of Indian philosophy and the first volume of his astonishing work of synthesis, *Indian Philosophy*, appeared in 1923, the second in 1927. Higher academic honours within India followed; the vicechancellorships of Andhra University, Waltair, 1931–6, and of Benares (Banaras) Hindu University, 1939–48. Now began Radhakrishnan's ambassadorship to the West, a series of invitations to lecture in England and America: the Upton lectures at Manchester College, Oxford, in 1926, which led to a more speculative if tentative work, *The Hindu View of Life* (1927), to Chicago also in 1926, and the Hibbert lectures at the University of London in 1929, which led to a more forceful assertion of Hindu values, *An Idealist View of Life* (1932). The generosity of a north Oxford philanthropist allowed Radhakrishnan to take up (1936–52) the Spalding professorship of Eastern religions and ethics at All Souls College, very much to be his second home from now on, and his Spalding lectures were published in 1939 as *Eastern Religions and Western Thought*, more

a work of comparative religion than of philosophy. His achievements as a philosopher had led to his appointment between 1931 and 1939 as the Indian delegate to the international committee on intellectual co-operation of the League of Nations, the viceroy, Lord Irwin (later earl of Halifax), gracing a somewhat embarrassed Radhakrishnan with a knighthood for the role, and thus Radhakrishnan was launched on a second and political career.

If always a patriot, Radhakrishnan did not join the Congress Party, but his foreign contacts, above all through All Souls, with such members of the English establishment as Sir John (later Viscount) Simon and Halifax, made him a useful contact man for Congress. He had met M. K. Gandhi as early as 1915 but did not meet Jawaharlal Nehru until the Calcutta Congress of 1928. Radhakrishnan's international reputation as an exponent of Indian culture was bound to make him attractive to Congress, but it was his resistance to the attempt by the marquess of Linlithgow to close down the Benares Hindu University as a centre for the freedom fighters of 1942 which finally gave him the seal of approval as a nationalist, and led to his election to the constituent assembly of 1947–8, when he sat on the 'backward classes' committee. The real breakthrough in his political career came, however, with his appointment as ambassador to the Soviet Union, 1949–52. His achievement there was not those famous friendly interviews with Stalin but his role in persuading the Russian government that Nehru was sincere in his policy of non-alignment, and more particularly in supporting India's case over Kashmir. He clearly had a way with heads of state, patting Chairman Mao on the cheeks, and clasping Elizabeth II with both hands in a special handshake. In 1952 he was elected vice-president, and, *ex officio*, chairman of the Rajya Sabha. These were to be years of much foreign travel. If disappointed at not becoming president in 1957, he was persuaded to run for a second term as vicepresident. In 1960, during the illness of Rajendra Prasad, who had been president since 1950, he was acting president, and on 12 May 1962 he was elected president of India. A man above parties, Radhakrishnan had always worked well with Nehru, believing that Nehru's were consensus politics and sharing much of his social idealism, but their relationship was to falter after the Indo-China border crisis of 1962, Nehru's seemingly perverse favouritism of Krishna Menon a large part of the cause. As president Radhakrishnan was to play an invaluable stabilizing role, steadying Indian nerve during two wars, with China in 1962 and Pakistan in 1965, and facilitating the peaceful succession to the prime ministership of Lal Bahadur Shastri in 1964, and of Indira Gandhi in 1966. He became, however, increasingly disaffected with the standards and performance of government and after his retirement in January 1967 he became a virtual recluse.

Radhakrishnan's political career had been combined with a continuing academic involvement, most noticeably a lecture tour to China in 1944, the chairmanship of the university education commission in 1948, and the chancellorship of the University of Delhi, 1953–62. He also made a valuable contribution to UNESCO as India's delegate, 1946–54, and as chairman of its executive board, 1948–9. Indeed, he had been considered as a possible successor to Trygve Lie as secretary-general of the United Nations.

Radhakrishnan's philosophy was the most eloquent reformulation in recent times of India's Vedantic tradition and an impressive contribution to comparative philosophy and religion. His idealism had been learnt as much from his Christian missionary teachers, Hegelianism being very much then in vogue, as from India's own idealist tradition. His was a non-dualist position, but with an acceptance of the world as itself a part of an absolute reality, an intellectual stance which made possible his dialogue with Western science, his passionate concern for social justice, and his marriage of the contemplative and the active in his dual career as philosopher and statesman. Some have doubted his Sanskritic learning but his prolonged contact with pandits in Mysore, Calcutta, and Benares gives the lie to this charge. Some have doubted his originality. More serious is the criticism that his Vedantism continued to saddle India with a reactionary philosophy. Radhakrishnan saw himself as offering some new transcendental philosophy which would steer mankind away from the muddle and confusion engendered by the twentieth-century ideologies of fascism and communism, by the destitution of wars and the threat of nuclear destruction. Yet his ultimate vision was mystical, a very Indian belief in the power of intuition to achieve beatitude, curiously optimistic and democratic, believing that history had meaning and that all could become liberated souls.

Numerous honours came the way of Radhakrishnan, among them the honorary DCL (Oxford, 1952), honorary LittD (Cambridge, 1943), LLD (London, 1948), the Bharat Rathna (1954), and honorary membership of the Order of Merit (1963). He was knighted in 1931 and became FBA in 1939 and honorary FBA in 1962.

In May 1903 Radhakrishnan had married Sivakamu (d. 1956), daughter of Talpuru Chenchurammiah, a railway station-master, with whom he had five daughters and one son, the distinguished historian Sarvepalli Gopal; but he was unfaithful, and his sexual philanderings deeply hurt his wife. He was a man of simple tastes, delighting in the company of friends, and a brilliant conversationalist. He was a discriminating but voracious reader. A fluent lecturer, he was, maybe, above all a teacher. In Derek Hill's 1967 portrait, in the hall of All Souls, Radhakrishnan looks out, quizzical, searching, with a would-be mystic's face, a touch of dourness—hardly the fun-loving extrovert personality many believed him to be. He died at his home in Madras on 16 April 1975.   ANTONY R. H. COPLEY

Sources *The Hindu* (17 April 1975) · K. I. Dutt, ed., *Sarvepalli Radhakrishnan: a study of the president of India* (1966) · P. A. Schilpp, ed., *The philosophy of Sarvepalli Radhakrishnan* (1952) · S. Gopal, *Radhakrishnan: a biography* (1989) · private information (2004)
Archives priv. coll. | FILM BFI NFTVA, current affairs footage
Likenesses photograph, *c.*1963 (with J. F. Kennedy), Hult. Arch. · D. Hill, portrait, 1967, All Souls Oxf. [*see illus.*]

Radical Dick. *See* Potter, Richard (1778–1842), *under* Potter, Thomas Bayley (1817–1898).

Radisson, Pierre-Esprit [*called* Oninga] (1639/40?–1710), explorer and trader, was born either in or near Avignon, then part of the Papal States, or in northern France of Avignonese parents, Pierre-Esprit Radisson (*b. c.*1590) and Madeleine Hénaut. In affidavits of 1697 and 1698 Radisson swore he was sixty-one and sixty-two (so born in 1636), but the census of New France in 1681 reports him as forty-one (thus born in 1639 or 1640); he describes himself as almost beardless in 1659, so the latter is more likely. Some Hudson's Bay Company records, perhaps confused by his Avignonese connection, call him an Italian; Radisson states he had visited Italy, but not when. Nothing is known of his early life: whatever his education, he wrote a confident hand, but his narratives exhibit few literary or historical allusions. He arrived in New France (modern Quebec) about 1651 to join his half-sister Marguerite Hayet Veron. In 1653 she married, as his second wife, **Médard Chouart** (1618–*c.*1695), sieur des Groseilliers (usually known as Groseilliers), who had been born in Charly-sur-Marne, the son of Médard Chouart and Marie Poirier and baptized on 31 July 1618; he had emigrated to New France about 1641. Radisson and Groseilliers were partners in exploration for most of their active lives.

Early journeys Radisson arrived in New France amid Iroquois attempts to eradicate Huron middlemen and dominate Native trade with Europeans; Iroquois raids had left the sparse settlers between Quebec and Montreal in daily fear for their lives. The youth was shortly captured by Mohawks while duck-hunting with foolhardy friends. As he recounts in his *Voyages* (begun about 1668), after an attempt to escape, he survived the ordeal of ritual torture (*Voyage I*), and was adopted by a Mohawk family, living for two years as a Native before reluctantly escaping to the Dutch at Fort Orange (Albany). (His name as a Mohawk was Oninga.) Groseilliers, after serving in the mid-1640s with the Jesuits to the west in Huronia (southern Ontario), settled at Trois Rivières and began laying plans, possibly on the basis of information from his first wife's relatives, to explore the resources of the interior. In 1654–6, with an unknown French companion, Groseilliers travelled beyond Huronia and possibly as far as the headwaters of the Mississippi. Radisson's controversial third *Voyage* is a suspiciously sketchy account of this journey, in which he claims to have taken part, but a document attests he was in Quebec in 1655. In 1657–8 Radisson accompanied Father Paul Rageneau and other Jesuits to a new mission among the Onondaga, who played an important role in the complex diplomatic life of the then Five Nations. *Voyage II* describes the violence-plagued journey and the ruses the Jesuits eventually used to evacuate their mission.

In August 1659 Radisson and Groseilliers left on the great journey chronicled in Radisson's superb fourth *Voyage*, which led directly to the founding of the Hudson's Bay Company. A French edict forbade independent trading for furs, so they left Trois Rivières stealthily with their Saulteaux companions, escaping marauding Iroquois whom they fought and, Radisson relates, whose flesh they consumed. Their journey took them past Sault St Marie, along Lake Superior's south shore, the beauty of which delighted Radisson, and beyond Chequamegon in Wisconsin. They met with Hurons dispersed by the war, spent a winter of famine, and participated in a great Feast of the Dead. This important Huron-Ojibwa ritual was also an opportunity for diplomacy; the explorers treated for peace, essential for a profitable fur trade, with 'eighten severall nations' (*Voyages*, 209), including the Lakota (Sioux). Later they travelled to the north shore of Lake Superior. Radisson maintains they reached James Bay, but lack of available time makes this doubtful; his vague account may be based on second-hand information from Natives. They returned to New France in August 1660 with a rich bounty of furs, only to be treated as outlaws by Governor D'Argenson.

The Hudson's Bay Company Groseilliers approached a French merchant at La Rochelle to exploit northern beaver, but the resulting expedition failed. Between 1662 and 1665 he and Radisson made other attempts to reach the Bay, seeking support in New England and New Holland. Two contemporaries claimed that the wily Groseilliers aided the English in their capture of Manhattan in 1664. In 1665 the British envoy in New England, Colonel George Cartwright, believing they had discovered a north-west passage, sent them to Charles II in London. News of the arrival of the explorers 'and of a great trade in beaver in that passage' (Rich, 1.24) circulated rapidly, as a letter to Robert Boyle shows. They arrived during the plague of 1665, and (though Radisson does not mention it) may have witnessed the great fire of London. The king, then at Oxford, was deeply interested in their news of riches in beaver (in great demand), their obvious experience, and their concept of a trade operating out of Hudson Bay independent of the heavily taxed overland route employed by the French at Quebec. He gave them an allowance, put them in contact with possible investors, and encouraged them to remain at court.

War with the Dutch frustrated quick action, but two ships attempted an experimental expedition to the Bay in 1668. Beaten by storm, Radisson's had to turn back, and he spent the winter alone in London, where internal evidence suggests he composed the first four of his *Voyages*, possibly at the king's command, or for members of the Royal Society (some were early shareholders in the Hudson's Bay Company), though evidence for either suggestion is lacking. The manuscript dedication is 'A la plus grande gloire de Dieu', but it is Radisson who is the centre of events. A lively narrator, at once self-aggrandizing and unashamed of his own fears, he concentrates on the shrewd observation of human action rather than the description of landscape. Writing in a vivacious Francophone English (the first four *Voyages* are not translations as once was thought), he planned the narratives with care, as textual cross-references show. Preserved in a scribal copy of about 1686–7 once owned by Samuel Pepys, they were discovered in the Bodleian Library in 1885.

On 2 May 1670 the Governor and Company of Adventurers of England Trading into Hudson's Bay received their royal charter, making the eighteen investors 'the True and absolute Lordes and Proprietors' (Rich, 1.53) of nearly 40 per cent of today's Canada. Radisson and Groseilliers spent 1670–74 advising the company and travelling to the Bay. During this time, in 1672 or 1674, Radisson married a daughter of Sir John Kirke, probably named Mary, from a family influential in the early history of Newfoundland; they had two children: a son, Matthew and a daughter, Hannah.

Later journeys However, in 1675 the partners, finding their advice rejected and persuaded by a captive Jesuit in London, returned to France with the assurance that Colbert would support their trading plans. Colbert, however, wanted Radisson to bring his wife to France as a testimony of good faith. Kirke and his brothers had many claims against France and he refused to let his daughter leave, possibly because the brothers, born in Dieppe, were regarded as French themselves. Further frustrated by inaction in New France, Radisson became a soldier of fortune, participating in Admiral Jean d'Estrée's 1677–8 naval expedition against the Dutch in Africa and the Caribbean and sending a closely written four-page report (his only known holograph) to his then patron, the geographically inclined Abbé Claude Bernou. About this time he wrote a remarkable deposition shrewdly setting forth the possibilities for trade in North America.

In 1682, supported by entrepreneurs in New France, Radisson and Groseilliers returned to the Bay, establishing a post on the Nelson River at Hudson Bay where the company had been trading. A three-way stalemate ensued when the Quebec party, a company ship, and traders from New England arrived almost simultaneously. 'I thought it better to surprise them than that they should me', Radisson wrote (*Voyages*, 251), and in a series of cunning manoeuvres swiftly gained control of the situation. But when he and Groseilliers, returning to Quebec, attempted to avoid tax on their booty they were packed off to France. There they found Colbert dead and the regime opposed to trading by colonists and increasingly sensitive to the claims of England in the north being urged by the English ambassador-extraordinary, Richard Graham, Viscount Preston. Possibly with the connivance of the French and certainly encouraged by Sir James Hayes, secretary of the Hudson's Bay Company, Radisson was persuaded to defect to English allegiance. Groseilliers sailed for New France, where he died about 1695; the two may never have met again. Radisson reached London in May 1684. Within weeks he took ship for the Bay, where the party from Quebec he had left behind under the leadership of Groseilliers's son was astounded by his return as an agent of the English. They submitted to his persuasions, and departed for England with a considerable cargo of furs.

London Returning to London Radisson—presumably now a widower—married, on 3 March 1685 in St Martin-in-the-Fields, Charlotte, the daughter of Gédéon Godet, Preston's go-between in his earlier negotiations; they had three sons, Peter-Espritt, John, and William. He defended his stratagems of 1682–4 in two insouciant *Voyages* in French; these, along with later depositions, became important testimony in the lengthy negotiations between France and England over territorial rights in Hudson Bay, eventually confirmed as England's by the treaty of Utrecht (1713). As a symbol of his fealty to England and the new regime, Radisson dedicated to James II two fine manuscripts of his fifth and sixth *Voyages*, now at Windsor Castle. For a time there was a price on his head in New France, but Radisson served the Hudson's Bay Company as superintendent of trade at Port Nelson in 1685–7 and then settled in London. When James II fled, the ageing explorer was left to the protection of Marlborough, but had to struggle for his company pension and stock dividends throughout the 1690s; between 1692 and 1697 he was pursuing a suit in chancery against the London committee of the company, whose deputy governor Sir Edward Dering seems to have opposed his just claims. Probably in or before 1692 he married for a third time; his new wife's name was Elizabeth (*d*. 1732) but her surname and parentage are unknown. They had at least one daughter, Elizabeth Sophia. Despite earlier prosperity Radisson left his family in poverty when he died. He made his will on 17 June 1710, and was buried at St Clement Danes on 21 June 1710, described by parish records as a decayed gentleman.

Reputation Radisson, a man of 'versatility and exuberance' (Nute, *DCB*, 2.539), lived precariously at the intersection of courtly, mercantile, and Native worlds. Regarded by English contemporaries as a rascal and by the French as a traitor, he was nevertheless a distinguished explorer, an innovative thinker on trade, and a significant figure in England's vexed relationship with France. Radisson acquired Native languages quickly, and few documents give such an authentic ethnographical account of Iroquois domestic and military life as his first two narratives. Whether he was present or not, his third *Voyage* reports on possibly the first European sighting of the Mississippi headwaters; his fourth *Voyage* provides the first written account of the area around Lake Superior; and the fifth and sixth document a critical episode in the seventeenth-century struggle over Hudson Bay. In maintaining England's ability to sustain its claim in the area, Radisson's actions of 1684 were decisive, confirming the Hudson's Bay Company—one of the smaller London trading companies—as an imperial actor in North America and in the formation of what was to become present-day Canada.

Radisson's modern reputation is fraught with ironies; little known after his death, he was much studied in the decades after the 1885 rediscovery of his first four *Voyages*, but chiefly by Americans who, because of his 1660 sojourn on the south shore of Lake Superior, honour him as a founder of the state of Wisconsin. Quebec historiography until recently has treated him with deep suspicion because of his defection to the English. To English-Canadian schoolchildren he and his companion traditionally were known as 'Radishes and Gooseberries', and Radisson was the hero of a popular young people's television

series in the 1960s. Early in the twentieth century a contest for the name of a new hotel in St Paul, Minnesota was won by a schoolgirl who proposed the name Radisson; from this the worldwide hotel chain evolved. His name has also been attached to La Radissonie, a remote area of northern Quebec which he never visited. Perhaps more fittingly, the London street where this gifted exploiter of international trading politics expired lies today beneath the Clare Court building of the London School of Economics. GERMAINE WARKENTIN

Sources *Voyages of Peter Esprit Radisson*, ed. G. Scull (1885) · G. L. Nute, 'Radisson, Pierre-Esprit', *DCB*, vol. 2 · G. L. Nute, *Caesars of the wilderness* (1943) · Hudson's Bay Company archives, Winnipeg · E. E. Rich, *The history of the Hudson's Bay Company, 1670–1870*, vol. 1, *1670–1763* (1958) · G. Warkentin, 'Discovering Radisson: a renaissance adventurer between two worlds', *Reading beyond words: contexts for Native history*, ed. J. S. H. Brown and E. Vibert (Peterborough, Ont., 1996) · G. Warkentin, 'Radisson's *Voyages* and their manuscripts', *Archivaria* (winter 2000) · G. Warkentin, 'Who was the scribe of the Radisson manuscript?', *Archivaria*, 53 (spring 2002) · M. Fournier, *Pierre-Esprit Radisson, coureur de bois et homme du monde (1652–1685)* (1996) · will, PRO, PROB 11/516, sig. 167 · parish register, St Clement Danes, City Westm. AC, 21 June 1710 [burial]
Archives BL, accounts of journeys for Hudson's Bay Co., Sloane MS 3527; Add. MS 11626 · Windsor Castle, Voyages V, VI | Bibliothèque Nationale, Paris, MS Clairambault 1016 · Hudson's Bay Company, Winnipeg, archives, Voyages V, VI, E1./1, E1./2
Wealth at death none or very little: will, PRO, PROB 11/516, sig. 167 · 'a decay'd gentleman': burial record, parish register, St Clement Danes, City Westm. AC

Radmilovic, Paolo Francesco [called Raddy] (**1886–1968**), water polo player and swimmer, was born on 5 March 1886 at 4 Bute Terrace, Cardiff, the son of Antonio Radmilovic, a boarding-house keeper, and his wife, Annie Dillon. His father was Greek and his mother was of Irish origin. Raddy was brought up in Cardiff and moved to Weston-super-Mare when he was eighteen. He was a versatile and dedicated sportsman, and participated in a range of sports throughout his life. As a youth, he was an outstanding footballer, a successful amateur boxer, and had won more than twenty prizes for track athletics by the age of eighteen. In later life he was a good golfer and bowler. He was a lifelong fitness enthusiast. 'Almost to the last, his day began with an early morning swim' (*Weston Mercury*, 4 Oct 1968).

Radmilovic was best-known as a versatile swimmer and the most outstanding water polo player of his generation. He competed in six consecutive Olympic games, a British record; he won a record four gold medals and captained the Great Britain water polo team on four occasions. He made his Olympic début at the intercalated games in Athens in 1906, when he reached the final of the 100 metres and 400 metres. Two years later, at the fourth Olympiad in London, he reached the semi-finals of the 100 metres, 400 metres, and 1500 metres, and won a gold medal in the 4 × 200 metres team race and another for water polo. He scored two goals in the final in a 9–2 victory over Belgium. After his Olympic successes in 1908 Radmilovic concentrated on water polo. He was the complete water polo player. He was 'extremely fast and powerful. There wasn't anything he lacked' (*Weston Mercury*, 4 Oct 1968). Moreover, he was very competitive, 'a great artist in water polo's "under water" tactics, and one remembers that innocent, beseeching look he used to give referees when the whistle went against him for a foul' (ibid.). Raddy was water polo team captain at the next four Olympiads. He won a third gold medal at the 1912 games in Stockholm, where he led the team to emphatic victories over Belgium, Sweden, and Austria. The team scored twenty-one goals and conceded only eight. Possibly his finest moment in an outstanding water polo career came when he scored the final goal in an ill-tempered 3–2 victory against Belgium in the 1920 Olympic final in Antwerp. Great Britain lost 6–7 to Hungary in the first round at the 1924 Olympiad in Paris, its first ever defeat in Olympic competition. Raddy was bitterly disappointed but bounced back by winning three British freestyle titles in 1925 (440 yards, 1 mile, and long distance) and another three in 1926 (880 yards, 1 mile, and long distance), at the age of forty. Moreover, when his selection for the 1928 Olympic team was in doubt, he changed his stroke from trudgen to freestyle and appeared at the Olympic trials in Blackpool in 1928, when he won the 440 yards and was selected subsequently for the 400 metres, 1500 metres, and the water polo team. He did not compete in the swimming events in Amsterdam but captained the water polo team, which lost 5–8 in the semi-final to Germany, the eventual winners. Trailing 5–6, the 'Great Britain team swept down on the German goal … ready to score …' when Radmilovic was ordered out of the water for a 'needless foul' (*Swimming Times*, September 1928, 260). Playing a man short, Great Britain lost another two goals and with them the game. It was a disappointing end to an unrivalled Olympic career.

With his wife, Margaret Georgina (1885–1971), Radmilovic had two sons and a daughter. He worked in the licensed trade, owning hotels in Minehead, Porlock, and Weston-super-Mare. He earned his last honour in 1967 when he became only the second Briton (after Captain Mathew Webb) to be selected for inclusion in the international swimming hall of fame, Fort Lauderdale, Florida. He died at the Mendip Hospital, Wells, Somerset, on 29 September 1968 and was buried on 3 October in Weston-super-Mare cemetery. PETER BILSBOROUGH

Sources R. D. Binfield, *The story of the Olympics* (1948) · I. Buchanan, *British Olympians: a hundred years of gold medallists* (1991) · British Olympic Council, *Official report of the Olympic games of 1908* (1909) · P. Besford, *Encyclopaedia of swimming* (1971) · K. Juba, *All about water polo* (1972) · *Swimming Hall of Fame Yearbook* (1968) · *Weston Mercury* (21 July 1968) · *Weston Mercury* (4 Oct 1968) · *Swimming Times* (Sept 1928) · b. cert. · d. cert. · *Western Daily Press* (10 Oct 1968) · *Bristol Evening Post* (23 Dec 1971)
Archives Weston Central Library, Weston-super-Mare, collection of newspaper cuttings
Likenesses group portrait, photograph, 1908 (with Great Britain water polo team), repro. in British Olympic Council, *Official report* · group portrait, photograph, 1912 (with Great Britain water polo team), repro. in *Olympiad Olympic Games Stockholm 1912 in pictures and words* (1912) · group portrait, photograph, 1920 (with Great Britain water polo team), repro. in *Weston Mercury* (21 May 1965) · group portrait, photograph, 1924 (with Great Britain water polo team), repro. in F. G. L. Fairlie, *Official report of the VIII Olympiad, 1924* (1925) · group portrait, photograph, 1928 (with Great Britain water polo team), repro. in H. Abrahams, *Official report of the IX Olympiad, 1928* (1929) · photograph (aged eighty-one), repro. in *Bristol Evening Post* (3 Nov 1967) · photograph, repro. in *South Wales Echo* (5 Sept 1972)
Wealth at death £50,029: probate, 10 Dec 1968, *CGPLA Eng. & Wales*

Radnor. For this title name *see* Robartes, John, first earl of Radnor (1606–1685); Bouverie, William Pleydell-, third earl of Radnor (1779–1869).

Rado, Richard (1906–1989), mathematician, was born on 28 April 1906 in Berlin, the second son of Leopold Rado from Budapest. He studied at the University of Berlin, and also spent some time in Göttingen. He took a DPh at Berlin with a thesis described as a 'mathematical jewel' (*Jahresbericht*, 128), under Issai Schur in 1933. On 16 March 1933 he married Luise Zadek, the elder daughter of Hermann Zadek, whom he had earlier come to know when he needed a partner to play piano duets. Their only son, Peter, was born in 1943.

As Hitler came to power in 1933, the Rados made their way to England. The decree on the civil service, issued soon after the National Socialists took power, made it impossible for those classified as Jewish to pursue academic careers in Germany, and Rado was interviewed at Berlin by Lindemann (Lord Cherwell) with a view to finding a place in England. On Lindemann's recommendation he was granted a scholarship of £300 per annum (by the chemist and philanthropist Sir Robert Mond) to enable him to study at Cambridge. He entered Fitzwilliam House in the same year and studied for a PhD under G. H. Hardy. During his stay at Cambridge he was closely associated with Harold Davenport and Hans Heilbronn, among others, and first met his later collaborator, Paul Erdős. After gaining his PhD in 1935 Rado was a temporary lecturer in Cambridge until 1936 when he was appointed assistant lecturer (and later lecturer) at the University of Sheffield. Among the refugee scientists living in Britain during the thirties, Rado's path to success was unusually straightforward, and he may have been assisted by the fact that he emigrated right at the beginning of his career. By 1939 he was able to assist his teacher, Issai Schur, to emigrate from Germany to Palestine.

After the war, in 1947, Rado was appointed to a readership at King's College, London, and in 1954 he became professor of mathematics at Reading, where he stayed until his retirement in 1971. He was active in the London Mathematical Society, which he served for a time as president, and he founded the British Combinatorial Committee, which he chaired until 1987. He was elected a fellow of the Royal Society in 1978. In 1981 he went to the Free University of Berlin to deliver lectures and to receive an honorary doctorate; this was described as perhaps 'the most moving experience of his life' (*The Times*, 2 Jan 1990). He was an extremely methodical person and was in the habit of making verbatim shorthand notes of lectures, seminars, and

Richard Rado (1906–1989), by Godfrey Argent, 1978

even senate meetings; his sixty-four extant diaries are likewise written in shorthand.

Rado had very wide mathematical interests and published 121 mathematical papers on an exceptionally varied range of topics. His main contribution was the development with Paul Erdős of the 'partition calculus'. A trivial example is the remark that if six people meet by chance, one can be sure that either at least three all know each other or there are at least three with no two knowing each other. A remarkable example (due to B. L. van der Waerden) shows that if k and l are given positive integers, then there is a large integer N, depending only on k and l, such that, if the numbers 1, 2, …, N are split up to form k sequences then at least one of the sequences contains an arithmetic progression of length l. Rado and Erdős, with some help from others, developed these and a few other isolated examples into a coherent theory, a partition calculus, with an amazing variety of applications in mathematics and mathematical logic. Rado was fascinated by mathematical beauty and sought after it. He always tried to formulate his results at their natural level of generality, so that their full power was exhibited, without their content being obscured by over-elaboration. His work with Erdős and others on partition relations is described in Erdős, Hajnal, Maté, and Rado, *Combinatorial Set Theory: Partition Relations for Cardinals* (1984).

Rado and his wife had a double partnership: she went with him to mathematical conferences and meetings and kept contact with his mathematical friends, he was an accomplished pianist and she was a singer of professional standard. They gave many recitals both public and private, often having musical evenings in their home in Reading. Rado was the kindest and gentlest of men. He died suddenly at the Thamesfield Nursing Home, Wargrave Road, Henley-on-Thames, on 23 December 1989, and his wife died a few months later (2 June 1990). Rado was cremated at Reading on 29 December 1989.

C. AMBROSE ROGERS

Sources C. A. Rogers, *Memoirs FRS*, 37 (1991), 412–26 · C. Richards, ed., 'Presentation ceremony to Professor Richard Rado, at the University of Reading, May 7, 1971', *Bulletin of the Institute of Mathematics and its Applications*, 7 (1971), 237–40 · P. Erdős, 'My joint work with Richard Rado', *Surveys in combinatorics*, ed. C. Whitehead (1987), 53–80 · H. Lenz, M. Aigner, and W. Deuber, *Jahresbericht der Deutschen Mathematiker-Vereinigung*, 93 (1991), 127–45 · personal knowledge (2004) · private information (2004) · P. Harper and T. E. Powell, *Catalogue of the papers and correspondence of Richard Rado* (1994)
Archives U. Reading L., corresp. and papers · University of Bath, National Cataloguing Unit for the Archives of Contemporary Scientists, catalogue of MSS and corresp. | Trinity Cam., corresp. with Harold Davenport
Likenesses G. Argent, photograph, 1978, RS [*see illus.*] · photograph, repro. in Lenz, Aigner, and Deuber, *Jahresbericht der Deutschen Mathematiker-Vereinigung*, 128
Wealth at death £137,124: probate, 1990, CGPLA Eng. & Wales

Radstock. For this title name *see* Waldegrave, William, first Baron Radstock (1753–1825); Waldegrave, George Granville, second Baron Radstock (1786–1857); Waldegrave, Granville Augustus William, third Baron Radstock (1833–1913).

Radzinowicz [*formerly* Rabinowicz], **Sir Leon** (1906–1999), criminologist, was born in Łódź, Russian Poland, on 15 August 1906, the elder son of David Boris Rabinowicz, physician and hospital administrator, and his wife Hinda Maria. The family were very well-to-do and, according to Radzinowicz (who changed his name about 1936 while in Poland) lived a 'cultivated social life' (Hood, 638). His younger brother died in his forties and his sister when a young child.

Leon Radzinowicz was educated at the *Gymnasium* in Łódź, where he showed early on his talent for languages: during his lifetime he mastered Russian, French, German, Italian, and English. After leaving school in 1924 he embarked on a European education with a very generous allowance from his father. First he went to the University of Paris to study law, history, and social sciences. Within a year he had moved to Geneva to complete his *licencié en droit* under the distinguished framer of the revised Swiss penal code, Professor Paul Logoz. But what fascinated him most was the radical transformation of criminal policy proposed by the Italian positivist school under the leadership of Enrico Ferri. This declared that social defence against crime would be much more effective if the courts assessed the future dangerousness of offenders rather than merely punishing them proportionately for past misdeeds. It embraced the policy of indeterminate sentences to be served until the offender was reformed or as a means of protecting society from the incorrigible. Radzinowicz went to study at Ferri's new Institute of Criminology at the University of Rome, where he was an outstanding student, graduating with the highest honours. His doctoral dissertation was published in Paris in 1929 under the title *Mesures de sûreté*. A revised version of the dissertation earned him a second doctorate, from the University of Cracow. After another spell in Geneva as a *Privat-dozent* he journeyed to Belgium as a private scholar to study its penal system, which had a positivist bent. He enjoyed the patronage of Count Carton de Wiat and so well received was his report that he was decorated chevalier de l'ordre de Léopold. By 1931 he had published another two books, one entitled *Crime passionel* (1931), and the other on an altogether different topic, *Le problème de la population en France* (1929).

In 1932 Radzinowicz returned to Poland to take up a post as lecturer at the Free University of Warsaw. In the following year he married Irena (Ira) Szereszewska; there were no children of the marriage. While at the Free University, Radzinowicz began to publish extensively (in Polish): most notably a book on the fundamentals of penitentiary science and a series of articles surveying the state of crime in Poland. In his intellectual autobiography *Adventures in Criminology* (1999), he described his growing disillusionment with positivism as he came to see, during the mid-1930s, how it could be used by authoritarian politicians to justify repressive penal policies, especially against minor repeat offenders. Fundamentally a liberal in politics he feared that Poland was going down the road of penal repression.

It was at this stage, in 1938, that Radzinowicz arrived with his wife in England with a letter of introduction from the Polish ministry of justice to study, again at his own expense, the English criminal justice and penal systems. He soon made contact with Sir Alexander Maxwell, permanent under-secretary at the Home Office. Although his report to the Polish ministry on the English penal system, as he put it, 'found its place amongst the ashes of Warsaw' (Radzinowicz, 130), several important articles appeared in journals such as the *Law Quarterly Review* and the *Cambridge Law Review*, and were subsequently republished in *The Modern Approach to Criminal Law* (1945). He was delighted when four articles based on his studies of the relationship between economic conditions and crime and on the sex ratio in criminality in Poland were accepted for publication by Morris Ginsberg between 1937 and 1941 in the *Sociological Review*.

Typically Radzinowicz made the most of his opportunities. At some time (probably in 1938), he introduced himself to J. W. C. (Cecil) Turner, fellow of Trinity Hall, Cambridge, and the only Cambridge lawyer known to the Howard League for Penal Reform. Their friendship and subsequent collaboration was the rock on which Radzinowicz's remarkable career in Cambridge was built. His financial independence allowed him and his wife to stay in Cambridge when the Second World War broke out. He was proud to be naturalized in 1947 and settled into the life of an English 'grand seigneur' (as he sometimes described himself). Always immaculately dressed in a bespoke suit and handmade shoes he never boarded a bus but travelled everywhere by taxi. He stayed in the best hotels—Browns in London and the Stanhope in New York were favourites—and enjoyed martinis and good restaurants. He had a reputation as a dynamic and witty conversationalist.

By 1940 Radzinowicz and Turner had clarified the role of criminology in relation to criminal law and criminal policy in an article entitled 'The language of criminal science' (published in the *Cambridge Law Journal*) and in the same year the first volume of English Studies of Criminal Science (jointly edited) appeared under the auspices of a committee established by the Cambridge law faculty to consider 'the promotion of research and teaching in criminal science'. From volume 7 to 40 Radzinowicz was the sole editor of the series, which later became the highly reputed Cambridge Studies in Criminology. In 1945 he obtained his first paid appointment as assistant director of research in criminal science and four years later, when a small department of criminal science was formally established, its first director.

Radzinowicz's study of the English penal system had made him aware that no one had written a social history of English criminal policy, and that no one had made much use, if any, of the vast amount of material on this subject to be found in the reports of commissioners and other bodies in the blue books, in parliamentary debates, in periodicals and newspapers, or in local record offices. He set about cataloguing them all and in 1943 published his findings in the *Cambridge Law Journal*. This was the beginning of his massive project for *A History of English Criminal Law and its Administration since 1750*. The title was misleading because there was very little about criminal law as such. Rather it was a study of changing attitudes towards the use of the penal law, and the development of policing and institutions of punishment in the late eighteenth and nineteenth centuries. The first volume, subtitled *The Movement for Reform* (1948), was awarded the James Barr Ames prize of Harvard law school and won for Radzinowicz a fellowship of Trinity College, Cambridge, and the Cambridge LLD in 1948. He had produced a remarkably readable account of the amelioration of capital statutes from the infamous Waltham Black Act to the restriction of capital punishment to murder in 1861. With the support of the Rockefeller Foundation three more volumes followed, mainly dealing with the development of the police. A fifth volume (written with Roger Hood) dealt with the emergence of penal policy in Victorian and Edwardian England. The work suffered some criticism, especially from Marxist historians, for being too whiggish and too concerned to show progress, but it has stood the test of time, not least for being a remarkable resource for other scholars.

For many, such a massive enterprise would have been sufficient. But when the call came to establish the first institute of criminology in England, in 1959, Radzinowicz grasped the opportunity with characteristic vigour. Appointed the first Wolfson professor of criminology, he began with a grand tour of universities and criminological institutes in Europe and the United States. His reflections, published as *In Search of Criminology* (1961), indicated his priorities for the Cambridge institute: solid empirical research on the phenomenon of crime and the workings of the criminal justice system rather than the pursuit of vague theories on the causes of crime. He recruited a young staff and set up a first-rate postgraduate course to help train the next generation of criminologists; promoted a vigorous programme of research; found funds for a first-class library; and forged close links with the leading practitioners. Younger criminologists later claimed that Cambridge criminology was too close to the Home Office establishment. Indeed it was close, but Radzinowicz fiercely maintained its academic independence. He was a professor of the old school: formal, rather remote, and an authoritarian director who could be very difficult if it looked as if he might not get his way, yet fiercely loyal when it mattered.

Radzinowicz was influential in public life, beginning with his membership of the royal commission on capital punishment (1949–53), and then on the Advisory Council on the Treatment of Offenders (1950–63) and its successor, the Advisory Council on the Penal System (1966–74). As chairman of its subcommittee on the treatment of prisoners in conditions of maximum security (1967–8) he opposed Lord Mountbatten's solution of building a 'British Alcatraz' in favour of dispersing the highest security risk prisoners between a number of prisons. His solution was accepted but was the subject of controversy thereafter. He also played a controversial role in bringing about the dissolution of the royal commission on the penal system (of which he was a member) in 1966, which he regarded as an ineffective 'talking shop'.

Radzinowicz's influence was also felt strongly in the international arena. In 1947 he spent a year with the United Nations at Lake Success as its first chief of the section on social defence. He chaired the Council of Europe's scientific committee on problems of crime from 1963 to 1970 and did much to stimulate interchange of ideas and the dissemination of research findings, especially among younger scholars. He was an adviser to President Johnson's commission on the causes and prevention of violence in 1968–9. In New York he tried, unsuccessfully, to bring about the establishment of a powerful institute of criminology through his report *The Need for Criminology* (1965), but he introduced the subject into the curriculum of Columbia Law School with the support of his close friend Herbert Wechsler. His Carpentier lectures, published as *Ideology and Crime* (1966), were a *tour de force*.

Radzinowicz retired from the Wolfson chair of criminology at Cambridge in 1973, honoured by a large Festschrift, *Crime, Criminology and Public Policy*. Yet he remained as busy as ever. His book (with Joan King) *The Growth of Crime* (1977) was followed up by several trenchant articles. In these he deplored the declining standards of criminal justice, which he stigmatized as 'penal regressions' not only in America but in England as well. He set about work on volume five of the *History*; and taught for several years at the law schools of Columbia, Virginia, Pennsylvania, and Rutgers as well as other places. He finally retired from

teaching in 1981, yet always kept in touch with developments in his subject, giving addresses to both the British and the American societies of criminology in his late eighties.

Radzinowicz's first marriage ended in divorce in 1955, and on 16 June 1958 he married Mary Ann Nevins (*b.* 1924/5), a Milton expert and fellow of Girton College, Cambridge, daughter of Arthur Seymour Nevins, a brigadier-general in the United States Army. They had a son and a daughter. This marriage was dissolved in 1979, and on 26 July 1979 he married Isolde Klarmann (*b.* 1915/16), widow of Professor Adolf Klarmann, scholar of German literature at the University of Pennsylvania, and daughter of Professor Emil Doernenburg, also a scholar of German literature. Radzinowicz was the most influential person in establishing criminology as an academic discipline in England, and his influence was also felt strongly in Europe and the United States of America. He was not merely a subject builder in the institutional sense. A distinguished scholar he also made significant contributions to the development of penal policy in his country of adoption. In 1970 he was knighted for his many contributions to criminology and in 1973 he was elected, many thought very belatedly, a fellow of the British Academy. He received honorary doctorates from Leicester and Edinburgh universities. The last twenty years of his life were spent very contentedly in Philadelphia with his wife, Isolde, and in 1999 he was delighted to be made an honorary QC. He died in Haverford, near Philadelphia, Pennsylvania, on 29 December 1999, and was survived by Isolde and by the two children of his second marriage. He never forgot the debt he owed to Cambridge and there his ashes lie in the city he called his 'harbour' (Radzinowicz, 163).

ROGER HOOD

Sources L. Radzinowicz, *Adventures in criminology* (1999) · R. Hood, 'Leon Radzinowicz, 1906–1999', *PBA*, 111 (2001), 637–55 · 'Professor Sir Leon Radzinowicz, LLD, FBA: a tribute to mark his 90th birthday', *British Journal of Criminology*, 37/1 (winter 1997), i–iv · *The Guardian* (1 Jan 2000); (11 Jan 2000); (24 Jan 2000) · *The Independent* (1 Jan 2000) · *The Times* (3 Jan 2000) · WWW · personal knowledge (2004) · private information (2004) · naturalization cert., PRO, HO 334/174 · m. certs. [Mary Ann Nevins, Isolde Klarmann]
Likenesses photograph, repro. in *The Times* · photograph, repro. in Hood, 'Leon Radzinowicz'

Rae, Alexander (1782–1820), actor, was born in London in May 1782. After the death of his father in 1787 he was educated under the Revd W. Lloyd, and in his sixteenth year entered the office of a Mr Campbell, an army and East India agent in the Adelphi. He was offered by his employer an appointment in India, which he declined. Instead he decided to adopt the theatrical profession, and made his first appearance at Huntingdon, Cambridgeshire. In 1806 he set out for Bath with an introduction from Richard Cumberland to Dimond, the manager of the Bath theatre. His first appearance there was on 28 January 1806 as Hamlet, a part which remained his favourite and which he was said to play with a beautiful settled melancholy. Rae also performed in Bath as Octavian in George Colman's *The Mountaineers*, Wilding in Samuel Foote's *The Liar*, and

Charles Surface in *The School for Scandal*. His good looks and pleasing style, rather than any conspicuous display of talent, recommended him to Colman, who engaged him for the Haymarket, where he appeared on 9 June 1806 as Octavian.

During the season, besides repeating Hamlet, Rae played Gondibert in *The Battle of Hexham*, Count Almaviva in *The Spanish Barber*, Captain Beldare in *Love Laughs at Locksmiths*, Frederick in *The Poor Gentleman*, and Sir Edward Mortimer in *The Iron Chest*, and was the original Edward in Dibdin's *Five Miles off is the Finger Post*, a part in which he was badly received. He was said at the time to have been genteel, with an expressive face but a bad voice, to have caught something from Kemble and more from Elliston, and to have the vice of expressing strong passion by hysterical 'guzzles' in the throat. At the close of the season he went to Liverpool, where he stayed for four years, declining invitations from the Lyceum and from America. In Liverpool he played the lead both in tragedy and comedy, except for a time when he supported John Kemble. Rae won some commendation from Sarah Siddons, with whom he frequently acted. In the slack season he often visited Dublin and Scotland.

In November 1812, as Rae from Liverpool, he made, on the introduction of Mrs Siddons, his first appearance at Drury Lane, playing Hamlet. Norval in *Douglas*, Romeo, George Barnwell, and Hastings in *Jane Shore* followed, and in January 1813 he was well received as the original Don Ordonio in Coleridge's *Remorse*. He was Bassanio to the Shylock of Edmund Kean on the latter's first appearance at Drury Lane, and also Othello to his Iago and Macduff to his Macbeth; when, in February 1814, Kean played Richard III for the first time, Rae was Richmond. Rae later played Horatio in Nicholas Rowe's *The Fair Penitent*, Orlando in *As You Like It*, Norfolk in *Richard II*, Hotspur, Alonzo in Edward Young's *The Revenge*, Ford in *The Merry Wives of Windsor*, Edgar in *King Lear*, Francesco in Philip Massinger's *The Duke of Milan*, and Rashleigh Osbaldistone in the first production of *Rob Roy the Greygaract*, Soame's adaptation from Scott (March 1818). He is last traced at Drury Lane on 19 June 1820, when he played Irwin in Elizabeth Inchbald's *Everyone has his Fault*.

On the death of Raymond some few years previously, Rae became stage-manager at Drury Lane. After the promotion he left his home and family to live with an actress who induced him to make what proved a crowning mistake. He quit Drury Lane and undertook in 1820 the management of the Royalty Theatre, Wellclose Square, where he opened as Sir Edward Mortimer in Colman's *The Iron Chest*. Here he played the tragic parts of which at Drury Lane Kean had dispossessed him. The experiment was a failure, salaries were unpaid, and Rae was ruined. He then underwent an operation from which he never recovered. Attended by his wife, he died on 8 September 1820. He left a son and two daughters, one of whom also went on the stage, working mainly in Edinburgh. A performance for the benefit of his widow and three children was given at Drury Lane in October 1820.

Rae's most pronounced gift was elegance; he had penetration and judgement, but lacked intensity and inspiration. He was handsome, about 5 feet 7 inches in height, dark-haired and a little bald, a fair singer, a good fencer, and from all accounts a fascinating companion.

JOSEPH KNIGHT, *rev.* NILANJANA BANERJI

Sources *Oxberry's Dramatic Biography*, 4/61 (1826) · T. Gilliland, *The dramatic mirror, containing the history of the stage from the earliest period, to the present time*, 2 vols. (1808) · Hall, *Dramatic ports.* · *Monthly Mirror* (June 1810) · *Theatrical Inquisitor, and Monthly Mirror*, 16 (1820) · Genest, *Eng. stage* · E. Stirling, *Old Drury Lane*, 2 vols. (1881)

Likenesses S. De Wilde, watercolour drawings, 1807–16, Garr. Club · portrait, repro. in *Memoirs of the green room* (1806) · portrait, repro. in Gilliland, *Dramatic mirror* · portrait, repro. in *Monthly Mirror* · portrait, repro. in *European Magazine* (1815) · portrait, repro. in Oxberry, *New English drama* (1818) · portrait, repro. in *Oxberry's Dramatic Biography* · prints, BM, NPG

Rae, Sir David, first baronet, Lord Eskgrove (1729–1804), judge, was the son of David Rae of St Andrews, an Episcopalian minister, and his wife, Agnes, daughter of Sir David Forbes, bt, of Newhall. He was educated at Haddington grammar school and at Edinburgh University, where he attended the law lectures of Professor John Erskine (1695–1768). He was admitted a member of the Faculty of Advocates on 11 December 1751, and quickly acquired a considerable practice. In 1753 he was retained in an appeal to the House of Lords, which took him to London, where he became acquainted with Lord Hardwicke and his son Charles Yorke.

Rae was appointed one of the commissioners for collecting evidence in the lengthy Douglas cause which established Archibald James Edward Stewart as the true son of Lady Jane Douglas and thus heir to the Douglas estates. In that capacity he accompanied James Burnett (afterwards Lord Monboddo) to France in September 1764. He was the leading advocate in the Scottish court of exchequer for many years. He succeeded Alexander Boswell, Lord Auchinleck, as an ordinary lord of session on 14 November 1782, taking the title Lord Eskgrove, from a small estate which he possessed near Inveresk. On 20 April 1785 he was appointed a lord of justiciary.

Among his famous cases, Eskgrove tried William Brodie (d. 1788) for robbing the general excise office in August 1788, the Revd Thomas Fyshe Palmer for seditious practices in September 1793, William Skirving and Maurice Margarot for sedition in January 1794, Joseph Gerrald for sedition in March 1794, and Robert Watt and David Downie for high treason in September 1794. He was promoted to the post of lord justice clerk on 1 June 1799, and was created a baronet on 27 June 1804.

Henry Cockburn declared of Eskgrove that 'never once did he do or say anything which had the slightest claim to be remembered for any intrinsic merit. The value of all his words and actions consisted in their absurdity', adding:

in the trial of Glengarry for murder in a duel, a lady of great beauty was called as a witness. She came into court veiled; but, before administering the oath, Eskgrove gave her this exposition of her duty: 'Young woman! you will now consider yourself as in the presence of Almighty God and of this High Court. Lift up your veil; throw off all modesty, and look me in the face'. (*Memorials … by Henry Cockburn*, 118–19, 122)

But in spite of his ludicrous appearance and his many eccentricities of manner, Eskgrove was a man of the greatest integrity, and one of the ablest Scottish lawyers of the day. He collaborated in publishing *Decisions of the Court of Session from the End of the Year 1756 to the End of the Year 1760* (1765).

For many years Eskgrove lived in a house in the Old Assembly Close, and afterwards at St John Street, Canongate, Edinburgh. From his marriage on 14 October 1761 to Margaret (*d.* 1770), youngest daughter of Dugald Stuart of Blairhall, Perthshire, there were two sons: David (*d.* 1815), who succeeded as the second baronet, but as he had no sons the baronetcy passed to his brother William *Rae (1769–1842). There was also one daughter, Margaret, who married, on 3 January 1804, Captain Thomas Phipps Howard of the 23rd light dragoons. Eskgrove died at Eskgrove on 23 October 1804, and was buried in Inveresk churchyard.   G. F. R. BARKER, rev. ANITA McCONNELL

Sources G. Brunton and D. Haig, *An historical account of the senators of the college of justice, from its institution in MDXXXII* (1832), 535–6 · J. Kay, *A series of original portraits and caricature etchings … with biographical sketches and illustrative anecdotes*, ed. [H. Paton and others], new edn [3rd edn], 1 (1877), 350–52 · *Journal of Henry Cockburn: being a continuation of the 'Memorials of his time', 1831–1854*, 1 (1874), 241–2 · [Clarke], *The Georgian era: memoirs of the most eminent persons*, 2 (1833), 287–8 · R. Douglas and others, *The baronage of Scotland* (1798), 244 · *N&Q*, 8th ser., 6 (1894), 188, 231, 358 · *N&Q*, 8th ser., 9 (1896), 136–7 · *Scots Magazine*, 23 (1761), 558 · *Scots Magazine*, 27 (1765), 502 · *Scots Magazine*, 29 (1767), 389 · *Scots Magazine*, 32 (1770), 343 · *Scots Magazine and Edinburgh Literary Miscellany*, 66 (1804), 78, 887 · *Scots Magazine and Edinburgh Literary Miscellany*, 77 (1815), 559 · *Memorials of his time, by Henry Cockburn* (1856), 118–19, 122

Likenesses J. Kay, caricature, etching, 1799, BM, NPG · H. Raeburn, oils, Faculty of Advocates, Parliament Hall, Edinburgh · miniature, watercolour on ivory, Scot. NPG

Rae, George (1817–1902), banker, was born in Aberdeen on 21 October 1817, the son of George Rae (1782–1867), messenger at arms, and his wife, Jean Edmond Rae (1785–1862). He was educated at the Classical and Commercial Academy, Aberdeen, then briefly apprenticed to a local lawyer. In 1836 Rae was recruited as branch accountant at the Peterhead office of the newly established North of Scotland Bank, Aberdeen, and was subsequently moved to that bank's new branches at Keith and Elgin. Rae then looked for opportunities in England and Wales, where provincial banking was expanding at a rapid rate. In April 1839 he successfully applied for the post of inspector at the North and South Wales Bank, Liverpool, at an annual salary of £130. The 'Wales Bank' was one of the more enterprising new banks, operating both in agricultural and industrial districts and claiming that it 'combined the best features of the Scotch system' (HSBC Group Archives, M139, March 1836). By 1839 the Wales Bank had opened thirteen branches, mostly in north Wales.

Rae's abilities and his experience of Scottish branch banking soon earned him promotion. On 13 March 1841 he married Elspet Kynoch of Keith, Banffshire. In 1842 he became manager at Oswestry, Shropshire, and in 1845 he was appointed general manager of the Wales Bank at the

age of only twenty-eight. Within two years, however, he faced the largest single crisis in the bank's career. In the commercial crisis of October 1847 the London money market suspended the discount of bills drawn on country banks. In Liverpool this suspension led to the failures of the Royal Bank and the Liverpool Banking Company and, on 22 October, a London newspaper reported that the Wales Bank had also stopped payment. The report was false but the panic was renewed and two days later the Wales Bank was forced to stop payments.

In the aftermath of the crisis Rae quickly set about the reconstruction of the bank. New preference shares were issued, depositors were asked to accept post-dated bills, and a number of Welsh branches were closed. These efforts allowed the bank to re-open in January 1848 and to begin a gradual recovery. In particular Rae sought new earnings from Liverpool business rather than from the branch network in Wales. 'Town branches' were opened in the Liverpool region—an early example of suburban branch banking outside London. Rae also pioneered a savings scheme for dockers in Birkenhead, giving the bank a local reputation as 'the tradesman's bank'. These initiatives, along with strict financial controls, stabilized earnings and allowed the Wales Bank to ride the severe banking crises of 1857 and 1865. Between 1850 and 1865, when Rae was promoted managing director at an annual salary of £2000, the bank's total deposits increased fivefold to £1.5 million.

Rae's first wife died about 1851, leaving two sons, George Bertram and Edward (chairman of the Liverpool stock exchange, 1894–1915), and a daughter, Alice. On 26 April 1855 he married his second wife, Julia (*b.* 1834/5), daughter of John Williams of Ferryside, Carmarthenshire.

Rae's career at the Wales Bank entered its most creative phase in the 1870s. In north Wales he negotiated the takeovers of the banking firms of Williams & Son in 1873, Cassons & Co. in 1875 and the Bala Banking Company in 1877. Then, as chairman and managing director from 1873, he upgraded the bank's financial systems and managerial structure. In the downturn after the City of Glasgow Bank collapse in 1878, he also reformed the Wales Bank's investment policies and took close control over advances and cash management. The bank's total deposits increased strongly from approximately £2 million in 1870 to £6.6 million by 1890, and shareholders received dividends of 17.5 per cent throughout that period. Meanwhile the bank's business continued to diversify away from its original agricultural base towards industrial, shipping, and commercial business in the Liverpool region.

In the 1890s Rae took a less active role in the management of the bank and he retired in March 1898. By then the bank had established a network of seventy-seven branches and held total deposits of £7.8 million, placing it among the largest provincial banks in England and Wales. The bank was acquired by the Midland Bank (now HSBC Bank plc) in 1908.

Rae was an authoritative figure in the Victorian banking community. In 1874 he was a founder of the Association of

Country Bankers, where he remained a dominant influence until his retirement. He was also a founder and trustee of the Institute of Bankers in 1879 and four years later, as a vice-president, he inaugurated an institute prize for the best essay on bank bookkeeping. In later life he remained committed to the development of the banking profession; in 1902 he established a prize in practical banking for entrants in the institute's examinations and also endowed a lectureship in banking and currency at the University College of North Wales, Bangor.

Rae was equally active as a spokesman for banking interests. He gave evidence to the 1875 parliamentary select committee on banks of issue and in 1879 he intervened to influence the 'reserved liability' legislation which was introduced after the City of Glasgow Bank failure, providing a bridge between limited liability and shareholder risk. He urged the more widespread publication of bank balance sheets as part of this legislation, believing that 'a strong balance sheet, I feel persuaded, attracts business' (HSBC Group Archives, M222, July 1891).

Rae's most durable influence on banking was as an author. His anonymous contributions to the *Bankers' Magazine* in the late 1840s were published as *The Internal Management of a Country Bank* (1850) and then reappeared (in his own name) as part of his classic textbook *The Country Banker: his Clients, Cares and Work* (1885). This guide to practical banking, written in a direct and persuasive style, won an international reputation—several pirate editions appeared in the USA—and it was published in ten editions between 1885 and 1976.

Rae was popular with staff, shareholders, customers, and other bankers. 'His dignified courtesy and kindliness were universal', a junior colleague recalled; 'he had the rare gift of placing any young man entirely at his ease and to make him feel that he counted for something' (R. O. Williams to T. B. Handley, 26 March 1930, HSBC Group Archives, Rae personal file). His portrait by Frank Holl (1884) shows a bearded figure with a relaxed, almost expansive bearing.

Outside banking, Rae's activities and interests were more colourful than those of many contemporary bankers. In the 1860s he was prominent in two companies which attempted to exploit shale and cannel deposits in Flintshire to produce paraffin oil. These enterprises had failed by the 1870s, costing Rae heavily in time and resources. In private life—despite poor health from the 1860s onwards—he was an enthusiastic traveller and student of the arts. He and his family undertook tours of Europe, Russia, and the Middle East and Rae's diary of these travels was published privately in 1891. He was also a champion of the Pre-Raphaelite school of painting. He was a friend and patron of Ford Madox Brown and Edward Burne-Jones and he was especially proud of his link with Dante Gabriel Rossetti: 'I was one of the few who recognized his genius from the first' (Macleod, 18). Rae's large collection included nineteen paintings by Rossetti (notably *The Beloved*, 1863), six by Madox Brown, and twenty-six by William Davis. The Raes' home, Redcourt, Devonshire Place, Claughton, Cheshire, was designed by Edmund Kirby and built between 1876 and 1879. Rae died there on 4 August 1902 and was buried at Flaybrick Hill cemetery on 6 August.   EDWIN GREEN

Sources W. F. Crick and J. E. Wadsworth, *A hundred years of joint stock banking* (1936); 3rd edn (1958); repr. (1964) · E. Green, 'Rae, George', *DBB* · E. Green, 'George Rae, 1817–1902', in G. Rae, *The country banker: his clients, cares, and work* (1976), xvii–xxxi · *Liverpool Daily Post* (5 Aug 1902) · *Liverpool Mercury* (5 Aug 1902) · D. S. Macleod, 'The identity of Pre-Raphaelite patrons', *Reframing the Pre-Raphaelites: historical and theoretical essays*, ed. E. Harding (1996), 7–26 · G. S. O. Rippon, 'The Flintshire Oil and Cannel Co. Ltd, 1864–1872', MA diss., U. Lond., 1977 · E. Green, *Debtors to their profession: a history of the Institute of Bankers, 1879–1979* (1979)

Archives HSBC Group Archives, London, North and South Wales Bank collection, class M

Likenesses F. Holl, oils, 1884, HSBC Group Archives, London · G. Rae, self-portraits, ink caricatures, HSBC Group archives, London

Wealth at death £192,000 net: Green, 'Rae, George'

Rae [*married name* Normand]**, Henrietta Emma Ratcliffe** (1856–1928), painter, was born at 1 Grove Villas, The Grove, Hammersmith, London, on 30 December 1856, the youngest daughter of Thomas Burbey Rae, clerk of the local board of guardians, and his wife, Anne Eliza Louisa, née Graves, a gifted amateur musician. Though her mother wished her to make a career in music, she eventually began to train in art at the Female School of Art, Bloomsbury, independently at the British Museum, and in the evenings at Heatherley's School of Art. In 1877 she gained access at her sixth attempt to the Royal Academy Schools, where she studied until 1884.

Henrietta Rae exhibited widely in London and the provinces from 1879, making her début at the Royal Academy in 1881 with *Miss Warman*, a portrait. Her 1884 exhibit, *Lancelot and Elaine*, marked her intention to become identified as a painter of the highest genre, which included literary and mythological subjects, and the following year *Ariadne Deserted by Theseus* and *A Bacchante* (Christopher Wood Gallery, London) signalled her commitment to the classical revival promoted by the Royal Academy as the path to high art. This became viable for female artists at this time because the artistic training accessible to them began to compare with that available to men. She became the first female artist in Britain since Angelica Kauffmann to establish herself at this level of the hierarchy of genres. In this ambition she was much influenced by her friendship with the leading artist and best-known neo-classicist of the day, Frederic (later Lord) Leighton, whom she freely acknowledged as her mentor, though she was never his student. On 26 May 1884 Rae married in Croydon fellow artist Ernest (1857–1923), son of George Barten Normand. She had met him while a student at the Royal Academy and they went to live near Leighton in the newly fashionable district of Kensington which became something of an artistic colony from the 1880s. They had a son in 1886 and a daughter in 1893.

Seeking to develop her work, Rae and her husband went to Paris in 1890, studying at the Académie Julian and in Brittany. This experience gave her work a new painterliness, to be seen in *La cigale* which she showed at the Royal Academy in 1891. In 1894 she exhibited a large multi-figure composition, *Psyche before the Throne of Venus*, which the artist intended as her *chef-d'oeuvre*: though attracting much attention, and finding a purchaser in the important collector of contemporary art George McCulloch, it was deprecated by critics who found it too 'feminine' to be sufficiently grand. This was a major disappointment for her and thenceforward she seems to have accepted that prejudice against women's artistic ambitions would dog her efforts and always limit her successes. She continued, however, in the same vein of subjects and style, with such works as *Apollo and Daphne* (1895), *Isabella* (1896) (ex Sothebys), and *Diana and Callisto* (1899). Interleaving these ambitious canvases with the more commercially reliable genre of portraiture, she continued to appear regularly at the Royal Academy exhibitions until 1919. Despite the advent of modernism she did not abandon her production of classical stories presented in narrative fashion—for example, *Hylas and the Nymphs* (1910; priv. coll.)—and symbolic nude female figures—as in *Songs of the Morning* (1904; priv. coll.)—which still found a ready audience in the gallery-goers and collectors of her own generation.

Rae gained an honourable mention at the Universal Exhibition in Paris in 1889 and a medal at the world fair in Chicago in 1893. Her painting *Ophelia* (Walker Art Gallery, Liverpool) was purchased by the Liverpool corporation in 1890 and she was the first woman to serve on the hanging committee of that city's important autumn exhibition at the Walker Art Gallery in 1893. She was one of the artists commissioned to produce frescoes for the Royal Exchange, London, completed in 1900, and was included in the Victorian Exhibition mounted at Earls Court, London, in 1897 to represent the art of the queen's reign, serving as president of the women's art section. She died on 26 March 1928 at her home, St Egberts, 4 Fox Hill Gardens, Upper Norwood, Surrey. PAMELA GERRISH NUNN

Sources A. Fish, *Henrietta Rae (Mrs Ernest Normand)* (1905) • F. Rinder, 'Henrietta Rae—Mrs Ernest Normand', *Art Journal*, new ser., 21 (1901), 303–7 • R. Treble, ed., *Great Victorian pictures: their paths to fame* (1978) [exhibition catalogue, Leeds, Leicester, Bristol, and London, 28 Jan – Sept 1978] • b. cert. • *CGPLA Eng. & Wales* (1928) • m. cert.
Archives V&A NAL, Dyce Library, autograph letters
Likenesses E. Normand, watercolour drawing, 1881–4, repro. in H. L. Postlethwaite, 'Some noted women-painters', *Magazine of Art* (1895), p. 20 • photographs, repro. in Fish, *Henrietta Rae*, facing pp. 16, 96
Wealth at death £5965 5s. 6d.: probate, 21 May 1928, *CGPLA Eng. & Wales*

Rae, James (1716–1791), surgeon, only son of John Rae (1677–1754), a writer and descendant of Stirlingshire landowners, was born in Edinburgh. His grandfather, also named James Rae, was appointed barber to Charles II in 1662 and in 1686 was given permission to build public baths in Edinburgh. On 27 August 1747 Rae became a member of the Incorporation of Surgeons of Edinburgh, where in 1764–5 he filled the office of deacon or president. He also served as auditor of accounts (1754), librarian (1756), and treasurer (1760–64). Rae was the first surgeon appointed to the Edinburgh Royal Infirmary, on 7 July

1766, and he immediately began to give a series of lectures. These lectures were so highly appreciated by his colleagues that in October 1776 they made a determined attempt to found a professorship of surgery in the university and to appoint Rae the first professor. This project was defeated by Alexander Monro secundus, who afterwards managed to convert his own chair of anatomy into one of anatomy and surgery.

Rae married, in 1744, Isobel, daughter of Ludovic Cant of Thurstan; they had two sons and several daughters. The elder son, William, joined the Incorporation of Surgeons on 18 July 1777, settled in London, where he married Isabella, sister of Sir Robert Dallas, and died young. John, the younger brother, was the first fellow of the Royal College of Surgeons of Edinburgh, admitted on 14 March 1781; he became president in 1804–5 and was well known in Edinburgh as a dentist. Among Rae's daughters was Elizabeth, wife of James Fleming of Kirkcaldy, whose daughter Margaret Fleming (1803–1811) was immortalized by John Brown in *Pet Marjorie*.

Rae did in Edinburgh what Percivall Pott did in London: he established the teaching of clinical surgery on a firm and broad platform. He died in 1791 and was buried, as was his wife, in the family tomb in Greyfriars Church, Edinburgh. D'A. POWER, *rev.* MICHAEL BEVAN

Sources J. Boyes, 'James Rae, 1716–1791', *Proceedings of the Royal Society of Medicine*, 46 (1953), 457–60 • *List of fellows of the Royal College of Surgeons of Edinburgh* (1874) • 'William Prout and the nature of matter, 1785–1985', J. Brown, *Horae subsecivae: John Leech and other papers*, 5th edn (1884) • *The Scotsman* (4 April 1988) • G. Stewart, 'Account of the history of the Royal Infirmary', *Edinburgh Hospital Reports*, 1 (1893) • private information (1896)

Rae, John (1813–1893), Arctic explorer, was born on 30 September 1813 at the Hall of Clestrain, near Stromness, Orkney Islands, the sixth of nine children of John Rae, factor, an Orcadian, and his wife, Margaret Glen, a Campbell from Argyll. He spent his boyhood in Orkney, being educated by a tutor at home, before going to Edinburgh to study medicine in 1829. He qualified in April 1833 as licentiate of the Royal College of Surgeons of Edinburgh and was appointed surgeon of the Hudson's Bay Company's ship *Prince of Wales* in June 1833. From 1834 to 1844 he was surgeon at Moose Factory, the company post on James Bay: 'the best place east of the Rocky Mountains … a very happy home to me for ten years' (Richards, 20). Here he took part in the general work of the post and tended patients among the company's employees and local Cree people. During his leisure time, he 'learned all the different methods of hunting, fishing, sledge-hauling, snowshoe walking and camping out … that were afterwards so useful to me in my Arctic exploration' (Richards, 22).

In 1844 Rae was chosen by the governor of the Hudson's Bay Company, Sir George Simpson, to lead an expedition to complete the survey of the northern coastline of North America, partly accomplished by the fur traders, Samuel Hearne, Sir Alexander Mackenzie, Peter Dease, and Thomas Simpson, and by naval parties led by Sir John Franklin. With ten men, Rae left York Factory (on the western coast of Hudson Bay) on 13 June 1846 in two small

John Rae (1813–1893), by Stephen Pearce, exh. RA 1853

boats, northward bound. At Churchill an Inuit interpreter named Ouligbuck and his son joined them. They reached Repulse Bay on 24 July and learned from a party of Inuit that the sea lay some 40 miles to the north-west, the route being partly taken up by deep lakes. This route was traversed with one of the boats, the *North Pole*. They reached Committee Bay, where Rae's attempts to survey the coast by boat were thwarted by ice and bad weather. He turned back on 8 August and established winter quarters on Repulse Bay, where Fort Hope was built. Game was shot for the winter, and store houses and two magnetic observatories constructed. During sledge journeys in the spring and summer of 1847, the party reached Lord Mayor's Bay, on the east coast of Boothia peninsula, connecting their survey with that of Sir John and Sir James Clark Ross in 1829–33, and explored the west coast of Melville peninsula, almost reaching Fury and Hecla Strait, explored by Sir William Edward Parry in 1821–3. They returned by boat to York Factory on 6 September 1847, when Rae heard of his promotion to chief trader. He wrote a *Narrative of an Expedition to the Shores of the Arctic Sea in 1846 and 1847* (1850). The expedition was significant, not only for its geographical and meteorological results, but because the party was able to winter in the Arctic by eating local game and fish and building igloos.

During 1848–9, Rae joined Sir John Richardson (at the latter's request) to search for Sir John Franklin. Richardson, Rae, and party made an extremely fast (possibly record long distance) canoe journey from Sault Ste Marie near Toronto to the mouth of the Mackenzie River on the Arctic Ocean in ninety-six days, arriving on 3 August 1848. They travelled east along the coast, but ice hampered their search. They wintered at Fort Confidence on Great Bear

Lake, making regular meteorological and magnetic observations. Richardson went back to England in 1849, while Rae returned down the Coppermine River to the Arctic Ocean. He explored the Rae River, which Richardson had named after him the previous year, but ice forced him to abandon attempts to travel westward along the coast and northward to 'Wollaston Land' (later peninsula). In September 1849 the party travelled up the Mackenzie River to Fort Simpson where Rae took up his post as chief trader. In his *Arctic Searching Expedition* (1851) Richardson paid generous tribute to Rae.

With his new appointment, Rae had responsibility for the Mackenzie River district, the company's largest, but found the unaccustomed business management and accounting difficult. In June 1850 he was promoted chief factor. He wintered at Fort Confidence in 1850–51 to resume the search for Franklin at the Admiralty's request. Two boats were built to Rae's specification and rigged by Rae himself. He left Fort Confidence on 25 April 1851, and with two men, sledges, and dogs, crossed over the ice of Dolphin and Union Strait, reaching Wollaston peninsula on 6 May. He then travelled eastward along the coast of Victoria Island, finding that no strait divided Wollaston 'Land' from Victoria 'Land' and linking his own explorations with those of Dease and Simpson in 1839. He retraced his steps westward along the shores of the Wollaston peninsula as far as Prince Albert Sound. The party reached Kendall River on 10 June, having covered some 824 miles in 42 days.

Rae set out again from Kendall River on 15 June with a party of eleven, in the two boats built at Fort Confidence, reaching the mouth of the Coppermine River on 5 July and the eastern end of the Kent peninsula on 24 July. They sailed to Victoria Island, exploring Cambridge Bay and the shores to the north-east, sighting Pelly Point on the Collinson peninsula. The walking was so rough that their footwear quickly wore out and every step 'was marked with blood' (Richards, 80). Unfortunately the ice in Victoria Strait was too closely packed for the boats to reach King William Island where the Franklin tragedy had been enacted in 1848. Rae did find two pieces of wood while returning along the south coast of Victoria Island, which probably came from the *Erebus* or the *Terror*. These he brought back to England. The party returned to Fort Confidence on 10 September 1851, having crossed the narrows at the junction of Dolphin and Union Strait with Coronation Gulf. Rae reached Fort Simpson on 26 September ending a highly successful exploring expedition, which none the less left the mystery of Franklin's disappearance unsolved. He arrived in London in April 1852 and in May was awarded the founder's gold medal of the Royal Geographical Society. The same month he proposed to the Hudson's Bay Company a further Arctic expedition to complete the survey of the north coast of America along the west coast of the Boothia peninsula. This they approved and Rae was appointed leader in June 1852. He reached York Factory on 18 June 1853, and with his party ascended the unexplored Quoich River from Chesterfield inlet in July and August and wintered at Repulse Bay, at first in tents, then in snow huts. In the spring, with sledges and four men, including Ouligbuck the younger as interpreter, Rae travelled to Pelly Bay, arriving on 17 April 1854. On 21 April, he met 'a very communicative and apparently intelligent Eskimo', who said that 'a number of Kabloonans, at least 35–40, had starved to death west of a large river a long way off'. This was the first news of the tragedy of the Franklin expedition. Rae bought a cap band from the Inuit, who had not seen the dead bodies himself, and 'could not or would not' explain the place on the chart (Richards, 98). Rae continued his survey, thinking the information too vague to act upon, but asking his informant to produce more evidence. On 27 April the party reached the cairn built by Dease and Simpson at the mouth of the Castor and Pollux River in 1839. They then travelled along the west coast of the Boothia peninsula, and on their return journey to Repulse Bay carefully examined the coast of Pelly Bay, finding no strait to the west. They reached Repulse Bay on 26 May.

From other Inuit, Rae obtained artefacts from the *Erebus* and *Terror*, received from yet others who had observed some forty white men on King William Island dragging a boat and sledges to the south, and had later found the bodies of about thirty men and some graves on the mainland and five bodies on an island (which Rae thought must be Montreal Island at the mouth of the Great Fish or Back River). He reached York Factory in time to sail for England in the *Prince of Wales* on 20 September, bringing the first news of Franklin's fate. Geographically, his discovery that King William 'Land' was separated from the Boothia peninsula by a strait (later called after him) was also important, and although he failed to complete the survey of the west coast of the Peninsula, he proved that it formed part of the mainland of North America.

Rae arrived in London on Sunday 22 October 1854 and his report to the Admiralty was published in full in *The Times* next day. It caused a sensation, mainly because it repeated the suggestion of the Inuit that the last survivors had resorted to cannibalism. A public controversy ensued and Rae was criticized for not having verified the Inuit reports himself and for having hurried home to claim the £10,000 offered to the discoverer of Franklin's fate; a reward of which he insisted he was ignorant until his return to England. In the end, he received £8000 and his findings were largely confirmed by Sir Leopold McClintock in 1857–9. Rae's biographer has commended his 'dignity and restraint' during the controversy (Richards, 131). He was awarded the honorary degree of MD by McGill University, Montreal, in 1853.

In 1857 (having retired the previous year), Rae appeared on behalf of the Hudson's Bay Company before a select committee of the House of Commons in London, which was convened to investigate the company's activities before the expiry of its charter in 1859. In Toronto in January 1860 Rae married Catherine Jane Alicia (Kate), third child of Major George Ash Thompson of Ardkill, co. Londonderry, and Munechrone, co. Tyrone, Ireland. The Raes made their home in Britain, although Rae travelled in Canada from time to time and took part in telegraph

surveys in 1860 and in 1864. He divided his last years (1870–93) between London and Orkney. In 1866 he had been made an honorary LLD by Edinburgh University and in 1880, having contributed articles to *Nature* and other learned journals, he was made fellow of the Royal Society. He died at his home, 4 Addison Gardens, Kensington, London, of a ruptured aneurism on 22 July 1893. He was buried in the churchyard of St Magnus Cathedral, Kirkwall, Orkney, where an impressive memorial was erected by public subscription in 1895.

Rae got on well with his superiors and fellow officers of the Hudson's Bay Company, and with Inuit and Indians. He spoke well of the naval explorers Parry, Franklin, and Richardson but felt later that neither he nor the Hudson's Bay Company was given sufficient credit for Arctic exploration by Sir Clements Markham and others, who championed the navy. In more recent times, Rae has attracted admirers such as Vilhjalmur Stefansson, not only for his discoveries, but for his ability to 'live off the land'.

ANN SAVOURS

Sources R. L. Richards, *Dr. John Rae* (1985) [incl. bibliography] · E. E. Rich and others, *John Rae's correspondence with the Hudson's Bay Company on Arctic exploration, 1844–1855* (1953) · J. Rae, *Narrative of an expedition to the shores of the Arctic sea in 1846 and 1847* (1850) · I. Bunyan and others, *No ordinary journey: John Rae, Arctic explorer, 1813–1893* (1993)
Archives McGill University, Montreal, McCord Museum, accounts and journal related to Arctic expedition · NA Canada, letters and papers · RGS, corresp., diary, and essays related to Arctic exploration · Scott Polar RI, corresp. and papers | CUL, letters to Sir George Stokes · NL Scot., letters to Gladys Holman-Hunt · Orkney Archives, Kirkwall, letters to David Balfour · Provincial Archives of Manitoba, Winnipeg, Hudson's Bay Company archives
Likenesses M. Brady, photograph, 1853?, Hudson's Bay Company Archives, Winnipeg · S. Pearce, oils, exh. RA 1853, NPG [*see illus.*] · G. Maccallum, statue, 1866, U. Edin. · J. Whitehead, statue, 1895, St Magnus Cathedral, Kirkwall, Orkney · E. W. Dallas, photograph, NPG · S. Hodges, portrait; copy, Stromness Museum, Orkney · S. Pearce, oils; second version, Scot. NPG · oils, Stromness town hall, Orkney · photograph (in old age), Hudson's Bay Company Archives, Winnipeg · wood-engraving (after daguerreotype by Beard), NPG; repro. in *ILN* (28 Oct 1854)
Wealth at death £2164 7s. 6d.: administration with will, 9 March 1894, *CGPLA Eng. & Wales*

Rae, Peter (*c.*1671–1748), printer and mechanic, was born probably at Burronhill in the parish of Mouswald near Dumfries; his father's name was probably Peter Rae. In February 1692 he is recorded as a student in the class of Master John Law at Glasgow University, from which he graduated MA on 4 April 1694. He held three posts of clerkship in Dumfries before marrying, on 19 July 1697, Agnes Corsane. Matrimony encouraged him to seek a parish, and following trials and delays he was ordained as minister by the parish of Kirkbride near Sanquhar on 22 April 1703. By this date Rae had already shown his interest in matters mechanical. The hammermen (metalworkers) of Dumfries made him a freeman of the incorporation on 31 July 1702; his essay piece, possibly the first grandfather clock to have been manufactured in the south of Scotland, still survived in the 1990s, as did an astronomical chime clock he presented to the third duke of Queensberry in the 1730s.

Rae's ministry at Kirkbride involved constant strife with his parishioners, but he still managed to construct a printing press, only the seventh operating in Scotland at the time. The first recorded production was a broadside against the Act of Union (1706), followed over the next fifteen years by at least eighteen further works ranging from religious tracts to chapbooks. *A History of the Late Rebellion* (1718), researched, written, and printed by Rae, is one of the main sources for the period. The *Dumfries Mercury* (1721), of which only the eighteenth and a portion of the twelfth numbers are known to survive, was the first newspaper in Scotland to be produced outside Edinburgh and Glasgow. A peculiarity of the press's productions was that Robert Rae was named as the printer. Robert, Peter's son, was eight years old when the press commenced operations, and although he later became involved with the family business (especially after 1714, when the press moved to Dumfries) it is likely that Peter used his son's name as a means of deflecting criticism within his parish. A hostile contemporary rhyme has no doubt of the printer's identity

> The printing trade he now does try
> The Minister trade he should lay by.
> (R. Ker, *Works*, 1719)

In 1721 Rae's wife, Agnes, inherited the extensive Corsane estates, and legal difficulties connected with the legacy persuaded him to cease printing. Nevertheless, other activities occupied this many-sided man. He was the agent at the Wanlockhead lead mines, surveyed the Lochar moss outside Dumfries, and in 1733 published his own sermon *Gospel Ministers Christ's Ambassadors*. Peter and Agnes had at least ten children; the surviving sons turned their father's hobbies into businesses, Robert as a printer, Alexander as a clockmaker in Dumfries, and James as agent at the lead mines and farmer. Rae was given the more substantial living of Kirkconnel parish in 1732, and in 1748 was awarded a timely tribute when he was elected moderator of Dumfries presbytery. He died at Kirkconnel manse on 29 December of that year, and was buried in Kirkconnel churchyard. *A Treatise of Lawful Oaths and Perjury* was published posthumously in 1749, and fragments of a manuscript history of Penpont presbytery survive.

GRAHAM ROBERTS

Sources G. W. Shirley, 'Mr. Peter Rae, V.D.M., printer', *Records of the Glasgow Bibliographical Society*, 1 (1914), 216–35 • G. W. Shirley, 'MSS notes for a life of Rev. Peter Rae, printer, and other notes, including some on the family of Corsares', Ewart Library, Dumfries, R. C. Reid MSS, vols. 123–4 • *Watson's preface to the 'History of printing'*, 1713, ed. W. J. Couper (1913) • G. W. Shirley, *Dumfries printers in the eighteenth century, with handlists of their books* (1934) • W. Stewart, *The Rae Press at Kirkbride and Dumfries* (1906) • A. E. Truckell, 'Supplementary chapter to the history of Dumfries', *History of the burgh of Dumfries, with notices of Nithsdale, Annandale and the western border*, 4th edn (1986) • G. W. Shirley, 'Kirkbride "where the Lord's redeemed ones lie": its legend examined', *Gallovidian Annual* (1926) • *Scots Magazine*, 11 (1749), 53 • parish records (marriage), Dumfries parish, 19 July 1697 • parish records (baptisms), Dumfries parish, 1671 • memorial inscriptions for Kirkconnel parish, Dumfriesshire, Scotland

Likenesses oils, *c*.1705, Gracefield Arts Centre, Dumfries

Wealth at death extensive stock of cattle and sheep, some acres of corn and barley, and an extensive library (about 400 volumes); large landed estate passed directly to Rae's son, Robert: will

Rae, Sir William, third baronet (1769–1842), judge, was born in Edinburgh on 14 April 1769, the younger son of Sir David *Rae, first baronet (1729–1804), judge, and his wife, Margaret, daughter of John Stuart of Blairhall, Perthshire. He was educated at Edinburgh high school (1779–82), at Glasgow University (*c*.1788), and then at Edinburgh University. On 9 September 1793 he married Mary (*d*. 1839), daughter of Lieutenant-Colonel Charles Stuart. They had no children.

Rae appears to have spent a convivial youth, and he retained convivial habits. At the age of nineteen he joined Walter Scott in founding 'The Club'. The two became lifelong friends. Scott referred to 'dear loved Rae' in the introduction to the fourth canto of *Marmion*, and later said that he was 'sensible, cool-headed, and firm, always thinking of his duty, and never of himself' (Lockhart, 1.207–8 n., 6.140). Rae followed his father's profession and became an advocate in 1791, but fifteen years later he was still described as 'not in great practice, of useful rather than shining abilities' (HoP, *Commons*, 5.2). He had, as a freeholder in Lanarkshire, whiggish connections with the duke of Hamilton and Lord Rosslyn. Through their influence he was appointed sheriff of Orkney in 1801. His politics remained, however, tory enough to win him promotion as sheriff of Edinburgh in 1809. On 22 May 1815 he succeeded his brother as third baronet.

Rae's tranquil career changed course abruptly in June 1819 when he was appointed lord advocate in place of the bungling Alexander Maconochie. The government needed a steadier hand to deal with the social upheavals after the end of the French wars. Lord Melville, the Scottish manager, described Rae as 'a most judicious adviser' (Fry, 339), and Lord President Hope found him a man 'of conciliatory manner and frank and open temper' (ibid.). Maconochie had tried harsh repression; Rae's line, while still firm, was markedly more moderate. He virtually ceased taking action against trades unions, because their illegality was by no means certain under Scots law, and because 'in none of the cases of simple combination which came before me was I satisfied that the masters were entirely without blame' (Fry, 336).

In April 1820 the 'radical war' broke out—an armed rebellion, if on a modest scale, by groups of industrial workers in the west of Scotland. Rae thought the authorities there indolent and panicky at once, and correctly predicted that the business would end in nothing. He went to Glasgow himself and remained unimpressed: 'Although we have had abundance of false alarms, all has continued quiet in Scotland' (Fry, 340). The radicals were cowed, he added, to such an extent that it might be difficult to bring them to justice. Rae disdained resort to the use of spies, turncoats, agents provocateurs, and other methods normal in Scottish forensic investigation. As he set about restoring order, he showed for the most part a good sense of public relations, tempered justice with mercy, and struck shrewd plea-bargains with prisoners and their counsel. Nevertheless, he led personally for the crown in the trials of Andrew Hardie and other radicals during the summer of 1820, on indictments of high treason; three of them were hanged.

On taking office, Rae had been elected MP for the Anstruther burghs. Much of his parliamentary career would be taken up with repelling reformers' attacks on the existing system of government of Scotland. In February 1822 he opposed Lord Archibald Hamilton's motion for a committee of the whole house on the notoriously corrupt councils of the royal burghs. Since they also elected MPs, Rae objected that any change in their constitutions would amount to 'a parliamentary reform of the burghs of Scotland' (*Hansard 2*). A few days afterwards, however, he introduced a bill to remedy at least the financial abuses in them. It became law but remained a dead letter. Later in the year he was embarrassed by the affair of the *Glasgow Sentinel*, a tory paper which the government subsidized. Libels published in it had led to a duel in which Alexander Boswell, son of the biographer, was shot dead. Rae prosecuted his killer, James Stuart, for murder. He was then himself heavily criticized for his part in supporting the newspaper. A motion in the House of Commons calling for an inquiry was defeated by an unusually small margin.

In other respects, Rae proved himself more liberal. He successfully resisted pressure for a tightening of the already parsimonious Scots poor law. He undertook a major series of legal reforms. The lord advocate nominated to the Scottish bench, and Rae made sure that some leading whig advocates were given the preferment that once would have been refused them. He ended the long-standing grievance that judges could themselves appoint juries in criminal cases, and replaced this practice with a ballot. He set up in 1824–5 a royal commission to look at the general structure of the judiciary, with special reference to procedure and appeals, both of which were too cumbrous and slow. As a result he was able to plan a thorough reorganization of the higher Scottish courts, which gave them more or less their modern shape. He carried this into law by an act of 1830. He also initiated a review of the state of Scottish prisons (1825). He set up a second royal commission on the universities in 1826 and served on it himself. This brought to light a number of weaknesses in a system of which Scotland was immensely proud, though no legislative remedy was to follow for many years.

In the general election of 1826, Rae lost his seat. The problems in his constituency appeared to be of no wider significance, but they gave startling evidence of decay in Melville's electoral machine. Rae was returned as MP for Harwich in 1827, soon after the political crisis at Westminster following the retirement of Lord Liverpool. Melville refused to serve under his successor, George Canning, but Rae, along with other officers of government in Scotland, agreed to stay on. This was a decisive break in the system of management under which the country had been ruled for fifty years and more.

Rae kept his post through further changes of ministry. One diversion from the rampant factionalism at Westminster was his leading the prosecution in December 1828 of William Burke, the 'resurrectionist', who was convicted and hanged. Higher political events caught up with Rae in 1830. Melville, by then back in office, refused to recommend him to the lucrative post of chief baron of exchequer, which he might reasonably have expected after eleven years in harness. His colleague John Hope, the solicitor-general, wrote: 'The treatment of the Advocate is scandalous. I think it the very harshest and most unfeeling thing any Government ever did … The cry against Lord Melville is louder and more general than any ever raised in my time as to any public or personal matter' (Fry, 377; Omond, 349).

Rae was made a privy councillor on 19 July 1830. He found another Scottish seat, in Bute, at the general election of that year, and resigned on the fall of the tory ministry in November. In the parliament of 1831–2 he represented Portarlington. He came back for Bute at a by-election in 1833, and sat for the county until his death. He was lord advocate again in Sir Robert Peel's government of 1834–5, and once more from 1841. Rae remained active until the end of his life, especially in some causes close to his heart: official aid for building new churches in Scotland, reform of the prisons, and erection of the Scott monument in Edinburgh. Often unfairly lampooned by the whig press as a dim and incompetent reactionary, his career rather showed his impartiality, quiet good sense, and capacity for sensible reform. He died a widower at his home, St Catherine's, near Edinburgh, on 19 October 1842, and was buried nearby at Inveresk.   MICHAEL FRY

Sources M. Fry, *The Dundas despotism* (1992) · G. W. T. Omond, *The lord advocates of Scotland from the close of the fifteenth century to the passing of the Reform Bill*, 2 vols. (1883) · *Hansard 2* (1822), 6.542–5 · HoP, Commons · J. G. Lockhart, *Memoirs of the life of Sir Walter Scott*, [2nd edn], 10 vols. (1839) · H. Cockburn, *Letters chiefly connected with the affairs of Scotland* (1888) · *Memorials of his time, by Henry Cockburn*, another edn, ed. H. A. Cockburn (1910) · NL Scot., SC 70/1/63/445 · DNB
Archives BL, corresp. with Sir Robert Peel, Add. MS 40339 · NA Scot., Home Office (Scotland) MSS · NA Scot., lord advocate's MSS · NA Scot., corresp. with Lord Melville · NL Scot., corresp. with Lord Melville · NL Scot., corresp. with Sir Walter Scott · NRA, priv. coll., corresp. with James Skene
Wealth at death £1431 7s. 2d.: inventory, 1843, NL Scot., SC 70/1/62/445

Rae, Sir William (1786–1873), naval surgeon, was the son of Matthew Rae of Park-end, Annandale, Dumfries. He was educated at Lochmaben and Dumfries schools, and afterwards graduated MD at Edinburgh University. In 1804 he entered the medical service of the East India Company, but in the following year was transferred as surgeon to the Royal Navy. He served first in the *Culloden* under Sir Edward Pellew. In 1807, when in the *Fox* (32 guns) he took part in the destruction of the Dutch ships at Gressic in Java. Subsequently, when the squadron was becalmed in the Bay of Bengal, he contrived an apparatus for distilling water. When attached to the *Leyden* in 1812–13 he was successful in his treatment of the troops suffering from yellow fever at Cartagena and Gibraltar, and received the thanks of the commander-in-chief and the medical board. In 1814 he married Mary, daughter of Robert Bell.

In 1824 Rae was appointed to the Bermuda station. He became MRCS in 1811, extra licentiate of the Royal College of Physicians in 1839, and FRCS in 1843. In 1831 he married Maria, daughter of Assistant Commissary-General R. Lee: she survived her husband. On 22 August 1840 he became deputy inspector of hospitals and fleets, and ultimately attained the rank of inspector-general of hospitals and fleets in January 1849. In 1855 he retired on a pension to a country practice near Barnstaple, Devon. He was created CB in July 1855, and knighted in June 1858. He died at his home, Hornby Lodge, Newton Abbot, Devon, on 8 April 1873, and was buried at Wolborough, near Newton Abbot.

G. Le G. Norgate, rev. Andrew Lambert

Sources *Navy List* · *The Times* (10 April 1873) · *ILN* (26 April 1873) · J. J. Colledge, *Ships of the Royal Navy: an historical index*, 1 (1969) · Boase, *Mod. Eng. biog.* · Walford, *County families* · Ward, *Men of the reign* · *CGPLA Eng. & Wales* (1873)
Wealth at death under £3000: probate, 5 May 1873, *CGPLA Eng. & Wales*

Rae, William Fraser (1835–1905), author, was born in Edinburgh on 3 March 1835, the elder son of George Rae and his wife, Catherine Fraser, both of Edinburgh. After education at Moffat Academy and at Heidelberg, where he studied German, Rae entered Lincoln's Inn as a student on 2 November 1857, and on 30 April 1861 was called to the bar. But he soon abandoned law for journalism.

On 29 August 1860 Rae married Sara Eliza, second daughter of James Fordati of the Isle of Man and London. About this time he edited the periodical *The Reader*, and joined the staff of the *Daily News* as a special correspondent in Canada and the United States. He was in complete sympathy with the Liberal views of that paper. He published books on Canada and other subjects.

Throat trouble led Rae to spend much time at Austrian health resorts, where he wrote articles about them for *The Times*, which were reprinted as *Austrian Health Resorts, and the Bitter Waters of Hungary* (1888). In *The Business of Travel* (1891) he described the methods of Thomas Cook & Son.

Rae was particularly interested in eighteenth-century English political history. In 1874 he brought out *Wilkes, Sheridan, and Fox, or, The Opposition under George III*, which echoed the style of Macaulay. He studied the question of the identity of Junius, on which he wrote in *The Athenaeum* (between 11 August 1888 and 6 May 1899, and occasionally later). He bolstered the argument that Junius was not Sir Philip Francis. He was never able to identify Junius, but eliminated many possible candidates from consideration. He also made a careful study of the career of Sheridan. With the aid of Lord Dufferin and others, he collected much unpublished material and sought to rehabilitate Sheridan's reputation. This resulted in *Sheridan, a Biography* (2 vols., 1896). Rae succeeded in proving many rumours false, but failed in his purpose of whitewashing

Sheridan. In 1902 he published from the original manuscripts *Sheridan's Plays, now Printed as he Wrote them* and *A Journey to Bath*, a previously unpublished comedy by Sheridan's mother. He also wrote four three-volume novels (published between 1887 and 1891).

Towards the end of his life Rae reviewed much for *The Athenaeum*, whose editor, Norman MacColl, was a close friend. He spent his time chiefly at the Reform Club, which he had joined in 1860, and where he was chairman of the library committee from 1873 until his death. He was an occasional contributor to the *Dictionary of National Biography*. Chronic ill health and his declining popularity tended somewhat to sour his last years. Sara died at Franzensbad, where she and Rae were frequent autumn visitors, on 29 August 1902, leaving two daughters. Rae died on 22 January 1905 at his residence, 13 South Parade, Bath, and was buried at Bath.

S. E. Fryer, rev. Joseph Coohill

Sources *The Times* (25 Jan 1905) · *WW* (1905) · Allibone, *Dict.*, suppl. · *The Athenaeum* (28 Jan 1905) · private information (1912) · *CGPLA Eng. & Wales* (1905)
Wealth at death £1405 10s. 3d.: administration with will, 7 March 1905, *CGPLA Eng. & Wales*

Raeburn, Harold Andrew (1865–1926), mountaineer, was born on 21 July 1865 at 12 Grange Loan, Edinburgh, the fourth son of William Raeburn (d. 1898), a brewer, and his wife, Jessie, née Ramsay. He grew up to enter his father's occupation as a brewer. It is not documented how or why he began climbing, but a fair guess would be that his deep interest in ornithology led him up steep places where he would not otherwise have ventured. Living under Edinburgh's Salisbury Crags and possessing a wiry, athletic build, he soon adapted to the vertical world of rock and ice.

Raeburn's other sport was sailing, and he raced yachts in the Firth of Forth; here too there may have been a connection with his passion for ornithology. With his uncle John he raced as a member of the Royal Forth Yachting Club, based in Granton. They were successful enough to win the club's Corinthian cup three times. After being presented with the cup, they in turn presented it back to the club, who renamed it the Raeburn trophy, the name under which it is still raced for. His diaries on the seabirds of the Shetland Islands are lodged with the National Library of Scotland.

In 1896 Raeburn joined the Scottish Mountaineering Club, which had been founded in 1889, and within a few years he became its leading climber, recording many classic routes throughout Scotland. There are quite a few 'Raeburn's gullies' scattered across the land. A mountaineer may well become a good writer, but in essence he or she will be remembered for the quality of the climbs made, either as first ascents or as repeat ascents. On Ben Nevis in particular Raeburn left a superb legacy of quality routes: a solo first ascent of Observatory Ridge in June 1901, Observatory Buttress solo in June 1902, his outstanding eponymous arête two days later on North-East Buttress, with Dr and Mrs Inglis Clark, and the first winter ascent of Green Gully in 1906. The latter ascent, with a Swiss alpinist,

Eberhard Phildius, was barely recognized in a later guide-book, as he had not climbed the rocks of the Comb on the left, but had instead followed snow and ice in the gully. Indeed, Raeburn's ascent was completely forgotten by 1937, when Jim Bell made the second winter ascent, thinking it was the first.

On the Buachaille in Glen Coe, Raeburn made the first three ascents of Crowberry Gully, including a wintry ascent in 1909, and the second ascent and first Scottish ascent of Crowberry Ridge Direct (1902), then the hardest rock climb in Scotland. His style of rock-climbing was very muscular, holding himself close to the rock, while his particular attention to the exact times of ascents could frequently drive his companions to exasperation. There is a humorous reference to this when a fellow club member called Newbigging made a first ascent on Ben Nevis and called it 'Newbigging's 80-minute route', this being an echo to 'Raeburn's 18-minute route' climbed the previous year.

In the greater ranges, too, Raeburn recorded fine climbs, including the first British guideless ascent of the Zmutt ridge of the Matterhorn in 1906, the ascent of the north face of the Disgrazia in 1910 with his friend Willie Ling, the first solo traverse of the Meije, as well as first ascents in Norway and the Caucasus. He made two interesting expeditions to the Caucasus, in 1913 and 1914. During the first he made first ascents of five mountains, and attempted Uschba, before being turned back by poor conditions. In 1914 four new mountains were climbed, with Raeburn descending to find that a world war had broken out. From 1902 onwards he climbed without guides. He sometimes climbed with women, including his sister Ruth, herself an expert climber. In 1904 he joined the Alpine Club (London).

Raeburn was vice-president of the Scottish Mountaineering Club from 1909 to 1911, but later turned down the presidency. His book *Mountaineering Art* was in manuscript when the First World War broke out, and long, hard hours in an aeroplane factory for the next six years stopped all climbing. (At forty-nine he was too old for the Royal Flying Corps.) As a celebration following the end of the war, in 1919 he returned to the Alps and made a solo traverse of the Meije ridges.

In 1920 Raeburn's book was finally published, having been postponed owing to the war. The timing was unlucky, as by then it was already becoming somewhat dated. At Easter 1920, during the Scottish Mountaineering Club meet at Fort William, he made what was probably his finest ascent in Scotland: the first winter ascent of Observatory Ridge on Ben Nevis. With fellow members W. A. Mounsey and F. S. Goggs, and using a 100 foot rope, the three finished the route in just under six hours. Equipped with just one long axe each, and no crampons, the mental and physical control required of all three climbers was astonishing.

In 1920 Raeburn was on an expedition to Kanchenjunga, and in 1921 he led an Everest reconnaissance party. He worked desperately hard at organizing and preparing the party while suffering from influenza. By the time the expedition reached Tibet, dysentery had broken out. One member of the party, Alexander Mitchell Kellas, died, and Raeburn himself had to be carried down and spent two months in hospital. Against common sense he returned to the expedition, but he was now exhausted and never really recovered. Declining health eventually led to his death five years later. He died, unmarried, at Craig House, Edinburgh, on 21 December 1926, and was buried in Warriston cemetery, Edinburgh.

Raeburn very obviously possessed the necessary determination and drive of any ambitious and hard mountaineer; Lord Mackay described him as 'physically and mentally hard as nails, trained by solitary sea-cliff climbing after birds' haunts, he was certain, unyielding and concise in every movement, both mental and physical', and commented on his remarkable capacity of grip: 'He was possessed of strong muscular fingers that could press firmly and in a straight downward contact upon the very smallest hold' (Mackay). The Scottish Mountaineering Club's Raeburn Hut, between Dalwhinnie and Newtonmore, was opened in 1988 and is named after him.

KEN CROCKET

Sources K. V. Crocket, *Ben Nevis: Britain's highest mountain* (1986) · W. N. Ling, 'In memoriam', *Scottish Mountaineering Club Journal*, 18 (1927), 26–31 · Lord Mackay, 'Vignettes of earlier climbers', *Scottish Mountaineering Club Journal*, 24 (1950), 169–80 · K. V. Crocket and J. R. R. Fowler, 'Of beer and boats', *Scottish Mountaineering Club Journal*, 36 (1997), 380–83 · 'Ben Nevis: Observatory Ridge', *Scottish Mountaineering Club Journal*, 15 (1920), 310–18 · *Alpine Club Journal*, 39 (May 1927), 126 · private information (2004) [Gerald Glancy] · H. A. Raeburn, *Mountaineering art* (1920) · b. cert. · d. cert.
Archives NL Scot., diaries, Acc. 11538
Likenesses photograph, c.1905, repro. in Ling, 'In memoriam' · photograph, repro. in *Alpine Club Journal*, 126 · photographs, repro. in Raeburn, *Mountaineering art*

Raeburn, Sir Henry (1756–1823), portrait painter, was born on 4 March 1756 in the village of Stockbridge, now a district of Edinburgh which lies about a mile north-west of Edinburgh Castle, at that time the westernmost limit of the city. He was baptized three days later in the parish church of St Cuthbert (the West Kirk), which lies beneath the castle rock. His parents were Robert Raeburn, a yarn boiler, who ran a successful business preparing raw yarn for the woollen trade, and Ann Elder. There were at least three other children of the marriage: William, who would work in the business; Charles, described in later life as a mariner; and Ann, who married a Robert Wemyss.

Childhood and apprenticeship Robert Raeburn was a man of some significance in his trade, holding office in the Incorporation of Weavers of his district on a number of occasions; but his reputation must have been tarnished when he was accused of forging a signature on a financial document and imprisoned for a period at the beginning of 1760. Accusations of sexual impropriety with his washerwoman were raised at the same time but these were not proved.

In the year before Henry Raeburn's birth, Robert Raeburn had erected a 114 foot-long boiling house on the east bank of the Water of Leith where it flowed north through Stockbridge, on land feued from the governors of George

Sir Henry Raeburn (1756–1823), self-portrait, *c.*1815

Heriot's Hospital. This was part of a complex of buildings that the elder Raeburn was erecting during the 1750s, and it was in one of these low-lying buildings that the future painter was born. The harnessed power of this river was the necessary condition for Raeburn's trade and for the other milling operations carried out in its vicinity, and for those brought up along its banks its constant sound must have seemed a natural part of their being.

At some time during the early 1760s Robert Raeburn and his wife both died, leaving Henry in the care of his brother William, some twelve years his senior. William took over the running of the family business (and continued in this role until his own death in 1810), while his younger brother entered George Heriot's Hospital in the spring of 1765. The school had been founded by James VI and I's jeweller, George Heriot, for the education of the orphaned children of tradesmen. The building had been erected between 1628 and the end of the seventeenth century in a Scots Renaissance style on a plateau of land above the Grassmarket, which lay to the south of the castle ramparts. The nine-year-old boy, after a quite long, uphill trek from his home, must initially have felt overwhelmed by the sheer presence of this immense, four-square building, still one of the most impressive in Edinburgh.

While pursuing a normal academic education Henry Raeburn, at some point during these years, must have demonstrated particular manual skills which seemed to suit him to the jewellery trade. Through a process begun by his school in the autumn of 1771, Raeburn was indentured to a goldsmith, James Gilliland, on 27 June 1772. He was now sixteen. At this time the jewellers of Edinburgh operated from the 'luckenbooths' (literally, locked-up shops) in Parliament Square, clustered round the medieval church of St Giles in the High Street. It is quite likely that Raeburn took up residence with his master, whose address is recorded as Blairs Luckenbooths. Gilliland had been in business as a jeweller from as early as 1752 and his activities are recorded until April 1790, when he probably died. His wife, Elizabeth, was the sister of the London publisher and bookseller John Murray (formerly McMurray), and they operated as agents for each other in their respective cities. The appearance of the jeweller and his wife is known, for in due course Raeburn painted their portraits in miniature.

The path that led Raeburn to portrait painting is not entirely clear, but at some time during his apprenticeship to Gilliland he seems to have graduated to painting miniatures, a class of object that would come quite naturally within his ken in a jeweller's workshop. Among his known subjects were Gilliland and his wife (both John Murray Publishers Ltd, London) and another goldsmith, and seal engraver, David Deuchar (NG Scot.). It is Deuchar who is traditionally credited with encouraging Raeburn to follow this course. These miniatures are accomplished in a descriptive sense but are formally rather naïve. Given the immense skills that Raeburn developed within the next decade as he turned to life-size portraiture, it is likely that this naïvety disappeared quite quickly and that many miniatures of a more sophisticated sort were painted during the 1770s and 1780s and are at present unrecognized. This possibility is borne out by a little watercolour portrait in miniature format of Sir John Clerk of Penicuik (priv. coll.), painted perhaps in the late 1780s and showing the precise control of light and shade that marks his mature work.

'Portrait Painter in Edinburgh'; Italian sojourn Within two years of the official end of his apprenticeship, Raeburn married, probably in 1780, a widow of some substance, Ann Leslie (*née* Edgar) (1744–1832), who was twelve years his senior. She had married the rather shadowy James Leslie in 1772 and through him had acquired Deanhaugh House, virtually opposite the Raeburn property on the other side of the Water of Leith. Besides two young daughters, Ann and Jacobina, she brought to the marriage not inconsiderable wealth inherited from her late father-in-law George Leslie, who had owned property in Paris as well as Edinburgh. A story in Allan Cunningham's life of Raeburn about how the painter met his future wife, and was enraptured by her when she came to sit for her portrait, has usually been dismissed as a romantic myth, but it has been given credence by the recent identification of an anonymous portrait of a widow as both Ann Leslie and Raeburn's earliest known full-scale portrait (NG Scot.).

The earliest years of the marriage were spent at Deanhaugh House, which was set in attractive grounds with close-cropped sward running to the river's edge. Despite the industrial activities on the other side of the river, the setting was virtually rural and the deep valley within yards to the south was a place of luxuriant natural growth.

In the next few decades as the classical New Town of Edinburgh spread in the fields above, the area acquired a degree of enlightened artificiality. On the south side of the river a temple to Hygieia, designed by the painter Alexander Nasmyth, was erected above a mineral spring, on land feued by Raeburn.

The Raeburns' marriage produced two sons: Peter, born on 18 May 1781, and Henry, born on 24 October 1783. Within months of the latter's birth Raeburn had turned his mind towards a prolonged visit to Rome, and the summer of 1784 saw him making financial arrangements for his wife's affairs during his absence and arranging letters of credit for himself. It is an indication of Raeburn's desire to succeed that he should undertake such a journey so soon after marriage and, especially, the birth of two children. In the course of these preparations Raeburn is designated 'Mr Raeburn the Painter' and refers unequivocally to himself as 'Portrait Painter in Edinburgh'. This must mean that he had already established himself in such a role and gained at least some public recognition. Surviving portraits that would bear this out are, however, rare. There is the presumed portrait of Ann Leslie, soon to be his wife, and a portrait of the young advocate and connoisseur John Clerk, who became a close friend. The latter portrait was destroyed before its significance was realized, but old photographs suggest a painter of great observational accomplishment, but one whose visual imagination was still to be released.

The friendship with Clerk, of whom Raeburn painted another portrait about 1815, one that is deeply eloquent (Scot. NPG), is likely to have had a significant effect on Raeburn's development. His collection of books, paintings, bronzes, and especially prints must have been a great stimulus. Among the prints was a complete set of Rembrandt etchings, whose humanity and tenebrism must have set him thinking. Sources of the practical skills that Raeburn was still developing in the years before he set off for Rome are likely to have been drawing classes of the kind that he is recorded as attending in 1781 where the older painter Alexander Runciman gave guidance. These comprised drawing from the antique and the draped figure—but not the nude, an inevitable restriction in a presbyterian country. This must account for the suspect anatomy in a number of Raeburn's mature portraits.

There is also a tradition that Raeburn was given some assistance by David Martin, who had once worked as an assistant to Raeburn's great Scottish predecessor, Allan Ramsay. Ramsay's method was one of careful planning and making preliminary drawings, quite the opposite of Raeburn's empirical approach. For Raeburn drawing was to be something done with a brush directly on the canvas and extended in a variety of visual responses. While Raeburn may have looked at Martin, none of Ramsay's genius had rubbed off on him, and Raeburn probably found his portraits stiff and uninspired.

Raeburn is likely to have reached Rome in the autumn of 1784. Almost inevitably he made contact with a countryman, James Byres, antiquary, *cicerone* (guide), and general entrepreneur, who provided a focus for Britons on the grand tour. Byres is credited with a piece of advice to Raeburn which, whatever the evidence, rings entirely true: this was always to paint with the object in front of him, and not to rely on memory or imagination. It was advice that Raeburn showed every sign of having accepted. Byres also found him a patron in the young second Earl Spencer, who commissioned a miniature of himself—not from life, but to be copied from a pastel drawing by the Irish artist Hugh Douglas Hamilton. Compared with Raeburn's early miniatures it is startlingly sophisticated and shows him working in a main-line British portrait tradition (priv. coll.).

The miniature was completed late in January 1786. Probably rather earlier, Raeburn had painted a life-size portrait of Byres's sixteen-year-old nephew Patrick Moir, in a melancholic pose, reading a book (on loan to NG Scot.). Not yet entirely accomplished, it has a carefully worked surface that may derive from the elderly Pompeo Batoni, pre-eminently the portraitist of young Britons, whom Raeburn must have met through Byres. His only other known works from this sojourn in Rome are two little copies, one of them a *David with the Head of Goliath* after the seventeenth-century painter Giovanni Francesco Romanelli. The conventional view has been that Raeburn learned little in Italy, but even this tiny copy disposes of that notion, for the way in which the light floods down the principal figure to illuminate the salient features became one of his major stylistic traits.

Early success Raeburn was probably back in Scotland by the summer of 1786. On both legs of his journey he must have spent some time in London. Tales of meeting Sir Joshua Reynolds are not strictly documented but some sort of contact is highly likely. That he had gathered first-hand evidence of the English portrait tradition, probably from a number of sources, is borne out by the portraits he painted shortly after his return to Edinburgh: a three-quarter length of the judge Lord Arniston (priv. coll.), and a pair of head-and-shoulders portraits of Sir William and Lady Forbes of Craigievar (Craigievar Castle), the first a rather solemn exercise in Reynolds's cerebral mode, the latter two suffused with his social sensibility.

It was with portraits like these that Raeburn very rapidly established his supremacy, brooking few rivals for the remainder of his life. It almost seemed that the vigorous society that he now entered, perceived as an 'Athens of the north', required a mediator like Raeburn and that this need was somehow a precondition of his genius.

Although a number of Raeburn's portraits of the late 1780s continued to show the influence of Reynolds, about 1790 he was developing a highly individual, indeed unique, form of lighting, where the figure was placed in front of a strong light source which scintillated around its contours and then spread in a series of reflections of differing strength within the dark forms. The most striking of these works, and one of the most beautiful he ever painted, was the double portrait of Sir John and Lady Clerk of Penicuik, standing in front of the low hills of their estate (NG Ire.). This portrait, for which he was able to charge 60 guineas, was sent to London for exhibition at the Royal Academy in 1792 but arrived too late for inclusion—an early misjudgment of the London art world. It was shown instead at Boydell's Shakspeare Gallery where its 'singular style' was noticed by an anonymous critic who found much in it to praise. He also suggested, however, that more attention should have been given to the foliage of the trees, one of the earliest accusations of lack of finish which were to follow Raeburn throughout his career.

The singular form of *contre-jour* lighting that Raeburn had devised had precedents of a sort in sixteenth- and seventeenth-century Italian painting but it had never been used in portraiture in quite this way and it seems that his patrons found it rather difficult to accept. Henry Mackenzie, for example—the 'man of feeling'—called it Raeburn's 'falsetto style' and hoped he would give it up. In effect, Raeburn did, although carefully angled sidelighting always remained part of his repertory. It was in the mid-1790s that his inventiveness, which might have had a freer rein in a different climate, led him to paint the unique little full length of his skating friend, the Revd Robert Walker, better known as *The Skating Minister* (NG Scot.). Its combination of poise, precision, and humour have made it by far Raeburn's most famous painting; indeed, by a quirk of taste, since its virtual rediscovery in 1949 it has gained a degree of popularity unique in British art.

Raeburn's studio in these years was on the south side of George Street, the central avenue of Edinburgh's burgeoning New Town. However, his success, and probably his aspirations, were such that he outgrew these premises and towards the turn of the century erected a grand terraced house in York Place (initially no. 16, now no. 34). The rooms included reception areas, a picture gallery, a workshop for a frame maker, and a studio which took up the whole of the first floor. This studio contained a greatly enlarged window to the north which gathered the light above the River Forth and the county of Fife. This pure light, which meant so much to him, he controlled by a series of complex shutters, probably of his own devising. Joseph Farington called to inspect this studio in 1801, but missed Raeburn himself. Viewing some of Raeburn's portraits, he speculated on their 'Camera Obscura effect' (Farington, *Diary*, 5.1631). It is highly unlikely, however, that Raeburn used any optical devices, and Farington may simply have failed to appreciate his observational acuity. As it happens, Raeburn later became aware of the camera lucida, and in 1818 he and Francis Chantrey made drawings of each other using one; but this was probably little more than a game. It is Raeburn's only known drawing (Scot. NPG).

One of the earliest portraits likely to have been completed in the York Place studio is the brilliantly coloured full-length portrait of Sir John Sinclair of Ulbster, dressed in highland-cum-military costume of his own design (NG Scot.). Both it and the full length of the immensely rich, self-made coppersmith William Forbes of Callendar, painted in 1798 (Scot. NPG), show Raeburn making use of the dramatic lighting effects he was now able to create.

The portrait of Sinclair was the earliest of a number of portraits of highland chiefs and lairds wearing the kind of exotic dress that raised eyebrows when paraded in London. They include *Francis MacNab* ('*the MacNab*') (priv. coll.) and *Colonel Alastair Macdonell of Glengarry* (NG Scot.), both probably painted about 1810 though stylistically quite different. The former has much of the broken, loose handling that is often seen as typifying Raeburn's painting, while the latter is carefully descriptive—of tartan, guns, dirks, and targe—which suggests that the sitter demanded this kind of record. The contrast illustrates Raeburn's sometimes disconcerting versatility, which raises difficult problems of dating as well as the unanswered question of studio participation. The theme here, which is of a new, self-assertive type of 'Scottishness' (reactionary in some respects), is perhaps completed by the Byronically romantic full length of the second marquess of Bute of 1820, the dark figure wrapped in a glowing tartan cloak (priv. coll.).

Bankruptcy and family tensions Worldly success seemed assured for Raeburn in the early years of the nineteenth century, but by 1808 things had gone badly wrong. His troubles seem to have stemmed from that entrepreneurial spirit that had created men like Forbes of Callendar. From 1805, and possibly earlier, he had been partner in a mercantile company, Henry Raeburn & Co., trading from the port of Leith. The other partners were his son Henry (his elder son Peter had died in 1798) and James Philip Inglis, husband of his stepdaughter Ann Leslie. The company owned a number of ships which seem to have traded mainly with London. In addition to his designation 'portrait painter' Raeburn now added 'underwriter', and in 1806 he was a director of the Caledonian Insurance Company. However, in January 1808 he was forced to seek a sequestration of his 'whole means and estate heritable and moveable' and his bankruptcy was announced in the *Edinburgh Gazette*. The 'unexpected misfortunes' that caused Raeburn's fall are not precisely known, but by July of the same year claims against him totalled more than £36,000. Set against these claims was his considerable heritable property in the districts of Stockbridge, Canonmills, and the Dean, as well as in Leith. There was also the spacious studio in York Place, ownership of which had to be relinquished and replaced by a leasing arrangement. In the course of the year arrangements were put in place for Raeburn to reimburse his creditors by a composition of 4s. in the pound, and the period of sequestration was ended in December. Against the securities involved, Raeburn pledged himself to 'task the remaining years of his life' until 'the trembling hand of age' overtook him (5 Dec 1808, NA Scot., CS/29/10). It was an affirmation that Walter Scott, that other great artist of the age (who in time was overwhelmed by similar misfortunes), recalled in the spring of 1819 when a second portrait of himself by Raeburn was proposed: 'he … works now chiefly for cash poor fellow as he can have but a few years to make money' (*Letters*, 5.349).

The complexities of Raeburn's financial affairs and the difficulties of disentangling them from those of the firm were such that attempts to unravel them continued long after his death. In the short term they created distinct strains within his family circle. This is confirmed in some recently discovered correspondence from the year 1813. These letters reveal a less idealized Raeburn than the one depicted by his early biographers. There was, of course, some evidence for the rosier picture of his personality. Writing to Sir Duncan Campbell in November 1812 to seek payment for his portrait (Fine Arts Museums of San Francisco), he launches his plea with a delicate and relaxed literary touch: 'Painters and poets and these sort of people, you know, are always poor, and … I am no exception to this general description' (NA Scot., GD/170/267). But writing in the following year to Daniel Vere, husband of his stepdaughter Jacobina, who had unwisely incurred financial liabilities on his behalf, Raeburn is revealed as someone easily hurt and inclined to hasty reactions. He believes that Jacobina (Bina) had looked at him 'oddly' when he last called, and concludes that she is 'as violent against' him (and Mrs Raeburn) as her sister Ann has been (Raeburn to Daniel Vere, 5 March 1813, NL Scot., acc. 11547). He will not call again until he is sure of a proper welcome. Three days later he makes the same point in a letter to Bina, regretting that he has lost her esteem. Vere (Dany) then replies that 'this unpleasant correspondence' has been quite unnecessary and that Bina had simply wished to warn her stepfather that his affairs were now a not 'inconsiderable topic of public conversation' (Vere to Raeburn, retained draft, March 1813, ibid.).

Raeburn's entrepreneurial spirit was not quashed by the bankruptcy. The same correspondence reveals him planning to encourage builders to erect terraced houses on his land with cash advances on the security of their houses. These plans led to the erection of houses in Raeburn Place, Dean Street, and, from 1817, Ann Street, one of the loveliest streets in classical Edinburgh. However, they led to more contention within the family. His stepdaughters now launched an attack on what they believed to be an extravagant mode of living in St Bernard's House, the rather grand dwelling next to Deanhaugh House into which the Raeburns had moved a few years earlier. New silver plate had been bought and old furniture had been replaced with unnecessarily fine pieces by William Trotter. Raeburn protests that such purchases will not need to be repeated in his lifetime—and he reminds Bina that 'there never was a thriftier or a more frugal woman' than her mother, even if she does occasionally like a 'little show' (Raeburn to Daniel Vere, 8 March 1813, NL Scot., acc. 11547). The 'little show' could refer to the over-lavish wedding presents bought for Charlotte White, who had recently married their son Henry, which had also raised hackles.

London afar Another way in which Raeburn thought he might revive his fortunes was to remove his practice to London. John Hoppner had died in January 1810 and Raeburn travelled to London in the spring to see if he might fill the gap that he had left. His visit was orchestrated by his fellow Scot David Wilkie, who had settled in London five years before. Wilkie introduced him to a number of artists, including William Beechey, Thomas Stothard, John Flaxman, and Benjamin West, but nothing came of his plans and he was back in Edinburgh by the end of June. From a national point of view it now seems just as well, for his definition of his time and place, which became part of his reputation, was incomplete. Effulgent statements like the glowing *Lord Newton* of 1811 (Dalmeny House, Edinburgh) or bravura parades of Scottish sentiment like the highland portraits would not have been made.

The episode can be seen as one of a number that illustrate a lack of ease in Raeburn's relationship with London. The earliest had been the late delivery of the Clerk of Penicuik portrait. Now came a misunderstanding with the Royal Academy of Arts, of which he had been made an associate member in 1812. Having been elected a full member, in place of Henry Tresham, in 1815, he sent in a self-portrait as his diploma picture, not knowing that portraits of members could not be accepted. Great effort had gone into the making of this Olympian image (NG Scot.), for its high seriousness was how he wished to be perceived in London. His disappointment must have been extreme. It was eventually replaced by the sentimental *Boy with a Rabbit*, a portrait of his step-grandson Henry Raeburn Inglis. The latest expression of this theme is found in a letter to Wilkie of 1819 in which he pleads for news of the 'famous London artists', including information on their prices. In a memorable *cri de coeur*, he writes: 'I … know almost as little about them as if I were living at the Cape of Good Hope' (Greig, xlvi). The most troubling part of this feeling of being cut off from the mainstream was his inability to see the works he had sent to the Royal Academy hanging alongside those of his peers.

There is little doubt that after 1808 Raeburn's work suffered from over-production, due partly to success but also to the promise he had made to himself about his duty to his creditors. There are many late portraits which are pedestrian or unresolved due to haste; and, surprisingly for a major painter, he was happy to make copies of other artists' works—ranging from quite minor painters, not always of his own time, to Ramsay and Reynolds. Nevertheless, some of his finest, most responsive portraits were produced during these years, among them, besides those already mentioned, the portrait of the seated huntsman William Hunt of Pittencrieff (priv. coll.), the equestrian full length of Major William Clunes (NG Scot.), and the superb military full length of Major James Lee Harvey, which is probably as late as 1820 (Louvre, Paris).

A marked characteristic of Raeburn's work had always been that some sitters, for not easily explained reasons, set his imagination alight, while others did not. This bore no relation to their worldly status and some of his most sympathetic portraits are of women neither beautiful nor young. Among earlier examples is the Rembrandtesque *Margaret Gerard, Mrs James Cruikshank*, painted about 1805 as a companion to the almost equally fine portrait of her West Indies merchant husband, James Cruikshank (both Frick Collection, New York). An example from the later period is the portrait of the elderly Mrs James Campbell (priv. coll.) which combines breathtaking freshness of colour and almost outrageously free handling with profound insight. There are also records that he was a man at ease with children, and in a number of group portraits he both contains and releases their wild energy; these range from the war-enacting *Allen Brothers* (priv. coll.) of the early 1790s to the playful trio in the painting known as *The Elphinston Children* (Cincinnati Art Museum, Ohio), which was painted about 1813.

In these later years a number of Raeburn's portraits were permeated by the influence of Sir Thomas Lawrence, not always to their advantage. There was some level of intermittent friendship between them, and the 'Cape of Good Hope' letter makes it clear that it was Lawrence who most interested him. He was attracted less by his methods than by his sentiment. Raeburn's own perceptual method continued but it often carried a new emotional charge, particularly in his female portraits, which he must have believed was in accordance with London taste. A kind of sweet ecstasy pervades portraits like *Mrs Scott Moncrieff* (NG Scot.), once regarded as the archetypal Raeburn, without entirely swamping them, as happens in the lost portrait of Lady Gordon Cumming, shown at the Royal Academy in 1817. Raeburn himself believed this almost ridiculously mannered portrait to be 'by much the best and handsomest female picture I have yet painted'—which it assuredly was not (Greig archive, Scot. NPG).

Honours and final days Honours came fast in Raeburn's final years: membership of the American Academy of Fine Arts in 1819, a fellowship of the Royal Society of Edinburgh in 1820, a knighthood in 1822, and the revived office of king's painter and limner in Scotland in 1823. The knighthood was bestowed personally by George IV in a ceremony at Hopetoun House, Edinburgh, the final act of the monarch on his famous visit to Scotland. It is a curiosity of simpler times that during the arrangements for the conferral of the knighthood the painter found himself in conversation with the secretary of state, Robert Peel, without realizing who he was. When he discovered the truth, he wrote of his dismay (with a request that he convey an apology) to a friend, the member of parliament John Maxwell of Pollok, whose portrait he was working on at the time—a portrait that, although left unfinished at his death, shows his essential powers undimmed (priv. coll.).

Another event connected with the knighthood offers one of the last glimpses of Raeburn the man. On the day following the ceremony, the painter and his wife gave a dinner party for a number of friends at St Bernard's House, within a virtual stone's throw of his much humbler place of birth. Among the guests were Sir Adam Ferguson, who had been knighted at the same time, and the artists William Collins and David Wilkie. In a letter to his sister, Wilkie described the boisterous evening of toasts and song. Raeburn 'made a very modest reply' to one of the toasts, and Lady Raeburn—despite her erstwhile liking of a 'little show'—'would not allow herself to be called *My Lady* on any account' (Andrew, 76–7).

Raeburn's death came quite suddenly. Late in June 1823 he took part in an excursion of an antiquarian sort into Fife with a number of friends who included Ferguson, Sir Samuel Shepherd, Lord Chief Commissioner William Adam, Walter Scott, and the diminutive Irish novelist Maria Edgeworth, who was visiting Scott at Abbotsford. They examined sites at Ravenscraig Castle, Pittenweem, and St Andrews. It was 'a very merry party' in the words of Scott, of whom Raeburn had recently completed his second portrait, greatly to Scott's satisfaction this time (Scot. NPG). The day after returning to Edinburgh, Raeburn attempted to resume his work—the 'task' he had set himself many years before—but felt too unwell to continue. He retired to bed and shortly afterwards, on 8 July, died of 'a total failure of the system'. Perhaps not surprisingly, he left no will. He was buried on 10 July 1823, not as might have been expected in the graveyard of St Cuthbert's, but in the dormitory of the adjacent episcopalian church of St John the Evangelist, which had only recently been erected at the west end of Princes Street.

Reputation Scott, because of urgent business at Abbotsford, was unable to attend 'the last obsequies of a friend whom he esteemd and respected so entirely', as he wrote in his apology to Raeburn's family (*Letters*, 8.35). He did, however, pay his respects in a practical way, by revising Hugh Murray's obituary, which appeared in *The Annual Biography* for 1823. This rather idealized view of the man and his art, given its association with Scott, was a strong signal to posterity. It was followed by a memorial exhibition in 1824. The next important exhibition, a very large one, did not come until 1876, but its impact was considerable and it evoked a review by Robert Louis Stevenson. It also had the effect of releasing many major paintings onto the market. From this time, and into the years preceding the First World War, Raeburn's popular reputation rose rapidly and at a critical level he seemed to be granted at least equal status with his great English contemporaries. He was then caught up in the great American love affair with British art, and many of his works were acquired by museums and private collectors in the United States, often for very high prices.

The picture during the remainder of the twentieth century has been less straightforward, caused in part by the economic and political upheavals of the inter-war years, but also because the kind of glamour and sentiment that Raeburn's work seemed to represent went out of fashion. As portraiture itself fell into disrepute his reputation inevitably suffered, because his range had been virtually confined to that form. He also began to become part of a distinctly Scottish agenda that had little to do with aesthetic values. There is no doubt that Raeburn's critical reputation has been affected by a Scottish tendency to imbue certain cultural figures with something like iconic status. This has meant that criticism which was already inherently Anglo-centric (and that problem remains) has tended to side-step him because of his perceived 'foreignness'. Even in the more objective exhibition held at the National Gallery of Scotland in 1956 there remained a certain collusion with notions of a picturesque Scottishness and a purely local sentiment. Nevertheless, towards the end of the century a view, represented by Denys Sutton writing in the journal *Apollo*, gained wide support that Raeburn's qualities as a painter were of such importance that they deserved to be re-examined in depth. This shift of opinion culminated in an exhibition confined to his finest works which was shown in both Edinburgh and London in 1997–8. By this time Raeburn's work had also been discovered, or, rather, rediscovered, in Europe—for example, a major painting, *Major James Lee Harvey*, had been acquired by the Louvre in 1995. In 2001 the National Gallery acquired its first painting by Raeburn, the double portrait known as *The Archers*—the kind of recognition in London which the painter had always craved.

DUNCAN THOMSON

Sources D. Thomson, '*Raeburn*': the art of Sir Henry Raeburn, 1756–1823 (1997) [exhibition catalogue, Royal Scot. Acad., 1 Aug 1997 – 5 Oct 1997, and NPG, 24 Oct 1997 – 1 Feb 1998] · D. Thomson, *Sir Henry Raeburn, 1756–1823*, National Galleries of Scotland, Scottish Masters, 21 (1994) · D. Mackie, 'Raeburn: life and art', PhD diss., U. Edin., 1994 · NL Scot., Acc. 11547 · D. Irwin and F. Irwin, *Scottish painters at home and abroad, 1700–1900* (1975) · J. Greig, *Sir Henry Raeburn, R.A.: his life and works, with a catalogue of his pictures* (1911) · A. Cunningham, 'Raeburn', *Lives of the most eminent British painters, sculptors and architects*, 6 vols. (1829–33) · A. Kerr, *A history of Ann Street* (1982) · W. R. Andrew, *Life of Sir Henry Raeburn* (1886) · *The letters of Sir Walter Scott*, ed. H. J. C. Grierson and others, centenary edn, 12 vols. (1932–79), vol. 5, p. 349; vol. 8, p. 35
Archives NL Scot., corresp.; corresp. and papers relating to bankruptcy and financial affairs | NA Scot., letters to George Home of Paxton · NRA, priv. coll., letters to William Adam
Likenesses H. Raeburn, self-portrait, paste medallion, 1792, Scot. NPG · J. Tossie, paste medallions, 1792, Scot. NPG · H. Raeburn, self-portrait, oils, *c*.1815, NG Scot. [*see illus.*] · F. Chantrey, camera lucida pencil drawing, 1818, Scot. NPG · T. Campbell, marble bust, 1822, Scot. NPG

Rædwald [Redwald] (*d.* 616x27), king of the East Angles, is known almost exclusively from Bede's *Historia ecclesiastica gentis Anglorum*. The first recorded East Anglian king, he may have had kingly predecessors, including Tytilus who Bede says was his father. He succeeded to the kingship in the late sixth or early seventh century. Bede says that he sheltered Eadwine as an exile, declined remunerative offers from Æthelfrith to surrender him, and attacked Æthelfrith who was defeated and killed in 616 or 617 in a battle on the River Idle (in modern Nottinghamshire) in which Rædwald's son, Rægenhere, also fell. Rædwald was converted to Christianity under the aegis of Æthelberht of Kent, but, according to Bede, adopted a syncretist mode, having a temple with a Christian altar and an idol. Bede lists him as fourth of the kings to hold overlordship over the kingdoms south of the Humber, adding 'qui etiam vivente Aedilbercto eidem suae genti ducatum praebebat' (Bede, *Hist. eccl.*, 2.5). The most convincing strict translation of this phrase would indicate that even in Æthelberht's time he gained independent military leadership of his people; but a broader interpretation relates it to his obtaining overlordship. It has been argued, more strongly than convincingly, that Rædwald must be the man buried in Mound 1 at Sutton Hoo. By 627 he had been succeeded as

king of the East Angles by his son Earpwald, whose successor but one, *Sigeberht, may also have been Rædwald's son.

J. CAMPBELL

Sources Bede, *Hist. eccl.*, 2.5, 12, 15 · F. M. Stenton, *Anglo-Saxon England*, 3rd edn (1971) · F. M. Stenton, 'The East Anglian kings of the seventh century', *Preparatory to 'Anglo-Saxon England': being the collected papers of Frank Merry Stenton*, ed. D. M. Stenton (1970), 394–402 · B. A. E. Yorke, *Kings and kingship in early England* (1990) · C. B. Kendall and P. S. Wells, eds., 'Voyage to the other world: the legacy of Sutton Hoo', *Medieval Studies at Minnesota*, 5 (1992)

Rædwulf (*d. c.*858). *See under* Eardwulf (*fl.* 796–*c.*830).

Rafael, Johanes Padre (*fl.* **1768–1770**). *See under* Indian visitors (*act. c.*1720–*c.*1810).

Raffald [*née* Whitaker], **Elizabeth** (*bap.* **1733**, *d.* **1781**), cook and writer on cookery, was born at Doncaster and baptized there on 8 July 1733. She was one of at least three daughters born to Joshua Whitaker, a man of some property in the town which the daughters inherited. After receiving a fair education, she passed about fifteen years (1748–63) in service, rising to become housekeeper at Arley Hall, Cheshire, to Lady Elizabeth Warburton. She married her employer's gardener, John Raffald, on 3 March 1763, at Great Budworth, Cheshire. They had at least nine children, all daughters; only three reportedly survived into adulthood. The daughters attracted much attention walking out, each in a clean white frock and each with her own nurse behind. The youngest, Anna, passed on this and many other anecdotes about her mother. Several sons of Mrs Raffald's sister Middleward lived with the Raffalds 'to be company for her Manchester sisters lasses' and to be apprenticed at the appropriate time (*Harland's Manchester collectanea*, 145).

A great publicist, Mrs Raffald recorded most of the highlights of her later career by advertisements in the *Manchester Mercury* and she is reported to have assisted Harrop in its publication, both with money and with advice. She opened a shop in Fennell Street, Manchester, near her husband's floristry shop, supplying 'cold Entertainments, Hot French Dishes, Confectionaries, &c.' (*Manchester Mercury*, 29 November 1763). In September 1766 she transferred her business to Exchange Alley by the Bull's Head in Market Place. This later became the Exchange Coffee House. She was a shrewd, tactful and strong-willed woman, with a good knowledge of French and an active concern for the poor. From her shop she ran a school of cookery and domestic economy, and what was probably the first register office for servants in Manchester.

In 1769 Mrs Raffald published her *Experienced English housekeeper, for the use and ease of ladies, housekeepers, cooks, &c., wrote purely from practice … consisting of near 800 original receipts*. Six more genuine editions were published during her lifetime, all, according to their title pages, 'printed for the author' and 'sold by R. Baldwin', the London printer. Baldwin reportedly paid Mrs Raffald £1400 for the copyright. Apparently when he suggested certain northern expressions in her work be altered, she replied: 'What I

Elizabeth Raffald (*bap.* 1733, *d.* 1781), by unknown engraver, pubd 1782 (after P. McMorland)

in 1773, and a third in 1781. She wrote a book on midwifery, with Charles White, but did not live to print it. Her husband is believed to have sold the manuscript in London, but if published it bore another name. She died suddenly on 19 April 1781, and was buried in the churchyard at Stockport on 23 April among her husband's ancestors. Raffald, an able botanist and florist, but of improvident and irregular habits, moved to London after her death, and lived extravagantly. He died in December 1809, aged eighty-five, and was buried at Sacred Trinity Chapel, Salford.   NANCY COX

Sources *Manchester Mercury* (1763–81) [numerous advertisements] · *Manchester Mercury* (24 April 1781) · J. Harland, ed., *Collectanea relating to Manchester and its neighbourhood at various periods*, 2, Chetham Society, 72 (1867), 144–73 · E. Raffald, dedication and preface, *The experienced English housekeeper* (1769) · *Manchester Directory for the year 1772* (1772), entry under Raffald · *Manchester and Salford Directory* (1773), entry under Raffald · *Manchester and Salford Directory* (1781), entry under Raffald · preface, E. Raffald, *The Manchester directory for the year 1772* (1889) · [C. W. S.], preface, in E. Raffald, *The Manchester directory for the year 1773* (1889) · private information (2004) · *Palatine Note-Book*, 1 (1881), 141 · V. Maclean, *A short-title catalogue of household and cookery books published in the English tongue, 1701–1800* (1981), 121–4 · M. Aylett and O. Orlish, *First catch your hare: a history of the recipe-makers* (1965), 126–38 · C. P. Hampson, *Salford through the ages: the 'fons et origo' of an industrial city* (1930), 192–3 · 'Raffald without applause', *Cheshire Life*, 52 (July 1986), 52–3 · *DNB*
Likenesses P. McMorland, portrait, repro. in E. Raffald, *Experienced English housekeeper*, 8th edn (1782) · line engraving (after P. McMorland), BM, NPG; repro. in E. Raffald, *Experienced English housekeeper*, 8th edn (1782) [*see illus.*] · print, repro. in *Manchester and Salford Directory*; copy, Manchester Central Library
Wealth at death she and her husband perhaps retained control over Exchange coffee house, Manchester: *Manchester and Salford Directory* (1781) · property in Doncaster; ran substantial Salford hostelry with husband; possibly retained rights to *Experienced English housekeeper* until late stage (title pages say 'printed for the author'), so perhaps retained £1400 supposedly paid for copyright; three children at boarding school suggests comfortable

have written I proposed to write at the time; it was written deliberately, and I cannot admit to any alteration' (*Harland's Manchester collectanea*, 147). The popularity of her work is shown by the many editions, mostly spurious, published in England and in Dublin during her lifetime and after. She is said to have refused to allow any portraits to be published, so that the first, from a painting by P. McMorland, appeared in the eighth edition in 1782, after her death.

For a time Mrs Raffald ran the Bull's Head near her shop but in 1772 the Raffalds took over the King's Head, Chapel Street, Salford, which they had 'fitted up in the neatest and most elegant manner' (*Manchester Mercury*, 25 August 1772). Within a month, they were advertising fortnightly 'Card assemblies' during the winter season (*Manchester Mercury*, 8 September 1772). The excellent cuisine and her ability to converse in French were said to have attracted many foreign visitors.

Mrs Raffald was instrumental in establishing a second Manchester newspaper, the *Prescott's Journal*, in 1771. The following year she published the first *Directory of Manchester*. A second extended edition including Salford followed

Raffles, Frances Rachel [Franki] (1955–1994), photographer and campaigner against violence against women, was born in Hope Hospital, Salford, Manchester, on 17 October 1955. She was the third daughter of four children, three sisters and a younger brother, of Gillian, *née* Posnansky (*b.* 1930), director of the Mercury Gallery, London and Edinburgh, and Eric Raffles (*b.* 1924), a businessman and textiles manufacturer, and later farmer in Somerset. The family moved to Ham Common, Richmond, when Franki was seven and she attended the Lady Eleanor Holles School. The family was Jewish; as an adult Franki was not a believer but retained a strong cultural identity as Jewish and kept the main festivals with her children.

After school Franki travelled in Israel before studying at St Andrews University (1973–7), where she graduated with honours (second-class) in philosophy. At university she was a strongly committed member of the women's liberation group and an active member of the student representative council, playing a leading role in several campaigns. Her Marxist-feminism and belief in the value of Soviet communism for women shaped her life and work. After graduating she made Scotland her home. In 1978 she moved to Lewis with her partner Martin Sime (*b.* 1953), director of the Scottish Council for Voluntary Organizations. With a small inheritance she bought an almost derelict 169 acre farm at Callanish, where they restored the house and kept sheep, learning farming and building skills on the job. Their daughter, Anna Raffles, was born on Lewis in 1979. Also on Lewis, Franki bought her first camera and taught herself photography. It led to her first exhibition, 'Lewis Women', in the Stills Gallery in Edinburgh.

The farm was not viable. Franki and Martin separated and she and Anna moved in 1982 to Edinburgh, where she began to build a career as a freelance photographer and designer, at the same time developing innovative work with children, and later adults, with learning difficulties. She taught the children at Pinewood special school in Blackburn, West Lothian, to take pictures of their daily lives, at first using instant-picture but graduating to basic compact cameras. This work was developed between 1985 and 1988 as Special Needs and Photography, in association with Community Service Volunteers, with photographic projects used to assist in learning practical skills and to address questions of self-image. It gave expression to Franki's concern that photography was more often used to objectify and exploit people than to benefit them.

Franki was a keen and intrepid traveller, which both enabled and developed her photography. Trips with her camera included one to Australia with the Scottish netball team and another to Mexico with her mother to photograph traditional masks. Franki had come out as lesbian while in Lewis, and in 1983 she met a teacher, Sandy Lunan (*b.* 1954), who remained her partner for the rest of her life. The following year Franki, Sandy, and Anna travelled, mainly by train and local buses, through the Soviet Union to China, Tibet, Nepal, and India, a journey again commemorated in an exhibition. Later journeys in Russia, Georgia, and Israel led to the unfinished photographic series 'Lot's Wife', on the lives of Soviet-Jewish women immigrants to Israel.

Franki's politics were at the core of her work, with women's working lives her major theme: Soviet women labouring on building sites or hawking potatoes, Chinese women running hand-in-hand, women traversing a vast, bleak mountain valley in Tibet; women's lives that are hard, enduring, but joyful. Eye, technical skill, and political purpose combined in remarkable photographic work that locates and directly engages with the subject. For people with special needs, Franki wrote, photography offers 'a unique opportunity to look closely at the world whilst retaining a measure of separateness from it' and is 'a way of challenging aspects of it' (Raffles, 16). That was also its importance for Franki Raffles.

Franki had great originality and very high standards, was strong-willed and tenacious, working long hours, surviving on black coffee and cigarettes. She could be impatient with those whose commitment differed but also generous with time and kindness. Her love for her children was the emotional focus of her life but work was its public face, taking pictures simultaneously an engagement with and distancing from life.

Franki's first work for Edinburgh district council was an exhibition, 'To Let You Understand', documenting women's working lives in the city and later exhibited by councils throughout the UK. It was followed, in 1992, by the Zero Tolerance campaign, a ground-breaking public awareness initiative challenging social attitudes to male violence against women and children. She was the campaign's image-maker; her ideas and arguments, the Z logo she designed, her photographs for the first posters, and the visual approach she established were integral from the outset and to the Zero Tolerance Trust's continuing work. The message of Zero Tolerance was radical, carried in the strapline 'Male abuse of power is a crime' and spelt out in bold black and white displays along Princes Street, on the sides of buses and posters in sports centres, pubs, and police stations. Its content and style aimed to empower women, eschewing images of abused women in favour of images of women and children in domestic settings, apparently comfortable and secure. The strong contrast between the everyday images and the message of the text underlined the familiar but hidden nature of abuse. The campaign was taken up by most other Scottish local authorities and elsewhere in Britain and Europe, and in South Australia. The Zero Tolerance Trust subsequently contributed to over 100 public education campaigns on domestic and sexual violence, in the UK and internationally.

Franki Raffles died in the Simpson Memorial Hospital, Edinburgh, on 6 December 1994, after giving birth to twin daughters. She was survived by her three daughters, a son, and the daughter she had brought up with Sandy Lunan. Her funeral was held at Mortonhall crematorium, Edinburgh, on 10 December. The day before she died she had been at work on the new images for the second stage of the Zero Tolerance campaign. The MP for Leith, Malcolm Chisholm, paid tribute to 'the brilliant designer of that [Zero Tolerance] campaign' in a debate on domestic violence in the House of Commons on 29 March 1995. 'She will be sorely missed', he said, 'but the work that she started goes on' (*Hansard 5C*, 29 March 1995, col. 944).

SUE INNES

Sources private information (2004) [Sandy Lunan, Greg Michaelson, Evelyn Gillan, Emma Feather] · personal knowledge (2004) · *Evening News* (8 Dec 1994), 1 · *The Scotsman* (9 Oct 1994) · E. Gillan, 'The strength of one voice', *The Scotsman* (28 Sept 1995) · E. Gillan and E. Samson, 'The Zero Tolerance campaign', *Home truths about domestic violence*, ed. J. Hamne and C. Ivein (2000) · K. Cosgrove, 'No man has the right', *Women in a violent world*, ed. C. Corrin (1996) · F. Mackay, 'The case of zero tolerance', *Women and contemporary Scottish politics*, ed. E. Breilenbach and F. Mackay (2001) · F. Raffles, *Photographers with special needs* (1998)
Archives priv. coll., archive of photographic work
Likenesses photograph, *c.*1994, priv. coll. · photograph, *c.*1994, Scotsman Publications library

Raffles, Sir (Thomas) Stamford Bingley (1781–1826), colonial governor and founder of Singapore, the eldest and only surviving son of Captain Benjamin Raffles (*d. c.*1797) and his wife, *née* Anne Lyde (*d.* 1824), was born off Port Morant, Jamaica, on 6 July 1781, aboard his father's ship, the West Indiaman *Ann*. He numbered a

Sir (Thomas) Stamford Bingley Raffles (1781–1826), by George Francis Joseph, 1817

seventeenth-century Sir Benjamin Raffles among his ancestors, and his paternal grandfather was a clerk for thirty years in the prerogative office, Doctors' Commons, London, but little is known about Raffles's childhood. He was christened for the second time—on this occasion as plain Thomas—by his uncle, the Revd John Lindeman, at Eaton Bishop in Herefordshire, on 4 July 1784. For two years he attended the reputable Mansion House boarding-school in Hammersmith, but had to leave in 1795 at the age of fourteen because of straitened financial circumstances. His father probably died about this time, leaving Anne to bring up Thomas and four younger sisters, and through a family connection she obtained him a temporary clerkship at East India House. A frail, diffident youth, Raffles's health suffered through the long hours of drudgery, but he also studied French in his own time, and his diligence impressed William Ramsay, secretary to the court of directors, whose son was Raffles's close friend. On 8 March 1805, on Ramsay's recommendation, Raffles was appointed assistant secretary to the government of the East India Company's newly elevated Penang presidency, with a salary leap from £70 to £1500 a year. One week later he married Olivia Mariamne Fancourt (1771–1814), *née* Devenish, a Madras assistant surgeon's penniless widow, of Irish and possibly Indian extraction, who was ten years his senior but strikingly beautiful, vivacious, and intelligent. Sailing in April, they reached Penang on 19 September 1805.

Early years On the voyage Raffles taught himself Malay and soon embarked on a lifetime study of the history,

flora, and fauna of the region. His meagre schooling left him with a passion for acquiring knowledge and cultivating the friendship of well-educated, clever men, such as Dr John Leyden, surgeon, naturalist, linguist, and Malay scholar, who was his house guest in Penang for three months in 1805–6, and William Marsden, secretary to the Royal Navy, linguist and historian of Sumatra, with whom Raffles initiated a long correspondence in 1806.

Appointed Malay translator and registrar of the recorder's court, in addition to assistant secretary, Raffles fell ill under the strain, and in 1807 he was sent on sick leave to Melaka, which the East India Company had seized from the Dutch during the French wars. Its splendid fortress had already been razed following the directors' orders to demolish Melaka's public buildings and transfer the population to Penang, but the rest of the town was saved on Raffles's recommendation. Indeed, in a report submitted in 1808 he urged its permanent retention, and in 1810 he visited Calcutta, hoping to be appointed governor of the Dutch Moluccas, which had also been occupied by the company. This bid failed, but he impressed Governor-General Lord Minto with his offer to turn local rulers against the Dutch to aid the company's planned invasion of Java. Minto appointed Raffles his agent in the Malay states, accepted his recommendation to use Melaka rather than Penang as the base to prepare for the Java campaign, and posted him back there in December 1810 to gather intelligence and collect supplies.

Invasion and administration of Java With his customary industry and attention to detail, Raffles amassed voluminous information, sent agents to Madura, Bali, and Java, and won over the sultan of Palembang. On arriving in Melaka in May 1811, Minto approved Raffles's recommended invasion route and took him on his own ship when the fleet set sail the following month. As a civilian Raffles took no direct part in the military operations, which were commanded by Colonel Robert Rollo Gillespie, a brave soldier and admired war hero. But, to Gillespie's chagrin, when the Dutch administration capitulated in September 1811 Minto appointed Raffles as lieutenant-governor, with far-reaching powers and a council comprising Gillespie as the senior member and two Dutch officials.

Unlike the company and the British government, Raffles regarded Java not as temporarily occupied territory but as the permanent base for extending British influence through the rest of the eastern archipelago, and he set out quickly to dismantle the Dutch system of monopoly, compulsory deliveries, and protective tariffs. Early in 1812 Raffles sent Gillespie to seize the tin islands of Banka and Billiton, appointed British residents at the courts of Javanese rulers, remodelled the judicial administration, introduced a jury system, and in 1813 abolished forced labour in favour of money rents in a large part of Java.

Travelling widely to gather information about the history, languages, and products of Java, Raffles enlisted the help and supported the researches of American botanist Thomas Horsfield, who had already spent more than ten years in Java before the British invasion. He arranged for

Horsfield to send specimens to the East India Company's museum in London and to Sir Joseph Banks, president of the Royal Society, who was collecting plants for the Royal Garden at Kew and for his own herbarium.

In February 1814 Raffles prepared a minute in council condemning the previous Dutch regime and claiming success for his land rent system, and that same month he recommended to Calcutta an ambitious scheme to extend British interests and appoint agents at all the leading ports in Borneo, Sulu, Riau-Lingga, Bali, east Sumatra, and as far afield as Siam, Cambodia, and Cochin China. Some modern-minded Dutch officials supported Raffles's land rent reform, but the unaccustomed new system resulted in a large financial loss of government revenue, and he resorted to selling government lands on his own authority to bolster a shaky paper currency.

Reducing the number of European troops as an economy measure brought conflict with Gillespie, who, on being posted back to Calcutta, brought charges before the governor-general in council in December 1813, attacking Raffles's whole administration and financial policy, accusing him of humiliating chiefs and regents, and of selling off government lands irresponsibly. Raffles submitted a detailed rebuttal in March 1814, which he also had privately printed in Batavia, and Gillespie was killed in action before judgment was given, but the accusations hung over Raffles for years. His remaining time in Java was fraught with troubles. Olivia's sudden death in November 1814 left Raffles distraught, and she was buried in the European cemetery at Batavia beside the grave of their friend John Leyden, who had died of malaria during the Java invasion. Meanwhile his patron, Minto, died in June 1814, and the new governor-general was critical of Raffles's financial record. In August 1814 Britain and the Netherlands signed a convention agreeing to return Java to Dutch rule. Excited by news of Napoleon's escape from Elba and the renewed outbreak of war, in August 1815 Raffles appealed to the British government to retain Java, but the directors had already issued a preliminary condemnation of his actions as injudicious and extravagant and demanded his recall. Accordingly, on 17 October 1815 the governor-general, reproving him for 'persevering imprudence', ordered Raffles's transfer to the company's ailing west Sumatra residency at Bencoolen, to which Minto had provisionally nominated him in 1813 as insurance in case Java was restored to Dutch rule.

History of Java Dispirited and ill, Raffles decided first to go to England and left Java on 25 March 1816, calling at St Helena, where he was disillusioned at meeting the exiled former emperor Napoleon, whom he had hitherto admired. Despite arriving home, in his own words 'wretchedly thin and sallow', in October 1816 he embarked on a two-volume *History of Java*, which was written and published within seven months. The spring of 1817 saw an uplift in his fortunes. On 13 February, although they still did not comment on his Java administration, the directors exonerated him from charges of dishonourable personal motives and confirmed his Bencoolen appointment. Nine days later, in a very quiet ceremony, he married Sophia

Hull (1786–1858), whom he had met while taking the waters at Cheltenham spa. Thirty years old and rather plain, Sophia appears to have appealed to Raffles as a mature, even-tempered, sensible match. She was to be a model of devotion and resilience, steadfast through personal and financial disasters, accompanying him uncomplaining on the most arduous journeys, and after his death publishing a glowing and detailed biography, but omitting any reference to Raffles's first marriage.

On 20 March 1817 Raffles was elected a fellow of the Royal Society, which brought him into contact with distinguished scientists and dignitaries, such as the duke and duchess of Somerset. On 10 April his *History of Java* was published, receiving mixed reviews and betraying hasty composition but causing a stir as the first English-language history. Raffles found himself lionized in London society, and from about this time he assumed the name of Stamford in place of the more pedestrian Thomas. He dined with Princess Charlotte, and on 29 May was knighted by the prince regent, who praised him in a twenty-minute speech at a Carlton House levee. The couple then toured Europe, dining with the Dutch colonial minister and also with King William, to whom Raffles offered advice about Java.

The Bencoolen residency In November 1817 Raffles and Sophia embarked for Bencoolen. Charlotte, their first child, was born at sea on 15 February 1818, and the voyage was enlivened by the company of Joseph Arnold, naval surgeon and botanist, who stimulated Raffles's already keen interest in natural history. He had high hopes for Bencoolen. In London he had tried in vain to persuade the East India Company to set up a chain of stations on the China route and develop British trade in the archipelago. At the end of the Napoleonic wars both the British government and the company wanted to reduce their commitments in south-east Asia and returned Melaka, the Moluccas, and Java to the Dutch, but, despite the failure of his Java dreams, Raffles hoped to use west Sumatra as the base to expand British influence. Because of his personal standing, he was dignified with the title of lieutenant-governor, rather than mere resident, and, through the influential contacts he had made in England, he nursed ambitions eventually to become governor-general of Bengal and a peer of the realm.

Raffles's arrival at malaria-ridden Fort Marlborough on 22 March 1818 was sobering. Recent earthquakes had destroyed most buildings, the administration had long been in chaos, pepper production (which represented Bencoolen's sole livelihood) was neglected, and Raffles was horrified to find slaves belonging to the East India Company. He immediately freed the company's slaves, prohibited gambling, and set about reorganizing the administration, improving pepper production, and introducing an enlightened convict labour system.

Raffles arranged for Horsfield to visit Bencoolen to accompany Sophia and himself on an arduous exploration of the Menangkabau territory of central Sumatra, where Horsfield identified many new plants. Raffles also undertook expeditions with Arnold, who discovered a five-petalled, mottled reddish parasite, the largest flower in the world, at Pulau Lebar in west Sumatra on 19 May 1818, shortly before he died of malaria. After Raffles reported the find to Sir Joseph Banks, a paper was presented to the Linnean Society of London in 1820, and the flower was assigned the generic name *Rafflesia*, and called *Rafflesia arnoldi*. Subsequently, in Singapore in February 1819 Raffles himself discovered a large, brilliant pitcher plant, which was named the *Nepenthes rafflesiana*.

But Raffles's primary concern was to establish friendly relations with neighbouring rulers in order to check the spread of Dutch power in Sumatra and the revival of their protectionist measures against British trade. He tried to prevent the Dutch return to Padang and Palembang, and established British posts in the Lampongs area of south Sumatra and islands off the west coast. Alarmed at the prospect of the Dutch dominating both the Melaka and Sunda straits, in September 1818 Raffles went to Calcutta to try to win the support of Governor-General Lord Hastings for a more aggressive policy. While Hastings vetoed Raffles's ambitious Sumatra schemes, he approved a more limited proposal to protect the Melaka Strait trade route by making a treaty with Aceh in north Sumatra and acquiring a trading station at Riau or some other southern point, provided this did not bring the company into collision with the Dutch. Hastings appointed Raffles his agent to undertake this enterprise, with the assistance of Colonel William Farquhar, who had been British resident of Melaka during the wartime occupation.

Founding Singapore Discovering that the Dutch had forestalled them in Riau, Raffles and Farquhar investigated the Karimun Islands but found them unsuitable, and on 29 January 1819 landed at Singapore, part of the Riau–Johor empire. The following day Raffles signed a preliminary treaty with the local chieftain, the *temenggong*, permitting the East India Company to set up a trading post on the Singapore River. Since the sultanate had been in dispute for some years between two half-brothers, with the Dutch supporting the younger claimant, Raffles invited the elder brother, Hussein, over from Riau, recognized him as sultan, and on 6 February 1819 signed a treaty with Hussein and the *temenggong* confirming the company's right to establish the post, subject to an annual payment. The next day Raffles departed for Penang to negotiate the treaty with Aceh, leaving Farquhar in charge as resident.

The new settlement's prospects looked precarious. The Dutch authorities in Batavia protested vigorously, and the governor of Penang urged Calcutta to repudiate Singapore, accusing Raffles of acting 'like a man who sets a house on fire and then runs away'. The day before he dropped anchor off Singapore, the company's Board of Control had dispatched instructions to the governor-general forbidding the proposed mission, but these did not reach Calcutta until March, and the embarrassing news of the acquisition got back to London only in August 1819. Raffles's actions in Sumatra and the Melaka Strait provoked a 'paper war' between Britain and the Netherlands, threatening to jeopardize wide-ranging diplomatic talks, which aimed to settle Anglo-Dutch differences in

the East in order to cement their friendship in Europe. But the Singapore issue was put in abeyance for years while the negotiations dragged on.

Meanwhile Raffles returned to Singapore at the end of May 1819, bringing immigrants from Penang, and he spent three weeks drafting plans for the settlement before returning to Bencoolen. Aspiring to gather under his own control all the British possessions in south-east Asia—Penang, Province Wellesley, Bencoolen, and Singapore—he hurried to Calcutta to push his claims when news of the sudden death of the governor of Penang reached Fort Marlborough in October 1819. While sympathetic in principle, Hastings refused to consider the matter further until the Anglo-Dutch negotiations were settled.

Somewhat disappointed, Raffles returned to Bencoolen in February 1820 and concentrated on making it a model colony. He settled his growing family in a country house at Dove's Rise, about 12 miles out of Fort Marlborough, where he kept a menagerie and indulged his passion for natural history. In this he was ably supported by a gifted young Scottish botanist, William Jack, whom he had met in Calcutta and appointed in November 1818 to succeed Arnold. Raffles kept up correspondence with experts in England and Calcutta, and amassed collections of manuscripts, natural history drawings, and paintings, together with botanical and zoological specimens, some of which he sent to Banks and Marsden.

This tranquil interlude was shattered by a series of cruel disasters. Within the space of six months, between July 1821 and January 1822, three of his four children died, and the surviving infant was sent to the safe care of Sophia's parents in England. William Jack died of tuberculosis in September 1822, while Raffles and Sophia themselves were seriously ill. Disheartened and prematurely aged, 'a little old man, all yellow and shrivelled', as he described himself at that time, Raffles decided to retire from the East.

Securing Singapore First Raffles resolved to pay a last visit to Singapore, about which he had received encouraging but only occasional reports over the last three years because of the poor communications with west Sumatra. On landing in October 1822 Raffles was thrilled with the spectacular commercial vigour of what he called 'this, my almost only child', but he became increasingly critical of the resident's old-fashioned ways: his deference to Hussein and the *temenggong*, his tolerance of slavery and legalized gambling, and his allocation of land. In January 1823 Raffles reported to Calcutta accusing Farquhar of incompetence, in April he took over as resident himself, and the following month he stripped Farquhar of his office as military commandant. On his return to England, Farquhar complained to the directors about wrongful dismissal, claiming that he himself had been primarily responsible for choosing the Singapore site and successfully nursing the infant settlement through its formative years.

Despite blinding headaches, which sometimes left Raffles prostrate for weeks on end, and ignoring the fact that the very survival of the settlement was still being debated in Europe, he hurried to lay down regulations for

Singapore's long-term administration. Absolute freedom of trade was declared a permanent principle, not merely a temporary expedient to build up commerce. Supported by a committee comprising European officials and merchants, with representatives of the various Asian ethnic groups, Raffles drew up a town plan and resettled a large part of the population according to their different communities. He established a magistracy administering English law, with Malay social custom where appropriate for the indigenous people. Prohibiting slave trading, he provided for existing debt slaves to work off their obligations in five years, and he introduced Bencoolen's liberal system of convict labour management. He banned the carrying of arms, gambling, and cock-fighting outright, and introduced deterrent taxation on other vices, such as alcohol and opium. In June 1823 he signed an agreement with the sultan and *temenggong*, commuting their commercial and judicial privileges to money payments. Most dear to Raffles's heart was the promotion of education, which he believed was the key to progress. His ideal was to revive Asian cultures in alliance with the best of Western tradition through a college which would attract the sons of the élite throughout the region, and, three days before leaving Singapore, he laid the foundation-stone for the Singapore Institution, with generous donations from himself and his wife and a pledge for annual funding from the East India Company.

Disasters and death Raffles departed from Singapore for the last time on 14 June 1823, returning to Bencoolen, where a fifth child was born but died within two months. On 2 February 1824 Raffles and Sophia set sail for England on the *Fame*, together with all their worldly possessions, worth between £20,000 and £30,000. That same night the ship caught fire. All on board were saved, but the *Fame* and its cargo were entirely destroyed, including a large collection of plants, fish, animals, and birds; between 2000 and 3000 unique natural history drawings and paintings; original Malay manuscripts and Raffles's notes about the history of Borneo, Sumatra, and the founding of Singapore; together with Raffles's irreplaceable scientific papers and those left by Arnold and Jack, the latter representing three years' unpublished research in Penang, Kedah, Singapore, and Sumatra.

The couple embarked again on 8 April, reaching Plymouth in August 1824. There Raffles was pleased to learn about the Anglo-Dutch treaty signed in London in March 1824, which recognized the British settlement at Singapore, to be followed by a treaty in August that year in which the Malay chiefs confirmed ceding the whole island to the East India Company. After living in London for a while, in July 1825 Raffles bought a country estate at High Wood, near Hendon, where he took up farming. Meanwhile, in November 1824 he published a *Statement of the Services of Sir Stamford Raffles*, justifying his administration over the past twelve years, and, after the author's death, he undertook the editing of George Finlayson's *Mission to Siam*, which was published in 1826. In the spring of 1825 he launched a long-cherished proposal for a zoo in London supported by a society to promote the science of zoology.

Enlisting the backing of Sir Humphry Davy, president of the Royal Society, Raffles issued a prospectus in March 1825 and was elected first president of the Zoological Society at a committee meeting of the proposers, which he chaired on 26 February 1826.

Raffles's hopes of obtaining a company pension became more pressing when most of his remaining capital was lost through a bank failure late in 1825. In April 1826 the directors finally came to a decision. They acknowledged Raffles's contribution to the successful invasion of Java and, despite questioning the propriety of his land sales, they accepted that he faced a financial crisis from the beginning of his administration in Java. While criticizing his aggressive external policy in Sumatra, they commended his internal administration in Bencoolen, and recognized his crucial role in acquiring and making sound administrative arrangements for Singapore. The overall judgment was favourable, but, so far from granting Raffles a pension, the directors now demanded £22,272 in alleged overpayments and interest going back to 1817.

The following month Raffles suffered an attack of apoplexy, and early in the morning of 5 July 1826 Sophia found him lying dead at the foot of the stairs. He was only forty-five, but an autopsy revealed an unsuspected brain tumour and showed that for years he had been receiving the wrong treatment for supposed digestive complaints. In March 1827 the directors accepted Sophia's offer of £10,000 to cancel her husband's debt. She lived on until 1858, but their only remaining daughter died in 1840 at the age of eighteen and it was left to Raffles's cousin to continue the family name. Raffles died an embittered man, prematurely broken in health, financially ruined, failing to acquire the honours and public recognition he craved, and apparently with little to show for the privations and tragedies he and his family had suffered. He was buried at Hendon church, but the grave was unmarked, allegedly because of family arguments with the vicar, who held investments in the West Indies and objected to Raffles's campaign against slavery. In 1887 his nephew installed a brass plaque, but the coffin was discovered only accidentally during building work in the vault in April 1914.

Assessment In many ways Raffles was a figure of contradictions and anomalies. His slight stature and sickly constitution masked an immense capacity for hard work and an agile mind. Gentle and soft-spoken, he commanded the devotion of friends and subordinates, but could be intolerant and vindictive towards those who crossed him personally or obstructed his policies. Despite his long years in the East in the service of an old-fashioned monopoly company, he sought to put into practice the most advanced Western views of his time on personal liberty, judicial equality, education, free trade, penal reform, and slave emancipation. A man of vision, with great ambitions for himself and his country, he saw Britain's mission to raise the people of the eastern archipelago from ignorance and poverty, not by means of territorial expansion but a combination of commercial and moral pre-eminence: reviving old cultures and spreading European enlightenment through economic progress, liberal education, and the rule of law.

Despite Raffles's scanty formal schooling, his intelligence and thirst for learning inspired respect among leading scientists of his day, and after his death he was singled out for praise by Sir Humphry Davy in his presidential address to the Royal Society. A statue by the eminent sculptor Sir Francis Chantrey was erected in Westminster Abbey in 1832, an oil portrait by G. F. Joseph was presented to the National Portrait Gallery, and another by Sir James Lonsdale hangs in the council room at the London Zoo.

But Raffles's most enduring monument was Singapore itself, which secured British supremacy in the eastern seas for more than a century and represented a triumph for the principles of free trade and *laissez-faire*. Educational dreams were slower to materialize, although eventually the renamed Raffles Institution became Singapore's premier school. Raffles's statue, which was first installed in Singapore in 1885 to celebrate Queen Victoria's golden jubilee, was torn down during the Japanese occupation but restored after the Second World War. Not only did it survive independence, but the republic of Singapore was unique among liberated colonies in erecting a second monument to honour the foresight of its imperial founder.

C. M. TURNBULL

Sources C. E. Wurtzburg, *Raffles of the eastern isles*, ed. C. Witting (1954); repr. (1984) · [S. Raffles], *Memoir of the life and public services of Sir Thomas Stamford Raffles* (1830) · T. S. Raffles, *Statement of the services of Sir Thomas Stamford Raffles* (privately printed, 1824); repr. with introduction by J. Bastin (1978) · T. S. Raffles, *Substance of a minute recorded by the Honourable Thomas Stamford Raffles, lieutenant governor of Java and its dependencies on the 11th February 1814 on the introduction of an improved system of internal management and the establishment of a land rental on the island of Java* (1814) · T. S. Raffles, *Charges preferred by Maj. Gen. Gillespie againt T. S. Raffles Esq, Lt. Gov. of Java, with Mr Raffles' defence* (privately printed, 1814) · T. S. Raffles, *The history of Java*, 2 vols. (1817); repr. with introduction by J. S. Bastin (1965) · J. Crawfurd, 'Raffles', *A descriptive dictionary of the Indian islands and adjacent countries* (1856); repr. (1971) · D. C. Boulger, *The life of Sir Stamford Raffles*, ed. A. Johnson, new edn (1973) · *GM*, 1st ser., 96/2 (1826) · Acts of a committee of the chapter of the Collegiate Church of St Peter, Westminster, 11 April 1832, Westminster Abbey · Abdullah bin Abdul Kadir, 'The Hikayat Abdullah', trans. A. H. Hill, *Journal of the Malayan Branch of the Royal Asiatic Society*, 28/3 (1955), 1–354 · H. T. Haughton, 'The landing of Raffles in Singapore by an eye witness (Wa Hakim)', *Journal of the Straits Branch of the Royal Asiatic Society*, 10 (1882), 285–6; repr. in *Journal of the Malaysian Branch of the Royal Asiatic Society*, 42/1 (1969), 78–9 · J. R. Logan, ed., 'Notes illustrative of the life and services of Sir Thomas Stamford Raffles', *Journal of the Indian Archipelago*, 9 (1855), 306–24 · J. R. Logan, 'Raffles and the Indian archipelago', *Journal of the Indian Archipelago*, new ser., 1 (1856) · J. S. Bastin, *The native policies of Sir Stamford Raffles in Java and Sumatra* (1957) · J. S. Bastin, 'Raffles's ideas on the land rent system in Java and the Mackenzie land tenure commission', *Verhandelingen van het Koninklijk Instituut voor Taal-, Land- en Volkenkunde*, 16 (1954), 72–92 · J. S. Bastin, 'Raffles's attempts to extend British power in Sumatra', *Essays on Indonesian and Malaysian history* (1961), 164–79 · J. S. Bastin, 'Raffles and British policy in the Indian archipelago, 1811–1816', *Journal of the Malayan Branch of the Royal Asiatic Society*, 27/1 (1954), 84–119 · J. S. Bastin, *Sir Thomas Stamford Raffles* (with an account of the Raffles–Minto manuscript collection presented to the India Office Library on 17 July 1969 by the Malaysia–Singapore Commercial Association) (1969) · R. Coupland, *Raffles, 1781–1826* (1926) [3rd edn repr. as *Raffles of Singapore* (1946)] · H. E. Egerton, *Sir Stamford Raffles: England in the Far East* (1900) · 'The letters of Sir Stamford Raffles to Nathaniel Wallich', ed. J. S. Bastin, *Journal of the Malaysian Branch of the Royal Asiatic Society*, 54/2 (1981), 1–73; pubd separately as J. Bastin, ed., *Letters of Sir Stamford Raffles to Nathaniel Wallich, 1819–1824* (Kuala Lumpur, 1981) · J. S. Bastin, *The journal of Thomas Otho Travers, 1813–1820* (1960) · J. S. Bastin, 'Dr Joseph Arnold and the discovery of Rafflesia arnoldii in west Sumatra in 1818', *Journal of the Society of the Bibliography of Natural History*, 6 (1971–4), 307–72 · J. S. Bastin, 'The first prospectus of the Zoological Society of London: new light on the society's origins', *Journal of the Society of the Bibliography of Natural History*, 5 (1968–71), 369–88 · J. S. Bastin, 'A further note on the origins of the Zoological Society of London', *Journal of the Society of the Bibliography of Natural History*, 6 (1971–4), 236–41 · J. S. Bastin, 'The Raffles–Minto manuscripts', *Straits Times' Annual* (1970) · J. S. Bastin, 'Raffles the naturalist', *Straits Times' Annual* (1971) · W. Thorn, *Memoir of the conquest of Java* (1815) · W. Thorn, *Memoir of Sir R. R. Gillespie* (1816) · Hussein Alatas, *Thomas Stamford Raffles, 1781–1826: schemer or reformer?* (1971) · *Journal of the Malaysian Branch of the Royal Asiatic Society* [Singapore: 150th anniverary commemorative issue], 42/1 (1969) · E. Hahn, *Raffles of Singapore: a biography* (1946); repr. (1968) · M. Collis, *Raffles* (1966) · J. A. B. Cook, *Sir Stamford Raffles* (1918) · D. Woodman, *Raffles of Java, 1781–1826* (1954) · G. C. Hough, 'The educational policy of Sir Stamford Raffles', *Journal of the Malayan Branch of the Royal Asiatic Society*, 11/2 (1933), 166–70

Archives BL, letter-books and papers, Add. MSS 45271–45273 · BL OIOC, corresp. and papers, MSS Eur. C 34–36, D 199–200, 742m E 104–110, F 31–33 · CUL, corresp. [mainly copies] · Duke U., Perkins L., papers · National Archives of Indonesia, official papers as lieutenant-governor of Java · Royal Asiatic Society, London, papers relating to Java | BL OIOC, W. Colin Mackenzie collection · BL OIOC, letters, etc., to Lord Minto · Botanic Garden, Calcutta, Dr Nathaniel Wallich, private letter-books · NL Scot., Leyden (Dr John) MSS · NL Scot., corresp. with Lord Minto · NMM, letters to Sir Samuel Hood · U. Aberdeen, letters to Major Forbes

Likenesses A. E. Chalon, miniature, 1817, repro. in Wurtzburg, *Raffles* · G. F. Joseph, oils, 1817, NPG [*see illus.*] · J. Lonsdale, oils, 1818, London Zoo, council room · F. Chantrey, marble statue, 1832, Westminster Abbey · F. Chantrey, marble bust; copies in BL OIOC, London Zoo, Singapore National Library · oils, Zoological Society, London · plaster cast, AM Oxf. · statue with memorial tablet, Empress Place, Singapore

Wealth at death in debt; lost £20,000–£30,000 of uninsured possessions on the *Fame* 1824; East India Company demanded £22,272 in 1826 of which his widow paid £10,000

Raffles, Thomas (1788–1863), Congregational minister, the only son of William Raffles, a Baptist and a solicitor (d. 1825), was born in Princes Street, Spitalfields, London, on 17 May 1788. His cousin was Sir Thomas Stamford *Raffles. His mother was a Wesleyan and he was brought up in that body. In 1800 he was sent to a boarding-school at Peckham run by a Baptist minister and attended the church pastored by William G. Collyer. For a short time in 1803 he was a clerk in Doctors' Commons but in October 1803 returned to Peckham to prepare for the ministry. Between 1805 and 1809 he studied at Homerton College under Dr Pye Smith. He declined a call to Hanover Street, Long Acre, but settled at George Yard Chapel, Hammersmith, and was ordained on 22 June 1809. On the sudden death of Thomas Spencer of Newington Chapel, Liverpool, Raffles was invited to succeed him. He began his Liverpool ministry on 19 April 1812, and moved on 27 May to the new Great George Street Chapel which had been built to accommodate Spencer's swelling congregation. Raffles married on 18 April 1815 Mary Catherine Hargreaves of Liverpool.

They had a daughter and three sons, two of whom became Liverpool worthies in their own right: Thomas S. Raffles, his father's biographer and the town's stipendiary magistrate, and William W. Raffles, a cotton broker.

Under Raffles the Great George Street Chapel grew rapidly and by 1841 his salary was £700 per annum. He at once began to occupy a leading role in Liverpool and Lancashire Congregationalism: he was known as the 'patriarch' of the body in Liverpool, where his influence was compared to that of Thomas Binney in London. A whig by principle he played no part in party politics except in the affairs of the Liverpool Slavery Abolition Society. In 1833 he declined an offer to succeed Rowland Hill at the Surrey Tabernacle, London, preferring to minister in the urban and rural chapels of Lancashire. He was chairman of the Congregational Union of England and Wales in 1839. On 19 February 1840 his Liverpool chapel was destroyed by fire, the day after it had been insured. A new building was quickly erected. Raffles was secretary of the Lancashire Congregational Union from 1826 to 1843. In 1816, in co-operation with the solicitor George Hadfield, he had promoted the Blackburn Academy for the training of ministers, and in 1843 saw to its successful removal to Manchester, as the Lancashire Independent college. He was chairman of the college education committee from 1839 to 1863. In the controversy over Samuel Davidson he took the conservative side. He was himself a moderate Calvinist and it is curious that his daughter married James Baldwin Brown, the leader of the liberal wing of Congregationalism. The Raffles scholarship and Raffles Library were founded at the Lancashire Independent college as a tribute to him in 1861. He had received an Aberdeen LLD in 1820 and a Union College, Connecticut, DD in 1830.

In Liverpool evangelical circles Raffles was well known, serving, among other causes, the Seaman's Friend Society, the Religious Tract Society, the Amicable Book Society, the Bible Society, Liverpool Infirmary, and the Liverpool Lunatic Asylum. His friendships were extensive: he was on good terms with Cardinal Wiseman and donned the white surplice over his cassock when he preached in Anglican pulpits. He was a great collector of original manuscripts relating to the history of nonconformity in Lancashire: these were subsequently used by Robert Halley and Benjamin Nightingale in their histories. He collected, too, vast numbers of autographs—forty volumes in all. He was also a poet and hymn writer, publishing in 1853 his own supplement to Watts's *Psalms and Hymns*. His *Original Hymns* were published posthumously in 1868 with a preface by his son-in-law, J. B. Brown. Josiah Conder chose one of Raffles's hymns for inclusion in his 1836 *Congregational Hymn-Book*. Besides his verse compositions and his translation of Klopstock's *Messiah* (1814), Raffles published his *Memoirs of Thomas Spencer* (1813), *Letters during a Tour through France, Savoy, etc.* (1818), *Lectures on Practical Religion* (1820), *Lectures on the Doctrines of the Gospel* (1822), *Hear the Church! A Word for All. By a Doctor of Divinity, but not of Oxford* (1839—a riposte to Pusey), *The Divine Command: a Jubilee Sermon to the London Missionary Society* (1844—interesting in that it produced a premillennialist backlash), *Internal Evidence of the Inspiration of Scripture* (1849), and *Independency at St Helens* (1856). He edited a new edition of John Brown's *Self-Interpreting Bible* (1815). He died at his home at Edge Hill on 18 August 1863 and was buried at the Liverpool necropolis, on 24 August.   ALEXANDER GORDON, *rev.* IAN SELLERS

Sources J. B. Brown, *Thomas Raffles: a sketch* (1863) · T. S. Raffles, *Memoirs of Thomas Raffles* (1864) · B. Nightingale, *Lancashire nonconformity*, 6 vols. [1890–93], vol. 6 · *Raffles centenary celebrations* (Liverpool, 1912) · G. S. Veitch, 'Thomas Raffles of Liverpool', *Transactions of the Congregational Historical Society*, 9 (1924–6), 100–21 · G. F. Nuttall, 'Autograph letters collected by Thomas Raffles', *Transactions of the Congregational Historical Society*, 21 (1971–2), 21–5 · JRL, Raffles Collection

Archives BL OIOC, corresp., MS Eur. D 742 · DWL, letters and papers · JRL, autograph collection, corresp., notes relating to Lancashire nonconformist churches, and sermons · NL Scot., corresp.

Likenesses T. Blood, stipple, BM, NPG; repro. in *Evangelical Magazine* (1812) · I. Jackson, marble bust, Walker Art Gallery, Liverpool · D. J. Pound, stipple, BM, NPG · J. Thomson, stipple (after Mosses), BM, NPG; repro. in *Imperial Magazine* (1822) · portrait, repro. in Raffles, *Memoirs*

Wealth at death under £8000: probate, 7 Oct 1863, CGPLA Eng. & Wales

Ragapo, Leonard (*fl.* 1595–1600). *See under* American Indians in England (*act. c.*1500–1609).

Ragg, Thomas (1808–1881), preacher and writer, was born at Nottingham on 11 January 1808, the son of George Ragg (1782–1836) and Jane, *née* Morrison (*d.* 1822), whose grandfather was a Jacobite. Ragg's father, also born at Nottingham, was great-grandson of Benjamin Ragg, brother-in-law and coadjutor of Richard Newsham, the inventor. He moved to Birmingham the year after his son's birth, and set up a bookshop in Bull Street selling radical political publications. He also continued his large lace and hosiery business for several years, but his political activities consumed so much time that this business ended in bankruptcy. George Ragg was one of the conveners of the meeting held at New Hall Hill on 22 January 1817 to petition for parliamentary reform. In 1818 he founded the *Birmingham Argus*, a reform newspaper. The following year he was prosecuted for selling Carlile's *Republican*, and was imprisoned in 1820 and again in 1821. After his release he was present at the dinner given to Henry Hunt on 14 July 1823 by the Birmingham Union Society of Radical Reformers.

Thomas Ragg attended various dame-schools and then the academy of the prominent radical George Edmonds, an associate of his father, who later served as town clerk. He left school at the age of eleven and went to work for his father at *The Argus*. During his father's imprisonments he helped to support the family. In 1822, after the death of his mother, he was apprenticed at Leicester to his uncle, a hosier. The uncle soon moved to the neighbourhood of Nottingham and set up a lace manufactory. Ragg, originally an infidel like his father, soon converted to Christianity, married Mary Ann Clark in 1832, and became an itinerant dissenting preacher in the Nottingham area. He also published three volumes of poetry and contributed verses to the *Nottingham Review*. His uncle strongly disapproved of Ragg's literary interests, and the birth of a son and heir late in his life further damaged his relations with his nephew. In 1834 Ragg published *The Deity*, a work of blank verse in twelve volumes that detailed his conversion from infidelity to Christianity. Ragg dedicated the work to the poet James Montgomery, who helped arrange its publication. The work received favourable reviews from the *Eclectic Review*, *The Times*, and other publications, but Ragg's uncle reacted with increased hostility, prompting Ragg to leave the business in 1834. He became an assistant to a bookseller named Dearden, in Nottingham, where he published other volumes of verse, wrote for local journals, and contributed an appeal on behalf of the weaver-poet Robert Millhouse to *Dearden's Miscellany*.

Ragg's religious poetry attracted notice from Anglicans and dissenters alike. He received an offer of a university education on condition that he take holy orders but he declined. He also refused the pulpits of three noncon-formist congregations. Instead, in 1839 he accepted the editorship of the Conservative *Birmingham Advertiser*, 'to bring about something like union and cordiality of feeling between Churchmen and Evangelical Dissenters' (Ragg, *God's Dealings*, xviii). For a short time he attended both an Anglican church and the prominent Carr's Lane Congre-gationalist Chapel, but left the latter after several chapel-goers accused him of hypocrisy in attending a dissenting chapel while editing a church publication. He was briefly a proprietor of *The Advertiser* and he also managed the *Midland Monitor* in 1841–2. He continued to write verse, pub-lishing seven volumes by 1843, and his poetry attracted the notice and friendship of Robert Southey. When *The Advertiser* failed in 1845, Ragg set up as a stationer and printer in Birmingham.

Frustrated by what he perceived as Birmingham's ani-mosity toward intellectual culture, in 1844 Ragg became a member of the Birmingham Polytechnic Institution (suc-cessor to the Birmingham Mechanics' Institution), taking part in meetings and debates. He also served as the insti-tution's official printer after 1845. In 1847 he founded the Birmingham branch of the Protestant Association of the Anglican church, and in 1849 founded its official organ, the *Protestant Watchman of the Midland District*, of which he was editor. The Protestant Association's pronounced anti-Catholicism was especially prominent in the 'papal aggression' agitation of 1850–51, and formed a counter-point to the local rise of Tractarianism. Ragg also used the pages of the *Watchman* to protest against what he felt were the dangerously humanistic tendencies of George Daw-son, an extremely popular local minister at the non-sectarian church of the Saviour. Later, in 1861, he debated with secularist George Jacob Holyoake in Birmingham's Temperance Hall.

In 1855 Ragg published *Creation's Testimony to its God, or the Accordance of Science, Philosophy, and Revelation*, an eviden-tial treatise dedicated to the Revd J. B. Owen. This work obtained wide popularity, reaching a thirteenth edition in 1877. Ragg updated each reissue, in order to keep it abreast of modern scientific progress. The 1858 'Teacher's Edi-tion' of this work was prefaced by an autobiography entitled *God's Dealings with an Infidel, or, Grace Triumphant.*

Ragg also published two additional works on the recon-ciliation of science and Christianity in 1857 and 1858. *Creation's Testimony* brought Ragg to the attention of Dr George Murray, bishop of Rochester, who induced him to accept ordination in 1858. He was appointed by the bishop to a curacy, the salary of which the bishop paid himself, at Southfleet in Kent. On the bishop's death he became cur-ate of Malin's Lee in Shropshire, and in 1865 was appoin-ted perpetual curate of the newly formed parish of Lawley in Shropshire, where he remained until his death there on 3 December 1881. He was buried in Lawley churchyard. He was survived by two sons of his first marriage, and two daughters and six sons of his second marriage, to Jane Sarah Barker.

G. LE G. NORGATE, rev. ANNE BALTZ RODRICK

Sources T. Ragg, *God's dealings with an infidel, or, Grace triumphant: being the autobiography of Thomas Ragg* (1858) · D. G. Paz, *Popular anti-Catholicism in mid-Victorian England* (1992) · *Annual Report* [Birming-ham Polytechnic Institution] (1844–55) · G. J. Barnsby, *Birmingham working people* (1989) · T. Ragg, *Creation's testimony to its God, or the accordance of science, philosophy and revelation* (1858) · F. W. Ragg, *Bir-mingham Weekly Post* (17 Nov 1894)
Likenesses photograph, c.1858, repro. in Ragg, *God's dealings with an infidel, or, Grace triumphant*, frontispiece
Wealth at death £272 19s. 3d.: probate, 16 March 1882, *CGPLA Eng. & Wales*

Raggi, Mario (1821–1907), sculptor, was born in Carrara, Italy, and studied art at the Accademia delle Belle Arti, Car-rara, first under Pietro Marchetti and later under Ferdi-nando Pelliccia. After winning all available prizes, at the age of seventeen he went to Rome, where he studied under Pietro Tenerani. In 1850 he moved to London, work-ing at first under Raffaelle Monti, afterwards for many years under Matthew Noble, and finally setting up his own studio about 1875. His principal works were memorial busts and statues. He executed the national memorial to the earl of Beaconsfield in Parliament Square, a jubilee memorial of Queen Victoria for Hong Kong, with replicas for Kimberley, in southern Africa, and Toronto, Canada, and statues of Lord Swansea for Swansea, Dr Tait for Edin-burgh, Dr Crowther for Hobart Town, Tasmania, Austra-lia, Sir Arthur Kennedy for Hong Kong, and W. E. Glad-stone for Manchester.

Raggi first exhibited at the Royal Academy in 1854, showing a work entitled *Innocence*, followed in 1878 by a marble bust of Admiral Henry Rous, which he executed for the Jockey Club, Newmarket, Suffolk. He afterwards exhibited intermittently until 1895, among other works busts of Cardinal Manning (1879), Cardinal Newman (1881), Lord John Manners, afterwards seventh duke of Rutland (1884), and the duchess of Rutland (1895). Raggi died at his home, The Mount, Boundstone, Farnham, Surrey, on 26 November 1907.

S. E. FRYER, rev. CHRISTOPHER WHITEHEAD

Sources V. Vicario, *Gli scultori italiani dal neoclassicismo al Liberty*, 2 (1990), 865 · A. Panzetta, *Dizionario degli scultori dell'ottocento e del primo novecento* (1993), 226 · J. A. Mackay, *The dictionary of western sculptors in bronze* (1977), 310 · Bénézit, *Dict.*, 3rd edn · B. Read, *Victor-ian sculpture* (1982) · M. H. Grant, *A dictionary of British sculptors from*

the XIIIth century to the XXth century (1953), 200 • Graves, RA exhibitors • CGPLA Eng. & Wales (1908) • The Times (29 Nov 1907)
Wealth at death £4690 6s. 3d.: resworn probate, 10 Jan 1908, CGPLA Eng. & Wales

Raglan. For this title name see Somerset, FitzRoy James Henry, first Baron Raglan (1788–1855); Somerset, FitzRoy Richard, fourth Baron Raglan (1885–1964).

Ragnall [Rægnald, Rögnvaldr] (d. 920/21), king of York, was one of the grandsons of the Danish viking Ívarr the Boneless. Information about him comes from English, Scottish, and Irish sources, and from coins. The written sources, though extensive, are often late and garbled and cannot be wholly reconciled one with another. Much remains uncertain.

After Ívarr's grandsons were evicted from Dublin in 902, Ragnall appears to have established a base in southern Scotland or the Isle of Man. He recruited from local settlers a band of Norwegian vikings, with whom he seized York, where the Danish leadership had been weakened following the battle of Tettenhall in 910. From there Ragnall sailed north to the River Tyne in 914, forcing Ealdred, the reeve of Bamburgh, to flee with his followers to King Constantine in Scotland. Ealdred and Constantine returned that year with an army of Scots and English to face Ragnall, who defeated them at the first battle of Corbridge. Ragnall then divided the eastern lands of the community of St Cuthbert (at Chester-le-Street) between two of his leaders, giving the southern half (from Castle Eden to Billingham on Tees) to Scule and the remainder (between Castle Eden and the River Wear) to Óláf Bald. After sailing north again, Ragnall crossed from the Forth to the Clyde and attacked Dumbarton in the kingdom of Strathclyde. Later in 914 his forces defeated the fleet of a rival viking leader named Bárd Óttarsson in a naval battle off the Isle of Man.

In the following years, with Waterford as his base, Ragnall harried southern Ireland, looting the monasteries of Munster. He was joined by his kinsman (probably his brother), *Sihtric Cáech, who recaptured Dublin in 919. Meanwhile Ragnall had invaded Scotland and sacked Dunblane. He turned south into Northumbria and with the aid of Guthfrith, another grandson of Ívarr, he fought a second battle at Corbridge in 918, defeating once again the king of the Scots and the English of Bamburgh. Among those killed there was Eadred, son of Ricsige, who had leased from the community of St Cuthbert much of their remaining territory. Ragnall gave the jurisdiction of these lands, lying south and west of Chester-le-Street, to Eadred's sons Esbriht and Earl Ælfstan, who appear to have supported him in the battle. With virtually the whole of Bernicia now in the hands of his nominees, Ragnall entered York early in 919 and ruled there as king until his death in late 920 or early 921. Ragnall submitted to King Edward the Elder as overlord some time before his death, but was allowed to keep his kingdom. He minted three issues of coinage bearing the name RAIENALT or RACNOLDT or a similar variant. At his death he was described in the annals of Ulster as 'king of the Finngaill

and the Dubhgaill', that is, the 'Fair Foreigners' and the 'Dark Foreigners', meaning the Norwegians and the Danes who had settled in Ireland and northern England. He was succeeded as king of York by Sihtric Cáech.

CYRIL HART

Sources W. F. Skene, ed., Chronicles of the Picts, chronicles of the Scots, and other early memorials of Scottish history (1867) • W. M. Hennessy, ed. and trans., Chronicum Scotorum: a chronicle of Irish affairs, Rolls Series, 46 (1866) • Symeon of Durham, Opera, 1.208–10 • ASC, s.a. 923–4 [texts A, D, E, F] • W. M. Hennessy and B. MacCarthy, eds., Annals of Ulster, otherwise, annals of Senat, 4 vols. (1887–1901), vol. 1 • F. T. Wainwright, Scandinavian England, ed. H. P. R. Finberg (1975) • A. P. Smyth, Scandinavian York and Dublin: the history of two related Viking kingdoms, 2 vols. (1975–9) • C. R. Hart, The early charters of northern England and the north midlands (1975) • C. E. Blunt, B. H. I. H. Stewart, and C. S. S. Lyon, Coinage in tenth-century England: from Edward the Elder to Edgar's reform (1989)
Likenesses coin, repro. in Blunt, Stewart, and Lyon, Coinage in tenth-century England, pl. 26, no. 12

Ragnall [Rægnald] **Guthfrithson** [Rögnvaldr Guðrøðarson] (fl. 943–944), viking king, was the son of *Guthfrith [see under Sihtric Cáech], who had ruled at York briefly in 927 and at Dublin for most of the period from 921 until his death in 934. Ragnall had at least three brothers: *Óláf Guthfrithson (d. 941), who succeeded his father as king in Dublin and was king at York from 939 to 941; Blacair (or Blacaire as he appears in Irish sources), who ruled Dublin intermittently from 940 until he was slain by Congalach mac Máele Mithig (d. 956) in 948; and Hálfdan, who was killed by Muirchertach mac Néill (d. 943) in 926. A 'son of Guthfrith' is also recorded as based at Waterford in 928. Inaccuracies in the dates given by different versions of the Anglo-Saxon Chronicle have led to confusion between Ragnall Guthfrithson and his namesake and predecessor, *Ragnall (d. 920/21).

Confusion also governs the scant evidence for Ragnall's career. The sources' first mention of him concerns his unnamed son, who in 942 raided Downpatrick, was attacked by rival vikings, and escaped, only to be slain by Matudán mac Áeda, king of Ulaid. Ragnall himself first comes to notice at York in connection with Óláf Sihtricson. The English king Edmund stood sponsor at the baptism of Óláf in, probably, 943. In the same year, 'after a fairly big interval' (ASC, s.a. 943, text D), Edmund stood sponsor at Ragnall's confirmation. The Anglo-Saxon Chronicle calls him 'king'. Whether Óláf and Ragnall ruled in co-operation or competition depends upon an interpretation of two further annals. The Historia regum, an eleventh-century compilation which may include older material, records that in 943 the Northumbrians drove Óláf Sihtricson from the kingdom. All versions of the Anglo-Saxon Chronicle, on the other hand, relate that in 944 'King Edmund reduced all Northumbria to his rule and drove out two kings, Olaf, Sihtric's son, and Rægnald, Guthfrith's son' (ASC, s.a. 944). One plausible explanation of these sources would envisage Óláf driven from York but remaining in the north to contest the rulership of the Scandinavian kingdom with Ragnall, until both were expelled by Edmund. Other scenarios are possible, however. Both Ragnall and Óláf seem at least to have been kings at York in this period, since both issued coins there. According to the chronicler Æthelweard (d. 998?), it was Bishop (that is, Archbishop) Wulfstan and an unnamed ealdorman of the Mercians who drove the two viking kings from York and forced them to submit to Edmund. Nothing more is heard of Ragnall, though he may have been the 'king of the Danes' who is reported by the later medieval annals of Clonmacnoise to have been killed at York by the English in 944 or 945.

MARIOS COSTAMBEYS

Sources ASC · Ann. Ulster · A. P. Smyth, Scandinavian York and Dublin: the history of two related Viking kingdoms, 2 (1979) · 'Historia regum', Symeon of Durham, Opera, vol. 2 · The chronicle of Æthelweard, ed. and trans. A. Campbell (1962) · AFM · D. Murphy, ed., The annals of Clonmacnoise, trans. C. Mageoghagan (1896); facs. edn (1993)

Ragnvald [Rögnvaldr, Reginald, Ragnall] (d. 1229), king of Man and the Isles, was the oldest but illegitimate son of *Godred, son of *Óláf [see under Godred Crovan]. Although his father had wished to be succeeded by his legitimate son Óláf, in 1187 the Manxmen brought Ragnvald from the Western Isles to be their king, 'since he was a sturdy man and of maturer years' (Cronica regum Mannie et Insularum, fol. 40v). He is said to have founded St Mary's Priory of Cistercian nuns at Douglas (Cowan and Easson, 238). The Irish author of a Gaelic poem in his honour describes him as the son of Sadb, possibly an Irishwoman, makes some exaggerated statements of his claim to the high-kingship of Ireland, and seeks patronage when Ragnvald establishes a footing in Dublin. His unnamed daughter married Rhodri ab Owain Gwynedd, who in 1193 subdued Anglesey with Ragnvald's help; after Rhodri's death Ragnvald sought unsuccessfully to secure her marriage to Rhodri's nephew, Llywelyn ab Iorwerth. It was perhaps in 1198 that William the Lion, king of Scots, granted him the earldom of Caithness for an annual rent, which Ragnvald, described in one source as 'the greatest warrior in the western lands', subdued with an army drawn from the Hebrides, Kintyre, and Ireland (Flateyjarbók, 2.515–17).

In 1204, when John de Courcy, married to Ragnvald's sister, Affreca, was forced from power in Ulster by Hugh de Lacy, he took refuge with Ragnvald in Man, but together they failed in an attempt to recover Ulster in the following year. In February 1205 Ragnvald was given letters of protection by King John, and was in England later that year when he was granted lands in Lancashire 'for his homage and service' (Oliver, 2.27). About 1208 Ragnvald captured his brother Óláf, who had ruled Lewis under him, and handed him over to William the Lion, in whose prison he remained until the latter's death in 1214. Ragnvald subsequently prevailed on Óláf to marry 'the daughter of a certain nobleman of Kintyre, the sister of his own wife' (Cronica regum Mannie et Insularum, fol. 42r). Following a Norse attack on the Isles in 1209–10 Ragnvald and his son Godred went to Norway, swore fealty to King Inge, and paid tribute. In 1210, when King John was in Ireland in pursuit of Hugh de Lacy and the family of William (III) de Briouze, they gained temporary refuge in the Isle of Man, and John responded by sending a fleet to ravage the island

in Ragnvald's absence. Two years later Ragnvald became King John's liegeman and was granted a knight's fee at Carlingford in Ireland, and an annual allowance of wheat, while the king's officials in Ireland were ordered to assist in destroying Ragnvald's enemies. In 1214 the mariners of Ireland were prohibited from entering the lands of Ragnvald. On several occasions in 1218 letters of safe conduct were granted to him to come to the English court 'to amend the excesses of his men done both in England and Ireland on the king's subjects' (Calendar … Ireland, 1.828), and by September of the following year he is recorded as having done homage to Henry III. At the same time, however, Ragnvald declared that he held the Isle of Man, his by hereditary right, as a fief of the papal see, an offer that resulted, in 1223, in Honorius III taking Ragnvald and his realm under papal protection, in return for an annual payment of 12 marks. Ragnvald reported to Henry III in November 1220 that the king of Norway 'lays snares for him and threatens his land with evil' (Calendar … Ireland, 1.976), whereupon the justiciar of Ireland was ordered to defend the kingdom of the Isles from Norse attack.

In the summer of 1224 Ragnvald's brother Óláf landed his fleet at Ronaldsway and forced Ragnvald to divide the kingdom between them, Ragnvald retaining Man, some of the Isles, and the title of king, Óláf being granted the rest. In the following year Ragnvald was joined by Alan of Galloway in an attempt to recover the entire kingdom which failed because the Manxmen were unwilling to oppose Óláf. Shortly afterwards Ragnvald gave his daughter in marriage to Alan's illegitimate son Thomas, and thereby so angered the inhabitants of Man that in 1226 they sent for Óláf and made him their king. In April 1228 Henry III issued a safe conduct for Óláf to come to him to make peace with Ragnvald, but in the same year, when Óláf was absent in the Isles, Ragnvald plundered Man in the company of Alan of Galloway, so that 'the southern part of Man was practically reduced to a desert' (Cronica regum Mannie et Insularum, fol. 43v). Óláf arrived, put them to flight, and regained the kingship, but in the following winter Ragnvald unexpectedly returned from Galloway, and won the allegiance of the men of the south of the island, while Óláf retained the support of those of the north. On 14 February 1229 the brothers did battle at Tynwald, during the course of which Ragnvald was assassinated. His body was brought by the monks of Rushen to St Mary's Abbey, Furness, and buried in the place he had chosen while living. He left at least one son, Godred Dond (Godred the Brown-haired) who, though mutilated by Óláf's men in 1223, briefly succeeded him.

SEÁN DUFFY

Sources G. Broderick, ed. and trans., Cronica regum Insularum / Chronicles of the kings of Man and the Isles (1979) · B. Ó Cuív, 'A poem in praise of Raghnall, king of Man', Éigse, 8 (1955–7), 283–301 · T. Jones, ed. and trans., Brut y tywysogyon, or, The chronicle of the princes: Peniarth MS 20 (1952) · CEPR letters, vol. 1 · A. O. Anderson, ed. and trans., Early sources of Scottish history, AD 500 to 1286, 2 vols. (1922) · Rymer, Foedera, new edn, vol. 1 · H. S. Sweetman and G. F. Handcock, eds., Calendar of documents relating to Ireland, 5 vols., PRO (1875–86) · CDS · A. W. Moore, A history of the Isle of Man, 2 vols. (1900) · C. R. Unger and G. Vigfússon, eds., Flateyjarbók (1859–68) ·

J. R. Oliver, ed., *Monumenta de Insula Manniae, or, A collection of national documents relating to the Isle of Man*, 3 vols., Manx Society, 4, 7, 9 (1860–62) • I. B. Cowan and D. E. Easson, *Medieval religious houses: Scotland*, 2nd edn (1976)

Rahere [Rayer] (*d.* 1143×5), founder of St Bartholomew's Hospital and priory, London, was of unknown origins. The one authoritative source for his life, *Liber fundacionis ecclesiae Sancti Bartholomei Londoniensis* written some forty years after his death but existing only in a fifteenth-century text, describes 'Rayer' as a man 'born of low lineage' (Moore, BL, Cotton Vespasian B.ix) and with little learning who, as a youth, sought the patronage of the nobility, and inveigled his way into their households with japes and flattery until he became a familiar figure with both king and courtiers through his prominence in courtly revels. At this time, about 1120, there was a canon of St Paul's Cathedral, prebendary of Chamberlainwood (Willesden, Middlesex), called Raherius. Bearing in mind the uncommon name without patronymic, and the strong links at that date between the royal court and St Paul's Cathedral chapter, it would seem probable that prebendary and courtier were one and the same. *The Book of the Foundation* continues that, suddenly penitent, Rahere made a pilgrimage to Rome to seek a full pardon. However, falling seriously ill while there, he promised God that he would found a hospital should he be granted recovery. His health was restored and, on the return journey to England, he had a vision of St Bartholomew, who instructed him to build a church at Smithfield. Rahere's friends welcomed him home, though, hearing of his vow, the barons of London advised him that Smithfield lay in the king's market and that Rahere should seek the king's favour. Henry I, impressed by the petitioner, granted him the land, which was consecrated by his supporter Richard de Belmeis, bishop of London (*d.* 1127). The building of the church caused no problem; but Rahere, anxious about opposition to his hospital, gathered together all the materials needed and, with everything ready, erected the building speedily. In the 1180s, when the early history of the priory was written down, the date of the foundation was remembered as March 1123. Rahere, who had chosen to follow the Augustinian rule, became the first prior.

The hospital soon won a reputation for miracles and healing, but disaffected people, seeing Rahere as an arbiter over life or death, planned to kill him. He again petitioned King Henry, who in 1133 granted a charter giving both royal protection and wide-ranging privileges to the young foundation. The author of *The Book of the Foundation* says that Rahere became 'rich in purity of conscience', diligent in divine service, sober and prudent, humble towards his brethren and benevolent to his enemies, while gently providing care to the sick and poor (Moore, fol. 41r). In succeeding centuries, however, his earlier reputation prevailed. John Stow reported that Rahere was 'a pleasant-witted gentleman and therefore in his time the king's minstrel' (Stow, 1.235). In Thomas Deloney's popular tale, *Thomas of Reading*, written in the sixteenth century, 'Reior' was 'the skilfullest musician that lived at that time whose wealth was very great' (Deloney, 452–3).

Rahere was thus frequently portrayed as the king's minstrel or jester. He remained in office as prior until his death. The prologue to book 2 of *The Book of the Foundation* states that he died on 20 September 'after the years of his prelacie xxii and vi months' (Moore, fol. 59r); but the writer also declares that the second prior (Thomas, from St Osyth's, Essex) was appointed in 1144 after the space of a year, which seems inconsistent with the earlier statement. Rahere was buried in the priory church, where his effigy, in the Augustinian habit of black cope and white surplice, under a decorated canopy, was placed about 1405. His two works of piety survive; after the Reformation, the choir of the priory church became the parish church of St Bartholomew-the-Great. The hospital, as a separate institution, became one of the world's most influential and respected medical establishments.

JUDITH ETHERTON

Sources N. Moore, ed., *The book of the foundation of St Bartholomew's church in London*, EETS, 163 (1923), 1–2, 33 • cartulary, St Bartholomew's Hospital, London, HC2/1 • N. J. M. Kerling, ed., *Cartulary of St Bartholomew's Hospital, founded 1123* (1973), 18 • N. Moore, *The history of St Bartholomew's Hospital*, 2 vols. (1918), vol. 1, pp. 6–49; vol. 2, pp. 23 • E. A. Webb, *The records of St Bartholomew's Priory and of the church and parish of St Bartholomew the Great, West Smithfield*, 1 (1921), 37–78 • *Fasti Angl., 1066–1300*, [St Paul's, London] • J. Stow, *A survey of the cities of London and Westminster and the borough of Southwark*, new edn, ed. J. Strype, 1/3 (1720), 235 • T. Deloney, 'Thomas of Reading', *Early English prose romances*, ed. W. J. Thomas (1907), 452–3 • C. N. L. Brooke, 'The composition of the chapter of St Paul's, 1086–1163', *Cambridge Historical Journal*, 10 (1950–52), 111–32 • N. Moore, *Ordnance of Richard of Ely, bishop of London, as to St Bartholomew's priory, 1198* (1886)

Likenesses stone effigy, *c.*1405, St Bartholomew the Great, West Smithfield, London

Raiftearaí, Antoine (1779–1835), poet, was born on 30 March 1779 at Cill Liadáin (Killedan), near Kiltimagh, co. Mayo, the son of a weaver; his mother's maiden name was Brennan. An attack of smallpox at five or nine years old left him blind for the rest of his life. With a view to eking out some kind of a living the young Raiftearaí learned to play the violin, some say tolerably, others poorly. In any event he was taken in tow by a local gentleman, Frank Taaffe, as a sort of family bard, musician, and story-teller, but Taaffe's patronage came to an end either because of Raiftearaí's involvement in the loss of a favourite horse or because of his too vocal support for the republican organization the United Irishmen.

Raiftearaí then migrated to south Galway, some 50 miles away, where the pickings were much better for one of his calling among the many well-off farmers of that area. The rest of his life he spent there, much in demand at house dances, weddings, and even wakes. While on such occasions the hat was invariably passed around for his benefit, there was also a deal of plying the blind bard with drink, with the result that he soon had a drink problem. There is no evidence that he ever married. However, it appears he lived with a woman named Siobhán for some years, the liaison producing a daughter and a son before they went their separate ways.

The nature of Raiftearaí's calling as an itinerant bard posited a very public dimension to his songs and poems, for no sooner had he composed a piece than he was in a position to sing or recite it in public. Satires on people who somehow or other incurred the bard's displeasure and an argle-bargle with local fellow poets, the brothers Callanan, were all grist to the mill of a self-publicist whose interest it was to stay in the public eye.

South Galway was in Raiftearaí's time a bilingual society, most people being fluent both in Irish and English. However, the problem with Irish was that it was not taught in the schools and while most people could speak it, there were few who could read it and even fewer who could write it. Raiftearaí's output of about forty-eight poems is considerable for a blind man. Lengthy poems such as *Seanchas na sceiche* ('The bush's history [of Ireland]'), a sort of potted history of Ireland up to the 1690s, could scarcely have been accomplished without the aid of an amanuensis, who no doubt doubled as an editor or adviser. The public recitation of Raiftearaí's work by himself and others and its circulation in manuscript copies led inevitably to the emergence of many different variations and additions, with the result that few poets in the Irish language have had their work interfered with to such an extent as Raiftearaí. The obverse of this is that some pieces, including the emotive *Mise Raiftearaí* ('I am Raiftearaí'), have been attributed to him which were not his.

Raiftearaí's work can be subdivided into poems about people and places, love songs, religious verse, and poems on current affairs and historical subjects. The poems about places characteristically develop into a listing over many stanzas of the flora and fauna of the place, a process which becomes tedious when repeated again and again. The well-known *Cill Liadáin* ('Killedan'), a celebration of Raiftearaí's native place, is no exception and would benefit from the dropping of four or five such stanzas. Similarly, poems about an assortment of tradesmen—shoemaker, weaver, blacksmith, carpenter, and so on—are little more than a stringing together in verse of the articles produced by such people. Seven or eight love songs, unlike many in that genre, have the merit that the subjects were real people, although Raiftearaí's efforts in that direction were not generally welcomed, for his love songs were said to bring bad luck.

Raiftearaí celebrated in verse many local and national events, including the victory in the Galway election of 1833 of the Catholic Sir John Burke, the proselytizing activities of the Hibernian Bible Society, agrarian agitation by a secret society called the Ribbonmen, Daniel O'Connell's great victory in the County Clare election of 1828 which led to Catholic emancipation, and the tithe war of the 1830s.

In the final analysis, however, Raiftearaí's claim to fame rests on perhaps half a dozen pieces. Arguably, first among these must be *Eanach Dhúin* ('Annaghdown'), a piteous dirge about the drowning of nineteen people in an unseaworthy craft on Lough Corrib, co. Galway, in 1828. Strangely, for a man whose private life was anything but exemplary, two long religious poems must be classed among his best, *Agallamh Raiftearaí agus an bháis* ('Raiftearaí's discourse with death') and *Achainí Raiftearaí ar Íosa Críost* ('Raiftearaí's petition to Jesus Christ'), a powerful call for repentance, not least by himself, in the face of a cholera epidemic. The latter was published posthumously in 1848 and accompanied by an English translation for the stated purpose of its being intelligible to the reading public. Also of lasting merit are some laments, notably that for Thomas Daly, piper and gentleman.

Raiftearaí died in the direst poverty in a barn near Craughwell, co. Galway, on Christmas day 1835, and was buried in nearby Killeenin graveyard, probably on 27 December. His name was rescued from obscurity towards the end of the century through the initiative of the newly established Gaelic League (for the revival of the Irish language) led by Douglas Hyde (Dubhghlas de híde) and the Irish literary movement led by Lady Gregory and Yeats. The two movements combined to erect a commemorative slab over Raiftearaí's grave in 1900. Gregory wrote a play about Raiftearaí and devoted a chapter of her *Poets and Dreamers* to him, while Hyde edited the first collection of his verse in 1903. PATRICK FAGAN

Sources C. Ó Coigligh, *Raiftearaí: amhráin agus dánta* (1987) · D. de híde, *Abhráin agus dánta an Reachtabhraigh* (1933) · A. Gregory, *Poets and dreamers* (1903) · S. Ó Ceallaigh, ed., *Filíocht na gCallanán* (1967) · Royal Irish Acad., MS 23.0.9 · Royal Irish Acad., MS 23.0.42 · NL Ire., MS G 751 · R. Welch, ed., *The Oxford companion to Irish literature* (1996)
Archives University College, Dublin, MS 1339 · University College, Cork, MS T36
Likenesses pen-and-ink drawing, Royal Irish Acad., MS 23.0.9; repro. in Ó Coigligh, *Raiftearaí*

Raikes, Charles (1812–1885), East India Company servant, was born at Theobalds Park, Cheshunt, Hertfordshire, on 9 December 1812, the son of Job Matthew Raikes (1767–1833), a merchant, formerly of Tunbridge Wells, and his wife, Charlotte Susannah, *née* Bayly. After a private education and a year at Haileybury College, in 1831 he arrived in Calcutta to take up a writership in the Bengal civil service. He married in 1834 Sophia Mary, daughter of Colonel Mathews of the 31st foot; she died in April the following year, shortly after giving birth to a daughter. On 21 March 1838, while on furlough, he married Justina Davidson, daughter of William Alves of Enham House, Hampshire; they had five sons and two daughters.

From 1831 until 1853 Raikes was based in the North-Western Provinces, becoming magistrate of Mainpuri in 1849 and publishing *Notes on the North-Western Provinces* in 1852. In 1853 he was appointed commissioner of Lahore. Three years later he returned to the North-Western Provinces as an officiating judge in the East India Company's chief court at Agra and remained there throughout the turmoil of 1857 until dispatched in December to Farrukhabad as civil commissioner in charge of areas liberated by Sir Colin Campbell. The uprising—which cost him a daughter, son-in-law (George Christian, commissioner of Sitapur), and two grandchildren—only strengthened his belief that Indians needed to be ruled despotically, a view he aired in *Notes on the Revolt in the North-Western Provinces*, published in 1858.

Raikes retired from the civil service in 1860. In 1866 he was made a CSI and in 1867 published a third volume, *The Englishman in India*. In retirement he served as a magistrate for Wiltshire and Sussex and commanded a corps of volunteers at Chichester. He died at his home, Mill Gap, Eastbourne, in Sussex, on 16 September 1885. His wife, Justina, had died in 1882. He was survived by several children, including Lieutenant-Colonel Frederick Duncan Raikes (1848–1915), commissioner in Upper Burma from 1896 until 1901.   KATHERINE PRIOR

Sources C. Raikes, *Notes on the revolt in the North-Western Provinces of India* (1858) · BL OIOC, Haileybury MSS · H. T. Prinsep and R. Doss, eds., *A general register of the Hon'ble East India Company's civil servants of the Bengal establishment from 1790 to 1842* (1844) · ecclesiastical records, East India Company, BL OIOC · *The Times* (19 Sept 1885) · Burke, *Gen. GB* (1914) · *CGPLA Eng. & Wales* (1885)
Wealth at death £9123 14s. 8d.: resworn probate, Aug 1886, *CGPLA Eng. & Wales* (1885)

Raikes, Henry (1782–1854), Church of England clergyman, was born in Broad Street, City of London, on 24 September 1782, the second son of Thomas Raikes (1741–1813), a merchant, who was governor of the Bank of England in 1797. His mother was Charlotte (d. 1810), daughter of the Hon. Henry Finch. The Raikes family was prominent in commercial, social, and evangelical circles. Thomas *Raikes, the dandy and diarist, was Henry's brother and Robert Raikes, the founder of the Sunday school movement, his uncle.

Educated at Eton College (1793–1800), Raikes entered St John's College, Cambridge, in 1800 and graduated BA in 1804; he proceeded MA in 1807. He spent most of 1805 travelling abroad. After visiting Austria and Hungary he sailed to Greece, where he met George Hamilton Gordon, fourth earl of Aberdeen, his fellow student at Cambridge, and spent the winter in exploring with him the sites of the temples and cities of Boeotia and the interior of the Peloponnese. The following year he accompanied the Mediterranean squadron for some months, as the guest of Lord Collingwood, on its cruise off the coasts of Sicily and Africa.

In 1807 Raikes was ordained deacon and in 1808 priest, becoming curate of Betchworth in Surrey. He was subsequently curate of Shillingstone, Dorset, Burnham, Buckinghamshire, and of Bognor, Sussex. On 16 March 1809 he married Augusta (d. 1820), eldest daughter of Jacob J. Whittington of Theberton Hall and Yoxford, Suffolk. They had one daughter and three sons, the eldest of whom, Henry *Raikes [see under Raikes, Henry Cecil], was the father of Henry Cecil *Raikes. In 1828 Raikes became examining chaplain to his early friend John Bird Sumner, bishop of Chester, and in 1830 chancellor of the diocese of Chester. His influence rapidly grew, and he became well known in the city and diocese as a preacher, a public speaker on religious occasions, and an active philanthropist. A leading evangelical, he was prominent in the activities of the Church Missionary Society. On 8 August 1844 he was named an honorary canon of the cathedral.

In Chester, Raikes encouraged a lively interest in the

Henry Raikes (1782–1854), by John Romney

city's historical remains and in the restoration of the cathedral. He was a president of the Architectural, Archaeological, and Historic Society of Chester, which he helped to found in 1849, and contributed many papers to its journal. He was also appointed historian to the society.

Raikes's most important published work was *Remarks on Clerical Education* (1831), which encouraged the universities to improve the theological examinations and the bishops to require a theological degree as a prelude to holy orders. His other works were mostly collected sermons. He was a member of the commission for the subdivision of parishes in 1849, a measure of church reform that he had long advocated.

Raikes died at his seat, Dee Side House, Chester, on 28 November 1854, and was buried in Chester cemetery on 5 December.   G. C. BOASE, *rev.* SIMON HARRISON

Sources *Journal of the Architectural, Archaeological and Historic Society for Chester*, 1 (1849–55), 414–21 · *GM*, 2nd ser., 43 (1855), 198–202 · Boase, *Mod. Eng. biog.* · Burke, *Gen. GB* · Venn, *Alum. Cant.* · burial register, Chester cemetery
Archives JRL, corresp. · U. Lpool, Sydney Jones Library, diary of a tour of Greece | BL, letters to W. E. Gladstone and others
Likenesses J. Romney, lithograph, NPG [see illus.]

Raikes, Henry (1811–1863). *See under* Raikes, Henry Cecil (1838–1891).

Raikes, Henry Cecil (1838–1891), politician, was born on 25 November 1838 at the deanery, Chester, the eldest son of **Henry Raikes** (1811–1863), barrister, of Llwynegrin Hall, Mold, Flintshire, and his wife, Lucy Charlotte (d. 1889), daughter of Archdeacon Francis Wrangham FRS. He had four brothers and five sisters. His father, the son of Henry *Raikes (1782–1854), Church of England clergyman, and his wife, Augusta, *née* Whittington, was high sheriff of Flintshire and registrar of the Chester diocese as well as being on the north Wales circuit; his two-volume

Popular sketch of the origin and development of the English constitution, from the earliest period to the present time was published between 1851 and 1854. He supervised the early education of his eldest son, who later recalled 'a diet of English Constitution' (Raikes, 8), but in 1846 sent him to Shrewsbury School where he thrived, entering the sixth form at the age of thirteen, excelling in classics, and becoming head of school. He went up to Trinity College, Cambridge, in 1856, and was elected a scholar in 1859, but his constant involvement with the university union, of which he became president in 1859, contributed to his taking a second in the classical tripos in 1860, a result he constantly rued. That same year he entered the Middle Temple and while studying for the law there, he married Charlotte Blanche Trevor Roper (d. 1922), fourth daughter of Charles Blayney Trevor Roper of Plas Teg, Flintshire, on 26 September 1861. He was called to the bar on 30 April 1863 and after a brief spell as a journalist he joined the north Wales circuit, but his interest in the law was minimal: politics was the abiding passion of his life.

Greatly influenced by Disraeli's concept of popular Conservatism, Raikes's desire to stand for parliament was constantly opposed by his father, who had twice unsuccessfully contested the Derby seat for the Conservatives. The latter's death left Raikes free to stand for Chester in 1865 and although defeated he was selected for the Devonport by-election in April 1866 but, again, was unsuccessful. In the following year, Raikes founded the short-lived *Imperial Review* and worked assiduously with Lord Nevill in the creation of a national union of local Conservative and constitutional associations. Raikes was convinced that any mass political party wishing either to gain or to retain power in the future would have to 'ascertain how far their proceedings were in harmony with the wishes of the people' (McKenzie, 158) and felt that this should be the union's major role, but he was not supported in this by the party leaders. He won the Chester seat in the 1868 general election despite the significant swing against the Conservative Party. Raikes remained chairman of the national union council until 1875 but found his role in party affairs being supplanted by J. E. Gorst, one colleague observing that the tall, thin Raikes, with 'his smiling eyes and soft deliberate voice … [was] a little indefinite in plan and careless in detail' whereas the short, prosaic Gorst possessed a 'genius for organisation … [an] inflexible will and untiring diligence' (Clarke, 95). Raikes's efforts were acknowledged by Disraeli's offer of the positions of chairman of ways and means and deputy speaker of the House of Commons following the Conservative success in the 1874 general election. Raikes knew that the offer reflected an intention to shelve his political aspirations, ironically because of his views and middle-class background, and he acquiesced only very reluctantly, being keenly aware of the likely consequences of refusal. His rather autocratic manner and substantial knowledge of procedure suited both positions and over the next six years he gained general acclaim for his firmness, courtesy, and discretion in the face of significant obstruction by Irish MPs in some debates. A cartoon in *Vanity Fair* (1875) signalled his growing political stature.

In the 1880 general election Raikes was stunned by the loss of his Chester seat and although the Conservatives petitioned to have the result overturned on the grounds of corruption he decided to sever his links with the town. The award of a privy councillorship in March 1880 provided some compensation for his loss, as did his election as a bencher of the Middle Temple two months later, but he had missed the chance of becoming speaker of the House of Commons. His return to the Commons in February 1882 as the MP for Preston reflected strong support from his party leaders in this instance, but this was not forthcoming when he resigned in the following November to contest the vacant University of Cambridge seat: this made his victory all the sweeter. A vociferous opponent of some of Gladstone's proposals for parliamentary reform, especially that of the closure of debates, Raikes was also highly critical of Sir Stafford Northcote's ineffective leadership of the opposition, being a supporter of Lord Salisbury. He used his considerable journalistic skills to publicize his views and also founded the *National Review* in March 1883, with Alfred Austin, in order to provide a public forum for the discussion of Conservatism. His independent stance and unwillingness to serve with Northcote, combined with an erroneous estimate of his own political standing, ensured his exclusion from office in Lord Salisbury's first administration of 1885–6. When Salisbury formed his second government in 1886, Raikes was only offered the minor position of postmaster-general, which he accepted.

Raikes did not enjoy his tenure as postmaster-general but he was determined to be the master of his department. He rapidly acquired a substantial knowledge of its operations, which, coupled with his despotic manner, enabled him to realize his aim but led to conflicts with his staff. His determination to secure the optimum provision of postal services generated confrontation with companies which had previously enjoyed monopolies in certain sectors. In two instances Raikes was able to secure considerable improvements to services, as well as substantial financial savings, by the negotiation of new contracts, in which he enjoyed the support of both the cabinet and the House of Commons. But in the conflict with Boy Messengers Limited in 1891 he was forced to compromise in the face of both cabinet and public pressure, and he found this an unpleasant experience. His belief that the Post Office should set an example by the liberal treatment of its staff was offset by his firm handling of unrest over conditions of service between January 1890 and April 1891, and the attendant conflict with the Postmen's Union. This earned him considerable public obloquy at the time, but ultimately respect for the improved conditions he managed to wrest from Treasury.

Lord Cranbrook believed Raikes had demonstrated significant administrative powers as postmaster-general, although another contemporary felt that he was essentially an official by nature and thus possessed the defect of his qualities. Edward Hamilton contended that Raikes's failure to achieve his political aims reflected his unpopularity within the Conservative Party as a result of his general conduct and his inability to 'say or do anything without saying it or doing it in the wrong manner' (Hamilton, BL, Add. MS 48656). Some later historians, notably Hanham, Feuchtwanger, and Shannon concur with Hamilton's analysis while acknowledging Raikes's contributions to the national union, party organization, and the post-Disraeli leadership struggle.

A committed lay member of the Anglican church, Raikes served as chairman of the Church Defence Institution (1868–74), president of the Central Council of Diocesan Conferences (1881–5), and from 1890 as chancellor of the diocese of St Asaph. His defence of the church in the Commons was notable, especially on the issue of Welsh disestablishment. He served as deputy lieutenant of Flintshire from 1864 until his death and received an honorary LLD from Cambridge University in 1888. He died suddenly on 24 August 1891 at his home, Llwynegrin Hall, Flintshire, and was buried on 27 August at St Mary's Church, Mold. He was survived by his wife.   N. D. DAGLISH

Sources H. St J. Raikes, The life and letters of Henry Cecil Raikes (1898) · R. Shannon, The age of Disraeli, 1868–1881: the rise of tory democracy (1992) · Bodl. Oxf., Dep. Hughenden · The diary of Gathorne Hardy, later Lord Cranbrook, 1866–1892: political selections, ed. N. E. Johnson (1981) · R. Shannon, The age of Salisbury, 1881–1902: unionism and empire (1996) · E. J. Feuchtwanger, Disraeli, democracy and the tory party: conservative leadership and organization after the second Reform Bill (1968) · E. W. Hamilton, diaries, 25 Aug 1891, BL, Add. MS 48656, fols. 63–4 · The diary of Sir Edward Walter Hamilton, 1880–1885, ed. D. W. R. Bahlman, 2 vols. (1972) · The Times (25 Aug 1891) · H. J. Hanham, Elections and party management: politics in the time of Disraeli and Gladstone (1959); repr. (1967) · J. Junior, VF (17 April 1875) · Burke, Gen. GB (1937) · Venn, Alum. Cant. · R. T. McKenzie, British political parties (1963) · E. Clarke, The story of my life (1918) · The Times (28 Aug 1891) · The Times (28 Oct 1863) · CGPLA Eng. & Wales (1891)
Archives BL, letters to T. H. S. Escott, Add. MS 58790 · Bodl. Oxf., Hughenden MSS · Ches. & Chester ALSS, letters to Thomas Hughes · Hatfield House, Hertfordshire, Salisbury MSS
Likenesses Ape [C. Pellegrini], caricature, watercolour study, NPG; repro. in Junior, 'Mr Henry Cecil Raikes' · engraving, repro. in Raikes, Life and letters, frontispiece · wood-engraving (after photograph by Fradelle), NPG; repro. in ILN (16 Dec 1882)
Wealth at death £15,853 15s. 11d.: probate, 12 Dec 1891, CGPLA Eng. & Wales · under £90,000—Henry Raikes: resworn probate, Aug 1866, CGPLA Eng. & Wales (1864)

Raikes, Humphrey Rivaz (1891–1955), chemist and university administrator, was born on 14 July 1891 at Ide Hill, Kent, the third son of Canon Walter Allan Raikes, vicar of Goudhurst, and his wife, Catherine Amelia, daughter of William Cotton *Oswell (1818–1893), an explorer and elephant hunter in southern Africa in the 1840s. Raikes, who remained an Anglican throughout his life, was educated first at St Clare's School, Walmer, then at Tonbridge School, Dulwich College, and Balliol College, Oxford, where he was a Williams exhibitioner in 1910 and Abbott scholar in 1911. A student of Harold Hartley, he attained a first class in the final honour school of chemistry in 1914.

At the outbreak of the First World War Raikes served in France as a second lieutenant in the Buffs, and in April 1915 he was wounded in the shoulder. In November 1915 he transferred to the Royal Flying Corps, and in January 1918 became chief experimental officer at the experimental station at Orford Ness with the rank of major. In June 1918 he was awarded the Air Force Cross, and joined the Royal Air Force mission to the United States to help train American personnel.

After the war Raikes returned to Oxford, and in June 1919 was elected to a tutorial fellowship at Exeter College. From 1920 to 1927 he again worked under Hartley, serving as demonstrator in physical chemistry at the Balliol and Trinity College laboratory, and from 1924 to 1927 he was sub-rector of Exeter College. He was a most stimulating teacher, his main interest being electrochemistry, and his colleagues in the growing school of physical chemistry owed much to his skilful administration of the Balliol and Trinity laboratory. On the formation of the Oxford University air squadron in 1925 Raikes was made chief instructor with the rank of wing commander.

In January 1928 Raikes succeeded Sir William Thomson to become the third principal of the University of the Witwatersrand, South Africa, then entering its seventh year as a full university. His appointment as principal was fortuitous. The university's London committee, visiting Exeter College to interview a favoured candidate and not finding him, happened upon Raikes, who so impressed them that they promptly nominated him for the post. Nevertheless, at first Raikes struggled to establish his position within the university. He had been appointed against the wishes of senate, which favoured an internal candidate (the philosopher R. F. A. Hoernlé), and often had difficulty in controlling senate meetings. Initially, the university council was not convinced that it had made the right appointment. A tall, gangling man, Raikes seemed shy, nervous, and lacking in drive. A narcoleptic, he also had the disconcerting habit of falling asleep during meetings. His position as principal was not confirmed until 1932, and it was not until 1948 that council appointed him to the largely ceremonial position of vice-chancellor. Although Raikes wished to identify himself with South Africa, he was long regarded by many as an alien transplant. This was compounded by his reticence and a natural reserve, which gave the impression of aloofness. In 1931 Raikes married Joan, daughter of Charles Mylne Mullaly of the Indian Civil Service; the marriage was soon annulled. In 1936 he returned to England to marry, on 8 December, Alice Joan (d. 1977), daughter of William Arthur Hardy, an accountant of Norwich; she became headmistress of Roedean School in Johannesburg. They had no children.

The Second World War enabled Raikes to come into his own, both within the university and in the wider community. He took the lead in involving the university in South Africa's war effort, including the formation of a university training corps, and in ensuring the provision by Wits, at the end of the war, of an accelerated programme for ex-volunteers. In August 1945 Raikes toured the South African forces in Italy and Egypt on a recruiting drive on behalf of all the country's universities; after the war twice as many ex-volunteers enrolled at Wits as in the other South African universities combined.

It was during Raikes's tenure that Wits developed,

together with the University of Cape Town, as an 'open' university in the South African context, by admitting black and white students to the same classes in defiance of the country's segregationist practices. In response to an external challenge, the university's council decided in 1934 to begin admitting black students, though this arrangement excluded them from clinical training in medicine and dentistry, leaving them with the option of going overseas for this; when the outbreak of war in 1939 rendered this impossible, Raikes played a central role in opening up the Wits medical school to the black students, on condition that their clinical training was confined to the non-European hospital. While Raikes strongly advocated the admission of all groups to Wits, he was reluctant to integrate the black students into formal social and sporting events—the university's policy of 'academic non-segregation and social segregation' encapsulated his own approach.

Following the accession of the National Party to power in 1948, Raikes found himself caught between a government committed to apartheid and a radicalized students' representative council pressing for an end to all forms of racial discrimination on campus. In March 1954 Raikes retired on the grounds of ill health, disheartened by the sheer complexity of the political pressures brought to bear on him after 1948 and frustrated by the financial constraints that had consistently obstructed his desire to develop Wits as a university of some international repute.

Raikes's style of leadership was unassertive and collegial. He lived on campus in the principal's lodgings, and took a personal interest in almost everything that happened at the university. It was a matter of regret to him that by the end of his tenure it was no longer possible for him to know all senior students by name, the student body having grown from 1476 in 1928 to 4277 by 1954.

Raikes was also active outside the university. He was president of the South African Chemical Institute in 1932–3; chairman of the board responsible for the aptitude testing of recruits to the South African Air Force during the Second World War; president of the Associated Scientific and Technical Societies of South Africa in 1947; and a long-serving member of the Johannesburg Hospital Board. Between 1948 and 1955 he was awarded five honorary doctorates, by the universities of Bristol, Cambridge, Toronto, Cape Town, and Wits. In 1960 the university's new chemistry building was named after him. Troubled by ill health since contracting dysentery on his way back from Egypt, Raikes died on 13 April 1955 in the Johannesburg General Hospital, following an operation; he was cremated on 14 April at Braamfontein crematorium. He was survived by his wife, and on her death the couple's estate went equally to the University of Witwatersrand and Balliol College, Oxford.   BRUCE K. MURRAY

Sources DNB · University of the Witwatersrand, Johannesburg, South Africa, Raikes MSS · The Times (22 April 1955) · H. Hartley, JCS (1956), 1922–3 · B. K. Murray, WITS, the early years: a history of the University of the Witwatersrand, Johannesburg, and its precursors, 1896–1939 (1982) · B. K. Murray, Wits, the 'open' years: a history of the University of the Witwatersrand, Johannesburg, 1939–1959 (1997) · Stapleton Magazine (Dec 1927), 162–3 · Stapleton Magazine (June 1955), 5–6 · private information (2004)
Archives University of the Witwatersrand, Johannesburg, archives, corresp. · University of the Witwatersrand, Johannesburg, archives, addresses and press clippings | Nuffield Oxf., corresp. with Lord Cherwell
Likenesses R. Broadley, oils, University of the Witwatersrand, Johannesburg, Senate Chamber · Graphart, photograph, University of the Witwatersrand, Johannesburg, archives
Wealth at death £1561 8s. 8d. in England: South African probate sealed in London, 19 May 1955, CGPLA Eng. & Wales

Raikes, Robert (*bap.* **1690**, *d.* **1757**), printer and newspaper proprietor, was baptized on 22 April 1690, the son of Timothy Raikes (1661–1722), vicar of Hessle, Yorkshire, and his wife, Sarah, *née* Partridge, of Gloucester. He was apprenticed to the London printer John Barber on 1 October 1705, was made a freeman of the Stationers' Company on 1 December 1712, and (presumably) worked as a journeyman. In 1718 Raikes was employed by Samuel Hasbart, a Norwich distiller, to print a newspaper in the tory interest in opposition to Henry Crossgrove's *Norwich Gazette*; there were already three established newspapers in the city, however, and the enterprise failed after a few weeks.

By 16 June 1718 Raikes had moved on to St Ives, Huntingdonshire, where he founded the *St Ives Post Boy* (possibly taking over the existing *St Ives Post* from John Fisher). In October 1719 William Dicey sought to establish a rival, the *St Ives Mercury*, but soon afterwards the two men formed a partnership and moved their enterprise to Northampton, where they introduced printing and founded the *Northampton Mercury* (2 May 1720), claiming that their new paper went 'further in length, than any other country newspaper in England', taking in nineteen counties (*Northampton Mercury*, 31 May 1720). In 1721 they also founded a literary magazine edited by Raikes, entitled the *Northampton Miscellany, or, Monthly Amusements*, which failed after six months. The following March the partners set up a second press, against The Swan inn, Northgate Street, Gloucester, again introducing their trade to the city. They announced a new newspaper, the *Gloucester Journal*, which appeared on 9 April 1722, Raikes taking responsibility for the new title and Dicey remaining in Northampton (where he successfully fought off the rival *Northampton Journal*). The following year the Gloucester press was moved to new premises in Southgate Street. In September 1725 the partners divided their business interests, Raikes retaining sole interest in the *Gloucester Journal* and the associated printing business while Dicey took over financial responsibility for the business in Northampton. Raikes also later became an agent for Berrow's *Worcester Journal* and Boddeley's *Bath Journal*.

In common with other provincial newspaper producers Raikes sought to reduce the impact of the changes in newspaper duties in April 1725 by changing the format of his newspaper from a sheet and a half to a half-sheet of large paper. In March 1728 he was summoned to appear before the House of Commons and was imprisoned for printing in his newspaper 'Votes of the House', taken from a written newsletter. He was freed a fortnight later upon payment of costs but his confession resulted in the arrest of several news writers. The following year he was again called upon to answer for an item in his paper but he was able to avoid attendance, pleading ill health and that the offending piece was printed without his knowledge. Thereafter he sought to avoid brushes with authority, although his 'Essay on riots', published in his newspaper in 1738, was regarded as provocative and was fiercely criticized by the *Salisbury Journal* for showing sympathy with the grievances of the Melksham rioters. Yet his printing business and newspaper continued to thrive, and in 1743 it was again moved to larger premises, in Blackfriars, Gloucester.

Raikes married, first, Sarah, the daughter of John Niblett of Fairford, Gloucestershire, in 1722; after her death he married, second, Ann Monk of London, on 16 May 1725; she also died young. The children from these marriages died in infancy. About 1735 he married, third, Mary (1713/14–1779), daughter of the Revd Richard Drew. Their elder son, Robert *Raikes (1736–1811), succeeded to his father's business and subsequently achieved fame as a philanthropist and founder of Sunday schools. A second son, Thomas (1741–1813), was apprenticed to the London printer William Bowyer and was the father of Thomas *Raikes (1777–1848) and of Henry *Raikes (1782–1854). A third son, Richard (*c.*1753–1823), was a clergyman.

Robert Raikes the elder died on 7 September 1757 and was buried with his third wife in the church of St Mary de Crypt, Gloucester. Little is known of his character other than his determination to succeed against all set-backs, in both professional and family life. He was, however, an important figure in the history of English journalism and in the gradual spread of printing from London into the provinces.

DAVID STOKER

Sources R. Austin, 'Robert Raikes the elder, and the *Gloucester Journal*', *The Library*, 3rd ser., 6 (1915), 1–24 • H. R. Plomer and others, *A dictionary of the printers and booksellers who were at work in England, Scotland, and Ireland from 1726 to 1775* (1932); repr. (1968), 20 • D. F. McKenzie, ed., *Stationers' Company apprentices*, [3]: *1701–1800* (1978) • D. Stoker, 'The Norwich book trades before 1800', *Transactions of the Cambridge Bibliographical Society*, 8 (1981–5), 79–125, esp. 82–3 • D. Dixon, 'Northamptonshire newspapers, 1720–1900', *Images and texts: their production and distribution in the eighteenth and nineteenth centuries*, ed. P. Isaac and B. McKay (1997) [1–10] • C. Y. Ferdinand, *Benjamin Collins and the provincial newspaper trade in the eighteenth century* (1997), 164–6 • A. Gregory, *Robert Raikes: journalist and philanthropist* (1877), 4–10 • G. A. Cranfield, *The development of the provincial newspaper press, 1700–1760* (1962) • R. M. Wiles, *Freshest advice: early provincial newspapers in England* (1965) • IGI • funeral monument, St Mary de Crypt Church, Gloucester

Raikes, Robert (1736–1811), promoter of Sunday schools, was born at Gloucester on 14 September 1736 and baptized on 24 September. He was the eldest of six sons, followed by one daughter, of Robert *Raikes (*bap.* 1690, *d.* 1757), printer, and his third wife, Mary (1713/14–1779), daughter of the Revd R. Drew. Robert Raikes senior had founded the *Gloucester Journal* in 1722, and Robert succeeded to the business on his father's death. In 1767 he married Anne (*d.* 1828), daughter of Thomas Trigge; three sons and seven daughters were born to them, of whom one son and one daughter died in infancy.

Robert Raikes (1736–1811), by George Romney, 1784–8

Raikes had a benevolent disposition, and was sensitive to the abuses that went on in Gloucester gaol. In 1768 his paper carried an appeal on behalf of the prisoners, for among other hardships no allowance was made for the support of lesser offenders, who were kept alive only by sharing the rations of their fellows. He offered hospitality to John Howard, the pioneer of prison reform, when he went to Gloucester in 1773 on his tour of prisons in the west of England to publicize these and other abuses.

The event which allegedly turned Raikes towards founding Sunday schools has grown much in the telling, but seems to have come about one Sunday when he was in St Catherine's Meadows, on the outskirts of Gloucester. There he saw the local children running wild, and was told that they had nothing else to do. Another version of the story tells that Raikes made up his newspaper on Sundays, and was annoyed by interruption from noisy children outside when reading his proofs. At much the same time, however, he heard of one dissenter named William King who had set up a Sunday school at Dursley, while another, Hannah Ball, had recently started a school at High Wycombe. There seems to have been a general movement towards the idea of religious instruction for children on Sundays, mostly promoted by dissenters.

Whatever the true inspiration or incentive for his actions, Raikes spoke to Thomas Stock (1749–1803), curate of a neighbouring parish, who had started a Sunday school at Ashbury, Berkshire. Raikes and Stock engaged and paid four women as teachers of children in their own homes, Stock drawing up the rules for their instruction. Raikes afterwards set up a school in his own parish of St

Mary le Crypt, which opened in July 1780, and on whose fortunes he thereafter concentrated. He visited the scholars at home, heard them read, and awarded prizes. Three years later he inserted in his paper a short anonymous notice of its success, which brought in many enquiries. An answer which he sent to Richard Towneley of Belfield, Rochdale, was published in the *Gentleman's Magazine* in June 1784, and a laudatory account of his proceedings, with his portrait, was printed in the *European Magazine* of November 1788. Such press notices generated further activity, with more schools opening in Leeds, Manchester, and the surrounding districts. John Wesley, preaching in Bingley, noted in his diary 'I find these schools springing up everywhere I go' (*Wesley's Journal*, 7.3, 18 July 1784). Wesley encouraged his followers to start similar schools.

Raikes had been eager that the Anglicans should lead. The bishops of Chester and Salisbury voiced their approval of his activities, and his friend Samuel Glasse, preaching a sermon at Painswick, Gloucestershire, in 1786, on behalf of its schools, claimed that 200,000 children were already being taught in England. Glasse added further momentum to the movement with his *The Piety, Wisdom, and Policy of Promoting Sunday Schools* (also 1786) and an essay in the *Gentleman's Magazine* (1788). The Baptist William Fox, who had been trying to start a system of day schools, thought Raikes's plan more practical and, after consulting him, formed the Sunday School Society in September 1786. Although he never attended a meeting, Raikes supported and encouraged Fox, and in 1787 he was admitted an honorary member in consideration of his zeal and his status as the perceived original founder of the Sunday school movement.

Before long, Sunday schools were flourishing in Wales, Scotland, Ireland, and the United States. At Christmas 1787 Raikes was granted an audience with Queen Charlotte. She spoke favourably of the plan to the educationist Sarah Trimmer, who established a school in Old Brentford, which attracted over 300 pupils within a year and was visited by George III. When the king visited Cheltenham in 1788 Miss Burney, then a maid of honour, went to Gloucester to meet Raikes, whom she revered, finding him however rather vain and voluble. She observed that he played an important role in all Gloucester's benevolent institutions, including the infirmary and the new model prison then under construction.

Raikes retired from business in 1802, receiving a life annuity of £100 from the *Gloucester Journal*. He died at Gloucester on 5 April 1811 and was buried in the church of St Mary le Crypt, where there are monuments to him and his parents. A statue of Raikes by Sir Thomas Brock was erected in 1880 on the Embankment, London.

ANITA MCCONNELL

Sources *DNB* · P. B. Cliff, *The rise and development of the Sunday school movement in England, 1780–1980* (1986) · *GM*, 1st ser., 54 (1784), 377, 410 · *GM*, 1st ser., 58 (1788), 11 · *GM*, 1st ser., 101/2 (1831), 132, 294, 391 · J. Lancaster, 'Memoir of Robert Raikes', *Imperial Magazine*, 10 (1828), 395–403 · J. H. Harris, *Robert Raikes: the man and his work* (1900) · F. Booth, *Robert Raikes of Gloucester* (1980) · R. Austin, 'Robert Raikes the elder, and the *Gloucester Journal*', *The Library*, 3rd ser., 6 (1915), 1–24 · D. Raikes, ed., *Pedigree of Raikes* (1980) · T. W. Laqueur, *Religion and respectability* (1976)

Likenesses G. Romney, oils, 1784–8, NPG [*see illus.*] · W. Bromley, line engraving, 1788 (after S. Drummond), BM, NPG; repro. in *European Magazine* (1788) · T. Brock, bronze statue, 1880, Victoria Embankment, London · token sculpture, 1880, NPG · W. Tassie, paste medallion, NPG

Raikes, Thomas (1777–1848), dandy and diarist, born on 3 October 1777, was the eldest son of Thomas Raikes (1741–1813) and his wife, Charlotte (d. 1810), daughter of the Hon. Henry Finch. He had three brothers, including the clergyman Henry *Raikes (1782–1854), and five sisters. His father was the brother of Robert Raikes, the promoter of Sunday schools, and was a merchant in London, governor of the Bank of England in the crisis of 1797, and personal friend of Wilberforce and the younger William Pitt.

Raikes was educated at Eton College, where he became a 'fair classical scholar' and made the acquaintance of many youths, including George Brummell, who were to be his friends in fashionable life. In 1795 he was sent abroad with a private tutor to study modern languages, and visited most of the German courts, including Berlin and Dresden. On his return to England he became a partner in his father's business, but he was more at home in the clubs of the West End. There he spent his time in the company of the 'dandies'. He was an early member of the Carlton Club, joined White's Club about 1810, and belonged to Watier's. As he was a City merchant as well as a dandy, his nickname was Apollo, 'because he rose in the east and set in the west'. He was a tall, large man, very much marked with the smallpox, and was caricatured by Dighton as *One of the Rake's of London*. His name appears with almost unequalled regularity in White's betting book. On 4 May 1802, he married Sophia Maria, daughter of Nathaniel Bayly, a proprietor in Jamaica. She died on 8 March 1822, leaving one son and three daughters.

Raikes was at The Hague in 1814, spending most of his time in the house of Lord Clancarty, the English ambassador; he visited Paris in 1814, 1819, and 1820, and he spent the winter of 1829–30 in Russia. But he still remained in business, and in 1832, at a meeting of City merchants at the London tavern, proposed the second resolution against the war with Holland. Financial troubles, however, forced him to leave for France in the summer of 1833, and for eight years he remained abroad. In October 1841, when the tories came into office, he returned to England, hoping for a post through the influence of the duke of Wellington, but his expectations were disappointed, and he found most of his old friends dead or in retirement. The following years were spent partly in London and partly in Paris. His health was failing and in May 1846 he went to Bath for its waters. He then took a house at Brighton, and died there on 3 July 1848.

Raikes's best book was his diary, comprising reminiscences of the leading men of fashion and politics—such as the duke of York, Brummell, Alvanley, and Talleyrand—in London and Paris during the earlier part of the nineteenth century. It was published in 1856–7. His other works included two volumes of foreign observations, and *Private*

Thomas Raikes (1777–1848), by Richard Dighton, pubd 1818 [*One of the Rake's of London*]

Correspondence with the Duke of Wellington and other Distinguished Contemporaries (1861), edited by his daughter, Harriet Raikes; most of the letters to the duke related to French politics from 1840 to 1844.

W. P. COURTNEY, *rev.* K. D. REYNOLDS

Sources Burke, *Gen. GB* · Allibone, *Dict.* · *A portion of the journal kept by Thomas Raikes esq. from 1831 to 1847: comprising reminiscences of social and political life in London and Paris during that period*, 4 vols. (1856–8) · R. H. Gronow, *The reminiscences of Captain Gronow* (1861) · *GM*, 2nd ser., 30 (1848), 332

Archives U. Southampton L., letters to first duke of Wellington

Likenesses R. Dighton, caricature, coloured etching, pubd 1818, BM, NPG, V&A [*see illus.*]

Railing, Sir Harry (1878–1963), electrical equipment manufacturer, was born on 10 December 1878, the son of Isaac Railing, a Jewish hop merchant of Munich, and his wife, Hannah, *née* Bing. His first name was originally Adolf, which he later changed to Harry when he settled in England. He attended Munich University and graduated as a doctor of engineering in 1901, before acquiring experience in the USA.

Sir Harry's elder brother, **Max John Railing** (*b.* 1868), had left Germany for England in 1892 and shortly after his arrival had joined the General Electric Company (GEC) in the accounts department. GEC was then a small but expanding electrical goods business run by two Bavarians, Gustav Byng and Hugo Hirst. With his quick grasp of figures and sound business sense, Max soon won promotion at GEC. He was particularly successful at winning orders from the electricity supply companies for GEC's heavy electrical machinery, and at the age of forty-two he became general manager at the firm's London head office—a post he retained until he was promoted to joint managing director in 1929. Max became the right-hand man of Hugo Hirst, who had emerged as the driving force behind GEC. Hirst described Max Railing as 'my alter ego' (Whyte, 143). They were not only close in business matters; in 1900 Max had married Amanda, daughter of Herman Hirsch, whose sister Leontine had married Hugo (her cousin) in 1892, the year both Leontine and Max had left Germany. Max Railing was the obvious choice as Hirst's successor, but he predeceased Hirst on 14 January 1942, at Whiteknights, Shinfield Road, Reading; he was survived by his wife. They had two daughters.

It was Harry who succeeded Hirst, at the age of sixty-three, having joined GEC in 1905 as chief of the test room at Witton, near Birmingham. His wide American and continental engineering experience marked him out for advancement, and in 1911 he joined the board of GEC. In 1933 he married, as a widower, his second wife, (Charlotte) Clare (1895/6–1959), an architect, and daughter of Joseph Ferdinand Nauheim, a bank clerk. There were no children. Nothing is known of his first wife. In 1942 he became vice-chairman, and then, on Hirst's death in 1942, chairman, of Britain's largest electrical manufacturing enterprise. At that time, the company had a capital of £7.8 million and nearly 40,000 employees. He was well suited to GEC's immediate task of responding to the war effort and, although company profits stagnated, he directed pioneering work on radar. He was knighted in 1944 and became an OBE in 1946.

Once the war was over, Railing greatly expanded the productive capacity of GEC to meet the booming demand for electrical goods of all kinds. Enormous sums of money were expended on re-equipment and extensions. Between 1947 and 1955, the company spent £20 million on plant and buildings alone, and in 1952 its authorized and issued capital was increased to £23.6 million. Much of the increased capital was spent on engineering, which was Harry's chief interest. A completely new generating shop with testing plant was added at Witton and opened in 1950, while at the same time a new heavy turbine shop was completed at Erith. In the mid-1950s, under Railing's guidance, GEC moved into the nuclear power field, not on a consortium basis—the means adopted by other electrical companies—but as an extension of its own heavy engineering interests. When GEC began winning major orders for nuclear power stations (as at Hunterston on the Ayrshire coast for £60 million) its prestige was assured, but more heavy expenditure was incurred, and the company became highly dependent on government contracts.

Harry Railing has been described as essentially a fine engineer, and his commitments outside GEC reflected that fact. He was president of the Institution of Electrical Engineers in 1944, for example, and served on the councils of several other professional bodies. But it has also been said that 'he did not have the broad outlook needed in the chairman of a large company' (Jones and Marriot, 198). Arguments with the other joint manager, Leslie Gamage, the autocratic GEC management style, the poor quality of executives below board level—all a legacy of the Hugo Hirst–Max Railing era—exacerbated these problems. GEC under Harry Railing was allowed to develop into a bloated, inefficient company, which unsuccessfully tried to mix both manufacturing and wholesaling functions. Harry Railing had boosted GEC's turnover to nearly £100 million by 1957, but, ominously, net profits had started to fall from £3.4 million in 1955 to £2.4 million in 1957. This decline was only remedied when the heavy loans of GEC's expansionist phase caused a major crisis and restructuring after Railing's retirement.

In 1957, Harry Railing, now almost seventy-nine, decided to step down. His wife was ill with a brain tumour and died in 1959. He handed over to his seventy-year-old successor, Leslie Gamage. Railing himself died at his London home, 12 Gloucester Square, on 16 October 1963.

GEOFFREY TWEEDALE

Sources R. Jones and O. Marriot, *Anatomy of a merger: a history of GEC, AEI, and English Electric* (1970) · A. Lindley, 'Development and organisation of the General Electric Company Ltd', *Business Growth*, ed. R. S. Edwards and H. Townsend (1966) · *The Times* (17 Oct 1963) · A. G. Whyte, *Forty years of electrical progress: the story of GEC* (1930) · G. Tweedale, 'Railing, Max John, and Railing, Sir Harry', *DBB* · d. cert. [M. J. Railing] · m. cert., 1933
Likenesses photograph, repro. in Tweedale, 'Max John Railing and Sir Harry Railing'
Wealth at death £424,840: probate, 14 Jan 1964, *CGPLA Eng. & Wales* · £291,186—gross; Max Railing: probate

Railing, Max John (*b.* 1868). *See under* Railing, Sir Harry (1878–1963).

Railton, David (1884–1955), Church of England clergyman and originator of the idea of the tomb of the unknown warrior, was born on 13 November 1884 at 48 Altham Road, Hackney, London, the son of **George Scott Railton** (*bap.* 1849, *d.* 1913), commissioner of the Salvation Army, and his wife, Marianne Deborah Lydia Ellen Parkyn.

George Scott Railton was baptized on 31 August 1849 at St Vigeans, Forfarshire, the son of Lancelot Railton, Methodist minister, and his wife, Margaret Scott, but he was left an orphan at the age of fifteen. In London he met William Booth and became his secretary, from which position he influenced Booth's and thus the Salvation Army's theology, particularly its views on the sacraments. In 1880 Booth's son took over as secretary, leaving Railton free to take up mission work. On 10 March 1880 Railton, the first officer to hold the rank of commissioner, arrived in New York to found the army's work. This was the first of many mission visits to Europe, North America, Africa, and the Far East. He was well suited to such work, being a skilled linguist, dedicated, and hard-working, and both he and his superiors felt more comfortable with him on the frontier than at headquarters. (At the celebration to mark the launch of the Salvation Army Assurance Society he sat on the platform barefoot and in sackcloth to register his disapproval of this worldly turn.) On 17 January 1884 he married Marianne Parkyn; the couple settled at Margate and had children, but Railton was there only rarely. His mission work and writing schedule took its toll on his health and he collapsed and died in Cologne, Germany, in 1913, while running for a train carrying heavy baggage, a manner of death which foreshadowed his son's. He was buried beside William Booth in Abney Park cemetery, London. A library and Salvation Army heritage centre in Toronto are named after him.

Although he saw little of him, David Railton shared his father's faith and concern for the poorest in society. He is reported as having been educated at Keble College, Oxford, though no record of this has been traced, and at Bishop's Hostel, Liverpool. Having joined the Church of England he was ordained in Liverpool in 1908 and took up the curacy of Edge Hill in Liverpool. In 1910 he moved to Ashford, Kent, and in the following year became temporary chaplain to the forces. He was curate of Folkestone in 1914–20, but had leave of absence to serve in France. He was awarded the MC in 1916 for saving an officer and two men under heavy fire.

Early in 1916 Railton was in Armentières, where he saw a grave in a garden marked with a rough wooden cross on which were pencilled the words 'An unknown British soldier'. This deeply impressed Railton, who realized that a similar monument was needed in Britain to honour the dead, but also to bring comfort to those who had only a bleak telegram to mark their loved one's death. In 1920 he suggested to Herbert Edward Ryle, dean of Westminster, that the body of an unknown soldier might be brought back to Britain and interred in Westminster Abbey. Ryle took up the idea and his and Lloyd George's enthusiasm won over the initially hesitant king. On 7 November 1920 six, or according to other accounts four, working parties visited the battlefields of Ypres, the Marne, Cambrai, Arras, the Somme, and the Aisne, where units of the Royal Naval division as well as the army had died: each party exhumed an unidentified body which was examined to ensure that it was British before being placed in a plain coffin. At midnight one of these coffins was chosen by Brigadier-General L. J. Wyatt, general officer commanding troops in France and Flanders, and thus became the official Unknown Warrior, placed in a new coffin bearing the inscription 'A British Warrior who fell in the Great War 1914–1918 for King and Country' [*see* Unknown Warrior, the].

A union flag, given to Railton by his mother and repeatedly darned by his wife, Ruby Marion Wilson, having been used by him as an altar cloth and funeral pall at the front, was wrapped around the coffin on its solemn journey to Britain. The flag long stood on a pillar by the tomb and is now in nearby St George's Chapel, marked simply 'the padre's flag'. On 11 November 1920 the coffin was borne through crowd-lined streets first to Whitehall, to the Cenotaph, which the king unveiled, and then, followed by the king as chief mourner, to Westminster Abbey, where it was interred in a solemn ceremony. The public ceremony was followed by an outpouring of personal grief which took the authorities quite by surprise: in the next seven days the grave was visited by more than one and a quarter million mourners from all over the British Isles, many of whom had travelled long distances and queued for many hours to reach the grave. The grave was covered by a permanent stone bearing inscriptions by the dean of Westminster one year later, on 11 November 1921.

After the war Railton returned briefly to Folkestone before being successively vicar of St John the Baptist, Margate (1920–25), curate of Christ Church, Westminster, vicar of St James's, Bolton, Yorkshire, vicar of Shalford, near Guildford (1931–5), rector of St Nicholas's, Liverpool, and archbishop's visitor to the RAF (1943–5) before his retirement in 1945. In addition he worked with the Revd (Geoffrey Anketell) Studdert Kennedy (better-known as the First World War padre poet Woodbine Willie) for the Church of England's industrial Christian fellowship, among workers at their places of work.

Railton made his home in retirement at Ard Rhu, Onich, Inverness-shire, and was returning there on 13 June 1955 from Battle, Sussex, where he had been helping the rural dean, when he accidentally fell from a moving train at Fort William railway station and died from his injuries. He was survived by his widow, one son, and four daughters; Dame Ruth Railton (1915–2001), the founder of the national youth orchestra, was one of his daughters.

Railton's idea of a tomb of the unknown soldier was echoed by similar developments in France. These were publicly expressed in 1916, the same year that Railton voiced his idea, and an unknown soldier was buried in the Arc de Triomphe on armistice day 1920, as in Westminster Abbey. Regardless of which country had priority, Railton's idea struck an immediate chord with a nation in mourning, and in particular with those who, with only vague information about the circumstances of their loved ones' deaths and without a body to bury, had no focal point at which to express their grief. His insight in realizing the comfort such a monument would bring was remarkable but characteristic, and his idea has been taken up in many lands (USA, 1921; Belgium, 1922). Commonly known as the 'tomb of the unknown soldier', the monument's official name is that of the 'unknown warrior', who represents all branches of the armed services. Railton's simpler and less bellicose vision, however, was of a monument to 'an unknown comrade' and this seems more effectively to capture its value in comforting individual mourners as well as in honouring the nation's dead.

ELIZABETH BAIGENT

Sources *The Times* (1 July 1955) · *The Times* (8 July 1955) · M. Gavaghan, *The story of the unknown warrior* (1997) · B. Watson, *Soldier saint: George Scott Railton, William Booth's first lieutenant* (1970) · *IGI* · Foster, *Alum. Oxon.* · www.westminster-abbey.org/library/burial/warrior.htm · www.aftermathww1.com/warrior2.asp · www.stephen-stratford.co.uk/uk.htm · T. Crilly, 'Remembering David Railton', www.cwgc.org · www.netspace.net.au/~finbarr/warior.htm · b. cert. · b. cert. [Ruth Railton, daughter of David Railton] · d. cert. · www.findagrave.com [George Scott Railton]

Wealth at death £2402 18s. 9d., eik to confirm £56 6s. 3d.: confirmation, 9 Aug 1955, *CCI*

Railton, George Scott (*bap.* 1849, *d.* 1913). *See under* Railton, David (1884–1955).

Railton, Herbert (1857–1910), illustrator, was born on 21 November 1857 at Brownlow House, Pleasington, near Blackburn, Lancashire, the fourth child in the Roman Catholic family of John Railton, an iron- and brass-founder and a JP. He was the eldest of his father's three children from his second marriage, to Eliza Ann Alexander, and was educated at Malines, Belgium, and at Ampleforth College in Yorkshire. He was then apprenticed to the Blackburn architect W. S. Varley, where he showed great promise as a draughtsman; in 1883 he had drawings published in a local guidebook. Realizing where his vocation lay, in 1885 he went to London, where he shared a studio with Louis Wain and John Jellicoe. Railton and Jellicoe jointly illustrated theatrical scenes for the *Illustrated Sporting and Dramatic News*, Jellicoe drawing the figures with Railton providing the scenery. This combination of talents found further outlet in reprints of the novels of Anne Manning, published between 1897 and 1899.

Railton became increasingly prominent in the 'black and white school' which flourished as a result of the introduction of photomechanical processes of reproduction into the commercial periodicals market: indeed, the crucial replacement of wood-engraving by the line-block (which allowed the draughtsman to reproduce his own lines on the page) occurred in 1886 in the *English Illustrated Magazine*, a journal which employed Railton extensively. Railton's illustration reflected his initial training, the architectural exterior being his speciality. Castles, cathedrals, great houses, and high streets came in profusion from his pen, although he was versatile enough to enjoy success with Macmillan's jubilee edition of *The Pickwick Papers* (1901). Railton also drew for *Good Words*, *The Graphic*, the *Illustrated London News*, *The Portfolio*, and the *Magazine of Art*. At the height of his career he was earning considerable sums, although he was frequently short of money. Some of the series of articles which he illustrated later appeared as monographs: W. J. Loftie's *Westminster Abbey* (1890), *The Inns of Court* (1893), and *Windsor* (1896) had first appeared in *The Portfolio*, and W. O. Tristram's *Coaching Days and Coaching Ways*, which he illustrated jointly with Hugh Thomson for the *English Illustrated Magazine*, was published in 1888 in book form by Macmillan with great success.

In 1887 Railton was fortunate enough to meet the fledgeling publisher J. M. Dent and was engaged to illustrate the Temple Library series. On 19 September 1891 he married the artist Frances (Fanny) Janetta Edney with whom he collaborated on Dent's elaborate gift books. Coloured lithographs in C. W. Stubbs's *Cambridge and its Story* (1903), Cecil Headlam's *Oxford and its Story* (1904), and W. O. Smeaton's *Edinburgh and its Story* (1904) were tinted by Mrs Railton, whose own drawings for *A Midsummer Night's Dream* (1901) reveal a delicacy of line. Herbert's lithographs, together with pen drawings from the texts, were reproduced in black and white in Dent's Mediaeval Towns series, for which he illustrated Bruges, Chartres, and London. Other work for Dent included the Temple Edition of the novels of Walter Scott (1897) and Boswell's *Life of Johnson* (1901). For the publisher Isbister he illustrated ten titles in the English Cathedrals series (1897–9). At this time he was also engaged on two de luxe editions for Freemantle, Gilbert White's *Natural History of Selborne* (1900) and Leigh Hunt's *The Old Court Suburb* (1902). Among other substantial projects were J. W. Brown's *The Builders of Florence* (1907) and W. O. Tristram's *Moated Houses* (1910), both published by Methuen.

Joseph Pennell claimed that Railton was influenced by the styles of Martin Rico y Ortega (1833–1908) and Daniel Urrabieta y Vierge (1851–1904), Spanish masters of pen drawing, but he rapidly developed his own, distinctive broken-line technique which enthused many followers, few of whom reached his standard. Because his style did not vary, critics found him boring, but the combination of picturesque subject matter and delicate penwork greatly appealed to the general public. According to the critic and novelist Frank Swinnerton, Railton was fond of a drink and drew better in a 'state of expansiveness'. During his final illness he was without money and asked J. M. Dent to help his wife and child. He died from pneumonia on 10 March 1910 in St Mary's Hospital, Paddington, and was buried in Kensal Green Roman Catholic cemetery. He was survived by his wife and daughter. Examples of his work, including a self-portrait, are held in Blackburn Art Gallery.

IAN ROGERSON

Sources M. Cross and D. Newbury, *Illustrations by Herbert Railton (1857–1910)* (1977) · I. Rogerson, 'Herbert Railton: an iconography of his published illustrations', MLS diss., Loughborough University, 1980 · *Blackburn Times* (19 March 1910) · *Northern Daily Telegraph* (17 March 1910) · *The Times* (18 March 1910) · C. G. Harper, *English pen artists of today* (1892) · J. Pennell, *Pen drawing and pen draughtsmen* (1889) · F. Swinnerton, *Swinnerton: an autobiography*, [new edn] (1937)
Likenesses group portrait, wood-engraving (*Our artists — past and present*), NPG; repro. in *ILN* (14 May 1892)
Wealth at death penniless: J. M. Dent MSS, Chapel Hill, University of North Carolina

Railton, William (*c*.1801–1877), architect, was a pupil of William Inwood and enrolled as a student in the Royal Academy Schools in 1823. From about 1825 to 1827 he visited Greece and Egypt, and on his way examined the then recently discovered temple at Cadachio in Corfu, his description of which was published in the supplementary volume of Stuart and Revett's *Antiquities of Athens* in 1830. He went into practice in Baker Street, London, and, from 1832 to 1851, at 12 Regent Street, and exhibited regularly at the Royal Academy between 1829 and 1851, obtaining fourth prize in the competition for the new houses of parliament in 1836. He subsequently lived with his wife, Amelia Knight Railton, at 65 Onslow Square, South Kensington. From 1838 to 1848 he held the appointment of architect to the ecclesiastical commissioners, specializing in the design of parsonages, and preparing two model designs which were criticized in *The Ecclesiologist* (*The Ecclesiologist*, 2, 1843, 145–7). He also designed a handful of country houses in the Gothic or Elizabethan styles, among

them Randalls, near Leatherhead, Surrey (1830; dem.), Grace-Dieu Manor, Leicestershire (1833–4), and Beaumanor Park, Leicestershire (1845–7). He was employed upon restorations at Ripon Cathedral in 1843–4, and he adapted and enlarged Riseholme Hall, Lincolnshire, as a palace for the bishop of Lincoln in 1840–45, and built the residence of the bishop of Ripon (later Spring Hill schools) in 1838–9, along with the chapel in 1848. His churches, most of them in the Early English Gothic style, include Copt Oak and Woodhouse Eaves, Leicestershire (both 1837), Holy Trinity, Hoxton, London (1846–8), and Meanwood, Leeds (1849). But his best-known work is Nelson's Column in Trafalgar Square, London, his design for which was accepted after two competitions in 1839, and carried out in spite of strong opposition. The column itself, 170 feet high, was erected between 1840 and 1843 and is surmounted by a bronze statue of Nelson by E. H. Baily (1842); the bas-reliefs which adorn the four sides of the plinth were added in 1849 and the lions at the four corners, by Sir Edwin Landseer, in 1867. Railton designed no buildings during the last twenty-seven years of his life, and he died at 140 Marine Parade, Brighton, while on a visit to Brighton on 13 October 1877. His wife survived him.

F. M. O'DONOGHUE, rev. GEOFFREY TYACK

Sources Colvin, *Archs.* · [W. Papworth], ed., *The dictionary of architecture*, 11 vols. (1853–92) · A. Savidge, *The parsonage in England* (1964) · Graves, *RA exhibitors* · J. Lever, ed., *Catalogue of the drawings collection of the Royal Institute of British Architects: O–R* (1976), 111 · IGI · d. cert.
Archives RIBA, nomination papers | RIBA BAL, drawings collection · Leics. RO, plans and drawings for Beaumanor Park, Leicestershire
Wealth at death under £40,000: probate, 14 Nov 1877, *CGPLA Eng. & Wales*

Railway King, the. See Hudson, George (1800–1871).

Raimbach, Abraham (1776–1843), engraver, was born in Cecil Court, St Martin's Lane, London, on 16 February 1776 and baptized on 28 March 1776 at St Martin-in-the-Fields, Westminster. His father, (John) Peter Raimbach, was a native of Switzerland, who went when a child to England, and married Martha Butler, a daughter of a Warwickshire farmer. Raimbach was educated at Archbishop Tenison's Grammar School, London, and in 1789 was articled to John Hall (1739–97), historical engraver to the king; in the following year he executed his first independent work, the key to Bartolozzi's plate of the *Death of Chatham* after J. S. Copley. On the expiration of his articles, Raimbach entered the Royal Academy Schools, and in 1799 gained a silver medal for a drawing from life. He studied at the academy for nine years, maintaining himself by engraving small plates for G. Cooke's editions of the poets and novelists, after R. H. Corbould, J. H. Thurston, and others; he also painted portraits in miniature which he exhibited at the Royal Academy from 1797 to 1805. In 1801 Raimbach executed three plates, after R. Smirke, for the Revd E. Forster's edition of *The Arabian Nights*. With the money thus earned he visited Paris in 1802 and stayed two months, studying in the Musée du Louvre. After his return he joined an Artists' volunteer corps in 1803; was a member of the Society of Engravers, 1804; and engraved the illustrations by Smirke for a new edition of Johnson's *Rasselas* (1805), doing similar work for J. Sharpe, Longman, and other publishers. In 1805 he married Juliet Harriet and went to live at 9 Warren Street, Fitzroy Square, London, where he remained until 1831, when he moved to Park Terrace, Greenwich. He engraved on steel plate for the Bank of England in 1811, and in 1819 he supported Jacob Perkins's siderographic process for the bank's competition to combat forgery.

In 1812 Sir David Wilkie proposed to Raimbach that they should undertake the publication of a series of large plates, and the scheme was arranged on terms very favourable to Raimbach. The first result was *The Village Politicians* (1814), a proof of which was exhibited at the Paris Salon and awarded a gold medal. This was followed by five others, upon all of which Raimbach's reputation mainly rests; these are excellent reproductions of the original pictures, the mode of execution being well suited to the subjects; they are entirely by his own hand, no assistants having been employed on them.

In 1824 and 1825 Raimbach paid further visits to Paris, where he was well received by the leading French engravers; in 1835 he was elected a corresponding member of the Institut de France and in 1836 signed the petition supporting the work of the House of Commons select committee on arts. After Wilkie's death in 1841 the six plates which were the joint property of himself and Raimbach were sold with the stock of prints at Christies. Most of his plates were in line and on copper, usually signed 'A. Raimbach'.

Raimbach died at his home in Park Terrace, Greenwich, Kent, of water on the chest, on 17 January 1843, and was buried beside his parents at Hendon, Middlesex, where a mural tablet to his memory was placed in St Mary's Church. His plates and so on were sold by auction on 15 March 1843. His *Memoirs and Recollections*, written in 1836, was privately printed in 1843 by his eldest son, Michael Thomson Scott Raimbach (*bap.* 26 July 1809), who at his death in 1887 bequeathed to the National Portrait Gallery, London, an excellent portrait of his father, painted by Wilkie. His second son, David Wilkie Raimbach (1820–1895), a godson of the painter, exhibited portraits at the Royal Academy from 1843 to 1855; he was for twenty years headmaster of the Birmingham School of Art, and, until within a few weeks of his death, an examiner for the Department of Science and Art. He died on 20 February 1895. There was a third son, Thomas Emmerson (*bap.* 9 July 1823), and daughters Eliza (*bap.* 10 Nov 1813), Julia Elizabeth (*bap.* 26 July 1809, *d.* 1816), and Emma Harriet (1810–*c.*1882) who exhibited miniatures at the Royal Academy between 1835 and 1855, and went into a French convent at Caen, where she died.   F. M. O'DONOGHUE, rev. B. HUNNISETT

Sources *Memoirs and recollections of the late Abraham Raimbach*, ed. M. T. S. Raimbach (1843) · J. Pye, *Patronage of British art: an historical sketch* (1845), 372 · Redgrave, *Artists* · *The Times* (22 Feb 1895) · *IGI* · will, PROB 11/1975, fol. 238*r–v* · J. C. Dyer, *Specimens of Perkins & Fairman's patented siderographic plan* (1819), 39 · *Art Union*, 5 (1843), 37 · *Art Union*, 5 (1843), 90 · *Catalogue of the whole of the remaining works in the possession of … A. Raimbach … which will be sold by auction by Messrs. Christie and Manson* [1843] [sale catalogue, Christies] · D. Foskett, *Miniatures: dictionary and guide* (1987), 624
Archives V&A NAL, letters
Likenesses D. Wilkie, oils, 1818, NPG · low relief, repro. in Raimbach, *Memoirs and recollections*
Wealth at death owned with his brother half of 9 Warren Street and 38 Poland Street, London; owned wholly 10 Warren Street, London: will, PRO, PROB 11/1975, fol. 238*r–v*

Rainborow, Thomas. *See* Rainborowe, Thomas (*d.* 1648).

Rainborow, William (*bap.* 1587, *d.* 1642), naval officer, was baptized at St Mary's, Whitechapel, on 11 June 1587, the eldest son of Thomas Rainborow (*d.* 1622) of Whitechapel, a prosperous mariner active in the Levant trade, and his wife, Martha More (*d.* 1631), and remained part of the close-knit Thameside community to the east of the City of London throughout his life. By 1618 he was sailing to the Mediterranean for the Levant Company, gaining its commendation for 'good service against pirates' (Hebb, 239): offered £25 as a reward, he asked instead to be made a member of the company. From his father he inherited shares in a number of merchant ships, among them the 400 ton *Royal Exchange*, and in or before 1625 was made an elder brother of Trinity House. Shortly afterwards he became co-owner and master of the *Sampson*, a heavily armed merchantman of 500 tons, newly built at Limehouse, which he regularly commanded on voyages for the Levant Company to and from Constantinople, sometimes carrying English diplomats. Sailing alone from Constantinople in 1628, with Sir Thomas Roe and his wife aboard, the *Sampson* was attacked by galleys of the knights of the order of St John when becalmed off Malta. Over the next seven hours Rainborow's obduracy broke the spirit of the Maltese. Roe, adept at redeeming British hostages by diplomatic means, was, as he later wrote, only saved from becoming one himself by the 'brave courage and temper', as well as the seamanship, of his captain (Strachan, 182). In the 1630s Rainborow was among the senior mariners consulted about manning the king's ships (1632), the Chatham chest (1635), and fraudulent timber imports (1638). He served as master of Trinity House in 1633–4, ending his term just as Charles I's standing navy came into being. Edward Nicholas, then drawing up a list of suitable officers for Lord Treasurer Portland, included Rainborow as one of only two professional seamen 'that have the command as captain and [have] performed good fyght at sea in merchant ships' (PRO, SP 16/270/65).

His contribution to the ship money fleets reflected Rainborow's determination to make the most of an overdue opportunity to rally England's maritime resources in the interests of its seafaring community. In 1635 he was Lindsey's flag captain, and bolstered the royal fleet by supplying both the *Sampson* and the *Royal Exchange* on charter as part of the contingent from the City of London. Afterwards he proposed the removal of galleries from the king's ships as a fire risk, but found that the officers of the navy considered that to do so would 'much diminish … [their] beauty' (PRO, SP 16/311/65). Northumberland selected him as flag captain in 1636 and quickly established a productive working relationship. At the end of the year Rainborow played a full part in Northumberland's detailed inquiry into the fleet's most serious deficiencies, and vetted his report, even though to limited effect, before it reached the king. The definitive proposal for a blockade of the port of Salé and its privateers in 1637 also came out of this association. Rainborow declared his 'extraordinary willingness to set forward that business' (PRO, SP 16/337/8) and Northumberland convinced Charles that he should take charge of it. Detailed advice was invited from Trinity House on the composition of his fleet, and four of its six captains were Trinity House brethren. Rainborow himself pressed for two pinnaces, to be built at once, for use in shallow waters inshore; and although his formal instructions still did not mention them, the admiralty accepted that without them 'the business cannot proceed' (PRO, SP 16/327/30). Writing to Wentworth at Dublin on 20 May, however, he made it clear that he would have preferred more than two, particularly as, to his growing irritation, the promised pair were proving to be so delayed that his four larger ships were left for more than two months to mount what blockade they could after Spain had failed to send any galleys. The turn of local politics within the port had as much to do with the successful outcome as had English seapower, a circumstance not lost on London commentators. After concluding a peace treaty with the king of Morocco in September 1637, and securing the release of 350 or so captives, Rainborow sailed home with the Moroccan ambassador and an English agent, Robert Blake. In what was a critical year for the future of ship money, from the submission of the king's case to the judges in February to the prosecution of Hampden in November, Charles was anxious to make the most of what might seem a happy demonstration of the practical benefits of the levy, hitherto less obvious to taxpayers than his concern for his sovereignty of the British seas. The ambassador was certainly extravagantly received, and fulsome accounts of his reception and of the expedition itself were soon in print; as Lord Conway observed, 'the reason of all … is the shipping money'. But Rainborow, offered a knighthood by Charles, preferred to accept no more than a gold chain and medal worth, it was said, £300 (*Earl of Strafforde's Letters and Dispatches*, 2.124, 129). At the same time onlookers in a crowded exchequer chamber daily disturbed the court by applauding the arguments of Hampden's defence counsel.

Rainborow had hopes in 1638 of undertaking a second stage in the campaign against the Mediterranean pirates; however, with Northumberland indisposed, his proposal in January for a more elaborate and expensive attack on Algiers found no favour, and instead he was given charge of the sea trials of the new great ship, the *Sovereign of the Seas*, which had been launched as he returned from Salé. According to her builder, Phineas Pett, who was aboard, three days in August 1638 proved enough to assess the 'condition and working of the ship in all respects' (*Autobiography*, 170). Thereafter it is unlikely that Rainborow went to sea again. He was among the founders of a poor seaman's fund, to be administered by Trinity House, in

September 1638, and in 1639 proposed a scheme for arming colliers as support craft for 'a great army'. During spring 1638 his daughter Martha and her husband, Thomas Coytmore, sailed for Massachusetts in a ship co-owned by Rainborow; and in time four of his six children lived for extended periods in New England, his sons William and Edward returning to fight for the parliamentarian side in the civil war. Rainborow was elected for Aldeburgh to both the parliaments of 1640, in April with Squire Bence and then in November with his tenant at Wapping, Alexander Bence, ending years of Howard influence. He was appointed to all the Commons' maritime committees, sometimes with Sir Thomas Roe, until 19 November 1641.

Rainborow died about 12 February 1642, and was buried on 17 February in St John's Chapel, Wapping. He had made his will in July 1638, and altered it little thereafter. He married twice. His first wife was a daughter of Rowland Coytmore of Wapping, an elder brother of Trinity House and a man of substance; the three elder children (Thomas *Rainborowe, with a turbulent career ahead, William *Rainborowe, and Martha, whose second husband was to be Governor John Winthrop) were all probably from this marriage. His second wife, whom he married about 1624, was Judith, daughter of Reynold Hoxton of Wapping; she died in March 1638 leaving three children (Judith, who later married Winthrop's son Stephen, Joan, and Edward). Rainborow's will was mainly concerned with his children, the five younger ones between them receiving the bulk of the £5500 he disposed in monetary bequests. He left to Thomas houses in Southwark, 'some of them latelie built' and bought from William Cambell, and to William houses in Gun Alley, Wapping. Other legacies were to the poor of Wapping (one by way of Trinity House) and Whitechapel; but he said nothing about his shares in ships.

Charles had recognized Rainborow's qualities as a professional seaman, but failed to give his inclination for reform the scope it needed, despite its moderate and conservative nature. Rainborow had little time for flights of fancy about sovereignty of the seas, and was much more concerned with finding ways of protecting merchant shipping and seamen, as ship money claimed to do, without damaging commercial interests. He recognized, better than the king, the urgent need to improve the versatility of the royal fleet as well as the quality of naval administration. In choosing to throw in their lot with the parliamentarian side in the months after his death, men who thought like Rainborow looked for a future beyond the misrepresentations and uncertainty of 1630s ship money. Prominent among them were three of the Trinity House captains who had served with him in the Salé expedition.   BRIAN QUINTRELL

Sources PRO, state papers domestic, 1625–42, esp. SP 16/270/65, SP 16/327/30, SP 16/337/8, SP 16/369/72 [Rainborow's journal for Salé expedition], SP 16/379/87 · Levant Company letter-books and court books, PRO, SP 105 · will, PRO, PROB 11/189, sig. 51 · Strafford papers, Sheff. Arch., Wentworth Woodhouse muniments, 17/67 · *Third report*, HMC, 2 (1872) · *The manuscripts of the Earl Cowper*, 3 vols., HMC, 23 (1888–9) · *Report on the manuscripts of Lord De L'Isle and Dudley*, 6, HMC, 77 (1966) · J. Dunton, *A true journal of the Sally fleet*

(1637) • *The arrivall and intertainements of the embassador, Alkaid Jaurar ben Abdella. From the emperor of Morocco* (1637) • *Two discourses of the navy, 1638 and 1659, by John Holland; also … 1660, by Sir Robert Slyngesbie*, ed. J. R. Tanner, Navy RS, 7 (1896) • G. Radcliffe, *The earl of Strafforde's letters and dispatches, with an essay towards his life*, ed. W. Knowler, 2 vols. (1739) • *The autobiography of Phineas Pett*, ed. W. G. Perrin, Navy RS, 51 (1918) • J. Finet, *Ceremonies of Charles I: the note books of John Finet, 1628–1641*, ed. A. J. Loomie (1987) • R. Scrope and T. Monkhouse, eds., *State papers collected by Edward, earl of Clarendon*, 3 vols. (1767–86) • K. R. Andrews, 'William Rainborowe and the Sallee rovers', *Ships, money, and politics: seafaring and naval enterprise in the reign of Charles I* (1991), chap. 7 • G. G. Harris, *The Trinity House of Deptford, 1514–1660* (1969) • W. R. Chaplin, 'William Rainsborough and his associates of the Trinity House', *Mariner's Mirror*, 31 (1945), 178–97 • D. D. Hebb, *Piracy and the English government, 1616–1642* (1994) • M. Strachan, *Sir Thomas Roe, 1581–1644: a life* (1989) • M. Strachan, '*Sampson's* fight with the Maltese galleys', *Mariner's Mirror*, 55 (1969), 281–9 • E. Peacock, 'Notes on the life of Thomas Rainborowe', *Archaeologia*, 46 (1881)

Wealth at death £5500 bequests; also substantial property in Southwark and more modest in Wapping: will, PRO, PROB 11/189, sig. 51

Rainborowe [Rainborow], **Thomas** (*d.* 1648), parliamentarian army officer and Leveller, was the first-born son of Captain William *Rainborow (*bap.* 1587, *d.* 1642), Levant merchant and naval officer. His mother, William's first wife, was a daughter of Captain Rowland Coytmore of Wapping. Martha, the first of his two sisters, was briefly married to John *Winthrop, governor of Massachusetts, as his fourth wife. His other sister, Judith, married the governor's fourth son, Stephen *Winthrop, who became a captain in the New Model Army, and later a colonel. His brother William *Rainborowe was a major in the New Model, but was dismissed in 1649 for his extremely radical opinions.

The first civil war Thomas Rainborowe grew up in Wapping, a Thameside parish east of the City. Raised to be a mariner like his father, he is known to have been a trader in currants with the Turkey Company before 1642. At his father's death in that year Thomas inherited all his property in Southwark and £1000. At the outbreak of the civil war it was therefore as a well-to-do young man that he joined the parliamentarian fleet under the earl of Warwick, guarding the Irish Sea to prevent Irish volunteers from joining the king's army in northern England. He had already established an economic stake in Ireland, investing £500 in the spring of 1642 in the Irish adventurers' scheme to reconquer the kingdom in return for land there. In the summer of the same year he was appointed by parliament one of the commissioners for the additional sea adventurers to Ireland, and invested a further £400 to fit out ships for an offensive against the south coast. In the summer of 1643, while commander of the *Lion*, he captured a ship off the east coast of Scotland bringing reinforcements to the king.

Shortly afterwards Rainborowe returned to land, and went to assist Ferdinando, Lord Fairfax, in the defence of Hull. On 11 October 1643 he led 500 musketeers in a sally against the enemy. After a fierce, see-saw struggle, during which Rainborowe was taken prisoner, the enemy were driven back, and the marquess of Newcastle was obliged to lift the siege. By this time Rainborowe had risen to the rank of colonel, and he remained with the land service for another four years. His next notable exploit was an amphibious assault on Crowland Castle in Lincolnshire, which resulted in the recapture of that fortress. Now an officer in the earl of Manchester's eastern association army, he raised a foot regiment largely officered by returning émigrés from New England.

At the formation of the New Model Army in the spring of 1645 Rainborowe, as a naval officer, was exempted from the terms of the Self-Denying Ordinance, and appointed colonel of foot, despite an attempt by the peers to reject him. With remarkable efficiency he pressed almost 1500 men, returning to the treasury more than half the money allotted to him for the purpose. On 1 June 1645 he captured Gaunt House near Oxford, and less than two weeks later fought at Naseby. At the New Model's second most important battle, Langport, on 10 July he led a party of 1500 musketeers 'with admirable resolution' across a stream and uphill through a narrow lane to the royalist position (Sprigge, 65). He also fought at the sieges of Bridgwater and Sherborne, and took Nunney Castle on 20 August and Berkeley Castle on 25 September. It was at the storming of Bristol on 10 September that, in Cromwell's words, he had 'the hardest task of all' (ibid., 115). The men of his brigade scaled the high walls of Prior's Hill Fort in the face of withering musket- and cannon-fire.

In December 1645 Rainborowe's regiment was sent to blockade Oxford, and on 25 April 1646 Woodstock surrendered to him. When Charles I attempted to negotiate his own reception by the army Rainborowe refused to get involved, and merely passed on the king's proposals to the Commons speaker. After the capitulation of the royalist headquarters at Oxford, Rainborowe was sent to reduce Worcester and was subsequently recommended for the governorship of the city by Sir Thomas Fairfax, who reminded parliament that Rainborowe had been 'very faithful, valiant, and successful in many undertakings' (Cary, 1.138). His career as governor lasted from July 1646 until the following April.

Putney and the navy In January 1647 Rainborowe was elected the recruiter MP for Droitwich, Worcestershire. But he did not give up his military career, for in May 1647 parliament ordered him to command the forces intended for the recovery of Jersey. His regiment mutinied, however, and threw in its lot with the other New Model regiments in their revolt against parliament. Rainborowe joined them soon afterwards. In recognition of his intelligence and military capability, army headquarters now assigned him increasingly important political and administrative responsibilities. At the end of July he was part of the delegation that presented the army's *The Heads of the Proposals* to the king. When Charles answered the officers with foolish intransigence Rainborowe quit the meeting and returned to Bedford where he spread the news of Charles's words among the soldiers.

Meanwhile in the City an attempted counter-revolution provoked the army to march on the capital to restore its friends to their places in parliament. On 4 August Rainborowe led an advance party of 4000 horse and foot that occupied Southwark. Later the same month Sir Thomas Fairfax appointed him to the committee of general officers to advise him on appointments and other policy matters. By now Rainborowe was becoming disillusioned with Oliver Cromwell and Henry Ireton for persisting in their negotiations with Charles. Cromwell for his part saw Rainborowe as the leader of the faction 'that were endeavouring to have no other power to rule but the sword' (Scrope and Monkhouse, 2, appx, xxxix). The antagonism between them also stemmed from Rainborowe's ambition to become vice-admiral of the navy, and Cromwell's desire to thwart him. The two men were at loggerheads, and in the army council Rainborowe blew up at Cromwell and thundered that 'one of them must not live' (Bodl. Oxf., MS Clarendon 30, fol. 67). In the event he obtained the appointment on 27 September 1647, perhaps because Cromwell appreciated that it would remove him from the centre of political power.

In the weeks before he took up his appointment Rainborowe continued to be a thorn in the side of the military grandees. In October and November he played a leading part in the army general council's debates at Putney on the Leveller *Agreement of the People*. He poured scorn on Cromwell and others who said of the projected constitution, 'Itt's a huge alteration, itt's a bringing in of New Lawes', commenting, 'if writinges bee true there hath bin many scufflinges betweene the honest men of England and those that have tyranniz'd over them' (*Clarke Papers*, 1.246). When the grandees sought to prolong the discussion of the army's engagements Rainborowe insisted that they move on to address the *Agreement of the People*. When Ireton attacked the principle of universal manhood suffrage Rainborowe took up the challenge in words that still ring in our ears after more than three-and-a-half centuries:

> really I thinke that the poorest hee that is in England hath a life to live as the greatest hee; and therefore truly, Sir, I thinke itt's cleare, that every man that is to live under a Government ought first by his owne consent to putt himself under that Government; and … I should doubt whether he was an Englishman or noe that should doubt of these thinges.   (ibid., 1.301)

Having, with Ireton, dominated the debates and won many waverers to his way of thinking, Rainborowe went on to persuade the army general council to write to parliament opposing any further addresses to the king. His next move was to demand that the *Agreement* be submitted to the whole body of the army at a rendezvous. By now the grandees had had enough. Adjourning the debate they summoned not one but three separate rendezvous of the army, at which they presented, not the *Agreement of the People*, but a much more limited remonstrance emphasizing army grievances. Rainborowe turned up uninvited to the first rendezvous at Corkbush field near Ware, and attempted to present a copy of the *Agreement* to General Fairfax, but he was brushed aside.

The consequence of all this radical political activity was that both houses of parliament immediately voted to revoke Rainborowe's appointment as vice-admiral. But with Charles having escaped to the Isle of Wight and a renewal of civil war imminent, the army officers closed ranks. Rainborowe apologized for what he had done and Fairfax urged the lords to reinstate him. They still refused, but the Commons, worried that the fleet might allow Charles to slip through their clutches and flee the kingdom, overrode the lords' veto and on 1 January 1648 ordered Rainborowe at once to take up his command.

The trouble was that neither the sailors nor their officers wanted Rainborowe to be their admiral. They resented having a man of such radical views and so identified with the army foisted upon them. Already by early 1648 the navy was rife with royalism and regarded Rainborowe as a man 'not wel-affected to the king, parliament and kingdome', whose 'insufferable pride, ignorance and insolency … [had] alienated the hearts of the seamen' (*The Declaration of the Navie*, 28 May 1648; Penn, 1.258). A royalist uprising in Kent in May quickly spread to the fleet. On 27 May the men of his own flagship, the *Constant Reformation*, expelled him and bundled him aboard a small vessel bound for London. They justified themselves by denouncing him as 'a man of most destructive principles both in religion and policy, and a known enemy to the peace and antient government of this kingdom' (*A Declaration of the Officers and Company of Sea-Men abord his Majesties Ships, the Constant Reformation …*, 1648). Rainborowe's authority in the navy was now at an end. Parliament appointed the earl of Warwick lord high admiral again and Rainborowe resumed his colonelcy in the army.

Murder and martyrdom Rainborowe joined Fairfax at the siege of Colchester, and was one of the commissioners who negotiated the royalists' surrender at the end of August 1648. In October Fairfax dispatched him northward to take command of the siege of Pontefract Castle. The officer whom he superseded, Sir Henry Cholmley, bitterly resented his displacement, and refused to recognize Rainborowe's authority. Rainborowe retired to Doncaster until parliament should settle the dispute. Perceiving his vulnerability there, a party of cavaliers crept out of Pontefract on 29 October and rode to Doncaster where they surprised the colonel in his quarters. Their intent was to ransom him for Sir Marmaduke Langdale, also a prisoner. But Rainborowe was not one to submit tamely to arrest. He tore himself loose from his captors in the street and brandished his sword crying 'armes, armes!' (Bodl. Oxf., MS Clarendon 34, fol. 27v). No one answered his cry, however, and in the ensuing struggle he was run through with a sword and killed.

The Levellers would later allege that Cromwell was somehow to blame for Rainborowe's assassination. However, the episode was thoroughly investigated at the time, and there is no evidence of Cromwell's being implicated. The body of the fallen hero was brought to London a fortnight after his death. There were reported to be 3000 in the funeral procession, which wound its way through the City, and out through the East End to Wapping where he was buried beside his father. Many elegies were printed demanding vengeance on the royalists for his death; a ballad was composed entitled 'Colonell Rainsborowes Ghost'; and his sea-green colours became a badge of Leveller allegiance.

Rainborowe left no will. Some years before his death he had married a woman called Margaret about whom little is known. Together they had a son, William, and at least one other child. Parliament was generous to his widow. She received his full arrears of pay, amounting to over £1300, in addition to £200 per year until land worth £3000 should be granted her. In 1653 and 1654 the treason trustees deeded her the manor of Somerset, Somerset, and the manor of West Derby and Trayles, Lancashire.

Thomas Rainborowe was one of the most vivid actors in the English revolution. A soldier of impressive professional competence and peerless courage, he led his men in a number of daring and successful engagements. During the political crisis of 1647–8 he stepped forward boldly as a tribune of the common soldiers and the poor people of England. He spoke eloquently for the Levellers' *Agreement of the People* and nearly won the army to their side. But his radicalism, as well as his truculent personality, offended many of the higher officers, who sought to remove him from the political debate, first by granting his request to be appointed to the navy, and then by assigning him to a siege in the north of England. Heedlessness of his own safety, combined with stubborn pride, brought about his end. In death he became the most prominent of the Leveller martyrs.   IAN J. GENTLES

Sources I. Gentles, *The New Model Army in England, Ireland, and Scotland, 1645–1653* (1992) • *The Clarke papers*, ed. C. H. Firth, 1, CS, new ser., 49 (1891) • E. Peacock, 'Notes on the life of Thomas Rainborowe', *Archaeologia*, 46 (1881), 9–64 • K. Lindley, 'Irish adventurers and godly militants in the 1640s', *Irish Historical Studies*, 29 (1994–5), 1–12 • B. Capp, *Cromwell's navy: the fleet and the English revolution, 1648–1660* (1989) • S. R. Gardiner, *History of the great civil war, 1642–1649*, new edn, 4 vols. (1893), vols. 3–4 • A. Woolrych, *Soldiers and statesmen: the general council of the army and its debates, 1647–1648* (1987) • J. Sprigge, *Anglia rediviva* (1647) • J. Rushworth, *Historical collections*, new edn, 7 (1721) • *The manuscripts of his grace the duke of Portland*, 10 vols., HMC, 29 (1891–1931), vol. 1 • J. Vicars, *The burning bush not consumed* (1646) • G. Penn, ed., *Memorials of the professional life and times of Sir William Penn*, 2 vols. (1833), vol. 1 • *JHC*, 3–5 (1642–8) • *JHL*, 5–10 (1642–8) • W. R. Chaplin, 'William Rainsborough and his associates of the Trinity House', *Mariner's Mirror*, 31 (1945), 178–97 • Bodl. Oxf., MS Tanner 57 • Bodl. Oxf., MS Clarendon 30, fol. 67; 31, fols. 17v–18v; 34, fol. 27v • New Model Army warrants, PRO, Commonwealth Exchequer papers, SP 28/34, fol. 365 • *A full and exact relation of the horrid murder committed upon the body of Col Rainsborough* (1648) • *The Moderate* (31 Oct–7 Nov 1648) • *Mercurius Militaris* (14–21 Nov 1648) • H. Cary, ed., *Memorials of the great civil war in England from 1646 to 1652*, 2 vols. (1842), vol. 1 • 'The Tower of London letter-book of Sir Lewis Dyve, 1646–47', ed. H. G. Tibbutt, *Bedfordshire Historical Record Society*, 38 (1958), 49–96 • R. Scrope and T. Monkhouse, eds., *State papers collected by Edward, earl of Clarendon*, 3 vols. (1767–86) • 10 March 1645, HLRO, main papers collection, fol. 146 • R. W. Stent, 'Thomas Rainsborough and the army Levellers', MPhil diss., U. Lond., 1975 • I. Gentles, 'Political funerals in the English revolution', *London and the civil war*, ed. S. Porter (1996), 205–23 • *The memoirs of Edmund Ludlow*, ed. C. H. Firth, 2 vols. (1894), vol. 1 • Greaves & Zaller, *BDBR* • G. E. Aylmer, *The Levellers in the English revolution* (1975) • M. A. E. Green, ed., *Calendar of the proceedings of the committee for compounding … 1643–1660*, 5 vols., PRO (1889–92) • J. R. Powell and E. K. Timings, eds., *Documents relating to the civil war, 1642–1648*, Navy RS, 105 (1963) • *Calendar of the manuscripts of the most hon. the marquess of Salisbury*, 22, HMC, 9 (1971) • R. Brenner, *Merchants and revolution: commercial change, political conflict, and London's overseas traders, 1550–1653* (1993)

Archives Worcester College, Oxford, Clarke papers, Putney debates

Likenesses etching, repro. in M. Stace, ed., *Cromwelliana* (1810) • portrait, Bodl. Oxf., Sutherland collection of portraits illustrating Clarendon's *History*

Rainborowe [Rainsborough], **William** (*fl.* 1639–1673), parliamentarian army officer and Leveller, was born, probably in Wapping, at a date unknown. He was a younger son of Captain William *Rainborow (*bap.* 1587, d. 1642), naval commander and merchant; his mother cannot be identified. According to the senior Rainborow's will, the family then included three sons and three daughters. The younger William migrated to New England in the late 1630s, bought land and became a member of the colonial militia company in 1639. Two of his sisters also migrated, both eventually marrying Winthrops.

At his father's death in 1642 Rainborowe inherited a house in Wapping. He returned to England that year, and married Margery Jenney of Suffolk in June. Parliament sent him and his elder brother, Thomas *Rainborowe, on a naval expedition to Ireland. William may have remained with his brother until the latter's tenure ended in summer 1643 but then he returned to New England briefly. By mid-1644 he was back in England and captain of a troop of horse in Essex's army. In the New Model Army he was a captain under Colonel Thomas Sheffield, although the Lords tried to disallow him on the grounds of his religious radicalism. In 1647, when the army was in crisis, Rainborowe attended a meeting with parliamentarian commissioners on 16 May, in which Sheffield said that his men were content and opposed the presentation of other views. Rainborowe, however, stated the grievances of his men, giving an account that contradicted that of his commander. Subsequently Rainborowe was promoted major under Thomas Harrison. Later that year, in the army debates at Putney (28 October – 1 November), William emerged as a radical Leveller. He asserted that the government ought to protect persons as well as property. Like his brother Thomas, and perhaps more consistently, he favoured manhood suffrage. After the murder of Thomas in 1648 he led the funeral procession which accompanied the body through London to Wapping. Subsequently a contemporary pamphlet described him as frustrated in his attempts to bring the killers to justice (*The Second Part of Englands New Chaines Discovered*, [1649], 11). Rainborowe's increasing radicalism was evident in the design of his cornets. Early in his military career his cornet combined the Bible, a sword, and the phrase 'Truth Conquers' with a Moor's head from his father's crest. The one in 1649 featured the bleeding, severed head of the late king, and the Latin motto, *Salus popul: suprema lex* ('the people's safety is the highest law').

After the 1649 Leveller mutiny, and possibly as a result of it, Rainborowe was removed from his command. That year he also became involved with the Ranters, reportedly hosting gatherings in his house in Fulham. Under a new anti-blasphemy ordinance, parliament arrested Rainborowe for financing Laurence Clarkson's *The Single Eye* (1650). He was discharged from his post as a Middlesex JP and disabled from holding such office in the future. Twice in the 1650s Rainborowe was nominated for a naval command; both times the council of state vetoed his candidacy. The will of Stephen Winthrop in 1658 mentions a daughter of William Rainborowe; nothing further is known of his children. While resident at Fulham he bought dean and chapter lands. From 1650 to 1654 he owned the former crown estate of Higham Park, Northamptonshire—a property he sold for £5498 15s. 2d.

The restored Rump Parliament commissioned Rainborowe colonel of a regiment of horse in the Northamptonshire militia in 1659. The regiment was never raised. Along with other radicals he protested against the overthrow of the Rump, signing *A Remonstrance and Protestation of the Well-Affected People* as a resident of Northamptonshire. Having purchased pistols to supply his regiment, Rainborowe attempted to sell them the following year. This caught the attention of the authorities, and Rainborowe was imprisoned on suspicion of treason in December 1660. When released on bail in February 1661 he was described as residing in Stepney. His movements thereafter cannot be traced, until 1673 when he was in Boston, Massachusetts.   CARLA GARDINA PESTANA

Sources Greaves & Zaller, *BDBR*, 78 · H. F. Waters, 'Genealogical gleanings in England', *New England Historical and Genealogical Register*, 40 (1886), 158–71 · J. J. Muskett, *Evidences of the Winthrops of Groton, co. Suffolk, England* (privately printed, Boston, MA, 1894–6), 157, 159 · *The Winthrop papers* (Boston, 1882), 393–5 · M. A. Kishlansky, *The rise of the New Model Army* (1979) · C. H. Firth and G. Davies, *The regimental history of Cromwell's army*, 2 vols. (1940) · I. Gentles, *The New Model Army in England, Ireland, and Scotland, 1645–1653* (1992) · B. Capp, *Cromwell's navy: the fleet and the English revolution, 1648–1660* (1989) · I. Gentles, 'The iconography of revolution: England, 1642–1649', *Soldiers, writers and statesmen of the English revolution*, ed. I. Gentles and others (1998), 91–113 · A. Woolrych, *Soldiers and statesmen: the general council of the army and its debates, 1647–1648* (1987) · A. S. P. Woodhouse, ed., *Puritanism and liberty: being the army debates (1647–9) from the Clarke manuscripts, with supplementary documents*, 2nd edn (1974) · O. A. Roberts, *History of the military company of the Massachusetts*, 1 (1895), 95

Rainbow, Bernarr Joseph George (1914–1998), historian of music education, was born on 2 October 1914 at 83 Silverthorne Road, Battersea, London, the only child of Ephraim James Rainbow (1888–1983) and his wife, Nellie Neal (1889–1965). His father was a cabinet-maker at Buckingham Palace and later curator of pictures at Hampton Court, so Rainbow grew up with a strong awareness of tradition through historic places and people. His father also was a keen amateur musician who played the cornet in brass bands and the trumpet in orchestras.

After the family moved to Clapham, Rainbow became a church chorister and was intrigued by watching the organist play; he also loved to explore London with his mother. Another move took him to Rutlish School,

Merton, and while still there he became organist and choirmaster at St James's Church; he later held similar posts at St Mary's, East Molesey, and St Andrew's, Wimbledon. He also gave piano recitals, admired for their maturity, and was active in local theatre. He formed the Merton Players' Guild, wrote a morality play for the group, and also directed and painted scenery.

In 1932 the family moved to Hampton Court. Rainbow was subsequently a part-time student at Trinity College of Music, while earning a living as a civil servant in the map branch of the Land Registry. The war interrupted his studies; he served with the army in north Africa and Italy.

On 9 August 1941 Rainbow married Olive Grace Still (1915–1996), a secretary, at the church of St Mary the Virgin, Merton; he composed the music for the service himself. In April 1944 he was discharged from the army on medical grounds after four years' service. In the following September he became organist of the parish church of All Saints, High Wycombe, and a few months later he was appointed senior music master at the Royal Grammar School there.

Rainbow made a considerable impact at High Wycombe by putting on concerts at the parish church and starting a week-long annual festival in 1946. In 1950 Benjamin Britten, who had started his own Aldeburgh Festival in 1948, encouraged him by writing the preface to the programme book. Rainbow's pupils won awards, and representatives from thirty local choirs joined in Handel's *Messiah*. Rainbow conducted the High Wycombe String Orchestra and was the soloist in his own piano concerto, which has not survived. In 1951 his parish church choir was chosen to sing evensong in the festival church on the new South Bank site in London.

At this stage Rainbow began to be concerned about the low quality of music teaching in schools nationally. So in 1952 he took the post of director of music at the College of St Mark and St John, Chelsea, the Church of England training college for teachers. He was interested in new initiatives in music education, and put together a team of lecturers who would 'revolutionise the country's music education' (*The Guardian*), encouraging children's improvisations and compositions. When the college moved to Plymouth in 1972, Rainbow decided to remain in London and became head of music at Gypsy Hill College (later Kingston University); he retired from there in 1978.

It was at Chelsea that Rainbow increasingly became a scholar and researcher. He had already acquired several music diplomas, but went on to gain three postgraduate degrees at the University of Leicester. His earlier publications, such as *Music in the Classroom* (1956) and the *Handbook for Music Teachers* (1964), were practical aids for teachers, but his most influential books were historical. His discovery of papers about John Pyke Hullah, a nineteenth-century predecessor at the College of St Mark and St John, aroused his interest in the social history of music education between 1800 and 1860 and led to *The Land without Music* (1967), in which he gave the lie to the German description of Britain. *The Choral Revival in the Anglican*

Church, 1839–1872 (1970) explored the movement to improve standards in church music, and gained Rainbow his doctorate from the University of Leicester. *Music in Educational Thought and Practice* (1989) was his most substantial book, covering his subject from the ancient Greeks to the mid-1980s. Rainbow also edited some twenty-five separate primers from originals in various languages as Classic Texts in Music Education, a series which promised to be a major landmark.

In 1978 Rainbow established the Curwen Institute to promote the work of John Curwen, the proponent of tonic sol-fa (whose brief biography Rainbow published in 1980). In the last two years of his life he became founder president of the Campaign for the Defence of the Traditional Cathedral Choir (opposing the introduction of girls into cathedral choirs) and established the Bernarr Rainbow award for school music teachers, subsequently supported by the Bernarr Rainbow Trust. His distinguished record was acknowledged when he was elected a fellow of the Royal Society of Arts in 1994 and made an honorary fellow of Trinity College of Music in the following year. The history of music education was brought alive by the detailed research that Rainbow undertook in order to communicate both his vivid awareness of the past and his concern for the present. He had no children, and died from cancer on 17 March 1998 at the Princess Alice Hospice, Esher, Surrey, two years after his wife's death. He was cremated at Mortlake on 25 March.

PETER DICKINSON

Sources Bernarr Rainbow MSS, U. Lond., Institute of Education · P. Dickinson, 'Bernarr Rainbow at 80', *Choir and Organ* (Oct–Nov 1994), 30 · P. Dickinson, 'In memoriam', *Philosophy of Music Education Review*, 6/2 (autumn 1998), 124 · *The Independent* (20 March 1998) · *The Guardian* (27 March 1998) · personal knowledge (2004) · b. cert. · m. cert. · d. cert.
Archives Hampton Court Palace, Surrey, family papers · U. Lond., Institute of Education, archive
Likenesses photograph, repro. in *The Independent* · photograph, repro. in *The Guardian* · photographs, priv. coll.
Wealth at death £468,400: probate, 22 May 1998, *CGPLA Eng. & Wales*

Rainbow [Rainbowe]**, Edward** (1608–1684), bishop of Carlisle, was born on 20 April 1608 at Blyton in Lindsey, Lincolnshire, son of Thomas Rainbow, the vicar, and his wife, Rebecca, daughter of David Allen, rector of the neighbouring parish of Ludborough. After a short time at school in Gainsborough he was sent in April 1620 to Peterborough to study under John Williams, then one of the prebendaries, and an old friend of his father. When, in 1621, Williams was preferred to the deanery of Westminster and bishopric of Lincoln, Rainbow transferred to Westminster School. In July 1623 Rainbow obtained a scholarship at Corpus Christi College, Oxford, where his brother was a fellow, but in July 1625, through the family of his godfather Edward Wray of Rycot, he received from Frances, dowager countess of Warwick, a nomination to one of the Wray scholarships founded at Magdalene College, Cambridge, by her father. He graduated BA in 1627 and

Edward Rainbow (1608–1684), by John Sturt, pubd 1688

His face you see, but not his noble mind
That like his fame was great and unconfin'd;
Yet humble too, and honors would prevent.
But's virtues built the greatest monument,
Which all devouring time cannot deface,
Till the world wants both gratitude and grace.

proceeded MA in 1630; during his time as a student he acquitted himself well when called on by the vice-chancellor to make a speech.

In July 1630 Wray accepted the mastership of a school at Kirton in Lindsey, but soon moved with some Cambridge contemporaries to London, settling first in Fuller's Rents, and afterwards at Sion College, so as to make use of the library. He was ordained in April 1632. After an unsuccessful application for the chaplaincy at Lincoln's Inn he was appointed curate at the Savoy Chapel by the minister, Thomas Hastler.

In November 1633 Rainbow was recalled to Cambridge. The master and fellows of Magdalene College elected him to a by-fellowship on Dr Goche's foundation, with a pre-election to the first open fellowship that should fall vacant. Four closed fellowships were to fall vacant before Rainbow joined the foundation. He became a successful tutor; two sons of the earl of Suffolk and two sons of Francis Leke, Baron Deincourt, became his pupils. On 23 September 1634 he preached at Paul's Cross a sermon published as *Labour Forbidden and Commanded* (1635). In 1637 he accepted the small vicarage of Childerley, near Cambridge, and became dean of Magdalene. In 1642 he was appointed master in succession to Henry Smyth by the earl of Suffolk, who had promised it to him some years earlier. He proved himself an effective master, putting college registers in order, ably managing finances and increasing student numbers.

The House of Lords granted Rainbow a pass into Holland on 16 May 1645. In 1648 he became rector of Great Easton, Essex, where there is evidence that he used the liturgy from the Book of Common Prayer, or a close adaptation of it. The preface to his *A Sermon … Preached at the Interring of the Corps of … Susanna Countess of Suffolk* (1649) was dated from Audley End on 11 September 1649. Ejected from his mastership in 1650 for refusal to swear to the engagement, he told the parliamentary committee for regulating the universities that his objection was on grounds of conscience but that he intended to live peaceably in the Commonwealth.

In 1652 Rainbow married Elizabeth Smyth (d. 1702), daughter of his predecessor at Magdalene, and accepted from the earl of Suffolk the small living of Little Chesterford, Essex. At the presentation of the earl of Warwick, and with the assistance of Lord Broghill, he became rector of Benefield, Northamptonshire, on 23 March 1659. At the Restoration, apparently to his surprise, Rainbow was restored to his mastership at Magdalene, and appointed chaplain to the king. In 1661 he was made dean of Peterborough, but returned to Cambridge on being appointed vice-chancellor in November 1662.

On the translation of Richard Sterne to the archbishopric of York, Rainbow was consecrated bishop of Carlisle on 10 July 1664 in Westminster Abbey by Archbishop Gilbert Sheldon. Having resigned his other preferments he had to borrow money to pay for his consecration, first-fruits, and costs of settlement in the diocese. The ruined state of his palace, Rose Castle, involved him in a heavy outlay on building a new parlour and chapel, and after protracted litigation with his predecessor and Archbishop Sterne, from whom he received £400 in dilapidations, he found much in his diocese that required reform. His visitation articles were published in 1667. Clergy found negligent did not hesitate to defy their bishop publicly, and his outspoken denunciation of immorality appears to have offended some great lady at court, once a friend, who revenged herself by blocking his translation to Lincoln in 1668. He was also rumoured for preferment on Sheldon's death in 1677, but received no offer. That year he published a funeral sermon for Anne, countess of Pembroke.

Rainbow's hospitality and charity were boundless. In years of scarcity, when his own stores were exhausted, he bought barley and distributed it to the poor; sometimes 150 were relieved in one day by the porter at Rose. To the poor at Carlisle and Dalston he made a monthly payment of 30s. He paid for the education of poor boys at Dalston School, and for putting them out as apprentices; he supported poor scholars at the universities; he subscribed generously to the French protestants and to foreign converts.

Rainbow's domestic life was a model of piety: prayers were read four times a day, swearing was banned, and servants were required to live blamelessly. He was an orthodox but moderate Anglican who was sympathetic to nonconformists. His strong eirenicism encouraged friendships with presbyterians such as Francis Tallents, and had enabled him at Cambridge to manage the restoration of ejected fellows without rancour. He was famous as a preacher, and in his later sermons abandoned the ornate rhetoric of his early days for exceptional plainness and perspicuity. He planned a treatise, to be called 'Verba Christi', a collection of Christ's sermons and sayings, but it was never completed.

Rainbow died at home on the morning of 26 March 1684 and was buried at Dalston church on 1 April. The sermon preached at his funeral by his chaplain and chancellor, Thomas Tullie, was published, together with some of his meditations and short poems, in Jonathan Banks's *The Life of … Edw. Rainbow* (1688). Elizabeth Rainbow, who after her husband's death lived mainly at Dalemain with her sister's son Sir Edward Hasell, died in 1702, and was also buried at Dalston.   R. S. FERGUSON, *rev.* WILLIAM GIBSON

Sources J. Banks, *The life of … Edw. Rainbow, DD, late lord bishop of Carlisle: to which is added, a sermon preached at his death by Thomas Tully* (1688) · R. S. Ferguson, *Carlisle* (1889) · Foster, *Alum. Oxon.* · Venn, *Alum. Cant.* · J. R. Magrath, ed., *The Flemings in Oxford*, 1, OHS, 44 (1904) · J. R. Magrath, ed., *The Flemings in Oxford*, 2, OHS, 62 (1913) · F. G. James, *North country bishop: a biography of William Nicholson* (1956) · P. Cunich and others, *A history of Magdalene College, Cambridge, 1428–1988* (1994) · K. L. Parker, *The English sabbath: a study of doctrine and discipline from the Reformation to the civil war* (1988) · J. Spurr, *The Restoration Church of England, 1646–1689* (1991), 14 · *Walker rev.*, 38

Likenesses J. Freeman (after unknown portrait), Magd. Cam. · J. Sturt, line engraving, BM, AM Oxf., NPG; repro. in J. Banks, *Life* (1688) [*see illus.*] · portrait, Rose Castle, near Carlisle

Raine, Allen. *See* Puddicombe, Anne Adalisa (1836–1908).

Raine, James (1791–1858), antiquary and topographer, son of James Raine (d. 1840), village blacksmith, and his wife, Anne, daughter of Edmund Moore, was born at Ovington in the parish of Wycliffe, Yorkshire, on 23 January 1791. He was from 1804 educated at the Kirby Hill Free Grammar School, then from 1809 at Richmond School under James Tate. After teaching at Richmond he was from 1812 to 1827 second master of Durham School. Raine was ordained deacon on 26 September 1814, and priest on 20 September 1818. In 1816, already known for his antiquarian tastes, he was appointed librarian by the dean and chapter of Durham, and in 1822 they presented him to the rectory of Meldon, near Morpeth, Northumberland. Litigation with the landowners, the Greenwich Hospital commissioners, over the Meldon rectory tithes continued until 1846, when the case was decided in Raine's favour. In 1825 he was instituted principal surrogate in the diocesan consistory court, and in 1828 presented to the living of St Mary in the South Bailey, in the city of Durham. These various preferments he held until his death. In November 1825, at Bishop Barrington's request, the archbishop of Canterbury conferred on him the Lambeth degree of MA, and he was in due course incorporated *ad eundem gradum* in the new University of Durham, which in 1857 awarded him an honorary DCL in recognition of his historical and ecclesiastical services.

In 1812 Raine first met Robert Surtees, of Mainsforth Hall, starting a collaboration that continued until Surtees's death in 1834. In 1819 Walter Scott wrote to Raine urging him to the study of 'a treasure of ancient papers preserved at Durham which wanted only the zeal and firmness of a northern Leland to examine and arrange them' (*Letters*). By then, as chapter librarian and with Surtees's example before him, he scarcely needed this further encouragement. His first efforts were in unselfishly assisting friends in the composition of their topographical works. The county historians John Hodgson, Sir Cuthbert Sharp, and Surtees himself, all paid tribute to Raine's unstinting assistance. Surtees stated that his *History of Durham* would never have been completed but for Raine's indefatigable industry (*History*, 1, 1816, x). Raine subsequently became his friend's literary executor and arranged and edited the fourth volume of Surtees's *History of Durham* (1840). In 1827 he had performed a similar service for John Hodgson, for whom during the author's absence abroad he saw through the press volume 3, part 2, of the *History of Northumberland*; he later wrote a two-volume memoir of Hodgson (1857).

In 1828 Raine published his first substantial independent work, a monograph on St Cuthbert, including an account of the saint's remains discovered in Durham Cathedral in 1827. In 1830 appeared the first part of Raine's *History of North Durham* (that is, those detached parts of the county palatine, including Norham and Holy Island, which after 1844 were statutorily united to Northumberland). The second part of Raine's *History* eventually appeared in 1852. Although some later writers have expressed reservations about Raine's charter scholarship, the history was important in its day and still remains useful.

Soon after Surtees's death in February 1834, Raine organized local commemorative effort into the formation of a society bearing his name, to publish unedited historical manuscripts relating to the area between the Humber and the Forth. Raine became first secretary of the Surtees Society, constituted on 27 May 1834, and was an industrious editor of seventeen of the volumes published between 1835 and 1858 by this pioneering society, whose scheme of operation was much copied.

While convalescing from heart stress in 1858, Raine began an autobiographical memoir (published by the Surtees Society in 1991), a charming though uncompleted account of a Teesdale rural upbringing. He died at his home, Crook Hall, near Durham, on 6 December 1858, and was buried in Durham Cathedral yard. He married on 28 January 1828 Margaret, eldest daughter of the Revd Thomas Peacock (1756–1851) and sister of George Peacock (1791–1858), dean of Ely. They had three daughters and one son, James (1830–1896), later chancellor of York Minster and the leading figure in the restoration of its library; he was also an editor for the Surtees Society and for the Rolls Series. The younger James's son Angelo Raine (1877–1962), historian of York, continued to a third generation the family's clerical and antiquarian tradition.

ALAN BELL

Sources A. Marsden, ed., *A Raine miscellany*, SurtS, 200 (1991) · 'Biographies of contributors to the society's literature', *Archaeologia Aeliana*, 3rd ser., 10 (1913), 146–9 · A. H. Thompson, *The Surtees Society, 1834–1934*, SurtS, 150 (1939) · *GM*, 3rd ser., 6 (1859), 156–62 · *The letters of Sir Walter Scott*, ed. H. J. C. Grierson and others, centenary edn, 12 vols. (1932–79), vol. 5, pp. 502–3 · *DNB*

Archives Durham Cath. CL, antiquarian notes, legal papers, and printed material · Keep and Blackgate Museum, Newcastle upon Tyne, notebooks · U. Durham L., archives and special collections, corresp. · W. Yorks. AS, Leeds, papers · York Minster Library, York Minster archive, historical papers | BL, letters to J. Hunter, Add. MS 24874 · Durham RO, letters to Edward Blore · U. Edin. L., special collections division, letters to David Laing · U. Newcastle, Robinson L., letters to Walter Trevelyan

Likenesses mezzotint (after engraving), NPG

Wealth at death under £2000: administration, 19 May 1859, CGPLA Eng. & Wales

Raine, Matthew (1760–1811), headmaster, was born on 20 May 1760 at Gilling in the North Riding of Yorkshire. His father, of the same name, was for many years vicar of St John's, Stanwick, and rector of Kirkby Wiske, and also master of a school at Hartforth, near Richmond, in the same county. His mother, Esther (d. 1803), was of a Cumberland family. After receiving the elements of education under his father, with William Beloe for a schoolfellow, he was admitted a scholar of the Charterhouse, on the king's nomination—obtained, it is said (Beloe, 1.10), through the interest of Lord Percy, a patron of his father—in June 1772. In 1778 he went up as an exhibitioner to Trinity College, Cambridge, where he became a scholar in 1779 and graduated as sixteenth wrangler in 1782 (MA 1785, BD 1794, DD 1799). In 1783 and 1784 he gained the members' university prize, and in the latter year was made fellow of his college. He was ordained deacon in 1782 and priest in 1784, and served as curate of Melford, Suffolk.

After some time spent in tuition at Cambridge, Raine was appointed headmaster of Charterhouse School on 7 June 1791, in succession to Samuel Berdmore. Charles Burney was one of his competitors. Here he remained until his death. The school enjoyed a high reputation, pupil numbers rose, and a new schoolroom was added in 1802. Raine was credited with the reform of providing a single bed for each scholar. In 1803 he was elected a fellow of the Royal Society, and in 1809 was chosen preacher of Gray's Inn. In July 1810 he was presented by the governors of the Charterhouse to the rectory of Hallingbury, Essex, in anticipation of his retirement.

Raine died, unmarried, at Charterhouse Square, London, on 17 September 1811. He was buried in the chapel of the Charterhouse, where a gravestone was placed in the south aisle inscribed M. R., and a mural tablet on the adjoining wall by Flaxman, with an epitaph by Samuel Parr. Parr and Richard Porson were his close friends. His choice collection of classical books, including many Aldines and rare editions, went by bequest, after the death of his brother Jonathan (1763–1831), to the library of Trinity College, Cambridge. This brother, a schoolfellow of

Porson's at Eton, and afterwards at Trinity (BA 1787, MA 1790), was a barrister and a member of parliament from 1802 to 1807 and again from 1812 to 1831.

Raine was described as eloquent in the pulpit and dignified in manner. The latter part of this description is borne out by his portrait, reputed to be by Hoppner, in the master's lodge at the Charterhouse. The Society of Schoolmasters owed much to his generosity. His only published works were two sermons.

J. H. LUPTON, *rev.* M. C. CURTHOYS

Sources GM, 1st ser., 81/2 (1811), 294, 461 · GM, 1st ser., 82/1 (1812), 403 · A. Chalmers, ed., *The general biographical dictionary*, new edn, 32 vols. (1812–17) · W. Beloe, *The sexagenarian, or, The recollections of a literary life*, ed. [T. Rennell], 2 vols. (1817) [annotated copy in British Museum] · Venn, *Alum. Cant.* · J. S. Watson, *The life of Richard Porson* (1861) · *The works of Samuel Parr ... with memoirs of his life and writings*, ed. J. Johnstone, 8 vols. (1828) · A. Quick, *Charterhouse: a history of the school* (1990) · F. Collins, ed., *The registers and monumental inscriptions of Charterhouse chapel*, Harleian Society, Register Section, 18 (1892), 67, 84 [registers; inscription] · private information (1896)
Likenesses J. Hoppner, oils, 1799, Trinity Cam. · J. Hoppner?, portrait, Charterhouse School, London

Raines, Francis Robert (1805–1878), antiquary, the descendant of an old Yorkshire family, third son of Isaac Raines MD, of Burton Pidsea in Holderness, and his wife, Ann, daughter of Joseph Robertson, was born at Whitby, Yorkshire, on 22 February 1805. He received his early education privately at Burton Pidsea, but at the age of thirteen was sent to Clitheroe, Lancashire, as apprentice to William Coultate, a surgeon, who afterwards moved to Burnley. During his apprenticeship Raines went to the Clitheroe and Burnley grammar schools. He later decided to enter the church, and in 1826 was admitted to St Bees Theological College in Cumberland. In 1828 he became assistant curate of Saddleworth on the Lancashire and Yorkshire border, and in 1829 was ordained and took the curacy at Rochdale parish church. In 1832 the vicar of Rochdale appointed him perpetual curate of the chapelry of St James, Milnrow. On 21 November 1836 he married Honora Elizabeth, eldest daughter of Major John Beswicke of Pike House, Littleborough, near Rochdale. They had three daughters.

Raines remained at Milnrow for the rest of his life, rebuilding the church there and providing schools and a parsonage. The earl of Dunmore appointed him his domestic chaplain in 1841, and in 1845 the archbishop of Canterbury awarded him an MA. He was rural dean of Rochdale from 1846 to 1877, and an honorary canon of Manchester Cathedral from 1849. On 30 March 1843 he was elected FSA. In the same year he was one of the founders, with Edward Holme, James Crossley, Richard Parkinson, and others, of the Chetham Society. He served from the first on the council, and succeeded Parkinson as vice-president in 1858. He was one of the most prominent nineteenth-century local historians in north-west England, an authority on genealogy, manorial and ecclesiastical history, and the documentary sources for the subject.

Raines was by far the most prolific of all the many authors and editors employed by the Chetham Society, and the quantity and scope of his work has remained unsurpassed. He was a careful and thorough antiquarian-historian, working so quickly and efficiently that the society relied heavily upon him to maintain a regular flow of publications. Between 1844 and 1878 he edited eighteen volumes and contributed eleven sections to the various Chetham miscellanies. A further eight volumes which he had partly completed were finished by others and published posthumously. The breadth of his interests was exceptionally wide, with works ranging from the 1845 edition of Bishop Gastrell's *Notitia Cestriensis*, a key source for the pre-1720 diocesan and educational history of Lancashire and Cheshire, through visitation returns, and detailed biographies of the rectors and wardens of Manchester and the vicars of Rochdale, to the delightful and always rewarding heavily annotated edition (1848) of the early seventeenth-century journal of Nicholas Assheton.

At the same time Raines was building up a remarkable collection of original manuscript material and detailed transcripts, which he housed in forty-four large volumes. On his death these, and his abundant correspondence with historians and antiquarians throughout the country, were given to Chetham's Library, Manchester, where they are now housed. This major collection of local history material is of particular importance in its coverage of the Rochdale area, but is Lancashire-wide in its scope. Other Raines material is held by the Archives and Local Studies department of Manchester Central Library.

Raines died after a short illness at Scarborough on 17 October 1878, survived by his wife; he was buried in Milnrow churchyard. A memorial was later erected to him in the church. C. W. SUTTON, *rev.* ALAN G. CROSBY

Sources H. Fishwick, *The Reliquary*, 19 (1878), 219–23 · *Manchester Guardian* (18 Oct 1878) · *Manchester Courier* (18 Oct 1878) · *Manchester Courier* (22 Oct 1878) · *Manchester Courier* (19 March 1879) · A. G. Crosby, *A society with no equal: the Chetham Society, 1843–1993*, Chetham Society, 3rd ser., 37 (1993) · CGPLA Eng. & Wales (1878)
Archives Chetham's Library, Manchester, corresp., papers, and MS collection | Man. CL, Manchester Archives and Local Studies, letters to William Longton
Likenesses portrait, repro. in W. Smith, *Old Yorkshire*, 4 (1881), 151
Wealth at death under £10,000: probate, 25 Nov 1878, CGPLA Eng. & Wales

Raines, Sir Julius Augustus Robert (1827–1909), army officer, was born at Rome on 9 March 1827, the only son of Colonel Joseph Robert Raines of Cork, of the 77th, 82nd, 95th, and 48th regiments, who had served in the Peninsular War, and his wife, Julia, daughter of Edward Jardine of Sevenoaks, Kent, banker. As a boy he lived with his mother's family at Sevenoaks, and attended the school there. He received his military education at the École Militaire, Brunswick (where an uncle by marriage, Baron von Girsewald, was master of horse to the duke), and at the Royal Military College, Sandhurst. He entered the army, as ensign in the 3rd foot (the Buffs), on 28 January 1842, and in the same year exchanged into the 95th regiment. He was promoted lieutenant on 5 April 1844, and captain on 13 April 1852.

Raines served throughout the Crimean War (1854–5).

For his services with the Turkish army in Silistria, before the invasion of the Crimea, he long after received the first-class gold medal of the Liakat. After the action at Bulganek he carried the queen's colour at the Alma. He was at Inkerman and Chernaya, and through the siege and fall of Sevastopol he served as an assistant engineer, being severely wounded in the trenches during the bombardment of 17 October 1854, and being present in the trenches at the attack on the Redan on 18 June 1855. He was mentioned in dispatches, and was awarded the Mejidiye (fifth class) and a brevet majority (24 April 1855). He became major on 1 May 1857.

Raines commanded the 95th throughout the Indian mutiny campaign in 1857–9. He was present at the assault and capture of Rewah on 6 January 1858, when he received the commendation of the governor of Bombay and the commander-in-chief for 'gallantry displayed and ably conducting these operations'. He led the left wing of the 95th at the siege and capture of Awa on 24 January, and at the siege and capture of Kotah on 30 March was in command of the third assaulting column. After the battle of Kotah-ki-sarai he was mentioned in dispatches. He was especially active during the capture of Gwalior on 19 June, when he was wounded by a musket ball in the left arm, after taking by assault two 18-pounders and helping to turn the captured guns on the enemy. For bravery in minor engagements he was four times mentioned in dispatches. The 95th, while under his command in central India, marched 3000 miles. He was promoted lieutenant-colonel on 17 November 1857, and brevet colonel on 20 July 1858, and was made CB on 21 March 1859. He married on 15 November 1859 his cousin, Catherine Elizabeth, eldest daughter and coheir of John Nicholas Wrixon of Killetra, Mallow, co. Cork. They had no children, and she survived him.

Raines next saw active service at Aden, where he commanded an expedition into the interior in 1865–6. The British troops captured and destroyed many villages and ports, including Assala, the Fadhlis' capital, and seven cannon. He was promoted major-general on 6 March 1868, lieutenant-general on 1 October 1877, and general (retired) on 1 July 1881, and was appointed colonel-in-chief of the Buffs (the East Kent regiment), in 1882. He was advanced to KCB on 3 June 1893 and GCB in 1906, and in the same year he received the grand cross of the Danish order of the Dannebrog. He published in 1900 *The 95th (the Derbyshire) Regiment in Central India*. He died on 11 April 1909 at his residence, 46 Sussex Gardens, Hyde Park, London, and was buried in the parish church, Sevenoaks.

H. M. VIBART, rev. JAMES LUNT

Sources *The Times* (13 April 1909) · *Dod's Peerage* · Walford, *County families* · *Hart's Army List* (1897) · J. A. R. Raines, *The 95th (the Derbyshire) regiment in central India* (1900) · T. Lowe, *Central India during the rebellion of 1857 and 1858* (1860) · J. H. Sylvester, *Recollections of the campaign in Malwa and central India* (Bombay, 1860) · R. J. Gavin, *Aden under British rule, 1839–1967* (1975) · Fortescue, *Brit. army*, vol. 13 · Marquess of Anglesey [G. C. H. V. Paget], *A history of the British cavalry, 1816 to 1919*, 2 (1975) · CGPLA Eng. & Wales (1909)
Wealth at death £91,501 1s. 10d.: probate, 12 May 1909, CGPLA Eng. & Wales

Rainey, George (*bap.* **1801**, *d.* **1884**), anatomist, the son of Robert and Mary Rainey, was baptized on 25 February 1801 at Spilsby, Lincolnshire, and was sent to school at Louth. He was apprenticed to a doctor first at Horncastle and afterwards at Spilsby, where he supplemented his schooling with a course of self-education in Latin, Greek, and mathematics, as well as in medicine. After serving as assistant to Thomas Barker, a surgeon at Spilsby, and adding to his income by private teaching, he entered with very low funds as a student of St Thomas's Hospital in 1824, still supporting himself chiefly by tuition. He obtained the membership of the Royal College of Surgeons in 1827.

For the next ten years Rainey was an active and very successful private teacher of anatomy. In 1837 his health broke down, and, being threatened with consumption, he travelled to the south of Europe, where he lived for five years, mainly in Italy. On returning to London he decided not to enter into medical practice, and was appointed curator of the museum and subsequently, in 1846, demonstrator of anatomy and of the microscope at St Thomas's Hospital, an appointment which he held until his death. For some years before his death he was in receipt of a government pension for his services to science.

Rainey was one of the old school of pure anatomists who had no other profession, and for many years was recognized as one of the ablest anatomical teachers in London. While closely occupied in teaching, scientific research was almost his sole recreation. One of his favourite subjects of enquiry was the production of organic or quasi-organic forms by physical processes, and the deposition of mineral substances in organized bodies. On this he published a book, *On the mode of formation of shells, of bone, and other structures by molecular coalescence, demonstrable by certain artificially formed products* (1858), as well as other works. These researches were important, not only as to their immediate object, but also in explaining the formation of urinary calculi, and leading to subsequent researches on this subject, especially those of Vandyke Carter and Ord.

Another of Rainey's early researches was published as *An experimental enquiry into the cause of the ascent and descent of the sap, with observations on endosmose and exosmose* (1847). To elucidate these and similar processes he made experiments extending over many years on 'the existence of continued currents in fluids, and their action in certain natural physical processes', described in four papers in the *St Thomas's Hospital Reports* (vols. 1, 2, 3, and 5).

Rainey also published several papers on points of minute anatomy, normal and pathological, in the *Philosophical Transactions* (140, 1850; 147, 1857), *Proceedings of the Royal Society* (5, 1846), the *Medico-Chirurgical Transactions* (vols. 28, 29, 31, and 32), *Transactions of the Pathological Society* (vols. 3, 4, 5, and 6), and elsewhere.

Rainey was an indefatigable observer with the microscope, and taught its use to students as early as 1846, when the instrument was little used in medicine. He was celebrated for his skill in the use of minute injections, and published some papers in the *Quarterly Journal of Microscopical Science*. His name was commemorated in 'Rainey's capsules', a term which was often quoted, especially in German pathological works, referring to minute parasites (later known as psorosperms) which he detected in the muscles. All his work was characterized by the most scrupulous accuracy and conscientiousness.

A man of simple habits, absorbed in scientific pursuits, Rainey lived a somewhat solitary life, but among his friends were Thomas Hodgkin, the physician, Richard Grainger, the physiologist, and Sir Richard Owen, who valued Rainey's work very highly. His own immediate pupils, among them John Syer Bristowe and William Ord, gratefully acknowledged the value of his stimulus and guidance in scientific research, and of his powerful moral influence, which was dominant over many generations of students. Rainey was married to Martha Dee; they had two sons, William (1852–1936) and James. Rainey died on 16 November 1884 at 86 Somerleyton Road, Brixton, London.   J. F. PAYNE, rev. MICHAEL BEVAN

Sources W. W. Wagstaffe, 'George Rainey: his life, work, and character', *St Thomas's Hospital Reports*, new ser., 22 (1894), xxiii–xl · personal knowledge (1896) · IGI · F. G. Parsons, *The history of St Thomas's Hospital*, 3 (1936) · b. cert. [William Rainey] · d. cert.
Likenesses W. Rainey, crayon drawings, 1896, St Thomas's Hospital, London · portrait, repro. in Wagstaffe, *St Thomas's Hospital Reports*

Rainforth, Elizabeth (1814–1877), singer, the daughter of Sampson Rainforth, a custom-house officer, was born on 23? November 1814. She studied singing with Tom Cooke, George Perry, and Crivelli. Her first public appearance was at a concert on 29 February 1836, when she sang an aria from *Der Freischütz*, and had great success. On 27 October of the same year she made her stage début as Mandane in Arne's *Artaxerxes* at the St James's Theatre. For many seasons she was a popular performer at this theatre, the English Opera House, Covent Garden, and Drury Lane; her roles included Zerlina in *Fra Diavolo* and Susanna and the Countess in *The Marriage of Figaro*. At the same time her services as a concert singer were in great demand, both in London and the provinces. In 1837 she appeared in oratorio with the Sacred Harmonic Society. On 18 March 1839 she sang at the Philharmonic Concerts, and in 1840 at the Concerts of Ancient Music. She also performed in Dublin during the 1840s. In 1845 she sang the soprano part in the first performance of Mendelssohn's 'Hear my prayer' in London. From 1852 to 1856 she lived in Edinburgh. She retired in 1859, and until 1871 taught singing at Old Windsor; thereafter she lived at Chatterton Villa, Greenway Road, Redland, Bristol, where she died, unmarried, on 22 September 1877.   R. H. LEGGE, rev. J. GILLILAND

Sources 'The Norwich festival', *Musical World* (30 Sept 1836), 38–46, esp. 43 · *Musical World* (29 Sept 1877), 653 · *The Spectator* (1836), 223 · *The Spectator* (2 Dec 1843), 1136 · *The Athenaeum* (5 March 1836), 179 · *New Grove* · Mrs C. Baron-Wilson, *Our actresses*, 2 vols. (1844) · H. S. Wyndham, *The annals of the Covent Garden Theatre: from 1732 to 1897*, 2 vols. (1906) · d. cert.
Likenesses portraits, repro. in *Actors by Gaslight*, 60 (1838), 1.201–2 · portraits, repro. in *Cumberland's British Theatre*, 43 (1837), 6 · two prints, Harvard TC

Wealth at death under £4000: probate, 20 Nov 1877, *CGPLA Eng. & Wales*

Rainier, Peter (1741–1808), naval officer, was born on 24 November 1741 at the parish of St Mary's, Sandwich, the son of Peter Rainier of Sandwich and Sarah (née Spratt). His grandfather was Daniel Rainier, a Huguenot refugee who settled in Ramsgate following the revocation of the edict of Nantes and established himself as a merchant in the surrounding area.

Rainier attended a school in Tonbridge in 1754. He entered the navy in 1756, joining the *Oxford* from which, in February 1758, he moved to the *Yarmouth* and, on her arrival in the East Indies in March 1758, to the *Tiger* (60 guns) in which he was present in the actions of 29 April and 3 August 1758 and 10 September 1759 fought off the Coromandel coast against the French admiral the comte d'Aché. In June 1760 he was moved to the *Norfolk*, flagship of Rear-Admiral Charles Steevens at the siege of Pondicherry. Steevens died in April 1761 and was succeeded by Vice-Admiral Samuel Cornish, who commanded at the reduction of Manila in September to October 1762, continuing to use the *Norfolk* as his flagship. The *Norfolk* returned to England in 1764 and was paid off. Rainier had no further service in the navy until 1774 and it is possible that he was employed by the East India Company during this time. He passed his lieutenant's examination on 2 February 1768 and was promoted lieutenant on 26 May 1768, and appointed to the *Maidstone* (under Captain Alan Gardner) in the West Indies in January 1774.

On 3 May 1777 Rainier was promoted by Vice-Admiral Clark Gayton to command the sloop *Ostrich* and in her he captured a large American privateer on 8 July 1778 after a hard fought action in which he was severely wounded. In approval of his conduct the Admiralty promoted him post captain on 29 October 1778 and appointed him to the *Burford* (64 guns) in January 1779. The *Burford* was part of Sir Edward Hughes's squadron which sailed for the East Indies on 7 March 1779. The *Burford* took part in all the operations of the war against Haidar Ali including the reduction of Negapatam in November 1781 and Trincomalee in January 1782, where a large quantity of military stores was captured. After the arrival of Admiral Suffren five major actions were fought against the French, a series unique in naval history where the same commanders and mostly the same ships confronted each other in this way. After the peace the *Burford* returned to England and Rainier went on half pay.

In 1790–91 Rainier commanded the *Monarch* in the channel and then, early in 1793, he commissioned the *Suffolk* (74 guns), in which, in the following year, he went to the East Indies as commodore and commander-in-chief. He took with him a large convoy completing a remarkable passage in which he arrived at Madras in November 1794 having made no landfall during the voyage. He remained on the East India station as commander-in-chief until 1805 during which time he assisted at the reduction of Trincomalee, which led to the surrender of all the Dutch posts in Ceylon, in August 1795, and took possession of Amboyna on 10 February 1796 and Banda Neira on 8 March. These captures produced vast booty, the admiral's share of which laid the foundation of his princely fortune. His principal duty in this command, which he discharged effectively, was to provide for the safety of the British settlements and the security of the British trade. Rainier was promoted vice-admiral of the blue on 14 February 1799 and vice-admiral of the red on 23 April 1804. Following his return to England in 1805 and retirement from active service, he continued to be consulted by the ministry on questions relating to the East India station. In the Trafalgar promotion of 9 November 1805 he was made admiral of the blue.

Rainier was returned to parliament in May 1807 as member for Sandwich. He died at his house in Great George Street, Westminster, on 7 April 1808 and was buried in Sandwich, probably at St Mary's Church. Rainier died an immensely wealthy man. Probate was given for £250,000 (PROB 11/1480) and, after some minor bequests, he gave one-tenth of his fortune towards a reduction of the national debt in gratitude for his service with the navy in the East Indies where he 'acquired the principal part of my fortune I now have which has far exceeded my merits and pretensions' (PROB 11/1480). Rainier was not married and he left the bulk of his fortune to his nephews, Admiral John Spratt Rainier (d. 1836) and Captain Peter Rainier CB (d. 1836).   KENNETH BREEN

Sources PRO, ADM 107, ADM 108, ADM 50, ADM 1, ADM 2 · will, PRO, PROB 11/1480 · R. Beatson, *Naval and military memoirs of Great Britain*, 3 vols. (1790) · W. James, *The naval history of Great Britain, from the declaration of war by France, in February 1793, to the accession of George IV in January 1820*, 5 vols. (1822–4) · *Letters and papers of Charles, Lord Barham*, ed. J. K. Laughton, 3 vols., Navy RS, 32, 38–9 (1907–11) · D. Syrett and R. L. DiNardo, *The commissioned sea officers of the Royal Navy, 1660–1815*, rev. edn, Occasional Publications of the Navy RS, 1 (1994) · *The private papers of John, earl of Sandwich*, ed. G. R. Barnes and J. H. Owen, 4 vols., Navy RS, 69, 71, 75, 78 (1932–8) · *GM*, 1st ser., 78 (1808), 373 · *IGI* · J. M. Collinge, 'Rainier, Peter', HoP, *Commons, 1790–1820*

Archives NMM, letter-books, logbooks, and papers · NRA Scotland, priv. coll., general orders | BL, letters to Lord Wellesley, Add. MSS 13757–13762

Likenesses T. Hickey, oils, *c.*1799–1804, NMM · Devis, portrait, 1805; in possession of W. S. Halliday in 1896

Wealth at death £250,000: will, 6 May 1808, PRO, PROB 11/1480

Rainier, (Ivy) Priaulx (1903–1986), composer, was born on 3 February 1903 at Howick, South Africa, a hamlet in the Natal midlands, the population of which was predominately Zulu. In 1913 she entered the South African College of Music, Cape Town, and studied violin. Her progress was quick and in 1920 she won a scholarship to attend the Royal Academy of Music, London, where she studied harmony and counterpoint with J. B. McEwen and violin with Rowsby Woof. She then worked as a violinist, chamber musician, and teacher until a grant from an anonymous benefactor in 1935 enabled her to concentrate on composing. But her interest in performance continued, and she later coached chamber music groups at the summer school of music at Bryanston.

By the late 1930s Rainier's potential as a composer was obvious and, after impressing Sir Arnold Bax with her talent, she spent three months in Paris with the renowned

teacher Nadia Boulanger in 1937. But by the end of her studies her portfolio was small, as she had written only a handful of works: an early string quartet in 1924, *Two Archaic Songs* for unaccompanied chorus in 1927, a duo for violin and piano in 1932, the *Incantation* for clarinet and orchestra in 1933, and the *Three Greek Epigrams* for soprano and piano in 1937. With the completion of her string quartet no. 1 in 1939, her career reached a watershed, and her reputation was secured. In the quartet she juxtaposed European techniques with an interest in African music; utilized a traditional four-movement plan; employed adventurous rhythmic repetition and alteration; limited her harmonic range; and emphasized the tritone, an interval that was common to many of her compositions. The Amadeus Quartet recorded the work with the support of the British Council in 1951 and later it was used as the basis for a ballet.

In 1943 Rainier was appointed professor of composition at the Royal Academy of Music and composed a suite for clarinet and piano. The suite elicited a poor critical response: some commentators argued that the work relied too heavily on rhythm and lacked melodic invention, while others suggested that the piano writing lacked skill. She responded quickly to these criticisms and tried to address some of them in her viola sonata of 1945. By employing extended melodic lines and by drawing upon her experiences as a string player, she produced a work of strength and beauty. But she never abandoned her interest in rhythm and the last movement of the sonata employs vital, dance-like structures. Rhythmic drive, small melodic units, and triadic harmony continued to dominate her style in the late 1940s, and these techniques can be found in *Sinfonia da camera*, broadcast by the BBC on 21 November 1947, and in the *Barbaric Dance Suite* for piano, written in 1949. The suite draws upon her early experiences in Natal, evoking the rhythms and melodies of the Zulu nation. Rainier claimed that her evocation of African music was subconscious and not the result of formal studies. But her assertion should be treated with caution, as her song *Ubunzima* (1948), a setting of Zulu words for voice and guitar, suggests a deeper understanding of the cultural practices of her homeland than that to which she admitted.

In the early 1950s Rainier moved to St Ives, Cornwall, and became friends with the artists Barbara Hepworth and Ben Nicholson. Her relationship with Hepworth and Nicholson affected her style, and their influence is apparent in the suite *Aequora lunae*. Dedicated to Hepworth, the piece is written for large orchestra and is divided into seven movements, each of which is named after a sea of the moon. The Cheltenham festival commissioned the work, and there it received its première on 18 July 1967. In 1952 Rainier was elected a fellow of the Royal Academy of Music and in 1953 she helped establish the St Ives festival of arts and composed *Cycle for Declamation*, a setting of words by John Donne for solo voice. The cycle was commissioned by Peter Pears, who also gave the first performance of *Requiem* for tenor and chorus at the Aldeburgh festival in 1956 and commissioned *The Bee Oracles* in 1969.

Rainier was made a freeman of the Worshipful Company of Musicians in 1955, and in 1960 she wrote *Phalaphala* for the tenth anniversary of Sir Adrian Boult's appointment as music director of the London Philharmonic Orchestra. Boult conducted the première on 17 January 1961 but was baffled by Rainier's style. In a letter to the author and violist Bernard Shore, he wrote:

> I'm afraid I have no opinion of Miss Rainier's effort—I can't make head or tail of it. It was rather good as we had been rehearsing some time, and went on and on with the stuff, when someone said 'When is the soloist coming?' A beautifully orchestral remark.   (Kennedy, 250)

Rainier retired from the Royal Academy of Music in 1961 but remained active as a composer. In the following year she composed the oboe quartet *Quanta*, which was recorded by Argo, and in 1963 she was commissioned by the BBC to compose her cello concerto. Performed by Jacqueline Du Pré at a Prom in September 1964, the work failed to excite the interest of other performers and promoters and it was soon moribund. But the reception of the concerto did not affect her relationship with the BBC and, with the support of her friend William Glock, the controller of music, her position was unassailable. It is unsurprising, therefore, that the BBC commissioned her *Ploërmel* for the 1973 Proms. In that year, *Vision and Prayer* was written with funds from the Arts Council of Great Britain, and four years later she completed *Due canti e finale* for violin and orchestra. Yehudi Menuhin commissioned the work and gave its first performance at the Edinburgh festival in September 1977. In 1981 Rainier's *Concertante duo* for oboe, clarinet, and chamber orchestra was given its première, and in June 1982 the University of Cape Town awarded her an honorary DMus. In that year she composed the *Grand Duo* for cello and piano, and in 1983 she became the first lady liveryman of the Worshipful Company of Musicians.

Rainier composed approximately thirty works. Though a relatively small *œuvre* for a career spanning six decades, some of her music was performed by leading musicians. Her works benefited from her originality and her strong musical personality. She did not excel when writing for the orchestra, but her chamber music is of a high standard. The Priaulx Rainier fund for young composers was established by the Royal Academy of Music and the University of Cape Town after her death, and many of her manuscripts and papers are held at those institutions. Priaulx Rainier died at Besse-en-Chandesse, Auvergne, France, on 10 October 1986.   RAYMOND HOLDEN

Sources J. Amis, 'Priaulx Rainier', *MT*, 96 (1955), 354–7 · T. Baxter, 'Priaulx Rainier: a study of her musical style', *Composer*, no. 60 (spring 1977), 19–26 · D. Cox, *The Henry Wood proms* (1980) · J. Frasier, *Women composers: a discography* (1983) · W. Glock, *Notes in advance* (1991) · W. Glock, 'The music of Priaulx Rainier', *The Listener*, xxxviii (1947), 872 · Grove, *Dict. mus.* (1954) · M. Kennedy, *Adrian Boult* (1987) · *The Macmillan dictionary of women's biography* (1999) · I. Kemp, 'Rainier, Priaulx', *New Grove* · *New Grove*, 2nd edn · J. Opie, *Come and listen to the stars singing: Priaulx Rainier, a pictorial biography* (1988) · E. Pirouet, *Heard melodies are sweet: a history of the London Philharmonic Orchestra* (1998) · *Baker's biographical dictionary of musicians*, rev. N. Slonimsky, 8th edn (1992) · H. H. van der Spuy, 'Priaulx Rainier', *Musicus*, vii/1 (1979), 7–14 · H. H. van der Spuy, 'Priaulx Rainier: 1903–86', *Musicus*, xxi/1 (1993), 47 · *CGPLA Eng. & Wales* (1986)
Archives Royal Academy of Music, London · University of Cape Town
Wealth at death £316,274: probate, 1986

Rainolds [Reynolds], **John** (1549–1607), theologian and college head, was born on 29 September 1549 in Pinhoe, Devon, the fifth of six sons of Richard Rainolds, a prosperous farmer. His uncle Thomas Rainolds (*d.* 1559) held numerous church positions as well as serving as warden of Merton College, Oxford, from 1545 to 1559 and vice-chancellor of the university from 1556 to 1557. His eldest brother was William *Rainolds (1544?–1594).

Early years and education, 1549–1572 All of Richard Rainolds's sons studied at Oxford University, and five of them held fellowships there. John Rainolds appears to have been sent to Oxford at eight, for an exhibition at Oriel College was bestowed on him on 11 December 1557. In all likelihood he was dispatched there so that Thomas Rainolds might oversee his education. However, as his uncle was ejected from Merton College following Elizabeth I's accession to the throne in November 1558 and imprisoned in the Marshalsea, John Rainolds was probably sent back home. He returned to Oxford in 1562, this time as a student of Merton College, but on 29 April 1563 he was admitted *discipulus* to Corpus Christi College, where his brothers Jerome and Edmund Rainolds were already fellows.

Upon his arrival at Oxford John Rainolds had been a Catholic, as were his father, his uncle, and his two brothers at Corpus. His conversion to protestantism was gradual and perhaps not completed until the late 1560s. According to Peter Heylin, he also studied in one of the English seminaries on the continent and, if true, this might explain why he was admitted a second time to Corpus on 12 February 1564 and why it took him five and a half years to complete his undergraduate course, for he graduated BA only on 15 October 1568. In any event, Rainolds appears to have been continually in residence by 1564. During Elizabeth's visit to Oxford (30 August to 3 September 1566), Rainolds presented her with verses and acted the part of the woman Hippolyta in the production at Christ Church of Richard Edward's *Palaemon and Arcyte*. Judging by the vehemence with which he criticized stage plays a quarter of a century later, this experience left an indelible impression on him. At the time, however, Rainolds's efforts were rewarded handsomely, and eight years later, when he presented Elizabeth with his translation of Plutarch's *De utilitate ex hostibus capienda* (BL, Royal MS 15 A. iii), he recalled her generosity towards him on that occasion.

Six weeks later, on 11 October 1566, Rainolds was elected probationary fellow of Corpus. His election coincided with the visitation of the college by George Acworth, chancellor and commissary to Robert Horne, bishop of Winchester, who investigated serious charges against Jerome Rainolds, which included not only his persistent adherence to Catholicism, but his concealment of church

John Rainolds (1549–1607), by unknown artist

plate, vestments, and various chapel furniture as well as his conspiring to alienate certain college property. Jerome Rainolds's countercharges against the college president, Thomas Greenway, were dismissed, and he was expelled with two other fellows. In July 1568 it was Edmund Rainolds's turn to be expelled from the college, for the role he played in opposing the installation of William Cole as the new president.

The extent to which John Rainolds sympathized with his brothers' religious and collegiate politics is not known. However, it was during that very period that his metamorphosis into puritanism occurred. William Alabaster, the Latin poet who had himself shifted from protestantism to Catholicism and back again, recounted in memorable verse how John and his then zealous Calvinist brother William Rainolds proselytized each other. It is often assumed that such an account of a mutual conversion is either apocryphal or a mistaken embellishment by Alabaster of the documented public disputation between John and his other brother Edmund Rainolds held during a visit of Robert Dudley, earl of Leicester, to Oxford almost twenty years later in January 1585. It should be noted, however, that Alabaster makes no mention of any spectacular public disputation and seems rather to use the battle imagery to invoke the far more drawn-out, painful, and private process of soul-searching that undoubtedly characterized the relations between members of the Rainolds family in general, and the eventual conversions of John and William Rainolds in particular. By whatever means

the conversion occurred, by 1569 the gifted John Rainolds had sufficiently demonstrated his protestant credentials to be entrusted with the tutorship of Richard Hooker.

Greek reader and lecturer, 1572–1580 Rainolds graduated MA on 14 July 1572, and shortly thereafter was elected Greek reader at Corpus. The lectureship was open to the university public at large and his lectures proved very popular. He began with Aristotle's *Rhetoric*, and the text of these lectures survives in the form of notes for two complete sets: the first on the *Rhetoric* alone, the second on dialectic and rhetoric. Both can be found with Rainolds's working copy of the Greek edition of the *Rhetoric* (1562). The lectures represent an advanced critical examination not only of Aristotle's rhetorical theory, but also of the relations between language, the passions, and the probity of the (Christian) orator. While the content of Rainolds's lectures during the latter part of his six years' tenure is not known, the exhortatory orations he was in the habit of delivering at the beginning of each term survive, and these further attest to his commitment to Christian humanism, though his endorsement of profane literature and philosophy is somewhat qualified by his nascent radical Calvinist sensibilities. These orations proved very popular and were printed several times, and in various forms, during the first half of the seventeenth century. Rainolds's lectures were also important in occasioning the rise of the short-lived erudite and ornamental literary style known as euphuism.

Rainolds resigned the lectureship so that he could devote himself to the study of theology, but he immediately became embroiled in a controversy over his successor. The choice fell on John Spenser, who was then only nineteen and not yet a master of arts. Rainolds judged the youth, who was neither a fellow nor even a scholar of the college, inexperienced—though not necessarily incompetent—for the task that he himself had performed with such distinction. He launched a public campaign to annul the election, appealing to both the visitor of the college, Horne, and to Sir Francis Walsingham—but in vain.

No sooner was the controversy settled than a far more divisive strife broke out. Towards the end of 1579 it was strongly rumoured that Cole was about to resign his office, and Rainolds became one of the two contenders for the position. His rival, John Barefoot, had been vice-president for the previous decade and, in addition, was backed by both Leicester and his brother, Ambrose Dudley, earl of Warwick. Rainolds was supported by Walsingham as well as by many members of the university who considered him by far the abler candidate. Though Leicester soon came round to support Rainolds, neither Barefoot nor Warwick gave way, and the ensuing impasse was resolved only by Cole's decision to remain president. The enraged Barefoot, however, in his capacity as vice-president, immediately expelled Rainolds, Hooker, and three other fellows on the grounds of infraction of college statutes. Fortunately for Rainolds, his powerful patrons quickly arranged for an *en bloc* reinstatement.

In the meantime Rainolds emerged in the forefront of the puritan party at Oxford. In addition to allying himself with Cole's reforming party at Corpus, in university politics Rainolds aligned himself with Laurence Humphrey. In 1575 he appears to have taken an active role in expelling Francesco Pucci, the opinionated Italian émigré who, with the support of Leicester, the chancellor of the university, petitioned for a licence to teach at Oxford while publicly denouncing key Calvinist doctrines. Rainolds led the university opposition against conferring, at Leicester's request, the degree of DTh on the Spaniard Antonio del Corro who, as Rainolds wrote to Humphrey on 7 June 1576, was actually Pucci's mentor. Rainolds protested that Corro's deliberately obscure writings concealed 'verie great heresies about predestination and justification by faith' (Wood, *Ath. Oxon.*, 2.182), and beseeched Humphrey to be as firm in refusing Corro's degree as he had been with Pucci. Three weeks earlier Rainolds had also been licensed to preach and at a later date, was ordained by Edmund Freake, bishop of Norwich.

Works and disputations, 1580–1598 Rainolds resigned his Greek lectureship, he later explained, so that he could devote himself to studying divinity. He was admitted BTh on 24 January 1580, having been chosen as respondent in the theology act of 13 July 1579, in the course of which he maintained three of the required six theses for the degree, completing his requirements four months later. The theses, exhibiting strong anti-Catholic sentiments and firm Calvinist attitudes on matters of scripture and the church, were immediately sent to press, appearing in March 1580 as *Sex theses de sacra scriptura et ecclesia*.

Having thus distinguished himself, Rainolds was charged the following year by Walsingham with the task of disputing with John Hart, an English Catholic who was to be executed alongside Edmund Campion on 1 December 1581. Shortly before the execution Hart recanted and was spared, but he soon reaffirmed his Catholic convictions and Walsingham sent him to Oxford, purposely to confer with Rainolds on the divisions between the English and Catholic churches, hoping thereby to offset the infelicitous outcome of the earlier debates between Campion and several protestant theologians. There followed a long series of conferences between Rainolds and Hart, first at Oxford and then in London. Despite his continued obstinacy, Hart finally conceded on one cardinal issue: the supremacy of the pope over secular rulers. Having been promised a reprieve from execution and banishment from England instead, Hart agreed to subscribe his name to the transcript of the debates that Rainolds prepared, which was published in 1584 as *The summe of the conference betweene John Rainoldes and John Hart: touching the head and the faith of the church*, with a dedication to Leicester. The book proved quite influential, and during the following quarter of a century it was reprinted four more times in English, and twice in Latin.

Partly to reward him, and partly in order to continue channelling his proven disputatious skills against the Catholic church, Walsingham resolved in 1586 to endow at Oxford a special lectureship in controversial theology earmarked for Rainolds—who had in the meantime been licensed for the degree of DTh on 14 June 1585—and convocation readily acquiesced. Walsingham promised to pay Rainolds £20 per annum and the latter, weary of the continued dissensions at Corpus, availed himself of the opportunity and resigned his fellowship in 1588, moving to Queen's College, where the provost, Henry Robinson, arranged room and board for him. Rainolds reciprocated by taking an active part in teaching at Queen's.

Rainolds lectured three times a week during term, drawing consistently large audiences: 'never were any lectures in our memory so frequented as in that university', wrote Daniel Featley, 'nor any in Cambridge, save those of Dr. [William] Whitaker' (*Abel redivivus*, 2.226). The lectures specifically targeted the Jesuit Robert Bellarmine, then a professor of theology at the Gregorian University in Rome. Walsingham instructed his agents at Rome to send him transcripts of the lectures that Bellarmine delivered there and, upon arrival, they were forwarded to Rainolds for immediate public rebuttal. Of particular interest to Rainolds was the refutation of Bellarmine's attempt to make the Apocryphal books an integral part of the Old Testament canon. True to his style and thoroughness, however, Rainolds left no stone unturned as he battled the Jesuit. The 250 lectures were not published during Rainolds's lifetime, but appeared in 1611 in two enormous quarto volumes under the title *Censura librorum apocryphorum veteris testamenti*.

In 1589 Rainolds also devoted a set of lectures to refute Hugh Broughton's *A Concent of Scripture* (1588). In his book the talented, though eccentric and opinionated, Broughton claimed to have constructed an exact chronology, based solely on the Bible, from Adam to Christ. Both Rainolds at Oxford and Edward Lively—regius professor of Hebrew at Cambridge University—had strong reservations concerning the plausibility and value of such an exercise, and they took Broughton to task in 1589. Relying on scriptures as well as on many 'heathen' authors, Rainolds pointed out various errors in Broughton's chronology. The latter, who was not the sort of person to take criticism lightly, was highly offended, especially since the objections of his formidable opponents seemed to have carried the day with university members as well as with many bishops. For the better part of the following decade, therefore, the irascible Broughton waged a stubborn campaign against Rainolds. He first attempted to force the Oxford scholar into submission through a series of conferences with him. Having failed in that, Broughton excoriated Rainolds in lectures he delivered in Stationers' Hall in London. At the same time he resorted to a campaign of letters and pamphlets addressed to, among others, the queen, William Cecil, Lord Burghley, and John Whitgift, archbishop of Canterbury. However, though Whitgift remained unwavering in his support of Rainolds's position, he was reluctant to allow the latter to publish his lectures against Broughton. It was not until 1631 that a modified version of some of these lectures was published by William Pemble.

While the debate with Broughton was still raging, Rainolds became inadvertently involved in a very different sort of controversy. In early February 1592 he was invited by Thomas Thornton of Christ Church to attend the performance of one of three plays by William Gager that the college staged between and 6 and 8 February. Rainolds, who was known for his objection even to academic drama, refused and when Thornton persisted he sent him a detailed letter enumerating his objections. For his part, Gager added to the last play in the series, a rendition of Seneca's *Hippolytus*, a speech spoken by Momus—highly suggestive of Rainolds—which was then promptly refuted in the epilogue. Gager immediately proceeded to publish both Momus's speech and his defence of academic drama as an appendix to his *Ulysses Redux*, sending Rainolds a complimentary copy in May 1592. An epistolary exchange between the two ensued, lasting until the following summer, at which time Alberico Gentili, regius professor of civil law, stepped in to take Gager's place. The main issues remained the same from the start—primarily Rainolds's claims of the unlawfulness of men wearing women's garb, his objections to breaching the sabbath, and the more generally puritan beliefs of the moral obloquy of plays and actors—but it quickly turned into an exercise of erudition and, with Gentili, it also descended into personal abuse. Again, Rainolds was apparently prohibited from publishing his letters, but in 1599 the puritan printing press of Richard Schilders at Middelburg in the Netherlands published *Th'Overthrow of Stage-Plays, by the Way of Controversie betwixt D. Gager and D. Rainoldes*, which included Rainolds's detailed letters to Gager as well as part of his exchange with Gentili.

Walsingham did not intend personally to support Rainolds in perpetuity, nor to endow the lectureship. As he wrote in 1586 to Sir Thomas Bromley, the acting chancellor of the university, he would pay Rainolds a salary until he 'maie be otherwise better called and enabled to doe good either there or elswhere oute of that Place' (Corpus Christi College, Oxford, MS 303, fol. 137). One such opportunity occurred in spring 1589, when the ailing Humphrey stepped down as regius professor of theology. On 9 May convocation petitioned the new chancellor, Sir Christopher Hatton, to appoint Rainolds as Humphrey's successor but, despite widespread support for such an appointment, Elizabeth would not consent and Thomas Holland was appointed instead. Walsingham died on 6 April 1590, but his son-in-law, Robert Devereux, second earl of Essex, took over supporting Rainolds's lectureship. Rainolds, however, was hoping for a more permanent arrangement. During 1593 fresh efforts were made to secure a church position for Cole that would facilitate Rainolds's election as president of Corpus. This time it was Anne Dudley, dowager countess of Warwick, who championed Rainolds's cause by attempting to secure for Cole the post of dean of Lincoln. But the queen remained obstinate in her refusal to allow for Rainolds's promotion within the university.

Elizabeth's objections stemmed from the continued extremism of Rainolds, who participated in several presbyterian meetings during the mid-1580s as well as becoming known for some radical preaching in Oxford. Equally alarming were his writings in support of various Calvinist positions which were at variance with the official position of the English church. Thus, for example, Rainolds was mobilized by Sir Francis Knollys to respond to Richard Bancroft's St Paul's sermon of 19 February 1589, in which the latter argued for the divine origin of episcopacy. Rainolds complied not only by refuting Bancroft's claim, but also by insisting that in upholding his own position he could not be considered a heretic. A year or two later Rainolds wrote a short treatise concerning the lawfulness of divorce and remarriage following adultery, and about the same time he challenged the established interpretation— embraced by Whitgift, and later by Thomas Bilson, bishop of Winchester—according to which Christ descended into hell in body as well as in soul, arguing instead that this descent was made only by the body of Christ, while the pains of hell were inflicted on Christ's soul only on the cross. Needless to add, none of these opinions was published during Rainolds's lifetime, though they were widely circulated in manuscript. Small wonder, then, that when Elizabeth visited Oxford in September 1592, she 'schooled Doctor Reynalds for his precisenes, willing him to follow her lawes and not to run before them' (J. Harrington, *A Supplie or Addicion to the Catalogue of Bishops to the Year 1608*, ed. R. H. Miller, Potomac, MD, 1979, 134).

What Elizabeth wanted, clearly, was for Rainolds to accept a position in the church. Cognizant of his stature, Elizabeth was loath to enhance Rainolds's influence at Oxford while a position in the church, by its very nature, would bring him much more in line with official religious policy. Indeed, the very acceptance of such a post would amount to a public declaration of conformity to the Church of England. Rainolds's patrons recognized the situation and convinced him to accept the deanery of Lincoln (he was appointed on 10 December 1593). Though he acquiesced, Rainolds remained resident in Oxford, invoking various technicalities in delaying his move. Only in 1598 was he finally installed as dean—and by then it was already certain that his patrons had managed to arrange for an exchange of positions with Cole. Rainolds was elected president on 11 December 1598.

President of Corpus Christi and final years, 1598–1607 The nine years of Rainolds's presidency greatly altered the fortunes of Corpus. Cole turned over to him a college plagued by internal conflicts and financial difficulties, and Rainolds set to work to rectify the situation. He introduced a more equitable system of distributing college revenues, which benefited the fellows as well as the college and allowed for the renovation of the hall, chapel, and library. The improved fortunes of the college also resulted in an increase in the number of students, who were subjected to the firm academic and religious discipline that Rainolds introduced.

With the accession of James I in 1603 Rainolds, like most English puritans, was buoyed by the hope that the new monarch would look more favourably upon the reformation of the English church. Indeed, he even contributed some verses to an Oxford volume commemorating James's accession—something he had not done for nearly forty years. In April 1603, while *en route* for London, James was presented with the celebrated millenary petition, in which the puritans set down their grievances against the established church. The relatively moderate tone of the petition worked well upon the new monarch, who soon announced his intention to hold a conference, over which he would preside, in which all grievances and disputes between the bishops and the puritans could be aired openly. The conference was scheduled for 14–18 January 1604 and Rainolds's name appeared on every list of puritan candidates that had been circulated the previous summer and autumn. When the historic occasion arrived, it was he who led the puritan delegation, which also included Laurence Chaderton, Thomas Sparke, and John Knewstub. Rainolds did most of the speaking, while Chaderton and Sparke were 'mute as any fish'. The outcome was disappointing, for though James listened favourably to the arguments against non-residency and consented to improve the state of preachers, he had no intention of compromising on matters of church discipline and ceremonies. Ultimately Rainolds's recommendation that the king establish a synod of bishops and presbyters to determine contested issues in the church so infuriated James that he brought the audience to a close, snapping 'No bishop, no king' and leaving the room.

In the aftermath of the conference, especially following Bancroft's elevation to the archbishopric of Canterbury, great pressure was brought to bear upon Rainolds to subscribe to the new book of canons. However, Rainolds put up a fight, using his old delaying tactics. He resorted to writing numerous letters to clarify his religious views in the hope that he would thereby privately satisfy the king and Bancroft in his conformity without the need to endure public subscription. Such a ploy was evidently successful, for it was not until the summer of 1605 that he was pushed for an immediate submission. No doubt the reason for this pressure was the impending visit of James to Oxford, scheduled for late August 1605. The king arrived at Oxford on 27 August, and Rainolds was one of the lecturers chosen in his honour. James was apparently determined to force the obstinate and slippery president of Corpus into submission, and he instructed the vicechancellor, George Abbot, to set Rainolds a deadline for submission, making it clear that failure to comply would lead to expulsion from the university. Rainolds, however, wrote a few more letters and, in the end, appears to have withstood the pressure.

By the time the subscription controversy subsided Rainolds was in failing health. Conscious of this, he tried to proceed in what he clearly regarded as the most important project of his career—and the only tangible result of the Hampton Court conference—the new translation of the Bible. The task was divided among six groups, and Rainolds was part of the one charged with translating both major and minor prophets. Although officially headed by John Harding, the regius professor of Hebrew, the group met at Rainolds's lodgings at Corpus three times a week, a practice that continued even during the last weeks of the president's life. It is difficult to judge just how far the translation of the Oxford group proceeded before Rainolds's death, but it appears that most of the work was accomplished, even though officially the task was completed only in 1609.

Rainolds died on Thursday 21 May 1607 of consumption. He had been in poor health for at least twenty years—suffering mostly from gout—and by the end of his life he was emaciated. His funeral on 25 May was attended by many drawn from all quarters of the university, as well as by the mayor and aldermen of Oxford, and he was mourned both at home and abroad. He was buried on 25 May in the college chapel where his pupil and successor, John Spenser, raised a monument to him. Rainolds left his large collection of books to various colleges and to friends. He did not marry. Joseph Hall, who seized the occasion to lament the great loss in recent years of eminent protestant divines such as William Fulke, William Whitaker, Hadrianus Junius, and Theodore Beza, added:

> Doctor Reynolds is the last; not in worth, but in the time of his loss. He alone was a well-furnished library, full of all faculties, full of all studies, of all learning; the memory, the reading of that man, were near to a miracle. (*The Works of the Right Reverend Joseph Hall*, ed. P. Wynter, 10 vols., 1863, 6.149–50)

In Leiden, Joseph Scaliger mourned the loss of not only a profoundly erudite scholar but a towering pillar of the reformed churches, writing on the subject in his *Illustriss; viri Iosephi Scaligeri … epistolae* (1627). That Rainolds's reputation remained high throughout the seventeenth century is manifest by the publication of many of his manuscripts, as well as by the frequency with which his judgement was invoked on both sides of the religious divide.

MORDECHAI FEINGOLD

Sources Wood, *Ath. Oxon.*, 2.12–19 · *Abel redivivus, or, The dead yet speaking* (1652); W. Nichols, ed., repr., 2 vols. (1867), vol. 2, pp. 219–45 · P. Heylin, *Cyprianus Anglicus, or, The history of the life and death of … William … archbishop of Canterbury* (1668), 50–51 · T. Fowler, *The history of Corpus Christi College*, OHS, 25 (1893) · C. M. Dent, *Protestant reformers in Elizabethan Oxford* (1983) · F. S. Boas, *University drama in the Tudor age* (1914) · K. Young, 'An Elizabethan defense of the stage', *Shakespeare studies by members of the department of English in the University of Wisconsin* (Madison, Wis, 1916), 103–24 · *DNB* · K. Young, 'William Gager's defence of the academic stage', *Transactions of the Wisconsin Academy of Sciences, Arts, and Letters*, 18 (1916), 593–638 · J. W. Binns, 'Women or transvestites on the Elizabethan stage? An Oxford controversy', *Sixteenth Century Journal*, 5 (1974), 95–119 · W. Ringler, 'The immediate source of euphuism', *Publications of the Modern Language Association of America*, 53 (1938), 678–86 · J. K. McConica, 'Humanism and Aristotle in Tudor Oxford', *EngHR*, 94 (1979), 291–317 · *John Rainolds's Oxford lectures on Aristotle's rhetoric*, ed. L. D. Green (Newark, NJ, 1986) · *Hist. U. Oxf.* 3: *Colleg. univ.* · CCC Oxf., MS 303
Archives BL, Royal MS 15 A.iii · BL, divinity lectures, Add. MS 30498 [copies] · Bodl. Oxf., MS Cherry 33 · CCC Oxf., MSS 280, 303 · Queen's College, Oxford, MSS 241, 354, 359
Likenesses Passe, line engraving (after painting), BM, NPG; repro. in H. Holland, *Heröologia* (1620) · frieze, Bodl. Oxf. · oils, CCC Oxf. [*see illus.*] · oils, second version, CCC Oxf. · painted stone bust, CCC Oxf.
Wealth at death personal belongings and money *c*.£500; library of over 2500 books: catalogue, Bodl. Oxf., MS Wood D.40

Rainolds [Reynolds], **William** (1544?–1594), Roman Catholic priest and author, was born at Pinhoe, Devon, the second son of Richard Rainolds, farmer, and elder brother of the puritan theologian John *Rainolds. In 1555 Rainolds was admitted to Winchester College, after which he proceeded to New College, Oxford, where he held a fellowship between 1560 and 1572. During Elizabeth I's visit to Oxford in 1566 he was one of the members of the university to mark the occasion with learned poems. He received his BA on 17 June 1563 and his MA on 4 June 1567. Subsequently he became rector of Lavenham, Suffolk.

There is a romantic story about Rainolds's conversion to Catholicism in Fuller's *Church History*: the protestant Rainolds and his Catholic brother John were both so successful in their attempts to convert one another that they both changed their faith. The truth is probably rather more prosaic: John Pits states in his *De illustribus Angliae scriptoribus* that William Rainolds's conversion was due to the influence of the famous controversy between Thomas Harding and John Jewel. However, Fuller's account neatly characterizes the complicated intellectual, theological, and moral choices that faced men at Oxford in the 1560s. In 1572 Rainolds resigned his fellowship and went to live in Hart Hall. In 1575 he made a public recantation at Rome and was received into the Catholic church. On 16 August 1577 he arrived at the English College, Douai. In 1578 and 1579 there were journeys to Rheims (the new location of the English College), Louvain, and Paris. On 31 March 1580 he was ordained priest at Châlons.

William Allen, the president of the English College at Rheims, appointed Rainolds professor of scriptures and Hebrew and on 11 April 1581 he started to lecture on the epistles of St Paul. However, Rainolds's precarious health prevented him from carrying out his teaching duties very regularly. Pits dramatically relates how over-exertion brought Rainolds close to death: Rainolds, having burst a blood-vessel and vomiting blood, made a solemn promise that, on recovery, he would devote the rest of his life to writing in defence of the Catholic church; and that, indeed, became his main occupation in life. Together with Gregory Martin, William Allen, and Richard Bristow, Rainolds was involved in the translation of the Rheims Bible (New Testament, 1582, Old Testament, 2 vols., 1609–10), although Rainolds's contribution mainly consisted in answering controversial works by opponents in England. Ironically, one of these opponents was William's brother John. William Rainolds replied to the attack on Gregory Martin's preface to the Old Testament by the Cambridge scholar William Whitaker. Whitaker's Latin treatise *Ad Nicolai Sanderi demonstrationes* (1583) provoked an English reply by Rainolds (*A Refutation of Sundry Reprehensions, Cavils, and False Sleights, by which M. Whitaker Laboureth to Deface the Late English Translation*, 1583), which, in its turn, elicited a reply by Whitaker in 1585. In 1584 Rainolds brought out a translation of William Allen's *Ad persecutores Anglos*. Under the pseudonym Guilielmus Rossaeus, Rainolds (probably with the co-operation of William Gifford) entered the debate about the future succession of Elizabeth I through his *De iusta reipub. christianae in reges impios et haereticos authoritate* (1590), in which he posits that 'heretics' cannot be legitimate monarchs. When the Scottish minister Robert Bruce attacked the Catholic position on attendance at Church of England services in his *Sermons upon the Sacrament* (1590) Rainolds replied with his *A Treatise Conteyning the True Catholick and Apostolike Faith* (1593). His final and most substantial publication is *Calvinoturcismus* (1597), a 1000-page treatise in which he compares protestant articles of faith to the—in his view—untenable ideas of infidels. The work was published posthumously by William Gifford.

During the last years of his life Rainolds served as chaplain to the Antwerp beguines. He died at Antwerp on 24 August 1594. J. BLOM and F. BLOM

Sources P. Milward, *Religious controversies of the Elizabethan age* (1977) · J. Pits, *Relationum historicarum de rebus Anglicis*, ed. [W. Bishop] (Paris, 1619), 817–18 · G. Anstruther, *The seminary priests*, 1 (1969) · A. C. Southern, *Elizabethan recusant prose, 1559–1582* (1950) · Gillow, *Lit. biog. hist.*, vol. 5 · T. F. Knox and others, eds., *The first and second diaries of the English College, Douay* (1878) · Wood, *Ath. Oxon.*, new edn, 1.613 · T. F. Kirby, *Winchester scholars: a list of the wardens, fellows, and scholars of … Winchester College* (1888) · Foster, *Alum. Oxon.* · A. F. Allison and D. M. Rogers, eds., *The contemporary printed literature of the English Counter-Reformation between 1558 and 1640*, 2 vols. (1989–94) · T. Fuller, *The church history of Britain*, ed. J. S. Brewer, new edn, 6 vols. (1845), vol. 5, pp. 201–2 · J. Loach, 'Reformation controversies', *Hist. U. Oxf.* 3: *Colleg. univ.*, 363–96

Rains, (William) Claude (1889–1967), actor, was born on 10 November 1889 at 26 Tregothnan Road in Clapham, London, the son of Frederick William Rains and his wife, Emily Eliza Cox. The family was not well off; he was one of a dozen siblings, nine of whom died in infancy. Frederick Rains had tried his hand at various jobs, including boilermaker and boxing instructor. At the time of Claude's birth he gave his occupation as 'Organ Builder (journeyman)'. Later in life he took up acting and film directing.

About the age of ten Claude Rains was sent to a boarding-school in Parsons Green in south-west London. Because he was small in stature, with a stammer and an inability to pronounce his Rs, his classmates made fun of him, and at least once he ran away from school. He was happier singing in the local church choir, an occupation which led to his stage début. A number of choristers were recruited to play street urchins in *Sweet Nell of Old Drury*, by Paul Kester, at the Theatre Royal, Haymarket. The play opened on 30 August 1900. Within a year Rains had persuaded his parents to let him quit school for the theatre, and was taken on as call-boy at the Duke of York's Theatre. He soon moved to His Majesty's Theatre, where he came under the wing of the actor–manager Sir Herbert Beerbohm Tree. As Tree's personal call-boy Rains had to prepare the great man's breakfast (including six plover's eggs) faultlessly each morning. 'He often used to fire me, but I never went', Rains recalled years later (*Daily Herald*, 3 April 1952). Noting Rains's eagerness to act, Tree helped him overcome his speech defects and lose his strong cockney accent. Promoted to assistant stage manager and prompter, Rains began to take bit parts on stage. In 1911–12 he toured Australia with Harley Granville Barker's company, and in 1914 Granville Barker entrusted him with taking the company on tour to the USA. The repertory damaged his vocal cords and cost him almost all the sight of his right eye. Having recuperated, he resumed his acting career in 1919, when he joined Henry Ainley's company at the St James Theatre. It was with Ainley that he made his first venture into cinema, eighth-billed in a now long-forgotten melodrama called *Build Thy House* (1920), directed by Fred Goodwins. Ainley took the lead role.

During the 1920s Rains built an impressive reputation as a stage actor, making up for his lack of physical stature (he was 5 feet 6 inches tall) with a commanding presence and a rich throaty voice that one critic described as 'like honey with some gravel in it' (Shipman, 451). He scored his first post-war success with the lead role in *Reparation* (1919), adapted from Tolstoy. Further critically acclaimed performances followed: as Cassius in *Julius Caesar* (1920), his only stage Shakespeare; in Gogol's *The Government Inspector* (1921); in the title role in Louis Verneuil's *Daniel* (1921), a part created for the seventy-year-old Sarah Bernhardt *en travesti*; in Clemence Dane's *A Bill of Divorcement* and *Will Shakespeare* (both 1921); as a sinister butler in the rip-roaring Gothic melodrama *The Bat* (1922); and in Karel Capek's *The Insect Play* (1923). Also in 1923 he played the lead in Bernard Shaw's *The Doctor's Dilemma*, which he followed with several more Shaw plays over the next few years, including *The Man of Destiny* (as Napoleon), *The Devil's Disciple*, *Misalliance*, *The Philanderer*, and *The Apple Cart*. Rains's 'impeccable timing, dry wit and fine sense of irony made him the perfect Shavian actor' (Richards, 13).

At this period Rains taught regularly at the Royal Academy of Dramatic Art, where his students included John Gielgud, Charles Laughton, and Rains's third wife, Beatrix Thomson. According to Gielgud, Rains was 'my first inspiration in the professional theatre … my principal and most inspiring teacher' (Soister and Wioskowski, 248). Gielgud remained a lifelong admirer of Rains's talents as an actor, and praised his 'virtuosity and timing and attack … [He had] a beautiful voice and spoke beautifully. … The moment he came on, he lit up the stage' (ibid.).

In 1927 Beatrix Thomson was offered a part in a New York production of *The Constant Nymph*, an adaptation of Margaret Kennedy's fashionable novel. Rains accompanied her and took a minor part in the same production, but soon went on to more prestigious roles on Broadway: as Samuel Pepys in J. B. Fagan's *And So to Bed*, the title role in Ben Jonson's *Volpone*, and the lead in Romain Rolland's *The Game of Love and Death*, in which his 'precise dominating acting', according to the *New York Times*, 'almost saved the play' (Soister and Wioskowski, 213). Rains realized he could earn far more as an actor in America than he could ever hope to in Britain, and decided to make the USA his permanent home.

Rains's growing fame on Broadway soon attracted the attention of Hollywood. According to his own account,

They told me they wanted to take me away from my art, the stage, to play in their beastly movies. I wouldn't listen; I resented the mere suggestion! Then they cabled me to say how much they would pay me. … I had my bags packed and was in Hollywood the next morning. (*Picturegoer*, 28 Dec 1940)

(**William) Claude Rains (1889–1967)**, by Russell Westwood, 1945 [as Julius Caesar in the film *Caesar and Cleopatra*]

included Bernard Shaw's *Androcles and the Lion* and Euripides' *Iphigenia in Tauris*. Rains took supporting roles in both, along with his managerial duties.

Among the company was actress Isabel Esther Jeans (*b. c.*1891), whom Rains had married on 27 March 1913. The marriage ended in divorce about five years later. This was the first of Rains's six marriages, all of which (except the last) ended in divorce. His other wives were: the actress Marie Foster Hemingway (*b. c.*1893), whom he married on 20 December 1920; a drama student, Beatrix Lindsay Thomson (*b. c.*1900), whom he married on 24 November 1924 (they divorced on 8 April 1935); Frances Propper (*b. c.*1910), whom he married on 9 April 1935 and with whom he had a daughter, Jennifer, in 1938, but whom he divorced about 1956; the Hungarian pianist Agi Jambor (*b. c.*1909), whom he married on 4 November 1959 and divorced on 29 July 1960; and the writer Rosemary Clark Schrode, *née* McGroarty (*b.* 1915/16), whom he married in August 1960 and who died in 1964. By all accounts Rains was not the easiest man to live with. His fifth wife, Agi Jambor, who divorced him after some nine months of marriage, claimed that he was 'vile and nasty' to her, that he kept her short of money and locked her out of the house. Against this, his daughter described him as 'loving, kind, and proud', though she added that he was 'frugal to a fault' (Soister and Wioskowski, 1–2).

Rains's stage appearances were starting to attract favourable notice when his career was interrupted by the war. On returning to Britain in 1915, he joined the London Scottish regiment—mainly, he later claimed, on account of their romantic kilts. He served in the trenches, and in 1917 suffered a poison gas attack at Vimy Ridge which

His first starring role, though, was essentially a radio performance. As H. G. Wells's *The Invisible Man* (1933), directed by James Whale, he appeared only in the final shot; the rest was special effects and Rains's sonorous voice. But it was enough to make his name in the film world, and after one final Broadway venture he forsook the stage for nearly two decades. His next few films were a mixed bag, but he hit his stride when he signed a contract with Warner Brothers in 1936. Now in his late forties, he was too old for romantic leads, but he rapidly established himself as one of the screen's finest character actors. He had no qualms about taking unsympathetic roles, and had few rivals when it came to playing suave sardonic villains, especially in costume dramas. He was a tetchy Spanish grandee plotting the downfall of *Anthony Adverse* (1936), the scheming earl of Hertford in *The Prince and the Pauper* (1937), a ruthless district attorney in the lynch-law melodrama *They Won't Forget* (1937), and, best-remembered of all his villains, Prince John in *The Adventures of Robin Hood* (1938). His John, peevish and effete, made an ideal foil for that other master of suave villainy, Basil Rathbone, as Sir Guy of Gisborne.

A Rains villain, nuanced and relishable, could often steal a picture from the nominal leads. *Juarez* (1939), a biopic of the Mexican revolutionary leader, starred Paul Muni in the title role, but it was Rains's malevolent Napoleon III who walked off with the film. This was the first of several teamings with Bette Davis. Davis, who could be scathing about her male co-stars (she reserved particular contempt for Errol Flynn), came to have the highest regard for Rains, both personally and professionally. 'Claude was enormously well read and extremely bright about scripts and his work', she later recalled: 'He was one of the really great actors' (Etheridge, 10).

Villainy was just one facet of Rains's screen persona; his range was extensive, and he avoided typecasting. He could equally play a harassed but charming widower bringing up his *Four Daughters* (1938), the prim celestial bureaucrat of the title in the supernatural fantasy *Here Comes Mr Jordan* (1941), the wise psychiatrist who helps Bette Davis liberate herself in *Now, Voyager* (1942), or the quiet, unassuming *Mr Skeffington* (1944), patiently putting up with his self-obsessed wife (Davis again). In Frank Capra's populist fable *Mr Smith Goes to Washington* (1939) he played a deeply corrupt senator while still hinting at the lost idealist the man might once have been. For this performance he was nominated for an Oscar; he was nominated thrice more, but never gained the award. Another nomination came for his Captain Renault in *Casablanca* (1942)—smooth as old cognac, the model of moral ambiguity.

Despite the tongue-in-cheek remarks quoted above, Rains—unlike many stage-trained actors—never disparaged the cinema. The English playwright Rodney Ackland, who visited Rains in America, reported, 'He would not hear a word against Hollywood … and furthermore, he *enjoyed* making films' (Richards, 13). This sense of enjoyment comes through strongly in all Rains's films, even the more preposterous ones. Though capable of the utmost subtlety, he could pull out the stops with the best of them

when the role invited it. In *Deception* (1946), high-class tosh set in the classical music world, his egomaniac composer acted both his co-stars—Bette Davis and Paul Henreid— right off the screen. *The Unsuspected* (1947) was unabashed Grand Guignol, filmed in deepest *noir*, as the criminologist-turned-killer Rains acted up a storm.

Regrettably, only one Shaw performance by Rains was captured on celluloid. Even more regrettably, it was in *Caesar and Cleopatra* (1945), directed (in Britain) without a trace of Shavian wit by the inept Gabriel Pascal. Rains's urbane Caesar was its sole saving grace. (His fee was $1 million, apparently the first time an actor had received such a sum for one film.) Back in Hollywood, he was much better served by a fellow British expatriate. Alfred Hitchcock's *Notorious* (1946) found him playing a Nazi whom Ingrid Bergman marries in order to spy on him. Touchingly vulnerable, his character was far more likeable than the film's nominal hero (played by Cary Grant). Rains returned to Britain for David Lean's love-triangle drama *The Passionate Friends* (1948); he was trenchant as the jealous husband, but this was one of Lean's lesser works.

Rains's contract with Warners expired in 1947. Thereafter he rarely lacked work, but the quality of the films offered him declined. In 1951 he made a triumphant return to the stage, playing the lead in Sidney Kingsley's adaptation of Arthur Koestler's political novel *Darkness at Noon*. His performance was showered with awards and critical plaudits. His co-star, Kim Hunter, remembered Kingsley, scared the play might be thought pro-communist,

> cutting out all of the 'grey' human tones and trying to make it all black and white. Claude fought him all the way and managed to bring the necessary humanity to the play. It was pure pleasure working with Claude. (Soister and Wioskowski, 219)

Though Rains liked making films, he had little time for Hollywood society. An essentially private person, he rarely socialized, and between films liked to retreat to his farm in Pennsylvania. He had started with a modest 40-acre spread in 1935. It was there that his daughter was born in 1938, and in that year Rains became an American citizen. In 1940 he bought a larger holding of some 330 acres, also in Pennsylvania, and he added further acreage over the years. He was no vanity farmer; for all his urban upbringing he took real pleasure—and acquired genuine skills—in tasks of routine farm labour. Not until 1957, when he was approaching seventy, did he reluctantly give up the farm.

Besides his stage and screen work, Rains often appeared on radio and television; between 1956 and 1962 he starred in five episodes of the long-running series *Alfred Hitchcock Presents*. His last notable film role was again for David Lean; a smaller part, but in a much more impressive film, as a drily calculating British diplomat in *Lawrence of Arabia* (1962). The death of his sixth wife, Rosemary, from cancer in 1964, at forty-eight, and his own increasingly poor health caused Rains to retire from acting in 1965. He died on 30 May 1967 from an internal haemorrhage at the

Lakes Region Hospital in Laconia, New Hampshire, and was buried in the nearby Red Hill cemetery, Sandwich, New Hampshire.   PHILIP KEMP

Sources J. T. Soister and J. Wioskowski, *Claude Rains: a complete illustrated reference to his work in film, stage, radio, television and recordings* (1999) · J. Richards, 'In praise of Claude Rains', *Films and Filming*, 329 (Feb 1982), 12–17; 330 (March 1982), 8–13 · A. Etheridge, 'Bette Davis and Claude Rains: two "opposites" that attracted', *American Classic Screen*, 5/3 (May–June 1981), 9–13 · J. Gielgud, *Distinguished company* (1972) · *Daily Herald* (3 April 1952) · *Picturegoer* (28 Dec 1940) · b. cert. · m. certs. · D. Shipman, *The great movie stars: the golden years* (1970)
Likenesses photographs, 1925–52, Hult. Arch. · R. Westwood, photograph, 1945, NPG [*see illus.*]

Rainsford, Charles (1728–1809), army officer, born at West Ham, Essex, on 3 February 1728, was the second son of Francis Rainsford (d. 1770), an alderman of Maldon, Essex, and influential in its parliamentary elections, and his wife, Isabella, daughter of William Bale of Foston, Derbyshire. He was educated at Great Clacton, Essex, by a clerical friend of his father, and in March 1744 was appointed second cornet in General Bland's 3rd dragoons through the influence of his uncle, Charles Rainsford (d. 1778), deputy lieutenant of the Tower of London. The regiment was then serving in the War of the Austrian Succession, in Flanders against the French; Rainsford joined it at once, and carried the standard at the battle of Fontenoy on 30 April 1745. On 1 May he was appointed ensign in the Coldstream Guards, and with them was ordered home on the news of the Jacobite rising. In 1751 he was gazetted lieutenant with the rank of captain, and when James O'Hara, second Baron Tyrawley (1690–1773), became colonel of the Coldstream Guards (April 1755), he made Rainsford successively adjutant to the battalion, major of brigade, and aide-de-camp. Rainsford was private secretary to Tyrawley, governor of Gibraltar (1756–7); he returned in 1760, and in 1761 was promoted captain and lieutenant-colonel, given a company, and sent to serve under Prince Ferdinand of Brunswick in Germany.

In 1762, when Spain threatened to invade Portugal, Rainsford again accompanied Tyrawley thither as aide-de-camp, and was shortly afterwards appointed brigadier-general and chief engineer in Portugal; he fortified many strongholds there. He was ordered home in 1763, and promoted second major in the Grenadier Guards. From 1766 to 1780 he was equerry to William, duke of Gloucester, brother of George III, and became his confidant. He commanded the army detachment at the king's bench prison, Southwark, following the May 1768 riot, and wrote of 'the difficulties the military are subject to in cases of riot, when not supported by the civil authority' (Hayter, 33).

A professional soldier, Rainsford ranked his parliamentary involvement beneath his army career, and regarded the former as a means of advancing the latter. From December 1772 to 1774 he was, with Gloucester's permission, through the influence of William Nassau de Zuylestein, fourth earl of Rochford, and pending the election of Rochford's nephew and heir, a safe stopgap MP for the freeman franchise borough of Maldon, Essex. Bamber Gascoyne, the other Maldon MP, wrote in November 1773

that Rainsford was 'a creature of the Duke of Gloucester, no fortune' and 'cannot be of consequence enough to hurt us when elected' (Namier, 346). Rainsford voted with the government and apparently did not speak in the house. A friend of the Percy family, he was through the influence of Algernon Percy, Lord Lovaine (brother of Hugh Percy, second duke of Northumberland), from February 1787 to December 1788 MP for the burgage borough of Bere Alston, Devon. He vacated the seat, presumably over the Regency Bill, on which Lovaine sided with the government, but Gloucester and Northumberland with the opposition. Northumberland recompensed him by returning him for Northumberland's burgage 'pocket borough', Newport, Cornwall, of which he was MP from 1790 to 1796. He followed his patron's line in voting for Grey's resolution on Ochakov (12 April 1791). In May 1796 he wrote that if parliament had been going to continue longer he would have 'begged leave to vacate my seat' (Thorne, 5.6), and he declined a seat in the next parliament. He took little part in parliamentary proceedings.

Promoted colonel in the army in August 1774, Rainsford was governor of Chester from 1776 to 1796. During 1776 and 1777 he was employed in raising troops in Germany for the American war, and in 1777 was appointed aide-de-camp to George III and in August promoted major-general. During the Gordon riots in June 1780 he commanded the camp established in Hyde Park and later at Blackheath. He provided cavalry escorts for infantry detachments sent from his Hyde Park camp, so that they could act in concert, while keeping a strong force to guard the camp with its supplies and six cannon. From May 1781 until his death he was colonel of the 44th regiment. In 1782 he was sent to take command of the garrison at Minorca, but before his arrival it surrendered to the Spaniards in February. He was promoted lieutenant-general in November 1782.

On the outbreak of the revolutionary war in February 1793, Rainsford was sent as second in command to Gibraltar, where he commanded following the death of Sir Robert Boyd and remained until March 1795. He was promoted general in May 1796 and appointed governor of Cliff Fort, Tynemouth, in the same year; he saw no further active service. He married, first, on 18 July 1775 Elizabeth (1758–1781), daughter of Edward Miles, and they had one son, Colonel William Henry Rainsford (*bap.* 1776, *d.* 1823), and two daughters, Julia Anne and Josephina; the latter, for whom Sir Joseph Yorke stood godfather, died in infancy. Rainsford married, second, on 16 February 1789 Ann Cornwallis (d. 1 Feb 1798), youngest daughter of Sir William More Molyneux of Loseley Park, Guildford; they had no children.

Rainsford had varied interests. He was elected a fellow of the Royal Society on 13 May 1779; he was also a fellow of the Society of Antiquaries, and a member of a society for making discoveries in Africa and of various benevolent institutions. He dabbled in alchemy, and was a Rosicrucian and a freemason. Rainsford died at his house, 29 Soho Square, London, on 24 May 1809. He was buried in a vault in the chancel of the chapel of St Peter ad Vincula in the

Tower of London, with his father, his uncle Charles, and his first wife.

Rainsford left nearly forty volumes of manuscript, which were purchased by the British Museum (BL, Add. MSS 23644–23680) and are an important historical source. They include autobiographical memoranda, papers, and letters referring to Portugal, 1762–4, to Gibraltar, 1793–6, and to raising of German mercenaries, 1776–8, a narrative of the expedition to the Mediterranean, 1781–2, correspondence with Lord Amherst, the duke and duchess of Northumberland, and others, papers on freemasonry, magnetism, and alchemical processes, copies of the correspondence and papers of Lord Tyrawley, and Rainsford's journal of his travels with the duke of Gloucester. The papers on the raising of German mercenaries for the American War of Independence were printed in the *Proceedings of the New York Historical Society* (1879).

A. F. POLLARD, rev. ROGER T. STEARN

Sources BL, Rainsford papers, Add. MSS 23644–23680 · *GM*, 1st ser., 79 (1809), 486 · L. B. Namier, 'Rainsford, Charles', HoP, *Commons, 1754–90* · R. G. Thorne, 'Rainsford, Charles', HoP, *Commons, 1790–1820* · P. Morant, *The history and antiquities of the county of Essex*, 2 vols. (1768) · *The record of the Royal Society of London*, Royal Society (1992) · T. Hayter, *The army and the crowd in mid-Georgian England* (1978) · A. Babington, *Military intervention in Britain: from the Gordon riots to the Gibraltar incident* (1990) · J. Black, *Britain as a military power, 1688–1815* (1999) · G. Rudé, *The crowd in history, 1730–1848* (1964) **Archives** BL, corresp. and papers, Add. MSS 23644–23680 · Wellcome L., alchemical notes and papers | PRO, corresp. with F. J. Jackson, FO 353 · RA, corresp. with Ozias Humphrey

Rainsford, Marcus (*b. c.*1750, *d.* in or after **1805**), author, was the younger son of Edward Rainsford of Sallins, co. Kildare. He obtained a commission and served in the 105th regiment during the American War of Independence. In 1794 he served under the duke of York in the Netherlands, and afterwards helped to raise black troops in the West Indies. In 1799 he visited Santo Domingo, and met Toussaint L'Ouverture, the black rebel leader and later governor of Santo Domingo. He was subsequently arrested and condemned to death as a spy, but was reprieved and eventually set free. He published an account of this adventure, entitled *A Memoir of Transactions that Took Place in St Domingo in the Spring of 1799* (1802). The book received severe reviews but a second edition, entitled *St Domingo, or, An Historical, Political, and Military Sketch of the Black Republic*, was published in the same year. He retired from the army with the rank of captain about 1803. He also published *An Historical Account of the Black Empire of Hayti* (1805), and a poem, *The Revolution, or, Britain Delivered* (1801). The date of Rainsford's death is uncertain. His sister Frances (*d.* 1809) married, first, in 1774, Major-General Wellbore Ellis Doyle (*d*, 1797), and, second, Count Joseph Grimaldi, brother of the prince of Monaco.

J. M. RIGG, rev. ELIZABETH BAIGENT

Sources Allibone, *Dict.* · *GM*, 1st ser., 102/2 (1832), 512 · M. Rainsford, *A memoir of transactions that took place in St. Domingo in the spring of 1799* (1802) · J. Foster, *The peerage, baronetage, and knightage of the British empire* [1880–83]

Rainsford, Sir Richard (1605–1680), judge and politician, was born at Staverton, near Daventry, Northamptonshire, the second son of Robert Rainsford and his second wife, Mary, daughter of Thomas Kirton of Thorpe Mandeville, Northamptonshire. He matriculated from Exeter College, Oxford, on 13 December 1622, but left the university before receiving a degree. On 24 May 1625 Rainsford was admitted to Lincoln's Inn. He was called to the bar on 16 October 1632, having been elected recorder of Daventry in the interval. On 30 May 1637 he married Catherine (*d.* 1698), daughter of Samuel Clerke, rector of St Peter's, Northampton, with whom he had eleven children. In 1653 Rainsford was elected deputy recorder of Northampton, a post he lost to a Cromwellian supporter during the protectorate.

At the Restoration Rainsford represented the Northampton borough in the Convention of 1660 and in Charles II's first parliament in 1661. In this capacity he delivered nine recorded speeches and was a member of thirty-two committees. He favoured increased regulation of the press, particularly unauthorized Anglican publications, supported King Charles's Worcester House declaration, and sought to scrutinize land purchases made during the interregnum. He became a serjeant-at-law on 26 October 1660, was made a knight in 1661, and was appointed a baron of the exchequer on 16 November 1663, under the tenure of Sir Matthew Hale. In 1665 Rainsford became a symbol of persecution for the Quakers, when he presided over the general quarter sessions in Northampton. After he tried many of the nonconformist religious group for refusing to take the oath of allegiance, they publicly denounced the 'unjust and illegal proceedings' of Rainsford and his fellow judges of the exchequer (*Another Outcry*, 1).

Rainsford sat in the exchequer for five years before being transferred to the king's bench on 6 February 1669. Henry Hyde, the earl of Clarendon, considered him 'a very extraordinary man and an excellent judge' (HoP, *Commons, 1660–90*, 309). Seven years later, when Hale resigned his post, Rainsford succeeded to the chief justiceship on 12 April 1676, despite gossip that it was he 'who most commonly slept on the bench' (Cromartie, 122). In his brief stint as lord chief justice, Rainsford's most significant constitutional case transpired in June 1677 after Anthony Ashley Cooper, the first earl of Shaftesbury, was imprisoned in the Tower by the House of Lords for treason. Shaftesbury claimed that the warrant to imprison him was illegal, but was denied a writ of habeas corpus. In a controversial decision, Rainsford found that the king's bench had no jurisdiction to allow a member of the House of Lords or Commons who had been sentenced and committed by parliament to be released from his sentence, even though such a writ would be valid in an ordinary tribunal. In June 1678 Rainsford was removed from office and replaced as lord chief justice by Sir William Scroggs. Whether he was dismissed for political reasons, as some biographers have suggested, or because of his age and declining health, cannot be determined (Campbell, 2.19; Foss, *Judges*, 7.157). Over the next eight months Rainsford's

Sir Richard Rainsford (1605–1680), by Gerard Soest, 1678

health deteriorated rapidly and he died on 17 February 1680 at his manor home in Dallington, Northamptonshire. Though his exact wealth at death is difficult to ascertain, he had inherited patrimonial property estimated at £600 a year on the death of his elder brother in the 1650s, and on retirement he received an annuity equal to his salary. A portion of his wealth helped to found an almshouse in Northamptonshire. A monument in his honour was erected at Dallington parish church, where his remains were interred.   SUSANNA CALKINS

Sources Foss, *Judges* · John, Lord Campbell, *The lives of the chief justices of England*, 2 (1851) · Foster, *Alum. Oxon.* · *Another outcry of the innocent and oppressed* (1665) · *CSP dom.*, 1663–4, 341; 1665–6, 496; 1670, 694 · R. West, *Profitableness of piety* (1671) · DNB · A. Cromartie, *Sir Matthew Hale, 1609–1676* (1995) · HoP, *Commons, 1660–90*, 3.309
Likenesses W. P. Claret, oils, *c.*1668, Gov. Art Coll. · G. Soest, oils, 1678, Lincoln's Inn, London [*see illus.*] · G. Soest, oils, copy, NPG · Tompson, engraving (after Claret) · M. Wright, oils; known to be at Guildhall, 1896
Wealth at death £600 from patrimonial property; plus annuity equivalent to salary: Campbell, *Lives of chief justices*, 2; Foss, *Judges*

Rainton, Sir Nicholas (1569–1646), mayor of London, was baptized on 10 June 1569 at Heighington in the parish of Washingborough, Lincolnshire, the third son of Robert Rainton and his wife, Margaret. From his marriage on 16 November 1602 at St Christopher-le-Stocks to Rebecca (*d.* 1640), daughter of Thomas Moulson, he was to have a son, Nicholas, and five grandchildren, who all predeceased him. He was free of the Haberdashers' Company and traded as a mercer in Lombard Street in satin and taffeta imported from Florence and velvet from Genoa. He came to enjoy considerable wealth and had a mansion house,

Forty Hall, built for him at Enfield by Inigo Jones in 1629–33. His portrait, painted by William Dobson in 1643, hangs over the fireplace. His 1636 enclosure of a considerable area of common land in Enfield encountered great local resentment, and a legal challenge by dispossessed commoners, and after his death there was anti-enclosure rioting.

During the 1620s and 1630s Rainton ascended the civic hierarchy: sheriff in 1621–2, alderman of the wards of Tower (1621–34) and Cornhill (1634–46), and lord mayor in 1632–3, with a knighthood conferred on 5 May 1633. He also served two terms, 1622–3 and 1632–3, as master of the Haberdashers' Company and was president of St Bartholomew's Hospital from 1634 until his death. Yet he was exceptional among his senior aldermanic colleagues for his undoubted puritan sympathies. In 1632 he was elected chairman by the London feoffees of impropriations, a puritan body (suppressed by Archbishop Laud in 1633) which aimed to install more godly clergy in the church by buying out lay owners of livings. He carried these religious sympathies with him to his final days, for among the clerical beneficiaries in his 1646 will were Thomas Foxley, former clerk to the feoffees and a principal victim of Laudian rule, and two other godly divines who had become leading city presbyterians. During his mayoralty Rainton also clashed with the bishop of London when the latter challenged the traditional practice of lord mayors having their sword of office carried before them into St Paul's Cathedral.

Along with most of his fellow aldermen Rainton refused the king's request for a loan in June 1639, more perhaps for practical than political objections. Despite close ties of family and friendship with two future parliamentarian aldermen, Richard Chambers and John Kendrick, his parliamentary sympathies appear to have declined in the early 1640s, or old age may have handicapped more active involvement. In May 1640 he was one of four aldermen committed to prison by the privy council for the defiant way they refused to draw up lists of ward inhabitants able to contribute to a royal loan. Yet in the disputed common council elections of December 1641 he clashed dramatically with some Cornhill ward electors who were determined to unseat two longstanding councillors and replace them with pro-parliamentary radicals. In the following month he was nominated to the new London militia committee but he made his excuses and was replaced by Alderman John Warner. During the trial of the pro-royalist lord mayor Richard Gurney in July, he gave evidence in Gurney's defence and visited him in the Tower. He was also one of three senior aldermen who pleaded ill health when asked by parliament to act as deputy mayor. However, after Gurney's conviction, he carried out parliament's instructions and called a common hall to elect a new lord mayor.

After the summer of 1642 Rainton faded from political view. He died on 19 August 1646 and was buried on 15 September in St Andrew's, Enfield. A spectacular funeral monument, grimly recording in effigy the deaths of Rainton and his wife, their son and daughter-in-law, and all their grandchildren, still survives in the church. His will, made on 2 May 1646 and proved on the following 11 September, bequeathed property in Middlesex, London, and Lincolnshire, made several charitable donations, and left a total of over £4000 in individual bequests to relatives and friends. His heir and executor was his great-nephew, Nicholas Rainton. KEITH LINDLEY

Sources D. Pam, *A parish near London: a history of Enfield, before 1837* (1990), vol. 1 of *A parish near London: a history of Enfield*, 36, 38, 109, 111, 114, 116, 146, 147 · PRO, PROB 11/197/130 · W. Robinson, *The history and antiquities of Enfield in the county of Middlesex*, 1 (1823), 109, 234–5, 239; 2 (1823), 31–2, 34 · A. B. Beaven, ed., *The aldermen of the City of London, temp. Henry III–[1912]*, 2 (1913), 55, 178 · V. Pearl, *London and the outbreak of the puritan revolution: city government and national politics, 1625–1643* (1961); repr. with corrections (1964), 304–5 · journals, CLRO, court of common council, vol. 40, fol. 21v · *CSP dom., 1640*, 142–3, 155 · parish register, St Christopher-le-Stocks, 16 Nov 1602, GL, MS 4421/1 [marriage] · M. A. E. Green, ed., *Calendar of the proceedings of the committee for advance of money, 1642–1656*, 2, PRO (1888), 722 · J. Foster, ed., *The visitation of Middlesex, 1663* (1887), 26 · *DNB* · *JHL*, 5 (1642–3), 284
Likenesses W. Dobson, oils, 1643, Forty Hall, Enfield, Middlesex · W. Dobson?, oils, 1643, St Bartholomew's Hospital, London; repro. in Robinson, *History and antiquities of Enfield*, 2.31–2 · funeral monument, St Andrew's Church, Enfield
Wealth at death over £4000 bequeathed to family and friends; plus Forty Hall and property in Middlesex, London, and Lincolnshire; also several charitable bequests; assessed (for levy purposes) at £2000 on 21 Aug 1646: will, PRO, PROB 11/197/130

Rainy, Adam Rolland (1862–1911). *See under* Rainy, Robert (1826–1906).

Rainy, Harry (1792–1876), expert in forensic medicine, was born at Creich, Sutherland, on 20 October 1792, the youngest son of George Rainy (*d.* 1810), minister of Creich, and his wife, Anne (*d.* 1833), daughter of the Revd Gilbert Robertson of Kincardine. Rainy matriculated at Glasgow University in 1806 and began medical studies there in 1808. In 1810 he transferred to the Edinburgh medical school, where he studied for a further two years. After a two-year stint as clerk to the Glasgow Royal Infirmary, he spent a year in Paris, from 1814 to 1815, to gain further experience in various hospitals. Rainy's stay in Paris brought him into contact with the great French medical and surgical figures of the day such as Dupuytren, Orfila, and Roux, and he also became interested in ophthalmology. Rainy witnessed the famous 'hundred days' of Napoleon, and on his return journey to Glasgow in 1815 via Germany and Belgium he crossed the field of Waterloo, shortly before the fateful battle.

Rainy's interest in eye surgery remained after his return to Glasgow and in 1824 he helped his friend William Mackenzie to open the city's first eye hospital. Rainy was directed at this point towards general practice, which provided a bedrock for his future finances. He married Barbara (*d.* 1854), daughter of Captain Robert Gordon of Invercharron, on 30 November 1818, the marriage ceremony being performed by Dr Thomas Chalmers. Their eldest son, Robert *Rainy (1826–1906), became principal of the New College, Edinburgh. Their second son, George (1832–1869), was surgeon to the Glasgow Eye Infirmary, and lecturer at the university in 1868.

In 1832 Rainy obtained a substitute university lectureship on the theory of physic, on behalf of the absent valetudinarian professor of the institutes of medicine, Charles Badham, who resided in the south of France. Badham retained his professorial stipend and took one quarter of the student fees, Rainy taking the remaining three-quarters. Rainy taught well from 1832 to 1839, but from 1839 to 1841 his politics and religious allegiance went against him: he was an ardent tory and a keen supporter of the Free Church of Scotland before and during the Disruption of 1843. In 1839 his subject was split by the whig government, which created a new regius chair for the theory of medicine. The chair went to a prominent whig, Andrew Buchanan.

At the same time, the government also instituted the first regius chair of medical jurisprudence and forensic medicine in the University of Glasgow, created for another staunch whig, Robert Cowan. Disappointed, Rainy then lectured on Badham's other string, the practice of medicine, until Badham retired entirely from the chair in 1840. Rainy was the university's choice for the vacant chair and had strong support, but he was deliberately excluded. The lord advocate appointed the whig William Thomson, son of the Edinburgh professor of pathology. The whig government fell in August 1841 and in October, after a long period of illness, Robert Cowan died. On Cowan's death, the university senate applied to Sir Robert Peel on behalf of Rainy. He was appointed within the month, aged almost fifty, as the second Glasgow professor of medical jurisprudence and forensic police.

Rainy was the last overt political appointment to a Scottish regius chair of public health and forensic medicine. Although by 1841 he was a man of wide experience, he was not a medical jurist cast in the mould of Robert Christison. Rainy's tall, erect figure and fine features rarely graced the witness box mainly because, according to a contemporary, 'he was not only cross looking, but was easily made cross. This was an unfortunate trait in a professor of medical jurisprudence … Counsel quickly discovered that they could make little of him' (Anderson, 8–9). Nevertheless, Rainy was a good teacher and an able chemist. In the first instance he took Christison's line and dropped Cowan's medical police (public health) string from lectures, and he styled himself professor of forensic medicine. Considering that the impetus for the chair's origins lay in Cowan's dedication to improving public health (Cowan styled himself professor of medical police), Rainy's decision was unfortunate for Glasgow and the west of Scotland, which was struggling with the worst excesses of industrialization. Medical students wishing to study public health subjects turned either to Glasgow's extramural schools or to Edinburgh.

Rainy taught forensic medicine to medical students and medical jurisprudence to law students. His lectures, which were delivered without notes, indicate the widening concerns of forensic medicine, and despite a well-recorded cold and forbidding demeanour he was held in warm and high regard. His main medical research contributions lay in toxicology, notably the study of arsenic, and the cooling time of dead bodies. The latter subject, undertaken in collaboration with Joseph Coates, then lecturer in pathology, resulted in a formula known as 'Rainy's curve', which provided a useful rule of thumb for this still inexact corner of medical science.

Rainy retired from the chair in 1862. The university bestowed on him the degree of LLD in 1876 on the installation of Disraeli as rector of the university. Rainy died in Glasgow on 6 August 1876.   BRENDA M. WHITE

Sources *BMJ* (19 Aug 1876), 251 · *The Times* (18 Aug 1876) · *The Scotsman* (8 Aug 1876) · *Fasti Scot.* · *The Lancet* (10 Aug 1839) · *The Lancet* (23 Oct 1842) · *The Lancet* (13 Nov 1842) · NA Scot., Dalhousie muniments, GD45/9/9/1 · senate minutes, U. Glas., Archives and Business Records Centre, GUA 89 · W. Anderson, *Four chiefs of the Glasgow Royal Infirmary* (1916) · M. A. Crowther and B. White, *On soul and conscience: the medical expert and crime* (1988) · D. Murray, *Memories of the old college of Glasgow: some chapters in the history of the university* (1927) · L. Davidson, 'Identities ascertained: British ophthalmology in the first half of the nineteenth century', *Social History of Medicine*, 9 (1996), 313–33 · parish register (marriage), Glasgow, 30 Nov 1818 · *CCI* (1877)
Archives U. Edin., New Coll. L., letters to Thomas Chalmers
Likenesses T. Annan, photograph, NPG · C. Holl and F. A. Roberts, stipple (after G. Richmond), NPG · portrait, U. Glas., department of forensic medicine and science · portrait, repro. in Crowther and White, *On soul and conscience*
Wealth at death £29,438 12s. 7d.: confirmation, 25 Jan 1877, *CCI*

Rainy, Robert (1826–1906), United Free Church of Scotland minister, elder son of Harry *Rainy MD (1792–1876), professor of forensic medicine in Glasgow University, and his wife, Barbara Gordon (d. July 1854), was born at 49 Montrose Street, Glasgow, on 1 January 1826. On 10 October 1835 he entered Glasgow high school, where Alexander Maclaren was his schoolfellow. In October 1838 he proceeded to Glasgow University, where he graduated MA in April 1844. He had been taken by his father's friend Robert Buchanan (1802–1875) to the debates in the general assembly of 1841 leading to the Disruption; when the Disruption came in 1843 he felt a vocation to the ministry of the Free Church. However, his father intended him for the medical profession, and on his father's advice he gave a year (1843–4) to medical study. In 1844 he entered the Divinity Hall of the Free Church (New College, Edinburgh), studying under Thomas Chalmers, David Welsh, William Cunningham, 'rabbi' John Duncan, and Alexander Campbell Fraser. He was at this time a member of the famous Speculative Society of Edinburgh University.

Rainy was licensed on 7 November 1849 by the Free Church presbytery of Glasgow, and for six months had charge of a mission at Inchinnan, near Renfrew. By Elizabeth, dowager duchess of Gordon, he was made chaplain at Huntly Lodge; declining other calls, he became minister of Huntly Free Church, ordained there by Strathbogie presbytery on 12 January 1851. His reputation was such that in 1854 he was called to Free High Church, Edinburgh, in succession to Robert Gordon. As he wished to remain in Huntly his presbytery declined (12 April 1854) to sustain the call, as did the synod; the general assembly (22 May 1854) transferred him to Edinburgh, henceforth his

Robert Rainy (1826–1906), by Sir George Reid

home. After moving to Edinburgh Rainy married one of his parishioners, Susan (b. 1835), daughter of Adam Rolland of Gask, on 2 December 1857. Their first son lived only briefly; they subsequently had three sons and three daughters. Susan Rainy was active in the Free Church and was convenor of the Women's Temporary Committee in 1903. She died on 30 September 1905. Rainy's pastorate lasted until 1862, when he was made professor of church history in New College, Edinburgh, delivering his inaugural lecture on 7 November 1862. In 1863 he received the degree of DD from Glasgow University. He became principal of the college in 1874, and retained this post until his death, resigning his chair in 1901.

Rainy's position soon became that of the ecclesiastical statesman of his church, of whose assembly he was moderator in 1887, 1900, and 1905. His aim appears to have been to permit gradual 'modernization' of Free Church theology on questions such as biblical criticism, evolution, and the Westminster confession, while simultaneously pursuing disestablishment of the Church of Scotland. During the prosecution of William Robertson Smith (1876–1881), he sought a diplomatic solution, and was successful in preventing the condemnation of Smith's teaching; the price for this was a formal condemnation of Smith on Rainy's motion on 23 May 1881, and Smith's consequent loss of his chair. In 1890 Rainy's diplomatic skills played an important part in the avoidance of prosecution of Marcus Dods and Alexander Balmain Bruce. Rainy gave no clear intellectual lead in these controversies. It has been said of him 'that he had practised the art of concealing his thoughts for so long that he had lost the ability to express them frankly and briefly' (Drummond and Bulloch, 8). His publications were mostly collected lectures and sermons. He also published *Presbyterianism as a Form of Church Life and Work* (1894) and *The Ancient Catholic Church* (1902). He edited *The Presbyterian* (1868–71) and contributed to collections of essays, including W. Wilson's *Memorials of R. S. Candlish* (1880) and F. Hastings's *The Atonement* (1883). Rainy pursued disestablishment with energy and resource, and succeeded in bringing pressure to bear on the Liberal Party leadership whose willingness to give the matter priority was vital. But Welsh rather than Scottish disestablishment took priority in the 1892–5 Liberal government.

Rainy also pursued the objective of a union of the various free churches. In 1876, after prolonged negotiations, he achieved the union of the Reformed Presbyterian synod with the Free Church (the Original Succession synod having been incorporated with the Free Church in 1852). In 1881 he became convenor of his church's Highland committee. His lack of Gaelic disadvantaged him, but between 1882 and 1893 he raised £10,795 for endowment and more than £10,000 for church building, mainly in the Outer Hebrides. Despite this, 'Black Rainy' was not much trusted in Gaelic-speaking areas. The Declaratory Act of 1892, largely passed as a result of his efforts, allowed for a more flexible interpretation of the Westminster confession and further encouraged the Free Church away from rigid Calvinism. Union with the United Presbyterian church was effected on 31 October 1900, with Rainy as the first moderator of the United Free Church. Discontented members of the old Free Church, mostly in Gaelic-speaking areas, won an action claiming for the dissentient minority the ownership of the pre-1900 Free Church property. Rainy co-ordinated the consequent negotiations and presentation of evidence to the royal commission chaired by Lord Elgin, which recommended that the Lords' verdict be reversed by statute; this was achieved by the Scottish Churches Bill (1905). Rainy achieved a fairly satisfactory amendment of the bill in the Commons in favour of the United Free Church. In good health hitherto, Rainy was operated on for an internal disorder and went on a recuperative voyage to Australia in October 1906. He reached Melbourne on 8 December 1906 and died there of lymphadenoma on 22 December. He was buried in the Dean cemetery, Edinburgh, on 7 March 1907.

Rainy's eldest son, **Adam Rolland Rainy** (1862–1911), MA, MB, and CM (Edinburgh), studied at Berlin and Vienna, and practised from 1887 to 1900 as a surgeon oculist in London. He travelled in Australia and New Zealand (1891), in the West Indies (1896), and in Spain and Algiers (1899 and 1903). Entering on political work he contested Kilmarnock burghs in 1900 as a radical, gained the seat in 1906, and held it until his sudden death at North Berwick on 26 August 1911. He married in 1887 Annabella, second daughter of Hugh Matheson of Ross-shire; she survived him with a son and two daughters.

H. C. G. MATTHEW

Sources P. C. Simpson, *The life of Principal Rainy*, 2 vols. (1909) · *The Times* (24 Dec 1906) · *The Highland Witness of the United Free Church of Scotland* (Feb 1907) · A. L. Drummond and J. Bulloch, *The church in late Victorian Scotland* (1978) · W. R. Nicoll, *Princes of the church* (1921) · R. Mackintosh, *Principal Rainy* (1907) · *DSCHT* · Gladstone, *Diaries*
Archives U. Edin., New Coll. L., corresp., lecture notes, etc. | BL, corresp. with W. E. Gladstone, Add. MSS 44444–44515 · NL Scot., corresp., mainly with Lord Rosebery
Likenesses G. Reid, portrait, before 1894, U. Edin., New College; replica, in family possession in 1912 · J. Bowie, oils, Scot. NPG · G. Reid, oils, Scot. NPG [*see illus.*] · eight portraits, repro. in *Highland Witness* · photographs, repro. in Simpson, *Life of Principal Rainy* · two portraits, repro. in Mackintosh, *Principal Rainy*
Wealth at death £5838 5s. 6d.: confirmation, 20 Feb 1907, CCI

Raisin, Catherine Alice (1855–1945), geologist and educationist, was born at 13 Camden Terrace, Camden New Town, London, on 24 April 1855, the daughter of (Daniel) Francis Raisin, pannierman at the Inner Temple, and his wife, Sarah Catherine, *née* Woodgate. She was educated at North London Collegiate School and at University College, London, which she entered in 1873, although she also taught at her old school until 1875. She studied botany, taking the honours examinations as a private student, and also geology and mineralogy. When University of London degrees were opened to women in 1878, she concentrated on botany, geology (studying under T. G. Bonney), and zoology (under T. H. Huxley). After taking her BSc in 1884, with second-class honours in geology and third-class in zoology, she stayed on at University College as voluntary research assistant to Professor Bonney. In 1898 she was awarded a DSc, only the second woman geologist to receive this degree from the University of London. She was elected a fellow of University College in 1902.

After serving as demonstrator in botany at Bedford College for Women from 1886 to 1890, Raisin succeeded Grenville A. J. Cole as head of the geology department, becoming the first woman head of a geology department in a British university. From 1907 she was also Norton Sumner lecturer in geology; she held both posts until her retirement in 1920. From 1890 to 1907 she also headed the botany department, and, from 1898 to 1901, was vice-principal of the college.

The Geological Society of London awarded Raisin the Lyell fund in 1893, the first such honour given a woman. It was accepted for her by Professor Bonney, since women were not then allowed to attend meetings of the society. She became one of the first women fellows in 1919, when women were finally admitted.

Much of Raisin's work was in microscopic petrology and mineralogy, interests she had developed when training under Bonney. She was known as an excellent microscopist. Her first research, an examination of the metamorphic rocks of south Devon, was notable as one of the early attempts to map metamorphic facies. Other work included field and laboratory studies of rocks from the Ardennes and Switzerland, and the petrography of rock collections from the Himalayas and many parts of Africa. She published twenty-four scientific papers between 1887 and 1905. Her best-known work was her detailed investigation of the microscopic structure of minerals forming

Catherine Alice Raisin (1855–1945), by unknown photographer [standing, in the botany library at Bedford College]

serpentine, published as a joint paper with Bonney in 1905 (*Quarterly Journal of the Geological Society*).

Remembered by colleagues as a strong, vigorous, and charming woman, Raisin was also a 'character', who ruled absolutely in her department and dealt summarily with opposition. An outstanding teacher, she paid close attention to the work of her assistants, and was always solicitous about her students; among them she was affectionately known as 'the Raisin', and (secretly) 'the Sultana'. In committee she could be a formidable opponent. One of Britain's first professional women geologists and a noted pioneer among late nineteenth-century women educationists, Raisin took a keen interest in all aspects of women's advancement. In the late 1870s she founded and organized a discussion group for women, the Somerville Club, which, when it opened in 1880, had 1000 members. She served as its honorary secretary and then as chair. After retiring, Raisin gave much time to various women's groups and to societies for the promotion of women's interests. She was a member of the Geologists' Association for sixty-seven years, and latterly its most senior member. She died on 12 July 1945, unmarried, at Ash Priors Nursing Home, Pitville Circus, Cheltenham and was buried on 17 July.   MARY R. S. CREESE

Sources D. L. Reynolds, 'Dr Catherine Alice Raisin', *Nature*, 156 (1945), 327–8 · [L. Hawkes], *Proceedings of the Geologists' Association*, 57 (1946), 53–4 · E. J. Garwood, *Quarterly Journal of the Geological Society of London*, 102 (1946), xliv–xlv · *The Times* (8 Aug 1945) · Bedford College personnel file, Royal Holloway College, Egham, Surrey, AR150/D168 · b. cert. · general register of graduates and undergraduates, 1900, U. Lond. · *The Times* (16 July 1945), 1 · CGPLA Eng. & Wales (1946) · d. cert.
Likenesses photograph, Royal Holloway College, Egham, Surrey [*see illus.*]
Wealth at death £12,117 8s. 4d.: probate, 3 Jan 1946, CGPLA Eng. & Wales

Raistrick, Arthur (1896–1991), industrial archaeologist and pacifist, was born in Saltaire, Yorkshire, on 16 August 1896, the son of George Raistrick, engineer, and his wife, Minnie, *née* Bell. This model industrial village had been built by manufacturer Titus Salt, in whose mill Arthur Raistrick's mother and several aunts and uncles were employed. His father was a founder member of the Independent Labour Party (ILP), formed in nearby Bradford in 1892. His four grandparents came from four different Yorkshire dales, their families involved in farming and lead mining. School holidays were spent visiting relatives in the dales, walking as far as Swaledale, some 50 miles away, sleeping in barns on the longer trips. This was his inheritance—socialist-pacifist, walker (he never had a car), and lover of the Pennine landscapes.

From Drummond Road elementary school in Shipley, he won a scholarship to Bradford grammar school. He left at the age of sixteen to become an engineering apprentice, continuing his education at evening classes. Passionately devoted to music, he played the organ in the local Wesleyan chapel. In 1915 he abandoned his work and study to travel with an uncle through the north of England, speaking at pacifist meetings. Refusing to do military service, he spent nearly three years in prison, in Wormwood Scrubs and Durham. His pacifism was rooted in the anti-war stance of the ILP, but some of his fellow prisoners were Quakers, and he joined the Society of Friends in 1919.

Released from prison in September 1919, Raistrick took up a scholarship at Leeds University which he had gained while an apprentice, and graduated in civil engineering. He stayed on to complete an MSc, followed by a PhD in geology, specializing in the composition of coal seams. His record as a conscientious objector was not helpful in the search for employment, and for a few years he survived on research grants, contract work for the Coal Mine Owners' Association and the modest rewards of teaching adult classes for the Workers' Educational Association (WEA). In 1929 he was appointed lecturer in applied geology at Armstrong (later King's) College, Newcastle, and was able on 17 April in the following year to marry fellow scholar (Sarah) Elizabeth Chapman (1891/2–1973). In addition to their home in Newcastle, the couple kept a cottage, later replaced by a house converted from a barn, in the Wharfedale village of Linton.

In the early 1930s the Raistricks planned to go as Quaker missionaries to China, but the sudden death of Arthur's father caused the trip to be cancelled. If Arthur Raistrick rarely travelled far physically—he would never have thought of holidaying away from the Pennines—his intellectual journeys went far beyond the range of most scholars. Five of his first seven published papers (1925–7) were on aspects of glaciation. His expertise in coalmining broadened into a general involvement in the history of technology, especially lead mining and smelting and ironworking. Glaciation led him to an interest in field archaeology, and he combined this with the history of technology to produce industrial archaeology, which he practised long before the term came into general use in

Arthur Raistrick (1896–1991), by W. R. Mitchell

the 1950s. He had published in all the above areas by 1929. Later he moved sideways again, into social history, with studies of the south Yorkshire ironmasters and the (Quaker) London Lead Company, the latter published as *Two Centuries of Industrial Welfare* (1938).

By that time another war was in prospect, and Raistrick helped to found the Pacifist Advisory Bureau. In 1939 he refused to add his name to a government register of engineering specialists whose skills might be used in the war effort, with the consequence, in his own words, that King's College 'just had to suspend me'—without pay (Joy, 13). He spent the war years at Linton, living partly off the produce of a small plot of land there, and taking WEA classes. For the benefit of WEA students he wrote *Teach yourself Geology* (1943). He normally had such readers, rather than academic specialists in mind when he wrote. He supplied many articles to the *Yorkshire Dalesman* on such topics as vernacular architecture, drystone walls, and green roads. He was the exact opposite of the kind of historian who researches the lives of people in the past without having the slightest interest in their counterparts in the present. During the depression of the early 1930s, for example, he toured the stricken south Wales coalfield, speaking at miners' welfare clubs and visiting camps for the unemployed.

After holding a fellowship at Woodbrooke, a Quaker college, in 1945–6, Raistrick was invited to return to King's College. His prolific output, including *Quakers in Science and Industry* (1950) and *Dynasty of Iron Founders: the Darbys and Coalbrookdale* (1953), led to his promotion to reader in 1954. He retired in 1956 to devote himself to activities in the Yorkshire dales, including membership of the national parks committee and his adult education work.

Raistrick conducted regular evening classes for the WEA and Leeds University extramural department until

he was well into his seventies. In addition he taught for the local adult schools (an educational movement with a Quaker flavour) and at residential centres including the West Riding Adult College at Grantley Hall and the Malham Tarn field centre. For the WEA he conducted linked weekend courses in youth hostels, a successful attempt to attract young workers into adult education. He aimed to turn curiosity into scholarship by encouraging his students to be active in fieldwork and careful in recording, and especially to use their eyes in reading the landscape as a historical document.

Raistrick's other activities were all of a piece with his research and teaching. He served as president of both the Holiday Fellowship and the Ramblers' Association, and was active in the campaign for wider access to moorland. He gave much attention to national parks, especially the two in Yorkshire. He edited and co-wrote the guide to the North York Moors Park. His involvement with the Society of Friends lasted for over seventy years, and he served for a time as clerk to the Settle monthly meeting.

Raistrick continued to publish on a broad front. In 1965, for example, his works included four pieces in the *Yorkshire Archaeological Journal* reporting on thirteen archaeological sites in Airedale and Wharfedale; *Vikings, Angles and Danes in Yorkshire*; *The Coalbrookdale Company, 1709–1959*; and, with B. Jennings, *A History of Lead Mining in the Pennines*. The publications of his seventies would have represented a respectable career achievement for most academics. They included three books deriving from his lifelong interest in the landscape as a record, *Old Yorkshire Dales* (1967), *The Pennine Dales* (1968), and a volume in the Making of the English Landscape series, *The West Riding of Yorkshire* (1970). One of his most important books is *Industrial Archaeology* (1972), designed to encourage 'a balanced investigation of industry from pre-Roman times to the present', instead of what he saw as an obsession with measuring textile mills. It was as well that he was so busy, as in 1973 his wife Elizabeth died, at the age of eighty-one.

As Raistrick was a broadbrush writer, in several disciplines, publishing over a period of sixty years, it is inevitable that some of his works have been, and others will be, overtaken by, for example, progress in archaeological techniques and in the range of sources used for local history. However, a book such as *The Pennine Dales* could survive periodic updating without the distinctive Raistrick quality being diminished. It is doubtful if anyone will ever match his combination of technical, economic, and social knowledge of the lead mining industry.

Raistrick received many honours, including medals and awards from the Geological Society and the Yorkshire Archaeological Society, and honorary doctorates from the universities of Leeds (1972) and Bradford (1974). The chancellor of Bradford was Harold Wilson, and after the Labour leader had won the general election of October 1974, he offered an OBE to Raistrick. The latter responded:

As a lifelong member of the Independent Labour Party I have frequently spoken against the system of the honours list. I feel that I cannot at this time break my principles and accept the prime minister's suggestion. My thanks for the thought so expressed are no less sincere and I shall value this gesture more than I could value the honour itself. (Correspondence in family possession)

A few days later Wilson wrote a friendly personal letter, regretting but respecting Raistrick's decision.

Throughout his life, Raistrick drew spiritual strength as well as intellectual stimulus from the Pennine hills, where 'quiet and healing solitude … refreshment of body, mind and spirit … can be found after the exertion of the climb' (Joy, 154). The hills inspired some of his finest writing, as in this description of the view from Cross Fell at sunset:

In the evening light the western edge of the long ridge, of which Cross Fell is the highest part, seems to plunge down at a fearful rate into the vale of Eden more than two thousand feet below, while far across the vale the Lake District mountains stand in glorious silhouette against the sunset sky. To the north, still more lightly sketched in, are the outlines of the Solway Firth, on rare occasions glowing like burnished gold under the last rays of the sun … To the east a wide extent of dusky moorlands steadily declines in broad ridges between shadow-filled valleys, until both are lost in the distance. (A. Raistrick, *The Pennine Dales*, 1972, 15)

Raistrick died in a nursing home at Skipton, Yorkshire, on 9 April 1991. BERNARD JENNINGS

Sources T. Croucher, *Boots and books: the work and writings of Arthur Raistrick* (1995) · D. Joy, ed., *Arthur Raistrick's Yorkshire dales* (1991) · M. W. Beresford, 'Dr Arthur Raistrick', *Yorkshire Archaeological Journal*, 64 (1992), 212–13 · private information (2004) [Mrs Elinor Rea, William Rea; U. Newcastle] · personal knowledge (2004) · *CGPLA Eng. & Wales* (1991)

Archives Craven Museum, Skipton, Yorkshire collections · Ironbridge Gorge Museum, Telford, research papers relating to Darby family, industry in Yorkshire and Shropshire · Skipton Reference Library, Yorkshire collections

Likenesses W. R. Mitchell, photograph, repro. in Croucher, *Boots and books* [see illus.] · photographs, repro. in Croucher, *Boots and books*

Wealth at death £193,723: probate, 24 May 1991, *CGPLA Eng. & Wales*

Raistrick, Harold (1890–1971), chemist, was born on 26 November 1890 at Pudsey in the West Riding of Yorkshire, the second of four children (and eldest surviving son) of Mark Walker Raistrick, an engineer in the local woollen mill, and his wife, Bertha Anne Galloway, a local elementary schoolteacher. The family was quite poor, and during Raistrick's childhood every penny had to be watched. Social intercourse centred on the local Primitive Methodist chapel. Attendance at the morning and evening services, and afternoon Sunday school, occupied most of Sunday. Indulgence in smoking and alcohol was prohibited as much from religious conviction as from financial necessity. Education was highly regarded as a means of improving status and financial prospects and also for assisting personal growth.

Raistrick went to the local elementary school where he obtained a scholarship at the age of eleven. This enabled him to enter Leeds central high school, which had a strong science tradition. A trusted and able pupil, he acted as a 'lab boy'. For this, he was paid 1s. per day and was permitted to experiment as he wished during, and sometimes after, school hours. At seventeen he secured a county major scholarship and progressed to Leeds University chemistry department where the professor, Julius Cohen, inspired in him an interest in unravelling the structures of organic molecules of biological significance.

Having gained in 1912 a first-class BSc and in 1913 an MSc, Raistrick decided to work with the German sugar chemist Emil Fischer. However, the war prevented this and Raistrick, debarred from active military service by ill health, went to Cambridge instead, working first in the agriculture department and transferring in 1915 to work under the supervision of the biochemist Frederick Gowland Hopkins. In 1917 he married Martha Louisa (d. 1945), daughter of Jonathan Coates, of Pudsey. They later had two daughters, both of whom became doctors of medicine. In 1920 (the same year in which he obtained his Leeds DSc) Raistrick became head of the biochemical department of Nobel's explosives company in Stevenston, Ayrshire. He left in 1929 to become professor of biochemistry at the London School of Hygiene and Tropical Medicine, a post he held until retirement in 1956.

Raistrick's approach to his scientific work was meticulous and persevering, reflecting the values inculcated in his youth. Undeterred by laborious bench procedures he applied existing methods of research to a greater effect than many of his contemporaries, though having fewer human and material resources. His output of high-quality scientific work was outstanding.

In his early work on the breakdown of amino acids by bacteria Raistrick was the first to show that they could be converted to unsaturated acids. His speculations on the mechanism of bacterial breakdown of simple organic acids contained elements of the famous citric acid cycle for which Hans Krebs received the Nobel prize thirty years later. There followed a long series of researches on the metabolic products of micro-organisms from pure strains of lower fungi grown in various media, some of which were antibiotics. His achievement in the isolation, structure identification, and synthesis of many of these important and often labile substances is remarkable. They included the mould tropolones, the tetronic acids, griseofulvin, and the fungal polyhydroxy benzoquinones and anthraquinones. His skill and reliability commanded the respect of both the biochemical fraternity and of organic chemists such as A. R. Todd and Robert Robinson, who collaborated and published with him. Raistrick was elected FRS in 1934. During the Second World War he was scientific adviser on penicillin production to the Ministry of Supply. He was Bakerian lecturer of the Royal Society in 1949 and Flintoff medallist of the Chemical Society in 1963.

Despite the evident high esteem of his colleagues Raistrick remained to the end the firm lipped, quiet Yorkshireman who drew refreshment from solitary fishing, and walking in the fells. Following the death of his first wife, in 1947 he married Betty Helen, daughter of Edward Young, of London. Raistrick died on 8 March 1971 at Felpham in Sussex.   FRED DAINTON, rev.

Sources J. H. Birkinshaw, *Memoirs FRS*, 18 (1972), 489–509 · personal knowledge (1986) · *The Times* (11 March 1971), 18h · *The Times* (19 March 1971), 22g · *CGPLA Eng. & Wales* (1971)
Archives Wellcome L., letters
Likenesses W. Stoneman, photograph, 1934, NPG
Wealth at death £12,692: probate, 26 April 1971, *CGPLA Eng. & Wales*

Rait, Sir Robert Sangster (1874–1936), historian and university principal, was born on 10 February 1874 at Narborough, Leicestershire, elder son and fourth child of David Rait and his wife, Elizabeth Sangster, who both came from Aberdeen. David Rait's service with the Inland Revenue took them back to Aberdeen, and Robert was educated at Old Meldrum parish school, Aberdeen grammar school, and King's College, Aberdeen, where he graduated MA in 1894. After acting as assistant to the professor of logic and attending classes in the Free Church Divinity Hall he won an exhibition in history at New College, Oxford, in 1896. H. A. L. Fisher was one of his teachers and among his friends was John Buchan, who nominated him for the post of secretary of the Oxford Union in 1898.

Rait was awarded a first class in modern history in 1899 and in the same year won the Stanhope essay prize for 'The Scottish parliament', published in 1901 as *The Scottish Parliament before the Union of the Crowns*. Elected to a fellowship at New College in 1900, he found life as a fellow, lecturer, and tutor congenial. For three years he was dean and for five years librarian. His students included Philip Kerr, later marquess of Lothian and ambassador to the USA. He published an edition of Acts of the Interregnum (1911) and biographies (1903, 1911) of two Victorian field marshals: Viscount Gough, who had served in the Peninsular War, Ireland, China, and India where his tactics during the Sikh wars in the 1840s had been controversial; and Sir Frederick Haines, a veteran of Crimea. In 1908 Rait married Ruth Edith Mary, elder daughter of John Charles Edward Bridge of Aylesbury. They had two daughters.

There had been extensive publication of Scottish historical sources, both officially and by private societies, during the nineteenth century, and with the foundation of the Sir William Fraser chair at Edinburgh in 1901 the subject became recognized by the universities. A decade later Glasgow University followed with its chair of Scottish history and literature, in which history dominated. Rait had a natural interest in the history of his native land—his first book (1895) was a history of the two universities of Aberdeen and he edited sources on Mary, queen of Scots (1899)—and he was appointed to the Glasgow post in 1913.

From 1915 to 1918 Rait served in the war trade intelligence department in London and was appointed CBE. As professor, he did not confine his writing to specialist readers: besides a one-volume history of Scotland (1915) and a history of the Union Bank (1930), he made many anonymous contributions to the *Glasgow Herald* and surveyed modern developments in the *Encyclopaedia*

Britannica new volumes (13th edition). He contributed to the *Scottish Review* under John Buchan's editorship in 1907 and to Nelson's The Teaching of History series under Buchan as general editor from 1928 to 1930. With a junior colleague, George Pryde, he wrote *Scotland* (1934), a collaboration which Pryde described as a command performance interrupting his editorial work for the Scottish History Society. Rait became president of the society in 1933 in succession to Buchan and took the opportunity to reproach English historians for their contemptuous attitude to Scottish history.

Rait's most important book, *The Parliaments of Scotland* (1924), returned to the subject of his Oxford Stanhope essay. Modifications in detail later emerged, for instance in regard to committees under the covenanters and the electoral system. At about the time of Rait's death the Scottish committee of the history of parliament began a study of burgh and shire commissioners which was eventually completed in 1992. It has been claimed that Rait, mesmerized by Stubbs's view of English history and taking an overly constitutional approach, exaggerated the subservience of parliament. Nevertheless the book has remained for remarkably long the standard work on the subject.

In 1929 Rait was appointed principal of Glasgow University by the secretary of state for Scotland. Some observers were surprised that he decided to resign as historiographer royal for Scotland, an office which went back to the time of the Restoration and which he had held for ten years in succession to Professor Hume Brown. He did so with regret, taking the view that, although no specific duties were required, the post of historiographer royal should pass to someone who would have more time for any necessary research work than his new responsibilities would allow.

Rait was principal and vice-chancellor of the University of Glasgow at a time of economic stringency. His main achievements were to introduce new arrangements for the faculty of divinity following the union of the Church of Scotland and the Free Church, to sell Queen Margaret College to the BBC, and to provide for a new chemistry building. Colleagues found him approachable, but to others he appeared increasingly distant. He was knighted in 1933, elected an honorary fellow of New College, Oxford, in the same year, and received honorary doctorates from the universities of Aberdeen (1921), Glasgow (1930), and Edinburgh and Lyons (1933). He was a justice of the peace and deputy lieutenant of Glasgow. From the time when the National Library of Scotland was founded by the transfer of the Advocates' Library in 1925 he had been a trustee, and he became chairman in 1932. In addition to his residence in Glasgow he owned a house at Blairmore on the Clyde coast.

In September 1935 Rait became ill, and in May 1936 he announced that he would resign at the end of September; his condition deteriorated, however, and he died at the Principal's Lodging, Glasgow University, on 25 May 1936; his wife survived him. His reputation as principal inevitably became somewhat overshadowed by the outstanding tenure of his successor, Sir Hector Hetherington, but the expansion of Scottish historical studies after the Second World War owed much to Rait's academic leadership.

D. M. ABBOTT

Sources *Aberdeen University Review*, 23 (1936), 253–4 • files on historiographer royal, NA Scot., HH1/1068-1070 • *DNB* • *WWW*, 1929–40 • M. Moss, J. F. Munro, and R. Trainor, *University, city and state: the University of Glasgow since 1870* (2000) • A. Lownie, *John Buchan: the Presbyterian cavalier* (1995) • J. Kirk, *Her majesty's historiographer: Gordon Donaldson, 1913–1993* (1996) • G. Donaldson, 'The Scottish History Society, 1886–1986', *Acts of the lords of the isles, 1336–1493*, ed. J. Munro and R. W. Munro, Scottish History Society, 4th ser., 22 (1986), 357–73 • C. Kidd, 'Constructions of the past', *SHR*, 76 (1997), 86–102 • W. Ferguson, 'The electoral system in the Scottish counties before 1832', *Miscellany two*, Stair Society (1984)
Archives NA Scot., letters • U. Glas., Archives and Business Records Centre, official archives • U. Glas. L., notebooks containing lectures on Scottish history and literature | NL Scot., letters to Alexander Campbell Fraser • U. Glas. L., letters to Mrs Barrett-Lennard
Likenesses J. Gunn, oils (posthumous), U. Glas. • photograph, repro. in *Aberdeen University Review* • photograph, U. Glas.; repro. in Moss, Munro, and Trainor, *University of Glasgow*, 182–3
Wealth at death £3037 5s. 7d.: confirmation, 4 Aug 1936, CCI

Raithby, John (1766–1826), lawyer, was the eldest son of Edmund Raithby of Edenham, Lincolnshire. Originally a law stationer in Chancery Lane, at the start of the French Revolution he apparently published anonymous pamphlets advocating democracy. On 26 January 1795 he was admitted a member of Lincoln's Inn, and was subsequently called to the bar. He practised in the court of chancery. His legal writings obtained for him a commissionership of bankruptcy; he was also nominated a subcommissioner on the public records. Raithby died at The Grove, Highgate, Middlesex, on 31 August 1826, leaving a widow; his only daughter died young.

Raithby published anonymously, in 1798, *The Study and Practice of the Law Considered*, which appeared in octavo form and was considered a work of great merit; for some time it was attributed to Sir James Mackintosh. An American edition appeared at Portland, Maine, in 1806, and the second English edition was issued at London in 1816 with the author's name. With Sir Thomas Edlyne Tomlins, Raithby issued a new edition in quarto form of the *Statutes at Large, from Magna Charta to the Union, 41 Geo. III* (10 vols., 1811). Tomlins co-operated in the edition down to 49 Geo. III, at which point he relinquished the task to Raithby and Nicholas Simons. Raithby compiled an index to the work, entitled *From Magna Charta to 49 Geo. III*, which appeared in 1814 in one volume in quarto form, and in three volumes in octavo form. He also compiled alphabetical and chronological indexes to the *Statutes of the Realm*, which were published by the record commissioners in 1824 and 1828, and he wrote *The Law and Principle of Money Considered* (1811). Apart from his work in the field of legal writing, Raithby also tried his hand at fiction and produced *Henry Bennet: a Novel*.

GORDON GOODWIN, rev. JOANNE POTIER

Sources *GM*, 1st ser., 96/2 (1826), 282 • Allibone, *Dict.* • [J. Watkins and F. Shoberl], *A biographical dictionary of the living authors of Great Britain and Ireland* (1816) • Watt, *Bibl. Brit.* • *A new biographical dictionary of 3000 cotemporary [sic] public characters, British and foreign, of all ranks and professions*, 2nd edn, 3 vols. in 6 pts (1825)

Rajagopalachari, Chakravarti (1878–1972), politician in India, was born on 8 December 1878, the third child of Chakravarti Venkatarya Iyengar and his wife, Singaramma, in the village of Thorappalli, near Hosur, then in the princely state of Mysore. His father was a moderately well-off landowner, *munsiff* (revenue official) of Hosur, and a recognized Sanskrit scholar. A natural conservative, C. R. or Rajaji as he was familiarly known, found himself invariably the dissident, a rebel against his father's strict Vaishnavite beliefs, against caste Hindu traditionalism, above all its oppression of the untouchables, and against the political authority of the raj, suffering frequent periods of imprisonment at its hand. This led to inner tension and may explain his chronic asthma, which only left him when he moved to his *ashram* at Tiruchengodu in 1925. His secondary education was at Bangalore Central College. He graduated in law from Presidency College, Madras, in 1897, and went on to enjoy great success, above all as a criminal lawyer, at the Salem bar. In 1897 he married Alarmelu Mangammal (d. 1916), daughter of an itinerant preacher; four of their children were to survive (two sons and two daughters), and her early death in 1916—bearing children too young was a possible cause, for which her husband never ceased to feel remorse—was one factor which drew Rajagopalachari, then only thirty-seven, to make a deeper commitment to politics. In 1918 he became chairman of the Salem municipal council. In 1919 he moved to Madras, and an almost chance encounter with M. K. Gandhi led to his being drawn into the new politics of civil disobedience. His becoming editor of Gandhi's mouthpiece, *Young India*, on his release from gaol in 1922 turned him into an all-India politician. He was always to see himself as Gandhi's disciple and friend. Rajagopalachari's daughter Lakshmi married Gandhi's son, Devadas, in an inter-caste marriage which caused both parents some concern. So close did C. R. and Gandhi become that, until Gandhi chose the young Jawarharlal Nehru as his successor, C. R. was widely viewed as his political heir apparent. But despite this closeness, at times his interpretations became too rigid, and he failed to grasp the subtlety of Gandhi's view, as for example over the no-change position on council entry in the 1920s, and in general he moved in a more conservative direction.

Rajagopalachari's was to be an extraordinary political career, straddling an enormous time-span, invariably in the front rank of national life. His power-base in the presidency of Madras was never strong, and he relied heavily on personal influence over the Congress triumvirate of Gandhi, Jawaharlal Nehru, and V. J. Patel to outwit his southern adversaries and sustain a role as an all Indian political figure. However, the numerous resignations in his Madras career were probably the result of depression and of a fear that he did not have long to live, rather than appeals for the help of his friends. After the deaths of Gandhi and Patel, Nehru ceased treating him as a friend and confidant, which does much to explain the end of his career at the centre and his return to provincial politics.

Rajagopalachari's exceptional talent for administration was given but brief opportunities for expression, in two periods as head of the Madras provincial government, 1937–9 and 1952–4, and at the centre, as successor to Earl Mountbatten of Burma as governor-general from 1948 to 1950, and to Patel, as home minister, in 1951. Most of his political career was in opposition, as a leading defendant of non-co-operation with the raj from 1919 to 1937 and, after 1954, as a critic of Congress rule, culminating in his founding in 1959 of an opposition conservative party, Swatantra. The contradictions in Rajagopalachari's political temperament were never more apparent than during the Second World War, when his statesmanlike search for some *modus vivendi* between Congress and the raj against the common enemy of Japan led to his advocacy of some concession to M. A. Jinnah and the Muslim League over a future state of Pakistan and to his resignation from Congress over its Quit India movement of August 1942. Many, however, saw Rajaji's formula as making partition more likely, and this was to dog his future career. Only Nehru's generosity was to rescue Rajagopalachari from political oblivion and give him a second chance as a Congress politician after 1946.

As a Tamil and a Brahman Rajagopalachari was peculiarly exposed in another dimension of his political career: his resistance to the forces of linguistic nationalism, in particular Andhra, and non-Brahman casteism. Here he had to accept defeat, with the setting up in 1953 of a new state of Andhra ((later Andhra Pradesh), breaking up the old presidency of Madras, and the coming to power in Tamil Nadu in 1967 of the non-Brahman party, the DMK. He considered that his greatest achievement in the south was the frustration of the rise of communism.

Rajagopalachari's was a highly distinctive contribution, in theory and practice, to India's continuing debate between the claims of tradition and modernization. He sought attitudinal rather than structural change in society, reflected in his endeavours to ease the burden of debt on the Madras peasantry in his Agricultural Debt Relief Act of March 1938 and to lessen the oppression of the untouchables by his Temple Entry Act of July 1939. Strikingly modern was his insistence on a clean administration, his fierce contempt for corruption and nepotism, but in later years, under Nehru's quasi-socialist administration, he came to distrust the excessive control by the state of the economy, licence-raj as he called it, and turned back to the caste system as an alternative source of authority to the modern state. He was much criticized for his seeming defence of caste in his craft-centred education scheme of 1953. His continuing preference lay in the simpler and more moral life, as he saw it, of village India. He was an ardent champion of prohibition, and his first act as head of the Madras administration was to introduce the Prohibition Act of October 1937.

Rajagopalachari had an immensely cultured intelligence, astonishingly widely versed in both Indian and Western culture. He was a superb craftsman of English prose. Among his many writings one might single out his Tamil versions, translated into English, of the *Mahabharata* and the *Ramayana*. He was not an easy political colleague, so unsparing were the moral demands he made both on himself and others; he was no less demanding of his children. He was a man of slight build, always immaculately dressed. In later years he mellowed, and his natural, aristocratic charm and simplicity of manner shone through. His was a far more Indian-based career than those of Gandhi or Nehru. His education was entirely home-based. His first journey outside India was, amazingly, as late as 1962, to visit President Kennedy. Maybe his was the most immediate and concrete involvement with the great debates within India on economic and social modernization and political change. He died in Madras on 25 December 1972.   ANTONY R. H. COPLEY

Sources *The Hindu* (26 Dec 1972) · R. Gandhi, *The Rajaji story*, 1: *The warrior from the south* (1978) · R. Gandhi, *The Rajaji story, 1937–1972* (1984) · C. R. Narasimhan, *Rajagopalachari: a biography* (1993) · A. R. H. Copley, *The political career of C. Rajagopalachari* (1978) · A. Copley, *C. Rajagopalachari: Gandhi's southern commander* (1986)
Archives Nehru Memorial Library, New Delhi | FILM IWM FVA, documentary footage | SOUND BL NSA, documentary recordings · BL NSA, oral history interview · BL NSA, performance recording
Likenesses statue, Law courts, Madras · statue, Col Parcha, New Delhi

Ralegh, Sir Carew (c.1550–1625/6). *See under* Ralegh, Sir Walter (1554–1618).

Ralegh, Carew (1605–1666). *See under* Ralegh, Sir Walter (1554–1618).

Ralegh, Sir Walter (1554–1618), courtier, explorer, and author, was born at Hayes, near East Budleigh, Devon, the second son and third surviving child of Walter Ralegh (1504/5–1581), landowner, of East Budleigh, and his third wife, Katherine (d. 1594), daughter of Sir Philip Champernowne of Modbury, Devon, and his wife, Catherine. The Raleghs were an old-established county family, recently traced with some caution back to the middle of the thirteenth century. The family was protestant. Walter Ralegh the elder was deputy vice-admiral in the south-west under Mary I from 1555 to 1558. Katherine Ralegh's children from her first marriage, to Otho Gilbert (d. 1547) of Compton, Devon, included the noted mariner and soldier Sir Humphrey *Gilbert (1537–1583), whose adventurous career greatly influenced the young Ralegh, and Adrian Gilbert (c.1541–1628).

Early years and education, 1554–1580 Although much has been conjectured, little is in fact known about Ralegh's early career. In particular, it is not understood for certain how he came to acquire the formidable learning displayed in later life. Sir Robert Naunton may give a lead when he writes that Ralegh was 'an indefatigable Reader, whether by sea or Land, and none of the least observers both of men and the times' (Naunton, 49). So far as can be discerned from the meagre clues to hand, some of them throwaway remarks in Ralegh's *History of the World* (1614), he served as a volunteer in France from 1569 with the Huguenot armies during the second phase of the wars of

Sir Walter Ralegh (1554–1618), by Nicholas Hilliard, c.1585

religion, and tasted an early military reverse at the battle of Moncontour in October. Campaigning took him across northern and south-western France, the barbarities and valour he witnessed making a deep impression on him. It appears that he returned to England after the peace of St Germain was concluded in 1570.

The date of Ralegh's matriculation at Oriel College, Oxford, remains uncertain, although he probably went up to the university in 1572. He was the youngest of four surviving sons—there were two half-brothers from his father's first marriage, John (d. 1588) and George (1527–1597), as well as an elder brother from his father's third marriage, Carew [see below]—and his means may accordingly have been somewhat limited. Thomas Child of Worcestershire told John Aubrey that Ralegh, pressed for money, 'borrowed a gowne of him when he was at Oxford … which he never restored, nor money for it' (Brief Lives, 2.179). Ralegh left Oxford without a degree, and was admitted to the Middle Temple on 27 February 1575. On admission he was described as being 'late of Lyons Inne' (H. A. C. Sturgess, ed., Register of Admissions to the Honourable Society of the Middle Temple, 3 vols., 1949, 1.39). His first published poem appeared in 1576, as a commendatory verse in George Gascoigne's The Steele Glass. He was living at Islington, Middlesex, in 1577, entering into a bond for one of his servants summoned to answer charges in December.

Records of Ralegh's early contacts with the court also remain elusive. His mother's elder sister, Katherine *Astley (d. 1565), was Princess Elizabeth's governess from 1544, became chief gentlewoman of the privy chamber in 1558 and of the bedchamber in 1559, and remained an intimate companion of the queen until her death in July 1565. This connection may have afforded Ralegh an initial

introduction, but it was perhaps through Gilbert's means that he first met leading courtiers, among them Sir Francis Walsingham and Robert Dudley, earl of Leicester. When in June 1578 Gilbert secured a patent to discover 'remote, heathen and barbarous lands … not actually possessed of any Christian prince', Ralegh sailed in his fleet as captain of the Falcon, a ship of 100 tons. To this day the precise purpose of Gilbert's expedition remains obscure, but he was in any case frustrated by storms, mischance, quarrels among the high command, and desertions. The Falcon, however, pressed on into the Atlantic, braving winter weather in a vain search for plunder and adventure. Ralegh eventually returned to Plymouth in May 1579.

The soldier in Ireland, 1580–1581 Ralegh turns up next in London. According to the not altogether trustworthy reports and assertions of Charles Arundell, Ralegh seems for a time to have moved in the circle of Edward de Vere, seventeenth earl of Oxford, Lord Henry Howard, and other Catholic courtiers, carrying a challenge from Oxford to Sir Philip Sidney after their tennis-court quarrel in August 1579. However, the association with Oxford— and more significantly with Howard—degenerated over time into mutual dislike. On 7 February 1580 Sir Thomas Perrot and Ralegh were committed to the Fleet prison by the privy council following a 'fraye' (APC, 1579–80, 384). Ill feeling between them was ongoing. A month later Ralegh was caught up in another brawl, and was on this occasion obliged to cool his heels in the Marshalsea prison. Through the good offices of other friends at court, he secured a captain's commission in the reinforcements then being dispatched to Ireland to counter the Desmond rebellion and its various offshoots. He served under the lord deputy, Arthur Grey, fourteenth Baron Grey de Wilton, at the bombardment of Smerwick, co. Kerry, where a force of Italian and Spanish adventurers had landed in support of the rebels. After four days the besieged garrison sought mercy, surrendered, were disarmed, and then methodically slaughtered, Ralegh overseeing the butchery. Searching through the possessions of the dead, he discovered letters which contained some unspecified matters of secrecy, and was sent to London with the documents in December 1580. This episode is frequently portrayed as the genesis of his career at court, even though he was ordered back to Ireland early in 1581. Until the summer Ralegh was quartered at Cork. Lobbying hard for a grant of Barry Castle, in Cork harbour, stronghold of the politically suspect David fitz James Barry, first Viscount Buttevant, he fought with considerable bravery in more than one guerrilla skirmish. His earliest surviving letter, written to William Cecil, Baron Burghley, lord treasurer, from Cork in February 1581, sought an allowance in respect of soldiers' pay, and adopted a degree of familiarity, naturally well mixed with deference. Certainly, his stock had risen to the extent that in the spring he was appointed to the commission, based at Lismore, co. Waterford, which governed Munster during the absence in London of the provost-marshal, Sir Warham St Leger.

At about this time Ralegh also fathered a child. Of the mother, Alice Goold, little is known beyond the fact that she appears to have been a daughter of Justice James Goold. Indeed, the very existence of this child rested on a single letter of disputed authenticity until the rediscovery of Ralegh's will in the 1960s revealed a bequest to his 'reputed daughter' of £333 6s. 8d. The girl's name is not known, but there is some reason to believe that Ralegh later betrothed her to Daniel Dumaresq, his page in Jersey, and that the young woman died of plague in London.

The favourite, 1581–1583 On returning to court, Ralegh began to attract Elizabeth I's attention. The well-worn tale of how he spread his cloak over a 'plashy place', thus allowing her to walk across, rests only on gossip recorded by Thomas Fuller. So too does the rather less credible, but also widely known, story that has Ralegh and his queen scratching couplets on a window pane (Fuller, *Worthies*, 1663, 262). Naunton, trying to account for Ralegh's influence, said that Elizabeth took him 'for a kind of oracle, which netled them all' (Naunton, 49). That is as may be; there was clearly a physical attraction too. Ralegh was tall (at 6 feet, taller than most of his contemporaries), dark-haired in youth, with somewhat pale and refined features. However apocryphal, Aubrey's raw tale of how Ralegh pleasured a scarcely reluctant maid of honour against the trunk of a convenient tree, gives a flavour of the man's power, and, ultimately, his weakness. The queen detained Ralegh for a time at court, making him an esquire of the body by 1581, but he eventually departed for the Low Countries in 1582 with François, duc d'Anjou, travelling with Leicester, Henry Carey, first Baron Hunsdon, and Sidney. While he was there, William of Orange entrusted him with a message intended for Elizabeth's ears only.

Ralegh rose rapidly in the queen's favour, playing the courtier to perfection and writing her elegant, at times innovative, poems—his 'Farewell false love' was read widely in court circles during the early 1580s. Corresponding with his half-brother in March 1583, he sent Gilbert 'a token from Her Majesty, an ancor guyded by a Lady … farther she cummandeth that yow leve your picture with mee' (*Letters*, 12). The intimacy, ostentatiously displayed, is unmistakable. On 27 December 1584 the Pomeranian traveller Leopold von Wedel, recounting a visit to the English court, offered further insight into this relationship. Chatting with her courtiers, the queen pointed 'with her finger at his face, that there was a smut [smudge] on it, and was going to wipe it off with her handkerchief; but before she could he wiped it off himself' (V. von Klarwill, ed., *Queen Elizabeth and some Foreigners*, trans. T. H. Nash, 1928, 336). Tangible rewards soon began to accrue. In April 1583 Ralegh secured leases reverting to the crown from All Souls College, Oxford, selling them on without delay. In the same year, Elizabeth granted him one of her favourite palaces, the handsome London dwelling, Durham Place on the Strand. It was blessed with a lantern tower that had a 'prospect which is pleasant perhaps as any in the world' (*Brief Lives*, 2.183). Views were important to him; Ralegh put the room to use as his study, and it is argued that he later used a similarly high attic room at Sherborne, Dorset, for the same purpose. Visitors to Durham Place spoke of its magnificence, of the splendour of its fabric and fittings. In May 1583 Ralegh received a patent for the sale of wine and the licensing of vintners, worth at a minimum over £700 per annum, and this remained the foundation-stone of his fortunes.

Although now at the heart of the court, Ralegh remained very much the Devon man. Apart from Aubrey's interesting assertion that Ralegh spoke 'broad Devonshire' to his dying day (*Brief Lives*, 2.182), it is known that the newly established courtier tried in July 1584 to purchase his birthplace, 'Hayes, a farme sumtyme in my fathers possession' (Devon RO, MS 2850Z/Z3). This attempt failed, but many of the honours bestowed upon him by the queen had a deliberate regional slant. Knighted on 6 January 1585, he was appointed vice-admiral of the west, lord lieutenant of Cornwall, and, with the death of Francis Russell, second earl of Bedford, lord warden of the stannaries in the same year. He also served as a knight of the shire for Devon in the parliaments of 1584 and 1586. In 1587 Ralegh was nominated to succeed Sir Christopher Hatton as captain of the guard, a post for which he appeared ideally suited, even to the most jaundiced of contemporaries. Ralegh duly took up his duties after Hatton's death in November 1591.

To support these new dignities Ralegh received extensive estates, including the Derbyshire properties of Anthony Babington, executed and attainted for a conspiracy in support of Mary, queen of Scots, in 1586. In the same year Ralegh also received from the queen a grant of three and a half seignories in the plantation of Munster, part of the confiscated Desmond patrimony, amounting to 42,000 acres. This was far larger than any other single grant in the plantation, almost three times larger than that given to Sir William Herbert, and four times more than the grant awarded to Hatton. Since each 'undertaker' was limited to 12,000 acres, the grant drew hostile comments from the lord deputy of Ireland, Sir John Perrot, Sir Thomas Perrot's father. Ralegh in turn accused Perrot of 'raising impertinent objections'. Perrot was then warned by Burghley that Ralegh 'is able to do you more harm in one hour than we are all able to do you good in a year', a striking tribute to the strength of the latter's position at court (M. MacCarthy-Morrogh, *The Munster Plantation: English Migration to Southern Ireland, 1583–1641*, 1986, 52, 102). Ralegh was not, however, prepared to stay in Ireland. He peopled his lands with tenants—148 of them by 1589—but leased out the seignories themselves to various Englishmen in 1594 for £200 per annum.

The colonist, 1583–1588 Ralegh's well-publicized initiatives to colonize North America began in earnest after the death of Gilbert in September 1583. Privateering and colonization had been a central element in his half-brother's grand design for the New World, and Ralegh eagerly took up the challenge, securing a patent for the purpose of colonization in 1584, and seeking practical advice from the mathematician and astronomer Thomas Harriot. Harriot, who became a close friend and one of the overseers of Ralegh's will in 1597, worked on a dictionary of the Algonquian language with the help of two native Americans brought back by members of Arthur Barlowe's reconnaissance expedition in 1584. Ralegh also enlisted both Richard Hakluyts to compose works supporting the colonizing initiative, Hakluyt senior in his *Inducements to the Liking of the Voyage Intended towards Virginia*, and his more famous younger cousin in the *Discourse of Western Planting* (written in summer 1584). Walsingham, Lord Charles Howard, Ralegh's cousin Sir Richard *Grenville (1542–1591), and many London merchants subscribed to his scheme. In 1585, having received his patent to colonize, he sent out an expedition of four ships and two pinnaces, with 600 men, under Grenville. Although Ralegh himself never went to Virginia, he was the mastermind behind this expedition and its successors. Grenville's men settled on Roanoke Island, while Grenville himself sailed into the Atlantic on a successful privateering voyage, leaving command of the infant colony to Ralph Lane, an army officer who had served in Ireland and equerry of the stables. By July of the following year the colonists were desperately short of food and welcomed the chance of a passage home when Sir Francis Drake put in at Roanoke on his return from the Caribbean. Grenville then arrived with a relief expedition, but, finding the colony deserted, sailed off, leaving behind fifteen unfortunate men. They were never seen again.

In 1587 Ralegh sent out yet another expedition, under John White. Unlike Lane's colony, whose purpose had been primarily a base for privateering, this was intended as a farming settlement. The planters were to have 500 acres each, more if their investment merited it. This venture was no more successful than its predecessor. After various catastrophes, White went home to organize relief. Unhappily for the colonists, Elizabeth was then involved in the Armada crisis and forbade the dispatch of further expeditions. When White did finally get two pinnaces to sea in 1588, they were diverted into piratical enterprises and were then themselves attacked. By the time a ship reached the colony in 1590 it was once again deserted, the settlers gone. Ralegh was blamed by some at the time, including Hakluyt, for neglecting the colony; and probably he must take some responsibility for the failure to relieve it. However, the main cause lies in the war with Spain, which distracted the attention of the queen and of her mariners.

There was a good deal of the courtier, if little of the politician, in Ralegh. His letter of 29 March 1586 to Leicester, who was concerned by the need to secure a contingent of tin-miners to serve as sappers in the Low Countries, overflows with tact and reassurance. He had, he declared, raised the matter with Elizabeth, and 'found her very willing in so mich as order was geven for a cummission, but since the matter is stayd, I know not for what cause'. If Leicester would only tell him of any grievances he would do his utmost to clear the misconceptions that must have given rise to them. He expanded upon his hatred for Spain, a passage which finds echoes in so many of his later writings:

> your lordshipe doth well understand my affection towards
> Spayn and how I have consumed the best part of my fortune

hating the tirranus sprosperety [*sic*] of that estate and it were now strange and monnsterous that I should becum an enemy to my countrey and conscience.   (BL, Harley MS 6994, fol. 2r)

The Low Countries again claimed his attention, along with those of the entire English political nation, when Sidney died in October 1586 as a result of the injury he received at the battle of Zutphen. Ralegh's honest, elegant epitaph, with more than a conscious element of *nisi nil bonum*, is arguably the best of his early work. Nevertheless, his talents as a courtier were perhaps limited. For all his success with the queen—and, indeed, because of that success—he made many enemies. Unlike Hatton, also raised from relative obscurity through royal favour alone, Ralegh lacked the patience and self-control of a conciliator. He occupied Hatton's lodgings at court in 1585, earning the sharp reprimand from Elizabeth that 'she had rather see him hanged than equal him with [Hatton] or that the world should think she did so' (HoP, *Commons, 1558–1603*, 3.273). Ralegh was, indeed, notoriously quick to denigrate. Shortly after Leicester's death in 1588 a derogatory epitaph began to circulate at court and beyond: 'Here lies the noble warrior that never drew a sword'. Rightly or wrongly, Ralegh was popularly given credit for its composition.

Ralegh was always, at heart, a man of action. In December 1587 he energetically assessed the defences of Devon and Cornwall, and pondered how best to pay for necessary precautions against the threat from Spain. In a thoughtful letter to Burghley he wrote that, so far as he could tell, 'if it might notwithstandinge stande withe Her Majesties likinge to beare the one half of the charge, beinge great, it would be very consonant to all good pollecy, and the countrey, as I judge, will willingly defray the rest' (PRO, SP 12/206/40). That was optimistic. Despite the danger, queen and privy council opted for economy and chose instead to forgo the mustering of any sizeable defence force. Ralegh did not confine his efforts to the south-west. He also surveyed the coastal defences of East Anglia, focusing everywhere on the need to protect deep-water harbours. William Camden maintained that he served with Charles Howard, second Baron Howard of Effingham, from 23 July 1588, but there is no other evidence for this. If Ralegh did see active service against the Armada, he was back in London by 2 August, when he was sent from court to the south coast to 'confer' with the lord admiral (APC, 16.212).

Potatoes and tobacco   A long tradition associates Ralegh with the introduction of both potatoes and tobacco into England. The potato originated in Peru and arrived in Seville by at least 1570: from there it spread to other parts of Europe. However, John Gerard, in his *Herball* of 1597, confused matters by writing that he received roots of the potato from Virginia, which grew in his garden, implying that this was a recent import and leading people to think that it had been brought over by one of the recent English expeditions. Ralegh's name is not, however, linked in print with the potato until 1699, when John Houghton claimed in a weekly bulletin that he first brought it to Ireland, whence it spread to Lancashire and then to the rest of England. Charles Smith's *History of Cork* (1750) relates a story of Ralegh's gardener at Myrtle Grove, his house at Youghal, co. Cork, finding tubers beneath the soil, growing them, and cooking the berries instead of the roots, with unhappy results. None of this is very convincing. More interesting evidence is provided in the manuscript journal of the Royal Society for December 1693, where the president, Sir Robert Southwell, writes that his grandfather brought potatoes into Ireland, having been given them by Ralegh. If that is so, Ralegh might be indirectly credited with importing the root into Ireland. However, most of the available evidence is thin and conclusions are speculative.

There was no reason at the time for anyone to have paid attention to the introduction of the potato; and the debate arose very much later. Tobacco was different. Smoking was a new, exotic, outlandish, and controversial habit; and credit or blame for it was soon bestowed. Tobacco was mentioned in the literature of discovery very early: by Christopher Columbus in 1492. It was introduced into Europe by André Thevet in mid-century, was growing in England by 1571, and was being smoked there by 1573. While Ralegh cannot have introduced it to this country, he probably helped to make it fashionable at court and in landed society. Aubrey claimed that Ralegh 'was the first that brought tobacco into England and into fashion' (*Brief Lives*, 2.181). He was certainly wrong on the first point, right on the second. Smoking was just the kind of habit—dramatic and new-fangled—that would appeal to a man as conscious of his image as Ralegh. Potatoes had—and have— no such cachet.

The propagandist, 1591 In 1591 there appeared the first of Ralegh's published works, *A report of the truth of the fight about the Isles of Azores, this last summer, betwixt the Revenge … and an Armada of the king of Spain* (generally known to historians as *The Last Fight of the Revenge*). Grenville died on 2 September 1591 in a disastrous encounter between ships under Howard of Effingham and a much larger fleet of fifty-three vessels dispatched from Spain. The English ships were caught unprepared, many of their men sick, others on shore. All save one, the *Revenge*, under Grenville, managed to escape. Grenville stayed and died with honour. It is not clear whether Ralegh was persuaded to write his account by the government to counter Spanish claims of victory, or whether he was moved to defend his cousin, Grenville, from charges of unnecessarily endangering himself and his men. Either or both are possible. Two principal objectives were pursued in his brief work: denying Spanish boasts and glorifying Grenville's conduct without, if possible, antagonizing the Howard clan. In following these Ralegh also wrote a bold, vivid, and moving account of the battle.

Ralegh described how Grenville rejected all pleas from the master of his ship to flee from the Spanish, and ordered the master gunner to 'split and sink the ship, that thereby nothing might remain of glory or victory to the Spaniards' (or, as Alfred, Lord Tennyson, put it in his 1878 reworking of the story, that the *Revenge* might 'fall into the hands of God, not into the hands of Spain'). In the end, the master and others of the ship's company overruled Grenville and negotiated a surrender. Mortally wounded, Grenville was carried onto the Spanish admiral's flagship, and there he died. Howard of Effingham would, according to Ralegh, have come to Grenville's aid, but was dissuaded by the rest of his fleet. As for the Spanish, they lost more ships than the English did, 'a manifest testimony how injust and displeasing their attempts are in the sight of God' (Ralegh, *Report*, sigs. A1r–D2r). Ralegh ended with a round condemnation of Spanish conduct in Europe and, above all in the Indies and Peru, thus declaring his allegiance to the protestant cause.

Marriage and disgrace, 1591–1595 Throughout the later 1580s Ralegh retained Elizabeth's confidence and so held the measure of her younger favourite, Robert Devereux, second earl of Essex. Ralegh and Essex were sometimes allies, occasionally friends, but for most of the following ten years they regarded one another warily, the relationship increasingly poisoned by distrust and suspicion. Blame for his failure to win over Ralegh, who at heart shared the same political and strategic philosophies, is conventionally laid squarely on the intransigent and irrational earl. However, Ralegh could be equally intransigent and, sometimes, just as irrational. His antagonism of the earl may have originated over his relationship with Essex's sister, Dorothy (d. 1619), who married Sir Thomas Perrot in July 1583. It was not, in any case, Essex who displaced him for ever from his central place in Elizabeth's affections. At the beginning of the 1590s, Ralegh began a liaison with Elizabeth (*bap.* 1565, *d. c.*1647), also known as Bess, one of the queen's maids of honour, and daughter of Sir Nicholas *Throckmorton (1515/16–1571) and his wife, Anne. At some point late in 1591, with Bess pregnant, she and Ralegh were married in secret, fully aware that news of this union, once it leaked out, would gravely displease the queen. All accounts agree that Bess was both determined and formidable. Her brother Sir Arthur Throckmorton (*c.*1557–1626), who was very fond of her, referred to her as 'Morgan le fay' in a diary entry of 1609 (Rowse, 276). The affection between husband and wife, however, was apparently strong and enduring. It had much to endure.

Ralegh perhaps felt that he would be able to ride the storm when it broke, but here he underestimated the intensity of Elizabeth's displeasure. Busying himself in preparations for a privateering venture, he made every effort to discount spreading rumours of the marriage, assuring Sir Robert Cecil as late as March 1592 that 'if any such thing weare I would have imparted it unto your sealf before any man livinge' (*Letters*, 63). He more than once resorted to blatant falsehood when he perceived his career to be at stake. The couple had a son on 29 March. Remarkably, Essex stood godfather when the child was baptized Damerei (1592–1593), after a prominent forebear on the Throckmorton side of the family. On 27 April Bess returned to court, taking up her duties as a maid of honour, still trying to hide the facts of marriage and motherhood, while Ralegh sailed on the first leg of an expedition in which a good part of his fortune was invested. He was back in Plymouth by mid-May, and then, belatedly, his secret came out. Elizabeth took his measure. On 28 May Damerei Ralegh was brought by his nurse to Durham Place, where his father saw him for perhaps the only time. Two days later Ralegh was committed to Cecil's charge, though by 2 June he was back at Durham Place. On the following day Bess was placed in the custody of the vice-chamberlain, Sir Thomas Heneage.

Still believing that the usual charades of courtly contrition would suffice, Ralegh lamented his wretchedness to Cecil. 'Do with mee now therfore what yow list', he wrote. 'I am more wery of life then they are desirus I should perishe, which if it had bynn for her, as it is by her, I had bynn to happelye borne' (Hatfield, Cecil MS 21/58). Later, Cecil himself recalled an occasion on which Ralegh, watching from Durham Place, noticed Elizabeth's barges on the river below, at Blackfriars. Wrestling theatrically with his keeper, George Carew, he shouted that he 'wolde disguyse hymselfe and gett into a pare of oares to ease his mynde butt with a syght of the Quene, or els, he protest, his harte wolde breake' (Bodl. Oxf., MS Ashmole 1729, fol. 177). Elizabeth was irritated rather than pacified by these gestures, smacking as they did of implicit defiance and a wholesale lack of remorse. It was a curious but somehow characteristic miscalculation, which provoked a venomous response from the queen. Husband and wife were both sent to the Tower of London on 7 August.

Ralegh chafed at the disgrace, sought solace in poetry, and begged their release with as much humility as he could muster. Happily for him, the fleet he had recently sent to the Azores succeeded in capturing a Portuguese carrack, the *Madre de Dios*, one of the greatest single prizes taken by Elizabethan seamen. The ship was brought home to Dartmouth in triumph, and exaggerated tales reached London of how the vast treasure on board was being rapidly plundered by those at the scene. In this administrative chaos lay Ralegh's opportunity. On 15 September, at the request of Sir John Hawkins and through the mediation of Burghley, he was sent to Dartmouth, still technically a prisoner, as he never tired of telling those he met on the way. Once there, under Cecil's observant eye, he worked hard, enjoying the welcome given him by mariners. When all was eventually divided up, Elizabeth allowed Ralegh only a small share of the spoils: a notional profit of £2000 on the £34,000 adventured by him and his associates. She did, however, begin to forgive. On 22 December Bess was released from the Tower.

It is possible, though now hard to prove, that the death of Bess's son helped prompt this charity. Damerei Ralegh vanishes from the record. On 1 November 1593 the couple's second child, Walter (1593–1618), was baptized at Lillington, Dorset, near the foundations of a fine new house Ralegh was beginning to build close by the old castle at Sherborne. In January 1592 the queen took a lease of ninety-nine years on all the estates of John Coldwell, bishop of Salisbury, in or near Sherborne, and immediately sublet these properties to Ralegh for the remainder of her term. The new 'Lodge', and its gardens, were substantially the work of Adrian Gilbert.

For the time being both Ralegh and his wife were banished from court—the ban on Ralegh was not lifted until 1597—but he was elected a burgess of Mitchell, Cornwall, in the parliament of 1593. He had been knight of the shire for Devon in the 1580s, and this borough seat was distinctly less exalted. Nevertheless, it was at least a stepping-stone back to favour, and in the next two parliaments he was returned for county seats: Dorset in 1597 and Cornwall in 1601. He was unique in Elizabeth's reign in sitting for three counties, a keen parliament man, actively concerned with borough patronage and with the business of the House of Commons. In 1593 he warned fellow MPs in ringing tones of the dangers posed by Spain, demanding pre-emptive action and, consequently, a grant of money sufficient for such a strike. These opinions were hardly unorthodox; and MPs duly granted the queen an unprecedented triple subsidy. However, he also strongly expressed hostility towards the Dutch. Early in 1593, perhaps, Ralegh wrote a treatise on the succession, arguing very correctly that the matter was for God and princes alone, beyond the remit of mere subjects, and beyond legislation. Again, however, he showed his lack of political common sense, wondering publicly about what James VI might do to press his claim if ever it were challenged.

The court poet Ralegh's poems present exceptional difficulties for his editors and biographers. He allowed very few, probably only five, to be printed; others circulated in manuscript, as was common enough at the time. Most probably, he did not want his authorship revealed to the generality and, consequently, there is no established canon of his poems. Many were attributed to him which were probably not his; others lay hidden for years. Many exist in anthologies edited by others and there is no certainty as to which words are his, which were interpolated by editors, or what was his final version, if such existed. The authorship of two of the best-known poems attributed to him has been questioned. Although 'The Lie' is now accepted as his by most, but not all, scholars, 'Sir Walter Raleighs Pilgrimage' ('Give me my scallop shell of quiet') usually is not. Few poems can be dated with any precision and attempts to relate individual pieces to specific events in his life are fraught with difficulty.

Ralegh's poems are essentially the work of a courtier, written very much within the context of the royal court. Some are commendations of the works of others, like his early verses praising Gascoigne's *The Steele Glass*, some are epitaphs, like that on Sidney. Most are concerned with love, especially his love for Elizabeth. His poetry is part, an important part, of his campaign to make a name for himself at court and, above all, to win the favour of the queen. That is not to say that the poems were cold or unemotional. On the contrary, they were passionate, angry, hyperbolic, cynical, pessimistic, and often despairing. 'Farewell, false love' is characteristic of his tone:

Farewell, false love, thou Oracle of Lyes,
A mortall Foe, an Enymy to reste,
An envious Boy, from whence all cares aryse,
A Bastard borne, a Beast with rage posseste.

A way of Error, a Temple full of Treason,
In all effectes, contrary unto reason.
(*Poems*, ed. Rudick, 12)

His early poems to Elizabeth are more straightforward:

Praysed be *Dianaes* faire and harmelesse light,
Praised be the dewes, where-with she moists the ground:
Praised be her beames, the glory of the night,
Prais'd be her power, by which all powers abound.
(ibid., 4)

Later, Ralegh became, or affected to become, less confident of the queen's love. In 'Fortune hath taken away my love', he complains directly to Elizabeth of her coldness. Her response tells much about the ease of their relationship. Ralegh complained that Fortune stole her affection from him. She replied to her 'silly pugge' that Fortune had no such power over her:

Revive againe and live without all drede,
the lesse afraid the better thou shalt spede.
(ibid., 19)

Ralegh was not so easily comforted and 'Farewell to the Court' may belong to the same period, the late 1580s, perhaps in response to Essex's rise to royal favour:

Like truthles dreames, so are my joyes expired,
And past returne, are all my dandled daies:
My love misled, and fancie quite retired,
Of all which past, the sorow only staies.
(ibid., 26)

'The Lie', a fierce indictment of the court, the church, and most other human institutions, may also belong to this phase of Ralegh's career, but although he is the most likely author of this poem, his title to it cannot be fully established.

Ralegh was, however, undoubtedly the author of four manuscript poems discovered at Hatfield House in the middle of the nineteenth century. Generally known as the 'Cynthia poems', they were first published in 1870. They are in Ralegh's 'best hand' and can be unequivocally counted as his. One, 'The 21st and Last Booke of the Ocean to Scinthia', is the longest poem by far that he ever wrote (522 lines). It is followed by a short fragment of 22 lines, 'The end of the boockes, of the oceans love to Scinthia, and the beginninge of the 22 boock, entreating of sorrow'.

Were these works part of a lost epic poem comparable to 'The Faerie Queene'? It seems unlikely that Ralegh could have found time to write such a mammoth piece in the course of Elizabeth's reign. (Some editors, particularly Agnes Latham, have deciphered the numbers in the titles as 11 and 12, causing some confusion, but Ralegh would have been hard pressed to have written even ten such books.) Did Ralegh start to write an epic, beginning, for some reason, at the twenty-second book? It is possible but only very slightly more probable. The truth is unknown, and it may not matter. What exists is a major poem, written about the time of, or a little later than, Ralegh's imprisonment in the Tower when Elizabeth learned of his marriage. It describes the desolation that he felt from the withdrawal of her affection for him. He describes the joy that she gave him during his years at court and his despair that she has deserted him:

My weery lymes, her memory imbalmed,
my darkest wayes her eyes make clear as day
what rage so feirce that love could not allay.
Twelve yeares intire I wasted in this warr
twelve yeares of my most happy younger dayes,
butt I in them, and they now wasted ar
of all which past the sorrow only stayes,
So wrate I once and my mishap fortolde.
(*Poems*, ed. Rudick, 52–3)

He finishes with the lines:

But be it so, or not, th'effects ar past,
her love hath end, my woe must ever last.
(ibid., 65)

The poem was evidently intended for the queen, to make her aware of his suffering and to relieve him from it. It was probably given to Cecil, so that he could present it to her. Instead, he placed it in his archive where it stayed, presumably unread, for nearly four hundred years: it is unlikely that it reached her. Rhetorical, exaggerated, and self-pitying as it is, 'The Ocean to Scinthia' is a work of tremendous poetic force.

The atheist Ralegh was, so far as can be discerned from his writings and his poetry, a conforming member of the Church of England. He was, however, prone to expressions of rational scepticism, a potentially dangerous trait given the company he sometimes kept and his inclination towards discussion and debate. His patronage of Thomas Harriot, and his contacts with Giordano Bruno, Christopher Marlowe, and Harriot's other patron, Henry Percy, ninth earl of Northumberland, tarred him with more radical notions. The belief that Ralegh was an atheist, that he denied God and advocated his own views to others, finds expression in Robert Persons's pseudonymous *Elizabethae … saevissimum in Catholicos sui regni edictum … cum responsione* (1592), and is echoed by other commentators during the seventeenth century and beyond. According to an English summary of Persons's work, Ralegh presided over a 'school of atheisme' in which, under Harriot's direction, 'both Moyses and our Savior, the olde, and the new Testamente are jested at, and the schollars taughte, among other thinges to spell God backwarde' (R. Persons, *An Advertisement Written to a Secretary of my Lord Treasurers of England, by an English Intelligencer as he Passed through Germany towards Italy*, 1592, 18). Persons's attacks—even his charges of atheism—were by no means confined to Ralegh, who was indeed something of a secondary target providing evidence to her Catholic enemies that Elizabeth governed through atheists.

Nevertheless, Persons's accusations here amounted to a little more than smoke without fire. Ralegh's still obscure links with Marlowe were viewed with suspicion, and on one notorious occasion he and his brother Carew quite deliberately ruffled the temper of Ralph Ironside, vicar of Winterborne, Dorset, during a supper hosted by Sir George Trenchard at Wolfeton, Dorset, in 1593, by enquiring deeply into the nature of the soul, and exposing what they saw as Ironside's circular theological arguments (BL, Harley MS 6849, fols. 183r–190r). This spat helped prompt an abortive investigation by the court of high commission in March 1594. Ralegh duly proved his religious credentials by overseeing a raid on Chideock, Dorset, and the arrest there of the Arundell family priest, John Cornelius, alias Mooney. 'He is', said Ralegh, 'a notable stout villain, and I think can say much' (Edwards, 2.91). It certainly seems that Cornelius had no compunction about talking to Ralegh, albeit on topics of his own choosing. According to a Catholic narrative Ralegh passed an entire night conversing with Cornelius and came away impressed by the man's sincerity. If, indeed, it ever took place, the long hours of talk did neither man any good. Cornelius was determined upon martyrdom, and nothing Ralegh or anyone else did or said could deflect him from his purpose.

The explorer, 1595–1596 In these years of disgrace Ralegh's preoccupation with the fabled empire of El Dorado took firm root. The power of Spain was, he observed, founded on its American silver and gold. A project to establish England's own source of wealth in the New World grew alongside his schemes to create a colonial empire on the north coast of South America. His dreams about the treasures of lost cities combined with an appreciation of Spain's present military weakness, sharpened by Spanish travellers' tales, and by the adventures of the governor of Trinidad, Antonio de Berrio, who had repeatedly travelled through the interior of Guiana in search of gold. The resulting voyage—financed largely on credit through the efforts of William Sanderson, Ralegh's nephew by marriage—was all very much a last resort; Bess, perhaps at her husband's suggestion, wrote to Cecil, hoping that he might 'draw Sir Walter towards the east than help him forward towards the sunset' (Rowse, 182). Cecil chose instead to invest in the new expedition, and Ralegh eventually sailed from Plymouth with four ships on 6 February 1595. When the Spanish colony on Trinidad was overwhelmed, amid considerable brutality, Ralegh focused on information provided at some length by a particularly valuable prisoner, the elderly Berrio. There followed an eventful voyage up the rising waters of the Orinoco. Like the Spaniards before him, Ralegh was beguiled all the way by tales of fantastic cities and wealth in the interior, and ultimately obliged to return to the coast empty-handed. Attempts to secure some plunder in the Caribbean were equally futile—costing several lives in an abortive assault on Cumana—and Ralegh arrived in Plymouth in September, his holds empty, to face the indifference of queen and privy council.

The scorn and derision of Ralegh's fellow countrymen grew intensely irksome. Some even suggested that he skulked in Cornwall for a year, making up the whole adventure. 'What becumes of Guiana', he wrote to Cecil on 10 November 1595, 'I miche desire to here, whether it pass for a history or a fable' (Hatfield, Cecil MS 36/4). 'Her majestye', he suggested two days later, would 'shortly bewayle her negligence therin, and the enemy by the addition of so mich wealth weare us out of all'. Once or twice in these fulminations he makes a telling point: 'wee must not looke to mayntyne warr upon the revenus of England' (ibid., MS 36/9).

Over the winter Ralegh wrote a report on the expedition, *The Discoverie of the Large, Rich and Bewtiful Empire of Guiana*. Dedicated to Cecil and Howard of Effingham, it was an elegant and memorable piece of travel writing, at once a self-justification and a call to exploit his discoveries. As they journeyed up the Orinoco:

> on both sides of the river we passed the most beautiful country that ever mine eyes beheld; and whereas all that we had seen before was nothing but woods, prickles, bushes and thorns, here we beheld plains of twenty miles in length, the grass short and green, and in divers parts groves of trees by themselves, as if they had been by all the art and labour in the world so made of purpose. (*Works*, 8.427)

However, the rapid rising of the rivers made it impossible to mine for gold in the time available and they lacked the necessary tools. Ralegh, though, was confident that 'the sun covereth not so much riches in any part of the earth' as in Guiana. He fully intended to return, because, as he wrote in conclusion:

> Guiana is a country that hath yet her maidenhead, never sacked, turned, nor wrought; the face of the earth hath not been torn, nor the virtue and salt of the soil spent by manurance, the graves not been opened for gold, the mines not broken with sledges, nor their images pulled down out of their temples.

Once conquered it could be easily defended. Ralegh had already made friends with the indigenous people and if the Spanish were once driven out the principal native chief would pay Elizabeth hundreds of thousands of pounds in tribute. At all events he convinced himself. More and more, the illusion of Guiana appeared—to a frustrated man—a means of re-establishing his own fortune and bolstering English war chests at one and the same time. The book was read widely, both at home and abroad. Latin, German, and Dutch editions all appeared within five years. Harriot drew a presentation map of Guiana, while his friend George Chapman waxed lyrical upon the fertility of the land and the friendliness of its inhabitants. Yet, all these tales of distant marvels failed to move the Cecils or the queen.

The rival, 1596–1600 Elizabeth and her privy councillors were, however, concerned at the dangers posed by a revived Spain. Virtually the entire privy council now recommended an attack on the Spanish coast, and in 1596 the interests of Essex and Cecil combined to pursue this goal. Ralegh's maritime knowledge was suddenly in demand, and he was closely involved in the labyrinthine discussions which, eventually, established who should take charge of what. He worked hard to raise the necessary troops and to prepare the fleet, under the direction of his friend Howard of Effingham, placating and cajoling suspicious courtiers and a queen reluctant to spend money in pursuit of campaigns abroad. When the commanders assembled, Ralegh and Sir Francis Vere quarrelled over the scope of their respective commands, and these arguments were never entirely resolved. This was all quite in character. Nevertheless, the ensuing expedition was one of the triumphs of Elizabethan arms. On 20 June 1596 the fleet arrived off Cadiz, taking the Spanish authorities there completely by surprise. Ralegh was sailing in the rearguard, patrolling the coast to surprise enemy shipping, but he was present for the main assault. In one of his longest surviving letters, written on the day after the assault to Arthur Gorges, he provided a vivid narrative of the action. He was wounded in the fighting, receiving 'a greevous blow in my legg, larded with manie splinters which I daylie pull out' (*Letters*, 149). Cadiz was sacked, but the wealth of the merchant fleet in the harbour was lost when the Spanish ships were scuttled. Essex busied himself in knighting sixty followers, but a great opportunity for plunder passed the victors by.

Ralegh's narrative was published in 1700 by his grandson as *A Relation of the Action at Cadiz*. It is one of the finest set-piece battle scenes in English literature. Writing of his own attack on the Spanish galleons, he described how the *Philip* ran aground:

> tumbling into the sea heaps of soldiers, so thick as if coals had been poured out of a sack in many ports at once, some drowned, some sticking in the mud. The Philip and the St Thomas burnt themselves. The St Matthew and the St Andrew were recovered with our boats ere they could get out to fire them. The spectacle was very lamentable on their side; for many drowned themselves; many, half burnt, leapt into the water, very many hanging by the ropes ends by the ship's side under the water even to the lips; many swimming with grievous wounds stricken under water, and put out of their pain; and withal, so huge a fire, and such tearing of the ordnance, in the great Philip and the rest, when the fire came to 'em, as if any man had a desire to see Hell itself, it was there most lively figured.   (W. Oakeshott, *The Queen and the Poet*, 1960, 214–15)

Weighing this triumph, Elizabeth inclined towards forgiveness. Ralegh was allowed to return to court the following year, and once again exercised his captaincy of the guard. As Essex's star waned, so Ralegh and his friends recaptured something of their old authority. For example, Henry Brooke, eleventh Baron Cobham, a rich if rather superficial young man, was appointed lord warden of the Cinque Ports, in succession to his altogether more worthy father, and in the face of a determined campaign by Essex to promote his own candidate. Ralegh acknowledged the influence of Cecil, now the queen's principal secretary, in restoring his own fortunes, flattering him and commiserating with him gracefully on the loss of his wife, Cobham's sister, in January 1597. 'Yow shall', he wrote:

> butt greve for that which now is as then it was when not yours, only bettered by the difference in this, that shee hath past the weresume jurney of this darke worlde and hath possession of her inheritance ... Sorrows draw not the dead to life butt the livinge to death.   (Hatfield, Cecil MS 37/97, fol. 2r)

Touching the melancholy of bereavement Ralegh was seldom lost for words. Possibly at the instigation of Burghley, he worked to foster better relations between the Cecils and Essex—passing on news from Cecil to the earl and recording by way of an intimate touch in July 1597 that Essex had been 'wonderfull merry att the consait of Richard the 2' (PRO, SP 12/264/10). He was recovering lost ground. Nevertheless, much of his former wealth had been eroded by expensive efforts to repair the breach with Elizabeth, and by his outlay on Sherborne. When he drew

up his will that same month, his estate appears relatively modest. Ralegh's own lands by now consisted only of the Irish estates—vast, but never profitable—and the leasehold on the manor of Sherborne. In this interesting document the queen was nowhere remembered. Indeed, the beneficiaries were exclusively members of his family, and his servants, although Cecil was given a residuary interest in a set of porcelain. Ralegh, it may be noted, had a liking for quality chinaware.

The will was drawn up for a purpose. Ralegh was sailing as Essex's second-in-command on a new expedition against Spain, the so-called 'islands voyage'. Beset by foul weather, incompetence, and deep divisions among the senior officers, the enterprise was a fiasco. It threatened to prove something worse when a Spanish fleet set sail in October 1597 for the undefended coasts of England, only to be swept away in turn by Biscayan storms. Ralegh's capture of the town of Fayal in the Azores was the sole achievement of any note, and here, so Essex maintained, the rear-admiral had flouted his direct orders.

This fresh quarrel gravely weakened the carefully nurtured amity between Essex and Ralegh, but Elizabeth chose to blame the earl, roundly and personally, for the expedition's shortcomings. The débâcle of Essex's expedition to Ireland in 1599, where a private parlay with Hugh O'Neill, second earl of Tyrone, touched on treason, and his precipitate return to court that autumn, completed the favourite's fall. Increasingly paranoid, Essex numbered Ralegh and Cobham among his bitterest foes: anyone who was not for him, stood against him. In the miserable finale Essex was condemned by the privy council in 1599, by commissioners at York House in 1600, and, after his desperate rebellion, by his peers in the court of the lord steward on a charge of high treason in February 1601. Ralegh, himself accused by the distracted earl of treason, and, fantastically, of plotting to divert the succession to Philip, infante of Spain, joined in the persecution. During spring 1600 he warned Cecil to ensure that the stricken favourite did not recover ground lost:

> the less yow make hyme the less he shalbe able to harme yow and yours ... for after revenges feare them not ... His soonn [son] shalbe the youngest earle of Ingland ... butt if the father continew he wilbe able to break the branches and pull up the tree, root and all. Lose not your advantage: if yow do I rede your destiney.   (Hatfield, Cecil MS 90/150)

That such a letter survives among Cecil's papers testifies to the anger Essex's insinuations aroused. It testifies as well to Ralegh's political naïvety. Elizabeth, noting his flaws, declined to have him sworn a privy councillor, despite repeated hints and requests. She did, however, appoint him governor of Jersey in August 1600, a post Ralegh had coveted ever since news of the fatal illness of the previous governor, Sir Anthony Paulet, was first made public, early in the year.

The suspect, 1600–1601 Cobham, something of a royal favourite in Elizabeth's final years, was assiduously courted as a friend and ally. Witty and capable, for all his shallowness, he proved congenial company for Ralegh, who regretted Cobham's failure to join him at Bath in a distinctly sycophantic letter of 29 April 1600: 'we can butt longe for yow and wyshe yow as owre lives whersoever' (PRO, SP 14/1/57). Cobham was at that moment preoccupied by his forthcoming marriage to Frances Fitzgerald, *née* Howard, dowager countess of Kildare, but the following summer he and Ralegh, along with Northumberland and other courtiers, visited the Low Countries to experience life on campaign. For Ralegh this was nothing new, and he was soon back in England. That autumn he travelled to Cornwall, and also to Jersey, surveying his new command. He took his oath of office on the island on 20 December. In his absence a fire, beginning in the stables, caused considerable damage to Durham Place. When Essex staged his rebellion on 8 February 1601, Ralegh was again in London. Early that morning he met his rebel kinsman Sir Ferdinando *Gorges (1568–1647) on boats in the middle of the Thames, counselling common sense, discretion, and reliance on the queen's clemency; but discretion and common sense were in short supply that day. Gorges refused, honouring his commitment to Essex and warning Ralegh of bloody times ahead. While they talked, Sir Christopher Blount aimed four bullets at Ralegh from Essex House, but the optimistic shots missed their target. Recognizing the futility of negotiation, Ralegh hurried to court and mobilized the guard. Essex's rising was crushed within hours. When he was brought to the executioner's block, seventeen days later, rumour had it that Ralegh gloated over his rival's fate, although the truth of the matter seems to have been that, obliged to attend the execution as captain of the guard, Ralegh withdrew to the armoury precisely to avoid such a charge. There was, for the moment, no means of restoring a reputation hopelessly tarnished:

> Raweleigh doth time bestride;
> He sits twixt winde and tide,
> Yet uppe hill hee cannot ride,
> For all his bloodie pride.
> (PRO, SP 12/278/23)

The popular ballad was a travesty—and Ralegh was by no means its only target—but the archetypal greedy and covetous upstart courtier struck a familiar chord. Although innocent of any open triumphalism, there is no question that Ralegh sought advantage from his rival's fall. He begged—and may have obtained—some of the lands of Essex's follower, the volatile Sir Edmund Baynham, who was sentenced to death for treason in February, only to be pardoned in August.

In September 1599 Ralegh also obtained from the queen a freehold title to his Sherborne estate, which he then proceeded to expand through further purchases. With Sherborne relatively secure there seemed little point in holding on to his Munster estate, long since a liability. In 1602 the Irish lands were sold to Sir Richard Boyle for £1500. Meanwhile, the courtier and captain of the guard had other roles to play. In September 1601 Ralegh escorted Charles de Gontaut, baron de Biron, Henri IV's emissary, 'to Westminster, to see the monuments' (Hatfield, Cecil MS 88/22). He disagreed openly with Cecil in the parliament of 1601 over the latter's call for further financial sacrifice in support of the war effort. In a quarrel fashioned on semantics, and again disclosing political ineptitude, Ralegh argued that to Spanish ears the very request would argue poverty in the state, and encourage a redoubling of their efforts against England. He is said to have blushed during the acrimonious debates over monopolies, defending the practice through his administration of the Cornish tin mines, and challenging his opponents to relinquish their own monopolistic interests if he did the same. The great silence that followed this typically theatrical gesture may signify embarrassment, or, more likely, open disagreement.

The traitor, 1601–1603 Ralegh's alienation of Cecil had serious consequences. Causes for the rift are still elusive. It may be that Ralegh felt disappointed that he was still not sworn a privy councillor, and that he somewhat unfairly blamed Cecil rather than Elizabeth for this frustration. That is conjecture. What is known is that Cecil, though outwardly correct and civil in all his dealings with Ralegh, felt increasingly abandoned by a former ally in the two years before Elizabeth's death. By summer 1601 he was writing to his client—and Ralegh's cousin—Sir George *Carew (1555–1629), lord president of Munster, that he had been so frustrated and irritated by 'the mutinys of those whom I do love and will (howsoever they do me)', that he had been 'left to seek new Freends' (*Letters*, ed. Maclean, 84–5, 89). Cecil duly found them. Over the next two years Ralegh's name was repeatedly blackened in the letters of Henry Howard, youngest brother of Thomas Howard, fourth duke of Norfolk, written to James in Edinburgh to assure him of Cecil's (and Howard's) loyalty, and to warn him against the intrigues of others. As Howard described him, Ralegh was once again an atheist, indiscreet, incompetent, hostile to the very idea of James's succession. More significantly, Howard's long-winded venom was clearly prompted by Cecil's own clandestine letters to James. All this is as crucial to understanding Ralegh's subsequent troubles as it is murky and unedifying. Given his significance at court, Cecil's dissociation from Ralegh, his insistence that he could never support a man of 'light and soddain humours' fundamentally opposed to a Stewart succession (Bruce, 18), was deeply damaging, and it is difficult to escape the conclusion that the latter's wilful part in this critical breach amounted to an entirely avoidable miscalculation.

Ralegh was still not entirely without friends. Northumberland, in his own secret correspondence, advised James that although Ralegh was certainly 'insolent, [and] extreamly heated' he was essentially powerless, unable to do the king 'muche good nor hearme'. Moreover, the earl felt compelled to add that there were 'excellent good parts of natur' in his old friend (Bruce, 67). However, Northumberland was himself subjected to Howard's insinuations, and these assurances probably did little to alter James's already low opinion of Ralegh.

When Elizabeth died on 24 March 1603, Ralegh's world began to fall apart. He hastened from the west country to meet the new king, only to receive the driest of welcomes. Aubrey puts the punning words into James's mouth, 'on my soule, Mon, I have heard rawly of thee' (*Brief Lives*, 2.186). Ralegh was present in his official capacity at the queen's funeral, but thereafter endured a series of telling rebuffs. He was stripped of his monopolies and captaincy of the guard in May, and was given notice to quit Durham Place, Tobias Matthew, bishop of Durham, having successfully petitioned James for the return of his London home. The decisive blow fell soon after. On 15 July, while at court, Ralegh was detained for questioning in connection with two tangled treasons, then coming to light. He was placed under house arrest in the charge of Sir Thomas Bodley, at Fulham, Middlesex. Implicated by Cobham in the so-called Main plot, which ostensibly hoped to foment rebellion and Spanish invasion, aiming thereby at the death of the king and the elevation of Arabella Stewart in his place, Ralegh was conveyed to the Tower on or about 20 July. There, overwhelmed with despair at the turn of events, he wrote a touching letter of farewell to Bess and made an unconvincing attempt at suicide on 27 July: he tried to stab himself to the heart using a table knife. Neither the theatricality of the gesture nor the essentially unchristian nature of the act were lost on hostile observers. Subsequently, however, his spirits returned. He perceived that the sole evidence of any substance laid against him was a statement made by Cobham on 20 July—made, moreover, in the heat of the moment, when Cobham was under the not wholly unfounded impression that Ralegh had betrayed *him*. Cobham withdrew his accusations almost as soon as they were made, but these fleeting charges had the two conspirators soliciting enormous sums of money from Spain—500,000 or 600,000 crowns. In this confession, Cobham admitted his intention to press for the money during a forthcoming visit to the continent. He had, he said, also planned to travel home via Jersey, where he and Ralegh proposed to discuss the distribution of this war chest, with a view to stirring revolt wherever the opportunity arose.

Cobham's curious, retracted testimony remained the most telling evidence against Ralegh when he was finally brought to trial at Winchester on 17 November. It was presented in court, not as a signed confession, but rather in the form of a 'certificate' attested by the examining counsellors and as an 'affirmation' from the lord chief justice, Sir John Popham. Cobham even smuggled letters of exoneration to Ralegh in October. The trial itself was an extraordinary affair, with Ralegh resolute and dignified, and with the attorney-general, Sir Edward Coke, losing his temper on more than one occasion and failing to present his case with any clarity. Coke did, however, manage to throw in an accusation of atheism, echoed by the lord chief justice at the end of the day, and he did trump Ralegh's letter from Cobham with a written confirmation from Cobham of previous accusations. The precise wording of this restatement is nevertheless interesting, for it departs from the charges allegedly made on 20 July. Cobham now declared that Ralegh had urged him to mediate with the former's friend Charles de Ligne, count of

Aremberg, in order to secure a general pension of £1500 for foreign intelligence. He added that 'coming from Greenewich one night', Ralegh passed on information on 'what was agreed upon betwixt the King and Low Countrymen' for transmission to Aremberg, insisting that Ralegh had been the principal cause of his own discontent. Though this is far from the broad sweep of treason embraced in his outburst of 20 July, the court seems to have interpreted Cobham's letter as an elaboration on that testimony, focusing upon the fact of accusation. At the end of a momentous day, this was sufficient to persuade a jury of Ralegh's guilt.

However, it is clear from Cobham's subsequent confessions, after Ralegh's conviction, and at his own arraignment, that these accusations should be seen as replacing those made in the heat of the moment, months earlier. Events on the night he returned from Greenwich seem to hold the key to Ralegh's subsequent actions. According to Cobham, Ralegh arrived full of 'discontent upon certeine woords that that day as he sayed had passed between the lord Cecill and him' (PRO, SP 14/4/91). He then pressed Cobham to negotiate with Aremberg 'that he should doe best to advertise and advise the king of Spaine [Philip III] to send an armie against England to Milford Haven'. Characteristically, Ralegh held that the bold approach was necessary in such situations: 'many more', he growled, in a prophetic utterance, 'had been hanged for words then for dedes' (ibid.). The picture that emerges from Cobham's later testimony, of a discontented Ralegh denouncing James and his ministers, conjuring visions of a Spanish descent on the nation that had treated him so poorly, and exploring the availability of a pension from any amenable foreign prince, offers a credible summary of his treason. Ralegh never denied that he lent 'a patient ear' to Cobham's 'unwise and lavish projects' (Hatfield, Cecil MS 102/51).

Legally if not morally, Ralegh's much maligned jury returned a correct verdict, even on the basis of Cobham's revised accusations, which they never heard. The most extraordinary aspect of Ralegh's political downfall was his simultaneous transformation in the popular imagination from upstart villain into popular hero. His composure at Winchester, the harshness of a technically accurate verdict, and Coke's loss of temper on so public a stage all combined to replace loathing with sympathy. As Dudley Carleton put it a few days later, 'never was a man so hated and so popular in so short a time' (Bodl. Oxf., MS Carte 80, fol. 622v).

The prisoner, 1603–1612 Despairing of mercy from James, Ralegh wrote another letter of farewell to his wife. Here is Ralegh at his doleful best: for all the obvious sentiment so characteristic of the man, and for all the common form, no one reading these lines can doubt that he loved his wife. James, however, ultimately allowed him his life on 9 December 1603, first putting Cobham, and the Bye conspirators Thomas Grey, fifteenth Baron Grey of Wilton, and Sir Griffin Markham, each in turn, through the grim charade of a reprieve on the scaffold. Ralegh dutifully thanked both king and Cecil, hoping that an early release might follow. That liberty was not forthcoming; Ralegh, like Cobham and Grey, was long to remain a prisoner in the Tower. Incarceration was comfortable enough. He was allowed his two rooms in the Bloody Tower, his books, a 'stilhows' (PRO, SP 14/19/112), or laboratory, a garden for his exercise, and congenial company. For most of this time his wife was allowed to come and go without significant restriction, and their third son, Carew [see below], was baptized at the church of St Peter ad Vincula on 15 February 1605. Lady Ralegh took a house on Tower Hill for its proximity to her husband's gaol. Nevertheless, confinement vexed a man of Ralegh's stamp. He suffered from some form of 'palsy' or paralysis (Hatfield, Cecil MS 109/13). Dr Leonard Poe, a royal physician, attended him in September 1604, and in March 1606 Peter Turner, another medical man, reported that Ralegh was complaining of a numbness in his left side, 'and his tong taken in sum parte, in so mych that he speketh wekely' (PRO, SP 14/19/112). Turner, perhaps taken in by another of Ralegh's theatrical performances, recommended a move to less chilly quarters.

The king did not at this stage act vindictively against Ralegh or his family, granting all his goods and chattels to his servants John Shelbury and Robert Smith on 14 February 1604 for the use of his wife and child, in order to settle his debts. Ralegh's wine licensees were ordered by the privy council to pay their arrears to the trustees one week later, and the right to grant wine licences was given to the earl of Nottingham (Howard of Effingham) and his son only in December 1604. Shelbury and Smith dutifully discharged their obligations. On 3 August 1604 the Sherborne estate was granted by letters patent to family trustees who held it on behalf of Lady Ralegh and young Walter for the duration of Ralegh's life. It may be that Ralegh held out for more, for the freehold to Sherborne, or it may be that here is the first intimation of a serious problem that blighted the Raleghs for years afterwards. By the following winter it had become apparent that a conveyance of the Sherborne estate to his son, dated 20 January and sealed on 12 April 1603, contained a fatal flaw, in that the clerk who had copied it from the draft had omitted ten crucial words. Legally, this left Ralegh in freehold possession of the estate at the time of his attainder, the manor being thus forfeit to the king. James at first inclined to confirm Ralegh's family in their possession, but by the end of 1609 Sherborne passed to his favourite, Sir Robert Carr. Intending it for his eldest son, the king purchased it back again in February 1610, Carr repurchasing it after the death of Henry, prince of Wales.

Quite early on, Ralegh's prospects for release appeared to turn on the feasibility of another voyage to Guiana. He was staking, and continued to stake, everything on the chimera of mountains of gold within a far-off continent. With support from a favoured Scot, John Ramsay, Viscount Haddington, Ralegh approached Cecil, by now earl of Salisbury, in summer 1607. He suggested that if the queen, Anne of Denmark, and Salisbury would each take a third stake in the venture (which he calculated would cost £5000) then he and his friends would cover the rest.

Ralegh himself would travel under another's command, as a private gentleman, so as to guarantee his return to England. 'Wee will break no peace, invade none of the Spanish towns. Wee will only trade with the Indiens and see none of that nation except they assayle us' (Hatfield, Cecil MS 124/121). Salisbury declined the bait. Later that year Ralegh is found cultivating James's eldest son, then thirteen years old, advising him on shipbuilding. The death of Henry on 6 November 1612—despite the application *in extremis* of a 'quintessence' supplied by Ralegh, 'which he sayes they shold have applied sooner'—was a grievous blow to his hopes of liberty (*Letters of John Chamberlain*, 1.389). This medicine, subsequently known as Ralegh's 'cordial', became famous, its properties passing into legend as the recipe itself was lost. Its concoction is again in character: Ralegh was long known to be dabbling in medicines and chemistry in the Tower. Earlier in 1612, reporting the death of Sidney's daughter Elizabeth Manners, dowager countess of Rutland, to Sir Ralph Winwood, John Chamberlain remarked that Ralegh had been 'slaundered to have geven her certain pilles that dispatcht her' (ibid., 1.374), and when Ralegh fell sick in February 1615 some, the ever cynical Chamberlain among them, put it down to his chemical experiments.

The Tower scholar, 1603–1618 During his years in the Tower Ralegh produced a great deal of prose but relatively little verse. His own situation and the conditions at court were now, of course, quite different from those during Elizabeth's reign. Only four poems from these years can be accepted as Ralegh's with any confidence. One compares the world to a theatre and men to actors, a favourite theme with Ralegh and other Elizabethans. 'Had Lucan hid the truth to please the time' is dedicated to Sir Arthur Gorges, translator of Lucan's *Pharsalia*. There are three versions of a petition to Anne of Denmark, which are confidently attributed to Ralegh but could have been written at any time between 1603 and 1618. Of several poems alleged to have been composed by him on the night before his execution, only one is likely to be genuine:

> Even such is Time who takes in trust
> Our youth, our Joyes and all we have,
> Then payes us bake with age and Dust,
> Who in a darke and silent Grave
> When wee have wandred all our wayes
> Shuts up the storie of our Dayes.
> But from Times rage, the Grave and Dust
> My God shall raise me up I trust.
> (*Poems*, ed. Rudick, 80)

The verse appeared in countless seventeenth-century collections and as an inscription upon at least three tombs of the period.

Ralegh's prose writings under James are much more numerous, varied, and wide-ranging than those written before 1603. However, like the poems, they present bibliographical problems. To begin with, some of them—*Maxims of State* and *The Cabinet Council* for instance—although they carry Ralegh's name, are not by him at all. The texts and contexts of others are uncertain. *Observations and Notes Concerning the Navy and Sea Service*, dedicated to Prince Henry in 1607, actually started life in 1597–8 as a manuscript presented to Elizabeth, was revised under James, but was not printed until 1625.

Ralegh was now denied direct participation in political or military life and, until his second expedition to Guiana, could maintain his reputation only with his pen. He reinvented himself as a kind of elder statesman, instructing Henry and advising James. Two tracts on proposed marriages between the children of James and the house of Piedmont-Savoy reveal his stance. They were probably written at Henry's instigation. The proposal made early in 1612 for a marriage between Princess Elizabeth and Victor Amadeus, eldest son of Charles Emmanuel (I), duke of Savoy, was adroitly criticized by Ralegh, on the grounds that it would be of no political advantage to Britain; might entangle the king in the impossible defence of Savoy against its powerful neighbours; and would not serve the comfort of the princess, who would be matched with a Catholic husband. Better, said Ralegh, for her to marry Frederich (V) Wittelsbach, prince palatine of the Rhine, who was a protestant and would strengthen the alliance with the Netherlands. (Ralegh's advice was taken, with unhappy results.) The companion piece, *A Discourse Touching a Marriage between Prince Henry of England and a Daughter of Savoy*, is rather more problematic, since some versions appear to have been addressed to Charles, duke of York. It was probably made to serve for both in turn. 'There is', said Ralegh, 'a kind of noble and royal deceiving in marriages between kings and princes' who bestow their daughters only for their own advantage. 'We do not need to fear Savoy, but it is the Spaniard whom we should fear, who layeth his pretences and practices with a long hand' (*Works*, 8.239). The duke of Savoy was firmly tied to Spain and to Rome, and might entangle James in their conflicts. The prince would do well to hold off marriage for the time being and then marry with a French princess. In *A Discourse Touching War with Spain*, probably written early in James's reign but not printed until 1702, Ralegh presented the king with general arguments for assisting the Netherlands against the Spanish. Without external help the Dutch would have to submit to the Spanish, which would provide the latter with a base for the invasion of England. If James did not assist them, the Dutch would look to the French, which would be equally disastrous: a familiar argument from the reign of Elizabeth, but cogently put by Ralegh.

About 1609—the year that his friend and fellow prisoner, Northumberland, was writing something very similar—Ralegh tried his hand at a familiar genre: the father's advice to his son. His version, known as *Instructions to his Son and to Posterity*, has a sharpness and cynicism that partly marks it out from the efforts of Shakespeare's Polonius and others. The first chapter, headed 'Virtuous persons to be made choice of for friends', turns out to be more self-seeking than the title suggests. A man should choose his betters for his friends and should shun the poor and needy. 'Such therefore as are thy inferiors will follow thee but to eat thee out'. While a man's betters are best for his friends, he should remember that 'great men forget such as have done them service' (*Works*, 8.557–8). Wise choice of a wife was crucial to the preservation of a man's estate: 'the only danger therein is beauty, by which all men in all ages, wise and foolish, have been betrayed'. It is better to choose beauty in a mistress rather than a wife, 'for when thy humour shall change, thou art yet free to choose again' (ibid., 8.559). On the other hand, it is inadvisable to marry an 'uncomely' woman, for the sake of the children, 'for comeliness in children is riches, if nothing else be left them' (ibid.). The *Instructions* circulated in manuscript until 1632, when they were printed: six more editions followed up to 1636.

Ralegh's major work during the years in the Tower was *The History of the World*. While most of his prose works up to then had been written for private circulation (the tracts on *The Revenge* and Guiana excepted) the *History* was intended for publication to a wide audience. Ralegh began writing it about 1607; the work was entered in the Stationers' register in 1611 and appeared towards the end of 1614. This copy did not have the 'Preface'. It was suppressed by George Abbot, archbishop of Canterbury, on 22 December and copies were seized by the king's agents for his own use. According to Chamberlain the suppression came about because it was 'too sawcie in censuring princes' (*Letters of John Chamberlain*, 1.568). The suppression order was soon lifted and the *History* was reprinted in 1617. It remained popular: there were at least eleven editions in the seventeenth century, one in the eighteenth, and one in the nineteenth.

The *History* is described as 'The first part of the general history of the world', implying, as Ralegh said, that other parts were to come. This, he admitted, was his intention and indeed he had 'hewn them out'. What exists is a substantial work, of about a million words, in five books, running from the creation of the world to 146 BC, the time of the second Macedonian war. The first two books are principally, though not wholly, concerned with biblical history, the last three mainly with the story of Greece and Rome. In the first two God's judgments are seen as the central determinants of events; in the latter three the role of man is more evident. History is regarded as moral exemplum, a classical concept appropriate to the treatment of ancient history but unusual for the subsequent discussion of Henry VIII. The juxtaposition of the discussion of Henry with that of James must have registered as ironic with the original readers, especially later when James's 'unstained sword of justice' had Ralegh's blood on it.

The *History* is far more than a chronology. Its opening chapters described the creation of the world and its nature, before Ralegh moved to the philosophical problems raised by the concepts of prescience, providence, free will, and fortune. He adopted the familiar distinction between first and second causes. God's will, he later wrote, determined everything: 'there is not therefore the smallest accident, which may seem unto men as falling out by chance, and of no consequence: but that the same is caused by God to effect somewhat else by' (Ralegh, *History*, 1736, 2.v.10, 175). Yet God works through second causes, 'instruments, causes and pipes', which carry his will to the world. The distinction is not clear or unambiguous, but it enabled Ralegh to focus upon human actions. Essentially, he wrote for a purpose, as a man of action: it was, he said, 'the end and scope of all History, to teach by example of times past, such wisdom as may guide our desires and actions' (ibid., 2.xxi.6, 307).

One principal theme of the work was the general wickedness of kings and the severity of God's judgment upon them:

> Oh by what plots, by what forswearings, betrayings, oppressions, imprisonments, tortures, poisonings, and under what reasons of state, and politic subtilty, have these forenamed Kings, both strangers and of our own nation, pulled the vengeance of God upon themselves, upon theirs, and upon their prudent ministers! (Ralegh, *History*, 1736, preface, xv)

The misdeeds of English kings were related in some detail. Of Henry VIII, Ralegh wrote that 'if all the pictures and patterns of a merciless prince were lost in the World, they might all again be painted to the life, out of the story of this king' (ibid., preface, viii). Only one ruler in the entire history of the world receives unstinted and unadulterated praise from Ralegh: Epaminondas of Thebes, with Hannibal as *proxime accessit*.

Although Ralegh believed that history could provide examples and precepts for rulers to follow, its events demonstrated only too clearly that they were unlikely to do so. His book ends with a paean of praise to Death:

> Oh eloquent, just and mighty Death! whom none could advise, thou has persuaded; that none has dared, thou hast done; and whom all the world hath flattered, thou only hath cast out of the world and despised: thou hast drawn together all the far stretched greatness, all the pride, cruelty, and ambition of man, and covered it over with these two narrow words, *Hic jacet*. (Ralegh, *History*, 1736, 5.vi.12, 815)

The bitterness, pessimism, and anger that marked so much of Ralegh's poetry remained to the end in his prose.

The next work that Ralegh wrote in the Tower, *A Dialogue betweene a Counsellor of State and a Justice of the Peace*, is very different in tone, style, and content. Written after the dissolution of the Addled Parliament in 1614, and presented in manuscript to James, it sought to persuade the king to call parliament. The counsellor took the part of those advising James against parliaments, which he claimed had always been dangerous to kings in the past. In reply the JP attacked the use of imprisonment without trial and argued that parliaments provided the king with the best way of raising money, which should be done by persuasion, not constraint. The argument proceeded by methodical examination of the relations of English kings with their subjects since the reign of John. It has none of the force or brilliance of the *History*; it is indeed often quite boring, yet it may have had in the short term the greater influence.

The last voyage, 1616–1618 With the advantage of hindsight, many commentators have dismissed Ralegh's final voyage to the Orinoco to try to find El Dorado as the hopeless pursuit of fantasy, but it is important to remember that friends and foes alike seriously questioned whether the enterprise was viable long before Ralegh set sail. For some, Ralegh deluded himself with daydreams. Locked away in the Tower, his vivid imagination simply got the better of him. Others, less charitable, wondered what the old fox was up to now. Surely he realized that Spanish settlements on the Orinoco had multiplied since 1595, and that, for all his disclaimers, the voyage would mean bloodshed? Was that perhaps what he wanted—one means to foment dissent between England and Spain being as good as any other? Here was a way to frustrate the carefully nurtured plans of James and the Spanish ambassador Diego Sarmiento de Acuna, count of Gondomar, who had long endeavoured to persuade a sceptical Philip that Charles, now prince of Wales, should marry his daughter, the Infanta Maria. And might not the frustration of these desires be encouraged by France? Ralegh certainly opened negotiations with the French ambassador, Count des Maretz, in 1616, apparently with the aim of securing a refuge in France if all went wrong, though evidence on the precise nature of these discussions remains obscure. In fact, the expedition may be taken at face value: it was Ralegh's final, personal gamble. He believed—he had to believe—that there was a mountain of gold or silver, deep in the jungles of Guiana, and he clung to proofs of its existence, gleaned over twenty years. The Spanish crown had no valid claim to unoccupied, undiscovered regions; the gold was there for the taking.

Ralegh was released on 19 March 1616, and at once set about planning his expedition. The planning was, of course, extensive, and little he said or did comforted those at court who were determined on a lasting peace with Spain. He discussed with Sir Francis Bacon, attorney-general, the possibility of seizing the silver fleet, brushing aside the latter's remarks that this would amount to an act of piracy: had Bacon, he asked rhetorically, ever heard 'of men being pirates for millions?' The Guiana fleet sailed from Plymouth on 12 June 1617, but storms and adverse winds detained it off the southern coast of Ireland for nearly two months. Finally, on 19 August, a fair wind allowed the ships to make their way south from Cork. It was to be a laborious voyage, with illness taking its usual toll. Never comfortable at sea, Ralegh himself succumbed to fever, and was unable to face solid food for nearly a month. The fleet did not arrive in harbour, at the mouth of the Cayenne River, until 14 November. An expedition under Lawrence Keymis, with Ralegh's nephew George Ralegh in command of the land forces, sailed up the Orinoco in five ships on 10 December. Carrying provisions for one month, the three vessels that survived the shoals of the delta battled against strong currents and arrived at the Spanish settlement San Thomé on 2 January 1618.

The English then took the town by storm. Fatalities in the brief, bitter struggle included the Spanish governor, Diego Palomeque, and Ralegh's elder son, Walter. There can be little doubt that the assault was pre-planned, and if so, that the action directly violated the commission by which they sailed. It is, however, uncertain whether the expedition acted under verbal orders from Ralegh, or whether they were rather following Keymis's own directions, given in an atmosphere of uncertainty and fear. Ralegh subsequently tried to excuse this aggression by claiming, in his *Apology for the Voyage to Guiana*, that quite another settlement had been stormed, but the characteristic evasion smacks of desperation.

Thereafter, Keymis visibly began to lose his nerve. The principal problem, of course, lay in the fact that no one knew for certain where the mine might be found. Three launches were eventually sent further up the Orinoco under George Ralegh's command. They travelled 300 miles upstream, but discovered neither gold nor silver. After an occupation of twenty-nine days San Thomé was burnt to the ground and the expedition returned to the river mouth. News proceeded ahead of the main party, and on 13 February Ralegh was told of his son's death. He met Keymis with accusations, refusing to accept any apology, and declaring that his lieutenant's obstinacy had undone him. Keymis took to his cabin. First he tried to put a bullet through his breast, but the shot was deflected by a rib. He then stabbed himself to the heart. Ralegh received the news of his suicide with contempt. Thereafter he blamed his dead subordinate for all his misfortunes. It is difficult not to reflect that Keymis had been charged with an impossible mission.

Faced with the crisis of his schemes, Ralegh planned another expedition to San Thomé. The mine, he reasoned, must have been overlooked, it might still be exploited. His men, however, refused to follow, and soon afterwards the fleet sailed north. Even then, Ralegh conjured with visions of revictualling and returning to Guiana, and he thought once more of plundering the Spanish treasure fleet. By now such hopes were vain; his demoralized troops were disinclined to adopt risky strategies. In the last week of March the rest of his fleet deserted, leaving Ralegh in the *Destiny*, alone off Nevis. With a mutinous crew he sailed north towards Newfoundland, then across the Atlantic to Kinsale, co. Cork, where a number of the company melted away. Ralegh, with the remnant of his force, sailed on to Plymouth.

Trial and execution, 1618 The failure of his expedition left Ralegh stunned. 'My braines are broken,' he wrote to Bess on 22 March 1618, 'and tis a torment to mee to write … as Sir Francis Drake and Sir John Hawkins died heart-broken when they failed of their enterprize, I could willinglie doe the like' (*Letters*, 353–4). Once home, he received no sympathy. A proclamation of 9 June denounced reports that the peace between England and Spain had been compromised by violence at San Thomé. Ralegh was placed under arrest by order of Howard of Effingham soon after his landing and conveyed to London by his cousin Sir Lewis *Stucley (1574/5–1620), vice-admiral of Devon, at the end of July, in accordance with directions from the privy council. While still at Plymouth he made an abortive attempt to escape by ship to France, but then changed his mind, resolving to see matters through at home. It can only be surmised that he was concerned for the fate of his wife and son, or that he believed James's anger to be essentially a diplomatic device. Perhaps he even hoped that the

Spanish alliance would soon come to grief. At Salisbury, Ralegh wrote an *Apology for the Voyage to Guiana*, insisting that Guiana was English territory, and the actions against Spanish authorities there were entirely justified. James arrived in the city on his summer progress, apparently rejected the *Apology*, and ordered Ralegh on to London. A second attempt to escape to France was frustrated by Stucley. As Chamberlain put it, Ralegh was:

> bewrayed, or in a sort betrayed by Sir Lewes Stukeley (who had the charge of him) and brought backe by certain boates that waited for him about Wolwich. Sir Lewes did nourish him in the humor with promise to assist and accompanie him, but yt was a fowle *pas de clerc* for an old cousener to be so cousened and overtaken. (*Letters of John Chamberlain*, 2.165)

The cozener again! Ralegh was conveyed to the Tower on 10 August, and appealed to George Villiers, marquess of Buckingham, for help two days later. His options had narrowed ominously. Buckingham was then actively supporting the Spanish alliance, and had little time for Ralegh's point of view.

James wished Ralegh dead; only the means to this end remained unresolved. A commission established to probe his offences first questioned Ralegh on 17 August, and members of his crew were also interrogated. Suspecting that stories of the silver mine were spurious, and half-believing that Ralegh's voyage was one element in an involved conspiracy fomented by France, the commissioners persevered. Ralegh was interviewed repeatedly by Sir Thomas Wilson, acting on behalf of the privy council under their commission dated 10 September. Wilson was no impartial examiner—he openly sought incriminating evidence from this 'arch-hypocrite', asking God to preserve James 'from having many such dangerous subjects' (Harlow, 272–3). Despite Wilson's efforts, the pickings were meagre. On 18 October the commissioners reported their findings to the king. James, however, was dissatisfied with their proposals. Simply issuing a warrant for executing the sentence of 1603 seemed unduly arbitrary, but he wanted no public hearing either. There was a risk that this 'would make [Ralegh] too popular, as was found by experiment at the arraignment at Winchester, where by his wit he turned the hatred of men into compassion for him' (ibid., 296). Mindful of Coke's bungling fifteen years earlier, the king wished rather to steer a middle course. Ralegh should be called before the commissioners alone, 'those who have been the examiners of him hitherto'. Examinations would be read out, Sir Henry Yelverton, the attorney-general, and Sir Thomas Coventry, the solicitor-general, would inform against him, the prisoner might speak, and 'others confronted with him, who were with him in this action' (ibid., 297). The conclusion was, of course, preordained.

The privy council duly summoned Ralegh before it on 22 October. Yelverton accused him of blatant lies—Ralegh had been ungenerous to a king who had pardoned his manifest treasons, he had known all along that there was no mine, he had planned to foment war between England and Spain, he had abandoned his men and betrayed

James. Ralegh in his reply also reached back across time to his finest hour, recalling the apparent harshness of the original verdict handed down at Winchester, 'he hath heard that the King said that he would not bee tried by a jury of Middlesex'. He had, he insisted, fully believed in the mine, he had not plotted with France, and he had not abandoned his own men in Guiana (Harlow, 299). His words were, of course, to no purpose; the commissioners informed him that they were satisfied of his guilt, and that he was therefore to be put to death.

Sentence was confirmed in his presence by Sir Henry Montagu, lord chief justice at the court of king's bench, Westminster, on 28 October. Again Ralegh tried to excuse his actions on the recent voyage, only to be stopped by Montagu, who told him that, since he had not been pardoned expressly in his commission, what he had or had not done in Guiana was quite irrelevant to the question at law, which was whether the king might indeed now confirm a sentence of execution passed in November 1603. Ralegh then took the only course open to him and threw himself on James's clemency. Montagu made a considered, and in the circumstances a rather courageous speech, affirming his own belief in Ralegh's character and religion, and praising his *History*. 'You must do', he said, 'as that valiant captain did, who perceiving himself in danger, said in defiance of death, *death thou expectest me, but maugre thy spite I expect thee*' (Harlow, 304). He concluded by granting execution.

Ralegh spent his last night in the Gatehouse and was executed on the morning of 29 October 1618, at Westminster. He made a long, moving speech, lasting three-quarters of an hour, welcoming the fact that he was to die in the light, forgiving his enemies and traducers, insisting that he had no ulterior motive in planning his expedition, that he had not plotted with France, and that he had never considered seeking refuge abroad. The execution of Essex still troubled him:

> There was a Report spread, that I should rejoice at the death of my Lord of Essex, and that I should take Tobacco in his presence; when I protest I shed Tears at his Death, though I was one of the contrary Faction.

He asked the onlookers to pray with him for divine forgiveness, summarizing his own career as he did so. He had been, he admitted, 'a Man full of all Vanity'; he had lived 'a sinful Life, in all sinful Callings, having been a Souldier, a Captain, a Sea-Captain, and a Courtier, which are all places of Wickedness and Vice' (Harlow, 309–10). Ralegh maintained his courage to the end, touching the edge of the axe and jesting with the sheriff that here was 'a sharp Medicine ... a Physitian for all Diseases'. His head, severed at the second blow, was placed into a 'Red-leather bag' (ibid., 310), and was carried away by Lady Ralegh, who kept it by her thereafter. The body was buried at St Margaret's, Westminster.

The legacy A. L. Rowse once remarked of Ralegh that his was a personality 'people could not let alone' (Rowse, 259). At the centre of gossip and romance when alive, Ralegh was no less a focus of interest in death. Throughout

November 1618 Chamberlain sent Carleton copies of letters, verses, and ballads. 'We are so full still of Sir Walter Raleigh', he wrote on 21 November, 'that almost every day brings foorth somwhat in this kind' (*Letters of John Chamberlain*, 2.185). There was no juicier topic for the newsmongers that side of Christmas.

During the 1620s Ralegh's posthumous career as a protestant and popular hero grew. In *Sir Walter Rawleighs Ghost, or, Englands Forewarner*, Thomas Scott presented him as the man to save England and addressed him as 'not borne for thy selfe but thy Countrie' (Beer, 120). Sir John Eliot possessed and used Ralegh's *Dialogue* as a source of arguments and precedents in his debates with the crown over forced loans and arbitrary imprisonment. In 1628 the *Dialogue* was printed and given a new and slightly misleading title, *The Prerogative of Parliaments*. It went into three editions that year.

There were two further editions of *The Prerogative* in 1640, and over the following twenty years radicals plundered Ralegh's *History* for examples of the workings of providence. The *History* was reprinted four times before 1640 and again in 1652 and 1666. In 1650 Oliver Cromwell recommended the work to his son Richard: 'recreate yourself with Sir Walter Raleigh's History: it's a Body of History; and will add much more to your understanding than fragments of Story' (Beer, 173 n. 12). In the course of the 1650s several of Ralegh's texts were published or republished, and some works by others were attributed to him, notably *Maxims of State* and *Cabinet Council*, the latter published by John Milton. Plainly his name carried a powerful attraction for writers and publishers, either to sell works which were not actually his or to validate a message; but it is not always easy to identify the message. It is far from clear, for instance, whether Milton published *Cabinet Council* because he was offering it as an ironic criticism of Cromwell or because it gave advice on how best to endure tyranny. Ralegh seems to be supplied with varying identities by writers of the Commonwealth and protectorate: for some the representative of corrupt monarchies, for others the advocate of aggressive commercialism. The one thing that seems quite certain is that his name attracted interest and helped to sell books.

Ralegh's name is still congenial to publishers, but with time the reasons for his enduring popularity have changed. The poem 'Britannia and Rawleigh', attributed to Andrew Marvell, ranked Ralegh in the 1670s with the steadfast puritans, while the 1719 *Tragedy of Sir Walter Raleigh*, by George Sewell, portrayed him not for the first or last time as a victim of perfidious Spanish intrigues. The nineteenth century, in turn, fashioned Ralegh as the archetypal heroic Englishman, the pioneer of empire, while adding a gloss derived from still earlier times. Suppressing with a shudder Aubrey's tale of the maid and the tree, Victorian popular histories, and even the assiduous Edward Edwards in his *Life and Letters*, turned him into something of a knight errant—the lad with his eyes fixed on distant horizons, as in Sir John Everett Millais's *Boyhood of Ralegh*, the gallant adventurer stepping forward in doublet and ruff to throw his cloak before an appreciative queen. And *in extremis*, of course, Ralegh played the man, fought and (in his own way) triumphed against immense odds, only to be duped, and at length cruelly murdered. A later, more cynical, age favoured his patronage of science and, particularly, his religious scepticism, detected the religious doubts that surfaced at Trenchard's dinner party as re-emerging in the *History*, and left Ralegh the politician and soldier alone, highlighting instead his scholarship and poetry. In the process he has been somehow sidelined. With Bacon he remains the Renaissance man *par excellence*, but Renaissance men now sit uneasily in a modern world of intense specialization. Significantly, the best biography of Ralegh remains that written by William Stebbing, published as long ago as 1891.

All these reworkings of the Ralegh persona touch on truth. He was indeed a victim of royal high-handedness, he was indeed the author of the most influential book published in the seventeenth century, he was indeed an accomplished courtier, a man fascinated both by the possibilities of distant new-found lands, and by those same new-found lands themselves. He certainly questioned some fundamental aspects in church doctrine. However, when these characteristics are added together the resulting creation must then be fleshed out with the judgement of contemporaries, many of whom found him a loquacious upstart, a compulsive liar given to insincere theatrical gestures, incapable of keeping a secret, a man who yearned to play some part—any part—in the high game of national politics but whose own shortcomings left that goal for ever beyond reach. Ralegh's overriding ambition was to advance himself and his family, and of this he made no bones. Again and again he urged his son to avoid poverty, to cultivate his betters, to get on in life, for poverty is shameful, the poor are despised and without the means to choose their own destiny. Nevertheless, he failed even here, at one point enjoying that free choice, but ultimately squandering both wealth and opportunity. Those who came after him, who never met him, have instinctively liked Ralegh, or their version of Ralegh. He was certainly a most astonishing and compelling man, in his writings as in the rest of his life, touched by genius, and greatness, the focus of legend. It should not be forgotten, however, that many of those who lived in the same small world of the Elizabethan court, after long association with Ralegh, either disliked him intensely or distrusted him profoundly. Their reservations must at least qualify our admiration.

Family and descendants Ralegh's elder brother, **Sir Carew Ralegh** (c.1550–1625/6), landowner, of Downton, Wiltshire, was, if anything, the more blunt in his conversation with Ralph Ironside at Wolfeton, but this isolated episode of vicar baiting had no lasting effect on a respectable county career. He represented Wiltshire in the parliaments of 1584 and 1586, Ludgershall, Wiltshire, in 1589, Fowey, Cornwall, in 1601, and Downton, Wiltshire, in 1603–4 and 1621. For some years gentleman of the horse to the wealthy Sir John Thynne of Longleat, Wiltshire, Ralegh in or after 1580 married Thynne's widow, Dorothy (d. 1616), daughter of Sir William Wroughton of Broad

Hinton, Wiltshire, and his second wife, Eleanor. The couple settled at Downton House, Salisbury. They had three sons and a daughter. Ralegh was knighted by Elizabeth at Basing House, Hampshire, on 14 September 1601. According to Aubrey he had 'a delicate clear voice, and played singularly well on the olpharion [orpharion]' (*Brief Lives*, 2.179). Although Ralegh did not desert his more famous younger brother during 1603–18, he remained largely a local gentleman, holding various county offices, including membership of the quorum of the peace in Dorset and Wiltshire from about 1583 and vice-admiral for Dorset in 1597. Ralegh died in 1625 or 1626. His second son was Walter *Ralegh (1586–1646), dean of Wells.

Sir Walter Ralegh's third son, **Carew Ralegh** (1605–1666), courtier, matriculated from Wadham College, Oxford, on 23 March 1621 at sixteen, his name remaining on the books there until 1623. According to Anthony Wood, Carew Ralegh was something of a poet in his student days, which is as may be. A single poem under his name is printed in Henry Lawes's *Ayres and Dialogues* (1653). William Herbert, third earl of Pembroke, presented him at court when he left Oxford, but James is said to have found him the reincarnation of his father, and he promptly set off for a year on the continent. Despite widespread sympathy he was restored in blood only in 1628, James having refused assent to an earlier private bill of restoration which had passed both houses of parliament in 1624. Charles I, for his part, insisted that in return Ralegh should renounce all remaining claims to the Dorset estates, Sherborne now resting in the hands of the family of John Digby, earl of Bristol, the former ambassador to Spain. For the moment, Ralegh looked elsewhere. In 1629 he bought from Thomas Wriothesley, third earl of Southampton, an estate at East Horsley, Surrey, and married Philippa (d. 1674), daughter of Sir Thomas Shelton and widow of Sir Anthony Ashley, at about the same time. The couple had at least two sons, Sir Walter (d. c.1663) and Philip (d. 1705), and a daughter, Anne. Ralegh danced in Ben Jonson's masque, *Love's Triumph* in 1630, and five years later became a gentleman of the privy chamber. His temper getting the better of him, he spent a week in the Fleet prison during 1639 for quarrelling with and striking Sir William St Ravee at court. He inherited his uncle Sir Nicholas Throckmorton's property at West Horsley, Surrey, in 1643.

Ralegh supported his king in the first civil war, but in time recognized that the English republic offered opportunities to the family of its foremost 'martyr'. Or, as the uncharitable Wood put it, he 'cringed afterwards to the men in power' (Wood, *Ath. Oxon.*, 1813–20, new edn, 2.244). It was rather more to the point that the Digbys, who had taken possession of Sherborne, remained determined royalists. Ralegh still coveted Sherborne, and saw opportunity in their misfortune. He sat as MP for Haslemere, Surrey, in the Rump Parliament from 1650 to 1653, petitioning time and again for the restoration of his father's lands in Dorset. But the Digbys' title was strong, and the most he secured was £500 a year out of the estate. One of these petitions was published in 1669, after his death, under the title *A Brief Relation of Sir Walter Ralegh's Troubles*. There is little doubt that he either wrote or else contributed information to the 1659 pamphlet *Observation upon some Particular Persons and Passages, Written by a Lover of the Truth*.

After Richard Cromwell's resignation Ralegh took his seat in the restored Rump, sitting frequently until its dissolution in March 1660. A supporter of General George Monck's efforts to reach an accommodation with Charles Stuart he was appointed to his father's former office, the governorship of Jersey, on 29 February 1660. At the Restoration he declined a knighthood; the honour was instead conferred upon his eldest son on 15 June, but young Walter Ralegh died in or about 1663. Two years later Carew Ralegh sold the West Horsley estate to Sir Edward Nicholas. He died at his London house in St Martin's Lane before the end of 1666 and was buried with his father at St Margaret's, Westminster, on 1 January 1667. It is said that Sir Walter Ralegh's head was interred at the same time. The register records that Carew Ralegh was 'kild', and without doubt his death was sudden, for a nuncupative will was subsequently registered in which he left his entire estate to his wife. Curiously, the parish register of West Horsley maintains that he was buried in the burial place of the manor in September 1680.

MARK NICHOLLS and PENRY WILLIAMS

Sources state papers domestic, PRO, SP 12; SP 13 · will, PRO, PROB 11/323, sig. 10 [Carew Ralegh] · Cecil MSS, Hatfield House, Hertfordshire · Sherborne Castle Estates, SHR/C/M · *The letters of Sir Walter Ralegh*, ed. A. Latham and J. Youings (1999) · HoP, *Commons, 1558–1603*, 3.271–6 · HoP, *Commons, 1509–58*, 3.173–4 · E. Edwards, *The life of Sir Walter Ralegh … together with his letters*, 2 vols. (1868) · P. Lefranc, *Sir Walter Ralegh, écrivain* (Quebec and Paris, 1968) · W. Stebbing, *Sir Walter Ralegh* (1891); repr. (1899) · *The works of Sir Walter Ralegh*, ed. W. Oldys and T. Birch, 8 vols. (1829) · V. T. Harlow, ed., *Sir Walter Ralegh's last voyage* (1932) · A. R. Beer, *Sir Walter Ralegh and his readers in the seventeenth century: speaking to the people* (1997) · *The poems of Sir Walter Ralegh: a historical edition*, ed. M. Rudick (Tempe, Arizona, 1999) · M. Nicholls, 'Sir Walter Ralegh's treason: a prosecution document', *EngHR*, 110 (1995), 902–24 · T. Brushfield, 'The history of the world, by Sir Walter Ralegh: a biographical study', *Report and Transactions of the Devonshire Association*, 36 (1904), 181–218 · T. Brushfield, 'Remarks on the ancestry of Sir Walter Ralegh', *Report and Transactions of the Devonshire Association*, 32 (1900), 309–40 · T. Brushfield, 'Three state documents relating to the arrest and execution of Sir Walter Ralegh in 1618', *Report and Transactions of the Devonshire Association*, 37 (1905), 284–324; 38 (1906), 416–90 · E. A. Strathmann, *Sir Walter Ralegh: a study in Elizabethan scepticism* (1951) · J. W. Shirley, *Thomas Harriot: a biography* (1983) · S. J. Greenblatt, *Sir Walter Ralegh: the Renaissance man and his roles* (New Haven, Conn., 1973) · J. Racin, *Sir Walter Ralegh as historian* (Salzburg, 1974) · *State trials* · *The letters of John Chamberlain*, ed. N. E. McClure, 2 vols. (1939) · *Correspondence of King James VI of Scotland with Sir Robert Cecil and others in England during the reign of Elizabeth*, ed. J. Bruce, CS, old ser., 78 (1861) · *Letters from Sir Robert Cecil to Sir George Carew*, ed. J. Maclean, CS, 88 (1864) · J. Youings, ed., *Ralegh in Exeter 1985: privateering and colonization in the reign of Elizabeth* (1985) · A. Latham, 'A birth-date for Sir Walter Ralegh', *Études Anglaises*, 3 (1956), 243–5 · *The poems of Sir Walter Ralegh*, ed. A. Latham (1962) · A. Latham, 'Sir Walter Ralegh's farewell letter to his wife in 1603: a question of authenticity', *Essays and Studies by Members of the English Association*, 25 (1939), 39–58 · A. Latham, 'Sir Walter Ralegh's will', *Review of English Studies*, new ser., 22 (1971), 129–36 · P. Lefranc, 'La date du marriage du Sir Walter Ralegh',

Études Anglaises, 9 (1956), 192–211 · W. Oakeshott, 'Sir Walter Ralegh's library', *The Library*, 23 (1968), 285–327 · M. J. G. Stanford, 'A history of the Raleigh family of Fardel and Budleigh in the early Tudor period', MA diss., U. Lond., 1955 · D. C. Peck, 'Raleigh, Sidney, Oxford, and the Catholics, 1579', *N&Q*, 223 (1978), 427–31 · A. L. Rowse, *Ralegh and the Throckmortons* (1962) · P. Edwards, *Sir Walter Ralegh* (1953) · R. Naunton, *Fragmenta regalia*, ed. E. Arber (1653); repr. (1870) · *Brief lives, chiefly of contemporaries, set down by John Aubrey, between the years 1669 and 1696*, ed. A. Clark, 2 vols. (1898) · P. Lefranc, 'Un inédit de Ralegh sur la succession', *Études Anglaises*, 13 (1960), 38–46 · P. Ahier, *The governorship of Sir Walter Ralegh in Jersey, 1600–1603* (St Helier, 1971) · J. W. Shirley, 'Sir Walter Ralegh's Guinea finances', *Huntington Library Quarterly*, 13 (1949–50), 55–69 · D. B. Quinn, *Raleigh and the British empire* (1947); rev. edn (1962) · A. M. C. Latham, 'Sir Walter Raleigh's gold mine', *Essays and Studies by Members of the English Association*, new ser., 4 (1951), 94–111 · W. S. Powell, 'John Pory on the death of Sir Walter Ralegh', *William and Mary Quarterly*, 3rd ser., 9 (1952), 532–8 · G. P. B. Naish, 'Raleigh's cloak: an historical revision', *Mariner's Mirror*, 41 (1955), 63 · R. N. Salaman, 'The introduction to Europe, the Raleigh and other legends', *The history and social influence of the potato*, ed. R. N. Salaman (1949), 142–58 · W. Ralegh, *The history of the world: to which is prefix'd the life of the author, by mr. [W.] Oldys*, 1st edn, 2 vols. (1614); 11th edn (1736) · C. Armitage, *Sir Walter Ralegh: an annotated bibliography* (Chapel Hill, 1987) · J. L. Mills, 'Recent studies in Ralegh', *English Literary Renaissance*, 15 (1985), 225–44 · T. Raleigh, *Sir Walter Raleigh* (2001)

Archives BL, corresp. and MSS, Add. MS 6177 · BL, journal, MS Cotton Titus B viii, fol. 153 · BL, commonplace book, Add. MS 57555 · Bodl. Oxf., letters and MSS · Carl H. Pforzheimer Library, New York, letters · Devon RO, prayer book · FM Cam., commonplace book · Folger, notes · Hatfield House, Hertfordshire, MSS · Longleat House, Wiltshire, corresp. and MSS · Queen's College, Oxford, letters to James I and others · University of North Carolina, Chapel Hill, MSS | BL, Sloane MSS, corresp. and MSS · BL, letters and speeches, Harley MSS

Likenesses N. Hilliard, watercolour miniature, *c*.1585, NPG [*see illus.*] · attrib. H., oils, 1588, NPG · portrait, *c*.1597, NG Ire. · oils, 1602 (with his son, Wat), NPG · Houbraken, line engraving, repro. in T. Birch, *Lives* · S. Passe, line engraving, BM, NPG; repro. in W. Ralegh, *History of the world* (1617) · R. Vaughan, line engraving, repro. in *Maxims of state* · oils (after portrait by unknown artist, *c*.1590), Colonial Williamsburg, Virginia

Ralegh, Walter (1586–1646), dean of Wells, was the second son of Sir Walter Ralegh's elder brother, Sir Carew *Ralegh (*c*.1550–1625/6) [see under Ralegh, Sir Walter (1554–1618)] of Downton, Wiltshire, and his wife, Dorothy (*d*. 1616), widow of Sir John Thynne of Longleat, Wiltshire, and daughter of Sir William Wroughton of Broad Hinton, Wiltshire. He was born at Downton and educated at Winchester College and at Magdalen College, Oxford, where he matriculated as commoner on 5 November 1602. He graduated BA in 1605 and MA in 1608. 'He was admired for his disputations in the schools, even when he was an undergraduate' (Patrick).

Ralegh took holy orders, and in 1618 became chaplain to William Herbert, third earl of Pembroke. In 1621 he was presented by his patron to the rectory of Chedzoy, near Bridgwater, Somerset, and in the following year received the rectory of Wilton St Mary, Wiltshire. Between 1620 and 1623 he married Maria, daughter of Sir Ralph Gibbs of Honington, Warwickshire. About 1630 he was chosen a chaplain-in-ordinary to Charles I, who admired his preaching. In 1632 he was made rector of Elingdon, otherwise Wroughton, Wiltshire, and in 1635 of Street-cum-

Walton, Somerset. In 1634 he was minor prebendary of Combe in Wells Cathedral, and in 1636 he was created DD. The next year he became rector of St Buryan, Cornwall, and in 1641 succeeded George Warburton as dean of Wells.

Before the civil war Ralegh was one of the circle associated with Lucius Cary, second Viscount Falkland, at Great Tew; among his friends were Henry Hammond, William Chillingworth, and Edward Hyde, earl of Clarendon. While he was attending the king during the civil war his rectory at Chedzoy was plundered by the parliamentarians, his property stolen, and his cattle driven away. His wife and children took refuge at Downton, where Ralegh joined them. After the royalist victories in 1643 Ralegh was able to return to Chedzoy and to live there in safety until the defeat of George Goring, Lord Goring, at Langport in 1645. Ralegh was reported to have been captured at Bridgwater on the fall of that town (21 July 1645), though another report says that he was taken when Raglan Castle surrendered in August 1646. He was placed under house arrest at Chedzoy and subsequently removed, first to the county gaol at Ilchester, then to the county committee's prison at Banwell, and eventually to his own deanery at Wells. His gaoler was David Barrett, a Baptist shoemaker who was marshal to the Somerset county committee. In the late summer of 1646 Ralegh was mortally wounded in a scuffle with Barrett and died, at his deanery, six weeks later. According to Simon Patrick the incident occurred when Ralegh tried to stop Barrett when he attempted to inspect a letter that Ralegh had written to his wife (cf. Walker, *Sufferings of the Clergy*, which, however, contains several inaccuracies, and Ryves, *Mercurius Rusticus*, 1647). Ralegh died on 10 October 1646, and was buried in the choir of Wells Cathedral, before the dean's stall.

Ralegh's papers were preserved in the family, and thirteen of his sermons were given by his widow to Simon Patrick (1626–1707), then dean of Peterborough, who published them in 1679, with a biographical notice and a Latin poem written in praise of Ralegh by a Cambridge admirer, probably Patrick himself. The volume is entitled *Reliquiae Raleighanae, being discourses and sermons on several subjects, by the Reverend Dr. Walter Raleigh*. The sermons, all apparently dating from before the outbreak of the civil war, show that Ralegh was moderate in his churchmanship, able to criticize both Calvinist and Arminian extremes, though usually in restrained language: 'the truth', he declared, 'lies between both' (*Reliquiae Raleighanae*, 156). A sermon, 'The original of wars', evidently preached at the time of the bishops' wars, is more emphatic in its denunciations of puritans as a 'viperous brood of error and contention' (ibid., 142) motivated by greed for the church's wealth, although in it Ralegh also attacks swaggering cavaliers as 'Ruffians and Rodotomantos, Brethren of the Sword that read Tavern Lectures' (ibid., 133). In 1719 Laurence Howell published *Certain Queries Proposed by Roman Catholicks, and Answered by Dr. Walter Raleigh*, with an account of Ralegh copied from Patrick. Of a tract on the millennium which Ralegh is said to have written, no trace remains.

E. C. MARCHANT, *rev.* DAVID UNDERDOWN

Sources *Walker rev.*, 318 • S. Patrick, 'A brief account of the author', in W. Ralegh, *Reliquiae Raleighanae*, ed. S. Patrick (1679) • J. Walker, *An attempt towards recovering an account of the numbers and sufferings of the clergy of the Church of England*, pt 2 (1714), 71 • D. Underdown, 'A case concerning bishops' lands: Cornelius Burges and the Corporation of Wells', *EngHR*, 78 (1963), 18–48 • D. Underdown, *Somerset in the civil war and interregnum* (1973) • B. Ryves, *Mercurius Rusticus* (1647) • Foster, *Alum. Oxon.* • G. D. Squibb, ed., *Wiltshire visitation pedigrees, 1623*, Harleian Society, 105–6 (1954) • F. W. Weaver, ed., *Somerset incumbents* (privately printed, Bristol, 1889), 193 • PRO, PROB 10/694 (20 June 1648) • *VCH Somerset*, 6.250

Wealth at death probably small; small legacies to family: will, proved 20 June 1648, PRO, PROB 10/694

Raleigh, Alexander (1817–1880), Congregational minister, was born at The Flock, a farm near Castle Douglas, Kirkcudbrightshire, on 3 January 1817. He was the fourth son and the fifth of the nine children born to Thomas and Isabella Raleigh. His parents were members of the Reformed Presbyterian church which maintained the ideals of the covenanter Richard Cameron. Alexander attended the high school at Castle Douglas, and in 1832 was apprenticed to a draper there; he continued in that trade in Liverpool after the family moved there in 1835. He joined the Congregational Crescent Chapel of which John Kelly (1801–1876) was minister, entered Blackburn Academy in March 1840, and moved to Manchester when the Lancashire Independent College took over the students of Blackburn Academy in 1843.

On 6 November 1844 Raleigh accepted a call to be minister of Greenock Congregational Church and was ordained there on 5 April 1845. Ill health compelled him to resign on 10 July 1848, but after a period of rest he began to minister to the church at Masborough Chapel, Rotherham, on 24 August 1850. On 10 August 1851, at Edinburgh, Raleigh married Mary Darling, only daughter of James Gifford of that city; they had four daughters and a son, Sir Walter Alexander *Raleigh (1861–1922). Raleigh subsequently moved to West George Street Congregational Church, Glasgow, and began his ministry there on 1 July 1855 in succession to Dr Ralph Wardlaw (1779–1853). He supervised the move to a new church at Elgin Place, opened in August 1856. Ill health still afflicted him and in December 1856 he moved south to Hare Court Chapel, Canonbury, London. His last move was to Kensington Congregational Church in 1875.

Alexander Raleigh was an attractive character, unassuming, tactful, and generous in his dealings with others. His rich, musical voice and polished sentences made him a powerful pulpit orator whose services were in constant demand. In May 1861 he preached the annual sermon of the London Missionary Society and was appointed one of the Merchants' lecturers. He was an exceptionally successful minister. The high regard in which he was held was shown by his being elected chairman of the Congregational Union of England and Wales on two occasions, in 1868 and 1879. In 1865 he represented the Congregational Union at the National Council of American Congregational Churches at Boston, together with Dr Robert Vaughan (1895–1868) and Dr George Smith (1803–1870), and his eirenic spirit did much to overcome the American hostility to Vaughan, who had been critical of the north during the civil war.

Some eighteen titles were published under Raleigh's name, most of them sermons. The most popular were *Quiet Resting Places* (1863), *The Book of Esther* (1880) (a series of meditations), and *Thoughts for the Weary and Sorrowful* (ed. Mary Raleigh, 3rd edn, 1886). A few of his publications were lectures and addresses, including *Questions and Duties of the Time*, his chairman's address at the Congregational Union meeting on 13 October 1868. Raleigh died at his home at 27 Ladbroke Grove, London, on 19 April 1880 and he was buried at Abney Park cemetery. His wife survived him and edited a life of Raleigh (1881) and collections of his sermons.   W. B. LOWTHER, *rev.* R. TUDUR JONES

Sources *Alexander Raleigh: records of his life*, ed. M. Raleigh (1881) · *Congregational Year Book* (1881), 387–8 · H. R. R. [H. R. Reynolds], 'Rev. Alexander Raleigh—in memoriam', *Evangelical Magazine and Missionary Chronicle*, [4th ser.], 10 (1880), 379–81 · H. Allon and J. G. Rogers, *Alexander Raleigh, D. D.: memorial sermons* (1880) · W. M. Statham, *In memoriam: a sermon … on the occasion of the decease of the Rev. Alexander Raleigh* (1880) · J. Smith, *Our Scottish clergy*, 1st ser. (1848), 145–8 · 'Alexander Raleigh', *The Congregationalist*, 11 (1882), 73–7 · J. G. Rogers, 'Later memorials of Dr. Raleigh', *The Congregationalist*, 13 (1884), 53–61

Likenesses photograph, 1880, repro. in Allon and Rogers, *Alexander Raleigh* · J. Cochran, stipple and line engraving (after photograph by Maull & Polyblank), NPG · oils; probably copy, Congregational Centre, Castle Gate, Nottingham · portrait, repro. in Raleigh, ed., *Alexander Raleigh*

Wealth at death under £12,000: probate, 7 May 1880, *CGPLA Eng. & Wales*

Raleigh, Sir Walter Alexander (1861–1922), literary scholar and university teacher, was born on 5 September 1861 at 4 Highbury Quadrant, London, the fifth child and only son of Alexander *Raleigh (1817–1880), then Congregational minister of Hare Court Chapel, Canonbury, London, and his wife, Mary Darling, the only daughter of James Gifford, of Edinburgh. After a short time at the City of London School he was sent in 1876 to Edinburgh, where he lived with his uncle, the judge Adam Gifford, Lord Gifford (1820–1887), and became a pupil at the Edinburgh Academy. On his return to London in 1877 he attended University College School and proceeded to University College, London, graduating with a BA in 1881. In October 1881 he entered King's College, Cambridge, and obtained a second class in the historical tripos of 1885. In the Lent term of 1883 he interrupted his residency at King's to travel by sea to Italy in the interest of his health; since childhood he had been subject to a nervous tremor in both arms, which he never wholly overcame. Upon his return he had shot up to 6 feet 6 inches in height. For some time he edited the *Cambridge Review*, and in Michaelmas term 1884 he was president of the Cambridge Union.

In the autumn of 1885 Raleigh went to India as the first professor of English literature at the Mohammedan Anglo-Oriental College in Aligarh, but he was invalided home in April 1887. His letters give a vivid picture of his Indian experience (*Letters*, 1.28–107), which he always spoke of with enthusiasm. Forbidden by his doctors to

Sir Walter Alexander Raleigh (1861–1922), by unknown photographer

return to India, he thought of becoming a journalist. During the winter of 1888–9 he lectured for the Oxford University extension delegacy, and in March 1889 he became personal assistant to Professor Adolphus William Ward at Victoria University, Manchester. In November of the same year he was appointed professor of modern literature at University College, Liverpool, in succession to A. C. Bradley, and began his work there in January 1890. On 8 July 1890 he married Lucie Gertrude Jackson (*b.* 1865/6), the only daughter of Mason Jackson, the art editor of the *Illustrated London News*. They had four sons, and one daughter, Philippa, who later married the scholar and journalist Charles Whibley (1859–1930).

At Liverpool Raleigh played a spirited part in college affairs, at a time when the college was developing into the university. He also began to write, his chief publication to this point having been a paper read to the Browning Society while he was still at Cambridge (Browning Society's *Papers*, no. 25, 1884). His first book was *The English Novel* (1894), which he soon came to regard as ''prentice' work, but it exhibits his gift for lucid and lively narrative, covering the period up to the publication of Scott's *Waverley*. It was followed by *Robert Louis Stevenson: an Essay* (1895), a brief appreciation based on a lecture delivered at the Royal Institution, and *Style* (1897), which he wrote with enthusiasm but afterwards disparaged as 'stuck up'—its prose is certainly highly affected. He was Clark lecturer in English literature at Trinity College, Cambridge, in 1899, and embodied his lectures in *Milton* (1900), a penetrating study, which includes interesting analyses of the poet's language. Its admirers have included William Empson, who called it a 'splendid handbook' (*Milton's God*, 1961, 9). The same year he edited, with a long introduction which broke new ground, Sir Thomas Hoby's *Book of the Courtier, from the Italian of Count Baldassare Castiglione* for the Tudor Translations, a series of reprints projected by W. E. Henley. In addition to these five books belonging to the ten years of his professorship at Liverpool, Raleigh also contributed to *English Prose Selections*, edited by Henry Craik, and to periodicals such as the *New Review* and the *Yellow Book*. Although his appointment to the professorship had been thought to be risky, by 1900 he was winning recognition as the most original and stimulating of the younger critics.

In June 1900 Raleigh was appointed by the crown to the chair of English language and literature at Glasgow University, again in succession to A. C. Bradley, and for the next four years he was one of the outstanding personalities there. Daily lectures to hundreds of students and continual administrative meetings left him less time for writing than he had enjoyed at Liverpool. But in the summer vacation of 1902, while staying at Stanford in the Vale, Berkshire, he wrote *Wordsworth* (1903), a companion to his *Milton* and a surprise to admirers of Wordsworth, who had not expected the author of *Style* to appraise the poet's language and themes so sympathetically. He intended that his next book should be on Chaucer, whom, in contrast to Milton and Wordsworth, he called 'my man', but only disjointed lecture notes remain. Having been consulted by the Glasgow publishing firm of MacLehose about their projected series of English voyages, Raleigh promised an essay for their edition of Richard Hakluyt's *Voyages*. This he wrote at Uffington, Berkshire, in the summer of 1904. It was published under the title of 'The English voyages of the sixteenth century' in *Hakluyt's Voyages* (12, 1905) and in 1906 was published separately. He said more than once that it was his 'best book', though modern readers may find unacceptable his tolerance of some of the actions of the English seamen.

In June 1904 Raleigh became the first holder of the new chair of English literature at Oxford, with a fellowship at Magdalen College. The school of English language and literature had been established in 1894, but its steady development began with Raleigh's appointment. His usual method as a lecturer was informal—a few facts, the reading of passages (admirably interpreted), and a running commentary. Much depended on his mood at the time, but when he was at his best no student forgot the impression he had made. Believing that system and dogma are unreliable guides in the study of literature, he invited his listeners to read and think for themselves. His audience contained men of all ages—during one term Robert Bridges attended regularly—and to one and all he seemed to speak as an equal. This was a rare attitude at the time for a professor to adopt, but it aroused enthusiasm among his students. An important part of his work at Oxford was his acting as an adviser to the Clarendon Press.

Raleigh's first essay written at Oxford was his introduction to *Lyrical Poems of William Blake* (1905). He wrote *Shakespeare* (1907) during the latter half of 1906, and of all his

books it was this one which he was most pleased to have finished. 'I think Falstaff is good', he said, 'so are Shakespeare's women'. He realized the book's inequalities; but the chapter entitled 'Story and character' is important for its insights into Shakespeare's methods. One vital point which he makes is that Shakespeare could not work on his characters until he had created a situation: 'His plays open with a postulate; then the characters begin to live' (pocket edn, 1925, 134).

Raleigh welcomed the relaxation offered by a voyage to South Africa in 1907, though during his two months there he lectured at Pretoria, Johannesburg, Durban, Grahamstown, Cape Town, and Stellenbosch. On his return he compiled a collection of Samuel Johnson's essays and notes on Shakespeare (*Johnson on Shakespeare*, 1908). In 1910 he brought out *Six Essays on Johnson*. This was his last book on a single author, and there are many critics who consider it his best. He was the Leslie Stephen lecturer at Cambridge in 1907 and went there as Clark lecturer for the second time, at Trinity College in 1911. In 1911 he was knighted on the occasion of the coronation of George V.

Raleigh had never overrated the importance of the academic study of literature, and from his first years at Oxford, and even earlier, he had an increasing desire to write on men and things directly. It was significant of this changing interest that his next book should have been an edition of the *Complete Works of George Savile, First Marquess of Halifax* (1912). His Henry Sidgwick memorial lecture on Dryden, delivered at Newnham College, Cambridge, in 1913, was largely on politics and the application of Dryden's satire to the present day. His essay on Burns (contributed to W. S. Douglas's edition of J. G. Lockhart's *Life of Burns*, 1914) he thought as good as anything he had written 'on a man'. But he had no heart for further literary criticism after the outbreak of war in 1914. He wrote only one more critical essay on a new subject, 'Don Quixote' (*TLS*, 27 April 1916). In October 1914, when his Oxford professorship was reconstituted as the Merton chair of English literature, he became a fellow of Merton College. Other academic honours which he received were honorary degrees from the universities of Glasgow and Durham and honorary fellowships of King's College, Cambridge (1912), and Magdalen College, Oxford (1916).

The war occupied Raleigh's thoughts for the rest of his life. *Might is Right*, written for the series of Oxford Pamphlets (October 1914), was followed by addresses on *The War of Ideas* (December 1916), *The Faith of England* (March 1917), *Some Gains of the War* (February 1918), and *The War and the Press* (March 1918), and by his British Academy lecture, *Shakespeare and England* (July 1918). These were collected into a volume entitled *England and the War* (1918), the main subject of which is the English character. In 1915 he was responsible for '*The Times* broadsheets for soldiers and sailors'. In that year he went to the United States to deliver at Princeton University the two lectures published under the title of *Romance* (1915); they were based on old material and delivered in the intervals of speaking about England and the war. His introduction to *Shakespeare's England* (1916), a book which he had planned many years earlier, is a glorification of the Elizabethan spirit and ends on a patriotic note.

Raleigh found a new interest in his lectures at Oxford after 1918, when men who had fought in the war crowded to hear him. At no time was he more sought after by the younger members of the university. These post-war years were busy, for in July 1918 he had accepted the invitation of the Air Ministry to write the official history of the Royal Air Force. He was able to complete only the first volume of *The War in the Air* (*History of the Great War Based on Official Documents*, 1922) but it remains his longest work. It was his first experience of writing history on a large scale, and he stated in his preface that 'The writer of this history has endeavoured to make his narrative intelligible to those who, like himself, are outsiders'. His style is here at its simplest, but the fervour of his admiration for the heroism of the air is everywhere apparent and finds memorable expression in the introduction. The volume was published a few weeks after his death.

On 16 March 1922 Raleigh set out for the Middle East in preparation for the second volume of *The War in the Air*. When he returned to London on 25 April he was in the grip of typhoid fever, contracted when his aeroplane was marooned for four or five days in the desert between Jerusalem and Baghdad. He died at the Acland Nursing Home, Oxford, on 13 May 1922 and was buried at Ferry Hinksey, Berkshire, the village near Oxford where he had lived since 1909 at The Hangings, the house designed for him by his friend A. H. Clough, the son of the poet. His wife survived him.

Raleigh was a fine conversationalist, equally at his ease in very different kinds of company. His letters show a wide range of mood and often disguise their purpose in their jocularity. Reviewing the letters, however, Virginia Woolf thought that the 'excitement, the adventure, the turmoil of creation was unknown to him' (Woolf, 87). As a critic he came to write most freely when dealing with an author's character and outlook. His aim, he once said briefly, was 'to explain people', and he was more interested in men than in movements or theories. Yet he taught the continuity of literature and maintained that the English school at Oxford must be a school of the history of English literature and language. With Joseph Wright, C. H. Firth, and others, Raleigh reformed the examination structure and oversaw a considerable expansion in the number of students. His aims were not completely realized, since it proved impossible fully to integrate philological and literary studies in the degree course.

A selection from Raleigh's lighter pieces in verse and prose, among them three 'little plays', was edited by his second son, Hilary Raleigh, in 1923 under the title *Laughter from a Cloud*, and in the same year fourteen of his occasional essays and addresses were collected in *Some Authors*, a volume which he had roughly planned. The longer passages in his notes for his lectures were edited in 1926 by George Gordon under the title *On Writing and Writers*. His *Letters* (2 vols.), edited by Lady Raleigh, also appeared in 1926. A memorial window to him by Laura Anning Bell was placed in the library of Merton College. The larger portion of the fund raised in his memory provides an income for the purchase of rare books for the English faculty library at Oxford, which he had been primarily responsible for founding in 1914.

D. N. SMITH, rev. DONALD HAWES

Sources G. S. G. [G. S. Gordon], 'Walter Raleigh', *TLS* (8 June 1922), 371 · O. Elton, *Liverpool Post* (15 May 1922) · H. W. Garrod, *Oxford Chronicle and Berks and Bucks Gazette* (19 May 1922) · R. W. Chapman, *Walter Raleigh* (1922) [privately printed] · H. A. Jones, *Sir Walter Raleigh and the air history: a personal recollection* (1922) · V. Crum, *Sir Walter Alexander Raleigh* (1923) · *Letters of Sir Walter Raleigh, 1879–1922*, ed. L. G. J. Raleigh, 2nd edn, 2 vols. (1926) · V. Woolf, 'Walter Raleigh', *The captain's deathbed* (1950) · A. A. Ansari, ed., *Essays on Walter Raleigh* (1988) · D. J. Palmer, *The rise of English studies* (1965) · m. cert. · d. cert. · *CGPLA Eng. & Wales* (1922)

Archives Bodl. Oxf., corresp. and MSS · Bodl. Oxf., notes · NRA, corresp. and literary papers · U. Lpool L., letters | BL, corresp. with Macmillans, MS 55029 · Bodl. Oxf., letters to R. W. Chapman and K. M. Chapman · Bodl. Oxf., letters to C. H. Firth · Bodl. Oxf., letters to Gilbert Murray · CUL, letters to M. R. James · Herts. ALS, letters to Lady Desborough · King's AC Cam., letters to Oscar Browning · King's AC Cam., letters to Sir J. T. Sheppard · NL Scot., letters to D. N. Smith · U. Birm. L., letters to Oliver Lodge · U. Glas. L., letters to W. Macneile Dixon · U. Glas. L., letters to D. S. MacColl · U. Leeds, Brotherton L., letters to Sir Edmund Gosse · U. Lpool L., letters to John Sampson · U. Southampton L., letters

Likenesses F. Dodd, oils, *c*.1896, King's Cam. · L. A. Bell, memorial window, Merton Oxf. · M. Egerton, lithograph (after photograph), NPG · W. Rothenstein, drawing, repro. in Raleigh, ed., *Letters of Sir Walter Raleigh* · photograph, NPG [*see illus.*] · prints (after L. A. Bell), NPG

Wealth at death £11,913 7s. 6d.: probate, 12 July 1922, *CGPLA Eng. & Wales*

Raleigh [Ralegh], **William of** (d. 1250), justice, administrator, and bishop of Winchester, came of a prominent Devon family which had several branches and whose members are sometimes difficult to distinguish from one another. In 1212 King John presented him to the church of Bratton Fleming in that county, when he was described as 'clerk'. He is first known to have served as a clerk of the bench in 1214, and there are numerous further references to him in that capacity from 1219 to 1229. For at least the latter part of that period, and certainly from 1225, he was the personal clerk of the bench and eyre justice Martin of Pateshull, and left the bench to go on eyre when Pateshull did so, including a circuit in the north in 1226–7, when he also acted as a commissioner for the assessment of tallage. It seems unlikely that he was the same William of Raleigh who was sheriff of Devon from 1225 to 1228; the sheriff was most likely the Devon knight of that name who had probably also served as a coroner immediately before 1225. William of Raleigh the clerk became a justice of the bench in May 1229, following Pateshull's retirement, second only to Stephen of Segrave in seniority, and above Robert of Lexinton, who had been a justice long before him. He inherited Pateshull's rolls, with the preparation of which he had been much concerned, and which later passed to Henry of Bracton, who handed them in to the exchequer in 1257/8. By December 1231 Raleigh's clerk was Roger of Thirkleby, a future justice.

Raleigh took part in an eyre in Middlesex in 1229, and then in seven more eyres elsewhere in 1232/3, in all but the first of which he was the senior justice. He became senior justice of the bench in Michaelmas term 1233, superseding Thomas of Muleton, and remained as such until his appointment in May 1234 as justice of the court *coram rege*, after the fall of his predecessor, the justiciar Stephen of Segrave. He thus became the most senior of all the king's judges, but without the title of justiciar, that office being allowed to lapse. For the whole of his tenure of office he was the only professional justice in the court, sitting with household stewards and members of the king's council as colleagues. By 1238 Bracton was probably his clerk, perhaps succeeding Thirkleby at about the time of the latter's marriage in 1235 or 1236.

During the next few years Raleigh was a trusted royal counsellor as well as a justice, and in fact between 1236 and 1239 he seems to have been the king's chief adviser, being responsible for at least some of the Statute of Merton in 1236 and for other legal reforms, and also for a programme of fiscal reforms which tried to lay secure foundations for the royal finances, culminating in 1237 in the grant of a thirtieth on movables. His position was shaken, however, by the revolt of Richard, earl of Cornwall, in January 1238, and was probably further undermined in the following August, when Henry III tried to persuade the monks of Winchester to elect as bishop another leading counsellor, the queen's uncle William de Valence. On the monks' stating a preference for Raleigh, the king remarked that Raleigh had killed more men with his tongue than Valence had with his sword. In February 1239 Raleigh was elected bishop of Coventry and Lichfield, but he declined; in April he was elected bishop of Norwich, and this time he accepted. As a result he ceased to be a justice, and he retired from the court about Whitsuntide.

On his appointment as bishop Raleigh gave up the lesser church livings he had acquired earlier. The most prestigious was the treasurership of Exeter Cathedral, which he had obtained by 1234; others included Blatherwycke in Northamptonshire, to which he had been presented in 1220, perhaps as a consequence of his association with Pateshull, and Whaplode in Lincolnshire, which he had received in 1231. As bishop of Norwich he punished Jews accused of conspiring to crucify a Christian boy. In 1241 the monks of Winchester still wanted him as their bishop, this time in preference to Boniface of Savoy, another of the queen's uncles and the king's candidate. The king again opposed Raleigh's candidature and urged him to renounce it, but he refused, upon which the king appealed to the pope. In September 1243 Innocent IV confirmed the choice of Raleigh by bull, which the strenuous efforts of the king and the persecution of Raleigh failed to reverse. Unable to obtain possession of his see, Raleigh placed Winchester under interdict and retired to France, where he enjoyed the favour of Louis IX. In 1244 the king had to relent and allow Raleigh to take possession of his bishopric, which was, however, ruined by the costs of the long dispute and by having been in the king's hands for six years.

As bishop of Winchester Raleigh continued to play a

wider public role, and in 1244 he was one of the joint committee of bishops, earls, and barons chosen to consider the royal demand for a subsidy. The next year he attended the Council of Lyons. In 1247 the king spent Christmas at Winchester and was reconciled with the bishop. In 1249 Raleigh went abroad again, this time to save money; he died at Tours on 1 September 1250. Matthew Paris wrote a touching account of his end. Earlier he had described him, in his annal for 1236, as a clerk who was the king's familiar, a discreet man and skilled in the laws of the land. One of the most notable of thirteenth-century justices, Raleigh has been plausibly credited with the authorship, or at least the patronage, of the treatise *De legibus et consuetudinibus Angliae*, traditionally ascribed to Bracton. Bracton probably worked under him in the court *coram rege* and may have made revisions to an existing text, based on the law as administered by Pateshull and Raleigh, in the years before 1239. The treatise and the compilation known as *Bracton's Notebook* provide between them a number of examples of legal innovations by Raleigh through the drafting of new writs, such as the action of cosinage in 1237, and contain many of the cases he heard, some from plea rolls which no longer survive. William of Raleigh had a brother called Robert, probably younger, who on one occasion acted as William's agent in the bench, but who seems to have died young in 1236.

DAVID CROOK

Sources C. A. F. Meekings, 'Martin Pateshull and William Raleigh', *BIHR*, 26 (1953), 157–80 · C. A. F. Meekings, 'Martin de Pateshull of good memory my sometime lord', *BIHR*, 47 (1974), 224–9 · *Curia regis rolls preserved in the Public Record Office* (1922–), vols. 7–16 · C. A. F. Meekings, unpublished notes on Raleigh · Paris, *Chron.*, vols. 3–5 · *Ann. mon.*, vol. 2 · *Henrici de Bracton de legibus et consuetudinibus Angliae / Bracton on the laws and customs of England*, ed. G. E. Woodbine, ed. and trans. S. E. Thorne, 4 vols. (1968–77) · A. M. S. Leys, ed., *The Sandford cartulary*, 1, Oxfordshire RS, 19 (1938) · *Roberti Grosseteste episcopi quondam Lincolniensis epistolae*, ed. H. R. Luard, Rolls Series, 25 (1861) · court of common pleas, feet of fines, PRO, CP 25/1 · Chancery records · plea rolls, PRO, KB26, JUST/1 · R. C. Stacey, *Politics, policy and finance under Henry III, 1216–1245* (1987) · *Bracton's note book*, ed. F. W. Maitland, 3 vols. (1887)

Ralfe, James (*fl.* 1820–1829), naval historian, was the author of *The Naval Chronology of Great Britain*, which covered the years 1803 to 1816 (3 vols., 1820): it was a useful compilation, intended to be a continuation of the *Naval Chronology* of Captain Isaac Schomberg, but more extensive. It was apparently issued in parts; the date on the title-page was that of its completion. Ralfe subsequently wrote *The Naval Biography of Great Britain, consisting of Historical Memoirs of Those Officers of the British Navy who Distinguished Themselves During the Reign of His Majesty George III* (4 vols., 1828), published in parts. In 1829 Ralfe issued a pamphlet vindicating Sir Edward Codrington's conduct at Navarino. The data in the *Naval Biography* seem to have been mostly contributed by the subjects, and may be accepted as largely correct as to facts: the inferences are less certain, and the style is very stilted and verbose. The work was reportedly financially unsuccessful, and in 1829 an attempt was made by some senior naval officers to raise a fund for the author's benefit, the subscriptions to be paid to his publishers, Messrs Whitmore and Fenn, 6 Charing Cross. J. K. LAUGHTON, *rev.* ANDREW LAMBERT

Sources BL cat.

Ralfs, John (1807–1890), surgeon and botanist, was born at Hill House, Millbrook, near Southampton, on 13 September 1807, the second son of Samuel Ralfs (*d.* 1808), yeoman, and his wife, Mary. Following the death of his father from typhus, John, his brother, and two sisters were brought up at Southampton by their mother.

Ralfs was educated at private schools in Southampton, Bishop's Waltham, and Romsey; he was then articled to his uncle, a Brentford surgeon, with whom he lived for two and a half years. He was also a student under Dr Lyford at Winchester Hospital, before further study at Guy's Hospital, London. His studies at Guy's were interrupted by typhus and it was not until 1832 that he passed the MRCS examination (specially commended for his botany). After a year as assistant at a practice in Towcester, Northamptonshire, he spent about two years in partnership with another surgeon at Shoreditch in London. In 1835 health problems (probably a tubercular lung infection) forced Ralfs to move to Torquay, where in the same year he married Laura Cecilia (*d.* 1848), daughter of Henry Newman of London. Although a son, John Henry, was born in 1836, the marriage failed within two years; Laura took her son and returned to her parents in France. No longer practising his profession, and very frail, Ralfs settled in Penzance in November 1837. As his health gradually improved he increasingly returned to his schoolboy love of botany.

In 1839 Ralfs published his *British Phaenogamous Plants and Ferns*. By the early 1840s a fascination with the smaller freshwater algae during field forays on Dartmoor led to the idea for a work on British Desmidieae. At about the same time, Arthur Hill Hassall was also planning a work on British freshwater algae. From extant correspondence it is clear that Hassall and Ralfs were fully aware of each other's intent to publish from before 1844. Later reports suggest Ralfs initially believed the works complemented each other and suggested co-operation. However, later correspondence (from 1844 onwards) indicates that Ralfs came to the decision personally to publish his original data before it could be used elsewhere. This may have been in part due to Hassall's demands for data, drawings, and other assistance from many contemporaries (including Ralfs and Jenner), which were on the grounds of priority of intent. Hassall's work, *A History of British Freshwater Algae*, was published in 1845. Ralfs's *The British Desmidieae* did not appear until 1848, yet eighteen months before publication Ralfs already had a subscription list greater than 220 names, with many of the subscribers requiring more than a single copy. A restricted print run (500, according to Marquand) has subsequently made the work, in its time considered unsurpassed for the beauty and accuracy of its plates, both rare and costly. German scientists bought many copies.

Comparisons between Ralfs's and Hassall's works, and approach to the subject, were inevitable. Ralfs is among those pioneers usually considered as founders of the critical approach to freshwater algology, Hassall as an acquisitive compiler, whose intent was to permit the leisured 'amateur' Victorian microscopist to identify his finds. Both contemporaries and later workers have tended to assess Hassall's algal work as largely second-hand and often careless, Ralfs's as both careful and original. Typical contemporary comment, in a letter of 9 October 1851 from David Landsborough I to Mrs Gatty (Sheffield City Library) is: 'Ralfs wrote an excellent book with exquisite plates, on the *Desmidieae* which I have. It is much more to be depended on than Hassall's which Arnott says is a bad book full of errors.'

Before publication of *The British Desmidieae* Ralfs's first paper, 'Desmids and diatoms', was read by the Revd M. J. Berkeley before the Edinburgh Botanical Society, in whose *Transactions* Ralfs's papers appeared over many years. He also published in the *Annals of Natural History*, in *The Phytologist* (1842), and in the *Report and Transactions of the Penzance Natural History and Antiquarian Society* (1851–1884?), the latter papers mostly about Cornish marine macroalgae.

In addition to his own works, Ralfs contributed strongly to the data provided (from 1838) by Amelia Warren Griffiths for the botanical texts in editions of Banfield's *A Guide to Ilfracombe* (retitled *A Guide to North Devon* from *c.*1850) and *The North Devon Handbook* (1857; 1860; 1877) of Tugwell and Stewart. Ralfs was also involved in writing botanical text for Courtney's *A Guide to Penzance* (1845), Besley's *The Hand-Book of Western Cornwall* (1873?; 1880?), J. T. Blight's *A Week at the Land's End* (1861; 1876; 1893; 1973), and *The Official Guide to Penzance* (1876; 1888). He contributed a desmid list for *The Flora of Tunbridge Wells* by Edward Jenner (who had drawn the illustrations for Ralfs's 1848 book). He also provided specimens which assisted in the production of academic works such as Sowerby's second edition of Smith's *English Botany* (the cryptogams described therein by Berkeley and Wilson were amplified by specimens sent by Ralfs) and Darwin's *Insectivorous Plants*. Andrew Pritchard's *History of Infusoria* was revised and enlarged (4th edn, 1861) by botanists including Ralfs, whose Diatomaceae section (pp. 756–940) was condensed by Pritchard (Ralfs, through illness, could neither further revise the Diatomaceae nor provide the desmid sections, as originally agreed).

In 1850 Ralfs visited the Dordogne château of Count Morambert (where his wife had died in 1848), during a six-month visit to France. He also then visited many French botanists, in Paris, Falaise, Caen, and Vire. However, letters from Lenormand and de Brébisson to the Revd M. J. Berkeley in 1851 suggest Ralfs proved no real correspondent following his return to England—possibly owing to continued ill health.

Through the misconduct of a trusted relative, it is said, Ralfs lost most of his 'moderate competency' (Marquand). In 1858 J. D. Hooker and T. H. Huxley initiated a charitable subscription fund to provide Ralfs with a small annuity. The fund, under the auspices of the Philosophical Society, was vastly oversubscribed and, in addition to providing

Ralfs an annuity, formed the basis of a second fund for general 'relief of necessitas Scientific Men'. An additional legacy from Ralfs's friend the Revd Henry Penneck (d. 1862) also provided some financial relief. Despite poor health and failing eyesight from the early 1850s onwards, Ralfs remained active in botanical research until he was at least seventy-five. For many years a committee member of the Penzance (Morrab Gardens) Library, he catalogued its books, did much of the buying of natural history stock, and prepared its printed catalogue. The library subsequently obtained Ralfs's unpublished manuscripts for his *Flora of West Cornwall* (8 vols., 1878–86), *Flora of the Scilly Isles* (1876), and *Fungi of West Cornwall* (2 vols., 1880–86).

In his final years Ralfs lived at 13 Clare Street, Penzance, in a house owned by a Miss Quick who cared well for him. He died there on 14 July 1890, and was buried in the local cemetery. A monument was erected to his memory by the Penzance Natural History and Antiquarian Society, of which he had been both vice-president and president (1883–4). He had been elected honorary fellow of the Royal Microscopical Society (1889) and, much earlier, had been proposed for (but had declined) associateship of the Linnean Society. His name is commemorated in taxa at many levels and in many plant groups.

JAMES H. PRICE

Sources E. D. Marquand, *Report and Transactions of the Penzance Natural History and Antiquarian Society*, new ser. (1890–91), 225–40 · H. Groves and J. Groves, *Journal of Botany, British and Foreign*, 28 (1890), 289–93 · Penzance Library, Ralfs MSS · A. G. Lewis, *John Ralfs, an old Cornish botanist* (1907) · F. H. Davey, *Flora of Cornwall* (1909) · J. H. Price, 'Goody two-shoes or a monument to industry? Aspects of the *Phycologia Britannica* of William Henry Harvey (1811 to 1866)', *Bulletin of the British Museum (Natural History)* [Historical Series], 16 (1988), 87–216 · J. Ruhrmund, 'Nature scene in Cornwall', *West Briton* (18 Dec 1986) · G. D. R. Bridson, V. C. Phillips, and A. P. Harvey, *Natural history manuscript resources in the British Isles* (1980) · *DNB* · F. A. Turk, 'Natural history studies in Cornwall, 1700–1900', *Journal of the Royal Institution of Cornwall*, new ser., 3 (1957–60), 229–79, esp. 274–6 · H. M. Clokie, *An account of the herbaria of the department of botany in the University of Oxford* (1964) · D. H. Kent and D. E. Allen, *British and Irish herbaria*, 2nd edn (1984) · *The correspondence of Charles Darwin*, ed. F. Burkhardt and S. Smith, 7 (1991), 531–2

Archives Manchester Museum, herbarium · Morrab Library, notebook and papers · NHM, herbarium · NMG Wales, herbarium · Penzance Library, notebooks and MSS · RBG Kew, herbarium · South London Botanical Institute, herbarium · U. Oxf., school of botany, corresp. and MSS associated with herbarium · U. Oxf., herbarium | Bolton Museum, Lancashire, natural history department, Mason collection, specimens of marine algae · Ludlow Museum, corresp. with Salwey · NHM, corresp. with Berkeley · NHM, corresp. with Broone · Norwich Castle Museum, Brightwell corresp.

Likenesses portrait (after photographs by R. H. Preston of Penzance, c.1882), repro. in Groves and Groves, *Journal of Botany* (1890) · portrait (after photographs by R. H. Preston of Penzance, c.1882), repro. in Lewis, *John Ralfs*

Wealth at death £96 7s.: administration, 21 Aug 1890, CGPLA Eng. & Wales

Ralli, Pantia Stephen [Pandias Stephen] (1793–1865), merchant, was born on the Turkish island of Chios, the third son of Stephen Ralli (1755–1827), a wealthy merchant of Chios, and his wife, Loula, daughter of Avgoustis and Virginia Sechiari. Pantia's eldest brother, Zannis (1785–1859), opened a branch house in London, trading as Ralli and Petrochino, and the second brother, Avgoustis (1792–1878), and Pantia followed soon after, to form Ralli Brothers. The firm was not the first Greek merchant house to trade in London, but it soon became the most successful.

Ralli Brothers' business records were destroyed during the Second World War, so details of their trade are scarce. It appears that their earliest trade was in silk, which no doubt included exports of raw silk from Asia Minor to England. The brothers then took an early lead in the export of Russian grain from the Black Sea ports to England. Here their success was due to the development of a system known as the cargo trade in which the merchant responsible for loading the grain in the Black Sea port dispatched the bill of lading and sample to his partner in London or Liverpool who sold the shipment in advance of its arrival. When the ship reached the first British port (Falmouth or Cork) the captain was informed where he was to discharge the cargo. Return cargoes to the Black Sea and the Middle East were increasingly British cottons, and to facilitate this trade the youngest of the five sons eventually in the firm, Eustratios (1800–1884), opened a branch in Manchester in 1827. Pantia married, on 25 September 1831 in London, Marietta (1810–1860), daughter of Petros Scaramanga, a Chian merchant, and his wife, Nina. Marietta had moved to London to live with her elder brothers and this connection cemented the Ralli and Scaramanga partnerships in Russia. They had two sons (one dying in infancy) and a daughter.

As Ralli Brothers' trade grew the firm spawned new partnerships and trading bases round the Mediterranean, Russia, and the Middle East, notably in Marseilles, Odessa, Constantinople, St Petersburg, Taganrog, and Tabriz (Persia). From these bases the firm's agents reached far into the interior, even as far as Turkestan, conducting a cash and barter trade, typically exchanging grain, wool, or raw silk for Manchester cottons. In 1851 Pantia Ralli attained his ultimate ambition as a merchant by opening a branch house in Calcutta, from which, as in Russia, his company reached out into the vast undeveloped interior of India. In the 1850s Ralli Brothers was employing some 4000 clerks and 15,000 workers for transporting and warehousing stock in their network of branches.

Pantia Ralli established an autocratic control and discipline which enabled Ralli Brothers to stamp its authority on the Levant trade and the Greek trading community. The system that he established included the rule that no partner or employee was allowed to 'lead a life unduly luxurious or extravagant' or to take part 'in any other combination or enterprise whatsoever' except Ralli Brothers. A second rule was established in 'the iron discipline which regulates the relations of superiors and inferiors, and which, indeed, pervades the entire organisation'. These rules, together with 'absolute probity in all transactions', were 'religiously maintained irrefragable for close upon an entire century', a Greek hagiographer wrote in 1902

(Gennadius). The London families from Chios, who constituted a large trading group in Victorian Britain, nicknamed Pantia Ralli 'Zeus', admitting the moral influence he exercised over them.

So anxious was Pantia to safeguard the reputation and credit of his firm that it never issued 'paper' (bills of exchange) but conducted a cash business to the extent of its available means. The system was reported to Baring Brothers in 1863:

> When they [Ralli Brothers] buy goods in New York and New Orleans, they pay cash and draw against them [Barings] on London; when they sell goods in America (this being an important branch of their business) they remit the net proceeds to the London firm.   (Baring Bros. MSS HC16.193)

This conservative policy protected the firm from the vulnerability of so many small trading houses in the recurrent trade crises. A partnership capital of £130,000 in 1827 had climbed to £500,000 in 1846, which meant that Ralli Brothers commanded more resources than any other merchant house in London at the period, so far as the record goes.

In 1835 Pantia Ralli was appointed Greek consul, which confirmed him as the leading Greek merchant in London. He proposed the building of a Greek church in London in 1843 when the Finsbury Square house used for worship became too small. Thirty Greek trading families that had settled in London subscribed £10,000 for an imposing Byzantine edifice, which was opened at the end of 1849. Ralli's leadership of the Greek trading community never restrained him from moving freely in English society; his surviving son was sent to Eton and his daughter married the son of the bishop of Gloucester, Charles Monk MP, another Etonian. He became friendly with W. E. Gladstone. In 1851 Ralli left the Finsbury Square Greek quarter for a mansion overlooking Marble Arch.

When Ralli died at his home, 5 Connaught Place West, London, on 9 July 1865 the Ralli partnerships were formally dissolved. However Stephen Augustus *Ralli (1829–1902), a nephew who had been trained in the London house (both of Pantia's sons having died in early life), constituted a new Ralli Brothers, based on India and the Anglo-American trade, leaving the Russian business to the Scaramangas. Stephen Ralli maintained Pantia Ralli's authority in the firm and leadership of the Greek community until the end of the century.   S. D. CHAPMAN

Sources T. Catsiyannis, *Pandias Stephen Rallis, 1793–1865: the founder of the Greek community in London* (privately printed, London, 1986) • J. Gennadius, *Stephen A. Ralli: a biographical memoir* (1902) • S. D. Chapman, *Merchant enterprise in Britain: from the industrial revolution to World War I* (1992), 154–61 • P. P. Argenti, *Libro d'oro de la noblesse de Chio*, 1 (1955), 101–4; 2 (1955), 143, 147 • Gladstone, *Diaries* • ING Barings, London, Barings archives, MS HC 16.193 • d. cert. **Archives** GL, Ralli Brothers, business records | Bank of England archive, London, discount office records • ING Barings, London, Barings archives, MS HC16.193 • PRO, corresp. with Kitchener, 30/57 WO/59 **Wealth at death** under £400,000: probate, 1 Aug 1865, *CGPLA Eng. & Wales*

Ralli, Stephen Augustus (1829–1902), merchant, was born in Marseilles, France, on 30 January 1829, the only son (there were two daughters) of Avgoustis (1792–1878) and Sozonga Ralli (d. 1878). His father was a Greek merchant. Stephen was educated in Marseilles. At the age of twenty-two, in 1851, he was summoned to London to assist his uncle Pantia Stephen *Ralli (1793–1865), the senior partner in Ralli Brothers, the foremost Anglo-Greek merchant house in London. Pantia Ralli's own sons had died in early life, so the nephew was evidently groomed for the succession. At Parkfield House, Clapham, he married on 27 October 1855 his cousin Marrietta (1838–1922), daughter of Antonio Theodore Ralli, merchant, and his wife, Catherine, née Mavrogordato, of Trieste. They had three sons and four daughters.

Before S. A. Ralli took entire control of Ralli Brothers he was responsible for a major new initiative in the firm, that of trade with the United States. A new interlinking partnership was created in 1860 based on London, Liverpool, and New York, with connections to New Orleans for the supply of raw cotton. The strategy and disposition of the new development was set in the mould of the parent house. S. A. Ralli explained that the:

> business is strictly commercial and legitimate; they [the partners] neither speculate in goods, nor on the stock exchanges, but confine themselves to the import and export trade with the U. States, and receive also consignments from Alexandria, Smyrna, and Syria. They have a good commission business besides the business for their own account.   (Guildhall Library, MS 23826)

Ralli Brothers also imported cotton from Egypt, installing the first steam-powered cotton gins in a factory there in 1860.

At the same time, Ralli Brothers' trade in India was being energetically pushed forward. New branches were opened in Bombay and Karachi about 1860 and connections 'up country' (with Indian traders in the interior) built up. Imports from India were mainly jute, cotton, indigo, rice, saltpetre, gunnies (sacking), and shellac; exports were 'Manchester goods', metals, and, later, petroleum. Perhaps this new development was partly to compensate for severe competition in the Russian grain trade, where Jewish houses (notably Dreyfus and Fribourg) were using their co-religionists to penetrate the interior. Rallis' Persian branch at Tabriz, a pioneer venture launched in 1837 to import silk, and for some years a prospering concern, had to be closed in 1871 after pebrine (silkworm disease) ruined the Persian silk trade. This closure was followed by that of the branches at Constantinople and Trebizond which had been sustained by it.

Notwithstanding the set-backs, S. A. Ralli drove his firm forward with single-minded commitment. According to a contemporary:

> the prestige and interest of the firm absorbed the very soul of the young Stephen Ralli, and filled it with a sort of religious cult. His devotion to work became a veritable passion. … He was austere … undisturbed by the accumulation of wealth … counting ostentation as a thing derogatory to the dignity of man.

He 'entirely abstained' from 'active politics', his only relaxation being the comfort of his home and his wife, herself a Ralli (Gennadius). He was utterly loyal to the system of strict discipline instituted by his uncle in the firm, and more financially successful with it. The partnership capital of Ralli Brothers rose from £500,000 in 1850 to £1.2 million in 1878, £2 million in 1880, and £3 million in 1901, according to the Bank of England records, keeping the firm at the top of the premier league of merchant houses in Britain. In India Ralli Brothers 'occupies commercially the first place: neither English nor German firms can compare with its ascendency there', Stephen Ralli's biographer fairly observed in 1902 (ibid.).

Ralli devoted his whole time and entire career to expanding the business, but, as his biographer insists, 'he did not labour for money, that he considered as an object quite secondary to the prestige of the firm' (Gennadius). The standing of the firm was not however the ultimate aim: that was unquestionably to raise the moral status of the Greek trading community in Britain. The large numbers of Greek small traders settling in London and Manchester in the 1840s and 1850s gave rise to widespread suspicions, which went as high as the Bank of England, of their probity. Publication of *The Bubbles of Finance* in 1865 featuring Mr Velardi, a Greek trader 'like the lowest Houndsditch Jew' (M. R. Laing-Meason, *The Bubbles of Finance*, 1865, 158), appeared to confirm the prejudices of many in the indigenous community. Stephen Ralli's achievement was to succeed his uncle, not only as head of Ralli Brothers, but more particularly as the doyen and mentor of the Anglo-Greek trading community.

Stephen Ralli died at Monte Carlo on 2 April 1902. His widow died at Brighton in 1922. Two of his sons having died young, he was succeeded as the head of the firm by a nephew, Sir Lucas Ralli (1846–1931). This third-generation head was born in Manchester and educated at Harrow School and Trinity College, Cambridge, which guaranteed his place, and that of his firm, in the English establishment. S. D. CHAPMAN

Sources T. Catsiyannis, *Pandias Stephen Rallis, 1793–1865: the founder of the Greek community in London* (privately printed, London, 1986) · J. Gennadius, *Stephen A. Ralli: a biographical memoir* (1902) · 'Committee to inquire into Indian currency', *Parl. papers* (1893–4), 65.133–4, C. 7060-II · S. D. Chapman, *Merchant enterprise in Britain: from the industrial revolution to World War I* (1992), 154–61 · *The Times* (30 April 1902), 4f · P. P. Argenti, *Libro d'oro de la noblesse de Chio*, 1 (1955), 101–4; 2 (1955), 143, 147 · m. cert. · Ralli Bros. business records, GL, MS 23826

Archives GL, Ralli Brothers, business records, MS 23826 | Bank of England archive, London, discount office records [unlisted] · ING Barings, London, Barings archives, MS HC16.193

Likenesses W. W. Ouless, oils, 1881, priv. coll.; photogravure, NPG [*see illus.*]

Wealth at death £1,068,000—value of unsettled estate: will, PRO

Ralph. *See also* Ranulf.

Ralph [*called* Ralph the Timid], **earl of Hereford** (*d.* **1057**), magnate, was the second son of Drogo, count of Amiens and the Vexin, and Godgifu (Gode), daughter of *Æthelred II and *Emma. His father died on pilgrimage to Jerusalem in 1035 and Godgifu married *Eustace (II), count of Boulogne (*d. c.*1087); she was dead by 1049. Ralph came to England with his uncle, Edward the Confessor, in 1041. He

Stephen Augustus Ralli (1829–1902), by Walter William Ouless, 1881

attested three charters of 1050 as earl (AS chart., S 1020–22); his sphere of authority was probably the east midlands, the region where the lands of his wife, Gytha, are to be found. Their distribution suggests that she was related to the local magnate Burgræd, whose lands lay in Bedfordshire, Buckinghamshire, and Northamptonshire; like Earl Ralph, he was a benefactor of Peterborough Abbey. Ralph himself held estates in Bedfordshire, Buckinghamshire, Leicestershire, Middlesex, Northamptonshire, and Rutland, as well as Berkshire, Gloucestershire, Warwickshire, and Worcestershire; but his full holding cannot now be recovered. Much of it must have come from the king, but he received a life-lease of Cranfield, Bedfordshire, from Ælfwine, abbot of Ramsey.

Ralph's tenure of the east midlands would have brought him into contact with Harold Godwineson, earl of East Anglia, and it is noteworthy that he named his son Harold. When, however, Earl Godwine and his family fell out with the king in 1051, Ralph raised the levies of his earldom for his uncle. In 1052 he and Earl Odda commanded the royal fleet assembled against Godwine at Sandwich, but they could not prevent the earl's triumphant return. Godwine and his sons were reinstated in lands and office, but Swein Godwineson died on pilgrimage to Jerusalem in 1052, and it was probably then that Ralph received Swein's earldom of Hereford, which included Oxfordshire (AS chart., S 1105). There was already a Norman presence in the shire, and at least one castle, at Hereford itself, though its builder, Osbern Pentecost, was driven out on Godwine's return.

In 1055 Ralph defended Herefordshire against the exiled Earl Ælfgar and his ally Gruffudd ap Llywelyn, but their encounter on 24 October was a disaster: 'before any spear had been thrown the English army fled because they were on horseback, and many were killed there—about four or five hundred men—and they killed none in return' (ASC, s.a. 1055, text C). The invaders sacked Hereford, burning down St Æthelberht's minster. Later sources accuse Ralph and his Frenchmen of starting the flight. It was this engagement which later earned Ralph his opprobrious nickname 'the timid' or, more properly, 'timorous' (timidus), in contrast to the 'vigorous' (strenuus) Earl Harold, who chased the invaders into Wales. Ralph probably lost Hereford to Earl Harold at this juncture. He died on 21 December 1057, not much above thirty, and was buried in the abbey at Peterborough. His elder brother Count Walter died in 1063, allegedly poisoned by Duke William of Normandy. His son Harold, a minor in 1066 in the care of his great-aunt, Edith, received part of his father's estate and later acquired the castle and honour of Ewias Harold, which preserves his name. His descendants are the Sudeleys of Toddington, Gloucestershire (for the early history of whom see Sudeley family).   ANN WILLIAMS

Sources ASC, s.a. 1051, 1055, 1057 [text D]; s.a. 1052 [text E]; s.a. 1055 [text C] · A. Farley, ed., Domesday Book, 2 vols. (1783), vol. 1 · F. E. Harmer, ed., Anglo-Saxon writs (1952) · D. Bates, 'Lord Sudeley's ancestors: the family of the counts of Amiens, Valois and the Vexin in France and England during the eleventh century', The Sudeleys: lords of Toddington, The Manorial Society (1987), 34–48 · A. Williams, 'The king's nephew: the family, career, and connections of Ralph, earl of Hereford', Studies in medieval history presented to R. Allen Brown, ed. C. Harper-Bill, C. J. Holdsworth, and J. L. Nelson (1989), 327–43 · S. Keynes, An atlas of attestations in Anglo-Saxon charters, c.670–1066 (privately printed, Cambridge, 1993) · P. A. Clarke, The English nobility under Edward the Confessor (1994) · John of Worcester, Chron. · The chronicle of Hugh Candidus, a monk of Peterborough, ed. W. T. Mellows (1949) · Ordericus Vitalis, Eccl. hist., vol. 2 · W. D. Macray, ed., Chronicon abbatiae Rameseiensis a saec. x usque ad an. circiter 1200, Rolls Series, 83 (1886)

Ralph [called Ralph de Gael, Ralph Guader], **earl** (d. 1097×9), magnate, was the elder son of *Ralph the Staller, earl of East Anglia (d. 1068×70), and his unnamed Breton wife. He seems to have been in Brittany in the reign of Edward the Confessor and to have come to England only after the conquest; Wace, indeed, represents him as leading a contingent of Bretons at the battle of Hastings. By 1069 he had succeeded his father as earl in East Anglia; he defended Norwich in that year against the Danish fleet sent to aid the English rebellion in the north. His English holdings were very extensive, for he received the lands of the English magnate Eadgifu the Fair as well as those of his father. His honour extended into Essex and Cambridgeshire as well as Lincolnshire, Norfolk, and Suffolk. Only in Cambridgeshire is he called Ralph Waders, Guader, or de Wather—that is, Ralph de Gael (Domesday Book, 1.196v; Chronicon abbatiae Rameseiensis, 174–5). Many Bretons accompanied him to take up land in England and it was probably he, rather than his father, who established the 'French borough' at Norwich (Domesday Book, 2.118).

In 1075 Ralph married Emma, daughter of *William fitz Osbern, and it was at their marriage-feast at Exning, Suffolk—the 'bride-ale that was many men's bale' (ASC, s.a. 1075, text D)—that Ralph and his brother-in-law, Roger de *Breteuil, earl of Hereford, planned a rebellion against King William. Earl Waltheof was also involved, and the plotters sought help from both Brittany and Denmark. Their motives are obscure, but it is probable that their powers were more circumscribed than those of their fathers had been: Ralph's authority seems to have been confined to East Anglia (and perhaps to Norfolk), whereas the earldom of East Anglia had once embraced the whole of the east midlands; Roger likewise held only the earldom of Hereford, whereas his father had authority over the whole of western Wessex; and Waltheof's power was confined to the lands north of the Tees, whereas his father, Earl Siward, had held all Northumbria.

It is clear that the earls had little support in England. The D version of the Anglo-Saxon Chronicle says that 'they plotted to drive their royal lord out of his kingdom' (ASC, s.a. 1075), highly pejorative language smacking of treason. Archbishop Lanfranc, too, did not hesitate to brand Ralph 'traitor' and describe his army of 'Breton dung' as 'oathbreakers', though he took a milder line with Earl Roger and (according to John of Worcester) with Waltheof. Waltheof, in fact, took no part in the revolt, but revealed all to the king and threw himself on William's mercy; and the Danes proved a broken reed, for their fleet (commanded by Cnut the Holy) arrived only when everything was over. Roger and Ralph attempted to raise their earldoms, but Roger was prevented from crossing the Severn by a force commanded by Wulfstan, bishop of Worcester, and other western magnates. In East Anglia both the castle garrisons and the local levies opposed Ralph and he was brought to bay at his manor of Fawdon by Geoffrey, bishop of Coutances, and other loyal magnates. His army was scattered and Ralph fled to Norwich, whence he escaped by ship. Emma held the castle against the king's men and eventually arranged safe conduct for herself and her men, joining her husband in Brittany. The prisoners taken after Fawdon were not so fortunate; at the Christmas court of 1075 those who were not exiled were blinded and mutilated. Roger de Breteuil was imprisoned for life and Waltheof was beheaded for treason in the following year.

Ralph was deprived of his office and of all his English lands, as was his brother Hardouin and his vassal Walter of Dol. His Breton lands of Montfort and Gael were beyond King William's reach and in 1076 Ralph joined a Breton revolt aimed against both Duke Hoel and William himself. He seized the castle of Dol and held it against William, who was forced to break off the siege by the approach of a relieving force commanded by King Philippe I of France and Foulques le Réchin, count of Anjou (d. 1109); it was the first serious reverse which William had suffered for many years. Ralph continued to prosper in Brittany. In 1095 the first crusade was preached and Ralph and Emma were among those who answered the call, in the following of Robert Curthose, duke of Normandy. Ralph fought at the siege of Nicaea and the battle of Dorylaeum in the summer of 1097, but died before the fall of Jerusalem in July 1099. Emma, too, died on crusade, as did one of their sons, Alan. Ralph's lands passed to his remaining sons, first to William de Gael (d. 1119) and then to Ralph. In 1103 William de Breteuil, the elder brother of Roger and Emma, died and William de Gael claimed the honour of Breteuil in right of his mother; but both he, and later his brother Ralph, had to fight both the illegitimate son of William de Breteuil and the barons of the honour. Eventually Breteuil passed to Robert, earl of Leicester (d. 1168), to whom Henry I gave, probably in 1121, the younger Ralph's daughter Amice in marriage.   ANN WILLIAMS

Sources ASC, s.a. 1075 [text D] · *The letters of Lanfranc, archbishop of Canterbury*, ed. and trans. H. Clover and M. Gibson, OMT (1979) · John of Worcester, *Chron.* · Ordericus Vitalis, *Eccl. hist.*, vols. 2–4 · F. Michel, ed., *Chroniques anglo-normandes: recueil d'extraits et d'écrits relatifs à l'histoire de Normandie et d'Angleterre* (Rouen, 1836–40) · K. S. B. Keats-Rohan, 'William I and the Breton contingent in the non-Norman conquest, 1060–1087', *Anglo-Norman Studies*, 13 (1990), 157–72 · C. P. Lewis, 'The early earls of Norman England', *Anglo-Norman Studies*, 13 (1990), 207–23 · A. Williams, *The English and the Norman conquest* (1995) · A. Farley, ed., *Domesday Book*, 2 vols. (1783) · D. C. Douglas, *William the Conqueror* (1964) · D. Crouch, *The Beaumont twins: the roots and branches of power in the twelfth century*, Cambridge Studies in Medieval Life and Thought, 4th ser., 1 (1986) · E. M. C. van Houts, 'Wace as historian and genealogist', *Family-trees and the roots of politics*, ed. K. S. B. Keats-Rohan (1996) · W. D. Macray, ed., *Chronicon abbatiae Rameseiensis a saec. x usque ad an. circiter 1200*, Rolls Series, 83 (1886) · C. P. Lewis, 'The formation of the honor of Chester, 1066–1100', *Journal of the Chester Archaeological Society*, 71 (1991), 37–68 [G. Barraclough issue, *The earldom of Chester and its charters*, ed. A. T. Thacker]

Ralph. *See* Ranulf (d. 1123).

Ralph [*called* Ralph Luffa] (d. 1123), bishop of Chichester, was considered by Orderic Vitalis to have been a court chaplain under William II before he became bishop in 1091, but his chief claims to fame are his establishment of the material basis of his cathedral church and chapter, and his model conduct as a diocesan according to the notions of the time. William of Malmesbury, in his *Gesta pontificum*, says that Ralph was alone among the bishops in resisting Henry I's pecuniary exactions from the clergy, thereby winning the king's respect; indeed, that as a result of his bemoaning the poverty of his bishopric and the fire that had burned down his cathedral (1114), he was actually helped by Henry's liberality to rebuild the church. One of the bishop's charters shows that, probably after 1114, he was also eliciting donations from the laity of his diocese towards the cathedral fabric. William of Malmesbury says that Ralph raised up his see from being humble and poor 'to the height of glory' (*De gestis pontificum*, 206). Ralph gathered together as many clergy as the means of the bishopric could sustain, thus creating canons for the cathedral, he donated valuables for the liturgy to the cathedral, he travelled around his diocese three times a year preaching, and he rebuked wrongdoers with good humour. Some of this picture is given colour by the admittedly sparse charter evidence. The main pattern of cathedral prebends in the vicinity of Chichester had been clearly established no later than 1147. Charters of Ralph stress the importance of priests' attendance at episcopal synods, not for the sake of financial dues but 'to hear the episcopal precepts' (*Acta*, 74), and the need to provide a secure material basis for the priest who would actually reside as pastor in a parish.

According to the chronicle of Battle Abbey the first rumblings of dispute between the bishop of Chichester and the abbey were felt in Ralph's time, over the bishop's right of hospitality and the abbot's liability to attend the bishop's synod. However, it is difficult to assess the trustworthiness of the charter and chronicle evidence, particularly on the latter issue, since it could be affected by hindsight from the certainly rancorous disputes of the mid-twelfth century. Ralph, abbot of Battle from 1107, and Bishop Ralph appear to have been the best of friends. Although not a central figure in politics, Ralph Luffa was a consistent supporter of Archbishop Anselm (d. 1109). He was not cowed by William II's bludgeoning, according to William of Malmesbury, but offered to resign his bishopric in support of Anselm's recognition of Pope Urban II (r. 1088–99) in 1095, even though he felt weakened by Anselm's subsequently going into exile. Again, according to Eadmer, he acted and spoke staunchly in favour of the archbishop of Canterbury's right to exact obedience from York in 1108–9. When Orderic says that of William II's chaplains who obtained bishoprics, some oppressed the weak and amassed wealth, while others, inspired by a deep sense of pastoral responsibility, devoted themselves to the welfare of their flocks and laudably amended their own lives, we must suppose that he thought of Ralph in the latter category. Ralph died on 14 December 1123, in circumstances of exemplary piety, having given all his possessions to the poor.　　　　　　　HENRY MAYR-HARTING

Sources H. Mayr-Harting, *The bishops of Chichester, 1075–1207: biographical notes and problems* (1963) · H. Mayr-Harting, ed., *The acta of the bishops of Chichester, 1075–1207*, CYS, 56 (1964) · M. Brett, *The English church under Henry I* (1975) · *Willelmi Malmesbiriensis monachi de gestis pontificum Anglorum libri quinque*, ed. N. E. S. A. Hamilton, Rolls Series, 52 (1870) · *Eadmeri Historia novorum in Anglia*, ed. M. Rule, Rolls Series, 81 (1884) · Ordericus Vitalis, *Eccl. hist.* · E. Searle, ed., *The chronicle of Battle Abbey*, OMT (1980) · Bodl. Oxf., MS Ashmole 1146, fols. 57–8
Wealth at death gave everything away on deathbed (incl. underwear): *Willelmi Malmesbiriensis monachi de gestis pontificum*, 206

Ralph [Ralph Nowell or Nouell] (*d.* in or after **1151**), bishop of Orkney, was a native of York, where he became a priest. York writers state that he was elected by 'men of Orkney' to the bishopric of Orkney (between June 1109 and February 1114) in the church of St Peter at York, and he was consecrated by Thomas (*d.* 1114), archbishop of York, to whom he made his formal profession. He is the third bishop known to have been formally consecrated by York to the see, which had been established by Earl Thorfinn *c.*1050. These appointments, however, were in opposition to those consecrated by authority of the archbishops of Hamburg-Bremen, and it is doubtful whether any of the three had full possession. The support registered for Ralph by 'men of Orkney' probably reflects the political disputes within the earldom at this date, and suggests that he was favoured by Magnus Erlendsson's party. After Earl Magnus's murder about 1115 Ralph must have faced increasing difficulty in getting possession, as is clearly perceived in the letter of 20 November 1119 from Calixtus II to the Norwegian kings Sigurd (*r.* 1103–30) and Eystein (*r.* 1103–23) requesting them to see that he remained in peaceable possession, and in that from Calixtus's successor, Honorius II, to King Sigurd in 1128, in which an intruder into the see is mentioned and the statement made that there can be only one bishop in possession. This must refer to the strong position of Bishop William (*d.* 1168) in the islands, and from this date onwards Ralph is active as a suffragan of York.

Ralph had already supported Thurstan (*d.* 1140), archbishop-elect of York, in the latter's struggle for the independence of the see of York against the claims of Canterbury, visiting him during his exile in France and being present at the archbishop's consecration at Rheims on 19 October 1119. He alone of the English and Norman bishops dared to take his seat beside the metropolitan for the opening next day of the general council at Rheims, and Thurstan must have secured the first papal bull on Ralph's behalf at this time. For his open support of the archbishop Ralph incurred the wrath of Henry I. In 1128 he assisted at the consecration of Robert (*d.* 1159), bishop of St Andrews, by Archbishop Thurstan; the chronicler of the occasion explains that he was assistant to the bishop of Durham and the archbishop of York because of his unacceptability to the people of his diocese, having been chosen by neither clergy, nor people, nor *princeps terrae*. Ralph represented the aged archbishop at the battle of the Standard, near Northallerton, on 22 August 1138. He played an active role in exhorting and absolving the English host, although he was probably not responsible for the speech ascribed to him by some authorities (but to Walter Espec by Ailred of Rievaulx). In 1143 he acted as suffragan of William de Ste Barbe (*d.* 1152), bishop of Durham, and represented him at the consecration of William Fitzherbert as archbishop of York in Winchester. Some time before this (1133–40) his sons (*Paulinus filius Rad. Orcadensis ep.* being named) were granted the land of Garmondsway, co. Durham, by Bishop Geoffrey Rufus. Ralph is last recorded in 1151; it is not known when he died.

　　　　　　ALICE M. COOKE, *rev.* BARBARA E. CRAWFORD

Sources B. E. Crawford, 'Bishops of Orkney in the eleventh and twelfth centuries: bibliography and biographical list', *Innes Review*, 47 (1996), 1–13 · D. E. R. Watt, ed., *Fasti ecclesiae Scoticanae medii aevi ad annum 1638*, [2nd edn], Scottish RS, new ser., 1 (1969) · O. Kolsrud, 'Den norske Kirkes Erkebiskoper og Biskoper indtil Reformationem', *Diplomatarium Norvegicum*, ed. G. Storm, 17B (Christiania, 1913), 177–360, esp. 198, 293–308 · *Hugh the Chanter: the history of the church of York, 1066–1127*, ed. and trans. C. Johnson, rev. edn, rev. M. Brett, C. N. L. Brooke, and M. Winterbottom, OMT (1990) · J. Raine, ed., *The historians of the church of York and its archbishops*, 3 vols., Rolls Series, 71 (1879–94) · G. V. Scammell, *Hugh du Puiset, bishop of Durham* (1956) · E. B. Fryde and others, eds., *Handbook of British chronology*, 3rd edn, Royal Historical Society Guides and Handbooks, 2 (1986) · R. Somerville, ed., *Scotia pontificia: papal letters to Scotland before the pontificate of Innocent III* (1982)

Ralph (*d.* **1174**), administrator and bishop of Bethlehem, was described by the historian William of Tyre, who succeeded him as chancellor of the Latin kingdom of Jerusalem, as 'a good-looking Englishman, who was well-educated but very worldly' (*Willelmi Tyrensis archiepiscopi chronicon*, 2.738). H. E. Mayer has argued persuasively that he should be identified with Ralph who between 1137 and 1141 was the chancellor of Matilda, the wife of King Stephen of England, but nothing certain is known about him until he was invested as chancellor of the kingdom of Jerusalem. This took place after 24 September 1143 (when Elias held that office) and before 1 February 1146, and the appointment was almost certainly made by Queen Melisende, co-ruler since November 1143 with her son Baudouin III. In 1146 when Fulcher, archbishop of Tyre, became patriarch of Jerusalem, the crown nominated Ralph to the vacant see, the most prestigious archbishopric in the kingdom. His candidacy was opposed, for unknown reasons, by a group of clergy led by Fulcher, and it has been conjectured that this led Melisende to dismiss Ralph as chancellor because she was unwilling to antagonize the hierarchy: his last act in her reign is dated July 1147.

Until June 1150 Ralph continued to style himself archbishop-elect and to enjoy the temporalities of Tyre, but Pope Eugenius III subsequently refused to ratify his appointment. Throughout this time, as relations between Baudouin III and Melisende deteriorated, Ralph remained a firm supporter of the young king, and he received his reward when Melisende was driven from power at Eastertide 1152. By 20 April Baudouin had reinstated him as chancellor, an office he retained for the rest of his life. In

1153 he and Frédéric, bishop of Acre, were sent by the king to Antioch to restore peace between Prince Reynaud de Châtillon and the patriarch, Aimery de Limoges, whom he had maltreated and imprisoned. Their mission was a success: Aimery was released and all confiscated church property was restored. Perhaps in recognition of his services, Baudouin nominated Ralph as bishop of Bethlehem when that see fell vacant, and Ralph's fellow countryman, Pope Adrian IV, ratified this appointment in the autumn of 1156. As suffragan of Jerusalem Ralph unsuccessfully opposed the election of Amaury de Nesle as patriarch in 1157–8, perhaps because he was Queen Melisende's candidate.

In King Amaury's reign (1163–74) the Byzantine emperor, Manuel I Komnenos, helped to fund an extensive programme of mosaic decoration in Ralph's cathedral, the church of the Holy Nativity: the nave mosaics depicting general and provincial councils of the church, with inscriptions in Latin and Greek, were designed to emphasize the unity of the Orthodox and Latin churches, and no doubt represented a view of the church that Ralph shared. Ralph took an active part in warfare against the Muslims. He was severely wounded in battle in 1167 in the course of King Amaury's Egyptian campaign; but he had recovered by the spring of 1170 when he carried the Holy Cross on a campaign in Transjordan, while in the following December he helped Amaury repel Saladin's attack on Darum. Although two western sources record the presence of a bishop of Bethlehem in northern France in the winter of 1169–70, the writers may have confused him with the bishop of Banias (Belinas in Latin) who is known to have been there. Ralph is last recorded in a document of 18 April 1174: he died soon after and was buried in the chapter house of the Augustinian canons at Bethlehem.

BERNARD HAMILTON

Sources Willelmi Tyrensis archiepiscopi chronicon, ed. R. B. C. Huygens, 2 vols. (Turnhout, Belgium, 1986) • E. de Rozière, ed., Cartulaire de l'église du Saint-Sépulcre de Jérusalem, Collection des Documents Inédits sur l'Histoire de France, 1st ser., 5 (1849) • H.-F. Delaborde, ed., Chartes de Terre Sainte (Paris, 1880) • J. Delaville Le Roulx, ed., Cartulaire général de l'ordre des hospitaliers de St Jean de Jérusalem (1100–1310), 4 vols. (1894–1906) • A. de Marsy, ed., 'Fragment d'un cartulaire de l'ordre de Saint-Lazare en Terre Sainte', Archives de l'Orient Latin, 2b (1884), 121–57 • R. Röhricht, Regesta regni Hierosolymitani, MXCVII–MCCXCI, 2 vols. (Innsbruck, 1893–1904) • Reg. RAN, 3.24, 157, 207, 239b, 586, 843, 921 • B. Hamilton, The Latin church in the crusader states: the secular church (1980) • P. Riant, Etudes sur l'histoire de l'église de Bethléem, 2 vols. (1889–96) • H. E. Mayer, 'Studies in the history of Queen Melisende of Jerusalem', Dumbarton Oaks Papers, 26 (1972), 93–182 • H. E. Mayer, Die Kanzlei der Lateinischen Könige von Jerusalem, 2 vols., MGH Schriften, 40 (Hanover, 1996) • J. Folda, The art of the crusaders in the Holy Land, 1098–1187 (1995), 347–78

Ralph d'Escures. See Escures, Ralph d' (c.1068–1122).

Ralph fitz Stephen (d. 1202), courtier and administrator, was probably the son of Stephen, a royal chamberlain who appears on the 1156/7 pipe roll. With his brothers William and Eustace he served Henry II in a number of capacities, in a manner characteristic of the familiares of that king. He frequently witnessed royal charters, often designated king's chamberlain; his deed confirming an agreement between Worcester Cathedral priory and the nuns of Westwood in 1178 uses this title. From Michaelmas 1171 to Michaelmas 1175, throughout the period of baronial rebellion, he was sheriff of Gloucestershire (his brother William accounted on his behalf each year, and then replaced him as sheriff, holding office until 1189). He received money from Henry II's chamber from 1156/7 onwards, and was concerned with the maintenance of the king and royal family, including provision for Queen Eleanor in her captivity in the last decade of Henry's reign. In 1170 he was among the 'tutors' of Henry, the Young King, with whom those wishing to approach the latter on Thomas Becket's behalf had to negotiate. In 1176 he was appointed a justice for the eyre in the south-west, and served as an assessor of tallage and a justice in several counties from then until 1190. He handled provisions and building works for the Carthusians at Witham (a royal foundation), accounted for Glastonbury Abbey's scutage in 1187/8, when the monastery was in the king's hand, and was probably the Ralph fitz Stephen who kept Guildford Castle in Surrey in 1192/3. Between 1176 and 1190 he accounted for the forest of Chippenham in Wiltshire, and from 1176 to 1197 for Sherwood Forest in Nottinghamshire and Derbyshire.

Ralph's rewards were as typical as his services. From 1161–2 onwards he received pardons of scutages in several counties, under both Henry II and Richard I. In 1163 he received Winterbourne and Wapley, both in Gloucestershire, from the king, in 1189/90 making fine to have tenure of them for life—Richard I confirmed him in them at Messina in April 1191. In 1184 or 1185 he married Maud, or Matilda, de Cauz, widow of Adam Fitzpeter and heir of half the Nottinghamshire barony of Shelford. John, count of Mortain, the future king, granted the hereditary forestership of Sherwood to Ralph, Maud, and their heirs. The returns to the 1166 inquest into feudal subtenancies had recorded him as holding one fee of the bishop of Exeter, half a fee of the honour of Totnes, and two fees of Hubert Fitzralph's honour of Crich in Derbyshire. He gave a fee held of Robert Fitzrandulf in Blackwell, Derbyshire, as a marriage portion with his niece Idonea to William Fitzrandulf. He was a benefactor of Haverholme Priory, Lincolnshire, Darley Abbey, Derbyshire, Gloucester Abbey, and Stanley Abbey, Wiltshire—his grants to the latter were also confirmed by Richard I in 1191. Ralph fitz Stephen died on 25 July 1202. When Maud died, in 1224, John of Birkin, the son of her first marriage, made fine to have her lands and forest custody; in 1225 the king took homage from Richard of Gloucester, perhaps the son of Ralph and an earlier wife, as Ralph's nearest heir for Winterbourne.

JULIA BOORMAN

Sources Pipe rolls • C. W. Foster and K. Major, eds., The registrum antiquissimum of the cathedral church of Lincoln, 7, Lincoln RS, 46 (1935), appx 209–25 • J. E. Lally, 'The court and household of Henry II', PhD diss., U. Lpool, 1969 • J. H. Round, ed., Rotuli de dominabus et pueris et puellis de XII comitatibus (1185), PRSoc., 35 (1913) [introduction and notes] • J. C. Holt and R. Mortimer, eds., Acta of Henry II and Richard I (1986) • R. W. Eyton, Court, household, and itinerary of King

Henry II (1878) · Tout, *Admin. hist.*, vol. 1 · D. M. Stenton, ed., *Pleas before the king or his justices, 1198–1212*, 3, SeldS, 83 (1967), appx 1 · *Chancery records* · R. R. Darlington, introduction, *The cartulary of Darley Abbey*, ed. R. R. Darlington, 2 vols. (1945) · *Materials for the history of Thomas Becket, archbishop of Canterbury*, 1, ed. J. C. Robertson, Rolls Series, 67 (1875), 108 · H. Hall, ed., *The Red Book of the Exchequer*, 3 vols., Rolls Series, 99 (1896), vol. 1, pp. 248, 247–8, 343–4 · L. Landon, *The itinerary of King Richard I*, PRSoc., new ser., 13 (1935), nos. 356–7 · R. R. Darlington, ed., *The cartulary of Worcester Cathedral Priory (register I)*, PRSoc., 76, new ser., 38 (1968), no. 163 · R. Howlett, ed., *Chronicles of the reigns of Stephen, Henry II, and Richard I*, 2, Rolls Series, 82 (1885)

Ralph of Bristol. *See* Bristol, Ralph of (*d.* 1232).

Ralph of Evesham. *See* Evesham, Randal of (*d.* 1229).

Ralph of Maidstone. *See* Maidstone, Ralph of (*d.* 1245).

Ralph of St Albans. *See* St Albans, Ralph of (*fl.* 1195x1214?).

Ralph of Shrewsbury. *See* Shrewsbury, Ralph (*c.*1286–1363).

Ralph the Staller, earl of East Anglia (*d.* 1068x70), magnate, was the son of a Breton father of the Montfort-Gael line. Since his brother was named Godwine, their mother may have been English and both Ralph himself and his son *Ralph de Gael are styled *anglicus* (Englishman) in Breton ducal charters. Ralph's first attestation is no later than 1034, and he may have been born *c.*1010, supposedly in Norfolk (though this may be an inference from his later tenure of the East Anglian earldom). His unnamed father perhaps came to England with Emma of Normandy when she married Æthelred II in 1002. Emma made a Frenchman her reeve in Exeter, and perhaps gave Ralph's father the single manor which Ralph held in Cornwall, for his other lands, at least some of which he received from Edward the Confessor, were concentrated in Norfolk, Suffolk, and Lincolnshire. From 1050 he attested both royal charters and private transactions as 'staller', the title borne by important members of the king's household. His precise position is unknown: he is described in charters as the king's steward (*regis dapifer*: AS chart., S 1029), courtier (*aulicus*: AS chart., S 1036), and steward of the king's hall (*procurator*: AS chart., S 1042).

Ralph's landed wealth in England can be reconstructed from Domesday Book, which also reveals the existence of his brother Godwine, who was living in 1069, and a nephew, Alsige, possibly Alsige of Landwade, Cambridgeshire, a benefactor of Ramsey Abbey. Ralph himself patronized the abbeys of St Riquier in Ponthieu and St Bene't of Holme, Norfolk, though the lands which he gave to the former did not belong to the church in 1086 and only one of his gifts to St Bene't was in its possession at that date.

Ralph was one of those French followers of King Edward who were classed as 'Englishmen' after 1066; thus the Anglo-Saxon Chronicle correctly describes him as English. He entered the service of William I, who gave him the earldom of Gyrth (*d.* 1066) in East Anglia. He is addressed as earl in a series of early writs relating to Bury St Edmunds and was charged, with William, bishop of London, and the royal priest Engelric, with overseeing the process by which the English redeemed their estates from

the Conqueror. He was alive in February 1068, when he attested a charter of William I for St Riquier, but died before the deposition of Æthelmær, bishop of East Anglia, at Easter, 1070. Ralph, styled *comes*, attests a charter of 1069 (*Reg. RAN*, 1.28) but whether this was the father or the son is unclear; Orderic Vitalis, however, says it was Ralph de Gael who defended Norwich in the summer of that year, when it was attacked by the Danish fleet sent to aid the English revolt in the north. Ralph the Staller left two sons, Ralph de Gael and Hardouin. It has been suggested that his wife was the Cambridgeshire magnate Eadgifu the Fair, but the Anglo-Saxon Chronicle specifically says that Ralph de Gael's mother was a Breton (*ASC*, s.a. 1075, texts D, E).   ANN WILLIAMS

Sources A. Farley, ed., *Domesday Book*, 2 vols. (1783), 2.119v, 127v, 144, 158, 158v, 194, 216, 367v · *Reg. RAN*, 1.28, 40, 43 · AS chart., S 1000, 1021, 1027, 1031, 1029, 1033, 1034, 1036, 1026, 1042, 1041 · *Chronica Johannis de Oxenedes*, ed. H. Ellis, Rolls Series, 13 (1859) · A. J. Robertson, ed. and trans., *Anglo-Saxon charters*, 2nd edn (1956) · S. Keynes, *An atlas of attestations in Anglo-Saxon charters, c.670–1066* (privately printed, Cambridge, 1993) · P. A. Clarke, *The English nobility under Edward the Confessor* (1994) · A. Williams, *The English and the Norman conquest* (1995) · K. S. B. Keats-Rohan, 'William I and the Breton contingent in the non-Norman conquest, 1060–1087', *Anglo-Norman Studies*, 13 (1990), 157–72 · *ASC*, s.a. 1075 [texts D, E] · H. M. Cam, 'The English lands of the abbey of St-Riquier', *EngHR*, 31 (1916), 443–7 · F. M. Stenton, 'St Benet of Holme and the Norman conquest', *EngHR*, 37 (1922), 225–35 · Ordericus Vitalis, *Eccl. hist.*, vol. 2 · C. R. Hart, *The early charters of eastern England* (1966)

Ralph, George Keith (*b.* 1752, *d.* in or after 1811), portrait and subject painter, was born in September 1752. He registered as a student at the Royal Academy in 1775 aged '23 last Sept' (Hutchison, 141) and exhibited thirty-five works there between 1778 and 1811 including one of Mr King, master of the ceremonies at Bath (1790). In 1794 he described himself as portrait painter to the duke of Clarence. He also exhibited at the Society of Artists and the British Institution. Although largely based in London, Ralph appears to have obtained considerable employment in the provinces, notably in the eastern counties. Several of his portraits were engraved including one of John Spink, alderman and banker of Bury St Edmunds. The original oil painting is in the town's Guildhall. His work is competent and straightforwardly painted, but lacks distinction. He was living in Covent Garden, London, in 1811, but is not heard of after that.

L. H. CUST, *rev.* JILL SPRINGALL

Sources Graves, *RA exhibitors* · S. C. Hutchison, 'The Royal Academy Schools, 1768–1830', *Walpole Society*, 38 (1960–62), 123–91, esp. 141 · B. Stewart and M. Cutten, *The dictionary of portrait painters in Britain up to 1920* (1997) · *Engraved Brit. ports.*

Ralph, James (*d.* 1762), historian and political writer, was probably born between 1695 and 1710 in or near Philadelphia, Pennsylvania, but may possibly have been born in England. Nothing is known of his parents. By 1724 he was married to Hannah Ogden and had a daughter, Mary, who was born that year. He was living in Philadelphia and worked there as a clerk. An aspiring poet, he belonged to a literary society which included Benjamin Franklin, whom he befriended. Many years later Franklin recalled that

Ralph was 'ingenious and shrewd, genteel in his manners, and extremely eloquent; I think I never knew a prettier talker' (Kenny, 219). In 1724, after what Franklin described as a falling-out with his wife's relatives, Ralph abandoned his family and left for London with Franklin. He never returned to America, but corresponded with his daughter, who remained there.

In December 1724 Ralph arrived in London. Living on money lent to him by Franklin, he set out to find work as an editor, as a copyist, and as an actor, but all without success. He had an affair with a milliner and lived with her for a time. He then moved to Berkshire in search of work, assumed Franklin's name, and found a job teaching at a village school. He wrote to Franklin asking him to look after his mistress in London. Franklin apparently misinterpreted Ralph's intentions and made sexual advances which were rebuffed. This put an end to their friendship and gave Ralph the opportunity to renege on the money he owed Franklin. In 1726 Franklin returned to Philadelphia.

Ralph now resumed his literary ambitions in London and in 1727 published a book of poetry, *The Tempest, or, The Terrors of Death*. This was followed by another, *Night* (1728), which sold well enough to go into a second edition. He now turned to literary polemics, for in 1728 he published an attack on Alexander Pope, *Sawney, an Heroic Poem Occasion'd by the Dunciad*. In this work of blank verse Ralph defended the Grub Street authors who had been ridiculed by Pope in the *Dunciad*. He provoked a withering counter-attack in a second edition of the *Dunciad*, in which Pope described him as a 'low writer' (*DNB*). Ralph believed that Pope's attacks turned the publishers against him and that his literary career suffered. At all events his career as a poet was over.

Ralph next tried his hand at drama and criticism. His *Touchstone* (1728) bemoaned the decline of high comedy and caught the attention of the young Henry Fielding. Ralph wrote the prologue to Fielding's *Temple Beau* (1730). Thus began a friendship and intermittent collaboration that lasted for more than twenty years. Fielding began managing the Haymarket Theatre in 1736 with Ralph as his assistant. Ralph owned shares in the theatre and advised him on his theatrical productions.

Ralph's *Fashionable Lady* was staged at the Goodman's Fields Theatre in April 1730. But he met little success as a playwright. In 1733 he was appointed surveyor of houses for Cambridgeshire, but apparently continued living in London; by the early 1750s, if not before, his home was in Chiswick. Fielding's plays satirized the Walpole ministry and led to the theatrical Licensing Act of 1737, which closed down the Haymarket Theatre and put Ralph in straitened circumstances. As he wrote in a plaintive begging letter to his friend Thomas Birch, 'all my schemes are broken as I feared' (Okie, 166).

Ralph now turned to political journalism and it was this that finally brought him a degree of financial security. He began writing occasionally for opposition newspapers in the early 1730s, contributing to the *Weekly Register* and *Daily Courant*. From 1737 to 1739 he covered parliament for the anti-ministerial *Universal Spectator*. In 1739 he resumed his collaboration with Fielding as co-editor of a new opposition journal, *The Champion*. Ralph wrote most of the political essays, attacking the government for its inept handling of the 'war of Jenkins' ear' and for an array of alleged court evils, such as corruption, vice, and standing armies. He continued these broadsides for *The Champion* until 1744. In 1743 Ralph edited *The Critical History of the Administration of Sir Robert Walpole*, a compilation of anti-ministerial tracts from newspapers and pamphlets. He wrote essays for *Common Sense* in 1739 and from 1743 to 1745 he and William Guthrie wrote *Old England, or, The Constitutional Journal*, co-sponsored by the earl of Chesterfield and George Bubb Dodington. Dodington became Ralph's patron for most of the next decade. From about 1743 Ralph was his personal secretary and stayed with him occasionally at his villa in Eastbury, Dorset. When Dodington joined the Broadbottom administration in 1744, Ralph was pensioned by the Treasury at £200 per year. Dodington, however, soon looked to rejoin the prince's opposition circle and in 1747 launched a new anti-court journal, *The Remembrancer*, with Ralph as editor. Ralph was the intermediary between Dodington and the prince of Wales in the negotiations that concluded with Dodington rejoining the opposition. Ralph conducted *The Remembrancer* until the death of Prince Frederick in 1751.

It was under Dodington's patronage that Ralph wrote his most important work, *The history of England during the reigns of King William, Queen Anne, and King George I, with an introductory review of the reigns of the royal brothers Charles and James* (1744–6). It was intended as a continuation of William Guthrie's *History of England*. Ralph's history, published serially in two volumes, contained long transcriptions of documents and ran to over 2000 folio pages in length. It was misleadingly titled because Ralph never, in fact, progressed beyond William's reign.

Ralph's history sold poorly and won its author few plaudits, but is a work of considerable merit and marked an advance in scholarship over the more popular English history of Paul de Rapin-Thoyras. Ralph examined far more documents than Rapin and used them meticulously. He was the first historian to examine the origins of the revolution of 1688 in detail and to explore its European background. In an age when historical writing was twisted by partisan politics, Ralph wrote from a 'country' viewpoint which allowed him to see through the special pleading of whig and tory historians, whose biases and errors he noted throughout. And Ralph wrote more about economics, in particular the financial revolution of the 1690s, than any previous historian of the period.

Another impressive work from this period was *The Other Side of the Question* (1742), Ralph's vivid critique of Sarah Churchill's *Account of the Conduct of the Dowager Duchess of Marlborough*. The book illustrates Ralph's country whig views. He presents Sarah and, to a lesser extent, her husband as archetypal courtiers, power-hungry self-seekers. Tory stalwarts like Henry Sacheverell fare no better in Ralph's account. In *Of the Use and Abuse of Parliaments* (2 vols., 1744) Ralph surveyed the history of parliament from the seventeenth century onwards, showing how 'through the craft and perfidy of kings, the degeneracy of mankind, and the extinction of that noble spirit which accompanies liberty', parliaments invariably become corrupt and tyrannical (Okie, 159).

After Prince Frederick's death in 1751 Ralph joined another opposition faction led by William Beckford and the duke of Bedford, and produced yet another propaganda journal, *The Protestor*. Ralph's new organ assailed the Jewish Naturalization Bill of 1753 and played a key role in having it repealed. Ralph was pensioned into silence by the Pelham ministry in 1753 at £300 per year. He stopped political pamphleteering but wrote occasional literary reviews for the *Monthly Review*. In 1758 he published anonymously his most popular and influential work, *The Case of the Authors by Profession or Trade Stated*. Drawing upon his own experiences as a Grub Street author, he argued that aristocratic patronage of literature had given way in the eighteenth century to a system in which writers were exploited by mercenary booksellers. Ralph's view of publishing in Augustan England became the conventional wisdom in the nineteenth century. His thesis was restated in books and essays by Oliver Goldsmith, Isaac Disraeli, and by Lord Macaulay.

In the late 1750s Ralph wisely ingratiated himself with the earl of Bute, from whom he received a pension when George III succeeded in 1760. Afflicted with gout, Ralph was about to edit yet another newspaper, this time one which was pro-Bute, when he died in Chiswick on 24 January 1762.   LAIRD OKIE

Sources R. W. Kenny, 'James Ralph: an eighteenth century Philadelphian in Grub Street', *Pennsylvanian Magazine of History and Biography*, 64 (1940), 218–42 · J. B. Shipley, 'James Ralph: pretender to Junius', PhD diss., Columbia University, 1963 · L. Okie, *Augustan historical writing: histories of England in the English Enlightenment* (1991) · DNB · F. Garrigues, *The Garrigues family in America* (Oceanside, California, 1982) · [H. Fielding], *Henry Fielding: The true patriot and related writings*, ed. W. B. Coley
Archives BL, letters to Thomas Birch, Add. MS 4317, fols. 82–107 · BL, letters to duke of Newcastle, Add. MSS 32737–32923, *passim*

Ralston, James Layton (1881–1948), politician in Canada, was born at Amherst, Cumberland county, Nova Scotia, Canada, on 27 September 1881, the eldest son of Burnett William Ralston, postmaster, and his wife, Bessie Chipman Layton. His father was of Scottish, his mother of united empire loyalist, descent. After attending the county academy at Amherst he studied at Dalhousie Law School, Halifax, and was called to the Nova Scotia bar in 1903. In 1907 he married Nettie Winnifred, daughter of John McLeod, a foreman iron moulder, of Amherst. They had one son, Stuart Bowman Ralston, who became a justice of the superior court of the province of Quebec for the district of Montreal.

In 1908, when a young practising barrister, Ralston ran as federal Liberal candidate for Cumberland county. He was defeated, but was elected to the legislative assembly of Nova Scotia in 1911 and again in 1916. He had rapidly attained eminence in his profession, first in Amherst and later in Halifax, and was in much demand as counsel. He was made a KC in 1914. A 'slight, distinguished looking man, with good features and thoughtful eyes' (Creighton, 39), he had considerable energy and physical stamina as well as a fine mind. He was noted for the thoroughness with which he prepared his cases and the forcefulness with which he presented them.

In 1915 Ralston enlisted as a lieutenant and in 1916 went overseas with the 85th Canadian infantry battalion as a major. He reached France early in 1917 and served continuously until the armistice, commanding the 85th from April 1918 to demobilization in June 1919. He was gazetted lieutenant-colonel in 1918, and colonel in 1924. He was wounded four times, mentioned twice in dispatches, and awarded the CMG (1918) and DSO with bar (1917 and 1918). The officers and men under Ralston's command were unusually devoted to him, a devotion not lessened by the exacting nature of his demands upon them, and which was enhanced by his well-earned reputation for personal bravery.

In 1919 Ralston returned to England and then to Canada, where he re-entered practice in the firm of Maclean and Ralston. He was defeated in provincial elections in 1920 and 1925 and in the federal election of 1926 at a time when the fortunes of his party were low in his province. In 1926 he was taken into W. L. Mackenzie King's cabinet as minister of national defence and never thereafter suffered a personal electoral defeat. In 1922 he had acted as chairman of a royal commission on pensions and soldiers' civil re-establishment, appointed by the dominion government, and in later years he was actively concerned with the well-being of former servicemen. This had important results in 1944 when the measures known as the veterans' charter were under consideration by the government in which he was then minister of defence. From 1930 to 1935 he was in opposition, and acted as Mackenzie King's 'chief English-speaking stand-by in debate' (*The Times*, 24 May 1948, 7e). He was a vigilant critic of the financial policies of the Conservative government and denounced the prime minister J. M. Bennett's 'New Deal' as a 'series of measures which prove to be only a hollow echo of the flow of fulsome rhetoric with which they were announced' (Thompson and Seager, 265). In 1931 he obtained admission to the Quebec bar and entered a firm in Montreal. After the death of his leading partner he had to choose between politics and the law, and for family reasons put law first. He retired from the Canadian House of Commons in 1935.

When war broke out in September 1939 Ralston offered his services in any capacity to the prime minister, Mackenzie King, and entered the cabinet as minister of finance. He gave his usual exhaustive—probably excessive—attention to detail, but he did not neglect broader considerations and quickly mastered the underlying principles of war finance. Mackenzie King recognized Ralston's value in establishing public confidence in his wartime administration and in July 1940 he appointed him minister of defence. In this capacity Ralston made a monumental contribution to Canada's war effort. His labours were prodigious, his determination irresistible—Canada's effort in mobilization of manpower met with striking success. In a sense he became the personification of Canada militant.

The winning of the war became the one purpose to which all his thoughts and energies were directed.

In winter 1940–41 Ralston visited Britain, where he had talks with Sir Archibald Sinclair about the Canadian contribution to the aerial war. The result was the Sinclair–Ralston agreement of January 1941, which provided for the eventual establishment of twenty-five Royal Canadian Air Force squadrons. In the meantime Canadian airmen would serve in the Royal Air Force. The agreement has been seen as a missed opportunity to create a Canadian air force, and Ralston's silence on this point as symptomatic of Canadian officials' lack of confidence in their dealings with British counterparts during the war. Vincent Massey, Canadian high commissioner in London, observed with regret that visiting Canadians 'frequently behaved like awkward and tongue-tied country cousins' (Creighton, 46).

In all that he did Ralston aimed to keep faith with the front-line soldier and this led him in autumn 1944 to advocate compulsion for overseas service. The government had statutory powers to send those conscripted for home service overseas, but for political reasons it preferred to rely on a flow of volunteers. In September 1944 Ralston visited Canadian forces in Italy. The corps commander there emphasized the need for reinforcements and when Ralston arrived in Brussels in early October a colleague observed: 'Much of his sparkle and good humour had disappeared and he could think or talk of little else but the reinforcement problem' (Soward, 36). Directly on his return to Canada he recommended to the war cabinet that 15,000 fully trained infantry be sent to Europe as soon as possible. But with the war seemingly won, his colleagues were reluctant to believe that this politically inexpedient step was necessary. The attitude was epitomized by Mackenzie King, who on 2 November accepted Ralston's resignation. Three weeks later, however, in a remarkable volte-face, the government tabled an order in council providing for the immediate dispatch of 16,000 men to Europe. Ralston had been vindicated and he quit politics with his reputation considerably enhanced.

Upon his retirement from the government, Ralston returned to his law practice in Montreal. He pursued his heavy labours with all his accustomed energy until stricken by a heart attack which resulted in his death in Montreal on 22 May 1948.

Ralston held numerous directorships, reflecting his eminence as a corporation lawyer. He was also a prominent Baptist layman, a governor of Acadia and McMaster universities, and the holder of seven honorary degrees. His friends, however, thought of him primarily as a simple, direct, devout man, generous and considerate. As a soldier, cabinet minister, and head of a law firm, Ralston drove himself and his subordinates hard. But it is a measure of his integrity that he retained the loyalty of those with whom he worked. After his death his picture remained in every office of his law firm, where colleagues continued to refer with deep respect and affection to 'the Colonel'.

MARK POTTLE

Sources private information (1959) · personal knowledge (1959) [*DNB*] · *The Times* (24 May 1948), 7e · *The Times* (25 Nov 1944), 3e · F. H. Soward, *Canada in world affairs: from Normandy to Paris, 1944–1946* (1950) · D. G. Creighton, *Canada, 1939–1957: the forked road* (1976) · J. Herd Thompson and A. Seager, *Canada, 1922–1939: decades of discord* (1985) · W. Stewart Wallace, *The Macmillan dictionary of Canadian biography* (1963) · *The Canadian who's who*, 3 (1938), 563 · *DNB*
Likenesses photograph, repro. in *The Times* (21 Jan 1930), 18 · photograph, repro. in *The Times* (14 Oct 1941), 6

Ralston, John (*d.* 1451/2), bishop of Dunkeld, was the illegitimate son of unknown parents. He is first recorded in 1426 as chaplain and secretary to James I's nephew Archibald Douglas, fifth earl of Douglas. He remained the earl's secretary until Douglas's death in 1439. Ralston, apparently educated at St Andrews University, was styled licensed in canon law and was about to obtain the degree of doctor of canon law when elevated to the episcopacy. There was another John Ralston, a notary, alive in the 1440s, and entries in sources about the two men could be confused; but it appears that the future bishop was rector of Douglas, Lanarkshire (in the patronage of the earls of Douglas), by 1429 until 1443, and dean of Dunkeld from late 1445 until he became bishop there by provision on 27 October 1447. He had been consecrated by 31 March 1448. He may have been in Rome in person briefly in 1446. A single reference to him as provost of Bothwell collegiate church, between 1424 and 1430, is thought to be unreliable.

By 1442 Ralston had begun to appear at the court of James II, possibly as a result of Douglas patronage. He was the king's secretary by January 1443 and occupied that post at least until mid-1448, when he and two others were sent on an embassy first to France, and then to Burgundy, in part to seek a suitable bride for the king. Mary of Gueldres, a kinswoman of the duke of Burgundy, was chosen, and the marriage negotiations were concluded in the spring of 1449. On his return Ralston was briefly king's treasurer, but he was relieved of his duties after the dramatic collapse in September 1449 of the Livingston faction which so dominated court politics in the late 1440s. He may have been connected with the Livingstons, as he had to apply to the king for a remission of rancour. Early in 1450 he resumed his regular appearances as witness to crown charters. Ralston was still alive on 26 October 1451, but he had died by 28 April 1452, when his successor as bishop was provided. He was buried in his cathedral, where he had continued the work of building the nave.

ALAN R. BORTHWICK

Sources J. M. Thomson and others, eds., *Registrum magni sigilli regum Scotorum / The register of the great seal of Scotland*, 11 vols. (1882–1914), vol. 2 · *CEPR letters*, vols. 9–10 · A. I. Dunlop, ed., *Calendar of Scottish supplications to Rome*, 4: 1433–1447, ed. D. MacLauchlan (1983) · *RotS*, vol. 2 · A. Myln, *Vitae Dunkeldensis ecclesiae episcoporum*, ed. T. Thomson, Bannatyne Club, 1 (1823) · G. Burnett and others, eds., *The exchequer rolls of Scotland*, 5 (1882) · *CDS*, vol. 4 · *The Asloan manuscript*, ed. W. A. Craigie, 2 vols., STS, new ser., 14, 16 (1923–5)

Ralston, William Ralston Shedden- (1828–1889), librarian and Russian scholar, was born on 4 April 1828 in York Terrace, Regent's Park, London, the only son of William

William Ralston Shedden-Ralston (1828–1889), by I. S.? Panov (after unknown artist, c.1875)

Patrick Ralston Shedden (1794–1880), merchant of Calcutta, and his wife, Frances Sophia, daughter of William Browne of that city. His grandfather William Ralston Shedden of Roughwood, Ayrshire, had had children from two unions in America, the second of which was confirmed on his deathbed in New York; but the Scottish estate passed none the less to relatives, and Ralston's father (as he afterwards maintained) was brought up ignorant of the facts. The Sheddens retired to England in 1833, settling at Palmyra Square in Brighton, where Ralston spent much of his childhood before being educated to university entrance level by the Revd John Roughton Hogg at Lower Brixham, Devon. Admitted to Trinity College, Cambridge, in 1846, he read mathematics, but was drawn to law, and before graduating in 1850 had entered Lincoln's Inn, London. His sensitive, warm-hearted nature was, however, distracted by London's squalor, and he gave himself to church charity work; he also became involved in the Working Men's College, and subsequently observed and commented on poverty in Paris.

The family's Indian wealth was meanwhile being exhausted by litigation. Shedden's claim to Roughwood was denied by a Scottish court and by the House of Lords, but the Legitimacy Declaration Act encouraged him to try again; insolvent as he now was, his case was brilliantly argued before the probate court in 1860 by his daughter Annabella Jean. Despite the emphatic judgment that Shedden was illegitimate and could not inherit British property, he appealed, and as late as 1869 reverted unsuccessfully to the House of Lords. By contrast his son, who loved and later succoured him, shrank from the notoriety and assumed the surname Ralston; in 1861 he formalized the name as Shedden-Ralston, preparatory to being called to the bar at the Inner Temple. Although he resided there in Fig Tree Court for many years, he never practised law, having already in 1853 joined the department of printed books at the British Museum. By diligent if often tedious work, he rose steadily to reach by 1867 the upper section

of the first class of assistants. Slim, more than 6 feet tall, with receding dark hair above a wistful face and flowing pepper-and-salt beard, he was an imposing but kindly figure; his presence was said to bring sunlight to the darkest room. He moved easily in the intellectual world, and was often at Macmillan's 'tobacco parliaments'; he enjoyed cordial if self-effacing relations with many leading writers, including Dante Gabriel Rossetti, Wilkie Collins, Tennyson, Carlyle, and George Eliot.

With the encouragement of Anthony Panizzi, Ralston developed a Slavonic speciality. He taught himself Russian to a very high level (by memorizing the pages of a dictionary), though he lamented his hesitancy when speaking it. He began to write about Russia and from the first exhibited his love of the common people, whose rich, lucid language, strong traditions, and unaffected religion he witnessed for himself in 1868 and 1870, when he also became acquainted with prominent linguists and folklorists such as V. I. Dal and A. N. Afanasyev. Among the earliest authors to excite him as translator were Koltsov (the 'Russian Burns'), the racy dramatist Ostrovsky, and the earthy fabulist Krylov. His study *Krilof and his Fables* (1869) was a landmark in the reception of Russian literature in Britain. As a translator and critic Ralston is, however, associated primarily with Turgenev, with whom he enjoyed a warm and productive friendship. Turgenev gave much practical help and advice, and Ralston enthusiastically championed the novelist in print, facilitated meetings with leading British authors, arranged a grand dinner for him in 1881, and translated—as *Liza*—Turgenev's *Dvoryanskoye gnezdo* ('A nest of the gentry'; 1869): Turgenev considered this the best translation ever made from any work of his.

Nicknamed the Russian Don Quixote, Ralston saw his vocation as tilting at British ignorance about Russia. Passionate in both praise and blame, he was constantly truthful and erred only by occasional extravagance. Already by 1875 he had published nearly a hundred items, including three authoritative books, *The Songs of the Russian People* (1872), *Russian Folk-Tales* (1873), and *Early Russian History* (1874). He lectured inimitably on Russian topics at the Royal Institution, at Oxford University, and throughout Britain. However, a crisis now occurred. For some years Ralston had protested that the museum constrained his time and energy, imposed on him unnecessary cataloguing chores, kept him from Slavonic books, and passed him over for promotion. As 'one of the rare just spirits in that academical Dotheboys Hall' (Gosse, 131), he became implicated in attacks on management and in April 1875 resigned his post, ostensibly on grounds of ill health.

Ralston was now a free agent, but needed to fill his life with work in order to survive. While he could, he did. He promoted Tolstoy's *War and Peace*, translated Lermontov's *Song of Ivan Vasilyevich*, contributed articles to the *Encyclopaedia Britannica*, wrote numerous reviews, and helped to found the Folklore Society. His regular public storytellings were extraordinarily popular and led to invitations to Marlborough House and Buckingham Palace. His researches were rewarded by membership of many Russian institutions, including the Geographical Society and the Academy of Sciences. But the lack of a daily routine drove Ralston in on himself and depression set in. He failed to carry through a planned monograph on Russian heroic poetry and a biography of Pushkin, and desisted from writing a general work on Russia, in favour of Mackenzie Wallace. His attempts at travel, to Russia and elsewhere, were generally aborted. He complained of rheumatism, dyspepsia, roaring in the ears, perpetual sleepiness; he perhaps had myalgic encephalomyelitis. Enforced inactivity brought no income, and most of what he did publish was unremunerative; his pension was mean, and he gave generously to friends and to charity. He increasingly shunned society, becoming almost a recluse.

Ralston no longer cared whether he lived or died: as early as 1882 he spoke of killing himself. In 1887 he nearly set his chimney on fire while burning his papers and diaries; all that survived was a large group of Turgenev's letters, and a few from Tolstoy and some English writers. Relief did sometimes come, as when late in 1888 Ralston became engaged to 26-year-old Annie, daughter of Henry Vizetelly. He hoped to obtain a post in Russia to support her, and placed such capital as he possessed—some £3000—in a trust for their marriage. Precisely at this period, however, he was twice arrested for disorderly behaviour, and his old Cambridge friend A. J. Munby had to intervene on his behalf at Bow Street and with the lunacy commission. Forced to move from his comfortable flat at 8 Alfred Place, Bedford Square, to cramped lodgings nearby at 11 North Crescent, Ralston attempted to control his despair with narcotics. On 6 August 1889 he was found dead, a gutta-percha sheet over his head and a bottle of chloroform in his hand. The coroner returned a verdict of misadventure. Ralston was buried in Brompton cemetery on 12 August.   PATRICK WADDINGTON

Sources M. P. Alekseyev and Yu. D. Levin, *Vil'yam Rol'ston—propagandist russkoy literatury i fol'klora* (1994) · W. Lauter, 'Die Bedeutung von W. R. S. Ralston als Vermittler russischer Literatur nach England', PhD diss., Philipps University, Marburg, 1962 · P. Waddington, 'A bibliography of the writings of W. R. S. Ralston (1828–89)', *New Zealand Slavonic Journal*, 1/1 (1980), 1–15 · P. Waddington, *Turgenev and England* (1980) · M. P. Alekseyev, 'William Ralston and Russian writers of the later nineteenth century', *Oxford Slavonic Papers*, 11 (1964), 83–93 · D. Hudson, *Munby, man of two worlds: the life and diaries of Arthur J. Munby, 1828–1910* (1972) · B. McCrimmon, 'W. R. S. Ralston, 1828–89: scholarship and scandal in the British Museum', *British Library Journal*, 14 (1988), 178–98 · E. W. Gosse, *Portraits and sketches* (1912) · *The letters of John Fiske*, ed. E. F. Fisk (1940) · M. P. Alekseyev, 'V. P. Gayevskiy i V. R. Rol'ston o Turgeneve', *Turgenevskiy Sbornik*, 1 (1964), 335–44 · R. E. Francillon, *Mid-Victorian memories* (1913) · ER, 164.958–80 · A. L. Tove, '"Dvoryanskoye gnezdo". Pervyy angliyskiy perevod', *Turgenevskiy Sbornik*, 2 (1966), 133–43 · A. Esdaile, *The British Museum Library: a short history and survey* (1946) · IGI
Archives NL Scot., corresp. and verses · U. Texas, corresp. | BL, letters to H. Wallis, Add. MS 38831, fols. 34, 52 · BL, letters to fourth Lord Carnarvon, Add. MS 61052, fols. 153–4 · Bodl. Oxf., letters, incl. to C. H. Pearson and to Vigfússon · Mitchell L., Glas., Strathclyde Regional archives, letters to Sir William Stirling-Maxwell of Keir
Likenesses I. S.? Panov, engraving (after photograph or sketch, c.1875), Novostí Press Agency, Moscow; repro. in Alekseyev and Levin, *Vil'yam Rol'ston*, frontispiece [*see illus.*]
Wealth at death £4025 7s. 11d.: resworn probate, March 1890, CGPLA Eng. & Wales (1889)

Ram, Sir (**Lucius Abel John**) **Granville** (1885–1952), parliamentary draftsman, was born on 24 June 1885 in Chester Square, Belgravia, London, the only surviving son of Abel John Ram (1842–1920), barrister, and his wife, Mary Grace O'Brien (d. 1912), daughter of the thirteenth Baron Inchiquin. The family was of Anglo-Irish descent. His father specialized in local government work at the parliamentary bar. Granville, who had two sisters, went to Eton College in 1898 and Exeter College, Oxford, in 1904 where he took a pass degree in 1909 before studying law with H. A. McCardie. He was called to the bar by the Inner Temple in 1910.

The First World War took Ram to Egypt, Gallipoli, and France as a captain in the Hertfordshire yeomanry, and he became adjutant of the South Irish horse. When demobilized in 1919 he entered the civil service as assistant solicitor to the Ministry of Labour, succeeding (Alfred) Clive Lawrence as solicitor in October 1923. His intention was to study government from inside as preparation for a parliamentary career. On 9 February 1924 he married Elizabeth Mitchell-Innes (b. 1901), daughter of a barrister. They had three sons and two daughters by 1938 and lived at Berkhamsted Place, an old mansion bought by his late father in Berkhamsted, Hertfordshire. A magistrate from 1923, Ram became deputy chairman (1932) and chairman (1946) of the Hertfordshire quarter sessions. Shooting and sailing were his hobbies.

In February 1925 Granville Ram was appointed to the office of the parliamentary counsel to the Treasury, the small yet high-powered department that drafted all government legislation. As the third counsel of three, he worked on the text of a variety of bills, notably the Trade Disputes Act of 1927, which outlawed sympathy strikes. Promotion to second parliamentary counsel in January 1929 and CB in January 1931 raised his expectations of the top job when Sir William Graham-Harrison resigned as first parliamentary counsel in November 1933; the selection of Maurice Gwyer came as an unwelcome surprise. Gwyer, who had no previous experience of drafting bills, tactfully allowed Ram a free hand with such important projects as the Unemployment Act of 1934 and the Public Order Act of 1936. The Abdication Bill engaged them both in December 1936, when Ram belatedly noticed a flaw. Conventionally, an act of parliament takes effect at the start of the day on which it receives the royal assent. Edward VIII could not therefore give the royal assent to the Abdication Bill (as it stood) without *ipso facto* invalidating that purported royal assent. A hasty addition specified that the abdication would take effect on the royal assent being signified.

Ram, 'a shortish bespectacled man with a suspicion of a paunch and a rather misleading air of Pickwickian benevolence' (Kent, 19), was perhaps less scholarly and certainly more rumbustious than the typical parliamentary counsel. He usually relied on his assistants to produce the first draft of a bill, before he pulled their work to pieces and comprehensively recast it. His pride in his own legal prose was such that he would repeatedly smother texts with stylistic alterations, some of them trivial. Subordinates, who favoured more functional wording, called him the Maestro behind his back. Not that Ram was indifferent to the content of legislation; on the contrary, he was remarkably free with opinions that went beyond the purely legal. Politics still fascinated him, and government ministers, once they grew used to his presumptuousness, came to appreciate an inventive draftsman who would readily consider how a particular form of words might play on the back benches.

Ram succeeded Gwyer as first parliamentary counsel in January 1937 with a salary of £3000 per annum and a knighthood (KCB) a year later. The office now consisted of five counsel and three assistants. Sir Granville ran it as though it were his own legal chambers. Other civil servants had always to come to see him; even assistant counsel never went out to meet anyone less than a permanent secretary. He stoutly defended his staff at all times: the only person with a right to criticize them was himself, and he exercised it to the full. At his worst, Ram could reduce his secretary to tears, yet colleagues learned to tolerate his moods, for he was basically good natured and keen to advance their careers. His excesses moreover caused amusement. Relations between the parliamentary counsel and ordinary departments were inevitably tense, for laymen failed to understand the technical difficulties faced by lawyers. Ram relished confrontation; his idea of success was to leave a meeting without having given an inch. Quick to form decided views, he was very slow to revise them.

For all his vigour, Granville Ram felt the strain of maintaining a full programme of legislation while also preparing a stream of emergency defence regulations for possible use in wartime. From late 1938 until 1940 he struggled to shake off a virus infection. Once back on form he drafted the Emergency Powers (Defence) Act of 1940, giving power to require persons 'to place themselves, their services, and their property at the disposal of His Majesty'. It was legally otiose but just what Churchill wanted to express the will of the nation. Bombed out of the Treasury, the office moved to Old Queen Street, where, while his expanded staff toiled away at wartime control orders, Ram took charge of the Education Act of 1944. He served as a governor of the Berkhamsted schools and the Francis Holland Church of England schools for girls and belonged to the Association of Governing Bodies of Public Schools. He was a king's counsel from June 1943.

Despite his antipathy to socialism, Ram enjoyed the professional challenge offered by the rush of major legislation that followed the election of a Labour government in 1945. He persuaded Jowitt, the lord chancellor, to endorse his ambitious plans for an ideal statute book, in which statute law on any given subject would be found in a single

act kept up to date by a continuous process of consolidation. The parliamentary counsel's office created a new branch to pursue this, and Ram took charge of it on retiring as first counsel in July 1947, combining the post with the chair of the statute law committee from December 1947.

Though he came to London only twice a month from his new home at Furze Park, Polruan by Fowey, Cornwall, Ram achieved twenty-nine consolidation acts in five years, thanks to the Consolidation of Enactments (Procedures) Act of 1949, which authorized the making of slight amendments. The purist doctrine of preserving ambiguities in the existing law had always struck him as absurd. He had time to become a lay preacher and a church commissioner from 1948. In spring 1952 Granville Ram developed leukaemia. The Magistrates' Court Act of 1952 nevertheless kept him busy in the private wing of University College Hospital, Gower Street, London. He died there on 23 December 1952, having been the dominant personality in the office of the parliamentary counsel for a generation.   JASON TOMES

Sources H. S. Kent, *In on the act* (1979) · *The Times* (27 Dec 1952) · *DNB* · Lord Jowitt, 'Sir Granville Ram: consolidation of statute law', *The Times* (8 Jan 1953) · Burke, *Gen. Ire.* (1976) · Burke, *Gen. GB* (1972)

Likenesses W. Stoneman, four photographs, NPG

Wealth at death £17,298 14s. 4d.: probate, 25 April 1953, CGPLA Eng. & Wales

Ram, James (1793–1870), lawyer and legal writer, was born in Essex, the son of James Ram of Monkwick, Essex. He was indentured to a London firm of solicitors, but later entered Pembroke College, Cambridge, where he graduated BA in 1817 and proceeded MA in 1823. After making what was then the grand tour between 1818 and 1822, he entered the Inner Temple, where he was called to the bar on 21 November 1823. A pupil of the conveyancer Richard Preston, he practised in London and Ipswich, where he lived in later life. He married the only daughter of Ralph Willett Adye, army officer, and had two sons.

As a legal author Ram obtained a reputation for painstaking research, methodical arrangement, and lucidity of style. He published works on jurisprudence, property, debt, and a father's custodial rights over his children. He died at 22 Silect Street, Ipswich, on 11 August 1870.

J. M. RIGG, *rev.* ERIC METCALFE

Sources Venn, *Alum. Cant.* · J. G. Marvin, *Legal bibliography, or, A thesaurus of American, English, Irish and Scotch law books* (1847) · *GM*, 1st ser., 80 (1810), 493 · private information (1896) · CGPLA Eng. & Wales (1870)

Wealth at death under £450: probate, 22 Dec 1870, CGPLA Eng. & Wales

Ram, Robert (d. **1657**). See under Ram, Thomas (1564–1634).

Ram, Thomas (1564–1634), Church of Ireland bishop of Ferns and Leighlin, was born at Windsor, the son of Dr Francis Ram (1537–1617) and his wife, Helen. He was educated at Eton College (c.1583–1588) and at King's College, Cambridge, where he matriculated in 1588, graduated BA in 1592–3, MA in 1596, and held a fellowship from 1591 to 1601. In 1599 he accompanied the earl of Essex on his ill-fated expedition to Ireland, subsequently becoming chaplain to his successor, Lord Deputy Mountjoy. In July 1600 he acquired the first of his many Irish benefices, the prebend of St John's, attached to Christ Church, Dublin, which he held until 1602. There followed, among others, the deanery of Cork (1601–5), the precentorship of Christ Church, Dublin (1601–34), the vicarage of Balrothery (1604), the deanery of Ferns (1604–26), and the rectory of Wexford (1605–22) and prebend of Fethard (1629–34), both in the diocese of Ferns. Though made bishop of Ferns and Leighlin in 1605 (nominated 6 February, consecrated 2 May), he retained a number of his benefices *in commendam* because of the poverty of the sees, the result of his sixteenth-century predecessors' habit of leasing valuable lands for low rents and high entry fines.

One of a number of committed English protestants appointed to Irish bishoprics at the start of the seventeenth century, Ram proved conscientious, residing in Ferns and Leighlin, travelling to Dublin to attend the chapter of Christ Church, and making an annual visitation of his diocese, as well as producing detailed reports for official inquiries in 1612, 1615, and 1622. But efforts to restore episcopal finances and spread protestantism made very slow progress. He began legal proceedings to recover illegally leased lands, and increased the value of Ferns from £66 when he was appointed to £120 by 1622, though it was not until after his death that the firm hand of Lord Deputy Wentworth forced the issue. He built a new episcopal residence at Leighlin, and bequeathed his library for the use of his clergy (it was destroyed in the 1641 rising). He improved the quality of the ministry by attracting local ordinands and educating them at the new University of Dublin (Trinity College), but made little headway with the lay population. In a revealing account written in 1612, he told of his efforts to use his legal powers to make the inhabitants come to church. Though some of the ordinary people confessed privately to him their desire to conform, their social superiors were, he concluded, so firmly committed to Catholicism that, together with the priests, they could ensure that Catholics shunned the established church and its institutions. Thus all those who attended the two protestant schools in his dioceses were warned by one local priest that they and their children risked damnation. Ram joined with most of the other Church of Ireland bishops in 1626 to sign a protest against the proposed toleration of Catholicism, and is recorded in 1631 implementing official policies to close down Catholic mass-houses. He died on 24 November 1634, reportedly of apoplexy, while attending convocation in Dublin, and was buried at Gorey, co. Wexford, in a chapel which he had built on his own estate, Ramsfort.

Ram founded an enduring dynasty. He had married first Jane Thompson, *née* Gilford (or Gifford), with whom he had one son and four daughters, and second, Anne Bowen, with whom he had three sons and one daughter. His eldest son, Thomas, inherited Ramsfort, and one of his descendants, Colonel Abel Ram, was the 'ram of Gorey' who fell foul of Swift in 1728. His second son, **Robert Ram** (*d.* 1657), Church of England clergyman, was educated at Trinity College, Dublin, where he graduated BA in 1611, MA in 1614 (incorporated Cambridge 1615), and was a fellow (1615), and where he was maintained by the income from a prebend in Ferns. After ordination he served first as rector of St James's Church, Colchester, then as minister of Spalding in Lincolnshire. In 1639 he married Anne, daughter of Tyringham Norwood. During the English civil war he came to prominence as a strong supporter of the parliamentary cause. In January 1643 he wrote to the people of the neighbouring town of Croyland condemning their folly in resisting parliament. They responded in March by launching a raid on Spalding, capturing Ram and some other inhabitants. These they deployed as hostages, twice tying Ram to the ramparts of Croyland in an effort to dissuade the attacking parliamentary forces. On 27 April the town was finally taken by Cromwell, and Ram freed after five weeks' imprisonment. Nothing daunted, he became chaplain to Colonel Edward Rossiter's regiment and is next found preaching to the soldiers in March 1646 before Newark, reassuring them that 'Your enemies are Gods enemies' since 'The Lord of Hosts is our *generalissimo*' (R. Ram, *A Sermon Preached at Balderton*, 1646, 11–12). His most popular work was *The Souldiers Catechism*, published in 1644, which reached its seventh edition by the following year. In it he defended the iconoclasm of the parliamentary soldiers, and attacked the prayer book as a brazen serpent, 'the most abominable idol in the land' (R. Ram, 21–2). In 1684 the *Catechism* was republished, but this time it was dedicated to Chief Justice Jeffries to serve as a warning of the dangers of those times 'when men were taught rebellion as a principle of religion … to fight against God's anointed' (R. Ram, eighth edn, sig. A1v). Theologically, Robert Ram was an orthodox Calvinist, a defender of presbyterianism and of infant baptism, concerned about the excesses of the religious radicals. On leaving the army he returned to Spalding and was buried there on 4 May 1657.

RICHARD BAGWELL, *rev.* ALAN FORD

Sources T. Ram, 'A true account of the bishop of Ferns and Leighlin', 1612, TCD, MS 1066, 135–50 · T. Ram, report to the commissioners on the diocese of Ferns, 1622, TCD, MS 2158, fols. 110r–120v · J. B. Leslie, *Ferns clergy and parishes* (1936), 7–8 · *The whole works of Sir James Ware concerning Ireland*, ed. and trans. W. Harris, 1 (1739), 447–8 · Burke, *Gen. Ire.* (1958) · Venn, *Alum. Cant.* · R. Ram, *The souldiers catechism composed for the parliaments army*, 7th edn, 1645; 8th edn, 1684 (1644) · A. Laurence, *Parliamentary army chaplains, 1642–1651*, Royal Historical Society Studies in History, 59 (1990), 168 · B. Donagan, 'Did ministers matter? War and religion in England, 1642–1649', *Journal of British Studies*, 33 (1994), 119–56 · *JHC*, 4 (1644–6), 593 · W. Sterry, ed., *The Eton College register, 1441–1698* (1943)

Archives TCD, MS 1066, 135–50

Ramabai, Pandita **Mary Saraswati** [*née* Ramabai Dongre] (**1858–1922**), social reformer and writer, was born on 23 April 1858 in Gangamul, near Mangalore, India, the youngest of the six children (of whom three survived infancy) of Anant Shastri Dongre, Sanskrit scholar, and his second wife, Lakshmibai, daughter of Madhavrao Abhyankar. Her father, who was a Marathi Brahman, had an unusual belief in the education of women. He taught his wife Sanskrit, in which Ramabai was instructed in the sacred books by both her parents. The family lived on a pilgrim route in a remote part of the Western Ghats, where her father spent so much in entertaining pilgrims and students that he had to sell off his rice fields and coconut plantations. He and his family then became travelling pilgrims, earning their living by reciting the Sanskrit *Puranas* in the villages. In the famine of 1876–7 all the family died except for Ramabai and her brother Shrinivas, who eventually arrived in Calcutta in 1878, where Ramabai studied the Hindu scriptures further. She was so disgusted with their treatment of women and of low castes that she became associated with the reforming Brahmo Samaj. Her lectures on the rise and fall of the Aryan race and on the position of women, as well as her knowledge of the sacred books, caused Calcutta University to confer on her the title Saraswati, after the goddess of learning; a gathering of scholars also awarded her the title of Pandita (learned woman). Her brother died in 1880. On 13 June in the same year she married, in a civil ceremony, a Bengali schoolteacher, Bipin Behari Das Medhavi, who was a member of the Brahmo Samaj. He died of cholera in 1881, leaving her with a daughter, Monorama, with whom she returned to Maharashtra, the home of her ancestors, where she earned a living by lecturing on social questions.

In 1883, hoping to study medicine, Ramabai went to England, where she and her daughter stayed with the community of St Mary the Virgin in Wantage while she improved her English. Impressed by the sisters' work, particularly among prostitutes, she was baptized with the name Mary and confirmed in the Church of England in 1883. When her defective hearing made a medical career impossible the sisters arranged for her to study at Cheltenham Ladies' College and to teach Sanskrit in return. Ramabai now came to question the Anglo-Catholic position of the community and was irritated by what she regarded as its patronizing attitude; it was a relief to all when in 1887 she accepted an invitation to visit the Women's Medical College in Philadelphia. There she decided to devote her life to the protection and the education for employment of Hindu widows, particularly those who were children. She prepared herself by taking a teaching course and by studying the school systems of America. At the same time she wrote *The Hindu High Caste Woman* (1887), the first book by an Indian woman to appear in English. Its vivid description of the cruelties suffered by Hindu widows and her lectures throughout America led to the formation of a Ramabai Association, which raised sufficient funds to enable her to return to India in 1889 and open a school for high-caste Hindu widows and orphans, first in Bombay, then in Poona, and finally in her Mukti Sadan (House of Salvation) near Poona. Rapidly becoming a public figure, in 1889 Ramabai was the first woman to address the Indian National Congress, recommending that Hindi should be used as the common language of India. At the Indian National Social Conference in the same year she urged that it should be made a legal offence to shave the heads of widows.

In 1896–7 and 1899 severe famines occurred in central India. With the memory of her parents' fate, Ramabai rescued hundreds of women and girls from starvation and prostitution and settled them at Mukti, where they were educated and set to work in fruit farming and small industries. A church was built with space for 5000 worshippers; services were usually conducted by American Methodist ministers. In 1905 a phenomenon occurred which has been variously treated with admiration, puzzlement, or reserve by Ramabai's biographers. As she was reading from the eighth chapter of St John, the whole congregation began to weep and speak in tongues, and waves of prayer swept through the church. Evangelical activity outside the settlement was now intensified. Though Ramabai dampened the manifestation of the revival when it verged on hysteria, it brought her a personal message to translate the Bible into a language which, unlike the current Marathi versions, could be understood by the people. For the remaining fifteen years of her life this translation from the original Hebrew and Greek became her main occupation, in addition to running her institution. She gave up travelling and public speaking.

Some 2000 people lived at Mukti, which was largely self-supporting, and where Ramabai had ten American and European helpers. In addition to the girls' school with its industrial and agricultural sides there was a rescue department for former prostitutes, homes for the elderly and sick, and a boys' orphanage which eventually provided Christian husbands for many of the girls. Despite occasional tussles with the British authorities, notably over insensitive plague control measures, Ramabai was awarded the kaisar-i-Hind medal in 1919. In 1921 she suffered a severe blow on the death of her only child, Monorama, who had been trained to succeed her. Shortly after completing her translation of the Bible she died in her sleep on 5 April 1922 at Mukti, where she was buried the following day. Her work was successfully continued by her foreign and Indian colleagues.

Ramabai was described by Sarojini Naidu as the first Christian to be enrolled in the calendar of Indian saints. In her twenties Max Müller found her 'truly heroic in appearance, small, delicate and timid, but in reality bold as a tigress' (Müller, 42). The timidity disappeared; later a visitor to Mukti described her as 'very charming and humble but imperious' (Dongre and Patterson, 123). She lived very simply, owning nothing but her books and clothes and wearing the white sari and cropped hair of a Hindu widow.

Ramabai's achievements were of many kinds. As an educationist she was a pioneer of methods which combined academic and practical work. Her girls operated and maintained the printing press, and as masons and carpenters did much of the construction of the Mukti buildings, organizing themselves and electing their own leaders. She also introduced kindergarten methods and braille into India. In modern India she was the first woman to become prominent in public life. She was a brilliant lecturer, earnest but witty. As a social reformer she aroused a strong sentiment against the cruel traditional treatment of widows. As a religious leader and evangelist she was closer to nonconformists than to Anglicans in later life, though she never formally renounced her membership of the Church of England. She was prophetic in calling for closer co-operation between Christian churches and for the acceptance by Christians of what was good in Hindu tradition and custom. She attributed all successes to God, in whose providence she was completely confident throughout the frequent financial crises at Mukti.

In addition to her *Hindu High Caste Woman* and her Bible translation, Ramabai was a prolific writer of books and articles on social and religious subjects in English and Marathi. Her many biographers draw largely on her own *Testimony* (1917), her recollections included in S. M. Adhav's *Pandita Ramabai* (1969), and her *Letters and Correspondence* (1977). The two latter contain bibliographies of her writings.   RICHARD SYMONDS

Sources S. M. Adhav, *Pandita Ramabai* (1970) · A. B. Shah, ed., *Letters and correspondence of Pandita Ramabai* (1977) · P. Sen Gupta, *Pandita Ramabai Saraswati: her life and work* (1970) · H. S. Dyer, *Pandita Ramabai* (1923) · N. MacNicol, *Pandita Ramabai* (1926) · F. M. Müller, *Auld lang syne*, 2nd ser. (1898–9) · R. Dongre and J. F. Patterson, *Ramabai remembered* (1969) · *Annual report prayer bell* [Ramabai Mukti Mission] (1903)

Archives Maharashtra state board for literature and culture, Bombay, notebooks of Sister Geraldine of the Community of St Mary the Virgin, Wantage

Likenesses photograph, repro. in Shah, ed., *Letters and correspondence*

Wealth at death on principle only clothes and books

Ramadge, Francis Hopkins (1793–1867), physician, was born in Dublin, the eldest son of Thomas Ramadge of that city. He was educated at Trinity College, Dublin, where he graduated BA in 1816 and MB and MA in 1819. He was incorporated on his MB degree at Oxford as a member of Magdalen Hall on 4 May 1821, and proceeded MD on 27 June in the same year. Ramadge was admitted an inceptor candidate of the Royal College of Physicians on 26 June 1820, a candidate on 1 October 1821, and a fellow on 30 September 1822. He was censor in 1825. Ramadge established himself in London, where he became physician to the Central Infirmary and Dispensary, lecturer there on the principles and practice of medicine and chemistry, and senior physician to the infirmary for asthma, consumption, and other diseases of the lungs. On 16 September 1826 he married Elizabeth Batts Bell at St Clement Danes, Westminster.

Besides contributions to *The Lancet*, *Medical Times*, and *Notes and Queries*, Ramadge wrote *Consumption Curable* (1834), which later appeared in two further editions and was also published in New York and translated into German and French. He also wrote *On Asthma and Diseases of the Heart* (1847). He translated R. T. H. Laennec's *De l'auscultation médiate*; *Treatise on Mediate Auscultation* (1846) appeared in an edition with Ramadge's own annotations and was seen through the press by Theophilus Herbert. Ramadge died at 12 Clarges Street, Piccadilly, London, on 8 June 1867, leaving a widow, Harriette, presumably his second wife.   GORDON GOODWIN, rev. KAYE BAGSHAW

Sources Munk, *Roll* · *London and Provincial Medical Directory* (1865) · *London and Provincial Medical Directory* (1868) · *CGPLA Eng. & Wales* (1867) · *N&Q*, 6th ser., 10 (1884), 478 · *A catalogue of all graduates ... in the University of Oxford, between ... 1659 and ... 1850* (1851) · Foster, *Alum. Oxon.* · IGI

Wealth at death under £1500: administration, 24 June 1867, *CGPLA Eng. & Wales*

Ramage, Craufurd Tait (1803–1878), writer, born at Annefield, near Newhaven, on 10 September 1803, was educated successively at Wallace Hall Academy, Dumfriesshire, at the Edinburgh high school, and from 1820 at Edinburgh University, where he graduated MA in 1825. While at the university he took private pupils, including Archibald Campbell Tait, afterwards archbishop of Canterbury, with whom he maintained a lifelong friendship. After leaving college Ramage became tutor in the family of Sir Henry Lushington, and spent three years with his pupils in Naples, afterwards making a tour of Italy. For fifteen years after his return he was tutor in the family of Thomas Spring-Rice, afterwards Lord Monteagle. He contributed to the *Quarterly Journal of Education*, the *Penny Cyclopaedia*, and the seventh edition of the *Encyclopaedia Britannica*.

In 1841 Ramage was appointed vice-master of Wallace Hall Academy; on the death of Dr Mundell he succeeded to the rectorship in 1842. He was a justice of the peace for Dumfriesshire from 1848, and in 1852 the University of Glasgow conferred on him the degree of LLD. He died at Wallace Hall on 29 November 1878. His wife, Mary, née Paterson, survived him. They had at least one son.

Ramage published four anthologies, from Greek (1864), Latin (1864), French and Italian (1866), and German and Spanish (1868). He also wrote a *Defence of the Parochial Schools of Scotland* (1854) (defending the established church), *The Nooks and Byways of Italy* (1868), and a history of Drumlanrig Castle (1876), and in addition contributed to *Notes and Queries*.

                    THOMPSON COOPER, rev. H. C. G. MATTHEW

Sources *Men of the time* (1875) · U. Edin. L., special collections division, university archives · *CCI* (1879)

Likenesses H. Adlard, stipple (after unknown portrait), NPG

Wealth at death £11,846 1s.: confirmation, 10 Feb 1879, *CCI*

Ramage, John (1788–1835), telescope maker and optician, born in Aberdeen on 2 November 1788, was probably the son of John Ramage, a horse currier or saddler of Aberdeen, and his wife, Jean Davidson. There was at least one other son, James, and two daughters, Mary and Elizabeth (the scanty parish records have another John Ramage born in Old Aberdeen to a James Ramage in 1783). His education and early life are unrecorded, but he appears to have followed the trade of currier and leather merchant at Ramage Court, 83–85 Broad Street, Aberdeen, as noted in the first city directory of 1824. In 1828 he is listed as an optician.

Ramage began making Gregorian reflecting telescopes about 1806, but was dissatisfied with their light grasp and changed over to the front-view Herschel type, which did not have a secondary speculum. In 1813 he made a telescope of 13½ inches aperture, later in the possession of the advocate Thomas Gordon of Buthlaw, then constructed three or four reflectors of 15 inches aperture and 25 feet focal length, mounted on elaborate altazimuth structures. In 1829 one of these was set up on an open space near his house, in the grounds of Robert Gordon's Hospital by permission of the governors. Dr Thomas Dick saw this telescope in 1833, and inspected several metal specula up to 18 inches aperture. Ramage claimed to have made more than a hundred specula entirely by hand. A second telescope was in the possession of the explorer Captain Sir John Ross RN, at Stranraer. He used it to make simultaneous observations of occultations of Jupiter and Uranus with Ramage in Aberdeen in 1824. The telescope later came into the hands of Andrew Barclay, a railway engineer and amateur astronomer of Kilmarnock.

A third telescope was owned by Dr Alexander Dauney, professor of civil law at King's College, and erected at Broadford, Aberdeen. He died in 1833 so the instrument may have been returned to the workshop. A telescope of this size was offered to the council of the Royal Astronomical Society for inspection, taken to London, and erected at the Royal Greenwich Observatory in 1825 in the hope that the Admiralty would purchase it. It is illustrated in W. Pearson's *Introduction to Practical Astronomy* (1829, 2.79–82) and in several contemporary works. The Herschel-type mounting on a circular iron ring had an arrangement of pulleys whereby the observer could move the telescope about 10 degrees in altitude and azimuth without assistance. Although Ramage pronounced it safe, Sir David Brewster fell off the structure. John Pond, the astronomer royal, and others extolled the brilliancy of the metal, but Sir James South, John F. W. Herschel, and George Biddell Airy found the figure poor, with aberrant zones which had to be masked out. Purchase was not forthcoming. After Ramage's death the telescope, and another by him—54 feet long and 22 inches aperture, which also lay at Greenwich—were bought by John Pringle Nichol, professor of astronomy at Glasgow, for what became the university's new observatory. Airy ordered the abandoned mounting to be demolished. The two universities at Aberdeen showed little interest in Ramage's telescopes—they were too big for the limited space at either observatory—but he was given a testimonial signed by eight professors. No speculum by him is known to survive.

Encouraged by his telescope making, Ramage appears to have taught himself sufficient physical sciences to enable him to extend his business to optical instrument making (he had premises at 39 Union Street and 29–32 George Street), then to expand into chemical apparatus, nautical instruments, firearms, fancy goods, and an agency for Admiralty charts. In 1835 he opened a branch in Inverness. After his death a vast stock was offered for sale, including the telescopes at Greenwich and Robert Gordon's Hospital, and a large transparent orrery which he used in his astronomy lectures. He was treasurer and trustee of the Aberdeen mechanics' institution, and in 1834 gave courses on natural philosophy and astronomy, 'of special interest to ladies'. In 1829 he was sponsored for fellowship of the Royal Astronomical Society by Sir John

Ross, and in 1834, at the Edinburgh meeting of the British Association for the Advancement of Science, he was a member of the mathematics and physics section committee.

Ramage married Jean King on 20 April 1806. They had at least four daughters and seven sons, some of whom carried on the businesses. Several members of his family were baptized and married in the Episcopal chapel. He died after a very short illness, possibly cholera which was epidemic in the city at the time, at his home, 29 George Street, on 26 December 1835, and was buried on 2 January 1836 in St Clement's churchyard in Aberdeen. His age at death was given as fifty-two in the *Aberdeen Journal* of 6 January 1836 but as forty-five in the parish record.

DAVID GAVINE

Sources *Memoirs of the Royal Astronomical Society*, 2 (1826), 413–18, 87, 91 · W. Pearson, *An introduction to practical astronomy*, 2 (1829), 79–82 · H. C. King, *The history of the telescope* (1955), 199–201 · T. Dick, *The practical astronomer* (1845), 310 · *The Northern Iris* [Aberdeen] (May 1826), 121, 137–8 · D. Brewster, *A treatise on optics* (1831), 357 · G. M. Fraser, *Aberdeen mechanics' institute* (1912), 5–11 · E. G. R. Taylor, *The mathematical practitioners of Hanoverian England, 1714–1840* (1966), 372 · *Glasgow Mechanics' Magazine*, 2 (1838), 444 · CUL, Airy MSS, M4.21, GRO/6 · *Aberdeen Journal* (5 Nov 1834) · *Aberdeen Journal* (6 Jan–17 Feb 1836) · parish records, Aberdeen · directories, Aberdeen, 1824–36 · *Report of the British Association for the Advancement of Science* (1834)
Likenesses miniature (of Ramage?), Rose Lipman Library, De Beauvoir Road, Hackney, London

Ramakrishna Paramahansa (1836–1886), Hindu religious leader, was born Gadadhar Chatterji on 18 February 1836, in the village of Kamarpukur, located in the Hooghly district of Bengal. His father, Kshudiram, and mother, Chandramani, were orthodox Brahmans, probably Vaishnavite sectarians. His father died in 1843, when Gadadhar was still a young child. At the age of nine Gadadhar received the sacred thread that denoted his place as a member of the Brahman caste and in 1852 he attended his elder brother Ramkumar's school in Calcutta. Here it is presumed he learned the necessary information and skills needed to conduct the rituals demanded by his inherited occupation as a Hindu priest. Upon completion of his education, he found employment at the newly established Dakshineshwar Temple 5 miles north of Calcutta. There he served as a pujari (priest), and conducted daily worship of Kali, the mother goddess of life and death. During his youth he demonstrated both a restlessness for and a fascination with mystical religion. The young Gadadhar neglected his ritual duties, and instead devoted increasing amounts of time to the search for spiritual enlightenment. He would sink into states of apparent unconsciousness and occasionally burst forth into extreme religious ecstasy. Such activity resulted in his dismissal from his position as a temple priest. In 1859 his family attempted to divert him from his preoccupation with personal religion by arranging his marriage to Sarada Devi. At the time of her marriage Sarada Devi was six years old and Gadadhar twenty-five. Following Hindu custom she returned home to live with her parents. In the intervening years Gadadhar was not to be dissuaded from continuing his search for a direct, mystical union with God.

During the 1860s Gadadhar studied with a series of ascetics, seeking their guidance in his search for ultimate truth, which, if found, would give him eternal freedom from the cycle of rebirth. His first guide was a Bhairavi Brahmani, a wandering female ascetic from East Bengal, who instructed him in the tantric texts and rituals that provided a path to spiritual power through magical and erotic rituals. Next he was instructed by Jatadhari, a Vaishnavite mystic from north India, and finally by Tota Puri, a devotee of Shankaracharya, the ninth-century religious thinker who created the philosophic foundation of orthodox Hinduism. Tota Puri initiated him into sanyas, the formal stage of a renunciant, and gave him the name Ramakrishna Paramahansa.

After his initiation as a sanyasi, Ramakrishna immersed himself in an exploration of Hinduism and other religions. He studied Sufism (Islamic mysticism), and even adopted Muslim dress, prayers, and religious behaviour. Using similar techniques, he explored Christianity, with the result that he received visions of both Christ and the Madonna. He also acted out other roles such as that of Radha, the wife of the Hindu deity Lord Krishna, for which he dressed and behaved as a Hindu woman. By 1871 he appears to have achieved a degree of inner peace. In 1872, when Sarada Devi reached the age of eighteen, she joined Ramakrishna, who still resided at the Dakshineshwar Temple but not as a practising priest. He proclaimed his wife to be the embodiment of the divine mother, thus transforming their marriage into a spiritual partnership. The attempt to draw the young Ramakrishna away from his preoccupation with a personal search for the divine had failed completely.

By the early 1870s Ramakrishna had attracted a small group of disciples who found in him an accessible, non-judgemental, and nurturing teacher. His new disciples came mostly from the growing number of young men who were educated in schools that taught a British curriculum through the English language. In addition, their urban experiences in Calcutta generated in them a sense of distance from their traditional culture. They questioned Hindu beliefs and customs, with which they were no longer comfortable. These disciples gathered, Ramakrishna talked, and occasionally they raised questions or spoke of their own doubts and needs. For them Ramakrishna was a guru, a spiritual guide to whom they gave increasing loyalty. Three interlinked themes ran through their discussions: the first was the universality of religions—all were true, for each followed its own road to the ultimate source of all being; a corresponding conclusion was that the doctrines and rituals of Hinduism should be preserved unchanged; and finally, since all religions were true there could be no justification for criticism of one religion by another or for conversion from one to another.

In 1882 one disciple, Mahendranath Gupta, began to record Swami Ramakrishna's conversations, thus producing the only written account of his doctrines. In October 1885, when Ramakrishna fell ill, his disciples embarked on the task of nursing their guru. In October they moved him to 55 Shyampur Street in Calcutta and in December transferred him to 90 Cossimpore Road. When he lay near death, he charged the young Narendra Nath to 'teach my boys' and 'keep them together'. On 16 August 1886 Ramakrishna Paramahansa died, leaving behind him a small group of disciples and no writings except for those recorded by Mahendranath Gupta.

Well before his death Ramakrishna's ideas were spread beyond the world of his disciples. After 1875 his message was popularized by Keshab Chandra *Sen, who met Ramakrishna in 1872 and accepted the concept of the universality of all religions. Sen was a Brahmo Samaj leader who broke with that reform society and established his own branch of this religious movement. Following Ramakrishna's death Sarada Devi became widely respected as a spiritual leader among those who followed her husband's doctrines and the wider public. The most famous of Ramakrishna's disciples, however, was Narendranath Datta, later known as Swami Vivekananda, who transmitted and transformed Ramakrishna's ideas and created the Ramakrishna Math and Mission, an international movement of religious action and social service. At a time when the impact of both Christian missions and imperial rule was causing questioning and turbulence in all of India's main religious traditions, Ramakrishna Paramahansa was among the most important leaders of the Hindu tradition.

KENNETH W. JONES

Sources Swami Gambhirananda, *History of the Ramakrishna Math and Mission* (1957) · J. N. Farquhar, *Modern religious movements in India* (1915); repr. (1919) · K. W. Jones, *Socio-religious reform movements in British India* (1989) · R. Rolland, *The life of Ramakrishna*, 6th edn (1960)

Raman, Sir (Chandrasekhara) Venkata (1888–1970), physicist, was born at Tiruvanaikkaval, near Trichinopoly, in the province of Madras, on 7 November 1888, the second of the eight children (five sons and three daughters) of Chandrasekhara Iyer (b. 1866) and his wife, Parvati Ammal (Saptarshi Parvati). His ancestors were Brahman landowners, exempt by their caste from manual labour, trade, and military service. Opportunities outside landowning depended on taking up English education and entering a profession. Raman's father taught at the local high school and, when Raman was four, moved to a lectureship in mathematics and physics at the Mrs A. V. Narashimha Rao College in Vizagapatam (Visakhapatnam).

Education and early career For ten years Raman studied at the high school, and then the college, in Vizagapatam. In 1903, aged only fourteen, he won a scholarship to the Presidency College in Madras. He graduated in 1904, being awarded the gold medal for both English and physics. With further education in England ruled out by delicate health Raman enrolled in the MA class at the Presidency College to study physics under R. Llewellyn Jones. Llewellyn Jones contributed little formally to his education but encouraged him to make free use of the laboratory. Raman was strongly influenced by the works of the third

Sir (Chandrasekhara) Venkata Raman (1888–1970), by
unknown photographer

Lord Rayleigh, and Hermann von Helmholtz's *The Sensations of Tone* which, he claimed, showed him how to conduct research. He worked within the tradition of classical wave theory established by these books throughout his life, using it to investigate and explain natural phenomena. This programme was well adapted both to Raman's strong aesthetic appreciation of natural beauty, and to the perennial lack of funds which dogged Indian science, for much could be achieved with little, and home improvised, apparatus. Raman's first publications, in the *Philosophical Magazine*, on the unsymmetrical diffraction of light and on the surface tension of drops, were published while he was still an MA student (1906, 1907).

Raman took the MA exam in January 1907, coming top. Scientific careers for Indians were virtually non-existent, so he followed his brother into the financial civil service. While awaiting a posting, aged eighteen, Raman met Lokasundari Ammal (*d.* 1980). Defying convention he insisted on marrying her, even though she belonged to a different Brahman sub-sect, and, even more remarkably, he refused a dowry. Intelligent, musical, and self-effacing, Lokasundari ensured that Raman enjoyed domestic peace. Throughout his life Raman worked long hours, typically 6 a.m. to 9 p.m. Lokasundari occupied herself in learning a number of languages and in social work. They had two sons.

In mid-1907 Raman was posted as assistant accountant-general in Calcutta. He rapidly discovered the existence

there of the Indian Association for the Cultivation of Science (IACS), established in 1876 to encourage native Indian science. Once again Raman was given free access to laboratories and devoted all his spare time to physics. As well as optics he studied acoustics and musical instruments, later the subject of an article in the *Handbuch der Physik* (vol. 8, 1927), and established violin research as a scientific discipline. The ensuing stream of papers raised the profile both of the IACS and of Raman, who emerged also as a superb popular lecturer.

Professor of physics In 1917 Sir Ausutosh Mookerjee, a member of the IACS and vice-chancellor of Calcutta University, offered Raman the newly created Palit professorship of physics. Raman accepted, even though it meant almost halving his salary and relinquishing a highly promising career. He described the next fifteen years as his golden era. His new duties included supervising research students, and he became an inspiring group leader with an infectious enthusiasm. Throughout, vibrations and optics remained the main themes of his group's work.

The discovery of the Raman effect, which established his position in modern science and won him the Nobel prize in 1930, was the culmination of nine years' interest in the molecular basis of refraction. That work started in 1919 with investigation of the Doppler effect in scattering, and was followed by extensive work on the blue colour of the sea, inspired by observations Raman made while returning from his first trip abroad, to England in 1921. Raman showed that, contrary to Rayleigh's suggestion that the sea reflected the sky colour, the blue was actually due to molecular scattering. His book *Molecular Diffraction of Light* (1922) recounted all his scattering work to date.

Following the discovery of the Compton effect in 1923, in which X-rays scattered by electrons suffered a discrete change in wavelength corresponding to absorption by the electrons of a quantum of radiation, Raman began to consider whether an optical analogue existed. His student Ramanathan had noticed that 'when sunlight filtered through a violet glass passed through certain liquids and solids … the scattered rays … contained certain rays not present in the incident beam' (C. V. Raman, presidential address to the Indian Science Congress, 1929). In 1925 another student, Krishnan, found that this 'feeble fluorescence' was partially polarized, unlike ordinary fluorescence. Further studies were hampered by lack of a sufficiently powerful light source. The problem was overcome in late 1927 when Raman redoubled his efforts to find evidence for optical scattering with a discrete wavelength change following the award to Compton of the Nobel prize. He used the IACS's new 18 cm refracting telescope coupled to a short focus lens to concentrate sunlight. Working with Venkateswaran and Krishnan, he found feeble fluorescence in a wide range of liquids and, on 7 February 1928, began interpreting this as the modified scattering predicted by the Kramers–Heisenberg dispersion theory. Experiments with a spectroscope on 28 February showed that wavelengths of modified scattered light did indeed differ from those of the incident light by discrete amounts, a result Raman rapidly published in *Nature* (vol. 121, 619). The differences were proved to correspond to absorption by molecules of a quantum of vibrational or rotational energy and the Raman effect became one of the main methods for elucidating molecular structure. Its importance was enhanced in the 1970s following the invention of lasers, which allowed Raman spectroscopy to be extended and pushed to new limits.

Institutional politics, 1933–1937 In 1932 Raman was offered the directorship of the prestigious Indian Institute of Science (IIS) in Bangalore, and was promised a new physics department there. He left Calcutta amid controversy over the appointment of a full time professor for the IACS. The Indian Institute was founded in 1911 following J. N. Tata's promotion of higher education and research as the key to solving India's technological, economic, and social problems. Bangalore was chosen largely for its climate, which proved so attractive to Raman that he remained there for the rest of his life. Yet once again he found himself embroiled in a power struggle. According to Max Born, who was visiting the Indian Institute, 'the deepest sources of the trouble are: the English group resented an Indian director, who, as a political principle, was wanted and pushed through by the powerful Tata group' (Born, cited in Venkataraman, 272). The Tatas apparently responded to commercial pressure from the English and soon turned against Raman, actively undermining his position. His personality made this easy.

> Raman is a very able physicist, full of enthusiasm … [His] European intensity alone would be enough to make Raman suspicious to the average Indian professor. Now Raman, far too much aware of his own superiority, likes to make other people seem small in his presence … Raman came to the Institute with the idea of making it a centre of science of international standard. What he found was a quiet sleepy place where little work was done by a number of well-paid people.   (ibid.)

Raman, who had spent four months at the California Institute of Technology in 1924, aimed at something similar for the IIS. Lack of additional funding for the new physics department forced him to reallocate money from other areas of the budget and in his pursuit of excellence he antagonized many staff. The climax was his proposal to create a chair of mathematical physics for Born, the first, Raman hoped, of many distinguished refugees from Nazi Germany whom he wished to bring to India. In 1937 Raman was forced to resign, following a government review.

A research school Raman retained his professorship of physics. With his desire to pursue nuclear physics and develop a theory group thwarted by lack of funds and support, Raman reverted to optics and scattering problems. Inevitably the work was mainly experimental and his group's thinking remained largely classical. Most important was the development of the Raman–Nath theory of the diffraction of light by high frequency sound waves (C. V. Raman and N. S. Nagendra Nath, *Proceedings of the*

Indian Academy of Science, 1935, 406, 413; 1936, 75, 119, 459). Raman and Nedungadi observed the vastly increased excitation of particular vibration modes at high temperatures, leading to deformation of the atomic arrangements and transition from the alpha to beta forms of quartz (C. V. Raman and T. M. K. Nedungadi, *Nature*, 1940, 147). This was twenty years before Cochran's well-known soft mode theory for such phase transitions.

Above all, Raman established a very active physics research school at the IIS, one of his most enduring contributions to Indian science. His influence convinced both Homi Bhabha and Vikram Sarabhai, later founders of Indian nuclear physics and space science respectively, that they should remain in India. Born had commented that 'The *clever* boys are very devoted to Raman, for he is most interested in their progress and asks very much of them' (Venkataraman, 274). He trained a number of students as first-class physicists, infecting them with his enthusiasm and accessibility. In a country where obtaining an interview with even minor dignitaries meant penetrating layers of officialdom, Raman was notable for leaving his office doors wide open to all, and for his willingness to help students with even the most mundane of manual tasks.

National role In 1934 Raman established the Indian Academy of Science, remaining president until his death in 1970. He aimed to improve communication between scientists, to promote science policy in India and to publish a national journal, thus stemming the flow of good papers to foreign periodicals. Monthly *Proceedings* appeared and, by hard work, Raman maintained his promise of punctual publication. The annual meeting became the high point of the year for Raman and many other scientists.

Before retiring from the IIS at the age of sixty Raman managed to obtain grants from private individuals and industry to build the Raman Research Institute at Bangalore, which he described as 'a haven where I could carry on my highly personal research work' (Venkataraman, 468). The Indian government elected him as the first national professor with an honorarium sufficient for his personal expenses. Determined, though, that the institute should remain independent of government control, Raman started some chemical companies and used the profits to finance the institute. He later gave most of his property for the same purpose. Raman devoted considerable care to designing the institute gardens and toured them twice a day. The inspiration for many of his later papers came from the flowers there.

Late research Raman's fascination with natural phenomena and aesthetics had led, at the IIS, to research on iridescence and the optics of stratified media, and the discovery of the speckles effect in coronae. He now examined the colours of flowers, birds, and insects, and how the eye perceives them, publishing a treatise on *The Physiology of Vision* in 1968 (when he was eighty). He built special galleries at the institute to display his specimens, pre-eminent among which were his diamonds and other gemstones.

Raman had a passionate interest in the physics of diamond. While at the IIS he had investigated X-ray diffraction in diamonds, discovering some unexpected reflections of a different kind from the well-known Laue patterns. Studies of the Raman spectra of diamond, which appeared to show sharp lines, now led to a controversy with Born over lattice dynamics, the origins of which lay in Raman's isolation from developments in quantum mechanics (C. V. Raman, *Proceedings of the Indian Academy of Science*, 1951, 61; 1955, 163; 1956, 327). Raman's interest stimulated research in many laboratories.

Bitter politics Raman's retirement coincided with India's independence and he became emotionally involved in efforts to transform society through science. Yet his views on how to do this differed markedly from those of the government. He deplored both the import of expensive foreign instruments that left India dependent on the West for instrumentation, and the emigration of good Indian scientists abroad. He feared that, despite the rhetoric, funding for universities and excellent fundamental research was still scarce and that mediocrity was becoming institutionalized. Raman expressed himself strongly and was bitterly attacked in the press. Deeply upset, he became a recluse. He erected a 'keep out' sign at the institute, resigned his fellowship of the Royal Society, to which he had been elected in 1924, and became estranged from his two sons. Raman recovered, at least as far as the company of children was concerned, a few years before his death. He had continued working throughout and expressed the wish that he might not survive his final illness if it left him unable to research. He died at his home at the institute on 21 November 1970, following a heart attack a few weeks earlier. He was cremated in its grounds.

Raman became a legendary figure in Indian science. He published more than 500 papers and four books. Of medium height with striking eyes, Raman always wore a turban and adhered to a Hindu diet. Yet he had little interest in organized religion but sought God through understanding nature. His temperament has been likened to that of a child, and was expressed in his enthusiasms, his angers, his supreme ego, and his lack of tact, which hurt many.

Raman travelled a number of times to Europe and North America, visiting colleagues in England, Canada, USA, Russia, Sweden, France, and Italy. He was knighted in 1929 and received the Nobel prize in 1930. He received honorary degrees from fifteen universities and was an honorary member of a number of scientific societies. He received the Matteuci medal of the Italian Academy (1928), the Hughes medal of the Royal Society (1930), the medal of the Franklin Institute of Philadelphia (1940), and the Lenin peace prize (1957). In 1954 the Indian government gave him the unique title of Bharat Ratna.

ISOBEL FALCONER

Sources G. Venkataraman, *Journey into light* (1988) [incl. bibliography] · A. Jayaraman, *Chandrasekhara Venkata Raman* (1989) · S. Bhagavantam, *Memoirs FRS*, 17 (1971), 565–92 · *DNB*
Archives FILM Indian government, films division

Likenesses oils, Raman Research Institute, Bangalore · photograph, Sci. Mus. [*see illus.*] · photographs, Raman Research Institute, Bangalore

Ramanujan, Srinivasa (1887–1920), mathematician, was born on 22 December 1887 in Erode, India, the third of five children (two older sisters died in infancy) of Kuppuswamy Srinivasa (*b.* 1863), a clerk in a silk merchant's shop, and his wife, Komalatammal (*b.* 1868), both Tamil-speaking south Indians. He grew up in Kumbakonam, a mid-sized temple town in Tanjore district, about 160 miles south of Madras. His family was of the Brahman, or priestly, caste but poor. To supplement his father's meagre income, Ramanujan's mother sang Hindu devotionals, and the family took in boarders to their small house, which stood within sight of a temple. Ramanujan attended the local high school, then briefly Government College in the same town and, later, also briefly, Pachaiyappa's College in Madras.

Early studies in India During his early school years Ramanujan showed marked mathematical ability but it was not until he was about sixteen, when a student boarding with the family showed him a copy of an English mathematics text, G. S. Carr's *Synopsis of Elementary Results in Pure and Applied Mathematics*, that he blossomed. Charging into the dense mathematical thicket of the book's 5000 theorems, Ramanujan, by now a first-year college student, lost interest in other subjects, failed them, and dropped out.

Ramanujan had first set out to prove the theorems in Carr's book—a workaday text used to prepare Cambridge students for the mathematical tripos examination—but soon left his remote mentor behind, going where Carr had never gone before or, in many cases, where no one had. Some time between about 1904 and 1907 he began keeping notebooks bearing the record of his mathematical discoveries. For the next few years he worked on his own, along the way reinventing large parts of Western mathematics.

On 14 July 1909 Ramanujan was married to Janaki, who was nine at the time of her betrothal (the institution of the child bride was still entrenched). Janaki did not go to live with Ramanujan or his family for another three years, but his marriage and the urgings of his parents apparently moved him to seek a livelihood. Soon the impoverished youth, notebooks under his arm, was shuttling up and down south India in search of a job or a patron. He found one in R. Ramachandra Rao, district collector of Nellore and sometime mathematician, who supported him modestly for about a year. In 1911 Ramanujan's first paper, on a class of numbers conceived by the Swiss mathematician Jacob Bernoulli, was published in an Indian mathematics journal.

His prodigious talents and a widening web of contacts at last brought Ramanujan to the attention of the British colonial administration in Madras. At first no one knew what to do with him but in 1912 he was given a sinecure in the Madras Port Trust, as a clerk, that let him work on mathematics largely unencumbered. His immediate superior, S. Narayana Iyer, something of a mathematician

Srinivasa Ramanujan (1887–1920), by unknown photographer, 1919

himself, befriended him, and encouraged him to write to England for help and support.

Several distinguished English mathematicians ignored Ramanujan's entreaties, but Godfrey Harold Hardy, of Trinity College, Cambridge, author of an important text on number theory and a leading figure in British mathematics, was intrigued by the pages of theorems he received from Ramanujan early in 1913. Some of them, he wrote later, 'defeated me completely; I had never seen anything in the least like them before' (Kanigel, 168). Conferring with a friend and colleague, J. E. Littlewood, he decided that this mathematics-strewn letter from a lowly Indian clerk was no hoax, a possibility he had first entertained; rather, it seemed to him, Ramanujan was a mathematician who, in raw ability, was on a par with Euler or Jacobi. In his reply he encouraged Ramanujan, but also urged him to prove some of the theorems he had blithely asserted as fact.

The Cambridge years The endorsement from Cambridge helped Ramanujan to obtain a research scholarship at the University of Madras. Ultimately Hardy prevailed on him to go to England, which he did in April 1914—in the face of a traditional proscription against voyages abroad. The mathematical collaboration between the two men lasted for five years and proved one of the most fruitful in the history of mathematics.

The onset of the First World War, a few months after Ramanujan's arrival, drained Cambridge of mathematicians, including Littlewood, and left Ramanujan almost wholly dependent on Hardy. Hardy introduced the self-taught genius to areas of mathematics about which he knew little but, as Hardy acknowledged later, 'I learnt

from him much more than he learnt from me' (Kanigel, 226). Teaching Ramanujan, another mathematician, Laurence Young, wrote later, 'was like writing on a blackboard covered with excerpts from a more interesting lecture' (Kanigel, 227).

Between 1914 and 1919 Ramanujan turned out paper after paper in the area of mathematics known as number theory, which seeks out patterns among ordinary whole numbers. Several grew out of problems Ramanujan had worked on in India that now, under Hardy's tutelage, he had been able to develop and refine. One was on highly composite numbers—numbers with numerous divisors (such as 24)—that were, in Hardy's phrasing, 'as unlike a prime [number] as a number can be' (Kanigel, 232), and among which Ramanujan had discerned subtle properties and patterns.

Perhaps the most notable product of the Hardy–Ramanujan collaboration lay in the area of 'partitions', which asks how one can add up whole numbers to get some other whole number: 3 can be viewed as the sum of 1 + 1 + 1, or 2 + 1, or 3 + 0, making for a total of three partitions. Hardy and Ramanujan discovered how to calculate the number of partitions for any number. Along the way they developed the 'circle method', a mathematically subtle approximating technique of broad application.

In 1918, at the age of thirty, Ramanujan was elected fellow of the Royal Society, only the second Indian so honoured. That forever secured his name in the national affections of India and helped to make him, both before independence and after, a veritable icon of Indian genius. After having been previously denied a Trinity fellowship—almost certainly on account of his race—he was granted one soon after being named a fellow of the Royal Society.

While in England, Ramanujan fell ill; cancer, vitamin deficiency, lead poisoning, and hepatic amoebiasis have been among the diagnoses advanced over the years, but he was treated mostly for tuberculosis. Ramanujan went from one sanitorium to another. At one point, poor health coupled with the absence of letters from home, loneliness in wartime England, and perhaps the suspicion that much of his earliest work had been for nought, drove him to a suicide attempt in the London Underground. He came away unscathed except for a bloodied shin. Soon after the end of the war, in March 1919, he returned to India to a hero's welcome.

Return to India Ramanujan's early relationship with his child bride had been limited at best and, apparently at the behest of his mother, he had not taken her with him to England, where he lived alone in rooms at Trinity College. On his return five years later, however, Janaki was a grown woman and they may have shared something like a real marriage, though they did not have children.

Ramanujan had a fleshy, pockmarked face, the vestige of a childhood bout of smallpox, and for most of his life, at least until his final illness, he was fat. Though immensely creative in higher mathematics, he was only modestly gifted at ordinary arithmetic manipulations. He took interest in philosophical matters. He could be charming and fun. He was not unmindful of society's plaudits; he was plainly delighted by his election to the Royal Society.

Ramanujan was a practising Hindu of the Vaishnavite sect—his caste name, Iyengar or Aiyangar, sometimes included as part of his name, indicates so—and a scrupulous vegetarian, but whether or not he was genuinely devout has been a matter of some controversy. Hardy maintained that he was not, but much other evidence suggests he was more than mechanical in his observance and that he could in one breath bring logic, reason, and deep insight to the defeat of a mathematical problem and in the next pay homage to his family deity, the goddess Namagiri, to whom some said he attributed his mathematical gifts.

In India Ramanujan's health continued to decline and, about a year after his return, on 26 April 1920, he died in Madras, where his body was cremated. Until just a few days before his death, he had continued his work, on a mathematical entity he called 'mock theta functions' that much impressed fellow mathematicians. In his brief life he made seminal contributions to several areas of mathematics, especially number theory, and he is deemed one of the most profoundly original figures in the history of mathematics.

Ramanujan's papers were later published in the *Collected Papers of Srinivasa Ramanujan* (1927), edited by Hardy, P. V. Seshu Iyer, and B. M. Wilson. His early *Notebooks*, brought out in 1957 in two volumes by Tata Institute (Bombay), have been the subject of a five-volume study, *Ramanujan's Notebooks* (1985–97), by the American mathematician Bruce Berndt. *The Lost Notebook and Other Unpublished Papers* (1988) was published by Narosa (New Delhi) in 1988.

In the years since Ramanujan's death, many have commented on the fiercely original nature of his contributions particularly his early notebooks, with some wondering whether a more conventional mathematical education would have enhanced, or crimped, his creativity. As it is, Ramanujan's work is still plumbed for its insights, and many mathematicians have attested to the inspiration furnished by his life and work.   ROBERT KANIGEL

Sources R. Kanigel, *The man who knew infinity: a life of the genius Ramanujan* (1991) · B. C. Berndt and R. A. Rankin, *Ramanujan: letters and commentary* (1995) · G. H. Hardy, *Ramanujan* (1940) · S. R. Ranganathan, *Ramanujan: the man and the mathematician* (1967) · P. K. Srinivasan, ed., *Ramanujan memorial number, vol. 1: letters and reminiscences* (1968) [Muthialpet High School, Madras] · P. V. Seshu Iyer and R. Ramachandra Rao, 'Srinivasa Ramanujan', *Collected papers of Srinivasa Ramanujan*, ed. G. H. Hardy, P. V. Seshu Iyer, and B. M. Wilson (1927), 11–19 · E. H. Neville, 'Srinivasa Ramanujan', *Nature*, 149 (1942), 292–5 · E. H. Neville, 'Srinivasa Ramanujan', typescript of radio broadcast, in or before 1938, U. Reading · S. Ram, *Srinivasa Ramanujan* (1972)

Archives CUL · National Archives of India, New Delhi · Trinity Cam.

Likenesses photograph, 1919, Trinity Cam. [*see illus.*]

Rambaut, Arthur Alcock (1859–1923), astronomer, was born at Waterford, Ireland, on 21 September 1859, the second of the three sons of Revd Edmund F. Rambaut (1827–1893), an ordained minister in the Church of Ireland, and

his wife, Madeleine, *née* Marlande (d. 1887). The Rambaut family in Ireland was descended from Edmund's Huguenot grandfather, Jean Rambaut (b. 1738), who arrived in Ireland at the age of sixteen, having been born in Duras, Bordeaux, and his wife, Marie Hautenville (d. 1810). An uncle of Arthur Rambaut, Revd William Hautenville Rambaut (1822–1873), was a graduate of Trinity College, Dublin, and had been an assistant to Revd Thomas Romney Robinson, director of Armagh observatory. Romney Robinson was uncle by marriage to Edmund and his siblings, which included one Romney Rambaut, who married Mary Anne Grubb, the daughter of Thomas Grubb of Dublin and the elder sister to Sir Howard Grubb, the renowned maker of telescopes.

Arthur Rambaut was educated at the Royal School, Armagh, and at Trinity College, Dublin, where he was gold medallist in mathematics and mathematical physics. After a brief period as senior science master at the Royal School, Armagh, he was appointed assistant to Robert Stawell Ball at Dunsink observatory, Dublin, in 1882. In 1892 he succeeded Ball as Andrews professor of astronomy and royal astronomer of Ireland, the only Dunsink assistant ever to be so promoted, and in 1897 he became Radcliffe observer at Oxford, probably without pecuniary advantage compared with his previous post. He had married Emily Longford in 1883, with whom he had three sons, all born at Dunsink, and he was elected fellow of the Royal Society in 1900.

At Dunsink, Rambaut was a stalwart and trusted assistant to Ball in the work with the transit circle, including execution of clock control for the Dublin Port and Docks Board, in the use of the 12 inch South refractor by Thomas Grubb dating from 1868, and in the initial work establishing Isaac Roberts's 15 inch reflector, adapted for photography. This telescope was remounted, modernized, and equipped with a new dome in 1895 during Rambaut's time by Howard Grubb. An early photographic survey of the chi Persei cluster, carefully carried out, was published in the *Transactions of the Royal Irish Academy*.

Having moved to Oxford, where the Radcliffe Observatory was not integrated with the university, Rambaut first worked on investigations of the large amount of work already carried out but not fully published, including that by Hornsby dating from the 1770s. He then turned to the task of modernizing the equipment, and by 1903, six years after he had arrived, he was able to start work with a fine Grubb 24 inch photographic refractor, equipped with a rising floor and coupled with an equally fine 18 inch visual refractor. This telescope was arguably the best of the large refractors made by Howard Grubb, a series beginning with the 1882 Vienna refractor and ending with the Johannesburg refractor of 1923. Starting in Rambaut's time, it was used extensively to determine stellar distances by measured parallaxes. W. M. H. Greaves described Rambaut's work as involving great patience and enthusiasm, undertaken with great thoroughness, but he also noted that Rambaut's work in this important field was done before it was understood that serious systematic errors would result from photographic spread of light, with non-linear response, if the light from bright 'parallax' stars were not dimmed by use of an occulting shutter.

Earlier in his career Rambaut had co-operated with W. E. Wilson in Ireland on spectroscopic work using other Grubb instruments. He derived orbital parameters of spectroscopic binaries, and in 1891 he had been among the first to point out that radial velocities of visual binaries with orbital motion would yield accurate parallax data. In 1900, with C. J. Joly at Dunsink, together with Sir Howard Grubb, he took part in the successful Royal Irish Academy–Royal Dublin Society total solar eclipse expedition to Plasencia, Spain. The Grubb coelostat built for this occasion later provided vital data in the famous eclipse of May 1919 that verified Einstein's theory of relativity.

There is good evidence that, up to his last years, Rambaut was a happy family man with a robust and cheerful disposition who was of great service to his colleagues and students. He died at Moorcroft, Hillingdon, Uxbridge, Middlesex, on 14 October 1923, after more than a year's illness.   P. A. WAYMAN

Sources *Monthly Notices of the Royal Astronomical Society*, 84 (1923–4), 220–21 · P. A. Wayman, *Dunsink observatory, 1785–1985: a bicentennial history* (1987) · I. Guest, *Dr John Radcliffe and his trust* (1991) · private information (2004) · MHS Oxf., Radcliffe MSS
Archives CUL, letters to Sir George Stokes · Dunsink observatory, Dublin · MHS Oxf., Radcliffe MSS · RAS, letters to Royal Astronomical Society
Likenesses photograph, Dunsink observatory, Dublin
Wealth at death £3562 15s. 1d.: administration with will, 5 Dec 1923, CGPLA Eng. & Wales

Ramberg, Johann Heinrich [John Henry] (1763–1840), painter and printmaker, was born at Hanover on 22 July 1763. His father, who was war secretary of the electorate and a lover of art, encouraged his son's early talent. In 1781 he came to England and was introduced to George III, for whom he made many humorous sketches and caricatures. He is said to have been a pupil of Sir Joshua Reynolds and Francesco Bartolozzi, and in November 1781 he entered the Royal Academy Schools, where he studied with Benjamin West under the special protection of George III. In 1784 he gained a silver medal for drawing from the life. He began to exhibit at the Royal Academy in 1782, when he sent five drawings, two of which—*The Embarkment* and *Good News*—were engraved. Between 1784 and 1788 he exhibited further historical and genre subjects. Ramberg made three drawings of the exhibition of 1784 (BM) including *Sir Joshua Reynolds showing the prince the paintings in the exhibition*; this, together with *The exhibition of the Royal Academy, 1787* and *Portraits of their majesties and the royal family viewing the exhibition of the Royal Academy, 1788*, was engraved in line by P. A. Martini. These works are of interest to historians for their record of exhibitions in the Great Room of the Royal Academy in the late eighteenth century. During the 1780s he gave his addresses as 19 Eaton Street, Pimlico, 85 Newman Street, and then 3 Frith Street, Soho.

In 1788, with the help of his royal patron, Ramberg visited the Netherlands, and afterwards Germany and Italy, returning to Hanover in 1792, when he was appointed electoral court painter. In 1789 he painted the curtain (destr.) for the court theatre in Hanover, which he himself etched in 1828, and of which sketches are preserved in the British Museum and in the Kupfertischkabinett, Berlin. While in Dresden in 1790–91 he met Goethe and painted, for the decoration of Carlton House, *Alexander Crossing the Granicus*. His other works include literary and historical subjects for book illustrations such as *Olivia, Maria, and Malvolio* from *Twelfth Night*, engraved by Thomas Ryder for Boydell's Shakspeare Gallery; *The Goldfinches* for Macklin's *British Poets*; *Public Amusement* and *Private Amusement*, engraved by William Ward; and *The Departure of Queen Marie-Antoinette and her Family*, engraved by J. F. Bolt. He also painted portraits of the princesses Mary, Elizabeth, and Sophia (daughters of George III), and a portrait of Baron Denon, etched by Denon himself. His work as a draughtsman for German almanacs and pocket books extended to more than twenty years, but his best illustrations are those which he himself etched for the narrative cycles *Reineke Fuchs* and *Tyll Eulenspiegel*, both published in 1826. He became one of the most popular illustrators in Germany and produced drawings for many contemporary writers. He made, from sketches by the Princess Elizabeth, landgravine of Hesse-Homburg, a series of twenty allegorical designs entitled *Genius, Imagination, Phantasie*, which were lithographed by Julius Giere and published at Hanover in 1834. Ramberg died at Hanover on 6 July 1840, and was buried in the Gartenkirchhof. Several studies of his satirical caricatures and book illustrations were published in German in the 1960s, and two exhibitions of his work were held in Hanover in 1973 and 1988–9.

R. E. GRAVES, rev. ANNETTE PEACH

Sources S. C. Hutchison, 'The Royal Academy Schools, 1768–1830', *Walpole Society*, 38 (1960–62), 123–91, esp. 246 · D. H. Solkin, ed., *Art on the line* (2001) · 'Johann Heinrich Ramberg', *The dictionary of art*, ed. J. Turner, 25 (1996), 871–2 · Redgrave, *Artists* · Graves, *RA exhibitors*
Likenesses D. V. Denon, etching, 1791, V&A · J. Gore, lithograph, 1838

Rambert, Dame Marie [née Cyvia Ramberg] (1888–1982), ballet dancer and founder of the Rambert Dance Company, was born in Poland on 20 February 1888 at Warsaw, then under Russian domination, the third of six children (four girls and two boys) of Yakov Ramberg, a bookseller of Jewish descent, and his wife, Yevgeniya Alapina. Originally her first name was Cyvia but she was known as Cesia. In France a friend and poet, Edmée Delebecque, suggested Rambert was like Myriam the prophetess dancing with joy (Pritchard, *Rambert*, 21) and Mim remained the name her friends used but in Britain she became Marie, which she considered more elegant. For political reasons her father and paternal uncles adopted different versions of the surname, originally Rambam. After her arrival in England in 1914 Ramberg chose to replace the 'g' with a 't' to enable the British to pronounce it more correctly. In France, in October 1907, she was baptized into the Christian faith as Cyvia Myriam Boleslass Emmanuèle. The first documented use of 'Marie Rambert' is in September 1915 when

Dame Marie Rambert (1888–1982), by Gordon Anthony, 1938

she danced at the Palladium Opera House, Brighton, between the screening of films.

Early years Marie Rambert received a good education at the *Gymnasium* in Warsaw. She developed a great passion for literature. Initially she read Russian books, falling in love with Aleksandr Pushkin, but as she conquered other languages she devoured volumes by Racine, Corneille, Hugo, Schiller, and Goethe. When she settled in London and became fluent in English, she studied Shakespeare and claimed to be able to recite thirty-one of his sonnets.

Rambert was an independent woman, and after graduating from school briefly became involved in the revolutionary movement against the tsarist domination of Poland. Fearing for her safety, Rambert's parents sent her to Paris to live with an uncle and aunt, who were both doctors, with a view to her joining their profession. Rambert was too young to enrol in medical college but took a *Certificat d'études français* at the Sorbonne in June 1906. By this time Rambert had been exposed to a variety of dance and she quickly developed a lifelong passion for movement. She had been unimpressed by her first glimpse of ballet, seeing *Swan Lake* at the Wielki Theatre about 1901, but was totally captivated by Isadora Duncan's performance at the Philharmonic Hall in Warsaw about four years later, in October 1904. Her initial experience of dance was the training in basic ballet and social dance that she received at school, where her teachers included Waslaw Slowacki of the Warsaw Opera House.

After she settled in Paris, Rambert's lively, impromptu performance of a mazurka with Kurylo (a dancer from the Warsaw Opera) at a fancy dress ball won terrific applause and among those who congratulated her was Isadora Duncan's brother, Raymond. Rambert was absorbed into the circle around Raymond Duncan, taking part (acting and dancing) in the productions he mounted and influenced by the group's neo-Grecian dress style. At this time Rambert also had some formal ballet training, taking classes with Mme Rat of the Paris Opéra, and performed solo dances of her own devising at society soirées and recitals.

Ballet teacher Ever curious about dance styles and dance's relationship with music, Rambert attended Émile Jaques-Dalcroze's eurhythmics summer school in Geneva in 1909. Eurhythmics is a system of movement designed to make musical structure and rhythm visible. She found this experience so inspiring she remained with Jaques-Dalcroze's organization for three years. Having been a pupil, Rambert was invited also to teach, arrange dances, and to serve as one of the group of dancers who travelled throughout Europe introducing Jaques-Dalcroze's ideas to new audiences. Rambert was also involved in the large productions designed by Adolph Appia (pioneer of the use of three-dimensional architectural stage environments enhanced by lighting) at Hellerau, the German garden city outside Dresden, where Jaques-Dalcroze established his school in 1911.

It was from Hellerau, in 1912, that Marie Rambert, already keen to spread her wings and travel, was engaged by Serge Diaghilev as assistant to the choreographer Vaslav Nijinsky with his radical ballet *Le sacre du printemps*. Rambert's primary function with the Ballets Russes was to help the dancers understand the complex rhythms of Igor Stravinsky's innovative score, which she would analyse for each of them. She also danced in *Le sacre du printemps* and performed in a number of other productions. Most were by Michel Fokine, whose choreography did not require strong classical technique. The majority of her roles, which may be identified from printed programmes, were performed only in South America, for which tour (from August to November 1913) the company was reduced in size. Rambert was with the Ballets Russes less than a year but, during that 1912–13 season, she was inspired by watching dancers of the calibre of Tamara Karsavina and fell in love with classical ballet. Her earlier experiences of seeing *Swan Lake* in Warsaw and works by Paris Opéra Ballet had not revealed the potential of the art to her. After the Ballets Russes returned to Europe and Nijinsky had been dismissed, Rambert had no further role with it and returned to her own programme of dances. In June 1914 she presented three showcase matinées at the Théâtre Impérial, Paris.

Thus, by her mid-twenties, Marie Rambert had a rich heritage of dance and theatre on which to draw. This encompassed Duncan's free dance and inspiring use of music; developments in central European dance and the work of the designer Adolph Appia with Dalcroze; and, from Diaghilev, a passion for ballet and admiration for his more pictorial designers and Nijinsky's innovative choreography. Few in the dance world had such a rich and varied background, which goes some way to explain her enthusiasm for such a wide variety of dance and why she was always willing to embrace new developments.

In 1914 at the outbreak of the First World War Rambert emigrated to England, finding work as a teacher of the then fashionable eurhythmics to society children (Peter Scott, son of the Antarctic explorer, who later became a naturalist, was one of her pupils). London became her home for the rest of her life and from 1920 she lived at 19 Campden Hill Gardens, Kensington, London; a blue plaque now records her long residence there.

Rambert continued to study ballet with the Russian teacher Serafina Astafyeva, and, after the Ballet Russes teacher, Enrico Cecchetti, established his school in London, she studied for his advanced certificate, which qualified her to teach classical ballet. In 1920 she opened her own school at Bedford Gardens, London, which would move the short distance to Ladbroke Road in 1927.

Dancers of Mercury In Britain Rambert also performed in theatres, music-halls, and in programmes which combined live entertainment with silent films, leaving the stage after twenty-five years when her company was becoming established. As an actress she was type-cast in soubrette roles, performing in either French plays or as a French character (usually a maid) in English drama, in which her vivacious personality delighted audiences. With her friend Vera Bowen (Donnet) she created and was involved with a range of ballets including the Renaissance-inspired *La pomme d'or* (1917), the Watteauesque *Fêtes galantes* (1917), *Les élégantes* (1918), and the cubist *Ballet philosophique* (1919). The contacts Rambert developed with theatres and impresarios (including Nigel Playfair and C. B. Cochran) would prove significant for the advancement of her company and the careers of her dancers, as they needed formal employment to subsidize their more experimental work with Rambert for which, in the 1930s, they only received expenses.

Through her involvement with the Stage Society, for which Rambert created *La pomme d'or* and *Fêtes galantes*, she met Ashley Dukes (1885–1959). She married him on 7 March 1918, after a very brief wartime courtship, thus becoming a British subject. They had two daughters: Angela, born in 1920, and Helena, born in 1923. Both became dancers, Helena having a successful career in musicals while Angela subsequently became a teacher taking over her mother's school. Dukes, the son of a Congregational minister, the Revd Edwin Joshua Dukes, was a playwright, translator of German plays, and critic. His success with *A Man with a Load of Mischief* at the Haymarket Theatre, London, in 1925 enabled him to buy the Horbury Hall at Notting Hill Gate, initially to provide a home for Marie Rambert's school. Dukes transformed the building into a small theatre, known from 1933 as the Mercury, which provided a venue for seasons of new choreography

from Rambert's students and the plays and other experimental and poetic drama which interested him. Although the building is no longer a theatre, the statue of Mercury still presides on its roof and two blue plaques record that it was both the birthplace of British ballet and the home of poetic drama. The appearance of the theatre is preserved in a reconstruction of the interior for Emerich Pressburger's and Michael Powell's film *The Red Shoes* (1948), in which Victoria Page (played by Moira Shearer) is allowed to guest in *Swan Lake*, act 2, there. The audience portrayed is, however, more working-class than the society and intelligentsia who supported the Ballet Club. Marie Rambert plays herself in that scene.

Marie Rambert is remembered as the self-styled 'midwife of British ballet' noted for discovering in others talent for dancing, for design, and, most significantly, for choreography. As a teacher her strength lay in instilling an understanding of style and theatricality in her dancers rather than in enabling them to analyse movement and develop technique. For those sophisticated enough to appreciate her talent she was a marvellous coach, able to inspire dancers to achieve desired effects. From her school developed a company, known successively as the Marie Rambert Dancers, the Ballet Club, Ballet Rambert (1935–87), and then Rambert Dance Company. It dates its existence from 1926 when Rambert encouraged Frederick Ashton to undertake the choreography of a short ballet, *A Tragedy of Fashion*, for a group of her dancers to insert into the long-running *Riverside Nights* when the revue returned to the Lyric Theatre, Hammersmith, London.

From the Mercury Theatre in the 1930s emerged the choreographers and designers nurtured by Rambert, the 'choreographic alchemist', who gave British ballet its individual style and character. This was her most significant role, for she never hesitated to give a chance to artists she sensed had talent, whether or not they conformed to preconceived ideas of a dancer. Among the choreographers she encouraged were Frederick Ashton, Antony Tudor, Andrée Howard, Frank Staff, and Walter Gore. Of the designers Sophie Fedorovitch was the most influential, but William Chappell, Hugh Stevenson, and (again) Andrée Howard played important roles.

Blueprint for ballet Just as Rambert's school was founded six years before Ninette de Valois opened her Institute of Choreographic Art, her company claims to have begun five years before the Vic-Wells (later Royal) Ballet was established and it was Rambert's blueprint for ballet in Britain that other organizations adopted. Rambert recognized the legacy of both Marius Petipa, acknowledging the heritage of the classics of Russia's Imperial Ballet, and the experimental activities of the breakaway Ballets Russes. She also encouraged original ballets, and those created for the minuscule Mercury stage were marked by their attention to detail which became a recognized characteristic of 'British ballet'. In the 1930s the fortunes of Rambert and de Valois were intermixed, with de Valois's Vic-Wells having access to larger stages and greater resources but needing to draw on the choreographers and particularly the male dancers Rambert developed (de Valois did not teach men until the mid-1930s).

Rambert thus prides itself on being Britain's oldest dance company, but it has never been insular, and its longevity reflects its constant readiness to respond to the changing world and present fresh and original dance works to new audiences. Its artists have always been encouraged to learn from different styles, and their openness and intellectual daring prevent performances from becoming in any way routine. Rambert's temperament was for artistic rather than business matters and she turned to others for help with administration. She was a brilliant producer and inspirer of artists but lacked long-term vision and ambition for developing her company. Fortunately her openness of mind enabled her and her company to weather radical changes and rise phoenix-like from misfortune. The company closed in 1941–3 after the impresario Harold Rubin, who had taken them on a long-term contract to the Arts Theatre, refused to pay Equity rates to the dancers (now employed by it full-time). It closed again in 1966 when it forsook performing larger-scale classical work requiring a *corps de ballet* (*Giselle*, *Coppélia*, *La sylphide*, *Don Quixote*) to return to its creative roots, becoming a smaller, more creative ensemble. Contemporary dance classes were introduced, alternating with ballet classes, which increased the range of the dancers.

The Second World War brought considerable changes for Rambert's company. It had outgrown the Mercury, for the ballets created for the larger theatres to which it toured could not be reduced to fit the tiny stage. Ballet Rambert had become, as it remains, a touring company with no performing home but being seen in a variety of London venues, most frequently Sadler's Wells. Proposals to build a new large dance house to replace the old Mercury absorbed a great deal of Rambert's energy from the 1950s onwards but the plans were never realized. Ballet Rambert was also no longer a private company funded by Rambert, Dukes, and their supporters at the Ballet Club. In 1943 Ballet Rambert was relaunched by the Council for the Encouragement of Music and the Arts (CEMA), which after the war developed into the Arts Council. The Arts Council relinquished direct management in 1947 but after Ballet Rambert's return from an eighteen-month tour of Australia in 1949 it became one of their clients.

Rambert encouraged her artists to move on to other, usually larger-scale, projects to develop their careers. She nevertheless felt hurt when they departed, and was frustrated by her inability to secure better working conditions for her company. In 1950 Walter Gore, the last remaining choreographer from the Ballet Club era, left Ballet Rambert to embark on a series of independent ventures. Briefly she gave opportunities to David Paltenghi, who proved a better producer than choreographer, and for a period in the 1950s had to bring in from outside young choreographers (including John Cranko and Kenneth MacMillan) whose talent she recognized. However, in 1958 a new in-house choreographer of talent and imagination, Norman Morrice, was launched. Morrice's *Two Brothers* reflected the aesthetic of 'the angry young man' and infused Ballet Rambert with a new purpose and creative energy linked to the mood of the period. It was Morrice who in 1966 encouraged Marie Rambert to restore the creative *raison d'être* to her company and, somewhat reluctantly, introduce contemporary dance technique, based on Martha Graham's teaching, to the company.

The reason for her reluctance was that, without a *corps de ballet*, Rambert's repertory could no longer include the romantic ballets which she loved. She had been introduced to *Giselle* by Diaghilev—and this was the first long work to enter Ballet Rambert's repertory in 1945–6, in a production carefully researched with help from the dance historian Cyril Beaumont. Rambert's production of *Giselle* always conveyed the essence of its 1840s period and, even without star dancers to perform the central roles, was always of the highest calibre and attracted great praise. The same was true of other ballets she supervised. They were never overplayed, vulgar, or dull; her standards of production were admired particularly when she was working in difficult conditions.

Final years Throughout her life Rambert retained an active interest in the fortunes of her company, although after 1966 she no longer concerned herself with day-to-day matters. Nevertheless choreographers would continue to welcome her perceptive remarks about their creations until the end of her life.

As an architect of British ballet Rambert received many awards and honours. She was appointed CBE in the 1953 coronation honours and DBE in the 1962 new year honours. In February 1957 she became a chevalier of the Légion d'honneur and in 1979 received the gold medal of the order of merit of the People's Republic of Poland. She was a fellow of the Royal Academy of Dancing and vice-president, receiving their Queen Elizabeth Coronation award for services to British ballet in 1956. She was also a member of the grand council of the Imperial Society of Teachers. She was awarded a Diploma of Associateship, College of Art, Manchester (1960); made honorary DLitt of the University of Sussex (1964); received the Composers' Guild award for services to British music (1978); and posthumously the Nijinsky medal (1996).

Rambert was a petite woman, only 5 ft 1 in. in height. She was cultivated, dynamic, alert, witty, and chic. Her *joie de vivre* never left her and in moments of delight she turned cartwheels or, if a partner was available, jumped into his arms in a 'fishdive'. She was fluent in many languages and, in spite of being a lifelong sufferer from insomnia, had boundless energy and ravenous curiosity. Her artistic instinct and unerring sense of theatre enabled her to discover and encourage generations of choreographers, dancers, designers, and composers. Tact was not one of her qualities but determination was. Some artists were unable to cope with her constant presence and were permanently scarred by the experience of working with Madam Wasp, as Agnes de Mille (a pupil in the 1930s) later described her; but the catalogue of those who benefited from her guidance—professionally as a teacher and personally as a mentor—is a who's who of British and Commonwealth dance in the mid-twentieth century from Frederick Ashton to Christopher Bruce.

Rambert died at her home in London, 19 Campden Hill Gardens, Kensington, on 12 June 1982 and was cremated at Golders Green crematorium. A service of thanksgiving was held at St Paul's Church, Covent Garden, on 30 September 1982 and a memorial gala at Sadler's Wells on 8 March 1983. A memorial plaque was unveiled in St Paul's on 27 March 1983.

On her eightieth birthday Rambert presented to the nation the fine Marie Rambert–Ashley Dukes collection of romantic ballet prints which had previously decorated the foyer of the Mercury Theatre. On her death she bequeathed her collection of set and costume designs to the Theatre Museum; she also gave a significant collection of ballet films, mostly recorded at the Ballet Club in the 1930s, to the National Film and Television Archive. Other material is in the Rambert Dance Company Archive.

JANE PRITCHARD

Sources A. de Mille, *Dance to the piper: memoirs of the ballet* (1951) · M. Clark, *Dancers of Mercury: the story of Ballet Rambert* (1962) · M. Rambert, *Quicksilver* (1972) [autobiography] · C. Crisp, A. Sainsbury, and P. Williams, *Ballet Rambert: 50 years and on* (1982) · J. Pritchard, 'Marie Rambert on stage', *Dance Theatre Journal*, 8/2 (1990), 40–44 · J. Pritchard, *Rambert: a celebration* (1996) · *Daily Telegraph* (14 June 1982) · *The Guardian* (14 June 1982) · *Financial Times* (14 June 1982) · *Classical Music* (3 July 1982), 29 · 'Rambert's achievement: a tribute from D & D to the midwife of British ballet', *Dance and Dancers*, 392 (Aug 1982), 20–25 · *CGPLA Eng. & Wales* (1982)
Archives Rambert Dance Company Archive, London | FILM 'Ballet Rambert', *Monitor*, interview with Huw Wheldon, BBC 17 Jan 1960 · 'Dame Marie Rambert', *This is your life*, BBC 26 Feb 1962 · 'Ballet Rambert struggles to survive', *Music on Two*, BBC2 14 Mar 1966 · 'Rambert remembers', BBC2 29 Nov 1970 | SOUND BBC Archives · NYPL, Dance Collection · Rambert Dance Company
Likenesses photographs, 1925–79, Hult. Arch. · G. Anthony, photograph, 1938, Theatre Museum, London [*see illus.*] · W. Bird, photograph, 1962, NPG · J. S. Lewinski, photograph, 1967, NPG · A. Zydower, bronze cast of bust, 1970, NPG · A. Zydower, bust, 1972, NPG · A. Newman, bromide print, 1978, NPG · J. Pannett, chalk drawing, NPG · photographs, Rambert Dance Company, London, archive · portraits, priv. colls.
Wealth at death £64,240: probate, 22 Oct 1982, *CGPLA Eng. & Wales*

Rambush, Niels Edward [*formerly* Niels Edvard Rambusch] (**1889–1957**), chemical engineer, was born on 25 March 1889 in Selde, Denmark, the eldest in the family of four sons and one daughter of Sigurd Harold Alfred Rambusch, medical practitioner and chief medical officer for northern Jutland, and his wife, Johanne Faartoft; both parents were sometime liberal members in the Danish parliament. He was sent away to school in Nykøbing Mors, living with grandparents for seven years. On leaving school he decided against entering university, preferring to study the practical side of engineering through an apprenticeship to a master blacksmith in Nykøbing Mors. At the age of fifteen he moved to Copenhagen to complete his practical engineering experience, and two years later he graduated as a mechanical engineer at the Copenhagen Technical College. Rambusch married Mavis, daughter of

John Henry Blackmore, grocer, in 1911. They had two sons, the elder of whom died at the age of nineteen, and two daughters.

In 1911, following six months' military service with the Danish infantry, Rambusch was invited to England by Arthur H. Lymn, who had formed a business in London to develop and exploit commercially the existing processes of gas production for industrial purposes. After a short period Lymn took Rambusch into partnership and formed the gas and chemical engineering firm of Lymn and Rambush. During his years in London, Rambusch expanded his knowledge of chemical processing, continuing his studies at Battersea Polytechnic under Professor J. W. Hinchley, who invited him to become a founding member of the Institution of Chemical Engineers in 1922. In 1930 Rambusch acquired British citizenship, having changed his name by deed poll to Rambush.

In 1918 Lymn and Rambush was taken over by the Power-Gas Corporation of Stockton-on-Tees. Rambush was appointed chief engineer and his boundless energy and leadership earned him rapid promotion with ever greater responsibilities. He was soon appointed chief engineer of the subsidiary company, Ashmore, Benson, Pease & Co., manufacturers of gas holders and iron and steelworks plant. He became general manager of both companies in 1931, managing director in 1938, and in 1951 executive chairman of the Power-Gas Corporation Ltd, which by then had acquired all the assets of the subsidiary company. He continued as chairman until his death.

Rambush travelled widely in connection with company business and contributed many technical papers, which earned him an international reputation. His 500 page *Modern Gas Producers* (1923) was for many years the standard work on the gasification of solid fuels in a fixed bed with a mixed blast of air and steam. In 1931 Rambush was awarded the Moulton medal of the Institution of Chemical Engineers and in 1954 he became a vice-president of the institution. In 1948 he received an honorary DSc from the University of Durham. Rambush died on 15 May 1957 at Barton House, Stockton-on-Tees. G. B. TAYLOR, *rev.*

Sources R. W. Rutherford, 'Famous men remembered', *Chemical Engineer*, 429 (Oct 1986), 50–51 · personal knowledge (1993) · d. cert.
Wealth at death £23,700 5s.: probate, 26 Aug 1957, *CGPLA Eng. & Wales*

Ramée, Marie Louise de la [*pseud.* Ouida] (**1839–1908**), novelist, was born on 1 January 1839, at 1 Union Terrace, Bury St Edmunds, Suffolk, the only child of Louis Ramé (d. 1872?) and his English wife, Susan Sutton (d. 1893), who named her Maria Louise. Her father was an enigmatic man, a native Frenchman; his marriage certificate records his occupations as tailor and gentleman, and in addition he is known to have taught French. Maria Louise's education apparently consisted completely of her father's tutoring. As her father's frequent absences grew longer and more mysterious, she romanticized him as a Napoleonic spy, changing her name to Marie de la Ramée to suggest a vague aristocratic background. Louis Ramé disappeared but is thought to have died in Paris street fighting in 1872.

Marie Louise de la Ramée [Ouida] (**1839–1908**), by Adolphe Beau, *c.*1872

Precocious as a child, de la Ramée began to write, producing *Idalia* (1867) at the age of sixteen. She published her first story, 'Dashwood's Drag, or, The Derby and What Came of It', in *Bentley's Miscellany* in 1859 under the auspices of her medical adviser's cousin, William Harrison Ainsworth. Seventeen stories later, her first novel, *Held in Bondage*, appeared in *Bentley's* in serial form in 1863, entitled *Granville de Vigne: a Tale of the Day* under the pseudonym Ouida, the childhood mispronunciation of Louise that had become her nickname. The pseudonym came to have a particular force, one that was seized upon by de la Ramée, as she strove throughout her life to distinguish between her private and public identities on its basis. This is made clear in a letter of January 1900 to her European publisher, Baron von Tauchnitz:

> I just see in your catalogue that you append another name to Ouida (Louise de la Ramée.) Please take it out. I have no other name in literature. And it should not be put in inverted commas … Besides, I *love* Ouida. It is my *very own*, as children say. I don't care for any of the other names I bear.
> (Jordan, 76)

After Sir Francis Burnand parodied her second novel, *Strathmore* (1865), in *Punch*, and Lord Strangford attacked it in the *Pall Mall Gazette*, Ouida became an established public figure. Her prolific, imaginative novels were admired for their fast-paced plots and atmospheric settings by such people as Bulwer-Lytton, Whyte Melville, and Sir Richard Burton. Many readers, however, criticized her factual inaccuracies, her redundancies, and her two-dimensional characters, including Byronic-type heroes. Her best-known work, *Under Two Flags* (1867), bears all of these hallmarks and went on to sell millions of copies in its single-volume 'cheap' format. The plot is certainly melodramatic, relating the adventures of the Hon. Bertie Cecil, a member of the Life Guards forced to fake his death and leave London to protect the honour of his younger brother. He enlists as a *chasseur d'Afrique* under the name Louis Victor, and his many acts of heroism are detailed at length. Having angered his commanding officer, he is about to be court-martialled when one of the camp followers, who has fallen in love with him, throws herself in front of the firing squad, saving his life, in time for the reprieve that follows as a result of his true identity becoming known. The effects of stirring plots such as these, combined with the popularity of Mudie's circulating library, the public appetite for Ouida's prurient romanticism, and her shocking revelations about upper-class and military life, ensured her success until her zenith in the mid-1870s.

De la Ramée lived and entertained lavishly at the Langham Hotel, London, on earnings averaging £5000 per year, until the eviction caused by her extravagances. Financial problems forced her to move to Italy with her beloved mother in 1871, living first in an apartment at the Palazzo Vagonville in Florence, then at the Villa Farinola at Scandicci, 3 miles from Florence. Mme Ramé died in 1893, to be buried in a pauper's grave at Allior cemetery in Florence, after which de la Ramée lived at the Villa Massonni, at Atna' Alessio near Lucca.

Probably her arrogance, vanity, idiosyncrasies, dramatic flair, and the other extreme oddities described in her biographies make as interesting reading as any of Ouida's novels. A woman whose slight build, large nose, undistinguished features, inauspicious colouring (brown hair, blue eyes), and diminutive stature detracted from her physical appearance, her vanity nevertheless caused her to order expensive dresses too short in the arms and skirt in an attempt to show off her small wrists and feet. The effort merely resulted in unfashionable and grotesque costumes. Often she would receive her visitors in the costume of the heroine of her latest novel, striking the artificial poses she imagined of her characters.

Snobbish, intolerant, and rude, de la Ramée became a difficult hostess and a demanding, insulting guest, yet she still attracted enough important people to hold a salon. As Lady Paget remarked of the quality of the guests at one of de la Ramée's parties: '[s]he has an extraordinary talent for forcing people to come' (Jordan, 84). Certain of the unusual merit of her amateurish paintings, she pressed them on unwitting guests or acquaintances including that practised observer of human nature, Henry James. To her first biographer, Elizabeth Lee, James remarked that de la Ramée 'was *curious*, in a common, little way … of a most uppish or dauntless little spirit of arrogance and independence … a little terrible and finally pathetic *grotesque*' (Lee, 231). However, Lee, the author of *Italian Hours*, also claimed to admire 'her original genuine perception of the beauty, the distinction and quality of Italy' (ibid., 234) demonstrated in such novels as *Signa* (1875), *Adriadne*

(1877), *In Maremma* (1881), *A Village Commune* (1882), and *The Massarenes* (1897). Most of Ouida's fiction was published in several editions and languages, as well as adapted for plays and operas.

In 1871 de la Ramée unwittingly initiated her own decline by engaging in a notorious ten-year affair with the marchese della Stuffa. This philandering member of an ancient Florentine family, a gentleman-in-waiting to the king, was also involved with Mrs Janet Ross, a society hostess of Florence, resulting in a series of embarrassing public scenes between de la Ramée and della Stuffa. As revenge for his refusal to marry her, Ouida published a *roman à clef*, *Friendship* (1878), vowing that every word of it was true. However, the negative public reaction to it diminished her already weak social currency, which was then permanently devalued by a direct snub from the prime minister, Lord Salisbury, in 1887. Her popularity as a novelist waned almost entirely after 1890.

Late in life, de la Ramée became passionate over various causes such as anti-feminism, the Second South African War, and animal vivisection. She also proclaimed her increasing disgust with the military, and with technological advances. Throughout her life she constantly avowed disbelief in any religion, writing to Lady Constance Leslie in 1907 that she regarded Christianity as an invention based on oriental myths in order to satisfy basic human needs and hopes, and that she deplored its claim to being the best or only religion.

From 1904 until her death de la Ramée lived in squalor with many adopted stray dogs in her tenement at Viareggio. Her dedication to these pets was perhaps the best index of her increasing eccentricity, as she indulged them with luxuries while starving herself; the local people called her 'Crazy Lady with the Dogs'. In these years she was humiliated by lawsuits, debts, and the well-meaning attempts of friends and readers to ease her poverty. When sympathizers made a public appeal to the subscribers of the *Daily Mail* to donate to her relief, de la Ramée issued a furious denial that she suffered any want. Her few remaining friends, including Lady Paget, Alfred Austin, and George Wyndham, persuaded the prime minister, Sir Henry Campbell-Bannerman, to offer her a pension. After considerable resistance, especially to the requirement of revealing her age for the purpose, in 1906 Winifred, Lady Howard of Glossop, finally persuaded her to accept the civil-list pension of £150 per year. Never strong, she contracted pneumonia and died of complications on 25 January 1908, unmarried and childless, at via Zanardelli 70, Viareggio, Italy. She was buried in the English cemetery at the Bagni di Lucca. There an anonymous female admirer erected a monument above her grave representing a reclining figure with a dog at her feet. A memorial drinking fountain with trough, designed by Ernest G. Gillick with a medallion portrait, and inscribed by Earl Curzon of Kedleston, was unveiled at Bury St Edmunds on 2 November 1909.

Ouida's last and incomplete novel, *Helianthus*, appeared posthumously in 1908. Although people read many of her forty-four works of fiction well into the twentieth century, it currently appears that only the essays in *Critical Studies* (1900) may retain lasting merit. *Under Two Flags*, however, was filmed three times in the early twentieth century, with the 1936 version, starring Ronald Colman and Claudette Colbert, best evoking the spirit of the novel. As Graham Greene put it:

> How Ouida would have loved the abandon of this picture, the thirty-two thousand rounds of ammunition shot off into the Arizona desert, the cast of more than ten thousand, [and] the five thousand pounds which insured the stars against camel bites. (Walker, 1129)

HELEN KILLORAN

Sources DNB · E. Lee, *Ouida: a memoir* (1914) · M. Stirling, *The fine and the wicked: the life and times of Ouida* (1958) · E. Bigland, *Ouida: the passionate Victorian* (1951) · Y. French, *Ouida: a study in ostentation* (1938) · J. Jordan, 'Ouida: the enigma of a literary identity', *Princeton University Library Chronicle*, 57 (1995), 75–105 · J. Walker, ed., *Halliwell's film guide*, 10th edn (1994)
Archives Harvard U., Houghton L., corresp. and literary papers · Morgan L., corresp. and literary papers · Suffolk RO, Bury St Edmunds, letters and papers · TCD, letters | BL, corresp. with Sir Sydney Cockerell, Add. MS 52744 · BL, corresp. with Macmillans, Add. MS 54964 · BL OIOC, corresp. with Lord Curzon, no. 95 · Hove Central Library, Sussex, letters to Viscount and Lady Wolseley · NL Scot., corresp. with Henry Drummond · U. Sussex, letters to Wilfrid Scawen Blunt
Likenesses photograph, 1870 · A. Beau, photograph, *c.*1872, Hult. Arch. [*see illus.*] · A. Beau, photograph, 1874 · A. Danyell, crayon, 1878, Harris's Picture Agency · lithograph, 1878 (after crayon drawing by A. Danyell), NPG · G. de Moraes Sarmento, chalk drawing, 1904, NPG · G. de Moraes Sarmento, chalk drawing, 1904, Moyse's Hall Museum, Bury St Edmunds, Suffolk · photograph, 1907, repro. in *Daily Mirror* (22 July 1907) · G. di Lucca, tomb effigy, 1908 · E. G. Gillick, medallion monument on drinking fountain, 1909, Bury St Edmunds, Suffolk · A. Beau, cabinet photograph, NPG · G. Norfini, plaster bust, priv. coll. · A. Weger senior, stipple (probably; after photograph by A. Beau), NPG

Ramensky, Johnny (1905–1972), safe-breaker and gaol-breaker, was born in Glenboig, Lanarkshire, on the outskirts of Glasgow, the only son in the family of three children of Lithuanian immigrants. His father, a Lanarkshire coalminer, died while Ramensky was still a child, and he was brought up in poverty by his mother, who had lost an arm in an accident. He left school at fourteen, and worked in the mines for a brief period before the family moved to Glasgow, settling in a tenement block in the Gorbals. He sold newspapers in the streets of Glasgow, but drifted into crime, and was sent to Polmont borstal, near Falkirk, in 1921, at the age of sixteen, and again in 1922, this time for eighteen months. When he came out, he and another former inmate turned to safe-breaking, putting to use the expertise he had acquired while handling explosives down the mines.

In 1934 Ramensky was caught breaking open a safe in a bakery in Aberdeen. As he began serving his prison sentence in Peterhead prison, his wife, Daisy (*née* McManus), died of a heart attack, in December 1934, and, refused permission to go to her funeral in Glasgow, Ramensky made the first of his five escapes from Peterhead. He was caught trying to cross the bridge at Ellon, 15 miles away, and as a punishment was shackled for weeks to the wall of his cell, in solitary confinement. John McGovern, MP for Shettle-ston, took up his case with the home secretary, and the shackles were removed: Ramensky was the last man in Scotland to be shackled in a prison cell, as well as the first to escape from Peterhead prison.

After his release Ramensky returned at once to safe-breaking, but his methods of blowing safes were easily identifiable, and he was convicted in 1938, and sentenced to five years in prison. However, in 1942, a few months before he was due to be released, he was taken to the War Office and asked to enlist in the army, as his skills with explosives were needed. He was trained as a commando at Achnacarry Castle, Inverness-shire, and, promoted to the rank of sergeant, he taught commandos how to blow safes, before being parachuted behind enemy lines sev-eral times to break open safes and steal military plans and secret documents. As the Eighth Army moved across north Africa he broke into safes ahead of the front line, including that at Rommel's headquarters, and when the allies captured Rome his commando unit blew fourteen safes in foreign embassies in one day. In Germany it was Ramensky who opened the strongroom and safes at Goering's headquarters in the Schorfheide.

Ramensky, who had changed his name to Ramsay, was demobilized in 1945 with the Military Medal. But within days he broke into a jeweller's shop in York, robbed the safe, and was sentenced to five years in prison. Freed in 1950, after seven days he was arrested again after blowing a safe at Cardonald post office, near Glasgow, and given another five-year sentence. At this point he began secretly writing his memoirs, although this was forbidden under the Official Secrets Act, and, hoping to find a publisher, he escaped from Peterhead in 1952 but was again captured at Ellon Bridge, and the manuscript was impounded and des-troyed.

When he was released in 1955, Ramensky married a widow from the Gorbals, Mrs Lilly Mulholland, but he then robbed a bank in Oban, and was arrested for a raid on a bank in Rutherglen. Although his war record had been taken into account before, this time Lord Carmont, in the Glasgow high court, imposed a sentence of ten years' pre-ventive detention, and he was sent back to Peterhead prison. In 1958 he escaped three times: after the third escape, which involved hiding under the floorboards of the doctor's surgery for a week before escaping over the wall, an inquiry was set up into how a known escaper could escape three times in one year.

Ramensky served nine years of this sentence. On his release in 1964 he got a job as a labourer, but after a break-in at Woolworths in Paisley he was sent back to gaol for two years. In 1967 he blew open a safe at Rutherglen and began a four-year gaol sentence, and in 1970 he fell off a roof while escaping from a safe-breaking in Stirling, and spent three months in hospital before going back to prison. Released in 1972, he was sentenced to twelve months' imprisonment after being caught hiding on the roof of a large shop in Ayr in an attempt to break in: dur-ing his final court appearance his solicitor said he had been on more roofs than the legendary fiddler.

Johnny Ramensky died on 4 November 1972 in Perth Royal Infirmary after collapsing in Perth prison. Hundreds of mourners attended his funeral in St Francis's Chapel in the Gorbals. He had become a legend. Two popular songs were written about him in the 1950s: the actor Roddy McMillan wrote and recorded 'Set Ramensky Free', and the Labour MP Norman Buchan wrote 'The Ballad of Johnny Ramensky'. He was known as Gentle Johnny because he was never violent, and his repeated prison escapes won him much public sympathy: at one point he was likened to Robin Hood escaping from the castle of the sheriff of Nottingham. A compulsive safe-breaker, Ram-ensky found it impossible to give up his safe-blowing activities after the war, driven by what his lawyer, Nich-olas Fairbairn QC, was to describe as a lifelong compulsion to break into whatever he was out of and out of whatever he was inside. Ramensky, sentenced to more than fifty-eight years in gaol, spent over forty years in prison: most of his adult life. ANNE PIMLOTT BAKER

Sources G. Forbes and P. Meehan, *Such bad company: the story of Glasgow criminality* (1982), chap. 8 · J. P. Bean, *Over the wall* (1994), chap. 2 · M. Rodgers, 'The Lanarkshire Lithuanians', *Odyssey: voices from Scotland's recent past*, ed. W. Kay (1980), 19–25 · K. E. Collins, *Glasgow jewry* (1993) · *Glasgow Herald* (6 Nov 1972) · *Daily Record* (6 Nov 1972) · *Glasgow Herald* (24 April 1934) · *Glasgow Herald* (22 Dec 1934) · *Glasgow Herald* (8 Nov 1955) · *Glasgow Herald* (27 Dec 1958) · *Glasgow Herald* (28 Jan 1959) · *Glasgow Herald* (28 April 1959)
Likenesses photograph, repro. in Bean, *Over the wall*, facing p. 122

Ramesey [Ramsay]**, William** (1627–1676?), physician and astrologer, was born on 13 March 1627 in Westminster, the son of David *Ramsay (c.1575–1660), a Scottish clock-maker, whom James I made keeper of his clocks and watches, and an English mother. Believing his paternal ancestors to have come from Egypt, Ramesey revised his surname in accord with what he thought to be its true spelling. He attended schools in and around London, including St Albans, Bushey, Westminster, and Mile End. He would have gone up to Oxford, but this intention was thwarted by the civil war, which also subsequently inter-rupted his studies at St Andrews. Moving to Edinburgh, he was obliged to leave by an outbreak of plague. He returned to London in April 1645.

Ramesey continued to study both physic and astrology. However, unlike most of his contemporaries combining these pursuits—notably Nicholas Culpeper—Ramesey was a royalist, unhappy with what he called 'this perverse and rebellious Age' (Ramesey, 29). But the increasing iden-tification of astrology itself as perverse and rebellious, on political as well as religious grounds, left him increasingly isolated. His *Lux veritatis, or, Christian Judicial Astrology Vindi-cated, and Demonology Confuted* (1651) was a reply to the criti-cisms of Nathanael Homes in *Daemonology and Theologie* (1650); it was answered in turn by another divine, William Rowland, in *Judiciall Astrologie, Judicially Condemned* (1652).

Ramesey's contribution to this debate was undistin-guished, being mostly a repetition of points made by Christopher Heydon half a century earlier. The main dif-ference between the two lies in Heydon's confident tones and Ramesey's defensive, petulant manner. He also signally failed to present a convincing case for astrology's religious probity; after arguing that it deals only with natural causes and transgresses neither God's secrets nor man's free will, he provided examples of astrology at its most magical, answering horary questions, such as 'Where is my husband?' and 'When shall I receive the money due me?'

In 1652 Ramesey produced another small astrological work, *Vox stellarum* (not to be confused with the better-known almanac of the same name by Francis Moore). By now he was living with his father 'in Holborn, within two doors of the wounded Heart, near the King's Gate' (Ramesey, preface). In that year he received his MD at Montpellier, and on 31 July 1661 was admitted as an extra licentiate to the College of Physicians.

Astrologia restaurata (1653) is Ramesey's principal work: it is a thorough if rather ponderous introduction to astrological theory and practice in all its branches, including horary, elections, nativities, and physic. Ramesey even included a section on 'Teaching how to judge of the permanency or durability of Kings, or such as are in Authority by any Revolution' (Ramesey, 225), exactly the sort of thing that was undermining the standing of his beloved subject.

Ramesey's subsequent publications include a theological tract, *Man's Dignity and Perfection* (1661), *De veneris, or, A Discourse of Poisons* (1663), and *Some Physical Considerations of … Wormes* (1668). By that time, astrology had almost disappeared from his work.

In June 1668 Ramesey was admitted MD at Cambridge by royal mandate; he is said to have by then become physician-in-ordinary to Charles II. He was now living in Plymouth, Devon. His last publication was *The Gentleman's Companion* (1676). According to Francis Bernard, he died that year while in prison—for debt, John Gadbury believed. PATRICK CURRY

Sources W. Ramesey, *Astrologia restaurata* (1653) · *DNB* · P. Curry, 'The decline of astrology in early modern England', PhD diss., U. Lond., 1986 · B. S. Capp, *Astrology and the popular press: English almanacs, 1500–1800* (1979), 326 · Munk, *Roll* · Venn, *Alum. Cant.* · BL, Sloane MS, 1683, fol. 39
Likenesses T. Cross, line engraving, BM; repro. in Ramesey, *Astrologia restaurata* · T. Cross, line engraving, BM; repro. in W. Ramesey, *Lux veritatis, or, Christian judicial astrology vindicated* (1651) · W. Sherwin, line engraving (aged forty-two), BM, NPG; repro. in W. Ramesey, *Some physical considerations of … wormes* (1668) · W. Sherwin, line engraving, BM, NPG; repro. in *Character of true nobility and gentility* (1672) · portrait, repro. in W. Ramesey, *Some physical considerations of … wormes* (1668)

Ramkins, Alexander (*supp. b.* **1671/2**, *d.* in or after **1719**), supposed Jacobite author, was once thought to have written *The Memoirs of Majr. Alexander Ramkins, a Highland-Officer, now in Prison at Avignon* (1719; reissued, 1720), an anti-Jacobite polemic attributed to Daniel Defoe, from which the *Dictionary of National Biography* article was solely derived. In the *Memoirs* Ramkins, a world-weary soldier, remembers when he, then an ardent young Scots-Catholic Jacobite, followed James II into exile in France; how he painfully became convinced that his host country was merely playing politics with the Stuarts; and how, despairing of the Stuarts ever regaining the monarchy, he has become so disillusioned with the Jacobite movement that, reconciled to the protestant succession, he is ready to return to his native land and accept Hanoverian rule.

Ramkins describes his participation in most of the contemporary Jacobite campaigns following the highlanders' victory at the battle of Killiecrankie, in July 1689, that inspired his abrupt departure from Aberdeen University and pointed him toward a military career in the Jacobite forces. He observed the French [*sic*] siege of Mainz, in September 1689, and after military college in Strasbourg and a brief Rhineland tour of duty with the grand musqueteers, fought in Ireland at the battle of the Boyne and in the first siege of Limerick in July and August 1690. Having been wounded at the battle of Aughrim he returned to France with the Irish troops under the articles of Limerick, late in 1691.

Ramkins chose not to join the projected Jacobite descent in the spring of 1692, but fought in the Piedmont campaign that summer. He participated in the battle of Landen, where he was severely wounded, in September 1693. He spent the winter of 1695–6 in St Germain, where he heard rumours of another proposed descent, and he agonized over his decision not to join it. He speaks critically of the peace of Ryswick (September 1697), but warmly of the prolonged visit to England it sanctioned. When Ramkins returned, he married. But having made what seemed an extraordinarily prudent choice, ironically he was ruined by her extravagance, and thus writes his putative memoirs from prison.

Apart from these *Memoirs*, no solid evidence exists attesting to Ramkins having actually lived. Except for those biographical dictionaries for which the *Dictionary of National Biography* is the source (his article was by Norman Moore), his name does not appear in any of the contemporary or later lists of eighteenth-century Scots, Roman Catholics, Jacobites, distinguished citizens, or even general obituaries. No Alexander Ramkins (or Rankine, unlike Ramkins an authentic Scottish, though lowland, name) appears among the admittedly scant list of 1688–9 students of King's or Marischal colleges, Aberdeen; nor is it likely that Roman Catholic Ramkins could have been enrolled there at that time because Principal John Row's regulations prohibiting the matriculation of Roman Catholics were still strictly enforced.

More significantly, neither Ramkins nor his brother can be traced through their military records, though Ramkins was purportedly on active or inactive duty with an Irish regiment of the French army for almost twenty-eight years, and his brother 'belong[ed] to the Guards of King James II. … and was kill'd in *Ireland*' (*Memoirs*, 10). Neither is listed in the Public Record Office, in Charles Dalton's *English Army Lists and Commission Registers, 1661–1714*, in the regimental Stuart papers at Windsor Castle, in the comprehensive regimental catalogue 'Jacobite army in Ireland, 1689', not even in the National Military History Society of Largs (Ayrshire) Scotland; nor is Ramkins's brother listed among the 1688 muster rolls for James's Scottish foot or life guards.

Ramkins's fictionality is confirmed by a number of mistakes in the *Memoirs* chronology that an actual participant simply could not have made; among them, the treaty of Ryswick is described as preceding the battle of Landen, the emperor's besiegers are confused with the French besieged at Mainz in 1689, and, especially, there is the chronological impossibility, given the details of the text, of Ramkins arriving in time to witness the Mainz siege.

BETH S. NEMAN

Sources B. S. Neman, introduction, in D. Defoe, *The memoirs of Major Alexander Ramkins*, ed. B. S. Neman (1976)
Wealth at death in debtor's prison while writing *Memoirs*: Defoe, *Memoirs*

Ramondon, Littleton [Lewis] (1684–1715x18), singer and composer, was born on 28 January 1684, in the parish of St Martin-in-the-Fields, London, the son of David Ramondon (*d.* after 1707) and his wife, Elizabeth, *née* Littletone. Charles Burney and John Hawkins both refer to him by his baptismal name, Lewis, but he appears as Littleton Ramondon in theatre documents and in the register of St Martin-in-the-Fields for his marriage to Barbara Collop (*bap.* 1688?) on 17 April 1706. At Drury Lane Theatre on 13 April 1705 Ramondon performed 'several Entertainments of Singing … all Compos'd by himself, it being the first time of his appearing on the Stage' (*Daily Courant*, 12 April 1705). He remained at Drury Lane until December 1707, singing between the acts of plays, in dramatic operas including Henry Purcell's *The Indian Queen* and *King Arthur*, in the English version of Giovanni Bononcini's *Camilla* (30 March 1706), and in a revival of Thomas Clayton's *Arsinoe*. In January 1708 he moved to John Vanbrugh's opera company at the Queen's Theatre, where he was paid £50 a year. Although he had occasionally performed songs in Italian at Drury Lane, he sang in English in the mixed-language performances of *Pyrrhus and Demetrius* (14 December 1708) and *Clotilda* (2 March 1709). Ramondon lost his roles when operas came to be performed completely in Italian and made his last advertised appearance on the London stage on 26 July 1710. He performed in a concert at Stationers' Hall in April 1712.

Ramondon also established himself as a composer and arranger. His arrangements from *Camilla* for harpsichord or spinet and for two flutes with a bass were published in July and September 1706, and he made instrumental arrangements of opera songs for *The Ladys Entertainment*, book 1 (1708). He was a prolific composer of songs. A dozen, mostly written for the theatre, appeared in the *Monthly Mask of Vocal Music* between April 1706 and July 1710, and his songs were also published as single sheets and in miscellaneous collections. He sometimes wrote the words for his songs, including all six in his *A New Book of Songs* (*c.*1713), published by Walsh and Hare. (His father, 'Mr Ramondon, Senior', produced a few songs by fitting words to popular ballad tunes.) Ramondon's fine tune 'All you that must take a leap in the dark', written on the execution of two criminals in May 1712, was used in *The Beggar's Opera* for the air 'Would I might be hanged'.

Ramondon's last known performance was as a singer with a theatre company at the Tennis Court, Edinburgh, in summer 1715. He must have died at some point during the next three years, as his widow married John Clarke at St Clement Danes, London, on 22 May 1718.

OLIVE BALDWIN and THELMA WILSON

Sources E. L. Avery, ed., *The London stage, 1660–1800*, pt 2: 1700–1729 (1960) • *Daily Courant* (12–13 April 1705) • J. Milhous and R. D. Hume, eds., *Vice Chamberlain Coke's theatrical papers, 1706–1715* (1982) • J. Milhous and R. D. Hume, eds., *A register of English theatrical documents, 1660–1737*, 1 (1991) • J. Hawkins, *A general history of the science and practice of music*, 5 (1776) • Burney, *Hist. mus.*, 4 • W. H. Logan and J. Maidment, eds., *Fragmenta Scoto-dramatica, 1715–1758* (1835) • M. Tilmouth, 'A calendar of references to music in newspapers, 1660–1719', *RMA Research Chronicle*, 1 (1961), i–vii, 1–107 • W. C. Smith, *A bibliography of the musical works published by John Walsh … 1695–1720* (1948); repr. (1968) • C. L. Day and E. B. Murrie, *English song books, 1651–1702* (1940) • D. Hunter, *Opera and song books published in England, 1703–1726* (1997) • C. M. Simpson, *The British broadside ballad and its music* (1966) • *The ladys entertainment*, book 1 (1708) [copy in Durham Cathedral Library] • *The ordinary of Newgate for … 27 May 1712* (1712) • parish register, St Martin-in-the-Fields, 31 Jan 1684 [baptism] • parish register, London, St James's, Duke's Place, 26 Oct 1682 [marriage; parents] • parish register, St Martin-in-the-Fields, 17 April 1706 [marriage] • parish register, London, St Margaret's, Westminster, 30 Sept 1688 [baptism: Barbara Collop] • parish register, London, St Clement Danes, 22 May 1718 [marriage: Barbara Ramondon, widow, and John Clarke]

Rampton, Sir Jack Leslie (1920–1994), civil servant, was born on 10 July 1920 in Ootacamund, India, the only son and elder child of Leonard Wilfrid Rampton (1891–1972), businessman, and his wife, Sylvia, *née* Davies (1891–1976). He was educated at Tonbridge School and Trinity College, Oxford, where despite defective vision which later led to his rejection by the armed forces he was proficient at cricket and captained the university squash team.

Rampton joined the Treasury in 1941 as a temporary civil servant. In 1942 he was appointed assistant private secretary to the chancellor of the exchequer, Sir Kingsley Wood, and later to his successor, Sir John Anderson. He remained in the Treasury after the war and progressed through a series of Treasury divisions, earning a reputation for outstanding work as principal and as assistant secretary. On 2 January 1950 he married Eileen Joan, *née* Hart (*b.* 1915); they had one son and one daughter. In 1959 he was seconded for two years to be economic and financial adviser to the commissioner-general in south-east Asia and British high commissioner in Malaya, a post which initiated his warm and enduring interest in the affairs of the people of the Far East and Australasia.

In 1964 Rampton was promoted to under-secretary in the public expenditure group of the Treasury, and in 1968 he was transferred as deputy secretary to the Ministry of Technology, where he became concerned with the problems of energy and of British industry, and showed a natural affinity and enthusiasm for the business of manufacturing, and an understanding of its problems. He moved to the Department of Trade and Industry when it absorbed the Ministry of Technology in 1970, and in 1972 became second permanent secretary with special responsibilities for industrial development. He was appointed CB in 1969 and KCB in 1973.

When, during the energy crisis of 1974, it was decided to create a separate energy department, Rampton was a natural choice to be its permanent secretary, a post he held until his retirement from the civil service in 1980. The department was born in the midst of crisis, and the many logistical problems that face new departments, such as key staff, premises, and telephone services, had to be dealt with at speed.

The new department's task was to cope with the disruption of Britain's energy supplies which had been brought about from within by the miners' overtime ban and from without by the OPEC oil price hike. The consequence had been the introduction of a three-day week for industry in order to conserve available energy supplies, and a major reduction of national income and output. The immediate problem of the overtime ban was almost at once removed by a change of government and a concession to the miners, but this only served to underline the importance of energy supply in the longer term. Rampton believed that dependence both on imported oil and on the domestic supply of coal had to be reduced as rapidly and efficiently as possible, and that this objective should guide the development of North Sea oil and gas resources. For the same reason he also had a firm belief in the importance of energy conservation and in the future of nuclear power, whose development in Britain had at that stage been stalled by internal arguments about the appropriate type of reactor for the next phase. Rampton considered that the American pressurized water reactor was the best design for Britain's needs, but the idea of relying on US technology for nuclear energy, in which Britain had been a pioneer, was strongly resisted in many quarters. On this and on several related policy issues Rampton and Tony Benn, his minister during the 1974–9 Labour government, had widely different views, and the relationship between them was often strained. None the less the department's role in the development of Britain's oil and gas resources in the North Sea was commendable.

Rampton was in many respects a shy man, viewing the world through thick spectacles, but always with shrewd judgement and quiet determination. He had a very even temperament and a great sense of humour. He was completely dedicated to his work and a very effective administrator, combining a willingness to delegate with attention to detail, which showed to best advantage in the work of his department in the development of North Sea energy resources. But he held throughout strong personal convictions about departmental policies, a characteristic which some politicians dislike in civil servants. He belonged to the Church of England, but was not very interested in religious affairs.

On retiring from the civil service Rampton became a director of several companies connected with energy, and was able to renew his relationship with Australia, which he visited frequently and where he made many friends. He was chairman of the British-Australia Society and of the Cook Society, and adviser to the Robert Menzies Memorial Trust. His work to shore up the long-established relationship between Britain and Australia was widely recognized in the latter country, and he received the rare distinction for a British civil servant of an obituary in the Australian press. He was a keen follower of cricket in both England and Australia, and an enthusiastic attender of the performances of the English National Opera company, of which he was a board member. He died in the medical centre, Tonbridge, Kent, of lung cancer on 30 March 1994, and was cremated on 8 April in the Kent and Sussex crematorium, Tunbridge Wells.   DOUGLAS CROHAM

Sources personal knowledge (2004) · private information (2004) [Lady Rampton; A. Howett, Tonbridge medical centre] · *The Times* (13 April 1994) · *The Independent* (18 April 1994)
Likenesses photograph, repro. in *The Times*
Wealth at death £430,346: probate, 4 July 1994, *CGPLA Eng. & Wales*

Ramsay family (*per. c.*1300–1513), landowners, was prominent locally in Fife, Lothian, and the borders, and intermittently important in national affairs. Sir William Ramsay of Dalhousie, Edinburghshire, swore fealty to Edward I in 1296 for his Lothian and Berwickshire lands. Thereafter the allegiances of family members fluctuated during the Anglo-Scottish wars; survival in disturbed conditions, if not great advancement, was achieved. National prominence was achieved by **Sir Alexander Ramsay of Dalhousie** (d. 1342), a highly successful border warrior in the 1330s and early 1340s. Ramsay was heavily involved in eroding the English occupation of southern Scotland and in a series of successful Scottish military operations against the Balliol faction and its English supporters. This included participation in the battle of Culblean in Aberdeenshire in 1335, an encounter that saw Edward Balliol's chief northern supporter, David Strathbogie, earl of Atholl, defeated and killed. Among many actions in the more familiar terrain of the eastern borders Ramsay's most important intervention was perhaps his relief by sea of the besieged garrison of Dunbar Castle in 1338, an achievement vital in ensuring the successful defence of an important Scottish border stronghold. These high-profile incidents are in a sense untypical, though, of Ramsay's military career. His regular mode of operation was as a guerrilla leader, continually harassing the English presence in southern Scotland with a relatively small armed retinue, which at one time had its base in a network of fortified caves.

One reward for Ramsay's military success was the renown of being regarded, according to Scottish accounts, as a paragon of chivalry. A genuine attachment to the chivalric ethos is certainly suggested by the jousts in which he led the Scots against a party of English knights under Henry of Grosmont, the future duke of Lancaster, at Berwick early in 1342, in which four of the participants were killed. But Ramsay, initially a relatively minor Lothian laird, also gained rewards more tangible than high contemporary esteem. In 1340 he was made warden of the east march, confirming his status as the chief war leader of the region. In 1342, moreover, he captured the powerful fortress of Roxburgh from the English.

Now in possession of the castle that dominated the area, Ramsay was made sheriff of Teviotdale by David II, an appointment which recognized the extension of Ramsay's influence into the central borders. These developments, though, marked an encroachment on the territorial interests of the other greatly successful Scottish border warlord of the era, Sir William Douglas of Liddesdale. At the height of his power Ramsay was seized by Douglas at Hawick in the central borders in June 1342, removed to the castle of Hermitage in Liddesdale, and starved to death. Ramsay's demise was not lightly accepted by his followers: in 1344 the Scottish parliament was still trying to prevent the Ramsay kindred from seeking revenge for the murder. The Dalhousie Ramsays would never again reach the heights of status that Sir Alexander had achieved. His illustrious career did, though, provide an imposing example of military endeavour and local leadership for his peers and future generations of the family. Ramsays were frequently involved in Anglo-Scottish warfare from Sir Alexander's time onwards, and as important aristocrats of the region they directed their ecclesiastical patronage firmly towards the Cistercian house of Newbattle, Edinburghshire.

It was a member of a Fife-based cadet branch of the family, **Sir William Ramsay of Colluthie** (d. in or after 1382), who next rose to prominence in national affairs. Ramsay of Colluthie, a minor laird, shared the developing family penchant for warfare. He was one of four Ramsays captured at the battle of Nevilles Cross in 1346. It was probably Colluthie also who took a retinue of ten on pilgrimage in the company of the future earl of Douglas in 1356, and fought at Poitiers in that year. These and other military ventures no doubt endeared Ramsay to David II, whose inner circle of retainers was a group of knights with shared chivalric leanings. Royal favour certainly propelled Ramsay from minor landed status into the top rank of the aristocracy in 1358 when David II awarded him the vacant earldom of Fife, in disregard of the rights of its heiress, Isabella. Magnate opposition to such flouting of rank, led by Robert the Steward (subsequently Robert II), resulted in 1359/60 in Ramsay's losing the earldom, which passed briefly to the Steward's family when Isabella married Robert's son Walter. Despite this setback Ramsay continued to prosper in the service of David II, and served as steward of the royal household in the later years of the reign. Ramsay's national prominence came to an end when his royal patron died suddenly in 1371, although his career appears to have stretched into the early 1380s.

Meanwhile the Dalhousie Ramsays remained prominent in Lothian and the borders, and in warfare. **Sir Alexander Ramsay of Dalhousie** (d. 1402) fought at the battle of Otterburn in 1388; his seat of Dalhousie was targeted during the invasion of Scotland by Henry IV in 1400; and he fought, along with two other Ramsays, and was killed at Homildon Hill on 14 September 1402. His grandson, also **Sir Alexander Ramsay of Dalhousie** (d. in or before 1465), who was knighted at James I's coronation in 1424, was one commander of a force which defeated a major English raid at Piperdean in 1435, and was appointed to the border office of conservator of the truce in 1451. The experience of the Ramsay family was ultimately one of moderate success amid the opportunities and dangers of regular warfare in lowland Scotland. A family tradition of militarism and local leadership developed, but the rewards of this rarely seem to have been outstanding after the mid-fourteenth century. Ramsay bellicosity can be seen as very much in the mainstream of European aristocratic behaviour, albeit tinged with the specifically Scottish edge of entrenched opposition to the English enemy. Unsurprisingly, a later Alexander Ramsay of Dalhousie was killed at Flodden in 1513.

ALASTAIR J. MACDONALD

Sources W. Bower, *Scotichronicon*, ed. D. E. R. Watt and others, new edn, 9 vols. (1987–98) · *Scots peerage*, vols. 3, 9 · S. I. Boardman, *The early Stewart kings: Robert II and Robert III, 1371–1406* (1996) · M. Brown, *The Black Douglases: war and lordship in late medieval Scotland, 1300–1455* (1998) · J. H. Ramsay, 'Notes on early Ramsay pedigrees … AD 1200–1600', *The Genealogist*, new ser., 31 (1915), 1–22 · J. M. Thomson and others, eds., *Registrum magni sigilli regum Scotorum / The register of the great seal of Scotland*, 11 vols. (1882–1914) · G. Burnett and others, eds., *The exchequer rolls of Scotland*, 1–4 (1878–80) · *CDS*, vols. 3–4 · Andrew of Wyntoun, *The orygynale cronykil of Scotland*, ed. D. Laing (1879) · G. W. S. Barrow and others, eds., *Regesta regum Scottorum*, 6, *Scalacronica by Sir Thomas Gray of Heton*, trans. H. Maxwell (1907) · *RotS* · C. Innes, ed., *Registrum S. Marie de Neubotle*, Bannatyne Club, 89 (1849)

Ramsay, Agnata Frances. *See* Butler, Agnata Frances (1867–1931).

Ramsay, Sir Alexander, of Dalhousie (d. 1342). *See under* Ramsay family (per. c.1300–1513).

Ramsay, Sir Alexander, of Dalhousie (d. 1402). *See under* Ramsay family (per. c.1300–1513).

Ramsay, Sir Alexander, of Dalhousie (d. in or before 1465). *See under* Ramsay family (per. c.1300–1513).

Ramsay, Alexander (1822–1909), newspaper editor, son of Alexander Ramsay, sheep farmer, was born in Glasgow on 22 May 1822. He was early orphaned and in 1824 his family removed to Edinburgh, where he was educated at Gillespie Free School and where, in 1836, he entered the printing office of Oliver and Boyd. The period 1843–4 he spent in London in the government printing office of T. and J. W. Harrison. Returning to Edinburgh in 1845 he took on literary work of different kinds until, in 1847, he was appointed editor of the *Banffshire Journal*, a post that he filled for sixty-two years. He greatly raised the position of that newspaper, in which he gave prominence to the subject of the sea fisheries, and made a special feature of agriculture, and the pure breeding of cattle. He wrote a life of Oliver Goldsmith (1858), and a *History of the Highland and Agricultural Society of Scotland* (1879). He was joint editor of volumes 2 (1872) and 3 (1875) of the *Aberdeen-Angus Herd Book*, and sole editor of volumes 4 to 33 (1876–1905). As such, he made an important contribution to Scottish agriculture, which was recognized in 1898 by a presentation from breeders of polled cattle throughout the United Kingdom and others, and later by the presentation of a cheque for £150 by members of the Herd Book Society.

A keen golfer, Ramsay was elected provost of Banff in 1894, and the next year received the honorary degree of LLD from Aberdeen University. He was twice married: first to Anne, daughter of John Chassar, engineer, of Auchinblae, and second to Jane, daughter of James Harper, commissary clerk of Banffshire. He died at his home, Earlhill, Banff, on 1 April 1909, his second wife surviving him.

J. C. HADDEN, rev. H. C. G. MATTHEW

Sources *Banffshire Journal* (April 1909) • *WWW*
Likenesses Miss Evans, portrait; in family possession in 1912 • portrait, repro. in *Banffshire Journal* [reprinted as a pamphlet]
Wealth at death £1623 12s. 6d.: probate, 22 June 1909, *CGPLA Eng. & Wales*

Ramsay, Allan (1684–1758), poet, was born on 15 October 1684 at Leadhills, in Crawfordmuir parish, Lanarkshire, the son of John Ramsay (*c.*1660–1685), factor to the Hope estate and superintendent of its lead mines, and the probably Scots-born Alice (*d.* 1700), daughter of Allan Bower, gentleman and mineralogist of Derbyshire. Ramsay has long been alleged to be a descendant of the Douglas family and a relative of the Ramsays of Dalhousie; there is little evidence for this, and even his status as the great-great-grandson of Ramsay, laird of Cockpen, is doubtful and may be a result of the search by one of his sons, the younger Allan Ramsay, for illustrious forebears.

Early years and marriage After the early death of his father, who died in debt, Ramsay was brought up by his mother and her second husband, Andrew Crichton, a local bonnet laird. He was possibly educated for at least some of the time up to the age of fifteen at Crawfordmuir parish school, and helped his stepfather on his farm. In his youth he was captivated by the folklore, poetry, and popular history of the Scottish past. According to Allan Ramsay the younger, Crichton opposed Ramsay's becoming a painter, and instead sent him into trade: in later life Ramsay clearly retained an interest in the visual and plastic arts, and also 'organized several sales of paintings and other works of art' (Brown, 12). Following his mother's death, about January 1701 Ramsay went to be apprenticed (as his brother Robert had been in 1695) to a wigmaker in Edinburgh, receiving back his indentures in either 1707 or 1709, after which he opened his own business (by tradition in the Grassmarket, though no firm evidence for this appears to exist). Ramsay was admitted a burgess of Edinburgh on 19 July 1710. In 1711 he moved to a shop trading under the sign of the Mercury; this was possibly in the north parish, where he was living in 1712–13. By 1714 he had moved to the north-east parish, but it is not until 1718 that there is firm evidence that Ramsay was at the Niddrie's Wynd address which is sometimes projected back into earlier years.

Depressed by what he regarded as the treachery of the Union, Ramsay threw himself for some years into the study of literature. William Hamilton of Gilbertfield, the translator of Blin Hary's patriotic *Wallace*, by his poem 'The Dying Words of Bonnie Heck' (printed in the first volume of Watson's *Choice Collection* of 1706) was said to have 'awakened within' Ramsay 'the desire to write in the dialect of his own country' (Smeaton, 37). By 1711 Ramsay was

Allan Ramsay (1684–1758), by Allan Ramsay, 1729

writing in the vernacular, and his 'Elegy on Maggy Johnston' dates from this time.

On 14 December 1712 Ramsay married Christian Ross (*d.* 1743), daughter of Robert Ross (*d.* 1699/1703), a writer, and his wife, Elizabeth Archibald. They had several children: Allan *Ramsay (1713–1784), who became a painter; Susanna (*b.* 1714), who was possibly later known as Anne (or there may have been a separate daughter of that name born between 1719 and 1724); Niell (*b.* 1715), Robert (*b.* 1716), Janet, Catherine, and Agnes (*b.* 1725); and another daughter, Christy, who died in infancy, probably in the 1720s. It appears that besides the eldest son only Janet, Anne, and Catherine survived into adulthood, since they were left their father's shop.

Literary career Shortly before his marriage Ramsay had become one of the original members of the Easy Club, founded on 12 May 1712. The club was a quasi-Jacobite grouping whose 'direct precursor' (Shuttleton, 52) was to be found among high-tory groups such as the Greppa, who met in Mistress Henderson's howff (tavern) after 1696; Archibald Pitcairne's Greppa Club was portrayed as Hades by his whig opponents, and Ramsay may have been taunting them in their own coin when his elegy on Pitcairne drew on Aeneas's journey there.

The Easy Club was typical of the convivial Scottish urban clubs of the eighteenth century which did so much to promote the Scottish Enlightenment. Such clubs were to some extent born out of social necessity, since there was little available living space for socializing at home in the huge twelve- or sixteen-storey lands within the narrow boundaries of the city wall. The club began with six members, and never had more than twelve. The idea that important figures such as Archibald Pitcairne, Patrick Abercrombie, and Thomas Ruddiman were members of the club has been largely disproved, but Ramsay certainly formed connections with Ruddiman, and in all probability Pitcairne, in these years. Ramsay's Latin (and quite possibly his French) probably benefited more from Ruddiman's circle than from his own schooling.

Pitcairne and Ramsay alike were fond of John Steill's tavern, the Cross Keys, which was to host Edinburgh's Musick Club. The subsequent Musical Society (supported by Ramsay) had Jacobite members and, according to at least one authority, sang Jacobite songs. Steill later subscribed to Ramsay's 1721 and 1728 volumes. The club was soon Ramsay's literary patron, on 2 February 1715 appointing him its poet laureate. Each member of the club took a fictitious name, usually that of a famous man of letters or literary mode: Ramsay first chose Isaac Bickerstaff. However, after the death of Pitcairne on 20 October 1713 and in common with other members of the club, he selected a Scots name, and from the meeting of 5 November onwards was known as Gavin Douglas. The *Aeneid*, which Douglas had translated into Scots and which had been published by Ruddiman and Robert Freebairn in 1710, was a widely recognized source of Jacobite code, and Ramsay drew on it freely in his elegy on Pitcairne, which was published in 1713 bearing the epigraph:

Sum yonder bene for reddy Gold in Hand
Sald and betrasit thare native Realme and Land.

This refers to a passage from *Aeneid*, vi, and is here a coded reference to the Union.

The club, which addressed an anti-Union manifesto to George I on 9 February 1715 (there is no evidence it was ever sent), dissolved at about the time of the Jacobite rising of that year, by which time Ramsay's career as a poet was taking off. His early work was traditionally thought to have been published in the broadside format used by the chapmen and balladeers of popular culture, and one early survivor in this format was: *A Scheme and Type of the Great and Terrible Eclipse of the Sun*, sold by James Watson near the Luckenbooths for 1*d*. in 1715. Subsequently Ramsay continued to publish in broadside form alongside more substantial publications.

Renowned poet and businessman In 1716–18 Ramsay completed the second and third cantos of the unfinished medieval poem *Christ's Kirk on the Green*, which was published first in two and then in three cantos in the latter year: by 1723 this had reached a fifth edition. Appointed constable in 1716, he received a commission in 1718 in the local militia. By then he had also begun working as a bookseller (as well as a dealer in prints, through which he became acquainted with Hogarth) and issuing his own work, including *Scots Songs* (1718), in which some compositions are probably adaptations rather than original pieces, following a practice which became standard in the

Scottish vernacular revival. Figures such as William Hamilton of Gilbertfield and Sir William Scott of Thirlestane congratulated the poet on his developing reputation. By 1719 Ramsay was complaining to the town council that his work was being pirated in London, and his status was further exemplified in the list of subscribers (among them Alexander Pope, Richard Steele, John Gay, and John Arbuthnot, as well as heavyweight Jacobites such as David Erskine of Dun and George Lockhart of Carnwath) to his quarto volume of *Poems* (1721), printed by Ruddiman, which followed an earlier gathering of 1720. The book realized 400 guineas for its author. By the early 1720s Ramsay had abandoned wigmaking in favour of bookselling, which also mushroomed not only into dealing in prints and engravings but also into the arrangement of auction sales in books, medals, jewellery, and silver. Some time before 1720 Ramsay had also become a member of the Whinbush Club (for Clydesdale men living in Edinburgh). Notwithstanding his networking and success in business, in 1722 he also pressed the duke of Roxburghe to help him secure a pension, 'the plea being that by writing Scots verse he is performing a national service' (Martin, 31).

In the same year Ramsay moved his shop near Edinburgh Cross, and produced his *Fables and Tales* and *A Tale of Three Bonnets*, a satire on the Union. His *Fair Assembly* (1723) attacked presbyterian attitudes to dancing, and following his admission to the Royal Company of Archers on 13 July 1724 he wrote several poems in praise of the royal company, at this time a nest of closet Jacobites, urging them to 'assert your King and Country's Cause' and to 'break … each disgraceful Link' of the chain which bound Scotland (*Works*, 6.25, 26, 28). The success of his *Tea-Table Miscellany: a Collection of Scots Songs*, published in three volumes in 1723, 1726, and 1727, set the seal on his reputation; a fourth volume appeared in 1737, by which time the original set had gone through ten editions. The *Miscellany* included work by Jacobites such as Hamilton of Bangour and Robertson of Struan, as well as traditional ballads and work by seventeenth-century writers, with pieces adapted or written by Ramsay himself; its format of setting new words to old airs was already established Jacobite practice. The year after the first volume appeared, Ramsay drew on the Bannatyne manuscripts, to which he had gained access through the good offices of William Carmichael, to publish *The Ever Green: being a Collection of Scots Poems, Wrote by the Ingenious before 1600* (1724). As a subsequent editor, Lord Hailes, pointed out, Ramsay was anything but scrupulous, freely altering his material for an eighteenth-century audience, in particular changing versification and spelling; his work does, however, predate later developments in scholarly editing. He altered William Dunbar's 'Lament for the Makaris' in order to include a prophecy of himself, and included poems of modern composition. Of these, one—'The Vision'—purported to be a medieval dream vision in which the narrator saw Scotland restored through the wars of independence; in fact it was yet another piece of anti-Union Jacobitism by Ramsay himself.

Ramsay's pastoral dialogues—*Patie and Roger* (1720) and

Jenny and Meggy (1723)—proved popular, and leading figures in Edinburgh society suggested that he write a longer drama. In *The Gentle Shepherd* (1725), a descendant of Gay's *Shepherd's Week* of 1714, Ramsay suggestively uses the pastoral form in a celebration of the revitalizing effects wrought by the return of the royalist exile Sir William Worthy, a thin disguise for James Stuart. The drama, which aimed to move classical patriotism into a Scottish landscape setting, was enormously successful, feeding Ramsay's reputation in England as well as north of the border. Following the appearance of Gay's *Beggar's Opera* in 1728, Ramsay's play was converted into a ballad opera at the instigation of the pupils of Haddington grammar school. In this guise it remained popular into the early nineteenth century; the play was performed at least 47 times in Scotland, 101 times in England, and 5 times in the United States before 1837.

The success of *The Gentle Shepherd* enabled Ramsay to flit in 1725–6 to the Luckenbooths, in the very centre of the High Street, with a fine view over Edinburgh Cross, the central afternoon rendezvous of society in the capital. Here he changed his sign to 'Hawthornden's and Ben Johnson's [*sic*] Heads' (Martin, 31). In his new premises Ramsay (probably in 1725) opened a circulating library, the first in Britain, though it is not clear whether it directly influenced the opening of the circulating libraries in Bristol, Birmingham, and London which followed; its contents were unsurprisingly condemned by Robert Wodrow. In 1726 Ramsay was deemed respectable enough to have his own pew in the Tron Kirk, and soon his poetic output had increased to the point that he was able to issue the third volume of the *Miscellany* and *A Collection of Thirty Fables* (1730). Thereafter he was content to prepare new editions and undertake editorial work such as his 1737 collection, *Scots Proverbs*. Although he wrote poetry, it was not for market; indeed, Ramsay opined that he would wish to destroy half his printed works, so that the other half would gain in value by their rarity. His fame was now growing apace, and by the 1730s he was the favourite of many of the great Scottish families. His reputation was also strong south of the border: Gay and Steele were likely visitors, and Ramsay was well known in London. In Dublin in 1727 'a broadside elegy … was hawked through the streets' on the false rumour of his death (Martin, 125).

Other enterprises, later years, and death Presbyterian opposition to his circulating library became increasingly manifest after Ramsay added to it a number of contemporary French plays in translation in 1736. When he also conceived the idea of developing a theatre in Edinburgh, opposition grew further. Ramsay, who wrote prologues, epilogues, and a masque, as well as publishing several editions of plays by other hands, was an enthusiast for the stage: in 1727–8 he had already 'defended the idea of staging plays in Edinburgh' (Murphy), and in 1733–5 he had managed the 'Edinburgh Company of Comedians at the Tailors' Hall' (ibid.). The theatre in Carrubber's Close was built in 1735–6 and opened on 8 November 1736, with annual tickets at 30s. or 2 guineas. It staged *The Recruiting Officer* on its first night, and it was also used for popular entertainments such as rope dancing. Unfortunately for Ramsay the 1737 statute of 10 Geo. II (passed in response to Henry Fielding's attacks on Walpole), banning stage plays outside London or Westminster except during the king's residence, was eagerly implemented by the local authority with clerical encouragement. Ramsay fought closure of his theatre until 1739 (on 27 February a number of his actors were fined £50 by the court of session). He was left with significant debts and had to sell the wood furnishings, and probably scenery and costumes too; none the less, he was later probably instrumental in the development of the Canongate Concert Hall, which opened in 1747 on land owned by Richard Cooper, a friend and collaborator. Ramsay's defence of a domestic Scottish theatre was matched by his interest in retaining native artistic talent in Scotland. He had also opened in 1729 the Edinburgh Academy of St Luke, where his son was a student (possibly under Ramsay's friend John Smibert) before it closed about five years later. In these areas Ramsay was thoroughly aware of the threat the metropolis posed to an indigenous Scottish culture.

In 1733 Ramsay bought some ground on the Castlehill, overlooking the Nor' Loch, and there built a house: the Goose Pie, constructed in the style of the Octagon at Twickenham (itself designed by the Jacobite architect James Gibbs for the secretary of state for Scotland), in a place still called Ramsay Garden, close up against Edinburgh Castle. As the inscription in 1704 shows, it was conceived as an explicitly Horatian 'House of the muses' of poetry and painting (Brown, 23). As this suggests, the house was shared by Ramsay and his son Allan, who took over its ownership in 1741 after Ramsay had retired from active business (his town house and shop having been put up for sale in the *Caledonian Mercury* in early 1739). In semi-retirement Ramsay lived in a kind of Horatian *rus in urbe*, though not in domestic felicity, for on 28 March 1743 his wife died. He did not fully retire from his business until 1755, though he left it largely in the hands of others. In 1745 his fame, central residence, and political opinions made him a prime focus for Jacobite interest during Charles Edward Stuart's occupation of Edinburgh. However, it has been claimed that Ramsay eluded disturbance by going to stay with his friend Sir John Clerk of Penicuik, where he experienced a serious indisposition which kept him out of town. The Jacobite army nevertheless used his house as a vantage point for firing on the castle garrison. Despite the poet's non-involvement at a time of risk, his nationalist work *The Vision* was republished in a separate edition in 1748, when there was considerable Jacobite unrest in Edinburgh.

Ramsay's health began to fail in the 1750s, scurvy in his gums affecting his jaw and as a result his speech. He died on 7 January 1758, and was buried two days later in Greyfriars kirkyard.

Legacy and reputation Ramsay was an early avatar of the primitivists and folklorists of the 1760s and thereafter, who wrote and collected at a time when it may yet have seemed possible to him that the preservation and defence of the culture of his native land might serve a political purpose rather than a cultural or literary one. Deeply interested in the visual arts, the theatre, and Scotland's historic literature, he sought to preserve the country's status as a cultural centre. It was Ramsay who helped a distinctive Scottish literature to survive by yoking the Jacobitical discourse of heroic valour to the poetic productions of the Scottish past, and through identifying the folk vernacular with the idea of a national literature in the present.

Ramsay was, as he put it himself, 'A black-a-vic'd, snod, dapper fellow … With phiz of a Morocco cut', whose 'tripping gait … earned for him the sobriquet of Denty Allan' (Smeaton, 13); later, he put on more weight than this picture suggests. He was regarded as amiable and kind to children: 'from pure kindness to the young, he would help to make dolls for them, and cradles wherein to place these little effigies' (Smeaton, 113). Canny in business, and in person short, fat, friendly, kind, hospitable, and vain, he was popular with his contemporaries. His achievement, which remains both historic and underestimated, was considerably more than the sum of its parts.

The best bibliography of Ramsay's works (of which 143 original and subsequent editions were published in his lifetime alone) is Burns Martin's 1931 list in *The Works of Allan Ramsay*, edited by Kinghorn and Law (vol. 6), which was updated in 1974.   MURRAY G. H. PITTOCK

Sources B. Martin, *Allan Ramsay: a study of his life and works* (1931); repr. (Westport, CT, [1973]) · *The works of Allan Ramsay*, ed. B. Martin, J. W. Oliver, A. M. Kinghorn, and A. Law, 6 vols., STS, 3rd ser., 19–20, 29; 4th ser., 6–8 (1945–74) · H. G. Brown, *Poet and painter: Allan Ramsay, father and son, 1684–1784* (1984) · A. Gibson, *New light on Allan Ramsay* (1927) · F. P. Lole, *A digest of the Jacobite clubs* (1999) · D. E. Shuttleton, '"A modest examination": John Arbuthnot and the Scottish Newtonians', *British Journal for Eighteenth-Century Studies*, 18 (1995), 47–62 · A. H. Maclaine, *Allan Ramsay* (1985) · M. Murphy, 'Edinburgh's first custom-built theatre auditorium', *Scottish Studies Review* (2001) · O. Smeaton, *Allan Ramsay* (1896)
Archives FM Cam. · Hunt. L., papers · NL Scot., 'The gentle shepherd' and MSS | NA Scot., poems and letters to Sir John Clerk · NA Scot., Dick-Cunyngham of Prestonfield muniments · NA Scot., Penicuik muniments
Likenesses J. Smibert, portrait, 1717, Scot. NPG · W. Aikman, oils, 1723, Scot. NPG · A. Ramsay, chalk drawing, 1729, Scot. NPG [*see illus.*] · A. Ramsay, chalk drawing, 1745 (after W. Aikman), Scot. NPG · A. Carse, wash drawing (after J. Smibert), Scot. NPG · R. Cooper, line engraving, NPG · G. Vertue, line engraving (after J. Smibert), BM, NPG; repro. in A. Ramsay, *Poems*, 2 vols. (1721) · G. White, mezzotint (after W. Aikman), BM, NPG · oils, Scot. NPG · oils (after J. Smibert), Scot. NPG

Ramsay, Allan, of Kinkell (1713–1784), portrait painter, was born in Edinburgh, in the parish of New Kirk, on 2 October 1713, the first of at least five surviving children of the Scottish poet and bookseller Allan *Ramsay (1684–1758) and his wife, Christian Ross (*d*. 1743).

Early training Ramsay grew up surrounded by books and from 1726 he attended the Edinburgh high school, where he acquired a good knowledge of Latin and French. To these would be added eventually Greek, Italian, and German. He was drawing 'since he was a dozen years old'

Allan Ramsay of Kinkell (1713–1784), self-portrait, *c*.1737–9

(Ramsay sen. to John Smibert, 10 May 1736, Brown, 'Ramsay's rise', 221) and before he was sixteen he drew a most accomplished head of his father (Scot. NPG) which was later engraved as the frontispiece for subsequent editions of his father's *Poems*. In 1729 he enrolled at the new (but short-lived) artists' Academy of St Luke in Edinburgh and by July 1732 he was in London studying under Hans Hysing. Although he had left by September 1733, Ramsay learned much of the painting of drapery and the use of gesture from his master.

Between 1732 and 1736 Ramsay was practising as a portrait painter in Edinburgh and of the few pictures which may now be identified from this period, *Kitty Hall of Dunglass, later Mrs Hamilton* (City Art Centre, Edinburgh) shows a lively professional competence. Ramsay benefited considerably from his father's connections. He met the virtuoso Sir John Clerk of Penicuik, who commissioned copies from him, and in 1733 and 1734 assisted with the design of the remarkable octagonal Guse-Pye (or Goose Pie) house (intended for his father's retirement, but transferred to his son in 1741), at the top of Castlehill in Edinburgh. In 1735 his father was soliciting the help of the provost of Edinburgh to send his son, now painting 'like a Raphael' (Ramsay sen. to John Smibert, 10 May 1736, Brown, 'Ramsay's rise', 221), to Italy to further his studies. Sir Peter Halkett Wedderburn of Gosford and Pitfirrane and his son Peter put up 2000 merks and Sir John Clerk supplied introductions to Dr Richard Mead and Dr Alexander Gordon in London who, in turn, gave further introductions and advice. By May 1736 Ramsay was ready to depart, accompanied by Alexander Cunyngham (1703–1785) (later Sir Alexander Dick, third baronet, of Prestonfield), a cultured and good-humoured Scottish physician of repute. They had resolved to speak only Italian in Italy 'as we had been well founded in it before we left Edinburgh' (Cunyngham's diary, Forbes, 99).

Italy, 1736–1739 Ramsay and Cunyngham were in Paris in July, when they met Cardinal de Polignac and the collector P.-J. Mariette, and proceeded south to Lyons and Marseilles in September. After a rough sea voyage from Genoa they arrived in Leghorn on 1 October. They spent three weeks in Florence, where Dr Mead had provided an introduction to the grand duke's physician and Ramsay was able to copy some of the antiquities in the ducal galleries. On 26 October they finally arrived in Rome and took lodgings on the piazza di Spagna. For three weeks they 'did little else than scamper about every day all over the streets of the City of Rome' (Cunyngham's diary, 15 Nov 1736, Forbes, 111). They met many of the Jacobite exiles and were introduced to the Pretender (James Stuart) and his exiled court; on 31 December they attended the birthday celebrations for Charles Edward Stuart, the Young Pretender, and in January 1737 they were admitted to the masonic lodge in the strada Paolina, whose membership was principally confined to Stuart sympathizers. Such conduct was, it appears, youthful extravagance, for both Ramsay and Cunyngham became staunch Hanoverians.

Ramsay was more serious concerning his professional advancement. He had initially been disappointed by Raphael's *Stanze* in the Vatican (an experience later shared by Reynolds), but he diligently pursued his studies under Francesco Imperiali and at the French Academy. After Cunyngham left Rome in March 1737, Ramsay visited Naples, where he studied briefly under the ageing Francesco Solimena, who was impressed with the portrait drawings he made of British travellers. In October he returned to Rome to stay a further six months, during which he bought, on commission from Dr Mead, a volume of seventeenth-century drawings after the antique by Pietro Santo Bartoli (probably that now in Glasgow University Library). In April 1738, accompanied by the Anglo-Italian Samuel Torriano (d. 1785), he set out north, passing through Venice, Parma, Milan, and Turin. Torriano left him at Marseilles and Ramsay arrived back in England in June 1738. Only one painting can now be associated with this first visit to Italy, the remarkable portrait of Torriano painted in Rome in 1738 (priv. coll.), which suggests Ramsay had thoroughly absorbed much of the Italian baroque convention.

London and Edinburgh, 1738–1754 By August 1738 Ramsay had taken apartments in the Great Piazza in Covent Garden, and had begun his London practice as a portrait painter. He soon achieved eminence within that crowded profession, due not only to his technical competence but also to his social and intellectual accomplishments. Dr Mead received him into the privileged circle of his dining club, and in 1740 Ramsay published in the *Philosophical Transactions of the Royal Society* descriptions of the recently discovered frescoes at Herculaneum, translated from the Italian of Camillo Paderni, who had been his fellow pupil under Imperiali in Rome. In 1743 he was elected a fellow of the Society of Antiquaries. Meanwhile in December 1738 Alexander Gordon ventured to suggest that young Ramsay was 'one of the first rate portrait painters in London, nay I may say Europe' (Gordon to Sir John Clerk, 7 Dec 1738, Smart, *Ramsay: Painter*, 42). Within a year he had made his mark in society with a series of imposing whole-length portraits: the second duke of Argyll, the duke of Buccleuch, the lord chancellor, the first earl of Hardwicke, and Rachel and Charles Hamilton, the children of Lord Binning, younger brother of Lord Haddington (all in priv. colls.). He had also married in 1739 Anne Bayne, the daughter of a law professor at Edinburgh; they had three children who did not survive childhood and it was in giving birth to the last, on 4 February 1743, that the first Mrs Ramsay died.

In the course of the 1740s Ramsay laid the foundation of his considerable fortune. He maintained a highly practical attitude to his profession, working extremely hard and choosing his moments for self-advertisement. He was always confident of success, telling Cunyngham in 1740 that he had put the visiting French and Italian painters (J. B. Van Loo, Andrea Soldi, and Carlo Rusca) to flight and now himself played 'the first fiddle' (Ramsay to Cunyngham, 10 April 1740, Forbes, 142). A self-portrait of this time (NPG) illustrates this self-belief, with its clear gaze and Italianate stylishness. A constant flow of commissions led him to employ a drapery painter, Joseph van Aken (or van Haeken; c.1699–1749), whose expert services he shared principally with Thomas Hudson, his only serious English rival. While this practice at times resulted in a certain monotony, particularly with modest half lengths, it enabled Ramsay to maintain an extraordinary level of production. From this first decade 300 portraits survive, more than half his total output. The decade closed, as it had begun, with outstanding whole-length portraits, three of which were destined for semi-public display. In 1747, following the example of Hogarth, he presented to Thomas Coram's Foundling Hospital in London a portrait of his patron Dr Mead; in 1748 he gave to the Edinburgh Royal Infirmary a whole length of the second earl of Hopetoun, and in 1749 he painted a dramatic portrait of the third duke of Argyll for the Glasgow city council. All three portraits remain *in situ*. A fourth imposing whole length, of the twenty-second chief of MacLeod painted in 1747 to 1748, in which the pose of the *Apollo Belvedere* is disguised with check trews, was dispatched to Dunvegan Castle on the Isle of Skye.

Ramsay never forgot Scotland and three visits he made between 1745 and 1748 may serve to chart his social progress. He was in Edinburgh when the Young Pretender entered on 16 September 1745 and when the Guse-Pye house was briefly threatened as a site of strategic importance; but during this visit of perhaps three months he displayed a practical tolerance towards his sitters, who included the wife of the solicitor-general, Mrs Robert Dundas, and Lord and Lady Ogilvy, the most enthusiastic

Jacobites (all in priv. colls.). Ramsay was next in Scotland in the late summer of 1747, staying until January 1748, during which time he bought a small estate in Fife, becoming known as a laird, Allan Ramsay of Kinkell. In the autumn of 1748 he spent three weeks at Inveraray Castle as the guest of the third duke of Argyll, 'the king of Scotland'.

In July 1749 Ramsay and Hudson acted as pall-bearers at van Aken's funeral. While the effect of his passing should not be exaggerated, the next five years saw pronounced changes in Ramsay's art and his emergence as a political essayist. He also married a second time, in Edinburgh on 1 March 1752, Margaret Lindsay (d. 1782), daughter of Sir Alexander Lindsay of Evelick, a kinsman of the earl of Balcarres, and his wife, born Amelia Murray, daughter of the fifth Viscount Stormont and sister of William Murray, who became the celebrated Lord Mansfield. They married without the consent of her parents who, despite the approval of Lord Balcarres, who told Ramsay he was 'very glad to hear you have got my fair cousin' (Balcarres to Ramsay, 12 March 1752, Smart, *Ramsay: Painter*, 95), remained opposed to the match. Ramsay was already maintaining a daughter from his previous marriage and helping his two surviving sisters, but he assured Sir Alexander that he could furnish his wife with an annual income of £100 which would grow 'as my affairs increase, and I thank God, they are in a way of increasing'; he had no motive for marriage 'but my love for your Daughter, who, I am sensible, is entitled to much more than ever I shall have to bestow upon her' (Ramsay to Lindsay, 31 March 1752, Smart, *Ramsay: Painter*, 96 n. 10). There were three surviving children from their long and happy marriage, Amelia (1755–1813), Charlotte (1758–1818?), and John (1768–1845).

The Ramsays were in London until the end of 1753 when they moved to Edinburgh until June 1754. Ramsay's portraiture now assumed a new informality, approaching Hogarth's naturalism, but also much affected by the contemporary French manner. When he painted the Wemyss sisters, Lady Helen and Lady Walpole, in 1753 (both priv. coll.), Ramsay remarked that 'les joues de My Lady Nelly Wemyss parlent Francois' (Smart, *Ramsay: Painter*, 110). Among other outstanding works from this time are *Thomas Lamb*, of 1753 (National Gallery of Scotland, Edinburgh), and *Hew Dalrymple, Lord Drummore*, of 1754 (Scot. NPG). David Hume also sat to him in Edinburgh in 1754 (priv. coll.), the portrait marking a friendship based on mutual intellectual respect. In 1754 Ramsay, Hume, and Adam Smith founded in Edinburgh an exclusive debating club, the Select Society. It first met on 22 May, with Hume as treasurer, and the rules laid down that the society could debate any subject 'except such as regard Revealed Religion, or which may give occasion to vent any Principles of Jacobitism' ('Rules and orders of the Select Society', MS, NL Scot.). At this time Ramsay was advising Hume on the first volume of his *History of England* (published in 1754), particularly on his assessment of Shakespeare. He was himself already beginning to publish essays which would

continue to appear as occasional and anonymous pamphlets throughout the rest of his life.

In 1753 there had appeared *On Ridicule* and *Concerning the Affair of Elizabeth Canning*. The former, concerning the use of ridicule as a test of truth, Ramsay advertised as 'tending to show the usefulness, and necessity of experimental reasoning in philological and moral enquiries'; while excusing himself as 'one whose necessary studies have been of a nature little connected with deep erudition', Ramsay reminded his readers that 'printing was discovered by a soldier, and gunpowder by a monk' (Smart, *Ramsay: Painter*, 98). *Elizabeth Canning* defended one Mary Squires against a sentence of death passed at the Old Bailey on evidence supplied by Elizabeth Canning, and it contained an impressive display of logic involving a discussion of the words 'improbability' and 'impossibility', much in the manner of Hume. The prisoner was afterwards released. Ramsay's pamphlet was to come to the notice of Voltaire, who was pleased to describe the author as a *philosophe*. In 1754 there appeared as *The Investigator: Number CCXXI* (a whimsical statistic) the *Essay on the Naturalization of Foreigners*, advocating that 'every man who lived in England would be an Englishman to all intents and purposes'.

In 1755 (when Ramsay was already in Italy) *The Investigator: Number CCXXII* (a further whimsy) published the most important of his writings, *A Dialogue on Taste*. It appeared two years after Hogarth's *Analysis of Beauty*, and was an altogether more disciplined performance. Ramsay described how fashion arose from the pleasures of the rich and powerful; how the eye is frequently pleased by what is 'the reverse of consistency'—as the darkening of the principal apartments of the new Mansion House in London 'by clapping before the windows stately pillars which support nothing or, which is much the same, nothing of any use'; on the other hand the 'vastly natural' quality of a portrait by Quentin de La Tour, a country house view by Lambert, or Hogarth's *March to Finchley* was appreciated by 'the lowest and most illiterate of the people'; he maintained the superiority of Greek architecture over the Roman (the Romans being mischievously described as 'a gang of meer plunderers, sprung from those who had been, but a little while before their conquest of Greece, naked thieves and runaway slaves') and of Gothic architecture over contrived post-Renaissance classicism (which was in effect a misapplication of Greek principles). In April or May 1755 Hume told Ramsay that his essay 'has met with a very good reception from the wits and the critics ... they told me it was very entertaining, and seemed very reasonable' (*The Letters of David Hume*, ed. J. Y. T. Greig, 1932, 1.221). Horace Walpole soon noticed Ramsay as 'a very agreeable writer' with 'a great deal of genuine wit and a very just manner of reasoning' (Walpole to Sir David Dalrymple, 25 Feb 1759, *Horace Walpole's Correspondence*, ed. W. S. Lewis, 1951, 15.47). Hogarth amicably announced that purchasers of his own *Analysis of Beauty* would be given copies of *A Dialogue on Taste*, 'written by A.R., a friend of Mr Hogarth and eminent portrait painter now at Rome' (Smart, *Ramsay: Painter*, 101).

Italy, 1754–1757 Ramsay, accompanied by his wife and sister Catherine, had left London in July 1754 and reached Italy in October. As on his previous visit to Italy, Ramsay spent two months in Florence, copying in the ducal galleries, before arriving in Rome in December. He took rooms on the Viminale Hill, 'to seclude myself a good deal from the English travellers without falling out with any of them, and to preserve the greater part of my time for painting, drawing and reading' (Fleming, 147). He held weekly *conversazioni* for British visitors and attended those given by the young and ambitious Robert Adam, who considered the Ramsays worthy company 'as Mrs Ramsay is of so good a family and Mumpy himself so rich' besides being 'generally known and regarded' (Fleming, 121, 174). Ramsay and Adam were quickly familiar with the Abbé Peter Grant, the Roman agent of the Scottish Catholic mission far better known for his unctuous attendance on wealthy tourists, and Robert Wood, the renowned eastern traveller then accompanying the duke of Bridgewater in Rome. Together they formed an unofficial Caledonian Club, gossiping in 'ain Mither tongue' (Fleming, 171).

Ramsay painted Robert Wood (NPG) and General John Burgoyne (priv. coll.), while the portrait of his wife holding a parasol (priv. coll.) must have been painted soon after the birth of their first child, Amelia, in March 1755. Ramsay also copied paintings by Domenichino and Batoni (whom he came to know well), and sketched Roman antiquities with the French artists Clérisseau and Pêcheux. He made a considerable number of life studies (National Gallery of Scotland, Edinburgh) at the French Academy which prompted Adam to observe that Ramsay 'knew less about the proportions of the human figure than any young boy about Rome' (Fleming, 174). There was always an element of striving about Ramsay's art and, perhaps to vindicate himself, Ramsay had his pupil David Martin bring out to Rome a number of his drawings to be shown at the Accademia di San Luca.

The study of antiquity increasingly occupied his time, and Ramsay formed an unlikely friendship with the Venetian engraver, designer, and antiquarian G. B. Piranesi ('the most extraordinary fellow I ever saw', said Adam; Fleming, 165). They argued about the respective merits of Greek and Roman classical architecture, but Piranesi saw fit to include a generous tribute to him in one of his *capricci* in *Le antichità Romane* (1756), in which a tomb appears (visibly) inscribed to Allan Ramsay: 'Scoti Pictor et in omni liberal artium facultae celeber'. Later in 1761 Piranesi attacked Ramsay in his *Della magnificenza ed architettura de' Romani* for having so wilfully misrepresented the achievements of the Romans and their architects in his *Dialogue on Taste*.

Ramsay paid a visit to Naples and sketched what was then thought to be Virgil's tomb at Posillipo, and while he stayed at the Villa d'Este in Tivoli in the summer of 1755 he began his search for the site of Horace's villa, a task which was to occupy him increasingly in later years. In the summer of 1756 Ramsay was taken ill and convalesced at Viterbo, but he was fit enough when he left Rome in May 1757. Again he stopped at Florence, where he copied the portrait of Galileo by Sustermans for the master of Trinity College, Cambridge. Late in August 1757 the Ramsays were back in London.

Royal patronage Ramsay now took up residence at 31 Soho Square, a fashionable area of Westminster, and entered upon the most distinguished episode of his professional career. His compatriot the third earl of Bute (a nephew of the third duke of Argyll) was now the prince of Wales's governor, and he commissioned from Ramsay a whole-length portrait of his royal pupil (Mount Stuart, Rothesay, Isle of Bute). Within weeks of his return from Italy, on 12 October 1757, Ramsay attended the prince at Kew for the first sitting. The portrait was admired and the prince in turn commissioned a whole length of Lord Bute (National Trust for Scotland, Edinburgh). After the prince ascended the throne in October 1760 as George III, with Bute as his favourite minister, he turned to Ramsay to paint his coronation portrait and that of his queen, Charlotte of Mecklenburg-Strelitz, whom he married in September 1761. These elegant state portraits (Royal Collection), the most impressive of British monarchs since Van Dyck, were completed by March 1762. Meanwhile Ramsay's position as painter to the king was criticized as a flagrant instance of undue Scottish influence, and was further complicated by the almost unnoticed survival of the previous, unimpressive incumbent, John Shackleton. In December 1761 Ramsay was appointed 'One of His Majesty's Painters in Ordinary', duly succeeding as 'Principal Painter in Ordinary to the King' upon Shackleton's death in March 1767. His relations with the king and queen were, it seems, relaxed, and he was the only courtier able to speak with them in German. In January 1762 he was ordering German books, 'matters of entertainment or Belles Lettres', by Lessing, Rabener, Gellert, Gessner, and Hagedorn (Ramsay to an unknown correspondent, 4 Jan 1762, Brown, *Ramsay's Rise*, 212).

From 1762 until his death in 1784 Ramsay was responsible for supplying at least 150 pairs of portraits of George III and his queen, either for the royal family, or for the lord chamberlain for distribution to government representatives abroad. He received 80 guineas for each portrait, so that his private fortune, already remarked upon by Adam in 1755, now increased considerably. He originally intended to 'give the last painting' of each replica himself but his resolve soon gave way. Joseph Moser recalled seeing his studio

> crowded with portraits of His Majesty in every stage of operation. The ardour with which these beloved objects were sought for by distant corporations and transmarine colonies was astonishing; the painter with all the assistance he could procure could by no means satisfy the diurnal demands that were made in Soho Square upon his talents and industry. (*European Magazine*, 64, 1813, 516)

In 1764 Ramsay acquired a more spacious house at 67 Harley Street where coachmen's rooms and haylofts were converted into a long gallery to facilitate production. His principal assistants were David Martin (1737–1797) and Philip Reinagle (1749–1833), who received up to 25 of the 80 guineas Ramsay was being paid for each picture.

Apart from the coronation portraits Ramsay painted profile half lengths of the king and queen, and a fine whole-length portrait of the queen with the two young princes, George and Frederick, between 1764 and 1767 (Royal Collection). For Lord Bute he painted, about 1764, a whole length of his particular friend, the king's mother, Augusta, the dowager princess of Wales (Mount Stuart, Rothesay, Isle of Bute). But royal portraiture was not an exclusive occupation, and many of Ramsay's finest portraits date from the ten years after his return from the second visit to Italy. Delicate colour and a French elegance lend them particular distinction. The beautiful picture of his wife holding a flower (National Gallery of Scotland, Edinburgh), his portraits of Lady Holland, Lady Coke, Mrs Elizabeth Montagu, and Lady Susan Fox-Strangways (all priv. coll.) provide ample evidence for Horace Walpole's comment that Ramsay, 'all delicacy', was 'formed to paint women', in contrast, he thought, to Reynolds, who seldom succeeded with them (Walpole to Sir David Dalrymple, 25 Feb 1759, *Horace Walpole's Correspondence*, ed. W. S. Lewis, 1951, 15.47). Ramsay's double portrait of Walpole's nieces, Laura Keppel and Lady Huntingtower (priv. coll., USA), painted in 1765, remains, perhaps, his masterpiece. In 1766 Ramsay painted the remarkable half lengths of his friend David Hume (Scot. NPG), full face in a bright scarlet coat, and Hume's temporary charge in England, the exiled Jean-Jacques Rousseau, dressed in dark Armenian fur and looking askance (National Gallery of Scotland, Edinburgh). These are profound studies of character and Rousseau's subsequent disenchantment with his portrait may be construed as a compliment to Ramsay's grasp of his instability.

Such elegant pictures lacked the grandiloquence which, as Reynolds understood, was becoming necessary for the effective exhibition picture. Ramsay never exhibited, although he had been elected a member of the Society of Arts in 1757 and became a vice-president of the Society of Artists in 1765; nor did he join in the various campaigns for annual exhibitions in London. Ultimately it was Reynolds who became the president of the Royal Academy in 1768. Ramsay's attitude to painting was very different from that of his earliest London years. Now he could choose his sitters; as the king's painter he was no longer a competitor, and he was financially independent. Moreover his ambitions were no longer wholly focused on his painting; travel, writing, and classical scholarship increasingly occupied his time.

Final years In September 1765, accompanied by his wife and eldest daughter, Amelia, Ramsay spent ten days in Geneva with Lord Stanhope, a mathematician of repute and a long-standing patron, and his wife, a sister of the earl of Haddington, who was suffering from a fractured thigh. From Geneva he took the opportunity of visiting Voltaire at Ferney. On their return journey they spent two weeks in Paris, where, apart from his familiarity with painters, Ramsay saw Hume, then attached to the British embassy, and Horace Walpole, confined to his rooms with gout. He was introduced to Baron d'Holbach and to Diderot, who called him *philosophe*—'on dit qu'il peint

mal, mais il raisonne très bien' (D. Diderot, *Œuvres complètes*, 19, 1876, 174); Ramsay entered into correspondence with him.

In 1766 Ramsay spent six months in Edinburgh where, as a freeholder in the shire of Kinross, he engaged in two minor legal disputes with his customary punctiliousness, a quality which continued to inform his essays. His previous pamphlets had been revised and reissued as *The Investigator* in 1762, and over the next ten years further political essays appeared essentially adhering to the king's high tory policies. *An Essay on the Constitution of England* appeared in 1765, a defence of the liberties enjoyed by the English people under Hanoverian rule. In an appendix he transcribed and discussed the original articles of the Magna Carta, showing how it was influenced by popery and concepts of arbitrary power. Ramsay had inspected the original articles through a manuscript he had discovered in a private collection and which, through his advocacy, was presented to the British Museum in 1769. Ramsay's essay was well received, being translated into German in 1767 with the author's name on the title-page. There followed in 1769 *Thoughts on the Origin and Nature of Government*, written in 1766, expressing serious concern over the threatened loss of the American colonies, but defending the right to tax them. In 1772 he published two essays on the necessity of government intervention in the affairs of the East India Company, of which he was a prominent shareholder: *An Enquiry into the Rights of the East India Company of Making War and Peace*, and *A Plan of the Government of Bengal*. The latter contained a letter from Ramsay to the prime minister Lord North, dated 20 March 1772, and the text of a speech given by Ramsay to the general court of the East India Company on 12 November 1772.

Early in 1773 Ramsay suffered a permanent injury to his right arm through a fall which effectively ended his career as a painter, although his activity had been reduced for several years. Later that year, with his sister Janet, he returned to Geneva to see Lady Stanhope, who was now disabled. Again he visited Voltaire at Ferney, this time accompanied by the young fifth earl of Chesterfield. Ramsay himself now began to suffer from rheumatic pains and in 1775, with his wife and daughter Amelia, he returned for a third time to Italy, hoping to effect a cure. But the waters at Pisa and Casiano proved ineffectual, the latter being like those of 'Tunbridge Wells, but twenty times stronger' (Ramsay to Sir John Pringe, 22 Nov 1775, Ingamells, 798). With more success he tried the baths on the island of Ischia and he began to draw again; drawings of himself and his wife dated 1776 are in the National Gallery of Scotland. But Ramsay was principally engrossed with antiquarian pursuits (Fuseli commenting on his fondness for 'tracing on dubious vestiges the haunts of ancient genius and learning'; Smart, *Ramsay: Painter*, 244) and soon became obsessed with the site of Horace's Sabine villa which he believed, probably correctly, to have been at Licenza. Count Orsini lent him rooms in his palace there, the young Jacob More made drawings for him, and his wife acted as amanuensis. 'An enquiry into the situation and circumstances of Horace's Sabine villa, written during travels through Italy in the years 1775, 1776 and 1777' is preserved in two manuscripts in the University Library, Edinburgh, and in the National Library of Scotland.

The Ramsays left Rome in June 1777 and were back in London by October. More essays followed. In 1777 appeared *Letters on the Present Disturbances in Great Britain and her American Provinces*, originally published in the *Public Advertiser* (18 April 1771; 25, 26 January 1775). *A Succinct Review of the American Contest* was first published in February 1778. *A Letter to Edmund Burke*, dated 13 March 1780, answered that statesman's speech concerning government expenditure and the need for economic reform; the present system, wrote Ramsay, was 'the popular or democratic system, and the most popular and democratic that was ever seen in any empire so rich and extended as ours'. The Gordon riots of 1780 induced *Observations on the Riot Act by a Dilettante in Law and Politics* in 1781, advocating a strengthening of legislation for the protection of life and property.

Ramsay was now part of London's intellectual society and there are glimpses of him in the Reynolds–Johnson–Boswell circle between 1778 and 1780. On 9 April 1778 Ramsay spoke at length on Horace's villa at a dinner given by Reynolds with Johnson, Boswell, and Edward Gibbon among the guests. Soon afterwards Boswell implored Ramsay to write the biography of his father the poet—but only a brief manuscript account survives (published in *The Works of Allan Ramsay, 1686–1758*, 4, ed. A. M. Kinghorn and A. Law, 1970, 71–5). On 29 April Ramsay hosted a dinner for Reynolds, Boswell, and Johnson, at which the conversation ranged over Alexander Pope, Homer, and Robert Adam; on the next day Johnson declared: 'I love Ramsay. You will not find a man in whose conversation there is more instruction, more information, and more elegance, than in Ramsay's' (Boswell, *Life*, 3.336). His conversation was more than once described as lively, and even his military son-in-law (who became Sir Alexander Campbell of Inverneil) described 'the famous Allan Ramsay' with some affection as the 'old Cadger' who was 'Rich and Highly respected; a most Sensible, Pleasing, Clever Old man' (Smart, *Ramsay: Painter*, 259).

Mrs Ramsay died on 4 March 1782 and that summer Ramsay resolved to return to Italy for his fourth and last visit, 'to alleviate his bodily infirmities, by change of climate, and to dissipate the melancholly occasioned by the loss of one valuable part of his family, and the dispersion of others' (advertisement to 'Horace's Sabine Villa' MS, Edinburgh University Library), both his daughters having gone to the West Indies with Amelia's military husband. Ramsay was accompanied by his son, the fourteen-year-old John Ramsay, who kept a journal (MS, NL Scot.), describing how he transcribed classical texts and read Latin texts to his now fragile and demanding father. In April 1783 he spent two months in Naples, where the distinguished British minister Sir William Hamilton played him Handel sonatas, receiving in return a copy of Ramsay's last pamphlet. The *Essay on the Right of Conquest*, just published in Florence, was a slightly jaded rationalization

of imperial expansion. Ramsay continued his study of Horace's villa, again staying in Count Orsini's palace at Licenza in September 1783, while the German artist Philipp Hackert, then painter to the king of Naples, made ten views, including a map, of the site. In October 1783 Ramsay and his son went to Florence, their visit marked by the attentions of the aged Sir Horace Mann and the rather unworthy verses which Ramsay was persuaded by the poetaster Robert Merry to have published in *The Arno Miscellany* in 1784. Horace Walpole told Mann this was the act of 'an old dotard ... sporting and playing at leap frog, with brats!' (Walpole to Mann, 8 Nov 1784, *Horace Walpole's Correspondence*, ed. W. S. Lewis, 1951, 25.540). In the summer of 1784 Ramsay resolved to return home, primarily to see his daughters, then about to return to England. But the journey proved too much, and he died on arrival at Dover, on 10 August 1784. He was buried in St Marylebone Church, Middlesex.

Conclusion Ramsay was a portrait painter of great distinction. Within the history of British art he appears a sophisticated artist, conversant with contemporary Italian and French practice, and at his best in the 1750s and 1760s. Both Reynolds and Gainsborough learned from his example. After his death British painting came to be dominated by the more imaginative, and often more heroic, paintings shown at the annual exhibitions of the Royal Academy, and it was only in the mid-twentieth century that Ramsay's refined elegance was again properly appreciated. Ramsay's other interests, his classical scholarship and his political essays, must now be accounted minor in comparison, but they set him apart from other painters of his time and showed the breadth of his understanding. One of the last portraits of Ramsay, the marble bust by Michael Foye carved in Rome from 1775 to 1777, shows a determined, level-headed elderly man with a set, down-turned mouth—the 'Old Mumpy' expression which Robert Adam had described (Scot. NPG); it seems a far cry from the handsome and ambitious self-portrait of his young manhood, but it is draped with a toga, suggestive of that Roman gravitas and steady spirit which characterized his life.

JOHN INGAMELLS

Sources A. Smart, *Allan Ramsay: painter, essayist, and man of the Enlightenment* (1992) • A. Smart, *Allan Ramsay: a complete catalogue of his paintings*, ed. J. Ingamells (1999) • I. G. Brown, 'Allan Ramsay's rise and reputation', *Walpole Society*, 50 (1984), 209–47 • I. G. Brown, 'The pamphlets of Allan Ramsay the younger', *Book Collector*, 37 (1988), 55–85 • J. Holloway, 'Two projects to illustrate Allan Ramsay's treatise on Horace's Sabine villa', *Master Drawings*, 14 (1976), 280–86 • J. Fleming, *Robert Adam and his circle in Edinburgh and Rome* (1962) • Mrs A. Forbes, ed., *Curiosities of a Scots charta chest, 1600–1800* (1897) • J. Ingamells, ed., *A dictionary of British and Irish travellers in Italy, 1701–1800* (1997)

Archives BL, autograph essay on the history of language and poetry, Add. MS 39999 • NL Scot., family corresp. • NL Scot., MS enquiry into Horace's Sabine villa • NL Scot., notes on his father's poem 'The gentle shepherd' • U. Edin. L., letters and papers | NL Scot., legal corresp. with John Davidson • NL Scot., corresp. with Sir Robert Strange

Likenesses A. Ramsay, self-portrait, drawing, c.1733, NG Scot. • A. Ramsay, self-portrait, oils, c.1737–1739, NPG [*see illus.*] • A. Ramsay, self-portrait, chalk, 1755, NG Scot. • A. Ramsay, self-portrait, oils, c.1756, priv. coll. • M. Foye, marble bust, 1775–7, Scot. NPG •

A. Ramsay, self-portrait, chalk, 1776, NPG • A. Nasmyth, oils, 1781 (after A. Ramsay), Scot. NPG • A. Wivell, mezzotint, pubd 1820 (after A. Ramsay), BM, NPG • A. Ramsay, self-portrait, chalk, Scot. NPG • A. Ramsay, self-portrait, drawing, Hunt. L. • A. Ramsay, self-portrait, pastels, Scot. NPG

Ramsay, Allen Beville (1872–1955), Latin poet and college head, was born at Croughton House, Brackley, Northamptonshire, on 3 August 1872, the second son, but the only son to survive to adulthood, in the family of two sons and eight daughters of Beville Ramsay (1833–1910), a country gentleman, and his wife, Sarah Maria (d. 1923), daughter of Matthew Carrier Tompson, rector of Woodstone, Northamptonshire. In 1886 he was elected a king's scholar at Eton College, where he was taught by Henry Elford Luxmoore and collaborated in editing *The Mayfly* (1891). After proceeding in 1891 to King's College, Cambridge, he was elected to a scholarship (1893), and was Browne's medallist for the Latin ode (1893) and for the Greek epigram (1894); he took a first in part one of the classical tripos in 1894. In 1895 he returned to teach at Eton as assistant master and then lower master from 1916 until 1925, when he became master of Magdalene College, Cambridge. An exacting tutor, he revitalized lower chapel, and in 1919 formed the first troop of boy scouts in a public school. He became a close friend of Montague Rhodes James, the provost of King's and then of Eton; the two men cycled together on the continent during the Easter vacations. In collaboration with Hugh Vibart Macnaghten, he edited Catullus's poems (1899).

Ramsay wrote much Latin verse at Eton, often commenting humorously on school life, but with 'a considerable residue of real poetry' (Bradner, 342). He demonstrated a fluent technique in both lyric and elegiac metres; the 'delicate sentiment' of some of his sapphics is singled out for praise by Bradner (who, as an American scholar, could admire the Etonian tradition from an independent perspective). Ramsay wrote movingly and perceptively on the effects of the First World War.

Throughout his career Ramsay published collections of Latin and English verse (in a uniform format, and with related, botanically inspired, titles). *Inter lilia* (1920) and *Ros rosarum* (1925) appeared while he was lower master at Eton, *Frondes salicis* (1935) and *Flos malvae* (1946) while master of Magdalene, and *Ros maris* (1954) in retirement. (The first two are discussed by Bradner, 341–3; the first four also by Money, 258–61.) He writes well on tea (he tended to ask 'Mr Kettle' if he was boiling), and on the Indian cricket team. He also explains the purpose of 'fagging': 'Ne mala vis fastus inflet inane caput' ('lest pride puff up an empty head'; *Inter lilia*, 52).

Ramsay was asked to join Rudyard Kipling and Charles Graves in an ingenious literary parody, purporting to be a newly discovered book of Horace. Kipling and Graves composed the English, Ramsay and others supplied elegant Latin 'originals': the whole appeared as *Q. Horati flacci carminum liber quintus* (1920). A few were fooled, many more were amused. Contemporary topics were covered (chemistry lessons, Lloyd George's sale of honours) in a lively Horatian spirit.

Ramsay had no pretensions to be a serious academic; he was therefore considered a suitable college master. He was appointed master of Magdalene College, Cambridge, on 27 October 1925, and took up the post in January 1926. He succeeded A. C. Benson, who had earlier been horrified at the thought of Ramsay being a candidate for Eton's headmastership: 'Ramsay is a poky, narrow-minded, parochial, stubborn, pig-headed little fellow … He knows nothing of the world except Eton' (Hyam, 235). It was a somewhat contentious appointment, made by the visitor, Henry Neville, seventh Baron Braybrooke (according to Magdalene's unusual system); the fellows were consulted, and would have preferred Ramsay's near namesake the mathematician Arthur Stanley Ramsey, a popular fellow and tutor, who felt betrayed at having been passed over for a schoolmaster. Ramsay was not Braybrooke's first choice: but Etonian opinion counted for more with Braybrooke than the college's preference.

Ramsay was chiefly responsible for the expulsion from Magdalene's fellowship of William Empson for sexual misconduct, on the discovery of 'engines of love' (that is, contraceptives) in Empson's possession. A colleague who regretted the decision (F. Salter) nevertheless thought that Ramsay had been fair, and 'behaved quite well' (Luckett and Hyam, 36); Empson called him 'shockingly unscrupulous' in a letter to I. A. Richards (ibid., 39). Many at Magdalene saw a positive side to Ramsay's personality: he was 'extraordinarily selfless', with 'fundamental modesty and simplicity' (Turner, 61); he presented a dignified, schoolmasterly appearance, 'his rubicund face adorned with a bushy white moustache' (Hyam, 236). Ramsay was vice-chancellor from 1929 to 1931, and the election of Stanley Baldwin as the university's chancellor fell within his period of office. He was also president of Cambridge University Cricket Club. Friends spoke of 'his love of the three Cs: classics, cricket, chess' (*The Times*, 22 Sept 1955).

Ramsay showed a strong preference for Old Etonians (whose numbers increased under his mastership to about 35 per cent of the college); many other undergraduates found 'the Ram', as he was generally known, something of an anachronism. He subjected the classicists to 'saying lessons': the learning and recitation of entire speeches of Demosthenes or Cicero, to teach 'his boys' (often undergraduates in their twenties, following military service) the virtues of 'Accuracy, Eloquence, and Deportment', together with 'Diligence and Obedience' (Ray, 43). A pupil learned deportment by standing still and reciting with the sun in his eyes. Ramsay remained unmarried. His sister Eva Ramsay kept house for him throughout his life. Ramsay retired in 1947 to Malvern; he busied himself with some preparatory school teaching, and had an 'instinctive rapport' with the boys (Hyam, 236).

Ramsay's final verse collection, *Ros maris* (1954), contained 'C. Licini Calvi poemata nuperrime inventa' ('Newly discovered poems of Gaius Licinius Calvus', an addressee of Catullus); no doubt inspired by his enjoyment of the fifth book of Horace, this is Ramsay's most sustained set of classical pastiches. There are nineteen 'Calvus' poems, including hendecasyllables on Catullus's death and scazontes (limping iambics), another character-istically Catullan verse form (though a man who could not bear the thought of undergraduate innocence being sullied by sex could never be wholly Catullan). To the end of his life he retained a simple charm; he wrote 'To a critic':

> I am sorry my verses tease you,
> When you take them from the shelf;
> But I didn't write them to please you;
> I wrote them to please myself.
> (*Ros maris*, 31)

Ramsay died at the Clanmere Nursing Home, Graham Road, Malvern, Worcestershire, on 20 September 1955. He was probably the most significant British Latin poet of the twentieth century; though he achieved far less than the major Latinists of past eras, such as John Owen or James Alban Gibbes in the seventeenth century, or Anthony Alsop or Vincent Bourne in the eighteenth, he continued to write Latin with natural elegance and enthusiasm.

D. K. MONEY

Sources D. K. Money, *The English Horace: Anthony Alsop and the tradition of British Latin verse* (1998) · L. Bradner, *Musae Anglicanae: a history of Anglo-Latin poetry, 1500–1925* (1940) · A. B. Ramsay, *Ros maris* (1954) · P. Cunich and others, *A history of Magdalene College, Cambridge, 1428–1988* (1994) · F. Turner, 'Allen Beville Ramsay', *Magdalene College Magazine and Record*, new ser., 43 (1998–9), 60–67 · C. Ray, 'The saying lesson', *Magdalene College Magazine and Record*, new ser., 35 (1990–91), 43–5 · R. Luckett and R. Hyam, 'Empson and the engines of love: the governing body decision of 1929', *Magdalene College Magazine and Record*, new ser., 35 (1990–91), 33–40 · *WWW* · Burke, *Gen. GB* (1937) · Venn, *Alum. Cant.* · *The Times* (22 Sept 1955) · d. cert. · R. W. Pfaff, *Montague Rhodes James* (1980) · *CGPLA Eng. & Wales* (1955)

Archives Magd. Cam., corresp. and literary papers

Likenesses G. Kelly, oils, 1927, Magd. Cam. · W. Stoneman, photograph, 1940, NPG

Wealth at death £56,772 9s. 3d.: probate, 11 Nov 1955, *CGPLA Eng. & Wales*

Ramsay, Andrew (1574–1659), Church of Scotland minister, was born at Fettercairn, the youngest son of David Ramsay of Balmain, Kincardineshire, and Katherine Carnegie, daughter of Sir Robert Carnegie of Kinnaird, Perthshire. He was educated at Marischal College, Aberdeen, whence he graduated MA. In common with many of his contemporaries Ramsay continued his schooling in France, where he studied theology. Latterly he occupied a professorial chair at the University of Saumur. An accomplished scholar, he published *Oratio* (1600) and *Paraenesis et orationes de laudibus academae Salmuriensis* (Saumur, n.d.) during his stay on the continent. He had returned to Scotland by 1606, when he was appointed minister of Arbuthnott, in the presbytery of Fordoun. Probably soon afterwards he married Marie Fraser; the couple had four sons, including Andrew *Ramsay (1620?–1688), later burgess and lord provost of Edinburgh.

Ramsay supported royal policy regarding the kirk, and was soon involved in religious controversy. He was appointed constant moderator of the presbytery of Fordoun, and in that capacity voted for the establishment of episcopacy in Scotland at the general assembly of 1610. On the authority of John Spottiswoode, archbishop of St Andrews, he was rewarded with a call to the ministry at Edinburgh in 1613, and was installed at the parish of Greyfriars on 28 April of the following year. He was named burgess of the city ('gratis') in 1615, and on 21 October of the same year was a member of the newly formed court of high commission (renewed on 15 June 1619). Despite his apparent conformity Ramsay (along with fifty-four others) appended his signature to the 'protestation for the liberties of the Kirk' of 1617, an action which frustrated James VI's plans to undermine the power of the general assembly. Following a personal audience with the king, however, Ramsay withdrew his protest. Consequently he retained the favour of James. He was appointed to the chair of divinity at the University of Edinburgh in 1620, and was subdean of the Chapel Royal in 1629.

Unsurprisingly, while Henry Guthrie, bishop of Dunkeld, knew him as a 'guid, modest, learned [and] godlie man' (*Fasti Scot.*, 1.70), presbyterian nonconformists took a dim view of Ramsay's support for episcopacy. His sole aim—according to the exiled minister David Calderwood in 1623—was to gain preferment by 'amazing the sillie people with griek & latine, [thereby] tickling the ears of the learned sort [and] flattering princes' (Calderwood, 'Answere', fol. 46r). There was some substance to these allegations, as Ramsay's preaching was widely regarded as tending towards Arminianism. In 1633 he was 'severely censured' by his brother-in-law, Sir John Carnegie, and Alexander Henderson, minister of Leuchars, for having adopted 'the modish Laudean doctrine of England' (Wodrow, fol. 12r–v). At the same time Ramsay was openly courting the patronage of William Laud, archbishop of Canterbury. His renowned *Poemata sacra … et epigrammata sacra* (a collection of Latin verse written in the style of Ovid) was published at Edinburgh to coincide with the coronation of Charles I, at which Laud was present. The work was highly commended by the contemporary Latinist Arthur Johnston, a client of the archbishop, who later reprinted the poems as part of a wider collection entitled *Deliciae poetarum Scotorum* (Amsterdam, 1637).

Notwithstanding his attempts to cultivate the patronage of Canterbury, Ramsay was passed over for the newly created bishopric of Edinburgh in 1634. Neither was he preferred during the extensive reshuffle of Scottish bishoprics—masterminded by Laud—which continued into the following year. Disillusioned, Ramsay's immediate thoughts were of 'dimitting his ministry and retiring to his own lairdship' (*DNB*). By 1637, however, he had sided with the nonconformist ministers of the capital, and—on the occasion of the riot at Edinburgh on 23 July—refused to read the service book from his pulpit. Subsequently Ramsay preached vehemently against the adoption of the new liturgy and canons, and successfully urged his congregation to sign the national covenant in February 1638. In *A warning to come out of Babylon … preached at the receiving of Mr T. Abernethie, sometime jesuite, into the church of Scotland* (Edinburgh, 1638), he demonstrated his own adherence to the covenant. Thereafter Ramsay supported the presbyterian administration in Scotland, and was moderator of the general assembly of 1640. In 1646 he was appointed rector of the University of Edinburgh, a position he held until 1648. In that year, however, he was accused of acting to the prejudice of the government, largely because of his refusal to preach against the engagement with Charles I. The decision to prosecute Ramsay over the issue was not unanimous. The presbyterian diarist Robert Baillie, for example, 'could not voyce to depose a man of such age and parts' (*Letters and Journals of Robert Baillie*, 3.92). Nevertheless, he was deprived of his ministry by the general assembly of 1649, and he retired to the family estate of Abbotshall, Fife. Later, in 1649, he composed an apology in which he objected to some of the innovations introduced into the kirk since 1638. His disapproval extended to all forms of set prayer in public worship, but especially the Lord's prayer; the repetition of the creed at baptism; and the practice whereby ministers knelt for private prayer on entering the pulpit. On 8 November 1655 the synod of Lothian—on account of his 'age and great esteem for piety and learning' (*DNB*)—voted in favour of his reinstatement, but he took no further active role in kirk affairs. Ramsay died at Abbotshall on 30 December 1659, and was buried there.

VAUGHAN T. WELLS

Sources D. Calderwood, *The history of the Kirk of Scotland*, ed. T. Thomson and D. Laing, 8 vols., Wodrow Society, 7 (1842–9) • D. Calderwood, 'Ane Answere … to the tripartite discourse entituled Calderwods Recantation', NL Scot., Wodrow MS Qto 76.5, fols. 37v–53r • R. Wodrow, 'Life of Andrew Ramsay', NL Scot. • *The letters and journals of Robert Baillie*, ed. D. Laing, 3 vols. (1841–2) • J. Row, *The history of the Kirk of Scotland, from the year 1558 to August 1637*, ed. D. Laing, Wodrow Society, 4 (1842) • Anderson, *Scot. nat.* • *Fasti Scot.*, new edn, vols. 1–2 • 'Johnston, Arthur', *DNB* • *Scots peerage*, vol. 8 • C. B. B. Watson, ed., *Roll of Edinburgh burgesses and guild-brethren, 1406–1700*, Scottish RS, 59 (1929) • M. Wood, ed., *Extracts from the records of the burgh of Edinburgh, 1604–1626*, [7] (1931) • *STC, 1475–1640* • Wing, *STC*

Ramsay, Sir Andrew, of Abbotshall and Waughton, first baronet, Lord Abbotshall (1620?–1688), provost of Edinburgh, was the third and eldest son of Andrew *Ramsay (1574–1659), professor of divinity in the University of Edinburgh and minister of Greyfriars Church, and his wife, Marie Fraser. Bred a merchant, he was admitted a burgess of Edinburgh on 10 August 1642 and a baillie in 1652. He bought the estate of Abbotshall, Fife, from the Scotts of Balwearie, and acquired the estate of Waughton, Haddingtonshire, by marriage to the heir of the Hepburns, whose name is unknown. He assented to the tender of union from the English parliament at Dalkeith in 1652. During Oliver Cromwell's government he was lord provost of Edinburgh from 1654 to 1657 and in 1655 was knighted by Cromwell. He was a member of the second protectorate parliament in 1656, and in 1658 went to London in an attempt to obtain from the protector some relief for the town's burdens.

At the Restoration Ramsay gained the friendship of John Maitland, second earl of Lauderdale, newly appointed secretary of state for Scotland, by prevailing on the city to give £5000 sterling to the government for the superiority of Leith, and another £5000 sterling for the new imposition granted to the town by the king on wine and ale. By ingratiating himself with Lauderdale he secured the favour of the new administration and was again knighted, by Charles II on 17 July 1660. Under Lauderdale's auspices he was again elected lord provost of Edinburgh in 1662 and he kept the chair for twelve successive years, defeating by complicated artifice or open violence any attempt of the council to remove him. He was elected to represent Edinburgh in the convention of estates in 1665 and 1667 and in the parliament from 1669 to 1674. In 1669 he was selected as one of the lords of the articles, and in 1670 he was appointed to the committee for considering union with England. In 1669 he was created a baronet. He was sworn of the privy council in 1671, and was admitted an ordinary lord of session on 23 November 1671, despite having no legal experience. According to Sir George Mackenzie his promotion, with that of three others who like him 'had not been bred lawyers', rendered the court of session 'the object of all men's contempt' (Mackenzie, 240). In recognition of Ramsay's services to the government, Lauderdale prevailed on the king to settle on the provost of Edinburgh £200 a year. In 1667 Ramsay procured from the king a letter ordaining that he as provost should have the same place and precedence as was due to the mayors of London and Dublin, and that no other provost could be called lord provost but he. Following a dispute with the university, at Ramsay's insistence, on 10 November 1667 the town council resolved that the lord provost should also hold the office of rector and governor of the college. By his corrupt and often tyrannical conduct as lord provost, Ramsay lost the support of many of the citizens of the city.

Through his influence in the town council, his presidency of the conventions of royal burghs, and the leading vote among the burghs in parliament, Ramsay was extremely useful to Lauderdale, so much so that the party opposed to Lauderdale resolved to remove him from his office. A motion to supersede him in March 1672 was lost by only two votes. In 1673 articles of impeachment were given in against him by the earl of Eglinton, which alleged that Ramsay had obtained a letter from the king to 'thrust Mr Rochead out of his employment as town clerk of Edinburgh without a formal and legal sentence' (Mackenzie, 262). Lauderdale, fearing recriminations due to his involvement in the ousting of Rochead, prevailed on Ramsay to resign the offices both of provost and of lord of session. In 1685 he was named a commissioner of trade. He died at his house at Abbotshall, Fife, on 17 January 1688. His son Andrew succeeded him in the baronetcy and estates.

GILLIAN H. MACINTOSH

Sources G. Mackenzie, *Memoirs of the affairs of Scotland* (1821) • G. Brunton and D. Haig, *An historical account of the senators of the college of justice, from its institution in MDXXXII* (1832) • *APS, 1661–9* • J. Nicoll, *A diary of public transactions and other occurrences, chiefly in Scotland, from January 1650 to June 1667*, ed. D. Laing, Bannatyne Club, 52 (1836) • M. Wood and T. B. Whitson, *The lord provosts of Edinburgh, 1296 to 1932* (1932) • C. S. Terry, ed., *The Cromwellian union: papers relating to the negotiations for an incorporating union between England and Scotland, 1651–1652*, Scottish History Society (1902) • Burke, *Gen. GB*

Archives BL, letters to duke of Lauderdale and Charles II, Add. MSS 23114–23135, 23243–23247 • Buckminster Park, Grantham, corresp. with duke of Lauderdale · NL Scot., letters to duke of Lauderdale · U. Edin. L., letters to duke of Lauderdale

Ramsay, Sir Andrew Crombie (1814–1891), geologist, was born on 31 January 1814 in Glasgow, third of the four children of William Ramsay and his wife, Elizabeth, *née* Crombie. His father was a manufacturing chemist and businessman associated with the dyeing industry, noted for his integrity and his scientific abilities; his mother is said to have been a woman of strong but gentle character. Ramsay was not a particularly healthy child, and he was sent to school at Saltcoats on the Ayrshire coast and then in Glasgow. However, his education was cut short by his father's death in 1827. Insufficient provision had been made for the family and his mother was forced to take in boarders, and Ramsay himself had to start work in a counting house.

Ramsay held a number of positions in business during a period of over ten years, not enjoying any of them. A venture in the cloth trade proved unsuccessful; but he began to develop an interest in science and literature, and met Lyon Playfair, who boarded in Ramsay's household. His scientific studies were encouraged by John Nichol (1804–1859) of Glasgow University, and he became interested in geology.

Ramsay developed a particular interest in the geology of Arran, and spent a number of vacations on the island. In 1839 a committee was established to prepare for the British Association's meeting in Glasgow in 1840, and Ramsay compiled a geological map, and geological model, of Arran. Nichol arranged for him to lecture to the association's geological section, and to conduct a field excursion to the island. The hope that this might bring Ramsay to the attention of the leaders of the geological community was dashed when Ramsay overslept and the geologists departed to Arran without him! However, Nichol came to the rescue and Ramsay's work was published the following year as *The Geology of the Island of Arran*.

Despite the Arran fiasco, Ramsay's abilities had been noticed by Roderick Murchison, who invited him as travelling companion on a visit to America. By the time Ramsay arrived in London to take up this offer, Murchison's plans had changed, but he induced the geological survey's director, Henry De la Beche, to offer Ramsay a position as assistant geologist; and he started work in Pembrokeshire in April 1841. He was highly successful in this new occupation and he was promoted to local director between 1844 and 1845; in 1848 he also became geology professor at University College, London. With the establishment of the Royal School of Mines at Kensington in 1851, Ramsay resigned from University College to take up the new chair of geology. He held his two appointments concurrently until 1872, when he succeeded Murchison as director general of the survey. This position Ramsay held until his retirement in 1881.

Ramsay's most important fieldwork was undertaken in Wales in the years 1848–51. There the surveyors' systematic work provided empirical information that eventually helped close the bitter controversy between Murchison

Sir Andrew Crombie Ramsay (1814–1891), by David Hains

and the Cambridge professor, Adam Sedgwick, concerning the Cambrian–Silurian boundary. Besides having responsibility for the mapwork, Ramsay was responsible for the geological sections of Wales. They had considerable aesthetic appeal as well as scientific significance. Yet Ramsay proposed a rather bizarre geological hypothesis, that certain major igneous masses near Bangor were responsible for metamorphosing not only the adjacent mainland rocks, but those of Anglesey too. So the island's gnarled rocks were construed by Ramsay as metamorphosed Cambrian, not Precambrian. This was in keeping with a view held for some years within the survey that Precambrian rocks were found in Britain only in the gneisses of north-west Scotland. In addition to the geological maps and sections of Wales, Ramsay produced a major survey memoir: *The Geology of North Wales* (1866; 2nd edn, 1881).

During his work in Anglesey, Ramsay stayed for a few days in 1850 at the home of James Williams, rector of Llanfair-yng-Nghornwy, whose daughter Louisa he married on 20 July 1852. They took their honeymoon in Europe, enabling Ramsay to see glaciers and glacial phenomena at first hand, as well as the contorted alpine rocks. He had previously been interested in geomorphology, especially with regard to the erosive powers of rivers and the development of river systems, on which topic he had published an important memoir (*On the Denudation of South Wales and the Adjacent Counties of England*) in 1846. Now, with his new alpine experiences, he developed a keen interest in glacial phenomena, and became one of the field's leading authorities.

Lakes had long troubled proponents of the origin of valleys by river action; and although the glacial theory of Louis Agassiz (which had been presented to the British Association in Glasgow in 1840) accounted for many surface phenomena observable in northern lands, the origin of lakes was still problematic. Could glaciers 'scoop' the hollows now occupied by lakes? In 1862 Ramsay presented his view to the Geological Society that glaciers could indeed hollow out lake-basins, without requiring earth movements to produce areas of weakness. His paper was controversial and led to numerous discussions over several decades. Ramsay's view eventually prevailed, though it is thought that earth movements may indeed play a part in basin formation. Ramsay also proposed (in 1854) that glacial conditions had existed in the Permian era, as well as in the geologically recent Pleistocene; and subsequently he contemplated other Palaeozoic glaciations. Initially, these ideas were coolly received, but in the light of the astronomical theory of James Croll, the hypothesis gathered strength, though it was not fully accepted in Ramsay's lifetime.

Following De la Beche's death in 1855, Ramsay might have hoped to assume the survey directorship, but the position went to Murchison, and it was only on his demise in 1872 that Ramsay succeeded to the leadership. Already in somewhat failing health, he was unable to achieve as much as director-general as he and his colleagues might have expected, and the affairs of the survey languished somewhat under Ramsay's leadership. He had had a serious breakdown in health in 1860, from which he only partly recovered. In 1878 his left eye was surgically removed following a severe infection. With such afflictions, he found that his administrative duties weighed upon him, and it was only with a struggle that he finished the second edition of his Welsh memoir.

In 1863 Ramsay published his *Physical Geology and Geography of Great Britain*, which reached its fifth edition in 1878. This book originated in six lectures for working men given at the School of Mines Museum, but it was developed and enlarged to become one of the standard nineteenth-century geological texts. By all accounts, Ramsay was an excellent lecturer, though he had to receive assistance in his lecturing work in his declining years.

As president of the Geological Society in 1863–4 Ramsay gave influential addresses on the problem of breaks in the stratigraphic record, arguing in terms of Charles Lyell's theory that such breaks might be attributed to the occurrence of continental conditions, for the existence of which Ramsay offered empirical evidence. For his presidential address to the British Association in 1880 he lectured 'On the recurrence of certain phenomena in geological time', which involved a wide survey of geological theory, seen through the lens of his uniformitarian beliefs. Ramsay claimed, for example, that metamorphism could occur at any geological epoch—contrary to a view held on the continent that certain rock types were associated with particular geological epochs.

Ramsay was elected a fellow of the Geological Society in 1844, and received its Wollaston medal in 1871. He was elected a fellow of the Royal Society in 1862 and received a royal medal in 1880. He received the Royal Society of Edinburgh's Neill prize in 1866. He was awarded an LLD by the University of Edinburgh in the same year, and by Glasgow University in 1880. He presided over the geological section of the British Association in 1856, 1866, and 1881, and was association president in 1880. Ramsay received the Italian award of the Cross of St Maurice and St Lazare in 1862, and was knighted shortly before his retirement in 1881.

Ramsay was a considerable traveller, visiting the continent several times, and North America in 1857. He was an active climber, admirable lecturer, lucid writer, and jovial raconteur. He was a devout Christian, but readily accepted the ideas of Darwin and Lyell. However, while an outstanding field geologist, Ramsay was somewhat unsympathetic towards laboratory studies and is recorded as saying that he didn't believe in looking at a mountain with a microscope. Sir Andrew and Lady Ramsay retired to Beaumaris in Anglesey but the geologist's old age was dogged by ill health. He died at his home in Beaumaris, 7 Victoria Terrace, on 9 December 1891, survived by his wife, four daughters, and a son; he was buried at Llansadwrn.

DAVID OLDROYD

Sources A. Geikie, *Memoir of Sir Andrew Crombie Ramsay* (1895) • J. Young, 'Memoir of the late Sir Andrew Ramsay, FRS, formerly director-general of the geological survey of Great Britain, and Ireland, and honorary member of the Philosophical Society', *Proceedings of the Philosophical Society of Glasgow*, 23 (1891–2), 281–90 • J. Young, 'The late Sir A. C. Ramsay, FGS, director-general of the geological survey of Great Britain', *Transactions of the Geological Society of Glasgow*, 9 (1893), 256–63 • J. Geikie, 'The late Sir Andrew Crombie Ramsay, LL.D., F.R.S.', *Transactions of the Edinburgh Geological Society*, 6 (1892), 233–40 [with photograph] • 'Andrew Crombie Ramsay', in E. Edwards, *Portraits of men of eminence in literature, science, and art, with biographic memoirs*, 5, ed. E. Walford (1866), 74–80 • A. Geikie, presidential address, *Quarterly Journal of the Geological Society*, 48 (1892), 14–23 • 'Eminent living geologists. Sir Andrew C. Ramsay', *Geological Magazine*, new ser., 2nd decade, 9 (1882), 289–93 • J. Pingree, 'Sir Andrew Crombie Ramsay, 1814–1891: list of papers', 1986, ICL, archives • *CGPLA Eng. & Wales* (1892)

Archives BGS, corresp. and papers • ICL, corresp., diaries, and papers • NL Wales, corresp. • U. Edin. L., corresp. | BGS, letters to William Aveline; letters to Trenham Reeks • Elgin Museum, letters to George Gordon • NMG Wales, letters to Sir Henry de la Ware • U. Edin. L., corresp. with Sir Charles Lyell

Likenesses W. Davis, bust, exh. RA 1864, GS Lond. • E. Edwards, photograph, repro. in E. Walford, ed., *Portraits of men of eminence*, 5 (1866) • D. Hains, photograph, NPG [*see illus.*] • bust, GS Lond. • caricature, ICL; repro. in Pingree, 'Sir Andrew Crombie Ramsay', frontispiece • engraving (after D. Hains), repro. in 'Eminent living geologists …', *Geological Magazine*, following p. 289 • photographs, BGS • portrait, repro. in Young, 'Memoir of the late Sir Andrew Ramsay …', following p. 281

Wealth at death £6919 6s. 3d.: probate, 23 Feb 1892, *CGPLA Eng. & Wales*

Ramsay, Andrew Michael [Jacobite Sir Andrew Ramsay, baronet] (1686–1743), philosopher and Jacobite sympathizer, was born in Ayr in 1686, probably on 29 May, the son of Andrew Ramsay (c.1660–c.1740) and his wife, Susanna. His father, a baker and burgess of the town of Ayr, was a staunch Calvinist; his mother was an Anglican. Ramsay was educated at the grammar school in Ayr and later described himself as having shown an early interest in study and the sciences. From the age of fifteen he was so taken with mathematics that he would spend twelve hours a day, without eating or drinking, in learning the calculus. With his mother's encouragement, he soon rejected the 'Dogme affreux de la predestination' (Bibliothèque Méjanes, MS 1188, p. 4). On his deathbed he recalled that his deep sense of piety at this time manifested itself in hours spent at prayer in a ruined Roman Catholic church. He entered Edinburgh University, perhaps with the intention of studying for the Episcopalian ministry, and seems also to have attended lectures in theology at Glasgow University. At the age of nineteen he encountered at Edinburgh a sceptical Episcopalian doctor who taught him the virtues of toleration and encouraged him to be critical of established religion. He abandoned his plans for a career in the Scottish Episcopal church and was at first drawn to deism, eventually discovering an interest in the mysticism of Madame Bourignon and, later, of Madame Guyon. Ramsay did not undertake this spiritual journey alone. He conversed and corresponded throughout this period with George Cheyne, James Cunningham, George and James Garden, Robert Keith, Lord Deskford of Cullen, and Lord Forbes of Pitsligo. This circle of friends, with whom Ramsay remained in contact for many years, constituted a distinct group of educated followers of mystical theology, several of them based in the north-east of Scotland, whose leanings were towards nonjuring and even Jacobitism.

Ramsay's first employment came from another Scottish follower of Madame Bourignon, Sir Thomas Hope of Craighall, but he soon moved to the service of the earl of Wemyss as tutor to his two children. This took Ramsay to London towards the end of 1708 and drew him closer to the world of the Jacobite nobility. Under the influence of James Keith, Ramsay took an interest in the Philadelphian movement and corresponded extensively with his Scottish friends about the activities of the French Prophets, both in London and Edinburgh. Ramsay was introduced to the Prophets by Nicolas Fatio de Duillier, who taught him mathematics for a time. He decided, however, to quit London and travel to the Netherlands in spring 1710. Encouraged by Scottish friends who were already in residence there, Ramsay settled briefly at Rijnsburg, the village between Leiden and The Hague which was the home of Madame Bourignon's disciple Pierre Poiret. At Leiden Ramsay attended some of Boerhaave's lectures, but he soon accepted Poiret's advice that he should travel to Cambrai to study with Archbishop Fénelon. Like Madame Bourignon or Madame Guyon, Fénelon preached the doctrine of disinterested love, but, unlike them, he encouraged his protestant pupils to convert to Catholicism. Ramsay arrived at Cambrai in August 1710 and embarked on six months of spiritual debate and confession, during the course of which he was received by Fénelon into the Catholic church.

Some time before Fénelon's death in 1715, Ramsay had moved with his encouragement to Blois, where he served as secretary to Madame Guyon herself, in particular maintaining a correspondence with her Scottish disciples.

Towards the end of 1716, however, he had moved to Paris, where he served as governor to the son of the comte de Sassenage, and began to become acquainted with the Jacobite court in exile and with the Benedictines of Scots College. He was devastated by the death of Madame Guyon, which he reported to his friends in Scotland. Ramsay's *Life of Fénelon*, which was published in French and in an English translation by Nathaniel Hooke in 1723, contained an extensive account of Madame Guyon as well as the story of his own conversion, and was in part a response to Poiret's edition of her autobiography (1720). By this time Ramsay had already published a discourse on epic poetry, extolling Fénelon's composition *Télémaque*, which was printed with a new edition of that poem in 1717, as well as an *Essay philosophique sur le gouvernement civil* (1721), according to Fénelon's principles, which was rapidly translated into English and appeared in editions at both London and Edinburgh in 1722. In the *Essay* Ramsay praised the virtues of monarchy, condemned rebellion, and argued that the proper practice of love for one's neighbour and one's self would overcome the danger of political revolution, which was caused by an excessive love of power on the part of rulers or of independence on the part of their subjects.

Ramsay's service with the comte de Sassenage terminated in September 1722. His friends arranged a pension for him from the abbey of Signy and his appointment as a chevalier of the ordre de Saint-Lazare on 20 May 1723. Through his acquaintance with the duke of Mar and with Lord Lansdowne, Ramsay was eventually able to find permanent employment with the Jacobite court. He was called to become tutor to the young prince, Charles Edward, in December 1723 and travelled to Rome in that capacity early in 1724. However, disunity and political intrigue in the Jacobite court at Rome soon led Ramsay to seek permission to return to Paris. The Old Pretender at this time described him as 'an odd body … yet I will be charitable enough to think him a madd man' (Henderson, *Chevalier Ramsay*, 106–7), and he did not rejoin the royal household. Instead Ramsay forged a literary career, in particular through the publication of *Les voyages de Cyrus* (1727), dedicated to his new patron, the duc de Sully, which was again translated into English by Hooke. In both its French and English editions Ramsay's *Cyrus* was a sensation. Deeply indebted to Fénelon's example, it told the story of Cyrus's adventures among the magi and the Greeks, drawing heavily on the tradition of a pristine ancient wisdom akin to Christianity, and arguing for the existence of three states of humanity: the innocent, the fallen, and the restored. It attacked the ideas of Spinoza and upheld the existence of a subtle fluid, through whose actions God produces physical effects. It also hinted at a doctrine of metempsychosis. In its pages Ramsay attempted to reconcile the philosophy of Descartes with that of Newton in a mystical Christian context.

In the wake of his success and at the request of English Catholics, Ramsay undertook a journey to London in 1729. In December he was elected a fellow of the Royal Society; he was also chosen as a member of the Spalding Gentlemen's Society, and on 10 April 1730 received the degree of DCL from Oxford University, where William King promoted his cause. He was, however, disappointed in his hope of meeting Jonathan Swift, whose writings had 'prepared [him] for relishing those principles of universal religion' (Ramsay to Swift, BL, Add. MS 4805, fols. 188–9). On his return to France Ramsay entered the service of the family of de Bouillon as a tutor, and moved to live first at Andresy and then at Pontoise. He was created a baronet in the Jacobite peerage on 23 March 1735. Although he was disappointed in his desire to become a member of the Académie he continued to publish widely. The most substantial of his works, the *Histoire du vicomte de Turenne*, which was based on extensive documentation that Ramsay printed, appeared in 1735, and celebrated the career of one of the heroes of the family that employed him. Its translation into English led to the falling out of Ramsay and Hooke.

In common with several of his Catholic Jacobite friends Ramsay became a leading figure in French freemasonry, as a member of the Lodge St Thomas. In 1737 he delivered *A Discourse Pronounced at the Reception of Freemasons*, which stressed the order's desire to unify humanity through the love of virtue, and argued that freemasonry had originated during the crusades. In June 1735 Ramsay married Marie (1701–*c*.1761), daughter of Sir David Nairne and his wife, Marie-Elizabeth de Compigny. Ramsay and his wife had a son, who died in infancy, and a daughter. In his last years he moved to St Germain-en-Laye, where he was nursed by his wife. He died there on 6 May 1743 NS and was buried the following day in the parish church; his heart was entombed at the convent of the Sisters of the Holy Sacrament, rue Casette, in Paris. On his deathbed Ramsay dictated 'Anecdotes' of his life, but he left unpublished his great work, *The Philosophical Principles of Natural and Revealed Religion*. His widow succeeded in placing the book with the Foulis brothers in Glasgow and it eventually appeared in two volumes in 1748–9. It reiterated many of the arguments of Ramsay's *Cyrus*, but made more explicit his attempt to reconcile Newtonian ideas to his own philosophy. SCOTT MANDELBROTE

Sources DNB · G. D. Henderson, *Chevalier Ramsay* (1952) · D. P. Walker, '"Mon cher Zoroastre" or the Chevalier Ramsay', *The ancient theology* (1972), 231–63 · Bibliothèque Méjanes, Aix-en-Provence, France, MS 1188 · G. D. Henderson, ed., *Mystics of the north-east* (1934) · NL Scot., MS Acc. 4796/104 · U. Edin. L., MS La. II 301/1–4 · BL, Add. MSS 4805–4806 · A. Cherel, *Un aventurier religieux au XVIIIe siècle* (1926)
Archives Bibliothèque Méjanes, Aix-en-Provence, MS 1188 · NL Scot., corresp. · U. Edin., MS La. II 301/1–4 | NL Scot., Fettercairn papers · Royal Arch., Stuart papers
Likenesses R. Carriera, portrait

Ramsay, Archibald Henry Maule (1894–1955), politician and wartime detainee, was born in India on 4 May 1894, the only son (and the eldest of three children) of Lieutenant-Colonel Henry Lushington Ramsay (1854–1928) of the Indian political department and his wife, Sophia (d. 1946), daughter of J. P. Thomas of Warneford Place, Wiltshire, and Calcutta. His paternal grandfather

was General the Hon. Sir Henry Ramsay, brother of the twelfth earl of Dalhousie.

Archibald (known to his friends as Jock) Ramsay was educated at Eton College and Sandhurst. In 1913 he joined the Coldstream Guards, and in 1914 was posted to France. Promoted captain in 1915, he was severely wounded in 1916, spending the rest of the war attached to the War Office. In 1919 he was invalided out of the army.

On 13 April 1917 he married the Hon. Ismay Lucretia Mary Crichton-Stuart (*née* Preston; 1882–1975), daughter of Jenico William Joseph Preston, the fourteenth Viscount Gormanston, and widow of Lord Ninian Crichton-Stuart MP (second son of the third marquess of Bute), who had been killed in action in 1915. After the war they settled down at Kellie Castle, near Arbroath, Forfarshire. In London they lived first at 7 Eaton Gate and then, from the late 1930s, at 24 Onslow Square. Four sons were born to them between 1918 and 1926.

Captain Ramsay became Unionist MP for Peebles and the southern division of Midlothian in 1931. At first his interventions were mainly about farming and constituency concerns. From 1937 onwards his political interests became more international. He spoke out in the House of Commons and elsewhere about the Spanish Civil War, which he saw as a crusade against an atheistic communist insurrection. He had become convinced 'that the Russian and Spanish revolutions, and the subversive societies in Britain, were part of the same Plan, secretly operated and controlled by World Jewry, exactly on the lines laid down in the Protocols of the Elders of Zion' (Ramsay, 95). In late 1938 he became a member of the Council of the Nordic League, an 'association of race-conscious Britons' (PRO, HO 144/21379/270–93). By now he was speaking publicly against the Jewish fomentation of war between Britain and Germany. This caused considerable concern in his Peebles constituency; but his local party gave him a resounding vote of confidence.

In May 1939 he formed a secret society, the Right Club, whose aim was to avert a war fomented by Jewish intrigue. It contained a number of MPs, peers, and other prominent members of society, alongside known extremists. At the outbreak of the Second World War most of the 'respectable' members of the club rallied to their country's cause, leaving an extremist rump to continue activities.

Ramsay was convinced that by proclaiming that the British had been misled into fighting a 'Jews' war', he was behaving as a true patriot. In the first nine months of the war he attended clandestine meetings with other leaders of subversive movements, including Sir Oswald Mosley and Admiral Sir Barry Domvile. The rump of the Right Club continued its anti-war and anti-Jewish propaganda, mainly by distributing subversive leaflets and pamphlets. Early in 1940, through his Right Club associate Anna Wolkoff, Ramsay became involved with Tyler Kent, a cipher clerk at the American embassy who smuggled out a number of confidential documents, including the correspondence between Roosevelt and Churchill. A 'sting' by MI5 in May revealed Wolkoff's contacts with the axis. Wolkoff and Kent were arrested, and a round-up of members of extremist movements took place under defence regulation 18B. Ramsay was detained on 23 May 1940 and sent to Brixton prison.

Ramsay continually protested his innocence, and when in July 1941 the *New York Times* produced an article alleging treason against him, he instituted a libel suit. Though the judgment was in his favour, the judge (Mr Justice Atkinson) awarded a farthing (without costs), declaring that 'Captain Ramsay was disloyal in heart and soul to his King, his Government, and the people' (*The Times*, 1 Aug 1941).

Ramsay (who had continued to present written parliamentary questions from prison) was released on 26 September 1944, and immediately went down to the House of Commons to resume his seat. In May 1945 he placed on the order paper a motion asking for the reinstatement of Edward I's Statute of Jewry. He was deselected from his seat for the general election of 1945. In 1952 he produced an apologia, *The Nameless War*, which traced the influence of the Jews through the ages, culminating in the injustice of his own treatment. He died at 46 Kensington Place, Kensington, London, on 11 March 1955.

Ramsay's main political achievement was to become, in 1936, parliamentary representative on the Potato Marketing Board. He was popular with his constituents and his fellow MPs, one of whom, the Liberal National whip, Sir (John) Henry Morris-Jones, after the war described him as 'a likeable character' whose 'sincerity, earnestness and depth of belief were unquestionable' (*Doctor in the Whips' Room*, 1955, 115). As with so many subscribers to the theory of the 'Judaeo-Bolshevik plot', however, his depth of belief led him into murky waters.

RICHARD GRIFFITHS

Sources R. Griffiths, *Patriotism perverted: Captain Ramsay, the Right Club and British anti-Semitism* (1998) · A. W. Brian Simpson, *In the highest degree odious: detention without trial in wartime Britain* (1992) · R. Bearse and A. Read, *Conspirator: the untold history of Churchill, Roosevelt and Tyler Kent* (1991) · A. H. M. Ramsay, *The nameless war* [1952] · diaries of Admiral Sir Barry Domvile, NMM · home office files, PRO · *Hansard* · membership list of the Right Club, Wiener Library · *The Times* (12 March 1955) · *Debrett's Peerage* · m. cert. · d. cert.

Likenesses two photographs, repro. in Griffiths, *Patriotism perverted*, following p. 116

Sir Bertram Home Ramsay (1883–1945), by Walter Stoneman, 1944

Ramsay, Sir Bertram Home (1883–1945), naval officer, was born at Hampton Court Palace on 20 January 1883, the third son of Captain William Alexander Ramsay and his wife, Susan, daughter of William Minchiner, of Clontarf, co. Dublin. He was born into an old established but long removed family from the highlands of Scotland, the Ramsays of Balmain. The Ramsays were also a service family and young Bertie lived the life of an officer's son, at one stage coming into contact with a young subaltern named Winston Churchill when the latter served under his father's command. Ramsay spent some time at Colchester grammar school, where he was remembered as a quiet but intense boy with, despite his relatively small stature, a natural talent for sports—riding, shooting, and running. Ramsay's older brothers followed the long family tradition by entering the army, but he followed a different path. It had become something of a tradition for youngest sons of larger families with some social position to enter the navy. An important reason for this was that the fees the navy charged for entry through the cadet ship *Britannia* were far lower than those demanded by the public schools. Two years after his parents were posted to India Ramsay entered the Royal Naval College, Dartmouth, in January 1898.

Early career Ramsay passed out in May 1899 and received his commission in September. A fairly typical career for a junior officer then ensued, marked by a taste of active service in the Somaliland expedition of 1903–4. There Ramsay earned a mention in dispatches for his work in a sphere where he was destined to make his mark: combined operations with the army. This brought him promotion to lieutenant and varied appointments over the next five years, including service in the first commission of the *Dreadnought*. The first promise of potential for great things came indirectly from Ramsay's decision to specialize as a signals officer, with a posting to the Royal Naval Signal School in Portsmouth for two years in 1909. One reason for this decision was an urge to defy the convention that gunnery was the road to flag rank; he cited a dislike of getting dirty hands as another! But the main reason was that Ramsay was more interested in moving fleets than ships, in grappling with bigger and broader naval problems. Signals training and sea duty brought him into contact with those parts of the navy dealing directly with new technology and the impact it would have on naval warfare.

The creation of a naval war staff in 1912 at last gave the service an arm devoted solely to preparing officers to identify, study, and cope with all manner of challenges the navy might face. It also began to promote modern methods of organization and command, reducing the emphasis on one commander running a fleet by himself in favour of sharing that load with a staff trained to manage and administer a large organization. This was a long difficult process destined to absorb the energies of a generation of naval officers. There was much resistance to the idea that the navy's acquired wisdom and time-honoured methods might no longer be enough to fight and win wars. But from the start it was clear where Ramsay stood.

Selected in 1913 for the second cohort of students at the Royal Naval War College, then at Portsmouth, Ramsay found the navy he was looking for. In some ways he personified its evolving blend, even as a junior officer just thirty years old. He was a stickler for observing customs and traditions which he felt contributed directly to efficiency and combat readiness: running a clean and well-organized ship, being well turned out in dress and deportment, looking aggressively to confront any challenges. But Ramsay's instincts and preferences led him to welcome the new emphasis on formal training, rather than reliance on the martial instincts of a supposedly superior social class to meet the challenge of war. He chafed at any method or procedure that was being followed only because it always had been. Passing out as a 'war staff officer' in spring 1914, promoted to the new rank of lieutenant-commander, Ramsay returned to the Dreadnought as one of the new breed of naval officers determined to bring modern methods to bear in order to wean the Royal Navy away from now outmoded practices. The challenge came very soon with the outbreak in August of the First World War, met by Ramsay on his war station at sea with the Grand Fleet.

Ramsay had mixed luck in his wartime service. Early in 1915 he turned down an offer to become flag lieutenant to commander cruisers, Grand Fleet, in the cruiser Defence, hoping to get his own command. After a short spell at the signal section of the Admiralty, he received his wish with the small monitor M.25 of the Dover patrol. Defence was blown up at Jutland. Ramsay had two collisions while serving in the Dover patrol, one of which earned him a reprimand from his commander, Vice-Admiral Roger Keyes, when Ramsay put Keyes's back up by bluntly rejecting any blame for the incident. But he lived through active and enterprising service which brought him command of the destroyer Broke, much experience of operations in the channel in collaboration with ground and air forces, and another mention in dispatches. At the war's end Ramsay was given the honour of transporting George V to France for a visit to the troops and made MVO for his own services.

In 1919 Lord Jellicoe selected Ramsay to be flag commander on his staff for an important tour of the dominions, to consider measures for future imperial defence. This exposure to the circles of power launched Ramsay on a post-war career path which, in the words of his biographer, 'might have been specially designed to fit him for the highest posts in the Navy' (Chalmers, 40). After two successive ship commands in the Mediterranean Ramsay was promoted captain in June 1923. This was followed by success in the senior officers' war and tactical courses, command of the cruiser Danae, then a spell as instructor at the War College. In 1929 Ramsay took command of the cruiser Kent as flag captain on the China station. He went from there to the Imperial Defence College in London in July 1931 to serve as the naval instructor on the staff; while there he struck up a lasting friendship with Alan Brooke which both later counted on in desperate times. In November 1933 Ramsay took command of the battleship Royal Sovereign, and in May 1935 he was promoted to flag rank.

Ramsay reached that exalted status after twenty-nine years of sea service and four staff postings, having had to endure only two shore billets despite his signals speciality. In large part this can be attributed to his early commitment to the war staff course and his strong support for the modernizing trends in the navy. With this blend of sea and staff experience he developed a broadness of vision on policy and strategy which reinforced his stature as a successful commander. Still only fifty-two, he had good reason to feel that the highest posts in the service were not out of reach.

Organizer *par excellence* Ramsay's character has been well described as 'a mass of well-controlled contradictions' (Stephen, 58). He loved the service and devoted himself to it, but also loved the life of a middle-class professional. Adding a passion for polo and the countryside to his earlier sporting pursuits, Ramsay worked hard to live up to his ideal image of the squire–sailor. When in London he dined in the right restaurants and clubs, patronized the theatre, and liked to mention being in the same places with famous and powerful people. But this was not empty socializing. Ramsay was ambitious—a meticulous organizer and systematic planner who never let himself drift along to no point or purpose. This is demonstrated by the story of his marriage. Reflecting contentedly on how well he was doing, he noted in his diary in 1925 that now all he needed was 'a charming wife and two good lieutenants'. An early romance in Australia on the Jellicoe tour had been cruelly cut short when the young woman died in the great influenza epidemic that swept the world in 1919. Home leave in 1925 led to an introduction to Helen Margaret, daughter of Colonel Charles T. Menzies. The Menzies came from the same border region of Scotland where Ramsay's own father had been raised. Helen was half his age, but shared his passion for life, horses, the countryside, and success. It took four years of determined courtship to win a proud and independent woman fully his equal in intelligence and ambition. They married in February 1929, by now devoted to each other. Two sons soon followed and Ramsay found in a happy and stable family an anchor in his life.

Not surprisingly, Ramsay was something of an authoritarian, typical for his time and social and professional milieu. Politically his views were certainly conservative but not unconventional. Professionally, he was seen to be a stickler, always commanding the respect but not always winning the affection of his subordinates. Ramsay was very intelligent indeed, with great confidence in his own ability. This sometimes led him to be brash and he was impatient with anything that seemed outmoded or inefficient. He was regarded as fair, but also often as difficult by both superiors and subordinates. Ramsay had immense powers of concentration, was a superb organizer, and was always able to master the detail without losing sight of the big picture. Living up to his own creed he was always willing to delegate and to listen to the ideas of others. The picture that emerges as he reaches flag rank is that of a well-rounded individual who lived life with zest, but was so determined to improve his service that he could be awkward when faced with something he felt hindered it. This trait very nearly ended his career.

Soon after reaching flag rank in 1935 Ramsay was invited by the incoming commander-in-chief, Home Fleet, Sir Roger Backhouse, to join him as his chief of staff. It was a prize posting and Backhouse was an old friend, their acquaintance stretching back nearly thirty years to when they were shipmates in the *Dreadnought*. Ramsay could not resist the opportunity, but took up his posting with well-founded apprehension. The problem was professional. He was a modernist who strongly believed the navy had to be run by delegation and decentralization; Backhouse was of the old school, equally convinced of the traditional, centralized method of command and determined to practise it. As Backhouse was also a workaholic with strong views on all matters great and small, and just as much pride and self-confidence as Ramsay, a clash was unavoidable. Ramsay joined his staff in August 1935. Within a few weeks, they were at loggerheads. Backhouse tried to do everything by himself, which left Ramsay frustrated and unimpressed by what he thought was outmoded practice. His attempts to act as a more responsible chief of staff were seen by Backhouse as efforts to run the fleet for him. In December Ramsay asked to be relieved and soon found himself idle and on half pay.

Their colleagues in the navy held both Backhouse and Ramsay responsible for this lamentable result—Backhouse because he clung to outmoded command methods, Ramsay because he quit in frustration rather than try to change the system one step at a time. To the credit of both men their friendship survived this failure, and Backhouse strongly endorsed Ramsay's fitness for future employment. But Ramsay rejected a command on the China station, one suspects out of lingering resentment that the Admiralty did not support his views against Backhouse. When he reached the top of the rear-admirals' list in October 1938 without having hoisted his flag at sea, the navy placed him on the retired list. Ramsay had in the end to go through almost four years of nearly total retirement and in the navy his career was generally considered over. This hurt him more than he allowed anyone but his family to realize, as was suggested by a lengthy paper he wrote to explain to them why he had resigned. But in the long run it turned out for the best.

Enforced idleness brought Ramsay closer to his wife and sons. They bought a property named Bughtrig in Berwickshire, and settled down to a happy life in the country. In the process there is no doubt that some of the rougher traits of his character faded considerably. In particular Ramsay seemed to become more patient with others, more aware of the need to get along with those he worked with and function effectively as a team player. In short it seems that in retirement Ramsay found the maturity which could make his great skill so much more effective. He also gained years of rest that would prove priceless in the coming trials. Those trials loomed even before he was officially retired, when the Munich crisis brought the country to the brink of war in September 1938. The Dover command was to be reactivated if war came but it had been dormant so long that a full investigation of what steps were to be taken was required. Backhouse, now first sea lord, nominated Ramsay to make the investigation, and to stand ready as potential flag officer, Dover. Ramsay's investigation revealed many deficiencies that needed to be made good and much progress was made in that direction before war finally did come in September 1939. He was the logical choice for an appointment which he took up, still officially retired, on 24 August—and in December he persuaded the Admiralty to make Dover an independent command, himself becoming vice-admiral, Dover.

The miracle of Dunkirk When the Germans attacked France and the Low Countries in May 1940 Dover immediately became a scene of much activity; when their breakthrough cut off the British expeditionary force, Ramsay was ordered to undertake the largest seaborne evacuation ever attempted. The stakes were the highest—without its trained soldiers the UK would be at the mercy of an invader. Ramsay had already anticipated the need and set to work with a will on 26 May. Over the next nine days he was directly responsible for the operation which successfully evacuated 338,266 allied soldiers—the 'miracle of Dunkirk'. His Dover command went from a small headquarters to the one with the largest staff of any flag officer ashore or afloat. As the man on the spot Ramsay commanded over 900 vessels of literally all types and sizes, from the fabled small boats to fleet destroyers. Luck played a part in his success. The weather co-operated, the German advance was for a time halted, the rearguards fought stubbornly. But equally important was Ramsay's own ability to rise to the challenge and inspire his team to do the same.

With no prior plans or preparations Ramsay and his staff had to improvise from the start, and then adjust to frequent changes in the situation and in policy. The original hope was to evacuate 45,000 troops in two days. Under Ramsay's command those targets were left behind. Indeed, this crisis showed just what Ramsay was made of. He selected the right people to handle the right jobs and left them to get on with it. He made bold decisions, such as using destroyers to lift troops directly off the harbour mole, which made the really big numbers possible. He was meticulous but flexible, organized but not rigid, drove his ships and men hard but knew when each had had enough. The heroism of many made the evacuation work, but the skill of Ramsay and his staff gave them the chance. Ramsay, seen as an orthodox admiral, brought off one of the navy's most unorthodox feats, earning the nation a fighting chance to survive and himself a well deserved KCB from George VI.

For the next two years Ramsay was occupied by the struggle to ward off German invasion and to dominate the channel, working closely again with the army and the air force. The mine barrier, coastal flotilla, coastal batteries and the air force made the channel a dangerous place for enemy submarines and surface vessels—and there was no invasion. On the other hand, Ramsay and the air force did fail to stop the 'channel dash', the embarrassing daylight run by German capital ships moving from danger in Brest to Germany in February 1942. Ramsay and nearly everyone else expected the enemy to run through the narrow Strait of Dover at night whereas they left Brest under cover of darkness and ran through at midday. This caught the available British forces off balance, but in any case those forces, naval and air, were woefully weak and not co-ordinated well enough to meet the challenge. None of this was Ramsay's fault, and he did not suffer from this one setback as a station commander. Indeed, very soon thereafter he took up the task that turned out to be his rendezvous with destiny—planning and preparing for the combined operations with the army and air force that would carry the war back to the enemy, culminating in the invasion of Europe.

Ramsay's experience in combined operations and his triumph at Dunkirk led to his appointment as flag officer, expeditionary force, in May 1942. As such he began to plan the invasion of Europe, working with the other services and with General Eisenhower, just arrived as commanding general, US army, in the European theatre of operations. Thus began a partnership and a mission that consumed almost all the rest of Ramsay's career. When allied grand strategy shifted the focus to an invasion of French north Africa in late 1942, Ramsay's task shifted accordingly. As a planner, Ramsay brought to bear his rare ability to master the detail but not lose the broad vision. This was invaluable in planning complicated amphibious invasions, which involved problems of movement, coordination, operations, and supply among three different services with different priorities, methods, and tasks. Equally necessary was the ability to issue clear instructions but delegate to others the job of executing them, and perhaps most important was the need to weld a team built from different services and different nations. Ramsay demonstrated all these qualities in abundance. He still fought his corner and drove his team hard, but now related much better to those with and for whom he worked. When it was decided that to reassure the Americans a more experienced and better known fleet commander must take charge, Ramsay was obliged to give way to

Admiral Sir Andrew Cunningham and become his stay-behind deputy, remaining in London. His work there and the success of the invasion and subsequent advance in north Africa redounded to Ramsay's credit, and he landed the job of eastern task force commander when it was decided in early 1943 to pursue the Mediterranean campaign by invading Sicily.

Ramsay's job was to plan and conduct the British portion of the invasion. In the process Ramsay scored one of the more remarkable naval triumphs of the war by winning both the friendship and the confidence of his army colleague, the notoriously difficult General Sir Bernard Montgomery. One of the very few commanders from any service able to work smoothly with the charismatic Monty, Ramsay achieved this by defending the navy's interests while being ready to meet the army's legitimate needs—plus a healthy dose of patience and diplomacy! He was in fact a master of combined operations, lauded by Montgomery as the only sailor who truly grasped the essential fact: the invasion was only the beginning, not the end, of the combined mission. This praise was well earned. Ramsay revelled in leading his fleet to sea in July 1943 and executing the invasion of Sicily, but the armies were barely ashore when such success brought him the ultimate challenge.

Masterminding invasion Ramsay returned to London that same month to rejoin the team preparing for the invasion of Europe. He gave an assessment of the problem of combined operations, written as a lecture, that was so masterful he was forbidden on security grounds to deliver it. In that text, Ramsay spelt out his concept:

> it must always be remembered that the guiding rule must be the operational plan first, and the administrative plan later, rather than the other way round. Once the Army have decided how they wish to fight the land battle it is necessary to examine how the troops can best be put ashore to give effect to the Army plan. In general it is the responsibility of the Navy to land the Army as they require, but as the plan develops Naval considerations will arise which must be discussed and agreed upon. (Ramsay MSS, file 8/22, CAC Cam.)

This spelt out the very essence of the problem now facing the allies: while effecting a landing against fierce German resistance was certainly going to be the most daunting amphibious invasion ever attempted, that would only begin the real struggle. From there the ground forces must be built up fast enough to repel a counter-attack, then made strong enough to drive back and finish off the German army in a continental campaign. The navy's role would merely change, not end, as the advance progressed. Ramsay was for many reasons the ideal choice for the appointment he received on 25 October 1943, allied naval commander, expeditionary force (ANCXF), followed the next day by promotion to the rank of acting admiral. His experience, character, and mastery of this most difficult operation of war had won him the confidence of his own boss, the army, the Americans, and above all the prime minister. Ramsay became the first service commander to start work on invasion preparations, taking responsibility for the assault plan code-named *NEPTUNE*.

Ramsay was joined in January 1944 by the rest of the command team that developed operation *OVERLORD*, finding himself working once again under Eisenhower as supreme commander and alongside Montgomery, who took command of Twenty-First Army group. If ever there was a right man in the right place at the right time, Ramsay was that man now. The task confronting the allies was to overcome the strongest coastal defences ever built, then mount a successful continental campaign. They had to master not just the defences but also the elements, their own differences between services, allies, and personalities, and debates over deployment of forces that dragged on long enough to make planning a nightmare. The naval commander had to draft the most complex assault plan ever conceived, marshal the largest armada ever assembled, work out sensible compromises with touchy peers and pull the whole gigantic task together in five months. Ramsay was certainly the only admiral in the Royal Navy who could have brought this off. Despite the enormous strain of the work, Ramsay inspired and directed an allied planning team which produced the most sophisticated staff work and operations plan in naval history. Ramsay kept Montgomery from sundering allied harmony, stood firm and won from Cunningham an allocation of forces the first sea lord considered excessive, demanded and received enough help from the US Navy to make the whole assault feasible, and submitted a plan that covered every contingency, including a full-scale action against the remainder of the German fleet. It assigned every vessel in the armada of over 3000 craft of all sizes specific orders on what to do and when to do it.

Ramsay's work earned him just rewards. In March 1944 Prime Minister Churchill compelled the Admiralty to reinstate Ramsay to the active list as a full admiral. It complied in lukewarm fashion, stating only that it was necessary to regularize his status as an allied commander in the forthcoming campaign. Did his 1935 complaints still rankle? If so, Ramsay won complete vindication in every respect with the success of the D-day invasion launched on 6 June. Four years after rescuing the army from the Germans, Ramsay sent it back to seek retribution. The success of the invasion, and the subsequent vital race to build the ground forces up so that they could consolidate that success, was compelling proof that Ramsay had been right: the modern navy needed more than fighting instructions and Nelsonian leadership. Ramsay's ability to help pull together an allied combined operation of vast complexity, sort out the essentials, and apply the plan effectively proved to be of far greater value to the nation, let alone the service, than relying on natural sailors preparing to fight another Jutland and win the war single-handedly.

As the campaign in north-west Europe progressed, Ramsay continued to play a vital role. When the allied armies advanced towards Germany in late August, he concentrated on keeping the supply lines flowing. Unlike Eisenhower and Montgomery, Ramsay kept his head in the euphoric days of early September and saw the greatest threat: if the enemy managed to block the channel to the massive port of Antwerp long enough, the allied armies would outrun their supply lines and grind to a halt. Unfortunately Ramsay's best efforts did not prevent the ground commanders from gambling that a quick strike could finish the enemy off. When it fell short, the naval forces were obliged to help clear the now heavily defended approaches to Antwerp along the River Scheldt, a job not completed until the end of November. This was the worst blunder Eisenhower's command team made in the campaign in north-west Europe; on that team, Ramsay stood out as the one senior commander who saw the danger and tried to head it off.

Death and reputation Neither this nor any other strains of such great responsibility impaired Ramsay's working relationships with his superiors, peers, and subordinates. All rightly regarded him as a tower of strength in the allied command. Privately, he felt the strain, securing leave when he could, writing incessantly to his wife, looking forward to the end of what he hoped was his last command. It was therefore with some reluctance that he agreed to a request from the first sea lord to take on the job of preparing to disarm the German navy when the enemy finally collapsed. That commission was a mark of the favour in which he now stood with his superiors. Unfortunately, fate kept him from ever completing it. The last enemy counter-offensive was in the end defeated, but at the time it seemed to threaten the supply line through Antwerp. Attentive as always to the focal point, Ramsay kept hard at work over the last week of 1944 lobbying his fellow commanders to stay on top of the problem. On 2 January 1945 he left his headquarters to attend a conference at Twenty-First Army group to discuss further operations. His aircraft crashed on take-off at Toussus-le-Noble, killing all on board. Ramsay was buried on 8 January at St Germain-en-Laye, mourned by a large number of allied political and military leaders led by Eisenhower and Cunningham.

Ramsay's reputation has soared as the war in which he fought so well becomes a distant memory. He became known before the war for his insistence that a modern navy must emphasize training over instincts, organization over reflexes, and be far better prepared to handle those campaigns in which it would co-operate with the other services and allies. The course of the war and his own service in it vindicated all those insights. Ramsay never led a fleet to victory in a conventional engagement for command of the sea, but the whole point of his career was that the navy now needed more than this. Friends and peers such as Alan Brooke and Montgomery knew at the time what most historians now accept, namely, that in the eyes of the army at least, Ramsay was the most successful fighting admiral in the Royal Navy in the Second World War.

BRIAN P. FARRELL

Sources CAC Cam., Ramsay MSS · W. S. Chalmers, *Full cycle: the biography of Admiral Sir Bertram Home Ramsay* (1959) · D. Woodward, *Ramsay at war: the fighting life of Admiral Sir Bertram Ramsay* (1959) · W. S. J. R. Gardner, 'Admiral Sir Bertram Ramsay', *Men of war: great naval leaders of World War II*, ed. S. Howarth (1992) · *The year of D-day: the 1944 diary of Admiral Sir Bertram Ramsay*, ed. R. W. Love and J. Major (1994) · C. Barnett, *Engage the enemy more closely: the Royal Navy in the Second World War* (1991) · S. W. Roskill, *The war at sea,*

1939–1945, 3 vols. in 4 (1954–61) • M. Stephen, *The fighting admirals: British admirals of the Second World War* (1991) • D. Divine, *The nine days of Dunkirk* (1959) • M. Simpson, ed., *The Somerville papers* (1995) • S. Roskill, *Churchill and the admirals* (1977) • S. W. Roskill, *Naval policy between the wars*, 2 vols. (1968–76) • *WWW*

Archives CAC Cam., corresp., diaries, reports | PRO, Admiralty MSS, incl. series ADM 1, ADM 116, ADM 196, ADM 199, ADM 205 | FILM BFI NFTVA, documentary footage • BFI NFTVA, news footage • IWM FVA, news footage | SOUND IWM SA, oral history interview

Likenesses W. Stoneman, photograph, 1944, NPG [*see illus.*] • O. Birley, oils, *c*.1945–1948, Royal Naval College, Greenwich • photographs, IWM • stained-glass windows, Portsmouth Cathedral

Wealth at death £17,228 17*s*. 7*d*.: confirmation, 4 May 1945, *CCI*

Ramsay, Charles Aloysius (*fl.* **1677–1680**), stenographer and translator, was descended from a younger branch of the noble Scottish family of Ramsay. He was thought to be related to Andrew Michael Ramsay and has been stated to be the son of Carl Ramsay (1617–1669), a municipal official of Elbing, Prussia, and author of travelogues and works on Polish and Russian history, which have been left in manuscript. Charles Aloysius Ramsay, who was living at Frankfurt in 1677 and at Paris in 1680, is identified in his own works as a 'Scottish gentleman'. A student of chemistry, medicine, and Latin, Ramsay became a wandering scholar and 'stenography's knight errant' ('*Stenografiens vandrande riddare*'; Melin, 1.344) on the European continent.

Ramsay's shorthand system is based on the popular *Tachy-Graphia* of Thomas Shelton. Ramsay may first have seen Shelton's system in its anonymous Latin translation (*Tachy-Graphia*, 1660) intended for a European market. Ramsay's adaptation of Shelton's system was disseminated on the continent in German (*Tacheographia, oder, Geschwinde Schreib-Kunst*, Frankfurt, 1678; translated presumably by Ramsay from a Latin original); in Latin (*Tacheographia*, Frankfurt, 1681); and in a French translation by the unidentified 'Sieur A. D. G.' (*Tachéographie, ou, L'art d'écrire aussi vite qu'on parle*, Paris, 1681, with accompanying Latin text). All had subsequent editions; claims that earlier editions existed, however, have not been verified. In its French translation Ramsay's system had great influence and was published at least four times between 1683 and 1693 (from 1690 with the title *Nouvelle méthode*). A copy of the 1690 *Nouvelle méthode* was in the library of Samuel Pepys, who himself used Shelton's shorthand (cf. *Catalogue of the Pepys Library at Magdalene College, Cambridge*, 1978, 1.119). In 1678 Ramsay translated into Latin as *Utiles observationes* (two parts, part 2 with the title *Observationes chymicae*) a German work by chemist and alchemist Johann Kunckel, dedicated to the Royal Society.

Ramsay's was not the first shorthand system published in Europe. The Abbé Jacques Cossard had published a French system in 1651, but few copies were printed and it had little circulation. Likewise, a German system has been attributed to Daniel Georg Morhof (1666). Shelton's system was known in Europe at this time and was discussed by Gaspard Schott in *Technica curiosa* (1664). A year after his German system was published, Ramsay was accused by Johann Christoph Mieth (*Die curiose Schreibe-Kunst*, 1679) of

plagiarizing Shelton's alphabet. Ramsay's German alphabet is indeed virtually identical to that of Shelton; two characters differ and two are dropped. His French alphabet, however, differs in eight characters, four being omitted. The differences among his German, Latin, and French alphabets suggest that Ramsay attempted to adapt his system to the linguistic requirements of each language and undermines the idea that he was a mere plagiarist. The question of plagiarism aside, the influence of the 'Ramsay literature' (M. Levy, *The History of Short-Hand Writing*, 1862, 58) was strong in Europe for a century after its first publication and was recognized in England. In 1736 Philip Gibbs remarked that the French 'have got a Short-hand Book, which was published a good while ago', citing the full title of Ramsay's *Tachéographie* though not giving his name (*An Historical Account of Compendious and Swift Writing*, 56).   PAGE LIFE

Sources J. W. Zeibig, 'Premiers pas à la sténographie en France', *Pantenographikon: Zeitschrift für Kunde der Stenographischen Systeme aller Nationen*, 1/3–4 (1874), 245–63 • O. F. Melin, *Stenographiens historia*, 2 vols. (1927–9) • C. G. Jöcher, *Allgemeines Gelehrten-Lexikon*, 3 (Leipzig, 1751); repr. (1961), 1894 • *Fortsetzung und Ergänzungen zu Christian Gottlieb Jöchers allgemeinem Gelehrten-Lexikon*, ed. J. C. Adelung, H. W. Rotermund, and O. Günther, 6 (Bremen, 1819); repr. (Hildesheim, 1961), col. 1314–15 • J. Michaud and L. G. Michaud, eds., *Biographie universelle ancienne et moderne*, new edn, 45 vols. (1860?), vol. 35, p. 158 • [J. C. F. Hoefer], ed., *Nouvelle biographie générale*, 41 (1862), col. 566 • J. W. Zeibig, 'Caroli Aloysii Ramsay *Tacheographia*', *Pantenographikon: Zeitschrift für Kunde der Stenographischen Systeme aller Nationen*, 1/3–4 (1874), 265–70 • H. Krieg, 'Carl Aloys Ramsay: Geschwindschreibkunst', *Pantenographikon: Zeitschrift für Kunde der Stenographischen Systeme aller Nationen*, 1/3–4 (1874), 271–8 • *DNB* • K. Brown and D. C. Haskell, *The shorthand collection in the New York Public Library* (1935); repr. (1971) • I. Pitman, *A history of shorthand*, 3rd edn (1891)

Ramsay [*née* Broun], **Christian**, countess of Dalhousie (**1786–1839**), hostess and botanical collector, was born on 28 February 1786, in the family seat of Coalstoun or Colstoun, near Lochmaben, Dumfriesshire, the only child and heir of Charles Broun. Her father was an advocate in Edinburgh, the son of Judge George Broun, Lord Coalstoun. On 14 May 1805 she married George *Ramsay (1770–1838), who became ninth earl of Dalhousie; they had three sons, the youngest of whom was James Andrew Broun *Ramsay, later the first marquess of Dalhousie. The two elder boys died as young men. At first she dedicated herself to furthering her husband's career. He succeeded to the earldom in 1815, and in 1816 was appointed lieutenant-governor of Nova Scotia.

While in Halifax Lady Dalhousie indefatigably promoted the foundation of educational institutions, particularly those concerned with science and agriculture, and collected unusual local plants. From 1817 she sent extensive collections of living plants and seeds back to Dalhousie Castle, near Edinburgh, to enrich the gardens. She also livened up tedious civic evenings by drawing caricatures of the Halifax élite, several of which are in the Dalhousie papers at the Nova Scotia Museum. In 1820 Dalhousie was appointed governor-in-chief of British North America and they moved to Quebec. They purchased an estate and leased another called Beauport, where she began arranging a botanical garden and farm. She was very active in organizing the foundation in 1824 of the Literary and Historical Society of Quebec and in 1827 she presented a paper on Canadian plants there. Her patronage extended widely, and the first work of fiction published by a native-born Canadian, Julia Catherine Beckwith's *St Ursula's Convent* (1824), was dedicated to her.

In 1824 the couple left Canada to return to Dalhousie Castle, making elaborate plans for extending the gardens. Joseph Archibald, their gardener, described these in the *Gardener's Magazine*, saying 'few … attained such proficiency as her ladyship in the science' (Archibald, 254). However, he also spoke of a 'reduction in the establishment'—in 1825 and 1826 they suffered great financial loss through the bankruptcy of their agent. For this reason they made an extended visit to Nova Scotia in 1826 to 1828. Dalhousie's political connections in England subsequently failed and they moved to India in July 1829 for him to take up a position as commander-in-chief of the British army there.

During the voyage out Lady Dalhousie collected plants on Madeira and St Helena and at the Cape of Good Hope. She worked hard collecting in India, including a new genus of tropical shrubs named *Dalhousiea* after her by Robert Graham. She corresponded with W. J. Hooker at Kew and presented an extensive collection of plants from Simla, and a smaller collection from Penang, made during a tour in Burma in 1831, to the Hooker family herbarium, which J. D. Hooker used in compiling his *Flora Indica*. She further presented a collection of Indian plants (some 1200 specimens) to the Botanical Society of Edinburgh, of which she was made an honorary member in 1837. She sent many interesting rhododendrons to the Dalhousie Gardens. Her husband's command in India lasted three years, after which they travelled on the continent until 1834, when they settled for good at Dalhousie. Lady Dalhousie soon became prominent in Edinburgh society. Edward Ramsay, dean of Edinburgh, who was unrelated, wrote that 'she was eminently distinguished for a fund of the most varied knowledge, for a clear and powerful judgement, for acute observation, a kind heart, a brilliant wit' (Ramsay, 257). She died suddenly in Dean Ramsay's house in Edinburgh on 22 January 1839, one year after her husband. The rhododendron known as Lady Dalhousie's rhododendron was named not after her, but after her daughter-in-law, Lady Susan. JANET BROWNE

Sources P. Burroughs, 'Ramsay, George', *DCB*, vol. 7 · J. Archibald, 'Dalhousie Castle and garden', *Gardener's Magazine*, 1 (1826), 251–8 · J. D. Hooker and T. Thomson, *Flora Indica*, 1 (1855) · M. Gunn and L. E. Codd, *Botanical exploration of southern Africa* (1981) · E. B. Ramsay, *Reminiscences of Scottish life and character*, [new edn] (1909) · Desmond, *Botanists*, rev. edn · Burke, *Peerage*
Archives NA Scot. · National Gallery of Canada, Ottawa · RBG Kew | Dalhousie University and Nova Scotia Museum, Halifax, Canada, Dalhousie MSS · Edinburgh Botanic Garden, herbarium
Likenesses portrait (Christian Ramsay?); copy, Royal Horticultural Society

Ramsay, David (*c*.1575–1660), clockmaker, was probably born in Fife, the second son of the three sons and two daughters of James Ramsay (*d.* 1580) and his wife, Elizabeth, eldest daughter of David Ramsay of Clatty. It appears that in the absence of his elder brother, George, David took possession of his brother's property in Lothian and court action was taken to evict him. He then went to France, where John Carnegie, writing to his brother from Paris on 10 January 1610, related how he had been through the palace and the town seeking clocks, which were both scarce and expensive; however, the king's clockmaker had promised to show him a very fine 'reveil-matin' clock, and Carnegie would take Ramsay's advice regarding its worth. Possible products of Ramsay's years in Paris are the very early watch by him, later housed in the Victoria and Albert Museum, with a small irregular octagonal case of gold and silver, with hinged covers, bearing engravings of the annunciation and nativity, and an oval gold watch in the French style, dated to between 1600 and 1610 and signed 'David Ramsay, scotus, me fecit', subsequently held in the British Museum. In later years he employed a French journeyman, Guillaume Petit. Some fourteen watches, all of fine quality and some with alarms or calendar dials, survive in various collections.

Writing long after the event, Ramsay's son, William, claimed that on the succession of James to the English crown in 1603:

> he sent into France for my father, who was then there, and made him page of the bedchamber and groom of the privy chamber, and keeper of all his majestie's clocks and watches. This I mention that by some he hath been termed no better than a watch maker. … It's confest his ingenuity led him to understand any piece of work in that nature … and therefore the king conferred that place upon him. (Ramesey, preface)

If correct, this would suggest that Ramsay returned to Paris. Certainly, however, David Ramsay made three watches for Henry, prince of Wales (*d.* 1612), between 1610 and 1612 (his bill of £61 was not paid until 1622), and the 'Book of ordinances made at the Establyshinge of Prince Henry … at Oatelands' named him as a groom of Henry's bedchamber (*Sixth Report*, HMC, 672b). In 1613 he was granted a pension of £200 per annum, and in the same year James I gave him a pension of £30. His 'clock watch with alarum', dating from about 1615, is remarkable for the smooth action of its hand-cut wheels and pinions. On 26 November 1618 he was appointed chief clockmaker to James, with fees and allowances. In July 1619 he was granted rights of residence in England.

Ramsay's interests in mechanics led him to apply for licences and patents for the manufacture and use of numerous inventions and engines: 'to plough without horses' in 1619; 'to make an engine invented by John Jack and David Ramsay, Page of the Bedchamber, to raise water', for draining land and mines; 'an engine to turn spits'; and others dealing with the manufacture of saltpetre and a scarlet dye. Ramsay's royal duties were evidently considerable. In 1616 he received £234 10s. for the supply and repair of clocks and watches for James I. In 1622 he received another payment of £232 15s. for repairing clocks at Theobalds, Oatlands, and Westminster, and for making a chime of bells at Theobalds.

No specific renewal of his appointment to Charles I has been found, but in January 1626 a warrant was issued to pay him £150 for coins to be given by the king on the day of his coronation. A large sum of money owing to him since the time of James I was paid in 1627—£441 3s. 4d. for work, plus £358 16s. 8d. 'in lieu of diet and bouche of court'—and in 1632 he received £219 for bills submitted during that year. At this time he was living variously in King Street and Cannon Row, running east from the parish church of St Margaret, Westminster. Ramsay's wife was English; her name is not recorded but their son William *Ramesey was born on 13 March 1627. William was schooled at St Albans, Bushy, Westminster, and other places. His father could not grant his request to go to St Andrews University so he attended Edinburgh, but had to leave that city because of the plague and from April 1645 he lived in London. By profession he was a physician and astrologer.

When Charles granted a charter of incorporation to the Clockmakers' Company he nominated Ramsay as its first master, an office he held for a year from October 1632. It seems, however, that he was mostly absent from town as a deputy was elected who presided at the court meetings during that time. An incident involving Ramsay was recounted by the astrologer William Lilly. Ramsay was told of treasure buried under the floor of Westminster Abbey and in 1632 he was given permission by the dean to search for it. He employed a diviner, John Scott, to ply his hazel rod through the cloisters and saw it twitch when they reached the west side. Their labourers excavated a coffin, but as this was deemed to be too light to contain anything of value, it was returned to its resting place unopened, no doubt disappointing the crowd of onlookers, Lilly among them, who had gathered for entertainment.

In his later years, Ramsay fell into poverty—perhaps having ventured his money in some barren mine—and in 1641 his creditors had him imprisoned in Westminster Gatehouse. He petitioned the House of Lords for payment of six years' arrears of his pension as groom of the privy chamber, but it was 1645 before the committee for the advancement of money granted him one-third of the money arising from his discovery of delinquents' estates. His petition of 1645 referred to arrears of bills and wages due to him from the king and prince amounting to £2000, payment of which he 'forbeares to request till times are better: yet having lost favour of the King … by his residence in London he had been cast into prison'. The petition is marked 'Nothing done in it' (*Sixth Report*, HMC, 41b–42a). In 1651 a further petition was referred to the mint committee; the outcome is unknown. It seems that he was still in prison in 1651 when he hoped to gain from the sale of some secret way of dyeing cloth scarlet. His son William, in the dedication to his father of his *Vox stellarum* (1652), alludes to this impoverishment having given 'occasion to some inferior-spirited people not to value you according to what you both are by nature and in yourself'. By this time David Ramsay was free and living in Holborn, by the Wounded Hart, near the King's Gate.

Ramsay died in 1660, being described as of the parish of St Martin-in-the-Fields in the administration granted to William on 20 August that year (PRO, PROB 6/203, fol. 113). A petition of 1661, from Mary, widow of David Ramsay, who stated that she raised troops for the king's service 'at Duke Hamilton's coming into England', since which time she had been sequestered and plundered, may refer to his widow. In 1660 Captain William Partridge petitioned for the appointment as king's clock- and watchmaker in succession to David Ramsay.   ANITA McCONNELL

Sources Scots peerage, 3.95–7 · Scots peerage, 6.494 · Sheffield University Library, Hartlib MSS, 7/12/4b; 14/4/18B; 3/2/125A; 28/2/12B · CSP dom., 1611–18, 211, 419, 598; 1619–23, 5, 67, 365, 430, 451, 525; 1627–8, 97; 1631–3, 484; 1651, 140 · SP, Cal. Cttee for the advancement of money (1642–56), 1.40 · Reg. PCS, 1st ser., 6.29 · Fourth report, HMC, 3 (1874), 110a · Fifth report, HMC, 4 (1876), 25b · Sixth report, HMC, 5 (1877–8), 41b–42a, 672b · C. Jagger, Royal clocks (1983) · F. J. Britten, Old clocks and watches and their makers, ed. G. H. Baillie, C. Ilbert, and C. Clutton, 9th edn (1982), 316–17 · W. Ramesey, Astrologia restaurata (1653), preface (unpag.); 28–9; postscript · W. Ramsey, Vox stellarum (1652) [dedication (unpag.)] · S. E. Atkins and W. H. Overall, Some account of the Worshipful Company of Clockmakers of the City of London (privately printed, London, 1881), 171–2 · E. J. Wood, Curiosities of clocks and watches (1866); repr. (1973), 266–7 · W. Lillie, Life and times (1715), 32–3 · administration, PRO, PROB 6/203, fol. 113
Wealth at death see administration, PRO, PROB 6/203, fol. 113

Ramsay [Ramsey], **David** (d. 1642), courtier, was born in Scotland, one of the nine children of Robert Ramsay of Wyliecleuch, Berwickshire, known as Sir Robert Ramsay. David Ramsay was kinsman to the Ramsays, earls of Dalhousie, and to John *Ramsay, Viscount Haddington and earl of Holdernesse (c.1580–1626). His brothers included Sir James *Ramsay (1589?–1638/9), groom of the bedchamber to Prince Henry and later a soldier in Swedish service, and George Ramsay, intruded by James I into a fellowship at Christ's College, Cambridge, in 1612. David Ramsay was also a beneficiary of royal favour. On 19 June 1604 a warrant was issued for the payment to David Ramsay of £26 13s. 4d. for a livery as groom of the bedchamber to Prince Henry. He is probably the 'Ramsey' reported by John Chamberlain to have been in the company of Prince Henry in March 1612. On 18 November 1613, following the death of the prince, he was awarded a pension of £200 per annum for his service as a groom.

In 1631 Donald Mackay, first Lord Reay, charged privately that Ramsay, unhappy with recent religious developments in England, had that spring sought Swedish support for a scheme to alter the frame of government by means of an army entrusted for use in the Thirty Years' War to James Hamilton, marquess of Hamilton. When this allegation became known, Ramsay challenged Reay to a duel, but then appears to have withdrawn his challenge. A difficulty for Reay was that his charge involved admitting to involvement in the plot, but it seems there was some truth in his allegations. Certainly Ramsay, who was in the Netherlands at the time alleged, had been fishing in dangerous waters, and seems to have been completely lacking in diplomatic skills. After the trial, in August 1632, Hamilton received from a servant in the Netherlands some frank advice to the effect that:

you will do yourself much right to provide some place for David Ramsay with the King of Sweden for he hath disobliged so many great men here and the King himself is so displeased with his behaviour that he is utterly lost in this place.

On 20 November 1631 Sir Thomas Roe had written from London to Princess Elizabeth of Bohemia, who had asked for information on the affair, that Ramsay had mentioned her name in connection with it, and was 'not a man on whose discretion to rely, being much transported by self-opinion' (*CSP dom.*, *addenda*, 1625–49, 421).

Given the seriousness of the issues, and the implications for Hamilton, the matter could not be ignored, but it was decided to hear them not in Star Chamber but in the court of chivalry. The case opened on Monday 28 November 1631 at the Painted Chamber in Westminster, before Robert, earl of Lindsay, lord high constable, and in the presence of the earl of Pembroke, the earl of Arundel, the earl of Dorset, and others. The dramatic case had taken on the appearance of a public spectacle; on 5 December 'the fame of the cause brought thither such a crowd of people as was not imaginable' and Ramsay appeared at each of the sessions in a new and expensive costume (*State trials*, 3.489). Progress in the trial was hampered by procedural wrangling over whether the several facts at issue were matters of honour or of treason, and over the respective roles in the case of judicial combat and the court's determination of the facts. When the facts proved impossible to establish with certainty, the court set the duel for 12 April, and issued instructions for the type and dimensions of the weapons to be used. Sir William Calley's son rode to London especially to see the contest, to be held at Tothill Fields. But he, and many others, were disappointed.

On 10 April the contest was deferred by the king until 17 May; on 12 May Lindsay announced a verdict: 'they had not found David Ramsey guilty of treason … yet they found that he had seditiously committed many contempts against his majesty, the reformation of which his majesty reserved to himself'. Ramsay and Reay were both committed to the Tower of London until they promised not to 'attempt any thing one against the other'. The king's direct influence is clear. He had 'revoked his letters patents, given to the said lords for the trial of this cause, not willing to have it decided by duel', and the official verdict in respect of Ramsay reads very like Charles's own conclusion, sent to James Hamilton and dated 8 May, four days earlier:

And for David Ramsey, though we must clear him of that treason in particular, yet not so far in the general, but that he might give occasion enough by his tongue of great accusation, if it had been rightly placed, as by his foolish presumptious carriage did appear;

and Charles was determined:

that you may know David Ramsey, that you may not have to do with such a pest as he is, suspecting he may seek to insinuate himself to you upon this occasion. Wherefore I must desire you, as you love me, to have nothing to do with him. (*State trials*, 3.513–14)

Despite this devastating judgment upon his character, Ramsay remained a recipient of royal largesse. He was still a groom of the privy chamber when in the late summer of 1633, in an effort to rehabilitate himself, he passed to the king information about Jesuits and other recusants then active in London, which was forwarded to the commissioners for recusants. It seems from a petition of 1643 on behalf of Fabian Phillips that Ramsay had been able to acquire an interest in the office of filazer, and that having 'had formerly a reversion of the same by letters patent' he had farmed it to Phillips in January 1640 (*CSP dom.*, 1643, 471). When he made his will on 13 May 1642 he was living in the fashionable new district of Covent Garden, and was able to dispose of considerable legacies, to his sister Agnes, his niece Barbara Forrett, his nephew David Forrett, and to Patrick Shawe, husband of his sister Barbara. Other beneficiaries included James Maxwell, usher of the black rod, and the patentee and army officer Sir John Meldrum, to whom he left £100 apiece and who, along with his nephew, he appointed his executors, though only the last was able to appear to prove the will on 3 August 1642.

STEPHEN WRIGHT

Sources *State trials*, 3.487–515 · *CSP dom.*, 1603–18; 1641–3; *addenda* 1625–49 · J. H. McMaster and M. Wood, eds., *Supplementary report on the manuscripts of his grace the duke of Hamilton*, HMC, 21 (1932) · will, PRO, PROB 11/190, sig. 101 · GEC, *Peerage* · *The letters of John Chamberlain*, ed. N. E. McClure, 2 vols. (1939)
Wealth at death substantial: will, PRO, PROB 11/190, sig. 101

Ramsay, David (1749–1815), historian and politician in the United States of America, was born on 2 April 1749 at Drumore township, Lancaster county, Pennsylvania, the son of James Ramsay and his wife, Jane, *née* Montgomery, who were protestant Irish farmers. He graduated from the College of New Jersey in 1765, and trained in medicine at the College of Philadelphia from 1770 to 1773 under Benjamin Rush. Professionally ambitious, he moved in 1774 to Charles Town (later Charleston), South Carolina, whose combination of a thriving economy and public health problems made it an ideal location for an ambitious young physician. Ramsay's rise was meteoric and aided by a series of successful marriages, beginning in 1775 with that to Sabina Ellis (d. 1776), daughter of a prosperous merchant family. Seven years after her death he married Frances (d. 1784), daughter of the Enlightenment thinker and president of the College of New Jersey, John *Witherspoon. In 1787 Ramsay was married for the final time, to Martha (d. 1811), daughter of Henry *Laurens, a prominent South Carolinian politician and merchant. These marriages produced seven daughters and five sons, as well as an impeccable social position.

Medicine was Ramsay's vocation, but revolutionary politics were his principal passion. He spent twenty-three years in the South Carolina legislature, including two terms in the confederation congress as its acting president and six years as president of the state's senate. From his college days in New Jersey he opposed interfering British policies. His whig values were nurtured by his college's capacity to blend Christian and classical values into a potent version of radical republicanism. Such views were strengthened during his studies with Rush who, like

David Ramsay (1749–1815), by Rembrandt Peale, 1796

Ramsay, was both a physician and an American patriot. In Charles Town his devotion to the American cause was absolute and undoubtedly aided his success. In pamphlets and orations, during his service in the legislature and as a physician in the revolutionary army, he steadfastly supported American independence. An active congregationalist, he encouraged William Tennent's successful campaign to disestablish the Church of England in South Carolina. As a member of the governor's council, he endured the British siege of Charles Town in 1780, suffering exile to St Augustine, Florida, after it capitulated.

A strong advocate of the federal constitution, Ramsay supported it both in his writings and as a member of South Carolina's state ratifying convention. Following its adoption, he ran for election to the United States house of representatives in 1788, but was defeated by William Loughton Smith in the midst of suspicion of his abolitionist sentiments. His connections with northern abolitionists such as Rush were well known, and he had been one of the few South Carolinian politicians to support John Laurens's bid to enlist large numbers of African-Americans in the continental army. His stance had implications for years to come, and lost him his bid for the United States senate in 1794.

Ramsay emerged as a leading figure in what might be called a 'second tier' of founding fathers, among them the historian Jeremy Belknap, the geographer Jedidiah Morse, Benjamin Rush, the painter Charles Willson Peale, the lexicographer Noah Webster, and the poet Philip Freneau. Despite their involvement in politics, this group is not so much noted for shaping American political institutions as

for influencing the ways in which subsequent generations saw late colonial and early republican America. All were guided by the belief that independence required a new intellectual agenda, and they aimed to define an identity, culture, political ideology, and set of institutions within the framework of an American nation.

Ramsay's lasting contribution was as the father of the American historical tradition. He stands out not only for his productivity—six major and numerous minor historical works—but also for having been the first person to compose histories addressed to the needs of a developing culture of revolutionary nationalism. Ramsay's *The History of the American Revolution* (1789) marked the beginnings of an American national historical consciousness. From 1789 to 1865 it went through six American editions, including a serialization in the *Columbian Magazine*, as well as two British, two French, and Irish, German, and Dutch editions. He remarked privately that 'We are too widely disseminated over an extensive country and too much diversified by different customs and forms of government to feel as one people'. Nevertheless, he contended that 'we really are one people' and 'should consider' the inhabitants 'of this country … as forming one whole'. 'Forming one whole' did not demand ethnic, cultural, or political homogeneity, but rather an understanding of 'America' which—rooted in republicanism—transcended geography, polity, and nationality; it meant a way of life, a credo, a novel society emancipated from the constraining customs and values of the past. Ramsay's paradigm—republican ideology as the basis of nationality—proved canonical to the historians of his generation. First, American history would be approached in a celebratory fashion, with American society itself the standard of achievement. Second, the revolution would be the benchmark of national character. All of American history, pre- and post-revolutionary, state, regional, and national, in Ramsay's canon, was to be viewed through the prism of the revolution. This meant focusing on narratives of the colonial era to create a republican genealogy, a succession of generations that, from the beginning of New World settlements, manifested the spirit of revolutionary republicanism. The story created by Ramsay and told in every national history could be summarized thus: English concepts of liberty, with its heritage of Magna Carta and the Revolution of 1688, had been exported to the New World, where a unique physical and civil environment had nurtured a freedom-loving people and societies republican in fact, if not always in form. By 1765 the American colonists had detected a conspiracy to enslave them; their resistance had been a defence of traditional freedoms and, driven to war, they had, under obligation, chosen independence. That heroic conflict had initiated a sense of nationhood, eventually secured by a convention of discerning statesmen who contrived an exemplary mechanism for a national government. Finally, and not least in Ramsay's nationalist canon, the local and unique was to be treated as a constituent part of the national whole, not a separate entity or character.

But if Ramsay's central aim was to 'reconcile to unite', its implementation proved problematic. During the 1790s Ramsay and others became increasingly frustrated with the prospects for a truly national society and a cultural renaissance, despite the ratification of the federal constitution. And while Ramsay's goal remained consistent, the stark nationalism of the *History of the American Revolution* later gave way to a concept of particularism within a nationalist framework, a perspective seen most clearly in his *History of South Carolina* (1809). These two works stood as prototypes for Ramsay's generation, and he became the nation's most respected historian and one of its premier literary figures. He died at his home in Broad Street, Charleston, on 8 May 1815, after being shot by a deranged patient.   ARTHUR H. SHAFFER

Sources R. Brunhouse, ed., 'David Ramsay, 1749–1815: selections from his writings', *Transactions of the American Philosophical Society*, new ser., 55 (1965) · A. H. Shaffer, *To be an American: David Ramsay and the making of the American consciousness* (1991) · P. Smith, 'David Ramsay and the causes of the American Revolution', *William and Mary Quarterly*, 17 (1960), 51–77 · L. Friedman, *Inventors of the promised land* (1975) · L. Cohen, *The revolutionary histories: contemporary narratives of the American Revolution* (1980) · A. H. Shaffer, *The politics of history: writing the history of the American Revolution* (1975)
Archives Charleston Library Society, letter-book · Duke U., papers · South Carolina Historical Society, Charleston, papers · University of South Carolina, Columbia, MSS | Library Company of Philadelphia, Rush papers · Mass. Hist. Soc., Belknap papers · University of South Carolina, Columbia, Henry Laurens papers
Likenesses C. W. Peale, oils, 1771 · R. Peale, oils, c.1796, Gibbes Museum of Art, Charleston, South Carolina · R. Peale, oils, 1796, Independence National Historical Park collections, Philadelphia [*see illus.*]
Wealth at death $500: Brunhouse, ed., 'David Ramsay', 27–8

Ramsay [*formerly* Burnett], **Edward Bannerman** (1793–1872), Scottish Episcopal dean of Edinburgh and author, was the fourth son of Alexander Burnett, advocate sheriff of Kincardineshire, and his second wife, Elizabeth, the eldest daughter of Sir Alexander Bannerman of Elsick; he was born at Aberdeen on 31 January 1793. His father (who was the second son of Sir Thomas Burnett, bt, of Leys, and his wife, Catherine Ramsay), after his succession in 1806 to the estates of Balmain and Fasque in Kincardineshire, left to him by his uncle, Sir Alexander Ramsay, assumed for himself and his family the name of Ramsay, was made a baronet by Fox (13 May 1806), resigned his sheriffship, and lived until his death in 1810 at Fasque, the estate later owned by the Gladstones.

Edward Ramsay spent much of his boyhood with his great-uncle, Sir Alexander, who lived on his Yorkshire estate. He was sent to the village school at Halsey after his uncle's death, and in 1806 to the cathedral grammar school at Durham. He completed his education at St John's College, Cambridge, where he graduated BA in 1816. In the same year he was ordained to the curacy of Rodden, near Frome in Somerset, and in 1817 became curate also of Buckland Denham in the same county, where the absence of the rector gave him the whole pastoral charge. In the *Sunday Magazine* of January 1865 he wrote

Edward Bannerman Ramsay (1793–1872), by Sir John Watson-Gordon, exh. RA 1845

'Reminiscences of a west of England curacy', in which he describes his life at this period and his friendship with the Wesleyan Methodists among his parishioners. His favourite studies were botany, architecture, and music. He became an accomplished player on the flute, and had a special admiration for Handel. In 1824 he went to Edinburgh as curate of St George's, York Place, where he remained for two years, and after a year's incumbency of St Paul's, Carrubbers Close, became in 1827 assistant to Bishop Sandford of St John's Church. He succeeded Sandford in 1830, and remained pastor of that congregation until his death.

Ramsay's English education had not made him a less patriotic Scot, but it enlarged his view of Scottish patriotism. He advocated consistently, and at last successfully, the removal of the barriers which separated the Scottish Episcopal from the English church. In 1841 he was appointed by Bishop Terrot dean of Edinburgh, and, having declined Peel's offer of the bishopric of New Brunswick, Nova Scotia, and at later periods the bishopric of Glasgow and the coadjutor-bishopric of Edinburgh, he became familiarly known in Scotland as 'the Dean' or Dean Ramsay. He was a vice-president of the Royal Society of Edinburgh, and delivered the opening address in 1861. His only other contribution to its *Proceedings* was a 'Memoir' of Thomas Chalmers, a friend for whose genius he had a high admiration. It was largely due to him that the statue of Chalmers was erected in George Street, Edinburgh.

The *Reminiscences of Scottish Life and Character* (1858), which gave Ramsay his widest reputation, had its origin in 'Two lectures on some changes in social life and habits', delivered at Ulbster Hall, Edinburgh, in 1857. It was rewritten and much enlarged in successive editions, of which twenty-one were published during his life; the twenty-second was issued after his death with a notice of his life by Professor Cosmo-Innes. The book has been recognized as the best collection of Scottish stories and one of the best answers to the charge of want of humour frequently made against the Scots. It is composed largely of stories and anecdotes furnished by his own recollection or that of his friends of all classes, supplemented by contributions from ministers of the various Scottish churches and others of his countrymen. Those who heard Ramsay tell Scottish stories maintained that print weakened their flavour, but they were woven together in the *Reminiscences* in an artless personal narrative, which has a charm of its own. The work did much to establish in the English mind an impression of Scotland being inhabited by pawky characters, revelling in their individuality and eccentricity, and they made Ramsay one of the best-known Scots of his time. In addition to the *Reminiscences* Ramsay published *A Catechism* (1835), at one time much used, and a number of volumes of sermons and lectures, of which *Pulpit Table-Talk* (1868) is characteristic.

Ramsay was the principal founder of the Scottish Episcopal Church Society, in 1876 absorbed in the Representative Church Council, a society which improved the still slender emoluments of the clergy of the Episcopal church. In theology his sympathy was with the evangelical rather than the high-church party, and in politics with the liberal Conservatives. He retained through life a warm friendship for W. E. Gladstone, with whom he was associated in the foundation of Trinity College, Glenalmond. But he was not a man of party, and the epithet 'unsectarian' might have been invented for him. His links with the clergy of other communions and his open-minded attitude did much to lessen the prejudice with which episcopacy was regarded in Scotland.

Ramsay married, in 1829, Isabella Cochrane, a Canadian, who predeceased him without children. Her nephews and nieces found a home in his house, where his brother, Admiral Sir W. Ramsay, resided after retiring from the navy. Dean Ramsay died in Edinburgh on 27 December 1872. A tablet was placed in St John's Church by his congregation, and an Iona cross in the adjoining burial-ground, facing Princes Street, was erected to his memory by public subscription. Ramsay left an autobiography of his ministry. It was bought by David Douglas at the sale of the effects of H. J. Rollo and was published privately by Douglas, edited by F. M. F. Skene, as *Reminiscences of a Scottish Episcopal Ministry* (1892).

A. J. G. Mackay, rev. H. C. G. Matthew

Sources personal knowledge (1896) • C. Innes, 'Memoir of Dean Ramsay', in E. B. Ramsay, *Reminiscences of Scottish life and character*, 22nd edn (1874), vii–xcix • M. Lochhead, *Episcopal Scotland in the nineteenth century* (1966) • Gladstone, *Diaries*
Archives NA Scot., letters | BL, corresp. with W. E. Gladstone, Add. MSS 44283–44284 • NA Scot., letters to Lord Dalhousie • NL Scot., corresp. with Blackwoods • St Deiniol's Library, Hawarden, letters to Sir John Gladstone • St Deiniol's Library, Hawarden, corresp. with Sir Thomas Gladstone • U. Edin., letters to Thomas Chalmers • U. St Andr., corresp. with James David Forbes
Likenesses J. Watson-Gordon, oils, exh. RA 1845, Scot. NPG [*see illus.*] • A. Edouart, paper silhouette, Scot. NPG • O. Leyde, lithograph, BM • J. Steell, oils, Scot. NPG • Steell, plaster bust, Scot. NPG
Wealth at death £4145 6s. 10d.: inventory, 6 March 1873, NA Scot., SC 70/1/161/277

Ramsay, George (*c.*1652–1705), army officer, was the third son of George Ramsay, second earl of Dalhousie (1633–1674), and his wife, Anne (*d.* 1661), daughter of John Fleming, second earl of Wigtown, and widow of Robert, Lord Boyd. Ramsay was a captain in the duke of Monmouth's Royal English regiment in the French army in 1674, transferring into the Anglo-Dutch brigade in 1676 before promotion to major of John Wachop's battalion in 1685 and lieutenant-colonel in 1687. When James II recalled the Anglo-Dutch brigade into England in March 1688, Ramsay remained loyal to the Dutch republic, although Colonel Wachop returned to the British Isles. It was Ramsay, with the rank of lieutenant-colonel, who led this regiment during William's invasion of England in November 1688. Shortly after the revolution of 1688 he was promoted to colonel and served with his regiment under Hugh Mackay during the campaign against the Scottish Jacobites in 1689. Although he displayed great personal bravery during the defeat at Killiecrankie (27 July 1689), rallying some of the broken troops, his own battalion fled. On 20 February 1691 he was promoted brigadier-general, and on 1 September 1691 he transferred to the colonelcy of the Scots guards. He served in Flanders from 1691 until 1697, fighting at Landen (1693), where he commanded the garrison of the village of Laar, and taking a leading role in the capture of the heights of Bouge during the early stages of the siege of Namur (1695). He was promoted major-general on 5 March 1694, and appointed commander-in-chief in Scotland on 12 May 1702. Marlborough considered him 'a very brave man and a good foot officer' (*The Marlborough–Godolphin Correspondence*, 1.201). He was raised to lieutenant-general on 11 February 1703 but died in Edinburgh on 2 September 1705 at fifty-two or fifty-three years of age.

John Childs

Sources raad van state 1928, Nationaal Archief, The Hague • J. Ferguson, ed., *Papers illustrating the history of the Scots brigade in the service of the United Netherlands, 1572–1782*, 3 vols., Scottish History Society, 32, 35, 38 (1899–1901) • J. MacLean, 'Huwelijken van militairen, behorende tot het derde regiment van de schotse brigade in Nederland ontleend aan de gereformeerde trouwboeken van 1674 tot 1708', *De Brabantse Leeuw*, 20 (1972), 140–59 • J. MacLean, 'Huwelijken van militairen, behorende tot het derde regiment van de schotse brigade in Nederland ontleend aan de gereformeerde trouwboeken van 1674 tot 1708', *De Brabantse*

Leeuw, 21 (1973), 90–113 • C. Dalton, ed., *English army lists and commission registers, 1661–1714*, 6 vols. (1892–1904) • *The Marlborough–Godolphin correspondence*, ed. H. L. Snyder, 3 vols. (1975)

Ramsay, George, ninth earl of Dalhousie (1770–1838), army officer and governor-in-chief of British North America, was born on 22 October 1770 at Dalhousie Castle, Edinburgh, the eldest son of George Ramsay, eighth earl of Dalhousie (d. 1787), and his wife, Elizabeth (1738/9–1807), the daughter of Andrew Glene. After being educated at the Royal High School and the University of Edinburgh, he became cornet in the 3rd dragoons in July 1788 and captain in January 1791; he joined the 1st foot and advanced to major in June 1792 and lieutenant-colonel in December 1794. He served in Gibraltar and in the West Indies (1795), in Ireland during the 1798 rebellion, and on the expedition to The Helder (Netherlands), rising to the brevet rank of colonel in January 1800. In 1801 he campaigned in Egypt, and two years later became brigadier-general on the staff in Scotland, where on 14 May 1805 he married Christian (1786–1839) [see Ramsay, Christian], the only child and heir of Charles Broun of Colstoun, East Lothian. They had three sons: George (1806–1832), Charles (1807–1817), and James Andrew Broun *Ramsay (1812–1860), a future governor-general of India.

Having been promoted major-general in April 1808, Dalhousie took part in the Walcheren expedition, and in August 1809 he was appointed colonel of the 6th garrison battalion. In 1812 he assumed command of the 7th division and served under the marquess of Wellington in Spain and France, with the local rank of lieutenant-general, confirmed as full rank in June 1813. The previous month he became colonel of the 26th foot, and that year was awarded a KB; in 1815 he was given a GCB, when he was also created Baron Dalhousie of Dalhousie Castle in the peerage of the United Kingdom, having since 1796 been a representative Scottish peer.

Keen to secure his post-war financial position, Dalhousie obtained appointment in July 1816 as lieutenant-governor of Nova Scotia. In a province he came to admire for its rugged scenery and hospitable people, he championed improved methods of farming and road-building to open up the countryside to the settlement of British immigrants. His enthusiasm for improvement extended to education and, by the foundation of a non-sectarian college in Halifax, modelled on the University of Edinburgh, he sought to release higher education from Anglican exclusiveness and denominational strife. Although a building was begun in 1820 with money from customs duties levied during the British wartime occupation of Castine (Maine) in 1814–15, Dalhousie College languished for lack of funding. As with this enterprise, the governor was increasingly drawn into conflict with the provincial assembly over financial affairs, and by the time of his departure in 1820 deadlock threatened. While he preserved cordial relations with his councillors and the deferential urban élite, he denounced the 'double faced Halifax Politicians, or Country Colonels, more addicted to Rum and preaching than to promote the welfare of the State'

(Dalhousie to Sir James Kempt, 16 Oct 1820, Dalhousie MSS, NA Scot., ED 45/3/27A).

Despite ambivalent feelings about a career of public service which entailed long absences from Scotland, Dalhousie had always aimed at becoming governor-in-chief of British North America. His ambition was finally gratified in November 1819, but he remained apprehensive about the violent political confrontation between English and French awaiting him in Lower Canada. Tactically, he determined to stay aloof from partisan squabbles, but this course left him bereft of experienced advisers and willing supporters, just as his sturdy Presbyterian aversion to priests who meddled in politics precluded him from cultivating the active backing of the influential hierarchy of the Roman Catholic church. Although at first he regarded the docile French Canadians with paternal benevolence, his prickly temperament and dislike of insubordination were soon inflamed by dealings with the scheming politicians of the French party. In disputes with the assembly, Dalhousie was handicapped by seeing himself as a latter-day Stuart king upholding the royal prerogative against parliamentary encroachment. This anachronistic conservatism was exacerbated by excessive sensitivity for his authority and dignity as the sovereign's representative, which personalized and inflated every criticism or challenge.

During the 1820s conflict centred around appropriation of crown and provincial revenues, control of which the assembly had for years been trying to wrest from the executive. Dalhousie insisted, in line with instructions from London, that any civil list voted must be unconditional and permanent. With the two houses of the legislature at loggerheads, he looked to the British parliament to intervene, a possibility momentarily glimpsed in 1822 when a bill to reunite the Canadas was introduced in the Commons but withdrawn. During Dalhousie's leave of absence in 1824–5, the lieutenant-governor, Sir Francis Burton, engineered a one-year vote of supplies, an apparent surrender of principle which Dalhousie persuaded the colonial secretary to disavow, though the censure was subsequently lifted and the earl himself blamed for having misled the imperial authorities. Since he rejected another bill in that form, no supplies were voted in 1826. When the same impasse occurred the following year, he dissolved the legislature and actively intervened in the ensuing election. Such blatant partisanship ensured an even more recalcitrant assembly, and Dalhousie petulantly refused to accept the election as speaker of Louis-Joseph Papineau, who had come to personify the truculent, power-hungry agitator.

Such extreme actions provoked alarm in London, and William Huskisson, the new colonial secretary, decided to hasten Dalhousie's transfer to India as commander-in-chief of the army. Meanwhile, in 1828, ministers conceded a parliamentary select committee on the civil administration of Lower Canada, which heard evidence from interested parties and belatedly received a Canadian petition with 87,000 signatures protesting against the governor's electoral tactics of purging the magistracy and militia of opponents. During his brief stay in Britain, Dalhousie sought to defend himself against the charges, which he read with 'the utmost astonishment' (letter to Sir George Murray, 23 Oct 1828, PRO CO/42/216) in the committee's highly critical report, but he obtained neither vindication nor sympathy from the then colonial secretary, Sir George Murray, even though he was a fellow Wellingtonian officer. For someone given to brooding, this sense of injustice continued to rankle. After a short tenure in India dogged by ill health, Dalhousie resigned his command and journeyed to Britain in 1832. Having then vainly sought recuperation in France and Germany, he returned to Dalhousie Castle in 1834 and passed his final years there an invalid, ultimately blind and senile. He died at Dalhousie Castle on 21 March 1838 and was buried on 29 March at Cockpen; his wife died the following January.

PETER BURROUGHS

Sources M. Whitelaw, ed., *The Dalhousie journals*, 3 vols. (1978–82) · R. Christie, *A history of the late province of Lower Canada*, 2–3 (1849–50) · R. Christie, *Memoirs of the administration of the government of Lower Canada by the Earl of Dalhousie* (1829) · H. T. Manning, *The revolt of French Canada, 1800–1835* (1962) · W. Lee-Warner, *The life of the Marquis of Dalhousie*, 2 vols. (1904) · H. J. Morgan, *Sketches of celebrated Canadians, and persons connected with Canada* (1862), 248–51 · J. MacGregor, *British America*, 2 (1832), 54–6 · *Army List* (1787–1838) · 'Select committee on the civil government of Lower Canada', *Parl. papers* (1828), 7.375, no. 569 · *Journals*, Nova Scotia, house of assembly (1816–20) · *Journals*, Lower Canada, house of assembly (1820–28) · register of births and baptisms, parish of Cockpen, Edinburgh, Scotland, General Register Office for Scotland, Edinburgh · GEC, *Peerage* · Burke, *Peerage* · register of deaths and burials, parish of Cockpen, Edinburgh, Scotland, General Register Office for Scotland, Edinburgh
Archives NA Scot., corresp. and papers · NRA Scotland, priv. coll., corresp. and papers | Derbys. RO, letters to Sir R. J. Wilmot-Horton · NA Canada, Burton MSS · NA Canada, Cochrane MSS · NA Canada, Kempt MSS · NA Canada, Neilson MSS · NA Canada, Papineau MSS · NA Canada, Ryland MSS · NA Canada, Sewell MSS · NA Canada, Viger MSS · PRO, CO 42/185–216; 43/25–27; 217/98–139; 218/29; 323/147–157; 324/73–90 · U. Nott. L., letters to Lord William Bentinck
Likenesses J. W. Gordon, oils, 1832?, NG Scot. · C. F. Comfort, oils, 1974 (after J. W. Gordon), Dalhousie University, Halifax · T. Lupton, engraving (after J. W. Gordon), Dalhousie University, Halifax · silhouette, NA Canada

Ramsay, Sir George, ninth baronet (1800–1871), philosopher, elder brother of William *Ramsay (1806–1865), professor of humanity at Glasgow University, was born at home on 19 March 1800. He was the second son of Sir William Ramsay, seventh baronet (d. 1807), of Bamff House, Aylth, Perthshire, and Agnata Frances, daughter of Vincent Biscoe of Hookwood, Surrey. He was educated at Harrow School and at Trinity College, Cambridge, where he graduated BA in 1823 and MB in 1826. On 9 October 1830 he married Emily Eugenia (1806–1885), youngest daughter of Captain Henry Lennon of co. Westmeath, with whom he had three sons. He succeeded his elder brother, Sir James Ramsay, as ninth baronet on 1 January 1859 and died at Bamff on 22 February 1871; the title passed to his eldest son, Sir James Henry *Ramsay, the historian. His youngest son, George Gilbert Ramsay LLD, was elected professor of humanity at Glasgow University in 1863.

Ramsay wrote voluminously on philosophy, psychology, and political economy from a standpoint firmly within the Scottish common-sense philosophical tradition. One of the most notable features of his writings is his determined opposition to utilitarianism, which in his *Enquiry into the Principles of Human Happiness and Human Duty* (1843) he criticizes for excessive emphasis on rationality and consequent neglect of sources of emotional satisfaction. In his writings Ramsay attempts to counteract philosophical rationality by the use of literary examples, a tendency most pronounced in his *The Philosophy and Poetry of Love* (1848), where excerpts from his philosophical writings are interspersed with a literary anthology. Ramsay's ethical philosophy chiefly distinguishes itself from that of his Scottish Enlightenment forebears through its romanticism; he strongly emphasizes the destructive effect of ennui on human happiness, and as an antidote recommends the state of continual emotion ensured by the cultivation of one 'prominent desire'. He also stresses the role of 'domestic happiness' and an ideal of affective marriage.

On political questions Ramsay was a Conservative. In *The Moralist and Politician, or, Many Things in Few Words* (1865), a collection of aphoristic writings, he characterizes aristocracy as the connecting link between 'monarchy' and 'democracy', without which the constitution 'falls to pieces', on the grounds that aristocrats represent local interests which would be ignored by the absolutist spirit of pure democracy. Ramsay attributes the condition of Ireland to the failure of the Irish aristocracy in *A Proposal for the Restoration of the Irish Parliament* (1845).

GAVIN BUDGE

Sources DNB · Burke, *Peerage*
Archives NA Scot.

Ramsay, George, twelfth earl of Dalhousie (1806–1880), naval officer, second son of John (1775–1842), the fourth son of George Ramsay, eighth earl of Dalhousie, was born on 26 April 1806. His mother was Mary (d. 1843), daughter of Philip Delisle of Calcutta. He entered the navy in December 1820 and served in the frigates *Cambrian* and *Euryalus* in the Mediterranean, and on the South American station in the *Doris*, from which, on 30 April 1827, he was promoted to be lieutenant of the *Heron*. He afterwards served in the *Ganges*, the flagship of Sir Robert Otway, at Rio de Janeiro, and in the *Orestes* on the coast of Ireland; his three years as first lieutenant of the *Nimrod* on the Lisbon station was followed by a period in the *Rodney* in the Mediterranean from November 1835 until his promotion to the rank of commander on 10 January 1837. From August 1838 to August 1842 he commanded the *Pilot* in the West Indies and on 20 March 1843 he was advanced to post rank. He married Sarah Frances (d. 1904), only daughter of William Robertson of Logan House, Midlothian, on 12 August 1845.

From August 1849 to the end of 1852 Ramsay commanded the *Alarm* (26 guns) on the North American and West Indian stations. In December 1853 he commissioned the *Euryalus*, a new screw frigate, then considered one of the finest ships in the navy, and during the two following years he commanded her in the Baltic. On 4 February 1856 he was nominated a CB, and on the conclusion of peace with Russia was sent, still in the *Euryalus*, to the West Indies, whence he returned in the spring of 1857. He was then appointed superintendent of Pembroke dockyard, where he continued until September 1862. On 22 November 1862 he was promoted to the rank of rear-admiral, and from 1866 to 1869, with the *Narcissus* as his flagship, he was commander-in-chief on the east coast of South America. He became vice-admiral on 17 March 1869 and admiral, on the retired list, on 20 July 1875. On 6 July 1874, on the death without issue of his cousin, Fox *Maule, eleventh earl of Dalhousie, he succeeded to the title. On 12 June 1875 he was also created Baron Ramsay in the peerage of the United Kingdom as a reward for his naval service and his tory principles. He died suddenly at his home, Dalhousie Castle, Midlothian, on 20 July 1880.

Dalhousie's eldest son, **John William Maule Ramsay**, thirteenth earl of Dalhousie (1847–1887), followed his father into the navy in January 1861 and, having passed his examination with unusual brilliance, was promoted to the rank of lieutenant on 12 April 1867. He was then appointed flag-lieutenant to his father in the *Narcissus*, but it is doubtful if he ever joined her, being lent to the *Galatea*, then commanded by Alfred, duke of Edinburgh, with whom he remained until the ship was paid off in the summer of 1871. In September 1872 he joined the *Lord Warden* as flag-lieutenant of Sir Hastings Yelverton, the commander-in-chief in the Mediterranean, and, on Yelverton's striking his flag, he was promoted commander on 4 March 1874. For the next three years he was equerry to the duke of Edinburgh, and in October 1875 he matriculated from Balliol College, Oxford, where he spent some months as an undergraduate. From April 1877 to August 1879 he was commander of the *Britannia* training ship of naval cadets. After this he virtually retired from the navy, and devoted himself to study and politics. He married Lady Ida Louisa Bennet (1857–1887), daughter of the sixth earl of Tankerville and his wife, Olivia, in December 1877; she was also active in political society.

In February 1880 Ramsay was a candidate for Liverpool in a by-election, as an advanced Liberal and a follower of Gladstone; he was defeated mainly, it was said, by the influence of his father, who was a staunch Conservative. In the general election of 1880 he was returned as the minority member for Liverpool unopposed with two Conservatives, but on his father's death on 20 July that year was called to the House of Lords. In September he was appointed one of Queen Victoria's lords-in-waiting and he was nominated a knight of the Thistle in November 1881. In January 1883 he spent some weeks in Ireland as one of a royal commission to inquire into the state of the country, and came back, in his own words, 'even more impressed than I was before I went with the serious state of discontent, quite apart from outrages, which seems to pervade all Ireland out of Ulster'. This impression led him—in contrast to the timidity of many of his colleagues in the Lords—to support Gladstone's home-rule policy in 1886,

and in March he joined the Liberal ministry as secretary for Scotland in succession to G. O. Trevelyan; he resigned with his colleagues in July. He was sworn of the privy council in April 1886.

In 1887 Dalhousie and his wife made an extensive tour of the United States. They arrived at Le Havre in poor health on their return voyage in November. On the 24th the countess's illness proved fatal, and Dalhousie, unable to bear the shock, died in Le Havre the next morning. The bodies were buried in the family vault in Cockpen parish church, Midlothian. They left two sons, the elder of whom, Arthur George Maule Ramsay, succeeded to the title.

J. K. LAUGHTON, rev. H. C. G. MATTHEW

Sources *The Times* (21 July 1880) · *The Times* (28 Nov 1887) [John William Maule Ramsay] · *The Times* (2 Dec 1887) [John William Maule Ramsay] · O'Byrne, *Naval biog. dict.* · *Navy List* · GEC, *Peerage* · Gladstone, *Diaries*
Archives CUL, journals as commander-in-chief of South American station · NA Scot., naval papers | BL, corresp. with W. E. Gladstone, Add. MSS 44466–44498 · BL, letters to G. D. Ramsay · LMA, Toynbee Hall MSS · Lpool RO, Holt MSS · U. Lpool L., Sydney Jones Library, Rathbone MSS

Ramsay, James [*known as* Sir James Ramsay; *called* Black Ramsay] (1589?–1638/9), army officer in the Swedish service, was born in Scotland probably in 1589. He was the eighth of nine children of Robert Ramsay of Wyliecleuch, known as Sir Robert; a brother was the courtier David *Ramsay and he was a kinsman of John *Ramsay, Viscount Haddington and earl of Holdernesse. In later life he became known as Black Ramsay to distinguish him from another James Ramsay in Swedish service at the time called the Fair. He is generally styled Sir James, though on what basis is not known.

James Ramsay accompanied King James to London in 1603, where he became an attendant in the privy chamber of the king and of Prince Henry. He is probably the same as the James Ramsay who was recommended for service at the court of Christian IV of Denmark–Norway by James VI and I in the first decade of the seventeenth century. In 1611 Ramsay was sent back to the Stuart kingdoms to levy recruits for the impending Kalmar War between Denmark–Norway and Sweden. However, he did not remain long in Danish service as in 1614 the Swedish chancellor, Axel Oxenstierna, entrusted a messenger known as Ramsay with carrying a letter to Colonel James *Spens, the Stuart ambassador to Sweden and Swedish ambassador to the Stuarts. Some time before 1614 Ramsay married Isobel Spens (*d.* after 1646), the ambassador's daughter. Little more is known of him during the next decade apart from his appointment as an ensign in the Swedish army in 1615. Ramsay next appears as a lieutenant-colonel in Colonel Spens's regiment from 1624 to 1626. The following year he became the colonel of his own recruited regiment of Scots.

Ramsay and his regiment were frequently considered by Oxenstierna and King Gustavus Adolphus for the Swedish campaigns in Germany during the Thirty Years' War. By 1630 Ramsay's regiment had suffered such a high mortality rate that Oxenstierna authorized the provision of new recruits from Courland, Lithuania, and Scotland. The Swedish chancellor was also quick to rectify Ramsay's shortage of funds for his troops, and wrote directly to the treasurer to release money to him. When the marquess of Hamilton's troops landed in Germany in 1631 Ramsay ensured the delivery of victuals to the starving and sickly men. In March 1631 Oxenstierna even recommended Ramsay as the only officer suitable to take over the occupation of Colberg with his regiment of 600 soldiers, revealing the high esteem he had for Ramsay's military leadership.

At the battle of Breitenfeld near Leipzig in September 1631 Ramsay's troops served in the vanguard whose actions helped bring victory to the Swedes, alongside those of Colonel Robert Monro of Foulis and Sir John Hamilton. Soon afterwards Ramsay's regiment was instrumental in forcing the fortified castle at Würzburg to surrender after the city had already capitulated to the Swedish king through the mediation of a Scottish priest named Ogilvie. During the manoeuvre Ramsay was incapacitated by a wound in the arm. Not only was he rewarded with a large land grant in the duchy of Mecklenburg, but he was also appointed the governor of Hanau. His regiment continued to undertake leading roles in Swedish army manoeuvres, such as the taking of Aschaffenberg, Oppenheim, and Creuznach. Shortly after this Ramsay's wife must have decided to leave Germany as in 1632 Oxenstierna requested that money be released for her removal along with her household to Stettin. Ramsay's favourable reputation was widespread and in 1634 the burgesses and town council of Nuremberg personally requested his appointment as commandant of their town upon the death of the former incumbent, Colonel Hastfer. Chancellor Oxenstierna had to refuse the request as Ramsay was still serving in Hanau. That year the Stuart ambassador to Poland, Sir George Douglas, visited Ramsay. During this period Ramsay was promoted major-general.

However, Ramsay's fortunes soon changed as imperial forces began to besiege Hanau in 1635, and the garrison barely survived until the following year when Swedish forces, led by Colonel Alexander Leslie, liberated the town. After a brief respite, during which Ramsay managed to send provisions to another garrison nearby, Hanau was again besieged and this time Philip Maurice, count of Hanau, made his peace with the emperor, and relinquished the Swedish cause. Seeing the impossibility of his situation, Ramsay agreed to evacuate the city on honourable terms. Oxenstierna wrote Ramsay a letter commending and congratulating him on his steadfast performance at Hanau, allowing him to retain his rank until he received full payment and compensation from the Swedish government to the value of 50,000 riksdaler (about £15,000). This was to cover several arrangements: to maintain his wife in Scotland, to secure an equivalent for his lands in Mecklenburg, and to obtain his safe conduct to Swedish quarters. However, Ramsay did not believe that this agreement would be honoured and in December 1637, to put pressure on the Swedes who would not want to give the Germans further cause to attack, he took the count of Hanau prisoner and re-occupied the town. Barely two months later, on 12 February 1638, Henry, Count Nassau Dillenburg, surprised, wounded, and captured Ramsay, who died a prisoner in the castle of Dillenburg on either 11 March 1638 or, according to T. Fischer, 29 June 1639. His widow lacked the means to bring his body back to Scotland and he was eventually buried at Dillenburg town church on 18 August 1650.

It is not known how many children Ramsay had, although a son, David, attained the rank of colonel in the Swedish service (his will is printed by Fischer, *Scots in Sweden*). Although Ramsay, unlike so many of his compatriots serving in the Swedish army, was never ennobled by the Swedes, he still proved a respectable and consistent soldier of the highest calibre, to the extent that he was actively sought after as governor by conquered German populations. A. N. L. GROSJEAN

Sources military muster rolls, Krigsarkivet, Stockholm, MR 1615/15, 1624/8, 1625/3, 5, 6, 1626/3–9, 1627/9, 12, 1628/6–15, 1629/5–10, 12, 14, 16, 18, 19, 1630/23, 24, 26, 1631/12, 15–18, 25, 27, 1632/22 · Danish state archives, Ra. TKUA Alm. del. 1, no.9 · Danish state archives, Latina 1600–15, fol. 262 · R. Monro, *Monro his expedition with the worthy Scots regiment (called Mac-Keyes regiment) levied in August 1626* (1637); new edn, with introduction by W. S. Brockington (1999) · *Rikskansleren Axel Oxenstiernas skrifter och brefvexling*, 15 vols. (Stockholm, 1888–1977), vols. 2, 4–7, 9/1, 12, 15 · *Scots peerage* · N. A. Kullberg, S. Bergh, and P. Sondén, eds., *Svenska riksrådets protokoll*, 18 vols. (Stockholm, 1878–1959), vols. 7, 9 · *CSP dom.*, 1631 · T. Riis, *Should auld acquaintance be forgot … Scottish–Danish relations, c.1450–1707*, 2 (1988), 2 · T. Fischer, *The Scots in Sweden* (1907) · J. Grant, *Memoirs and adventures of Sir John Hepburn* (1851) · J. Grant, *The Scottish soldiers of fortune, their adventures and achievements in the armies of Europe* (1890) · O. Donner, *A brief sketch of the Scottish families in Finland and Sweden* (1884) · *DNB* · T. Fischer, *The Scots in Germany* (1902)

Likenesses S. Fürck, line engraving (aged forty-seven), BM, NPG · S. Fürck, line engraving, BM, NPG

Wealth at death was owed 50,000 riksdaler: *DNB* · approx. £15,000: *DNB*

Ramsay, James (*c.*1624–1696), bishop of Ross, was born in Irvine, the son of Robert Ramsay (*c.*1598–1651), principal of Glasgow University, and his wife, Janet Campbell. He entered Glasgow University on 31 March 1645 and was laureated in 1647. About 1648 he married Mary Gartshore, with whom he raised a large family. The resolutioner party in the church ordained him to his first charge at Kirkintilloch on 19 February 1653. During the English occupation his parishioners defied the prohibition against attending his services, which the protester clergy had obtained after having failed to stop his admission. In 1655 he was translated to Linlithgow, where, despite obstructions to his call, the synod declared him legally called and admitted. A respected member of the resolutioner party, he preached in thanksgiving for Charles II's restoration (*Moses Returned from Midian*, 1660), and on 29 May 1661 officiated at the anniversary pageant in Linlithgow at which symbols of the solemn league and covenant and the interregnum were burned. In 1664 he was appointed to the charge of Hamilton and *ex officio* to the deanery of Glasgow. From 1665 to 1667 he was rector of Glasgow University, heading the subscriptions of the oath of allegiance to episcopacy on 6 January 1666. Accompanying the duke of Hamilton with Thomas Dalziel's forces at the skirmish at Pentland on 28 November 1666, he protected him from a rebel's blow.

Ramsay's views on dissenting presbyterians became intolerant as he and many brethren grew aghast at the undermining of the diocese of Glasgow by the indulged ministers and the prevalence of conventicles. In September 1669 in a bold remonstrance to the king, drawn up by Ramsay and Arthur Ross, parson of Glasgow, the diocesan synod lamented the state of the church and criticized government policy for not enacting uniformity of worship and discipline. Summoned before the council, they were both confined to their parishes for a year. The remonstrance was suppressed, but it provided a reason for the dismissal of Alexander Burnet as archbishop of Glasgow. Under his successor, Robert Leighton, Ramsay supported measures for conciliation and accommodation of presbyterian dissenters, but John Paterson, dean of Edinburgh, reported that he was oppressive towards the conforming clergy. He earned sufficient favour to be recommended to the vacant diocese of the Isles in 1672. The chapter completed the formalities of his election on 31 July, but the clergy objected that although otherwise qualified, he could not fulfil his episcopal duties without knowing Gaelic, and requested the king to nominate another man. The objections were heeded, for on 22 July 1673 Ramsay was instead nominated bishop of Dunblane and *ex officio* dean of the Chapel Royal.

During 1674 a movement for the calling of a national synod arose among Edinburgh and Glasgow clergy, supported by Bishop Laurie of Brechin and by Ramsay. Archbishop Sharp of St Andrews and others opposed it vehemently, fearing its destabilizing influence and suspecting it was intended to lead to demands for the recall of parliament. On 8 July 1674 at a conference of the bishops and some clergy, Ramsay was alone in pressing the case for a synod to settle the church. For disobeying his metropolitan the king ordered Sharp to translate him to the Isles. On 28 July Ramsay petitioned the privy council, which forwarded his petition to the king. Sharp suspended him from his episcopal functions. In April 1675 Ramsay followed the primate to court 'where they fall a scolding in their letters' (Wodrow, 2.304). A commission of Scottish bishops arbitrated in September, and after Ramsay's submission to authority in December he resumed his see of Dunblane in April 1676, holding the charge of Culross *in commendam*. In 1676–7 his rights to an annuity due to the deanery of the Chapel Royal were disputed in an important case for church revenues.

After the death of Bishop Young of Ross, Ramsay was named his successor on 14 April 1684; he served his diocese diligently for five years, residing also at Culross. Although he accepted the royal prerogative and obeyed the Test Act, in May 1686 he again stood up for his principles in a sermon to parliament against the act for the toleration of Roman Catholics. In order to overawe other opponents of the toleration, he was summoned before Alexander Burnet, now archbishop of St Andrews, and

John Paterson, now bishop of Edinburgh, for defamatory remarks about the earls of Perth and Melfort, and remarks offensive to Lord Moray. Melfort remarked that because of previous kindnesses, Ramsay was 'the only one amongst the Bishops I regrate' (earl of Moray papers, 7/619). The bishop held out for a synodical trial but there being no proof the case was dropped. Ramsay also narrowly escaped the dismissal that befell Bishop Bruce of Dunkeld on 3 June. During 1687–8 Ramsay was keen to assist Robert Boyle's abortive project for the distribution of Gaelic bibles and catechisms in his predominantly Gaelic-speaking diocese. However, because of the difficulties inherent in expounding scripture and doctrine from books in the Irish form of Gaelic, which was not fully understood in Scotland, Ramsay was unable to condemn those who designed to have 'the language quite worn out of this country', along with 'the barbarity of the manners of some of our highlanders' (NL Scot., MS 821, fol. 89r). Nevertheless, Ramsay commissioned a Gaelic translation of a catechism, and ensured there was a school in every parish, even if its language was English.

At the revolution this opponent of the excesses of Stuart church policy displayed the same loyalty to the crown as his brethren; Ramsay was deprived of his see on 22 July 1689, retiring into obscurity in Edinburgh. When on 9 August 1694 he ordained James Greenshields a presbyter, it was conditional on an oath 'to the same King for whom the Bishop professed to suffer' (Christ Church library, Oxford, Wake papers, vol. 19, fol. 189r). On 22 October 1696 Ramsay died at Edinburgh 'in very low circumstances' (Keith and Spottiswoode, 517); he was buried in Canongate churchyard.

TRISTRAM CLARKE

Sources J. Kirkton, *A history of the Church of Scotland, 1660–1679*, ed. R. Stewart (1992) · R. Wodrow, *The history of the sufferings of the Church of Scotland from the Restoration to the revolution*, ed. R. Burns, 2 (1829) · *The Lauderdale papers*, ed. O. Airy, 3 vols., CS, new ser., 34, 36, 38 (1884–5) · *Reg. PCS*, 3rd ser., vol. 4 · papers concerning Ramsay's election, 1672, NL Scot., MS 10285, fols. 62–6 · letters of John Paterson to Archbishop Sharp, 1674–5, NA Scot., CH12/12/1366–1371 · letters to earl of Moray, 1686, priv. coll., earl of Moray's papers, 7/619 · J. Kirkwood, correspondence, 1687–8, NL Scot., MS 821, fols. 79–91 · R. Keith and J. Spottiswoode, *An historical catalogue of the Scottish bishops, down to the year 1688*, new edn, ed. M. Russel [M. Russell] (1824) · E. B. Fryde and others, eds., *Handbook of British chronology*, 3rd edn, Royal Historical Society Guides and Handbooks, 2 (1986) · G. Grub, *An ecclesiastical history of Scotland*, 4 vols. (1861), vol. 3 · W. L. Mathieson, *Politics and religion: a study in Scottish history from the Reformation to the revolution*, 2 (1902) · *Fasti Scot.*, new edn, vol. 7 · *DNB* · *The letters and journals of Robert Baillie*, ed. D. Laing, 3 (1842) · C. S. Terry, *The Pentland rising and Rullion Green* (1905) · Christ Church Oxf., Wake MSS

Archives NL Scot., letters and MSS | NA Scot., corresp. with Archbishop Sharp, CH12/12/1789 · NL Scot., letters to Forbes of Culloden, MS 2963

Ramsay, James (1733–1789), surgeon and slavery abolitionist, was born on 25 July 1733 at Fraserburgh, Aberdeenshire, the only son of William Ramsay (1683–1754), ship's carpenter, and his wife, Margaret Ogilvie (1696–1772) of Powrie. After attending Fraserburgh grammar school he was apprenticed to Dr Alexander Findlay, a local surgeon. A bursary enabled him to enter King's College, Aberdeen,

James Ramsay (1733–1789), by Carl Fredrik von Breda, 1789

and brought Ramsay under the teaching of Dr Thomas Reid (1710–1796), professor of moral philosophy, who exercised a profound influence on his thinking. After obtaining the degree of MA on 9 April 1753, he continued his surgical training in London with Dr George Macaulay, physician and treasurer of the British Lying-in Hospital. He passed his examination to enter the navy on 2 June 1757 and was appointed to the *Arundel*, a sixth rate of 24 guns and 160 men, on the West Indies station, where he came under the command of Sir Charles Middleton. The *Arundel* intercepted the British slave ship *Swift*, ravaged by dysentery, on 27 November 1759 and, on boarding her, Ramsay found over 100 slaves wallowing in blood and excreta, a scene of human degradation which remained for ever in his memory and so distracted his attention that, on returning to his ship, he fell and fractured his thigh bone. It was the more serious of two such accidents and he remained lame for life.

With an end to his naval service in prospect, Ramsay sought ordination in the Anglican church to enable him to work among slaves. He returned to Britain in July 1761, left the navy in September, and was ordained by the bishop of London in November. He departed almost immediately for St Kitts, where he was appointed to St John's, Capisterre (1762), and to Christ Church, Nicola Town (1763). In 1763 he married Rebecca Akers (*d.* 1804), daughter of a well-connected planter; they had a son, who predeceased him, and three daughters. Responding to a local need, he practised his skills in surgery and midwifery, but provided a free service to the poor. He was also appointed surgeon

to several plantations and this enabled him to see the conditions under which slaves laboured, the brutality of many owners and overseers, and the mutilating punishments and cruel injustice meted out to them. His sympathy for disadvantaged settlers led to involvement in local government and he proposed a more equitable taxation system, while his naval experience was reflected in his *Essay on the Duty and Qualifications of a Sea Officer* (1765), which was highly acclaimed and translated into a number of other languages.

Ramsay's interest in the welfare of slaves was encouraged by people of integrity, but aroused the antagonism of influential planters and local government officials who, facing ruin, attempted to manipulate the interest rate in their favour to the detriment of honest and thrifty citizens. Ramsay felt it his duty to challenge this illegal scheme and became the target of verbal abuse, scurrilous pamphlets, and letters to newspapers. He was deprived of his magistracy, privileges of the clergy were curtailed, and church-going discouraged. His letters to the bishop of London disclose serious disaffection among colonists at this period. They marked the beginning of his relationship with British politicians.

On returning to Britain in 1777 Ramsay visited his married sister Jean in Fraserburgh, adopted his nephew James Ramsay Walker, and paid for the boy's education. Walker subsequently became bishop of Edinburgh and primus of the Scottish Episcopal church. Ramsay was then received into the family of Sir Charles Middleton at Barham Court, Teston, Kent, where Lady Middleton immediately warmed to the cause of slaves. In April 1778 he rejoined the navy as chaplain to Admiral Barrington on the West Indies station. His knowledge of West Indies affairs may have influenced the appointment for he had been introduced to Lord George Germain, secretary of state for the American department, who arranged for him to supply private intelligence. Ramsay saw action against the French off St Lucia in December 1778 and off Grenada and St Kitts in July 1779. He was subsequently based in St Kitts gathering intelligence for Admiral G. B. Rodney, formed a lasting friendship with Sir Gilbert Blane, Rodney's physician, and rendered valuable service to the Jews when Rodney captured St Eustatius. During this time he prepared the material for his book *Sea Sermons for the Royal Navy* (1781), which revealed a genuine affection for the sailor, an understanding of his character, and an appreciation of his contribution to the nation. 'You and your fellow-combatants were a band of brothers engaged in one cause', he said (*Sea Sermons*, 7). It was a phrase later adopted by Nelson.

Early in 1779 Ramsay had been invited by Middleton, then a rear-admiral and comptroller of the navy, to assist him with a radical reform of the Navy Board and he returned to Britain with his wife and family during the latter part of 1781, to be awarded a Lambeth MA and, in January 1782, installed as vicar of Teston and rector of Nettleshead. The livings were in Middleton's gift and the rectory adjoined Barham Court, where Ramsay acted as Middleton's confidential secretary. He also appears to have initiated policy, for several papers are in his handwriting and preliminary drafts appear in his private diary. In 1782 he also took the new diploma of the Company of Surgeons, which suggests an intention eventually to resume his practice in St Kitts.

At Barham Court and the Middleton's London home in Hertford Street, Ramsay found himself among an influential circle of philanthropists, intelligentsia, and politicians where his account of the iniquities of the slave trade aroused vehement indignation, and Lady Middleton urged him to lay his evidence before the nation. His *Essay on the Treatment and Conversion of African Slaves in the British Sugar Colonies* appeared in 1784 and was the most important event in the early history of the anti-slavery movement. In this work he reviewed the status of slaves in history, their moral rights, their ill treatment in British colonies, and the influence of nutritional deficiency, overwork, and mutilating punishments upon morbidity, mortality, and output, with examples of the benefits of enlightened management. Nevertheless he foresaw the problems of precipitate emancipation and proposed a programme of preparation which would encompass education, Christian teaching, the inculcation of family and social values, and the passing of equitable laws. The book received immediate acclaim but was followed by a flood of vituperation from the planter community in anonymous letters to national and colonial newspapers, which Ramsay countered effectively in his *Reply to Personal Invectives* (1785). Meanwhile, in *An Inquiry into the Effects of Putting a Stop to the African Slave Trade* (1784) he advocated the development of a mixed economy on the African coast for emancipated slaves who would trade their produce for British manufactures. This book impressed Pitt and William Wilberforce.

During this period Ramsay was acting as Middleton's secretary and, in addition to the reorganization of the Navy Board, was involved in the settlement of Australia. He appears to have chosen the surgeons of the first fleet (1787), who achieved a remarkable health record and provided the medical establishment of the colony. He also collaborated with Sir Gilbert Blane in his book *Diseases of Seamen* (1785) and Blane was impressed by his warm and disinterested zeal for the service.

Initially, Ramsay bore the acrimony of the planters alone until Wilberforce, whom he had met in 1783, and T. Clarkson, his curate in 1787, rallied to the abolitionist cause. He was thereafter consulted by Pitt as the Middletons co-ordinated the anti-slavery campaign. In the run-up to the first Commons debate on abolition (May 1789)—a response to the deluge of petitions following the controversy over Ramsay's books—Ramsay prepared briefs for Wilberforce and other politicians containing many of the moral arguments and much of the evidence which Wilberforce used in his speech. During the debate Crisp Molyneux, a planter from St Kitts, impugned Ramsay's character and professional reputation. Although Middleton leapt to his defence and Olaudah Equiano, an emancipated slave acquainted with St Kitts, confirmed all that Ramsay had written, Ramsay never recovered from this attack. He developed increasingly severe abdominal pain

and died from a massive gastric haemorrhage on 20 July 1789 in the Middleton's London home in Hertford Street. He was buried in Teston churchyard on 25 July and a memorial near to that of his black servant Nestor is in Teston church. He was survived by his wife.

C. I. La Trobe paid tribute to Ramsay's diligence, benevolence, and urbanity and to his mild and charitable disposition (La Trobe, 17), while Clarkson admired his insight, coolness, courage, patriotism, public spirit, amiability, and the personal example which characterized his ministry (Clarkson, 2.117). Even his enemies acknowledged his exemplary qualities, while deploring the intemperate language of his books; and the abolition of the British slave trade in 1807 probably owed more to James Ramsay's personal integrity, ethical arguments, and constructive proposals than to any other influence.   J. WATT

Sources F. Shyllow, *James Ramsay: the unknown abolitionist* (1977) • *The interesting narrative of the life of Olaudah Equiano, or Gustavus Vassa, the African*, 2 vols. (1789) • J. Ramsay, *Sea sermons, or, A series of discourses for the use of the Royal Navy*, 1st edn (1781) • T. Clarkson, *The history of the rise, progress, and accomplishment of the abolition of the African slave trade by the British parliament*, 2 vols. (1808) • *Letters and papers of Charles, Lord Barham*, ed. J. K. Laughton, 3 vols., Navy RS, 32, 38–9 (1907–11) • C. I. La Trobe, *Letters to my children* (1851) • R. I. Wilberforce and S. Wilberforce, *Life of William Wilberforce*, 5 vols. (1838), vols. 1–2 • J. Pollock, *Wilberforce* (1977) • J. Watt, 'James Ramsay, 1733–1789: naval surgeon, naval chaplain and morning star of the anti-slavery movement', *Mariner's Mirror*, 81 (1995), 156–70 • J. A. Henderson, *Epitaphs and inscriptions*, 1 (1907) • *DNB* • *Encyclopaedia Britannica*, 6th edn (1823), vol. 17, pp. 632–5 • LPL, Fulham MSS • J. Lloyd-Phillips, 'The evangelical administrator, Sir Charles Middleton, at the navy board, 1778–1790', DPhil diss., U. Oxf., 1974 • parish records, Teston and Nettleshead, CKS [probate, copy] • parish register, Yalding, CKS • private information (2004)
Archives BL, essay on slavery, Add. MS 27621 • Bodl. RH, account of abolitionist work in St Kitts; holograph diary | LPL, Fulham MSS, xx, fols. 33–102; xxx, fols. 186–91 • PRO, Admiralty records, Muster lists, HMS *Arundel*, captain's log, masters' logs, ADM36/4774–4776 and 7901; ADM51/3771; ADM52/787 and 1160
Likenesses C. F. von Breda, oils, 1789, NPG [see illus.]
Wealth at death approx. £2200, to be divided between widow and three daughters: will, CKS, Teston and Nettleshead parish records

Ramsay, James (1786–1854), portrait painter, was the son of Robert Ramsay (1754–1828) of Sheffield, a carver and gilder who later became a dealer in prints and plaster models. Thus Ramsay was brought up in an atmosphere of artistic activity, this being intensified when Francis Chantrey, then a precociously talented youth, became an apprentice to Ramsay's father in 1797. In the following year his father published two mezzotint portraits of well-known Sheffield men painted by the Chesterfield artist E. Needham. The engravings were produced by John Raphael Smith and, possibly influenced by Needham and Smith, Ramsay became attracted to a career in art himself. By the age of fifteen, when he joined the family business, he was already a talented artist, his father announcing in *The Iris* (Sheffield), on 12 February 1801, that the services of 'Ramsay Junior' were available as a 'Portrait and Miniature Painter'. In 1803 Ramsay left Sheffield, taking with him a self-portrait, and, after showing it to an old friend of his father, Robert Pollard, in London, was successful in having it accepted by the Royal Academy. He was then only seventeen and, uncertain of his future in London, returned to Sheffield on a number of occasions over the next four years for what he advertised locally as 'short stays'. He was probably the James Ramsey who entered the Royal Academy Schools in March 1805 when his age was given as twenty-one. However, he soon established himself as a successful portrait painter in London, and three years after his first arrival there exhibited at the Royal Academy a portrait of Henry Grattan which was engraved in mezzotint by Charles Turner; in 1810 one of John Townley, and in 1813 that of Lord Brougham. In 1814 at the Royal Academy he varied his exhibits for the first time by showing two scriptural subjects: *Peter Denying Christ*, and *Peter's Repentance*, and in 1819 sent views of Tynemouth Abbey, and of North and South Shields. He also exhibited at the British Institution and the Society of British Artists. His main work for the remainder of his life, however, was portraiture of well-known people. One of the most notable of these was his friend and fellow artist Thomas Bewick, of whom he painted at least three portraits; the earliest of these was exhibited at the Royal Academy in 1816 and engraved by John Burnet (National History Society of Northumbria, Newcastle); the remaining two at the Royal Academy in 1823. One of these 1823 exhibits showed Bewick alone (NPG); the other consisted of a group portrait including Ramsay and his wife (Laing Gallery, Newcastle). His other sitters included James Northcote RA and Charles, second Earl Grey (1824). Although he once contemplated practising as a portrait painter in Scotland following the death of Raeburn (letter to Reid, the Leith bookseller, quoted by Jane Bewick in a letter to her brother Robert Elliott Bewick, 12 Aug 1823, Huntington MSS HM 17315), Ramsay remained based in London for some forty years. In 1848, however, he decided to move with his wife to practise in Newcastle upon Tyne, a town with which he had long been connected through his several portrait commissions in the north-east of England, his friendships with brother artists in the area, and his regular appearances at various exhibitions there. He continued to exhibit at the Royal Academy while at Newcastle, showing several portraits of local celebrities, including George Hawkes, first mayor of Gateshead (1848), and William Armstrong (1854). He died after a long illness, at 40 Blackett Street, Newcastle, on 23 June 1854. Examples of Ramsay's work are in the Carlisle Art Gallery, Hull Art Gallery, and Newcastle Central Library, and in the collections of the Literary and Philosophical Society of Newcastle and the Natural History Society of Northumbria.   R. E. GRAVES, *rev.* MARSHALL HALL

Sources W. T. Freemantle, collection of newspaper cuttings from *Sheffield Telegraph*, 2 May 1922, Sheffield Central Library, 942.74SF, vol. 5, p. 82 • *Newcastle Journal* (24 June 1854) • M. Hall, *The artists of Northumbria*, 2nd edn (1982) • Graves, *RA exhibitors* • J. Bewick, letter to R. E. Bewick, 12 Aug 1823, Hunt. L., Huntington papers, HM 17315 • S. C. Hutchison, 'The Royal Academy Schools, 1768–1830', *Walpole Society*, 38 (1960–62), 123–91, esp. 162 • Farington, *Diary* • R. Walker, *National Portrait Gallery: Regency portraits*, 2 vols. (1985)

Likenesses J. Ramsay, self-portrait, oils, exh. RA 1823, Laing Art Gallery, Newcastle upon Tyne • J. Ramsay, self-portrait, oils, 1848, Laing Art Gallery, Newcastle upon Tyne

Ramsay, James Andrew Broun, first marquess of Dalhousie (1812–1860), governor-general of India, was born at Dalhousie Castle, Bonnyrigg, Midlothian, on 22 April 1812, the youngest of three sons of George *Ramsay, ninth earl of Dalhousie (1770–1838), soldier, and colonial governor, and his wife, Christian *Ramsay (1786–1839), only daughter and heiress of Charles Broun of Colstoun in East Lothian.

Education, politics, and marriage James accompanied his parents to Canada in 1816 but returned home in 1822 and entered Harrow School in 1825. In 1829 he went to Christ Church, Oxford, where his career was not outstanding. Gladstone, Canning, and Elgin were among his contemporaries. He showed some signs of youthful intolerance— his diary notes, 'We certainly are immensely cocky but then, hang it, we have reason' (K. Fieling, *In Christ Church Hall*, 1960, 164)—but was also prone to self-examination and the desire to do better. When he came of age he resolved 'to act solely by a consideration of what will most conduce to the interests and happiness of my countrymen … In my private life … I will hope and pray that I ever shall be all that an honest and good man could wish to see me' (Warner, 1.24). The death of his elder brother, Lord Ramsay, in 1832 (the second brother had died some years before) prevented him from obtaining honours although he was awarded an honorary fourth (then regarded as equivalent to a second class) at his examination a year later.

Ramsay's political views evolved along Conservative lines; in 1831 he was unhappy about the Reform Bill and the clamour of its partisans. At the 1835 general election as Lord Ramsay he stood as a tory candidate for Edinburgh with 'no wish to perpetuate abuses or to preserve blots' (Warner, 1.34). He was defeated, but his good humour, determination, and the spirit in which he accepted defeat were remembered, and the election served to introduce him to public life. He subsequently became a JP for Haddington, joined several political and philanthropic committees, and resisted calls to come forward for an English seat, preferring to remain in Scotland. On 21 January 1836 he married Lady Susan Georgiana Hay (1817–1853), eldest daughter of the marquess of Tweeddale, a family friend. It was a love match and Ramsay came to depend much on his wife's support; her premature death at thirty-five overshadowed the remainder of his life. Their first child, Susan Georgiana, was born in 1837 and a second daughter, Edith Christian, in 1839.

In 1837 Ramsay was elected MP for East Lothian, but his father's death the following year called him to the Lords as the tenth earl of Dalhousie. It seems he saw little chance of early advancement in the upper house (where he joined the group of Peelite tory peers) and so devoted his energies to specifically Scottish issues. In 1839 he became a member of the general assembly of the Church of Scotland, representing the presbytery of Dalkeith, in which lay his own parish of Cockpen. He took an active part in

James Andrew Broun Ramsay, first marquess of Dalhousie
(1812–1860), by Sir John Watson-Gordon, 1847

the assembly at a time when the great questions which resulted in the Disruption four years later were already stirring. Dalhousie was in favour of church reform but later resigned his seat in disagreement that the assembly should persist with a measure against a ruling of the court of session confirmed by the House of Lords.

President of the Board of Trade Dalhousie soon attracted the notice of the duke of Wellington and Sir Robert Peel, who, after the fall of Melbourne in 1841, became Conservative prime minister. Dalhousie declined an appointment to the queen's household (although his wife briefly served as a lady of the bedchamber) and was considered for the governorships of Madras and Bombay. In 1843 his chance came with the offer of the post of vice-president of the Board of Trade when Gladstone became president.

Dalhousie took up office with a vigour that would become characteristic of his tenure in India; he was usually first and last at his desk each day, often working into the early hours. His appointment was soon followed by the onset of the 'railway mania' which confronted the board with a huge workload. Gladstone gave Dalhousie a free hand, allowing him an insight into railway business of great value later when he dealt with schemes in India.

In 1845 he succeeded Gladstone as president, and eventually joined the cabinet. If Dalhousie had had his way, he would have subjected the construction and management of railway schemes to the co-ordinating control of government. He failed, however, to win Peel's support and devised instead a mechanism for the close scrutiny of each new scheme before sanction was given.

Dalhousie, when president, also had to deal with a wide range of other issues including banking, the coal trade, land matters, and sugar duties. His abilities and capacity for work were recognized not only by his own party but also by the opposition. After Peel's fall in 1846 Lord John Russell tried and failed to secure Dalhousie for the whig cabinet.

Governor-general of India In the following year, however, Dalhousie accepted Russell's offer of the governor-generalship of India in succession to Viscount Hardinge, on the understanding that it would not compromise his political loyalties. A factor in his decision was the insecure financial position he inherited (a debt by now of £48,000): the governor-general commanded a substantial salary. He sailed for India in November 1847 and was sworn as governor-general in Calcutta on 12 January 1848. At thirty-five he was the youngest man to have held the appointment; small and short but well made in stature, with dark brown hair and a rich resonant voice, he had a quiet dignity coupled with a nervous force backed by obvious strength of mind and character.

Dalhousie faced problems of consolidating East India Company rule without jeopardizing its essential dynamism. His policy came to have two closely interwoven strands: economic and administrative 'modernization', and strategic territorial expansion within India's 'natural frontiers'. The two strands were linked by the immediate and practical need to strengthen the company's hold on India and to create a state capable of providing the resources both for its own occupation and for the underpinning of British economic and military power throughout the East. The problems were not new (the concerns of his predecessors such as Bentinck and Ellenborough show this), but Dalhousie's combination of political and administrative skills, energy, and sheer determination to become thoroughly acquainted with the Indian system of government and administration and its condition and resources was. The consistent pursuit of this dual policy has given Dalhousie the credit for laying the foundations of modern India through modernization and consolidation but also the blame for the most serious crisis of the whole period of British control—the uprising of 1857.

Dalhousie's style of government in India From the outset Dalhousie established a rigorous official routine in Calcutta. He rose at about 6 a.m., read a Bible chapter, and then devoted himself to office boxes until breakfast over the Indian newspapers at 8 a.m. At 9.30 a.m. he went to his desk and usually stayed there until 5.30 p.m., consuming lunch while at work. While away from Calcutta on tour he worked equally hard to keep up with the necessary business. As at the Board of Trade, he put immense effort into mastering the details of questions with which he had to deal and used this as a means of enforcing considerable personal authority throughout the entire Indian government. For example, only sixteen days after taking up his duties he refused to continue established practice of autographing blank dispatches for the government secretaries to draft over, so that in future 'I may see what I am signing' (Dalhousie MSS). His arduous days meant he preferred quiet evenings with his wife rounded off with another Bible chapter before bed; he much disliked the official functions, many of them after normal working hours, that were inseparable from his official position.

Dalhousie considered the governor-general 'the beginning, middle and end of all', and his style made it the more so; he confided to his diary in 1854 on the departure of Sir Henry Elliot, 'I have myself done the chief part of the work in his, as in every other, department of Govt.' Dalhousie's almost obsessive attention to detail shows he saw this as the only safe way to get things done and his frustrations were revealed in another document of 1854 when he advised, 'if you want anything done which *must* be done, follow my plan viz Order it to be done, see that it is done and *circulate* the papers afterwards' (Dalhousie MSS).

Despite his forceful style it is equally clear, however, that Dalhousie accepted advice, did not generally allow personal considerations to influence his judgement (although he was involved in some acrimonious wrangles with other key figures, such as the commander-in-chief Sir Charles Napier, when this resolve was tested to the full), was prepared to forgive mistakes, and was keen to give credit to subordinates where credit was due. Overall, Dalhousie's example and efforts improved the conduct of the company's administration. Canning, his successor (1856–62), observed that 'Dalhousie, though he did more than was necessary in some matters, made business shorter and smoother' (M. Maclagan, *Clemency Canning*, 1962, 47). Dalhousie's thoroughgoing administrative background was important in his selection as governor-general and, arriving after the defeat of the Sikhs, he seemed destined to undertake the final pacification of India. In April 1848, however, two events occurred that would mould the course of Dalhousie's incumbency: the death of the raja of Satara, which raised the question of the 'lapse' of princely states to the direct rule of the East India Company, and the outbreak of revolt in Multan, which initiated a train of events leading to the annexation of the Punjab, the last of the major native powers within the 'natural frontiers'.

The lapse of Satara Dalhousie has been credited with invention of the doctrine of lapse, which featured so strongly in the territorial expansion of his years in India. The doctrine was, in fact, first promulgated in 1834 and formalized in 1841, and Dalhousie was not alone in India or in London in wishing to use it to give both order and legitimacy to the 'falling-in' of princely states. In this way the company's rule could be extended gradually and methodically, with each case being carefully considered on its merits and its contribution to company resources, and in a way designed to avoid overstretching Calcutta's capacity to deal effectively with new acquisitions. Dalhousie later wrote that he was 'for the extension of territory by way of consolidation' (Wood MSS). He noted in relation to Satara that,

> while I would not seek to lay down any inflexible rule with respect to adoption, I hold that on all occasions where heirs natural shall fail, the territory shall be made to lapse and adoption should not be permitted, excepting in those cases in which some strong political reason may render it expedient to depart from this general rule.   (S. N. Prasad, *Paramountcy under Dalhousie*, 1964, 106)

Dalhousie hoped incorporation of princely states would rationalize administration, broaden company revenue, and consolidate its geographical hold on the subcontinent. Such reasoning was the reality of Indian politics, and talk of any moral responsibility for the welfare of the population at large was 'nothing else than ambitious and hypothetical humbug' (India home miscellaneous series, vol. 828). Satara, therefore, 'lapsed' and established the outline of Dalhousie's policy towards the princely states, although its presentation was moulded, in each case, by reaction to the policy both at home and in India.

The annexation of the Punjab The Punjab was even more crucial; it came to exemplify Dalhousie's concern to link strategic and improving policies in a co-ordinated way to consolidate company power and provide a model for effective administration elsewhere in the subcontinent. In 1848 the Punjab lay beyond formal British authority but within the company's sphere of interest. The revolt at Multan, therefore, presented Dalhousie with a major crisis within ten months of arriving in India; he saw that a solution must allow military savings and some addition to company revenue, although initially he resisted annexation. A second Anglo-Sikh war had not been unexpected, but the difficulties the company forces experienced in gaining a decisive victory were a surprise and it was not until January 1849 that Multan was taken.

In the meantime Dalhousie had left Calcutta for the Punjab and exercised close, though not unchallenged, supervision over Lord Gough, the commander-in-chief. Victory was achieved only after considerable effort, and in March 1849 Dalhousie decided to annex the Punjab to reinforce company standing against its enemies within India. Drawing on the advice of those with experience of the Punjab during its period of company supervision after 1846, he was convinced that the province would be a paying proposition. The young Sikh maharaja Duleep Singh was deposed, and the famous Koh-i-noor diamond was confiscated and sent to Queen Victoria (it remains part of the British crown jewels). Dalhousie was created a marquess in recognition of his role in the campaign and, characteristically, noted in his diary that 'I of course prefer to be a Scottish Earl of 1633 to being an English Marquis of 1849', although he was still 'most deeply grateful for it and gratified by it' (Warner, 1.230–31).

Consolidation and conciliation in the Punjab Dalhousie was fully aware that annexation was only the start of the Punjab problem; it was the largest and most powerful state to be absorbed by the company since the final defeat of the Marathas in 1818. Contemporaries drew a distinction between it and previous conquests; annexation had not just overturned a dynasty but clashed with a nationality, so British policy had to be more comprehensive, persuasive, and assertive than ever before. Dalhousie was, therefore, concerned to frame a civil policy pitched towards the local sources of influence while maintaining a firm grip on military security. His response was to devise a mixed form of military and civilian government under his own supervision, so the Punjab became a new form of non-regulation province under a board of administration until 1853. Boards, which divided authority and responsibility, were not generally favoured by Dalhousie, but it provided a way of managing Henry Lawrence (hitherto the British resident in Lahore), whom he thought 'plus Sikh que les Sikhs'. The governor-general also wanted to make the best use of the available official talent, and made appointments without regard to the usual rules of seniority. In contrast to the older established territories, the new administration was to be 'rough and ready ... until revenues mend' (Dalhousie MSS). Dalhousie also identified the need for a co-ordinated scheme of pacification and development to stitch the Sikhs to company rule, and was therefore keen to use 'Native Agency united with Europeans' because 'policy would dictate our doing so, even if finance should not compel it' (Henry Lawrence MSS).

Dalhousie was equally keen that annexation should not mean full-scale, and therefore unsettling, change for the Punjab. The authority of the local chiefs (*sardars*) had already been undermined by the military and political changes that had swept the province since the death of Ranjit Singh in 1839. Where *sardars* were effective collaborators with company rule, they were retained. Where resumption by the new rulers of chiefly authority was deemed necessary, extremes of leniency or harshness were avoided and the decisions made with certainty and quietness to consolidate British control. The major problems facing the board were in the extraction of revenue from powerful village brotherhoods, which held sway in most of the province, and in settling the men of the defeated Sikh army back to the plough. Dalhousie was anxious to preserve village rights so far as possible and to establish effective arbitration procedures; settlement officers were vested with full civil and revenue powers. Revenue demands were cut by 25 per cent and it is clear that Dalhousie was carefully balancing immediate needs against longer-term political security. Mistakes occurred, but settlement officers trod as carefully as possible. John Lawrence was petitioned by some headmen in Butala; he sent them away but told the assessing officer that 'You might quietly take a look at your statements' (John Lawrence MSS). The care with which these detailed problems were approached owed much to the influence of the governor-general himself.

The Punjab pacification also necessitated dealing with about 40,000 Sikh soldiers. Dalhousie decided, despite misgivings from London, to recruit local corps and

regarded 'the free enlistment of the young Sikhs from the Manjha [area] as a measure of great political value' (Dalhousie MSS), thereby establishing a key component of the future military history of India. The Manjha benefited from Dalhousie's blend of civil and military policy because he considered it

> of the utmost moment to provide means of subsistence and employment for the Sikhs of the Manjha who have been the most turbulent in the recent proceedings and have been most affected by the results of the war ... To this end the opening of new branches from the Irrigation Canal which traverses the upper Manjha ... was very early urged upon me on Political and Financial grounds.   (Dalhousie MSS)

This combined policy was crucial to the stability of the Punjab during the tumult of 1857.

The annexation of Pegu   The Punjab problem came early in Dalhousie's Indian career and did much to develop his ideas for consolidating company rule. Ideally, such consolidation would concentrate on civil and economic measures, but Dalhousie soon concluded that the company 'could not, consistently with its own safety, appear in an attitude of inferiority ... among the numberless princes and peoples embraced within the vast circuit of the Empire' (Dalhousie MSS) in India. External difficulties always posed dangers. Trouble in Burma during 1851 was, therefore, unwelcome to Dalhousie; it gave no opportunity to consolidate within the natural frontiers, nor did it promise much for the company's coffers. The grievances of British mercantile interests in Rangoon were old and unproven, but they were skilfully manipulated. Dalhousie tried hard to avoid war but failed: the new province of Pegu was added to the empire on 20 December 1852. Dalhousie decided that Pegu should be entrusted to a commissioner with an administration similar to that developed for the Punjab. Initial optimism about a swift settlement proved unfounded, and the governor-general characteristically brought his direct authority to bear. The commissioner was asked to prepare a comprehensive plan for future government of the province; he was told that 'order internally I must have, and at whatever cost' (*The Dalhousie–Phayre Correspondence, 1852–56*, ed. D. G. E. Hall, 1932, 100). Effective British authority was gradually imposed from 1854, and Pegu also remained quiet in 1857.

Absorption of princely states within India   Dalhousie had reservations about the annexation of both the Punjab and Pegu; both threatened to pose major problems for his concept of an ordered consolidation of company rule. This was not the case, however, in relation to the absorption of many of the 'internal' princely states: he advocated

> taking advantage of every just opportunity which presents itself for consolidating the territories which already belong to us, by taking possession of States which may lapse in the midst of them; for getting rid of those petty intervening principalities which may be a means of annoyance, but which can never, I venture to think, be a source of strength. (Hunter, 128–9)

The outcome at Satara has been noted, as has the fact that

Dalhousie did not invent the doctrine of lapse. It was typical of the man that he applied the doctrine in a more rigorous and uniform way than his predecessors; he presumed in favour of annexation if it could be done 'legitimately'. Even so, not all princely states could have lapsed to company rule in this way; Dalhousie generally recognized the right to adopt of those rulers whose sovereignty predated company paramountcy.

Financial and security factors form a thread through Dalhousie's absorptions of internal princely states. The nizam of Hyderabad lost territory through the long-standing question of the financing of the Hyderabad contingent, a body of native troops provided for company use. Dalhousie, concerned as always to make the most of scarce resources, wished to see the contingent's cost cut and its troops used more flexibly. He did not want the full-scale annexation of Hyderabad; instead, he wanted a portion of Hyderabad to be held against the costs of the contingent. This was achieved in 1853. Nagpur was next to be absorbed, in 1854; Dalhousie wrote, 'To sum up in one sentence, the possession of Nagpur would combine our military strength and would enlarge our commercial resources—and would materially tend to consolidate our power' (Dalhousie MSS). The lapse, however, did not take place without heirs coming forward, and a contemporary noted that 'the real law by which Nagpur was added to our dominions was the law of the strongest' (E. Arnold, *The Marquess of Dalhousie's Administration of British India*, 2 vols., 1862–5, 2.164–6). Nagpur was to Dalhousie a classic case of consolidation; it added 40 lakhs of rupees to the company's annual revenue and 80,000 square miles of valuable territory in central India, and it straddled the routes from Bombay to Calcutta and the north.

The same principle of lapse on failure of heirs was applied to several other princely states by Dalhousie. In Jhansi (1853) he decided that

> the British Government would not derive any material advantage from the annexation … for it was very small and its revenue inconsiderable; but since it lay in the midst of other British districts its possession … would tend to the improvement of the general internal administration of British possessions in Bundlekund, beside greatly benefiting the people of Jhansi. (Rahim, 210)

Jaitpur and Sambalpur (1849), Baghpat (1850), and Udaipur (1852) were also incorporated under lapse. Absorption of these smaller states caused concern among some native rulers about the company's long-term intentions, and the home government refused Dalhousie's desire to absorb Karauli, one of the oldest Rajput states. After the mutiny the annexation of Baghpat and Udaipur was reversed. Dalhousie was convinced, however, that his policy was the correct way to consolidate the reality of company power behind its extended frontier.

Dalhousie also abolished several titular sovereignties that had ceased to have any real substance and yet remained as a distraction to company supremacy. In 1853 he supported the wish of the Madras government to avoid designating an heir as nawab of the Carnatic, and in 1855

the raj of Tanjore was suppressed. Dalhousie also contemplated abolishing the Mughal emperor's title at Delhi but was overruled by caution in London.

The annexation of Oudh Just as Dalhousie's Indian career opened with exceptional events in the Punjab, so it closed with an exceptional problem in Oudh. The annexation of Oudh was not undertaken on the basis of conquest, lapse, or suppression of titular sovereignty. Since 1801 it had been a protected state with full internal autonomy but had become racked by increasing internal political strife. Dalhousie was reluctant to intervene if it would cost rather than raise company revenues. Yet Oudh was both economically productive and strategically important, straddling as it did the trading and military routes from Bengal to the north-west. The nawabs had also provided useful loans to the company during moments of crisis such as the First Anglo-Afghan War (1838–42), and many of their wealthier citizens held company stock.

The loyalty of the nawabs over many years forced Dalhousie to admit that he could not 'find a pretext' for annexation and to decide to preserve the nawab's title and royal status, a line inconsistent with his general views. In February 1856, however, the king refused to sign a new treaty, or to abdicate, thereby breaking the loyalty that had protected him for so long; Oudh was consequently annexed. The transition to British rule had all the appearance of ease and order backed by the co-operation of the nawab. It was decided that the new administration should be modelled on that of the Punjab, and the same attempts were made to balance company control with the adherence of locals with power and influence. Unlike the Punjab, however, the measures did not work as well, and arguably contributed to the uprising of 1857. The long-standing question of Oudh was tackled very late in the day by Dalhousie, and absorption of the province was rushed. Dalhousie was unable to devote the detailed attention he applied to the Punjab: he was preoccupied with handover arrangements for his successor, and was in increasingly poor health.

The material improvement of India Traditionally, territorial acquisitions occupy centre stage of Dalhousie's Indian career. From his own perspective internal reforms were equally important, not as agents of deliberate 'Westernizing', but as practical steps for the consolidation of British power in India. Temperament and previous experience fitted him well for a career devoted to 'improvement' in the mid-Victorian sense. As with India's external and princely state affairs, financial difficulties were also central to domestic policies. Dalhousie strove after the most cost-effective administration possible for India's development as a modern state. This would hinge as much on railways, posts and telegraphs, streamlined bureaucracy, and reformed education as on improved military and territorial measures.

Dalhousie's annexations added to revenue and, although charges initially increased in a higher proportion than income, strenuous efforts were made to keep costs to a minimum. Besides, he saw territorial accretion as an inevitable process to be regulated and assessed in the longer term; only when company rule was securely established on a wider revenue base throughout India could real returns be expected. His aim was not uniform centralization but local responsiveness. Ideally the government of India should not control local affairs, and fully centralized departments like the post office should be the exception rather than the rule. Dalhousie wanted secure administration and attacked what he saw as proven abuses. For instance, he said Bombay's administrative problems were worsened by the presidency government's tendency to correspond on little slips of paper 'like an electric telegraph' (Dalhousie MSS). He also reduced courses at Fort William College from twenty-two to six months, supplementing them with in-service training, and pressed for competitive entry designed to produce a more professional service. If India was not understood, she could not be administered safely: 'There never was a mutiny in this army except from our own injustice or ill management' (Dalhousie, *Letters*, 344). He also took steps to enlarge the legislative council and to include more expert opinion; there were already Indians who could contribute to policy. In 1854 the appointment of an Indian judge to the bench of the *sadr adalat* was recommended.

The changes made in the administration of the law sprang from the same desire for more effective, impartial, and therefore secure rule, for example by bringing Europeans within the jurisdiction of local criminal courts (they already came under local civil courts), although Indian law needed modification to be acceptable to Europeans. Dalhousie undertook some of the most important domestic reforms ever introduced into modern India. Most significant was probably his railway scheme, contained in a seminal minute of 1853 which drew much on his previous British ministerial experience and was heralded by the *Friend of India* newspaper as 'the text book for all future Railway projects in India' (8 Sept 1853). The minute also embodied proposals that had been impossible at home. Dalhousie wished to establish a strategic scheme for the whole country, embracing a rational assessment of political, military, and commercial needs and, while making the most of private capital, reserved the right of the government of India to take over lines after twenty-five or thirty years. He was also careful to decide on only one gauge—of 5 ft 6 in.—after careful weighing of the technical and financial arguments, rather than the standard of 4 ft 8½ in. established after the Stockton and Darlington Railway in 1825. Dalhousie took care to make the best use possible of expert opinion and worked closely with Colonel John Pitt Kennedy, who had been appointed consulting engineer for railways in 1850. In 1853 the first line in India was opened over the 20 miles from Bombay to Thana. In 1855 Dalhousie himself inaugurated the first section of the East Indian Railway from Calcutta to Raniganj. By 1858 there were 400 miles of railway open and another 3600 planned throughout the subcontinent.

Dalhousie supplemented railways with the electric telegraph, which revolutionized the tempo of both commercial and official business. He also established a public works department and colleges of engineering, key agents in development policy, especially of roads and irrigation. Social measures included the initiation of a complete scheme of public education in both English and the vernaculars (framed before Sir Charles Wood's famous Education Despatch of 1854), action against thuggee, suttee, dacoity, and infanticide, concern to improve the lot of Indian women, and reform of prison administration. In social policy he was generally careful to avoid disturbing deeply held Indian beliefs; for example, it was 'the duty of the Government to maintain in Calcutta, as heretofore, the Seminaries of that peculiar oriental learning which is cultivated by the great sects of Hindus and Musalmans respectively' (S. C. Ghosh, 'The utilitarianism of Dalhousie and the material improvement of modern India', *Modern Asian Studies*, Feb 1978). He also held that 'no British subject should suffer penalties in his person or in his property by reason of the religious creed that he professes' (Dalhousie MSS), and he was keen that the Taj Mahal, as a symbol of historic India, should not have a railway viaduct built in too close proximity. Increased social change was fostered, nevertheless, and contributed to the outbreak of 1857.

The three quasi-autonomous presidency governments sometimes frustrated Dalhousie in his quest for efficiency although, as noted, he was aware of the dangers of over-centralization. He reorganized the workings of the central secretariat and the governor-general's council in Calcutta through the division of the work and the introduction of more specific accountability. He was also called upon to implement the changes required by the company's new charter passed by the British parliament in 1853 and to institute the new legislative council and the lieutenant-governorship of Bengal. One of his last acts was to put forward proposals for military reforms, including a case for increasing the company's European strength and reducing dependence on native troops. The Indian army had for a long time diverted some of its best officers to civil administration, and Dalhousie's concern increased when British troops withdrew for service in the Crimean War (1854–6), despite his objections, because the European force was 'not more than adequate for preserving the Empire in security and tranquillity even in ordinary times' (C. Jackson, *A Vindication of the Marquis of Dalhousie's Indian Administration*, 1865, 160–61). Again he was concerned that the responsibilities of company power fell short of the means to fulfil them.

After India: retirement and death Dalhousie's tenure as governor-general was twice extended, so that he served for three years beyond his allotted time. At a personal level his career in India was immensely stressful (he referred to it as a form of 'transportation'), and his habit of hard work together with the climate soon took its toll on his health. From 1853 his life was also seriously overshadowed by the death of his wife *en route* to Britain to convalesce, although he received immense support from his elder daughter, Lady Susan, who joined him in 1854. In 1855 he spent time in the Nilgiri hills in a vain attempt to restore his energies and was glad to hand over his responsibilities to Canning on 29 February 1856, leaving India 'exhausted with fatigue, agitation and pain', telling his friend Couper that 'Opus exegi—my work is done', and determined on retirement (Dalhousie, *Letters*, 371).

He arrived at Spithead on 13 May 1856, having, typically, spent the voyage composing a major review of his Indian administration. Dalhousie travelled to London and, although very ill, received a number of friends at Claridge's, including Gladstone. Dalhousie received a letter of thanks for his services from Queen Victoria, and the directors of the East India Company voted him a pension of £5000 per year. In August he moved north to Arrochar and from there to Edinburgh (Dalhousie Castle being in the hands of builders). His health remained precarious; in December 1856 he wrote, 'My progress is so slow and my condition such, that there is no probability of my return to public life, under any circumstances, for a long time to come, if ever' (Warner, 2.400). During 1857 his health was further eroded by the news of the mutiny in India; a sea cruise to Malta brought little improvement. In September 1857 he recorded that 'I can hardly bear to think of the horrible scenes that have been acted' (ibid., 401). A year later he was back in Edinburgh and, as the alterations to Dalhousie Castle were by then complete, he took an interest in the running of the estate. India was never far away, however, and the factor on the estate recorded how Dalhousie often talked of the mutiny and considered that, if he had still been in Calcutta, the turmoil would not have happened.

Dalhousie's health remained poor, and in 1860 he gave up the duties of lord warden of the Cinque Ports (assumed after the death of the duke of Wellington in 1852). In September he was presented with a granddaughter by Lady Edith, who had married Sir James Fergusson in 1859. His strength now declined steadily; he died peacefully at home on 19 December 1860 from Bright's disease of the kidney. He was buried next to his wife in the Dalhousie vault in the old churchyard at Cockpen.

Dalhousie's career assessed In 1865 the duke of Argyll concluded, 'When the records of our Empire in the East are closed, Lord Dalhousie's administration will be counted with the greatest that have gone before it' (Campbell). It is a measure of Dalhousie's achievement that this verdict still holds true, and his career is seen as crucially important both by historians of the British empire in the East and by those of the emergence of India as a modern nation. Fittingly, Dalhousie Road still remains in New Delhi as a reminder to both traditions.

Dalhousie was frustrated in developing a political career at home, and India gave him the opportunity to make his mark from a sense of both patriotic duty and ambition for his family tradition. He proved himself a superb, lucid, and indefatigable administrator who was at once a master of detail but also a strategic thinker. He did not set out for India with any preconceived ideas of 'modernization', 'Westernization', or 'annexation'. Instead he used his immense skills and energy in a pragmatic way to tackle the fundamental problem of closing the gap between the reality and fragility of company power on the one hand and the expectations vested in it on the other. It is for this that Dalhousie should be remembered and not for the supposed application of abstract nostrums or for a *post hoc* responsibility for the mutiny.   DAVID J. HOWLETT

Sources NA Scot., Dalhousie MSS • W. W. Hunter, *The marquess of Dalhousie* (1890) • W. L. Warner, *The life of the marquess of Dalhousie*, 2 vols. (1904) • J. A. B. Ramsay, marquess of Dalhousie, *Private letters*, ed. J. G. A. Baird (1910) • M. A. Rahim, *Lord Dalhousie's administration of the conquered and annexed states* (1963) • G. D. Campbell, *India under Dalhousie and Canning ... from the 'Edinburgh Review'* (1865) • H. Parris, *Government and the railways in nineteenth-century Britain* (1965) • S. C. Ghosh, *Dalhousie in India, 1848–56* (1975) • C. A. Bayly, *Indian society and the making of the British empire* (1988), vol. 2/1 of *The new Cambridge history of India*, ed. G. Johnson • Marquess of Dalhousie's diary, priv. coll. • BL OIOC, Wood MSS • BL OIOC, Home misc. • BL OIOC, Henry Lawrence MSS • BL OIOC, John Lawrence MSS • d. cert. • Gladstone, *Diaries* • GEC, *Peerage*

Archives NA Scot., corresp. and papers • NRA Scotland, priv. coll., corresp. and journals [copies] • priv. coll., diary | BL, corresp. with W. E. Gladstone, Add. MSS 44359–44650, *passim* • BL, corresp. with John Charles Herries, Add. MS 57411 • BL, corresp. with Sir J. C. Hobhouse, Add. MSS 36476–36477 • BL, letters to Sir Herbert Maddock, Add. MS 46186 • BL, corresp. with Sir Charles Napier, Add. MS 49106 • BL, corresp. with Sir Robert Peel, Add. MSS 40422–40601, *passim* • BL, letters to Colonel H. T. Tucker, Add. MS 48590 • BL OIOC, corresp. with Sir George Clerk, MSS Eur. D 538 • BL OIOC, letters to F. F. Courtenay, MSS Eur. C 204 • BL OIOC, corresp. with Sir Bartle Frere, MSS Eur. F 81 • BL OIOC, letters to Sir J. P. Grant, MSS Eur. F 127 • BL OIOC, corresp. with Sir J. C. Hobhouse, MSS Eur. F 213 • BL OIOC, letters to Sir J. W. Hogg, MSS Eur. E 342 • BL OIOC, corresp. with Sir Henry Lawrence, MSS Eur. F 85 • BL OIOC, letters to John Lawrence, MSS Eur. F 90 • BL OIOC, Wood MSS • Bodl. Oxf., Napier MSS • Duke U., Perkins L., letters to Sir W. R. Gilbert • Lpool RO, letters to fourteenth earl of Derby • NA Scot., letters to G. W. Hope • NL Scot., letters to Lord Tweeddale • NRA Scotland, priv. coll., letters to Sir George Couper • PRO, letters to Sir Charles Napier, PRO 30/64 • PRO, corresp. with Lord John Russell, PRO 30/22 • U. Nott. L., letters to fifth duke of Newcastle • U. Southampton L., letters to duke of Wellington • W. Yorks. AS, Leeds, corresp. with Lord Canning

Likenesses J. Watson-Gordon, oils, *c.*1835, Archers' Hall, Edinburgh • H. Robinson, stipple, pubd 1845 (after G. Richmond), BM, NPG • J. Watson-Gordon, oils, 1847, NPG [*see illus.*] • J. Watson-Gordon, oils, 1857, Scot. NPG • J. Watson-Gordon, oils, *c.*1858, legislative council chamber, Calcutta • J. Steell, marble statue, 1864, Victoria Memorial Hall, Calcutta • G. Harvey, group portrait, oils, Scot. NPG • G. Richmond, portrait, Dalhousie Castle, Midlothian • J. Steell, plaster cast, Scot. NPG • J. Watson-Gordon, pencil drawing, Scot. NPG • bust, Dalhousie Castle, Midlothian

Ramsay, Sir James Henry, tenth baronet (1832–1925), historian, was the eldest son of Sir George *Ramsay, ninth baronet (1800–1871), a philosopher, and Emily Eugenia (1806–1885), daughter of Captain Henry Lennon, of co. Westmeath. William *Ramsay (1806–1865), the classicist, was his uncle. He was born at Versailles on 21 May 1832, and educated at Rugby School and at Christ Church, Oxford. He was awarded a second class in classical moderations in 1853, a first in *literae humaniores* in 1854, and a first in law and modern history in 1855. He was elected a student of Christ Church in 1854, but gave up that position in 1861 on his marriage on 24 July to Mary (*d.* 1868), daughter of William Scott Kerr, of Chatto and Sunlaws, Roxburghshire. There were three daughters of the marriage. Ramsay was called to the bar by Lincoln's Inn in 1863, but he does not appear to have practised.

In 1867–9 Ramsay was appointed as an examiner in the Oxford school of law and modern history, and this experience convinced him that the current books on English political history were unsatisfactory. He records in his diary that in December 1869 he consulted Dean Henry Liddell, of Christ Church, on his intention to write a history of England. The necessary leisure and financial support were supplied in 1871, when he succeeded to the baronetcy and estates of Bamff, near Alyth in Perthshire.

For a while, Ramsay was tempted to enter politics, and in 1872 he stood unsuccessfully for Forfarshire in the Liberal interest. Thereafter, although he continued to take a keen interest in politics, his activity was limited to local affairs. He had by this time settled down to writing a history of England from 55 BC to 1485—the period covered, from a different angle, by William Stubbs. However, while Stubbs lived an active academic and ecclesiastical life, in contact with other scholars and with practical problems, Ramsay was a solitary scholar. However despite his dedication to his work, he enjoyed and excelled in outdoor recreations. With a short sturdy figure, he was an admirable walker, skater, and mountaineer. With his brother George, Ramsay was a keen member of the Alpine Club, and he became a pioneer in ascending Mont Blanc from the Italian side. On 20 August 1873 Ramsay married Charlotte Fanning (d. 1904), daughter of Major William Stewart, of Ardvorlich; there were two sons and three more daughters of the marriage, and Ramsay's elder daughters later gave him valuable assistance in his historical work.

For twenty years the only visible products of Ramsay's labours were a series of articles in *The Antiquary*. Then, in 1892, the first two volumes of Ramsay's work were issued. This instalment was, curiously, the concluding part, entitled *Lancaster and York: a Century of English History, 1399–1485*. Six years later, in 1898, two further volumes appeared, under the title *The Foundations of England*, covering the period from 55 BC to AD 1154. Succeeding volumes followed in chronological order: *The Angevin Empire, 1154–1216*, in 1903; *The Dawn of the Constitution, 1216–1307*, in 1908; and *The Genesis of Lancaster, 1307–1399*, in 1913.

Ramsay's avowed intention was to provide a verified and chronological narrative of political history, written around the king as the central figure. He gave, as far as possible, exact, authenticated references to the original authorities on which each statement rested, so that readers might have the material for forming independent judgements. This was the kind of guidance provided by the *Jahrbücher des deutschen Reiches*, differing in that he had less charter material, but made use of the invaluable financial rolls in the Public Record Office. His books had the defects as well as the qualities of good annals; lucid and concise, they were somewhat arid. Although he kept abreast of the work of other British scholars as it appeared, he failed to give attention to the findings of German and French historians; and inevitably there were

misconceptions, especially in the early volumes. His books found a place in university and college libraries principally as works of reference, though some private scholars found the clarity and directness of the narrative enjoyable. One of his special interests was military history, and he based his battle narratives on personal visits to the sites. In this field his principal contribution was his insistence on the small size of medieval armies. A contemporary who heard him speak on the subject in 1913 remembered with admiration 'the vigour and vivacity with which the octogenarian scholar upheld his views' (Tout, 482).

Ramsay's most original contribution to knowledge was the work he did on the revenues of the kings of England, based on his study of the issue rolls, receipt rolls, and enrolled customs accounts in the Public Record Office. Although he did not make use of all the available records, such as the calendars of chancery rolls, and was only partly familiar with the technicalities of exchequer accounting, his work was an important pioneering attempt to break into a new area of study. He achieved his aim of opening up the subject for further research by other scholars. This proved to be his most lasting historical achievement.

After the completion of his *magnum opus* Ramsay employed his leisure in editing, largely from the family charter box, *The Bamff Charters and Papers* (1915). He also put together his researches on medieval finance, which were published as *A History of the Revenues of the Kings of England, 1066–1399* (1925).

Ramsay's work received some public recognition. The University of Glasgow conferred upon him the honorary degree of LLD in 1906. Cambridge gave him an honorary DLitt two years later, and he was elected a fellow of the British Academy in 1915.

Apart from his historical work, Ramsay's chief interest was in his family. He was a resolute advocate of the education of women, and a keen supporter of St Leonard's Girls' School at St Andrews, to which he sent four of his daughters. He was immensely gratified by the success of his third daughter by his first marriage, Agnata Frances *Butler (1867–1931), who was placed by the examiners above the senior classic at Cambridge in 1887. Ramsay's last appearance at a political meeting took place when his daughter Katharine Stewart-*Murray, duchess of Atholl (1874–1960), was nominated as candidate for the division of Kinross and West Perthshire in 1923. He died at Bamff on 17 February 1925, and was buried at Alyth on 21 February. He was succeeded as eleventh baronet by his only surviving son, James Douglas (b. 1878).

RICHARD LODGE, rev. MARJORIE CHIBNALL

Sources T. F. Tout, 'Sir James Henry Ramsay, 1832–1925', *PBA*, 11 (1924–5), 479–85 · private information (1937) · personal knowledge (1937) · Burke, *Peerage* · WWW
Archives LUL, letters to J. H. Round
Likenesses portrait, repro. in *Royal Academy Pictures* (1922)
Wealth at death £13,563 17s. 4d.: confirmation, 28 May 1925, CCI

Ramsay, John, Lord Bothwell and Lord Balmain (c.1464–1513), administrator and conspirator, was reputedly the son of Sir John Ramsay of Corstoun and his wife, Janet Napier. Evidence for his early career is found only in late sixteenth-century chronicles, which describe him as a page of James III who survived the execution of the royal familiars at Lauder Bridge in July 1482 by leaping onto James's horse and clinging to the king. His life was spared at James's 'earnest sollicitatione, being bot a zouthe of 18 zeires of age, and a courte pimpe' (*Historical Works*, 206). The trustworthiness of the details of this episode cannot be taken for granted, but the unanimity of the sources makes it appear likely that Ramsay was indeed threatened with execution in 1482 and saved by the king's intercession. What is certain is that he became squire of the chamber, gaining the lands formerly held by Alexander Kennedy of Irwell on 6 September 1483, then the barony of Bothwell and a 40 merk annuity from Lord Monypenny's lands in February 1484. About 1484 Ramsay married a widow, Isabel Cant of Dunbar, and on 20 July they received a twenty-year lease on half the lands of the Two Kinkells in Strathearn, Perthshire, and part of a mill at Strathmiglo, Fife. Knighted at an unknown date, by May 1485 Ramsay had been raised to the peerage as Lord Bothwell, and his official duties increased: he was auditor of the exchequer (1484–7), commissioner for leasing crown lands in Ettrick and Menteith (during 1486), master of the royal household (November 1486), custodian of Dunbar Castle (from June 1486), and royal justiciar south of Forth (from 1487). On 30 October 1485 Ramsay, with Bishop William Elphinstone and others, represented James III at Henry VII's coronation at Westminster, and he was closely involved in negotiations for an Anglo-Scottish truce in May–July 1486 and November 1487.

As a royal familiar, however, Ramsay became the scapegoat for James III's politically unpopular policies and the focus of rebel propaganda, held responsible for the pro-English foreign policy, and even accused of having poisoned Queen Margaret (who had died in July 1486). Such accusations helped to give the rebels justification for the overthrow and murder of James III in June 1488. Seeking help against the rebels, Ramsay spent Easter 1488 at Windsor with Henry VII, from whom he received £13 6s. 8d. as a gift, and subsequently became one of several Scottish exiles at the English court. On 6 August 1488 he was among ten of James III's supporters summoned by James IV to answer the charge of treason; in their absence, on 8 August, they were forfeited by parliament. The barony of Bothwell was granted to Patrick, Lord Hailes (elevated to earl of Bothwell on 17 October).

Though the apparent nadir of Ramsay's career, the years 1488–97 marked the most interesting phase of his life as client and agent of Henry VII; he had an annuity of 100 merks from Easter 1488 to Michaelmas 1496, in return for which Henry expected intelligence reports and loyal service. In April 1491 Henry entered into an agreement with James Stewart, earl of Buchan, and Sir Thomas Tod, with Ramsay acting as their guarantor, to try to capture James IV and his brother James, duke of Ross, one of a number of unsuccessful English schemes to preserve the Anglo-Scottish peace by undermining James IV. Ramsay's favour

with Henry VII is evident from his joining the king's expedition to France in October–November 1492.

Ramsay proved particularly useful to Henry VII when James IV sheltered Perkin Warbeck from November 1495 to July 1497. About March 1495 Ramsay accompanied Richard Fox, bishop of Durham, into northern England on a diplomatic–intelligence mission, and the Scot returned home in late 1495 or early 1496, presumably as Henry's agent to uncover the details of the Warbeck plot. Despite being 'ondir respit and assurans within the realm of Scotland' (Ellis, 1.25), Ramsay was given considerable freedom to move around the country and travel to Berwick, and he received £10 from Henry VII on 24 May and 15 July 1496. Two of Ramsay's letters to Henry in 1496 have survived, one written between 28 August and 2 September and the second dated 8 September; both allude to negotiations for an Anglo-Scottish treaty held at Berwick and involving Ramsay and Bishop Fox. The letters combine self-promotion, concerning Ramsay's plots to kidnap Warbeck and his efforts to persuade James to abandon the 'fenyt boy' and make peace, with fairly accurate factual information on the Scottish military preparations (including the precise date of attack and James's shortages of money, supplies, and ordnance) and on Warbeck's treasonable dealings with various Englishmen, the French envoy, and Margaret of Burgundy's representative. The reports also contain more speculative and fanciful opinions on James IV's unpopularity with his subjects—Ramsay asserts that an English military victory was assured if Henry took the offensive by land and sea. Perhaps the only remarkable aspect about the activities of Ramsay, who is vilified by Scottish historians for betraying James IV, is that he was so successful, managing to repay Henry VII's patronage while ingratiating himself with James IV. Any man who serves three kings and survives plots, rebellion, and exile has to possess some degree of tenacity, charisma, and an appearance of loyalty.

Ramsay accompanied James IV to Norham and Kintyre during 1497, being restored to royal favour by grant of remission and rehabilitation on 18 April. Between 27 April 1497 and 6 November 1500 he was rewarded for his good service with lands in Tealing and Polgavie in Angus, Terringzeane in Ayrshire, Kirkandrews, and Wigtown, and a house, garden, and other land in Cowgate, Edinburgh. In 1507 he inherited the ward, relief, and non-entries of the Corstoun lands by Janet Ramsay's death, while on 13 May 1510 James gave his knight of the body the barony of Balmain, and lands in Ely and Westir Strathe, 'for his good service and special favour'. Ramsay was auditor of the exchequer in the early sixteenth century and a trusted privy councillor, and his knowledge of English affairs led to his appointment as envoy to Henry VIII on 24 January 1513. He was present on various occasions during Nicholas West's embassy to Scotland from March to April 1513. Given his earlier career, it is ironic that Ramsay died at Flodden on 9 September 1513; the exchequer rolls record the lease of land to William Ramsay, son of John Ramsay of Balmain, *qui obiit in bello*.   DAVID DUNLOP

Sources M. McKerracher, 'John Ramsay of Balmain: Tudor agent?', *The Ricardian*, 4/61 (1976–8), 2–11 • N. Macdougall, *James III: a political study* (1982) • N. Macdougall, *James IV* (1989) • G. Burnett and others, eds., *The exchequer rolls of Scotland*, 8–14 (1885–93) • T. Dickson and J. B. Paul, eds., *Compota thesaurariorum regum Scotorum / Accounts of the lord high treasurer of Scotland*, 1–4 (1877–1902) • J. M. Thomson and others, eds., *Registrum magni sigilli regum Scotorum / The register of the great seal of Scotland*, 11 vols. (1882–1914), vol. 2 • *CDS*, vol. 4 • *LP Henry VIII* • H. Ellis, ed., *Original letters illustrative of English history*, 2nd edn, 1st ser., 1 (1825), pp. 22–33, nos. 12–13 [Ramsay's letters to Henry VII] • *APS*, 1424–1567 • PRO, E. 404/79, 80, 81, 82, 86; E. 405/75, 77, 78, 79; E. 36/124, 125, 130; E. 101/414/6; E. 403/2558 • Exchequer Scots documents, PRO, E. 39 • BL, Add. MS 7099 • J. Leslie, *The historie of Scotland*, ed. E. G. Cody and W. Murison, trans. J. Dalrymple, 2/2, STS, 34 (1895) [Lat. and Scot. orig.] • *The historie and cronicles of Scotland … by Robert Lindesay of Pitscottie*, ed. A. J. G. Mackay, 1, STS, 42 (1899) • *The historical works of Sir James Balfour*, ed. J. Haig, 1 (1824) • Rymer, *Foedera*, 3rd edn • *RotS*, vol. 2
Archives BL, Cotton MS Vespasian C.xvi, fols. 154–156

Ramsay, John. *See* Ramsey, John (d. 1551).

Ramsay, John, earl of Holdernesse (c.1580–1626), courtier, was the second son of Sir Robert Ramsay of Wyliecleuch. He had at least six siblings, for four brothers and two sisters were named in his will, dated 6 January 1626, not long before his death. He first makes an appearance in the historical record in June 1599, when he was in the service of James VI and I, in somewhat unedifying circumstances. On the tenth of that month John Ramsay, one of the king's 'familiar serwands' (Pitcairn, 2.91–3), was struck by one Patrick Myrtoun, one of the king's carvers, after a verbal quarrel in the king's own chamber at Falkland Palace in Fife. On the following day they encountered each other in the courtyard of the palace and once again exchanged heated words. Myrtoun drew his sword on Ramsay who responded in kind, but both were restrained by other royal servants and no blood was shed. Because these violent encounters took place while the king was in residence in the palace, the two were formally convicted of treason. They submitted themselves to the king's will and were pardoned and once more received into his favour.

The following year Ramsay more than redeemed himself and set his career at court on a firmly upward path. On 5 August 1600 he was in the company of the king when James was apparently lured to Perth by John Ruthven, third earl of Gowrie, son of William, the second earl, who had been executed in 1584. This was the so-called 'Gowrie conspiracy', the precise object and circumstances of which remain a mystery. The king was taken to Gowrie House, the Ruthvens' Perth residence, which he entered in the company of nobody else but the two Ruthven brothers. The official version, first given a public airing six days after the event, has it that soon afterwards James VI broke an upstairs window to call to his retinue for help because his life was threatened. The first person to arrive 'by the providence of God' was 'his Majesteis peadge and trustie servand', John Ramsay (Moysie, 142). He is said to have found the king tussling with Alexander Ruthven, the earl's younger brother, whom he killed. He then encountered the earl himself on the stairs and told him that the king had been killed. The earl, carrying two swords, put their points to the floor in what seems to have been a gesture of submission but he too was thereupon killed by Ramsay. Having thus apparently saved his sovereign's life Ramsay found almost instant favour from a grateful monarch. On 13 November that year he was knighted and given the lands of East Barns, near Dunbar in Haddingtonshire, the charter for which even narrated the details of the incident at Perth by way of an explanation for the gift.

After accompanying James VI to England in 1603 Ramsay spent most of the rest of his life at court. He did, however, maintain links with his homeland, and was appointed between 1610 and 1623 to various commissions for the peace for the constabulary of Haddington, where his principal Scottish lands lay. He was given further lands in England and a number of pensions from the English crown, as well as royal gifts to help him to settle his debts. On 11 June 1606 he was raised to the Scottish peerage with the title of Viscount Haddington and Lord Ramsay of Barns. To commemorate his deeds of 1600 he was allowed to incorporate within the coat of arms which he was granted a crown and a right arm holding a sword, at the point of which was a heart, and the motto *Haec dextra vindex principis et patriae* ('This right arm saved the king and the nation').

On 20 February 1609 Haddington married Lady Elizabeth Ratcliffe (d. 1618), daughter of Robert, earl of Sussex. At the wedding celebrations the couple were honoured by the performance of a masque, specially written by Ben Jonson and performed by five English and twelve Scottish men of 'noble birth or high position' (*Scots peerage*, 4.301). The marriage produced two sons, both of whom predeceased their father. On 28 August 1609 Haddington received a charter of the lands formerly belonging to the Cistercian abbey of Melrose, which were erected into a temporal lordship carrying the title Lord Ramsay of Melrose. In 1618, however, he resigned these lands with their title into the hands of Sir George Ramsay of Dalhousie, a kinsman.

Haddington certainly returned to Scotland in 1617, probably as part of the king's retinue on his only return visit to his kingdom after 1603. He must have stayed on after the king's journey back to England, for he served in November as one of the king's commissioners at the general assembly at St Andrews which rejected the liturgical reforms which would come to be known as the five articles of Perth. In 1619 he appears to have retired from court to France in protest at having been refused an English peerage, being passed over for the earldom of Montgomery. In 1621 he must have returned to favour, for on 22 January that year he was made baron of Kingston and earl of Holdernesse. With the title came the right to carry the English sword of state before the king every year on 5 August at the celebrations to mark the anniversary of his rescue of the king from the Gowrie conspiracy in 1600. His vote was counted at the notorious Scottish parliament of 1621 which approved the five articles of Perth, although he attended only by proxy.

Holdernesse's first wife having died in 1618, in July 1624 he married Martha Cockayne, daughter of Sir William

Cockayne and sister of Charles, first Viscount Cullen. The marriage produced no children and she survived her husband, marrying Montagu Bertie, later second earl of Lindsey, in 1627. She died in July 1641. Holdernesse died in London in February 1626 and was, according to a request in his will, buried on 28 February in Westminster Abbey beside his sons James, who had died in 1618, and Charles, who had died in 1621. As he had no surviving children his titles died with him.   ALAN R. MACDONALD

Sources *Scots peerage*, vol. 4 · R. Pitcairn, ed., *Ancient criminal trials in Scotland*, 7 pts in 3, Bannatyne Club, 42 (1833) · *CSP dom.*, 1603–25 · *Reg. PCS*, 1st ser. · *APS*, 1593–1625 · D. Moysie, *Memoirs of the affairs of Scotland, 1577–1603*, ed. J. Dennistoun, Bannatyne Club, 39 (1830) · D. Calderwood, *The history of the Kirk of Scotland*, ed. T. Thomson and D. Laing, 8 vols., Wodrow Society, 7 (1842–9) · will, PRO, PROB 11/151, sig. 13
Archives Berks. RO, letter to Sir Nicholas Carew of Beddington
Wealth at death debts: will, PRO, PROB 11/151, sig. 13

Ramsay, John, of Ochtertyre (1736–1814), writer on Scotland, was born on 26 August 1736, the elder son of James Ramsay of Ochtertyre, near Stirling (*d.* 1748), writer to the signet, and Anne Dundas, daughter of Ralph Dundas of Manor. Educated at the grammar school at Dalkeith and then at the University of Edinburgh, he passed as advocate by 1753. He was a moderate Presbyterian in his earlier years and attended various meetings of the general assembly of the Church of Scotland between 1753 and 1760, before shifting to a more traditional outlook. He never married: according to a friend this was owing to an early attachment to Mary Dundas, his cousin, killed in the collapse of the North Bridge in Edinburgh on 3 August 1769. Ramsay visited England twice; otherwise he remained in Scotland, either at home or visiting his friends and relatives.

In 1787 Ramsay was visited by Robert Burns, to whom he gave a great deal of excellent advice (which was not taken), and, six years later, by Walter Scott. He looked after his small estate, really no more than a farm, read, gardened, engaged in literary composition, and conducted a voluminous correspondence. Few of his letters have survived, with the exception of a series written to Elizabeth Graham, wife of James Dundas, clerk to the signet. He eventually left the estate of Ochtertyre to Dundas. In these letters Ramsay frequently refers to his 'lucubrations', a series of essays on the state of eighteenth-century Scotland, along with brief biographies of deceased friends and relatives. As one trained in the law, he may have thought it wiser not to comment on the living, though this is unfortunate from the point of view of posterity. No portrait of Ramsay has been found, but there is a good description by George Robert Gleig, son of George Gleig, bishop of Brechin, Ramsay's friend. He says that Ramsay insisted on reading his essays to any available audience, willing or otherwise, and mentions the possibility that Ramsay was partly the model for Jonathan Oldbuck in Scott's novel *The Antiquary*; Scott himself claimed that his model was based on George Constable and John Clerk of Eldin.

Ramsay's literary remains were bound in ten volumes,

deposited in the National Library of Scotland in 1936, and purchased by the library in 1993. A selection edited by Alexander Allardyce for publication in 1888 under the title *Scotland and Scotsmen in the Eighteenth Century* has become a standard source for Scottish political, religious, and social history. Allardyce managed to get most of the material into two printed volumes, but he broke up the essays and rearranged them. However, as Ramsay was prone to repeat himself, not that much was lost. The work was reprinted in 1996 with a new introduction by David J. Brown. The manuscripts contain much of interest: Ramsay was well placed to comment, and since he had only a small estate to manage and lived alone, with few other activities apart from an avuncular interest in various young ladies with whom he corresponded, he had leisure to consider his contemporaries and his surroundings, and the effect of changes upon them. Writing only for his own private entertainment and that of his friends, he was able to concentrate on what he described as 'minute revolutions in manners and sentiments which other historians think below their notice' (NL Scot., MS 1639, fol. 135), often with fascinating results.

Although a firm whig and a lowlander, Ramsay sympathized with the plight of his Jacobite neighbours and was deeply interested in the effect of the rising of 1745 on the highlands in general. He was also interested in the beginnings of the agricultural revolution, and believed that the Anglicization of Scottish manners, language, politics, agriculture, and industry threatened to be carried too far; on this point as on others he became increasingly wary of change as he grew older. He thought little of George III but had a great admiration, mixed with alarm, for Napoleon. He did not live to see the latter's defeat. He died at Ochtertyre on 2 March 1814, and is said to have been buried in the family burial-ground in the old churchyard of Kincardine in Menteith: there is a monument to his memory in the new church there (built 1814–16), with a Latin epitaph of his own composition.   B. L. H. HORN

Sources *Scotland and Scotsmen in the eighteenth century: from the MSS of John Ramsay, esq., of Ochtertyre*, ed. A. Allardyce, 2 vols. (1888) · D. J. Brown, introduction, in *Scotland and Scotsmen in the eighteenth century: from the MSS of John Ramsay, esq., of Ochtertyre*, ed. A. Allardyce, 2 vols. (1888); repr. (1996) · *Letters of John Ramsay of Ochtertyre, 1799–1812*, ed. B. L. H. Horn, Scottish History Society, 4th ser., vol. 3 (1966) · NL Scot., MS 1639, fol. 135
Archives NL Scot., corresp. and literary MSS
Wealth at death approx. £250—incl. furniture, linen, and books valued at £147 19s. 1d.; cattle and horses valued at £77 10s. 10d.; farm utensils valued at £23 16s. 11d.: NA Scot., comm. of Dunblane testaments, recorded 11 Oct 1814, vol. 27, fol. 365

Ramsay, John (1802–1879), poet, was born on 16 August 1802 in Kilmarnock, the son of James Ramsay, carpet weaver, and his wife, Jean, *née* Fulton. He received a limited education, during which he resided occasionally with a grandfather at Gulillard, near the village of Dundonald, Ayrshire. He was apprenticed in carpet weaving in Kilmarnock, and soon began to compose verses while working at the loom. Subsequently he became a grocer in Kilmarnock, by which time he is described as 'married [with] a rising family' (Paterson, 405). His entry in the

Scottish register of deaths gives his wife's name as Elizabeth Templeton. However, meeting with reverses he relinquished the business, and for fifteen years he travelled through Scotland selling his poems. Finally he became the agent of a benevolent society in Edinburgh.

While a carpet weaver Ramsay contributed verses to the *Edinburgh Literary Journal*, then edited by Henry Glassford Bell. In 1836 he published his collected poems under the title of *Woodnotes of a Wanderer*, which reached a second edition in 1839. 'The Eglinton Park Meeting', the leading piece in the volume, is a humorous description in *ottava rima* of a review of the Ayrshire yeomanry by the marquess of Hastings in 1823. 'Address to Dundonald Castle', in somewhat laboured heroic couplets, is energetic and picturesque. As late as 1871 Ramsay published a volume entitled *Gleanings of the Gloamin*. He died at 495 St Vincent Street, Glasgow, on 11 May 1879.

T. W. Bayne, *rev.* James How

Sources J. Paterson, *The contemporaries of Burns and the more recent poets of Ayrshire* (1840) · J. Ramsay, 'Introduction', *Gleanings of the gloamin* (1871) · J. Ramsay, 'Notes', *Gleanings of the gloamin* (1871) · Irving, *Scots.* · Boase, *Mod. Eng. biog.* · J. G. Wilson, ed., *The poets and poetry of Scotland*, 2 vols. in 4 (1876–7) · C. Rogers, *The modern Scottish minstrel, or, The songs of Scotland of the past half-century*, 6 vols. (1855–7) · IGI · bap. reg. Scot. · d. reg. Scot.
Archives Ayrshire Archives, travel diary

Ramsay, John William Maule, thirteenth earl of Dalhousie (1847–1887). *See under* Ramsay, George, twelfth earl of Dalhousie (1806–1880).

Ramsay, Katherine (1720s–1808), milliner and shopkeeper, was one of eight children of Gilbert Ramsay (*d.* before 1743), solicitor, and factor to the duke of Roxburghe, and of Katherine Kerr, daughter of Andrew Kerr of Kippilaw, near Kelso, Roxburghshire. Katherine Ramsay and her five sisters were involved in selling millinery and haberdashery, and all seem to have been in business together initially. Katherine, however, separated and set up in business with the help of her sister Ann (1730–1804), dealing in millinery goods. They ran a thriving and fashionable business from a house and shop, which appear in the Edinburgh stent (tax) book from 1749 and which were in Lyon Close, opposite the city guardhouse, on the north side of Edinburgh's High Street. The shop was entered from the High Street; the house had five 'fire rooms'. The millinery goods were made in the shop, and Katherine herself helped with this work. House and shop were advertised for sale on 20 December 1765. It is not known where Katherine operated after this time but she and Ann may have joined up with the company of Ramsay and Cramond in Gray's Close, where their sister Mary was one of the partners. However, surviving bills, headed 'Katherine Ramsay and Sister', show that Katherine continued to merchandise until at least 1771, when she sold goods to the family of Clerk of Penicuik.

With her sister Ann, Katherine took many debtors to court, and she appeared personally in court when suing them. The evidence of witnesses in these cases shows that girls were trained by Katherine and Ann as apprentices and eventually became journeywomen; Isobel Colvin, for example, was in Katherine's employment for ten years. This evidence is significant in that it has been thought that most women in this period had intermittent employment, whereas the pattern in the eighteenth-century Edinburgh retail trade suggests otherwise. Katherine's bills show that her clientele were from the aristocracy and the gentry, although the middle classes in the burgh, business and professional, were also represented. Her business appears to have been sufficiently prosperous for her to employ the services of a resident clerk, James Mushet.

In 1769 Katherine and Ann acquired a piece of ground at Restalrig, near Edinburgh, known as the Kilnacre, from their brother-in-law James Ramsay, a slater and builder, on which they built a house which still stands today. They called it Viewfrith (Viewfirth); in his *Traditions of Edinburgh*, Robert Chambers, referring to Katherine and Ann as well-known personalities of their day, says that their neighbours called the new house, derisively, 'Lappet Ha'. They sold the house in 1783 to Captain James McCrae, who gave it the name Marionville, which it still bears, and moved to Antigua Street in Edinburgh's New Town. Katherine also owned property in the town from which she drew income in rents.

Although the Ramsay family was baptized in the Church of Scotland Katherine appears to have become an Episcopalian; she bequeathed her prayer book, with her Bible, to her niece Katherine, daughter of her sister Christian and James Ramsay. She died, unmarried, on 28 January 1808 in Edinburgh, probably in Antigua Street. Her testament records that she had £4000 Scots of capital stock in the Bank of Scotland at the time of her death.

Elizabeth C. Sanderson

Sources E. C. Sanderson, *Women and work in eighteenth-century Edinburgh* (1996) · Edinburgh register of testaments, NA Scot., CC 8/8/138, 29 March 1810 · Edinburgh register of sasines, NA Scot., RS 27, vol. 275, fols. 21, 25 · Edinburgh stent book, 1749, Edinburgh City Archives · NA Scot., Clerk of Penicuik MSS, GD 18/2180 · NA Scot., Hamilton-Bruce MSS, GD 34/559a · NA Scot., Hall of Dunglass MSS, GD 206, portfolio 2/1 · NA Scot., Leven and Melville MSS, GD 26/6/123/32 · NA Scot., Murray of Lintrose MSS, GD 68/72/74 · Edinburgh commissary court, processes, NA Scot., CC 8/4/503 [1758] · Edinburgh commissary court, processes, NA Scot., CC 8/4/519 [1767] · Edinburgh commissary court, decreets, NA Scot., CC 8/2/68; CC 8/2/128 · *Edinburgh Advertiser* (20 Dec 1765)
Wealth at death £4000 Scots—capital stock in Bank of Scotland: Edinburgh register of testaments, 29 March 1810, NA Scot., CC 8/8/138

Ramsay, Laurence (*fl. c.*1577–1588), poet, consistently used his verses to castigate puritan sectarians and Catholics alike. About 1577 he venomously attacked 'the pestilent Pelagians, Arians, and Anabaptists, besides Atheists, & Papists' in a poem of eighty-two seven-line stanzas in the form of a monologue spoken by Satan entitled *The practise of the divell … in his papistes, against the true professors of Gods holie worde, in these our latter dayes*, published in London by J. Charlewood for Timothie Rider. In 1579 the same bookseller distributed a broadside by Ramsay, entitled 'A Short Discourse of Mans Fatall End with an Unfaygned, Commendation of Syr Nicholas Bacon', which begins 'Since God hath fyxt our dayes and yeares, to live and else to dye'. This thirty-six-line poem, written in couplets and commemorating the death of Bacon, celebrates the dead knight in part for the fact that 'no patch of popish mynde in him was ever found'. In later life Ramsay seems to have been attached to the household of Robert Dudley, earl of Leicester, who favoured an aggressively anti-Catholic foreign policy. After Leicester's death, Ramsay wrote 'Ramsies farewell to his late lorde and master therle of Leicester, which departed this worlde at Cor'burye the 4 Sept. 1588', which was licensed to Edward Aggas on 7 October 1588. No copy is now known. Also lost is Ramsay's 'Wisshinge and Wouldynge', for which Edward White obtained a licence on 5 August 1583. It was possibly a poem resembling 'I would and I would not' by Nicholas Breton.

The *Dictionary of National Biography* identifies Ramsay with the Laurence Ramsay who joined a body of sectarians meeting at Faversham, Kent, in 1550 and who advocated Anabaptism and Pelagianism (Strype, *Ecclesiastical Memorials*, 2/1, 370). However, in the light of Ramsay's explicit attacks on 'Anabaptistes and … Pelagians' as 'sectes diabolicall', either this identification seems unlikely, or represents a religious position that (twenty years later) Ramsay had come to regret (Ramsay, *Practise of the Divell*).

CATHY SHRANK

Sources J. Strype, *Ecclesiastical memorials*, 3 vols. (1822) · J. Strype, *Annals of the Reformation and establishment of religion … during Queen Elizabeth's happy reign*, new edn, 2 (1824) · E. Brydges, *Restituta, or, Titles, extracts, and characters of old books in English literature*, 4 vols. (1814–16) · L. Ramsay, *The practise of the divell* (c.1577) · J. Ritson, *Bibliographia poetica* (1802) · W. T. Lowndes, *The bibliographer's manual of English literature*, ed. H. G. Bohn, [new edn], 6 vols. (1864) · W. C. Hazlitt, *Hand-book to the popular, poetical and dramatic literature of Great Britain* (1867) · Watt, *Bibl. Brit.* · J. P. Collier, 'The registers of the Stationers' Company', *N&Q*, 2nd ser., 12 (1861), 142–4, esp. 142 · *STC, 1475–1640* · *DNB* · Arber, *Regs. Stationers*

Ramsay [*née* Venniker], **Margaret Francesca** [Peggy] (1908–1991), play agent, was born on 27 May 1908 in Bank Street, Molong, New South Wales, Australia, the first of the two children of John Charles (Jack) Venniker (1869–1958), doctor and army officer, and Annie Rhoda, *née* Adams (1882–1963), known as Nancy, who were on a trip abroad when Peggy was born. Her parents were both English but had emigrated to South Africa, where Jack converted from Judaism to Christianity and changed his surname from Velenski. Peggy's brother, Tony (1921–1989), became a popular radio doctor in South Africa. Peggy attended the Collegiate School, Port Elizabeth, Girton School, Johannesburg, and Rhodes University, Grahamstown, where she studied zoology, botany, English, and psychology but left within a year without completing her BSc. Nine months later, on 29 September 1927, she married—disastrously—the university's senior lecturer in psychology, (Charles) Norman Matheson Ramsay (*b.* 1891), and the following year they left for England. The marriage collapsed as soon as they arrived and Peggy Ramsay had to start a new life from scratch.

It was like the story-books Ramsay had avidly devoured in the Great Karoo: she took singing lessons, joined a touring opera company, and then turned to acting. She had many affairs, and in the cast of one production she met matinée idol William Roderick, who later lived with her and took care of all her domestic arrangements for the final three decades of her life. She stumbled on the path that would ultimately lead her to becoming Britain's most powerful play agent when, in 1945, she became the director Hugh Hunt's right-hand woman at the newly created Bristol Old Vic Theatre. She helped him in many tasks, including that of choosing the repertory, and so began her move away from performing towards being a 'backstage' influence. In the early 1950s, with two others, she briefly ran the west London Q Theatre, one of the capital's leading little theatres, and there developed her interest in new plays while demonstrating a rare ability to judge a script on the page.

Disillusioned with acting, Ramsay was reading plays for several theatre managers, and when it became apparent to friends that she had recommended a number of West End successes but without receiving any commission, they offered to set her up in her own play agency. After an initial refusal, she agreed and by the end of 1953 had founded Margaret Ramsay Ltd in a converted brothel in Goodwin's Court, one of the oldest alleyways in the city of Westminster, off St Martin's Lane. Her immediate problem was to find clients; she represented playwrights she knew from her play-reading days and took on the then little known Romanian-French absurdist Eugène Ionesco when he left his previous agent. She built a reputation for herself quickly because of her unconventional and uncompromising behaviour. (She was known to shock many a prospective client by pointing to the chaise longue on which they were sitting and declaiming, 'That's where Ionesco fucked me.')

Writers and their art came first, before managers, directors, actors, and even the writers' partners and families. Although Ramsay enjoyed the cut-and-thrust of negotiating and the gamble of the box office, the business side of the firm was secondary. She would turn work down for clients—often without recourse to the playwrights themselves—if she felt it was not right for them. Developing talent was what ignited her, and she was a practical yet hard taskmistress. The first writer to come to prominence through her 'tough love' was Robert Bolt, whom she first met when he was a teacher writing radio dramas. She tackled the structural shortcomings of his writing and after several efforts which she rejected she secured an Oxford Playhouse production of one of his plays. This was followed by his triumphant West End début, *Flowering Cherry* (1957). Ironically, the commercial success of this and subsequent of his plays such as *A Man for All Seasons* (1960) secured the future of the agency, allowing Ramsay's anti-materialistic approach to flourish and make its unique contribution to British playwriting.

Ramsay was a confidante of the director Peter Hall from the mid-1950s when he was running the Arts Theatre and sought her advice about the author of *Waiting for Godot*, the English-language première of which he was about to direct, through his creation of the Royal Shakespeare

Company (RSC) to his stewardship of the National Theatre (NT) which he invited her—unsuccessfully—to join as his literary manager. Her clients John Whiting and David Rudkin featured in the early RSC repertory and Howard Brenton, David Hare, Edward Bond, Alan Ayckbourn, and Stephen Poliakoff were prominent at the NT, a list that reveals her catholic taste which could embrace John Arden as well as Willy Russell. She enjoyed a close and long association with Britain's main new writing theatre, the Royal Court, which promoted numerous clients of hers, such as Ann Jellicoe, Christopher Hampton, and Caryl Churchill. In commercial theatre she found a kindred spirit in the producer Michael Codron; among her clients whose work he presented were John Mortimer, Henry Livings, Frank Marcus, Charles Wood, James Saunders, David Mercer, and Joe Orton, who, through his infamous death at the hand of his male lover, was the most notorious of her protégés. Ramsay figures in the film based on Orton's diaries, *Prick up your Ears* (1987), played by Vanessa Redgrave, and in 1999 she was brought to life by Maureen Lipman in the play *Peggy for you*, written by her client Alan Plater. Several of her authors used aspects of her personality in the make-up of their own fictional characters, most notably Marion in Ayckbourn's *Absurd Person Singular* (1972), Valentina Nrovka in Hare's *The Bay at Nice* (1986), and Nancy Fraser in Peter Nichols's *A Piece of my Mind* (1987). In recognition of the wider impact of her writers, the British Film Institute in 1984 gave her an award for her contribution to the film and television industries.

A swift and cutting intelligence combined with excoriating candour, legendary indiscretion, and a swooping voice that could deliver wisdom and profanity in equal measure made Ramsay's presence as formidable as it was alluring. She *was* the firm, and, battling through Alzheimer's disease, she went to work every day until shortly before her death at a central London hospital on 4 September 1991 at the age of eighty-three. She was cremated at Golders Green on 10 September.

Ramsay's executors used her wealth to establish the Peggy Ramsay Foundation to nurture new playwriting. With Ramsay gone, the agency merged with another and finally moved out of Goodwin's Court, nearly forty years after this idiosyncratic, indefatigable lady with piercing, hawk-like eyes, a gangling, lolloping walk, and a fondness for flowing hats had taken a gamble there that turned her dilapidated offices festooned with posters of clients' successes into one of the most influential addresses in the British theatrical landscape.   COLIN CHAMBERS

Sources C. Chambers, *Peggy: the life of Margaret Ramsay, play agent* (1997) · S. Callow, *Love is where it falls* (1999) · M. Gussow, *New Yorker* (23 May 1988), 35–60 · '"Better food for critics": a talk with Margaret Ramsay', *Encore*, 10/3 (May–June 1963), 35–8 · J. Lahr, *Prick up your ears: the biography of Joe Orton* (1978) · J. Lahr, ed., *The Orton diaries* (1986)
Archives BL, archive | FILM BBC-TV Archive of BBC-TV, *Arena*, programme about her 26 March 1990
Likenesses J. Bratby, portrait, priv. coll.
Wealth at death £2,862,244: probate, 6 Nov 1991, *CGPLA Eng. & Wales*

Ramsay, Lady Patricia [*formerly* Princess Patricia of Connaught] (1886–1974), artist, was born Victoria Patricia Helena Elizabeth in London at Buckingham Palace on St Patrick's day, 17 March 1886. She was the third and youngest child and younger daughter of Prince *Arthur William Patrick Albert, duke of Connaught and Strathearn (1850–1942), the third son of Queen Victoria, and his wife, Princess Louise Margaret Alexandra Victoria Agnes (1860–1917), third daughter of Prince Frederick Charles Nicholas of Prussia. The duchess of Connaught, the dominant partner in the marriage, who had herself spent an unhappy childhood, was an undemonstrative and sometimes neglectful parent. The young princess, Patsy, as she was called in the family, had to wear her elder sister's cast-off clothing, and to the end of her life suffered from painful feet, the result of her mother's refusal to buy her well-fitting shoes.

Although Princess Patricia of Connaught grew up to be tall, handsome, and intelligent, she was handicapped by an inculcated lack of self-confidence that made her feel unwanted and helped delay her acceptance of a suitor in marriage until she was nearly thirty-three. Alfonso XIII of Spain, who in 1906 married her cousin Princess Victoria Eugénie, was among those who sought her hand in vain.

Meanwhile, Princess Patricia travelled the world in the wake of her father, who held a succession of military appointments in India, the Mediterranean, Canada, and Ireland. During the duke's years as governor-general of Canada, 1911–16, his wife was in declining health and Princess Patricia acted as his hostess. The Canadians appreciated her beauty, her charm, and her devotion to war work. She was persuaded to sign innumerable miniature portraits of herself to be sold in aid of the Red Cross, and embroidered the original colour of Princess Patricia's Canadian light infantry which was carried into battle on the western front. Immensely proud at being appointed their colonel-in-chief, she visited her regiment many times over the years, even after her retirement from public duties. Canada also paid the princess the compliment of naming after her an extension to Ontario's boundaries and a bay in British Columbia.

On 27 February 1919 Princess Patricia was married in Westminster Abbey to Captain the Hon. Sir Alexander Robert Maule Ramsay (1881–1972), a younger son of John William *Ramsay, thirteenth earl of Dalhousie [*see under* Ramsay, George, twelfth earl of Dalhousie] and a serving naval officer. It was a love match born of a friendship that had begun even before Ramsay's attachment to the duke of Connaught's staff in Canada; impossible during her mother's lifetime, it also marked the more relaxed postwar attitude of the royal family towards marriage with a commoner, and was to bring the princess the first real happiness she knew. There was one child of the marriage, Alexander Arthur Alfonso David, born on 21 December 1919, who fought in the Grenadier Guards during the Second World War and was severely wounded. Admiral Ramsay died in 1972. Two days before the wedding George V gave his permission for the bride to relinquish, at her own wish, her royal title, style, and rank and to assume the style of Lady Patricia Ramsay, with precedence immediately before the marchionesses of England. She nevertheless chose to wear at the coronations of 1937 and of 1953 the robes and coronet of a princess of the blood.

After her marriage Lady Patricia scarcely ever emerged from the seclusion of her private life except to attend an exhibition of her own paintings; even then she would not submit her work to the Royal Academy, although willing to become patron of the less publicized Royal West of England Academy. In 1931 she joined the New English Art Club, and was an honorary member of the Royal Institute of Painters in Water Colours. She found much fulfilment in her art, insisting always that it be judged only by exacting professional standards. The earliest of her 600 paintings were of flowers. During travels abroad, her imagination was caught by marine life and tropical vegetation, and in later years she turned to abstracts. Lady Patricia experimented boldly with bright colours and bold contrasts that owed something to the influence of Gauguin and Van Gogh, whose work was introduced to her by A. S. Hartrick, with whom she studied. She was equally deft in oils, watercolours, pen and ink, and gouache. Most of her works were in the possession of her son.

As the wife of a naval officer, Lady Patricia had no house of her own until 1942, when she took possession of Ribsden Holt, Windlesham, bequeathed to her by her aunt and fellow artist Princess Louise, duchess of Argyll. It was there that she died on 12 January 1974 in her eighty-eighth year. The funeral took place in St George's Chapel, Windsor, and the burial at Frogmore.   KENNETH ROSE, *rev.*

Sources *The Times* (14 Jan 1974) · private information (1986) [Captain Alexander Ramsay of Mar]
Likenesses W. & D. Downey, double portrait, photograph, *c.*1906 (with her sister), NPG · W. & D. Downey, group portrait, photograph, 1907 (with royal family), NPG · J. Lavery, oils, before 1910, National Gallery of Canada, Ottawa · C. Shannon, oils, 1917–18, National Gallery of Canada, Ottawa · A. S. Hartrick, portrait, *c.*1920, priv. coll. · A. McEvoy, portrait, 1926, priv. coll. · C. Shannon, portrait, Currie barracks, Edmonton, Alberta · C. Sims, portrait, Bagshot Park, Surrey
Wealth at death £917,199: probate, 17 April 1974, *CGPLA Eng. & Wales*

Ramsay, Robert. *See* Ramsey, Robert (*c.*1595–1644).

Ramsay, Robert (1842–1882), lawyer and politician in Australia, the eldest son of Andrew Mitchell Ramsay (1809–1869), a minister of the United Presbyterian church, and his wife, Isabella Milne, was born at Hawick, Roxburghshire, on 16 February 1842. The family emigrated in 1847 to Melbourne (one of the three children died on the voyage), and Robert was educated at Robert Campbell's and John Macgregor's school in the Melbourne suburb of St Kilda, and then at Scotch College, Melbourne. He studied law at Melbourne University, graduating in 1861, and was admitted a solicitor in 1862. He began practice on his own account, but in January 1866 John Macgregor, jun., to whom he had been articled, took him into partnership in the firm of Macgregor, Ramsay, and Brahe of Melbourne.

He married, on 16 April 1868, at Yangery, near Warrnambool, Isabella Catherine, the daughter of Roderick Urquhart of Yangery Park, Victoria.

Ramsay began his political career as secretary to a committee for abolishing state aid to religion, a cause to which his father devoted much of his life. From 1870 to 1882 he represented East Bourke in the legislative assembly, where state education initially absorbed his attention. He was a moderate protectionist, generally supporting Sir James McCulloch's ministry. In the frequent changes of Victorian ministries Ramsay served as minister without portfolio from 1872 to 1874, as postmaster-general from 1874 to 1877 (when, by introducing long terms of contract for the mail service, he saved the colony considerable sums of money), and as minister of public instruction from 1875 to 1877. In this last post he vigorously administered the Education Act, which he had introduced in 1872, and in two years opened more schools in country districts than any predecessor. He firmly believed in national education and ardently supported the separation of church and state. His tenure of office ended on 11 May 1877, but in 1878 he represented Victoria at the telegraphic conference in Sydney. On 5 March 1880 he joined James Service's ministry, where as chief secretary he was responsible for the controversial police actions which eventually led to the capture of Ned Kelly's gang, and, as minister for public instruction again, he tackled the problems of country schools and insisted on removing the name of Christ from school readers. After the government's defeat in August 1880, he left office, but continued active in parliamentary affairs until he died suddenly of pleurisy at his residence in Gipps Street, East Melbourne, on 23 May 1882. He was buried at Melbourne general cemetery, and was survived by his widow, two sons, and two daughters. He left an estate of about £40,000, largely in pastoral properties. His main legacy to the colony was the firm establishment of secular education, the culmination of his and his father's campaign.   C. A. HARRIS, *rev.* ELIZABETH BAIGENT

Sources *AusDB* · 'Ramsay, Andrew Mitchell', *AusDB*, vol. 6 · *The Argus* [Melbourne] (24 May 1882) · A. Henderson, ed., *Early pioneer families of Victoria and Riverina* (1936)
Wealth at death approx. £40,000 in Australia: *AusDB*

Ramsay [Ramsey], **Thomas** (*fl. c.*1647–1653), Roman Catholic agent, was the son of the émigré Scot Dr Alexander Ramsay. According to the *Dictionary of National Biography* he was born in the parish of St Dunstan-in-the-West in the neighbourhood of Temple Bar and was sent by his father about 1647 to study in the University of Leiden under the care of an uncle, who in fact opposed this plan and instead encouraged Ramsay to take up studies in Greek and philosophy at Glasgow, graduating MA there. Apparently fleeing the plague in Glasgow, Ramsay resumed the study of philosophy in Edinburgh, taking a second MA degree there. To improve himself further he travelled to Bremen, headed south for Würzburg, and proceeded to Rome, where he spent some time in a Dominican friary and in a Jesuit college. The pope then sent him, he recalled, to Germany on a mission which involved work among Baptist communities. Returning to Rome he was circumcised in order to appear convincingly as a Jew. Adopting the alias Thomas Horsley, he left Hamburg for the port of Shields in April 1652 and established himself in Newcastle upon Tyne as a Jew, using the name Joseph ben Israel. From Newcastle he moved to nearby Hexham, where he arrived on 4 June 1653, claiming to have been born in Mantua. At Hexham Thomas Tillam had been building up a Baptist congregation in the early 1650s, separate from the Baptist community in Newcastle and in conflict with its ministers. It was this that led to 'one of the most bizarre episodes in the religious history of the North' (Howell, 249)—the case of the 'false Jew'. When the apparent Jew ben Israel converted to the Baptist faith, it seemed a triumph for Tillam's ministry in a period of mounting excitement, not least among Baptists, about the possible readmission of the Jews to England, with the prospect, some thought, of their conversion to Christianity as a heralding of the second coming of Christ.

It soon emerged, though, that the Jew ben Israel was in fact the English-born Catholic convert Ramsay, perhaps sent to the north-east by forces unnamed to sow confusion among Baptists there. And if that was his mission he succeeded brilliantly. Tillam's reputation was brought down and that of the Newcastle ministers rehabilitated. Ramsay was summoned to a church hearing in Newcastle, travelling there in company with Tillam and being confronted with the captain who had transported Ramsay to Shields as Horsley. The extraordinary case next came to the government's attention; on 8 July 1653 the keeper of the Gatehouse prison was issued with a warrant by the council of state to take into custody Thomas Ramsay, 'suspected of being a Romish priest' (*CSP dom.*, 1653–4, 428); on 13 July a warrant was issued for Ramsay's arrest and he was sent to London for examination by the council which, on 4 August 1653, appointed Commissary-General Whalley to head a committee for investigating Ramsay concerning his entry into England. On 23 August it was ordered by the council that the information delivered to it about Ramsay be written up for publication by Secretary Thurloe.

The sensational and serpentine case made ideal journalistic diet, and a work published in Newcastle in 1653 neatly captured the multiple identities of Ramsay as Anglo-Scot, Catholic-Jew and bogus Baptist. If Ramsay was the Thomas Ramsay issued with a pass by the council of state just before the Restoration in March 1660, that is our last glimpse of the 'false Jew'. MICHAEL MULLETT

Sources R. Howell, *Newcastle upon Tyne and the puritan revolution: a study of the civil war in north England* (1967) • J. Jacobs and L. Wolf, eds., *Magna bibliotheca Anglo-Judaica: a bibliographical guide to Anglo-Jewish history*, rev. C. Roth, rev. edn (1937) • *CSP dom.*, 1653–4 • D. S. Katz, *Philo-Semitism and the re-admission of the Jews to England, 1603–1655* (1982)

Ramsay, Thomas Kennedy (1826–1886), judge and jurist in Canada, born in Ayr on 2 September 1826, was the third son of David Ramsay, writer to the signet, of Grimmat in the parish of Straiton, Ayrshire. His mother was the daughter of Thomas Kennedy of Kirkmechan House, Ayr; she died in 1878. The family moved to St John's, Maryhill, where Ramsay began his education under private tutors;

later he attended Madras College, St Andrews, then Ayr Academy, and completed his education in France. In 1847 he and his family migrated to Canada and settled on the estate of St Hugues in Quebec. After studying law in the office of Meredith, Bethune, and Dunkin, solicitors, he was admitted to the bar in 1852, and soon had a thriving practice. He was also an active contributor to the press; for a time he helped manage *La Patrie*, in which he fought the battle of the seigneurs (landed proprietors) with substantial success. He was himself owner of part of the Ramezay seigneury. He was co-founder and editor of the *Law Reporter* in 1854, and aided in establishing the *Lower Canada Jurist* in 1857. In 1859, because of his sound knowledge of French and English, he was appointed secretary of the commission for the codification of the civil law of Lower Canada, but in 1862 he was dismissed, allegedly because his very conservative political views were unacceptable. He taught civil law briefly in Morrin College, Quebec City, and in 1863 and 1867 he stood unsuccessfully as a Conservative in elections to the assembly. From 1864 to 1868 he was crown prosecutor at Montreal, and in this capacity in 1866 he prosecuted the Fenian raiders charged with invading Lower Canada at Sweetsburg. In 1867 he became QC.

In 1870 Ramsay was appointed an assistant justice of the superior court of Quebec, and in 1873 a puisne judge of the court of queen's bench for the dominion. His industry was immense and he spent great pains upon his judgments, invariably writing them out. Especially well read in Roman law, he wrote various pamphlets on legal subjects. His only relaxation was farming his estate at St Hugues. He died suddenly while still serving on the bench on 22 December 1886. He was unmarried. He was buried at the Mount Royal cemetery, Montreal. In an obituary he was described as 'one of [Canada's] ablest lawyers and its most irascible judge' (*Montreal Daily Star*).

C. A. HARRIS, rev. ELIZABETH BAIGENT

Sources DCB, vol. 11 • *Montreal Daily Star* (23 Dec 1886) • *The Gazette* [Montreal] (23 Dec 1886) • *The Gazette* [Montreal] (25 Dec 1886) • *Montreal Legal News* (1 Jan 1887)

Ramsay, William. *See* Ramesey, William (1627–1676?).

Ramsay, Sir William, of Colluthie (*d*. in or after **1382**). *See under* Ramsay family (*per. c.*1300–1513).

Ramsay, William, first earl of Dalhousie (*d*. 1672), politician and army officer, was the eldest son of George Ramsay, first Lord Ramsay of Dalhousie (*d*. 1629) and Margaret Douglas, daughter and heir of George Douglas of Helenhill, brother of William, earl of Morton, and Robert, earl of Douglas. Ramsay's parents were married in 1593. Ramsay himself married in 1617 Margaret Carnegie (*d*. 1661), eldest daughter of David *Carnegie, first earl of Southesk. They had four sons and three daughters: George (the second earl), John, James, and William; Marjory, who married James Erskine, earl of Buchan; Anne, who married first John, earl of Dundee, and second Sir Henry Bruce of Clackmannan; and Magdalene, who died unmarried. After Margaret's death in April 1661 Ramsay married

Jocosa (*d.* 1663), the daughter of Sir Allen *Apsley and widow of Lyster Blunt of Maple Durham.

Ramsay was chosen to represent the burgh of Montrose in the Scottish parliament in 1617 and 1621. On 21 July 1618 he obtained from the king a charter of the barony of Dalhousie and of the lands of Carrington, Edinburghshire. He succeeded his father as Lord Ramsay of Dalhousie in 1629, and on the occasion of the coronation of Charles I in Scotland was created earl of Dalhousie and Lord Ramsay and Carrington by patent dated 29 June 1633.

Dalhousie was among those of the commissioners appointed for the subscription of the king's covenant who were covenanters, and he subscribed the libel against the bishops presented the same year to the presbytery of Edinburgh. In late March 1639 he had a horse regiment from Edinburghshire, which went to secure the eastern borders with Balmerino's, Cranston's, Home's, and Lothian's cavalry regiments, and Sir Robert Munro's infantry regiment. He also signed the letter of the covenanting lords to the earl of Essex and served as colonel in the covenanting army which took up a position on the Duns Law to bar the progress of the king's army northwards. His regiment disbanded on 20 June.

In 1640 Dalhousie raised 800 foot from Lothian for a regiment in which his eldest son served as lieutenant-colonel. On 20 August 1640 Dalhousie's foot was part of the covenanting army which crossed the Tweed and invaded England. Dalhousie's unit brigaded with Lord Boyd's and Dundas of Dundas's infantry at Newcastle. It left England on 21 August 1641, disbanding six days later. At the parliament held in Edinburgh in November 1641 Dalhousie's name was inserted in a new list of privy councillors, to displace certain others chosen by the king. He served as president of parliament in 1641, 1644, and 1645. In the politics of the 1640s Dalhousie has been identified as one of the 'Royalist or pragmatic' nobles among the covenanters (Young, 62).

Dalhousie was engaged in the campaign in England in 1644, in command of a horse regiment levied from Berwickshire, Lothian, and Stirlingshire. Dalhousie's horse served at the siege of York and broke with the other allied cavalry regiments at Marston Moor, but rallied to assist the siege of Newcastle. He was called out of England with his regiment to proceed to the north of Scotland to aid Argyll against Montrose, but his son held the field command. The regiment saw active service in England and Scotland until August 1646 when it became a reserve force; it was disbanded on 9 February 1647. Montrose's second son, James, Lord Graham, who had been confined in Edinburgh Castle, was delivered over to Dalhousie to be educated.

On 24 October 1646 Dalhousie was appointed high sheriff of the county of Edinburgh (this was to be confirmed by parliament on 12 July 1661). On 4 May 1648 he was nominated colonel of horse for Edinburghshire, with his son as alternate colonel, for the engagement on behalf of Charles I. He did not accept the offices, but he did support the engagement, which he had been constrained to

repudiate by 1 June 1649. In 1651 he or his heir was nominated by Charles II colonel for Edinburghshire but due to the English occupation they could not levy any men. For having sided with Charles II he was fined £1500 on 12 April 1654, which was reduced to £400 on 6 April 1655. Dalhousie died, 'a very old man', in November 1672 (GEC, *Peerage*).   T. F. HENDERSON, *rev.* EDWARD M. FURGOL

Sources J. Balfour, *Works*, 4 vols. (1823–5) · *The letters and journals of Robert Baillie*, ed. D. Laing, 3 vols., Bannatyne Club, 73 (1841–2) · M. Napier, ed., *Memorials of Montrose and his times*, 2 vols., Maitland Club, 66 (1848–50) · J. Gordon, *History of Scots affairs from 1637–1641*, ed. J. Robertson and G. Grub, 3 vols., Spalding Club, 1, 3, 5 (1841) · J. Spalding, *Memorialls of the trubles in Scotland and in England, AD 1624 –AD 1645*, ed. J. Stuart, 2 vols., Spalding Club, [21, 23] (1850–51) · A. F. Mitchell and J. Christie, eds., *The records of the commissions of the general assemblies of the Church of Scotland*, 3 vols., Scottish History Society, 11, 25, 58 (1892–1909) · *Scots peerage* · J. R. Young, *The Scottish parliament, 1639–1661: a political and constitutional analysis* (1996) · GEC, *Peerage* · *The memoirs of Henry Guthry, late bishop*, 2nd edn (1747)

Ramsay, William (1806–1865), classical scholar, was born in Edinburgh on 6 February 1806, the third son of Sir William Ramsay, seventh baronet, and his wife, Agnata Frances, daughter of Vincent Biscoe of Hookwood, Surrey. Sir George *Ramsay, the ninth baronet, was his elder brother. He was educated at Edinburgh high school and at Glasgow University from 1823 to 1826, before going to Cambridge, where he matriculated at Trinity College in 1826. He was made a scholar in 1828 and proceeded BA in 1831 and MA in 1836. His anonymous obituarist in the *Gentleman's Magazine* claims that he was appointed a professor of mathematics at Glasgow while an undergraduate at Cambridge. In 1831 Ramsay was elected professor of humanity (Latin) at Glasgow. In 1834 he married Catherine, daughter of Robert Davidson LLD, professor of civil law in the university. They had one daughter.

Ramsay's colleague as professor of Greek was E. L. Lushington, brother-in-law of Tennyson. C. J. Fordyce, a more recent occupant of Ramsay's chair, described them as 'a pair of professors who not only outshone all their predecessors but vastly outshone their contemporaries in the other [Scottish] universities'. Their pupils included a number of men who later became prominent classical scholars: W. Y. Sellar, L. Campbell, D. B. Monro, and J. Frazer. Ramsay resigned his chair because of ill health in 1863. He was succeeded by his nephew, G. G. Ramsay.

Ramsay produced a variety of classical works, of which *Elegiac Extracts from Tibullus and Ovid* (1840) and an *Elementary Manual of Roman Antiquities* (1859) went through several editions. He also wrote a *Manual of Roman Antiquities* in the third division of the *Encyclopaedia metropolitana* (1848) and contributed many articles to William Smith's classical dictionaries. He spent some time after his retirement in Rome collating manuscripts of Plautus, and, according to Fordyce, his edition of *Mostellaria* (1869) 'laid the foundation of Plautine studies in Britain'. He died at San Remo on 12 February 1865.

W. W. WROTH, *rev.* RICHARD SMAIL

Sources *GM*, 3rd ser., 18 (1865), 652 · Venn, *Alum. Cant.* · C. J. Fordyce, 'Classics', *Fortuna domus: a series of lectures delivered in the University of Glasgow in commemoration of the fifth centenary of its foundation*, ed. [J. B. Neilson] (1952), 21–40 · W. I. Addison, ed., *The matriculation albums of the University of Glasgow from 1728 to 1858* (1913) · *CGPLA Eng. & Wales* (1865)
Archives U. Lpool L., Sydney Jones Library, notebook on classical philology
Likenesses A. Edouart, silhouette, Scot. NPG · portrait, repro. in J. Maclehose, *Glasgow men*, 2 (1886), 265–6
Wealth at death £41,433 12s. 3d.: probate, 22 July 1865, NA Scot., SC49/31/79, 1522

Ramsay, Sir William (1852–1916), physical chemist, was born on 2 October 1852 at 2 Queen's Crescent, Glasgow, the only child of William Ramsay (1811–1887), civil engineer and later surveyor to the Scottish Union Insurance Company, and his wife, Catherine (d. 1891), daughter of Dr Archibald Robertson of Edinburgh, who was a governess before her marriage. On his father's side he was descended from a long line of chemist-dyers, and on his mother's side, physicians; both of his grandfathers published works on chemistry. His father had a good general knowledge of science and mathematics, while his uncle was the well-known geologist Sir Andrew Crombie Ramsay (1814–1891). Ramsay's own scientific interests developed at an early age, and despite his mother's initial intention that he should enter the Calvinist ministry, he had by the age of sixteen decided to become a chemist.

When he was about six Ramsay was sent to a preparatory school kept by a Mr Stark. In 1862 he entered the Glasgow Academy, and four years later he matriculated at the University of Glasgow, where he studied classics, English literature, logic, and mathematics. In May 1869 he began to work in the laboratory of the city analyst, Robert Tatlock, as the university could not provide a full course of instruction for students who wished to take up chemistry as a profession. During the next eighteen months he continued as a pupil of Tatlock, while attending university lectures on physics, chemistry, anatomy, and geology; he did not take a degree.

In October 1870 Ramsay went to Heidelberg, intending to study under Robert Bunsen, but decided to return to Glasgow for the winter. In April of the following year he entered the laboratory of the organic chemist Rudolf Fittig, in Tübingen, where he worked on the toluic and nitrotoluic acids; in August 1872 he received the PhD degree at Tübingen. In October he was appointed assistant in the Young Laboratory of Technical Chemistry at Anderson's College, Glasgow. In 1874 he became tutorial assistant to Professor John Ferguson in the chemistry department of the University of Glasgow, and carried out research in organic chemistry. He synthesized pyridine and a variety of pyridinic acids (*Philosophical Magazine*, 1876, 1877), and showed the connection between the alkaloids and pyridine (*Journal of the Chemical Society*, 1877, 1879).

Ramsay's interest in physico-chemical problems grew out of his studies of the molecular volumes of elements at their boiling points, begun in 1879, and he continued this work after he was appointed professor of chemistry at

Sir William Ramsay (1852–1916), by unknown photographer

University College, Bristol, in 1880. In 1882 Sydney Young became his assistant, and together they published over thirty papers on vapour pressure, the critical states of liquids, evaporation, and dissociation. The work required the design and construction of novel apparatus and a high degree of manipulative skill, and helped to establish the foundations for Ramsay's later experimental researches on gases.

On 3 August 1881 Ramsay married Margaret Johnstone Marshall (d. 1936), daughter of George Stevenson Buchanan of Glasgow. They had two children: Elizabeth Catherine (1883–1960), known as Elska, who married H. L. Tidy in 1906; and William George (1886–1927), who died early of disseminated sclerosis. In September 1881 Ramsay was appointed principal of University College, Bristol, in succession to Alfred Marshall. In that capacity he was instrumental in the successful movement to obtain government funding for the university colleges. He combined the post with his duties as professor until 1887 when, at the retirement of A. W. Williamson, he was elected to the chair of general chemistry at University College, London.

In London Ramsay continued his research on critical states, with John Shields and others. He studied the variation of surface tension with temperature, confirming a linear relationship between them, and used the results to deduce the molecular complexity of associating liquids. During this period he became a strong proponent of the osmotic-ionic theories of van't Hoff, Arrhenius, and Ostwald, and helped to ease the introduction of the new physical chemistry to Britain. By 1894 his laboratory had become a centre of research activity and he had firmly established his reputation as a physical chemist.

In 1894 Ramsay began his most important research, on the seemingly chemically inert, monatomic, elemental gases. The physicist J. W. Strutt (Lord Rayleigh) had found that the density of atmospheric nitrogen was consistently higher than that of chemically pure nitrogen, a discrepancy first noted by Henry Cavendish in 1785. Ramsay thought that this might be due to a heavy gas in atmospheric nitrogen, while Rayleigh ascribed it to a light gas in chemical nitrogen. Throughout the summer of 1894 they worked to find the source of the anomaly, using two different methods. Ramsay removed oxygen, water vapour, carbon dioxide, and nitrogen from air, the crucial step being the absorption of nitrogen by red-hot magnesium, and was left with a residue which appeared to be a new element. Rayleigh too had been partially successful, and in August 1894 they made a joint announcement at the meeting of the British Association for the Advancement of Science. They named the new gas argon, from the Greek word meaning 'idle', and formally presented their results to the Royal Society in January 1895 (*PRS*, 1895). Later that year they were awarded the Smithsonian Institution's Hodgkins prize, given for the most important discovery concerning atmospheric air.

In February 1895 Henry Miers called Ramsay's attention to the work of W. F. Hillebrand of the United States Geological Survey, who had found that two uranite minerals, pitchblende and cleveite, gave off a considerable amount of gas when heated. Ramsay, seeking to determine whether the gas contained argon, repeated the experiments with cleveite and was able to isolate another inert elementary gas in March (*Journal of the Chemical Society*, 1895). Spectrum analysis showed that it was identical with the element helium, which had in 1868 been spectroscopically detected in the sun's atmosphere by the astronomer J. N. Lockyer (who named it) and the chemist Edward Frankland, but had hitherto been terrestrially unknown.

It had earlier occurred to Ramsay that there was room in the periodic table for a new, eighth, group of elements. The discovery of helium increased the likelihood that further 'inert' gases might exist, and in his book *The Gases of the Atmosphere* (1896; 4th edn., 1915), he reproduced the periodic table with spaces reserved for several new elements. He made his ideas public in his presidential address, entitled 'An undiscovered gas', to the Chemistry Section of the 1897 British Association meeting in Toronto, predicting the existence of at least one other gaseous element whose atomic weight would lie between those of helium and argon. Working with his student Morris W. Travers from April 1895, Ramsay searched for further sources of both gases, and attempted to make them combine with other substances; J. N. Collie, Ramsay's assistant, worked with them until he left University College in 1896. Their discovery that thorium and uranium minerals produce helium was explained by subsequent developments in the study of radioactivity.

Ramsay refined his experimental techniques during the work on helium, learning to manipulate increasingly small quantities of gas; he and Travers, both skilled glassblowers, designed and constructed all the apparatus that they used. In 1898 they began to look for a third new element by liquefying argon and subjecting it to fractional distillation, a method made possible by William Hampson's independent development of a liquefaction process; Ramsay was on bad terms with James Dewar, who had pioneered the technology of liquid air.

In May 1898, as a preliminary trial, Ramsay and Travers allowed a small quantity of liquid air to evaporate slowly, and collected the least volatile fraction. After removal of oxygen and nitrogen, spectroscopic examination of the residue showed the presence of an unknown gas, which they named krypton (hidden). It was heavier than argon, and was thus not the gas they had been looking for. They then condensed 15 litres of argon and collected the most volatile fraction; spectrum analysis revealed that they had found the light gas, which they named neon (new). In July they found that the heavy fraction of liquid air contained a gas more dense than krypton; in September they announced the discovery of xenon (stranger). Ramsay and Travers spent the next two years isolating the gases and determining their properties, thereby confirming the existence of a new group of elements in the periodic table (*PTRS*, 1901). In 1904 Ramsay became the first British recipient of the Nobel prize for chemistry, in recognition of this unique achievement.

In 1903, working with Frederick Soddy, Ramsay observed the spectrum of helium in the gaseous emanation from radium (radon), thus providing experimental evidence for Rutherford's theory of radioactive disintegration. Rutherford and Soddy had earlier shown that radon was probably a sixth member of the family of inert gases; in 1910 Ramsay and Robert Whytlaw-Gray confirmed this by determining its physical properties from minute samples (*PRS*, 1911). In showing that its atomic weight differed from that of radium by the mass of one helium atom, they provided further proof that α-particles emitted during radioactive decay were helium nuclei. Ramsay's research in the field of radioactivity was not always so fruitful: after 1905 he performed many unsuccessful experiments in attempts to discover whether chemical or physical means could cause the transmutation of elements.

Ramsay was a man of many interests. He was concerned by the state of science education in Britain and was the first to write textbooks based on the periodic system of classification—*A System of Inorganic Chemistry* and *Elementary Systematic Chemistry for the Use of Schools and Colleges* (both 1891). Throughout the 1890s he was involved in the movement to reorganize the University of London, which had been an examining body independent of the London colleges; he was a strong supporter of the role of research and teaching in a modern university. In 1900 he went to India at the invitation of J. N. Tata, who proposed to endow a technical research institution; he advised that it be sited in Bangalore, where the Indian Institute of Science was eventually established with Travers as its first director.

At about this time Ramsay began to write magazine articles of a semi-popular nature, a selection of which were published in his *Essays Biographical and Chemical* (1908). For many years he acted as a consultant to industry, advising on a wide range of chemical matters and appearing as an expert witness in several court cases. He was a member of the royal commission on sewage disposal (1898–1915), chemical adviser to the British Radium Corporation (1909–12), and a director on the boards of two short-lived chemical companies. After the turn of the century these commitments took up increasing amounts of his time.

Ramsay received many awards and honorary degrees, and was elected a member of scientific societies in twenty countries. He was elected a fellow of the Royal Society in 1888 and awarded its Davy medal in 1895; in 1897 he received the Longstaff medal from the Chemical Society, of which he was president in 1907–9. He served three terms as a vice-president of the Institute of Chemistry, and was president of the Society of Chemical Industry (1903–4), the International Congress of Applied Chemistry (1909), and the British Association (1911). He was created KCB in 1902, was awarded the Prussian order of merit (1911), was an officer of the French Légion d'honneur, and a commander of the order of the Corona d'Italia.

Ramsay was loved by his students, who affectionately called him 'the Chief'. He was unfailingly optimistic and enthusiastic; colleagues found him charming, witty, and generous. He had an aptitude for languages and music, and enjoyed travel and outdoor activities. At his retirement, in 1912, he was the most famous British chemist of the day. After moving to Hazlemere, near High Wycombe, Buckinghamshire, he continued to work from his home, Beechcroft, and was engaged in work connected to the war effort when he died there of cancer on 23 July 1916. He was buried at Holy Trinity Church, Hazlemere, on 26 July.

K. D. WATSON

Sources M. W. Travers, *A life of Sir William Ramsay, KCB, FRS* (1956) · W. A. Tilden, *Sir William Ramsay, KCB, FRS: memorials of his life and work* (1918) · K. D. Watson, 'Aspects of a career in science: Sir William Ramsay and the chemical community, 1880–1915', DPhil diss., U. Oxf., 1994 · R. B. Moore, 'Sir William Ramsay', *Journal of the Franklin Institute*, 186 (1918), 29–55 · T. J. Trenn, 'Ramsay, William', *DSB* · J. N. C. [J. N. Collie], *PRS*, 93A (1916–17), xlii–liv · O. Hehner, *The Analyst*, 41 (1916), 329–33 · F. Soddy and A. M. Worthington, 'Sir William Ramsay', *Nature*, 97 (1916), 482–5 · M. W. Travers, *The discovery of the rare gases* (1928) · F. G. Donnan, 'Introduction', in W. Ramsay, *Life and letters of Joseph Black, MD* (1918), ix–xix · *Morning Post* (24 July 1916) · M. W. Travers, 'William Ramsay', *British chemists*, ed. A. Findlay and W. H. Mills (1947), 146–75 · *CGPLA Eng. & Wales* (1917)

Archives Cornell University, Ithaca, New York, corresp. relating to *Journal of Physical Chemistry* · RS · UCL, corresp., notebooks, and papers · University of Strathclyde, Glasgow, report on waters of Bath | Air Force Research Laboratories, Cambridge, Massachusetts, corresp. with Lord Rayleigh · CUL, letters to Lord Kelvin · CUL, corresp. with Lord Rutherford · CUL, letters to Sir George Stokes · Sci. Mus., corresp. with Oswald John Silberrad · U. Cal., Berkeley, Bancroft Library, Emil Fischer MSS · U. Leeds, Brotherton L., letters to Arthur Smithells · UCL, corresp. with Sir Oliver Lodge · UCL, Rayleigh MSS

Likenesses photographs, *c.*1862–1913, UCL, Ramsay MSS · M. Milbanke, oils, 1913, UCL, Christopher Ingold Laboratories · M. Milbanke, oils, 1913, Sci. Mus. · C. L. Hartwell, relief memorial tablet, *c.*1922, Westminster Abbey · Spy [L. Ward], caricature, Mentschel-colourtype, NPG; repro. in *VF* (2 Dec 1908) · photogravure, NPG [*see illus.*] · two photographs, RS

Wealth at death £17,896: K. D. Watson, 'Aspects of a career in science: Sir William Ramsay and the chemical community, 1880–1915', DPhil diss., Oxford University, 1994, 203

Ramsay, Sir William Mitchell (1851–1939), classical scholar and archaeologist, was born in Glasgow on 15 March 1851, the youngest son of Thomas Ramsay and his wife, Jane, daughter of William Mitchell, both of Alloa. Ramsay came from a family of lawyers, his father, grandfather, and great-grandfather having all been advocates, his grandfather also procurator-fiscal of Clackmannanshire. His father died in 1857, and the family returned to live in the country near Alloa. In his education his eldest brother and his maternal uncle, Andrew Mitchell, of Alloa, took an active interest. From the Gymnasium, Old Aberdeen, he went on to the University of Aberdeen and then won a scholarship at St John's College, Oxford, where he obtained a first class in classical moderations (1874) and in *literae humaniores* (1876). In 1874, through his uncle's generosity, he was able to spend the long vacation at Göttingen, studying Sanskrit under a great scholar, Theodor Benfey. This was a critical period of his life: then for the first time, in his own words, he 'gained some insight into modern methods of literary investigation', and his 'thoughts ever since turned towards the border lands between European and Asian civilization'. A further stimulus was received from Henry Jardine Bidder, of St John's, who introduced him to the diverse elements which made up Hellenistic culture.

The opportunity to begin what was to become Ramsay's life work—exploration in Asia Minor for the study of its antiquities and history, with special reference to the influence of Asia on Greek civilization and the Graeco-Roman administration—was provided by his election in 1880 to an Oxford studentship for travel and research in Greek lands. At Smyrna he met Sir C. W. Wilson, then British consul-general in Anatolia, who advised him to explore the unknown inland regions of the country and in whose company he made two long journeys in 1881–2. So started an exploration that was to be continued, save for one considerable break (from 1891 to 1899), until 1914. Further funds were provided by his election to a research fellowship at Exeter College, Oxford, in 1882, and by the establishment of an Asia Minor Exploration Fund supported by individuals and societies. From 1885 to 1886 he held the newly created Lincoln and Merton professorship of classical archaeology and art at Oxford and became a fellow of Lincoln College; he was then appointed regius professor of humanity at Aberdeen, where he remained until 1911. After his retirement he continued to devote himself to Anatolian studies up to the very end of his long life.

Ramsay was knighted in 1906 and received many academic distinctions: three honorary fellowships of Oxford colleges (Exeter, 1898, Lincoln, 1899, and St John's, 1912) and honorary degrees from six British universities and

Sir William Mitchell Ramsay (1851–1939), by James Russell & Sons

historical study. Topography and history are combined in his local history of Phrygia (*The Cities and Bishoprics of Phrygia*, 1895, 1897), uncompleted for lack of adequate evidence. The value of his historical work as a whole, largely scattered in journals and elsewhere (listed down to 1923 in W. H. Buchler and W. M. Calder, eds., *Anatolian Studies*, presented to him), cannot be discussed here. In his lifetime he was best known for his contributions to early Christian history, beginning with *The Church in the Roman Empire before A.D. 170* (1893) and continuing in a series of books devoted mainly to St Paul and St Luke. His basic contention that St Luke was a first-class historian of the first century AD, remains a controversial issue and with it the value of the Acts of the Apostles as a historical source. However, his view that the Galatians to whom St Paul addressed his epistle were those, not of Galatia proper, but of the southern part of the Roman province has gained general acceptance. The judgements and polemics expressed in his New Testament studies have often been questioned subsequently, but not so the value of his topographical work and the stimulus which he gave to the exploration of Asia Minor in the early twentieth century.

J. G. C. Anderson, *rev.* Peter W. Lock

Sources *The Times* (22 April 1939) · S. Mitchell, *Anatolia*, 2 (1993) · W. H. Buchler and W. M. Calder, eds., *Anatolian studies* (1923) · D. G. Hogarth, *The wandering scholar in the Levant* (1898) · B. Levick, *Roman colonies in southern Asia Minor* (1967)

Archives AM Oxf., corresp., notebooks, and papers | JRL, letters to the *Manchester Guardian* · U. Aberdeen, archives of three expeditions Monumenta Asiae Minoris with retrospective (?) to Ramsay · U. Aberdeen, MSS relevant to university membership

Likenesses J. Russell & Sons, photograph, NPG [*see illus.*] · photograph, repro. in Buchler and Calder, eds., *Anatolian studies*, frontispiece · portrait, U. Aberdeen, Marischal Museum

Wealth at death £1404 18s. 9d.: confirmation, 23 June 1939, CCI · £220 11s. 8d.: further grant, 6 Sept 1939, CCI

from New York, Bordeaux, and Marburg. He was an original fellow of the British Academy but resigned in 1924. In 1893 he was awarded the gold medal of Pope Leo XIII, and in 1906 the Victoria medal of the Royal Geographical Society. He paid several visits to the United States of America to deliver courses of lectures, most of which were afterwards published.

Ramsay married first, in 1878, Agnes Dick (d. 1927), second daughter of the Revd William Marshall, of Leith, and granddaughter of the Revd Dr Andrew Marshall, of Kirkintilloch, Dunbartonshire, one of the original seceders from the Church of Scotland. She shared with her husband the discomforts of travel in Turkey and aided him in his work. They had two sons, the younger of whom was killed in action in 1915, and four daughters. He married second, in 1928, Phyllis Eileen, daughter of Alfred Ernest Thorowgood, of Old Bosham, Sussex, who survived him. He died at his home, 34 Wentworth Avenue, Bournemouth, on 20 April 1939.

Ramsay's enduring claim to distinction is the immense advance, based upon a rich harvest of new evidence, which he achieved in the knowledge of the geography and topography of Asia Minor and of its political, social, and cultural (including religious) history. In his *Historical Geography of Asia Minor* (1890) and in subsequent articles he worked out a topographical scheme which, while leaving much to be settled by discovery, laid a sure foundation for

Ramsay, William Norman (1782–1815), army officer, was the eldest son of Captain David Ramsay RN (d. 1818) and belonged to the family of the Ramsays of Balmain in Kincardineshire. He entered the Royal Military Academy, Woolwich, on 17 January 1797, was commissioned second lieutenant, Royal Artillery, on 27 October 1798, became first lieutenant on 1 August 1800, and second captain on 24 April 1806. He served in the Egyptian campaign in 1800–01. On 14 June 1808 he married Mary Emilia, eldest daughter of Lieutenant-General Norman McLeod, twentieth chief of McLeod; she died on 10 August 1809.

In 1809 Ramsay was posted to I troop (Bull's), Royal Horse Artillery, and went with it to Portugal. This troop was engaged at Busaco in 1810 and was specially thanked by Sir Stapleton Cotton for its conduct while covering the retreat to Torres Vedras.

When the British army again advanced in 1811 the troop equally distinguished itself. It was mentioned by Wellington in dispatches (14 and 16 March, 9 April) for its conduct in the actions of Cazal Nova, Foz d'Aronce, and Sabugal. At Fuentes d'Oñoro (5 May) the British cavalry on the right wing was driven back by the French cavalry, which was in much greater strength, and I troop, or part of it, was cut off. It was supposed that the guns were lost, but soon a commotion was observed among the French cavalry:

> an English shout pealed high and clear, the mass was rent asunder, and Norman Ramsay burst forth, sword in hand, at the head of his battery, his horses breathing fire, stretched like greyhounds along the plain, the guns bounded behind them like things of no weight, and the mounted gunners followed close, with heads bent low and pointed weapons in desperate career. (Napier, 3.150, 151)

In 1812 I troop took part in the battle of Salamanca, and in the advance on (and retreat from) Burgos, distinguishing itself in the action of Venta de Pozo on 23 October. Major Bull was wounded during the retreat, and had to leave the army. Command of the troop fell temporarily to Ramsay, and though Major Frazer assumed it at the beginning of 1813 his appointment to command the whole of the horse artillery three months afterwards left I troop in Ramsay's hands throughout the 1813 campaign.

At Vitoria (21 June 1813) the troop was attached to Graham's corps, and contributed largely to the capture of Abechuco, by which the French army was cut off from the Bayonne Road, its best line of retreat. Ramsay rode a couple of 6 pounders over a hedge and ditch, in order to get them up in time to act against the retreating enemy. Frazer wrote that 'Bull's troop (which I have no hesitation in saying is much the best in this country) had, under Ramsay's command, been of unusual and unquestionable service' (Fraser, 186). Two days after the battle (23 June) Ramsay was ordered forward in pursuit of the French. Wellington met him at a neighbouring village and, as he had some thought of sending him with Graham's corps by another road, told him, according to his own account, to halt there

> and not to move from it till he should receive further orders from myself, knowing that he would be sent to from the advanced posts. Notwithstanding these orders, Ramsay left the village in the morning before the orders reached him to join Graham; and he got forward into the defile, and it was not possible to bring him back till the whole column had passed. (Dispatches, 10.539)

For this alleged disobedience Wellington put Ramsay under arrest.

Ramsay's act was due to some misunderstanding. He supposed that he was to wait at the village for the night, and that if orders for the troop were issued in the course of the night, Wellington would forward them. None came; and next morning Ramsay, acting on the verbal directions of a staff-officer and a written order from the quartermaster-general, advanced to rejoin the cavalry brigade, to which he belonged. As his friend and chief, Frazer, wrote: 'Admitting, contrary to all evidence, that he had mistaken the verbal orders he received, this, surely, is a venial offence, and one for which long-tried and faithful services should not be forgotten.' There was a strong feeling in the army that he was hardly used, but Sir Thomas Graham's intercession on his behalf only irritated Wellington. A distorted account of this affair was given in Samuel Lover's novel Handy Andy (1842). Ramsay was soon released, but was not recommended for promotion.

In mid-July 1813 Ramsay was allowed to resume command of his troop, and on 22 November he received a brevet majority. In the advance of the army over the Pyrenees his troop was attached to Sir John Hope's corps, and he was one of the officers specially mentioned by Hope in his report of the actions near Biarritz on 10–12 December. Ramsay was twice wounded slightly in these actions.

On 17 December he became captain in the regiment, and had to return to England to take command of K troop. In the spring of 1815 he was transferred to H troop, which formed part of Wellington's army in the Netherlands. A week before Waterloo, Frazer speaks of him as 'adored by his men; kind, generous, and manly, he is more than the friend of his soldiers'. At Waterloo (18 June 1815) his troop was at first with the cavalry division, but, like the rest of the horse artillery, it was soon brought into action in the front line. It was placed a little to the left rear of Hougoumont, and there before the end of the day it had lost four officers out of five. Ramsay himself was killed at about 4 p.m., during the heavy fire of artillery and skirmishers which was the prelude to the French cavalry charges. A bullet, passing through a snuff-box which he carried, entered his heart.

Ramsay's friend Frazer buried the body immediately behind in a hollow during a momentary lull in the battle, and afterwards erected a monument in the church at Waterloo. The body was a few weeks afterwards sent to Scotland, where on 8 August it was reinterred in the churchyard of Inveresk, near Edinburgh, his family burial-place, beneath a sarcophagus, supported by a cannon and shot, and surmounted by a helmet, sword, and accoutrements.

The elder of Ramsay's two brothers, Lieutenant Alexander Ramsay RA, was killed in the attack on New Orleans on 1 January 1815; his other brother, Lieutenant David Ramsay RN, died in Jamaica on 31 July 1815.

E. M. LLOYD, rev. ROGER T. STEARN

Sources records of the royal horse artillery, Royal Artillery Institution, Woolwich · F. Duncan, ed., *History of the royal regiment of artillery*, 2 vols. (1873) · A. Fraser, *Letters of Colonel Sir Augustus Frazer* (1859) · W. Tomkinson, *The diary of a cavalry officer in the Peninsular and Waterloo campaigns, 1809–1815*, ed. J. Tomkinson (1894) · W. F. P. Napier, *History of the war in the Peninsula and in the south of France*, new edn, 6 vols. (1886) · *The dispatches of … the duke of Wellington … from 1799 to 1818*, ed. J. Gurwood, 13 vols. in 12 (1834–9) · C. Dalton, *The Waterloo roll call*, 2nd edn (1904) · *Edinburgh Evening Courant* (10 Aug 1815) · *Edinburgh Evening Courant* (28 Sept 1815) · private information (1896) · E. Longford [E. H. Pakenham, countess of Longford], *Wellington*, 1: *The years of the sword* (1969) · R. Muir, *Britain and the defeat of Napoleon, 1807–1815* (1996)
Archives Royal Artillery Institution, Woolwich, London, papers

Ramsbotham, Francis Henry (1801–1868), obstetrician, was born on 9 December 1801 at Richmond, Surrey, son of John Ramsbotham, lecturer on obstetric medicine at the London Hospital and physician to the Royal Maternity Charity, who also had a large obstetric practice in east London. Ramsbotham was educated at St Paul's School and apprenticed to a druggist in Cheapside before he entered in 1818 the London Hospital, and in 1819 Edinburgh University, where he graduated MD in 1822. He became a licentiate of the Royal College of Physicians in 1822, and fellow in 1844. At first his assistant, he eventually succeeded to his father's practice, which he continued successfully for many years. In 1825 the Royal Maternity Charity, the Tower Hamlets Dispensary, and the Eastern Dispensary appointed him their physician. He was obstetric physician and lecturer on obstetric and forensic medicine at the London Hospital from 1854 to 1863. In 1826 he helped to found, and became secretary of, the Obstetric Society of London. He was also president of the Harveian and Hunterian societies, and vice-president of the Pathological Society. At an unknown date he married Mary, daughter of Henry Lindsay of Perth. They had two sons.

As a practitioner Ramsbotham's chief rival was David Daniel Davis, with whom he vied for pre-eminence in English midwifery. Ramsbotham was an enthusiastic and popular teacher, but could be dogmatic, and his fixed opposition to the use of chloroform in childbirth led to a decline in his practice in his later years. Ultimately he moved from New Broad Street to Portman Square, but this failed to lift his professional prospects. Ill health obliged him to relinquish his practice and retire to Wood End, near Perth, the home of his son Francis John, where he died on 7 July 1868.

Ramsbotham's main publication was *The Principles and Practice of Obstetric Medicine and Surgery* (1844), a rival to Davis's *Principles and Practice of Obstetric Medicine* (1836). Ramsbotham's was one of the first medical books brought out with expensive illustrations, and was very successful, running to many editions in Britain and the USA. He also published two other monographs and journal articles for the medical press, mainly on midwifery.

GORDON GOODWIN, rev. ELIZABETH BAIGENT

Sources *The Lancet* (18 July 1868), 100 · *BMJ* (18 July 1868), 62 · review, *Medical Times and Gazette* (4 Jan 1868), 22 · *Medical Register* (1859), 246 · *London and Provincial Medical Directory* (1865), 480 · review, *The Athenaeum* (18 July 1857), 910 · Munk, *Roll* · S. P. Chippingdale, 'Byegone members of the hospital staff', *London Hospital Gazette*, 22 (1917–19), 219–23, esp. 221 · CGPLA Eng. & Wales (1868) · P. M. Dunn, 'Dr Francis Ramsbotham (1801–1868) and obstetric practice in London', *Archives of Disease in Childhood: Fetal and Neonatal Edition*, 73/2 (Sept 1995), F118–F120
Archives National Library of Medicine, Bethesda, Maryland, corresp. and papers
Wealth at death £4761 1s. 9d.: confirmation, 10 Sept 1868, CCI · £6304 17s. 3d.: additional estate, 21 April 1869, CCI

Ramsbotham, Herwald, first Viscount Soulbury (1887–1971), politician and governor-general of Ceylon, was born on 6 March 1887 at Winterbrook, Cholsey, Berkshire, the son of Herwald Ramsbotham (1859–1941), and his wife, Ethel Margaret Bevan (d. 1943), daughter of T. Bevan of Stone Park, Greenhithe, Kent. He came from a distinguished wealthy Lancashire family noted for public service. He was educated at Uppingham School, and at University College, Oxford, where he graduated with a first class in moderations and Greats. In 1911 he was called to the bar, and subsequently practised as a barrister. He married Doris Violet (d. 1954), the daughter of S. de Stein, a wealthy banker, in 1911. They had two sons and a daughter.

In the First World War, Ramsbotham commanded a company of the 7th battalion of the Bedfordshire regiment, before becoming staff-captain of the 53rd infantry brigade and deputy assistant adjutant-general. He was mentioned in dispatches three times, awarded the Military Cross, and appointed an OBE. Following the end of hostilities he worked in the City of London. Intent on a career in politics he contested Lancaster in 1910 and 1928 as a Conservative. He was finally elected for the constituency in 1929, and remained an MP until his elevation to the peerage in 1941. He became parliamentary secretary to Lord Halifax, president of the Board of Education, in 1931. His responsibilities were great, as Lord Halifax was employed in other duties and took little interest in public education. In 1935 Ramsbotham became parliamentary secretary to the board of agriculture before becoming minister of pensions, an office in which he continued to assist the minister of agriculture in the House of Commons. In 1939 he was appointed first commissioner of works and was sworn of the privy council. In April 1940 he became president of the Board of Education following the resignation of Lord De La Warr. This position was widely regarded as a political backwater.

Unlike his immediate predecessors, who had been keen to move on to more prestigious positions, Ramsbotham remained at the ministry and initiated important reforms. One of his priorities was to restore the coherence of the educational system, which had become fragmented by the process of evacuation. He was also instrumental in developing plans for its long-term reorganization. The board's proposals were embodied in the so-called green book. Although confidential, this was distributed 'in such a blaze of secrecy that it achieved an unusual degree of publicity' (McKibbin, 221). This pioneering document, although based on an administrative approach to the educational service, was firmly based on the premise that the reforms must meet the educational requirements of the children. It highlighted the unfairness and indefensible inequalities of the educational system after the age of eleven. According to Nigel Middleton and Sophia Weitzman's *A Place for Everyone* this innovation was instrumental in establishing a new constitutional approach based on a more open form of constructive debate. However, Ramsbotham 'was moving too fast for Churchill' (McKibbin, 221), and he was replaced by R. A. Butler in July 1941. The latter nevertheless continued the process of reform initiated by Ramsbotham. In July 1941 as compensation for relinquishing his position at the Board of Education he was raised to the peerage as Baron Soulbury of Soulbury. He was also appointed chairman of the recently renamed Assistance Board. The functions of its predecessor, the Unemployment Assistance Board, had been radically extended the previous year following the transfer to it of the administration of pensions relief, war distress, and allowances to families of men in the forces. In addition it had become responsible for the care of evacuees and air-raid victims. In 1942 Soulbury was appointed chairman of the standing joint committee on teachers' salaries (the Burnham committee), a position he retained until 1949.

In November 1944 Soulbury became chairman of the commission on constitutional reform for Ceylon. The Soulbury commission report, issued in October 1945, drafted a constitution for Ceylon which provided self-government while retaining some imperial safeguards in defence and external affairs. Ceylonese leaders pressed for the removal of these safeguards, demanding the grant of dominion status. This was affirmed with the Ceylon Independence Act of 1947, which was widely portrayed as a bold experiment in Western-style parliamentary government in a plural society. Soulbury was subsequently appointed governor-general of Ceylon, arriving in Colombo in June 1949. Within a month he was fluent enough to make his first speech in Sinhalese to the Ceylon National Congress. It was a testing appointment for Soulbury as the path to independence proved considerably more challenging than expected: Soulbury had to cope with the effects of the unexpected death of the prime minister, D. S. Senanayake, in March 1952, the general election later that year, and also a visit to Ceylon by Elizabeth II and the duke of Edinburgh. Early in 1954, moreover, shortly before the formal end of Soulbury's period of office, his wife died after being run down by a London bus.

Following his return to England in July 1954 Soulbury was raised to a viscountcy. He continued to intervene occasionally in the House of Lords, and in August 1956, at the invitation of the archbishop of Canterbury, he was appointed chairman of the National Society. He was also chairman of the board of governors of the Royal Ballet School, from 1956 to 1964. On 10 November 1962 he married (Carmen) Ursula, widow of Frederick Wakeham and daughter of Armand and Helen Jerome. She died two years later on 12 November 1964.

Soulbury is best remembered for his contribution to educational reform in Britain, and for his role in guiding Ceylon to independence. He had an impressive capacity for hard work, coupled with ability for common sense and shrewd judgement. His popularity among his departmental colleagues was a testimony to his good humour and charm. As leader of the commission which reported on Ceylon's future he played a key role in formulating a workmanlike constitution and made strenuous efforts during his period as governor-general to run the country in an effective way. A lucid if not inspirational orator, he gained a reputation as an honest broker and a safe pair of hands. Soulbury died on 30 January 1971 at Stoke House, Stoke Fleming, near Newton Abbot, Devon.

JOHN MARTIN

Sources *The Times* (14 Nov 1971) · C. J. Jeffries, *Ceylon: the path to independence* (1962) · P. H. J. H. Gosden, *Education in the Second World War: a study in policy and administration* (1976) · N. Middleton and S. Weitzman, *A place for everyone: a history of education from the end of the eighteenth century to the 1970s* (1976) · A. Calder, *The people's war: Britain, 1939–45*, [new edn] (1971) · R. M. Titmuss, *Problems of social policy* (1950) · J. M. Brown and W. R. Louis, eds., *The twentieth century* (1999), vol. 4 of *The Oxford history of the British empire* · R. McKibbin, *Classes and cultures: England 1918–1951* (1998) · C. R. De Silva, *Sri Lanka: a history* (New York, 1988) · K. M. De Silva, ed., *Sri Lanka*, 2 vols. (1997) · Burke, *Peerage* (1999) · b. cert. · m. cert. · d. cert.

Archives NRA, papers | BLPES, corresp. with Violet Markham
Likenesses W. Stoneman, three photographs, 1937–56, NPG · E. Halliday, oils, 1965, Carlton Club, London

Ramsbottom, John (1814–1897), railway engineer, was born at Todmorden, Lancashire, on 11 September 1814, the son of a cotton spinner who owned the only steam-driven mill in the area. He was educated by local schoolmasters and Baptist ministers. His practical training started at his father's mill, where he was given a lathe and built small working steam engines. He then rebuilt and re-erected the beam engine at his father's mill and invented the weft fork, later adopted universally, which enabled looms to be worked at high speed. He was an active and enthusiastic member of the Todmorden Mechanics' Institute, showing quick perception and ability in all mechanical matters.

About 1839 Ramsbottom went to Manchester and joined Sharp, Roberts & Co., who already had a high reputation as builders of locomotives and cotton-spinning machinery. Here he gained experience in locomotive building and his ability sufficiently impressed Charles F. Beyer, who ran the locomotive department, that, in 1842, he recommended Ramsbottom as locomotive superintendent of the Manchester and Birmingham Railway; in 1846 the latter company became part of the London and North Western Railway (LNWR), of which Ramsbottom was then appointed district superintendent of the north-east division. In 1857 he was promoted to locomotive superintendent of the northern division, covering all routes of the LNWR north of Rugby, at Crewe works, where in the following year the first of almost 1000 of his DX 0–6–0 type freight locomotives were built. Some of these were still running over sixty years later. In 1859 he built the first of his 2–2–2 type express locomotives, two of which took part in the railway 'race' between east- and west-coast companies from London to Edinburgh in 1888, and in 1863 he developed the 2–4–0 type for use over more heavily graded routes.

In 1862 Ramsbottom became all-line chief mechanical engineer of the LNWR, Britain's largest railway, with locomotive construction concentrated at Crewe works. His mechanical and organizing abilities were given full scope during the rapid development of these works, where he introduced Bessemer open-hearth steel-making. In 1868 he installed Siemens-Martin furnaces. He reduced the number of individual locomotive types and standardized their components to the greatest possible extent; and new machine tools and equipment ensured accuracy in manufacture, and facilitated transfer of components within the works. The result was a more than twofold increase in the rate of locomotive production. He was the inventor of water pick-up troughs laid between the rails, whereby a scoop lowered into the trough from the locomotive or tender allowed additional water to be picked up while the train was running, thus making possible much longer non-stop runs. First applied in 1860, this was rapidly extended to most British and some American and French main-line railways. His other inventions included narrow spring piston rings (1852), tamper-proof safety valves

(1856), and locomotive screw reverse (1858). In 1870, locomotive haulage replaced steel-rope haulage of trains up the steep gradient from Liverpool, and Ramsbottom designed ventilating extractor fans to remove foul air and smoke from the tunnel.

In 1871 Ramsbottom retired from the LNWR. In 1883 he became consulting engineer and in 1885 a director of the Lancashire and Yorkshire Railway, where he was responsible for the design and construction of their Horwich locomotive works near Bolton and was chairman of the rolling-stock and locomotive workshop committees. He was also a director of Beyer, Peacock & Co., locomotive builders, a firm in which his two sons held important positions.

A modest and kindly man, Ramsbottom took a great interest in technical education and was a governor of Owens College, Manchester, where, in 1873, he endowed the Ramsbottom scholarship for young men in the locomotive department of LNWR. He was a founder member of the Institution of Mechanical Engineers in 1847 and its president in 1870–71. He was a member of the Institution of Civil Engineers from 1866 and in 1868 received the honorary degree of MEng from the University of Dublin. Ramsbottom died on 20 May 1897 at Fernhill, his home in Alderley Edge, Cheshire, and was buried in Macclesfield cemetery.   GEORGE W. CARPENTER, rev.

Sources Institution of Mechanical Engineers: Proceedings (April 1897) · Locomotive, Railway Carriage and Wagon Review (July 1941) · Locomotive, Railway Carriage and Wagon Review (Aug 1941) · H. A. V. Bulleid, The Aspinall era (1967) · J. N. Westwood, Locomotive designers in the age of steam (1977) · W. K. V. Gale, The British iron and steel industry: a technical history (1967), 80 · F. C. Hambleton, John Ramsbottom: the father of the modern locomotive (1937) · The Oxford companion to British railway history (1997) · d. cert.
Likenesses bust, 1872, Institution of Mechanical Engineers, London · photograph, Institution of Mechanical Engineers, London · two photographs, repro. in Locomotive, Railway Carriage and Wagon Review (July–Aug 1941)
Wealth at death £144,372 5s. 5d.: resworn probate, Jan 1898, CGPLA Eng. & Wales

Ramsbottom, John (1885–1974), mycologist, was born on 25 October 1885 in Manchester, the second of the five children and eldest of four sons of Stephen Ramsbottom, letter carrier in the leather trade, and his wife, Hannah Crosdale. After elementary schooling and four years as a pupil teacher in Manchester he entered Emmanuel College, Cambridge, in 1905, obtaining a first class in part one of the natural science tripos (1908) and a second class in part two (botany, 1909). He then returned to Manchester to take up the Robert Platt scholarship in botany and zoology at the university under Professor F. E. Weiss.

Ramsbottom entered the civil service in 1910 as assistant in the cryptogamic section of the British Museum (Natural History), South Kensington. In 1917 he married Beatrice (d. 1957), daughter of Henry Westwood Broome of Cambridge; they later had one daughter. Also in 1917, Ramsbottom went on war service to Salonika as a civilian protozoologist. While there he became a captain attached to the Royal Army Medical Corps, was thrice mentioned in dispatches, and was appointed MBE (1918) and OBE (1919).

In 1919 he returned to the museum, where he worked until his retirement in 1950, having become a deputy keeper in 1928 and keeper of botany in 1930.

Under Ramsbottom's keepership the department of botany began a collaboration with Portuguese botanists, and Ramsbottom was awarded an honorary doctorate by Coimbra University in 1938. Later, a major preoccupation was salvaging the collections and organizing the rebuilding of the department after the disastrous fire at the museum caused by incendiary bombs in September 1940. (Damage was such that the botanical gallery did not reopen until 1962.) It was, however, through his activities outside the museum that Ramsbottom exerted his greatest influence.

Ramsbottom was sociable, and served in diverse societies and organizations. He received many honours: the Royal Horticultural Society elected him an honorary fellow in 1912 and awarded him the Veitch memorial gold medal in 1944 and the Victoria medal of honour in 1950. Also in 1950 he received the Dean Hole medal from the National Rose Society. Other societies which he supported included the Quekett Microscopical Club, the Essex Field Club, the Society for the Bibliography of Natural History (president, 1942–72), the British Society for Mycopathology, and the Société Mycologique de France. He was also associated with the South London Botanical Institute (president, 1938–68) and the Haslemere Educational Museum, and presided over section K of the British Association for the Advancement of Science in 1936, and section X in 1947. He was in demand at international congresses of botany and microbiology and by working parties on international botanical nomenclature. It was, however, to the Linnean Society and the British Mycological Society that Ramsbottom was most loyal, being an active member of both for more than sixty years and holding office in each for a quarter of a century. In 1957 Uppsala University conferred on him an honorary doctorate for his interest in Linnaeus.

Ramsbottom is remembered both as a mycologist and a popularizer of mycology. As a mycologist he surveyed developments in the cytology of fungus reproduction and made summaries of the British Discomycetes, Uredinales, and phycomycetes. He rewrote W. G. Smith's Guide to [James] Sowerby's Models of British Fungi as A Handbook of the Larger British Fungi (1923), which remained popular for the next fifty years. As a popularizer of mycology, his Fungi, an Introduction to Mycology (Benn's Sixpeny Library, 1929) was a model of lucidity.

One of Ramsbottom's long-standing interests was the history of mycology and his presidential address to the Linnean Society, 'The expanding knowledge of mycology since Linnaeus', set a standard for mycological historians. Other interests included orchid mycorrhiza and medical mycology. Finally, Ramsbottom distilled his wide knowledge of fungi into Mushrooms and Toadstools (1953), his most enduring work.

Ramsbottom was a complex, erudite, genial, loquacious, and cultured man, well read, well connected, and with a very retentive memory. He liked teaching and gave advice willingly, though he often exasperated people by procrastination. He had a fund of stories, both proper and improper. Much anecdote (some self-generated) became associated with his name and for long he was a familiar figure at fungus 'forays' in conventional dark city clothes as though he had just stepped from the museum into the woods. He died on 14 December 1974 at King's Ride Nursing Home, 289 Sheen Road, Richmond, Surrey.

G. C. AINSWORTH, rev.

Sources The Times (1 June 1938) · The Times (17 Dec 1974) · The Times (28 Dec 1974) · Transactions of the British Mycological Society, 49 (1966), 1–2 · P. H. Gregory, Transactions of the British Mycological Society, 65 (1975), 1–6 · personal knowledge (1986) · private information (1986) · CGPLA Eng. & Wales (1975)
Archives RBG Kew
Likenesses photograph, repro. in Transactions of the British Mycological Society, 49 · photograph, repro. in Gregory, Transactions of the British Mycological Society
Wealth at death £30,916: probate, 21 March 1975, CGPLA Eng. & Wales

Ramsden, Harry (1888–1963), fish and chip restaurateur, was born on 10 February 1888 at 64 Chatham Street, Bradford, the sixth child of seven born to Henry Ramsden and his wife, Emily Gledhill, formerly Holroyd. His father was then a police constable, but later became a stage-door manager, publican, and fish frier. Shortly after Harry's birth his father was running a fish and chip shop at 22 Manchester Road, Bradford, a main thoroughfare in a working-class district. At this time the fish and chip trade was developing rapidly from its small and often disreputable origins in the 1870s and becoming an important provider of main meals as well as late-night snacks for working-class families in London and the northern industrial towns. It was a labour-intensive, invariably family-run business, using coal-fired ranges and ingredients prepared by hand, and it recruited mainly from skilled workers and their families, with limited capital saved or borrowed from relatives and friends. Children were usually pressed into service, but Ramsden took evasive action, working half-time in a mill in the mornings and as a lather boy in a barber's shop after school. In his late teens he borrowed heavily, and successfully, to set up a small taxi business, and at twenty-one he leased the Craven Heifer in Bolton Road, reputed to be a publican's graveyard, and made it pay by introducing (unlicensed) piano music. Then war service intervened.

It was after the First World War that Harry Ramsden followed his father into the fish and chip trade, combining it with theatrical lodgings. The latter were managed by his first wife, Bridget (b. 1888/9), daughter of James Murphy, a farmer; they had married on 13 June 1911. He subsequently traded up from small beginnings and opened the Cosy Café in Westgate, which his lodgers promoted by introducing it into their stage patter. In 1928 he moved to White Cross, Guiseley, at the edge of the Leeds–Bradford conurbation, in search of cleaner air for his wife and son. The former died within a few months; but the move was to make Ramsden famous. In 1931, in the depths of the depression, he opened a full-scale restaurant at White Cross, with chandeliers, wall lighting, leaded lights in the windows, piano music, and a conspicuous clock. This was not the first attempt to propel fish and chips up market: there had been several since the turn of the century, in Leeds as well as London, Manchester, and indeed Reading. In 1917 a restaurant in Wigan had given tripe the same treatment. But Harry Ramsden's became a famous success. It was solidly based in the established lunch-time take-away trade of the surrounding factories; but the restaurant soon became a destination for evenings out, and also captured the returning weekend motor traffic from the Lake District and Yorkshire dales. Above all, it was stimulated by Ramsden's obsessive attention to detail and eye for improvement, and his flair for populist advertising. He created and propagated his own myth, and was sometimes referred to as 'the uncrowned king of fish and chips'. Through his nephew the television puppeteer Harry *Corbett he made contact with a world of Blackpool showmanship with which he had much in common.

Ramsden took pride in dressing well but without pretension. But his own roots remained resolutely local, and after he handed over management of the restaurant to Eddie Stokes in 1954 he set up two more fish and chip restaurants, before terminal illness set in. It is in many ways ironical that his name should be attached to the Harry Ramsden restaurant chain which spread its wings internationally in the 1990s, because he himself exemplified the local entrepreneur who knew his market well enough to respect his customers, in a trade where such local knowledge was at a premium. His career belongs to a tradition of extrovert populist showmanship which also flourished in the music-hall, and his personal success was a product of that era.

Harry Ramsden died from cancer on 7 January 1963 at the hospital, Middleton, Wharfedale, Yorkshire. He was survived by his second wife, I. M. Ramsden.

JOHN K. WALTON

Sources D. Mosey and H. Ramsden, Harry Ramsden: the uncrowned king of fish-and-chips (1989) · M. Houlihan, A most excellent dish: tales of the Lancashire tripe trade (1988) · S. Priestland, Frying tonight (1972) · H. T. Reeves, The modern fish frier, 2 vols. (1933) · J. K. Walton, Fish and chips and the British working class (1992) · CGPLA Eng. & Wales (1963) · b. cert. · m. cert. · d. cert.
Wealth at death £44,177 4s. 6d.: probate, 1963, CGPLA Eng. & Wales

Ramsden, Sir James (1822–1896), civil engineer and civic leader, was probably born on 25 February 1822, at Bolton, Lancashire, and was baptized there on 31 March 1822, one of several children of William Ramsden (d. 1840) and his wife, Jane Grandage. His father, a millwright and afterwards described as an engineer, subsequently moved to Liverpool; his mother later ran a tavern on behalf of her husband. Little is known of Ramsden's early years until he was apprenticed to the Liverpool firm of Bury, Curtis, and Kennedy. Edward Bury, a distinguished locomotive engineer, enabled him to gain further experience as assistant engineer in the works at Wolverton, Buckinghamshire.

In January 1846 Ramsden was appointed locomotive superintendent of the new Furness Railway, which had ordered engines from Bury's works. He found the first line under construction: this was to carry slate from Kirkby in Furness to the coastal hamlet of Barrow. Ramsden's great energy and versatility soon enabled him to make progress in the railway's hierarchy: by December he had assumed the role of company secretary and he was soon delegated further different managerial responsibilities. He served as managing director from 1866 to 1895. He became a member of the Institution of Civil Engineers in 1856.

Ramsden recognized the area's many opportunities for economic and municipal development, and he was to be pre-eminent among those responsible for the impressive growth of Barrow in Furness. He advocated the building of new housing to support the expanding population, and he drew up a detailed plan for new streets. By the 1860s he had inspired the creation of the town's early schools, churches, library, and other institutions. He supported the exploitation of local iron ore resources, and when the town's new iron and steel companies were amalgamated in 1866 he remained a director of the new firm. Ramsden promoted the building of the town's dock system, commencing with the Devonshire Dock, opened in 1867. As a logical development he encouraged the establishment of Barrow's shipbuilding company in 1870. Prosperity in other ventures was sometimes less evident, but the creation of a jute works served to stabilize the immigrant population by providing work for women.

On 9 June 1853 Ramsden married Hannah Mary (c.1822–1899), daughter of Robert Edwards, gentleman, at Wallasey, Cheshire. Their unmarried only child, Frederic James (1859–1941), served as superintendent of the Furness railway. about 1859 Ramsden moved into Abbots Wood, a new mansion leased from the Furness railway.

By the later 1860s Barrow's population had risen from a few hundred to about 20,000, and Ramsden successfully petitioned for its incorporation as a borough. From 1867 to 1872 he served as its first mayor. In 1870 the corporation launched an appeal to recognize his services; a statue by Matthew Noble was unveiled in 1872, in what became known as Ramsden Square. Ramsden was knighted in the same year and became high sheriff of Lancashire in 1873.

Besides being a benefactor of hospitals, public baths, and numerous other local institutions, Sir James was an active member of the Barrow yacht club. While his original vision of a town that would rival Liverpool proved over-ambitious, he witnessed the diversification of shipping services from the port. Involved in civic affairs until the 1890s, he served five successive terms as mayor of the borough.

Even though Ramsden was an extremely gifted municipal administrator and a competent engineer, he remained a purely local figure. When the borough selected its first MP in 1885, he declined calls to stand for the Liberals. He was a notable example of an energetic but perhaps opportunistic Victorian entrepreneur. His patron, the duke of Devonshire, together with other local luminaries—such as the politician and industrialist H. W. Schneider—undoubtedly viewed him with respect, but

without obvious warmth. The local populace plainly regarded him with deference. Much of the documentary evidence for his life comes from newspaper reports or official records; the virtual disappearance of his private papers inevitably impedes assessment of his personality. In later life Ramsden suffered from diabetes, and following long infirmity he died of a diabetic coma at Abbots Wood, Barrow in Furness, on 19 October 1896. He was buried in Barrow cemetery four days later; his mausoleum bears the family arms but has no external inscription.

AIDAN C. J. JONES

Sources PICE, 129 (1896–7), 385–9 · J. Kellett, *James Ramsden: Barrow's man of vision* (1990) · J. D. Marshall, *Furness and the industrial revolution* (1958) · 'Biographical sketches of local worthies: Sir James Ramsden', *North Lonsdale Magazine and Furness Miscellany*, 2/5 (Feb 1897), 95–101 · *The Engineer* (23 Oct 1896) · *Westmorland Gazette* (23 Oct 1896) · *Biograph and Review*, 3 (1880), 140–45 · will of William Ramsden of Liverpool, engineer, Consistory Court of Chester; probate issued, 29 April 1841 · will of Sir James Ramsden of Abbots Wood, Barrow in Furness, Lancashire, knight; probate issued London, 22 Dec 1896 · candidate circular, 1856, Inst. CE · directors' minutes, 1844–95, Furness Railway Company · Barrow Corporation Bill, minutes of evidence to the House of Commons, 1 May 1873 · census returns for Vulcan Street, Liverpool, 1841 · census returns for Abbots Wood, Barrow in Furness, 1861, 1871, 1881, 1891 · *Gore's Directory of Liverpool* (1829–41) · parish register (baptisms), St Peter's Bolton-le-Moors, Lancashire, 31 March 1822 · parish register (burials), Barrow in Furness, Lancashire, 23 Oct 1896 · m. cert. · d. cert. · parish register (burials), Barrow in Furness, Lancashire, 1899 · M. Levey, 'Abbots Wood, Barrow-in-Furness: furniture by Gillow for Sir James Ramsden', *Apollo*, 137 (1993), 384–8 · P. Lucas, 'Publicity and power: James Ramsden's experiment with daily journalism', *Transactions of the Cumberland and Westmorland Antiquarian and Archaeological Society*, new ser., 75 (1975), 352–75 · *Slater's directory of Lancashire* (1855)

Archives Cumbria AS, Barrow, Furness collection, minor mementoes

Likenesses M. Noble, statue, 1872, Ramsden Square, Barrow in Furness · J. P. Knight, portrait, 1875, Town Hall, Barrow in Furness · engraving (after photograph by Taphouse), repro. in J. Richardson, *Furness past and present*, 2 (1880), 194–5 · photographs, repro. in Marshall, *Furness and the industrial revolution*, 224–5 · photographs, repro. in 'Biographical sketches of local worthies', 95 · portraits, Cumbria AS, Barrow, Furness collection

Wealth at death £69,402 7s. 6d.: probate, 22 Dec 1896, CGPLA Eng. & Wales

Ramsden, Jesse (1735–1800), maker of scientific instruments, was born at Salterhebble, near Halifax, Yorkshire, the son of Thomas Ramsden, innkeeper, probably on 6 October 1735, though his baptism on 3 November is the earliest surviving record. Between the ages of nine and twelve he attended the free school in Halifax. He was then sent to live with his uncle, a Mr Craven, in the North Riding, where for four years he studied mathematics with the Revd Mr Hall, after which he was apprenticed to a Halifax clothworker. In 1755, having completed his apprenticeship, he went to London and found employment as a clerk in a cloth warehouse. By this time, however, his interests had clearly been drawn to scientific instrument making, for in 1756, at the mature age of twenty-one, he bound himself apprentice to Mark Burton, mathematical instrument maker, of Denmark Street, Strand, for a fee of £12.

Jesse Ramsden (1735–1800), by Robert Home, in or before 1791

Ramsden soon acquired such a reputation as a mathematical scale engraver that other instrument makers sought his services, and in 1763 he began trading under his own name, in the Strand. To improve his knowledge of optical instruments he spent his evenings and leisure hours in the nearby house of the *Dollond family, one of the most famous and prosperous families in the profession. On 16 August 1766 he married Sarah (1743–1796), only daughter of John *Dollond, FRS [see under Dollond family (per. 1750–1871)] at St Martin-in-the-Fields. Dollond had developed, and in 1758 patented, the achromatic lens, which allowed an image free of the coloured rings which hampered vision. Ramsden acquired a share in this lucrative patent as part of his bride's dowry. He took a shop in Haymarket, near Little Suffolk Street, trading under the sign of the Golden Spectacles. Two sons and two daughters were born to the Ramsdens between 1767 and 1771, but only John (1768–1841) survived infancy.

Heavenly measurements The foundation of Ramsden's reputation lay in the advances that he made in the design of astronomical instruments used for measuring exact angles in the heavens. By 1760 such instruments stood at the forefront of research in the physical sciences as astronomers across Europe, and especially in England, sought to obtain data that would enable them to refine their understanding of the moon's orbit, the solar, and (they hoped) the stellar, parallaxes, and to map the stars to an error of less than a single arc second. The application of astronomical research to navigation was of pressing importance to Britain as a maritime power. To find a ship's

longitude at sea with the aid of tables of the moon's motion, newly compiled by Tobias Mayer and Nevil Maskelyne, seamen needed sextants which were small and light enough to be handy, yet accurately divided, and affordable. This demand led Ramsden to develop his first dividing engine, with its 30 inch wheel, in 1767. The dividing engine was a machine devised for the fast precision graduation of mathematical instruments with circular scales, such as octants, sextants, and theodolites; the mechanical concepts involved were similar to those embodied in an earlier and smaller engine constructed by Henry Hindley, a prominent clockmaker of York, which, according to tradition within the mathematical instrument making world, had been described to Ramsden by John Stancliffe. Ramsden's first engine did not measure up to his expectations, leading him to build a second, superior, machine which became operational about 1775. The old engine was used by Sarah and the apprentices for less accurate work before it was sold to the Frenchman Bochart de Saron and illegally exported (England being then at war with France), hidden in a piece of furniture. At the Revolution it was confiscated from de Saron, and it is now preserved in the Conservatoire des Arts et Métiers in Paris. The second machine consisted of a horizontal bell-metal wheel 45 inches in diameter, its rim incised with 2160 precision teeth. The teeth were engaged by an accurate lead-screw, which, turned by means of a treadle and cord, rotated the wheel through an exact, pre-selected angle. A sextant body was centred upon the wheel, and by alternately depressing the treadle and moving a radially sliding cutter, a semi-skilled operative could divide the 120° of a sextant scale in 30 minutes, to a far higher degree of accuracy than a master scale divider could have done by hand in as many hours. The engine could graduate sextants as small as 8 inches in radius, thus pioneering the development of precision miniaturization.

In 1777 the commissioners of longitude awarded Ramsden £300 for this invention, and bought rights in the engine for a further £315, on condition that he wrote a full description of its construction, and that they could nominate other craftsmen to be taught to make and use other engines of the same kind. Ramsden also agreed to divide sextants brought to him, at 6s. each. His *Description of an Engine for Dividing Mathematical Instruments* was published in 1777. The book was translated into French by Jérôme de Lalande and published in Paris in 1790. Having developed the circular dividing engine, Ramsden then applied the precision lead-screw to divide fractional parts in his straight line dividing engine, with which he could calibrate linear mathematical scales with an accuracy of one four-thousandth part of an inch. His description of this engine was published in 1779.

Domestic difficulties It seems that the Ramsdens did not enjoy a happy marriage, for in or soon after 1773, when Ramsden moved to larger premises at 199 Piccadilly, alongside St James's Church, Sarah and her son went to live in the Haymarket, probably at no. 55, a house owned by the Dollonds. She did not entirely sever her contacts with former associates. Ramsden's contacts with Matthew Boulton in Birmingham may have begun prior to their separation, for records from 1777 disclose exchange of workmen and each man supplying goods to the other; in 1786–7 Sarah Ramsden was corresponding from the Haymarket with Boulton on behalf of an official of the king of Naples who was negotiating for a steam engine from Boulton and Watt. She was living at Hercules Buildings, off Westminster Road, Lambeth, at her death on 29 August 1796, and was buried at St Mary's, Lambeth, on 1 September.

Expansion and further inventions   Ramsden further expanded his premises in 1780, taking 196 Piccadilly and the large, high wooden sheds behind these properties, previously occupied by a coach builder and reached from Piccadilly through a wide passageway under the intervening houses. Here he had both space and headroom to construct the large astronomical apparatus for which he became renowned. The sale of smaller instruments (some of which were imported from outside London) and sundries, together with repairs and resale of instruments, generated sufficient income to pay his workforce of sixty men.

The dividing engine, in both its circular and linear forms, became one of the key inventions of the industrial revolution, foreshadowing as it did the replacement of hand craftsmen by labourers operating complex precision apparatus. Before Ramsden, astronomical instrument makers had approached precision division through geometry; his instincts were essentially those of an engineer who sought exactitude not through draughtsmanship but by mechanical generation. Without Ramsden's dividing engine, sextants could not have been made in sufficient numbers, or cheaply enough, to transform navigational practice. By 1789 he had graduated more than a thousand sextants, not to mention numerous surveying instruments.

In the 1770s Ramsden began to experiment with the graduation of full circles for astronomical observatories, as an alternative to the large mural quadrants which were then in use throughout Europe. He was aware, probably from the work of the duc de Chaulnes in France in the 1760s, that a circle was thermally and mechanically more stable than a quadrant, and hence less prone to error when carrying a set of precision graduations. The circles forming part of Ramsden's own observatory apparatus were not divided on the engine, which was incapable of graduating such large arcs to the accuracy demanded by astronomers for fundamental research and star mapping; rather, he used an elaborate procedure of bisection and trisection, where each fraction was laid off and subjected to multiple checks and corrections by means of micrometer microscopes. The errors which inevitably remained on the finished circle were known and could be compensated for. In this way, Ramsden's efforts transformed the accuracy of precision astronomy from between one and two seconds of arc to half a second, a breakthrough of fundamental importance.

A perfectionist   Ramsden's notorious slowness in completing major observatory commissions largely derived from his pioneering work on the circle. Quite simply, it was a new technology and Ramsden was a perfectionist, reluctant to finish an instrument if any suspected faults in its design were likely to rebound to his discredit once it was in the client's hands. The division of a full circle by hand took about 150 days and could only be performed in equable temperatures, and that did not take into account the resolution of any engineering problems encountered in mounting the circle and telescope for use. Ramsden's clients became exasperated with the delays, often amounting to years, between placing an order and taking delivery of an instrument, their irritation made worse by the knowledge that he was by far the best craftsman of his day. The first originally divided (that is, not engine-divided) instrument that he delivered, in 1787, was a 36 inch theodolite for General William Roy's project to remeasure the longitude between the Greenwich and Paris observatories, and out of which the Ordnance Survey developed. Two years later he had to be harassed into completing the first astronomical apparatus bearing a full circle ever constructed, of 5 feet in diameter, ordered by Giuseppe Piazzi, and installed at Palermo observatory in Sicily, where it is preserved. A mural circle 6 feet in diameter ordered for Dunsink observatory in Ireland was twenty-eight years in the making, being completed only after Ramsden's death.

Ramsden was the first instrument maker seriously to tackle the structural problems inherent in the design of equatorially mounted telescopes. In 1774 he published an account of his *New Universal Equatorial* and instruments of his design were constructed for George III and other prominent persons. He also built small clockwork-driven equatorials, and he remodelled the large and defective equatorial sectors which Jeremiah Sisson had built for the Royal Observatory, Greenwich, in 1775. Ramsden's truly innovative equatorial instrument was that completed for Sir George Shuckburgh in 1793. Transforming the unsuccessful equatorial sectors with which Bird and Sisson had experimented in the early 1770s, Ramsden produced a far more stable design. Using conical load bearing supports and compensating for the changing weight distribution inherent in a large 'English' equatorial mounting, he brought engineering skills to the resolution of problems of building large instruments with ponderous moving parts.

In addition to the work discussed above, Ramsden made numerous other improvements to scientific instruments. For telescopes he developed the reduced aberration 'Ramsden eyepiece', as well as two new micrometers. He made zenith sectors, barometers, levels, precision balances, and pyrometers for detecting slight changes of heat in metals, and in 1795 received the Royal Society's Copley medal for his 'various inventions and improvements to philosophical instruments'. Specimens of his craftsmanship can be found in the national collections of most countries affected by western science. Yet he was more than a superb craftsman, being acknowledged as an equal member within the international scientific community.

Reputation, character, and death Ramsden was elected fellow of the Royal Society on 12 January 1786, and to membership of the Imperial Academy of St Petersburg in 1794. He enjoyed cordial relations with the leading scientists of the age, including such aristocratic amateurs as the duke of Marlborough, whose apparatus he had made and installed at Blenheim, and which he continued to maintain. He corresponded widely with foreign astronomers and scientists, and they called on him when in London; men from those more feudal parts of Europe were sometimes struck by the easy social acceptance of a craftsman by England's scientific gentry. Ramsden learned to read French with sufficient fluency as to enjoy Molière and Boileau, while his favourite scientific authors were Euler and Bouguer.

Ramsden's personal appearance was, according to the Revd Louis Dutens:

> above the middle size, slender, but extremely well-made, and to a late period of life, possessed of great activity. His countenance was a faithful index of his mind, full of intelligence and sweetness. His forehead was open, and high, with a very projecting and expressive brow. His eyes were dark hazel, sparkling with animation. He had a good musical voice.   (Aikin, 454)

Ramsden lived simply and, said Dutens, spent his evenings in the kitchen with his apprentices, eating bread and butter, discussing ideas, and perfecting designs. Several of his apprentices went on to distinguished careers in their own right, notably Thomas Jones (1775–1852), who was bound for seven years on 14 March 1789. A few foreign apprentices and journeymen are also known; Georg Dreschler of Hamburg spent five years with Ramsden, as did François Antoine Jecker, who on his return to Paris constructed a straight line dividing engine on Ramsden's pattern and was noted for adopting, as Ramsden had done, a strict division of labour in his workshop [see Industrial spies]. Richard Lovell Edgeworth, in his *Memoirs* (1820, 1.191–2) recorded a famous episode when Ramsden drove down to Kew palace with an instrument which George III had ordered. He asked if the king was at home, and insisted on being admitted. The king received him graciously, and, after examining the instrument, said to him: 'I have been told, Mr Ramsden, that you are considered to be the least punctual of any man in England; you have brought home this instrument on the very *day* that was appointed. You have only mistaken the year.'

Ramsden died on 5 November 1800 at Brighton, where he had gone for the benefit of his health; his body was brought back for burial at St James's, Piccadilly, on 13 November. His foreman, Matthew Berge, who had been with him upwards of thirty years, completed the major unfinished instruments and continued to live and trade at 196 Piccadilly until his own death in 1819. Ramsden's estate passed to his son John, by this time a commander in the East India Company's navy. His uncles, Peter and John

Dollond, were called in to make an inventory of Ramsden's assets, including his stock and machinery, which came to under £5000. Of the considerable sums owing to him, only £1300 appeared to be recoverable.

ALLAN CHAPMAN

Sources J. Aikin and others, *General biography, or, Lives, critical and historical of the most eminent persons*, 10 vols. (1799–1815), vol. 8 · W. Pearson, *An introduction to practical astronomy*, 2 (1829) · E. Troughton, 'An account of a method of dividing astronomical and other instruments', *PTRS*, 99 (1809), 105–45 · W. Pearson, 'Graduation', in A. Rees and others, *The cyclopaedia, or, Universal dictionary of arts, sciences, and literature*, 45 vols. (1819–20) · D. Brewster, 'Graduation', *The Edinburgh encyclopaedia*, ed. D. Brewster and others, 3rd edn, 18 vols. (1830), vol. 10 · A. Chapman, *Dividing the circle: the development of critical angular measurement in astronomy, 1500–1850*, 2nd edn (1995) · A. McConnell, 'From craft workshop to big business', *London Journal*, 19 (1994), 36–53 · J. Ramsden, *Description of an engine for dividing mathematical instruments* (1777) · J. Ramsden, *Description of an engine for dividing straight lines on mathematical instruments* (1779) · Birm. CL, Boulton and Watt collection · private information (1995) · parish register (baptisms), Halifax, Yorkshire, 3 Nov 1735

Archives RS | Birm. CA, letters to Matthew Boulton · PRO, crown estates MSS

Likenesses R. Home, oils, in or before 1791, RS [*see illus.*] · engraving, 1791 (after R. Home) · C. Turner, mezzotint, pubd 1801 (after H. Edridge), BM

Wealth at death under £5000: inventory, 1800

Ramsden, Omar (1873–1939), silver designer, was born on 21 August 1873 at 16 Fir Street, Nether Hallam, Walkley, Sheffield, the only son of Benjamin Woolhouse Ramsden (1833–c.1898), engraver and cutlery manufacturer, and his wife, Norah (1850–1929), née Ibbotson, whose family dealt in ivory.

Ramsden was apprenticed to a silver manufacturer in Sheffield by 1887, learning basic skills and workshop practice. From 1894 he won annual scholarships to study design at Sheffield School of Art, where he met Alwyn Charles Ellison Carr (1872–1940). They attended summer schools at the Royal College of Art, and studied in the Victoria and Albert Museum. In 1897 Ramsden won an open competition for a civic mace for the city of Sheffield, but he and Carr spent a year travelling in Europe before moving to London to set up a workshop and begin work on the mace. A joint mark for Ramsden and Carr was registered in 1898. The partnership prospered until 1914, and work of this period shows close study of Renaissance silver, with both arts and crafts and art nouveau influences. Their most important commission, in 1906, was a monstrance for Westminster Cathedral.

In 1914 Carr joined the army, and Ramsden continued independently, building up a team of specialist workers for the increasing volume of commissions, registering his own mark in 1918. The partnership was formally dissolved in 1919. Ramsden kept the Chelsea studio, St Dunstan's, and the workshop in Maxwell Road, Fulham, and over the next two decades maintained a reputation as a fashionable designer of domestic, ceremonial, and church plate catering to the conservative taste of a moneyed inter-war society. His designs drew on Renaissance metalwork, and showed an awareness of the work of George Jensen (1866–1935).

During the early 1920s Ramsden became interested in mazers, turned burr-maple bowls with silver mounts. He made a large number, culminating in the *Three Kings Mazer* of 1937. The following year he published privately an illustrated booklet tracing the history of mazers. In addition to larger pieces of silver Ramsden produced quantities of personal objects, including jewellery, in silver with cabochons and enamel in medieval or art nouveau styles. In 1928 he designed an elaborate crown for a Madonna in Westminster Cathedral, reusing stones from jewellery given as votive offerings. He also made an 'everyday' crown, and in 1935 a morse or clasp for a bishop's cope. He was commissioned in 1929 by the Honourable Company of Master Mariners for a spectacular ceremonial collar, one of several such orders from City livery companies.

At his Maxwell Road workshop Ramsden employed up to twenty men, including apprentices. Some spent nearly forty years in the spartan shop under the taciturn Ramsden's strict discipline. Surviving workbooks and working drawings record orders carried out between 1921 and 1939, costed in code. Despite the claim 'Omar Ramsden me fecit' on every piece, Ramsden worked only rarely at the bench and his role was principally to interpret customers' requirements for execution by the workshop. His championship of hand craftsmanship is challenged in that production pieces were usually spun by external contractors for finishing in the workshop.

From the beginning St Dunstan's Studio had acted as a showroom where customers were received and stock displayed, and studio sales became a social event. Ramsden's genial charm towards his customers and skill as a salesman ensured the momentum of his success, helped by his flair for publicity and the business skills of his wife, Annie Emily Downes-Butcher, *née* Berrif (1871–1950), whom he married in 1927. He died at St Dunstan's on 9 August 1939 and was buried in Eccleshall, near Sheffield. There were no children.

Ramsden was regarded as an authority on his craft, and frequently participated in professional debates. In 1928 he contributed articles on modern silver design to the *Goldsmiths' Journal*. Acclaimed in his day by his patrons and by the press as almost a latterday Cellini, and awarded many professional honours, Ramsden was later regarded as no more than a brilliant entrepreneur. Today he is recognized as influential in the revival of public taste in silver design, evocatively combining traditional and modern styles. Collections of Ramsden's work are held at Goldsmiths' Hall, the Victoria and Albert Museum, St Bartholomew-the-Great, Smithfield, and Westminster Cathedral, London; Birmingham City Museum, Graves Art Gallery, Sheffield, and the Campbell Collection, Toronto. Other examples are in public and private collections including churches and City livery companies.

ANNE SHANNON and MURIEL WILSON

Sources P. Cannon-Brookes, *Omar Ramsden, 1873–1939* (1973) [exhibition catalogue, Birmingham City Museum and Art Gallery] · E. Turner and L. Springer Roberts, *English silver: masterpieces by Omar Ramsden from the Campbell collection* (1992) [exhibition catalogue, Art Institute of Chicago, 30 May – 16 Aug 1992 and elsewhere] · private information (1997, 2004) [L. Durbin; G. Wild, Birmingham City Museum and Art Gallery; R. Baker] · Omar Ramsden Archive, Goldsmiths' Hall, Foster Lane, London · J. Fleming and H. Honour, *Penguin dictionary of decorative art* (1989) · C. G. L. Du Cann, 'Omar Ramsden, salesman extraordinary', *Art and Antiques*, 19, no. 12 (19 July 1975), 22–4 · *CGPLA Eng. & Wales* (1939)
Archives Goldsmiths' Hall, Foster Lane, London, archive of workbooks, drawings, photographs, albums, etc.
Likenesses van Duindsson, pencil drawing, priv. coll. · photograph, repro. in Cannon-Brookes, *Omar Ramsden*
Wealth at death £13,208 12s. 10d.: probate, 21 Nov 1939, *CGPLA Eng. & Wales*

Ramsey, Agnes (*d.* in or after **1399**). *See under* Women traders and artisans in London (*act. c.*1200–*c.*1500).

Ramsey, Sir Alfred Ernest [Alf] (**1920–1999**), footballer and football manager, was born at Five Elms Farm, Dagenham, on 22 January 1920, the fourth son of Herbert Henry Ramsey, a hay and straw dealer, and his wife, Florence Bixby. He attended Becontree Heath elementary school, and though small in size proved a tenacious centre-half, playing representative football for Essex schools. After leaving school in 1934 he failed to get a job at the Ford car factory and went instead to the local Co-operative Society to work in the grocery department, first as a delivery boy and later behind the counter. During the winter he played football for Five Elms United, a club formed by a local shopkeeper to cater for sixteen-year-olds who had been prominent in local football but who could find nowhere to play. Here he was spotted by a scout from Portsmouth and it was suggested that Ramsey should sign amateur forms for the club, but Portsmouth never replied to his letters.

In June 1940 Ramsey joined the army, where he served in the Duke of Cornwall's light infantry, before eventually becoming a quartermaster sergeant in an anti-aircraft unit in Britain. He was also soon playing for the battalion football team both with and against professionals. Ramsey played well enough against Southampton reserves to get himself noticed and to play a few games for the club. There is some suggestion that he told the club that he was younger than he was (twenty-two rather than twenty-four), doubtless anxious that they might have thought twenty-four too old to begin a professional career. In August 1944 Ramsey signed as a professional for Southampton at £2 a match. After demobilization in June 1946 he was retained for the 1946–7 season. Ramsey was still thinking he might return to his old job at the Co-op, especially when Southampton offered only £6 a week in the season, but when that was increased to £7 in winter, £6 in summer, and £8 if he made the first team, he signed.

By this time Ramsey had played in several positions but the Southampton manager, Bill Dodgin, converted him to full-back. He played his first league game in the second division against Plymouth Argyle in October 1946, three months short of his twenty-seventh birthday. He was determined to make a success of it. Inclined to be heavy and slow on the turn, he trained hard and practised harder, returning in the afternoons to improve his passing and his weaker left foot. He also worked to improve both

Sir Alfred Ernest Ramsey (1920–1999), by unknown photographer, 1966

his movement and positional play. A non-smoker and only an occasional drinker, Ramsey was a quiet man who was certainly not 'one of the boys' and was in bed most nights by ten o'clock. The hard work paid off: Ramsey became a stylish full-back when most were rough types who tackled anything that moved and asked questions afterwards. He won his first cap for England against Switzerland in 1948, but then lost form and his place for both club and country to Bill Ellerington and in 1949 was transferred to Tottenham Hotspur.

This move showed that Ramsey possessed either an extraordinary ability to be in the right place at the right time or prodigious good fortune. Arthur Rowe had assembled a Tottenham side whose push-and-run style was about to run away with the second division. Ramsey's thoughtful and constructive defence, his intelligent passing, and his willingness to begin attacks from deep in his own half, combined with an aura of calm authority that he appeared to exude, meant that he fitted into the team so perfectly that he almost became Rowe's representative on the pitch. Ramsey became known to the other players as the General. Not only was the second division won in 1949–50, but it was followed in the very next season by the first division title. Rowe admired Ramsey's calm and described him later as a perfectionist with a thirst for footballing knowledge. On 10 December 1951 Ramsey married Victoria Phyllis Answorth (Rita) Norris, *née* Welch (b. 1920/21), hairdresser, daughter of William Answorth Welch, lift attendant. They adopted a daughter, Tania.

The move to Tottenham revived Ramsey's England career and he made twenty-nine consecutive appearances for his country between November 1949 and October 1953. He was a member of the England team which lost to the USA in the world cup of 1950 in Belo Horizonte and also of the one demolished 6–3 by Hungary at Wembley in November 1953, his last appearance for the national team. Ramsey remained with Tottenham, becoming team captain before injury led to his retirement in 1955.

Ramsey made a quick return to football by being appointed manager of the third division south club Ipswich Town just before the start of the 1955–6 season. Ipswich were an unsung club with no long tradition in the game, having turned professional only in the late 1930s. The club was not rich, but by making the best of a not very promising job Ramsey blended a few local youngsters, some more experienced players cast aside by other clubs, and a few others who were thought to be past their best, into a side whose tactics puzzled most opponents. In his second season Ipswich were champions of division three south, as their superior goal average pushed Torquay United into the runners-up position. Three mid-table seasons in the second division followed. Then in 1960–61 the championship was won and 100 goals scored. Critics believed that first division teams would quickly identify the weakest links of these unfashionable upstarts. But they did not and Ramsey's side emulated the Tottenham team for whom he had played by winning the first division in their first season with the élite. Ramsey became one of only nine men to win the championship as both player and manager. By playing Jimmy Leadbetter, a 33-year-old who could easily pass for fifty, wide and deep on the left, and two big forwards, Ray Crawford and Ted Phillips, Ramsey found tactics to confound the best of English football. His talent for getting the maximum out of players with limited ability, together with tactical shrewdness, made Ramsey's reputation as a manager.

After England's defeat in 1962 in the world cup in Chile, the Football Association (FA) began to look for a manager to replace Walter Winterbottom. This was far from being a vacancy which attracted many applicants. For one thing the international selection committee of the FA, made up of men with little experience of professional football, was still influential in selecting the team, in spite of Winterbottom's reforms. Moreover, it was clear how far behind world playing standards England was. In addition, the skills needed to manage a club side were not the same as those required for the national team. In the league, loss of an individual match could be made up over a forty-two-game season. In international competitions defeat often meant immediate elimination. The national manager also missed out on the day-to-day contact with players which club managers so prized. Jimmy Adamson was the FA's favourite for the post but Burnley were reluctant to release him. Ramsey, then, was not the first choice, but neither was he the last resort. He was qualified enough and in September 1962, when he was interviewed by the *Daily Mail*, he intriguingly laid out what should be done by whoever was appointed. First, the new man must be allowed to pick his team alone and to decide how the players would play.

> I think an England manager must make up his mind what players he has and then find a rigid method for them to play to. If any player, no matter how clever an individual is not prepared to accept the discipline of the team's method then I can see no advantage in selecting him.

As for the idea that great players did not need a plan, Ramsey said 'Well, I played with many of these [great] players and I would say England's team was good then, but it would have been many times better if we had also had a rigid plan.' He also pointed out that this England team had failed to score against Spain and the USA in the 1950 world cup. However, Ramsey emphasized the value of home advantage in the world cup of 1966 and suggested that if the Football League and FA would co-operate and allow proper time for preparation, 'I think we could win'. Ramsey was offered the job in October 1962 but asked for time to think about it. He accepted on the condition that only he was responsible for team selection and tactics. This marked the end of selection by amateur committee and was an important moment in the development of the post of England team manager. Ramsey eventually accepted the job on 25 October 1962 and began work full-time on 1 May 1963.

Ramsey's career as England manager got off to an inauspicious start, when the team lost 5–2 to France. However, by 1966 he believed that England were in a position to win the world cup. The opening group matches were not encouraging: performances were mediocre, star goal-scorer Jimmy Greaves was injured, and Ramsey was under pressure from the English football authorities to drop Nobby Stiles from the team because of his rough play. In the event performances improved, and the team reached the final after victories over Argentina and Portugal; Geoff Hurst proved to be a more than successful replacement for Greaves, and Ramsey's loyalty to Stiles further strengthened team spirit. Ramsey's strength of mind enabled him to ignore criticism of his 'wingless wonders' and to reject calls for Greaves to be reinstated to the team after he had recovered from his injury. He also had to overcome the furore surrounding his comments after the tempestuous quarter-final against Argentina, when he likened the South Americans' behaviour to that of 'animals'.

Ramsey's decisions were vindicated in glorious fashion. England's 4–2 victory, including a hat-trick from Hurst, over a talented West German team in the final at Wembley on 30 July 1966 proved to be a pinnacle which, with the possible exception of the 1970 side, no other English team has since seemed remotely capable of reaching. The nation basked in glory. Only the French, Scots, and South Americans were disappointed. Ramsey had remained extraordinarily calm throughout the final. After West Germany had scored a last-minute equalizer to take the match into extra time Ramsey told his team, 'You've won it once. Now you must win it again.' They did, and at the final whistle Ramsey alone stayed seated as the rest of the players and staff leapt for joy. Nobby Stiles was probably correct when he said: 'You did it Alf! We'd have been nothing without you' (*The Guardian*, 1 May 1999). Ramsey was knighted in 1967.

If Ramsey's on-field management was excellent, he was not so assured off it. The England football team had a higher profile than any club side, and in the 1960s media appetites were expanding. No manager would have found it easy to cope with the demands of press, radio, and television, and Ramsey found it particularly difficult. He had come from a working-class family, had left school at fourteen and, although he was determined to make himself a better life through football, he was aware of his lack of formal educational qualifications. The course of self-improvement he began as a player continued as a manager. Before taking the manager's job at Ipswich, Ramsey took elocution lessons in an attempt to remove the sharper edges of his Essex accent. The lessons changed the way he spoke but he remained self-conscious of vowels and aitches. His speaking voice became curiously strangulated. Ramsey mistrusted his own spontaneity and was particularly suspicious of journalists, and indeed all outsiders. He was sensitive to criticism and in public he often appeared aloof and graceless, even downright rude. What Ramsey did possess was something no successful football manager can do without: the loyalty of his players.

Ramsey's sometimes curt way with the English football authorities and media was not helpful when results began to go against him. Third place in the European championships of 1968 was seen as an underachievement and the 3–2 defeat by West Germany in the quarter-final of the 1970 world cup in Mexico after being two goals up was a major disappointment when a Brazil–England final had been widely predicted. Ramsey's use of substitutes that day came in for particular criticism. England lost again to West Germany in the quarter-final of the 1972 European championship. Worse was to follow during qualification for the 1974 world cup. A mistake by Bobby Moore and Alan Ball's sending-off led to defeat in Poland, and in the return at Wembley, England could only draw after dominating the match. The campaign to remove him was as tumultuous as the cheers of 1966 and on 1 May 1974 he was sacked.

Football managers usually do not enjoy much public affection; Matt Busby, Bill Shankly, and Jock Stein are probably exceptions. Few had a good word to say about Sir Alf. His apparent hauteur, his disregard for the opinions of others, and his failure ever to be diplomatic had upset many during his eleven years in charge of the England team. It is hard to believe that he was not hurt by his dismissal but he refused to give his side of the story and was not tempted to produce an autobiography. But what a record England had under him: played 113, won 69, drawn 27, lost 17; goals for 224, against 99. Ramsey's initial salary had been £4500, about the same as he had been getting at Ipswich, but rose later to £7000 and then £9500. His world cup-winning bonus was only £5000. He left the England job with a pay-off of £8000 and a pension of £1200 a year.

After eighteen months out of football Ramsey joined the board of Birmingham City, and did well as caretaker manager between September 1977 and March 1978. Poor health precipitated early retirement. Thereafter he lived quietly in Ipswich. He died at 248 Sidegate Lane, Ipswich, on 28 April 1999. He was survived by his wife. A statue of Ramsey was later erected in Ipswich. According to one obituarist, Ramsey was 'a flawed hero if ever there was one. But a hero nevertheless' (*The Independent*, 1 May 1999).

The events at Wembley on that Saturday afternoon in the summer of 1966 are now deeply embedded in the national consciousness, and as long as those events continue to be recalled the memory of Sir Alf Ramsey, the man to whom English football owes its finest achievement, will live on.   TONY MASON

Sources D. Bowler, *Winning isn't everything: a biography of Sir Alf Ramsey* (1998) · H. McIlvanney, *World cup '66* (1966) · D. Miller, *The boys of '66* (1996) · A. Hopcraft, *The football man* (1968) · D. Thomson, *4–2* (1996) · *The Guardian* (1 May 1999) · *The Independent* (1 May 1999) · *The Times* (1 May 1999) · *Daily Telegraph* (1 May 1999) · b. cert. · m. cert. · d. cert.
Archives SOUND BL NSA, documentary recordings
Likenesses photograph, 1966, Hult. Arch. [*see illus.*] · Wesley, photograph, 1971, Hult. Arch.

Ramsey, Benedict of. *See* Benedict of Ramsey (*d.* in or after 1211).

Ramsey, Byrhtferth of. *See* Byrhtferth of Ramsey (*fl. c.*986–*c.*1016).

Ramsey, (Mary) Dorothea Whiting (1904–1989), social worker, was born on 10 January 1904 in Kensington, London, the only child of Robert William Ramsey, solicitor, and his wife, Anna Whiting Brown, of Clarendon Road, in the Notting Hill area of London. Of well-to-do parents, she was educated at St Paul's Girls' School, London, and at Newnham College, Cambridge, where she obtained third classes in both parts of the classical tripos (1926 and 1928). She then taught Greek and Latin in London until the outbreak of the Second World War in 1939. It was as a voluntary worker with the Bristol Council of Social Service in the war emergency bureau that she became alerted to the social problems of elderly people, and, henceforward, her career concentrated on that area.

In 1941 Dorothea Ramsey helped to form the Bristol Old People's Welfare Committee and became its secretary. Just as wartime threw into vivid perspective the needs of deprived children when they were evacuated, so was the distress of many old people made more apparent. Dorothea Ramsey was one of the first to stress the value of residential care for older people, especially compared with the isolation of living, often in a feeble condition, at home or floundering in the large dormitories of the workhouse or the chronic sick wards of the former poor-law and other hospitals. She was to the fore in establishing, in 1942, the West Town House residential care home in Bristol, a small, model facility, only the second of its kind in the country.

Returning to London, in 1943 Dorothea Ramsey became a member of the advisory case subcommittee of social service, a body dealing with old people in distress and the mobilization of people likely to care for them. This had been set up not least as a consequence of the bombing, involving both injury and homelessness. This small-scale agency received 2000 requests for help each year, and was much pressed to find adequate residential and allied amenities for its needy elderly clients. As early as 1940 the National Council of Social Service, aware of the manifest difficulties of many older people, had convened a group of representatives of the major voluntary and statutory providers. Out of this initiative grew the National Old People's Welfare Committee, its remit the campaigning for and provision of decent social services for impoverished and sick old people. Soon it was to abandon its lengthy title, redolent of 1940s officialdom, in favour of the more user-friendly Age Concern.

Dorothea Ramsey became secretary of this new charity in 1945, and she fought hard and vigorously to improve conditions for its elderly clientele. During her seven-year secretaryship—she resigned in 1952—the number of groups grew rapidly from eight regional or county and eighty local committees to sixty-two regional or county and 831 local committees. Given her experience, it is not surprising that she concentrated on residential care, persuading both local old people's welfare groups and local authorities to build and sustain homes. She urged the value of professional training, successfully pressed for chiropody services, and sought for older people a reasonable degree of dignity and independence. Because of the work of men and women like Dorothea Ramsey during the post-war decades, a less negative attitude towards ageing began to develop. She was one of the first to take a more personal and less paternalist stand on social provision, insisting—at a time when welfare was granted grudgingly in rather chilling vein—that the criterion should be 'what you would like in similar circumstances'. Her pioneering work led to recognition overseas, particularly in the USA, which she toured with a Smith—Mundt scholarship in 1952.

On retirement to the Lake District, Dorothea Ramsey devoted herself to what had been a lifelong affection for music—she had studied the flute under Gustav Holst as a girl—and she applied her considerable administrative skills to the furtherance of orchestral and choral activity in Cumberland. She also played in and became chairman of the Cumberland Symphony Orchestra. Severe eye problems, arthritis, and diabetes constrained her life over thirty years, but she bore these handicaps with admirable fortitude. She was dark, of medium height, with intelligent, bright looks, and penetrating eyes. A woman of committed conscience, if somewhat shy, she never married. In retirement she lived with a friend, Frances M. Birkett. She had lived latterly at High Rigg Grange, Borrowdale, near Keswick, Cumberland, and died in Keswick on 27 September 1989.   ERIC MIDWINTER, *rev.*

Sources N. Roberts, *Our future selves* (1970) · *The Independent* (5 Oct 1989) · CGPLA Eng. & Wales (1990)
Wealth at death £454,594: probate, 17 Jan 1990, CGPLA Eng. & Wales

Ramsey, Frank Plumpton (1903–1930), mathematician and philosopher, was born on 22 February 1903 at 71 Chesterton Road, Chesterton, Cambridge, the eldest of the two sons and two daughters of Arthur Stanley Ramsey (1867–1954), fellow and later president of Magdalene College, Cambridge, and his wife, Agnes Mary Wilson (1875–1927). He was baptized at Horbling church, Horbling, at Easter 1903, but rejected religion in his teens.

As a child Ramsey lived with his parents in Howfield, Buckingham Road, Cambridge. He was educated at Winchester College (1915–20), and at Trinity College, Cambridge (1920–23), where he read mathematics, winning an entrance scholarship, and becoming a senior scholar in 1921 and a wrangler in 1923. In 1924 he became a fellow of King's College, Cambridge (only the second non-Kingsman to do so), and in 1926 a university lecturer in mathematics, a post he held until his death. On 21 August 1925 he married Lettice Cautley Baker (1898–1985), a psychologist, at the St Pancras register office in London. They lived in Cambridge, first in a flat in Hoop Chambers, Bridge Street, and then, from about April 1927, at 4 Mortimer Road. They had two daughters.

Ramsey was tall (6 feet 3 inches), bulky, and shortsighted. He appeared clumsy but was not—he was, for example, a good tennis player. He produced his extraordinary output of major contributions to mathematics, logic, philosophy, and economics by working for about four hours a day, mostly in the mornings, since he found it too exacting to work longer. His afternoons and evenings were often spent walking and listening to records. He listened a lot to classical music, both live and recorded, went to the opera in London, and was a keen hill-walker. He was a quiet, modest man, easy-going and uninhibited. His tolerance and good humour enabled him to disagree strongly without giving or taking offence, for example with his brother Michael *Ramsey whose ordination (he went on to become archbishop of Canterbury) Ramsey, as a militant atheist, naturally regretted.

Ramsey's main interest in mathematics was in its foundations. His 'The foundations of mathematics', read to the London Mathematical Society on 12 November 1925, was the culmination of the reduction of mathematics to logic undertaken in Russell's and Whitehead's *Principia mathematica* (1913). On mathematics itself he published only eight pages, 'On a problem of formal logic' (read to the London Mathematical Society on 13 December 1928), but this has since become the basis of a branch of mathematics known as Ramsey theory. He also worked on economics, encouraged by his friend and contemporary John Maynard Keynes, who edited the *Economic Journal*. His economics papers 'A contribution to the theory of taxation' (1927) and 'A mathematical theory of saving' (1928), which were published there, founded two branches of the subject—optimal taxation and optimal accumulation—which took off in the 1960s and 1970s.

Keynes also helped to persuade King's College to make Ramsey a fellow, despite his attacks on the concept of probability (as an a priori measure of the extent to which evidence supports a hypothesis) developed in Keynes's *A*

Treatise on Probability (1921). After criticizing this concept so effectively that Keynes himself abandoned it, Ramsey worked out his own ideas on the subject in 'Truth and probability', written at the end of 1926. This classic paper, only published after his death, laid the foundations of modern subjective interpretations of probability, and related theories of games and decision making, foundations which were not rediscovered and built on until the 1940s.

Ramsey's real vocation, however, was philosophy, influenced especially by Russell and the early Wittgenstein of the *Tractatus logico-philosophicus* (1922), which he was the first to translate into English from the German. He visited Wittgenstein in Austria in 1923 and in 1924 and established a lasting friendship with him. After Wittgenstein's return to Cambridge in January 1929 the two used to meet several times a week for long philosophical discussions. As Wittgenstein later acknowledged in his preface to *Philosophical Investigations*, Ramsey's criticisms of the *Tractatus* were a primary influence in bringing him to reject its key doctrines, such as its claim to have shown a relation (of language to the world) which cannot be stated: for, as Ramsey remarked, 'What we can't say we can't say, and we can't whistle it either' (Ramsey, 146)—Wittgenstein was a famous whistler.

Ramsey's own work in philosophy, besides the pieces mentioned above, included published papers—'Universals' (1925) and 'Facts and propositions' (1927)—and notes on 'Universals of law and of fact', written in 1928, as well as 'Theories' and 'Knowledge', written in 1929. Like his work on economics and probability, all these notes and papers were way ahead of their time. 'Universals', for example, challenges the a priori status, still unquestioned by most philosophers, of the distinction between universal properties (such as being wise) and the particular entities (such as Socrates) which have them.

'Universals of law and of fact' has had more, if still belated, success. In it Ramsey advocated a new theory of what distinguishes laws of nature such as 'all men are mortal' from universal statements that are only accidentally true. This theory, which Ramsey himself rejected a year later in 'General propositions and causality', is now widely accepted as the best account of natural laws in the empiricist tradition of David Hume. 'Theories', similarly, has revolutionized our understanding of how scientific theories—identified with what are now called their 'Ramsey sentences'—are related to the laws and observations they explain.

'Facts and propositions' is no less famous for its new and still contested reduction of the analysis of truth to that of belief, via the fact that (in Ramsey's example) 'It is true that Caesar was murdered' means no more than that Caesar was murdered. It also anticipates much later and equally contentious theories of the mind by trying to define our beliefs by how they make us act—just as his fragmentary note 'Knowledge' does by equating knowledge with true beliefs that have been reliably formed, as opposed to ones their holders could justify.

Several of Ramsey's papers were prepared for publication only after his death, in *The Foundations of Mathematics* (1930), edited by his friend R. B. Braithwaite. All the philosophical works mentioned here are contained in his *Philosophical Papers* (1990), which also includes his work on the foundations of mathematics and a bibliography of his writings.

The present influence of Ramsey's work in mathematics, logic, economics, and philosophy makes it hard to understand why it took so long to be taken up. There seem to have been several reasons for this. One is that he was no controversialist, and never pressed his own views. Another is the sheer difficulty of the topics he tackled and his original and unorthodox conclusions and arguments. A third is the fact that the very simplicity of his writing tends to conceal its originality and importance. And finally, those in Cambridge who understood his ideas and might have developed them were, for many years after his death, seduced into following the more charismatic character and enigmatic doctrines of Wittgenstein. More recently, however, Ramsey has come into his own, and is recognized as the founder of whole areas of mathematics and economics besides major theories in philosophy.

After a long attack of jaundice, Ramsey died on 19 January 1930 in Guy's Hospital, London, of a combination of the undiagnosed hepatitis that had caused his symptoms and the effects of an operation designed to deal with their supposed cause. He was buried alongside his mother in the St Giles' and St Peter's burial-ground, Cambridge.

D. H. MELLOR

Ian Thomas Ramsey (1915–1972), by Godfrey Argent, 1968

Sources D. H. Mellor, 'F. P. Ramsey', *Philosophy*, 70 (1995), 243–62 · F. P. Ramsey, *Philosophical papers*, ed. D. H. Mellor (1990) · R. B. Braithwaite, 'Introduction', in F. P. Ramsey, *The foundations of mathematics and other logical essays*, ed. R. B. Braithwaite (1931), ix–xiv · D. H. Mellor, L. Mirsky, T. J. Smiley, and R. Stone, 'Introductions', in F. P. Ramsey, *Foundations: essays in philosophy, logic, mathematics and economics*, ed. D. H. Mellor (1978), 1–16 · private information (2004) **Archives** King's AC Cam., corresp. with his wife and parents [copies] · King's AC Cam., diaries and papers · University of Pittsburgh, Pennsylvania | King's AC Cam., Keynes MSS · King's AC Cam., letters to W. J. H. Sprott | SOUND CUL, D. H. Mellor, 'Better than the stars', 1978, a radio biography of Ramsey with contributions by Ramsey's relatives, friends and colleagues, Ua.1.73 (transcript), CT1507 (sound cassette) **Likenesses** L. Ramsey, photograph, U. Cam., faculty of philosophy; repro. in Ramsey, *Philosophical papers* **Wealth at death** £1400 9s. 9d.: probate, 10 March 1930, *CGPLA Eng. & Wales*

Ramsey, Ian Thomas (1915–1972), bishop of Durham, was born on 31 January 1915 in Kearsley, Lancashire, the only child of Arthur Ramsey, who worked in the Post Office and ended up as postmaster of Norwich, and his wife, May Cornthwaite. He won a scholarship to Farnworth grammar school at the age of ten and another to Christ's College, Cambridge, at the age of eighteen. He was placed in the first class in the mathematical tripos, part one (1936), and in moral sciences (philosophy), part two(a) (1938), and to the end of his life maintained a keen interest in mathematics and science. But during his first year as an undergraduate he contracted tuberculosis. During eight months in hospital, followed by long restrictions on his activity, he pondered the use to which he ought to put the life which had been spared, formed close friendships with other young men with Christian convictions, and began to read widely.

Ramsey emerged from his ordeal with the desire to be ordained and the third 'first' which he gained (in 1939) was in the philosophical section of the theological tripos, part two. He won the Burney prize in 1938 and became Burney student in 1939. He prepared for ordination in 1940 at Ripon Hall, choosing a modernist college in an Oxford environment because he recognized the challenge of the anti-metaphysical philosophy then flourishing in the university. It was already his ambition to try to build a bridge between theology and philosophy. He was always, however, more devout than most modernists and avoided disputes about the Bible.

After a curacy at Headington Quarry near Oxford, Ramsey returned to Christ's College in 1943. In that year he married Margretta (Margaret), daughter of John McKay, from Coleraine near Londonderry; they had two sons. Ramsey quietly shared the pacifism of the master of Christ's, Charles Raven, but had a more eirenic personality and quickly became a popular figure, first as the chaplain and then as a tutor. He was soon appointed a university lecturer and began the attempt to rescue what seemed valid in the insights of Christian metaphysical philosophers while recognizing the validity in the demand of most of the academic philosophers of his own age for logical analysis and linguistic rigour. Behind this academic discussion lay the tension between the religious and scientific values which he had absorbed in his Lancashire boyhood. His rare equipment for a difficult debate was recognized by his election as Nolloth professor of the philosophy of the Christian religion at Oxford in 1951.

The chair carried with it a fellowship of Oriel College and Ramsey again played an active role in college life. He was also now busy in wider administration, in the divinity faculty, and as chairman of the Warneford and Park hospitals management committee (1954–66). He became fascinated by contemporary ethical dilemmas, particularly on the frontiers between religion, medicine, and law, and was prominent in groups which on behalf of the Church of England's board for social responsibility studied problems such as suicide, sterilization, punishment, doctors' decisions about life and death, and abortion. Above all he developed as an energetic and stimulating teacher, in lectures and seminars which attracted a growing number of students, and as director (1964–7) of the Lambeth diploma in theology for part-time students outside Oxford.

A stream of publications began to appear, mostly arising out of lectures. The most important were *Religious Language* (1957) and *Freedom and Immortality* (1960). Ramsey admitted that all religious language was 'odd' and consisted largely of the use of 'models', all of which needed 'qualifiers' since no one model could fully describe the ineffable God or his actions in time or eternity. Such admissions about the fallibility of traditional dogmas often alarmed Ramsey's fellow Christians, while non-Christian philosophers tended to rate him as prejudiced if not amateurish; they were astonished that in 1963 he could entitle a book *On being Sure in Religion*. Thus despite his personal popularity with colleagues and his appeal to students in America as well as the United Kingdom, his intellectual position was not widely shared.

However, Ramsey felt compelled to argue for the importance of religious worship and belief, and of the demand of the conscience acknowledged in ethics, because on the basis of his own experience he maintained that human life included certain situations which constituted 'disclosures' of a more than everyday reality and which led to 'commitments' to beliefs and to devout and moral actions. To him, religion's 'characteristic claim is that there are situations which are spatio-temporal and more' (Edwards, 28).

Ramsey admired the philosophical theology of past Anglicans such as Bishop George Berkeley (to whom the world was essentially persons perceiving) and Bishop Joseph Butler (to whom the person's most important perception was of duty), while also insisting on the empiricism enshrined in Butler's phrase: 'Everything is what it is, and not another thing.' (Edwards, 31) He was encouraged when Oxford philosophers paid an attention subtler than in earlier periods to the significance of personality and duty, and between 1961 and 1971 he edited five symposia designed to promote such developments and a wider awareness of them. Many of his own essays were collected posthumously under the title *Christian Empiricism* (1974).

But the question whether Ramsey could have constructed a convincing system of modern metaphysics, given leisure, cannot be answered, for in 1966 he accepted a call to be bishop of Durham. As such Ramsey had a seat in the House of Lords and there he fulfilled the hope that he would take the lead in expressing the Church of England's reactions to moral problems of the day. He criticized the Conservative government, pleading for a new recognition of the multiracial world and for a new spirit in industry. His episcopal activities were, however, far wider. He threw himself enthusiastically into his mainly industrial diocese, making up for his lack of experience of the church's ordinary life by the warmth of his affection and the energy of his calls for modernization. In his enthronement sermon he declared that 'words, persons, institutions, possess genuine authority as and when they are vehicles of a vision' (Edwards, 62); and his strongly personal episcopate in the north-east was such a vehicle.

One of Ramsey's many assets was that he was totally unprelatical. He was short and stocky in appearance, his accent retained traces of his Lancashire boyhood, and his friendliness was outgoing. The Durham miners invited him to speak on their gala day; when he was criticized for one of his many controversial comments, Durham students demonstrated in his favour; the clergy knew that their bishop was a man of prayer who was able to relate prayer to the age of science and industry; and in the Church of England at large he was soon being talked about as the inevitable successor to Archbishop Michael Ramsey at Canterbury.

Ramsey was chairman of the doctrine commission appointed in 1967 (producing in 1968 *Subscription and Assent to the 39 Articles*); of a national commission on religious education in schools (producing *The Fourth R*, 1970); of the Institute of Religion and Medicine; of William Temple College; and of the Central Religious Advisory Council relating to the BBC and the Independent Broadcasting Authority. He was in demand as a bishop able to talk sense about modern problems and as a chairman whose sunny temperament was combined with a tireless attention to detail and a total honesty in wrestling with problems which were often slippery and dark. And he had a vision of a 'new culture' where science and religion, industrial technology, and humane ethics, were reconciled. He was able to create an atmosphere of excitement and hope.

Because his life was poured out in the service of his pupils, his diocese, and the church and nation in a time of widespread perplexity, Ramsey's best legacy lay in thousands of memories of the quality of his mind and character, rather than in any substantial literary or administrative achievement. It is absurdly inadequate to identify him with the relaxation of the terms of the clergy's assent to the historic Anglican formularies, or with the decrease in the hostility of secular humanists to religious education in state schools, or with any other one point that he made, since once he had helped to vindicate a place for metaphysics in the English academic world many looked to him for leadership of a spiritual movement which might have halted the splitting asunder of English theology into radicalism and conservatism and the secularization of English life and schools.

It is by no means certain that had he lived Ramsey would have been chosen as archbishop of Canterbury, since, balancing his appeal to the labour movement (and Labour was in power when the vacancy occurred in 1974), there was disquiet both about his theological and political outspokenness and about his eagerness to speak whenever the opportunity arose, dissipating his energies and diluting his wisdom. Perhaps the highest office would not have been wrong for him. But the Church of England had not been given a leader marked by his combination of intellectual power with a cheerful populism since the death of Archbishop William Temple in 1944—and, unlike Temple, he shared the interests of scientists and technologists. The gap which he left was not filled.

Ramsey was an honorary fellow of Oriel (1967) and Christ's (1967) and had honorary doctorates from the universities of Oxford (1966), Durham (1967), and Glasgow (1968). He died after a heart attack in Broadcasting House, London, on 6 October 1972, survived by his wife, Margretta, and their two sons. He had worn himself out because, in Archbishop Ramsey's words, 'it had become a deep and inseparable part of his character never to say "no"' (Edwards, 100). Although he always tried to be accessible to troubled individuals, his willingness to lecture to, or to take the chair at, meetings outside his own diocese consumed much of his time.

DAVID L. EDWARDS, *rev.*

Sources D. L. Edwards, *Ian Ramsey, bishop of Durham: a memoir* (1973) · J. H. Gill, *Ian Ramsey: to speak responsibly of God* (1976) · personal knowledge (1986) · *The Times* (7 Oct 1972) · *CGPLA Eng. & Wales* (1973)
Archives Durham Cath. CL, papers | SOUND BL NSA, Bow dialogues, 14 Feb 1967, C812/16C5 · BL NSA, Bow dialogues, 14 Feb 1967, C812/27C10
Likenesses G. Argent, photograph, 1968, NPG [*see illus.*]
Wealth at death £41,895: probate, 22 Jan 1973, *CGPLA Eng. & Wales*

Ramsey, Joan Alice Chetwode, Lady Ramsey (1909–1995). *See under* Ramsey, (Arthur) Michael, Baron Ramsey of Canterbury (1904–1988).

Ramsey [Ramsay, Bowle], **John** (d. 1551), prior of Merton and religious pamphleteer, is first recorded in 1513, when, as an Augustinian canon, he attended St Mary's College, Oxford. He supplicated for his BA in 1514, and for his BTh in 1522, being admitted to the latter degree on 26 June. In 1528 he was *prior studentium* at St Mary's, but two years later, on 18 February 1530, he became prior of Merton, Surrey, an office he held until the dissolution of the house on 13 April 1538. On 9 May following Ramsey—under the name of John Bowle (probably his family name)—received an annual pension of 200 marks, together with the promise for life of the prior's London house in Trinity Lane. On 3 July 1545 he was admitted rector of Woodchurch, Kent, a benefice he held until his death in September 1551.

It is not surprising that Ramsey should have adapted easily to monastic dissolution and protestant reformation, for he had clearly come to hold advanced literary and religious opinions. Among the eight books which survive from his library is Erasmus's *Enchiridion*, and while he was still prior of Merton, in 1537 his fellow canon Thomas Paynell dedicated to him 'Comparation of a vyrgin and a martyr', the translation of another of Erasmus's works which Ramsey had commissioned. Ramsey subsequently became the author of at least three pamphlets. One of these, *Communication Betw. a Poore Man and his Wife*, recorded in 1595, is now lost. Of the other two, *A Plaister for a Galled Horse*, published in 1548, may have been the first, since it promises another plaster if this one proves too cold. One of a group of attacks on the mass produced in this period, it derides Romish priests as 'blynde owles', and denounces them as traitors and heretics, while the mass itself is represented as an exercise in hypocrisy and superstition.

Ramsey's other tract, *A Corosyfe to be Layed Hard unto the Hartes of all Faythfull Professours of Cristes Gospel*, is less knockabout in style. It calls on all to remember the full and final sacrifice of Christ, urging them to remember their battleaxe (Christ's cross), to keep their armour bright, and never again to lust after the fleshpots of Egypt. They should love their neighbours, have a care for the poor, and obey the magistrates, who are God's ministers on earth. Ramsey concludes by commending the king, wishing him long life. By this time Ramsey's own religious position was such that he had become one of Archbishop Cranmer's chaplains.

JOHN FINES

Sources Emden, *Oxf.*, 4.473 · *Report of the Deputy Keeper of the Public Records*, 8 (1847) · *LP Henry VIII*, vols. 13/1, 16/1 · F. B. Williams, 'Lost books of Tudor England', *The Library*, 5th ser., 33 (1978), 1–14 · E. Hasted, *The history and topographical survey of the county of Kent*, 3 (1790)

Ramsey, (Arthur) Michael, Baron Ramsey of Canterbury (1904–1988), archbishop of Canterbury, was born at 71 Chesterton Road, Chesterton, Cambridgeshire, on 14 November 1904, the younger son in the family of two sons and two daughters of Arthur Stanley Ramsey (1867–1954), mathematics fellow of Magdalene College, Cambridge, and his wife, (Mary) Agnes (1875–1927), daughter of Plumpton Stravenson Wilson, vicar of Horbling, Lincolnshire. His elder brother, Frank Plumpton *Ramsey, became an outstanding mathematical economist.

Early life Though Ramsey's father, a Congregational deacon, could be stern and oppressive, Ramsey was fond of him and inherited something of his nonconformist conscience. His mother was an Anglican, a socialist, suffragist, and writer. Ramsey inherited her humour, her love for history, her ability to hold an audience, her concern for society, her indifference to dress, and her desire for a simple life. The family regularly attended Emmanuel Congregational Church. Ramsey disliked its austerity but enjoyed the sermons. He had been baptized by his Anglican grandfather, and his mother continued as an Anglican communicant.

The brilliant Frank overshadowed his less able and very odd brother. Ramsey reacted by becoming intensely shy (a lifelong trial) and by withdrawing into a fantasy world: he was bishop to his toy soldiers and conducted their funerals, wrote to King John in hell to tell him he was 'a very bad man', and composed his own epitaph, 'for many years Bishop of Peking' (Simpson, 36). After painful false starts in schooling, he went to King's College choir school, where he met the first Anglican priest to influence him, Eric Milner-White, later dean of York. He began to blossom academically. From his preparatory school he won a scholarship to Repton School, where Geoffrey Fisher (later archbishop of Canterbury) was headmaster and prepared him for confirmation. Ramsey forsook his father's protestantism and became an Anglo-Catholic. Though physically clumsy and generally strange, he won a name through his eloquence in the debating society, supporting liberal causes against the prevailing toryism. In later life Ramsey relished quoting Fisher's final report: 'A boy with plenty of force of character, who, in spite of certain uncouthness, has done good service on his own lines' (Chadwick, 15).

In 1923 Ramsey went up to Magdalene College, Cambridge, with a classics scholarship. In 1926 he became president of the union. While he was still a second-year undergraduate, the Cambridgeshire Liberals wanted Ramsey as their candidate for the next election, and Asquith prophesied from a Cambridge platform that he would be leader of the Liberal Party. But when he went to mass at a local Anglo-Catholic church, Ramsey discovered another world of mystery, awe, and the supernatural. In 1926 he chaired the university mission. He found the evangelical missioner dogmatic, vulgar, and emotional; by contrast Bishop William Temple (later archbishop of Canterbury), the chief missioner, grappled with the complexity of the world and the difficulties of belief. For the rest of his life Ramsey admired Temple and distrusted populist evangelism. He became convinced that he could do more

good as a priest than as a politician, abandoned law in favour of theology, and after only four terms instead of the usual six took first-class honours. In Edwyn Hoskyns, Ramsey found a theological mentor who introduced him to Karl Barth, the foe of modernist theology, and convinced him of the identity between the historical Jesus and the Christ of the church.

Ordination A fortnight after Ramsey arrived at Cuddesdon College, near Oxford, in July 1927 for a year's ordination preparation, his mother was killed in a motor accident. The death of the most important person in his life brought long-standing problems to the surface and plunged him into mental turmoil. During the first four months of 1928 he lived in a London settlement and saw a psychiatrist three times a week. The treatment continued when he returned to Cuddesdon. Years later he told how someone with a problem might go to a pastor who would try to resolve it by talking about God, but the problem remained, while another professional, without mentioning God, might largely relieve it. In June the Commons for the second time rejected the revised prayer book. Ramsey, the Anglo-Catholic with nonconformist roots, convinced that the church's authority derived from God rather than the state, was horrified. On 23 September 1928 Ramsey was made deacon to serve in the parish of Our Lady and St Nicholas, near Liverpool quayside, which introduced him to the ordinary life of humanity. Charles Raven, the passionate modernist, was his post-ordination tutor. They frequently disagreed. In retreat before his priesting on 22 September 1929 Ramsey wrote, 'this will be utter joy; no man can take it away' (Chadwick, 41).

(Arthur) **Michael Ramsey, Baron Ramsey of Canterbury** (1904–1988), by Godfrey Argent, 1969 [with a photograph of Archbishop William Temple]

Ramsey's reputation as priest and preacher spread. Temple asked him to help on a mission. But on 19 January 1930 Ramsey suffered another terrible bereavement when his brother died, not yet twenty-seven. He conducted the funeral and said a requiem in King's College, where Frank was fellow, and he and his father gave money for a prize in his memory. The fact that someone as brilliant as Frank could be an atheist made him always sympathetic to doubters. Later in life he disturbed some by saying he expected to meet atheists in heaven. (He also believed that the divine light shone in the people of other faiths.) After only eighteen months in Liverpool he moved to Lincoln Theological College, where he became sub-warden. For the last few weeks of his curacy he had to move lodgings because his tory landlady was scandalized by his support for the Labour Party.

At Lincoln the students were enthralled by Ramsey's lectures and amused by his eccentricities. They could hear him pacing his room as he wrestled with problems. In vacations he still saw the psychiatrist. A prospective student's interview consisted of fifteen minutes' silence which concluded with Ramsey murmuring 'You will find Lincoln rather a quiet place'. Father George Florovsky came to stay and awakened a lifelong devotion to Eastern Orthodoxy. In 1936 Ramsey published his first and most influential book, *The Gospel and the Catholic Church*, which established him as a mature theologian at the age of thirty-one. He attempted nothing less than the reconciliation of the Catholic and evangelical traditions, and alerted Anglicans to developments in Roman Catholic, Orthodox, and protestant theology and to the importance of F. D. Maurice. It set the ecumenical agenda for the next half-century. Adrian Hastings, the Roman Catholic theologian, regarded it as an anticipation, thirty years early, of the approach of the Second Vatican Council. Among the congratulatory letters Ramsey received was one from Temple: 'you have done the Church great service by your book, and have ... given to me personally a re-direction and enrichment in devotional life' (LPL, Ramsey papers, 2/49).

Invited to be principal of St Chad's, Durham, Ramsey met Hensley Henson, the acerbic bishop, who noted in his diary: 'Ramsey is a heavy fellow with a fat face, and a cumbrous manner, not prepossessing, but improving on acquaintance' (Chadwick, 50). The bishop of Lincoln, realizing that Ramsey was an exceptional priest, in 1936 offered him the senior curacy of Boston parish church to extend his experience. Ramsey's eccentricities continued. Disliking processions, he developed a limp, and it was thought he had been wounded in the war. He explored the possibility of a vocation to the monastic life with the Community of the Resurrection, Mirfield. In January 1939 he became vicar of the small parish of St Benet's, Cambridge, which provided him academic contacts and nearness to his father. That autumn he was invited to become professor of divinity at Durham and canon of the cathedral.

Professor of divinity In his inaugural lecture, 'Jesus Christ in faith and history', Ramsey rejected the modernist belief that it was possible to discover the true Jesus apart from the church, and that the church had misunderstood Jesus from the apostles onwards until nineteenth-century professors discovered the truth. But Henson criticized Ramsey for subordinating history to theology. Under Ramsey the faculty became the most respected in England. Hitherto an Anglican preserve, it was enriched with Free Church scholars. Ramsey was still odd—he was once observed walking along with one foot in the gutter and one on the pavement—but the students worshipped him. Wherever he preached, whether in the cathedral or in mining parishes, the congregation was gripped, for he took his hearers into his struggle for truth. He spoke not from a prepared text but from a few notes and from the heart.

Soon after arriving in Durham, Ramsey met his future wife. **Joan Alice Chetwode Ramsey** [*née* Hamilton], Lady Ramsey (1909–1995). was born on 16 September 1909 at Inwoods, Cargate Hill, Aldershot, Hampshire, the daughter of Lieutenant-Colonel Francis Alexander Chetwode Hamilton and his wife, Ouida Mary Tryon. Her uncle Eric Hamilton was bishop of Shrewsbury from 1940 and dean of Windsor from 1944. A former social worker, she became secretary and driver for Leslie Owen, bishop of Jarrow (Ramsey's former warden at Lincoln), and lived near by with the Owen family. She was no academic but had a lively mind and a penetrating wit and she shared Ramsey's sense of the ridiculous. Both had a remarkable memory for people and places. They were married on 8 April 1942 in the Galilee chapel of the cathedral. She helped Ramsey to be less eccentric and saw that his clothes were tidier. When in company he fell silent, she drew him back with 'Tell them Michael about ...'. Once, over coffee with the staff at Chichester Theological College after a strenuous morning and with another session to come, she saw him withdrawing. 'Michael', she said, 'you could do with a little solitude and silence'. 'Solitude and silence, what a good idea', he replied, and then asked the principal, 'Have you a bed?' In his turn Ramsey kept a close eye on his wife's health. She suffered illnesses of a nervous origin. It is impossible to imagine that he would have become a bishop, let alone an archbishop, without her close companionship and guidance. She made homes out of huge draughty official residences and expressed the gratitude and appreciation to hosts and to his staff which he often forgot. They were fulfilled in each other, although their failure to have children was a source of grief to her. Her faith, like his, was focused on the eucharist.

Ramsey disliked the large-scale assemblies of the World Council of Churches, but at the first in Amsterdam (1948) he met Barth. Barth had never before encountered an Anglo-Catholic: 'with strange views', he reported, 'concerning tradition, succession, ontology and so on ... the outstanding figure in the picture of my first ecumenical experience!' (Chadwick, 67). Ramsey reached a wider public through three books: *F. D. Maurice and the Conflicts of Modern Theology* (1951) and two biblical studies, *The Resurrection of Christ* (1945) and *The Glory of God and the Transfiguration of Christ* (1949). Glory and transfiguration, great

Orthodox themes, were central to his spirituality. Theology was never just academic: 'There is no holiness apart from the theology which [Jesus] reveals, and there is no imparting of the theology except by consecrated lives', he wrote in the last (1967 edn, p. 79).

In 1950 Ramsey was appointed regius professor of divinity at Cambridge, proposed and seconded by Free Churchmen. Ramsey became a fellow of Magdalene. His lectures were popular across the university. He showed how theology and devotion belonged together. The Ramseys had just moved into their third house in less than two years (some said they enjoyed moving) when Ramsey received a letter from Churchill, the prime minister, offering to recommend him as bishop of Durham. Ramsey hesitated. An acceptance would anger Cambridge, which had so recently elected him, and would end his academic career. Archbishop Geoffrey Fisher worried that Ramsey would be bad at administration, and he and Garbett of York thought he should stay at Cambridge longer. But Durham was pressing for his return. Ramsey accepted, largely because he believed that a bishop should be an apostolic teacher and that the church lacked such bishops.

Bishop of Durham Ramsey was consecrated in York Minster on 29 September 1952 and enthroned in Durham Cathedral on 18 October. He rejoiced to be in fellowship with the northern saints—Aidan, Cuthbert, Bede—and Westcott and Lightfoot more recently. He was more at ease with them than with modern industrial Durham. His sense of history led him to remain in Auckland Castle. Its awesome butler asked Mrs Ramsey for their silver, and she replied that it was in the bank (in fact they had none); he did not approve of the townspeople being invited to tea. Ramsey enjoyed wandering into the market place and listening to the retired miners. When children saw him coming they led him to Woolworths, where he bought them sweets. Ramsey wanted the people to think about their faith, and revived the diocesan journal, *The Bishoprick*. He criticized the attitude of Billy Graham to the Bible, so gladdening the thoughtful and dismaying evangelicals. He called for a more contemplative church, more monks and nuns, more devotion to the saints. The 1953 coronation brought him to national attention. Millions watching on television saw this kind old bishop on the queen's right hand, not knowing he was only forty-eight.

In 1955 Garbett of York was eighty and ill. Fisher and Garbett wondered whether the revered G. K. A. Bell of Chichester might go to York until Ramsey gained more episcopal experience. But Eden, like Churchill before him, refused to give recognition to Bell, who had taken up controversial positions during the war. Fisher saw Ramsey as his possible successor and wondered whether he should go to London, which would be good preparation. Garbett wanted Ramsey to succeed him at York. Fisher agreed.

Archbishop of York Ramsey was enthroned in York Minster on 25 April 1956. The Ramseys were determined to stay in Bishopthorpe. Mrs Ramsey made it welcoming for large numbers of clergy, their families, and other visitors. In 1956 Ramsey led an Anglican delegation to Russia, where he was moved by Orthodox worship. At the 1958 Lambeth conference he was the outstanding figure. In 1960 he toured central Africa, where he was amused to hear that most Africans thought him well over seventy. At home Ramsey continued his teaching ministry. He revived the *York Quarterly*, in which he discussed nuclear weapons as well as biblical criticism. He was in great demand to conduct retreats, particularly for religious orders. *From Gore to Temple* (1960), Ramsey's masterly exposition of fifty years of Anglican theology, concluded that Gore and Temple achieved theological coherence, not through a quest for tidiness but by 'wrestling with the truth for truth's own sake' (p. 170). He was popular with students. His clear elucidations of faith in several universities were published as *Introducing the Christian Faith* (1961).

Ramsey's relationship with Fisher became strained as Fisher, now in his seventies, became more domineering. At a bishops' meeting when Fisher was absent and Ramsey was in the chair the bishops expressed their pent-up frustrations, and Fisher's domestic chaplain courageously told him he should resign. Fisher no longer thought Ramsey should succeed him—he was too eccentric, not a good administrator, too Anglo-Catholic, too lukewarm about establishment, too academic, and Ramsey was not among the names he recommended to Harold Macmillan, the prime minister. But Macmillan and his advisers thought Ramsey the obvious choice for Canterbury. Macmillan was also a high-churchman, liked *From Gore to Temple*, and admired F. D. Maurice. When Macmillan said to Ramsey that Fisher did not seem to approve of him, Ramsey (who had never got over having been Fisher's pupil) replied that Fisher, as his headmaster, knew his deficiencies. 'Well,' replied Macmillan, 'he's not going to be *my* headmaster'. Macmillan later remarked, 'we have had enough of Martha and it was time for some Mary' (Chadwick, 107). Ramsey felt keenly Fisher's lack of confidence in him.

Appointed archbishop of Canterbury On the eve of his formal election Ramsey gave a remarkable television interview. 'If disestablishment were to come we would remember that our credentials come not from the State but from Christ'. The church must be free to revise its own liturgy. The method of episcopal appointments must be reformed. He went on:

> People ask me, sometimes, if I am in good heart about being Archbishop … My answer is 'Yes' … But the phrase 'in good heart', gives me pause, because after all, we are here as a church to represent Christ crucified and the compassion of Christ crucified before the world. And, because that is so, it may be the will of God that our church should have its heart broken and perhaps the heart of its Archbishop broken with it. (*Church Times*, 9 June 1961)

Here at last was a great priest who could speak convincingly about God and was prepared to stand up against the state. Ramsey's abandonment of quaint gaiters in favour of a cassock (other bishops followed) indicated that the Church of England was going to be less insular. His thirteen years in office coincided with great moral, social, and theological ferment. Ramsey was a liberal reformer who, unlike the statist Temple, had no overall social blueprint, but because be bravely tackled emotional questions such as race and sexuality, horrified conservative opinion much more than Temple. A bishop-to-be and his family were kept up late, the evening before his consecration, by Ramsey's passionate conversation about race, armaments, and radical theology.

Church and society Ramsey powerfully supported the campaign of the 1960s for homosexual law reform, while maintaining that homosexual practice was sinful. Throughout, Lambeth officials co-ordinated bishops' attendances in the Lords and kept in close touch with the Homosexual Law Reform Society. Ramsey received many abusive letters from opponents; he was bitterly attacked by certain peers, one of whom accused him of contributing pornography to *Hansard*. The success in the Lords of the Sexual Offences Bill (1967), which decriminalized homosexuality, owed much to episcopal support. Ramsey also appointed a church commission to frame a more just divorce law. *Putting Asunder* (1966) continued to be influential on divorce law into the twenty-first century. In 1962 all but one bishop in the convocations voted against capital punishment. At one stage Ramsey accepted an invitation to steer the bill for abolition through the Lords (an indication of how strongly he felt), but he had to withdraw.

Ramsey had grown up without racial prejudice, a very unusual thing at that time. 'I should love to think of a black Archbishop of York holding a mission to the University of Oxford', he told students in 1960 (*Introducing the Christian Faith*, 75). Ramsey was asked by Harold Wilson, the prime minister, to chair the National Committee for Commonwealth Immigrants. He opposed restrictions on Kenyan Asian immigration, but supported the Race Relations Bill (1968). Enoch Powell and others were scathing. Threats were made against Ramsey's life. In October 1965, when Rhodesia was moving towards a unilateral declaration of independence, Ramsey declared that if the British government thought it practicable to use force for the protection of the majority, Christians should support it. He was congratulated by Liberal and Labour MPs, but both pacifists and the right were outraged: that an archbishop should support black people rather than white people was incomprehensible. He received many denunciatory letters. A placard was placed on the cenotaph, reading 'Ramsey warmonger and traitor', and Canterbury Cathedral was defaced. Owen Chadwick described it as the greatest storm endured by an archbishop since 1688. Ramsey was deeply concerned about other areas of Africa. He opposed World Council of Churches grants for medical purposes to guerrilla groups, but he and 100 other bishops wrote to Edward Heath, the prime minister, asking him not to sell arms to South Africa. Visiting South Africa in 1970, he described all people as God's children and condemned apartheid but said that change, not violence, was the answer. He characterized his confrontational interview with the dour, aggressive prime minister, B. J. Vorster, as the 'worst day' of his life (Chadwick, 259).

Fisher had been the first archbishop to travel beyond Europe. As the patriarchal role of Canterbury developed, so did requests for overseas visits. Abroad Ramsey was overjoyed to be treated primarily as a priest and not as an establishment figure. Late one night, as he was removing his vestments in a New York church, a young woman came and asked him to bless her crucifix. He became totally absorbed in her and the prayers. 'Truly you are a child of God!' she exclaimed (De-la-Noy, *A Day*, 42). In North America the civil rights and charismatic movements caused Ramsey to rethink his dislike of emotional religion. In Chile it was rumoured that he was going to be assassinated because of his critical remarks about the Pinochet regime. In Rio, Billy Graham invited him to join him on his platform: Ramsey told his largely protestant audience that they could not come to Christ without their Roman Catholic fellows and that Christ was with the poor. Continental protestantism was not his natural world, but he made several visits to Lutherans. He moved a vast congregation in Leipzig by placing three roses on the tomb of Bach. He wept in Buchenwald and prayed in the cell of the martyr Paul Schneider.

Church and state 'Establishment has never been one of my enthusiasms', Ramsey wrote. Christianity was 'passing into a post-Constantinian phase' (*Canterbury Pilgrim*, 1974, 176). He was not at ease with the royal family. He corrected the queen mother when she referred to her daughter as head of the church. At a royal occasion at St Paul's he first bowed to the altar, muttering 'God first' and only then bowed to the queen (Chadwick, 142). He secured abolition of the severe penalties payable by those who refused the crown's nominee. An archbishops' commission on church and state recommended in 1970 that worship and doctrine should be decided by the synod (which that year replaced the less representative church assembly) and that bishops should be nominated by the church, not the prime minister. On the day of Ramsey's retirement in 1974, to his great satisfaction, the Lords approved the Church of England (Worship and Doctrine) Measure. In 1975 a canon under that measure replaced subscription to the Thirty-Nine Articles with a simpler declaration. The Crown Appointments Commission, created in 1976, gave the church a more decisive say in the choice of bishops. Ramsey did a great deal to exorcize the ghost of Henry VIII.

Ecumenism Ramsey warned against a 'defensive Catholicism which supposes that no risks must be taken in the process of Christian unity' (M. Ramsey, *The Christian Priest Today*, 1972, 26). He also came to believe with the Roman Catholic Yves Congar that a united church would be in a form which was as yet unknown. The Second Vatican Council transformed ecumenical relations. The editor of the *Catholic Herald* interviewed Ramsey about it, and commented on 'the rich texture of his personality, his candour, his generosity, his immense good will, his infectious humour. Above all his deep spirituality' (*Catholic Herald*, 12 Oct 1962). Ramsey had learned more from Roman Catholic theologians than any other senior Anglican bishop: he regarded his meeting with Pope Paul VI in March 1966 as the highlight of his life. A minority vehemently objected, particularly from Northern Ireland. Whereas Fisher's visit in 1960 was low-key (no photographs were allowed), when Ramsey arrived to stay at the English College, seminarians crowded around him and kissed his ring. The day after their mutual discussions, pope and archbishop gave the blessing together at a joint service. The pope slipped off his episcopal ring and put it on Ramsey's finger, where it remained until the day of his death. A joint theological commission was created which produced a remarkable convergence between the churches. Ramsey and Cardinal Suenens wrote two books together, the first time that Anglican and Roman Catholic prelates had engaged in joint teaching. Ramsey himself grew to favour the ordination of women, but wanted delay for ecumenical reasons.

To Ramsey the fundamental schism was that between East and West. He felt deeply akin to Orthodox worship and theology, and believed that it could help the Western church with some of its problems. In 1964 the patriarch of Moscow came to Lambeth, in 1966 the patriarch of Romania, and in 1967 the ecumenical patriarch himself.

The healing of the schism between Methodists and Anglicans through a union scheme was dear to Ramsey's heart. That it would modify the church–state relationship was for him an added attraction. He kept in touch with the Vatican about the proposals. But despite his passionate speeches, the scheme failed to gain the required majorities from Anglicans. Ramsey was deeply distressed and ashamed. He wrote to Father Geoffrey Curtis at Mirfield, an old friend, 'Our church has "made an ass of itself"' (Borth. Inst., Mir/6/D13). What made it much worse for Ramsey was that Fisher, now released from the constraints of office, publicly campaigned against the scheme and bombarded Ramsey with long, heated letters on this and other subjects.

Theological ministry Surprisingly it was not a political but a theological controversy which (initially) knocked Ramsey off balance. Radicals had rooted for him as someone who wanted change. Later they accused him of only being able to do theology to the sound of church bells. John Robinson, bishop of Woolwich, an individualist who relished publicity, was already notorious for defending *Lady Chatterley's Lover* at its trial. In 1963 he published *Honest to God*. A missionary book, it sold over 1 million copies. *The Observer* ran Robinson's summary of the book under its own title, 'Our image of God must go', which made Robinson sound destructive and insensitive. Ramsey's immediate reaction was a statement that it was right to seek for other helpful images but utterly wrong to denounce images held by ordinary Christians. Ramsey had always disliked modernism for its shallowness and rationalism. He was receiving mail attacking Robinson for blasphemy. However, he prevented a motion in convocation accusing Robinson of heresy, and within a fortnight he produced a booklet, *Image Old and New*, which calmly and sympathetically examined new ways of looking at faith, worship, and morality, and concluded that since the war the church had been concerned with its own life and assumed that the faith could be taken for granted. 'But we state and commend the faith only in so far as we go out and put ourselves with loving sympathy inside the doubts of the doubting' (p. 14). After he retired, Ramsey was publicly self-critical about his handling of this controversy and for not grasping that the book was bringing to the boil a number of issues which had been simmering for some time. At the time he wrote books about these issues, notably *Sacred and Secular* (1965) and *God, Christ and the World* (1969), and contributed to *The Charismatic Christ* (1974). *The Christian Priest Today* (1972) became a spiritual classic. In *Canterbury Pilgrim* (1974) he humbly confessed that he came to Canterbury as a teacher and found himself a learner.

Retirement When Ramsey retired in 1974 he went round exclaiming 'I'm free', 'I'm happy as a sandboy'. Significantly, warm tributes came as often from politicians as from churchpeople. At the bishops' farewell dinner Ramsey mused on his predecessors, including Anselm, to whom he felt closest: 'We embraced each other because here I felt there was a man who was primarily a don, who tried to say his prayers and who cared nothing for the pomp and glory of his position' (Chadwick, 381). He was unhappy about accepting the traditional peerage and wanted to be simply 'Bishop Ramsey', but acquiesced and became Baron Ramsey of Canterbury. He was amused as much as pleased when the queen gave him the Royal Victorian Chain. The Ramseys moved frequently during retirement: first to Cuddesdon, then to a house in Durham, then to another nearer to the cathedral. Becoming more frail, they moved to a flat in Bishopthorpe. Finally they came to rest with the nuns at All Saints' Convent, Oxford.

Until he became too elderly Ramsey exercised a vigorous priestly ministry, teaching and preaching both in Britain and abroad. The Ramseys felt particularly at home at Nashotah House (an American Anglo-Catholic seminary in Wisconsin), where he ministered as priest and teacher for several years. A priest who stayed with them in Durham described it as 'like a country weekend with saints' (Chadwick, 391). Some afternoons Ramsey would amble into the market place: 'You could see the eyes of the Durham folk watching him with deep affection', a vicar observed (De-la-Noy, *Ramsey*, 233). He continued his writing ministry in *Holy Spirit* (1977) and *Jesus and the Living Past* (1980). *Be Still and Know* (1982) sold over 60,000 copies. His themes were that prayer is wanting God; sacramental confession can be a meeting with Jesus as wonderful as communion; nearness to God is nearness to the world's suffering; the passivity of contemplation expresses 'by faith alone'. Two voices speak from the eucharist: 'Join with me and my mother and my friends in the heavenly supper' and 'Come, I am here in this world in those who suffer' (1993 edn, p. 106). In the Oxford convent the Ramseys had just a sitting-room and bedroom. Ramsey made friends with a Muslim at the post office. When he heard that Ramsey had been ordained nearly sixty years he responded, to Ramsey's delight, 'That's a very long friendship' (Chadwick, 398).

Michael Ramsey died on 23 April 1988 at St John's Home,

St Mary's Road, Oxford. During his funeral on 3 May in Canterbury Cathedral the choir appropriately sang the Russian *kontakion*. He was cremated and was buried, as he wished, near Temple in the cloisters. He hoped his stone would not be too small, lest people might think he was Temple's cat. It was inscribed with the words of Irenaeus: 'The Glory of God is the living man; And the life of man is the Vision of God'. Joan, Lady Ramsey, died, also at St John's Home, Oxford, on 13 February 1995 and after a funeral service in Canterbury Cathedral on 17 February her ashes were buried with those of her husband.

Assessment Ramsey has been rightly estimated the greatest twentieth-century archbishop of Canterbury (Temple made his name at York). How was it that someone who seemed such a funny old thing at first sight, with a sing-song voice, who was ill at ease with modernity, who unnerved people by his silences, his repeated 'yes, yes', and his eccentricities, could become the most loved and admired twentieth-century archbishop? His very hesitancy of speech as he pondered questions marked him off from glib ecclesiastical salesmen. Study to be simple, he told the clergy, and behind everything he said was both scholarship and prayer. 'The bishop is still a priest, and unless he retains the heart and mind of a priest he will be a bad bishop', he wrote (*The Christian Priest Today*, 97). Ramsey looked like a medieval carving of God the Father, but drew upon timeless wisdom. He warned against the tyranny of the contemporary, but his antennae were surprisingly alert to contemporary issues. He was uninterested in administration—he took an adolescent delight in secreting interesting letters. He saw the priest as an epiphany not as a manager. He disliked chit-chat and could seem uninterested in people unless they sought his counsel or could talk theology or politics. But he often spoke arrestingly. A journalist asked him what troubled him most as head of the church. Ramsey replied, 'I sometimes lie awake at night and wonder if I am acceptable to God' (Chadwick, 125). He believed clergy should be uninterested in status and Christians should live simply. As archbishop he sometimes turned up in a chauffeur-driven Morris 1000. He was awarded honorary DDs by at least seventeen institutions (including Durham and Cambridge universities and the Institut Catholique, Paris), five doctorates of law (including Oxford and Nashotah House), and three DLitt degrees. Deep down there was a lightness of heart, humility, and much laughter. Apart from daily liturgical prayers, his devotions included the repetition of the Jesus prayer and the recitation of the Angelus.

No archbishop has ever reviewed his own ministry so critically in public on retirement. Clifford Longley wrote that Ramsey was 'a man hard on himself for his own mistakes, and with little sense of his own greatness' (*The Times*, 15 Dec 1975). He showed that the Church of England had a soul, that it was possible to be both an explorer and a believer. The church's purpose was to keep 'alive in the midst of the world the creature's longing towards his Creator' (M. Ramsey, *Introducing the Christian Faith*, 1961, 73). Michael Ramsey believed that longing was fulfilled only with the saints in heaven.   ALAN WILKINSON

Sources DNB · E. Carpenter and A. Hastings, *Cantuar* (1997) · O. Chadwick, *Michael Ramsey* (1990) · M. De-la-Noy, *Michael Ramsey: a portrait* (1990) · M. De-la-Noy, *A day in the life of God* (1971) · R. Gill and L. Kendall, eds., *Michael Ramsey as theologian* (1995) · C. Martin, ed., *Great Christian centuries to come: essays in honour of A. M. Ramsey* (1974) · J. B. Simpson, *The hundredth archbishop of Canterbury* (1962) · LPL, Ramsey papers · LPL, Fisher papers · LPL, Bell papers · *The Times* (25 April 1988) · *The Independent* (25 April 1988) · *The Times* · *The Independent* · WWW · b. cert. · b. cert. [Joan Hamilton, Lady Ramsey] · m. cert. · d. cert. · d. cert. [Lady Ramsey] · personal knowledge (2004) · private information (2004)
Archives LPL, corresp. and official papers | LPL, Bell papers · LPL, Fisher papers
Likenesses G. Bruce, oils, 1865, Auckland Castle, co. Durham · Ramsey & Muspratt, photograph, 1951, NPG · G. Bruce, oils, 1958, Bishopthorpe, York · photographs, 1961–71, Hult. Arch. · P. Greenham, oils, 1964, LPL · Y. Karsh, photograph, 1964, NPG · R. Spear, oils, 1965, Magd. Cam. · G. Argent, bromide print, 1969, NPG [*see illus.*] · G. Roddon, oils, 1970, LPL · J. Worsley, oils, 1971, priv. coll. · J. Doubleday, bronze bust, 1974, Ripon College, Cuddesdon, Oxfordshire · B. Kulik, bust, *c.*1974, Council of Christians and Jews, London · G. Bruce, oils, 1982, LPL · J. Sorrell, oils, 1982, NPG · L. Ramsey, photograph, NPG · photographs, repro. in Chadwick, *Michael Ramsey*
Wealth at death £16,226—Lord Ramsey: probate, 29 Jan 1990, CGPLA Eng. & Wales · under £125,000—Lady Ramsey: probate, 1995, CGPLA Eng. & Wales

Ramsey, Robert (*c.*1595–1644), composer and organist, was born of unknown parents. He apparently passed his adult musical career at Trinity College, Cambridge, where he was organist and master of the choristers, and from where he supplicated for the MusB degree, having spent seven years in the study of music. A grace was granted on 10 June 1616 on condition that he compose and perform a motet in the university church of St Mary the Great: this work, the eight-part *Inclina domine*, is still extant. His acceptance of these duties may in fact have antedated the award of his degree, and it was probably in a musical capacity that he justified his first recorded payment by the college in 1616 when, styled simply Mr Ramsey, he was allowed 20s. 'for extra commons at the tyme of the Kinges being here' (Payne, *Provision and Practice*, 283). This suggests a much earlier date of appointment than has been accepted by most commentators and almost certainly refers to royal visits that had taken place in Easter term of the previous year. An additional commons payment followed in 1619 but, owing to lacunae in the archives, no further payments to him appear until June 1629.

On 5 August 1622 Ramsey married Elizabeth Ryding at Great St Mary's, Cambridge, and the couple moved to the parish of Holy Trinity, where, between 1623 and 1626, three children were born to them. Ramsey is styled master of the choristers in January 1632, though at Trinity these duties and those of organist were discharged by one man. Further 'rewards' followed in the 1630s and early 1640s, possibly for the composition of music. These include payments of 10s. made in July 1638 by Peterhouse, very probably for music delivered to that college for inclusion in its so-called 'Caroline' partbooks, and of 5s. 'for one werke' (Payne, *Provision and Practice*, 284) unfortunately not specified.

Ramsey's music, though variable in quality, is important for its experimental, Italianate features typical of the early baroque. His most adventurous music is contained in his continuo songs and monodies, such as 'What Tears, Dear Prince', which laments the death in 1612 of Henry, prince of Wales, and the highly expressive 'In Guilty Night'. Such settings cater to the taste for Italianate music which Thomas Mace says was prevalent in Cambridge at the time, and the composer's royalist sympathies would have been much appreciated at Trinity. Ramsey mourned Prince Henry's death with another work—the 'Dialogues of Sorrow', dated 1615 in its manuscript source and probably meant for publication. This work uses a consort of viols and was probably intended, together with a number of English madrigals, for domestic use at Trinity and, like the majority of them, is both scored in six parts and fragmentary.

Ramsey is perhaps best-known for his settings of English and Latin liturgical texts, which, while embracing Italian practice, are generally more conservative than his solo vocal pieces in the new monodic style. His Latin music employs devices found, for example, in Monteverdi's sacred music; but he is at his best when combining the madrigal and anthem, as in his masterpiece, the six-part 'How are the mighty fallen'. Some of his madrigals and anthems, including a fine six-part elegy, probably on the death of Prince Henry, entitled 'Sleep fleshly birth', are preserved in a set of autograph partbooks (Euing Collection, Glasgow University Library).

Ramsey died in 1644 and was buried at Holy Trinity, Cambridge, on 12 February; at Michaelmas of the same year the college paid 6s. 8d. towards his funeral expenses. 'Widdow Ramsey', very probably the composer's widow, was buried on 2 August 1667 (Payne, *Provision and Practice*, 284–5). IAN PAYNE

Sources I. Payne, *The provision and practice of sacred music at Cambridge colleges and selected cathedrals, c.1547–c.1646* (1993) · I. Payne, 'The musical establishment at Trinity College, Cambridge, 1546–1644', *Proceedings of the Cambridge Antiquarian Society*, 74 (1985), 53–69 · E. Thompson, 'Ramsey, Robert', *New Grove* · I. Payne, 'Instrumental music at Trinity College, Cambridge, c.1594–c.1615: archival and biographical evidence', *Music and Letters*, 68 (1987), 128–40 · E. Thompson, 'Robert Ramsey', *Musical Quarterly*, 49 (1963), 210–24

Ramsey, William of (*fl.* 1219), Benedictine monk and poet, may have been born at Ramsey, Huntingdonshire, and belonged to the community at Crowland Abbey in Lincolnshire. Modern scholarship has deprived him of most of the works attributed to him by the antiquaries. John Bale, building on John Leland's list, credited him with the following: verse lives of saints Guthlac, Edmund, and Birinus (all by Henry d'Avranches); excerpts from pagan philosophers, addressed to a friend Guthlac (in fact, William of Malmesbury's *Polyhistor*); *De vita et moribus philosophorum* (by Walter Burley); and commentaries on Bede's *De temporibus* and Isidore's *Computus* (both by Byrhtferth of Ramsey). Consequently J. C. Russell proclaimed him a 'literary ghost' (J. C. Russell, *Dictionary of Thirteenth-Century Writers*, 1936, 198–9), but a case can be made for two other verse works.

Leland and Bale credited him with lives of Earl Waltheof in verse and prose: a verse epitaph of Waltheof, printed by Michel, written after the translation of 1219, is signed internally 'William', and the other associated works in the Douai manuscript (Douai, Bibliothèque Municipale, MS 852) may be his. Further, Bale attributed to him prose and verse lives of St Neot. The prose lives are too early for William, but the verse life could be his. Admittedly, the marginal ascription to William in the one extant manuscript (Magd. Oxf., MS Lat. 53) is in Bale's own hand, and Bale was notoriously speculative; nevertheless, the *Acta sanctorum* volume on St Neot independently cites William as testimony for the presence of Neot's relics at Ramsey. The extant text of the poem is incomplete (675 lines of elegiac couplets); it is based on the *Vita secunda* (a second prose life) and, when retranscribed from the manuscript, is seen to be more grammatical and fluent than its editor supposed.

Bale confused the poet with **William of Crowland** (d. 1179), abbot of Ramsey. Ramsey was a thriving community and doubtless produced several literary Williams: another of this name wrote a prose treatise on the Song of Songs. A. G. RIGG

Sources F. Michel, ed., *Chroniques anglo-normandes: recueil d'extraits et d'écrits relatifs à l'histoire de Normandie et d'Angleterre*, 2 (Rouen, 1836), 99–142 · J. Whitaker, *The life of St Neot, the oldest of all the brothers to King Alfred* (1809), 317–38 · *Commentarii de scriptoribus Britannicis, auctore Joanne Lelando*, ed. A. Hall, 1 (1709), 215–16 · Bale, *Cat.*, 1.216–7 · Bale, *Index*, 122–3, 144–5 · J. C. Russell, 'The *Dictionary of National Biography*: William of Ramsey', *BIHR*, 8 (1930–31), 107–9 · A. G. Rigg, *A history of Anglo-Latin literature, 1066–1422* (1992), 177–8 · 'Vita S. Neoti confessoris', *Acta sanctorum: Julius*, 7 (Antwerp, 1731), 319–30 · J. Leclercq, 'Les *Distinciones super Cantica* de Guillaume de Ramsey', *Sacris Erudiri*, 10 (1958), 329–52

Archives Bibliothèque Municipale, Douai, MS 852 · Magd. Oxf., MS lat. 53

Ramsey, William (d. 1349), master mason, belonged to a family which included several master masons active in Norwich and London in the first half of the fourteenth century. He is first documented in 1323 and 1325 working as an ordinary cutting mason at St Stephen's Chapel in Westminster Palace. Between 1326 and 1336 he and his brother John visited the works of the cloister at Norwich Cathedral priory as consultant master masons. On 23 November 1331 William and his wife, Christina, along with others including two other men named Ramsey and a priest, were accused of going to the house of John Spray without Aldersgate for the purpose of abducting Spray's ward Robert Huberd and marrying him to William's daughter Agnes. William and the rest were acquitted of the abduction and the fourteen-year-old Huberd, heir to the considerable property of his father, a minter, chose to stay with Ramsey, who became his guardian in succession to Spray. Within a few months Ramsey had been appointed master mason of the new chapter house and cloister of St Paul's Cathedral, and on 13 July 1332 the city exempted him from sitting on assizes and from jury service in order to enable him to concentrate wholly on that work. Along with the remodelling of the south transept of what is now Gloucester Cathedral (c.1331–7), these destroyed but fairly well recorded buildings were the earliest example of the Perpendicular style of architecture. The influence of the cloister was to be felt in London and south-east England for at least the next half-century, most obviously in the south cloister walk of Westminster Abbey (begun in 1344), which is merely an enlarged copy of the St Paul's design, and most notably in the nave of Canterbury Cathedral (begun after 1381), whose piers are a most ingenious application of the system embodied in the St Paul's vault responds.

Ramsey's position, that of master mason of the most prestigious building then in progress in the city of London, probably accounts for his being appointed in 1335 to a commission to inquire into the state of the Tower of London. The impending war with France was the background to this investigation and to Ramsey's appointment for life on 1 June 1336 as both chief mason in the Tower of London and chief surveyor of the king's works of masonry there and at all the other king's castles south of the River Trent. His most architecturally significant contribution to the Tower was the remodelling in 1336–8 of the great hall (destroyed). From February 1344 he had charge of the masonry work at Windsor Castle, where a 'Round Table' 200 feet in diameter was under construction for Edward III's projected order of chivalry. This work ceased in November of the same year and was subsequently destroyed. By 1337, when Ramsey took charge of the works of St Stephen's Chapel, Westminster, his royal responsibilities were evidently regarded as extending beyond castles to encompass all masonry work south of the Trent. The main opportunity for executing a new design at St Stephen's was the upper storey of the west porch (destroyed after 1834). Although in the Perpendicular style, this structure matched in its exceptional richness the fifty-year-old design of the main chapel to which it led. In the field of decorative architecture it was to exert an influence as powerful and enduring as that which the cloister of St Paul's had exercised on the more monumental genres. As late as the 1450s the London mason Richard Beke incorporated numerous quotations from the St Stephen's porch into the choir screen of Canterbury Cathedral.

Ramsey's royal work coexisted with a private practice which may well have been extensive, like that of other leading royal architects of the late middle ages. Unfortunately, the only documented episode is his appointment on 23 May 1337 to advise on the works of the eastern arm of Lichfield Cathedral. The resulting design of the main vessel of the presbytery took account of the earlier work on the site and did not include the innovatory Perpendicular tracery used at St Paul's. Ramsey may also have been heavily involved in the profitable business of tomb making, but his only documented works of this kind are the marble tomb-chest of Blanche of the Tower (an infant daughter of Edward III) in 1343, and the now-destroyed monumental brass over the grave of Abbot Thomas Henley (d. 1344), both in Westminster Abbey. Stylistic evidence indicates that Ramsey was the designer of the outstandingly splendid canopied tombs of Edward III's younger brother John of Eltham (d. 1336), at Westminster, and Archbishop John Stratford (d. 1348), at Canterbury.

Ramsey died at the height of the black death, within a few days of 29 May 1349. His daughter Agnes, the child of his marriage to Christina, later submitted accounts to the exchequer which showed that over half the fees and robes due to him as king's chief mason had never been paid. This indication that Ramsey was prosperous enough to be able to live and conduct his business without depending on his official pay, is borne out by the size of his contribution—£10—to the £5000 loan made by the city of London to Edward III in 1340. In 1347 he served as a common councillor for Aldersgate Ward.   CHRISTOPHER WILSON

Sources J. Harvey and A. Oswald, *English mediaeval architects: a biographical dictionary down to 1550*, 2nd edn (1984), 242–5 · H. M. Colvin and others, eds., *The history of the king's works*, 6 vols. (1963–82), vol. 1, pp. 174, 177, 182 n, 187, 207; vol. 2 · C. Wilson, 'The origins of the Perpendicular style and its development to c.1360', PhD diss., U. Lond., 1980, 172–258, 349–52 · J. H. Harvey, 'The origin of the Perpendicular style', *Studies in building history*, ed. E. M. Jope [1961], 134–65, esp. 139–41, 150–52 · Westminster Abbey Muniment Room, London, WAM 5467A · E. C. Fernie and A. B. Whittingham, eds., *The early communar and pitancer rolls of Norwich Cathedral priory with an account of the building of the cloister*, Norfolk RS, 41 (1972), 33–8, 104, 115

Rana, Karnabahadur (1898–1973), soldier, was born at Mangalthan Gulmi, Litung, in the Baglung district of Nepal. He was of the Magar people. Nothing is known of his parents and even his exact date of birth is unknown. He was one of the first Gurkha soldiers to win the Victoria Cross, Britain's highest award for valour. He joined the 3rd Queen Alexandra's Own Gurkha rifles of the Indian army during the First World War and was posted as a young rifleman, the lowest rank in the rifle regiments of the Indian army, to the 2nd battalion of his regiment in Palestine, where they were part of 232 infantry brigade in 75 infantry division. On 10 April 1918 the battalion was ordered to carry out an attack on a German position on top of a rocky slope at al-Qefr, Palestine. The ground was broken and scrub-covered, which offered considerable advantage to the defending enemy forces. All movement by the Gurkha troops and their British senior officers was under observation and fire from the German position, making the advance extremely difficult and hazardous. Rana's sub-unit, 'B' company, suffered heavy casualties, including the company commander.

During the attack Rana, together with a few other men, succeeded under intense fire, in creeping forward with a Lewis gun in order to engage an enemy machine gun which had caused severe casualties to officers and other ranks who had attempted to put it out of action. Number 1 of the Lewis gun opened fire, and was shot immediately. Without a moment's hesitation Rana pushed the dead man off the gun, and in spite of bombs thrown at him and heavy fire from both flanks, he opened fire and knocked out the enemy machine-gun crew; then, switching his fire on to the enemy bombers and riflemen in front of him, he silenced their fire. He kept his gun in action and showed the greatest coolness in removing defects which on two occasions prevented the gun from firing. During the remainder of the day he performed further heroic acts, and when a withdrawal was ordered he assisted with covering fire until the enemy was close on him.

Rana displayed throughout a very high standard of valour and devotion to duty, for which he was awarded the Victoria Cross by George V at Buckingham Palace in 1919. According to the citation published in the *London Gazette*, this was 'for most conspicuous bravery, resource in action under adverse conditions, and utter contempt of danger' (21 June 1918).

Very little is known of Rana's later life; his old regiment, 3rd Queen Alexandra's Own Gurkha rifles, transferred to the army of India upon independence in 1947 and no records were kept by the British army of subsequent events. It is, however, known that he died at Litung, Bharse Gulmi, in Nepal on 25 July 1973, aged seventy-four.　　　　　R. A. PETT

Sources *The story of Gurkha VCs*, Gurkha Museum (1993) · J. B. R. Nicholson, *The Gurkha rifles* (1974) · J. Parker, *The Gurkhas: the inside story of the world's most feared soldiers* (1999) · A. Gould, *Imperial warriors: Britain and the Gurkhas* (1999) · *LondG* (21 June 1918)

Ranade, Mahadev Govind (1842–1901), judge and Indian nationalist, was born in Niphad in the Bombay presidency on 18 January 1842, the first of two surviving children of Govindrao Amrita Ranade (*d.* 1877), head clerk in a district office in the Nasik district of the Bombay presidency, and later administrative officer in Kolhapur state, and his first wife, Gopikabai (*d.* 1853). He had two surviving half-brothers from his father's second marriage.

Although an apparently indifferent scholar at the Kolhapur English school (1851–6) he performed brilliantly at the Elphinstone Institution in Bombay (1857) and the Elphinstone College (1858–62) of the new University of Bombay. He graduated BA in 1862 and won a gold medal in history and economics, and became the university's first MA in 1864. He passed his LLB with first-class honours in 1866 and his advocates' examination in 1871. From 1860 to 1863 he had been junior fellow in the college, and senior fellow and assistant professor of history and English from 1868 to 1871. He entered the Bombay government's education department as acting Marathi translator in 1866 while obtaining his advocate's qualifications, and began his judicial career in 1871 as third presidency judge in Bombay. After a variety of positions he became first-class judge in Poona in 1873 until he was transferred under a political cloud to Nasik (1878) and Dhulia (1879). He became additional presidential magistrate in Bombay in 1881, judge of the small cases court in Poona (1884), special judge under the Deccan Ryots' Relief Act (1887), and was judge of the Bombay high court from 1893 until his death in 1901. He served on the Bombay legislative council (1885–6, 1890–91, and 1893–4) and was a member of the finance commission from 1886 to 1887, for which he was created CIE.

Ranade profoundly shaped the intellectual and political discourses of the day. He edited the English columns of a Bombay Anglo-Marathi daily, the *Indu Prakash* (1864–71), and from 1878 guided and wrote much of the *Quarterly Journal of the Poona Sarvajanik Sabha*, a Poona-based association which he was instrumental in founding in 1870. Through a reinterpretation of Maratha history, *Rise of the Maratha Power* (1900), and numerous essays, many initially presented as public addresses, he argued for a social, political, economic, and moral regeneration of the Indian people, achievable through a rethinking of Indian values, much as he saw the protestant Reformation as having transformed Europe. In the contours of his thought he prefigured a Weberian view of the interrelationship between value systems and societal development.

Ranade also fought for change. He participated in a reform movement to permit Hindu widows to remarry, which culminated in a debate in 1870 between reformers and religious conservatives, resulting in the reformers' defeat. His reinterpretation of Hinduism on theist lines was expressed through the Prarthana Samaj ('prayer society'), founded in 1867. Ranade and the Samaj tried to influence Hindu society from within, rather than moving outside it as a marginalized reform sect. He promoted the development of Indian industries and the use of Indian-made goods through his writings and the convening of industrial conferences in the 1890s. He was most influential politically during the 1870s in the Poona Sarvajanik Sabha's campaigns to educate Indian opinion and organize opposition against government measures, such as its land revenue policies and its inept handling of the disastrous Deccan famine crisis of the late 1870s. Suspected by the government of complicity in the rural and political unrest in the late 1870s, he was transferred from Poona to lessen his influence. Of necessity as a judge he worked from behind the scenes. He played a critical role in the founding of the Indian National Congress in 1885 and in guiding its subsequent deliberations, though he did not participate in its public sessions. In 1887 he established the Indian National Social Conference to promote social reform but, since the meetings were held immediately after the Congress and in its tent, the conference also enabled his attendance at Congress sessions. In 1895 conservative Hindus, led by B. G. Tilak, opposed the reformers and broke the link between Congress and conference. The following year Ranade lost control of the Poona Sarvajanik Sabha and formed the Deccan Sabha to maintain his political approach.

Ranade's indirect tactics derived partly from judicial exigencies but may have been equally the product of his physical persona: he was large and ungainly, socially inept and diffident. His stand on social reform had been compromised after the death of his first wife, Sakubai Dandekar, whom he had married in 1854. Within a month of her death in 1873 he bowed to pressure from his father and remarried. His new wife, Ramabai Kurlekar (*d.* 1924), was then eleven years old. His allies on the issue of the remarriage of widows were annoyed that he had not married a widow, and his ability to influence social reform debates was thereby reduced. He taught Ramabai to read and write English, and after his death, from a heart attack, on 16 January 1901 in Bombay, she became an important social reformer and public figure in her own right. There were no children from either marriage. Ranade was cremated and his ashes were spread at the Triveni at Allahabad.

JIM MASSELOS

Sources R. P. Tucker, *Ranade and the roots of Indian nationalism* (1977) · J. Kellock, *Mahadev Govind Ranade: patriot and social servant* (1926) · R. Ranade, *Ranade: his wife's reminiscences* (1963) · J. C. Masselos, *Towards nationalism: group affiliations and the politics of public associations in nineteenth century western India* (1974) · P. J. Jagirdar, *Studies in the social thought of M. G. Ranade* (1963) · D. G. Karve, *Ranade: the prophet of liberated India* (1942) · *Bombay Gazette* (18 Jan 1901), 5
Likenesses Mhatre, statue, Veer Nariman Road, Churchgate, Bombay, India

Ranby, John (1703–1773), surgeon, the son of Joseph Ranby of St Giles-in-the-Fields, London, innkeeper, was apprenticed to Edward Barnard, foreign brother of the Company of Barber–Surgeons, on 5 March 1715, paying him the sum of £32 5s. On 5 October 1722 Ranby's surgical skills were examined. His answers were approved, and he was ordered the seal of the Barber–Surgeons' Company as a foreign brother. He was elected a fellow of the Royal Society on 30 November 1724. He married, in 1729, Jane, the elder daughter of the Hon. Dacre Barrett-Lennard. Queen Caroline, according to Lord Hervey, 'once asked Ranby whilst he was dressing her wound if he would not be glad to be officiating in the same manner to his own old cross wife that he hated so much' (Hervey). Ranby was appointed surgeon-in-ordinary to the king's household in 1738, and in 1740 he was promoted sergeant–surgeon to George II. He became principal sergeant–surgeon in May 1743, and in this capacity accompanied the king during the German campaign of that year. Ranby was present at the battle of Dettingen, where the duke of Cumberland, the king's second son, was one of his patients.

In 1745 Ranby's influence with the king and the government of the day was sufficient to ensure the passing of the act of parliament constituting a Company of Surgeons distinct from that of the barbers. His exertions in promoting this separation were rewarded by his nomination as the first master of the newly founded surgeons' company, a special favour, as he had never held any office in the old and united Company of Barber–Surgeons. Joseph Sandford, the senior warden of the old company, and William Cheselden, the junior warden, took office under him as the first wardens. Ranby presented a silver loving cup to the company to mark his year of office, and it is still in the possession of the Royal College of Surgeons of England. He was re-elected master of the company in 1751, when the company entered into occupation of their new theatre in the Old Bailey, and for a third time in 1752. Ranby was appointed surgeon to the Chelsea Hospital on 13 May 1752 in succession to Cheselden. He became a controversial figure as a result of his role during the last illnesses of Queen Caroline, in 1737, and of Robert Walpole, earl of Orford, in 1745 (see *A Narrative of the Last Illness of the Earl of Orford*, 1745). Ranby had a large surgical practice, and the surgeon introduced by Fielding into his novel *Tom Jones* (1749) is said to be him. He is also mentioned in Fielding's *Journal of a Voyage to Lisbon* (1755). It has also been claimed that Ranby

served as the model for the hero in Hogarth's *Rake's Progress* (*N&Q*, 29). Ranby was a man of strong passions, harsh voice, and inelegant manners. Queen Caroline called him 'the blockhead' before submitting to the operation from which she died.

Ranby's writings include *The Method of Treating Gunshot Wounds* (1744), an account of some of the surgical cases which came under Ranby's care when he served under Lord Stair in the German campaign, terminating at the battle of Dettingen, and 'Three curious dissections by John Ranby, esq., surgeon to his majesty's household and F.R.S. 1728', printed in William Beckett's *Collection of Chirurgical Tracts* (1740).

Ranby died on 28 August 1773, after a few hours' illness, at his apartments in Chelsea Hospital, and was buried in the south-west portion of the burying-ground attached to the hospital, in a square sandstone tomb with a simple inscription.

A natural son of the surgeon, **John Ranby** (1743–1820), pamphleteer, assumed the name of Ranby by royal licence in exchange for that of George Osborne, in 1756. Educated at Eton College, he stated that he knew Richard Watson, afterwards bishop of Llandaff, at Trinity College, Cambridge, where he was admitted on 26 May 1761; however, he did not graduate. Ranby, who was admitted at Lincoln's Inn in 1762, 'huzzaed after Mr. Wilkes' in 1763, but developed into a partisan pamphleteer on the tory side. In 1791 he published *Doubts on the Abolition of the Slave Trade*, which James Boswell (who called Ranby his 'learned and ingenious friend') highly commended. In 1794, in his *Short Hints on a French Invasion*, he deprecated the general tendency to panic. Three years later he supported Bishop Watson in his controversy with Gilbert Wakefield, and in 1811 he attempted to explode the theory of the increasing influence of the crown. In later life he lived first at Woodford in Essex, where he befriended Thomas Maurice, the orientalist, and then at Bury St Edmunds, where he died on 31 March 1820. He was buried at Brent Eleigh in Suffolk, and a monument was placed there commemorating him and his wife, Mary, daughter of Edward Grote and Mary Barnardiston. Mary Ranby died on 3 January 1814.

D'A. POWER, rev. MICHAEL BEVAN

Sources D'A. Power and J. F. South, eds., *Memorials of the craft of surgery in England* (1886) · private information (1896) · *N&Q* (9 July 1928), 29–30 · Z. Cope, *The Royal College of Surgeons of England: a history* (1959) · Venn, *Alum. Cant.* · J. Hervey, *Memoirs of the reign of George the Second*, ed. J. W. Croker, 2 vols. (1848) · *GM*, 1st ser., 43 (1773), 415 · P. J. Wallis and R. V. Wallis, *Eighteenth century medics*, 2nd edn (1988)

Ranby, John (1743–1820). *See under* Ranby, John (1703–1773).

Rance, Patrick Lowry Cole Holwell (1918–1999), cheesemonger and writer on cheese, was born on 18 March 1918 at 65 Boscombe Road, Southend-on-Sea, son of Frederick Ernest Rance, vicar of All Saints' Church, and of his wife, Mary May Cole. They subsequently moved to St Margaret's, Leytonstone, where Patrick's father held an early morning mass for the local milkmen, the family's only known connection with the dairy industry. The youngest of five children, at the age of nine Patrick followed his brothers to Christ's Hospital, at Horsham, Sussex, where the masters obtusely condemned the nascent polymath as 'not university material' (*The Times*). He instead opted for a military career.

After beginning his training at the Royal Military College, Sandhurst, in 1936 Rance was commissioned in the Northhamptonshire regiment in 1938, was seconded when war broke out to the Buffs, as adjutant of a wartime battalion, and was promoted to major at twenty-four. He served at the Anzio landings in 1944. Immediately after the war he was employed in intelligence in Vienna. Touring Europe with friends in the summer of 1948 he met Janet Maxtone Graham (*d.* 1996), the daughter of Jan Struther, author of *Mrs Miniver* (1939), a book (and later Hollywood film) which helped to keep up morale at home and impressed the allies. He resigned his commission in 1949 and worked for two years at Conservative central office, pioneering the new department that did research into public opinion. Janet's domineering father, the golfing laird Anthony Maxtone Graham, insisted that the marriage could not take place in 1951 until the rhododendrons were out at his Perthshire home. The bride's relations were not pleased when, in February 1954, the couple moved from Rance's serviced flat in Mayfair to Jessamine Cottage in Streatley, Oxfordshire, for it was attached to Wells Stores, where he intended to become a shopkeeper. (The shop was named after the Misses Wells who had previously owned it.)

The new owner, Major Patrick Rance, as he was still described, was unforgettable (the name 'rhymes with pants, not France', the monocled and usually smiling Rance would tell new acquaintances). He spoke French, German, Italian, Polish, and Swedish; could win bets by quoting lengthy passages of Shakespeare; and knew a great deal about music, butterflies, and the behaviour of bacteria on milk and cheese. In the 1960s he made an alphabetical inventory of the goods he stocked: Alka Seltzer, Bombay duck, crumpets, dog food, elastic, French butter, greeting cards, hot-water bottles, ice cream, Jersey milk, Kleenex, lychees, mushrooms, nylons … as well as 'over 16 cheeses from different countries' (*The Times*). By 1980 he stocked over 150 cheeses. A visit to Wells Stores became a Saturday-morning institution for people from all over Berkshire and Oxfordshire. Hosts would bring their house guests with them, and if you were known to them, Rance and Janet might invite you to take a glass of wine with them in the cottage, jammed to the rafters with their seven children and ten grandchildren who, at Christmas, competed for space in the corridors with rows of Stilton cheeses awaiting dispatch.

Rance served in the shop himself, wearing his blue-striped apron and monocle either screwed into his right eye or dangling from its black cord, with his pint mug of tepid tea beside him on the counter. His benign, eccentric appearance was a draw, especially to those who had seen him on television or heard his good-natured drawl on the radio. He insisted on customers tasting the 200 cheeses that by the mid-1980s had taken over the shop completely,

and was adamant that you should eat the rind of soft-ripened and washed cheeses such as Camembert. He loved telling the story of Charlemagne discovering Brie in 744 and being reprimanded for removing the rind by the monks at the priory of Reuil-en-Brie. It was Rance's dislike of refrigerating cheese that produced the distinctive smell of the shop. His goods were not behind glass but on open tables, where customers could not only smell them, but touch and prod them to see if they were ripe. This practice would not meet present-day hygiene requirements, but he regarded his cheeses as living organisms that rewarded intimate attention.

The shop never made much money. Prices were low, as Rance felt certain that his customers would not pay London prices. Though the shop had a huge turnover and supplied more than thirty restaurants, the profit in 1990 was a mere £7000. Janet made up the difference needed to bring up the children, by working as a journalist at *Good Housekeeping* and later writing as Janet Graham in *Reader's Digest*. They also had the *Mrs Miniver* royalties after her mother's death in 1953.

In 1982 Rance became a writer as well. He had done a prodigious amount of research for *The Great British Cheese Book*, finding a wealth of artisan cheeses in many areas of the country, noting farmers and small dairies who continued to produce the superior Cheddar, Lancashire, Stilton, and Cheshire cheeses that can only be made from unpasteurized milk, encouraging those who wanted to develop new cow, sheep, or goat's milk cheeses, and supporting dairy farmers who wanted to revive older cheeses. One of his coups was to discover that Dorset blue vinny was not extinct, but continued to be made at a location he kept secret 'between Dorchester and Puddletown' (*The Independent*). He later found someone able to supply it in commercial quantities, and it is now widely available from specialist shops.

Rance was an inspiration to cheesemakers and retailers in conflict with the stupidities of the Milk Marketing Board, the overzealousness of functionaries responsible for enforcing (sometimes ridiculous) hygiene regulations, and the complexity of EC directives. His worst battle concerned pasteurization when, in the mid-1980s, there was a *Listeria monocytogenes* scare because a large number of people died (it was claimed) from eating Vacherin made from unpasteurized milk. In fact the deadly cheeses had been made from pasteurized milk, but the damage had been done. Supermarkets (for whose cheese retailing practices Rance never felt much sympathy) shunned cheeses made from unpasteurized milk, various governmental agencies tried to ban them, and Colston Bassett (the world's last maker of unpasteurized Stilton), went over to pasteurization—so Britain lost its greatest cheese.

None the less, Rance had presided over a part of the sea change in the food culture of the country, acting as a mentor to Randolph Hodgson of Neal's Yard Dairy in London, and encouraging scores of other conscientious cheesemakers and retailers. Rance and Janet moved to a house in Provence, where he undertook the even bigger, six-year project of researching for his *French Cheese* (1989). Their son Hugh took over the Streatley shop in 1990, and expanded with a second one at Abingdon, but the new business rates made it impossible for him to carry on. Janet's death in 1996 devastated Rance, but during the last few days before he died in Brompton Hospital, Fulham Road, Chelsea, of pneumonia and accelerated pulmonary fibrosis on 22 August 1999, he was still solving arcane crossword-puzzle clues for the children and grand-children that crowded around his bed.   PAUL LEVY

Sources personal knowledge (2004) · *The Times* (27 Aug 1999) · *The Independent* (13 Sept 1999) · *The Guardian* (31 Aug 1999) · b. cert. · d. cert. · *CGPLA Eng. & Wales* (1999)
Wealth at death £312,078—gross; £307,161—net: probate, 17 Dec 1999, *CGPLA Eng. & Wales*

Rand, Isaac (1674–1743), botanist, was probably the son of James Rand, who in 1674 agreed, with thirteen other members of the Society of Apothecaries, to build a wall round the Chelsea Physic Garden. Isaac Rand was already an apothecary practising in the Haymarket, London, in 1700, though his apprenticeship formally ended in 1702. In Plukenet's *Mantissa* (1700) he is mentioned as the discoverer, in Tothill Fields, Westminster, of the dock now known as *Rumex palustris*, and described as a diligent investigator and a botanist of great promise. He seems to have had a particular interest in inconspicuous plants, and is credited by fellow botanists such as Doody and Buddle with new discoveries including the goosefoot 'Rand's oak blite' (*Chenopodium glaucum*). He is known to have botanized with James Sherard, and with Petiver, with whom he was not on good terms, being somewhat critical of his work. He was a member of the Botanical Society that met weekly between 1721 and 1726 in a coffee house in Watling Street. Rand had a wife, Ann, about whom nothing more is known.

In 1707 Rand and nineteen other members of the Society of Apothecaries, including Petiver and Joseph Miller, took a lease of the Chelsea garden (owned by the manor of Chelsea) and were made trustees. For some time before Petiver's death in 1718 Rand seems either to have assisted him or to have succeeded him in the office of demonstrator of plants. In 1725 he was appointed to the newly created office of *praefectus horti* or director of the garden. Among other duties he had to give at least two demonstrations in the garden in each of the six summer months, and to transmit each year to the Royal Society the fifty specimens required by the terms of Sir Hans Sloane's new lease of 1722 (in his capacity as lord of the manor of Chelsea). Rand himself delivered the plants on many occasions. Lists of the plants sent for several years are at the Royal Society and in the Sloane MSS (British Library). Rand was in charge when Linnaeus, who was not impressed by his understanding, visited the garden. Dillenius's edition of Ray's *Synopsis* (1724) contains several records by Rand, whose assistance is acknowledged in the preface. William Sherard proposed that Rand's name, rather than that of the foreigner Dillenius, should appear as editor, but Rand declined. He also is mentioned by Elizabeth Blackwell as having instructed her and assisted with specimens for her *Curious Herbal* (1737–9), which she produced at Chelsea. He

is one of those who put their names to a certificate of accuracy, and a copy in the British Library has manuscript notes by him.

By 1727 relations between Rand and Philip Miller, gardener to the Society of Apothecaries, seem to have been strained, and it has been inferred that rivalry was the reason why each produced a catalogue of the garden in 1730. Publication of Rand's *Index plantarum officinalium ... in horto Chelseiano*, a list of 518 plants used in medicine, was ordered by the society, and 1000 copies printed, as was pointed out by Rand in a letter to Samuel Brewer. The two publications may, however, have been intended for different audiences. In 1739 Rand published *Horti medici Chelseiani index compendiarius*, a longer alphabetical list of all the plants in the garden. He was succeeded as demonstrator by Joseph Miller in 1738 or 1740. Rand died in the parish of St James, Westminster, in 1743, some time before 11 May. His widow presented his botanical books and extensive herbarium to the society, and bequeathed 50s. a year for replacing twenty decayed specimens. His books remained at Chelsea. His herbarium was preserved there, with those of Ray and Dale, until 1862, when all three were presented to the British Museum (and thus later were moved to the Natural History Museum, London). Important specimens, particularly British species, were incorporated in the general herbarium, and many of Rand's specimens are in the Sloane herbarium. Rand was elected a fellow of the Royal Society in 1719. Linnaeus retained the name *Randia*, applied by Houston in Rand's honour to a genus of tropical Rubiaceae.

RUTH STUNGO

Sources Desmond, *Botanists*, rev. edn, 572 · H. Field, *Memoirs of the botanic garden at Chelsea belonging to the Society of Apothecaries of London*, rev. R. H. Semple (1878), 41–63 · J. Britten and J. E. Dandy, eds., *The Sloane herbarium* (1958), 188–9 · C. Wall, *A history of the Worshipful Society of Apothecaries of London*, ed. H. C. Cameron and E. A. Underwood (1963), 169–71, 176 · B. Henrey, *British botanical and horticultural literature before 1800*, 2 (1975), 52, 210–11, 230, 231, 235 · H. Trimen and W. T. Thiselton Dyer, *Flora of Middlesex* (1869), 388–9 · Nichols, *Illustrations*, 1.322 · L. Plukenet, *Almagesti botanici mantissa* (1700), 112 · E. Blackwell, *A curious herbal: containing five hundred cuts, of the most useful plants, which are now used in the practice of physick*, 2 vols. (1737–9) · P. I. Edwards, 'The Botanical Society [of London], 1721–26', *Proceedings of the Botanical Society of the British Isles*, 5 (1963), 117 · P. Miller, *The gardener's and botanist's dictionary*, rev. T. Martyn, 2 vols. in 4 (1797–1807), viii · A. L. A. Fée, *Vie de Linné* (1832), 249 · J. Ray, *Synopsis methodica stirpium Britannicarum*, 3rd edn (1724); facs edn with introduction by W. T. Stearn, Ray Society, 148 (1973) · private information (2004) · *N&Q*, 8th ser., 10 (1896), 193 · E. J. L. Scott, *Index to the Sloane manuscripts in the British Museum* (1904), 443 · P. J. Wallis and R. V. Wallis, *Eighteenth century medics*, 2nd edn (1988) · D. H. Kent and D. E. Allen, *British and Irish herbaria*, 2nd edn (1984), 226
Archives BL, Sloane MSS · GL, Society of Apothecaries archives · NHM, herbarium · NHM, Sloane herbarium · RS, classified MSS
Likenesses oils, 1737 (after G. Kneller), Society of Apothecaries, London
Wealth at death see *N&Q*

Rand, Samuel (*bap.* 1588, *d.* 1654), physician, the eldest surviving son of the Revd James Rand (*d.* 1621), vicar of

Norton, co. Durham (1578–1621) and prebend of Durham Cathedral (1606–20), and his wife, Margery, daughter of the Revd Edward Banckes, rector of Long Newton, co. Durham, was baptized at Norton on 18 August 1588. His early schooling was probably in Stockton. He matriculated as a pensioner at Christ's College, Cambridge, his father's college, at Easter 1606, and became BA in 1610, and MA in 1613. He may also have studied at St Andrew's in 1612; his cousin, Ralph Rand, took an MA at St Andrew's in that same year. Samuel Rand was admitted on the medical line at Leiden on 2 September 1616, but he took his MD from Groningen in the following year, on 18 August 1617. He dedicated his thesis on vertigo to his uncle, the Revd Ralph Rand, rector and 'minister of the word of God' at Oxted, Surrey. There is no record that Rand ever incorporated his foreign degree at either Oxford or Cambridge.

Rand did not begin to practise medicine in London until 1624. It is likely that prior to that date he practised near his family's home district in the north-east of England. On 3 February 1626 Rand was reprimanded for abusing his College of Physicians licence to practise outside London, by doing so within the City. By 6 July 1626 he had somehow satisfied the requirement of incorporation and was elected a candidate; he became a fellow on 22 December 1630.

While practising as a prominent London physician, Rand also became an investor in the colonization of the British West Indies and in particular in the plantation of the island of Tortuga, which was organized by a relative, Anthony Hilton, a shipmaster from Durham. On the death of Hilton in 1635, Rand purchased his estate for Hilton's widow, in order to keep it out of the hands of her late husband's creditors. On 8 August 1631 he consulted with John Clarke of the College of Physicians during the terminal illness of William Nethersole. Rand and Clarke were both products of the intensely puritan Christ's College, Cambridge, and their relationship may well have gone back to their Cambridge days. They were also both signatories to a college petition in 1632 to Charles I, which implored the king to curb the improper medical activities of London apothecaries who prescribed without the direction of a physician. In 1633 Rand purchased a pedigree from the College of Arms on its visitation of London. In September 1635, along with Dr Othowell Meverell and Dr William Clement of the College of Physicians, he attended the mother of John Evelyn in her final illness.

Rand is listed in the annals of the Royal College of Physicians as practising in Newcastle by 13 January 1637. The ostensible reason for his departure was to take up the position as town physician to Newcastle upon Tyne. He held this post until 21 April 1643, when he was removed by royalist sympathizers. However, in September 1644 parliament appointed him master of Greatham Hospital, Durham. A strong puritan as well as a parliamentarian, Rand was elected an elder in the Presbyterian classis at Stockton, co. Durham, in December 1645. In 1647 he was elected by town authorities at Newcastle as one of four elders to assist the Presbyterian minister, Richard Prideaux, at All Saints' parish, in the city. He was restored as town physician to Newcastle in 1652. Rand died in 1654 and was buried at Gateshead, co. Durham, on 8 March.

WILLIAM BIRKEN

Sources assessment, CLRO, Box 31, MS 4, fols. 1–2 • Munk, *Roll* • R. Surtees, *The history and antiquities of the county palatine of Durham*, 3 (1823), 417 • Evelyn, *Diary* • C. Webster, 'English medical reformers of the puritan revolution: a background to the "Society of Chymical Physitians"', *Ambix*, 14 (1967), 16–41 • C. Webster, *The great instauration: science, medicine and reform, 1626–1660* (1975) • will, PRO, PROB 11/235, sig. 122 • *CSP dom., 1631–3* • R. Howell, *Newcastle upon Tyne and the puritan revolution: a study of the civil war in north England* (1967) • A. P. Newton, *The colonising activities of the English puritans* (1914) • annals, RCP Lond. • J. Peile, *Biographical register of Christ's College, 1505–1905, and of the earlier foundation, God's House, 1448–1505*, ed. [J. A. Venn], 1 (1910) • Venn, *Alum. Cant.* • R. W. Innes Smith, *English-speaking students of medicine at the University of Leyden* (1932) • *The visitation of London, anno Domini 1633, 1634, and 1635, made by Sir Henry St George*, 2, ed. J. J. Howard, Harleian Society, 17 (1883)
Wealth at death moderate estate: will, PRO, PROB 11/235, sig. 122

Randall, John (1570–1622), Church of England clergyman, was born in 1570 at Great Missenden, Buckinghamshire, and sent 'by his relations' (Wood, *Ath. Oxon.*, 2.319) to St Mary Hall, Oxford, matriculating aged eleven on 27 November 1581. Following a move to Trinity College, Randall graduated BA on 9 February 1585, was elected a fellow of Lincoln College on 6 July 1587, and proceeded MA on 9 July 1589. Among his pupils at Lincoln in the early 1590s was the impoverished future puritan Robert Bolton (1572–1631), to whom he lent many books. Tutor Randall was 'of no great note then, but afterward became a learned divine and godly preacher at London' (Bagshawe, 6–7). When Queen Elizabeth visited Oxford in August 1592 Randall was appointed to 'frame and oversee the stage for the academical performance given' in her honour (*DNB*). Afterwards Randall studied divinity, and was admitted BD on 28 June 1598.

On 31 January 1599 Randall was presented by Gilbert Talbot, seventh earl of Shrewsbury (1553–1617), to the rectory of St Andrew Hubbard, London; he applied for his preaching licence on 14 May. There he made a reputation as a staunch puritan and effective preacher; he married a wife and had a daughter, but outlived both. When he began to draw up his will on 11 January 1622, he had been afflicted by a serious illness. Randall bequeathed property to the poor of the parishes of Great Missenden, All Hallows, Oxford, and St Andrew; a tenement called Ship Hall to Lincoln College, Oxford; and property in Southwark and Oxford, as well as money, to various relations including eight married sisters. His brother Edward Randall and nephew Joshua Randall were named executors. The will was signed on 13 April and Randall died at his house in the Minories in May, probably at the end of the month since he was buried in St Andrew Hubbard in June. In the same year William Holbrooke, who seems to have been his curate from about 1613, published his mentor's *The Description of Fleshly Lusts*, *The Necessitie of Righteousnes*, and *The Great Mystery of Godliness*. The dedications, to Mary, Lady Weld, Lady Bennet, and Mistress Thomasin Owefield, reveal the godly circles of which Randall was a respected member.

Further works followed: *St Pauls Triumph* (1623) (Sermons on Romans 8: 38–9); *Three and Twenty Sermons, or, Catechisticall Lectures upon … the Lords Supper* (1630), dedicated to Lady Boys, another friend; and *Twenty-Nine Lectures of the Church* (1631), dedicated to Richard Knightley of Preston Capes.   STEPHEN WRIGHT

Sources Wood, *Ath. Oxon.*, new edn, 2.319 • Foster, *Alum. Oxon.* • will, PRO, PROB 11/139, sig. 57 • G. Hennessy, *Novum repertorium ecclesiasticum parochiale Londinense, or, London diocesan clergy succession from the earliest time to the year 1898* (1898) • E. B. [E. Bagshaw], 'The life and death of the author', *Mr Bolton's last and learned worke of the four last things*, ed. E. B. [E. Bagshawe] (1632) • *DNB*
Likenesses portrait, Lincoln College, Oxford
Wealth at death see will, PRO, PROB 11/139, sig. 57

Randall, John (1717–1799), organist and composer, born on 26 February 1717, was a chorister of the Chapel Royal under Bernard Gates. On 23 February 1732 at the Crown and Anchor tavern in the Strand Randall sang the part of Esther in the dramatic representation of Handel's oratorio. At Christmas 1742 he was appointed organist to King's College chapel, Cambridge. There he graduated MusB in 1744 and in 1755 he succeeded Maurice Greene as professor of music in the University of Cambridge. In 1756 he proceeded MusD. He was also organist at Trinity College, St John's College, and Pembroke College. Assisted by his pupil, William Crotch, from 1786 to 1788, Randall retained his appointments until his death at Cambridge on 18 March 1799. His wife, Grace Pattison, whom he married on 5 October 1756, predeceased him on 27 April 1792.

Randall set to music Thomas Gray's 'Ode for the Installation of the Duke of Grafton as Chancellor of the University' (1 July 1769). He published *A collection of psalm & hymn tunes, some of which are new & others by permission of the authors, with six chants and Te Deums, calculated for the use of congregations in general* (1794). Of these Randall is best known by his two double chants and the hymn tune 'University'. Four published songs and three anthems in manuscripts in Cambridge complete his known compositions.

L. M. MIDDLETON, *rev.* ROBERT J. BRUCE

Sources Highfill, Burnim & Langhans, *BDA*, 12.254–5 • C. Hogwood, 'Randall, John', *New Grove* • H. W. Shaw, *The succession of organists of the Chapel Royal and the cathedrals of England and Wales from c.1538* (1991) • O. E. Deutsch, *Handel: a documentary biography* (1955) • Brown & Stratton, *Brit. mus.* • Burney, *Hist. mus.*, 4.360 • *GM*, 1st ser., 62 (1792), 480
Likenesses R. Clamp, stipple, pubd 1794 (after S. Harding), BM [*see illus.*]

Randall, John (1755–1802), shipbuilder, was the son of John Randall, shipbuilder, of Rotherhithe. He received a classical education. On the death of his father, about 1776, he successfully continued the shipbuilding business, applying himself at the same time to the study of mathematics and the principles of naval construction. In the course of his career, as well as building a large number of ships for the mercantile marine and the East India Company, he built over forty for the government, including several 74-gun ships and large frigates. He took a prominent part in founding the Society of Naval Architects, and collected materials for a treatise on naval architecture, which he abandoned on the publication of some French works.

Randall died at his house in Great Cumberland Street, Hyde Park, London, in 1802. His death occurred towards the end of a strike by shipwrights, who worked along the Thames, against a reduction of their wages from a war to a peace rate. It was alleged that he died from a fever resulting from a slight wound incurred in his attempt to quell a riot. However, the charge of wounding him was denied by a spokesman for the shipwrights, who claimed he was highly respected by his employees as more of a parent than a master. Randall was survived by his wife and children.   J. K. LAUGHTON, *rev.* ROGER MORRISS

Sources *GM*, 1st ser., 72 (1802), 79–80 • 'Memoirs of the late John Randall', *European Magazine and London Review*, 42 (1802), 193–6 • J. Gast, *Calumny defeated, or, A compleat vindication of the conduct of the working shipwrights during the late disputes with their employers* (1802) • P. Banbury, *Shipbuilders of the Thames and Medway* (1971), 133–5

Randall, Sir John Turton (1905–1984), physicist and biophysicist, was born on 23 March 1905 at Newton-le-Willows, Lancashire, the only son and the first of the three children of Sidney Randall, nurseryman and seedsman, and his wife, Hannah Cawley, daughter of John Turton, colliery manager in the area. He was educated at the grammar school at Ashton in Makerfield and at the University of Manchester, where he was awarded a first-class honours degree in physics and a graduate prize in 1925, and an MSc in 1926. He married Doris, daughter of Josiah John Duckworth, a colliery surveyor, in 1928. They had one son.

From 1926 to 1937 Randall was employed on research by

John Randall (1717–1799), by R. Clamp, pubd 1794 (after Sylvester Harding)

the General Electric Company at its Wembley laboratories, where he took a leading part in developing luminescent powders for use in discharge lamps. He also took an active interest in the mechanisms of such luminescence. By 1937 he was recognized as the leading British worker in the field, and was awarded a Royal Society fellowship to Birmingham University, where he worked on the electron trap theory of phosphorescence. When war began in 1939 Randall transferred to the large group working on centimetre radar. By 1940 he had, with H. A. H. Boot, invented the cavity magnetron, which gave a higher output of centimetre wave power and overcame the greatest obstacle in the development of radar. The magnetron was probably one of the most significant scientific advances of the war.

In 1944 Randall was appointed professor of natural philosophy at St Andrews University and began planning research in biophysics. In 1946 he moved to the Wheatstone chair of physics at King's College, London, where the Medical Research Council set up the Biophysics Research Unit with Randall as honorary director. A wide-ranging programme of research was begun by physicists, biochemists, and biologists. The use of new types of light microscopes led to the important proposal in 1954 of the sliding filament mechanism for muscle contraction. At the same time X-ray diffraction studies aided the development of the double helix model of DNA by Francis Crick and J. D. Watson in 1953 at Cambridge. Randall was also successful in integrating the teaching of biosciences at King's College.

In 1951 he set up a large multidisciplinary group working under his personal direction to study the structure and growth of the connective tissue protein collagen. Their contribution helped to elucidate the three-chain structure of the collagen molecule. Randall himself specialized in using the electron microscope, first studying the fine structure of spermatozoa and then concentrating on collagen. In 1958 he began to study the structure of protozoa. He set up a new group to use the cilia of protozoa as a model system for the analysis of morphogenesis by correlating the structural and biochemical differences in mutants. In 1970 he retired to Edinburgh University, where he formed a group which applied a range of new biophysical methods to study various biological problems. He continued that work with characteristic vigour until his death.

In science Randall was not only original but even maverick. He made extremely important contributions to biological science when he set up, at the right time, a large multidisciplinary biophysical laboratory where his staff were able to achieve much success. His contributions as an individual worker in biophysics were possibly not so outstanding as those in physics. In science and elsewhere he showed good judgement. He had unusual capacity to see the essentials of a situation and had outstanding skill in obtaining funds and buildings for research. He was ambitious and liked power, but his ambition worked very largely for the common good. The informal and democratic side of his character contrasted strongly with his self-assertion. He showed great dedication and enthusiasm in his scientific work, just as he did in the extensive gardening he much enjoyed.

In 1938 Randall was awarded a DSc by the University of Manchester. In 1943 he was awarded (with H. A. H. Boot) the Thomas Gray memorial prize of the Royal Society of Arts for the invention of the cavity magnetron. In 1945 he became Duddell medallist of the Physical Society of London and shared a payment from the Royal Commission on Awards to Inventors for the magnetron invention, and in 1946 he was made a fellow of the Royal Society and became its Hughes medallist. Further awards (with Boot) for the magnetron work were, in 1958, the John Price Wetherill medal of the Franklin Institute of the state of Pennsylvania and, in 1959, the John Scott award of the city of Philadelphia. In 1962 he was knighted, and in 1972 he became a fellow of the Royal Society of Edinburgh. Randall died on 16 June 1984 at Edinburgh. He was survived by his wife. M. H. F. WILKINS, *rev.*

Sources M. H. F. Wilkins, *Memoirs FRS*, 33 (1987), 491–535 · personal knowledge (1990) · *The Times* (20 June 1984)
Archives CAC Cam., papers · Inst. EE, papers relating to development of cavity magnetron · King's Lond., papers · Medical Research Council, London, papers relating to biophysics research unit | CAC Cam., corresp. with A. V. Hill
Wealth at death £152,142.87: confirmation, 31 July 1984, NA Scot., SC 70/1/3925/77–112

Randall, Joseph (*d.* 1789), schoolmaster and agriculturist, is of unknown origins. In 1740 he started a boarding-school for boys at Heath, near Wakefield, which he described in detail in *An Account of the Academy at Heath* (1750). His school could accommodate 130 boarders, with a further 30 or 40 pupils boarded out in the village. The staff of ten masters and assistants taught an extensive range of subjects that included English, Latin, and history, mathematics, geography, astronomy, and natural and experimental philosophy. Randall's particular interests are demonstrated in the textbooks that he published for his pupils, the first of which, *A System of Geography* (1744), contained a brief history of the Quakers in North America, which was published separately in several editions. In 1750 he published a course of lectures on geography, astronomy, chronology, and pneumatics, and he clearly taught the practical as well as theoretical aspects of these subjects, for the school possessed apparatus for scientific experiments, including an orrery.

By June 1763 Randall had given up the school and moved to York, where he advertised places for six private boarders for a basic fee of 15 guineas a year. Here he also professed to resolve all questions relating to annuities, leases, reversions, livings, and matters of intricate accounts, and he interested himself in practical agriculture. His main interest was in the system of seed-drill husbandry devised by Jethro Tull and the associated need to prepare a good, well-drained seedbed. He designed four implements for this work: a drill (seed-furrow plough), a spiky roller to pulverize the soil, a potato planter, and a draining plough. They were not especially original (Randall cited William Ellis as the inspiration for his spiky roller) and they were criticized as complicated and poorly constructed. From the brief published descriptions they do not seem to have been very effective. Randall's influence, rather, lay in his contribution to disseminating knowledge about the new drill husbandry. He did this principally in two publications, published in 1764. The first was dedicated to the Society of Arts and entitled *The semi-Virgilian husbandry, deduced from various experiments, or, An essay towards a new course of national farming*; the second was *Construction and extensive use of a new invented seed-furrow plough, of a draining plough, and of a potato-drill machine, with a theory of a common plough*. Though verbose and diffuse these works did play their part in spreading the news of drill husbandry. Randall also claimed: 'I do, and will continue to instruct young gentlemen … in the mechanical and geometrical principles of all the implements of husbandry' (*Museum Rusticum*, 440–41). Here, again, was his contribution to the spread of new ideas. Randall died at York on 8 August 1789, 'aged upwards of 80' (*GM*, 59/2).

M. G. WATKINS, rev. JONATHAN BROWN

Sources G. E. Fussell, *More old English farming books* (1950) • *Museum Rusticum*, 6 (1766), 371–6, 438–41 • *GM*, 1st ser., 34 (1764), 460, 515–16, 532 • *GM*, 1st ser., 59 (1789), 768 • J. Donaldson, *Agricultural biography* (1854) • G. E. Fussell, *The farmer's tools* (1952) • G. E. Fussell, *Jethro Tull: his influence on mechanised agriculture* (1973) • J. Randall, *An account of the academy at Heath, near Wakefield, Yorkshire* (1750)

Randall, Richard William (1824–1906), dean of Chichester, born at Bloomsbury Square, London, on 13 April 1824, was the eldest son of James Randall (1789/90–1882), archdeacon of Berkshire, and his wife, Rebe, only daughter of Richard Lowndes of Rose Hill, Dorking. A younger brother, James Leslie, was appointed suffragan bishop of Reading in 1889. Randall was educated at Winchester College from 1836 to 1842, and then at Christ Church, Oxford. He graduated BA in 1846, with an honorary fourth class in classics, and proceeded MA in 1849 and DD in 1892. In 1847 he was ordained curate to his father, the rector of Binfield, Berkshire. On 6 November 1849 Randall married Wilhelmina, daughter of George Augustus Bruxner, originally a merchant of St Petersburg, who had settled in the Manor House at Binfield. They had three sons and three daughters.

In 1851 Randall was nominated to the rectory of Lavington-cum-Graffham, Sussex, in succession to Archdeacon Manning who had just seceded to Rome. Manning had already become his model and was influential in his adoption of Tractarian practices. At Lavington, Randall's innovations in high-church doctrine and ritual excited some opposition in 1858 and 1859, led by his own curate and taken up by the evangelical press.

In 1868 Randall was presented by the trustees to the new parish church of All Saints, Clifton, designed by G. E. Street and intended as a centre of Tractarian worship and teaching in Bristol. Daily services as well as daily celebrations of the holy communion were instituted, and lectures, Bible classes, guilds, and confraternities were organized in the parish. Randall showed himself a capable administrator, and raised large sums in support of church work. He gained a wide reputation as a preacher, was

chosen by Bishop Samuel Wilberforce as preacher of Lenten sermons at Oxford, and became a well-known director of retreats. His few published works, mainly devotional, originated in this Clifton period. Randall was always a ritualist and a supporter of the English Church Union, and in 1873, owing to complaints as to certain practices at All Saints, Charles John Ellicott, bishop of Gloucester, refused to license curates to the church; however, he declined to allow proceedings to be taken against Randall under the Public Worship Regulation Act. In 1889 the bishop resumed confirmations in the church, and in 1891 bestowed on Randall an honorary canonry in the cathedral, where he occupied the stall formerly held by his father.

In February 1892 Randall was appointed dean of Chichester by Lord Salisbury. Here he introduced a daily celebration of holy communion, and undertook restoration work at his own expense. Despite suspicion and hostility he effectively began the long high-church tradition at Chichester Cathedral. Owing to ill health he retired in 1902, and settled for a time in London, before moving to Bournemouth. He died at his home, Pelham, Lindsay Road, Bournemouth, on 23 December 1906, and was buried nearby at Branksome.

G. S. WOODS, rev. GEORGE HERRING

Sources J. F. Briscoe and H. F. B. Mackay, *A Tractarian at work: a memoir of Dean Randall* (1932) • *The Times* (24 Dec 1906) • *The Guardian* (27 Dec 1906) • *Church Times* (27 Dec 1906) • Foster, *Alum. Oxon.*
Archives Pusey Oxf., corresp., diaries, and papers | W. Sussex RO, letters to duke of Richmond
Likenesses Captain Bates, photograph (after engraving by W. Henderson; after painting by H. Herkomer), repro. in Briscoe and Mackay, *Tractarian at work*, frontispiece • photograph, repro. in Briscoe and Mackay, *Tractarian at work*, 110 • wood-engraving, NPG; repro. in *ILN* (13 Feb 1892)
Wealth at death £27,678 13s. 9d.: probate, 1 Feb 1907, CGPLA Eng. & Wales

Randall, Thomas (1711–1780). *See under* Davidson, Thomas Randall (1747–1827).

Randall, William (*fl.* 1585–1604), musician and composer, was born of unknown parents and began his career at Exeter Cathedral, where he was certainly a vicar-choral and possibly previously a chorister. By 15 February 1585, however, he had left Devon for London, for on this date he was sworn epistoler at the Chapel Royal. He is next recorded as a lay clerk at St George's Chapel, Windsor, in 1586–7 and 1600–01, but had left by 1602–3. In the meantime Randall continued his association with the Chapel Royal: on 26 July 1592 he was referred to as an organist, and between June of that year and April 1598 he witnessed numerous entries in the cheque book.

At some time before January 1601 Randall tried to secure readmission to his Exeter vicar's stall, of which he claimed to have been unjustly dispossessed by the dean and chapter, for on the 23rd of that month Queen Elizabeth wrote on his behalf, accusing the canons of penalizing him for his service at court and insisting he be reinstated forthwith. But the Exeter canons, in their reply dated 28 March, firmly denied any unfairness and pointed out that Randall, who had clearly resigned his place, had not in fact been 'sent for' to serve the chapel, 'but made great sute & frindes to obtayne the place' (Payne). Despite an entry in the Exeter accounts dated 16 October of the same year, showing that the vicars-choral paid Randall 33s. 4d., however, there is no evidence that he was ever reinstated.

Randall's few surviving compositions comprise a good consort In nomine for five viols, three very accomplished keyboard pieces, and the music for three anthems, two of which are fragmentary. (A service setting sometimes attributed to him is actually by Greenwood Randall, another Exeter musician and possibly a relative.)

Having attended both the funeral of Elizabeth I and the coronation of James I in April and July 1603 respectively, Randall had either died or resigned by 1 March of the following year, when he was succeeded by another émigré Exonian, Edmund Hooper.   IAN PAYNE

Sources I. Payne, *The provision and practice of sacred music at Cambridge colleges and selected cathedrals, c.1547–c.1646* (1993), 290 • H. W. Shaw, *The succession of organists of the Chapel Royal and the cathedrals of England and Wales from c.1538* (1991), 4–5 • A. Ashbee and D. Lasocki, eds., *A biographical dictionary of English court musicians, 1485–1714*, 2 (1998), 945–6 • *New Grove*, 15.581 • *DNB*

Randegger, Alberto (1832–1911), music teacher and composer, was born in Trieste on 13 April 1832. His father was a German schoolmaster and his mother, an amateur musician, was Tuscan. At the age of thirteen he was taught by Tivoli, of Trieste Cathedral, and then studied piano with Lafont and composition with Luigi Ricci. In 1850 he made the acquaintance of Verdi, who visited Trieste for the production of his opera *Stiffelio* (which was to become *Aroldo*), first performed on 16 November 1850. In 1852–4 he conducted at several theatres in Italy and Dalmatia, composed ballets and church music, and collaborated with other pupils of Ricci in the opera buffa *Il lazzarone* (Trieste, 1852). His tragic opera *Bianca Capello* was produced at Brescia in 1854, and its success brought him an offer to conduct it in America, but he was prevented from doing this by a cholera outbreak in New York. Later that year he stayed in Paris for a month and then, at the invitation of his eldest brother, visited London. He decided to stay, and established himself as a singing teacher, conductor, and composer.

Randegger had never heard an oratorio, and is said to have been daunted by the huge number of performers at a performance at Exeter Hall of Handel's *Messiah*, and the strangeness of the style soon sent him to sleep. But on the advice of Sir Michael Costa he persevered, mastered the English language, and in 1855 published his first composition set to English words, a song entitled 'The Meadow Gate'. He took further lessons in composition in London from Bernhard Molique, and in 1857 conducted an opera season at St James's Theatre. From 1854 to 1870 he was organist at St Paul's, Regent's Park, and on the death of Prince Albert he composed an anthem performed there.

Randegger was most successful as a teacher of singing, and in 1868 was appointed professor of singing at the

Royal Academy of Music. It has been said that his compositions were distinguished by practical qualities, were always tasteful and externally effective, but had no deep originality, and soon fell into disuse. The most notable are the comic opera *The Rival Beauties* (Leeds, 2 May 1864), dedicated to Costa, and a dramatic cantata *Fridolin* (Birmingham festival, 28 August 1873). The trio *I naviganti* (1862) was also popular. For Novello's series of primers he contributed *Singing* (1893), which had an exceptionally wide circulation. He worked at the Carl Rosa Theatre (1879–85) and also at Covent Garden and Drury Lane (1887–98), conducting Italian opera for Sir Augustus Harris as well as many choral concerts. He also conducted the Queen's Hall Choral Society and the first two seasons of symphony concerts at Queen's Hall (1895–7), and he introduced many important novelties, mainly English, at the Norwich festival, which he conducted from 1881 to 1905 (taking over from Benedict). In addition he appeared at the Wolverhampton festival from 1868. He attended the Beethoven centenary festival in Bonn in 1870. He edited numerous collections of classical airs, including works by Handel and Mendelssohn, collaborated with T. J. H. Marzials on the libretto for Goring Thomas's *Esmeralda* (1883), actively promoted Wagner's early operas, and was admired for his interpretations of Verdi's works. Besides his extensive practice at the Royal Academy of Music he also became in 1896 a teacher at the Royal College, sharing in the management of both institutions. He was much in request as an adjudicator in competitions, including various eisteddfods, and was an honorary member of the Philharmonic Society of Madrid. In 1892 the king of Italy made him a cavaliere. In 1897 he married Louise Nancy Baldwin of Boston, USA.

To the end of his life Randegger remained an indefatigable worker, and he attended the performance of new works with a score which he marked with all details of the performance. He was still actively engaged, and a familiar figure at London musical functions, in 1911, when, after a short illness, he died at his residence, 5 Nottingham Place, Marylebone, London, on 18 December; his wife survived him. He was described as a very kind man, and his memorial service, held at St Pancras Church by Canon Sheppard of the Chapel Royal on 21 December, was attended by many prominent musicians. He was cremated at Golders Green crematorium.

HENRY DAVEY, rev. DAVID J. GOLBY

Sources *MT*, 53 (1912), 17 • *MT*, 40 (1899), 653–8 • J. Warrack, 'Randegger, Alberto', *New Grove* • *Musical Herald* (Jan 1912) • *Musical News* (23 Dec 1911) • *Musical Standard* (23 Dec 1911)
Likenesses P. Naumann, woodcut (after photograph), BM • photograph, repro. in *MT*, 40, 653 • photograph, repro. in *MT*, 53, 17
Wealth at death £34,931 12s. 6d.: resworn probate, 4 Jan 1912, *CGPLA Eng. & Wales*

Randle, Frank [*real name* Arthur Hughes; *known as* Arthur McEvoy] (1901–1957), music-hall comedian and film actor, was born in 50 Wigan Road, Aspull, Wigan, Lancashire, on 30 January 1901, the illegitimate son of Rhoda Hughes, a domestic servant; his father is unrecorded. He was baptized Arthur Hughes, but was raised by Annie Heath and her family and was known at that time as Arthur Heath. He was educated at St George's School, Wigan, which he left at thirteen to enter the cotton mills. However, he rapidly left the mills and travelled to Blackpool to rejoin his natural mother, by now married to a former soldier, Dick McEvoy; Arthur took his name, becoming known as Arthur McEvoy. After short spells as waiter, bottle washer, and tram conductor, he took to the stage, joining an acrobatic troupe at fifteen and renaming himself Arthur Twist. Later he joined another acrobatic act, the Bouncing Randles, and settled on the name he was to employ for the rest of his career, Frank Randle.

Leaving the Bouncing Randles, Randle began in 1928 to tour the music-halls as a character comedian. He became a fixture on the northern circuits and in due course created his own show, *Randle's Scandals*, in which he toured for the rest of his life with a regular company including comic stooges Gus Aubrey and Ernie Dale. He interspersed these tours with appearances in pantomime and regular summer seasons at Blackpool. In addition to this he made ten films, eight of them for the Manchester-based film company Mancunian, run by John E. Blakeley, in which Randle himself invested.

Randle was a great regional success in the north of England, though never nationally. He was not taken up by a national film company as were Gracie Fields and George Formby because he was too disreputable and subversive. Gracie, the big-sister figure, and George, the overgrown urchin, were lovable, safe, and essentially respectable: Randle embodied the 'rough' working-class ethic of instant gratification, especially in sex and drink, insubordination, and violence. This is indicated by his catchphrases—which included 'I'll fight anyone', 'I'll spifflicate the lot of you', 'Bah, I've supped some ale toneet', and 'I bet you're a hot'un'—and was embodied in his gallery of characters who included the Vulgar Boatman, Private Sans Grey Matter, the Hiker, and, perhaps most popular, Grandpa, a scrofulous old man frothing with ale and senile lust, toothless, lecherous, and combative. The essence of Randle's act was to defy all the established canons of propriety and decorum and this brought him into regular conflict with the authorities. He fought a running battle with Harry Barnes, the Blackpool police chief, in the 1940s and 1950s and was regularly censured, censored, and banned from the stage for the use of bad language and suggestive material. He was known to take out his false teeth and throw them into the audience, and after being banned for one such misdemeanour he bombarded Blackpool with toilet-rolls from an aeroplane.

Randle became a film star during the Second World War. Having failed the medical to join the RAF he had to settle for a spell in the Home Guard, but he embarked on a film career which saw him overtaking his fellow Wigan-born comic George Formby in popularity in Lancashire cinemas. His films preserve an archive of his persona and routines; they consist of a succession of sketches, many of them improvised before camera, highlighting various aspects of his anarchic personality. He is totally disrespectful, showing contempt for authority, giving two-fingered salutes to officers, and being generally bloody-minded, scrimshanking, and obstructive. In his earliest films, *Somewhere in England* (1940), *Somewhere in Camp* (1942), and *Somewhere on Leave* (1942), which put him in a service context, he can be found disrupting pay parades, medical parades, and drills, and permanently baiting and defying a long-suffering sergeant-major. He returned to a service setting for his final film, *It's a Grand Life* (1953). The appeal lay in the fact that for some he was a comic anti-hero, a celebration of the rough working class, and for others a safety valve, mocking authority at a time of restriction and regulation.

The comedy is physical, destructive, sometimes surreal, often funny, and expertly choreographed. Randle's films regularly included scenes of him wrecking rooms, trying to get upstairs while drunk, taking a bath fully clothed, and amorously pursuing pretty girls, his rubber-limbed contortions reflecting his earlier acrobatic experience. Much of the character and activity reflected the real Randle, who was given to punishing drinking bouts, outbursts of violence, wrecking dressing rooms and, once, setting fire to a hotel whose service had displeased him. In 1952 he was convicted of drunken driving after his car hit a stationary tram.

In the 1950s, as variety was overtaken by television and music-halls closed, Randle was beset by financial problems of debts and tax arrears, and health problems (the onset of tuberculosis and cirrhosis of the liver). He was made bankrupt by the Inland Revenue in 1955 but continued to work almost to the end. He died in Blackpool of gastroenteritis on 7 July 1957, and was buried in Carlton cemetery, Blackpool. He was survived by his wife, May Annie Victoria, known as Queenie, whom he had married in 1924; there were no children of the marriage. There was, however, allegedly an illegitimate son, Arthur Delaney, whose mother was a fellow stage performer, Genevieve Willis (also known as Delaney); Queenie denied the paternity. Arthur Delaney became a well-known painter of Manchester street scenes and died in 1987 aged fifty-nine.   JEFFREY RICHARDS

Sources J. Nuttall, *King Twist* (1978) • J. Fisher, *Funny way to be a hero* (1973) • B. Band, *Blackpool's comedy greats* (1995) • J. Richards, *Stars in our eyes* (1994) • J. Montgomery, *Comedy films* (1954) • G. J. Mellor, *They made us laugh* (1982) • b. cert. • *CGPLA Eng. & Wales* (1957)
Archives FILM BFI NFTVA, performance footage
Wealth at death £3799 0s. 3d.: administration, 29 Oct 1957, *CGPLA Eng. & Wales*

Randles, Marshall (1826–1904), Wesleyan Methodist minister, was born at Over Darwen, Lancashire, on 7 April 1826, the son of John Randles of Derbyshire and his wife, Mary Maguire. He was educated at a private school, and after engaging in business at Haslingden he was accepted as a candidate for the Wesleyan Methodist ministry in 1850; he studied at Didsbury College, Manchester. He commenced his ministry in 1853, and was stationed successively at Montrose, Clitheroe, Boston, Nottingham, Lincoln, Halifax, Cheetham Hill, Altrincham, Bolton, and

Leeds. In August 1856 he married Sarah Dewhurst, second daughter of John Scurrah of Padiham; their son, Sir John Scurrah Randles, was Conservative MP for North-West Manchester.

In 1882 Randles was elected a member of the legal conference, and in 1886 succeeded William Burt Pope as tutor in systematic theology at Didsbury. For many years he was chairman of the Manchester district, and in 1896 was elected president of the conference. In 1891 he received the degree of DD from the Wesleyan Theological College, Montreal. He retired in 1902 from the active ministry, and died at his home, 16 Brownsville Road, in Heaton Chapel, Lancashire, on 4 July 1904; he was buried in Cheetham Hill Wesleyan churchyard in the same county.

A strong advocate of total abstinence, Randles first dealt with the question in *Britain's Bane and Antidote* (1864). But his pen was mainly devoted to theology on conservative lines: 'the deposit of evangelical truth was sacred to him, in its form and expression, as well as its substance' (*Minutes*, 155). In his best-known work, *For Ever, an Essay on Everlasting Punishment* (1871; 4th edn, 1895), he defended the eternity of future punishment. Of kindred character was *After Death: is there a Post-Mortem Probation?* (1904), in which he sought to refute *Man's Immortality* (1903) by Robert Percival Downes. The view that God is incapable of suffering he strongly maintained, against James Baldwin Brown, A. M. Fairbairn, George Matheson, George Adam Smith, and others, in *The Blessed God: Impassibility* (1900). His ablest criticism of scepticism is found in his *First Principles of Faith* (1884), in which he dealt with the views of John Stuart Mill, Herbert Spencer, and Henry Mansel. He also published *Substitution: a Treatise on the Atonement* (1877), and *The Design and Use of Holy Scripture* (Fernley lecture, 1892), in which he incidentally acknowledged the service of the higher criticism. C. H. IRWIN, *rev.* MARTIN WELLINGS

Sources *Minutes of several conversations at the yearly conference of the people called Methodists* (1904), 154–6 · *Methodist Recorder* (23 July 1896) · private information (1912) · *CGPLA Eng. & Wales* (1904)
Likenesses A. Nowell, oils, Didsbury College, Manchester · P. N., wood-engraving (after photograph by Ball), NPG; repro. in *ILN* (1 Aug 1896)
Wealth at death £14,620 9s. 7d.: probate, 26 Aug 1904, *CGPLA Eng. & Wales*

PICTURE CREDITS

Pott, Percivall (1714–1788)—St Bartholomew's Hospital Archives and Museum. Photograph: Photographic Survey, Courtauld Institute of Art, London

Potter, (Helen) Beatrix (1866–1943)—© National Portrait Gallery, London

Potter, Christopher (1590/91–1646)—reproduced by permission of the Provost and Fellows of the Queen's College, Oxford

Potter, Dennis Christopher George (1935–1994)—© Trevor Leighton / Camera Press; collection National Portrait Gallery, London

Potter, Thomas Bayley (1817–1898)—© National Portrait Gallery, London

Pottinger, Sir Henry, first baronet (1789–1856)—Crown copyright in photograph: UK Government Art Collection

Pound, Sir (Alfred) Dudley Pickman Rogers (1877–1943)—The Imperial War Museum, London

Pound, Ezra Loomis (1885–1972)—© National Portrait Gallery, London

Povey, Thomas (b. 1613/14, d. in or before 1705)—National Trust Photographic Library

Powell, Cecil Frank (1903–1969)—© National Portrait Gallery, London

Powell, (Elizabeth) Dilys (1901–1995)—© National Portrait Gallery, London

Powell, (John) Enoch (1912–1998)—© Jane Bown

Powell, Foster (bap. 1734, d. 1793)—private collection

Powell, Frederick Smith (1850–1904)—© Estate of Sir William Rothenstein / National Portrait Gallery, London

Powell, Sir George Smyth Baden- (1847–1898)—private collection; photograph National Portrait Gallery, London

Powell, Michael Latham (1905–1990)—© National Portrait Gallery, London

Powell, Dame Muriel Betty (1914–1978)—© National Portrait Gallery, London

Powell, Olave St Clair Baden-, Lady Baden-Powell (1889–1977)—© reserved; collection National Portrait Gallery, London

Powell, Robert Stephenson Smyth Baden-, first Baron Baden-Powell (1857–1941)—© National Portrait Gallery, London

Power, Eileen Edna Le Poer (1889–1940)—British Library of Political and Economic Science

Power, (William Grattan) Tyrone (1797–1841)—photograph © Ulster Museum. Photograph reproduced with the kind permission of the Trustees of the National Museums & Galleries of Northern Ireland

Powicke, Sir (Frederick) Maurice (1879–1963)—© National Portrait Gallery, London

Powlett, Thomas Orde-, first Baron Bolton (1746–1807)—© National Portrait Gallery, London

Pownall, Sir Henry Royds (1887–1961)—© National Portrait Gallery, London

Pownall, Thomas (1722–1805)—National Portrait Gallery, Smithsonian Institution

Powys, Caroline (1738–1817)—© National Portrait Gallery, London

Powys, John Cowper (1872–1963)—© reserved; Bissell Collection; photograph National Portrait Gallery, London

Poynder, John Poynder Dickson-, Baron Islington (1866–1936)—© National Portrait Gallery, London

Poynter, Sir Edward John, first baronet (1836–1919)—© National Portrait Gallery, London

Praed, Winthrop Mackworth (1802–1839)—© National Portrait Gallery, London

Prain, Sir David (1857–1944)—© National Portrait Gallery, London

Pratt, Anne (1806–1893)—by permission of the Linnean Society of London

Pratt, Charles, first Earl Camden (1714–1794)—© National Portrait Gallery, London

Pratt, Hodgson (1824–1907)—© National Portrait Gallery, London

Pratt, John Jeffreys, first Marquess Camden (1759–1840)—© National Portrait Gallery, London

Pratt, John Tidd (1797–1870)—© National Portrait Gallery, London

Pratt, Josiah (1768–1844)—© National Portrait Gallery, London

Pratt, Samuel Jackson (1749–1814)—photograph by courtesy Sotheby's Picture Library, London

Preece, Sir William Henry (1834–1913)—Heritage Images Partnership

Prendergast, Sir Harry North Dalrymple (1834–1913)—courtesy of the Director, National Army Museum, London

Preston, John (1587–1628)—© National Portrait Gallery, London

Price, Bonamy (1807–1888)—© National Portrait Gallery, London

Price, Dennis (1915–1973)—© National Portrait Gallery, London

Price, Henry Habberley (1899–1984)—photograph reproduced by courtesy of The British Academy

Price, Richard (1723–1791)—© National Portrait Gallery, London

Price, Robert (1655–1733)—© National Portrait Gallery, London

Price, William (1800–1893)—unknown collection; photograph © National Portrait Gallery, London

Price, William Charles (1909–1993)—Godfrey Argent Studios / Royal Society

Prideaux, John (1578–1650)—© Copyright The British Museum

Priestley, Joseph (1733–1804)—© National Portrait Gallery, London

Primrose, Sir Archibald, first baronet, Lord Carrington (1616–1679)—private collection / Scottish National Portrait Gallery

Primrose, Archibald Philip, fifth earl of Rosebery and first earl of Midlothian (1847–1929)—private collection

Pringle, Sir John, first baronet (1707–1782)—© The Royal Society

Prinsep, Henry Thoby (1792–1878)—© National Portrait Gallery, London

Prinsep, Valentine Cameron (1838–1904)—Aberdeen Art Gallery and Museums Collections

Prior, Edward Schroder (1852–1932)—© National Portrait Gallery, London

Prior, Matthew (1664–1721)—The Master and Fellows, Trinity College, Cambridge

Pritchard, Charles (1808–1893)—© National Portrait Gallery, London

Pritchard, George (1796–1883)—unknown collection / Christie's; photograph National Portrait Gallery, London

Pritchard, Hannah (1709–1768)—Garrick Club / the art archive

Pritchard, Sir John Michael (1918–1989)—© Derek Allen; collection National Portrait Gallery, London

Pritchett, Sir Victor Sawdon (1900–1997)—© National Portrait Gallery, London

Pritt, Denis Nowell (1887–1972)—© National Portrait Gallery, London

Probyn, Sir Edmund (1678–1742)—© National Portrait Gallery, London

Procter, Adelaide Anne (1825–1864)—© National Portrait Gallery, London

Procter, Bryan Waller (1787–1874)—© National Portrait Gallery, London

Proops, (Rebecca) Marjorie (1911–1996)—Dezo Hoffman / Rex Features

Prothero, Sir George Walter (1848–1922)—© Estate of Sir William Rothenstein / National Portrait Gallery, London

Prothero, Rowland Edmund, first Baron Ernle (1851–1937)—© National Portrait Gallery, London

Prout, Ebenezer (1835–1909)—© National Portrait Gallery, London

Pryde, James Ferrier (1866–1941)—Estate of the Artist; City Art Centre: City of Edinburgh Museums and Galleries

Prynne, William (1600–1669)—© National Portrait Gallery, London

Psalmanazar, George (1679–1763)—© National Portrait Gallery, London

Pugin, Auguste Charles (1768/9–1832)—private collection; photograph National Portrait Gallery, London

Pugin, Augustus Welby Northmore (1812–1852)—RIBA Library Photographs Collection

Pugin, Edward Welby (1834–1875)—© reserved

Pullen, Josiah (1631–1714)—© National Portrait Gallery, London

Pulteney, (Henrietta) Laura, suo jure countess of Bath (1766–1808)—© The Trustees of the Holburne Museum of Art, Bath

Pulteney, Richard (1730–1801)—© National Portrait Gallery, London

Pulteney, William, earl of Bath (1684–1764)—private collection. Photograph: Photographic Survey, Courtauld Institute of Art, London

Punnett, Reginald Crundall (1875–1967)—© National Portrait Gallery, London

Purcell, Henry (1659–1695)—© National Portrait Gallery, London

Purchas, Samuel (bap. 1577, d. 1626)—© Copyright The British Museum

Purdey, James (1784–1863)—by courtesy of James Purdey & Sons Ltd.

Pusey, Edward Bouverie (1800–1882)—© National Portrait Gallery, London

Pusey, Philip (1799–1855)—© National Portrait Gallery, London

Pye, Henry James (1745–1813)—© National Portrait Gallery, London

Pye, John (1782–1874)—© National Portrait Gallery, London

Pyke, Magnus Alfred (1908–1992)—© Kyffin Williams

Pym, Barbara Mary Crampton (1913–1980)—© Mark Gerson; collection National Portrait Gallery, London

Pym, John (1584–1643)—© National Portrait Gallery, London

Pynchon, William (1590–1662)—photography courtesy Peabody Essex Museum

Quain, Sir Richard, baronet (1816–1898)—by permission of the Royal College of Physicians, London

Quaritch, Bernard Alexander Christian (1819–1899)—Bernard Quaritch Ltd

Quarles, Francis (1592–1644)—© Copyright The British Museum

Quarrier, William (1829–1903)—© National Portrait Gallery, London

Quayle, Sir (John) Anthony (1913–1989)—© National Portrait Gallery, London

Quelch, Henry [Harry] (1858–1913)—by permission of the People's History Museum

Quick, Sir John (1852–1932)—© reserved; photograph by permission of the National Library of Australia

Quick, Robert Hebert (1831–1891)—© National Portrait Gallery, London

Quilter, Roger Cuthbert (1877–1953)—© National Portrait Gallery, London

Quin, James (1693–1766)—© Tate, London, 2004

Quin, Windham Thomas Wyndham-, fourth earl of Dunraven and Mount Earl (1841–1926)—© National Portrait Gallery, London

Quincey, Thomas Penson De (1785–1859)—© National Portrait Gallery, London

Quincy, Saer de, earl of Winchester (d. 1219)—The British Library

Rachman, Peter (1920?–1962)—© Popperfoto

Rackham, Arthur (1867–1939)—Art Workers' Guild; photograph by Bridgeman Art Library

Radcliffe, Cyril John, Viscount Radcliffe (1899–1977)—© National Portrait Gallery, London

Radcliffe, Frances, countess of Sussex (1531?–1589)—by permission of the Master and Fellows of Sidney Sussex College, Cambridge

Radcliffe, John (*bap.* 1650, *d.* 1714)—© Bodleian Library, University of Oxford

Radcliffe, Thomas, third earl of Sussex (1526/7–1583)—private collection

Radhakrishnan, Sir Sarvepalli (1888–1975)—All Souls College, Oxford

Rado, Richard (1906–1989)—Godfrey Argent Studios / Royal Society

Rae, John (1813–1893)—© National Portrait Gallery, London

Raeburn, Sir Henry (1756–1823)—National Gallery of Scotland

Raffald, Elizabeth (*bap.* 1733, *d.* 1781)—© National Portrait Gallery, London

Raffles, Sir (Thomas) Stamford Bingley (1781–1826)—© National Portrait Gallery, London

Raikes, Henry (1782–1854)—© National Portrait Gallery, London

Raikes, Robert (1736–1811)—© National Portrait Gallery, London

Raikes, Thomas (1777–1848)—© National Portrait Gallery, London

Rainbow, Edward (1608–1684)—Ashmolean Museum, Oxford

Rainolds, John (1549–1607)—by permission of the President and Scholars, Corpus Christi College, Oxford

Rains, (William) Claude (1889–1967)—© Estate of Russell Westwood / National Portrait Gallery, London

Rainsford, Sir Richard (1605–1680)—The Honourable Society of Lincoln's Inn. Photograph: Photographic Survey, Courtauld Institute of Art, London

Rainy, Robert (1826–1906)—Scottish National Portrait Gallery

Raisin, Catherine Alice (1855–1945)—Royal Holloway College; photograph National Portrait Gallery, London

Raistrick, Arthur (1896–1991)—© W. R. Mitchell MBE

Ralegh, Sir Walter (1554–1618)—© National Portrait Gallery, London

Raleigh, Sir Walter Alexander (1861–1922)—© National Portrait Gallery, London

Ralli, Stephen Augustus (1829–1902)—© National Portrait Gallery, London

Ralston, William Ralston Shedden- (1828–1889)—© National Portrait Gallery, London

Raman, Sir (Chandrasekhara) Venkata (1888–1970)—Heritage Images Partnership

Ramanujan, Srinivasa (1887–1920)—The Master and Fellows, Trinity College, Cambridge

Rambert, Dame Marie (1888–1982)—V&A Images, The Victoria and Albert Museum

Ramée, Marie Louise de la [Ouida] (1839–1908)—Getty Images – Adolphe Beau

Ramsay, Allan (1684–1758)—Scottish National Portrait Gallery

Ramsay, Allan, of Kinkell (1713–1784)—© National Portrait Gallery, London

Ramsay, Sir Andrew Crombie (1814–1891)—© National Portrait Gallery, London

Ramsay, Sir Bertram Home (1883–1945)—© National Portrait Gallery, London

Ramsay, David (1749–1815)—Independence National Historical Park

Ramsay, Edward Bannerman (1793–1872)—Scottish National Portrait Gallery

Ramsay, James (1733–1789)—© National Portrait Gallery, London

Ramsay, James Andrew Broun, first marquess of Dalhousie (1812–1860)—© National Portrait Gallery, London

Ramsay, Sir William (1852–1916)—© National Portrait Gallery, London

Ramsay, Sir William Mitchell (1851–1939)—© National Portrait Gallery, London

Ramsden, Jesse (1735–1800)—© The Royal Society

Ramsey, Sir Alfred Ernest (1920–1999)—Getty Images – Hulton Archive

Ramsey, Ian Thomas (1915–1972)—© National Portrait Gallery, London

Ramsey, (Arthur) Michael, Baron Ramsey of Canterbury (1904–1988)—© National Portrait Gallery, London

Randall, John (1717–1799)—© Copyright The British Museum